BASEBALL GUIDE

1990 EDITION

Editor/Baseball Guide
DAVE SLOAN

Associate Editor/Baseball Guide
MIKE NAHRSTEDT

Contributing Editors/Baseball Guide
CRAIG CARTER
BARRY SIEGEL
LARRY WIGGE

President-Chief Executive Officer
THOMAS G. OSENTON

Book Publisher
GREGORY WILEY

Editorial Director of Books and Periodicals
RON SMITH

Published by

The Sporting News

1212 North Lindbergh Boulevard
P.O. Box 56 — St. Louis, MO 63166

Copyright © 1990
The Sporting News Publishing Company

▼▼ A Times Mirror
◼ Company

ISBN 0-89204-337-7   ISSN 0078-3838

TABLE OF CONTENTS

For Index to Contents See Page 536

(Index to Minor League Cities on Page 531)

ON THE COVER: Kansas City righthander Bret Saberhagen won his second American League Cy Young Award in five years in 1989 after leading the league in wins (23), earned-run average (2.16), innings pitched (262.1) and complete games (12).

—Photo by Tom DiPace

The Unusual and Unexpected Became the Norm in Tragic '89

By CLIFFORD KACHLINE

No previous year in the long history of professional baseball witnessed as many troublesome and tragic events as did 1989. It was a year of the unexpected, the unusual and the bizarre.

There were moments of triumph, to be sure. However, few of the successes qualified among the sport's all-time great accomplishments.

Developments beyond the playing arena often overshadowed action on the field. Some drew a positive, enthusiastic response; others cast a long, dark shadow. Among off-the-field incidents commanding media headlines with a frequency rivaling achievements on the diamond were: two changes in the position of commissioner within five months—one planned, the other necessitated by death; the election by National League club owners of a black as league president; a six-month investigation that led to the lifetime suspension of one of the game's best-known figures; a $10.5 million fine levied against the 26 big-league clubs by an arbitrator for collusion; and an earthquake that disrupted the World Series.

Despite all the commotion, heartache and havoc, one constant stood out in '89: The fans generally focused on the same aspects of the game as in past years—the performances of the athletes, the division races and the postseason battles. Not even the various negative notes on which the season began—the investigation of Pete Rose's gambling activities, the admission of Wade Boggs to extramarital indiscretions, Jose Canseco's involvement in several automobile-related infractions and the booing of Roger Clemens and Frank Viola by fans at their clubs' home openers —could dampen the public's interest.

Instead, the enthusiasm of the game's followers was stirred to new heights by the highly successful debut of Jim Abbott, a one-handed pitcher fresh out of college; the unbelievable turnaround of the Baltimore Orioles, who a year earlier posted the majors' worst record; the continuing wizardry of strikeout artist Nolan Ryan at age 42; the opening of Toronto's palatial SkyDome; the comeback of Dave Dravecky from surgery for a cancerous tumor in his pitching arm, a heartwarming development that was short-lived (the

Pete Rose's problems dominated the headlines in 1989.

San Francisco lefthander soon fractured the arm while delivering a pitch); and the tight races in all four divisions, at least for much of the season.

As a consequence, the major leagues established a regular-season attendance record for the fifth year in succession and the seventh time in the last eight years. The combined total of 55,173,096 amounted to a 4.1 percent increase over the high set a year earlier, and a record 15 teams attained the 2,000,000 level in home attendance. Two clubs—the Toronto Blue Jays and St. Louis Cardinals—topped 3,000,000.

All four divisions enjoyed spirited races, but only the American League East went down to the last weekend of the season. The stunning comeback of the Orioles, together with a sudden shift of strength from the A.L. East to the A.L. West, figured in the division's exciting battle. For the first time since 1977, the West emerged victorious in head-to-head competition with the long-dominant East, posting a 41-game edge (314-273). As late as the morning of May 24, with each team having played 40-plus games, all seven teams in the East Division were under .500; the A.L. West had five above the break-even mark at that point.

The Orioles, embarking on a rebuilding program with a roster laden with young talent, took advantage of the malaise and nearly pulled off a miracle. Frank Robinson's crew began a three-month stay in first place on May 26. The euphoria produced by the surprising performance erased memories of Baltimore's nightmarish 0-21 start a year earlier. At the All-Star break, the Orioles were 48-37 and owned the biggest lead of any division front-runner, 5½ games. They boosted it to 7½ lengths on July 18 before encountering a slump. The skid reached 13 losses in 14 games when they dropped a double-header at Boston on August 1. This slashed the Baltimore lead to one game over the Red Sox; even the sixth-place New York Yankees, seven games below .500, were only five games back.

The Orioles rebounded, clinging to the undisputed lead for the next four weeks. But during Baltimore's tightrope act, Cleveland, Milwaukee and Toronto joined the Red Sox in challenging for the No. 1 spot. Only the Blue Jays were able to sustain their drive. After getting off to a dismal start, the Jays fired Manager Jimy Williams on May 15 and elevated coach Cito Gaston to the helm. The team's record at that point was 12-24, and it wasn't until August 8 that Toronto edged over the .500 mark for the first time since opening day. The addition of veterans Mookie Wilson (via trade with the New York Mets) and Lee Mazzilli (on waivers from the Mets) early in August helped energize the Blue Jays. On August 31, they ended Baltimore's 97-day sole occupancy of first place by tying for the lead. Toronto gained undisputed leadership the next night and never relinquished it.

The Blue Jays proceeded to hike their lead to 2½ games on two occasions but were just one in front when the Orioles arrived at the SkyDome on September 29 for a three-game, season-ending showdown. Gaston's club took the Friday night encounter, 2-1, in 11 innings. When the Jays came from behind to win again the next day, 4-3, they wrapped up the last of the division titles.

The N.L. East also experienced a dramatic race. Until the last three weeks, the top four teams often were separated by no more than three or four games. The surprise club in that group was the Chicago Cubs. A horrid 9-23 record in spring exhibitions led many experts to consign the Cubs to fifth place. Don Zimmer's team fooled them. By contrast, the New York Mets, a top-heavy choice to repeat as East champions, were a prime disappointment. Starting May 23, the Cubs spent 24 consecutive days—and 32 of 33—in first place. Still, the All-Star layoff found the Montre-

al Expos on top at 49-38, followed by Chicago (47-39), New York (45-39) and St. Louis (44-39).

Montreal's surge coincided with the deal that brought lefthander Mark Langston from Seattle on May 25. Before his arrival, the Expos were 23-23, but they won 40 of their next 61 games and enjoyed a 42-day stay on top. After dropping three straight August 4-6 in New York (games in which the Mets briefly revived their flagging hopes), the Expos found themselves in a first-place tie with Chicago. When Montreal lost again the following night in Chicago—the start of another three-game sweep that extended the Expos' skid to seven straight—the Cubs regained the undisputed lead and held it to the finish.

The Cardinals provided the Cubs with their last serious threat. Winning the opener of a series at Wrigley Field September 8, St. Louis climbed within one-half game of the lead, but the Cubs copped the last two games of the series and then began pulling away from the field. They became the first team to clinch division honors by winning, 3-2, at Montreal on September 26. With 93 victories, the Cubs wound up six games ahead of the second-place Mets and seven in front of the Cardinals.

Like Toronto, the Oakland Athletics had to ward off an unexpected challenger in capturing their second successive A.L. West crown. The California Angels, who finished 29 games out a year earlier, kept pace with the A's for much of the summer and even led the division for most of July (and at various other points as well). At the All-Star interlude, the Angels boasted the majors' best record, 52-33, and had a 1½-game edge over the A's. The return to action of outfielder Jose Canseco, who missed the entire first half because of a wrist injury, and relief ace Dennis Eckersley, idled six weeks with a strained rotation cuff, following the midsummer break gave Manager Tony La Russa and Oakland followers a big lift.

The A's nudged the Angels from the lead on August 21, taking over first place for keeps despite late threats by California and Kansas City. With two weeks remaining, both the Angels and Royals were within 2½ lengths of the lead. Neither succeeded in getting any closer as the A's won 11 of their last 14 games. The clincher came on September 27 when Mike Moore and two relievers shut out Texas, 5-0. Winning twice in their closing series with the Royals, the Athletics finished with the finest record (99-63) in the majors in 1989. For the first time since 1977, the West Division could boast three teams with 90 victories each as Kansas City wound up with 92 and California with 91.

In the N.L. West, the San Francisco Giants withstood a late surge by San Diego to earn their second division title in three years. Roger Craig's club occupied the top rung all alone continuously from June 17 on. The Houston Astros hung tough during the first five months of the campaign, trailing by just one game as July ended and by only four as August drew to a close. Although the Giants played at only a .500 clip (14-14) in August, they increased their lead when the Astros could do no better than 11-17 for the month.

The Padres, 12 lengths back on the morning of July 25, finally found the combination and performed at a .667 clip (42-21) the balance of the way. The spurt lifted them into contention in mid-September, but came a bit late. Going into the final week of the season, the Padres had won 26 of their last 33 games while the Giants had captured 17 of their last 24. Then, four games back with four remaining, the Padres saw their flickering hopes vanish in a 13-inning, 2-1 loss to Cincinnati on September 27. The Padres' defeat clinched the crown for San Francisco and made the Giants' visit to San Diego on the final weekend meaningless. The Padres finished three games behind and Houston wound up six off the pace.

Both Oakland and San Francisco made quick work of the opposition in League Championship Series play. Each won in five games. The Athletics' power and pitching proved too much for Toronto, while the Cubs' dream season fell victim to the sensational hitting of the Giants' Will Clark. In winning the American League pennant, the A's earned the distinction of being the first team to reach the World Series in successive years since the Yankees of 1977 and 1978; meanwhile, the Giants' victory gave them their first National League flag in 27 years.

The bat and legs of Rickey Henderson and the arms of Moore, Dave Stewart, Bob Welch and reliever Eckersley sparked the Oakland success. Henderson reached base on 14 of 23 plate appearances with six hits, seven walks and one hit-by-pitch for a .400 batting average and .609 on-base percentage. He also had team-leading totals of eight stolen bases, eight runs scored and five runs batted in. Stewart notched two of the A's victories—in the opener and the finale.

Starting with a bases-loaded home run and six RBIs in the opener and ending with a winning two-run single in the fifth game, Clark established N.L. playoff records for hits (13), average (.650), runs (8), total bases (24) and slugging average (1.200) in San Francisco's romp. His 13 hits included three doubles, a triple and two homers and accounted for eight RBIs (thereby matching the N.L. playoff mark). Clark's first-base counterpart, Mark Grace, was almost as productive for the Cubs. He had 11 hits in 17 at-bats and a 1.118 slugging percentage while driving in eight of his club's 22 runs.

The World Series, the first all-Bay Area fall classic, probably will always be remembered more for Mother Nature's role than for the four-game sweep registered by Oakland. The earthquake that struck that section of Northern California less than 30 minutes before Game 3 was to begin at Candlestick Park stunned the fans and general populace to a far greater degree than the A's bats and arms rocked the Giants.

The Battle of the Bay—also called the "BART Series" by some because of the Bay Area Rapid Transportation system that connects the two cities and as the "Bart Series" by others because it was dedicated to the memory of the late commissioner, A. Bartlett Giamatti—began routinely enough. Game 1 at Oakland-Alameda County Coliseum saw Stewart handcuff the Giants on five hits, 5-0. Moore and two relievers followed with a four-hit, 5-1 victory.

After the customary day off, the Series moved across the Bay to San Francisco. Most of the 62,000 ticket-holders already were seated in Candlestick when at 5:04 p.m., Pacific Daylight Time, on Tuesday, October 17, the temblor occurred. The quake, centered about 60 miles south of San Francisco and measuring 7.1 on the Richter scale, shook the stadium for an estimated 15 or 20 seconds. The upper deck and light towers swayed, and the park's power supply was cut off, dousing the lights and interrupting ABC-TV's national pregame show.

The rumbling shocked most of the crowd. Fortunately, no one panicked, and except for a few places where some concrete crumbled, mostly along expansion joints, Candlestick Park suffered little noticeable damage. A project begun in 1984 to strengthen the upper deck during quakes probably prevented a major tragedy at the park. Once the vibrations ceased, many in the crowd, unaware of the devastation caused elsewhere, began chanting "Play ball." Commissioner Fay Vincent, in only his second month on the job, immediately began conferring with stadium and club officials and other authorities. About 45 minutes after the tremor, having learned there was no possibility that electric service could soon be restored and that surrounding areas had suffered heavy damage, he decided to postpone the game. The move assured that everyone could vacate the stadium before darkness set in.

The fans and players, many in a state of semi-shock, began an orderly exit. Some had portable radios and television sets and already were aware of the widespread havoc. The quake cut off electric power throughout the city and caused billions of dollars of property damage over a wide area. Not only were many businesses and homes badly damaged, but one section of the upper deck of the Bay Bridge, the major link between Oakland and San Francisco, had dropped onto the lower level, and a 1½-mile stretch of the Nimitz Freeway (Interstate 880) in Oakland had collapsed. Early estimates pegged the death toll at more than 250, including possibly 200 when the upper level of the Nimitz crashed onto the lower level, crushing trucks and cars. Luckily, the final fatality count was only 67 for the entire area. Authorities theorized that many motorists who might normally have been on the Nimitz at the time of the earthquake may have left work early either to attend the game or to watch it on television.

Less than 24 hours after the quake, Vincent conducted a press conference at the St. Francis Hotel in San Francisco. It was held amid candlelight because the city was still without power. Having met most of the day with stadium engineers and representatives of both leagues, both teams, the players' association and the city, he announced that the Series—or "our modest little sporting event," as he termed it in light of the tragedy—was being postponed for one week, with October 24 the tentative date for Game 3. Plans were further revised on October 22. Vincent finally had an opportunity to meet that day with San Francisco's besieged mayor, Art Agnos, who urged a further delay. Vincent then established a new schedule calling for games at Candlestick on October 27 and 28 and, if needed October 29, plus games—also if needed—at Oakland on October 31 and November 1.

The 10-day postponement was the longest in World Series history and the first ever for anything other than inclement weather. Following several days off, both teams resumed working out in their home parks. When rain threatened, the A's flew to Phoenix for their last two days of practice on October 25 and 26. An estimated 6,000 fans attended each session there and donated nearly $20,000 to the Red Cross earthquake fund. Meanwhile, the 26 major league clubs voted to contribute at least $40,000 apiece, with the A's and Giants making larger contributions, to provide $1.4 million to assist in earthquake relief efforts.

When the Series resumed on October 27, it was business as usual, especially for the A's. With a throng of 62,038 on hand at Candlestick, La Russa's bashers smashed five home runs, including two by Dave Henderson, and walloped the Giants, 13-7. In the process, Stewart became the first pitcher to win two games in both the playoffs and World Series in the same year. One night later, Oakland completed the sweep with a 9-6 victory behind Moore and four relievers.

For Stewart, the four postseason victories capped a tremendous season. The 32-year-old Oakland ace chalked up a 21-9 record in the regular campaign. He thus became the first pitcher to have three consecutive 20-victory seasons since Jim Palmer had four straight with Baltimore from 1975 through 1978. The year's only other 20-game winners were Bret Saberhagen of Kansas City and Mike Scott of Houston. Saberhagen won 14 of his last 15 starts to notch a 23-6 record. He also led the American League with a 2.16 earned-run average. Scott finished at 20-10. Scott Garrelts of San Francisco emerged as the National League ERA leader at 2.28.

Mark Davis of San Diego topped all relief pitchers in saves with 44, one shy of the National League record and two under the major league mark. Jeff Russell of Texas was the American League leader with 38. The Los Angeles Dodgers' Tim Belcher paced all pitchers in shutouts with eight.

Two other pitchers who occupied the spotlight all season were Texas veteran Ryan and California rookie Abbott. Ryan qualified as the majors' oldest player at 42 when the Yankees released 46-year-old Tommy John on Memorial Day, but the fireballing righthander demonstrated in his first season with the Rangers that he still ranked among the best. He twice took bids for a sixth career no-hitter into the ninth inning and three times pitched hitless ball into the eighth. With two complete-game one-hitters, he raised his career total of nine-inning no-hit and one-hit performances to 16, breaking the record of 14 he previously shared with Bob Feller.

Ryan's crowning achievements, however, came in two other appearances. On August 22, with a crowd of 42,869 cheering him on in Arlington Stadium, the all-time strikeout king registered career No. 5,000 by fanning Oakland's Rickey Henderson in the fifth inning. On the next-to-last day of the season, September 30, Ryan struck out 13 in a three-hit, 2-0 victory over the Angels at Anaheim Stadium. This gave him 301 strikeouts and made him the oldest pitcher by 11 years to fan 300 in a season. He came within five outs of a perfect game that night while notching win No. 16, which equaled his best victory total since 1977. Allowing only 162 hits in 239⅓ innings for the year, Ryan held the opposition to a .187 batting average, lowest in the majors among starting pitchers. He also averaged 11.3 strikeouts per nine innings, high among big-league starters.

Abbott, a 21-year-old lefthander with no previous professional experience, also created considerable excitement. Born without a right hand, the University of Michigan product went to spring training as a non-roster player with the California Angels and proceeded to win a spot in the Angels' rotation. Although Abbott had pitched the United States to victory in the gold-medal game at the Seoul Olympics the previous fall, critics wondered if the Angels were engaged in a publicity gimmick. Abbott quickly proved his physical disability was no handicap and chalked up a 12-12 record, including two shutouts.

Another player who overcame extreme adversity was the Giants' Dravecky. A few days after the 1988 season ended, the lefthander underwent surgery for removal of a cancerous tumor from the upper part of his pitching arm. Because the tumor was attached to the bone, his doctor had to remove half of the deltoid muscle. Medical experts and teammates thought the pitcher's career was over, but Dravecky, 33, thought otherwise. Late in July, following extensive therapy and hard work, he was assigned to the Giants' Class A San Jose (California) farm team. He promptly reeled off two complete-game victories.

Recalled by the Giants, Dravecky made a storybook return. With an emotional crowd of 34,810 watching at Candlestick Park on August 10, he limited Cincinnati to one hit over seven innings. The Reds solved him for three runs in the eighth, but he won, 4-3.

Five nights later at Montreal, Dravecky carried a three-hit shuout into the sixth inning before his remarkable comeback was halted. Damaso Garcia led off the Expos' sixth with a homer, and Andres Galarraga then was hit by a pitch. On his next delivery, with Tim Raines at bat, Dravecky crashed to the ground as if shot by a sniper.

"It sounded like a firecracker," commented Hubie Brooks, who was in the on-deck circle. Members of both teams rushed to the pitcher, who was writhing in pain and gripping his left arm.

Taken to a hospital, Dravecky was found to have suffered a stress fracture of the humerus, the large bone between the elbow and shoulder. During the October '88 operation, doctors had applied a freezing agent to the bone, leaving it susceptible to such a break.

Adding to the misfortune, Dravecky suffered a hairline fracture of the same arm the day of the Giants' playoff-clinching victory over the Cubs. The mishap occurred when he was shoved from behind during the postgame mob scene on the Candlestick Park infield. In November, following discovery of another lump in his pitching arm, Dravecky announced his retirement.

Kevin Mitchell, San Francisco outfielder, was the year's most explosive hitter. He walloped 22 home runs in the Giants' first 57 games and finished with 47 round-trippers, 11 more than his nearest major league rivals. In addition, Mitchell topped both leagues in RBIs, 125; total bases, 345, and slugging percentage, .635. Fred McGriff of Toronto led the American League in home runs with 36, while Ruben Sierra of Texas took A.L. honors in RBIs (119), total bases (344) and slugging percentage (543).

The battle for the league batting championships went down to the wire.

By stinging San Francisco pitchers for six hits in eight at-bats in the last two games, Tony Gwynn of San Diego edged the Giants' Will Clark, .336 to .333, for the National League title. It was Gwynn's third successive N.L. crown and his fourth in six years. The last previous N.L. player to win three consecutive batting titles was Stan Musial, who led the league in 1950, 1951 and 1952.

Minnesota's Kirby Puckett captured the American League batting championship when he went 2 for 5 at Seattle on closing day to wind up at .339, three points ahead of Carney Lansford of Oakland, who was 0 for 3 against Kansas City that afternoon. Puckett became the first righthanded batter to win a full-season A.L. batting title since California's Alex Johnson accomplished the feat in 1970 (the right-handed-hitting Lansford was the A.L.

champion in the strike-shortened 1981 season).

With 215 hits, Puckett led the majors in that department. Wade Boggs of Boston, A.L. batting champion the four previous seasons, came in third this time at .330, but had his seventh consecutive 200-hit season, breaking his own league record.

Rickey Henderson, who was traded by the Yankees to Oakland on June 21, ran away with American League basestealing honors for the ninth time in 10 years with 77 thefts. Vince Coleman of St. Louis led the National League for the fifth consecutive season with 65. Coleman owned a streak of 50 consecutive steals over two seasons—a major league record—before Montreal catcher Nelson Santovenia threw him out on July 28. Henderson also paced A.L. batters in walks with 126, while Jack Clark of San Diego topped the N.L. by drawing 132 bases on balls.

For the second successive season, home run production decreased, providing further evidence that the baseballs being used were less lively than in 1987. The two league combined for 3,083 homers in 1989, compared with 3,180 in 1988 and the astounding total of 4,458 in '87.

The number of balks also dropped abruptly. American League umpires called only 168—a year earlier, the total was a record 558. In the National League, balks dropped from a record 366 in '88 to 239. The steep decreases followed a request by the players' association to abandon the strict interpretation on balks that was approved on a one-year trial basis in '88 and to return to the policy that previously was in effect. In another change approved by the Rules Committee, it was decided to drop the game-winning RBI as an official statistic.

Other noteworthy on-field developments during the '89 season:

• The Griffeys became the first father-son duo ever to play in the majors simultaneously. Ken Griffey Sr., 39, participated in 106 games with Cincinnati, batting .263; Ken Jr., the majors' youngest player at 19, became Seattle's regular center fielder and hit .264 in 127 games. Ken Jr. quickly became a celebrity in Seattle and found himself the subject of a candy bar, four posters and an upcoming book. Royalties from the Ken Griffey Jr. chocolate bars, with the wrappers showing the rookie at bat, amounted to approximately half of his baseball salary (the major league minimum of $68,000), and more than 80,000 of the posters were sold.

• Kevin Elster of the New York Mets extended his string of errorless games to 88, a record for major league shortstops, before he misplayed a grounder in the ninth inning of a 3-1 Mets victory in Cincinnati on May 9. Elster handled 294 chances during the streak.

• Benny Distefano, reserve first baseman with Pittsburgh, became the third lefthanded catcher in the majors in this century—joining Dale Long (1958 Chicago Cubs) and Mike Squires (1980 Chicago White Sox)—when he took over behind the plate in the ninth inning against Atlanta on May 14. Distefano caught in two other games.

• In an emotional and tearful news conference at San Diego's Jack Murphy Stadium on May 29, third baseman Mike Schmidt of the Philadelphia Phillies announced his retirement. The 39-year-old slugger smashed 548 home runs in his 18-year career, but batted only .203 in 42 games in his final season.

• Tom Browning, who tossed a perfect game a year earlier, came within three outs on July 4 of becoming the first major league pitcher to hurl a second perfect game. The Cincinnati lefthander retired the first 24 batters at Philadelphia's Veterans Stadium before Dickie Thon opened the ninth inning with a double to right-center. One out later, Steve Jeltz singled Thon home. Reliever John Franco then came on to wrap up Browning's 2-1 victory.

• The Cincinnati Reds established several records when they cracked out 16 hits and scored 14 runs in the first inning—all before out No. 2 was recorded—on the way to an 18-2 drubbing of Houston at Riverfront Stadium on August 3. Victims of the 38-minute half-inning were pitchers Jim Clancy and Bob Forsch. A record seven Reds collected two hits each during the inning.

• For the third time in less than a year, Dave Stieb of Toronto came within one out of a no-hitter. This time, with 48,789 fans watching in the SkyDome on August 4, he owned a perfect game—having retired the first 26 Yankees—before Roberto Kelly doubled and Steve Sax singled on successive pitches to spoil his bid as the Blue Jays won, 2-1. Back on April 10 in New York, Stieb had yielded just one hit—a fifth-inning single by Jamie Quirk—while blanking the Yankees, 8-0. The Toronto righthander, who missed no-hitters with two away in the ninth in his last two starts of 1988, was deprived of yet another gem on August 26 when Robin Yount's sixth-inning one-hopper bounced off the glove of third baseman Kelly Gruber for the lone Milwaukee hit in a 7-0 victory in the SkyDome.

• Howard Johnson of the New York Mets became the third player in major league history to hit 30 home runs and steal 30 bases in the same season more than once. A 36-homer, 32-steal man in 1987, Johnson cracked 36 homers and stole 41 bases last year. Bobby Bonds had five 30-30 seasons and Willie Mays had two.

• Jerome Walton, rookie outfielder, went on a 30-game hitting streak—the longest by a Chicago Cub in this century and the best string in the majors last year. The streak ended when he went 0 for 4 in a 10-inning, 6-5 loss to Cincinnati at Wrigley Field on August 21.

• Ryne Sandberg of the Chicago Cubs erased the record of 89 consecutive errorless games in a season by a big-league second baseman, set by Manny Trillo with Philadelphia in 1982, when he turned in his 90th straight flawless effort in the regular-season finale on October 1. Sandberg made only six errors all year, none after June 20.

• Closing day of the season also found shortstop Cal Ripken Jr. completing his seventh successive year of appearing in every Baltimore Orioles game, extending his consecutive-game streak to 1,250. The skein began on May 30, 1982. Only Lou Gehrig with 2,130 and Everett Scott with 1,307 had longer playing streaks in the majors.

The formal opening on June 5 of the SkyDome, the Blue Jays' new space-age home in downtown Toronto, was another high point of the season. The glitzy stadium, as tall as a 31-story building, became major league baseball's fifth enclosed facility and its first with a fully retractable roof, one that can be closed during a game if the need arises. The ballpark drew rave reviews from players and fans alike. A near-capacity crowd of 48,378 attended the inaugural game, but the visiting Milwaukee Brewers spoiled the evening by winning, 5-3.

The world's most technologically advanced stadium, the SkyDome was built at an estimated cost of $450 million in Canadian funds ($375 million U.S.)—more than three times the original projection. It was underwritten by a combination of public and private money and is operated by the Stadium Corp. of Ontario. The governments of both the province and the Toronto metropolitan area made sizable contributions, while 28 companies chipped in $5 million each and $60 million was raised from the sale of private boxes. Referred to as "a city within a city," the facility includes a 364-room hotel (with 70 rooms overlooking the playing field), five restaurants and bars with views of the field, shopping boutiques, a 150-seat movie theater, a health club with sauna, a 25-meter swimming pool and a running track.

With its movable roof, the SkyDome marks the third generation of domed stadiums, following the so-called hard tops (Houston and Seattle) and the soft top (Minneapolis). The roof, weighing 11,000 tons and covering almost eight acres, consists of four panels. One engineer termed it "a quantum leap" in technology. When the roof is open, the four panels stack over each other above the center-field area. Three panels sit on carts and travel on rails to close the roof. It was designed to be able to open or close in 20 minutes on as many as 200 occasions a year.

The Toronto stadium can seat 53,000 for baseball, including 40,000 between the foul lines; 55,000 for football, and 60,000 or more for concerts and other events. Included are 161 luxury boxes that sold for up to $2.5 million each for 10 years, not counting the cost of season tickets. The field has artificial turf and dimensions of 328 feet down the foul lines, 375 in the power alleys and 400 in straightaway center, with a 10-foot fence across the outfield.

The SkyDome roof received its first real test during the Blue Jays' third game there on June 7. When clouds moved in quickly, officials decided to close the roof in the fifth inning. Because of mechanical bugs that were still being ironed out, it took 34 minutes—instead of the scheduled 20—to get all the panels in place. Before the process was completed, a heavy downpour began and umpire Rich Garcia halted play for six minutes, but the game then resumed.

By contrast, the Montreal Expos continued to be plagued by problems with the umbrella-type roof at Olympic Stadium. More than a year after the roof was installed, a ceremony was held on July 17 to mark its first public lifting. The following night, rain began falling shortly before game time, but the wind was deemed too strong for the roof to be lowered safely. As a consequence, the start of the Expos-Atlanta game had to be delayed an hour and 57 minutes. Besides the wind factor, the absence of government employees to operate the roof-moving mechanism on weekends and holidays posed a problem for the Expos.

Plans for new stadiums were moving ahead in two cities, but for the second time in three years San Francisco voters rejected an initiative for a new park. Ground was broken in Chicago on May 7 for a $119.4 million, 45,000-seat facility across from 79-year-old Comiskey Park. The new White Sox home was expected to be ready by opening day in 1991. In Baltimore, the Maryland Stadium Authority was pushing efforts on a $246 million, 46,800-seat downtown stadium for the Orioles. It is scheduled to open in 1992.

With nearly 171,500 votes cast, the proposal to build a $115 million, 45,000-seat park in downtown San Francisco lost by fewer than 2,000 votes in the November 7 balloting. Afterward, Giants Owner Bob Lurie said his team would remain at Candlestick Park at least one more season, but the San Jose-Santa Clara-Sunnyvale area some 40 miles south of San Francisco was expected to make another bid to lure the team to a new stadium.

The combination of a new stadium and a division-winning team proved to be a powerful box-office magnet in Toronto. Each of the Blue Jays' last 38 regular-season games in the SkyDome was a sellout. This enabled Toronto to lead the majors in attendance with 3,375,883, an American League record. Only the Los Angeles Dodgers have ever exceeded that total. In addition to the Blue Jays, five other American League teams broke their previous attendance highs—Baltimore, with 2,535,208; Boston, 2,510,012; Kansas City, 2,477,700; Oakland, 2,667,225, and Texas, 2,043,993.

Three National League teams also established attendance records. There were the St. Louis Cardinals, who led the league with 3,080,980; Chicago Cubs, 2,491,942, and San Francisco Giants, 2,059,701. For the second successive year, Atlanta was the lone city to fail to draw at least a million fans, with the Braves attracting just 984,930.

Only four clubs switched managers during the year. A fifth team—Detroit—operated under the leadership of one of its coaches for several weeks during the absence of skipper Sparky Anderson.

The Tigers' collapse and a heavy schedule of charity appearances exacted their toll on Anderson. Suffering from physical exhaustion, he was sent home to Thousand Oaks, Calif., on May 19 by Dr. Clarence Livingood, team physician and Anderson's personal doctor. The Tigers were 13-24 at the time. Coach Dick Tracewski was named interim manager. Anderson, 55, returned to the helm on June 5. During his absence, the Tigers won nine of 17 games.

The first manager to feel the ax was Jimy Williams of Toronto. With the Blue Jays off to a disappointing start, General Manager Pat Gillick decided to take action on May 15. The team, in sixth place and victim of a 13-1 thumping at Minnesota the previous day, had just returned home. Dismissing Williams, Gillick named batting coach Cito Gaston as interim manager, emphasizing that Gaston was not a candidate to head the club on a permanent basis.

Gillick interviewed several candidates and settled on Lou Piniella. Because Piniella was on the Yankees' payroll as a consultant and part-time broadcaster, the Blue Jays needed permission from Yankees Owner George Steinbrenner to pursue him. Finding New York's demands for player compensation too high, Gillick was forced to resume his search. In the meantime, the Blue Jays had begun to play better. Although Gaston initially said he didn't want to manage on a permanent basis, he later had a change of mind, and on May 31 he was officially appointed manager for the remainder of the season. Gaston, 45, thus became the fourth black manager in major league history, joining Frank Robinson, Larry Doby and Maury Wills. When the Blue Jays went on to nose out Robinson's Orioles for the A.L. East crown, Gaston was rewarded with a new one-year contract.

Dallas Green of the Yankees became the second skipper to get the gate. Carrying out his ritual of dumping the manager, Steinbrenner dismissed Green and four of his coaches—Charlie Fox, Lee Elia, Frank Howard and Pat Corrales—on August 18 in Detroit. To replace Green, Steinbrenner brought in Bucky Dent, who had been guiding the Yankees' Columbus (International) farm team. It was the 17th managerial change—and ninth during the season—made by Steinbrenner since he assumed control of the New York club in 1973.

Green had been hired the previous October under a two-year, $700,000 contract. The honeymoon between him and Steinbrenner, both strong-willed individuals with large egos, ended shortly before the start of spring training when the Yankees' boss re-signed veteran free-agent pitchers Tommy John and Ron Guidry over Green's objections. Steinbrenner subsequently promised not to interfere with the manager and coaches, but by midseason he began criticizing them through the media and Green responded in kind. Steinbrenner tried to induce Piniella to return for a third fling as Yankee skipper, but Dent was brought in when Piniella declined. The Yankees were in sixth place with a 56-65 ledger when the switch was made. They lost 11 of their first 13 games under Dent, but then posted a winning record in September.

Doc Edwards' tenure as Cleveland manager came to a close September 12 when he was fired by Indians President Hank Peters. John Hart, a special-assignment scout for the Indians, took over as temporary skipper. Under Hart, the team lost 11 of 19 games and remained in sixth place. John McNamara was hired as the Indians' new manager on November 3. McNamara, who previously piloted Oakland, San Diego, Cincinnati, California and Boston, received a two-year contract.

The other club to change managers was Cincinnati. When Commissioner Bart Giamatti announced the lifetime suspension of Pete Rose on August 24, Rose's longtime friend and dugout associate, coach Tommy Helms, assumed the reins on an interim basis. Helms had guided the Reds to victories in their last two games in Chicago after Rose left the team to be with his wife Carol following the August 22 birth of their daughter. Earlier, Helms also had directed the team in four games in Montreal and New York, May 1-4, when chest congestion, headaches, high blood pressure and a 101.5-degree fever forced Rose to return home to Cincinnati for treatment. Helms also managed the club during Rose's 30-day suspension in 1988.

The Reds were in fourth place with a 61-66 record when Rose was banished. They dropped 21 of their remaining 35 games and slipped to fifth place.

On the same day that Cleveland hired McNamara, the Reds named Lou Piniella as their new manager. Piniella, who had two years at $400,000 annually remaining on his personal-services contract with the Yankees, was given a two-year pact reportedly worth $350,000 per season by Cincinnati.

The banishment of Rose climaxed what was baseball's biggest gambling controversy since the 1919 Black Sox scandal. Several other incidents, including the Ty Cobb-Tris Speaker situation that surfaced late in 1926 and the Leo Durocher affair of 1947, also were the cause of much concern, but none became the focus of as much media scrutiny. Giamatti's ruling capped five months of almost-daily disclosures, rumors and innuendoes and also brought to an end three months of legal maneuvering by Rose's attorneys to block the commissioner from acting.

Reports that Rose had wagered on baseball games began circulating late in March. Rose long had been known as an avid bettor at the horse and dog tracks. Like the general public, baseball personnel are allowed to engage in legal betting at the tracks, and it has become a common pastime for players and managers. However, under professional baseball's rules, anyone employed by the sport who is found guilty of betting on a baseball game is subject to being declared ineligible for one year. If the wager involves a game in which the person has a duty to perform, he faces permanent ineligibility. A copy of the regulation—Rule 21—is posted in every clubhouse in the major and minor leagues.

The August 24 news conference at which Rose's suspension was announced took place in the New York Hilton Hotel beginning at 10 a.m. Although the subject to be discussed was not revealed in advance, the certainty that it involved Rose brought out the media en masse. Network television arranged to air the proceedings. As the session got under way, copies of a five-page, double-spaced document titled "Agreement and Resolution" were handed to the assembled writers and broadcasters. Signed the previous day by both Rose and Giamatti, it stated: "Peter Edward Rose is hereby declared permanently ineligible in accordance with Major League Rule 21 and placed on the Ineligible List."

The action was based on a report prepared by John M. Dowd, a trial lawyer with the Washington legal firm of Heron, Burchette, Ruckert & Rothwell. He had been hired by the commissioner's office as special counsel to conduct an investigation after Kevin Hallinan, baseball's security director, learned of possible wrongdoing on Rose's part. Dowd at one time headed a federal task force on organized crime.

"The banishment for life of Pete Rose from baseball is the sad end of a sorry episode," declared Giamatti as he read a prepared statement to the assembled media. "One of the game's greatest players has engaged in a variety of acts which have stained the game, and he must now live with the consequences of those acts."

Without detailing the acts, the commissioner then described the investigative procedure that was followed and the reasoning behind it before concluding his statement with: "The matter of Mr. Rose is now closed. It will be debated and discussed. Let no one think that it did not hurt baseball. That hurt will pass, however, as the great glory of the game asserts itself and a resilient institution goes forward. Let it also be clear that no individual is superior to the game."

Besides declaring Rose permanently ineligible, the "Agreement and Resolution" stated Rose "acknowledges that the commissioner has treated him fairly in this agreement" and "Rose will conclude these proceedings before the commissioner without a hearing and the commissioner will not make any formal findings or determinations on any matter including without limitation the allegation that Peter Edward Rose bet on any major league baseball games."

In addition, the agreement stipulated that counsel for Rose, upon his authority, had taken steps to dismiss a civil suit filed against Giamatti and that Rose "acknowledges that the commissioner has a factual basis to impose the penalty provided herein, and hereby accepts the penalty . . . and agrees not to challenge that penalty in court or otherwise. He also agrees he will not institute any legal proceedings of any nature against the commissioner or any of his representatives, either major league or any major league club."

The document also contained the following provisions: "Nothing in this agreement shall deprive Peter Edward Rose of the rights under Major League Rule 15(c) to apply for reinstatement (and he) agrees not to challenge, appeal or otherwise contest the decision of, or the procedure employed by, the commissioner or any future commissioner in the evaluation of any application for reinstatement" and "Nothing in this agreement shall be deemed either an admission or denial by Peter Edward Rose of the allegation that he bet on any major league baseball game."

After reading his 891-word statement, Giamatti opened the session to questions. Although the "Agreement and Resolution" stated the commissioner would "not make any formal findings" on allegations that Rose bet on games, Giamatti responded to a direct query on the subject by saying: "In the absence of a hearing and therefore in the absence of any evidence to the contrary, I am confronted by the factual record of the Dowd report, and on the basis of that, yes, I have concluded that he (Rose) bet on baseball." And, he was asked, on the Reds? "Yes," the commissioner replied. He said he considered Rose's acceptance of permanent ineligibility as a no-contest plea to the charges.

Asked about the possibility of reinstatement, Giamatti commented: "Is there a deal, a secret number? No. Is there anything automatic? Absolutely not . . . There

is a standing major league rule on the subject . . . The burden to show a redirected, reconfigured, rehabilitated life is entirely Pete Rose's."

The rule to which Giamatti referred— Major League Rule 15(c)—states: "No application for reinstatement from the Ineligible List may be made until the lapse of one year from the date of placement on the Ineligible List." Reuven Katz, one of Rose's lawyers, later confirmed there was no deal about reinstatement.

Shortly after the Giamatti news conference finished in New York, Rose was afforded an opportunity to discuss the situation with the media in Cincinnati. The interview room at Riverfront Stadium was packed to overflowing to hear Rose's side of the agreement that could keep him out of the sport for life. Like the commissioner's session, the Rose news conference was carried live on national television.

"As your can imagine, it's a very sad day," an ashen-faced, solemn Rose began as his lawyers looked on. Showing no emotion but with his voice wavering, he continued: "I've been in baseball for three decades, and to think I'm going to be out of baseball for a very short period of times hurts . . . I've made some mistakes, and I'm being punished for those mistakes . . . However, the settlement is fair. Especially the wording that says there's no finding that I bet on baseball . . . Regardless of what the commissioner said today, I did not bet on baseball."

The game's all-time hit leader, who in the past seldom lacked for the right answer or a witty comment, became clearly uncomfortable at times during the questioning that ensued. Asked if he expected to be reinstated, he replied: "Absolutely. Without a doubt." He added he would apply for reinstatement as soon as the rules permit.

On a question about the Hall of Fame, Rose commented: "I did my part to get in the Hall of Fame. It's up to you people who vote (members of the Baseball Writers' Association)." As for his gambling habits, he said: "I don't think I have a gambling problem—not at all . . . I won't be seeking help of any kind."

Another person asked: "If you're innocent, why did you agree to this (the commissioner's ruling)?" Rose stood silent for several seconds before stepping aside to let Katz respond. In a carefully worded answer, Rose's lawyer noted that Rose had confessed during a meeting with Dowd to certain indiscretions, such as betting with bookmakers and consorting with felons, that likewise fall under Major League

Rule 21. (Rule 21(f) says that "conduct not in the best interests of baseball"—whatever that conduct may be—is subject to penalty, including permanent ineligibility.)

The formal conclusion of the investigation, as enunciated in the "Agreement and Resolution," was viewed by baseball officials and the legal community as a reaffirmation of the authority of the commissioner as spelled out in the Professional Baseball Rules. Federal courts had upheld this authority on several previous occasions, but it was threatened for a time by the suit that Rose's attorneys had filed.

The 225-page report prepared by Dowd, together with seven volumes of exhibits containing depositions, statements, documents, etc., had been turned over to Giamatti on May 9. Two days later, copies of all the material were hand-delivered to the offices of Rose's attorney, Katz, by a representative of the commissioner. In a covering letter, Giamatti stressed that the report, which he had copyrighted, was to be kept confidential. It wasn't until June 26, when the court released the documents, that the media had access to them. In the meantime, publications throughout the country carried stories about some of Rose's alleged activities following investigations by their writers. Many of the articles dealt with the same incidents that were investigated by Dowd and his staff.

The Dowd report was based largely on the sworn, voluntary, corroborated testimony of Ronald Peters and Paul Janszen. Peters, a bookmaker and owner of Jonathan's Cafe in Franklin, O., 40 miles north of Cincinnati, was sentenced to two years in prison on June 16 for cocaine distribution and failure to report $80,000 in gambling and bookmaking income on his 1985 tax return. Janszen, a body-builder friend of Rose's, was sentenced to six months in a Cincinnati halfway house after pleading guilty in January to evading taxes on the sale of steroids.

Numerous others among the 40 persons interviewed by Dowd and his investigative team corroborated the testimony of Peters and Janszen. The list included Danita Marcum, Janszen's girlfriend; Dave Morgan, an associate of Peters'; Michael Fry, former co-owner of Gold's Gym, where Rose and Janszen worked out; David Bernstein, a friend of Janszen's, and Mark Stowe, assistant clubhouse attendant with the Reds. Also supporting the charges were betting records kept by Peters and Janszen, three betting sheets in Rose's handwriting, telephone records, checks signed by Rose and Katz, a tape-recorded conversation that Peters had with another Rose counsel (Robert Pitcairn) and a tape-recorded conversation between Janszen and Michael Bertolini, an associate of Rose's and a baseball memorabilia dealer in Brooklyn, N.Y.

Some of the salient points contained in the Dowd report:

• Conclusions reached by Dowd were that Rose bet on baseball games, including games played by the Reds, in 1985, 1986 and 1987, and that Rose usually had some other person place his bets. Most of Rose's bets in 1985 and 1986 were placed with Peters by Tommy Gioiosa. In a 359-page deposition taken by Dowd on April 20-21, Rose acknowledged that Gioiosa lived with him for about five years starting in 1978 and that he placed bets with Gioiosa on football and basketball games in the 1984-1988 time frame, but under oath Rose denied ever betting on baseball games. (Gioiosa, who declined on the advice of counsel to cooperate in the investigation, was convicted by a federal jury in Cincinnati on September 12 of conspiring to distribute cocaine and to hide Rose's racetrack winnings from the IRS.)

• Fry testified he made cash loans of $17,000 and $30,000 to Rose to pay his gambling debts in the fall of 1985. (Five weeks prior to the April 11 interview, Fry was sentenced to eight years in prison on cocaine-distribution and income-tax charges.)

• Early in 1986, Peters claimed Rose owned him $24,000 in gambling debts. Rose's bank records show he wrote four checks for $8,000 each in February 1986, one to Gioiosa, one to Fry and two to "cash." Peters identified three of the checks as the ones presented to him by Gioiosa to pay off the debt.

• Peters testified that late in 1986 he refused to take any more bets because Rose owed him $34,000 in gambling debts and refused to pay. Rose subsequently began placing bets with an unidentified New York bookmaker through Bertolini. Records of Rose's account at a Cincinnati savings and loan show he wrote 29 checks in amounts ranging from $5,000 to $9,000—and totaling $227,000—in a three-month period beginning early in October 1986. When the report was written, Dowd had received photocopies of only 11 of the checks; each was for $8,000, each was made out to a fictitious payee, and Rose admitted all had been sent to Bertolini. Other bank records revealed Rose signed on loans for Bertolini of $43,000 in May 1987 and $50,000 in September 1987, both with the same Cincinnati bank. In a tape-recorded conversation in April 1988, Bertolini told Janszen that Rose owed him and the New York bookie around $200,000 and that Rose arranged the loans to pay off the gambling debts. (Upon advice of counsel, Bertolini declined to submit to an interview by Dowd's staff or to produce records of his two companies, Sports Images Inc., and Pete Rose Hit King Marketing Inc.)

• In 1987, Rose also placed bets through Janszen with a Staten Island, N.Y., bookmaker known at the time only as "Val." Janszen's records indicated Rose lost $67,900 to Val from April 7 to May 13 that year. When Rose failed to pay, Val refused to take any more of his bets. Janszen said he personally paid Val approximately $30,000 of his own money on Rose's behalf because of concern Val might otherwise expose Rose and his baseball gambling. (Early in July, the commissioner's investigators learned that "Val" was Richard Troy, who was among 33 persons arrested in October 1988 in a series of gambling raids in Staten Island, Brooklyn and Queens. Records found in Troy's home included Janszen's telephone number and next to it the names Janszen and Rose. Troy was indicted on charges of promoting gambling.)

• Before Peters would agree to resume taking Rose's bets in May 1987, he told Janszen that he wanted the $34,000 he said Rose still owned him. After relaying the message to Rose, Janszen said Rose responded that he had authorized Katz during spring training of 1987 to issue a check for $34,000 to Gioiosa to pay off a debt to Peters. Janszen obtained a copy of the canceled check, dated March 12, 1987, from Rose and showed it to Peters to demonstrate Rose's good faith.

• There were three pages of handwritten records covering bets from April 8-11, 1987, which an expert determined were in Rose's handwriting; 22 pages from a notebook that Janszen testified reflected the bets he and his girlfriend (Marcum) placed for Rose from April 8 to May 12, 1987, and copies of Peters' betting records covering bets by Rose from May 17 to July 3, 1987, that listed bets totaling $852,600 on 390 baseball games, including 52 games involving the Reds. The sheets showed Rose bet $2,000 per game most of the time, but listed 69 games on which he wagered more than $2,500 each. The largest wager was shown as $4,800 on the Mets vs. Atlanta on April 12, 1987—a game won by the Braves. The biggest bets on the Reds were $4,000 on the April 28-29, 1987, games against Atlanta; again, the Braves

won on both occasions. All of the bets on the Reds were for them to win.

• Bernstein testified he visited Janszen at his apartment every Friday night for a period early in 1987 and that on each occasion Rose called, instructing Janszen on which teams to bet, and that Janszen then phoned the bets to Peters. Bernstein also said he went to several Reds games with Janszen and witnessed him give hand signals—from their seats behind home plate —to Rose to indicate how he stood on his bets because the Riverfront Stadium scoreboard that normally carried scores of other games was out of order. He explained that Janszen kept abreast of the scores by calling a sports hot line from a stadium pay phone. (When the allegation appeared in the April 3 issue of Sports Illustrated and a newspaper reporter subsequently asked Rose about it, he said it was preposterous because "the scoreboard has never not worked." However, a Reds official confirmed the scoreboard was out of order for 18 games from April 17 to May 28, 1987.)

• When Rose's betting with Peters stopped in July 1987, Janszen estimated he was owed approximately $44,000 by Rose. Janszen said he met some months later with Rose's attorney, Katz, told him about the gambling he had done for Rose and said he "needed some of the money he loaned Rose." Subsequently, Janszen received a check drawn on Rose's account for $10,000. The check, dated March 18, 1988, bore the notation "for loan."

• Upon Rose's return from a meeting in the commissioner's office on February 20, 1989, Stowe said Rose told him that he was betting with Janszen and that Janszen claimed Rose owned him money.

The February 20 meeting was the first indication that Rose might be in trouble. In response to a summons from then-Commissioner Peter Ueberroth, the Cincinnati manager flew from the Reds' Plant City, Fla., training base to New York. Besides Ueberroth and Rose, those attending the session at Major League Baseball's headquarters were Commissioner-elect Giamatti and his new deputy, Fay Vincent; Edwin Durso, executive vice president and chief operating officer in the commissioner's office, and two of Rose's attorneys, Katz and Pitcairn. No details of what transpired during the one-hour meeting were released, but within days reports circulated that Rose's gambling was the subject.

A Cincinnati television station had disclosed that Rose was rumored to have been a betting partner in a $265,669.20

Pik-Six payoff on January 25 at Turfway Park in Florence, Ky., across the Ohio River from Cincinnati. Arnold Metz, a former Riverfront Stadium employee and friend of Rose's, had signed for the two winning tickets. Questioned about the incident by the media, the Reds' manager denied any involvement, but a few days later Jerry Carroll, co-owner of Turfway Park, confirmed that he and Rose had shared the winning tickets.

According to the Dowd report, Rose likewise denied he was a winner on the Pik-Six tickets during the February 20 meeting in the commissioner's office, but then admitted in his April 20-21 deposition that it was true. During the interview with Dowd, Rose disputed an account given earlier by Janszen that Rose owned 75 percent of a $47,646 Pik-Six ticket at Turfway Park on January 16, 1987. Janszen further claimed he and Gioiosa split ownership of the remaining 25 percent and that Gioiosa represented himself as the sole owner when he cashed the ticket. In his meeting with Dowd, Rose said he did not recall being at the track on that date, but when he was shown two $10,000 checks signed by him, dated January 16, 1987, and cashed the same day at Turfway, he acknowledged they established he was at the track on that occasion.

After simmering quietly for several weeks, the Rose situation reached a boil on March 20. In a carefully worded statement issued jointly by Ueberroth and Giamatti, the commissioner's office acknowledged for the first time that it was investigating "serious allegations" involving Rose. A few days later, the newest issue of Sports Illustrated hit the newsstands and in a one-page story reported it had been told "the commissioner has information that Rose may have bet on baseball games." It added: "One man linked to possible baseball betting with Rose is Ron Peters . . . Another is Paul Janszen . . . but he (Rose) told SI he has never wagered with bookies on any sport . . . (and) denied knowing Peters." The article also said that both Alan Statman, Peters' attorney, and Janszen had offered to sell their stories of how they placed bets for Rose, but that Sports Illustrated declined to buy them.

The revelations set off a firestorm of investigative stories that tantalized the public. Cincinnati's two major newspapers began publishing one or more front-page stories daily on Rose, and he became the prime topic of local television news reports and radio talk shows. Other newspapers in the area, as well as in New York,

Washington, Boston, Chicago and other cities, quickly joined in the probe. The upshot was that more than 100 reporters and cameramen frequently surrounded Rose in the dugout prior to spring exhibition games.

Rose broke his silence during a 20-minute meeting March 25 with four writers who regularly cover the Reds. He responded to numerous questions they posed, but when one asked if he had ever bet on baseball he said: "I'm not saying anything about that . . . My best comment is no comment." He denied rumors he owed around $500,000 in gambling debts when he left the Reds as a free agent in 1978, saying: "I have no idea what they're talking about." As for reports he sold some prized memorabilia, he acknowledged that Steve Wolter, his insurance agent, had the bat with which he made hit No. 4,192 in 1985 to break Ty Cobb's record. Wolter reportedly paid $175,000 for the historic bat and the ball. He also bought the red Corvette with the "PR 4192" vanity plates that Reds Owner Marge Schott gave Rose following the record hit. (According to the Dowd report, Rose testified he sold the Corvette to Wolter for $55,000, even though he valued it at $30,000, and claimed the car was given to him by General Motors, not by Schott. Rose contended Schott "manipulated the press to make it look like she had given him the car.")

Speculation that the Rose issue might be resolved before opening day—and possibly by March 31, Ueberroth's last day as commissioner—was squelched on March 28 when Dowd said the investigation would take "at least several more weeks." As a result, the rumors—and the media circus —continued into the season.

In mid-April, two Boston newspapers reported that Joseph Cambra, a convicted gambler from Somerset, Mass., had a 1975 Cincinnati World Series ring that he said was given him by Rose. Asked about it, the embattled Reds manager said he arranged for the Balfour Co. of Indianapolis, which made the rings, to produce a duplicate for Cambra. He added that Cambra, whom he described as a dear friend, "sent them a check for $3,150" in payment. A few days later, to counter rumors he had sold his '75 ring, Rose put his Series championship rings of 1975, 1976 and 1980 on display at Kentucky National Bank's downtown Cincinnati office. (The Dowd report revealed that Rose said he traded his original 1975 World Series ring to Barry Halper, a memorabilia collector and limited partner in the New York Yankees, for a bust of Ty Cobb and later had a new ring made. And although Rose denied in his deposition with Dowd that he ever placed any bets with Cambra, the Boston Globe on August 16 disclosed that a tape-recorded conversation between Cambra and another bookmaker on November 12, 1984, which was legally wiretapped as part of a gambling probe, contained mention of Rose contacting Cambra to place illegal sports bets and betting $6,000 on a pro football game.)

As the investigation dragged on, a few writers and broadcasters criticized Giamatti for the delay. They contended Rose was left to twist in the wind. Others in the media pointed out that in this litigious era, the delay demonstrated that the commissioner was proceeding cautiously because of awareness that his verdict had to be unassailable lest Rose be tempted to sue.

A decision announced by Giamatti on May 11, the day the Dowd report was delivered to Rose's attorney, appeared finally to set the stage for resolution of the investigation. Declaring Rose "is owed, in my opinion, an opportunity to review the report and its accompanying materials, and thereafter to respond to me if he wishes to do so," Giamatti set a hearing date for May 25 at 9 a.m. in his office.

In short order, Rose's battery of attorneys—Katz, Pitcairn, Roger Makley and Robert Stachler—began a series of legal maneuvers that lasted three months. The first came on May 19 when the lawyers asked for a 30-day postponement of the May 25 hearing, citing the need for additional preparation time. Giamatti granted the request and rescheduled the hearing for June 26.

The Rose legal team next filed a lawsuit against Giamatti in Hamilton County, O., Common Pleas Court on June 19. Claiming the commissioner's investigation wasn't "fair and impartial" and that he had prejudged the case, the 36-page suit sought to prevent Giamatti from deciding the case. It also confirmed publicly for the first time that Ron Peters had accused Rose of betting on Reds games and asked for unspecified monetary damages "which will fairly compensate him (Rose) for the destruction of his reputation as one of baseball's foremost living participants."

By taking the commissioner to court, Rose entered territory that four club owners had previously ventured into without success. Each of the four—George Steinbrenner in 1983, Ted Turner and Charles Finley in 1977 and Phil Ball in 1931—took legal action against decisions by commissioners. Steinbrenner obtained a temporary restraining order but later dropped his bid for an injunction. Judges upheld the authority of the commissioner in the case of the three others.

The hearing on Rose's suit opened in Hamilton County Court, located just four blocks from Riverfront Stadium, on June 22. Judge Norbert A. Nadel presided. More than 100 reporters, cameramen and fans jammed the courtroom. Two days of hearings provided the public with its first glimpse into the Dowd report when witnesses discussed portions of the testimony. Two expert witnesses hired by Rose's lawyers—Sam Dash, the No. 1 Senate investigator of the Watergate scandal, and George Palmer, former Ohio Court of Appeals judge—attacked the Dowd report as "flawed" and essentially "a prosecutor's brief." Because Rose's lawyers made portions of the Dowd report public as part of their lawsuit, Louis Hoynes, Major League Baseball's attorney, requested that the entire document be made public, but Nadel declined to do so.

Rose emerged victorious in that initial legal skirmish. On June 25, with the courtroom again packed, Nadel, in an unusual Sunday session that lasted just five minutes, issued a landmark ruling. Holding the commissioner had prejudged the Reds' manager, he granted a 14-day restraining order blocking the hearing that Giamatti had set for the next day. The ruling, described by some observers as a "hometown decision," also prohibited the commissioner and the Reds from taking any disciplinary action against Rose during the two-week period. A letter sent in April to Judge Carl B. Rubin, who was to preside at Ron Peters' trial, was cited by Nadel as "the strongest evidence" that Giamatti was not impartial. The letter, written by Dowd but signed by Giamatti, noted that Peters had provided "significant and truthful cooperation" in the Rose investigation and had been "candid, forthright and truthful with my special counsel."

One day after his ruling, Nadel released the Dowd report and accompanying material to the media under pressure from the Ohio Supreme Court, which said he had no reason to keep it sealed. This quickly set off another round of stories detailing the charges against Rose.

Over the next eight weeks the legal maze became even more tangled. On July 3, attorneys for the commissioner filed a petition for removal of the case to U.S. District Court in Columbus, O. Two days later, U.S. District Judge John D. Holschuh gave Rose's lawyers until July 17 to present arguments for keeping the lawsuit before a state judge in Cincinnati. Counsel for both sides agreed the protection given Rose against suspension or firing would remain in effect until three days after Holschuh's decision on jurisdiction.

While the judge pondered, Rose himself made a decision: Several days before the Reds' scheduled July 24 appearance in Cooperstown for the annual Hall of Fame exhibition game, he announced he was going to pass up the visit. One of those to be inducted into the Hall of Fame on July 23 was his longtime former teammate, Johnny Bench, and Rose said he didn't want the "media circus" that was trailing him to intrude. As it turned out, the Cincinnati players didn't make it to Cooperstown, either; the plane that was to fly them out of Montreal that morning was grounded because of mechanical problems. Their absence forced the Boston Red Sox to stage an intrasquad game instead.

Holschuh effectively put the Rose lawsuit on hold on July 31. In a 47-page opinion, he ruled the suit belonged in federal court and set August 14 as the date on which he would hear Rose's request for a preliminary injunction to bar a hearing by Giamatti. He also extended the protection given Rose from disciplinary action to the same date and gave the manager's attorneys 10 days to appeal to the U.S. Court of Appeals in Cincinnati.

On August 17, a three-judge panel of the federal appeals court rejected the Rose petition appealing Holschuh's ruling and agreed Holschuh had applied "settled law" in deciding to keep the suit in federal court rather than returning it to Hamilton County Common Pleas Court. The following day, Holschuh set August 28 for the start of the hearing on Rose's request for a preliminary injunction.

Shortly after learning of the appeals-court decision, Katz phoned Giamatti's deputy, Vincent, to seek to negotiate a settlement. It later was disclosed that they previously had met three times in hopes of striking a deal—on April 29 in Dayton, O., and in New York on July 16 and July 27. Vincent originally proposed that Rose agree to wait seven years before applying for reinstatement. Later, he decided Rule 15(c) was applicable. Once the formal wording of the "Agreement and Resolution" was finally hammered out by attorneys representing both sides, Rose signed the document in Cincinnati at 4 p.m. on August 23, and the next day Giamatti announced the verdict.

For Rose, the commissioner's decision not only terminated his tenure as manager of the Reds, but also meant he was barred from any association with professional baseball as long as his name is on the Ineligible List. The 48-year-old legend known as Charlie Hustle is prohibited from visiting the clubhouse or playing field, from participating in old-timer games and from accepting any position in baseball, even as a broadcaster.

Rose was the 15th man to be placed on the permanently ineligible roll since the office of commissioner was established late in 1920. All of the others were banned by baseball's first commissioner, Kenesaw M. Landis. None ever was reinstated. Prior to Rose, the last person to draw a lifetime suspension was William D. Cox. Shortly after Cox bought the Philadelphia Phillies in 1943, Landis banished him for betting on his own team. Most prominent of those declared permanently ineligible by Landis were the eight members of the Chicago White Sox who were implicated in the 1919 World Series scandal—Shoeless Joe Jackson, Ed Cicotte, Happy Felsch, Chick Gandil, Swede Risberg, Buck Weaver, Claude Williams and Fred McMullin. Others tossed out were Gene Paulette and Benny Kauff in 1921, Phil Douglas in 1922 and Jimmy O'Connell and coach Cozy Dolan in 1924.

Curiously, in the midst of the Rose investigation, Giamatti was petitioned by the South Carolina Senate to reinstate Joe Jackson, the majors' third leading hitter of all time with a career .356 average and a South Carolina native. Jackson, who died in 1951, was the best-known player to be banned prior to Rose. In a July 31 letter to a South Carolina state legislator, Giamatti turned down the request, declaring he did "not wish to play God with history."

In the aftermath of his banishment, Rose said he felt Giamatti had double-crossed him with his public comment that he believed Rose had bet on baseball.

"I was dumbfounded that he would say that," Rose said in an interview. "The only reason I signed that agreement was that it had no finding that I bet on baseball."

Upon learning of the comment, Giamatti said Rose apparently was misinformed about the agreement.

"I'm saddened to hear this view (by Rose)," Giamatti declared. "I was very clear about the fact that I was not going to be constrained from saying what I thought was the case. The agreement was reached to acquiesce in their desire to avoid a hearing. The document says I have a formal basis for the sanction I imposed."

Legal costs incurred by Major League

Baseball and Rose during the legal skirmishing were estimated at nearly $3 million, including around $500,000 by Rose. The termination of his contract with Cincinnati, which was to run through October 30, 1990, and pay $500,000 per season, cost Rose roughly $678,000. Several sponsors also dropped him.

Rose offset some of his losses with an appearance as a pitchman on the Cable Value Network in Minneapolis less than 12 hours after his suspension was announced. He made another appearance on the home shopping network the following night and then again several weeks later to hawk a "Pete Rose Autographed Plaque" at $79.92, autographed baseballs at $39.94, bats and other memorabilia. Rose claimed that in four hours on the first two appearances he generated $1.2 million in products sold and was paid $100,000.

Disclosures about Rose's betting continued even after his suspension. In a story in the New York Times on August 27, Murray Chass reported that a source close to baseball's investigation revealed that telephone records indicated Rose made calls to Dominick Basso, a Chicago bookmaker, from September 1987 through January 8, 1989. At the news conference the day he was banned, Rose denied he knew anyone in Chicago named Basso.

Appearing on the nationwide Phil Donahue television show on November 8, Rose admitted during a conversation about his gambling: "It's difficult to swallow, with the evidence, that you never bet on baseball." A few days later in a telephone interview with an Associated Press writer, Rose said he had done some reflecting, had decided he might indeed have been a compulsive gambler and planned to begin a treatment program for the problem.

Meantime, there were indications that Rose's troubles might not yet be over. U.S. postal inspectors raided the Pete Rose Hit King Marketing offices in Brooklyn in October following receipt of approximately 70 complaints from people who sent for Rose autographs or sent items to be autographed and never received responses. Rose's publicist, Barbara Pinzkla, said Rose had no financial interest in the firm.

In addition, a federal grand jury in Cincinnati was studying Rose's tax returns to determine whether he hid income from gambling, autograph shows and sales of baseball memorabilia. One reason he sought to avoid a hearing before Giamatti, some observers speculated, was because his testimony could have been turned over to federal investigators and would have been admissible in court proceedings.

Baseball was still reeling from the lifetime suspension of Rose when it suffered another shocking blow—the death on September 1 of Giamatti. He succumbed to a massive heart attack that afternoon at his vacation home in a secluded, rustic area near Edgartown, Mass., on the popular resort island of Martha's Vineyard. Giamatti and his deputy, Vincent, had left New York City in the morning via chartered plane to get an early start on a Labor Day weekend break with their families.

"I dropped him off at noon on Martha's Vineyard and he seemed OK," recounted Vincent, who continued on to his home on nearby Cape Cod. Both Giamatti's wife Toni and their son Paul were at the vacation retreat. They found him unconscious and in full cardiac arrest before 3 p.m. Efforts by doctors to revive him were unsuccessful.

Giamatti, 51, was a chain smoker who once described cigarettes as his "primary vice." Medical experts declined to speculate whether his smoking or stress from the prolonged Rose case contributed to the heart attack. When Vincent was asked whether the ordeal might have affected his friend's health, he responded: "Obviously that's a medical question. If you asked me to guess, I would say no . . . I don't think it got to him at all." An autopsy revealed the commissioner had suffered a minor heart attack years earlier.

Giamatti's death came exactly five months to the day after he succeeded Ueberroth to become the game's seventh commissioner. His 154-day reign was the shortest of any of the seven. The only other commissioner to die in office was Landis.

Giamatti spent a good portion of his life at Yale University, first as a student followed by 12 years as a professor and then almost eight years as president. He was elected president of the National League in June 1986 and took office in the following December, succeeding Chub Feeney.

In his relatively short time in baseball, Giamatti demonstrated a strong belief in tradition, championed the interests of the fans and was a vigorous defender of the sport's integrity. He will be, of course, forever linked with Rose. In his second season as N.L. president in 1988 he suspended the Cincinnati manager for 30 days for bumping an umpire and nearly inciting a riot by the fans, and his entire tenure as commissioner was dominated by the Rose gambling investigation.

Angelo Bartlett Giamatti, who went from Renaissance scholar and Yale president to commissioner of baseball, was laid to rest on September 6 in the Grove Street Cemetery near the Yale campus in New Haven, Conn., the traditional burial site for Yale presidents. Attendance at the private ceremony was limited to his family and closest friends. Besides his widow, he was survived by three children.

Baseball honored Giamatti's memory by dedicating the World Series to him. The baseballs used in the fall classic carried his signature; the players, managers and coaches wore black arm bands; the umpires wore patches with the initials "ABG"; the stadium flags flew at half-staff, and the World Series program reprinted his baseball essay, "The Green Fields of the Mind." In addition, a 90-minute memorial titled "Celebration of Bart Giamatti and Baseball" was held in New York City's Carnegie Hall on November 15. An invitation-only audience of owners, general managers, scouts, agents, arbitrators, lawyers and television executives filled the facility to say a final goodbye.

To fill the void left by Giamatti's death, the 10-member major league Executive Council held a conference call on September 2 and agreed to name Vincent acting commissioner. Eleven days later, at their regular quarterly meeting in Milwaukee, the 26 club owners unanimously elected Vincent to serve as commissioner through March 31, 1994, when Giamatti's term was due to expire.

A graduate of Williams College and Yale Law School, Francis T. (Fay) Vincent Jr was baseball's first deputy commissioner. Giamatti appointed him late in 1988 to occupy that role once he moved into the commissioner's office. Although they attended Yale at the same time, they had been close friends only since the 1970s. Vincent, 51, quickly impressed club executives with his business and financial acumen. His quiet gentility, especially while serving as the commissioner's confidant and liaison in the Rose investigation, also made a strong impression.

Upon graduation from Yale, Vincent practiced corporate law for 15 years in Washington and New York. He then served briefly as an associate director of corporate finance for the Securities and Exchange Commission in 1978. Later that year, he was appointed chairman and chief executive officer of Columbia Pictures. When Coca-Cola acquired the firm in 1983, Vincent became executive vice president and held that position until he left the company in July 1988. During his tenure, Columbia released such highly acclaimed motion pictures as "Gandhi,"

"Tootsie" and "Kramer vs. Kramer."

Besides establishing the position of deputy commissioner, Giamatti restructured the office of commissioner shortly after taking over from Ueberroth. The move followed a two-month review that he and Vincent conducted with the help of a consulting firm, Strategy Associates. The new table of organization created three separate departments in baseball's headquarters. Giamatti himself assumed responsibility for overseeing baseball operations, player relations and public relations; Vincent was put in charge of broadcasting, special events, corporate sponsorship, licensing and publishing, and Edwin Durso, executive vice president, became responsible for legal, financial and security affairs. The trio also served as the decision-making council.

Giamatti's death and the departure two weeks later of Durso necessitated a further reorganization of the office. Durso, 36, left to join the ESPN cable network as senior vice president and legal counsel. He had held legal and management positions in the commissioner's office for 10 years. On November 1, Vincent filled one vacancy by announcing the appointment of Stephen Greenberg, son of the late Hall of Famer Hank Greenberg, to the position of deputy commissioner, effective January 1. Greenberg, 41, was managing partner of the Los Angeles law firm of Phelps, Rothenberg & Phillips and served as an agent for more than 100 baseball players. A Yale graduate and former student of Giamatti's, he played baseball in college and rose as high as Class AAA in the Texas Rangers' organization.

While the elevation of Giamatti in 1986 to head the National League and his subsequent elevation to commissioner were regarded as historic, the selection of his replacement as N.L. president likewise was precedent-shattering. The league's club owners broke the racial barrier in the game's top-echelon ranks by picking William D. White, veteran baseball broadcaster and six-time All-Star first baseman. White thus earned the distinction of becoming the highest-ranking black executive in the history of professional sports. He was elected unanimously during a February 3 conference call and officially assumed office on April 1 when Giamatti moved up to commissioner.

The National League's choice of White came just two years after remarks by Al Campanis, then vice president of player personnel for the Los Angeles Dodgers, on ABC-TV's "Nightline" left the sport awash in racial controversy. Ironically,

Campanis' former boss, Dodgers President Peter O'Malley, headed the five-man committee that recommended White to the owners. O'Malley denied that race was a factor in the decision, but three of the four others who reportedly were approached about the job also were black. They were Simon Gourdine, who had served as deputy commissioner of the National Basketball Association for 12 years; Gilroy A. Griffin Jr., an executive with the Bristol-Myers pharmaceutical firm, and Joe Morgan, former standout second baseman. Morgan reportedly declined candidacy because of lucrative business interests. The other person considered was Louis Hoynes, the National League's legal counsel for 19 years. He informed the committee he wasn't interested in the position.

As it turned out, White was an eleventh-hour candidate. A representative of Heidrick & Struggles, a New York-based executive search firm hired by the league, approached White about the job just 10 days before he was elected. In accepting, he gave up a lucrative contract as a television announcer with the Yankees and his role as broadcaster for CBS Radio. He received a four-year contract as league president with a starting salary estimated at around $200,000. This was said to represent roughly a $100,000 cut in pay.

White, 55, spent 13 years in the National League as a player. Upon his retirement after the 1969 season, he turned to broadcasting. He had been an announcer with the Yankees for the last 18 years. Yankees Owner George Steinbrenner had tried on more than one occasion to induce White to become the club's manager or general manager, but he declined. In accepting the National League presidency, he joined another former major league player, Dr. Bobby Brown, head of the American League, in the game's executive suite.

Two other black ex-players were appointed to new roles in baseball in September. Don Baylor, who retired following the 1988 season, was hired as special assistant to General Manager Harry Dalton by the Milwaukee Brewers on September 5. Nine days later, Joe Black, former pitcher, was named as special consultant on a part-time basis to the committee newly created by the commissioner's office to help players deal with personal problems and issues.

The sport's financial health received both some additional boosts and several sharp jolts during the year. On January 5, Commissioner Ueberroth announced the signing of a four-year, $400 million cable

package with ESPN to take effect in 1990, and CBS Radio renewed its tieup with major league baseball in May by agreeing to a four-year, $50 million contract, also effective in 1990. The deal with ESPN promised to revolutionize the presentation of the sport on cable TV. It calls for games to be shown four nights a week, with single games on Sunday and Wednesday evenings and doubleheaders on Tuesday and Friday nights. In addition, games on opening day, all holidays and during spring training also will be shown, bringing the total carried by ESPN each year to 175. The CBS Radio package includes the regular Game of the Week schedule plus the All-Star Game and postseason games.

The ESPN and CBS Radio deals, coming on top of the four-year, $1.06 billion contract signed with CBS-TV in December 1988, assured the 26 clubs of approximately $377.5 million a year in national television and radio revenue. This comes to around $14.5 million per team each season —double the amount received under the expiring contracts.

When Ueberroth became commissioner in October 1984, all except five teams reportedly were losing money. A report prepared by his office revealed the 26 teams enjoyed combined profits of $100 million in 1988 and $209 million for the 1986-1988 period. Besides increased revenue from television and radio, both nationally and locally, the clubs also were benefiting from baseball's corporate sponsorship and licensing programs. Eight of the biggest U.S. corporations were paying $1 million each annually in direct fees to be official corporate sponsors, and Major League Baseball Properties reported that gross sales of licensed merchandise in 1988 topped $1 billion—a gain of more than 50 percent over the previous year.

Taking note of the improved financial ledgers, Ueberroth, in his farewell address to the owners at their quarterly meetings in March, proposed the clubs freeze ticket prices. "We have had incredibly good luck in TV and radio negotiations," he said. "Let's pass that to the fans and have a voluntary situation (on a ticket freeze)." The suggestion was greeted with something less than enthusiasm by many owners, and a number of clubs increased ticket prices for 1990.

Not all of ownership's fiscal fortunes were good, of course. The clubs experienced a stiff financial blow with the announcement of monetary damages to be assessed in the first of three collusion cases filed by the Major League Players Association. In his August 31 ruling, arbitrator

Thomas Roberts awarded $10,528,086.71 to 139 players he decided were financially damaged for the 1986 season because of collusion by the owners. The 139 included players who were eligible for free agency after the 1985 season or were eligible for salary arbitration in 1986 but signed contracts instead of going to arbitration. The clubs immediately said they would place an amount equal to the award, representig $404,926 per team, in an escrow account. The players' association asked that interest on the money involved be added to the award. Roberts held out the possibility of additional damage awards for other elements of the case. These included the conspiracy's possible effect on multiyear contracts and on special covenant losses such as option buyouts, signing bonuses, performance and award bonuses and no-trade provisions.

Roberts' decision came almost two years after his initial ruling of September 21, 1987, in what came to be known as Collusion I. In that ruling he held that management had violated the collective bargaining agreement by substituting "a common understanding that no club would bid on the services of a free agent until and unless his former club no longer desired to sign that free agent." Four months later, he awarded free-look free agency to seven players—Kirk Gibson, Carlton Fisk, Joe Niekro, Donnie Moore, Tom Brookens, Butch Wynegar and Juan Beniquez.

During the 38 days in which Roberts heard evidence and arguments in the remedy phase of Collusion I, lawyers for the players' union offered three methods of computing the salary shortfall of the 139 affected athletes. The complex calculations produced totals ranging from $15,047,202 down to $7,265,295.63. By contrast, the clubs argued the total should be from $2.2 million to $4.4 million. After taking into account the clubs' challenges and averaging the players' figures, Roberts arrived at $10,528,086.71. The amount each player will receive was expected to be determined in additional hearings.

The award by Roberts was actually the second financial penalty levied in the collusion cases. Oddly, the first involved Collusion II and affected only one player and one team. On June 29, George Nicolau, who succeeded Roberts as baseball's impartial arbitrator, ordered the New York Yankees to pay $91,758.24 to Ron Guidry as salary he missed in 1987 because of the owners' collusion. Nicolau ruled in effect that the Yankees had docked Guidry that amount when he re-signed on May 1 for

an $825,000 salary for each of two seasons.

Guidry and seven other free agents had gone past the January 8 deadline in 1987 without signing with their old teams and consequently, under the rules, had to wait until May 1 to re-sign. Bob Boone, Rich Gedman and Doyle Alexander, who were in that same class of free agents, also lost pay because they didn't re-sign with their teams until May 1 or later. Nicolau said he would hear further arguments before deciding their cases. Another of the eight—Tim Raines—re-signed with Montreal on May 1 but did not lose any pay. The three others—Andre Dawson, Lance Parrish and Bob Horner—all joined new teams.

In a followup ruling on November 28, Nicolau granted Parrish, who by now was on California's roster, free agency until January 8. The arbitrator announced his decision after the owners' Player Relations Committee decided to no longer contest Parrish's free agency. Parrish was with Detroit when he opted for free agency after the 1986 season; he wound up signing with Philadelphia the following spring and was traded to California in October 1988. Two weeks after Nicolau's ruling, Parrish re-signed with the Angels after being offered $6.75 million for three years.

Still pending at year's end was a decision on the damages phase of Collusion II involving players who became free agents after the 1986 season. Twelve players from that group were awarded free-look free agency by Nicolau in October 1987. The players' association was seeking $60 million in damages in that case. Also pending was a verdict on Collusion III covering 1987 free agents. Nicolau had completed hearings in the liability phase of the case.

The inability of many club owners to control their checkbooks—the factor that led to collusion in the first place—returned to haunt management again late in the year when the newest crop of free agents became available. A total of 91 players who were eligible to do so filed for free agency by the November 13 deadline. This eclipsed the record of 89, set in 1977, the second year of free agency. Once the two-week filing period ended, a number of owners threw fiscal caution to the wind and, in an effort to land the cream of the available talent, resumed the bidding wars that once prevailed.

The full list of 91 players who opted for free agency follows:

American League: Baltimore—Keith Moreland, Dave Schmidt, Mark Thurmond. Boston—Oil Can Boyd, Nick

Esasky, Greg Harris, Dennis Lamp, Joe Price, Mike Smithson. California—Dan Petry. Chicago—Richard Dotson. Cleveland—Pete O'Brien. Detroit—Charles Hudson, Fred Lynn, Gary Pettis, Frank Tanana. Kansas City—Floyd Bannister, Bill Buckner, Steve Crawford, Frank White, Willie Wilson. Milwaukee—Terry Francona, Ed Romero, Robin Yount. Minnesota—Wally Backman, Carmen Castillo, Kent Hrbek, Shane Rawley, Jeff Reardon. New York—Rich Gossage, Mel Hall, Walt Terrell. Oakland—Chris Bando, Storm Davis, Rickey Henderson, Dave Parker, Ken Phelps, Tony Phillips, Matt Young. Texas—Rick Leach, Craig McMurtry. Toronto—Sal Butera, Tom Lawless, Lee Mazzilli, Lloyd Moseby, Mookie Wilson.

National League: Atlanta—Darrell Evans. Chicago—Scott Sanderson. Cincinnati—Dave Collins, Bo Diaz, Joel Youngblood. Houston—Kevin Bass, Bob Forsch, Greg Gross, Rick Rhoden, Dan Schatzeder, Harry Spilman. Los Angeles—Dave Anderson, John Shelby, John Tudor, Fernando Valenzuela. Montreal—Hubie Brooks, Damaso Garcia, Mark Langston, Pascual Perez, Bryn Smith. New York—Don Aase, Keith Hernandez, Tim Teufel (Teufel re-signed before the filing period ended). Philadelphia—Bob Dernier, Steve Lake. Pittsburgh—Doug Bair, Jim Gott, Neal Heaton. St. Louis—Danny Cox, Frank DiPino, Leon Durham, Rick Horton, Tony Pena, Ted Power. San Diego—Mark Davis, Carmelo Martinez. San Francisco—Bob Brenly, Terry Kennedy, Bob Knepper, Mike Krukow, Craig Lefferts, Candy Maldonado, Ken Oberkfell, Pat Sheridan, Chris Speier.

The first of the '89 free agents to switch clubs and benefit from the owners' new generosity was Kevin Bass, Houston outfielder. He signed a three-year, $5.25 million contract with San Francisco on November 16. One day later, Atlanta lured first baseman Nick Esasky from Boston with a three-year, $5.7 million package. During the next few weeks the free-agent sweepstakes pushed salary offers to new heights. The fattest contract went to Mark Langston when the California Angels landed the Montreal lefthander with a guaranteed five-year, $16 million deal.

Two other free-agent pitchers were lured away from Montreal. The Yankees grabbed Pascual Perez with a guaranteed three-year, $5.1 million pact, while St. Louis signed Bryn Smith to a three-year, $6 million contract.

Outfielder Kirby Puckett of Minnesota, who wasn't eligible for free agency, became the sport's first $3 million-a-season performer when he signed a three-year, $9 million contract on November 23. Six days later, Rickey Henderson, Oakland's free-agent outfielder, accepted a four-year, $12 million deal to remain with the A's.

Other free agents receiving new contracts worth at least $3 million a season were Robin Yount of Milwaukee (three years, $9.6 million), who remained with the Brewers, and Mark Davis, former San Diego relief ace, who signed a four-year, $13 million package with Kansas City on December 11. Four days earlier, the Royals landed another free agent, former Oakland pitcher Storm Davis, with a three-year, $6 million package.

Also, Minnesota's Kent Hrbek, a free agent, and Kansas City's Bret Saberhagen signed contracts that came close to the $3 million-a-year mark. For Saberhagen, the deal was an extension of his current contract.

A total of 110 players earned $1 million or more in '89, including 21 who were paid at least $2 million. For the first time ever, all 26 teams had at least one performer in the $1 million category. According to a study by the New York Times, which was made before postseason awards were announced, the average major league salary for the year was $490,829. With the acquisition of pitcher Frank Viola late in July, the New York Mets had four $2 million players and the highest average salary, $858,575. Oakland was next at $711,375. Viola and pitcher Orel Hershiser of Los Angeles were the year's highest-paid players at $2,766,667 each. Dan Quisenberry of St. Louis was next at $2,494,200, but the Cardinals paid him only the $68,000 minimum since Kansas City, his former club, was obligated for the remainder.

Others in the $2 million salary class, according to the New York Times' study, were Cal Ripken, Baltimore; Jim Rice and Roger Clemens, Boston; Willie Wilson, Kansas City; Kirby Puckett, Minnesota; Don Mattingly, New York Yankees; Rickey Henderson, Oakland; Dale Murphy, Atlanta; Rick Sutcliffe and Andre Dawson, Chicago Cubs; Eddie Murray, Los Angeles; Tim Raines, Montreal; Dwight Gooden, Gary Carter and Keith Hernandez, New York Mets; Andy Van Slyke, Pittsburgh; Ozzie Smith, St. Louis, and Jack Clark, San Diego.

The salary-arbitration process remained a prime factor in pushing up payrolls. A total of 135 players filed for arbitration in January. Only 12 of the cases actually went to arbitration, but the salaries for which the 135 eventually settled rose a collective 71 percent over their '88 pay. Hershiser wound up receiving the biggest raise ever. After asking for $2,425,000 in an arbitration filing, he agreed to a three-year contract that increased his remuneration from $1,100,000 to $2,766,667 annually.

Of the 12 salary disputes that went to arbitration, the players won seven. It marked the first time since 1981—and only the fourth time in 14 years of the procedure—that the athletes came away with more victories than the owners. The players who won their cases, with the team's offer in parentheses, were: Joe Carter, Cleveland, $1,630,000 ($1,150,000); Danny Jackson, Cincinnati, $1,150,000 ($865,000); Glenn Davis, Houston, $1,085,000 ($875,000); Steve Balboni, Seattle, $800,000 ($500,000); Tim Leary, Los Angeles, $670,000 ($525,000); Tim Teufel, Mets, $590,000 ($470,000), and Len Dykstra, Mets, $575,000 ($455,000).

The salaries of the five players who lost in arbitration, with the player's rejected figure in parentheses: Vince Coleman, St. Louis, $775,000 ($950,000); Walt Terrell, San Diego, $775,000 ($941,000); Pete Incaviglia, Texas, $475,000 ($828,000); Dion James, Atlanta, $400,000 ($540,000), and Albert Hall, Atlanta, $250,000 ($310,000).

Despite the prosperity being enjoyed by owners and players alike, a storm cloud hovered over the sport as the year drew to a close. The five-year Basic Agreement expired December 31, 1989, and the 1990 season was threatened by the possibility of another player strike or owner lockout unless terms could be reached quickly on a new industry code. Negotiations on a new collective bargaining agreement got under way on November 28. Shortly before the session began, it was disclosed that Barry Rona had resigned as executive director and general counsel of management's Player Relations Committee. Charles P. (Chuck) O'Connor, who had served as the PRC's outside labor counsel, took over as interim executive director.

Two franchises underwent changes in ownership during the year, the sale of a third club received formal approval and still another team was officially put on the block. The three teams operating under new management—all in the American League—were the Baltimore Orioles, Texas Rangers and Seattle Mariners. The club placed on the market was the National League's San Diego Padres.

American League owners formally ratified deals involving Baltimore and Texas in an April 18 conference call. The Orioles'

transaction actually was completed in December 1988. A partnership headed by New York businessman Eli S. Jacobs bought the club from the estate of the late Edward Bennett Williams for $70 million. Jacobs is chairman of the board of Memorex Telex Corp., the world's second largest manufacturer of computer peripheral equipment. Joining him in the purchase were Larry Lucchino, who worked nearly 15 years for Williams and recently had served as the team's acting president, and R. Sargent Shriver, brother-in-law of the late President John F. Kennedy.

After several earlier attempts failed, Eddie Chiles finally sold his 58 percent controlling interest in the Rangers on March 18. George W. Bush, chief stockholder of Harken Energy Corp. and son of President George Bush, headed a group of 15 investors, mostly Texas businessmen, who purchased the club.

The Rangers' minority owners included Ed (Rusty) Rose, Dallas banker; Richard Rainwater, Fort Worth investment banker; Bill DeWitt Jr., Cincinnati businessman whose father once owned the Reds, and Dudley Taft, a former part-owner of the Philadelphia Phillies. The purchase price of Chiles' holdings reportedly was $46 million.

George Argyros, who bought the Seattle team for $13.1 million in 1981, reached agreement August 22 to sell the Mariners for a record $77 million to a group of Indianapolis investors led by Jeff Smulyan and Michael Browning. The transaction was approved by owners of the other clubs at their quarterly meeting three weeks later. Smulyan heads the Emmis Broadcasting Corp., which owns 11 radio stations, making it the largest privately held chain in the United States. Browning is an Indianapolis real estate developer.

Under the new setup, Emmis Broadcasting owns the largest share of the Mariners—just under 50 percent—while Morgan Stanley & Co., Emmis' investment banker, holds 25 percent. Smulyan and Browning each took 10 percent, and the remainder is held by other Emmis executives. Two stipulations in the deal were that the team would not be moved and that one of the owners would establish residence in Seattle.

For the second time in three years, Joan Kroc announced October 17 that she was putting the San Diego Padres up for sale. Declaring "there's a lot of aggravation owning the Padres," she said she wanted to devote her time to other priorities. Mrs. Kroc, 61, has headed up the club since the death in January 1984 of her husband, Ray Kroc, founder of the McDonald's hamburger chain, who bought the team in 1974. She designated her son-in-law, player agent Jerry Kapstein, to handle discussions with prospective purchasers and said any buyer would have to agree to keep the team in San Diego.

Concerns over the Padres' front-office leadership added to Mrs. Kroc's problems. In February, Tal Smith, former Houston general manager, was brought in to oversee the club's daily operations until a permanent administrator could be hired. His firm, Tal Smith Enterprises, had served as a consultant to the club since the end of the '88 season, when Dick Freeman was named interim president following the resignation of Chub Feeney. Kroc took steps to solidify the organization by appointing Freeman president on a permanent basis March 14 and then inducing Tony Siegle, who was vice president of baseball administration with the Phillies, to take over the Padres' newly created position of vice president of player personnel on April 16.

Two other clubs welcomed new presidents during the year. The Toronto Blue Jays, who had left the position vacant since 1981, promoted Paul Beeston from executive vice president to president/chief operating officer in January. The death on September 29 of August A. Busch Jr., 90-year-old board chairman, president and chief executive officer of the St. Louis Cardinals, led to changes in that club's hierarchy. On October 30, August A. Busch III was elected chairman of the board, Fred Kuhlmann was elevated to president and chief executive officer and Mark Sauer was named executive vice president and chief operating officer.

The New York Yankees again experienced the biggest turnover in high-level executive personnel. In a two-month span, three executives quit. The departures began on August 29 when Syd Thrift resigned after barely five months on the job. He had joined the club as senior vice president of baseball operations on March 21 under a four-year contract calling for a reported $350,000 starting salary and had assumed some of the duties formerly handled by General Manager Bob Quinn.

Following Thrift's departure, Owner George Steinbrenner announced that George Bradley, vice president in charge of player development and scouting, was being given additional authority. Bradley and Quinn, Steinbrenner said, would be the club's "top two decision-makers." In October, both Quinn and John Ertmann,

the club's general counsel, resigned. Quinn immediately signed a two-year contract as vice president and general manager at Cincinnati, where he replaced Murray Cook, while Ertmann took a position with NBC Sports. Harding (Pete) Peterson, like Thrift a former Pittsburgh general manager, was named to succeed Quinn as the Yankees' general manager.

With the NBC and ABC television contracts with baseball expiring at the close of the year, reports circulated in mid-May that a group of individuals was seeking to established a new league in 1990 and had approached the two networks about their possible interest in televising games of the proposed circuit. The organizers later were identified as Richard Moss, a prominent player agent, and David LeFevre, former minority partner in the Houston Astros. Although nothing concrete developed on the proposed league, the National League announced in June following a two-day meeting of major league club owners that it would reveal a timetable for adding two teams within three months after a new Basic Agreement was reached with the players' association.

Approximately 200 former major league players returned to uniform late in the year to participate in the newly formed Senior Professional Baseball Association. Players had to be at least 35 years of age except for catchers, who could be no younger than 32. The eight-team league, operating in Florida spring-training cities, began its season on November 1. Each team was scheduled to play 72 games, with the regular season ending on January 31. Salaries were set at a maximum of $15,000 and minimum of $2,000, with a team salary cap of $550,000. Curt Flood was appointed commissioner of the league, which was the brainchild of real estate developer Jim Morley.

Prominent names among the players who joined the league included Bill Madlock, Bert Campaneris, Luis Tiant, George Foster, Paul Blair, Al Oliver, Rick Manning, Ferguson Jenkins, Rollie Fingers, Vida Blue and Mickey Rivers.

In another innovative move, the Class AA Eastern League sent a squad of 20 players to the Soviet Union in the fall on a 17-day "Diamond Diplomacy" tour. The trip was arranged by league President Charles Eshbach.

Only three of the eight postseason awards made to major league players and managers by the Baseball Writers' Association went to members of first-place teams. Outfielder Kevin Mitchell of San Francisco was a landslide winner of the

National League's Most Valuable Player prize, outfielder Jerome Walton of the Chicago Cubs gained N.L. Rookie of the Year honors and Don Zimmer, who led the Cubs to the N.L. East title, was voted the league's Manager of the Year.

Mitchell received 20 of the 24 first-place votes in beating his teammate, Will Clark, 314 points to 225, in the senior-circuit MVP poll. The voting for Most Valuable Player in the American League was much closer and saw outfielder Robin Yount of Milwaukee edge Texas outfielder Ruben Sierra, 256 to 228. Yount, who also gained MVP honors in 1982 as a shortstop, was the first A.L. winner to play on a team that had only a .500 record. Results of the MVP balloting in the two leagues, with 14 points for a first-place vote, nine for second and on down to one for 10th, follow:

American League

Player—Club	1	2	3	4	5	6	7	8	9	10	Pts.
Robin Yount, Milwaukee	8	6	5	4	1	1	2	1	—	—	256
Ruben Sierra, Texas	6	5	7	4	1	—	—	2	1	1	228
Cal Ripken, Baltimore	6	3	3	7	1	4	—	2	—	—	216
George Bell, Toronto	4	9	4	1	2	2	1	—	1	1	205
Dennis Eckersley, Oakland	3	—	1	2	6	1	—	3	1	—	116
Fred McGriff, Toronto	—	1	—	1	2	6	4	3	5	3	96
Kirby Puckett, Minnesota	—	—	3	3	—	2	5	1	3	—	84
Bret Saberhagen, Kansas City	—	3	1	1	4	1	—	2	2	1	82
Rickey Henderson, N.Y.-Oak.	—	—	—	1	2	3	8	—	—	1	67
Bo Jackson, Kansas City	—	—	—	—	2	2	4	2	1	—	46
Dave Parker, Oakland	—	—	1	2	3	—	—	1	—	1	44
Gregg Olson, Baltimore	—	—	—	—	—	3	1	3	1	5	35
Bert Blyleven, California	—	—	—	2	1	—	2	3	3	32
Dave Stewart, Oakland	—	—	1	1	1	1	—	—	1	2	30
Don Mattingly, New York	—	—	2	—	—	—	—	1	2	2	25
Joe Carter, Cleveland	—	—	—	1	—	—	3	—	2	—	23
Carney Lansford, Oakland	1	—	—	—	—	—	—	1	1	1	20
Nick Esasky, Boston	—	—	—	—	—	1	—	3	1	3	19
Tony Fernandez, Toronto	—	1	—	—	—	—	—	—	—	—	9
Mike Moore, Oakland	—	—	—	—	1	—	—	—	—	—	6
Wade Boggs, Boston	—	—	—	—	—	—	—	1	1	3
Steve Sax, New York	—	—	—	—	—	—	—	1	—	—	3
Alvin Davis, Seattle	—	—	—	—	—	—	—	—	1	—	2
Nolan Ryan, Texas	—	—	—	—	—	—	—	—	1	—	2
Chili Davis, California	—	—	—	—	—	—	—	—	—	1	1
Mark McGwire, Oakland	—	—	—	—	—	—	—	—	—	1	1
Mookie Wilson, Toronto	—	—	—	—	—	—	—	—	—	1	1

National League

Player—Club	1	2	3	4	5	6	7	8	9	10	Pts.
Kevin Mitchell, San Fran.	20	2	2	—	—	—	—	—	—	—	314
Will Clark, San Fran.	3	15	6	—	—	—	—	—	—	—	225
Pedro Guerrero, St. Louis	1	4	10	6	3	—	—	—	—	—	190
Ryne Sandberg, Chicago	—	1	4	9	6	2	1	1	—	—	157
Howard Johnson, New York	—	2	2	6	8	5	1	—	—	—	153
Mark Davis, San Diego	—	—	—	1	4	5	1	3	3	1	76
Glenn Davis, Houston	—	—	—	—	—	5	6	2	4	1	64
Tony Gwynn, San Diego	—	—	—	—	1	4	5	3	—	2	57
Eric Davis, Cincinnati	—	—	—	—	—	—	5	3	7	1	44
Mitch Williams, Chicago	—	—	—	2	—	2	1	2	2	3	41
Lonnie Smith, Atlanta	—	—	—	—	1	1	—	2	3	11	34
Jack Clark, San Diego	—	—	—	—	—	1	—	2	1	2	16
Jerome Walton, Chicago	—	—	—	—	—	—	2	1	1	1	14
Mark Grace, Chicago	—	—	—	—	—	—	2	—	—	1	9
Mike Scott, Houston	—	—	—	—	—	—	—	1	1	1	6
Bobby Bonilla, Pittsburgh	—	—	—	—	—	—	—	1	1	—	5
Brett Butler, San Fran.	—	—	—	—	—	—	—	1	—	—	3
Tim Raines, Montreal	—	—	—	—	—	—	—	1	—	—	3
Milt Thompson, St. Louis	—	—	—	—	—	—	—	1	—	—	3
Scott Garrelts, San Fran.	—	—	—	—	—	—	—	—	1	—	2

Baltimore's Frank Robinson (above) and the Cubs' Don Zimmer were baseball's best managers in 1989.

Bret Saberhagen, Kansas City ace, and Mark Davis, lefthanded relief specialist with San Diego, captured the Cy Young Awards in their respective leagues. Saberhagen, who also won in 1985, was given 27 of the 28 first-place votes in the A.L. poll and easily outdistanced Oakland ace Dave Stewart. Davis collected 19 of 24 first-place votes in becoming only the fourth reliever to gain the Cy Young prize in the N.L. A breakdown of the voting, with five points for a first-place vote, three for second and one for third, follows:

American League

Pitcher—Team	1	2	3	Pts.
Bret Saberhagen, K.C.	27	1	0	138
Dave Stewart, Oakland	1	24	3	80
Mike Moore, Oakland	0	2	4	10
Bert Blyleven, California	0	0	9	9
Nolan Ryan, Texas	0	0	5	5
Jeff Ballard, Baltimore	0	1	0	3
Dennis Eckersley, Oak.	0	0	3	3
Gregg Olson, Baltimore	0	0	3	3
Jeff Russell, Texas	0	0	1	1

National League

Pitcher—Team	1	2	3	Pts.
Mark Davis, S.D.	19	4	0	107
Mike Scott, Houston	4	14	3	65
Greg Maddux, Chicago	0	3	8	17
Orel Hershiser, L.A.	1	0	2	7
Joe Magrane, St. Louis	0	1	4	7
Tim Belcher, L.A.	0	1	1	4
Scott Garretts, S.F.	0	0	4	4
Rick Reuschel, S.F.	0	1	0	3
Mike Bielecki, Chicago	0	0	1	1
Mitch Williams, Chicago	0	0	1	1

Zimmer received 23 of 24 first-place votes in the BBWAA's National League Manager of the Year poll in winning handily over runner-up Roger Craig of San Francisco. In the American League balloting, Frank Robinson of Baltimore was the No. 1 pick of 23 of the 28 voters and edged Cito Gaston of Toronto. Tony La Russa of the World Series champion Oakland A's finished third.

Walton and Gregg Olson, Baltimore reliever, were runaway winners in the writers' Rookie of the Year balloting. Each received all but two of the first-place votes in his league. Walton finished with 116 points compared with 68 for teammate Dwight Smith, who drew the two other first-place votes and wound up second. Olson accumulated 136 points in the American League balloting, while runner-up Tom Gordon of Kansas City ended with 67.

AMERICAN LEAGUE

Including

Team Reviews of 1989 Season

Team Day-by-Day Scores

1989 Standings, Home-Away Records

1989 Pitching Against Each Club

1989 Official A.L. Batting Averages

1989 Official A.L. Fielding Averages

1989 Official A.L. Pitching Averages

Dave Stewart recorded his third straight 20-victory season (21-9) and then added four more wins in the A's American League Championship Series victory over Toronto and their World Series triumph over San Francisco.

A's Overcome Big Injury Jinx

By KIT STIER

Driven by the desire to win the world championship they had failed to capture the year before, the 1989 Oakland Athletics found the going much rougher the second time around. But when it was over, they left no doubt that they were the best team in baseball.

The A's, who had thoroughly dominated the opposition before running up against an overachieving Los Angeles club in the 1988 World Series, added a quality starter (Mike Moore) to the American League's best pitching staff before the '89 season. Already a juggernaut, the A's looked virtually invincible.

And then, as early as spring training, the A's began to break into little pieces.

The first to fall was right fielder Jose Canseco, the league's defending Most Valuable Player. Early in the spring he suffered a stress fracture in his left wrist that eventually required surgery. He missed Oakland's first 88 games.

Shortly thereafter, the disabled list became a gathering spot for former Rookies of the Year. First baseman Mark McGwire was next, missing 14 April games with a back injury. In May, shortstop Walt Weiss suffered a knee injury that shelved him for 65 games and kept him at less than full speed even after his return.

Then bullpen stopper Dennis Eckersley was lost for 40 games before the All-Star break. The A's went 20-20 during his recovery period. Starters Bob Welch and Storm Davis and reliever Gene Nelson also missed time.

But Oakland never fell far off the pace. In fact, the A's led the race for most of May and June, and at the All-Star break they were in second, 1½ games behind California.

By August 21, the A's had taken over first place for good. But it wasn't until they survived a test of their mettle in mid-September that their eighth A.L. West crown was assured.

On September 15-17, Boston swept the A's in a three-game series at Fenway Park, reducing Oakland's lead to 2½ games. The A's had looked awful in Boston, and they were faced with a three-game series at Cleveland and a four-game set at Minnesota, where they had lost three straight in June. If either of Oakland's top pursuers, California or Kansas City, was going to make its move, this was

the time.

But the A's rose to the challenge, sweeping the Indians and taking three of four from the Twins. Over the same weekend that Oakland was at the Metrodome, the Angels were swept in four games at Cleveland while the Royals were at home splitting four games with lowly Seattle. The A's returned home with their magic number at two and a 5½-game lead—at that point, the biggest advantage by any A.L. West team all summer.

"They could have come out of Boston on a real downer, especially since they were headed to a place they don't like to play," A's executive Bill Rigney said. "That's the sign of a real good team."

The best in baseball for a second straight season, if regular-season records are the barometer. The A's finished with a 99-63 mark, seven games ahead of Kansas City and only five games behind their phenomenal '88 pace. But this time they finished the job, beating Toronto in the A.L. playoffs in five games and sweeping San Francisco in the World Series.

"It's been so much nicer this time because of the adversity we had to face," third baseman Carney Lansford said. "When Jose went down in spring training, my heart stopped, and I know a lot of others did, too. He's a lot of offense and we had to battle, battle, battle. Then Mark went down and Walter and Dennis.

"It showed the character and the depth of this team. We had depth last year, but it didn't show as much. I can't say enough about the job Dunc (pitching coach Dave Duncan) and (Manager) Tony (La Russa) have done keeping us motivated day in, day out. It's a tough thing to do to convince players they can win after losing their top players."

La Russa, in turn, credited his players for their determination.

"You can take any part of this season and there was this guy missing, that guy missing, these guys missing, and we kept finding ways to win games," the manager said. "The one constant is our players."

The A's did make one key personnel move to improve the situation while their casualty list grew. On June 21, three young players were sent to the New York Yankees for former Oakland star Rickey Henderson. He arrived with a paltry .247 average and 25 stolen bases but went on to bat .294 and steal 52 bases for the A's, providing the offensive spark they needed at

SCORES OF OAKLAND ATHLETICS' 1989 GAMES

APRIL

Date		Score	Winner	Loser
3—Seattle	W	3-2	Stewart	Langston
5—Seattle	W	11-1	Welch	Bankhead
6—Seattle	W	11-3	Davis	Campbell
7—Chicago	L	1-7	Long	C. Young
8—Chicago	L	4-7	Perez	Moore
9—Chicago	W	4-2	Stewart	Reuss
10—At Calif.	W	4-0	Welch	Finley
11—At Calif.	L	1-7	Blyleven	Davis
12—At Calif.	L	0-5	McCaskill	C. Young
13—At Calif.	W	5-0	Moore	Abbott
14—At Chicago	W	7-4	Stewart	Perez
15—At Chicago	L	4-7	Reuss	Welch
16—At Chicago	W	3-2	Eckersley	King
17—At Seattle	L	2-7	Hanson	C. Young
18—At Seattle	W	5-3	Plunk	Reed
19—At Seattle	W	7-5	Stewart	Langston
21—California	W	10-6	Welch	Finley
22—California	W	4-3	C. Young	Blyleven
23—California	W	2-0	Moore	McCaskill
24—Toronto	W	5-4	Nelson	Henke
25—Toronto	W	3-1	Davis	Cerutti
26—Baltimore	L	1-2	Bautista	Welch
27—Baltimore	W	9-4	Burns	Thurmond
28—Detroit	W	2-1	Moore	Gibson
29—Detroit	W	3-2	Stewart	Alexander
30—Detroit	L	2-7	Tanana	Davis

Won 18, Lost 8

MAY

Date		Score	Winner	Loser
2—At Toronto	W	8-5	Honeycutt	Ward
3—At Toronto	L	0-2	Flanagan	Moore
5—At Detroit	W	5-3	Stewart	Tanana
6—At Detroit	L	3-6	Morris	Davis
7—At Detroit	W	5-4	Welch	Hudson
8—At Balt.	W	6-1	Moore	Milacki
11—At Balt.	L	2-6	Ballard	Stewart
12—Milwaukee	W	5-4	Burns	Plesac
13—Milwaukee	W	4-3	Welch	Bosio
14—Milwaukee	L	1-2	Crim	Moore
15—Milwaukee	W	12-2	Stewart	August
16—New York	L	2-3	Parker	C. Young
17—New York	W	8-3	Davis	Dotson
18—New York	W	6-2	Welch	John
19—Boston	L	4-7*	Stanley	Nelson
20—Boston	W	6-3	Stewart	Gardner
21—Boston	W	5-4	Burns	Clemens
23—At Milw.	L	1-9	Bosio	Welch
24—At Milw.	W	6-2	Moore	Birkbeck
25—At Milw.	L	1-4	Clutterbuck	Stewart
26—At N.Y.	W	4-0	Burns	Hawkins
27—At N.Y.	W	3-0	C. Young	LaPoint
28—At N.Y.	W	4-3	Moore	Parker
29—At Bos.	W	2-3*	Smith	Welch
30—At Bos.	W	4-2	Stewart	Smithson
31—At Bos.	L	3-4*	Smith	Plunk

Won 16, Lost 10

JUNE

Date		Score	Winner	Loser
2—Cleveland	L	3-5	Swindell	Moore
3—Cleveland	W	7-0	Welch	Candiotti
4—Cleveland	W	4-0	Stewart	Farrell
5—Minnesota	L	1-2	Oliveras	C. Young
6—Minnesota	W	1-0	Moore	Anderson
7—Minnesota	W	3-2	Welch	Viola
9—At Texas	L	8-11	Guante	Nelson
10—At Texas	W	5-1	Davis	Witt
11—At Texas	W	5-1	Moore	Brown
12—At K.C.	L	1-2†	Gordon	Burns
13—At K.C.	L	3-5	Appier	C. Young
14—At K.C.	W	2-1	Stewart	Leibrandt
16—At Balt.	W	7-5	Davis	Holton
16—At Balt.	L	1-5	Tibbs	Moore
17—At Balt.	L	2-4	Bautista	M. Young
18—At Balt.	L	2-4	Schmidt	C. Young
19—Detroit	L	4-6	Tanana	Stewart
20—Detroit	W	6-4	Nelson	Havens
21—Detroit	W	6-3	Moore	Schwabe
22—Toronto	L	2-4‡	Hernandez	Corsi
23—Toronto	L	8-10	Buice	C. Young
24—Toronto	W	7-1	Stewart	Stieb
25—Toronto	W	6-3	Davis	Key
26—At Minn.	L	3-4*	Reardon	Burns
27—At Minn.	L	5-11	Wayne	Nelson
28—At Minn.	L	0-2	Viola	Stewart
30—At Cleve.	W	5-0	Welch	Swindell

Won 13, Lost 14

JULY

Date		Score	Winner	Loser
1—At Cleve.	W	6-4	Moore	Yett
2—At Cleve.	W	11-3	Davis	Farrell
3—Kan. City	W	1-0	Stewart	Gubicza
4—Kan. City	L	1-10	Saberhagen	M. Young
5—Kan. City	L	9-12†	Crawford	Honeycutt
6—Kan. City	W	3-1	Moore	Aquino
7—Texas	L	3-6	Witt	Davis
8—Texas	L	4-5*	Russell	M. Young
9—Texas	W	7-1	Welch	Hough
13—At Toronto	W	11-7	Burns	Key
14—At Toronto	L	1-4	Stieb	Welch
15—At Toronto	L	1-6	Flanagan	Stewart
16—At Toronto	W	6-2	Moore	Cerutti
17—At Detroit	L	1-2	Henneman	Nelson
18—At Detroit	W	7-2	Davis	Beard
20—Baltimore	W	5-2	Stewart	Schmidt
21—Baltimore	W	3-2	Moore	Olson
22—Baltimore	W	3-1	Welch	Harnisch
23—Baltimore	W	3-2	Davis	Ballard
24—California	L	4-5	Fraser	Nelson
25—California	L	0-4	Finley	Stewart
26—California	W	9-5	M. Young	Witt
28—Seattle	W	8-7†	Burns	Harris
29—Seattle	L	6-14	Johnson	Davis
30—Seattle	W	5-3	Stewart	Holman
31—Chicago	W	3-2	Moore	Thigpen

Won 16, Lost 10

AUGUST

Date		Score	Winner	Loser
1—Chicago	W	2-0	C. Young	Hibbard
2—Chicago	W	2-0	Davis	Perez
3—Chicago	L	4-6	Pall	Welch
4—At Seattle	W	5-3	Stewart	Holman
5—At Seattle	L	5-11	Bankhead	Moore
6—At Seattle	W	2-1	Davis	Dunne
7—At Seattle	L	1-5	Zavaras	Welch
8—At Chicago	W	3-2*	Honeycutt	Pall
9—At Chicago	L	2-3†	McCarthy	Corsi
10—At Chicago	W	4-1	Davis	Rosenberg
11—At Calif.	W	5-0	Moore	Witt
12—At Calif.	W	8-3	Welch	Abbott
13—At Calif.	L	3-4	Blyleven	Stewart
15—Cleveland	W	5-2	Davis	Nichols
16—Cleveland	L	3-6	Olin	Honeycutt
17—Cleveland	W	1-0	Welch	Farrell
18—Minnesota	L	3-4	Smith	Stewart
19—Minnesota	W	5-4*	Davis	Wayne
20—Minnesota	W	5-0	Moore	Anderson
21—At Detroit	W	6-1	C. Young	Tanana
22—At Texas	W	2-0	Welch	Ryan
23—At Texas	W	5-4	Stewart	Brown
24—At Texas	L	2-6	Jeffcoat	Davis
25—At K.C.	L	1-3	Gubicza	Moore
26—At K.C.	L	0-2	Saberhagen	C. Young
27—At K.C.	W	6-0	Welch	Gordon
28—At N.Y.	W	7-3	Stewart	Hawkins
29—At N.Y.	W	19-5	Davis	Cary
30—At N.Y.	L	5-8	Plunk	Moore

Won 18, Lost 11

SEPTEMBER

Date		Score	Winner	Loser
1—At Milw.	L	5-6*	Crim	Burns
2—At Milw.	W	7-2	Stewart	Filer
3—At Milw.	W	5-0	Davis	Navarro
4—Boston	L	5-8	Dopson	Moore
5—Boston	W	13-1	C. Young	Clemens
6—Boston	W	7-5	Welch	Smithson
8—New York	L	1-5	Mohorcic	Stewart
9—New York	W	7-0	Moore	Parker
10—New York	W	6-2	Davis	Plunk
12—Milwaukee	L	6-7	August	M. Young
13—Milwaukee	W	7-6	Eckersley	Crim
15—At Bos.	L	2-7	Clemens	Moore
16—At Bos.	L	2-5	Dopson	Davis
17—At Bos.	L	6-7	Harris	Welch
18—At Cleve.	W	4-2*	Eckersley	Olin
19—At Cleve.	W	5-1	Moore	Nichols
20—At Cleve.	W	8-6	Davis	Swindell
21—At Minn.	W	2-1	Welch	Aguilera
22—At Minn.	W	5-2	Stewart	Dyer
23—At Minn.	L	3-5	Anderson	Moore
24—At Minn.	W	9-3	Davis	Tapani
25—Texas	L	2-3	Hall	Burns
26—Texas	W	4-3	Eckersley	Jeffcoat
27—Texas	W	5-0	Moore	Moyer
28—Texas	W	5-3	Stewart	Arnsberg
29—Kan. City	W	4-3	Nelson	Luecken
30—Kan. City	L	1-6	Saberhagen	Burns

Won 17, Lost 10

OCTOBER

Date		Score	Winner	Loser
1—Kan. City	W	4-3†	Corsi	Leach

Won 1, Lost 0

*10 innings. †11 innings. ‡13 innings.

Despite a long stint on the disabled list, Dennis Eckersley saved 33 games and headed the A's talented bullpen corps.

the top of the lineup. The left fielder wound up leading the league in steals for the ninth time with 77 and also was tops in walks (126) and runs (113, tied with Boston's Wade Boggs).

Oakland also got a big lift from designated hitter Dave Parker, who was hurt much of 1988 but came back to hit 22 home runs and drive in a team-high 97 runs. The other big guns for the A's were McGwire, who produced 33 homers and 95

runs batted in despite hitting just .231; Lansford, who just missed out on the A.L. batting crown with a .336 average; center fielder Dave Henderson (15 homers, 80 RBIs), and Canseco, whose wrist healed in time for him to muscle up for 17 homers and 57 RBIs in just 65 games.

Until Canseco returned and Rickey Henderson arrived, the outfield corners were virtually devoid of power, but the A's got by using such players as Stan Javier (.248), rookie Lance Blankenship (.232) and Luis Polonia, who hit .286 before leaving in the Henderson deal.

La Russa made good use of his entire roster. Mike Gallego (.252) stepped in for Weiss at shortstop and played so well, Weiss (.233) couldn't get the full-time job back after he returned. Tony Phillips (.262) was La Russa's most frequent choice at second base, but he played the outfield and the other three infield spots, too. Catcher Terry Steinbach batted .273 and was solid behind the plate, but backup Ron Hassey also contributed, particularly when Welch was pitching.

Welch was one of four Oakland pitchers who won at least 17 games and helped the A's lead the league in ERA a second straight year. They were even more dominant in '89, lowering their ERA from 3.44 to 3.09.

The ace of the staff again was Dave Stewart, who went 21-9 with a 3.32 ERA and became the only player in the '80s to win 20 games three times. Moore, a free-agent acquisition from Seattle, posted career highs with 19 wins and a 2.61 ERA, while Davis won 19 games despite a 4.36 ERA. Welch went 17-8 with a 3.00 ERA while working almost exclusively with Hassey behind the plate. The only soft spot in the rotation was Curt Young (5-9).

Led by Eckersley, the bullpen was the league's best. Eckersley saved 33 games despite his 40-game layoff, while Rick Honeycutt, Todd Burns and Nelson combined for 23 saves. When Eckersley was healthy, the others provided fine middle relief.

"We've always been a pitching-strong club," Stewart said.

That the pitching staff excelled even with Eckersley, Welch, Davis and Nelson doing time on the disabled list was typical of the A's in '89.

"This team has gone through a lot of adversity by playing short and never flinched," La Russa said. "Take out Jose, Walter and Dennis and that's only part of the story. We played short one way or the other the whole time."

Not that you could tell.

Bo Jackson got off to a blazing start in 1989 and finished with 32 home runs and 105 RBIs despite tapering off in the second half.

Royals Win 92, Come Up Short

By STEVE CAMERON

A season cannot be defined solely with arithmetic, of course, but when the Kansas City Royals review 1989, they find a few numbers clinging to them like soot.

The first is 92, as in victories, equaling the third-highest win total in franchise history. The Royals won a world championship in 1985 with fewer regular-season victories than that.

But the next number is seven, as in the number of games the second-place Royals finished behind Oakland in the American League West.

And, finally, there is 18, the number of times the Royals were shut out in 1989. Manager John Wathan didn't need a calculator to figure out that Kansas City's unusually high shutout total had much to do with the gap between his team and the Athletics.

"You can't expect to be shut out that many times and contend for a division championship," Wathan said. "It comes down to striking out too much, failing to make contact when we needed to keep rallies alive. That and injuries kept us from battling Oakland right to the last day."

The Royals, who got off to a club-record start by going 16-8 in April, weren't actually eliminated until the last Wednesday of the season. But their inability to win on the road (37-44), on grass (25-37) and during the daytime (20-20) made it almost impossible for them to keep up with the A's. On the bright side, the Royals posted the best home record (55-26) in the major leagues, and their flair for come-from-behind victories (22 in their last at-bat) made them a more exciting team than in recent years.

Kansas City again had one of the league's top pitching staffs, producing a 3.55 earned-run average that ranked third. Bret Saberhagen led the majors with a 23-6 record, 2.16 ERA, 12 complete games and 262⅓ innings pitched and won his second A.L. Cy Young Award. His solid fielding also brought him his first Gold Glove. Mark Gubicza won 15 games and posted a 3.04 ERA despite a September shoulder injury. Tom Gordon won 10 games as a reliever, then joined the rotation and won seven more to capture A.L. Rookie Pitcher of the Year honors from The Sporting News. The bullpen, which had been a big question mark for the Royals, turned out to be a strength as both

Steve Farr and Jeff Montgomery (1.37 ERA) showed closer's mettle with 18 saves apiece.

The Royals also had some sock in the middle of their lineup. Left fielder Bo Jackson racked up career-best statistics with 32 home runs and 105 runs batted in, both team highs. Despite off-years from first baseman George Brett (.282, 12 homers, 80 RBIs) and right fielder Danny Tartabull (.268, 18 homers, 62 RBIs), the Royals were 50-25 in games with all three in the starting lineup. Obviously, the problem was that for more than half the season, injuries to all three prevented Wathan from playing them simultaneously. Another drawback was that Jackson struck out 172 times, Tartabull 123.

The catching was solid as 41-year-old Bob Boone not only helped the pitching staff and tutored young backup Mike Macfarlane, but also hit .274, drove in a bushel of key runs and added a seventh Gold Glove to his collection.

Another pleasant surprise was Jim Eisenreich, the onetime Minnesota prospect whose career was resurrected when proper medication arrested the symptoms of Tourette syndrome, a nervous disorder. Eisenreich led the team with a .293 average and 27 stolen bases, drove in 59 runs and played solid defense at all three outfield positions. From outsider in spring training to consistent No. 5 hitter behind Jackson down the stretch, Eisenreich made himself one of the most important Royals in planning for 1990 and beyond.

Eisenreich solidified his spot in the lineup after center fielder Willie Wilson went on the disabled list with a shoulder injury in May. Wilson, who had been hitting .192 at the time, came back in June and raised his average to .253 by the end of the season. Various injuries also allowed versatile Pat Tabler (.259) and rookie Matt Winters (.234) to see some outfield action.

The infield was steady, if not spectacular. Brett, who is underrated defensively, got the 2,500th hit of his career in September. Frank White was still smooth at second base, even with a nagging knee injury, but his 36 RBIs was his lowest total since 1977. Kurt Stillwell hit .261 with some decent pop (54 RBIs) and provided a good glove at shortstop, but third baseman Kevin Seitzer's 20 errors detracted a bit from a .281 average, his all-around toughness and a decent transition to the leadoff role.

SCORES OF KANSAS CITY ROYALS' 1989 GAMES

APRIL

Date	W/L	Score	Winner	Loser
3—Toronto	L	3-4	Key	Gubicza
5—Toronto	W	2-1	Gordon	Stottlemyre
6—Toronto	W	3-2	Montgomery	Ward
7—Boston	W	9-8	Montgomery	Smith
8—Boston	W	2-1‡	Aquino	Murphy
9—Boston	L	6-8	Dopson	Montgomery
10—Baltimore	W	3-0	Saberhagen	Harnisch
11—Baltimore	W	6-5	Bannister	Bautista
12—Baltimore	L	4-5z	Olson	Farr
14—At Toronto	L	0-3	Key	Leibrandt
15—At Toronto	W	10-5	Aquino	Ward
16—At Toronto	L	8-15	Wells	Saberhagen
18—At Balt.	W	7-4y	Gordon	Williamson
19—At Balt.	L	5-6	Schmidt	Leibrandt
20—At Balt.	L	0-2	Ballard	Saberhagen
21—At Bos.	W	7-4	Bannister	Dopson
22—At Bos.	W	7-3	Gubicza	Boddicker
23—At Bos.	W	10-0	Leibrandt	Gardner
25—New York	W	5-3	Saberhagen	Candelaria
26—New York	W	5-3	Gordon	Leiter
27—New York	L	2-3	John	Gubicza
28—Milwaukee	W	8-1	Leibrandt	Wegman
29—Milwaukee	W	4-3‡	Gordon	Plesac
30—Milwaukee	W	2-0	Bannister	Birkbeck

Won 16, Lost 8

MAY

Date	W/L	Score	Winner	Loser
2—At N.Y.	W	5-3	Gubicza	John
3—At Cleve.	L	2-6	Candiotti	Leibrandt
4—At Cleve.	L	1-3	Farrell	Saberhagen
5—At Milw.	W	5-4‡	Montgomery	Knudson
6—At Milw.	L	0-1‡	Krueger	Gordon
7—At Milw.	L	2-8	Bosio	Leibrandt
9—Cleveland	W	3-1	Saberhagen	Candiotti
10—Cleveland	W	3-2	Montgomery	Farrell
11—Texas	L	3-6	Ryan	Gubicza
12—Texas	W	4-3	Leibrandt	Witt
13—Texas	W	4-1	Aquino	Moyer
14—Texas	W	3-2‡	Montgomery	Guante
15—At Minn.	W	4-3	Bannister	Berenguer
16—At Minn.	W	8-1	Gubicza	Oliveras
17—At Minn.	L	3-4‡	Berenguer	Farr
19—At Detroit	L	0-2	Henneman	Saberhagen
20—At Detroit	L	1-2	Henneman	Gordon
21—At Detroit	L	2-4	Gibson	Gubicza
22—At Texas	L	1-4	Hough	Leibrandt
23—At Texas	L	8-10	Ryan	Aquino
24—At Texas	W	6-4	Saberhagen	Moyer
26—Detroit	W	6-3	Montgomery	Henneman
27—Detroit	W	5-1	Gubicza	Nosek
28—Detroit	W	9-5	Gordon	Trujillo
29—Minnesota	W	7-1	Saberhagen	Viola
30—Minnesota	L	1-7	Smith	Clarke
31—Minnesota	L	1-7*	Oliveras	Bannister

Won 14, Lost 13

JUNE

Date	W/L	Score	Winner	Loser
2—At Calif.	W	4-0	Gubicza	Finley
3—At Calif.	L	3-4	McCaskill	Leibrandt
4—At Calif.	L	1-5	Blyleven	Appier
5—At Seattle	W	5-3y	Gordon	Niedenfuer
6—At Seattle	L	2-5	Bankhead	Clarke
7—At Seattle	W	9-6	Gubicza	Swift
9—California	W	6-1	Leibrandt	McCaskill
10—California	W	5-4	Gordon	Minton
11—California	W	5-3	Leach	Abbott
12—Oakland	W	2-1§	Gordon	Burns
13—Oakland	W	5-3	Appier	C. Young
14—Oakland	L	1-2	Stewart	Leibrandt
15—At Cleve.	W	5-4	Saberhagen	Jones
16—At Cleve.	L	0-1	Black	Leach
17—At Cleve.	L	3-4	Bailes	Gubicza
18—At Cleve.	L	1-4	Swindell	Appier
20—At Milw.	W	8-2§	Gordon	Knudson
21—At Milw.	W	6-0	Saberhagen	August
22—At Milw.	L	2-3‡	Crim	Farr
23—New York	W	3-0	Gubicza	Eiland
24—New York	L	5-12	McCullers	Appier
25—New York	L	4-5	Hawkins	Leibrandt
27—Seattle	L	0-8	Holman	Aquino
28—Seattle	W	12-7	Gubicza	Harris
29—At Chicago	L	5-12	Perez	Leach
30—At Chicago	W	6-3	Leibrandt	Reuss

Won 14, Lost 12

JULY

Date	W/L	Score	Winner	Loser
1—At Chicago	L	4-6	Hillegas	Aquino
2—At Chicago	L	3-7	Hibbard	Appier
3—At Oak.	L	4-6	Stewart	Gubicza
4—At Oak.	W	10-1	Saberhagen	M. Young
5—At Oak.	W	12-9§	Crawford	Honeycutt
6—At Oak.	L	1-3	Moore	Aquino
7—Chicago	W	4-2	Leach	Dotson
8—Chicago	W	4-3§	Montgomery	Davis
9—Chicago	W	5-4	Gordon	Hillegas
13—At N.Y.	L	0-6	Hawkins	Gubicza
14—At N.Y.	W	14-5	Saberhagen	Eiland
14—At N.Y.	L	7-9	Guetterman	Farr
15—At N.Y.	W	7-1	Aquino	Guetterman
16—At N.Y.	L	1-10†	Cadaret	Leach
17—Milwaukee	W	3-2	Gordon	Filer
18—Milwaukee	W	9-4	Gubicza	August
19—Milwaukee	L	1-7	Bosio	Leibrandt
20—Cleveland	L	0-4	Swindell	Saberhagen
21—Cleveland	W	6-1	Aquino	Bailes
22—Cleveland	L	0-1	Candiotti	Gordon
23—Cleveland	L	5-17	Black	Gubicza
25—At Bos.	L	0-10	Boddicker	Leibrandt
26—At Bos.	W	7-4	Saberhagen	Price
27—At Bos.	L	2-7	Dopson	Gordon
28—Baltimore	L	3-4y	Williamson	Montgomery
29—Baltimore	W	5-0	Aquino	Schmidt
30—Baltimore	W	7-6	Farr	Olson

Won 13, Lost 14

AUGUST

Date	W/L	Score	Winner	Loser
1—At Toronto	W	2-1	Saberhagen	Stottlemyre
2—At Toronto	L	0-8	Cerutti	Gubicza
3—At Toronto	W	5-0	Gordon	Key
4—At Minn.	L	1-5	Anderson	Aquino
5—At Minn.	L	4-6	Berenguer	Farr
6—At Minn.	W	3-2	Saberhagen	Rawley
7—Boston	W	6-4	Gubicza	Harris
8—Boston	W	8-1	Gordon	Bolton
9—Boston	L	2-6	Boddicker	Aquino
11—Toronto	W	6-2	Saberhagen	Flanagan
12—Toronto	L	0-2	Stottlemyre	Gubicza
13—Toronto	W	8-3	Gordon	Cerutti
14—At Chicago	L	3-4	Patterson	Aquino
15—At Chicago	W	10-6	Leach	McCarthy
16—At Chicago	W	5-4	Saberhagen	Thigpen
17—At Seattle	W	4-2	Gubicza	Dunne
18—At Seattle	W	3-1	Gordon	Zavaras
19—At Seattle	W	13-5	Leach	Johnson
20—At Seattle	W	5-4	Crawford	Holman
21—California	W	4-2	Saberhagen	Fraser
22—California	W	4-2	Leach	Witt
23—California	W	6-4	Gordon	Abbott
24—California	L	0-5	Blyleven	Aquino
25—Oakland	W	3-1	Gubicza	Moore
26—Oakland	W	2-0	Saberhagen	C. Young
27—Oakland	L	0-6	Welch	Gordon
29—Detroit	W	12-8	Crawford	Searcy
30—Detroit	W	6-1	Gubicza	Alexander
31—Detroit	W	3-0	Saberhagen	Ritz

Won 21, Lost 8

SEPTEMBER

Date	W/L	Score	Winner	Loser
1—At Texas	W	5-3x	Luecken	Rogers
2—At Texas	L	3-6	Ryan	Leach
3—At Texas	W	13-2	Gubicza	Brown
4—At Detroit	L	1-5	Alexander	Saberhagen
5—At Detroit	L	2-10	Ritz	Gordon
6—At Detroit	L	5-11	Nunez	Leibrandt
8—Minnesota	W	6-0	Gubicza	Smith
9—Minnesota	W	3-1	Saberhagen	Aguilera
10—Minnesota	L	2-8	Anderson	Gordon
11—Minnesota	W	6-1	McWilliams	Dyer
12—Texas	W	6-5	Luecken	Rogers
13—Texas	W	3-2	Saberhagen	Hough
14—Texas	L	4-10	Jeffcoat	Gordon
15—At Balt.	L	2-5	Milacki	Crawford
16—At Balt.	L	5-7	Olson	Leach
17—At Balt.	W	7-0	Saberhagen	Johnson
18—Chicago	L	2-4	Jones	Montgomery
19—Chicago	W	5-3	McWilliams	Dotson
20—Chicago	L	2-7	Perez	Gubicza
22—Seattle	W	9-2	Saberhagen	Holman
22—Seattle	L	0-2	Swift	Gordon
23—Seattle	L	0-8	Bankhead	McWilliams
24—Seattle	W	4-1	Farr	Zavaras
26—At Calif.	W	4-0	Saberhagen	McCaskill
27—At Calif.	W	8-3	Gordon	Abbott
28—At Calif.	L	0-2	Blyleven	McWilliams
29—At Oak.	L	3-4	Nelson	Luecken
30—At Oak.	W	6-1	Saberhagen	Burns

Won 14, Lost 14

OCTOBER

Date	W/L	Score	Winner	Loser
1—At Oak.	L	3-4§	Corsi	Leach

Won 0, Lost 1

*5½ innings. †6½ innings. ‡10 innings. §11 innings. x12 innings. y13 innings. z15 innings.

Jeff Montgomery emerged in the second half as the Royals' stopper and finished with 18 saves and a sparkling 1.37 ERA.

The Royals got a .249 average from their designated hitters, 10th in the league. The most frequently used DH was Tartabull (55 games), followed by Tabler, Jackson and Bill Buckner. Tabler, Buckner (.216) and Brad Wellman (.230) also provided backup infield help.

The whole package produced the third-best record in the major leagues (tied with National League champion San Francisco), but it wasn't enough to win in the tough A.L. West. Wathan will always wonder how many wins he lost because of injuries.

"I'll remember all the guys we lost more than any other single thing about the season," Wathan said. "Every time we seemed to have it going, another key guy got hurt."

One of the first was Floyd Bannister, who was expected to win 13 to 17 games as a regular starter. But Bannister had shoulder surgery in June and was lost for the season. The Royals had gone 11-3 in games he started. And when the club's

other veteran lefthander, Charlie Leibrandt, went sour—he did not win another game after posting his fifth victory June 30—Wathan ran out all sorts of people as stopgap starters. Gordon and Luis Aquino had some strong games as starters, but both had long stretches of ineffectiveness.

Farr opened the season as the bullpen stopper, then was forced to undergo knee surgery after saving 17 games. Montgomery became a fine closer in his stead, but that switch and the use of Gordon and Aquino in the rotation left the Royals' middle-relief corps decimated.

As for the assorted injuries that dogged the everyday lineup, one statistic stands out: Seitzer was the only Royal who played in more than 135 games. And even when they were in the lineup, such players as Jackson, Tartabull, White and Brett often played at less than full speed.

"In a lot of ways," Wathan said, "it was a good year. But for a team which was thinking pennant from day one, it wasn't good enough."

Lefthander Chuck Finley blossomed in his second year as a starter, posting a 16-9 record and the league's second-best earned-run average (2.57).

Angels Rise Up From the Ashes

By TOM SINGER

In any other season, the California Angels would have been the year's Cinderella story. But in 1989, when unheralded San Francisco and Chicago realized their National League dreams and lowly Baltimore performed American League miracles that came up just short, the Angels were almost an afterthought. And yet it was only a late slide that kept the Angels from stealing the game's strongest division from its defending champion and producing the biggest upset of a surprise-filled year.

Given little chance of escaping the A.L. West's second division, California led the race for a total of 49 days, including July 7-31. The Angels played tag with Oakland for 4½ months, the two teams seldom more than one game apart, but spent their last day on top August 20.

There, California's charge hit a wall. A streaky team all year, the Angels hit a final skid from which they couldn't emerge and slipped to third, eight games behind the first-place Athletics. As a result, the season's achievements and the job Doug Rader did managing the revival were somewhat obscured by the team's finish. After all, when a franchise ends its 29th season still looking for its first pennant, embracing minor triumphs is hard.

"We haven't yet been in a World Series," General Manager Mike Port said. "That's still the goal. A lot of good can be said about the season, but the bottom line is we didn't win. We aren't satisfied, by any means."

At least they weren't embarrassed, as they had been in going 75-87 the previous two seasons. The Angels compiled the fifth-best record in the major leagues (91-71) and regained both their respect and their fans, increasing their home attendance by more than 306,000 (to 2.65 million).

The improvement was concentrated on the mound, where the Angels' staff earned-run average dropped more than a run in one season, from 4.32 in 1988 to 3.28 in 1989. The starters made the greatest strides, improving from 50-68 in '88 to 70-55 in '89.

The dramatic upswing was led by Bert Blyleven, who had been acquired from Minnesota in the off-season following the worst year of his career (10-17, 5.43 ERA). But the 38-year-old righthander rebounded to go 17-5 with a 2.73 ERA and

Veteran Bert Blyleven turned around his sagging fortunes by delivering a 17-5 record to California's 1989 cause.

a league-high five shutouts and was named The Sporting News' A.L. Comeback Player of the Year.

Three other spots in the rotation were solid. Kirk McCaskill overcame a history of injuries to improve from 8-6 to 15-10 with four shutouts. Chuck Finley blossomed in his second year as a starter, posting a 16-9 mark and finishing second in the league in ERA (2.57). And Jim Abbott skipped directly from college ball to the majors and turned in a fine rookie season (12-12). The weak link among the starters was former ace Mike Witt, who continued his premature decline with a 9-15 record.

It was a workhorse rotation, averaging 211 innings per man, but then it had to be in front of an erratic bullpen. Bryan Harvey's 25 saves reflected an increase of eight over his rookie total, but control problems made him unreliable. Of the bullpen's other 13 saves, eight belonged to equally inconsistent Greg Minton. Former starter Willie Fraser was adequate in

SCORES OF CALIFORNIA ANGELS' 1989 GAMES

APRIL			Winner	Loser
4—Chicago	L	2-9	Reuss	Witt
5—Chicago	W	6-2	Finley	King
6—Chicago	L	2-3	Patterson	Fraser
7—Seattle	W	2-1	McCaskill	Hanson
8—Seattle	L	0-7	Langston	Abbott
9—Seattle	W	13-5	Witt	Trout
10—Oakland	L	0-4	Welch	Finley
11—Oakland	W	7-1	Blyleven	Davis
12—Oakland	W	5-0	McCaskill	C. Young
13—Oakland	L	0-5	Moore	Abbott
14—At Seattle	L	5-9	Langston	Witt
15—At Seattle	W	9-2	Finley	Reed
16—At Seattle	W	10-0	Blyleven	Campbell
17—At Chicago	W	3-0	McCaskill	Hillegas
19—At Chicago	W	7-2	Witt	Long
21—At Oak.	L	6-10	Welch	Finley
22—At Oak.	L	3-4	C. Young	Blyleven
23—At Oak.	L	0-2	Moore	McCaskill
24—Baltimore	W	3-2	Abbott	Schmidt
25—Baltimore	L	1-8	Ballard	Witt
26—Detroit	W	1-0	Finley	Morris
27—Detroit	W	10-3	Blyleven	Hudson
28—Toronto	W	9-0	McCaskill	Stottlemyre
29—Toronto	W	4-3†	Minton	Ward
30—Toronto	W	1-0‡	McClure	Henke
Won 15, Lost 10				

MAY			Winner	Loser
2—At Balt.	L	3-4	Olson	Fraser
3—At Balt.	W	2-0	Monteleone	Milacki
4—At Toronto	W	3-2†	Harvey	Ward
5—At Toronto	W	5-3	Abbott	Cerutti
6—At Toronto	W	5-4	McClure	Ward
8—At Detroit	W	9-2	Finley	Alexander
9—At Detroit	W	5-1	Blyleven	Gibson
10—At Detroit	L	2-3	Hernandez	Harvey
12—New York	L	2-5	Dotson	Abbott
13—New York	W	6-1	Witt	John
14—New York	W	5-0	Finley	Hawkins
15—New York	W	4-3‡	Fraser	McCullers
16—Boston	W	7-2	McCaskill	Smithson
17—Boston	W	5-0	Abbott	Clemens
18—Boston	L	2-5	Dopson	Witt
19—Milwaukee	W	3-1	Finley	Clutterbuck
20—Milwaukee	L	3-5	August	Blyleven
21—Milwaukee	W	12-9	Petry	Wegman
24—At N.Y.	W	11-4	Abbott	Dotson
25—At N.Y.	L	6-8	Mohorcic	Fraser
26—At Bos.	W	5-0	Finley	Clemens
28—At Bos.	W	3-0	McCaskill	Dopson
29—At Milw.	W	12-3	Blyleven	Birkbeck
30—At Milw.	W	3-2	Abbott	Clutterbuck
31—At Milw.	L	1-4	August	Witt
Won 18, Lost 7				

JUNE			Winner	Loser
2—Kan. City	L	0-4	Gubicza	Finley
3—Kan. City	W	4-3	McCaskill	Leibrandt
4—Kan. City	W	5-1	Blyleven	Appier
5—Cleveland	L	3-7	Black	Witt
6—Cleveland	W	2-1	Petry	Yett
7—Cleveland	L	0-1	Swindell	Finley
9—At K.C.	L	1-6	Leibrandt	McCaskill
10—At K.C.	L	4-5	Gordon	Minton
11—At K.C.	L	3-5	Leach	Abbott
12—At Texas	L	0-4	Jeffcoat	Witt
14—At Texas	L	1-5	Ryan	Finley
14—At Texas	L	3-6	Hough	McCaskill
16—At Detroit	W	9-4	Blyleven	Schwabe
17—At Detroit	W	6-3	Abbott	Alexander
18—At Detroit	W	3-1	Witt	Palmer
19—Toronto	L	1-8	Stieb	Finley
20—Toronto	L	2-6	Key	McCaskill
21—Toronto	L	1-6§	Henke	Minton
22—Baltimore	L	5-6	Williamson	Fraser
23—Baltimore	W	5-1	Witt	Schmidt
24—Baltimore	W	8-3	Finley	Milacki
25—Baltimore	W	7-6	McCaskill	Ballard
27—At Cleve.	W	2-1†	Monteleone	Allen
28—At Cleve.	L	1-2	Bailes	Abbott
29—At Minn.	W	10-3	Witt	Dyer
30—At Minn.	W	7-2	Finley	Anderson
Won 12, Lost 14				

JULY			Winner	Loser
1—At Minn.	W	6-1	McCaskill	Rawley
2—At Minn.	L	1-2	Viola	Monteleone
3—Texas	W	5-2	Abbott	Jeffcoat
4—Texas	W	5-2	Fraser	Brown
5—Texas	W	2-1	Finley	Hough
6—Texas	L	0-3	Ryan	McCaskill
7—Minnesota	W	5-2	Blyleven	Viola

JULY			Winner	Loser
8—Minnesota	W	4-1	Abbott	Smith
9—Minnesota	W	9-3	Witt	Anderson
13—At Balt.	W	13-5	Blyleven	Thurmond
14—At Balt.	L	4-6	Holton	McCaskill
15—At Balt.	L	9-11	Williamson	Harvey
16—At Balt.	L	2-3‡	Smith	Fraser
17—At Toronto	L	4-6	Wells	Abbott
17—At Toronto	L	4-5	Wells	McClure
18—At Toronto	W	1-0	Blyleven	Key
20—Detroit	W	4-3	Finley	Henneman
21—Detroit	W	8-7	Harvey	Beard
22—Detroit	W	5-4x	Petry	Hudson
23—Detroit	W	5-4	McClure	Henneman
24—At Oak.	W	5-4	Fraser	Nelson
25—At Oak.	W	4-0	Finley	Stewart
26—At Oak.	L	5-9	M. Young	Witt
27—Chicago	W	8-5	Abbott	Perez
28—Chicago	W	6-5	Harvey	Pall
29—Chicago	W	2-1	McCaskill	Rosenberg
30—Chicago	L	2-3	Reuss	Finley
31—At Seattle	L	5-6	Comstock	Harvey
Won 18, Lost 10				

AUGUST			Winner	Loser
1—At Seattle	L	1-8	Dunne	Abbott
2—At Seattle	W	7-0	Blyleven	Reed
3—At Seattle	W	6-0	McCaskill	Johnson
4—At Milw.	W	6-2	Finley	Reuss
5—At Milw.	L	2-5	Higuera	Witt
6—At Milw.	W	6-0	Abbott	Navarro
8—Seattle	L	4-6†	Reed	Minton
9—Seattle	W	4-1	McCaskill	Holman
10—Seattle	L	2-3†	Jackson	Finley
11—Oakland	L	0-5	Moore	Witt
12—Oakland	L	3-8	Welch	Abbott
13—Oakland	W	4-3	Blyleven	Stewart
14—Minnesota	L	3-6	Anderson	McCaskill
15—Minnesota	W	3-2	Finley	Dyer
16—Minnesota	W	7-3	Witt	Rawley
18—Cleveland	W	6-5	Minton	Olin
19—Cleveland	W	7-4	Blyleven	Nichols
20—Cleveland	W	1-0	McCaskill	Black
21—At K.C.	L	2-4	Saberhagen	Fraser
22—At K.C.	L	2-4	Leach	Witt
23—At K.C.	L	4-6	Gordon	Abbott
24—At K.C.	W	5-0	Blyleven	Aquino
25—At Texas	W	4-1	McCaskill	Witt
26—At Texas	L	2-3	Hough	Clark
27—At Texas	W	5-4	McClure	Ryan
29—At Bos.	L	4-8	Lamp	Blyleven
29—At Bos.	L	5-13*	Stanley	Petry
30—At Bos.	W	4-0	Abbott	Dopson
31—At Bos.	L	2-5	Clemens	McCaskill
Won 15, Lost 14				

SEPTEMBER			Winner	Loser
1—At N.Y.	L	5-11	Terrell	Clark
2—At N.Y.	L	1-2	Cadaret	Witt
3—At N.Y.	L	2-5	Hawkins	Blyleven
4—At N.Y.	L	1-2	Parker	Abbott
5—Milwaukee	W	8-4	McCaskill	Knudson
6—Milwaukee	L	4-7	Bosio	Petry
7—Milwaukee	L	1-7	Filer	Witt
8—Boston	W	2-1	Blyleven	Boddicker
9—Boston	W	8-5	Fraser	Murphy
10—Boston	W	2-1§	McClure	Lamp
12—New York	W	7-6	McClure	Cary
13—New York	W	4-3†	Minton	Righetti
15—At Chicago	L	1-3	Perez	Abbott
15—At Chicago	W	2-1	Finley	Dotson
16—At Chicago	L	1-2	Hillegas	McCaskill
17—At Chicago	W	6-3	Witt	King
18—At Minn.	W	6-3	Blyleven	West
19—At Minn.	W	7-3	Finley	Tapani
20—At Minn.	W	9-1	Abbott	Guthrie
21—At Cleve.	L	4-5y	Bailes	Monteleone
23—At Cleve.	L	3-4	Black	Witt
23—At Cleve.	L	2-6	Candiotti	Blyleven
24—At Cleve.	L	4-5	Orosco	Fraser
26—Kan. City	L	0-4	Saberhagen	McCaskill
27—Kan. City	L	3-8	Gordon	Abbott
28—Kan. City	W	2-0	Blyleven	McWilliams
29—Texas	L	0-5	B. Witt	M. Witt
30—Texas	L	0-2	Ryan	Finley
Won 12, Lost 16				

OCTOBER			Winner	Loser
1—Texas	W	4-3	Minton	Akerfelds
Won 1, Lost 0				

*7½ innings. †10 innings. ‡11 innings. §14 innings. x16 innings. y17 innings.

First baseman Wally Joyner batted .282 and produced another steady performance for the Angels.

middle relief, posting a 3.24 ERA in 91⅔ innings.

The key to the pitching upsurge was Blyleven, who also was a leader in the clubhouse, an important role on a team that had had a grave attitude problem for years. His judgeship of the Angels' kangaroo court and irreverent wit helped unite the team and make Rader's job easier.

"What he did was absolutely sensational," Rader said. "You can't put into words what he meant to the team."

Blyleven, acquired for three minor leaguers, turned into an accidentally brilliant stroke by Port, who had thought little enough of the Dutchman that he had tried desperately to sign free agents Nolan Ryan and Bruce Hurst. Low-risk moves involving other veterans paid similar dividends. For instance, free-agent signee Bob McClure (6-1, 1.55 ERA) gave the bullpen a valuable lefthanded setup man. Catcher Lance Parrish, who was obtained in the off-season from Philadelphia, and right fielder Claudell Washington, another free-agent acquisition, patched holes in the lineup, though neither put together a complete year. Parrish finished with 17

home runs but had only two homers and six runs batted in after August 5, while Washington (.273, 13 homers, 42 RBIs) was often unavailable because of a leg injury and two long absences to tend to family matters.

Three incumbent veterans paced the offense, with left fielder Chili Davis leading the Angels in homers (22) and RBIs (90), second baseman Johnny Ray in average (.289) and designated hitter Brian Downing in on-base percentage (.354). Downing produced his lowest home run total (14) since 1981 but raised his average 41 points in one season to .283.

The Angels' younger players got mixed grades. First baseman Wally Joyner wound up with typically solid numbers (.282, 16 homers, 79 RBIs) but had only two homers and 34 RBIs at the All-Star break. Third baseman Jack Howell (20 homers) and center fielder Devon White (44 stolen bases, 13 triples and a Gold Glove) remained hopelessly undisciplined at bat, combining for 254 strikeouts and only 83 walks in 1,211 plate appearances. And shortstop Dick Schofield (.228) was limited to 91 games by chest and hand injuries.

Rookie shortstop Kent Anderson minimized Schofield's loss, batting .229 in 86 games. Another important reserve was outfielder Tony Armas, who in only 60 games popped 11 homers, one of a team-record eight players to reach double figures in home runs.

The Angels led the league in homers with 145 but somehow finished 12th in runs. They also posted A.L. highs in a couple of key pitching categories (32 complete games, 20 shutouts) and finished a close second in fielding percentage (.985, a club record). California set another club mark by winning 50 games against the A.L. East. But the Angels took themselves out of the race with a 1-11 road record against that division late in the season.

Perhaps the most bizarre set of numbers, however, was this one: California was 90-62 playing 'em one at a time and 1-9 in doubleheaders. Five twin bills did them in.

"I can't explain that one, but there was no escaping the fact," said Rader, the one-time managerial terror of the Texas Rangers who upheld his new, gentler image right to the end by praising, rather than scolding, his collapsed club.

"The way we finished isn't something we're proud of, but 91 wins is," he said. "These people deserve to be commended for their effort. I'm very proud of them. There was more good than bad."

Outfielder Ruben Sierra put together an outstanding 1989 season, batting .305 with 29 homers and a league-leading 119 RBIs.

Rangers Start Fast, Finish Slow

By PHIL ROGERS

Like a sprinter in a marathon, the Texas Rangers sprang to the front early in 1989 but found nothing left for the long haul. Three teams passed them before they struggled to the finish line in the middle of the pack.

For a franchise in search of its first American League West title, first place was fun while it lasted—even if it was only through May 4. Texas won 10 of its first 11 games and finished April with a 17-5 record, tops in the major leagues. It was the Rangers' fastest start ever.

"Your imagination wanders a little bit when you're 17-5," General Manager Tom Grieve said. "You say, 'Wow,' but on the other hand you look at all the indicators that go into good teams, and there were still some question marks at that time. I still judge the season a success."

In many ways, it was. The Rangers went 83-79, only their third winning season of the 1980s, and posted 13 more victories than the year before. Though they finished fourth, 16 games behind division-winning Oakland, the Rangers were a much better team than in recent years.

"Other than the fact we were 17-5 at the beginning, it was satisfying because of the things we accomplished and the growth that we've made individually," Manager Bobby Valentine said. "Our future is in place, defined. From where we came, from last year, the feeling of almost despair we had at the end of last year, to the feeling I have right now, it is satisfying."

There were three keys to the Rangers' improvement: the coming of age of right fielder Ruben Sierra, the transformation of Jeff Russell from All-Star starter to the league's top reliever and the free-agent signing of Nolan Ryan.

Ryan provided an amazing return on the Rangers' $2 million investment. He paced the staff with a 16-10 record and a 3.20 earned-run average, led the majors with 301 strikeouts, held opponents to a .187 batting average, went at least five innings in all 32 starts and flirted with no-hitters five times. At 42, he was a true marvel.

The Rangers had signed Ryan in December 1988, two days after obtaining pitchers Jamie Moyer and Drew Hall and outfielder Rafael Palmeiro from the Chicago Cubs for six players. At that point, Grieve declared the organization to be deeper in starting pitching than ever be-

Jeff Russell made the switch from starter to reliever and led the A.L. with 38 saves.

fore. But the Rangers' rotation failed to live up to expectations because of bad seasons by Charlie Hough (10-13, 4.35 ERA), who spent time on the disabled list with shoulder problems, and Bobby Witt (12-13), whose 5.14 ERA was the highest in the majors among pitchers who hurled at least 162 innings. It also didn't help that Texas lost Moyer (4-9, 4.86) for three months and Jose Guzman for the season, both with shoulder injuries.

"We had really only one consistent starter from day one—Nolan," Grieve said. "Kevin Brown had a nice season, but start to finish, Nolan was the only one. You can't compete, expect to win a division, with one starting pitcher."

Besides Ryan, the only bright spots in the rotation were Brown, who went 12-9 with a 3.35 ERA in his rookie season, and Mike Jeffcoat (9-6, 3.58), who was a nice surprise when injuries forced Valentine to start him 22 times.

Russell was another pleasant surprise. A former reliever who had been switched to the rotation in 1988, Russell was returned to the bullpen in spring training and handed the job of stopper. The results were tremendous. He led the league with a club-record 38 saves, fashioned a 1.98 ERA and won the A.L. Rolaids Relief Man Award.

Russell didn't get much help. Rookie

SCORES OF TEXAS RANGERS' 1989 GAMES

APRIL

Date		Score	Winner	Loser
4—Detroit	W	4-0	Hough	Morris
6—Detroit	W	5-4	Guante	Williams
7—Toronto	L	9-10	Castillo	Guante
8—Toronto	W	5-4	Moyer	Key
9—Toronto	W	3-2	Rogers	Henke
10—At Milw.	W	6-4*	Russell	Crim
12—At Milw.	W	8-1	Ryan	Wegman
13—At Milw.	W	6-1	Witt	August
14—At Detroit	W	4-2	Moyer	Williams
15—At Detroit	W	4-1	Brown	Tanana
16—At Detroit	W	9-6	Hough	Morris
17—Milwaukee	L	1-8	Wegman	Ryan
18—Milwaukee	W	6-2	Witt	August
19—Milwaukee	W	5-1	Moyer	Birkbeck
21—At Toronto	L	3-6	Stieb	Brown
22—At Toronto	L	2-4	Ward	Hough
23—At Toronto	W	4-1	Ryan	Stottlemyre
25—At Cleve.	W	11-7	Witt	Bailes
26—At Cleve.	W	3-2*	Russell	Jones
28—Boston	W	7-6‡	Guante	Murphy
29—Boston	L	5-8	Gardner	Hough
30—Boston	W	2-1	Ryan	Clemens

Won 17, Lost 5

MAY

Date		Score	Winner	Loser
1—Cleveland	L	1-11	Yett	Witt
2—Cleveland	L	3-8	Swindell	Moyer
3—New York	W	4-1	Brown	Hawkins
4—New York	L	7-11	LaPoint	Hough
5—At Bos.	L	6-7	Clemens	Ryan
6—At Bos.	L	0-7	Smithson	Witt
7—At Bos.	L	5-9	Dopson	Moyer
8—At N.Y.	W	13-2	Brown	Hawkins
9—At N.Y.	L	3-5	LaPoint	Hough
11—At K.C.	W	6-3	Ryan	Gubicza
12—At K.C.	L	3-4	Leibrandt	Witt
13—At K.C.	L	1-4	Aquino	Moyer
14—At K.C.	L	2-3*	Montgomery	Guante
17—Baltimore	L	2-8	Schmidt	Hough
18—Minnesota	W	6-5†	Russell	Gonzalez
19—Minnesota	W	4-2	Rogers	Viola
20—Minnesota	L	3-19	Smith	Witt
21—Minnesota	L	1-6	Oliveras	Russell
22—Kan. City	W	4-1	Hough	Leibrandt
23—Kan. City	W	10-8	Ryan	Aquino
24—Kan. City	L	4-6	Saberhagen	Moyer
26—At Minn.	W	5-3	Witt	Smith
27—At Minn.	W	5-3	Brown	Anderson
28—At Minn.	W	8-6	Guante	Reardon
29—At Balt.	L	1-6	Holton	Ryan
30—At Balt.	L	2-6	Williamson	Moyer
31—At Balt.	L	5-8	Williamson	Witt

Won 10, Lost 17

JUNE

Date		Score	Winner	Loser
1—At Seattle	L	2-3	Schooler	Brown
2—At Seattle	W	9-5	Jeffcoat	Swift
3—At Seattle	W	6-1	Ryan	Zavaras
4—At Seattle	L	1-2	Johnson	Hough
5—Chicago	W	4-2	Witt	Hibbard
6—Chicago	W	3-1	Brown	Perez
7—Chicago	L	4-6	Patterson	Guante
8—Chicago	W	11-7	Ryan	King
9—Oakland	W	11-8	Guante	Nelson
10—Oakland	L	1-5	Davis	Witt
11—Oakland	L	1-5	Moore	Brown
12—California	W	4-0	Jeffcoat	Witt
14—California	W	5-1	Ryan	Finley
14—California	W	6-3	Hough	McCaskill
16—At N.Y.	L	3-8	Hawkins	Witt
16—At N.Y.	L	1-6	Jones	Brown
17—At N.Y.	L	3-5	Eiland	Jeffcoat
18—At N.Y.	W	5-2	Hough	LaPoint
20—At Bos.	L	3-6	Boddicker	Russell
21—At Bos.	W	10-3	Mielke	Clemens
22—At Bos.	W	9-1	Brown	Smithson
23—Cleveland	W	4-0	Jeffcoat	Bailes
24—Cleveland	L	3-7	Swindell	Hough
25—Cleveland	W	4-2	Ryan	Candiotti
26—Cleveland	L	3-4	Farrell	Witt
27—At Chicago	W	5-1	Brown	Hibbard
28—At Chicago	W	10-5	Jeffcoat	Rosenberg
29—Seattle	L	0-2	Bankhead	Hough
30—Seattle	L	3-4	Swift	Ryan

Won 16, Lost 13

JULY

Date		Score	Winner	Loser
1—Seattle	W	1-0	Witt	Johnson
3—At Calif.	L	2-5	Abbott	Jeffcoat
4—At Calif.	L	2-5	Fraser	Brown
5—At Calif.	L	1-2	Finley	Hough
6—At Calif.	W	3-0	Ryan	McCaskill
7—At Oak.	W	6-3	Witt	Davis
8—At Oak.	W	5-4*	Russell	M. Young
9—At Oak.	L	1-7	Welch	Hough
13—At Cleve.	W	9-3†	Russell	Nichols
14—At Cleve.	L	5-11	Orosco	Guante
15—At Cleve.	L	1-7	Swindell	Ryan
16—At Cleve.	L	5-11	Yett	Brown
17—Boston	W	12-6	Guante	Gardner
18—Boston	W	8-1	Witt	Clemens
19—Boston	L	0-4	Boddicker	Hough
20—New York	W	6-2	Ryan	Hawkins
21—New York	W	5-2	Brown	Cadaret
22—New York	W	2-1	Jeffcoat	LaPoint
23—New York	W	5-4*	Witt	Righetti
24—Toronto	L	3-6	Stottlemyre	Alvarez
25—Toronto	L	0-4	Stieb	Ryan
26—Toronto	W	11-1	Brown	Flanagan
28—Milwaukee	L	3-15	Filer	Jeffcoat
29—Milwaukee	L	2-8	Bosio	Witt
30—Milwaukee	W	9-3	Ryan	August

Won 13, Lost 12

AUGUST

Date		Score	Winner	Loser
1—At Detroit	W	4-3	Brown	Gibson
2—At Detroit	L	4-6	Ritz	Jeffcoat
3—At Detroit	L	6-9	Henneman	Guante
4—At Balt.	W	6-4	Hough	Schmidt
5—At Balt.	L	2-5	Milacki	Ryan
6—At Balt.	L	2-3*	Williamson	Russell
7—At Toronto	L	1-2	Cerutti	Jeffcoat
8—At Toronto	L	0-7	Gozzo	Witt
9—At Toronto	W	4-3	Hough	Stieb
10—Detroit	W	4-1	Ryan	Alexander
11—Detroit	W	7-3	Brown	Tanana
12—Detroit	L	5-6	Gibson	Rogers
13—Detroit	L	2-4	Henneman	Rogers
15—At Seattle	L	0-2	Holman	Hough
16—At Seattle	W	3-1	Ryan	Bankhead
17—At Chicago	L	1-6	Hibbard	Brown
18—At Chicago	W	6-5	Jeffcoat	Perez
19—At Chicago	W	7-6	Witt	Dotson
20—At Chicago	W	7-1	Hough	Rosenberg
22—Oakland	L	0-2	Welch	Ryan
23—Oakland	L	4-5	Stewart	Brown
24—Oakland	W	6-2	Jeffcoat	Davis
25—California	L	1-4	McCaskill	Witt
26—California	W	3-2	Hough	Clark
27—California	L	4-5	McClure	Ryan
29—At Minn.	W	4-2	Hall	Aguilera
30—At Minn.	L	3-7	Dyer	Russell
31—At Minn.	L	6-8	West	Witt

Won 12, Lost 16

SEPTEMBER

Date		Score	Winner	Loser
1—Kan. City	L	3-5§	Luecken	Rogers
2—Kan. City	W	6-3	Ryan	Leach
3—Kan. City	L	2-13	Gubicza	Brown
4—Minnesota	W	8-5	Arnsberg	Dyer
5—Minnesota	L	4-8	Tapani	Moyer
6—Minnesota	W	3-2	Hough	West
7—Baltimore	L	3-8	Ballard	Ryan
7—Baltimore	L	6-9	Harnisch	Witt
8—Baltimore	W	3-1	Brown	Johnson
9—Baltimore	L	2-4*	Olson	Hall
10—Baltimore	W	8-1	Moyer	Schmidt
12—At K.C.	L	5-6	Luecken	Rogers
13—At K.C.	L	2-3	Saberhagen	Hough
14—At K.C.	W	10-4	Jeffcoat	Gordon
15—At Milw.	L	2-6	Navarro	Moyer
16—At Milw.	L	3-5	August	Barfield
17—At Milw.	W	4-2	Witt	Bosio
18—Seattle	W	5-2	Guante	Jackson
19—Seattle	W	5-3	Arnsberg	Reed
20—Seattle	W	3-2	Jeffcoat	Comstock
21—Seattle	L	3-8	Johnson	Moyer
22—Chicago	L	6-9	Jones	Guante
23—Chicago	W	6-4	Rogers	Segura
24—Chicago	W	5-4*	Russell	Rosenberg
25—At Oak.	W	3-2	Hall	Burns
26—At Oak.	L	3-4	Eckersley	Jeffcoat
27—At Oak.	L	0-5	Moore	Moyer
28—At Oak.	L	3-5	Stewart	Arnsberg
29—At Calif.	W	5-0	B. Witt	M. Witt
30—At Calif.	W	2-0	Ryan	Finley

Won 15, Lost 15

OCTOBER

Date		Score	Winner	Loser
1—At Calif.	L	3-4	Minton	Akerfelds

Won 0, Lost 1

*10 innings. †11 innings. ‡12-inning suspended game, completed April 29. §12 innings.

Second baseman Julio Franco batted .316 and drove in 92 runs in his first season with the Rangers.

Kenny Rogers made 73 appearances as a middle reliever and posted a 2.93 ERA, but Hall (3.70 ERA), Cecilio Guante (3.91) and Craig McMurtry (7.43) left much to be desired.

Grieve's top off-season priority had been to improve an offense that slumped from 5.08 runs per game in 1987 to 3.96 in 1988. But moves that added second baseman Julio Franco, designated hitter Harold Baines and Palmeiro might have had no impact if Sierra hadn't raised his game a notch after a winter in the weight room.

Sierra, 23, put together the best offensive year in Rangers history, setting club records and leading the league with 119 runs batted in, 14 triples, 78 extra-base hits, 344 total bases and a .543 slugging percentage. He also smacked 29 home runs while batting .306 and was named The Sporting News' A.L. Player of the Year. Nevertheless, the Rangers' scoring average rose only slightly, to 4.29 runs per game.

When not prodding Sierra into being more selective at the plate, Franco had the best season of his seven-year career after being obtained from Cleveland for three players the previous December. He had hit leadoff for the Indians, but Valentine moved him to the fifth spot in the order and he responded with a team-high .316 average and career highs in homers

(13) and RBIs (92). Left fielder Pete Incaviglia also had a surprisingly productive year, managing to hit 21 homers and drive in 81 runs despite hitting just .236.

The rest of the Texas offense was disappointing.

Baines was hitting .321 when he was acquired from the White Sox (along with infielder Fred Manrique) in a July 29 trade that sent infielder Scott Fletcher and two other players to Chicago. But Baines knocked in only 16 runs in 172 at-bats while batting .285 for Texas. Manrique, who started at second, third and shortstop, hit .288 after the deal, 11 points below his White Sox average.

Palmeiro, who had played outfield for the Cubs but was switched to first base by the Rangers, was leading the league with a .361 average in late May. He collapsed after trying to hit for more power, however, and finished at .275 with eight homers and 64 RBIs. Center fielder Cecil Espy failed to take charge in the leadoff spot, raising his on-base percentage from .288 in 1988 to just .313 and leading the league with 20 failures in 65 stolen-base attempts. Third baseman Steve Buechele had his typical year (.235, 16 homers, 59 RBIs). Backup outfielder/DH Rick Leach hit .272, his lowest average in a full major league season since 1983.

Shortstop was unsettled after Fletcher went to the White Sox. Jeff Kunkel and Manrique had trouble making routine plays, contributing to a weakness up the middle. But Kunkel, who also played six other positions, did bat a career-high .270.

Injuries to Geno Petralli exposed a major weakness at catcher, where rookie Chad Kreuter batted .152 and led the league with 21 passed balls. Petralli hit .304 in 70 games, but backup Jim Sundberg was batting .197 when he retired September 24.

Defense was a shortcoming all season, evident more in the 91 unearned runs charged to Texas pitchers than the team's 136 errors.

The season was a financial, if not aesthetic, success. The club set a home attendance record, breaking 2 million for the first time. The fans, it seemed, believed the Rangers were headed in the right direction.

"I think this team's mission is to be a contender," said George W. Bush, the Rangers' managing general partner and a son of President Bush. "Next year is a year for us to contend. Hopefully, for the next decade, every year we're in contention."

For more than one month.

Kirby Puckett's run production dropped, but his .339 average was good enough to win the American League batting championship.

Pitching-Poor Twins Fall Hard

By TOM POWERS

It was supposed to be a season in which the Minnesota Twins made a run at returning to the top of the American League West, a division they had taken by storm en route to the 1987 World Series championship.

They weren't even close.

Instead, the Twins took a big step down in 1989. After improving from 85 victories in '87 to 91 wins the next year, the Twins stumbled to their seventh losing season of the decade. They finished fifth with an 80-82 record, 19 games behind division-winning Oakland.

Offensively, Minnesota ranked second in the league in both batting (.276) and runs (740). But it was feast or famine for the Twins, who would score eight runs one game, one the next. Production was down at almost every position as such veterans as Kent Hrbek, Gary Gaetti and Tim Laudner were limited by injuries. And the pitching was awful. The Twins compiled a 4.28 earned-run average, the league's third-worst mark.

That was a surprise considering the Twins' staff included Frank Viola, who had won the 1988 A.L. Cy Young Award, and Allan Anderson, the league's ERA champion that year. But Viola got off to a rocky start in the wake of a contract dispute that prompted him to announce he would leave the club via free agency after the season. He was booed regularly while losing his first five decisions, and clubhouse turmoil, a rarity the previous two years, took up permanent residence at the Metrodome in April.

Midway through that stretch, the Twins tore up the final year of Viola's contract and signed him to a three-year, $7.9 million deal. But on July 31, with the Twins well out of contention and the lefthander sporting a meager 8-12 record, Viola was sent to the New York Mets for five pitchers: Rick Aguilera, Dave West, Kevin Tapani, Tim Drummond and Jack Savage. It was clear that the Twins were conceding defeat in '89 and looking to the future.

By season's end, Manager Tom Kelly's rotation consisted of Anderson, Aguilera and four rookies: West (3-2, 6.41 ERA), Tapani (2-2, 3.86), Mike Dyer (4-7, 4.82) and Mark Guthrie (2-4, 4.55). All four were terrific at times. And all four were horrible at times.

"They all showed they can pitch in the major leagues," General Manager Andy

Allan Anderson became the ace of Minnesota's staff and recorded a 17-10 record and 3.80 ERA.

MacPhail said. "But it seemed like when they struggled, they all struggled at the same time."

The offense was just as streaky.

"Due to a lack of playing time on the field, we didn't get the production we are accustomed to out of Gaetti and Hrbek," MacPhail said. "I think we picked up a lot from the fringe-type players. But we did not get as much out of the middle of the lineup."

Hrbek separated a shoulder on the Metrodome turf in May while diving for a ground ball. He also had some nagging problems with muscle pulls and appeared in just 109 games, many as a designated hitter. Hrbek still managed to hit .272 with 25 home runs and 84 runs batted in.

When Hrbek was out of the lineup for six weeks from mid-May until late June—a period in which the Twins struggled to score runs—backup Gene Larkin had a

SCORES OF MINNESOTA TWINS' 1989 GAMES

APRIL

Date		Score	Winner	Loser
4—New York	L	2-4	John	Viola
5—New York	W	12-2	Anderson	Hawkins
6—New York	W	7-1	Rawley	LaPoint
7—Baltimore	W	8-3	Smith	Milacki
8—Baltimore	W	6-5	Gonzalez	Holton
9—Baltimore	L	1-8	Ballard	Viola
11—At Detroit	W	14-0	Anderson	Morris
13—At Detroit	L	0-3	Robinson	Rawley
14—At N.Y.	L	5-8	Leiter	Cook
16—At N.Y.	W	9-4	Anderson	John
18—Detroit	W	9-8	Toliver	Robinson
19—Detroit	L	2-3	Alexander	Viola
20—Detroit	W	7-2	Gonzalez	Tanana
21—At Balt.	W	7-1	Anderson	Bautista
22—At Balt.	L	1-4	Olson	Toliver
23—At Balt.	L	0-3	Milacki	Rawley
24—At Milw.	L	4-5	Plesac	Reardon
25—At Milw.	L	4-10	Clutterbuck	Smith
26—At Milw.	L	0-12	Bosio	Anderson
28—Cleveland	L	7-9	Candiotti	Rawley
29—Cleveland	L	1-4	Farrell	Viola
30—Cleveland	W	2-1	Smith	Black
Won 10, Lost 12				

MAY

Date		Score	Winner	Loser
1—Boston	L	6-13	Boyd	Anderson
2—Boston	L	2-4	Dopson	Gonzalez
3—Milwaukee	L	2-7	Wegman	Rawley
4—Milwaukee	L	2-3	August	Viola
5—At Cleve.	W	3-2§	Gonzalez	Jones
7—At Cleve.	L	4-5	Jones	Oliveras
7—At Cleve.	L	1-12	Yett	Toliver
8—At Bos.	W	4-2	Rawley	Boddicker
9—At Bos.	W	6-2	Viola	Gardner
12—Toronto	W	6-5	Berenguer	Wells
13—Toronto	W	10-8	Rawley	Stieb
14—Toronto	W	13-1	Viola	Flanagan
15—Kan. City	L	3-4	Bannister	Berenguer
16—Kan. City	L	1-8	Gubicza	Oliveras
17—Kan. City	W	4-3†	Berenguer	Farr
18—At Texas	L	5-6‡	Russell	Gonzalez
19—At Texas	L	2-4	Rogers	Viola
20—At Texas	W	19-3	Smith	Witt
21—At Texas	W	6-1	Oliveras	Russell
22—At Toronto	W	6-2	Anderson	Stieb
23—At Toronto	L	1-2	Wells	Berenguer
24—At Toronto	W	10-4	Viola	Flanagan
26—Texas	L	3-5	Witt	Smith
27—Texas	L	3-5	Brown	Anderson
28—Texas	L	6-8	Guante	Reardon
29—At K.C.	L	1-7	Saberhagen	Viola
30—At K.C.	W	7-1	Smith	Clarke
31—At K.C.	W	7-1*	Oliveras	Bannister
Won 13, Lost 15				

JUNE

Date		Score	Winner	Loser
2—At Chicago	W	8-0	Anderson	Perez
3—At Chicago	L	5-4	Viola	King
3—At Chicago	L	1-2	Hillegas	Rawley
4—At Chicago	L	1-2	Reuss	Smith
5—At Oak.	W	2-1	Oliveras	C. Young
6—At Oak.	L	0-1	Moore	Anderson
7—At Oak.	L	2-3	Welch	Viola
9—Chicago	L	3-8	Reuss	Rawley
10—Chicago	W	11-8	Berenguer	Thigpen
11—Chicago	W	5-2	Anderson	Perez
13—Seattle	W	4-3‡	Wayne	Reed
14—Seattle	W	10-8	Berenguer	Niedenfuer
15—Seattle	L	5-9	Powell	Shields
16—Milwaukee	L	6-8	Crim	Berenguer
17—Milwaukee	W	7-3	Tunnell	Knudson
18—Milwaukee	W	8-6	Reardon	Crim
19—Milwaukee	L	8-11	Krueger	Oliveras
20—At Cleve.	W	7-4	Anderson	Candiotti
21—At Cleve.	W	5-1	Rawley	Farrell
22—At Cleve.	W	9-8	Wayne	Orosco
23—At Bos.	W	10-0	Viola	Price
24—At Bos.	L	2-6	Dopson	Oliveras
24—At Bos.	L	2-11	Smithson	Toliver
25—At Bos.	W	7-0	Anderson	Boddicker
26—Oakland	W	4-3†	Reardon	Burns
27—Oakland	W	11-5	Wayne	Nelson
28—Oakland	W	2-0	Viola	Stewart
29—California	L	3-10	Witt	Dyer
30—California	L	2-7	Finley	Anderson
Won 17, Lost 12				

JULY

Date		Score	Winner	Loser
1—California	L	1-6	McCaskill	Rawley
2—California	W	2-1	Viola	Monteleone
4—At Seattle	L	2-3	Bankhead	Anderson

JULY

Date		Score	Winner	Loser
5—At Seattle	L	3-7	Harris	Dyer
6—At Seattle	L	5-7	Jackson	Wayne
7—At Calif.	L	2-5	Blyleven	Viola
8—At Calif.	L	1-4	Abbott	Smith
9—At Calif.	L	3-9	Witt	Anderson
13—Boston	L	1-3	Clemens	Viola
14—Boston	L	0-5	Boddicker	Anderson
15—Boston	W	3-2	Berenguer	Smithson
16—Boston	W	4-3‡	St. Claire	Murphy
17—Cleveland	W	5-2	Berenguer	Jones
18—Cleveland	W	5-4	Viola	Jones
19—Cleveland	L	1-10	Farrell	Anderson
21—At Milw.	L	3-5	Higuera	Rawley
22—At Milw.	W	6-1	Smith	Navarro
23—At Milw.	L	1-4	Filer	Viola
25—Baltimore	W	9-3	Anderson	Schmidt
26—Baltimore	W	5-4	Reardon	Williamson
27—Baltimore	W	10-6	Smith	Harnisch
28—At Detroit	L	4-6	Ritz	Viola
28—At Detroit	W	7-3	Dyer	Robinson
29—At Detroit	L	2-3†	Henneman	Wayne
30—At Detroit	W	14-3	Anderson	Alexander
Won 11, Lost 14				

AUGUST

Date		Score	Winner	Loser
1—At N.Y.	W	5-4	Rawley	Terrell
2—At N.Y.	L	6-7	McCullers	Wayne
2—At N.Y.	W	4-3†	Reardon	Plunk
3—At N.Y.	L	1-8	Cary	Aguilera
4—Kan. City	W	5-1	Anderson	Aquino
5—Kan. City	W	6-4	Berenguer	Farr
6—Kan. City	L	2-3	Saberhagen	Rawley
7—At Balt.	W	4-2	Smith	Ballard
8—At Balt.	L	1-6	Johnson	Aguilera
9—At Balt.	W	7-0	Anderson	Thurmond
11—New York	L	3-11	Terrell	Rawley
12—New York	W	6-3	Smith	Cadaret
13—New York	L	7-9	Guetterman	Reardon
14—At Calif.	W	6-3	Anderson	McCaskill
15—At Calif.	L	2-3	Finley	Dyer
16—At Calif.	L	3-7	Witt	Rawley
18—At Oak.	W	4-3	Smith	Stewart
19—At Oak.	L	4-5†	Davis	Wayne
20—At Oak.	L	0-5	Moore	Anderson
22—Chicago	L	2-10	King	Rawley
23—Chicago	W	8-7	Smith	Hibbard
24—Chicago	W	6-4	Berenguer	Hillegas
25—Seattle	W	2-1	Dyer	Johnson
26—Seattle	W	1-0	West	Holman
27—Seattle	W	8-5	Guthrie	Bankhead
28—Seattle	W	5-4†	Reardon	Schooler
29—Texas	L	2-4	Hall	Aguilera
30—Texas	W	7-3	Dyer	Russell
31—Texas	W	8-6	West	Witt
Won 17, Lost 12				

SEPTEMBER

Date		Score	Winner	Loser
1—At Toronto	L	3-7	Stottlemyre	Guthrie
2—At Toronto	L	2-4	Cerutti	Smith
3—At Toronto	W	9-4	Aguilera	Flanagan
4—At Texas	L	5-8	Arnsberg	Dyer
5—At Texas	W	8-4	Tapani	Moyer
6—At Texas	L	2-3	Hough	West
8—At K.C.	L	0-6	Gubicza	Smith
9—At K.C.	L	1-3	Saberhagen	Aguilera
10—At K.C.	W	8-2	Anderson	Gordon
11—At K.C.	L	1-6	McWilliams	Dyer
12—Toronto	W	8-2	West	Stottlemyre
13—Toronto	W	3-2	Tapani	Cerutti
14—Toronto	W	2-0	Guthrie	Flanagan
15—Detroit	W	8-4	Aguilera	DuBois
16—Detroit	W	8-7	Anderson	Alexander
17—Detroit	L	2-9	Searcy	Dyer
18—California	L	3-6	Blyleven	West
19—California	L	3-7	Finley	Tapani
20—California	L	1-9	Abbott	Guthrie
21—Oakland	L	1-2	Welch	Aguilera
22—Oakland	L	2-5	Stewart	Dyer
23—Oakland	W	5-3	Anderson	Moore
24—Oakland	L	3-9	Davis	Tapani
25—At Chicago	L	2-10	Dotson	Guthrie
26—At Chicago	W	7-1	Aguilera	Perez
27—At Chicago	W	6-1	Dyer	Hillegas
29—At Seattle	W	10-7‡	Berenguer	Schooler
30—At Seattle	L	1-2†	Reed	Reardon
Won 12, Lost 16				

OCTOBER

Date		Score	Winner	Loser
1—At Seattle	L	1-3	Hanson	Guthrie
Won 0, Lost 1				

*5½ innings. †10 innings. ‡11 innings. §12 innings.

Kent Hrbek played only 109 games but still checked in with 25 homers and 84 RBIs.

terrible time. Larkin, a highly touted hitter, wound up batting .267, but only because he raised his average about 40 points after Hrbek returned. As an everyday first baseman, Larkin—who also filled in at DH and in the outfield—left the Twins wanting.

Gaetti, bothered by knee, back and stomach problems, did a short stint on the disabled list and finished at .251 with 19 homers in 130 games. By year's end he was so beat up he was spending more time on the bench than in the lineup. But he continued to play good defense, winning his fourth consecutive Gold Glove.

Shortstop Greg Gagne (.272) was streaky at the plate but solid in the field. He did not have a regular double-play partner, however, as second base remained a problem for the Twins.

After Tom Herr flopped at second base in 1988, the Twins acquired Wally Backman from the New York Mets. Backman was even worse. He was sidelined for long stretches with a bum shoulder and hit .231

in 87 games, stole only one base and demonstrated no range in the field. Al Newman, on the other hand, took advantage of the opportunity to play fairly regularly, hitting .253 with a team-high 25 stolen bases. But the Twins' preference to use Newman, who also played shortstop and third base, as a utilityman meant the second-base problem still was unsolved.

The steadiest part of the Twins' game in '89 was their outfield play. Left fielder Dan Gladden, who had hamstring problems, hit .295 with 23 steals. The amazing Kirby Puckett won the A.L. batting title with a .339 average, led Minnesota with 85 RBIs and played his usual Gold Glove defense in center field. His home run production did slip, though, from the mid-20s to nine. In right, the platoon of Randy Bush and Carmen Castillo provided decent punch (a combined 22 homers and 87 RBIs) if little defense. Fourth outfielder John Moses hit .281.

The biggest surprise was Brian Harper, a career journeyman who had established himself as the No. 1 catcher by the end of the season. Harper wound up hitting .325, second on the team to Puckett and more than 100 points higher than Laudner, whose season ended in early September because of a knee injury. Minnesota's other .300 hitter was DH Jim Dwyer, who was hitting .316 when he was traded to Montreal in August.

The only impressive member of the pitching rotation was Anderson, who went 17-10 with a 3.80 ERA and, following Viola's departure, became the ace of the staff. But, like the team, Anderson was inconsistent.

Roy Smith won 10 of 16 decisions in his first full major league season, while Aguilera went 3-5 with a 3.21 ERA after being obtained from the Mets. The weakest link in the rotation was Shane Rawley (5-12, 5.21), who didn't win after August 1.

In the bullpen, Jeff Reardon saved 31 games, making him the only reliever ever to save 30 or more in five straight seasons. But his ERA was 4.07 and he blew 11 save opportunities.

Setup man Juan Berenguer (9-3) gave Minnesota the same decent 100 innings he always does. After a disastrous start, rookie Gary Wayne (3-4, 3.30) became a steady bullpen contributor.

The bright spots for the Twins, however, were few and far between. As Hrbek said, the '89 season "isn't a good one to remember, that's for sure."

Said Gaetti: "I hope I remember something (about the season). I hope I remember how difficult it was."

First baseman Alvin Davis quietly enjoyed another outstanding offensive season, batting .305 with 21 homers and 95 RBIs.

Mariners Fail to Break Even

By JIM STREET

Every year is a building year for the Seattle Mariners, a franchise that has never enjoyed so much as a break-even season, much less a winning one. But 1989 was supposed to be different. This was the year the record would reflect the Mariners' improvement. It was the year to reach .500.

That was how General Manager Woody Woodward and Manager Jim Lefebvre had it figured. Obviously, they miscalculated.

The Mariners finished sixth in the American League West with a 73-89 record, 26 games out of first place. It was a fairly typical season—16 games under .500—for the major leagues' losingest organization.

"As young as this club was," Woodward said, "I feel that it should have played .500 baseball. I thought that was a realistic goal."

Realistic? Perhaps. But the club definitely was young. Eleven rookies played for the Mariners in 1989, including two starting outfielders, the starting shortstop and two starting pitchers.

The best rookie, of course, was 19-year-old center fielder Ken Griffey Jr., who was such a hit that he had a candy bar named after him and wound up making more money off the field than on it. He became a star on a team that has had few.

A shower in a Chicago hotel room gave Griffey more trouble than some of the best pitchers in the league. "Junior" was well on his way to becoming the league's Rookie of the Year when he slipped coming out of the shower July 24 and broke a bone in his right hand. The injury knocked him out for a month, and when he came back he wasn't the same, struggling to bat .200. His defense didn't miss a beat, though, and he finished with a .264 average, 16 home runs and 61 runs batted in. He came in third in the A.L. Rookie of the Year voting.

Seattle's other talented rookie outfielder was Greg Briley, little in stature (5-foot-9, 170 pounds) but big in potential. The left fielder hit .266 and contributed 13 homers and 52 RBIs.

Shortstop Omar Vizquel was forced to make the jump from Class AAA Calgary to the majors when Rey Quinones was traded to Pittsburgh in April. Vizquel was steady on defense but became "Omar the Outmaker" on offense, hitting just .220.

Two rookies were among the top four Seattle pitchers in starts, and one had a fine season interrupted by a shoulder injury. Erik Hanson was shelved for three months after getting off to a 4-4 start. He came back strong, winning five of seven starts to finish with a 9-5 record and a 3.18 earned-run average. The other rookie starter, Randy Johnson, was 7-9.

Injuries such as Hanson's and Griffey's were largely responsible for the Mariners' failure to win at least half of their games. Seattle just wasn't deep enough to compensate.

"There is no doubt in my mind that if this team had stayed healthy, it would have finished at or above .500," Lefebvre said. "We lost Alvin Davis (for two weeks with a calf injury), Dave Valle (for five weeks with a knee injury), Griffey and Hanson. Some teams can overcome injuries to key players. We couldn't."

The Mariners also struggled while trade rumors regarding Mark Langston, the best pitcher in Mariners history, enveloped the club from spring training through the first eight weeks of the season. "From day one, that was a distraction," Lefebvre said.

Langston, who was likely to leave Seattle via free agency after the season, finally was traded to the Montreal Expos on May 25 for three young guns: Johnson, Brian Holman and Gene Harris. The trade did not provide many immediate benefits—Johnson and Holman combined for a 15-19 record—but Lefebvre was convinced that they have what it takes to be consistent winners.

"I like their arms and I like their makeup," the manager said. "They are going to be instrumental in this team's future."

So, once again, a Mariners season ended with more talk about future achievements than current ones. But the season was not without its bright spots.

Scott Bankhead won a career-high 14 games, including a club-record nine straight, and fashioned a 3.34 ERA. With Langston's departure, Bankhead stamped himself as the new ace of the starting staff.

Reliever Mike Schooler emerged as the kind of stopper the Mariners have lacked since Bill Caudill saved 26 games in both 1982 and '83. In only his second big-league season, Schooler had a club-record 33 saves in 40 opportunities. Mike Jackson, also a second-year reliever, added seven

SCORES OF SEATTLE MARINERS' 1989 GAMES

APRIL

Date	W/L	Score	Winner	Loser
3—At Oak.	L	2-3	Stewart	Langston
5—At Oak.	L	1-11	Welch	Bankhead
6—At Oak.	L	3-11	Davis	Campbell
7—At Calif.	L	1-2	McCaskill	Hanson
8—At Calif.	W	7-0	Langston	Abbott
9—At Calif.	L	5-13	Witt	Trout
10—Chicago	W	6-5	Reed	King
11—Chicago	L	6-8	Jones	Niedenfuer
12—Chicago	W	9-1	Hanson	Long
14—California	W	9-5	Langston	Witt
15—California	L	2-9	Finley	Reed
16—California	L	0-10	Blyleven	Campbell
17—Oakland	W	7-2	Hanson	C. Young
18—Oakland	L	3-5	Plunk	Reed
19—Oakland	L	5-7	Stewart	Langston
20—At Chicago	W	5-2	Bankhead	Jones
21—At Chicago	W	11-1	Campbell	Reuss
22—At Chicago	L	0-1	King	Hanson
23—At Chicago	W	10-6	Trout	Hillegas
24—At Detroit	L	0-1	Alexander	Langston
25—At Detroit	L	2-5	Tanana	Bankhead
26—Toronto	W	7-6	Trout	Wells
27—Toronto	L	1-6	Flanagan	Dunne
28—Baltimore	W	11-5	Reed	Holton
29—Baltimore	W	4-3	Langston	Schmidt
30—Baltimore	L	3-4	Ballard	Trout

Won 11, Lost 15

MAY

Date	W/L	Score	Winner	Loser
1—Detroit	W	5-3	Powell	Morris
2—Detroit	W	7-2	Dunne	Hudson
3—Detroit	W	3-2	Hanson	Alexander
6—At Balt.	W	2-1	Langston	Schmidt
6—At Balt.	W	6-5	Bankhead	Ballard
7—At Balt.	W	5-3	Swift	Bautista
8—At Toronto	L	1-10	Stieb	Dunne
9—At Toronto	W	4-3	Hanson	Flanagan
10—At Toronto	L	2-3	Key	Langston
12—Boston	L	0-2	Clemens	Bankhead
13—Boston	W	14-6	Reed	Dopson
14—Boston	W	4-3	Trout	Boddicker
16—Milwaukee	W	6-5	Jackson	Wegman
17—Milwaukee	L	6-9	Crim	Bankhead
18—Milwaukee	W	9-5	Swift	Bosio
19—New York	L	5-9	Hawkins	Hanson
20—New York	W	6-4	Trout	LaPoint
21—New York	L	2-6	Parker	Langston
23—At Bos.	L	5-6	Smith	Reed
24—At Bos.	L	5-6	Boddicker	Hanson
25—At Bos.	L	0-10	Smithson	Dunne
26—At Milw.	W	7-2	Jackson	August
27—At Milw.	L	2-3	Plesac	Holman
28—At Milw.	L	4-6	Crim	Powell
29—At N.Y.	L	3-6	Dotson	Powell
30—At N.Y.	W	3-2	Johnson	Jones
31—At N.Y.	L	5-9	Hawkins	Trout

Won 14, Lost 13

JUNE

Date	W/L	Score	Winner	Loser
1—Texas	W	3-2	Schooler	Brown
2—Texas	L	5-9	Jeffcoat	Swift
3—Texas	L	1-6	Ryan	Zavaras
4—Texas	W	2-1	Johnson	Hough
5—Kan. City	W	3-5x	Gordon	Niedenfuer
6—Kan. City	W	5-2	Bankhead	Clarke
7—Kan. City	L	6-9	Gubicza	Swift
9—At Cleve.	L	4-5	Candiotti	Zavaras
10—At Cleve.	W	3-1	Johnson	Farrell
11—At Cleve.	W	6-3	Holman	Black
13—At Minn.	L	3-4‡	Wayne	Reed
14—At Minn.	L	8-10	Berenguer	Niedenfuer
15—At Minn.	W	9-5	Powell	Shields
16—At Toronto	L	3-4	Henke	Schooler
17—At Toronto	L	2-3	Ward	Jackson
18—At Toronto	W	8-2	Bankhead	Wills
19—Baltimore	L	5-9	Milacki	Jackson
20—Baltimore	L	6-8	Weston	Reed
21—Baltimore	L	6-8	Tibbs	Holman
23—Detroit	L	4-5	Henneman	Schooler
24—Detroit	W	3-1	Bankhead	Tanana
25—Detroit	W	5-3	Swift	Palmer
27—At K.C.	W	8-0	Holman	Aquino
28—At K.C.	L	7-12	Gubicza	Harris
29—At Texas	W	2-0	Bankhead	Hough
30—At Texas	W	4-3	Swift	Ryan

Won 12, Lost 14

JULY

Date	W/L	Score	Winner	Loser
1—At Texas	L	0-1	Witt	Johnson
4—Minnesota	W	3-2	Bankhead	Anderson
5—Minnesota	W	7-3	Harris	Dyer
6—Minnesota	W	7-5	Jackson	Wayne
7—Cleveland	L	3-4§	Jones	Jackson
8—Cleveland	W	4-3‡	Swift	Orosco
9—Cleveland	W	8-0	Bankhead	Bailes
13—At Detroit	W	5-4§	Swift	Schwabe
14—At Detroit	W	13-0	Holman	Alexander
15—At Detroit	W	9-3	Bankhead	Ritz
16—At Detroit	L	5-8	Hudson	Harris
17—At Balt.	L	4-8	Harnisch	Dunne
18—At Balt.	L	3-4	Ballard	Johnson
19—At Balt.	W	7-0	Holman	Holton
20—Toronto	W	5-2	Bankhead	Stieb
21—Toronto	L	1-8	Flanagan	Harris
22—Toronto	L	1-7	Cerutti	Dunne
23—Toronto	W	5-2	Johnson	Key
24—At Chicago	L	4-5	Hillegas	Jackson
25—At Chicago	L	6-7	Pall	Jackson
26—At Chicago	L	3-5	Hibbard	Swift
28—At Oak.	L	7-8‡	Burns	Harris
29—At Oak.	W	14-6	Johnson	Davis
30—At Oak.	L	3-5	Stewart	Holman
31—California	W	6-5	Comstock	Harvey

Won 13, Lost 12

AUGUST

Date	W/L	Score	Winner	Loser
1—California	W	8-1	Dunne	Abbott
2—California	L	0-7	Blyleven	Reed
3—California	L	0-6	McCaskill	Johnson
4—Oakland	L	3-5	Stewart	Holman
5—Oakland	W	11-5	Bankhead	Moore
6—Oakland	L	1-2	Davis	Dunne
7—Oakland	W	5-1	Zavaras	Welch
8—At Calif.	W	6-4†	Reed	Minton
9—At Calif.	L	1-4	McCaskill	Holman
10—At Calif.	W	3-2†	Jackson	Finley
11—Chicago	L	6-9†	Thigpen	Schooler
12—Chicago	W	4-3†	Reed	Pall
13—Chicago	L	4-6	Long	Comstock
15—Texas	W	2-0	Holman	Hough
16—Texas	L	1-3	Ryan	Bankhead
17—Kan. City	L	2-4	Gubicza	Dunne
18—Kan. City	L	1-3	Gordon	Zavaras
19—Kan. City	L	5-13	Leach	Johnson
20—Kan. City	L	4-5	Crawford	Holman
22—At Cleve.	L	2-3†	Jones	Schooler
23—At Cleve.	L	3-5	Candiotti	Dunne
24—At Cleve.	L	2-5	Davis	Zavaras
25—At Minn.	L	1-2	Dyer	Johnson
26—At Minn.	L	0-1	West	Holman
27—At Minn.	L	5-8	Guthrie	Bankhead
28—At Minn.	L	4-5†	Reardon	Schooler
29—At Milw.	W	5-3	Hanson	Navarro
30—At Milw.	W	7-3	Johnson	Peterek
31—At Milw.	L	1-6	Knudson	Holman

Won 9, Lost 20

SEPTEMBER

Date	W/L	Score	Winner	Loser
1—At Bos.	W	7-2	Bankhead	Smithson
2—At Bos.	L	5-6	Lamp	Dunne
3—At Bos.	W	3-2	Hanson	Boyd
5—New York	L	2-12	Plunk	Johnson
6—New York	L	3-5	Terrell	Holman
7—New York	L	4-6	Gossage	Schooler
8—Milwaukee	L	3-7	Navarro	Zavaras
9—Milwaukee	L	3-7	Reuss	Hanson
10—Milwaukee	L	1-7	Knudson	Johnson
11—Boston	W	2-1	Holman	Dopson
12—Boston	W	5-3	Bankhead	Hetzel
13—Boston	W	7-4	Reed	Boddicker
15—At N.Y.	W	3-1	Hanson	Hawkins
16—At N.Y.	L	1-4*	Plunk	Johnson
17—At N.Y.	W	3-0	Holman	Terrell
18—At Texas	L	2-5	Guante	Jackson
19—At Texas	L	3-5	Arnsberg	Reed
20—At Texas	L	2-3	Jeffcoat	Comstock
21—At Texas	W	8-3	Johnson	Moyer
22—At K.C.	L	2-9	Saberhagen	Holman
22—At K.C.	W	2-0	Swift	Gordon
23—At K.C.	W	8-0	Bankhead	McWilliams
24—At K.C.	L	1-4	Farr	Zavaras
26—Cleveland	W	3-2	Hanson	Jones
27—Cleveland	L	1-4	Farrell	Johnson
28—Cleveland	W	6-2	Holman	Olin
29—Minnesota	L	7-10‡	Berenguer	Schooler
30—Minnesota	W	2-1†	Reed	Reardon

Won 13, Lost 15

OCTOBER

Date	W/L	Score	Winner	Loser
1—Minnesota	W	3-1	Hanson	Guthrie

Won 1, Lost 0

*6 innings. †10 innings. ‡11 innings. §12 innings. x13 innings.

Although Ken Griffey Jr. missed a month of the 1989 season with a broken hand, the Mariners liked what they saw of the talented rookie.

saves.

Davis, one of the league's overlooked stars, turned in another strong season, hitting 21 homers and leading the team with a .305 average and 95 RBIs. He also had 101 walks, helping him post the league's second-best on-base percentage (.424).

Designated hitter Jeffrey Leonard found the Kingdome to his liking in his first year in Seattle. He enjoyed his most productive season, hitting 24 homers and knocking in 93 runs.

Second baseman Harold Reynolds hit .300 for the first time in his career and led the club with 87 runs scored. He also won his second consecutive Gold Glove, despite assessing his defensive performance (17 errors) thusly: "I stunk."

A few players had adequate seasons. Darnell Coles (.252, 59 RBIs) played right field, left field, third base, first base and DH while appearing in a career-high 146 games. Henry Cotto batted .264 and started at all three outfield spots. Backup catcher Scott Bradley led the league in pinch-hitting with a .360 average. Reliever Jerry Reed established career bests with seven victories, a 3.19 ERA and 101⅔ innings pitched.

For the most part, the other Mariners struggled. Slugging third baseman Jim Presley had his worst full major league season, managing only 12 homers and 41

RBIs. Valle was hitting .285 and playing well behind the plate until May 28, when Milwaukee's Bill Spiers slid into his knee. Valle suffered torn ligaments and hit just .194 after returning from the disabled list. Outfielder Jay Buhner hit .275 but was sidelined twice with injuries. Bill Swift (4.43 ERA) was effective in middle relief but erratic as a spot starter. Mike Dunne, one of three players obtained from Pittsburgh in the Quinones deal, and rookie Clint Zavaras combined for only three wins in 25 starts.

The Mariners still had a shot at a .500 season as late as mid-August, when they were 57-61. But they then lost 12 straight games, putting a winning season out of reach.

The difference between a winning and a losing season for Seattle probably was its record in close games. The Mariners were involved in 86 games decided by one or two runs (tops in the league) and went 38-48 in those games.

"The number of close games we played tells me that we're close, but not yet over the hump," Woodward said. "To get where we want to get, we somehow have to learn how to win those games."

Even if "where we want to get" is just the .500 level. In the meantime, the tally of the Mariners' losing efforts is at 13—and counting.

Relief ace Bobby Thigpen was one of Chicago's few pitching bright spots, tying his own club record with 34 saves.

Optimistic Sox Drop to Cellar

By JOE GODDARD

General Manager Larry Himes was so optimistic about the Chicago White Sox in 1989, he predicted that they would win 87 games. But they won only 69, their worst full-season total in 13 years.

"It was a struggle for us," said Manager Jeff Torborg, whose first White Sox club never left the American League West cellar after May 12 and finished 29½ games behind Oakland. "I kind of overrated us, but it was based on what I was told by other people. I was new, and we made a big turnover in personnel."

Himes also had set goals of a .262 team batting average, a 3.99 earned-run average for the pitchers and 120 errors for the defense. The White Sox achieved only the first of those goals.

The batters made a quantum leap under new coach Walt Hriniak, improving from .244 in 1988 to .271. Although home runs fell from 132 to 94 because of the trade of designated hitter Harold Baines and injuries to four other power hitters, the White Sox scored 693 runs, up from 631.

The pitching and defense, however, were still poor. The White Sox ranked 11th in the league with a 4.23 ERA, while their 151 errors ranked 13th.

"I'm not disappointed with my predictions," Himes said. "I hope it let them know I had confidence in them."

The White Sox showed confidence in Torborg by going 37-36 after the All-Star break, even with injured sluggers Ron Kittle, Dan Pasqua and Greg Walker contributing little or nothing in the second half. That over-.500 stretch was an encouraging sign.

"We can go into next year knowing that this team has a chance to be a winning ball club," Torborg said.

Himes made a bold move in late July to further that cause. He traded Baines—who was so popular with Jerry Reinsdorf that the team's co-owner had Baines' number retired—to the Texas Rangers for veteran infielder Scott Fletcher and prospects Sammy Sosa and Wilson Alvarez. The White Sox were tying their 1990 plans to that trade and the development of third baseman Robin Ventura, a product of a farm system that had the top winning percentage (.582) in baseball in '89.

Torborg installed Fletcher at second base, where he teamed with shortstop Ozzie Guillen to give the White Sox one of their few defensive strong points. "I'll

Sammy Sosa, obtained in the trade that sent Harold Baines to Texas, played a smooth center field and showed good offensive promise.

match up our double-play combination with any in the league," Torborg said.

Sosa also provided a good glove in center field the last month of the season. But overall, the defense was porous, especially in the first half. "It was the worst defense I've ever seen, just horrible," Torborg said.

The most noticeable defensive improvement was in the outfield. Chicago opened the season with Pasqua in left, Dave Gallagher in center and Ivan Calderon in right, an alignment that promised a lot of wallop but little speed. Injuries prompted changes that left the White Sox with little wallop, but some offensive punch and good range.

Pasqua missed almost six weeks early in the year with a broken wrist, then suffered a season-ending knee injury in August. In just 73 games, he had hit 11 homers with 47 runs batted in. Meanwhile, first baseman Walker spent a couple of weeks on the disabled list with a hip

SCORES OF CHICAGO WHITE SOX' 1989 GAMES

APRIL

			Winner	Loser
4—At Calif.	W	9-2	Reuss	Witt
5—At Calif.	L	2-6	Finley	King
6—At Calif.	W	3-2	Patterson	Fraser
7—At Oak.	W	7-1	Long	C. Young
8—At Oak.	W	7-4	Perez	Moore
9—At Oak.	L	2-4	Stewart	Reuss
10—At Seattle	L	5-6	Reed	King
11—At Seattle	W	8-6	Jones	Niedenfuer
12—At Seattle	L	1-9	Hanson	Long
14—Oakland	L	4-7	Stewart	Perez
15—Oakland	W	7-4	Reuss	Welch
16—Oakland	L	2-3	Eckersley	King
17—California	L	0-3	McCaskill	Hillegas
19—California	L	2-7	Witt	Long
20—Seattle	L	2-5	Bankhead	Jones
21—Seattle	L	1-11	Campbell	Reuss
22—Seattle	W	1-0	King	Hanson
23—Seattle	L	6-10	Trout	Hillegas
25—At Bos.	L	0-11	Clemens	Perez
26—At Bos.	L	4-5*	Stanley	Jones
27—At Bos.	W	3-1‡	Pall	Smithson
28—At N.Y.	L	1-3	Hawkins	Hillegas
29—At N.Y.	L	2-8	LaPoint	Long
30—At N.Y.	L	2-5	Candelaria	Perez

Won 8, Lost 16

MAY

			Winner	Loser
1—Milwaukee	W	6-0	Reuss	Higuera
2—Milwaukee	W	6-1	King	Bosio
3—Boston	L	4-8	Boddicker	Hillegas
4—Boston	W	5-4	Long	Gardner
5—New York	L	5-7	McCullers	Pall
6—New York	L	2-5	Righetti	Rosenberg
7—New York	W	6-2	King	John
9—At Milw.	W	10-1	Hillegas	Wegman
10—At Milw.	W	12-2	Perez	Higuera
12—At Balt.	L	6-9	Thurmond	McCarthy
13—At Balt.	W	8-2	King	Milacki
14—At Balt.	W	8-5	Rosenberg	Williamson
15—At Detroit	L	2-3	Tanana	Long
16—At Detroit	L	7-9	Williams	Perez
17—At Detroit	W	10-7	Patterson	Hernandez
19—Toronto	L	3-9	Flanagan	King
20—Toronto	L	1-11	Key	Hillegas
21—Toronto	L	3-9	Cerutti	Perez
22—Baltimore	L	1-5	Schmidt	Rosenberg
23—Baltimore	L	3-9	Milacki	Long
24—Baltimore	L	0-8	Tibbs	King
26—At Toronto	L	3-11	Key	Hillegas
27—At Toronto	W	5-3	Perez	Cerutti
28—At Toronto	L	5-7*	Henke	Thigpen
29—Detroit	L	2-4	Alexander	King
30—Detroit	L	3-10	Tanana	Bittiger
31—Detroit	L	3-4	Henneman	Thigpen

Won 10, Lost 17

JUNE

			Winner	Loser
2—Minnesota	L	0-8	Anderson	Perez
3—Minnesota	L	4-5	Viola	King
3—Minnesota	W	2-1	Hillegas	Rawley
4—Minnesota	W	2-1	Reuss	Smith
5—At Texas	L	2-4	Witt	Hibbard
6—At Texas	L	1-3	Brown	Perez
7—At Texas	W	6-4	Patterson	Guante
8—At Texas	L	7-11	Ryan	King
9—At Minn.	W	8-3	Reuss	Rawley
10—At Minn.	L	8-11	Berenguer	Thigpen
11—At Minn.	L	2-5	Anderson	Perez
12—Cleveland	W	5-3	Rosenberg	Yett
13—Cleveland	L	6-9	Swindell	Peterson
14—Cleveland	W	3-1	Reuss	Candiotti
16—Boston	L	0-2	Clemens	Patterson
17—Boston	L	1-6	Smithson	Perez
18—Boston	L	4-7	Price	Rosenberg
19—Boston	W	8-2	Hillegas	Dopson
20—At N.Y.	W	13-6	Reuss	Dotson
21—At N.Y.	W	7-3	Pall	Hawkins
22—At N.Y.	L	7-10	Cadaret	Hillegas
23—At Milw.	L	5-17	Bosio	Rosenberg
23—At Milw.	W	6-4	Perez	Clutterbuck
24—At Milw.	W	5-3	Long	Krueger
25—At Milw.	L	1-3	Navarro	Reuss
27—Texas	L	1-5	Brown	Hibbard
28—Texas	L	5-10	Jeffcoat	Rosenberg
29—Kan. City	W	12-5	Perez	Leach
30—Kan. City	L	3-6	Leibrandt	Reuss

Won 12, Lost 17

JULY

			Winner	Loser
1—Kan. City	W	6-4	Hillegas	Aquino
2—Kan. City	W	7-3	Hibbard	Appier
3—At Cleve.	L	2-4	Black	Hillegas

JULY

			Winner	Loser
4—At Cleve.	L	2-3	Bailes	Perez
5—At Cleve.	L	2-4	Swindell	Reuss
7—At K.C.	L	2-4	Leach	Dotson
8—At K.C.	L	3-4†	Montgomery	Davis
9—At K.C.	L	4-5	Gordon	Hillegas
13—Milwaukee	W	5-4	Thigpen	Fossas
14—Milwaukee	W	6-4	Long	Bosio
15—Milwaukee	W	2-1	Perez	Higuera
16—Milwaukee	W	2-0	Dotson	Navarro
17—New York	W	7-3	Rosenberg	LaPoint
19—New York	W	11-5	Hillegas	Guetterman
21—At Bos.	W	1-0	Perez	Hetzel
22—At Bos.	W	10-6	Patterson	Murphy
23—At Bos.	L	2-8	Clemens	Rosenberg
24—Seattle	W	5-4	Hillegas	Jackson
25—Seattle	W	7-6	Pall	Jackson
26—Seattle	W	5-3	Hibbard	Swift
27—At Calif.	L	5-8	Abbott	Perez
28—At Calif.	L	5-6	Harvey	Pall
29—At Calif.	L	1-2	McCaskill	Rosenberg
30—At Calif.	W	3-2	Reuss	Finley
31—At Oak.	L	2-3	Moore	Thigpen

Won 14, Lost 11

AUGUST

			Winner	Loser
1—At Oak.	L	0-2	C. Young	Hibbard
2—At Oak.	L	0-2	Davis	Perez
3—At Oak.	W	6-4	Pall	Welch
4—Detroit	W	5-4	Patterson	Gibson
5—Detroit	W	7-6	King	Alexander
6—Detroit	L	3-4	Tanana	Hibbard
8—Oakland	L	2-3*	Honeycutt	Pall
9—Oakland	W	3-2†	McCarthy	Corsi
10—Oakland	L	1-4	Davis	Rosenberg
11—At Seattle	W	9-6*	Thigpen	Schooler
12—At Seattle	L	3-4*	Reed	Pall
13—At Seattle	W	6-4	Long	Comstock
14—Kan. City	W	4-3	Patterson	Aquino
15—Kan. City	L	6-10	Leach	McCarthy
16—Kan. City	L	4-5	Saberhagen	Thigpen
17—Texas	W	6-1	Hibbard	Brown
18—Texas	L	5-6	Jeffcoat	Perez
19—Texas	L	6-7	Witt	Dotson
20—Texas	L	1-7	Hough	Rosenberg
22—At Minn.	W	10-2	King	Rawley
23—At Minn.	L	7-8	Smith	Hibbard
24—At Minn.	L	4-6	Berenguer	Hillegas
25—At Cleve.	W	5-4	Dotson	Orosco
26—At Cleve.	W	4-3	Rosenberg	Black
27—At Cleve.	W	9-3	Hibbard	Farrell
29—At Toronto	L	2-3	Flanagan	Pall
30—At Toronto	L	1-2	Key	Dotson
31—At Toronto	L	1-5	Stieb	Rosenberg

Won 12, Lost 16

SEPTEMBER

			Winner	Loser
1—Baltimore	W	10-1	King	Milacki
2—Baltimore	L	1-2	Holton	Hibbard
3—Baltimore	W	4-2	Perez	Ballard
4—Toronto	L	2-5	Key	Dotson
5—Toronto	L	1-6	Stieb	Rosenberg
6—Toronto	L	2-4	Stottlemyre	King
8—At Detroit	L	5-7	Morris	Hibbard
9—At Detroit	W	13-3	Perez	Robinson
10—At Detroit	L	5-6	Henneman	Thigpen
11—At Balt.	L	3-6	Ballard	Rosenberg
12—At Balt.	W	11-3	King	Harnisch
13—At Balt.	W	3-0	Hibbard	Johnson
15—California	W	3-1	Perez	Abbott
15—California	L	1-2	Finley	Dotson
16—California	W	2-1	Hillegas	McCaskill
17—California	L	3-6	Witt	King
18—At K.C.	W	4-2	Jones	Montgomery
19—At K.C.	L	3-5	McWilliams	Dotson
20—At K.C.	W	7-2	Perez	Gubicza
22—At Texas	W	9-6	Jones	Guante
23—At Texas	L	4-6	Rogers	Segura
24—At Texas	L	4-5*	Russell	Rosenberg
25—Minnesota	W	10-2	Dotson	Guthrie
26—Minnesota	L	1-7	Aguilera	Perez
27—Minnesota	L	1-6	Dyer	Hillegas
29—Cleveland	W	2-1	King	Candiotti
30—Cleveland	W	8-2	Hibbard	Nichols

Won 13, Lost 14

OCTOBER

			Winner	Loser
1—Cleveland	L	0-1	Orosco	Dotson

Won 0, Lost 1

*10 innings. †11 innings. ‡16 innings.

Right fielder Ivan Calderon enjoyed a solid offensive season, batting .286 and leading the White Sox in homers (14) and RBIs (87).

injury, then languished on the bench for much of the year as a chronic shoulder problem curtailed his power (five homers, 26 RBIs). With Calderon moving to first base and then DH to replace Walker, two outfield spots eventually opened up.

The White Sox called up Lance Johnson from Class AAA Vancouver in late July and put him in left field, moving Pasqua to right. Then when Pasqua went down, Sosa was called up and placed in center, with Gallagher moving to right field. Johnson hit .300 and stole 16 bases after his promotion, while Sosa hit .273 for Chicago.

Calderon had a solid year, batting .286 with team highs in homers (14) and RBIs (87). Still, his 14 homers was the White Sox's lowest team-leading total since 1976. Gallagher suffered offensively, dropping from .303 as a 1988 rookie to .266. Daryl Boston, a part-time outfield starter, hit .252.

The White Sox lost a big gun when a back injury ended Kittle's season in June. The first baseman/DH was hitting .302 with 11 homers at the time.

Before Kittle went down, the White Sox already had lost catcher Carlton Fisk, who broke his hand. But Fisk returned after seven weeks and finished with a .293 average, 13 homers and 68 RBIs. And even when Fisk was gone, the backup catching situation was improved as Ron Karkovice, a career .168 hitter entering the season, vaulted to .264 under Hriniak.

Like the outfield, the infield started to jell in the second half. Rookie Carlos Martinez hit .300 in 350 at-bats and showed that he could play first and third base. Fletcher hit .272 after being obtained from Texas, while Guillen hit .253 and stole 36 bases. Versatile Steve Lyons (.264) performed well everywhere.

Bullpen closer Bobby Thigpen was the only bright spot on a dismal pitching staff. Thigpen saved 34 games, tying his own club record.

The White Sox had just one double-digit winner, Melido Perez, and he had to put on a late rush to reach 11-14. His 5.01 ERA was the rotation's second highest, behind Jerry Reuss' 5.06 mark. Reuss went 8-5 before being traded to Milwaukee in late July.

The rest of the rotation was a patchwork job that included Eric King, who was obtained from Detroit in March and sandwiched a 9-10 record around a stint on the disabled list; rookie Greg Hibbard, who won six games and led the staff with a 3.21 ERA; Richard Dotson, who was signed after being released by the New York Yankees in June and went 3-7 in 17 starts, and Shawn Hillegas (7-11) and Steve Rosenberg (4-13), both of whom struggled while flip-flopping between the rotation and long relief.

Besides Reuss, the only pitchers above .500 were in the bullpen: rookie Ken Patterson (6-1, 4.52 ERA) and Barry Jones (3-2, 2.37). But Jones was lost for much of the season after undergoing elbow surgery in May. Long reliever Bill Long (5-5, 3.92) refined a slider under coach Sammy Ellis to finally get his ERA under 4.00, while rookie Donn Pall (3.31 ERA) showed promise.

If there was a bright side to the '89 season, it was that Torborg was able to experiment with various combinations and see how his players would respond.

"We've been through a storm," Himes said, "but we paid the price (of rebuilding) and we know what we're doing is right."

First baseman Fred McGriff slumped over the final month of the 1989 season, but his 36 home runs still led the American League.

Blue Jays Soar Under Gaston

By NEIL MacCARL

If George Steinbrenner achieved the same success with in-season managerial changes as the Toronto Blue Jays, the New York Yankees would still be a dynasty. After all, Toronto is batting 1.000 in that department.

Until 1989, the Blue Jays had never changed managers during a season. But on May 15, Jimy Williams got the ax after Toronto had struggled to a 12-24 start in the American League East. He was replaced on an interim basis by batting coach Cito Gaston, who had no previous managerial experience and expressed no interest in the permanent job.

Nor did the Blue Jays seem interested in letting Gaston manage the rest of the year. They talked to several other candidates, including Yankees broadcaster Lou Piniella. But after Steinbrenner, the Yankees' principal owner, refused to release Piniella from his contract and no other leads panned out, both the Blue Jays and Gaston had a change of heart. The interim tag was removed May 31.

The move couldn't have worked out any better for the Blue Jays. Under Gaston, Toronto went 77-49—tops in the majors during his tenure—and ran down Baltimore to capture the A.L. East title by two games with an 89-73 record. The Blue Jays got thumped by Oakland in the A.L. Championship Series, but that defeat did little to tarnish their major accomplishment of the season: They didn't choke.

The Blue Jays had earned a reputation as chokers in 1985, when they blew a three-games-to-one lead in the playoffs against Kansas City, and reinforced it in 1987, when they watched a 3½-game lead disappear by losing their last seven games. But in '89, Toronto moved ahead of Baltimore on September 1 and never surrendered the lead. The division championship came down to a season-ending series against the Orioles at Toronto, and the Blue Jays won the first two games to clinch the title.

"We've proved everybody wrong; we've erased everything," center fielder Lloyd Moseby said. "People said we were too far back. People said we'd choke against the Orioles. We took it to the brink, but we didn't choke."

The key change that sparked the Blue Jays' resurgence was the appointment of Gaston, the fourth black manager in major league history and the first to take

Toronto third baseman Kelly Gruber established career highs with a .290 average and 18 home runs.

his team to the playoffs. Inheriting a team with a definite attitude problem, Gaston was advised that he would need to come down hard on some players. But that wasn't his style. "I treat people the way I would like to be treated," he said.

The Blue Jays made a few other important changes during the season. The first was on April 30, when they traded right fielder Jesse Barfield to the Yankees for pitcher Al Leiter. Barfield was batting only .200, and though Leiter made only one start for Toronto before a shoulder injury ended his season, the trade still worked out well for the Blue Jays.

Junior Felix was called up from Class AAA Syracuse to replace Barfield. The speedy rookie had eight home runs and 41

SCORES OF TORONTO BLUE JAYS' 1989 GAMES

APRIL			Winner	Loser
3—At K.C.	W	4-3	Key	Gubicza
5—At K.C.	L	1-2	Gordon	Stottlemyre
6—At K.C.	L	2-3	Montgomery	Ward
7—At Texas	W	10-9	Castillo	Guante
8—At Texas	L	4-5	Moyer	Key
9—At Texas	L	2-3	Rogers	Henke
10—At N.Y.	W	8-0	Stieb	Hawkins
11—At N.Y.	W	11-6*	Henke	Righetti
12—At N.Y.	L	3-5	Candelaria	Castillo
14—Kan. City	W	3-0	Key	Leibrandt
15—Kan. City	L	5-10	Aquino	Ward
16—Kan. City	W	15-8	Wells	Saberhagen
17—New York	L	2-7	Hawkins	Flanagan
18—New York	L	0-2	LaPoint	Musselman
19—New York	L	2-4	Candelaria	Key
21—Texas	W	6-3	Stieb	Brown
22—Texas	W	4-2	Ward	Hough
23—Texas	L	1-4	Ryan	Stottlemyre
24—At Oak.	L	4-5	Nelson	Henke
25—At Oak.	L	1-3	Davis	Cerutti
26—At Seattle	L	6-7	Trout	Wells
27—At Seattle	W	6-1	Flanagan	Dunne
28—At Calif.	L	0-9	McCaskill	Stottlemyre
29—At Calif.	L	3-4*	Minton	Ward
30—At Calif.	L	0-1†	McClure	Henke

Won 9, Lost 16

MAY			Winner	Loser
2—Oakland	L	5-8	Honeycutt	Ward
3—Oakland	W	2-0	Flanagan	Moore
4—California	L	2-3*	Harvey	Ward
5—California	L	3-5	Abbott	Cerutti
6—California	L	4-5	McClure	Ward
8—Seattle	W	10-1	Stieb	Dunne
9—Seattle	L	3-4	Hanson	Flanagan
10—Seattle	W	3-2	Key	Langston
12—At Minn.	L	5-6	Berenguer	Wells
13—At Minn.	L	8-10	Rawley	Stieb
14—At Minn.	L	1-13	Viola	Flanagan
15—Cleveland	W	5-3	Key	Farrell
16—Cleveland	W	7-6	Henke	Atherton
17—Cleveland	L	3-6	Black	Stieb
19—At Chicago	W	9-3	Flanagan	King
20—At Chicago	W	11-1	Key	Hillegas
21—At Chicago	W	9-3	Cerutti	Perez
22—Minnesota	L	2-6	Anderson	Stieb
23—Minnesota	W	2-1	Wells	Berenguer
24—Minnesota	L	4-10	Viola	Flanagan
26—Chicago	W	11-3	Key	Hillegas
27—Chicago	L	3-5	Perez	Cerutti
28—Chicago	W	7-5*	Henke	Thigpen
29—At Cleve.	L	3-5	Candiotti	Flanagan
30—At Cleve.	L	2-6	Farrell	Sanchez
31—At Cleve.	L	4-7	Black	Key

Won 11, Lost 15

JUNE			Winner	Loser
2—At Bos.	W	7-2	Cerutti	Dopson
3—At Bos.	W	10-2	Stieb	Boddicker
4—At Bos.	W	13-11‡	Ward	Lamp
5—Milwaukee	L	3-5	August	Key
6—Milwaukee	L	4-6	Aldrich	Ward
7—Milwaukee	W	4-2	Cerutti	Bosio
9—Detroit	W	2-0	Stieb	Tanana
10—Detroit	L	8-11	Williams	Key
11—Detroit	W	4-0	Flanagan	Schwabe
12—Detroit	W	5-4†	Henke	Gibson
13—At Milw.	W	4-3	Ward	Plesac
14—At Milw.	W	6-1	Stieb	Krueger
15—At Milw.	L	4-6	Fossas	Key
16—Seattle	W	4-3	Henke	Schooler
17—Seattle	W	3-2	Ward	Jackson
18—Seattle	L	2-8	Bankhead	Wills
19—At Calif.	W	8-1	Stieb	Finley
20—At Calif.	W	6-2	Key	McCaskill
21—At Calif.	W	6-1x	Henke	Minton
22—At Oak.	W	4-2§	Hernandez	Corsi
23—At Oak.	W	10-8	Buice	C. Young
24—At Oak.	L	1-7	Stewart	Stieb
25—At Oak.	L	3-6	Davis	Key
27—At Balt.	L	6-16	Tibbs	Flanagan
28—At Balt.	L	1-2	Hickey	Cerutti
29—At Balt.	W	11-1	Cummings	Schmidt
30—Boston	L	1-3	Boddicker	Wells

Won 17, Lost 10

JULY			Winner	Loser
1—Boston	L	1-3	Hetzel	Stottlemyre
2—Boston	L	1-4†	Murphy	Wells
3—Boston	W	3-2	Cerutti	Smithson
4—Baltimore	L	0-8	Schmidt	Stieb

JULY			Winner	Loser
5—Baltimore	L	4-5	Milacki	Key
6—Baltimore	W	4-1	Stottlemyre	Ballard
7—At Detroit	W	6-4	Cummings	Hernandez
8—At Detroit	W	8-3	Cerutti	Alexander
9—At Detroit	W	2-0	Stieb	Tanana
13—Oakland	L	7-11	Burns	Key
14—Oakland	W	4-1	Stieb	Welch
15—Oakland	W	6-1	Flanagan	Stewart
16—Oakland	L	2-6	Moore	Cerutti
17—California	W	6-4	Wells	Abbott
17—California	W	5-4	Wells	McClure
18—California	L	0-1	Blyleven	Key
20—At Seattle	L	2-5	Bankhead	Stieb
21—At Seattle	W	8-1	Flanagan	Harris
22—At Seattle	W	7-1	Cerutti	Dunne
23—At Seattle	L	2-5	Johnson	Key
24—At Texas	W	6-3	Stottlemyre	Alvarez
25—At Texas	W	4-0	Stieb	Ryan
26—At Texas	L	1-11	Brown	Flanagan
28—At N.Y.	W	6-2	Cerutti	LaPoint
29—At N.Y.	L	2-7	Cary	Key
30—At N.Y.	L	6-7	Guetterman	Ward
31—At N.Y.	W	6-5	Wells	Hawkins

Won 15, Lost 12

AUGUST			Winner	Loser
1—Kan. City	L	1-2	Saberhagen	Stottlemyre
2—Kan. City	W	8-0	Cerutti	Gubicza
3—Kan. City	L	0-5	Gordon	Key
4—New York	W	2-1	Stieb	Parker
5—New York	L	4-5	Hawkins	Ward
6—New York	W	6-5	Stottlemyre	Terrell
7—Texas	W	2-1	Cerutti	Jeffcoat
8—Texas	W	7-0	Gozzo	Witt
9—Texas	L	3-4	Hough	Stieb
11—At K.C.	L	2-6	Saberhagen	Flanagan
12—At K.C.	W	2-0	Stottlemyre	Gubicza
13—At K.C.	L	3-8	Gordon	Cerutti
14—At Bos.	W	4-2	Gozzo	Boddicker
15—At Bos.	W	7-2	Stieb	Smithson
16—At Bos.	W	7-3	Wells	Murphy
17—At Balt.	L	6-11	Ballard	Cerutti
18—At Balt.	W	9-2	Gozzo	Johnson
19—At Balt.	W	5-1	Key	Milacki
20—At Balt.	L	2-7	Harnisch	Stieb
22—Detroit	W	3-2x	Gozzo	Nunez
23—Detroit	W	11-4	Wills	Robinson
24—Detroit	W	11-3	Flanagan	Morris
25—Milwaukee	W	3-1	Key	Peterek
26—Milwaukee	W	7-0	Stieb	Higuera
27—Milwaukee	W	5-4	Stottlemyre	Bosio
28—Milwaukee	L	2-8	Filer	Cerutti
29—Chicago	W	3-2	Flanagan	Pall
30—Chicago	W	2-1	Key	Dotson
31—Chicago	W	5-1	Stieb	Rosenberg

Won 20, Lost 9

SEPTEMBER			Winner	Loser
1—Minnesota	W	7-3	Stottlemyre	Guthrie
2—Minnesota	W	4-2	Cerutti	Smith
3—Minnesota	L	4-9	Aguilera	Flanagan
4—At Chicago	W	5-2	Key	Dotson
5—At Chicago	W	6-1	Stieb	Rosenberg
6—At Chicago	W	4-2	Stottlemyre	King
7—At Cleve.	W	12-4	Cerutti	Candiotti
8—At Cleve.	L	4-5	Jones	Acker
9—At Cleve.	W	7-5y	Wills	Kaiser
10—At Cleve.	W	5-4*	Acker	Olin
12—At Minn.	L	2-8	West	Stottlemyre
13—At Minn.	L	2-3	Tapani	Cerutti
14—At Minn.	L	0-2	Guthrie	Flanagan
15—Cleveland	W	5-2	Key	Swindell
16—Cleveland	W	3-2†	Wells	Jones
17—Cleveland	W	2-1*	Acker	Bailes
18—Boston	L	3-6	Boddicker	Cerutti
19—Boston	W	6-5§	Henke	Harris
20—Boston	L	3-10	Clemens	Key
22—At Milw.	W	7-3	Stieb	Reuss
23—At Milw.	L	1-4	August	Stottlemyre
24—At Milw.	L	3-8	Filer	Cerutti
25—At Detroit	W	2-0	Key	DuBois
26—At Detroit	L	3-4	Henneman	Ward
27—At Detroit	W	8-1	Stieb	Alexander
29—At Baltimore	W	2-1†	Henke	Williamson
30—At Baltimore	W	4-3	Wills	Williamson

Won 17, Lost 10

OCTOBER			Winner	Loser
1—Baltimore	L	5-7	McDonald	Gozzo

Won 0, Lost 1

*10 innings. †11 innings. ‡12 innings. §13 innings. x14 innings. y16 innings.

runs batted in at the All-Star break, but he slumped badly after injuring a shoulder in a collision with an outfield fence July 30.

Even so, the Blue Jays were in good shape—thanks to another trade. On August 1, Mookie Wilson was obtained from the New York Mets in exchange for two pitchers. Wilson quickly became the fan favorite in Toronto with his aggressive baserunning (12 stolen bases) and solid hitting (.298) while starting at all three outfield positions. About the same time, Toronto picked up Lee Mazzilli from the Mets on waivers, and the veteran responded with four homers and 11 RBIs in limited duty as a designated hitter and pinch-hitter.

"Thank you for showing us how to win," N.E. (Peter) Hardy, the club's chief executive officer, told the two former Mets after the Blue Jays shot to the front of the pack by winning 20 of 29 games in August.

The Blue Jays also seemed to get a boost from a change of address. After starting the season with a 12-14 home record at Exhibition Stadium, they moved into the SkyDome—with its retractable roof and huge video scoreboard—on June 5 and won 34 of 55 games at their new home. The Blue Jays benefited from tremendous support at the SkyDome as they sold out 50 games and set an A.L. attendance record with more than 3.3 million fans.

The Toronto faithful had a number of good performances to watch, including several by Dave Stieb, the Blue Jays' top winner with a 17-8 record. Stieb tossed a pair of one-hit shutouts and came within one out of a perfect game against the Yankees on August 4, finally giving up two hits and earning a 2-1 victory.

Stieb's 3.35 earned-run average ranked second among the starters to John Cerutti's 3.07 ERA. But Cerutti was winless in his first seven starts and finished at 11-11.

Jimmy Key got off to a 6-2 start, then lost 11 of his next 12 decisions before going on the disabled list with a shoulder injury. He won six of his last seven decisions to finish at 13-14 with a 3.88 ERA.

Mike Flanagan (8-10, 3.93 ERA) also was inconsistent. Todd Stottlemyre (7-7, 3.88) fizzled in relief, but after a demotion to Syracuse he established himself as a solid starter in the second half.

Tom Henke headed an effective bullpen with 20 saves and a 1.92 ERA. He came on strong after a terrible first month, and in the second half there wasn't a better closer in the league. Toronto had another stopper in Duane Ward, who lost 10 games but saved 15. David Wells (7-4, 2.40) provided solid middle relief, while the acquisition of Jim Acker (2-1, 1.59) from Atlanta in late August added bullpen depth.

The two biggest bats in the Toronto lineup belonged to first baseman Fred McGriff and left fielder/DH George Bell.

McGriff was the A.L. home run king with 36, and his .525 slugging percentage and 119 walks both ranked second in the league. But he slumped down the stretch, batting only .223 after August 31 and going the last 24 games without a homer. He also made 17 errors at first base.

Bell batted .297 and led the club with 104 RBIs. But his home run output dipped to a career-low 18.

Moseby continued his slide, batting .221 with 11 homers and 43 RBIs. But in the two key victories over the Orioles in late September, Moseby drove in the winning run in one and keyed Toronto's winning rally with a sacrifice bunt in the other. And with 24 stolen bases—his lowest total in seven years—he still led the club.

Third baseman Kelly Gruber established career highs with a .290 average and 18 homers despite suffering a hand injury in a freak accident August 9 when he collided with umpire Don Denkinger. He went on the disabled list, and his hand was sore for the rest of the season. He finished with 73 RBIs, eight shy of his career best.

Rance Mulliniks filled in at third when Gruber was injured and spent the rest of the season as Toronto's primary DH. But in 273 at-bats, he knocked in only 29 runs.

Shortstop Tony Fernandez bounced back after missing most of April when a pitched ball fractured his cheekbone. His .257 average was his lowest ever, but he hit a career-high 11 homers and won his fourth Gold Glove, committing just six errors in 140 games.

The No. 1 second baseman was Nelson Liriano, who batted .263 and, in the span of six days, spoiled a pair of no-hitters with ninth-inning hits. Down the stretch, Gaston platooned Liriano with Manny Lee (.260), who also started at third base and shortstop.

Catcher Ernie Whitt was batting .300 at the All-Star break, but he slumped to a .262 finish and threw out only 19 of 75 runners trying to steal. Backup Pat Borders gunned down 17 of 48 runners.

Overall, it was a solid year for the Blue Jays, though not an overpowering one. They ranked fourth in the league in pitching (3.58 ERA) and eighth in batting (.260), yet still won the division. Clearly, much of the credit for that must go to Gaston, the manager who didn't even want the job.

Gregg Olson established a rookie record with 27 saves and captured the American League's Rookie of the Year award.

O's Fall Just Short of Miracle

By JIM HENNEMAN

The 1989 Baltimore Orioles will long be remembered as one of the most celebrated non-championship teams of all time.

While teams that finish second seldom etch themselves into the sports public's memory, the Orioles did. After all, this was a team that had lost 107 games the year before and was almost universally picked to finish last in the American League East.

But this also was a young team that had little interest in history. The Orioles were more concerned with their present. So what if no team in the modern era had ever gone from last place to first in one season? The Orioles had nothing to lose by giving it their best shot.

It was almost good enough. The Orioles held first place for 98 consecutive days, enjoying a run longer than many Broadway plays. They built a 7½-game lead by mid-July and tried to nurse it to the wire. Even a disastrous stretch in which they lost 13 of 14 games from July 19-August 1 wasn't enough to knock the Orioles out of first place. They recovered gamely and held onto the lead for the rest of the month before falling behind the Toronto Blue Jays for good September 1.

They lagged no more than 2½ games off the pace over the next four weeks, however, as the division title came down to a season-ending three-game series at Toronto. The Blue Jays came from behind to win the first two games, eliminating the Orioles on the next-to-last day of their storybook season.

"I'm more proud than I am disappointed," said Manager Frank Robinson, whose team finished with an 87-75 record, two games behind Toronto.

But Robinson was disappointed, as were his players, who were not happy to settle for a surprisingly good season. They wanted to win it all.

"You get this close, you can taste it," said Robinson, the A.L. Manager of the Year. "This hurts a little bit, but in time it will be something to look back on with pride.

"If you could guarantee that managing would be like this every year, I'd manage for the rest of my life. I'm not talking about results, but the total effort the players gave me."

Had it not been for a late-season injury to catcher Mickey Tettleton, the Orioles might have done even better than their

Catcher Mickey Tettleton hit 26 home runs and was a key figure in Baltimore's dramatic turnaround.

32½-game turnaround—the second-best one-year improvement in A.L. history. Tettleton symbolized Baltimore's first-half rise to prominence, hitting 20 home runs by the All-Star break after collecting no more than 11 in any previous major league season. But a knee injury that required surgery in early August limited him to six homers in the second half.

Tettleton and shortstop Cal Ripken (21 homers, a team-high 93 runs batted in) were Baltimore's only big-number guys in the lineup. The Orioles worked their magic with an opportunistic offense, a defense that was spectacular throughout the season and a pitching staff anchored by closer Gregg Olson, the league's Rookie of the Year.

Olson failed in only six of 33 save opportunities and did not allow a run after July 31, finishing with a 1.69 earned-run average. His 27 saves established a new A.L. rookie record. Mark Williamson (10-5, 2.93 ERA, nine saves) was brilliant most of the year as Olson's setup man, giving the Orioles a solid finishing act. Mark Thurmond (3.90 ERA) and spot starter Brian Holton (5-7, 4.02) provided adequate long relief.

While the bullpen was one of the league's best, the rotation was just good enough to

SCORES OF BALTIMORE ORIOLES' 1989 GAMES

APRIL			Winner	Loser
3—Boston	W	5-4†	Holton	Stanley
6—Boston	W	6-4	Bautista	Smithson
7—At Minn.	L	3-8	Smith	Milacki
8—At Minn.	L	5-6	Gonzalez	Holton
9—At Minn.	W	8-1	Ballard	Viola
10—At K.C.	L	0-3	Saberhagen	Harnisch
11—At K.C.	L	5-6	Bannister	Bautista
12—At K.C.	W	5-4§	Olson	Farr
14—At Bos.	L	4-7	Dopson	Schmidt
15—At Bos.	W	12-4	Ballard	Boddicker
17—At Bos.	L	4-6	Smith	Holton
18—Kan. City	L	4-7‡	Gordon	Williamson
19—Kan. City	W	6-5	Schmidt	Leibrandt
20—Kan. City	W	2-0	Ballard	Saberhagen
21—Minnesota	L	1-7	Anderson	Bautista
22—Minnesota	W	4-1	Olson	Toliver
23—Minnesota	W	3-0	Milacki	Rawley
24—At Calif.	L	2-3	Abbott	Schmidt
25—At Calif.	W	8-1	Ballard	Witt
26—At Oak.	W	2-1	Bautista	Welch
27—At Oak.	L	4-9	Burns	Thurmond
28—At Seattle	L	5-11	Reed	Holton
29—At Seattle	L	3-4	Langston	Schmidt
30—At Seattle	W	4-3	Ballard	Trout
Won 12, Lost 12				

MAY			Winner	Loser
2—California	W	4-3	Olson	Fraser
3—California	L	0-2	Monteleone	Milacki
6—Seattle	L	1-2	Langston	Schmidt
6—Seattle	L	5-6	Bankhead	Ballard
7—Seattle	L	3-5	Swift	Bautista
8—Oakland	L	1-6	Moore	Milacki
11—Oakland	W	6-2	Ballard	Stewart
12—Chicago	W	9-6	Thurmond	McCarthy
13—Chicago	L	2-8	King	Milacki
14—Chicago	L	5-8	Rosenberg	Williamson
17—At Texas	W	8-2	Schmidt	Hough
18—Cleveland	W	3-2*	Williamson	Atherton
19—Cleveland	L	1-4	Candiotti	Bautista
20—Cleveland	W	5-1	Ballard	Farrell
21—Cleveland	L	0-2	Yett	Holton
22—At Chicago	W	5-1	Schmidt	Rosenberg
23—At Chicago	W	9-3	Milacki	Long
24—At Chicago	W	8-0	Tibbs	King
26—At Cleve.	W	5-2	Ballard	Yett
27—At Cleve.	W	5-1	Schmidt	Black
28—At Cleve.	L	0-1	Swindell	Milacki
29—Texas	W	6-1	Holton	Ryan
30—Texas	W	6-2	Williamson	Moyer
31—Texas	W	8-5	Williamson	Witt
Won 14, Lost 10				

JUNE			Winner	Loser
1—At Detroit	W	8-3	Schmidt	Nosek
2—At Detroit	W	4-1	Milacki	Trujillo
3—At Detroit	W	4-2	Hickey	Alexander
4—At Detroit	W	7-4	Tibbs	Tanana
5—At N.Y.	W	16-3	Ballard	Hawkins
6—At N.Y.	L	0-4	LaPoint	Schmidt
8—Milwaukee	L	2-6	Knudson	Milacki
9—Milwaukee	W	7-1	Williamson	Clutterbuck
10—Milwaukee	L	0-6	August	Ballard
11—Milwaukee	L	1-3	Crim	Hickey
13—New York	W	5-2	Schmidt	LaPoint
14—New York	L	1-2	Guetterman	Hickey
15—New York	W	3-2*	Thurmond	McCullers
16—Oakland	L	5-7	Davis	Holton
16—Oakland	W	5-1	Tibbs	Moore
17—Oakland	W	4-2	Bautista	M. Young
18—Oakland	W	4-2	Schmidt	C. Young
19—At Seattle	W	9-5	Milacki	Jackson
20—At Seattle	W	8-6	Weston	Reed
21—At Seattle	W	8-6	Tibbs	Holman
22—At Calif.	W	6-5	Williamson	Fraser
23—At Calif.	L	1-5	Witt	Schmidt
24—At Calif.	L	3-8	Finley	Milacki
25—At Calif.	L	6-7	McCaskill	Ballard
27—Toronto	W	16-6	Tibbs	Flanagan
28—Toronto	W	2-1	Hickey	Cerutti
29—Toronto	L	1-11	Cummings	Schmidt
30—Detroit	W	5-16	Schwabe	Milacki
Won 17, Lost 11				

JULY			Winner	Loser
1—Detroit	W	8-1	Ballard	Hudson
2—Detroit	L	3-7	Nunez	Thurmond
3—Detroit	W	11-4	Smith	Alexander
4—At Toronto	W	8-0	Schmidt	Stieb
5—At Toronto	W	5-4	Milacki	Key
6—At Toronto	L	1-4	Stottlemyre	Ballard

JULY			Winner	Loser
7—At Milw.	L	4-6	August	Harnisch
8—At Milw.	W	5-2	Holton	Higuera
9—At Milw.	L	2-7	Bosio	Schmidt
13—California	L	5-13	Blyleven	Thurmond
14—California	W	6-4	Holton	McCaskill
15—California	W	11-9	Williamson	Harvey
16—California	W	3-2†	Smith	Fraser
17—Seattle	W	8-4	Harnisch	Dunne
18—Seattle	W	4-3	Ballard	Johnson
19—Seattle	L	0-7	Holman	Holton
20—At Oak.	L	2-5	Stewart	Schmidt
21—At Oak.	L	2-3	Moore	Olson
22—At Oak.	L	1-3	Welch	Harnisch
23—At Oak.	L	2-3	Davis	Ballard
25—At Minn.	L	3-9	Anderson	Schmidt
26—At Minn.	L	4-5	Reardon	Williamson
27—At Minn.	L	6-10	Smith	Harnisch
28—At K.C.	W	4-3‡	Williamson	Montgomery
29—At K.C.	L	0-5	Aquino	Schmidt
30—At K.C.	L	6-7	Farr	Olson
31—At Bos.	L	6-9	Stanley	Milacki
Won 11, Lost 16				

AUGUST			Winner	Loser
1—At Bos.	L	3-5	Murphy	Harnisch
1—At Bos.	L	2-6	Gardner	Johnson
2—At Bos.	W	9-8	Williamson	Hetzel
4—Texas	L	4-6	Hough	Schmidt
5—Texas	W	5-2	Milacki	Ryan
6—Texas	W	3-2*	Williamson	Russell
7—Minnesota	L	2-4	Smith	Ballard
8—Minnesota	W	6-1	Johnson	Aguilera
9—Minnesota	L	0-7	Anderson	Thurmond
11—Boston	L	4-6	Clemens	Milacki
11—Boston	W	4-1	Harnisch	Smithson
12—Boston	L	8-10‡	Stanley	Hickey
13—Boston	W	6-1	Johnson	Bolton
14—At Detroit	W	4-1*	Schmidt	Morris
15—At Detroit	W	2-0	Milacki	Alexander
16—At Detroit	L	0-4	Tanana	Harnisch
17—Toronto	W	11-6	Ballard	Cerutti
18—Toronto	L	2-9	Gozzo	Johnson
19—Toronto	L	1-5	Key	Milacki
20—Toronto	W	7-2	Harnisch	Stieb
21—Milwaukee	W	5-0	Ballard	Reuss
22—Milwaukee	W	4-2	Johnson	Bosio
23—Milwaukee	W	3-1	Milacki	Filer
24—At N.Y.	L	1-5	Cary	Harnisch
24—At N.Y.	W	9-2	Schmidt	Plunk
25—At N.Y.	W	3-1	Ballard	Parker
26—At N.Y.	W	6-4	Johnson	Terrell
27—At N.Y.	W	8-5	Milacki	Cadaret
29—At Cleve.	L	1-3	Jones	Harnisch
30—At Cleve.	W	7-4	Ballard	Swindell
31—At Cleve.	L	0-11	Farrell	Johnson
Won 18, Lost 13				

SEPTEMBER			Winner	Loser
1—At Chicago	L	1-10	King	Milacki
2—At Chicago	W	2-1	Holton	Hibbard
3—At Chicago	W	2-4	Perez	Ballard
4—Cleveland	W	5-4	Williamson	Nichols
5—Cleveland	W	3-1	Milacki	Farrell
6—Cleveland	L	0-9	Black	Schilling
7—At Texas	W	8-3	Ballard	Ryan
7—At Texas	W	9-6	Harnisch	Witt
8—At Texas	L	1-3	Brown	Johnson
9—At Texas	W	4-2*	Olson	Hall
10—At Texas	L	1-8	Moyer	Schmidt
11—Chicago	W	6-3	Ballard	Rosenberg
12—Chicago	L	1-11	King	Harnisch
13—Chicago	L	0-3	Hibbard	Johnson
15—Kan. City	W	5-2	Milacki	Crawford
16—Kan. City	W	7-5	Olson	Leach
17—Kan. City	L	0-7	Saberhagen	Johnson
19—Detroit	W	6-2	Milacki	Morris
20—Detroit	W	9-2	Ballard	Tanana
22—New York	L	4-5	Terrell	Holton
23—New York	W	10-2	Milacki	Plunk
24—New York	L	0-2	Cary	Ballard
25—At Milw.	W	5-3	Harnisch	Higuera
26—At Milw.	L	3-7	Navarro	Johnson
27—At Milw.	W	4-0	Milacki	Reuss
29—At Toronto	L	1-2†	Henke	Williamson
30—At Toronto	L	3-4	Wills	Williamson
Won 14, Lost 13				

OCTOBER			Winner	Loser
1—At Toronto	W	7-5	McDonald	Gozzo
Won 1, Lost 0				

*10 innings. †11 innings. ‡13 innings. §15 innings.

Jeff Ballard came out of nowhere to lead all A.L. lefthanders with 18 victories.

keep the Orioles in contention. But depth was a big problem down the stretch as Robinson tried to juggle his staff around two strong starters, Jeff Ballard and rookie Bob Milacki. In the end, the Orioles simply didn't have enough able arms.

But their top two were impressive. Ballard, who had spent parts of the last two seasons at Class AAA Rochester, led all A.L. lefthanders with 18 wins and fashioned a 3.43 ERA. Milacki went 14-12 with a 3.74 ERA and shared the A.L. lead with 36 starts, becoming the first rookie in 71 years to lead the league in that category.

Dave Schmidt was the No. 1 starter when the season opened, but the last two months he was almost lost in the bullpen. He finished with a 10-13 record and a 5.69 ERA, by far the highest of his career. Jose Bautista (3-4, 5.31) opened as the No. 2 man but spent the year bouncing back and forth between Baltimore and Rochester. Rookie Pete Harnisch (5-9, 4.62) also did a stint at Rochester and was the club's hard-luck pitcher, getting the lowest run support from his teammates while holding opponents to a .249 average, lowest among Baltimore starters. Rookie Dave Johnson, a late-blooming local hero, won four games in August after being called up from the minors.

But it was the defense that was the heart

and soul of the Orioles. The outfield, with Phil Bradley, Mike Devereaux, Steve Finley and Joe Orsulak leading the way, provided the most dramatic contrast, vastly improving an area that had been a glaring weakness in recent years. Ripken had the best defensive year of his career, making only eight errors and stabilizing an infield that included brother Bill at second base and rookie Craig Worthington at third. Tettleton was a workhorse catcher until his injury, which reduced him to the designated hitter role in the final weeks. Bob Melvin assumed most of the burden the final two months, despite a nagging back injury. Melvin was dependable behind the plate and adequate offensively (.241).

The Orioles hit only .252 as a team (12th in the league) but used their speed to score 708 runs, more than all but four A.L. teams. The outfield was particularly swift, with Devereaux, Bradley, Finley and Brady Anderson combining for 75 stolen bases.

The outfield did not pack much punch, though, as left fielder Bradley and right fielder Orsulak led that group with 55 RBIs each. At .285, Orsulak was Baltimore's top hitter. Devereaux (.266) and Finley (.249), who each played all three outfield positions, enjoyed solid rookie seasons, while Anderson (.207) slumped after a promising start.

Worthington played 145 games at third base, nailing down a position that had been a longtime problem for the Orioles. He was often spectacular in the field and a good run producer at the plate (15 homers, 70 RBIs) despite a slow start that had him under .200 as late as June 15.

The Orioles' offense was lacking on the right side of the infield, particularly at second base. Injury-plagued Bill Ripken batted .239, while backup Rene Gonzales hit only .217. First baseman Randy Milligan hit .268 with 12 homers in his first full major league season, but backup Jim Traber (.209) contributed almost nothing in the second half.

The Orioles got little production from the DH spot. Led by Larry Sheets (.243), Baltimore DHs batted only .237, the league's second-lowest average.

Obviously, the Orioles left some room for improvement. But their '89 performance ended the club's horrendous three-year skid and showed that the foundation of the franchise no longer is on the verge of collapse.

"We'll be back," Robinson said. "We proved that we could play with the big boys."

Veteran Dwight Evans continued to defy his age, batting .285 with 20 home runs and 100 RBIs in 1989.

Red Sox Lose Success Formula

By JOE GIULIOTTI

The so-called "Morgan magic" that sparked the Boston Red Sox to the 1988 American League East title vanished in 1989. The glitter was gone before the club ever left spring camp, and the problems between Joe Morgan and his players only got worse as the year dragged on.

At the '88 All-Star break, Morgan—Boston's third-base coach and previously a longtime manager in the minor leagues——had replaced John McNamara as manager. The Red Sox then went on a tear, winning 19 of their first 20 games and capturing their second division title in three years. Naturally, Morgan received much of the credit and became a local hero.

The '89 season, however, was a different story.

The Red Sox were never serious contenders, although they stayed close to the top for five months simply because the division was so weak. An eight-game losing streak in mid-September ended their slim championship hopes, and the Red Sox had to win 13 of their last 16 games just to finish third with an 83-79 record, six games out of first place. It was a poor showing all the way around.

Privately, many players claimed the manager lost control of the team—a charge Morgan and the front office strongly denied. But Boston was a team in disarray even before the season started.

Spring training was a circus. There were the Margo Adams kiss-and-tell articles in Penthouse magazine that detailed her four-year affair with third baseman Wade Boggs and mentioned several Boston players in an unfavorable light. There was Boggs' rebuttal to Adams' allegations on ABC's "20/20." There were clubhouse meetings to clear the air between Boggs and peeved teammates. And there were Morgan's two departures from camp—first for a Communion breakfast at his alma mater (Boston College), then for a St. Patrick's Day parade in his hometown of Walpole, Mass.

It was the second defection that opened the gap between the manager and players. Morgan had ripped the Red Sox, calling them "a dead team," just before boarding the plane home—a move that did not sit well with the players.

Morgan had several problems with his pitching staff during the season. Bob Stanley blasted Morgan after being ig-

nored in the bullpen. Between June 22 and July 31, Stanley worked only three innings and endured 10- and 13-day stretches without pitching. Morgan denied losing confidence in the veteran reliever, but Stanley wasn't convinced. "I want to pitch and (Morgan) won't use me," he said. "If he's got no confidence in me, then let me go somewhere else."

The Red Sox appeared willing to give him that opportunity when they showed no interest in picking up his option for 1990. But Stanley, who finished with a 4.88 earned-run average, decided to retire.

Joe Price criticized Morgan for his handling of a game in Oakland, then cursed the manager in the dugout after being lifted following a poor performance in Anaheim. That outburst cost Price, another reliever who struggled (4.35 ERA), a four-day suspension.

"I know the relievers don't like me," Morgan said, "but I can't help that. They don't like me because I won't keep a guy out there when he's not doing the job."

Another unhappy camper was designated hitter Jim Rice, who didn't like the manner in which he was released after more than 15 years with the Red Sox. Rice said the organization "showed me no class," adding that the lack of class "starts upstairs and goes right down to the man who puts the names in the lineups." His assessment of Morgan's managerial ability was not kind.

Other players voiced complaints, but Morgan shrugged them off. "Some (players) don't do the job and they keep making excuses for the way they are," he said. "I believe that's just a little babyness coming out in them."

The Red Sox had all kinds of problems on the field, too, primarily with injuries. The pitching staff was hit particularly hard. John Dopson missed a month with an arm injury and finished at 12-8 with a 3.99 ERA. Oil Can Boyd made only 10 starts (five in September) because of another life-threatening blood clot near his shoulder. A third starter, Wes Gardner (3-7, 5.97 ERA), was both injured and inconsistent and made only 16 starts.

Elbow surgery limited Rice, who had enjoyed a great spring, to only 56 games, three home runs and 28 runs batted in. Center fielder Ellis Burks, the team's best all-around player, suffered two shoulder injuries that sidelined him for 65 games. He played well when healthy, batting .303

SCORES OF BOSTON RED SOX' 1989 GAMES

APRIL

Date		Score	Winner	Loser
3—At Balt.	L	4-5‡	Holton	Stanley
6—At Balt.	L	4-6	Bautista	Smithson
7—At K.C.	L	8-9	Montgomery	Smith
8—At K.C.	L	1-2†	Aquino	Murphy
9—At K.C.	W	8-6	Dopson	Montgomery
10—Cleveland	W	5-2	Boddicker	Skalski
12—Cleveland	L	6-10	Black	Boyd
13—Cleveland	W	9-1	Clemens	Yett
14—Baltimore	W	7-4	Dopson	Schmidt
15—Baltimore	L	4-12	Ballard	Boddicker
17—Baltimore	W	6-4	Smith	Holton
19—At Cleve.	W	8-4	Clemens	Black
20—At Cleve.	W	5-2	Boyd	Yett
21—Kan. City	L	4-7	Bannister	Dopson
22—Kan. City	L	3-7	Gubicza	Boddicker
23—Kan. City	L	0-10	Leibrandt	Gardner
25—Chicago	W	11-0	Clemens	Perez
26—Chicago	W	5-4†	Stanley	Jones
27—Chicago	L	1-3a	Pall	Smithson
28—At Texas	W	6-7x	Guante	Murphy
29—At Texas	W	8-5	Gardner	Hough
30—At Texas	L	1-2	Ryan	Clemens

Won 10, Lost 12

MAY

Date		Score	Winner	Loser
1—At Minn.	W	13-6	Boyd	Anderson
2—At Minn.	W	4-2	Dopson	Gonzalez
3—At Chicago	W	8-4	Boddicker	Hillegas
4—At Chicago	L	4-5	Long	Gardner
5—Texas	W	7-6	Clemens	Ryan
6—Texas	W	7-0	Smithson	Witt
7—Texas	W	9-5	Dopson	Moyer
8—Minnesota	L	2-4	Rawley	Boddicker
9—Minnesota	L	2-6	Viola	Gardner
12—At Seattle	W	2-0	Clemens	Bankhead
13—At Seattle	L	6-14	Reed	Dopson
14—At Seattle	L	3-4	Trout	Boddicker
16—At Calif.	L	2-7	McCaskill	Smithson
17—At Calif.	L	0-5	Abbott	Clemens
18—At Calif.	W	5-2	Dopson	Witt
19—At Oak.	W	7-4†	Stanley	Nelson
20—At Oak.	L	3-6	Stewart	Gardner
21—At Oak.	L	4-5	Burns	Clemens
23—Seattle	W	6-5	Smith	Reed
24—Seattle	W	6-5	Boddicker	Hanson
25—Seattle	W	10-0	Smithson	Dunne
26—California	L	0-5	Finley	Clemens
28—California	L	0-3	McCaskill	Dopson
29—Oakland	W	3-2†	Smith	Welch
30—Oakland	L	2-4	Stewart	Smithson
31—Oakland	W	4-3†	Smith	Plunk

Won 14, Lost 12

JUNE

Date		Score	Winner	Loser
2—Toronto	L	2-7	Cerutti	Dopson
3—Toronto	L	2-10	Stieb	Boddicker
4—Toronto	L	11-13§	Ward	Lamp
5—At Detroit	W	5-2	Clemens	Palmer
6—At Detroit	L	1-5	Schwabe	Price
7—At Detroit	W	6-1	Dopson	Alexander
8—At N.Y.	L	7-8‡	McCullers	Stanley
10—At N.Y.	W	14-8	Clemens	Dotson
11—At N.Y.	L	2-4	Hawkins	Price
11—At N.Y.	L	7-8	Nielsen	Murphy
13—Detroit	W	8-7	Gardner	Williams
14—Detroit	L	3-7	Tanana	Boddicker
16—At Chicago	W	2-0	Clemens	Patterson
17—At Chicago	W	6-1	Smithson	Perez
18—At Chicago	W	7-4	Price	Rosenberg
19—At Chicago	L	2-8	Hillegas	Dopson
20—Texas	W	6-3	Boddicker	Russell
21—Texas	L	3-10	Mielke	Clemens
22—Texas	L	1-9	Brown	Smithson
23—Minnesota	L	0-10	Viola	Price
24—Minnesota	W	6-2	Dopson	Oliveras
24—Minnesota	W	11-2	Smithson	Toliver
25—Minnesota	L	0-7	Anderson	Boddicker
27—At Milw.	L	4-5	August	Clemens
28—At Milw.	L	5-12	Higuera	Smithson
29—At Milw.	W	2-1	Dopson	Bosio
30—At Toronto	W	3-1	Boddicker	Wells

Won 12, Lost 15

JULY

Date		Score	Winner	Loser
1—At Toronto	W	3-1	Hetzel	Stottlemyre
2—At Toronto	W	4-1‡	Murphy	Wells
3—At Toronto	L	2-3	Cerutti	Smithson
4—Milwaukee	L	3-4	Bosio	Price
6—Milwaukee	W	5-4	Boddicker	Navarro
7—New York	W	6-4	Clemens	Cadaret
8—New York	L	5-7	Plunk	Smithson
9—New York	W	10-5	Smith	Schulze
13—At Minn.	W	3-1	Clemens	Viola
14—At Minn.	W	5-0	Boddicker	Anderson
15—At Minn.	L	2-3	Berenguer	Smithson
16—At Minn.	L	3-4‡	St. Claire	Murphy
17—At Texas	L	6-12	Guante	Gardner
18—At Texas	L	1-8	Witt	Clemens
19—At Texas	W	4-0	Boddicker	Hough
21—Chicago	L	0-1	Perez	Hetzel
22—Chicago	L	6-10	Patterson	Murphy
23—Chicago	W	8-2	Clemens	Rosenberg
25—Kan. City	W	10-0	Boddicker	Leibrandt
26—Kan. City	L	4-7	Saberhagen	Price
27—Kan. City	W	7-2	Dopson	Gordon
28—At Cleve.	L	2-3	Candiotti	Clemens
28—At Cleve.	L	1-2	Nichols	Gardner
29—At Cleve.	W	5-0	Smithson	Black
30—At Cleve.	W	5-2	Lamp	Farrell
31—Baltimore	W	9-6	Stanley	Milacki

Won 14, Lost 12

AUGUST

Date		Score	Winner	Loser
1—Baltimore	W	5-3	Murphy	Harnisch
1—Baltimore	W	6-2	Gardner	Johnson
2—Baltimore	L	8-9	Williamson	Hetzel
3—Cleveland	L	2-4	Nichols	Bolton
4—Cleveland	L	3-4	Black	Boddicker
5—Cleveland	W	10-2	Smithson	Farrell
6—Cleveland	W	6-4	Murphy	Orosco
7—At K.C.	L	4-6	Gubicza	Harris
8—At K.C.	L	1-8	Gordon	Bolton
9—At K.C.	W	6-2	Boddicker	Aquino
11—At Balt.	W	6-4	Clemens	Milacki
11—At Balt.	L	1-4	Harnisch	Smithson
12—At Balt.	W	10-8y	Stanley	Hickey
13—At Balt.	L	1-6	Johnson	Bolton
14—Toronto	L	2-4	Gozzo	Boddicker
15—Toronto	L	2-7	Stieb	Smithson
16—Toronto	L	3-7	Wells	Murphy
17—At Milw.	L	4-8	Bosio	Gardner
18—At Milw.	L	2-5	Filer	Bolton
19—At Milw.	W	3-1z	Harris	Knudson
20—At Milw.	L	3-6	Navarro	Smithson
21—At N.Y.	L	4-6	Terrell	Clemens
22—At N.Y.	W	4-3	Murphy	Candelaria
23—At N.Y.	W	4-1	Boddicker	Hawkins
25—Detroit	W	4-2	Smithson	Alexander
25—Detroit	W	11-3	Lamp	Ritz
26—Detroit	W	5-2	Clemens	Tanana
27—Detroit	W	7-1	Price	DuBois
28—Detroit	W	6-3	Boddicker	Robinson
29—California	W	8-4	Lamp	Blyleven
29—California	W	13-5*	Stanley	Petry
30—California	L	0-4	Abbott	Dopson
31—California	W	5-2	Clemens	McCaskill

Won 18, Lost 15

SEPTEMBER

Date		Score	Winner	Loser
1—Seattle	L	2-7	Bankhead	Smithson
2—Seattle	W	6-5	Lamp	Dunne
3—Seattle	L	2-3	Hanson	Boyd
4—At Oak.	W	8-5	Dopson	Moore
5—At Oak.	L	1-13	C. Young	Clemens
6—At Oak.	L	5-7	Welch	Smithson
8—At Calif.	L	1-2	Blyleven	Boddicker
9—At Calif.	L	5-8	Fraser	Murphy
10—At Calif.	L	1-2z	McClure	Lamp
11—At Seattle	L	1-2	Holman	Dopson
12—At Seattle	L	3-5	Bankhead	Hetzel
13—At Seattle	L	4-7	Reed	Boddicker
15—Oakland	W	7-2	Clemens	Moore
16—Oakland	W	5-2	Dopson	Davis
17—Oakland	W	7-6	Harris	Welch
18—At Toronto	W	6-3	Boddicker	Cerutti
19—At Toronto	L	5-6y	Henke	Harris
20—At Toronto	W	10-3	Clemens	Key
22—At Detroit	W	9-7	Murphy	Nunez
23—At Detroit	W	6-1	Boddicker	Ritz
24—At Detroit	W	4-2	Boyd	Morris
25—New York	W	7-4	Clemens	Mmahat
26—New York	W	9-5	Hetzel	Hawkins
27—New York	L	0-3	Terrell	Dopson
28—Milwaukee	W	12-6	Boddicker	August
29—Milwaukee	W	5-4	Smith	Crim
30—Milwaukee	L	1-3	Knudson	Clemens

Won 14, Lost 13

OCTOBER

Date		Score	Winner	Loser
1—Milwaukee	W	5-1	Dopson	Navarro

Won 1, Lost 0

*7½ innings. †10 innings. ‡11 innings. §12 innings. x12-inning suspended game, completed April 29. y13 innings. z14 innings. a16 innings.

First baseman Nick Esasky followed his sensational first season with the Red Sox (30 homers, 108 RBIs) by signing a lucrative free-agent contract with Atlanta.

with 12 homers and 61 RBIs. Second baseman Marty Barrett missed two months with a knee injury that required surgery and never was the same when he returned. He had his worst offensive year, batting .256.

The Red Sox also suffered from subpar years by other players.

Rich Gedman, the No. 1 catcher coming out of spring training, was awful. He hit only .212 with four homers and 16 RBIs. Rick Cerone, a .243 hitter with 48 RBIs in

'89, handled most of the catching duties and did a solid job.

Boggs and left fielder Mike Greenwell had fine seasons, although a bit below their usual high standards. Boggs, who entered the season with a career .356 average, was hitting only .292 after the first two months of the season. He eventually raised his average to .330 by season's end and led the league in doubles (51), on-base percentage (.430) and runs (113, tied with Rickey Henderson), but for the first time in five years he failed to win the A.L. batting title. Greenwell hit .308 with 14 homers and 95 RBIs but could have been more productive. His batting average with men in scoring position dropped from .332 in '88 to .289 in '89. His 70 RBIs in those situations, however, was the team high.

Roger Clemens never won more than three straight starts and was not as effective as his 17-11 record, 3.13 ERA and 230 strikeouts might indicate. Mike Boddicker got off to a slow start, winning only four of his first 16 starts, before finishing at 15-11 with a 4.00 ERA. Mike Smithson (7-14, 4.95 ERA) and rookie Eric Hetzel (2-3, 6.26) both struggled.

On the bright side, first baseman Nick Esasky, right fielder/DH Dwight Evans and relievers Rob Murphy, Dennis Lamp and Lee Smith all performed at or above expectations.

Esasky had a sensational year. He hit .277 and led the team with 30 homers and 108 RBIs, all career highs. And the 37-year-old Evans continued to produce big numbers, hitting .285 with 20 homers and 100 RBIs.

Murphy, who was obtained the previous December along with Esasky from Cincinnati, became the team's most valuable pitcher. He made a team-high 74 appearances, struck out 107 batters in 105 innings, won five games, saved nine more and posted a 2.74 ERA. Middle man Lamp (4-2, 2.32) had his best season since going 11-0 for Toronto in 1985, while Smith had a team-high 25 saves in 31 opportunities.

There were a few other positive performances. Outfielders Danny Heep (.300), Kevin Romine (.274) and Randy Kutcher (.225) were great off the bench. Shortstop Jody Reed, who was moved to second base when Barrett was injured, had a big second half and finished with a .288 average and 42 doubles (third in the league). Luis Rivera played good shortstop in Reed's place and hit .257.

But the bad easily outweighed the good in 1989, which was anything but a magical year for Red Sox fans.

Righthander Chris Bosio posted a solid 15-10 record last season and emerged as the Brewers' No. 2 starter behind Teddy Higuera.

Unhealthy Brewers Finish 81-81

By CLIFF CHRISTL

Nothing summarized the Milwaukee Brewers' 1989 season better than their 81-81 record.

"That's the way we played," Manager Tom Trebelhorn said. "Sometimes, I think, we overachieved. At other times, I think, we underachieved. I'm still not sure what we did."

The standings told Trebelhorn his club finished fourth, eight games behind division-winning Toronto, in a year it was picked to win the American League East title. But those lofty expectations were based on having a healthy Teddy Higuera, a starting rotation that included Juan Nieves and Bill Wegman and a lineup that included first baseman Greg Brock for more than 107 games and second baseman Jim Gantner for more than 116.

"The talent we evaluated to make us think we could be a contending club has never been there," Trebelhorn said.

In all, 15 Brewers spent time on the disabled list. The only starters who didn't were center fielder Robin Yount, left fielder Glenn Braggs and catcher B.J. Surhoff. Nieves, who had won 32 games over the previous three years, missed the entire season with a shoulder injury. Shoulder problems forced Wegman, who had averaged more than 200 innings per season over the previous three years, to miss all but two months of '89. And starting shortstop Dale Sveum spent the year recovering from a broken leg.

On the bright side, rookies Bill Spiers, Jaime Navarro and Greg Vaughn arrived in the major leagues a year ahead of schedule and displayed considerable promise.

Spiers didn't nail down the full-time job at shortstop until mid-July, but it became apparent early in the season that he was a slicker fielder than Gary Sheffield, a more highly touted rookie. And the Brewers were 40-37 with Spiers, a .255 hitter, as their starting shortstop.

After starting the year at Class AA El Paso, Navarro advanced to Class AAA Denver and then to Milwaukee in June. His poise, 90-mph-plus fastball and 3.12 earned-run average made a bigger impression than his 7-8 record might suggest. Vaughn, a slugging outfielder, joined the Brewers on August 10 and hit home runs off Bob Welch, Dave Stewart and Dennis Eckersley in a two-game series at Oakland in mid-September.

Milwaukee closer Dan Plesac recorded a club-record 33 saves.

Another positive development was the emergence of Chris Bosio as a bona fide No. 2 starter. Armed with a new split-finger fastball, he went 15-10, posted a 2.95 ERA (sixth in the league) and completed eight of his 33 starts.

The pitching staff featured some other pleasant surprises, too. Rookie Tony Fossas, a 10-year veteran of the minor leagues, made 51 appearances as a setup man and allowed only 10 of 54 inherited runners to score. Ignoring his five starts, Bill Krueger had a 3.36 ERA as a long reliever. Tom Filer was called up from Denver in July and won seven of 10 decisions. Mark Knudson, a spot starter and middle reliever, was 8-5 with a 3.35 ERA.

Injuries forced Trebelhorn to use 13 different starters, including Bryan Clutterbuck (2-5, 4.14 ERA) and Jerry Reuss (1-4, 5.35). The most serious casualty was Higuera, the ace of the staff. He missed the first month while recovering from January back surgery and most of the last month while suffering from a variety of other injuries. He had some strong performances in between, but the end result was Higuera's worst major league season (9-6, 3.46).

Despite the injuries and the league's worst defense, the Brewers' pitching held up remarkably well. The staff compiled a

SCORES OF MILWAUKEE BREWERS' 1989 GAMES

APRIL

Date		Score	Winner	Loser
3—At Cleve.	L	1-2	Swindell	August
6—At Cleve.	W	3-0	Bosio	Black
7—At Detroit	L	3-10	Alexander	Wegman
8—At Detroit	W	5-2	August	Tanana
10—Texas	L	4-6*	Russell	Crim
12—Texas	L	1-8	Ryan	Wegman
13—Texas	L	1-6	Witt	August
14—Cleveland	W	8-4	Knudson	Skalski
15—Cleveland	W	5-1	Bosio	Candiotti
16—Cleveland	W	4-3*	Crim	Atherton
17—At Texas	W	8-1	Wegman	Ryan
18—At Texas	L	2-6	Witt	August
19—At Texas	L	1-5	Moyer	Birkbeck
21—Detroit	W	2-1	Bosio	Morris
22—Detroit	L	3-6	Williams	Crim
23—Detroit	L	3-11	Gibson	August
24—Minnesota	W	5-4	Plesac	Reardon
25—Minnesota	W	10-4	Clutterbuck	Smith
26—Minnesota	W	12-0	Bosio	Anderson
28—At K.C.	L	1-8	Leibrandt	Wegman
29—At K.C.	L	3-4*	Gordon	Plesac
30—At K.C.	L	0-2	Bannister	Birkbeck

Won 10, Lost 12

MAY

Date		Score	Winner	Loser
1—At Chicago	L	0-6	Reuss	Higuera
2—At Chicago	L	1-6	King	Bosio
3—At Minn.	W	7-2	Wegman	Rawley
4—At Minn.	W	3-2	August	Viola
5—Kan. City	L	4-5*	Montgomery	Knudson
6—Kan. City	W	1-0*	Krueger	Gordon
7—Kan. City	W	8-2	Bosio	Leibrandt
9—Chicago	L	1-10	Hillegas	Wegman
10—Chicago	L	2-12	Perez	Higuera
12—At Oak.	L	4-5	Burns	Plesac
13—At Oak.	L	3-4	Welch	Bosio
14—At Oak.	W	2-1	Crim	Moore
15—At Oak.	L	2-12	Stewart	August
16—At Seattle	L	5-6	Jackson	Wegman
17—At Seattle	W	9-6	Crim	Bankhead
18—At Seattle	L	5-9	Swift	Bosio
19—At Calif.	L	1-3	Finley	Clutterbuck
20—At Calif.	W	5-3	August	Blyleven
21—At Calif.	L	9-12	Petry	Wegman
23—Oakland	W	9-1	Bosio	Welch
24—Oakland	L	2-6	Moore	Birkbeck
25—Oakland	W	4-1	Clutterbuck	Stewart
26—Seattle	L	2-7	Jackson	August
27—Seattle	W	3-2	Plesac	Holman
28—Seattle	W	6-4	Crim	Powell
29—California	L	3-12	Blyleven	Birkbeck
30—California	L	2-3	Abbott	Clutterbuck
31—California	W	4-1	August	Witt

Won 12, Lost 16

JUNE

Date		Score	Winner	Loser
1—New York	W	5-0	Higuera	LaPoint
2—New York	L	2-3*	Righetti	Crim
3—New York	W	2-0	Krueger	Dotson
4—New York	L	9-12	Jones	Clutterbuck
5—At Toronto	W	5-3	August	Key
6—At Toronto	W	6-4	Aldrich	Ward
7—At Toronto	L	2-4	Cerutti	Bosio
8—At Balt.	W	6-2	Knudson	Milacki
9—At Balt.	L	1-7	Williamson	Clutterbuck
10—At Balt.	W	6-0	August	Ballard
11—At Balt.	W	3-1	Crim	Hickey
13—Toronto	L	3-4	Ward	Plesac
14—Toronto	L	1-6	Stieb	Krueger
15—Toronto	W	6-4	Fossas	Key
16—At Minn.	W	8-6	Crim	Berenguer
17—At Minn.	L	3-7	Tunnell	Knudson
18—At Minn.	L	6-8	Reardon	Crim
19—At Minn.	W	11-8	Krueger	Oliveras
20—Kan. City	L	2-8†	Gordon	Knudson
21—Kan. City	L	0-6	Saberhagen	August
22—Kan. City	W	3-2*	Crim	Farr
23—Chicago	W	17-5	Bosio	Rosenberg
23—Chicago	L	4-6	Perez	Clutterbuck
24—Chicago	L	3-5	Long	Krueger
25—Chicago	W	3-1	Navarro	Reuss
27—Boston	W	5-4	August	Clemens
28—Boston	W	12-5	Higuera	Smithson
29—Boston	L	1-2	Dopson	Bosio
30—At N.Y.	L	3-4	Hawkins	Crim

Won 15, Lost 14

JULY

Date		Score	Winner	Loser
1—At N.Y.	L	1-5	Parker	Veres
2—At N.Y.	W	10-2	August	McCullers
3—At N.Y.	W	8-5	Higuera	Eiland

JULY

Date		Score	Winner	Loser
4—At Bos.	W	4-3	Bosio	Price
6—At Bos.	L	4-5	Boddicker	Navarro
7—Baltimore	W	6-4	August	Harnisch
8—Baltimore	L	2-5	Holton	Higuera
9—Baltimore	W	7-2	Bosio	Schmidt
13—At Chicago	L	4-5	Thigpen	Fossas
14—At Chicago	L	4-6	Long	Bosio
15—At Chicago	L	1-2	Perez	Higuera
16—At Chicago	L	0-2	Dotson	Navarro
17—At K.C.	L	2-3	Gordon	Filer
18—At K.C.	L	4-9	Gubicza	August
19—At K.C.	W	7-1	Bosio	Leibrandt
21—Minnesota	W	5-3	Higuera	Rawley
22—Minnesota	L	1-6	Smith	Navarro
23—Minnesota	W	4-1	Filer	Viola
24—Detroit	W	10-0	Bosio	Morris
25—Detroit	L	2-7	Alexander	August
26—Detroit	W	3-2	Higuera	Nunez
27—Detroit	W	11-1	Navarro	Gibson
28—At Texas	W	15-3	Filer	Jeffcoat
29—At Texas	W	8-2	Bosio	Witt
30—At Texas	L	3-9	Ryan	August
31—Cleveland	W	6-1	Higuera	Bailes

Won 14, Lost 12

AUGUST

Date		Score	Winner	Loser
1—Cleveland	W	4-2	Navarro	Jones
2—Cleveland	L	0-1	Candiotti	Bosio
4—California	L	2-6	Finley	Reuss
5—California	W	5-2	Higuera	Witt
6—California	L	0-6	Abbott	Navarro
7—At Detroit	L	3-5	Ritz	Fossas
7—At Detroit	W	5-2	Filer	Gibson
8—At Detroit	L	3-6	Robinson	August
9—At Detroit	W	6-1	Crim	Morris
10—At Cleve.	W	10-3	Higuera	Black
11—At Cleve.	L	0-5	Farrell	Navarro
11—At Cleve.	W	8-7	Knudson	Wojna
12—At Cleve.	W	5-1	Bosio	Bailes
13—At Cleve.	W	5-4*	Plesac	Jones
14—New York	W	5-4	Fossas	Righetti
15—New York	W	1-0	Higuera	Parker
16—New York	W	5-1	Knudson	Terrell
17—Boston	W	8-4	Bosio	Gardner
18—Boston	W	5-2	Filer	Bolton
19—Boston	L	1-3‡	Harris	Knudson
20—Boston	W	6-3	Navarro	Smithson
21—At Balt.	L	0-5	Ballard	Reuss
22—At Balt.	L	2-4	Johnson	Bosio
23—At Balt.	L	1-3	Milacki	Filer
25—At Toronto	L	1-3	Key	Peterek
26—At Toronto	L	0-7	Stieb	Higuera
27—At Toronto	L	4-5	Stottlemyre	Bosio
28—At Toronto	W	8-2	Filer	Cerutti
29—Seattle	L	3-5	Hanson	Navarro
30—Seattle	L	3-7	Johnson	Peterek
31—Seattle	W	6-1	Knudson	Holman

Won 16, Lost 15

SEPTEMBER

Date		Score	Winner	Loser
1—Oakland	W	6-5*	Crim	Burns
2—Oakland	L	2-7	Stewart	Filer
3—Oakland	L	0-5	Davis	Navarro
5—At Calif.	L	4-8	McCaskill	Knudson
6—At Calif.	W	7-4	Bosio	Petry
7—At Calif.	W	7-1	Witt	Witt
8—At Seattle	W	7-3	Navarro	Zavaras
9—At Seattle	W	7-3	Reuss	Hanson
10—At Seattle	W	7-1	Knudson	Johnson
12—At Oak.	W	7-6	August	M. Young
13—At Oak.	L	6-7	Eckersley	Crim
15—Texas	W	6-2	Navarro	Moyer
16—Texas	W	5-3	August	Barfield
17—Texas	L	2-4	Witt	Bosio
21—At N.Y.	W	14-1	Knudson	Cadaret
21—At N.Y.	L	4-5*	Guetterman	Plesac
22—Toronto	L	3-7	Stieb	Reuss
23—Toronto	W	4-1	August	Stottlemyre
24—Toronto	W	8-3	Filer	Cerutti
25—Baltimore	L	3-5	Harnisch	Higuera
26—Baltimore	W	7-3	Navarro	Johnson
27—Baltimore	L	0-4	Milacki	Reuss
28—At Bos.	L	6-12	Boddicker	August
29—At Bos.	L	4-5	Smith	Crim
30—At Bos.	W	3-1	Knudson	Clemens

Won 14, Lost 11

OCTOBER

Date		Score	Winner	Loser
1—At Bos.	L	1-5	Dopson	Navarro

Won 0, Lost 1

*10 innings. †11 innings. ‡14 innings.

Third baseman Paul Molitor batted .315 and continued in his role as Milwaukee's catalyst.

3.80 ERA, ranking sixth in the league. Of course, it helped that the bullpen was largely free of injuries. Setup man Chuck Crim led the league in appearances for the second straight year with 76, won nine games and saved seven others. And closer Dan Plesac set a club record with 33 saves, making good on all but seven opportunities.

Offensively, Gantner, Yount and third baseman Paul Molitor had banner years.

Gantner was Milwaukee's hottest hitter when he suffered a season-ending knee injury August 15. Losing Gantner down the stretch was as serious as losing Higuera at the start of the year. "Those were the bookend injuries that were the biggest," Trebelhorn said.

Gantner was hitting .385 in August when he went down, finishing at .274 with 20 stolen bases. His replacements—Gus Polidor (.194), Billy Bates (.214) and Ed Romero (.200)—could not provide Gantner's offense or his fearless defense around the bag at second.

Once again, Yount was a model of consistency. He smacked 21 homers, led the club with a .318 average, 103 runs batted in and 101 runs scored and collected the 2,500th hit of his career in July. Molitor wasn't as steady—he raised his average 30

points by hitting .458 the last month of the season—but his final numbers (.315, 11 homers and a team-high 27 steals) were quite respectable. As usual, Molitor and Yount were the backbone of the team.

"If they didn't play as well as they did, we'd have been fortunate to win 60 games," Plesac said.

That was because of injuries, of course, but also because several young products of Milwaukee's flourishing farm system turned in disappointing performances.

After winning 13 games as a 1988 rookie, pitcher Don August won 12 but finished with a 5.31 ERA. Joey Meyer (.224) didn't cut it as the designated hitter. Braggs finished with 15 homers and 66 RBIs, but only four homers and 24 RBIs after the All-Star break.

In addition, Surhoff was outplayed by defensive specialist Charlie O'Brien. The Brewers were 47-53 in games Surhoff started, 34-28 in games O'Brien started. Surhoff hit .248 (14 points higher than O'Brien) and threw out only 26 percent of the runners who tried to steal on him, compared to 35 percent for O'Brien.

And, most notably, Sheffield was a flop. Sheffield, the preseason pick to be the league's Rookie of the Year, was a defensive liability at shortstop and a disappointment at the plate (.247). He hit just .208 with runners in scoring position.

A pair of seasoned veterans also had subpar years. After missing the first two months following shoulder surgery, Brock returned but didn't hit with the pop expected from a first baseman. He finished with 52 RBIs, while backup Terry Francona knocked in just 23 runs.

Right fielder Rob Deer, the team leader with 26 homers, was even worse than Braggs after the All-Star break, when he had a .161 average, five homers and 16 RBIs. Deer finished the year playing behind Mike Felder, who was one of only two Brewer reserves (O'Brien was the other) who made any kind of contribution. Felder stole 26 bases, helping Milwaukee to a league-leading total of 165.

The Brewers had only one stretch in which they played inspiring ball. From July 19 through August 20, they won 23 of 33 games and climbed from 12 games behind the leader to half a game out. But they promptly lost six straight to Baltimore and Toronto and finished the year with a number of players clamoring for some changes.

"With the injuries, it's a little tough to gauge where we are," Molitor said, "but the record indicates it was a year of decline."

In a season of disenchantment for the Yankees, first baseman Don Mattingly was a rock, batting .303 with 113 RBIs.

Yankees Sputter, Fans Protest

By BILL MADDEN

It was late September 1989, and the scene was all too familiar to New York Yankee fans. Another manager had been fired, another general manager was preparing to pack his bags, another Yankee season was going down in flames. And the mudslinging was only beginning.

In 1989, however, there was one difference: This time the fans joined in, directing their wrath at George Steinbrenner, the Yankees' principal owner. Exasperated over yet another disappointing season, the fans began chanting "George must go! George must go!" at Yankee Stadium night after night. Then they began waving banners expressing similar sentiments. And when Steinbrenner's security people began confiscating the banners, the American Civil Liberties Union stepped in and threatened legal action if the protests were further thwarted.

The fans had every right to be upset. The Yankees' 74-87 record was their worst in 22 years and marked the fourth straight season in which their record declined from the previous year. Although Steinbrenner and his supporters point out that the Yankees won more games (854) during the 1980s than any other team, the fact is that the '80s was the first decade since 1910-19 in which the team did not win a World Series.

Naturally, Steinbrenner sacked another skipper. The victim this time was Dallas Green, the 17th Yankee manager in Steinbrenner's 17 years of ownership to get the ax. Green and four coaches were shown the door August 18 with the team in sixth place with a 56-65 record.

Steinbrenner, who said that hiring Green "was one of the biggest mistakes I ever made," named former Yankee shortstop Bucky Dent as the new manager. The Yankees went 18-22 under Dent and finished fifth in the American League East, 14½ games out of first place.

Green, who reacted to his ouster by saying "George Steinbrenner doesn't know anything about baseball," was virtually guaranteed a brief tenure when he inherited a team devoid of most of its firepower from the year before. Except for first baseman Don Mattingly, who hit .303, led the Yankees with 23 home runs and 113 runs batted in and won his fifth Gold Glove, the squad Green took over in October 1988 had been gutted of its best hitters.

After the '88 season, Steinbrenner traded slugger Jack Clark to the San Diego Padres for pitchers Lance McCullers and Jimmy Jones and outfielder Stan Jefferson. Three months later, outfielder Claudell Washington left via free agency for the California Angels. Then in spring training, right fielder Dave Winfield underwent back surgery and was lost for the season.

The departure of Clark, Washington and Winfield represented a total of 264 RBIs that Green would have to replace. And to make matters worse, incumbent shortstop Rafael Santana was felled for the season with an elbow injury in spring training.

Green and Syd Thrift, who came aboard in spring training as the Yankees' new front office chief, eventually found replacements for all the missing parts. The biggest addition was right fielder Jesse Barfield, who was acquired from Toronto on April 30 in exchange for pitcher Al Leiter. Although he batted just .240 as a Yankee, Barfield contributed 18 homers and led all major league outfielders with 20 assists (16 for New York).

Spring-training trades brought the Yankees two other power hitters. Designated hitter/first baseman Steve Balboni (obtained from Seattle) and left fielder/DH Mel Hall (Cleveland) each hit 17 homers. Balboni knocked in 59 runs, Hall 58. The Yankees' other first baseman/DH, Ken Phelps, had 29 RBIs when he was traded to Oakland on August 31.

The most unexpected contribution came from Alvaro Espinoza, a former career minor leaguer who in 1989 became perhaps the best all-around Yankee shortstop since Tony Kubek. Espinoza batted .282 and laid down 23 sacrifice bunts, ranking second in the majors. His fielding, however, was inconsistent (22 errors).

An even bigger bonus was second baseman Steve Sax, the former Los Angeles Dodger signed as a free agent the previous winter. Sax, who played more games (158) at second than any other player in '89, led the Yankees in batting (.315), hits (205), runs (88) and stolen bases (43). He also dispelled questions about his defense by leading all A.L. second basemen with a .987 fielding percentage.

Not every transaction, however, worked to the Yankees' benefit. On June 21, they traded left fielder Rickey Henderson to Oakland for pitchers Eric Plunk and Greg Cadaret and outfielder Luis Polonia.

SCORES OF NEW YORK YANKEES' 1989 GAMES

APRIL			Winner	Loser
4—At Minn.	W	4-2	John	Viola
5—At Minn.	L	2-12	Anderson	Hawkins
6—At Minn.	L	1-7	Rawley	LaPoint
7—Cleveland	L	2-4	Yett	Candelaria
8—Cleveland	L	1-11	Swindell	Leiter
9—Cleveland	L	3-4	Candiotti	John
10—Toronto	L	0-8	Stieb	Hawkins
11—Toronto	L	6-11‡	Henke	Righetti
12—Toronto	W	5-3	Candelaria	Castillo
14—Minnesota	W	8-5	Leiter	Cook
16—Minnesota	L	4-9	Anderson	John
17—At Toronto	W	7-2	Hawkins	Flanagan
18—At Toronto	W	2-0	LaPoint	Musselman
19—At Toronto	W	4-2	Candelaria	Key
21—At Cleve.	L	5-6	Jones	Mohorcic
22—At Cleve.	L	1-3	Bailes	John
23—At Cleve.	W	5-0	Hawkins	Farrell
24—At Cleve.	W	6-3	LaPoint	Black
25—At K.C.	L	3-5	Saberhagen	Candelaria
26—At K.C.	L	3-5	Gordon	Leiter
27—At K.C.	W	3-2	John	Gubicza
28—Chicago	W	3-1	Hawkins	Hillegas
29—Chicago	W	8-2	LaPoint	Long
30—Chicago	W	5-2	Candelaria	Perez

Won 12, Lost 12

MAY			Winner	Loser
2—Kan. City	L	3-5	Gubicza	John
3—At Texas	L	1-4	Brown	Hawkins
4—At Texas	W	11-7	LaPoint	Hough
5—At Chicago	W	7-5	McCullers	Pall
6—At Chicago	W	5-2	Righetti	Rosenberg
7—At Chicago	L	2-6	King	John
8—Texas	L	2-13	Brown	Hawkins
9—Texas	W	5-3	LaPoint	Hough
12—At Calif.	W	5-2	Dotson	Abbott
13—At Calif.	L	1-6	Witt	John
14—At Calif.	L	0-5	Finley	Hawkins
15—At Calif.	L	3-4§	Fraser	McCullers
16—At Oak.	W	3-2	Parker	C. Young
17—At Oak.	L	3-8	Davis	Dotson
18—At Oak.	L	2-6	Welch	John
19—At Seattle	W	9-5	Hawkins	Hanson
20—At Seattle	L	4-6	Trout	LaPoint
21—At Seattle	W	6-2	Parker	Langston
24—California	L	4-11	Abbott	Dotson
25—California	W	8-6	Mohorcic	Fraser
26—Oakland	L	0-4	Burns	Hawkins
27—Oakland	L	0-3	C. Young	LaPoint
28—Oakland	L	3-4	Moore	Parker
29—Seattle	W	6-3	Dotson	Powell
30—Seattle	L	2-3	Johnson	Jones
31—Seattle	W	9-5	Hawkins	Trout

Won 11, Lost 15

JUNE			Winner	Loser
1—At Milw.	L	0-5	Higuera	LaPoint
2—At Milw.	W	3-2‡	Righetti	Crim
3—At Milw.	L	0-2	Krueger	Dotson
4—At Milw.	W	12-9	Jones	Clutterbuck
5—Baltimore	L	3-16	Ballard	Hawkins
6—Baltimore	W	4-0	LaPoint	Schmidt
8—Boston	W	8-7§	McCullers	Stanley
10—Boston	L	8-14	Clemens	Dotson
11—Boston	W	4-2	Hawkins	Price
11—Boston	W	8-7	Nielsen	Murphy
13—At Balt.	L	2-5	Schmidt	LaPoint
14—At Balt.	W	2-1	Guetterman	Hickey
15—At Balt.	L	2-3‡	Thurmond	McCullers
16—Texas	W	8-3	Hawkins	Witt
16—Texas	W	6-1	Jones	Brown
17—Texas	W	5-3	Eiland	Jeffcoat
18—Texas	L	2-5	Hough	LaPoint
20—Chicago	L	6-13	Reuss	Dotson
21—Chicago	L	3-7	Pall	Hawkins
22—Chicago	W	10-7	Cadaret	Hillegas
23—At K.C.	L	0-3	Gubicza	Eiland
24—At K.C.	W	12-5	McCullers	Appier
25—At K.C.	W	5-4	Hawkins	Leibrandt
27—At Detroit	L	5-6	Havens	Guetterman
28—At Detroit	L	5-6‡	Henneman	Righetti
29—At Detroit	W	7-6	Plunk	Nunez
30—Milwaukee	W	4-3	Hawkins	Crim

Won 15, Lost 12

JULY			Winner	Loser
1—Milwaukee	W	5-1	Parker	Veres
2—Milwaukee	L	2-10	August	McCullers
3—Milwaukee	L	5-8	Higuera	Eiland
4—Detroit	W	1-0	Schulze	Tanana
5—Detroit	W	9-0	Hawkins	Havens
6—Detroit	W	6-5§	Plunk	Henneman
7—At Bos.	L	4-6	Clemens	Cadaret
8—At Bos.	W	7-5	Plunk	Smithson
9—At Bos.	L	5-10	Smith	Schulze
13—Kan. City	W	6-0	Hawkins	Gubicza
14—Kan. City	L	5-14	Saberhagen	Eiland
14—Kan. City	W	9-7	Guetterman	Farr
15—Kan. City	L	1-7	Aquino	Guetterman
16—Kan. City	W	10-1†	Cadaret	Leach
17—At Chicago	L	3-7	Rosenberg	LaPoint
19—At Chicago	L	5-11	Hillegas	Guetterman
20—At Texas	L	2-6	Ryan	Hawkins
21—At Texas	L	2-5	Brown	Cadaret
22—At Texas	L	1-2	Jeffcoat	LaPoint
23—At Texas	L	4-5‡	Witt	Righetti
24—At Cleve.	L	3-7	Farrell	Guetterman
25—At Cleve.	W	5-1	Hawkins	Swindell
26—At Cleve.	L	7-9	Jones	Guetterman
28—Toronto	L	2-6	Cerutti	LaPoint
29—Toronto	W	7-2	Cary	Key
30—Toronto	W	7-6	Guetterman	Ward
31—Toronto	L	5-6	Wells	Hawkins

Won 11, Lost 16

AUGUST			Winner	Loser
1—Minnesota	L	4-5	Rawley	Terrell
2—Minnesota	W	7-6	McCullers	Wayne
2—Minnesota	L	3-4‡	Reardon	Plunk
3—Minnesota	W	8-1	Cary	Aguilera
4—At Toronto	L	1-2	Stieb	Parker
5—At Toronto	W	5-4	Hawkins	Ward
6—At Toronto	L	5-6	Stottlemyre	Terrell
7—Cleveland	W	9-0	Cadaret	Bailes
8—Cleveland	L	1-3	Candiotti	Cary
9—Cleveland	L	4-7	Nichols	Hawkins
11—At Minn.	W	11-3	Terrell	Rawley
12—At Minn.	L	3-6	Smith	Cadaret
13—At Minn.	W	9-7	Guetterman	Reardon
14—At Milw.	L	4-5	Fossas	Righetti
15—At Milw.	L	0-1	Higuera	Parker
16—At Milw.	L	1-5	Knudson	Terrell
17—At Detroit	W	2-1	Cadaret	DuBois
18—At Detroit	L	3-7	Robinson	Cary
19—At Detroit	L	4-5	Morris	Righetti
20—At Detroit	L	6-7	Nunez	Plunk
21—Boston	W	6-4	Terrell	Clemens
22—Boston	L	3-4	Murphy	Candelaria
23—Boston	L	1-4	Boddicker	Hawkins
24—Baltimore	W	5-1	Cary	Harnisch
24—Baltimore	L	2-9	Schmidt	Plunk
25—Baltimore	L	1-3	Ballard	Parker
26—Baltimore	L	4-6	Johnson	Terrell
27—Baltimore	L	5-8	Milacki	Cadaret
28—Oakland	L	3-7	Stewart	Hawkins
29—Oakland	L	5-19	Davis	Cary
30—Oakland	W	8-5	Plunk	Moore

Won 10, Lost 21

SEPTEMBER			Winner	Loser
1—California	W	11-5	Terrell	Clark
2—California	W	2-1	Cadaret	Witt
3—California	W	5-2	Hawkins	Blyleven
4—California	W	2-1	Parker	Abbott
5—At Seattle	W	12-2	Plunk	Johnson
6—At Seattle	W	5-3	Terrell	Holman
7—At Seattle	W	6-4	Gossage	Schooler
8—At Oak.	W	5-1	Mohorcic	Stewart
9—At Oak.	L	0-7	Moore	Parker
10—At Oak.	L	2-6	Davis	Plunk
12—At Calif.	L	6-7	McClure	Cary
13—At Calif.	L	3-4‡	Minton	Righetti
15—Seattle	L	1-3	Hanson	Hawkins
16—Seattle	W	4-1*	Plunk	Johnson
17—Seattle	L	0-3	Holman	Terrell
21—Milwaukee	L	1-14	Knudson	Cadaret
21—Milwaukee	W	5-4‡	Guetterman	Plesac
22—At Balt.	W	5-4	Terrell	Holton
23—At Balt.	L	2-10	Milacki	Plunk
24—At Balt.	W	2-0	Cary	Ballard
25—At Bos.	L	4-7	Clemens	Mmahat
26—At Bos.	L	5-9	Hetzel	Hawkins
27—At Bos.	W	3-0	Terrell	Dopson
29—Detroit	W	5-1	Plunk	Morris
30—Detroit	W	9-2	Hawkins	Ritz

Won 15, Lost 10

OCTOBER			Winner	Loser
1—Detroit	L	3-5	Tanana	Mmahat

Won 0, Lost 1

*6 innings. †6½ innings. ‡10 innings. §11 innings.

Free-agent signee Steve Sax led the Yankees with a .315 average and led A.L. second basemen with a .987 fielding percentage.

Henderson, who was hitting just .247 for the Yankees, went on a tear for the Athletics and helped them win a World Series championship. Cadaret and Plunk had only moderate success (a combined 12-10 record as spot starters and long relievers) in New York, while Polonia hit .313 for the Yankees but was arrested in Milwaukee in August for having sexual relations with a 15-year-old girl. After finishing the season, he was sentenced to 60 days in jail.

The July 22 trade of third baseman Mike Pagliarulo to San Diego for pitcher Walt Terrell was a toss-up for New York. Pagliarulo was hitting just .197 at the time, but Terrell had a whopping 5.20 earned-run average in 13 Yankee starts. On the bright side, infielder Randy Velarde, who was called up from Class AAA Columbus shortly after the Pagliarulo deal, hit .340 in 100 at-bats.

Another bright spot was Roberto Kelly, who batted .302, stole 35 bases and gave the Yankees a good glove in center field. And the catching tandem of Don Slaught and rookie Bob Geren combined for 14 homers and 65 RBIs.

Overall, the Yankee offense wasn't that bad. It produced 698 runs, the league's seventh-best total. In the final analysis, it was lousy pitching that doomed the Yan-

kees again. Among A.L. clubs, only Detroit had an ERA higher than New York's 4.50 mark.

Andy Hawkins and Dave LaPoint, who were signed to lucrative free-agent contracts before the season, helped little. Hawkins, slightly better than a .500 pitcher (60-58) before 1989, was just that (15-15, 4.80 ERA) for the Yankees. LaPoint, who missed the last two months with a shoulder injury, was a disappointing 6-9 with a 5.62 ERA.

Green and Dent used 16 different starting pitchers, including Tommy John (2-7), Richard Dotson (2-5), Clay Parker (4-5) and Chuck Cary (4-4). In the bullpen, Dave Righetti and Lee Guetterman combined for 38 saves, while McCullers struggled (4.57 ERA). At season's end, Steinbrenner was talking about venturing once again into the free-agent market for more pitchers.

By that time, Thrift had resigned and General Manager Bob Quinn was about to leave for a similar position with the Cincinnati Reds. Those moves prompted Steinbrenner to announce that he would get more involved than ever in the future day-to-day operations of the team.

That's precisely what disgruntled Yankee fans didn't want to hear.

Cleveland closer Doug Jones enjoyed his second straight outstanding season, posting 32 saves and a 2.34 earned-run average.

Indians Fade Down the Stretch

By SHELDON OCKER

Normally when the Cleveland Indians finish sixth in the American League East, the hometown fans shrug and ask, "So what else is new?"

But 1989 was different. Oh, the results were basically the same—the Tribe finished sixth or seventh for the 11th time in 12 years—but this time the fans and the front office hardly took the club's second-half swoon in stride.

The reason was simple: On August 4, Cleveland was in second place, only 1½ games behind the division-leading Baltimore Orioles. Granted, the Indians' record was a modest 54-54, but there was no denying that they had been presented with their first chance to join a pennant race since 1959. As Tribe President Hank Peters reminded the fans when attendance failed to keep pace with the Indians' position in the standings, "We are in the race, and that's more significant than our record."

Maybe the fans knew something. Cleveland was unable to sustain even a .500 winning percentage and compiled a dismal 19-35 record the rest of the year. That left the Indians with a final mark of 73-89, 16 games off the pace.

Along the way, Manager Doc Edwards was fired and an obscure special assignment scout, John Hart, was hired as interim skipper for the last 19 games of the year. Hart had no better luck than Edwards, posting an 8-11 mark in his brief stint as manager.

Ostensibly, Edwards was dismissed because of the team's alleged lack of intensity and emotion. But there was a more obvious problem. The Indians were last in the league in scoring with 604 runs, compiling their lowest team batting average (.245) since 1972. And this from a club with a reputation for strong hitting.

But that reputation was earned with a lineup that bore little resemblance to the '89 squad. In a span of 16 months, Julio Franco, Pat Tabler, Carmen Castillo and Mel Hall were traded and Brett Butler and Ron Kittle fled as free agents. It didn't help when Cleveland's major off-season trade turned sour.

At the 1988 winter meetings, Cleveland sent Franco to the Texas Rangers for left fielder Oddibe McDowell, first baseman Pete O'Brien and second baseman Jerry Browne. Peters was hoping that McDowell would become a legitimate

Jerry Browne, obtained in the off-season from Texas, blossomed into one of the A.L.'s top young second basemen.

leadoff hitter, something the Indians lacked in 1988 after Butler signed with San Francisco. O'Brien was expected to give the Tribe lefthanded punch and solid defense, while Browne was obtained to take Franco's place at second.

It soon became evident that McDowell was not the answer at the top of the lineup. He struggled to get his average over .200 and failed to draw walks. Finally, McDowell was dealt to Atlanta on July 2 for Dion James, who took over in left field and batted .306 for the Indians.

A month before that trade, Browne took McDowell's place in the leadoff spot. As it turned out, Browne saved the Franco deal by blossoming into an excellent all-purpose hitter. He batted .299, led the club with 14 stolen bases and accepted 68 walks, giving him the team's top on-base percentage (.370). And though he had only 45 runs batted in, Browne did an exceptional job of getting runners home from third base with less than two out.

"If Jerry is this good of a hitter at age 23," Edwards said, "he's going to be one of the best by the time he's 25."

Only two other starters had solid sea-

SCORES OF CLEVELAND INDIANS' 1989 GAMES

APRIL

Date	W/L	Score	Winner	Loser
3—Milwaukee	W	2-1	Swindell	August
6—Milwaukee	L	0-3	Bosio	Black
7—At N.Y.	W	4-2	Yett	Candelaria
8—At N.Y.	W	11-1	Swindell	Leiter
9—At N.Y.	W	4-3	Candiotti	John
10—At Bos.	L	2-5	Boddicker	Skalski
12—At Bos.	W	10-6	Black	Boyd
13—At Bos.	L	1-9	Clemens	Yett
14—At Milw.	L	4-8	Knudson	Skalski
15—At Milw.	L	1-5	Bosio	Candiotti
16—At Milw.	L	3-4*	Crim	Atherton
19—Boston	L	4-8	Clemens	Black
20—Boston	L	2-5	Boyd	Yett
21—New York	W	6-5	Jones	Mohorcic
22—New York	W	3-1	Bailes	John
23—New York	L	0-5	Hawkins	Farrell
24—New York	L	3-6	LaPoint	Black
25—Texas	L	7-11	Witt	Bailes
26—Texas	L	2-3*	Russell	Jones
28—At Minn.	W	9-7	Candiotti	Rawley
29—At Minn.	W	4-1	Farrell	Viola
30—At Minn.	L	1-2	Smith	Black

Won 9, Lost 13

MAY

Date	W/L	Score	Winner	Loser
1—At Texas	W	11-1	Yett	Witt
2—At Texas	W	8-3	Swindell	Moyer
3—Kan. City	W	6-2	Candiotti	Leibrandt
4—Kan. City	W	3-1	Farrell	Saberhagen
5—Minnesota	L	2-3‡	Gonzalez	Jones
7—Minnesota	W	5-4	Jones	Oliveras
7—Minnesota	W	12-1	Yett	Toliver
9—At K.C.	L	1-3	Saberhagen	Candiotti
10—At K.C.	L	2-3	Montgomery	Farrell
12—Detroit	L	3-6	Morris	Black
13—Detroit	W	3-1	Swindell	Alexander
14—Detroit	W	8-3	Candiotti	Gibson
15—At Toronto	L	3-5	Key	Farrell
16—At Toronto	L	6-7	Henke	Atherton
17—At Toronto	W	6-3	Black	Stieb
18—At Balt.	L	2-3*	Williamson	Atherton
19—At Balt.	W	4-1	Candiotti	Bautista
20—At Balt.	L	1-5	Ballard	Farrell
21—At Balt.	W	2-0	Yett	Holton
22—At Detroit	W	7-3	Black	Morris
23—At Detroit	L	2-7	Trujillo	Swindell
24—At Detroit	L	1-2*	Hernandez	Bailes
25—At Detroit	L	5-9	Tanana	Farrell
26—Baltimore	L	2-5	Ballard	Yett
27—Baltimore	L	1-5	Schmidt	Black
28—Baltimore	W	1-0	Swindell	Milacki
29—Toronto	W	5-3	Candiotti	Flanagan
30—Toronto	W	6-2	Farrell	Sanchez
31—Toronto	W	7-4	Black	Key

Won 16, Lost 13

JUNE

Date	W/L	Score	Winner	Loser
2—At Oak.	W	5-3	Swindell	Moore
3—At Oak.	L	0-7	Welch	Candiotti
4—At Oak.	L	0-4	Stewart	Farrell
5—At Calif.	W	7-3	Black	Witt
6—At Calif.	L	1-2	Petry	Yett
7—At Calif.	W	1-0	Swindell	Finley
9—Seattle	W	5-4	Candiotti	Zavaras
10—Seattle	L	1-3	Johnson	Farrell
11—Seattle	L	3-6	Holman	Black
12—At Chicago	L	3-5	Rosenberg	Yett
13—At Chicago	W	9-6	Swindell	Peterson
14—At Chicago	L	1-3	Reuss	Candiotti
15—Kan. City	L	4-5	Saberhagen	Jones
16—Kan. City	W	1-0	Black	Leach
17—Kan. City	W	4-3	Bailes	Gubicza
18—Kan. City	W	4-1	Swindell	Appier
20—Minnesota	L	4-7	Anderson	Candiotti
21—Minnesota	L	1-5	Rawley	Farrell
22—Minnesota	L	8-9	Wayne	Orosco
23—At Texas	L	0-4	Jeffcoat	Bailes
24—At Texas	W	7-3	Swindell	Hough
25—At Texas	L	2-4	Ryan	Candiotti
26—At Texas	W	4-3	Farrell	Witt
27—California	L	1-2*	Monteleone	Allen
28—California	W	2-1	Bailes	Abbott
30—Oakland	L	0-5	Welch	Swindell

Won 11, Lost 15

JULY

Date	W/L	Score	Winner	Loser
1—Oakland	L	4-6	Moore	Yett
2—Oakland	L	3-11	Davis	Farrell
3—Chicago	W	4-2	Black	Hillegas
4—Chicago	W	3-2	Bailes	Perez
5—Chicago	W	4-2	Swindell	Reuss
7—At Seattle	W	4-3‡	Jones	Jackson
8—At Seattle	L	3-4†	Swift	Orosco
9—At Seattle	L	0-8	Bankhead	Bailes
13—Texas	L	3-9†	Russell	Nichols
14—Texas	W	11-5	Orosco	Guante
15—Texas	W	7-1	Swindell	Ryan
16—Texas	W	11-5	Yett	Brown
17—At Minn.	L	2-5	Berenguer	Jones
18—At Minn.	L	4-5	Viola	Jones
19—At Minn.	W	10-1	Farrell	Anderson
20—At K.C.	W	4-0	Swindell	Saberhagen
21—At K.C.	L	1-6	Aquino	Bailes
22—At K.C.	W	1-0	Candiotti	Gordon
23—At K.C.	W	17-5	Black	Gubicza
24—New York	W	7-3	Farrell	Guetterman
25—New York	L	1-5	Hawkins	Swindell
26—New York	W	9-7	Jones	Guetterman
28—Boston	W	3-2	Candiotti	Clemens
28—Boston	W	2-1	Nichols	Gardner
29—Boston	L	0-5	Smithson	Black
30—Boston	L	2-5	Lamp	Farrell
31—At Milw.	L	1-6	Higuera	Bailes

Won 15, Lost 12

AUGUST

Date	W/L	Score	Winner	Loser
1—At Milw.	L	2-4	Navarro	Jones
2—At Milw.	W	1-0	Candiotti	Bosio
3—At Bos.	W	4-2	Nichols	Bolton
4—At Bos.	W	4-3	Black	Boddicker
5—At Bos.	L	2-10	Smithson	Farrell
6—At Bos.	L	4-6	Murphy	Orosco
7—At N.Y.	L	0-9	Cadaret	Bailes
8—At N.Y.	W	3-1	Candiotti	Cary
9—At N.Y.	W	7-4	Nichols	Hawkins
10—Milwaukee	L	3-10	Higuera	Black
11—Milwaukee	W	5-0	Farrell	Navarro
11—Milwaukee	L	7-8	Knudson	Wojna
12—Milwaukee	L	1-5	Bosio	Bailes
13—Milwaukee	L	4-5*	Plesac	Jones
15—At Oak.	L	2-5	Davis	Nichols
16—At Oak.	W	6-3	Olin	Honeycutt
17—At Oak.	L	0-1	Welch	Farrell
18—At Calif.	L	5-6	Minton	Olin
19—At Calif.	L	4-7	Blyleven	Nichols
20—At Calif.	L	0-1	McCaskill	Black
22—Seattle	W	3-2*	Jones	Schooler
23—Seattle	W	5-3	Candiotti	Dunne
24—Seattle	W	5-2	Davis	Zavaras
25—Chicago	L	4-5	Dotson	Orosco
26—Chicago	L	3-4	Rosenberg	Black
27—Chicago	L	3-9	Hibbard	Farrell
29—Baltimore	W	3-1	Jones	Harnisch
30—Baltimore	L	4-7	Ballard	Swindell
31—Baltimore	W	11-0	Farrell	Johnson

Won 12, Lost 17

SEPTEMBER

Date	W/L	Score	Winner	Loser
1—At Detroit	L	1-2‡	Gibson	Jones
2—At Detroit	L	4-10	Robinson	Davis
3—At Detroit	L	3-12	Morris	Candiotti
4—At Balt.	L	4-5	Williamson	Nichols
5—At Balt.	L	1-3	Milacki	Farrell
6—At Balt.	W	9-0	Black	Schilling
7—Toronto	L	4-12	Cerutti	Candiotti
8—Toronto	W	5-4	Jones	Acker
9—Toronto	L	5-7§	Wills	Kaiser
10—Toronto	L	4-5*	Acker	Olin
12—Detroit	W	1-0	Black	Tanana
13—Detroit	L	1-3	Morris	Candiotti
14—Detroit	W	4-0	Nichols	Ritz
15—At Toronto	L	2-5	Key	Swindell
16—At Toronto	L	2-3†	Wells	Jones
17—At Toronto	L	1-2*	Acker	Bailes
18—Oakland	L	2-4*	Eckersley	Olin
19—Oakland	L	1-5	Moore	Nichols
20—Oakland	L	6-8	Davis	Swindell
21—California	W	5-4x	Bailes	Monteleone
23—California	W	4-3	Black	Witt
23—California	W	6-2	Candiotti	Blyleven
24—California	W	5-4	Orosco	Fraser
26—At Seattle	L	2-3	Hanson	Jones
27—At Seattle	W	4-1	Farrell	Johnson
28—At Seattle	L	2-6	Holman	Olin
29—At Chicago	L	1-2	King	Candiotti
30—At Chicago	L	2-8	Hibbard	Nichols

Won 9, Lost 19

OCTOBER

Date	W/L	Score	Winner	Loser
1—At Chicago	W	1-0	Orosco	Dotson

Won 1, Lost 0

*10 innings. †11 innings. ‡12 innings. §16 innings. x17 innings.

Lefthander Greg Swindell jumped off to another blazing start before falling victim to elbow problems.

sons. Center fielder Joe Carter, despite struggling defensively (nine errors) and posting his lowest major league batting average (.243), was a big run producer, hitting a career-high 35 home runs and driving in 105 runs. And third baseman Brook Jacoby rallied from a 1988 slump to bat .272 with 13 homers and 64 RBIs.

But that was not enough to offset poor seasons by right fielder Cory Snyder, catcher Andy Allanson, O'Brien and Cleveland's platoon of designated hitters, Dave Clark and rookie Luis Medina.

Snyder's career-worst season was most devastating. He was slowed by a sore back in June and July and finished with a .215 average, 18 homers and 59 RBIs. Edwards benched Snyder briefly in August, and when the manager was fired a month later, Snyder was not one of his defenders. "I thought Doc could have done more," Snyder said.

By contrast, O'Brien, who got off to a hot start but had cooled off by the All-Star break, maintained that the responsibility for any player's failure rests with the player alone.

"Anybody who blames the manager for his bad season is in for a long, hard career," said O'Brien, who finished with his lowest numbers in six years (.260, 12 homers, 55 RBIs).

Allanson, a .263 hitter with 50 RBIs in '88, fell to .232 with 17 RBIs. Clark knocked in 29 runs, while Medina had just eight RBIs when he was returned to Class AAA Colorado Springs in June. And shortstop Felix Fermin knocked in only 21 runs in 156 games, though he rarely struck out and was adept at dropping sacrifice bunts. He had 32, the highest single-season total by an A.L. player since 1977.

The bench provided little help. Among outfielders Clark, Brad Komminsk and Joey Belle, catcher Joel Skinner and infielder Luis Aguayo, Clark and Komminsk had the top batting average at .237.

The Indians' slumbering offense neutralized their best pitching performance since 1976. Cleveland hurlers compiled a 3.65 earned-run average, ranking fifth in the league, and walked a league-low 452 batters.

Cleveland may have had the best starting rotation in the division. For the first time since 1968, four Tribe pitchers—Greg Swindell, John Farrell, Tom Candiotti and Bud Black—worked at least 180 innings. None of the four had an ERA higher than 3.63, but because of poor offensive support, Candiotti and Swindell tied for the staff high with only 13 wins each.

Injuries sidelined three starters. Swindell (13-6) missed five weeks with a damaged elbow, while Candiotti (13-10) and Farrell (9-14) also spent time on the disabled list. Only Black, who enjoyed his finest season (12-11) in five years, escaped injury.

When Swindell went down, the Indians recalled Rod Nichols from Colorado Springs to take his place. Nichols posted a 4-6 record with a 4.40 ERA. Cleveland's other starters included Scott Bailes (5-9, 4.28 ERA) and Rich Yett (5-6, 5.00), both of whom also worked in long relief.

Bullpen closer Doug Jones suffered no letdown after setting a franchise record with 37 saves in 1988. He posted 32 saves with a 2.34 ERA and was limited only by his teammates' inability to get a lead late in the game.

Free-agent signee Jesse Orosco did a good job as Jones' setup man. His 2.08 ERA was the lowest by a Cleveland reliever since 1968.

Teams with quality pitching are supposed to win, and Cleveland had that in 1989. But the fact was that a lack of run production cost the Indians a rare opportunity to contend for a title.

Second baseman Lou Whitaker rebounded from a bad 1988 season to hit 28 home runs for the lowly Tigers.

Tigers Pull a 103-Loss Stunner

By TOM GAGE

Several weeks before the Detroit Tigers went home for the winter, Manager Sparky Anderson already had determined the best way to handle future questions about the club's disastrous 1989 season.

"Amnesia," he said. "When my grandchildren ask me someday about my career and I start talking about the different seasons, I'll skip 1989. 'Sorry, kids, don't remember a thing about it.'"

It was indeed a forgettable season for Detroit, a team that was plagued by injuries while making a clumsy transition from a veteran-laden to a youth-oriented squad. The Tigers' record of 59-103 was the worst in the major leagues. They sank into sole possession of the American League East cellar on June 7 and stayed there, finishing 30 games out of first place.

Nothing went right for the Tigers in 1989. The youth movement didn't work and most of the trades flopped. Every time there was even the slightest glimmer of hope, someone else got hurt.

"By the end of the season," Anderson said, "I'd be listening to the injuries other teams had, knowing I could triple it. I've never seen a season with more injuries. They don't exist."

The Tigers put players on the disabled list 20 times in 1989, including Jack Morris, the ace of their pitching staff, for the first time in his career. Morris missed two months with an elbow fracture and closed out the '80s—a decade in which he won more games (162) than any other major league pitcher—with his worst season ever (6-14, 4.86 earned-run average).

Along with Morris, Jeff Robinson had been expected to be one of the workhorses of the rotation. But injuries to his side and elbow limited him to only 16 starts in which he went 4-5 with a 4.73 ERA.

The bullpen wasn't spared, either. An elbow injury ended Guillermo Hernandez's season August 19. He still led the Tigers with 15 saves, followed by Mike Henneman with eight. Henneman, who led the club with 11 victories despite working solely in relief, was relatively lucky in that he was disabled only three weeks of the season. Frank Williams (3.64 ERA) and Charles Hudson (6.35) joined Hernandez and Robinson as two-time residents on the disabled list in '89.

Detroit's everyday lineup was ravaged by injuries, too.

Matt Nokes, the Tigers' power-hitting catcher, was out for seven weeks with a knee injury. He later hurt his shoulder and was limited to duty as the designated hitter, finishing with only nine home runs and 39 runs batted in.

The Tigers lost shortstop Alan Trammell for various amounts of time that added up to 41 games. He hit a career-low .243 with five homers and 43 RBIs, but didn't blame his injuries entirely.

"Because of my back, I couldn't swing the way I wanted most of the year," he said, "but I didn't do a whole lot even when I could."

Left fielder/DH Fred Lynn did a short stint on the disabled list with a sore side and suffered through his worst season (.241, 11 homers, 46 RBIs) since 1981. A spring thumb injury kept center fielder Gary Pettis out of action until May 15, although he came back to post some solid numbers (a team-high .257 average and 43 stolen bases) and win his fourth Gold Glove. But he knocked in only 18 runs.

The Tigers even lost a player who began the season with another team. Left fielder Tracy Jones, who produced 26 RBIs in 46 games after being acquired from San Francisco for outfielder Pat Sheridan in June, underwent knee surgery in mid-August and did not return.

"I'm not saying we would have been a contending team with a normal amount of injuries," Anderson said. "I wouldn't deceive people that way. But we would have been better than what we were."

From the start, it was a transitional year as the aging Tigers toyed with a youth movement. It didn't work.

After being handed the starting first baseman's job based only on a good spring, rookie Torey Lovullo hit .115 the first six weeks of the season and was returned to the minors to stay. Rookie infielder Mike Brumley, who was obtained from San Diego in March, hit only .198. Acquired the same day from the Chicago White Sox was Ken Williams, who opened the season as Pettis' replacement in center field but batted just .205 for the season.

The Brumley and Williams deals were among several that did not work out for Detroit in '89. Another was the October 1988 trade that sent pitcher Walt Terrell to San Diego for third baseman Chris Brown and infielder/DH Keith Moreland. Brown lasted only until mid-May before the Tigers unloaded his .193 average and myriad injuries by releasing him. More-

SCORES OF DETROIT TIGERS' 1989 GAMES

APRIL

Date		Score	Winner	Loser
4—At Texas	L	0-4	Hough	Morris
6—At Texas	L	4-5	Guante	Williams
7—Milwaukee	W	10-3	Alexander	Wegman
8—Milwaukee	L	2-5	August	Tanana
11—Minnesota	L	0-14	Anderson	Morris
13—Minnesota	W	3-0	Robinson	Rawley
14—Texas	L	2-4	Moyer	Williams
15—Texas	L	1-4	Brown	Tanana
16—Texas	L	6-9	Hough	Morris
18—At Minn.	L	8-9	Toliver	Robinson
19—At Minn.	W	3-2	Alexander	Viola
20—At Minn.	L	2-7	Gonzalez	Tanana
21—At Milw.	L	1-2	Bosio	Morris
22—At Milw.	W	6-3	Williams	Crim
23—At Milw.	W	11-3	Gibson	August
24—Seattle	W	1-0	Alexander	Langston
25—Seattle	W	5-2	Tanana	Bankhead
26—At Calif.	L	0-1	Finley	Morris
27—At Calif.	L	3-10	Blyleven	Hudson
28—At Oak.	L	1-2	Moore	Gibson
29—At Oak.	L	2-3	Stewart	Alexander
30—At Oak.	W	7-2	Tanana	Davis

Won 8, Lost 14

MAY

Date		Score	Winner	Loser
1—At Seattle	L	3-5	Powell	Morris
2—At Seattle	L	2-7	Dunne	Hudson
3—At Seattle	L	2-3	Hanson	Alexander
5—Oakland	L	3-5	Stewart	Tanana
6—Oakland	W	6-3	Morris	Davis
7—Oakland	L	4-5	Welch	Hudson
8—California	L	2-9	Finley	Alexander
9—California	L	1-5	Blyleven	Gibson
10—California	W	3-2	Hernandez	Harvey
12—At Cleve.	W	6-3	Morris	Black
13—At Cleve.	L	1-3	Swindell	Alexander
14—At Cleve.	L	3-8	Candiotti	Gibson
15—Chicago	W	3-2	Tanana	Long
16—Chicago	W	9-7	Williams	Perez
17—Chicago	L	7-10	Patterson	Hernandez
19—Kan. City	W	2-0	Henneman	Saberhagen
20—Kan. City	W	2-1	Henneman	Gordon
21—Kan. City	W	4-2	Gibson	Gubicza
22—Cleveland	L	3-7	Black	Morris
23—Cleveland	W	7-2	Trujillo	Swindell
24—Cleveland	W	2-1*	Hernandez	Bailes
25—Cleveland	W	9-5	Tanana	Farrell
26—At K.C.	L	3-6	Montgomery	Henneman
27—At K.C.	L	1-5	Gubicza	Nosek
28—At K.C.	L	5-9	Gordon	Trujillo
29—At Chicago	W	4-2	Alexander	King
30—At Chicago	W	10-3	Tanana	Bittiger
31—At Chicago	W	4-3	Henneman	Thigpen

Won 14, Lost 14

JUNE

Date		Score	Winner	Loser
1—Baltimore	L	3-8	Schmidt	Nosek
2—Baltimore	L	1-4	Milacki	Trujillo
3—Baltimore	L	2-4	Hickey	Alexander
4—Baltimore	L	4-7	Tibbs	Tanana
5—Boston	L	2-5	Clemens	Palmer
6—Boston	W	5-1	Schwabe	Price
7—Boston	L	1-6	Dopson	Alexander
9—At Toronto	L	0-2	Stieb	Tanana
10—At Toronto	W	11-8	Williams	Key
11—At Toronto	L	0-4	Flanagan	Schwabe
12—At Toronto	L	4-5†	Henke	Gibson
13—At Boston	L	7-8	Gardner	Williams
14—At Boston	W	7-3	Tanana	Boddicker
16—California	L	4-9	Blyleven	Schwabe
17—California	L	3-6	Abbott	Alexander
18—California	L	1-3	Witt	Palmer
19—At Oak.	W	6-4	Tanana	Stewart
20—At Oak.	L	4-6	Nelson	Havens
21—At Oak.	L	3-6	Moore	Schwabe
23—At Seattle	W	5-4	Henneman	Schooler
24—At Seattle	L	1-3	Bankhead	Tanana
25—At Seattle	L	3-5	Swift	Palmer
27—New York	W	6-5	Havens	Guetterman
28—New York	W	6-5*	Henneman	Righetti
29—New York	L	6-7	Plunk	Nunez
30—At Balt.	W	16-5	Schwabe	Milacki

Won 8, Lost 18

JULY

Date		Score	Winner	Loser
1—At Balt.	L	1-8	Ballard	Hudson
2—At Balt.	W	7-3	Nunez	Thurmond
3—At Balt.	L	4-11	Smith	Alexander
4—At N.Y.	L	0-1	Schulze	Tanana
5—At N.Y.	L	0-9	Hawkins	Havens
6—At N.Y.	L	5-6†	Plunk	Henneman
7—Toronto	L	4-6	Cummings	Hernandez
8—Toronto	L	3-8	Cerutti	Alexander
9—Toronto	L	0-2	Stieb	Tanana
13—Seattle	L	4-5‡	Swift	Schwabe
14—Seattle	L	0-13	Holman	Alexander
15—Seattle	L	3-9	Bankhead	Ritz
16—Seattle	W	8-5	Hudson	Harris
17—Oakland	W	2-1	Henneman	Nelson
18—Oakland	L	2-7	Davis	Beard
20—At Calif.	L	3-4	Finley	Henneman
21—At Calif.	L	7-8	Harvey	Beard
22—At Calif.	L	4-5x	Petry	Hudson
23—At Calif.	L	4-5	McClure	Henneman
24—At Milw.	L	0-10	Bosio	Morris
25—At Milw.	W	7-2	Alexander	August
26—At Milw.	L	2-3	Higuera	Nunez
27—At Milw.	L	1-11	Navarro	Gibson
28—Minnesota	W	6-4	Ritz	Viola
28—Minnesota	L	3-7	Dyer	Robinson
29—Minnesota	W	3-2*	Henneman	Wayne
30—Minnesota	L	3-14	Anderson	Alexander

Won 6, Lost 21

AUGUST

Date		Score	Winner	Loser
1—Texas	L	3-4	Brown	Gibson
2—Texas	W	6-4	Ritz	Jeffcoat
3—Texas	W	9-6	Henneman	Guante
4—At Chicago	L	4-5	Patterson	Gibson
5—At Chicago	L	6-7	King	Alexander
6—At Chicago	W	4-3	Tanana	Hibbard
7—Milwaukee	W	5-3	Ritz	Fossas
7—Milwaukee	L	2-5	Filer	Gibson
8—Milwaukee	W	6-3	Robinson	August
9—Milwaukee	L	1-6	Crim	Morris
10—At Texas	L	1-4	Ryan	Alexander
11—At Texas	L	3-7	Brown	Tanana
12—At Texas	W	6-5	Gibson	Rogers
13—At Texas	W	4-2	Henneman	Rogers
14—Baltimore	L	1-4*	Schmidt	Morris
15—Baltimore	L	0-2	Milacki	Alexander
16—Baltimore	W	4-0	Tanana	Harnisch
17—New York	L	1-2	Cadaret	DuBois
18—New York	W	7-3	Robinson	Cary
19—New York	W	5-4	Morris	Righetti
20—New York	W	7-6	Nunez	Plunk
21—Oakland	L	1-6	C. Young	Tanana
22—At Toronto	L	2-3§	Gozzo	Nunez
23—At Toronto	L	4-11	Wills	Robinson
24—At Toronto	L	3-11	Flanagan	Morris
25—At Boston	L	2-4	Smithson	Alexander
25—At Boston	L	3-11	Lamp	Ritz
26—At Boston	L	2-5	Clemens	Tanana
27—At Boston	L	1-7	Price	DuBois
28—At Boston	L	3-6	Boddicker	Robinson
29—At K.C.	L	8-12	Crawford	Searcy
30—At K.C.	L	1-6	Gubicza	Alexander
31—At K.C.	L	0-3	Saberhagen	Ritz

Won 11, Lost 22

SEPTEMBER

Date		Score	Winner	Loser
1—Cleveland	W	2-1‡	Gibson	Jones
2—Cleveland	W	10-4	Robinson	Davis
3—Cleveland	W	12-3	Morris	Candiotti
4—Kan. City	W	5-1	Alexander	Saberhagen
5—Kan. City	W	10-2	Ritz	Gordon
6—Kan. City	W	11-5	Nunez	Leibrandt
8—Chicago	W	7-5	Morris	Hibbard
9—Chicago	L	3-13	Perez	Robinson
10—Chicago	W	6-5	Henneman	Thigpen
12—At Cleve.	L	0-1	Black	Tanana
13—At Cleve.	W	3-1	Morris	Candiotti
14—At Cleve.	L	0-4	Nichols	Ritz
15—At Minn.	L	4-8	Aguilera	DuBois
16—At Minn.	L	7-8	Anderson	Alexander
17—At Minn.	W	9-2	Searcy	Dyer
19—At Balt.	L	2-6	Milacki	Morris
20—At Balt.	L	2-9	Ballard	Tanana
22—Boston	L	7-9	Murphy	Nunez
23—Boston	L	1-6	Boddicker	Ritz
24—Boston	L	2-4	Boyd	Morris
25—Toronto	L	0-2	Key	DuBois
26—Toronto	W	4-3	Henneman	Ward
27—Toronto	L	1-8	Stieb	Alexander
29—At N.Y.	L	1-5	Plunk	Morris
30—At N.Y.	L	2-9	Hawkins	Ritz

Won 11, Lost 14

OCTOBER

Date		Score	Winner	Loser
1—At N.Y.	W	5-3	Tanana	Mmahat

Won 1, Lost 0

*10 innings. †11 innings. ‡12 innings. §14 innings. x16 innings.

One of the few bright spots in Detroit's dismal season was the offensive and defensive play of veteran catcher Mike Heath.

land did better, batting .299 in 90 games for Detroit, but the Tigers shipped him to Baltimore for rookie pitcher Brian DuBois in late July.

Brown was followed at third base by a succession of players that ended with a platoon of Rick Schu and rookie Doug Strange. But both players batted only .214, contributing to Detroit's league-low .242 average.

The Tigers also finished last in the league in pitching with a 4.53 ERA, although the club's difficulty scoring runs made the situation worse. Frank Tanana thought he pitched his best in more than a decade, but his record was only 10-14 despite a 3.58 ERA.

"The injuries we had were only a small part of what happened to this team," Tanana said. "It's tough to go out there time after time knowing you don't have much chance to win."

Doyle Alexander lost a career-high 18 games and won only six, while Paul Gibson went 4-8 with a 4.64 ERA as a spot starter and long reliever. The Tigers finished the year with rookies Kevin Ritz (4-6, 4.38 ERA in 12 games) and DuBois (0-4, 1.75 ERA in six games) as part of their rotation.

The Tigers didn't end the season with every position in a shambles, however. In Nokes' absence, Mike Heath established himself as the starting catcher by batting .263 with 10 homers and nailing 33 of 105 would-be basestealers.

"I know we couldn't have been much worse," Anderson said, "but we would have been without Heath."

First baseman Dave Bergman enjoyed his busiest year ever (385 at-bats) and one of his best (.268 average). After being released by the New York Yankees in April, Gary Ward was signed by Detroit and hit nine homers while filling in at first base, DH and in the outfield. Second baseman Lou Whitaker had excellent production numbers for a last-place team (a club-high 28 homers and 85 RBIs), although his .251 average was his lowest since 1980.

While Whitaker was shattering the club season record for homers by a second baseman, another Tiger veteran, right fielder Chet Lemon, was enduring his worst season (.237, 47 RBIs) since 1976.

"There was never a time I got hot and stayed hot," he said. "This wasn't a good year for many of us, though. Every time we looked around, there was someone new in the lineup. We never got to know each other, we never played as a unit, which is what we'd become known for the last several years—playing as a team and getting the most of ourselves."

The Tigers' problems were most evident on the road. Their 21-60 record away from home was the worst in the majors.

"We have a long way to go, but Baltimore showed what can be done in a year," Henneman said. "At least we have that to be encouraged about."

But little else.

American League Averages for 1989

CHAMPIONSHIP WINNERS IN PREVIOUS YEARS

Year	Team	Pct.
1900—Chicago*		.607
1901—Chicago		.610
1902—Philadelphia		.610
1903—Boston		.659
1904—Boston		.617
1905—Philadelphia		.622
1906—Chicago		.616
1907—Detroit		.613
1908—Detroit		.588
1909—Detroit		.645
1910—Philadelphia		.680
1911—Philadelphia		.669
1912—Boston		.691
1913—Philadelphia		.627
1914—Philadelphia		.651
1915—Boston		.669
1916—Boston		.591
1917—Chicago		.649
1918—Boston		.595
1919—Chicago		.629
1920—Cleveland		.636
1921—New York		.641
1922—New York		.610
1923—New York		.645
1924—Washington		.597
1925—Washington		.636
1926—New York		.591
1927—New York		.714
1928—New York		.656
1929—Philadelphia		.693
1930—Philadelphia		.662
1931—Philadelphia		.704
1932—New York		.695
1933—Washington		.651
1934—Detroit		.656
1935—Detroit		.616
1936—New York		.667
1937—New York		.662
1938—New York		.651
1939—New York		.702
1940—Detroit		.584
1941—New York		.656
1942—New York		.669
1943—New York		.636
1944—St. Louis		.578
1945—Detroit		.575
1946—Boston		.675
1947—New York		.630
1948—Cleveland†		.626
1949—New York		.630
1950—New York		.636
1951—New York		.636
1952—New York		.617
1953—New York		.656
1954—Cleveland		.721
1955—New York		.623
1956—New York		.630
1957—New York		.636
1958—New York		.597
1959—Chicago		.610
1960—New York		.630
1961—New York		.673
1962—New York		.593
1963—New York		.646
1964—New York		.611
1965—Minnesota		.630
1966—Baltimore		.606
1967—Boston		.568
1968—Detroit		.636
1969—Baltimore (East)		.673
1970—Baltimore (East)		.667
1971—Baltimore (East)		.639
1972—Oakland (West)		.600
1973—Oakland (West)		.580
1974—Oakland (West)		.556
1975—Boston (East)		.594
1976—New York (East)		.610
1977—New York (East)		.617
1978—New York (East)		.613
1979—Baltimore (East)		.642
1980—Kansas City (West)		.599
1981—New York (East)		.551
1982—Milwaukee (East)		.586
1983—Baltimore (East)		.605
1984—Detroit (East)		.642
1985—Kansas City (West)		.562
1986—Boston (East)		.590
1987—Minnesota (West)		.525
1988—Oakland (West)		.642

*Not recognized as major league in 1900. †Defeated Boston in one-game playoff for pennant.

STANDING OF CLUBS AT CLOSE OF SEASON

EAST DIVISION

Club	Tor.	Bal.	Bos.	Mil.	N.Y.	Cle.	Det.	Oak.	K.C.	Cal.	Tex.	Min.	Sea.	Chi.	W.	L.	Pct.	G.B.
Toronto	..	6	8	7	6	8	11	5	5	5	7	3	7	11	89	73	.549	......
Baltimore	7	..	6	7	8	7	10	5	6	6	9	4	6	6	87	75	.537	2
Boston	5	7	..	6	7	8	11	7	4	4	6	6	5	7	83	79	.512	6
Milwaukee	6	6	7	..	8	10	7	5	4	5	5	9	7	2	81	81	.500	8
New York	7	5	6	5	..	4	7	3	6	6	5	6	8	6	74	87	.460	14½
Cleveland	5	6	5	3	9	..	5	2	8	7	7	5	6	5	73	89	.451	16
Detroit	2	3	2	6	6	8	..	4	6	1	4	5	4	8	59	103	.364	30

WEST DIVISION

Club	Oak.	K.C.	Cal.	Tex.	Min.	Sea.	Chi.	Tor.	Bal.	Bos.	Mil.	N.Y.	Cle.	Det.	W.	L.	Pct.	G.B.
Oakland	..	6	8	8	7	9	8	7	7	5	7	9	10	8	99	63	.611	......
Kansas City	7	..	9	8	7	9	7	7	6	8	8	6	4	6	92	70	.568	7
California	5	4	..	6	11	7	8	7	6	8	7	6	5	11	91	71	.562	8
Texas	5	5	7	..	8	7	10	5	3	6	7	7	5	8	83	79	.512	16
Minnesota	6	6	2	5	..	7	8	9	8	6	3	6	7	7	80	82	.494	19
Seattle	4	4	6	6	6	..	6	5	6	7	5	4	6	8	73	89	.451	26
Chicago	5	6	5	3	5	7	..	1	6	5	10	5	7	4	69	92	.429	29½

Championship Series—Oakland defeated Toronto, four games to one.

SHUTOUT GAMES

Club	Oak.	Tor.	Cal.	Cle.	Min.	Sea.	Bos.	N.Y.	Tex.	Mil.	K.C.	Chi.	Bal.	Det.	W.	L.	Pct.
Oakland	..	0	4	4	2	0	0	3	2	1	2	2	0	0	20	5	.800
Toronto	1	..	0	0	0	0	0	1	2	1	3	0	0	4	12	7	.632
California	2	3	..	1	0	3	4	1	0	1	2	1	1	1	20	12	.625
Cleveland	0	0	1	..	0	0	0	0	0	2	3	1	4	2	13	11	.542
Minnesota	1	1	0	0	..	1	2	0	0	0	0	1	1	1	8	7	.533
Seattle	0	0	1	1	0	..	0	1	2	0	3	1	1	1	10	9	.526
Boston	0	0	0	1	1	2	..	0	2	0	1	2	0	0	9	9	.500
New York	0	1	0	2	0	0	1	..	0	0	1	0	2	2	9	10	.474
Texas	0	0	4	1	0	1	0	0	..	0	0	0	1	7	8	.467
Milwaukee	0	0	0	1	1	0	0	3	0	..	1	0	1	1	8	11	.421
Kansas City	1	1	2	0	1	0	1	1	0	2	..	0	3	1	13	18	.419
Chicago	0	0	0	0	0	1	1	0	2	0	2	..	1	0	5	8	.385
Baltimore	0	1	0	0	1	0	0	0	0	2	1	1	..	1	7	15	.318
Detroit	0	0	0	0	1	0	0	0	0	0	1	0	1	..	4	15	.211

RECORD AT HOME
EAST DIVISION

Club	Balt.	Bos.	Tor.	Mil.	Cle.	N.Y.	Det.	K.C.	Oak.	Cal.	Min.	Tex.	Sea.	Chi.	W.	L.	Pct.
Baltimore	....	4-2	4-3	4-3	4-3	3-3	4-2	4-2	4-2	4-2	3-3	5-1	2-4	2-4	47	34	.580
Boston	5-2	....	0-6	4-2	4-3	4-2	6-1	2-4	5-1	3-3	2-4	4-2	4-2	4-2	46	35	.568
Toronto	3-3	2-5	....	4-3	5-1	2-4	6-1	3-3	3-3	2-4	3-3	4-2	4-2	5-1	46	35	.568
Milwaukee	3-3	5-2	3-3	....	5-1	5-2	4-3	3-3	3-3	2-4	5-1	2-4	3-3	2-4	45	36	.556
Cleveland	3-3	2-4	4-3	2-5	....	4-3	4-2	5-1	0-6	5-1	2-4	3-3	4-2	3-3	41	40	.506
New York	2-5	4-3	3-4	3-3	1-5	....	5-1	3-3	1-5	5-1	3-3	4-2	3-3	4-2	41	40	.506
Detroit	1-6	1-5	1-5	3-3	6-1	5-2	....	6-0	2-4	1-5	3-3	2-4	3-3	4-2	38	43	.469

WEST DIVISION

Club	K.C.	Oak.	Cal.	Min.	Tex.	Sea.	Chi.	Balt.	Bos.	Tor.	Mil.	Cle.	N.Y.	Det.	W.	L.	Pct.
Kansas City	....	4-2	6-1	4-3	5-2	3-3	4-2	4-2	4-2	4-2	5-1	3-3	3-3	6-0	55	26	.679
Oakland	4-3	....	4-2	4-2	4-3	5-1	4-3	5-1	4-2	4-2	4-2	4-2	4-2	4-2	54	27	.667
California	3-3	3-4	....	5-1	4-3	3-3	4-3	4-2	5-1	3-3	3-3	4-2	5-1	6-0	52	29	.642
Minnesota	3-3	4-3	1-6	....	2-4	6-1	4-2	5-1	2-4	6-0	2-4	3-3	3-3	4-2	45	36	.556
Texas	3-3	2-4	2-4	4-3	....	4-3	5-2	2-4	4-2	3-3	3-3	2-4	5-1	4-2	45	36	.556
Seattle	1-6	3-4	3-4	5-1	3-3	....	3-3	2-4	5-1	3-3	2-4	4-2	1-5	5-1	40	41	.494
Chicago	4-3	2-4	2-4	3-4	1-5	4-3	....	2-4	2-4	0-6	6-0	4-2	3-2	2-4	35	45	.438

RECORD ABROAD
EAST DIVISION

Club	Tor.	Balt.	Bos.	Mil.	N.Y.	Cle.	Det.	Oak.	Cal.	Tex.	K.C.	Min.	Chi.	Sea.	W.	L.	Pct.
Toronto	....	3-4	6-0	3-3	4-3	3-4	5-1	2-4	3-3	3-3	2-4	0-6	6-0	3-3	43	38	.531
Baltimore	3-3	....	2-5	3-3	5-2	3-3	6-1	1-5	2-4	4-2	2-4	1-5	4-2	4-2	40	41	.494
Boston	5-2	2-4	....	2-5	3-4	4-2	5-1	2-4	1-5	2-4	2-4	4-2	4-2	1-5	37	44	.457
Milwaukee	3-4	3-4	2-4	....	3-3	5-2	3-3	2-4	3-3	3-3	1-5	4-2	0-6	4-2	36	45	.444
New York	4-2	3-3	2-4	2-5	....	3-4	2-5	2-4	1-5	1-5	3-3	3-3	2-3	5-1	33	47	.413
Cleveland	1-5	3-4	3-4	1-5	5-1	....	1-6	2-4	2-4	4-2	3-3	3-3	2-4	2-4	32	49	.395
Detroit	1-6	2-4	1-6	3-4	1-5	2-4	....	2-4	0-6	2-4	0-6	2-4	4-2	1-5	21	60	.259

WEST DIVISION

Club	Oak.	Cal.	Tex.	K.C.	Min.	Chi.	Sea.	Tor.	Balt.	Bos.	Mil.	N.Y.	Cle.	Det.	W.	L.	Pct.
Oakland	....	4-3	4-2	2-4	3-4	4-2	4-3	3-3	2-4	1-5	3-3	5-1	6-0	4-2	45	36	.556
California	2-4	....	2-4	1-6	6-1	4-2	4-3	4-2	2-4	3-3	4-2	1-5	5-1	4-2	39	42	.481
Texas	3-4	3-4	....	2-5	4-2	5-1	3-3	2-4	1-5	2-4	4-2	2-4	3-3	4-2	38	43	.469
Kansas City	3-4	3-3	3-3	....	3-3	3-4	6-1	3-3	2-4	4-2	3-3	3-3	1-5	0-6	37	44	.457
Minnesota	2-4	1-5	3-4	3-4	....	4-3	1-5	3-3	3-3	4-2	1-5	3-3	4-2	3-4	35	46	.432
Chicago	3-4	3-4	2-5	2-4	2-4	....	3-3	1-5	4-2	3-3	4-2	2-4	3-3	2-4	34	47	.420
Seattle	1-5	3-3	3-4	3-3	1-6	3-4	....	2-4	4-2	2-4	3-3	3-3	2-4	3-3	33	48	.407

1989 A.L. Pitching Against Each Club

BALTIMORE—87-75

Pitcher	Bos. W-L	Cal. W-L	Chi. W-L	Clev. W-L	Det. W-L	K.C. W-L	Mil. W-L	Minn. W-L	N.Y. W-L	Oak. W-L	Sea. W-L	Tex. W-L	Tor. W-L	Totals W-L
Ballard	1-0	1-1	1-1	3-0	2-0	1-0	1-1	1-1	2-1	1-1	2-1	1-0	1-1	18-8
Bautista	1-0	0-0	0-0	0-1	0-0	0-1	0-0	0-1	0-0	2-0	0-1	0-0	0-0	3-4
Harnisch	1-1	0-0	0-1	0-1	0-1	0-1	1-1	0-1	0-1	0-1	1-0	1-0	1-0	5-9
Hickey	0-1	0-0	0-0	0-0	1-0	0-0	0-1	0-0	0-1	0-0	0-0	0-0	1-0	2-3
Holton	1-1	1-0	1-0	0-1	0-0	0-0	1-0	0-1	0-1	0-1	1-0	0-0	0-1	5-7
Johnson	1-1	0-0	0-1	0-1	0-0	0-1	1-1	1-0	1-0	0-0	0-0	0-1	0-1	4-7
McDonald	0-0	0-0	0-0	0-0	0-0	0-0	0-0	0-0	0-0	0-0	0-0	0-0	1-0	1-0
Milacki	0-2	0-2	1-2	1-1	3-1	1-0	2-1	1-1	2-0	0-1	1-0	1-0	1-1	14-12
Olson	0-0	1-0	0-0	0-0	0-0	0-0	0-0	2-1	0-0	0-1	0-0	0-0	0-0	5-2
Schilling	0-0	0-0	0-0	0-1	0-0	0-0	0-0	0-0	0-0	0-0	0-0	0-0	0-0	0-1
Schmidt	0-1	0-2	1-0	1-0	1-0	1-1	0-1	0-1	2-1	1-1	0-2	1-2	1-1	10-13
Smith	0-0	1-0	0-0	0-0	1-0	0-0	0-0	0-0	0-0	0-0	0-0	0-0	0-0	2-0
Thurmond	0-0	0-1	1-0	0-0	0-1	0-0	0-0	0-1	1-0	0-1	0-0	0-0	0-0	2-4
Tibbs	0-0	0-0	1-0	1-0	0-0	0-0	0-0	0-0	0-0	1-0	0-0	1-0	1-0	5-0
Weston	0-0	0-0	0-0	0-0	0-0	0-0	0-0	0-0	0-0	0-0	1-0	0-0	0-0	1-0
Williamson	1-0	2-0	0-1	2-0	0-0	1-1	1-0	0-1	0-0	0-0	0-0	3-0	0-2	10-5
Totals	6-7	6-6	6-6	7-7	10-3	6-6	7-6	4-8	8-5	5-7	6-6	9-3	7-6	87-75

No Decisions—Huismann.

BOSTON—83-79

Pitcher	Balt. W-L	Cal. W-L	Chi. W-L	Clev. W-L	Det. W-L	K.C. W-L	Mil. W-L	Minn. W-L	N.Y. W-L	Oak. W-L	Sea. W-L	Tex. W-L	Tor. W-L	Totals W-L
Boddicker	0-1	0-1	1-0	1-1	2-1	2-1	2-0	1-2	1-0	0-0	1-2	2-0	2-2	15-11
Bolton	0-1	0-0	0-0	0-1	0-0	0-1	0-1	0-0	0-0	0-0	0-0	0-0	0-0	0-4
Boyd	0-0	0-0	0-0	1-1	1-0	0-0	0-0	1-0	0-0	0-0	0-1	0-0	0-0	3-2
Clemens	1-0	1-2	3-0	2-1	2-0	0-0	0-2	1-0	3-1	1-2	1-0	1-3	1-0	17-11

BOSTON—83-79

Pitcher	Balt. W-L	Cal. W-L	Chi. W-L	Clev. W-L	Det. W-L	K.C. W-L	Mil. W-L	Minn. W-L	N.Y. W-L	Oak. W-L	Sea. W-L	Tex. W-L	Tor. W-L	Totals W-L
Dopson	1-0	1-2	0-1	0-0	1-0	2-1	2-0	2-0	0-1	2-0	0-2	1-0	0-1	12-8
Gardner	1-0	0-0	0-1	0-1	1-0	0-1	0-1	0-1	0-0	0-1	0-0	1-1	0-0	3-7
Harris	0-0	0-0	0-0	0-0	0-0	0-1	1-0	0-0	0-0	1-0	0-0	0-0	0-1	2-2
Hetzel	0-1	0-0	0-1	0-0	0-0	0-0	0-0	0-0	1-0	0-0	0-1	0-0	1-0	2-3
Lamp	0-0	1-1	0-0	1-0	1-0	0-0	0-0	0-0	0-0	0-0	1-0	0-0	0-1	4-2
Murphy	1-0	0-1	0-1	1-0	1-0	0-1	0-0	0-1	1-1	0-0	0-0	0-1	1-1	5-7
Price	0-0	0-0	1-0	0-0	1-1	0-1	0-1	0-1	0-1	0-0	0-0	0-0	0-0	2-5
Smith	1-0	0-0	0-0	0-0	0-0	0-0	1-0	0-0	1-0	2-0	1-0	0-0	0-0	6-1
Smithson	0-2	0-1	1-1	2-0	1-0	0-0	0-2	1-1	0-1	0-2	1-1	1-1	0-2	7-14
Stanley	2-1	1-0	1-0	0-0	0-0	0-0	0-0	0-0	0-1	1-0	0-0	0-0	0-0	5-2
Totals	7-6	4-8	7-5	8-5	11-2	4-8	6-7	6-6	7-6	7-5	5-7	6-6	5-8	83-79

No Decisions—Rochford.

CALIFORNIA—91-71

Pitcher	Balt. W-L	Bos. W-L	Chi. W-L	Clev. W-L	Det. W-L	K.C. W-L	Mil. W-L	Minn. W-L	N.Y. W-L	Oak. W-L	Sea. W-L	Tex. W-L	Tor. W-L	Totals W-L
Abbott	1-0	2-0	1-1	0-1	1-0	0-3	2-0	2-0	1-2	0-2	0-2	1-0	1-1	12-12
Blyleven	1-0	1-1	0-0	1-1	3-0	3-0	1-1	2-0	0-1	2-1	2-0	0-0	1-0	17-5
Clark	0-0	0-0	0-0	0-0	0-0	0-0	0-0	0-0	0-1	0-0	0-0	0-1	0-0	0-2
Finley	1-0	1-0	2-1	0-1	3-0	0-1	2-0	3-0	1-0	1-2	1-1	1-2	0-1	16-9
Fraser	0-3	1-0	0-1	0-1	0-0	0-1	0-0	0-0	1-1	1-0	0-0	1-0	0-0	4-7
Harvey	0-1	0-0	1-0	0-0	1-1	0-0	0-0	0-0	0-0	0-0	0-1	0-0	1-0	3-3
McCaskill	1-1	2-1	2-1	1-0	0-0	1-2	1-0	1-1	0-0	1-1	3-0	1-2	1-1	15-10
McClure	0-0	1-0	0-0	0-0	1-0	0-0	0-0	0-0	1-0	0-0	0-0	1-0	2-1	6-1
Minton	0-0	0-0	0-0	1-0	0-0	0-0	0-0	0-0	1-0	0-0	0-1	1-0	1-1	4-3
Monteleone	1-0	0-0	0-0	0-1	0-0	0-0	0-0	0-1	0-0	0-0	0-0	0-0	0-0	2-2
Petry	0-0	0-1	0-0	1-0	1-0	0-0	1-1	0-0	0-0	0-0	0-0	0-0	0-0	3-2
Witt	1-1	0-1	2-1	0-2	1-0	0-1	0-3	3-0	1-1	0-2	1-1	0-2	0-0	9-15
Totals	6-6	8-4	8-5	5-7	11-1	4-9	7-5	11-2	6-6	5-8	7-6	6-7	7-5	91-71

No Decisions—Corbett, Fetters, Lovelace.

CHICAGO—69-92

Pitcher	Balt. W-L	Bos. W-L	Cal. W-L	Clev. W-L	Det. W-L	K.C. W-L	Mil. W-L	Minn. W-L	N.Y. W-L	Oak. W-L	Sea. W-L	Tex. W-L	Tor. W-L	Totals W-L
Bittiger	0-0	0-0	0-0	0-0	0-1	0-0	0-0	0-0	0-0	0-0	0-0	0-0	0-0	0-1
Davis	0-0	0-0	0-0	0-0	0-0	0-1	0-0	0-0	0-0	0-0	0-0	0-0	0-0	0-1
Dotson	0-0	0-0	0-0	1-1	0-0	0-2	1-0	1-0	0-0	0-0	0-0	0-1	0-2	3-7
Hibbard	1-1	0-0	0-0	2-0	0-2	1-0	0-0	0-1	0-0	0-1	1-0	1-2	0-0	6-7
Hillegas	0-0	1-1	1-1	0-1	0-0	1-1	1-0	1-2	1-2	0-0	1-1	0-0	0-2	7-11
Jones	0-0	0-1	0-0	0-0	0-0	0-0	0-0	0-0	0-0	0-0	1-1	1-0	0-0	3-2
King	3-1	0-0	0-2	1-0	1-1	0-0	1-0	1-1	1-0	0-1	1-1	0-1	0-0	9-10
Long	0-0	1-0	0-1	0-0	0-1	0-0	2-0	0-0	0-1	1-0	1-1	0-0	0-0	5-5
McCarthy	0-1	0-0	0-0	0-0	0-0	0-1	0-0	0-0	1-0	0-0	0-0	0-0	0-0	1-2
Pall	0-0	1-0	0-1	0-0	0-0	0-0	0-0	0-0	1-1	1-1	1-1	0-0	0-1	4-5
Patterson	0-0	1-1	1-0	0-0	2-0	1-0	0-0	0-0	0-0	0-0	1-0	0-0	0-0	6-1
Perez	1-0	1-2	1-1	0-1	1-1	2-0	3-0	0-3	0-1	1-2	0-0	0-2	1-1	11-14
Peterson	0-0	0-0	0-0	0-1	0-0	0-0	0-0	0-0	0-0	0-0	0-0	0-0	0-0	0-1
Reuss	0-0	0-0	2-0	1-1	0-0	0-1	1-1	2-0	1-0	1-1	0-1	0-0	0-0	8-5
Rosenberg	1-2	0-2	0-1	2-0	0-0	0-0	0-1	0-0	1-1	0-1	0-0	0-3	0-2	4-13
Segura	0-0	0-0	0-0	0-0	0-0	0-0	0-0	0-0	0-0	0-0	0-0	0-1	0-0	0-1
Thigpen	0-0	0-0	0-0	0-0	0-2	0-1	1-0	0-1	0-0	0-1	1-0	0-0	0-1	2-6
Totals	6-6	5-7	5-8	7-5	4-8	6-7	10-2	5-8	5-6	5-8	7-6	3-10	1-11	69-92

No Decisions—Edwards, Hardy.

CLEVELAND—73-89

Pitcher	Balt. W-L	Bos. W-L	Cal. W-L	Chi. W-L	Det. W-L	K.C. W-L	Mil. W-L	Minn. W-L	N.Y. W-L	Oak. W-L	Sea. W-L	Tex. W-L	Tor. W-L	Totals W-L
Allen	0-0	0-0	0-1	0-0	0-0	0-0	0-0	0-0	0-0	0-0	0-0	0-0	0-0	0-1
Atherton	0-1	0-0	0-0	0-0	0-0	0-0	0-1	0-0	0-0	0-0	0-0	0-0	0-1	0-3
Bailes	0-0	0-0	2-0	1-0	0-1	1-1	0-2	0-0	1-1	0-0	0-1	0-2	0-1	5-9
Black	1-1	2-2	2-1	1-1	2-1	2-0	0-2	0-1	0-1	0-0	0-1	0-0	2-0	12-11
Candiotti	1-0	1-0	1-0	0-2	1-2	2-1	1-1	1-1	2-0	0-1	2-0	0-0	1-1	13-10
Davis	0-0	0-0	0-0	0-0	0-1	0-0	0-0	0-0	0-0	0-0	1-0	0-0	0-0	1-1
Farrell	1-2	0-2	0-0	0-1	0-1	1-1	1-0	2-1	1-1	0-3	1-1	1-0	0-1	9-14
Jones	1-0	0-0	0-0	0-0	0-1	0-1	0-2	1-3	2-0	0-0	2-1	0-1	1-1	7-10
Kaiser	0-0	0-0	0-0	0-0	0-0	0-0	0-0	0-0	0-0	0-0	0-0	0-1	0-1	0-3
Nichols	0-1	2-0	0-1	0-1	1-0	0-0	0-0	0-0	1-0	0-2	0-0	0-1	0-0	4-6
Olin	0-0	0-0	0-1	0-0	0-0	0-0	0-0	0-0	0-0	1-1	0-1	0-0	0-1	1-4
Orosco	0-0	0-1	1-0	1-1	0-0	0-0	0-1	0-0	0-0	0-0	0-0	1-0	0-0	3-4
Skalski	0-0	0-1	0-0	0-0	0-0	0-0	0-1	0-0	0-0	0-0	0-0	0-0	0-0	0-2
Swindell	1-1	0-0	1-0	2-0	1-1	2-0	1-0	0-0	1-1	1-2	0-0	3-0	0-1	13-6
Wojna	0-0	0-0	0-0	0-0	0-0	0-0	0-1	0-0	0-0	0-0	0-0	0-0	0-0	0-1
Yett	1-1	0-2	0-1	0-1	0-0	0-0	0-0	1-0	1-0	0-1	0-0	2-0	0-0	5-6
Totals	6-7	5-8	7-5	5-7	5-8	8-4	3-10	5-7	9-4	2-10	6-6	7-5	5-8	73-89

No Decisions—Havens, Seanez, Stoddard, Wickander.

DETROIT—59-103

Pitcher	Balt. W-L	Bos. W-L	Cal. W-L	Chi. W-L	Clev. W-L	K.C. W-L	Mil. W-L	Minn. W-L	N.Y. W-L	Oak. W-L	Sea. W-L	Tex. W-L	Tor. W-L	Totals W-L
Alexander...	0-3	0-2	0-2	1-1	0-1	1-1	2-0	1-2	0-0	0-1	1-2	0-1	0-2	6-18
Beard	0-0	0-0	0-1	0-0	0-0	0-0	0-0	0-0	0-0	0-1	0-0	0-0	0-0	0-2
DuBois	0-0	0-1	0-0	0-0	0-0	0-0	0-0	0-1	0-1	0-0	0-0	0-0	0-1	0-4
Gibson........	0-0	0-0	0-1	0-1	1-1	1-0	1-2	0-0	0-0	0-1	0-0	1-1	0-1	4-8
Havens.......	0-0	0-0	0-0	0-0	0-0	0-0	0-0	0-0	1-1	0-1	0-0	0-0	0-0	1-2
Henneman ..	0-0	0-0	0-2	2-0	0-0	2-1	0-0	1-0	1-1	1-0	1-0	2-0	1-0	11-4
Hernandez..	0-0	0-0	1-0	0-1	1-0	0-0	0-0	0-0	0-0	0-0	0-0	0-0	0-1	2-2
Hudson	0-1	0-0	0-2	0-0	0-0	0-0	0-0	0-0	0-0	0-1	1-1	0-0	0-0	1-5
Morris........	0-2	0-1	0-1	1-0	3-1	0-0	0-3	0-1	1-1	1-0	0-1	0-2	0-1	6-14
Nosek	0-1	0-0	0-0	0-0	0-0	0-1	0-0	0-0	0-0	0-0	0-0	0-0	0-0	0-2
Nunez	1-0	0-1	0-0	0-0	0-0	1-0	0-1	0-0	1-1	0-0	0-0	0-0	0-1	3-4
Palmer.......	0-0	0-1	0-1	0-0	0-0	0-0	0-0	0-0	0-0	0-0	0-1	0-0	0-0	0-3
Ritz..........	0-0	0-2	0-0	0-0	0-1	1-1	1-0	1-0	0-1	0-0	0-1	1-0	0-0	4-6
Robinson.....	0-0	0-1	0-0	0-1	1-0	0-0	1-0	1-2	0-0	0-0	0-0	0-0	0-1	4-5
Schwabe	1-0	1-0	0-1	0-0	0-0	0-0	0-0	0-0	0-0	0-1	0-1	0-0	0-1	2-4
Searcy.......	0-0	0-0	0-0	0-0	0-0	0-1	0-0	1-0	0-0	0-0	0-0	0-0	0-0	1-1
Tanana	1-2	1-1	0-1	3-0	1-1	0-0	0-1	0-1	1-1	2-2	1-1	0-2	0-2	10-14
Trujillo........	0-1	0-0	0-0	0-0	1-0	0-1	0-0	0-0	0-0	0-0	0-0	0-0	0-0	1-2
F. Williams .	0-0	0-1	0-0	1-0	0-0	0-0	1-0	0-0	0-0	0-0	0-0	0-2	1-0	3-3
Totals	3-10	2-11	1-11	8-4	8-5	6-6	6-7	5-7	6-7	4-8	4-8	4-8	2-11	59-103

No Decisions—Bockus, Holman, Pena.

KANSAS CITY—92-70

Pitcher	Balt. W-L	Bos. W-L	Cal. W-L	Chi. W-L	Clev. W-L	Det. W-L	Mil. W-L	Minn. W-L	N.Y. W-L	Oak. W-L	Sea. W-L	Tex. W-L	Tor. W-L	Totals W-L
Appier	0-0	0-0	0-1	0-1	0-1	0-0	0-0	0-0	0-1	1-0	0-0	0-0	0-0	1-4
Aquino	1-0	1-1	0-1	0-2	1-0	0-0	0-0	0-1	1-0	0-1	0-1	1-1	1-0	6-8
Bannister.....	1-0	1-0	0-0	0-0	0-0	0-0	1-0	1-1	0-0	0-0	0-0	0-0	0-0	4-1
Clarke........	0-0	0-0	0-0	0-0	0-0	0-0	0-0	0-1	0-0	0-0	0-1	0-0	0-0	0-2
Crawford.....	0-1	0-0	0-0	0-0	0-0	1-0	0-0	0-0	0-0	1-0	1-0	0-0	0-0	3-1
Farr...........	1-1	0-0	0-0	0-0	0-0	0-0	0-1	0-2	0-1	0-0	1-0	0-0	0-0	2-5
Gordon	1-0	1-1	3-0	1-0	0-1	1-2	3-1	0-1	1-0	1-1	2-1	0-1	3-0	17-9
Gubicza......	0-0	2-0	1-0	0-1	0-2	2-1	1-0	2-0	2-2	1-1	3-0	1-1	0-3	15-11
Leach	0-1	0-0	2-0	2-1	0-1	0-0	0-0	0-0	0-1	0-1	1-0	0-1	0-0	5-6
Leibrandt ...	0-1	1-1	1-1	1-0	0-1	0-1	1-2	0-0	0-1	0-1	0-0	1-1	0-1	5-11
Luecken	0-0	0-0	0-0	0-0	0-0	0-0	0-0	0-0	0-0	0-0	0-1	2-0	0-0	2-1
McWilliams.	0-0	0-0	0-1	1-0	0-0	0-0	0-0	1-0	0-0	0-0	0-1	0-0	0-0	2-2
M'ntgmry ...	0-1	1-1	0-0	1-1	1-0	1-0	1-0	0-0	0-0	0-0	0-0	1-0	1-0	7-3
S'brhagen...	2-1	1-0	2-0	1-0	2-2	1-2	1-0	3-0	2-0	3-0	1-0	2-0	2-1	23-6
Totals	6-6	8-4	9-4	7-6	4-8	6-6	8-4	7-6	6-6	7-6	9-4	8-5	7-5	92-70

No Decisions—Buchanan, DeJesus, Gleaton.

MILWAUKEE—81-81

Pitcher	Balt. W-L	Bos. W-L	Cal. W-L	Chi. W-L	Clev. W-L	Det. W-L	K.C. W-L	Minn. W-L	N.Y. W-L	Oak. W-L	Sea. W-L	Tex. W-L	Tor. W-L	Totals W-L
Aldrich........	0-0	0-0	0-0	0-0	0-0	0-0	0-0	0-0	0-0	0-0	0-0	0-0	1-0	1-0
August........	2-0	1-1	2-0	0-0	0-1	1-3	0-2	1-0	1-0	1-1	0-1	1-3	2-0	12-12
Birkbeck.....	0-0	0-0	0-1	0-0	0-0	0-0	0-1	0-0	0-0	0-1	0-0	0-1	0-0	0-4
Bosio	1-1	2-1	1-0	1-2	3-1	2-0	2-0	1-0	0-0	1-1	0-1	1-1	0-2	15-10
Clutterbuck .	0-1	0-0	0-2	0-1	0-0	0-0	0-0	0-0	0-1	1-0	0-0	0-0	0-0	2-5
Crim..........	1-0	0-1	0-0	0-0	1-0	1-1	1-0	1-1	0-2	2-1	2-0	0-1	0-0	9-7
Filer...........	0-1	1-0	1-0	0-0	0-0	1-0	0-1	1-0	0-0	0-1	0-0	1-0	2-0	7-3
Fossas........	0-0	0-0	0-0	0-1	0-0	0-1	0-0	0-0	1-0	0-0	0-0	0-0	1-0	2-2
Higuera......	0-2	1-0	1-0	0-3	2-0	1-0	0-0	1-0	3-0	0-0	0-0	0-0	0-1	9-6
Knudson	1-0	1-1	0-1	0-0	2-0	0-0	0-2	0-1	2-0	0-0	2-0	0-0	0-1	8-5
Krueger......	0-0	0-0	0-0	0-1	0-0	0-0	1-0	1-0	0-0	0-0	0-0	0-0	0-1	3-2
Navarro	1-0	1-2	0-1	1-1	1-1	1-0	0-0	0-1	0-0	0-1	1-1	1-0	0-0	7-8
Peterek	0-0	0-0	0-0	0-0	0-0	0-0	0-0	0-0	0-0	0-0	0-1	0-0	0-1	0-2
Plesac........	0-0	0-0	0-0	0-0	1-0	0-0	0-1	1-0	0-1	0-1	1-0	0-0	0-1	3-4
Reuss.........	0-2	0-0	0-1	0-0	0-0	0-0	0-0	0-0	0-0	0-0	1-0	0-0	0-1	1-4
Veres.........	0-0	0-0	0-0	0-0	0-0	0-0	0-0	0-0	0-1	0-0	0-0	0-0	0-0	0-1
Wegman......	0-0	0-0	0-1	0-1	0-0	0-1	0-1	1-0	0-0	0-0	0-1	1-1	0-0	2-6
Totals	6-7	7-6	5-7	2-10	10-3	7-6	4-8	9-3	8-5	5-7	7-5	5-7	6-7	81-81

No Decisions—Francona, Krawczyk, Mirabella.

MINNESOTA—80-82

Pitcher	Balt. W-L	Bos. W-L	Cal. W-L	Chi. W-L	Clev. W-L	Det. W-L	K.C. W-L	Mil. W-L	N.Y. W-L	Oak. W-L	Sea. W-L	Tex. W-L	Tor. W-L	Totals W-L
Aguilera.....	0-1	0-0	0-0	1-0	0-0	1-0	0-1	0-0	0-1	0-1	0-0	0-1	1-0	3-5
Anderson....	3-0	1-2	1-2	2-0	1-1	3-0	2-0	0-1	2-0	1-2	0-1	0-1	1-0	17-10
Berenguer ..	0-0	1-0	0-0	2-0	1-0	0-0	2-1	0-1	0-0	0-0	2-0	0-0	1-1	9-3
Cook	0-0	0-0	0-0	0-0	0-0	0-0	0-0	0-0	0-1	0-0	0-0	0-0	0-0	0-1
Dyer...........	0-0	0-0	0-2	1-0	0-0	1-1	0-1	0-0	0-0	0-1	1-1	1-1	0-0	4-7

MINNESOTA—80-82

Pitcher	Balt. W-L	Bos. W-L	Cal. W-L	Chi. W-L	Clev. W-L	Det. W-L	K.C. W-L	Mil. W-L	N.Y. W-L	Oak. W-L	Sea. W-L	Tex. W-L	Tor. W-L	Totals W-L
Gonzalez	1-0	0-1	0-0	0-0	1-0	1-0	0-0	0-0	0-0	0-0	0-0	0-1	0-0	3-2
Guthrie	0-0	0-0	0-1	0-1	0-0	0-0	0-0	0-0	0-0	0-0	1-1	0-0	1-1	2-4
Oliveras	0-0	0-1	0-0	0-0	0-1	0-0	1-1	0-1	0-0	1-0	0-0	1-0	0-0	3-4
Rawley	0-1	1-0	0-2	0-3	1-1	0-1	0-1	0-2	2-1	0-0	0-0	0-0	1-0	5-12
Reardon	1-0	0-0	0-0	0-0	0-0	0-0	0-0	1-1	1-1	1-0	1-1	0-1	0-0	5-4
Shields	0-0	0-0	0-0	0-0	0-0	0-0	0-0	0-0	0-0	0-0	0-0	0-0	0-0	0-1
Smith	3-0	0-0	0-1	1-1	1-0	0-0	1-1	1-1	1-0	1-0	0-0	1-1	0-1	10-6
St. Claire	0-0	1-0	0-0	0-0	0-0	0-0	0-0	0-0	0-0	0-0	0-0	0-0	0-0	1-0
Tapani	0-0	0-0	0-1	0-0	0-0	0-0	0-0	0-0	0-0	0-1	0-0	1-0	1-0	2-2
Toliver	0-1	0-1	0-0	0-0	0-1	1-0	0-0	0-0	0-0	0-0	0-0	0-0	0-0	1-3
Tunnell	0-0	0-0	0-0	0-0	0-0	0-0	0-0	1-0	0-0	0-0	0-0	0-0	0-0	1-0
Viola	0-1	2-1	1-1	1-0	1-1	0-2	0-1	0-2	0-1	1-1	0-0	0-1	2-0	8-12
Wayne	0-0	0-0	0-0	0-0	1-0	0-1	0-0	0-0	0-1	1-1	1-1	0-0	0-0	3-4
West	0-0	0-0	0-1	0-0	0-0	0-0	0-0	0-0	0-0	0-0	1-0	1-1	1-0	3-2
Totals	8-4	6-6	2-11	8-5	7-5	7-5	6-7	3-9	6-6	6-7	7-6	5-8	9-3	80-82

No Decisions—Booker, Drummond, Gladden, Moses.

NEW YORK—74-87

Pitcher	Balt. W-L	Bos. W-L	Cal. W-L	Chi. W-L	Clev. W-L	Det. W-L	K.C. W-L	Mil. W-L	Minn. W-L	Oak. W-L	Sea. W-L	Tex. W-L	Tor. W-L	Totals W-L
Cadaret	0-1	0-1	1-0	1-0	1-0	1-0	1-0	0-1	0-1	0-0	0-0	0-1	0-0	5-5
Candelaria	0-0	0-1	0-0	1-0	0-1	0-0	0-1	0-0	0-0	0-0	0-0	0-0	2-0	3-3
Cary	2-0	0-0	0-1	0-0	0-1	0-1	0-0	0-0	1-0	0-1	0-0	0-0	1-0	4-4
Dotson	0-0	0-1	1-1	0-1	0-0	0-0	0-0	0-1	0-0	0-1	1-0	0-0	0-0	2-5
Eiland	0-0	0-0	0-0	0-0	0-0	0-0	0-2	0-1	0-0	0-0	0-0	1-0	0-0	1-3
Gossage	0-0	0-0	0-0	0-0	0-0	0-0	0-0	0-0	0-0	0-0	1-0	0-0	0-0	1-0
Guetterman	1-0	0-0	0-0	0-1	0-2	0-1	1-1	1-0	1-0	0-0	0-0	0-0	1-0	5-5
Hawkins	0-1	1-2	1-1	1-1	2-1	2-0	2-0	1-0	0-1	0-2	2-1	1-3	2-2	15-15
John	0-0	0-0	0-1	0-1	0-2	0-0	1-1	0-0	1-1	0-1	0-0	0-0	0-0	2-7
Jones	0-0	0-0	0-0	0-0	0-0	0-0	0-0	1-0	0-0	0-0	0-1	1-0	0-0	2-1
LaPoint	1-1	0-0	0-0	1-1	1-0	0-0	0-0	0-1	0-1	0-1	0-1	2-2	1-1	6-9
Leiter	0-0	0-0	0-0	0-0	0-1	0-0	0-1	0-0	1-0	0-0	0-0	0-0	0-0	1-2
McCullers	0-1	1-0	0-1	1-0	0-0	0-0	1-0	0-1	1-0	0-0	0-0	0-0	0-0	4-3
Mmahat	0-0	0-1	0-0	0-0	0-0	0-0	0-1	0-0	0-0	0-0	0-0	0-0	0-0	0-2
Mohorcic	0-0	0-0	1-0	0-0	0-1	0-0	0-0	0-0	0-0	1-0	0-0	0-0	0-0	2-1
Nielsen	0-0	1-0	0-0	0-0	0-0	0-0	0-0	0-0	0-0	0-0	0-0	0-0	0-0	1-0
Parker	0-1	0-0	1-0	0-0	0-0	0-0	0-0	1-1	0-0	1-2	1-0	0-0	0-1	4-5
Plunk	0-2	1-0	0-0	0-0	0-0	3-1	0-0	0-0	0-1	1-1	2-0	0-0	0-0	7-5
Righetti	0-0	0-0	0-1	1-0	0-0	0-0	0-2	0-0	1-1	0-0	0-0	0-1	0-1	2-6
Schulze	0-0	0-1	0-0	0-0	0-0	1-0	0-0	0-0	0-0	0-0	0-0	0-0	0-0	1-1
Terrell	1-1	2-0	1-0	0-0	0-0	0-0	0-0	0-1	1-1	0-0	1-1	0-0	0-1	6-5
Totals	5-8	6-7	6-6	6-5	4-9	7-6	6-6	5-8	6-6	3-9	8-4	5-7	7-6	74-87

No Decisions—Davidson.

OAKLAND—99-63

Pitcher	Balt. W-L	Bos. W-L	Cal. W-L	Chi. W-L	Clev. W-L	Det. W-L	K.C. W-L	Mil. W-L	Minn. W-L	N.Y. W-L	Sea. W-L	Tex. W-L	Tor. W-L	Totals W-L
Burns	1-0	1-0	0-0	0-0	0-0	0-0	0-2	1-1	0-1	1-0	1-0	0-1	1-0	6-5
Corsi	0-0	0-0	0-0	0-1	0-0	0-0	1-0	0-0	0-0	0-0	0-0	0-0	0-1	1-2
Davis	2-0	0-1	0-1	2-0	3-0	1-2	0-0	1-0	2-0	3-0	2-1	1-2	2-0	19-7
Eckersley	0-0	0-0	0-0	1-0	1-0	0-0	0-0	1-0	0-0	0-0	0-0	1-0	0-0	4-0
Honeycutt	0-0	0-0	0-0	1-0	0-1	0-0	0-1	0-0	0-0	0-0	0-0	0-0	1-0	2-2
Moore	2-1	0-2	3-0	1-1	2-1	2-0	1-1	1-1	2-1	2-1	0-1	2-0	1-1	19-11
Nelson	0-0	0-1	0-1	0-0	0-0	1-1	1-0	0-0	0-1	0-0	0-0	0-1	1-0	3-5
Plunk	0-0	0-1	0-0	0-0	0-0	0-0	0-0	0-0	0-0	0-0	1-0	0-0	0-0	1-1
Stewart	1-1	2-0	0-2	2-0	1-0	2-1	2-0	2-1	1-2	1-1	4-0	2-0	1-1	21-9
Welch	1-1	1-2	3-0	0-2	3-0	1-0	1-0	1-1	2-0	1-0	1-1	2-0	0-1	17-8
C. Young	0-1	1-0	1-1	1-1	0-0	1-0	0-2	0-0	0-1	1-1	0-1	0-0	0-1	5-9
M. Young	0-0	0-0	1-0	0-0	0-0	0-0	0-1	0-1	0-0	0-0	0-0	0-1	0-0	1-4
Totals	7-5	5-7	8-5	8-5	10-2	8-4	6-7	7-5	7-6	9-3	9-4	8-5	7-5	99-63

No Decisions—Cadaret, Dawley, Otto, Snyder.

SEATTLE—73-89

Pitcher	Balt. W-L	Bos. W-L	Cal. W-L	Chi. W-L	Clev. W-L	Det. W-L	K.C. W-L	Mil. W-L	Minn. W-L	N.Y. W-L	Oak. W-L	Tex. W-L	Tor. W-L	Totals W-L
Bankhead	1-0	2-1	0-0	1-0	1-0	2-1	2-0	0-1	1-1	0-0	1-1	1-1	2-0	14-6
Campbell	0-0	0-0	0-1	1-0	0-0	0-0	0-0	0-0	0-0	0-0	0-1	0-0	0-0	1-2
Comstock	0-0	0-0	1-0	0-1	0-0	0-0	0-0	0-0	0-0	0-0	0-0	0-1	0-0	1-2
Dunne	0-1	0-2	1-0	0-0	0-1	0-1	0-1	0-0	0-0	0-0	0-0	0-0	0-3	2-9
Hanson	0-0	1-1	0-1	1-1	1-0	1-0	0-0	1-1	1-0	1-1	1-0	0-0	1-0	9-5
Harris	0-0	0-0	0-0	0-0	0-1	0-1	0-0	1-0	0-0	0-1	0-0	0-0	0-1	1-4
Holman	1-1	1-0	0-1	0-0	2-0	1-0	1-2	0-2	0-1	1-1	0-2	1-0	0-0	8-10
Jackson	0-1	0-0	1-0	0-2	0-1	0-0	0-0	2-0	1-0	0-0	0-0	0-1	0-1	4-6
Johnson	0-1	0-0	0-1	0-0	1-1	0-0	0-1	1-1	0-1	1-2	1-0	2-1	1-0	7-9
Langston	2-0	0-0	2-0	0-0	0-0	0-1	0-0	0-0	0-0	0-1	0-2	0-0	0-0	4-5
Niedenfuer	0-0	0-0	0-0	0-1	0-0	0-0	0-1	0-0	0-1	0-0	0-0	0-0	0-0	0-3

SEATTLE—73-89

Pitcher	Balt. W-L	Bos. W-L	Cal. W-L	Chi. W-L	Clev. W-L	Det. W-L	K.C. W-L	Mil. W-L	Minn. W-L	N.Y. W-L	Oak. W-L	Tex. W-L	Tor. W-L	Totals W-L
Powell	0-0	0-0	0-0	0-0	0-0	1-0	0-0	0-1	1-0	0-1	0-0	0-0	0-0	2-2
Reed	1-1	2-1	1-2	2-0	0-0	0-0	0-0	0-0	1-1	0-0	0-1	0-1	0-0	7-7
Schooler	0-0	0-0	0-0	0-1	0-1	0-1	0-0	0-0	0-2	0-1	0-0	1-0	0-1	1-7
Swift	1-0	0-0	0-0	0-1	1-0	2-0	1-1	1-0	0-0	0-0	0-0	1-1	0-0	7-3
Trout	0-1	1-0	0-1	1-0	0-0	0-0	0-0	0-0	0-0	1-1	0-0	0-0	1-0	4-3
Zavaras	0-0	0-0	0-0	0-0	0-2	0-0	0-2	0-1	0-0	0-0	1-0	0-1	0-0	1-6
Totals	6-6	7-5	6-7	6-7	6-6	8-4	4-9	5-7	6-7	4-8	4-9	6-7	5-7	73-89

No Decisions—DeLeon, Solano.

TEXAS—83-79

Pitcher	Balt. W-L	Bos. W-L	Cal. W-L	Chi. W-L	Clev. W-L	Det. W-L	K.C. W-L	Mil. W-L	Minn. W-L	N.Y. W-L	Oak. W-L	Sea. W-L	Tor. W-L	Totals W-L
Akerfelds	0-0	0-0	0-1	0-0	0-0	0-0	0-0	0-0	0-0	0-0	0-0	0-0	0-0	0-1
Alvarez	0-0	0-0	0-0	0-0	0-0	0-0	0-0	0-0	0-0	0-0	0-0	0-0	0-1	0-1
Arnsberg	0-0	0-0	0-0	0-0	0-0	0-0	0-0	0-0	1-0	0-0	0-1	1-0	0-0	2-1
Barfield	0-0	0-0	0-0	0-0	0-0	0-0	0-0	0-1	0-0	0-0	0-0	0-0	0-0	0-1
Brown	1-0	1-0	0-1	2-1	0-1	3-0	0-1	0-0	1-0	3-1	0-2	0-1	1-1	12-9
Guante	0-0	2-0	0-0	0-2	0-1	1-1	0-1	0-0	1-0	0-0	1-0	0-0	0-1	6-6
Hall	0-1	0-0	0-0	0-0	0-0	0-0	0-0	0-0	1-0	0-0	1-0	0-0	0-0	2-1
Hough	1-1	0-2	2-1	1-0	0-1	2-0	1-1	0-0	1-0	1-2	0-1	0-3	1-1	10-13
Jeffcoat	0-0	0-0	1-1	2-0	1-0	0-1	1-0	0-1	0-0	1-1	1-1	2-0	0-1	9-6
Mielke	0-0	1-0	0-0	0-0	0-0	0-0	0-0	0-0	0-0	0-0	0-0	0-0	0-0	1-0
Moyer	1-1	0-1	0-0	0-0	0-1	1-0	0-2	1-1	0-1	0-0	0-1	0-1	1-0	4-9
Rogers	0-0	0-0	0-0	1-0	0-0	0-2	0-2	0-0	1-0	0-0	0-0	0-0	1-0	3-4
Russell	0-1	0-1	0-0	1-0	2-0	0-0	0-0	1-0	1-2	0-0	1-0	0-0	0-0	6-4
Ryan	0-3	1-1	3-1	3-1	1-1	1-0	3-0	2-1	0-0	0-1	0-1	2-1	1-1	16-10
Witt	0-2	1-1	1-1	2-0	1-2	0-0	0-1	3-1	1-2	1-1	1-1	1-0	0-1	12-13
Totals	3-9	6-6	7-6	10-3	5-7	8-4	5-8	7-5	8-5	7-5	5-8	7-6	5-7	83-79

No Decisions—Kunkel, McMurtry, Wilmet.

TORONTO—89-73

Pitcher	Balt. W-L	Bos. W-L	Cal. W-L	Chi. W-L	Clev. W-L	Det. W-L	K.C. W-L	Mil. W-L	Minn. W-L	N.Y. W-L	Oak. W-L	Sea. W-L	Tex. W-L	Totals W-L
Acker	0-0	0-0	0-0	0-0	2-1	0-0	0-0	0-0	0-0	0-0	0-0	0-0	0-0	2-1
Buice	0-0	0-0	0-0	0-0	0-0	0-0	0-0	0-0	0-0	0-0	1-0	0-0	0-0	1-0
Castillo	0-0	0-0	0-0	0-0	0-0	0-0	0-0	0-0	0-0	0-1	0-0	0-0	1-0	1-1
Cerutti	0-2	2-1	0-1	1-1	1-0	1-0	1-1	1-2	1-1	1-0	0-2	1-0	1-0	11-11
Cummings	1-0	0-0	0-0	0-0	0-0	1-0	0-0	0-0	0-0	0-0	0-0	0-0	0-0	2-0
Flanagan	0-1	0-0	0-0	2-0	0-1	2-0	0-1	0-0	0-4	0-1	2-0	2-1	0-1	8-10
Gozzo	1-1	1-0	0-0	0-0	0-0	1-0	0-0	0-0	0-0	0-0	0-0	0-0	1-0	4-1
Henke	1-0	1-0	1-1	1-0	1-0	1-0	0-0	0-0	0-0	1-0	0-1	1-0	0-1	8-3
Hernandez	0-0	0-0	0-0	0-0	0-0	0-0	0-0	0-0	0-0	1-0	0-0	0-0	0-0	1-0
Key	1-1	0-1	1-1	4-0	2-1	1-1	2-1	1-2	0-0	0-2	0-2	1-1	0-1	13-14
Musselman	0-0	0-0	0-0	0-0	0-0	0-0	0-0	0-0	0-0	0-1	0-0	0-0	0-0	0-1
Sanchez	0-0	0-0	0-0	0-0	0-1	0-0	0-0	0-0	0-0	0-0	0-0	0-0	0-0	0-1
Stieb	0-2	2-0	1-0	2-0	0-1	3-0	0-0	3-0	0-2	2-0	1-1	1-1	2-1	17-8
Stottlemyre	1-0	0-1	0-1	1-0	0-0	0-0	1-2	1-1	1-1	1-0	0-0	0-0	1-1	7-7
Ward	0-0	1-0	0-3	0-0	0-0	0-1	0-2	1-1	0-0	0-2	0-1	1-0	1-0	4-10
Wells	0-0	1-2	2-0	0-0	1-0	0-0	1-0	0-0	1-1	1-0	0-0	0-1	0-0	7-4
Wills	1-0	0-0	0-0	0-0	1-0	1-0	0-0	0-0	0-0	0-0	0-0	0-1	0-0	3-1
Totals	6-7	8-5	5-7	11-1	8-5	11-2	5-7	7-6	3-9	6-7	5-7	7-5	7-5	89-73

No Decisions—Leiter, Nunez.

OFFICIAL AMERICAN LEAGUE BATTING AVERAGES

(Compiled by the MLB-IBM Baseball Information Service)

CLUB BATTING

Club	AVG	G	AB	R	H	TB	2B	3B	HR	RBI	SH	SF	HP	BB	IBB	SO	SB	CS	GI DP	LOB	SHO	SLG	OBP
Boston	.277	162	5666	774	1571	2281	326	30	108	716	52	58	36	643	57	755	56	57	169	1308	9	.403	.351
Minnesota	.276	162	5581	740	1542	2241	278	35	117	691	51	58	39	478	40	743	111	53	126	1170	7	.402	.334
Chicago	.271	161	5504	693	1493	2109	262	36	94	661	85	51	28	464	51	873	97	52	113	1141	8	.383	.328
New York	.269	161	5458	698	1470	2135	229	23	130	657	58	40	27	502	48	831	137	60	130	1139	10	.391	.331
Texas	.263	162	5458	695	1433	2151	260	46	122	654	63	40	34	503	28	989	101	49	151	1105	8	.394	.326
Oakland	.261	162	5416	712	1414	2065	220	25	127	659	36	62	34	562	37	855	157	55	163	1110	5	.381	.331
Kansas City	.261	162	5475	690	1428	2040	227	41	101	653	42	60	29	554	50	897	154	51	141	1147	18	.373	.329
Toronto	.260	162	5581	731	1449	2220	265	40	142	685	30	53	31	521	32	923	144	58	124	1102	7	.398	.323
Milwaukee	.259	162	5473	707	1415	2092	235	32	126	660	51	54	50	455	41	791	165	62	108	1076	11	.382	.318
Seattle	.257	162	5512	694	1417	2114	237	29	134	653	35	52	45	489	40	838	81	55	109	1113	9	.384	.320
California	.256	162	5545	669	1422	2139	208	37	145	624	54	46	28	429	48	1011	89	40	114	1090	12	.386	.311
Baltimore	.252	162	5440	708	1369	2060	238	33	129	659	63	47	30	593	44	957	118	55	140	1135	15	.379	.326
Cleveland	.245	162	5463	604	1340	1994	221	26	127	567	72	41	35	499	52	934	74	51	109	1126	11	.365	.310
Detroit	.242	162	5432	617	1315	1909	198	24	116	564	35	43	37	585	25	899	103	50	138	1167	15	.351	.318
Totals	.261	1133	77004	9732	20078	29550	3404	457	1718	9103	727	704	483	7277	593	12296	1587	726	1835	15929	145	.384	.326

INDIVIDUAL BATTING

(Top Fifteen Qualifiers for Batting Championship—502 or More Plate Appearances)

(★Lefthanded Batter   †Switch-Hitter)

Player, Club	AVG	G	AB	R	H	TB	2B	3B	HR	RBI	SH	SF	HP	BB	IBB	SO	SB	CS	GI DP	SLG	OBP
Puckett, Kirby, Min.	.339	159	635	75	215	295	45	4	9	85	0	5	3	41	9	59	11	4	21	.465	.379
Lansford, Carney, Oak.	.336	148	551	81	185	223	28	2	2	52	1	4	9	51	2	25	37	15	21	.405	.398
Boggs, Wade, Bos.★	.330	156	621	113	205	279	51	7	3	54	0	7	7	107	19	51	2	6	19	.449	.430
Yount, Robin, Mil.	.318	160	614	101	195	314	38	9	21	103	3	6	6	63	9	71	19	3	9	.511	.384
Franco, Julio, Tex.	.316	150	548	80	173	253	31	5	13	92	0	4	6	66	11	69	21	3	27	.462	.386
Molitor, Paul, Mil.	.315	155	615	84	194	270	35	4	11	56	4	9	1	64	4	67	27	11	11	.439	.379
Sax, Stephen, N.Y.	.315	158	651	88	205	252	26	3	5	63	8	5	1	52	2	44	43	17	19	.387	.364
Baines, Harold, Chi.-Tex.★	.309	146	505	72	156	235	29	1	16	72	0	4	0	73	13	73	0	3	15	.465	.395
Greenwell, Michael, Bos.★	.308	145	578	87	178	256	36	0	14	95	0	4	3	56	15	44	13	5	21	.443	.370
Sierra, Ruben, Tex.†	.306	162	634	101	194	344	35	14	29	119	14	10	2	43	2	82	8	5	7	.543	.347
Davis, Alvin, Sea.★	.305	142	498	84	152	247	30	1	21	95	0	6	6	101	15	49	0	1	15	.496	.424
Mattingly, Donald, N.Y.★	.303	158	631	79	191	301	37	2	23	113	0	10	1	51	18	30	0	0	15	.477	.351
Reynolds, Harold, Sea.†	.300	153	613	87	184	226	24	9	0	43	3	3	3	55	1	45	25	18	4	.369	.359
Browne, Jerome, Cle.†	.299	153	598	88	179	233	31	4	5	45	14	1	1	68	10	64	14	6	9	.390	.370
Bell, George, Tor	.297	153	613	88	182	281	41	2	18	104	0	14	2	33	3	60	4	3	18	.458	.330

DEPARTMENTAL LEADERS: G—Carter, Clev., C. Ripken, Balt. and Sierra, Tex., 162; AB—Carter, Clev. and Sax, N.Y., 651; R—Boggs, Bos. and R. Henderson, N.Y.-Oak. 113; H—Puckett, Minn., 215; TB—Sierra, Tex., 344; 2B—Boggs, Bos., 51; 3B—Sierra, Tex., 14; HR—McGriff, Tor., 36; RBI—Sierra, Tex., 119; SH—Fermin, Clev., 32; SF—Bell, Tor., 14; HP—Gantner, Mil., 10; BB—R. Henderson, N.Y.-Oak., 126; IBB—Boggs, Bos., 19; SO—Jackson, K.C., 172; SB—R. Henderson, N.Y.-Oak., 77; CS—Espy, Tex., 20; GIDP—Franco, Tex., 27; Slg. Pct.—Sierra, Tex., 543; OB. Pct.—Boggs, Bos., .430.

INDIVIDUAL BATTING
ALL PLAYERS LISTED ALPHABETICALLY
(* Lefthanded Batter † Switch-Hitter)

Player, Club	AVG	G	AB	R	H	TB	2B	3B	HR	RBI	SH	SF	HP	BB	IBB	SO	SB	CS	GIDP	SLG	OBP
Aguayo, Luis, Clev.	.175	47	97	7	17	26	4	1	1	8	3	3	2	7	1	19	0	0	4	.268	.239
Allanson, Andrew, Clev.	.232	111	323	30	75	95	9	1	3	17	6	1	4	23	0	47	4	4	7	.294	.289
Allred, Dale, Clev.	.250	13	24	0	6	9	3	0	0	1	0	0	0	2	0	10	0	0	0	.375	.308
Anderson, Allan, Minn.*	.000	34	1	0	0	0	0	0	0	0	5	0	0	0	0	1	0	0	0	.000	.000
Anderson, Brady, Balt.*	.207	94	266	44	55	83	12	2	4	16	5	1	3	43	0	45	16	4	4	.312	.324
Anderson, Kent, Cal.	.229	86	223	27	51	59	6	1	0	17	6	2	1	17	0	42	0	2	2	.265	.285
Armas, Antonio, Cal.	.257	60	202	22	52	94	7	0	11	30	0	2	0	7	2	48	0	0	2	.465	.280
Arndt, Larry, Oak.	.167	2	6	0	1	1	0	0	0	1	1	0	0	0	0	1	0	0	0	.167	.167
Backman, Walter, Minn.†	.231	87	299	33	69	85	9	2	1	26	4	1	1	32	0	45	1	0	4	.284	.306
Baines, Harold, Chi.-Tex.*	.309	146	505	73	156	235	29	1	16	72	0	4	1	73	13	79	0	3	15	.465	.395
Baker, Douglas, Minn.†	.295	43	78	17	23	30	5	1	0	9	2	1	2	9	0	18	1	0	0	.385	.378
Balboni, Stephen, N.Y.	.237	110	300	33	71	138	12	2	17	59	0	6	3	25	5	67	0	0	10	.460	.296
Bando, Christopher, Oak.†	.500	1	2	0	1	1	0	0	0	1	0	0	0	0	0	1	0	0	0	.500	.500
Barfield, Jesse, Tor.-N.Y.	.234	150	521	79	122	216	23	1	23	67	1	3	3	87	6	150	5	5	8	.415	.345
Barrett, Martin, Bos.	.256	86	336	31	86	107	18	0	1	27	15	5	2	32	0	12	4	1	12	.318	.320
Bates, William, Mil.*	.214	7	14	3	3	3	0	0	0	0	0	0	0	0	0	1	3	0	0	.214	.214
Batiste, Kevin, Tor.†	.250	6	8	1	2	2	0	0	0	0	0	0	0	0	0	5	3	0	0	.250	.250
Bean, William, Det.*	.000	6	11	0	0	0	0	0	0	0	0	1	0	0	0	3	0	1	0	.000	.000
Bell, David, Tex.	.241	37	79	8	19	24	5	0	0	11	2	1	0	7	0	13	1	0	2	.304	.238
Bell, George, Tor.	.297	153	613	88	182	281	41	2	18	104	0	14	4	33	3	60	4	3	18	.458	.330
Bell, Juan, Balt.†	.183	34	82	4	15	19	2	1	0	3	0	0	0	7	0	10	1	0	4	.232	.247
Belle, A. Jojuan, Clev.	.225	62	218	22	49	86	8	0	7	37	0	2	2	12	0	55	2	1	5	.394	.269
Bergman, David, Det.*	.268	137	385	38	103	139	13	1	7	37	4	1	2	44	3	44	3	3	0	.361	.345
Bichette, A. Dante, Cal.	.210	48	138	13	29	45	7	0	3	15	0	0	1	6	0	24	3	1	1	.326	.240
Blankenship, Lance, Oak.	.232	58	125	22	29	39	5	1	1	4	3	0	0	8	0	31	5	1	0	.312	.276
Blowers, Michael, N.Y.	.263	13	38	2	10	10	0	0	0	3	0	1	0	3	0	13	0	0	1	.263	.317
Boggs, Wade, Bos.*	.330	156	621	113	205	279	51	7	3	54	0	7	7	107	19	51	2	6	19	.449	.430
Boone, Robert, K.C.	.274	131	405	33	111	131	13	1	1	43	8	5	2	49	4	37	3	2	16	.323	.351
Borders, Patrick, Tor.	.257	94	241	22	62	84	11	1	3	29	1	2	1	11	2	45	2	1	7	.349	.290
Bosley, Thaddis, Tex.*	.225	37	40	5	9	14	2	0	1	9	0	0	0	3	1	11	2	2	1	.350	.273
Boston, Daryl, Chi.*	.252	101	218	34	55	81	3	4	5	23	4	0	7	24	3	31	7	2	12	.372	.325
Bradley, Philip, Balt.	.277	144	545	83	151	227	23	10	11	55	0	6	0	59	3	82	20	6	12	.417	.364
Bradley, Scott, Sea.*	.274	103	270	21	74	99	16	0	3	37	4	6	7	21	4	23	1	2	5	.367	.322
Brady, Brian, Cal.*	.500	2	2	0	1	1	0	0	0	0	0	0	0	0	0	0	0	0	0	.500	.500
Braggs, Glenn, Mil.	.247	144	514	77	127	190	12	5	15	66	3	7	4	42	4	111	17	5	13	.370	.305
Brantley, Michael, Sea.	.157	34	108	14	17	22	5	0	0	8	3	0	0	7	0	7	1	2	2	.204	.207
Brenly, Robert, Tor.	.170	48	88	9	15	23	3	1	1	6	0	0	0	10	0	17	1	1	2	.261	.255
Brett, George, K.C.*	.282	124	457	67	129	197	26	3	12	80	1	5	3	59	14	47	14	4	18	.431	.362
Briley, Greg, Sea.*	.266	115	394	52	105	174	22	4	13	52	0	5	0	39	1	82	11	5	2	.442	.336
Brock, Gregory, Mil.*	.265	107	373	40	99	151	22	0	12	52	5	5	3	43	8	49	6	3	10	.405	.336
Brookens, Thomas, N.Y.	.226	66	168	14	38	56	6	0	4	14	2	1	1	11	1	27	1	1	3	.333	.272
Brower, Robert, N.Y.	.232	26	69	9	16	25	6	0	1	14	3	1	1	6	0	11	3	0	0	.362	.293
Brown, J. Christopher, Det.	.193	17	57	3	11	14	3	0	0	4	0	0	0	1	0	17	0	0	3	.246	.203
Browne, Jerome, Clev.†	.299	153	598	83	179	233	31	4	5	45	14	4	1	68	10	64	14	6	9	.390	.370
Brumley, A. Michael, Det.†	.198	92	212	33	42	54	5	2	1	11	3	0	1	14	0	45	8	4	4	.255	.251
Buckner, William, K.C.*	.216	79	176	7	38	47	4	1	1	16	0	1	0	6	2	11	1	0	4	.267	.240

Player, Club	AVG	G	AB	R	H	TB	2B	3B	HR	RBI	SH	SF	HP	BB	IBB	SO	SB	CS	GI DP	SLG	OBP
Buechele, Steven, Tex.	.235	155	486	60	114	188	22	2	16	59	2	1	5	36	0	107	1	3	21	.387	.294
Buhner, Jay, Sea.	.275	58	204	27	56	100	15	1	9	33	0	1	1	19	0	55	21	5	3	.490	.341
Burks, Ellis, Bos.	.303	97	399	73	121	188	19	6	12	61	2	4	5	36	2	52	5	8	8	.471	.365
Bush, R. Randall, Minn.*	.263	141	391	60	103	170	17	4	14	54	0	2	3	48	6	73	7	1	16	.435	.347
Cabrera, Francisco, Tor.	.167	3	12	2	2	3	1	0	0	0	2	0	0	1	0	3	0	0	0	.250	.231
Calderon, Ivan, Chi.	.286	157	622	83	178	272	34	9	14	87	0	6	3	43	7	94	7	1	20	.437	.332
Canale, George, Mil.*	.192	13	26	5	5	9	1	0	1	3	1	0	0	5	0	3	0	0	0	.346	.250
Canseco, Jose, Oak.	.269	65	227	40	61	123	9	1	17	57	0	6	2	23	4	69	6	3	4	.542	.333
Carter, Joseph, Clev.	.243	162	651	84	158	303	32	4	35	105	2	5	8	39	8	112	13	5	6	.465	.292
Castillo, Juan, Mil.	.000	3	4	0	0	0	0	0	0	0	0	2	0	0	0	0	1	0	0	.000	.000
Castillo, M. Carmelo, Minn.	.257	94	218	23	56	99	13	3	8	33	4	2	1	15	1	40	0	2	5	.454	.305
Cerone, Richard, Bos.	.243	102	296	28	72	102	16	1	4	48	4	2	0	34	0	40	0	0	10	.345	.320
Clark, David, Clev.*	.237	102	253	21	60	96	12	0	8	29	4	1	1	30	5	63	0	0	2	.379	.317
Cochrane, David, Sea.†	.235	54	102	13	24	39	4	3	3	7	2	0	0	14	3	27	5	2	7	.382	.333
Coles, Darnell, Sea.	.252	146	535	54	135	192	21	3	10	59	1	3	6	27	3	61	5	4	13	.359	.294
Coolbaugh, Scott, Tex.	.275	25	51	7	14	21	1	0	2	7	0	0	0	1	0	12	0	0	2	.412	.321
Cotto, Henry, Sea.	.264	100	295	44	78	120	11	2	9	33	2	1	3	12	3	44	10	4	4	.407	.300
Dalena, Peter, Clev.*	.143	5	7	0	1	2	0	0	0	0	0	0	0	0	0	3	0	0	0	.286	.173
Datz, Jeffrey, Det.	.200	7	10	0	2	2	0	0	0	0	0	0	1	1	0	1	0	1	1	.200	.333
Daugherty, John, Tex.†	.302	52	106	15	32	43	4	2	1	10	0	3	6	11	0	21	0	0	4	.406	.364
Davis, Alvin, Sea.*	.305	142	498	84	152	247	30	1	21	95	0	6	6	101	15	49	0	0	15	.496	.424
Davis, Charles, Cal.†	.271	154	560	81	152	244	24	1	22	90	3	6	0	61	12	109	3	8	21	.436	.340
Davis, Wallace, Balt.	.167	5	6	0	1	2	1	0	0	0	0	0	0	0	0	3	0	0	0	.333	.167
de los Santos, Luis, K.C.	.253	28	87	6	22	27	3	0	0	6	2	0	0	5	0	14	0	0	2	.310	.293
Deer, Robert, Mil.	.210	130	466	72	98	198	18	2	26	65	0	4	4	60	5	158	4	8	8	.425	.305
Devereaux, Michael, Balt.	.266	122	391	55	104	148	14	3	8	46	2	3	2	36	5	60	22	11	7	.379	.329
Diaz, Mario, Sea.	.135	52	74	9	10	13	0	0	1	7	5	0	0	7	0	7	0	0	2	.176	.210
Disarcina, Gary, Cal.	....	2	0	0	0	0	0	0	0	0	0	0	0	0	0	0	0	0	0	....	....
Dorsett, Brian, N.Y.	.364	8	22	3	8	9	1	0	0	4	0	0	0	1	0	3	0	0	0	.409	.391
Downing, Brian, Cal.	.283	142	544	59	154	225	25	2	14	59	0	4	6	56	3	87	0	0	6	.414	.354
Ducey, Robert, Tor.*	.211	41	76	5	16	20	4	0	0	7	1	0	1	9	1	25	2	1	2	.263	.294
Dwyer, James, Minn.*	.316	88	225	34	71	91	11	0	3	23	0	0	2	28	2	23	2	0	6	.404	.390
Eisenreich, James, K.C.*	.293	134	475	64	139	213	33	7	9	59	3	4	3	37	9	44	27	8	8	.448	.341
Engle, R. David, Mil.	.215	27	65	14	14	23	3	0	3	8	1	0	0	4	0	13	0	0	1	.354	.261
Eppard, James, Cal.*	.250	12	12	0	3	3	0	0	0	2	0	0	0	1	0	4	0	0	0	.250	.308
Esasky, Nicholas, Bos.	.277	154	564	79	156	282	26	5	30	108	0	3	3	66	9	117	1	2	11	.500	.355
Espinoza, Alvaro, N.Y.	.282	146	503	51	142	167	23	1	0	41	23	2	1	14	1	60	3	3	14	.332	.301
Espy, Cecil, Tex.†	.257	142	475	65	122	157	12	7	3	31	10	7	2	38	2	99	45	20	0	.331	.313
Evans, Dwight, Bos.	.285	146	520	82	148	241	27	3	20	100	1	9	2	99	8	84	3	3	16	.463	.397
Felder, Michael, Mil.†	.241	117	315	50	76	102	11	3	3	23	7	0	0	23	2	38	26	5	4	.324	.293
Felix, Junior, Tor.†	.258	110	415	62	107	164	14	8	9	46	0	3	3	33	2	101	18	12	5	.395	.315
Fermin, Felix, Clev.	.238	156	484	50	115	126	9	1	0	21	32	1	4	41	2	27	6	8	15	.260	.302
Fernandez, O. Antonio, Tor.†	.257	140	573	64	147	223	25	9	11	64	2	2	3	29	3	51	22	6	9	.389	.291
Fields, Bruce, Sea.*	.333	3	3	2	1	2	1	0	0	0	1	0	0	0	0	1	1	0	0	.667	.333
Finley, Steven, Balt.*	.249	81	217	35	54	69	5	2	2	25	0	3	3	15	0	30	17	3	3	.318	.298
Fisk, Carlton, Chi.	.293	103	375	47	110	178	25	2	13	68	6	5	5	36	8	60	1	1	15	.475	.356
Fletcher, Scott, Tex.-Chi.	.253	142	546	77	138	170	25	2	1	43	11	6	3	64	1	60	0	1	12	.311	.332
Franco, Julio, Tex.	.316	150	548	80	173	253	31	5	13	92	1	6	6	66	3	69	21	3	27	.462	.386
Francona, Terry, Mil.*	.232	90	233	26	54	75	10	5	0	23	1	2	0	8	0	20	2	1	4	.322	.255
Freeman, LaVel, Mil.*	.000	2	3	1	0	0	0	0	0	0	0	0	0	0	0	2	0	0	0	.000	.000

Player, Club	AVG	G	AB	R	H	TB	2B	3B	HR	RBI	SH	SF	HP	BB	IBB	SO	SB	CS	GI DP	SLG	OBP
Gaetti, Gary, Minn.	.251	130	498	63	125	201	11	4	19	75	1	9	3	25	5	87	6	2	12	.404	.286
Gagne, Gregory, Minn.	.272	149	460	69	125	195	29	7	9	48	7	5	2	17	1	80	11	4	10	.424	.298
Gallagher, David, Chi.	.266	161	601	74	160	189	22	2	1	46	16	5	2	46	0	79	5	6	9	.314	.320
Gallego, Michael, Oak.	.252	133	357	45	90	117	14	2	3	30	8	3	6	35	1	43	7	5	10	.328	.327
Gantner, James, Mil.★	.274	116	409	51	112	136	18	3	0	34	8	5	2	21	2	33	20	5	10	.333	.321
Gedman, Richard, Bos.★	.212	93	260	24	55	76	9	0	4	16	6	3	1	23	1	47	0	6	8	.292	.273
Geren, Robert, N.Y.	.288	65	205	26	59	93	5	0	9	27	5	5	0	12	3	44	0	1	10	.454	.329
Gladden, C. Daniel, Minn.	.295	121	461	69	136	189	23	3	8	46	6	5	1	23	0	53	23	7	6	.410	.331
Gonzales, Rene, Balt.	.217	71	166	16	36	43	4	0	1	11	6	1	5	12	3	30	3	3	6	.259	.268
Gonzalez, Denio, Clev.	.294	8	17	3	5	6	1	0	0	1	2	0	0	0	0	4	0	0	0	.353	.333
Gonzalez, Juan, Tex.	.150	24	60	6	9	15	3	0	1	7	0	0	0	6	0	17	0	0	4	.250	.227
Greenwell, Michael, Bos.★	.308	145	578	87	178	256	36	0	14	95	0	4	3	56	15	44	13	5	21	.443	.370
Griffey, G. Kenneth Jr., Sea.★	.264	127	455	61	120	191	23	0	16	61	1	5	2	44	1	83	16	5	4	.420	.329
Gruber, Kelly, Tor.	.290	135	545	83	158	244	24	4	18	73	6	3	3	30	0	60	10	7	13	.448	.328
Guillen, Oswaldo, Chi.★	.253	155	597	63	151	190	20	8	1	54	11	3	0	15	3	48	36	17	8	.318	.270
Hairston, Jerry, Chi.†	.333	3	3	0	1	1	0	0	0	0	0	0	0	0	0	0	0	0	0	.333	.333
Hale, Walter, Minn.★	.209	28	67	6	14	17	3	0	0	4	1	0	0	1	0	6	0	0	0	.254	.214
Hall, Melvin, N.Y.★	.260	113	361	54	94	154	23	0	17	58	0	8	0	21	4	37	0	0	9	.427	.295
Harper, Brian, Minn.	.325	126	385	43	125	173	24	0	8	57	1	4	1	13	3	16	2	4	11	.449	.353
Hassey, Ronald, Oak.★	.228	97	268	29	61	88	12	0	5	23	4	2	0	24	2	45	1	0	9	.328	.290
Heath, Michael, Det.	.263	122	396	38	104	154	16	2	10	43	1	4	4	24	2	71	7	0	18	.389	.308
Heep, Daniel, Bos.★	.300	113	320	36	96	128	17	2	5	49	4	4	4	29	4	26	0	0	13	.400	.356
Hemond, Scott, Oak.	----	4	0	2	0	0	0	0	0	0	0	0	0	0	0	0	0	0	0	----	----
Henderson, David, Oak.	.250	152	579	77	145	220	24	3	15	80	0	6	3	54	1	131	8	5	13	.380	.315
Henderson, Rickey, N.Y.-Oak.	.274	150	541	113	148	216	26	3	12	57	1	4	0	126	5	68	77	14	8	.399	.411
Hengel, David, Clev.	.120	12	25	2	3	4	1	0	0	0	1	0	0	2	0	6	0	0	1	.160	.185
Higgins, Mark, Clev.	.100	6	10	1	1	1	0	0	0	0	0	0	0	1	0	6	0	0	0	.100	.182
Hill, Glenallen, Tor.	.288	19	52	4	15	18	0	0	1	7	0	0	0	3	0	12	2	1	0	.346	.327
Hinzo, Thomas, Clev.†	.000	18	17	4	0	0	0	0	0	0	0	2	0	0	0	6	1	2	0	.000	.105
Hoffman, Glenn, Cal.	.212	48	104	9	22	28	3	0	1	11	3	0	0	3	0	13	0	2	1	.269	.241
Hoiles, Christopher, Balt.	.111	6	9	1	1	2	1	0	0	0	1	0	0	1	0	3	0	0	0	.222	.200
Horn, Samuel, Bos.★	.148	33	54	8	8	10	2	0	0	4	0	0	0	8	0	16	0	0	0	.185	.258
Howell, Jack, Cal.★	.228	144	474	56	108	195	19	4	20	52	3	1	1	52	9	125	3	3	8	.411	.308
Howitt, Dann, Oak.★	.000	3	3	1	0	0	0	0	0	0	0	0	0	0	0	3	0	0	0	.000	.000
Hrbek, Kent, Minn.★	.272	109	375	59	102	194	17	0	25	84	1	4	1	53	4	35	3	0	6	.517	.360
Hubbard, Glenn, Oak.	.198	53	131	12	26	41	6	0	3	12	7	2	1	19	0	20	2	3	3	.313	.296
Hulett, Timothy, Balt.	.278	33	97	12	27	41	5	0	3	18	4	1	0	10	0	17	0	4	3	.423	.343
Incaviglia, Peter, Tex.	.236	133	453	48	107	205	27	4	21	81	0	6	6	32	0	136	5	7	12	.453	.293
Infante, Alexis, Tor.	.167	20	12	1	2	2	0	0	0	0	1	0	0	1	0	1	0	0	0	.167	.167
Jackson, Vincent, K.C.	.256	135	515	86	132	255	15	6	32	105	0	4	6	39	8	172	26	9	10	.495	.310
Jacoby, Brook, Clev.	.272	147	519	49	141	216	26	5	13	64	0	8	3	62	3	90	2	5	15	.416	.348
James, Dion, Clev.★	.306	71	245	29	75	98	11	3	1	29	2	8	0	24	1	26	5	4	5	.400	.368
Javier, Stanley, Oak.†	.248	112	310	42	77	98	12	3	1	28	4	2	1	31	4	45	12	4	6	.316	.317
Jefferson, Stanley, N.Y.-Balt.†	.245	45	139	20	34	53	7	3	2	21	4	0	2	4	0	26	10	4	1	.381	.267
Jennings, J. Douglas, Oak.★	.000	4	4	0	0	0	0	0	0	0	0	0	0	1	0	2	0	0	0	.000	.000
Johnson, K. Lance, Chi.★	.300	50	180	28	54	66	8	2	0	16	3	3	0	17	1	24	16	3	1	.367	.360
Jones, Tracy, Det.	.259	46	158	17	41	60	10	0	3	26	1	2	1	16	1	16	1	0	1	.380	.326
Jorgensen, Terry, Minn.	.174	10	23	1	4	5	1	0	0	2	0	0	0	4	0	5	0	0	0	.217	.296
Jose, D. Felix, Oak.†	.193	20	57	3	11	13	2	0	0	5	0	1	0	4	0	13	0	0	2	.228	.246
Joyner, Wallace, Cal.★	.282	159	593	78	167	249	30	2	16	79	1	8	6	46	7	58	3	2	15	.420	.335

Player, Club	AVG	G	AB	R	H	TB	2B	3B	HR	RBI	SH	SF	HP	BB	IBB	SO	SB	CS	GIDP	SLG	OBP
Karkovice, Ronald, Chi.	.264	71	182	21	48	70	9	2	3	24	7	2	2	10	0	56	0	0	0	.385	.306
Keedy, C. Patrick, N.Y.	.214	9	14	3	3	5	2	0	0	1	0	0	0	2	0	5	0	0	0	.357	.313
Kelly, Roberto, N.Y.	.302	137	441	65	133	184	18	3	9	48	8	0	6	41	3	89	35	12	9	.417	.369
Kiefer, Steven, N.Y.	.125	5	8	0	1	1	0	0	0	0	0	0	0	1	0	5	1	1	0	.125	.125
Kingery, Michael, Sea.*	.224	31	76	14	17	26	3	0	2	6	0	1	0	7	0	14	0	0	2	.342	.286
Kittle, Ronald, Chi.	.302	51	169	26	51	94	10	0	11	37	0	4	1	22	1	42	8	2	4	.556	.378
Komminsk, Brad, Clev.	.237	71	198	27	47	83	8	2	8	33	1	3	3	24	0	55	8	1	2	.419	.319
Kreuter, Chad, Tex.†	.152	87	158	16	24	42	3	0	5	9	6	1	0	27	1	40	0	2	4	.266	.274
Kunkel, Jeffrey, Tex.	.270	108	293	39	79	128	21	3	8	29	9	2	3	20	0	75	3	1	6	.437	.274
Kutcher, Randy, Bos.	.225	77	160	28	36	58	10	2	2	18	10	0	3	11	0	46	3	2	5	.363	.323
Lansford, Carney, Oak.	.336	148	551	81	185	223	28	2	2	52	3	4	9	51	1	25	37	15	21	.405	.398
Larkin, Eugene, Minn.†	.267	136	446	61	119	164	25	1	6	46	1	6	9	54	2	57	5	2	13	.368	.353
Laudner, Timothy, Minn.	.222	100	239	24	53	84	11	0	6	27	5	2	0	25	6	65	1	1	7	.351	.293
Lawless, Thomas, Tor	.229	59	70	20	16	17	1	0	0	3	4	0	0	12	0	12	5	0	0	.243	.295
Lawton, Marcus, N.Y.†	.214	10	14	1	3	3	0	0	0	0	0	0	0	0	0	5	1	1	1	.214	.214
Leach, Richard, Tex.*	.272	110	239	32	65	84	14	1	1	23	0	1	0	32	7	33	2	0	7	.351	.358
Lee, Manny, Tor.†	.260	99	300	27	78	100	9	2	3	34	4	4	1	20	1	60	4	2	8	.333	.305
Leonard, Jeffrey, Sea.	.254	150	566	69	144	238	20	1	24	93	0	2	8	38	2	125	5	5	12	.420	.301
Liriano, Nelson, Tor.†	.263	132	418	51	110	157	26	3	5	53	4	5	1	43	2	51	16	7	10	.376	.331
Lovullo, Salvatore, Det.†	.115	29	87	8	10	15	2	0	1	4	1	2	0	14	0	20	0	0	3	.172	.233
Lusader, Scott, Det.★	.252	40	103	15	26	33	4	0	1	8	0	1	0	9	0	21	3	0	2	.320	.310
Lynn, Frederic, Det.★	.241	117	353	44	85	131	11	1	11	46	0	5	1	47	1	71	2	1	5	.371	.328
Lyons, Stephen, Chi.★	.264	140	443	51	117	150	21	3	2	50	12	3	2	35	0	68	9	6	3	.339	.317
Macfarlane, Michael, K.C.	.223	69	157	13	35	47	6	0	2	19	0	2	1	7	0	27	0	0	8	.299	.263
Magrann, Thomas, Clev.	.000	9	10	0	0	0	0	0	0	0	0	0	0	0	0	4	0	0	0	.000	.000
Manrique, R. Fred, Chi.-Tex.	.294	119	378	46	111	150	25	1	4	52	13	1	2	17	1	63	4	5	9	.397	.326
Martinez, Carlos, Chi.	.300	109	350	44	105	142	22	2	5	32	6	5	3	21	2	57	4	1	14	.406	.340
Martinez, Edgar, Sea.	.240	65	171	20	41	52	5	0	2	20	3	2	3	17	0	26	2	1	3	.304	.314
Marzano, John, Bos.	.444	7	18	5	8	14	3	0	1	3	1	0	0	2	0	6	0	0	1	.778	.421
Mattingly, Donald, N.Y.★	.303	158	631	79	191	301	37	2	23	113	0	10	1	51	18	30	3	3	15	.477	.351
Mazzilli, Lee, Tor.†	.227	28	66	12	15	30	3	0	4	11	0	1	2	17	1	16	3	0	1	.455	.395
McDowell, Oddibe, Clev.★	.222	69	239	33	53	71	5	3	2	22	3	2	1	25	1	36	12	5	3	.297	.296
McGriff, Frederick, Tor.★	.269	161	551	98	148	289	27	3	36	92	0	5	4	119	12	132	7	5	14	.525	.399
McGuire, William, Sea.	.179	14	28	2	5	8	0	0	1	4	0	0	0	2	0	6	0	0	2	.286	.233
McGwire, Mark, Oak.	.231	143	490	74	113	229	17	0	33	95	0	11	3	83	5	94	1	0	23	.467	.339
McLemore, Mark, Cal.†	.243	32	103	12	25	30	3	1	0	14	3	0	3	7	0	19	6	1	3	.291	.295
Medina, Luis, Clev.	.205	30	83	8	17	30	3	2	2	8	0	0	2	6	0	35	1	0	3	.361	.258
Melendez, Francisco, Balt.★	.273	9	11	1	3	3	0	0	0	0	0	0	0	1	0	2	0	1	1	.273	.308
Melvin, Robert, Balt.	.241	85	278	22	67	82	10	0	1	32	7	1	0	15	3	53	0	4	10	.295	.279
Mercado, Orlando, Minn.	.105	19	38	1	4	4	0	0	0	1	2	0	0	4	0	3	0	0	0	.105	.190
Merullo, Matthew, Chi.★	.222	31	81	5	18	22	1	0	1	8	0	1	0	6	0	14	0	1	2	.272	.273
Meulens, Hensley, N.Y.	.179	8	28	2	5	5	0	0	0	1	0	0	0	2	0	8	0	0	0	.179	.233
Meyer, T. Joey, Mil.	.224	53	147	13	33	60	6	0	7	29	0	5	0	12	3	36	0	0	2	.408	.274
Milligan, Randy, Balt.	.268	124	365	56	98	167	23	2	12	45	0	3	4	74	5	75	9	5	11	.458	.394
Molitor, Paul, Mil.	.315	155	615	84	194	270	35	4	11	56	4	9	2	67	4	67	27	11	11	.439	.379
Moreland, B. Keith, Det.-Balt.	.278	123	425	45	118	156	20	0	6	45	0	6	2	31	5	45	3	2	21	.367	.330
Morman, Russell, Chi.	.224	37	58	5	13	15	2	0	0	8	1	1	0	6	1	16	1	1	1	.259	.292
Morris, Harold, N.Y.★	.278	15	18	5	5	5	0	0	0	0	2	0	0	1	0	4	0	0	0	.278	.316
Moseby, Lloyd, Tor.★	.221	135	502	72	111	175	25	3	11	43	7	1	6	56	1	101	24	7	7	.349	.306

Player, Club	AVG	G	AB	R	H	TB	2B	3B	HR	RBI	SH	SF	HP	BB	IBB	SO	SB	CS	GIDP	SLG	OBP
Moses, John, Minn.†	.281	129	242	33	68	89	12	3	1	31	3	2	1	19	1	23	14	7	5	.368	.333
Mulliniks, S. Rance, Tor.★	.238	103	273	25	65	89	11	2	2	29	0	2	0	34	6	40	0	0	2	.326	.320
Myers, Gregory, Tor.★	.114	17	44	0	5	7	1	0	0	1	1	0	0	2	0	9	0	1	1	.159	.152
Newman, Albert, Minn.†	.253	141	446	62	113	135	18	2	0	38	10	4	2	59	1	46	25	12	3	.303	.341
Nokes, Matthew, Det.★	.250	87	268	15	67	104	10	0	9	39	1	2	2	17	1	37	1	0	7	.388	.298
O'Brien, Charles, Mil.	.234	62	188	22	44	72	10	0	6	35	8	0	9	21	1	11	0	0	11	.383	.339
O'Brien, Peter, Clev.★	.260	155	554	75	144	206	24	1	12	55	2	5	0	83	17	48	3	0	10	.372	.356
Olerud, John, Tor.★	.375	6	8	2	3	3	0	0	0	0	0	0	0	0	0	1	0	0	0	.375	.375
Olson, Gregory W. Minn.	.500	3	2	0	1	1	0	0	0	0	0	0	0	0	0	0	0	0	0	.500	.500
Orsulak, Joseph, Balt.★	.285	123	390	59	111	164	22	5	7	55	7	6	2	41	6	35	5	3	8	.421	.351
Orton, John, Cal.	.179	16	39	4	7	8	1	0	0	4	1	0	0	6	0	17	0	0	0	.205	.220
Pagliarulo, Michael, N.Y.★	.197	74	223	19	44	66	10	1	2	16	2	0	2	19	0	43	1	1	2	.296	.266
Palacios, R. Rey, K.C.	.170	55	47	12	8	13	2	0	1	8	1	0	0	2	0	14	1	0	1	.277	.216
Palmeiro, Rafael, Tex.★	.275	156	559	76	154	209	23	4	8	64	2	2	6	63	3	48	4	3	18	.374	.354
Palmer, Dean, Tex.	.105	16	19	0	2	4	2	0	0	1	0	1	0	0	0	12	0	0	0	.211	.100
Parker, David, Oak.★	.264	144	553	56	146	239	27	1	22	97	0	8	1	38	13	91	4	0	21	.432	.308
Parrish, Lance, Cal.	.238	124	433	48	103	168	12	0	17	50	1	5	2	42	6	104	1	1	10	.388	.306
Pasqua, Daniel, Chi.★	.248	73	246	26	61	105	9	4	11	47	0	4	1	25	1	58	1	2	4	.427	.315
Pecota, William, K.C.	.205	65	83	21	17	34	4	3	0	5	2	0	0	7	0	9	5	0	5	.410	.275
Pedrique, Alfredo, Det.	.203	31	69	1	14	17	3	0	0	5	2	0	0	2	0	15	0	0	5	.246	.225
Petralli, Eugene, Tex.★	.304	70	184	18	56	75	7	0	4	23	1	1	0	17	1	24	0	0	5	.408	.368
Pettis, Gary, Det.†	.257	119	444	77	114	137	8	6	1	18	8	0	1	84	0	106	43	15	14	.309	.375
Phelps, Kenneth, N.Y.-Oak.★	.242	97	194	26	47	72	6	0	7	29	0	3	2	31	2	47	0	0	2	.371	.342
Phillips, K. Anthony, Oak.†	.262	143	451	48	118	157	15	0	4	47	5	7	3	58	2	66	3	8	17	.348	.345
Polidor, Gustavo, Mil.	.194	79	175	15	34	41	7	0	0	14	3	4	0	6	1	18	1	0	6	.234	.230
Polonia, Luis, Oak.-N.Y.★	.300	125	433	70	130	168	16	8	3	46	2	2	1	25	1	44	22	8	13	.388	.338
Presley, James, Sea.	.236	117	390	42	92	150	20	1	12	41	4	5	0	21	9	107	4	2	12	.385	.275
Puckett, Kirby, Minn.	.339	159	635	75	215	295	45	4	9	85	3	5	3	41	21	59	11	4	21	.465	.379
Quinones, Rey, Sea.	.105	7	19	2	2	2	0	0	0	0	2	0	0	7	0	1	0	0	0	.105	.150
Quintana, Carlos, Bos.	.208	34	77	6	16	21	5	0	0	6	2	1	1	12	0	12	0	0	5	.273	.274
Quirk, James, N.Y.-Oak-Balt.★	.176	47	85	6	15	20	2	0	1	10	3	0	0	7	0	20	0	4	0	.235	.276
Ray, Johnny, Cal.†	.289	134	530	52	153	190	26	2	5	62	4	5	2	36	3	30	6	3	14	.358	.327
Reed, Jody, Bos.	.288	146	524	76	151	206	42	2	3	40	13	5	2	73	0	44	4	5	12	.393	.376
Reimer, Kevin, Tex.★	.000	3	5	0	0	0	0	0	0	0	0	0	0	0	0	1	0	0	4	.000	.000
Rice, James, Bos.	.234	56	209	22	49	72	10	0	3	28	1	3	0	13	1	39	1	1	4	.344	.276
Richie, Robert, Det.★	.265	19	49	6	13	24	2	0	3	10	0	0	0	5	0	10	0	0	4	.490	.333
Ripken, Calvin, Balt.	.257	162	646	80	166	259	30	0	21	93	0	6	3	57	5	72	3	3	22	.401	.317
Ripken, William, Balt.	.239	115	318	31	76	97	11	2	2	26	19	5	1	22	0	53	1	2	12	.305	.284
Rivera, Luis, Bos.	.257	93	323	35	83	117	17	3	5	29	4	1	2	20	0	60	3	3	7	.362	.301
Robidoux, William J., Chi.★	.128	16	39	2	5	7	2	0	0	3	0	0	1	4	0	9	0	0	2	.179	.209
Rodriguez, Victor, Minn.	.455	6	11	2	5	7	2	0	0	0	2	0	0	0	1	1	0	0	0	.636	.455
Romero, Edgardo, Bos.-Mil.	.209	61	163	17	34	41	2	2	1	9	2	0	0	7	1	17	0	0	4	.252	.243
Romine, Kevin, Bos.	.274	92	274	30	75	91	13	0	1	23	3	3	2	21	0	53	6	5	11	.332	.327
Rose, Robert, Cal.	.211	14	38	4	8	16	1	0	1	3	0	0	1	2	0	10	0	0	2	.421	.268
Saberhagen, Bret, K.C.	.221	39	77	7	17	29	4	0	2	7	3	0	0	5	1	13	0	0	2	.377	.277
Salas, Mark, Clev.★	.234	30	47	4	11	19	4	2	0	7	1	0	2	3	2	8	0	0	2	.404	.280
Sanders, Deion, N.Y.★	.234	14	47	7	11	19	2	0	2	7	0	0	0	3	0	8	1	0	0	.404	.280
Sax, Stephen, N.Y.	.315	158	651	88	205	252	26	3	5	63	8	5	1	52	2	44	43	17	19	.387	.364
Schaefer, Jeffrey, Chi.	.100	15	10	2	1	1	0	0	0	0	1	0	0	0	0	2	1	1	0	.100	.100

Player, Club	AVG	G	AB	R	H	TB	2B	3B	HR	RBI	SH	SF	HP	BB	IBB	SO	SB	CS	GI DP	SLG	OBP
Schofield, Richard, Cal.	.228	91	302	42	69	96	11	2	4	26	11	2	3	28	0	47	9	3	4	.318	.299
Schroeder, A. William, Cal.	.203	41	138	16	28	48	2	0	6	15	3	0	0	3	0	44	0	0	3	.348	.220
Schu, Richard, Balt.-Det.	.214	99	266	25	57	89	11	0	7	21	2	1	0	24	0	37	1	2	6	.335	.278
Schulz, Jeffrey, K.C.★	.222	7	9	0	2	2	0	0	0	1	0	0	0	0	0	2	0	0	0	.222	.222
Scott, Richard, Oak.	.000	3	2	0	0	0	0	0	0	0	0	0	0	0	0	0	0	0	0	.000	.000
Seitzer, Kevin, K.C.	.281	160	597	78	168	201	17	2	4	48	4	7	5	102	7	76	17	8	16	.337	.387
Sheaffer, Danny, Clev.	.063	7	16	1	1	1	0	0	0	1	0	0	0	0	0	2	1	1	0	.063	.167
Sheets, Larry, Balt.★	.243	102	304	33	74	109	12	1	7	33	0	5	3	26	7	58	1	1	4	.359	.305
Sheffield, Gary, Mil.	.247	95	368	34	91	124	18	0	5	32	3	3	4	27	0	33	10	6	4	.337	.303
Sheridan, Patrick, Det.★	.242	50	120	16	29	41	3	3	1	15	3	1	0	17	0	21	4	2	2	.342	.333
Sierra, Ruben, Tex.†	.306	162	634	101	194	344	35	14	29	119	0	10	2	43	13	82	8	2	7	.543	.347
Sinatro, Matthew, Det.	.120	13	25	2	3	3	0	0	0	1	1	0	1	3	0	3	0	0	1	.120	.185
Skinner, Joel, Clev.	.230	79	178	10	41	54	10	0	1	13	2	0	1	9	0	42	1	1	3	.303	.271
Slaught, Donald, N.Y.	.251	117	350	34	88	130	21	3	5	38	2	5	5	30	3	57	0	5	9	.371	.315
Snyder, J. Cory, Clev.	.215	132	489	49	105	176	17	0	18	59	0	4	2	23	1	134	6	5	11	.360	.251
Sorrento, Paul, Minn.★	.238	14	21	2	5	5	0	0	0	0	0	0	0	5	0	4	0	1	0	.238	.370
Sosa, Samuel, Tex.-Chi.	.257	58	183	27	47	67	8	0	4	13	1	2	2	11	1	47	7	5	6	.366	.303
Spiers, William, Mil.★	.255	114	345	44	88	115	9	3	4	33	5	2	1	21	2	63	10	2	8	.333	.298
Stanley, R. Michael, Tex.	.246	67	122	9	30	38	3	1	1	11	4	0	1	12	1	29	0	1	2	.311	.324
Steinbach, Terry, Oak.	.273	130	454	37	124	160	13	0	7	42	2	3	2	30	0	66	3	2	14	.352	.319
Stillwell, Kurt, K.C.†	.261	130	463	52	121	176	20	7	7	54	5	3	2	42	2	64	9	6	3	.380	.325
Stone, Jeffrey, Tex.-Bos.★	.176	40	51	8	9	14	1	2	0	6	2	0	0	4	0	7	9	3	0	.275	.246
Strange, J. Douglas, Det.†	.214	64	196	16	42	51	7	1	0	14	3	1	1	17	0	36	3	3	6	.260	.280
Sundberg, James, Tex.	.197	76	147	13	29	44	4	1	2	8	7	0	0	23	0	37	0	0	3	.299	.304
Surhoff, William J., Mil.★	.248	126	436	32	108	148	17	4	5	55	8	10	1	25	0	29	14	12	8	.339	.287
Tabler, Patrick, K.C.	.259	123	390	36	101	120	11	1	2	42	3	2	0	37	1	42	4	0	14	.308	.325
Tartabull, Danilo, K.C.	.268	133	441	54	118	194	22	2	18	62	0	1	3	69	2	123	4	2	12	.440	.369
Tettleton, Mickey, Balt.†	.258	117	411	72	106	209	21	2	26	65	0	3	1	73	4	117	3	8	8	.509	.369
Thurman, Gary, K.C.	.195	72	87	24	17	21	2	1	0	5	5	1	0	15	0	26	16	0	0	.241	.311
Tingley, Ronald, Cal.	.333	4	3	1	1	1	0	0	0	0	2	0	0	0	0	0	0	0	0	.333	.500
Tolleson, J. Wayne, N.Y.†	.164	80	140	16	23	35	5	2	1	9	3	0	0	16	0	23	0	1	3	.250	.255
Traber, James, Balt.★	.209	86	234	14	49	69	8	0	4	26	1	3	0	19	3	41	0	3	7	.295	.266
Trammell, Alan, Det.	.243	121	449	54	109	150	20	3	5	43	1	5	4	45	1	45	10	3	9	.334	.314
Valle, David, Sea.	.237	94	316	32	75	112	10	0	9	34	1	2	6	29	2	32	0	1	13	.354	.311
Vaughn, Gregory, Mil.	.265	38	113	18	30	48	4	1	5	23	0	3	3	13	0	23	4	3	0	.425	.336
Velarde, Randy, N.Y.	.340	33	100	12	34	48	4	2	2	11	3	0	0	7	0	14	0	0	3	.480	.389
Venable, W. McKinley, Cal.★	.358	20	53	7	19	23	4	0	0	4	1	0	0	1	0	16	13	3	0	.434	.370
Ventura, Robin, Chi.★	.178	16	45	5	8	11	3	0	0	7	0	0	0	8	0	6	0	0	1	.244	.298
Virgil, Osvaldo, Tor.	.182	9	11	2	2	6	1	0	1	2	0	0	0	0	0	3	0	0	0	.545	.400
Vizquel, Omar, Sea.†	.220	143	387	45	85	101	7	3	1	20	13	2	1	28	2	40	1	4	6	.261	.273
Walker, Gregory, Chi.†	.210	77	233	25	49	78	14	0	5	26	0	3	0	23	0	50	0	0	8	.335	.286
Ward, Gary, N.Y.-Det.	.253	113	292	27	74	116	11	2	9	30	1	4	3	24	0	59	5	3	11	.397	.306
Washington, Claudell, Cal.★	.273	110	418	74	114	179	18	4	13	42	0	2	2	27	3	84	13	5	7	.428	.319
Webster, Leonard, Minn.	.300	14	20	7	6	8	2	0	0	4	0	0	0	3	0	2	0	0	0	.400	.391
Weiss, Walter, Oak.†	.233	84	236	30	55	75	11	0	3	21	5	0	1	21	0	39	6	1	5	.318	.298
Wellman, Brad, K.C.	.230	103	178	30	41	51	4	0	2	12	3	0	1	7	0	36	5	3	7	.287	.263
Whitaker, Louis, Det.★	.251	148	509	77	128	235	21	1	28	85	1	9	3	89	6	59	6	3	7	.462	.361
White, Devon, Cal.†	.245	156	636	86	156	236	18	13	12	56	7	2	2	31	3	129	44	8	12	.371	.282
White, Frank, K.C.	.256	135	418	34	107	137	22	1	2	36	5	3	2	30	0	52	3	2	7	.328	.307
Whitt, L. Ernest, Tor.★	.262	129	385	42	101	160	24	1	11	53	1	2	0	52	2	53	5	4	9	.416	.349

Player, Club	AVG	G	AB	R	H	TB	2B	3B	HR	RBI	SH	SF	HP	BB	IBB	SO	SB	CS	GI DP	SLG	OBP
Williams, Dana, Bos.	.200	8	5	1	1	2	1	0	0	0	0	0	1	0	0	1	0	0	0	.400	.333
Williams, Edward, Chi.	.274	66	201	25	55	72	8	1	3	10	3	3	4	18	3	31	2	2	4	.358	.341
Williams, Kenneth, Det.	.205	94	258	29	53	78	5	1	6	23	2	2	5	18	0	63	9	4	6	.302	.269
Wilson, James, Sea.	.000	5	8	0	0	0	0	0	0	0	0	0	0	0	0	3	0	1	0	.000	.000
Wilson, William, Tor.†	.298	54	238	32	71	88	9	1	2	17	3	1	2	3	0	37	12	1	5	.370	.311
Wilson, Willie, K.C.†	.253	112	383	58	97	137	17	7	3	43	6	6	1	27	0	78	24	6	8	.358	.300
Winters, Matthew, K.C.★	.234	42	107	14	25	37	6	0	2	9	0	1	0	14	1	23	1	1	3	.346	.320
Worthington, Craig, Balt.	.247	145	497	57	123	191	23	0	15	70	3	6	4	61	2	114	1	2	10	.384	.334
Young, Michael, Clev.†	.186	32	59	2	11	14	0	0	1	5	0	1	1	6	1	13	1	2	0	.237	.273
Yount, Robin, Mil.	.318	160	614	101	195	314	38	9	21	103	3	4	6	63	8	71	19	3	9	.511	.384
Zuvella, Paul, Clev.	.276	24	58	10	16	24	2	0	2	6	3	0	0	11	0	11	0	0	0	.414	.300

AWARDED FIRST BASE ON INTERFERENCE—Kelly, N.Y. 2 (Skinner, Heath); Gantner, Mil. 2 (Steinbach, Slaught); Hengel, Clev. (Fisk); Buckner, K.C. (Steinbach); Daugherty, Tex. (Hassey); Strange, Det. (Sundberg); Coles, Sea. (Harper).

PLAYERS WITH TWO OR MORE CLUBS DURING 1989 SEASON
(Listed Alphabetically, First Club on Top)

Player, Club	AVG	G	AB	R	H	TB	2B	3B	HR	RBI	SH	SF	HP	BB	IBB	SO	SB	CS	GI DP	SLG	OBP
Baines, Harold, Chi.★	.321	96	333	55	107	168	20	1	13	56	0	3	1	60	13	52	0	2	11	.505	.423
Baines, Harold, Tex.★	.285	50	172	18	49	67	9	0	3	16	1	1	0	13	0	27	0	1	4	.390	.333
Barfield, Jesse, Tor.	.200	21	80	8	16	35	4	1	5	11	1	0	1	5	0	28	0	2	0	.438	.256
Barfield, Jesse, N.Y.	.240	129	441	71	106	181	19	1	18	56	0	3	2	82	6	122	5	3	8	.410	.360
Cadaret, Gregory, Oak.★	.000	26	0	0	0	0	0	0	0	0	0	0	0	0	0	0	0	0	0	.000	.000
Cadaret, Gregory, N.Y.★	.000	20	0	0	0	0	0	0	0	0	0	0	0	0	0	0	0	0	0	.000	.000
Dotson, Richard, N.Y.	.000	11	0	0	0	0	0	0	0	0	0	0	0	0	0	0	0	0	0	.000	.000
Dotson, Richard, Chi.	.000	17	0	0	0	0	0	0	0	0	0	0	0	0	0	0	0	0	0	.000	.000
Fletcher, Scott, Tex.	.239	83	314	47	75	91	14	1	0	22	2	2	2	38	1	41	1	0	8	.290	.323
Fletcher, Scott, Chi.	.272	59	232	30	63	79	11	1	1	21	9	3	2	26	0	19	1	1	4	.341	.344
Havens, Bradley, Clev.★	.000	7	0	0	0	0	0	0	0	0	0	0	0	0	0	0	0	0	0	.000	.000
Havens, Bradley, Det.★	.000	13	0	0	0	0	0	0	0	0	0	0	0	0	0	0	0	0	0	.000	.000
Henderson, Rickey, N.Y.	.247	65	235	41	58	82	13	3	3	22	0	1	0	56	0	29	25	8	0	.349	.392
Henderson, Rickey, Oak.	.294	85	306	72	90	134	13	2	9	35	0	3	2	70	5	39	52	6	8	.438	.425
Jefferson, Stanley, N.Y.†	.083	10	12	1	1	1	0	0	0	1	0	0	0	4	0	4	1	1	0	.083	.083
Jefferson, Stanley, Balt.†	.260	35	127	19	33	52	7	0	4	20	0	2	0	4	0	22	9	3	1	.409	.284
Leiter, Alois, N.Y.★	.000	4	0	0	0	0	0	0	0	0	0	0	0	0	0	0	0	0	0	.000	.000
Leiter, Alois, Tor.★	.000	1	0	0	0	0	0	0	0	0	0	0	0	0	0	0	0	0	0	.000	.000
Manrique, R. Fred, Chi.	.299	65	187	23	56	77	13	1	2	30	4	4	1	8	1	30	0	4	6	.412	.333
Manrique, R. Fred, Tex.	.288	54	191	23	55	73	12	0	2	22	9	1	0	8	0	33	4	1	3	.382	.318
Moreland, Keith, Det.	.299	90	318	34	95	126	16	0	5	35	0	0	2	27	5	33	3	2	14	.396	.357
Moreland, Keith, Balt.	.215	33	107	11	23	30	4	0	1	10	0	0	0	4	0	12	0	0	7	.280	.243
Phelps, Kenneth, N.Y.★	.249	86	185	26	46	70	3	0	7	29	0	3	0	27	2	47	0	0	2	.378	.340
Phelps, Kenneth, Oak.★	.111	11	9	0	1	2	1	0	0	0	0	0	0	4	0	0	0	0	0	.222	.385
Plunk, Eric, Oak.	.000	23	0	0	0	0	0	0	0	0	0	0	0	0	0	0	0	0	0	.000	.000
Plunk, Eric, N.Y.	.000	27	0	0	0	0	0	0	0	0	0	0	0	0	0	0	0	0	0	.000	.000

Player, Club	AVG	G	AB	R	H	TB	2B	3B	HR	RBI	SH	SF	HP	BB	IBB	SO	SB	CS	GI DP	SLG	OBP
Polonia, Luis, Oak.*	.286	59	206	31	59	76	6	4	1	17	2	1	0	9	0	15	13	4	5	.369	.315
Polonia, Luis, N.Y.*	.313	66	227	39	71	92	11	2	2	29	0	3	2	16	1	29	9	4	8	.405	.359
Quirk, James, N.Y.*	.083	13	24	0	2	2	0	0	0		0	0	0	3	0	5	0	1	1	.083	.185
Quirk, James, Oak.*	.200	9	10	1	2	5	0	0	1	1	0	0	0	0	0	4	0	0	0	.500	.200
Quirk, James, Balt.*	.216	25	51	5	11	13	2	0	0	9	1	0	0	9	0	11	0	1	3	.255	.328
Reuss, Jerry, Chi.*	.000	23	0	0	0	0	0	0	0	0	0	0	0	0	0	0	0	0	0	.000	.000
Reuss, Jerry, Mil.*	.000	7	0	0	0	0	0	0	0	0	0	0	0	0	0	0	0	0	0	.000	.000
Romero, Edgardo, Bos.	.212	46	113	14	24	28	4	0	0	6	0	2	1	7	1	7	0	2	1	.248	.260
Romero, Edgardo, Mil.	.200	15	50	3	10	13	3	0	0	3	2	0	0	0	0	10	0	0	3	.260	.200
Schu, Richard, Balt.	.000	1	0	0	0	0	0	0	0	0	0	0	0	0	0	0	0	0	0	.000	.000
Schu, Richard, Det.	.214	98	266	25	57	89	11	0	7	21	2	1	0	24	0	37	1	2	6	.335	.278
Sosa, Samuel, Tex.	.238	25	84	8	20	26	3	0	1	3	4	2	0	0	0	20	0	3	3	.310	.238
Sosa, Samuel, Chi.	.273	33	99	19	27	41	5	0	3	10	1	0	0	11	2	27	7	3	3	.414	.351
Stone, Jeffrey, Tex.*	.167	22	36	5	6	11	1	2	0	5	0	1	0	3	0	5	2	1	2	.306	.250
Stone, Jeffrey, Bos.*	.200	18	15	3	3	3	0	0	0	1	0	1	0	1	1	2	1	0	1	.200	.235
Ward, Gary, N.Y.	.294	8	17	3	5	6	1	0	0	1	1	0	0	3	1	5	0	1	1	.353	.400
Ward, Gary, Det.	.251	105	275	24	69	110	10	2	9	29	1	4	0	21	1	54	1	3	10	.400	.300

OFFICIAL AMERICAN LEAGUE DESIGNATED HITTING

CLUB DESIGNATED HITTING

Club	AVG	G	AB	R	H	TB	2B	3B	HR	RBI	SH	SF	HP	BB	IBB	SO	SB	CS	GI DP	SLG	OBP
Minnesota	.291	162	594	82	173	240	40	0	9	59	5	5	1	65	7	77	3	2	15	.404	.359
California	.277	162	629	67	174	260	32	3	16	72	1	5	6	61	4	105	2	1	8	.413	.344
Chicago	.264	161	613	90	162	278	41	3	23	99	1	5	3	81	18	115	2	2	21	.454	.349
New York	.263	161	609	84	160	272	27	2	27	106	1	13	3	57	11	114	5	1	16	.447	.323
Detroit	.262	162	621	66	163	237	31	4	13	83	0	6	1	52	13	87	5	3	15	.382	.318
Oakland	.262	162	641	73	168	276	30	2	26	107	0	8	2	48	3	110	4	0	23	.431	.312
Seattle	.259	162	633	74	164	254	25	1	21	96	1	11	6	45	3	114	6	2	11	.401	.309
Boston	.257	162	627	83	161	244	35	3	14	98	2	9	3	73	2	103	0	2	20	.389	.333
Texas	.252	162	591	60	149	202	29	3	6	53	6	5	3	55	2	118	4	4	27	.342	.317
Kansas City	.249	162	618	75	154	237	21	1	20	86	0	7	3	59	1	128	6	4	18	.383	.314
Cleveland	.242	162	608	59	147	229	23	1	19	66	3	15	2	62	6	137	8	6	16	.377	.314
Milwaukee	.238	162	588	68	140	196	23	0	10	67	1	10	3	66	8	98	18	8	15	.333	.311
Baltimore	.237	162	603	85	143	223	28	2	16	71	3	4	4	65	12	123	6	2	15	.370	.311
Toronto	.216	162	589	67	127	182	23	4	8	55	1	4	6	69	7	105	10	0	18	.309	.302
Totals	.255	1133	8564	1033	2185	3330	411	25	228	1118	20	106	46	858	96	1534	76	36	231	.389	.323

TOP 10 DESIGNATED HITTERS
(Minimum: 100 At-Bats)

Player, Club	AVG	G	AB	R	H	TB	2B	3B	HR	RBI	SH	SF	HP	BB	IBB	SO	SB	CS	GI DP	SLG	OBP
Molitor, P., Mil.	.354	28	113	15	40	56	10	0	2	11	1	0	1	12	0	17	4	4	1	.496	.417
James, D., Cle.*	.343	27	102	18	35	49	5	0	3	16	0	0	0	15	1	11	1	1	3	.480	.427

Player, Club	AVG	G	AB	R	H	TB	2B	3B	HR	RBI	SH	SF	HP	BB	IBB	SO	SB	CS	GI DP	SLG	OBP
Dwyer, J., Min.*	.324	74	216	33	70	90	11	1	3	22	1	0	1	26	0	22	2	0	5	.417	.397
Baines, H., Chi.-Tex.*	.312	115	414	63	129	201	28	1	14	58	1	4	1	57	12	70	0	0	13	.486	.393
Evans, D., Bos.	.299	69	254	43	76	122	14	1	10	54	1	3	2	45	1	37	1	1	9	.480	.405
Leach, R., Tex.	.298	44	114	17	34	47	8	1	1	11	1	1	0	14	0	19	1	1	4	.412	.372
Hall, M., N.Y.	.288	34	111	15	32	45	4	0	3	16	0	2	0	14	1	18	0	0	2	.405	.296
Downing, B., Cal.	.284	141	543	59	154	225	25	2	14	59	0	4	6	56	3	87	0	2	6	.414	.355
Larkin, G., Min.†	.281	41	146	24	41	63	13	0	3	11	0	2	1	13	4	19	1	0	4	.432	.340
Lynn, F., Det.*	.277	46	137	19	38	58	8	0	4	20	0	2	0	16	0	22	0	0	2	.423	.348

INDIVIDUAL DESIGNATED HITTING
(* Bats Lefthanded   †Switch Hitter)

Player, Club	AVG	G	AB	R	H	TB	2B	3B	HR	RBI	SH	SF	HP	BB	IBB	SO	SB	CS	GI DP	SLG	OBP
Parker, D., Oak.*	.265	140	547	56	145	238	27	1	22	97	0	8	1	37	13	89	0	2	21	.435	.309
Downing, B., Cal.	.284	141	543	59	154	225	25	2	14	59	0	4	6	56	3	87	0	1	6	.414	.355
Leonard, J., Sea.	.241	123	473	55	114	185	18	1	17	71	0	9	4	29	12	102	5	1	7	.391	.285
Baines, H., Chi.Tex.*	.312	116	414	63	129	201	28	1	14	58	0	4	1	57	9	70	0	0	13	.486	.393
Sheets, L., Bal.*	.241	88	291	33	70	105	12	1	7	31	0	5	3	25	1	54	2	1	3	.361	.302
Moreland, K., Det.-Bal.	.252	80	278	26	70	92	10	0	10	28	1	3	2	20	5	26	1	0	15	.331	.304
Evans, D., Bos.	.299	69	254	43	76	122	14	1	10	54	0	6	2	45	0	37	0	0	9	.480	.405
Balboni, S., N.Y.	.255	82	235	27	60	118	12	0	14	52	0	6	0	18	5	50	1	1	9	.502	.307
Dwyer, J., Min.*	.324	74	216	33	70	90	10	0	3	22	1	0	2	26	0	22	0	0	5	.417	.397
Rice, J., Bos.	.236	55	208	22	49	72	10	0	3	28	0	5	1	13	0	38	1	0	4	.346	.278
Tartabull, D., K.C.	.267	55	195	27	52	88	9	2	9	25	0	1	0	32	0	56	0	0	4	.451	.368
Mulliniks, R., Tor.*	.242	73	186	15	45	54	5	0	3	14	0	1	0	26	3	23	0	0	10	.290	.333
Clark, D., Cle.*	.232	55	168	12	39	58	7	0	4	19	0	1	1	19	3	41	1	0	6	.345	.309
Larkin, G., Min.*	.281	41	146	24	41	63	13	0	0	11	0	2	0	13	4	19	0	0	7	.432	.340
Calderon, I., Chi.	.241	36	145	19	35	61	7	0	5	24	0	1	0	12	2	25	1	1	2	.421	.297
Phelps, K., N.Y.-Oak.*	.236	56	144	20	34	48	2	0	4	17	0	3	0	26	2	35	0	0	7	.333	.347
Tabler, P., K.C.	.248	39	141	11	35	43	5	0	1	14	0	2	0	9	0	15	0	0	6	.305	.291
Lynn, F., Det.*	.277	46	137	16	38	58	8	0	4	20	0	2	0	16	2	22	2	1	2	.423	.348
Tettleton, M., Bal.†	.219	43	137	24	30	63	7	0	8	22	0	2	0	31	0	41	0	0	3	.460	.363
Leach, R., Tex.*	.298	44	114	17	34	47	8	0	1	11	0	1	1	14	2	19	2	4	4	.412	.372
Molitor, P., Mil.	.354	28	113	15	40	56	10	1	2	11	1	1	0	12	0	17	4	4	1	.496	.417
Hall, M., N.Y.*	.288	34	111	15	32	45	4	0	3	16	0	2	0	15	1	18	0	0	2	.405	.296
James, D., Cle.*	.343	27	102	18	35	49	5	0	3	16	0	0	1	10	1	11	3	1	3	.480	.427
Meyer, J., Mil.	.184	31	98	7	18	33	4	0	4	17	0	5	0	4	0	30	0	0	1	.337	.248
Nokes, M., Det.*	.286	33	98	5	28	38	5	0	2	11	0	0	0	8	1	11	3	1	0	.388	.314
Jackson, B., K.C.	.290	24	93	20	27	53	2	0	8	27	0	3	0	3	0	35	3	0	0	.570	.349
Bell, G., Tor.	.288	19	80	11	23	27	4	0	0	13	0	2	0	3	2	11	0	2	1	.338	.306
Francona, T., Mil.*	.213	23	75	6	16	24	2	0	2	8	0	1	0	7	1	3	0	1	1	.320	.241
Walker, G., Chi.*	.147	23	75	3	11	17	3	0	1	10	0	0	0	5	0	16	1	0	0	.227	.221
Medina, L., Cle.	.216	25	74	7	16	26	5	0	3	6	0	0	0	5	2	32	0	0	2	.351	.266
Yount, R., Mil.	.282	17	71	7	20	28	5	0	1	9	0	1	0	5	0	11	1	2	2	.394	.325
Buckner, B., K.C.*	.217	19	69	4	15	22	2	0	1	8	0	2	0	1	2	12	0	0	2	.319	.229
Brett, G., K.C.*	.176	17	68	7	12	18	3	0	1	9	0	0	0	4	0	10	0	2	4	.265	.227
Salas, M., Cle.*	.242	20	66	13	16	28	4	0	2	7	0	2	1	5	0	7	0	1	1	.424	.306
Mattingly, D., N.Y.*	.262	17	65	17	17	38	3	0	6	14	0	1	1	7	4	1	0	0	1	.585	.329
Kittle, R., Chi.	.222	17	63	8	14	28	5	0	3	9	0	0	1	7	1	18	0	0	2	.444	.310

Player, Club	AVG	G	AB	R	H	TB	2B	3B	HR	RBI	SH	SF	HP	BB	IBB	SO	SB	CS	GI DP	SLG	OBP
Hrbek, K., Min.*	.194	18	62	6	12	20	5	0	1	3	0	1	0	11	1	7	0	0	3	.323	.311
Ward, G., N.Y.-Det.	.194	27	62	5	12	21	1	1	2	8	0	1	0	5	0	15	0	0	3	.339	.250
Belle, J., Cle.	.224	17	58	5	13	27	5	0	4	8	0	0	0	6	0	14	1	0	4	.466	.297
Brenly, B., Tor.	.185	28	54	5	10	14	2	0	1	3	1	0	3	7	0	12	1	0	1	.259	.279
Moseby, L., Tor.*	.185	14	54	4	10	17	2	1	1	3	0	0	0	3	0	10	3	0	1	.315	.267
Bell, B., Tex.	.135	22	52	2	7	10	1	1	0	2	1	0	1	5	0	6	0	0	3	.192	.211
Davis, A., Sea.*	.333	14	51	6	17	25	4	0	2	11	0	0	0	10	2	5	0	0	1	.490	.444
Fisk, C., Chi.	.280	13	50	7	14	22	3	0	1	8	0	1	0	7	0	14	0	0	1	.440	.368
Mazzilli, L., Tor.†	.160	19	50	10	8	20	3	0	3	5	0	0	1	14	1	12	0	0	1	.400	.358
Borders, P., Tor.	.245	18	49	5	12	18	3	0	1	7	1	0	0	4	0	15	0	0	0	.367	.315
Laudner, T., Min.	.333	19	48	5	16	29	3	0	2	8	1	0	0	5	0	9	0	0	3	.604	.396
Petralli, G., Tex.*	.313	16	48	5	15	24	7	1	0	7	0	1	0	4	0	9	1	0	2	.500	.370
Coles, D., Sea.	.319	12	47	3	15	19	1	0	1	7	0	0	1	5	0	2	0	0	2	.404	.347
Harper, B., Min.	.340	19	47	5	16	18	3	0	0	2	0	1	0	3	1	2	0	0	4	.383	.373
Stanley, M., Tex.	.190	21	42	2	8	8	0	0	0	6	0	0	1	5	0	13	0	1	0	.190	.292
Lemon, C., Det.	.220	13	41	3	9	15	3	0	1	4	0	1	0	3	0	10	2	0	0	.366	.273
Surhoff, B., Mil.*	.268	12	41	1	11	12	1	0	0	2	0	3	0	5	0	11	3	2	1	.293	.340
Braggs, G., Mil.	.103	13	39	3	4	7	0	0	1	6	0	2	0	10	0	7	2	1	1	.179	.275
Young, M., Cle.†	.205	15	39	4	8	11	0	0	1	4	1	0	0	6	1	7	0	0	0	.282	.326
Horn, S., Bos.*	.132	14	38	2	5	7	0	0	0	2	0	0	0	5	1	9	0	0	4	.184	.233
Franco, J., Tex.	.194	10	36	6	7	9	2	0	0	1	0	0	0	4	0	6	0	0	5	.250	.275
Vaughn, G., Mil.	.194	13	36	4	7	7	0	0	0	3	0	0	0	3	0	10	0	0	0	.194	.333
Carter, J., Cle.	.212	18	33	8	7	15	2	0	2	4	0	0	1	1	0	7	2	0	2	.455	.278
Stone, J., Tex.-Bos.*	.212	18	33	5	7	12	1	0	1	5	0	0	0	2	0	3	0	0	0	.364	.278
Heep, D., Bos.*	.194	9	31	3	6	6	0	0	0	4	0	1	1	3	0	4	1	0	2	.194	.265
Polonia, L., N.Y.*	.333	9	30	1	10	12	0	1	0	1	0	1	0	1	0	4	2	1	2	.400	.364
Eisenreich, J., K.C.*	.310	10	29	4	9	9	0	0	0	1	0	1	0	4	0	4	2	1	0	.310	.394
Castillo, C., Min.	.214	16	28	3	6	6	0	0	0	4	0	0	0	2	0	6	0	0	1	.214	.267
Washington, C., Cal.*	.214	7	28	2	6	8	0	0	0	1	0	0	0	2	1	5	0	0	0	.286	.267
Brock, G., Mil.*	.259	7	27	1	7	8	1	0	0	3	0	0	0	4	0	0	1	0	1	.296	.355
Schu, R., Det.	.280	9	25	4	7	11	4	0	0	2	0	0	0	1	0	3	0	0	0	.440	.308
Whitt, E., Tor.*	.160	8	25	3	4	4	0	0	0	0	0	0	1	3	1	5	0	0	1	.160	.192
Melvin, B., Bal.	.292	9	24	2	7	9	2	0	0	2	0	0	1	0	0	3	0	0	1	.375	.292
Brantley, M., Sea.	.217	7	23	3	5	7	2	0	0	3	0	0	0	2	0	5	1	0	1	.304	.240
Davis, C., Cal.†	.227	6	22	1	5	8	3	0	0	6	0	2	0	1	0	7	0	0	0	.364	.292
Jones, T., Det.	.227	8	22	2	5	7	2	0	0	4	0	0	0	1	0	1	0	0	2	.318	.240
Quintana, C., Bos.	.182	7	22	2	4	5	1	0	0	2	0	0	0	0	0	6	0	0	1	.227	.250
Sheridan, P., Det.*	.273	8	22	3	6	7	1	0	0	1	1	0	0	3	0	2	1	0	2	.318	.360
Greenwell, M., Bos.*	.381	5	21	2	8	14	3	0	1	6	0	0	0	2	0	1	1	0	0	.667	.381
Lee, M., Tor.†	.143	13	21	3	3	5	0	0	0	3	1	0	0	0	0	5	0	0	2	.238	.217
Canseco, J., Oak.	.211	8	19	2	4	13	0	0	3	3	0	0	0	2	0	4	0	0	0	.684	.286
Daugherty, J., Tex.†	.316	8	19	3	6	6	0	0	0	2	0	1	0	2	0	3	0	0	2	.316	.364
Armas, T., Cal.	.278	6	18	4	5	13	2	0	2	4	0	0	1	0	0	4	0	0	0	.722	.300
Barrett, M., Bos.	.278	4	18	1	5	6	1	0	0	3	0	0	0	2	0	3	0	0	0	.333	.278
Felder, M., Mil.†	.111	11	18	4	2	2	0	0	0	0	0	0	0	1	0	2	1	0	0	.111	.200
Bradley, S., Sea.*	.353	6	17	3	6	10	1	0	1	3	0	0	0	2	0	5	0	0	1	.588	.421
Traber, J., Bal.*	.235	5	17	0	4	5	1	0	0	3	0	0	0	0	0	4	0	0	1	.294	.316
Gonzalez, D., Cle.	.313	6	16	3	5	6	1	0	0	2	0	0	0	0	0	6	0	0	0	.375	.313
Incaviglia, P., Tex.	.188	5	16	0	3	3	0	0	0	2	0	0	0	1	0	4	0	0	0	.188	.188
Sheffield, G., Mil.	.313	4	16	2	5	6	1	0	0	3	1	0	0	1	0	1	2	0	0	.375	.333

Player, Club	AVG	G	AB	R	H	TB	2B	3B	HR	RBI	SH	SF	HP	BB	IBB	SO	SB	CS	GI DP	SLG	OBP
Deer, R., Mil.	.067	5	15	1	1	2	1	0	0	1	0	0	0	1	0	5	0	0	0	.133	.125
Pasqua, D., Chi.★	.200	5	15	3	3	10	1	0	2	4	0	0	0	1	0	5	0	0	1	.667	.250
Sosa, S., Chi.	.200	6	15	0	3	3	0	0	0	1	0	0	0	0	0	8	0	0	0	.200	.200
Steinbach, T., Oak.★	.067	4	15	1	1	1	0	0	0	0	0	0	0	1	0	3	0	0	1	.067	.125
Myers, G., Tor.★	.000	6	14	0	0	0	0	0	0	0	0	0	0	1	0	2	0	0	1	.000	.067
Sorrento, P., Min.★	.286	5	14	1	4	4	0	0	0	0	0	0	0	2	0	3	0	0	0	.286	.375
Spiers, B., Mil.★	.231	4	13	3	3	4	1	0	0	0	0	0	0	3	0	3	2	0	0	.308	.375
Cabrera, F., Tor.	.167	3	12	2	2	3	1	0	0	2	0	0	0	1	0	3	0	0	0	.250	.231
Orsulak, J., Bal.★	.417	5	12	2	5	6	1	0	0	0	0	1	0	0	0	3	1	0	1	.500	.385
Bergman, D., Det.★	.273	7	11	3	3	3	0	0	0	1	0	0	0	2	0	2	0	0	0	.273	.385
Macfarlane, M., K.C.	.091	3	11	0	1	1	0	0	0	0	0	0	0	1	0	3	0	0	1	.091	.167
Sheaffer, D., Cle.	.091	3	11	0	1	1	0	0	0	1	0	0	0	0	0	1	0	0	0	.091	.091
Henderson, R., Oak.	.300	3	10	2	3	4	1	0	0	0	0	0	0	2	0	0	1	0	0	.400	.417
Lansford, C., Oak.	.600	3	10	2	6	7	1	0	0	1	0	0	0	2	0	2	0	0	0	.700	.667
Liriano, N., Tor.†	.100	5	10	2	1	1	0	0	0	0	0	0	0	1	0	3	2	0	0	.100	.182
Virgil, O., Tor.	.200	3	10	2	2	6	1	0	1	1	0	0	0	3	0	2	1	0	0	.600	.385
Winters, M., K.C.	.300	6	10	0	3	3	0	0	0	1	0	0	0	1	0	1	0	0	0	.300	.364
Blankenship, L., Oak.	.222	10	9	5	2	5	2	0	1	1	0	0	0	4	0	2	2	0	0	.556	.429
Boggs, W., Bos.★	.222	3	9	1	2	4	2	0	0	1	0	0	0	1	0	2	0	0	2	.444	.300
Bush, R., Min.★	.000	5	9	1	0	0	0	0	0	0	0	0	0	0	0	3	0	0	0	.000	.000
Espy, C., Tex.†	.222	3	9	1	2	3	1	0	0	2	0	0	0	0	0	3	2	0	0	.333	.222
Palmeiro, R., Tex.★	.222	6	9	1	2	2	0	0	0	0	0	0	0	5	0	1	0	0	0	.222	.500
Zuvella, P., Cle.	.444	3	9	0	4	5	1	0	0	3	0	1	0	0	0	2	0	0	0	.556	.400
Engle, D., Mil.	.250	3	8	0	2	2	0	0	0	0	0	0	0	1	0	4	0	0	0	.250	.333
Henderson, D., Oak.	.125	3	8	2	1	1	0	0	0	2	0	0	0	1	0	2	0	0	1	.125	.222
Hubbard, G., Oak.	.125	5	8	0	1	1	0	0	0	0	0	0	0	0	0	5	0	0	0	.125	.111
Jacoby, B., Cle.	.000	3	8	0	0	0	0	0	0	1	0	0	0	2	0	1	0	0	0	.000	.222
Palmer, D., Tex.	.125	6	8	1	1	2	1	0	0	2	0	0	0	0	0	0	0	0	1	.250	.125
Parrish, L., Cal.	.250	2	8	0	2	4	2	0	0	0	0	0	0	0	0	3	0	0	1	.500	.250
Polidor, G., Mil.	.250	2	8	0	2	3	1	0	0	1	0	0	0	0	0	1	0	0	0	.375	.250
Wilson, J., Sea.	.000	5	7	0	0	0	0	0	0	0	0	0	0	0	0	0	1	0	0	.000	.000
Bosley, T., Tex.★	.286	5	7	2	2	2	0	0	0	2	0	0	0	0	0	0	0	0	1	.286	.286
Brookens, T., N.Y.	.286	3	7	1	2	3	1	0	0	2	0	0	0	1	0	1	0	0	0	.429	.375
Devereaux, M., Bal.	.286	5	7	2	2	3	1	0	0	1	0	0	0	0	1	0	2	0	1	.429	.333
Gantner, J., Mil.★	.286	2	7	0	2	2	0	0	0	0	0	0	1	0	0	0	0	0	1	.286	.375
Hill, G., Tor.	.286	3	7	0	2	2	0	0	0	1	0	0	0	0	0	3	0	0	0	.286	.286
McGriff, F., Tor.★	.143	2	7	3	1	1	0	0	0	3	0	0	0	2	0	0	0	0	0	.143	.333
Trammell, A., Det.	.571	9	7	2	4	7	0	0	1	2	0	0	0	0	0	0	1	0	1	1.000	.571
Boston, D., Chi.★	.167	2	6	1	1	1	0	0	0	1	0	0	0	0	0	4	0	0	0	.167	.286
Browne, J., Cle.†	.333	2	6	2	2	2	0	0	0	2	0	0	0	1	0	0	1	0	0	.333	.333
Hale, C., Min.★	.333	2	6	0	2	2	0	0	0	0	0	0	0	0	0	0	0	0	0	.333	.286
Hassey, R., Oak.★	.167	5	6	1	1	1	0	0	0	1	0	0	0	1	0	1	0	0	0	.167	.286
Kunkel, J., Tex.	.167	5	6	0	1	2	0	0	0	2	0	0	0	1	0	0	0	0	0	.333	.286
Puckett, K., Min.	.500	2	6	1	3	4	0	0	0	0	0	0	0	0	0	1	0	0	0	.667	.500
Romine, K., Bos.	.333	2	6	1	2	2	0	0	0	2	0	0	0	0	0	0	0	0	0	.333	.333
Briley, G., Sea.★	.400	1	5	1	2	2	0	0	0	1	0	0	0	1	0	1	0	0	0	.400	.400
Fletcher, S., Chi.	.400	3	5	0	2	2	1	0	0	2	0	0	0	0	0	0	0	0	0	.400	.400
Gaetti, G., Min.	.400	2	5	1	2	3	0	0	0	2	0	0	0	1	0	1	0	0	0	.600	.500
Karkovice, R., Chi.	.400	2	5	1	2	3	1	0	0	0	0	0	0	0	0	1	0	0	0	.600	.400
Richie, R., Det.★	.200	4	5	2	1	3	0	0	1	2	0	0	0	1	0	1	0	0	0	.600	.333

Player, Club	AVG	G	AB	R	H	TB	2B	3B	HR	RBI	SH	SF	HP	BB	IBB	SO	SB	CS	GIDP	SLG	OBP
Slaught, D., N.Y.	.400	3	5	1	2	4	2	0	0	0	1	0	0	0	0	1	0	0	0	.800	.400
Beane, B., Oak.	1.000	4	4	1	4	5	1	0	0	1	0	0	0	0	0	0	0	0	0	1.250	1.000
Bradley, P., Bal.	.250	4	4	1	1	2	1	0	0	1	0	0	0	1	0	0	0	0	0	.500	.400
Brumley, M., Det.†	.250	8	4	5	1	2	1	0	0	0	0	0	0	0	0	2	1	0	0	.500	.250
Coolbaugh, S., Tex.	.250	2	4	3	1	1	0	0	0	0	0	0	0	1	0	1	0	0	0	.250	.400
Gladden, D., Min.	.250	2	4	0	1	1	0	0	0	0	1	0	0	0	0	0	0	0	0	.250	.250
Hoffman, G., Cal.	.000	1	4	0	0	0	0	0	0	0	0	0	0	0	0	1	0	0	0	.000	.000
Hoiles, C., Bal.	.000	3	4	0	0	0	0	0	0	0	0	0	0	1	0	2	0	0	1	.000	.200
Keedy, P., Cle.	.000	4	4	0	0	0	0	0	0	0	1	0	0	1	0	2	0	0	0	.000	.200
Kutcher, R., Bos.	.250	6	4	3	1	1	0	0	0	1	0	0	0	1	0	3	0	0	0	.250	.400
Lawless, T., Tor.	.500	12	4	6	2	2	0	0	0	0	0	0	0	0	0	0	4	0	0	.500	.500
McGwire, M., Oak.	.000	1	4	0	0	0	0	0	0	0	0	0	0	0	0	3	0	0	0	.000	.000
Presley, J., Sea.	.500	2	4	0	2	2	0	0	0	3	0	0	0	0	0	0	0	0	0	.500	.500
Whitaker, L., Det.*	.250	2	4	1	1	1	0	0	0	0	0	0	0	0	0	1	0	0	0	.250	.250
Williams, D., Bos.	.250	2	4	0	1	2	1	0	0	1	1	0	0	0	0	0	0	0	0	.500	.250
Allred, B., Cle.*	.333	1	3	0	1	1	0	0	0	0	0	0	0	0	0	2	0	0	0	.333	.333
Anderson, K., Cal.	.333	2	3	0	1	1	0	0	0	1	0	0	0	0	0	2	0	0	0	.333	.333
Dalena, P., Cle.*	.000	1	3	0	0	0	0	0	0	0	1	0	0	0	0	2	0	0	0	.000	.000
Felix, J., Tor.†	.333	2	3	2	1	4	0	0	1	1	0	0	0	1	0	1	0	0	0	1.333	.500
Freeman, L., Tex.*	.000	2	3	0	0	0	0	0	0	0	0	0	0	0	0	2	0	0	0	.000	.000
Heath, M., Det.	.000	3	3	0	0	0	0	0	0	0	0	0	0	0	0	0	0	0	0	.000	.000
Hengel, D., Cle.	.000	1	3	0	0	0	0	0	0	0	0	0	0	1	0	1	0	0	1	.000	.250
Morris, H., N.Y.*	.333	3	3	0	1	1	0	0	0	1	0	0	0	0	0	0	0	0	0	.333	.333
Reimer, K., Tex.*	.000	1	3	0	0	0	0	0	0	0	0	0	0	1	0	1	0	0	0	.000	.250
Reynolds, H., Sea.†	.333	2	3	1	1	1	0	0	0	1	0	0	0	0	0	0	1	0	0	.333	.333
Schaefer, J., Chi.	.333	3	3	0	1	1	0	0	0	0	0	0	0	0	0	1	0	0	0	.333	.333
Snyder, C., Cle.	.000	2	3	0	0	0	0	0	0	0	0	0	0	0	0	2	0	0	0	.000	.000
Strange, D., Det.†	.333	10	3	1	1	1	0	0	0	0	0	0	0	2	0	1	1	0	0	.333	.600
Tolleson, W., N.Y.†	.000	8	3	0	0	0	0	0	0	0	0	0	0	1	0	0	0	0	0	.000	.250
Anderson, B., Bal.*	.000	2	2	0	0	0	0	0	0	0	0	0	0	0	0	1	0	0	0	.000	.000
Bichette, D., Cal.	.500	1	2	0	1	3	0	1	0	1	0	0	0	0	0	0	0	0	0	1.500	.500
Buechele, S., Tex.	.000	2	2	0	0	0	0	0	0	0	0	0	0	0	0	1	0	0	0	.000	.000
Cerone, R., Bos.	.000	2	2	0	0	0	0	0	0	0	0	0	0	0	0	0	0	0	0	.000	.000
Cotto, H., Sea.	1.000	2	2	0	2	2	0	0	0	0	0	0	0	0	0	0	0	0	0	1.000	1.000
Datz, J., Det.	.000	1	2	0	0	0	0	0	0	0	0	0	0	0	0	1	0	0	0	.000	.000
Geren, R., N.Y.	.000	2	2	0	0	0	0	0	0	0	0	0	0	1	0	0	0	0	0	.000	.333
Hairston, J., Chi.†	.500	2	2	0	1	1	0	0	0	0	0	0	0	0	0	1	0	0	0	.500	.500
Jefferson, S., N.Y.-Bal.†	1.000	3	2	0	2	2	0	0	0	1	0	0	0	0	0	0	0	0	0	1.000	1.000
Pagliarulo, M., N.Y.*	.500	1	2	0	1	2	1	0	0	0	0	0	0	0	0	0	0	0	0	1.000	.500
Rivera, L., Bos.	.000	2	2	0	0	0	0	0	0	0	0	0	0	0	0	1	0	0	0	.000	.000
Romero, E., Mil.	.000	1	2	0	0	0	0	0	0	0	0	0	0	0	0	0	0	0	0	.000	.000
Wilson, W., K.C.†	.000	2	2	1	0	0	0	0	0	0	0	0	0	0	0	0	1	0	0	.000	.000
Aguayo, L., Cle.	.000	2	1	0	0	0	0	0	0	0	0	0	0	1	0	0	0	0	0	.000	.500
Backman, W., Min.†	1.000	1	1	0	1	1	0	0	0	0	0	0	0	0	0	0	0	0	0	1.000	1.000
Burks, E., Bos.	.000	1	1	1	0	0	0	0	0	1	0	0	0	0	0	0	0	0	0	.000	.000
Ducey, R., Tor.*	.000	1	1	0	0	0	0	0	0	0	0	0	0	0	0	0	0	0	0	.000	.000
Gallagher, D., Chi.	.000	1	1	0	0	0	0	0	0	0	0	0	0	0	0	0	0	0	0	.000	.000
Gallego, M., Oak.	1.000	1	1	0	1	1	0	0	0	0	0	0	0	1	0	0	0	0	0	1.000	1.000
Gruber, K., Tor.	1.000	1	1	0	1	4	0	0	1	1	0	0	0	0	0	0	0	0	0	4.000	1.000
Lusader, S., Det.*	.000	1	1	0	0	0	0	0	0	0	0	0	0	0	0	0	0	0	0	.000	.000

Player, Club	AVG	G	AB	R	H	TB	2B	3B	HR	RBI	SH	SF	HP	BB	IBB	SO	SB	CS	GI DP	SLG	OBP
McLemore, M., Cal.†	.000	1	1	0	0	0	0	0	0	0	0	0	0	0	0	1	0	0	0	.000	.000
Moses, J., Min.†	.000	3	1	0	0	0	0	0	0	0	0	0	0	0	0	1	0	0	0	.000	.000
Newman, A., Min.†	.000	2	1	0	0	0	0	0	0	0	0	0	0	0	0	0	0	0	0	.000	.500
O'Brien, P., Cle.*	.000	1	1	0	0	0	0	0	0	0	0	0	0	0	0	1	0	0	0	.000	.000
Olerud, J., Tor.*	.000	1	1	0	0	0	0	0	0	0	0	0	0	0	0	0	0	0	0	.000	.000
Quirk, J., Bal.*	.000	1	1	0	0	0	0	0	0	0	0	0	0	1	0	0	0	0	0	.000	.500
Reed, J., Bos.	.000	1	1	0	0	0	0	0	0	0	0	0	0	0	0	1	1	0	0	.000	.000
Sundberg, J., Tex.	.000	4	0	2	0	0	0	0	0	0	0	0	0	0	0	0	0	0	0	.000	.000
Bell, J., Bal.	.000	3	0	1	0	0	0	0	0	1	0	0	0	0	0	0	0	0	0	.000	.000
Filer, T., Mil.	.000	3	0	1	0	0	0	0	0	0	0	0	0	0	0	0	1	0	0	.000	.000
Finley, S., Bal.*	.000	3	0	2	0	0	0	0	0	0	0	0	0	0	0	0	0	0	0	.000	.000
Hemond, S., Oak.	.000	1	0	0	0	0	0	0	0	0	0	0	0	0	0	0	0	0	0	.000	.000
Hinzo, T., Cle.†	.000	1	0	0	0	0	0	0	0	0	0	0	0	0	0	0	0	0	0	.000	.000
Johnson, L., Chi.*	.000	1	0	0	0	0	0	0	0	0	0	1	0	0	0	0	0	0	0	.000	.000
Lawton, M., N.Y.†	.000	1	0	0	0	0	0	0	0	0	0	0	0	0	0	0	1	0	0	.000	.000
Martinez, C., Chi.	.000	2	0	1	0	0	0	0	0	0	0	0	0	0	0	0	0	0	0	.000	.000
McDowell, O., Cle.*	.000	4	0	1	0	0	0	0	0	0	0	0	0	1	0	0	0	0	0	.000	1.000
Thurman, G., K.C.	.000	1	0	1	0	0	0	0	0	0	0	0	0	0	0	0	0	1	0	.000	.000
Wellman, B., K.C.	.000	1	0	1	0	0	0	0	0	0	0	0	0	0	0	0	1	0	0	.000	.000
White, D., Cal.†	.000	1	0	1	0	0	0	0	0	0	0	0	0	0	0	0	1	0	0	.000	.000
Williams, K., Det.	.000	1	0	0	0	0	0	0	0	0	0	0	0	0	0	0	1	0	0	.000	.000

DESIGNATED HITTERS WITH TWO OR MORE CLUBS

Player, Club	AVG	G	AB	R	H	TB	2B	3B	HR	RBI	SH	SF	HP	BB	IBB	SO	SB	CS	GI DP	SLG	OBP
Baines, H., Chi.*	.323	70	248	45	80	134	19	1	11	44	0	3	1	45	12	44	0	0	9	.540	.424
Baines, H., Tex.*	.295	46	166	18	49	67	9	0	3	14	0	1	0	12	1	26	0	2	4	.404	.341
Moreland, K., Det.	.274	51	175	15	48	64	7	0	3	20	0	0	1	16	0	15	2	1	8	.366	.339
Moreland, K., Bal.	.214	29	103	11	22	28	3	0	1	8	0	0	0	4	0	11	0	0	7	.272	.243
Phelps, K., N.Y.*	.236	55	144	20	34	48	2	0	4	17	0	3	0	25	2	35	0	0	2	.333	.343
Phelps, K., Oak.*	.000	1	1	0	0	0	0	0	0	0	0	0	0	0	0	0	0	0	0	.000	1.000
Ward, G., N.Y.	.000	1	1	0	0	0	0	0	0	0	0	0	0	1	0	1	0	0	0	.000	.500
Ward, G., Det.	.197	26	61	5	12	21	1	1	2	7	0	1	0	4	0	14	1	0	4	.344	.242
Stone, J., Tex.*	.207	15	29	4	6	11	1	0	0	5	1	0	0	2	0	3	2	1	2	.379	.281
Stone, J., Bos.*	.250	3	4	1	1	2	0	0	0	0	0	0	0	0	0	0	0	0	0	.250	.250
Jefferson, S., N.Y.†	.000	1	2	1	0	0	0	0	0	1	0	0	0	0	0	0	0	0	0	.000	.000
Jefferson, S., Bal.†	1.000	2	2	2	2	2	0	0	0	0	0	0	0	0	0	0	0	0	0	1.000	1.000

OFFICIAL AMERICAN LEAGUE FIELDING AVERAGES
CLUB FIELDING

Club	PCT	G	PO	A	E	TC	DP	TP	PB
Baltimore	.986	162	4345	1795	87	6227	163	1	8
California	.985	162	4363	1887	96	6346	173	0	14
Minnesota	.982	162	4288	1598	107	5993	141	0	8
Kansas City	.982	162	4355	1761	114	6230	139	0	12
Cleveland	.981	162	4359	1750	118	6227	126	0	17
Toronto	.980	162	4401	1864	127	6392	164	0	16
New York	.980	161	4244	1743	122	6109	183	0	7
Boston	.980	162	4381	1709	127	6217	162	0	11
Detroit	.979	162	4282	1762	130	6174	153	0	10
Oakland	.979	162	4345	1640	129	6114	159	0	13
Texas	.978	162	4303	1651	136	6090	137	0	42
Seattle	.977	162	4314	1777	143	6234	168	0	10
Chicago	.975	161	4266	1718	151	6135	176	0	16
Milwaukee	.975	162	4297	1803	155	6255	164	0	11
Totals	.980	1133	60543	24458	1742	86743	2208	1	195

INDIVIDUAL FIELDING
(*Throws Lefthanded)
FIRST BASEMEN

Leader, Club	PCT	G	PO	A	E	TC	DP
JOYNER, CAL.*	.997	159	1487	99	4	1590	146

Player, Club	PCT	G	PO	A	E	TC	DP
Armas, Cal.	.833	2	4	1	1	6	2
Arndt, Oak.	1.000	1	8	1	0	9	2
Balboni, N.Y.	.994	20	150	7	1	158	15
Bean, Det.*	.875	2	7	0	1	8	1
Beane, Oak.	.938	4	13	2	1	16	1
Bell, Tex.	1.000	1	7	1	0	8	0
Bergman, Det.*	.993	123	912	85	7	1004	88
Bradley, Sea.	.917	2	10	1	1	12	2
Brenly, Tor.	1.000	5	24	3	0	27	1
Brett, K.C.	.998	104	896	80	2	978	71
Brock, Mil.	.995	100	850	58	5	913	86
Buckner, K.C.*	.985	24	181	13	3	197	19
Bush, Minn.*	1.000	25	139	7	0	146	13
Calderon, Chi.	.978	26	167	9	4	180	21
Canale, Mil.	.989	11	86	4	1	91	4
Carter, Clev.	.991	11	93	14	1	108	4
Cochrane, Sea.	1.000	9	57	5	0	62	4
Coles, Sea.	.977	18	118	8	3	129	11
Crim, Mil.	....	1	0	0	0	0	0
Daugherty, Tex.*	1.000	23	129	13	0	142	11
Davis, Sea.	.992	125	1106	81	10	1197	119
de los Santos, K.C.	.986	27	203	16	3	222	23
Engle, Mil.	.973	18	133	12	4	149	11
Eppard, Cal.*	1.000	4	12	0	0	12	2
Esasky, Bos.	.996	153	1317	107	6	1430	129
Francona, Mil.*	.989	46	320	25	4	349	32
Gaetti, Minn.	1.000	2	11	2	0	13	1
Harper, Minn.	1.000	2	2	0	0	2	0
Hassey, Oak.	1.000	1	4	0	0	4	0
Heep, Bos.*	.986	19	124	12	2	138	17
Higgins, Clev.	1.000	5	18	3	0	21	1
Hoffman, Cal.	1.000	1	7	1	0	8	0
Horn, Bos.*	1.000	2	5	0	0	5	0
Howitt, Oak.	1.000	1	2	0	0	2	0
Hrbek, Minn.	.995	89	723	60	4	787	66
James, Clev.*	.750	2	3	0	1	4	0
Javier, Oak.	1.000	1	1	0	0	1	1
Joyner, Cal.*	.997	159	1487	99	4	1590	146
Keedy, Clev.	1.000	1	1	0	0	1	0
Kittle, Chi.	.982	27	208	11	4	223	28
Lansford, Oak.	1.000	15	91	5	0	96	9
Larkin, Minn.	.992	67	463	28	4	495	45

Player, Club	PCT	G	PO	A	E	TC	DP
Laudner, Minn.	1.000	11	19	0	0	19	2
Leach, Tex.*	1.000	4	17	1	0	18	2
Lovullo, Det.	1.000	18	128	4	0	132	12
Lyons, Chi.	.988	40	230	24	3	257	24
Martinez, Chi.	.991	34	217	13	2	232	13
Mattingly, N.Y.*	.995	145	1274	87	7	1368	143
Mazzilli, Tor.	.944	2	16	1	1	18	1
McGriff, Tor.*	.989	159	1460	115	17	1592	148
McGwire, Oak.	.995	141	1170	114	6	1290	122
Medina, Clev.*	1.000	1	2	0	0	2	0
Melendez, Balt.*	1.000	5	25	2	0	27	4
Meyer, Mil.	.982	18	100	7	2	109	14
Milligan, Balt.	.995	117	914	83	5	1002	92
Moreland, Balt.	1.000	31	241	12	0	253	21
Morman, Chi.	.988	35	157	13	2	172	21
Morris, N.Y.*	1.000	2	8	0	0	8	2
Moses, Minn.*	1.000	2	12	0	0	12	0
O'Brien, Clev.*	.994	154	1359	114	9	1482	111
Olerud, Tor.*	1.000	5	19	2	0	21	0
Palacios, K.C.	.984	18	59	4	1	64	8
Palmeiro, Tex.*	.991	147	1167	119	12	1298	106
Pecota, K.C.	1.000	4	8	0	0	8	1
Phelps, N.Y.-Oak.*	.983	9	56	2	1	59	5
Phillips, Oak.	....	1	0	0	0	0	0
Presley, Sea.	.995	30	168	15	1	184	16
Quintana, Bos.	1.000	1	6	0	0	6	0
Quirk, Balt.	1.000	1	3	0	0	3	0
Robidoux, Chi.	.990	15	93	7	1	101	17
Schroeder, Cal.	.984	8	58	5	1	64	8
Schu, Det.	1.000	3	2	1	0	3	0
Seitzer, K.C.		2	0	0	0	0	0
Sorrento, Minn.	1.000	5	13	0	0	13	1
Spiers, Mil.	.909	2	10	0	1	11	3
Stanley, Tex.	.973	7	35	1	1	37	2
Steinbach, Oak.	.983	10	55	3	1	59	7
Tabler, K.C.	.993	20	126	13	1	140	10
Traber, K.C.*	.998	69	514	54	1	569	59
Walker, Chi.	.987	48	373	17	5	395	38
Ward, Det.	.986	26	126	14	2	142	14
K. Williams, Det.	....	1	0	0	0	0	0

FIRST BASEMAN WITH TWO OR MORE CLUBS

Player, Club	PCT	G	PO	A	E	TC	DP
Phelps, N.Y.*	.980	8	47	1	1	49	4
Phelps, Oak.*	1.000	1	9	1	0	10	1

SECOND BASEMEN

Leader, Club	PCT	G	PO	A	E	TC	DP
SAX, N.Y.	.987	158	312	460	10	782	117

Player, Club	PCT	G	PO	A	E	TC	DP
Aguayo, Clev.	1.000	10	17	28	0	45	7
Anderson, Cal.	1.000	7	3	7	0	10	2
Backman, Minn.	.982	84	146	187	6	339	37
Baker, Minn.	.982	25	22	32	1	55	4

Player, Club	PCT	G	PO	A	E	TC	DP
Barrett, Bos.	.975	80	152	245	10	407	53
Bates, Mil.	.938	7	14	16	2	32	7
Bell, Balt.	1.000	1	3	0	4	1	
Blankenship, Oak.	.987	24	26	48	1	75	10
Briley, Sea.	.981	10	18	33	1	52	6
Brookens, N.Y.	1.000	5	4	7	0	11	1
Browne, Clev.	.979	151	305	380	15	700	67

SECOND BASEMEN—Continued

Player, Club	PCT	G	PO	A	E	TC	DP
Brumley, Det.	.932	24	31	51	6	88	10
Buechele, Tex.	1.000	18	21	23	0	44	6
Castillo, Mil.	1.000	3	6	5	0	11	1
Cochrane, Sea.	1.000	4	4	5	0	9	1
Diaz, Sea.	1.000	14	8	14	0	22	4
Felder, Mil.	.966	10	12	16	1	29	4
Fermin, Clev.	1.000	2	6	5	0	11	0
Fletcher, Chi.	1.000	53	108	161	0	269	38
Franco, Tex.	.980	140	256	386	13	655	70
Gallego, Oak.	.970	41	58	106	5	169	18
Gantner, Mil.	.987	114	241	362	8	611	88
Gonzales, Balt.	.978	54	93	125	5	223	35
Hale, Minn.	.980	16	14	36	1	51	8
Hinzo, Clev.	.867	6	6	7	2	15	1
Hoffman, Cal.	1.000	4	6	7	0	13	2
Hubbard, Oak.	.968	48	82	132	7	221	34
Hulett, Balt.	.976	23	61	59	3	123	12
Infante, Tor.	1.000	1	3	3	0	6	1
Javier, Oak.	1.000	1	1	4	0	5	1
Kunkel, Tex.	1.000	8	14	12	0	26	6
Lawless, Tor.	1.000	7	17	13	0	30	5
Lee, Tor.	.985	40	103	96	3	202	29
Liriano, Tor.	.980	122	267	330	12	609	76
Lyons, Chi.	.982	70	142	185	6	333	46
Manrique, Chi.-Tex.	.952	74	118	160	14	292	36
McLemore, Cal.	.966	27	55	88	5	148	24
Molitor, Mil.	.986	16	28	44	1	73	9
Newman, Minn.	.980	84	116	171	6	293	37
Pecota, K.C.	1.000	12	8	19	0	27	3
Pedrique, Det.	.973	8	15	21	1	37	7

Leader, Club	PCT	G	PO	A	E	TC	DP
Phillips, Oak.	.985	84	140	252	6	398	46
Polidor, Mil.	.964	29	34	46	3	83	5
Ray, Cal.	.984	130	279	403	11	693	98
Reed, Bos.	.978	70	143	209	8	360	46
Reynolds, Sea.	.980	151	311	506	17	834	109
W. Ripken, Balt.	.985	114	255	335	9	599	81
Rivera, Bos.	1.000	1	1	0	0	1	0
Romero, Bos.-Mil.	.988	33	68	93	2	163	22
Rose, Cal.	1.000	3	3	5	0	8	0
Sax, N.Y.	.987	158	312	460	10	782	117
Schaefer, Chi.	1.000	4	1	2	0	3	1
Schu, Balt.-Det.	1.000	6	4	5	0	9	2
Spiers, Mil.	1.000	4	6	11	0	17	1
Strange, Det.	.968	9	16	14	1	31	5
Tabler, K.C.	1.000	3	2	4	0	6	0
Tolleson, N.Y.	1.000	13	6	15	0	21	5
Wellman, K.C.	.995	64	74	128	1	203	27
Whitaker, Det.	.985	146	327	393	11	731	99
White, K.C.	.985	132	238	407	10	655	64

TRIPLE PLAY: W. Ripken, Balt.

SECOND BASEMEN WITH TWO OR MORE CLUBS

Player, Club	PCT	G	PO	A	E	TC	DP
Manrique, Chi.	.961	57	94	127	9	230	30
Manrique, Tex.	.919	17	24	33	5	62	6
Romero, Bos.	.983	21	52	67	2	121	17
Romero, Mil.	1.000	11	16	26	0	42	5
Schu, Balt.	1.000	1	1	0	0	1	0
Schu, Det.	1.000	5	3	5	0	8	2

THIRD BASEMEN

Leader, Club	PCT	G	PO	A	E	TC	DP
HOWELL, CAL.	.974	142	95	322	11	428	27

Player, Club	PCT	G	PO	A	E	TC	DP
Aguayo, Clev.	.950	19	9	29	2	40	1
Anderson, Cal.	.929	5	2	11	1	14	2
Arndt, Oak.	1.000	1	0	1	0	1	1
Beane, Oak.	1.000	1	0	1	0	1	0
Bell, Tex.	1.000	9	3	12	0	15	0
Blowers, N.Y.	.852	13	9	14	4	27	3
Boggs, Bos.	.958	152	123	264	17	404	29
Brookens, N.Y.	.926	51	17	70	7	94	4
Brown, Det.	.909	17	15	25	4	44	4
Brumley, Det.	.813	11	0	13	3	16	1
Buechele, Tex.	.969	145	106	264	12	382	22
Cochrane, Sea.	.889	9	1	7	1	9	0
Coles, Sea.	.949	26	15	59	4	78	6
Coolbaugh, Tex.	.958	23	7	39	2	48	3
Diaz, Sea.	1.000	3	1	0	0	1	1
Gaetti, Minn.	.973	125	104	251	10	365	23
Gallego, Oak.	1.000	3	1	2	0	3	0
Gonzales, Balt.	.923	17	8	16	2	26	1
Gonzalez, Clev.	.000	1	0	0	1	1	0
Gruber, Tor.	.945	119	86	291	22	399	15
Hale, Minn.	1.000	9	1	4	0	5	0
Harper, Minn.	1.000	2	1	1	0	2	0
Heath, Det.	.750	4	1	2	1	4	0
Hoffman, Cal.	.957	18	14	30	2	46	2
Howell, Cal.	.974	142	95	322	11	428	27
Hulett, Balt.	.955	11	9	12	1	22	1
Infante, Tor.	1.000	4	0	1	0	1	0
Jacoby, Clev.	.955	144	92	268	17	377	15
Jorgensen, Minn.	.958	9	4	19	1	24	3
Keedy, Clev.	.857	2	0	6	1	7	1
Kiefer, N.Y.	1.000	5	1	1	0	2	0
Kunkel, Tex.	.600	4	1	5	4	10	0
Kutcher, Bos.	.917	6	3	8	1	12	0
Lansford, Oak.	.957	136	104	183	13	300	11
Lawless, Tor.	.842	12	4	12	3	19	1
Lee, Tor.	.891	17	9	32	5	46	4
Lovullo, Det.	.963	11	6	20	1	27	3
Lyons, Chi.	.895	28	16	35	6	57	3
Manrique, Chi.-Tex.	.875	7	5	9	2	16	1
Martinez, Chi.	.912	68	45	121	16	182	12
Martinez, Sea.	.949	61	40	72	6	118	9

Player, Club	PCT	G	PO	A	E	TC	DP
Meulens, N.Y.	.875	8	5	23	4	32	1
Molitor, Mil.	.950	112	78	243	17	338	18
Moreland, Balt.	.846	12	2	20	4	26	2
Mulliniks, Tor.	.985	29	15	50	1	66	9
Newman, Minn.	.954	37	32	51	4	87	5
Pagliarulo, N.Y.	.936	69	25	122	10	157	6
Palacios, K.C.	.958	21	13	10	1	24	0
Palmer, Tex.	.667	6	1	3	2	6	0
Pecota, K.C.	.889	7	2	6	1	9	2
Pedrique, Det.	.960	12	7	17	1	25	1
Phillips, Oak.	.900	49	19	44	7	70	3
Polidor, Milw.	.923	30	14	34	4	52	3
Presley, Sea.	.924	90	54	154	17	225	13
Quirk, Balt.	.500	3	0	1	1	2	0
Reed, Bos.	1.000	4	3	1	0	4	0
Rodriguez, Minn.	.900	5	3	6	1	10	1
Romero, Bos.-Mil.	.933	18	10	18	2	30	4
Rose, Cal.	.920	10	7	16	2	25	1
Schaefer, Chi.	.000	4	0	0	1	1	0
Schu, Det.	.934	83	52	119	12	183	11
Seitzer, K.C.	.950	159	112	272	20	404	28
Sheaffer, Clev.	....	2	0	0	0	0	0
Sheffield, Mil.	.937	21	15	44	4	63	4
Spiers, Mil.	.882	12	10	20	4	34	1
Stanley, Tex.	1.000	3	0	1	0	1	0
Steinbach, Oak.	1.000	3	2	1	0	3	1
Strange, Det.	.878	54	33	96	18	147	11
Surhoff, Mil.	.917	6	4	7	1	12	1
Tabler, K.C.	....	1	0	0	0	0	0
Tolleson, N.Y.	.912	28	14	38	5	57	5
Velarde, N.Y.	.954	27	18	44	3	65	7
Ventura, Chi.	.962	16	17	33	2	52	2
Wellman, K.C.	....	3	0	0	0	0	0
Williams, Chi.	.909	65	37	123	16	176	21
Worthington, Balt.	.951	145	113	277	20	410	22
Zuvella, Clev.	.923	5	4	8	1	13	0

THIRD BASEMEN WITH TWO OR MORE CLUBS

Player, Club	PCT	G	PO	A	E	TC	DP
Manrique, Chi.	.833	1	3	2	1	6	0
Manrique, Tex.	.900	6	2	7	1	10	1
Romero, Bos.	.957	14	7	15	1	23	4
Romero, Mil.	.857	4	3	3	1	7	0

106

SHORTSTOPS

Leader, Club	PCT	G	PO	A	E	TC	DP
FERNANDEZ, TOR...	.992	140	260	475	6	741	93

Player, Club	PCT	G	PO	A	E	TC	DP
Aguayo, Clev.	.912	15	8	23	3	34	3
Anderson, Cal.	.972	70	96	215	9	320	52
Baker, Minn.	.981	19	20	31	1	52	5
Bell, Balt.	1.000	2	1	3	0	4	0
Brookens, N.Y.	1.000	7	2	7	0	9	2
Brumley, Det.	.980	42	48	96	3	147	13
Buechele, Tex.	1.000	1	1	1	0	2	1
Cochrane, Sea.	.905	30	14	24	4	42	9
Diaz, Sea.	.930	37	26	40	5	71	5
Disarcina, Cal.	....	1	0	0	0	0	0
Espinoza, N.Y.	.970	146	237	471	22	730	114
Fermin, Clev.	.967	153	247	512	26	785	84
Fernandez, Tor.	.992	140	260	475	6	741	93
Fletcher, Tex.-Chi.	.957	89	133	201	15	349	50
Gagne, Minn.	.971	146	218	389	18	625	66
Gallego, Oak.	.967	94	152	255	14	421	68
Gonzales, Balt.	1.000	1	2	5	0	7	1
Gruber, Tor.	1.000	1	0	2	0	2	0
Guillen, Chi.	.973	155	272	512	22	806	106
Hinzo, Clev.	.750	1	3	0	1	4	0
Hoffman, Cal.	.982	23	18	37	1	56	8
Infante, Tor.	1.000	9	3	9	0	12	2
Keedy, Clev.	1.000	1	0	1	0	1	0
Kunkel, Tex.	.936	59	68	150	15	233	21
Lee, Tor.	.974	28	40	73	3	116	18
Lyons, Chi.	1.000	3	2	1	0	3	0
Manrique, Chi.-Tex.	.964	39	54	81	5	140	24
Newman, Minn.	.940	31	35	59	6	100	16
Palmer, Tex.	1.000	1	1	1	0	2	0
Pecota, K.C.	.988	29	27	54	1	82	8
Pedrique, Det.	.974	12	13	24	1	38	6
Phillips, Oak.	.947	17	11	25	2	38	5

Player, Club	PCT	G	PO	A	E	TC	DP
Polidor, Mil.	.936	21	30	43	5	78	12
Quinones, Sea.	.889	7	5	19	3	27	3
Quirk, Balt.	....	1	0	0	0	0	0
Reed, Bos.	.967	77	107	213	11	331	42
C. Ripken, Balt.	.990	162	276	531	8	815	119
Rivera, Minn.	.958	90	126	240	16	382	59
Romero, Bos.-Mil.	1.000	11	4	16	0	20	3
Schaefer, Chi.	.900	5	4	5	1	10	3
Schofield, Cal.	.983	90	118	276	7	401	56
Schu, Det.	1.000	3	1	1	0	2	1
Scott, Oak.	....	3	0	0	0	0	0
Seitzer, K.C.	1.000	6	5	5	0	10	2
Sheffield, Mil.	.959	70	85	194	12	291	40
Snyder, Clev.	1.000	7	6	14	0	20	2
Spiers, Mil.	.962	89	138	264	16	418	57
Stillwell, K.C.	.970	130	179	334	16	529	65
Strange, Det.	1.000	9	4	8	0	12	1
Tolleson, N.Y.	.975	28	25	54	2	81	10
Trammell, Det.	.985	117	188	396	9	593	71
Velarde, N.Y.	.962	9	8	17	1	26	9
Vizquel, Sea.	.971	143	208	388	18	614	102
Weiss, Oak.	.953	84	106	195	15	316	44
Wellman, K.C.	.989	34	30	56	1	87	15
Zuvella, Clev.	.963	15	10	16	1	27	1

TRIPLE PLAY: C. Ripken, Balt.

SHORTSTOPS WITH TWO OR MORE CLUBS

Player, Club	PCT	G	PO	A	E	TC	DP
Fletcher, Tex.	.960	81	124	190	13	327	45
Fletcher, Chi.	.909	8	9	11	2	22	5
Manrique, Chi.	1.000	2	2	2	0	4	2
Manrique, Tex.	.963	37	52	79	5	136	22
Romero, Bos.	1.000	10	4	13	0	17	3
Romero, Mil.	1.000	1	0	3	0	3	0

OUTFIELDERS

Leader, Club	PCT	G	PO	A	E	TC	DP
SNYDER, CLEV.	.997	125	291	18	1	310	5

Player, Club	PCT	G	PO	A	E	TC	DP
Allred, Clev.*	1.000	5	11	1	0	12	1
Anderson, Balt.*	.985	79	191	3	3	197	0
Anderson, Cal.	1.000	2	1	0	0	1	0
Armas, Cal.	.990	47	97	4	1	102	1
Baines, Chi.-Tex.*	.964	26	54	0	2	56	0
Barfield, Tor.-N.Y.	.973	150	340	20	10	370	4
Batiste, Tor.	1.000	5	7	0	0	7	0
Bean, Det.*	.833	6	5	0	1	6	0
Beane, Oak.	1.000	25	44	0	0	44	0
Bell, Tor.	.963	134	258	4	10	272	1
Belle, Clev.	.979	44	92	3	2	97	1
Bergman, Det.*	....	1	0	0	0	0	0
Bichette, Cal.	.990	40	95	6	1	102	2
Blankenship, Oak.	1.000	25	43	1	0	44	1
Bosley, Tex.*	1.000	8	12	1	0	13	1
Boston, Chi.*	.971	75	134	2	4	140	0
Bradley, Balt.	.990	140	284	4	3	291	0
Bradley, Sea.	1.000	1	2	0	0	2	0
Brady, Cal.*	....	1	0	0	0	0	0
Braggs, Mil.	.972	132	267	6	8	281	1
Brantley, Sea.	1.000	23	50	1	0	51	0
Brett, K.C.	1.000	2	2	0	0	2	0
Briley, Sea.	.958	105	179	5	8	192	1
Brookens, N.Y.	1.000	3	4	1	0	5	0
Brower, N.Y.	.970	25	62	2	2	66	1
Brumley, Det.	1.000	4	1	0	0	1	0
Buhner, Sea.	.966	57	106	6	4	116	3
Burks, Bos.	.977	95	245	7	6	258	3
Bush, Minn.*	.986	109	200	7	3	210	1
Calderon, Chi.	.978	103	217	8	5	230	3
Canseco, Oak.	.976	56	119	5	3	127	2
Carter, Clev.	.978	146	350	6	8	364	3
Castillo, Minn.	.976	67	119	3	3	125	1
Cerone, Bos.	1.000	1	1	0	0	1	0
Clark, Clev.	.964	21	27	0	1	28	0
Cochrane, Sea.	1.000	3	2	0	0	2	0

Player, Club	PCT	G	PO	A	E	TC	DP
Coles, Sea.	.975	89	184	9	5	198	3
Cotto, Sea.	.988	90	153	9	2	164	3
Daugherty, Tex.*	1.000	5	3	1	0	4	1
Davis, Cal.	.979	147	270	5	6	281	0
Davis, Balt.	1.000	3	3	0	0	3	0
Deer, Mil.	.972	125	267	10	8	285	1
Devereaux, Balt.	.983	112	288	1	5	294	0
Ducey, Tor.	1.000	35	56	3	0	59	2
Dwyer, Minn.*	....	1	0	0	0	0	0
Eisenreich, K.C.*	.989	123	273	4	3	280	0
Esasky, Bos.	1.000	1	2	0	0	2	0
Espy, Tex.	.990	133	281	5	3	289	2
Evans, Bos.	.981	77	153	5	3	161	1
Felder, Mil.	.985	93	191	8	3	202	3
Felix, Tor.	.966	107	243	9	9	261	0
Fields, Sea.	....	1	0	0	0	0	0
Finley, Balt.*	.986	76	144	1	2	147	0
Francona, Mil.*	1.000	16	19	1	0	20	0
Gagne, Minn.	....	1	0	0	0	0	0
Gallagher, Chi.	.993	160	390	8	3	401	4
Gladden, Minn.	.966	117	245	8	9	262	3
Gonzalez, Tex.	.964	24	53	0	2	55	0
Greenwell, Bos.	.967	139	220	11	8	239	1
Griffey, Sea.*	.969	127	302	12	10	324	6
Gruber, Tor.	1.000	16	35	2	0	37	1
Hall, N.Y.*	.993	75	141	3	1	145	2
Harper, Minn.	1.000	3	3	0	0	3	0
Heath, Det.	1.000	3	1	0	0	1	0
Heep, Bos.*	.989	75	92	2	1	95	1
D. Henderson, Oak.	.977	149	385	5	9	399	1
R. H'derson, NY-Oak.*	.988	147	335	6	4	345	1
Hengel, Clev.	.909	9	12	1	0	13	0
Hill, Tor.	.964	16	27	0	1	28	0
Howell, Cal.	1.000	4	2	0	0	2	0
Howitt, Oak.	....	1	0	0	0	0	0
Incaviglia, Tex.	.973	125	213	7	6	226	2
Jackson, K.C.	.967	110	224	11	8	243	2
James, Clev.*	.976	37	82	1	2	85	0
Javier, Oak.	.991	107	219	4	2	225	0

OUTFIELDERS—Continued

Player, Club	PCT	G	PO	A	E	TC	DP		Player, Club	PCT	G	PO	A	E	TC	DP
Jefferson, N.Y.-Balt. ...	.988	39	82	3	1	86	1		Sanders, N.Y.★	.969	14	30	1	1	32	0
Jennings, Oak.★	1.000	3	2	0	0	2	0		Schulz, K.C.	1.000	5	6	0	0	6	0
Johnson, Chi.★	.983	45	113	0	2	115	0		Seitzer, K.C.	1.000	3	1	0	0	1	0
Jones, Det.	.986	36	72	0	1	73	0		Sheaffer, Clev.	1.000	1	4	0	0	4	0
Jose, Oak.	.974	19	35	2	1	38	0		Sheridan, Det.	.982	35	52	2	1	55	1
Keedy, Clev.	1.000	3	3	0	0	3	0		Sierra, Tex.	.973	162	313	13	9	335	2
Kelly, N.Y.	.984	137	353	9	6	368	2		Snyder, Clev.	.997	125	291	18	1	310	5
Kingery, Sea.★	1.000	23	70	0	0	70	0		Sosa, Tex.-Chi.	.960	52	94	2	4	100	0
Kittle, Chi.	1.000	5	8	1	0	9	0		Steinbach, Oak.	.963	14	26	0	1	27	0
Komminsk, Clev.	.995	68	181	3	1	185	1		Stone, Tex.-Bos.	1.000	14	8	0	0	8	0
Kunkel, Tex.	.952	30	59	1	3	63	0		Tabler, K.C.	.970	55	89	8	3	100	1
Kutcher, Bos.	.982	57	108	0	2	110	0		Tartabull, K.C.	.982	71	108	3	2	113	0
Larkin, Minn.	1.000	32	61	0	0	61	0		Thurman, K.C.	.949	60	54	2	3	59	0
Lawless, Tor.	1.000	16	17	0	0	17	0		Vaughn, Mil.	.943	24	32	1	2	35	0
Lawton, N.Y.	.818	8	9	0	2	11	0		Venable, Cal.	1.000	13	21	0	0	21	0
Leach, Tex.★	.951	41	57	1	3	61	0		Ward, N.Y.-Det.	.991	57	108	2	1	111	1
Lee, Tor.	....	1	0	0	0	0	0		Washington, Cal.★	.975	100	187	6	5	198	2
Lemon, Det.	.985	111	189	6	3	198	0		White, Cal.	.989	154	430	10	5	445	3
Leonard, Sea.	.982	26	54	2	1	57	0		White, K.C.	....	1	0	0	0	0	0
Lusader, Det.★	.933	33	56	0	4	60	0		Williams, Bos.	1.000	1	0	1	0	1	0
Lynn, Det.★	.992	68	119	5	1	125	0		K. Williams, Det.	.979	87	180	11	4	195	3
Lyons, Chi.	1.000	20	24	0	0	24	0		Wilson, Tor.	.991	54	111	2	1	114	1
Martinez, Chi.	.913	10	21	0	2	23	0		Wilson, K.C.	.977	108	252	2	6	260	0
Mattingly, N.Y.★	1.000	1	2	0	0	2	0		Winters, K.C.	.939	31	45	1	3	49	0
Mazzilli, Tor.	1.000	2	3	0	0	3	0		Young, Clev.	1.000	1	1	0	0	1	0
McDowell, Clev.★	.992	64	124	5	1	130	1		Yount, Mil.	.981	143	361	8	7	376	2
Medina, Clev.★	.500	3	2	0	2	4	0									
Morris, N.Y.★	1.000	5	4	0	0	4	0		**OUTFIELDERS WITH TWO OR MORE CLUBS**							
Moseby, Tor.	.986	120	288	3	4	295	1									
Moses, Minn.★	.988	108	156	3	2	161	0		Player, Club	PCT	G	PO	A	E	TC	DP
Newman, Minn.	1.000	4	8	1	0	9	0		Baines, Chi.★	.981	25	52	0	1	53	0
Orsulak, Balt.★	.985	109	250	10	4	264	2		Baines, Tex.★	.667	1	2	0	1	3	0
Palacios, K.C.	....	1	0	0	0	0	0		Barfield, Tor.	.979	21	43	4	1	48	1
Palmer, Tex.	1.000	1	1	0	0	1	0		Barfield, N.Y.	.972	129	297	16	9	322	3
Parker, Oak.	1.000	1	2	0	0	2	0		R. Henderson, N.Y.★	.993	65	144	3	1	148	0
Pasqua, Chi.★	.993	66	149	3	1	153	2		R. Henderson, Oak.★	.985	82	191	3	3	197	1
Pecota, K.C.	1.000	15	5	0	0	5	0		Jefferson, N.Y.	1.000	7	3	0	0	3	0
Pettis, Det.	.988	119	325	1	4	330	0		Jefferson, Oak.	.988	32	79	3	1	83	1
Phillips, Oak.	1.000	16	14	0	0	14	0		Polonia, Oak.*	.985	55	126	3	2	131	1
Polonia, Oak.-N.Y.★	.984	108	231	9	4	244	2		Polonia, N.Y.*	.982	53	105	6	2	113	1
Puckett, Minn.	.991	157	438	13	4	455	3		Sosa, Tex.	.944	19	33	1	2	36	0
Quintana, Bos.	.926	21	25	0	2	27	0		Sosa, Chi.	.969	33	61	1	2	64	0
Quirk, Balt.	1.000	1	2	0	0	2	0		Stone, Tex.	.000	3	0	0	0	0	0
Reed, Bos.	1.000	1	2	0	0	2	0		Stone, Bos.	1.000	11	8	0	0	8	0
Richie, Det.	.917	13	21	1	2	24	0		Ward, N.Y.	1.000	6	7	0	0	7	0
Robidoux, Chi.	....	1	0	0	0	0	0		Ward, Det.	.990	51	101	2	1	104	1
Romine, Bos.	.982	89	157	9	3	169	4									

CATCHERS

Leader, Club	PCT	G	PO	A	E	TC	DP	PB		Player, Club	PCT	G	PO	A	E	TC	DP	PB
FISK, CHI.	.993	90	419	37	3	459	1	9		Lyons, Chi.	....	1	0	0	0	0	0	0
										Macfarlane, K.C. ..	.996	59	249	17	1	267	4	9
Player, Club	PCT	G	PO	A	E	TC	DP	PB		Magrann, Clev.	1.000	9	30	2	0	32	0	0
Allanson, Clev.	.986	111	570	53	9	632	4	12		Marzano, Bos.	1.000	7	29	4	0	33	0	1
Bando, Oak.	1.000	1	8	0	0	8	0	0		McGuire, Sea.	1.000	14	62	6	0	68	0	2
Beane, Oak.	1.000	1	1	0	0	1	0	0		Melvin, Balt.	.991	75	303	20	3	326	1	1
Boone, K.C.	.991	129	752	64	7	823	6	3		Mercado, Minn.	1.000	19	73	9	0	82	2	1
Borders, Tor.	.980	68	261	27	6	294	1	3		Merullo, Chi.	.973	27	100	10	3	113	0	3
Bradley, Sea.	.993	70	388	25	3	416	4	2		Moreland, Balt.	....	1	0	0	0	0	0	0
Brenly, Tor.	.975	13	37	2	1	40	0	1		Myers, Tor.	1.000	11	46	6	0	52	1	0
Cerone, Bos.	.984	97	578	41	10	629	5	4		Nokes, Det.	.978	51	235	26	6	267	3	7
Cochrane, Sea.	....	2	0	0	0	0	0	0		O'Brien, Mil.	.986	62	314	36	5	355	5	1
Datz, Det.	1.000	6	17	1	0	18	0	0		Olson, Minn.	1.000	3	4	0	0	4	0	0
Dorsett, N.Y.	1.000	8	29	3	0	32	1	0		Orton, Cal.	.988	16	76	7	1	84	3	0
Engle, Mil.	1.000	3	1	0	0	1	0	0		Palacios, K.C.	1.000	13	24	1	0	25	0	0
Fisk, Chi.	.993	90	419	37	3	459	1	9		Parrish, Cal.	.993	122	638	63	5	706	7	12
Gedman, Bos.	.981	91	486	36	10	532	6	6		Petralli, Tex.	.989	49	258	15	3	276	3	7
Geren, N.Y.	.991	60	308	24	3	335	4	3		Quirk, NY-Ok-Bal.	1.000	32	124	14	0	138	3	4
Harper, Minn.	.978	101	456	35	11	502	7	5		Salas, Clev.	1.000	5	3	1	0	4	0	0
Hassey, Oak.	.991	78	421	25	4	450	4	4		Schroeder, Cal.	.991	33	194	27	2	223	2	2
Heath, Det.	.986	117	582	66	9	657	10	2		Sinatro, Det.	1.000	13	42	2	0	44	0	1
Hoiles, Balt.	1.000	3	11	0	0	11	0	0		Skinner, Clev.	.990	79	280	22	3	305	1	5
Karkovice, Chi.	.986	68	299	47	5	351	6	4		Slaught, N.Y.	.991	105	493	44	5	542	8	4
Kreuter, Tex.	.992	85	453	26	4	483	4	21		Stanley, Tex.	.978	25	82	6	2	90	1	4
Kutcher, Bos.	1.000	1	1	0	0	1	0	0		Steinbach, Oak.	.985	103	529	43	9	581	6	9
Laudner, Minn. ...	.991	68	328	16	3	347	3	2		Sundberg, Tex.	.992	73	353	27	3	383	3	10
Lawless, Tor.	1.000	1	1	1	0	2	0	0		Surhoff, Mil.	.985	106	526	51	9	586	6	10

CATCHERS —Continued

Player, Club	PCT	G	PO	A	E	TC	DP	PB
Tettleton, Balt.....	.994	75	297	42	2	341	1	3
Tingley, Cal.	.889	4	7	1	1	9	0	0
Valle, Sea.	.993	93	496	52	4	552	3	6
Virgil, Tor.	1.000	1	1	0	0	1	0	0
Webster, Minn.	1.000	14	32	0	0	32	0	0
Whitt, Tor.	.992	115	550	43	5	598	5	12

CATCHER WITH TWO OR MORE CLUBS

Player, Club	PCT	G	PO	A	E	TC	DP	PB
Quirk, N.Y.	1.000	6	28	4	0	32	2	0
Quirk, Oak.	1.000	2	0	1	0	1	0	0
Quirk, Balt.	1.000	24	96	9	0	105	1	4

PITCHERS

Leader, Club	PCT	G	PO	A	E	TC	DP
TANANA, DET.*	1.000	33	16	41	0	57	2

Player, Club	PCT	G	PO	A	E	TC	DP
Abbott, Cal.*	.914	29	6	26	3	35	1
Acker, Tor.	.917	14	1	10	1	12	0
Aguilera, Minn.	1.000	11	4	13	0	17	2
Akerfelds, Tex.	1.000	6	0	2	0	2	0
Aldrich, Mil.	1.000	16	4	4	0	8	1
Alexander, Det.	.982	33	23	32	1	56	1
Allen, Clev.	1.000	3	2	0	0	2	0
Alvarez, Tex.*	...	1	0	0	0	0	0
Anderson, Minn.*	.975	33	12	27	1	40	5
Appier, K.C.	1.000	6	1	0	0	1	0
Aquino, K.C.	1.000	34	11	23	0	34	3
Arnsberg, Tex.	1.000	16	5	10	0	15	2
Atherton, Clev.	1.000	32	4	1	0	5	0
August, Mil.	.950	31	13	25	2	40	5
Bailes, Clev.*	.923	34	4	20	2	26	2
Ballard, Balt.*	.971	35	13	55	2	70	6
Bankhead, Sea.	1.000	33	14	19	0	33	2
Bannister, K.C.*	1.000	14	3	15	0	18	3
Barfield, Tex.*	1.000	4	1	1	0	2	0
Bautista, Balt.	.929	15	3	10	1	14	0
Beard, Det.	1.000	2	1	1	0	2	0
Berenguer, Minn.	1.000	56	2	11	0	13	1
Birkbeck, Mil.	.750	9	4	5	3	12	0
Bittiger, Chi.	...	2	0	0	0	0	0
Black, Clev.*	.958	33	13	33	2	48	3
Blyleven, Cal.	1.000	33	14	38	0	52	6
Bockus, Det.	...	2	0	0	0	0	0
Boddicker, Bos.	.943	34	14	36	3	53	2
Bolton, Bos.*	1.000	4	1	2	0	3	0
Booker, Minn.	1.000	6	0	5	0	5	1
Bosio, Mil.	.962	33	16	35	2	53	2
Boyd, Bos.	1.000	10	7	10	0	17	1
Brown, Tex.	.966	28	15	41	2	58	6
Buchanan, K.C.*	...	2	0	0	0	0	0
Buice, Tor.	1.000	7	0	3	0	3	0
Burns, Oak.	.857	50	9	9	3	21	1
Cadaret, Oak.-N.Y.*	.938	46	9	21	2	32	2
Campbell, Sea.	1.000	5	2	1	0	3	0
Candelaria, N.Y.*	1.000	10	1	6	0	7	0
Candiotti, Clev.	.986	31	28	41	1	70	1
Cary, N.Y.*	.800	22	4	4	2	10	0
Castillo, Tor.*	1.000	17	2	1	0	3	0
Cerutti, Tor.*	.984	33	16	45	1	62	3
Clark, Cal.	1.000	4	0	2	0	2	0
Clarke, K.C.*	1.000	2	0	1	0	1	0
Clemens, Bos.	1.000	35	17	27	0	44	1
Clutterbuck, Mil.	1.000	14	2	3	0	5	0
Comstock, Sea.*	.800	31	0	4	1	5	0
Cook, Minn.	1.000	15	2	0	0	2	0
Corbett, Cal.*	...	4	0	0	0	0	0
Corsi, Oak.	1.000	22	3	5	0	8	0
Crawford, K.C.	1.000	25	7	13	0	20	1
Crim, Mil.	.947	76	5	13	1	19	2
Cummings, Tor.	.800	5	0	4	1	5	0
Davidson, N.Y.	...	1	0	0	0	0	0
Davis, Oak.	.935	31	12	17	2	31	0
J. Davis, Chi.	1.000	4	0	1	0	1	0
S. Davis, Clev.*	1.000	12	1	3	0	4	0
Dawley, Oak.	1.000	4	0	1	0	1	0
DeJesus, K.C.	1.000	3	0	1	0	1	0
DeLeon, Sea.	...	1	0	0	0	0	0
Dopson, Bos.	.982	29	20	34	1	55	1
Dotson, N.Y.-Chi.	.929	28	5	21	2	28	3
Drummond, Minn.	1.000	8	0	1	0	1	0
DuBois, Det.*	1.000	6	2	5	0	7	0
Dunne, Sea.	.955	15	7	.14	1	22	2
Dyer, Minn.	1.000	16	6	3	0	9	1

Player, Club	PCT	G	PO	A	E	TC	DP
Eckersley, Oak.	1.000	51	4	4	0	8	1
Edwards, Chi.*	1.000	7	0	1	0	1	1
Eiland, N.Y.	1.000	6	2	2	0	4	0
Farr, K.C.	1.000	51	7	4	0	11	0
Farrell, Clev.	.950	31	18	20	2	40	1
Fetters, Cal.	1.000	1	0	1	0	1	0
Filer, Mil.	.909	13	4	16	2	22	4
Finley, Cal.*	.909	29	4	16	2	22	0
Flanagan, Tor.*	1.000	30	8	33	0	41	4
Fossas, Mil.*	.867	51	1	12	2	15	0
Francona, Mil.*	...	1	0	0	0	0	0
Fraser, Cal.	1.000	44	6	14	0	20	1
Gardner, Bos.	.917	22	3	8	1	12	1
Gibson, Det.*	.929	45	6	20	2	28	0
Gladden, Minn.	...	1	0	0	0	0	0
Gleaton, K.C.	1.000	15	0	2	0	2	0
Gonzalez, Minn.	1.000	22	4	2	0	6	0
Gordon, K.C.	1.000	49	15	26	0	41	7
Gossage, N.Y.	1.000	11	2	1	0	3	1
Gozzo, Tor.	1.000	9	3	3	0	6	0
Guante, Tex.	1.000	50	4	5	0	9	0
Gubicza, K.C.	.931	36	18	49	5	72	0
Guetterman, N.Y.*	.909	70	6	24	3	33	4
Guthrie, Minn.*	1.000	13	2	8	0	10	0
Hall, Tex.*	1.000	38	2	8	0	10	1
Hanson, Sea.	1.000	17	8	16	0	24	0
Hardy, Chi.	1.000	5	3	4	0	7	1
Harnisch, Balt.	1.000	18	7	9	0	16	2
Harris, Bos.	.857	15	2	4	1	7	0
Harris, Sea.	1.000	10	2	2	0	4	0
Harvey, Cal.	.889	51	1	7	1	9	0
Havens, Clev.-Det.*	1.000	20	4	7	0	11	3
Hawkins, N.Y.	.933	34	8	20	2	30	1
Henke, Tor.	.929	64	3	10	1	14	0
Henneman, Det.	1.000	60	5	12	0	17	2
Hernandez, Tor.	.750	7	1	2	1	4	0
Hernandez, Det.*	1.000	32	2	4	0	6	1
Hetzel, Bos.	1.000	12	3	1	0	4	1
Hibbard, Chi.*	1.000	23	5	27	0	32	4
Hickey, Balt.*	1.000	51	2	6	0	8	0
Higuera, Mil.*	.938	22	5	10	1	16	0
Hillegas, Chi.	.857	50	5	13	3	21	1
Holman, Sea.	.974	23	9	28	1	38	3
Holman, Det.	1.000	5	0	1	0	1	0
Holton, Balt.	.969	39	22	9	1	32	1
Honeycutt, Oak.*	.952	64	4	16	1	21	1
Hough, Tex.	.969	30	13	18	1	32	3
Hudson, Det.	.923	18	7	5	1	13	1
Huismann, Balt.	1.000	8	3	3	0	6	0
Jackson, Sea.	.875	65	3	11	2	16	0
Jeffcoat, Tex.*	.969	22	13	18	1	32	1
John, N.Y.*	1.000	10	3	21	0	24	0
Johnson, Balt.	1.000	14	6	5	0	11	0
Johnson, Sea.*	.848	22	7	21	5	33	1
Jones, Chi.	.833	22	1	9	2	12	1
Jones, Clev.	1.000	59	3	14	0	17	1
Jones, N.Y.	1.000	11	2	14	0	16	1
Kaiser, Clev.*	...	6	0	0	0	0	0
Key, Tor.*	.965	33	11	44	2	57	2
King, Chi.	.921	25	15	20	3	38	2
Knudson, Mil.	1.000	40	12	10	0	22	2
Krawczyk, Mil.	...	1	0	0	0	0	0
Krueger, Mil.*	1.000	34	5	11	0	16	0
Kunkel, Tex.	1.000	1	1	0	0	1	0
Lamp, Bos.	1.000	42	12	20	0	32	3
Langston, Sea.*	1.000	10	7	6	0	13	1
LaPoint, N.Y.*	1.000	20	2	10	0	12	1
Leach, K.C.	.857	30	5	19	4	28	0
Leibrandt, K.C.*	.941	33	6	26	2	34	0

PITCHERS—Continued

Player, Club	PCT	G	PO	A	E	TC	DP
Leiter, N.Y.-Tor.★	1.000	5	1	2	0	3	0
Long, Chi.	1.000	30	9	15	0	24	0
Lovelace, Cal.★	....	1	0	0	0	0	0
Luecken, K.C.	1.000	19	2	2	0	4	0
McCarthy, Chi.	1.000	31	4	13	0	17	2
McCaskill, Cal.	.951	32	16	42	3	61	5
McClure, Cal.★	1.000	48	2	4	0	6	0
McCullers, N.Y.	.882	52	5	10	2	17	0
McDonald, Balt.	1.000	6	0	2	0	2	0
McMurtry, Tex.	.857	19	1	5	1	7	0
McWilliams, K.C.★	1.000	8	1	4	0	5	0
Mielke, Tex.	.900	43	3	6	1	10	0
Milacki, Balt.	.965	37	27	28	2	57	5
Minton, Cal.	1.000	62	8	20	0	28	0
Mirabella, Mil.★	.750	13	0	6	2	8	0
Mmahat, N.Y.★	.500	4	0	1	1	2	0
Mohorcic, N.Y.	1.000	32	5	10	0	15	2
Monteleone, Cal.	.909	24	1	9	1	11	1
Montgomery, K.C.	.895	63	11	6	2	19	1
Moore, Oak.	.969	35	25	37	2	64	5
Morris, Det.	.975	24	17	22	1	40	3
Moses, Minn.★	....	1	0	0	0	0	0
Moyer, Tex.★	1.000	15	5	14	0	19	2
Murphy, Bos.★	1.000	74	7	15	0	22	1
Musselman, Tor.★	.667	5	0	2	1	3	0
Navarro, Mil.	.917	19	6	16	2	24	0
Nelson, Oak.	1.000	50	6	3	0	9	0
Nichols, Clev.	1.000	15	4	8	0	12	0
Niedenfuer, Sea.	.846	25	6	5	2	13	0
Nielsen, N.Y.	....	2	0	0	0	0	0
Nosek, Det.	....	2	0	0	0	0	0
Nunez, Det.	1.000	27	3	9	0	12	2
Nunez, Tor.	.500	6	1	0	1	2	0
Olin, Clev.	1.000	25	2	5	0	7	0
Oliveras, Minn.	.857	12	0	6	1	7	2
Olson, Balt.	.944	64	5	12	1	18	0
Orosco, Clev.★	1.000	69	6	13	0	19	1
Otto, Oak.★	1.000	1	0	1	0	1	0
Pall, Chi.	.857	53	5	7	2	14	0
Palmer, Det.	.750	5	2	1	1	4	0
Parker, N.Y.	1.000	22	7	20	0	27	1
Patterson, Chi.★	1.000	50	3	4	0	7	1
Pena, Det.	1.000	8	1	5	0	6	1
Perez, Chi.	.966	31	9	19	1	29	3
Peterek, Mil.	1.000	7	3	4	0	7	0
Peterson, Chi.	.500	3	1	0	1	2	0
Petry, Cal.	1.000	19	5	7	0	12	0
Plesac, Mil.★	1.000	52	2	8	0	10	0
Plunk, Oak.-N.Y.	.900	50	2	7	1	10	0
Powell, Sea.★	1.000	43	2	11	0	13	0
Price, Bos.★	1.000	31	2	5	0	7	0
Rawley, Minn.★	.923	27	4	20	2	26	2
Reardon, Minn.	1.000	65	1	3	0	4	0
Reed, Sea.	1.000	52	10	12	0	22	1
Reuss, Chi.-Mil.★	1.000	30	4	14	0	18	1
Righetti, N.Y.★	1.000	55	0	9	0	9	0
Ritz, Det.	1.000	12	4	10	0	14	0
Robinson, Det.	1.000	16	3	6	0	9	1
Rochford, Bos.★	....	4	0	0	0	0	0
Rogers, Tex.★	1.000	73	1	22	0	23	0
Rosenberg, Chi.★	.903	38	8	20	3	31	5
Russell, Tex.	1.000	71	6	14	0	20	3
Ryan, Tex.	.909	32	11	19	3	33	0
Saberhagen, K.C.	.934	36	21	36	4	61	1
Sanchez, Tor.	1.000	4	1	6	0	7	1
Schilling, Balt.	1.000	5	1	0	0	1	0
Schmidt, Balt.	.939	38	18	28	3	49	2
Schooler, Sea.	1.000	67	4	14	0	18	3
Schulze, N.Y.	1.000	2	1	1	0	2	0
Schwabe, Det.	1.000	13	7	8	0	15	1
Seanez, Clev.	....	5	0	0	0	0	0
Searcy, Det.★	.800	8	2	2	1	5	0
Segura, Chi.	1.000	7	0	2	0	2	0
Shields, Minn.	1.000	11	0	3	0	3	1
Skalski, Clev.	1.000	2	0	1	0	1	0
Smith, Bos.	1.000	64	1	1	0	2	0
Smith, Minn.	1.000	32	9	13	0	22	1
Smith, Balt.	1.000	13	1	4	0	5	0
Smithson, Bos.	.966	40	9	19	1	29	3
Snyder, Oak.★	....	2	0	0	0	0	0
Solano, Sea.	1.000	7	1	3	0	4	0
St. Claire, Minn.	1.000	14	4	2	0	6	1
Stanley, Bos.	.952	43	3	17	1	21	0
Stewart, Oak.	.926	36	22	28	4	54	4
Stieb, Tor.	1.000	33	18	29	0	47	1
Stoddard, Clev.	1.000	14	0	4	0	4	0
Stottlemyre, Tor.	.821	27	7	16	5	28	1
Swift, Sea.	.966	37	18	39	2	59	5
Swindell, Clev.★	1.000	28	7	25	0	32	1
Tanana, Det.★	1.000	33	16	41	0	57	2
Tapani, Minn.	1.000	5	3	3	0	6	1
Terrell, N.Y.	1.000	13	6	11	0	17	1
Thigpen, Chi.	1.000	61	7	7	0	14	0
Thurmond, Balt.★	1.000	49	4	10	0	14	0
Tibbs, Balt.	1.000	10	5	5	0	10	0
Toliver, Minn.	1.000	7	3	11	0	14	0
Trout, Sea.★	1.000	19	2	5	0	7	1
Trujillo, Det.	1.000	8	0	5	0	5	0
Tunnell, Minn.	....	10	0	0	0	0	0
Veres, Mil.	1.000	3	0	1	0	1	0
Viola, Minn.★	.917	24	7	26	3	36	1
Ward, Tor.	.963	66	5	21	1	27	2
Wayne, Minn.★	.929	60	2	11	1	14	1
Wegman, Mil.	1.000	11	3	11	0	14	0
Welch, Oak.	.922	33	26	21	4	51	3
Wells, Tor.★	.952	54	9	11	1	21	0
West, Minn.★	.750	10	2	1	1	4	0
Weston, Balt.	1.000	7	0	1	0	1	0
Wickander, Clev.★	....	2	0	0	0	0	0
F. Williams, Det.	1.000	42	3	10	0	13	0
Williamson, Balt.	1.000	65	9	10	0	19	1
Wills, Tor.	1.000	24	5	10	0	15	0
Wilmet, Tex.	1.000	3	0	1	0	1	0
Witt, Cal.	.944	33	18	49	4	71	4
Witt, Tex.	.972	31	13	22	1	36	1
Wojna, Clev.	1.000	9	4	7	0	11	1
Yett, Clev.	1.000	32	9	7	0	16	0
C. Young, Oak.★	1.000	25	2	14	0	16	0
M. Young, Oak.★	1.000	26	3	6	0	9	0
Zavaras, Sea.	.889	10	0	8	1	9	0

PITCHERS WITH TWO OR MORE CLUBS

Player, Club	PCT	G	PO	A	E	TC	DP
Cadaret, Oak.★	1.000	26	3	7	0	10	0
Cadaret, N.Y.★	.909	20	6	14	2	22	2
Dotson, N.Y.	1.000	11	1	5	0	6	1
Dotson, Chi.	.909	17	4	16	2	22	2
Havens, Clev.★	1.000	7	2	4	0	6	2
Havens, Det.★	1.000	13	2	3	0	5	1
Leiter, N.Y.★	1.000	4	1	2	0	3	0
Leiter, Tor.★	.000	1	0	0	0	0	0
Plunk, Oak.	1.000	23	1	3	0	4	0
Plunk, N.Y.	.833	27	1	4	1	6	0
Reuss, Chi.★	1.000	23	3	9	0	12	1
Reuss, Mil.★	1.000	7	1	5	0	6	0

OFFICIAL AMERICAN LEAGUE PITCHING AVERAGES

CLUB PITCHING

Club	W-L	ERA	G	CG	SHO	SV	IP	H	TBF	R	ER	HR	SH	SF	HB	TBB	IBB	SO	WP	BK
Oakland	99-63	3.09	162	17	20	57	1448.1	1287	6026	576	497	103	46	44	28	510	23	930	71	6
California	91-71	3.28	162	32	20	38	1454.1	1384	6068	578	530	113	54	50	29	465	19	897	51	9
Kansas City	92-70	3.55	162	27	13	38	1451.2	1415	6081	635	572	86	50	43	45	455	56	978	56	7
Toronto	89-73	3.58	162	12	12	38	1467.0	1408	6159	651	584	99	61	62	44	478	56	849	58	8
Cleveland	73-89	3.65	162	23	13	38	1453.0	1423	6128	654	589	107	58	48	24	452	36	844	43	17
Milwaukee	81-81	3.80	162	16	8	45	1432.1	1463	6106	679	604	129	49	49	29	457	43	812	35	8
Texas	83-79	3.91	162	26	7	44	1434.1	1279	6161	714	623	119	47	50	42	654	42	1112	65	16
Seattle	73-89	4.00	162	15	10	44	1438.0	1422	6187	728	639	114	56	49	50	560	44	897	65	13
Baltimore	87-75	4.00	162	16	7	44	1448.1	1518	6189	686	644	134	53	42	42	486	43	676	47	13
Boston	83-79	4.01	162	14	7	42	1460.1	1448	6248	735	650	131	51	59	25	548	43	1054	38	13
Chicago	69-92	4.23	161	9	9	46	1422.0	1472	6168	750	668	144	60	56	35	539	23	778	40	18
Minnesota	80-82	4.28	162	19	5	38	1429.1	1495	6180	738	680	139	51	43	35	500	26	851	55	15
New York	74-87	4.50	161	15	8	44	1414.2	1550	6169	792	708	150	45	45	37	521	52	787	46	13
Detroit	59-103	4.53	162	24	4	26	1427.1	1514	6334	816	719	150	52	64	43	652	91	831	42	18
Totals	1133-1133	3.88	1133	265	145	582	20181.0	20078	86204	9732	8707	1718	727	704	483	7277	593	12296	697	168

NOTE—Totals for earned runs for several clubs do not agree with the composite totals for all pitchers of each respective club due to instance in which provisions of Section 10.18 (i) of the Scoring Rules were applied. The following differences are to be noted: Chicago pitchers add to 671, Cleveland pitchers add to 590, Detroit pitchers add to 720, New York pitchers add to 713, Oakland pitchers add to 504, Seattle pitchers add to 641, Texas pitchers add to 624, Toronto pitchers add to 585.

PITCHERS' RECORDS

(Top Fifteen Qualifiers for Earned-Run Average Championship—162 or More Innings)

(* Lefthanded Pitcher)

Pitcher, Club	W	L	ERA	G	GS	CG	SHO	GF	SV	IP	H	R	ER	HR	SH	SF	HB	TBB	IBB	SO	WP	BK
Saberhagen, Bret, K.C.	23	6	2.16	36	35	12	4	0	0	262.1	209	74	63	13	8	6	2	43	6	193	8	1
Finley, Charles, Cal.*	16	9	2.57	29	29	9	1	0	0	199.2	171	64	57	13	7	3	2	82	1	156	4	2
Moore, Michael, Oak.	19	11	2.61	35	35	6	3	0	0	241.2	193	82	70	14	5	6	2	83	1	172	17	0
Blyleven, R. Aalbert, Cal.	17	5	2.73	33	33	8	5	0	0	241.0	225	76	73	14	7	7	8	44	2	131	2	0
McCaskill, Kirk, Cal.	15	10	2.93	32	32	8	4	0	0	212.0	202	73	69	16	5	4	6	59	1	107	7	2
Bosio, Christopher, Mil.	15	10	2.95	33	33	8	2	0	0	234.2	225	90	77	16	5	5	3	48	1	173	4	0
Welch, Robert, Oak.	17	8	3.01	33	33	6	0	0	0	209.2	191	82	70	13	5	5	6	78	3	137	5	2
Gubicza, Mark, K.C.	15	11	3.04	36	36	8	3	0	0	255.0	252	100	86	10	11	8	6	63	2	173	9	0
Cerutti, John, Tor.*	11	11	3.07	33	31	4	1	1	0	205.1	214	90	87	19	6	5	5	53	2	69	4	2
Candiotti, Thomas, Cle.	13	10	3.10	31	31	4	0	0	0	206.0	188	80	71	10	7	6	5	55	2	124	4	8
Clemens, W. Roger, Bos.	17	11	3.13	35	35	8	3	0	0	253.1	215	101	88	20	8	9	8	93	5	230	7	0
Ryan, L. Nolan, Tex.	16	10	3.20	32	32	6	2	0	0	239.1	162	96	85	17	9	9	6	98	3	301	19	1
Stewart, David, Oak.	21	9	3.32	36	36	8	3	0	0	257.2	260	105	95	23	9	9	3	69	0	155	13	0
Bankhead, M. Scott, Sea.	14	6	3.34	33	33	8	2	0	0	210.1	187	84	78	19	9	3	6	63	0	140	7	0
Brown, J. Kevin, Tex.	12	9	3.35	28	28	7	0	0	0	191.0	167	81	71	10	3	6	4	70	2	104	7	2

DEPARTMENTAL LEADERS: W—Saberhagen, K.C., 23; L—Alexander, Det., 18; G—Crim, Mil., 76; GS—Gubicza, K.C., Milacki, Balt. and Stewart, Oak., 36; CG—Saberhagen, K.C., 12; ShO—Blyleven, Cal., 5; GF—Russell, Stewart, Oak., 66; Sv.—Russell, Tex., 38; IP—Saberhagen, K.C., 262.1; H—Stewart, Oak., 260; TBF—Stewart, Oak., 1,081; R—Hawkins, N.Y., 127; ER—Hawkins, N.Y., Witt, Tex. and Witt, Cal., 111; HR—Alexander, Det. and Hough, Tex., 28; SH—Ward, Tor., 12; SF—Witt, Cal., 13; HB—Stieb, Tor., 13; TBB—Witt, Tex., 114; IBB—Henneman, Det., 15; SO—Ryan, Tex., 301; WP—Ryan, Tex., 19; Bk.—Dopson, Bos., 15.

INDIVIDUAL PITCHING
(* Throws Lefthanded)

Pitcher, Club	W	L	ERA	G	GS	CG	SHO	SV	GF	IP	H	TBF	R	ER	HR	SH	SF	HB	TBB	IBB	SO	WP	BK
Abbott, James, Cal.*	12	12	3.92	29	29	4	2	0	0	181.1	190	788	95	79	13	1	5	4	74	3	115	8	2
Acker, James, Tor.	2	1	1.59	14	0	0	0	3	3	28.1	24	116	7	5	1	1	0	1	12	3	24	1	0
Aguilera, Richard, Minn.	3	5	3.21	11	11	3	0	0	0	75.2	71	310	32	27	5	2	1	1	17	2	57	1	0
Akerfelds, Darrel, Tex.	0	1	3.27	6	0	0	0	0	2	11.0	11	50	6	4	1	1	0	0	5	2	9	1	0
Aldrich, Jay, Mil.	1	0	3.81	16	0	0	0	2	8	26.0	24	110	6	11	3	0	1	1	13	3	12	2	1
Alexander, Doyle, Det.	6	18	4.44	33	33	5	1	0	0	223.0	245	977	118	110	28	9	11	5	76	3	95	4	0
Allen, Neil, Clev.	0	0	15.00	1	0	0	0	1	1	3.0	3	17	5	5	1	0	0	0	0	0	0	0	0
Alvarez, Wilson, Tex.*	0	1		1	1	0	0	0	0	0.0	8	5	3	3	2	0	0	0	2	1	0	5	0
Anderson, Allan, Minn.*	17	10	3.80	33	33	4	1	0	0	196.2	214	846	97	83	15	4	5	7	53	1	69	5	1
Appier, R. Kevin, K.C.	1	4	9.14	6	5	0	0	0	0	21.2	34	106	22	22	3	0	3	2	12	1	10	0	1
Aquino, Luis, K.C.	6	8	3.50	34	16	2	0	0	7	141.1	148	591	62	55	6	2	4	4	35	4	68	4	2
Arnsberg, Bradley, Tex.	2	1	4.13	16	1	0	0	0	0	48.0	45	209	27	18	6	1	1	4	13	4	26	6	0
Atherton, Keith, Clev.	0	3	4.15	32	0	0	0	2	14	39.0	48	178	22	18	7	1	0	0	13	4	13	0	0
August, Donald, Mil.	12	12	5.31	31	25	2	0	0	2	142.1	175	648	93	84	17	2	7	3	58	4	51	3	1
Bailes, Scott, Clev.*	5	9	4.28	34	11	1	1	0	9	113.2	116	473	57	54	7	5	5	2	29	4	47	3	0
Ballard, Jeffrey, Balt.*	18	8	3.43	35	35	4	2	0	0	215.1	240	912	95	82	16	10	5	4	57	5	62	3	0
Bankhead, M. Scott, Sea.	14	6	3.34	33	33	3	2	0	0	210.1	187	862	84	78	19	4	8	3	63	1	140	2	0
Bannister, Floyd, K.C.*	4	1	4.66	14	14	2	0	0	0	75.1	87	323	40	39	8	8	2	1	18	0	35	1	0
Barfield, John, Tex.*	0	1	6.17	15	2	0	0	0	4	15.0	15	52	10	8	0	1	0	0	4	0	9	0	0
Bautista, Jose, Balt.	3	4	5.31	15	10	0	0	0	4	78.0	84	325	46	46	17	0	7	1	15	0	30	0	0
Beard, David, Det.	9	2	5.06	2	1	0	0	0	0	5.1	9	27	7	3	2	0	0	1	2	0	1	0	3
Berenguer, Juan, Minn.	9	3	3.48	56	0	0	0	3	17	106.0	96	452	44	41	11	7	5	2	47	2	93	5	0
Birkbeck, Michael, Mil.	0	1	5.44	9	9	1	0	0	0	44.2	57	214	32	27	7	2	3	3	22	2	31	1	3
Bittiger, Jeffrey, Chi.	0	4	6.52	2	1	0	0	0	0	9.2	9	41	7	7	2	0	0	0	6	0	7	0	0
Black, Harry, Clev.*	12	11	3.36	33	32	6	3	0	0	222.1	213	912	95	83	14	9	5	1	52	0	88	13	5
Blyleven, R. Aalbert, Cal.	17	5	2.73	33	33	8	5	0	0	241.0	225	973	76	73	10	7	7	8	44	2	131	2	0
Bockus, Randy, Det.	0	0	5.06	2	0	0	0	0	0	5.1	7	23	3	3	0	0	0	0	2	1	3	0	1
Boddicker, Michael, Bos.	15	11	4.00	34	34	3	2	0	0	211.2	217	912	101	94	19	8	10	10	71	4	145	4	0
Bolton, Thomas, Bos.*	0	0	8.31	6	4	0	0	0	0	17.1	21	83	18	16	1	0	0	0	10	2	9	2	0
Booker, Gregory, Minn.	0	4	4.15	6	0	0	0	0	2	8.2	11	38	4	4	1	0	0	0	10	0	3	2	0
Bosio, Christopher, Mil.	15	10	2.95	33	33	8	2	0	0	234.2	225	969	90	77	16	5	5	6	48	1	173	4	0
Boyd, Dennis, Bos.	3	2	4.42	10	10	0	0	0	0	59.0	57	246	31	29	8	0	2	4	19	0	26	2	2
Brown, J. Kevin, Tex.	12	9	3.35	28	28	7	0	0	0	191.0	167	798	81	71	10	0	6	4	70	2	104	7	2
Buice, DeWayne, Tor.	0	0	16.20	2	0	0	0	0	0	3.1	5	18	6	6	2	0	0	0	3	2	3	0	0
Buchanan, Robert, K.C.*	6	5	5.82	7	2	0	0	0	3	17.0	13	74	12	11	3	7	2	0	13	5	10	4	0
Burns, Todd, Oak.	5	5	2.24	50	0	0	0	8	22	96.1	66	374	24	24	7	3	1	1	28	4	49	4	2
Cadaret, Gregory, Oak-N.Y.*	5	5	4.05	46	13	3	0	0	0	120.0	130	531	62	54	13	0	5	2	57	5	80	6	1
Campbell, Michael, Sea.	3	3	7.29	5	5	0	0	0	0	21.0	28	103	22	17	8	6	2	0	10	1	6	2	8
Candelaria, John, N.Y.*	13	10	5.14	10	6	0	0	0	0	49.0	49	206	28	28	8	1	0	0	12	1	37	2	1
Candiotti, Thomas, Clev.	4	4	3.10	31	31	4	0	0	0	206.0	188	847	80	71	10	2	4	4	55	5	124	4	8
Cary, Charles, N.Y.*	4	1	3.26	22	11	2	0	0	4	99.1	78	404	42	36	13	6	4	1	29	6	79	6	1
Castillo, Antonio, Tor.*	1	1	6.11	17	0	0	0	0	8	17.2	23	86	14	12	2	7	5	6	10	5	10	3	0
Cerutti, John, Tor.*	11	11	3.07	33	31	3	0	0	1	205.1	214	856	90	70	19	2	5	0	53	2	69	4	2
Clark, Terry, Cal.	0	2	4.91	4	2	0	0	0	2	11.0	13	48	8	6	2	0	0	0	3	0	7	2	1
Clarke, Stanley, K.C.*	0	2	15.43	2	2	0	0	0	0	7.0	14	36	12	12	2	0	5	8	4	0	2	1	0
Clemens, W. Roger, Bos.	17	11	3.13	35	35	8	3	0	0	253.1	215	1044	101	88	20	9	4	5	93	5	230	7	0
Clutterbuck, Bryan, Mil.	2	5	4.14	14	11	1	0	0	0	67.1	73	291	39	31	11	0	2	4	16	1	29	2	0
Comstock, Keith, Sea.*	1	2	2.81	31	0	0	0	0	7	25.2	26	111	8	8	2	2	2	0	10	2	22	2	0

Pitcher, Club	W	L	ERA	G	GS	CG	SHO	GF	SV	IP	H	TBF	R	ER	HR	SH	SF	HB	TBB	IBB	SO	WP	BK
Cook, Michael, Minn.	0	1	5.06	15	0	0	0	5	0	21.1	22	102	12	12	1	0	0	1	17	1	15	0	0
Corbett, Sherman, Cal.*	0	2	3.38	4	0	0	0	1	0	5.1	3	20	2	2	1	0	0	0	1	0	3	0	0
Corsi, James, Oak.	1	2	1.88	22	0	0	0	14	0	38.1	26	149	8	8	2	2	2	2	10	3	21	0	0
Crawford, Steve, K.C.	3	1	2.83	25	0	0	0	5	0	54.0	48	224	19	17	2	3	1	1	19	3	33	5	0
Crim, Charles, Mil.	9	7	2.83	76	0	0	0	31	7	117.2	114	487	42	37	7	3	6	3	36	9	59	5	0
Cummings, Steven, Tor.	2	0	3.00	5	2	0	0	2	0	21.0	18	90	9	7	1	0	0	2	11	0	8	0	1
Davidson, Robert, N.Y.*	0	1	18.00	5	0	0	0	1	0	1.0	1	5	2	1	0	0	0	0	1	0	0	0	0
Davis, George, Oak.	19	7	4.36	31	31	1	1	0	0	169.1	187	733	91	82	19	5	7	3	68	1	91	8	1
Davis, John, Chi.	0	1	4.50	4	0	0	0	3	1	6.0	5	25	4	3	3	5	0	0	2	0	5	0	0
Davis, Steven, Clev.*	1	1	8.06	12	2	0	0	2	0	25.2	34	121	24	23	2	0	7	0	14	1	12	2	0
Dawley, William, Oak.	0	0	4.00	4	0	0	0	2	0	9.0	11	41	5	4	2	0	0	1	5	2	3	2	0
DeJesus, Jose, K.C.	0	0	4.50	3	2	0	0	0	0	8.0	7	37	4	4	0	0	0	0	8	0	3	0	0
DeLeon, Luis, Sea.	0	0	2.25	1	1	0	0	0	0	4.0	5	18	1	1	1	0	0	1	1	0	2	0	0
Dopson, John, Bos.	12	8	3.99	29	28	2	0	0	0	169.1	166	727	84	75	14	5	4	2	69	0	95	7	0
Dotson, Richard, N.Y.-Chi.	5	12	4.46	28	26	2	2	2	0	151.1	181	685	84	75	16	6	4	1	58	3	69	3	15
Drummond, Timothy, Minn.	0	4	3.86	8	0	0	0	1	1	16.1	16	75	7	7	4	0	0	2	8	1	9	1	3
DuBois, Brian, Det.*	0	4	1.75	6	0	0	0	0	1	36.0	29	153	14	7	2	0	3	1	17	3	13	0	1
Dunne, Michael, Sea.	2	9	5.27	15	15	2	1	0	0	85.1	104	386	61	50	7	3	5	2	37	1	38	1	1
Dyer, Michael, Minn.	4	7	4.82	16	12	1	1	0	0	71.0	74	317	43	38	2	5	5	2	37	3	37	1	1
Eckersley, Dennis, Oak.	4	0	1.56	51	0	0	0	46	33	57.2	32	206	10	10	5	0	1	2	3	0	55	0	0
Edwards, Wayne, Chi.*	0	0	3.68	7	0	0	0	2	0	7.1	7	30	3	3	1	1	2	0	13	3	9	0	0
Eiland, David, N.Y.	1	3	5.77	6	6	0	0	0	0	34.1	44	152	25	22	5	2	3	1	3	0	11	0	0
Farr, Steven, K.C.	2	5	4.12	51	0	0	0	40	18	63.1	75	279	35	29	5	3	6	1	22	5	56	2	0
Farrell, John, Clev.	9	14	3.63	31	16	7	2	0	0	208.0	196	895	97	84	14	2	3	7	71	4	132	4	0
Fetters, Michael, Cal.	7	3	8.10	13	0	0	0	0	0	3.1	5	16	4	3	1	8	4	0	1	0	4	2	0
Filer, Thomas, Mil.	3	3	3.61	29	13	0	0	0	0	72.1	74	302	30	29	3	0	2	4	23	0	20	1	0
Finley, Charles, Cal.*	16	9	2.57	30	29	9	0	0	0	199.2	171	827	64	57	13	6	3	2	82	4	156	4	2
Flanagan, Michael, Tor.*	8	10	3.93	30	30	3	1	0	0	171.2	186	726	82	75	10	7	8	5	47	2	47	4	3
Fossas, Tony, Mil.*	2	2	3.54	51	0	0	0	16	1	61.0	57	256	27	24	3	8	3	0	22	7	42	0	3
Francona, Terry, Mil.*	0	0	0.00	1	0	0	0	1	0	1.0	2	3	0	0	0	0	0	0	0	0	1	0	0
Fraser, William, Cal.	4	7	3.24	44	0	0	0	21	2	91.2	80	375	33	33	6	4	3	5	23	1	46	5	0
Gardner, Wesley, Bos.	3	7	5.97	22	16	2	0	0	0	86.0	97	393	64	57	8	0	4	4	47	7	81	3	0
Gibson, Paul, Det.*	4	8	4.64	45	13	2	0	16	1	132.0	129	573	71	68	11	3	7	6	57	12	77	4	1
Gladden, C. Daniel, Minn.	0	0	9.00	1	0	0	0	0	0	1.0	2	6	1	1	0	1	0	0	1	0	0	1	1
Gleaton, Jerry, K.C.*	0	0	5.65	15	0	0	0	5	0	14.1	20	66	10	9	2	7	0	1	6	1	9	0	1
Gonzalez, German, Minn.	3	0	4.66	22	0	0	0	9	1	29.0	32	134	17	15	2	0	1	4	11	0	25	2	3
Gordon, Thomas, K.C.	17	9	3.64	49	16	1	1	16	1	163.0	122	677	67	66	10	4	1	1	86	1	153	12	0
Gossage, Richard, N.Y.	1	0	3.77	11	0	0	0	6	1	14.1	14	56	6	6	1	2	2	4	6	1	6	0	0
Gozzo, Mauro, Tor.	0	0	4.83	9	3	0	0	2	0	31.2	35	133	19	17	2	0	4	0	9	0	10	0	0
Guante, Cecilio, Tex.	4	6	3.91	50	0	0	0	19	2	69.0	66	311	35	30	7	1	2	4	36	3	69	1	0
Gubicza, Mark, K.C.	15	11	3.04	36	36	8	2	0	0	255.0	252	1060	100	86	10	11	8	5	63	10	173	9	0
Guetterman, A. Lee, N.Y.*	5	5	2.45	70	8	0	0	38	13	103.0	98	412	31	28	6	4	2	0	26	8	51	1	0
Guthrie, Mark, Minn.*	2	1	4.55	13	17	1	0	0	0	57.1	66	254	32	29	7	2	4	3	21	1	38	3	1
Hall, Andrew, Tex.*	2	3	3.70	38	0	0	0	8	0	58.1	42	242	24	40	3	1	2	1	33	3	45	1	0
Hanson, Erik, Sea.	9	5	3.18	17	17	0	2	0	0	113.1	103	465	44	40	7	2	8	5	32	1	75	3	0
Hardy, John, Chi.	0	0	6.57	5	0	0	0	4	0	12.1	14	56	9	9	0	1	0	1	5	3	4	1	0
Harnisch, Peter, Balt.	5	9	4.62	18	17	2	0	1	0	103.1	97	468	55	53	3	0	3	5	64	3	70	5	1
Harris, Greg A., Bos.	2	2	2.57	15	0	0	0	7	0	28.0	21	118	12	8	1	4	1	5	15	2	25	2	0
Harris, T. Eugene, Cal.	2	4	6.48	10	6	0	0	2	1	33.1	47	152	27	24	3	1	3	0	15	2	14	0	0
Harvey, Bryan, Cal.	3	3	3.44	51	0	0	0	42	25	55.0	36	245	21	21	6	5	2	3	41	7	78	5	0
Havens, Bradley, Clev.-Det.*	1	2	5.00	20	1	0	0	11	0	36.0	46	170	20	20	6	0	4	3	21	4	21	2	0

Pitcher, Club	W	L	ERA	G	GS	CG	SHO	GF	SV	IP	H	TBF	R	ER	HR	SH	SF	HB	TBB	IBB	SO	WP	BK
Hawkins, M. Andrew, N.Y.	15	15	4.80	34	34	5	2	0	0	208.1	238	908	127	111	23	3	3	6	76	6	98	1	2
Henke, Thomas, Tor.	8	3	1.92	64	0	0	0	56	20	89.0	66	356	20	19	5	4	3	2	25	4	116	2	0
Henneman, Michael, Det.	11	4	3.70	60	0	0	0	35	8	90.0	84	401	46	37	4	7	3	5	51	15	69	1	1
Hernandez, F. Xavier, Tor.	1	0	4.76	7	0	0	0	2	0	22.2	25	101	15	12	2	1	2	1	8	0	7	1	0
Hernandez, Guillermo, Det.*	2	2	5.74	32	0	0	0	25	15	31.1	36	141	21	20	4	0	1	1	16	2	30	2	1
Hetzel, Eric, Bos.	2	3	6.26	12	11	0	0	0	0	50.1	61	239	39	35	7	1	2	2	28	0	33	4	0
Hibbard, J. Gregory, Chi.*	6	7	3.21	23	23	0	0	0	0	137.1	142	581	58	49	5	5	4	1	41	2	55	3	2
Hickey, Kevin, Balt.*	2	3	2.92	51	0	0	0	17	0	49.1	38	199	16	16	3	5	5	2	23	4	28	4	1
Higuera, Teodoro, Mil.*	9	6	3.46	22	22	2	1	0	0	135.1	125	567	56	52	9	2	2	4	48	1	91	5	2
Hillegas, Shawn, Chi.	7	11	4.74	50	13	2	0	12	3	119.2	132	533	67	63	12	6	5	3	51	6	76	4	1
Holman, Brian, Sea.	8	10	3.44	23	22	6	2	1	0	159.2	160	688	68	61	9	4	2	6	62	4	82	5	0
Holton, Brian, Balt.	5	7	1.80	5	0	0	0	2	0	10.0	8	50	2	2	0	0	0	0	11	1	9	6	1
Honeycutt, Frederick, Oak.*	2	2	2.35	64	0	0	0	24	12	76.2	56	305	26	20	5	0	6	6	26	3	52	6	5
Hough, Charles, Tex.	10	13	4.35	30	30	5	1	0	0	182.0	168	795	97	88	28	5	5	2	95	3	94	7	0
Hudson, Charles, Det.	1	5	6.35	18	7	0	0	4	1	66.2	75	297	49	47	14	3	1	6	31	3	23	3	2
Huismann, Mark, Balt.	4	0	6.35	8	0	0	0	1	0	11.1	13	48	8	8	0	1	2	2	0	0	13	1	1
Jackson, Michael, Sea.*	4	6	3.17	65	0	0	0	27	7	99.1	81	431	43	35	8	2	5	0	54	6	94	4	0
Jeffcoat, J. Michael, Tex.*	9	6	3.58	22	22	2	2	0	0	130.2	139	559	65	52	7	5	3	6	33	0	64	1	2
John, Thomas, N.Y.*	2	7	5.80	10	10	2	0	0	0	63.2	87	290	45	41	6	3	3	4	22	2	18	3	0
Johnson, David W., Balt.	4	7	4.23	14	14	4	2	0	0	89.1	90	378	44	42	11	3	3	3	28	1	26	0	2
Johnson, Randall, Sea.*	7	9	4.40	22	22	2	1	0	0	131.0	118	572	75	64	11	7	9	1	70	2	104	5	5
Jones, Barry, Chi.	3	2	2.37	22	0	0	0	8	1	30.1	22	121	12	8	2	4	2	0	8	2	17	0	1
Jones, Douglas, Clev.	2	1	2.34	59	0	0	0	53	32	80.2	76	331	25	21	8	8	6	1	13	4	65	0	0
Jones, James, N.Y.	1	10	5.25	11	6	0	0	3	0	48.0	56	211	29	28	7	1	8	2	16	1	25	1	0
Kaiser, Jeffrey, Clev.*	0	2	7.36	6	0	0	0	1	0	3.2	5	22	5	3	1	0	0	0	5	1	4	1	0
Key, James, Tor.*	13	14	3.88	33	33	5	1	0	0	216.0	226	886	99	93	18	9	9	3	27	2	118	1	4
King, Eric, Chi.	9	10	3.35	25	25	1	1	0	0	159.1	144	666	69	60	13	3	4	4	64	3	72	4	0
Knudson, Mark, Mil.	8	5	3.35	40	7	1	0	16	0	123.2	110	499	50	46	15	2	1	3	29	0	47	2	0
Krawczyk, Raymond, Mil.	0	2	13.50	1	0	0	0	0	0	2.0	4	11	3	3	0	1	0	0	1	0	6	0	0
Krueger, William, Mil.*	3	2	3.84	34	5	0	0	8	3	93.2	96	403	43	40	9	9	0	0	33	3	72	1	1
Kunkel, Jeffrey, Tex.	0	1	21.60	1	0	0	0	1	0	1.2	4	12	4	4	1	0	2	0	3	0	0	0	1
Lamp, Dennis, Bos.	4	2	2.32	42	0	0	0	14	0	112.1	96	445	37	29	4	5	0	0	27	6	61	1	2
Langston, Mark, Sea.*	4	5	3.56	10	10	2	1	0	0	73.1	60	297	30	29	3	2	5	4	19	0	60	2	1
LaPoint, David, N.Y.*	6	9	5.62	20	20	0	0	0	0	113.2	146	524	73	71	12	6	4	1	45	9	51	2	1
Leach, Terry, K.C.	5	6	4.15	30	3	0	0	6	0	73.2	78	328	46	34	4	4	3	2	36	4	34	3	2
Leibrandt, Charles, K.C.*	5	11	5.14	33	27	3	0	3	0	161.0	196	712	98	92	13	5	4	1	54	9	73	2	0
Leiter, Alois, N.Y.-Tor.*	1	2	5.67	5	5	0	0	0	0	33.1	32	154	23	21	2	0	2	2	23	4	26	1	1
Lovelace, Vance, Cal.*	0	0	3.92	30	8	1	0	3	0	98.2	101	432	49	43	8	8	1	3	37	0	51	3	0
Luecken, Richard, K.C.	0	0	0.00	1	0	0	0	1	0	1.0	0	4	0	0	0	0	0	0	1	0	1	0	0
McCarthy, Thomas, Chi.	2	1	3.42	19	0	0	0	12	1	23.2	23	104	9	9	3	0	1	0	13	1	16	1	1
McCaskill, Kirk, Cal.	15	10	3.51	31	32	6	0	14	0	66.2	72	285	32	26	3	2	4	2	20	0	27	5	2
McClure, Robert, Cal.*	6	1	2.93	32	0	0	0	0	0	212.0	202	864	73	69	16	3	3	3	59	1	107	7	0
McCullers, Lance, N.Y.	4	3	1.55	48	1	0	0	27	3	52.1	39	205	14	9	2	4	4	1	15	0	36	2	2
McDonald, L. Benard, Balt.	1	0	4.57	52	0	0	0	20	3	84.2	83	373	46	43	9	5	5	3	37	2	82	2	0
McMurtry, J. Craig, Tex.	0	0	8.59	6	0	0	0	4	0	7.1	8	33	7	7	2	0	0	0	4	1	3	1	1
McWilliams, Larry, K.C.*	2	2	7.43	19	0	0	0	0	0	23.0	29	111	21	19	3	2	1	2	13	0	14	2	0
Mielke, Gary, Tex.	1	0	4.13	8	5	1	0	8	0	32.2	31	136	15	15	4	3	2	3	8	1	24	2	1
Milacki, Robert, Balt.	14	12	3.74	37	36	3	2	1	0	243.0	233	1022	105	101	21	7	6	2	88	4	113	1	1

Pitcher, Club	W	L	ERA	G	GS	CG	SHO	GF	SV	IP	H	TBF	R	ER	HR	SH	SF	HB	TBB	IBB	SO	WP	BK
Minton, Gregory, Cal.	4	3	2.20	62	0	0	0	24	8	90.0	76	373	22	22	4	2	1	2	37	7	42	3	0
Mirabella, Paul, Mil.*	0	0	7.63	13	0	0	0	7	0	15.1	18	74	14	13	1	1	3	1	7	3	6	0	0
Mmahat, Kevin, N.Y.*	2	1	12.91	4	2	0	0	1	0	7.2	13	44	12	11	2	0	0	1	8	0	3	0	1
Mohorcic, Dale, N.Y.	2	2	4.99	32	0	0	0	10	0	57.2	65	254	41	32	8	1	2	6	18	3	24	4	0
Monteleone, Richard, Cal.	2	3	3.18	24	0	0	0	8	0	39.2	39	170	15	14	3	5	1	1	13	1	27	2	1
Montgomery, Jeffrey, K.C.	7	3	1.37	63	0	0	0	39	18	92.0	66	363	16	14	4	6	2	2	25	4	94	6	1
Moore, Michael, Oak.	19	11	2.61	35	35	6	3	0	0	241.2	193	976	82	70	14	5	6	2	83	3	172	9	1
Morris, John, Det.	6	14	4.86	24	24	10	0	0	0	170.1	189	743	102	92	23	6	7	0	59	1	115	12	0
Moses, John, Minn.*	0	0	0.00	1	0	0	0	1	0	1.0	0	3	0	0	0	0	0	0	1	0	0	0	1
Moyer, Jamie, Tex.*	4	9	4.86	15	15	1	0	0	0	76.0	84	337	51	41	10	7	4	1	33	0	44	1	1
Murphy, Robert, Bos.*	5	7	2.74	74	0	0	0	27	9	105.0	97	438	38	32	7	7	3	3	41	8	107	6	0
Musselman, Jeffrey, Tor.*	1	0	10.64	5	3	0	0	2	0	11.0	19	58	15	13	2	5	1	0	9	0	3	1	0
Navarro, Jaime, Mil.	7	8	3.12	19	17	1	0	0	0	109.2	119	470	47	38	6	5	2	3	32	0	56	3	0
Nelson, W. Eugene, Oak.	3	5	3.26	50	0	0	0	15	3	80.0	60	335	33	29	5	3	4	2	30	3	70	5	0
Nichols, Rooney, Clev.*	4	6	4.40	15	11	0	0	0	0	71.2	81	315	42	35	9	4	2	2	24	0	42	0	0
Niedenfuer, Thomas, Sea.	0	3	6.69	25	0	0	0	14	0	36.1	46	171	29	27	7	0	0	0	15	5	15	0	0
Nielsen, J. Scott, N.Y.*	1	0	13.50	2	0	0	0	0	0	0.2	2	6	1	1	0	0	0	0	1	0	1	0	1
Nosek, Randall, Det.	0	2	13.50	6	2	0	0	0	0	5.1	7	31	8	8	2	0	0	0	10	0	4	2	1
Nunez, Edwin, Det.	3	4	4.17	27	2	0	0	12	1	54.0	49	238	33	25	6	6	2	0	36	13	41	2	0
Nunez, Jose, Tor.	1	0	2.53	6	2	0	0	3	0	10.2	8	42	3	3	2	1	0	1	2	0	14	2	0
Olin, Steven, Clev.	1	4	3.75	25	1	0	0	1	1	36.0	35	152	16	15	6	6	4	2	14	2	24	2	0
Oliveras, Francisco, Minn.	3	4	4.53	25	8	1	0	0	0	55.2	64	239	28	28	8	1	2	2	15	2	24	9	3
Olson, Gregg W., Balt.	5	2	1.69	64	0	0	0	52	27	85.0	57	356	17	16	5	4	2	0	46	10	90	0	0
Orosco, Jesse, Clev.*	3	4	2.08	69	0	0	0	29	3	78.0	54	312	20	18	7	8	2	1	26	4	79	0	3
Otto, David, Oak.*	0	0	2.70	1	1	0	0	0	0	6.2	6	26	2	2	0	0	0	0	2	0	4	0	0
Pall, Donn, Chi.	4	5	3.31	53	0	0	0	27	6	87.0	90	370	35	32	9	8	2	2	19	3	58	4	1
Palmer, David, Det.	4	5	7.79	5	5	0	0	0	0	17.1	25	85	19	15	2	0	0	2	11	0	12	2	0
Parker, J. Clayton, N.Y.	4	5	3.68	22	17	2	0	1	0	120.0	123	507	53	49	12	6	4	2	31	3	53	3	2
Patterson, Kenneth, Chi.*	6	1	4.52	50	0	0	0	18	2	65.2	64	284	37	33	11	4	4	2	28	3	43	3	1
Pena, Ramon, Det.	0	0	6.00	8	0	0	0	6	0	18.0	26	88	14	12	3	1	2	2	8	3	12	0	0
Perez, Melido, Chi.	11	14	5.01	31	31	2	1	0	0	183.1	187	810	106	102	23	4	4	3	90	3	141	12	5
Peterek, Jeffrey, Mil.	0	2	4.02	7	4	0	0	1	0	31.1	31	137	14	14	3	1	0	2	14	0	16	1	0
Peterson, Adam, Chi.	0	2	15.19	3	2	0	0	0	0	5.1	13	31	9	9	2	0	1	0	2	0	3	0	0
Petry, Daniel, Cal.	3	4	5.47	19	4	0	0	3	0	51.0	53	223	32	31	6	4	3	4	23	0	21	2	0
Plesac, Daniel, Mil.*	3	4	2.35	52	0	0	0	51	33	61.1	47	242	16	16	8	5	3	2	17	1	52	2	0
Plunk, Eric, Oak.-N.Y.	8	6	3.28	50	7	0	0	17	1	104.1	82	445	43	38	6	0	3	2	64	2	85	3	3
Powell, Dennis, Sea.*	2	2	5.00	43	0	0	0	9	2	45.0	49	201	25	24	10	8	5	1	21	1	27	1	0
Price, Joseph, Bos.*	5	5	4.35	31	5	0	0	10	7	70.1	71	305	35	34	8	1	2	0	30	3	52	1	0
Rawley, Shane, Minn.*	5	12	5.21	27	25	2	1	0	0	145.0	167	638	89	84	19	5	5	3	60	3	68	6	3
Reardon, Jeffrey, Minn.	5	4	4.07	65	0	0	0	61	31	73.0	68	297	33	33	3	0	3	0	12	6	46	5	0
Reed, Jerry, Sea.	4	7	3.19	30	12	1	0	14	2	101.2	89	432	44	36	10	3	1	0	43	1	50	6	0
Reuss, Jerry, Chi-Mil.*	9	9	5.13	30	26	1	0	0	0	140.1	171	617	88	80	19	5	5	4	34	2	40	5	0
Righetti, David, N.Y.*	2	6	3.00	55	0	0	0	53	25	69.0	73	300	32	23	3	3	1	1	26	10	51	6	1
Ritz, Kevin, Det.	4	6	4.38	12	12	0	0	0	0	74.0	75	334	47	36	8	7	5	3	44	1	56	6	0
Robinson, Jeffrey M., Det.	4	5	4.73	16	16	1	0	0	0	78.0	76	347	41	41	10	0	1	1	46	3	40	5	0
Rochford, Michael, Bos.*	0	0	6.75	4	0	0	0	4	0	4.0	4	20	3	3	2	0	0	0	4	0	1	1	0
Rogers, Kenneth, Tex.*	3	4	2.93	73	0	0	0	24	2	73.2	60	314	28	24	1	2	3	4	42	9	63	3	1
Rosenberg, Steven, Chi.*	4	13	4.94	38	21	2	0	0	0	142.0	148	617	92	78	14	6	3	1	58	5	77	6	2
Russell, Jeffrey, Tex.	6	4	1.98	71	0	0	0	66	38	72.2	45	278	16	16	4	7	5	9	24	5	77	7	0
Ryan, L. Nolan, Tex.	16	10	3.20	32	32	6	2	0	0	239.1	162	988	96	85	17	9	3	9	98	3	301	19	1
Saberhagen, Bret, K.C.	23	6	2.16	36	35	12	4	0	0	262.1	209	1021	74	63	13	9	6	2	43	6	193	8	1

Pitcher, Club	W	L	ERA	G	GS	CG	SHO	GF	SV	IP	H	TBF	R	ER	HR	SH	SF	HB	TBB	IBB	SO	WP	BK
Sanchez, Alex, Tor.	0	1	10.03	4	3	0	0	0	0	11.2	16	61	13	13	1	0	2	0	4	0	6	1	0
Schilling, Curt, Balt.	0	1	6.23	5	1	0	0	0	0	8.2	10	38	6	6	2	0	0	2	3	0	4	1	1
Schmidt, David, Balt.	10	13	5.69	38	26	2	0	5	0	156.2	196	686	102	99	24	9	7	2	36	2	46	3	1
Schooler, Michael, Sea.	1	7	2.81	67	0	0	0	60	33	77.0	81	329	27	24	2	3	1	2	19	3	69	6	1
Schulze, Donald, N.Y.	1	1	4.09	2	2	0	0	0	0	11.0	12	49	5	5	1	1	2	0	5	0	5	0	0
Schwabe, Michael, Det.	2	4	6.04	13	4	0	0	6	0	44.2	58	209	33	30	6	0	3	3	16	5	13	1	0
Seanez, Rudy, Clev.	0	1	3.60	5	0	0	0	3	0	5.0	1	20	4	2	0	0	0	1	4	1	7	0	0
Searcy, W. Stephen, Det.*	1	1	6.04	8	2	0	0	2	0	22.1	27	100	16	15	3	2	1	0	12	1	11	0	1
Segura, Jose, Chi.	0	0	15.00	7	0	0	0	2	0	6.0	13	34	11	10	0	1	0	2	3	1	4	0	0
Shields, Stephen, Minn.	0	1	7.79	11	1	0	0	0	0	17.1	28	86	18	15	3	2	3	0	6	0	12	2	0
Skalski, Joseph, Clev.	0	2	6.75	6	0	0	0	2	0	6.2	7	33	6	5	2	1	1	0	4	0	3	1	0
Smith, Lee, Bos.	6	1	3.57	64	0	0	0	50	25	70.2	53	290	30	28	6	0	0	2	33	6	96	1	1
Smith, Leroy, Minn.	2	6	3.92	32	2	2	0	9	1	172.1	180	733	82	75	22	2	3	5	51	5	92	5	0
Smith, Michael A., Balt.	0	0	7.65	3	1	0	0	1	0	20.0	25	97	19	17	3	2	0	1	14	2	12	2	1
Smithson, B. Mike, Bos.*	7	14	4.95	40	19	1	0	3	0	143.2	170	632	84	79	21	5	9	10	35	5	61	0	0
Snyder, Brian, Oak.*	0	0	27.00	2	0	0	0	1	0	0.2	6	6	2	2	0	0	0	1	2	0	0	1	0
Solano, Julio, Sea.	0	0	5.59	7	0	0	0	5	0	9.2	19	39	8	6	1	0	0	0	4	0	6	0	0
St. Claire, Randy, Minn.	1	5	5.24	14	0	0	0	8	1	22.1	19	98	13	13	2	2	1	2	10	2	14	1	1
Stanley, Robert, Bos.	5	2	4.88	43	0	0	0	22	4	79.1	102	356	54	43	4	4	4	1	26	3	32	1	0
Stewart, David, Oak.	21	9	3.32	36	36	8	0	0	0	257.2	260	1081	105	95	23	9	10	6	69	2	155	13	1
Stieb, David, Tor.	17	8	3.35	33	33	3	2	0	0	206.2	164	850	83	77	12	10	3	13	76	0	101	3	0
Stoddard, Timothy, Clev.	0	0	2.95	14	0	0	0	7	0	21.1	25	91	9	7	2	1	7	0	7	1	12	1	1
Stottlemyre, Todd, Tor.	7	7	3.88	27	18	0	0	4	0	127.2	137	545	56	55	11	3	3	5	44	4	63	4	0
Swift, William, Sea.	7	3	4.43	37	16	0	0	7	1	130.0	140	551	72	64	7	4	7	2	38	4	45	3	1
Swindell, F. Gregory, Clev.*	13	6	3.37	28	28	5	2	0	0	184.1	170	749	71	69	16	4	10	0	51	1	129	3	0
Tanana, Frank, Det.*	10	14	3.58	33	33	6	1	0	0	223.2	227	955	105	89	21	7	4	8	74	8	147	8	0
Tapani, Kevin, Minn.	2	2	3.86	5	5	0	0	0	0	32.2	34	138	15	14	2	1	1	0	8	0	21	0	0
Terrell, C. Walter, N.Y.	6	5	5.20	13	13	0	0	0	0	83.0	102	362	52	48	9	2	2	2	24	1	30	2	1
Thigpen, Robert, Chi.	2	6	3.76	61	0	0	0	56	34	79.0	62	336	34	33	3	5	5	1	40	3	47	2	0
Thurmond, Mark, Balt.*	2	4	3.90	49	0	0	0	12	4	90.0	102	375	43	39	10	2	2	0	17	0	34	3	1
Tibbs, Jay, Balt.	2	5	2.82	10	8	1	0	0	0	54.1	62	238	17	17	6	1	2	1	20	0	30	3	0
Toliver, Freddie, Minn.	1	3	7.76	7	5	0	0	0	0	29.0	39	140	26	25	5	3	2	0	15	0	11	0	0
Trout, Stephen, Sea.*	4	3	6.60	19	8	0	0	3	0	30.0	43	148	27	22	2	1	1	0	17	2	17	5	0
Trujillo, Michael, Det.	4	1	5.96	8	4	0	0	1	0	25.2	35	122	17	17	3	0	1	0	13	1	13	1	0
Tunnell, B. Lee, Minn.	1	0	6.00	10	1	0	0	4	0	12.0	18	59	8	8	1	3	3	0	6	0	7	0	0
Veres, Randolph, Mil.	0	1	4.32	3	0	0	0	1	0	8.1	9	36	5	4	0	0	0	1	4	0	8	1	0
Viola, Frank, Minn.*	8	12	3.79	24	24	7	0	0	0	175.2	171	731	80	74	17	9	4	3	47	1	138	5	1
Ward, R. Duane, Tor.	4	10	3.77	66	0	0	0	39	15	114.2	94	494	55	48	4	12	11	5	58	11	122	13	0
Wayne, Gary, Minn.*	3	4	3.30	60	0	0	0	21	1	71.0	55	302	28	26	4	4	2	1	36	4	41	7	0
Wegman, William, Mil.	2	6	6.71	11	8	0	0	0	0	51.0	69	240	44	38	6	3	4	6	21	2	27	2	0
Welch, Robert, Oak.	17	8	3.00	33	33	3	1	0	0	209.2	191	884	82	70	13	4	4	0	78	3	137	5	3
Wells, David, Tor.*	7	4	2.40	54	0	0	0	19	2	86.1	66	352	25	23	5	3	2	4	28	7	78	6	0
Weston, Michael, Balt.	2	2	6.41	10	5	0	0	4	0	39.1	48	182	29	28	5	3	5	2	19	1	31	1	3
West, David, Minn.*	1	3	5.54	7	5	0	0	2	0	13.0	18	55	8	8	1	2	0	1	7	0	7	1	0
Wickander, Kevin, Clev.*	0	0	3.38	7	0	0	1	1	0	2.2	6	15	1	1	0	0	0	0	2	1	0	0	0
Williams, Frank, Det.	3	3	3.64	42	0	0	0	16	1	71.2	70	330	37	29	5	5	4	3	46	10	33	0	0
Williamson, Mark, Balt.	10	5	2.93	65	0	0	0	38	9	107.1	105	445	35	35	4	7	3	2	30	9	55	2	0
Wills, Frank, Tor.	3	1	3.66	24	4	0	0	6	0	71.1	65	302	31	29	4	1	0	1	30	1	41	4	0
Wilmet, Paul, Tex.	0	0	15.43	3	0	0	0	2	0	2.1	5	14	4	4	0	0	3	0	2	1	1	1	0
Witt, Michael, Cal.	9	15	4.54	33	33	5	0	0	0	220.0	252	937	119	111	26	10	13	2	48	1	123	0	0
Witt, Robert, Tex.	12	13	5.14	31	31	5	1	0	0	194.1	182	869	123	111	14	11	8	2	114	3	166	7	4

Pitcher, Club	W	L	ERA	G	GS	CG	SHO	GF	SV	IP	H	TBF	R	ER	HR	SH	SF	HB	TBB	IBB	SO	WP	BK
Wojna, Edward, Clev.	0	1	4.09	9	3	0	0	0	0	33.0	31	139	17	15	0	2	1	0	14	1	10	1	1
Yett, Richard, Clev.	5	6	5.00	32	12	1	0	5	0	99.0	111	446	56	55	10	1	2	1	47	1	47	7	0
Young, Curtis, Oak.*	5	9	3.73	25	20	1	1	2	0	111.0	117	495	56	46	10	1	3	3	47	2	55	7	4
Young, Matthew, Oak.*	5	4	6.75	26	4	0	0	0	0	37.1	42	183	31	28	2	4	0	0	31	2	27	4	0
Zavaras, Clinton, Sea.	1	6	5.19	10	10	0	0	0	0	52.0	49	231	33	30	4	4	1	2	30	1	31	5	0

PITCHERS WITH TWO OR MORE CLUBS IN 1989
(Listed Alphabetically, First Club on Top)

Pitcher, Club	W	L	ERA	G	GS	CG	SHO	GF	SV	IP	H	TBF	R	ER	HR	SH	SF	HB	TBB	IBB	SO	WP	BK
Cadaret, Gregory, Oak.*	0	0	2.28	26	0	0	0	6	0	27.2	21	119	9	7	0	0	2	0	19	3	14	1	0
Cadaret, Gregory, N.Y.*	5	5	4.58	20	13	3	1	1	0	92.1	109	412	53	47	7	3	3	1	38	0	66	6	2
Dotson, Richard, N.Y.	2	5	5.57	11	9	1	0	2	0	51.2	69	239	33	32	8	6	2	1	17	0	14	0	3
Dotson, Richard, Chi.	3	7	3.88	17	17	1	0	0	0	99.2	112	446	51	43	8	0	2	0	41	3	55	2	0
Havens, Bradley, Cle.*	0	0	4.05	7	0	0	0	4	0	13.1	18	60	6	6	3	0	2	0	7	2	6	1	0
Havens, Bradley, Det.*	0	2	5.56	13	0	0	0	7	0	22.2	28	110	14	14	3	1	2	3	14	0	15	1	0
Leiter, Alois, N.Y.*	1	2	6.08	4	4	0	0	0	0	26.2	23	123	20	18	1	1	1	0	21	0	22	1	1
Leiter, Alois, Tor.*	0	0	4.05	1	1	0	0	0	0	6.2	9	31	3	3	0	0	2	0	2	0	4	1	0
Plunk, Eric, Oak.	1	7	2.20	23	0	0	0	12	1	28.2	17	113	7	7	1	1	2	0	12	0	24	4	0
Plunk, Eric, N.Y.	7	5	3.69	27	7	0	0	5	0	75.2	65	332	36	31	9	0	4	4	52	2	61	6	3
Reuss, Jerry, Chi.*	8	5	5.06	23	19	1	1	0	0	106.2	135	470	65	60	12	2	6	3	21	1	27	1	0
Reuss, Jerry, Mil.*	1	4	5.35	7	7	0	0	0	0	33.2	36	147	23	20	7	1	0	1	13	1	13	0	0

NOTE—Following pitchers combined to pitch shutout games: Baltimore (4)—Ballard and Williamson; Tibbs and Williamson; Schmidt and Williamson; Milacki, Hickey and Williamson. Boston (3)—Smithson and Stanley; Boddicker and Murphy; Smithson and Murphy. California (8)—Finley and Minton 2; McCaskill, Minton and Harvey; McCaskill and Harvey; Finley, Minton and Harvey; Witt and McClure; Blyleven and Monteleone; Abbott, Minton and Harvey. Chicago (3)—Dotson, Pall and Thigpen; Perez and Thigpen; Hibbard and Thigpen. Cleveland (6)—Swindell, Orosco and Jones 2; Yett, Bailes and Jones; Candiotti and Jones; Candiotti and Orosco; Nichols and Orosco. Detroit (1)—Alexander, Williams and Henneman. Kansas City (4)—Bannister and Farr; Saberhagen and Montgomery; Gubicza, Crawford and Montgomery; Saberhagen, Gleaton and Montgomery. Milwaukee (4)—Clutterbuck and Krueger; Higuera and Aldrich; Krueger, Knudson and Plesac; Bosio, Knudson and Fossas. Minnesota (6)—Anderson, Gonzalez and Wayne; Anderson, Berenguer and Reardon; Viola and St. Claire; Anderson and Reardon; West and Reardon; Guthrie and Reardon. New York (5)—LaPoint and Righetti 2; Hawkins and Righetti; Schulze and Guetterman; Cary, Guetterman, McCullers and Righetti. Oakland (17)—Welch and Eckersley 3; Welch and Plunk 2; Moore and Eckersley; Moore, Honeycutt and Eckersley; Burns, Honeycutt and Plunk; C. Young, Nelson, Eckersley and Honeycutt; Stewart, Burns and Honeycutt; Welch, Nelson and Eckersley; Stewart, Burns and Honeycutt; C. Young, Burns, Honeycutt and Eckersley; Davis, Nelson and Honeycutt; Moore and Burns; Davis and Nelson; Moore, Honeycutt and Nelson. Seattle (5)—Holman and Schooler 2; Bankhead and Schooler; Holman, Reed and Comstock; Swift, Jackson and Schooler. Texas (1)—Witt and Russell. Toronto (7)—Stieb and Wells; Flanagan and Ward; Stieb and Henke; Stieb, Wells and Ward; Gozzo and Ward; Stottlemyre and Henke; Key and Henke.

NATIONAL LEAGUE

Including

Team Reviews of 1989 Season

Team Day-by-Day Scores

1989 Standings, Home-Away Records

1989 Pitching Against Each Club

1989 Official N.L. Batting Averages

1989 Official N.L. Fielding Averages

1989 Official N.L. Pitching Averages

**San Francisco first baseman Will Clark fell just short of a batting title in
1989 while hitting .333 with 23 home runs and 111 RBIs.**

A Giant Step Into the Spotlight

By NICK PETERS

Long before the California earthquake jolted the World Series into a 10-day delay, the San Francisco Giants shook up the National League Western Division with a blend of power, pitching and defense.

Sluggers Kevin Mitchell and Will Clark stole the spotlight with their robust hitting, but the Giants' N.L. pennant in 1989 stemmed more from their remarkable consistency and balance, especially after a rash of injuries to their pitching staff.

The Giants did a lot of things right and everything well in winning 92 games en route to their second division title in three seasons and their first World Series appearance in 27 years.

"We did all the little things you need to do to become a champion," said Manager Roger Craig, who has guided the club to 354 victories in slightly more than four seasons at the helm. He is just 14 victories shy of becoming San Francisco's all-time winningest manager.

As a tribute to their consistency, the Giants didn't lose more than three games in a row last year until Oakland swept them in the World Series. And they never relinquished the lead after taking over sole possession of first place in the N.L. West on June 14. They posted a 17-11 record in September to finish three games ahead of San Diego, which won 29 of its final 39 games.

The team's individual star was Mitchell, who never had more than 22 home runs or 80 runs batted in during any previous season. He led the major leagues with a whopping 47 home runs (11 more than any other player) and 125 RBIs en route to N.L. Most Valuable Player honors.

Mitchell gave a hint of things to come by batting .455 with seven homers and 21 RBIs in spring training. And once the regular season began, he didn't miss a beat. Mitchell had 31 homers and 81 RBIs when the All-Star break rolled around in early July. No National League player had ever hit more home runs before the All-Star break.

"I keep thinking it's never going to stop," Mitchell said at the time. "I'm going to the plate and thinking about hitting the ball hard. I have the confidence to think I can do it every time."

Mitchell's 47 homers were the most by a Giant since Willie Mays belted a club-record 52 in 1965 and his 125 RBIs were the most for the club since Willie McCovey had 126 in 1969.

Almost as impressive was Clark, who sacrificed power for average to stay in contention for the N.L. batting crown until his final at-bat of the season. He finished the year at .333 (second to San Diego's Tony Gwynn) and drove in 111 runs (third best in the league).

Clark, who is regarded by some as the best player in the National League, compiled the highest batting average by a Giant since Mays hit .347 in 1958.

Although Silver Slugger recipients Mitchell and Clark were the individual standouts, the Giants' championship was a team effort in every sense. That was never more evident than in September, when non-regulars fueled a flurry of late-inning comebacks.

Players like Mike Laga, Bill Bathe, Chris Speier and Ernie Camacho—all called up when rosters were expanded the final month— were the heroes of a 9-8 victory at Cincinnati on September 4 after the Giants had fell behind 8-0 after six innings.

In a home game against the Dodgers on September 20, the Giants scored five times in the bottom of the ninth inning to pull out an 8-7 victory. The Giants lashed out seven straight hits in the inning before making their first out.

When Mitchell slowed down some after the All-Star break, Matt Williams returned from Triple A Phoenix (Pacific Coast) and promptly picked up the slack. He hit 11 homers in August and finished the season with 18. Counting the 26 he hit at Phoenix, Williams' total of 44 homers was exceeded only by Mitchell in professional baseball.

The Giants' new Murderers' Row was complemented by a solid supporting cast. Leadoff man Brett Butler led the league with 23 bunt hits and scored 100 runs for the second straight year. Robby Thompson, batting second, led the league with 11 triples.

Utilityman Ernest Riles anchored a strong bench, batting .353 in September to finish with a .278 average. Ken Oberkfell, who arrived on May 10 in a trade with Pittsburgh, finished with a club-record 18 pinch-hits and batted .319 with San Francisco.

Catcher Terry Kennedy, acquired from Baltimore, was the only newcomer to the starting lineup and provided more punch

SCORES OF SAN FRANCISCO GIANTS' 1989 GAMES

APRIL

Date	W/L	Score	Winner	Loser
3—At S.D.	W	5-3	Reuschel	Show
4—At S.D.	W	8-3	Downs	Hurst
5—At S.D.	L	3-4	Whitson	Robinson
7—At Cin.	W	3-4x	Birtsas	Price
9—At Cin.	W	9-1	Reuschel	Jackson
10—Los Ang.	L	4-7	Hershiser	LaCoss
11—Los Ang.	W	8-3	Downs	Leary
12—Los Ang.	W	3-1	Garrelts	Valenzuela
14—Atlanta	W	7-5	Reuschel	Z. Smith
15—Atlanta	W	1-0	Hammaker	P. Smith
16—Atlanta	L	2-7	Smoltz	Downs
16—Atlanta	W	6-1	Price	Puleo
17—San Diego	W	9-0	Garrelts	Rasmussen
18—San Diego	L	2-4	Terrell	Reuschel
19—San Diego	L	3-4	Show	Hammaker
21—At L.A.	L	2-8	Hershiser	Downs
22—At L.A.	W	5-4	Lefferts	Howell
23—At L.A.	L	6-7*	Howell	Hammaker
25—At St. L.	W	4-0	Robinson	Hill
26—At St. L.	L	1-3	DeLeon	Downs
27—At St. L.	L	1-10	Terry	Garrelts
28—At Pitts.	L	0-1	Smiley	Reuschel
29—At Pitts.	W	4-3	LaCoss	Robinson
30—At Pitts.	L	1-11	Walk	Robinson

Won 12, Lost 12

MAY

Date	W/L	Score	Winner	Loser
1—Chicago	L	3-4‡	Pico	LaCoss
2—Chicago	W	4-0	Reuschel	Maddux
3—Pittsburgh	L	3-5	Smiley	Robinson
4—Pittsburgh	W	6-3	Krukow	Kramer
5—St. Louis	L	1-3	DiPino	LaCoss
6—St. Louis	W	9-0	Reuschel	DeLeon
7—St. Louis	W	5-1	Robinson	Terry
9—At Chicago	W	4-2	Krukow	Kilgus
10—At Chicago	W	4-3	LaCoss	Williams
12—At Mon.	W	2-1	Reuschel	Perez
13—At Mon.	L	4-5	Burke	Hammaker
14—At Mon.	L	3-4	Martinez	Krukow
15—At Phila.	L	2-3‡	Bedrosian	Lefferts
16—At Phila.	W	13-5	Hammaker	Maddux
17—At Phila.	W	6-0	Reuschel	Howell
19—At N.Y.	L	2-3*	Myers	Lefferts
20—At N.Y.	W	3-0	Krukow	Ojeda
21—At N.Y.	W	10-6	Hammaker	McDowell
23—Montreal	W	4-2	Reuschel	Holman
24—Montreal	L	0-1	Gross	Robinson
25—Montreal	L	0-2	Martinez	Krukow
26—Phila.	W	6-1	Garrelts	Sebra
27—Phila.	W	6-2	Hammaker	Madrid
28—Phila.	W	8-5	Reuschel	Howell
29—New York	W	3-2	Robinson	Darling
30—New York	W	10-3	Krukow	Cone
31—New York	L	1-3*	Myers	Lefferts

Won 17, Lost 10

JUNE

Date	W/L	Score	Winner	Loser
2—At Atlanta	W	7-6	Reuschel	Glavine
3—At Atlanta	W	4-0	Hammaker	Z. Smith
4—At Atlanta	L	3-6	Lilliquist	Krukow
5—At Cin.	W	11-8	Garrelts	Rijo
6—At Cin.	L	3-4	Franco	LaCoss
6—At Cin.	W	3-2	Reuschel	Dibble
7—At Cin.	L	5-12	Mahler	Hammaker
8—At Cin.	L	2-3	Dibble	LaCoss
9—San Diego	W	12-2	Robinson	Hurst
10—San Diego	W	1-0	Garrelts	Whitson
11—San Diego	W	3-1‡	Gossage	Davis
13—Atlanta	W	3-2	Hammaker	Z. Smith
14—Atlanta	W	10-1	Robinson	Lilliquist
15—Atlanta	L	1-2	Smoltz	Garrelts
16—Cincinnati	L	4-5	Charlton	Gossage
17—Cincinnati	W	8-1	Cook	Jackson
18—Cincinnati	W	2-1	LaCoss	Rijo
19—Houston	W	3-2	Robinson	Knepper
20—Houston	W	4-0	Garrelts	Forsch
21—Houston	W	2-0	Reuschel	Clancy
23—At S.D.	W	8-7	Gossage	Harris
24—At S.D.	W	3-1	Robinson	Terrell
25—At S.D.	L	7-10	Grant	Garrelts
26—At Hous.	W	4-3	Lefferts	Agosto
27—At Hous.	L	5-7	Darwin	Bedrosian
28—At Hous.	L	3-7	Deshaies	Robinson
29—Chicago	W	12-2	Brantley	Kilgus
30—Chicago	L	4-6	Sanderson	Wilson

Won 18, Lost 10

JULY

Date	W/L	Score	Winner	Loser
1—Chicago	L	2-3	Maddux	Reuschel
2—Chicago	W	4-3	Brantley	Sutcliffe
4—At Pitts.	L	3-5	Kramer	Robinson
5—At Pitts.	W	6-4	Wilson	Walk
6—At Pitts.	W	2-1*	Brantley	Smiley
7—At St. L.	L	4-6	DiPino	LaCoss
8—At St. L.	W	8-5	Brantley	Power
9—At St. L.	L	4-6	Magrane	Wilson
13—Pittsburgh	W	3-2§	Brantley	Garcia
14—Pittsburgh	L	4-7	Drabek	Reuschel
15—Pittsburgh	W	8-3	LaCoss	Smiley
16—Pittsburgh	W	3-1	Garrelts	Robinson
17—St. Louis	W	8-4	McCament	Power
18—St. Louis	W	7-3	Robinson	Hill
19—St. Louis	W	7-5	Brantley	Terry
20—At Chicago	L	3-4†	Lancaster	McCament
21—At Chicago	W	4-3	Garrelts	Sutcliffe
22—At Chicago	L	2-5	Sanderson	Hammaker
23—At Chicago	L	5-9	Maddux	Robinson
24—At Atlanta	W	2-0	Reuschel	Smoltz
25—At Atlanta	W	5-4	LaCoss	Lilliquist
26—At Atlanta	L	4-5	Boever	Bedrosian
27—At Atlanta	L	1-10	Glavine	Hammaker
28—At Hous.	W	3-2	Robinson	Clancy
29—At Hous.	L	1-8	Portugal	Reuschel
30—At Hous.	L	2-6	Scott	LaCoss

Won 14, Lost 12

AUGUST

Date	W/L	Score	Winner	Loser
1—At L.A.	W	5-2	Garrelts	Valenzuela
2—At L.A.	L	4-7	Martinez	Wilson
3—At L.A.	L	3-6	Hershiser	Swan
4—Houston	W	4-2	Robinson	Darwin
5—Houston	W	7-0	LaCoss	Scott
6—Houston	L	2-3	Agosto	Lefferts
7—Cincinnati	L	2-10	Robinson	Brantley
8—Cincinnati	L	4-10	Browning	Swan
9—Cincinnati	W	10-1	Robinson	Mahler
10—Cincinnati	W	4-3	Dravecky	Scudder
11—Los Ang.	W	10-2	LaCoss	Belcher
12—Los Ang.	L	1-5	Valenzuela	Knepper
13—Los Ang.	L	2-3‡	Howell	Robinson
15—At Mon.	W	3-2	Dravecky	B. Smith
16—At Mon.	L	2-4	Burke	Bedrosian
17—At Mon.	W	10-5	Knepper	Hesketh
18—At Phila.	W	5-2	Reuschel	Ruffin
19—At Phila.	L	0-1	Mulholland	Downs
20—At Phila.	W	5-2	Brantley	McDowell
21—At N.Y.	L	1-4	Darling	LaCoss
22—At N.Y.	W	5-0	Knepper	Viola
23—At N.Y.	W	5-0	Reuschel	Cone
25—Montreal	L	2-3	Martinez	Downs
26—Montreal	W	8-3	Garrelts	Langston
27—Montreal	L	3-6	B. Smith	LaCoss
28—Phila.	L	1-9	Howell	Reuschel
29—Phila.	L	1-6	Ruffin	Robinson
30—Phila.	W	3-2	Downs	Mulholland

Won 14, Lost 14

SEPTEMBER

Date	W/L	Score	Winner	Loser
1—New York	W	7-1	Garrelts	Darling
2—New York	W	6-2	Reuschel	Viola
3—New York	W	4-0	Robinson	Ojeda
4—At Cin.	W	9-8	Camacho	Franco
5—At Cin.	L	5-6	Armstrong	LaCoss
6—At Atlanta	W	7-2	Garrelts	Lilliquist
7—At Atlanta	W	7-5	Bedrosian	Stanton
8—At Hous.	L	2-5	Portugal	Robinson
9—At Hous.	L	1-4	Scott	Downs
10—At Hous.	W	5-3	Knepper	Rhoden
11—Atlanta	W	3-2	Garrelts	Castillo
12—Atlanta	L	5-6	Aldrich	Bedrosian
13—Cincinnati	W	8-7§	Camacho	Rodriguez
14—Cincinnati	W	4-3‡	Camacho	Charlton
15—San Diego	L	3-5	Rasmussen	Knepper
17—San Diego	W	5-3	Garrelts	Harris
17—San Diego	L	1-6	Hurst	Reuschel
19—Los Ang.	W	3-2	LaCoss	Hershiser
20—Los Ang.	W	8-7	Wilson	Hartley
21—Los Ang.	W	4-3	Downs	Martinez
22—Houston	L	1-3	Portugal	Garrelts
23—Houston	W	3-1	Reuschel	Scott
24—Houston	W	10-2	LaCoss	Clancy
25—At L.A.	L	2-5	Wetteland	Robinson
26—At L.A.	L	1-2	Martinez	Downs
27—At L.A.	L	0-1	Belcher	Garrelts
29—At S.D.	W	7-2	LaCoss	Benes
30—At S.D.	L	5-11	Grant	Reuschel

Won 17, Lost 11

OCTOBER

Date	W/L	Score	Winner	Loser
1—At S.D.	L	0-3	Harris	Downs

Won 0, Lost 1

*10 innings. †11 innings. ‡12 innings. §13 innings. x16 innings.

The ace of San Francisco's 1989 pitching staff was 40-year-old Rick Reuschel, who posted a 17-8 record and 2.94 ERA.

than his .239 average would suggest. And he was credited with deft handling of a surprisingly successful pitching staff.

The staff was led by 40-year-old Rick Reuschel, alias Big Daddy, who posted a 17-8 record and 2.94 earned-run average in 32 starts. The big righthander didn't lose in either May or June and his nine-game winning streak those two months represented a career best. Although his postseason performance was mediocre at best (1-2 record, 7.11 ERA), Reuschel has compiled a 41-22 record in 76 starts with San Francisco since August 1987.

Scott Garrelts· was a pleasant surprise in his first year as a starter. He finished with a 14-5 record, including an eight-game winning streak from July 16 through September 17, and a league-leading 2.28 ERA. Don Robinson won 12 games as the No. 3 man in the rotation.

An assortment of others filled in the remainder of the starting rotation. Mike La-Coss won his last three starts to finish 10-10. Dave Dravecky, making a courageous comeback from cancer surgery, was 2-0. Bob Knepper, a former Houston Astro signed as a free agent, won three games.

Atlee Hammaker contributed six wins and Mike Krukow added four.

Lefthander Craig Lefferts, Garrelts' successor in the bullpen, had a career-high 20 saves. Righthander Steve Bedrosian was acquired June 18 from Philadelphia to shore up the bullpen and finished with 17 saves as a Giant.

Rookie Jeff Brantley (7-0) and Camacho (3-0) were a combined 10-0 in relief for a bullpen that finished the season with a 24-21 record and 3.08 ERA.

Defense was another key to San Francisco's success. Led by an infield of third baseman Williams, shortstop Jose Uribe, second baseman Thompson and first baseman Clark, the Giants established a franchise record by making only 114 errors and tied for the league lead with a .982 fielding percentage.

The Giants weren't perfect in 1989, but their few blemishes couldn't obscure what was an enjoyable season. They filled Candlestick Park with a team-record attendance of 2,059,701 and their motto during most of the season was "I Feel Good." Before long, however, it was changed to an emphatic "I Feel Great."

Mark Davis saved 44 games in 48 opportunities for the Padres last season before signing a free-agent contract with Kansas City in the off-season.

Padres Finish With a Big Rush

By BARRY BLOOM

A name for the highlight film of the San Diego Padres' 1989 season? That's easy. Call it "The Agony and the Ecstasy."

It was the agony of watching the Padres, who had been a popular preseason choice to win the National League West title, struggle for the first 4½ months of the season. It was the ecstasy of the final six weeks, when they played .744 ball (29-10) to crawl back into the race and finish three games behind division-winning San Francisco. It was the agony of watching the Padres eliminate themselves in a heartbreaking extra-inning loss to Cincinnati just before the Giants came to town for the final three games of the season. It was the ecstasy of watching Tony Gwynn edge out San Francisco's Will Clark in head-to-head competition in the season finale to win his third straight N.L. batting crown.

It was a season of mixed blessings. On the one hand, San Diego's 89-73 record became the second-best mark in the club's 21-year history. But on the other hand, the $3.75 million spending spree that brought in first baseman Jack Clark and pitcher Bruce Hurst obviously was not enough to produce a division title.

"I thought it was a good year," said Manager Jack McKeon, whose .563 winning percentage after one-plus seasons on the job is the best in club history. "We made a lot of improvement. We certainly found out about a few guys."

McKeon found out that catcher Benito Santiago and second baseman Roberto Alomar were his top men in the heat of a pennant race. Santiago, who won his second Gold Glove, hit 10 of his 16 home runs —many of them game-deciding blows— after the Padres began to turn it around in mid-August, when their record had dipped to 60-63. Alomar tied for second in the league with 42 stolen bases and hit at a .381 clip after August 22. He finished with a .295 average, providing ample spark at the top of the lineup between leadoff hitter Bip Roberts and Gwynn.

Roberts was a major discovery. A disappointment in 1986 when he failed to make the jump from Class AA Nashua in the Pittsburgh organization to second base in San Diego, Roberts became the offensive catalyst in 1989.

"He made it happen," Gwynn said of the 5-foot-7 Roberts, who batted .301 in 117 games. "For weeks and weeks and weeks,

Versatile Bip Roberts emerged last season as the Padres' catalyst.

he set the table for us."

Roberts also was San Diego's most versatile player, manning three infield and all three outfield positions and performing capably everywhere. McKeon used him primarily in left field and at third base.

McKeon also found out that Ed Whitson, who won a club-high 16 games and paced the starters with a 2.66 earned-run average, has become a solid pitcher and that Mark Davis, the league's Cy Young Award winner, may be the premier left-handed reliever in the league.

Davis had saved 28 games in 1988, his first season in the closer role, and upped that total in 1989 to 44—one shy of the N.L. record set by Bruce Sutter. He recorded saves in his first 17 opportunities and blew only four chances all season. So, despite Gwynn winning his third Gold Glove and hitting .336 to capture his fourth batting title in his sixth full major league season, Davis was clearly the club's most valuable player.

"Without M.D., I don't know where we would have been," said Hurst, who left Boston as a free agent after the '88 season and overcame a slow start to go 15-11 with 10 complete games (tied for first in

SCORES OF SAN DIEGO PADRES' 1989 GAMES

APRIL			Winner	Loser		JULY			Winner	Loser
3—San Fran.	L	3-5	Reuschel	Show		4—At Chicago	L	1-5	Bielecki	Whitson
4—San Fran.	L	3-8	Downs	Hurst		5—At Chicago	L	3-5	Sanderson	Rasmussen
5—San Fran.	W	4-3	Whitson	Robinson		6—At Chicago	L	3-7	Maddux	Terrell
7—At Hous.	W	5-3	Rasmussen	Rhoden		7—At Pitts.	L	0-3	Drabek	Hurst
8—At Hous.	L	2-6	Clancy	Terrell		8—At Pitts.	W	2-0	Whitson	Robinson
9—At Hous.	W	5-4	Show	Scott		9—At Pitts.	W	5-3	Grant	Kramer
10—Atlanta	W	5-2	Hurst	P. Smith		13—Chicago	L	3-7	Maddux	Hurst
11—Atlanta	W	3-2	Whitson	Smoltz		14—Chicago	W	7-4	Whitson	Bielecki
12—Atlanta	L	0-5	Glavine	Rasmussen		15—Chicago	W	3-2	Terrell	Kilgus
13—Atlanta	L	1-4	Lilliquist	Terrell		16—Chicago	W	4-3	Rasmussen	Sutcliffe
14—Cincinnati	W	6-5	Show	Jackson		17—Pittsburgh	L	1-4	Kramer	Harris
15—Cincinnati	L	3-6*	Charlton	Booker		18—Pittsburgh	W	17-4	Hurst	Walk
16—Cincinnati	L	0-5	Mahler	Whitson		19—Pittsburgh	W	9-1	Whitson	Drabek
17—At S.F.	L	0-9	Garrelts	Rasmussen		20—St. Louis	L	1-7	Magrane	Terrell
18—At S.F.	W	4-2	Terrell	Reuschel		21—St. Louis	L	0-5	DeLeon	Rasmussen
19—At S.F.	W	4-3	Show	Hammaker		22—St. Louis	L	2-5	Power	Harris
21—At Atlanta	W	5-3	Hurst	Boever		23—St. Louis	L	2-3	Hill	Hurst
22—At Atlanta	L	1-5	Smoltz	Whitson		25—At Cin.	W	6-2	Whitson	Browning
23—At Atlanta	L	4-9	Glavine	Rasmussen		26—At Cin.	W	5-3	Grant	Franco
24—At Atlanta	W	5-2	Terrell	Lilliquist		27—At Cin.	L	1-6	Leary	Harris
25—At Pitts.	W	1-0	Show	Walk		28—Los Ang.	W	2-1	Hurst	Hershiser
26—At Pitts.	W	3-1	Hurst	Drabek		29—Los Ang.	W	9-4	Schulze	Wetteland
27—At Pitts.	W	8-1	Whitson	Heaton		30—Los Ang.	L	1-10	Belcher	Whitson
28—At Chicago	L	1-3	Kilgus	Rasmussen				**Won 12, Lost 13**		
29—At Chicago	W	5-4	Terrell	Bielecki						
30—At Chicago	L	3-7	Sanderson	Show		AUGUST			Winner	Loser
		Won 14, Lost 12				1—At Atlanta	W	5-2†	Grant	Acker
						2—At Atlanta	W	9-7	Hurst	Eichhorn
MAY			Winner	Loser		3—At Atlanta	W	6-5	Schulze	Smoltz
1—St. Louis	L	0-6	DeLeon	Hurst		4—At L.A.	L	3-6	Wetteland	Whitson
2—St. Louis	W	7-1	Whitson	Terry		5—At L.A.	W	4-2	Harris	Belcher
3—Chicago	L	4-5	Kilgus	Grant		6—At L.A.	L	2-4	Valenzuela	Rasmussen
4—Chicago	L	0-4	Bielecki	Terrell		7—Houston	W	5-2	Hurst	Deshaies
5—Pittsburgh	L	2-4	Walk	Show		8—Houston	L	3-12	Clancy	Schulze
6—Pittsburgh	W	4-2	Hurst	Drabek		9—Houston	W	2-1	Davis	Smith
7—Pittsburgh	W	3-1	Whitson	Heaton		10—Houston	W	13-3	Harris	Forsch
9—At St. L.	L	3-4	Dayley	Harris		11—Atlanta	L	5-6	Eichhorn	Benes
10—At St. L.	L	1-3	Magrane	Terrell		11—Atlanta	W	2-0	Rasmussen	Clary
11—At St. L.	L	5-6	DeLeon	Show		12—Atlanta	L	4-5	Glavine	Hurst
12—At N.Y.	W	4-3‡	Davis	McDowell		15—At N.Y.	L	2-3	Musselman	Whitson
13—At N.Y.	L	3-4†	Myers	Harris		16—At N.Y.	L	2-7	Darling	Rasmussen
14—At N.Y.	L	1-2	McDowell	Leiper		17—At N.Y.	W	6-2	Hurst	Viola
15—At Mon.	W	6-5†	Davis	McGaffigan		18—At Mon.	L	2-5	Perez	Benes
16—At Mon.	W	5-2	Show	Holman		19—At Mon.	L	4-6	Martinez	Harris
17—At Mon.	W	6-5	Grant	Perez		20—At Mon.	W	5-2	Whitson	B. Smith
19—At Phila.	W	8-2	Whitson	McWilliams		21—At Phila.	W	8-2	Rasmussen	Carman
20—At Phila.	W	3-2	Rasmussen	Carman		22—At Phila.	L	2-4	Howell	Grant
21—At Phila.	L	1-3	Sebra	Terrell		23—At Phila.	W	7-3	Benes	Ruffin
23—New York	W	3-2	Show	Gooden		25—New York	W	5-3†	Harris	Myers
24—New York	L	0-3	Darling	Hurst		26—New York	W	9-4	Rasmussen	Darling
25—New York	W	2-1	Whitson	Cone		27—New York	W	13-7	Clements	Mitchell
26—Montreal	L	0-5	B. Smith	Rasmussen		28—Montreal	W	9-4	Benes	Gross
27—Montreal	W	5-0	Terrell	Gardner		29—Montreal	W	2-1	Grant	Thompson
28—Montreal	L	2-10	Langston	Show		30—Montreal	L	1-5	Martinez	Whitson
29—Phila.	W	1-0	Hurst	McWilliams		31—Phila.	W	5-1	Rasmussen	Carman
30—Phila.	W	9-3	Whitson	Carman				**Won 18, Lost 11**		
31—Phila.	W	2-1	Harris	Parrett						
		Won 15, Lost 13				SEPTEMBER			Winner	Loser
						2—Phila.	W	3-2	Hurst	Howell
JUNE			Winner	Loser		3—Phila.	W	9-5	Benes	Cook
2—At Cin.	L	4-9	Browning	Terrell		4—At Atlanta	W	10-9	Clements	Boever
3—At Cin.	L	2-6	Mahler	Show		5—At Atlanta	W	7-5*	Grant	Boever
4—At Cin.	L	3-5	Jackson	Hurst		6—At Hous.	W	3-2	Schiraldi	Deshaies
5—At Hous.	W	10-2	Whitson	Portugal		7—At Hous.	L	1-2	Clancy	Hurst
6—At Hous.	L	7-8*	Smith	Davis		8—Los Ang.	W	1-0	Benes	Hershiser
7—At Hous.	L	2-3	Scott	Terrell		9—Los Ang.	W	3-1	Whitson	Wetteland
8—At Hous.	L	6-7*	Darwin	Davis		10—Los Ang.	L	8-14	Martinez	Rasmussen
9—At S.F.	L	2-12	Robinson	Hurst		11—Houston	W	7-3	Schiraldi	Deshaies
10—At S.F.	L	0-1	Garrelts	Whitson		12—Houston	W	9-0	Hurst	Clancy
11—At S.F.	L	1-3‡	Gossage	Davis		13—Atlanta	W	3-2	Davis	Henry
13—Cincinnati	L	6-9	Jackson	Terrell		14—Atlanta	L	4-13	Glavine	Whitson
14—Cincinnati	W	4-2	Show	Rijo		15—At S.F.	W	5-3	Rasmussen	Knepper
15—Cincinnati	W	1-0‡	Harris	Birtsas		17—At S.F.	L	3-5	Garrelts	Harris
16—Houston	L	1-3	Clancy	Whitson		17—At S.F.	W	6-1	Hurst	Reuschel
17—Houston	W	2-1	Harris	Darwin		19—At Cin.	W	5-1	Benes	Scudder
18—Houston	L	2-5	Scott	Terrell		20—At Cin.	W	3-1*	Harris	Charlton
19—Los Ang.	W	5-1	Show	Hershiser		21—At Cin.	W	11-7	Clements	Franco
20—Los Ang.	W	2-0	Hurst	Belcher		22—At L.A.	L	1-2	Belcher	Hurst
21—Los Ang.	L	2-6	Leary	Whitson		23—At L.A.	W	7-1	Schiraldi	Valenzuela
23—San Fran.	L	7-8	Gossage	Harris		24—At L.A.	W	1-0	Benes	Hershiser
24—San Fran.	L	1-3	Robinson	Terrell		25—Cincinnati	L	3-5	Dibble	Harris
25—San Fran.	W	10-7	Grant	Garrelts		26—Cincinnati	W	3-1	Rasmussen	Armstrong
27—At L.A.	W	5-3x	Clements	Belcher		27—Cincinnati	L	1-2§	Charlton	Schiraldi
28—At L.A.	W	2-1	Whitson	Morgan		29—San Fran.	L	2-7	LaCoss	Benes
29—At L.A.	W	5-3	Rasmussen	Valenzuela		30—San Fran.	W	11-5	Grant	Reuschel
30—At St. L.	L	3-4	Terry	Terrell				**Won 19, Lost 8**		
		Won 10, Lost 16								
						OCTOBER			Winner	Loser
JULY			Winner	Loser		1—San Fran.	W	3-0	Harris	Downs
1—At St. L.	L	3-9	Power	Clements				**Won 1, Lost 0**		
2—At St. L.	W	5-2	Hurst	DeLeon						

*10 innings. †11 innings. ‡12 innings. §13 innings. x17 innings.

After a tough first half, Jack Clark rebounded to hit 26 homers and drive in 94 runs for his new team.

the league) and a career-low 2.69 ERA. "We would have been down near the cellar. That's where we would have been."

The Padres also would have finished lower if not for players acquired in three midseason trades. The first cost San Diego local favorites John Kruk and Randy Ready, but the June 2 deal netted Chris James from Philadelphia. James answered the Padres' need for both a steady left fielder—incumbent Carmelo Martinez sputtered to a .221 finish—and a No. 5 hitter behind Clark, who languished in the cleanup spot for almost half a season. At the All-Star break, Clark was batting .227 with just nine homers and 40 runs batted in. But with James providing punch behind him (11 homers, 46 RBIs for the Padres), the righthanded-hitting slugger finished with 26 homers and 94 RBIs.

"I think we found out a lot about ourselves this year. I know I sure did," said Clark, who was so down on himself during the first half of the season that he openly wondered about retiring. "People keep asking if it was frustrating. But you know, it really wasn't. We were the ones who burned ourselves early. I'm just surprised we jelled as well as we did by the end of

the season."

That happened in no small part because of McKeon's ability to arrange trades. McKeon, who earned the moniker "Trader Jack" as the Padres' general manager for most of the '80s, was the moving force behind two other deals in 1989. After the James trade, he sent pitcher Walt Terrell and his 13 losses to the New York Yankees for Mike Pagliarulo, who solidified third base and shored up the infield defensively alongside veteran shortstop Garry Templeton. Templeton hit .255, his highest average in four years, but Pagliarulo struggled at the plate, hitting .196 with only three homers and 14 RBIs in 50 games.

McKeon made his last swap of the season when he shipped Marvell Wynne and Luis Salazar to the Chicago Cubs on August 31 for pitcher Calvin Schiraldi, outfielder Darrin Jackson and a player to be named. Schiraldi went 3-0 as a starter during the stretch run, while Jackson provided the best defensive play the Padres had seen all season by a center fielder. In addition, he enabled Gwynn to move from center field back to right to put less pressure on a constantly aching left Achilles tendon and his sore legs.

Schiraldi was a welcome addition to a pitching staff that saw only two of its five season-opening starters perform up to expectations. Whitson and Hurst were fine, but Eric Show, Dennis Rasmussen and Terrell fell short. Show was 8-6 in 16 starts when a back injury that required surgery ended his season. Rasmussen struggled until he found a way to keep the ball in the park, and he needed a late rush to even his record at 10-10.

A couple of rookie pitchers made promising contributions in '89. Andy Benes was promoted from Class AAA Las Vegas in August and went 6-3 in 10 starts, including a pair of 1-0 decisions over the Dodgers' Orel Hershiser. Benes was named The Sporting News' N.L. Rookie Pitcher of the Year. Fellow rookie Greg Harris was effective as a spot starter and reliever, winning eight games and saving six. Joining Harris as a solid middle reliever was Mark Grant, who enjoyed the best year of his career (8-2, 3.33 ERA).

Though the Padres made it a close race with their late surge, they certainly left room for improvement. They were inconsistent for too long before finally getting hot.

"You have to strive for consistency," McKeon said. "That's the whole thing. The Giants were consistent. We weren't. That's why they kept playing and we went home."

First baseman Glenn Davis posted his typical power numbers in 1989, hitting 34 homers and driving in 89 runs.

September Fade Ruins Astros

By NEIL HOHLFELD

For the fourth straight season in 1989, the Houston Astros went into September with a legitimate chance of winning the National League Western Division title.

And for the third straight year, the team's shortcomings became obvious in the final month, leaving them again on the sidelines when postseason play began.

But the difference last season was that Houston's biggest liability was starting pitching, usually a strong spot on Astro teams. Aside from righthander Mike Scott, who fought off a recurring hamstring injury to post his first 20-win season, and 15-game winner Jim Deshaies, the Astros' starting rotation was a major disappointment.

Scott, Deshaies and second-half sensation Mark Portugal (7-1 after being called up from the minors in July) were a combined 42-21. The other starters were 15-34, and that statistic more than any other tells why the Astros finished six games off the pace in the N.L. West.

At the crux of the team's pitching problems were righthanders Jim Clancy and Rick Rhoden, who were brought to Houston after Nolan Ryan went to the Texas Rangers as a free agent the previous winter.

Clancy, a former Toronto Blue Jay who was signed as a free agent, posted a 7-14 record with a 5.08 earned-run average in his first National League season. Rhoden, who came from the New York Yankees for three minor-league players, missed almost two months with a back injury and was 2-6 with a 4.28 ERA.

"It's easy to see that if I had had even an average year, we'd have been much better off," Clancy said. "Coming to a new team and having a year like this was hard for me to accept."

But Clancy and Rhoden weren't the only veteran pitchers who had disappointing seasons. Bob Knepper, Houston's all-time winningest lefthander, was 4-10 when he was released in late July.

The bulk of the Astros' pitching success in '89 came from the bullpen. And had the relievers not come through as they did, even Houston's modest third-place finish would not have been possible.

At age 36, Larry Andersen had his best season as a middle reliever. His ERA was under 1.00 the majority of the year and he finished with a 1.54 mark in 87⅔ innings.

Danny Darwin, a former starter, may have been the Astros' most valuable player. He appeared in 68 games and pitched 122 innings, the most of any reliever in the league. His 11 wins and 104 strikeouts set Astro relief-pitching records.

Dave Smith saved 25 games in 29 chances (an 86.2 percent success rate) and has saved 136 games (out of 159) since 1985.

"I think it's pretty obvious that the main reason we were in a position to contend was the bullpen," said Art Howe, who finished 86-76 in his first season as a big-league manager. "They gave us a chance to win all those one-run games."

The Astros played in 59 one-run games, the most in the majors. They were 35-24, with 11 of those one-run wins coming during a 16-1 stretch from May 26-June 11 that jumped the Astros from fifth place to first in the division.

It was during that hot streak that 23-year-old catcher Craig Biggio began to show that he could handle the pressure of playing full-time in the major leagues. He stole 21 bases to become only the seventh catcher since 1900 to swipe 20 or more in a season.

Biggio hit in every spot in the lineup except cleanup and ninth. In the last week of the season, he showed additional versatility by playing five games in the outfield.

Third baseman Ken Caminiti was another pleasant surprise. He played in a team-high 161 games and was second on the club with 72 runs batted in. His aggressive style of play helped inspire the rest of the Astros.

"Sometimes, you're so close to the situation that you don't realize you've become complacent," veteran second baseman Bill Doran said. "It was only after I saw how the kids were playing that I realized we needed some fresh blood."

Doran's own 1989 season was a mystery. On June 25, he was hitting .280 with seven homers and 46 RBIs. But after the All-Star break, he hit just .131 (23 for 176) with no home runs and nine runs batted in. His last home run was on June 29 and he drove in just three runs after July 29.

Doran, however, was not the only Astro regular to suffer through a sub-par season. Center fielder and leadoff man Gerald Young hit just .233 with an on-base percentage of .326. His stolen-base total dropped off dramatically from 1988, from 65 to just 34 last year. Young was caught stealing 25 times and had a paltry 57.6

SCORES OF HOUSTON ASTROS' 1989 GAMES

APRIL			Winner	Loser
4—Atlanta	W	10-3	Scott	Z. Smith
5—Atlanta	L	4-8	Alvarez	Knepper
6—Atlanta	L	2-3	Smoltz	Deshaies
7—San Diego	L	3-5	Rasmussen	Rhoden
8—San Diego	W	6-2	Clancy	Terrell
9—San Diego	L	4-5	Show	Scott
10—Cincinnati	L	3-8	Browning	Knepper
11—Cincinnati	W	5-3	Deshaies	Mahler
12—Cincinnati	L	1-3	Dibble	Smith
13—At L.A.	W	4-2y	Forsch	Searage
14—At L.A.	W	3-2	Scott	Morgan
15—At L.A.	L	1-3	Hershiser	Knepper
16—At L.A.	L	1-2	Leary	Deshaies
18—At Atlanta	L	4-5†	Boever	Smith
19—At Atlanta	L	3-4	Alvarez	Clancy
20—At Atlanta	W	4-3	Darwin	Assenmacher
21—At Cin.	W	7-0	Deshaies	Mahler
22—At Cin.	L	4-5*	Birtsas	Darwin
23—At Cin.	W	5-2	Knepper	Jackson
24—Phila.	L	4-8	Harris	Forsch
25—Phila.	W	4-1	Scott	Howell
26—Phila.	W	6-5	Darwin	Parrett
28—New York	L	3-7	Fernandez	Rhoden
29—New York	L	1-5	Darling	Knepper
30—New York	W	7-6	Scott	Cone
Won 11, Lost 14				

MAY			Winner	Loser
2—At Phila.	W	12-4	Deshaies	Youmans
3—At Mon.	L	5-6†	Burke	Agosto
4—At Mon.	W	5-4*	Darwin	Hesketh
6—At N.Y.	L	1-2	Cone	Clancy
7—At N.Y.	W	5-0	Deshaies	Gooden
8—Montreal	L	1-4	Gross	Knepper
9—Montreal	L	2-4	Martinez	Scott
10—Montreal	L	1-10	B. Smith	Clancy
12—At Chicago	W	3-1	Deshaies	Sutcliffe
13—At Chicago	W	1-0	Knepper	Maddux
14—At Chicago	W	5-1	Scott	Kilgus
16—St. Louis	W	8-7†	Schatzeder	Carpenter
17—St. Louis	W	3-2	Andersen	Magrane
18—St. Louis	L	3-4*	Dayley	Andersen
19—Pittsburgh	W	3-0	Scott	Walk
20—Pittsburgh	W	5-4‡	Agosto	Kipper
21—Pittsburgh	L	5-17	Heaton	Clancy
22—Chicago	L	3-5	Sutcliffe	Deshaies
23—Chicago	L	4-5	Sanderson	Scott
24—Chicago	L	1-3	Maddux	Knepper
26—At Pitts.	W	4-2	Clancy	Heaton
27—At Pitts.	W	5-4‡	Schatzeder	Robinson
28—At Pitts.	W	9-2	Scott	Smiley
29—At St. L.	W	3-2	Knepper	Hill
30—At St. L.	W	8-4	Darwin	Terry
31—At St. L.	W	4-3	Schatzeder	Carpenter
Won 16, Lost 10				

JUNE			Winner	Loser
1—Los Ang.	W	7-2	Deshaies	Morgan
2—Los Ang.	W	1-0	Scott	Valenzuela
3—Los Ang.	W	5-4z	Clancy	Hamilton
4—Los Ang.	W	7-6§	Scott	Pena
5—San Diego	L	2-10	Whitson	Portugal
6—San Diego	W	8-7*	Smith	Davis
7—San Diego	W	3-2	Scott	Terrell
8—San Diego	W	7-6*	Darwin	Davis
9—Atlanta	W	6-5	Agosto	Alvarez
10—Atlanta	W	1-0	Clancy	Smoltz
11—Atlanta	W	10-6	Deshaies	Glavine
13—At L.A.	L	2-3	Valenzuela	Scott
14—At L.A.	L	0-3	Hershiser	Knepper
15—At L.A.	L	1-2†	Wetteland	Agosto
16—At S.D.	W	3-1	Clancy	Whitson
17—At S.D.	L	1-2	Harris	Darwin
18—At S.D.	W	5-2	Scott	Terrell
19—At S.F.	L	2-3	Robinson	Knepper
20—At S.F.	L	0-4	Garrelts	Forsch
21—At S.F.	L	0-2	Reuschel	Clancy
23—At Atlanta	W	5-2	Darwin	Assenmacher
24—At Atlanta	W	5-4	Scott	Alvarez
25—At Atlanta	W	12-6	Schatzeder	Acker
26—San Fran.	L	3-4	Lefferts	Agosto
27—San Fran.	W	7-5	Darwin	Bedrosian
28—San Fran.	W	7-3	Deshaies	Robinson
29—At Mon.	W	8-3	Scott	Gross
30—At Mon.	L	1-6	Martinez	Knepper
Won 18, Lost 10				

JULY			Winner	Loser
1—At Mon.	W	4-1	Andersen	Perez
2—At Mon.	L	2-13	B. Smith	Clancy
3—New York	L	1-3	Cone	Deshaies
4—New York	W	10-3	Scott	Ojeda

JULY			Winner	Loser
5—New York	W	6-5	Darwin	Darling
7—Montreal	L	8-11*	Hesketh	Agosto
8—Montreal	W	3-2	Darwin	McGaffigan
9—Montreal	L	1-6	Langston	Scott
13—At Phila.	L	4-11	Ruffin	Knepper
13—At Phila.	W	3-0	Forsch	Cook
14—At Phila.	L	2-4	Parrett	Andersen
15—At Phila.	W	9-6	Portugal	McWilliams
17—At N.Y.	W	6-0	Deshaies	Darling
17—At N.Y.	W	12-3	Knepper	West
18—At N.Y.	L	0-9	Fernandez	Forsch
19—At N.Y.	L	2-8	Cone	Clancy
21—Phila.	W	4-2	Scott	Mulholland
22—Phila.	W	1-0	Deshaies	Howell
22—Phila.	W	4-3	Darwin	McWilliams
23—Phila.	W	3-2	Forsch	Ruffin
25—Los Ang.	L	0-6	Belcher	Rhoden
26—Los Ang.	W	6-2	Scott	Valenzuela
27—Los Ang.	L	5-7	Morgan	Andersen
28—San Fran.	L	2-3	Robinson	Clancy
29—San Fran.	W	8-1	Portugal	Reuschel
30—San Fran.	W	6-2	Scott	LaCoss
Won 15, Lost 11				

AUGUST			Winner	Loser
1—At Cin.	W	5-0	Rhoden	Leary
2—At Cin.	L	2-5	Robinson	Deshaies
3—At Cin.	L	2-18	Browning	Clancy
4—At S.F.	L	2-4	Robinson	Darwin
5—At S.F.	L	0-7	LaCoss	Scott
6—At S.F.	W	3-2	Agosto	Lefferts
7—At S.D.	L	2-5	Hurst	Deshaies
8—At S.D.	W	12-3	Clancy	Schulze
9—At S.D.	L	1-2	Davis	Smith
10—At S.D.	L	3-13	Harris	Forsch
11—Cincinnati	L	1-6	Leary	Rhoden
12—Cincinnati	W	6-5	Smith	Franco
13—Cincinnati	L	0-5	Browning	Clancy
15—Pittsburgh	W	3-2†	Andersen	Smith
16—Pittsburgh	L	4-5‡	Heaton	Andersen
17—Pittsburgh	W	5-3	Deshaies	Robinson
18—Chicago	W	6-5	Smith	Schiraldi
19—Chicago	W	8-4	Portugal	Maddux
20—Chicago	W	8-4	Darwin	Lancaster
22—At Pitts.	L	1-4	Smiley	Deshaies
23—At Pitts.	L	1-6	Walk	Clancy
24—At Pitts.	L	2-3x	Bair	Agosto
25—St. Louis	L	4-7	DeLeon	Scott
26—St. Louis	L	3-5	Hill	Rhoden
27—St. Louis	W	6-3	Forsch	Power
28—At Chicago	L	1-6	Maddux	Cano
29—At Chicago	L	9-10*	Assenmacher	Smith
30—At Chicago	W	8-4	Scott	Sutcliffe
Won 11, Lost 17				

SEPTEMBER			Winner	Loser
1—At St. L.	W	6-3	Deshaies	Costello
2—At St. L.	L	5-13	Power	Forsch
3—At St. L.	L	3-4	Worrell	Darwin
4—Los Ang.	L	5-7	Morgan	Scott
5—Los Ang.	W	3-2	Agosto	Pena
6—San Diego	L	2-3	Schiraldi	Deshaies
7—San Diego	W	2-1	Clancy	Hurst
8—San Fran.	W	5-2	Portugal	Robinson
9—San Fran.	W	4-1	Scott	Downs
10—San Fran.	L	3-5	Knepper	Rhoden
11—At S.D.	L	3-7	Schiraldi	Deshaies
12—At S.D.	L	0-9	Hurst	Clancy
13—At L.A.	W	3-1	Portugal	Hershiser
14—At L.A.	W	11-3	Scott	Wetteland
15—Cincinnati	W	4-1	Rhoden	Armstrong
16—Cincinnati	W	3-1	Deshaies	Robinson
17—Cincinnati	W	1-0	Portugal	Browning
19—At Atlanta	L	0-3	Eave	Scott
20—At Atlanta	W	7-6x	Andersen	Boever
21—At Atlanta	L	0-3	Greene	Deshaies
22—At S.F.	W	3-1	Portugal	Garrelts
23—At S.F.	L	1-3	Reuschel	Scott
24—At S.F.	L	2-10	LaCoss	Clancy
25—Atlanta	L	3-5	Puleo	Schatzeder
26—Atlanta	W	3-2	Deshaies	Greene
27—Atlanta	L	4-5	Eichhorn	Clancy
29—At Cin.	L	3-4	Dibble	Meyer
30—At Cin.	W	9-2	Cano	Scudder
Won 14, Lost 14				

OCTOBER			Winner	Loser
1—At Cin.	W	2-0	Deshaies	Leary
Won 1, Lost 0				

*10 innings. †11 innings. ‡12 innings. §13 innings. x14 innings. y15 innings. z22 innings.

Veteran Mike Scott fought off recurring hamstring problems to post his first 20-victory campaign.

percent success rate.

The one player the Astros could count on again last season was first baseman Glenn Davis, who hit a career-high 34 homers (the second best single-season total in club history). He has hit at least 30 home runs in three of the last four seasons.

And once again, Davis amassed those numbers without protection in the lineup. Outfielder Kevin Bass was sidelined with a broken leg in late May and didn't return until mid-August. Right fielder Glenn Wilson, acquired in August from Pittsburgh for Billy Hatcher, suffered a hamstring injury shortly after becoming an Astro and wasn't a factor last year.

Though the Astros' team batting average was .239—second worst in the league—they scored the fourth highest number of runs (647) in the N.L. Howe was able to patch together enough offense to support a declining pitching staff and keep Houston in the race until the final month. The Astros were just 1½ games out of first place as late as August 21.

But when it came to crunch time in September, the Astros once again didn't have enough of a kick left. And for the third straight year since winning the N.L. West in 1986, they simply faded away.

Although Orel Hershiser managed only a 15-15 record, his other numbers compared favorably to his Cy Young-winning effort of 1988.

Punchless Dodgers Hit Skids

By GORDON VERRELL

One year after a championship season they hope to always remember, the Los Angeles Dodgers suffered through a campaign they'd just as soon forget.

The Dodgers were futile last season trying to defend their 1988 World Series title. The main problem was hitting, or lack thereof, as the punchless Dodgers were shut out a staggering 17 times, the most of any National League team. Los Angeles was 10th in the N.L. in hitting, last in runs scored, last in runs batted in and next to last in home runs.

And largely because of their inability to hit, the Dodgers were 9½ games out of first place in the National League West by the end of June before stumbling to a 77-83 finish, 14 games behind division champion San Francisco. Los Angeles was officially eliminated 2½ weeks before the end of the season, its earliest ouster in 22 years.

It wasn't supposed to be that way. After the addition of former Baltimore slugger Eddie Murray and former Yankee second baseman Willie Randolph, the Los Angeles offense was expected to improve on the .248 average, 628 runs scored, 99 home runs and 587 RBIs compiled in 1988. Instead, the Dodgers regressed in all four categories, to .240, 554, 89 and 513, respectively.

Manager Tommy Lasorda was bubbling over in the spring at the prospect of Kirk Gibson, Murray and Mike Marshall batting 3-4-5 in the L.A. lineup. But the bubble burst early when Gibson, the 1988 N.L. Most Valuable Player, never fully recovered from the knee injury he sustained in the '88 playoffs. Gibson played in only 71 games because of his injuries while Marshall, who has had persistent back ailments for most of his career, ended up playing in only 105 games.

All told, the Gibson-Murray-Marshall trio started only 35 games together, forcing Lasorda to use 110 different lineups.

Although Murray played in every game and started all but one, he was largely a disappointment. He went more than a month without a homer in one stretch and had only one in 51 games between May 14-July 7. It is no small wonder that the Dodgers went from 3½ games out of first place to 11 behind in that span.

Nevertheless, Murray led the Dodgers with 20 homers and 88 RBIs, impressive stats for most players but not what the Dodgers expected.

Eddie Murray collected 20 homers and 88 RBIs but fell short of Dodger expectations.

The outfield was supposed to consist of Gibson, John Shelby and Marshall, a trio that combined for 222 RBIs in 1988. Those three players combined for only 82 last year, a paltry 12 by Shelby.

Driving in runs was a problem all year. The Dodgers led the league in runners left on base (1,171) and were last in runs batted in. After Murray's 88, the team's next-highest RBI total was 56 by third baseman Jeff Hamilton.

The Dodgers' inability to score runs would have made more sense if the batters were taking their swings against the team's pitchers. The Dodgers led all major league teams with a 2.95 staff earned-run average, the only club with an ERA lower than 3.00.

Even though '88 Cy Young Award winner Orel Hershiser finished with a .500 record (15-15) for the third time in four years, he was hardly to blame. The

SCORES OF LOS ANGELES DODGERS' 1989 GAMES

APRIL

Date		Score	Winner	Loser
3—At Cin.	L	4-6	Jackson	Belcher
5—At Cin.	L	3-4	Browning	Hershiser
6—At Cin.	W	4-1	Leary	Mahler
7—At Atlanta	L	1-6	Glavine	Valenzuela
9—At Atlanta	W	4-2‡	Pena	Eichhorn
10—At S.F.	W	7-4	Hershiser	LaCoss
11—At S.F.	L	3-8	Downs	Leary
12—At S.F.	L	1-3	Garrelts	Valenzuela
13—Houston	L	2-4x	Forsch	Searage
14—Houston	L	2-3	Scott	Morgan
15—Houston	W	3-1	Hershiser	Knepper
16—Houston	W	2-1	Leary	Deshaies
17—Cincinnati	L	2-3*	Dibble	Howell
18—Cincinnati	W	6-0	Belcher	Jackson
19—Cincinnati	W	3-0	Morgan	Browning
21—San Fran.	W	8-2	Hershiser	Downs
22—San Fran.	L	4-5	Lefferts	Howell
23—San Fran.	W	7-6*	Howell	Hammaker
25—At Chicago	W	4-0	Belcher	Sanderson
26—At Chicago	W	3-1	Morgan	Sutcliffe
27—At Chicago	L	0-1	Maddux	Hershiser
28—At St. L.	L	3-6	Heinkel	Leary
29—At St. L.	L	0-1†	Carpenter	Searage
30—At St. L.	L	3-4	Magrane	Belcher

Won 11, Lost 13

MAY

Date		Score	Winner	Loser
1—Pittsburgh	W	1-0	Howell	Drabek
2—Pittsburgh	W	7-0	Hershiser	Heaton
3—St. Louis	W	4-3	Searage	Dayley
4—St. Louis	L	0-12	Hill	Valenzuela
5—Chicago	L	2-4	Sanderson	Belcher
6—Chicago	W	3-0	Morgan	Sutcliffe
7—Chicago	L	2-4	Wilson	Hershiser
12—At Phila.	L	0-3	Howell	Leary
13—At Phila.	L	0-2	McWilliams	Belcher
14—At Phila.	W	9-0	Hershiser	Madrid
15—At N.Y.	W	3-1	Searage	McDowell
17—At N.Y.	W	4-3*	Pena	Aguilera
18—At N.Y.	L	3-5	Gooden	Pena
19—At Mon.	W	8-0	Belcher	Gross
20—At Mon.	W	3-2*	Hershiser	Perez
21—At Mon.	L	1-3	B. Smith	Morgan
23—Phila.	L	1-4	Howell	Valenzuela
24—Phila.	W	4-2	Leary	McWilliams
25—Phila.	W	7-6	Belcher	Carman
26—New York	L	2-8	Ojeda	Hershiser
27—New York	W	2-1	Morgan	Fernandez
28—New York	W	4-3‡	Searage	McDowell
29—Montreal	L	2-3	Perez	Leary
30—Montreal	L	4-5	Hesketh	Howell
31—Montreal	W	9-4	Hershiser	Hesketh

Won 14, Lost 11

JUNE

Date		Score	Winner	Loser
1—At Hous.	L	2-7	Deshaies	Morgan
2—At Hous.	L	0-1	Scott	Valenzuela
3—At Hous.	L	4-5z	Clancy	Hamilton
4—At Hous.	L	6-7§	Scott	Pena
5—At Atlanta	W	7-0	Martinez	P. Smith
5—At Atlanta	W	5-2	Leary	Smoltz
6—At Atlanta	L	0-3	Glavine	Morgan
7—At Atlanta	W	5-4	Valenzuela	Z. Smith
9—Cincinnati	L	0-4	Rijo	Hershiser
10—Cincinnati	L	0-5	Browning	Belcher
11—Cincinnati	W	3-1	Leary	Scudder
12—Cincinnati	W	9-2	Morgan	Mahler
13—Houston	W	3-2	Valenzuela	Scott
14—Houston	W	3-0	Hershiser	Knepper
15—Houston	W	2-1†	Wetteland	Agosto
16—Atlanta	L	1-6	Glavine	Leary
17—Atlanta	L	1-2	P. Smith	Morgan
18—Atlanta	W	5-3	Valenzuela	Z. Smith
19—At S.D.	L	1-5	Show	Hershiser
20—At S.D.	L	0-2	Hurst	Belcher
21—At S.D.	W	6-2	Leary	Whitson
23—At Cin.	L	1-3	Rijo	Morgan
24—At Cin.	W	10-3	Valenzuela	Birtsas
25—At Cin.	W	7-0	Hershiser	Browning
26—At Cin.	L	3-5	Dibble	Belcher
27—San Diego	L	3-5y	Clements	Belcher
28—San Diego	L	1-2	Whitson	Morgan
29—San Diego	L	3-5	Rasmussen	Valenzuela
30—Pittsburgh	L	3-4	Walk	Hershiser

Won 12, Lost 17

JULY

Date		Score	Winner	Loser
1—Pittsburgh	W	1-0	Belcher	Smiley
2—Pittsburgh	W	3-2	Wetteland	Drabek
3—Pittsburgh	L	2-4	Robinson	Morgan
4—At St. L.	L	1-2	Magrane	Valenzuela
5—At St. L.	L	2-3	Costello	Wetteland
6—At St. L.	L	2-14	Hill	Leary
7—At Chicago	L	4-6	Sutcliffe	Wetteland
8—At Chicago	W	8-2	Morgan	Pico
9—At Chicago	L	4-11	Bielecki	Valenzuela
13—St. Louis	W	3-2	Hershiser	Hill
14—St. Louis	L	2-7	Terry	Morgan
15—St. Louis	L	0-2	Magrane	Valenzuela
16—St. Louis	W	3-2	Belcher	DeLeon
17—Chicago	L	3-6	Lancaster	Leary
18—Chicago	W	4-1	Hershiser	Maddux
19—Chicago	L	0-4	Bielecki	Morgan
21—At Pitts.	L	1-4	Smiley	Belcher
21—At Pitts.	W	7-3	Valenzuela	Heaton
22—At Pitts.	W	8-4	Martinez	Robinson
23—At Pitts.	W	4-3	Hershiser	Kramer
23—At Pitts.	L	1-2*	Kipper	Crews
24—At Pitts.	L	4-7	Walk	Morgan
25—At Hous.	W	6-0	Belcher	Rhoden
26—At Hous.	L	2-6	Scott	Valenzuela
27—At Hous.	W	7-5	Morgan	Andersen
28—At S.D.	L	1-2	Hurst	Hershiser
29—At S.D.	L	4-9	Schulze	Wetteland
30—At S.D.	W	10-1	Belcher	Whitson

Won 12, Lost 16

AUGUST

Date		Score	Winner	Loser
1—San Fran.	L	2-5	Garrelts	Valenzuela
2—San Fran.	W	7-4	Martinez	Wilson
3—San Fran.	W	6-3	Hershiser	Swan
4—San Diego	W	6-3	Wetteland	Whitson
5—San Diego	L	2-4	Harris	Belcher
6—San Diego	W	4-2	Valenzuela	Rasmussen
7—Atlanta	L	0-1	Glavine	Martinez
8—Atlanta	W	10-2	Hershiser	Smoltz
9—Atlanta	L	3-6	P. Smith	Wetteland
11—At S.F.	L	2-10	LaCoss	Belcher
12—At S.F.	W	5-1	Valenzuela	Knepper
13—At S.F.	W	3-2‡	Howell	Robinson
15—At Phila.	L	6-7	Parrett	Searage
16—At Phila.	L	2-6	Carman	Belcher
17—At Phila.	W	10-4	Valenzuela	Howell
18—At N.Y.	L	2-3	Cone	Hershiser
19—At N.Y.	L	1-4	Ojeda	Wetteland
20—At N.Y.	W	5-4	Pena	Aase
21—At Mon.	W	6-1	Belcher	Langston
22—At Mon.	L	2-4	Gross	Valenzuela
23—At Mon.	W	1-0z	Wetteland	Martinez
25—Phila.	L	2-3	Mulholland	Martinez
26—Phila.	W	4-0	Belcher	Cook
27—Phila.	W	8-1	Valenzuela	Carman
28—New York	L	0-1	Viola	Hershiser
29—New York	L	1-2	Cone	Wetteland
30—New York	L	3-9	Fernandez	Martinez

Won 13, Lost 14

SEPTEMBER

Date		Score	Winner	Loser
1—Montreal	W	2-0	Belcher	Langston
2—Montreal	W	4-3	Howell	Burke
3—Montreal	L	0-4	Gross	Hershiser
4—At Hous.	W	7-5	Morgan	Scott
5—At Hous.	L	2-3	Agosto	Pena
6—At Cin.	L	5-9	Rodriguez	Searage
7—At Cin.	W	8-2	Valenzuela	Browning
8—At S.D.	L	0-1	Benes	Hershiser
9—At S.D.	L	1-3	Whitson	Wetteland
10—At S.D.	W	14-8	Martinez	Rasmussen
11—Cincinnati	W	8-2	Belcher	Robinson
12—Cincinnati	W	5-4	Howell	Dibble
13—Houston	L	1-3	Portugal	Hershiser
14—Houston	L	3-11	Scott	Wetteland
15—Atlanta	W	5-0	Martinez	Greene
16—Atlanta	W	1-0	Belcher	Boever
17—Atlanta	W	4-3†	Pena	Boever
19—At S.F.	L	2-3	LaCoss	Hershiser
20—At S.F.	L	7-8	Wilson	Hartley
21—At S.F.	L	3-4	Downs	Martinez
22—San Diego	W	2-1	Belcher	Hurst
23—San Diego	L	1-7	Schiraldi	Valenzuela
24—San Diego	L	0-1	Benes	Hershiser
25—San Fran.	W	5-2	Wetteland	Robinson
26—San Fran.	W	2-1	Martinez	Downs
27—San Fran.	W	1-0	Belcher	Garrelts

Won 14, Lost 12

OCTOBER

Date		Score	Winner	Loser
1—At Atlanta	W	3-1‡	Hershiser	Aldrich

Won 1, Lost 0

*10 innings. †11 innings. ‡12 innings. §13 innings. x15 innings. y17 innings. z22 innings.

Righthander Tim Belcher enjoyed an outstanding season, winning 15 games, striking out 200 batters and leading the N.L. with eight shutouts.

Dodgers scored only 17 runs in his 15 defeats and—in a seven-game Hershiser losing streak between August 18 and September 24—the team scored just six runs in eight starts. The Dodgers were shut out four times.

"I really feel I'm pitching as well as I did last year," Hershiser said during the streak. His 2.31 ERA ranked second in the National League in 1989 and his final numbers in games pitched (35), innings pitched (256.2), earned runs allowed (66), walks (77) and strikeouts (178) were amazingly similar to those he had the year before.

Righthander Tim Belcher was just the opposite of Hershiser, winning his last seven decisions to match Hershiser as the Dodgers' top winner with 15. Belcher also struck out a team-high 200, compiled a 2.82 ERA and led the major leagues with eight shutouts.

The Dodgers also saw the emergence of two young righthanders: Ramon Martinez (6-4), who hurled two shutouts and struck out 89 in 98⅔ innings, and John Wetteland, who fanned 96 in 102⅔ innings and was impressive despite a 5-8 record.

The team was also helped by the comeback of Fernando Valenzuela, who was lost for virtually all of the second half of 1988 due to shoulder problems. The veteran lefthander lost his first five decisions of 1989 before winning his next four and finishing at 10-13, including three complete games.

In the bullpen, closer Jay Howell established a franchise record with 28 saves and had a span of 28 appearances from June 4 through September 4 in which gave up just two runs in 41⅓ innings, saved 15 games and won two others.

Alejandro Pena and Mike Morgan provided strong middle relief after the latter was dropped from the starting rotation in late July. Morgan led the league in ERA for much of the first half of the season—he was at 1.79 after a win in Chicago on July 8—before losing his next three starts.

The Dodgers ended their disappointing season with two rainouts in a scheduled three-game series in Atlanta. As Executive Vice President Fred Claire surveyed the handful of rain-soaked fans in attendance and the Dodgers' rookie-filled lineup for the final game of the season, he remarked, "I'd have to say this is certainly different from our last game in 1988."

Indeed. That one was a World Series winner.

Shortstop Barry Larkin was batting .340 and en route to an outstanding season when he was sidelined by an arm injury suffered during an All-Star Game skills competition.

Distracted Reds Fall to Fifth

By HAL McCOY

Yes, the Cincinnati Reds did play baseball in 1989. But that was easily the most overlooked part of their season.

Most of the news emanating from Riverfront Stadium in '89 dealt with two things: The trials and tribulations of Manager Pete Rose and the daily medical bulletins listing injuries. In a year in which Cincinnati was supposed to be a frontrunner in the race for the National League West title, doctors and lawyers seemed to be the biggest sources of news about the Reds.

Baseball? Well, there wasn't much to say. After four straight second-place finishes, the Reds stumbled home fifth with a 75-87 record, 17 games out of first. They completed the decade as the only N.L. West team not to win at least one division championship.

It would have been a miracle if the Reds had won considering the distractions caused by the ongoing investigation of their manager, who spent most of his time denying a flood of allegations against him concerning gambling on sports (including baseball), consorting with shady characters and the like. But the Reds successfully divorced themselves from Rose's problems early in the season, and as late as June 10 they were in first place.

Then the injuries began to mount, however, and the Reds sank slowly in the West. By the time Rose was banned from baseball for life by Commissioner Bart Giamatti on August 24, the Reds were uncomfortably mired in fourth place. Coach Tommy Helms was named interim manager, and under him the Reds went 14-21, falling to fifth on September 16 and staying there.

The Reds would have struggled even without the Rose investigation diverting their attention. Of the eight regular position players, all but first baseman Todd Benzinger spent time on the disabled list. And the pitching staff was decimated. Before the inglorious season concluded, 12 different players were disabled, two of them twice. As a result, Rose and Helms filled out lineup cards that seemed more appropriate for the Reds' Class AAA affiliate at Nashville than the parent club.

The situation got so bad that relief pitcher Kent Tekulve, who had signed with Cincinnati as a free agent "because I wanted to pitch for a contender," retired July 17. "The team is going nowhere and it

Right fielder Paul O'Neill enjoyed a solid season despite missing six weeks with a broken thumb.

isn't any fun," said Tekulve, who broke Hoyt Wilhelm's major league record for relief appearances (1,018) and extended it to 1,050 before bowing out.

The biggest loss was shortstop Barry Larkin, who was hitting .340 at the All-Star break before injuring his elbow while making a throw during an All-Star skills competition. He was sidelined for all but 10 pinch-hitting appearances in the final month.

"I learned a lesson," Larkin said. "If I ever make the All-Star Game again, I won't participate in any extracurricular competition."

Other than first base, where Benzinger hit .245 with 17 home runs and 76 runs batted in, every position was hit in '89.

In right field, Paul O'Neill was en route to a great season when he broke his thumb trying for a diving catch July 20. Despite missing six weeks, O'Neill hit 15 homers, drove in 74 runs and stole 20 bases. Third baseman Chris Sabo, the 1988 N.L. Rookie of the Year, injured his knee in a home-plate collision with Los Angeles Dodgers catcher Mike Scioscia. Sabo kept playing for a while but eventually was disabled and finished with a .260 average.

SCORES OF CINCINNATI REDS' 1989 GAMES

APRIL

Date		Score	Winner	Loser
3—Los Ang.	W	6-4	Jackson	Belcher
5—Los Ang.	W	4-3	Browning	Hershiser
6—Los Ang.	L	1-4	Leary	Mahler
7—San Fran.	W	4-3x	Birtsas	Price
9—San Fran.	L	1-9	Reuschel	Jackson
10—At Hous.	W	8-3	Browning	Knepper
11—At Hous.	L	3-5	Deshaies	Mahler
12—At Hous.	W	3-1	Dibble	Smith
14—At S.D.	L	5-6	Show	Jackson
15—At S.D.	W	6-3†	Charlton	Booker
16—At S.D.	W	5-0	Mahler	Whitson
17—At L.A.	W	3-2†	Dibble	Howell
18—At L.A.	L	0-6	Belcher	Jackson
19—At L.A.	L	0-3	Morgan	Browning
21—Houston	L	0-7	Deshaies	Mahler
22—Houston	W	5-4†	Birtsas	Darwin
23—Houston	L	2-5	Knepper	Jackson
25—Montreal	W	6-1	Browning	Martinez
26—Montreal	W	6-5	Mahler	Perez
28—At Phila.	W	3-0	Rijo	Carman
29—At Phila.	L	0-8*	Maddux	Jackson
30—At Phila.	W	5-3	Dibble	McWilliams

Won 13, Lost 9

MAY

Date		Score	Winner	Loser
1—At Mon.	W	19-6	Mahler	Perez
2—At Mon.	L	4-6	Burke	Tekulve
3—At N.Y.	W	6-4	Rijo	Fernandez
4—At N.Y.	L	2-3†	Myers	Dibble
5—Phila.	L	0-7	Howell	Browning
6—Phila.	W	7-4	Mahler	McWilliams
7—Phila.	L	0-5	Madrid	Armstrong
8—New York	W	3-0	Rijo	Ojeda
9—New York	L	1-3	Fernandez	Jackson
10—New York	L	4-11	Darling	Browning
12—At St. L.	W	5-0	Mahler	Power
13—At St. L.	W	3-2	Rijo	Carpenter
14—At St. L.	W	5-2	Jackson	Hill
15—Pittsburgh	W	6-5	Charlton	Robinson
16—Pittsburgh	L	0-5	Kramer	Mahler
17—Pittsburgh	W	5-4†	Franco	Landrum
19—Chicago	L	2-8	Maddux	Jackson
20—Chicago	L	3-7	Kilgus	Browning
21—Chicago	W	7-2	Mahler	Bielecki
23—St. Louis	W	6-4	Jackson	Kinzer
24—St. Louis	W	5-1	Browning	Hill
26—At Chicago	W	10-8‡	Dibble	Schiraldi
27—At Chicago	L	3-5	Sutcliffe	Rijo
28—At Chicago	L	1-6	Bielecki	Jackson
29—At Pitts.	L	3-12	Walk	Browning
30—At Pitts.	L	0-2	Drabek	Mahler
31—At Pitts.	W	4-3	Rijo	Heaton

Won 14, Lost 13

JUNE

Date		Score	Winner	Loser
2—San Diego	W	9-4	Browning	Terrell
3—San Diego	W	6-2	Mahler	Show
4—San Diego	W	5-3	Jackson	Hurst
5—San Fran.	L	8-11	Garrelts	Rijo
6—San Fran.	W	4-3	Franco	LaCoss
6—San Fran.	L	2-3	Reuschel	Dibble
7—San Fran.	W	12-5	Mahler	Hammaker
8—San Fran.	W	3-2	Dibble	LaCoss
9—At L.A.	W	4-0	Rijo	Hershiser
10—At L.A.	W	5-0	Browning	Belcher
11—At L.A.	L	1-3	Leary	Scudder
12—At L.A.	L	2-9	Morgan	Mahler
13—At S.D.	W	9-6	Jackson	Terrell
14—At S.D.	L	2-4	Show	Rijo
15—At S.D.	L	0-1‡	Harris	Birtsas
16—At S.F.	W	5-4	Charlton	Gossage
17—At S.F.	L	1-8	Cook	Jackson
18—At S.F.	L	1-2	LaCoss	Rijo
21—At Atlanta	L	3-4	Eichhorn	Franco
21—At Atlanta	L	0-1	Smoltz	Mahler
22—At Atlanta	W	6-1	Scudder	Glavine
23—Los Ang.	W	3-1	Rijo	Morgan
24—Los Ang.	L	3-10	Valenzuela	Birtsas
25—Los Ang.	L	0-7	Hershiser	Browning
26—Los Ang.	W	5-3	Dibble	Belcher
27—Atlanta	W	9-3	Scudder	Smoltz
28—Atlanta	L	3-4	Glavine	Rijo
29—Atlanta	L	1-2	Clary	Dibble
30—New York	L	1-11	Darling	Mahler

Won 14, Lost 15

JULY

Date		Score	Winner	Loser
1—New York	W	6-2	Armstrong	Gooden
2—New York	L	2-7	Fernandez	Scudder
3—At Phila.	L	1-2	Howell	Rijo
4—At Phila.	W	2-1	Browning	Mulholland
5—At Phila.	L	2-3†	McDowell	Franco
6—At N.Y.	W	10-2	Jackson	West
7—At N.Y.	L	1-7	Fernandez	Scudder
8—At N.Y.	L	3-8	Cone	Browning
9—At N.Y.	L	3-6	Aguilera	Charlton
13—Montreal	L	3-6	Martinez	Tekulve
14—Montreal	L	0-1	B. Smith	Browning
15—Montreal	W	5-3	Mahler	Langston
16—Montreal	L	3-6‡	Frey	Tekulve
17—Phila.	L	1-4	Howell	Robinson
18—Phila.	L	5-6	Frohwirth	Jackson
19—Phila.	L	4-9	Cook	Browning
20—At Mon.	L	1-4	Langston	Mahler
21—At Mon.	L	1-3	Gross	Leary
22—At Mon.	L	5-6	McGaffigan	Franco
23—At Mon.	L	4-12	Martinez	Jackson
25—San Diego	L	2-6	Whitson	Browning
26—San Diego	L	3-5	Grant	Franco
27—San Diego	W	6-1	Leary	Harris
28—At Atlanta	W	4-2y	Charlton	Valdez
29—At Atlanta	W	4-1	Browning	Smoltz
30—At Atlanta	L	1-3	Lilliquist	Mahler

Won 7, Lost 19

AUGUST

Date		Score	Winner	Loser
1—Houston	L	0-5	Rhoden	Leary
2—Houston	W	5-2	Robinson	Deshaies
3—Houston	W	18-2	Browning	Clancy
4—Atlanta	W	5-4†	Franco	Boever
5—Atlanta	L	1-7	Lilliquist	Scudder
6—Atlanta	W	3-2	Charlton	Boever
7—At S.F.	W	10-2	Robinson	Brantley
8—At S.F.	W	10-4	Browning	Swan
9—At S.F.	L	1-10	Robinson	Mahler
10—At S.F.	L	3-4	Dravecky	Scudder
11—At Hous.	W	6-1	Leary	Rhoden
12—At Hous.	L	5-6	Smith	Franco
13—At Hous.	W	5-0	Browning	Clancy
15—Chicago	L	2-5‡	Williams	Roesler
16—Chicago	L	1-5	Bielecki	Leary
17—Chicago	L	2-3	Sutcliffe	Franco
18—St. Louis	W	6-2	Browning	Hill
18—St. Louis	W	8-3	Dibble	Worrell
19—St. Louis	L	1-5	Magrane	Mahler
20—St. Louis	L	1-8	DeLeon	Leary
21—At Chicago	W	6-5†	Charlton	Schiraldi
22—At Chicago	W	7-2	Browning	Kraemer
23—At Chicago	W	8-5	Scudder	Maddux
25—Pittsburgh	L	3-12	Robinson	Mahler
26—Pittsburgh	W	6-4	Robinson	Reed
27—Pittsburgh	W	1-0	Browning	Kramer
28—At St. L.	L	2-3	Costello	Dibble
29—At St. L.	L	2-4	Magrane	Leary
30—At St. L.	W	2-0§	Dibble	Worrell

Won 16, Lost 13

SEPTEMBER

Date		Score	Winner	Loser
1—At Pitts.	W	11-5	Robinson	Patterson
2—At Pitts.	W	6-2	Browning	Walk
3—At Pitts.	L	1-3	Drabek	Scudder
4—San Fran.	L	8-9	Camacho	Franco
5—San Fran.	W	6-5	Armstrong	LaCoss
6—Los Ang.	W	9-5	Rodriguez	Searage
7—Los Ang.	L	2-8	Valenzuela	Browning
8—Atlanta	W	5-1	Scudder	P. Smith
9—Atlanta	L	1-2	Glavine	Leary
10—Atlanta	W	5-4	Franco	Henry
11—At L.A.	L	2-8	Belcher	Robinson
12—At L.A.	L	4-5	Howell	Dibble
13—At S.F.	L	7-8§	Camacho	Rodriguez
14—At S.F.	L	3-4‡	Camacho	Charlton
15—At Hous.	L	1-4	Rhoden	Armstrong
16—At Hous.	L	1-3	Deshaies	Robinson
17—At Hous.	L	0-1	Portugal	Browning
19—San Diego	L	1-5	Benes	Scudder
20—San Diego	L	1-3†	Harris	Charlton
21—San Diego	L	7-11	Clements	Franco
22—At Atlanta	W	8-3	Robinson	Lilliquist
23—At Atlanta	W	11-5	Charlton	Aldrich
24—At Atlanta	L	2-6	Eave	Scudder
25—At S.D.	W	5-3	Dibble	Harris
26—At S.D.	L	1-3	Rasmussen	Armstrong
27—At S.D.	W	2-1§	Charlton	Schiraldi
29—Houston	W	4-3	Dibble	Meyer
30—Houston	L	2-9	Cano	Scudder

Won 11, Lost 17

OCTOBER

Date		Score	Winner	Loser
1—Houston	L	0-2	Deshaies	Leary

Won 0, Lost 1

*5 innings. †10 innings. ‡12 innings. §13 innings. x16 innings. y17 innings.

Eric Davis was Cincinnati's biggest offensive weapon, hitting 34 homers and driving in 101 runs.

A hamstring injury kept second baseman Ron Oester (.246) out for almost six weeks. Catcher Bo Diaz (.205) missed all but 43 games with a knee injury. Left fielder Kal Daniels was sidelined for six weeks with a knee injury and was batting just .218 when he was traded with infielder Lenny Harris to Los Angeles for shortstop Mariano Duncan and pitcher Tim Leary in July. Even center fielder Eric Davis, the team's top offensive threat, was out for part of May with a hamstring injury. But Davis, by comparison one of the healthier members of the club, still led Cincinnati with 34 homers, 101 RBIs and 21 steals.

Of the many call-ups from Nashville, only rookie catcher Joe Oliver displayed major league talent. Oliver was called up July 15 and platooned with Jeff Reed until August 23, when he became the regular catcher. Oliver batted .272, showed a strong arm and handled the pitchers well, while Reed hit .223.

Rookie outfielder Rolando Roomes had his moments despite striking out 100 times in 315 at-bats. He was hitting .305 through August 3 but slipped to .263. Infielder Luis Quinones hit .244 and blasted a surprising 12 homers after being summoned from

Nashville on May 26, but infielders Jeff Richardson (.168) and Scotti Madison (.173) were less productive.

Except for 39-year-old Ken Griffey, the veterans on the bench weren't much help, either. Griffey helped plug the left-field hole by starting 52 games there and batting .263. Outfielders Herm Winningham, Dave Collins and Joel Youngblood combined for only 33 RBIs in 475 at-bats. Duncan batted .247 after being obtained from the Dodgers but was slowed by hamstring problems.

Among the pitchers, no one suffered more injuries than Danny Jackson. After winning 23 games in 1988, Jackson was plagued by shoulder, wrist and toe problems that sidelined him for the season in July. He finished with a 6-11 record and a 5.60 earned-run average.

Another fallen starter was Jose Rijo, who was 7-6 with a 2.84 ERA when a fractured vertebra ended his season in July. Rijo was replaced by Ron Robinson, who had opened the season on the disabled list but came back to go 5-3 with a 3.35 ERA.

Reliever Rob Dibble also was disabled for two weeks, but he became the bullpen star with a 10-5 record, a 2.09 ERA and 141 strikeouts in only 99 innings. Dibble and roommate Norm Charlton (8-3, 2.93 ERA) combined for more victories than any Cincinnati starter. "Me and my roomie combined for 18," Dibble said. "We almost got 20 out of our room."

In fact, Dibble ranked second on the club in victories behind Tom Browning (15-12, 3.39 ERA). Browning, who led the league in starts (37) for the second straight season and completed nine of them, was limited by poor run support. Rick Mahler (9-13, 3.83), Leary (2-7, 3.71 in 14 starts with the Reds) and rookie Scott Scudder (4-9, 4.49) suffered from the same problem.

While bullpen stopper John Franco recorded 32 saves, third best in the league, he lost eight games and blew seven save opportunities, including five after the All-Star break.

Oh, the Reds had their moments. On August 3, they scored 14 runs on 16 hits in the first inning against Houston, setting three major league records and tying two more en route to an 18-2 victory. They also pulled off a triple play—the club's first since 1967—against Atlanta on June 28.

But such moments were rare for the '89 Reds, who will be remembered less for their disappointing performance than for the turmoil that surrounded them all year long.

Atlanta's best 1989 performance was turned in by Lonnie Smith, who batted .315, hit 21 homers and won N.L. Comeback Player of the Year honors.

Futility Continues for Braves

By JOE STRAUSS

The 1989 season was a case of good news and bad news for the Atlanta Braves. The good news was that because of two rainouts, the Braves played 160 games last year. The bad news was that the Braves had to play 160.

Aside from a young and promising pitching staff, an old Atlanta team got even older. The starting lineup included four players 32 or older, including the league's oldest player, 42-year-old infielder Darrell Evans. And when the season ended, Manager Russ Nixon's team had the National League's worst record (63-97) and their third last-place finish in four years.

The Braves broke spring camp confident they could compete with anybody. And they were right—for 34 games. But following a 17-17 start built mainly on solid starting pitching, Atlanta won only seven of its next 30 games to topple into familiar territory—the cellar.

The Braves failed to win more than two games in a row after June 17 and finished 28 games behind San Francisco and 11 behind fifth-place Cincinnati in the National League West.

The Braves' futility extended to the box office. They drew just 984,930 fans to Atlanta-Fulton County Stadium in 1989 and are the only major-league team to draw fewer than one million fans the past two seasons.

The brightest spot on a dismal team was left fielder Lonnie Smith, voted N.L. Comeback Player of the Year after batting .315, bashing a team-high 21 home runs with a .533 slugging percentage, and leading the league with a .415 on-base percentage.

The 33-year-old Smith, who was signed by the Braves as a minor league free-agent in March 1988, had spent most of the '88 season at Triple A Richmond (International).

"I really don't know where we would have been without Lonnie this year," right fielder Dale Murphy said. "I don't know if I want to think about it."

Murphy himself was disappointing for a second straight year, hitting only .228 with 20 home runs and 84 runs batted in. In one stretch of 64 games, Murphy hit only one homer.

General Manager Bobby Cox helped the club significantly on July 2 when he acquired center fielder and leadoff hitter

Righthander John Smoltz recorded a 12-11 record and established himself as a key member of Atlanta's young and talented staff.

Oddibe McDowell from Cleveland for outfielder Dion James. Labeled as disinterested and passive while in the American League, McDowell became a catalyst with the Braves. In 76 games, he scored 56 runs and stole 15 bases, second most on the team.

But there were far more negatives than positives. Catcher Jody Davis went from Atlanta's fifth-place hitter on opening day to its third-string catcher by August. As a group, Braves catchers hit only seven home runs with 35 RBIs in 582 at-bats.

Shortstop Andres Thomas was a perplexing figure in 1989. He hit 10 home runs with 43 RBIs before the All-Star break before going into a second-half funk that included only three homers, 14 RBIs and a .176 average. Thomas' slide left management pondering whether to trade him and have Jeff Blauser assume the shortstop job.

A converted shortstop who opened the year at second base, Blauser shocked club officials with his consistent power (38

SCORES OF ATLANTA BRAVES' 1989 GAMES

APRIL

Date	W/L	Score	Winner	Loser
4—At Hous.	L	3-10	Scott	Z. Smith
5—At Hous.	W	8-4	Alvarez	Knepper
6—At Hous.	W	3-2	Smoltz	Deshaies
7—Los Ang.	W	6-1	Glavine	Valenzuela
9—Los Ang.	L	2-4§	Pena	Eichhorn
10—At S.D.	L	2-5	Hurst	P. Smith
11—At S.D.	L	2-3	Whitson	Smoltz
12—At S.D.	W	5-0	Glavine	Rasmussen
13—At S.D.	W	4-1	Lilliquist	Terrell
14—At S.F.	L	5-7	Reuschel	Z. Smith
15—At S.F.	L	0-1	Hammaker	P. Smith
16—At S.F.	W	7-2	Smoltz	Downs
16—At S.F.	L	1-6	Price	Puleo
18—Houston	W	5-4‡	Boever	Smith
19—Houston	W	4-3	Alvarez	Clancy
20—Houston	L	3-4	Darwin	Assenmacher
21—San Diego	L	3-5	Hurst	Boever
22—San Diego	W	5-1	Smoltz	Whitson
23—San Diego	W	9-4	Glavine	Rasmussen
24—San Diego	L	2-5	Terrell	Lilliquist
25—At N.Y.	L	1-2	Cone	Z. Smith
26—At N.Y.	L	1-6	Gooden	P. Smith
28—At Mon.	L	4-10	Gross	Smoltz
29—At Mon.	L	7-9	Hesketh	Acker
30—At Mon.	L	6-9	Holman	Lilliquist

Won 10, Lost 15

MAY

Date	W/L	Score	Winner	Loser
1—New York	L	1-3	Gooden	Z. Smith
2—New York	L	1-7	Ojeda	P. Smith
3—Phila.	W	6-3	Smoltz	Carman
4—Phila.	W	3-0	Glavine	Maddux
5—Montreal	W	6-1	Lilliquist	B. Smith
6—Montreal	W	13-3	Z. Smith	Perez
7—Montreal	W	7-1	P. Smith	Johnson
9—At Phila.	W	7-2	Smoltz	Carman
11—At Phila.	W	8-3	Glavine	O'Neal
12—At Pitts.	L	2-10	Smiley	Z. Smith
13—At Pitts.	L	3-8	Walk	P. Smith
14—At Pitts.	W	5-2	Smoltz	Drabek
15—At Chicago	L	0-1	Bielecki	Lilliquist
16—At Chicago	L	3-4	Sanderson	Glavine
17—At Chicago	L	0-4	Pico	Z. Smith
19—St. Louis	W	3-2	Boever	Quisenberry
20—St. Louis	L	0-1x	Dayley	Boever
21—St. Louis	L	1-6†	DiPino	Alvarez
23—Pittsburgh	L	2-5	Smiley	Z. Smith
24—Pittsburgh	L	1-4y	Landrum	Acker
25—Pittsburgh	L	3-7	Drabek	P. Smith
26—At St. L.	L	0-3	Terry	Smoltz
27—At St. L.	W	4-1	Alvarez	DeLeon
28—At St. L.	T	3-3*	.....	.....
29—Chicago	W	2-1	Lilliquist	Sanderson
30—Chicago	L	2-3	Maddux	P. Smith
31—Chicago	W	3-2	Smoltz	Kilgus

Won 12, Lost 14

JUNE

Date	W/L	Score	Winner	Loser
2—San Fran.	L	6-7	Reuschel	Glavine
3—San Fran.	L	0-4	Hammaker	Z. Smith
4—San Fran.	W	6-3	Lilliquist	Krukow
5—Los Ang.	L	0-7	Martinez	P. Smith
5—Los Ang.	L	2-5	Leary	Smoltz
6—Los Ang.	W	3-0	Glavine	Morgan
7—Los Ang.	L	4-5	Valenzuela	Z. Smith
9—At Hous.	L	5-6	Agosto	Alvarez
10—At Hous.	L	0-1	Clancy	Smoltz
11—At Hous.	L	6-10	Deshaies	Glavine
13—At S.F.	L	2-3	Hammaker	Z. Smith
14—At S.F.	L	1-10	Robinson	Lilliquist
15—At S.F.	W	2-1	Smoltz	Garrelts
16—At L.A.	W	6-1	Glavine	Leary
17—At L.A.	W	2-1	P. Smith	Morgan
18—At L.A.	L	3-5	Valenzuela	Z. Smith
21—Cincinnati	W	4-3	Eichhorn	Franco
21—Cincinnati	W	1-0	Smoltz	Mahler
22—Cincinnati	L	1-6	Scudder	Glavine
23—Houston	L	2-5	Darwin	Assenmacher
24—Houston	L	4-5	Scott	Alvarez
25—Houston	L	6-12	Schatzeder	Acker
27—At Cin.	L	3-9	Scudder	Smoltz
28—At Cin.	W	4-3	Glavine	Rijo
29—At Cin.	W	2-1	Clary	Dibble
30—At Phila.	L	2-4	Mulholland	Z. Smith
30—At Phila.	W	3-1	Lilliquist	McWilliams

Won 10, Lost 17

JULY

Date	W/L	Score	Winner	Loser
1—At Phila.	L	2-4	Ruffin	P. Smith
2—At Phila.	W	3-1	Smoltz	Cook
3—Montreal	L	0-3	Langston	Glavine
4—Montreal	W	9-3	Clary	Gross
5—Montreal	L	5-7	Martinez	Eichhorn
6—Phila.	L	0-4	Ruffin	P. Smith
7—Phila.	W	5-3	Smoltz	Cook
8—Phila.	W	4-3	Assenmacher	Parrett
9—Phila.	L	3-4x	Parrett	Boever
13—New York	L	1-5	Darling	P. Smith
14—New York	W	3-2	Boever	Fernandez
15—New York	L	4-6	Aguilera	Assenmacher
16—New York	W	6-2	Clary	Ojeda
17—At Mon.	L	2-5	Perez	Glavine
18—At Mon.	W	7-6	Eichhorn	Frey
19—At Mon.	W	3-2§	Eichhorn	Hesketh
20—At N.Y.	L	1-4	Ojeda	Lilliquist
21—At N.Y.	L	4-6	Darling	Clary
22—At N.Y.	L	5-7	Aguilera	Acker
23—At N.Y.	L	2-7	Cone	Valdez
24—San Fran.	L	0-2	Reuschel	Smoltz
25—San Fran.	L	4-5	LaCoss	Lilliquist
26—San Fran.	W	5-4	Boever	Bedrosian
27—San Fran.	W	10-1	Glavine	Hammaker
28—Cincinnati	L	2-4z	Charlton	Valdez
29—Cincinnati	L	1-4	Browning	Smoltz
30—Cincinnati	W	5-2	Lilliquist	Mahler

Won 11, Lost 16

AUGUST

Date	W/L	Score	Winner	Loser
1—San Diego	L	2-5‡	Grant	Acker
2—San Diego	L	7-9	Hurst	Eichhorn
3—San Diego	L	5-6	Schulze	Smoltz
4—At Cin.	L	4-5†	Franco	Boever
5—At Cin.	W	7-1	Lilliquist	Scudder
6—At Cin.	L	2-3	Charlton	Boever
7—At L.A.	W	1-0	Glavine	Martinez
8—At L.A.	L	2-10	Hershiser	Smoltz
9—At L.A.	W	6-3	P. Smith	Wetteland
11—At S.D.	W	6-5	Eichhorn	Benes
11—At S.D.	L	0-2	Rasmussen	Clary
12—At S.D.	W	5-4	Glavine	Hurst
14—At St. L.	L	4-7	Magrane	Smoltz
14—At St. L.	L	2-5	Costello	P. Smith
15—At St. L.	L	1-9	DeLeon	Lilliquist
16—At St. L.	L	2-3	DiPino	Acker
18—Pittsburgh	W	13-6	Glavine	Walk
19—Pittsburgh	W	4-3	Smoltz	Drabek
20—Pittsburgh	L	6-7	Reed	P. Smith
22—St. Louis	L	5-10	Power	Lilliquist
23—St. Louis	W	3-0	Clary	Horton
24—St. Louis	L	1-4	Magrane	Glavine
25—At Chicago	L	3-4§	Williams	Eichhorn
26—At Chicago	W	5-3	Valdez	Sutcliffe
27—At Chicago	L	2-3†	Williams	Eichhorn
28—At Pitts.	W	5-2	P. Smith	Walk
29—At Pitts.	L	4-5	Drabek	Glavine
30—At Pitts.	L	5-7	Kramer	Boever

Won 10, Lost 18

SEPTEMBER

Date	W/L	Score	Winner	Loser
1—Chicago	W	5-1	Lilliquist	Wilson
2—Chicago	L	3-10	Maddux	Clary
3—Chicago	W	8-5	P. Smith	Bielecki
4—San Diego	L	9-10	Clements	Boever
5—San Diego	L	5-7†	Grant	Boever
6—San Fran.	L	2-7	Garrelts	Lilliquist
7—San Fran.	L	5-7	Bedrosian	Stanton
8—At Cin.	L	1-5	Scudder	P. Smith
9—At Cin.	W	2-1	Glavine	Leary
10—At Cin.	L	4-5	Franco	Henry
11—At S.F.	L	2-3	Garrelts	Castillo
12—At S.F.	W	6-5	Aldrich	Bedrosian
13—At S.D.	L	2-3	Davis	Henry
14—At S.D.	W	13-4	Glavine	Whitson
15—At L.A.	L	0-5	Martinez	Greene
16—At L.A.	L	0-1	Belcher	Boever
17—At L.A.	L	3-4‡	Pena	Boever
19—Houston	W	3-0	Eave	Scott
20—Houston	L	6-7y	Andersen	Boever
21—Houston	W	3-0	Greene	Deshaies
22—Cincinnati	W	3-8	Robinson	Lilliquist
23—Cincinnati	L	5-11	Charlton	Aldrich
24—Cincinnati	W	6-2	Eave	Scudder
25—At Hous.	W	5-3	Puleo	Schatzeder
26—At Hous.	L	2-3	Deshaies	Greene
27—At Hous.	W	5-4	Eichhorn	Clancy

Won 10, Lost 16

OCTOBER

Date	W/L	Score	Winner	Loser
1—Los Ang.	L	1-3§	Hershiser	Aldrich

Won 0, Lost 1

*9½ innings. †10 innings. ‡11 innings. §12 innings. x13 innings. y14 innings. z17 innings.

Lefthander Tom Glavine finished his second full big-league season with a 14-8 record and 3.68 ERA.

extra-base hits in 456 at-bats). He was moved to third in June when '88 rookie sensation Ron Gant was demoted to Class A Sumter (South Atlantic). Gant, who hit 19 homers and stole 19 bases in his rookie year, was batting just .172 before his demotion and finished the year with only nine homers, nine steals and a .177 average.

The Braves got lucky with former Cincinnati second baseman Jeff Treadway. The Columbus, Ga., native amassed solid numbers—.277 batting average, 58 runs scored and a 16-game hitting streak.

The season's best news was the blossoming of righthander John Smoltz into an All-Star, a solid 14-win season by lefthander Tom Glavine and the unexpected consistency of 27-year-old righthander Marty Clary, who was not even invited to major-league camp in spring training.

The Braves were dismayed by the struggles of No. 2 starter Pete Smith, who was 5-14 with a 4.75 ERA and had just one complete game in 27 starts.

A year after reaching All-Star status,

first baseman Gerald Perry suffered a disastrous season in which he went 169 at-bats without an RBI, suffered a season-ending dislocated shoulder and dropped from a .300 average to .252.

The bullpen retained its rank as the worst in baseball. Along with a gruesome 16-35 record, the Braves' pen saved just 33 games while blowing 23 other save opportunities. Middle reliever Jose Alvarez suffered cartilage damage to his right knee and did not pitch after June 18.

Righthander Joe Boever, who converted 16 of his first 19 opportunities—including 13 in a row—collapsed down the stretch. The beefy Boever finished with only 21 saves and lost his closer's role to rookie lefthander Mike Stanton (0-1, seven saves).

Entering the last year of a five-year contract in 1990, Cox is under pressure to produce something more than another last-place product for Owner Ted Turner and his WTBS Superstation.

The down-trodden Braves have nowhere to go but up.

Cubs second baseman Ryne Sandberg hit a career-high 30 home runs and captured his seventh straight Gold Glove.

'Chemistry' Helps Cubs Prosper

By DAVE VAN DYCK

When the Chicago Cubs left their 1989 spring-training camp in Mesa, Ariz., with a 9-23 record, General Manager Jim Frey and Manager Don Zimmer had a private dinner conversation.

"We agreed that if we won 81 games, we'd go out and celebrate," Zimmer said.

The two celebrated victory No. 81 on September 11, then celebrated again 15 days later after the Cubs clinched their second National League Eastern Division title in six years.

"If there is such a thing as chemistry, this team had it," said Zimmer, who was voted the N.L. Manager of the Year in a near-unanimous vote. "This team was something special. . . .they played hard every game. They may not always have played good, but they played hard."

And despite a disappointing five-game loss to San Francisco in the League Championship Series, Zimmer had nothing but praise for a team that won a league-high 93 games.

"I couldn't be more proud of a ball club than this one, in all my 41 years in baseball," he said. "This has been my most satisfying season."

The Cubs led the N.L. in hitting (.261) for the second straight year and had the best road record (45-36) in the league. Their staff earned-run average was 3.43, just sixth best in the circuit, but it was the best for a Cubs team since 1972.

It is a cliche that winning teams to cite a team effort for their success, but in the Cubs' case, it's true. A major-league leading nine Chicago batters drove in 40 or more runs and three pitchers won at least 16 games, the first time the latter has happened on the Cubs since 1970.

"I've never seen a team where so many guys have contributed," Zimmer said.

The Cubs' pitching leader was righthander Greg Maddux, who won 19 games, including a 5-2 decision over Montreal on August 7 that put the team in first place to stay. At age 23, Maddux replaced 33-year-old Rick Sutcliffe as the ace of the staff. Righthanded batters hit just .213 against Maddux last year.

Sutcliffe was troubled by shoulder stiffness the entire second half of the season. After pitching in the All-Star game, Sutcliffe was only 6-5 after the break.

If Maddux came of age, fellow starter Mike Bielecki got better with age. A 30-year-old journeyman, Bielecki was just happy to break spring camp with the major league team. By the time the season was over, he was 18-7 with a 3.14 ERA, all because of a split-finger fastball he developed in winter ball.

The fourth and fifth starting roles were passed around from Paul Kilgus to Scott Sanderson to Jeff Pico to Steve Wilson. Zimmer even experimented with a four-man rotation during August.

Perhaps the biggest surprise of the pitching staff, however, was righthander Les Lancaster. After starting the '89 season at Triple A Iowa (American Association), Lancaster was called to the big club on June 24 when reliever Pat Perry experienced arm trouble. Lancaster didn't allow a run for a club record 30⅔ innings.

Lancaster's role was to set up Mitch Williams, the self-proclaimed "Wild Thing" obtained from Texas in an off-season trade. The enigmatic lefthander fit right in with the overachieving Cubs.

Williams had 22 saves at the All-Star break and finished the season with 36, one short of Bruce Sutter's team record. And he excited the Wrigley Field faithful, who set an all-time attendance record of 2,491,942.

Among the Cubs' everyday players, probably the best was second baseman Ryne Sandberg, who hit .346 with 18 homers and 38 runs batted in after July 28. Sandberg finished with a career-high 30 homers and set a major-league record with 90 consecutive errorless games at second base, a mark he achieved on the last day of the regular season. He made just six errors all season and won a Gold Glove for the seventh straight year.

First baseman Mark Grace was another big contributor, even before a phenomenal playoff series against the Giants. In only his second full season, Grace batted both third and cleanup in the lineup and led the team in RBIs (79) and batting average among full-time players (.314).

Another key performer in 1989 was rookie outfielder Jerome Walton, who made a successful jump from Double A ball to the major leagues in just one year.

Walton provided spark to the offense from the leadoff spot and had a major-league high 30-game hitting streak from July 21 to August 20. Just as important to Zimmer, he filled a huge void defensively in center field.

Walton's roommate and fellow rookie Dwight Smith did the same thing in left

SCORES OF CHICAGO CUBS' 1989 GAMES

APRIL

Date		Score	Winner	Loser
4—Phila.	W	5-4	Sutcliffe	Youmans
5—Phila.	L	4-12	Howell	Maddux
6—Phila.	L	3-8	Ontiveros	Kilgus
7—Pittsburgh	W	6-5	Wilson	Taylor
8—Pittsburgh	W	5-3	Bielecki	Heaton
9—Pittsburgh	W	8-3	Sutcliffe	Walk
11—St. Louis	W	5-4	Schiraldi	DeLeon
12—St. Louis	W	3-2	Kilgus	Terry
14—At Phila.	W	6-4	Sanderson	Ruffin
16—At Phila.	W	5-3	Sutcliffe	Youmans
17—At Mon.	L	1-2	Gross	Maddux
18—At Mon.	L	2-11	B. Smith	Kilgus
19—At Mon.	L	2-3	Martinez	Sanderson
20—At N.Y.	L	3-4	Gooden	Williams
21—At N.Y.	W	8-4	Sutcliffe	Ojeda
22—At N.Y.	L	1-3	Fernandez	Maddux
23—At N.Y.	L	2-4	Aguilera	Schiraldi
25—Los Ang.	L	0-4	Belcher	Sanderson
26—Los Ang.	L	1-3	Morgan	Sutcliffe
27—Los Ang.	W	1-0	Maddux	Hershiser
28—San Diego	W	3-1	Kilgus	Rasmussen
29—San Diego	L	4-5	Terrell	Bielecki
30—San Diego	W	7-3	Sanderson	Show

Won 12, Lost 11

MAY

Date		Score	Winner	Loser
1—At S.F.	W	4-3§	Pico	LaCoss
2—At S.F.	L	0-4	Reuschel	Maddux
3—At S.D.	W	5-4	Kilgus	Grant
4—At S.D.	W	4-0	Bielecki	Terrell
5—At L.A.	W	4-2	Sanderson	Belcher
6—At L.A.	L	0-3	Morgan	Sutcliffe
7—At L.A.	W	4-2	Wilson	Hershiser
9—San Fran.	L	2-4	Krukow	Kilgus
10—San Fran.	L	3-4	LaCoss	Williams
12—Houston	L	1-3	Deshaies	Sutcliffe
13—Houston	L	0-1	Knepper	Maddux
14—Houston	L	1-5	Scott	Kilgus
15—Atlanta	W	4-0	Bielecki	Lilliquist
16—Atlanta	W	4-3	Sanderson	Glavine
17—Atlanta	W	4-0	Pico	Z. Smith
19—At Cin.	W	8-2	Maddux	Jackson
20—At Cin.	W	7-3	Kilgus	Browning
21—At Cin.	L	2-7	Mahler	Bielecki
22—At Hous.	W	5-3	Sutcliffe	Deshaies
23—At Hous.	W	5-4	Sanderson	Scott
24—At Hous.	W	3-1	Maddux	Knepper
26—Cincinnati	L	8-10§	Dibble	Schiraldi
27—Cincinnati	W	5-3	Sutcliffe	Rijo
28—Cincinnati	W	6-1	Bielecki	Jackson
29—At Atlanta	L	1-2	Lilliquist	Sanderson
30—At Atlanta	W	3-2	Maddux	P. Smith
31—At Atlanta	L	2-3	Smoltz	Kilgus

Won 16, Lost 11

JUNE

Date		Score	Winner	Loser
2—At St. L.	W	5-2	Sutcliffe	Magrane
3—At St. L.	L	5-6†	Quisenberry	Schiraldi
4—At St. L.	W	11-3	Sanderson	Terry
5—New York	W	15-3	Maddux	Cone
6—New York	W	8-4	Kilgus	Ojeda
7—New York	L	5-10	Gooden	Sutcliffe
8—New York	W	5-4†	Williams	Aase
9—St. Louis	L	0-1	DeLeon	Sanderson
10—St. Louis	L	0-6	Magrane	Maddux
11—St. Louis	L	7-10	Carpenter	Schiraldi
12—St. Louis	W	10-3	Wilson	Terry
13—At N.Y.	W	4-2	Bielecki	Darling
14—At N.Y.	L	0-2*	Gooden	Sanderson
15—At N.Y.	L	3-4§	Aguilera	Perry
16—At Mon.	L	5-8	B. Smith	Kilgus
17—At Mon.	W	3-2	Sutcliffe	Perez
18—At Mon.	W	5-4	Bielecki	Langston
20—At Pitts.	W	5-4‡	Schiraldi	Garcia
21—At Pitts.	W	1-0‡	Maddux	Bair
22—At Pitts.	W	8-0	Sutcliffe	Kramer
23—Montreal	L	1-5	Langston	Bielecki
24—Montreal	L	0-5	Gross	Kilgus
25—Montreal	L	0-5	Martinez	Sanderson
26—Pittsburgh	L	1-2	Drabek	Maddux
27—Pittsburgh	L	4-5	Kramer	Sutcliffe
28—Pittsburgh	L	1-3	Robinson	Bielecki
29—At S.F.	L	2-12	Brantley	Kilgus
30—At S.F.	W	6-4	Sanderson	Wilson

Won 13, Lost 15

JULY

Date		Score	Winner	Loser
1—At S.F.	W	3-2	Maddux	Reuschel
2—At S.F.	L	3-4	Brantley	Sutcliffe
4—San Diego	W	5-1	Bielecki	Whitson
5—San Diego	W	5-3	Sanderson	Rasmussen
6—San Diego	W	7-3	Maddux	Terrell
7—Los Ang.	W	6-4	Sutcliffe	Wetteland
8—Los Ang.	L	2-8	Morgan	Pico
9—Los Ang.	W	11-4	Bielecki	Valenzuela
13—At S.D.	W	7-3	Maddux	Hurst
14—At S.D.	L	4-7	Whitson	Bielecki
15—At S.D.	L	2-3	Terrell	Kilgus
16—At S.D.	L	3-4	Rasmussen	Sutcliffe
17—At L.A.	W	6-3	Lancaster	Leary
18—At L.A.	L	1-4	Hershiser	Maddux
19—At L.A.	W	4-0	Bielecki	Morgan
20—San Fran.	W	4-3‡	Lancaster	McCament
21—San Fran.	L	3-4	Garrelts	Sutcliffe
22—San Fran.	W	5-2	Sanderson	Hammaker
23—San Fran.	W	9-5	Maddux	Robinson
24—At St. L.	W	3-2	Bielecki	Terry
25—At St. L.	W	4-2	Kilgus	Magrane
26—At St. L.	L	0-2	DeLeon	Sutcliffe
28—New York	W	6-5	Schiraldi	Aguilera
29—New York	W	10-3	Maddux	Whitehurst
30—New York	W	6-4	Lancaster	Aguilera
31—At Phila.	W	10-2	Sutcliffe	Mulholland
31—At Phila.	L	4-7	Carman	Kilgus

Won 18, Lost 9

AUGUST

Date		Score	Winner	Loser
1—At Phila.	W	4-1	Wilson	McWilliams
2—At Phila.	L	0-6	Howell	Sanderson
3—At Phila.	W	2-0	Maddux	Ruffin
4—At Pitts.	W	3-2	Bielecki	Drabek
5—At Pitts.	W	4-2	Wilson	Landrum
6—At Pitts.	L	4-5x	Drabek	Sanderson
7—Montreal	W	5-2	Maddux	Perez
8—Montreal	W	4-2	Bielecki	Martinez
9—Montreal	W	3-0	Sutcliffe	B. Smith
10—Phila.	L	13-16	Parrett	Wilson
11—Phila.	W	9-2	Maddux	Carman
12—Phila.	W	9-7	Bielecki	Howell
13—Phila.	L	3-5	Parrett	Wilson
15—At Cin.	W	5-2§	Williams	Roesler
16—At Cin.	W	5-1	Bielecki	Leary
17—At Cin.	W	3-2	Sutcliffe	Franco
18—At Hous.	L	5-6	Smith	Schiraldi
19—At Hous.	L	4-8	Portugal	Maddux
20—At Hous.	L	4-8	Darwin	Lancaster
21—Cincinnati	L	5-6†	Charlton	Schiraldi
22—Cincinnati	L	2-7	Browning	Kraemer
23—Cincinnati	L	5-8	Scudder	Maddux
25—Atlanta	W	4-3§	Williams	Eichhorn
26—Atlanta	L	3-5	Valdez	Sutcliffe
27—Atlanta	W	3-2†	Williams	Eichhorn
28—Houston	W	6-1	Maddux	Cano
29—Houston	W	10-9†	Assenmacher	Smith
30—Houston	L	4-8	Scott	Sutcliffe

Won 16, Lost 12

SEPTEMBER

Date		Score	Winner	Loser
1—At Atlanta	L	1-5	Lilliquist	Wilson
2—At Atlanta	W	10-3	Maddux	Clary
3—At Atlanta	L	5-8	P. Smith	Bielecki
4—At N.Y.	W	7-3	Sutcliffe	Cone
5—At N.Y.	L	2-3	Fernandez	Williams
6—At Phila.	L	1-9	Ruffin	Maddux
7—At Phila.	W	6-2	Bielecki	Howell
8—St. Louis	L	8-11	Carpenter	Williams
9—St. Louis	W	3-2†	Assenmacher	Dayley
10—St. Louis	W	4-1	Sanderson	Hill
11—Montreal	W	4-3	Maddux	Langston
12—Montreal	W	2-0	Bielecki	B. Smith
13—Montreal	W	3-1	Sanderson	Gross
15—At Pitts.	W	7-2	Sutcliffe	Belinda
16—At Pitts.	L	6-8	Smiley	Maddux
17—At Pitts.	L	0-2	Drabek	Bielecki
18—New York	W	10-6	Wilkins	Viola
19—New York	L	2-5	Ojeda	Wilson
20—Phila.	W	8-9	Carman	Lancaster
21—Phila.	W	9-1	Maddux	Mulholland
22—Pitts.	W	4-2	Bielecki	Drabek
23—Pitts.	W	3-2	Lancaster	Bair
24—Pitts.	W	4-2	Wilson	Robinson
25—At Mon.	L	3-4†	Burke	Sanderson
26—At Mon.	W	3-2	Maddux	Martinez
27—At Mon.	W	7-2	Bielecki	Thompson
29—At St. L.	L	5-7	Dayley	Assenmacher
30—At St. L.	W	6-4	Pico	Costello

Won 17, Lost 11

OCTOBER

Date		Score	Winner	Loser
1—At St. L.	W	5-1	Sutcliffe	Hill

Won 1, Lost 0

*6½ innings. †10 innings. ‡11 innings. §12 innings. x18 innings.

Talented youngster Jerome Walton took over in center field and batted .293 from the Cubs' leadoff spot en route to N.L. Rookie of the Year honors.

field. Although he was not called up from the minors until May 1, Smith hit .324 in 343 at-bats while platooning with Lloyd McClendon. Smith's was the highest average for a Cub rookie since 1922.

McClendon, a journeyman obtained from Cincinnati in an off-season trade, was more than either Frey or Zimmer could have hoped for. He hit .286 in 92 games, filled in at first base when Grace was disabled, and played at third base and catcher in addition to platooning with Smith.

The 1989 season was one right fielder Andre Dawson would just as soon forget. The former N.L. Most Valuable Player got into just 118 regular-season games because of knee troubles and concluded the year with a poor postseason performance against San Francisco. Dawson hit 21 homers with 77 RBIs despite his injury problems, however, and the Cubs renewed the option year on his contract for $2.1 million.

"There's no doubt he had a struggling year," Zimmer said. "But there's still no better right fielder in the league."

Management's patience with shortstop

Shawon Dunston finally paid off late last season. Despite constant trade rumors swirling around him, the 26-year-old Dunston hit .329 with 25 RBIs in 50 games after hitting just .215 with 17 RBIs in his first 50 games. And he made just one throwing error after July 1.

Dunston watched a parade beside him at third base. It started with Vance Law, who finally was platooned with Domingo Ramos and Curtis Wilkerson. In the end, the Cubs traded with San Diego for Luis Salazar, who hit .325 with 12 RBIs in just 26 games with Chicago.

The catching job was also passed around like an offering plate on Sunday morning. Damon Berryhill (89 games) got the bulk of the playing time there despite opening and closing the season on the disabled list with an injured right shoulder. That left the job to rookies Joe Girardi (58 games) and Rick Wrona (37), who filled in capably defensively if not offensively.

"It was a funny year," Zimmer said. "We had a lot of ups and downs. But I said it best with a month to go in the season: Regardless of what happens, this will be the best year I've ever had."

A 36-homer, 101-RBI performance in 1989 established Howard Johnson as one of the game's elite third basemen.

Mets Fall Short of Expectations

By DAN CASTELLANO

Just how far short of the expectations of others did the 1989 New York Mets fall? Consider: The Baltimore Orioles won 87 games last season and their city threw them a parade. The Mets won the same number of games and the people of New York sneered at them in disgust.

"Expectations," said former Met Mookie Wilson with a big smile on his face. "That's the difference. A record that was a success for one team was a failure for another."

That about sums up the story of the 1989 Mets, the consensus choice to win the National League Eastern Division title when the season began and a near-unanimous pick as the season's biggest underachiever when the year ended.

Manager Dave Johnson, whose job security became the subject of much speculation as the season wound down, was saved from extinction four days after the campaign ended. General Manager Frank Cashen said Johnson would return in 1990 to complete the final two years of his contract. Johnson had been expecting the worst.

"It's a little frustrating for me, after nine years in the organization, not to know my status," the Mets manager said after the season's final game.

The Mets finished in second place, six games behind the Chicago Cubs, but their 87-75 record was their worst in Johnson's six years at the helm. Johnson's teams had won at least 90 games in each of his previous five seasons.

Johnson's six-year record with the Mets is 575-395—for an average season of 96-66 — and includes four second-place finishes, two division titles and one World Series championship.

Why would management consider firing this man?

"We didn't win," Cashen said. "When you don't win, you have to re-evaluate."

"Frank made the ultimate decision," said Vice President Joe McIlvaine. "It was an organizational decision, one we all stand by."

Cashen also made changes in the coaching staff. Batting instructor Bill Robinson and third-base coach Sam Perlozzo were fired in late October, but pitching coach Mel Stottlemyre, dugout coach Bud Harrelson and bullpen coach Greg Pavlick were all retained.

Robinson, who had often been men-

Lefty Sid Fernandez posted a 14-5 record and emerged as the Mets' most dependable 1989 starter.

tioned as a possible manager on the big-league level, first joined the Mets when Johnson came aboard as manager in 1984.

"I'm disappointed," Robinson said, "but I'm confident in my ability as a teacher to be able to land another job."

The Mets, who had nine players make at least $1 million in salary last season, cut loose two of those players two days after the '89 season ended. Co-captains Keith Hernandez and Gary Carter, both 35, were told they would not be offered contracts for the 1990 season.

Certainly, these two players could not be held solely responsible for the team's disappointing showing last year. But their own failures—caused at least in part by injuries—had a lot to do with everything that went wrong.

"We were clearly a team in transition," Johnson said. "Keith and Gary were the heart and soul of this team. Without them in the lineup most of the year, we had to break in new people and, when you do that, your execution suffers."

Hernandez, a former Gold Glove first baseman, batted only .233 in 75 games while Carter, a former All-Star catcher, hit just .183 in 50 games. Both players

148

SCORES OF NEW YORK METS' 1989 GAMES

APRIL

Date		Score	Winner	Loser
3—St. Louis	W	8-4	Gooden	Magrane
5—St. Louis	L	1-3	DeLeon	Ojeda
7—At Mon.	L	3-7	Gross	Darling
8—At Mon.	L	2-3	Harris	Cone
9—At Mon.	W	2-1	Gooden	McGaffigan
11—At Pitts.	L	3-4‡	Robinson	Myers
13—At Pitts.	L	2-4	Smiley	Darling
14—At St. L.	W	9-4	Cone	Magrane
15—At St. L.	L	2-3†	Quisenberry	Aase
16—At St. L.	L	3-5	DeLeon	Ojeda
17—Phila.	W	5-2	Fernandez	Carman
18—Phila.	L	1-7	McWilliams	Darling
19—Phila.	W	4-2	Myers	Bedrosian
20—Chicago	W	4-3	Gooden	Williams
21—Chicago	L	4-8	Sutcliffe	Ojeda
22—Chicago	W	3-1	Fernandez	Maddux
23—Chicago	W	4-2	Aguilera	Schiraldi
25—Atlanta	W	2-1	Cone	Z. Smith
26—Atlanta	W	6-1	Gooden	P. Smith
28—At Hous.	W	7-3	Fernandez	Rhoden
29—At Hous.	W	5-1	Darling	Knepper
30—At Hous.	L	6-7	Scott	Cone

Won 12, Lost 10

MAY

Date		Score	Winner	Loser
1—At Atlanta	W	3-1	Gooden	Z. Smith
2—At Atlanta	W	7-1	Ojeda	P. Smith
3—Cincinnati	L	4-6	Rijo	Fernandez
4—Cincinnati	W	3-2†	Myers	Dibble
6—Houston	W	2-1	Cone	Clancy
7—Houston	L	0-5	Deshaies	Gooden
8—At Cin.	L	0-3	Rijo	Ojeda
9—At Cin.	W	3-1	Fernandez	Jackson
10—At Cin.	W	11-4	Darling	Browning
12—San Diego	L	3-4§	Davis	McDowell
13—San Diego	W	4-3‡	Myers	Harris
14—San Diego	W	2-1	McDowell	Leiper
15—Los Ang.	L	1-3	Searage	McDowell
17—Los Ang.	L	3-4†	Pena	Aguilera
18—Los Ang.	W	5-3	Gooden	Pena
19—San Fran.	W	3-2†	Myers	Lefferts
20—San Fran.	L	0-3	Krukow	Ojeda
21—San Fran.	L	6-10	Hammaker	McDowell
23—At S.D.	L	2-3	Show	Gooden
24—At S.D.	W	3-0	Darling	Hurst
25—At S.D.	L	1-2	Whitson	Cone
26—At L.A.	W	8-2	Ojeda	Hershiser
27—At L.A.	L	1-2	Morgan	Fernandez
28—At L.A.	L	3-4§	Searage	McDowell
29—At S.F.	L	2-3	Robinson	Darling
30—At S.F.	L	3-10	Krukow	Cone
31—At S.F.	W	3-1†	Myers	Lefferts

Won 13, Lost 14

JUNE

Date		Score	Winner	Loser
2—Pittsburgh	W	3-2‡	Aguilera	Kramer
3—Pittsburgh	W	9-3	Darling	Walk
4—Pittsburgh	W	4-3	Aase	Kipper
5—At Chicago	L	3-15	Maddux	Cone
6—At Chicago	L	4-8	Kilgus	Ojeda
7—At Chicago	W	10-5	Gooden	Sutcliffe
8—At Chicago	L	4-5†	Williams	Aase
9—At Pitts.	L	3-4†	Landrum	McDowell
10—At Pitts.	L	5-6	Kipper	Myers
11—At Pitts.	W	6-1	Ojeda	Fisher
13—Chicago	L	2-4	Bielecki	Darling
14—Chicago	W	2-0*	Gooden	Sanderson
15—Chicago	W	4-3§	Aguilera	Perry
16—At Phila.	W	15-11	Myers	Bedrosian
17—At Phila.	W	1-0	Ojeda	McWilliams
18—At Phila.	L	5-6	Parrett	Myers
19—Montreal	W	5-3	Gooden	Gross
20—Montreal	L	5-8	Burke	Aguilera
21—Montreal	W	2-0	Cone	B. Smith
23—Phila.	W	9-3	Ojeda	Howell
24—Phila.	W	4-2	Darling	Youmans
25—Phila.	W	5-1	Fernandez	Mulholland
26—At Mon.	L	1-5	Perez	Gooden
27—At Mon.	L	2-3x	Frey	Aguilera
28—At Mon.	L	3-4	Langston	Ojeda
30—At Cin.	W	11-1	Darling	Mahler

Won 15, Lost 11

JULY

Date		Score	Winner	Loser
1—At Cin.	L	2-6	Armstrong	Gooden
2—At Cin.	W	7-2	Fernandez	Scudder
3—At Hous.	W	3-1	Cone	Deshaies
4—At Hous.	L	3-10	Scott	Ojeda
5—At Hous.	L	5-6	Darwin	Darling
6—Cincinnati	L	2-10	Jackson	West
7—Cincinnati	W	7-1	Fernandez	Scudder
8—Cincinnati	W	8-3	Cone	Browning
9—Cincinnati	W	6-3	Aguilera	Charlton
13—At Atlanta	W	5-1	Darling	P. Smith
14—At Atlanta	L	2-3	Boever	Fernandez
15—At Atlanta	W	6-4	Aguilera	Assenmacher
16—At Atlanta	L	2-6	Clary	Ojeda
17—Houston	L	0-6	Deshaies	Darling
17—Houston	L	3-12	Knepper	West
18—Houston	W	9-0	Fernandez	Forsch
19—Houston	W	8-2	Cone	Clancy
20—Atlanta	W	4-1	Ojeda	Lilliquist
21—Atlanta	W	6-4	Darling	Clary
22—Atlanta	W	7-5	Aguilera	Acker
23—Atlanta	W	7-2	Cone	Valdez
25—Pittsburgh	L	2-4	Drabek	Aguilera
26—Pittsburgh	L	2-3	Smiley	Darling
27—Pittsburgh	L	8-10	Kipper	Aase
28—At Chicago	L	5-6	Schiraldi	Aguilera
29—At Chicago	L	3-10	Maddux	Whitehurst
30—At Chicago	L	4-6	Lancaster	Aguilera
31—At St. L.	L	2-3	DeLeon	Darling

Won 13, Lost 15

AUGUST

Date		Score	Winner	Loser
1—At St. L.	W	11-0	Fernandez	Terry
2—At St. L.	W	4-3	Viola	Worrell
3—At St. L.	L	5-6	Quisenberry	Musselman
4—Montreal	W	11-5	Ojeda	B. Smith
5—Montreal	W	3-2	Darling	Burke
6—Montreal	W	2-1x	Musselman	Frey
7—At Phila.	L	1-2	McDowell	Musselman
8—At Phila.	W	9-0	Cone	Ruffin
9—At Phila.	W	6-0	Ojeda	Cook
10—St. Louis	W	5-1	Darling	DeLeon
10—St. Louis	W	6-4	Musselman	Costello
11—St. Louis	L	0-3	Terry	Viola
12—St. Louis	W	3-1	Cone	Power
13—St. Louis	W	3-2	Ojeda	Hill
15—San Diego	W	3-2	Musselman	Whitson
16—San Diego	W	7-2	Darling	Rasmussen
17—San Diego	L	2-6	Hurst	Viola
18—Los Ang.	W	3-2	Cone	Hershiser
19—Los Ang.	W	4-1	Ojeda	Wetteland
20—Los Ang.	L	4-5	Pena	Aase
21—San Fran.	W	4-1	Darling	LaCoss
22—San Fran.	L	0-5	Knepper	Viola
23—San Fran.	L	0-5	Reuschel	Cone
25—At S.D.	L	3-5‡	Harris	Myers
26—At S.D.	L	4-9	Rasmussen	Darling
27—At S.D.	L	7-13	Clements	Mitchell
28—At L.A.	W	1-0	Viola	Hershiser
29—At L.A.	W	2-1	Cone	Wetteland
30—At L.A.	W	9-3	Fernandez	Martinez

Won 19, Lost 10

SEPTEMBER

Date		Score	Winner	Loser
1—At S.F.	L	1-7	Garrelts	Darling
2—At S.F.	L	2-6	Reuschel	Viola
3—At S.F.	L	0-4	Robinson	Ojeda
4—Chicago	L	3-7	Sutcliffe	Cone
5—Chicago	W	3-2	Fernandez	Williams
6—St. Louis	L	2-3	DiPino	Darling
7—St. Louis	W	13-1	Viola	Power
8—Pittsburgh	W	7-2	Ojeda	Drabek
9—Pittsburgh	L	5-8§	Taylor	Innis
10—Pittsburgh	L	1-4	Smiley	Fernandez
11—At Phila.	W	5-2	Darling	Ruffin
12—At Phila.	L	1-2	McDowell	Aase
13—At Phila.	W	10-4	Ojeda	Grimsley
15—At Mon.	W	5-0	Cone	Martinez
16—At Mon.	L	1-10	Perez	Fernandez
17—At Mon.	L	0-1	Langston	Darling
18—At Chicago	L	6-10	Wilkins	Viola
19—At Chicago	W	5-2	Ojeda	Wilson
20—At St. L.	L	3-5	DiPino	Cone
21—At St. L.	W	6-1	Fernandez	Horton
22—Montreal	W	3-2	Darling	Candelaria
23—Montreal	W	13-6	Viola	Langston
24—Montreal	L	5-6	Hesketh	Machado
25—Phila.	L	1-2	Combs	Ojeda
26—Phila.	W	3-0	Fernandez	Grimsley
27—Phila.	L	3-5	Howell	Darling
29—At Pitts.	W	6-2	Viola	Kramer
29—At Pitts.	W	7-0	Cone	Robinson
30—At Pitts.	W	7-2‡	Myers	Landrum

Won 14, Lost 15

OCTOBER

Date		Score	Winner	Loser
1—At Pitts.	W	7-3	Fernandez	Patterson

Won 1, Lost 0

*6½ innings. †10 innings. ‡11 innings. §12 innings. x14 innings.

Young Gregg Jefferies got off to a horrible start and never really got untracked in his rookie season.

spent roughly two months on the disabled list last year.

Offensively, their replacements were adequate. Dave Magadan took over at first base and batted .286 but hit only four home runs and drove in just 41 runs. Barry Lyons, who succeeded Carter behind the plate, hit .247 with three homers and 27 RBIs.

Another problem was Gregg Jefferies, the overwhelming preseason favorite for rookie of the year honors based on his hot finish (.321 average in 29 games) in 1988. Jefferies got off to a horrible start in '89, however, and his teammates became more than a little upset when the 21-year-old, perceived to be getting preferential treatment, wasn't benched. Johnson stuck with him and Jefferies wound up the season with a .258 average.

Perhaps the team's biggest disappointment was rightfielder Darryl Strawberry. The Mets' cleanup hitter batted just .225 with 29 home runs and 77 RBIs and caused Johnson more than a few headaches with his on- and off-field antics. Leftfielder Kevin McReynolds also dropped from an MVP-caliber year in 1988 (.288 average, 27 home runs, 99

RBIs) to a .272 average with 22 home runs and 85 RBIs.

The Mets' troubles in center field gave them a Triple Crown of sorts for outfield disappointments. They broke up their longtime platoon of Lenny Dykstra and Wilson by trading the former to the Phillies in June and the latter to the Blue Jays a month later. The job was given to Juan Samuel, acquired in the Dykstra deal, but the seven-year veteran was a disappointment who ended his first season in New York by asking for a trade.

The only two everyday players who weren't disappointments in 1989 were third baseman Howard Johnson, who had the best year of his career (.287 average, 36 home runs and 101 RBIs), and shortstop Kevin Elster, who rebounded from a bad first half by hitting .231 with 10 home runs and 55 RBIs. Elster also established a major-league record of 88 consecutive errorless games at shortstop.

Mark Carreon (10 of 27 with four home runs as a pinch-hitter), Keith Miller and Mackey Sasser helped out off the bench.

The Mets have an impressive array of pitchers who, for the most past, didn't get the job done in '89. Dwight Gooden (9-4, 2.89 earned-run average) suffered a torn muscle in his right shoulder on July 1 and didn't start another game. Ron Darling went from 17-9 in 1988 to 14-14; David Cone went from 20-3 to 14-8; and Frank Viola, the American League Cy Young Award winner in 1988 with the Minnesota Twins, dropped from 24-7 to 13-17, including a 5-5 record with the Mets.

The team's best starter was Sid Fernandez, who posted a 14-5 record in 32 starts with a 2.83 ERA.

The New York bullpen suffered through a transition year. Lefthander Randy Myers (7-4, 24 saves and a 2.35 ERA) anchored a crew that saw Roger McDowell, Rick Aguilera and Terry Leach all depart via trades. Veteran Don Aase (1-5, two saves and a 3.94 ERA) showed little. Rookie Julio Machado, who came up in September, was impressive and probably will be given a shot at the righthanded closer job in 1990.

"It was a total, systematic breakdown," said Darling, who won a Gold Glove for fielding excellence. "Only two players, HoJo and Sid, had great years. Who knows what's going to happen here? With Keith and Gary gone and a few trades, the foundation of the club could be totally different."

For those who don't already know it, finishing second in New York is not allowed.

Cardinal first baseman Pedro Guerrero drove in 117 runs last season and batted .311 overall and .406 with runners in scoring position.

Injured Cardinals Run in Place

By RICK HUMMEL

In any team's championship season, a single moment often can be identified as the precise instant when the club irrevocably turned the tide in its favor. At that moment, it seems, destiny takes control and the victories just fall into place.

By all indications, that moment had come for the 1989 St. Louis Cardinals on September 8 when slugger Pedro Guerrero blasted a three-run home run to shock first-place Chicago at Wrigley Field. Trailing 7-1, the Cardinals stormed back to beat the Cubs, 11-8, and move within half a game of the National League East lead. With two games left in the weekend series between the two clubs, St. Louis was poised to take the top spot in the division race for the first time since May 12.

As it turned out, the pivotal moment came the next day, and it wasn't the Cardinals who were destiny's darlings. With St. Louis protecting a 2-1 lead in the eighth inning, right fielder Tom Brunansky hesitated a second too long and allowed Dwight Smith to take an extra base on a single. Smith later scored the tying run and Chicago came back to register a dramatic 3-2 win in 10 innings. The Cubs then won the rubber game of the series and never looked back. The Cardinals, meanwhile, stumbled to third place, seven games behind Chicago with an 86-76 record.

It was a disappointing finish for a team that had come so close in September, but the Cardinals had not been a particularly imposing squad in 1989. And given the customary banged-up shape of their pitching staff, they did about as well as could have been expected.

Neither Danny Cox nor Greg Mathews threw a pitch in '89. Manager Whitey Herzog had hoped that one or both of the starters would be healthy after injury-plagued 1988 seasons, but such was not the case. The major pitching loss, however, was reliever Todd Worrell, who missed the last four weeks with an elbow problem and four more earlier in the year with a groin injury. Worrell finished with 20 saves, giving him four straight years of 20 or more, but the Cardinals could have used him in key late-season situations. Ken Dayley had a career-high 12 saves but is better when he and Worrell are a two-headed monster in the eighth and ninth innings.

Scott Terry, who went 8-10 with a 3.57 earned-run average, also was lost for almost a month, leaving Herzog to make do with Joe Magrane, Jose DeLeon and a cast of extras in the rotation. Magrane seemed headed for the N.L. Cy Young Award but ran out of steam in September, when he didn't win a game, and finished at 18-9 with a 2.91 ERA. DeLeon won the league strikeout title with 201, breaking 200 for the second straight year, and had a career-high 16 victories. No other St. Louis starter had more than eight wins.

Ken Hill, who was rushed to the majors to fill a spot in the rotation, started 33 games but lost 15 of them, including nine losses in his last 10 decisions. Down the stretch, the Cardinals were starting one rookie (Hill) and two pitchers who had been released by other clubs (Ted Power and Rick Horton). Power gave the Cardinals a lift with seven victories, while Horton pitched reasonably well in his eight starts but didn't win a game.

Following Magrane and DeLeon on the victory list was middle reliever Frank DiPino, who reeled off nine straight victories and had a team-leading 2.45 ERA. Dan Quisenberry and John Costello combined for nine saves but generally were used in long relief.

While the Cardinals' pitching overall was adequate, their offense was a season-long problem. Despite posting the league's second-best batting average (.258), they finished tied for seventh in runs (632).

"We just didn't have enough guys capable of driving in runs," Herzog said. "There were a lot of guys who were slashers. You didn't have to play them very deep."

The Cardinals' only consistent threat was Guerrero, who showed skeptics in Los Angeles and elsewhere that he was far from finished. Guerrero drove in 117 runs, second in the league only to San Francisco's Kevin Mitchell, and batted .406 with men in scoring position. He also hit .311 with 17 homers in a career-high 162 games and played better-than-expected defense at first base.

Only a shade less consistent was center fielder Milt Thompson. Presumed to be a backup when he arrived from Philadelphia in the off-season, Thompson wound up playing 155 games, batting .290 and driving in a career-high 68 runs. His contributions were especially important because of the myriad injuries that limited

SCORES OF ST. LOUIS CARDINALS' 1989 GAMES

APRIL

Date		Score	Winner	Loser
3—At N.Y.	L	4-8	Gooden	Magrane
5—At N.Y.	W	3-1	DeLeon	Ojeda
8—At Phila.	L	4-5§	Parrett	Costello
9—At Phila.	W	15-3	Magrane	Ruffin
11—At Chicago	L	4-5	Schiraldi	DeLeon
12—At Chicago	L	2-3	Kilgus	Terry
14—New York	L	4-9	Cone	Magrane
15—New York	W	3-2‡	Quisenberry	Aase
16—New York	W	5-3	DeLeon	Ojeda
17—Pittsburgh	W	4-2	Terry	Fisher
18—Pittsburgh	L	3-4	Madden	Worrell
19—Pittsburgh	L	5-7	Walk	Heinkel
20—Montreal	W	5-2	Hill	Johnson
21—Montreal	W	1-0	DeLeon	Burke
22—Montreal	W	5-2	Terry	Gross
23—Montreal	L	3-9	B. Smith	Carpenter
25—San Fran.	L	0-4	Robinson	Hill
26—San Fran.	W	3-1	DeLeon	Downs
27—San Fran.	W	10-1	Terry	Garrelts
28—Los Ang.	W	6-3	Heinkel	Leary
29—Los Ang.	W	1-0§	Carpenter	Searage
30—Los Ang.	W	4-3	Magrane	Belcher

Won 13, Lost 9

MAY

Date		Score	Winner	Loser
1—At S.D.	W	6-0	DeLeon	Hurst
2—At S.D.	L	1-7	Whitson	Terry
3—At L.A.	L	3-4	Searage	Dayley
4—At L.A.	W	12-0	Hill	Valenzuela
5—At S.F.	W	3-1	DiPino	LaCoss
6—At S.F.	L	0-9	Reuschel	DeLeon
7—At S.F.	L	1-5	Robinson	Terry
9—San Diego	W	4-3	Dayley	Harris
10—San Diego	W	3-1	Magrane	Terrell
11—San Diego	W	6-5	DeLeon	Show
12—Cincinnati	L	0-5	Mahler	Power
13—Cincinnati	L	2-3	Rijo	Carpenter
14—Cincinnati	L	2-5	Jackson	Hill
16—At Hous.	L	7-8§	Schatzeder	Carpenter
17—At Hous.	L	2-3	Andersen	Magrane
18—At Hous.	W	4-3‡	Dayley	Andersen
19—At Atlanta	L	2-3	Boever	Quisenberry
20—At Atlanta	W	1-0y	Dayley	Boever
21—At Atlanta	W	6-1‡	DiPino	Alvarez
23—At Cin.	L	4-6	Jackson	Kinzer
24—At Cin.	L	1-5	Browning	Hill
26—Atlanta	W	3-0	Terry	Smoltz
27—Atlanta	L	1-4	Alvarez	DeLeon
28—Atlanta	T	3-3†	.....	.....
29—Houston	L	2-3	Knepper	Hill
30—Houston	L	4-8	Darwin	Terry
31—Houston	L	3-4	Schatzeder	Carpenter

Won 10, Lost 16

JUNE

Date		Score	Winner	Loser
2—Chicago	L	2-5	Sutcliffe	Magrane
3—Chicago	W	6-5‡	Quisenberry	Schiraldi
4—Chicago	L	3-11	Sanderson	Terry
5—At Mon.	W	5-4	DeLeon	B. Smith
6—At Mon.	L	2-3	Perez	Magrane
7—At Mon.	W	5-2	Hill	Langston
8—At Mon.	W	7-2	DiPino	Gross
9—At Chicago	W	1-0	DeLeon	Sanderson
10—At Chicago	W	6-0	Magrane	Maddux
11—At Chicago	W	10-7	Carpenter	Schiraldi
12—At Chicago	L	3-10	Wilson	Terry
13—Montreal	L	0-2	Langston	DeLeon
14—Montreal	W	10-0	Magrane	Gross
15—Montreal	W	4-3‡	Worrell	McGaffigan
16—Pittsburgh	W	6-2	Terry	Kramer
17—Pittsburgh	L	2-7	Robinson	DeLeon
18—Pittsburgh	L	4-12	Madden	Magrane
20—At Phila.	W	6-4	Hill	Mulholland
20—At Phila.	W	5-3	DiPino	Ontiveros
22—At Phila.	L	2-11	Cook	DeLeon
23—At Pitts.	W	3-2	Magrane	Madden
24—At Pitts.	L	2-5	Walk	Terry
25—At Pitts.	L	3-5	Smiley	Power
26—Phila.	L	4-5	Parrett	Worrell
27—Phila.	L	2-4	Cook	DeLeon
28—Phila.	W	2-1	Magrane	Howell
30—San Diego	W	4-3	Terry	Terrell

Won 15, Lost 12

JULY

Date		Score	Winner	Loser
1—San Diego	W	9-3	Power	Clements
2—San Diego	L	2-5	Hurst	DeLeon
4—Los Ang.	W	2-1	Magrane	Valenzuela
5—Los Ang.	W	3-2	Costello	Wetteland
6—Los Ang.	W	14-2	Hill	Leary
7—San Fran.	W	6-4	DiPino	LaCoss
8—San Fran.	L	5-8	Brantley	Power
9—San Fran.	W	6-4	Magrane	Wilson
13—At L.A.	L	2-3	Hershiser	Hill
14—At L.A.	W	7-2	Terry	Morgan
15—At L.A.	W	2-0	Magrane	Valenzuela
16—At L.A.	L	2-3	Belcher	DeLeon
17—At S.F.	L	4-8	McCament	Power
18—At S.F.	L	3-7	Robinson	Hill
19—At S.F.	L	5-7	Brantley	Terry
20—At S.D.	W	7-1	Magrane	Terrell
21—At S.D.	W	5-0	DeLeon	Rasmussen
22—At S.D.	W	5-2	Power	Harris
23—At S.D.	W	3-2	Hill	Hurst
24—Chicago	L	2-3	Bielecki	Terry
25—Chicago	L	2-4	Kilgus	Magrane
26—Chicago	W	2-0	DeLeon	Sutcliffe
28—At Mon.	W	2-0	Power	Perez
29—At Mon.	L	0-2	Martinez	Hill
30—At Mon.	W	8-3	Magrane	B. Smith
31—New York	W	3-2	DeLeon	Darling

Won 16, Lost 10

AUGUST

Date		Score	Winner	Loser
1—New York	L	0-11	Fernandez	Terry
2—New York	L	3-4	Viola	Worrell
3—New York	W	6-5	Quisenberry	Musselman
4—Phila.	W	6-3	Magrane	Cook
5—Phila.	L	3-7	Mulholland	DeLeon
6—Phila.	W	5-4‡	Worrell	Parrett
7—At Pitts.	W	4-0	Power	Reed
8—At Pitts.	L	3-7	Walk	Hill
9—At Pitts.	W	5-2	Magrane	Drabek
10—At N.Y.	L	1-5	Darling	DeLeon
10—At N.Y.	L	4-6	Musselman	Costello
11—At N.Y.	W	3-0	Terry	Viola
12—At N.Y.	L	1-3	Cone	Power
13—At N.Y.	L	2-3	Ojeda	Hill
14—Atlanta	W	7-4	Magrane	Smoltz
14—Atlanta	W	5-2	Costello	P. Smith
15—Atlanta	W	9-1	DeLeon	Lilliquist
16—Atlanta	W	3-2	DiPino	Acker
18—At Cin.	L	2-6	Browning	Hill
18—At Cin.	L	3-8	Dibble	Worrell
19—At Cin.	W	5-1	Magrane	Mahler
20—At Cin.	W	8-1	DeLeon	Leary
22—At Atlanta	W	10-5	Power	Lilliquist
23—At Atlanta	L	0-3	Clary	Horton
24—At Atlanta	W	4-1	Magrane	Glavine
25—At Hous.	W	7-4	DeLeon	Scott
26—At Hous.	W	5-3	Hill	Rhoden
27—At Hous.	L	3-6	Forsch	Power
28—Cincinnati	W	3-2	Costello	Dibble
29—Cincinnati	W	4-2	Magrane	Leary
30—Cincinnati	L	0-2y	Dibble	Worrell

Won 18, Lost 13

SEPTEMBER

Date		Score	Winner	Loser
1—Houston	L	3-6	Deshaies	Costello
2—Houston	W	13-5	Power	Forsch
3—Houston	W	4-3	Worrell	Darwin
4—Montreal	W	4-1	DeLeon	Martinez
5—Montreal	L	2-6	Perez	Hill
6—At N.Y.	W	3-2	DiPino	Darling
7—At N.Y.	L	1-13	Viola	Power
8—At Chicago	W	11-8	Carpenter	Williams
9—At Chicago	L	2-3‡	Assenmacher	Dayley
10—At Chicago	L	1-4	Sanderson	Hill
11—Pittsburgh	L	1-3	Heaton	Horton
12—Pittsburgh	L	2-5	Walk	Magrane
13—Pittsburgh	T	0-0*	.....	.....
14—Pittsburgh	L	3-4	Patterson	Dayley
15—At Phila.	L	0-2	Combs	Hill
15—At Phila.	W	7-6	Costello	McDowell
17—At Phila.	L	5-9x	Cook	Kinzer
17—At Phila.	W	2-0	Carpenter	Howell
18—At Mon.	W	3-2	DeLeon	B. Smith
19—At Mon.	W	5-0	Tewksbury	Gardner
20—New York	W	5-3	DiPino	Cone
21—New York	L	1-6	Fernandez	Horton
22—Phila.	W	2-1‡	Costello	McDowell
23—Phila.	W	11-5	DiPino	Cook
24—Phila.	W	2-1	Power	Parrett
25—At Pitts.	L	2-4	Heaton	DeLeon
26—At Pitts.	L	1-4	Patterson	Hill
27—At Pitts.	L	0-1	Drabek	Magrane
29—Chicago	W	7-5	Dayley	Assenmacher
30—Chicago	L	4-6	Pico	Costello

Won 14, Lost 15

OCTOBER

Date		Score	Winner	Loser
1—Chicago	L	1-5	Sutcliffe	Hill

Won 0, Lost 1

*5 innings. †9½ innings. ‡10 innings. §11 innings. x12 innings. y13 innings.

Jose Oquendo batted a solid .291 and established himself as one of the N.L.'s top defensive second basemen.

Willie McGee to 58 games and 17 runs batted in.

Vince Coleman struggled both offensively and defensively. The left fielder won his fifth straight stolen-base crown, but his total dropped from 81 to 65 as he showed less aggressiveness on the basepaths. He also hit a weak .254 (only 28 RBIs), and on the occasions when McGee was healthy in the final two months, Coleman sat on the bench while Thompson played left field.

Brunansky drove in 85 runs and hit 20 homers in a streaky campaign. Had he been consistent, he easily could have surpassed 100 RBIs for the first time in his career.

Catcher Tony Pena, popular with the pitchers but a notoriously bad RBI man, drove in just 37 runs in 424 at-bats. By the end of the season he was sharing time with the Cardinals' top minor league prospect, Todd Zeile, who hit .256 in limited duty but had trouble throwing out baserunners.

On the left side of the infield, the Cardinals were unsurpassed defensively as shortstop Ozzie Smith and third baseman Terry Pendleton both won Gold Gloves. Smith may have lost a step over the years, but he hit a solid .273 with 50 RBIs and was second on the team in stolen bases with 29. For the first time in eight seasons the Cardinals did not steal 200 bases, nor did they lead the league in steals.

Pendleton had an up-and-down year,

although he finished with a flurry to total 74 RBIs and a career-high 13 homers. Jose Oquendo turned in his second consecutive solid year as a regular, batting .291 and playing a club-record 163 games. (St. Louis had two tie games in '89.) Oquendo drove in 48 runs despite hitting just one homer and established himself as one of the league's best defensive second basemen.

The Cardinals' bench was weak, especially from the right side, where Tom Pagnozzi and Jim Lindeman combined for just four pinch hits in 41 tries. Left-handed-hitting Denny Walling and John Morris were more productive, getting 20 hits in 73 pinch-hit at-bats, although Morris, after a fast start, dropped to .239 for the season.

The thin bench was one reason why six players appeared in 155 or more games. Infielder Tim Jones, a .293 hitter in 42 games, probably could start for most teams, but he had little chance to play because Oquendo and Smith were so tireless.

Overall, though, the Cardinals looked a bit worn, especially when it came to running the bases, previously a Cardinal specialty.

"We didn't play the daring baseball we used to play—I mean hellbent for leather, daring them to throw us out like they used to," Herzog said. "We're getting to be a much more refined club. A more intelligent club, but less efficient."

Dennis Martinez was the rock of Montreal's 1989 pitching staff, fashioning a 16-7 record and 3.18 earned-run average.

Expos Lose Their Big Gamble

By IAN MacDONALD

The Montreal Expos made one blockbuster deal in 1989 and went for broke. That's about how they ended up.

On May 25, the Expos sent three talented pitching prospects—Randy Johnson, Brian Holman and Gene Harris—to the Seattle Mariners for Mark Langston, one of the most coveted pitchers in the game. Because Langston was eligible for free agency after the season and had shown no interest in making Montreal his new home, it was clear that the Expos had mortgaged the future of their pitching staff in an effort to win the National League East title immediately.

They didn't, through no fault of Langston's. He won 12 of 24 starts, led the staff with four shutouts, a 2.39 earned-run average and 175 strikeouts and provided the spark that lifted Montreal from fourth place to first for 42 consecutive days through August 6. But the Expos collapsed over the last two months, falling from 63-44 and a three-game lead to 81-81 and a 12-game deficit in the standings. That 18-37 slide landed them in fourth place with the same .500 record as the year before.

"It was devastating to see the thing go down the drain," Manager Buck Rodgers said after many sleepless nights down the stretch.

So, the Expos gambled and lost. They wound up with neither a division title nor Langston. As expected, the star lefthander ignored Montreal's offer of $10.5 million over three years and declared for free agency, leaving the Expos empty-handed.

But while Langston was there, Montreal had an excellent rotation. Dennis Martinez went 16-7 and posted a 3.18 ERA. Bryn Smith had an even better ERA (2.84) but was 10-11. Pascual Perez, who had entered a drug rehabilitation center in February but returned before the season opener, also had a losing record (9-13) despite a solid ERA (3.31). Among the starters, only Kevin Gross (11-12) had a high ERA (4.38).

The problem was a scoring slump over the last two months and a bullpen that was virtually non-existent beyond closer Tim Burke, who saved 28 games, won nine more and fashioned a 2.55 ERA.

"The guys we hoped would help Tim Burke this year, didn't," General Manager David Dombrowski said.

The missing element in the bullpen was Jeff Parrett, who had been sent to Phila-

The Expos took a big gamble when they traded for Seattle lefty Mark Langston, who gave them a 12-9 record before taking the free-agent trail to California.

delphia in an off-season deal that brought Gross to Montreal. Parrett had been a crucial link between the starters and Burke, and the Expos never found an adequate replacement. Joe Hesketh (6-4, 5.77 ERA) and Andy McGaffigan (3-5, 4.68) both slipped following fine '88 seasons, exposing the bullpen as a major weakness. The only bright spot was Zane Smith, who posted a 1.50 ERA in 31 relief appearances after being obtained from Atlanta in July.

SCORES OF MONTREAL EXPOS' 1989 GAMES

APRIL

Date	W/L	Score	Winner	Loser
4—Pittsburgh	W	6-5	McGaffigan	Robinson
5—Pittsburgh	L	0-3	Drabek	Johnson
6—Pittsburgh	W	3-2	Burke	Smiley
7—New York	W	7-3	Gross	Darling
8—New York	W	3-2	Harris	Cone
9—New York	L	1-2	Gooden	McGaffigan
10—At Phila.	L	6-7	Bedrosian	Harris
11—At Phila.	L	2-6	Ontiveros	Perez
12—At Phila.	L	3-6	Carman	Gross
14—At Pitts.	W	7-6	Hesketh	Medvin
15—At Pitts.	L	4-6	Dunne	Johnson
16—At Pitts.	W	5-4†	Hesketh	Robinson
17—Chicago	W	2-1	Gross	Maddux
18—Chicago	W	11-2	B. Smith	Kilgus
19—Chicago	W	3-2	Martinez	Sanderson
20—At St. L.	L	2-5	Hill	Johnson
21—At St. L.	L	0-1	DeLeon	Burke
22—At St. L.	L	2-5	Terry	Gross
23—At St. L.	W	9-3	B. Smith	Carpenter
25—At Cin.	L	1-6	Browning	Martinez
26—At Cin.	L	5-6	Mahler	Perez
28—Atlanta	W	10-4	Gross	Smoltz
29—Atlanta	W	9-7	Hesketh	Acker
30—Atlanta	W	9-6	Holman	Lilliquist

Won 13, Lost 11

MAY

Date	W/L	Score	Winner	Loser
1—Cincinnati	L	6-19	Mahler	Perez
2—Cincinnati	W	6-4	Burke	Tekulve
3—Houston	W	6-5†	Burke	Agosto
4—Houston	L	4-5*	Darwin	Hesketh
5—At Atlanta	L	1-6	Lilliquist	B. Smith
6—At Atlanta	L	3-13	Z. Smith	Perez
7—At Atlanta	L	1-7	P. Smith	Johnson
8—At Hous.	W	4-1	Gross	Knepper
9—At Hous.	W	4-2	Martinez	Scott
10—At Hous.	W	10-1	B. Smith	Clancy
12—San Fran.	L	1-2	Reuschel	Perez
13—San Fran.	W	5-4	Burke	Hammaker
14—San Fran.	W	4-3	Martinez	Krukow
15—San Diego	L	5-6†	Davis	McGaffigan
16—San Diego	L	2-5	Show	Holman
17—San Diego	L	5-6	Grant	Perez
19—Los Ang.	L	0-8	Belcher	Gross
20—Los Ang.	L	2-3*	Hershiser	Perez
21—Los Ang.	W	3-1	B. Smith	Morgan
23—At S.F.	L	2-4	Reuschel	Holman
24—At S.F.	W	1-0	Gross	Robinson
25—At S.F.	W	2-0	Martinez	Krukow
26—At S.D.	W	5-0	B. Smith	Rasmussen
27—At S.D.	L	0-5	Terrell	Gardner
28—At S.D.	W	10-2	Langston	Show
29—At L.A.	W	3-2	Perez	Leary
30—At L.A.	W	5-4	Hesketh	Howell
31—At L.A.	L	4-9	Hershiser	Hesketh

Won 14, Lost 14

JUNE

Date	W/L	Score	Winner	Loser
2—At Phila.	W	2-1§	Frey	Harris
3—At Phila.	W	7-5	Gross	McWilliams
4—At Phila.	W	7-4	Martinez	Carman
5—St. Louis	L	4-5	DeLeon	B. Smith
6—St. Louis	W	3-2	Perez	Magrane
7—St. Louis	L	2-5	Hill	Langston
8—St. Louis	L	2-7	DiPino	Gross
9—Phila.	W	5-0	Martinez	Youmans
10—Phila.	W	9-1	B. Smith	Ruffin
11—Phila.	W	7-2	Perez	Sebra
13—At St. L.	W	2-0	Langston	DeLeon
14—At St. L.	L	0-10	Magrane	Gross
15—At St. L.	L	3-4*	Worrell	McGaffigan
16—Chicago	W	8-5	B. Smith	Kilgus
17—Chicago	L	2-3	Sutcliffe	Perez
18—Chicago	L	4-5	Bielecki	Langston
19—At N.Y.	L	3-5	Gooden	Gross
20—At N.Y.	W	8-5	Burke	Aguilera
21—At N.Y.	L	0-2	Cone	B. Smith
23—At Chicago	W	5-1	Langston	Bielecki
24—At Chicago	W	5-0	Gross	Kilgus
25—At Chicago	W	5-0	Martinez	Sanderson
26—New York	W	5-1	Perez	Gooden
27—New York	W	3-2x	Frey	Aguilera
28—New York	W	4-3	Langston	Ojeda
29—Houston	L	3-8	Scott	Gross
30—Houston	W	6-1	Martinez	Knepper

Won 17, Lost 10

JULY

Date	W/L	Score	Winner	Loser
1—Houston	L	1-4	Andersen	Perez
2—Houston	W	13-2	B. Smith	Clancy
3—At Atlanta	W	3-0	Langston	Glavine
4—At Atlanta	L	3-9	Clary	Gross
5—At Atlanta	W	7-5	Martinez	Eichhorn
7—At Hous.	W	11-8*	Hesketh	Agosto
8—At Hous.	L	2-3	Darwin	McGaffigan
9—At Hous.	W	6-1	Langston	Scott
13—At Cin.	W	6-3	Martinez	Tekulve
14—At Cin.	W	1-0	B. Smith	Browning
15—At Cin.	L	3-5	Mahler	Langston
16—At Cin.	W	6-3‡	Frey	Tekulve
17—Atlanta	W	5-2	Perez	Glavine
18—Atlanta	L	6-7	Eichhorn	Frey
19—Atlanta	L	2-3‡	Eichhorn	Hesketh
20—Cincinnati	W	4-1	Langston	Mahler
21—Cincinnati	W	3-1	Gross	Leary
22—Cincinnati	W	6-5	McGaffigan	Franco
23—Cincinnati	W	12-4	Martinez	Jackson
24—Phila.	W	4-3‡	McGaffigan	Harris
25—Phila.	W	2-0	Langston	Carman
26—Phila.	L	3-4	Parrett	Z. Smith
28—St. Louis	L	0-2	Power	Perez
29—St. Louis	W	2-0	Martinez	Hill
30—St. Louis	L	3-8	Magrane	B. Smith
31—At Pitts.	W	4-2	Langston	Smiley

Won 17, Lost 9

AUGUST

Date	W/L	Score	Winner	Loser
1—At Pitts.	W	5-4†	Burke	Bair
2—At Pitts.	W	3-1	Perez	Reed
3—At Pitts.	L	0-1‡	Bair	McGaffigan
4—At N.Y.	L	5-11	Ojeda	B. Smith
5—At N.Y.	L	2-3	Darling	Burke
6—At N.Y.	L	1-2x	Musselman	Frey
7—At Chicago	L	2-5	Maddux	Perez
8—At Chicago	L	2-4	Bielecki	Martinez
9—At Chicago	L	0-3	Sutcliffe	B. Smith
11—Pittsburgh	W	4-1	Langston	Smiley
12—Pittsburgh	W	5-2	Gross	Robinson
13—Pittsburgh	L	4-6	Walk	Perez
14—Pittsburgh	L	1-6	Drabek	Martinez
15—San Fran.	L	2-3	Dravecky	B. Smith
16—San Fran.	W	4-2	Burke	Bedrosian
17—San Fran.	L	5-10	Knepper	Hesketh
18—San Diego	W	5-2	Perez	Benes
19—San Diego	W	6-4	Martinez	Harris
20—San Diego	L	2-5	Whitson	B. Smith
21—Los Ang.	L	1-6	Belcher	Langston
22—Los Ang.	W	4-2	Gross	Valenzuela
23—Los Ang.	L	0-1y	Wetteland	Martinez
25—At S.F.	W	12-2	Martinez	Downs
26—At S.F.	L	3-8	Garrelts	Langston
27—At S.F.	W	6-3	B. Smith	LaCoss
28—At S.D.	L	4-9	Benes	Gross
29—At S.D.	L	1-2	Grant	Thompson
30—At S.D.	W	5-1	Martinez	Whitson

Won 11, Lost 17

SEPTEMBER

Date	W/L	Score	Winner	Loser
1—At L.A.	L	0-2	Belcher	Langston
2—At L.A.	L	3-4	Howell	Burke
3—At L.A.	W	4-0	Gross	Hershiser
4—At St. L.	L	1-4	DeLeon	Martinez
5—At St. L.	W	6-2	Perez	Hill
6—Pittsburgh	W	11-6	Langston	Kramer
7—Pittsburgh	L	4-7	Walk	Candelaria
8—Phila.	L	3-4	Grimsley	Gross
9—Phila.	W	6-5	Burke	Parrett
10—Phila.	L	2-4	Combs	Perez
11—At Chicago	L	3-4	Maddux	Langston
12—At Chicago	L	0-2	Bielecki	B. Smith
13—At Chicago	L	1-3	Sanderson	Gross
15—New York	L	0-5	Cone	Martinez
16—New York	W	10-1	Perez	Fernandez
17—New York	W	1-0	Langston	Darling
18—St. Louis	L	2-3	DeLeon	B. Smith
19—St. Louis	L	0-5	Tewksbury	Gardner
20—At Pitts.	L	1-9	Heaton	Gross
21—At Pitts.	W	6-5	Martinez	Smiley
22—At N.Y.	L	2-3	Darling	Candelaria
23—At N.Y.	L	6-13	Viola	Langston
24—At N.Y.	W	6-5	Hesketh	Machado
25—Chicago	W	4-3*	Burke	Sanderson
26—Chicago	L	2-3	Maddux	Martinez
27—Chicago	L	2-7	Bielecki	Thompson
29—At Phila.	L	0-2	Cook	Langston
30—At Phila.	L	3-6	Ruffin	Gardner

Won 9, Lost 19

OCTOBER

Date	W/L	Score	Winner	Loser
1—At Phila.	L	3-5	Combs	B. Smith

Won 0, Lost 1

*10 innings. †11 innings. ‡12 innings. §13 innings. x14 innings. y22 innings.

Third baseman Tim Wallach was the Expos' most consistent performer in 1989, both offensively and defensively.

The bullpen was not the Expos' only problem. Their defense and ability to hit in the clutch also suffered down the stretch. In August, when the Expos went 11-17 and fell behind Chicago, St. Louis and New York, the club's composite batting average for the month was .225—and with men in scoring position it was below .200. The Expos batted .245 in the last month but committed 24 errors while winning only nine of 29 games.

"Sure, the offense didn't come through over the last seven weeks," third baseman Tim Wallach said. "But the defense wasn't there, either. Even the pitchers weren't up to par. We played badly as a team."

Wallach was the Expos' most consistent player both offensively and defensively. He made 18 errors at third and hit .277

with 13 home runs, 77 runs batted in and 42 doubles (tied for the league high).

The Expos were strong defensively at the other infield corner as well—first baseman Andres Galarraga won his first Gold Glove—but his career-low .257 average was a disappointment. Galarraga led the team with 23 homers, 85 RBIs and a team-record 158 strikeouts.

Left fielder Tim Raines led Montreal with 41 stolen bases and a .286 average. It was, however, his second consecutive year under .300 after four straight above that level. Also suffering a bit of an off season was right fielder Hubie Brooks, who raised his final numbers to .268, 14 homers and 70 RBIs with a hot September.

The Expos platooned in center field with Dave Martinez and Otis Nixon. Martinez hit .274 but, with 103 more at-bats, scored the same number of runs (41) as Nixon, who hit .217. They combined for 60 stolen bases.

Shortstop Spike Owen and second baseman Tom Foley supplied solid defense up the middle. Both players lost their hitting touch after being sidelined with midseason injuries, however, and Owen finished at .233, Foley .229. Damaso Garcia also played second base and batted .271.

Catcher Nelson Santovenia struggled while trying to reach the offensive potential he showed as a rookie in 1988. In fact, Mike Fitzgerald, who was scheduled for a utility role, did much of the work behind the plate. Fitzgerald batted .238 with seven homers and 42 RBIs, while Santovenia hit .250 with five homers and 31 RBIs.

The Expos didn't get as much help from their bench as they had anticipated. Wallace Johnson led the team in pinch hits with 14. That represented a drop, however, from 22 the year before. Mike Aldrete was to be a lefthanded-hitting savior, but he batted just .221. Utilityman Rex Hudler hit .245 in 92 games.

The Expos' failure to win the division championship left many of the players upset and bewildered.

"This is the most frustrated I've been as a player," Wallach said. "I really felt we were going to win it earlier. I still feel we should have."

So did Rodgers, who watched in agony while the team collapsed. But he said he doesn't plan to let the Expos' horrible finish haunt him forever.

"If my grandchildren or great-grandchildren ever ask me about the final two months of the 1989 season," he said, "I'll tell them I had amnesia and don't remember."

Righthander Bill Landrum replaced injured Jim Gott as Pittsburgh's stopper last season and recorded 26 saves in 29 opportunities.

Injured Pirates Take a Tumble

By JOHN MEHNO

The Pittsburgh Pirates played more games than ever (164) and more extra-inning games (21) than any other major league team in 1989.

That only prolonged the agony of a disappointing season.

After finishing second to the New York Mets in the National League Eastern Division in 1988, the Pirates entered last season with high expectations. But those hopes were dashed quickly after injuries to key players and subpar seasons from others. The '89 Pirates dropped three rungs in the division and finished the year with a 74-88 record, a 12-game decline from the previous year.

The season was a lost one for reliever Jim Gott, first baseman Sid Bream and starting pitcher Brian Fisher. Gott, who set a team record with 34 saves in 1988, was limited to two-thirds of an inning last year after blowing out his elbow on April 6. He underwent surgery a month later.

Bream played only 19 games last year due to recurring problems with his right knee. He twice had arthroscopic surgery before undergoing reconstructive surgery on July 21.

Fisher had an incredible run of bad luck. In less than a year, he had surgery on his right shoulder, both knees and also put a 17-stitch gash in his left forearm in a spring-training miniature golf mishap. Fisher was 0-3 with a 7.94 earned-run average in nine appearances, the last coming on June 11.

Pittsburgh had at least two players on the disabled list every day last season. Catcher Mike LaValliere was lost for nearly three months after suffering a knee injury in a collision with Montreal's Rex Hudler on April 16.

Center fielder Andy Van Slyke, who was fourth in N.L. Most Valuable Player balloting in 1988, spent a month on the disabled list with a strained rib cage muscle and suffered with lingering shoulder and knee problems as well. His offensive production took a huge nosedive from 1988, going from a .288 average, 25 home runs and 100 RBIs to .237, nine and 53.

The Pirates used 11 pitchers in their starting rotation but only three—Doug Drabek, John Smiley and Bob Walk—were consistent. Drabek's 2.80 ERA was sixth-best in the National League and he led the Pirates in wins (14), shutouts (5), and innings (244.1) despite having the worst run support on the staff.

Smiley allowed three earned runs or less in 22 of his 28 starts, tied Drabek for the staff lead in complete games (8) and strikeouts (123) and had a 2.81 ERA before he developed bone chips in his elbow and missed his last five starts.

Walk won a career-high 13 games but his ERA rose from 2.71 to 4.41. Neal Heaton, who finished the season with a 6-7 record and 3.05 ERA, was 3-0 with a 1.59 ERA after rejoining the rotation in September.

It took a costly two months for Manager Jim Leyland to find a suitable replacement for Gott, but the trial-and-error method finally led the Pittsburgh skipper to 30-year-old righthander Bill Landrum. Landrum, signed as a minor-league free agent after pitching in seven games for the Cubs in 1988, had 26 saves in 29 chances, including a team-record streak of nine in as many appearances from June 24 to July 17.

Righthander Jeff Robinson, who failed in the closer's role, became a starter by default in mid-June and finished with a 7-13 record and 4.58 ERA in 141.1 innings. Lefthander Bob Kipper (2.93 ERA in 83 innings) was effective in a limited relief role. The Pirates used a league-high 22 pitchers.

Among the regulars, only third baseman Bobby Bonilla came close to duplicating his 1988 season. Bonilla actually played more consistently en route to a .281 average, 24 home runs and 86 RBIs. But he also had 35 errors—the most of any major-league third baseman—and was playing first base on a part-time basis by the end of the season. The Pirates had the National League's worst defense, committing 160 errors and 19 passed balls.

Jeff King, the top pick in the June 1986 free-agent draft, played all four infield positions (primarily first base) but batted just .195 with five home runs and 19 RBIs in 75 games.

The Pirates, who have been plagued for a decade by the lack of a shortstop, thought they had solved their dilemma after acquiring Jay Bell from the Cleveland Indians during spring training. But Bell started the season in a 1-for-20 slump, a performance that earned him a ticket to Triple A Buffalo (American Association). He was recalled on July 22 and hit .275 the remainder of the season.

Second baseman Jose Lind declined sig-

SCORES OF PITTSBURGH PIRATES' 1989 GAMES

APRIL

Date		Score	Winner	Loser
4—At Mon.	L	5-6	McGaffigan	Robinson
5—At Mon.	W	3-0	Drabek	Johnson
6—At Mon.	L	2-3	Burke	Smiley
7—At Chicago	L	5-6	Wilson	Taylor
8—At Chicago	L	3-5	Bielecki	Heaton
9—At Chicago	L	3-8	Sutcliffe	Walk
11—New York	W	4-3§	Robinson	Myers
13—New York	W	4-2	Smiley	Darling
14—Montreal	L	6-7	Hesketh	Medvin
15—Montreal	W	6-4	Dunne	Johnson
16—Montreal	L	4-5§	Hesketh	Robinson
17—At St. L.	L	2-4	Terry	Fisher
18—At St. L.	W	4-3	Madden	Worrell
19—At St. L.	W	7-5	Walk	Heinkel
20—Phila.	L	4-9	Howell	Dunne
21—Phila.	L	2-3	Youmans	Drabek
22—Phila.	W	4-3	Robinson	Carman
23—Phila.	W	6-4	Easley	Bedrosian
25—San Diego	L	0-1	Show	Walk
26—San Diego	L	1-3	Hurst	Drabek
27—San Diego	L	1-8	Whitson	Heaton
28—San Fran.	W	1-0	Smiley	Reuschel
29—San Fran.	L	3-4	LaCoss	Robinson
30—San Fran.	W	11-1	Walk	Robinson

Won 10, Lost 14

MAY

Date		Score	Winner	Loser
1—At L.A.	L	0-1	Howell	Drabek
2—At L.A.	L	0-7	Hershiser	Heaton
3—At S.F.	W	5-3	Smiley	Robinson
4—At S.F.	L	3-6	Krukow	Kramer
5—At S.D.	W	4-2	Walk	Show
6—At S.D.	L	2-4	Hurst	Drabek
7—At S.D.	L	1-3	Whitson	Heaton
12—Atlanta	W	10-2	Smiley	Z. Smith
13—Atlanta	W	8-3	Walk	P. Smith
14—Atlanta	L	2-5	Smoltz	Drabek
15—At Cin.	L	5-6	Charlton	Robinson
16—At Cin.	W	5-0	Kramer	Mahler
17—At Cin.	L	4-5‡	Franco	Landrum
19—At Hous.	L	0-3	Scott	Walk
20—At Hous.	L	4-5x	Agosto	Kipper
21—At Hous.	W	17-5	Heaton	Clancy
23—At Atlanta	W	5-2	Smiley	Z. Smith
24—At Atlanta	W	4-1z	Landrum	Acker
25—At Atlanta	W	7-3	Drabek	P. Smith
26—Houston	L	2-4	Clancy	Heaton
27—Houston	L	4-5x	Schatzeder	Robinson
28—Houston	L	2-9	Scott	Smiley
29—Cincinnati	W	12-3	Walk	Browning
30—Cincinnati	W	2-0	Drabek	Mahler
31—Cincinnati	L	3-4	Rijo	Heaton

Won 11, Lost 14

JUNE

Date		Score	Winner	Loser
2—At N.Y.	L	2-3§	Aguilera	Kramer
3—At N.Y.	L	3-9	Darling	Walk
4—At N.Y.	L	3-4	Aase	Kipper
5—At Phila.	T	3-3†	.....	.....
6—At Phila.	L	4-9	Sebra	Fisher
7—At Phila.	L	5-7	Parrett	Kipper
8—At Phila.	L	11-15	Carman	Robinson
9—New York	W	4-3‡	Landrum	McDowell
10—New York	W	6-5	Kipper	Myers
11—New York	L	1-6	Ojeda	Fisher
13—Phila.	L	2-10	Howell	Madden
14—Phila.	W	6-4	Smiley	Carman
15—Phila.	W	5-3	Drabek	Sebra
16—At St. L.	L	2-6	Terry	Kramer
17—At St. L.	W	7-2	Robinson	DeLeon
18—At St. L.	W	12-4	Madden	Magrane
20—Chicago	L	4-5§	Schiraldi	Garcia
21—Chicago	L	0-1§	Maddux	Bair
22—Chicago	L	0-8	Sutcliffe	Kramer
23—St. Louis	L	2-3	Magrane	Madden
24—St. Louis	W	5-2	Walk	Terry
25—St. Louis	W	5-3	Smiley	Power
26—At Chicago	W	2-1	Drabek	Maddux
27—At Chicago	W	5-4	Kramer	Sutcliffe
28—At Chicago	W	3-1	Robinson	Bielecki
30—At L.A.	W	4-3	Walk	Hershiser

Won 12, Lost 13

JULY

Date		Score	Winner	Loser
1—At L.A.	L	0-1	Belcher	Smiley
2—At L.A.	L	2-3	Wetteland	Drabek
3—At L.A.	W	4-2	Robinson	Morgan
4—San Fran.	W	5-3	Kramer	Robinson
5—San Fran.	L	4-6	Wilson	Walk
6—San Fran.	L	1-2‡	Brantley	Smiley
7—San Diego	W	3-0	Drabek	Hurst
8—San Diego	L	0-2	Whitson	Robinson
9—San Diego	L	3-5	Grant	Kramer
13—At S.F.	L	2-3y	Brantley	Garcia
14—At S.F.	W	7-4	Drabek	Reuschel
15—At S.F.	L	3-8	LaCoss	Smiley
16—At S.F.	L	1-3	Garrelts	Robinson
17—At S.D.	W	4-1	Kramer	Harris
18—At S.D.	L	4-17	Hurst	Walk
19—At S.D.	L	1-9	Whitson	Drabek
21—Los Ang.	W	4-1	Smiley	Belcher
21—Los Ang.	L	3-7	Valenzuela	Heaton
22—Los Ang.	L	4-8	Martinez	Robinson
23—Los Ang.	L	3-4	Hershiser	Kramer
23—Los Ang.	W	2-1‡	Kipper	Crews
24—Los Ang.	W	7-4	Walk	Morgan
25—At N.Y.	W	4-2	Drabek	Aguilera
26—At N.Y.	W	3-2	Smiley	Darling
27—At N.Y.	W	10-8	Kipper	Aase
28—At Phila.	W	10-5	Heaton	Howell
28—At Phila.	L	1-6	Harris	Reed
29—At Phila.	L	2-6	Parrett	Walk
30—At Phila.	L	6-8	Cook	Kipper
31—Montreal	L	2-4	Langston	Smiley

Won 12, Lost 18

AUGUST

Date		Score	Winner	Loser
1—Montreal	L	4-5§	Burke	Bair
2—Montreal	L	1-3	Perez	Reed
3—Montreal	W	1-0x	Bair	McGaffigan
4—Chicago	L	2-3	Bielecki	Drabek
5—Chicago	L	2-4	Wilson	Landrum
6—Chicago	W	5-4a	Drabek	Sanderson
7—St. Louis	L	0-4	Power	Reed
8—St. Louis	W	7-3	Walk	Hill
9—St. Louis	L	2-5	Magrane	Drabek
11—At Mon.	L	1-4	Langston	Smiley
12—At Mon.	L	2-5	Gross	Robinson
13—At Mon.	W	6-4	Walk	Perez
14—At Mon.	W	6-1	Drabek	Martinez
15—At Hous.	L	2-3§	Andersen	Smith
16—At Hous.	W	5-4x	Heaton	Andersen
17—At Hous.	L	3-5	Deshaies	Robinson
18—At Atlanta	L	6-13	Glavine	Walk
19—At Atlanta	L	3-4	Smoltz	Drabek
20—At Atlanta	W	7-6	Reed	P. Smith
22—Houston	W	4-1	Smiley	Deshaies
23—Houston	W	6-1	Walk	Clancy
24—Houston	W	3-2z	Bair	Agosto
25—At Cin.	W	12-3	Robinson	Mahler
26—At Cin.	L	4-6	Robinson	Reed
27—At Cin.	L	0-1	Browning	Kramer
28—Atlanta	L	2-5	P. Smith	Walk
29—Atlanta	W	5-4	Drabek	Glavine
30—Atlanta	W	7-5	Kramer	Boever

Won 13, Lost 15

SEPTEMBER

Date		Score	Winner	Loser
1—Cincinnati	L	5-11	Robinson	Patterson
2—Cincinnati	L	2-6	Browning	Walk
3—Cincinnati	W	3-1	Drabek	Scudder
4—At Phila.	W	7-5	Patterson	Maddux
5—At Phila.	L	2-3	Parrett	Patterson
6—At Mon.	L	6-11	Langston	Kramer
7—At Mon.	W	7-4	Walk	Candelaria
8—At N.Y.	L	2-7	Ojeda	Drabek
9—At N.Y.	W	8-5x	Taylor	Innis
10—At N.Y.	W	4-1	Smiley	Fernandez
11—At St. L.	W	3-1	Heaton	Horton
12—At St. L.	W	5-2	Walk	Magrane
13—At St. L.	T	0-0*	.....	.....
14—At St. L.	W	4-3	Patterson	Dayley
15—Chicago	L	2-7	Sutcliffe	Belinda
16—Chicago	W	8-6	Smiley	Maddux
17—Chicago	W	2-0	Drabek	Bielecki
18—Phila.	W	6-2	Patterson	Grimsley
19—Phila.	W	4-2	Robinson	Ruffin
20—Montreal	W	9-1	Heaton	Gross
21—Montreal	L	5-6	Martinez	Smiley
22—At Chicago	L	2-4	Bielecki	Drabek
23—At Chicago	L	2-3	Lancaster	Bair
24—At Chicago	L	2-4	Wilson	Robinson
25—St. Louis	W	4-2	Heaton	DeLeon
26—St. Louis	W	4-1	Patterson	Hill
27—St. Louis	W	1-0	Drabek	Magrane
29—New York	L	2-6	Viola	Kramer
29—New York	L	0-7	Cone	Robinson
30—New York	L	2-7§	Myers	Landrum

Won 16, Lost 13

OCTOBER

Date		Score	Winner	Loser
1—New York	L	3-7	Fernandez	Patterson

Won 0, Lost 1

*5 innings. †7½ innings. ‡10 innings. §11 innings. x12 innings. y13 innings. z14 innings. a18 innings.

Bobby Bonilla hit 24 homers and drove in 86 runs for the Pirates, but he also led major league third basemen with 35 errors.

nificantly from the previous season, dropping from .262 to .232 and rarely showing the spectacular defense that characterized his first season as a regular.

Veteran Gary Redus played out of position at first base in place of the injured Bream. He batted .283, hit for the cycle on August 25 against Cincinnati and recovered fully after being hit in the face by a fastball from Dodgers righthander Tim Crews on July 24.

Left fielder Barry Bonds saw his average drop 35 points from 1988 and his homer total decline from 24 to 19. Right field was staffed by a committee that included Glenn Wilson, who started 81 games before his August 22 trade to Houston for Billy Hatcher, and R.J. Reynolds, a prototype fourth outfielder who batted .270. Hatcher was limited to 19 starts by a late-season knee injury.

LaValliere, the Pirates' only productive catcher, batted a career-best .316 in 68 games. The others to man the spot behind the plate for Pittsburgh included Dann Bilardello, who batted .225, Junior Ortiz (.217) and Tom Prince (.135).

General Manager Larry Doughty had a shaky rookie season. On April 21 he traded pitcher Mike Dunne and two prospects to Seattle for shortstop Rey Quinones. Quinones batted .209 with 19 errors in 71 games and was released on July 22 after his erratic play had exasperated Leyland and Doughty.

Doughty, however, was also responsible for acquiring Landrum, Heaton and Bell.

Doughty and Leyland are convinced that injuries were the reason a team expected to contend for N.L. East honors fell well short of expectations in 1989. The two men can only hope that the real Pittsburgh Pirates were those of 1988, not those of last year.

Despite a .259 batting average, outfielder Von Hayes hit a career-high 26 home runs and had five multi-homer games.

Quick-Change Phils Last Again

By BILL BROWN

Even though some of the names had changed from the year before, change alone wasn't enough to alter the fortunes of the Philadelphia Phillies in 1989.

Coming off their first last-place finish since 1973, the Phils again ended up in the National League Eastern Division basement, posting a 67-95 record in Manager Nick Leyva's first year at the helm.

Although General Manager Lee Thomas moved early and often to reverse the team's slide, the '89 Phils managed to win just two more games than the year before.

The first sign of trouble came April 18, when promising rookie outfielder Ron Jones, who was batting .290 with two home runs, was lost for the season after tearing up his knee running into the right-field fence at Shea Stadium.

By the time the Phillies slipped into last place for good on May 25, they had already lost three starting pitchers. Bruce Ruffin was sent to Triple-A after an 0-2 start, Steve Ontiveros was disabled with a sore elbow after going 2-0, and Marvin Freeman went down with a season-ending shoulder injury after his first start of the year.

On May 29, third baseman Mike Schmidt retired from the game in an emotional farewell played out in a spare football locker room at San Diego's Jack Murphy Stadium.

Trying to come back from a partial tear of the rotator cuff in his right shoulder, the future Hall of Famer played well for a week before watching his once-formidable skills dissolve with almost incredible haste.

"I look at the Will Clarks and the Kevin Mitchells and I see the player I used to be," said a sobbing Schmidt, who was 39 when he called it quits. "It hurts to know that I'm no longer that player."

On June 3, the Phillies traded outfielder-third baseman Chris James, Schmidt's best friend on the team, to the Padres in exchange for John Kruk and Randy Ready.

It was considered a bold move because James, who led the team with 19 home runs in 1988, appeared to be Schmidt's most likely successor at third base.

But a couple weeks later, on June 18, Thomas engineered two more blockbuster trades that shed some light on the James deal.

First, Thomas dealt 1987 Cy Young

First baseman Ricky Jordan rebounded with a strong second half to bat .285 and drive in 75 runs.

Award winner Steve Bedrosian to the Giants for lefthanders Terry Mulholland and Dennis Cook and third baseman Charlie Hayes.

Next, the Phils sent popular infielder-outfielder Juan Samuel, a two-time All Star, to the Mets in exchange for outfielder Lenny Dykstra and relief pitcher Roger McDowell.

The immediate impact on the team was positive. Between June 18 and July 19, the Phils were 15-13 and starting to feel optimistic about the future.

But then the Phils lost six in a row—four of those defeats by one run—and the momentum came to a grinding halt. The Phils didn't win four games in a row until the final four games of the season.

Despite the last-place finish, not all the news was bad last year. Rookie lefthander Pat Combs, the Phillies' No. 1 draft pick in 1988, won four games without a loss in six starts after a September call-up.

Thomas and Leyva were also upbeat about the sophomore year of first baseman Ricky Jordan, who batted .302 in the second half of the season after struggling

SCORES OF PHILADELPHIA PHILLIES' 1989 GAMES

APRIL

Date		Score	Winner	Loser
4—At Chicago	L	4-5	Sutcliffe	Youmans
5—At Chicago	W	12-4	Howell	Maddux
6—At Chicago	W	8-3	Ontiveros	Kilgus
8—St. Louis	W	5-4§	Parrett	Costello
9—St. Louis	L	3-15	Magrane	Ruffin
10—Montreal	W	7-6	Bedrosian	Harris
11—Montreal	W	6-2	Ontiveros	Perez
12—Montreal	W	6-3	Carman	Gross
14—Chicago	L	4-6	Sanderson	Ruffin
16—Chicago	L	3-5	Sutcliffe	Youmans
17—At N.Y.	L	2-5	Fernandez	Carman
18—At N.Y.	W	7-1	McWilliams	Darling
19—At N.Y.	L	2-4	Myers	Bedrosian
20—At Pitts.	L	9-4	Howell	Dunne
21—At Pitts.	W	3-2	Youmans	Drabek
22—At Pitts.	L	3-4	Robinson	Carman
23—At Pitts.	L	4-6	Easley	Bedrosian
24—At Hous.	W	8-4	Harris	Forsch
25—At Hous.	L	1-4	Scott	Howell
26—At Hous.	L	5-6	Darwin	Parrett
28—Cincinnati	L	0-3	Rijo	Carman
29—Cincinnati	W	8-0*	Maddux	Jackson
30—Cincinnati	L	3-5	Dibble	McWilliams

Won 11, Lost 12

MAY

Date		Score	Winner	Loser
2—Houston	L	4-12	Deshaies	Youmans
3—At Atlanta	L	3-6	Smoltz	Carman
4—At Atlanta	L	0-3	Glavine	Maddux
5—At Cin.	W	7-0	Howell	Browning
6—At Cin.	L	4-7	Mahler	McWilliams
7—At Cin.	W	5-0	Madrid	Armstrong
9—Atlanta	L	2-7	Smoltz	Carman
11—Atlanta	L	3-8	Glavine	O'Neal
12—Los Ang.	W	3-0	Howell	Leary
13—Los Ang.	W	2-0	McWilliams	Belcher
14—Los Ang.	L	0-9	Hershiser	Madrid
15—San Fran.	W	3-2x	Bedrosian	Lefferts
16—San Fran.	L	5-13	Hammaker	Maddux
17—San Fran.	L	0-6	Reuschel	Howell
19—San Diego	L	2-8	Whitson	McWilliams
20—San Diego	L	2-3	Rasmussen	Carman
21—San Diego	W	3-1	Sebra	Terrell
23—At L.A.	W	4-1	Howell	Valenzuela
24—At L.A.	L	2-4	Leary	McWilliams
25—At L.A.	L	6-7	Belcher	Carman
26—At S.F.	L	1-6	Garrelts	Sebra
27—At S.F.	L	2-6	Hammaker	Madrid
28—At S.F.	L	5-8	Reuschel	Howell
29—At S.D.	L	0-1	Hurst	McWilliams
30—At S.D.	L	3-9	Whitson	Carman
31—At S.D.	L	1-2	Harris	Parrett

Won 7, Lost 19

JUNE

Date		Score	Winner	Loser
2—Montreal	L	1-2y	Frey	Harris
3—Montreal	L	5-7	Gross	McWilliams
4—Montreal	L	4-7	Martinez	Carman
5—Pittsburgh	T	3-3†	.....	.....
6—Pittsburgh	W	9-4	Sebra	Fisher
7—Pittsburgh	W	7-5	Parrett	Kipper
8—Pittsburgh	W	15-11	Carman	Robinson
9—At Mon.	L	0-5	Martinez	Youmans
10—At Mon.	L	1-9	B. Smith	Ruffin
11—At Mon.	L	2-7	Perez	Sebra
13—At Pitts.	W	10-2	Howell	Madden
14—At Pitts.	L	4-6	Smiley	Carman
15—At Pitts.	L	3-5	Drabek	Sebra
16—New York	L	11-15	Myers	Bedrosian
17—New York	L	0-1	Ojeda	McWilliams
18—New York	W	6-5	Parrett	Myers
20—St. Louis	L	4-6	Hill	Mulholland
20—St. Louis	L	3-5	DiPino	Ontiveros
22—St. Louis	W	11-2	Cook	DeLeon
23—At N.Y.	L	3-9	Ojeda	Howell
24—At N.Y.	L	2-4	Darling	Youmans
25—At N.Y.	L	1-5	Fernandez	Mulholland
26—At St. L.	W	5-4	Parrett	Worrell
27—At St. L.	W	4-2	Cook	DeLeon
28—At St. L.	L	1-2	Magrane	Howell
30—Atlanta	W	4-2	Mulholland	Z. Smith
30—Atlanta	L	1-3	Lilliquist	McWilliams

Won 9, Lost 17

JULY

Date		Score	Winner	Loser
1—Atlanta	W	4-2	Ruffin	P. Smith
2—Atlanta	L	1-3	Smoltz	Cook
3—Cincinnati	W	2-1	Howell	Rijo
4—Cincinnati	L	1-2	Browning	Mulholland
5—Cincinnati	W	3-2‡	McDowell	Franco
6—At Atlanta	W	4-0	Ruffin	P. Smith
7—At Atlanta	L	3-5	Smoltz	Cook
8—At Atlanta	L	3-4	Assenmacher	Parrett
9—At Atlanta	W	4-3y	Parrett	Boever
13—Houston	W	11-4	Ruffin	Knepper
13—Houston	L	0-3	Forsch	Cook
14—Houston	W	4-2	Parrett	Andersen
15—Houston	L	6-9	Portugal	McWilliams
17—At Cin.	W	4-1	Howell	Robinson
18—At Cin.	W	6-5	Frohwirth	Jackson
19—At Cin.	W	9-4	Cook	Browning
21—At Hous.	L	2-4	Scott	Mulholland
22—At Hous.	L	0-1	Deshaies	Howell
22—At Hous.	L	3-4	Darwin	McWilliams
23—At Hous.	L	2-3	Forsch	Ruffin
24—At Mon.	L	3-4x	McGaffigan	Harris
25—At Mon.	L	0-2	Langston	Carman
26—At Mon.	W	4-3	Parrett	Z. Smith
28—Pittsburgh	L	5-10	Heaton	Howell
28—Pittsburgh	W	6-1	Harris	Reed
29—Pittsburgh	W	6-2	Parrett	Walk
30—Pittsburgh	W	8-6	Cook	Kipper
31—Chicago	L	2-10	Sutcliffe	Mulholland
31—Chicago	W	7-4	Carman	Kilgus

Won 15, Lost 14

AUGUST

Date		Score	Winner	Loser
1—Chicago	L	1-4	Wilson	McWilliams
2—Chicago	W	6-0	Howell	Sanderson
3—Chicago	L	0-2	Maddux	Ruffin
4—At St. L.	L	3-6	Magrane	Cook
5—At St. L.	W	7-3	Mulholland	DeLeon
6—At St. L.	L	4-5‡	Worrell	Parrett
7—New York	W	2-1	McDowell	Musselman
8—New York	L	0-9	Cone	Ruffin
9—New York	L	0-6	Ojeda	Cook
10—At Chicago	W	16-13	Parrett	Wilson
11—At Chicago	L	2-9	Maddux	Carman
12—At Chicago	L	7-9	Bielecki	Howell
13—At Chicago	W	5-3	Parrett	Wilson
15—Los Ang.	W	7-6	Parrett	Searage
16—Los Ang.	W	6-2	Carman	Belcher
17—Los Ang.	L	4-10	Valenzuela	Howell
18—San Fran.	L	2-5	Reuschel	Ruffin
19—San Fran.	W	1-0	Mulholland	Downs
20—San Fran.	L	2-5	Brantley	McDowell
21—San Diego	L	2-8	Rasmussen	Carman
22—San Diego	W	4-2	Howell	Grant
23—San Diego	L	3-7	Benes	Ruffin
25—At L.A.	W	3-2	Mulholland	Martinez
26—At L.A.	L	0-4	Belcher	Cook
27—At L.A.	L	1-8	Valenzuela	Carman
28—At S.F.	W	9-1	Howell	Reuschel
29—At S.F.	W	6-1	Ruffin	Robinson
30—At S.F.	L	2-3	Downs	Mulholland
31—At S.D.	L	1-5	Rasmussen	Carman

Won 12, Lost 17

SEPTEMBER

Date		Score	Winner	Loser
2—At S.D.	L	2-3	Hurst	Howell
3—At S.D.	L	5-9	Benes	Cook
4—Pittsburgh	L	5-7	Patterson	Maddux
5—Pittsburgh	W	3-2	Parrett	Patterson
6—Chicago	W	9-1	Ruffin	Maddux
7—Chicago	L	2-6	Bielecki	Howell
8—At Mon.	W	4-3	Grimsley	Gross
9—At Mon.	L	5-6	Burke	Parrett
10—At Mon.	W	4-2	Combs	Perez
11—New York	L	2-5	Darling	Ruffin
12—New York	W	2-1	McDowell	Aase
13—New York	W	4-10	Ojeda	Grimsley
15—St. Louis	W	2-0	Combs	Hill
15—St. Louis	L	6-7	Costello	McDowell
17—St. Louis	W	9-5x	Cook	Kinzer
17—St. Louis	L	0-2	Carpenter	Howell
18—At Pitts.	L	2-6	Patterson	Grimsley
19—At Pitts.	L	2-4	Robinson	Ruffin
20—At Chicago	W	9-8	Carman	Lancaster
21—At Chicago	L	1-9	Maddux	Mulholland
22—At St. L.	L	1-2‡	Costello	McDowell
23—At St. L.	L	5-11	DiPino	Cook
24—At St. L.	L	1-2	Power	Parrett
25—At N.Y.	W	2-1	Combs	Ojeda
26—At N.Y.	L	0-3	Fernandez	Grimsley
27—At N.Y.	W	3-5	Howell	Darling
29—Montreal	W	2-0	Cook	Langston
30—Montreal	W	6-3	Ruffin	Gardner

Won 12, Lost 16

OCTOBER

Date		Score	Winner	Loser
1—Montreal	W	5-3	Combs	B. Smith

Won 1, Lost 0

*5 innings. †7½ innings. ‡10 innings. §11 innings. x12 innings. y13 innings.

Ken Howell finished 12-12 and was the only Philadelphia starter to record a .500-or-better record.

with badly strained hand and wrist in the first half.

It was also a good year at shortstop, where Dickie Thon rediscovered his old batting stroke and Steve Jeltz finally came alive.

Thon, who hit .271 for the season, led N.L. shortstops with 15 home runs and appeared to rebound completely from being hit in the eye by a Mike Torrez pitch in 1984.

"Dickie's back," said Leyva. "You've got be excited for a young man who's worked so hard and long to make it."

Jeltz, who was Thon's caddy for much of the year, batted .243 with four home runs.

McDowell finished the year with 23 saves and a 1.96 earned run average, helping to make the Samuel deal look better in light of Dykstra's lackluster .237 batting average.

Kruk helped make the James trade look good by hitting an even .300, the only Phillies regular to reach that level.

The Phils also got a good season from righthanded reliever Jeff Parrett, who was 12-6 with a 2.98 ERA in 72 appearances.

Second baseman Tom Herr hit .287 and made only seven errors in his first year with the Phillies.

Beyond those bright spots, however, remained dark clouds.

Outfielder Von Hayes, the N.L.'s Player of the Month for April, signed a new three-year contract worth roughly $9 million on June 14 before finishing the season with his worst batting average (.259) since joining the team in 1983. Hayes did, however, hit a career-high 26 home runs and had five multi-homer games.

Charlie Hayes made a whopping 22 errors in 84 games at third base to make no one forget about Schmidt. At the plate, he was hot and cold for most of the year and finished with eight homers and a .257 average.

Catching was a disaster area last year. Darren Daulton hit just .201 in 368 at-bats and backup Steve Lake drove in only 14 runs in 58 games.

The pitchers weren't any better. Righthander Ken Howell won his final start of the season to finish 12-12, making him the only regular starter to finish .500 or better.

The two arrivals in the Bedrosian trade, Mulholland and Cook, were both disappointing. Mulholland ended the year with a 4-7 record and 4.92 ERA while Cook was 7-8 with a 3.72 ERA.

Ruffin came back from the minor leagues in June to finish 6-10. Don Carman, pitching in and out of the rotation, was the staff's big loser with a 5-15 mark.

Change was the order of the day for the 1989 Phillies, and if a third straight last-place finish is to be avoided in 1990, even more changes will have to be made.

National League Averages for 1989

CHAMPIONSHIP WINNERS IN PREVIOUS YEARS

Year		Pct.	Year		Pct.	Year		Pct.
1876—Chicago		.788	1914—Boston		.614	1952—Brooklyn		.627
1877—Boston		.646	1915—Philadelphia		.592	1953—Brooklyn		.682
1878—Boston		.683	1916—Brooklyn		.610	1954—New York		.630
1879—Providence		.705	1917—New York		.636	1955—Brooklyn		.641
1880—Chicago		.798	1918—Chicago		.651	1956—Brooklyn		.604
1881—Chicago		.667	1919—Cincinnati		.686	1957—Milwaukee		.617
1882—Chicago		.655	1920—Brooklyn		.604	1958—Milwaukee		.597
1883—Boston		.643	1921—New York		.614	1959—Los Angeles‡		.564
1884—Providence		.750	1922—New York		.604	1960—Pittsburgh		.617
1885—Chicago		.777	1923—New York		.621	1961—Cincinnati		.604
1886—Chicago		.726	1924—New York		.608	1962—San Francisco§		.624
1887—Detroit		.637	1925—Pittsburgh		.621	1963—Los Angeles		.611
1888—New York		.641	1926—St. Louis		.578	1964—St. Louis		.574
1889—New York		.659	1927—Pittsburgh		.610	1965—Los Angeles		.599
1890—Brooklyn		.667	1928—St. Louis		.617	1966—Los Angeles		.586
1891—Boston		.630	1929—Chicago		.645	1967—St. Louis		.627
1892—Boston		.680	1930—St. Louis		.597	1968—St. Louis		.599
1893—Boston		.662	1931—St. Louis		.656	1969—New York (East)		.617
1894—Baltimore		.695	1932—Chicago		.584	1970—Cincinnati (West)		.630
1895—Baltimore		.669	1933—New York		.599	1971—Pittsburgh (East)		.599
1896—Baltimore		.698	1934—St. Louis		.621	1972—Cincinnati (West)		.617
1897—Boston		.705	1935—Chicago		.649	1973—New York (East)		.509
1898—Boston		.685	1936—New York		.597	1974—Los Angeles (West)		.630
1899—Brooklyn		.677	1937—New York		.625	1975—Cincinnati (West)		.667
1900—Brooklyn		.603	1938—Chicago		.586	1976—Cincinnati (West)		.630
1901—Pittsburgh		.647	1939—Cincinnati		.630	1977—Los Angeles (West)		.605
1902—Pittsburgh		.741	1940—Cincinnati		.654	1978—Los Angeles (West)		.586
1903—Pittsburgh		.650	1941—Brooklyn		.649	1979—Pittsburgh (East)		.605
1904—New York		.693	1942—St. Louis		.688	1980—Philadelphia (East)		.562
1905—New York		.686	1943—St. Louis		.682	1981—Los Angeles (West)		.573
1906—Chicago		.763	1944—St. Louis		.682	1982—St. Louis (East)		.568
1907—Chicago		.704	1945—Chicago		.636	1983—Philadelphia (East)		.556
1908—Chicago		.643	1946—St. Louis*		.628	1984—San Diego (West)		.568
1909—Pittsburgh		.724	1947—Brooklyn		.610	1985—St. Louis (East)		.623
1910—Chicago		.675	1948—Boston		.595	1986—New York (East)		.667
1911—New York		.647	1949—Brooklyn		.630	1987—St. Louis (East)		.586
1912—New York		.682	1950—Philadelphia		.591	1988—Los Angeles (West)		.584
1913—New York		.664	1951—New York†		.624			

*Defeated Brooklyn, two games to none, in playoff for pennant. †Defeated Brooklyn, two games to one, in playoff for pennant. ‡Defeated Milwaukee, two games to none, in playoff for pennant. §Defeated Los Angeles, two games to one, in playoff for pennant.

STANDING OF CLUBS AT CLOSE OF SEASON

EAST DIVISION

Club	Chi.	N.Y.	St.L.	Mon.	Pitt.	Phil.	S.F.	S.D.	Hou.	L.A.	Cin.	Atl.	W.	L.	Pct.	G.B.
Chicago	..	10	11	10	12	10	6	5	5	7	7	7	93	69	.574	....
New York	8	..	10	9	9	12	3	5	6	7	8	10	87	75	.537	6
St. Louis	7	8	..	13	5	11	5	10	5	9	4	9	86	76	.531	7
Montreal	8	9	5	..	11	9	7	5	8	5	8	6	81	81	.500	12
Pittsburgh	6	9	13	7	..	8	5	3	5	5	5	8	74	88	.457	19
Philadelphia	8	6	7	9	10	..	4	2	3	6	8	4	67	95	.414	26

WEST DIVISION

Club	S.F.	S.D.	Hou.	L.A.	Cin.	Atl.	Chi.	N.Y.	St.L.	Mon.	Pitt.	Phil.	W.	L.	Pct.	G.B.
San Francisco	..	10	10	8	10	12	6	9	7	5	7	8	92	70	.568	....
San Diego	8	..	10	12	9	11	4	7	2	7	9	10	89	73	.549	3
Houston	8	8	..	10	10	10	7	6	7	4	7	9	86	76	.531	6
Los Angeles	10	6	8	..	10	10	5	5	3	7	7	6	77	83	.481	14
Cincinnati	8	9	8	8	..	10	5	4	8	4	7	4	75	87	.463	17
Atlanta	6	7	8	6	8	..	5	2	3	6	4	8	63	97	.394	28

Championship Series—San Francisco defeated Chicago, four games to one.
Tie Games—Atlanta vs. St. Louis; Pittsburgh vs. Philadelphia; Pittsburgh vs. St. Louis.

SHUTOUT GAMES

Club	S.F.	St.L.	N.Y.	Hou.	L.A.	S.D.	Mon.	Chi.	Pitt.	Phil.	Cin.	Atl.	W.	L.	Pct.
San Francisco...	..	2	4	3	0	2	0	1	0	1	0	3	16	6	.727
St. Louis	0	..	1	0	3	2	4	3	1	1	0	2	17	10	.630
New York	0	1	..	1	1	1	2	1	1	4	0	0	12	9	.571
Houston	0	0	2	..	1	0	0	1	1	2	4	1	12	10	.545
Los Angeles	1	0	0	2	..	0	3	2	3	2	3	3	19	17	.528
San Diego	1	0	0	1	3	..	1	0	2	1	1	1	11	10	.524
Montreal	2	2	1	0	1	1	..	2	0	2	1	1	13	15	.464
Chicago	0	0	0	2	2	1	2	..	2	1	0	2	10	12	.455
Pittsburgh	1	1	0	0	0	1	2	1	..	0	2	0	8	11	.421
Philadelphia	1	1	0	0	2	0	1	1	0	..	3	1	10	16	.385
Cincinnati	0	2	1	1	2	1	0	0	1	1	..	0	9	15	.375
Atlanta	0	1	0	2	2	1	0	0	0	1	1	..	8	14	.364

RECORD AT HOME

EAST DIVISION

Club	N.Y.	Chi.	St.L.	Mon.	Pitt.	Phil.	S.D.	Hou.	S.F.	Cin.	L.A.	Atl.	W.	L.	Pct.
New York	....	6-3	6-3	7-2	4-5	6-3	2-4	3-3	4-2	3-3	4-2	6-0	51	30	.630
Chicago	7-2	....	5-4	6-3	6-3	4-5	3-3	2-4	5-1	3-3	2-4	5-1	48	33	.593
St. Louis	5-4	3-6	....	6-3	2-7	6-3	4-2	2-4	5-1	6-0	2-4	5-1	46	35	.568
Montreal	7-2	5-4	2-7	....	5-4	6-3	3-3	3-3	2-4	2-4	5-1	4-2	44	37	.543
Pittsburgh	4-5	3-6	6-3	3-6	....	6-3	3-3	3-3	1-5	3-3	3-3	4-2	39	42	.481
Philadelphia	3-6	3-6	4-5	6-3	7-2	....	2-4	2-3	2-4	4-2	3-3	2-4	38	42	.475

WEST DIVISION

Club	S.F.	Hou.	S.D.	L.A.	Cin.	Atl.	N.Y.	Chi.	St.L.	Mon.	Pitt.	Phil.	W.	L.	Pct.
San Francisco...	....	7-2	5-4	6-3	6-3	6-3	5-1	3-3	5-1	2-4	4-2	4-2	53	28	.654
Houston	6-3	....	5-4	6-3	5-4	5-4	3-3	3-3	3-3	1-5	4-2	6-1	47	35	.573
San Diego	4-5	6-3	....	6-3	4-5	4-5	5-1	3-3	1-5	3-3	4-2	6-0	46	35	.568
Los Angeles	7-2	5-4	3-6	....	6-3	5-4	2-4	2-4	3-3	3-3	4-2	4-2	44	37	.543
Cincinnati	5-4	4-5	4-5	5-4	....	5-4	2-4	4-2	1-5	4-2	4-2	1-5	38	43	.469
Atlanta	3-6	4-5	2-7	2-5	4-5	....	2-4	4-2	2-4	4-2	4-2	4-2	33	46	.418

RECORD ABROAD

EAST DIVISION

Club	Chi.	St.L.	Mon.	N.Y.	Pitt.	Phil.	S.D.	Hou.	S.F.	Cin.	L.A.	Atl.	W.	L.	Pct.
Chicago	....	6-3	4-5	3-6	6-3	3-3	3-3	3-3	3-3	5-1	4-2	2-4	45	36	.556
St. Louis	4-5	....	7-2	3-6	3-6	5-4	5-1	3-3	1-5	2-4	3-3	4-2	40	41	.494
Montreal	3-6	3-6	....	2-7	6-3	3-6	3-3	5-1	4-2	3-3	3-3	2-4	37	44	.457
New York	2-7	4-5	2-7	....	5-4	6-3	1-5	3-3	1-5	4-2	4-2	4-2	36	45	.444
Pittsburgh	3-6	7-2	4-5	5-4	....	2-7	2-4	2-4	2-4	2-4	2-4	4-2	35	46	.432
Philadelphia	5-4	3-6	3-6	3-6	3-6	....	0-6	1-6	2-4	5-1	2-4	2-4	29	53	.354

WEST DIVISION

Club	S.D.	Hou.	S.F.	Cin.	L.A.	Atl.	N.Y.	Chi.	St.L.	Mon.	Pitt.	Phil.	W.	L.	Pct.
San Diego...	....	4-5	4-5	5-4	6-3	7-2	1-5	1-5	4-2	2-4	5-1	4-2	43	38	.531
Houston	3-6	....	2-7	5-4	4-5	5-4	4-2	4-2	3-3	3-3	3-3	3-2	39	41	.488
San Francisco...	5-4	3-6	....	4-5	2-7	6-3	3-3	2-4	3-3	4-2	3-3	4-2	39	42	.481
Cincinnati	5-4	4-5	3-6	....	3-6	5-4	4-2	4-2	1-5	2-4	3-3	3-3	37	44	.457
Los Angeles	3-6	3-6	3-6	4-5	....	5-2	3-3	0-6	4-2	3-3	3-3	2-4	33	46	.418
Atlanta	5-4	4-5	3-6	4-5	4-5	....	1-5	1-5	2-4	0-6	2-4	4-2	30	51	.370

1989 N.L. Pitching Against Each Club

ATLANTA—63-97

Pitcher	Chi. W—L	Cin. W—L	Hou. W—L	L.A. W—L	Mtl. W—L	N.Y. W—L	Phil. W—L	Pitt. W—L	St.L. W—L	S.D. W—L	S.F. W—L	Totals W—L
Acker	0—0	0—0	0—1	0—0	0—1	0—1	0—0	0—1	0—0	0—1	0—0	0—6
Aldrich	0—0	0—1	0—0	0—1	0—0	0—0	0—0	0—0	0—0	0—0	1—0	1—2
Alvarez	0—0	0—0	2—2	0—0	0—0	0—0	0—0	0—0	1—1	0—0	0—0	3—3
Assenmacher	0—0	0—0	0—2	0—0	0—0	0—1	1—0	0—0	0—0	0—0	0—0	1—3
Boever	0—0	0—2	1—1	0—2	0—0	1—0	0—1	0—1	1—1	0—3	1—0	4—11
Castillo	0—0	0—0	0—0	0—0	0—0	0—0	0—0	0—0	0—0	0—0	0—1	0—1
Clary	0—1	1—0	0—0	0—0	1—0	1—1	0—0	0—0	1—0	0—1	0—0	4—3
Eave	0—0	1—0	1—0	0—0	0—0	0—0	0—0	0—0	0—0	0—0	0—0	2—0
Eichhorn	0—2	1—0	1—0	0—0	2—1	0—0	0—0	0—0	1—1	0—0	0—0	5—5
Glavine	0—1	2—1	0—1	4—0	0—2	0—0	2—0	1—1	0—1	4—0	1—1	14—8
Greene	0—0	0—0	1—1	0—0	0—0	0—0	0—0	0—0	1—0	0—0	0—0	1—2
Henry	0—0	0—1	0—0	0—0	0—0	0—0	0—0	0—0	0—0	0—1	0—0	0—2
Lilliquist	2—1	2—1	0—0	0—0	1—1	0—1	1—0	0—0	0—2	1—1	1—3	8—10
Puleo	0—0	0—0	1—0	0—0	0—0	0—0	0—0	0—0	0—0	0—0	0—1	1—1
P. Smith	1—1	0—1	0—0	2—1	1—0	0—3	0—2	1—3	0—1	0—1	0—1	5—14
Z. Smith	0—1	0—0	0—1	0—2	1—0	0—0	0—1	0—2	0—0	0—0	0—3	1—12
Smoltz	1—0	1—2	1—1	0—2	0—1	0—0	4—0	2—0	0—2	1—2	2—1	12—11
Stanton	0—0	0—0	0—0	0—0	0—0	0—0	0—0	0—0	0—0	0—1	0—1	0—1
Valdez	1—0	0—1	0—0	0—0	0—0	0—0	0—0	0—0	0—0	0—0	0—0	1—2
Totals	5—7	8—10	8—10	6—10	6—6	2—10	8—4	4—8	3—9	7—11	6—12	63—97

No Decisions—Blocker, Mercker, Richards, Russell.

CHICAGO—93-69

Pitcher	Atl. W—L	Cin. W—L	Hou. W—L	L.A. W—L	Mtl. W—L	N.Y. W—L	Phil. W—L	Pitt. W—L	St.L. W—L	S.D. W—L	S.F. W—L	Totals W—L
Assenmacher	0—0	0—0	1—0	0—0	0—0	0—0	0—0	0—0	1—1	0—0	0—0	2—1
Bielecki	1—1	2—1	0—0	2—0	4—1	1—0	2—0	3—2	1—0	2—2	0—0	18—7
Kilgus	0—1	1—0	0—1	0—0	0—3	1—0	0—2	0—0	2—0	2—1	0—2	6—10
Kraemer	0—0	0—1	0—0	0—0	0—0	0—0	0—0	0—0	0—0	0—0	0—0	0—1
Lancaster	0—0	0—0	0—1	1—0	0—0	1—0	0—1	1—0	0—0	0—0	1—0	4—2
Maddux	2—0	1—1	2—2	1—1	3—1	2—1	3—2	1—2	0—1	2—0	2—1	19—12
Perry	0—0	0—0	0—0	0—0	0—0	0—0	0—1	0—0	0—0	0—0	0—0	0—1
Pico	1—0	0—0	0—0	0—1	0—0	0—0	0—0	0—0	1—0	0—0	1—0	3—1
Sanderson	1—1	0—0	1—0	1—1	1—3	0—1	1—1	0—1	2—1	2—0	2—0	11—9
Schiraldi	0—0	0—2	0—1	0—0	0—0	1—1	0—0	1—0	1—2	0—0	0—0	3—6
Sutcliffe	0—1	2—0	1—2	1—2	2—0	2—1	3—0	3—1	2—1	0—1	0—2	16—11
Wilkins	0—0	0—0	0—0	0—0	0—0	1—0	0—0	0—0	0—0	0—0	0—0	1—0
Williams	2—0	1—0	0—0	0—0	0—0	1—2	0—0	0—0	0—1	0—0	0—1	4—4
Wilson	0—1	0—0	0—0	1—0	0—0	0—1	1—2	3—0	1—0	0—0	0—0	6—4
Totals	7—5	7—5	5—7	7—5	10—8	10—8	10—8	12—6	11—7	8—4	6—6	93—69

No Decision—Blankenship.

CINCINNATI—75-87

Pitcher	Atl. W—L	Chi. W—L	Hou. W—L	L.A. W—L	Mtl. W—L	N.Y. W—L	Phil. W—L	Pitt. W—L	St.L. W—L	S.D. W—L	S.F. W—L	Totals W—L
Armstrong	0—0	0—0	0—1	0—0	0—0	1—0	0—1	0—0	0—0	0—1	1—0	2—3
Birtsas	0—0	0—0	1—0	0—1	0—0	0—0	0—0	0—0	0—0	0—1	1—0	2—2
Browning	1—0	1—1	3—1	2—3	1—1	0—2	1—2	2—1	2—0	1—1	1—0	15—12
Charlton	3—0	1—0	0—0	0—0	0—0	0—1	0—0	1—0	0—0	2—1	1—1	8—3
Dibble	0—1	1—0	2—0	2—1	0—0	0—1	1—0	0—0	2—1	1—0	1—1	10—5
Franco	2—1	0—1	0—1	0—0	0—1	0—0	0—1	1—0	0—0	0—2	1—1	4—8
Jackson	0—0	0—2	0—1	1—1	0—1	1—1	0—2	0—0	2—0	2—1	0—2	6—11
Leary	0—1	0—1	1—2	0—0	0—1	0—0	0—0	0—0	0—2	1—0	0—0	2—7
Mahler	0—2	1—0	0—2	0—2	3—1	0—1	1—0	0—3	1—1	2—0	1—1	9—13
Rijo	0—1	0—1	0—0	2—0	0—0	2—0	1—1	1—0	1—0	0—1	0—2	7—6
Robinson	1—0	0—0	1—1	0—0	0—0	0—0	2—0	0—0	0—0	0—0	1—0	5—3
Rodriguez	0—0	0—0	0—0	1—0	0—0	0—0	0—0	0—0	0—0	0—0	0—1	1—1
Roesler	0—0	0—1	0—0	0—0	0—0	0—0	0—0	0—0	0—0	0—0	0—0	0—1
Scudder	3—2	1—0	0—1	0—1	0—0	0—2	0—0	0—1	0—0	0—1	0—1	4—9
Tekulve	0—0	0—0	0—0	0—0	0—3	0—0	0—0	0—0	0—0	0—0	0—0	0—3
Totals	10—8	5—7	8—10	8—10	4—8	4—8	4—8	7—5	8—4	9—9	8—10	75—87

No Decisions—Griffin, Sebra.

HOUSTON—86-76

Pitcher	Atl. W—L	Chi. W—L	Cin. W—L	L.A. W—L	Mtl. W—L	N.Y. W—L	Phil. W—L	Pitt. W—L	St.L. W—L	S.D. W—L	S.F. W—L	Totals W—L
Agosto	1—0	0—0	0—0	1—1	0—2	0—0	0—0	1—1	0—0	0—0	1—1	4—5
Andersen	1—0	0—0	0—0	0—1	1—0	0—0	0—1	1—1	1—1	0—0	0—0	4—4
Cano	0—0	0—1	1—0	0—0	0—0	0—0	0—0	0—0	0—0	0—0	0—0	1—1
Clancy	1—2	0—0	0—2	1—0	0—2	0—2	0—0	1—2	0—0	4—1	0—3	7—14
Darwin	2—0	1—0	0—1	0—0	2—0	1—0	2—0	0—0	1—1	1—1	1—1	11—4
Deshaies	2—2	1—1	4—1	1—1	0—0	2—1	2—0	1—1	1—0	0—3	1—0	15—10
Forsch	0—0	0—0	0—0	1—0	0—0	0—1	2—1	0—0	1—1	0—1	0—0	4—5
Knepper	0—1	1—1	1—1	0—2	0—2	1—1	0—1	0—0	1—0	0—0	0—1	4—10
Meyer	0—0	0—0	0—1	0—0	0—0	0—0	0—0	0—0	0—0	0—0	0—0	0—1
Portugal	0—0	1—0	1—0	1—0	0—0	0—0	1—0	0—0	0—0	0—1	3—0	7—1
Rhoden	0—0	0—0	2—1	0—1	0—0	0—1	0—0	0—0	0—1	0—1	0—1	2—6
Schatzeder	1—1	0—0	0—0	0—0	0—0	0—0	0—0	1—0	2—0	0—0	0—0	4—1
Scott	2—1	2—1	0—0	5—2	1—2	2—0	2—0	2—0	0—1	2—1	2—2	20—10
Smith	0—1	1—1	1—1	0—0	0—0	0—0	0—0	0—0	0—0	1—1	0—0	3—4
Totals	10—8	7—5	10—8	10—8	4—8	6—6	9—3	7—5	7—5	8—10	8—10	86—76

No Decisions—Gross, Mason, Reynolds.

LOS ANGELES—77-83

Pitcher	Atl. W—L	Chi. W—L	Cin. W—L	Hou. W—L	Mtl. W—L	N.Y. W—L	Phil. W—L	Pitt. W—L	St.L. W—L	S.D. W—L	S.F. W—L	Totals W—L
Belcher	1—0	1—1	2—3	1—0	3—0	0—0	2—2	1—1	1—1	2—3	1—1	15—12
Crews	0—0	0—0	0—0	0—0	0—0	0—0	0—1	0—0	0—0	0—0	0—0	0—1
Hamilton	0—0	0—0	0—0	0—1	0—0	0—0	0—0	0—0	0—0	0—0	0—0	0—1
Hartley	0—0	0—0	0—0	0—0	0—0	0—0	0—0	0—0	0—0	0—0	0—1	0—1
Hershiser	2—0	1—2	1—2	2—1	2—1	0—3	1—0	2—1	1—0	0—4	3—1	15—15
Howell	0—0	0—0	1—1	0—0	1—1	0—0	0—0	1—0	0—0	0—0	2—1	5—3
Leary	1—1	0—1	2—0	1—0	0—0	0—0	1—1	0—0	0—2	1—0	0—1	6—7
Martinez	2—1	0—0	0—0	0—0	0—0	0—1	0—1	1—0	0—0	1—0	2—1	6—4
Morgan	0—2	3—1	2—1	2—2	0—1	1—0	0—0	0—2	0—1	1—0	0—0	8—11
Pena	2—0	0—0	0—0	0—2	0—0	2—1	0—0	0—0	0—0	0—0	0—0	4—3
Searage	0—0	0—0	0—1	0—1	1—0	0—0	2—0	0—1	1—0	0—0	0—0	3—4
Valenzuela	2—1	0—1	2—0	1—2	0—0	1—0	0—0	0—3	1—2	1—2	1—2	10—13
Wetteland	0—1	0—1	0—0	1—1	1—0	0—2	0—0	1—0	0—1	1—2	1—0	5—8
Totals	10—6	5—7	10—8	8—10	7—5	5—7	6—6	7—5	3—9	6—12	10—8	77—83

No Decisions—Fischer, Hatcher, Horton, Munoz, Tudor.

MONTREAL—81-81

Pitcher	Atl. W—L	Chi. W—L	Cin. W—L	Hou. W—L	L.A. W—L	N.Y. W—L	Phil. W—L	Pitt. W—L	St.L. W—L	S.D. W—L	S.F. W—L	Totals W—L
Burke	0—0	1—0	1—0	1—0	0—1	1—1	1—0	2—0	0—1	0—0	2—0	9—3
Candelaria	0—0	0—0	0—0	0—0	0—0	0—1	0—0	0—1	0—0	0—0	0—0	0—2
Frey	0—1	0—0	1—0	0—0	0—0	1—1	1—0	0—0	0—0	0—0	0—0	3—2
Gardner	0—0	0—0	0—0	0—0	0—0	0—0	0—1	0—0	0—1	0—1	0—0	0—3
Gross	1—1	2—1	1—0	1—1	2—1	1—1	1—2	1—1	0—3	0—1	1—0	11—12
Harris	0—0	0—0	0—0	0—0	0—0	1—0	0—1	0—0	0—0	0—0	0—0	1—1
Hesketh	1—1	0—0	0—0	1—1	1—1	1—0	0—0	2—0	0—0	0—0	0—1	6—4
Holman	1—0	0—0	0—0	0—0	0—0	0—0	0—0	0—0	0—0	0—1	0—1	1—2
R. Johnson	0—1	0—0	0—0	0—0	0—0	0—0	0—0	0—2	0—1	0—0	0—0	0—4
Langston	1—0	1—2	1—1	1—0	0—2	2—1	1—1	3—0	1—1	1—0	0—1	12—9
Den. Martinez	1—0	2—2	2—1	2—0	0—1	0—1	2—0	1—1	1—1	2—0	3—0	16—7
McGaffigan	0—0	0—0	1—0	0—1	0—0	0—1	1—0	1—1	0—1	0—1	0—0	3—5
Perez	1—1	0—2	0—2	0—1	1—1	2—0	1—2	1—1	2—1	1—1	0—1	9—13
B. Smith	0—1	2—2	1—0	2—0	1—0	0—2	1—1	0—0	1—3	1—1	1—1	10—11
Z. Smith	0—0	0—0	0—0	0—0	0—0	0—0	0—1	0—0	0—0	0—0	0—0	0—1
Thompson	0—0	0—1	0—0	0—0	0—0	0—0	0—0	0—0	0—0	0—1	0—0	0—2
Totals	6—6	8—10	8—4	8—4	5—7	9—9	9—9	11—7	5—13	5—7	7—5	81—81

No Decisions—Foley, Gideon, Lugo, Wallach.

NEW YORK—87-75

Pitcher	Atl. W—L	Chi. W—L	Cin. W—L	Hou. W—L	L.A. W—L	Mtl. W—L	Phil. W—L	Pitt. W—L	St.L. W—L	S.D. W—L	S.F. W—L	Totals W—L
Aase	0—0	0—1	0—0	0—0	0—1	0—0	0—1	1—1	0—1	0—0	0—0	1—5
Aguilera	2—0	2—2	1—0	0—0	0—1	0—2	0—0	1—1	0—0	0—0	0—0	6—6
Cone	2—0	0—2	1—0	3—1	2—0	2—1	1—0	1—0	2—1	0—1	0—2	14—8
Darling	2—0	0—1	2—0	1—2	0—0	2—2	2—2	1—2	1—2	2—1	1—2	14—14
Fernandez	0—1	2—0	3—1	2—0	1—1	0—1	3—0	1—1	2—0	0—0	0—0	14—5
Gooden	2—0	3—0	0—1	0—1	1—0	2—1	0—0	0—0	1—0	0—1	0—0	9—4
Innis	0—0	0—0	0—0	0—0	0—0	0—0	0—0	0—1	0—0	0—0	0—0	0—1
Machado	0—0	0—0	0—0	0—0	0—0	0—1	0—0	0—0	0—0	0—0	0—0	0—1
McDowell	0—0	0—0	0—0	0—0	0—2	0—0	0—0	0—1	0—0	1—1	0—1	1—5
Mitchell	0—0	0—0	0—0	0—0	0—0	0—0	0—0	0—0	0—0	0—1	0—0	0—1
Musselman	0—0	0—0	0—0	0—0	0—0	1—0	0—0	1—0	1—1	1—0	0—0	3—2
Myers	0—0	0—0	1—0	0—0	0—0	0—0	2—1	1—2	0—0	0—1	2—0	7—4
Ojeda	2—1	1—2	0—1	0—1	2—0	1—1	4—1	2—0	1—2	0—0	0—2	13—11
Viola	0—0	0—1	0—0	0—0	1—0	1—0	0—0	1—0	2—1	0—1	0—2	5—5
West	0—0	0—0	0—1	0—0	0—0	0—0	0—0	0—0	0—0	0—0	0—0	0—2
Whitehurst	0—0	0—1	0—0	0—0	0—0	0—0	0—0	0—0	0—0	0—0	0—0	0—1
Totals	10—2	8—10	8—4	6—6	7—5	9—9	12—6	9—9	10—8	5—7	3—9	87—75

No Decisions—Beatty, M. Hernandez, Leach, Tapani.

PHILADELPHIA—67-95

Pitcher	Atl. W—L	Chi. W—L	Cin. W—L	Hou. W—L	L.A. W—L	Mtl. W—L	N.Y. W—L	Pitt. W—L	St.L. W—L	S.D. W—L	S.F. W—L	Totals W—L
Bedrosian	0—0	0—0	0—0	0—0	0—0	1—0	0—2	0—1	0—0	0—0	1—0	2—3
Carman	0—2	2—1	0—1	0—0	1—2	1—2	0—1	1—2	0—0	0—4	0—0	5—15
Combs	0—0	0—0	0—0	0—0	0—0	2—0	1—0	0—0	1—0	0—0	0—0	4—0
Cook	0—2	0—0	1—0	0—1	0—1	1—0	0—1	1—0	3—2	0—1	0—0	6—8
Frohwirth	0—0	0—0	1—0	0—0	0—0	0—0	0—0	0—0	0—0	0—0	0—0	1—0
Grimsley	0—0	0—0	0—0	0—0	0—0	1—0	0—2	0—1	0—0	0—0	0—0	1—3
Harris	0—0	0—0	0—0	0—0	0—0	0—0	0—2	0—0	1—0	0—0	0—0	2—2
Howell	0—0	2—2	3—0	0—2	2—1	0—0	1—1	2—1	0—2	1—1	1—2	12—12
Maddux	0—1	0—0	1—0	0—0	0—0	0—0	0—0	0—1	0—0	0—0	0—1	1—3
Madrid	0—0	0—0	1—0	0—0	0—1	0—0	0—0	0—0	0—0	0—0	0—1	1—2
McDowell	0—0	0—0	1—0	0—0	0—0	0—0	2—0	0—0	0—2	0—0	0—1	3—3
McWilliams	0—1	0—1	0—2	0—2	1—1	0—1	1—1	0—0	0—0	0—2	0—0	2—11
Mulholland	1—0	0—2	0—1	0—1	1—0	0—0	0—1	0—0	1—1	0—0	1—1	4—7
O'Neal	0—1	0—0	0—0	0—0	0—0	0—0	0—0	0—0	0—0	0—0	0—0	0—1
Ontiveros	0—0	1—0	0—0	0—0	0—0	0—0	0—0	0—0	1—0	0—0	0—0	2—1
Parrett	1—1	2—0	0—0	1—1	1—0	1—1	1—0	3—0	2—2	0—1	0—0	12—6
Ruffin	2—0	1—2	0—0	1—1	0—0	1—1	0—2	0—1	0—1	0—1	1—1	6—10
Sebra	0—0	0—0	0—0	0—0	0—0	0—1	0—0	1—1	0—0	1—0	0—1	2—3
Youmans	0—0	0—2	0—0	0—0	0—1	0—0	0—1	1—0	0—0	0—0	0—0	1—5
Totals	4—8	8—10	8—4	3—9	6—6	9—9	6—12	10—8	7—11	2—10	4—8	67—95

No Decisions—Dillard, Freeman, McElroy.

PITTSBURGH—74-88

Pitcher	Atl. W—L	Chi. W—L	Cin. W—L	Hou. W—L	L.A. W—L	Mtl. W—L	N.Y. W—L	Phil. W—L	St.L. W—L	S.D. W—L	S.F. W—L	Totals W—L
Bair	0—0	0—2	0—0	1—0	0—0	1—1	0—0	0—0	0—0	0—0	0—0	2—3
Belinda	0—0	0—1	0—0	0—0	0—0	0—0	0—0	0—0	0—0	0—0	0—0	0—1
Drabek	2—2	3—2	2—0	0—0	0—2	2—0	1—1	1—1	1—1	1—3	1—0	14—12
Dunne	0—0	0—0	0—0	0—0	0—0	1—0	0—0	0—1	0—0	0—0	0—0	1—1
Easley	0—0	0—0	0—0	0—0	0—0	0—0	0—0	1—0	0—0	0—0	0—0	1—0

PITTSBURGH—74-88

Pitcher	Atl. W—L	Chi. W—L	Cin. W—L	Hou. W—L	L.A. W—L	Mtl. W—L	N.Y. W—L	Phil. W—L	St.L. W—L	S.D. W—L	S.F. W—L	Totals W—L
Fisher	0—0	0—0	0—0	0—0	0—0	0—0	0—1	0—1	0—1	0—0	0—0	0—3
Garcia	0—0	0—1	0—0	0—0	0—0	0—0	0—0	0—0	0—0	0—0	0—1	0—2
Heaton	0—0	0—1	0—1	2—1	0—2	1—0	0—0	1—0	2—0	0—2	0—0	6—7
Kipper	0—0	0—0	0—0	0—1	1—0	0—0	2—1	0—2	0—0	0—0	0—0	3—4
Kramer	1—0	1—1	1—1	0—0	0—1	0—1	0—2	0—0	0—1	1—1	1—1	5—9
Landrum	1—0	0—1	0—1	0—0	0—0	0—0	1—1	0—0	0—0	0—0	0—0	2—3
Madden	0—0	0—0	0—0	0—0	0—0	0—0	0—0	0—1	2—1	0—0	0—0	2—2
Medvin	0—0	0—0	0—0	0—0	0—0	0—1	0—0	0—0	0—0	0—0	0—0	0—1
Patterson	0—0	0—0	0—1	0—0	0—0	0—0	0—1	2—1	2—0	0—0	0—0	4—3
Reed	1—0	0—0	0—1	0—0	0—0	0—1	0—0	0—1	0—1	0—0	0—0	1—4
Robinson	0—0	1—1	1—1	0—2	1—1	0—3	1—1	2—1	1—0	0—1	0—2	7—13
Smiley	2—0	1—0	0—0	1—1	1—1	0—4	3—0	1—0	1—0	0—0	2—2	12—8
Smith	0—0	0—0	0—0	0—1	0—0	0—0	0—0	0—0	0—0	0—0	0—0	0—1
Taylor	0—0	0—1	0—0	0—0	0—0	0—0	1—0	0—0	0—0	0—0	0—0	1—1
Walk	1—2	0—1	1—0	1—1	2—0	2—0	0—1	0—1	4—0	1—2	1—1	13—10
Totals	8—4	6—12	5—7	5—7	5—7	7—11	9—9	8—10	13—5	3—9	5—7	74—88

No Decisions—Gott, Samuels.

ST. LOUIS—86-76

Pitcher	Atl. W—L	Chi. W—L	Cin. W—L	Hou. W—L	L.A. W—L	Mtl. W—L	N.Y. W—L	Phil. W—L	Pitt. W—L	S.D. W—L	S.F. W—L	Totals W—L
Carpenter	0—0	2—0	0—1	0—2	1—0	0—1	0—0	1—0	0—0	0—0	0—0	4—4
Costello	1—0	0—1	1—0	0—1	1—0	0—0	0—1	2—1	0—0	0—0	0—0	5—4
Dayley	1—0	1—1	0—0	1—0	0—1	0—0	0—0	0—0	0—1	1—0	0—0	4—3
DeLeon	1—1	2—1	1—0	1—0	0—1	4—1	3—1	0—3	0—2	3—1	1—1	16—12
DiPino	2—0	0—0	0—0	0—0	0—0	1—0	2—0	2—0	0—0	0—0	2—0	9—0
Heinkel	0—0	0—0	0—0	0—0	1—0	0—0	0—0	0—0	0—1	0—0	0—0	1—1
Hill	0—0	0—2	0—3	1—1	2—1	2—2	0—1	1—1	0—2	1—0	0—2	7—15
Horton	0—1	0—0	0—0	0—0	0—0	0—0	0—0	0—1	0—0	0—0	0—0	0—3
Kinzer	0—0	0—0	0—1	0—0	0—0	0—0	0—0	0—1	0—0	0—0	0—0	0—2
Magrane	2—0	1—2	2—0	0—1	3—0	2—1	0—2	3—0	2—3	2—0	1—0	18—9
Power	1—0	0—0	0—1	1—1	0—0	1—0	0—2	1—0	1—1	2—0	0—2	7—7
Quisenberry	0—1	1—0	0—0	0—0	0—0	0—0	2—0	0—0	0—0	0—0	0—0	3—1
Terry	1—0	0—4	0—0	0—1	1—0	1—0	1—1	0—0	2—1	1—1	1—2	8—10
Tewksbury	0—0	0—0	0—0	0—0	0—0	1—0	0—0	0—0	0—0	0—0	0—0	1—0
Worrell	0—0	0—0	0—2	1—0	0—0	0—0	1—0	0—1	1—1	0—0	0—0	3—5
Totals	9—3	7—11	4—8	5—7	9—3	13—5	8—10	11—7	5—13	10—2	5—7	86—76

No Decisions—None.

SAN DIEGO—89-73

Pitcher	Atl. W—L	Chi. W—L	Cin. W—L	Hou. W—L	L.A. W—L	Mtl. W—L	N.Y. W—L	Phil. W—L	Pitt. W—L	St.L. W—L	S.F. W—L	Totals W—L
Benes	0—1	0—0	1—0	0—0	2—0	1—1	0—0	2—0	0—0	0—0	0—1	6—3
Booker	0—0	0—0	0—1	0—0	0—0	0—0	0—0	0—0	0—0	0—0	0—0	0—1
Clements	1—0	0—0	1—0	0—0	0—0	0—0	1—0	0—0	0—0	1—0	0—0	4—1
Davis	1—0	0—0	0—0	1—2	0—0	1—0	1—0	0—0	0—0	0—0	0—1	4—3
Grant	2—0	0—1	1—0	0—0	0—0	2—0	0—0	0—1	1—0	0—0	2—0	8—2
Harris	0—0	0—0	2—2	2—0	1—0	0—1	1—1	0—0	0—1	0—2	1—2	8—9
Hurst	3—1	0—1	0—1	2—1	2—1	0—0	1—1	2—0	3—1	1—2	1—2	15—11
Leiper	0—0	0—0	0—0	0—0	0—0	0—0	0—1	0—0	0—0	0—0	0—0	0—1
Rasmussen	1—2	1—2	1—0	1—0	1—2	0—1	1—1	3—0	0—0	0—1	1—1	10—10
Schiraldi	0—0	0—0	0—1	2—0	1—0	0—0	0—0	0—0	0—0	0—0	0—0	3—1
Schulze	1—0	0—0	0—0	0—1	1—0	0—0	0—0	0—0	0—0	0—0	0—0	2—1
Show	0—0	0—1	2—1	1—0	1—0	1—1	1—0	0—0	1—1	0—1	1—1	8—6
Terrell	1—1	2—2	0—2	0—3	0—0	1—0	0—0	0—1	0—0	0—3	1—1	5—13
Whitson	1—2	1—1	1—1	1—1	2—3	1—1	1—1	2—0	4—0	1—0	1—1	16—11
Totals	11—7	4—8	9—9	10—8	12—6	7—5	7—5	10—2	9—3	2—10	8—10	89—73

No Decisions—Murphy, Nolte, Toliver.

SAN FRANCISCO—92-70

Pitcher	Atl. W—L	Chi. W—L	Cin. W—L	Hou. W—L	L.A. W—L	Mtl. W—L	N.Y. W—L	Phil. W—L	Pitt. W—L	St.L. W—L	S.D. W—L	Totals W—L
Bedrosian	1—2	0—0	0—0	0—1	0—0	0—1	0—0	0—0	0—0	0—0	0—0	1—4
Brantley	0—0	2—0	0—1	0—0	0—0	0—0	0—0	1—0	2—0	2—0	0—0	7—1
Camacho	0—0	0—0	3—0	0—0	0—0	0—0	0—0	0—0	0—0	0—0	0—0	3—0
Cook	0—0	0—0	1—0	0—0	0—0	0—0	0—0	0—0	0—0	0—0	0—0	1—0
Downs	0—1	0—0	0—0	0—1	2—2	0—1	0—0	1—1	0—0	0—1	1—1	4—8
Dravecky	0—0	0—0	1—0	0—0	0—0	1—0	0—0	0—0	0—0	0—0	0—0	2—0
Garrelts	2—1	1—0	1—0	1—1	2—1	1—0	1—0	1—0	1—0	0—1	3—1	14—5
Gossage	0—0	0—0	0—1	0—0	0—0	0—0	0—0	0—0	0—0	2—0		2—1
Hammaker	3—1	0—1	0—1	0—0	0—1	0—1	1—0	2—0	0—0	0—0	0—1	6—6
Knepper	0—0	0—0	0—0	1—0	0—1	1—0	1—0	0—0	1—0	0—0	0—0	3—2
Krukow	0—1	1—0	0—0	0—0	0—0	0—2	2—0	0—0	1—0	0—0	0—0	4—3
LaCoss	1—0	1—1	1—3	2—1	2—1	0—1	0—1	0—0	2—0	0—2	1—0	10—10
Lefferts	0—0	0—0	0—0	1—1	1—0	0—0	0—2	0—1	0—0	0—0		2—4
McCament	0—0	0—1	0—0	0—0	0—0	0—0	0—0	0—0	0—0	1—0	0—0	1—1

Ten months after a cancerous tumor was removed from his pitching arm, Giants pitcher Dave Dravecky allowed just four hits in eight innings in a 4-3 victory over the Cincinnati Reds on August 10. It was Dravecky's first major-league appearance since May 28, 1988.

SAN FRANCISCO—92-70

Pitcher	Atl. W—L	Chi. W—L	Cin. W—L	Hou. W—L	L.A. W—L	Mtl. W—L	N.Y. W—L	Phil. W—L	Pitt. W—L	St.L. W—L	S.D. W—L	Totals W—L
Price	1—0	0—0	0—1	0—0	0—0	0—0	0—0	0—0	0—0	0—0	0—0	1—1
Reuschel	3—0	1—1	2—0	2—1	0—0	2—0	2—0	3—1	0—2	1—0	1—3	17—8
Robinson	1—0	0—1	1—0	3—2	0—2	0—1	2—0	0—1	0—3	3—0	2—1	12—11
Swan	0—0	0—0	0—1	0—0	0—1	0—0	0—0	0—0	0—0	0—0	0—0	0—2
Wilson	0—0	0—1	0—0	0—0	1—1	0—0	0—0	0—0	1—0	0—1	0—0	2—3
Totals	12—6	6—6	10—8	10—8	8—10	5—7	9—3	8—4	7—5	7—5	10—8	92—70

No Decisions—Mulholland, Tate.

OFFICIAL NATIONAL LEAGUE BATTING AVERAGES

(Compiled by the MLB-IBM Baseball Information Service)

CLUB BATTING

Club	AVG	G	AB	R	H	TB	2B	3B	HR	RBI	SH	SF	HP	BB	IBB	SO	SB	CS	GIDP	LOB	SHO	SLG	OBP
Chicago	.261	162	5513	702	1438	2135	235	45	124	653	80	50	26	472	75	921	136	57	114	1093	12	.387	.319
St. Louis	.258	164	5492	632	1418	1994	263	47	73	587	78	43	21	507	59	848	155	54	120	1143	11	.363	.321
San Diego	.251	162	5422	642	1360	1999	215	32	120	598	95	41	9	552	79	1013	155	67	115	1134	10	.369	.319
San Francisco	.250	162	5469	699	1365	2133	241	52	141	647	82	39	40	508	83	1071	87	54	84	1113	6	.390	.316
Montreal	.247	162	5482	632	1353	1980	267	30	100	587	71	46	35	572	83	958	160	70	119	1166	15	.361	.319
Cincinnati	.247	162	5520	632	1362	2045	243	28	128	588	66	49	30	493	67	1028	128	71	96	1115	15	.370	.309
New York	.246	162	5489	683	1351	2114	280	21	147	633	56	48	33	504	69	934	158	53	87	1103	9	.385	.311
Philadelphia	.243	163	5447	629	1324	1980	215	36	123	594	57	42	24	558	57	926	106	50	107	1152	16	.364	.314
Pittsburgh	.241	164	5539	637	1334	1988	263	53	95	584	83	51	22	563	51	914	155	69	115	1143	12	.359	.311
Los Angeles	.240	160	5465	554	1313	1855	241	17	89	513	83	41	27	507	77	885	81	54	98	1171	17	.339	.306
Houston	.239	162	5516	647	1316	1902	239	28	97	598	65	44	24	530	62	860	144	62	80	1125	10	.345	.306
Atlanta	.234	161	5463	584	1281	1910	201	22	128	544	65	42	24	485	51	996	83	54	94	1096	14	.350	.298
Totals	.246	973	65817	7673	16215	24035	2903	411	1365	7126	899	536	318	6251	853	11354	1529	715	1229	13554	147	.365	.312

INDIVIDUAL BATTING

(Top Fifteen Qualifiers for Batting Championship—502 or More Plate Appearances)

(*Lefthanded Batter †Switch-Hitter)

Player, Club	AVG	G	AB	R	H	TB	2B	3B	HR	RBI	SH	SF	HP	BB	IBB	SO	SB	CS	GIDP	SLG	OBP
Gwynn, Anthony, S.D.*	.336	158	604	82	203	256	27	7	4	62	11	4	1	56	16	30	40	16	12	.424	.389
Clark, William, S.F.*	.333	159	588	104	196	321	38	9	23	111	0	8	5	74	14	103	8	3	6	.546	.407
Smith, Lonnie, Atl.	.315	134	482	89	152	257	34	4	21	79	1	3	11	76	13	95	25	12	7	.533	.415
Grace, Mark, Chi.*	.314	142	510	74	160	233	28	3	13	79	3	7	0	80	13	42	14	7	13	.457	.405
Guerrero, Pedro, St.L.	.311	162	570	60	177	272	42	1	17	117	0	12	4	79	13	84	2	0	17	.477	.391
Alomar, Roberto, S.D.	.295	158	623	82	184	234	27	5	7	56	17	5	1	53	4	76	42	17	10	.376	.347
Walton, Jerome, Chi.	.293	116	475	64	139	183	23	3	5	46	2	5	6	27	1	77	24	7	6	.385	.335
Oquendo, Jose, St.L.†	.291	163	556	59	162	207	28	1	7	48	7	8	0	79	7	53	3	5	12	.372	.375
Mitchell, Kevin, S.F.	.291	154	543	100	158	345	34	6	47	125	1	8	3	87	32	115	3	4	9	.635	.388
Sandberg, Ryne, Chi.	.290	157	606	104	176	301	25	5	30	76	6	2	4	59	5	85	15	5	6	.497	.356
Thompson, Milton, St.L.*	.290	155	545	60	158	214	28	8	8	68	5	6	4	39	8	91	27	8	12	.393	.340
Johnson, Howard, N.Y.†	.287	153	571	104	164	319	41	3	36	101	0	6	1	77	8	126	41	8	8	.559	.369
Herr, Thomas, Phil.†	.287	151	561	65	161	204	25	6	2	37	6	6	1	54	8	63	10	7	9	.364	.352
Raines, Timothy, Mtl.†	.286	145	517	76	148	216	29	6	9	60	3	5	3	93	18	48	41	9	8	.418	.395
Jordan, Paul, Phil.	.285	144	523	63	149	213	22	3	12	75	0	8	5	23	5	62	3	3	19	.407	.317

DEPARTMENTAL LEADERS: G—Bonilla, Pitt. and Oquendo, St.L., 163; AB—Benzinger, Cin., 628; R—Clark, S.F., Johnson, N.Y., and Sandberg, Chi., 104; H—Gwynn, S.D., 203; TB—Mitchell, S.F., 345; 2B—Wallach, Mtl. and Guerrero, St.L., 42; 3B—Thompson, S.F., 11; HR—Mitchell, S.F., 47; RBI—Mitchell, S.F., 125; SH—R. Alomar, S.D., 17; SF—Guerrero, St.L., 12; HP—Galarraga, Mtl. and Thompson, S.F., 13; BB—Ja. Clark, S.D., 132; IBB—Mitchell, S.F., 32; SO—Galarraga, Mtl., 158; SB—Coleman, St.L., 65; CS—Young, Hou., 25; GIDP—Wallach, Mtl., 25; Slg. Pct.—Mitchell, S.F., .635; OB. Pct.—L. Smith, Atl., .415.

INDIVIDUAL BATTING
ALL PLAYERS LISTED ALPHABETICALLY
(*Lefthanded Batter †Switch-Hitter)

Player, Club	AVG	G	AB	R	H	TB	2B	3B	HR	RBI	SH	SF	HP	BB	IBB	SO	SB	CS	GIDP	SLG	OBP
Aase, Donald, N.Y.	.000	49	5	0	0	0	0	0	0	0	0	0	0	0	0	3	0	0	0	.000	.000
Abner, Shawn, S.D.	.176	57	102	13	18	28	4	0	2	14	0	1	0	5	2	20	1	0	1	.275	.213
Acker, James, Atl.	.143	59	7	0	1	1	0	0	0	0	1	0	0	0	0	2	0	0	1	.143	.143
Adduci, James, Phil.*	.368	13	19	1	7	8	1	0	0	0	0	0	0	0	0	4	0	0	0	.421	.368
Agosto, Juan, Hou.*	.200	71	5	0	1	1	0	0	0	0	1	0	0	0	0	2	0	0	0	.200	.200
Aguilera, Richard, N.Y.	.000	36	7	1	0	0	0	0	0	0	2	0	0	1	0	2	0	0	0	.000	.125
Aldrete, Michael, Mtl.*	.221	76	136	12	30	43	8	1	1	12	0	2	0	19	4	30	1	3	4	.316	.316
Aldrich, Jay, Atl.	.000	8	1	0	0	0	0	0	0	0	0	0	0	0	0	1	0	0	0	.000	.000
Alomar, Roberto, S.D.†	.295	158	623	82	184	234	27	1	7	56	17	8	1	53	4	76	42	17	10	.376	.347
Alomar, Santos, S.D.	.211	7	19	4	4	8	1	0	1	6	0	0	0	3	1	3	0	0	1	.421	.318
Alvarez, Jose, Atl.	.000	30	3	0	0	0	0	0	0	0	2	0	0	0	0	3	0	0	0	.000	.000
Andersen, Larry, Hou.	.333	60	3	0	1	1	0	0	0	0	1	0	0	0	0	2	0	0	1	.333	.333
Anderson, David, L.A.	.229	87	140	15	32	37	2	0	1	14	2	1	0	17	1	26	2	0	0	.264	.310
Anthony, Eric, Hou.*	.180	25	61	7	11	25	2	0	4	7	0	0	0	9	2	16	0	0	1	.410	.286
Armstrong, John, Cin.	.000	10	8	0	0	0	0	0	0	0	3	0	0	0	0	5	0	0	1	.000	.111
Ashby, Alan, Hou.†	.164	22	61	4	10	13	1	0	0	3	1	1	0	7	1	8	0	0	2	.213	.257
Assenmacher, Paul, Atl-Chi.*	.000	63	5	0	1	1	0	0	0	0	0	0	0	0	0	3	0	0	1	.000	.000
Bair, C. Douglas, Pitt.	.200	44	5	0	1	2	0	0	0	0	1	0	0	0	0	2	0	0	0	.400	.200
Barnes, William, Cin.	.000	5	3	1	0	0	0	0	0	0	0	0	0	0	0	0	0	0	0	.000	.000
Barrett, Thomas, Phil.†	.222	14	27	3	6	6	0	0	0	0	0	0	0	1	0	7	0	0	0	.222	.250
Bass, Kevin, Hou.†	.300	87	313	42	94	136	19	4	5	44	1	4	1	29	3	44	11	4	2	.435	.357
Bathe, William, S.F.	.281	30	32	3	9	10	1	0	0	6	0	1	0	0	0	7	0	0	2	.313	.273
Bean, William, L.A.*	.197	51	71	7	14	18	4	0	0	3	1	0	0	4	0	10	2	2	0	.254	.250
Beatty, G. Blaine, N.Y.*	.500	5	2	0	1	1	0	0	0	0	0	0	0	0	0	0	0	0	0	.500	.500
Bedrosian, Stephen, Phil.-S.F.	.167	68	6	0	1	1	0	0	0	0	0	0	0	4	0	3	0	0	0	.167	.167
Belcher, Timothy, L.A.	.100	39	70	3	7	8	1	0	0	6	10	0	1	2	0	26	0	0	2	.114	.137
Belinda, Stanley, Pitt.		8	0	0	0	0	0	0	0	0	0	0	0	0	0	0	0	0	0		
Bell, Jay, Pitt.	.258	78	271	33	70	95	13	3	2	27	10	2	1	19	0	47	5	3	9	.351	.307
Belliard, Rafael, Pitt.	.214	67	154	10	33	37	4	0	0	8	8	1	0	8	2	22	5	2	1	.240	.253
Benedict, Bruce, Atl.	.194	66	160	12	31	37	3	0	1	6	2	2	1	23	4	18	0	1	1	.231	.299
Benes, Andrew, S.D.	.250	10	24	2	6	9	0	0	1	2	1	0	0	0	0	12	0	0	0	.375	.250
Benjamin, Michael, S.F.	.167	14	6	2	1	1	0	0	0	1	1	0	0	0	0	1	0	0	1	.167	.167
Benzinger, Todd, Cin.†	.245	161	628	79	154	239	28	3	17	76	4	8	2	44	13	120	3	7	5	.381	.293
Berroa Geronimo, Atl.	.265	81	136	7	36	46	4	0	2	9	0	0	2	7	1	32	0	1	2	.338	.301
Berryhill, Damon, Chi.†	.257	91	334	37	86	114	13	0	5	41	9	5	1	16	4	54	1	0	13	.341	.291
Bielecki, Michael, Chi.	.043	33	70	1	3	3	0	0	0	3	6	0	0	3	0	35	0	0	0	.043	.082
Biggio, Craig, Hou.	.257	134	443	64	114	178	21	2	13	60	6	5	2	49	8	64	21	3	7	.402	.336
Bilardello, Dann, Pitt.	.225	33	80	11	18	30	6	0	2	8	1	6	0	2	0	18	1	0	3	.375	.244
Birtsas, Timothy, Cin.*	.250	42	4	1	1	1	0	0	0	0	0	0	0	0	0	1	0	0	0	1.000	.250
Blankenship, Kevin, Chi.	.000	2	1	0	0	4	0	0	1	1	0	0	0	0	0	1	0	0	0	.000	.000
Blauser, Jeffrey, Atl.	.270	142	456	63	123	187	24	2	12	46	8	4	1	38	2	101	5	2	7	.410	.325
Blocker, Terry, Atl.*	.226	26	31	2	7	8	1	0	0	1	0	0	0	1	0	5	1	1	0	.258	.250
Boever, Joseph, Atl.	.000	66	1	0	0	0	0	0	0	0	1	0	0	0	0	1	0	0	0	.000	.000
Bonds, Barry, Pitt.*	.248	159	580	96	144	247	34	6	19	58	0	4	1	93	22	93	32	10	9	.426	.351
Bonilla, Roberto, Pitt.†	.281	163	616	96	173	302	37	10	24	86	0	5	0	76	20	93	8	8	10	.490	.358
Booker, Gregory, S.D.		11	0	0	0	0	0	0	0	0	0	0	0	0	0	0	0	0	0		

Player, Club	AVG	G	AB	R	H	TB	2B	3B	HR	RBI	SH	SF	HP	BB	IBB	SO	SB	CS	GI DP	SLG	OBP
Booker, Roderick, St.L.★	.250	10	8	1	2	2	0	0	0	0	0	0	0	0	0	1	0	0	0	.250	.250
Brantley, Jeffrey, S.F.	.083	59	12	1	1	1	0	0	0	0	3	0	0	0	0	8	0	0	0	.083	.083
Bream, Sidney, Pitt.★	.222	19	36	3	8	11	3	0	0	4	2	0	0	12	1	10	0	4	1	.306	.417
Brenly, Robert, S.F.	.182	12	22	2	4	6	1	0	0	3	0	1	0	1	0	7	0	0	1	.273	.208
Brooks, Hubert, Mtl.	.268	148	542	56	145	219	30	1	14	70	0	8	4	39	2	108	6	11	15	.404	.317
Brown, Marty, Cin.	.167	16	30	2	5	6	1	0	0	4	0	1	0	4	0	9	0	0	0	.200	.257
Browning, Thomas, Cin.★	.090	41	78	2	7	7	0	0	0	2	14	0	0	4	0	32	0	1	1	.090	.134
Brunansky, Thomas, St.L.	.239	158	556	67	133	228	29	3	20	85	0	5	2	59	3	107	5	9	10	.410	.312
Bullock, Eric, Phil.★	.000	6	4	1	0	0	0	0	0	0	0	0	0	0	0	2	0	0	0	.000	.000
Burke, Timothy, Mtl.	.000	68	3	0	0	0	0	0	0	0	0	0	0	1	0	3	0	0	0	.000	.250
Butler, Brett, S.F.★	.283	154	594	100	168	210	22	4	4	36	13	3	3	59	2	69	31	16	4	.354	.349
Cabrera, Francisco, Atl.	.214	13	14	0	3	5	2	0	0	0	0	0	0	0	0	3	0	0	0	.357	.214
Camacho, Ernie, S.F.	.000	12	1	0	0	0	0	0	0	0	0	0	0	0	0	0	0	0	0	.000	.000
Caminiti, Kenneth, Hou.†	.255	161	585	71	149	216	31	3	10	72	3	4	3	51	9	93	4	1	8	.369	.316
Candelaria, John, Mtl.	—	12	0	0	0	0	0	0	0	0	0	0	0	0	0	0	0	0	0	—	—
Cangelosi, John, Pitt.†	.219	112	160	18	35	43	4	0	0	9	1	0	2	35	2	20	11	0	1	.269	.365
Cano, Joselito, Hou.	.000	6	6	0	0	0	0	0	0	0	0	0	0	0	0	5	0	0	0	.000	.000
Carman, Donald, Phil.★	.029	49	34	1	1	1	0	0	0	1	7	0	0	0	0	13	0	0	2	.029	.029
Carpenter, Cris, St.L.	.444	36	9	0	4	4	0	0	0	0	0	0	0	0	0	2	0	0	1	.444	.444
Carreon, Mark, N.Y.	.308	68	133	20	41	65	6	0	6	16	0	1	0	12	0	17	2	3	0	.489	.370
Carter, Gary, N.Y.	.183	50	153	14	28	42	8	0	2	15	0	0	1	12	1	15	0	3	5	.275	.241
Carter, Steven, Pitt.	.125	12	16	2	2	2	0	0	0	3	0	0	0	2	0	5	0	0	0	.125	.222
Castillo, Antonio, Atl.★	.000	9	1	0	0	0	0	0	0	0	0	0	0	0	0	1	0	0	0	.000	.000
Charlton, Norman, Cin.†	.000	69	5	3	0	0	0	0	0	0	7	0	0	0	0	4	2	0	0	.000	.000
Clancy, James, Hou.	.146	33	41	3	6	7	1	0	0	0	0	0	0	1	0	14	0	0	0	.171	.167
Clark, Jack, S.D.	.242	142	455	76	110	209	19	1	26	94	0	5	1	132	18	145	6	2	10	.459	.410
Clark, Jerald, S.D.	.195	17	41	5	8	13	2	0	1	7	0	0	0	3	0	9	0	1	1	.317	.250
Clark, William, S.F.★	.333	159	588	104	196	321	38	9	23	111	5	8	5	74	14	103	8	3	6	.546	.407
Clary, Martin, Atl.	.161	18	31	3	5	5	0	0	0	1	1	0	0	3	0	7	0	0	0	.161	.235
Clements, Patrick, S.D.	.000	23	6	0	0	0	0	0	0	0	5	0	0	0	0	4	0	0	0	.000	.000
Coleman, Vincent, St.L.†	.254	145	563	94	143	188	21	9	2	28	7	2	2	50	0	90	65	10	4	.334	.316
Collins, David, Cin.†	.236	78	106	12	25	29	4	0	0	7	2	0	0	10	0	17	3	1	2	.274	.302
Combs, Patrick, Phil.★	.167	6	12	0	2	3	1	0	0	0	1	0	0	0	0	4	0	0	1	.250	.167
Cone, David, N.Y.★	.234	34	77	4	18	20	2	0	0	4	6	0	0	2	0	13	1	0	1	.260	.253
Cook, Dennis, S.F.-Phil.★	.214	24	42	5	9	12	1	1	0	3	4	0	0	0	0	6	0	0	2	.286	.214
Cora, Jose, S.D.†	.316	12	19	0	6	7	1	0	0	1	2	0	0	1	0	5	0	0	0	.368	.350
Costello, John, St.L.	.000	48	6	0	0	0	0	0	0	0	0	0	0	0	0	0	0	0	0	.000	.000
Crews, S. Timothy, L.A.	—	44	0	0	0	0	0	0	0	0	0	0	0	0	0	0	0	0	0	—	—
Daniels, Kalvoski, Cin.-L.A.★	.246	55	171	33	42	67	13	1	2	17	0	5	2	43	1	33	9	4	2	.392	.399
Darling, Ronald, N.Y.	.123	35	73	8	9	16	1	1	0	5	8	0	0	2	0	28	0	0	0	.219	.147
Darwin, Danny, Hou.	.118	68	17	1	2	2	0	0	0	2	3	1	0	0	0	8	0	0	0	.118	.111
Dascenzo, Douglas, Chi.†	.165	47	139	20	23	27	2	1	0	12	1	1	0	13	0	13	6	3	4	.194	.234
Daulton, Darren, Phil.★	.201	131	368	29	74	114	12	2	8	44	1	2	2	52	8	58	2	4	7	.310	.303
Davidson, J. Mark, Hou.	.200	33	65	7	13	20	2	1	1	5	0	0	0	7	0	14	1	1	1	.308	.278
Davis, Eric, Cin.	.281	131	462	74	130	250	14	2	34	101	0	11	6	68	12	116	21	7	16	.541	.367
Davis, Glenn, Hou.	.269	158	581	87	156	286	26	1	34	89	0	6	7	69	17	123	4	0	9	.492	.350
Davis, Jody, Atl.	.169	78	231	12	39	56	5	0	4	19	0	1	1	23	3	61	0	0	8	.242	.246
Davis, Mark, S.D.★	.000	70	13	0	0	0	0	0	0	0	0	0	0	0	0	7	0	0	0	.000	.000
Davis, Michael, L.A.★	.249	67	173	21	43	67	7	1	5	19	0	2	1	16	1	28	6	5	2	.387	.309

Player, Club	AVG	G	AB	R	H	TB	2B	3B	HR	RBI	SH	SF	HP	BB	IBB	SO	SB	CS	GI DP	SLG	OBP
Dawson, Andre, Chi.	.252	118	416	62	105	198	18	6	21	77	0	7	1	35	13	62	8	5	16	.476	.307
Dayley, Kenneth, St.L.*	.000	71	5	0	0	0	0	0	0	0	0	0	0	0	0	2	0	0	1	.000	.000
DeLeon, Jose, St.L.	.096	36	83	3	8	8	0	0	0	1	9	0	0	2	0	37	0	0	1	.096	.118
Dempsey, J. Rikard, L.A.	.179	79	151	16	27	46	7	0	4	16	1	0	1	30	3	37	1	0	5	.305	.319
Denson, Andrew, Atl.†	.250	12	36	1	9	10	0	0	0	5	0	0	0	3	0	9	0	0	1	.278	.308
Dernier, Robert, Phil.	.171	107	187	26	32	40	5	0	1	13	9	3	0	14	0	28	4	3	1	.214	.225
Deshaies, James, Hou.*	.120	35	75	2	9	9	0	0	0	2	9	0	0	1	0	26	0	0	3	.120	.132
Diaz, Baudilio, Cin.	.205	43	132	6	27	35	5	0	1	8	0	0	0	6	3	7	0	2	3	.265	.239
Dibble, Robert, Cin.*	.000	74	8	0	0	0	0	0	0	0	3	0	0	0	0	3	0	0	0	.000	.000
Dillard, Gordon, Phil.*	....	5	0	0	0	0	0	0	0	0	0	0	0	0	0	0	0	0	0	....	....
DiPino, Frank, St.L.*	.077	67	13	2	1	1	0	0	0	0	9	0	0	0	0	9	1	0	0	.077	.077
Distefano, Benito, Pitt.*	.247	96	154	12	38	52	8	2	2	15	3	2	3	17	3	30	1	0	6	.338	.333
Doran, William, Hou.†	.219	142	507	65	111	164	25	2	8	58	6	3	2	59	2	63	22	3	8	.323	.301
Downs, Kelly, S.F.	.091	18	22	2	2	2	0	0	0	0	6	0	0	0	0	14	0	0	0	.091	.091
Drabek, Douglas, Pitt.	.104	40	77	1	8	9	1	0	0	3	6	0	1	3	0	14	0	1	3	.117	.148
Dravecky, David, S.F.	.333	2	3	0	1	1	0	0	0	0	2	0	0	2	0	1	0	0	0	.333	.600
Duncan, Mariano, L.A.-Cin.	.248	94	258	32	64	92	15	2	3	21	2	0	5	8	2	51	9	5	3	.357	.284
Dunne, Michael, Pitt.*	.250	13	4	1	1	1	0	0	0	0	6	0	1	1	0	2	0	0	0	.250	.400
Dunston, Shawon, Chi.	.278	138	471	52	131	190	20	6	9	60	6	4	4	30	15	86	19	11	7	.403	.320
Durham, Leon, St.L.*	.056	29	18	2	1	2	1	0	0	1	1	0	1	2	0	4	0	0	1	.111	.182
Dwyer, James, Mtl.*	.300	13	10	1	3	4	1	0	0	2	0	1	0	1	1	1	0	0	0	.400	.364
Dykstra, Lenny, N.Y.-Phil.*	.237	146	511	66	121	182	32	4	7	32	10	5	3	60	1	53	30	12	7	.356	.318
Easley, K. Logan, Pitt.	.000	10	6	0	0	0	0	0	0	0	1	0	0	0	0	1	0	0	0	.000	.000
Eave, Gary, Atl.	.000	3	2	0	0	0	0	0	0	0	0	0	0	0	0	1	0	0	0	.000	.000
Eichhorn, Mark, Atl	.000	45	6	0	0	0	0	0	0	0	1	0	0	3	0	3	0	0	0	.000	.000
Elster, Kevin, N.Y.	.231	151	458	52	106	165	25	2	10	55	6	8	2	34	11	77	4	3	13	.360	.283
Evans, Darrell, Atl.*	.207	107	276	31	57	98	6	1	11	39	0	6	1	41	6	46	4	3	1	.355	.303
Fernandez, C. Sid, N.Y.*	.211	35	71	2	15	21	3	0	1	8	10	0	0	1	0	25	2	0	0	.296	.233
Fischer, Jeffrey, L.A.	....	2	0	0	0	0	0	0	0	0	0	0	0	0	0	0	0	0	0	....	....
Fisher, Brian, Pitt.	.000	9	5	0	0	0	0	0	0	0	2	0	0	0	0	2	0	0	0	.000	.000
Fitzgerald, Michael R. Mtl.	.238	100	290	33	69	112	18	2	7	42	2	1	2	35	3	61	3	4	8	.386	.322
Flannery, Timothy, S.D.*	.231	73	130	9	30	35	5	0	0	8	6	1	1	13	5	20	2	2	8	.269	.299
Fletcher, Darrin, L.A.*	.500	8	8	1	4	7	0	0	1	2	0	0	0	1	0	0	0	0	0	.875	.556
Foley, Thomas, Mtl.*	.229	122	375	34	86	130	19	2	7	39	4	4	3	45	4	53	5	3	2	.347	.314
Ford, Curtis, Phil.*	.218	108	142	13	31	41	5	1	1	13	2	1	1	16	0	33	5	3	4	.289	.298
Forsch, Robert, Hou.	.167	37	24	1	4	4	0	0	0	0	2	0	0	0	0	6	0	0	0	.167	.167
Franco, John, Cin.*	.333	60	3	1	1	1	0	0	0	0	6	0	0	3	0	2	0	0	0	.333	.333
Freeman, Marvin, Phil.	....	1	0	0	0	0	0	0	0	0	0	0	0	0	0	0	0	0	0	....	....
Frey, Steven, Mtl.*	....	20	0	0	0	0	0	0	0	0	0	0	0	0	0	0	0	0	0	....	....
Frohwirth, Todd, Phil.	.000	45	2	0	0	0	0	0	0	0	0	0	0	3	0	1	0	1	0	.000	.000
Galarraga, Andres, Mtl.	.257	152	572	76	147	248	30	1	23	85	1	3	13	48	10	158	12	5	12	.434	.327
Gant, Ronald, Atl.	.177	75	260	26	46	87	8	3	9	25	3	2	1	20	1	63	9	6	0	.335	.237
Garcia, Damaso, Mtl.	.271	80	203	26	55	75	9	1	3	18	1	3	0	15	1	20	5	4	6	.369	.317
Garcia, Miguel, Pitt.*	1.000	11	1	0	1	1	0	0	0	0	0	0	0	0	0	0	0	0	0	1.000	1.000
Gardner, Mark, Mtl.	.167	7	6	0	1	1	0	0	0	0	2	0	0	0	0	4	0	0	0	.167	.167
Garrelts, Scott, S.F.	.136	32	66	3	9	13	0	2	0	0	2	2	2	3	0	30	0	1	0	.197	.174
Gibson, Kirk, L.A.*	.213	71	253	35	54	93	8	2	9	28	0	2	2	35	5	55	12	3	5	.368	.312
Gideon, B. Brett, Mtl.	.000	4	4	0	0	0	0	0	0	0	0	0	0	0	0	0	0	0	0	.000	.000
Girardi, Joseph, Chi.	.248	59	157	15	39	52	10	0	1	14	10	1	2	11	5	26	2	1	4	.331	.304

Player, Club	AVG	G	AB	R	H	TB	2B	3B	HR	RBI	SH	SF	HP	BB	IBB	SO	SB	CS	GIDP	SLG	OBP
Glavine, Thomas, Atl.*	.149	30	67	6	10	12	1	0	0	4	4	1	0	5	0	20	0	0	0	.179	.208
Gonzalez, Jose, L.A.	.268	95	261	31	70	94	11	1	3	18	1	1	0	23	5	53	9	3	2	.360	.326
Gooden, Dwight, N.Y.	.200	19	40	1	8	11	1	0	0	0	3	0	0	0	0	7	0	0	1	.275	.195
Gossage, Richard, S.F.	.000	31	1	0	0	0	0	0	0	0	0	0	0	0	0	0	0	0	0	.000	.000
Gott, James, Pitt.			0	0	0	0	0	0	0	0	0	0	0	0	0	0	0	0	0		
Grace, Mark, Chi.*	.314	142	510	74	160	233	28	3	13	79	3	3	0	80	13	42	14	7	13	.457	.405
Grant, Mark, S.D.	.050	50	20	5	1	1	0	0	0	0	3	0	0	4	0	10	0	0	0	.050	.050
Green, Gary, S.D.	.259	15	27	4	7	10	3	0	0	0	0	0	0	1	0	1	0	1	1	.370	.286
Greene, I. Thomas, Atl.	.100	4	10	1	1	1	0	0	0	0	0	0	0	0	0	3	0	0	0	.100	.208
Gregg, W. Thomas, Atl.*	.243	102	276	24	67	93	8	0	6	23	0	3	0	18	2	45	3	4	4	.337	.288
Griffey, G. Kenneth, Cin.*	.263	106	236	26	62	100	8	0	8	30	3	0	1	29	3	42	4	2	4	.424	.346
Griffin, Alfredo, L.A.†	.247	136	506	49	125	156	27	3	0	29	11	1	0	29	2	57	10	7	5	.308	.287
Griffin, Michael, Cin.	1.000	3	1	1	1	1	0	0	0	0	0	0	0	0	0	0	0	0	0	1.000	1.000
Grimsley, Jason, Phil.	.000	4	5	0	0	0	0	0	0	0	2	0	0	0	0	2	0	0	1	.000	.000
Grissom, Marquis, Mtl.	.257	26	74	16	19	24	2	0	1	2	1	0	1	12	0	21	1	0	0	.324	.360
Gross, Gregory, Hou.*	.200	60	75	2	15	15	0	0	0	4	0	0	0	11	2	6	0	0	3	.200	.310
Gross, Kevin, Mtl.	.141	32	64	5	9	11	2	0	0	4	6	0	0	6	0	32	0	0	0	.172	.214
Guerrero, Pedro, St.L.	.311	162	570	60	177	272	42	1	17	117	0	12	4	79	13	84	2	0	17	.477	.391
Gwynn, Anthony, S.D.*	.336	158	604	82	203	256	27	7	4	62	0	7	1	56	16	30	40	16	12	.424	.389
Gwynn, Christopher, L.A.*	.235	32	68	8	16	22	4	1	0	7	2	1	0	2	0	9	1	0	0	.324	.254
Hall, Albert, Pitt.†	.182	32	33	4	6	10	2	1	0	2	2	0	0	3	0	5	0	0	0	.303	.250
Hamilton, Jeffrey, L.A.	.245	151	548	45	134	207	35	1	12	56	4	6	6	20	5	71	0	0	10	.378	.272
Hammaker, C. Atlee, S.F.†	.368	28	19	3	7	8	1	0	0	3	4	0	0	0	0	3	0	0	0	.421	.368
Harris, Gregory A., Phil.†	.167	44	6	1	1	1	0	0	0	0	1	0	0	0	0	2	0	0	0	.167	.167
Harris, Gregory W., S.D.	.053	56	19	3	1	3	0	0	0	1	4	0	0	2	0	10	0	0	0	.053	.143
Harris, Leonard, Cin.-L.A.*	.236	115	335	36	79	100	10	3	2	26	1	6	2	20	2	33	14	9	14	.299	.283
Harris, T. Eugene, Mtl.	.000	11	1	0	0	0	0	0	0	0	0	0	0	0	0	1	0	0	0	.000	.000
Hartley, Michael, L.A.	.000	5	6	0	0	0	0	0	0	0	0	0	0	0	0	0	0	0	0		
Hatcher, Michael, L.A.	.295	94	224	18	66	85	9	3	2	25	2	6	1	13	3	16	2	1	7	.379	.328
Hatcher, William, Hou.-Pitt.	.231	135	481	59	111	148	19	2	4	51	3	4	6	30	2	62	24	7	4	.308	.277
Hayes, Charles, S.F.-Phil.	.257	87	304	26	78	119	15	1	8	43	2	3	1	11	1	50	3	7	6	.391	.280
Hayes, Von, Phil.*	.259	154	540	93	140	249	27	2	26	78	0	7	4	101	14	103	28	7	7	.461	.376
Heaton, Neal, Pitt.*	.214	44	42	2	9	9	0	0	0	2	2	0	0	2	0	16	0	1	0	.214	.214
Heinkel, Donald, St.L.*	.000	7	6	0	0	0	0	0	0	0	0	0	0	0	0	3	0	0	0	.000	.000
Henry, Dwayne, Atl.	.000	12	12	0	0	0	0	0	0	0	0	0	0	2	0	0	0	0	0		
Hernandez, Keith, N.Y.*	.233	75	215	18	50	70	8	0	4	19	6	1	2	27	3	39	0	3	4	.326	.324
Hernandez, Manuel, N.Y.		1	1	0	0	0	0	0	0	0	0	0	0	0	0	0	0	0	0		
Herr, Thomas, Phil.†	.287	151	561	65	161	204	25	6	2	37	6	1	3	54	2	63	10	7	9	.364	.352
Hershiser, Orel, L.A.	.182	35	77	4	14	20	4	0	0	2	10	1	3	4	0	25	0	0	0	.260	.220
Hesketh, Joseph, Mtl.*	.500	43	2	1	1	1	0	0	0	0	0	0	0	0	0	1	0	0	0	.500	.500
Hill, Kenneth, St.L.	.153	33	59	4	9	10	0	0	0	3	8	0	0	2	0	21	0	0	0	.169	.180
Holman, Brian, Mtl.	.125	10	8	1	1	1	0	0	0	0	0	0	0	0	0	3	0	0	0	.125	.125
Horton, Ricky, L.A.-St.L.*	.250	34	12	1	3	4	1	0	0	1	2	0	0	2	0	2	0	0	0	.333	.250
Howell, Jay, L.A.	.092	56	3	0	0	0	0	0	0	0	0	0	0	0	0	0	0	0	0	.000	.000
Howell, Kenneth, Phil.	.245	33	65	6	6	8	2	0	0	2	10	1	1	2	0	25	0	1	3	.123	.132
Hudler, Rex, Mtl.	.245	92	155	21	38	63	7	0	6	13	0	1	1	6	2	23	15	4	2	.406	.278
Huff, Michael, L.A.	.200	12	25	4	5	9	1	0	0	2	8	1	1	3	0	6	0	1	1	.360	.310
Hurst, Bruce, S.D.*	.071	33	70	4	5	5	0	0	0	0	8	0	0	9	3	47	0	0	1	.071	.177
Huson, Jeffrey, Mtl.*	.162	32	74	1	12	17	5	0	0	2	3	0	0	6	0	6	3	0	6	.230	.225
Innis, Jeffrey, N.Y.	.000	29	2	0	0	0	0	0	0	0	0	0	0	0	0	0	0	0	0	.000	.000

Player, Club	AVG	G	AB	R	H	TB	2B	3B	HR	RBI	SH	SF	HP	BB	IBB	SO	SB	CS	GIDP	SLG	OBP
Jackson, Danny, Cin.	.222	21	36	4	8	9	1	0	0	4	4	0	0	0	0	22	0	0	0	.250	.222
Jackson, Darrin, Chi.-S.D.	.218	70	170	17	37	56	7	0	4	20	0	2	0	13	5	34	1	2	2	.329	.270
James, D. Chris, Phil.-S.D.	.243	132	482	55	117	177	17	2	13	65	0	3	1	26	2	68	5	2	20	.367	.281
James, Dion, Atl.*	.259	63	170	15	44	54	7	0	1	11	4	1	1	25	2	23	5	3	0	.318	.355
Jefferies, Gregory, N.Y.†	.258	141	508	72	131	199	28	2	12	56	2	5	5	39	8	46	21	6	16	.392	.314
Jeltz, L. Steven, Phil.†	.243	116	263	28	64	89	7	3	4	25	6	0	1	45	6	44	4	6	6	.338	.356
Johnson, Howard, N.Y.†	.287	153	571	104	164	319	41	3	36	101	0	6	1	77	8	126	41	8	4	.559	.369
Johnson, Randall, Mtl.	.143	7	7	0	1	1	0	0	0	0	0	0	0	0	0	3	0	0	0	.143	.143
Johnson, Wallace, Mtl.†	.272	85	114	9	31	42	3	1	2	17	0	2	0	7	3	12	1	0	2	.368	.309
Jones, Ronald, Phil.*	.290	12	31	7	9	15	0	0	2	4	0	2	1	0	0	1	1	0	4	.484	.450
Jones, Tracy, S.F.	.186	42	97	5	18	22	4	0	0	12	2	0	1	7	1	14	2	0	2	.227	.233
Jones, W. Timothy, St.L.*	.293	42	75	11	22	28	6	0	0	7	1	2	1	5	0	8	1	4	2	.373	.353
Jordan, Paul, Phil.	.285	144	523	63	149	213	22	3	12	75	1	8	5	23	5	62	4	3	19	.407	.317
Jurak, Edward, S.F.	.238	30	42	2	10	10	3	0	0	1	1	0	0	5	1	5	2	0	1	.238	.319
Justice, David, Atl.*	.235	16	51	7	12	18	3	0	1	3	0	3	0	3	0	9	2	1	0	.353	.291
Kennedy, Terrence, S.F.*	.239	125	355	19	85	115	13	0	5	34	0	2	0	35	7	56	1	3	6	.324	.306
Kilgus, Paul, Chi.*	.073	35	41	1	3	3	0	0	0	2	4	0	0	1	1	11	0	0	3	.073	.095
King, Jeffrey, Pitt.	.195	75	215	31	42	76	13	3	5	19	1	4	2	20	1	34	4	2	3	.353	.266
Kinzer, Matthew, St.L.	.000	8	1	0	0	0	0	0	0	0	0	0	0	0	0	0	0	0	0	.000	.000
Kipper, Robert, Pitt.	.111	52	9	0	1	1	0	0	0	0	3	0	2	0	1	2	0	0	1	.111	.200
Knepper, Robert, Hou.-S.F.*	.186	35	43	5	8	16	5	0	0	1	3	0	0	9	0	9	0	0	0	.372	.327
Kraemer, Joseph, Chi.*	.000	11	1	0	0	0	0	0	0	0	2	0	0	0	0	1	0	0	0	.000	.000
Kramer, Randall, Pitt.	.152	8	33	1	5	6	1	0	0	3	2	0	0	0	0	12	0	0	1	.182	.152
Kruk, John, S.D.-Phil.*	.300	112	357	53	107	156	13	6	8	44	0	3	2	44	2	53	3	1	6	.437	.374
Krukow, Michael, S.F	.063	8	16	0	1	1	0	0	0	0	3	0	0	1	0	6	0	0	0	.063	.063
LaCoss, Michael, S.F.	.073	45	41	1	3	5	2	0	0	1	4	0	0	0	1	16	0	0	1	.122	.156
Laga, Michael, S.F.*	.200	17	20	1	4	8	1	0	1	7	0	0	0	0	0	6	0	0	0	.400	.238
Lake, Stephen, Phil.	.252	58	155	9	39	52	5	1	2	14	3	1	0	12	4	20	0	0	6	.335	.304
Lancaster, T. William, Pitt.	.182	42	11	0	2	3	1	0	0	0	4	0	0	0	0	7	0	0	0	.273	.182
Landrum, Mark, Mtl.	.000	56	3	0	0	0	0	0	0	0	1	0	0	0	0	0	0	0	0	.000	.000
Langston, Mark, Mtl.	.172	24	64	4	11	13	2	0	0	3	13	0	0	0	0	26	0	0	1	.203	.169
Larkin, Barry, Cin.	.342	97	325	47	111	145	14	4	4	36	0	8	2	20	5	23	10	5	7	.446	.375
LaValliere, Michael, Pitt.*	.316	68	190	15	60	76	10	0	2	23	0	7	0	29	7	23	0	2	4	.400	.406
Law, Vance, Chi.	.235	130	408	38	96	145	22	3	7	42	4	5	2	38	7	73	2	2	11	.355	.296
Leach, Terry, N.Y.	.000	33	4	0	0	0	0	0	0	0	0	0	0	0	0	3	0	0	0	.000	.000
Leary, Timothy, L.A.-Cin.	.119	33	59	2	7	9	2	0	0	4	9	0	0	4	1	23	0	0	1	.153	.175
Lefferts, Craig, S.F.*	.000	70	7	0	0	0	0	0	0	0	0	0	0	0	0	5	0	0	0	.000	.000
Leiper, David, S.D.*	.000	22	1	0	0	0	0	0	0	0	0	0	0	0	0	1	0	0	0	.000	.000
Lemke, Mark, Atl.†	.182	14	55	4	10	20	2	1	2	10	1	0	1	5	0	7	0	0	1	.364	.250
Lilliquist, Derek, Atl.*	.190	36	63	5	12	13	1	0	0	2	3	0	0	0	0	18	0	0	0	.206	.190
Lind, Jose, Pitt.	.232	153	578	52	134	167	21	3	2	48	13	0	1	39	7	64	15	4	13	.289	.280
Lindeman, James, St.L.	.111	73	45	8	5	6	1	0	0	2	2	0	0	3	0	18	0	0	0	.133	.163
Little, Dennis, Pitt.	.250	3	4	0	1	1	0	0	0	0	0	0	0	1	0	1	0	0	0	.250	.250
Litton, J. Gregory, S.F.	.252	71	143	12	36	59	5	3	4	17	0	0	0	7	1	29	0	0	3	.413	.291
Lombardi, Phillip, N.Y.†	.229	18	48	4	11	15	1	0	1	3	0	0	0	5	0	8	0	0	2	.313	.302
Lombardozzi, Stephen, Hou.	.216	21	37	5	8	16	3	1	1	3	0	0	0	4	1	9	0	1	3	.432	.293
Lugo, Urbano, Mtl.	......	10	0	0	0	0	0	0	0	0	0	0	0	0	0	0	0	0	0	......	......
Lyons, Barry, N.Y.	.247	79	235	15	58	80	13	0	3	27	1	3	2	11	1	28	0	0	7	.340	.283
Machado, Julio, N.Y.	......	10	0	0	0	0	0	0	0	0	0	0	0	0	0	0	0	0	0	......	......
Madden, Morris, Pitt.*	.000	10	1	0	0	0	0	0	0	0	3	0	0	0	0	1	0	0	0	.000	.000

Player, Club	AVG	G	AB	R	H	TB	2B	3B	HR	RBI	SH	SF	HP	BB	IBB	SO	SB	CS	GIDP	SLG	OBP
Maddux, Gregory, Chi	.210	35	81	6	17	19	2	0	0	4	8	0	1	1	0	22	1	0	0	.235	.229
Maddux, Michael, Phil.*	.000	16	10	2	0	0	0	0	0	0	1	0	0	1	0	1	0	0	0	.000	.091
Madison, C. Scott, Cin.†	.173	40	98	13	17	27	7	0	1	7	0	1	1	8	2	9	0	1	4	.276	.241
Madrid, Alexander, Phil	.000	6	6	0	0	0	0	0	0	0	1	0	0	0	0	3	0	0	0	.000	.143
Magadan, David, N.Y.*	.286	127	374	47	107	147	22	3	4	41	1	4	0	49	6	37	0	1	2	.393	.367
Magrane, Joseph, St.L.*	.138	38	80	6	11	17	3	0	1	4	8	0	1	4	0	18	1	0	0	.213	.179
Mahler, Richard, Cin.	.177	40	62	4	11	13	2	0	0	4	3	0	0	4	0	8	0	0	2	.210	.239
Maldonado, Candido, S.F.	.217	129	345	39	75	125	23	0	9	41	1	3	3	37	4	69	4	0	8	.362	.296
Mann, Kelly, Atl.	.208	7	24	1	5	7	2	0	0	1	0	0	1	0	1	6	0	0	1	.292	.240
Manwaring, Kirt, S.F.	.210	85	200	14	42	50	4	2	0	18	7	1	4	11	1	28	2	0	5	.250	.264
Marshall, Michael, L.A.	.260	105	377	41	98	154	21	1	11	42	0	4	5	33	4	78	2	5	8	.408	.325
Martinez, Carmelo, S.D.	.221	111	267	23	59	93	12	0	6	39	0	2	1	32	3	54	0	0	12	.348	.302
Martinez, David, Mtl.*	.274	126	361	41	99	138	16	7	3	27	7	1	0	27	2	57	23	4	1	.382	.324
Martinez, J. Dennis, Mtl.	.125	34	72	5	9	9	0	0	0	3	9	0	0	5	0	19	1	0	1	.125	.182
Martinez, Ramon, L.A.	.162	16	37	4	6	7	1	0	0	3	2	0	0	1	0	14	0	0	0	.189	.184
Mason, Roger, Hou.		2	0	0	0	0	0	0	0	0	2	0	0	0	0	0	0	0	0		
Mazzilli, Lee, N.Y.†	.183	48	60	10	11	19	2	0	2	7	0	0	0	17	0	19	3	0	1	.317	.364
McCament, L. Randall, S.F.	.333	25	3	0	1	1	0	0	0	0	1	0	0	0	0	1	0	0	0	.333	.333
McClendon, Lloyd, Chi.	.286	92	259	47	74	124	12	1	12	40	1	7	1	37	3	31	6	4	3	.479	.368
McDowell, Oddibe, Atl.*	.304	76	280	56	85	132	18	4	7	24	1	0	0	27	3	37	15	10	0	.471	.365
McDowell, Roger, N.Y.-Phil.	.333	69	3	0	1	1	0	0	0	0	1	0	0	0	0	1	0	0	0	.333	.333
McElroy, Charles, Phil.*		11	0	0	0	0	0	0	0	0	0	0	0	0	0	0	0	0	0		
McGaffigan, Andrew, Mtl.	1.000	57	1	0	1	1	0	0	0	0	1	0	0	0	0	0	0	0	0	1.000	1.000
McGee, Willie, St.L.†	.236	58	199	23	47	70	10	1	3	17	2	1	1	10	0	34	8	6	2	.352	.275
McGriff, Terence, Cin.	.273	6	11	1	3	3	0	0	0	2	0	0	0	2	1	3	0	0	1	.273	.385
McKnight, Jefferson, N.Y.†	.250	6	12	2	3	3	0	0	0	2	0	0	0	2	0	1	0	0	0	.250	.357
McReynolds, W. Kevin, N.Y.	.272	148	545	74	148	245	25	0	22	85	0	3	1	46	10	74	15	7	8	.450	.326
McWilliams, Larry, Phil.*	.111	41	27	1	3	5	2	0	0	3	3	0	0	0	0	14	0	0	1	.185	.111
Meadows, Michael, Hou.*	.176	31	51	5	9	18	0	0	3	10	3	0	0	1	0	14	1	2	0	.353	.189
Medvin, Scott, Pitt.		6	0	0	0	0	0	0	0	0	0	0	0	0	0	0	0	0	0		
Mercker, Kent, Atl.*	.000	2	1	0	0	0	0	0	0	0	0	0	0	0	0	0	0	0	0	.000	.000
Meyer, Brian, Hou.		12	0	0	0	0	0	0	0	0	0	0	0	0	0	0	0	0	0		
Miller, Keith A., N.Y.	.231	57	143	15	33	43	7	0	1	7	3	0	1	5	0	27	6	0	3	.301	.262
Miller, N. Keith, Phil.†	.300	8	10	0	3	4	1	0	0	0	0	0	0	0	0	3	0	0	0	.400	.300
Mitchell, John, N.Y.		2	0	0	0	0	0	0	0	0	0	0	0	0	0	0	0	0	0		
Mitchell, Kevin, S.F.	.291	154	543	100	158	345	34	6	47	125	0	7	3	87	32	115	3	4	6	.635	.388
Mizerock, John, Atl.*	.222	11	27	1	6	6	0	0	0	2	1	0	0	0	0	3	0	0	1	.222	.222
Morgan, Michael, L.A.*	.083	40	36	1	3	3	0	0	0	2	12	0	0	1	0	12	0	0	1	.083	.108
Morris, John, St.L.*	.239	96	117	8	28	40	4	0	2	14	1	1	0	4	1	17	0	0	2	.342	.264
Mulholland, Terence, S.F.-Phil	.056	25	36	1	2	3	1	0	0	0	3	0	0	0	0	17	0	0	0	.083	.056
Munoz, Michael, L.A.*		3	0	0	0	0	0	0	0	0	0	0	0	0	0	0	0	0	0		
Murphy, Dale, Atl	.228	154	574	60	131	207	16	0	20	84	0	6	2	65	10	142	3	0	14	.361	.306
Murphy, Daniel, S.D.		7	0	0	0	0	0	0	0	0	0	0	0	0	0	0	0	0	0		
Murphy, Dwayne, Phil.*	.218	98	156	20	34	66	5	0	9	27	0	0	2	29	2	44	0	1	2	.423	.341
Murray, Eddie, L.A.†	.247	160	594	66	147	238	29	1	20	88	0	7	2	87	24	85	7	2	11	.401	.342
Musselman, Jeffrey, N.Y.*		20	0	0	0	0	0	0	0	0	1	0	0	1	0	0	0	0	0		1.000
Myers, Randall, N.Y.*	.000	65	3	1	0	0	0	0	0	0	0	0	0	0	0	3	0	0	0	.000	.000
Nelson, Robert, S.D.*	.195	42	82	6	16	27	5	0	2	7	0	1	0	20	1	29	0	0	2	.329	.353
Nichols, Carl, Hou.	.077	11	13	0	1	1	0	0	0	2	0	0	0	0	0	3	0	0	0	.077	.077
Nieto, Thomas, Phil	.150	20	20	1	3	3	0	0	0	2	1	0	1	6	0	7	0	0	0	.150	.370

Player, Club	AVG	G	AB	R	H	TB	2B	3B	HR	RBI	SH	SF	HP	BB	IBB	SO	SB	CS	GIDP	SLG	OBP
Nixon, Otis, Mtl.†	.217	126	258	41	56	67	7	2	0	21	2	0	0	33	1	36	37	12	4	.260	.306
Nixon, R. Donell, S.F.	.265	95	166	23	44	49	2	0	1	15	0	0	0	11	1	30	10	3	4	.295	.311
Noboa, Milciades, Mtl.	.227	21	44	3	10	10	0	0	0	1	0	0	0	1	0	3	0	1	0	.227	.244
Nolte, Eric, S.D.★	.000	3	2	0	0	0	0	0	0	0	2	0	0	0	0	1	0	0	0	.000	.000
Oberkfell, Kenneth, Pitt.-S.F.★	.269	97	156	19	42	56	6	1	0	17	2	3	2	10	0	10	0	1	4	.359	.316
O'Malley, Thomas, N.Y.★	.545	9	11	2	6	8	2	0	0	8	0	0	0	0	0	2	0	0	0	.727	.545
O'Neal, Randall, Phil.	.000	20	5	1	0	0	0	0	0	0	0	4	0	2	0	0	0	0	0	.000	.000
O'Neill, Paul, Cin.★	.276	117	428	49	118	191	24	2	15	74	0	4	2	46	8	64	20	5	7	.446	.346
Oester, Ronald, Cin.†	.246	109	305	23	75	93	15	2	0	14	6	0	0	32	8	47	0	5	10	.305	.318
Ojeda, Robert, N.Y.★	.106	32	66	3	7	7	0	0	0	0	6	0	0	3	0	14	0	0	0	.106	.145
Oliver, Joseph, Cin.	.272	49	151	13	41	58	8	0	3	23	1	2	1	6	1	28	0	0	3	.384	.300
Ontiveros, Steven, Phil.	.083	6	12	2	1	2	1	0	0	3	0	0	0	1	0	5	0	0	0	.167	.154
Oquendo, Jose, St.L.†	.291	163	556	59	162	207	28	7	1	48	7	8	0	79	7	59	3	5	12	.372	.375
Ortiz, Adalberto, Pitt.	.217	91	230	16	50	61	6	1	1	22	3	3	3	20	4	20	0	2	9	.265	.282
Owen, Spike, Mtl.†	.233	142	437	52	102	145	17	4	6	41	3	3	1	76	25	44	3	2	11	.332	.349
Pagliarulo, Michael, S.D.★	.196	50	148	12	29	45	7	0	3	14	0	1	1	18	4	39	0	0	3	.304	.287
Pagnozzi, Thomas, St.L.	.150	52	80	3	12	14	2	0	0	3	0	0	0	6	2	19	0	0	7	.175	.216
Pardo, Al, Phil.†	.000	1	1	0	0	0	0	0	0	0	0	0	0	0	0	0	0	0	0	.000	.000
Parent, Mark, S.D.	.191	52	141	12	27	52	4	0	7	21	1	0	2	8	2	34	0	0	5	.369	.229
Parrett, Jeffrey, Phil.	.000	72	5	0	0	0	0	0	0	0	0	2	0	0	0	2	0	0	0	.000	.000
Patterson, Robert, Pitt.	.000	12	3	0	0	0	0	0	0	0	0	3	0	1	0	2	0	0	0	.000	.250
Pena, Alejandro, L.A.	1.000	53	1	0	1	1	0	0	0	0	1	0	0	0	0	0	0	0	0	1.000	1.000
Pena, Antonio, St.L.	.259	141	424	36	110	143	17	2	4	37	2	4	2	35	19	33	5	5	19	.337	.318
Pendleton, Terry, St.L.†	.264	162	613	83	162	239	28	5	13	74	5	2	1	44	3	81	9	5	16	.390	.313
Perez, Pascual, Mtl.	.204	35	54	2	11	14	3	0	0	8	9	0	0	2	0	19	0	0	0	.259	.228
Perry, Gerald, Atl.★	.252	72	266	24	67	90	11	0	4	21	0	2	3	32	5	28	10	6	5	.338	.337
Perry, W. Patrick, Chi.★	.167	19	6	1	1	1	0	0	0	0	1	0	0	0	0	8	0	0	1	.167	.167
Pevey, Marty, Mtl.★	.220	13	41	2	9	12	1	1	0	3	0	0	0	0	0	4	1	0	0	.293	.220
Pico, Jeffrey, Chi.	.100	53	10	0	1	1	0	0	0	0	3	0	0	0	0	6	0	0	0	.100	.100
Portugal, Mark, Hou.	.206	20	34	3	7	13	3	0	1	2	3	0	0	1	0	16	0	0	0	.382	.229
Power, Ted, St.L.	.091	23	33	1	3	3	0	0	0	1	3	0	0	0	0	10	0	0	0	.091	.091
Price, Joseph, S.F.	.000	7	2	0	0	0	0	0	0	0	0	1	0	1	0	1	0	0	1	.000	.333
Prince, Thomas, Pitt.	.135	21	52	1	7	11	4	0	0	5	0	1	0	6	1	12	1	1	1	.212	.220
Puhl, Terrance, Hou.★	.271	121	354	41	96	129	25	4	0	27	4	2	1	45	3	39	9	8	7	.364	.353
Puleo, Charles, Atl.	.000	15	1	0	0	0	0	0	0	0	0	0	0	0	0	1	0	0	0	.000	.000
Quinones, Luis, Cin.†	.244	97	340	43	83	140	13	2	12	34	8	2	3	25	0	46	2	2	3	.412	.300
Quinones, Rey, Pitt.	.209	71	225	21	47	67	11	0	3	29	4	8	1	15	2	40	0	0	5	.298	.253
Quisenberry, Daniel, St.L.	.250	63	4	0	1	1	0	0	0	1	0	0	0	0	0	1	0	0	0	.250	.250
Raines, Timothy, Mtl.†	.286	145	517	76	148	216	29	6	9	60	0	5	3	93	18	48	41	9	8	.418	.395
Ramirez, Rafael, Hou.	.246	151	537	46	132	174	20	2	6	54	6	6	0	29	3	64	3	1	8	.324	.283
Ramos, Domingo, Chi.	.263	85	179	18	47	60	8	1	1	19	6	5	4	17	4	23	1	1	10	.335	.333
Randolph, William, L.A.	.282	145	549	62	155	179	18	0	2	36	3	4	2	71	1	20	7	6	6	.326	.366
Rasmussen, Dennis, S.D.★	.169	33	65	1	11	14	3	0	0	2	18	1	0	1	0	37	0	0	1	.215	.182
Ready, Randy, S.D.-Phil.	.264	100	254	37	67	108	13	2	8	26	1	3	1	42	0	35	4	3	6	.425	.368
Redus, Gary, Pitt.	.283	98	279	42	79	129	18	7	6	33	7	4	2	40	3	51	25	6	5	.462	.372
Reed, Jeffrey, Cin.★	.223	102	287	16	64	84	11	0	3	23	3	4	2	34	5	46	0	0	6	.293	.306
Reed, Richard, Pitt.	.077	15	13	2	1	1	0	0	0	0	4	0	0	2	0	5	0	0	2	.077	.200
Reuschel, Ricky, S.F.	.164	32	61	0	10	11	1	0	0	3	16	1	0	5	0	16	0	0	0	.180	.224
Reyes, Gilberto, Mtl.	.200	4	5	0	1	1	0	0	0	1	0	0	0	0	0	1	0	0	1	.200	.200
Reynolds, G. Craig, Hou.★	.201	101	189	16	38	48	4	0	2	14	5	0	0	19	5	18	1	0	2	.254	.274

Player, Club	AVG	G	AB	R	H	TB	2B	3B	HR	RBI	SH	SF	HP	BB	IBB	SO	SB	CS	GI DP	SLG	OBP
Reynolds, Robert J., Pitt.†	.270	125	363	45	98	136	16	2	6	48	1	4	1	34	8	66	22	5	13	.375	.331
Rhoden, Richard, Hou.	.207	20	29	0	6	7	1	0	0	6	2	0	0	3	0	2	0	0	0	.241	.207
Richards, Russell, Atl.*	.000	2	3	0	0	0	0	0	0	0	1	0	0	0	0	2	1	0	0	.000	.000
Richardson, Jeffrey, Cin.	.168	53	125	10	21	31	4	0	2	11	3	1	0	10	0	23	1	0	3	.248	.234
Rijo, Jose, Cin.	.211	19	38	0	8	9	1	0	0	0	4	0	2	1	0	11	1	0	0	.237	.231
Riles, Ernest, S.F.*	.278	122	302	43	84	122	13	2	7	40	1	4	2	28	3	50	0	6	7	.404	.339
Roberts, Leon, S.D.†	.301	117	329	81	99	139	15	3	3	25	6	0	1	49	0	45	21	11	3	.422	.391
Robinson, Don, S.F.	.185	40	81	7	15	25	1	0	3	7	6	0	0	1	0	23	0	0	0	.309	.195
Robinson, Jeffrey D., Pitt.	.229	50	35	2	8	11	0	0	1	3	5	0	0	0	0	11	0	0	0	.314	.229
Robinson, Ronald, Cin.	.214	15	28	3	6	7	1	0	0	0	2	0	0	1	0	14	0	0	1	.250	.241
Rodriguez, Rosario, Cin.	…	7	0	0	0	0	0	0	0	0	0	0	0	0	0	0	0	0	0	…	…
Roesler, Michael, Cin.	…	17	0	0	0	0	0	0	0	0	0	0	0	0	0	0	0	0	0	…	…
Romero, Edgardo, Atl.	.263	7	19	1	5	9	1	0	1	1	0	0	0	0	0	0	0	0	1	.474	.263
Roomes, Rolando, Cin.	.263	107	315	36	83	132	18	5	7	34	1	0	3	13	1	100	12	8	2	.419	.296
Ruffin, Bruce, Phil.†	.176	24	34	1	6	7	1	0	0	1	6	0	0	6	0	15	0	0	4	.206	.300
Russell, John, Atl.	.182	74	159	14	29	37	2	0	2	9	3	0	0	8	1	53	0	0	0	.233	.225
Ryal, Mark, Phil.*	.242	29	33	2	8	10	2	0	0	5	1	0	0	1	0	6	0	0	6	.303	.265
Sabo, Christopher, Cin.	.260	82	304	40	79	120	21	1	6	29	4	2	1	25	2	33	14	9	7	.395	.316
Salazar, Luis, S.D.-Chi.	.282	121	326	34	92	135	12	2	9	34	7	2	3	15	3	57	4	4	6	.414	.316
Samuel, Juan, Phil.-N.Y.	.235	137	532	69	125	178	16	5	11	48	2	2	11	42	2	120	42	12	7	.335	.303
Samuels, Roger, Pitt.*	…	5	0	0	0	0	0	0	0	0	1	0	0	0	0	0	0	0	0	…	…
Sandberg, Ryne, Chi.	.290	157	606	104	176	301	25	5	30	76	6	2	4	59	8	85	15	5	9	.497	.356
Sanderson, Scott, Chi.	.047	37	43	1	2	2	0	0	0	1	3	0	0	5	0	22	0	0	0	.047	.146
Santiago, Benito, S.D.	.236	129	462	50	109	179	16	3	16	62	2	4	3	26	6	89	11	6	9	.387	.277
Santovenia, Nelson, Mtl.	.250	97	304	30	76	107	14	1	5	31	4	3	1	24	6	37	0	1	12	.352	.307
Sasser, Mackey, N.Y.*	.291	72	182	17	53	74	14	0	1	22	0	1	0	7	4	15	0	0	3	.407	.316
Schatzeder, Daniel, Hou.*	…	36	0	0	0	0	0	0	0	0	1	0	0	0	0	3	0	0	0	…	…
Schiraldi, Calvin, Chi.-S.D.	.063	59	16	0	1	4	0	0	1	4	4	0	0	1	0	9	0	0	0	.250	.111
Schmidt, Michael, Phil.	.203	42	148	19	30	55	7	0	6	28	0	3	0	21	4	17	0	3	6	.372	.297
Schulze, Donald, S.D.	.000	7	1	0	0	0	0	0	0	0	1	0	0	0	0	3	0	0	0	.000	.000
Scioscia, Michael, L.A.*	.250	133	408	40	102	148	16	0	10	44	3	0	3	52	14	29	0	4	4	.363	.338
Scott, Michael, Hou.	.133	33	75	2	10	13	0	0	1	10	7	1	0	2	0	31	0	1	1	.173	.154
Scudder, W. Scott, Cin.	.167	23	24	1	4	4	0	0	0	2	9	0	0	4	0	13	0	0	0	.167	.286
Searage, Raymond, L.A.*	…	41	0	0	0	0	0	0	0	0	4	0	0	0	0	0	0	0	0	…	…
Sebra, Robert, Phil.-Cin.	.182	21	11	2	2	2	0	0	0	0	1	0	0	0	0	6	0	0	1	.182	.154
Sharperson, Michael, L.A.	.250	27	28	3	7	10	3	0	0	5	0	1	0	2	1	7	0	1	6	.357	.333
Shelby, John, L.A.†	.183	108	345	28	63	79	11	2	1	12	4	0	1	25	5	92	10	7	1	.229	.237
Sheridan, Patrick, S.F.*	.205	70	161	20	33	53	3	4	3	14	7	0	0	13	1	45	4	0	6	.329	.264
Shipley, Craig, N.Y.	.143	4	7	3	1	1	0	0	0	0	0	0	0	0	0	1	0	0	1	.143	.143
Show, Eric, S.D.	.235	17	34	3	8	9	1	0	0	7	4	0	0	1	0	12	0	0	6	.265	.257
Smiley, John, Pitt.*	.138	28	65	4	9	13	4	0	0	4	7	0	0	3	0	19	0	0	1	.200	.176
Smith, Bryn, Mtl.	.065	33	62	4	4	5	1	0	0	4	10	0	2	7	0	23	0	0	3	.081	.159
Smith, David, Hou.	.000	52	1	0	0	0	0	0	0	0	0	0	0	0	0	1	0	0	0	.000	.000
Smith, Gregory, Chi.†	.400	4	5	1	2	2	0	0	0	2	4	0	0	0	0	0	0	0	0	.400	.500
Smith, J. Dwight, Chi.*	.324	109	343	52	111	169	19	6	9	52	1	1	1	31	3	51	9	4	4	.493	.382
Smith, Lonnie, Atl.	.315	134	482	89	152	257	34	4	21	79	7	7	11	76	3	95	25	12	7	.533	.415
Smith, Michael, Pitt.	.000	16	3	0	0	0	0	0	0	0	0	0	0	0	0	1	0	0	0	.000	.000
Smith, Osborne, St.L.†	.273	155	593	82	162	214	30	8	2	50	11	3	0	55	3	37	29	7	10	.361	.335
Smith, Peter, Atl.	.098	29	41	2	4	6	0	1	0	3	5	0	0	4	0	9	0	0	1	.146	.178
Smith, Zane, Atl.-Mtl.*	.188	53	32	4	6	7	1	0	0	3	4	0	0	0	0	3	0	0	0	.219	.188

Player, Club	AVG	G	AB	R	H	TB	2B	3B	HR	RBI	SH	SF	HP	BB	IBB	SO	SB	CS	GI DP	SLG	OBP
Smoltz, John, Atl.	.113	33	62	6	7	13	1	0	1	6	6	0	0	6	0	23	0	0	0	.210	.191
Snider, Van, Cin.*	.143	8	7	1	1	1	0	0	0	0	0	0	0	0	0	5	0	0	0	.143	.143
Speier, Chris, S.F.	.243	28	37	7	9	13	4	0	0	2	2	0	0	5	1	9	0	0	2	.351	.333
Spilman, W. Harry, Hou.*	.278	32	36	7	10	13	3	0	0	3	0	0	0	7	1	2	0	0	1	.361	.395
Stanicek, Stephen, Phil.	.111	9	9	0	1	1	0	0	0	1	0	0	0	2	0	3	0	0	0	.111	.111
Stanton, W. Michael, Atl.*		20	0	0	0	0	0	0	0	0	0	0	0	0	0	0	0	0	0		
Steels, James, S.F.*	.083	13	12	0	1	1	0	0	0	0	0	0	0	2	1	4	1	4	0	.083	.214
Stephenson, Phillip, Chi.-S.D.*	.237	27	38	4	9	15	0	1	2	2	0	0	0	5	1	5	1	0	4	.395	.326
Strawberry, Darryl, N.Y.*	.225	134	476	69	107	222	26	0	29	77	1	3	1	61	13	105	11	4	4	.466	.312
Stubbs, Franklin, L.A.*	.291	69	103	11	30	48	6	0	4	15	1	0	1	16	2	27	3	2	3	.466	.387
Sutcliffe, Richard, Chi.*	.143	37	70	5	10	12	2	0	0	5	5	0	0	0	0	19	0	0	1	.171	.250
Swan, Russell, S.F.*	.000	2	2	0	0	0	0	0	0	0	1	0	0	0	0	0	0	0	0	.000	.000
Tapani, Kevin, N.Y.	.000	3	2	0	0	0	0	0	0	0	0	0	0	0	0	1	0	0	0	.000	.000
Tate, Stuart, S.F.		2	0	0	0	0	0	0	0	0	0	0	0	0	0	0	0	0	0		
Taylor, Donald, Pitt.	.000	10	1	0	0	0	0	0	0	0	0	0	0	0	0	0	0	0	0	.000	.000
Tekulve, Kenton, Cin.	.500	37	2	1	1	1	0	0	0	0	0	0	0	0	0	1	0	0	0	.500	.500
Templeton, Garry, S.D.†	.255	142	506	43	129	179	26	3	6	40	4	3	0	23	12	80	1	3	15	.354	.286
Terrell, C. Walter, S.D.*	.100	19	40	2	4	6	2	0	0	2	1	0	1	3	0	22	0	0	0	.150	.163
Terry, Scott, St.L.	.156	35	45	3	7	14	1	2	2	4	4	3	2	1	0	11	1	3	4	.311	.191
Teufel, Timothy, N.Y.	.256	83	219	27	56	73	7	2	15	15	4	0	1	32	1	50	1	1	4	.333	.350
Tewksbury, Robert, St.L.	.111	7	9	0	1	1	0	0	0	1	1	0	0	0	0	5	0	0	0	.111	.111
Thomas, Andres, Atl.	.213	141	554	41	118	175	18	8	13	57	1	4	0	12	3	62	3	3	17	.316	.228
Thompson, Milton, St.L.*	.290	155	545	60	158	214	28	8	4	68	8	3	4	39	5	91	27	8	12	.393	.340
Thompson, Richard N., Mtl.	.000	19	2	0	0	0	0	0	0	0	0	0	0	1	0	1	0	0	0	.000	.333
Thompson, Robert, S.F.	.241	148	547	91	132	219	26	11	13	50	9	3	13	51	6	133	12	3	6	.400	.321
Thon, Richard, Phil.	.271	136	435	45	118	189	18	4	15	60	1	3	0	33	6	81	6	3	6	.434	.321
Thornton, Louis, N.Y.*	.308	13	13	5	4	5	1	0	0	1	0	0	0	0	0	0	2	1	0	.385	.308
Toliver, Freddie, S.D.		9	0	0	0	0	0	0	0	0	0	0	0	0	0	1	0	0	0		
Treadway, H. Jeffrey, Atl.*	.277	134	473	58	131	179	18	3	8	40	6	5	0	30	3	38	3	2	9	.378	.317
Trevino, Alejandro, Hou.	.290	59	131	15	38	53	7	1	2	16	7	1	1	7	0	18	0	0	3	.405	.329
Trillo, J. Manuel, Cin.	.205	17	39	3	8	8	0	0	0	0	1	0	1	2	0	9	0	0	0	.205	.262
Tudor, John, L.A.*	.000	6	2	0	0	0	0	0	0	0	1	0	0	0	0	0	0	0	0	.000	.000
Uribe, Jose, S.F.†	.221	151	453	34	100	127	12	6	1	30	4	4	0	34	12	74	6	6	7	.280	.273
Valdez, Sergio, Atl.	1.000	19	1	0	1	1	0	0	0	0	0	0	0	0	0	0	0	0	0	1.000	1.000
Valenzuela, Fernando, L.A.*	.182	34	66	3	12	14	2	0	0	6	7	0	0	0	0	11	0	0	0	.212	.182
Van Slyke, Andrew, Pitt.*	.237	130	476	64	113	176	18	9	9	53	1	3	3	47	3	100	16	4	13	.370	.308
Varsho, Gary, Chi.*	.184	61	87	10	16	24	4	2	0	6	5	0	0	4	1	13	3	0	0	.276	.220
Viola, Frank, N.Y.*	.130	12	23	0	3	3	0	0	0	1	0	0	0	1	0	7	0	0	0	.130	.167
Vizcaino, Jose, L.A.†	.200	7	10	2	2	2	0	0	0	0	1	0	0	0	0	1	1	0	0	.200	.200
Walk, Robert, Pitt.	.186	33	70	2	13	19	2	2	0	9	5	3	0	5	0	18	1	1	2	.271	.197
Walker, Larry, Mtl.*	.170	47	47	4	8	8	0	0	0	4	0	0	1	1	0	13	3	7	0	.170	.264
Wallach, Timothy, Mtl.	.277	154	573	76	159	240	42	0	13	77	0	7	1	58	10	81	1	3	21	.419	.341
Walling, Dennis, St.L.*	.304	69	79	9	24	34	7	3	0	11	2	0	1	14	1	12	3	7	6	.430	.409
Walton, Jerome, Chi.	.293	116	475	64	139	183	23	3	5	46	3	2	6	27	1	77	24	7	2	.385	.335
Washington, Ronald, Hou.	.143	12	7	1	1	2	1	0	0	2	0	0	0	0	0	4	1	0	0	.286	.143
Weaver, James, S.F.*	.200	7	20	0	4	7	1	1	0	0	2	0	0	0	0	7	0	0	0	.350	.200
Webster, Mitchell, Chi.†	.257	98	272	40	70	99	12	4	3	19	3	2	1	30	5	55	14	2	3	.364	.331
West, David, N.Y.*	.200	11	5	0	1	1	0	0	0	0	1	0	0	0	0	2	0	0	2	.200	.200
Wetherby, Jeffrey, Atl.*	.208	52	48	5	10	17	2	1	1	7	2	1	0	4	0	6	1	0	0	.354	.264
Wetteland, John, L.A.	.143	31	21	1	3	4	1	0	0	3	5	0	0	0	0	10	0	0	0	.190	.143

Player, Club	AVG	G	AB	R	H	TB	2B	3B	HR	RBI	SH	SF	HP	BB	IBB	SO	SB	CS	GIDP	SLG	OBP
Whited, Edward, Atl.	.162	36	74	5	12	18	3	0	1	4	1	0	0	6	2	15	1	0	2	.243	.222
Whitehurst, Walter, N.Y.	.000	9	1	1	0	0	0	0	0	0	1	0	0	0	0	1	0	0	0	.000	.500
Whitson, Eddie, S.D.	.139	36	72	4	10	14	4	0	0	4	7	1	0	5	0	19	0	0	3	.194	.195
Wilkerson, Curtis, Chi.†	.244	77	160	18	39	50	4	2	1	10	1	1	0	8	1	33	4	2	3	.313	.278
Wilkins, Dean, Chi.	.000	11	1	0	0	0	0	0	0	0	1	0	0	1	0	1	0	0	0	.000	.000
Williams, Matthew, S.F.	.202	84	292	31	59	133	18	1	18	50	0	2	2	14	1	72	1	1	5	.455	.242
Williams, Mitchell, Chi.*	.200	76	5	1	1	4	0	0	0	3	1	0	0	0	0	2	0	0	0	.800	.200
Wilson, Craig, St.L.	.250	6	4	1	1	1	0	0	0	0	0	0	0	1	0	1	0	0	0	.250	.400
Wilson, Glenn, Pitt.-Hou.	.266	128	432	50	115	182	26	4	11	64	0	6	1	37	5	53	1	5	11	.421	.321
Wilson, Stephen, Chi.*	.063	53	16	1	1	2	0	0	0	1	6	0	0	1	0	3	0	5	0	.063	.118
Wilson, Trevor, S.F.*	.250	14	8	1	2	2	0	0	0	0	3	0	0	1	0	3	1	1	0	.250	.400
Wilson, William, N.Y.†	.205	80	249	22	51	72	10	1	3	18	0	2	1	10	3	47	7	4	5	.289	.237
Winningham, Herman, Cin.*	.251	115	251	40	63	89	11	3	3	13	3	0	0	24	1	50	14	5	2	.355	.316
Woodson, Tracy, L.A.	.000	4	6	0	0	0	0	0	0	0	0	0	0	0	0	1	0	0	0	.000	.000
Worrell, Todd, St.L.	.000	47	4	0	0	0	0	0	0	0	0	0	0	0	0	1	0	0	0	.000	.000
Wrona, Rick, Chi.	.283	38	92	11	26	36	2	1	2	14	0	1	1	2	2	21	0	1	3	.391	.299
Wynne, Marvell, S.D.-Chi.*	.243	125	342	27	83	121	13	2	7	39	7	2	1	13	0	48	6	1	2	.354	.274
Yelding, Eric, Hou.	.233	70	90	19	21	23	2	0	0	9	2	2	0	7	0	19	11	5	0	.256	.290
Youmans, Floyd, Phil.†	.077	10	13	1	1	1	0	0	0	0	0	0	0	0	0	6	0	0	0	.077	.077
Young, Gerald, Hou.†	.233	146	533	71	124	147	17	3	0	38	6	5	2	74	4	60	34	25	7	.276	.326
Youngblood, Joel, Cin.	.212	76	118	13	25	39	5	1	3	13	0	2	0	13	2	21	0	1	6	.331	.299
Zeile, Todd, St.L.	.256	28	82	7	21	29	3	1	1	10	1	0	0	14	1	14	0	1	6	.354	.326

AWARDED FIRST BASE ON INTERFERENCE—Carreon, N.Y. (Bilardello, Pitt.); Ja. Clark, S.D. (Fitzgerald, Mtl.); Daulton, Phil. (Fitzgerald); Herr, Phil. (Benedict, Atl.); Hudler, Mtl. (Biggio, Hou.); Huff, L.A. (Lake, Phil.); Sheridan, S.F. (Berryhill, Chi.); Van Slyke, Pitt. (Girardi, Chi.).

PLAYERS WITH TWO OR MORE CLUBS DURING 1989 SEASON
(Listed Alphabetically)

Player, Club	AVG	G	AB	R	H	TB	2B	3B	HR	RBI	SH	SF	HP	BB	IBB	SO	SB	CS	GIDP	SLG	OBP
Assenmacher, Paul, Atl.*	.000	49	2	0	0	0	0	0	0	0	0	0	0	0	0	1	0	0	0	.000	.000
Assenmacher, Paul, Chi.*	.000	14	3	0	0	0	0	0	0	0	0	0	0	0	0	1	0	0	0	.000	.000
Bedrosian, Stephen, Phil.	.000	28	6	0	0	0	0	0	0	0	0	0	0	0	0	3	0	0	0	.000	.000
Bedrosian, Stephen, S.F.	.167	40	6	1	1	1	0	0	0	0	0	0	0	0	0	0	0	0	0	.167	.167
Cook, Dennis, S.F.*	.167	2	6	0	1	3	0	1	0	1	0	0	0	0	0	2	0	0	0	.500	.167
Cook, Dennis, Phil.*	.222	22	36	3	8	9	1	0	0	2	2	0	0	0	0	4	0	0	0	.250	.222
Daniels, Kalvoski, Cin.*	.218	44	133	26	29	46	11	0	2	9	0	1	2	36	1	28	6	4	1	.346	.390
Daniels, Kalvoski, L.A.*	.342	11	38	7	13	21	2	0	2	8	0	0	0	7	0	5	3	0	1	.553	.435
Duncan, Mariano, L.A.	.250	49	84	9	21	28	5	1	0	8	1	0	0	0	0	15	6	3	1	.333	.267
Duncan, Mariano, Cin.	.247	45	174	23	43	64	10	1	3	13	0	0	3	8	0	36	3	2	2	.368	.292
Dykstra, Lenny, N.Y.*	.270	56	159	27	43	66	12	1	3	13	4	4	2	23	0	15	13	1	2	.415	.362
Dykstra, Lenny, Phil.*	.222	90	352	39	78	116	20	3	4	19	1	1	1	37	1	38	17	11	5	.330	.297
Harris, Leonard, Cin.*	.223	61	188	17	42	52	4	3	1	11	0	0	1	9	0	20	10	6	2	.277	.263
Harris, Leonard, L.A.*	.252	54	147	19	37	48	6	1	1	15	1	0	1	11	0	13	4	3	5	.327	.308
Hatcher, William, Hou.	.228	108	395	49	90	120	15	3	3	44	3	4	1	30	2	53	22	6	3	.304	.281
Hatcher, William, Pitt.	.244	27	86	10	21	28	4	0	1	7	0	0	1	0	0	9	2	1	1	.326	.253

Player, Club	AVG	G	AB	R	H	TB	2B	3B	HR	RBI	SH	SF	HP	BB	IBB	SO	SB	CS	GI DP	SLG	OBP
Hayes, Charles, S.F.	.200	3	5	0	1	1	0	1	0	0	0	0	0	0	0	1	0	1	0	.200	.200
Hayes, Charles, Phil.	.258	84	299	26	77	118	15	1	8	43	2	3	0	11	1	49	3	1	6	.395	.281
Horton, Ricky, L.A.*	.000	23	1	0	0	0	0	0	0	0	0	0	0	0	0	1	0	0	0	.000	.000
Horton, Ricky, St.L.*	.273	11	11	0	3	4	1	0	0	0	2	0	0	0	0	1	0	0	0	.364	.273
Jackson, Darrin, Chi	.229	45	83	7	19	26	4	0	1	8	0	2	0	6	1	17	1	2	1	.313	.281
Jackson, Darrin, S.D.	.207	25	87	10	18	30	3	0	3	12	0	0	0	7	4	17	0	2	1	.345	.260
James, D. Chris, Phil	.207	45	179	14	37	47	4	0	2	19	1	1	0	4	0	23	3	3	9	.263	.223
James, D. Chris, S.D.	.264	87	303	41	80	130	13	2	11	46	3	2	1	22	2	45	2	1	11	.429	.314
Knepper, Robert, Hou.*	.226	22	31	3	7	14	4	0	1	3	2	1	0	6	0	6	0	0	1	.452	.351
Knepper, Robert, S.F.*	.083	13	12	2	1	2	1	0	0	0	1	2	0	3	0	3	0	0	1	.167	.267
Kruk, John, S.D.*	.184	31	76	7	14	23	0	0	3	6	6	3	0	17	2	14	0	0	5	.303	.333
Kruk, John, Phil.*	.331	81	281	46	93	133	13	6	5	38	1	3	0	27	2	39	3	0	5	.473	.386
Leary, Timothy, L.A.	.061	19	33	1	2	2	0	0	0	0	6	0	0	0	0	14	0	0	1	.061	.061
Leary, Timothy, Cin.	.192	14	26	1	5	7	2	0	0	4	3	0	0	4	0	9	0	0	0	.269	.300
McDowell, Roger, N.Y.	.500	25	2	0	1	1	0	0	0	0	1	0	0	0	0	0	0	0	0	.500	.500
McDowell, Roger, Phil.	.000	44	1	0	0	0	0	0	0	0	0	0	0	0	0	1	0	0	0	.000	.000
Mulholland, Terence, S.F.	.000	5	2	0	0	0	0	0	0	0	0	0	0	0	0	2	0	0	0	.000	.000
Mulholland, Terence, Phil.	.059	20	34	1	2	3	1	0	0	1	2	0	0	0	0	15	0	0	1	.088	.059
Oberkfell, Kenneth, Pitt.*	.125	14	40	2	5	6	1	0	0	2	0	1	0	2	0	8	0	1	4	.150	.163
Oberkfell, Kenneth, S.F.*	.319	83	116	17	37	50	5	1	2	15	1	2	2	8	0	8	0	0	4	.431	.367
Ready, Randy, S.D.	.254	28	67	4	17	21	2	1	0	5	1	1	0	11	0	6	0	0	2	.313	.354
Ready, Randy, Phil.	.267	72	187	33	50	87	11	1	8	21	0	3	2	31	3	31	4	3	2	.465	.372
Salazar, Luis, S.D.	.268	95	246	27	66	101	7	2	8	22	7	0	1	11	1	44	0	3	3	.411	.302
Salazar, Luis, Chi.	.325	26	80	7	26	34	5	1	2	12	0	0	1	4	0	13	1	0	4	.425	.357
Samuel, Juan, Phil.	.246	51	199	32	49	78	3	1	8	20	0	1	1	18	1	45	11	3	2	.392	.311
Samuel, Juan, N.Y.	.228	86	333	37	76	100	13	1	3	28	2	0	10	24	1	75	31	9	5	.300	.299
Schiraldi, Calvin, Chi.	.000	54	9	0	0	0	0	0	0	0	4	0	0	0	0	7	0	0	0	.000	.000
Schiraldi, Calvin, S.D.	.143	5	7	1	1	4	0	0	1	3	0	0	0	2	0	2	0	0	0	.571	.250
Sebra, Robert, Phil.	.000	6	10	0	0	0	0	0	0	0	1	0	0	2	0	5	0	0	0	.000	.167
Sebra, Robert, Cin.	.000	15	1	0	0	0	0	0	0	0	0	0	0	0	0	1	0	0	0	.000	.000
Smith, Zane, Atl.*	.179	21	28	3	5	5	0	0	0	0	4	0	0	0	0	1	0	0	0	.179	.179
Smith, Zane, Mtl.*	.250	32	4	0	1	2	1	0	0	0	0	0	0	2	0	2	0	0	0	.500	.250
Stephenson, Phillip, Chi.*	.143	17	21	3	3	3	0	0	0	0	0	0	1	2	0	3	1	0	0	.143	.217
Stephenson, Phillip, S.D.*	.353	10	17	4	6	12	0	2	1	2	2	0	1	3	0	2	0	0	0	.706	.450
Wilson, Glenn, Pitt.	.282	100	330	42	93	148	20	1	9	49	0	5	0	32	5	39	1	4	8	.448	.342
Wilson, Glenn, Hou.	.216	28	102	8	22	34	6	2	0	15	2	1	0	5	1	14	0	1	3	.333	.250
Wynne, Marvell, S.D.*	.252	105	294	19	74	105	11	4	6	35	6	1	1	12	1	41	4	2	3	.357	.282
Wynne, Marvell, Chi.*	.188	20	48	8	9	16	2	1	1	4	1	0	1	1	0	7	2	0	0	.333	.220

OFFICIAL NATIONAL LEAGUE FIELDING AVERAGES

CLUB FIELDING

Club	PCT	G	PO	A	E	TC	DP	TP	PB
St. Louis	.982	164	4383	1856	112	6351	134	0	12
San Francisco	.982	162	4371	1725	114	6210	135	0	11
Los Angeles	.981	160	4390	1668	118	6176	153	0	10
Cincinnati	.980	162	4393	1671	121	6185	108	1	8
Chicago	.980	162	4381	1722	124	6227	130	0	12
Montreal	.979	162	4405	1822	136	6363	126	1	11
Philadelphia	.979	163	4300	1771	133	6204	136	0	6
Houston	.977	162	4438	1653	142	6233	121	0	14
New York	.976	162	4363	1462	144	5969	110	1	11
San Diego	.976	162	4372	1822	154	6348	147	1	14
Atlanta	.976	161	4343	1722	152	6217	124	0	14
Pittsburgh	.975	164	4463	1756	160	6379	130	0	19
Totals	.978	973	52602	20650	1610	74862	1554	4	142

INDIVIDUAL FIELDING

(★ Throws Lefthanded)

FIRST BASEMEN

Leader, Club	PCT	G	PO	A	E	TC	DP
MURRAY, L.A.	.996	159	1316	137	6	1459	122

Player, Club	PCT	G	PO	A	E	TC	DP
Adduci, Phil.★	1.000	4	25	3	0	28	1
Aldrete, Mtl.★	1.000	10	62	7	0	69	8
Benzinger, Cin.	.995	158	1417	73	7	1497	96
Bonilla, Pitt.	1.000	8	65	4	0	69	6
Bream, Pitt.★	.992	13	111	7	1	119	5
Brunansky, St.L.	....	1	0	0	0	0	0
Cabrera, Atl.	1.000	2	24	1	0	25	1
Carter, N.Y.	....	1	0	0	0	0	0
Ja. Clark, S.D.	.988	131	1135	88	15	1238	99
Clark, S.F.★	.994	158	1445	111	10	1566	117
Davis, Hou.	.992	156	1347	113	12	1472	101
Davis, Atl.	1.000	2	12	0	0	12	3
Denson, Atl.	.988	12	71	11	1	83	3
Distefano, Pitt.★	.981	48	302	16	6	324	21
Durham, St.L.★	.961	18	44	5	2	51	7
Evans, Atl.	.985	50	358	49	6	413	32
Ford, Phil.	1.000	1	0	1	0	1	0
Galarraga, Mtl.	.992	147	1335	91	11	1437	97
Grace, Chi.★	.996	142	1230	126	6	1362	93
Gregg, Atl.★	1.000	37	264	16	0	280	18
Griffey, Cin.★	.979	9	46	0	1	47	3
Gross, Hou.★	1.000	6	24	1	0	25	2
Guerrero, St.L.	.990	160	1445	72	15	1532	99
Hatcher, L.A.	1.000	5	16	2	0	18	3
V. Hayes, Phil.	.995	30	182	16	1	199	20
K. Hernandez, N.Y.★	.991	58	405	31	4	440	22
James, Atl.★	1.000	8	39	7	0	46	5
W. Johnson, Mtl.	.972	18	130	7	4	141	8
Jordan, Phil.	.993	140	1271	61	9	1341	99
Jurak, S.F.	1.000	1	11	0	0	11	0
Kennedy, S.F.	1.000	2	3	0	0	3	0
King, Pitt.	.995	46	384	22	2	408	32
Kruk, Phil.★	1.000	7	53	1	0	54	2
Laga, S.F.★	1.000	4	16	1	0	17	0
Lindeman, St.L.	.989	42	88	6	1	95	7
Lombardi, N.Y.	1.000	1	1	0	0	1	0
Magadan, N.Y.	.991	87	574	59	6	639	50

Player, Club	PCT	G	PO	A	E	TC	DP
Martinez, N.Y.	1.000	32	122	13	0	135	10
Mazzilli, N.Y.	1.000	8	39	1	0	40	2
McClendon, Chi.	1.000	28	225	12	0	237	20
McKnight, N.Y.	1.000	1	3	0	0	3	0
Meadows, Hou.★	1.000	1	1	0	0	1	0
Murray, L.A.	.996	159	1316	137	6	1459	122
Nelson, S.D.★	.991	31	201	23	2	226	17
Oberkfell, Pitt.-S.F.	.992	16	110	7	1	118	8
Oquendo, St.L.	1.000	1	1	0	0	1	0
Pagnozzi, St.L.	1.000	2	1	0	0	1	0
Parent, S.D.	1.000	1	5	0	0	5	0
Perry, Atl.	.987	72	618	51	9	678	49
Puhl, Hou.	1.000	3	8	0	0	8	1
Redus, Pitt.	.987	72	567	54	8	629	42
Reynolds, Hou.	1.000	5	13	4	0	17	0
Russell, Atl.	1.000	2	6	0	0	6	0
Ryal, Phil.★	1.000	4	14	0	0	14	0
Salazar, Chi.	1.000	2	2	0	0	2	2
Santovenia, Mtl.	1.000	1	3	0	0	3	1
Sharperson, L.A.	1.000	2	4	1	0	5	0
Speier, S.F.	1.000	1	4	1	0	5	1
Spilman, Hou.	1.000	9	47	4	0	51	2
Steels, S.F.★	1.000	3	14	2	0	16	0
Stephenson, S.D.★	.977	8	39	4	1	44	3
Stubbs, L.A.★	1.000	7	18	2	0	20	2
Teufel, N.Y.	.983	33	205	25	4	234	16
Trevino, Hou.	1.000	2	9	1	0	10	0
Trillo, Cin.	1.000	3	6	0	0	6	0
Valenzuela, L.A.★	1.000	1	2	0	0	2	0
Van Slyke, Pitt.	1.000	2	6	0	0	6	1
Walling, St.L.	.969	20	58	4	2	64	4
Whited, Atl.	1.000	3	3	0	0	3	1
Wilson, Hou.	1.000	10	36	3	0	39	1

TRIPLE PLAYS: Benzinger, Cin.; Ja. Clark, S.D.; Galarraga, Mtl.; Magadan, N.Y.

FIRST BASEMAN WITH TWO OR MORE CLUBS

Player, Club	PCT	G	PO	A	E	TC	DP
Oberkfell, Pitt.	.908	9	75	5	1	81	4
Oberkfell, S.F.	1.000	7	35	2	0	37	4

SECOND BASEMEN

Leader, Club	PCT	G	PO	A	E	TC	DP
OQUENDO, ST.L.	.994	156	346	500	5	851	106

Player, Club	PCT	G	PO	A	E	TC	DP
R. Alomar, S.D.	.967	157	341	472	28	841	91
Anderson, L.A.	1.000	7	6	13	0	19	1
Barrett, Phil.	.978	9	26	18	1	45	9
Belliard, Pitt.	1.000	20	23	46	0	69	7
Blauser, Atl.	.970	39	58	71	4	133	14
Booker, St.L.	.867	5	4	9	2	15	2
Cora, S.D.	1.000	1	1	0	0	1	0
Doran, Hou.	.980	138	254	345	12	611	64

Player, Club	PCT	G	PO	A	E	TC	DP
Duncan, L.A.-Cin.	.944	13	13	21	2	36	5
Flannery, S.D.	1.000	1	0	1	0	1	0
Foley, Mtl.	.988	108	188	295	6	489	53
Ford, Phil.	1.000	1	0	1	0	1	0
Garcia, Mtl.	.972	62	86	157	7	250	25
Hamilton, L.A.	....	1	0	0	0	0	0
Harris, Cin.-L.A.	.975	46	95	103	5	203	27
Herr, Phil.	.990	144	281	415	7	703	80
Hudler, Mtl.	.958	38	27	42	3	72	9
Huson, Mtl.	1.000	9	18	23	0	41	4
Jefferies, N.Y.	.975	123	223	254	12	489	41

SECOND BASEMEN—Continued

Player, Club	PCT	G	PO	A	E	TC	DP	Player, Club	PCT	G	PO	A	E	TC	DP
Jeltz, Phil.	1.000	23	32	40	0	72	12	Reynolds, Hou.	.979	29	35	60	2	97	11
Jones, St.L.	1.000	12	18	28	0	46	3	Riles, S.F.	.962	18	20	31	2	53	2
Jurak, S.F.	.778	4	1	6	2	9	0	Roberts, S.D.	.976	9	17	23	1	41	7
King, Pitt.	1.000	7	10	14	0	24	2	Romero, Atl.	.947	4	6	12	1	19	2
Lemke, Atl.	1.000	14	25	40	0	65	7	Sandberg, Chi.	.992	155	294	466	6	766	80
Lind, Pitt.	.976	151	309	438	18	765	81	Sharperson, L.A.	1.000	4	7	4	0	11	2
Litton, S.F.	1.000	15	18	20	0	38	4	G. Smith, Chi.	.778	2	4	3	2	9	1
Lombardozzi, Hou.	.922	18	20	27	4	51	5	Speier, S.F.	1.000	4	7	7	0	14	4
McKnight, N.Y.	1.000	4	1	5	0	6	1	Teufel, N.Y.	.960	40	56	87	6	149	14
Miller, N.Y.	.967	23	49	38	3	90	7	Thompson, S.F.	.989	148	307	425	8	740	88
Noboa, Mtl.	1.000	13	15	39	0	54	6	Treadway, Atl.	.981	123	271	336	12	619	80
Oberkfell, Pitt.-S.F.	.933	10	13	15	2	30	2	Trillo, Cin.	1.000	10	21	18	0	39	2
Oester, Cin.	.985	102	211	239	7	457	42	Washington, Hou.	....	1	0	0	0	0	0
Oquendo, St.L.	.994	156	346	500	5	851	106	Wilkerson, Chi.	.987	15	26	50	1	77	7
Quinones, Cin.	.979	53	81	107	4	192	20	Yelding, Hou.	.962	13	20	30	2	52	5
Randolph, L.A.	.987	140	260	412	9	681	85								
Ready, S.D.-Phil.	.864	9	7	12	3	22	3								

TRIPLE PLAYS: R. Alomar, S.D.; Harris, Cin.

SECOND BASEMEN WITH TWO OR MORE CLUBS

Player, Club	PCT	G	PO	A	E	TC	DP	Player, Club	PCT	G	PO	A	E	TC	DP
Duncan, L.A.	.917	8	9	13	2	24	3	Oberkfell, Pitt.	1.000	3	5	5	0	10	1
Duncan, Cin.	1.000	5	4	8	0	12	2	Oberkfell, S.F.	.900	7	8	10	2	20	1
Harris, Cin.	.980	32	74	75	3	152	19	Ready, S.D.	.000	2	0	0	0	0	0
Harris, L.A.	.961	14	21	28	2	51	8	Ready, Phil.	.864	7	7	12	3	22	3

THIRD BASEMEN

Leader, Club	PCT	G	PO	A	E	TC	DP	Player, Club	PCT	G	PO	A	E	TC	DP
PENDLETON, ST.L.	.971	161	113	392	15	520	25	McKnight, N.Y.	....	1	0	0	0	0	0
								Miller, N.Y.	1.000	2	0	1	0	1	0
Player, Club	PCT	G	PO	A	E	TC	DP	Mitchell, S.F.	1.000	2	0	2	0	2	0
Anderson, L.A.	1.000	18	9	11	0	20	1	Murray, L.A.	....	2	0	0	0	0	0
Belliard, Pitt.	1.000	6	2	2	0	4	0	Noboa, Mtl.	....	1	0	0	0	0	0
Blauser, Atl.	.929	78	42	128	13	183	9	Oberkfell, S.F.	.971	38	8	25	1	34	1
Bonilla, Pitt.	.929	156	125	330	35	490	31	O'Malley, N.Y.	1.000	3	2	1	0	3	0
Booker, St.L.	....	1	0	0	0	0	0	Pagliarulo, S.D.	.936	49	19	83	7	109	3
M. Brown, Cin.	.913	11	2	19	2	23	2	Pagnozzi, St.L.	....	1	0	0	0	0	0
Caminiti, Hou.	.954	160	126	335	22	483	27	Pendleton, St.L.	.971	161	113	392	15	520	25
Cora, S.D.	.500	2	0	1	1	2	1	Quinones, Cin.	.956	50	31	99	6	136	5
Evans, Atl.	.931	28	13	41	4	58	5	Ramos, Chi.	.879	30	6	23	4	33	0
Fitzgerald, Mtl.	1.000	8	0	7	0	7	0	Ready, S.D.-Phil.	.953	32	26	56	4	86	7
Flannery, S.D.	.920	33	14	55	6	75	3	Reynolds, Hou.	.905	10	2	17	2	21	2
Foley, Mtl.	.913	16	5	16	2	23	1	Richardson, Cin.	1.000	8	2	5	0	7	1
Gant, Atl.	.887	53	23	103	16	142	8	Riles, S.F.	.962	83	45	107	6	158	13
Garcia, Mtl.	....	1	0	0	0	0	0	Roberts, S.D.	.974	37	15	59	2	76	3
Green, S.D.	....	1	0	0	0	0	0	Romero, Atl.	1.000	1	0	1	0	1	0
Hamilton, L.A.	.951	147	139	233	19	391	29	Russell, Atl.	1.000	2	0	3	0	3	0
Harris, Cin.-L.A.	.955	24	11	31	2	44	2	Sabo, Cin.	.943	76	36	145	11	192	12
Hatcher, L.A.	.950	16	5	14	1	20	2	Salazar, S.D.-Chi.	.959	97	45	143	8	196	11
C. Hayes, S.F.-Phil.	.911	85	51	174	22	247	15	Sasser, N.Y.	....	1	0	0	0	0	0
V. Hayes, Phil.	.909	10	8	22	3	33	3	Schmidt, Phil.	.918	42	18	71	8	97	8
Huson, Mtl.	1.000	1	1	1	0	2	0	Sharperson, L.A	....	2	0	0	0	0	0
James, Phil.-S.D.	.882	17	9	21	4	34	4	Shipley, N.Y.	1.000	2	0	2	0	2	0
Jefferies, N.Y.	.957	20	19	26	2	47	3	Speier, S.F.	1.000	9	2	4	0	6	0
Jeltz, Phil.	.945	30	8	44	3	55	6	Treadway, Atl.	1.000	6	2	5	0	7	0
Johnson, N.Y.	.910	143	63	180	24	267	15	Trevino, Hou.	1.000	2	1	1	0	2	0
Jones, St.L.	.889	5	4	4	1	9	1	Wallach, Mtl.	.958	153	113	302	18	433	20
Jurak, S.F.	.833	5	3	7	2	12	1	Walling, St.L.	.714	9	0	5	2	7	0
King, Pitt.	.941	13	9	23	2	34	2	Washington, Hou.	1.000	1	0	1	0	1	0
Law, Chi.	.949	119	76	168	13	257	13	Whited, Atl.	.914	29	20	33	5	58	2
Litton, S.F.	.953	34	19	42	3	64	1	Wilkerson, Chi.	.881	26	14	38	7	59	2
Lombardozzi, Hou.	1.000	1	0	1	0	1	0	Williams, S.F.	.961	73	71	126	8	205	10
Madison, Cin.	1.000	26	19	44	0	63	3	Wilson, St.L.	.500	2	1	0	1	2	0
Magadan, N.Y.	.977	28	13	30	1	44	4	Woodson, L.A.	1.000	1	1	1	0	2	0
McClendon, Chi.	.750	6	3	3	2	8	1								

TRIPLE PLAY: Salazar, S.D.

THIRD BASEMEN WITH TWO OR MORE CLUBS

Player, Club	PCT	G	PO	A	E	TC	DP	Player, Club	PCT	G	PO	A	E	TC	DP
Harris, Cin.	.944	16	7	27	2	36	1	James, S.D.	.857	6	4	8	2	14	2
Harris, L.A.	1.000	8	4	4	0	8	1	Ready, S.D.	.963	18	16	36	2	54	4
C. Hayes, S.F.	1.000	3	2	1	0	3	0	Ready, Phil.	.938	14	10	20	2	32	3
C. Hayes, Phil.	.910	82	49	173	22	244	15	Salazar, S.D.	.968	72	37	116	5	158	10
James, Phil.	.900	11	5	13	2	20	2	Salazar, Chi.	.921	25	8	27	3	38	1

SHORTSTOPS

Leader, Club	PCT	G	PO	A	E	TC	DP	Player, Club	PCT	G	PO	A	E	TC	DP
OWEN, MTL.	.979	142	232	388	13	633	65	Noboa, Mtl.	1.000	4	2	6	0	8	1
								Oester, Cin.	1.000	2	4	10	0	14	2
Player, Club	PCT	G	PO	A	E	TC	DP	Oquendo, St.L.	.970	7	9	23	1	33	2
Anderson, L.A.	.990	33	46	49	1	96	13	Owen, Mtl.	.979	142	232	388	13	633	65
Bell, Pitt.	.968	78	109	197	10	316	41	Quinones, Cin.	1.000	5	0	7	0	7	0
Belliard, Pitt.	.978	40	46	90	3	139	13	Quinones, Pitt.	.934	69	94	174	19	287	24
Benjamin, S.F.	1.000	8	4	4	0	8	0	Ramirez, Hou.	.945	149	189	326	30	545	60
Blauser, Atl.	.958	30	37	55	4	96	5	Ramos, Chi.	.959	42	43	119	7	169	20
Cora, S.D.	.960	7	10	14	1	25	2	Reynolds, Hou.	.957	26	35	54	4	93	10
Duncan, L.A.-Cin.	.952	60	84	134	11	229	25	Richardson, Cin.	.969	39	48	76	4	128	15
Dunston, Chi.	.972	138	213	379	17	609	76	Riles, S.F.	1.000	7	1	6	0	7	1
Elster, N.Y.	.976	150	235	374	15	624	63	Roberts, S.D.	.930	14	25	28	4	57	7
Foley, Mtl.	1.000	14	10	6	0	16	4	Romero, Atl.	1.000	2	1	12	0	13	1
Green, S.D.	.921	11	6	29	3	38	7	Salazar, Chi.	.958	9	13	10	1	24	6
Griffin, L.A.	.975	131	208	333	14	555	69	Sharperson, L.A.	1.000	1	0	3	0	3	0
Hamilton, L.A.	....	1	0	0	0	0	0	Shipley, N.Y.	1.000	3	0	2	0	2	0
Harris, Cin.-L.A.	.846	18	11	33	8	52	3	Smith, St.L.	.976	153	209	483	17	709	73
Hudler, Mtl.	.892	18	16	17	4	37	4	Speier, S.F.	.933	9	6	8	1	15	1
Huson, Mtl.	.886	20	21	41	8	70	7	Templeton, S.D.	.970	140	232	409	20	661	74
Jeltz, Phil.	.985	63	71	121	3	195	15	Thomas, Atl.	.956	138	231	400	29	660	81
Johnson, N.Y.	1.000	31	34	37	0	71	7	Thon, Phil.	.972	129	174	380	16	570	65
Jones, St.L.	.963	12	10	16	1	27	0	Trillo, Cin.	.000	1	0	0	1	1	0
Jurak, S.F.	.875	6	3	4	1	8	1	Uribe, S.F.	.973	150	225	436	18	679	85
King, Pitt.	....	1	0	0	0	0	0	Vizcaino, L.A.	.882	5	6	9	2	17	2
Larkin, Cin.	.976	82	142	267	10	419	31	Wilkerson, Chi.	1.000	7	2	3	0	5	1
Litton, S.F.	1.000	9	0	4	0	4	0	Williams, S.F.	.968	30	19	42	2	63	5
McKnight, N.Y.	.000	1	0	0	1	1	0	Yelding, Hou.	1.000	15	10	26	0	36	4
Miller, N.Y.	.960	8	11	13	1	25	1								

TRIPLE PLAYS: Elster, N.Y.; Huson, Mtl.; Larkin, Cin.

SHORTSTOPS WITH TWO OR MORE CLUBS

Player, Club	PCT	G	PO	A	E	TC	DP	Player, Club	PCT	G	PO	A	E	TC	DP
Duncan, L.A.	.943	16	19	31	3	53	8	Harris, Cin.	.843	17	11	32	8	51	3
Duncan, Cin.	.955	44	65	103	8	176	17	Harris, L.A.	1.000	1	0	1	0	1	0

OUTFIELDERS

Leader, Club	PCT	G	PO	A	E	TC	DP	Player, Club	PCT	G	PO	A	E	TC	DP
YOUNG, HOU.	.998	143	412	15	1	428	5	Gonzalez, L.A.	.968	87	171	8	6	185	2
								Gregg, Atl.★	.967	48	57	1	2	60	0
								Griffey, Cin.★	.987	58	76	2	1	79	1
Player, Club	PCT	G	PO	A	E	TC	DP	Grissom, Mtl.	.943	23	32	1	2	35	0
Abner, S.D.	1.000	51	67	0	0	67	0	Gross, Hou.★	.929	12	13	0	1	14	0
Adduci, Phil.★	....	1	0	0	0	0	0	Gwynn, S.D.★	.984	157	353	13	6	372	1
Aldrete, Mtl.★	.980	37	47	2	1	50	0	Gwynn, L.A.★	1.000	19	26	1	0	27	1
Anthony, Hou.★	1.000	21	34	1	0	35	0	Hall, Pitt.	.909	12	10	0	1	11	0
Bass, Hou.	.985	84	186	6	3	195	0	Harris, L.A.	1.000	21	30	1	0	31	0
Bean, L.A.★	1.000	44	49	0	0	49	0	Hatcher, L.A.	.961	48	68	5	3	76	2
Berroa, Atl.	.971	34	67	1	2	70	0	Hatcher, Hou.-Pitt.	.992	124	250	1	2	253	1
Biggio, Hou.	.933	5	14	0	1	15	0	V. Hayes, Phil.	.980	128	236	9	5	250	1
Blauser, Atl.	....	2	0	0	0	0	0	Hudler, Mtl.	1.000	23	16	0	0	16	0
Blocker, Atl.★	1.000	8	7	0	0	7	0	Huff, L.A.	1.000	9	18	0	0	18	0
Bonds, Pitt.★	.984	156	365	14	6	385	1	Jackson, Chi.-S.D.	.962	63	121	5	5	131	4
Bonilla, Pitt.	....	1	0	0	0	0	0	James, Phil.-S.D.	.986	116	206	6	3	215	0
Brooks, Mtl.	.964	140	234	6	9	249	2	James, Atl.	1.000	46	87	0	0	87	0
Brunansky, St.L.	.977	155	291	9	7	307	2	Jeltz, Phil.	....	1	0	0	0	0	0
Bullock, Phil.★	1.000	3	2	0	0	2	0	Jones, Phil.	1.000	12	27	1	0	28	1
Butler, S.F.★	.986	152	407	11	6	424	3	Jones, S.F.	1.000	30	35	0	0	35	0
Cangelosi, Pitt.	.973	46	71	1	2	74	0	Jones, St.L.	1.000	1	1	0	0	1	0
Carreon, N.Y.★	.983	39	57	0	1	58	0	Jurak, S.F.	1.000	2	2	0	0	2	0
Carter, Pitt.	1.000	5	4	0	0	4	0	Justice, Atl.★	1.000	16	24	0	0	24	0
Ja. Clark, S.D.	1.000	12	22	1	0	23	0	Kruk, S.D.-Phil.★	.977	99	159	8	4	171	2
Je. Clark, S.D.	.947	14	16	2	1	19	0	Law, Chi.	....	1	0	0	0	0	0
Coleman, St.L.	.962	142	247	5	10	262	1	Lindeman, St.L.	1.000	5	5	0	0	5	0
Collins, Cin.★	1.000	16	41	0	0	41	0	Little, Pitt.	1.000	1	1	1	0	2	1
Daniels, Cin.-L.A.	1.000	49	88	4	0	92	1	Litton, S.F.	1.000	6	5	0	0	5	0
Dascenzo, Chi.★	1.000	45	96	0	0	96	0	Maldonado, S.F.	.974	116	181	6	5	192	1
Davidson, Hou.	1.000	23	36	0	0	36	0	Marshall, L.A.	.978	102	179	2	4	185	0
Davis, Cin.	.984	125	298	2	5	305	1	Martinez, S.D.	.982	65	103	5	2	110	1
Davis, L.A.★	.987	48	74	1	1	76	1	Da. Martinez, Mtl.★	.967	118	199	7	7	213	1
Dawson, Chi.	.987	112	227	4	3	234	0	Mazzilli, N.Y.	.889	10	8	0	1	9	0
Dernier, Phil.	.970	74	95	1	3	99	0	McClendon, Chi.	.962	45	75	2	3	80	0
Distefano, Pitt.★	1.000	1	1	0	0	1	0	McDowell, Atl.★	.978	68	179	2	4	185	0
Duncan, Cin.	.800	7	4	0	1	5	0	McGee, St.L.	.976	47	118	2	3	123	0
Dykstra, N.Y.-Phil.★	.988	139	332	10	4	346	0	McReynolds, N.Y.	.969	145	307	10	10	327	3
Fitzgerald, Mtl.	1.000	6	6	2	0	8	0	Meadows, Hou.★	1.000	14	12	0	0	12	0
Ford, Phil.	1.000	52	46	3	0	49	0	Miller, N.Y.	.968	14	30	0	1	31	0
Gant, Atl.	.979	14	47	0	1	48	0	Miller, Phil.	1.000	2	2	0	0	2	0
Gibson, L.A.★	.980	70	146	3	3	152	2	Mitchell, S.F.	.978	147	305	8	7	320	0

OUTFIELDERS—Continued

Player, Club	PCT	G	PO	A	E	TC	DP
Morris, St.L.★	1.000	51	45	0	0	45	0
Murphy, Atl.	.985	151	331	5	5	341	1
Murphy, Phil.	.986	52	69	1	1	71	1
Nixon, Mtl.	.988	98	160	2	2	164	0
Nixon, S.F.	.967	64	87	0	3	90	0
O'Neill, Cin.★	.983	115	223	7	4	234	1
Pena, St.L.	1.000	1	1	0	0	1	0
Pevey, Mtl.	....	1	0	0	0	0	0
Puhl, Hou.	1.000	103	204	3	0	207	0
Raines, Mtl.	.996	139	253	7	1	261	0
Ready, S.D.-Phil.	.962	37	47	4	2	53	3
Redus, Pitt.	.944	16	16	1	1	18	1
Reynolds, Hou.	1.000	1	1	1	0	2	1
Reynolds, Pitt.	.990	98	200	6	2	208	3
Riles, S.F.	.750	5	3	0	1	4	0
Roberts, S.D.	.976	54	77	3	2	82	0
Roomes, Cin.	.981	100	201	4	4	209	0
Russell, Atl.	.867	14	12	1	2	15	0
Ryal, Phil.★	1.000	4	3	0	0	3	0
Salazar, S.D.-Chi.	.952	16	19	1	1	21	0
Samuel, Phil.-N.Y.	.989	134	339	6	4	349	3
Shelby, L.A.	.991	98	220	3	2	225	1
Sheridan, S.F.	.983	66	111	2	2	115	0
D. Smith, Chi.	.975	102	188	7	5	200	3
L. Smith, Atl.	.993	132	289	3	2	294	0
Snider, Cin.	1.000	6	6	0	0	6	0
Steels, S.F.★	1.000	1	1	0	0	1	0
Stephenson, S.D.★	1.000	3	3	0	0	3	0
Strawberry, N.Y.★	.972	131	272	4	8	284	2
Stubbs, L.A.★	.948	28	52	3	3	58	3
Thompson, St.L.	.978	147	348	5	8	361	1
Thornton, N.Y.	1.000	6	9	0	0	9	0
Van Slyke, Pitt.	.989	123	338	9	4	351	5
Varsho, Chi.	.929	21	25	1	2	28	0
Walker, Mtl.	1.000	15	19	2	0	21	1
Walling, St.L.	1.000	6	9	0	0	9	0
Walton, Chi.	.990	115	289	2	3	294	1
Weaver, S.F.★	1.000	8	7	0	0	7	0
Webster, Chi.★	.965	74	161	3	6	170	0
Wetherby, Atl.★	1.000	9	8	0	0	8	0
Wilkerson, Chi.	....	1	0	0	0	0	0
Wilson, Pitt.-Hou.	.974	110	213	10	6	229	1
Wilson, N.Y.	.975	71	152	2	4	158	0
Winningham, Cin.	.980	85	146	3	3	152	0
Worrell, St.L.	....	1	0	0	0	0	0
Wynne, S.D.-Chi.★	.968	109	177	7	6	190	2
Yelding, Hou.	.889	8	7	1	1	9	0
Young, Hou.	.998	143	412	15	1	428	5
Youngblood, Cin.	.970	45	31	1	1	33	1

OUTFIELDERS WITH TWO OR MORE CLUBS

Player, Club	PCT	G	PO	A	E	TC	DP
Daniels, Cin.	1.000	38	67	4	0	71	1
Daniels, L.A.	1.000	11	21	0	0	21	0
Dykstra, N.Y.★	.984	51	124	1	2	127	0
Dykstra, Phil.★	.991	88	208	9	2	219	0
Hatcher, Hou.	.991	104	223	1	2	226	1
Hatcher, Pitt.	1.000	20	27	0	0	27	0
Jackson, Chi.	.970	39	61	3	2	66	2
Jackson, S.D.	.954	24	60	2	3	65	2
James, Phil.	.985	37	61	3	1	65	0
James, S.D.	.987	79	145	3	2	150	0
Kruk, S.D.★	.962	27	48	3	2	53	0
Kruk, Phil.★	.983	72	111	5	2	118	2
Ready, S.D.	.000	1	0	0	0	0	0
Ready, Phil.	.962	36	47	4	2	53	3
Salazar, S.D.	.947	14	18	0	1	19	0
Salazar, Chi.	1.000	2	1	1	0	2	0
Samuel, Phil.	.993	50	133	2	1	136	0
Samuel, N.Y.	.986	84	206	4	3	213	3
Wilson, Pitt.	.977	85	163	4	4	171	0
Wilson, Hou.	.966	25	50	6	2	58	1
Wynne, S.D.★	.971	96	160	7	5	172	2
Wynne, Chi.★	.944	13	17	0	1	18	0

CATCHERS

Leader, Club	PCT	G	PO	A	E	TC	DP	PB
PENA, St.L.	.997	134	674	70	2	746	13	5

Player, Club	PCT	G	PO	A	E	TC	DP	PB
S. Alomar, S.D.	1.000	6	33	1	0	34	1	0
Ashby, Hou.	1.000	19	101	4	0	105	0	1
Bathe, S.F.	1.000	7	13	0	0	13	0	0
Benedict, Atl.	.995	65	361	40	2	403	2	5
Berryhill, Chi.	.992	89	473	41	4	518	4	5
Biggio, Hou.	.990	125	728	56	8	792	6	9
Bilardello, Pitt.	.970	33	150	14	5	169	1	4
Brenly, S.F.	1.000	12	31	5	0	36	0	2
Cabrera, Atl.	.750	1	3	0	1	4	0	0
Carter, N.Y.	.980	47	266	31	6	303	6	3
Daulton, Phil.	.984	126	627	56	11	694	8	5
Davis, Atl.	.985	72	364	40	6	410	1	6
Dempsey, L.A.	.984	62	265	35	5	305	4	3
Diaz, Cin.	.984	43	237	14	4	255	1	2
Distefano, Pitt.★	1.000	3	2	0	0	2	0	1
Fitzgerald, Mtl.	.984	77	459	35	8	502	5	6
Fletcher, L.A.	1.000	5	16	1	0	17	0	1
Girardi, Chi.	.981	59	332	28	7	367	1	5
Jones, St.L.	....	1	0	0	0	0	0	0
Kennedy, S.F.	.986	121	516	47	8	571	6	2
Lake, Phil.	.990	55	262	33	3	298	1	0
LaValliere, Pitt.	.991	65	306	24	3	333	3	4
Litton, S.F.	1.000	2	2	0	0	2	0	0
Lombardi, N.Y.	.980	16	92	5	2	99	1	1
Lyons, N.Y.	.980	76	463	29	10	502	4	5
Mann, Atl.	1.000	7	48	5	0	53	0	0
Manwaring, S.F.	.982	81	289	32	6	327	3	7
McClendon, Chi.	.889	5	7	1	1	9	0	0
McGriff, Cin.	.929	6	23	3	2	28	0	0
Mizerock, Atl.	1.000	11	48	4	0	52	0	1
Nichols, Hou.	1.000	6	16	1	0	17	0	0
Nieto, Phil.	1.000	11	63	2	0	65	0	1
Oliver, Cin.	.986	47	260	21	4	285	1	1
Ortiz, Pitt.	.995	84	334	32	2	368	2	9
Pagnozzi, St.L.	.982	38	99	9	2	110	1	2
Pardo, Phil.	1.000	1	3	0	0	3	0	0
Parent, S.D.	1.000	41	241	17	0	258	2	0
Pena, St.L.	.997	134	674	70	2	746	13	5
Pevey, Mtl.	.985	11	58	7	1	66	0	1
Prince, Pitt.	.960	21	85	11	4	100	1	1
Reed, Cin.	.988	99	504	50	7	561	2	5
Reyes, Mtl.	1.000	4	10	1	0	11	0	0
Russell, Atl.	.990	45	178	24	2	204	1	2
Santiago, S.D.	.975	127	685	81	20	786	10	14
Santovenia, Mtl.	.981	89	561	66	12	639	7	4
Sasser, N.Y.	.992	62	335	19	3	357	3	2
Scioscia, L.A.	.988	130	822	82	11	915	12	6
Spilman, Hou.	....	1	0	0	0	0	0	0
Trevino, Hou.	.989	32	163	11	2	176	2	4
Wrona, Chi.	.983	37	158	15	3	176	1	2
Zeile, St.L.	.971	23	125	10	4	139	1	5

TRIPLE PLAY: Parent, S.D.

PITCHERS

Leader, Club	PCT	G	PO	A	E	TC	DP
HURST, S.D.★	1.000	33	8	42	0	50	2

Player, Club	PCT	G	PO	A	E	TC	DP
Aase, N.Y.	1.000	49	6	8	0	14	0
Acker, Atl.	1.000	59	12	14	0	26	0
Agosto, Hou.★	.885	71	4	19	3	26	2
Aguilera, N.Y.	.909	36	2	8	1	11	0
Aldrich, Atl.	.500	8	0	1	1	2	0

PITCHERS—Continued

Leader, Club	PCT	G	PO	A	E	TC	DP
Alvarez, Atl.	1.000	30	5	8	0	13	1
Andersen, Hou.	.852	60	10	13	4	27	0
Armstrong, Cin.	1.000	9	1	9	0	10	0
As'nmacher, Atl-Chi★	1.000	63	3	13	0	16	0
Bair, Pitt.	.947	44	8	10	1	19	0
Beatty, N.Y.★	1.000	2	2	0	0	2	0
Bedrosian, Phil.-S.F.	.875	68	2	5	1	8	1
Belcher, L.A.	.929	39	21	18	3	42	3
Belinda, Pitt.	....	8	0	0	0	0	0
Benes, S.D.	1.000	10	4	8	0	12	1
Bielecki, Chi.	.975	33	18	21	1	40	0
Birtsas, Cin.★	.900	42	0	9	1	10	0
Blankenship, Chi.	1.000	2	1	0	0	1	0
Blocker, Atl.★	....	1	0	0	0	0	0
Boever, Atl.	1.000	66	7	15	0	22	0
Booker, S.D.	1.000	11	3	2	0	5	0
Brantley, S.F.	1.000	3	3	16	0	19	0
Browning, Cin.★	1.000	37	8	35	0	43	3
Burke, Mtl.	1.000	68	4	16	0	20	0
Camacho, S.F.	1.000	13	2	5	0	7	0
Candelaria, Mtl.★	.667	12	1	1	1	3	0
Cano, Hou.	.800	6	2	2	1	5	1
Carman, Phil.★	.960	49	4	20	1	25	0
Carpenter, St.L.	1.000	36	3	10	0	13	1
Castillo, Atl.★	1.000	12	0	2	0	2	0
Charlton, Cin.★	.842	69	3	13	3	19	0
Clancy, Hou.	.731	33	9	10	7	26	2
Clary, Atl.	1.000	18	10	18	0	28	1
Clements, S.D.★	1.000	23	1	8	0	9	1
Combs, Phil.★	1.000	6	1	3	0	4	0
Cone, N.Y.	.972	34	21	14	1	36	0
Cook, S.F.-Phil.★	.870	23	4	16	3	23	0
Costello, St.L.	1.000	48	3	4	0	7	0
Crews, L.A.	1.000	44	3	7	0	10	0
Darling, N.Y.	.929	33	15	37	4	56	5
Darwin, Hou.	.875	68	2	12	2	16	2
Davis, S.D.★	.800	70	1	11	3	15	0
Dayley, St.L.★	.875	71	2	5	1	8	0
DeLeon, St.L.	.833	36	9	16	5	30	0
Deshaies, Hou.★	.929	34	8	31	3	42	2
Dibble, Cin.	.889	74	3	5	1	9	0
Dillard, Phil.★	1.000	5	0	1	0	1	0
DiPino, St.L.★	1.000	67	6	13	0	19	0
Downs, S.F.	.938	18	7	8	1	16	1
Drabek, Pitt.	.967	35	24	34	2	60	0
Dravecky, S.F.★	1.000	2	0	3	0	3	0
Dunne, Pitt.	1.000	3	0	3	0	3	0
Easley, Pitt.	.667	10	0	2	1	3	0
Eave, Atl.	1.000	3	1	0	0	1	0
Eichhorn, Atl.	1.000	45	9	17	0	26	1
Fernandez, N.Y.★	1.000	35	4	13	0	17	2
Fischer, L.A.	....	2	0	0	0	0	0
Fisher, Pitt.	1.000	9	2	1	0	3	0
Foley, Mtl.	....	1	0	0	0	0	0
Forsch, Hou.	.957	37	13	9	1	23	1
Franco, Cin.★	.955	60	2	19	1	22	1
Freeman, Phil.	....	1	0	0	0	0	0
Frey, Mtl.★	1.000	20	1	2	0	3	0
Frohwirth, Phil.	1.000	45	5	8	0	13	0
Garcia, Pitt.★	1.000	11	1	3	0	4	0
Gardner, Mtl.	1.000	7	1	3	0	4	0
Garrelts, S.F.	.977	30	18	24	1	43	0
Gideon, Mtl.	....	4	0	0	0	0	0
Glavine, Atl.★	.917	29	7	37	4	48	4
Gooden, N.Y.	.889	19	8	16	3	27	0
Gossage, S.F.	.889	31	5	3	1	9	0
Gott, Pitt.	....	1	0	0	0	0	0
Grant, S.D.	.958	50	9	14	1	24	1
Greene, Atl.	1.000	4	2	2	0	4	0
Griffin, Cin.	1.000	3	0	1	0	1	0
Grimsley, Phil.	.833	4	1	4	1	6	1
Gross, Hou.★	....	1	0	0	0	0	0
Gross, Mtl.	.952	31	15	25	2	42	1
Hamilton, L.A.	1.000	1	0	1	0	1	0
Hammaker, S.F.★	.923	28	3	9	1	13	0
Harris, Phil.	.900	44	2	16	2	20	0
Harris, S.D.	1.000	56	12	21	0	33	2
Harris, Mtl.	1.000	11	0	11	0	11	0
Hartley, L.A.	1.000	5	2	0	0	2	0

Player, Club	PCT	G	PO	A	E	TC	DP
Hatcher, L.A.	....	1	0	0	0	0	0
Heaton, Pitt.★	.971	42	6	28	1	35	1
Heinkel, St.L.	1.000	7	3	3	0	6	1
Henry, Atl.	.500	12	1	0	1	2	0
M. Hernandez, N.Y.	....	1	0	0	0	0	0
Hershiser, L.A.	.949	35	24	51	4	79	2
Hesketh, Mtl.★	.923	43	3	9	1	13	3
Hill, St.L.	.977	33	12	31	1	44	1
Holman, Mtl.	.833	10	2	3	1	6	0
Horton, L.A.-St.L.★	1.000	34	2	13	0	15	2
Howell, L.A.	.938	56	5	10	1	16	2
Howell, Phil.	1.000	33	13	19	0	32	2
Hurst, S.D.★	1.000	33	8	42	0	50	2
Innis, N.Y.	.938	29	7	8	1	16	0
Jackson, Cin.★	1.000	20	5	15	0	20	0
R. Johnson, Mtl.★	.750	7	1	5	2	8	0
Kilgus, Chi.	.946	35	10	25	2	37	0
Kinzer, St.L.	....	8	0	0	0	0	0
Kipper, Pitt.★	.867	52	3	10	2	15	1
Knepper, Hou.-S.F.★	.949	35	8	29	2	39	1
Kraemer, Chi.★	....	1	0	0	0	0	0
Kramer, Pitt.	1.000	35	10	10	0	20	0
Krukow, S.F.	1.000	8	4	6	0	10	1
LaCoss, S.F.	.889	45	12	20	4	36	1
Lancaster, Chi.	1.000	42	8	5	0	13	1
Landrum, Pitt.	1.000	56	8	10	0	18	0
Langston, Mtl.★	.938	24	8	22	2	32	1
Leach, N.Y.	1.000	10	2	6	0	8	0
Leary, L.A.-Cin.	.962	33	20	31	2	53	2
Lefferts, S.F.★	1.000	70	5	9	0	14	2
Leiper, S.D.★	.917	22	4	7	1	12	0
Lilliquist, Atl.★	.935	32	9	20	2	31	1
Lugo, Mtl.	1.000	3	1	0	0	1	0
Machado, N.Y.	1.000	10	2	0	0	2	0
Madden, Pitt.★	.333	9	1	0	2	3	0
Maddux, Chi.	.962	35	35	41	3	79	4
Maddux, Phil.	1.000	16	7	12	0	19	1
Madrid, Phil.	1.000	6	0	2	0	2	0
Magrane, St.L.★	.955	34	11	31	2	44	1
Mahler, Cin	.977	40	8	35	1	44	2
De. Martinez, Mtl.	.968	34	11	50	2	63	6
Martinez, L.A.	1.000	15	11	14	0	25	1
Mason, Hou.	1.000	2	1	0	0	1	0
McCament, S.F.	.917	25	3	8	1	12	1
McDowell, N.Y.-Phil.	.933	69	17	25	3	45	3
McElroy, Phil.★	1.000	11	1	0	0	1	0
McGaffigan, Mtl.	.846	57	3	8	2	13	0
McWilliams, Phil.	.933	40	6	22	2	30	2
Medvin, Pitt.	1.000	6	1	2	0	3	0
Mercker, Atl.★	....	2	0	0	0	0	0
Meyer, Hou.	1.000	12	2	2	0	4	0
Mitchell, N.Y.	....	2	0	0	0	0	0
Morgan, L.A.	.968	40	20	41	2	63	2
Mulholland, S.F.-Phil.★	.871	25	2	25	4	31	1
Munoz, L.A.★	1.000	3	1	1	0	2	0
Murphy, S.D.	1.000	7	0	1	0	1	0
Musselman, N.Y.★	.941	20	6	10	1	17	0
Myers, N.Y.★	1.000	65	3	11	0	14	0
Nolte, S.D.★	1.000	3	0	3	0	3	0
O'Neal, Phil.	.917	20	2	9	1	12	0
Ojeda, N.Y.★	.981	31	16	36	1	53	3
Ontiveros, Phil.	1.000	6	4	9	0	13	2
Parrett, Phil.	1.000	72	2	9	0	11	0
Patterson, Pitt.★	1.000	12	1	2	0	3	0
Pena, L.A.	.857	53	1	5	1	7	0
Perez, Mtl.	.956	33	17	26	2	45	1
Perry, Chi.★	.833	19	2	3	1	6	0
Pico, Chi.	.897	53	4	22	3	29	2
Portugal, Hou.	.929	20	11	15	2	28	0
Power, St.L.	1.000	23	5	8	0	13	0
Price, S.F.★	1.000	7	0	3	0	3	1
Puleo, Atl.	1.000	15	2	1	0	3	0
Quisenberry, St.L.	1.000	63	7	22	0	29	1
Rasmussen, S.D.★	1.000	33	6	27	0	33	3
Reed, Pitt.	1.000	15	6	5	0	11	0
Reuschel, S.F.	1.000	32	8	33	0	41	0
Reynolds, Hou.	....	1	0	0	0	0	0
Rhoden, Hou.	1.000	20	6	20	0	26	0
Richards, Atl.	1.000	2	1	3	0	4	0

PITCHERS—Continued

Player, Club	PCT	G	PO	A	E	TC	DP	Player, Club	PCT	G	PO	A	E	TC	DP
Rijo, Cin.	1.000	19	6	14	0	20	0	Swan, S.F.★	1.000	2	1	1	0	2	0
Robinson, S.F.	1.000	34	6	12	0	18	1	Tapani, N.Y.	1.000	3	1	1	0	2	0
Robinson, Pitt.	.886	50	13	26	5	44	2	Tate, S.F.	....	2	0	0	0	0	0
Robinson, Cin.	.944	15	4	13	1	18	0	Taylor, Pitt.	1.000	9	0	1	0	1	0
Rodriguez, Cin.★	1.000	7	1	1	0	2	0	Tekulve, Cin.	1.000	37	2	9	0	11	1
Roesler, Cin.	1.000	17	0	1	0	1	0	Terrell, S.D.	1.000	19	13	30	0	43	3
Ruffin, Phil.★	.902	24	3	34	4	41	0	Terry, St.L.	.951	31	6	33	2	41	2
Russell, Atl.	....	1	0	0	0	0	0	Tewksbury, St.L.	1.000	7	1	3	0	4	0
Samuels, Pitt.★	....	5	0	0	0	0	0	Thompson, Mtl.	1.000	19	0	4	0	4	0
Sanderson, Chi.	1.000	37	10	12	0	22	1	Toliver, S.D.	1.000	9	1	1	0	2	0
Schatzeder, Hou.★	.846	36	2	9	2	13	1	Tudor, L.A.★	1.000	6	0	3	0	3	0
Schiraldi, Chi.-S.D.	1.000	59	9	5	0	14	0	Valdez, Atl.	1.000	19	2	2	0	4	0
Schulze, S.D.	.900	7	4	5	1	10	0	Valenzuela, L.A.★	.914	31	18	35	5	58	4
Scott, Hou.	.909	33	15	25	4	44	0	Viola, N.Y.★	.923	12	3	9	1	13	2
Scudder, Cin.	.933	23	5	9	1	15	0	Walk, Pitt.	.943	33	19	31	3	53	3
Searage, L.A.★	.929	41	5	8	1	14	0	Wallach, Mtl.	....	1	0	0	0	0	0
Sebra, Phil.-Cin.	.769	21	2	8	3	13	0	West, N.Y.★	1.000	11	0	1	0	1	0
Show, S.D.	.933	16	4	10	1	15	1	Wetteland, L.A.	.867	31	5	8	2	15	0
Smiley, Pitt.★	.882	28	7	23	4	34	2	Whitehurst, N.Y.	1.000	9	1	1	0	2	0
B. Smith, Mtl.	.983	33	16	42	1	59	2	Whitson, S.D.	.951	33	17	22	2	41	1
Smith, Hou.	1.000	52	6	10	0	16	1	Wilkins, Chi.	1.000	11	1	3	0	4	0
Smith, Pitt.	1.000	16	2	8	0	10	0	Williams, Chi.★	.786	76	0	11	3	14	0
P. Smith, Atl.	.957	28	11	11	1	23	2	Wilson, Chi.★	.909	53	6	14	2	22	0
Z. Smith, Atl.-Mtl.★	.939	48	7	39	3	49	0	Wilson, S.F.★	.875	14	0	7	1	8	0
Smoltz, Atl.	.887	29	23	32	7	62	2	Worrell, St.L.	1.000	47	0	11	0	11	1
Stanton, Atl.★	.750	20	1	2	1	4	0	Youmans, Phil.	1.000	10	4	6	0	10	1
Sutcliffe, Chi.	.981	35	22	31	1	54	3								

PITCHERS WITH TWO OR MORE CLUBS

Player, Club	PCT	G	PO	A	E	TC	DP	Player, Club	PCT	G	PO	A	E	TC	DP
Assenmacher, Atl.★	1.000	49	2	9	0	11	0	Leary, Cin.	.950	14	4	15	1	20	0
Assenmacher, Chi.★	1.000	14	1	4	0	5	0	McDowell, N.Y.	.957	25	10	12	1	23	2
								McDowell, Phil.	.909	44	7	13	2	22	1
Bedrosian, Phil.	.833	28	2	3	1	6	1								
Bedrosian, S.F.	1.000	40	0	2	0	2	0	Mulholland, S.F.★	1.000	5	0	3	0	3	0
								Mulholland, Phil.★	.857	20	2	22	4	28	1
Cook, S.F.★	1.000	2	0	3	0	3	0	Schiraldi, Chi.	1.000	54	6	5	0	11	0
Cook, Phil.★	.850	21	4	13	3	20	0	Schiraldi, S.D.	1.000	5	3	0	0	3	0
Horton, L.A.★	1.000	23	1	4	0	5	0								
Horton, St.L.★	1.000	11	1	9	0	10	2	Sebra, Phil.	.857	6	1	5	1	7	0
Knepper, Hou.★	.938	22	6	24	2	32	1	Sebra, Mtl.	.667	15	1	3	2	6	0
Knepper, S.F.★	1.000	13	2	5	0	7	0	Z. Smith, Atl.★	.939	17	4	27	2	33	0
Leary, L.A.	.970	19	16	16	1	33	2	Z. Smith, Mtl.★	.938	31	3	12	1	16	0

OFFICIAL NATIONAL LEAGUE PITCHING AVERAGES

CLUB PITCHING

Club	W-L	ERA	G	CG	SHO	SV	IP	H	TBF	R	ER	HR	SH	SF	HB	TBB	IBB	SO	WP	BK
Los Angeles	77-83	2.95	160	25	19	36	1463.1	1278	6034	536	479	95	74	39	27	504	73	1052	53	14
New York	87-75	3.29	162	24	12	38	1454.1	1260	6098	595	532	115	51	46	26	532	45	1108	50	24
San Francisco	92-70	3.30	162	12	16	47	1457.0	1320	6041	600	535	120	69	52	24	471	54	802	37	26
St. Louis	86-76	3.36	164	18	18	43	1461.0	1330	6090	608	546	84	64	46	30	482	89	844	40	16
San Diego	89-73	3.38	162	21	11	52	1457.1	1359	6095	626	547	133	84	44	21	481	51	933	42	15
Chicago	93-69	3.43	162	18	10	55	1460.1	1369	6163	623	556	106	76	45	25	532	70	918	44	24
Montreal	81-81	3.48	162	20	13	35	1468.1	1344	6152	630	567	120	42	32	31	519	62	1059	40	20
Pittsburgh	74-88	3.64	164	19	9	40	1487.2	1394	6309	680	602	121	76	44	29	539	78	827	55	20
Houston	86-76	3.64	162	19	12	38	1479.1	1379	6290	669	599	105	90	44	25	551	94	965	50	23
Atlanta	63-97	3.70	161	15	8	33	1447.2	1370	6088	680	595	114	89	44	16	468	57	966	48	17
Cincinnati	75-87	3.73	162	16	9	37	1464.1	1404	6265	691	607	125	83	50	33	559	105	981	39	22
Philadelphia	67-95	4.04	163	10	10	33	1433.1	1408	6204	735	644	127	74	40	31	613	75	899	91	18
Totals	970-970	3.49	973	218	147	487	17534.0	16215	73829	7673	6809	1365	899	536	318	6251	853	11354	589	239

NOTE—Totals of earned runs for several clubs do not agree with the composite totals for all pitchers of each respective club due to instances in which provisions of Section 10.18 (i) of the Scoring Rules were applied. The following differences are to be noted: Atlanta pitchers add to 597 earned runs, Cincinnati pitchers add to 609, Houston pitchers add to 601, Montreal pitchers add to 568, New York pitchers add to 533, Philadelphia pitchers add to 648, St. Louis pitchers add to 547, San Diego pitchers add to 548.

PITCHERS' RECORDS

(Top Fifteen Qualifiers for Earned-Run Average Leadership—162 or More Innings)

(*Lefthanded Pitcher)

Pitcher, Club	W	L	ERA	G	GS	CG	SHO	GF	SV	IP	H	TBF	R	ER	HR	SF	SH	HB	TBB	IBB	SO	WP	BK
Garrelts, Scott, S.F.	14	5	2.28	30	29	2	1		0	193.1	149	766	58	49	11	9	9	3	46	3	119	7	2
Hershiser, Orel, L.A.	15	15	2.31	35	33	8	4		0	256.2	226	1047	75	66	13	6	19	0	77	14	178	8	4
Langston, Mark, Mtl.*	12	9	2.39	24	24	6	4		0	176.2	138	740	57	47	13	9	9	0	93	6	175	5	2
Whitson, Eddie, S.D.	16	11	2.66	33	33	6	4		0	227.0	198	914	77	67	22	8	12	5	48	7	117	2	3
Hurst, Bruce, S.D.*	15	11	2.69	33	33	10	2		0	244.2	214	990	84	73	16	3	18	0	66	7	179	8	0
Drabek, Douglas, Pitt.	14	12	2.80	35	34	8	1		0	244.1	215	994	83	76	21	13	13	3	69	3	123	5	0
Smiley, John, Pitt.*	12	8	2.81	28	28	8	0		1	205.1	174	835	78	64	22	5	5	7	49	3	123	2	2
Belcher, Timothy, L.A.	15	12	2.82	39	30	10	8		1	230.0	182	937	81	72	20	7	7	4	80	5	200	7	3
Fernandez, C. Sid, N.Y.*	14	5	2.83	35	32	6	2		0	219.1	157	883	73	69	21	4	4	6	75	3	198	3	1
Smith, Bryn, Mtl.	10	11	2.84	34	34	6	3		0	215.2	177	864	76	68	16	7	5	4	54	8	129	3	1
Deshaies, James, Hou.*	15	10	2.91	34	33	3	1		0	225.2	180	928	80	73	15	5	11	5	79	8	153	8	5
Magrane, Joseph, St.L.*	18	9	2.92	34	33	9	3		0	234.2	219	971	81	76	15	14	8	6	72	7	127	14	0
Reuschel, Ricky, S.F.	17	8	2.94	32	32	5	2		0	208.1	195	860	75	68	18	8	7	2	54	2	111	1	0
Smoltz, John, Atl.	12	11	2.94	29	29	5	0		0	208.0	160	847	79	68	15	10	10	2	72	2	168	8	3
Maddux, Gregory, Chi.	19	12	2.95	35	35	7	1		0	238.1	222	1002	90	78	13	18	18	6	82	13	135	5	3

DEPARTMENTAL LEADERS: W—Scott, Hou., 20; L—Carman, Phil., Hershiser, L.A. and Hill, St.L., 15; G—Williams, Chi., 76; GS—Browning, Cin., 37; CG—Belcher, L.A. and Hurst, S.D., 10; SHO—Belcher, L.A., 8; GF—Davis, S.D., 65; Sv—Davis, S.D., 44; IP—Hershiser, L.A., 256.2; H—Mahler, Cin., 242; TBF—Hershiser, L.A., 1,047; R—Mahler, Cin., 113; ER—Gross, Mtl., 98; HR—Browning, Cin., 31; SH—Hershiser, L.A., 19; SF—Darling, N.Y., 13; HB—Mahler, Cin., 10; BB—Hill, St.L., 99; IBB—Clancy, Hou. and Leary, L.A.-Cin., 15; SO—DeLeon, St.L., 201; WP—Howell, Phil., 21; Bk.—P. Smith, Atl., 7.

INDIVIDUAL PITCHING
(*Throws Lefthanded)

Pitcher, Club	W	L	ERA	G	GS	CG	SHO	GF	SV	IP	H	TBF	R	ER	HR	SH	SF	HB	TBB	IBB	SO	WP	BK
Aase, Donald, N.Y.	1	5	3.94	49	0	0	0	22	2	59.1	56	261	27	26	5	2	3	1	26	3	34	0	1
Acker, James, Atl.	0	6	2.67	59	0	0	0	23	1	97.2	84	383	32	29	5	5	5	1	20	8	68	1	0
Agosto, Juan, Hou.*	4	5	2.93	71	0	0	0	28	7	83.0	81	361	32	27	3	5	6	2	32	10	46	4	1
Aguilera, Richard, N.Y.	6	6	2.34	36	0	0	0	19	7	69.1	59	284	19	18	3	5	1	1	21	3	80	3	1
Aldrich, Jay, Atl.	1	3	2.19	8	0	0	0	2	0	12.1	7	50	5	3	0	1	1	0	6	1	7	3	3
Alvarez, Jose, Atl.	3	3	2.86	30	0	0	0	12	2	50.1	44	217	18	16	4	4	1	1	24	2	45	0	0
Andersen, Larry, Hou.	4	4	1.54	60	0	0	0	21	3	87.2	63	351	19	15	4	2	5	0	24	4	85	2	1
Armstrong, John, Cin.	2	3	4.64	9	8	0	0	1	0	42.2	40	187	24	22	5	2	3	1	21	4	23	3	0
Assenmacher, Paul, Atl.-Chi.*	3	4	3.99	63	0	0	0	17	1	76.2	74	331	37	34	3	2	1	0	28	8	79	7	0
Bair, C. Douglas, Pitt.	3	3	2.27	44	0	0	0	17	0	67.1	52	276	19	17	4	1	0	0	28	10	56	3	0
Beatty, G. Blaine, N.Y.*	0	2	1.50	2	1	0	0	0	0	6.0	5	25	1	1	1	0	4	0	2	0	3	0	0
Bedrosian, Stephen, Phil.-S.F.	3	7	2.87	68	0	0	0	60	23	84.2	56	342	31	27	12	6	0	1	39	5	58	2	0
Belcher, Timothy, L.A.	15	12	2.82	39	30	10	8	0	0	230.0	182	937	81	72	20	6	2	7	80	5	200	7	3
Belinda, Stanley, Pitt.	0	1	6.10	8	0	0	0	6	1	10.1	13	46	8	7	0	0	2	1	2	0	8	0	0
Benes, Andrew, S.D.	6	3	3.51	10	10	0	0	0	0	66.2	51	280	28	26	6	6	0	0	31	8	66	0	3
Bielecki, Michael, Chi.	18	7	3.14	33	33	4	3	1	0	212.1	187	882	82	74	16	3	3	1	81	8	147	9	4
Birtsas, Timothy, Cin.*	2	2	3.75	42	1	0	0	12	1	69.2	68	300	33	29	5	3	6	0	27	8	57	3	3
Blankenship, Kevin, Chi.	0	0	1.69	2	0	0	0	0	0	5.1	4	22	1	1	0	0	0	3	2	0	2	0	0
Blocker, Terry, Atl.*	0	0	0.00	1	0	0	0	1	0	1.0	0	4	0	0	0	0	0	0	2	1	0	0	0
Boever, Joseph, Atl.	4	11	3.94	66	0	0	0	53	21	82.1	78	349	37	36	6	5	0	3	34	5	68	5	5
Booker, Gregory, S.D.	0	1	4.26	11	1	0	0	4	0	19.0	15	79	10	9	2	2	0	0	10	1	8	1	1
Brantley, Jeffrey, S.F.	7	1	4.07	59	1	0	0	15	0	97.1	101	422	50	44	10	7	3	2	37	8	69	3	2
Browning, Thomas, Cin.*	15	12	3.39	37	37	9	2	0	0	249.2	241	1031	109	94	31	12	6	3	64	10	118	1	1
Burke, Timothy, Mtl.	9	3	2.55	68	0	0	0	52	28	84.2	68	333	24	24	6	2	5	3	22	7	54	1	0
Camacho, Ernie, S.F.	3	2	2.76	13	0	0	0	5	0	16.1	10	70	5	5	1	4	1	0	11	2	14	3	1
Candelaria, John, Mtl.*	0	2	3.31	12	6	0	0	2	0	16.1	17	68	8	6	3	2	3	0	4	1	14	0	0
Cano, Joselito, Hou.	0	0	5.09	6	3	0	0	5	0	23.0	24	99	13	13	1	1	0	3	7	1	8	0	3
Carman, Donald, Phil.*	5	15	5.24	49	20	0	0	0	0	149.1	152	683	98	87	21	5	5	3	86	6	81	7	3
Carpenter, Cris, St.L.	4	4	3.18	36	5	0	0	10	3	68.0	70	303	30	24	4	4	4	0	26	9	35	0	0
Castillo, Antonio, Atl.*	1	1	4.82	12	0	0	0	0	0	9.1	8	41	5	5	1	4	2	0	9	1	5	0	4
Charlton, Norman, Cin.*	8	3	2.93	69	0	0	0	27	2	95.1	67	393	38	31	5	9	2	2	40	7	98	6	3
Clancy, James, Hou.	7	14	5.08	33	26	1	0	3	1	147.0	155	655	100	83	13	9	4	2	66	15	91	5	3
Clary, Marty, Atl.	4	3	3.15	18	17	2	1	1	0	108.2	103	452	47	38	6	4	3	1	31	5	30	1	0
Clements, Patrick, S.D.*	4	3	3.92	23	1	0	0	8	2	39.0	39	167	17	17	4	5	1	3	15	5	18	5	4
Combs, Patrick, Phil.*	4	0	2.09	6	6	1	1	0	0	38.2	36	153	10	9	2	2	0	0	6	1	30	0	0
Cone, David, N.Y.	14	8	3.52	34	33	7	2	1	0	219.2	183	910	92	86	20	6	4	4	74	6	190	14	4
Cook, Dennis, S.F.-Phil.*	7	8	3.72	23	18	2	0	1	1	121.0	110	499	59	50	18	5	2	2	38	6	67	4	0
Costello, John, St.L.	5	4	3.32	48	0	0	0	16	3	62.1	48	252	24	23	5	2	5	2	20	7	40	1	4
Crews, S. Timothy, L.A.	0	1	3.21	44	0	0	0	11	1	61.2	69	275	27	22	8	5	13	3	23	9	56	1	0
Darling, Ronald, N.Y.	14	14	3.52	33	33	4	0	0	0	217.1	214	922	100	85	19	3	5	3	70	7	153	2	3
Darwin, Danny, Hou.	11	4	2.36	68	0	0	0	26	7	122.0	92	482	34	32	8	8	4	0	33	9	104	8	1
Davis, Mark, S.D.*	4	3	1.85	70	0	0	0	65	44	92.2	66	370	21	19	6	3	1	6	31	1	92	2	0
Dayley, Kenneth, St.L.*	4	3	2.87	71	0	0	0	28	12	75.1	63	310	26	24	6	3	3	4	30	10	40	8	1
DeLeon, Jose, St.L.	16	12	3.05	36	36	5	3	0	0	244.2	173	972	96	83	15	11	5	6	80	5	201	8	1
Deshaies, James, Hou.*	15	10	2.91	34	34	6	3	0	0	225.2	180	928	80	73	15	5	5	4	79	11	153	7	1
Dibble, Robert, Cin.	10	5	2.09	74	0	0	0	18	2	99.0	62	401	23	23	4	3	0	3	39	8	141	1	0
Dillard, Gordon, Phil.*	0	0	6.75	5	0	0	0	1	0	4.0	7	19	3	3	0	0	0	1	0	0	2	1	0
DiPino, Frank, St.L.*	9	0	2.45	67	0	0	0	8	0	88.1	73	347	26	24	6	1	5	0	20	7	44	2	0

Pitcher, Club	W	L	ERA	G	GS	CG	SHO	GF	SV	IP	H	TBF	R	ER	HR	SH	SF	HB	TBB	IBB	SO	WP	BK
Downs, Kelly, S.F.	4	8	4.79	18	15	0	0	0	0	82.2	82	349	47	44	7	4	4	1	26	4	49	3	3
Drabek, Douglas, Pitt.	14	12	2.80	35	34	8	1	0	0	244.1	215	994	83	76	21	13	7	3	69	3	123	3	0
Dravecky, David, S.F.*	2	1	3.46	2	2	0	0	0	0	13.0	8	50	5	5	2	1	0	1	4	0	5	1	0
Dunne, Michael, Pitt.	1	0	7.53	3	3	0	0	0	0	14.1	21	75	12	12	1	1	0	1	9	0	5	1	1
Easley, K. Logan, Pitt.	1	0	4.38	10	0	0	0	4	0	12.1	6	51	6	6	1	1	0	1	7	0	4	1	1
Eave, Gary, Atl.	2	0	1.31	3	3	0	0	0	0	20.2	15	88	3	3	0	0	4	0	12	0	6	1	1
Eichhorn, Mark, Atl.	5	5	4.35	45	0	0	0	13	0	68.1	70	286	36	33	6	7	4	4	19	8	49	0	3
Fernandez, C. Sid, N.Y.*	14	5	2.83	35	32	6	2	0	0	219.1	157	883	73	69	21	4	4	6	75	3	198	1	0
Fischer, Jeffrey, L.A.	0	0	13.50	2	0	0	0	0	0	3.1	7	17	5	5	2	1	1	0	0	0	2	0	0
Fisher, Brian, Pitt.	0	3	7.94	9	3	0	0	3	1	17.0	25	88	17	15	1	1	4	0	10	0	8	1	0
Foley, Thomas, Mtl.	0	0	27.00	1	0	0	0	1	0	0.1	1	3	1	1	0	0	0	0	0	0	0	0	0
Forsch, Robert, Hou.	4	5	5.32	37	15	0	0	5	0	108.1	133	494	68	64	10	4	4	4	46	6	40	4	5
Franco, John, Cin.*	4	8	3.12	60	0	0	0	50	32	80.2	77	345	35	28	3	7	3	0	36	8	60	3	2
Freeman, Marvin, Phil.*	0	2	6.00	20	1	0	0	11	0	30.0	29	136	22	20	4	0	0	3	17	3	9	1	1
Frey, Steven, Mtl.*	3	2	5.48	45	0	0	0	11	0	21.1	25	103	15	13	4	0	2	0	11	3	15	1	1
Frohwirth, Todd, Phil.	0	2	3.59	11	0	0	0	6	0	62.2	56	258	26	25	5	3	1	2	18	3	39	0	1
Garcia, Miguel, Pitt.*	0	0	8.44	7	0	0	0	1	0	16.0	25	78	16	15	2	0	0	0	11	0	7	0	0
Gardner, Mark, Mtl.	0	3	5.13	4	4	0	0	0	0	26.1	26	117	16	15	2	0	0	2	7	3	21	1	2
Garrelts, Scott, S.F.	14	5	2.28	30	29	2	2	0	0	193.1	149	766	58	49	11	9	7	0	46	3	119	2	2
Gideon, B. Brett, Mtl.	0	0	1.93	4	0	0	0	1	0	4.2	5	22	1	1	0	0	0	0	5	0	5	0	0
Glavine, Thomas, Atl.*	14	8	3.68	29	29	6	0	0	0	186.0	172	766	88	76	20	11	4	2	40	3	90	5	5
Gooden, Dwight, N.Y.	9	4	2.89	19	17	2	0	0	0	118.1	93	497	42	38	9	4	3	0	47	6	101	2	2
Gossage, Richard, S.F.	2	2	2.68	31	0	0	0	22	4	43.2	32	182	16	13	2	2	2	0	27	3	24	1	0
Gott, James, Pitt.	0	0	0.00	2	0	0	0	0	0	0.2	1	4	0	0	0	0	0	0	1	0	1	0	0
Grant, Mark, S.D.	8	2	3.33	50	0	0	0	19	2	116.1	105	466	45	43	11	5	5	3	32	6	69	3	5
Greene, I. Thomas, Atl.	1	0	4.10	4	4	0	0	0	0	26.1	22	103	12	12	5	1	2	0	6	1	17	1	2
Griffin, Michael, Cin.	0	0	12.46	3	0	0	0	0	0	4.1	10	26	6	6	0	2	0	0	3	1	2	1	0
Grimsley, Jason, Phil.	2	3	5.89	4	4	0	0	0	0	18.1	19	91	13	12	2	0	0	0	19	1	7	2	4
Gross, Gregory, Hou.*	0	0	18.00	1	0	0	0	0	0	1.0	3	6	2	2	0	0	0	0	1	0	1	0	0
Gross, Kevin, Mtl.	11	12	4.38	31	31	4	1	0	0	201.1	188	867	105	98	20	10	3	6	88	6	158	5	5
Hamilton, Jeffrey, L.A.	0	1	5.40	1	1	0	0	0	0	1.2	2	6	1	1	0	0	0	0	1	0	2	1	2
Hammaker, C. Atlee, S.F.*	6	6	3.76	28	9	0	0	5	0	76.2	78	322	34	32	5	6	4	1	23	2	30	1	0
Harris, Gregory A., Phil.	6	2	3.58	44	0	0	0	17	1	75.1	64	324	34	30	7	4	2	2	43	7	51	7	3
Harris, Gregory W., S.D.	2	9	2.60	56	0	0	0	25	6	135.0	106	554	43	39	8	3	5	2	52	9	106	10	3
Harris, T. Eugene, Mtl.	8	1	4.95	11	3	0	0	7	0	20.0	16	84	11	11	1	1	1	0	11	0	11	1	1
Hartley, Michael, L.A.	1	0	1.50	5	0	0	0	3	0	6.0	6	20	1	1	0	0	0	0	3	0	4	0	2
Hatcher, Michael, L.A.	0	1	9.00	1	0	0	0	0	0	1.0	2	6	1	1	0	0	0	0	0	1	0	0	1
Heaton, Neal, Pitt.*	6	7	3.05	42	18	1	0	5	0	147.1	127	620	55	50	12	12	3	3	55	12	67	4	0
Heinkel, Donald, St.L.	1	1	5.81	7	5	0	0	0	0	26.1	40	125	19	17	2	1	2	0	7	1	16	1	5
Henry, Dwayne, Atl.	0	2	4.26	12	0	0	0	6	1	12.2	12	55	6	6	0	2	0	0	5	0	16	1	2
Hernandez, Manuel, N.Y.	0	0	0.00	1	0	0	0	0	0	1.0	2	6	0	0	0	0	0	0	0	0	0	0	0
Hershiser, Orel, L.A.	15	15	2.31	35	33	15	4	0	0	256.2	226	1047	75	66	9	19	6	3	77	14	178	8	4
Hesketh, Joseph, Mtl.*	6	4	5.77	43	0	0	0	17	0	48.1	54	219	34	31	5	6	6	0	26	6	44	6	3
Hill, Kenneth, St.L.	7	5	3.80	33	33	2	1	0	0	196.2	186	862	92	83	9	14	5	5	99	6	112	11	1
Holman, Brian, Mtl.	1	3	4.83	10	3	0	0	0	0	31.2	34	145	18	17	2	2	1	4	15	0	23	3	2
Horton, Ricky, L.A.-St.L.*	5	3	4.85	34	8	0	0	7	0	72.1	85	314	45	39	3	4	4	0	21	4	26	1	0
Howell, Jay, L.A.	5	3	1.58	56	0	0	0	41	28	79.2	60	312	15	14	3	2	2	2	22	6	55	4	1
Howell, Kenneth, Phil.	12	12	3.44	33	32	5	1	0	0	204.0	155	827	84	78	11	8	9	0	86	6	164	8	5
Hurst, Bruce, S.D.*	15	11	2.69	33	33	10	2	0	0	244.2	214	990	84	73	16	18	3	1	66	7	179	8	0
Innis, Jeffrey, N.Y.	0	1	3.18	29	0	0	0	12	0	39.2	38	160	16	14	1	2	1	1	8	0	16	0	0

Pitcher, Club	W	L	ERA	G	GS	CG	SHO	GF	SV	IP	H	TBF	R	ER	HR	SH	SF	HB	TBB	IBB	SO	WP	BK
Jackson, Danny, Cin.*	6	11	5.60	20	20	0	0	0	0	115.2	122	519	78	72	10	6	4	1	57	7	70	3	2
Johnson, Randall, Mtl.*	7	10	6.67	7	6	0	0	0	2	29.2	29	143	25	22	2	3	4	0	26	1	26	2	2
Kilgus, Paul, Chi.*	6	10	4.39	35	23	0	0	5	0	145.2	164	642	90	71	9	5	1	5	49	6	61	3	2
Kinzer, Matthew, St.L.	0	2	12.83	8	1	0	0	3	0	13.1	25	67	20	19	3	0	0	0	4	1	8	1	2
Kipper, Robert, Pitt.*	3	4	2.93	52	0	0	0	15	4	83.0	55	334	29	27	5	5	6	3	33	6	58	5	0
Knepper, Robert, Hou.-S.F.*	7	12	5.13	35	26	1	0	2	0	165.0	190	746	98	94	16	12	0	3	75	6	64	5	2
Kraemer, Joseph, Chi.*	0	0	4.91	1	0	0	0	1	0	3.2	7	21	6	2	0	0	0	0	2	1	5	0	4
Kramer, Randall, Pitt.	5	5	3.96	35	15	1	1	7	0	111.1	90	482	53	49	10	9	4	7	61	4	52	1	0
Krukow, Michael, S.F.	4	3	3.98	8	8	0	0	0	0	43.0	37	177	20	19	5	0	1	1	18	3	18	0	0
LaCoss, Michael, S.F.	10	10	3.17	45	18	1	1	16	0	150.1	143	647	62	53	8	8	7	7	65	1	78	1	5
Lancaster, Lester, Chi.	4	2	1.36	42	0	0	0	15	8	72.2	60	288	12	11	2	3	2	0	15	5	51	2	1
Landrum, T. William, Pitt.	2	3	1.67	56	0	0	0	40	26	81.0	60	325	18	15	2	3	2	0	28	8	51	5	0
Langston, Mark, Mtl.*	12	9	2.39	24	24	6	4	0	0	176.2	138	740	57	47	13	9	4	2	93	6	175	5	2
Leach, Terry, N.Y.	0	0	4.22	10	0	0	0	4	0	21.1	19	85	11	10	1	7	8	1	4	0	2	0	0
Leary, Timothy, L.A.-Cin.	8	14	3.52	33	31	4	0	0	0	207.0	205	874	84	81	17	4	4	5	68	15	123	10	1
Lefferts, Craig, S.F.*	2	4	2.69	70	0	0	0	32	20	107.0	93	430	38	32	11	2	4	1	22	5	71	2	1
Leiper, David, S.D.*	1	0	5.02	22	0	0	0	11	0	28.2	40	143	19	16	2	1	3	2	20	4	7	2	3
Lilliquist, Derek, Atl.*	8	10	3.97	32	30	2	0	0	0	165.2	202	718	87	73	16	8	3	0	34	5	79	4	0
Lugo, Urbano, Mtl.	0	0	6.75	3	0	0	0	2	0	4.0	9	16	4	3	1	0	0	0	0	0	3	0	0
Machado, Julio, N.Y.	1	1	3.27	10	0	0	0	9	0	11.0	17	45	5	4	0	1	6	0	13	3	14	0	0
Madden, Morris, Pitt.*	2	2	7.07	9	3	0	0	2	0	14.0	14	67	14	11	3	0	1	6	13	0	6	5	3
Maddux, Gregory, Chi.	19	12	2.95	35	35	7	3	0	0	238.1	222	1002	90	78	13	18	6	2	82	13	135	5	1
Maddux, Michael, Phil.	1	3	5.15	16	4	0	0	1	0	43.2	52	191	29	25	3	3	1	1	14	3	26	3	1
Madrid, Alexander, Phil.	1	2	5.47	6	3	0	0	1	0	10.1	12	46	16	15	3	1	0	3	14	1	13	1	0
Magrane, Joseph, St.L.*	18	9	2.91	34	33	9	3	0	0	234.2	219	971	81	76	11	14	8	6	72	7	127	14	5
Mahler, Richard, Cin.	9	13	3.83	40	31	6	2	1	0	220.2	242	940	113	94	15	15	5	10	51	13	102	4	4
Martinez, J. Dennis, Mtl.	16	7	3.18	34	33	5	1	0	0	232.0	227	950	88	82	21	8	7	5	49	4	142	5	2
Martinez, Ramon, L.A.	6	4	3.19	15	15	2	2	0	0	98.2	79	410	39	35	11	0	0	5	41	0	89	1	0
Mason, Roger, Hou.	0	0	20.25	2	0	0	0	1	0	1.1	2	8	3	3	0	0	0	0	2	0	3	0	0
McCament, L. Randall, S.F.	1	0	3.93	25	0	0	0	10	0	36.2	32	159	22	16	4	8	1	1	23	2	12	1	1
McDowell, Roger, N.Y.-Phil.	4	8	1.96	69	0	0	0	56	23	92.0	79	387	36	20	3	6	3	3	38	8	47	3	1
McElroy, Charles, Phil.*	0	1	1.74	11	0	0	0	4	0	10.1	12	46	4	2	1	7	1	0	4	1	8	0	0
McGaffigan, Andrew, Mtl.	3	5	4.68	57	0	0	0	23	2	75.0	85	333	40	39	6	6	4	4	30	6	40	3	0
McWilliams, Larry, Phil.*	2	11	4.10	16	16	2	1	0	0	120.2	123	531	67	55	9	9	4	3	49	4	54	6	3
Medvin, Scott, Pitt.	0	0	5.68	6	0	0	0	2	0	6.1	6	30	5	4	1	0	0	0	5	2	4	1	1
Mercker, Kent, Atl.*	0	0	12.46	2	1	0	0	0	0	4.1	8	26	6	6	1	0	2	0	6	0	4	0	0
Meyer, Brian, Hou.	1	0	4.50	12	0	0	0	6	0	18.0	16	82	13	9	1	6	1	1	13	3	13	1	1
Mitchell, John, N.Y.	1	1	6.00	7	2	0	0	2	0	3.0	12	17	7	2	0	2	0	0	4	1	4	0	0
Morgan, Michael, L.A.	8	11	2.53	40	19	0	0	7	0	152.1	130	604	51	43	8	8	6	4	33	8	72	6	1
Mulholland, Terence, S.F.-Phil.*	4	7	4.92	25	18	2	0	4	0	115.1	137	513	66	63	8	7	0	3	36	3	66	3	0
Munoz, Michael, L.A.*	0	0	16.88	3	0	0	0	1	0	2.2	5	14	5	5	1	0	0	4	2	1	3	0	0
Murphy, Daniel, S.D.	0	0	5.68	7	0	0	0	2	0	6.1	6	30	5	4	0	0	0	0	4	1	1	0	0
Musselman, Jeffrey, N.Y.*	3	2	3.08	20	0	0	0	4	0	26.1	27	119	11	9	1	4	0	1	14	3	11	1	0
Myers, Randall, N.Y.*	7	4	2.35	65	0	0	0	47	24	84.1	62	349	23	22	4	6	2	0	40	4	88	3	0
Nolte, Eric, S.D.*	0	0	11.00	1	1	0	0	0	0	9.0	15	49	12	11	1	0	6	1	7	1	8	0	0
Ojeda, Robert, N.Y.*	13	11	3.47	31	31	5	2	0	0	192.0	179	824	83	74	16	7	7	2	78	5	95	5	2
O'Neal, Randall, Phil.	2	1	6.23	20	6	0	0	2	0	39.0	46	167	28	27	6	2	3	0	9	2	29	0	1
Ontiveros, Steven, Phil.	2	1	3.82	6	5	0	0	0	0	30.2	34	134	15	13	5	1	0	3	15	1	12	5	0
Parrett, Jeffrey, Phil.	12	6	2.98	72	0	0	0	34	6	105.2	90	444	43	35	6	7	5	0	44	13	98	7	3
Patterson, Kenneth, Pitt.*	4	3	4.05	12	3	0	0	2	1	26.2	23	109	13	12	3	1	1	0	8	2	20	0	0

Pitcher, Club	W	L	ERA	G	GS	CG	SHO	GF	SV	IP	H	TBF	R	ER	HR	SH	SF	HB	TBB	IBB	SO	WP	BK
Pena, Alejandro, L.A.	4	3	2.13	53	0	0	0	28	5	76.0	62	306	20	18	8	3	1	2	18	4	75	1	1
Perez, Pascual, Mtl.	9	13	3.31	33	28	2	0	3	1	198.1	178	811	85	73	15	6	4	4	45	13	152	6	1
Perez, W. Patrick, Chi.*	1	1	1.77	19	0	0	0	6	2	35.2	23	141	8	7	2	6	1	4	16	3	20	1	0
Pico, Jeffrey, Chi.	3	1	3.77	53	5	0	0	17	0	90.2	99	394	43	38	7	5	2	0	31	10	38	2	0
Portugal, Mark, Hou.	7	1	2.75	20	15	2	1	1	1	108.0	91	440	34	33	8	8	1	0	37	3	86	3	0
Power, Ted, St.L.	7	7	3.71	23	15	0	0	2	0	97.0	96	407	47	40	7	5	3	0	21	3	43	1	0
Price, Joseph, S.F.*	1	1	5.79	7	1	0	0	3	0	14.0	16	59	9	9	3	3	1	0	4	2	10	1	0
Puleo, Charles, Atl.	3	1	4.66	15	1	0	0	2	0	29.0	26	128	15	15	2	2	4	0	16	1	17	0	1
Quisenberry, Daniel, St.L.	1	3	2.64	63	0	0	0	35	6	78.1	78	317	25	23	2	3	1	3	14	9	37	1	0
Rasmussen, Dennis, S.D.*	10	10	4.26	33	33	1	0	0	0	183.2	190	799	100	87	18	9	11	3	72	6	87	4	2
Reed, Richard, Pitt.	1	1	5.60	15	7	0	0	2	0	54.2	62	232	35	34	5	2	7	1	11	3	34	1	3
Reuschel, Ricky, S.F.	17	8	2.94	32	32	2	2	0	0	208.1	195	860	75	68	18	9	7	1	54	4	111	1	0
Reynolds, G. Craig, Hou.	0	0	27.00	1	0	0	0	0	0	1.0	3	9	4	3	0	0	0	1	2	0	0	0	0
Rhoden, Richard, Hou.	0	6	4.28	20	17	0	0	2	0	96.2	108	432	49	46	7	11	3	3	41	8	41	1	2
Richards, Russell, Atl.	0	0	4.82	2	2	0	0	0	0	9.1	10	41	5	5	0	0	0	1	6	0	4	1	0
Rijo, Jose, Cin.	12	6	2.84	19	19	1	1	0	0	111.0	101	464	39	35	6	3	5	2	48	3	86	4	3
Robinson, Don, S.F.	7	13	3.43	34	32	5	0	0	0	197.0	184	793	80	75	22	6	6	2	37	6	96	4	4
Robinson, Jeffrey D., Pitt.	7	13	4.58	50	19	0	0	18	4	141.1	161	643	92	72	14	7	7	3	59	11	95	14	2
Robinson, Ronald, Cin.*	5	3	3.35	15	15	0	0	4	0	83.1	80	353	36	31	8	5	1	2	28	2	36	2	0
Rodriguez, Rosario, Cin.*	0	0	4.15	7	0	0	0	4	0	4.1	3	19	2	2	0	1	0	0	3	1	3	0	0
Roesler, Michael, Cin.	0	1	3.96	7	0	0	0	6	0	25.0	22	102	11	11	4	1	0	0	9	1	14	0	0
Ruffin, Bruce, Phil.*	6	10	4.44	24	23	1	0	0	0	125.2	152	576	69	62	10	8	1	2	62	6	70	8	0
Russell, John, Atl.	0	0	0.00	1	0	0	0	1	0	0.1	0	1	0	0	0	0	0	0	0	0	0	0	0
Samuels, Roger, Pitt.*	0	0	9.82	5	0	0	0	4	0	3.2	9	23	4	4	1	0	0	0	4	2	2	0	3
Sanderson, Scott, Chi.	11	9	3.94	37	23	0	0	2	1	146.1	155	611	69	64	16	8	3	3	31	6	86	1	1
Schatzeder, Daniel, Hou.*	4	7	4.45	36	4	0	0	7	1	56.2	64	259	33	28	2	5	3	1	28	6	46	7	1
Schiraldi, Calvin, Chi.-S.D.	6	1	3.51	59	4	0	0	25	4	100.0	72	429	40	39	8	2	2	2	63	6	71	4	0
Schulze, Donald, S.D.	1	1	5.55	7	4	0	0	2	0	24.1	38	118	20	15	6	1	2	0	6	3	15	1	0
Scott, Michael, Hou.	20	10	3.10	33	32	9	8	0	0	229.0	180	924	87	79	23	7	4	3	62	12	172	7	0
Scudder, W. Scott, Cin.	4	9	4.49	23	17	0	0	3	0	100.1	91	451	54	50	14	2	7	0	61	11	66	0	1
Searage, Raymond, L.A.*	3	3	3.53	41	0	0	0	17	1	35.2	29	152	15	14	1	5	2	1	18	6	24	2	1
Sebra, Robert, Phil.-Cin.	0	6	5.20	21	5	0	0	4	0	55.1	65	263	36	32	8	6	3	0	28	3	35	2	2
Show, Eric, S.D.	8	6	4.23	16	16	0	0	0	0	106.1	113	464	59	50	9	5	5	7	39	3	66	2	1
Smiley, John, Pitt.*	12	8	2.81	28	28	8	3	0	0	205.1	174	835	78	64	22	6	5	4	49	5	123	5	2
Smith, Bryn, Mtl.	10	11	2.84	32	32	8	1	0	0	215.2	177	864	76	68	16	7	7	4	54	9	129	3	1
Smith, David, Hou.	3	4	2.64	52	0	0	0	44	25	58.0	49	239	20	17	4	8	1	3	19	7	31	1	0
Smith, Michael, Pitt.	0	0	3.75	16	0	0	0	8	0	24.0	28	107	12	10	1	1	2	0	10	1	12	1	0
Smith, Peter, Atl.	5	14	4.75	27	27	0	0	0	0	142.0	144	613	83	75	13	5	5	3	57	3	115	3	1
Smith, Zane, Atl-Mtl.*	1	13	3.49	48	17	0	0	10	2	147.0	141	634	76	57	7	15	5	5	52	7	93	4	0
Smoltz, John, Atl.	12	11	2.94	29	29	5	0	0	0	208.0	160	847	79	68	15	10	7	2	72	2	168	8	3
Stanton, W. Michael, Atl.*	0	1	1.50	20	0	0	0	10	7	24.0	17	94	4	4	1	0	0	0	8	0	27	1	0
Sutcliffe, Richard, Chi.	16	11	3.66	35	34	5	0	0	0	229.0	202	938	98	93	18	15	10	2	69	8	153	12	6
Swan, Russell, S.F.*	0	0	3.66	2	0	0	0	1	0	6.2	11	34	10	8	4	2	0	0	4	0	2	0	0
Tapani, Kevin, N.Y.	0	0	10.80	3	0	0	0	1	0	7.1	5	31	3	1	0	2	0	0	4	0	4	0	0
Tate, Stuart, S.F.	0	1	3.68	9	0	0	0	0	0	2.2	3	12	3	1	6	0	0	0	0	0	2	1	0
Taylor, Donald, Pitt.	1	3	5.06	7	0	0	0	5	0	10.2	14	47	6	6	0	4	2	0	5	2	3	0	0
Tekulve, Kenton, Cin.	0	3	3.38	37	0	0	0	20	1	52.0	56	235	29	25	5	8	3	2	23	8	31	0	1
Terrell, C. Walter, S.D.	5	13	5.02	29	19	4	0	0	0	123.1	134	520	65	59	14	8	2	0	26	6	63	4	1
Terry, Scott, St.L.	8	10	4.01	31	24	1	0	5	2	148.2	142	619	65	59	14	8	4	3	43	6	69	2	2
Tewksbury, Robert, St.L.	1	0	3.30	7	4	0	0	2	0	30.0	25	125	12	11	2	1	2	0	10	3	17	0	0

Pitcher, Club	W	L	ERA	G	GS	CG	SHO	GF	SV	IP	H	TBF	R	ER	HR	SH	SF	HB	TBB	IBB	SO	WP	BK
Thompson, Richard, Mtl	0	0	2.18	19	1	1	0	9	0	33.0	27	129	11	8	2	1	2	1	11	2	15	0	1
Toliver, Freddie, S.D.	0	0	7.07	9	0	0	0	3	0	14.0	17	65	14	11	5	1	1	0	9	1	14	0	0
Tudor, John, L.A.★	0	2	3.14	6	3	0	0	1	0	14.1	17	62	5	5	1	1	0	0	6	3	9	2	0
Valdez, Sergio, Atl.	1	2	6.06	19	1	0	0	8	0	32.2	31	145	24	22	5	1	2	0	17	3	26	2	4
Valenzuela, Fernando, L.A.★	10	13	3.43	31	31	3	3	0	0	196.2	185	852	89	75	11	7	7	2	98	6	116	6	0
Viola, Frank N.Y.★	5	5	3.38	12	12	2	1	0	0	85.1	75	351	35	32	5	7	2	1	27	3	73	3	4
Walk, Robert, Pitt.	13	10	4.41	33	31	2	0	0	0	196.0	208	843	106	96	15	3	4	0	65	0	83	7	1
Wallach, Timothy, Mtl	0	0	9.00	1	0	0	0	1	0	1.0	2	4	1	1	0	0	0	0	0	0	0	0	0
West, David, N.Y.★	0	2	7.40	11	2	0	0	0	0	24.1	25	112	20	20	4	0	2	1	14	4	19	0	1
Wetteland, John, L.A.	5	8	3.77	31	12	0	0	7	1	102.2	81	411	46	43	8	4	0	0	34	4	96	16	1
Whitehurst, Walter, N.Y.	0	1	4.50	9	1	0	0	4	0	14.0	17	64	7	7	2	0	1	0	5	0	9	1	0
Whitson, Eddie, S.D.	16	11	2.66	33	33	5	5	0	0	227.0	198	914	77	67	22	12	8	5	48	6	117	2	3
Wilkins Dean, Chi.	0	0	5.17	11	0	0	0	1	0	15.2	13	67	9	9	2	0	0	0	9	2	14	0	0
Williams, Mitchell, Chi.★	4	4	2.64	76	0	0	0	61	36	81.2	71	365	27	24	6	2	5	8	52	4	67	6	4
Wilson, Stephen, Chi.★	6	4	4.20	53	8	0	0	9	2	85.2	83	364	43	40	6	5	4	1	31	5	65	0	1
Wilson, Trevor, S.F.★	2	3	4.35	14	4	0	0	4	0	39.1	28	167	20	19	2	3	1	4	24	0	22	0	1
Worrell, Todd, St.L.	3	5	2.96	47	0	0	0	39	20	51.2	42	219	21	17	4	3	0	2	26	13	41	3	3
Youmans, Floyd, Phil.	1	5	5.70	10	10	0	0	0	0	42.2	40	200	27	27	7	3	2	2	25	3	20	2	2

NOTE—Following pitchers combined to pitch shutout games: Atlanta (2)—Smoltz, Assenmacher, Eichhorn and Boever; Eave, Henry and Stanton. Chicago (5)—Bielecki and Schiraldi; Pico and Perry; Maddux and Williams; Maddux, Williams and Lancaster; Sutcliffe and Williams. Cincinnati (4)—Rijo, Dibble and Franco; Rijo, Charlton and Franco; Browning and Franco; Mahler, Dibble and Franco. Houston (6)—Knepper, Andersen and Smith; Clancy, Agosto and Smith; Forsch, Darwin and Smith; Deshaies and Andersen; Deshaies, Agosto, Andersen and Smith; Rhoden, Andersen and Smith. Los Angeles (5)—Morgan and Howell 2; Morgan, Crews, Searage and Howell; Leary and Belcher; Hershiser, Howell, Pena, Crews and Wetteland. Montreal (3)—De. Martinez and Burke; De. Martinez, McGaffigan and Burke; Smith and Hesketh. New York (5)—Darling and Aguilera; Gooden and Aguilera; Cone and Myers; Fernandez, Innis and Myers; Cone and Innis. Philadelphia (4)—Howell and Dillard; Madrid, Dillard and Bedrosian; Howell and Bedrosian; Ruffin and Parrett. Pittsburgh (2)— Drabek and Kramer; Walk, Landrum and Bair. St. Louis (10)—DeLeon, Dayley and Worrell 2; Hill, Dayley, Worrell and Carpenter; Terry, Kinzer, Carpenter, Dayley and Quisenberry; Terry, Dayley and Quisenberry; DeLeon and Dayley; Power, Dayley and Worrell; Power and Dayley; Terry and Dayley; Carpenter, DiPino and Costello. San Diego (7)—Benes and Davis 2; Show and Davis; Hurst and Harris; Rasmussen and Davis; Harris and Davis. San Francisco (13)—Robinson and Hammaker; Robinson and Lefferts; Reuschel and Gossage; Reuschel and LaCoss; Reuschel and Brantley; Krukow and LaCoss; Robinson, Hammaker and LaCoss; Garrelts, Gossage and Lefferts; Garrelts and Lefferts; Reuschel and Bedrosian; Reuschel, Brantley, Lefferts and Bedrosian; LaCoss, Camacho and Bedrosian; Reuschel, Lefferts and Bedrosian.

PITCHERS WITH TWO OR MORE CLUBS IN 1989
(Listed Alphabetically, First Club on Top)

Pitcher, Club	W	L	ERA	G	GS	CG	SHO	GF	SV	IP	H	TBF	R	ER	HR	SH	SF	HB	TBB	IBB	SO	WP	BK
Assenmacher, Paul, Atl.★	1	3	3.59	49	0	0	0	14	0	57.2	55	247	26	23	2	7	2	1	16	7	64	3	1
Assenmacher, Paul, Chi.★	2	1	5.21	14	0	0	0	3	0	19.0	19	84	11	11	1	2	1	0	12	1	15	0	0
Bedrosian, Stephen, Phil.	2	3	3.21	28	0	0	0	27	6	33.2	21	135	13	12	7	1	2	1	17	1	24	0	0
Bedrosian, Stephen, S.F.	1	4	2.65	40	0	0	0	33	17	51.0	35	207	18	15	5	1	2	0	22	4	34	2	0
Cook, Dennis, S.F.★	1	0	1.80	2	2	1	0	1	0	15.0	13	58	3	3	1	0	2	0	5	0	9	1	0
Cook, Dennis, Phil.★	6	8	3.99	21	16	1	1	1	0	106.0	97	441	56	47	17	5	2	3	33	6	58	3	2
Horton, Ricky, L.A.★	0	0	5.06	23	0	0	0	6	0	26.2	35	120	15	15	1	4	2	1	11	2	12	0	0
Horton, Ricky, St.L.★	0	3	4.73	11	8	0	0	1	0	45.2	50	194	24	24	2	2	3	3	10	2	14	0	0
Knepper, Robert, Hou.★	4	10	5.89	22	20	2	0	0	0	113.0	135	520	78	74	12	9	3	2	60	4	45	4	3
Knepper, Robert, S.F.★	3	2	3.46	13	6	1	1	2	0	52.0	55	226	20	20	4	3	3	0	15	2	19	1	1
Leary, Timothy, L.A.	6	7	3.38	19	17	2	0	0	0	117.1	107	481	45	44	9	4	4	2	37	7	59	4	0
Leary, Timothy, Cin.	2	7	3.71	14	14	0	0	0	0	89.2	98	393	39	37	8	3	4	3	31	8	64	6	1
McDowell, Roger, N.Y.	1	5	3.31	25	0	0	0	15	4	35.1	34	156	21	13	1	1	0	2	16	3	15	3	0
McDowell, Roger, Phil.	3	3	1.11	44	0	0	0	41	19	56.2	45	231	15	7	2	3	0	1	22	5	32	0	0
Mulholland, Terence, S.F.★	0	0	4.09	5	1	0	0	2	0	11.0	15	51	5	5	0	0	0	0	4	0	6	0	0
Mulholland, Terence, Phil.★	4	7	5.00	20	17	2	0	2	0	104.1	122	462	61	58	8	7	1	4	32	3	60	3	0
Schiraldi, Calvin, Chi.	3	6	3.78	54	0	0	0	24	4	78.2	60	342	34	33	7	2	2	0	50	2	54	3	1
Schiraldi, Calvin, S.D.	3	1	2.53	5	4	0	0	1	0	21.1	12	87	6	6	1	0	0	0	13	0	17	1	1
Sebra, Robert, Phil.	2	3	4.46	6	5	0	0	0	1	34.1	41	157	20	17	6	3	1	4	10	2	21	1	0
Sebra, Robert, Cin.	0	0	6.43	15	0	0	0	4	0	21.0	24	106	16	15	2	2	3	3	18	1	14	1	1
Smith, Zane, Atl.★	1	12	4.45	17	17	0	0	0	0	99.0	102	432	65	49	5	10	5	2	33	3	58	3	0
Smith, Zane, Mtl.★	0	1	1.50	31	0	0	0	10	2	48.0	39	202	11	8	2	5	0	1	19	4	35	1	0

1989 CHAMPIONSHIP SERIES

Including

American League Review

American League Box Scores

American League Composite Box Score

National League Review

National League Box Scores

National League Composite Box Score

The American League Championship Series was a showcase for Oakland's Rickey Henderson, who punched a big hole in Toronto's pennant plans with his baserunning (above) and hitting. Henderson earned a big post-series hug (below) from teammate Dennis Eckersley and everybody's vote as the series MVP.

Henderson Shoots Down Jays

By DAVE NIGHTINGALE

Probably because he had never played on a pennant winner during his 10 previous seasons, 30-year-old Rickey Lee Henderson didn't realize that he was fielding a tough question after the Oakland Athletics' 4-3 victory had closed out the Toronto Blue Jays in the American League Championship Series.

The pint-sized Oakland left fielder was the main man in Oakland's four games to one victory in the best-of-seven postseason classic. The question put to Henderson was tough because it sought the impossible answer: "Rickey, what can you do for an encore in the World Series?"

Considering that the 5-foot-10, 185-pound Henderson had just destroyed the Blue Jays with his legs, his bat and, yes, even his brain (to win the ALCS Most Valuable Player trophy), what could he say?

In five games against Toronto, Henderson compiled a .400 batting average and a .609 on-base percentage. He also led his team in walks (7), runs batted in (5), stolen bases (8) and runs scored (8).

A post-ALCS question that had a much easier answer was this:

"Tell us, Oakland, what can you do for an encore?"

Last year, the self-styled "Best Team in Baseball" blew away the Boston Red Sox in four straight in the playoffs, then folded like a cheap accordion in the World Series, losing to the Los Angeles Dodgers in five games.

"We didn't allow ourselves to dwell on the past during the 1989 season, because just repeating as division champion is the toughest thing in baseball," said Oakland Manager Tony La Russa.

Indeed, the Athletics were the first team to win back-to-back divisional championships and reach the World Series since the New York Yankees and the Los Angeles Dodgers of 1977 and '78.

"But the 1988 Series gave us something to keep in the back of our minds for '89," said Mark McGwire, the big first baseman, who led the A's in home runs (33) during the regular season.

"We had a great team last year, but we didn't get the whole job done. Against the Dodgers, we forgot some of the little things that made it possible to get to the Series. We all tried to hit the ball out of the park against the Dodgers. And we lost.

"Now, we're back in the Series. And this time around, we won't forget the little

Oakland ace Dave Stewart picked up right where he left off in the regular season, winning both of his starts in the A.L. Championship Series against Toronto.

things. We're stronger than we were in 1988. We've got some new parts for our engine. We have a more complete team than we did a year ago."

The first of the A's new parts was pitcher Mike Moore, signed as a free agent in December 1988 after he left Seattle. Moore's 20th victory of the season came in the second ALCS game. He was 19-11 in the regular campaign.

But the addition Toronto fans will never forget is Henderson, who returned to the club that originally hired him on June 21, via a deal with the Yankees.

Rickey had 90 hits, 70 walks, 52 stolen bases and 35 RBIs in half a season with the A's, helping them to fight off September

Designated hitter Dave Parker watches his long Game 2 blast sail over the right-center-field wall in Oakland's 6-3 victory over the Blue Jays.

divisional challenges from both Kansas City and California.

"There's just nobody like him in our league," La Russa said. "The opponents' pitchers, catchers and infielders all have to alter their approach to the game when he's involved. I remember that when we were opposing him, we always thought we'd had a helluva game if we held him to one run."

Henderson was not too modest to disagree.

"I think I helped this team win some games because I can create things," he said. "Last year, they didn't have a real leadoff hitter, a guy who could get on base and run and get into scoring position—which is what I do. They depended almost entirely on their big guys—(Jose) Canseco, McGwire, Dave Henderson. If the other team's pitchers stopped the big guys, like in the ('88) Series, then they didn't win."

La Russa added, "I don't think the series Rickey had against Toronto can be topped. He has all of these abilities and he brings them to the park and uses them every day."

And here, by way of review, is what Rickey brought to the park in the series against Toronto:

• In Game 1, a 7-3 A's victory in the Oakland Coliseum, Henderson broke up a possible double play by upending Toronto second baseman Nelson Liriano. The crash, and subsequent wild throw, provided the two runs that put the A's ahead to stay.

"The only guy in the league who could have got to me fast enough to make that happen is Rickey Henderson," said Liriano.

• In Game 2, a 6-3 Oakland victory at home, Rickey stole four bases, scored two runs and had Blue Jays catcher Ernie Whitt and the Toronto pitchers in a state of shellshock.

• In Game 3, Henderson's speed led to two early runs in the SkyDome, but the Blue Jays came from behind for their only ALCS victory, 7-3.

• In Game 4, also in Toronto, Henderson hit two home runs and drove in four runs in Oakland's 6-5 victory.

• In Game 5, the ALCS finale on October 8, Henderson stole second in the first inning to set up the A's first run, then tripled home Walt Weiss two innings later. The 4-3 victory put the A's in the World Series.

As for using his brain to beat the Blue Jays, well, Rickey was just being Rickey. And that drove some previously sane Toronto players batty.

Center fielder Dave Henderson (right) is greeted by teammate Mark McGwire after his second-inning solo home run in Oakland's 7-3 Game 1 victory.

Henderson had help in that department from 38-year-old teammate Dave Parker.

In Game 2, Henderson got such a big lead against Jays reliever David Wells that he was able to steal second base standing up.

In the same game, Parker hit his first postseason homer in 93 times at bat, and meandered only 15 feet toward first base before pausing to watch the ball land in the seats. Then, he completed the remainder of his journey in a slow trot.

After the game, Henderson observed with complete candor: "I probably have them intimidated. Their pitchers seem to be worrying about me and not our hitters. It's my job to make pitchers aware that I'm on base; to keep the pressure on them and not let them off the hook."

Oakland relief ace Dennis Eckersley lets out a triumphant yell after recording the final out in the A's 6-5 Game 4 triumph over the Blue Jays.

Toronto Manager Cito Gaston tried to treat Henderson's four-theft performance in Game 2 with levity.

"Maybe we can get him out if we throw the ball to third base when he's trying to steal second," said Cito.

But Blue Jays catcher Ernie Whitt and third baseman Kelly Gruber flipped over the antics of Henderson and Parker.

"If we give you a base, don't tiptoe around," said Whitt. "Steal it. Slide in to it. Don't show up our club. That's bush."

Henderson laughed and stuck in the needle a bit deeper.

"Show him up? I don't need to show him up. I can beat him," said Rickey. "If he wants me to slide just for the hell of it, then the next time he should just yell over: 'Slide, Rickey, slide!'

"I don't think he can throw me out. If they want to win, maybe they should put some other catcher back there."

"He's a hotdog," growled Whitt.

"If I was the pitcher, I'd have some guys decked—like Parker and Henderson," Gruber said. "And I don't care if they know. I wouldn't hit the next guy up. I'd wait until they came up again the next time and I'd get 'em."

That sent Parker's mouth into motion.

The Cobra put on his broadest grin and said, "Kelly Gruber is at the present time overexaggerating his importance on Earth. Who is he to tell me how to do a home run trot? I was hitting homers before he was conceived. I've got kids his age. Is there a Kelly Gruber school of baseball etiquette? And if there is, did he graduate?"

Toronto's Lloyd Moseby expressed the feelings of many Blue Jays when he said: "We should stop worrying about the A's, slap ourselves upside the head and start playing some baseball ourselves."

The Jays did salvage Game 3, of course, even though Henderson managed two runs with his legs and even though Parker homered again and mumbled to Gruber, as he went past third base, "Hey, am I running hard enough for you?"

But Henderson's pair of two-run homers in Game 4—one of which traveled 420 feet, the other 328 feet, one inch—put Oakland in command. That left the crowd to "oooh" and "aaah" about a baseball that Canseco drove into the SkyDome's fifth deck during the same game.

An IBM computer estimated that the hit

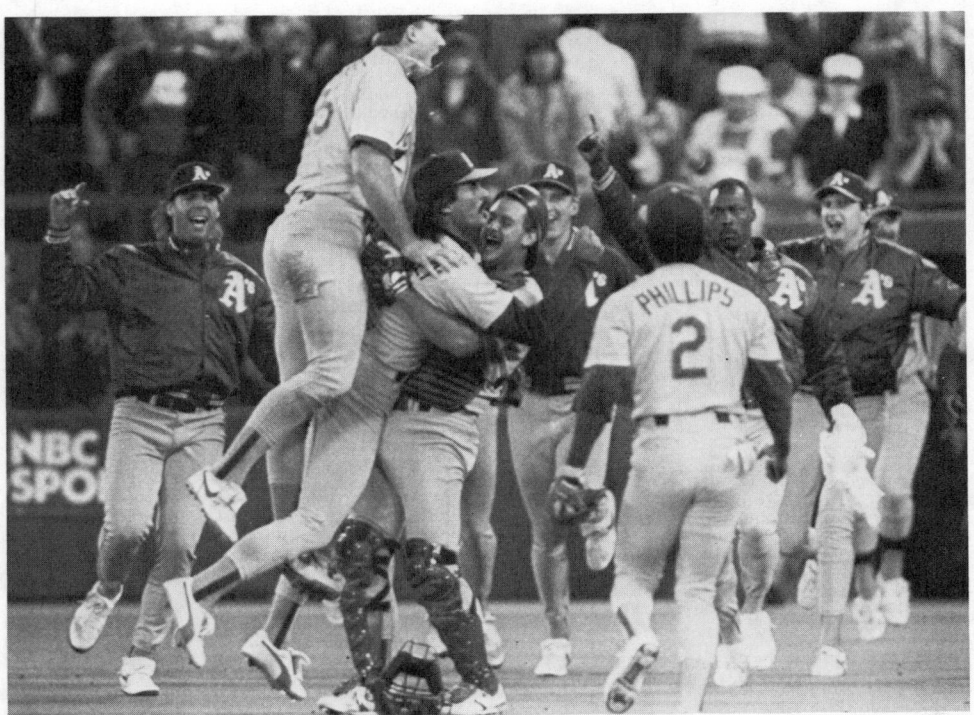

Triumphant Oakland players congregate near the pitcher's mound after the final out was recorded in the A's pennant-winning Game 5 victory.

traveled 480 feet. Others put it in the range of 500 to 600 feet, and they recalled the remark by Toronto pitcher John Cerutti that IBM stands for "Improper Baseball Measurements."

Canseco himself said that, distance-wise, the blow didn't rank among his career top 10.

About the only other noteworthy ALCS moment was sparked by an 11th-hour complaint by Gaston that Dennis Eckersley, the A's relief ace, was doctoring the ball and that he had stuffed something (like sandpaper?) into his pants just before pitching the ninth inning of the finale.

"I couldn't prove it because the umpires aren't allowed to look inside his pants," said Gaston.

"That was just gamesmanship and I hate it," snarled La Russa. "Nobody ever turned in a scuffed ball they said that Eck threw. If only two people in the country think Eck's efforts over the last few years are tainted by this incident, then I think it's horsefeathers.

"I was going to congratulate Gaston on a fine job this season. Now, I don't know whether I will or not."

Gaston wasn't waiting for congratula-tions, just revenge.

"All I know is that I didn't care for what Eckersley said to me when I went out to the mound with the umps," the Toronto manager said. "If you're going to call me something like that, then don't do it between the lines where you've got protec-tion. Do it out on the street where we real-ly can 'discuss' things—which is something Eckersley will never do."

Eckersley kept his cool during the entire brouhaha and proceeded to record his third save of the ALCS, sending the A's home for the start of the World Series.

GAME OF TUESDAY, OCTOBER 3
AT OAKLAND (N)

Toronto	AB.	R.	H.	RBI.	PO.	A.
Moseby, cf	4	0	0	0	2	0
Wilson, rf	3	0	1	0	3	0
McGriff, 1b	4	0	0	0	6	0
Bell, lf	4	1	1	0	2	1
Fernandez, ss	4	1	1	0	0	3
Whitt, c	3	1	1	2	10	0
Gruber, 3b	3	0	0	0	0	1
Mazzilli, dh	3	0	0	0	0	0
Liriano, 2b	2	0	1	1	1	0
Stieb, p	0	0	0	0	0	1
Acker, p	0	0	0	0	0	0
Ward, p	0	0	0	0	0	0
Totals	30	3	5	3	24	6

Oakland	AB.	R.	H.	RBI.	PO.	A.
R. Henderson, lf	2	1	0	0	2	0
Lansford, 3b	5	1	2	2	1	1
Canseco, rf	4	0	0	0	2	0
Parker, dh	4	0	1	1	0	0
D. Henderson, cf	4	1	2	1	7	0
McGwire, 1b	4	1	1	1	5	0
Steinbach, c	4	0	1	0	7	0
Phillips, 2b	3	1	2	0	2	2
Gallego, ss	4	2	2	0	1	1
Stewart, p	0	0	0	0	0	0
Eckersley, p	0	0	0	0	0	0
Totals	34	7	11	5	27	4

Toronto .... 020 100 000—3
Oakland .... 010 013 02x—7

Toronto	IP.	H.	R.	ER.	BB.	SO.
Stieb (Loser)	5⅓	8	4	4	2	6
Acker	1⅔	1	1	0	0	1
Ward	1	2	2	2	2	2

Oakland	IP.	H.	R.	ER.	BB.	SO.
Stewart (Winner)	8	5	3	3	3	6
Eckersley	1	0	0	0	0	0

Error—Liriano. Double play—Oakland 1. Left on bases—Toronto 4, Oakland 8. Two-base hits—Phillips, Gallego. Home runs—D. Henderson, Whitt, McGwire. Stolen bases—R. Henderson 2, Fernandez, Liriano, Wilson, Lansford, Phillips. Sacrifice fly—Whitt. Hit by pitcher—By Acker (R. Henderson). Wild pitch—Ward. Passed ball—Whitt. Umpires—Phillips, Morrison, Ford, Cousins, Palermo and Reed. Time—2:52. Attendance—49,435.

GAME OF WEDNESDAY, OCTOBER 4
AT OAKLAND

Toronto	AB.	R.	H.	RBI.	PO.	A.
Moseby, cf	3	2	1	0	3	0
Wilson, rf	3	0	1	0	0	0
McGriff, 1b	4	0	1	2	9	1
Bell, lf	4	0	1	0	1	0
Fernandez, ss	3	0	0	0	5	4
Whitt, c	4	0	0	0	5	0
Gruber, 3b	4	0	0	0	1	1
Mazzilli, dh	4	0	0	0	0	0
Liriano, 2b	2	1	1	0	0	3
Stottlemyre, p	0	0	0	0	0	0
Acker, p	0	0	0	0	0	0
Wells, p	0	0	0	0	0	0
Henke, p	0	0	0	0	0	0
Cerutti, p	0	0	0	0	0	1
Totals	31	3	5	2	24	10

Oakland	AB.	R.	H.	RBI.	PO.	A.
R. Henderson, lf	2	2	2	0	3	0
Lansford, 3b	3	1	1	1	0	1
Parker, dh	4	1	1	1	0	0
McGwire, 1b	4	1	3	1	15	0
D. Henderson, cf	4	1	1	0	3	0
Hassey, c	2	0	0	1	3	0
Phillips, 2b	4	0	1	1	0	8
Javier, rf	2	0	0	0	1	0
Canseco, ph-rf	1	0	0	0	0	0
Weiss, ss	3	0	0	0	2	2
Moore, p	0	0	0	0	0	0
Honeycutt, p	0	0	0	0	0	1
Eckersley, p	0	0	0	0	0	0
Totals	29	6	9	5	27	12

Toronto .... 001 000 020—3
Oakland .... 000 203 10x—6

Toronto	IP.	H.	R.	ER.	BB.	SO.
Stottlemyre (Loser)	5*	7	4	4	2	3
Acker	⅓	2	1	1	0	0
Wells	1	0	1	0	2	1
Henke	⅔	0	0	0	0	1
Cerutti	1	0	0	0	1	0

Oakland	IP.	H.	R.	ER.	BB.	SO.
Moore (Winner)	7	3	1	0	2	3
Honeycutt	0†	1	2	2	2	0
Eckersley (Save)	2	1	0	0	0	0

*Pitched to two batters in sixth.
†Pitched to three batters in eighth.

Errors—McGwire, McGriff. Double plays—Toronto 2, Oakland 1. Left on bases—Toronto 5, Oakland 5. Two-base hits—McGwire, D. Henderson. Home run—Parker. Stolen bases—Fernandez, R. Henderson 4, Liriano, Phillips, Lansford. Sacrifice fly—Hassey. Passed ball—Hassey. Umpires—Morrison, Ford, Cousins, Palermo, Reed and Phillips. Time—3:20. Attendance—49,444.

GAME OF FRIDAY, OCTOBER 6
AT TORONTO (N)

Oakland	AB.	R.	H.	RBI.	PO.	A.
R. Henderson, lf	4	2	1	0	3	0
Lansford, 3b	3	0	2	1	0	0
Blankenship, 2b	0	0	0	0	0	1
Canseco, rf	4	0	2	0	1	1
McGwire, 1b	2	0	0	1	8	0
D. Henderson, cf	4	0	1	0	3	0
Steinbach, c	4	0	0	0	6	0
Parker, dh	4	1	1	1	0	0
Phillips, 2b-3b	4	0	0	0	1	1
Gallego, ss	2	0	0	0	2	4
Phelps, ph	1	0	1	0	0	0
Weiss, pr-ss	1	0	0	0	0	0
Davis, p	0	0	0	0	0	0
Honeycutt, p	0	0	0	0	0	0
Nelson, p	0	0	0	0	0	0
M. Young, p	0	0	0	0	0	0
Totals	33	3	8	3	24	7

Toronto	AB.	R.	H.	RBI.	PO.	A.
Moseby, cf	2	1	0	0	4	0
Wilson, lf	4	1	2	1	4	0
McGriff, 1b	4	1	1	0	7	0
Bell, dh	3	0	0	1	0	0
Fernandez, ss	4	2	2	1	1	2
Whitt, c	3	0	1	1	4	0
Gruber, 3b	2	1	0	0	0	3
Lee, 2b	4	1	1	0	2	1
Felix, rf	3	0	1	1	5	0
Key, p	0	0	0	0	0	0
Acker, p	0	0	0	0	0	1
Henke, p	0	0	0	0	0	0
Totals	29	7	8	6	27	7

Oakland .... 101 100 000—3
Toronto .... 000 400 30x—7

Oakland	IP.	H.	R.	ER.	BB.	SO.
Davis (Loser)	6⅓	5	6	5	2	3
Honeycutt	0*	2	1	1	0	0
Nelson	1⅓	1	0	0	0	2
M. Young	⅓	0	0	0	2	0

Toronto	IP.	H.	R.	ER.	BB.	SO.
Key (Winner)	6	7	3	3	2	2
Acker	2	1	0	0	1	1
Henke	1	0	0	0	0	1

*Pitched to three batters in seventh.

Error—Canseco. Double plays—Oakland 1, Toronto 1. Left on bases—Oakland 7, Toronto 4. Two-base hits—R. Henderson, Fernandez 2, D. Henderson, Phelps. Home run—Parker. Stolen base—R. Henderson. Sacrifice flies—McGwire, Bell. Umpires—Ford, Cousins, Palermo, Reed, Phillips and Morrison. Time—2:54. Attendance—50,268.

GAME OF SATURDAY, OCTOBER 7
AT TORONTO

Oakland	AB.	R.	H.	RBI.	PO.	A.
R. Henderson, lf	4	2	2	4	2	0
D. Henderson, cf	4	1	1	0	4	0

Oakland	AB.	R.	H.	RBI.	PO.	A.
Canseco, rf	5	1	2	2	1	0
McGwire, 1b	4	0	2	0	8	0
Steinbach, dh	3	0	1	0	0	0
Phillips, 3b	3	0	0	0	1	2
Hassey, c	4	0	1	0	7	0
Gallego, 2b	4	1	1	0	2	5
Weiss, ss	3	1	1	0	1	1
Welch, p	0	0	0	0	1	0
Honeycutt, p	0	0	0	0	0	0
Eckersley, p	0	0	0	0	0	1
Totals	34	6	11	6	27	9

Toronto	AB.	R.	H.	RBI.	PO.	A.
Moseby, cf	3	0	2	0	3	0
Wilson, lf	5	1	1	1	1	0
McGriff, 1b	5	0	1	1	7	0
Bell, dh	5	0	0	0	0	0
Fernandez, ss	5	2	2	0	2	4
Whitt, c	2	0	0	0	6	0
Borders, ph-c	1	0	1	1	1	0
Mulliniks, ph	1	0	0	0	0	0
Gruber, 3b	5	1	4	0	1	1
Lee, 2b	4	1	1	0	2	0
Mazzilli, ph	1	0	0	0	0	0
Felix, rf	4	0	1	2	1	0
Flanagan, p	0	0	0	0	2	3
Ward, p	0	0	0	0	1	0
Cerutti, p	0	0	0	0	0	1
Acker, p	0	0	0	0	0	0
Totals	41	5	13	5	27	9

```
Oakland ................. 003 020 100—6
Toronto ................. 000 101 120—5
```

Oakland	IP.	H.	R.	ER.	BB.	SO.
Welch (Winner)	5⅔	8	2	2	1	4
Honeycutt	1⅔	3	3	2	2	1
Eckersley (Save)	1⅔	2	0	0	0	1

Toronto	IP.	H.	R.	ER.	BB.	SO.
Flanagan (Loser)	4⅓	7	5	5	1	3
Ward	2⅔	4	1	1	1	3
Cerutti	1⅔	0	0	0	2	1
Acker	⅓	0	0	0	0	0

Error—R. Henderson. Double plays—Toronto 2. Left on bases—Oakland 6, Toronto 12. Two-base hits—Weiss, Felix, D. Henderson, Fernandez. Home runs—R. Henderson 2, Canseco. Stolen bases—Moseby, Gruber, Weiss, Fernandez. Sacrifice hit—Weiss. Wild pitch—Honeycutt. Umpires—Cousins, Palermo, Reed, Phillips, Morrison and Ford. Time—3:29. Attendance—50,076.

GAME OF SATURDAY, OCTOBER 8
AT TORONTO

Oakland	AB.	R.	H.	RBI.	PO.	A.
R. Henderson, lf	3	1	1	1	3	0
Phillips, 3b	4	0	0	0	0	1
Canseco, rf	3	0	1	1	2	0
Parker, dh	4	0	0	0	0	0
D. Henderson, cf	3	1	0	0	5	0
McGwire, 1b	4	1	1	0	10	1
Steinbach, c	4	0	1	1	4	0
Weiss, ss	2	1	0	0	2	6
Gallego, 2b	1	0	0	1	1	4
Stewart, p	0	0	0	0	0	1
Eckersley, p	0	0	0	0	0	0
Totals	28	4	4	4	27	13

Toronto	AB.	R.	H.	RBI.	PO.	A.
Moseby, cf	4	1	2	1	3	0
Wilson, lf	4	0	0	0	2	0
McGriff, 1b	4	0	0	0	6	1
Bell, dh	4	1	2	1	0	0
Fernandez, ss	4	1	2	0	1	2
Whitt, c	4	0	0	0	7	2
Gruber, 3b	3	0	1	1	2	2
Felix, rf	4	0	1	0	2	0
Liriano, 2b	3	0	1	0	3	0
Stieb, p	0	0	0	0	0	0
Acker, p	0	0	0	0	1	0
Henke, p	0	0	0	0	0	1
Totals	34	3	9	3	27	8

```
Oakland ................. 101 000 200—4
Toronto ................. 000 000 012—3
```

Oakland	IP.	H.	R.	ER.	BB.	SO.
Stewart (Winner)	8†	8	2	2	0	3
Eckersley (Save)	1	1	1	1	0	1

Toronto	IP.	H.	R.	ER.	BB.	SO.
Stieb (Loser)	6*	4	4	4	4	4
Acker	2	0	0	0	0	2
Henke	1	0	0	0	0	1

*Pitched to three batters in seventh.
†Pitched to one batter in ninth.

Double play—Oakland 1. Left on bases—Oakland 3, Toronto 5. Two-base hit—Gruber. Three-base hit—R. Henderson. Home runs—Moseby, Bell. Stolen bases—R. Henderson, Liriano, Fernandez 2. Sacrifice hits—Gallego 2. Sacrifice fly—Gruber. Umpires—Palermo, Reed, Phillips, Morrison, Ford and Cousins. Time—2:52. Attendance—50,024.

OAKLAND ATHLETICS' BATTING AND FIELDING AVERAGES

Player—Position	G.	AB.	R.	H.	TB.	2B.	3B.	HR.	RBI.	B.A.	PO.	A.	E.	F.A.
Phelps, ph	1	1	0	1	2	1	0	0	0	1.000	0	0	0	.000
Lansford, 3b	3	11	2	5	5	0	0	0	4	.455	1	2	0	1.000
R. Henderson, lf	5	15	8	6	15	1	1	2	5	.400	13	0	1	.929
McGwire, 1b	5	18	3	7	11	1	0	1	3	.389	46	1	1	.979
Canseco, rf-ph	5	17	1	5	8	0	0	1	3	.294	6	1	1	.875
Gallego, ss-2b	4	11	3	3	4	1	0	0	1	.273	6	14	0	1.000
D. Henderson, cf	5	19	4	5	11	3	0	1	1	.263	22	0	0	1.000
Steinbach, c-dh	4	15	0	3	3	0	0	0	1	.200	17	0	0	1.000
Parker, dh	4	16	2	3	9	0	0	2	3	.188	0	0	0	.000
Phillips, 2b-3b	5	18	1	3	4	1	0	0	1	.167	4	14	0	1.000
Hassey, c	2	6	0	1	1	0	0	0	0	.167	10	0	0	1.000
Weiss, ss-pr	4	9	2	1	2	1	0	0	0	.111	5	9	0	1.000
Blankenship, 2b	1	0	0	0	0	0	0	0	0	.000	0	1	0	1.000
Davis, p	1	0	0	0	0	0	0	0	0	.000	0	0	0	.000
Eckersley, p	4	0	0	0	0	0	0	0	0	.000	0	1	0	1.000
Honeycutt, p	3	0	0	0	0	0	0	0	0	.000	0	0	0	.000
Moore, p	1	0	0	0	0	0	0	0	0	.000	0	1	0	1.000
Nelson, p	1	0	0	0	0	0	0	0	0	.000	0	0	0	.000
Stewart, p	2	0	0	0	0	0	0	0	0	.000	0	1	0	1.000
Welch, p	1	0	0	0	0	0	0	0	0	.000	1	0	0	1.000
M. Young, p	1	0	0	0	0	0	0	0	0	.000	0	0	0	.000
Javier, rf	1	2	0	0	0	0	0	0	0	.000	1	0	0	1.000
Totals	5	158	26	43	75	9	1	7	23	.272	132	45	3	.983

TORONTO BLUE JAYS' BATTING AND FIELDING AVERAGES

Player—Position	G.	AB.	R.	H.	TB.	2B.	3B.	HR.	RBI.	B.A.	PO.	A.	E.	F.A.
Borders, ph-c	1	1	0	1	1	0	0	0	1	1.000	1	0	0	1.000
Liriano, 2b	3	7	1	3	3	0	0	0	1	.429	4	3	1	.875
Fernandez, ss	5	20	6	7	10	3	0	0	1	.350	9	15	0	1.000
Moseby, cf	5	16	4	5	8	0	0	1	2	.313	15	0	0	1.000
Gruber, 3b	5	17	2	5	6	1	0	0	1	.294	4	8	0	1.000
Felix, rf	3	11	0	3	4	1	0	0	3	.273	8	0	0	1.000
Wilson, rf-lf	5	19	2	5	5	0	0	0	2	.263	10	0	0	1.000
Lee, 2b	2	8	2	2	2	0	0	0	0	.250	4	1	0	1.000
Bell, lf-dh	5	20	2	4	7	0	0	1	2	.200	3	1	0	1.000
McGriff, 1b	5	21	1	3	3	0	0	0	3	.143	35	2	1	.974
Whitt, c	5	16	1	2	5	0	0	1	3	.125	32	2	0	1.000
Acker, p	5	0	0	0	0	0	0	0	0	.000	1	1	0	1.000
Cerutti, p	2	0	0	0	0	0	0	0	0	.000	0	2	0	1.000
Flanagan, p	1	0	0	0	0	0	0	0	0	.000	2	3	0	1.000
Henke, p	3	0	0	0	0	0	0	0	0	.000	0	1	0	1.000
Key, p	1	0	0	0	0	0	0	0	0	.000	0	0	0	.000
Stieb, p	2	0	0	0	0	0	0	0	0	.000	0	1	0	1.000
Stottlemyre, p	1	0	0	0	0	0	0	0	0	.000	0	0	0	.000
Ward, p	2	0	0	0	0	0	0	0	0	.000	1	0	0	1.000
Wells, p	1	0	0	0	0	0	0	0	0	.000	0	0	0	.000
Mulliniks, ph	1	1	0	0	0	0	0	0	0	.000	0	0	0	.000
Mazzilli, dh-ph	3	8	0	0	0	0	0	0	0	.000	0	0	0	.000
Totals	5	165	21	40	54	5	0	3	19	.242	129	40	2	.988

OAKLAND ATHLETICS' PITCHING RECORDS

Pitcher	G.	GS.	CG.	IP.	H.	R.	ER.	BB.	SO.	HB.	WP.	W.	L.	Pct.	ERA.
Moore	1	1	0	7	3	1	0	2	3	0	0	1	0	1.000	0.00
Nelson	1	0	0	1⅓	1	0	0	2	0	0	0	0	0	.000	0.00
M. Young	1	0	0	⅓	0	0	0	2	0	0	0	0	0	.000	0.00
Eckersley	4	0	0	5⅔	4	1	1	0	2	0	0	0	0	.000	1.59
Stewart	2	2	0	16	13	5	5	3	9	0	0	2	0	1.000	2.81
Welch	1	1	0	5⅔	8	2	2	1	4	0	0	1	0	1.000	3.18
Davis	1	1	0	6⅓	5	6	5	2	3	0	0	0	1	.000	7.11
Honeycutt	3	0	0	1⅔	6	6	6	5	1	0	1	0	0	.000	32.40
Totals	5	5	0	44	40	21	19	15	24	0	1	4	1	.800	3.89

No shutouts. Saves—Eckersley 3.

TORONTO BLUE JAYS' PITCHING RECORDS

Pitcher	G.	GS.	CG.	IP.	H.	R.	ER.	BB.	SO.	HB.	WP.	W.	L.	Pct.	ERA.
Cerutti	2	0	0	2⅔	0	0	0	3	1	0	0	0	0	.000	0.00
Henke	3	0	0	2⅔	0	0	0	3	3	0	0	0	0	.000	0.00
Wells	1	0	0	1	0	1	0	2	1	0	0	0	0	.000	0.00
Acker	5	0	0	6⅓	4	2	1	1	4	1	0	0	0	.000	1.42
Key	1	1	0	6	7	3	3	2	2	0	0	1	0	1.000	4.50
Stieb	2	2	0	11⅓	12	8	8	6	10	0	0	0	2	.000	6.35
Stottlemyre	1	1	0	5	7	4	4	2	3	0	0	0	1	.000	7.20
Ward	2	0	0	3⅔	6	3	3	3	5	0	1	0	0	.000	7.36
Flanagan	1	1	0	4⅓	7	5	5	1	3	0	0	0	1	.000	10.38
Totals	5	5	0	43	43	26	24	20	32	1	1	1	4	.200	5.02

No shutouts or saves.

COMPOSITE SCORE BY INNINGS

Oakland	2	1	5	3	3	6	4	2	0	— 26
Toronto	0	2	1	6	0	1	4	5	2	— 21

Sacrifice hits—Weiss, Gallego 2.

Sacrifice flies—Whitt, Hassey, McGwire, Bell, Gruber.

Stolen bases—R. Henderson 8, Fernandez 5, Liriano 3, Lansford 2, Phillips 2, Wilson, Moseby, Gruber, Weiss.

Caught stealing—Canseco 2.

Double plays—Phillips and McGwire; Fernandez (unassisted); Liriano, Fernandez and McGriff; Phillips, Weiss and McGwire; Gruber, Lee and McGriff; Gallego and McGwire; Flanagan and Fernandez; Flanagan and McGriff; McGwire, Weiss, McGwire and Gallego.

Left on bases—Oakland 8, 5, 7, 6, 3—29; Toronto 4, 5, 4, 12, 5—30.

Hit by pitcher—By Acker (R. Henderson).

Passed balls—Whitt, Hassey.

Time of games—First game, 2:52; second game, 3:20; third game, 2:54; fourth game, 3:29; fifth game, 2:52.

Attendance—First game, 49,435; second game, 49,444; third game, 50,268; fourth game, 50,076; fifth game, 50,024.

Umpires—Phillips, Morrison, Ford, Cousins, Palermo and Reed.

Official scorers—John Hickey, Hayward (Calif.) Review; Roy Lefevre, Toronto official scorer; Bob Stevens, San Francisco Chronicle—retired.

Will Clark, Giants Pound Cubs

San Francisco relief ace Steve Bedrosian jumps for joy after recording the final out in the Giants' Game 5 pennant-clinching victory over the Chicago Cubs in the National League Championship Series.

By PAUL ATTNER

There comes a moment in the career of every baseball star when he crosses the line that separates mere public awareness from true athletic greatness. For Will Clark, that time came during a wonderful five-game performance in the National League Championship Series.

Clark already was a two-time all-star but, before this series, perhaps Joe Fan didn't consider him, as the San Francisco Giants do, the best active player around. After Clark finished destroying the Chicago Cubs in five stunning games to set up a World Series by the Bay against the Oakland Athletics, there was no question how talented he really is.

"Will The Thrill," as Clark is called, certainly gave this best-of-seven series a magnificent thrill. Starting with six RBIs (including a grand slam) in Game 1 and ending with a two-out, bases loaded, series-winning two-run single in the eighth inning of Game 5, Clark was an unending headache for Chicago. He had set NLCS records for average (.650), hits (13), runs (eight), total bases (24) and slugging percentage (1.200) by the time the series ended. He hit two homers, three doubles, a triple and drove in eight runs. He also fielded his first base position flawlessly and helped to cut down the Cubs' aggressiveness on the bases with his pinpoint throwing.

All this came despite an ailing knee and shin that inhibited his running. But the way he barreled into second base trying to break up a double play in Game 4, you wouldn't have known that he was slowed. Nor could you have told after watching him steam into third base with a triple that set up the Giants' first run in Game 5. It was the type of intensity that his teammates say forms the basis of his success.

"You saw the best today," Manager Roger Craig said of Clark, after the Giants had wrapped up the series with a 3-2 victory in the finale. "They don't get any better than that."

The Cubs, down 3-1 in the series, did about everything they could to send the series back to Chicago for Game 6. Starting pitcher Mike Bielecki was nearly flawless for six innings, giving up just two hits while his teammates scratched out a 1-0 lead. That came in the third inning, courtesy of a dropped fly ball in left by Kevin Mitchell and a double by Ryne Sandberg.

Chicago righthander Greg Maddux was a lonely figure in Game 1 after surrendering a third-inning home run to San Francisco's Will Clark—the first of two homers Clark would hit in the game.

But in the seventh, Clark led off with a curving line drive to right field that Andre

Dawson, after stumbling, caught up to but couldn't hold. He then overran the ball and Clark wound up on third. Mitchell flied deep to center for a sacrifice and a 1-1 tie. That's how it stood until the bottom of the eighth when, with two out, Bielecki suddenly fell apart. He walked three straight batters—his first walks of the afternoon—to bring up you-know-who. Cubs Manager Don Zimmer turned to his premier reliever, lefthander Mitch Williams, to face Clark.

Williams immediately got ahead, no balls and two strikes, before a ball and three fouls set up a fastball that Clark said got over the plate a little too much. "I was trying to hang in there and fight him off," he said. He smashed the pitch through the middle, driving in Candy Maldonado and Brett Butler.

As Clark stood at first, clapping his hands and thrusting his fist, he said his heart was "racing just a bit." Even for someone as cocky as Clark, it was a moment to treasure.

The Cubs put three successive two-out singles together to get one run back in the top of the ninth against reliever Steve Bedrosian but, finally, Sandberg grounded weakly to second and the Giants could celebrate their first pennant since 1962.

It was a sad end to a surprisingly successful season for Chicago, which seemed a good bet to finish last in the East but instead scrambled to a title. In this series, though, the Cubs suffered from poor pitching, inconsistent fielding and some puzzling tactical decisions by Zimmer, who kept making the wrong move at the wrong time for his team.

Even in the final game, the Cubs couldn't get the hit they needed. Four times, they had runners on first and third and came up empty. Dawson, once the foundation of the team, completed a dreadful series by leaving six runners on base in Game 5 and 14 for the playoff.

Yet in the end, they were outmanned by the Giants, who really didn't pitch or field that well themselves. But the Giants did hit. Clark obviously was the most dominant slugger, but both Matt Williams and Robby Thompson won games with late home runs and Mitchell drove in seven runs and had two homers. The Giants had eight homers in all; the Cubs' offense consisted mainly of first baseman Mark Grace, who batted .647 and had 19 total bases but still was overshadowed by Clark.

This also was a series in which the weather, which was expected to be windy and cold in both cities, turned mild and be-

The N.L. Championship Series was a showcase for Will Clark, who shot down the Cubs with a .650 batting average, two homers and eight RBIs.

Giants second baseman Robby Thompson, shown receiving congratulations from teammates Brett Butler and Will Clark, muscled up and hit two Championship Series home runs that helped dash the Cubs' pennant hopes.

nign in each. And it was a series in which these teams pounded out, in the first inning alone, 18 runs, 24 hits, five doubles, a triple, a homer and eight walks. No wonder Craig was relieved when Rick Reuschel, who had lasted only 18 pitches in the Cubs' 9-5 triumph in Game 2, came back to give him eight strong innings in Game 5, walking away with the victory.

Still, the Cubs have to wonder how things might have turned out if some of Zimmer's strange maneuverings hadn't backfired in his face.

• In Game 1, Zimmer was faced with a two-out, bases-loaded situation in the top of the fourth. Starter Greg Maddux was laboring and had already given up a third-inning homer to Clark, who now was batting again. In the bullpen, Cub lefty Paul Assenmacher was ready to face the lefthanded Clark. Zimmer, who had intentionally walked Butler two batters earlier to load the bases, now decided to stay with Maddux, who had just retired Thompson on a pop fly to shortstop.

"I got the answers to my questions," Zimmer said of his trip to the mound prior to Clark stepping into the batter's box. "I already had said to myself, if Maddux gets Thompson out, he's going to pitch to Clark."

A man of his word, Zimmer let Maddux do just that. One pitch later, Clark, who claims he doesn't like to hit in Wrigley Field, made him regret the decision. He lifted a Maddux fastball out of the park for an 8-3 lead.

• In Game 2, Zimmer would bring in Assenmacher to face Clark in the fifth with two on and the Cubs up, 6-2. Assenmacher got Clark to ground out on his initial pitch, the first time Clark had been retired in the series, and Chicago went on to a 9-5 triumph. But Zimmer, of course, said he would still make the same Game 1 move.

"He had quite a week," Zimmer said of Clark's first-game effort.

• In Game 3, Zimmer yanked Assenmacher, who had a 1-0 count on Thompson in the seventh with the Cubs ahead, 4-3. Les Lancaster came in despite having worked four innings in Game 2. Lancaster mistakenly thought the count was 2-0 (it was actually 1-0) and, after throwing another ball, grooved what he figured was a 3-0 fastball down the middle. Thompson yanked it over the left-field fence with Butler on base and the Giants won, 5-4.

Lancaster already had given up a home run to Thompson in the second game while the Cubs' other stellar reliever, Williams, was sitting in the bullpen, still

San Francisco also got excellent offensive production from third baseman Matt Williams, who connected twice for homers and drove in a series-high nine runs.

waiting to make his first appearance in the series.

• In Game 4, Zimmer had another opportunity to go the intentional-walk route. Earlier, in the third inning, he had ordered a free pass to Mitchell to load the bases for Williams, who responded with a bloop hit over second for two runs and a 3-2 lead. Now, in the fifth with the game tied at four, Clark led off with a double, his third straight hit. After Mitchell flied out, Williams came up against lefthander Steve Wilson with first base open and two lefthanded hitters to follow.

"I went out and talked to our pitcher (Wilson) and told him what we wanted," said Zimmer, who instructed Wilson to pitch inside and not leave anything over the plate. Wilson pitched well against Williams, but the Giant third baseman forced 11 offerings until pitch No. 12 came over the plate. He launched it over the left-field fence for a 6-4 lead.

"I made one mistake and he made me pay for it," said a distraught Wilson.

Just as they would in Game 5, the Cubs had a chance to win this one in the ninth. Bedrosian found himself in a bases-loaded situation against Dawson, but he fanned the Chicago slugger on a wicked slider to preserve the victory.

GAME OF WEDNESDAY, OCTOBER 4
AT CHICAGO (N)

San Francisco	AB.	R.	H.	R.BI.	PO.	A.
Butler, cf	4	2	1	0	4	0
Thompson, 2b	4	1	1	0	1	3
Clark, 1b	4	4	4	6	8	0
Mitchell, lf	5	2	2	3	1	0
Matt Williams, 3b	4	0	1	2	2	4
Kennedy, c	4	0	1	0	7	0
Manwaring, ph-c	1	0	0	0	0	0
Sheridan, rf	4	1	2	0	2	0
Maldonado, ph-rf	1	0	0	0	1	0
Uribe, ss	4	1	1	0	1	1
Garrelts, p	3	0	0	0	0	0
Bathe, ph	1	0	0	0	0	0
Brantley, p	0	0	0	0	0	0
Hammaker, p	0	0	0	0	0	0
Totals	39	11	13	11	27	8

Chicago	AB.	R.	H.	R.BI.	PO.	A.
Walton, cf	4	0	1	0	1	0
Wilson, p	0	0	0	0	0	1
Ramos, ph	1	0	0	0	0	0
Sandberg, 2b	5	2	3	1	1	4
Smith, lf	4	0	0	0	0	0
Grace, 1b	4	1	3	2	13	0
Dawson, rf	3	0	0	0	1	0
Salazar, 3b	4	0	2	0	1	2
Dunston, ss	4	0	0	0	3	6
Wrona, c	4	0	0	0	7	1
Maddux, p	1	0	0	0	0	0
Law, ph	1	0	0	0	0	0
Kilgus, p	0	0	0	0	0	0
Wynne, ph-cf	1	0	0	0	0	0
McClendon, ph	1	0	1	0	0	0
Totals	37	3	10	3	27	14

San Francisco	3 0 1	4 0 0	0 3 0—11
Chicago	2 0 1	0 0 0	0 0 0— 3

San Francisco	IP.	H.	R.	ER.	BB.	SO.
Garrelts (Winner)	7	8	3	3	1	6
Brantley	1	1	0	0	0	1
Hammaker	1	1	0	0	0	0

Chicago	IP.	H.	R.	ER.	BB.	SO.
Maddux (Loser)	4	8	8	8	1	3
Kilgus......................	3	4	0	0	1	1
Wilson	2	1	3	0	1	2

Error—Salazar. Left on bases—San Francisco 6, Chicago 8. Two-base hits—Clark, Matt Williams, Sandberg. Three-base hits—Salazar, Sheridan. Home runs—Grace, Clark 2, Sandberg, Mitchell. Stolen bases—Grace, Uribe. Sacrifice hit—Thompson. Hit by pitcher—By Maddux (Matt Williams). Wild pitch—Wilson. Passed ball—Wrona. Umpires—Harvey, Froemming, Tata, Quick, Williams and Marsh. Time—2:51. Attendance—39,195.

GAME OF THURSDAY, OCTOBER 5
AT CHICAGO (N)

San Francisco	AB.	R.	H.	RBI.	PO.	A.
Butler, cf....................	4	0	0	0	1	0
Thompson, 2b	4	1	1	1	1	1
Clark, 1b....................	4	1	1	0	5	2
Mitchell, lf.................	4	2	3	2	1	0
Matt Williams, 3b-ss	4	1	2	2	1	0
Kennedy, c	2	0	1	0	6	0
Bathe, ph	0	0	0	0	0	0
Oberkfell, ph-3b	2	0	0	0	0	1
Bedrosian, p	0	0	0	0	0	0
Sheridan, rf	3	0	0	0	3	0
Lefferts, p	0	0	0	0	0	0
Brantley, p	0	0	0	0	0	0
Litton, ph-3b	1	0	1	0	0	0
Uribe, ss	2	0	1	0	0	0
Riles, ph	1	0	0	0	0	0
Manwaring, c	1	0	0	0	4	0
Reuschel, p	0	0	0	0	0	0
Downs, p	1	0	0	0	0	1
Nixon, rf	2	0	0	0	2	0
Totals	35	5	10	5	24	5

Chicago	AB.	R.	H.	RBI.	PO.	A.
Walton, cf	4	2	3	1	4	0
Sandberg, 2b................	3	2	1	1	2	1
Smith, lf.....................	4	1	1	0	6	0
Grace, 1b....................	4	1	3	4	9	0
Dawson, rf...................	4	0	0	0	1	0
Salazar, 3b..................	3	1	1	1	0	1
Lancaster, p.................	1	0	0	0	0	1
Dunston, ss..................	3	1	1	0	0	1
Girardi, c....................	3	1	0	0	5	0
Bielecki, p...................	2	0	1	2	0	1
Assenmacher, p	0	0	0	0	0	0
Law, 3b......................	2	0	0	0	0	0
Totals	33	9	11	9	27	5

San Francisco........................ 000 200 021—5
Chicago................................ 600 003 00x—9

San Francisco	IP.	H.	R.	ER.	BB.	SO.
Reuschel (Loser)	⅔	5	5	5	0	1
Downs.........................	4⅔	5	3	3	5	5
Lefferts........................	⅔	1	1	1	2	1
Brantley	1	0	0	0	1	1
Bedrosian	1	0	0	0	0	1

Chicago	IP.	H.	R.	ER.	BB.	SO.
Bielecki.....................	4⅔	4	2	2	3	3
Assenmacher	⅓*	2	0	0	0	0
Lancaster (Winner) ...	4	4	3	3	0	2

*Pitched to two batters in sixth.

Double plays—San Francisco 2. Left on bases—San Francisco 7, Chicago 8. Two-base hits—Grace 2, Kennedy, Smith. Three-base hit—Sandberg. Home runs—Mitchell, Matt Williams, Thompson.

Stolen base—Dunston. Sacrifice hit—Downs. Passed ball—Manwaring. Umpires—Froemming, Tata, Quick, Williams, Marsh and Harvey. Time —3:08. Attendance—39,195.

GAME OF SATURDAY, OCTOBER 7
AT SAN FRANCISCO (N)

Chicago	AB.	R.	H.	RBI.	PO.	A.
Walton, cf	5	0	0	0	2	0
Sandberg, 2b................	3	1	1	1	2	3
Smith, lf.....................	5	1	1	0	3	0
Grace, 1b....................	3	0	2	0	8	2
Dawson, rf...................	4	0	1	2	1	0
Salazar, 3b..................	4	0	1	0	1	1
Wilkerson, pr-3b	0	0	0	0	0	0
Dunston, ss..................	4	1	2	0	4	1
Girardi, c....................	2	1	0	0	2	0
Wynne, ph	0	0	0	0	0	0
McClendon, ph-c..........	1	0	0	0	1	0
Sutcliffe, p..................	2	0	1	0	0	2
Maddux, pr..................	0	1	0	0	0	0
Assenmacher, p	0	0	0	0	0	0
Lancaster, p.................	0	0	0	0	0	0
Webster, ph	1	0	0	0	0	0
Totals	34	4	10	3	24	9

San Francisco	AB.	R.	H.	RBI.	PO.	A.
Butler, cf....................	4	2	2	0	1	0
Thompson, 2b	4	2	2	4	4	2
Clark, 1b....................	4	0	2	0	10	3
Mitchell, lf.................	3	1	1	0	6	1
Matt Williams, 3b	4	0	1	0	4	4
Kennedy, c	3	0	0	0	4	1
Maldonado, rf	2	0	0	1	1	0
Robinson, p.................	0	0	0	0	0	0
Lefferts, p	0	0	0	0	0	0
Oberkfell, ph	1	0	0	0	0	0
Bedrosian, p	0	0	0	0	0	0
Uribe, ss	4	0	1	1	1	2
LaCoss, p...................	1	0	0	0	0	0
Brantley, p	0	0	0	0	0	0
Nixon, rf	1	0	0	0	0	0
Sheridan, rf	0	0	0	0	0	0
Totals	31	5	8	5	27	13

Chicago........................... 200 100 100—4
San Francisco................... 300 000 20x—5

Chicago	IP.	H.	R.	ER.	BB.	SO.
Sutcliffe	6	5	3	3	4	2
Assenmacher	⅓	1	1	1	0	0
Lancaster (Loser)	1⅔	2	1	1	0	1

San Francisco	IP.	H.	R.	ER.	BB.	SO.
LaCoss	3*	7	3	3	0	2
Brantley	3	0	0	0	1	1
Robinson (Winner)	1⅔	3	1	0	0	0
Lefferts	⅓	0	0	0	0	0
Bedrosian (Save)	1	0	0	0	1	0

*Pitched to three batters in fourth.

Errors—LaCoss, Uribe, Nixon. Double plays—Chicago 1, San Francisco 1. Left on bases—Chicago 8, San Francisco 6. Two-base hits—Grace, Sutcliffe. Home run—Thompson. Sacrifice hits—Sutcliffe, Girardi. SF—Sandberg. Wild pitches—LaCoss, Brantley. Balk—Sutcliffe. Umpires—Tata, Quick, Williams, Marsh, Harvey and Froemming. Time—2:48. Attendance—62,065.

GAME OF SUNDAY, OCTOBER 8
AT SAN FRANCISCO (N)

Chicago	AB.	R.	H.	RBI.	PO.	A.
Walton, cf....................	5	1	2	0	2	0
Sandberg, 2b................	5	1	2	0	2	3
Smith, lf.....................	2	0	1	0	1	0
McClendon, lf-c............	1	0	1	0	2	0
Grace, 1b....................	3	1	1	2	8	0
Dawson, rf....................	5	0	1	1	1	0

Chicago	AB.	R.	H.	RBI.	PO.	A.
Salazar, 3b	4	1	2	1	1	1
Dunston, ss	4	0	2	0	1	2
Wrona, c	1	0	0	0	2	0
Wynne, ph	1	0	0	0	0	0
Girardi, c	2	0	0	0	4	0
Mitch Williams, p	0	0	0	0	0	0
Maddux, p	2	0	0	0	0	0
Wilson, p	0	0	0	0	0	0
Wilkerson, ph	1	0	0	0	0	0
Sanderson, p	0	0	0	0	0	0
Webster, lf	1	0	0	0	0	0
Totals	37	4	12	4	24	6

San Francisco	AB.	R.	H.	RBI.	PO.	A.
Butler, cf	4	1	1	0	2	0
Thompson, 2b	3	1	1	0	3	2
Clark, 1b	4	2	3	0	6	1
Mitchell, lf	3	0	0	1	6	0
Matt Williams, 3b	4	1	2	4	1	2
Kennedy, c	4	0	1	0	4	0
Nixon, pr	0	0	0	0	0	0
Manwaring, c	0	0	0	0	1	0
Sheridan, rf	4	0	0	0	3	0
Uribe, ss	4	1	1	0	1	2
Garrelts, p	1	0	0	0	0	1
Downs, p	2	0	0	0	0	0
Bedrosian, p	0	0	0	0	0	0
Totals	33	6	9	5	27	8

Chicago .... 1 1 0 0 2 0 0 0 0—4
San Francisco .... 1 0 2 1 2 0 0 0 x—6

Chicago	IP.	H.	R.	ER.	BB.	SO.
Maddux	3⅓	5	4	3	3	2
Wilson (Loser)	1⅔	2	2	2	0	2
Sanderson	2*	2	0	0	0	1
Mitch Williams	1	0	0	0	2	0

San Francisco	IP.	H.	R.	ER.	BB.	SO.
Garrelts	4⅔	8	4	4	1	2
Downs (Winner)	4	3	0	0	1	1
Bedrosian (Save)	⅓	1	0	0	1	1

*Pitched to one batter in eighth.

Errors—Uribe, Maddux. Double play—San Francisco 1. Left on bases—Chicago 10, San Francisco 6. Two-base hits—Sandberg, Clark 2, Uribe, Dawson. Three-base hit—Grace. Home runs—Salazar, Matt Williams. Stolen bases—Smith, Nixon. Sacrifice hit—Grace. Wild pitches—Garrelts, Maddux. Umpires—Quick, Williams, Marsh, Harvey, Froemming and Tata. Time—3:13. Attendance—62,078.

GAME OF MONDAY, OCTOBER 9
AT SAN FRANCISCO

Chicago	AB.	R.	H.	RBI.	PO.	A.
Walton, cf	4	1	2	1	2	0
Sandberg, 2b	4	0	1	1	0	0
Wynne, lf	4	0	1	0	3	0
Grace, 1b	3	0	2	0	6	1
Dawson, rf	3	0	0	0	0	0
Mitch Williams, p	0	0	0	0	0	0
Lancaster, p	0	0	0	0	0	0
Salazar, 3b	4	0	1	0	1	0
Dunston, ss	4	0	1	0	2	4
Girardi, c	3	0	0	0	9	0
Wilkerson, ph	1	1	1	0	0	0
Bielecki, p	3	0	0	0	1	1
Webster, rf	1	0	1	0	0	0
Totals	34	2	10	2	24	6

San Francisco	AB.	R.	H.	RBI.	PO.	A.
Butler, cf	3	1	0	0	1	0
Thompson, 2b	3	0	0	0	1	5
Clark, 1b	4	1	3	2	14	0
Mitchell, lf	2	0	0	1	1	0
Matt Williams, 3b	4	0	1	0	1	2
Kennedy, c	3	0	0	0	5	0
Sheridan, rf	2	0	0	0	1	1
Oberkfell, ph	1	0	0	0	0	0
Bedrosian, p	0	0	0	0	0	0
Uribe, ss	3	0	0	0	3	4
Reuschel, p	2	0	0	0	0	3
Maldonado, ph-rf	0	1	0	0	0	0
Totals	27	3	4	3	27	15

Chicago .... 0 0 1 0 0 0 0 0 1—2
San Francisco .... 0 0 0 0 0 0 1 2 x—3

Chicago	IP.	H.	R.	ER.	BB.	SO.
Bielecki (Loser)	7⅔	3	3	3	3	8
Mitch Williams	0*	1	0	0	0	0
Lancaster	⅓	0	0	0	1	0

San Francisco	IP.	H.	R.	ER.	BB.	SO.
Reuschel (Winner)	8	7	1	0	2	4
Bedrosian (Save)	1	3	1	1	0	0

*Pitched to one batter in eighth.

Errors—Mitchell, Dunston. Double plays—San Francisco 2. Left on bases—Chicago 9, San Francisco 5. Two-base hit—Sandberg. Three-base hit—Clark. Sacrifice hit—Sandberg. Sacrifice fly—Mitchell. Hit by pitcher—By Reuschel (Dawson). Passed ball—Girardi. Umpires—Williams, Marsh, Harvey, Froemming, Tata and Quick. Time—2:47. Attendance—62,084.

SAN FRANCISCO GIANTS' BATTING AND FIELDING AVERAGES

Player—Position	G.	AB.	R.	H.	TB.	2B.	3B.	HR.	RBI.	B.A.	PO.	A.	E.	F.A.
Litton, ph-3b	1	1	0	1	1	0	0	0	0	1.000	0	0	0	.000
Clark, 1b	5	20	8	13	24	3	1	2	8	.650	43	6	0	1.000
Mitchell, lf	5	17	5	6	12	0	0	2	7	.353	15	1	1	.941
Matt Williams, 3b-ss	5	20	2	6	13	1	0	2	9	.300	5	12	0	1.000
Thompson, 2b	5	18	5	5	11	0	0	2	3	.278	10	13	0	1.000
Uribe, ss	5	17	2	4	5	1	0	0	1	.235	6	9	2	.882
Butler, cf	5	19	6	4	4	0	0	0	0	.211	9	0	0	1.000
Kennedy, c	5	16	0	3	4	1	0	0	0	.188	26	1	0	1.000
Sheridan, rf	5	13	1	2	4	0	1	0	0	.154	9	1	0	1.000
Bedrosian, p	4	0	0	0	0	0	0	0	0	.000	0	0	0	.000
Brantley, p	3	0	0	0	0	0	0	0	0	.000	0	0	0	.000
Hammaker, p	1	0	0	0	0	0	0	0	0	.000	0	0	0	.000
Lefferts, p	2	0	0	0	0	0	0	0	0	.000	0	0	0	.000
Robinson, p	1	0	0	0	0	0	0	0	0	.000	0	0	0	.000
Bathe, ph	2	1	0	0	0	0	0	0	0	.000	0	0	0	.000
LaCoss, p	1	1	0	0	0	0	0	0	0	.000	0	1	0	1.000
Riles, ph	1	1	0	0	0	0	0	0	0	.000	0	0	0	.000
Manwaring, ph-c	3	2	0	0	0	0	0	0	0	.000	5	0	0	1.000
Reuschel, p	2	2	0	0	0	0	0	0	0	.000	0	3	0	1.000
Downs, p	2	3	0	0	0	0	0	0	0	.000	0	1	0	1.000
Maldonado, ph-pr	3	3	1	0	0	0	0	0	1	.000	2	0	0	1.000
Nixon, rf-pr	3	3	0	0	0	0	0	0	0	.000	2	0	1	.667
Garrelts, p	2	4	0	0	0	0	0	0	0	.000	0	1	0	1.000
Oberkfell, ph-3b	3	4	0	0	0	0	0	0	0	.000	0	1	0	1.000
Totals	5	165	30	44	78	6	2	8	29	.267	132	49	5	.973

CHICAGO CUBS' BATTING AND FIELDING AVERAGES

Player—Position	G.	AB.	R.	H.	TB.	2B.	3B.	HR.	RBI.	B.A.	PO.	A.	E.	F.A.
McClendon, ph-c-lf	3	3	0	2	2	0	0	0	0	.667	3	0	0	1.000
Grace, 1b	5	17	3	11	19	3	1	1	8	.647	44	3	0	1.000
Sutcliffe, p	1	2	0	1	2	1	0	0	0	.500	0	2	0	1.000
Wilkerson, pr-3b-ph	3	2	1	1	1	0	0	0	0	.500	0	0	0	.000
Sandberg, 2b	5	20	6	8	16	3	1	1	4	.400	7	11	0	1.000
Salazar, 3b	5	19	2	7	12	0	1	1	2	.368	4	5	1	.900
Walton, cf	5	22	4	8	8	0	0	0	2	.364	11	0	0	1.000
Webster, ph-lf-rf	3	3	0	1	1	0	0	0	0	.333	0	0	0	.000
Dunston, ss	5	19	2	6	6	0	0	0	0	.316	10	14	1	.960
Smith, lf	4	15	2	3	4	1	0	0	0	.200	10	0	0	1.000
Bielecki, p	2	5	0	1	1	0	0	0	2	.200	1	2	0	1.000
Wynne, ph-cf-lf	4	6	0	1	1	0	0	0	0	.167	3	0	0	1.000
Dawson, rf	5	19	0	2	3	1	0	0	3	.105	4	0	0	1.000
Girardi, c	4	10	1	1	1	0	0	0	0	.100	20	0	0	1.000
Assenmacher, p	2	0	0	0	0	0	0	0	0	.000	0	0	0	.000
Kilgus, p	1	0	0	0	0	0	0	0	0	.000	0	0	0	.000
Sanderson, p	1	0	0	0	0	0	0	0	0	.000	0	0	0	.000
Mitch Williams, p	2	0	0	0	0	0	0	0	0	.000	0	0	0	.000
Wilson, p	2	0	0	0	0	0	0	0	0	.000	0	1	0	1.000
Lancaster, p	3	1	0	0	0	0	0	0	0	.000	0	1	0	1.000
Ramos, ph	1	1	0	0	0	0	0	0	0	.000	0	0	0	.000
Law, ph-3b	2	3	0	0	0	0	0	0	0	.000	0	0	0	.000
Maddux, p-pr	3	3	1	0	0	0	0	0	0	.000	0	0	1	.000
Wrona, c	2	5	0	0	0	0	0	0	0	.000	9	1	0	1.000
Totals	5	175	22	53	77	9	3	3	21	.303	126	40	3	.982

SAN FRANCISCO GIANTS' PITCHING RECORDS

Pitcher	G.	GS.	CG.	IP.	H.	R.	ER.	BB.	SO.	HB.	WP.	W.	L.	Pct.	ERA.
Brantley	3	0	0	5	1	0	0	2	3	1	0	0	0	.000	0.00
Robinson	1	0	0	1⅔	3	1	0	0	0	0	0	1	0	1.000	0.00
Hammaker	1	0	0	1⅓	1	0	0	0	0	0	0	0	0	.000	0.00
Bedrosian	4	0	0	3⅓	4	1	1	2	2	0	0	0	0	.000	2.70
Downs	2	0	0	8⅔	8	3	3	6	6	0	0	1	0	1.000	3.12
Reuschel	2	2	0	8⅔	12	6	5	2	5	1	0	1	1	.500	5.19
Garrelts	2	2	0	11⅔	16	7	7	2	8	0	1	1	0	1.000	5.40
LaCoss	1	1	0	3	7	3	3	0	2	0	1	0	0	.000	9.00
Lefferts	2	0	0	1	1	1	1	2	1	0	0	0	0	.000	9.00
Totals	5	5	0	44	53	22	20	16	27	1	3	4	1	.800	4.09

No shutouts. Saves—Bedrosian 3.

CHICAGO CUBS' PITCHING RECORDS

Pitcher	G.	GS.	CG.	IP.	H.	R.	ER.	BB.	SO.	HB.	WP.	W.	L.	Pct.	ERA.
Kilgus	1	0	0	3	4	0	0	1	1	0	0	0	0	.000	0.00
Sanderson	1	0	0	2	2	0	0	1	1	0	0	0	0	.000	0.00
Mitch Williams	2	0	0	1	1	0	0	0	2	0	0	0	0	.000	0.00
Bielecki	2	2	0	12⅓	7	5	5	6	11	0	0	0	1	.000	3.65
Sutcliffe	1	1	0	6	5	3	3	4	2	0	0	0	0	.000	4.50
Wilson	2	0	0	3⅔	3	5	2	1	4	0	1	0	1	.000	4.91
Lancaster	3	0	0	6	6	4	4	1	3	0	1	1	1	.500	6.00
Maddux	2	2	0	7⅓	13	12	11	4	5	1	0	1	1	.000	13.50
Assenmacher	2	0	0	⅔	3	1	1	0	0	0	0	0	0	.000	13.50
Totals	5	5	0	42	44	30	26	17	29	1	2	1	4	.200	5.57

No shutouts or saves.

COMPOSITE SCORE BY INNINGS

San Francisco	7	0	3	7	2	0	3	7	1 — 30
Chicago	11	1	2	1	2	3	1	0	1 — 22

Sacrifice hits—Thompson, Downs, Sutcliffe, Girardi, Sandberg.
Sacrifice flies—Sandberg, Grace, Mitchell.
Stolen bases—Grace, Uribe, Dunston, Smith, Nixon.
Double plays—Thompson, Clark and Matt Williams; Downs, Clark and Kennedy; Clark, Kennedy and Clark; Sandberg, Dunston and Grace; Mitchell and Thompson; Matt Williams, Thompson and Clark; Thompson, Uribe and Clark; Uribe and Clark.
Left on bases—San Francisco 6, 7, 6, 6, 5—30; Chicago 8, 8, 8, 10, 9—43.
Hit by pitcher—By Maddux (Matt Williams); by Reuschel (Dawson).
Passed balls—Wrona, Manwaring, Girardi.
Balk—Sutcliffe.
Time of games—First game, 2:51; second game, 3:08; third game, 2:48; fourth game, 3:13; fifth game, 2:47.
Attendance—First game, 39,195; second game, 39,195; third game, 62,065; fourth game, 62,078; fifth game, 62,084.
Umpires—Harvey, Froemming, Tata, Quick, Williams and Marsh.
Official scorers—Don Friske, Arlington Heights (Ill.) Herald; Dick O'Connor, San Francisco official scorer; Bob Stevens, San Francisco Chronicle—retired.

1989 WORLD SERIES

Including

Review of 1989 Series

Official Play-by-Play, Each Game

Official Composite Box Score

The four-game 1989 World Series, interrupted by a devastating earth-quake and thus played over a two-week span, ended with the triumphant Oakland Athletics mobbing each other near the pitcher's mound at San Francisco's Candlestick Park.

A's Overcome Quake, Giants

By PAUL ATTNER

When the 1989 World Series came to a merciful end on October 28, the Oakland Athletics had clearly established themselves as one of the best baseball teams of the last two decades. Their easy four-game sweep of the outmanned San Francisco Giants, perpetrated with cold, calculated precision, was glaring proof that this was no ordinary championship squad.

But the talented A's were destined to be remembered more for their part in one of Mother Nature's greatest shows of force than for their expertise on the baseball field. What opened as the "Battle of the Bay" on October 14 ended its two-week run as the great "Earthquake Series"—a twist of fate that played cruelly on the A's 1989 accomplishments.

The A's season of vindication began in April and resulted in the major leagues' best 1989 record—99 victories and a seven-game cushion in the American League West Division over second-place Kansas City. Then the A's, trying to exorcise the ghosts of their five-game 1988 World Series loss to the seemingly inferior Los Angeles Dodgers, dispatched the Toronto Blue Jays in neat fashion in the American League Championship Series, capturing four of five games to set up the first-ever all-Bay Area showdown in baseball's fall classic.

And the Athletics indeed appeared to be a team on a mission as they jumped to a 2-0 lead against the Giants by recording easy victories in Games 1 and 2 at the Oakland Coliseum.

Game 1 clearly belonged to Oakland starter Dave Stewart, who pitched a five-hit shutout. Stewart was aptly supported by Dave Parker and Walt Weiss, who contributed home runs to the A's 5-0 victory. Stewart, who had won 21 regular-season games in his third straight 20-victory campaign before beating Toronto twice in the Championship Series, was in control all the way and never was seriously threatened after Oakland had jumped to a 3-0 second-inning lead.

That lead was produced by Tony Phillips' run-scoring single, an error by San Francisco catcher Terry Kennedy and a single by Rickey Henderson. Kennedy's error occurred when Giants first baseman Will Clark fielded Weiss' grounder and threw home ahead of sliding Oakland catcher Terry Steinbach. The throw clearly had him beat, but Steinbach slid

Oakland righthander Dave Stewart, who beat the Giants twice in the four-game fall classic, holds aloft his Most Valuable Player award as he stands behind the A's World Series trophy.

Allegiances were divided when the first-ever Bay Area World Series opened and fans sported their diplomatic Athletics-Giants caps.

into Kennedy's glove and the ball rolled free. The Giants could never recover.

Parker's solo home run made it 4-0 in the third and Weiss, who had hit just three regular-season homers, made it 5-0 in the fourth off losing pitcher Scott Garrelts. Stewart took care of the rest.

Game 2 followed an amazingly similar course, with Mike Moore in control rather than Stewart. The A's jumped to a 1-0 lead in the first when Henderson singled, stole second and scored on Carney Lansford's double, and then broke a 1-1 tie in the fourth with a four-run outburst that felled Giants starter Rick Reuschel. The big blow of the inning was Steinbach's long three-run homer into the left-field stands.

Moore, a 19-game winner during the regular season, stopped the Giants on four hits through seven innings before giving way to Rick Honeycutt and closer Dennis Eckersley. As the teams moved to San Francisco's Candlestick Park for Game 3, it was painfully apparent to Giants fans

that it would take something out of the ordinary to stop the A's express.

And that's exactly what happened.

At 5:04 p.m. San Francisco time, as more than 60,000 fans awaited the introduction of the Game 3 lineups at Candlestick Park, a large earthquake (7.1 on the Richter Scale) rolled through the Bay Area, causing serious destruction and the loss of dozens of lives. The atmosphere at Candlestick remained amazingly calm as officials tried to determine exactly what had happened.

With reports rolling in of widespread destruction and building and highway collapses throughout San Francisco and Oakland, Candlestick was calmly evacuated and the Series postponed indefinitely. And in the ensuing 24-hour period, as the scope of the disaster became known, the fate of the 1989 classic hung by a thread.

New baseball Commissioner Fay Vincent walked softly and explored all sides

Oakland pitcher Storm Davis takes a baby from an unidentified woman after the earthquake had struck before the scheduled start of Game 3.

of the issue. Many called for the first-ever cancellation of a World Series in deference to the dead and homeless earthquake victims. But Vincent patiently waited, postponing the event indefinitely. Candlestick and the Coliseum were checked thoroughly for structural damage before Vincent consulted with the mayors of the stricken communities. He finally decided to continue the Series on October 27—12 days after Oakland's Game 2 victory—with the blessing of all participants and city officials from both San Francisco and Oakland.

The A's used every dimension at their disposal when the Series resumed. Most noticeable, of course, was the Oakland power, especially in Game 3.

But the victors also received seven strong innings from Stewart, on a night when every other hurler in the park was looking for a flak jacket. And they also got a gem of a defensive play from first baseman Mark McGwire when they most

needed it—in the fourth inning when the outcome was still in doubt.

Prior to Game 3, all hands on both sides tried to peer into a crystal ball and predict who would be affected the most by the 12-day layoff. Giants batting coach Dusty Baker stamped himself as the absolute worst of all the forecasters.

"A long layoff is much harder on power hitters than on singles hitters," Baker said. "When a power hitter is out of sync, he has a tougher time getting straightened out because he has a longer stroke than a singles hitter and there is a lot more that can go wrong with his swing. So, since the A's have more true power hitters than the Giants, the layoff should work to our advantage."

It was a nice theory, except that San Francisco hurlers Garrelts, Kelly Downs and Jeff Brantley kept hanging those high sliders. And the A's kept hitting them over the fence.

Dave Henderson hit two home runs—

Oakland players (above) watch proceedings in the wake of the major earthquake that struck the Bay Area on October 17 and forced delay of the World Series. After taking stock of the serious destruction and loss of lives caused by the quake, San Francisco Mayor Art Agnos (below left) and baseball Commissioner Fay Vincent appeared together at an October 22 press conference to announce that the Series would resume on October 24. The date later was changed to October 27.

and missed a third by two inches—as he drove across four runs. A Jose Canseco homer in the fifth inning was worth three runs and put the game out of the Giants' reach. And Lansford and Phillips also knocked the ball out of the park.

The five-homer effort tied a Series record set by the 1928 New York Yankees. And it helped the A's take a 13-3 lead into the bottom of the ninth, when four insignificant Giants runs—all coming as the result of hits by San Francisco benchwarmers—made the final score more respectable.

The most notable hit of the Giants' ninth was a three-run homer by backup catcher Bill Bathe. That was No. 7 for the game, a high-water mark in World Series annals.

While the A's were taking batting practice against Garrelts et al, Stewart was just slogging along in what he said was his same old mode: "I don't walk people; I put the ball in play; I try for an occasional strikeout. There's no secret about the way I pitch."

Stewart gave up a solo home run to Matt Williams in the second inning before yielding a two-run single to Terry Kennedy in the fourth as the Giants pulled within one run at 4-3. A diving stop by McGwire, however, prevented a fourth run and produced the final out. After Canseco's three-run blast and Dave Henderson's second homer provided a five-run cushion in the top of the fifth, Stewart coasted through the seventh before retiring.

"I was told I've now done something that no one ever has done before—win two games in a League Championship Series and two games in a World Series in the same year," Stewart said. "So I guess I've got something that I can stick out my chest about."

For nearly seven innings, Game 4 was little more than an exercise in numbers.

Rickey Henderson led off the contest with a homer—the 41st time he's done that in his career—and the Athletics never trailed, just as they had never trailed at any point in the three previous Series games.

It was Oakland's ninth Series homer, enabling the A's to match the 1928 Yanks for the most homers in a four-game title match. (The A's and Giants combined for 13 homers in the four contests, shattering the previous four-game mark of 11, by the 1932 Yanks and Chicago Cubs.)

The straw that broke the Giants' back, though, came in the top of the second when the A's had two on with two out and Oakland starting pitcher Moore at the

Game 4 got off to an ominous start for the Giants, who watched Oakland's Rickey Henderson belt a leadoff home run and then signal his feelings to the crowd.

plate.

San Francisco starter Don Robinson whistled a pair of fastballs past Moore, who had batted just once in his big-league career (unsuccessfully). But Moore lined Robinson's next fastball 380 feet over the glove of center fielder Brett Butler for a two-run double.

It was the first, last and only Series hit by an American League pitcher during the decade of the 1980s (in 73 times at the plate).

Rickey Henderson singled home Moore to make it 4-0. Steinbach's two-run double made it 6-0 in the fifth and Steinbach scored on Phillips' double. A triple by Rickey Henderson and Lansford's single made it 8-0 in the sixth.

Strictly a yawner. That is, until Moore gave up a two-run homer to Giants slugger Kevin Mitchell in the sixth and until the Giants climbed all over Gene Nelson and Honeycutt for four runs in the seventh to make it an 8-6 game. Mitchell's bid for a game-tying two-run homer in that same

San Francisco Manager Roger Craig takes the ball from starter Don Robinson in the second inning of Game 4 after the righthander had surrendered four runs to the relentless Athletics.

San Francisco (N.L.)	AB.	R.	H.	RBI.	PO.	A.
Kennedy, c	3	0	0	0	8	0
Uribe, ss	2	0	1	0	1	2
aOberkfell, 3b	0	0	0	0	0	0
Garrelts, p	0	0	0	0	0	1
Hammaker, p	0	0	0	0	0	0
Brantley, p	0	0	0	0	0	0
LaCoss, p	0	0	0	0	0	0
Totals	33	0	5	0	24	9

Oakland (A.L.)	AB.	R.	H.	RBI.	PO.	A.
R. Henderson, lf	5	0	2	1	2	0
Lansford, 3b	5	0	1	0	3	1
Gallego, 2b	0	0	0	0	0	0
Canseco, rf	3	0	0	0	0	0
Parker, dh	4	1	1	1	0	0
D. Henderson, cf	3	1	0	0	2	0
McGwire, 1b	4	0	3	0	7	1
Steinbach, c	4	1	1	0	7	0
Phillips, 2b-3b	4	1	2	1	3	5
Weiss, ss	4	1	1	1	1	3
Stewart, p	0	0	0	0	2	0
Totals	36	5	11	4	27	10

```
San Francisco.................. 000  000  000—0
Oakland.......................... 031  100  00x—5
```

San Francisco	IP.	H.	R.	ER.	BB.	SO.
Garrelts (L)	4	7	5	4	1	5
Hammaker	1⅔	3	0	0	0	2
Brantley	1⅓	1	0	0	1	0
LaCoss	1	0	0	0	0	1

Oakland	IP.	H.	R.	ER.	BB.	SO.
Stewart (W)	9	5	0	0	1	6

Bases on balls—Off Garrelts 1 (D. Henderson), off Brantley 1 (Canseco), off Stewart 1 (Oberkfell).

Strikeouts—By Garrelts 5 (Canseco 2, Steinbach, Phillips, R. Henderson), by Hammaker 2 (Parker, Weiss), by LaCoss 1 (R. Henderson), by Stewart 6 (Williams 2, Maldonado, Thompson, Mitchell, Riles).

aWalked for Uribe in eighth. Errors—Stewart, Kennedy. Left on bases—San Francisco 7, Oakland 9. Two-base hit—Clark. Home runs—Parker, Weiss. Passed ball—Steinbach. Umpires—Garcia (A.L.) plate, Runge (N.L.) first base, Voltaggio (A.L.) second base, Rennert (N.L.) third base, Clark (A.L.) left field, Gregg (N.L.) right field. Time—2:45. Attendance—49,385.

FIRST INNING

Giants—Butler flied to D. Henderson in left-center field. Stewart fielded Thompson's tapper in front of the mound, but threw the ball past first base for an error, Thompson going to second base on the play. Clark flied to D. Henderson in left-center. Mitchell grounded to Phillips. No runs, no hits, one error, one left.

A's—R. Henderson grounded to Thompson. Lansford grounded a single to center field. Canseco struck out. Garrelts knocked down Parker's smash to the mound and threw to Clark at first base for the out. No runs, one hit, no errors, one left.

SECOND INNING

Giants—Williams struck out. Riles bounced to Phillips. Maldonado struck out. No runs, no hits, no errors, none left.

A's—D. Henderson walked. McGwire flied to Butler. Steinbach lined a single to center, D. Henderson stopping at second base. Phillips grounded a single through the hole into right field, scoring D. Henderson and sending Steinbach to third. Weiss bounced to Clark, who threw home, but Steinbach was safe when he knocked the ball out

There wasn't any doubt in the mind of Oakland slugger Jose Canseco as to the outcome of the A's 9-6 Game 4 victory as the end drew near.

inning died on the left-field warning track.

"Todd Burns retiring Mitchell was the key to the game, that and the fact that Todd pitched a clean eighth inning so we could give the ball to Eck (relief ace Eckersley) for the last three outs," said A's Manager Tony La Russa.

The A's closed the scoring in the eighth off Steve Bedrosian, when Steinbach coaxed the Giants ace for a bases-loaded walk.

The 9-6 final score gave the A's the championship they had missed a year earlier and closed out one of the most bizarre World Series in history—and one that most of baseball's officials would like to forget.

Game 1

**At Oakland
October 14**

San Francisco (N.L.)	AB.	R.	H.	RBI.	PO.	A.
Butler, cf	4	0	0	0	2	0
Thompson, 2b	4	0	0	0	0	4
Clark, 1b	4	0	2	0	9	1
Mitchell, lf	4	0	2	0	3	0
Williams, 3b-ss	4	0	0	0	0	1
Riles, dh	4	0	0	0	0	0
Maldonado, rf	4	0	0	0	1	0

of Kennedy's glove with a hard slide. Phillips stopped at second on the play. An error was charged to Kennedy. R. Henderson lined a single to right, Phillips scoring to give the A's a 3-0 lead and Weiss advancing to third on Maldonado's throw to the plate. Lansford flied to Mitchell in short left field. Canseco struck out. Three runs, three hits, one error, two left.

THIRD INNING

Giants—Kennedy grounded to Weiss. Uribe was credited with a single when his bouncer to the mound went off Stewart's glove. Butler popped to Weiss. Thompson struck out. No runs, one hit, no errors, one left.

A's—Parker belted an 0-2 pitch into the right-field bleachers for his first World Series home run, giving the A's a 4-0 lead. D. Henderson grounded to Uribe. McGwire blooped a single to right. Steinbach struck out. Phillips also struck out. One run, two hits, no errors, one left.

FOURTH INNING

Giants—Clark fouled out to Lansford. Mitchell lined a single to right field. Williams fouled out to Lansford. Riles forced Mitchell at second base, Weiss to Phillips. No runs, one hit, no errors, one left.

A's—Weiss, who had only three homers all season, smacked a 1-1 pitch over the right-field wall for a home run to boost the A's lead to 5-0. R. Henderson was called out on strikes. Lansford flied to Mitchell in short left field. Canseco fouled out to Clark. One run, one hit, no errors, none left.

FIFTH INNING

Giants—Maldonado fouled out to McGwire. Kennedy grounded to Phillips, who threw to Stewart covering first base for the out. Uribe bounced to Weiss, who made the play behind second base and threw to McGwire for the out. No runs, no hits, no errors, none left.

A's—Hammaker replaced Garrelts on the mound for the Giants. Parker struck out. D. Henderson grounded to Uribe. McGwire got a broken bat single to right field. Steinbach flied to Mitchell. No runs, one hit, no errors, one left.

SIXTH INNING

Giants—Butler fouled out to Lansford. Thompson popped to Phillips. Clark doubled off the wall in right field. Mitchell struck out. No runs, one hit, no errors, one left.

A's—Phillips lined a single to right. Weiss was called out on strikes. R. Henderson lined a single to right, Phillips stopping at second base. Lansford flied to Maldonado. Brantley replaced Hammaker on the mound for the Giants. Canseco walked on four pitches to load the bases. Parker forced Canseco at second, Thompson to Uribe. No runs, two hits, no errors, three left.

SEVENTH INNING

Giants—Williams flied to R. Henderson. Riles grounded to McGwire, who threw to Stewart covering first base for the out. Maldonado fouled out to Steinbach just in front of the screen behind home plate. No runs, no hits, no errors, none left.

A's—D. Henderson bounced to Williams. McGwire lined a single to left field. Steinbach fouled out to Clark, who made a fine backhanded grab while on the run, McGwire holding at first base. Phillips flied to Butler. No runs, one hit, no errors, one left.

EIGHTH INNING

Giants—Kennedy grounded to Phillips. Oberkfell batted for Uribe and walked. Butler flied to R.

Henderson. Thompson forced Oberkfell at second base, Lansford to Phillips. No runs, no hits, no errors, one left.

A's—Oberkfell stayed in the game at third base, Williams moved to shortstop and LaCoss came in to pitch for the Giants. Weiss grounded to Thompson. R. Henderson struck out. Lansford bounced to Thompson, who made the play behind second base and threw to Clark for the out. No runs, no hits, no errors, none left.

NINTH INNING

Giants—Gallego came in to play second base and Phillips moved to third for the A's. Clark singled to center. Mitchell was credited with a single to right when Canseco attempted to make a sliding catch but couldn't hold on for the out, Clark stopping at second base. Williams struck out. On a 1-2 pitch to Riles, Clark went to third and Mitchell to second on a passed ball. Riles then struck out. Phillips backhanded Maldonado's bouncer near the third-base bag and made a long throw to McGwire for the out, giving Stewart his first shutout since August 30, 1988, when he beat Boston. It was the fourth World Series shutout for the A's and the first since George Earnshaw blanked St. Louis, 3-0, in the fourth game of the 1931 Series. No runs, two hits, no errors, two left.

Game 2

At Oakland
October 15

San Francisco (N.L.)	AB.	R.	H.	RBI.	PO.	A.
Butler, cf	2	0	1	0	0	0
Thompson, 2b	3	0	0	1	1	3
Clark, 1b	4	0	0	0	9	0
Mitchell, lf	4	0	1	0	3	0
Williams, 3b-ss	4	0	0	0	1	4
Riles, dh	3	0	0	0	0	0
Maldonado, rf	3	0	0	0	3	0
Kennedy, c	3	0	1	0	7	1
Uribe, ss	2	1	0	0	0	1
aOberkfell, 3b	1	0	1	0	0	0
Reuschel, p	0	0	0	0	0	0
Downs, p	0	0	0	0	0	0
Lefferts, p	0	0	0	0	0	1
Bedrosian, p	0	0	0	0	0	0
Totals	29	1	4	1	24	10

Oakland (A.L.)	AB.	R.	H.	RBI.	PO.	A.
R. Henderson, lf	3	1	3	0	1	0
Lansford, 3b	3	0	1	1	1	2
Canseco, rf	2	1	0	0	2	0
Parker, dh	4	1	1	1	0	0
D. Henderson, cf	3	1	0	0	2	0
McGwire, 1b	4	0	1	0	10	0
Steinbach, c	4	1	1	3	7	1
Phillips, 2b	3	0	0	0	1	3
Weiss, ss	3	0	0	0	3	2
Moore, p	0	0	0	0	0	1
Honeycutt, p	0	0	0	0	0	0
Eckersley, p	0	0	0	0	0	0
Totals	29	5	7	5	27	9

San Francisco.......... 0 0 1   0 0 0   0 0 0—1
Oakland.................. 1 0 0   4 0 0   0 0 x—5

San Francisco	IP.	H.	R.	ER.	BB.	SO.
Reuschel (L)	4*	5	5	5	4	2
Downs	2	1	0	0	0	2
Lefferts	1	1	0	0	1	1
Bedrosian	1	0	0	0	0	2

Oakland	IP.	H.	R.	ER.	BB.	SO.
Moore (W)	7†	4	1	1	2	7
Honeycutt	1⅓	0	0	0	0	1
Eckersley	⅔	0	0	0	0	0

*Pitched to two batters in fifth.
†Pitched to one batter in eighth.

Bases on balls—Off Reuschel 4 (R. Henderson, Canseco, D. Henderson, Lansford), off Lefferts 1 (Canseco), off Moore 2 (Butler 2).

Strikeouts—By Reuschel 2 (D. Henderson, McGwire), by Downs 2 (Canseco, Parker), by Lefferts 1 (Weiss), by Bedrosian 2 (D. Henderson, McGwire), by Moore 7 (Williams 2, Maldonado, Clark, Thompson, Kennedy 2), by Honeycutt 1 (Butler).

aSingled for Uribe in eighth. Errors—None. Double plays—Williams, Thompson and Clark; Kennedy and Williams; Weiss, Phillips and McGwire. Left on bases—San Francisco 4, Oakland 5. Two-base hits—Lansford, Parker, McGwire. Three-base hit—R. Henderson. Home run—Steinbach. Stolen bases—R. Henderson, Butler 2. Caught stealing—R. Henderson. Sacrifice fly—Thompson. Wild pitches—Moore 2. Umpires—Runge (N.L.) home plate, Voltaggio (A.L.) first base, Rennert (N.L.) second base, Clark (A.L.) third base, Gregg (N.L.) left field, Garcia (A.L.) right field. Time—2:47. Attendance—49,388.

FIRST INNING

Giants—Butler walked. With Butler running, Thompson bounced to McGwire, who made the play unassisted at first base for the out, Butler stopping at second base on the play. Clark flied to R. Henderson just in front of the warning track in left field. Mitchell popped to Weiss. No runs, no hits, no errors, one left.

A's—R. Henderson walked on four pitches. With a 1-0 count on Lansford, R. Henderson stole second base for his ninth steal of the postseason. Lansford then looped a double just inside the right-field line, scoring R. Henderson to give the A's a 1-0 lead. Canseco bounced to Williams, Lansford holding at second. Parker lined to Maldonado in short right field. D. Henderson struck out. One run, one hit, no errors, one left.

SECOND INNING

Giants—Williams struck out. Riles flied to Canseco on the warning track in right field. Maldonado struck out. No runs, no hits, no errors, none left.

A's—McGwire bounced to Williams. Steinbach flied to Mitchell on the warning track in left-center field. Phillips grounded to Clark, who made the play unassisted at first base. No runs, no hits, no errors, none left.

THIRD INNING

Giants—Kennedy lined a single to right field. Uribe hit a comebacker to Moore, who threw to Weiss to force Kennedy at second base, with Uribe beating Weiss' throw to first in an attempt to complete the double play. With Uribe running on the pitch, Butler grounded a single through the hole into left field, Uribe advancing to third on the play. Butler stole second base on the first pitch to Thompson. Thompson then lined to D. Henderson in right-center field for a sacrifice fly, Uribe coming home to enable the Giants to tie the score, 1-1. Butler went to third on a wild pitch. Clark struck out, but had to be retired, Steinbach to McGwire, when the third strike was in the dirt. One run, two hits, no errors, one left.

A's—Weiss flied to Maldonado. R. Henderson looped a single to right field. Lansford grounded into a double play, Williams to Thompson to Clark. No runs, one hit, no errors, none left.

FOURTH INNING

Giants—Mitchell singled to center field. Williams struck out. With Mitchell running, Riles bounced out to Weiss behind the mound, Mitchell taking second base on the play. With an 0-1 count on Maldonado, Mitchell advanced to third on a wild pitch. Maldonado bounced to Lansford. No

runs, one hit, no errors, one left.

A's—Canseco walked. Parker doubled high off the wall down the right-field line, scoring Canseco to give the A's a 2-1 lead. Parker was safe at second by sliding under the tag of Uribe. D. Henderson walked. McGwire struck out. Steinbach belted a 2-0 delivery from Reuschel into the left-field seats, scoring Parker and D. Henderson to boost the A's lead to 5-1. Phillips flied to Maldonado. Weiss flied to Mitchell. Four runs, two hits, no errors, none left.

FIFTH INNING

Giants—Kennedy struck out. Uribe popped to Weiss. Butler walked. On the second pitch to Thompson, Butler stole second base. Thompson then struck out. No runs, no hits, no errors, one left.

A's—R. Henderson singled past a diving Williams into left field. Lansford walked. Downs replaced Reuschel on the mound for the Giants. Canseco struck out. Parker also struck out and R. Henderson was out at third base, Kennedy to Williams, on a steal attempt. No runs, one hit, no errors, one left.

SIXTH INNING

Giants—Clark grounded to McGwire, who made the play unassisted at first base for the out. Mitchell flied to Canseco in short right field. Williams popped to McGwire. No runs, no hits, no errors, none left.

A's—D. Henderson grounded to Uribe. McGwire doubled down the left-field line. Steinbach bounced to Williams, who looked McGwire back to second and threw to Clark at first base for the out. Phillips flied to Mitchell. No runs, one hit, no errors, one left.

SEVENTH INNING

Giants—Riles flied to D. Henderson. Maldonado grounded sharply to Lansford. Kennedy struck out. No runs, no hits, no errors, none left.

A's—Lefferts came in to pitch for the Giants. Weiss was called out on strikes. R. Henderson tripled down the third-base line, going to third when the ball rolled under the A's bullpen bench before Mitchell could retrieve it. Lansford grounded out, Lefferts to Thompson to Clark, after the ball went off the pitcher's glove. R. Henderson held third base on the play. Canseco was walked intentionally. Parker bounced to Clark, who made the play unassisted at first base for the out. No runs, one hit, no errors, two left.

EIGHTH INNING

Giants—Oberkfell, pinch-hitting for Uribe, lined a single to left field. Honeycutt replaced Moore on the mound for the A's. Butler struck out. Thompson grounded into a double play Weiss to Phillips to McGwire. No runs, one hit, no errors, none left.

A's—Oberkfell stayed in the game at third base, Williams moved to shortstop and Bedrosian came in to pitch for the Giants. D. Henderson struck out. McGwire was called out on strikes. Steinbach grounded to Thompson. No runs, no hits, no errors, none left.

NINTH INNING

Giants—Clark grounded sharply to Phillips, who made a diving stop to his left and threw to McGwire at first base for the out. Eckersley replaced Honeycutt on the mound for the A's. Mitchell fouled out to Lansford. Williams grounded to Phillips, who bobbled the ball, but threw to McGwire at first base for the out. No runs, no hits, no errors, none left.

Game 3

At San Francisco
October 27

Oakland (A.L.)	AB.	R.	H.	RBI.	PO.	A.
R. Henderson, lf	5	1	1	0	2	0
Nelson, p	0	0	0	0	0	0
Burns, p	0	0	0	0	0	0
Lansford, 3b	4	4	3	2	1	0
Honeycutt, p	0	0	0	0	0	0
eGallego, 3b	1	0	0	0	0	0
Canseco, rf	5	3	3	3	1	0
Javier, rf	0	0	0	0	0	0
McGwire, 1b	4	0	0	1	3	1
D. Henderson, cf	4	2	3	4	6	0
Steinbach, c	4	0	1	1	10	0
Phillips, 2b-3b-lf	5	1	1	1	1	3
Weiss, ss	5	1	1	0	1	1
Stewart, p	3	0	0	0	1	0
bBlankenship, 2b	2	1	1	0	0	0
Totals	42	13	14	12	27	5

San Francisco (N.L.)	AB.	R.	H.	RBI.	PO.	A.
Butler, cf	3	0	0	0	3	0
cNixon, cf	2	1	1	0	0	0
Thompson, 2b	3	0	0	0	3	3
dLitton, 2b	2	0	2	1	1	0
Clark, 1b	4	1	1	0	11	1
Mitchell, lf	5	1	1	0	2	0
Oberkfell, 3b	2	1	1	0	0	4
Williams, ss	4	1	1	1	0	3
Kennedy, c	3	0	1	2	5	0
Manwaring, c	1	1	1	0	0	0
Sheridan, rf	2	0	0	0	0	0
Brantley, p	0	0	0	0	1	0
aRiles	1	0	0	0	0	0
Hammaker, p	0	0	0	0	0	1
Lefferts, p	0	0	0	0	0	0
fBathe	1	1	1	3	0	0
Garrelts, p	1	0	0	0	0	1
Downs, p	0	0	0	0	0	0
Maldonado, rf	3	0	0	0	1	0
Totals	37	7	10	7	27	13

Oakland	2 0 0	2 4 1	0 4 0—13
San Francisco	0 1 0	2 0 0	0 0 4— 7

Oakland	IP.	H.	R.	ER.	BB.	SO.
Stewart (W)	7	5	3	3	1	8
Honeycutt	1	1	0	0	0	1
Nelson	⅔	3	4	4	1	1
Burns	⅓	1	0	0	1	0

San Francisco	IP.	H.	R.	ER.	BB.	SO.
Garrelts (L)	3⅓	6	4	4	0	3
Downs	1	2	4	4	2	1
Brantley	2⅔	1	1	1	2	1
Hammaker	⅔	5	4	4	0	0
Lefferts	1⅓	0	0	0	0	0

Bases on balls—Off Stewart 1 (Oberkfell), off Nelson 1 (Oberkfell), off Burns 1 (Clark), off Downs 2 (R. Henderson, Lansford), off Brantley 2 (Steinbach, McGwire). Strikeouts—By Stewart 8 (Thompson 2, Clark, Mitchell, Kennedy, Garrelts, Williams, Maldonado), by Honeycutt 1 (Clark), by Nelson 1 (Maldonado), by Garrelts 3 (Phillips, Stewart, Lansford), by Downs 1 (McGwire), by Brantley 1 (Phillips).

aFlied out for Brantley in seventh. bSingled for Stewart in eighth. cGrounded out for Butler in eighth. dSingled for Thompson in eighth. eFlied out for Honeycutt in ninth. fHit three-run homer for Lefferts in ninth. Errors—Oberkfell, Mitchell, Lefferts. Double play—Oberkfell, Thompson and Clark. Left on bases—Oakland 7, San Francisco 6. Two-base hits—D. Henderson, R. Henderson, Manwaring, Litton. Home runs—Williams, D. Henderson 2, Phillips, Canseco, Lansford, Bathe. Stolen bases—R. Henderson 2. Hit by pitcher—By Hammaker (D. Henderson). Balk—Brantley. Umpires—Voltaggio (A.L.) plate, Rennert (N.L.)

first base, Clark (A.L.) second base, Gregg (N.L.) third base, Garcia (A.L.) left field, Runge (N.L.) right field. Time—3:03. Attendance—62,038.

FIRST INNING

A's—R. Henderson grounded to Williams. Lansford lined a single to center field. Canseco ended an 0-for-23 Series slump when he singled to left, Lansford stopping at second base. With the runners going, McGwire grounded to Williams, who threw to Clark at first base for the out. D. Henderson doubled off the top of the fence in right field, scoring Lansford and Canseco to give the A's a 2-0 lead. Steinbach grounded to Oberkfell. Two runs, three hits, no errors, one left.

Giants—Butler flied to R. Henderson. Thompson struck out. Clark struck out on a pitch in the dirt. No runs, no hits, no errors, none left.

SECOND INNING

A's—Phillips struck out. Weiss flied to Butler in left-center field. Stewart was called out on strikes. No runs, no hits, no errors, none left.

Giants—Mitchell fanned, becoming Stewart's third straight strikeout victim. Oberkfell flied to Canseco. Williams smashed Stewart's 1-1 delivery over the left-field fence for a home run, cutting the A's lead to 2-1. Kennedy struck out. One run, one hit, no errors, none left.

THIRD INNING

A's—R. Henderson lined a double to the fence in left-center field. Lansford was called out on strikes. On the first pitch to Canseco, R. Henderson stole third base. Canseco then bounced to Oberkfell on a ball that appeared to have hit off Canseco's foot while he was still in the batter's box, R. Henderson holding at third on the play. McGwire bounced hard to the mound off Garrelts' right arm, but the pitcher recovered in time to throw to Clark at first base for the out. No runs, one hit, no errors, one left.

Giants—Sheridan bounced to Phillips. Garrelts was called out on strikes. Butler flied to D. Henderson. No runs, no hits, no errors, none left.

FOURTH INNING

A's—D. Henderson belted Garrelts' 2-0 pitch over the right-center field fence to boost the A's lead to 3-1. Steinbach bounced to Williams. Phillips hit the first pitch over the right-field fence, giving the A's a 4-1 lead. Downs replaced Garrelts on the mound for the Giants. Weiss grounded to Clark, who made the play unassisted at first base. Stewart hit a soft liner to Thompson. Two runs, two hits, no errors, none left.

Giants—Thompson struck out on a pitch in the dirt. Clark lined a single to center field. Mitchell singled to left, Clark stopping at second base. Oberkfell walked on four pitches to load the bases. Williams was called out on strikes. Kennedy lined a single to center, scoring Clark and Mitchell to cut the A's lead to 4-3, with Oberkfell stopping at second. McGwire made a diving stop to his right and threw to Stewart covering first base to retire Sheridan on a close play. Two runs, three hits, no errors, two left.

FIFTH INNING

A's—R. Henderson walked. On a 1-1 pitch to Lansford, R. Henderson stole second base to break Davey Lopes' record of 10 postseason stolen bases, set in 1981. Lansford also walked. Canseco slugged Downs' 2-2 pitch over the fence in left-center field for a three-run homer, sending the A's to a 7-3 lead. McGwire struck out. D. Henderson hit an 0-1 delivery over the fence in center field for his second homer of the game, giving the A's an 8-3 lead. Brantley replaced Downs on the mound and Maldonado went in to play right field for the Giants. Steinbach walked. Brantley was charged with a balk, enabling Steinbach to advance to second base. Phillips was called out on strikes. Weiss bounced to Clark, who threw to Brantley covering first base for the out. Four runs, two hits, no errors, one left.

Giants—Maldonado bounced to Phillips. Butler flied to D. Henderson. Thompson flied to R. Henderson, who made a fine running catch near the left-field line. No runs, no hits, no errors, none left.

SIXTH INNING

A's—Stewart popped to Thompson in short right field. R. Henderson grounded hard to Oberkfell. Lansford hit Brantley's first pitch over the fence in left field for the A's fifth home run of the game, giving Oakland a 9-3 lead. The round-tripper tied a record for most homers in one game by one team, set by the New York Yankees in Game 4 of the 1928 World Series against the St. Louis Cardinals, and equalled a two-team record of six homers in one game. Canseco flied to Mitchell on the warning track in left field. One run, one hit, no errors, none left.

Giants—Clark popped to Weiss. Mitchell flied to D. Henderson in right-center field. Oberkfell singled to right. Williams flied to D. Henderson. No runs, one hit, no errors, one left.

SEVENTH INNING

A's—McGwire walked. D. Henderson grounded into a double play, Oberkfell to Thompson to Clark. Steinbach reached base safely on Oberkfell's error. Phillips grounded to Thompson, who went to his left to make the play and threw to Clark at first base for the out. No runs, no hits, one error, one left.

Giants—Kennedy popped to Lansford. Riles, batting for Brantley, flied to D. Henderson. Maldonado struck out. No runs, no hits, no errors, none left.

EIGHTH INNING

A's—Hammaker came in to pitch for the Giants. Weiss hit a high chop off home plate for a single. Blankenship batted for Stewart and lined a single to center, Weiss stopping at second base. R. Henderson flied to Butler, Weiss advancing to third after the catch. Lansford chopped a single over the head of Oberkfell, Weiss scored and Blankenship also scored when Mitchell overran the ball in left field for an error. Lansford wound up at second base on the misplay as the A's increased their lead to 11-3. Canseco beat out a high chopper to Williams, Lansford advancing to third on the play. McGwire's bouncer back to the mound deflected off Hammaker's glove to Thompson, who made a fine play behind second base and threw to Clark at first for the out, Lansford scoring and Canseco stopping at second on the play. D. Henderson was hit by a pitch. Steinbach lined a single to left, scoring Canseco for a 13-3 lead. Lefferts replaced Hammaker on the mound for the Giants. Phillips flied to Butler. Four runs, five hits, one error, two left.

Giants—Blankenship stayed in the game at second base, Phillips moved to third, Javier came in to play right field and Honeycutt took over on the mound for the A's. Nixon, batting for Butler, grounded to Weiss. Litton batted for Thompson and singled to center. Clark struck out. Mitchell forced Litton at second base, Phillips to Blankenship. No runs, one hit, no errors, one left.

NINTH INNING

A's—Nixon stayed in the game in right field,

Litton stayed in at second base and Manwaring went in to catch for the Giants. Weiss popped to Litton in short right field. Blankenship reached base safely when Lefferts failed to field his tapper down the first-base line for an error. R. Henderson flied to Mitchell just in front of the fence in left field. Gallego, batting for Honeycutt, flied to Maldonado. No runs, no hits, one error, one left.

Giants—Gallego stayed in the game at third base, Phillips moved to left field and Nelson came in to pitch for the A's. Oberkfell walked. Williams flied to D. Henderson in left-center field. Manwaring blooped a double down the right-field line just in front of Javier, Oberkfell advancing to third. Bathe batted for Lefferts and became the 21st player to hit a homer in his first Series at-bat —second as a pinch-hitter— when he hit for the circuit over the left-field fence with two men aboard to cut the A's lead to 13-6. The seven homers by both teams broke a record of six set by the Yankees in 1932 and 1953 and by the Cincinnati Reds in 1975. Maldonado was called out on strikes. Nixon singled to center. Burns replaced Nelson on the mound for the A's. Litton doubled down the left-field line, plating Nixon to make the score 13-7. Clark walked. Mitchell flied to Phillips in left field. Four runs, four hits, no errors, two left.

Game 4

At San Francisco
October 28

Oakland (A.L.)	AB.	R.	H.	RBI.	PO.	A.
R. Henderson, lf	6	2	3	2	4	0
Lansford, 3b	4	1	2	1	0	2
Canseco, rf	4	1	2	0	3	0
McGwire, 1b	5	0	1	0	8	0
D. Henderson, cf	3	2	1	0	3	0
Steinbach, c	4	1	1	3	3	1
Phillips, 2b	5	0	1	1	3	4
Weiss, ss	3	1	0	0	2	2
Moore, p	3	1	1	2	0	2
bPhelps	1	0	0	0	0	0
Nelson, p	0	0	0	0	0	0
Honeycutt, p	0	0	0	0	0	0
Burns, p	0	0	0	0	0	0
fParker	1	0	0	0	0	0
Eckersley, p	0	0	0	0	1	0
Totals	39	9	12	9	27	11

San Francisco (N.L.)	AB.	R.	H.	RBI.	PO.	A.
Butler, cf	5	1	3	1	4	0
Oberkfell, 3b	3	0	0	0	0	1
eThompson, 2b	1	0	1	1	0	0
Bedrosian, p	0	0	0	0	0	0
Clark, 1b	4	1	1	0	11	0
Mitchell, lf	4	1	1	2	2	0
Williams, ss-3b	4	0	1	0	3	4
Kennedy, c	3	1	0	0	3	0
Litton, 2b-3b-2b	4	1	1	2	1	3
Nixon, rf	3	0	0	0	2	0
Robinson, p	0	0	0	0	1	0
LaCoss, p	1	0	0	0	0	0
aBathe	1	0	0	0	0	0
Brantley, p	0	0	0	0	0	0
Downs, p	0	0	0	0	0	0
cRiles	0	0	0	0	0	0
dMaldonado	1	1	1	0	0	0
Lefferts, p	0	0	0	0	0	0
Uribe, ss	0	0	0	0	1	0
Totals	35	6	9	6	27	8

Oakland	1 3 0	0 3 1	0 1 0—9
San Francisco	0 0 0	0 0 2	4 0 0—6

Oakland	IP.	H.	R.	ER.	BB.	SO.
Moore (W)	6	5	2	2	1	3
Nelson	⅓	1	2	2	1	0
Honeycutt	⅓	3	2	2	0	0

Oakland	IP.	H.	R.	ER.	BB.	SO.
Burns	1⅓	0	0	0	0	0
Eckersley (S)	1	0	0	0	0	0

San Francisco	IP.	H.	R.	ER.	BB.	SO.
Robinson (L)	1⅔	4	4	4	1	0
LaCoss	3⅓	4	3	3	3	1
Brantley	⅓	3	1	1	0	0
Downs	1⅔	0	0	0	0	1
Lefferts	⅓	1	1	1	1	0
Bedrosian	1⅔	0	0	0	2	0

Bases on balls—Off Moore 1 (Nixon), off Nelson 1 (Kennedy), off Robinson 1 (Weiss), off LaCoss 3 (Lansford, D. Henderson, Weiss), off Lefferts 1 (Canseco), off Bedrosian 2 (D. Henderson, Steinbach).

Strikeouts—By Moore 3 (Nixon, Mitchell, Williams), by LaCoss 1 (Moore), by Downs 1 (D. Henderson).

aHit into forceout for LaCoss in fifth. bPopped out for Moore in seventh. cAnnounced as pinch-hitter for Downs in seventh. dTripled for Riles in seventh. eSingled home one run for Oberkfell in seventh. fPopped out for Burns in ninth. Errors—None. Left on bases—Oakland 10, San Francisco 4. Two-base hits—D. Henderson, Moore, Phillips, Butler. Three-base hits—Steinbach, R. Henderson, Maldonado. Home runs—R. Henderson, Mitchell, Litton. Stolen base—Canseco. Caught stealing—Butler. Umpires—Rennert (N.L.) plate, Clark (A.L.) first base, Gregg (N.L.) second base, Garcia (A.L.) third base, Runge (N.L.) left field, Voltaggio (A.L.) right field. Time—3:07. Attendance —62,032.

FIRST INNING

A's—R. Henderson belted Robinson's 2-0 pitch over the left-field fence to give the A's a 1-0 lead. It was the 15th time in Series history that a player had homered to lead off the game. Lansford flied to Butler. Canseco fouled out to Clark. McGwire grounded to Williams, who made the play behind second base. One run, one hit, no errors, none left.

Giants—Butler beat out a bunt down the first-base line. Oberkfell forced Butler at second base, Weiss to Phillips. Clark flied to D. Henderson in right-center field. Mitchell forced Oberkfell at second base, Lansford to Phillips. No runs, one hit, no errors, one left.

SECOND INNING

A's—D. Henderson doubled down the left-field line. Steinbach flied to Nixon, D. Henderson advancing to third base after the catch. With the infield drawn in, Phillips grounded sharply to Litton, D. Henderson holding at third. Weiss was walked intentionally. Moore lined an 0-2 pitch over Butler's head in center field for a double, scoring D. Henderson and Weiss to give the A's a 3-0 lead. A.L. pitchers had been hitless in 70 at-bats in Series competition since Tim Stoddard turned the trick in 1979 and without an extra-base hit since Ken Holtzman in 1974. R. Henderson singled to left, scoring Moore to boost the A's lead to 4-0, R. Henderson advancing to second on the throw to the plate. LaCoss replaced Robinson on the mound for the Giants. Lansford walked. Canseco beat out a high chop to Oberkfell, loading the bases. McGwire forced Canseco at second, Williams to Litton. Three runs, four hits, no errors, three left.

Giants—Williams lined a single to center. McGwire fielded Kennedy's high chop and made the play unassisted at first base, Williams moving to second on the play. Litton bounced to Moore, who knocked the ball down and then threw to McGwire at first for the out, Williams going to third on the play. Nixon struck out. No runs, one hit, no errors, one left.

THIRD INNING

A's—D. Henderson fouled out to Mitchell on the warning track in the left-field corner. Steinbach grounded to Litton. Phillips flied to Nixon on the warning track in right-center field. No runs, no hits, no errors, none left.

Giants—LaCoss hit a high chopper off home plate and was out, Moore to McGwire. Butler singled to right field. Oberkfell flied to R. Henderson. With a 1-2 count on Clark, Butler was out stealing, Steinbach to Weiss. No runs, one hit, no errors, none left.

FOURTH INNING

A's—Weiss flied to Butler. Moore lined hard to LaCoss. R. Henderson grounded to Litton. No runs, no hits, no errors, none left.

Giants—Clark hit a high chopper to McGwire, who tagged Clark coming down the first-base line for the out. Mitchell struck out on a pitch in the dirt. Williams was called out on strikes. No runs, no hits, no errors, none left.

FIFTH INNING

A's—Lansford bounced to Oberkfell. Canseco looped a single to left field. McGwire flied to Butler. On the first pitch to D. Henderson, Canseco stole second base. D. Henderson then walked. Steinbach lined a triple into the right-field corner, scoring Canseco and D. Henderson to increase the A's lead to 6-0. Phillips doubled over Mitchell's head in left field, scoring Steinbach for a 7-0 lead. Weiss was walked intentionally. Moore struck out. Three runs, three hits, no errors, two left.

Giants—Kennedy lined hard to R. Henderson in left field. Litton flied to Canseco on the warning track in right field. Nixon walked. Bathe, batting for LaCoss, forced Nixon at second base, Phillips to Weiss, with Phillips making a diving stop behind second. No runs, no hits, no errors, one left.

SIXTH INNING

A's—Brantley took over on the mound for the Giants. R. Henderson tripled to the fence in right-center field. Lansford lined a single to center, scoring R. Henderson to give the A's an 8-0 lead. Canseco fouled out to Mitchell. McGwire lined a single to center, Lansford stopping at second base. Downs replaced Brantley on the mound for the Giants. D. Henderson struck out. Steinbach flied to Butler in right-center field. One run, three hits, no errors, two left.

Giants—Butler grounded to Phillips. Oberkfell grounded to Weiss. Clark lined a single to right field. Mitchell smashed Moore's 1-0 pitch over the left-field fence for a two-run homer, cutting the A's lead to 8-2. Williams bounced to Lansford, who made the play behind the third-base bag. Two runs, two hits, no errors, none left.

SEVENTH INNING

A's—Phillips popped to Williams, who made the catch in front of Butler in short left-center field. Weiss bounced to Clark, who made the play unassisted at first base. Phelps, batting for Moore, popped to Williams just behind the pitching mound. No runs, no hits, no errors, none left.

Giants—Nelson came in to pitch for the A's. Kennedy walked. Litton belted Nelson's 2-1 pitch into the left-field bleachers for a two-run homer to cut the Giants lead to 8-4. Nixon flied to Canseco in short right-center field. Riles was announced as a pinch-hitter for Downs. Honeycutt replaced Nelson on the mound for the A's. Maldonado then batted for Riles and tripled high off the fence in right field. Butler lined a double to left, scoring Maldonado. R. Henderson overran the ball, but the play was ruled a double. Thompson, batting for Oberkfell, singled to left past a diving Weiss to plate Butler and cut the A's lead to 8-6. Clark flied to Canseco in short right field. Burns replaced Honeycutt on the mound for the A's. Mitchell flied to R. Henderson just in front of the fence in left field. Four runs, four hits, no errors, one left.

EIGHTH INNING

A's—Thompson stayed in the game at second base, Litton moved to third and Lefferts came in to pitch for the Giants. R. Henderson grounded to Williams, who made the play behind second base. Lansford singled to third, beating the throw to first base after Litton made a diving stop to his left. Canseco walked on four pitches. Bedrosian replaced Lefferts on the mound, Uribe came in to play shortstop with Williams moving to third base and Litton back to second. McGwire fouled out to Kennedy near the first-base dugout. D. Henderson walked to load the bases. Steinbach also walked on a 3-2 pitch, forcing home Lansford to increase the A's lead to 9-6. Phillips fouled out to Clark, who fell into the auxiliary stands near the Commissioner's box after making the catch. One run, one hit, no errors, three left.

Giants—Williams lined to Phillips. Kennedy flied to D. Henderson. Litton flied to D. Henderson in right-center field. No runs, no hits, no errors, none left.

NINTH INNING

A's—Clark fielded Weiss' one-hopper and made the play unassisted at first base. Parker, batting for Burns, popped to Williams at third. R. Henderson grounded to Williams. No runs, no hits, no errors, none left.

Giants—Eckersley came in to pitch for the A's. Nixon was out at first base on a close play when Phillips charged in to field his bunt and shoveled the ball to McGwire at first base for the out. Uribe flied to R. Henderson. Butler grounded to Phillips, who ranged far to his left and tossed to Eckersley covering first base for the out. The victory enabled the A's to gain the first Series sweep since 1976 when the Cincinnati Reds won four straight games from the New York Yankees. No runs, no hits, no errors, none left.

OAKLAND ATHLETICS' BATTING AND FIELDING AVERAGES

Player—Position	G.	AB.	R.	H.	TB.	2B.	3B.	HR.	RBI.	BB.	IBB.	SO.	B.A.	PO.	A.	E.	F.A.
Blankenship, ph-2b	1	2	1	1	1	0	0	0	0	0	0	0	.500	1	0	0	1.000
R. Henderson, lf	4	19	4	9	17	1	2	1	3	2	0	2	.474	9	0	0	1.000
Lansford, 3b	4	16	5	7	11	1	0	1	4	3	0	1	.438	5	5	0	1.000
Canseco, rf	4	14	5	5	8	0	0	1	3	4	1	3	.357	6	0	0	1.000
Moore, p	2	3	1	1	2	1	0	0	2	0	0	1	.333	0	3	0	1.000
D. Henderson, cf	4	13	6	4	12	2	0	2	4	4	0	3	.308	13	0	0	1.000
McGwire, 1b	4	17	0	5	6	1	0	0	1	1	0	3	.294	28	2	0	1.000
Steinbach, c	4	16	3	4	9	0	1	1	7	2	0	1	.250	27	2	0	1.000
Phillips, 2b-3b-lf	4	17	2	4	8	1	0	1	3	0	0	3	.235	8	15	0	1.000
Parker, dh-ph	3	9	2	2	6	1	0	1	2	0	0	2	.222	0	0	0	.000
Weiss, ss	4	15	3	2	5	0	0	1	1	2	2	2	.133	7	8	0	1.000
Burns, p	2	0	0	0	0	0	0	0	0	0	0	0	.000	0	0	0	.000
Eckersley, p	2	0	0	0	0	0	0	0	0	0	0	0	.000	0	1	0	1.000
Honeycutt, p	3	0	0	0	0	0	0	0	0	0	0	0	.000	0	0	0	.000
Javier, rf	1	0	0	0	0	0	0	0	0	0	0	0	.000	0	0	0	.000
Nelson, p	2	0	0	0	0	0	0	0	0	0	0	0	.000	0	0	0	.000
Gallego, 2b-ph-3b	2	1	0	0	0	0	0	0	0	0	0	0	.000	0	0	0	.000
Phelps, ph	1	1	0	0	0	0	0	0	0	0	0	0	.000	0	0	0	.000
Stewart, p	2	3	0	0	0	0	0	0	0	0	0	1	.000	3	0	1	.750
Totals	4	146	32	44	85	8	3	9	30	18	3	22	.301	108	35	1	.993

Blankenship—Singled for Stewart in eighth inning of third game.
Gallego—Flied out for Honeycutt in ninth inning of third game.
Parker—Popped out for Burns in ninth inning of fourth game.
Phelps—Popped out for Moore in seventh inning of fourth game.

SAN FRANCISCO GIANTS' BATTING AND FIELDING AVERAGES

Player—Position	G.	AB.	R.	H.	TB.	2B.	3B.	HR.	RBI.	BB.	IBB.	SO.	B.A.	PO.	A.	E.	F.A.
Manwaring, c	1	1	1	1	2	1	0	0	0	0	0	0	1.000	0	0	0	.000
Litton, ph-2b-3b	2	6	1	3	7	1	0	1	3	0	0	0	.500	2	3	0	1.000
Bathe, ph	2	2	1	1	4	0	0	1	3	0	0	0	.500	0	0	0	.000
Oberkfell, ph-3b	4	6	1	2	2	0	0	0	3	0	0	0	.333	0	5	1	.833
Mitchell, lf	4	17	2	5	8	0	0	1	2	0	0	3	.294	10	0	1	.909
Butler, cf	4	14	1	4	5	1	0	0	1	2	0	1	.286	9	0	0	1.000
Clark, 1b	4	16	2	4	5	1	0	0	0	1	0	3	.250	40	2	0	1.000
Nixon, ph-cf-rf	2	5	1	1	1	0	0	0	0	1	0	1	.200	2	0	0	1.000
Uribe, ss	3	5	1	1	1	0	0	0	0	0	0	0	.200	1	3	0	1.000
Kennedy, c	4	12	1	2	2	0	0	0	2	1	0	3	.167	23	1	1	.960
Williams, 3b-ss	4	16	1	2	5	0	0	1	1	0	0	6	.125	4	12	0	1.000
Maldonado, rf-ph	4	11	1	1	3	0	1	0	0	0	0	4	.091	5	0	0	1.000
Thompson, 2b-ph	4	11	0	1	1	0	0	0	0	0	0	4	.091	4	10	0	1.000
Bedrosian, p	2	0	0	0	0	0	0	0	0	0	0	0	.000	0	0	0	.000
Brantley, p	3	0	0	0	0	0	0	0	0	0	0	0	.000	1	0	0	1.000
Downs, p	3	0	0	0	0	0	0	0	0	0	0	0	.000	0	0	0	.000
Hammaker, p	2	0	0	0	0	0	0	0	0	0	0	0	.000	0	1	0	1.000
Lefferts, p	3	0	0	0	0	0	0	0	0	0	0	0	.000	0	1	1	.500
Reuschel, p	1	0	0	0	0	0	0	0	0	0	0	0	.000	0	0	0	.000
Robinson, p	1	0	0	0	0	0	0	0	0	0	0	0	.000	0	2	0	1.000
Garrelts, p	2	1	0	0	0	0	0	0	0	0	0	1	.000	0	0	0	.000
LaCoss, p	2	1	0	0	0	0	0	0	0	0	0	0	.000	1	0	0	1.000
Sheridan, rf	1	2	0	0	0	0	0	0	0	0	0	0	.000	0	0	0	.000
Riles, dh-ph	4	8	0	0	0	0	0	0	0	0	0	0	.000	0	0	0	.000
Totals	4	134	14	28	46	4	1	4	14	8	0	27	.209	102	40	4	.973

Bathe—Homered for Lefferts in ninth inning of third game; forced Nixon at second for LaCoss in fifth inning of fourth game.

Litton—Singled for Thompson in eighth inning of third game.

Maldonado—Tripled for Riles in seventh inning of fourth game.

Nixon—Grounded out for Butler in eighth inning of third game.

Oberkfell—Walked for Uribe in eighth inning of first game; singled for Uribe in eighth inning of second game.

Riles—Flied out for Brantley in seventh inning of third game; announced as pinch-hitter for Downs in seventh inning of fourth game.

Thompson—Singled for Oberkfell in seventh inning of fourth game.

OAKLAND ATHLETICS' PITCHING RECORDS

Pitcher	G.	GS.	CG.	IP.	H.	R.	ER.	HR.	BB.	IBB.	SO.	HB.	WP.	W.	L.	Pct.	ERA.
Burns	2	0	0	1⅔	1	0	0	0	1	0	0	0	0	0	0	.000	0.00
Eckersley	2	0	0	1⅔	0	0	0	0	0	0	0	0	0	0	0	.000	0.00
Stewart	2	2	1	16	10	3	3	1	2	0	14	0	0	2	0	1.000	1.69
Moore	2	2	0	13	9	3	3	1	3	0	10	0	2	2	0	1.000	2.08
Honeycutt	3	0	0	2⅔	4	2	2	0	0	0	2	0	0	0	0	.000	6.75
Nelson	2	0	0	1	4	6	6	2	2	0	1	0	0	0	0	.000	54.00
Totals	4	4	1	36	28	14	14	4	8	0	27	0	2	4	0	1.000	3.50

Shutout—Stewart. Save—Eckersley.

SAN FRANCISCO GIANTS' PITCHING RECORDS

Pitcher	G.	GS.	CG.	IP.	H.	R.	ER.	HR.	BB.	IBB.	SO.	HB.	WP.	W.	L.	Pct.	ERA.
Bedrosian	2	0	0	2⅔	0	0	0	0	2	0	2	0	0	0	0	.000	0.00
Lefferts	3	0	0	2⅔	2	1	1	0	2	1	1	0	0	0	0	.000	3.38
Brantley	3	0	0	4⅓	5	2	2	1	3	0	1	0	0	0	0	.000	4.15
LaCoss	2	0	0	4⅓	4	3	3	0	3	1	2	0	0	0	0	.000	6.23
Downs	3	0	0	4⅔	3	4	4	2	2	0	4	0	0	0	0	.000	7.71
Garrelts	2	2	0	7⅓	13	9	8	4	1	0	8	0	0	0	2	.000	9.82
Reuschel	1	1	0	4	5	5	5	1	4	0	2	0	0	0	1	.000	11.25
Hammaker	2	0	0	2⅓	8	4	4	0	0	0	2	1	0	0	0	.000	15.43
Robinson	1	1	0	1⅔	4	4	4	1	1	1	0	0	0	0	1	.000	21.60
Totals	4	4	0	34	44	32	31	9	18	3	22	1	0	0	4	.000	8.21

No shutouts or saves.

COMPOSITE SCORE BY INNINGS

Oakland	4	6	1	7	7	2	0	5	0	—	32
San Francisco	0	1	1	2	0	2	4	0	4	—	14

Sacrifice fly—Thompson.

Stolen bases—R. Henderson 3, Butler 2, Canseco.

Caught stealing—R. Henderson, Butler.

Double plays—Williams, Thompson and Clark; Kennedy and Williams; Weiss, Phillips and McGwire; Oberkfell, Thompson and Clark.

Passed ball—Steinbach.

Hit by pitcher—By Hammaker (D. Henderson).

Balk—Brantley.

Bases on balls—Off Moore 3 (Butler 2, Nixon), off Nelson 2 (Kennedy, Oberkfell), off Stewart 2 (Oberkfell 2), off Burns 1 (Clark), off Reuschel 4 (Canseco, D. Henderson, R. Henderson, Lansford), off Brantley 3 (Canseco, McGwire, Steinbach), off LaCoss 3 (D. Henderson, Lansford, Weiss), off Bedrosian 2 (D. Henderson, Steinbach), off Downs 2 (R. Henderson, Lansford), off Lefferts 2 (Canseco 2), off Garrelts 1 (D. Henderson), off Robinson 1 (Weiss).

Strikeouts—By Stewart 14 (Thompson 3, Williams 3, Maldonado 2, Mitchell 2, Clark, Garrelts, Kennedy, Riles), by Moore 10 (Williams 3, Kennedy 2, Clark, Maldonado, Mitchell, Nixon, Thompson), by Honeycutt 2 (Butler, Clark), by Nelson 1 (Maldonado), by Garrelts 8 (Canseco 2, Phillips 2, R. Henderson, Lansford, Steinbach, Stewart), by Downs 4 (Canseco, D. Henderson, McGwire, Parker), by Bedrosian 2 (D. Henderson, McGwire), by Hammaker 2 (Parker, Weiss), by LaCoss 2 (R. Henderson, Moore), by Reuschel 2 (D. Henderson, McGwire), by Brantley 1 (Phillips), by Lefferts 1 (Weiss).

Left on bases—Oakland 9, 5, 7, 10—31; San Francisco 7, 4, 6, 4—21.

Time of games—First game, 2:45; second game, 2:47; third game, 3:03; fourth game, 3:07.

Attendance—First game, 49,385; second game, 49,388; third game, 62,038; fourth game, 62,032.

Umpires—Garcia (A.L.), Runge (N.L.), Voltaggio (A.L.), Rennert (N.L.), Clark (A.L.), Gregg (N.L.).

Official scorers—Chuck Dybdal, Contra Costa (Cal.) Times; Phil Pepe, New York Daily News; Nick Peters, Sacramento Bee; Gordon Verrell, Long Beach Press Telegram.

1989 ALL-STAR GAME

Including

Review of 1989 Game

Official Box Score

Official Play-by-Play

Results of Previous Games

Kansas City outfielder Bo Jackson was the center of attention upon receiving the Most Valuable Player Award after the American League's 5-3 victory in the All-Star Game.

Jackson Leads A.L. to Victory

By DAVE SLOAN

When American League Manager Tony La Russa put together his starting lineup for the 1989 All-Star Game, he was looking for a leadoff hitter who could get his team off to a fast start.

The obvious choice was Boston third baseman Wade Boggs, a five-time A.L. batting champion who has often led off during his career with the Red Sox. But La Russa opted for an unconventional choice—Kansas City outfielder Bo Jackson, a power hitter who had never before batted leadoff in his brief major league career.

"I think (Jackson) gives us a great chance to get on the board early and, hopefully, often," La Russa said on the eve of the July 11 game. "I think it will make for a lot of excitement right away."

Jackson made La Russa look like a genius when he smashed the second pitch he saw from San Francisco's Rick Reuschel over the center-field fence at Anaheim Stadium to cut a 2-0 National League lead in half. More importantly, Jackson's 448-foot blast swung the momentum back to the American League after the N.L. had scratched out two first-inning runs against starter Dave Stewart.

"There were butterflies when I was in the on-deck circle, but once you get into the batter's box, there's no time to think," said Jackson, who was making his first All-Star appearance. "You just put your tunnel vision on the pitcher and do what comes naturally."

What comes natural to Jackson is hitting home runs, some of prodigious length. He had hit 47 in his first two full seasons (1987 and '88) with the Royals and entered the All-Star Game with a league-leading 21 in 1989.

The 26-year-old Jackson became only the fifth player—the first since Cincinnati's Joe Morgan in 1977—to lead off an All-Star Game with a home run.

"I thought I made a good pitch," Reuschel said. "He just went down and got it. I heard about his power and strength and I saw it first-hand tonight."

Reuschel also saw the next batter, Boggs, hit a home run, the first time in All-Star history that the first two batters in a game had homered. Boggs' left-center-field clout tied the game at 2-2 and helped the American League to a 5-3 victory, the A.L.'s third All-Star triumph in the last four years and the first time the

Bo Jackson watches his leadoff homer sail over the center-field wall in the 1989 All-Star Game.

junior circuit had won back-to-back All-Star Games since 1957-58.

The victory cut the N.L.'s advantage in the series to 37-22-1 and quieted, at least for another year, talk of National League superiority.

"That's so much nonsense," La Russa said. "I watch National League games on TV and they're no more aggressive than (we) are in our league. We have guys who slide into second just as hard as their guys. We have guys who throw just as many fastballs as their guys. I know one thing, they're no better than we are."

Certainly no one was better than Vincent Edward Jackson on this night. The Kansas City star drove in another run in the second inning when he beat out a routine double-play relay to score Texas' Ruben Sierra from third base and singled cleanly to right in his next at-bat. Jackson finished with two hits in four at-bats, two runs batted in, one stolen base and one run scored.

He became only the second player (Willie Mays in 1960 was the other) to hit a home run and steal a base in the same All-Star Game. Jackson also ran down a broken-bat blooper by St. Louis' Pedro Guerrero in the first inning with runners on second and third with two out, preventing at least one more National League run. He was a unanimous choice as the game's Most Valuable Player.

"I'm a believer," said San Diego's Tony

Gwynn, who, like many N.L. players, was watching Jackson play for the first time. "He can do everything they say he can."

One thing the National League failed to do for a second straight year is get an extra-base hit. All nine of their safeties were singles, with hits by San Francisco's Kevin Mitchell and the Mets' Howard Johnson (both in the first inning) and Philadelphia's Von Hayes (in the eighth) accounting for the only N.L. runs.

"I was impressed," Johnson said of the American League pitchers. "The guys they threw were quality pitchers. Very high quality."

La Russa used a record-tying eight pitchers, but none was better than Nolan Ryan of the Texas Rangers. Ryan relieved Stewart and allowed just one hit while striking out three in two innings to become the oldest pitcher (42) ever to win an All-Star Game.

"This one means the most because of coming back to Anaheim, all the games I've pitched here, all the fond memories and the fact that there is a good chance this could be my last All-Star Game," said Ryan, who pitched for the Angels from 1972-79. He was participating in his seventh All-Star Game in his 23rd major league season.

"He's an amazing man," N.L. Manager Tom Lasorda said of baseball's all-time strikeout king. "If he continues to go out and pitch the way he does, they ought to send his arm to the Smithsonian Institute."

But while Ryan's past is amazing to many, Jackson's future looks awesome to all.

"I really didn't think about the MVP until I came back to the dugout after the homer," Jackson said. "The guys were saying, 'You got this thing locked up.' Then when Wade followed with his homer, they said the same thing to him. Really, I was just out there trying to have fun. That's what I always do."

NATIONALS	AB.	R.	H.	RBI.	PO.	A.
Smith, (Cardinals) ss...	4	0	1	0	1	3
Gwynn, (Padres) rf......	2	1	1	0	2	0
Dawson, (Cubs) rf........	1	0	0	0	1	0
Clark, (Padres) 1b	2	0	0	0	5	0
G. Davis, (Astros) 1b ...	1	1	1	0	7	0
Mitchell, (Giants) lf	4	1	2	1	0	0
eColeman, (Cards) lf ...	0	0	0	0	0	0
E. Davis, (Reds) cf.......	2	0	0	0	1	0
Hayes, (Phillies) cf......	1	0	1	1	0	0
Johnson, (Mets) 3b.......	3	0	1	1	0	0
Wallach, (Expos) 3b	1	0	0	0	0	0
Guerrero, (Cards) dh ...	2	0	0	0	0	0
bBonilla, (Pirates) dh..	2	0	2	0	0	0
Sandberg, (Cubs) 2b....	3	0	0	0	2	4
Randolph, (Dod.) 2b....	1	0	0	0	0	0
Santiago, (Padres) c....	1	0	0	0	0	0
Scioscia, (Dodgers) c ...	1	0	0	0	3	0

NATIONALS	AB.	R.	H.	RBI.	PO.	A.
cPena, (Cardinals) c....	2	0	0	0	2	0
Reuschel, (Giants) p....	0	0	0	0	0	1
Smoltz, (Braves) p........	0	0	0	0	0	0
Sutcliffe, (Cubs) p........	0	0	0	0	0	1
Burke, (Expos) p.........	0	0	0	0	0	0
M. Davis, (Padres) p....	0	0	0	0	0	0
Howell, (Dodgers) p.....	0	0	0	0	0	0
Williams, (Cubs) p.......	0	0	0	0	0	1
Totals	33	3	9	3	24	10

AMERICANS	AB.	R.	H.	RBI.	PO.	A.
Jackson, (Royals) lf.....	4	1	2	2	2	0
Greenwell, (R. Sox) lf..	0	0	0	0	1	0
Boggs, (Red Sox) 3b....	3	1	1	1	1	1
Gaetti, (Twins) 3b........	1	0	0	0	1	0
Puckett, (Twins) cf......	3	1	1	0	0	0
White, (Angels) cf	1	0	0	0	0	0
Baines, (White Sox) dh	3	1	1	0	0	0
dLeonard, (Mariners)..	1	0	0	0	0	0
Franco, (Rangers) 2b..	3	0	1	0	1	1
Mattingly, (Yanks) 1b	1	0	1	0	4	0
C. Ripken, (Orioles) ss..	3	0	1	0	0	0
aF'r'nd'z, (B. Jays) ss..	1	0	0	0	2	2
Sierra, (Rangers) rf.....	3	1	2	1	0	0
McGwire, (A's) 1b........	3	0	1	0	5	0
Sax, (Yankees) 2b........	1	0	0	0	1	3
Steinbach, (A's) c	3	0	1	0	6	1
Tettleton, (Orioles) c....	1	0	0	0	2	0
Stewart, (A's) p	0	0	0	0	0	0
Ryan, (Rangers) p	0	0	0	0	0	0
Gubicza, (Royals) p......	0	0	0	0	0	0
Moore, (A's) p	0	0	0	0	0	0
Swindell, (Indians) p....	0	0	0	0	0	0
Russell, (Rangers) p....	0	0	0	0	0	0
Plesac, (Brewers) p......	0	0	0	0	0	0
Jones, (Indians) p.........	0	0	0	0	0	1
Totals	35	5	12	5	27	9

Nationals	2 0 0	0 0 0	0 1 0—3
Americans	2 1 2	0 0 0	0 0 x—5

NATIONALS	IP.	H.	R.	ER.	BB.	SO.
Reuschel (Giants)	1	3	2	2	0	0
Smoltz (Braves)	1	2	1	1	0	0
Sutcliffe (Cubs)	1	4	2	2	0	0
Burke (Expos)	2	2	0	0	0	1
M. Davis (Padres)	1	0	0	0	0	2
Howell (Dodgers)	1	1	0	0	0	1
Williams (Cubs)	1	0	0	0	1	1

AMERICANS	IP.	H.	R.	ER.	BB.	SO.
Stewart (A's)	1	3	2	2	2	0
Ryan (Rangers)	2	1	0	0	0	3
Gubicza (Royals)	1	0	0	0	0	1
Moore (A's)	1	0	0	0	0	1
Swindell (Indians)	1⅔	2	0	0	0	3
Russell (Rangers)	1	1	1	1	1	0
Plesac (Brewers)	0*	1	0	0	0	0
Jones (Indians)	1⅓	1	0	0	0	0

*Pitched to one batter in eighth.

Winning pitcher—Ryan. Losing pitcher—Smoltz. Save—Jones.

aRan for C. Ripken in fifth. bSingled for Guerrero in seventh. cGrounded out for Scioscia in seventh. dStruck out for Baines in seventh. eRan for Mitchell in eighth. Error—Santiago. Double plays—Fernandez, Sax and Mattingly; Jones, Fernandez and Mattingly. Left on bases—Nationals 6, Americans 7. Two-base hits—C. Ripken, Mattingly. Home runs—Jackson, Boggs. Stolen bases—E. Davis, Johnson, Jackson, Gwynn. Caught stealing—Smith. Wild pitch—Sutcliffe. Bases on balls—Off Williams 1 (Sierra), off Stewart 2 (Gwynn, E. Davis), off Russell 1 (G. Davis). Strikeouts—By Burke 1 (Baines), by M. Davis 2 (Jackson, Gaetti), by Howell 1 (Leonard), by Williams 1 (Tettleton), by Ryan 3 (Santiago, Clark, Mitchell), by Gubicza 1 (Sandberg), by Moore 1 (Gwynn), by Swindell 3 (Mitchell, John-

Boston's Wade Boggs (above) homers in the first inning to tie the All-Star Game at 2-2 before winning pitcher Nolan Ryan came on to hurl two scoreless innings in the American League's 5-3 victory.

son, Sandberg). Umpires—Evans (A.L.) plate, Engle (N.L.) first, Cooney (A.L.) second, Crawford (N.L.) third, Hirschbeck (A.L.) left field, Davis (N.L.) right field. Official scorers—Phil Pepe (New York Daily News), Wayne Monroe (Los Angeles Dodgers), Ed Munson (California Angels).

Players listed on rosters but not used: N.L.—Larkin, Jo. Franco, Hershiser. A.L.—Gruber, Finley, Henneman. Time—2:48. Attendance—64,036.

FIRST INNING

Nationals—Smith lined a single to center. Smith was caught stealing, Steinbach to Franco. Gwynn walked. Clark hit a high chopper to McGwire, who made the play unassisted at first base, Gwynn advancing to second on the play. Mitchell hit a checked-swing single to center, scoring Gwynn to give the Nationals a 1-0 lead. Eric Davis walked. Johnson lined Stewart's first pitch to left field for a single, Mitchell scoring for a 2-0 National League lead and Davis stopping at second. With 0-2 count on Guerrero, Davis stole third and Johnson second. Guerrero then flied to Jackson, who made a nice running catch in left-center field. Two runs, three hits, no errors, two left.

Americans—Jackson slugged 1-0 delivery from Reuschel over the center-field wall for a home run, becoming only the ninth player in history to hit a homer in his first All-Star Game at-bat and cutting the Nationals' lead to 2-1. Boggs followed with another homer, belting a 3-2 pitch over the left-center-field fence to tie the game at 2-2. The last time back-to-back homers were hit in an All-Star Game was 1975, when Steve Garvey and Jim Wynn accomplished the feat. Puckett hit a high chopper to Sandberg. Baines bounced back to the mound, Reuschel to Clark. Franco grounded a single to left. Ripken forced Franco at second base, Smith to Sandberg. Two runs, three hits, no errors, one left.

SECOND INNING

Nationals—Ryan came in to pitch for the Americans. Sandberg fouled to McGwire. Santiago struck out. Smith popped to Boggs just in front of home plate. No runs, no hits, no errors, none left.

Americans—Smoltz came in to pitch for the Nationals. Sierra lined a single to right. McGwire flied to Gwynn. Steinbach lined a single to center, sending Sierra to third. Jackson forced Steinbach at second base, Smith to Sandberg, with Sierra scoring on the play to give the Americans a 3-2 lead. With a 1-1 count on Boggs, Jackson stole second and advanced to third when Santiago's errant throw went into center field. Boggs popped to Smith in short left field. One run, two hits, one error, one left.

THIRD INNING

Nationals—Gwynn singled off Ryan's glove. With 1-1 count on Clark, Gwynn stole second base. Clark struck out. Mitchell was called out on strikes. Eric Davis flied to Sierra. No runs, one hit, no errors, one left.

Americans—Sutcliffe came in to pitch for the Nationals. Puckett lined a single to left. With Baines batting, Puckett went to second on a wild pitch. Baines grounded a single to right, scoring Puckett to give the Americans a 4-2 lead. Franco bounced to Sutcliffe, who went to his right to make the play and threw to Clark at first base for the out, Baines advancing to second on the play. Ripken bounced to Sandberg, Baines advancing to third on the play. Clark went far to his right to get a glove on Sierra's bouncer, but couldn't make a play, Baines scoring to give the Americans a 5-2 lead. McGwire grounded a single to center, Sierra

stopping at second. Steinbach flied to Gwynn. Two runs, four hits, no errors, two left.

FOURTH INNING

Nationals—Gubicza came in to pitch for the Americans. Johnson grounded hard to McGwire, who raced to first base and made the play unassisted. Guerrero bounced to Boggs. Sandberg was called out on strikes. No runs, no hits, no errors, none left.

Americans—Scioscia went in to catch and Burke took over on the mound for the Nationals. Jackson lined a single to center. With Jackson running, Boggs bounced to Sandberg, who threw to Clark at first base for the out. Puckett flied to Eric Davis in left-center field, Jackson tagging and going to third after the catch. Baines struck out. No runs, one hit, no errors, one left.

FIFTH INNING

Nationals—Gaetti went in to play third base and Moore took over on the mound for the Americans. Scioscia flied to Jackson. Smith grounded to Franco. Gwynn was called out on strikes. No runs, no hits, no errors, none left.

Americans—Dawson went in at third base and Glenn Davis took over at first for the Nationals. Franco flied to Dawson. Ripken sliced a double down the right-field line. Fernandez went in to run for Ripken. Sierra grounded to Glenn Davis, who made the play unassisted at first base with Ripken advancing to third on the play. Smith went to his right to knock down McGwire's grounder and recovered in time to nip McGwire at first base. No runs, one hit, no errors, one left.

SIXTH INNING

Nationals—Fernandez stayed in the game at shortstop, Mattingly went in at first base, Sax at second and Swindell to pitch for the Americans. Glenn Davis lined a single to center. Mitchell struck out. Eric Davis grounded into a double play, Fernandez to Sax to Mattingly. No runs, one hit, no errors, none left.

Americans—Mark Davis went in to pitch for the Nationals. Steinbach bounced to Sandberg. Jackson struck out. Gaetti was called out on strikes. No runs, no hits, no errors, none left.

SEVENTH INNING

Nationals—Tettleton took over at catcher, Greenwell went into the game in left field and White took over in center for the Americans. Johnson struck out. Bonilla, batting for Guerrero, looped a single to left. Sandberg struck out. Russell came in to replace Swindell on the mound after Pena was announced as a pinch-hitter for Scioscia. Pena broke his bat and sent a grounder to Mattingly, who made the play unassisted at first base. No runs, one hit, no errors, one left.

Americans—Pena stayed in the game to catch, Randolph went in at second, Wallach at third, Hayes went in to play in center and Howell went in to pitch for the Nationals. White bounced to Glenn Davis, who made the play unassisted at first base. Leonard batted for Baines and was called out on strikes. Mattingly smashed a double just inside the first-base line. Fernandez bounced to Glenn Davis, who made the play unassisted at first base. No runs, one hit, no errors, one left.

EIGHTH INNING

Nationals—Smith grounded to Sax. Dawson fouled to Gaetti. Glenn Davis walked. Mitchell grounded a single to left, Davis stopping at second. Coleman went into the game to run for Mitchell. Plesac replaced Russell on the mound for the Americans. Hayes lined a single to left, scoring Davis to cut the Americans' lead to 5-3 with Coleman advancing to third. Jones replaced Plesac on the mound for the Americans. Wallach lined hard to Greenwell in left. One run, two hits, no errors, two left.

Americans—Coleman stayed in the game to play left and Williams went in to pitch for the Nationals. Sierra walked. Sierra was picked off first, Williams to Glenn Davis. Sax popped to Glenn Davis. Tettleton struck out. No runs, no hits, no errors, none left.

NINTH INNING

Nationals—Bonilla singled hard past Mattingly, but was prevented from taking an extra base when the ball struck third-base umpire Engel. Randolph forced Bonilla at second base, Sax to Fernandez. Pena bounced into a double play, Jones to Fernandez to Mattingly. No runs, one hit, no errors, none left.

RESULTS OF PREVIOUS GAMES

1933—At Comiskey Park, Chicago, July 6. Americans 4, Nationals 2. Managers—Connie Mack, John McGraw. Winning pitcher—Lefty Gomez. Losing pitcher—Bill Hallahan. Attendance —47,595.

1934—At Polo Grounds, New York, July 10. Americans 9, Nationals 7. Managers—Joe Cronin, Bill Terry. Winning pitcher—Mel Harder. Losing pitcher—Van Mungo. Attendance—48,363.

1935—At Municipal Stadium, Cleveland, July 8. Americans 4, Nationals 1. Managers—Mickey Cochrane, Frankie Frisch. Winning pitcher—Lefty Gomez. Losing pitcher—Bill Walker. Attendance— 69,831.

1936—At Braves Field, Boston, July 7. Nationals 4, Americans 3. Managers—Charlie Grimm, Joe McCarthy. Winning pitcher—Dizzy Dean. Losing pitcher—Lefty Gomez. Attendance—25,556.

1937—At Griffith Stadium, Washington, July 7. Americans 8, Nationals 3. Managers—Joe McCarthy, Bill Terry. Winning pitcher—Lefty Gomez. Losing pitcher—Dizzy Dean. Attendance—31,391.

1938—At Crosley Field, Cincinnati, July 6. Nationals 4, Americans 1. Managers—Bill Terry, Joe McCarthy. Winning pitcher—Johnny Vander Meer. Losing pitcher—Lefty Gomez. Attendance— 27,067.

1939—At Yankee Stadium, New York, July 11. Americans 3, Nationals 1. Managers—Joe McCarthy, Gabby Hartnett. Winning pitcher—Tommy Bridges. Losing pitcher—Bill Lee. Attendance— 62,892.

1940—At Sportsman's Park, St. Louis, July 9. Nationals 4, Americans 0. Managers—Bill McKechnie, Joe Cronin. Winning pitcher—Paul Derringer. Losing pitcher—Red Ruffing. Attendance— 32,373.

1941—At Briggs Stadium, Detroit, July 8. Americans 7, Nationals 5. Managers—Del Baker, Bill McKechnie. Winning pitcher—Ed Smith. Losing pitcher—Claude Passeau. Attendance—54,674.

1942—At Polo Grounds, New York, July 6. Americans 3, Nationals 1. Managers—Joe Cronin, Leo Durocher. Winning pitcher—Spud Chandler. Losing pitcher—Mort Cooper. Attendance—34,178.

1943—At Shibe Park, Philadelphia, July 13 (night). Americans 5, Nationals 3. Managers—Joe McCarthy, Billy Southworth. Winning pitcher— Dutch Leonard. Losing pitcher—Mort Cooper. Attendance—31,938.

1944—At Forbes Field, Pittsburgh, July 11 (night). Nationals 7, Americans 1. Managers— Billy Southworth, Joe McCarthy. Winning pitcher —Ken Raffensberger. Losing pitcher—Tex Hughson. Attendance—29,589.

1945—No game played.

1946—At Fenway Park, Boston, July 9. Americans 12, Nationals 0. Managers—Steve O'Neill, Charlie Grimm. Winning pitcher—Bob Feller. Losing pitcher—Claude Passeau. Attendance—34,906.

1947—At Wrigley Field, Chicago, July 8. Americans 2, Nationals 1. Managers—Joe Cronin, Eddie Dyer. Winning pitcher—Frank Shea. Losing pitcher—Johnny Sain. Attendance—41,123.

1948—At Sportsman's Park, St. Louis, July 13. Americans 5, Nationals 2. Managers—Bucky Harris, Leo Durocher. Winning pitcher—Vic Raschi. Losing pitcher—Johnny Schmitz. Attendance— 34,009.

1949—At Ebbets Field, Brooklyn, July 12. Americans 11, Nationals 7. Managers—Lou Boudreau, Billy Southworth. Winning pitcher—Virgil Trucks. Losing pitcher—Don Newcombe. Attendance—32,577.

1950—At Comiskey Park, Chicago, July 11. Nationals 4, Americans 3 (14 innings). Managers— Burt Shotton, Casey Stengel. Winning pitcher— Ewell Blackwell. Losing pitcher—Ted Gray. Attendance—46,127.

1951—At Briggs Stadium, Detroit, July 10. Nationals 8, Americans 3. Managers—Eddie Sawyer, Casey Stengel. Winning pitcher—Sal Maglie. Losing pitcher—Ed Lopat. Attendance—52,075.

1952—At Shibe Park, Philadelphia, July 8. Nationals 3, Americans 2 (five innings—rain). Managers—Leo Durocher, Casey Stengel. Winning pitcher—Bob Rush. Losing pitcher—Bob Lemon. Attendance—32,785.

1953—At Crosley Field, Cincinnati, July 14. Nationals 5, Americans 1. Managers—Chuck Dressen, Casey Stengel. Winning pitcher—Warren Spahn. Losing pitcher—Allie Reynolds. Attendance— 30,846.

1954—At Municipal Stadium, Cleveland, July 13. Americans 11, Nationals 9. Managers—Casey Stengel, Walter Alston. Winning pitcher—Dean Stone. Losing pitcher—Gene Conley. Attendance— 68,751.

1955—At Milwaukee County Stadium, Milwaukee, July 12. Nationals 6, Americans 5 (12 innings). Managers—Leo Durocher, Al Lopez. Winning pitcher—Gene Conley. Losing pitcher—Frank Sullivan. Attendance—45,643.

1956—At Griffith Stadium, Washington, July 10. Nationals 7, Americans 3. Managers—Walter Alston, Casey Stengel. Winning pitcher—Bob Friend. Losing pitcher—Billy Pierce. Attendance—28,843.

1957—At Busch Stadium, St. Louis, July 9. Americans 6, Nationals 5. Managers—Casey Stengel, Walter Alston. Winning pitcher—Jim Bunning. Losing pitcher—Curt Simmons. Attendance— 30,693.

1958—At Memorial Stadium, Baltimore, July 8. Americans 4, Nationals 3. Managers—Casey Stengel, Fred Haney. Winning pitcher—Early Wynn. Losing pitcher—Bob Friend. Attendance—48,829.

1959 (first game)—At Forbes Field, Pittsburgh, July 7. Nationals 5, Americans 4. Managers—Fred Haney, Casey Stengel. Winning pitcher—Johnny Antonelli. Losing pitcher—Whitey Ford. Attendance—35,277.

1959 (second game)—At Memorial Coliseum, Los Angeles, August 3. Americans 5, Nationals 3. Managers—Casey Stengel, Fred Haney. Winning pitcher—Jerry Walker. Losing pitcher—Don Drysdale. Attendance—55,105.

1960 (first game)—At Municipal Stadium, Kansas City, July 11. Nationals 5, Americans 3. Managers—Walter Alston, Al Lopez. Winning pitcher— Bob Friend. Losing pitcher—Bill Monbouquette.

238

Attendance—30,619.

1960 (second game)—At Yankee Stadium, New York, July 13. Nationals 6, Americans 0. Managers —Walter Alston, Al Lopez. Winning pitcher—Vernon Law. Losing pitcher—Whitey Ford. Attendance—38,362.

1961 (first game)—At Candlestick Park, San Francisco, July 11. Nationals 5, Americans 4 (10 innings). Managers—Danny Murtaugh, Paul Richards. Winning pitcher—Stu Miller. Losing pitcher—Hoyt Wilhelm. Attendance—44,115.

1961 (second game)—At Fenway Park, Boston, July 31. Americans 1, Nationals 1 (nine-inning tie, stopped by rain). Managers—Paul Richards, Danny Murtaugh. Attendance—31,851.

1962 (first game)—At District of Columbia Stadium, Washington, July 10. Nationals 3, Americans 1. Managers—Fred Hutchinson, Ralph Houk. Winning pitcher—Juan Marichal. Losing pitcher—Camilo Pascual. Attendance—45,480.

1962 (second game)—At Wrigley Field, Chicago, July 30. Americans 9, Nationals 4. Managers—Ralph Houk, Fred Hutchinson. Winning pitcher—Ray Herbert. Losing pitcher—Art Mahaffey. Attendance—38,359.

1963—At Municipal Stadium, Cleveland, July 9. Nationals 5, Americans 3. Managers—Alvin Dark, Ralph Houk. Winning pitcher—Larry Jackson. Losing pitcher—Jim Bunning. Attendance—44,160.

1964—At Shea Stadium, New York, July 7. Nationals 7, Americans 4. Managers—Walter Alston, Al Lopez. Winning pitcher—Juan Marichal. Losing pitcher—Dick Radatz. Attendance—50,850.

1965—At Metropolitan Stadium, Bloomington (Minnesota), July 13. Nationals 6, Americans 5. Managers—Gene Mauch, Al Lopez. Winning pitcher—Sandy Koufax. Losing pitcher—Sam McDowell. Attendance—46,706.

1966—At Busch Memorial Stadium, St Louis, July 12. Nationals 2, Americans 1 (10 innings). Managers—Walter Alston, Sam Mele. Winning pitcher—Gaylord Perry. Losing pitcher—Pete Richert. Attendance—49,936.

1967—At Anaheim Stadium, Anaheim (California), July 11. Nationals 2, Americans 1 (15 innings). Managers—Walter Alston, Hank Bauer. Winning pitcher—Don Drysdale. Losing pitcher—Jim Hunter. Attendance—46,309.

1968—At Astrodome, Houston, July 9 (night). Nationals 1, Americans 0. Managers—Red Schoendienst, Dick Williams. Winning pitcher—Don Drysdale. Losing pitcher—Luis Tiant. Attendance —48,321.

1969—At Robert F. Kennedy Memorial Stadium, Washington, July 23. Nationals 9, Americans 3. Managers—Red Schoendienst, Mayo Smith. Winning pitcher—Steve Carlton. Losing pitcher—Mel Stottlemyre. Attendance—45,259.

1970—At Riverfront Stadium, Cincinnati, July 14 (night). Nationals 5, Americans 4 (12 innings). Managers—Gil Hodges, Earl Weaver. Winning pitcher—Claude Osteen. Losing pitcher—Clyde Wright. Attendance—51,838.

1971—At Tiger Stadium, Detroit, July 13 (night). Americans 6, Nationals 4. Managers—Earl Weaver, George (Sparky) Anderson. Winning pitcher—Vida Blue. Losing pitcher—Dock Ellis. Attendance—53,559.

1972—At Atlanta Stadium, Atlanta, July 25 (night). Nationals 4, Americans 3 (10 innings). Managers—Danny Murtaugh, Earl Weaver. Winning pitcher—Tug McGraw. Losing pitcher—Dave McNally. Attendance—53,107.

1973—At Royals Stadium, Kansas City, July 24 (night). Nationals 7, Americans 1. Managers—George (Sparky) Anderson, Dick Williams. Winning pitcher—Rick Wise. Losing pitcher—Bert Blyleven. Attendance—40,849.

1974—At Three Rivers Stadium, Pittsburgh, July 23 (night). Nationals 7, Americans 2. Managers—Yogi Berra, Dick Williams. Winning pitcher—Ken Brett. Losing pitcher—Luis Tiant. Attendance —50,706.

1975—At Milwaukee County Stadium, Milwaukee, July 15 (night). Nationals 6, Americans 3. Managers—Walter Alston, Alvin Dark. Winning pitcher—Jon Matlack. Losing pitcher—Jim Hunter. Attendance—51,480.

1976—At Veterans Stadium, Philadelphia, July 13 (night). Nationals 7, Americans 1. Managers—George (Sparky) Anderson, Darrell Johnson. Winning pitcher—Randy Jones. Losing pitcher—Mark Fidrych. Attendance—63,974.

1977—At Yankee Stadium, New York, July 19 (night). Nationals 7, Americans 5. Managers—Alfred (Billy) Martin, George (Sparky) Anderson. Winning pitcher—Don Sutton. Losing pitcher—Jim Palmer. Attendance—56,683.

1978—At San Diego Stadium, San Diego, July 11 (night). Nationals 7, Americans 3. Managers—Alfred (Billy) Martin, Thomas Lasorda. Winning pitcher—Bruce Sutter. Losing pitcher—Rich Gossage. Attendance—51,549.

1979—At Kingdome, Seattle, July 17. Nationals 7, Americans 6. Managers—Chuck Tanner, Bob Lemon. Winning pitcher—Bruce Sutter. Losing pitcher—Jim Kern. Attendance—58,905.

1980—At Dodger Stadium, Los Angeles, July 8. Nationals 4, Americans 2. Managers—Chuck Tanner, Earl Weaver. Winning pitcher—Jerry Reuss. Losing pitcher—Tommy John. Attendance—56,088.

1981—At Municipal Stadium, Cleveland, August 9 (night). Nationals 5, Americans 4. Managers—Dallas Green, Jim Frey. Winning pitcher—Vida Blue. Losing pitcher—Rollie Fingers. Attendance—72,086.

1982—At Olympic Stadium, Montreal, July 13 (night). Nationals 4, Americans 1. Managers—Thomas Lasorda, Alfred (Billy) Martin. Winning pitcher—Steve Rogers. Losing pitcher—Dennis Eckersley. Attendance—59,057.

1983—At Comiskey Park, Chicago, July 6 (night). Americans 13, Nationals 3. Managers—Harvey Kuenn, Dorrel (Whitey) Herzog. Winning pitcher—Dave Stieb. Losing pitcher—Mario Soto. Attendance—43,801.

1984—At Candlestick Park, San Francisco, July 10 (night). Nationals 3, Americans 1. Managers—Paul Owens, Joseph Altobelli. Winning pitcher—Charlie Lea. Losing pitcher—Dave Stieb. Attendance—57,756.

1985—At Metrodome, Minneapolis, July 16 (night). Nationals 6, Americans 1. Managers—Dick Williams, George (Sparky) Anderson. Winning pitcher—LaMarr Hoyt. Losing pitcher—Jack Morris. Attendance—54,960.

1986—At Astrodome, Houston, July 15 (night). Americans 3, Nationals 2. Managers—Dick Howser, Dorrel (Whitey) Herzog. Winning pitcher—Roger Clemens. Losing pitcher—Dwight Gooden. Attendance—45,774.

1987—At Oakland-Alameda County Coliseum, July 14 (night). Nationals 2, Americans 0 (13 innings). Managers—Dave Johnson, John McNamara. Winning pitcher—Lee Smith. Losing pitcher —Jay Howell. Attendance—49,671.

1988—At Riverfront Stadium, Cincinnati, July 12 (night). Americans 2, Nationals 1. Managers—Tom Kelly, Dorrel (Whitey) Herzog. Winning pitcher—Frank Viola. Losing pitcher—Dwight Gooden. Attendance—55,837.

BATTING, PITCHING FEATURES

Including

Low-Hit Pitching Performances

Top Strikeout Performances

Baseball's Top Firemen

Pitchers Winning 1-0 Games

Multi-Home Run Performances

Batters Hitting Grand Slams

Top One-Game Hitting Performances

Baseball's Top Pinch-Hitters

Top Performances in Debuts

Homers by Parks

Award Winners

Hall of Fame Electees

Hall of Famers List, Years Selected

Major League Draft

Toronto Tops in Low-Hit Games

By DAVE SLOAN

The 1989 Toronto Blue Jays fell short in their bid for an American League pennant, but nobody could deny Toronto its title as king of low-hit (one- and two-hit) games.

The Jays were involved in 10 such contests, the most of any major league team. On six occasions Toronto pitchers held the opposition to one or two hits. In four other games, Blue Jay batters were stymied by the opposition's low-hit effort.

Righthander Dave Stieb, who had lost no-hit bids with two out in the ninth inning in his final two 1988 starts, picked up right where he left off in 1989. In his second start of the season (April 10), Stieb allowed only a fifth-inning single by Jamie Quirk in a one-hit, 8-0 victory over the New York Yankees. And Stieb flirted with perfection August 4 against the Yankees before seeing his dream die on a two-out, ninth-inning double by Roberto Kelly and a single by Steve Sax.

For the second consecutive year, Stieb led all major league pitchers in low-hit pitching performances. The Toronto star recorded four such efforts—three complete games—including another one-hitter in which he allowed only a sixth-inning single to Milwaukee's Robin Yount in a 7-0 Toronto victory August 26.

Second baseman Nelson Liriano, Stieb's Toronto teammate, proved almost as adept at spoiling no-hitters in 1989. He broke up a bid by Texas righthander Nolan Ryan with a one-out, ninth-inning triple April 23 and, just five days later, he smacked the first pitch of the ninth inning from California's Kirk McCaskill for a double to ruin yet another no-hit attempt.

There were 66 low-hit performances in the major leagues—39 in the American League and 27 in the National. All clubs had a pitcher throw at least one such game, with only the Oakland Athletics and Texas Rangers never being on the receiving end.

The Rangers led all pitching staffs with eight low-hit performances, Ryan and Bobby Witt pitching three apiece. The only other pitcher to be involved in three low-hit games was St. Louis righthander Jose DeLeon, who in addition pitched 11 innings of one-hit ball August 30 against Cincinnati before retiring without a decision.

Toronto finished second to Texas in the A.L. with six low-hit pitching performances while San Diego paced the N.L. with five such games. On the other side of the ledger, the Kansas City Royals were victims of six low-hit games to lead the A.L. while the Atlanta Braves and Philadelphia Phillies were victimized four times each to pace the N.L.

Toronto's Nelson Liriano broke up two no-hitters in the ninth inning within five days last year.

On three occasions, the team throwing the low-hit game lost. On August 15, in one of the year's more bizarre games, Charlie Hough of the Rangers yielded only a sixth-inning single to Harold Reynolds in a 2-0 loss to Seattle. What made the game unusual was that the Rangers collected 13 hits themselves but failed to score.

For Hough, the game probably was a case of deja vu. In the only other one-hit game of his 20-year major league career (1986), he lost, 2-1, to the California Angels.

Fourteen of the 66 low-hit games were one-hitters.

A complete list of one- and two-hit games for the 1989 season follows:

Bobby Witt's three low-hit gems in 1989 tied with teammate Nolan Ryan and helped the Rangers lead all clubs with eight such games.

AMERICAN LEAGUE
One-Hit Games

April 10—Stieb, Toronto vs. New York, 8-0—Quirk, single in fifth.

April 23—Ryan, Texas vs. Toronto, 4-1—Liriano, triple in ninth.

April 28—McCaskill, California vs. Toronto, 9-0—Liriano, double in ninth.

May 4—Farrell (eight innings) and Jones (one inning), Cleveland vs. Kansas City, 3-1—Seitzer, single in ninth.

May 26—Burns (6⅔ innings), Honeycutt (⅓ inning) and Plunk (two innings), Oakland vs. New York, 4-0—Henderson, single in fourth.

May 26—Finley, California vs. Boston, 5-0—Reed, single in eighth.

June 3—Ryan, Texas vs. Seattle, 6-1—Reynolds, single in first.

Aug. 15—Hough, Texas vs. Seattle, 0-2—Reynolds, single in sixth.

Aug. 26—Stieb, Toronto vs. Milwaukee, 7-0—Yount, single in sixth.

Two-Hit Games

April 14—Key, Toronto vs. Kansas City, 3-0—Seitzer, single in seventh; Tartabull, single in seventh.

April 28—Moore (six innings), Honeycutt (two innings) and Eckersley (one inning), Oakland vs. Detroit, 2-1—Nokes, double in fifth; Whitaker, single in sixth.

May 3—Brown, Texas vs. New York, 4-1—Pagliarulo, single in second; Henderson, double in sixth.

May 12—Clemens, Boston vs. Seattle, 2-0—Reynolds, single in first; Presley, double in eighth.

May 23—Rawley (eight innings) and Berenguer (⅔ inning), Minnesota vs. Toronto, 1-2—Liriano, single in sixth; McGriff, single in seventh.

June 2—Milacki (8⅓ innings) and Hickey (⅔ inning), Baltimore vs. Detroit, 4-1—Lynn, homer in fourth; Whitaker, single in fourth.

June 7—Swindell, Cleveland vs. California, 1-0—White, single in fourth; Joyner, single in fifth.

June 16—Clemens, Boston vs. Chicago, 2-0—Lyons, single in fourth; Guillen, single in ninth.

July 1—Witt (7⅔ innings) and Russell (1⅓ innings), Texas vs. Seattle, 1-0—Coles, single in fifth; Reynolds, single in eighth.

July 4—Schmidt (6¼ innings) and Williamson (2⅔ innings), Baltimore vs. Toronto, 8-0—Fernandez, single in seventh; Gruber, single in seventh.

July 9—Stieb (seven innings) and Henke (two innings), Toronto vs. Detroit, 2-0—Whitaker, single in sixth; Lynn, single in seventh.

July 16—Dotson (7⅓ innings), Pall (one inning) and Thigpen (⅔ inning), Chicago vs. Milwaukee, 2-0—Yount, single in sixth; Surhoff, single in ninth.

July 18—Witt, Texas vs. Boston, 8-1—Romine, single in fourth; Greenwell, single in eighth.

July 19—Farrell, Cleveland vs. Minnesota, 10-1 —Dwyer, double in second and single in fourth.

July 20—Swindell, Cleveland vs. Kansas City, 4-0—Jackson, single in second; Tartabull, double in fifth.

July 29—Smithson (eight innings) and Murphy (one inning), Boston vs. Cleveland, 5-0—O'Brien, single in fourth; Browne, single in ninth.

Aug. 1—Navarro (eight innings) and Plesac (one inning), Milwaukee vs. Cleveland, 4-2—Allanson, single in third; Carter, homer in seventh.

Aug. 2—Cerutti, Toronto vs. Kansas City, 8-0—Brett, double in seventh; Wilson, double in ninth.

Aug. 4—Stieb, Toronto vs. New York, 2-1—Kelly, double in ninth; Sax, single in ninth.

Aug. 7—Cadaret, New York vs. Cleveland, 9-0—Jacoby, single in eighth; Aguayo, double in ninth.

Aug. 10—Ryan (8⅓ innings) and Russell (⅔ inning), Texas vs. Detroit, 4-1—Bergman, single in ninth; Nokes, double in ninth.

Aug. 16—Tanana, Detroit vs. Baltimore, 4-0—Melvin, single in third; C. Ripken, single in fourth.

Sept. 10—Knudson, Milwaukee vs. Seattle, 7-1—Vizquel, single in third; Griffey, single in seventh.

Sept. 15—Hanson, Seattle vs. New York, 3-1—Hall, single in fourth; Kelly, homer in eighth.

Sept. 15—Perez, Chicago vs. California, 3-1—White, single in sixth; Downing, double in seventh.

Sept. 17—Saberhagen (seven innings), Gleaton (one inning) and Montgomery (one inning), Kansas City vs. Baltimore, 7-0—Milligan, single in third; Gonzales, single in ninth.

Sept. 19—Moore (eight innings) and Nelson (one inning), Oakland vs. Cleveland, 5-1 —Belle, single in second; Snyder, single in seventh.

Sept. 22—Swift (six innings), Jackson (two innings) and Schooler (one inning), Seattle vs. Kansas City, 2-0—Seitzer, singles in first and sixth.

Sept. 23—Bankhead, Seattle vs. Kansas City, 8-0 —Boone, single in fifth; Wilson, double in sixth.

Sept. 29—Witt, Texas vs. California, 5-0—Downing, single in fourth; Parrish, single in fifth.

NATIONAL LEAGUE
One-Hit Games

April 10—Hurst, San Diego vs. Atlanta, 5-2—L. Smith, homer in third.

May 16—Kramer, Pittsburgh vs. Cincinnati, 5-0 —Oester, double in eighth.

May 17—Reuschel (eight innings) and Brantley (one inning), San Francisco vs. Philadelphia, 6-0—Herr, single in seventh.

May 19—Scott, Houston vs. Pittsburgh, 3-0—Wilson, single in eighth.

Sept. 13—DeLeon (5⅓ innings), St. Louis vs. Pittsburgh, 0-0—Drabek, double in third.

Two-Hit Games

April 5—Drabek, Pittsburgh vs. Montreal, 3-0— Brooks, single in first; Galarraga, single in seventh.

April 15—Robinson (five innings) and Hammaker (four innings), San Francisco vs. Atlanta, 1-0—Thomas, single in second; Gregg, single in second.

April 21—DeLeon, St. Louis vs. Montreal, 1-0— Nixon, single in first; Aldrete, single in ninth.

April 29—Maddux (five innings), Philadelphia vs. Cincinnati, 8-0—Sabo, single in first; Larkin, single in fourth.

May 4—Glavine, Atlanta vs. Philadelphia, 3-0— Herr, single in fourth; Daulton, triple in fifth.

May 10—Magrane (8⅔ innings) and Worrell (⅓ inning), St. Louis vs. San Diego, 3-1 —Martinez, double in seventh; Ja. Clark, single in ninth.

May 14—Hershiser, Los Angeles vs. Philadelphia, 9-0—Jordan, single in third; Jeltz, double in eighth.

June 1—Deshaies (8⅔ innings) and Agosto (⅓ inning), Houston vs. Los Angeles, 7-2—Hatcher, single in eighth; Murray, single in ninth.

June 10—Whitson (six innings) and Harris (two innings), San Diego vs. San Francisco, 0-1—Jones, single in second; Thompson, triple in third.

July 3—Langston, Montreal vs. Atlanta, 3-0—Perry, single in second; Murphy, single in ninth.

July 4—Browning (8⅓ innings) and Franco (⅔ inning), Cincinnati vs. Philadelphia, 2-1—Thon, double in ninth; Jeltz, single in ninth.

July 16—Garrelts (six innings), Brantley (two innings) and Bedrosian (one inning), San Francisco vs. Pittsburgh, 3-1—Bonds, single in first; Bonilla, single in seventh.

July 17—Deshaies (eight innings) and Andersen (one inning), Houston vs. New York, 6-0—Magadan, single in first; Teufel, single in first.

July 20—Ojeda (5⅔ innings) and Aguilera (3⅓ innings), New York vs. Atlanta, 4-1 —Thomas, singles in second and sixth.

July 26—DeLeon (eight innings), Dayley (⅓ inning) and Worrell (⅔ inning), St. Louis vs. Chicago, 2-0—Walton, single in third; Berryhill, single in seventh.

Aug. 9—Whitson (eight innings) and Davis (one inning), San Diego vs. Houston, 2-1 —Anthony, homer in first; Davis, single in fourth.

Aug. 12—Valenzuela, Los Angeles vs. San Francisco, 5-1—Manwaring, single in fifth; Williams, double in sixth.

Aug. 19—Mulholland, Philadelphia vs. San Francisco, 1-0—Williams, single in second; Uribe, single in sixth.

Sept. 8—Benes (7⅓ innings) and Davis (1⅔ innings), San Diego vs. Los Angeles, 1-0—Hamilton, single in fifth; Murray, double in sixth.

Sept. 12—Bielecki, Chicago vs. Montreal, 2-0—Raines, single in first; Wallach, single in second.

Sept. 12—Hurst, San Diego vs. Houston, 9-0—Caminiti, single in fourth; Davidson, double in fifth.

Sept. 21—Fernandez, New York vs. St. Louis, 6-1 —Pendleton, triple in fifth; Zeile, single in fifth.

Ryan Extends 10-K Records

By DAVE SLOAN

As the television commercial says, Texas righthander Nolan Ryan is not getting older, he's getting better.

Ryan, baseball's all-time strikeout king (5,076) at age 43, again led the major leagues in 10-strikeout games last season, fanning 10 or more batters in a whopping 18 of the 32 games he pitched. Ryan's total was 12 better than any other pitcher and increased his career total to 199, another record. The big Texan struck out 301 batters for the season, 71 more than Boston runner-up Roger Clemens in the American League and 100 more than the Cardinals' Jose DeLeon, the pacesetter in the National League.

Ryan's performance enabled the Rangers to lead all major league teams with 22 10-strikeout games. Bobby Witt (three) and Jamie Moyer (one) were the other Ranger pitchers to accomplish the feat.

Overall, there were 109 such performances last season, with the feat being accomplished 63 times in the A.L. and 46 times in the N.L. A total of 48 pitchers did it at least once, with lefthanders Frank Viola and Mark Langston turning the trick for two different teams. Viola did it three times with the Minnesota Twins before his July 31 trade to the Mets, while Langston did it once with the Seattle Mariners before being traded to Montreal on May 26. Viola and Langston did it one and five more times, respectively, for their new teams.

Langston's season total of six was the highest for any pitcher other than Ryan.

All teams except Baltimore, Pittsburgh and San Francisco had at least one 10-strikeout performance. The two New York teams—the Mets and Yankees—had five different pitchers perform the feat while 10 pitchers held the distinction of being the only hurler on their team to strike out at least 10 batters in one game.

The Mets led the National League with 10 such performances and were the only team other than Texas to reach double figures.

Following is a list of all pitchers who recorded at least 10 strikeouts in a game in 1989, with the number of times the feat

Texas righthander Nolan Ryan.

was accomplished:

AMERICAN LEAGUE: Baltimore—None. Boston (5)—Clemens 5. California (3)—Finley 3. Chicago (2)—Perez 2. Cleveland (5)—Farrell 3, Nichols, Swindell. Detroit (2)—Tanana 2. Kansas City (7)—Gordon 3, Saberhagen 3, Gubicza. Milwaukee (1)—Bosio. Minnesota (3)—Viola 3. New York (6)—Cary 2, Candelaria, Leiter, Parker, Plunk. Oakland (1)—Moore. Seattle (4)—Johnson 3, Langston. Texas (22)—Ryan 18, Witt 3, Moyer. Toronto (2)—Key, Stieb.

NATIONAL LEAGUE: Atlanta (2)—P. Smith, Smoltz. Chicago (5)—Sutcliffe 3, Bielecki, Wilson. Cincinnati (3)—Charlton, Leary, Rijo. Houston (2)—Deshaies, Scott. Los Angeles (8)—Belcher 4, Martinez 2, Hershiser, Wetteland. Montreal (8)—Langston 5, Perez 2, Gross. New York (10)—Cone 4, Fernandez 3, Darling, Gooden, Viola. Philadelphia (2)—Howell 2. Pittsburgh—None. St. Louis (4)—DeLeon 4. San Diego (2)—Hurst 2. San Francisco—None.

1989 Games With 15 or More Strikeouts

Date	Pitcher—Club—Opp.	Place	IP.	H.	R.	ER.	BB.	SO.	Result
July 14—Fernandez, Mets vs. Braves		Atlanta	8	6	3	3	0	16	L 2-3
April 12—Ryan, Rangers vs. Brewers		Milwaukee	8	1	0	0	2	15	W 8-1
June 24—Finley, Angels vs. Orioles		California	9	7	3	2	1	15	W 8-3

Davis Cops Fireman Award

By LARRY WIGGE

At one point early in the 1989 season, Mark Davis, San Diego's relief ace, told reporters not to talk to him about numbers. That, he said, usually gets him into trouble.

Numbers, however, became very important to Davis in 1989. He converted 44 of 48 save opportunities and added four victories to become only the seventh reliever to capture a Cy Young Award while easily winning The Sporting News Fireman of the Year Award as the top relief pitcher in the National League. Those numbers also earned Davis, a free agent, a four-year contract worth more than $3 million per year with the Kansas City Royals.

After years of trying to find his niche as a starter or reliever, Davis had become the Padres' closer after a July 1987 trade in which slugger Kevin Mitchell was sent to San Francisco. After compiling 28 saves in 1988, he exploded into the upper echelon of relief pitchers with his 44 saves and outstanding 1.85 earned-run average.

American League Fireman of the Year honors went to hard-throwing Texas righthander Jeff Russell, who recorded 38 saves and six victories for 44 points.

With one point being awarded for each save or relief win, Davis edged Chicago's Mitch Williams (36 saves, four wins), Montreal's Tim Burke (28 saves, nine wins) and Cincinnati's John Franco, the 1988 Fireman of the Year who had 32 saves and four wins last season.

Ironically, Russell volunteered to go from the starting rotation to the bullpen when the Rangers traded Williams to the Cubs prior to the 1989 season and he went on to convert 38 of 44 save opportunities.

Cleveland's Doug Jones (32 saves, seven wins) finished second, with Oakland's Dennis Eckersley, the A.L.'s 1988 Fireman of the Year, finishing third (33 saves, four wins). Milwaukee's Dan Plesac, Chicago's Bobby Thigpen and Minnesota's Jeff Reardon were tied for fourth with 36 points apiece.

Davis, whose 44 saves were two short of the major league record set by New York Yankee lefthander Dave Righetti in 1986, joined Mike Marshall of the Los Angeles Dodgers (1974), Sparky Lyle of the Yankees ('77), Bruce Sutter of the Cubs ('79), Rollie Fingers of the Milwaukee Brewers (1981), Willie Hernandez of the Detroit Tigers ('84) and Steve Bedrosian of the

Cub reliever Mitch Williams finished second in the N.L. with 40 points.

Philadelphia Phillies ('87) as the only relief pitchers to capture a Cy Young Award.

Following is a complete list of major league players who recorded saves or relief wins in 1989:

AMERICAN LEAGUE

Pitcher—Club	Saves	Relief Wins	Tot. Pts.
Russell, Texas	38	6	44
Jones, Cleveland	32	7	39
Eckersley, Oakland	33	4	37
Plesac, Milwaukee	33	3	36
Thigpen, Chicago	34	2	36
Reardon, Minnesota	31	5	36
Schooler, Seattle	33	1	34
Olson, Baltimore	27	5	32
Smith, Boston	25	6	31
Harvey, California	25	3	28
Henke, Toronto	20	8	28
Righetti, New York	25	2	27
Montgomery, Kansas City	18	7	25
Farr, Kansas City	18	1	19
Henneman, Detroit	8	11	19
Ward, Toronto	15	4	19
Williamson, Baltimore	9	10	19
Guetterman, New York	13	5	18
Hernandez, Detroit	15	2	17
Crim, Milwaukee	7	9	16
Honeycutt, Oakland	12	2	14
Murphy, Boston	9	5	14
Burns, Oakland	8	5	13
Berenguer, Minnesota	3	9	12
Minton, California	8	4	12
Gordon, Kansas City	1	10	11
Jackson, Seattle	7	4	11
Pall, Chicago	6	4	10
McClure, California	3	6	9
Stanley, Boston	4	5	9

Pitcher—Club	Saves	Relief Wins	Tot. Pts.	Pitcher—Club	Saves	Relief Wins	Tot. Pts.
Wells, Toronto	2	7	9	Gonzalez, Minnesota	0	3	3
Guante, Texas	2	6	8	Long, Chicago	1	2	3
Hillegas, Chicago	3	5	8	Luecken, Kansas City	1	2	3
McCullers, New York	3	4	7	Smithson, Boston	2	1	3
Reed, Seattle	0	7	7	Swift, Seattle	1	2	3
Fraser, California	2	4	6	Trout, Seattle	0	3	3
Lamp, Boston	2	4	6	Wills, Toronto	0	3	3
Nelson, Oakland	3	3	6	Acker, Toronto	0	2	2
Orosco, Cleveland	3	3	6	Aldrich, Milwaukee	1	1	2
Patterson, Chicago	0	6	6	Aquino, Kansas City	0	2	2
Thurmond, Baltimore	4	2	6	Atherton, Cleveland	2	0	2
Plunk, Oakland-New York	1	4	5	August, Milwaukee	0	2	2
Rogers, Texas	2	3	5	Bailes, Cleveland	0	2	2
Hickey, Baltimore	2	2	4	Castillo, Toronto	1	1	2
Jones, Chicago	1	3	4	Gossage, New York	1	1	2
Krueger, Milwaukee	3	1	4	Hall, Texas	0	2	2
Leach, Kansas City	0	4	4	Harris, Boston	0	2	2
Mohorcic, New York	2	2	4	Holton, Baltimore	0	2	2
Nunez, Detroit	1	3	4	Knudson, Milwaukee	0	2	2
Powell, Seattle	2	2	4	Mielke, Texas	1	1	2
Wayne, Minnesota	1	3	4	Monteleone, California	0	2	2
F. Williams, Detroit	1	3	4	Olin, Cleveland	1	1	2
Arnsberg, Texas	1	2	3	Petry, California	0	2	2
Crawford, Kansas City	0	3	3	Smith, Baltimore	0	2	2
Fossas, Milwaukee	1	2	3	St. Claire, Minnesota	1	1	2
Gibson, Detroit	0	3	3	Weston, Baltimore	1	1	2

One save—J. Davis, Chicago; Drummond, Minnesota; DuBois, Detroit; Harris, Seattle; Huismann, Baltimore; Smith, Minnesota.

One relief win—Black, Cleveland; Buice, Toronto; Cadaret, Oakland-New York; Comstock, Seattle; Corsi, Oakland; Cummings, Toronto; Dopson, Boston; Gardner, Boston; Gozzo, Toronto; Havens, Cleveland-Detroit; Hernandez, Toronto; McCarthy, Chicago; McDonald, Baltimore; Navarro, Milwaukee; Nielsen, New York; Price, Boston; Rosenberg, Chicago; Schmidt, Baltimore; Schwabe, Detroit; Toliver, Minnesota; Tunnell, Minnesota; Yett, Cleveland; M. Young, Oakland.

NATIONAL LEAGUE

Pitcher—Club	Saves	Relief Wins	Tot. Pts.	Pitcher—Club	Saves	Relief Wins	Tot. Pts.
Davis, San Diego	44	4	48	Robinson, Pittsburgh	4	2	6
Williams, Chicago	36	4	40	Agosto, Houston	1	4	5
Burke, Montreal	28	9	37	Alvarez, Atlanta	2	3	5
Franco, Cincinnati	32	4	36	Eichhorn, Atlanta	0	5	5
Howell, Los Angeles	28	5	33	McGaffigan, Montreal	2	3	5
Myers, New York	24	7	31	Schatzeder, Houston	1	4	5
Landrum, Pittsburgh	26	2	28	Wilson, Chicago	2	3	5
Smith, Houston	25	3	28	Clements, San Diego	0	4	4
McDowell, New York-Philadelphia	23	4	27	Patterson, Pittsburgh	1	3	4
Bedrosian, Phila.-San Francisco	23	3	26	Pico, Chicago	2	2	4
Boever, Atlanta	21	4	25	Wetteland, Los Angeles	1	3	4
Worrell, St. Louis	20	3	23	Aase, New York	2	1	3
Lefferts, San Francisco	20	2	22	Assenmacher, Atlanta-Chicago	0	3	3
Darwin, Houston	7	11	18	Bair, Pittsburgh	1	2	3
Parrett, Philadelphia	6	12	18	Birtsas, Cincinnati	1	2	3
Dayley, St. Louis	12	4	16	Camacho, San Francisco	0	3	3
Aguilera, New York	7	6	13	Carpenter, St. Louis	0	3	3
Dibble, Cincinnati	2	10	12	Frey, Montreal	0	3	3
Lancaster, Chicago	8	4	12	Hammaker, San Francisco	0	3	3
Harris, San Diego	6	5	11	Harris, Philadelphia	1	2	3
Grant, San Diego	2	8	10	Kramer, Pittsburgh	2	1	3
DiPino, St. Louis	0	9	9	Musselman, New York	0	3	3
Hesketh, Montreal	3	6	9	Searage, Los Angeles	0	3	3
LaCoss, San Francisco	6	3	9	Acker, Atlanta	2	0	2
Pena, Los Angeles	5	4	9	Belcher, Los Angeles	1	1	2
Quisenberry, St. Louis	6	3	9	Carman, Philadelphia	0	2	2
Charlton, Cincinnati	0	8	8	Easley, Pittsburgh	1	1	2
Costello, St. Louis	3	5	8	Heaton, Pittsburgh	0	2	2
Andersen, Houston	3	4	7	Kilgus, Chicago	2	0	2
Brantley, San Francisco	0	7	7	Morgan, Los Angeles	0	2	2
Kipper, Pittsburgh	4	3	7	Power, St. Louis	0	2	2
Schiraldi, Chicago-San Diego	4	3	7	Z. Smith, Atlanta-Montreal	2	0	2
Stanton, Atlanta	7	0	7	Terry, St. Louis	2	0	2
Gossage, San Francisco	4	2	6				

One save—Crews, Los Angeles; Fisher, Pittsburgh; Gooden, New York; Henry, Atlanta; Maddux, Philadelphia; Meyer, Houston; Perry, Chicago; Sebra, Philadelphia-Cincinnati; Tekulve, Cincinnati.

One relief win—Aldrich, Atlanta; Clancy, Houston; Cook, San Francisco-Philadelphia; Drabek, Pittsburgh; Forsch, Houston; Frohwirth, Philadelphia; Harris, Montreal; Knepper, Houston-San Francisco; Leary, Los Angeles-Cincinnati; Madden, Pittsburgh; McCament, San Francisco; Perez, Montreal; Puleo, Atlanta; Rodriguez, Cincinnati; Sanderson, Chicago; Scott, Houston; Taylor, Pittsburgh; Valdez, Atlanta; Wilkins, Chicago; Wilson, San Francisco.

Hershiser Loses 4 1-0 Games

By DAVE SLOAN

Any 1989 pitcher who wants to file a grievance against his teammates for non-support will have to get in line behind Los Angeles Dodger ace Orel Hershiser.

Although his final statistics were virtually identical to those he compiled in winning the 1988 Cy Young Award, Hershiser watched his record plummet from 23-8 to 15-15. And nowhere was the Dodgers' lack of run support for Hershiser more evident than in 1-0 games.

Hershiser lost four games by that score while no other big-league hurler lost more than two. Hershiser lost a pair of 1-0 decisions to San Diego rookie Andy Benes in September and another to Mets lefthander Frank Viola on August 28.

Whereas Hershiser was 0-4 in 1-0 games, teammate Tim Belcher won all three of his 1-0 decisions. He was the only pitcher in baseball to win three such contests. Two of Belcher's 1-0 victories were complete games, a feat accomplished by only two other pitchers—Cleveland lefthanders Greg Swindell and Bud Black.

Fifty-seven major league games ended in 1-0 scores, 35 of those contests occurring in the National League and 22 in the American. All clubs were involved in at least one, with the Dodgers posting a 5-7 mark in their major league-leading total of 12. The Indians won more 1-0 games than any other team (seven) and paced the A.L. with nine 1-0 games.

Ironically, only three A.L. pitchers won two 1-0 games last year and all three played for the Indians—Swindell, Black and righthander Tom Candiotti. Belcher, Benes, the Cubs' Greg Maddux and the Cardinals' Jose DeLeon all recorded at least two 1-0 victories in the N.L.

Nine 1-0 games were decided by a home run, the most dramatic coming August 23 when Dodger catcher Rick Dempsey hit a leadoff blast in the 22nd inning to beat Montreal. Dempsey's homer off Expos righthander Dennis Martinez decided the longest 1-0 game in baseball history and the second-longest shutout game ever.

The Orioles, Red Sox, Royals, Mariners and Blue Jays did not win any 1-0 games while the Astros, Athletics and Rangers did not lose.

The complete list of 1-0 games, including the winning and losing pitchers and the inning in which the run was scored, follows:

AMERICAN LEAGUE (22)

APRIL—

Date	Winner	Loser	Inning
22 —	King, Chi.	*Hanson, Sea.	3
24 —	Alexander, Det.	*Langston, Sea.	7
26 —	*Finley, Cal.	Morris, Det.	2
30 —	*McClure, Cal.	*Henke, Tor.	11

MAY—

| 6 — | *Krueger, Mil. | *Gordon, K.C. | 10 |
| 28 — | Swindell, Cle. | *Milacki, Bal. | 9 |

JUNE—

6 —	Moore, Oak.	Anderson, Minn.	2
7 —	Swindell, Cle.	Finley, Cal.	7
16 —	Black, Cle.	*Leach, K.C.	9

JULY—

1 —	*Witt, Tex.	Johnson, Sea.	3
3 —	*Stewart, Oak.	Gubicza, K.C.	3
4 —	*Schulze, N.Y.	Tanana, Det.	4
18 —	Blyleven, Cal.	Key, Tor.	6
21 —	*Perez, Chi.	*Hetzel, Bos.	8
22 —	*Candiotti, Cle.	*Gordon, K.C.	9

AUGUST—

2 —	*Candiotti, Cle.	Bosio, Mil.	3
15 —	Higuera, Mil.	Parker, N.Y.	4
17 —	*Welch, Oak.	Farrell, Cle.	5
20 —	McCaskill, Cal.	Black, Cle.	7
26 —	*West, Minn.	Holman, Sea.	3

SEPTEMBER—

| 12 — | Black, Cle. | Tanana, Det. | 8 |

OCTOBER—

| 1 — | *Orosco, Cle. | *Dotson, Chi. | 8 |

NATIONAL LEAGUE (35)

APRIL—

Date	Winner	Loser	Inning
15 —	*Hammaker, S.F.	P. Smith, Atl.	7
21 —	DeLeon, St. L.	*Burke, Mon.	9
25 —	*Show, S.D.	*Walk, Pitt.	5
27 —	Maddux, Chi.	*Hershiser, L.A.	5
28 —	Smiley, Pitt.	*Reuschel, S.F.	6
29 —	*Carpenter, St.L.	*Searage, L.A.	11

MAY—

1 —	*Howell, L.A.	Drabek, Pitt.	9
13 —	*Knepper, Hou.	Maddux, Chi.	8
20 —	*Dayley, St.L.	*Boever, Atl.	13
24 —	Gross, Mon.	*Robinson, S.F.	1
29 —	*Hurst, S.D.	*McWilliams, Phil.	1

JUNE—

2 —	Scott, Hou.	*Valenzuela, L.A.	7
9 —	*DeLeon, St.L.	*Sanderson, Chi.	1
10 —	*Garrelts, S.F.	*Whitson, S.D.	3
10 —	*Clancy, Hou.	*Smoltz, Atl.	6
15 —	*Harris, S.D.	*Birtsas, Cin.	12
17 —	*Ojeda, N.Y.	McWilliams, Phil.	1
21‡ —	*Smoltz, Atl.	*Mahler, Cin.	1
21 —	*Maddux, Chi.	*Bair, Pitt.	11

JULY—

1 —	*Belcher, L.A.	Smiley, Pitt.	9
14 —	*B. Smith, Mon.	*Browning, Cin.	2
22† —	*Deshaies, Hou.	*Howell, Phil.	2

AUGUST—

3 —	*Bair, Pitt.	*McGaffigan, Mon.	12
7 —	*Glavine, Atl.	*Martinez, Pitt.	3
19 —	Mulholland, Phil.	*Downs, S.F.	9
23 —	*Wetteland, L.A.	*Martinez, Mon.	22
27 —	*Browning, Cin.	*Kramer, Pitt.	3
28 —	Viola, N.Y.	*Hershiser, L.A.	3

SEPTEMBER—

8 —	*Benes, S.D.	*Hershiser, L.A.	7
16 —	Belcher, L.A.	*Boever, Atl.	9
17 —	Portugal, Hou.	Browning, Cin.	5
17 —	Langston, Mon.	*Darling, N.Y.	5
24 —	*Benes, S.D.	*Hershiser, L.A.	7
27 —	Drabek, Pitt.	*Magrane, St.L.	4
27 —	Belcher, L.A.	*Garrelts, S.F.	1

*Did not pitch complete game.
†First game of doubleheader.
‡Second game of doubleheader.

Carter Led Multi-HR Parade

By DAVE SLOAN

When Joe Carter gets hot, he will hit home runs in bunches. And that was particularly true in 1989, when the former Cleveland outfielder belted 35 homers to finish second in the American League behind Toronto's Fred McGriff (36).

Carter, who was traded to San Diego in the off-season, hit two or more home runs in six games and tied a major league record by homering three times in two different games. Carter homered in three consecutive at-bats to lead Cleveland to a 7-3 victory at Texas on June 24 and enjoyed a three-homer, six-RBI performance in Cleveland's 10-1 victory over Minnesota on July 19. His second three-homer effort gave him five home runs in two games.

Philadelphia's Von Hayes was the only other player to hit three homers in one game last season. He accomplished the feat in a 6-1 Phillies' victory over San Francisco on August 29.

Carter and San Francisco's Kevin Mitchell, who led the major leagues with 47 home runs, topped all players with six multi-homer performances. A total of 82 players had at least one multi-homer game and the feat was accomplished 129 times overall—70 times in the American League and 59 in the National. All 26 teams had at least one player with a multi-homer game.

The Chicago Cubs led all teams with 11 multi-homer performances, five different Cubs contributing to the total. Outfielder Andre Dawson did it three times to increase his 14-year career total to 32, second only to Boston's Jim Rice (35) among active players.

The Cubs, Brewers, Twins and Mariners each had five players with at least one multi-homer game while the Cardinals and Padres had only one player each perform the feat.

The Twins, who paced the majors with a dozen multi-homer games in 1988, led the A.L. last season with 10.

Two players managed multi-homer performances in the same game on seven occasions. Teammates did it in the same game three times. Harold Baines hit two homers for the White Sox and Ruben Sierra hit two for the Rangers in an 11-7 Texas victory June 8. The two players became teammates after Baines' July 29 trade to the Rangers.

Atlanta's Dale Murphy enjoyed two multi-homer performances last season and now has 30 in his 14-year big-league career. One came July 27 in a 10-1 Braves' victory over the Giants—a game in which Atlanta scored all its runs in the sixth inning. Murphy, who tied a record with six RBIs in the frame, became only the 14th player in history to hit two home runs in the same inning.

The last player to perform the feat was the Phillies' Hayes against the Mets in 1985.

Following is a list of players who had multi-homer games in '89 and the number of times:

AMERICAN LEAGUE: Baltimore (3) —Orsulak, Sheets, Tettleton. Boston (2)— Burks, Greenwell. California (4)—C. Davis 2, Schroeder, Washington. Chicago (2)—Baines, Pasqua. Cleveland (9)—Carter 6, Belle, Jacoby, Snyder. Detroit (3)— Heath 2, Lynn. Kansas City (3)—Jackson, Pecota, Stillwell. Milwaukee (7)—Deer 3, Braggs, Molitor, Vaughn, Yount. Minnesota (10)—Gaetti 3, Hrbek 3, Castillo 2, Bush, Laudner. New York (6)—Barfield 2, Mattingly 2, Balboni, Hall. Oakland (6) —McGwire 3, Canseco, Parker, Weiss. Seattle (7)—Briley 2, Griffey 2, Coles, Cotto, Leonard. Texas (3)—Incaviglia, Kunkel, Sierra. Toronto (5)—McGriff 4, Fernandez.

NATIONAL LEAGUE: Atlanta (6)— Evans 2, Murphy 2, Blauser, McDowell. Chicago (11)—Sandberg 5, Dawson 3, Dunston, Grace, Law. Cincinnati (6)— Davis 3, Griffey, O'Neill, Quinones. Houston (4)—Davis 2, Bass, Biggio. Los Angeles (3)—Murray 2, Hamilton. Montreal (3)—Fitzgerald 2, Da. Martinez. New York (4)—Strawberry 2, Jefferies, Johnson. Philadelphia (8)—V. Hayes 5, Jeltz, Jordan, Thon. Pittsburgh (3)—Bonds, Bonilla, Wilson. St. Louis (1)—Brunansky. San Diego (2)—Ja. Clark 2. San Francisco (8)—Mitchell 6, Maldonado, Williams.

A recap of the three-homer games:

Date	Player—Club—Opp.	Place	AB.	R.	H.	2B.	3B.	HR.	RBI.	Result
June 24	Carter, Indians vs. Rangers	Texas	4	3	3	0	0	3	3	W 7-3
July 19	Carter, Indians vs. Twins	Minnesota	3	3	3	0	0	3	6	W 10-1
Aug. 29	V. Hayes, Phillies vs. Giants	San Francisco	4	3	3	0	0	3	6	W 6-1

Blue Jays Belt 8 Grand Slams

By DAVE SLOAN

The Toronto Blue Jays have beaten the Boston Red Sox an amazing 15 straight times at Fenway Park. The Red Sox's frustration was punctuated in 1989 by a June 4 game in which catcher Ernie Whitt's ninth-inning grand slam keyed a Toronto rally that resulted in a 13-11 victory.

The Red Sox led that game, 10-0, after six innings and held a 10-7 lead with one out in the ninth when Whitt took a Lee Smith delivery over the right-field fence to give the Jays an 11-10 lead. Boston tied the game in the bottom of the ninth, but Toronto won in the 12th on Junior Felix's two-run homer.

Whitt's grand slam was one of 71 hit by major leaguers last season and one of 40 in the American League. The Blue Jays led all teams with eight, all coming from different players. The Houston Astros led the National League with six grand slams. Every team with the exception of Atlanta, Pittsburgh and St. Louis hit at least one.

Eight players hit two slams, including outfielder Chris James, who connected for both the Philadelphia Phillies and San Diego Padres. Other players to hit two slams were Houston's Kevin Bass, Cincinnati's Todd Benzinger, Boston's Dwight Evans, Seattle's Jeffrey Leonard, Oakland's Mark McGwire, Los Angeles' Mike Scioscia and San Francisco's Matt Williams.

No team had more than one player hit two grand slams last season, but two Detroit pitchers—Guillermo Hernandez and Charles Hudson—gave up two apiece. Not surprisingly, the Tigers led all teams with six slams allowed, a fate that befell every team except San Diego at least once.

Besides Hernandez and Hudson, pitchers allowing two slams last year were Los Angeles' Tim Belcher, Atlanta's Mark Eichhorn, Cincinnati's Danny Jackson and Toronto's Duane Ward. Veteran lefthander Frank Viola also gave up two, one as a member of the Minnesota Twins on April 14 and another on September 23 following his trade to the New York Mets.

Eddie Murray, whose 15 career grand slams are the most of any active player, hit his only 1989 slam on April 10 against the Giants. It was the 13-year veteran's first home run of the season and it came in only his sixth game as a member of the Los Angeles Dodgers.

The fastest slam of the year was hit

Chris James was the only player to hit a grand slam for two different teams last year.

June 24 at Kansas City. After the first three Yankees reached base against Royals starter Kevin Appier, cleanup hitter Mel Hall homered on the youngster's first pitch.

The most popular dates for grand slams in 1989 were May 2, June 4 and August 27. Three slams were hit on each of those days.

The complete list of grand slams, with the inning in which each was hit in parentheses, follows:

Oakland's Mark McGwire was one of eight major league players to hit two grand slams in 1989.

AMERICAN LEAGUE (40)

APRIL—
7 —Fernandez, Toronto vs. Witt, Texas .... (2)
8 —Calderon, Chicago vs. Honeycutt, Oakland .... (6)
11 —Castillo, Minnesota vs. Hernandez, Detroit .... (8)
14 —Balboni, New York vs. Viola, Minnesota.............. (5)
14 —Leonard, Seattle vs. Witt, California .... (3)
17 —Spiers, Milwaukee vs. Arnsberg, Texas .... (9)
26 —Surhoff, Milwaukee vs. Wayne, Minnesota .... (7)
28 —Esasky, Boston vs. Brown, Texas .... (1)

MAY—
2 —Mulliniks, Toronto vs. Welch, Oakland .... (1)
2 —McGwire, Oakland vs. Henke, Toronto .... (9)
2 —Leonard, Seattle vs. Hudson, Detroit .... (3)
19 —Evans, Boston vs. Eckersley, Oakland .... (10)
21 —Schroeder, California vs. Wegman, Milwaukee.. (3)
29 —Nokes, Detroit vs. King, Chicago .... (4)
31 —Gladden, Minnesota vs. Gordon, Kansas City ..... (6)

JUNE—
2 —Felix, Toronto vs. Stanley, Boston .... (9)
4 —Whitt, Toronto vs. Smith, Boston .... (9)
5 —Finley, Baltimore vs. Cary, New York .... (3)
9 —McGwire, Oakland vs. Hough, Texas .... (1)
10 —Dwyer, Minnesota vs. Thigpen, Chicago .... (8)
15 —Davis, Seattle vs. Shields, Minnesota .... (7)
17 —Evans, Boston vs. Perez, Chicago .... (3)
24 —Hall, New York vs. Appier, Kansas City .... (1)

JULY—
7 —Borders, Toronto vs. Hernandez, Detroit............. (8)
16 —Steinbach, Oakland vs. Ward, Toronto................ (7)
17 —Incaviglia, Texas vs. Gardner, Boston................. (1)
21 —McGriff, Toronto vs. Harris, Seattle .... (3)
22 —Moseby, Toronto vs. Powell, Seattle .... (9)
24 —Belle, Cleveland vs. Plunk, New York .... (7)
27 —Deer, Milwaukee vs. Hudson, Detroit.................. (6)

AUGUST—
5 —Coles, Seattle vs. Moore, Oakland .... (3)
19 —Eisenreich, Kansas City vs. Johnson, Seattle ...... (4)
27 —Burks, Boston vs. DuBois, Detroit .... (5)
27 —Karkovice, Chicago vs. Farrell, Cleveland.......... (3)

SEPTEMBER—
1 —Boston, Chicago vs. Milacki, Baltimore .... (1)
1 —Hill, Toronto vs. Guthrie, Minnesota................... (4)
6 —Parker, Oakland vs. Smithson, Boston .... (3)

9 —Lyons, Chicago vs. Williams, Detroit................... (8)
12 —Hrbek, Minnesota vs. Ward, Toronto................... (7)
27 —Jackson, Kansas City vs. Fraser, California .... (7)

NATIONAL LEAGUE (31)

APRIL—
9 —Williams, San Fran. vs. Jackson, Cincinnati....... (1)
10 —Murray, Los Angeles vs. LaCoss, San Francisco (9)
27 —Martinez, San Diego vs. Easley, Pittsburgh .... (8)
29 —James, Philadelphia vs. Jackson, Cincinnati...... (4)

MAY—
19 —Hamilton, Los Angeles vs. Gross, Montreal .... (7)
28 —Clark, San Francisco vs. Maddux, Philadelphia (4)

JUNE—
4 —Scioscia, Los Angeles vs. Forsch, Houston .... (1)
4 —Meadows, Houston vs. Belcher, Los Angeles........ (5)
7 —O'Neill, Cincinnati vs. Brantley, San Francisco . (2)
11 —Doran, Houston vs. Puleo, Atlanta .... (2)
27 —Benzinger, Cincinnati vs. Clary, Atlanta .... (7)

JULY—
18 —James, San Diego vs. Walk, Pittsburgh .... (5)
31 —Smith, Chicago vs. Harris, Philadelphia .... (7)

AUGUST—
8 —Scioscia, Los Angeles vs. Smoltz, Atlanta.............. (2)
11 —Williams, San Fran. vs. Belcher, Los Angeles..... (1)
18 —Benzinger, Cincinnati vs. Worrell, St. Louis .... (8)
20 —Bass, Houston vs. Williams, Chicago................... (9)
20 —Riles, San Fran. vs. McDowell, Philadelphia ...... (9)
27 —Galarraga, Montreal vs. Lefferts, San Fran........ (7)
29 —Ramirez, Houston vs. Wilkins, Chicago............... (5)
30 —McReynolds, New York vs. Crews, Los Angeles . (7)

SEPTEMBER—
3 —Santiago, San Diego vs. Parrett, Philadelphia..... (7)
4 —Ja. Clark, San Diego vs. Eichhorn, Atlanta......... (7)
5 —Wallach, Montreal vs. Hill, St. Louis .... (7)
11 —Templeton, San Diego vs. Darwin, Houston .... (6)
14 —Biggio, Houston vs. Wetteland, Los Angeles .... (2)
15 —Dunston, Chicago vs. Patterson, Pittsburgh .... (6)
17 —Kruk, Philadelphia vs. Kinzer, St. Louis.............. (12)
20 —Bass, Houston vs. Eichhorn, Atlanta................... (7)
21 —Fitzgerald, Montreal vs. Smiley, Pittsburgh....... (1)
23 —Brooks, Montreal vs. Viola, New York .... (3)

Boggs, Sax Set Multi-Hit Pace

By DAVE SLOAN

Although his 1989 season was shadowed by off-field controversy, Boston's Wade Boggs again proved that he's one of the game's best hitters. The Red Sox third baseman led the major leagues with a .430 on-base percentage, topped the American League with 51 doubles and ranked among the league leaders in runs scored (113), hits (205) and batting average (.330).

Boggs also shared the major league lead for multi-hit (four or more) games with New York Yankee second baseman Steve Sax. Two of Boggs' six multi-hit performances came in consecutive games against New York on June 8-10. He also had three doubles and a triple in a 10-0 Boston victory over Kansas City on July 25.

There were 254 multi-hit performances in 1989, 39 fewer than the year before. American League players produced 143 multi-hit games, National Leaguers 111. A total of 161 players, 86 in the A.L., 76 in the N.L. (Tracy Jones did it in each league), accomplished the feat at least once.

Every team had at least one multi-hit performance, with Boggs' Boston team leading the American League with 17. The Cincinnati Reds led all teams with 18, a major league-high 11 Reds players doing it at least once. Cincinnati outfielder Eric Davis had four multi-hit games, a National League-leading total he shared with Chicago's Ryne Sandberg and San Diego's Tony Gwynn.

Milwaukee's Paul Molitor and Texas' Ruben Sierra had five multi-hit games each to finish behind Boggs and Sax for A.L. individual honors.

Chicago's Andre Dawson had only two multi-hit games last season but they came in consecutive games May 4 and 5. The Cub outfielder hit safely in eight straight at-bats in games against the Padres and Los Angeles Dodgers.

Seventeen players had five hits in one game, a feat accomplished 10 times in the A.L. and seven times in the N.L. The Minnesota Twins (Gene Larkin and Dan Gladden), Rangers (Geno Petralli and Cecil Espy) and Philadelphia Phillies (Ricky Jordan and Darren Daulton) all had two players with five-hit performances. Only four times did the team of the player with five hits lose.

Four players hit for the cycle (a single, double, triple and homer in the same game) last season. Toronto's Kelly Gruber did it April 16 against Kansas City; Cincinnati's Davis did it June 2 against San Diego; the New York Mets' Kevin McReynolds did it August 1 against St. Louis, and Pittsburgh's Gary Redus did it August 25 against Cincinnati. Each performance came in a winning effort—the Blue Jays won 15-8, the Reds 9-4, the Mets 11-0 and the Pirates 12-3.

Twenty-four players compiled hitting streaks of 15 or more games—17 in the American League and seven in the National. The season's longest streak belonged to Cubs rookie Jerome Walton, who hit safely in 30 consecutive games between July 21 and August 20.

Besides Walton, the following players compiled hitting streaks of 15 or more games: 23 games—Jose Oquendo, Cardinals; 22 games—George Bell, Blue Jays; 21 games—Mike Greenwell, Red Sox; 19 games—Carney Lansford, Athletics; Paul Molitor, Brewers; Robin Yount, Brewers; 18 games—Ozzie Guillen, White Sox; Luis Quinones, Reds; 17 games—Roberto Alomar, Padres; Don Mattingly, Yankees; Steve Sax, Yankees; 16 games—Phil Bradley, Orioles; Tony Fernandez, Blue Jays; Harold Reynolds, Mariners; Jeff Treadway, Braves; 15 games—Ellis Burks, Red Sox; Kelly Gruber, Blue Jays; Barry Larkin, Reds; Johnny Ray, Angels; Jim Rice, Red Sox; Kevin Seitzer, Royals; Terry Steinbach, Athletics; Milt Thompson, Cardinals.

The complete list of players with four or more hits in one game follows:

AMERICAN LEAGUE: Baltimore (7) —Bradley 2, Devereaux, Hulett, Milligan, B. Ripken, C. Ripken. Boston (17)—Boggs 6, Reed 3, Esasky 2, Greenwell 2, Barrett, Evans, Rivera, Romine. California (7)— Parrish 3, Downing, Joyner, Venable, Washington. Chicago (8)—Fisk 2, Guillen 2, Baines, Calderon, Gallagher, Kittle. Cleveland (14)—Browne 2, Clark 2, James 2, O'Brien 2, Snyder 2, Carter, Jacoby, Skinner, Zuvella. Detroit (11)— Heath 2, Nokes 2, Pettis 2, Trammell 2, Jones, Lynn, Moreland. Kansas City (4)— Boone, Brett, Seitzer, Wilson. Milwaukee (8)—Molitor 5, Francona, Surhoff, Yount. Minnesota (13)—Gagne 3, Gladden 2, Larkin 2, Puckett 2, Dwyer, Gaetti, Harper, Hrbek. New York (16)—Sax 6, Mattingly 4, Kelly 2, Hall, Phelps, Polonia, Slaught. Oakland (6)—Lansford 3, Canse-

The Red Sox's Wade Boggs (left) and the Yankees' Steve Sax tied for individual honors with six multi-hit games in 1989.

co, Polonia, Steinbach. Seattle (3)—Griffey, Reynolds, Valle. Texas (14)—Sierra 5, Espy 3, Palmeiro 2, Baines, Incaviglia, Petralli, Sosa. Toronto (15)—Felix 3, Gruber 3, Whitt 2, Wilson 2, Barfield, Bell, Lee, Liriano, McGriff.

NATIONAL LEAGUE: Atlanta (10)— Blauser 2, McDowell 2, Murphy 2, Gregg, Perry, L. Smith, Thomas. Chicago (16)— Sandberg 4, Dawson 2, D. Smith 2, Walton 2, Berryhill, Dunston, Grace, Salazar, Webster, Wilkerson. Cincinnati (18)— Davis 4, Benzinger 3, Oliver 2, Reed 2, Larkin, Oester, O'Neill, Roomes, Sabo, Winningham, Youngblood. Houston (7)— Ramirez 2, Bass, Davis, Doran, Trevino, Young. Los Angeles (9)—Griffin 2, Harris 2, Gibson, Hamilton, Murray, Randolph, Shelby. Montreal (8)—Brooks 2, Foley 2, Garcia, Grissom, Raines, Wallach. New York (7)—Jefferies 2, Johnson 2, Carter, McReynolds, Teufel. Philadelphia (7)— Herr 2, Kruk 2, Daulton, Jeltz, Jordan. Pittsburgh (5)—Bonilla 2, Bonds, Redus, Van Slyke. St. Louis (9)—Pendleton 3, Smith 2, Guerrero, Oquendo, Pena, Thompson. San Diego (12)—Gwynn 4, R. Alomar 2, Ja. Clark 2, Santiago 2, James, Roberts. San Francisco (3)—Clark, Jones, Mitchell.

The records of all players with five hits in a game follows:

Date	Player—Club—Opp.	Place	AB.	R.	H.	2B.	3B.	HR.	RBI.	Result
April 18	Gregg, Braves vs. Astros (11 innings)	H	5	1	5	2	0	0	2	W 5-4
April 23	Clark, Giants vs. Dodgers (10 innings)	A	5	3	5	1	0	1	3	L 6-7
May 1	Reed, Reds vs. Expos	A	6	3	5	1	0	1	3	W 19-6
June 11	Smith, Cardinals vs. Cubs	A	6	2	5	2	0	0	2	W 10-7
June 12	Gruber, Blue Jays vs. Tigers (11 innings)	H	6	0	5	1	0	0	3	W 5-4
June 12	Heath, Tigers vs. Blue Jays (11 innings)	A	6	0	5	0	0	0	2	L 4-5
June 21	Petralli, Rangers vs. Red Sox	A	5	1	5	1	0	0	2	W 10-3
June 27	Sax, Yankees vs. Tigers	A	5	1	5	1	0	1	1	L 5-6
July 2	Romine, Red Sox vs. Blue Jays (11 inn.)	A	5	2	5	2	0	0	0	W 4-1
July 9	Bradley, Orioles vs. Brewers	A	5	0	5	1	0	0	1	L 2-7
July 13	Espy, Rangers vs. Indians (11 innings)	A	6	1	5	0	0	0	3	W 9-3
July 18	Larkin, Twins vs. Indians	H	5	2	5	0	0	0	1	W 5-4
July 19	Jordan, Phillies vs. Reds	A	5	3	5	1	0	1	3	W 9-4
Aug. 23	Harris, Dodgers vs. Expos (22 innings)	A	9	0	5	0	0	0	0	W 1-0
Sept. 9	Molitor, Brewers vs. Mariners	A	5	0	5	0	0	0	1	W 7-3
Sept. 20	Daulton, Phillies vs. Cubs	A	5	0	5	1	0	0	0	W 9-8
Sept. 29	Gladden, Twins vs. Mariners (11 innings)	A	5	0	5	0	0	1	1	W 10-7

Cubs' Smith Excelled in Pinch

Rookie Dwight Smith of the Chicago Cubs hit safely in eight of his 15 pinch at-bats last season.

By DAVE SLOAN

While teammate Jerome Walton was garnering the bulk of the headlines en route to National League Rookie of the Year honors, Cubs outfielder Dwight Smith was enjoying a fine rookie season of his own in 1989.

Smith, whose overall .324 average was the highest for a Cubs rookie since 1922, compiled the best pinch-hitting average in the majors last year among those players with 10 or more pinch at-bats. Smith was 8 for 15 (.533) as a pinch-hitter in '89, the only player to finish the year with an average above .500.

Veteran infielder Ken Oberkfell, who played for both Pittsburgh and San Francisco, led all players with 18 pinch-hits. All 18 of Oberkfell's hits came as a Giant, helping San Francisco lead all clubs with 72.

The Chicago White Sox compiled the highest average among all teams (.282), but the New York Mets, who paced the N.L. with a .255 team mark, drove in more runs (39) with pinch-hits than any other club. Mets rookie Mark Carreon led all players with four pinch-hit home runs, the highest major league total since Danny Heep hit four for the Mets in 1983.

The American League home run leader was Ken Phelps, whose three homers, 13 RBIs and 11 hits all represented league highs. Phelps hit his three pinch homers with the Yankees before he was traded to the Oakland Athletics on August 30. Ironically, the only other player to hit three pinch homers in 1989—infielder Luis Salazar—hit all of them with San Diego before he, too, was traded August 30—to the Chicago Cubs.

Six other players hit two pinch homers last year, including Lee Mazzilli and Oddibe McDowell. Both hit their pinch-hit homers for two different teams. Mazzilli hit round-trippers for the Mets and Blue Jays while McDowell did it for the Indians and Braves.

The Cubs' Smith and Minnesota's Carmen Castillo were the only players to hit pinch grand slams last year.

Following is a list of all pinch-hitters with at least 10 at-bats in 1989:

NATIONAL LEAGUE PINCH-HITTING

Club Pinch-Hitting

Club	AB.	H.	HR.	RBI.	Pct.	Club	AB.	H.	HR.	RBI.	Pct.
New York	200	51	5	39	.255	Cincinnati	275	58	5	25	.211
Chicago	201	50	2	23	.249	Philadelphia	286	57	3	30	.199
San Francisco	300	72	2	37	.240	Atlanta	256	50	5	20	.195
Los Angeles	255	60	3	38	.235	St. Louis	192	37	0	25	.193
San Diego	173	38	5	26	.220	Houston	233	43	1	22	.185
Montreal	251	54	4	36	.215	Totals	2879	625	36	354	.217
Pittsburgh	257	55	1	33	.214						

Individual Pinch-Hitting
(10 or More At-Bats)

Player—Club	AB.	H.	HR.	RBI.	Pct.	Player—Club	AB.	H.	HR.	RBI.	Pct.
Smith, Chi.	15	8	1	8	.533	Murphy, Phil.	43	9	2	8	.209
Ramos, Chi.	14	6	0	2	.429	Dempsey, L.A.	24	5	0	2	.208
Harris, Cin.-L.A.	20	8	0	4	.400	Jones, St.L.	10	2	0	0	.200
Jordan, Phil.	10	4	0	3	.400	King, Pitt.	15	3	0	2	.200
Larkin, Cin.	10	4	0	4	.400	Mazzilli, N.Y.	25	5	1	5	.200
Salazar, S.D.-Chi.	15	6	3	6	.400	McGee, St.L.	10	2	0	2	.200
Wilkerson, Chi.	28	11	0	0	.393	Nixon, S.F.	25	5	0	1	.200
Duncan, L.A.-Cin.	18	7	0	3	.389	Sharperson, L.A.	15	3	0	3	.200
Carreon, N.Y.	27	10	4	6	.370	Griffey, Cin.	42	8	1	5	.190
Roomes, Cin.	11	4	0	1	.364	Davis, L.A.	16	3	0	1	.188
Oberkfell, Pitt.-S.F.	50	18	1	8	.360	James, Atl.	16	3	0	2	.188
Gonzalez, L.A.	14	5	0	0	.357	Gross, Hou.	38	7	0	2	.184
Roberts, S.D.	17	6	0	0	.353	Collins, Cin.	55	10	0	2	.182
Walling, St.L.	32	11	0	6	.344	Daulton, Phil.	11	2	0	3	.182
Hatcher, Hou.-Pitt.	15	5	0	4	.333	Laga, S.F.	11	2	0	4	.182
Litton, S.F.	27	9	1	6	.333	Wilson, N.Y.	22	4	0	3	.182
McClendon, Chi.	16	5	1	1	.313	Ford, Phil.	62	11	0	3	.177
Aldrete, Mon.	26	8	0	10	.308	Cangelosi, Pitt.	68	12	0	2	.176
Dwyer, Mon.	10	3	0	2	.300	Hatcher, L.A.	34	6	0	10	.176
Fitzgerald, Mon.	10	3	0	1	.300	Blocker, Atl.	18	3	0	0	.167
Speier, S.F.	10	3	0	2	.300	Davidson, Hou.	12	2	0	2	.167
Sasser, N.Y.	17	5	0	6	.294	Foley, Mon.	12	2	1	1	.167
Reynolds, Pitt.	31	9	0	5	.290	Evans, Atl.	31	5	0	1	.161
Kennedy, S.F.	11	3	0	5	.273	Anderson, L.A.	25	4	0	1	.160
D. Martinez, Mon.	11	3	0	0	.273	Garcia, Mon.	26	4	1	1	.154
Treadway, Atl.	11	3	0	0	.273	Jeltz, Phil.	13	2	0	2	.154
Distefano, Pitt.	48	13	0	7	.271	Hudler, Mon.	27	4	2	4	.148
Puhl, Hou.	15	4	0	0	.267	Stephenson, Chi.-S.D.	14	2	0	0	.143
Wilson, Pitt.-Hou.	15	4	0	6	.267	Varsho, Chi.	36	5	0	2	.139
Flannery, S.D.	35	9	0	3	.257	Reynolds, Hou.	37	5	1	5	.135
Redus, Pitt.	12	3	0	1	.250	Pagnozzi, St.L.	15	2	0	2	.133
Teufel, N.Y.	12	3	0	0	.250	Webster, Chi.	30	4	0	4	.133
Yelding, Hou.	16	4	0	0	.250	Hernandez, N.Y.	17	2	0	2	.118
Winningham, Cin.	29	7	1	2	.241	Wynne, S.D.-Chi.	17	2	0	1	.118
Johnson, Mon.	59	14	0	8	.237	Meadows, Hou.	20	2	0	2	.100
Riles, S.F.	38	9	0	2	.237	Thompson, St.L.	10	1	0	0	.100
Berroa, Atl.	47	11	0	4	.234	Van Slyke, Pitt.	10	1	0	2	.100
Maldonado, S.F.	30	7	0	4	.233	Dernier, Phil.	41	4	0	1	.098
Bathe, S.F.	26	6	0	4	.231	Nixon, Mon.	21	2	0	0	.095
Stubbs, L.A.	26	6	1	3	.231	Durham, St.L.	11	1	0	1	.091
Jurak, S.F.	18	4	0	0	.222	Nelson, S.D.	11	1	0	0	.091
Wetherby, Atl.	36	8	1	6	.222	Lindeman, St.L.	26	2	0	2	.077
Morris, St.L.	41	9	0	6	.220	Ortiz, Pitt.	13	1	0	2	.077
Martinez, S.D.	32	7	1	9	.219	Jackson, Chi.-S.D.	14	1	0	1	.071
Magadan, N.Y.	23	5	0	5	.217	Madison, St.L.	16	1	0	1	.063
Gregg, Atl.	28	6	2	5	.214	Russell, Atl.	17	1	0	0	.059
Gwynn, L.A.	14	3	0	3	.214	Trevino, Hou.	21	1	0	1	.048
Ready, S.D.-Phil.	28	6	1	3	.214	Law, Chi.	10	0	0	0	.000
Ryal, Phil.	19	4	0	2	.211	Shelby, L.A.	11	0	0	0	.000
Spilman, Hou.	19	4	0	1	.211	Sheridan, S.F.	11	0	0	0	.000
Youngblood, Cin.	38	8	1	3	.211						

PINCH-HOMERS FOR 1989

NATIONAL LEAGUE: Atlanta (5)—Gregg 2, Lemke, McDowell, Wetherby. Chicago (2)—McClendon, Smith. Cincinnati (5)—Davis, Griffey, Richardson, Winningham, Youngblood. Houston (1)—Reynolds. Los Angeles (3)—Fletcher, Murray, Stubbs. Montreal (4)—Hudler 2, Foley, Garcia. New York (5)—Carreon 4, Mazzilli. Philadelphia (3)—Murphy 2, Ready. Pittsburgh (1)—Bonds. San Diego (5)—Salazar 3, Martinez, Parent. San Francisco (2)—Litton, Oberkfell.

AMERICAN LEAGUE: Baltimore (2)—Orsulak, Traber. Boston (3)—Greenwell, Heep, Reed. California (1)—Washington. Chicago (1)—Boston. Cleveland (4)—Clark 2, McDowell, Young. Kansas City (2)—Eisenreich, Tabler. Milwaukee (1)—Meyer. Minnesota (2)—Castillo, Hrbek. New York (3)—Phelps 3. Oakland (1)—Steinbach. Seattle (3)—Cotto, Griffey, Presley. Texas (3)—Bosley, Incaviglia, Petralli. Toronto (3)—Gruber, Liriano, Mazzilli.

Ken Phelps hit three pinch homers for the Yankees prior to his trade to the Athletics.

AMERICAN LEAGUE PINCH-HITTING

Club Pinch-Hitting

Club	AB.	H.	HR.	RBI.	Pct.	Club	AB.	H.	HR.	RBI.	Pct.
Chicago	85	24	1	11	.282	Kansas City	102	23	2	14	.225
Milwaukee	45	12	1	5	.267	Baltimore	118	25	2	17	.212
Boston	92	24	3	22	.261	California	63	13	1	9	.206
Toronto	121	32	3	13	.264	Oakland	102	21	1	12	.206
Seattle	127	33	3	20	.260	Cleveland	131	24	4	15	.183
Texas	184	45	3	30	.245	Detroit	180	28	0	26	.156
Minnesota	170	39	2	29	.229	Totals	1674	378	29	251	.226
New York	154	35	3	28	.227						

Individual Pinch-Hitting
(10 or More At-Bats)

Player—Club	AB.	H.	HR.	RBI.	Pct.	Player—Club	AB.	H.	HR.	RBI.	Pct.
Espy, Tex.	13	6	0	0	.462	Clark, Clev.	29	7	2	4	.241
Laudner, Minn.	11	5	0	2	.455	Balboni, N.Y.	25	6	0	2	.240
Brenly, Tor.	14	6	0	2	.429	Young, Clev.	21	5	1	4	.238
Polonia, Oak.-N.Y.	14	6	0	1	.429	Horn, Bos.	17	4	0	3	.235
Orsulak, Balt.	15	6	1	6	.400	Moreland, Det.-Balt.	17	4	0	2	.235
Daugherty, Tex.	18	7	0	2	.389	Heep, Bos.	20	4	1	6	.200
Cotto, Sea.	19	7	1	4	.368	Leach, Tex.	30	6	0	6	.200
Bradley, Sea.	25	9	0	5	.360	Schu, Balt.-Det.	10	2	0	4	.200
Lyons, Chi.	14	5	0	1	.357	Hassey, Oak.	16	3	0	1	.188
Sheets, Balt.	18	6	0	2	.333	Traber, Balt.	16	3	1	5	.188
Lemon, Det.	13	4	0	5	.308	Ward, N.Y.-Det.	32	6	0	4	.188
Phillips, Oak.	10	3	0	1	.300	Whitt, Tor.	16	3	0	2	.188
Cochrane, Sea.	17	5	0	2	.294	Milligan, Balt.	11	2	0	0	.182
Phelps, N.Y.-Oak.	38	11	3	13	.289	Lynn, Det.	17	3	0	3	.176
Castillo, Minn.	29	8	1	7	.276	James, Clev.	12	2	0	3	.167
Briley, Sea.	11	3	0	1	.273	Macfarlane, K.C.	12	2	0	2	.167
Brookens, N.Y.	11	3	0	1	.273	Mulliniks, Tor.	18	3	0	1	.167
Heath, Det.	11	3	0	0	.273	Tabler, K.C.	13	2	1	4	.154
Larkin, Minn.	11	3	0	4	.273	K. Williams, Det.	10	1	0	0	.100
Moses, Minn.	30	8	0	5	.267	Nokes, Det.	11	1	0	1	.091
Petralli, Tex.	15	4	1	4	.267	Quirk, NY-Oak-Balt.	11	1	0	0	.091
Buckner, K.C.	38	10	0	4	.263	Stone, Tex.-Bos.	12	1	0	0	.083
Dwyer, Minn.	19	5	0	2	.263	Lee, Tor.	13	1	0	0	.077
Stanley, Tex.	23	6	0	0	.261	Bergman, Det.	18	1	0	1	.056
Borders, Tor.	20	5	0	2	.250	Bush, Minn.	18	1	0	0	.056
Bosley, Tex.	28	7	1	9	.250	Devereaux, Balt.	14	0	0	1	.000
Boston, Chi.	16	4	1	3	.250	Salas, Clev.	11	0	0	0	.000
Hall, N.Y.	16	4	0	2	.250	Tolleson, N.Y.	10	0	0	0	.000
Slaught, N.Y.	12	3	0	4	.250						

Abbott Debut an Inspiring One

By DAVE SLOAN

One hundred and fifty players made their first appearances as major leaguers in 1989, but no debut was anticipated as much or scrutinized more closely than that of California pitcher Jim Abbott.

Abbott, a member of the 1988 Gold Medal-winning U.S. Olympic team, was inserted into the Angels' starting rotation in late March by Manager Doug Rader—an unusual promotion for a player who had never played professional baseball. But what made Abbott so newsworthy was the fact that he was born without a right hand. It was a handicap that many believed he would not be able to overcome on the big-league level.

But not the Angels. They selected the 21-year-old former University of Michigan star with the eighth pick in the first round of the 1988 free-agent draft. And although Abbott's '89 spring-training stats were not that impressive—24 hits and 10 runs in 17 innings—Rader announced in the final week of camp that Abbott would open the season in the team's starting rotation.

Marcel Lachemann, the Angels' pitching coach, convinced Rader that the rookie could handle a starting job after the manager saw the pitcher rocked in his only spring-training start (six hits and two runs in four innings against San Diego). Rader believed that putting Abbott in the bullpen would help him cope better with what figured to be a media onslaught.

But Abbott handled the media better than he did the Seattle Mariners in his April 8 debut. Seattle's first two batters, Harold Reynolds and Henry Cotto, both singled. After Abbott threw a wild pitch, both runners scored.

Abbott allowed six hits, six runs and walked three without striking out a batter before being lifted by Rader with two out in the fifth inning. He finished the season with a 12-12 record and 3.92 earned-run average in 29 games, all starts. Abbott's 12 victories shattered the previous record of wins by a pitcher (six) going straight from the amateur draft to the major leagues.

Another player to make a huge leap into the major leagues was Jerome Walton of the Chicago Cubs, who nailed down the club's center-field job in spring training and proceeded to help the Cubs win the National League East Division crown. Walton, who won a Class AA batting title

at Pittsfield (Eastern) in 1988, had never played a game at the Triple-A level before opening the '89 season with Chicago.

Walton's April 4 debut against the Phillies was a preview of things to come. Filling the Cubs' dire need for a leadoff man, he singled twice in four at-bats and drove in one run in a 5-4 Chicago victory. Despite missing nearly a month because of a hamstring injury, Walton finished the season with a .293 average, 64 runs scored and 24 stolen bases. He was an easy choice for N.L. Rookie of the Year.

Abbott and Walton were just two of the 150 players to debut last season, 90 in the American League and 60 in the National. Non-pitchers accounted for 80 of the debuts and pitchers for 70. Five players—including Walton—debuted in their club's season-opening game.

Outfielder Ken Griffey Jr. debuted with the Mariners in their 3-2 opening-day loss to Oakland on April 3. The debut was historic because, at the same time, Griffey's father, Ken Sr., was beginning his 17th major league season with the Cincinnati Reds. It marked the first time in baseball history that a father-son duo had played in the major leagues at the same time.

The younger Griffey had one double in three at-bats and scored once in his debut game. The 19-year-old played well in the following 3½ months and was the odds-on favorite for the A.L. Rookie of the Year award before suffering a broken hand in late July. The injury put the youngster on the disabled list for a month. Griffey, who was batting .287 with 13 home runs and 45 runs batted in at the time of the injury, finished the '89 season with a .264 average, 16 homers and 61 RBIs.

Another debut that created headlines came on May 31 when the Yankees called up outfielder Deion Sanders from their Class AAA affiliate in Columbus (International) and started him in center field in that night's game against Seattle. Sanders singled once in four at-bats in a 9-5 New York victory.

An All-America cornerback at Florida State and the 1989 No. 1 draft choice of the National Football League's Atlanta Falcons, Sanders was hoping to follow in Bo Jackson's footsteps as a two-sport standout. However, the Yankees sent Sanders back to Columbus after just nine games and, although he was later recalled for the final month of the season, Sanders finished the '89 campaign with only 11 hits in 14 games and a .234 batting average.

As usual, California led all 50 states in the number of players making debuts, with 25 players hailing from the nation's most populous state. Texas (12), Florida (eight) and Louisiana (seven) also ranked high. Thirteen states, however, did not produce a single player.

Six foreign countries produced at least one major league player in 1989, with the Dominican Republic (eight) leading the way.

An alphabetical list of the players who made their debuts in '89 follows:

Player	Pos.	Club	Date and Place of Birth	Debut
Abbott, James Anthony	P	California	9-19-67—Flint, Mich.	4- 8
Allred, Dale LeBeau	PH-OF	Cleveland	6- 4-65—Mesa, Ariz.	9- 7
Alvarez, Wilson E.	P	Texas	3-24-70—Maracaibo, Venez.	7-24
Anderson, Kent McKay	SS	California	8-12-63—Florence, S.C.	4-15
Anthony, Eric Todd	OF	Houston	11- 8-67—San Diego, Calif.	7-28
Appier, Robert Kevin	P	Kansas City	12- 6-67—Lancaster, Calif.	6- 4
Arndt, Larry Wayne	3B	Oakland	2-25-63—Fremont, O.	6- 6
Barfield, John David	P	Texas	10-15-64—Little Rock, Ark.	9- 7
Bates, William Derrick	2B	Milwaukee	12- 7-63—Houston, Tex.	8-17
Batiste, Kevin Wade	PR	Toronto	10-21-66—Galveston, Tex.	6-13
Beatty, Gordon Blaine	P	New York N.L.	4-25-64—Victoria, Tex.	9-16
Belinda, Stanley Peter	P	Pittsburgh	8- 6-66—Huntingdon, Pa.	9- 8
Bell, Juan	2B	Baltimore	3-29-68—S.P. de Macoris, D.R.	9- 6
Belle, Albert Jojuan	OF	Cleveland	8-25-66—Shreveport, La.	7-15
Benes, Andrew Charles	P	San Diego	8-20-67—Evansville, Ind.	8-11
Benjamin, Michael Paul	PR	San Francisco	11-22-65—Euclid, O.	7- 7
Berroa, Geronimo Emiliano	OF	Atlanta	3-18-65—Santo Domingo, D.R.	4- 5
Blowers, Michael Roy	PH-3B	New York A.L.	4-24-65—Wurzburg, W. Germany	9- 1
Brady, Brian Phelan	PH-OF	California	7-11-62—Queens, N.Y.	4-16
Cabrera, Francisco	DH	Toronto	10-10-66—Santo Domingo, D.R.	7-24
Canale, George Anthony	PR	Milwaukee	8-11-65—Memphis, Tenn.	9- 3
Cano, Joselito Soriano	P	Houston	3- 7-62—Boca Del Soco, D.R.	8-28
Carter, Steven Jerome	PH	Pittsburgh	12- 3-64—Charlottesville, Va.	4-16
Combs, Patrick Dennis	P	Philadelphia	10-29-66—Newport, R.I.	9- 5
Coolbaugh, Scott Robert	3B	Texas	6-13-66—Binghamton, N.Y.	9- 2
Cummings, Steven Brent	P	Toronto	7-15-66—Houston, Tex.	6-24
Dalena, Peter Martin	PH	Cleveland	6-26-60—Fresno, Calif.	7- 7
Datz, Jeffrey William	C	Detroit	11-28-59—Camden, N.J.	9- 5
Davidson, Robert Banks	P	New York A.L.	1- 6-63—Bad Kurznach, W. Ger.	7-15
Denson, Andrew, Jr.	1B	Atlanta	11-16-65—Cincinnati, O.	9-13
Disarcina, Gary Thomas	SS	California	11-19-67—Malden, Mass.	9-23
DuBois, Brian Andrew	P	Detroit	4-18-67—Joliet, Ill.	8-17
Dyer, Michael Lawrence	P	Minnesota	9- 8-66—Upland, Calif.	6-29
Edwards, Wayne Maurice	P	Chicago A.L.	3- 7-64—Burbank, Calif.	9-11
Felix, Junior Francisco	OF	Toronto	10- 3-67—Laguna Sabada, D.R.	5- 3
Fetters, Michael Lee	P	California	12-19-64—Van Nuys, Calif.	9- 1
Finley, Steven Allen	OF	Baltimore	5-12-65—Union City, Tenn.	4- 3
Fletcher, Darrin Glen	C	Los Angeles	10- 3-66—Elmhurst, Ill.	9-10
Freeman, LaVel Maurice	DH	Milwaukee	2-18-63—Oakland, Calif.	4- 7
Frey, Steven Francis	P	Montreal	7-29-63—Meadowbrook, Pa.	5-10
Gardner, Mark Allan	P	Montreal	3- 1-62—Los Angeles, Calif.	5-16
Girardi, Joseph Elliott	C	Chicago N.L.	10-14-64—Peoria, Ill.	4- 4
Gonzalez, Juan Alberto	OF	Texas	10-16-69—Vega Baja, P.R.	9- 1
Gozzo, Mauro Paul	P	Toronto	3- 7-66—New Britain, Conn.	8- 8
Greene, Ira Thomas	P	Atlanta	4- 6-67—Lumberton, N.C.	9-10
Griffey, George Kenneth, Jr.	OF	Seattle	11-21-69—Charleroi, Pa.	4- 3
Grimsley, Jason Alan	P	Philadelphia	8- 7-67—Cleveland, Tex.	9- 8
Grissom, Marquis Dean	OF	Montreal	4-17-67—Atlanta, Ga.	8-22
Guthrie, Mark Andrew	P	Minnesota	9-22-65—Buffalo, N.Y.	7-25
Hale, Walter William	2B	Minnesota	12- 2-64—Santa Clara, Calif.	8-27
Hardy, John Graydon	P	Chicago A.L.	10- 8-59—St. Petersburg, Fla.	5-23
Harris, Tyrone Eugene	P	Montreal	12- 5-64—Sebring, Fla.	4- 5
Hartley, Michael Edward	P	Los Angeles	8-31-61—Hawthorne, Calif.	9-10
Hemond, Scott Mathew	PR	Oakland	11-18-65—Taunton, Mass.	9- 9
Hernandez, Francis Xavier	P	Toronto	8-16-65—Port Arthur, Tex.	6- 4
Hetzel, Eric Paul	P	Boston	9-25-63—Crowley, La.	7- 1
Hibbard, James Gregory	P	Chicago A.L.	9-13-64—New Orleans, La.	5-31
Higgins, Mark Douglas	1B	Cleveland	7- 9-63—Miami, Fla.	9- 7
Hill, Glenallen	OF	Toronto	3-22-65—Santa Cruz, Calif.	7-31
Hoiles, Christopher Allen	PH	Baltimore	3-20-65—Bowling Green, O.	4-25
Holman, Shawn LeRoy	P	Detroit	11-10-64—Sewickley, Pa.	9- 5
Howitt, Dann Paul	PH	Oakland	2-13-64—Battle Creek, Mich.	9-15
Huff, Michael Kale	PH	Los Angeles	8-11-63—Honolulu, Haw.	8- 7
Jorgensen, Terry Allen	3B	Minnesota	9- 2-66—Kewaunee, Wis.	9-10
Justice, David Christopher	OF	Atlanta	4-14-66—Cincinnati, O.	5-24
King, Jeffrey Wayne	PH-1B	Pittsburgh	12-26-64—Marion, Ind.	6- 2
Kinzer, Matthew Roy	P	St. Louis	6-17-63—Indianapolis, Ind.	5-18
Kraemer, Joseph Wayne	P	Chicago N.L.	9-10-64—Olympia, Wash.	8-22
Lawton, Marcus Dwayne	PH-OF	New York A.L.	8-18-65—Gulfport, Miss.	8-11
Lilliquist, Derek Jansen	P	Atlanta	2-20-66—Winter Park, Fla.	4-13

Player	Pos.	Club	Date and Place of Birth	Debut
Little, Dennis Scott	PH	Pittsburgh	1-19-63—East St. Louis, Ill.	7-27
Litton, Jon Gregory	2B	San Francisco	7-13-64—New Orleans, La.	5- 2
Luecken, Richard Fred	P	Kansas City	11-15-60—McAllen, Tex.	6- 6
Machado, Julio S.	P	New York N.L.	12- 1-65—Zulia, Venezuela	9- 7
Magrann, Thomas Joseph	C	Cleveland	12- 9-63—Hollywood, Fla.	9- 7
Mann, Kelly John	C	Atlanta	8-17-67—Santa Monica, Calif.	9- 4
McCament, Larry Randall	P	San Francisco	7-29-62—Albuquerque, N.M.	6-28
McDonald, Larry Benard	P	Baltimore	11-24-67—Baton Rouge, La.	9- 6
McElroy, Charles Dwayne	P	Philadelphia	10- 1-67—Galveston, Tex.	9- 4
McKnight, Jefferson Alan	PH	New York N.L.	2-18-63—Conway, Ark.	6- 6
Mercker, Kent Franklin	P	Atlanta	2- 1-68—Dublin, O.	9-22
Merullo, Matthew Bates	C	Chicago A.L.	8- 4-65—Winchester, Mass.	4-12
Meulens, Hensley Filemon	3B	New York A.L.	6-23-67—Curacao, Neth. Ant.	8-23
Mmahat, Kevin Paul	P	New York A.L.	11- 9-64—Memphis, Tenn.	9- 9
Munoz, Michael Anthony	P	Los Angeles	7-12-65—Baldwin Park, Calif.	9- 6
Murphy, Daniel Lee	P	San Diego	9-18-64—Artesia, Calif.	8-10
Navarro, Jaime	P	Milwaukee	3-27-67—Bayamon, P.R.	6-20
Nosek, Randall William	P	Detroit	1- 8-67—Omaha, Neb.	5-27
Olerud, John Garrett	1B	Toronto	8- 5-68—Bellevue, Wash.	9- 3
Olin, Steven Robert	P	Cleveland	10-10-65—Portland, Ore.	7-29
Oliver, Joseph Melton	C	Cincinnati	7-24-65—Memphis, Tenn.	7-15
Oliveras, Francisco Javier	P	Minnesota	1-31-63—Santurce, P.R.	5- 3
Olson, Gregory William	C	Minnesota	9- 6-60—Marshall, Minn.	6-27
Orton, John Andrew	C	California	12- 8-65—Santa Cruz, Calif.	8-20
Palmer, Dean William	PR-DH	Texas	12-27-68—Tallahassee, Fla.	9- 1
Pena, Ramon Arturo	P	Detroit	5- 5-62—Santiago, D.R.	4-27
Peterek, Jeffrey Allen	P	Milwaukee	9-22-63—Michigan City, Ind.	8-14
Pevey, Marty A.	C	Montreal	9-18-61—Statesboro, Ga.	5-16
Richards, Russell Earl	P	Atlanta	1-27-65—Houston, Tex.	9-20
Richardson, Jeffrey Scott	SS	Cincinnati	8-26-65—Grand Island, Neb.	7-14
Richie, Robert Eugene	OF	Detroit	9- 5-65—Reno, Nev.	8-19
Ritz, Kevin D.	P	Detroit	6- 8-65—Eatonstown, N.J.	7-15
Rodriguez, Rosario	P	Cincinnati	7- 8-69—Los Mochis, Mex.	9- 1
Roesler, Michael Joseph	P	Cincinnati	9-12-63—Fort Wayne, Ind.	8- 9
Rogers, Kenneth Scott	P	Texas	11-10-64—Savannah, Ga.	4- 6
Rose, Robert Richard	PH	California	3-15-67—Covina, Calif.	8-12
Sanchez, Alex Anthony	P	Toronto	4- 8-66—Antioch, Calif.	5-23
Sanders, Deion Luwynn	OF	New York A.L.	8- 9-67—Fort Myers, Fla.	5-31
Schaefer, Jeffrey Scott	2B	Chicago A.L.	5-31-60—Patchogue, N.Y.	4- 7
Schulz, Jeffrey Alan	PH	Kansas City	6- 2-61—Evansville, Ind.	9- 2
Schwabe, Michael Scott	P	Detroit	7-12-64—Fort Dodge, Ia.	5-27
Scott, Richard Edward	SS	Oakland	7-19-62—Ellsworth, Me.	5-19
Scudder, William Scott	P	Cincinnati	2-14-68—Paris, Tex.	6- 6
Seanez, Rudy Caballero	P	Cleveland	10-20-68—Brawley, Calif.	9- 7
Skalski, Joseph Douglas	P	Cleveland	9-26-64—Chicago, Ill.	4-10
Smith, Gregory Allen	2B	Chicago N.L.	4- 5-67—Baltimore, Md.	9- 2
Smith, John Dwight	OF	Chicago N.L.	11- 8-63—Tallahassee, Fla.	5- 1
Smith, Michael Anthony	P	Baltimore	10-31-63—San Antonio, Tex.	6-30
Sorrento, Paul Anthony	PH	Minnesota	11-17-65—Somerville, Mass.	9- 8
Sosa, Samuel	OF	Texas	11-10-68—S.P. de Macoris, D.R.	6-16
Spiers, William James III	3B	Milwaukee	6- 5-66—Orangeburg, S.C.	4- 7
Stanton, William Michael	P	Atlanta	6- 2-67—Houston, Tex.	8-24
Stephenson, Phillip Raymond	PH	Chicago N.L.	9-19-60—Guthrie, Okla.	4- 5
Strange, Joseph Douglas	3B	Detroit	4-13-64—Greenville, S.C.	7-13
Swan, Russell Howard	P	San Francisco	1- 3-64—Fremont, Calif.	8- 3
Tapani, Kevin Ray	P	New York N.L.	2-18-64—Des Moines, Ia.	7- 4
Tate, Stuart Douglas	P	San Francisco	6-17-62—Huntsville, Ala.	9-20
Vaughn, Gregory Lamont	PR	Milwaukee	7- 3-65—Sacramento, Calif.	8-10
Ventura, Robin Mark	3B	Chicago A.L.	7-14-67—Santa Maria, Calif.	9-12
Veres, Randolph Ruhland	P	Milwaukee	11-25-65—San Francisco, Calif.	7- 1
Vizcaino, Jose Luis	SS	Los Angeles	3-26-68—Palenque, D.R.	9-10
Vizquel, Omar Enrique	SS	Seattle	5-15-67—Caracas, Venezuela	4- 3
Walker, Larry K. Robert	OF	Montreal	12- 1-66—Maple Ridge, B.C.	8-16
Walton, Jerome O'Terrell	OF	Chicago N.L.	7- 8-65—Newnan, Ga.	4- 4
Wayne, Gary Anthony	P	Minnesota	11-30-62—Dearborn, Mich.	4- 7
Webster, Leonard Irell	C	Minnesota	2-10-65—New Orleans, La.	9- 1
Weston, Michael Lee	P	Baltimore	3-26-61—Flint, Mich.	6-18
Wetherby, Jeffrey Barrett	PH	Atlanta	10-18-63—Granada Hills, Calif.	6- 7
Wetteland, John Karl	P	Los Angeles	8-22-66—San Mateo, Calif.	5-31
Whited, Edward Morris	PH	Atlanta	2- 9-64—Bristol, Pa.	7- 5
Whitehurst, Walter Richard	P	New York N.L.	4-11-64—Shreveport, La.	7-17
Wickander, Kevin Dean	P	Cleveland	1- 5-65—Fort Dodge, Ia.	8-10
Wilkins, Dean Allan	P	Chicago N.L.	8-24-66—Blue Island, Ill.	8-21
Williams, Dana Lamont	PH	Boston	3-20-63—Weirton, W.Va.	6-19
Wilmet, Paul Richard	P	Texas	11- 8-60—Green Bay, Wis.	7-25
Wilson, Craig	PH	St. Louis	11-28-64—Anne Arundel Cty., Md.	9- 6
Winters, Matthew Littleton	PH	Kansas City	3-18-60—Buffalo, N.Y.	5-30
Yelding, Eric Girard	PR	Houston	2-22-65—Montrose, Ala.	4- 9
Zavaras, Clinton Wayne	P	Seattle	1- 4-67—Denver, Colo.	6- 3
Zeile, Todd Edward	PH	St. Louis	9- 9-65—Van Nuys, Calif.	8-18

Homers by Parks for 1989

American League

	At Balt.	At Bos.	At Cal.	At Chi.	At Clev.	At Det.	At K.C.	At Mil.	At Min.	At N.Y.	At Oak.	At Sea.	At Tex.	At Tor.	Totals 1989	1988
Baltimore	61	7	10	6	2	9	3	3	5	9	3	3	4	4	129	137
Boston	5	52	3	4	6	3	4	3	4	9	4	1	5	5	108	124
California	9	3	73	3	5	4	2	7	9	8	7	12	0	3	145	124
Chicago	6	4	5	36	4	8	1	6	5	7	1	3	7	1	94	132
Cleveland	7	6	6	1	56	9	3	4	10	5	2	4	8	6	127	134
Detroit	5	3	5	10	1	74	0	3	5	1	2	2	1	4	116	143
Kansas City	4	2	7	4	3	2	38	3	8	9	4	9	7	1	101	121
Milwaukee	0	5	8	1	1	7	1	69	5	7	7	4	6	5	126	113
Minnesota	3	4	4	6	7	6	4	1	59	6	2	3	9	3	117	151
New York	3	7	5	5	5	8	2	5	5	64	5	10	2	4	130	148
Oakland	4	8	6	2	4	5	1	5	5	8	65	2	4	8	127	156
Seattle	8	7	6	5	6	3	5	5	5	5	5	68	3	3	134	148
Texas	3	4	5	3	2	6	0	6	1	2	5	7	75	3	122	112
Toronto	8	10	5	8	5	5	2	3	2	12	4	7	7	64	142	158
1989 Totals	126	122	148	94	107	151	64	123	128	152	116	135	138	114	1718	......
1988 Totals	147	141	129	119	114	159	92	125	155	152	114	178	125	151	......	1901

AT BALTIMORE (126): Baltimore (61)—Tettleton 15, C. Ripken 13, Worthington 12, Milligan 6, Devereaux 4, Bradley 3, Jefferson 3, Anderson 2, Hulett 2, Sheets. **Boston (5)**—Esasky 2, Greenwell 2, Burks. **California (9)**—Howell 3, Parrish 2, Schofield 2, Downing, Joyner. **Chicago (6)**—Calderon 2, Fisk, Fletcher, Kittle, Manrique. **Cleveland (7)**—Jacoby 2, Snyder 2, Carter, James, Komminsk. **Detroit (5)**—Heath 2, Lemon, Schu, Whitaker. **Kansas City (4)**—Brett, Eisenreich, Jackson, Wellman. **Milwaukee**—None. **Minnesota (3)**—Harper 2, Bush. **New York (3)**—Balboni, Hall, Velarde. **Oakland (4)**—McGwire 2, Hassey, Polonia. **Seattle (8)**—Briley 3, Bradley, Coles, Davis, Martinez, Presley. **Texas (3)**—Buechele, Franco, Incaviglia. **Toronto (8)**—Bell 2, Gruber 2, McGriff 2, Mazzilli, Wilson.

AT BOSTON (122): Baltimore (7)—Anderson, Bradley, Milligan, Moreland, Orsulak, Sheets, Tettleton. **Boston (52)**—Esasky 15, Evans 8, Burks 6, Greenwell 6, Rivera 4, Boggs 2, Cerone 2, Gedman 2, Reed 2, Heep, Kutcher, Marzano, Rice, Romine. **California (3)**—Armas, Parrish, Washington. **Chicago (4)**—Calderon, Fisk, Kittle, Martinez. **Cleveland (5)**—Snyder 2, Belle, Carter, Clark, Jacoby. **Detroit (3)**—Lynn, Schu, Whitaker. **Kansas City (2)**—Jackson 2. **Milwaukee (5)**—Yount 2, Meyer, Molitor, Spiers. **Minnesota (4)**—Gaetti 2, Backman, Gladden. **New York (7)**—Barfield 3, Hall, Kelly, Sax, Slaught. **Oakland (8)**—Parker 3, McGwire 2, Canseco, D. Henderson, Steinbach. **Seattle (7)**—Davis 2, Leonard 2, Cotto, Presley, Valle. **Texas (4)**—Petralli 3, Sosa. **Toronto (10)**—Felix 2, Moseby 2, Mulliniks 2, Bell, Lee, McGriff, Whitt.

AT CALIFORNIA (148): Baltimore (10)—Sheets 2, Traber 2, Devereaux, Finley, Milligan, Orsulak, B. Ripken, Tettleton. **Boston (3)**—Barrett, Evans, Greenwell. **California (73)**—Downing 10, Howell 9, Washington 9, White 9, Joyner 8, Parrish 8, Davis 6, Armas 5, Ray 3, Bichette 2, Schroeder 2, Rose, Schofield. **Chicago (5)**—Fisk 2, Baines, Calderon, Walker. **Cleveland (4)**—Browne 2, Carter, Medina, O'Brien, Snyder. **Detroit (5)**—Whitaker 2, Lemon, Schu, Trammell. **Kansas City (7)**—Jackson 2, Tartabull 2, Brett, Buckner, Seitzer. **Milwaukee (8)**—Yount 2, Braggs, Brock, Canale, Deer, Spiers, Surhoff. **Minnesota (4)**—Hrbek 2, Gaetti, Laudner. **New York (5)**—Barfield, Brookens, Kelly, Mattingly, Pagliarulo. **Oakland (6)**—D. Henderson, Hubbard, Lansford, McGwire, Parker, Phillips. **Seattle (6)**—Leonard 2, Coles, Cotto, Diaz, Presley. **Texas (5)**—Buechele, Coolbaugh, Incaviglia, Kreuter, Sierra. **Toronto (5)**—Fernandez 2, Barfield, Felix, Liriano.

AT CHICAGO (94): Baltimore (6)—Tettleton 2, Anderson, Devereaux, B. Ripken, Sheets. **Boston (4)**—Esasky 2, Cerone, Evans. **California (3)**—Armas, Parrish, White. **Chicago (36)**—Kittle 6, Pasqua 5, Baines 4, Fisk 4, Walker 4, Boston 3, Calderon 2, Martinez 2, Williams 2, Gallagher, Manrique, Merullo, Sosa. **Cleveland (1)**—Snyder. **Detroit (10)**—Whitaker 3, Moreland 2, Heath, Nokes, Schu, Trammell, Ward. **Kansas City (4)**—Tartabull 2, Brett, Macfarlane. **Milwaukee (1)**—Deer. **Minnesota (6)**—Bush, Castillo, Gaetti, Gladden, Larkin, Puckett. **New York (5)**—Brookens 2, Balboni, Barfield, Henderson. **Oakland (2)**—D. Henderson, McGwire. **Seattle (5)**—Davis 2, Leonard 2, Valle. **Texas (3)**—Buechele 2, Sierra. **Toronto (5)**—Fernandez 2, McGriff 2, Whitt 2, Bell, Gruber.

AT CLEVELAND (107): Baltimore (2)—Sheets, Tettleton. **Boston (6)**—Esasky 3, Evans, Heep, Rice. **California (5)**—Howell 2, Armas, Bichette, Davis. **Chicago (4)**—Pasqua 2, Fisk, Karkovice. **Cleveland (56)**—Carter 16, Jacoby 7, Komminsk 6, Snyder 6, O'Brien 5, Clark 4, Belle 3, Zuvella 2, Aguayo, Allanson, Browne, James, McDowell, Medina, Salas. **Detroit (1)**—Moreland. **Kansas City (3)**—Jackson, Palacios, Stillwell. **Milwaukee (1)**—Sheffield. **Minnesota (7)**—Laudner 3, Castillo, Gladden, Hrbek, Larkin. **New York (5)**—Barfield, Brookens, Mattingly, Phelps, Polonia. **Oakland (4)**—R. Henderson 2, Parker, Quirk. **Seattle (6)**—Leonard 2, Buhner, Cotto, McGwire, Presley. **Texas (2)**—Incaviglia 2. **Toronto (5)**—Bell 2, Liriano, Mazzilli, Moseby.

AT DETROIT (151): Baltimore (9)—C. Ripken 2, Bradley, Gonzales, Jefferson, Milligan, Orsulak, Traber, Worthington. **Boston (3)**—Evans, Gedman, Greenwell. **California (4)**—Howell 2, Davis, Washington. **Chicago (8)**—Calderon 3, Baines, Boston, Guillen, Lyons, Martinez. **Cleveland (9)**—Jacoby 2, O'Brien 2, Allanson, Carter, McDowell, Salas, Young. **Detroit (74)**—Whitaker 17, Lynn 9, Nokes 7, Bergman 6, Ward 6, Heath 5, Lemon 4, Jones 3, Schu 3, K. Williams 3, Moreland 2, Sheridan 2, Trammell 2, Brumley, Lusader, Pettis, Richie, Strange. **Kansas City (2)**—Brett, Jackson. **Milwaukee (7)**—Braggs 2, Deer, Engle, Felder, Molitor, Yount. **Minnesota (6)**—Bush, Castillo, Dwyer, Gagne, Hrbek, Puckett. **New York (8)**—Barfield 2, Balboni, Geren, Kelly, Sax, Slaught, Tolleson. **Oakland (5)**—McGwire 3, D. Henderson, Parker. **Seattle (5)**—Coles, Davis, Leonard, Presley, Valle. **Texas (6)**—Baines, Buechele, Franco, Incaviglia, Manrique, Palmeiro. **Toronto (5)**—Felix 2, Borders, Fernandez, Gruber.

AT KANSAS CITY (64): Baltimore (3)—Bradley, Milligan, Orsulak. **Boston (4)**—Burks, Greenwell, Heep, Rice. **California (2)**—Downing, Joyner. **Chicago (1)**—Fisk. **Cleveland (3)**—Jacoby, James, Komminsk. **Detroit**—None. **Kansas City (38)**—Jackson 11, Tartabull 9, Eisenreich 4, Brett 3, Seitzer 2, Stillwell 2, Tabler 2, Winters 2, Boone, White, Wilson. **Milwaukee (1)**—Deer. **Minnesota (4)**—Bush 2, Gladden, Hrbek. **New York (2)**—Balboni, Hall. **Oakland (1)**—R. Henderson. **Seattle (3)**—Coles, Cotto, Leonard. **Texas**—None. **Toronto (2)**—Barfield, McGriff.

AT MILWAUKEE (123): Baltimore (3)—Orsulak, C. Ripken, Tettleton. **Boston (3)**—Esasky 2, Heep. **California (7)**—Davis 2, Joyner 2, Parrish 2, Washington. **Chicago (6)**—Calderon 2, Pasqua 2, Karkovice, Kittle. **Cleveland (4)**—Belle, Browne, Carter, O'Brien. **Detroit (3)**—Lynn, Sheridan, Ward. **Kansas City (3)**—Jackson 2, Tartabull. **Milwaukee (69)**—Deer 15, Yount 14, Braggs 8, Brock 7, Molitor 6, Meyer 5, O'Brien 4, Surhoff 3, Sheffield 2, Engle, Felder, Francona, Spiers, Vaughn. **Minnesota (1)**—Gladden. **New York (5)**—Barfield 2, Balboni, Hall, Sanders. **Oakland (5)**—Canseco 2, McGwire 2, Parker. **Seattle (5)**—Griffey 2, Leonard 2, Bradley. **Texas (6)**—Incaviglia 2, Buechele, Franco, Palmeiro, Sierra. **Toronto (3)**—Bell, Brenly, Gruber.

AT MINNESOTA (128): Baltimore (5)—Bradley, Devereaux, Milligan, C. Ripken, Worthington. **Boston (4)**—Burks, Esasky, Evans, Greenwell. **California (9)**—Davis 4, Armas 2, Downing, Joyner, Washington. **Chicago (5)**—Baines 2, Calderon, Fisk, Sosa. **Cleveland (10)**—Carter 5, Belle, Browne, Clark, McDowell, Medina. **Detroit (5)**—Lovullo, Nokes, Trammell, Whitaker, K. Williams. **Kansas City (8)**—Tartabull 3, Stillwell 2, Jackson, Seitzer, Wilson. **Milwaukee (5)**—Deer 2, Braggs, Brock, Sheffield. **Minnesota (59)**—Hrbek 17, Gaetti 10, Puckett 7, Bush 6, Gagne 5, Harper 4, Larkin 3, Castillo 2, Dwyer 2, Laudner 2, Gladden. **New York (5)**—Balboni 2, Geren, Kelly, Phelps. **Oakland (5)**—McGwire 3, Canseco, Gallego. **Seattle (5)**—Briley, Buhner, Davis, Griffey, Valle. **Texas (1)**—Leach. **Toronto (2)**—Bell, Fernandez.

AT NEW YORK (152): Baltimore (9)—Orsulak 2, Finley, Hulett, Melvin, C. Ripken, Sheets, Tettleton, Traber. **Boston (9)**—Esasky 2, Evans 2, Boggs, Cerone, Gedman, Kutcher, Rivera. **California (8)**—Davis 2, Schroeder 2, Downing, Joyner, Parrish, Ray. **Chicago (7)**—Baines 3, Boston, Fisk, Karkovice, Pasqua. **Cleveland (5)**—Carter 2, Snyder 2, O'Brien. **Detroit (1)**—Whitaker. **Kansas City (9)**—Pecota 3, Brett 2, Macfarlane, Tartabull, Wellman, Wilson. **Milwaukee (7)**—Brock, Deer, Felder, Francona, Meyer, Molitor, Yount. **Minnesota (6)**—Gaetti 3, Bush, Gagne, Hrbek. **New York (64)**—Mattingly 19, Hall 11, Balboni 7, Barfield 6, Geren 4, Phelps 4, Pagliarulo 3, Slaught 3, Kelly 2, Sax 2, Henderson, Polonia, Velarde. **Oakland (8)**—Canseco 3, Parker 2, Hassey, McGwire, Weiss. **Seattle (5)**—Griffey 2, Briley, Coles, Leonard. **Texas (2)**—Incaviglia, Palmeiro. **Toronto (12)**—McGriff 4, Bell 2, Gruber 2, Moseby 2, Barfield, Fernandez.

AT OAKLAND (116): Baltimore (3)—Bradley, C. Ripken, Tettleton. **Boston (4)**—Evans 3, Reed. **California (7)**—Davis 3, Howell 2, Hoffman, Schofield. **Chicago (1)**—Calderon. **Cleveland (2)**—Carter, Snyder. **Detroit (2)**—Heath, Whitaker. **Kansas City (4)**—Jackson 2, Brett, Eisenreich. **Milwaukee (7)**—Deer 3, Vaughn 3, Braggs. **Minnesota (2)**—Gaetti, Gladden. **New York (5)**—Balboni, Barfield, Hall, Henderson, Kelly. **Oakland (65)**—McGwire 12, D. Henderson 10, Parker 10, Canseco 8, R. Henderson 6, Steinbach 5, Hassey 3, Gallego 2, Hubbard 2, Phillips 2, Weiss 2, Blankenship, Javier, Lansford. **Seattle (5)**—Briley, Coles, Davis, Leonard, Valle. **Texas (5)**—Buechele 2, Sierra 2, Manrique. **Toronto (4)**—McGriff 2, Gruber, Moseby.

AT SEATTLE (135): Baltimore (3)—Tettleton 2, C. Ripken. **Boston (1)**—Burks. **California (12)**—Davis 2, Howell 2, Schroeder 2, White 2, Armas, Joyner, Parrish, Ray. **Chicago (3)**—Fisk, Lyons, Williams. **Cleveland (4)**—Carter, James, Skinner, Snyder. **Detroit (2)**—Bergman, K. Williams. **Kansas City (9)**—Eisenriech 3, Jackson 3, Brett, Stillwell, White. **Milwaukee (4)**—Braggs, Francona, Molitor, O'Brien. **Minnesota (3)**—Hrbek 2, Harper. **New York (10)**—Geren 3, Balboni, Brower, Hall, Kelly, Mattingly, Sanders, Sax. **Oakland (2)**—Parker, Phillips. **Seattle (68)**—Davis 13, Griffey 10, Leonard 9, Buhner 7, Presley 7, Briley 5, Cotto 5, Coles 4, Cochrane 3, Kingery 2, Bradley, Valle, Vizquel. **Texas (7)**—Kreuter 2, Sierra 2, Espy, Franco, Palmeiro. **Toronto (7)**—McGriff 5, Borders, Moseby.

AT TEXAS (138): Baltimore (4)—Bradley, Devereaux, Milligan, Tettleton. **Boston (5)**—Burks 2, Esasky, Evans, Greenwell. **California**—None. **Chicago (7)**—Baines 2, Kittle 2, Calderon, Pasqua, Sosa. **Cleveland (8)**—Carter 3, Snyder 2, Allanson, Clark, O'Brien. **Detroit (1)**—Heath. **Kansas City (7)**—Jackson 5, Brett, Stillwell. **Milwaukee (6)**—Brock, Molitor, O'Brien, Sheffield, Spiers, Surhoff. **Minnesota (9)**—Bush 2, Castillo 2, Gaetti, Gagne, Harper, Larkin, Moses. **New York (2)**—Balboni, Kelly. **Oakland (4)**—McGwire 3, Parker. **Seattle (3)**—Briley, Griffey, Leonard. **Texas (75)**—Sierra 21, Incaviglia 13, Franco 9, Kunkel 8, Buechele 7, Palmeiro 4, Espy 2, Kreuter 2, Sundberg 2, Baines, Bosley, Coolbaugh, Daugherty, Gonzalez, Petralli, Stanley. **Toronto (7)**—Fernandez 2, Gruber 2, Barfield, Lee, McGriff.

AT TORONTO (114): Baltimore (4)—Bradley 2, C. Ripken, Worthington. **Boston (5)**—Esasky 2, Evans, Greenwell, Heep. **California (3)**—Davis, Joyner, Parrish. **Chicago (1)**—Martinez. **Cleveland (6)**—Carter 2, Belle, Clark, Medina, O'Brien. **Detroit (4)**—Lemon, Ward, Whitaker, K. Williams. **Kansas City (1)**—Jackson. **Milwaukee (5)**—Braggs, Brock, Deer, Vaughn, Yount. **Minnesota (3)**—Castillo, Gagne, Gladden. **New York (4)**—Barfield, Brower, Mattingly, Phelps. **Oakland (8)**—McGwire 3, Canseco 2, D. Henderson, Parker, Steinbach. **Seattle (3)**—Briley, Martinez, Valle. **Texas (3)**—Baines, Buechele, Sierra. **Toronto (64)**—McGriff 18, Bell 8, Gruber 8, Whitt 8, Felix 4, Moseby 4, Liriano 3, Fernandez 2, Mazzilli 2, Barfield, Borders, Hill, Lee, Mulliniks, Virgil, Wilson.

NOTE: Toronto totals include the following home runs hit at Exhibition Stadium: Baltimore—None. Boston—None. California (2)—Davis, Parrish. Chicago (1)—Martinez. Cleveland (3)—Carter, Medina, O'Brien. Detroit—None. Kansas City (1)—Jackson. Milwaukee—None. Minnesota—None. New York (1)—Brower. Oakland (1)—McGwire. Seattle (1)—Valle. Texas (1)—Sierra. Toronto (19)—McGriff 4, Bell 3, Moseby 3, Felix 2, Gruber 2, Whitt 2, Barfield, Liriano, Mulliniks.

260

National League

	At Atl.	At Chi.	At Cin.	At Hou.	At L.A.	At Mont.	At N.Y.	At Phil.	At Pitt.	At St.L.	At S.D.	At S.F.	Totals 1989	1988
Atlanta	55	6	6	8	8	5	5	4	6	3	14	8	128	96
Chicago	5	61	5	5	4	5	4	10	8	10	5	2	124	113
Cincinnati	5	8	59	4	8	7	7	5	5	1	9	10	128	122
Houston	7	2	7	42	5	4	3	3	6	2	11	5	97	96
Los Angeles	3	2	6	4	37	2	4	7	4	1	12	7	89	99
Montreal	4	7	2	6	1	55	4	7	5	2	2	5	100	107
New York	6	12	6	5	2	4	78	10	9	7	6	2	147	152
Philadelphia	4	15	7	4	2	5	6	61	5	3	5	6	123	106
Pittsburgh	4	2	8	3	1	8	8	5	45	1	6	4	95	110
St. Louis	2	6	6	3	2	6	4	6	3	27	4	4	73	71
San Diego	9	3	7	5	5	6	2	5	4	0	66	8	120	94
San Francisco	12	1	11	3	8	8	9	5	7	6	8	63	141	113
1989 Totals	116	125	130	92	83	115	134	128	107	63	148	124	1365	....
1988 Totals	112	129	146	83	87	109	101	126	106	68	112	100	....	1279

AT ATLANTA (116): Atlanta (55)—L. Smith 10, Murphy 9, Blauser 5, Evans 5, Gant 5, Thomas 5, Gregg 2, McDowell 2, Perry 2, Treadway 2, Berroa, Davis, Justice, Lemke, Russell, Smoltz, Wetherby, Whited. Chicago (5)—Dawson 3, Sandberg, Wrona. Cincinnati (5)—Benzinger 2, Davis 2, Larkin. Houston (7)—Bass, Biggio, Caminiti, Doran, Hatcher, Ramirez, Trevino. Los Angeles (3)—Gibson, Hamilton, Shelby. Montreal (4)—Foley, Galarraga, Hudler, Wallach. New York (6)—Strawberry 3, Jefferies, Johnson, McReynolds. Philadelphia (4)—C. Hayes, Murphy, Ready, Samuel. Pittsburgh (4) —Wilson 2, Bonds, Hatcher. St. Louis (2)—Brunansky, Guerrero. San Diego (9)—Ja. Clark 4, Martinez 2, R. Alomar, Jackson, Santiago. San Francisco (12)—Mitchell 6, Thompson 2, Clark, Litton, Maldonado, Nixon.

AT CHICAGO (125): Atlanta (6)—Blauser 2, McDowell, Murphy, L. Smith, Thomas. Chicago (61) —Sandberg 16, McClendon 9, Grace 8, Dawson 6, D. Smith 5, Law 4, Dunston 3, Walton 3, Berryhill 2, Ramos, Salazar, Webster, Wilkerson, Williams. Cincinnati (8)—Benzinger 2, Sabo 2, Davis, Oliver, Roomes, Youngblood. Houston (2)—Bass, Ramirez. Los Angeles (2)—Murray 2. Montreal (1)—Da. Martinez 2, Brooks, Fitzgerald, Grissom, Raines, Wallach. New York (12)—Johnson 3, McReynolds 3, Strawberry 2, Carter, Elster, Jefferies, Mazzilli, Miller. Philadelphia (15)—V. Hayes 3, Daulton 2, Schmidt 2, Dykstra, C. Hayes, James, Jeltz, Jones, Jordan, Kruk, Ready. Pittsburgh (2)—Bonilla, Wilson. St. Louis (6)—Brunansky 2, Guerrero 2, Coleman, Pendleton. San Diego (3)—Kruk, Parent, Wynne. San Francisco (1)—Maldonado.

AT CINCINNATI (130): Atlanta (6)—Murphy 2, Treadway 2, Evans, Gregg. Chicago (5)—Dawson 2, Jackson, McClendon, D. Smith. Cincinnati (59)—Davis 15, O'Neill 11, Benzinger 6, Quinones 5, Roomes 5, Sabo 3, Duncan 2, Griffey 2, Birtsas, Daniels, Diaz, Larkin, Oester, Oliver, Reed, Richardson, Winningham, Youngblood. Houston (7)—Davis 4, Biggio, Doran, Reynolds. Los Angeles (6)—Gibson 2, Murray, Randolph, Scioscia, Stubbs. Montreal (2)—Wallach 2. New York (6)—Johnson 3, Darling, Lyons, Strawberry. Philadelphia (7)—Ready 2, Samuel 2, V. Hayes, Jordan, Thon. Pittsburgh (8)— Bonds 3, Bell, Bonilla, King, Quinones, Redus. St. Louis (6)—Brunansky 3, Pendleton, Walling, Zeile. San Diego (7)—Salazar 2, Abner, Ja. Clark, Gwynn, Jackson, Santiago. San Francisco (11)—Mitchell 3, Kennedy 2, Williams 2, Clark, Laga, Maldonado, Uribe.

AT HOUSTON (92): Atlanta (9)—Gant 2, Benedict, Berroa, Blauser, Gregg, McDowell, Russell. Chicago (5)—Grace 2, Sandberg 2, Dunston. Cincinnati (4)—Davis 4. Houston (42)—Davis 15, Biggio 6, Caminiti 3, Doran 3, Meadows 3, Ramirez 3, Anthony 2, Bass 2, Wilson 2, Lombardozzi, Portugal, Trevino. Los Angeles (4)—Scioscia 2, Gibson, Murray. Montreal (6)—Aldrete, Brooks, Foley, Galarraga, W. Johnson, Raines. New York (5)—Carreon, K. Hernandez, Johnson, Strawberry, Teufel. Philadelphia (4)—Daulton 2, Murphy, Samuel. Pittsburgh (3)—Bonilla 2, Van Slyke. St. Louis (3)—Guerrero, McGee, Pendleton. San Diego (5)—R. Alomar 2, Ja. Clark, Santiago, Wynne. San Francisco (3)—Clark 2, Maldonado.

AT LOS ANGELES (83): Atlanta (8)—Murphy 2, Blauser, Gregg, James, L. Smith, Thomas, Treadway. Chicago (4)—Dawson 2, Grace, Sandberg. Cincinnati (8)—Benzinger 2, Davis, Griffey, Harris, Larkin, Oliver, Winningham. Houston (5)—Biggio 2, Caminiti 2, Davis. Los Angeles (37)—Hamilton 8, Marshall 6, Gibson 4, Murray 4, Scioscia 4, Davis 2, Dempsey 2, Gonzalez 2, Anderson, Daniels, Fletcher, Harris, Stubbs. Montreal (1)—Hudler. New York (2)—Johnson, McReynolds. Philadelphia (2)—Daulton, Murphy. Pittsburgh (1)—Bonilla. St. Louis (2)—Brunansky, Thompson. San Diego (5)—Ja. Clark, James, Santiago, Schiraldi, Wynne. San Francisco (8)—Clark 3, Williams 3, Mitchell, Sheridan.

AT MONTREAL (115): Atlanta (5)—Evans 2, Davis, Gregg, Murphy. Chicago (5)—Dawson 3, Sandberg 2. Cincinnati (7)—Griffey 3, Benzinger, Davis, O'Neill, Reed. Houston (4)—Doran 2, Biggio, Hatcher. Los Angeles (2)—Dempsey, Hamilton. Montreal (55)—Galarraga 13, Brooks 7, Raines 6, Wallach 6, Owen 5, Foley 4, Santovenia 4, Fitzgerald 3, Garcia 3, Hudler 3, Da. Martinez 3. New York (4)—Elster, K. Hernandez, Johnson, Lombardi. Philadelphia (5)—C. Hayes, V. Hayes, Herr, Murphy, Thon. Pittsburgh (8)—Bonds 3, Bonilla 2, Van Slyke 2, Bilardello. St. Louis (6)—Brunansky 3, Guerrero, Pena, Thompson. San Diego (6)—Ja. Clark 3, James, Nelson, Pagliarulo. San Francisco (8)— Maldonado 3, Mitchell 2, Clark, Thompson, Williams.

AT NEW YORK (134): Atlanta (5)—Gant 2, Murphy, L. Smith, Treadway. Chicago (4)—Sandberg 2, Dawson, Dunston. Cincinnati (7)—Quinones 3, Benzinger, Davis, Harris, Roomes. Houston (3) —Davis 3. Los Angeles (4)—Murray 2, Davis, Randolph. Montreal (4)—Galarraga 2, Brooks, W. Johnson. New York (78)—Johnson 19, Strawberry 15, McReynolds 12, Jefferies 7, Elster 5, Carreon 4, Magadan 3, Dykstra 2, K. Hernandez 2, Samuel 2, Carter, Darling, Lyons, Mazzilli, Sasser, Teufel, Wilson. Philadelphia (6)—Daulton, V. Hayes, Herr, Jordan, Schmidt, Thon. Pittsburgh (8)—Bonilla 2, Reynolds 2, King, Redus, Robinson, Van Slyke. St. Louis (4)—Guerrero 3, McGee. San Diego (2)—James, Salazar. San Francisco (9)—Mitchell 3, Clark, Maldonado, Riles, Sheridan, Thompson, Williams.

AT PHILADELPHIA (128): Atlanta (4)—L. Smith 2, Blauser, Thomas. **Chicago (10)**—Berryhill 2, Sandberg 2, Dascenzo, Grace, McClendon, D. Smith, Walton, Wynne. **Cincinnati** (5)—Davis 2, Daniels, Griffey, O'Neill. **Houston** (3)—Davis 2, Davidson. **Los Angeles** (7)—Marshall 2, Murray 2, Hamilton, Huff, Scioscia. **Montreal** (7)—Fitzgerald 2, Galarraga 2, Brooks, Hudler, Wallach. **New York (10)**—Jefferies 2, Johnson 2, Strawberry 2, Lyons, Magadan, McReynolds, Samuel. **Philadelphia (61)**—V. Hayes 15, Thon 8, Jordan 7, Kruk 4, Murphy 4, Dykstra 3, C. Hayes 3, Jeltz 3, Ready 3, Samuel 3, Daulton 2, Schmidt 2, Dernier, James, Jones, Lake. **Pittsburgh** (5)—Bonds 3, Ortiz, Van Slyke. **St. Louis** (6)—Brunansky 2, Guerrero 2, Pendleton, Smith. **San Diego** (5)—Ja. Clark, Martinez, Roberts, Santiago, Templeton. **San Francisco** (5)—Clark 2, Mitchell, Riles, Williams.

AT PITTSBURGH (107): Atlanta (6)—McDowell 2, Blauser, Davis, L. Smith, Thomas. **Chicago** (8)—Dawson 3, Dunston, Grace, Sandberg, D. Smith, Walton. **Cincinnati** (5)—Quinones 2, Benzinger, Sabo, Youngblood. **Houston** (6)—Davis 4, Bass, Caminiti. **Los Angeles** (4)—Marshall 2, Daniels, Scioscia. **Montreal** (5)—Brooks, Fitzgerald, Galarraga, Owen, Santovenia. **New York** (9)—Johnson 3, McReynolds 2, Dykstra, Jefferies, Strawberry, Wilson. **Philadelphia** (5)—V. Hayes, Ready, Samuel, Schmidt, Thon. **Pittsburgh** (45)—Bonilla 13, Bonds 7, Van Slyke 4, King 3, Redus 3, Reynolds 3, Distefano 2, LaValliere 2, Lind 2, Wilson 2, Bell, Bilardello, Carter, Quinones. **St. Louis** (3)—Guerrero, Magrane, Oquendo. **San Diego** (4)—Ja. Clark, James, Martinez, Nelson. **San Francisco** (7)—Mitchell 3, Butler, Kennedy, Sheridan, Thompson.

AT ST. LOUIS (63): Atlanta (3)—Romero, Thomas, Treadway. **Chicago** (10)—Dunston 3, Law 2, Sandberg 2, Webster 2, Wrona. **Cincinnati** (1)—Richardson. **Houston** (2)—Caminiti, Reynolds. **Los Angeles** (1)—Murray. **Montreal** (2)—Brooks, Wallach. **New York** (7)—Strawberry 3, Elster, Fernandez, McReynolds, Wilson. **Philadelphia** (3)—Jordan 2, Thon. **Pittsburgh** (1)—Redus. **St. Louis** (27)—Pendleton 8, Brunansky 4, Guerrero 3, Pena 3, Morris 2, Terry 2, Thompson 2, Coleman, McGee, Smith. **San Diego**—None. **San Francisco** (6)—Mitchell 3, Butler, Clark, Robinson.

AT SAN DIEGO (148): Atlanta (14)—Evans 3, Murphy 3, L. Smith 2, Blauser, Davis, Lemke, McDowell, Perry, Thomas. **Chicago** (5)—Dawson, Law, McClendon, Sandberg, D. Smith. **Cincinnati** (9)—Davis 3, Benzinger 2, Griffey, Larkin, Reed, Winningham. **Houston** (11)—Davis 4, Biggio 2, Caminiti 2, Anthony, Doran, Hatcher. **Los Angeles** (12)—Murray 4, Davis 2, Hatcher 2, Stubbs 2, Dempsey, Hamilton. **Montreal** (2)—Galarraga, Raines. **New York** (6)—McReynolds 2, Carreon, Elster, Johnson, Strawberry. **Philadelphia** (5)—Thon 2, Ford, V. Hayes, Murphy. **Pittsburgh** (6)—Wilson 3, Bonilla, Quinones, Reynolds. **St. Louis** (4)—Brunansky 2, Guerrero 2. **San Diego** (66)—Ja. Clark 11, Santiago 8, James 6, Parent 6, Salazar 5, Templeton 5, R. Alomar 3, Gwynn 3, Wynne 3, Kruk 2, Martinez 2, Pagliarulo 2, Roberts 2, Stephenson 2, Abner, S. Alomar, Benes, Je. Clark, Jackson, Nelson. **San Francisco** (8)—Mitchell 3, Clark 2, Kennedy, Oberkfell, Thompson.

AT SAN FRANCISCO (124): Atlanta (8)—L. Smith 3, Thomas 2, Murphy, Perry, Treadway. **Chicago** (2)—Berryhill, Girardi. **Cincinnati** (10)—Davis 4, O'Neill 2, Quinones 2, Duncan, Madison. **Houston** (5)—Anthony, Davis, Knepper, Ramirez, Scott. **Los Angeles** (7)—Murray 3, Gibson, Gonzalez, Marshall, Scioscia. **Montreal** (5)—Galarraga 2, Brooks, Foley, Wallach. **New York** (2)—Elster, Johnson. **Philadelphia** (6)—V. Hayes 3, C. Hayes 2, Lake. **Pittsburgh** (4)—Bonds 2, Bonilla, Wilson. **St. Louis** (4)—Brunansky 2, Guerrero, Pendleton. **San Diego** (8)—Ja. Clark 3, Santiago 3, R. Alomar, James. **San Francisco** (63)—Mitchell 22, Williams 10, Clark 9, Thompson 7, Riles 5, Litton 3, Butler 2, Robinson 2, Kennedy, Maldonado, Oberkfell.

Major League Attendance for 1989

NATIONAL LEAGUE			AMERICAN LEAGUE		
	Home	Road		Home	Road
Atlanta	984,930	1,936,802	Baltimore	2,535,208	2,041,702
Chicago	2,491,942	2,271,855	Boston	2,510,012	2,394,851
Cincinnati	1,979,320	2,163,186	California	2,647,291	1,970,796
Houston	1,834,908	1,996,660	Chicago	1,045,651	2,082,105
Los Angeles	2,944,653	2,169,015	Cleveland	1,285,542	2,059,189
Montreal	1,783,533	2,083,227	Detroit	1,543,656	2,165,594
New York	2,918,710	2,498,323	Kansas City	2,477,700	2,120,050
Philadelphia	1,861,985	1,929,699	Milwaukee	1,970,735	2,219,397
Pittsburgh	1,374,141	2,135,671	Minnesota	2,277,438	1,988,012
St. Louis	3,080,980	1,963,976	New York	2,170,485	2,508,085
San Diego	2,009,031	1,944,761	Oakland	2,667,225	2,283,228
San Francisco	2,059,701	2,230,659	Seattle	1,298,443	1,943,841
			Texas	2,043,993	2,101,701
			Toronto	3,375,883	1,970,711
Total	25,323,834	25,323,834	Total	29,849,262	29,849,262

THE SPORTING NEWS AWARDS
THE SPORTING NEWS MVP AWARDS

	AMERICAN LEAGUE			NATIONAL LEAGUE	
Year	Player Club	Points		Player Club	Points
1929	Al Simmons, Philadelphia, of	40		No selection	
1930	Joseph Cronin, Washington, ss	52		William Terry, New York, 1b	47
1931	H. Louis Gehrig, New York, 1b	40		Charles Klein, Philadelphia, of	40
1932	James Foxx, Philadelphia, 1b	46		Charles Klein, Philadelphia, of	46
1933	James Foxx, Philadelphia, 1b	49		Carl Hubbell, New York, p	64
1934	H. Louis Gehrig, New York, 1b	51		Jerome Dean, St. Louis, p	57
1935	Henry Greenberg, Detroit, 1b	64		J. Floyd Vaughan, Pittsburgh, ss	42
1936	H. Louis Gehrig, New York, 1b	55		Carl Hubbell, New York, p	61
1937	Charles Gehringer, Detroit, 2b	78		Joseph Medwick, St. Louis, of	70
1938	James Foxx, Boston, 1b	304		Ernest Lombardi, Cincinnati, c	229
1939	Joseph DiMaggio, New York, of	280		William Walters, Cincinnati, p	303
1940	Henry Greenberg, Detroit, of	292		Frank McCormick, Cincinnati, 1b	274
1941	Joseph DiMaggio, New York, of	291		Adolph Camilli, Brooklyn, 1b	300
1942	Joseph Gordon, New York, 2b	270		Morton Cooper, St. Louis, p	263
1943	Spurgeon Chandler, New York, p	246		Stanley Musial, St. Louis, of	267
1944	Robert Doerr, Boston, 2b			Martin Marion, St. Louis, ss	
1945	Edward J. Mayo, Detroit, 2b			Thomas Holmes, Boston, of	

THE SPORTING NEWS PLAYER, PITCHER OF YEAR

AMERICAN LEAGUE	NATIONAL LEAGUE
1948—Louis Boudreau, Cleveland, ss Robert Lemon, Cleveland, p	1948—Stanley Musial, St. Louis, of-1b John Sain, Boston, p
1949—Theodore Williams, Boston, of Ellis Kinder, Boston, p	1949—Enos Slaughter, St. Louis, of Howard Pollet, St. Louis, p
1950—Philip Rizzuto, New York, ss Robert Lemon, Cleveland, p	1950—Ralph Kiner, Pittsburgh, of C. James Konstanty, Philadelphia, p
1951—Ferris Fain, Philadelphia, 1b Robert Feller, Cleveland, p	1951—Stanley Musial, St. Louis, of Elwin Roe, Brooklyn, p
1952—Luscious Easter, Cleveland, 1b Robert Shantz, Philadelphia, p	1952—Henry Sauer, Chicago, of Robin Roberts, Philadelphia, p
1953—Albert Rosen, Cleveland, 3b Erv (Bob) Porterfield, Washington, p	1953—Roy Campanella, Brooklyn, c Warren Spahn, Milwaukee, p
1954—Roberto Avila, Cleveland, 2b Robert Lemon, Cleveland, p	1954—Willie Mays, New York, of John Antonelli, New York, p
1955—Albert Kaline, Detroit, of Edward Ford, New York, p	1955—Edwin Snider, Brooklyn, of Robin Roberts, Philadelphia, p
1956—Mickey Mantle, New York, of W. William Pierce, Chicago, p	1956—Henry Aaron, Milwaukee, of Donald Newcombe, Brooklyn, p
1957—Theodore Williams, Boston, of W. William Pierce, Chicago, p	1957—Stanley Musial, St. Louis, 1b Warren Spahn, Milwaukee, p
1958—Jack Jensen, Boston, of Robert Turley, New York, p	1958—Ernest Banks, Chicago, ss Warren Spahn, Milwaukee, p
1959—J. Nelson Fox, Chicago, 2b Early Wynn, Chicago, p	1959—Ernest Banks, Chicago, ss Samuel Jones, San Francisco, p
1960—Roger Maris, New York, of Charles Estrada, Baltimore, p	1960—Richard Groat, Pittsburgh, ss Vernon Law, Pittsburgh, p
1961—Roger Maris, New York, of Edward Ford, New York, p	1961—Frank Robinson, Cincinnati, of Warren Spahn, Milwaukee, p
1962—Mickey Mantle, New York, of Richard Donovan, Cleveland, p	1962—Maurice Wills, Los Angeles, ss Donald Drysdale, Los Angeles, p
1963—Albert Kaline, Detroit, of Edward Ford, New York, p	1963—Henry Aaron, Milwaukee, of Sanford Koufax, Los Angeles, p
1964—Brooks Robinson, Baltimore, 3b Dean Chance, Los Angeles, p	1964—Kenton Boyer, St. Louis, 3b Sanford Koufax, Los Angeles, p
1965—Pedro (Tony) Oliva, Minnesota, of James Grant, Minnesota, p	1965—Willie Mays, San Francisco, of Sanford Koufax, Los Angeles, p
1966—Frank Robinson, Baltimore, of James Kaat, Minnesota, p	1966—Roberto Clemente, Pittsburgh, of Sanford Koufax, Los Angeles, p
1967—Carl Yastrzemski, Boston, of Jim Lonborg, Boston, p	1967—Orlando Cepeda, St. Louis, 1b Mike McCormick, San Francisco, p
1968—Ken Harrelson, Boston, of Denny McLain, Detroit, p	1968—Pete Rose, Cincinnati, of Bob Gibson, St. Louis, p
1969—Harmon Killebrew, Minnesota, 1b-3b Denny McLain, Detroit, p	1969—Willie McCovey, San Francisco, 1b Tom Seaver, New York, p
1970—Harmon Killebrew, Minnesota, 3b Sam McDowell, Cleveland, p	1970—Johnny Bench, Cincinnati, c Bob Gibson, St. Louis, p
1971—Pedro (Tony) Oliva, Minnesota, of Vida Blue, Oakland, p	1971—Joe Torre, St. Louis, 3b Ferguson Jenkins, Chicago, p
1972—Richie Allen, Chicago, 1b Wilbur Wood, Chicago, p	1972—Billy Williams, Chicago, of Steve Carlton, Philadelphia, p
1973—Reggie Jackson, Oakland, of Jim Palmer, Baltimore, p	1973—Bobby Bonds, San Francisco, of Ron Bryant, San Francisco, p

PLAYER, PITCHER OF YEAR—Continued

AMERICAN LEAGUE	NATIONAL LEAGUE
1974—Jeff Burroughs, Texas, of	1974—Lou Brock, St. Louis, of
Jim Hunter, Oakland, p	Mike Marshall, Los Angeles, p
1975—Fred Lynn, Boston, of	1975—Joe Morgan, Cincinnati, 2b
Jim Palmer, Baltimore, p	Tom Seaver, New York, p
1976—Thurman Munson, New York, c	1976—George Foster, Cincinnati, of
Jim Palmer, Baltimore, p	Randy Jones, San Diego, p
1977—Rod Carew, Minnesota, 1b	1977—George Foster, Cincinnati, of
Nolan Ryan, California, p	Steve Carlton, Philadelphia, p
1978—Jim Rice, Boston, of	1978—Dave Parker, Pittsburgh, of
Ron Guidry, New York, p	Vida Blue, San Francisco, p
1979—Don Baylor, California, of	1979—Keith Hernandez, St. Louis, 1b
Mike Flanagan, Baltimore, p	Joe Niekro, Houston, p
1980—George Brett, Kansas City, 3b	1980—Mike Schmidt, Philadelphia, 3b
Steve Stone, Baltimore, p	Steve Carlton, Philadelphia, p
1981—Tony Armas, Oakland, of	1981—Andre Dawson, Montreal, of
Jack Morris, Detroit, p	Fernando Valenzuela, Los Angeles, p
1982—Robin Yount, Milwaukee, ss	1982—Dale Murphy, Atlanta, of
Dave Stieb, Toronto, p	Steve Carlton, Philadelphia, p
1983—Cal Ripken, Baltimore, ss	1983—Dale Murphy, Atlanta, of
LaMarr Hoyt, Chicago, p	John Denny, Philadelphia, p
1984—Don Mattingly, New York, 1b	1984—Ryne Sandberg, Chicago, 2b
Willie Hernandez, Detroit, p	Rick Sutcliffe, Chicago, p
1985—Don Mattingly, New York, 1b	1985—Willie McGee, St. Louis, of
Bret Saberhagen, Kansas City, p	Dwight Gooden, New York, p
1986—Don Mattingly, New York, 1b	1986—Mike Schmidt, Philadelphia, 3b
Roger Clemens, Boston, p	Mike Scott, Houston, p
1987—George Bell, Toronto, of	1987—Andre Dawson, Chicago, of
Jimmy Key, Toronto, p	Rick Sutcliffe, Chicago, p
1988—Jose Canseco, Oakland, of	1988—Andy Van Slyke, Pittsburgh, of
Frank Viola, Minnesota, p	Orel Hershiser, Los Angeles, p
1989—Ruben Sierra, Texas, of	1989—Kevin Mitchell, San Francisco, of
Bret Saberhagen, Kansas City, p	Mark Davis, San Diego, p

FIREMAN (Relief Pitcher) OF THE YEAR

Year	Player	Club	Player	Club
1960—Mike Fornieles, Boston			Lindy McDaniel, St. Louis	
1961—Luis Arroyo, New York			Stu Miller, San Francisco	
1962—Dick Radatz, Boston			Roy Face, Pittsburgh	
1963—Stu Miller, Baltimore			Lindy McDaniel, Chicago	
1964—Dick Radatz, Boston			Al McBean, Pittsburgh	
1965—Eddie Fisher, Chicago			Ted Abernathy, Chicago	
1966—Jack Aker, Kansas City			Phil Regan, Los Angeles	
1967—Minnie Rojas, California			Ted Abernathy, Cincinnati	
1968—Wilbur Wood, Chicago			Phil Regan, L.A.-Chicago	
1969—Ron Perranoski, Minnesota			Wayne Granger, Cincinnati	
1970—Ron Perranoski, Minnesota			Wayne Granger, Cincinnati	
1971—Ken Sanders, Milwaukee			Dave Giusti, Pittsburgh	
1972—Sparky Lyle, New York			Clay Carroll, Cincinnati	
1973—John Hiller, Detroit			Mike Marshall, Montreal	
1974—Terry Forster, Chicago			Mike Marshall, Los Angeles	
1975—Rich Gossage, Chicago			Al Hrabosky, St. Louis	
1976—Bill Campbell, Minnesota			Rawly Eastwick, Cincinnati	
1977—Bill Campbell, Boston			Rollie Fingers, San Diego	
1978—Rich Gossage, New York			Rollie Fingers, San Diego	
1979—Mike Marshall, Minnesota			Bruce Sutter, Chicago	
Jim Kern, Texas				
1980—Dan Quisenberry, Kansas City			Rollie Fingers, San Diego	
			Tom Hume, Cincinnati	
1981—Rollie Fingers, Milwaukee			Bruce Sutter, St. Louis	
1982—Dan Quisenberry, Kansas City			Bruce Sutter, St. Louis	
1983—Dan Quisenberry, Kansas City			Al Holland, Philadelphia	
			Lee Smith, Chicago	
1984—Dan Quisenberry, Kansas City			Bruce Sutter, St. Louis	
1985—Dan Quisenberry, Kansas City			Jeff Reardon, Montreal	
1986—Dave Righetti, New York			Todd Worrell, St. Louis	
1987—Dave Righetti, New York			Steve Bedrosian, Philadelphia	
Jeff Reardon, Minnesota				
1988—Dennis Eckersley, Oakland			John Franco, Cincinnati	
1989—Jeff Russell, Texas			Mark Davis, San Diego	

THE SPORTING NEWS ROOKIE AWARDS

1946—Combined selection—Delmer Ennis, Philadelphia, N. L., of
1947—Combined selection—Jack Robinson, Brooklyn, 1b
1948—Combined selection—Richie Ashburn, Philadelphia, N. L., of

AMERICAN LEAGUE	NATIONAL LEAGUE
Year Player Club	Player Club
1949—Roy Sievers, St. Louis, of	Donald Newcombe, Brooklyn, p
1950—Combined selection—Edward Ford, New York, A. L., p	
1951—Orestes Minoso, Chicago, of	Willie Mays, New York, of
1952—Clinton Courtney, St. Louis, c	Joseph Black, Brooklyn, p
1953—Harvey Kuenn, Detroit, ss	James Gilliam, Brooklyn, 2b
1954—Robert Grim, New York, p	Wallace Moon, St. Louis, of
1955—Herbert Score, Cleveland, p	William Virdon, St. Louis, of
1956—Luis Aparicio, Chicago, ss	Frank Robinson, Cincinnati, of
1957—Anthony Kubek, New York, inf-of	Edward Bouchee, Philadelphia, 1b
(No pitcher named)	Jack Sanford, Philadelphia, p
1958—Albert Pearson, Washington, of	Orlando Cepeda, San Francisco, 1b
Ryne Duren, New York, p	Carlton Willey, Milwaukee, p
1959—W. Robert Allison, Washington, of	Willie McCovey, San Francisco, 1b
1960—Ronald Hansen, Baltimore, ss	Frank Howard, Los Angeles, of
1961—Richard Howser, Kansas City, ss	Billy Williams, Chicago, of
Donald Schwall, Boston, p	Kenneth Hunt, Cincinnati, p
1962—Thomas Tresh, New York, of-ss	Kenneth Hubbs, Chicago, 2b
1963—Peter Ward, Chicago, 3b	Peter Rose, Cincinnati, 2b
Gary Peters, Chicago, p	Raymond Culp, Philadelphia, p
1964—Pedro (Tony) Oliva, Minnesota, of	Richard Allen, Philadelphia, 3b
Wallace Bunker, Baltimore, p	William McCool, Cincinnati, p
1965—Curtis Blefary, Baltimore, of	Joseph Morgan, Houston, 2b
Marcelino Lopez, California, p	Frank Linzy, San Francisco, p
1966—Tommie Agee, Chicago, of	Tommy Helms, Cincinnati, 3b
James Nash, Kansas City, p	Donald Sutton, Los Angeles, p
1967—Rod Carew, Minnesota, 2b	Lee May, Cincinnati, 1b
Tom Phoebus, Baltimore, p	Dick Hughes, St. Louis, p
1968—Del Unser, Washington, of	Johnny Bench, Cincinnati, c
Stan Bahnsen, New York, p	Jerry Koosman, New York, p
1969—Carlos May, Chicago, of	Coco Laboy, Montreal, 3b
Mike Nagy, Boston, p	Tom Griffin, Houston, p
1970—Roy Foster, Cleveland, of	Bernie Carbo, Cincinnati, of
Bert Blyleven, Minnesota, p	Carl Morton, Montreal, p
1971—Chris Chambliss, Cleveland, 1b	Earl Williams, Atlanta, c
Bill Parsons, Milwaukee, p	Reggie Cleveland, St. Louis, p
1972—Carlton Fisk, Boston, c	Dave Rader, San Francisco, c
Dick Tidrow, Cleveland, p	Jon Matlack, New York, p
1973—Al Bumbry, Baltimore, of	Gary Matthews, San Francisco, of
Steve Busby, Kansas City, p	Steve Rogers, Montreal, p
1974—Mike Hargrove, Texas, 1b	Greg Gross, Houston, of
Frank Tanana, California, p	John D'Acquisto, San Francisco, p
1975—Fred Lynn, Boston, of	Gary Carter, Montreal, of-c
Dennis Eckersley, Cleveland, p	John Montefusco, San Francisco, p
1976—Butch Wynegar, Minnesota, c	Larry Herndon, San Francisco, of
Mark Fidrych, Detroit, p	Butch Metzger, San Diego, p
1977—Mitchell Page, Oakland, of	Andre Dawson, Montreal, of
Dave Rozema, Detroit, p	Bob Owchinko, San Diego, p
1978—Paul Molitor, Milwaukee, 2b	Bob Horner, Atlanta, 3b
Rich Gale, Kansas City, p	Don Robinson, Pittsburgh, p
1979—Pat Putnam, Texas, 1b	Jeff Leonard, Houston, of
Mark Clear, California, p	Rick Sutcliffe, Los Angeles, p
1980—Joe Charboneau, Cleveland, of	Lonnie Smith, Philadelphia, of
Britt Burns, Chicago, p	Bill Gullickson, Montreal, p
1981—Rich Gedman, Boston, c	Tim Raines, Montreal, of
Dave Righetti, New York, p	Fernando Valenzuela, Los Angeles, p
1982—Cal Ripken, Baltimore, ss-3b	Johnny Ray, Pittsburgh, 2b
Ed Vande Berg, Seattle, p	Steve Bedrosian, Atlanta, p
1983—Ron Kittle, Chicago, of	Darryl Strawberry, New York, of
Mike Boddicker, Baltimore, p	Craig McMurtry, Atlanta, p
1984—Alvin Davis, Seattle, 1b	Juan Samuel, Philadelphia, 2b
Mark Langston, Seattle, p	Dwight Gooden, New York, p
1985—Ozzie Guillen, Chicago, ss	Vince Coleman, St. Louis, of
Teddy Higuera, Milwaukee, p	Tom Browning, Cincinnati, p
1986—Jose Canseco, Oakland, of	Robby Thompson, San Francisco, 2b
Mark Eichhorn, Toronto, p	Todd Worrell, St. Louis, p
1987—Mark McGwire, Oakland, 1b	Benito Santiago, San Diego, c
Mike Henneman, Detroit, p	Mike Dunne, Pittsburgh, p
1988—Walt Weiss, Oakland, ss	Mark Grace, Chicago, 1b
Bryan Harvey, California, p	Tim Belcher, Los Angeles, p
1989—Craig Worthington, Baltimore, 3b	Jerome Walton, Chicago, of
Tom Gordon, Kansas City, p	Andy Benes, San Diego, p

MAJOR LEAGUE EXECUTIVE

Year	Executive	Club
1936	Branch Rickey, St. Louis NL
1937	Edward Barrow, New York AL
1938	Warren Giles, Cincinnati NL
1939	Larry MacPhail, Brooklyn NL
1940	W. O. Briggs, Sr., Detroit AL
1941	Edward Barrow, New York AL
1942	Branch Rickey, St. Louis NL
1943	Clark Griffith, Washington AL
1944	Wm. O. DeWitt, St. Louis AL
1945	Philip K. Wrigley, Chicago NL
1946	Thomas A. Yawkey, Boston AL
1947	Branch Rickey, Brooklyn NL
1948	Bill Veeck, Cleveland AL
1949	Robt. Carpenter, Phila'phia NL
1950	George Weiss, New York AL
1951	George Weiss, New York AL
1952	George Weiss, New York AL
1953	Louis Perini, Milwaukee NL
1954	Horace Stoneham, N. York NL
1955	Walter O'Malley, Brooklyn NL
1956	Gabe Paul, Cincinnati NL
1957	Frank Lane, St. Louis NL
1958	Joe L. Brown, Pittsburgh NL
1959	E. J. (Buzzie) Bavasi, L.A. NL
1960	George Weiss, New York AL
1961	Dan Topping, New York AL
1962	Fred Haney, Los Angeles AL
1963	Vaughan (Bing) Devine, St.L.NL
1964	Vaughan (Bing) Devine, St.L.NL
1965	Calvin Griffith, Minnesota AL
1966	Lee MacPhail, Commissioner's Office
1967	Dick O'Connell, Boston AL
1968	James Campbell, Detroit AL
1969	John Murphy, New York NL
1970	Harry Dalton, Baltimore AL
1971	Cedric Tallis, Kansas City AL
1972	Roland Hemond, Chicago AL
1973	Bob Howsam, Cincinnati NL
1974	Gabe Paul, New York AL
1975	Dick O'Connell, Boston AL
1976	Joe Burke, Kansas City AL
1977	Bill Veeck, Chicago AL
1978	Spec Richardson, San Fran. NL
1979	Hank Peters, Baltimore AL
1980	Tal Smith, Houston NL
1981	John McHale, Montreal NL
1982	Harry Dalton, Milwaukee AL
1983	Hank Peters, Baltimore AL
1984	Dallas Green, Chicago NL
1985	John Schuerholz, Kansas City AL
1986	Frank Cashen, New York NL
1987	Al Rosen, San Francisco NL
1988	Fred Claire, Los Angeles NL
1989	Roland Hemond, Baltimore AL

MAJOR LEAGUE MANAGER

Year	Manager	Club
1936	Joe McCarthy, New York AL
1937	Bill McKechnie, Boston NL
1938	Joe McCarthy, New York AL
1939	Leo Durocher, Brooklyn NL
1940	Bill McKechnie, Cincinnati NL
1941	Billy Southworth, St. Louis NL
1942	Billy Southworth, St. Louis NL
1943	Joe McCarthy, New York AL
1944	Luke Sewell, St. Louis AL
1945	Ossie Bluege, Washington AL
1946	Eddie Dyer, St. Louis NL
1947	Bucky Harris, New York AL
1948	Bill Meyer, Pittsburgh NL
1949	Casey Stengel, New York AL
1950	Red Rolfe, Detroit AL
1951	Leo Durocher, New York NL
1952	Eddie Stanky, St. Louis NL
1953	Casey Stengel, New York AL
1954	Leo Durocher, New York NL
1955	Walter Alston, Brooklyn NL
1956	Birdie Tebbetts, Cincinnati NL
1957	Fred Hutchinson, St. Louis NL
1958	Casey Stengel, New York AL
1959	Walter Alston, Los Angeles NL
1960	Danny Murtaugh, Pitts. NL
1961	Ralph Houk, New York AL
1962	Bill Rigney, Los Angeles AL
1963	Walter Alston, Los Angeles NL
1964	Johnny Keane, St. Louis NL
1965	Sam Mele, Minnesota AL
1966	Hank Bauer, Baltimore AL
1967	Dick Williams, Boston AL
1968	Mayo Smith, Detroit AL
1969	Gil Hodges, New York NL
1970	Danny Murtaugh, Pittsb'gh NL
1971	Charlie Fox, San Francisco NL
1972	Chuck Tanner, Chicago AL
1973	Gene Mauch, Montreal NL
1974	Bill Virdon, New York AL
1975	Darrell Johnson, Boston AL
1976	Danny Ozark, Philadelphia NL
1977	Earl Weaver, Baltimore AL
1978	George Bamberger, Milw'kee AL
1979	Earl Weaver, Baltimore AL
1980	Bill Virdon, Houston NL
1981	Billy Martin, Oakland AL
1982	Whitey Herzog, St. Louis NL
1983	Tony LaRussa, Chicago AL
1984	Jim Frey, Chicago NL
1985	Bobby Cox, Toronto AL
1986	John McNamara, Boston AL; Hal Lanier, Houston NL
1987	Sparky Anderson, Detroit AL; Buck Rodgers, Montreal NL
1988	Tony LaRussa, Oakland AL; Tom Lasorda, Los Angeles NL (tie); Jim Leyland, Pittsburgh NL (tie)
1989	Frank Robinson, Baltimore AL; Don Zimmer, Chicago NL

MAJOR LEAGUE PLAYER

Year	Player	Club
1936	Carl Hubbell, New York NL
1937	Johnny Allen, Cleveland AL
1938	Johnny Vander Meer, Cinn. NL
1939	Joe DiMaggio, New York AL
1940	Bob Feller, Cleveland AL
1941	Ted Williams, Boston AL
1942	Ted Williams, Boston AL
1943	Spud Chandler, New York AL
1944	Marty Marion, St. Louis NL
1945	Hal Newhouser, Detroit AL
1946	Stan Musial, St. Louis NL
1947	Ted Williams, Boston AL
1948	Lou Boudreau, Cleveland AL
1949	Ted Williams, Boston AL
1950	Phil Rizzuto, New York AL
1951	Stan Musial, St. Louis NL
1952	Robin Roberts, Philadelphia NL
1953	Al Rosen, Cleveland AL
1954	Willie Mays, New York NL
1955	Duke Snider, Brooklyn NL
1956	Mickey Mantle, New York AL
1957	Ted Williams, Boston AL
1958	Bob Turley, New York AL
1959	Early Wynn, Chicago AL
1960	Bill Mazeroski, Pittsburgh NL
1961	Roger Maris, New York AL

MAJOR LEAGUE PLAYER—Continued

Year	Player	Club	Year	Player	Club
1962	—Maury Wills, Los Angeles NL		1976	—Joe Morgan, Cincinnati NL	
	Don Drysdale, Los Angeles NL		1977	—Rod Carew, Minnesota AL	
1963	—Sandy Koufax, Los Angeles NL		1978	—Ron Guidry, New York AL	
1964	—Ken Boyer, St. Louis NL		1979	—Willie Stargell, Pittsburgh NL	
1965	—Sandy Koufax, Los Angeles NL		1980	—George Brett, Kansas City AL	
1966	—Frank Robinson, Baltimore AL		1981	—Fernando Valenzuela, Los Angeles NL	
1967	—Carl Yastrzemski, Boston AL		1982	—Robin Yount, Milwaukee AL	
1968	—Denny McLain, Detroit AL		1983	—Cal Ripken, Baltimore AL	
1969	—Willie McCovey, San Fran. NL		1984	—Ryne Sandberg, Chicago NL	
1970	—Johnny Bench, Cin. NL		1985	—Don Mattingly, New York AL	
1971	—Joe Torre, St. Louis NL		1986	—Roger Clemens, Boston AL	
1972	—Billy Williams, Chicago NL		1987	—George Bell, Toronto AL	
1973	—Reggie Jackson, Oakland AL		1988	—Orel Hershiser, Los Angeles NL	
1974	—Lou Brock, St. Louis NL		1989	—Kevin Mitchell, San Francisco NL	
1975	—Joe Morgan, Cincinnati NL				

MINOR LEAGUE EXECUTIVE (HIGHER CLASSIFICATIONS)
(Restricted to Class AAA Starting in 1963)

Year	Executive	Club	Year	Executive	Club
1936	—Earl Mann, Atlanta, Southern		1963	—Lewis Matlin, Hawaii, PCL	
1937	—Robt. LaMotte, Savannah, Sally		1964	—Ed. Leishman, San Diego, PCL	
1938	—Louis McKenna, St. Paul, A.A.		1965	—Harold Cooper, Columbus, Int.	
1939	—Bruce Dudley, Louisville, A.A.		1966	—John Quinn, Jr., Hawaii, PCL	
1940	—Roy Hamey, Kansas City, A.A.		1967	—Hillman Lyons, Richmond, Int.	
1941	—Emil Sick, Seattle, PCL		1968	—Gabe Paul, Jr., Tulsa, PCL	
1942	—Bill Veeck, Milwaukee, A.A.		1969	—Bill Gardner, Louisville, Int.	
1943	—Clar. Rowland, Los Angeles, PCL		1970	—Dick King, Wichita, A.A.	
1944	—William Mulligan, Seattle, PCL		1971	—Carl Steinfeldt, Jr., Roch'ter, Int.	
1945	—Bruce Dudley, Louisville, A.A.		1972	—Don Labbruzzo, Evansville, A.A.	
1946	—Earl Mann, Atlanta, Southern		1973	—Merle Miller, Tucson, PCL	
1947	—Wm. Purnhage, Waterloo, I.I.I.		1974	—John Carbray, Sacramento, PCL	
1948	—Ed. Glennon, Bir'ham, Southern		1975	—Stan Naccarato, Tacoma, PCL	
1949	—Ted Sullivan, Indianapolis, A.A.		1976	—Art Teece, Salt Lake City, PCL	
1950	—Cl. (Brick) Laws, Oakland, PCL		1977	—George Sisler, Jr., Col'bus, Int.	
1951	—Robert Howsam, Denver, West.		1978	—Willie Sanchez, Albu'que, PCL	
1952	—Jack Cooke, Toronto, Int.		1979	—George Sisler, Jr., Col'bus, Int.	
1953	—Richard Burnett, Dallas, Texas		1980	—Jim Burris, Denver, A.A.	
1954	—Edward Stumpf, Indpls., A.A.		1981	—Pat McKernan, Albuquerque, PCL	
1955	—Dewey Soriano, Seattle, PCL		1982	—A. Ray Smith, Louisville, A.A.	
1956	—Robert Howsam, Denver, A.A.		1983	—A. Ray Smith, Louisville, A.A.	
1957	—John Stiglmeier, Buffalo, Int.		1984	—Mike Tamburro, Pawtucket, Int.	
1958	—Ed. Glennon, Bir'ham, Southern		1985	—Patty Cox Hampton, Okla City, A.A.	
1959	—Ed. Leishman, Salt Lake, PCL		1986	—Bob Goughan, Rochester, Int.	
1960	—Ray Winder, Little Rock, Sou.		1987	—Stu Kehoe, Vancouver PCL	
1961	—Elten Schiller, Omaha, A.A.		1988	—Bob Rich, Buffalo, A.A.	
1962	—Geo. Sisler, Jr., Rochester, Int.		1989	—Larry Schmittou, Nashville, A.A.	

MINOR LEAGUE EXECUTIVE (LOWER CLASSIFICATIONS)
(Separate Awards for Class AA and Class A Started in 1963; for Short Class A in 1988)

Year	Executive	Club	Year	Executive	Club
1950	—H. Cooper, Hutch'son, West. A.		1969	—Charlie Blaney, Albuq., Texas	
1951	—O. W. (Bill) Hayes, T'ple, B.S.			Bill Gorman, Visalia, Calif.	
1952	—Hillman Lyons, Danville, MOV		1970	—Carl Sawatski, Arkansas, Texas	
1953	—Carl Roth, Peoria, III			Bob Williams, Bakersfield, Calif.	
1954	—James Meaghan, Cedar R., III		1971	—Miles Wolff, Savannah, Dixie A.	
1955	—John Petrakis, Dubuque, MOV			Ed Holtz, Appleton, Midwest	
1956	—Marvin Milkes, Fresno, Calif.		1972	—John Begzos, S. Antonio, Texas	
1957	—Richard Wagner, L'coln, West.			Bob Piccinini, Modesto, Calif.	
1958	—Gerald Waring, Macon, Sally		1973	—Dick Kravitz, Jacksonville, Sou.	
1959	—Clay Dennis, Des Moines, III			Fritz Colschen, Clinton, Midw.	
1960	—Hubert Kittle, Yakima, Northw.		1974	—Jim Paul, El Paso, Texas	
1961	—David Steele, Fresno, California			Bing Russell, Portland, N'west	
1962	—John Quinn, Jr., S. Jose, Calif.		1975	—Jim Paul, El Paso, Texas	
1963	—Hugh Finnerty, Tulsa, Texas			Cordy Jensen, Eugene, N'west	
	Ben Jewell, M. Valley, Pioneer		1976	—Woodrow Reid, Chat'ooga, Sou.	
1964	—Glynn West, Birmingham, Sou.			Don Buchheister, Ced. Rap., Mid.	
	Jas. Bayens, Rock Hill, W. Car.		1977	—Jim Paul, El Paso, Texas	
1965	—Dick Butler, Dallas-Ft.W., Tex.			Harry Pells, Quad Cities, Midw.	
	Ken. Blackman, Quad C., Midw.		1978	—Larry Schmittou, Nashville, Sou.	
1966	—Tom Fleming, Evansville, South.			Dave Hersh, Appleton, Midwest	
	Cappy Harada, Lodi, California		1979	—Bill Rigney Jr., Midland, Tex.	
1967	—Robt. Quinn, Reading, East.			Tom Romenesko, G'sboro, W.C.	
	Pat Williams, Spar'burg, W. C.		1980	—Frances Crockett, C'lotte, Sou.	
1968	—Phil Howser, Charlotte, South.			Tom Romenesko, G'sboro, W.C.	
	Merle Miller, Burlington, Midw.				

MINOR LEAGUE EXECUTIVE (LOWER CLASSIFICATIONS)—Cont.

Year	Executive	Club
1981—	Allie Prescott, Memphis, Southern	
	Dan Overstreet, Hagerstown, Caro.	
1982—	Art Clarkson, Birmingham, Sou.	
	Bob Carruesco, Stockton, Calif.	
1983—	Edward Kenney, New Britain, East.	
	Terry Reynolds, Vero Beach, Fla. St.	
1984—	Bruce Baldwin, Greenville, Sou.	
	Dave Tarrolly, Beloit, Midwest	
1985—	Ben Bernard, Albany-Colonie, Eastern	
	Pete Vonachen, Peoria, Midwest	
1986—	Bill Davidson, Midland, Texas	
	Rob Dlugozima, Durham, Carolina	

Year	Executive	Club
1987—	Joe Preseren, Tulsa, Texas	
	Skip Weisman, Greensboro, So. Atl.	
1988—	Bill Valentine, Arkansas, Texas	
	Dennis Bastien, Charleston, W.V., S. At.	
	Bob Beban, Eugene, Northwest	
1989—	Chuck Domino, Reading, Eastern	
	John Baxter, South Bend, Midwest	
	Bill Pereira, Boise, Northwest	

MINOR LEAGUE MANAGER

Year	Manager	Club
1936—	Al Sothoron, Milwaukee, A.A.	
1937—	Jake Flowers, Salis'y, East. Sh.	
1938—	Paul Richards, Atlanta, South.	
1939—	Bill Meyer, Kansas City, A.A.	
1940—	Larry Gilbert, Nashville, South.	
1941—	Burt Shotton, Columbus, A.A.	
1942—	Eddie Dyer, Columbus, A.A.	
1943—	Nick Cullop, Columbus, A.A.	
1944—	Al Thomas, Baltimore, Int.	
1945—	Lefty O'Doul, San Fran., PCL	
1946—	Clay Hopper, Montreal, Int.	
1947—	Nick Cullop, Milwaukee, A.A.	
1948—	Casey Stengel, Oakland, PCL	
1949—	Fred Haney, Hollywood, PCL	
1950—	Rollie Hemsley, Columbus, A.A.	
1951—	Charlie Grimm, Milw., A.A.	
1952—	Luke Appling, Memphis, South.	
1953—	Bobby Bragan, Hollywood, PCL	
1954—	Kerby Farrell, Indpls., A.A.	
1955—	Bill Rigney, Minneapolis, A.A.	
1956—	Kerby Farrell, Indpls., A.A.	
1957—	Ben Geraghty, Wichita, A.A.	
1958—	Cal Ermer, Birmingham, South.	
1959—	Pete Reiser, Victoria, Texas	
1960—	Mel McGaha, Toronto, Int.	
1961—	Kerby Farrell, Buffalo, Int.	
1962—	Ben Geraghty, Jackson'le, Int.	

Year	Manager	Club
1963—	Rollie Hemsley, Indpls., Int.	
1964—	Harry Walker, Jacks'vle., Int.	
1965—	Grady Hatton, Okla. City, PCL	
1966—	Bob Lemon, Seattle, PCL	
1967—	Bob Skinner, San Diego, PCL	
1968—	Jack Tighe, Toledo, Int.	
1969—	Clyde McCullough, Tide., Int.	
1970—	Tom Lasorda, Spokane, PCL	
1971—	Del Rice, Salt Lake City, PCL	
1972—	Hank Bauer, Tidewater, Int.	
1973—	Joe Morgan, Charleston, Int.	
1974—	Joe Altobelli, Rochester, Int.	
1975—	Joe Frazier, Tidewater, Int.	
1976—	Vern Rapp, Denver, A.A.	
1977—	Tommy Thompson, Arkan., Tex.	
1978—	Les Moss, Evansville, A.A.	
1979—	Vern Benson, Syracuse, Int.	
1980—	Hal Lanier, Springfield, A.A.	
1981—	Del Crandall, Albuquerque, PCL	
1982—	George Scherger, Indianapolis, A.A.	
1983—	Bill Dancy, Reading, East.	
1984—	Bob Rodgers, Indianapolis, A.A.	
1985—	Jim Fregosi, Louisville, A.A.	
1986—	Joe Sparks, Indianapolis, A.A.	
1987—	Terry Collins, Albuquerque, PCL	
1988—	Joe Sparks, Indianapolis, A.A.	
1989—	Bob Bailor, Syracuse, Int.	

MINOR LEAGUE PLAYER

Year	Player	Club
1936—	Jn. Vander Meer, Durham, Pied.	
1937—	Charlie Keller, Newark, Int.	
1938—	Fred Hutchinson, Seattle, PCL	
1939—	Lou Novikoff, Tulsa-Los A'les.	
1940—	Phil Rizzuto, Kansas City, A.A.	
1941—	John Lindell, Newark, Int.	
1942—	Dick Barrett, Seattle, PCL	
1943—	Chet Covington, Scranton, East.	
1944—	Rip Collins, Albany, Eastern	
1945—	Gil Coan, Chattanooga, South.	
1946—	Sibby Sisti, Indianapolis, A.A.	
1947—	Hank Sauer, Syracuse, Int.	
1948—	Gene Woodling, S. F., PCL	
1949—	Orie Arntzen, Albany, Eastern	
1950—	Frank Saucier, San Ant'o, Tex.	
1951—	Gene Conley, Hartford, Eastern	
1952—	Bill Skowron, Kans. City, A.A.	
1953—	Gene Conley, Toledo, A.A.	
1954—	Herb Score, Indianapolis, A.A.	
1955—	John Murff, Dallas, Texas	
1956—	Steve Bilko, Los Angeles, PCL	
1957—	Norm Siebern, Denver, A.A.	
1958—	Jim O'Toole, Nashville, South.	
1959—	Frank Howard, Victoria-Spok.	
1960—	Willie Davis, Spokane, PCL	
1961—	Howie Koplitz, Bir'ham, South.	
1962—	Bob Bailey, Columbus, Int.	
1963—	Don Buford, Indianapolis, Int.	

Year	Player	Club
1964—	Mel Stottlemyre, Richm'd., Int.	
1965—	Joe Foy, Toronto, International	
1966—	Mike Epstein, Rochester, Int.	
1967—	Johnny Bench, Buffalo, Int.	
1968—	Merv Rettenmund, Roch'ter, Int.	
1969—	Danny Walton, Okla. City, A.A.	
1970—	Don Baylor, Rochester, Int.	
1971—	Bobby Grich, Rochester, Int.	
1972—	Tom Paciorek, Albuq'que, PCL	
1973—	Steve Ontiveros, Phoenix, PCL	
1974—	Jim Rice, Pawtucket, Int.	
1975—	Hector Cruz, Tulsa, A.A.	
1976—	Pat Putnam, Asheville, W. Car.	
1977—	Ken Landreaux, S.L.C., PCL-El Paso, Tex.	
1978—	Champ Summers, Indi'polis, A.A.	
1979—	Mark Bomback, Vancouver, PCL	
1980—	Tim Raines, Denver, A.A.	
1981—	Mike Marshall, Albuquerque, PCL	
1982—	Ron Kittle, Edmonton, PCL	
1983—	Kevin McReynolds, Las Vegas, PCL	
1984—	Alan Knicely, Wichita, A.A.	
1985—	Jose Canseco, Hunt., Sou.-Tac., PCL	
1986—	Tim Pyznarski, Las Vegas, PCL	
1987—	Randy Milligan, Tidewater, Int.	
1988—	Sandy Alomar, Jr., Las Vegas, PCL (tie)	
	Gary Sheffield, Denver, A.A. (tie)	
1989—	Sandy Alomar, Jr., Las Vegas, PCL	

Major League All-Star Teams

1925
Bottomley, St. Louis NL	1B
Hornsby, St. Louis NL	2B
Wright, Pittsburgh NL	SS
Traynor, Pittsburgh NL	3B
Cuyler, Pittsburgh NL	OF
Carey, Pittsburgh NL	OF
Goslin, Washington AL	OF
Cochrane, Philadelphia AL	C
Johnson, Washington AL	P
Rommel, Philadelphia AL	P
Vance, Brooklyn NL	P

1926
G. Burns, Cleve. AL
Hornsby, St. Louis NL
J. Sewell, Cleve. AL
Traynor, Pittsburgh NL
Goslin, Wash'ton AL
Mostil, Chicago AL
Ruth, New York AL
O'Farrell, St. Louis NL
Pennock, N. Y. AL
Uhle, Cleveland AL
Alexander, St. L. NL

1927
1B—Gehrig, N. Y. AL
2B—Hornsby, N. Y. AL
SS—Jackson, N. Y. NL
3B—Traynor, Pitts. NL
OF—Ruth, New York AL
OF—Simmons, Phila. AL
OF—P. Waner, Pitts. NL
C—Hartnett, Chicago NL
P—Root, Chicago NL
P—Lyons, Chicago AL

1928
Gehrig, New York AL	1B
Hornsby, Boston NL	2B
Jackson, New York NL	SS
Lindstrom, N. Y. NL	3B
Ruth, New York AL	OF
Manush, St. Louis AL	OF
P. Waner, Pittsburgh NL	OF
Cochrane, Philadelphia AL	C
Grove, Philadelphia AL	P
Hoyt, New York AL	P

1929
Foxx, Phila'phia AL
Hornsby, Chicago NL
Jackson, N. Y. NL
Traynor, Pittsb'gh NL
Simmons, Phila. AL
L. Wilson, Chi. NL
Ruth, New York AL
Cochrane, Phila. AL
Grove, Phila'phia AL
Grimes, Pittsburgh NL

1930
1B—Terry, New York NL
2B—Frisch, St. Louis NL
SS—Cronin, Wash'ton AL
3B—Lindstrom, N. Y. NL
OF—Simmons, Phila. AL
OF—L. Wilson, Chi. NL
OF—Ruth, New York AL
C—Cochrane, Phila AL
P—Grove, Phila'phia AL
P—W. Ferrell, Cleve. AL

1931
Gehrig, New York AL	1B
Frisch, St. Louis NL	2B
Cronin, Washington AL	SS
Traynor, Pittsburgh NL	3B
Simmons, Philadelphia AL	OF
Averill, Cleveland AL	OF
Ruth, New York AL	OF
Cochrane, Philadelphia AL	C
Grove, Philadelphia AL	P
Earnshaw, Philadelphia AL	P

1932
Foxx, Phila'phia AL
Lazzeri, N. Y. AL
Cronin, Wash'ton AL
Traynor, Pittsb'gh NL
O'Doul, Brooklyn NL
Averill, Cleveland AL
Klein, Philadelphia NL
Dickey, New York AL
Grove, Phila'phia AL
Warneke, Chicago NL

1933
1B—Foxx, Phila'phia AL
2B—Gehringer, Det. AL
SS—Cronin, Wash'ton AL
3B—Traynor, Pitts. NL
OF—Simmons, Chi. AL
OF—Berger, Boston NL
OF—Klein, Phila'phia NL
C—Dickey, N. Y. AL
P—Crowder, Wash. AL
P—Hubbell, N. Y. NL

1934
Gehrig, New York AL	1B
Gehringer, Detroit AL	2B
Cronin, Washington AL	SS
Higgins, Philadelphia AL	3B
Simmons, Chicago AL	OF
Averill, Cleveland AL	OF
Ott, New York NL	OF
Cochrane, Detroit AL	C
Gomez, New York AL	P
Rowe, Detroit AL	P
J. Dean, St. Louis NL	P

1935
Greenberg, Det. AL
Gehringer, Det. AL
Vaughan, Pitts. NL
J. Martin, St. L. NL
Medwick, St. L. NL
Cramer, Phila. AL
Ott, New York NL
Cochrane, Detroit AL
Hubbell, N. Y. NL
J. Dean, St. Louis NL

1936
1B—Gehrig, New York AL
2B—Gehringer, Det. AL
SS—Appling, Chicago AL
3B—Higgins, Phila. AL
OF—Medwick, St. L. NL
OF—Averill, Cleve. AL
OF—Ott, New York NL
C—Dickey, N. Y. AL
P—Hubbell, N. Y. NL
P—J. Dean, St. Louis NL

1937
Gehrig, New York AL	1B
Gehringer, Detroit AL	2B
Bartell, New York NL	SS
Rolfe, New York AL	3B
Medwick, St. Louis NL	OF
J. DiMaggio, New York AL	OF
P. Waner, Pittsburgh NL	OF
Hartnett, Chicago NL	C
Hubbell, New York NL	P
Ruffing, New York AL	P

1938
Foxx, Boston AL
Gehringer, Detroit AL
Cronin, Boston AL
Rolfe, New York AL
Medwick, St. Louis NL
J. DiMaggio, N. Y. AL
Ott, New York NL
Dickey, New York AL
Ruffing, New York AL
Gomez, New York AL
Vander Meer, Cin. NL

1939
1B—Foxx, Boston AL
2B—Gordon, N. Y. AL
SS—Cronin, Boston AL
3B—Rolfe, New York AL
OF—Medwick, St. L. NL
OF—J. DiMaggio, N. Y. AL
OF—Williams, Boston AL
C—Dickey, N. Y. AL
P—Ruffing, N. Y. AL
P—Feller, Cleveland AL
P—Walters, Cin. NL

1940
F. McCormick, Cin. NL	1B
Gordon, New York AL	2B
Appling, Chicago AL	SS
Hack, Chicago NL	3B
Greenberg, Detroit AL	OF
J. DiMaggio, New York AL	OF
Williams, Boston AL	OF
Danning, New York NL	C
Feller, Cleveland AL	P
Walters, Cincinnati NL	P
Derringer, Cincinnati NL	P

1941
Camilli, Brooklyn NL
Gordon, N. Y. AL
Travis, Wash'ton, AL
Hack, Chicago NL
Williams, Boston AL
J. DiMaggio, N. Y. AL
Reiser, Brooklyn NL
Dickey, New York AL
Feller, Cleveland AL
Wyatt, Brooklyn NL
Lee, Chicago NL

1942
1B—Mize, New York NL
2B—Gordon, N. Y. AL
SS—Pesky, Boston AL
3B—Hack, Chicago NL
OF—Williams, Boston AL
OF—J. DiMaggio, N. Y. AL
OF—Slaughter, St. L. NL
C—Owen, Brooklyn NL
P—M. Cooper, St. L. NL
P—Bonham, N. Y. AL
P—Hughson, Boston AL

1943
York, Detroit AL........................ 1B
Herman, Brooklyn NL.............. 2B
Appling, Chicago AL .... SS
Johnson, New York AL.............. 3B
Wakefield, Detroit AL............... OF
Musial, St. Louis NL.................. OF
Nicholson, Chicago NL .... OF
W. Cooper, St. Louis NL   C
Chandler, New York AL............. P
M. Cooper, St. Louis NL............ P
Sewell, Pittsburgh NL .... P

1944
Sanders, St. Louis NL
Doerr, Boston AL
Marion, St. Louis NL
Elliott, Pittsburgh NL
Musial, St. Louis NL
Wakefield, Detroit AL
F. Walker, Brkn, NL
W. Cooper, St. L. NL
Newhouser, Det. AL
M. Cooper, St. L. NL
Trout, Detroit AL

1945
1B—Cavarretta, Chi. NL
2B—Stirnweiss, N. Y. AL
SS—Marion, St. Louis NL
3B—Kurowski, St. L. NL
OF—Holmes, Boston NL
OF—Pafko, Chicago NL
OF—Rosen, Brooklyn NL
C—Richards, Detroit AL
P—Newhouser, Det. AL
P—Ferriss, Boston AL
P—Borowy, Chicago NL

1946
Musial, St. Louis NL.................. 1B
Doerr, Boston AL 2B
Pesky, Boston AL...................... SS
Kell, Detroit AL 3B
Williams, Boston AL .... OF
D. DiMaggio, Boston AL........... OF
Slaughter, St. Louis NL .... OF
Robinson, New York AL........... C
Newhouser, Detroit AL............. P
Feller, Cleveland AL .... P
Ferriss, Boston AL..................... P

1947
Mize, New York NL
Gordon, Cleveland AL
Boudreau, Cleve. AL
Kell, Detroit AL
Williams, Boston AL
J. DiMaggio, N. Y. AL
Kiner, Pittsburgh NL
W. Cooper, N. Y. NL
Blackwell, Cin. NL
Feller, Cleveland AL
Branca, Brooklyn NL

1948
1B—Mize, New York NL
2B—Gordon, Cleve. AL
SS—Boudreau, Cleve. AL
3B—Elliott, Boston NL
OF—Williams, Boston AL
OF—J. DiMaggio, N. Y. AL
OF—Musial, St. Louis NL
C—Tebbetts, Boston AL
P—Sain, Boston NL
P—Lemon, Cleveland AL
P—Brecheen, St. L. NL

1949
Henrich, New York AL............. 1B
Robinson, Brooklyn NL 2B
Rizzuto, New York AL.............. SS
Kell, Detroit AL 3B
Williams, Boston AL .... OF
Musial, St. Louis NL.................. OF
Kiner, Pittsburgh NL................. OF
Campanella, Brooklyn NL........ C
Parnell, Boston AL..................... P
Kinder, Boston AL .... P
Page, New York AL .... P

1950
Dropo, Boston AL
Robinson, Brkn. NL
Rizzuto, New York AL
Kell, Detroit AL
Musial, St. Louis NL
Kiner, Pittsburgh NL
Doby, Cleveland AL
Berra, New York AL
Raschi, New York AL
Lemon, Cleveland AL
Konstanty, Phila. NL

1951
1B—Fain, Phila. AL
2B—Robinson, Brkn. NL
SS—Rizzuto, N. Y. AL
3B—Kell, Detroit AL
OF—Musial, St. Louis NL
OF—Williams, Boston AL
OF—Kiner, Pittsburgh NL
C—Campanella, Brkn. NL
P—Maglie, N. Y. NL
P—Roe, Brooklyn NL
P—Reynolds, N. Y. AL

1952
Fain, Philadelphia AL 1B
Robinson, Brooklyn NL 2B
Rizzuto, New York AL.............. SS
Kell, Boston AL 3B
Musial, St. Louis NL.................. OF
Sauer, Chicago NL..................... OF
Mantle, New York AL .... OF
Berra, New York AL C
Roberts, Philadelphia NL .... P
Shantz, Philadelphia AL........... P
Reynolds, New York AL........... P

1953
Vernon, Wash'ton AL
Schoendienst, St. L. NL
Reese, Brooklyn NL
Rosen, Cleveland AL
Musial, St. Louis NL
Snider, Brooklyn NL
Furillo, Brooklyn NL
Campanella, Brkn. NL
Roberts, Phila'phia NL
Spahn, Milwaukee NL
Porterfield, Wash. AL

1954
1B—Kluszewski, Cin. NL
2B—Avila, Cleveland AL
SS—Dark, New York NL
3B—Rosen, Cleveland AL
OF—Mays, New York NL
OF—Musial, St. Louis NL
OF—Snider, Brooklyn NL
C—Berra, New York AL
P—Lemon, Cleveland AL
P—Antonelli, N. Y. NL
P—Roberts, Phila. NL

1955
Kluszewski, Cincinnati NL 1B
Fox, Chicago AL 2B
Banks, Chicago NL.................... SS
Mathews, Milwaukee NL......... 3B
Snider, Brooklyn NL .... OF
Williams, Boston AL .... OF
Kaline, Detroit AL..................... OF
Campanella, Brooklyn NL........ C
Roberts, Philadelphia NL .... P
Newcombe, Brooklyn NL......... P
Ford, New York AL .... P

1956
Kluszewski, Cin. NL
Fox, Chicago AL
Kuenn, Detroit AL
Boyer, St. Louis NL
Mantle, New York AL
Aaron, Milwaukee NL
Williams, Boston AL
Berra, New York AL
Newcombe, Brkn. NL
Ford, New York AL
Pierce, Chicago AL

1957
1B—Musial, St. Louis NL
2B—Scho'st, N.Y.-Mil. NL
SS—McDougald, N. Y. AL
3B—Mathews, Milw. NL
OF—Mantle, N. Y. AL
OF—Williams, Boston AL
OF—Mays, New York NL
C—Berra, New York AL
P—Spahn, Milw. NL
P—Pierce, Chicago NL
P—Bunning, Detroit AL

1958
Musial, St. Louis NL.................. 1B
Fox, Chicago AL 2B
Banks, Chicago NL.................... SS
Thomas, Pittsburgh NL 3B
Williams, Boston AL .... OF
Mays, San Francisco NL .... OF
Aaron, Milwaukee NL .... OF
Crandall, Milwaukee NL C
Turley, New York AL .... P
Spahn, Milwaukee NL .... P
Friend, Pittsburgh NL............... P

1959
Cepeda, San Fran. NL
Fox, Chicago AL
Banks, Chicago NL
Mathews, Milw. NL
Minoso, Cleveland AL
Mays, San Fran. NL
Aaron, Milwaukee NL
Lollar, Chicago AL
Wynn, Chicago AL
S. Jones, S. Fran. NL
Antonelli, S. Fran. NL

1960
1B—Skowron, N. Y. AL
2B—Mazeroski, Pitts. NL
SS—Banks, Chicago NL
3B—Mathews, Milw. NL
OF—Minoso, Chicago AL
OF—Mays, San Fran. NL
OF—Maris, New York AL
C—Crandall, Milw. NL
P—Law, Pittsburgh NL
P—Spahn, Milw. NL
P—Broglio, St. Louis NL

1961—National
1B—Orlando Cepeda, S.F.
2B—Frank Bolling, Milw.
SS—Maury Wills, L.A.
3B—Ken Boyer, St. Louis
OF—Willie Mays, S.F.
OF—Frank Robinson, Cin.
OF—Roberto Clemente, Pitts.
C—Smoky Burgess, Pitts.
P—Joey Jay, Cincinnati
P—Warren Spahn, Milw.

1961—American
1B—Norm Cash, Detroit
2B—Bobby Richardson, N.Y.
SS—Tony Kubek, N.Y.
3B—Brooks Robinson, Balt.
OF—Mickey Mantle, N.Y.
OF—Roger Maris, N.Y.
OF—Rocky Colavito, Detroit
C—Elston Howard, N.Y.
P—Whitey Ford, N.Y.
P—Frank Lary, Detroit

1962—National
1B—Orlando Cepeda, S.F.
2B—Bill Mazeroski, Pitts.
SS—Maury Wills, L.A.
3B—Ken Boyer, St. Louis
OF—Tommy Davis, L.A.
OF—Willie Mays, S.F.
OF—Frank Robinson, Cin.
C—Del Crandall, Milw.
P—Don Drysdale, L.A.
P—Bob Purkey, Cin.

1962—American
1B—Norm Siebern, K.C.
2B—Bobby Richardson, N.Y.
SS—Tom Tresh, N.Y.
3B—Brooks Robinson, Balt.
OF—Leon Wagner, L.A.
OF—Mickey Mantle, N.Y.
OF—Al Kaline, Detroit
C—Earl Battey, Minnesota
P—Ralph Terry, N.Y.
P—Dick Donovan, Cleve.

1963—National
1B—Bill White, St. Louis
2B—Jim Gilliam, L.A.
SS—Dick Groat, St. Louis
3B—Ken Boyer, St. Louis
OF—Tommy Davis, L.A.
OF—Willie Mays, S.F.
OF—Hank Aaron, Milw.
C—John Edwards, Cin.
P—Sandy Koufax, L.A.
P—Juan Marichal, S.F.

1963—American
1B—Joe Pepitone, N.Y.
2B—Bobby Richardson, N.Y.
SS—Luis Aparicio, Balt.
3B—Frank Malzone, Boston
OF—Carl Yastrzemski, Boston
OF—Albie Pearson, L.A.
OF—Al Kaline, Detroit
C—Elston Howard, N.Y.
P—Whitey Ford, N.Y.
P—Gary Peters, Chicago

1964—American
1B—Dick Stuart, Boston
2B—Bobby Richardson, N.Y.
SS—Jim Fregosi, L.A.
3B—Brooks Robinson, Balt.
OF—Harmon Killebrew, Minn.
OF—Mickey Mantle, N.Y.
OF—Tony Oliva, Minn.
C—Elston Howard, N.Y.
P—Dean Chance, L.A.
P—Gary Peters, Chicago

1964—National
1B—Bill White, St. Louis
2B—Ron Hunt, New York
SS—Dick Groat, St. Louis
3B—Ken Boyer, St. Louis
OF—Billy Williams, Chicago
OF—Willie Mays, San Fran.
OF—Roberto Clemente, Pitts.
C—Joe Torre, Milwaukee
P—Sandy Koufax, L.A.
P—Jim Bunning, Phila.

1965—American
1B—Fred Whitfield, Cleveland
2B—Bobby Richardson, N.Y.
SS—Zoilo Versalles, Minnesota
3B—Brooks Robinson, Balt.
OF—Carl Yastrzemski, Boston
OF—Jimmie Hall, Minnesota
OF—Tony Oliva, Minnesota
C—Earl Battey, Minnesota
P—Jim Grant, Minnesota
P—Mel Stottlemyre, N.Y.

1965—National
1B—Willie McCovey, S.F.
2B—Pete Rose, Cincinnati
SS—Maury Wills, Los Angeles
3B—Deron Johnson, Cincinnati
OF—Willie Stargell, Pitts.
OF—Willie Mays, San Fran.
OF—Hank Aaron, Milwaukee
C—Joe Torre, Milwaukee
P—Sandy Koufax, L.A.
P—Juan Marichal, S.F.

1966—American
1B—Boog Powell, Baltimore
2B—Bobby Richardson, N.Y.
SS—Luis Aparicio, Baltimore
3B—Brooks Robinson, Balt.
OF—Frank Robinson, Balt.
OF—Al Kaline, Detroit
OF—Tony Oliva, Minnesota
C—Paul Casanova, Wash.
P—Jim Kaat, Minnesota
P—Earl Wilson, Detroit

1966—National
1B—Felipe Alou, Atlanta
2B—Pete Rose, Cincinnati
SS—Gene Alley, Pittsburgh
3B—Ron Santo, Chicago
OF—Willie Stargell, Pittsburgh
OF—Willie Mays, San Fran.
OF—Roberto Clemente, Pitts.
C—Joe Torre, Atlanta
P—Sandy Koufax, L.A.
P—Juan Marichal, S.F.

1967—American
1B—Harmon Killebrew, Minn.
2B—Rod Carew, Minnesota
SS—Jim Fregosi, California
3B—Brooks Robinson, Balt.
OF—Carl Yastrzemski, Boston
OF—Al Kaline, Detroit
OF—Frank Robinson, Balt.
C—Bill Freehan, Detroit
P—Jim Lonborg, Boston
P—Earl Wilson, Detroit

1967—National
1B—Orlando Cepeda, St. Louis
2B—Bill Mazeroski, Pittsburgh
SS—Gene Alley, Pittsburgh
3B—Ron Santo, Chicago
OF—Hank Aaron, Atlanta
OF—Jim Wynn, Houston
OF—Roberto Clemente, Pitts.
C—Tim McCarver, St. Louis
P—Mike McCormick, S.F.
P—Ferguson Jenkins, Chi.

1968—American
1B—Boog Powell, Baltimore
2B—Rod Carew, Minnesota
SS—Luis Aparicio, Chicago
3B—Brooks Robinson, Balt.
OF—Ken Harrelson, Boston
OF—Willie Horton, Detroit
OF—Frank Howard, Wash.
C—Bill Freehan, Detroit
P—Dave McNally, Balt.
P—Denny McLain, Detroit

1968—National
1B—Willie McCovey, S.F.
2B—Tommy Helms, Cincinnati
SS—Don Kessinger, Chicago
3B—Ron Santo, Chicago
OF—Billy Williams, Chicago
OF—Curt Flood, St. Louis
OF—Pete Rose, Cincinnati
C—Johnny Bench, Cincinnati
P—Bob Gibson, St. Louis
P—Juan Marichal, S.F.

1969—American
1B—Boog Powell, Baltimore
2B—Rod Carew, Minnesota
SS—Rico Petrocelli, Boston
3B—Harmon Killebrew, Minn.
OF—Frank Howard, Wash.
OF—Paul Blair, Baltimore
OF—Reggie Jackson, Oak.
C—Bill Freehan, Detroit
RHP—Denny McLain, Detroit
LHP—Mike Cuellar, Baltimore

1969—National
1B—Willie McCovey, S.F.
2B—Glenn Beckert, Chicago
SS—Don Kessinger, Chicago
3B—Ron Santo, Chicago
OF—Cleon Jones, New York
OF—Matty Alou, Pittsburgh
OF—Hank Aaron, Atlanta
C—Johnny Bench, Cincinnati
RHP—Tom Seaver, New York
LHP—Steve Carlton, St. Louis

1970—American
1B—Boog Powell, Baltimore
2B—Dave Johnson, Baltimore
SS—Luis Aparicio, Chicago
3B—Harmon Killebrew, Minn.
OF—Frank Howard, Wash.
OF—Reggie Smith, Boston
OF—Tony Oliva, Minnesota
C—Ray Fosse, Cleveland
RHP—Jim Perry, Minnesota
LHP—Sam McDowell, Cleve.

1970—National
1B—Willie McCovey, S.F.
2B—Glenn Beckert, Chicago
SS—Don Kessinger, Chicago
3B—Tony Perez, Cincinnati
OF—Billy Williams, Chicago
OF—Bobby Tolan, Cincinnati
OF—Hank Aaron, Atlanta
C—Johnny Bench, Cincinnati
RHP—Bob Gibson, St. Louis
LHP—Jim Merritt, Cincinnati

1971—American
1B—Norm Cash, Detroit
2B—Cookie Rojas, K.C.
SS—Leo Cardenas, Minnesota
3B—Brooks Robinson, Balt.
OF—Merv Rettenmund, Balt.
OF—Bobby Murcer, N.Y.
OF—Tony Oliva, Minnesota
C—Bill Freehan, Detroit
RHP—Jim Palmer, Baltimore
LHP—Vida Blue, Oakland

1971—National
1B—Lee May, Cincinnati
2B—Glenn Beckett, Chicago
SS—Bud Harrelson, New York
3B—Joe Torre, St. Louis
OF—Willie Stargell, Pittsburgh
OF—Willie Davis, Los Angeles
OF—Hank Aaron, Atlanta
C—Manny Sanguillen, Pitts.
RHP—Ferguson Jenkins, Chi.
LHP—Steve Carlton, St. Louis

1972—American
1B—Dick Allen, Chicago
2B—Rod Carew, Minnesota
SS—Luis Aparicio, Boston
3B—Brooks Robinson, Balt.
OF—Joe Rudi, Oakland
OF—Bobby Murcer, N.Y.
OF—Richie Scheinblum, K.C.
C—Carlton Fisk, Boston
RHP—Gaylord Perry, Cleveland
LHP—Wilbur Wood, Chicago

1972—National
1B—Willie Stargell, Pittsburgh
2B—Joe Morgan, Cincinnati
SS—Chris Speier, San Fran.
3B—Ron Santo, Chicago
OF—Billy Williams, Chicago
OF—Cesar Cedeno, Houston
OF—Roberto Clemente, Pitts.
C—Johnny Bench, Cincinnati
RHP—Ferguson Jenkins, Chi.
LHP—Steve Carlton, Phila.

1973—American
1B—John Mayberry, K.C.
2B—Rod Carew, Minnesota
SS—Bert Campaneris, Oak.
3B—Sal Bando, Oakland
OF—Reggie Jackson, Oak.
OF—Amos Otis, Kansas City
OF—Bobby Murcer, N.Y.
C—Thurman Munson, N.Y.
RHP—Jim Palmer, Baltimore
LHP—Ken Holtzman, Oakland

1973—National
1B—Tony Perez, Cincinnati
2B—Dave Johnson, Atlanta
SS—Bill Russell, Los Angeles
3B—Darrell Evans, Atlanta
OF—Bobby Bonds, San Fran.
OF—Cesar Cedeno, Houston
OF—Pete Rose, Cincinnati
C—Johnny Bench, Cincinnati
RHP—Tom Seaver, New York
LHP—Ron Bryant, San Fran.

1974—American
1B—Dick Allen, Chicago
2B—Rod Carew, Minnesota
SS—Bert Campaneris, Oak.
3B—Sal Bando, Oakland
OF—Joe Rudi, Oakland
OF—Paul Blair, Baltimore
OF—Jeff Burroughs, Texas
C—Thurman Munson, N.Y.
DH—Tommy Davis, Baltimore
RHP—Jim Hunter, Oakland
LHP—Mike Cuellar, Baltimore

1974—National
1B—Steve Garvey, Los Angeles
2B—Joe Morgan, Cincinnati
SS—Dave Concepcion, Cin.
3B—Mike Schmidt, Phila.
OF—Lou Brock, St. Louis
OF—Jim Wynn, Los Angeles
OF—Richie Zisk, Pittsburgh
C—Johnny Bench, Cincinnati
RHP—Andy Messersmith, L.A.
LHP—Don Gullett, Cincinnati

1975—American
1B—John Mayberry, K.C.
2B—Rod Carew, Minnesota
SS—Toby Harrah, Texas
3B—Graig Nettles, New York
OF—Jim Rice, Boston
OF—Fred Lynn, Boston
OF—Reggie Jackson, Oakland
C—Thurman Munson, N.Y.
DH—Willie Horton, Detroit
RHP—Jim Palmer, Baltimore
LHP—Jim Kaat, Chicago

1975—National
1B—Steve Garvey, Los Ang.
2B—Joe Morgan, Cincinnati
SS—Larry Bowa, Philadelphia
3B—Bill Madlock, Chicago
OF—Greg Luzinski, Phila.
OF—Al Oliver, Pittsburgh
OF—Dave Parker, Pittsburgh
C—Johnny Bench, Cincinnati
RHP—Tom Seaver, New York
LHP—Randy Jones, San Diego

1976—American
1B—Chris Chambliss, N.Y.
2B—Bobby Grich, Baltimore
3B—George Brett, K.C.
SS—Mark Belanger, Balt.
OF—Joe Rudi, Oakland
OF—Mickey Rivers, N.Y.
OF—Reggie Jackson, Balt.
C—Thurman Munson, N.Y.
DH—Hal McRae, Kansas City
RHP—Jim Palmer, Baltimore
LHP—Frank Tanana, Calif.

1976—National
1B—Willie Montanez, S.F.-Atl.
2B—Joe Morgan, Cincinnati
3B—Mike Schmidt, Phila.
SS—Dave Concepcion, Cin.
OF—George Foster, Cincinnati
OF—Cesar Cedeno, Houston
OF—Ken Griffey, Cincinnati
C—Bob Boone, Philadelphia
RHP—Don Sutton, Los Angeles
LHP—Randy Jones, San Diego

1977—American
1B—Rod Carew, Minn.
2B—Willie Randolph, N.Y.
3B—Graig Nettles, N.Y.
SS—Rick Burleson, Boston
OF—Jim Rice, Boston
OF—Larry Hisle, Minn.
OF—Bobby Bonds, Calif.
C—Carlton Fisk, Boston
DH—Hal McRae, K.C.
RHP—Nolan Ryan, Calif.
LHP—Frank Tanana, Calif.

1977—National
1B—Steve Garvey, L.A.
2B—Joe Morgan, Cincinnati
3B—Mike Schmidt, Phila.
SS—Garry Templeton, St. L.
OF—George Foster, Cin.
OF—Dave Parker, Pitts.
OF—Greg Luzinski, Phila.
C—Ted Simmons, St. Louis
RHP—Rick Reuschel, Chicago
LHP—Steve Carlton, Phila.

1978—American
1B—Rod Carew, Minnesota
2B—Frank White, K.C.
3B—Graig Nettles, N.Y.
SS—Robin Yount, Milw.
OF—Jim Rice, Boston
OF—Larry Hisle, Milw.
OF—Fred Lynn, Boston
C—Jim Sundberg, Texas
DH—Rusty Staub, Detroit
RHP—Jim Palmer, Balt.
LHP—Ron Guidry, N.Y.

1978—National
1B—Steve Garvey, L.A.
2B—Dave Lopes, Los Angeles
3B—Pete Rose, Cincinnati
SS—Larry Bowa, Phila.
OF—George Foster, Cin.
OF—Dave Parker, Pitts.
OF—Jack Clark, San Fran.
C—Ted Simmons, St. Louis
RHP—Gaylord Perry, S.D.
LHP—Vida Blue, San Fran.

1979—American
1B—Cecil Cooper, Milw.
2B—Bobby Grich, Calif.
3B—George Brett, K.C.
SS—Roy Smalley, Minn.
OF—Jim Rice, Boston
OF—Fred Lynn, Boston
OF—Ken Singleton, Balt.

C—Darrell Porter, K.C.
DH—Don Baylor, Calif.
RHP—Jim Kern, Texas
LHP—Mike Flanagan, Balt.

1979—National
1B—Keith Hernandez, St. L.
2B—Dave Lopes, Los Angeles
3B—Mike Schmidt, Phila.
SS—Garry Templeton, St. L.
OF—Dave Kingman, Chicago
OF—Omar Moreno, Pittsburgh
OF—Dave Winfield, San Diego

C—Ted Simmons, St. Louis
RHP—Joe Niekro, Houston
LHP—Steve Carlton, Phila.

1980—American
1B—Cecil Cooper, Milw.
2B—Willie Randolph, N.Y.
3B—George Brett, K.C.
SS—Robin Yount, Milw.
OF—Ben Oglivie, Milw.
OF—Al Bumbry, Baltimore
OF—Reggie Jackson, N.Y.
DH—Reggie Jackson, N.Y.
C—Rick Cerone, N.Y.
RHP—Steve Stone, Balt.
LHP—Tommy John, N.Y.

1980—National
1B—Keith Hernandez, St. L.
2B—Manny Trillo, Phila.
3B—Mike Schmidt, Phila.
SS—Garry Templeton, St. L.
OF—Dusty Baker, L.A.
OF—Cesar Cedeno, Houston
OF—George Hendrick, St. L.
C—Gary Carter, Montreal
RHP—Jim Bibby, Pittsburgh
LHP—Steve Carlton, Phila.

1981—American
1B—Cecil Cooper, Milw.
2B—Bobby Grich, Calif.
3B—Buddy Bell, Texas
SS—Rick Burleson, Calif.
OF—Rickey Henderson, Oak.
OF—Dwayne Murphy, Oak.
OF—Tony Armas, Oak.
C—Jim Sundberg, Texas
DH—Richie Zisk, Seattle
RHP—Jack Morris, Detroit
LHP—Ron Guidry, N.Y.

1981—National
1B—Pete Rose, Phila.
2B—Manny Trillo, Phila.
3B—Mike Schmidt, Phila.
SS—Dave Concepcion, Cin.
OF—George Foster, Cin.
OF—Andre Dawson, Mon.
OF—Pedro Guerrero, L.A.
C—Gary Carter, Montreal
RHP—Tom Seaver, Cincinnati
LHP—Fernando Valenzuela, L.A.

1982—American
1B—Cecil Cooper, Milw.
2B—Damaso Garcia, Tor.
3B—Doug DeCinces, Calif.
SS—Robin Yount, Milw.
OF—Dave Winfield, N.Y.
OF—Gorman Thomas, Milw.
OF—Dwight Evans, Boston
C—Lance Parrish, Detroit
DH—Hal McRae, K.C.
RHP—Dave Stieb, Toronto
LHP—Geoff Zahn, Calif.

1982—National
1B—Al Oliver, Montreal
2B—Manny Trillo, Phila.
3B—Mike Schmidt, Phila.
SS—Ozzie Smith, St. Louis
OF—Lonnie Smith, St. Louis
OF—Dale Murphy, Atlanta
OF—Pedro Guerrero, L.A.
C—Gary Carter, Montreal
RHP—Steve Rogers, Montreal
LHP—Steve Carlton, Phila.

1983—American
1B—Eddie Murray, Balt.
2B—Lou Whitaker, Detroit
3B—Wade Boggs, Boston
SS—Cal Ripken, Balt.
OF—Jim Rice, Boston
OF—Dave Winfield, N.Y.
OF—Lloyd Moseby, Toronto
C—Carlton Fisk, Chicago
DH—Greg Luzinski, Chicago
RHP—LaMarr Hoyt, Chicago
LHP—Ron Guidry, New York

1983—National
1B—George Hendrick, St. L.
2B—Glenn Hubbard, Atlanta
3B—Mike Schmidt, Phila.
SS—Dickie Thon, Houston
OF—Dale Murphy, Atlanta
OF—Andre Dawson, Montreal
OF—Tim Raines, Montreal
C—Tony Pena, Pittsburgh
RHP—John Denny, Phila.
LHP—Larry McWilliams, Pitts.

1984—American
1B—Don Mattingly, N.Y.
2B—Lou Whitaker, Detroit
3B—Buddy Bell, Texas
SS—Cal Ripken, Baltimore
OF—Tony Armas, Boston
OF—Dwight Evans, Boston
OF—Dave Winfield, N.Y.
C—Lance Parrish, Detroit
DH—Dave Kingman, Oak.
RHP—Mike Boddicker, Balt.
LHP—Willie Hernandez, Det.

1984—National
1B—Keith Hernandez, N.Y.
2B—Ryne Sandberg, Chicago
3B—Mike Schmidt, Phila.
SS—Ozzie Smith, St. Louis
OF—Dale Murphy, Atlanta
OF—Jose Cruz, Houston
OF—Tony Gwynn, S.D.
C—Gary Carter, Montreal
RHP—Rick Sutcliffe, Chicago
LHP—Mark Thurmond, S.D.

1985—American
1B—Don Mattingly, N.Y.
2B—Damaso Garcia, Tor.
3B—Wade Boggs, Boston
SS—Cal Ripken, Balt.
OF—Rickey Henderson, N.Y.
OF—Harold Baines, Chicago
OF—Phil Bradley, Seattle
C—Carlton Fisk, Chicago
DH—Don Baylor, New York
RHP—Bret Saberhagen, K.C.
LHP—Ron Guidry, New York

1985—National
1B—Keith Hernandez, N.Y.
2B—Tom Herr, St. Louis
3B—Tim Wallach, Mon.
SS—Ozzie Smith, St. L.
OF—Dave Parker, Cin.
OF—Willie McGee, St. L.
OF—Dale Murphy, Atlanta
C—Gary Carter, N.Y.
RHP—Dwight Gooden, N.Y.
LHP—John Tudor, St. Louis

1986—American
1B—Don Mattingly, N.Y.
2B—Tony Bernazard, Cleve.
3B—Wade Boggs, Boston
SS—Tony Fernandez, Tor.
OF—Jim Rice, Boston
OF—George Bell, Toronto
OF—Kirby Puckett, Minn.
C—Rich Gedman, Boston
DH—Don Baylor, Boston
RHP—Roger Clemens, Boston
LHP—Teddy Higuera, Milw.

1986—National
1B—Keith Hernandez, N.Y.
2B—Steve Sax, L.A.
3B—Mike Schmidt, Phila.
SS—Ozzie Smith, St. Louis
OF—Tim Raines, Montreal
OF—Tony Gwynn, San Diego
OF—Dave Parker, Cincinnati
C—Gary Carter, New York
RHP—Mike Scott, Hou.
LHP—Fernando Valenzuela, L.A.

1987—American
1B—Don Mattingly, N.Y.
2B—Willie Randolph, N.Y.
3B—Wade Boggs, Boston
SS—Alan Trammell, Det.
OF—George Bell, Toronto
OF—Kirby Puckett, Minn.
OF—Dwight Evans, Bos.
C—Matt Nokes, Detroit
DH—Paul Molitor, Milw.
RHP—Roger Clemens, Bos.
LHP—Jimmy Key, Toronto

1987—National
1B—Jack Clark, St. Louis
2B—Juan Samuel, Philadelphia
3B—Tim Wallach, Montreal
SS—Ozzie Smith, St. Louis
OF—Andre Dawson, Chicago
OF—Tony Gwynn, San Diego
OF—Eric Davis, Cincinnati
C—Benito Santiago, S.D.
RHP—Rick Sutcliffe, Chicago
LHP—Zane Smith, Atlanta

1988—American
1B—George Brett, K.C.
2B—Johnny Ray, Calif.
3B—Wade Boggs, Boston
SS—Alan Trammell, Det.
OF—Kirby Puckett, Minn.
OF—Mike Greenwell, Bos.
OF—Jose Canseco, Oakland
C—Ernie Whitt, Toronto
DH—Harold Baines, Chi.
RHP—Dave Stewart, Oak.
LHP—Frank Viola, Minn.

1988—National
1B—Will Clark, S.F.
2B—Ryne Sandberg, Chi.
3B—Bobby Bonilla, Pitt.
SS—Barry Larkin, Cin.
OF—Darryl Strawberry, N.Y.
OF—Andy Van Slyke, Pitt.
OF—Kevin McReynolds, N.Y.
C—Mike LaValliere, Pitt.

RHP—Orel Hershiser, L.A.
LHP—Danny Jackson, Cin.

1989—American
1B—Fred McGriff, Tor.
2B—Julio Franco, Tex.
3B—Carney Lansford, Oak.
SS—Cal Ripken, Balt.
OF—Ruben Sierra, Tex.
OF—Kirby Puckett, Minn.
OF—Robin Yount, Milw.
C—Mickey Tettleton, Balt.
DH—Harold Baines, Chi.-Tex.
RHP—Bret Saberhagen, K.C.
LHP—Chuck Finley, Calif.

1989—National
1B—Will Clark, S.F.
2B—Ryne Sandberg, Chi.
3B—Howard Johnson, N.Y.
SS—Shawon Dunston, Chi.
OF—Tony Gwynn, San Diego
OF—Kevin Mitchell, S.F.
OF—Eric Davis, Cincinnati
C—Benito Santiago, S.D.
RHP—Mike Scott, Houston
LHP—Mark Davis, San Diego

Gold Glove Fielding Teams

1957 Majors
P—Shantz, N.Y. AL
C—Lollar, Chicago AL
1B—Hodges, Brooklyn
2B—Fox, Chicago AL
3B—Malzone, Boston
SS—McMillan, Cin.
OF—Minoso, Chicago AL
OF—Mays, N.Y. NL
OF—Kaline, Detroit

1958 American
P—Shantz, New York
C—Lollar, Chicago
1B—Power, Cleveland
2B—Bolling, Detroit
3B—Malzone, Boston
SS—Aparicio, Chicago
OF—Siebern, New York
OF—Piersall, Boston
OF—Kaline, Detroit

1958 National
P—Haddix, Cincinnati
C—Crandall, Milwaukee
1B—Hodges, Los Angeles
2B—Mazeroski, Pitt.
3B—Boyer, St. Louis
SS—McMillan, Cin.
OF—Robinson, Cin.
OF—Mays, San Fran.
OF—Aaron, Milwaukee

1959 American
P—Shantz, New York
C—Lollar, Chicago
1B—Power, Cleveland
2B—Fox, Chicago
3B—Malzone, Boston
SS—Aparicio, Chicago
OF—Minoso, Cleveland
OF—Kaline, Detroit
OF—Jensen, Boston

1959 National
P—Haddix, Pittsburgh
C—Crandall, Milwaukee
1B—Hodges, Los Angeles
2B—Neal, Los Angeles
3B—Boyer, St. Louis
SS—McMillan, Cincinnati
OF—Brandt, San Fran.
OF—Mays, San Francisco
OF—Aaron, Milwaukee

1960 American
P—Shantz, New York
C—Battey, Washington
1B—Power, Cleveland
2B—Fox, Chicago
3B—Robinson, Baltimore
SS—Aparicio, Chicago
OF—Minoso, Chicago
OF—Landis, Chicago
OF—Maris, New York

1960 National
P—Haddix, Pittsburgh
C—Crandall, Milwaukee
1B—White, St. Louis
2B—Mazeroski, Pittsburgh
3B—Boyer, St. Louis
SS—Banks, Chicago
OF—Moon, Los Angeles
OF—Mays, San Francisco
OF—Aaron, Milwaukee

1961 American
P—Lary, Detroit
C—Battey, Chicago
1B—Power, Cleveland
2B—Richardson, N.Y.
3B—Robinson, Baltimore
SS—Aparicio, Chicago
OF—Kaline, Detroit
OF—Piersall, Cleveland
OF—Landis, Chicago

1961 National
P—Shantz, Pittsburgh
C—Roseboro, Los Angeles
1B—White, St. Louis
2B—Mazeroski, Pittsburgh
3B—Boyer, St. Louis
SS—Wills, Los Angeles
OF—Mays, San Francisco
OF—Clemente, Pittsburgh
OF—Pinson, Cincinnati

1962 American
P—Kaat, Minnesota
C—Battey, Minnesota
1B—Power, Minnesota
2B—Richardson, N.Y.
3B—Robinson, Baltimore
SS—Aparicio, Chicago
OF—Landis, Chicago
OF—Mantle, New York
OF—Kaline, Detroit

1962 National
P—Shantz, St. Louis
C—Crandall, Milwaukee
1B—White, St. Louis
2B—Hubbs, Chicago
3B—Davenport, S.F.
SS—Wills, Los Angeles
OF—Mays, San Francisco
OF—Clemente, Pittsburgh
OF—Virdon, Pittsburgh

1963 American
P—Kaat, Minnesota
C—Howard, New York
1B—Power, Minnesota
2B—Richardson, N.Y.
3B—Robinson, Baltimore
SS—Versalles, Minnesota
OF—Kaline, Detroit
OF—Yastrzemski, Boston
OF—Landis, Chicago

1963 National
P—Shantz, St. Louis
C—Edwards, Cincinnati
1B—White, St. Louis
2B—Mazeroski, Pittsburgh
3B—Boyer, St. Louis
SS—Wine, Philadelphia
OF—Mays, San Francisco
OF—Clemente, Pittsburgh
OF—Flood, St. Louis

1964 American
P—Kaat, Minnesota
C—Howard, New York
1B—Power, Los Angeles
2B—Richardson, N.Y.
3B—Robinson, Baltimore
SS—Aparicio, Baltimore
OF—Kaline, Detroit
OF—Landis, Chicago
OF—Davalillo, Cleveland

1964 National
P—Shantz, Philadelphia
C—Edwards, Cincinnati
1B—White, St. Louis
2B—Mazeroski, Pittsburgh
3B—Santo, Chicago
SS—Amaro, Philadelphia
OF—Mays, San Francisco
OF—Clemente, Pittsburgh
OF—Flood, St. Louis

1965 American
P—Kaat, Minnesota
C—Freehan, Detroit
1B—Pepitone, New York
2B—Richardson, N.Y.
3B—Robinson, Baltimore
SS—Versalles, Minnesota
OF—Kaline, Detroit
OF—Tresh, New York
OF—Yastrzemski, Boston

1965 National
P—Gibson, St. Louis
C—Torre, Atlanta
1B—White, St. Louis
2B—Mazeroski, Pittsburgh
3B—Santo, Chicago
SS—Cardenas, Cincinnati
OF—Mays, San Francisco
OF—Clemente, Pittsburgh
OF—Flood, St. Louis

1966 American
P—Kaat, Minnesota
C—Freehan, Detroit
1B—Pepitone, New York
2B—Knoop, California
3B—B. Robinson, Balt.
SS—Aparicio, Baltimore
OF—Kaline, Detroit
OF—Agee, Chicago
OF—Oliva, Minnesota

1966 National
P—Gibson, St. Louis
C—Roseboro, Los Angeles
1B—White, Philadelphia
2B—Mazeroski, Pittsburgh
3B—Santo, Chicago
SS—Alley, Pittsburgh
OF—Mays, San Francisco
OF—Flood, St. Louis
OF—Clemente, Pittsburgh

1967 American
P—Kaat, Minnesota
C—Freehan, Detroit
1B—Scott, Boston
2B—Knoop, California
3B—B. Robinson, Balt.
SS—Fregosi, California
OF—Yastrzemski, Boston
OF—Blair, Baltimore
OF—Kaline, Detroit

1967 National
P—Gibson, St. Louis
C—Hundley, Chicago
1B—Parker, Los Angeles
2B—Mazeroski, Pittsburgh
3B—Santo, Chicago
SS—Alley, Pittsburgh
OF—Clemente, Pittsburgh
OF—Flood, St. Louis
OF—Mays, San Francisco

1968 American
P—Kaat, Minnesota
C—Freehan, Detroit
1B—Scott, Boston
2B—Knoop, California
3B—B. Robinson, Balt.
SS—Aparicio, Chicago
OF—Stanley, Detroit
OF—Yastrzemski, Boston
OF—Smith, Boston

1968 National
P—Gibson, St. Louis
C—Bench, Cincinnati
1B—Parker, Los Angeles
2B—Beckert, Chicago
3B—Santo, Chicago
SS—Maxvill, St. Louis
OF—Mays, San Francisco
OF—Clemente, Pittsburgh
OF—Flood, St. Louis

1969 American
P—Kaat, Minnesota
C—Freehan, Detroit
1B—Pepitone, New York
2B—Johnson, Baltimore
3B—B. Robinson, Balt.
SS—Belanger, Baltimore
OF—Blair, Baltimore
OF—Stanley, Detroit
OF—Yastrzemski, Boston

1969 National
P—Gibson, St. Louis
C—Bench, Cincinnati
1B—Parker, Los Angeles
2B—Millan, Atlanta
3B—Boyer, Atlanta
SS—Kessinger, Chicago
OF—Clemente, Pittsburgh
OF—Flood, St. Louis
OF—Rose, Cincinnati

1970 American
P—Kaat, Minnesota
C—Fosse, Cleveland
1B—Spencer, California
2B—Johnson, Baltimore
3B—B. Robinson, Balt.
SS—Aparicio, Chicago
OF—Stanley, Detroit
OF—Blair, Baltimore
OF—Berry, Chicago

1970 National
P—Gibson, St. Louis
C—Bench, Cincinnati
1B—Parker, Los Angeles
2B—Helms, Cincinnati
3B—Rader, Houston
SS—Kessinger, Chicago
OF—Clemente, Pittsburgh
OF—Agee, New York
OF—Rose, Cincinnati

1971 American
P—Kaat, Minnesota
C—Fosse, Cleveland
1B—Scott, Boston
2B—Johnson, Baltimore
3B—B. Robinson, Balt.
SS—Belanger, Baltimore
OF—Blair, Baltimore
OF—Otis, Kansas City
OF—Yastrzemski, Boston

1971 National
P—Gibson, St. Louis
C—Bench, Cincinnati
1B—Parker, Los Angeles
2B—Helms, Cincinnati
3B—Rader, Houston
SS—Harrelson, New York
OF—Clemente, Pittsburgh
OF—Bonds, San Francisco
OF—Davis, Los Angeles

1972 American
P—Kaat, Minnesota
C—Fisk, Boston
1B—Scott, Milwaukee
2B—Griffin, Boston
3B—Robinson, Baltimore
SS—Brinkman, Detroit
OF—Blair, Baltimore
OF—Murcer, New York
OF—Berry, California

1972 National
P—Gibson, St. Louis
C—Bench, Cincinnati
1B—Parker, Los Angeles
2B—Millan, Atlanta
3B—Rader, Houston
SS—Bowa, Philadelphia
OF—Clemente, Pittsburgh
OF—Cedeno, Houston
OF—Davis, Los Angeles

1973 American
P—Kaat, Chicago
C—Munson, New York
1B—Scott, Milwaukee
2B—Grich, Baltimore
3B—Robinson, Baltimore
SS—Belanger, Baltimore
OF—Blair, Baltimore
OF—Otis, Kansas City
OF—Stanley, Detroit

1973 National
P—Gibson, St. Louis
C—Bench, Cincinnati
1B—Jorgensen, Montreal
2B—Morgan, Cincinnati
3B—Rader, Houston
SS—Metzger, Houston
OF—Bonds, San Francisco
OF—Cedeno, Houston
OF—Davis, Los Angeles

1974 American
P—Kaat, Chicago
C—Munson, New York
1B—Scott, Milwaukee
2B—Grich, Baltimore
3B—Robinson, Baltimore
SS—Belanger, Baltimore
OF—Blair, Baltimore
OF—Otis, Kansas City
OF—Rudi, Oakland

1974 National
P—Messersmith, L.A.
C—Bench, Cincinnati
1B—Garvey, Los Angeles
2B—Morgan, Cincinnati
3B—Rader, Houston
SS—Concepcion, Cincinnati
OF—Cedeno, Houston
OF—Geronimo, Cincinnati
OF—Bonds, San Francisco

1975 American
P—Kaat, Chicago
C—Munson, New York
1B—Scott, Milwaukee
2B—Grich, Baltimore
3B—Robinson, Baltimore
SS—Belanger, Baltimore
OF—Blair, Baltimore
OF—Rudi, Oakland
OF—Lynn, Boston

1975 National
P—Messersmith, L.A.
C—Bench, Cincinnati
1B—Garvey, Los Angeles
2B—Morgan, Cincinnati
3B—Reitz, St. Louis
SS—Concepcion, Cincinnati
OF—Cedeno, Houston
OF—Geronimo, Cincinnati
OF—Maddox, Philadelphia

1976 American
P—Palmer, Baltimore
C—Sundberg, Texas
1B—Scott, Milwaukee
2B—Grich, Baltimore
3B—Rodriguez, Detroit
SS—Belanger, Baltimore
OF—Rudi, Oakland
OF—Evans, Boston
OF—Manning, Cleveland

1976 National
P—Kaat, Philadelphia
C—Bench, Cincinnati
1B—Garvey, Los Angeles
2B—Morgan, Cincinnati
3B—Schmidt, Philadelphia
SS—Concepcion, Cincinnati
OF—Cedeno, Houston
OF—Geronimo, Cincinnati
OF—Maddox, Philadelphia

1977 American
P—Palmer, Baltimore
C—Sundberg, Texas
1B—Spencer, Chicago
2B—White, Kansas City
3B—Nettles, New York
SS—Belanger, Baltimore
OF—Beniquez, Texas
OF—Yastrzemski, Boston
OF—Cowens, Kansas City

1977 National
P—Kaat, Philadelphia
C—Bench, Cincinnati
1B—Garvey, Los Angeles
2B—Morgan, Cincinnati
3B—Schmidt, Philadelphia
SS—Concepcion, Cincinnati
OF—Geronimo, Cincinnati
OF—Maddox, Philadelphia
OF—Parker, Pittsburgh

1978 American
P—Palmer, Baltimore
C—Sundberg, Texas
1B—Chambliss, New York
2B—White, Kansas City
3B—Nettles, New York
SS—Belanger, Baltimore
OF—Lynn, Boston
OF—Evans, Boston
OF—Miller, California

1978 National
P—Niekro, Atlanta
C—Boone, Philadelphia
1B—Hernandez, St. Louis
2B—Lopes, Los Angeles
3B—Schmidt, Philadelphia
SS—Bowa, Philadelphia
OF—Maddox, Philadelphia
OF—Parker, Pittsburgh
OF—Valentine, Montreal

1979 American
P—Palmer, Baltimore
C—Sundberg, Texas
1B—Cooper, Milwaukee
2B—White, Kansas City
3B—Bell, Texas
SS—Burleson, Boston
OF—Evans, Boston
OF—Lezcano, Milwaukee
OF—Lynn, Boston

1979 National
P—Niekro, Atlanta
C—Boone, Philadelphia
1B—Hernandez, St. Louis
2B—Trillo, Philadelphia
3B—Schmidt, Philadelphia
SS—Concepcion, Cincinnati
OF—Maddox, Philadelphia
OF—Parker, Pittsburgh
OF—Winfield, San Diego

1980 American
P—Norris, Oakland
C—Sundberg, Texas
1B—Cooper, Milwaukee
2B—White, Kansas City
3B—Bell, Texas
SS—Trammell, Detroit
OF—Lynn, Boston
OF—Murphy, Oakland
OF—Wilson, Kansas City

1980 National
P—Niekro, Atlanta
C—Carter, Montreal
1B—Hernandez, St. Louis
2B—Flynn, New York
3B—Schmidt, Philadelphia
SS—Smith, San Diego
OF—Dawson, Montreal
OF—Maddox, Philadelphia
OF—Winfield, San Diego

1981 American
P—Norris, Oakland
C—Sundberg, Texas
1B—Squires, Chicago
2B—White, Kansas City
3B—Bell, Texas
SS—Trammell, Detroit
OF—Murphy, Oakland
OF—Evans, Boston
OF—Henderson, Oakland

1981 National
P—Carlton, Philadelphia
C—Carter, Montreal
1B—Hernandez, St. Louis
2B—Trillo, Philadelphia
3B—Schmidt, Philadelphia
SS—Smith, San Diego
OF—Dawson, Montreal
OF—Maddox, Philadelphia
OF—Baker, Los Angeles

1982 American
P—Guidry, New York
C—Boone, California
1B—Murray, Baltimore
2B—White, Kansas City
3B—Bell, Texas
SS—Yount, Milwaukee
OF—Evans, Boston
OF—Winfield, New York
OF—Murphy, Oakland

1982 National
P—Niekro, Atlanta
C—Carter, Montreal
1B—Hernandez, St. Louis
2B—Trillo, Philadelphia
3B—Schmidt, Philadelphia
SS—O. Smith, St. Louis
OF—Dawson, Montreal
OF—Murphy, Atlanta
OF—Maddox, Philadelphia

1983 American
P—Guidry, New York
C—Parrish, Detroit
1B—Murray, Baltimore
2B—Whitaker, Detroit
3B—Bell, Texas
SS—Trammell, Detroit
OF—Evans, Boston
OF—Winfield, New York
OF—Murphy, Oakland

1983 National
P—Niekro, Atlanta
C—Pena, Pittsburgh
1B—Hernandez, St.L.-N.Y.
2B—Sandberg, Chicago
3B—Schmidt, Philadelphia
SS—O. Smith, St. Louis
OF—Dawson, Montreal
OF—Murphy, Atlanta
OF—McGee, St. Louis

1984 American
P—Guidry, New York
C—Parrish, Detroit
1B—Murray, Baltimore
2B—Whitaker, Detroit
3B—Bell, Texas
SS—Trammell, Detroit
OF—Evans, Boston
OF—Winfield, New York
OF—Murphy, Oakland

1984 National
P—Andujar, St. Louis
C—Pena, Pittsburgh
1B—Hernandez, New York
2B—Sandberg, Chicago
3B—Schmidt, Philadelphia
SS—O. Smith, St. Louis
OF—Murphy, Atlanta
OF—Dernier, Chicago
OF—Dawson, Montreal

1985 American
P—Guidry, New York
C—Parrish, Detroit
1B—Mattingly, New York
2B—Whitaker, Detroit
3B—Brett, Kansas City
SS—Griffin, Oakland
OF—Pettis, California
OF—Winfield, New York
OF—Evans, Boston (tie)
　　Murphy, Oakland (tie)

1985 National
P—Reuschel, Pittsburgh
C—Pena, Pittsburgh
1B—Hernandez, New York
2B—Sandberg, Chicago
3B—Wallach, Montreal
SS—O. Smith, St. Louis
OF—McGee, St. Louis
OF—Murphy, Atlanta
OF—Dawson, Montreal

1986 American
P—Guidry, New York
C—Boone, California
1B—Mattingly, New York
2B—White, Kansas City
3B—Gaetti, Minnesota
SS—Fernandez, Toronto
OF—Pettis, California
OF—Barfield, Toronto
OF—Puckett, Minnesota

1986 National
P—Valenzuela, Los Angeles
C—Davis, Chicago
1B—Hernandez, New York
2B—Sandberg, Chicago
3B—Schmidt, Philadelphia
SS—Smith, St. Louis
OF—Gwynn, San Diego
OF—Murphy, Atlanta
OF—McGee, St. Louis

1987 American
P—Langston, Seattle
C—Boone, California
1B—Mattingly, New York
2B—White, Kansas City
3B—Gaetti, Minnesota
SS—Fernandez, Toronto
OF—Barfield, Toronto
OF—Puckett, Minnesota
OF—Winfield, New York

1987 National
P—Reuschel, Pitt.-S.F.
C—LaValliere, Pittsburgh
1B—Hernandez, New York
2B—Sandberg, Chicago
3B—Pendleton, St. Louis
SS—Smith, St. Louis
OF—Davis, Cincinnati
OF—Gwynn, San Diego
OF—Dawson, Chicago

1988 American
P—Langston, Seattle
C—Boone, California
1B—Mattingly, New York
2B—Reynolds, Seattle
3B—Gaetti, Minnesota
SS—Fernandez, Toronto
OF—Puckett, Minnesota
OF—White, California
OF—Pettis, Detroit

1988 National
P—Hershiser, L.A.
C—Santiago, S.D.
1B—Hernandez, New York
2B—Sandberg, Chicago
3B—Wallach, Montreal
SS—Smith, St. Louis
OF—Van Slyke, Pitt.
OF—Davis, Cincinnati
OF—Dawson, Chicago

1989 American
P—Saberhagen, Kansas City
C—Boone, Kansas City
1B—Mattingly, New York
2B—Reynolds, Seattle
3B—Gaetti, Minnesota
SS—Fernandez, Toronto
OF—Puckett, Minnesota
OF—White, California
OF—Pettis, Detroit

1989 National
P—Darling, New York
C—Santiago, San Diego
1B—Galarraga, Montreal
2B—Sandberg, Chicago
3B—Pendleton, St. Louis
SS—Smith, St. Louis
OF—Van Slyke, Pittsburgh
OF—Gwynn, San Diego
OF—Davis, Cincinnati

Silver Slugger Teams

1980 American
1B—Cecil Cooper, Milw.
2B—Willie Randolph, N.Y.
3B—George Brett, K.C.
SS—Robin Yount, Milw.
OF—Ben Oglivie, Milw.
OF—Al Oliver, Texas
OF—Willie Wilson, K.C.
C—Lance Parrish, Detroit
DH—Reggie Jackson, N.Y.

1980 National
1B—Keith Hernandez, St.L.
2B—Manny Trillo, Phila.
3B—Mike Schmidt, Phila.
SS—Garry Templeton, St.L.
OF—Dusty Baker, Los Angeles
OF—Andre Dawson, Montreal
OF—George Hendrick, St.L.
C—Ted Simmons, St. Louis
P—Bob Forsch, St. Louis

1981 American
1B—Cecil Cooper, Milw.
2B—Bobby Grich, Calif.
3B—Carney Lansford, Bos.
SS—Rick Burleson, Calif.
OF—Rickey Henderson, Oak.
OF—Dwight Evans, Boston
OF—Dave Winfield, N.Y.
C—Carlton Fisk, Chicago
DH—Al Oliver, Texas

1981 National
1B—Pete Rose, Philadelphia
2B—Manny Trillo, Phila.
3B—Mike Schmidt, Phila.
SS—Dave Concepcion, Cin.
OF—Andre Dawson, Montreal
OF—George Foster, Cincinnati
OF—Dusty Baker, Los Angeles
C—Gary Carter, Montreal
P—Fernando Valenzuela, L.A.

1982 American
1B—Cecil Cooper, Milw.
2B—Damaso Garcia, Tor.
3B—Doug DeCinces, Calif.
SS—Robin Yount, Milw.
OF—Dave Winfield, N.Y.
OF—Willie Wilson, K.C.
OF—Reggie Jackson, Calif.
C—Lance Parrish, Detroit
DH—Hal McRae, K.C.

1982 National
1B—Al Oliver, Montreal
2B—Joe Morgan, S.F.
3B—Mike Schmidt, Phila.
SS—Dave Concepcion, Cin.
OF—Dale Murphy, Atlanta
OF—Pedro Guerrero, L.A.
OF—Leon Durham, Chicago
C—Gary Carter, Montreal
P—Don Robinson, Pittsburgh

1983 American
1B—Eddie Murray, Balt.
2B—Lou Whitaker, Detroit
3B—Wade Boggs, Boston
SS—Cal Ripken, Baltimore
OF—Jim Rice, Boston
OF—Dave Winfield, N.Y.
OF—Lloyd Moseby, Toronto
C—Lance Parrish, Detroit
DH—Don Baylor, New York

1983 National
1B—George Hendrick, St.L.
2B—Johnny Ray, Pittsburgh
3B—Mike Schmidt, Phila.
SS—Dickie Thon, Houston
OF—Andre Dawson, Montreal
OF—Dale Murphy, Atlanta
OF—Jose Cruz, Houston
C—Terry Kennedy, San Diego
P—Fernando Valenzuela, L.A.

1984 American
1B—Eddie Murray, Balt.
2B—Lou Whitaker, Detroit
3B—Buddy Bell, Texas
SS—Cal Ripken, Baltimore
OF—Tony Armas, Boston
OF—Jim Rice, Boston
OF—Dave Winfield, N.Y.
C—Lance Parrish, Detroit
DH—Andre Thornton, Cleve.

1984 National
1B—Keith Hernandez, N.Y.
2B—Ryne Sandberg, Chicago
3B—Mike Schmidt, Phila.
SS—Garry Templeton, S.D.
OF—Dale Murphy, Atlanta
OF—Jose Cruz, Houston
OF—Tony Gwynn, San Diego
C—Gary Carter, Montreal
P—Rick Rhoden, Pittsburgh

1985 American
1B—Don Mattingly, N.Y.
2B—Lou Whitaker, Detroit
3B—George Brett, K.C.
SS—Cal Ripken, Baltimore
OF—Rickey Henderson, N.Y.
OF—Dave Winfield, N.Y.
OF—George Bell, Toronto
C—Carlton Fisk, Chicago
DH—Don Baylor, New York

1985 National
1B—Jack Clark, St. Louis
2B—Ryne Sandberg, Chi.
3B—Tim Wallach, Montreal
SS—Hubie Brooks, Montreal
OF—Willie McGee, St. Louis
OF—Dale Murphy, Atlanta
OF—Dave Parker, Cincinnati
C—Gary Carter, New York
P—Rick Rhoden, Pittsburgh

1986 American	1986 National	1987 American
1B—Don Mattingly, N.Y.	1B—Glenn Davis, Houston	1B—Don Mattingly, N.Y.
2B—Frank White, K.C.	2B—Steve Sax, L.A.	2B—Lou Whitaker, Det.
3B—Wade Boggs, Boston	3B—Mike Schmidt, Phila.	3B—Wade Boggs, Boston
SS—Cal Ripken, Baltimore	SS—Hubie Brooks, Montreal	SS—Alan Trammell, Det.
OF—George Bell, Toronto	OF—Tony Gwynn, San Diego	OF—George Bell, Toronto
OF—Kirby Puckett, Minn.	OF—Tim Raines, Montreal	OF—Dwight Evans, Boston
OF—Jesse Barfield, Toronto	OF—Dave Parker, Cincinnati	OF—Kirby Puckett, Minn.
C—Lance Parrish, Detroit	C—Gary Carter, New York	C—Matt Nokes, Detroit
DH—Don Baylor, Boston	P—Rick Rhoden, Pittsburgh	DH—Paul Molitor, Milw.

1987 National	1988 American	1988 National
1B—Jack Clark, St. Louis	1B—George Brett, K.C.	1B—Andres Galarraga, Mon.
2B—Juan Samuel, Philadelphia	2B—Julio Franco, Clev.	2B—Ryne Sandberg, Chi.
3B—Tim Wallach, Montreal	3B—Wade Boggs, Boston	3B—Bobby Bonilla, Pitt.
SS—Ozzie Smith, St. Louis	SS—Alan Trammell, Det.	SS—Barry Larkin, Cin.
OF—Andre Dawson, Chicago	OF—Kirby Puckett, Minn.	OF—Darryl Strawberry, N.Y.
OF—Eric Davis, Cincinnati	OF—Jose Canseco, Oak.	OF—Andy Van Slyke, Pitt.
OF—Tony Gwynn, San Diego	OF—Mike Greenwell, Bos.	OF—Kirk Gibson, L.A.
C—Benito Santiago, S.D.	C—Carlton Fisk, Chicago	C—Benito Santiago, S.D.
P—Bob Forsch, St. Louis	DH—Paul Molitor, Milw.	P—Tim Leary, L.A.

1989 American	1989 National
1B—Fred McGriff, Tor.	1B—Will Clark, S.F.
2B—Julio Franco, Tex.	2B—Ryne Sandberg, Chi.
3B—Wade Boggs, Boston	3B—Howard Johnson, N.Y.
SS—Cal Ripken, Balt.	SS—Barry Larkin, Cin.
OF—Kirby Puckett, Minn.	OF—Kevin Mitchell, S.F.
OF—Ruben Sierra, Tex.	OF—Tony Gwynn, S.D.
OF—Robin Yount, Milw.	OF—Eric Davis, Cin.
C—Mickey Tettleton, Balt.	C—Craig Biggio, Hou.
DH—H. Baines, Chi.-Tex.	P—Don Robinson, S.F.

Baseball Writers' Association Awards
Most Valuable Player Citations
CHALMERS AWARD

AMERICAN LEAGUE				NATIONAL LEAGUE		
Year	Player	Club	Points	Player	Club	Points
1911—Tyrus Cobb, Detroit, of			64	Frank Schulte, Chicago, of		29
1912—Tristram Speaker, Boston, of			59	Lawrence Doyle, New York, 2b		48
1913—Walter Johnson, Washington, p			54	Jacob Daubert, Brooklyn, 1b		50
1914—Edward Collins, Philadelphia, 2b			63	John Evers, Boston, 2b		50

LEAGUE AWARDS

AMERICAN LEAGUE				NATIONAL LEAGUE		
Year	Player	Club	Points	Player	Club	Points
1922—George Sisler, St. Louis, 1b			59	No selection		
1923—George Ruth, New York, of			64	No selection		
1924—Walter Johnson, Washington, p			55	Arthur Vance, Brooklyn, p		74
1925—Roger Peckinpaugh, Washington, ss			45	Rogers Hornsby, St. Louis, 2b		73
1926—George Burns, Cleveland, 1b			63	Robert O'Farrell, St. Louis, c		79
1927—H. Louis Gehrig, New York, 1b			56	Paul Waner, Pittsburgh, of		72
1928—Gordon Cochrane, Philadelphia, c			53	James Bottomley, St. Louis, 1b		76
1929—No selection				Rogers Hornsby, Chicago, 2b		60

BASEBALL WRITERS' ASSOCIATION MVP AWARDS

AMERICAN LEAGUE				NATIONAL LEAGUE		
Year	Player	Club	Points	Player	Club	Points
1931—Robert Grove, Philadelphia, p			78	Frank Frisch, St. Louis, 2b		65
1932—James Foxx, Philadelphia, 1b			75	Charles Klein, Philadelphia, of		78
1933—James Foxx, Philadelphia, 1b			74	Carl Hubbell, New York, p		77
1934—Gordon Cochrane, Detroit, c			67	Jerome Dean, St. Louis, p		78
1935—Henry Greenberg, Detroit, 1b			*80	Charles Hartnett, Chicago, c		75
1936—H. Louis Gehrig, New York, 1b			73	Carl Hubbell, New York, p		60
1937—Charles Gehringer, Detroit, 2b			78	Joseph Medwick, St. Louis, of		70
1938—James Foxx, Boston, 1b			305	Ernest Lombardi, Cincinnati, c		229
1939—Joseph DiMaggio, New York, of			280	William Walters, Cincinnati, p		303
1940—Henry Greenberg, Detroit, of			292	Frank McCormick, Cincinnati, 1b		274
1941—Joseph DiMaggio, New York, of			291	Adolph Camilli, Brooklyn, 1b		300
1942—Joseph Gordon, New York, 2b			270	Morton Cooper, St. Louis, p		263
1943—Spurgeon Chandler, New York, p			246	Stanley Musial, St. Louis, of		267
1944—Harold Newhouser, Detroit, p			236	Martin Marion, St. Louis, ss		190
1945—Harold Newhouser, Detroit, p			236	Philip Cavaretta, Chicago, 1b		279

BASEBALL WRITERS' ASSOCIATION MVP AWARDS—Cont.

AMERICAN LEAGUE | NATIONAL LEAGUE

Year	Player Club	Points	Player Club	Points
1946	Theodore Williams, Boston, of	224	Stanley Musial, St. Louis, 1b	319
1947	Joseph DiMaggio, New York, of	202	Robert Elliott, Boston, 3b	205
1948	Louis Boudreau, Cleveland, ss	324	Stanley Musial, St. Louis, of	303
1949	Theodore Williams, Boston, of	272	Jack Robinson, Brooklyn, 2b	264
1950	Philip Rizzuto, New York, ss	284	C. James Konstanty, Philadelphia, p	286
1951	Lawrence Berra, New York, c	184	Roy Campanella, Brooklyn, c	243
1952	Robert Shantz, Philadelphia, p	280	Henry Sauer, Chicago, of	226
1953	Albert Rosen, Cleveland, 3b	*336	Roy Campanella, Brooklyn, c	297
1954	Lawrence Berra, New York, c	230	Willie Mays, New York, of	283
1955	Lawrence Berra, New York, c	218	Roy Campanella, Brooklyn, c	226
1956	Mickey Mantle, New York, of	*336	Donald Newcombe, Brooklyn, p	223
1957	Mickey Mantle, New York, of	233	Henry Aaron, Milwaukee, of	239
1958	Jack Jensen, Boston, of	233	Ernest Banks, Chicago, ss	283
1959	J. Nelson Fox, Chicago, 2b	295	Ernest Banks, Chicago, ss	232½
1960	Roger Maris, New York, of	225	Richard Groat, Pittsburgh, ss	276
1961	Roger Maris, New York, of	202	Frank Robinson, Cincinnati, of	219
1962	Mickey Mantle, New York, of	234	Maurice Wills, Los Angeles, ss	209
1963	Elston Howard, New York, c	248	Sanford Koufax, Los Angeles, p	237
1964	Brooks Robinson, Baltimore, 3b	269	Kenton Boyer, St. Louis, 3b	243
1965	Zoilo Versalles, Minnesota, ss	275	Willie Mays, San Francisco, of	224
1966	Frank Robinson, Baltimore, of	*280	Roberto Clemente, Pittsburgh, of	218
1967	Carl Yastrzemski, Boston, of	275	Orlando Cepeda, St. Louis, 1b	*280
1968	Dennis McLain, Detroit, p	*280	Robert Gibson, St. Louis, p	242
1969	Harmon Killebrew, Minnesota, 1-3b	294	Willie McCovey, San Francisco, 1b	265
1970	John (Boog) Powell, Baltimore, 1b	234	Johnny Bench, Cincinnati, c	326
1971	Vida Blue, Oakland, p	268	Joseph Torre, St. Louis, 3b	318
1972	Richie Allen, Chicago, 1b	321	Johnny Bench, Cincinnati, c	263
1973	Reggie Jackson, Oakland, of	*336	Pete Rose, Cincinnati, of	274
1974	Jeff Burroughs, Texas, of	248	Steve Garvey, Los Angeles, 1b	270
1975	Fred Lynn, Boston, of	326	Joe Morgan, Cincinnati, 2b	321½
1976	Thurman Munson, New York, c	304	Joe Morgan, Cincinnati, 2b	311
1977	Rod Carew, Minnesota, 1b	273	George Foster, Cincinnati, of	291
1978	Jim Rice, Boston, of	352	Dave Parker, Pittsburgh, of	320
1979	Don Baylor, California, of	347	Willie Stargell, Pittsburgh, 1b	216
			Keith Hernandez, St. Louis, 1b	216
1980	George Brett, Kansas City, 3b	335	Mike Schmidt, Philadelphia, 3b	*336
1981	Rollie Fingers, Milwaukee, p	319	Mike Schmidt, Philadelphia, 3b	321
1982	Robin Yount, Milwaukee, ss	385	Dale Murphy, Atlanta, of	283
1983	Cal Ripken, Baltimore, ss	322	Dale Murphy, Atlanta, of	318
1984	Willie Hernandez, Detroit, p	306	Ryne Sandberg, Chicago, 2b	326
1985	Don Mattingly, New York, 1b	367	Willie McGee, St. Louis, of	280
1986	Roger Clemens, Boston, p	339	Mike Schmidt, Philadelphia, 3b	287
1987	George Bell, Toronto, of	332	Andre Dawson, Chicago, of	269
1988	Jose Canseco, Oakland, of	*392	Kirk Gibson, Los Angeles, of	272
1989	Robin Yount, Milwaukee, of	256	Kevin Mitchell, San Francisco, of	314

*Unanimous selection.

BASEBALL WRITERS' ASSOCIATION ROOKIE AWARDS

1947—Combined selection—Jack Robinson, Brooklyn, 1b.
1948—Combined selection—Alvin Dark, Boston, N. L., ss.

AMERICAN LEAGUE | NATIONAL LEAGUE

Year	Player Club	Votes	Player Club	Votes
1949	Roy Sievers, St. Louis, of	10	Donald Newcombe, Brooklyn, p	21
1950	Walter Dropo, Boston, 1b	15	Samuel Jethroe, Boston, of	11
1951	Gilbert McDougald, New York, 3b	13	Willie Mays, New York, of	18
1952	Harry Byrd, Philadelphia, p	9	Joseph Black, Brooklyn, p	19
1953	Harvey Kuenn, Detroit, ss	23	James Gilliam, Brooklyn, 2b	11
1954	Robert Grim, New York, p	15	Wallace Moon, St. Louis, of	17
1955	Herbert Score, Cleveland, p	18	William Virdon, St. Louis, of	15
1956	Luis Aparicio, Chicago, ss	22	Frank Robinson, Cincinnati, of	*24
1957	Anthony Kubek, New York, inf-of	23	John Sanford, Philadelphia, p	16
1958	Albert Pearson, Washington, of	14	Orlando Cepeda, San Francisco, 1b	*†21
1959	W. Robert Allison, Washington, of	18	Willie McCovey, San Francisco, 1b	*24
1960	Ronald Hansen, Baltimore, ss	22	Frank Howard, Los Angeles, of	12
1961	Donald Schwall, Boston, p	7	Billy Williams, Chicago, of	10
1962	Thomas Tresh, New York, of-ss	13	Kenneth Hubbs, Chicago, 2b	19
1963	Gary Peters, Chicago, p	10	Peter Rose, Cincinnati, 2b	17
1964	Pedro (Tony) Oliva, Minnesota, of	19	Richard Allen, Philadelphia, 3b	18
1965	Curtis Blefary, Baltimore, of	12	James Lefebvre, Los Angeles, 2b	13
1966	Tommie Agee, Chicago, of	16	Tommy Helms, Cincinnati, 3b	12
1967	Rod Carew, Minnesota, 2b	19	Tom Seaver, New York, p	11
1968	Stan Bahnsen, New York, p	17	Johnny Bench, Cincinnati, c	10½
1969	Lou Piniella, Kansas City, of	9	Ted Sizemore, Los Angeles, 2b	14
1970	Thurman Munson, New York, c	23	Carl Morton, Montreal, p	11
1971	Chris Chambliss, Cleveland, 1b	11	Earl Williams, Atlanta, c	18

BASEBALL WRITERS' ASSOCIATION ROOKIE AWARDS—Continued

	AMERICAN LEAGUE				NATIONAL LEAGUE		
Year	Player	Club	Votes		Player	Club	Votes
1972—Carlton Fisk, Boston, c			*24		Jon Matlack, New York, p		19
1973—Al Bumbry, Baltimore, of			13½		Gary Matthews, San Francisco, of		11
1974—Mike Hargrove, Texas, 1b			16½		Bake McBride, St. Louis, of		16
1975—Fred Lynn, Boston, of			23		John Montefusco, San Francisco, p		12
1976—Mark Fidrych, Detroit, p			22		Butch Metzger, San Diego, p		11
					Pat Zachry, Cincinnati, p		11
1977—Eddie Murray, Baltimore, dh-1b			12½		Andre Dawson, Montreal, of		10
1978—Lou Whitaker, Detroit, 2b			21		Bob Horner, Atlanta, 3b		12½
1979—John Castino, Minnesota, 3b			7		Rick Sutcliffe, Los Angeles, p		20
Alfredo Griffin, Toronto, ss			7				
1980—Joe Charboneau, Cleveland, of			103		Steve Howe, Los Angeles, p		80
1981—Dave Righetti, New York, p			127		Fernando Valenzuela, Los Angeles, p		107
1982—Cal Ripken, Baltimore, ss-3b			132		Steve Sax, Los Angeles, 2b		63
1983—Ron Kittle, Chicago, of			104		Darryl Strawberry, New York, of		109
1984—Alvin Davis, Seattle, 1b			134		Dwight Gooden, New York, p		118
1985—Ozzie Guillen, Chicago, ss			101		Vince Coleman, St. Louis, of		*120
1986—Jose Canseco, Oakland, of			110		Todd Worrell, St. Louis, p		118
1987—Mark McGwire, Oakland, 1b			*140		Benito Santiago, San Diego, c		*120
1988—Walt Weiss, Oakland, ss			103		Chris Sabo, Cincinnati, 3b		79
1989—Gregg Olson, Baltimore, p			136		Jerome Walton, Chicago, of		116

*Unanimous selection. †Three writers did not vote.

CY YOUNG MEMORIAL AWARD

Year	Pitcher	Club	Votes		Year	Pitcher	Club	Votes
1956—Donald Newcombe, Brooklyn			10		1976—A. L.—Jim Palmer, Baltimore			108
1957—Warren Spahn, Milwaukee			15		N. L.—Randy Jones, San Diego			96
1958—Robert Turley, New York, A.L.			5		1977—A. L.—Sparky Lyle, New York			56½
1959—Early Wynn, Chicago, A.L.			13		N. L.—Steve Carlton, Philadelphia			*104
1960—Vernon Law, Pittsburgh			8		1978—A. L.—Ron Guidry, New York			*140
1961—Edward Ford, New York, A.L.			9		N. L.—Gaylord Perry, San Diego			116
1962—Don Drysdale, Los Angeles, N.L.			14		1979—A. L.—Mike Flanagan, Baltimore			136
1963—Sanford Koufax, Los Angeles, N.L.			*20		N. L.—Bruce Sutter, Chicago			72
1964—Dean Chance, Los Angeles, A.L.			17		1980—A. L.—Steve Stone, Baltimore			100
1965—Sanford Koufax, Los Angeles, N.L.			*20		N. L.—Steve Carlton, Philadelphia			118
1966—Sanford Koufax, Los Angeles, N.L.			*20		1981—A. L.—Rollie Fingers, Milwaukee			126
1967—A. L.—Jim Lonborg, Boston			18		N. L.—Fernando Valenzuela, Los Ang.			70
N. L.—M. McCormick, San Francisco			18		1982—A. L.—Pete Vuckovich, Milwaukee			87
1968—A. L.—Dennis McLain, Detroit			*20		N. L.—Steve Carlton, Philadelphia			112
N. L.—Bob Gibson, St. Louis			*20		1983—A. L.—LaMarr Hoyt, Chicago			116
1969—A. L.—Dennis McLain, Detroit			10		N. L.—John Denny, Philadelphia			103
Mike Cuellar, Baltimore			10		1984—A. L.—Willie Hernandez, Detroit			88
N. L.—Tom Seaver, New York			23		N. L.—Rick Sutcliffe, Chicago			*120
1970—A. L.—Jim Perry, Minnesota			55		1985—A. L.—Bret Saberhagen, Kansas City			127
N. L.—Bob Gibson, St. Louis			118		N. L.—Dwight Gooden, New York			*120
1971—A. L.—Vida Blue, Oakland			98		1986—A. L.—Roger Clemens, Boston			*140
N. L.—Fergy Jenkins, Chicago			97		N. L.—Mike Scott, Houston			98
1972—A. L.—Gaylord Perry, Cleveland			64		1987—A. L.—Roger Clemens, Boston			124
N. L.—Steve Carlton, Philadelphia			*120		N. L.—Steve Bedrosian, Philadelphia			57
1973—A. L.—Jim Palmer, Baltimore			88		1988—A. L.—Frank Viola, Minnesota			138
N. L.—Tom Seaver, New York			71		N. L.—Orel Hershiser, Los Angeles			*120
1974—A. L.—Jim Hunter, Oakland			90		1989—A. L.—Bret Saberhagen, Kansas City			138
N. L.—Mike Marshall, Los Angeles			96		N. L.—Mark Davis, San Diego			107
1975—A. L.—Jim Palmer, Baltimore			98					
N. L.—Tom Seaver, New York			98					

*Unanimous selection.

Palmer, Morgan Voted to Hall

By LARRY WIGGE

Joe Morgan and Jim Palmer joked about who got the better of it in the three or four times the two faced each other on their way to being inducted into baseball's Hall of Fame in 1990.

"I don't remember the first time I pitched against him," said Palmer, who spent his entire 19-year major league career with the Baltimore Orioles. "But the second time, he hit a home run against me in the 1977 All-Star Game."

Morgan led off the 1977 All-Star Game at Yankee Stadium with a long drive into the right-field stands. But Palmer retired Morgan on a liner to second base one inning later.

The two players met again in Game 3 of the 1983 World Series, when Palmer hurled two scoreless innings in relief to help Baltimore to a 3-2 victory over the Philadelphia Phillies. Morgan popped to second base.

One-on-one duels aside, there's little doubt that Palmer and Morgan helped make the Orioles and Cincinnati Reds, respectively, two of the game's most successful franchises in the 1970s. The Orioles won three World Series titles during Palmer's career (1966, '70 and '83) while the Reds won two crowns (1975 and '76) during Morgan's tenure with the team.

Palmer, who won 268 games and lost 152 from 1965-84, was named on 411 of 444 ballots (92.6 percent) cast by members of the Baseball Writers' Association of America. The only pitcher to win election with a higher percentage was Bob Feller, who garnered 93.8 percent of the vote in 1962.

In his 22-year major league career, Morgan batted .271 and hit more home runs (266) than any other second baseman in history. He combined power, speed and slick fielding to become the most complete player on the Reds' 1975-76 World Series champions. Morgan earned 363 votes (81.7 percent) to join Palmer as the 20th and 21st players elected to the Cooperstown, N.Y., shrine in their first year of eligibility.

The addition of Palmer and Morgan swelled the membership in the Hall of Fame to 206.

Gaylord Perry, who was 314-265 during his 22-year career, received 320 votes—13 short of the required 75 percent needed for induction.

Ferguson Jenkins, a seven-time 20-game winner en route to a 284-226 career record, was fourth with 296 votes. Jim Bunning, who pitched no-hitters in both leagues and compiled a record of 224-184, had 257 votes. Bunning, who missed election by just four votes in 1988, has just one more year of eligibility remaining before being passed on to the Veterans Committee.

Palmer won an American League-record three Cy Young Awards (1973, '75 and '76) after compiling 22-9, 23-11 and 22-13 records those three seasons. He was a 20-game winner eight times between 1970-78 and his 2.86 career earned-run average ranks fourth among pitchers with at least 3,000 innings.

Palmer became the youngest player (at age 20) to pitch a shutout in World Series history when his four-hitter beat Los Angeles, 6-0, in Game 2 of the 1966 Series. In the process, he handed Hall of Famer Sandy Koufax a defeat in his final major league appearance.

Palmer led the American League with a 2.40 ERA in 1973 and a 2.09 mark in '75. He pitched a no-hitter against Oakland in 1969 and won four Gold Glove awards. Like many of the game's greats, Palmer was at his best when it mattered most, compiling a 4-1 record in Championship Series play and a 4-2 mark in the World Series.

Morgan was The Sporting News' N.L. Rookie Player of the Year in 1965 when he hit .271 for the Houston Astros. His career, however, really took off after he was traded to Cincinnati in an eight-player deal on November 29, 1971.

Morgan played eight seasons with the Reds and won the National League's Most Valuable Player award in both 1975 and 1976. He is the only second baseman to win back-to-back MVP awards and one of nine players overall.

Morgan delivered a two-out single in the ninth inning of Game 7 that drove in the winning run against the Boston Red Sox in the 1975 World Series.

"I would say this—he was just a good major league player when it didn't mean anything," said Sparky Anderson, Morgan's manager with the Reds. "But when it meant something, he was a Hall of Famer."

Morgan hit .327 with 17 homers, 94 RBIs and 67 stolen bases in 1975. He followed with a .320 average, 27 homers, 111 RBIs and 60 steals the next year. That made

Joe Morgan (above) hits a leadoff homer against fellow Hall of Famer Jim Palmer in the 1977 All-Star Game but Palmer (left) pitched in relief to beat Morgan's Phillies team in Game 3 of the 1983 World Series.

him only the fifth second baseman in N.L. history to drive in more than 100 runs in a season.

He hit 268 homers overall, won five Gold Glove awards and ranks third (with 1,865) in career walks behind Babe Ruth and Ted Williams. He played in the All-Star Game in each of his eight seasons with the Reds, from 1972-79, and nine times overall.

A series of injuries in the late '70s caused Morgan's production to drop off. And Cincinnati's decision to dismantle the Big Red Machine came at Morgan's expense in 1980, when he signed as a free agent with Houston and helped the Astros win an N.L. Western Division title in his first season. He spent two seasons with San Francisco (1981-82) before reuniting with former Cincinnati teammates Pete Rose and Tony Perez in Philadelphia, where the trio helped the Phillies win an N.L. pennant in 1983. Morgan retired after playing the 1984 season with Oakland.

The election of Palmer and Morgan marked only the fourth time since 1936 that two players were elected in their first year of eligibility. Jackie Robinson and Feller did it in 1962; Hank Aaron and Frank Robinson in 1982 and Johnny Bench and Carl Yastrzemski in 1989.

The complete 1990 Hall of Fame voting totals follow: Palmer, 411; Morgan, 363; Perry, 320; Jenkins, 296; Bunning, 257; Orlando Cepeda, 211; Tony Oliva, 142; Bill Mazeroski, 131; Harvey Kuenn, 107; Ron Santo, 96; Maury Wills, 95; Jim Kaat, 79; Ken Boyer, 78; Dick Allen, 58; Joe Torre, 55; Minnie Minoso, 51; Elroy Face, 50; Luis Tiant, 42; Vada Pinson, 36; Curt Flood, 35; Thurman Munson, 33; Bobby Bonds, 30; Mickey Lolich, 27; Sparky Lyle, 25; Tug McGraw, 6; Bucky Dent and Bob Watson, 3 each; Rick Monday, Lou Piniella and Mickey Rivers, 2 each; Jim Bibby, Greg Luzinski, Jerry Remy and Mike Torrez, 1 each.

Failing to receive votes: Mike Caldwell, Roy Howell, Jose Morales, Amos Otis, Tony Scott, Ken Singleton, Paul Splittorff, John Stearns, Champ Summers and Dick Tidrow.

Following is a complete list of those enshrined in the Hall of Fame prior to 1990 with the vote by which each enrollee was elected:

1936—Tyrus Cobb (222), John (Honus) Wagner (215), George (Babe) Ruth (215), Christy Mathewson (205), Walter Johnson (189), named by Baseball Writers' Association of America. Total ballots cast, 226.

1937—Napoleon Lajoie (168), Tristram Speaker (165), Denton (Cy) Young (153), named by the BBWAA. Total ballots cast, 201. George Wright, Morgan G. Bulkeley, Byron Bancroft Johnson, John J. McGraw, Cornelius McGillicuddy (Connie Mack), named by Centennial Commission.

1938—Grover C. Alexander (212), named by BBWAA. Total ballots, 262. Henry Chadwick, Alexander J. Cartwright, named by Centennial Commission.

1939—George Sisler (235), Edward Collins (213), William Keeler (207), Louis Gehrig, named by BBWAA (Gehrig by special election after retirement from game was announced). Total ballots cast, 274. Albert G. Spalding, Adrian C. Anson, Charles A. Comiskey, William (Buck) Ewing, Charles Radbourn, William A. (Candy) Cummings, named by committee of old-time players and writers.

1942—Rogers Hornsby (182), named by BBWAA. Total ballots cast, 233.

1944—Judge Kenesaw M. Landis, named by committee on old-timers.

1945—Hugh Duffy, Jimmy Collins, Hugh Jennings, Ed Delahanty, Fred Clarke, Mike Kelly, Wilbert Robinson, Jim O'Rourke, Dennis (Dan) Brouthers and Roger Bresnahan, named by committee on old-timers.

1946—Jesse Burkett, Frank Chance, Jack Chesbro, Johnny Evers, Clark Griffith, Tom McCarthy, Joe McGinnity, Eddie Plank, Joe Tinker, Rube Waddell and Ed Walsh, named by committee on old-timers.

1947—Carl Hubbell (140), Frank Frisch (136), Gordon (Mickey) Cochrane (128) and Robert (Lefty) Grove (123), named by BBWAA. Total ballots, 161.

1948—Herbert J. Pennock (94) and Harold (Pie) Traynor (93), named by BBWAA. Total ballots cast, 121.

1949—Charles Gehringer (159), named by BBWAA in runoff election. Total ballots cast, 187. Charles (Kid) Nichols and Mordecai (Three-Finger) Brown, named by committee on old timers.

1951—Mel Ott (197) and Jimmie Foxx (179), named by BBWAA. Total ballots cast, 226.

1952—Harry Heilmann (203) and Paul Waner (195), named by BBWAA. Total ballots cast, 234.

1953—Jerome (Dizzy) Dean (209) and Al Simmons (199), named by BBWAA. Total ballots cast, 264. Charles Albert (Chief) Bender, Roderick (Bobby) Wallace, William Klem, Tom Connolly, Edward G. Barrow and William Henry (Harry) Wright, named by the new Committee on Veterans.

1954—Walter (Rabbit) Maranville (209), William Dickey (202) and William Terry (195), named by BBWAA. Total ballots cast, 252.

1955—Joe DiMaggio (223), Ted Lyons (217), Arthur (Dazzy) Vance (205) and Charles (Gabby) Hartnett (195), named by BBWAA. Total ballots cast, 251. J. Franklin (Home Run) Baker and Ray Schalk, named by Committee on Veterans.

1956—Hank Greenberg (164) and Joe Cronin (152), named by BBWAA. Total ballots cast, 193.

1957—Joseph V. McCarthy and Sam Crawford, named by Committee on Veterans.

1959—Zachariah (Zack) Wheat, named by Committee on Veterans.

1961—Max Carey and William Hamilton, named by Committee on Veterans.

1962—Bob Feller (150) and Jackie Robinson (124), named by BBWAA. Total ballots cast, 160. Bill McKechnie and Edd Roush, named by Committee on Veterans.

1963—Eppa Rixey, Edgar (Sam) Rice, Elmer Flick and John Clarkson, named by Committee on Veterans.

1964—Luke Appling (189), named by BBWAA in runoff election. Total ballots cast, 225. Urban (Red) Faber, Burleigh Grimes, Tim Keefe, Heinie Manush, Miller Huggins and John Montgomery Ward, named by Committee on Veterans.

1965—James (Pud) Galvin, named by Committee on Veterans.

1966—Ted Williams (282), named by BBWAA. Total ballots cast, 302. Casey Stengel, named by Committee on Veterans.

1967—Charles (Red) Ruffing (266), named by BBWAA in runoff election. Total ballots cast, 306. Branch Rickey and Lloyd Waner, named by Committee on Veterans.

1968—Joseph (Ducky) Medwick (240), named by BBWAA. Total ballots cast, 283. Leon (Goose) Goslin and Hazen (Kiki) Cuyler, named by Committee on Veterans.

1969—Stan (The Man) Musial (317) and Roy Campanella (270), named by BBWAA. Total ballots cast, 340. Stan Coveleski and Waite Hoyt, named by Committee on Veterans.

1970—Lou Boudreau (232), named by BBWAA. Total ballots cast, 300. Earle Combs, Jesse Haines and Ford Frick, named by Committee on Veterans.

1971—Chick Hafey, Rube Marquard, Joe Kelley, Dave Bancroft, Harry Hooper, Jake Beckley and George Weiss, named by Committee on Veterans. Satchel Paige, named by Special Committee on Negro Leagues.

1972—Sandy Koufax (344), Yogi Berra (339) and Early Wynn (301), named by BBWAA. Total ballots cast, 396. Lefty Gomez, Will Harridge and Ross Youngs, named by Committee on Veterans. Josh Gibson and Walter (Buck) Leonard, named by Special Committee on Negro Leagues.

1973—Warren Spahn (316), named by BBWAA. Total ballots cast, 380. Roberto Clemente (393), in special election by BBWAA in which 424 ballots were cast. Billy Evans, George Kelly and Mickey Welch, named by Committee on Veterans. Monte Irvin, named by Special Committee on Negro Leagues.

1974—Mickey Mantle (322) and Whitey Ford (284), named by BBWAA. Total ballots cast, 365. Jim Bottomley, Sam Thompson and Jocko Conlan, named by Committee on Veterans. James (Cool Papa) Bell, named by Special Committee on Negro Leagues.

1975—Ralph Kiner (273), named by BBWAA. Total ballots cast, 362. Earl Averill, Bucky Harris and Billy Herman, named by Committee on Veterans. William (Judy) Johnson, named by Special Committee on Negro Leagues.

1976—Robin Roberts (337) and Bob Lemon (305), named by BBWAA. Total ballots cast, 388. Roger Connor, Cal Hubbard and Fred Lindstrom, named by Committee on Veterans. Oscar Charleston, named by Special Committee on Negro Leagues.

1977—Ernie Banks (321), named by BBWAA. Total ballots cast, 383. Joe Sewell, Al Lopez and Amos Rusie, named by Committee on Veterans. Martin Dihigo and John Henry Lloyd, named by Special Committee on Negro Leagues.

1978—Eddie Mathews (301), named by BBWAA. Total ballots cast, 379. Larry MacPhail and Addie Joss, named by Committee on Veterans.

1979—Willie Mays (409), named by BBWAA. Total ballots cast, 432. Hack Wilson and Warren Giles, named by Committee on Veterans.

1980—Al Kaline (340) and Duke Snider (333), named by BBWAA. Total ballots cast, 385. Chuck Klein and Tom Yawkey, named by Committee on Veterans.

1981—Bob Gibson (337), named by BBWAA. Total ballots cast, 401. Johnny Mize and Rube Foster, named by Committee on Veterans.

1982—Henry Aaron (406) and Frank Robinson (370), named by BBWAA. Total ballots cast, 415. Albert B. (Happy) Chandler and Travis Jackson, named by Committee on Veterans.

1983—Brooks Robinson (344) and Juan Marichal (313), named by BBWAA. Total ballots cast, 374. George Kell and Walter Alston, named by Committee on Veterans.

1984—Luis Aparicio (341), Harmon Killebrew (335) and Don Drysdale (316), named by BBWAA. Total ballots cast, 403. Rick Ferrell and Pee Wee Reese, named by Committee on Veterans.

1985—Hoyt Wilhelm (331) and Lou Brock (315), named by BBWAA. Total ballots cast, 395. Enos Slaughter and Joseph (Arky) Vaughan, named by Committee on Veterans.

1986—Willie McCovey (346), named by BBWAA. Total ballots cast, 425. Bobby Doerr and Ernie Lombardi, named by Committee on Veterans.

1987—Billy Williams (354) and Jim (Catfish) Hunter (315), named by BBWAA. Total ballots cast, 413. Ray Dandridge, named by Committee on Veterans.

1988—Willie Stargell (352), named by BBWAA. Total ballots cast, 427.

1989—Johnny Bench (431) and Carl Yastrzemski (423), named by BBWAA. Total ballots cast, 447. Al Barlick and Albert (Red) Schoendienst, named by Committee on Veterans.

Owners Spend Freely in Draft

By DAVE SLOAN

When baseball's owners decided to loosen their purse strings in the off-season, they didn't just spend their money in the free-agent market.

Fourteen teams spent a record $900,000 to claim 18 unprotected players in the major league draft held December 4 in Nashville, Tenn. The total of 18 draftees was just one shy of the record set in 1980, when the drafting price was $25,000 per player. This time around the price was $50,000, but the drafting team will get half that amount back if the prospect fails to make the season-opening roster.

Twelve of the 18 players chosen were pitchers, with righthander Steve Wapnick going to the Detroit Tigers with the No. 1 choice. The 24-year-old Wapnick was a second-round pick of San Diego in January 1985 who was subsequently drafted by the Oakland and Toronto organizations. He compiled a combined 6-0 record, 1.57 earned-run average and nine saves in 42 games with three different Blue Jays farm clubs last year.

Wapnick was the first of three Toronto prospects taken in the draft, the heaviest loss of any team. The Padres, Pirates and Yankees lost two players each while the Astros, Giants, Phillies and Tigers each drafted two apiece. Four clubs—the Angels, Brewers, Cardinals and Cubs—did not draft or lose any players.

The 1989 draft choices in order of selection:

Tigers—Pitcher Steve Wapnick from Syracuse (International) of the Blue Jays' organization.

Phillies—Outfielder Sil Campusano from Syracuse (International) of the Blue Jays' organization.

Indians—Pitcher Doug Robertson from Phoenix (Pacific Coast) of the Giants' organization.

Reds—Pitcher Tim Layana from Columbus (International) of the Yankees' organization.

Twins—Outfielder Shane Mack from Las Vegas (Pacific Coast) of the Padres' organization.

Expos—Pitcher Bill Sampen from Buffalo (American Association) of the Pirates' organization.

Rangers—Pitcher Ramon Manon from Columbus (International) of the Yankees' organization.

Astros—Pitcher Francis Hernandez from Syracuse (International) of the Blue Jays' organization.

Mets—Pitcher Brad Knackert from Vancouver (Pacific Coast) of the White Sox's organization.

Orioles—Infielder Marty Brown from Nashville (American Association) of the Reds' organization.

Padres—Pitcher Mike Dunne from Calgary (Pacific Coast) of the Mariners' organization.

Giants—Pitcher Jose Alvarez from Richmond (International) of the Braves' organization.

Royals—Pitcher Bill Wilkinson from Buffalo (American Association) of the Pirates' organization.

Athletics—Pitcher Reggie Harris from Pawtucket (International) of the Red Sox's organization.

Tigers—Infielder Johnny Paredes from Indianapolis (American Association) of the Expos' organization.

Phillies—Infielder David Hollins from Las Vegas (Pacific Coast) of the Padres' organization.

Astros—Pitcher Bill Brennan from Albuquerque (Pacific Coast) of the Dodgers' organization.

Giants—Infielder Chuck Jackson from Tucson (Pacific Coast) of the Astros' organization.

MAJOR LEAGUE TRANSACTIONS

NECROLOGY

Expos' Big Deal Was a Bust

By DAVE SLOAN

Depending on the talent on his own club and the talent on other teams in the same division, a major league general manager must decide early in a season whether to play for the short or long term. Should he go all-out for a division title in the current season or shoot for a few years down the road?

It's an important decision with ramifications that can be felt for years.

On May 25, 1989, with his team four games behind the Chicago Cubs in the National League East, Montreal Vice President of Player Personnel David Dombrowski sent three promising young pitchers—Randy Johnson, Brian Holman and Gene Harris—to the Seattle Mariners for much-coveted lefthander Mark Langston. Langston, who was due to become a free agent at the end of the '89 season, had been on the trading block for months after letting it be known that he would not resign with Seattle.

The trade was a gamble that didn't work out. Although Langston won 12 games and posted a 2.39 earned-run average in 24 starts for his new team, Montreal ended the season with the same 81-81 record it had compiled the previous year. The Expos led the N.L. East for 42 consecutive days through August 6 before losing 37 of their final 55 games to finish 12 lengths behind the division-winning Cubs.

To add insult to injury, the Expos lost Langston's future services when the 29-year-old signed a five-year, $16 million contract with the California Angels on December 1. And Johnson, Holman and Harris figure to be members of the Seattle Mariners for years to come.

The Langston deal, however, was not the only trade of a big-name pitcher that failed to pay dividends last year. On July 31, with his team six games behind Montreal in the N.L. East, New York Mets General Manager Frank Cashen sent five players to Minnesota for lefthander Frank Viola, the 1988 American League Cy Young Award winner who had been embroiled in a contract dispute with the Twins and had won just eight of his 24 starts in 1989.

But Viola, a native of Hempstead, N.Y., and a former St. John's University standout, wasn't much better with the Mets. He posted a 5-5 record in 12 National League starts as the Mets—heavy preseason favorites to win the division—failed to gain a

Although he pitched well, Mark Langston could not deliver an N.L. East flag to Montreal in 1989.

game in the standings after the trade. New York finished the year with an 87-75 record, six games behind the Cubs.

As a whole, big-league general managers proved more adept last season at trading for leadoff men than pitchers.

Needing a sparkplug at the top of their lineup to set the table for the power hitters that follow, the Oakland Athletics reacquired outfielder Rickey Henderson from the New York Yankees on June 21. Although the defending A.L. champions had a two-game lead over Kansas City in the A.L. West at the time of the trade, there is little doubt that Henderson was an important figure in the team's drive to a World Series championship.

Henderson, who grew up in Oakland and played for the Athletics from 1979-84, was outstanding in postseason play. He won the Most Valuable Player award in the A.L. Championship Series after batting .400, driving in five runs, stealing eight bases and making life miserable for the Toronto Blue Jays in a five-game Oakland triumph. He followed that performance by hitting .474 and stealing three bases in the Athletics' four-game World Series sweep of the San Francisco Giants.

Fittingly, Henderson led off Game 4 with a home run against the Giants' Don Robinson, only the 15th time in Series history that a player had led off a game with a round-tripper.

The Blue Jays might not have advanced to the ALCS were it not for the acquisition of center fielder Mookie Wilson on August 1. Wilson, who was trapped in a platoon situation for most of his nine-plus seasons with the New York Mets, became an everyday player and Toronto's leadoff man in the final two months of the regular season.

And what a final two months they were. The Jays, who trailed Baltimore by three games in the A.L. East at the time of the trade, wound up winning the division by two games in the closest race of the '89 season. And Wilson, who had hit just .205 with seven stolen bases in 80 games with the Mets, batted .298 and stole 12 bases in 54 games with Toronto.

The N.L. West-champion Giants solidified their bullpen with the acquisition of righthander Steve Bedrosian from the Philadelphia Phillies on June 18. Bedrosian, who won the N.L. Cy Young Award in 1987 after saving 40 games for a fourth-place Phillies team, saved 17 for the Giants to help San Francisco win its first pennant in 27 years.

The Chicago Cubs, who lost to the Giants in a five-game N.L. Championship Series, nabbed their first division crown since 1984 with the help of three players acquired through trades in late August. Pitcher Paul Assenmacher (from Atlanta), infielder Luis Salazar and outfielder Marvell Wynne (both from San Diego) all made late contributions to the Cubs' cause. Salazar, a 10-year veteran, hit .325 in 26 games following the trade and solidified a weak spot at third base.

Once the season ended, a number of prominent players switched teams, most of them via the free-agent route. The same club owners who were found guilty of conspiring against the 1985 and '86 free-agent crops showed no hesitancy in handing out big-money contracts following the 1989 season.

Among the most notable free-agent signings, in addition to Langston, were, in alphabetical order: outfielder Kevin Bass, who left Houston for San Francisco; outfielder Hubie Brooks (Montreal to Los Angeles); first baseman Nick Esasky (Boston to Atlanta); Cy Young Award-winning reliever Mark Davis (San Diego to Kansas City); pitcher Storm Davis (Oakland to Kansas City); designated hitter Dave Parker (Oakland to Milwaukee); catcher Tony Pena (St. Louis to Boston); pitcher Pascual Perez (Montreal to the New York Yankees); reliever Jeff Reardon (Minnesota to Boston), and pitcher Bryn Smith (Montreal to St. Louis).

The most bizarre signing was probably that of Perez, who agreed to a guaranteed three-year, $5.7 million contract with the pitching-poor Yankees on November 21. The 32-year-old Perez has a 64-62 record in eight-plus major league seasons and was 9-13 with a 3.31 ERA in 1989. He began last season in a drug rehabilitation program and his off-field antics have gained the free-spirited pitcher more notoriety than anything he has done on the mound.

Ironically, three former All-Star players were given their unconditional releases during 1989 on successive days.

On November 13, the Boston Red Sox bid adieu to outfielder Jim Rice, who replaced Hall of Famer Carl Yastrzemski as the team's regular left fielder in 1975 and went on to play in seven All-Star Games during a 16-year major league career. Rice, who clubbed 382 homers and drove in 1,451 runs, spent his entire big-league career with Boston.

One day later, the New York Mets said goodbye to catcher Gary Carter, who spent the first 10 full seasons of his career with the Montreal Expos before being traded to the Mets after the 1984 season. Carter, who holds the major league records for both total chances accepted (11,701) and putouts (10,626) for catchers, played in 10 All-Star Games during his career. He won the All-Star Game MVP award in both 1981 and 1984.

On November 15, relief pitcher Bruce Sutter, who didn't pitch last season because of shoulder problems, was given his release by the Atlanta Braves. Sutter, who won the National League's Cy Young

Award in 1979 while with the Chicago Cubs, enjoyed his best success with the St. Louis Cardinals from 1981-84. Sutter helped the Cardinals to a World Series triumph in 1982 and established the N.L. record for most saves in a season (45) in 1984. Sutter also holds the career record (300) for most saves in the National League.

Three major off-season deals were completed late in 1989:

• The Cleveland Indians sent power-hitting outfielder Joe Carter to the San Diego Padres on December 6 for catcher Sandy Alomar Jr., outfielder Chris James and third baseman Carlos Baerga. The Indians were forced to make a trade because Carter, who had hit 151 home runs in five-plus seasons with Cleveland, would have been a free agent following the 1990 season and had shown no interest in re-signing with the team. The key player in the deal for the Indians is Alomar, who has been selected Minor League Player of the Year the last two years by The Sporting News but has been unable to dislodge All-Star Benito Santiago from the San Diego lineup.

• Also on December 6, the New York Mets and Cincinnati Reds swapped left-handed relief pitchers, with Randy Myers going from the Mets to the Reds and John Franco, a Brooklyn native, returning to his hometown. Franco, 29, is two years older than Myers and has saved 148 games for Cincinnati over the last six seasons. Myers, who has considerably fewer saves (56) on the major league level, also commands a salary considerably less than Franco's.

• Two weeks after acquiring Franco, the Mets picked up another reliever in a trade with the Los Angeles Dodgers. Righthander Alejandro Pena, who had only 32 saves in eight-plus seasons with the Dodgers, was acquired by New York along with outfielder Mike Marshall for infielder-outfielder Juan Samuel. Pena and Marshall both have long histories of injury problems but Samuel—who was acquired by the Mets from Philadelphia in June—was a huge disappointment in his half-season with New York. He had requested a trade and the Mets obliged.

Following is a list of all player transactions for the 1989 calendar year:

January 4—Reds' Nashville affiliate signed catcher Scotti Madison, a free agent.

January 4—Expos' Indianapolis affiliate signed second baseman Junior Noboa and outfielder Darryl Motley, both free agents.

January 6—Twins re-signed pitcher Charlie Lea, a free agent.

January 6—Rangers re-signed catcher Jim Sundberg and pitcher Cecilio Guante, both free agents.

January 6—Braves re-signed pitcher Jim Acker, a free agent, and assigned him to Richmond.

January 9—Rangers signed third baseman Buddy Bell, a free agent.

January 10—Yankees traded pitcher Rick Rhoden to Astros for outfielder John Fishel and pitchers Pedro DeLeon and Mike Hook; Astros assigned DeLeon and Hook to Albany.

January 11—Phillies' Scranton/Wilkes-Barre affiliate signed outfielder Steve Stanicek, a free agent.

January 12—Pirates signed pitcher Bill Landrum, a free agent.

January 12—Angels signed pitcher Bob McClure, a free agent.

January 13—Athletics' Tacoma affiliate signed catcher Chris Bando, a free agent.

January 13—Tigers re-signed pitcher Doyle Alexander, a free agent.

January 16—Tigers signed pitcher Frank Williams, a free agent.

January 17—Angels signed outfielder Claudell Washington, a free agent formerly with the Yankees.

January 17—Indians signed pitcher Neil Allen, a free agent formerly with the Yankees.

January 17—Giants signed outfielder Jim Steels, a free agent.

January 18—Blue Jays signed catcher Bob Brenly, a free agent.

January 18—Indians signed pitcher Tim Stoddard, a free agent.

January 19—Cardinals' Louisville affiliate signed pitcher Don Heinkel, a free agent.

January 19—Expos' Indianapolis affiliate signed second baseman Damaso Garcia, a free agent.

January 21—Brewers' Denver affiliate signed pitcher Tony Fossas, a free agent.

January 22—Pirates' Buffalo affiliate signed outfielders Tito Landrum and Reggie Williams, both free agents.

January 23—Indians traded infielder Eddie Williams to White Sox for pitchers Joel Davis and Ed Wojna.

January 23—Rangers signed outfielder Rick Leach, a free agent formerly with the Blue Jays.

January 23—Blue Jays signed infielder Tom Lawless, a free agent.

January 24—Orioles traded catcher Terry Kennedy to Giants for catcher Bob Melvin.

January 25—Pirates' Buffalo affiliate signed catcher Dann Bilardello, a free agent.

January 27—Phillies purchased shortstop Dickie Thon from Padres.

January 28—Angels signed pitcher Mark Clear, a free agent.

January 30—Phillies signed pitcher Larry McWilliams, a free agent formerly with the Cardinals.

January 30—Astros signed pitcher Dan Schatzeder, a free agent formerly with the Twins.

January 31—Angels signed shortstop Dave Concepcion, a free agent.

February 3—Yankees re-signed pitcher Ron Guidry, a free agent.

February 6—Red Sox signed outfielder Danny Heep, a free agent.

February 6—Pirates signed pitcher Bill Scherrer, a free agent, and assigned him to Buffalo.

February 7—Astros' organization signed infielder Ron Washington, a free agent formerly with the Indians, and Harry Spilman, a free agent formerly with the Astros.

February 13—Yankees re-signed pitcher Tommy John, a free agent.

February 13—Twins' Portland affiliate signed pitcher Lee Tunnell, a free agent.

February 14—Pirates signed outfielder Steve Henderson, a free agent, and assigned him to Buffalo.

February 15—Cardinals signed first baseman Leon Durham, a free agent, and assigned him to Louisville.

February 15—Brewers traded pitcher Dan Murphy to Padres for pitchers Todd Simmons and James Austin.

February 16—Phillies' organization signed pitcher Steve Ontiveros, a free agent.

February 17—Blue Jays' Syracuse affiliate re-signed pitcher Doug Bair, a free agent.

February 20—Mets signed pitcher Don Aase, a free agent, and assigned him to Tidewater.

February 22—Tigers released pitcher Mark Huismann.

February 22—Pirates signed infielder Jim Pankovits, a free agent, and assigned him to Buffalo.

February 25—Red Sox' New Britain affiliate signed pitcher Bill Laskey, a free agent.

February 25—Tigers signed pitcher David Palmer, a free agent.

February 25—Rangers' Oklahoma City affiliate signed outfielder Jeff Stone, a free agent.

March 1—Orioles' Rochester affiliate signed pitcher Mark Huismann, a free agent.

March 9—Angels traded pitcher DeWayne Buice to Blue Jays for pitcher Cliff Young.

March 9—White Sox released infielder Donnie Hill.

March 12—Orioles traded pitcher Mike Morgan to Dodgers for outfielder Mike Devereaux.

March 17—Indians released pitcher Jeff Dedmon.

March 17—Pirates traded catcher Ruben Rodriguez to Brewers for a player to be named; Pirates acquired outfielder Lou Thornton on March 26.

March 18—Indians released pitcher Don Gordon.

March 19—Indians traded outfielder Mel Hall to Yankees for catcher Joel Skinner and outfielder Turner Ward.

March 20—Twins traded pitcher Balvino Galvez to Yankees for pitcher Steve Shields.

March 21—Twins traded second baseman Steve Lombardozzi to Astros for a player to be named; Twins acquired outfielder Ramon Cedeno and pitcher Gordon Farmer on September 16.

March 23—Tigers traded pitcher Eric King to White Sox for outfielder Kenny Williams.

March 23—Indians' Colorado Springs affiliate signed pitcher Don Gordon, a free agent.

March 23—Tigers traded infielder Tom Brookens to Yankees for pitcher Charles Hudson.

March 23—Tigers traded infielder Luis Salazar to Padres for shortstop Mike Brumley.

March 23—Royals released catcher Larry Owen.

March 23—Brewers released outfielder Mike Young.

March 23—Twins released pitcher Charlie Lea.

March 25—Braves purchased second baseman Jeff Treadway from Reds.

March 25—Braves purchased catcher John Russell from Phillies.

March 25—Pirates traded shortstop Felix Fermin to Indians for shortstop Jay Bell.

March 25—Tigers released pitcher Ted Power.

March 26—Orioles traded outfielder Ken Gerhart to Giants for first baseman Francisco Melendez; Orioles assigned Melendez to Rochester and Giants assigned Gerhart to Phoenix.

March 26—Twins traded pitcher Keith Atherton to Indians for outfielder Carmen Castillo.

March 26—Twins released pitcher Jeff Calhoun.

March 26—Giants released outfielder Jessie Reid.

March 27—Mets reclaimed outfielder Marcus Lawton from Angels, who had selected him from Tidewater in the 1988 major league draft; Mets assigned Lawton to Tidewater.

March 27—Mariners traded designated hitter Steve Balboni to Yankees for pitcher Dana Ridenour.

March 27—Braves released infielder Paul Runge and catcher Matt Stark.

March 27—Angels released catcher Darrell Miller.

March 27—Indians released pitcher Neil Allen.

March 27—Tigers released outfielder Dwayne Murphy.

March 27—Dodgers traded catcher Gil Reyes to Expos for pitcher Jeff Fischer; Expos assigned Reyes to Indianapolis and Dodgers assigned Fischer to Albuquerque.

March 28—Braves released outfielder Albert Hall.

March 28—Cubs released pitchers Rich Gossage and Al Nipper.

March 28—White Sox released catcher Mark Salas.

March 28—Reds released pitcher Randy St. Claire.

March 28—Expos traded pitcher Neal Heaton to Pirates for a player to be named; Expos acquired pitcher Brett Gideon on March 30.

March 28—Mets released pitcher Edwin Nunez.

March 28—Mets traded pitcher Steve Frey to Expos for catcher Mark Bailey and third baseman Tom O'Malley; Mets assigned Bailey and O'Malley to Tidewater and Expos assigned Frey to Indianapolis.

March 28—Pirates released pitcher Bill Krueger.

March 28—Cardinals signed pitcher Ted Power, a free agent, and assigned him to Louisville.

March 28—Rangers released pitcher Ed Vande Berg and shortstop Bobby Meacham.

March 28—Angels released shortstop Dave Concepcion.

March 29—Braves purchased pitcher Mark Eichhorn from Blue Jays.

March 30—Braves traded pitcher David Miller and cash to Rangers for pitcher Dwayne Henry.

March 30—Reds signed pitcher Kent Tekulve, a free agent, and re-signed outfielder Ken Griffey, Sr., a free agent.

March 30—Brewers signed catcher Dave Engle, a free agent, and outfielder Terry Francona, a free agent formerly with the Indians.

March 31—Brewers reclaimed pitcher Dave Stapleton from Astros, who had selected him from Denver in the 1988 major league draft; Brewers assigned him to Denver.

March 31—Blue Jays reclaimed pitcher Chris Jones from Dodgers, who had selected him from Syracuse in the 1988 major league draft; Blue Jays assigned him to Syracuse.

March 31—Pirates released outfielder Tito Landrum.

March 31—Orioles traded catcher Carl Nichols to Astros for pitcher Dave Johnson and outfielder Victor Hithe.

March 31—Angels released pitcher Urbano Lugo.

April 1—Indians' Colorado Springs affiliate re-signed pitcher Neil Allen and signed catcher Mark Salas, a free agent.

April 1—Red Sox released pitcher Bill Laskey.

April 1—Twins signed pitcher Randy St. Claire, a free agent, and assigned him to Portland.

April 1—Mariners traded outfielder Dave Hengel to Indians for infielders Paul Noce and Chuck Baldwin; Mariners assigned Noce to Calgary and Baldwin to San Bernardino.

April 1—Tigers' Toledo affiliate signed pitcher Edwin Nunez, a free agent.

April 2—Phillies signed outfielder Dwayne Murphy, a free agent.

April 3—Astros claimed outfielder Eric Yelding on waivers from Cubs.

April 4—Indians' Colorado Springs affiliate signed outfielder Mike Young, a free agent.

April 4—Yankees signed catcher Darrell Miller, a free agent, and assigned him to Columbus.

April 4—Expos' Indianapolis affiliate signed pitcher Urbano Lugo, a free agent.

April 5—Astros signed pitcher Greg Gross, a free agent formerly with the Phillies.

April 5—Pirates signed infielder Bobby Meacham, a free agent, and assigned him to Buffalo.

April 6—Athletics traded catcher Matt Sinatro to Astros for catcher-outfielder Troy Afenir; Astros assigned Sinatro to Tucson and Athletics assigned Afenir to Huntsville.

April 7—Brewers' Denver affiliate signed pitcher Bill Krueger, a free agent.

April 14—Giants signed pitcher Rich Gossage, a free agent.

April 16—Yankees released outfielder Gary Ward.

April 21—Mariners traded shortstop Rey Quinones and pitcher Bill Wilkinson to Pirates for pitchers Mike Dunne and Mike Walker and outfielder Mark Merchant; Pirates assigned Wilkinson to Buffalo.

April 23—Tigers signed outfielder Gary Ward, a free agent.

April 30—Blue Jays traded outfielder Jesse Barfield to Yankees for pitcher Al Leiter.

May 1—Giants released pitcher Joe Price.

May 5—Red Sox signed pitcher Joe Price, a free agent.

May 10—Pirates traded infielder Ken Oberkfell to Giants for pitcher Roger Samuels.

May 10—Reds' Nashville affiliate signed outfielder Tito Landrum, a free agent.

May 11—Astros released catcher Alan Ashby.

May 13—Indians released pitcher Brad Havens.

May 16—Twins traded outfielder Mark Davidson to Astros for a player to be named; Astros assigned Davidson to Tucson. Twins acquired pitcher Greg Johnson on September 6.

May 16—Yankees released catcher Jamie Quirk.

May 18—Pirates sold first baseman Orestes Destrade to Seibu Lions of Japanese Baseball League.

May 19—Tigers released third baseman Chris Brown.

May 19—Tigers purchased infielder Rick Schu from Orioles' Rochester affiliate.

May 23—Dodgers' Albuquerque affiliate purchased infielder Jim Pankovits from Pirates' Buffalo affiliate.

May 23—Tigers' Toledo affiliate signed pitcher Brad Havens, a free agent.

May 25—Mariners traded pitcher Mark Langston and a player to be named to Expos for pitchers Randy Johnson, Brian Holman and Gene Harris; Mariners assigned Harris to Calgary. Expos' Indianapolis affiliate acquired pitcher Mike Campbell on July 31.

May 25—Reds released infielder Manny Trillo.

May 27—Athletics signed catcher Jamie Quirk, a free agent, and assigned him to Tacoma.

May 30—Yankees released pitcher Tommy John.

June 2—Padres traded infielder Randy Ready and outfielder John Kruk to Phillies for outfielder Chris James.

June 2—Pirates' Buffalo affiliate signed third baseman Chris Brown, a free agent.

June 9—Mets traded pitcher Terry Leach to Royals for a player to be named; Mets acquired pitcher Agueado Vasquez on October 1.

June 12—Mariners released pitcher Steve Trout.

June 16—Pirates purchased pitcher Doug Bair from Blue Jays' Syracuse affiliate.

June 18—Tigers traded outfielder Pat Sheridan to Giants for outfielder Tracy Jones.

June 18—Phillies traded pitcher Steve Bedrosian and a player to be named to Giants for pitchers Dennis Cook and Terry Mulholland and third baseman Charlie Hayes; Phillies assigned Hayes to Scranton/Wilkes-Barre. Giants acquired infielder Rick Parker on August 7 and assigned him to Phoenix.

June 18—Phillies traded outfielder Juan Samuel to Mets for outfielder Lenny Dykstra, pitcher Roger McDowell and a player to be named; Phillies acquired pitcher Tom Edens on July 27 and assigned him to Scranton.

June 19—Tigers purchased catcher Matt Sinatro from Astros' Tucson affiliate.

June 20—Mariners signed pitcher Keith Comstock, a free agent.

June 21—Yankees traded outfielder Rickey Henderson to Athletics for pitchers Greg Cadaret and Eric Plunk and outfielder Luis Polonia.

June 22—Yankees released pitcher Richard Dotson.

June 22—Pirates traded outfielder Tony Chance to Orioles for pitcher Mike 'Mississippi' Smith; Pirates assigned Smith to Buffalo.

June 23—Reds released outfielder Dave Collins.

June 24—Blue Jays signed catcher Ozzie Virgil, a free agent formerly with the Braves, and assigned him to Syracuse.

June 26—Red Sox purchased outfielder Jeff Stone from Rangers.

June 29—Padres traded pitcher Greg Booker to Twins for pitcher Fred Toliver; Twins assigned Booker to Portland.

June 29—Rangers traded pitcher Scott May and outfielder Mike Wilson to Brewers for outfielder LaVel Freeman and pitcher Todd Simmons;

Brewers assigned May and Wilson to Denver and Rangers assigned Freeman and Simmons to Oklahoma City.

July 1—White Sox signed pitcher Richard Dotson, a free agent.

July 2—Braves traded pitcher Zane Smith to Expos for pitchers Sergio Valdez and Nate Minchey and outfielder Kevin Dean.

July 2—Braves traded outfielder Dion James to Indians for outfielder Oddibe McDowell.

July 10—Yankees traded pitcher Scott Nielsen to Mets for outfielder Marcus Lawton; Mets assigned Nielsen to Tidewater and Yankees assigned Lawton to Columbus.

July 12—Indians released pitcher Tim Stoddard.

July 13—Tigers released pitcher David Palmer.

July 13—Phillies traded pitcher Bob Sebra to Reds for a player to be named; Phillies acquired pitcher Jeff Gray on September 6 and assigned him to Scranton/Wilkes-Barre.

July 16—Dodgers released pitcher Rick Horton.

July 17—Tigers traded outfielder-first baseman Billy Bean to Dodgers for outfielder Steve Green and first baseman-outfielder Domingo Michel; Tigers assigned Green to Lakeland and Michel to Toledo and Dodgers assigned Bean to Albuquerque.

July 18—Dodgers traded pitcher Tim Leary and shortstop Mariano Duncan to Reds for outfielder Kal Daniels and infielder Lenny Harris.

July 20—Cardinals' Louisville affiliate signed pitcher Rick Horton, a free agent.

July 20—Orioles traded pitcher John Habyan to Yankees for outfielder Stanley Jefferson; Yankees assigned Habyan to Columbus and Orioles assigned Jefferson to Rochester.

July 22—Yankees traded third baseman Mike Pagliarulo and pitcher Don Schulze to Padres for Pitcher Walt Terrell and a player to be named; Yankees acquired pitcher Fred Toliver on September 27.

July 22—Pirates released shortstop Rey Quinones.

July 24—Blue Jays released catcher Bob Brenly.

July 24—Athletics released catcher Jamie Quirk.

July 27—Athletics released pitcher Bill Dawley.

July 28—Tigers traded first baseman Keith Moreland to Orioles for pitcher Brian DuBois; Tigers assigned DuBois to Toledo.

July 28—Astros released pitcher Bob Knepper.

July 29—White Sox traded outfielder Harold Baines and infielder Fred Manrique to Rangers for shortstop Scott Fletcher, outfielder Sammy Sosa and pitcher Wilson Alvarez; White Sox assigned Sosa to Vancouver and Alvarez to Birmingham.

July 30—Reds re-signed outfielder Dave Collins, a free agent.

July 31—White Sox traded pitcher Jerry Reuss to Brewers for pitcher Brian Drahman.

July 31—Twins traded pitcher Frank Viola to Mets for pitchers Rick Aguilera and David West and three players to be named; Twins acquired pitchers Kevin Tapani and Tim Drummond on August 1 and assigned them to Portland and acquired pitcher Jack Savage on October 16.

July 31—Athletics released second baseman Glenn Hubbard.

July 31—Blue Jays traded pitchers Jeff Musselman and Mike Brady to Mets for a player to be named; Mets assigned Brady to Columbia. Blue

Jays acquired outfielder Mookie Wilson on August 1.

July 31—Blue Jays claimed outfielder Lee Mazzilli on waivers from Mets.

August 1—Mets' Tidewater affiliate purchased pitchers Manny Hernandez and Ray Soff from Twins.

August 2—Brewers released catcher Dave Engle.

August 2—Giants' Phoenix affiliate signed catcher Bob Brenly, a free agent.

August 4—Giants signed pitcher Bob Knepper, a free agent.

August 5—Red Sox released infielder Ed Romero.

August 5—Orioles signed catcher Jamie Quirk, a free agent.

August 5—Mariners' Calgary affiliate purchased catcher Matt Sinatro from Tigers.

August 6—Mets' Tidewater affiliate purchased pitcher Mike Trujillo from Tigers' Toledo affiliate.

August 7—Red Sox claimed pitcher Greg A. Harris on waivers from Phillies.

August 7—Indians released pitcher Keith Atherton.

August 10—Yankees claimed pitcher Rich Gossage on waivers from Giants.

August 12—Braves signed infielder Ed Romero, a free agent.

August 18—Astros traded outfielder Billy Hatcher to Pirates for outfielder Glenn Wilson.

August 23—Braves traded infielder Ed Romero to Brewers for a player to be named; Braves acquired pitcher Jay Aldrich on September 1.

August 24—Braves traded pitcher Jim Acker to Blue Jays for pitcher Tony Castillo and a player to be named; Braves acquired catcher Francisco Cabrera on August 24 and assigned him to Richmond.

August 24—Braves traded pitcher Paul Assenmacher to Cubs for two players to be named; Braves acquired catcher Kelly Mann and pitcher Pat Gomez on September 1.

August 28—Twins traded outfielder Jim Dwyer to Expos for a player to be named; Twins acquired outfielder Alonzo Powell on September 16.

August 29—Yankees traded pitcher John Candelaria to Expos for a player to be named; Yankees acquired third baseman Mike Blowers on August 31

August 30—Yankees traded designated hitter-first baseman Ken Phelps to Athletics for pitcher Scott Holcomb.

August 30—Cubs traded pitcher Calvin Schiraldi, outfielder Darrin Jackson and a player to be named to Padres for outfielder Marvell Wynne and infielder Luis Salazar; Padres acquired first baseman Phil Stephenson on September 5.

August 30—Giants traded outfielder James Steels to Expos for a player to be named; Expos assigned Steels to Indianapolis.

September 1—White Sox re-signed designated hitter Jerry Hairston, a free agent.

September 2—Phillies traded pitcher Larry McWilliams to Royals for a player to be named; Phillies acquired catcher Jeff Hulse on October 21 and assigned him to Reading.

September 4—Giants traded infielder Ed Jurak to Expos for a player to be named; Expos assigned Jurak to Indianapolis.

September 6—Indians' Colorado Springs affiliate traded catcher Ron Tingley to Angels for a player to be named.

September 29—Mets released infielder Jeff McKnight.

October 2—Rangers released pitcher Cecilio Guante and outfielder Thad Bosley.

October 2—White Sox released designated hitter Jerry Hairston.

October 3—Orioles released pitcher Mark Huismann.

October 3—Twins released pitcher Steve Shields.

October 3—Mets released pitcher Manny Hernandez.

October 4—Yankees released third baseman Steve Kiefer.

October 4—Phillies released pitcher Randy O'Neal.

October 4—Indians released pitcher Neil Allen and infielder Luis Aguayo.

October 4—Tigers released pitcher Dave Beard.

October 5—Cardinals released infielder Rod Booker.

October 6—Angels released pitcher Terry Clark and outfielder Jim Eppard.

October 9—Giants released pitcher Karl Best.

October 11—Phillies released catcher Al Pardo and first baseman Steve Stanicek.

October 12—Cardinals released pitcher Don Heinkel.

October 12—Red Sox released outfielder Jeff Stone.

October 16—Brewers released designated hitter Joey Meyer.

October 20—Blue Jays released catcher Ozzie Virgil.

October 31—Angels released infielder Glenn Hoffman.

November 2—Orioles released catcher Jamie Quirk.

November 8—Indians sold outfielder Mike Young to Hiroshima Toyo Carp of Japanese Baseball League.

November 8—Brewers released pitcher Jerry Reuss.

November 8—Yankees released outfielder Marcus Lawton and pitcher Dale Mohorcic.

November 9—Brewers released pitcher Paul Mirabella.

November 9—White Sox traded pitcher Jeff Bittiger to Dodgers for infielder Tracy Woodson.

November 13—Red Sox released outfielder Jim Rice.

November 14—Mets released catcher Gary Carter.

November 14—Pirates re-signed pitcher Doug Bair, a free agent.

November 15—Braves released pitchers Bruce Sutter, Charlie Puleo and Jay Aldrich.

November 16—Padres released pitcher Don Schulze.

November 16—Giants signed outfielder Kevin Bass, a free agent formerly with the Astros.

November 16—Pirates released infielder Sammy Khalifa and pitchers Logan Easley and Mike 'Mississippi' Smith.

November 17—Braves signed first baseman Nick Esasky, a free agent formerly with the Red Sox.

November 20—Yankees released infielders Tom Brookens and Rafael Santana.

November 20—White Sox released first baseman Russ Morman.

November 20—Tigers re-signed pitcher Frank Tanana, a free agent.

November 20—Pirates signed pitcher Ted Power, a free agent formerly with the Cardinals.

November 20—Braves purchased infielder Alexis Infante from Blue Jays.

November 20—Braves released pitcher Mark Eichhorn.

November 20—Indians traded outfielder Dave Clark to Cubs for outfielder Mitch Webster.

November 20—Phillies released outfielder Dwayne Murphy and pitcher Mike Maddux.

November 21—Indians signed pitcher Cecilio Guante, a free agent.

November 21—Yankees signed pitcher Pascual Perez, a free agent formerly with the Expos.

November 21—Pirates released catcher Dann Bilardello and pitcher Morris Madden.

November 21—Tigers released pitcher Frank Williams.

November 24—Rangers signed outfielder Gary Pettis, a free agent formerly with the Tigers.

November 27—Red Sox signed catcher Tony Pena, a free agent formerly with the Cardinals.

November 27—Blue Jays re-signed outfielder Mookie Wilson, a free agent.

November 28—Indians signed outfielder Candy Maldonado, a free agent formerly with the Giants.

November 28—Athletics re-signed outfielder Rickey Henderson, a free agent.

November 28—Cardinals signed pitcher Bryn Smith, a free agent formerly with the Expos.

November 29—Giants signed shortstop Dave Anderson, a free agent formerly with the Dodgers.

November 29—Pirates signed pitcher Walt Terrell, a free agent formerly with the Yankees.

November 29—Pirates released pitcher Brian Fisher.

November 30—Orioles released first baseman Jim Traber, who was signed by Kintetsu Buffaloes of Japanese Baseball League.

November 30—Yankees re-signed outfielder Mel Hall, a free agent.

November 30—Cardinals re-signed pitcher Danny Cox, a free agent.

December 1—Phillies signed outfielder-first baseman Carmelo Martinez, a free agent formerly with the Padres.

December 1—Angels signed pitcher Mark Langston, a free agent formerly with the Expos.

December 1—Indians released catcher Mark Salas.

December 3—Brewers signed designated hitter Dave Parker, a free agent formerly with the Athletics.

December 4—Yankees traded catcher Don Slaught to Pirates for pitchers Jeff Robinson and Willie Smith.

December 4—Indians released pitcher Ed Wojna.

December 4—Yakult Swallows of Japanese Baseball League signed pitcher Floyd Bannister, a free agent formerly with the Royals.

December 5—Mets traded pitcher John Mitchell and outfielder Joaquin Contreras to Orioles for outfielder Keith Hughes and pitcher Cesar Mejia.

December 5—Orioles' Rochester affiliate signed pitcher Jay Aldrich and infielder Jeff McKnight, both free agents.

December 5—Tigers signed infielder Tony Phillips, a free agent formerly with the Athletics.

December 5—Royals re-signed pitcher Steve Crawford, a free agent, and signed pitcher Richard Dotson, a free agent formerly with the White Sox.

December 6—Astros signed infielder Ken Oberkfell, a free agent formerly with the Giants.

December 6—Red Sox signed pitcher Jeff Reardon, a free agent formerly with the Twins.

December 6—Cardinals traded first baseman-outfielder Jim Lindeman and pitcher Matt Kinzer to Tigers for second baseman Pat Austin, catcher Bill Henderson and pitcher Marcos Betances.

December 6—Cardinals re-signed pitcher Rick Horton, a free agent.

December 6—Red Sox re-signed pitcher Dennis Lamp, a free agent.

December 6—Indians traded outfielder Joe Carter to Padres for catcher Sandy Alomar, outfielder Chris James and third baseman Carlos Baerga.

December 6—Astros signed pitcher Bill Gullickson, a free agent formerly with the Yankees.

December 6—Twins re-signed first baseman Kent Hrbek, a free agent.

December 6—Reds traded pitcher John Franco and outfielder Don Brown to Mets for pitchers Randy Myers and Kip Gross.

December 6—Phillies re-signed catcher Steve Lake, a free agent.

December 6—Pirates re-signed pitcher Neal Heaton, a free agent.

December 6—Pirates released first baseman Benny Distefano.

December 6—Padres signed outfielder Fred Lynn, a free agent formerly with the Tigers, and signed pitcher Craig Lefferts, a free agent formerly with the Giants.

December 7—Expos signed pitcher Dennis Boyd, a free agent formerly with the Red Sox.

December 7—Royals re-signed second baseman Frank White and outfielder Willie Wilson, both free agents, and signed pitcher Storm Davis, a free agent formerly with the Athletics.

December 7—Indians signed first baseman Keith Hernandez, a free agent formerly with the Mets.

December 7—Tigers signed outfielder Lloyd Moseby, a free agent formerly with the Blue Jays.

December 7—Mariners signed first baseman Pete O'Brien, a free agent formerly with the Indians.

December 7—Dodgers signed pitcher Jim Gott, a free agent formerly with the Pirates.

December 7—Blue Jays traded pitcher Jose Nunez to Cubs for pitcher Paul Kilgus.

December 7—Expos' Indianapolis affiliate signed pitchers Dale Mohorcic and Keith Atherton, both free agents.

December 8—Giants re-signed catcher Terry Kennedy, a free agent.

December 8—Athletics re-signed first baseman Ken Phelps, a free agent.

December 8—Indians signed infielder Tom Brookens, a free agent.

December 11—Royals signed pitcher Mark Davis, a free agent formerly with the Padres.

December 12—Reds traded pitcher Tim Leary and outfielder Van Snider to Yankees for first baseman Hal Morris and pitcher Rodney Imes.

December 12—Brewers re-signed first baseman-outfielder Terry Francona, a free agent.

December 12—Indians traded pitcher Steve Davis to Dodgers for infielder Manny Francois

and outfielder Joe Kesselmark.

December 12—Mets' Tidewater affiliate signed catcher Orlando Mercado, a free agent.

December 13—Cardinals re-signed pitcher Frank DiPino, a free agent.

December 13—Red Sox' Pawtucket affiliate signed outfielder Jeff Stone and first baseman Billy Jo Robidoux, both free agents.

December 13—Cubs released pitcher Pat Perry.

December 13—Expos signed pitcher Dave Schmidt, a free agent formerly with the Orioles.

December 13—Athletics signed catcher Jamie Quirk, a free agent, and pitcher Scott Sanderson, a free agent formerly with the Cubs.

December 14—Cardinals signed pitcher John Tudor, a free agent formerly with the Dodgers.

December 14—Phillies' Scranton/Wilkes-Barre affiliate signed infielder Rod Booker, a free agent.

December 15—Braves traded first baseman Gerald Perry and pitcher Jim Lemasters to Royals for pitchers Charlie Leibrandt and Rick Luecken.

December 15—Mariners signed pitcher Matt Young, a free agent formerly with the Athletics.

December 15—Dodgers re-signed pitcher Fernando Valenzuela, a free agent.

December 17—Blue Jays traded catcher Ernie Whitt and outfielder Kevin Batiste to Braves for pitcher Rick Trlicek.

December 19—Red Sox released catcher Rick Cerone.

December 19—Angels' Edmonton affiliate signed pitcher Mark Eichhorn, a free agent.

December 19—Padres released pitcher Dave Leiper.

December 19—Brewers re-signed outfielder Robin Yount, a free agent.

December 19—Rangers re-signed outfielder Thad Bosley, a free agent.

December 19—Astros re-signed infielder Harry Spilman and pitcher Dan Schatzeder, both free agents.

December 19—Dodgers re-signed outfielder John Shelby and catcher Rick Dempsey, both free agents.

December 20—Orioles released outfielder Butch Davis.

December 20—Red Sox released first baseman Sam Horn and pitcher Bob Stanley.

December 20—Angels released pitcher Mark Clear and outfielder Tony Armas.

December 20—Tigers released pitchers Guillermo Hernandez and Doyle Alexander.

December 20—Dodgers released outfielder Mike Davis.

December 20—Mets traded outfielder Juan Samuel to Dodgers for pitcher Alejandro Pena and outfielder Mike Marshall.

December 20—Yankees signed catcher Rick Cerone, a free agent.

December 21—Dodgers signed outfielder Hubie Brooks, a free agent formerly with the Expos.

December 21—Angels signed pitcher Mike Smithson, a free agent formerly with the Red Sox.

December 21—Indians released pitcher Rich Yett.

December 21—Athletics released outfielder Billy Beane.

December 22—Yankees signed infielder Damaso Garcia, a free agent formerly with the Expos.

December 29—Twins signed pitcher Rich Yett, a free agent.

Giamatti's Death Stuns Game

By DAVE SLOAN

The 1989 season produced its share of sad stories, but none was more shocking than the September 1 death of baseball Commissioner A. Bartlett Giamatti.

Giamatti, who possessed a deep love for the game that many believed would translate into great success during a long tenure as commissioner, died five months to the day after succeeding Peter Ueberroth to baseball's highest office. He was stricken by a massive heart attack at his summer home in Edgartown, Mass., on Martha's Vineyard and died after efforts by paramedics and doctors to revive him were unsuccessful. He was 51.

Giamatti was an academician by trade and a sportsman at heart. He was graduated magna cum laude from Yale University in 1960 and later served as president of the school from 1978 through 1986. He left Yale at that time to become president of the National League, a position he held until succeeding Ueberroth on April 1.

Most of the media's attention during Giamatti's 154-day tenure—the shortest in baseball history—was focused on Cincinnati Reds Manager Pete Rose, baseball's all-time hit leader who was accused of gambling on baseball and other sports. Ironically, Giamatti's death came just eight days after he announced that Rose would be banned from baseball for life as a result of his gambling activities.

Giamatti was born in Boston on April 4, 1938, and developed an early allegiance to the Boston Red Sox. His affection for the Red Sox caused him some discomfort in 1986 when, as N.L. president, they faced off against the New York Mets in the World Series.

Giamatti decided to follow the academic trail and, after earning a Ph.D. in comparative literature from Yale in 1964, taught for two years at Princeton University before returning to Yale as an assistant professor of English in 1966. He became a full professor at age 31 and in 1978 became Yale's 19th president and its youngest (age 40) since the 18th century.

After his eight-year term had expired, Giamatti made a dramatic career change that shocked his Yale colleagues. He received a telephone call from Los Angeles Dodger President Peter O'Malley, then chairman of the N.L. presidential search committee, and considered the offer carefully before being elected National League president June 10, 1986. He officially took office December 11.

During his two-plus years as president, Giamatti gained a reputation as one who would go to great lengths to preserve the integrity of the game. He dealt severely with batters who were discovered using corked bats and pitchers found doctoring baseballs. He also tried to curb alcohol consumption at N.L. ball parks by directing clubs to set policies that would restrict beer sales late in the game while policing their parking lots and training their ushers and security guards on what to look for in potential troublemakers.

Giamatti, whose given first name was Angelo, was unanimously elected as baseball's seventh commissioner on September 8, 1988. Of the six men who had preceded him, only Judge Kenesaw Mountain Landis, baseball's first commissioner (1920-44), died in office.

The baseball world was shocked again on Christmas Day when Billy Martin, a fiery competitor for 11 years as a big-league infielder and 16 more as an on-again, off-again big-league manager, died in an automobile accident near Johnson City, N.Y. He was 61.

Martin, who compiled a .257 average in 1,021 major league games in an 11-year playing career that began with the Yankees in 1952, made up for what he lacked in natural ability with hustle, determination and a win-at-all-costs attitude. The feisty little second baseman, who carried only 165 pounds on his 5-foot-11 frame, refused to back down from anyone. That attitude led to several publicized on-field brawls and a number of off-field incidents that would haunt him throughout his long association with baseball.

Two of his most celebrated on-field fights came against St. Louis Browns catcher Clint Courtney in 1951 and '52. His part in a 1957 brawl at New York's Copacabana nightclub—Yankees Yogi Berra, Mickey Mantle, Johnny Kucks and Hank Bauer also were involved—led to a $1,000 fine and his 1957 trade to the Kansas City Athletics.

He went on to play for the Detroit Tigers, Cleveland Indians, Cincinnati Reds, Milwaukee Braves and Minnesota Twins before concluding his playing career in 1961. The high point of that career came in 1953 when he batted .500 and won MVP honors in the Yankees' six-game World Series victory over the Brooklyn Dodgers.

Commissioner A. Bartlett Giamatti died only eight days after announcing at a New York press conference (above) that Cincinnati Reds Manager Pete Rose would be banned from baseball for life.

Martin's first big-league managing job came with the Twins in 1969 and he was an immediate success. He guided the talent-laden club to an American League West Division title, but the Twins fell to Baltimore in three straight games in the A.L. Championship Series and Martin, whose relationship with Owner Calvin Griffith had become strained, was fired.

That was the pattern Martin's managing career would follow. He was a master at turning around a team's fortunes, only to wear out his welcome and lose his job.

He did that with both the Detroit Tigers and Texas Rangers in the early 1970s before finally renewing his association with the Yankees in 1976 and beginning what would develop into a love-hate relationship with George Steinbrenner—the unpredictable Yankee owner who would hire and fire Martin five times in 13 years.

Martin's first Yankee stint was easily his longest and most successful. He guided the team to a 30-26 finish in the final two months of the 1975 season and then guided the Yankees to an A.L. pennant in 1976 and a six-game World Series triumph over the Los Angeles Dodgers the following year—the Yankees' first Series triumph since 1962. A much-publicized feud with Steinbrenner and a dugout confrontation with star outfielder Reggie Jackson during a nationally televised game in 1977, however, contributed to his first Yankee firing on July 25, 1978.

Martin's second term with the Yankees began on June 18, 1979, when Steinbrenner fired Bob Lemon—the man who had succeeded Martin the previous July—with the team in fourth place. Martin managed the team for only the final 95 games of the '79 season, however, before Steinbrenner fired him again on October 29 for punching a marshmallow salesman in a Minneapolis bar. The following February, Martin agreed to become the manager of the Oakland A's—a job he held for three seasons before returning again to New York.

Martin's third Yankee stint lasted just one season, his fourth term consisted of 145 games in 1985 and his finale lasted 68 games in 1988. Martin and the Yankees parted ways for the final time on June 23, 1988, when Steinbrenner brought in Lou Piniella, another former Yankee manager, to finish out the year.

Martin, who saw his Yankee uniform No. 1 retired in 1986, compiled a 1,258-

Bill Terry, shown here in a 1930 photo, batted .401 for the New York Giants that year, the last time a National League player has hit .400.

1,018 big-league managerial record that included six division championships and one World Series title. He managed five A.L. teams, a league record he shares with Jimmy Dykes.

The 1989 calendar year also marked the passing of four members of baseball's Hall of Fame.

Bill Terry, the last N.L. player to bat .400 in a season and the man who succeeded the legendary John McGraw as manager of the New York Giants, died January 9 at Jacksonville, Fla., at age 90; Lefty Gomez, a four-time 20-game winner and the ace of outstanding New York Yankee teams in the 1930s, died February 17 at Larkspur, Calif., at age 80; Jocko Conlan, one of the giants among major league umpires, died April 1 at Scottsdale, Ariz., at age 89, and Judy Johnson, a former star third baseman in the old Negro leagues, died June 14 at Wilmington, Del., at age 88.

Terry began his professional career as a 16-year-old pitcher in the old Georgia-Alabama League in 1915. He did not have much success, however, in three minor league seasons and retired to Memphis, where he worked at a filling station. McGraw got word of a young lefthanded-hitting phenom in a Memphis semipro league and signed Terry to a contract in 1922.

Terry compiled .336 and .377 averages in the 1922 and '23 seasons with the Giants' Toledo (American Association) farm club and then was promoted to the Giants roster late in the 1923 campaign. By 1925, he was working as the team's regular first baseman, a job he held regularly for the next 12 years. He batted .300 or better in 11 of those campaigns and drove in 100-plus runs in a six-season stretch from 1927-32. He also led N.L. first basemen in putouts and assists five times.

His .401 average in 1930 led the league and his .3486 mark the following year was just a fraction off Chick Hafey's league-leading .3489 figure. Terry's 254 hits in 1930 (tying a mark set by Philadelphia's Frank O'Doul one year earlier) still stands as a National League record.

Terry became the Giants' playing manager on June 3, 1932, after the 59-year-old McGraw—who had managed the club since 1902—could no longer continue because of poor health. Terry guided the team to a World Series championship in his first full season (1933) and N.L. pennants in 1936 and '37. He continued at the helm for four mediocre seasons (1938-41) before giving way to another future Hall of Famer, Mel Ott, in 1941.

Known for his high leg kick, Lefty Gomez was one of baseball's premier pitchers in the 1930s.

Terry, who later served on the Hall of Fame's Veterans Committee, was not elected to the shrine himself until 1954—18 years after he first became eligible. That might well have been the result of the long-running feud he carried on throughout his long career with the media in general and Eastern sportswriters in particular. His final statistics as a player included 154 home runs, 1,078 runs batted in and a .341 batting average in 1,721 games.

Gomez, who like Terry spent 14 years as a player in New York, helped the Yankees to five World Series championships (1932 and 1936-39) in the decade. He was 6-0 in seven Series games, a record for Series victories without defeat that still stands.

Gomez, known for his high leg kick and keen sense of humor, both on and off the mound, signed his first professional contract with the San Francisco Seals (Pacific Coast) in 1927. He was released, however, because management thought he was too skinny (at 6-2, 151 pounds) to withstand the rigors of pro ball. But Gomez was back with the team two years later and proved his durability by pitching 267 innings and compiling an 18-11 record for the Seals, a performance that attracted the Yankees' attention.

Gomez struggled to a 2-5 record in his first season in New York (1930) before finishing the campaign with the Yankees' St. Paul (American Association) farm team. He returned to the majors the following year and went 21-9. The fun-loving lefthander's best season came in 1934, when he won 26 of 31 decisions and led the A.L. in wins, innings pitched (281⅓), winning percentage (.839), strikeouts (158) and earned-run average (2.33).

Gomez was as much a fixture in All-Star Games during the '30s as he was in the World Series. He started five games for the A.L. in the decade and won three of them—including the first All-Star Game in 1933 in which he also drove in the first run. He also was the winning pitcher in the 1935 and '37 midsummer classics and the losing pitcher in 1938. His three victories in All-Star competition are a record.

Gomez posted some outstanding single-season winning percentages in a career that saw him win 189 games and lose 102. His .839 mark in 1934 was his career best, but he also had winning percentages of .700 or better in three seasons and .600 or better six other times. His .750 (15-5) mark in 1941 led the American League.

Except for a one-game, five-inning fling with the Washington Senators in 1943, Gomez's entire major league career was spent with the Yankees. He pitched 2,503 innings in 368 games and had 1,468 strikeouts with an ERA of 3.34. Gomez, who was much in demand as a banquet speaker in later life, was elected to the Hall of Fame by the Veterans Committee in 1972.

Among the other baseball personalities who died in 1989 were, alphabetically, Nick Bremigan, an A.L. umpire since 1974; August Adolphus (Gussie) Busch, the last of America's old-style beer barons and the man most responsible for the success of the St. Louis Cardinals after his purchase of the team in 1953; Murry Dickson, a wiry righthander who won 172 games in a big-league career that lasted 21 years; Bibb Falk, a .314 hitter in 12 major league seasons and the man who replaced Shoeless Joe Jackson in the Chicago White Sox lineup after the Black Sox scandal of 1919; Carl Furillo, a strong-armed outfielder for 15 seasons with the Brooklyn and Los Angeles Dodgers and one of author Roger Kahn's Boys of Summer; Stan Isle, a member of The Sporting News' editorial staff since 1965 known for his weekly feature "Caught on the Fly" as well as a popular notes column, and

Truett (Rip) Sewell, a Pittsburgh Pirates righthander who enjoyed several successful seasons after developing a blooper pitch that confounded N.L. hitters.

An alphabetical list of baseball deaths in 1989 follows:

Earl J. (Sparky) Adams, 94, a 5-foot-5, 150-pound infielder who batted .286 in a 13-year career with four National League teams, at Pottsville, Pa., on February 24; was a slick fielder who played second base, shortstop and third base during stints with the Chicago Cubs, Pittsburgh Pirates, St. Louis Cardinals and Cincinnati Reds from 1922 through '34; began career with the Cubs and led the N.L. in at-bats for three straight seasons (1925 to '27) before being traded to Pittsburgh; spent two seasons with the Pirates before getting traded to St. Louis, where he batted a career-high .314 in 1930 and helped the Cardinals win the N.L. pennant; batted only .143 in the 1930 World Series as the Cardinals fell to the Philadelphia A's in six games; batted .293 in 1931 and led the league in doubles before suffering a late-season ankle injury that limited him to two World Series appearances in St. Louis' seven-game victory over the A's; played only 31 games in 1932 because of a leg injury and was traded to Cincinnati in May of 1933; was sent to the minor leagues in May of 1934 and retired a year later.

J. Kyle Anderson, 83, the baseball coach at the University of Chicago from 1933 to '71 and one of the founders of the College World Series, at Crown Point, Ind., on November 15; earned three varsity letters in both baseball and football at Chicago and signed a professional baseball contract with Pittsburgh; quit after one season and returned to his alma mater, where he became an assistant football coach under Amos Alonzo Stagg in 1929; took over the school's baseball program in 1933 and managed the U.S. Pan American Games baseball team in 1959; was a founder of the American Association of Baseball Coaches and was elected to that group's hall of fame in 1969.

Richard Lee Anderson, 35, a righthander who pitched six games in relief for the 1979 New York Yankees and 1980 Seattle Mariners, at Wilmington, Calif., on June 23; spent six seasons in the Yankee farm system as a starter before converting to the bullpen in 1979; enjoyed excellent success with the Yankees' Columbus (Class AAA) affiliate before being called up in 1979 and pitching in one game; was traded to Seattle and spent most of the 1980 season with the Mariners' Spokane (Class AAA) affiliate, although he did appear in five games with the big-league club; developed serious arm problems and was released in 1982; ended major league career with no wins, losses or saves.

Joseph Edmund Batchelder, 90, a lefthander who compiled a 1-0 record in three short trials with the Boston Braves from 1923 to '25, at Beverly, Mass., on May 5; spent only five seasons in professional baseball and made only 11 major league appearances while compiling a 5.66 ERA.

Carlos Rodriguez Bernier, 60, a fleet-footed outfielder who stole 89 and 94 bases in the second and third years of his professional career but was unsuccessful in a one-year stay with the Pittsburgh Pirates in 1953, at Juana Diaz, Puerto Rico, on April 6; stole 89 bases for Bristol (Colonial) in 1949 and 94 the following season for Bristol and St. Jean (Provincial); swiped almost 600 bases in his minor league career before retiring after the 1965 season; was struck by a pitched ball in his first professional season and suffered a fractured skull that led to chronic headaches; that was blamed for a quick temper that often kept the youngster in hot water with umpires and management; was Pacific Coast League's top rookie in 1952 when he stole 65 bases for Hollywood and he earned the circuit's player of the year citation nine years later when he batted .351; excited Pirates fans in 1953 when he tied a modern major league record by hitting three triples in one game, but he never could find a groove that season and wound up with a .213 average in 105 games.

Nick G. Bremigan, 43, an American League umpire since 1974 and a veteran of one World Series, four Championship Series games and two All-Star Games, at Garland, Tex., on March 28; was a University of Buffalo graduate who taught high school social studies and physical education before deciding to become an umpire; took a specialization course and was assigned to the Florida State League in 1969; also umpired in the Florida Instructional League and the Puerto Rican winter league while coaching and refereeing high school hockey; progressed quickly through the Eastern and International leagues before the A.L. purchased his contract after the 1973 season; had served as an instructor at umpiring schools since 1971 and wrote a weekly syndicated newspaper column on sports rules.

James Ehrenfeld Brideweser, 62, an infielder who spent parts of seven seasons with four American League teams in the 1950s and later coached college baseball in California, at El Toro, Calif., on August 25; was the starting shortstop for the 1948 Southern Cal baseball team that captured the school's first NCAA championship; signed with the New York Yankees and played three minor league seasons before reaching the major leagues in 1951; appeared in 51 games for the Yankees from 1951 to '53 before his contract was sold to Baltimore; played for the Orioles, the Chicago White Sox, the Detroit Tigers and the Orioles again over the next four seasons and then played and managed in the minor leagues until 1972, when he returned to California to teach and coach at the high school level; eventually became coach at Saddleback College in Mission Viejo and led his teams to two conference championships; finished his 329-game big-league career with a .252 average.

K.O. (Buddy) Burbage, 84, a 5-foot-6 outfielder whose career in the Negro baseball leagues spanned three decades, at Philadelphia on August 30; was blessed with great speed that he put to good use as a high school sprinter; did not play high school baseball because he already was being paid to perform for a semipro baseball team in Philadelphia at age 15; began his professional career in 1929 with the Mohawk Giants and later played with the Baltimore Black Sox, the Homestead Grays, the Pittsburgh Crawfords, the Washington Black Senators and the Brooklyn Royal Giants before ending his career in 1942.

August Adolphus (Gussie) Busch, 90, the last of America's old-style beer barons, a driving force in the expansion of his family's brewing business and the man most responsible for the success of the St. Louis Cardinals over the past 35 years, at St. Louis on September 29; was born into a wealthy family and was the son of August A. Busch Sr., whose father was a co-founder of Anheuser-Busch brewery prior to the Civil War; learned the beer brewing business from the ground up and developed his business acumen during Prohibition when the company survived by diversifying into everything from soda pop to the manufacturing of truck bodies; inherited the brewery with his brother in 1934 when his father committed suicide after a long illness; was married four times and fathered 11 children; began an aggressive expansion of Anheuser-Busch after the death of his brother in 1946; by 1954, Anheuser-Busch was the largest brewery in America and by

the time of his death, it was the largest in the world; rescued the Cardinals in 1953 when owner Fred Saigh was on the verge of selling the franchise to interests who planned to move their operation to Milwaukee; convinced his brewery's board of directors to buy the club and paid $3.75 million; pushed for the construction of a new ball park and the brewery paid $5 million of the estimated $20 million in private funds needed to build Busch Stadium in downtown St. Louis; became president of the redevelopment corporation responsible for the stadium's operation and the new facility served as the hub of a downtown revitalization program; the Cardinals did not give Busch a championship until 11 years after the purchase, but they went on to win National League pennants in 1964, '67, '68, '82, '85 and '87 and world championships in '64, '67 and '82; was also a great horse lover who raised the Clydesdales that became the symbol of his brewing empire; seated atop a red beer wagon pulled by a hitch of Clydesdales, Busch would circle the field inside Busch Stadium before every playoff and World Series game involving the Cardinals; was a magnetic, rough-hewn personality who also dabbled in politics and fund-raising projects and he was always visible in the progressive activities of St. Louis.

Robert E. (Bob) Caffery, 59, a former minor league infielder who briefly reached the Triple-A level during an 11-year playing career in the late 1940s and '50s, at Wood River, Ill., on January 20; broke in with the St. Louis Browns organization and played four seasons in the Class AA Texas League with San Antonio.

Joseph Carroll, 80, whose career as a minor league trainer spanned four decades, at Pompano Beach, Fla., on November 8; was a native New Yorker who got his start as a trainer for the New York Giants of the National Football League; moved to baseball in the 1940s and went on to make stops at Burlington and Greensboro in North Carolina, Charleston, W.Va., Syracuse, Buffalo, Portland, Ore., Richmond, Va., Vancouver, B.C., Macon, Ga., and Denver; was an active member of the Association of Professional Baseball Players of America, the benevolent organization that aids ill and indigent former players, umpires and trainers.

George Washington Case, 73, a six-time American League stolen base champion who spent most of his 11-year career with the Washington Senators, at Trenton, N.J., on January 23; was an outstanding track athlete and pitcher during his schoolboy days who switched to the outfield on the advice of Philadelphia A's Manager Connie Mack during a 1936 tryout; spent one season with Washington's Trenton farm team in 1937 before joining the Senators at age 21; became a regular in 1938 and captured his first stolen base title the next season with 51; topped the .300 mark three times during his career and set a league record in 1943 with 61 steals; tied a major league record in 1940 by collecting nine hits in a doubleheader; regarded as the fastest runner in the game, he relied mostly on his outstanding speed, rather than instincts, to swipe bases; was also known as an excellent drag bunter; began suffering from leg, ankle, shoulder and back problems as his career progressed and was traded to Cleveland prior to the 1946 season; batted only .225 that year with the Indians but won the last of his stolen base titles with 28; was reacquired by the Senators in 1947 and retired at the end of the campaign at age 31; finished his major league career with 1,415 hits in 1,226 games, 349 stolen bases and a .282 career average; began a second career in 1951 as Rutgers baseball coach, a position he held for 10 years; went on to coach at both the minor and major league levels, managed in the minors for both Washington and the New York Yankees, scouted for both of those organizations and served as a minor league instructor for both the Texas Rangers and Seattle Mariners.

James Buster (Buzz) Clarkson, 70, an infielder who spent the major portion of his career in the Negro leagues but appeared in 14 games with the 1952 Boston Braves, at Jeannette, Pa., on January 21; played Negro league baseball from 1937 to '50 with the Pittsburgh Crawfords, Newark Eagles, Philadelphia Stars and Baltimore Elite Giants before spending another six seasons in the minor leagues, primarily with Milwaukee in the American Association; topped the .300 mark five times for the Class AAA Brewers and played in the Little World Series after the 1951 and '52 seasons; reached the big leagues with Boston as a 34-year-old rookie in 1952 and batted just .200; later played in the minors with Dallas, Beaumont, Tulsa and Des Moines before retiring in 1956.

Joseph Edward (Joe) Collins, 66, a first baseman who played in seven World Series with the New York Yankees in the 1950s, at Union, N.J., on August 30; was signed by the Yankees at age 16 and kicked around their minor league system for nine years before getting a brief look in 1948; became the team's regular first baseman in 1950 and held the job for the next seven seasons; batted a career-high .286 in 1951 but was a versatile performer and a favorite of Manager Casey Stengel; was a streak-hitting lefthander who played excellent defense, both at first and occasionally in the outfield; batted only .163 in 36 World Series games from 1950 to '57; biggest thrill came in the 1955 Series opener when he hit two home runs off Brooklyn's Don Newcombe; batted only .256 in a career that ended in 1957 when he lost his job to young Bill Skowron; retired with the distinction of having played more games at first base (715) than any Yankee player except Lou Gehrig (2,136).

Paul G. Compton, 75, a former minor league coach and business manager and an associate scout for the Baltimore Orioles, at Lynchburg, Va., on February 28; played briefly in the minors before starting his coaching career in the old Class-C Virginia League and the Class-D Appalachian League.

John Bertrand (Jocko) Conlan, 89, considered one of the giants of the umpiring profession and a member of baseball's Hall of Fame, at Scottsdale, Ariz., on April 1; was a 5-foot-7, 160-pound reserve outfielder for the Chicago White Sox when he accidently stumbled into his calling as an umpire, a job he would perform with intense pride, honesty and dedication for a quarter of a century; a .263 career hitter in two partial seasons with the White Sox after a 14-year minor league career, Conlan was sitting on the bench nursing a sprained thumb in 1935 when umpire Red Ormsby was overcome by heat during a doubleheader in St. Louis; filled in for Ormsby and called the bases effectively in that game and again the next day as Ormsby recovered; was paid $50 for his trouble and was offered $300 a month to umpire in the New York-Penn League the following campaign; polished his skills for two seasons before earning promotion to the American Association in 1938; was scouted by the American League in 1940 but was judged to be too small to ever reach the major leagues; received a strong recommendation, however, from another Hall of Fame umpire, Bill Klem, who took Conlan under his wing when he got the call from the National League and taught him the ropes; armed with excellent patience and a strong Irish wit, he quickly established himself as a no-nonsense, common-sense arbitrator; would eject anybody who cursed during an argument, a policy that resulted in 26 ejections during his rookie N.L. season; was par-ticularly remembered for his on-field battles with Leo Durocher, whom Conlan later called "king of the complainers, troublemakers, arguers and moaners"; was chosen as a member of the umpiring crew for each of the N.L. pennant-deciding playoff games (1946, '51, '59 and '62), worked in six All-Star Games and was a World Series umpire five times; when leg problems affected his mobility in the early 1960s and he developed a painful bone spur on one heel in 1963, Conlan announced that 1964 would be his last season; attracted much attention and adulation during his retirement swing and won election to the Hall of Fame in 1974; published his autobiography, entitled "Jocko," in 1967.

Joseph Consoli, 64, a former minor league player and manager who later worked as a scouting supervisor for the Pittsburgh Pirates, at Baltimore on January 10; became a part-time scout for the Pirates in 1954 while serving as a player-manager at Erie; became a full-time scout for Pittsburgh in 1966 and aided in the signings of such stars as Al Oliver and Bob Robertson before leaving to join the Major League Scouting Bureau in 1975; rejoined the Pirates' scouting staff in 1982 and was one of the club's area scouting supervisors at the time of his death.

Dale Roger Coogan, 58, a first baseman who spent part of the 1950 season with the Pittsburgh Pirates, at Mission Viejo, Calif., on March 8; signed a professional contract in 1948 and played two seasons in the minor leagues before making the spring training cut with the Pirates in 1950; batted just .240 while playing a reserve role; was sent back to the minors the next season, where he played until his retirement in 1958; later managed the Los Alamitos Naval Air Station team that won the All-Service baseball title in 1953; went back to school and earned a doctorate in education from Southern Cal and eventually became superintendent of the Ocean View (Calif.) School District.

George S. (Chick) Cooper, 94, the retired sports editor of the Johnstown (Pa.) Tribune-Democrat and a former minor league executive in the city, at Johnstown on March 18; was sports editor for 39 years and used his influence with the Brooklyn Dodgers to help the city acquire a Middle Atlantic League franchise after the St. Louis Browns had ended their affiliation in 1939; served as president and general manager of the Class-C team for nine seasons before its demise in 1951; also was active in amateur baseball, securing a number of national tournaments for Johnstown; was executive sports editor of the Tribune-Democrat until his retirement in 1958.

Delbert Leon Culberson, 71, a former Boston Red Sox outfielder who was involved in the play that decided the 1946 World Series in favor of the St. Louis Cardinals, at Rome, Ga., on September 24; was a righthanded hitter who was called up by the Red Sox in 1943 as a potential replacement of military service-bound regulars; batted .272 in 80 games that season and went on to play four more seasons with Boston before finishing his big-league career in 1948 with Washington; compiled a .266 career average in 370 major league games and batted .222 in the 1946 Series; was playing center field in the eighth inning of Game 7 with the score tied 3-3 and St. Louis' Enos Slaughter on first; fielded Harry Walker's hit to left-center field cleanly and relayed the ball to shortstop Johnny Pesky who, surprised to see that Slaughter had not stopped at third, hesitated and then threw the ball badly to the plate; Slaughter's run proved to be the Series winner.

John Peter (Jack) Cusick, 61, a former shortstop with the Chicago Cubs and Boston Braves in the early 1950s, at Edgewood, N.J., on November

17; began his professional career in 1946 at age 17 with the Philadelphia Phillies' Americus club in the old Class-D Georgia-Florida League; also played at Utica, Houston, Columbus, Beaumont and Kansas City before being drafted by the Cubs in 1950; appeared in 65 games with Chicago, 56 of them at shortstop, in 1951 and then was traded the next winter to Boston; batted .167 in 49 games with the Braves in 1952 and retired from baseball the following year with a .174 career average.

Murry Monroe Dickson, 73, a wiry 155-pound righthander who won 172 big-league games and pitched more than 3,000 innings in a career that ran from 1939 to '59, at Kansas City, Kan., on September 21; fashioned a 172-181 record and 3.66 ERA while pitching for the St. Louis Cardinals, Pittsburgh Pirates, Philadelphia Phillies, Kansas City Athletics and New York Yankees; won 20 games in 1951 for the Pirates and led the National League in winning percentage in 1946 when he compiled a 15-6 record for the Cardinals; pitched in three World Series (two with St. Louis and one with the Yankees), recording an 0-1 record and 3.86 ERA; lost 40 games in two seasons (1952 and '53) with the last-place Pirates and 20 more the next year with the Phillies; had a well-earned reputation as a tinkerer on the mound and employed an unorthodox style that led batterymate Joe Garagiola to refer to him as "the Thomas Edison of the toeplate"; would continually vary his location on the rubber, his windup and his angle of delivery for a repertoire that included a fastball, curveball, sinker, slider, knuckleball and screwball, most of which he could throw overhand, sidearm or underhand; finished his career in 1959 with the A's, having pitched 3,052 innings in 625 games; he had a 42-32 record as a reliever and logged 23 saves.

Edna Dreisewerd, 74, the wife of former major league pitcher Clem Dreisewerd who wrote a book describing her experiences as a "warmup catcher" for her husband during his 15-year professional career, at New Orleans on May 24; detailed the couple's travels along the minor league trail in a trailer during the early days of her husband's career, when she acted as cook, housewife, pitching coach and warmup catcher; her husband, who pitched for the Boston Red Sox, St. Louis Browns and New York Giants in a 46-game major league career, credited her with helping him develop a screwball and taming his control.

Elzie Clise Dudley, 85, a righthanded pitcher who compiled a 17-33 record over five National League seasons with the Brooklyn Dodgers, Philadelphia Phillies and Pittsburgh Pirates from 1929 to '33, at Moncks Corner, S.C., on January 12; his best season was 1931, when he compiled an 8-14 record and 3.52 ERA for the Phillies; retired with a career 5.03 ERA.

Bibb August Falk, 90, an excellent big-league outfielder who is best remembered as the man who replaced Joe Jackson in the Chicago White Sox lineup on the heels of the Black Sox scandal and later a highly successful baseball coach at the University of Texas, at Austin, Tex., on June 8; was the last surviving member of the 1920 White Sox; became an important figure to the team in 1920 when it was being rebuilt because of the lifetime ban imposed on most of its regulars, including Jackson, for their part in the conspiracy to throw the 1919 World Series to the Cincinnati Reds; went on to compile a .314 career average in 12 major league seasons, eight with Chicago and four with Cleveland; batted a career-high .352 in 1924 but lost the batting title to New York's Babe Ruth; topped the .300 mark in seven other seasons; was an above-average defensive player with an excellent throwing arm that produced 26 assists in 1924; led the American League in pinch-hitting

in both 1930 and '31 with Cleveland before retiring; managed in the minor leagues for the Indians before coaching at the big-league level with Cleveland and the Boston Red Sox; scouted for the Red Sox from 1935 to '40, when he returned to Austin to take over as Texas' baseball coach; guided his Longhorn teams to a 478-176 record over the next 25 years—with two years out for military service—and his teams won or shared 20 Southwest Conference championships and captured two NCAA titles (1949 and '50); retired following the 1967 season; was the brother of the late Chester Falk, a relief pitcher who compiled a 5-4 record in 40 appearances with the St. Louis Browns from 1925-27.

Earl Flora, 70, a former director of publicity and promotions for the Chicago White Sox and former sports editor of the old Ohio State Journal and sports director of WBNS-TV in Columbus, O., at Columbus on September 27; after working at the Journal while attending school and then serving in the Army Air Corps during World War II, he became public relations director for the American Association from 1945 through '47 and then joined the White Sox the following year; returned to Columbus as sports editor of the Journal in 1951 and later served as a columnist for the Columbus Dispatch before joining the TV station.

Richard T. (Dick) Foley, 64, a baseball scout for almost 30 years even though he was confined to a wheelchair because of wounds he suffered following the Normandy invasion of 1944, at Needham, Mass., on May 29; when his baseball aspirations were wiped out because of his injuries, he turned to scouting on a part-time basis with Brooklyn in the 1950s and then joined the New York Mets on a full-time basis in 1961; later worked for the Pittsburgh Pirates and Philadelphia Phillies and served as a member of the Major League Scouting Bureau from its inception, covering the New York State and New England areas for the combine; lost the use of his legs as the result of wounds he suffered in Holland on Thanksgiving Day in 1944 while a member of the 101st Airborne Division; insisted on working independently and traveled alone most of the time on his scouting assignments.

Lewis Albert Fonseca, 90, a player, manager and coach on the professional level for 60 years and the originator of World Series and All-Star Game highlight films that promoted baseball for more than 30 years, at Ely, Iowa, on November 26; joined the Cincinnati Reds in 1921 as one of baseball's original bonus babies and proceeded to hit .316 over a 12-year career that also included stops with the Philadelphia Phillies, the Cleveland Indians and the Chicago White Sox; was an excellent righthanded hitter and a versatile defensive performer who could play any infield or outfield position; was also injury prone, a problem that led to his nickname of "Fractures"; was sidelined at various times during his career by broken shoulders (four times), a fractured wrist, a chipped bone in an ankle, a dislocated hip, a concussion, a broken nose, a severed artery in his leg from a spike wound and a severe case of scarlet fever; played more than 100 games in only four seasons, one of which, 1929 with Cleveland, he captured an American League batting title with a .369 average; became player-manager of a weak White Sox team in 1931 and continued in that capacity until he was fired in 1934 with a 120-198 record; seeking a way to maintain his connections with baseball, Fonseca, who had filmed many of the game's better hitters while he was managing, took the idea for an American League motion picture bureau to league President Will Harridge; began producing a league highlights film and soon got A.L. club owners' approval and commercial financing to expand his idea; produced his first sound film in 1935 and began making World Series and All-Star Game films during World War II; was estimated that 10 million military personnel saw the films between 1943 and '45; N.L. joined in the plan to make baseball's Motion Picture Division a cooperative venture in 1946 and, by 1965, he had produced 53 baseball films, including historical documentaries; as popularity of films increased, commercial sponsorship became available and Major League Baseball Promotion Corporation was formed in 1968; went back to the field in the early 1970s as a hitting instructor for the Chicago Cubs and Cincinnati, tutoring such rising stars as Billy Williams, Johnny Bench, Rick Monday and Bill Madlock; later served as a consultant with the San Francisco Giants, Atlanta Braves and Texas Rangers before retiring in 1981; was awarded the J. Louis Comiskey Award for long and meritorious service to baseball in 1960.

Joseph Anthony Foy, 46, who spent six seasons as a major league third baseman after being named The Sporting News' Minor League Player of the Year in 1965, at New York City on October 12; won the International League batting title with a .302 average and was named the circuit's most valuable player, leading to TSN's 1965 citation; played next three seasons with the Boston Red Sox before being selected by the Kansas City Royals in the draft to stock the Kansas City and Seattle expansion rosters in '69; played one year in Kansas City and enjoyed his best big-league season, batting .262 and driving in 71 runs; was traded to the New York Mets for Amos Otis and Bob Johnson and lasted there just one season before moving on to Washington; played only 41 games with the 1971 Senators in his last season and finished his career with a .248 average, 58 home runs and 291 RBIs; batted .133 for Boston in six games of the 1967 World Series.

Fredrick Meloy (Fred) Frankhouse, 85, a righthander who compiled a 106-97 record with the St. Louis Cardinals, Boston Braves and Brooklyn Dodgers over a 13-year career that started in 1927, at Port Royal, Pa., on August 17; started his career as a relief pitcher for the Cardinals and did not become a starter until after he was traded to Boston in 1930; enjoyed his best success in 1934 when he compiled a 17-9 record and 3.20 ERA for the Braves while pitching 233⅔ innings; was traded to the Dodgers after the 1935 campaign and pitched three seasons in Brooklyn before being traded back to Boston for his final season; coached and pitched in the minor leagues at Newark until he entered the Army in 1943; finished his big-league career with a 3.92 ERA.

Robert (Bob) Freitas, 72, a longtime minor league front-office official and a field representative for the National Association of Professional Baseball Leagues for 19 years, at Aptos, Calif., on September 19; took his first baseball job in 1941 as a part-time scout for Cincinnati; held position as business manager at a string of minor league stops before finally moving to Vancouver (Pacific Coast) as general manager and public relations director in 1960; was a strong proponent of ball park promotions and had a well-earned reputation as a man who could put an ailing franchise back on its feet; was persuaded to put those talents to use as the National Association's chief troubleshooter in the West, a job he held from 1961 to '67 and again from 1971 to '81; worked between those stints in the front office for Charlie Finley's Oakland A's and as president of the short-season Class-A Northwest League; moved back to the latter job again in 1982 and was made chairman of the Northwest League's board of directors; received George Trautman Award in 1984 for long and distinguished service to professional baseball; was working as a minor league baseball franchise broker at the time of his death.

Carl Anthony Furillo, 66, an excellent outfielder who enjoyed an outstanding 15-year career with the Brooklyn and Los Angeles Dodgers and was one of Roger Kahn's Boys of Summer, at Stony Creek Mills, Pa., on January 21; was known as the Reading Rifle, a reference to both his Pennsylvania birthplace and the fine throwing arm he exhibited as one of the best outfielders ever to play at Ebbets Field; was a strong righthanded hitter who posted a career .299 average in 1,806 games while hitting 192 home runs and driving in 1,058 runs; captured a National League batting title with a .344 mark in 1953; broke in as a 24-year-old Dodger rookie in 1946 after three years of service in the Army; batted .284 that season and became the team's regular right fielder the next year; went on to top the .300 mark five times and hit .314 for the 1955 Dodgers, the team that ended years of Brooklyn frustration by bringing the city its first World Series championship; played for six pennant winners in Brooklyn and one in Los Angeles; batted .266 with 13 RBIs in 40 World Series games; reached the end of his playing career in 1960 when, after appearing in only eight games, he severely injured a leg muscle and was sidelined; balked when the team tried to assign him to its Class AAA Spokane team (Pacific Coast) and the Dodgers responded by cutting his salary from $33,000 to $12,000; ended his association with the Dodgers on a bitter note, suing to collect the balance of that salary—a settlement he finally won in 1962; refused any association with baseball in the following years but finally softened his feelings and began participating in Dodger old-timers' games and even served as an instructor at several of the club's fantasy camps.

Nicholas (Nick) Furillo, 70, a former minor league player and the older brother of former Brooklyn star Carl Furillo, at Coatesville, Pa., on January 4; played in the Eastern Shore League in the early 1940s.

Angelo Bartlett Giamatti, 51, a scholar and former president of Yale University who served three years as National League president and five months as baseball's seventh commissioner, of a massive heart attack at Edgartown, Mass., on September 1; died only eight days after announcing that Pete Rose, baseball's all-time hit leader and acting manager of the Cincinnati Reds, would be banned from baseball for life because of his alleged gambling on baseball games and other sports; that decision invited comparisons to another baseball commissioner, Judge Kenesaw Mountain Landis, who had taken a similar action 69 years earlier against members of the 1919 Chicago White Sox team that conspired to throw the World Series against Cincinnati and Landis, ironically, was the only other commissioner to die in office; was Boston-born and raised and formed an early allegiance to the Boston Red Sox, a situation that caused him some embarrassment in 1986 when, as the N.L. president, he watched the Red Sox battle the New York Mets in the World Series; was graduated magna cum laude from Yale in 1960 and earned his Ph.D. in comparative literature four years later; taught for two years at Princeton before returning to Yale as an assistant professor of English in 1966; developed a reputation as a scholar of the Italian Renaissance and became a full professor at age 31; became Yale's 19th president in 1978 and its youngest (at age 40) since the 18th century; spent a turbulent eight years in that job during which time he handled a faculty strike while struggling to balance the school's budget; continued to closely follow baseball and his 1981 treatise pleading for the end to the players' strike appeared in the New York Times; after his term ran out in 1986, he received an unexpected call from Los Angeles Dodger President Peter O'Malley, who was chairman of the N.L.'s presidential search committee; considered the prospect carefully before deciding to make a dramatic career change; was elected N.L. president June 10, 1986, and took office December 11 of that year; waged a strong war against corked bats and other forms of "cheating" that he perceived as detrimental to the game; suspended Rose for 30 days in 1988 for a bumping incident with umpire Dave Pallone; took positive steps by convincing club owners to restrict overconsumption of alcohol at their ball parks and by introducing guidelines aimed at curtailing scoreboard gimmicks, loud music as the batter was getting ready to hit and live-action replays that made the umpires look bad; was an easy choice by the owners to replace Commissioner Peter Ueberroth, who decided to step down and pursue other interests; the Rose affair received most of the publicity during his brief tenure, which started April 1, but much of Giamatti's time was actually spent trying to formulate a game plan in the event of a 1990 players' strike; his 154-day tenure as commissioner was by far the shortest in baseball history.

Charles Franklin (Whitey) Glazner, 95, a righthanded pitcher who spent most of his short career with Pittsburgh in the early 1920s and the second-oldest surviving former Pirates player, at Orlando, Fla., on June 6; compiled a 41-48 record in a five-year career that culminated in 1924 when he finished with a 7-16 mark for the Philadelphia Phillies; enjoyed his most success in 1921 when he fashioned a 14-5 record and 2.77 ERA for the Pirates; returned to the minor leagues in 1925 and pitched for Los Angeles, Mobile and Dallas before retiring from baseball to pursue a career as a professional golfer; the only older surviving former Pirate at the time of Glazner's death was 96-year-old Erving L. Kantlehner, also a pitcher.

Vernon (Lefty) Gomez, 80, a fun-loving lefthander who epitomized the success of the great New York Yankee teams of the 1930s as a four-time 20-game winner and later won election to baseball's Hall of Fame, at Larkspur, Calif., on February 17; compiled a 189-102 record, a 3.34 ERA and 1,468 strikeouts while pitching 2,503 innings over a 14-year big-league career; also compiled a 6-0 record while pitching in five World Series and was 3-1 in five All-Star Game appearances, all of them as the American League's starting pitcher; was the winning pitcher in the first All-Star Game ever played (1933) and drove in the first run in that game; was particularly known for his high leg kick and his on- and off-field sense of humor, which earned him the nickname "Goofy"; signed his first professional contract with the San Francisco Seals (Pacific Coast) in 1927 but was soon released because officials considered him too skinny (he was 6-foot-2 and 151 pounds); was back with the Seals two years later and proved his durability by pitching 267 innings and recording an 18-11 record, a performance that resulted in the Yankees purchasing his contract; won his first start for the Yankees in 1930 but then struggled and finished the season at St. Paul (American Association); returned to New York in 1931 and proceeded to top the 20-victory mark in three of the next four seasons; was 21-9 in 1931, 24-7 in '32 and 26-5 in '34, a season in which he led the A.L. in innings pitched (281⅔), ERA (2.33), complete games (25) and strikeouts (158); recorded his last 20-victory season (he was 21-11) in 1937, but he continued to post winning records through the remainder of his career and led the A.L. with a .750 winning percentage (15-5) in 1941; used an outstanding fastball as his chief weapon early in his career and added a slow curveball that helped him remain effective later on; his charming personality was an excellent fit with the glitter of New York City;

courted New York musical comedy actress June O'Dea and married her prior to the opening of the 1933 season—a marriage that endured for more than 55 years; was also a former roommate of Babe Ruth, who took a strong liking to Gomez when he arrived in the majors in 1930 and enjoyed trading banter with the youngster; was plagued by arm problems in his later years and became primarily a six-inning pitcher who relied heavily on Yankee relief ace Johnny Murphy; was pretty much burned out by the age of 33 and was sold to the Boston Braves after the 1942 season; earned a spot on the Braves' roster in spring training, but did not pitch an inning during the regular season; hooked up briefly with the Washington Senators in 1943 and made one start (a loss) before calling it quits; was coaxed back into the game three years later as the manager of the Yankees' Binghampton club in the Eastern League; put himself on the roster and pitched two games that season; managed one more season before retiring; became an unofficial goodwill ambassador for baseball while working as a representative for Wilson Sporting Goods Co.; was in much demand as a banquet speaker and attended the winter meetings as late as 1988; was elected to the Hall of Fame by the Veterans Committee in 1972.

Louis Joseph (Lou) Guisto, 94, a first baseman who appeared in 156 games with the Cleveland Indians between 1916 and 1923 and later served as the baseball coach at St. Mary's College, at Napa, Calif., on October 15; was believed to be the oldest living former Indians player; was signed by Portland (Pacific Coast) in 1915 and was sold to Cleveland the following year, appearing in six games; batted .185 in 73 games in 1917 and then took time out for service in the Army during World War I; returned to the Indians in 1921 and played three more seasons before being sent to Oakland (Pacific Coast), where he played until 1929; managed briefly in the minor leagues before hooking on with St. Mary's in 1931, a job he held until the mid-1950s; finished his big-league career with a .196 average.

Edward P. (Ed) Hamman, 81, former owner and manager of the Indianapolis Clowns Negro league baseball team and former business manager of the Harlem Globetrotters, at Gainesville, Fla., on January 9; played shortstop with barnstorming baseball teams—Jim Thorpe's Nebraska Indians and the House of David—while developing and perfecting the comedy routines that would serve him later as a talented baseball and basketball clown; joined Syd Pollock in 1935 to operate the Clowns, a group that provided comic relief at major and minor league games, including World Series; Hamman and the Clowns traveled the circuit with a portable lighting system that he boasted could be set up anywhere in 45 minutes; trucked the lights from park to park while giving many fans their first taste of night baseball in the 1930s; managed the Harlem Globetrotters in the 1940s, providing halftime entertainment himself; was responsible for the adoption of "Sweet Georgia Brown" as the team's theme song; retired after a 50-year association with sports and wrote an autobiography that was eventually made into a movie, "Bingo Long and His Traveling All-Stars."

Rodney J. Hampton, 35, who scouted for the Detroit Tigers after a brief playing career in the Montreal Expos organization, of cancer at Detroit on November 24; was one of three brothers who played professional baseball; was an outfielder-first baseman with the Sarasota (Gulf Coast) Expos in 1974 and became a part-time scout in '75; formed his own college and pro baseball and basketball scouting service in Detroit a year before his death.

John M. (Jack) Hand, 75, clubhouse man for

the Detroit Tigers from 1943 until his retirement in 1975, at Lakeland, Fla., on March 21; joined the Tigers as a member of their groundcrew in 1935 and became clubhouse man eight years later.

Donald Henry Heffner, 78, a major league second baseman for 11 years (1934 to '44) and later the manager of the Cincinnati Reds for half a season, at Pasadena, Calif., on August 1; batted .241 in 743 big-league games; opened his major league career with the New York Yankees in 1934 and later played for the St. Louis Browns, Philadelphia Athletics and Detroit Tigers before a shoulder injury forced the end of his playing career; managed 12 years in the minor leagues, winning pennants in 1947 with Aberdeen (Northern), in 1948 with Globe (Arizona-Texas) and in 1962 with San Diego (Pacific Coast); coached in the major leagues for Kansas City, Detroit, the New York Mets and the California Angels; became the oldest person ever to be named a major league manager for the first time when the Reds tabbed him before the 1966 campaign; guided the Reds to a 37-46 record and was fired at the All-Star break, giving way to Dave Bristol; left baseball and worked for the Santa Anita racetrack near his home in Arcadia, Calif.; was obsessed throughout his career with what he perceived to be a weight problem; was a 130-pounder when he signed a professional contract in 1929 and never got above 155, despite the various milk-eggs-meat diets he tried over the years to increase his weight.

Otto Huber, 74, a righthanded-hitting infielder who appeared in 11 games with the Boston Braves in 1939, at Garfield, N.J., on April 9; played professional baseball for nine seasons beginning in 1936 and batted .273 in his 11-game 1939 fling with the Braves; his career was interrupted in the 1940s by military service and he returned for a brief stint as player-manager in the minor leagues before retiring from baseball.

John Stanley (Stan) Isle, 66, a member of The Sporting News' editorial staff since 1965, of cancer at St. Louis on December 28; was a lifelong sports fan who turned to sportswriting at an early age and served as sports editor at the Moberly (Mo.) Monitor Index and the Wisconsin Rapids Daily Tribune before answering an ad to join the TSN staff as an associate editor; worked at a variety of assignments, the most notable of which were the assembly and editing of minor league notes and the weekly feature "Caught on the Fly"; began writing a popular notes column in 1979 that appeared weekly until just before his death; was promoted to senior editor in 1984; was a member of the Society of Professional Journalists and a past St. Louis chairman of the Baseball Writers' Association of America; was a familiar face at baseball functions and in press boxes around the country and attended every session of baseball's winter meetings for 22 years prior to 1989, taking great delight in making the annual awards presentations to TSN's minor league executives of the year; was a graduate of the University of Missouri and a veteran of both World War II and the Korean War; succeeded former Missouri football coach Don Faurot as executive director of the Missouri Sports Hall of Fame in 1980, a labor of love at which he worked until his death; was enshrined in the Missouri Basketball Hall of Fame in 1989 and was to be inducted into the University of Missouri Media Hall of Fame, the eighth inductee overall to that group.

William J. (Judy) Johnson, 88, an outstanding third baseman who in 1975 became the sixth black player to be named to baseball's Hall of Fame by the Committee on the Negro Leagues, at Wilmington, Del., on June 14; was a scrawny youngster who played baseball and football for integrated teams in Wilmington; was playing for the Madison Stars in 1920 when postwar expansion of the Negro leagues gave him an opportunity to join the Philadelphia Hilldale Daisies; quickly developed into one of the best third basemen in Negro league history; was a fine fielder with an excellent arm and a line-drive hitter with occasional power; participated in the first Negro World Series in 1924 (against the Kansas City Monarchs) and led all players in the series with a .341 average over 10 games; left Philadelphia to join the Homestead Grays in 1929 after the league folded; returned to Philadelphia a year later to manage the Darby Daisies, a short-lived successor to the Hilldales; joined the Pittsburgh Crawfords in 1932 and closed out his playing-managing career in 1937 with that club; was credited with a .340 career average and recorded a one-season high of .416 (1929), although that average was only fourth-highest in the league; often barnstormed during the fall months with various teams and usually played winter ball in Mexico; was hired to scout black players by the Philadelphia A's after Jackie Robinson broke the color barrier with Brooklyn in 1951; began scouting for the Philadelphia Phillies in 1961 and helped sign Dick Allen to his first contract; also signed former Milwaukee star Bill Bruton, who later became his son-in-law; remained with the Phillies until 1974 and then worked part-time with the Los Angeles Dodgers as a scout until his retirement in 1977.

Anton Andrew (Andy) Karl, 75, a righthander who compiled a 19-23 record in five big-league seasons in the 1940s, at San Diego on April 8, his birthday; pitched for the Boston Red Sox, the Philadelphia Phillies and Boston Braves in a career that started in 1943; enjoyed his best success in 1945 when he compiled a 9-8 record and 2.99 ERA in a National League-leading 67 appearances for the Phillies; spent most of his career working out of the bullpen, making only four big-league starts.

Eugene G. Kavanagh, 68, a former minor league outfielder and the son of former major league second baseman Marty Kavanagh, at Detroit on March 9; signed his first professional contract in 1940 and moved as high as Triple-A with Sacramento (Pacific Coast); his father played for Detroit, Cleveland and the St. Louis Cardinals from 1914 to '18.

Howard Wilbur (Spud) Krist, 73, a righthander who compiled a 37-11 record over six seasons between 1937 and '46 with the St. Louis Cardinals, at Buffalo on April 23; was a two-time 20-game winner in the minors—both before and between his stints with the Cardinals—who was used primarily in relief during his major league career; was hampered by a series of illnesses and injuries that kept him from ever really reaching his full potential; was 10-0 despite his 4.03 ERA in 1941 and then enjoyed seasons of 13-3 and 11-5 the next two years, the second of which he worked 17 games as a starter; entered the Army in 1944 and suffered leg wounds during infantry action in France; returned to the Cardinals in 1946 but went 0-2 in 15 games and was sent to the minor leagues; retired after that season; compiled a 3.32 ERA to go along with his .771 winning percentage and appeared once in relief for the Cardinals in the 1943 World Series.

Francis X. Leary, 74, a vice-president and treasurer for the California Angels from the formation of the franchise until 1982, at Orange, Calif., on November 2; began his association with baseball in 1947 when he joined the Boston Braves as public accountant; went with the Braves to Milwaukee in 1953 and was named assistant treasurer as well as a member of the team's board of directors; was hired for the Angels' front office when the expansion team was formed in 1961 and ramained a member of the team's executive staff until his retirement.

Harold Burnham (Sheriff) Lee, 84, a right-handed-hitting outfielder who compiled a .275 batting average with three National League teams between 1930 and '36, at Pascagoula, Miss., on September 4; was a Mississippi native who signed with the Brooklyn Dodgers in 1928; spent entire 1930 season with the Dodgers but played only 22 games before being traded to the Philadelphia Phillies; enjoyed his best season in 1932 as part of a .300-hitting outfield with Chuck Klein and Kiddo Davis; batted .303 with 18 home runs and 85 RBIs; was traded the next season to the Boston Braves, the team with which he finished his big-league career in 1936; was sent to Jersey City and was batting in the .340 range when he suffered a broken leg, an injury that ended his hopes of returning to the majors; continued as a good hitter on the minor league level until 1941, but his inability to run well finally forced his retirement.

Stephen Neal Lembo, 63, a reserve catcher who played seven major league games for the Brooklyn Dodgers in 1950 and '52 and later a scout for that organization, at Flushing, N.Y., on December 4; appeared in five games with Brooklyn in 1950 and two more in '52 as a backup for Hall of Famer Roy Campanella; played for eight different Brooklyn farm clubs during his nine-year professional career and then began working as a Dodger scout in 1955, a job he held for 20 years.

Anthony (Tony) Lucadello, 76, a longtime major league scout who signed Philadelphia Phillies great Mike Schmidt to his first professional contract, of an apparent suicide at Fostoria, O., on May 8; was a former minor league player who scouted 11 years for the Chicago Cubs before joining the Phillies in 1957; signed at least 50 major leaguers-to-be to professional contracts, including such stars as Ferguson Jenkins, Toby Harrah, Larry Hisle and Grant Jackson; covered the Ohio, Michigan and Indiana areas for the Phillies; had a younger brother, John Lucadello, who played 239 games as an infielder with the St. Louis Browns and New York Yankees between 1938 and '47.

E. Vernon Luse, 66, a former minor league catcher and an early member of the Society for American Baseball Research, at La Jolla, Calif., on January 22; played for Palatka (Florida State) and Dayton (Middle Atlantic) prior to World War II; attended Wichita State and earned a degree in engineering after the war; worked as a professional engineer with several firms until his retirement two years ago; had been a member of SABR since 1972 and served as one of its board members and officers; was honored by the organization for his pioneer research of 19th century minor leagues.

Max Cullen Macon, 73, a lefthanded pitcher who also played the outfield and first base during a six-year National League career from 1938 to '47 before turning to managing and scouting, at Jupiter, Fla., on August 5; compiled a 17-19 record in 81 games as a pitcher; recorded a .265 batting average in 226 games as a position player; earned his first shot with the St. Louis Cardinals in 1938 after recording a 21-12 record with Columbus (American Association) the previous season; was 4-11 with the Cardinals and returned to the minors before resurfacing with Brooklyn in 1940; pitched three seasons with the Dodgers before finishing his career in 1944 and 1947 with the Boston Braves; played 106 games as a position player with the Braves in 1944, batting .273 with three homers and 36 RBIs; later managed the Dodgers' St. Paul (American Association) farm club from 1956 to '59 before turning to scouting;

lived for most of his retirement days in Louisville, where he was well known as a high school and college basketball referee.

Joseph Charles Malay, 83, a lefthanded-hitting first baseman who played nine big-league games for the New York Giants in 1933 and '35, at Bridgeport, Conn., on March 19; batted 25 times in his brief major league career and batted .160; was the son of Charlie Malay, a big-league infielder-outfielder who played 102 games for the 1905 Brooklyn Dodgers.

Alfred Manuel (Billy) Martin, 61, a fiery, controversial competitor for 11 years as a major league infielder and then for more than 16 years as an on-again, off-again big-league manager, in an automobile accident near Johnson City, N.Y., on December 25; will be best remembered for his confrontational personality, quick fists and celebrated run-ins with everybody he worked for, most notably New York Yankee Owner George Steinbrenner, who hired and fired him as Yankee manager five times; blessed with only average natural ability, Martin compensated with hustle, determination and his win-at-all-costs mentality; started his professional career in 1946 with Idaho Falls (Pioneer) and worked his way onto the Yankee roster by 1950; became their regular second baseman in 1952, batting .267, his career high, in 109 games; took part in several celebrated on-field fights with St. Louis Browns catcher Clint Courtney (1951 and '52) and, despite his slight 5-foot-11, 165-pound build, refused to back down from anybody; played with the Yankees until 1957 when he became the scapegoat in a well-documented off-field brawl at the Copacabana nightclub in New York; Yankee teammates Yogi Berra, Mickey Mantle, Johnny Kucks and Hank Bauer also were involved, but Martin was fined $1,000 and he was traded to the Kansas City Athletics midway through the 1957 season; went on to play for the A's, Detroit Tigers, Cleveland Indians, Cincinnati Reds, Milwaukee Braves and Minnesota Twins in a career that ended in 1961 with a .257 career average in 1,021 games; was known as an excellent clutch performer and he supported that notion by batting .333 in five World Series with the Yankees; won a citation as the outstanding player in the 1953 Series when he batted .500 and set a six-game Series record with 12 hits in the Yankees' victory over the Brooklyn Dodgers; stayed on with the Twins as a scout following his 1961 retirement and became a Minnesota coach three years later; was talked into managing the Twins' Denver (Pacific Coast) farm club in 1968 by Owner Calvin Griffith and immediately took to the new job, leading his team to a 65-50 record; was named to replace Cal Ermer as Twins' manager in 1969 and guided them to the A.L. West Division championship with a 97-65 record; was fired five days after the Twins were swept in the A.L. Championship Series by Baltimore because of a growing rift with Griffith; that same pattern—immediate success followed by owner-manager disenchantment—followed Martin through the rest of his career; managed Detroit to an A.L. East championship in 1972 and was fired the next season; led the Texas Rangers to a surprising second-place finish in the West in 1974 and was fired the next year; took his first job as Yankee manager in 1975 and led his team to an A.L. pennant in 1976 and a World Series championship in '77; a much-publicized feud with Steinbrenner and a dugout confrontation with Yankee star Reggie Jackson during a nationally-televised game led to his firing in July 1978; four days after his tearful resignation, Steinbrenner announced that Martin would return as Yankee manager in 1980, a second term that actually began in June 1979 when Steinbrenner fired Bob Lemon; got into a celebrated barroom fight with a marshmallow salesman in late 1979, an altercation that ended with one Martin punch and his eventual firing; enjoyed more success in three seasons as manager of the Oakland A's before returning for his third term with the Yankees in 1983; became embroiled in numerous incidents during the season and was fired in December; took over as Yankee manager again 16 games into the 1985 season and lasted through the campaign before more off-field incidents led to his firing; began last term as Yankee manager in 1988, lasting just halfway through the season because of another alleged barroom fight; finished his managing career with a 1,258-1,018 record that included six division championships and one World Series title; managed the Yankees for 942 games, exactly half of them in his first tenure; was still on the Yankee payroll as a consultant at the time of his death; his uniform No. 1 was retired before a sellout crowd at Yankee Stadium in 1986 and a Billy Martin plaque was added to those in the stadium's Monument Park.

Jim McLaughlin, 74, a baseball executive with the St. Louis Browns, Baltimore Orioles and Cincinnati Reds, at Baltimore on January 1; began his career with the Browns in 1937 as an assistant to General Manager Bill DeWitt and became the team's farm director in 1945, a job he continued to hold after the team's transfer to Baltimore in 1954; remained there until 1961 when he rejoined DeWitt, who had taken over as president of the Reds; when DeWitt was replaced by Bob Howsam in 1967, McLaughlin returned to Baltimore; was coordinator of scouting and player development when he retired in 1980; was credited with the signing of such players as Johnny Bench, Boog Powell, Brooks Robinson and Dave McNally.

Glenn Richard (Red) McQuillen, 73, a former outfielder for the St. Louis Browns who batted .274 in five seasons between 1938 and '47, at Gardenville, Md., on June 8; jumped from the campus of Western Maryland College to the Browns in 1938, but was sent to the minors for seasoning after just 43 games; returned for seven games in 1941 before batting .283 in 100 games with the Browns in 1942; spent next three years in the military service before returning to play 59 games in 1946; made one pinch-hitting appearance in 1947, his last season at the major league level; was sent to Toledo and won the American Association batting title in 1948; made several more minor league stops as a player before turning to managing; lasted nearly another decade in the minors before retiring permanently from baseball.

Donnie Ray Moore, 35, a righthander who set a California Angels record in 1985 with 31 saves only to become the "goat" in the team's disappointing 1986 Championship Series loss to Boston, of a self-imposed gunshot wound at Anaheim, Calif., on July 18; was a journeyman pitcher through most of his early career that included stints with the Chicago Cubs (four years), St. Louis Cardinals (one year), Montreal Expos (one year) and Atlanta Braves (three years); armed with a newly perfected forkball and renewed confidence after being drafted off the Braves roster in January 1985, Moore enjoyed his best season, recording his record 31 saves while making a club-record 65 appearances and helping the Angels compile a 30-13 record in one-run decisions; signed a big free-agent contract with the Angels following the season and underwent successful knee surgery; began to experience a series of problems with his right shoulder and rib cage early in 1986, however, and was limited to 45 appearances and 21 saves; fighting back problems during the Championship Series that season, Moore was called into the game to protect a 5-4 ninth-inning California lead that would have

given the Angels their first-ever World Series berth; facing Boston's Dave Henderson with two out and a man on base, Moore got two strikes before surrendering a crushing two-run homer that gave Boston new life; the Angels tied the game in the bottom of the inning, but the Red Sox won in the 11th and then won the next two games in Boston to wrap up the series; underwent back surgery following the season and then spent much of 1987 on the disabled list with a series of different maladies; was released by California in 1988 and signed a contract with the Omaha Royals (American Association) before being released in June 1989; finished his career with a 43-40 record, 89 saves and a 3.66 ERA; appeared in five playoff games, two with Atlanta in 1982 and three with California in '86, compiling an 0-1 record and 4.70 ERA.

Euel Walton (Chief) Moore, 80, a full-blooded Chickasaw Indian who compiled a 9-16 record in three major league seasons with the Philadelphia Phillies and New York Giants in the 1930s, at Tishomingo, Okla., on February 12; was a burly righthander who turned from wrestling to baseball in his youth; his vast potential was diminished considerably in 1929 when he broke his pitching arm while sliding into second in a minor league game; reached the major leagues in 1934 and made 61 appearances, 29 as a starter, over the next three seasons with the Phillies, the Giants and the Phillies again in 1936, his last big-league campaign; pitched in the minors until seeing duty during World War II and settling in Tishomingo as a game warden.

Raymond Anderson Morehart, 89, a utility infielder with the 1927 New York Yankees and one of only two surviving members of what many consider the finest major league baseball team of all time, at Dallas on January 13; played only the one season with the Yankees, batting .256 in 73 games as a late-inning replacement for second baseman Tony Lazzeri; did not get to play in the Yankees' four-game sweep of Pittsburgh in the World Series; played two other seasons, 1924 and '26, in the major leagues—both with the Chicago White Sox; compiled a career .269 average in 177 big-league games and once collected nine hits in a doubleheader (1926), a major league record that has been tied several times, but never broken; left baseball in 1934 to work in the Texas oil fields; Morehart's death leaves shortstop Mark Koenig as the last survivor of the 1927 Yankees.

Howard Glenn Moss, a righthanded hitter who played 22 major league games with three teams in parts of the 1942 and '46 seasons, at Baltimore on May 7; played seven games with the 1942 New York Giants and then spent time in the military service before dividing his 1946 campaign between the Cincinnati Reds and Cleveland Indians; batted .097 in 72 big-league at-bats.

Edward (Eddie) Neville, 66, a well-traveled minor league pitcher who set several club records for the Durham Bulls (Carolina) but never reached the major leagues, at Durham, N.C., on January 24; was a lefthander who tied a Carolina League record when he won 25 games for a sixth-place Durham team in 1949; was ineffective at the Triple-A level and returned to Durham in 1952 to set a record for earned-run average (1.72); was also 21-8 in 1953.

Sherry O'Brien, 81, a former Philadelphia sports announcer whose biggest contribution to his profession came when he decided to personalize the introduction of baseball players in his position as field announcer for the Athletics and Phillies at old Shibe Park, at Philadelphia on April 10; broke with tradition in 1944 by reciting the full name and average of each player as he came to the plate; previously, field announcers had read the starting lineups, using only the players' last names; began adding more information about players, an idea that quickly became popular around the country; also used his position to explain complicated umpiring decisions to the crowd; began his career as a sports writer and helped found the National Football League's Frankford Yellowjackets, a forerunner to the Philadelphia Eagles, before beginning a new career as a sports announcer; worked in both television and radio as well as his field announcing before retiring from sports in the early 1970s to work as a clerk and librarian for the state supreme court in Philadelphia.

James C. (Jim) Odom, 72, an American League umpire for 11 seasons in the 1960s and '70s and a member of the crews that worked the first night All-Star and World Series games, at Bennettsville, S.C., on January 18; after striking out as a minor league player, he turned to umpiring in 1948 when he enrolled in George Barr's umpire school in Sanford, Fla.; began working in the Class D West Texas-New Mexico League and rose through the ranks to the Class AAA International League in 1960; his contract was purchased by the A.L. in 1963; owned the distinction of being the only umpire to work the first night All-Star Game (Houston, 1968) and the first night World Series game (Baltimore, 1971); also umpired in the A.L. playoffs in 1970 and '73; retired after the 1974 season and later did some work as a staff member at the Al Somers umpiring school in Daytona Beach, Fla.

Vern Jarl Olsen, 71, a lefthander who compiled a 30-26 record in all or parts of five seasons with the Chicago Cubs between 1939 and '46, at Chicago on July 13; was a rookie sensation in his first professional season when he won 23 games for Ponca City (Western Association) in 1937; posted 37 victories in the next two seasons with Tulsa (Texas) and joined the Cubs at the end of the 1939 campaign; enjoyed his best major league season in 1940 when he started 20 games and posted a 13-9 record and 2.97 ERA; won 16 games over the next two campaigns before serving in the Navy during World War II; was overweight and bothered by arm problems when he returned in 1946 to make five appearances with the Cubs; was sent back to the minors and retired the following spring.

Oliver Edward (Ollie) O'Mara, 98, an slightly-built infielder who made his major league debut in 1912 as the shortstop on the team that replaced striking Detroit Tigers players for one game, at Reno, Nev., on October 24; was among a group of college and amateur players hastily recruited by the Tigers and signed to contracts in Philadelphia for a May 18, 1912, game against the Athletics; the team was recruited because the Tiger regulars had staged a one-game walkout to protest the suspension of teammate Ty Cobb, who had been banned indefinitely by American League President Ban Johnson for going into the stands in New York after a heckler; went 0 for 4 in the game and the Tigers lost, 24-2; never played another game for Detroit; spent the rest of the season in the minors and was drafted by the Dodger organization; was called up by Brooklyn in 1914 and appeared in 67 games, batting .263; was the club's regular shortstop in 1915 and batted .244 in 149 games; was up and down between Brooklyn and the minor leagues the next three seasons but appeared on the Dodgers' World Series roster in 1916, striking out in one pinch-hitting appearance against the Boston Red Sox; compiled a .231 average in 412 big-league games; kicked around in the minor leagues until the late 1920s before settling in Kenosha, Wis., where he ran a billiards parlor and semipro baseball operation.

Stanwood Wendell (Stan) Partenheimer, 66, a lefthander who pitched briefly with the Boston Red Sox and St. Louis Cardinals in 1944 and '45, at Wilson, N.C., on January 28; suffered a badly broken leg in a sandlot football game as a youth and was told by doctors that he would never participate in competitive sports again; proved them wrong and was pitching in the minor leagues by the early 1940s before being drafted into the Army; was discharged because of his leg and resumed his minor league career, finally reaching the major leagues for one start with the Red Sox in 1944; made eight appearances for the Cardinals the next season without a decision; his bad leg continued to give him problems and adversely affected his control, eventually leading to his retirement; coached baseball and lacrosse and served as athletic director at Sewickley Academy outside Pittsburgh for 25 years before his retirement in 1984.

Pat Penafeather, 18, a member of the Auburn (New York-Penn) office staff who was thought to have been the youngest administrative assistant in professional baseball, of a viral infection at Auburn, N.Y., on February 18; had been with the club since the Houston affiliate move to Auburn in 1982, working as a vendor, a member of the groundcrew and, finally, in the club's front office; was a freshman at Niagara University at the time of his death.

William John (Bill) Posedel, 83, a righthander who compiled a 41-43 record in five seasons with the Brooklyn Dodgers and Boston Braves between 1938 and '46 before serving as a longtime pitching coach and scout, at Livermore, Calif., on November 28; was nicknamed "Sailor Bill," "Porthole" and "Chief" because of his two stints in the Navy; spent most of his pitching career in the minor leagues but was called up by Brooklyn in 1938 and posted an 8-9 record; enjoyed his best success the next season at Boston, where he finished 15-13 with a 3.92 ERA for the Braves; pitched two more seasons for Boston before fulfilling his military commitment during World War II; returned to Boston in 1946 and posted a 2-0 record in 19 games in what would be his final major league season; went on to serve as pitching coach for seven major league teams; was credited with playing a big role in the development of an Oakland staff that helped the A's to World Series championships in 1972, '73 and '74; also scouted for several big-league teams prior to his retirement in 1974.

Albert Allen (Al) Reiss, 80, a shortstop who appeared in nine games with the Philadelphia Athletics in 1932, at Red Bank, N.J., on May 13; was signed by Connie Mack off the Seton Hall University campus and batted .200 in his brief stay with the A's; went on to play another four seasons in the minor leagues before retiring from the game.

Chester James (Chet) Ross, 72, a righthanded-hitting outfielder who compiled a .241 average in 413 big-league games with the Boston Braves from 1939 to '44, at Buffalo on February 21; enjoyed his best major league season in 1940 when he batted .281 with 17 home runs and 89 RBIs for the Braves; never reached that performance level again, however, and after serving his military commitment in 1945 and '46, he kicked around the minor leagues for five more years before retiring.

Arthur C. (Art) Routzong, 76, a farm system and front-office employee of the St. Louis Cardinals for 28 of the 42 years he spent in baseball, at Spring, Tex., on January 10; received a law degree from the University of Dayton in 1936 but chose instead to pursue a sportswriting career, landing a job with the Dayton Herald; impressed Cardinals General Manager Branch Rickey during an interview and was offered a job in the Cardinals' publicity department; became business manager at Pocatello (Pioneer) in 1939 and supervised the construction of a new park there; moved on to Asheville (Piedmont) in the same capacity and, after serving for the Army during World War II, went to Allentown (Inter-State) where he oversaw the erection of another new park; became business manager of St. Louis' Houston (Texas) club in 1952 and was named general manager of the club three years later; returned to St. Louis in 1958 to serve as business manager under new General Manager Bing Devine; left the Cardinal organization in 1964 when Devine was fired and returned to Houston, where he served as director of stadium operations for the Astros when the Astrodome was opened; went to Pittsburgh in 1969 and served as treasurer until 1976; spent one more year as treasurer of the Three Rivers Management Corp. before retiring to the Houston area.

George Rulon, 67, the national director of the American Legion junior baseball program for a quarter of a century, at Bay Pines, Fla., on January 20; was a North Dakota native who worked as a sportswriter for the Fargo Forum and in public relations with the Fargo-Moorhead Twins of the Northern League from 1948 to '54; was a service officer with the North Dakota Legion for seven years and was appointed to the national staff of the veterans' organization in 1958, at which time he moved to Indianapolis; served as national director of membership and post activities for three years before being selected as successor to former major league pitcher Lou Brissie as director of the baseball program in 1961; coordinated the program's activities, including its national tournament, and the American Legion system grew to involve more than half a million youths playing on more than 20,000 teams; retired in 1986 but quickly accepted a job as coordinator of the 1987 Pan American Games, which were held in Indianapolis; retired after that task was completed.

Harold (Bus) Saidt, a sportswriter who covered three major league baseball teams during his 20-year career with the Trenton (N.J.) Times, at Trenton; covered the Philadelphia Phillies, New York Mets and New York Yankees; had written a feature article on newly elected National League President Bill White that appeared in The Sporting News a few weeks before his death; also did play-by-play work for the Trenton Giants when they were a farm club for the New York Giants.

Steve Leonard Senteney, 33, a righthander who made 11 relief appearances with the Toronto Blue Jays in 1982 without getting a decision, in an automobile accident near Colusa, Calif., on June 19; began pitching professionally in 1979 with Medicine Hat of the Pioneer League; after his brief fling in the majors, he pitched in the New York Mets and Pittsburgh organizations before retiring from baseball in 1985; remained active in baseball as a coach and player with two semipro teams in California.

Truett Banks (Rip) Sewell, 82, a Pittsburgh Pirates righthander who enjoyed several successful seasons after developing a blooper pitch that confounded National League hitters and delighted baseball fans, at Plant City, Fla., on September 3; was signed off the Vanderbilt University campus by Detroit and pitched five games for the Tigers in 1932 before a fight with star first baseman Hank Greenberg resulted in his demotion to the minor leagues; labored there for six seasons before resurfacing with the Pirates in 1938; compiled a 10-9 record in '39, his first full season with Pittsburgh, at age 32; went 16-5 the next season with a 2.80 ERA but fell to 14-17 in 1941 before a fall hunting accident in which he suffered buckshot

wounds to the abdomen, thighs, legs and feet; most of the shot was removed during surgery, but several pellets remained in the foot—a problem that would come back to haunt him in later years; returned healthy in 1942 and recorded a 17-15 record; began experimenting in the bullpen with a slow, high-arcing pitch to complement his average fastball and curve; threw it for the first time during a 1943 spring training game to Detroit rookie Dick Wakefield, who swung from the heels, missed the ball and fell down laughing; Pirates outfielder Maurice Van Robays coined the nonexistent word "eephus" to describe the pitch and that's what it was fondly called as Sewell continued using it in regular competition; aided by the "eephus," Sewell began making a mockery of some of the league's free swingers and recorded 21 victories in each of the next two seasons; fans came to the park to see him throw the pitch and no N.L. hitter ever was able to hit it out of the park; suffered a mild stroke in the Pirates' clubhouse in May 1946 and went on to record an 8-12 record; appeared in the 1946 All-Star Game and, with the National Leaguers trailing 12-0, fed his blooper to Boston Red Sox slugger Ted Williams, who promptly deposited it in the right-field seats; was involved in two other important events in '46: helped Cardinal shortstop Marty Marion work out the framework of a plan that was to lead to establishment of baseball's player pension fund, and he thwarted an attempt to unionize the Pirates clubhouse by speaking out against the idea; posted a combined 19-4 record in 1948 and '49 before retiring at age 43; managed in the minor leagues until 1955 and then coached for the Kansas City Athletics in 1956 before leaving baseball; doctors had to amputate both legs below the knees in 1973 because of life-threatening circulatory problems and one leg was eventually amputated at the hip; finished his baseball career with a 143-97 record with a 3.48 ERA and 137 complete games; made three appearances in All-Star Games.

Ernesto (Ernie) Sierra Jr., 66, a former minor league player who had served recently as a farm system instructor and scout for the San Diego Padres, at San Jose, Calif., on May 5; was a slightly built infielder who played for San Jose, Pocatello and Idaho Falls in the 1940s and '50s with military service sandwiched between; worked as a brewer following his retirement and returned to baseball with the Padres in 1984.

Steven Edward Simpson, 41, a righthander who pitched briefly for the San Diego Padres in 1972 during a five-year professional career, at Omaha, Neb., on November 2; was drafted by the Padres in 1970 and pitched his first couple of seasons as a starter before converting to the bullpen; made nine appearances for the 1972 Padres in relief, compiling an 0-2 record, a 4.76 ERA and two saves in 11⅓ innings of work; was sent back to the minor leagues where he stayed until his retirement in 1975.

George Truitt (Pappy) Smith, 79, who spent more than 20 years in the minor leagues as a player and manager, at Atlantic City, N.J.; was a little righthander who played under the name of George T. Kline when he broke in with Hagerstown in 1927; made it to the Boston Red Sox's roster but never played in a big-league game; also played and/or managed at Montreal, Jamestown, Ottawa, Winston-Salem and Sherbrooke before retiring from baseball in 1947.

Thomas Virgil (Red) Stallcup, 67, a shortstop with the Cincinnati Reds and St. Louis Cardinals between 1947 and '53, of a self-inflicted gunshot wound at Greenville, S.C., on May 2; compiled a .241 career average in 587 big-league games in his seven-year career; was signed by the Boston Red

Sox in 1941 but his career was interrupted by military service in World War II; was drafted by the Reds after his return in 1946 and reached the major leagues at the end of the '47 campaign; served as the Reds' regular shortstop from 1948 through '51 before being traded early in the 1952 season to St. Louis; played 29 games with the Cardinals that season and made one appearance in 1953 before being shipped to the minors; finished his career as a player-manager in the minor leagues in 1954 and '55.

Joseph Valentine (Jersey Joe) Stripp, 87, a righthanded-hitting infielder who compiled a .294 average in 11 major league seasons in the late 1920s and '30s, at Orlando, Fla., on June 10; broke in with the Cincinnati Reds in 1928 and batted .288 in 42 games; topped the .300 mark in six of seven seasons from 1930 through '36 while playing with the Reds and Brooklyn Dodgers, primarily at third base; played 1,146 major league games and collected 1,238 hits in a career that ended in 1938 after he had divided time between the St. Louis Cardinals and Boston Braves; opened a school for professional baseball prospects and those players already signed by big-league clubs; was a six-week program that utilized the facilities at Tinker Field in Orlando, Fla., and featured instruction from former major league players and coaches; enrolled upward of 175 students each January during its heyday and major league clubs sent a lot of signees to the school; the school shut its doors in 1943 and '44 because of World War II but was back in business in 1945 and stayed that way until the early 1950s.

Tommy V. Tatum, 70, an outfielder who played briefly with the Brooklyn Dodgers and Cincinnati Reds in the 1940s and played in the game in which Jackie Robinson broke the major league color barrier, at Oklahoma City on November 7; began his 19-year professional career with Harlingen (Texas Valley) under the name Tommy Mays; earned his first look with Brooklyn in 1941 but appeared in only eight games and was shipped back to the minors; after serving three years in the Army Air Corps, returned to play for the Montreal Royals, who won the 1946 Junior World Series; earned another promotion to Brooklyn but played in only four 1947 games, one of which marked the big-league debut of Robinson; was traded to Cincinnati and batted .273 in 69 games; returned the next season to the minor leagues and stayed there, both as a player and manager, until 1955; became a scout for Baltimore in 1956 and eventually retired to Oklahoma City.

William Harold (Bill) Terry, 90, a Hall of Fame first baseman in his 14-year playing career with the New York Giants, the last National Leaguer to bat over .400 and the man who succeeded the legendary John McGraw as Giants manager, at Jacksonville, Fla., on January 9; played 14 major league seasons and batted .341 with 154 home runs, 1,078 RBIs and 2,193 hits; was an aloof, sometimes arrogant man who was known for his run-ins with the Eastern press and McGraw, his longtime manager; began his professional career at age 16 as a wild lefthanded pitcher in the old Georgia-Alabama League in 1915; labored with little success for three years before deciding to give up the game; married at age 18 and began pumping gas at a Memphis filling station while continuing to play baseball as a pitcher-outfielder in a semipro league; developed a reputation as a powerful lefthanded hitter and attracted the attention of McGraw, who signed him to a contract and then watched him hit .336 and .377 in two seasons at Toledo (American Association); arrived in New York at the end of the 1923 campaign and backed up regular first baseman George (Highpockets) Kelly in 1924; became a regular in 1925 and batted .319, the first of 11 .300-

plus seasons he would produce at the major league level; nicknamed Memphis Bill, Terry began a string of six consecutive 100-plus RBI seasons in 1927 when he drove in 121; was outstanding in 1930, when he led the National League with a .401 average and 254 hits while hitting 23 homers and driving in 139 runs; also led the league that season in putouts and assists; narrowly missed a second straight batting title in 1931 when his .3486 mark fell just short of Chick Hafey's .3489; continued to hit for average after 1932, but his run production tapered off considerably; was offered the job of Giants manager, held for more than 30 years by McGraw, in 1932 because of McGraw's illness; led the Giants to a World Series championship in 1933 and the N.L. pennant in 1936—his last active season as a player; guided the Giants to another pennant in '37 and then watched them flounder through the next four campaigns before, under a barrage of criticism, he handed the managerial reins over to Mel Ott; remained one more season with the Giants as farm director before returning to Memphis to establish a successful automobile dealership; spurned later managerial offers from Brooklyn and Cincinnati as his business dealings flourished; relocated in Jacksonville in 1949 and served briefly as president of the Class A South Atlantic League, which had its headquarters in the city at that time; later served on the Baseball Hall of Fame Veterans Committee, a post he resigned 10 years prior to his death; was elected to the Hall of Fame in 1954, 18 years after becoming eligible.

George (Specs) Toporcer, 90, the first nonpitcher to wear eyeglasses in a major league game and a 30-year baseball man before going blind in 1952, at Huntington Station, N.Y., on May 17; was a boyhood friend and schoolmate of the late actor James Cagney who was signed by the Syracuse Stars off the New York sandlots in 1921; wore thick glasses—he could barely see beyond the end of his nose without them—that couldn't hide the fact that he was a talented player; joined the St. Louis Cardinals late in 1921 and spent eight years serving the club as a utility infielder; enjoyed best success in 1922 when he batted .324 in 116 games while playing all four infield defensive positions; appeared as a late-inning defensive replacement in the 1926 World Series; was sent to the minor leagues in 1928 with a career .279 average in 546 big-league games; played for Rochester (International) for four seasons and then managed the club from mid-1932 through '34; continued to manage in the minors and served in various front-office capacities both at the minor and major league levels; lost sight in his left eye in 1948 because of a detached retina and then went totally blind in 1952; wrote an autobiography, "Baseball From Backlots to Big League," and was a much-sought speaker who delivered inspirational messages about overcoming handicaps.

Frank Adam Trechock, 73, an infielder who played one game with the 1937 Washington Senators in a professional career that stretched to 1951, at Minneapolis on January 16; played a good part of his career with the Minneapolis Millers (American Association), joining them in 1940 and playing for them until 1948; also played in Louisville, Milwaukee and Buffalo.

Don Unferth, 75, who served the Chicago White Sox in a variety of front-office positions for 32 years before his retirement in 1980, at North Port, Fla., on December 4; was a standout lefthanded pitcher for Stevens Point Teachers College in the early 1930s before injuring his arm in a semipro game; turned to teaching at the high school level before becoming sports editor of the Wisconsin Rapids Daily Tribune in 1942 and a sports announcer for the University of Wisconsin network;

was hired by the White Sox in 1948 to assist farm director John Rigney and went on to serve the White Sox as publicity director, club statistician and traveling secretary; became the team's director of public relations in 1976, a job he held until his retirement; was known as a master at compiling and presenting statistical matter; spent almost an entire decade compiling material for a thick volume that contained the baseball history of every player to wear a Chicago uniform during the first 75 years of the club's existence; completed that work in 1973.

Emil Matthew Verban, 73, an infielder who played seven major league seasons with the St. Louis Cardinals, Philadelphia Phillies, Chicago Cubs and Boston Braves, at Lincoln, Ill., on June 8; was a righthanded spray hitter who compiled a .272 average in his big-league career; led all Cardinals in the 1944 all-St. Louis World Series, batting .412 in the Redbirds' six-game victory over the Browns; teamed with shortstop Marty Marion to give the wartime Cardinals the best double play combination in the National League; led N.L. second basemen in double plays in 1944 and in fielding average in 1945, when he played every inning of every game; with the return of Chuck Klein from military service in 1946, Verban was traded to Philadelphia, where he batted .275 in 138 games; went to the Cubs midway through the 1948 campaign and joined the Braves in '49, playing his last major league season in 1950; returned to the minor leagues and retired in 1952.

Fred Warren Waters, 62, a manager, scout and coach in the Minnesota Twins' farm system for 25 years after a brief stint as a lefthanded pitcher for the Pittsburgh Pirates in the mid-1950s, at Pensacola, Fla., on August 28; was a 1950 Mississippi Southern graduate who spent seven years in the minors with 12 different teams before getting his chance with the Pirates in 1955; appeared in two games with no record that season and made 23 appearances, most of them in relief, in 1956, compiling a 2-2 record and 2.82 ERA; was sent back to the minors in 1957 and pitched another seven years before turning to managing in the Twins' organization; also scouted for the Twins and served as an instructor in their minor league system; coached baseball at three high schools in the Pensacola area over an 18-year period.

Harrison P. Wickel, 76, who spent more than 50 years in baseball as a minor league player, manager and general manager and a big-league scout and farm director, at Sherman Oaks, Calif., on March 25; played shortstop, second base and outfield and batted above .300 in eight of the 10 seasons he was active as a player or player-manager; earned a degree in education from Ohio State University and was signed by the St. Louis Cardinals following graduation; never reached the major leagues but his ability as a teacher led to roles as a player-manager, which he filled from 1936 until a stint with the Navy during World War II; returned to the Cardinal organization as a minor league manager in 1946 and then spent five years as the Cardinals' senior West Coast scout before joining the Chicago Cubs as farm director, a post he held from 1952 to '54; scouted for the Detroit Tigers from 1955 to '59 before serving one year as president of the Fort Worth (Texas) club; scouted for the Cubs, Cardinals and Houston Astros through the remainder of his career; was Stan Musial's manager at Williamson (Mountain States) in 1939 and strongly urged the Cardinals to convert the pitcher to an everyday player; also was credited with signing Cardinal third baseman Whitey Kurowski to his first professional contract.

Theodore (Ted) Wilks, 73, a 5-foot-10, 200-pound righthander who led the National League in winning percentage as a St. Louis Cardinal rookie in 1944 when he compiled a 17-4 record and later went on to become the Cardinals' top bullpen performer, at Houston on August 21; was signed by the Cardinals in 1938 and spent six seasons in the minors before bursting onto the major league scene with his big rookie campaign; started 21 games that season and pitched twice in the 1944 World Series, compiling an 0-1 record; started 16 times in 1945 before moving to the bullpen, where he spent most of his remaining career; used an assortment of deliveries that varied from straight overhand to submarine; led N.L. relievers with 10 victories in 1949 while appearing in a league-high 59 games; missed most of the 1950 season after having bone chips removed from his elbow and then made only 17 appearances for the Cardinals in 1951 before being traded to Pittsburgh; was traded to the Cleveland Indians in 1952 and made four relief appearances in '53 before being placed on waivers, two months short of the 10-year service goal that would have qualified him for a full major league pension; embittered, Wilks pitched three more seasons as a reliever in the minor leagues; retired from baseball with a 59-30 career major league record and 3.26 ERA in 912⅔ innings; also made one appearance for the Cardinals in the 1946 World Series.

Willie (Devil) Wells, 82, an outstanding shortstop in the old Negro leagues whose professional career spanned three decades, at Austin, Tex., on January 21; was a stocky 5-foot-7, 160-pounder who had excellent hands, good range and a mediocre throwing arm, the result of a basketball injury; was credited with a .326 career batting average and set an all-time league mark in 1929 when he hit 27 home runs in an 88-game schedule; remembered primarily for his play with the St. Louis Stars and Newark Eagles; also performed for the Detroit Wolves, Kansas City Monarchs, Chicago American Giants and Baltimore Elite Giants while playing winter ball in Mexico and Cuba; managed the Newark team for several years and was credited with helping the careers of Larry Doby, Monte Irvin and Don Newcombe, all of whom became major league stars after the color barrier was broken; Irvin, a standout player with the New York Giants and a member of the Hall of Fame's Veterans Committee that has placed 11 former Negro league stars into the shrine, long has campaigned for Wells, whom he once called "the greatest living shortstop not in the Hall of Fame."

Hy Zimmerman, 74, a Seattle Times baseball writer and sports columnist who campaigned to bring major league baseball and a major league stadium to the city, at Seattle on April 22; was a longtime beat writer for Seattle's Pacific Coast League baseball team and covered both the ill-fated expansion Pilots and the Mariners prior to his retirement; also covered ice hockey, hydroplane racing and boxing in addition to writing a regular column after joining the Times in 1953; campaigned through his column for a major league franchise, but suffered a heart attack near the end of the Pilots' only spring training in 1969; returned to cover the team during the season but was devastated when the Pilots fled to Milwaukee in bankruptcy after only one year; began another editorial campaign for an expansion franchise; when voters finally approved a bond issue funding the Kingdome, which resulted in the establishment of the Mariners' franchise in 1977, there was a push to name the stadium in his honor; was a former president of the Seattle chapter of the Baseball Writers' Association of America.

Edward J. Zipay, 72, a first baseman who batted .300 or better in six of his 11 professional seasons but never rose above the Triple-A level, at Scranton, Pa., on May 25.

LEAGUE AND CLUB INFORMATION

Including

Major League Directory

American League Directory

American League Team Directories

National League Directory

National League Team Directories

Major League Farm Systems

Minor League Presidents

MAJOR LEAGUE BASEBALL

OFFICE OF THE COMMISSIONER
Commissioner—Francis T. Vincent, Jr.
Deputy Commissioner & Chief Operating Officer—Steven D. Greenberg
BASEBALL OPERATIONS
Director—Bill Murray
Assistant Director—George Pfister
Manager, Player Records—Janice Micale
DATA PROCESSING
Director—Dave Alworth
Operations Manager—Brian Vieira
FINANCE, PERSONNEL & OFFICE MANAGEMENT
Chief Financial Officer—Don Marr
Controller—Frank Simio
Office Manager—Mary Ann Burns
LEGAL
Director, Legal Affairs—Tom Ostertag
Assistant Counsel—Don Gibson
Records Manager—Charlyne Sanders
LICENSING
Director, Licensing & Pres., MLBP—Rick White
Account Managers—Karyn Donohue, Marla Miller, Mary Pierson
PUBLIC RELATIONS
Director—Richard Levin
Assistant Director—Jim Small
Manager, Club Relations—Susan Aglietti
Manager, Media Relations—Carole Coleman
Manager, Community Relations—Wally Weibel
SECURITY/FACILITY MANAGEMENT
Director—Kevin Hallinan
Regional Director, Central—Al Williams
**BROADCASTING, MARKETING SUPPORT,
PUBLISHING, SPECIAL EVENTS**
Senior Vice-President/Broadcasting—Bryan Burns
Director, Publications/Information—Dave Alworth
Director, Broadcast Administration—Leslie Lawrence
Marketing Manager—Steve McKelvey
Publishing Manager—Cindy McManus
Special Events Manager—David Dziedzic

Headquarters—350 Park Avenue, New York, N.Y. 10022
Telephone—371-7800 (area code 212)
Teletype—910-380-9482

American League
Organized 1900

ROBERT W. BROWN, M.D.
President

JOHN E. FETZER, GENE AUTRY
Vice-Presidents

DICK WAGNER
Special Assistant to Baseball

MARTIN J. SPRINGSTEAD
Supervisor of Umpires

RICHARD BUTLER
Special Assistant to the President

PHYLLIS MERHIGE
Director of Public Relations

JOHN C. MAROON
Assistant Director of Public Relations

TIM McCLEARY
Director, Waivers & Player Records

TESS BASTA
Administrator of Umpires/Travel

CAROLYN COEN
Administrative Assistant

Headquarters—350 Park Avenue, New York, N. Y. 10022

Telephone—371-7600 (area code 212)

ASSISTANT SUPERVISORS OF UMPIRES—Henry Soar, Larry Napp, Jerry Neudecker.

UMPIRES—Lawrence Barnett, Joseph Brinkman, Alan Clark, Drew Coble, Terrance Cooney, Derryl Cousins, Donald Denkinger, James Evans, Dale Ford, Richard Garcia, Ted Hendry, John Hirschbeck, Mark Johnson, Jim Joyce, Kenneth Kaiser, Greg Kosc, Tim McClelland, Larry McCoy, James McKean, Durwood Merrill, Dan Morrison, Stephen Palermo, David Phillips, Rick Reed, Michael Reilly, John (Rocky) Roe, Dale Scott, John Shulock, Tim Tschida, Vic Voltaggio, Tim Welke, Larry Young.

OFFICIAL STATISTICIANS—Elias Sports Bureau, Inc., 500 5th Ave., Suite 2114, New York, N.Y. 10036. Telephone—(212) 869-1530.

BALTIMORE ORIOLES

Chairman—Eli S. Jacobs
President—Lawrence Lucchino

Exec. Vice-President & General Manager—Roland A. Hemond
Vice-President, Finance—Joseph P. Hamper, Jr.
Vice-President, Administrative Personnel—Calvin Hill
Vice-President, Business Affairs—Robert R. Aylward
Vice-President/Sales—Louis I. Michaelson
Vice-President & Club Counsel—Lon Babby
Vice-President, Planning & Development—Janet Marie Smith
Vice-President—Sven Erik Holmes
Vice-President, Marketing—Martin B. Conway
Asst. G.M./Director of Player Personnel—R. Douglas Melvin
Director of Scouting—John Barr
Special Assistants to the Vice President—Gordon Goldsberry, Fred Uhlman Sr.
Director of Publications—Robert W. Brown
Traveling Secretary—Philip E. Itzoe
Director of Public Relations—Richard L. Vaughn
Director of Stadium Services—Roy A. Sommerhof
Director of Research & Statistics—Eddie Epstein
Director of Orioles Productions—Charles A. Steinberg, DDS
Director of Sales Operations—Vince Dunbar
Director, Community Relations—Julia A. Wagner
Director, Computer Services—James L. Kline
Special Projects/Baseball Operations—Kenneth E. Nigro
Ticket Office Manager—Audrey Brown
Assistant Director of Public Relations—Bob Miller
Assistant Director of Marketing—Julie Dryer
Assistant Director of Sales Operations—Matt Dryer
Asst. Director, Player Development/Scouting—Roy H. Krasik
Assistant Director of Scouting—Fred Uhlman Jr.
Assistant Director of Community Relations—Stephanie Kelly
Assistant Ticket Office Manager—Joseph B. Codd
Manager—Frank Robinson
Club Physicians—Drs. Sheldon Goldgeier and Charles E. Silberstein
Trainers—Richie Bancells, Jamie Reed
Executive Offices—Memorial Stadium, Baltimore, Md. 21218
Telephone—243-9800 (area code 301)

SCOUTS—Rick Arnold, Carlos Bernhardt, Jesus Carmona, John Cox, Ray Crone, Ed Farmer, Jim Gilbert, Jesus Halabi, Jim Howard, Leo Labossiere, Mike Ledna, Ed Liberatore, Tim Luginbuhl, Miguel Machado, Lamar North, Camilo Nunez, Jim Pamlanye, Ed Sprague, Birdie Tebbetts, Logan White, Bennett Williams, Jerry Zimmerman.

PARK LOCATION—Memorial Stadium, 33rd Street, Ellerslie Avenue, 36th Street and Ednor Road.

Seating capacity—54,017.

FIELD DIMENSIONS—Home plate to left field at foul line, 309 feet; to center field, 405 feet; to right field at foul line, 309 feet.

BOSTON RED SOX

Owner
General Partner—JRY Corporation:
Majority Owner & Chairwoman of the Board—Jean R. Yawkey
President—John L. Harrington
Vice-President & Treasurer—William B. Gutfarb

Owner
General Partner—Haywood C. Sullivan

Senior V.P. & General Manager—James (Lou) Gorman
Executive V.P. & Counsel—John F. Donovan, Jr.
Exec. Asst. to the General Partners & Dir. of Personnel Admin.—Linda G. Ezell
V.P. & Chief Financial Officer—Robert C. Furbush
V.P., Player Development—Edward F. Kenney
Assistant General Manager—Elaine C. Weddington
Manager—Joseph M. Morgan
Director of Scouting—Edward M. Kasko
Director of Minor League Operations—Edward P. Kenney
Vice President Transportation—John J. Rogers
Special Assistant to the General Manager—John M. Pesky
Team Physician—Arthur M. Pappas, M.D.
Vice President Public Relations—Richard L. Bresciani
Vice-President Broadcasting & Advertising—James P. Healey
Director of Ticket Operations—Joseph P. Helyar
Vice-President Property Management—Joseph F. McDermott
Director of Functions and Food Services—Thomas L. Queenan, Jr.
Director of Marketing—Lawrence C. Cancro
Exec. Asst. & Dir. of Community Relations—Michael L. Silva
Director of Publicity—Josh S. Spofford
Treasurer—John J. Reilly
Controller—Stanley H. Tran
Coordinator of Publications—Debra A. Matson
Superintendent of Grounds & Maintenance—Joseph Mooney
Manager of Group Sales—Leslie A. Leary
Director of Statistics—James A. Samia
Executive Offices—4 Yawkey Way, Boston, Mass. 02215
Telephone—267-9440 (area code 617)

SCOUTS—Rafael Batista, Milton Bolling, Ray Boone, Wayne Britton, Erwin Bryant, George Digby, Howard (Danny) Doyle, Bill Enos, Larry Flynn, Charles Koney, Jack Lee, Wilfrid (Lefty) Lefebvre, Don Lenhardt, Howard McCullough, Felix Maldonado, Frank Malzone, Sam Mele, Willie Paffen, Phillip Rossi, Edward Scott, Matt Sczesny, Joe Stephenson, Larry Thomas, Fay Thompson, Charlie Wagner.

PARK LOCATION—Fenway Park, Yawkey Way, Lansdowne Street and Ipswich Street.

Seating capacity—34,182.

FIELD DIMENSIONS—Home plate to left field at foul line, 315 feet; to center field, 420 feet; to right field at foul line, 302 feet; average right-field distance, 382 feet.

CALIFORNIA ANGELS

President/Chairman of the Board—Gene Autry

Board of Directors—Gene Autry, Jackie Autry, Mike Port, Stanley B. Schneider, Michael M. Schreter, Richard M. Brown
Exec. V.P./General Manager/Chief Operating Officer—Mike Port
Vice-President, Baseball Operations—Dan O'Brien
Executive Vice-President—Jackie Autry
Exec. V.P. Treasurer/Asst. Secretary—Michael Schreter
Sr. Vice-President, Marketing—John Hays
Sr. Vice-President, Finance and Administration—James Wilson
Vice-President, Public Relations—Tom Seeberg
Secretary & Legal Counsel—Richard M. Brown
Assistant to the General Manager—Preston Gomez
Director Minor League Operations—Bill Bavasi
Director Scouting—Bob Fontaine Jr.
Controller—Jim Kaczmarek
Admin. Assistant (Baseball)—Tom Osowski
Admin. Assistant (Minors)—Cathy Carey
Admin. Assistant (Scouting)—Roberta Mazur
Traveling Secretary—Frank Sims
Director Public Relations—Tim Mead
Director Publications—John Sevano
Public Relations Assistants—Jan Newton, Larry Babcock
Director, Marketing—Bob Wagner
Asst. Director, Marketing—Jann Mueller
Director, Group Sales & Promotions—Lynn Biggs
Manager, Group Sales & Promotions—Marianne Zambrano
Director, Special Projects—Corky Lippert
Director, Stadium Operations—Kevin Uhlich
Director, Ticket Department—Carl Gordon
Medical Director—Dr. Robert Kerlan
General Medicine—Dr. Jules Rasinski
Orthopedist—Dr. Lewis Yocum
Trainers—Rick Smith, Ned Bergert
Physical Therapist—Roger Williams
Manager—Doug Rader
Executive Offices—Anaheim Stadium, 2000 State College Blvd.,
Anaheim, Calif. 92806
Telephone—937-6700 (area code 714) or 625-1123 (area code 213)

SCOUTS—Edmundo Borrome, Ty Brown, Ted Brzenk, Joe Carpenter, Loyd Christopher, Ray Crone, Pompeyo Davalillo, Orlando Estevez, Roger Ferguson, Bob Gardner, Lin Garrett, Red Gaskill, Rosey Gilhousen, Jose Gomez, Dean Gruwell, Steve Gruwell, Fred Hatfield, Rick Ingalls, Nick Kamzic, Tim Kelly, Kris Kline, Tom Kotchman, Jim McLaughlin, Bobby Myrick, Jon Neiderer, Eusebio Perez, Vic Power, Paul Robinson, Cookie Rojas, Rich Schlenker, Duane Shaffer, Woody Smith, Brian York.

PARK LOCATION—Anaheim Stadium, 2000 State College Blvd.

Seating capacity—64,573.

FIELD DIMENSIONS—Home plate to left field at foul line, 333 feet; to center field, 404 feet; to right field at foul line, 333 feet.

CHICAGO WHITE SOX

Chairman—Jerry M. Reinsdorf

President—Eddie M. Einhorn
Executive Vice-President—Howard C. Pizer
Senior Vice-President/General Manager—Larry Himes
Senior Vice-President/Marketing & Broadcasting—Rob Gallas
Senior Vice-President, Baseball—Jack Gould
Vice-President, Finance—Timothy L. Buzard
Vice-President, Stadium Operations—Terry Savarise
V.P., Public Relations/Community Affairs—Chuck Adams
General Counsel—Allan B. Muchin
Assistant Vice-President, Broadcast Sales—Edwin M. Doody
Director of Marketing & Broadcasting—Mike Budek
Director of Advertising & Promotions—Bob Grim
Director of Scouting & Player Development—Al Goldis
Director of Baseball Administration—Dan Evans
Special Assistants to the General Manager—Bart Johnson, Larry Monroe
Asst. Director of Scouting & Player Development—Steve Noworyta
Minor League Administrator—Chuck Bizzell
Director of Park Operations—David Schaffer
Director of Ticket Administration—Millie Johnson
Director of Ticket Sales—Bob Voight
Director of Purchasing—Don Esposito
Ticket Manager—Bob Devoy
Major League Scouting & Video Analyst—Jeff Chaney
Major League Computer Scouting Analyst—Mike Maziarka
Traveling Secretary—Glen Rosenbaum
Manager of Merchandising & Special Events—Sharon Sreniawski
Manager of Media Relations—Dana Noel
Coordinator of Broadcasting—Dan Fabian
Coordinator of Publications—Sue Selig
Coord. of Public Relations/Community Affairs—Adelle Powell
Trainers—Herman Schneider, Mark Anderson
Team Physicians—Drs. James B. Boscardin,
Hugo Cuadros, David Orth, Bernard Feldman, Scott Price
Manager—Jeff Torborg
Executive Offices—Comiskey Park, 324 W. 35th Street, Chicago, Ill. 60616
Telephone—924-1000 (area code 312)

SCOUTS—(Major League)—Ed Brinkman, Bart Johnson, Larry Monroe, Joe Nossek. (Supervisors/National Cross Checkers)—Mark Bernstein, Dan Monzon, Lou Snipp. (Full-time)—Juan Bernhardt, Tom Calvano, Alex Cosmidis, Preston Douglas, Jesse Flores, Ed Ford, Rod Fridely, Mike Harris, Miguel Ibarra, Ed Pebley, Gary Pellant, Orlando Pena, Mike Powers, Mike Rizzo, Phil Rizzo, Alberto Rondon, Mark Snipp, Mike Taylor, Ron Vaughn. (Part-time)—Warren Hughes, Joe Ingalls, Reggie Lewis, Guy Mader, Jose Ortega, Victor Puig, Bob Sloan, Richard Taylor, John Tumminia.

PARK LOCATION—Comiskey Park, 324 W. 35th Street, Chicago, Ill. 60616

Seating capacity—43,951.

FIELD DIMENSIONS—Home plate to left field at foul line, 347 feet; to center field, 409 feet; to right field at foul line, 347 feet.

CLEVELAND INDIANS

Board of Directors—Richard E. Jacobs, Chairman; David H. Jacobs, Vice-Chairman; Martin J. Cleary, Gary L. Bryenton

Chairman of the Board and Chief Executive Officer—Richard E. Jacobs
Vice-Chairman of the Board—David H. Jacobs
President and Chief Operating Officer—Hank Peters
Senior Vice President, Business—Dennis Lehman
Vice-President, Baseball Operations—Tom Giordano
Vice-President, Finance—Gregg Olson
V.P., Public Relations/Community Relations—Bob DiBiasio
Vice-President, Stadium Operations—Carl Hoerig
Vice-President—Martin J. Cleary
Manager—John McNamara
Director, Publications/Advertising Sales—Valerie Arcuri
Director, Merchandising/Licensing—Jayne Churchmack
Director, Ticket Services—Connie Minadeo
Director, Scouting—Chet Montgomery
Director, Player Development—Dan O'Dowd
Director, Team Travel—Mike Seghi
Director, Ticket Sales—Gary Sherwood
Director, Promotions/Sales—Jon Starrett
Controller—Diane Stuczynski
Assistant Director, Media Relations—Susie Gharrity
Assistant Director, Player Personnel—Phil Thomas
Administrator, Player Personnel—Wendy Hoppel
Manager, Promotions/Sales—Nadine Glinski
Manager, Season/Group Sales—Tony Seghy
Manager, Community Relations—Glen Shumate
Manager, Box Office—Tom Sullivan
Manager, Operations—Kerry Wimsatt
Marketing Representative—Chris Previte
Account Executives, Ticket Sales—Scott Sterneckert, Devore Whitt
Speakers Bureau—Bob Feller
Indians Equipment & Clubhouse Manager—Cy Buynak
Medical Director—William T. Wilder, M.D.
Orthopedic Specialists—John Bergfeld, M.D., Tom Anderson, M.D.
Trainer—Jim Warfield
Assistant Trainer—Paul Spicuzza
Team Physicians—Drs. James R. Conforto, Godofredo Domingo,
K.V. Gopal, David Schultz, Chris Ruszkowski
Executive Offices—Cleveland Stadium, Cleveland, Ohio 44114
Telephone—861-1200 (area code 216)

SCOUTS—(Special Assignments)—Dan Carnevale, Gordie MacKenzie, Bill Werle. Regular—Luis Aponte, Steve Avila, Tom Chandler, Ramon Conde, Tom Couston, Ed Crosby, Joe DeLucca, Dave Koblentz, George Lauzerique, Bill Lawlor, Winston Llenas, Bobby Malkmus, Buddy Mercado, Jim Miller, Don Mitchell, Mike Piatnik, Jim Richardson, Dave Roberts, Doug Takaragawa, Paul Tinnell.

PARK LOCATION—Cleveland Stadium, Boudreau Blvd.

Seating capacity—74,483.

FIELD DIMENSIONS—Home plate to left field at foul line, 320 feet; to center field, 400 feet; to right field at foul line, 320 feet.

DETROIT TIGERS

Board of Directors
Thomas S. Monaghan, James A. Campbell, Douglas J. Dawson,
Glenn E. (Bo) Schembechler, George Kell

Chairman Emeritus—John E. Fetzer
Vice-Chairman and Owner—Thomas S. Monaghan
Chairman & Chief Executive Officer—James A. Campbell
President & Chief Operating Officer—Glenn E. (Bo) Schembechler
Vice-President & General Manager—William R. Lajoie
Vice-President, Operations—William E. Haase
V.P., Player Procurement & Development—Joseph A. McDonald
V.P., Secretary/Treasurer—Alexander C. Callam
V.P., Marketing, Communications & P.R.—Jeff Odenwald
Assistant Secretary/Controller—Michael Wilson
Director of Press & Public Relations—Dan Ewald
Director of Radio & TV—Neal Fenkell
Director of Stadium Operations—Ralph E. Snyder
Director of Ticket Sales—William H. Willis
Director, Minor League Administration—Dave Miller
Director, Special Projects—Lew Matlin
Director, Marketing Services—Scott Nickle
Executive Secretary/Baseball—Alice Sloane
Executive Secretary/Operations—Hazel McLane
Data Processing Manager—Richard Roy
Traveling Secretary—Bill Brown
Executive Consultant—Rick Ferrell
Special Assignment Scouts—Walter A. Evers, Jerry Walker,
Hal Keller, Jim Davenport
Scouting Director—Jax Robertson
Western Scouting Supervisor—Dick Wiencek
Assistant Director of Public Relations—Greg Shea
Manager, Promotions—Mike Pyle
Community Affairs Coordinator—Vince Desmond
Group Sales Coordinator—Irwin Cohen
Assistant Director of Stadium Operations/Grounds Maintenance—Frank Feneck
Assistant Director of Stadium Operations/Grounds Maintenance—Ed Goward
Manager—Sparky Anderson
Club Physicians—Clarence S. Livingood M.D., David Collon M.D., Louis Saco, M.D.
Executive Offices—Tiger Stadium, Detroit, Mich. 48216
Telephone—962-4000 (area code 313)

SCOUTS—Ruben Amaro, Wayne Blackburn, Charlie Gault, Richard Henning, Joe Lewis, Dave Littlefield, Jeff Malinoff, Ramon Pena, Dee Phillips, Joe Robinson, Donnie Rowland, Bill Schudlich, Steve Souchock, Clyde Weir, Rob Wilfong, Richard Wilson, Gary York.

PARK LOCATION—Tiger Stadium, Michigan Avenue, Cochrane Avenue, Kaline Drive and Trumbull Avenue.

Seating capacity—52,416.

FIELD DIMENSIONS—Home plate to left field at foul line, 340 feet; to center field, 440 feet; to right field at foul line, 325 feet.

KANSAS CITY ROYALS

Board of Directors
Joe Burke, Avron Fogelman, Charles Hughes,
Ewing Kauffman, Mrs. Ewing Kauffman, Earl Smith

Chairman of the Board (co-owner)—Ewing Kauffman
Vice Chairman of the Board (co-owner)—Avron Fogelman
President—Joe Burke
Executive Vice-President and General Manager—John Schuerholz
Executive Vice-President, Administration—Spencer (Herk) Robinson
Vice-President, Treasurer—Charles Hughes
Vice-President, Finance—Dale Rohr
Vice-President, Government & Consumer Affairs—Merle Wood
Vice-President, Public Relations—Dean Vogelaar
Vice-President, Marketing and Broadcasting—Dennis Cryder
Vice-President, Player Personnel—Joe Klein
Director of Scouting—Art Stewart
Assistant to General Manager—Dean Taylor
Director of Stadium Operations—Jay Hinrichs
Director of Ticket Operations—Glenn Loest
Director of Season Ticket Sales—Joe Grigoli
Director of Group Sales/Lancer Coordinator—Chris Muehlbach
Director of Data Processing—Loretta Kratzberg
Director of Benefits & Compensation—Tom Pfannenstiel
Director of Accounting—Ken Willeke
Ticket Office Manager—Stacy Sherrow
Traveling Secretary—Dave Witty
Adm. Asst., Scouting & Player Development—Bob Hegman
Assistant Directors of Public Relations—Steve Fink, Phil Dixon
Assistant Directors of Marketing—Mike Behymer, Laura Collins
Accountant—Lisa Collins
Stadium Engineers—Duane Robinson, Chris Frank
Executive Secretary/Baseball—Peggy Mathews
Manager—John Wathan
Equipment Manager—Mike Wallace
Team Physician—Dr. Paul Meyer
Trainers—Mickey Cobb, Nick Swartz
Executive Offices—Royals Stadium, Harry S Truman Sports Complex
Mailing Address—P. O. Box 419969, Kansas City, Mo. 64141
Telephone—921-2200 (area code 816)

SCOUTS—Allard Baird, Carl Blando, Gary Blaylock, Bob Carter, Floyd Chandler, Balos Davis, Tom Ferrick, Steve Flores, Ken Gonzales, Dave Herrera, Gary Johnson, Ken Kravec, Al Kubski, Tony Levato, Jeff McKay, Chuck McMichael, Jim Moran, Brian Murphy, Buck O'Neil, Wil Rutenschroer, Luis Silverio, Jerry Stephens, Terry Wetzel.

PARK LOCATION—Royals Stadium, Harry S Truman Sports Complex.

Seating capacity—40,625.

FIELD DIMENSIONS—Home plate to left field at foul line, 330 feet; to center field, 410 feet; to right field at foul line, 330 feet.

MILWAUKEE BREWERS

President, Chief Executive Officer—Allan H. (Bud) Selig

Executive Vice-President, General Manager—Harry Dalton
Vice-President, Marketing—Richard Hackett
Vice-President, Broadcast Operations—William Haig
Vice-President, Finance—Richard Hoffmann
Vice-President, Stadium Operations—Gabe Paul, Jr.
Director of Market Research—John Cordova
Asst. General Manager & Farm Director—Bruce Manno
Senior Advisor, Baseball Operations—Walter Shannon
Special Assistants to the General Manager—Dee Fondy, Sal Bando
Traveling Secretary—Jimmy Bank
Scouting Coordinator—Dick Foster
V.P., International Baseball Oper.—Ray Poitevint
Dir. of Latin American Baseball Operations—Hiram Cuevas
Coord. of Player Development—Bob Humphreys
Asst. Dir., Spring Training Operations—Freddie Frederico
Director of Publicity—Tom Skibosh
Assistant Director of Stadium Operations and Advertising—Jack Hutchinson
Director of Publications and Assistant Director of Publicity—Mario Ziino
Director of Special Projects—Jake Frego
Promotions Director—Tim Van Wagoner
Promotions Manager—Karen Brooks
Group Sales Director—Tim Trovato
Season Ticket Sales Director—Rich Fromstein
Ticket Office Manager—John Barnes
Director of Season Ticket Account Services—Alice Boettcher
Manager—Tom Trebelhorn
Club Physicians—Dr. Paul Jacobs, Dr. Dennis Sullivan
Trainers—John Adam, Al Price
Superintendent of Grounds and Maintenance—Harry Gill
Equipment Manager—Tony Migliaccio
P.A. Announcer—Bob Betts
Executive Offices—Milwaukee Brewers Baseball Club
Milwaukee County Stadium, Milwaukee, Wis. 53214
Telephone—933-4114 (area code 414)

SCOUTS—National crosschecker: Ken Bracey. Special Assignment: Nelson Burbrink, Dave Garcia, Cal McLish, Danny Menendez, Ben Oglivie, Charlie Silvera, Paul Tretiak. Supervisors: Fred Beene, Julio Blanco-Herrera, Ken Califano, Felix Delgado, Roland LeBlanc, Lee Sigman, Walter Youse. Regulars: Al Bleser, Derek Bryant, Kevin Christman, Lou Cohenour, Del Crandall, Ed Durkin, Al Geddes, Harvey Kuenn, Jr., Terry Laschen, Phil Long, Steve McAllister, Jim McCray, Ed Mathes, Gus Mureo, Tony Muser, Johnny Neun, Al Otto, Frank Pena, Reuben Rodriguez, Art Schuerman, Harry Smith, Mike Stafford, Sam Suplizio, Tommy Thompson, Rip Tutor, Red Whitsett, David Young, George Zabala.

PARK LOCATION—Milwaukee County Stadium, S. 46th St. off Bluemound Rd.

Seating capacity—53,192.

FIELD DIMENSIONS—Home plate to left field at foul line, 315 feet; to center field, 402 feet; to right field at foul line, 315 feet.

MINNESOTA TWINS

Owner—Carl R. Pohlad

President—Jerry Bell
Chairman of Executive Committee—Howard Fox
Directors—Donald E. Benson, Paul R. Christen, James O. Pohlad, Robert C. Pohlad,
William M. Pohlad, Robert E. Woolley
Exec. Vice-President, Baseball Operations—Andy MacPhail
Vice-President, Player Personnel—Bob Gebhard
Director of Finance—Kevin Mather
Vice-President, Operations—Dave Moore
Director of Minor Leagues—Jim Rantz
Director of Scouting—Terry Ryan
Director of Baseball Administration—Bill Smith
Director of Marketing—Laurel Prieb
Director of Media Relations—Tom Mee
Traveling Secretary—Remzi Kiratli
Manager—Tom Kelly
Club Physicians—Dr. Leonard J. Michienzi, Dr. John Steubs
Executive Offices—Hubert H. Humphrey Metrodome, 501 Chicago Ave. South,
Minneapolis, Minn. 55415
Telephone—375-1366 (area code 612)

SCOUTS—Floyd Baker, Vern Borning, Enrique Brito, Ellsworth Brown, Larry
Corrigan, Gene Deboer, Edward Dunn, Dan Durst, Cal Ermer, Marty Esposito, Vern
Followell, Earl Frishman, Angelo Giuliani, Bill Lohr, Kevin Malone, Mike Radcliff,
Clair Reirson, Jay Robertson, Edwin Rodriguez, Mike Ruth, Cobby Saatzer, Jeff
Schugel, Johnny Sierra, Herb Stein, Jerry Terrell, Steve Williams.

PARK LOCATION—Hubert H. Humphrey Metrodome, 501 Chicago Ave. South.

Seating capacity—55,883.

FIELD DIMENSIONS—Home plate to left field at foul line, 343 feet; to center
field, 408 feet; to right field at foul line, 327 feet.

NEW YORK YANKEES

Principal Owner—George M. Steinbrenner

Directors—Harold M. Bowman, Daniel M. Crown, James S. Crown, Lester Crown, Michael Friedman, Marvin Goldklang, Barry Halper, Harvey Leighton, Daniel McCarthy, Harry Nederlander, James Nederlander, Robert Nederlander, William Rose Sr., Edward Rosenthal, Jack Satter, Joan Z. Steinbrenner, Charlotte Witkind, Richard Witkind

Exec. Vice-President & Chief Operating Officer—Leonard L. Kleinman
Senior Vice-President—Arthur Richman
Vice-President & General Manager—Harding Peterson
V.P., Player Personnel, Development & Scouting—George W. Bradley
Vice-President, Marketing—John C. Fugazy
Vice-President, Community Relations—Richard Kraft
Vice-President, Ticket Operations—Frank Swaine
Vice President—Ed Weaver
Secretary/Treasurer—Joseph A. Molloy
General Counsel—David Sussman
Chief Controller—Harry Rabb
Special Advisor—Clyde King
Director of Scouting—Brian Sabean
Assistant to General Manager—Peter Jameson
Director of Minor League Operations—Mitch Lukevics
Controller/Player Development & Scouting—Mike Macaluso
Traveling Secretary—Bill Emslie
Assistant Director of Scouting—Kevin Elfering
Asst. Dir. of Minor League Operations—Les Parker
Director of Stadium Operations—William D. Squires
Director of Customer Services—Joel S. White
Executive Director of Ticket Operations—Jeff Kline
Ticket Director—Jim Hodge
Director of Group & Season Sales—Debbie Tymon
Director of Media Relations & Publicity—Jeff Idelson
Asst. Dir. of Media Relations & Publicity—Kara Waxman
Director of Scoreboard Operations—Betsy Leesman
Assistant Directors of Public Relations—Ed Angelino, Patrick McGrew
Director of Publications—Tom Bannon
Director of Television & Video Production—Joe Violone
Editor-in-Chief, Yankees Magazine—Gregg Mazzola
Diamond Vision Director—John Franzone
Director of Special Events—Bob Pelegrino
Team Physician—Dr. Stuart Hershon
Trainers—Gene Monahan, Steve Donohue
Manager—Bucky Dent
Executive Offices—Yankee Stadium, Bronx, N.Y. 10451
Telephone—293-4300 (area code 212)

SCOUTS—(Cross-checkers)—Dick Groch, Jack Gillis, Don Lindeberg, Bill Livesey, Stan Saleski. (Supervisors)—Mark Batchko, Hop Cassady, Joe DiCarlo, Walt Dixon, Carl Moesche, Greg Orr, Joe Robison, Rudy Santin, Bill Schmidt, Tim Schmidt, Ken Stauffer, Jeff Taylor, Paul Turco, Marti Wolever, Leon Wurth. (Special Assignments)—Bill Haller, Jack Lewellyn, Jim Naples. (Associates)—Jack Carroll, Kermit Damont, Joe Ross, Chip Smith, Bob Stead, Joe Thurman.

PARK LOCATION—Yankee Stadium, E. 161st St. and River Ave., Bronx, N.Y. 10451.

Seating capacity—57,545.

FIELD DIMENSIONS—Home plate to left field at foul line, 312 feet; to center field, 410 feet; to right field at foul line, 310 feet.

OAKLAND ATHLETICS

Owner/Managing General Partner—Walter A. Haas, Jr.
Chief Operating Officer—Walter J. Haas
Executive Vice-President—Roy Eisenhardt
Vice-President, Baseball Operations—Sandy Alderson
Vice-President, Business Operations—Andy Dolich
Vice-President, Finance—Kathleen McCracken
Vice-President, Administration & Personnel—Raymond B. Krise Jr.
Assistant to the Exec. V.P., Baseball Matters—Bill Rigney
Assistant to the V.P., Baseball Operations—Ron Schueler
Director of Player Development—Karl Kuehl
Director of Scouting—Dick Bogard
Asst. Director of Scouting—Eric Kubota
Director of Baseball Administration—Walt Jocketty
Director of Latin American Scouting—Juan Marichal
Director of Team Travel—Mickey Morabito
Director of Baseball Information—Jay Alves
Asst. Director, Baseball Administration—Pamela Pitts
Admin. Assistant, Baseball Operations—Suzanne Davis
Admin. Assistant, Baseball Relations—Doreen Alves
Director of Broadcasting—David Rubinstein
Director of Media Relations—Kathy Jacobson
Director of Community Affairs/Speakers Bureau—Dave Perron
Director of Stadium Operations—Kevin Kahn
Director of Publications—Rob Kelly
Director of Broadcast Operations—Bill King
Director of Business Administration—Alan Ledford
Director of Sales—Tom Cordova
Director of Special Projects—Steve Page
Director of Season Tickets—Barbara Reilly
Director of Group Sales—Bettina Flores
Director of Outreach Activities—Sharon Jones
Director of Promotions—Sharon Kelly
Manager—Tony La Russa
Team Physician—Dr. Allan Pont
Team Orthopedist—Dr. Rick Bost
Trainers—Barry Weinberg, Larry Davis
Equipment Manager—Frank Ciensczyk
Visiting Clubhouse Manager—Steve Vucinich
Executive Offices—Oakland-Alameda County Coliseum,
P.O. Box 2220, Oakland, Calif. 94621
Telephone—638-4900 (area code 415)

SCOUTS—Tony Arias, Mark Conkin, Dan Ford, Frank Franchi, Grady Fuson, Bill Gayton, James Guinn, Mike Jones, John Kazanas, Billy Merkel, Bill Meyer, Marty Miller, Steve Nichols, J.P. Ricciardi, Jeff Scott, Mike Sgobba, Pat Sullivan, Craig Wallenbrock.

PARK LOCATION—Oakland-Alameda County Coliseum, Nimitz Freeway and Hegenberger Road.

Seating capacity—48,219.

FIELD DIMENSIONS—Home plate to left field at foul line, 330 feet; to center field, 400 feet; to right field at foul line, 330 feet.

SEATTLE MARINERS

General Managing Partner—Jeff Smulyan

Executive Vice President—Gary Kaseff
Vice President, Baseball Operations—Woody Woodward
Vice President, Finance & Administration—Brian Beggs
Vice President, Marketing—Stuart Layne
Vice President, Sales—John Thomas
V.P., Scouting & Player Development—Roger Jongewaard
Sr. Director of Communications—Randy Adamack
Director of Baseball Administration—Lee Pelekoudas
Assistant to V.P., Baseball Operations—George Zuraw
Farm Director—Jim Beattie
Coordinator of Minor League Instruction—Fred Stanley
Director of Team Travel—Craig Detwiler
Director of Community Relations—Randy Stearnes
Director of Promotional Sales—Larry Sindall
Director of Public Relations—Dave Aust
Director of Ticketing & Stadium Services—Jeff Klein
Controller—Denise Podosek
Assistant Director of Marketing—Ross Skinner
Assistant Director of Public Relations—Ethan Kelly
Assistant Director of Ticketing—John Ross Karnoski
Exec. Asst. to General Managing Partner—Janet Croft
Accounting Assistant—Shirley Shreve
Player Development & Scouting Assistant—Larry Beinfest
Public Relations Assistants—Pete Vanderwarker, David Venneri
Manager—Jim Lefebvre
Trainer—Rick Griffin
Home Clubhouse & Equipment Manager—Henry Genzale
Club Physicians—Dr. Larry Pedegana, Dr. Mitchel Storey
Club Dentist—Dr. Richard Leshgold
Head Groundskeeper—Wilbur Loo
P.A. Announcer—Tom Hutyler
Executive Offices—P.O. Box 4100
411 First Ave. S., Seattle, Washington 98104
Telephone—628-3555 (area code 206)

SCOUTS—(Special Assignments)—Bob Harrison, Bill Kearns, Eddie Robinson. (Regulars)—Bill Barkley, Gordon Blakeley, John Burden, Ken Compton, Ramon de los Santos, Ken Duzich, Matt Hall, Joe Henderson, Angel Hermosa, Ron Hopkins, Dan Jennings, Pete Jones, Dave Karaff, Bobby Lawrence, Benny Looper, Gary McGraw, Mark McKnight, Ken Madeja, Jerry Marik, Marty Martinez, Omer Munoz, Joe Nigro, Fran Oneto, Cliff Pastornicky, Myron Pines, Ron Rizzi, Jack Webber, Mickey White, Luke Wrenn, Phil Zelman.

PARK LOCATION—The Kingdome, 201 King Street, Seattle, Washington.

Seating capacity—58,150.

FIELD DIMENSIONS—Home plate to left field at foul line, 324 feet; to center field, 410 feet; to right field at foul line, 313 feet.

TEXAS RANGERS

General Partners—George W. Bush, Edward W. (Rusty) Rose

President, Chief Operating Officer—Michael H. Stone
Vice President, General Manager—Thomas A. Grieve
Vice President, Business Operations—John F. McMichael
Vice President, Administration—Charles F. Wangner
General Counsel—Gerald W. Haddock
Assistant G.M., Player Personnel and Scouting—Sandy Johnson
Assistant General Manager—Wayne Krivsky
Director, Player Development—Marty Scott
Director, Public Relations—John Blake
Director, Sales, Broadcasting and Producer, Diamond Vision—Chuck Morgan
Director, Promotions and Director, Diamond Vision—Dave Fendrick
Director, Stadium Administration—Jay Miller
Director, Stadium Operations—Mat Stolley
Traveling Secretary—Dan Schimek
Controller—Steve McNeill
Manager, Group Sales—Rich Billings
Manager, Telemarketing—Randy Chappel
Manager, Community Services—Taunee Paur
Manager, Ticket Operations—John Schriever
Major League Scout/Special Assignments—John Young
General Manager, Charlotte County Operations—Ted Guthrie
Assistant to the President, Special Projects—Bobby Bragan
Assistant Director, Public Relations—Larry Kelly
Assistant Manager, Ticket Operations—Ben Marthaler
Medical Director—Dr. Mike Mycoskie
Manager—Bobby Valentine
Field Superintendent—Jim Anglea
Assistant Field Superintendent—Brad Richards
Spring Training Director—John Welaj
Home Clubhouse and Equipment Manager—Joe Macko
Visiting Clubhouse Manager—Zack Minasian
Executive Offices—1250 Copeland Road, 11th Floor, Arlington, Tex. 76011
Arlington Stadium—1500 Copeland Road, Arlington, Tex. 76010
Mailing Address—P.O. Box 1111, Arlington, Tex. 76004
Telephone—273-5222 (area code 817)

SCOUTS—Hector Acevedo, Manuel Batista, Ray Blanco, Joe Branzell, Paddy Cottrell, Dick Coury, Antonio Cruz, Mike Daughtry, Amado Dinzey, Jim Dreyer, Bill Earnhart, Doug Gassaway, Mark Giegler, Mike Grouse, Tim Hallgren, Andy Hancock, Jack Hays, Bryan Lambe, Robert Lavallee, Jim Lentine, Omar Minaya, Jose Offerman, Sergio Robles, Bill Schmidt, Al Schoenberger, Rick Schroeder, Len Strelitz, Charles Taylor, Randy Taylor, Rudy Terrasas, Danilo Troncoso, Gorge Urribarri, Boris Villa, Mac D. Whitaker.

PARK LOCATION—Arlington Stadium, 1500 Copeland Road, Arlington, Tex.

Seating capacity—43,508.

FIELD DIMENSIONS—Home plate to left field at foul line, 330 feet; to center field, 400 feet; to right field at foul line, 330 feet.

TORONTO BLUE JAYS

Board of Directors—John Craig Eaton, L. G. Greenwood,
N. E. Hardy, William Ferguson, P. N. T. Widdrington
Honorary Chairman—R. Howard Webster
Chairman & Chief Executive Officer—N. E. Hardy
President & Chief Operating Officer—Paul Beeston
Executive Vice-President, Baseball—Pat Gillick
Vice-Presidents, Baseball—Bob Mattick, Al LaMacchia
Vice-President, Finance & Administration—Bob Nicholson
Assistant General Manager—Gord Ash
Director, Public Relations—Howard Starkman
Director, Stadium & Ticket Operations—George Holm
Director, Marketing—Paul Markle
Director, Finance—Susan Quigley
Director, Canadian Scouting—Bob Prentice
Director, Minor League Business—Ken Carson
Administrator, Player Personnel—Bob Nelson
Assistant Director, Public Relations—Gary Oswald
Assistant Director, Ticket Operations—Randy Low
Assistant Director, Operations—Len Frejlich
Manager, Group Sales—Maureen Haffey
Manager, Team Travel—John Brioux
Manager, Promotions and Advertising—Rick Amos
Manager, Community Relations—Mark Edwards
Manager, Employee Compensation—Catherine Elwood
Manager, Information Systems—Kevin Worth
Manager, Ticket Vault—Paul Goodyear
Manager, Ticket Revenue—Mike Maunder
Managers, Ticket Mail Services—Allan Koyanagi, Doug Barr
Manager, Security—Fred Wootton
Manager, Event Personnel—Mario Coutinho
Systems Administrator—Mark Graham
Coordinator, Group Sales—Dave Cox
Supervisor, Grounds—Brad Bujold
Supervisor, Office & Game Services—Mick Bazinet
Trainers—Tommy Craig, Brent Andrews
Manager—Cito Gaston
Team Physician—Dr. Ron Taylor
Executive Offices—SkyDome, 300 The Esplanade West, Gate #9,
Toronto, Ontario M5V 3B3
Mailing Address—SkyDome, 300 The Esplanade West, Box 3200,
Toronto, Ontario M5V 3B3
Telephone—341-1000 (area code 416)

SCOUTS—David Blume, Chris Bourjos, Chris Buckley, John Cole, Ellis Dungan,
Bob Engle (Eastern Regional Scouting Director), Joe Ford, Epy Guerrero (Coordina-
tor, Latin American Scouting & Player Development), Tom Hinkle, Jim Hughes,
Moose Johnson (Special Assignment), Gordon Lakey (Special Assignment), Duane
Larson, Ted Lekas, Ben McLure, Steve Minor, Wayne Morgan (Western Regional
Scouting Director), Andy Pienovi, Neil Summers, Don Welke, Tim Wilken (Special
Assignment), Dave Yoakum (Advance).

PARK LOCATION—SkyDome, 300 The Esplanade West, Between Lakeshore
Boulevard and Front Street, east of Spadina Avenue.

Seating capacity—50,000.

FIELD DIMENSIONS—Home plate to left field at foul line, 330 feet; to center
field, 400 feet; to right field at foul line, 330 feet.

National League
Organized 1876

WILLIAM D. WHITE
President and Treasurer

PHYLLIS B. COLLINS
Vice-President & Secretary

KATY FEENEY
Director of Media & Public Affairs

NANCY CROFTS
Assistant Secretary

VALERIE DIETRICH
Executive Secretary

CATHY DAVIS
Administrative Assistant

Headquarters—350 Park Avenue, New York, N. Y. 10022

Telephone—339-7700 (area code 212)

UMPIRES—Greg Bonin, Fred Brocklander, Gerald Crawford, Gary Darling, Robert Davidson, Gerry Davis, Dana DeMuth, Robert Engel, Bruce Froemming, Eric Gregg, Tom Hallion, H. Douglas Harvey, Mark Hirschbeck, Bill Hohn, Jerry Layne, Randall Marsh, John McSherry, Edward Montague, Frank Pulli, James Quick, Lawrence (Dutch) Rennert, Steve Rippley, Paul Runge, Terry Tata, Harry Wendelstedt, Joseph West, Charles Williams.

OFFICIAL STATISTICIANS—Elias Sports Bureau, Inc., 500 5th Ave., Suite 2114, New York, N.Y. 10036. Telephone—(212) 869-1530.

ATLANTA BRAVES

Chairman of the Board—William C. Bartholomay

President—Stan Kasten
Senior V.P. & Asst. to President—Henry L. Aaron
Vice-President & General Manager—Robert J. Cox
Vice-President & Asst. General Manager—John W. Mullen
Senior Vice-President, Administration & Finance—Charles S. Sanders
Director of Player Development—Bobby Dews
Asst. Vice-President & Director of Scouting—Paul L. Snyder, Jr.
Assistant Scouting Director—Rod Gilbreath
V.P., Director of Marketing & Broadcasting—Wayne Long
Director of Team Travel & Equipment Manager—Bill Acree
Director of Public Relations—Jim Schultz
Director of Community Relations—Danny Goodwin
Director of Promotions—Miles McRea
Director of Ticket Sales—Jack Tyson
Assistant Director of Ticket Sales—Peter Serrano
Director of Ticket Operations—Ed Newman
Assistant Director of Ticket Operations—Sam Willliams
Director of Advertising—Peter Diffin
Director of Merchandising—Robert A. Hope
Director of Stadium Operations & Security—Terri Brennan
Assistant Controller—Chip Moore
Public Relations Assistants—Glen Serra, Mike Ringering
Manager—Russ Nixon
Trainer—Dave Pursley
Assistant Trainer—Jeff Porter
Club Physician—Dr. David T. Watson
Associate Physicians—Dr. John Cantwell, Dr. Robert Crow
Club Orthopedist—Dr. Joe Chandler
Executive Offices—P.O. Box 4064, Atlanta, Ga. 30302
Telephone—522-7630 (area code 404)

SCOUTS—Mike Arbuckle, Ray Belanger, Sam Berry, Forrest (Smoky) Burgess, Joe Campise, Stu Cann, Joe Caputo, Bill Clark, Roy Clark, Harold Cronin, Tony DeMacio, Bob Dunning, Lou Fitzgerald, John Flannery, Ralph Garr, Pedro Gonzalez, Larry Grefer, John Groth, John Hageman, Gene Hassell, Ray Holton, Jim Johnson, Dean Jongewaard, Steve Jongewaard, Robyn Lynch, Burney R. (Dickey) Martin, Bob Mavis, Red Murff, Arthur Neal, Umberto Oropeza, Ernie Pedersen, Jack Pierce, Rance Pless, Jorge Posada, Harry Postove, Paul Ricciarini, Carlos Rios, Jose Salado, Bill Serena, Fred Shaffer, Charles Smith, Ted Sparks, Andy Stewart, Tony Stiel, Bob Turzilli, Wesley Westrum, William R. Wight, Don Williams, H.F. (Red) Wooten.

PARK LOCATION—Atlanta-Fulton County Stadium, on Capitol Avenue at the junction of Interstate Highways 20, 75 and 85.

Seating capacity—52,007.

FIELD DIMENSIONS—Home plate to left field at foul line, 330 feet; to center field, 402 feet; to right field at foul line, 330 feet.

CHICAGO CUBS

Board of Directors—Thomas G. Ayers, Charles T. Brumback, Stanton R. Cook,
Donald C. Grenesko, Andrew J. McKenna, Walter E. Massey
President and Chief Executive Officer—Donald C. Grenesko
Executive Vice-President, Baseball Operations—Jim Frey
Vice-President, Business Operations—Mark McGuire
Director, Human Resources—Wendy Lewis
Director, Marketing—John McDonough
Director, Media Relations—Ned Colletti
Director, Minor League Operations—Bill Harford
Director, Finance & Information—Keith Bode
Director, Scouting—Dick Balderson
Director, Stadium Operations—Tom Cooper
Director, Ticket Operations—Frank Maloney
Consultant—E.R. Saltwell
Corporate Secretary—Joyce Hutchinson
General Counsel—Geoffrey A. Anderson
Special Player Consultants—Hugh Alexander, Scott Reid
Traveling Secretary—Peter Durso
Assistant Director, Media Relations—Sharon Pannozzo
Assistant Director, Promotions and Community Services—Conrad Kowal
Assistant Director, Scouting—Scott Nelson
Assistant Director, Stadium Operations/Event Personnel—Paul Rathje
Assistant Director, Stadium Operations/Facilities—Lubie Veal
Assistant Director, Ticket Operations/Sales—Bill Galante
Assistant Director, Ticket Operations/Sales—Joe Kirchen
Manager, Event Personnel and Security—Paul Gerlach
Speakers Bureau Coordinator—Billy Williams
P.A. Announcer—Wayne Messmer
Team Photographer—Steve Green
Team Physician—John F. Marquardt, M.D.
Trainer—John Fierro
Equipment Manager—Yosh Kawano
Manager—Don Zimmer
Executive Offices—Wrigley Field, 1060 West Addison Street, Chicago, Ill. 60613
Telephone—281-5050 (area code 312)

SCOUTS—(Regional Supervisors)—Frank DeMoss, Doug Mapson, Earl Winn. (Latin American Coordinator)—Luis Rosa. (Area Scouts)—Billy Blitzer, Bill Capps, Billy Champion, Tom Davis, Ed DiRamio, Lou Garcia, Bobby Gardner, John Gracio, Gene Handley, John Hennessy, Toney Howell, John (Spider) Jorgensen, Jeff Kahn, Gil Kubski, Doug Lauman, Paul Provas. (Part-Time Scouts)—Keith Bailey, Bob Beck, Jeff Brookens, Lane Decker, Morley Freitas, Roger Harris, Rich Jeffries, Pat Kane, Noe Maduro, Tony Malara, Larry Maxie, Bill Perry, Lee Phillips, Joe Sayers, Harry Von Suskil, Wally Walker, Larry Watts, Gary York.

PARK LOCATION—Wrigley Field, Addison Street, N. Clark Street, Waveland Avenue and Sheffield Avenue.

Seating capacity—39,012.

FIELD DIMENSIONS—Home plate to left field at foul line, 355 feet; to center field, 400 feet; to right field at foul line, 353 feet.

CINCINNATI REDS

General Partner—Marge Schott

President and Chief Executive Officer—Marge Schott
Executive Vice President—Stephen Schott
Vice-President & General Manager—Bob Quinn
Vice-President, Publicity—Jim Ferguson
Director, Player Development—Howie Bedell
Director, Scouting—Julian Mock
Special Player Consultant—Sheldon Bender
Controller—Timothy A. Sabo
Director, Stadium Operations—Tim O'Connell
Director, Ticket Department—Bill Stewart
Director, Season Ticket Sales—Pat McCaffrey
Director, Group Sales—Susan Toomey
Director, Marketing—Chip Baker
Director, Information & Publications—Jon Braude
Director, Speakers Bureau—Gordy Coleman
Traveling Secretary—Joel Pieper
Advance Scout—Jim Stewart
Coordinator, Scouting—Brad Del Barba
Assistant Ticket Director—John O'Brien
Admin. Asst., Player Development & Scouting—Jim Bowden
Chief Administrative Assistant—Joyce Pfarr
Manager—Lou Piniella
Executive Offices—100 Riverfront Stadium, Cincinnati, O. 45202
Telephone—421-4510 (area code 513)

SCOUTS—Jeff Barton, Larry Barton, Jr., Ray Bellino, Gene Bennett, Dave Calaway, Ray Corbett, Paul Faulk, Fred Ferreira, Les Houser, Eddie Kolo, Tom McDevitt, Tom Roberts, Tom Severtson, Bob Szymkowski, Randy Wilson, Tom Wilson, Jeff Zimmerman.

PARK LOCATION—Riverfront Stadium, downtown Cincinnati, bounded by Pete Rose Way to the Ohio River and from Walnut Street to Broadway.

Seating capacity—52,392.

FIELD DIMENSIONS—Home plate to left field at foul line, 330 feet; to center field, 404 feet; to right field at foul line, 330 feet.

HOUSTON ASTROS

Board of Directors—Dr. John J. McMullen, Chairman. Owners—Dr. John J. McMullen, Mrs. Thomas E. (Mimi) Dompier, James A. Elkins, Jr., Alfred C. Glassell, Jr., Bob Marco, Don Sanders, Jack T. Trotter, H.L. Brown and Jacqueline, Peter, Catherine and John McMullen, Jr.

General Manager—William J. Wood
Assistant General Manager—Bob Watson
Special Assistant to the G.M.—Donald Davidson
Director of Minor League Operations—Fred Nelson
Director of Scouting—Dan O'Brien
Director of Public Relations—Rob Matwick
Traveling Secretary—Barry Waters
Assistant to Dirs., Minor Leagues/Scouting—Lew Temple
Assistant Director of Public Relations—Chuck Pool
Assistant to General Manager—Tim Hellmuth
Admin. Asst., Minor Leagues/Scouting—David Rawnsley
Vice-President, Marketing—Ted Haracz
Director of Broadcasting—Jamie Hildreth
Director, Season Ticket Services—Mike Levy
Director, Group Sales—Debra Treffalls
Director of Advertising Sales—Norm Miller
Director of Communications—Pam Gardner
Director of Promotions—Mark Guion
Director, Community Services—John Sorrentino
Scoreboard Operations—Paul Darst
Club Physicians—Dr. William Bryan, Dr. Michael Feltovich
Manager—Art Howe
Executive Offices—The Astrodome, P.O. Box 288
Houston, Tex. 77001
Telephone—799-9500 (area code 713)
HOUSTON SPORTS ASSOCIATION, INC.
President and Chief Operating Officer—Robert G. Harter
Executive Vice-President—Neal Gunn
Vice-President, Astrodome-Astrohall Stadium Corporation—John Elsner
Vice-President, Finance—Gary Brooks
Vice-President, Operations—W. Gary Keller
Vice-President, Public Affairs—Jim Weidler
General Counsel—Frank Rynd
Treasurer—Adam C. Richards
Controller—Robert McBurnett

SCOUTS—Stan Benjamin, Bob Blair, Jack Bloomfield, Ralph Bratton, George Brophy, Gerry Craft, Clark Crist, Jug DeFord, Doug Deutsch, Chuck Edmondson, Charlie Fox, Ben Galante, Carl Greene, Howie Haak, Bill Hallauer, Sterling Housley, Dan Hutson, Marc Johnson, Brian Keegan, Bill Kelso, Bob King, David Lakey, Julio Linares, Mike Maggart, Walter Mathews, Domingo Mercedes, Walter Millies, Tom Mooney, Carlos Muro, Hal Newhouser, Cotton Nix, Shawn Pender, Ramon Perez, Joe Pittman, Pico Prado, Andres Reiner, O.H. Robertson, Adriano Rodriguez, Ross Sapp, Lynwood Stallings, Kevin Stein, Frankie Thon, Bo Trumbo, Reggie Waller, Paul Weaver, Gene Wellman, Tom Wheeler.

PARK LOCATION—The Astrodome, Kirby and Interstate Loop 610

Seating capacity—54,816.

FIELD DIMENSIONS—Home plate to left field at foul line, 330 feet; to center field, 400 feet; to right field at foul line, 330 feet.

LOS ANGELES DODGERS

Board of Directors—Peter O'Malley, President; Harry M. Bardt;
Roland Seidler, Vice-President and Treasurer;
Mrs. Roland (Terry) Seidler, Secretary

President—Peter O'Malley
Executive Vice-President, Player Personnel—Fred Claire
Vice-President, Communications—Tom Hawkins
Vice-President, Finance—Bob Graziano
Vice-President, Marketing—Merritt Willey
Vice-President, Treasurer—Roland Seidler
Assistant to the President—Ike Ikuhara
Assistant Secretary & General Counsel—Santiago Fernandez
Controller and Assistant Treasurer—Ken Hasemann
Director, Community Relations—Don Newcombe
Community Relations—Roy Campanella
Director, Human Resources—Irene Tanji
Director, Data Processing—Mike Mularky
Director, Stadium Operations—Bob Smith
Director, Ticket Department—Walter Nash
Director, Minor League Operations—Charlie Blaney
Director, Scouting—Ben Wade
Assistant Scouting Director—Terry Reynolds
Director of Publicity—Mike Williams
Assistant Director of Publicity—Jay Lucas
Director of Publications—Brent Shyer
Director, Marketing and Promotions—Barry Stockhamer
Asst. Dir., Marketing & Promotions—Paul Kalil
Traveling Secretary—Bill DeLury
Manager—Tom Lasorda
Club Physicians—Dr. Frank W. Jobe, Dr. Michael F. Mellman
Executive Offices—Dodger Stadium, 1000 Elysian Park Avenue,
Los Angeles, Calif. 90012
Telephone—224-1500 (area code 213)

SCOUTS—Eleodoro Arias, Ralph Avila, Eddie Bane, Boyd Bartley, Gil Bassetti, Bob Bishop, Gib Bodet, Flores Bolivar, Mike Brito, Joe Campbell, Bob Darwin, Eddie Fajardo, Ossie Alvarez Gonzalez, Rafael Gonzalez, Michael Hankins, Dick Hanlon, Dennis Haren, Gail Henley, Hank Jones, John Keenan, Gary LaRocque, Juan Lantigua, Don LeJohn, Carl Loewenstine, Teodoro Martinez, Teodoro Mata, Dale McReynolds, Bob Miske, Tommy Mixon, Luis Angel Montalvo, Danny Montgomery, Ruben Morales, Victor Nazario, Deni Pacini, Camilo Pasqual, Pablo Peguero, Bill Pleis, Silvano Quesada, Mark Sheehy, Dick Teed, Glen Van Proyen, Corito Varona, Miguel Angel Villaran. Special Assignment Scouts—Mel Didier, Phil Regan, Jerry Stephenson, Gary Sutherland.

PARK LOCATION—Dodger Stadium, 1000 Elysian Park Avenue.

Seating capacity—56,000.

FIELD DIMENSIONS—Home plate to left field at foul line, 330 feet; to center field, 395 feet; to right field at foul line, 330 feet.

MONTREAL EXPOS

Board of Directors—Charles R. Bronfman, Lorne C. Webster, Claude R. Brochu, Hugh Hallward, Sen. E. Leo Kolber, Arnold Ludwick

Honorary Directors—Louis R. Desmarais, Sydney Maislin

Chairman of the Board—Charles R. Bronfman
President & Chief Operating Officer—Claude R. Brochu
Honorary Treasurer—Arnold Ludwick
Vice-President, Baseball Operations—Bill Stoneman
Vice-President, Player Personnel—David Dombrowski
Director, Player Development—Dan Duquette
Director, Scouting—Gary Hughes
Director, Team Travel—Erik Ostling
Assistant Director, Scouting—Frank Wren
Senior Consultant, Player Personnel—Whitey Lockman
Special Consultant, Baseball Operations—Jim Fanning
Special Consultant to V.P., Player Personnel—Angel Vazquez
Admin. Assistant, Player Development—Kent Qualls
G.M., West Palm Beach Operations—Rob Rabenecker
Vice-President, Business Operations—Gerry Trudeau
Controller—Raymond St. Pierre
Director, Ticket Department—Claude Delorme
Director, Retailing—Catherine Goldner
Director, Ticket Sales—Michel Heneault
Director, Stadium Operations—Monique Lacas
Director, Marketing—Michel Lagace
Director, Public Relations—Pierre Vidal
Media Relations—Monique Giroux, Richard Griffin
Manager—Buck Rodgers
Club Physician—Dr. Robert Brodrick
Club Orthopedist—Dr. Larry Coughlin
Mailing Address—P. O. Box 500, Station M, Montreal, Quebec,
Canada H1V 3P2
Telephone—253-3434 (area code 514)

SCOUTS—Jesus Alou, Kelvin Bowles, Pepito Centeno, Ed Creech, Pat Daugherty, Richard DeHart, Manny Estrada, Orrin Freeman, Joseph Frisina, Eddie Haas, Herb Hippauf, Jim Holden, Bert Holt, Juan Joa, Carlos Loreto, Bill MacKenzie, Rene Marchand, Jethro McIntyre, Roy McMillan, Levy Ochoa, Bob Oldis, Mark Servais, Keith Snider, Ron Walters, Stan Zielinski, Greg Zunino.

PARK LOCATION—Olympic Stadium, 4545 Pierre de Coubertin St., Montreal, Quebec, Canada H1V 3N7.

Seating capacity—60,011.

FIELD DIMENSIONS—Home plate to left field at foul line, 325 feet; to center field, 404 feet; to right field at foul line, 325 feet.

NEW YORK METS

Chairman of the Board—Nelson Doubleday

President & Chief Executive Officer—Fred Wilpon
Directors—Nelson Doubleday, Fred Wilpon, J. Frank Cashen,
Saul Katz, Marvin Tepper
Special Consultant to the Board of Directors—Richard Cummins
Exec. Vice-President, G.M. & Chief Operating Officer—J. Frank Cashen
Vice-President, Operations—Bob Mandt
Vice-President, Baseball Administration—Alan E. Harazin
Vice-President, Baseball Operations—Joseph McIlvaine
Vice-President, Treasurer—Harold W. O'Shaughnessy
Vice-President, Marketing—James Ross
Vice-President, Broadcasting—Mike Ryan
Director of Public Relations—Jay Horwitz
Promotions Director—James Plummer
Executive Asst. to General Manager—Jean Coen
Ticket Manager—Bill Ianniciello
Controller—Rick Iandoli
Traveling Secretary—Bob O'Hara
Director of Minor League Operations—Gerry Hunsicker
Director of Scouting—Roland Johnson
Stadium Manager—John McCarthy
Director of Amateur Baseball Relations—Tommy Holmes
Manager—Dave Johnson
Club Physician—Dr. James C. Parkes II
Team Trainer—Steve Garland
Executive Offices—William A. Shea Stadium, Roosevelt
Avenue and 126th Street, Flushing, N.Y. 11368
Telephone—507-6387 (area code 718)

SCOUTS—Paul Baretta, Eric Broersma, Phil Favia, Dick Gernert, Rob Guzik, Marty Harvat, Reginald Jackson, Buddy Kerr, Craig Kornfeld, Joe Mason, Bob Minor, Harry Minor, Carlos Pascual, Jim Reeves, Junior Roman, Marv Scott, Daraka Shaheed, Eddy Toledo, Terry Tripp, Bob Wellman, Jim Woodward, Jack Zduriencik.

PARK LOCATION—William A. Shea Stadium, Roosevelt Avenue and 126th Street, Flushing, N. Y. 11368.

Seating capacity—55,300.

FIELD DIMENSIONS—Home plate to left field at foul line, 338 feet; to center field, 410 feet; to right field at foul line, 338 feet.

PHILADELPHIA PHILLIES

President/General Partner—Bill Giles

Partners—John Drew Betz, Claire S. Betz
Tri-Play Associates (Alexander K. Buck, J. Mahlon Buck Jr.,
William C. Buck); Fitz Eugene Dixon; Mrs. Rochelle Levy
Executive Vice-President—David Montgomery
Vice-President, General Manager—Lee Thomas
Vice-President, Finance—Jerry Clothier
Vice-President, Public Relations—Larry Shenk
Director of Player Development—Del Unser
Director of Scouting—Jay Hankins
Secretary and Counsel—William Y. Webb
Player Personnel Administrator—Ed Wade
Assistant to President—Paul Owens
Director of Planning, Development & Super Boxes—Tom Hudson
Director of Promotions—Frank Sullivan
Traveling Secretary—Eddie Ferenz
Director of Sales and Ticket Operations—Richard Deats
Asst. to Dirs. of Player Development & Scouting—Jack Pastore
Director of Community Relations—Chris Wheeler
Director of Marketing—Dennis Mannion
Director of Stadium Operations—Mike DiMuzio
Director of Operations—Pat Cassidy
Controller—Mike Kent
Public Relations Assistants—Gene Dias, Leigh McDonald
Director of Group Sales—Bettyanne Joyce
Director of Season Ticket Sales—Rory McNeil
Assistant Director of Promotions—Chris Legault
Assistant Director of Marketing—Jo-Anne Levy
Administrative Asst., Minor Leagues—Bill Gargano
Club Physician—Dr. Phillip Marone
Club Trainer—Jeff Cooper
Strength and Flexibility Instructor—Gus Hoefling
Manager—Nick Leyva
Executive Offices—Philadelphia Veterans Stadium
Mailing Address—P.O. Box 7575, Philadelphia, Pa. 19101
Telephone—463-6000 (area code 215)

SCOUTS—(National Cross-Checkers)—Tony Roig and Randy Waddill. (Regional Cross-Checkers)—Jim Baumer, Ron King, Dick Lawlor and Bob Reasonover. (Special Assignment, Major Leagues)—Ray Shore. (Advance Scout, Major Leagues)—Hank King. (Special Assignment)—Eddie Bockman, Bing Devine and Larry Rojas. (Regular)—Oliver Bidwell, Jim Bierman, Wilfredo Calvino, Carlos Cuervo, Tom Ferguson, Bill Harper, Ken Hultzapple, Jerry Jordan, Jerry Lafferty, Terry Logan, Fred Mazuca, Lance Nichols, Cotton Nye, Arthur Parrack, Bob Poole, Larry Reasonover, Joe Reilly, Roy Tanner, Scott Trcka.

PARK LOCATION—Philadelphia Veterans Stadium, Broad Street and Pattison Avenue.

Seating capacity—62,382.

FIELD DIMENSIONS—Home plate to left field at foul line, 330 feet; to center field, 408 feet; to right field at foul line, 330 feet.

PITTSBURGH PIRATES

Board of Directors—Carl F. Barger, Joe L. Brown, Frank V. Cahouet, Richard M. Cyert, Douglas D. Danforth, Eugene Litman, Howard M. Love, John Marous, Sophie Masloff, John H. McConnell, Thomas H. O'Brien, Paul H. O'Neill, David M. Roderick, Vincent A. Sarni, Dwight C. Schar, Harvey M. Walken.

Chairman & Chief Executive Officer—Douglas D. Danforth
President—Carl F. Barger
Senior V.P. & G.M./Baseball Operations—Larry Doughty
Senior Vice-President, Business Operations—Bernard J. Mullin
Vice-President, Finance & Secretary—Kenneth C. Curcio
Vice-President, Administration & Operations—Richard L. Andersen
Vice-President, Public Relations—Richard J. Cerrone
Vice-President, Marketing—Steven N. Greenberg
Asst. Vice-President, Finance—Patti Mistick
Traveling Secretary—Greg Johnson
Director of Broadcasting & Advertising Sales—Dean Jordan
Director of Community Relations—Patty Paytas
Director of Community Services & Sales—Al Gordon
Director of Corporate Sales—Nellie Briles
Director of Diamond Club—Bob Derda
Director of Group Sales—Karin Kmetz
Director of In-Game Entertainment—Mike Gordon
Director of Media Relations—Jim Lachimia
Director of Merchandising—Bruce Stephen
Director of Minor League Operations—Chuck LaMar
Director of Scouting—Cam Bonifay
Director of Stadium Operations—Dennis DaPra
Director of Telemarketing—Mark Norelli
Director of Ticket Operations—Gary Remlinger
Asst. Director of Media Relations—Jim Trdinich
Asst. Director of Public Relations—Sally O'Leary
Asst., Baseball Operations—Scott Proefrock
Guest Relations Coordinator—Elliot Falcione
Promotions Coordinator—Nanci Rich
Manager—Jim Leyland
Club Physician—Dr. Joseph Coroso
Team Orthopedist—Dr. Jack Failla
Trainers—Kent Biggerstaff, Dave Tumbas
Equipment Manager—John Hallahan
Executive Offices—Three Rivers Stadium, 600 Stadium Circle, Pittsburgh, Pa. 15212
Telephone—323-5000 (area code 412)

SCOUTS—(Coordinators)—Bart Braun, Jerry Gardner, Buzzy Keller. (Supervisors)—Gene Baker, Jack Bowen, Sonny Bowers, Joe L. Brown, Bill Bryk, Pablo Cruz, Larry D'Amato, Steve Demeter, Angel Figueroa, Steve Fleming, Jesse Flores, Dave Holliday, Rene Mons, Boyd Odom, George Ortiz, Ed Roebuck, Bob Rossi. (Major League Scout)—Lenny Yochim.

PARK LOCATION—Three Rivers Stadium, 600 Stadium Circle.

Seating capacity—58,729.

FIELD DIMENSIONS—Home plate to left field at foul line, 335 feet; to center field, 400 feet; to right field at foul line, 335 feet.

ST. LOUIS CARDINALS

Chairman of the Board—August A. Busch, III

President & Chief Executive Officer—Fred L. Kuhlmann
Exec. Vice-President & Chief Operating Officer—Mark Sauer
Senior Vice-President—Stan Musial
Vice-President, Finance & Administration—Mark Gorris
Controller—Brad Wood
Board of Directors—Adolphus A. Busch, IV,
August A. Busch, III, Frederic E. Giersch, Jr., Louis B. Hager, John Hayward,
Ben Kerner, Fred L. Kuhlmann, Stanley F. Musial, W.R. Persons,
Walter C. Reisinger, Louis B. Susman, John Valentine
Vice-President, General Manager—Dal Maxvill
Manager—Whitey Herzog
Admin. Asst. to President & Chief Executive Officer—Jacqueline Hunter
Admin. Asst. to Vice-President, General Manager—Judy Carpenter Barada
Admin. Asst. to Vice-President, Finance & Administration—Bernadine Hogan
Vice-President, Marketing—Marty Hendin
Manager, Promotions & Advertising—Nancy McElroy
Director of Player Development—Ted Simmons
Director of Scouting—Fred McAlister
Assistant Director of Scouting—Marty Maier
Asst. to Player Development & Scouting—Scott Smulczenski
Director of Public Relations—Jeff Wehling
Public Relations Manager—Brian Bartow
Director of Promotions—Dan Farrell
Promotions Assistant—John Kendall
Director of Community Relations & Group Sales—Joe Cunningham
Director of Season Ticket Sales—Sue Ann McClaren
Manager of Group Sales—Bridget Wynn
Manager, Special Projects—Ted Savage
Director of Tickets and Stadium Operations—Mike Bertani
Assistant Director of Tickets—Josephine Arnold
Exec. Asst. to V.P., Finance & Administration—Marian Rhodes
Office Manager—Kevin Wade
Dir. of Information Services—Colin Allsop
Traveling Secretary—C.J. Cherre
Club Physician—Dr. Stan London
Secretary and Treasurer—John L. Hayward
Assistant Secretary—Richard Schwartz
Executive Offices—Busch Stadium, 250 Stadium Plaza,
St. Louis, Mo. 63102
Telephone—421-4040 (area code 314)

SCOUTS—(Supervisors)—Jim Belz, Vern Benson, Jim Johnston, Marty Keough, Tom McCormack, Joe Morlan, Mel Nelson, Joe Rigoli, Mike Roberts, Hal Smith, Roger Smith, Charles (Tim) Thompson, Rube Walker (special assignment). (Part-time)—Jorge Aranzamendi (special assignment), James Brown, Roy Cromer, Roberto Diaz, Manuel Espinosa, Cecil Espy, Manuel Guerra (special assignment), Juan Melo, Virgil Melvin, Charles Menzhuber, Ramon Ortiz, Joe Popek, Kenneth Thomas.

PARK LOCATION—Busch Stadium, Broadway, Walnut Street, Stadium Plaza and Spruce Street.

Seating capacity—54,224.

FIELD DIMENSIONS—Home plate to left field at foul line, 330 feet; to center field, 414 feet; to right field at foul line, 330 feet.

SAN DIEGO PADRES

Board of Directors—Joan Kroc, Dick Freeman,
Anthony J. Zulfer, Jr., Beth Benes, Mel Etter, Dick Starmann

President—Dick Freeman
Vice-President, Baseball Operations—Jack McKeon
Vice-President, Business Operations—Bill Adams
Vice-President, Communications—Chuck Gelman
Director of Finance—Bob Wells
Major League Scout, Special Assignments—Dick Hager
Major League Scout, Special Assignments—Bill McKeon
Director of Minor Leagues—Tom Romenesko
Director of Scouting—Randy Smith
Media Relations—Mike Swanson
Director of Broadcasting—Jim Winters
Director of Marketing—Andy Strasberg
Director of Stadium Operations—Doug Duennes
Director of Ticket Sales—Dave Gilmore
Traveling Secretary—John Mattei
Manager—Jack McKeon
Club Physician—Scripps Clinic
Executive Offices—P. O. Box 2000, San Diego, Calif. 92120
Telephone—283-7294 (area code 619)

SCOUTS—Dave Bartosch, Billy Castell, Rich Chiles, Dave Freeland, Denny Galehouse, Ronquito Garcia, Al Hargesheimer, Randy Johnson, Benny Jones, Harvey Koepf, John Kosciak, Don La Bossiere, Manny Lantigua, Joe Lutz, Jim Marshall, Abraham Martinez, Darryl Milne, Damon Oppenheimer, Hosken Powell, Sonny Siebert, Earl Smith, Dale Sutherland, Kevin Towers, Vince Valecce, Jose Valentin, Bob Warner, Bob Willis, Hank Zacharias. (National Cross Checkers)—Ray Coley, Brian Granger, Brad Sloan.

PARK LOCATION—San Diego Jack Murphy Stadium, 9449 Friars Road.

Seating capacity—59,022.

FIELD DIMENSIONS—Home plate to left field at foul line, 327 feet; to center field, 405 feet; to right field at foul line, 327 feet.

SAN FRANCISCO GIANTS

Chairman—Robert A. Lurie

President & General Manager—Al Rosen
Executive Vice-President, Administration—Corey Busch
Vice-President, Baseball Operations—Bob Kennedy
Senior Vice-President—Pat Gallagher
V.P., Assistant General Manager—Ralph Nelson Jr.
Vice President, Scouting—Bob Fontaine
Director of Player Development—Carlos Alfonso
Director of Minor Leagues—Dave Nahabedian
Director of Scouting Operations—Larry Harper
Director of Travel—Dirk Smith
Special Assistants to the President and G.M.—Willie Mays, Willie McCovey
Administrative Assistant—Florence Myers
Vice President, Public Relations—Duffy Jennings
Director of Marketing—Mario Alioto
Director of Sales—Pennie Lundberg
Vice President, Stadium Operations—Jorge Costa
Director of Retail Sales—Bob Tolifson
Vice President, Tickets—Arthur Schulze
Director of Ticket Operations—Judy Jones
Controller—Jeannie Hurley
Promotions Manager—Valerie McGwire
Director Community Services—Dave Craig
Director of Media Relations—Matt Fischer
Asst. Dir. of Media Relations—Robin Carr
Assistant Director of Stadium Operations—Gene Telucci
Staff Counsel—Michael Shapiro, Esq.
Community Representative—Mike Sadek
Gov't Affairs, Broadcast Coordinator—Bob Hartzell
Producer, Broadcast Services—Jeff Kuiper
Manager—Roger Craig
Executive Offices—Candlestick Park, San Francisco, Calif. 94124
Telephone—468-3700 (area code 415)

SCOUTS—Harry Craft, Bob Cummings, Nino Escalera, Jim Fairey, George M. Genovese, Larry Harper, Grady Hatton, Herman Hannah, Al Heist, Elvio Jiminez, Bob Kennedy Jr., Richard Klaus, Andy Korenek, Alan Marr, Bob Miller, Bill Parese, Ken (Squeaky) Parker, Mike Russell, Hank Sauer, John Shafer, Bill Teed, Todd Thomas, Gene Thompson, Mike Toomey, Jack Uhey, John Van Ornum, Tom Zimmer.

PARK LOCATION—Candlestick Point, Bayshore Freeway.

Seating capacity—58,000.

FIELD DIMENSIONS—Home plate to left field at foul line, 335 feet; to center field, 400 feet; to right field at foul line, 330 feet.

Minor League Presidents for '90

CLASS AAA

American Association—Randy Mobley, P.O. Box 608, Grove City, Ohio 43123

International League—Harold Cooper, P.O. Box 608, Grove City, Ohio 43123

Mexican League—Pedro Treto Cisneros, Angel Pola No. 16 Col. Periodista C.P. 11220, Mexico, D.F.

Pacific Coast League—Bill Cutler, 2101 E. Broadway Rd., Tempe, Ariz. 85282

CLASS AA

Eastern League—Charles Eshbach, P.O. Box 716, Plainville, Conn. 06062

Southern League—Jimmy Bragan, 235 Main St., Suite 103, Trussville, Ala. 35173

Texas League—Carl Sawatski, 10201 W. Markham St., Little Rock, Ark. 72205

CLASS A

California League—Joe Gagliardi, P.O. Box 26400, San Jose, Calif. 95159

Carolina League—John Hopkins, 4241 United Street, Greensboro, N.C. 27407

Florida State League—To Be Announced

Midwest League—George Spelius, P.O. Box 936, Beloit, Wis. 53511

New York-Pennsylvania League—Leo A. Pinckney, 168 E. Genesee St., Auburn, N.Y. 13021

Northwest League—Jack Cain, P.O. Box 30025, Portland, Ore. 97230

South Atlantic League—John H. Moss, P.O. Box 49, Kings Mountain, N.C. 28086

ROOKIE CLASSIFICATION

Appalachian League—Bill Halstead, 157 Carson Lane, Bristol, Va. 24201

Arizona League—Bob Richmond, 8340 E. San Benito, Scottsdale, Ariz. 85258

Gulf Coast League—Thomas J. Saffell, 11 Sunset Drive, Suite 501, Sarasota, Fla. 33577

Pioneer League—Ralph C. Nelles, P.O. Box 1144, Billings, Mont. 59103

Major League Farm Systems for '90

AMERICAN LEAGUE

BALTIMORE (5): AAA—Rochester. AA—Hagerstown. A—Frederick, Wausau. Rookie—Bluefield.

BOSTON (6): AAA—Pawtucket. AA—New Britain, Conn. A—Elmira, Lynchburg, Winter Haven. Rookie—Winter Haven.

CALIFORNIA (6): AAA—Edmonton. AA—Midland. A—Boise, Quad City, Palm Springs. Rookie—Mesa.

CHICAGO (6): AAA—Vancouver. AA—Birmingham. A—Sarasota, South Bend, Utica. Rookie—Gulf Coast.

CLEVELAND (6): AAA—Colorado Springs. AA—Canton-Akron. A—Kinston, Watertown. Rookie—Burlington, N.C., Gulf Coast.

DETROIT (6): AAA—Toledo. AA—London, Ont. A—Lakeland, Fayetteville, Niagara Falls. Rookie—Bristol, Va.

KANSAS CITY (6): AAA—Omaha. AA—Memphis. A—Appleton, Baseball City, Fla., Eugene. Rookie—Boardwalk.

MILWAUKEE (6): AAA—Denver. AA—El Paso. A—Beloit, Stockton. Rookie—Helena, Peoria, Ariz.

MINNESOTA (6): AAA—Portland. AA—Orlando. A—Kenosha, Visalia. Rookie—Elizabethton, Gulf Coast.

NEW YORK (7): AAA—Columbus, O. AA—Albany-Colonie, N.Y. A—Fort Lauderdale, Greensboro, Oneonta, Prince William. Rookie—Sarasota.

OAKLAND (6): AAA—Tacoma. AA—Huntsville. A—Modesto, Madison, Medford. Rookie—Scottsdale.

SEATTLE (6): AAA—Calgary. AA—Williamsport. A—Peninsula, San Bernardino, Bellingham. Rookie—Tempe.

TEXAS (6): AAA—Oklahoma City. AA—Tulsa. A—Port Charlotte, Gastonia. Rookie—Butte, Gulf Coast.

TORONTO (6): AAA—Syracuse. AA—Knoxville. A—Myrtle Beach, Dunedin, St. Catharines, Ont. Rookie—Medicine Hat.

NATIONAL LEAGUE

ATLANTA (8): AAA—Richmond. AA—Greenville. A—Burlington, Ia., Durham, Sumter. Rookie—Bradenton, Idaho Falls, Pulaski.

CHICAGO (6): AAA—Iowa. AA—Charlotte. A—Geneva, Peoria, Ill., Winston-Salem. Rookie—Huntington.

CINCINNATI (6): AAA—Nashville. AA—Chattanooga. A—Cedar Rapids, Charleston, W. Va. Rookie—Billings, Plant City.

HOUSTON (6): AAA—Tucson. AA—Columbus, Ga. A—Asheville, Auburn, Osceola, Fla. Rookie—Gulf Coast.

LOS ANGELES (7): AAA—Albuquerque. AA—San Antonio. A—Bakersfield, Salem, Ore., Vero Beach. Rookie—Great Falls, Gulf Coast.

MONTREAL (6): AAA—Indianapolis. AA—Jacksonville. A—Jamestown, Rockford, West Palm Beach. Rookie—Bradenton.

NEW YORK (7): AAA—Tidewater. AA—Jackson. A—Columbia, S.C., Pittsfield, Port St. Lucie. Rookie—Kingsport, Sarasota.

PHILADELPHIA (6): AAA—Scranton/Wilkes-Barre. AA—Reading. A—Batavia, Clearwater, Spartanburg. Rookie—Martinsville.

PITTSBURGH (6): AAA—Buffalo. AA—Harrisburg. A—Salem, Va., Augusta, Ga., Welland, Ont. Rookie—Bradenton.

ST. LOUIS (8): AAA—Louisville. AA—Arkansas. A—Hamilton, Ont., St. Petersburg, Savannah, Springfield, Ill. Rookie—Johnson City, Peoria, Ariz.

SAN DIEGO (7): AAA—Las Vegas. AA—Wichita. A—Charleston, S.C., Riverside, Spokane, Waterloo. Rookie—Scottsdale.

SAN FRANCISCO (5): AAA—Phoenix. AA—Shreveport. A—Clinton, Everett, San Jose.

OFFICIAL MINOR LEAGUE AVERAGES

Including

Official Averages of All Class AAA, Class AA, Class A and Rookie Leagues

American Association

CLASS AAA

**Leading Batter
JUNIOR NOBOA
Indianapolis**

**League President
RANDY MOBLEY**

**Leading Pitcher
RICH THOMPSON
Indianapolis**

CHAMPIONSHIP WINNERS IN PREVIOUS YEARS

Year	Team	Avg.
1902—Indianapolis		.683
1903—St. Paul		.657
1904—St. Paul		.646
1905—Columbus		.658
1906—Columbus		.615
1907—Columbus		.584
1908—Indianapolis		.601
1909—Louisville		.554
1910—Minneapolis		.637
1911—Minneapolis		.600
1912—Minneapolis		.636
1913—Milwaukee		.599
1914—Milwaukee		.590
1915—Minneapolis		.597
1916—Louisville		.605
1917—Indianapolis		.588
1918—Kansas City		.589
1919—St. Paul		.610
1920—St. Paul		.701
1921—Louisville		.583
1922—St. Paul		.641
1923—Kansas City		.675
1924—St. Paul		.578
1925—Louisville		.635
1926—Louisville		.629
1927—Toledo		.601
1928—Indianapolis		.593
1929—Kansas City		.665
1930—Louisville		.608
1931—St. Paul		.623
1932—Minneapolis		.595
1933—Columbus*		.604
Minneapolis		.562
1934—Minneapolis		.570
Columbus*		.556
1935—Minneapolis		.591
1936—Milwaukee†		.584
1937—Columbus†		.584
1938—St. Paul		.596
Kansas City (2nd)‡		.556
1939—Kansas City		.695
Louisville (4th)‡		.490

Year	Team	Avg.
1940—Kansas City		.625
Louisville (4th)‡		.500
1941—Columbus†		.621
1942—Kansas City		.549
Columbus (3rd)‡		.532
1943—Milwaukee		.596
Columbus (3rd)‡		.532
1944—Milwaukee		.667
Louisville (3rd)‡		.574
1945—Milwaukee		.604
Louisville (3rd)‡		.545
1946—Louisville†		601
1947—Kansas City		.608
Milwaukee (3rd)‡		.513
1948—Indianapolis		.649
St. Paul (3rd)‡		.558
1949—St. Paul		.608
Indianapolis (2nd)‡		.604
1950—Minneapolis		.584
Columbus (3rd)‡		.549
1951—Milwaukee†		.623
1952—Milwaukee		.656
Kansas City (2nd)‡		.578
1953—Toledo		.584
Kansas City (2nd)‡		.571
1954—Indianapolis		.625
Louisville (2nd)‡		.556
1955—Minneapolis†		.597
1956—Indianapolis†		.597
1957—Wichita		.604
Denver (2nd)‡		.584
1958—Charleston		.589
Minneapolis (3rd)‡		.536
1959—Louisville§		.599
Omaha§		.516
Minneapolis (2nd)‡		.586
1960—Denver		.571
Louisville (2nd)‡		.556
1961—Indianapolis		.573
Louisville (2nd)‡		.533
1962—Indianapolis		.605
Louisville (4th)‡		.486

Year	Team	Avg.
1963-1968—Did not operate.		
1969—Omaha		.607
1970—Omaha*		.529
Denver		.504
1971—Indianapolis		.604
Denver*		.521
1972—Wichita		.621
Evansville*		.593
1973—Iowa		.610
Tulsa*		.504
1974—Indianapolis		.578
Tulsa*		.567
1975—Evansville*		.566
Denver		.596
1976—Denver*		.632
Omaha		.574
1977—Omaha		.563
Denver*		.522
1978—Indianapolis		.578
Omaha*		.489
1979—Evansville*		.574
Oklahoma City		.533
1980—Denver		.676
Springfield*		.551
1981—Omaha		.581
Denver*		.559
1982—Indianapolis*		.551
Omaha		.518
1983—Louisville		.578
Denver‡		.545
1984—Denver		.513
Louisville‡		.510
1985—Oklahoma City		.556
Louisville*		.521
1986—Indianapolis*		.563
Denver		.535
1987—Denver		.564
Indianapolis‡		.536
1988—Indianapolis*		.627
Omaha		.570

*Won playoff (East vs. West). †Won championship and four-team playoff. ‡Won four-team playoff. §Respective Eastern and Western division winners.

STANDING OF CLUBS AT CLOSE OF SEASON, SEPTEMBER 1

EASTERN DIVISION

Club	W.	L.	T.	Pct.	G.B.
Indianapolis (Expos)	87	59	0	.596	......
Buffalo (Pirates)	80	62	0	.563	5
Nashville (Reds)	74	72	0	.507	13
Louisville (Cardinals)	71	74	0	.490	15½

WESTERN DIVISION

Club	W.	L.	T.	Pct.	G.B.
Omaha (Royals)	74	72	0	.507	......
Denver (Brewers)	69	77	0	.473	5
Iowa (Cubs)	62	82	0	.431	11
Oklahoma City (Rangers)	59	86	0	.407	14½

COMPOSITE STANDING OF CLUBS AT CLOSE OF SEASON, SEPTEMBER 1

Club	Ind.	Buf.	Oma.	Nash.	Lou.	Den.	Iowa	O.C.	W.	L.	T.	Pct.	G.B.
Indianapolis (Expos)	...	12	10	10	12	8	7	9	87	59	0	.596	......
Buffalo (Pirates)	6	...	9	10	11	5	5	5	80	62	0	.563	5
Omaha (Royals)	2	3	...	5	6	10	11	11	74	72	0	.507	13
Nashville (Reds)	8	8	7	...	4	10	7	6	74	72	0	.507	13
Louisville (Cardinals)	6	7	6	14	...	6	6	6	71	74	0	.490	15½
Denver (Brewers)	4	7	8	2	6	...	5	13	69	77	0	.473	18
Iowa (Cubs)	5	6	7	5	6	13	...	6	62	82	0	.431	24
Oklahoma City (Rangers)	3	7	7	6	6	5	11	...	59	86	0	.407	27½

Major league affiliations in parentheses.

Iowa club represented Des Moines, Ia.

Playoffs—Indianapolis defeated Omaha, three games to two, to win league championship. Indianapolis defeated Richmond (International League), four games to none, to win Alliance championship.

Regular-Season Attendance—Buffalo, 1,132,183; Denver, 346,300; Indianapolis, 303,143; Iowa, 260,404; Louisville, 580,270; Nashville, 457,845; Oklahoma City, 251,480; Omaha, 335,517. Total, 3,667,142. Playoffs (5 games)—25,070. Alliance Playoffs (4 games)—13,341. AAA All-Star Game—14,131.

Managers—Buffalo, Terry Collins; Denver, Dave Machemer; Indianapolis, Tom Runnells; Iowa, Pete Mackanin; Louisville, Mike Jorgensen; Nashville, Frank Lucchesi; Oklahoma City, Jim Skaalen; Omaha, Sal Rende.

All-Star Team—1B—Luis DeLos Santos, Omaha; 2B—Junior Noboa, Indianapolis; 3B—Scott Coolbaugh, Oklahoma City; SS—Jeff Huson, Indianapolis; OF—Skeeter Barnes, Nashville; Greg Vaughn, Denver; Larry Walker, Indianapolis; C—Todd Zeile, Louisville; DH—Steve Henderson, Buffalo; RHP—Mark Gardner, Indianapolis; LHP—Morris Madden, Buffalo; Most Valuable Player—Greg Vaughn, Denver; Rookie of the Year—Todd Zeile, Louisville; Manager of the Year—Tom Runnells, Indianapolis.

(Compiled by Howe Sportsdata International, Boston, Mass.)

CLUB BATTING

Club	Pct.	G.	AB.	R.	OR.	H.	TB.	2B.	3B.	HR.	RBI.	SH.	SF.	HP.	BB.	Int. BB.	SO.	SB.	CS.	LOB.
Denver	.261	146	4790	651	674	1251	1828	212	37	97	593	55	47	34	490	27	866	122	67	964
Buffalo	.259	142	4595	599	574	1192	1649	193	48	56	540	61	47	40	449	29	820	157	66	960
Louisville	.259	145	4866	624	628	1259	1827	223	39	89	575	52	41	29	494	17	780	94	44	1042
Indianapolis	.258	146	4713	624	489	1214	1816	225	49	93	561	50	46	32	494	42	946	148	74	976
Omaha	.254	146	4895	609	582	1244	1792	249	46	69	546	44	35	38	492	29	880	130	68	1033
Nashville	.253	146	4882	593	622	1234	1832	250	30	96	554	59	47	39	422	26	844	89	30	1022
Iowa	.243	144	4725	549	652	1148	1708	201	46	89	493	73	30	27	409	29	813	164	84	911
Oklahoma City	.238	145	4800	544	656	1143	1599	210	33	60	487	47	39	28	483	21	821	82	47	999

INDIVIDUAL BATTING

(Leading Qualifiers for Batting Championship—394 or More Plate Appearances)

*Bats lefthanded. †Switch-hitter.

Player and Club	Pct.	G.	AB.	R.	H.	TB.	2B.	3B.	HR.	RBI.	SH.	SF.	HP.	BB.	Int. BB.	SO.	SB.	CS.
Noboa, Milciades, Indianapolis	.340	117	467	61	159	202	21	8	2	62	7	8	3	21	4	34	14	11
Huson, Jeffrey, Indianapolis*	.304	102	378	70	115	149	17	4	3	35	2	2	1	50	1	26	30	17
Barnes, William, Nashville	.303	124	472	57	143	206	39	3	6	55	5	8	5	32	2	59	15	6
Delos Santos, Luis, Omaha	.297	99	387	45	115	161	31	3	3	62	1	6	0	29	1	53	1	4
Capra, Nick, Omaha	.290	128	500	84	145	199	27	3	7	44	5	1	4	70	1	67	31	18
Baine, Thomas, Louisville	.289	125	380	53	110	137	14	5	1	37	5	2	4	76	2	48	9	5
Zeile, Todd, Louisville	.289	118	453	71	131	220	26	3	19	85	0	7	1	45	1	78	0	1
Hamilton, Darryl, Denver*	.286	129	497	72	142	180	24	4	2	40	5	5	5	42	3	58	20	13
Cole, Alexander, Louisville*	.281	127	455	75	128	149	5	5	2	29	4	1	1	71	1	76	47	19
Dascenzo, Douglas, Iowa†	.281	111	431	59	121	159	18	4	4	33	9	2	0	51	3	41	34	21

Departmental Leaders: G—Canale, Coolbaugh, 144; AB—Coolbaugh, 527; R—Capra, 84; H—Noboa, 159; TB—Canale, 245; 2B—W. Barnes, 39; 3B—Canale, Guinn, Snider, 9; HR—Vaughn, 26; RBI—Vaughn, 92; SH—Roenicke, 12; SF—W. Barnes, Noboa, Snider, 8; HP—J. Mitchell, 11; BB—Baine, 76; IBB—Stephenson, 9; SO—Canale, 134; SB—Cole, 47; CS—Dascenzo, 21.

(All Players—Listed Alphabetically)

Player and Club	Pct.	G.	AB.	R.	H.	TB.	2B.	3B.	HR.	RBI.	SH.	SF.	HP.	BB.	Int. BB.	SO.	SB.	CS.
Alba, Gibson, Louisville*	.231	50	13	2	3	5	2	0	0	3	2	0	0	1	0	2	0	0
Aldrete, Michael, Indianapolis*	.129	10	31	4	4	5	1	0	0	2	0	0	0	8	0	10	0	1
Alicea, Luis, Louisville†	.248	124	412	53	102	152	20	3	8	48	3	4	4	59	1	55	13	5
Anderson, Scott, Indianapolis	.083	30	24	0	2	2	0	0	0	0	1	0	0	1	0	13	0	0
Armstrong, Jack, Nashville	.032	25	31	1	1	1	0	0	0	0	7	0	0	1	0	16	0	0
Arnold, Scott, Louisville	.091	34	22	3	2	2	0	0	0	0	5	0	0	1	0	8	0	0
Bafia, Robert, Iowa	.226	35	106	13	24	48	4	1	6	17	2	0	0	8	0	24	2	0
Baine, Thomas, Louisville	.289	125	380	53	110	137	14	5	1	37	5	2	4	76	2	48	9	5
Baller, Jay, Indianapolis	.500	62	2	0	1	2	1	0	0	1	0	0	0	0	0	1	0	0
Barnes, Brian, Indianapolis*	.000	1	2	0	0	0	0	0	0	0	0	0	0	0	0	0	0	0
Barnes, William, Nashville	.303	124	472	57	143	206	39	3	6	55	5	8	5	32	2	59	15	6
Barrett, Timothy, Indianapolis*	.667	8	3	3	2	3	1	0	0	0	0	0	0	1	0	0	0	0
Bates, William, Denver*	.273	95	363	50	99	117	11	2	1	38	5	2	2	36	1	26	13	5
Belinda, Stanley, Buffalo	.000	19	1	0	0	0	0	0	0	0	0	0	0	0	0	0	0	0
Bell, Jay, Buffalo	.285	86	298	49	85	136	15	3	10	54	3	2	3	38	1	55	12	5
Benavides, Alfredo, Nashville	.170	31	94	9	16	23	4	0	1	12	1	0	0	6	0	24	0	0
Berger, Michael, Oklahoma City	.220	114	354	41	78	125	13	2	10	42	2	3	3	30	1	90	2	3
Berryhill, Damon, Iowa†	.200	7	30	4	6	13	1	0	2	4	0	0	0	1	0	8	0	0
Bilardello, Dann, Buffalo	.206	66	180	11	37	54	8	0	3	17	5	1	1	14	3	26	3	2
Blankenship, Kevin, Iowa	.136	35	22	0	3	3	0	0	1	3	0	0	2	0	0	7	0	0
Blowers, Michael, Indianapolis	.267	131	461	49	123	206	29	6	14	56	1	3	2	41	4	109	3	2

Player and Club	Pct.	G.	AB.	R.	H.	TB.	2B.	3B.	HR.	RBI.	SH.	SF.	HP.	BB.	Int. BB.	SO.	SB.	CS.
Booker, Roderick, Louisville*	.232	94	276	37	64	83	9	2	2	30	5	1	0	38	0	39	9	1
Bosley, Thaddis, Oklahoma City*	.307	30	101	17	31	44	7	0	2	12	0	1	0	13	1	21	3	3
Braun, Randall, Indianapolis*	.248	109	331	39	82	136	17	2	11	46	0	2	0	25	4	59	2	0
Brown, Christopher, Buffalo	.343	57	181	28	62	85	8	0	5	32	3	1	1	19	2	19	0	0
Brown, Keith, Nashville	.167	29	24	1	4	4	0	0	0	1	1	0	0	1	0	8	0	0
Brown, Marty, Nashville	.244	120	422	61	103	164	21	2	12	46	2	4	2	41	1	85	15	6
Bruno, Joseph, Nashville	.000	4	1	0	0	0	0	0	0	0	0	0	0	0	0	0	0	0
Bundy, Lorenzo, Indianapolis*	.281	19	32	3	9	13	1	0	1	3	0	1	0	3	1	4	0	0
Burdick, Kevin, Buffalo	.293	36	147	24	43	55	6	3	0	27	2	4	2	5	1	5	1	0
Burrell, Kevin, Omaha	.217	84	281	28	61	84	11	3	2	22	2	3	3	17	1	64	4	1
Byers, Randell, Louisville*	.259	94	316	30	82	118	12	3	6	53	0	6	0	14	3	50	1	1
Campbell, Michael, Indianapolis	.000	9	3	0	0	0	0	0	0	0	0	0	0	0	0	1	0	0
Canale, George, Denver*	.278	144	503	80	140	245	33	9	18	71	2	6	2	71	1	134	5	8
Capel, Michael, Iowa	.333	64	3	0	1	1	0	0	0	0	0	0	0	0	0	2	0	0
Capra, Nick, Omaha	.290	128	500	84	145	199	27	3	7	44	5	1	4	70	1	67	31	18
Carrasco, Norman, Iowa	.178	66	219	10	39	52	8	1	1	16	3	1	0	6	0	26	3	4
Carrillo, Matías, Denver*	.260	125	400	46	104	156	14	4	10	43	7	2	2	24	1	90	22	6
Carter, Steven, Buffalo*	.295	100	356	53	105	144	24	6	1	43	1	3	2	27	5	62	17	9
Castaneda, Nick, Omaha*	.268	52	149	18	40	72	11	0	7	29	0	1	0	36	5	37	0	1
Castillo, Juan, Denver†	.170	13	53	4	9	10	1	0	0	2	0	0	0	1	0	5	1	0
Castro, Jose, Omaha	.248	106	367	20	91	116	17	1	2	33	0	2	4	29	1	38	1	3
Coffman, Kevin, Iowa	.000	14	1	0	0	0	0	0	0	0	0	0	0	0	0	1	0	0
Cole, Alexander, Louisville*	.281	127	455	75	128	149	5	5	2	29	4	1	1	71	1	76	47	19
Cook, Jeffrey, Buffalo†	.248	97	315	35	78	95	7	5	0	20	3	1	1	25	2	41	21	8
Coolbaugh, Scott, Oklahoma City	.260	144	527	66	137	219	28	0	18	74	2	3	2	57	5	93	1	2
Crabbe, Bruce, Iowa	.265	50	147	20	39	56	8	0	3	14	2	1	3	11	0	22	4	1
Crawford, Steven, Omaha	.000	22	0	0	0	0	0	0	0	0	0	0	0	1	0	0	0	0
Cruz, Luis, Iowa	.154	10	13	4	2	2	0	0	0	0	0	0	0	3	0	3	0	0
Cucjen, Romulo, Louisville	.276	105	348	42	96	145	19	3	8	38	0	5	2	24	0	50	0	2
Damian, Leonard, Iowa	.250	41	20	0	5	5	0	0	0	0	1	0	0	0	0	5	0	1
Dascenzo, Douglas, Iowa†	.281	111	431	59	121	159	18	4	4	33	9	2	0	51	3	41	34	21
Daugherty, John, Oklahoma City†	.251	82	311	28	78	108	15	3	3	32	2	3	0	39	5	35	2	2
Dean, Kevin, Indianapolis	.215	74	233	36	50	77	10	7	1	23	1	3	2	44	1	68	9	8
Dedmon, Jeffrey, Indianapolis*	.000	51	6	0	0	0	0	0	0	0	0	0	0	0	0	4	0	0
Delos Santos, Luis, Omaha	.297	99	387	45	115	161	31	3	3	62	1	6	0	29	1	53	1	4
DeShields, Delino, Montreal*	.260	47	181	29	47	69	8	4	2	14	1	0	0	16	0	53	16	7
Destrade, Orestes, Buffalo†	.230	33	100	8	23	32	6	0	1	17	1	1	3	13	2	13	0	1
Diaz, Edgar, Denver	.215	105	316	29	68	81	8	1	1	22	6	3	1	44	1	29	4	2
Distefano, Benito, Buffalo*	.235	5	17	2	4	5	1	0	0	3	0	0	1	2	0	3	0	0
Dixon, Edward, Indianapolis	.000	27	2	0	0	0	0	0	0	0	0	0	0	0	0	1	0	0
Dodd, Thomas, Omaha	.252	130	461	52	116	196	24	7	14	63	2	5	1	35	1	108	2	5
Duke, Douglas, Indianapolis	.169	27	77	4	13	20	4	0	1	5	0	2	0	5	0	23	0	0
Dunbar, Thomas, Omaha*	.280	34	125	21	35	53	13	1	1	18	0	1	0	14	0	10	4	2
Durham, Leon, Louisville*	.287	59	178	31	51	91	10	0	10	30	0	2	4	20	3	38	0	0
Easley, Logan, Buffalo	.500	28	2	0	1	1	0	0	0	1	0	0	0	0	0	1	0	0
Erickson, Roger, Louisville	.000	27	5	0	0	0	0	0	0	0	1	0	0	0	0	0	0	0
Escobar, Jose, Omaha	.079	23	76	3	6	6	0	0	0	1	0	1	0	2	0	19	0	0
Farmer, Howard, Indianapolis	.333	1	3	0	1	1	0	0	0	1	0	0	0	0	0	1	0	0
Fassero, Jeffrey, Louisville*	.048	23	21	1	1	1	0	0	0	1	4	0	0	1	0	10	0	0
Ficklin, Winston, Iowa	.223	68	188	20	42	55	7	0	2	9	1	1	0	7	0	33	7	4
Figueroa, Bienvenido, Louisville	.217	74	221	18	48	51	3	0	0	14	5	1	0	12	0	22	0	1
Fisher, Brian, Buffalo	.000	5	5	0	0	0	0	0	0	0	0	0	0	0	0	4	0	0
Fitzgerald, Michael, Louisville	.219	103	343	22	75	109	13	0	7	38	0	2	4	10	0	47	0	1
Fowlkes, Alan, Iowa	.056	13	18	2	1	1	0	0	0	1	0	0	0	0	0	4	0	0
Fox, Michael, Louisville	.177	19	62	4	11	14	3	0	0	6	0	2	1	2	0	14	0	0
Freeman, Lavell, 46 Den.-52 OKC*	.238	98	302	32	72	101	14	3	3	27	2	2	0	24	1	64	7	5
Frey, Steven, Indianapolis	.000	21	1	0	0	0	0	0	0	0	0	0	0	0	0	0	0	0
Gakeler, Daniel, Indianapolis	.000	11	12	0	0	0	0	0	0	0	2	0	0	0	0	7	0	0
Garcia, Miguel, Buffalo*	.200	31	5	0	1	1	0	0	0	0	0	0	0	0	0	2	0	0
Garcia, Victor, Iowa	.195	47	123	16	24	48	3	0	7	16	0	2	2	11	1	28	1	0
Gardner, Mark, Indianapolis	.115	24	26	2	3	4	1	0	0	1	3	0	0	1	0	12	0	0
Garman, Patrick, Oklahoma City	.293	43	133	19	39	51	6	0	2	18	0	1	2	23	0	30	0	1
Germann, Mark, Nashville	.067	10	15	0	1	1	0	0	0	1	0	0	0	3	0	1	0	0
Gibbons, John Michael, Oklahoma City	.218	59	188	26	41	65	7	1	5	24	1	6	1	24	1	47	1	0
Girardi, Joseph, Iowa	.245	32	110	12	27	41	4	2	2	11	0	0	5	1	1	19	3	1
Gray, Jeffrey, Nashville	.000	44	2	0	0	0	0	0	0	0	1	0	0	0	0	2	0	0
Griffin, Michael, Nashville	.000	41	3	0	0	0	0	0	0	0	0	0	0	0	0	0	0	0
Grissom, Marquis, Indianapolis	.278	49	187	28	52	76	10	4	2	21	0	1	0	14	0	23	16	4
Guinn, Brian, Iowa†	.239	120	380	43	91	143	16	9	6	39	8	3	1	52	2	65	9	10
Gwosdz, Douglas, Nashville	.293	24	41	6	12	15	3	0	0	7	1	0	0	10	0	11	0	0
Hall, Albert, Buffalo†	.304	90	345	63	105	140	13	5	4	33	6	4	5	28	1	53	31	8
Hall, D. Andrew, Buffalo	.262	20	42	4	11	15	2	1	0	7	0	1	0	9	0	18	0	0
Hamilton, Darryl, Denver*	.286	129	497	72	142	180	24	4	2	40	5	5	5	42	3	58	20	13
Hammond, Christopher, Nashville*	.125	24	24	1	3	3	0	0	0	1	4	0	0	4	0	10	0	0
Harkey, Michael, Iowa	.143	12	7	0	1	1	0	0	0	1	0	0	0	0	0	1	0	0
Harris, Leonard, Nashville*	.265	8	34	6	9	20	2	0	3	6	0	0	0	0	0	5	0	2
Harris, Eugene, Indianapolis	.000	6	1	0	0	0	0	0	0	0	0	0	0	0	0	0	0	0
Hayden, Alan, Nashville*	.246	73	191	29	47	50	3	0	0	12	3	0	2	15	0	23	13	4
Hearn, Edward, Omaha	.281	67	228	18	64	74	8	1	0	15	3	2	1	16	0	39	1	0
Heinkel, Donald, Louisville*	.000	2	2	0	0	0	0	0	0	0	1	0	0	1	0	0	0	0
Henderson, Stephen, Buffalo	.298	100	319	53	95	147	21	5	7	45	0	2	5	46	3	62	4	1
Hesketh, Joseph, Indianapolis*	.000	5	1	0	0	0	0	0	0	0	0	0	0	0	0	0	0	0
Hill, Kenneth, Louisville	.250	3	8	1	2	2	0	0	0	0	0	0	0	0	0	0	0	0
Hill, Orsino, Iowa*	.255	30	94	9	24	32	6	1	0	11	0	1	0	9	1	19	0	2
Hilton, Howard, Louisville	.500	70	4	0	2	3	1	0	0	0	0	0	0	0	0	2	0	0
Horton, Ricky, Louisville*	.500	2	2	0	1	1	0	0	0	1	0	0	0	0	0	0	0	0
House, Bryan, Iowa†	.250	138	503	64	126	182	24	7	6	48	8	3	9	43	0	83	37	17
Houston, Melvin, Indianapolis	.000	1	1	0	0	0	0	0	0	0	0	0	0	0	0	0	0	0
Huson, Jeffrey, Indianapolis*	.304	102	378	70	115	149	17	4	3	35	2	2	1	50	1	26	30	17
Jackson, Charles, Omaha	.299	28	97	16	29	38	0	3	1	12	1	0	1	12	1	10	1	1
Jackson, Darrin, Iowa	.258	30	120	18	31	58	4	1	7	17	0	0	2	7	2	22	4	0

Player and Club	Pct.	G.	AB.	R.	H.	TB.	2B.	3B.	HR.	RBI.	SH.	SF.	HP.	BB.	Int. BB.	SO.	SB.	CS.
Jackson, Kenneth, Oklahoma City	.038	13	26	3	1	1	0	0	0	0	0	0	0	8	0	8	0	0
Jelks, Gregory, Louisville	.240	113	375	57	90	157	24	5	11	48	1	4	5	39	1	73	6	2
Jirschele, Michael, Omaha	.091	16	44	1	4	5	1	0	0	0	2	0	0	1	0	20	0	0
Johnson, Randall, Indianapolis	.000	3	2	0	0	0	0	0	0	0	0	0	0	0	0	1	0	0
Jones, Christopher, Nashville	.163	21	49	8	8	15	1	0	2	5	1	0	0	0	0	16	2	0
Jones, James, Denver	.225	39	80	9	18	21	3	0	0	6	0	0	1	8	0	25	1	0
Jones, Ruppert, Oklahoma City*	.200	27	80	7	16	25	6	0	1	12	0	3	0	7	0	25	1	1
Jurak, Edward, Indianapolis	.000	1	3	0	0	0	0	0	0	0	0	0	0	0	0	0	0	0
Kemp, Hubert, Nashville*	.083	37	24	5	2	2	0	0	0	0	5	0	0	1	0	9	0	0
Khalifa, Sam, Louisville	.276	87	283	45	78	105	14	5	1	20	3	2	2	57	1	60	11	10
Kilgus, Paul, Iowa*	.250	1	4	1	1	1	0	0	0	0	0	0	0	0	0	2	0	0
King, Jeffrey, Buffalo	.254	51	169	26	43	70	5	2	6	29	2	5	0	13	0	22	7	1
Kinzer, Matthew, Louisville	.250	51	4	0	1	1	0	0	0	0	0	0	0	0	0	0	0	0
Kraemer, Joseph, Iowa*	.043	27	23	1	1	1	0	0	0	0	2	0	0	0	0	7	0	0
Kramer, Randall, Buffalo	.000	5	4	0	0	0	0	0	0	0	0	0	0	0	0	2	0	0
Kreuter, Chad, Oklahoma City†	.253	26	87	10	22	25	3	0	0	6	1	1	0	13	0	11	1	1
Lancaster, Lester, Iowa	.000	17	12	0	0	0	0	0	0	0	0	0	0	0	0	5	0	0
Landrum, William, Buffalo	.200	5	5	0	1	1	0	0	0	0	0	0	0	0	0	1	0	0
Landrum, Terry, Nashville	.221	68	226	31	50	68	7	1	3	20	4	1	3	20	0	40	7	2
Larkin, Barry, Nashville	1.000	2	5	2	5	6	1	0	0	0	0	0	0	0	0	0	0	0
Laskey, William, Omaha	.000	14	1	0	0	0	0	0	0	0	0	0	0	0	0	0	0	0
LaValliere, Michael, Buffalo*	.111	7	18	0	2	2	0	0	0	1	0	1	0	3	0	4	0	0
Lee, Terry, Nashville	.234	13	47	5	11	15	4	0	0	3	1	0	1	3	0	8	0	0
Lind, Orlando, Buffalo	.000	32	9	0	0	0	0	0	0	0	0	0	0	0	0	4	0	0
Lindeman, James, Louisville	.303	29	109	18	33	58	8	1	5	20	0	0	0	14	2	17	3	0
Little, Scott, Buffalo	.295	107	298	38	88	116	11	4	3	43	1	5	3	18	0	53	9	3
Lockhart, Keith, Nashville*	.267	131	479	77	128	203	21	6	14	58	2	4	6	61	4	41	4	3
Loggins, Michael, Omaha†	.264	103	311	57	82	114	14	6	2	29	7	0	2	33	2	68	29	10
Lopez, Robert, Nashville*	.429	26	7	0	3	4	1	0	0	1	0	0	1	0	2	0	0	0
Loy, Darren, Oklahoma City	.206	48	155	10	32	39	4	0	1	10	2	0	2	20	0	20	0	0
Lugo, Urbano, Indianapolis	.000	22	20	3	0	0	0	0	0	3	5	0	0	2	0	5	0	0
Madden, Morris, Buffalo*	.111	26	27	1	3	3	0	0	0	0	3	0	0	1	0	5	0	0
Madison, Scott, Nashville†	.267	79	266	26	71	103	14	0	6	38	1	4	0	31	3	33	3	1
Masters, David, Iowa	.500	4	4	1	2	2	0	0	0	1	0	0	0	0	0	0	0	0
Mattox, Frank, Denver†	.333	9	33	4	11	11	0	0	0	1	1	1	1	0	0	1	1	1
McClendon, Lloyd, Iowa	.321	34	109	18	35	57	10	0	4	13	0	1	0	21	1	19	4	1
McGee, Willie, Louisville†	.407	8	27	5	11	15	4	0	0	4	0	2	0	3	1	4	3	0
McGrath, Charles, Louisville	.063	21	16	0	1	1	0	0	0	0	2	0	0	0	0	9	0	0
McGriff, Terence, Nashville	.281	102	335	42	94	135	24	1	5	28	1	0	1	29	3	68	1	1
Meacham, Robert, Buffalo	.218	94	271	23	59	72	13	0	0	25	5	1	4	31	3	64	4	2
Medvin, Scott, Buffalo	.500	54	2	0	1	1	0	0	0	0	0	0	0	0	0	0	0	0
Melton, Lawrence, Buffalo	.000	9	2	0	0	0	0	0	0	0	0	0	0	0	0	2	0	0
Mendez, Jesus, Louisville*	.216	10	37	4	8	11	3	0	0	4	0	0	0	2	0	4	0	1
Merced, Orlando, Buffalo†	.341	35	129	18	44	58	5	3	1	16	2	1	0	7	1	26	0	1
Mesh, Michael, Omaha	.247	101	299	45	74	93	5	4	2	26	8	0	5	32	0	54	11	3
Meyer, Joe, Denver	.281	41	146	20	41	78	10	0	9	37	0	1	2	16	1	42	1	0
Mitchell, Charles, Nashville	.600	40	5	0	3	3	0	0	0	0	1	0	0	0	0	1	0	0
Mitchell, Joseph, Denver	.249	138	486	75	121	210	24	4	19	76	5	7	11	34	6	119	5	3
Monico, Mario, Denver*	.266	72	241	32	64	78	11	0	1	27	0	5	4	26	3	30	3	3
Moore, William, Indianapolis	.159	14	44	1	7	11	1	0	1	8	0	2	0	6	0	19	0	1
Moreno, Armando, Indianapolis	.275	113	316	45	87	139	19	3	9	43	6	3	5	45	2	52	5	3
Motley, Darryl, Indianapolis	.254	76	236	33	60	81	10	1	3	23	2	2	3	23	1	41	2	0
Murphy, John, Louisville	.000	1	1	0	0	0	0	0	0	0	0	0	0	0	0	0	0	0
Nichols, Howard, Iowa	.242	55	178	19	43	60	7	2	2	15	1	0	2	8	0	35	2	1
Noboa, Milciades, Louisville	.340	117	467	61	159	202	21	8	2	62	7	8	3	21	4	34	14	11
Norman, Nelson, Indianapolis	.083	8	12	1	1	1	0	0	0	0	3	0	0	2	0	1	0	0
O'Neill, Paul, Nashville*	.333	4	12	1	4	4	0	0	0	0	0	0	0	3	0	1	1	1
Oelkers, Bryan, Louisville*	.143	18	14	2	2	2	0	0	0	1	3	0	1	0	0	2	0	0
Oliver, Joseph, Nashville	.292	71	233	22	68	99	13	0	6	31	1	5	3	13	1	35	0	0
Owen, Dave, Iowa†	.247	79	227	30	56	78	9	5	1	22	7	2	0	32	1	42	4	5
Pacillo, Patrick, Indianapolis	.190	22	21	3	4	4	0	0	0	0	2	0	0	3	0	6	0	0
Palacios, Rey, Omaha	.178	34	90	13	16	25	6	0	1	6	1	0	0	14	0	29	1	2
Pankovits, James, Buffalo	.181	30	83	5	15	25	2	1	2	8	0	2	0	12	0	15	3	2
Paris, Kelly, Omaha†	.250	49	176	26	44	71	10	1	5	28	2	3	1	19	0	32	4	1
Parker, Stephen, Iowa*	.000	19	2	0	0	0	0	0	0	0	0	0	0	0	0	0	0	0
Patterson, Robert, Buffalo	.154	31	26	2	4	5	1	0	0	1	8	0	0	0	0	10	0	0
Pearson, Kevin, Nashville	.247	68	190	20	47	73	12	1	4	22	0	4	12	0	34	0	1
Pecota, William, Nashville	.254	64	248	34	63	86	12	1	3	40	1	5	2	29	2	29	10	5
Peters, Steven, Louisville*	.000	65	4	0	0	0	0	0	0	0	0	0	0	0	0	3	0	0
Pevey, Marty, Indianapolis*	.259	34	108	12	28	39	4	2	1	14	2	0	0	8	1	20	3	3
Pico, Jeffrey, Iowa	.000	2	2	0	0	0	0	0	0	0	0	0	0	0	0	0	0	0
Potestio, Frank, Louisville	.231	22	13	0	3	3	0	0	0	0	0	0	0	1	0	2	0	0
Powell, Alonzo, Indianapolis	.232	121	423	50	98	173	26	5	13	59	1	2	2	38	2	106	9	6
Power, Ted, Louisville	.000	8	4	0	0	0	0	0	0	0	0	0	0	0	0	4	0	0
Prince, Thomas, Buffalo	.202	65	183	21	37	65	8	1	6	33	1	4	2	22	1	30	2	3
Pryor, Buddy, Indianapolis	1.000	1	1	0	1	1	0	0	0	0	0	0	0	0	0	0	0	0
Pulliam, Harvey, Omaha	.182	7	22	3	4	6	2	0	0	2	0	0	0	3	0	6	0	0
Puzey, James, Louisville*	.301	36	103	15	31	47	7	0	3	20	0	0	18	2	6	0	0
Pyznarski, Timothy, Omaha	.071	5	14	0	1	1	0	0	0	0	0	0	0	2	0	10	0	0
Quinones, Luis, Nashville†	.227	45	176	19	40	65	9	2	4	24	3	5	1	8	1	22	1	0
Reed, Richard, Buffalo	.188	20	16	0	3	3	0	0	0	0	2	0	0	0	0	4	0	0
Reimer, Kevin, Oklahoma City*	.267	133	514	59	137	218	37	7	10	73	1	4	2	33	3	91	4	1
Reyes, Gilberto, Indianapolis	.226	106	314	35	71	106	8	0	9	35	2	1	3	30	4	69	0	2
Reynolds, Jeffrey, Nashville	.229	65	188	23	43	79	10	1	8	32	1	1	4	15	1	45	0	0
Reynolds, Ronn, Denver	.267	10	30	1	8	11	3	0	0	1	0	0	2	0	5	0	0
Richardson, Jeffrey, Nashville	.273	88	286	36	78	104	19	2	1	25	6	3	1	17	4	42	3	1
Ritter, Reggie, Iowa*	.000	12	0	0	0	0	0	0	0	0	1	0	0	0	0	0	0	0
Robertson, Andre, Oklahoma City	.177	64	164	23	29	36	5	1	0	6	1	1	1	19	0	33	6	2
Robinson, Ronald, Nashville	.000	3	3	0	0	0	0	0	0	0	0	0	0	0	0	0	0	0
Rodriguez, Ruben, Denver	.195	12	41	2	8	8	0	0	2	2	0	1	2	0	13	0	0
Roenicke, Ronald, Oklahoma City†	.230	105	352	47	81	107	13	2	3	31	12	4	2	70	2	65	23	4

Player and Club	Pct.	G.	AB.	R.	H.	TB.	2B.	3B.	HR.	RBI.	SH.	SF.	HP.	BB.	Int. BB.	SO.	SB.	CS.
Roesler, Michael, Nashville	.000	40	2	0	0	0	0	0	0	0	0	0	0	1	0	2	0	0
Rohn, Daniel, Oklahoma City*	.238	117	395	48	94	117	15	4	0	26	7	0	4	44	1	51	3	3
Romano, Thomas, Buffalo	.241	60	166	18	40	52	4	1	2	22	2	2	1	6	0	22	6	1
Rood, Nelson, Denver	.259	63	174	22	45	49	4	0	0	21	3	2	0	21	0	27	8	4
Roomes, Rolando, Nashville	.272	25	92	13	25	42	3	1	4	10	1	1	2	9	1	30	6	1
Rossy, Elam, Buffalo	.193	38	109	11	21	26	5	0	0	10	1	2	1	18	1	11	4	0
Rucker, David, Buffalo*	1.000	24	1	0	1	1	0	0	0	0	1	0	0	0	0	0	0	0
Sabo, Christopher, Nashville	.167	7	30	0	5	7	2	0	0	3	0	0	0	0	0	0	0	0
Sanchez, Rey, Oklahoma City	.224	134	464	38	104	125	10	4	1	39	5	3	2	21	0	50	4	4
Sauveur, Richard, Indianapolis*	.000	9	1	0	0	0	0	0	0	0	0	0	0	0	0	1	0	0
Schulz, Jeffrey, Omaha*	.278	95	331	31	92	127	19	5	2	37	1	1	2	28	6	47	2	0
Scott, Donald, Denver†	.255	111	330	36	84	108	15	0	3	31	4	3	1	42	4	37	4	1
Scudder, Scott, Nashville	.167	12	6	0	1	1	0	0	0	0	0	0	0	2	0	5	0	0
Sebra, Robert, Nashville	.000	11	1	0	0	0	0	0	0	0	0	0	0	0	0	0	0	0
Sellers, Jeffrey, Nashville	.000	1	2	0	0	0	0	0	0	0	0	0	0	0	0	1	0	0
Sheffield, Gary, Denver*	.138	7	29	3	4	7	1	1	0	0	1	0	0	2	0	0	0	0
Shepherd, Ronald, Louisville	.250	99	304	35	76	123	20	6	5	30	0	1	1	25	0	73	2	2
Shines, Raymond, Indianapolis†	.305	77	226	37	69	102	16	1	5	33	0	5	1	42	8	48	3	3
Shumpert, Terrance, Omaha	.248	113	355	54	88	133	29	2	4	22	7	1	10	25	0	63	23	7
Simmons, Nelson, Louisville†	.316	5	19	3	6	11	2	0	1	3	0	0	0	1	0	3	0	0
Small, Jeffrey, Iowa	.214	84	295	20	63	82	8	1	3	25	8	4	2	7	1	38	4	1
Smith, Brick, Indianapolis	.159	27	69	3	11	13	2	0	0	6	0	1	1	9	1	15	0	0
Smith, David, Denver	.231	5	13	1	3	3	0	0	0	2	1	1	0	0	0	2	1	0
Smith, Dwight, Iowa*	.325	21	83	11	27	46	7	3	2	7	1	0	0	7	0	11	6	2
Smith, Michael, Buffalo	.000	9	2	0	0	0	0	0	0	0	0	0	0	0	0	1	0	0
Snider, Van, Nashville*	.222	119	442	48	98	169	17	9	12	64	0	8	4	32	2	117	7	0
Sosa, Samuel, Oklahoma City	.103	10	39	2	4	6	2	0	0	3	0	0	2	0	0	8	4	2
Spiers, William, Denver*	.362	14	47	9	17	27	2	1	2	8	1	0	0	5	0	6	1	0
Spratke, Kenneth, Omaha	.000	33	1	0	0	0	0	0	0	0	0	0	0	0	0	1	0	0
St. Laurent, James, Oklahoma City*	.243	115	374	31	91	115	14	5	0	36	5	3	3	16	2	46	6	6
Steels, James, Indianapolis*	.556	2	9	3	5	11	0	0	2	3	0	0	0	0	0	2	0	0
Stephenson, Phillip, Iowa*	.300	84	290	52	87	149	17	3	13	62	0	4	1	58	9	41	28	3
Stone, Jeffrey, Oklahoma City*	.179	13	39	4	7	9	2	0	0	1	0	0	1	0	0	10	1	0
Tanner, Edwin, Nashville*	.266	113	323	30	86	117	17	1	4	38	1	2	0	47	3	29	3	1
Taylor, Donald, Buffalo	.032	25	31	1	1	1	0	0	0	1	1	0	0	0	0	14	0	0
Tewksbury, Robert, Louisville	.189	28	37	4	7	7	0	0	0	2	6	0	0	2	0	14	0	0
Thompson, Richard, Indianapolis†	.000	23	17	0	0	0	0	0	0	0	2	0	0	4	0	11	0	0
Thornton, Louis, Buffalo*	.208	28	96	8	20	28	3	1	1	7	0	2	0	7	0	15	3	2
Threadgill, George, Oklahoma City	.227	50	141	21	32	38	3	0	1	10	0	1	3	20	0	33	6	4
Thurman, Gary, Omaha	.219	17	64	5	14	21	3	2	0	3	0	0	0	7	0	18	5	4
Tullier, Michael, Iowa*	.218	83	174	23	38	46	3	1	1	24	7	1	1	10	1	23	2	4
Valdez, Sergio, Indianapolis	.000	19	16	0	0	0	0	0	0	0	2	0	0	1	0	1	0	0
Varsho, Gary, Iowa*	.232	31	112	13	26	37	3	1	2	13	0	2	2	9	2	21	6	3
Vasquez, Luis, Nashville	.257	34	35	5	9	11	2	0	0	3	4	0	0	0	0	5	0	0
Vaughn, Gregory, Denver	.276	110	387	74	107	212	17	5	26	92	2	1	0	62	4	94	20	3
Villanueva, Hector, Iowa	.252	120	444	46	112	175	25	1	12	57	1	2	1	32	2	95	1	1
Walker, Bernard, Nashville*	.250	22	64	9	16	20	1	0	1	8	0	1	0	4	0	14	7	0
Walker, Larry, Indianapolis*	.270	114	385	68	104	162	18	2	12	59	5	7	9	50	8	87	36	6
Walker, Michael, Buffalo	.400	3	5	0	2	2	0	0	0	0	0	0	0	0	0	0	0	0
Walters, Darryel, Denver	.230	34	113	18	26	42	3	2	3	15	1	1	0	6	0	30	2	1
Walton, Jerome, Iowa	.333	4	18	4	6	10	1	0	1	3	0	0	0	1	0	5	2	1
Wilkins, Dean, Iowa	.100	38	10	0	1	1	0	0	0	0	7	0	0	0	0	7	0	0
Wilkinson, William, Buffalo	.000	21	12	1	0	0	0	0	0	0	1	0	0	0	0	9	0	0
Williams, Reginald, Buffalo	.243	107	321	51	78	102	11	2	3	25	2	0	3	28	2	86	19	7
Williams, Roger, Iowa	.143	28	14	1	2	2	0	0	0	1	0	0	0	1	0	7	0	0
Wilson, Craig, Louisville	.291	75	278	37	81	108	18	3	1	30	3	1	2	14	0	25	1	3
Wilson, Michael, 53 OKC-48 Den	.267	101	348	46	93	126	21	3	2	46	8	2	4	47	0	37	12	14
Wine, Robert, Indianapolis	.200	11	25	1	5	8	0	0	1	3	0	0	0	1	0	11	0	0
Winters, Matthew, Omaha*	.224	75	268	33	60	111	6	3	13	54	1	4	1	38	8	58	0	1
Wrona, Richard, Iowa	.217	60	189	15	41	61	8	3	2	13	0	1	7	2	40	1	1	
Xavier, Joseph, Denver*	.262	84	214	30	56	73	13	2	0	17	5	5	0	17	1	47	5	5
York, Michael, Buffalo	.071	8	14	0	1	1	0	0	0	0	0	0	0	0	0	5	0	0
Zeile, Todd, Louisville	.289	118	453	71	131	220	26	3	19	85	0	7	1	45	1	78	0	1

The following pitchers, listed alphabetically by club, with games in parentheses, had no plate appearances, primarily through use of designated hitters:

BUFFALO—Conroy, Timothy (3); Palacios, Vicente (2); Samuels, Roger (18).

DENVER—Aldrich, Jay (31); August, Donald (4); Birkbeck, Michael (5); Costello, Michael (18); Dawley, William (11); Filer, Thomas (12); Fossas, Anthony (24); Jones, Odell (28); Kinnunen, Michael (3); Krawczyk, Raymond (43); Krueger, William (2); May, Scott (12); Navarro, Jaime (3); Nieves, Juan (3); Peterek, Jeffrey (23); Puig, Edward (12); Sadler, Alan (28); Simmons, Todd (26); Stapleton, David (34); Stoddard, Robert (12); Veres, Randolf (17); Waddell, Thomas (6); Watkins, Timothy (7).

INDIANAPOLIS—Gideon, Brett (47); McKeon, Joel (28); Waddell, Thomas (1).

IOWA—Parmenter, Gary (1); Perry, Patrick (5); Scheid, Richard (7); Vande Berg, Edward (69).

LOUISVILLE—Carpenter, Cris (27); Costello, John (4); Mathews, Gregory (1); Worrell, Todd (1).

OKLAHOMA CITY—Akerfelds, Darrel (33); Arnsberg, Bradley (18); Barfield, John (28); Cliburn, Stewart (4); Hagen, Kevin (4); Hall, Andrew C. (11); Jeffcoat, Michael (11); Lankard, Steven (10); Lynch, David (11); May, Scott (18); McMurtry, Craig (1); Mielke, Gary (18); Miller, David (27); Pavlas, David (29); Petkovsek, Mark (6); Scherrer, William (5); Simmons, Todd (13); Whitaker, Darrell (38); Wilmet, Paul (55).

OMAHA—Appier, Kevin (22); Buchanan, Robert (27); Clarke, Stanley (27); Crouch, Matthew (8); DeJesus, Jose (31); Encarnacion, Luis (31); Fireovid, Stephen (29); Gleaton, Jerry Don (24); Luecken, Richard (36); Moore, Donnie (7); Olwine, Edward (53); Stottlemyre, Melvin (7).

GRAND SLAM HOME RUNS—Alicea, Bell, Braun, Canale, Destrade, Dodd, Al. Hall, Hamilton, T. Landrum, Loggins, Mesh, Prince, Reyes, J. Reynolds, Stephenson, Snyum, Zeile, 1 each.

AWARDED FIRST BASE ON CATCHER'S INTERFERENCE—Daugherty (Villanueva); J. Mitchell (R. Palacios); Paris (J. Mitchell); Reimer (Marzano); Threadgill (Little); L. Walker (Berger).

CLUB FIELDING

Club	Pct.	G.	PO.	A.	E.	DP.	PB.	Club	Pct.	G.	PO.	A.	E.	DP.	PB.
Oklahoma City	.973	145	3821	1633	151	171	9	Omaha	.971	146	3871	1565	165	130	14
Louisville	.973	145	3810	1522	150	120	22	Indianapolis	.970	146	3779	1432	163	111	15
Denver	.972	146	3788	1596	155	148	23	Nashville	.969	146	3834	1541	173	119	14
Buffalo	.971	142	3666	1439	154	128	17	Iowa	.968	144	3771	1650	178	127	10

Triple Plays—Denver, Louisville.

INDIVIDUAL FIELDING

*Throws lefthanded.

FIRST BASEMEN

Player and Club	Pct.	G.	PO.	A.	E.	DP.	Player and Club	Pct.	G.	PO.	A.	E.	DP.
Aldrete, Indianapolis*	1.000	5	35	3	0	3	King, Buffalo	.996	27	205	21	1	18
Bafia, Iowa	1.000	3	24	1	0	0	Lee, Nashville	.985	13	118	13	2	12
Barnes, Nashville	.990	11	95	9	1	11	Lindeman, Louisville	.929	5	13	0	1	1
Berger, Oklahoma City	.986	24	184	21	3	26	Little, Buffalo	.988	22	151	17	2	11
Bilardello, Buffalo	1.000	1	13	0	0	1	Madison, Nashville	.993	60	491	53	4	38
Braun, Indianapolis	.977	59	474	33	12	37	McClendon, Iowa	.967	12	83	6	3	4
C. Brown, Buffalo	1.000	1	3	1	0	1	Merced, Buffalo	.994	21	155	10	1	16
M. Brown, Nashville	.961	17	111	11	5	14	Meyer, Denver	1.000	1	8	1	0	3
Bundy, Indianapolis	1.000	2	12	4	0	2	Mitchell, Denver	.972	4	31	4	1	3
Burrell, Omaha	1.000	10	79	6	0	1	Moore, Indianapolis*	.960	4	23	1	1	2
CANALE, Denver	.993	141	1287	94	10	122	Oliver, Indianapolis	1.000	2	4	0	0	0
Carrillo, Denver*	1.000	1	1	0	0	0	Owen, Iowa	1.000	2	11	1	0	0
Castaneda, Omaha	.978	16	127	7	3	15	Paris, Omaha	.973	5	36	0	1	1
Crabbe, Iowa	1.000	3	16	0	0	0	Pearson, Nashville	.971	15	127	8	4	6
Cucjen, Louisville	.979	6	41	6	1	6	Powell, Indianapolis	.972	20	133	8	4	8
Daugherty, Oklahoma City*	.992	77	715	54	6	71	J. Reynolds, Nashville	1.000	8	29	5	0	3
DeLos Santos, Omaha	.991	94	841	56	8	74	R. Reynolds, Denver	1.000	1	7	0	0	0
Destrade, Buffalo	.989	19	163	9	2	20	Roenicke, Oklahoma City*	.981	19	141	13	3	16
Distefano, Buffalo*	.976	5	37	3	1	6	Shines, Indianapolis	.992	62	467	35	4	33
Dodd, Omaha	.992	29	236	17	2	21	Smith, Indianapolis	1.000	12	95	9	0	8
Durham, Louisville*	.992	32	240	23	2	24	Stephenson, Iowa*	.991	68	639	51	6	62
Fitzgerald, Louisville	.988	76	601	41	8	46	Tanner, Nashville	.978	38	250	22	6	12
Freeman, Denver*	1.000	2	1	0	0	0	Tullier, Iowa*	1.000	3	9	0	0	0
Garcia, Iowa	.989	27	172	9	2	16	Villanueva, Iowa	.991	39	299	27	3	24
Garman, Oklahoma City	.991	36	307	23	3	44	Williams, Buffalo	.875	1	7	0	0	0
Henderson, Buffalo	.987	54	445	27	6	37	Wrona, Iowa	1.000	5	48	4	0	5
Jelks, Louisville	.992	40	351	19	3	30	Zeile, Louisville	1.000	2	15	1	0	0

Triple Plays—Canale, Jelks.

SECOND BASEMEN

Player and Club	Pct.	G.	PO.	A.	E.	DP.	Player and Club	Pct.	G.	PO.	A.	E.	DP.
Alicea, Louisville	.972	115	240	310	16	62	Lockhart, Nashville	.973	127	279	335	17	63
Bates, Denver	.973	93	192	285	13	65	Mattox, Denver	.982	8	17	39	1	7
Booker, Louisville	1.000	1	0	2	0	0	Meacham, Buffalo	.966	39	58	82	5	14
Burdick, Buffalo	.971	35	79	91	5	20	Mesh, Omaha	.986	32	64	81	2	19
Capra, Omaha	1.000	2	0	1	0	0	Moreno, Indianapolis	.949	48	90	115	11	21
Carrasco, Iowa	.922	26	46	72	10	13	NOBOA, Indianapolis	.986	101	150	262	6	51
Castillo, Denver	.958	5	10	13	1	2	Owen, Iowa	.926	5	10	15	2	2
Castro, Omaha	1.000	2	1	1	0	0	Pankovits, Buffalo	.964	24	48	59	4	19
Coolbaugh, Oklahoma City	1.000	1	3	1	0	1	Pearson, Nashville	.969	9	14	17	1	4
Crabbe, Iowa	1.000	3	8	12	0	2	Pecota, Omaha	.981	12	22	30	1	6
Cruz, Iowa	1.000	1	4	3	0	0	Quinones, Nashville	1.000	3	6	8	0	1
Cucjen, Louisville	1.000	8	7	13	0	3	Robertson, Oklahoma City	.958	49	74	109	8	28
Figueroa, Louisville	1.000	3	2	2	0	0	Rohn, Oklahoma City	.973	110	218	313	15	93
Germann, Nashville	1.000	3	1	1	0	0	Romano, Buffalo	1.000	1	1	0	0	0
Guinn, Iowa	.950	4	5	14	1	3	Rood, Denver	.974	26	46	66	3	14
Harris, Nashville	1.000	8	23	20	0	6	Rossy, Buffalo	1.000	2	1	1	0	1
House, Iowa	.963	31	64	93	6	13	Shumpert, Omaha	.959	112	218	295	22	88
Huson, Indianapolis	.909	3	5	5	1	1	Small, Iowa	.977	84	188	243	10	54
Jackson, Oklahoma City	1.000	7	11	16	0	5	Tanner, Nashville	1.000	8	8	17	0	4
Jirschele, Omaha	1.000	1	1	0	0	0	Wilson, Louisville	.963	38	98	84	7	22
Khalifa, Buffalo	.988	57	128	122	3	39	Xavier, Denver	.991	21	44	65	1	15

Triple Plays—Bates, Wilson.

THIRD BASEMEN

Player and Club	Pct.	G.	PO.	A.	E.	DP.	Player and Club	Pct.	G.	PO.	A.	E.	DP.
Bafia, Iowa	.978	30	16	74	2	10	Madison, Nashville	1.000	3	1	3	0	0
Barnes, Nashville	.833	4	2	3	1	0	Meacham, Buffalo	.800	6	1	11	3	2
Bell, Buffalo	.924	39	33	64	8	5	Merced, Buffalo	1.000	1	0	2	0	0
Berger, Oklahoma City	1.000	4	3	3	0	2	Mesh, Omaha	.000	2	0	0	1	0
BLOWERS, Indianapolis	.930	127	91	214	23	12	Mitchell, Denver	.870	112	66	148	32	18
Booker, Louisville	1.000	8	4	5	0	0	Moreno, Indianapolis	.871	16	9	18	4	2
C. Brown, Buffalo	.907	52	28	69	10	9	Nichols, Iowa	.881	25	22	30	7	2
M. Brown, Nashville	.888	78	45	138	23	7	Owen, Iowa	.931	27	12	42	4	6
Burdick, Buffalo	1.000	2	0	4	0	1	Palacios, Omaha	1.000	5	1	4	0	1
Capra, Omaha	1.000	1	0	2	0	0	Paris, Omaha	.879	12	5	24	4	1
Carrasco, Iowa	.930	39	25	82	8	3	Pearson, Nashville	.938	7	2	13	1	1
Castillo, Denver	1.000	8	2	13	0	2	Pecota, Omaha	1.000	14	12	26	0	6
Castro, Omaha	.941	89	53	172	14	9	Pevey, Indianapolis	1.000	2	0	5	0	0
Coolbaugh, Oklahoma City	.927	140	105	278	30	32	Quinones, Nashville	.883	36	28	63	12	8
Crabbe, Iowa	.926	38	22	78	8	6	Reynolds, Nashville	.750	2	1	2	1	0
Cucjen, Louisville	.945	63	38	116	9	8	Robertson, Oklahoma City	.800	3	0	4	1	0
DeLos Santos, Omaha	.667	2	1	1	1	0	Rohn, Oklahoma City	1.000	1	0	1	0	1
Garcia, Iowa	1.000	2	1	2	0	1	Rood, Denver	.949	23	17	39	3	2
Garman, Oklahoma City	1.000	2	1	2	0	0	Sabo, Nashville	.923	5	7	5	1	0
Germann, Nashville	1.000	1	0	1	0	0	Scott, Denver	.833	4	3	2	1	0
Jackson, Omaha	.899	25	12	50	7	2	Shines, Indianapolis	.917	4	1	10	1	0
Jelks, Louisville	.872	47	31	85	17	3	Small, Iowa	1.000	1	1	0	0	0
Jirschele, Omaha	.971	9	7	26	1	0	Smith, Denver	1.000	5	5	7	0	0
Jurak, Indianapolis	1.000	1	0	6	0	1	Tanner, Nashville	.970	19	9	23	1	3
Khalifa, Buffalo	.976	15	15	25	1	3	Wilson, Louisville	.900	38	32	67	11	9
King, Buffalo	.873	18	8	40	7	3	Xavier, Denver	1.000	13	4	17	0	2
Little, Buffalo	.853	33	15	43	10	3	Zeile, Louisville	.900	5	3	6	1	1

Triple Play—Mitchell.

SHORTSTOPS

Player and Club	Pct.	G.	PO.	A.	E.	DP.
Bell, Buffalo	.967	55	77	159	8	27
Benavides, Nashville	.942	29	40	73	7	13
Booker, Louisville	.961	85	119	225	14	42
Brown, Nashville	1.000	5	8	9	0	3
Capra, Omaha	.929	17	26	53	6	9
Carrasco, Iowa	1.000	1	0	1	0	0
Castro, Omaha	.867	5	5	8	2	1
Cucjen, Louisville	.929	20	29	50	6	9
DeShields, Indianapolis	.930	46	73	101	13	21
Diaz, Denver	.955	104	198	307	24	70
Escobar, Omaha	.957	23	22	66	4	13
Figueroa, Louisville	.955	68	85	172	12	24
Germann, Nashville	1.000	4	0	3	0	0
Guinn, Iowa	.940	113	165	334	32	64
Huson, Indianapolis	.955	85	134	209	16	46
C. Jackson, Omaha	1.000	1	2	4	0	0
K. Jackson, Oklahoma City	1.000	6	6	10	0	1
Khalifa, Buffalo	.965	21	24	58	3	11
Larkin, Nashville	1.000	2	1	3	0	2
Mattox, Denver	1.000	1	0	1	0	0
Meacham, Buffalo	.944	50	76	127	12	38
Mesh, Omaha	.938	40	66	115	12	26
Mitchell, Denver	1.000	2	0	1	0	0
Noboa, Indianapolis	.940	16	20	43	4	4
Norman, Indianapolis	1.000	3	6	9	0	4
Owen, Iowa	.933	38	58	96	11	16
Paris, Omaha	.933	31	45	80	9	18
Pearson, Nashville	.936	20	32	41	5	10
Pecota, Omaha	.968	43	61	150	7	22
Quinones, Nashville	.889	3	4	4	1	1
Richardson, Nashville	.956	88	132	218	16	47
Robertson, Oklahoma City	.977	12	11	31	1	9
Rood, Denver	.875	4	8	6	2	1
Rossy, Buffalo	.961	31	54	93	6	11
SANCHEZ, Oklahoma City	.958	133	237	418	29	104
Sheffield, Denver	1.000	2	2	6	0	1
Small, Iowa	1.000	1	1	1	0	0
Spiers, Denver	.970	14	32	33	2	10
Tanner, Nashville	.952	16	17	23	2	4
Xavier, Denver	.958	28	45	69	5	12

OUTFIELDERS

Player and Club	Pct.	G.	PO.	A.	E.	DP.
Aldrete, Indianapolis*	1.000	5	6	0	0	0
Bafia, Iowa	1.000	3	4	1	0	1
Baine, Louisville	.987	112	220	12	3	2
Barnes, Nashville	.978	105	208	12	5	0
Berger, Oklahoma City	.965	50	80	3	3	0
Bosley, Oklahoma City*	.974	20	35	2	1	0
Braun, Indianapolis	.978	25	42	3	1	0
Brown, Nashville	1.000	20	38	4	0	1
Bundy, Indianapolis	1.000	3	2	0	0	0
Byers, Louisville	.983	69	119	0	2	0
Capra, Omaha	.973	113	210	8	6	2
Carrillo, Denver*	.973	118	235	15	7	3
Carter, Buffalo	.970	90	188	3	6	0
Castro, Omaha	1.000	1	1	0	0	0
Cole, Louisville*	.977	127	320	14	8	2
Cook, Buffalo	.978	81	173	4	4	0
Dascenzo, Iowa*	.980	110	273	15	6	4
Daugherty, Oklahoma City*	1.000	5	13	0	0	0
Dean, Indianapolis	.977	73	169	3	4	2
Destrade, Buffalo	1.000	2	2	0	0	0
Dodd, Omaha	.964	60	101	5	4	0
Dunbar, Omaha*	1.000	25	41	1	0	0
Durham, Louisville*	1.000	6	6	0	0	0
Ficklin, Iowa	.980	56	96	3	2	1
Freeman, 28 Den-49 OKC	.953	77	111	10	6	3
Grissom, Indianapolis	1.000	48	106	5	0	0
Hall, Buffalo	.985	86	191	2	3	0
HAMILTON, Denver	1.000	128	263	11	0	2
Hayden, Nashville*	.979	59	92	2	2	0
Henderson, Buffalo	1.000	16	19	1	0	0
Hill, Iowa	.980	29	48	2	1	0
House, Iowa	.959	97	159	3	7	0
Huson, Indianapolis	1.000	10	33	0	0	0
Jackson, Iowa	1.000	29	66	12	0	3
Jelks, Louisville	1.000	16	21	1	0	0
C. Jones, Nashville	.962	17	25	0	1	0
R. Jones, Oklahoma City*	1.000	11	10	1	0	0
Landrum, Nashville	.984	57	118	2	2	1
Lindeman, Louisville	.978	28	39	5	1	1
Little, Buffalo	.981	33	43	8	1	0
Loggins, Omaha*	.982	100	209	10	4	2
Madison, Nashville	1.000	4	5	0	0	0
McClendon, Iowa	.880	8	22	0	3	0
McGee, Louisville	.955	8	20	1	1	0
Mendez, Louisville*	1.000	9	14	0	0	0
Merced, Buffalo	.913	15	18	3	2	0
Mesh, Omaha	.968	19	29	1	1	1
Monico, Denver*	.926	34	49	1	4	0
Moore, Indianapolis*	1.000	12	12	0	0	0
Moreno, Indianapolis	.926	13	21	4	2	0
Motley, Indianapolis	.983	68	113	4	2	1
Nichols, Iowa	.963	18	24	2	1	0
O'Neill, Nashville*	1.000	4	7	1	0	1
Palacios, Omaha	1.000	1	4	0	0	0
Pearson, Nashville	.933	14	14	0	1	0
Pecota, Omaha	1.000	1	1	0	0	0
Powell, Indianapolis	.994	95	167	7	1	1
Pulliam, Omaha	1.000	7	12	1	0	1
Reimer, Oklahoma City	.926	44	73	2	6	0
Reynolds, Nashville	.968	43	58	3	2	0
Roenicke, Oklahoma City*	.981	88	193	9	4	2
Romano, Buffalo	.951	35	77	1	4	1
Rood, Denver	1.000	2	1	0	0	0
Roomes, Nashville	.983	25	57	2	1	1
Schulz, Omaha	.979	77	132	6	3	2
Shepherd, Louisville	.975	96	152	4	4	1
Simmons, Louisville	1.000	5	10	0	0	0
Smith, Iowa	.911	21	39	2	4	0
Snider, Nashville	.970	107	244	15	8	5
Sosa, Oklahoma City	.917	10	22	0	2	0
St. Laurent, Oklahoma City	.989	104	176	9	2	1
Steels, Indianapolis*	1.000	2	4	0	0	1
Stephenson, Iowa*	.900	8	9	0	1	0
Stone, Oklahoma City	.857	4	6	0	1	0
Tanner, Nashville	.933	11	13	1	1	0
Thornton, Buffalo	.981	27	48	3	1	0
Threadgill, Oklahoma City	.959	39	71	0	3	0
Thurman, Omaha	.946	15	34	1	2	1
Tullier, Iowa*	.958	43	87	5	4	1
Varsho, Iowa	.959	31	67	4	3	3
Vaughn, Denver	.980	89	140	4	3	2
B. Walker, Nashville	.962	17	24	1	1	0
L. Walker, Indianapolis	.959	110	241	18	11	2
Walters, Denver	1.000	23	36	2	0	0
Walton, Iowa	1.000	4	8	0	0	0
Williams, Buffalo	.977	80	167	4	4	1
Wilson, 53 OKC-44 Den	.980	97	194	7	4	1
Winters, Omaha	.981	54	100	3	2	0

CATCHERS

Player and Club	Pct.	G.	PO.	A.	E.	DP.	PB.
Berger, Oklahoma City	.982	30	153	9	3	0	1
Berryhill, Iowa	.957	7	40	5	2	0	0
Bilardello, Buffalo	.982	65	351	33	7	5	2
Burrell, Indianapolis	.978	68	413	22	10	1	4
Duke, Indianapolis	.968	22	110	10	4	2	0
Fox, Louisville	.991	19	103	5	1	2	3
Garcia, Iowa	1.000	2	5	1	0	0	0
Gibbons, Oklahoma City	.983	56	303	45	6	7	5
Girardi, Iowa	.995	30	172	21	1	0	2
Gwosdz, Nashville	.935	11	23	6	2	1	0
Hall, Buffalo	.961	19	70	3	3	2	0
Hearn, Omaha	.980	62	409	30	9	8	8
Jones, Denver	.978	33	125	10	3	1	5
Kreuter, Oklahoma City	.988	21	146	14	2	2	2
LaValliere, Buffalo	1.000	5	15	1	0	0	0
Little, Buffalo	.971	12	56	11	2	2	5
Loy, Oklahoma City	.992	48	223	29	2	3	1
McClendon, Iowa	1.000	2	10	0	0	0	0
McGriff, Nashville	.985	88	534	74	9	10	8
Mitchell, Denver	.951	18	89	8	5	0	2
Oliver, Nashville	.970	62	384	37	13	5	6
Palacios, Omaha	.972	28	159	16	5	3	2
Pevey, Indianapolis	.982	26	151	12	3	1	3
Prince, Buffalo	.985	62	312	22	5	1	2
Pryor, Indianapolis	1.000	1	2	0	0	0	0
Puzey, Louisville	.991	32	199	15	2	1	2
Reyes, Indianapolis	.988	103	647	86	9	10	11
Reynolds, Denver	1.000	5	24	3	0	0	0
Rodriguez, Denver	1.000	12	71	7	0	1	1
Rohn, Oklahoma City	1.000	1	7	2	0	1	0
Rossy, Buffalo	1.000	4	30	4	0	0	5
Scott, Denver	.983	103	543	80	11	9	15
Villanueva, Iowa	.989	61	319	40	4	3	3
Wine, Indianapolis	.981	11	46	5	1	2	1
Wrona, Nashville	.982	54	292	37	6	8	5
ZEILE, Louisville	.992	101	565	64	5	6	17

PITCHERS

Player and Club	Pct.	G.	PO.	A.	E.	DP.
Akerfelds, Oklahoma City	.909	33	9	11	2	2
Alba, Louisville*	.875	50	6	15	3	1
Aldrich, Denver	1.000	31	4	8	0	0
Anderson, Indianapolis	.926	29	14	11	2	0
Appier, Omaha	.935	22	9	20	2	0
Armstrong, Nashville	.918	25	15	41	5	1

PITCHERS—Continued

Player and Club	Pct.	G.	PO.	A.	E.	DP.
Arnold, Louisville	.842	34	9	7	3	0
Arnsberg, Oklahoma City	1.000	18	12	23	0	1
August, Denver	1.000	4	3	3	0	1
Baller, Indianapolis	.857	62	6	6	2	1
Barfield, Oklahoma City*	.966	28	15	41	2	4
Barnes, Indianapolis	1.000	1	0	3	0	0
Barrett, Indianapolis	1.000	8	3	1	0	0
Belinda, Buffalo	.800	19	1	7	2	1
Birkbeck, Denver	1.000	5	2	5	0	1
Blankenship, Iowa	.907	35	9	30	4	2
Brown, Nashville	.981	29	19	32	1	1
Buchanan, Omaha*	.917	27	4	40	4	1
Capel, Iowa	.840	64	7	14	4	0
Carpenter, Louisville	1.000	27	1	4	0	0
Clarke, Omaha*	1.000	26	5	20	0	1
Cliburn, Oklahoma City	1.000	4	2	0	0	0
Coffman, Iowa	.800	14	0	4	1	1
Conroy, Buffalo*	1.000	3	1	4	0	0
M. Costello, Denver	1.000	18	4	10	0	0
Crawford, Omaha	1.000	22	4	6	0	0
Crouch, Omaha	1.000	8	3	3	0	0
Damian, Iowa	1.000	41	12	20	0	1
Dawley, Denver	.750	11	1	2	1	0
Dedmon, Indianapolis	.971	51	11	23	1	0
DeJesus, Omaha	.882	31	5	10	2	0
Dixon, Indianapolis	.833	27	3	7	2	0
Easley, Buffalo	1.000	28	3	8	0	0
Encarnacion, Omaha	1.000	31	3	4	0	0
Erickson, Louisville	1.000	27	6	13	0	1
Farmer, Indianapolis	.667	1	2	0	1	0
Fassero, Louisville	1.000	22	5	18	0	0
Figueroa, Louisville	1.000	1	1	0	0	0
Filer, Denver	.971	12	8	25	1	2
Fireovid, Omaha	.979	26	12	35	1	2
Fisher, Buffalo	1.000	5	2	4	0	0
Fossas, Denver*	1.000	24	2	6	0	1
Fowlkes, Iowa	1.000	13	9	15	0	0
Frey, Indianapolis*	1.000	21	2	0	0	0
Gakeler, Indianapolis	.833	11	5	10	3	0
Garcia, Buffalo*	1.000	31	5	10	0	1
Gardner, Indianapolis	.857	24	8	22	5	2
Gideon, Indianapolis	.941	47	5	11	1	1
Gleaton, Omaha*	.900	24	1	8	1	0
Gray, Nashville	1.000	44	11	13	0	1
Griffin, Nashville	.971	41	5	29	1	3
Hagen, Oklahoma City	1.000	4	0	2	0	0
Hall, Oklahoma City*	1.000	11	2	3	0	0
Hammond, Nashville*	.941	24	6	26	2	2
Harkey, Iowa	.938	12	6	9	1	1
Harris, Indianapolis	.750	6	0	3	1	0
Heinkel, Louisville	1.000	2	2	0	0	0
Hill, Louisville	1.000	3	0	3	0	0
Hilton, Louisville	.944	70	9	8	1	0
Horton, Louisville*	1.000	2	0	6	0	1
Jeffcoat, Oklahoma City*	.917	11	1	10	1	0
Johnson, Indianapolis*	1.000	3	0	2	0	0
Jones, Denver	.958	28	7	16	1	1
Kemp, Nashville	1.000	28	10	17	0	0
Kilgus, Iowa*	1.000	1	0	1	0	0
Kinnunen, Denver*	1.000	3	0	1	0	0
Kinzer, Louisville	.900	51	5	4	1	1
Kraemer, Iowa*	.969	27	8	23	1	1
Kramer, Buffalo	.833	5	0	5	1	0
Krawczyk, Denver	.846	43	5	17	4	1
Krueger, Denver*	1.000	2	2	1	0	0
Lancaster, Iowa	.962	17	8	17	1	2
Landrum, Buffalo	1.000	5	1	3	0	0
Lankard, Oklahoma City	1.000	10	1	2	0	0
Laskey, Omaha	1.000	14	8	5	0	1
Lind, Buffalo	1.000	31	4	15	0	2
Lopez, Nashville	.900	26	6	12	2	1
Luecken, Omaha	1.000	36	2	10	0	0
Lugo, Indianapolis	1.000	22	4	21	0	3
Lynch, Oklahoma City*	1.000	11	2	1	0	0
Madden, Buffalo*	.976	26	16	24	1	3
Masters, Iowa	1.000	4	1	2	0	0
May, 18 OkC-12 Den	.935	30	9	20	2	0
McGrath, Louisville	.941	21	7	9	1	0
McKeon, Indianapolis*	1.000	28	2	2	0	0
McMurtry, Oklahoma City	1.000	1	0	2	0	0
Medvin, Oklahoma City	.938	54	3	12	1	0
Melton, Buffalo	1.000	9	3	2	0	0
Mielke, Oklahoma City	.929	18	3	10	1	0
Miller, Oklahoma City	.979	27	17	29	1	2
Mitchell, Nashville	1.000	39	10	21	0	0
Moore, Omaha	1.000	7	0	1	0	0
Navarro, Denver	1.000	3	1	3	0	0
Nieves, Denver*	1.000	3	0	1	0	0
Oelkers, Louisville*	.857	18	7	17	4	0
Olwine, Omaha*	.957	53	9	13	1	2
Pacillo, Indianapolis	.931	20	9	18	2	2
Palacios, Buffalo	1.000	2	0	2	0	0
Parker, Iowa*	1.000	19	2	6	0	0
Patterson, Buffalo*	1.000	31	10	34	0	4
Pavlas, Oklahoma City*	.960	29	6	18	1	1
Peterek, Denver	1.000	23	6	32	0	0
Peters, Louisville*	.933	65	1	13	1	0
Petkovsek, Oklahoma City	.909	6	5	5	1	2
Pico, Iowa	1.000	2	1	0	0	0
Potestio, Louisville	1.000	22	2	7	0	0
Power, Iowa*	.833	8	1	4	1	0
Puig, Denver*	1.000	12	0	1	0	0
Reed, Buffalo	.778	20	6	8	4	1
Ritter, Iowa	.875	12	0	7	1	0
Robinson, Nashville	1.000	3	1	4	0	0
Roesler, Nashville	.667	40	2	2	2	0
Rucker, Buffalo*	1.000	24	1	5	0	1
Sadler, Denver	.929	28	16	36	4	3
Samuels, Denver*	1.000	19	1	6	0	0
Sauveur, Indianapolis*	1.000	8	0	1	0	0
Scherrer, Oklahoma City*	1.000	5	0	2	0	1
Scudder, Nashville	1.000	12	3	10	0	1
Sebra, Nashville	1.000	11	2	2	0	0
Sellers, Nashville	1.000	1	1	1	0	0
Simmons, 26 Den-13 OkC	.917	39	1	10	1	0
Smith, Buffalo	1.000	9	0	2	0	0
Spratke, Omaha	.944	33	7	10	1	1
Stapleton, Denver*	.947	34	3	15	1	0
Stoddard, Denver	.926	42	7	18	2	2
Stottlemyre, Omaha	1.000	7	1	1	0	0
Taylor, Buffalo	.935	25	16	27	3	1
TEWKSBURY, Louisville	1.000	28	11	46	0	1
Thompson, Indianapolis	.957	23	11	34	2	1
Valdez, Indianapolis	.813	19	4	9	3	1
Vande Berg, Iowa*	.885	69	6	17	3	0
Vasquez, Nashville	.976	29	13	28	1	1
Veres, Denver	.900	17	3	15	2	1
Waddell, 1 Ind-6 Den	1.000	7	0	1	0	0
Walker, Buffalo	.750	3	1	2	1	0
Watkins, Denver	1.000	7	0	2	0	1
Whitaker, Oklahoma City	1.000	38	9	10	0	1
Wilkins, Iowa	.974	38	10	27	1	2
Wilkinson, Buffalo*	1.000	21	6	11	0	2
Williams, Iowa	.944	27	3	14	1	2
Wilmet, Oklahoma City	.920	55	7	16	2	1
York, Buffalo	1.000	8	1	7	0	0

The following players did not have any fielding statistics at the positions indicated or appeared only as a designated hitter, pinch-hitter or pinch-runner: Bates, of; Berger, ss; Blowers, ss; Bruno, p; Campbell, p; Canale, 3b; Castro, p; J. Costello, p; Cruz, of; Dodd, 3b; Fox, 1b; Hearn, 1b; Hesketh, p; Houston, 2b; Jirschele, ss; J. Jones, 3b; Little, 2b; Mathews, p; Meacham, 1b; Murphy, ph; Norman, 3b; Owen, of; Parmenter, p; Perry, p; Pevey, 1b; Puzey, p; Pyznarski, dh, ph; Scheid, p; Tanner, p; Tullier, p; Villanueva, 3b, of, p; Worrell, p; Wrona, of; Xavier, of, p.

CLUB PITCHING

Club	ERA.	G.	CG.	ShO.	Sv.	IP.	H.	R.	ER.	HR.	HB.	BB.	Int. BB.	SO.	WP.	Bk.
Indianapolis	2.80	146	11	10	50	1259.2	1070	489	392	57	40	455	20	912	50	10
Omaha	3.44	146	19	12	37	1290.1	1212	582	493	75	29	418	20	946	62	23
Buffalo	3.57	142	17	8	45	1222.0	1155	574	485	97	32	475	24	800	69	20
Louisville	3.76	145	6	11	39	1270.0	1228	628	530	86	40	493	32	822	56	25
Nashville	3.82	146	30	17	27	1278.0	1192	624	542	78	28	563	35	905	58	17
Iowa	3.89	144	19	11	23	1257.0	1263	652	544	82	44	492	29	794	74	20
Oklahoma City	3.96	145	31	12	27	1273.2	1297	656	561	78	48	467	41	800	65	19
Denver	4.18	146	15	7	42	1262.2	1345	674	587	88	31	533	31	831	65	19

PITCHERS' RECORDS
(Leading Qualifiers for Earned-Run Average Leadership — 117 or More Innings)

*Throws lefthanded.

Pitcher—Club	W.	L.	Pct.	ERA.	G.	GS.	CG.	GF.	ShO.	Sv.	IP.	H.	R.	ER.	HR.	HB.	BB.	Int. BB.	SO.	WP.
Thompson, Indianapolis	9	6	.600	2.06	23	23	3	0	2	0	161.1	146	46	37	3	4	37	0	73	1
Gardner, Indianapolis	12	4	.750	2.37	24	23	4	1	2	0	163.1	122	51	43	3	5	59	1	175	7
Tewksbury, Louisville	13	5	.722	2.43	28	28	2	1	1	0	189.0	170	63	51	9	2	34	1	72	1
Taylor, Buffalo	10	8	.556	2.58	25	25	5	0	2	0	170.2	145	61	49	15	4	51	2	103	4

Pitcher—Club	W.	L.	Pct.	ERA.	G.	GS.	CG.	GF.	ShO.	Sv.	IP.	H.	R.	ER.	HR.	HB.	BB.	Int. BB.	SO.	WP.
Armstrong, Nashville	13	9	.591	2.91	25	24	12	0	6	0	182.2	144	63	59	10	6	58	2	152	5
Lugo, Indianapolis	12	4	.750	2.94	22	21	0	0	0	0	122.1	100	53	40	8	1	41	1	79	3
Anderson, Indianapolis	7	8	.467	3.17	29	19	1	3	0	0	127.2	139	62	45	7	4	44	1	88	5
Buchanan, Omaha*	8	9	.471	3.35	27	24	3	1	2	0	164.0	150	70	61	8	0	49	2	104	8
Patterson, Buffalo*	12	6	.667	3.35	31	25	4	3	1	1	177.1	177	69	66	13	2	35	2	103	3
Hammond, Nashville*	11	7	.611	3.38	24	24	3	0	1	0	157.1	144	69	59	7	3	96	1	142	9

Departmental Leaders: G—Hilton, 70; W—Armstrong, Blankenship, Fireovid, Tewksbury, 13; L—Pavlas, 14; Pct.—Gardner, Lugo, .750; GS—Vasquez, 29; CG—Armstrong, 12; GF—Baller, 59; ShO—Armstrong, 6; Sv.—Baller, 34; IP—Tewksbury, 189.0; H—Miller, 188; R—May, 107; ER—May, 89; HR—Taylor, 15; HB—Arnold, 12; BB—DeJesus, 98; IBB—Medvin, 9; SO—Gardner, 175; WP—Medvin, 18.

(All Pitchers—Listed Alphabetically)

Pitcher—Club	W.	L.	Pct.	ERA.	G.	GS.	CG.	GF.	ShO.	Sv.	IP.	H.	R.	ER.	HR.	HB.	BB.	Int. BB.	SO.	WP.
Akerfelds, Oklahoma City	5	5	.500	3.33	33	11	1	15	0	4	108.0	89	45	40	5	4	59	5	75	5
Alba, Louisville*	7	6	.538	3.61	50	11	0	12	0	1	104.2	68	45	42	6	6	65	2	109	5
Aldrich, Denver	2	4	.333	2.74	31	0	0	29	0	15	42.2	44	15	13	3	4	13	2	24	0
Anderson, Indianapolis	7	8	.467	3.17	29	19	1	3	0	0	127.2	139	62	45	7	4	44	1	88	5
Appier, Omaha	8	8	.500	3.95	22	22	3	0	2	0	139.0	141	70	61	6	2	42	1	109	5
Armstrong, Nashville	13	9	.591	2.91	25	24	12	0	6	0	182.2	144	63	59	10	6	58	2	152	5
Arnold, Louisville	8	10	.444	3.97	34	22	2	5	1	0	147.1	130	78	65	11	12	61	0	88	7
Arnsberg, Oklahoma City	6	8	.429	4.06	18	18	4	0	1	0	115.1	117	58	52	6	6	34	1	61	4
August, Denver	1	1	.500	4.94	4	4	0	0	0	0	23.2	35	18	13	3	1	5	0	12	1
Baller, Indianapolis	1	5	.167	2.02	62	0	0	59	0	34	62.1	49	19	14	3	1	20	2	53	1
Barfield, Oklahoma City*	10	8	.556	4.06	28	28	7	0	3	0	175.1	178	93	79	14	2	68	2	58	11
Barnes, Indianapolis*	1	0	1.000	1.50	1	1	0	0	0	0	6.0	5	1	1	0	0	2	0	5	0
Barrett, Indianapolis	1	3	.250	9.56	8	3	0	1	0	0	16.0	19	17	17	5	1	19	1	8	2
Belinda, Buffalo	2	2	.500	0.95	19	0	0	15	0	9	28.1	13	5	3	1	2	13	3	28	1
Birkbeck, Denver	2	2	.500	3.04	5	5	0	0	0	0	23.2	26	9	8	2	0	10	1	9	2
Blankenship, Iowa	13	7	.650	3.72	35	26	5	2	1	0	162.0	155	79	67	10	4	79	5	110	12
Brown, Nashville	8	13	.381	4.80	29	27	4	0	2	0	161.1	171	99	86	13	1	51	2	85	5
Bruno, Nashville	0	1	.000	9.00	4	0	0	1	0	1	5.0	6	5	5	0	0	2	0	4	0
Buchanan, Omaha*	8	9	.471	3.35	27	24	3	1	2	0	164.0	150	70	61	8	0	49	2	104	8
Campbell, Indianapolis	1	0	1.000	4.00	9	3	0	0	0	0	27.0	23	12	12	3	0	4	0	18	1
Capel, Iowa	4	7	.364	3.25	64	0	0	28	0	5	97.0	87	43	35	9	3	41	6	62	7
Carpenter, Louisville	5	3	.625	3.19	27	0	0	23	0	11	36.2	39	17	13	3	0	9	3	29	1
Castro, Omaha	0	0	.000	4.50	2	0	0	2	0	0	2.0	2	1	1	0	0	1	0	0	1
Clarke, Omaha*	12	6	.667	3.51	26	24	8	1	1	0	171.2	157	72	67	12	3	31	1	145	4
Cliburn, Oklahoma City	0	0	.000	4.63	4	1	0	0	0	0	11.2	16	6	6	0	0	1	0	8	2
Coffman, Iowa	0	2	.000	8.15	14	1	0	5	0	0	17.2	17	19	16	3	0	26	1	11	3
Conroy, Buffalo*	0	1	.000	7.71	3	3	0	0	0	0	11.2	15	10	10	0	1	9	0	5	4
J. Costello, Louisville	0	0	.000	1.80	4	0	0	2	0	1	5.0	5	1	1	0	0	1	0	4	0
M. Costello, Denver	1	7	.125	6.03	18	10	0	5	0	1	68.2	85	50	46	6	1	36	2	32	5
Crawford, Omaha	3	1	.750	2.93	22	0	0	6	0	2	43.0	41	18	14	6	2	9	1	32	1
Crouch, Omaha	0	5	.000	6.69	8	8	0	0	0	0	39.0	49	31	29	2	1	11	0	19	5
Damian, Iowa	4	12	.250	4.36	41	19	1	10	0	2	150.2	173	88	73	12	2	27	1	95	3
Dawley, Denver	0	0	.000	6.05	11	0	0	4	0	0	19.1	30	15	13	4	0	6	0	12	0
Dedmon, Indianapolis	8	6	.571	2.71	51	1	0	19	0	2	83.0	71	32	25	3	4	33	3	41	8
DeJesus, Omaha	8	11	.421	3.78	31	21	2	7	0	1	145.1	112	78	61	9	6	98	1	158	11
Dixon, Indianapolis	3	2	.600	2.48	27	4	0	7	0	1	54.1	45	20	15	2	0	18	0	31	0
Easley, Buffalo	4	1	.800	4.28	28	0	0	21	0	13	33.2	37	16	16	2	1	7	0	19	1
Encarnacion, Omaha	3	5	.375	1.78	31	0	0	25	0	5	50.2	39	10	10	2	0	18	6	41	1
Erickson, Louisville	1	2	.333	3.59	27	3	0	9	0	0	57.2	66	27	23	3	3	12	2	26	0
Farmer, Indianapolis	1	0	1.000	0.00	1	1	0	0	0	0	7.0	3	1	0	0	0	3	0	3	0
Fassero, Louisville*	3	10	.231	5.22	22	19	0	0	0	0	112.0	136	79	65	13	2	47	1	73	8
Figueroa, Louisville	0	0	.000	9.00	1	0	0	1	0	0	1.0	2	2	1	0	1	1	0	1	0
Filer, Denver	5	1	.833	2.80	12	12	1	0	0	0	83.2	77	28	26	3	4	14	1	34	3
Fireovid, Omaha	13	8	.619	3.45	26	26	3	0	1	0	154.0	164	70	59	9	3	27	0	59	4
Fisher, Buffalo	3	0	1.000	5.14	5	5	0	0	0	0	28.0	30	17	16	5	0	7	0	15	0
Fossas, Denver*	5	1	.833	2.04	24	1	0	7	0	6	35.1	27	9	8	0	1	11	1	35	2
Fowlkes, Iowa	4	4	.500	2.93	13	13	2	0	0	0	86.0	77	37	28	7	8	16	0	55	1
Frey, Indianapolis*	2	1	.667	1.78	21	0	0	8	0	3	25.1	18	7	5	1	0	6	0	23	0
Gakeler, Indianapolis	3	6	.333	3.12	11	11	1	0	0	0	66.1	53	29	23	1	3	28	1	41	4
Garcia, Buffalo*	6	2	.750	4.37	31	1	0	10	0	0	59.2	64	39	29	3	0	29	1	54	4
Gardner, Indianapolis	12	4	.750	2.37	24	23	4	1	2	0	163.1	122	51	43	3	5	59	1	175	7
Gideon, Indianapolis	7	2	.778	2.26	47	0	0	20	0	5	71.2	41	24	18	4	6	23	4	71	4
Gleaton, Omaha*	3	3	.500	1.11	24	1	0	9	0	4	56.2	40	12	7	0	0	22	1	57	3
Gray, Nashville	4	4	.500	3.66	44	0	0	33	0	7	66.1	76	33	27	3	0	12	3	58	3
Griffin, Nashville	2	3	.400	2.30	41	0	0	14	0	6	74.1	66	25	19	2	3	28	6	54	4
Hagen, Oklahoma City	0	0	.000	14.54	4	0	0	3	0	0	4.1	7	7	7	0	1	3	0	2	0
Hall, Oklahoma City*	1	0	1.000	1.53	11	0	0	7	0	5	17.2	7	3	3	0	1	6	0	18	1
Hammond, Nashville*	11	7	.611	3.38	24	24	3	0	1	0	157.1	144	69	59	7	3	96	1	142	9
Harkey, Iowa	2	7	.222	4.43	12	12	0	0	0	0	63.0	67	37	31	7	3	25	0	37	3
Harris, Indianapolis	2	0	1.000	0.00	6	0	0	4	0	2	11.0	4	0	0	0	0	10	1	9	0
Heinkel, Louisville	1	1	.500	4.38	2	2	0	0	0	0	12.1	11	7	6	2	0	6	0	12	1
Hesketh, Indianapolis*	0	0	.000	3.86	5	1	0	3	0	1	9.1	11	4	4	0	0	5	0	9	1
Hill, Louisville	0	2	.000	3.50	3	3	0	0	0	0	18.0	13	8	7	1	0	10	0	18	1
Hilton, Louisville	12	5	.706	3.74	70	0	0	22	0	1	96.1	86	44	40	7	1	42	7	77	2
Horton, Louisville*	1	0	1.000	1.00	2	2	0	0	0	0	9.0	8	1	1	0	0	2	0	7	0
Jeffcoat, Oklahoma City*	4	4	.500	3.22	11	11	0	0	0	0	72.2	81	31	26	1	1	21	1	50	1
Johnson, Indianapolis*	1	1	.500	2.00	3	3	0	0	0	0	18.0	13	5	4	0	1	9	0	17	0
Jones, Denver	6	6	.500	4.11	28	14	0	11	0	4	100.2	102	50	46	9	3	59	5	77	4
Kemp, Nashville	6	9	.400	5.34	28	21	2	4	0	1	123.0	121	87	73	8	3	71	5	64	9
Kilgus, Iowa	1	0	1.000	3.00	1	1	1	0	0	0	9.0	9	3	3	0	2	0	0	5	2
Kinnunen, Denver*	0	1	.000	5.40	3	0	0	1	0	0	1.2	2	1	1	0	0	3	0	2	0
Kinzer, Louisville	1	4	.200	3.25	51	0	0	30	0	15	72.0	69	28	26	5	1	14	3	62	2
Kraemer, Iowa*	8	10	.444	3.47	27	27	7	0	3	0	181.2	180	81	70	7	4	50	0	113	5
Kramer, Buffalo	1	0	1.000	1.26	5	2	0	2	0	0	14.1	15	5	2	0	0	7	1	8	2
Krawczyk, Denver	2	6	.250	3.47	43	2	1	15	0	4	93.1	109	45	36	5	0	34	2	85	4
Krueger, Denver*	1	1	.500	2.03	2	2	0	0	0	0	13.1	10	4	3	1	0	6	0	9	0
Lancaster, Iowa	5	7	.417	2.66	17	14	3	0	2	0	91.1	76	38	27	6	3	43	0	56	2
Landrum, Buffalo	3	0	1.000	0.71	5	3	1	1	0	0	25.1	16	2	2	0	0	8	0	20	0
Lankard, Oklahoma City	0	0	.000	7.41	10	0	0	9	0	0	17.0	24	14	14	0	0	8	1	6	0
Laskey, Omaha	4	4	.500	3.38	14	13	0	1	0	0	77.1	83	38	29	3	1	20	0	53	0
Lind, Buffalo	3	4	.429	5.43	31	5	0	8	0	2	71.1	80	50	43	11	3	33	2	45	8

Pitcher—Club	W.	L.	Pct.	ERA.	G.	GS.	CG.	GF.	ShO.	Sv.	IP.	H.	R.	ER.	HR.	HB.	BB.	Int. BB.	SO.	WP.
Lopez, Nashville	4	3	.571	4.61	26	4	0	5	0	0	68.1	67	39	35	5	2	26	2	39	2
Luecken, Omaha	4	1	.800	2.31	36	0	0	29	0	16	46.2	33	14	12	0	1	22	0	39	6
Lugo, Indianapolis	12	4	.750	2.94	22	21	0	0	0	0	122.1	100	53	40	8	1	41	1	79	3
Lynch, Oklahoma City*	0	2	.000	6.17	11	0	0	5	0	0	11.2	12	8	8	1	0	8	1	10	3
Madden, Buffalo*	12	8	.600	3.39	26	20	2	1	1	1	130.0	117	66	49	9	3	63	0	94	5
Masters, Iowa	0	1	.000	6.52	4	4	0	0	0	0	19.1	21	17	14	1	0	18	0	22	3
Mathews, Louisville*	0	0	.000	Infin.	1	1	0	0	0	0	0.0	0	1	1	0	0	1	0	0	0
May, 17 OkC-12 Den	9	13	.409	4.44	29	28	5	0	2	0	180.1	180	107	89	10	7	79	7	129	9
McGrath, Louisville	6	7	.462	3.63	21	18	0	0	0	0	111.2	129	58	45	5	4	36	4	51	5
McKeon, Indianapolis*	4	2	.667	3.96	28	0	0	2	0	0	25.0	26	11	11	1	0	13	1	22	1
McMurtry, Oklahoma City	0	0	.000	3.00	1	0	0	1	0	0	3.0	2	1	1	0	1	0	1	0	0
Medvin, Buffalo	7	6	.538	2.30	54	1	0	34	0	16	86.0	65	29	22	6	3	46	9	84	18
Melton, Buffalo	1	2	.333	6.65	9	1	0	3	0	0	21.2	25	18	16	4	4	15	0	8	1
Mielke, Oklahoma City	3	3	.500	1.11	18	0	0	11	0	4	40.2	28	7	5	2	1	10	3	40	1
Miller, Oklahoma City	9	13	.409	4.13	27	27	10	0	3	0	176.1	188	88	81	13	9	43	6	98	7
Mitchell, Nashville	1	3	.250	3.81	39	1	0	21	0	0	85.0	79	42	36	9	3	26	8	48	7
Moore, Omaha	1	2	.333	6.39	7	0	0	3	0	0	12.2	17	11	9	3	0	3	1	12	2
Navarro, Denver	1	1	.500	3.60	3	3	1	0	0	0	20.0	24	8	8	0	0	7	2	17	0
Nieves, Denver*	2	1	.667	6.43	3	3	0	0	0	0	14.0	9	10	10	1	0	11	0	8	0
Oelkers, Louisville*	6	6	.500	5.68	18	18	1	0	0	0	101.1	107	73	64	9	1	48	0	49	12
Olwine, Omaha*	3	4	.429	2.85	53	0	0	22	0	6	88.1	84	37	28	3	5	22	4	61	4
Pacillo, Indianapolis	6	5	.545	3.36	20	20	2	0	0	0	101.2	91	45	38	7	5	48	1	56	7
Palacios, Buffalo	0	2	.000	7.20	2	2	0	0	0	0	10.0	9	8	8	2	1	8	0	8	1
Parker, Iowa*	2	2	.500	2.58	19	2	0	7	0	1	38.1	32	13	11	1	2	20	2	21	1
Parmenter, Iowa	0	1	.000	9.00	1	0	0	1	0	0	1.0	1	1	1	0	0	0	0	0	2
Patterson, Buffalo*	12	6	.667	3.35	31	25	4	3	1	1	177.1	177	69	66	13	2	35	2	103	3
Pavlas, Oklahoma City	2	14	.125	4.70	29	21	4	4	0	0	143.2	175	89	75	7	7	67	4	94	8
Perry, Iowa*	1	0	1.000	6.23	5	0	0	1	0	0	4.1	3	3	3	1	1	6	0	4	1
Peterek, Denver	9	9	.500	3.61	23	22	7	0	1	0	149.2	146	73	60	11	2	52	0	77	7
Peters, Louisville*	1	7	.125	2.93	65	0	0	30	0	10	83.0	81	38	27	2	2	49	4	72	7
Petkovsek, Oklahoma City	0	4	.000	7.34	6	6	0	0	0	0	30.2	39	27	25	3	3	18	1	8	2
Pico, Iowa	1	0	1.000	0.00	2	1	0	1	0	1	6.1	5	0	0	0	0	2	0	2	0
Potestio, Louisville	3	2	.400	4.74	22	10	0	2	0	0	74.0	78	45	39	7	3	39	4	41	3
Power, Louisville	4	3	.571	3.16	8	7	1	0	1	0	37.0	29	13	13	3	2	15	1	36	1
Puig, Denver*	1	1	.500	6.75	12	0	0	4	0	2	13.1	30	13	10	1	1	8	2	12	1
Puzey, Louisville	0	0	.000	0.00	2	0	0	2	0	0	1.0	1	0	0	0	0	0	0	0	0
Reed, Buffalo	9	8	.529	3.72	20	20	3	0	0	0	125.2	130	58	52	9	1	28	0	75	3
Ritter, Iowa	1	0	1.000	1.72	12	0	0	7	0	0	15.2	13	5	3	0	1	4	0	7	2
Robinson, Nashville	2	0	1.000	1.89	3	3	0	0	0	0	19.0	12	5	4	1	0	6	0	11	0
Roesler, Nashville	6	4	.600	3.25	40	0	0	30	0	10	69.1	63	30	25	2	1	39	4	53	5
Rucker, Buffalo*	1	1	.500	4.35	24	0	0	13	0	2	31.0	39	20	15	1	3	14	1	18	3
Sadler, Denver	8	10	.444	4.25	28	27	2	0	1	0	171.1	169	96	81	11	1	85	1	113	9
Samuels, Buffalo*	1	1	.500	2.36	19	0	0	7	0	2	26.2	23	11	7	0	2	8	1	18	2
Sauveur, Indianapolis*	0	1	.000	7.45	8	0	0	4	0	1	9.2	10	8	8	1	0	6	0	8	0
Scheid, Iowa*	0	0	.000	4.91	7	0	0	2	0	0	7.1	8	6	4	0	0	10	1	7	0
Scherrer, Oklahoma City*	0	0	.000	8.44	5	0	0	3	0	0	5.1	6	6	5	2	2	8	0	4	0
Scudder, Nashville	6	2	.750	2.68	12	12	3	0	3	0	80.2	54	27	24	6	3	48	0	64	1
Sebra, Nashville	0	0	.000	2.50	11	0	0	7	0	2	18.0	15	6	5	0	0	10	1	15	1
Sellers, Nashville	0	1	.000	5.40	1	1	0	0	0	0	3.1	3	2	2	0	0	6	0	1	0
Simmons, 26 Den-13 OkC	4	8	.333	5.58	39	0	0	17	0	0	61.1	73	40	38	3	1	31	5	47	5
Smith, Buffalo	0	0	.000	2.65	9	0	0	6	0	5	17.0	15	5	5	1	0	5	0	11	1
Spratke, Omaha	3	4	.429	4.19	33	7	0	15	0	2	92.1	94	46	43	11	4	41	2	47	7
Stapleton, Denver*	2	6	.250	5.10	34	10	0	13	0	1	72.1	86	46	41	4	2	32	3	46	6
Stoddard, Denver	6	2	.750	3.92	42	1	0	23	0	9	80.1	77	39	35	8	4	31	4	56	6
Stottlemyre, Omaha	1	1	.500	2.35	7	0	0	6	0	1	7.2	6	4	2	1	0	3	0	9	1
Tanner, Nashville	0	0	.000	4.50	1	0	0	1	0	0	2.0	1	1	1	0	0	0	0	0	0
Taylor, Buffalo	10	8	.556	2.58	25	25	5	0	2	0	170.2	145	61	49	15	4	51	2	103	4
Tewksbury, Louisville	13	5	.722	2.43	28	28	2	1	1	0	189.0	170	63	51	9	2	34	1	72	1
Thompson, Indianapolis	9	6	.600	2.06	23	23	3	0	2	0	161.1	146	46	37	3	4	37	0	73	1
Tullier, Iowa*	0	0	.000	0.00	1	0	0	1	0	0	1.0	0	0	0	0	0	1	0	0	0
Valdez, Indianapolis	6	3	.667	3.28	19	12	0	3	0	1	90.2	78	38	33	4	5	26	2	81	5
Vande Berg, Iowa*	6	6	.500	3.74	69	0	0	36	0	10	86.2	87	43	36	4	3	30	6	65	8
Vasquez, Nashville	11	13	.458	4.60	29	29	6	0	2	0	162.1	170	91	83	11	3	84	1	115	7
Veres, Denver	6	7	.462	3.95	17	17	2	0	1	0	107.0	108	57	47	6	4	38	0	80	4
Villanueva, Iowa	0	0	.000	18.00	1	0	0	1	0	0	1.0	3	2	2	0	1	0	0	0	0
Waddell, 1 Ind-6 Den	0	1	.000	7.00	7	0	0	3	0	0	9.0	16	13	7	1	0	11	1	2	2
Walker, Buffalo	0	1	.000	5.29	3	3	0	0	0	0	17.0	12	13	10	2	0	13	0	5	2
Watkins, Denver	2	1	.667	5.93	7	1	0	4	0	0	13.2	13	9	9	2	0	6	0	10	1
Whitaker, Oklahoma City	6	4	.600	4.15	38	6	1	10	0	1	104.0	125	63	48	13	2	23	4	75	6
Wilkins, Iowa	8	11	.421	4.24	38	16	0	17	0	3	138.0	149	74	65	5	4	58	5	82	15
Wilkinson, Buffalo*	4	6	.400	3.57	21	18	2	1	0	0	95.2	80	43	38	10	1	53	2	51	5
Williams, Iowa	2	5	.286	6.21	27	8	0	6	0	1	79.2	100	63	55	11	3	35	2	40	6
Wilmet, Oklahoma City	7	8	.467	2.33	55	0	0	40	0	13	100.1	71	32	26	5	4	40	3	94	7
Worrell, Louisville	0	0	.000	0.00	1	0	0	1	0	0	1.0	0	0	0	0	0	0	0	1	0
Xavier, Denver	0	0	.000	9.00	1	0	0	1	0	0	1.0	2	1	1	0	0	0	0	1	0
York, Buffalo	1	3	.250	5.93	8	8	0	0	0	0	41.0	48	29	27	3	1	25	0	28	1

BALKS—Erickson, 7; Alba, Arnsberg, 6 each; Stapleton, 5; Armstrong, Clarke, Fassero, Kraemer, Lancaster, Laskey, May, Valdez, 4 each; Crouch, Fowlkes, Lopez, Madden, Medvin, 3 each; Anderson, Brown, Buchanan, Capel, DeJesus, Gleaton, Hammond, Melton, Miller, Peters, Rucker, Sadler, Samuels, Simmons, Stoddard, Stottlemyre, Taylor, Veres, Wilmet, 2 each; Akerfelds, Appier, Baller, Barfield, Belinda, Birkbeck, Blankenship, Coffman, Dedmon, Easley, Fireovid, Fossas, Gardner, Gideon, Hall, Harkey, Hilton, Jones, Kemp, Kinzer, Landrum, Lind, McGrath, Mitchell, Nieves, Oelkers, Olwine, Palacios, Parker, Pavlas, Peterek, Potestio, Ritter, Roesler, Scheid, Scudder, Sellers, Spratke, Tewksbury, Vasquez, Watkins, Whitaker, Wilkins, Wilkinson, 1 each.

COMBINATION SHUTOUTS—Madden-Samuels-Medvin, Reed-Medvin, Taylor-Easley, Taylor-Lind, Buffalo; Krueger-Krawczyk, Filer-Stoddard-Aldrich, Nieves-Simmons-Fossas-Krawczyk-Aldrich, May-Aldrich, Denver; Thompson-Gideon-Baller, Valdez-Gideon, Dixon-McKeon, Gakeler-Dedmon-Baller, Thompson-McKeon-Dedmon, Lugo-Dedmon-Baller, Indianapolis; Blankenship-Vande Berg 2, Harkey-Damian, Parker-Capel-Williams-Vande Berg, Pico-Vande Berg, Iowa; Power-Alba-Arnold, Arnold-Kinzer, Tewksbury-Costello, Fassero-Peters-Hilton, Tewksbury-Carpenter, Alba-Hilton-Peters-Carpenter, Horton-McGrath-Carpenter, Alba-Peters-Carpenter, Louisville; Vasquez-Kemp, Hammond-Roesler-Kemp, Brown-Griffin, Nashville; Barfield-Akerfelds, Miller-Wilmet, Arnsberg-Wilmet, Oklahoma City; Appier-Spratke, Laskey-Moore, Fireovid-Olwine, Laskey-Gleaton-Luecken, DeJesus-Gleaton, DeJesus-Spratke, Omaha.

NO-HIT GAMES—None.

International League

CLASS AAA

**Leading Batter
HAL MORRIS
Columbus**

**League President
HAROLD COOPER**

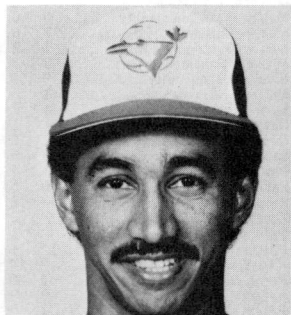

**Leading Pitcher
JOSE NUNEZ
Syracuse**

CHAMPIONSHIP WINNERS IN PREVIOUS YEARS

1884—Trenton	.520	1931—Rochester	.601
1885—Syracuse	.584	1932—Newark	.649
1886—Utica	.646	1933—Newark	.622
1887—Toronto	.644	Buffalo (4th)†	.494
1888—Syracuse	.723	1934—Newark	.608
1889—Detroit	.649	Toronto (3rd)†	.559
1890—Detroit	.617	1935—Montreal	.597
1891—Buffalo (reg. season)	.727	Syracuse (2nd)†	.565
Buffalo (supplem'l)	.680	1936—Buffalo‡	.610
1892—Providence	.615	1937—Newark‡	.717
Binghamton*	.667	1938—Newark‡	.684
1893—Erie	.606	1939—Jersey City	.582
1894—Providence	.696	Rochester (2nd)†	.556
1895—Springfield	.687	1940—Rochester	.611
1896—Providence	.602	Newark (2nd)†	.594
1897—Syracuse	.632	1941—Newark	.649
1898—Montreal	.586	Montreal (2nd)†	.584
1899—Rochester	.624	1942—Newark	.601
1900—Providence	.616	Syracuse (3rd)†	.513
1901—Rochester	.642	1943—Toronto	.625
1902—Toronto	.669	Syracuse (3rd)†	.536
1903—Jersey City	.642	1944—Baltimore‡	.553
1904—Buffalo	.657	1945—Montreal	.621
1905—Providence	.638	Newark (2nd)†	.582
1906—Buffalo	.607	1946—Montreal‡	.649
1907—Toronto	.619	1947—Jersey City	.610
1908—Baltimore	.593	Syracuse (3rd)†	.575
1909—Rochester	.596	1948—Montreal‡	.614
1910—Rochester	.601	1949—Buffalo	.584
1911—Rochester	.645	Montreal (3rd)†	.545
1912—Toronto	.595	1950—Rochester	.609
1913—Newark	.625	Baltimore (3rd)†	.556
1914—Providence	.617	1951—Montreal‡	.617
1915—Buffalo	.632	1952—Montreal	.629
1916—Buffalo	.586	Rochester (3rd)†	.619
1917—Toronto	.604	1953—Rochester	.630
1918—Toronto	.693	Montreal (2nd)†	.586
1919—Baltimore	.671	1954—Toronto	.630
1920—Baltimore	.719	Syracuse (4th)§	.510
1921—Baltimore	.717	1955—Montreal	.617
1922—Baltimore	.689	Rochester (4th)†	.497
1923—Baltimore	.677	1956—Toronto	.566
1924—Baltimore	.709	Rochester (2nd)†	.553
1925—Baltimore	.633	1957—Toronto	.575
1926—Toronto	.657	Buffalo (2nd)†	.571
1927—Buffalo	.667	1958—Montreal‡	.588
1928—Rochester	.549	1959—Buffalo	.582
1929—Rochester	.613	Havana (3rd)†	.523
1930—Rochester	.629	1960—Toronto‡	.649

1961—Columbus	.597
Buffalo (3rd)†	.559
1962—Jacksonville	.610
Atlanta (3rd)†	.539
1963—Syracuse x	.533
Indianapolis‡	.562
1964—Jacksonville	.589
Rochester (4th)†	.532
1965—Columbus	.582
Toronto (3rd)†	.556
1966—Rochester	.565
Toronto (2nd-tied)†	.558
1967—Richmond	.574
Toledo (3rd)†	.525
1968—Toledo	.565
Jacksonville (4th)†	.514
1969—Tidewater	.563
Syracuse (3rd)†	.536
1970—Syracuse‡	.600
1971—Rochester‡	.614
1972—Louisville	.563
Tidewater (3rd)†	.545
1973—Charleston	.586
Pawtucket y†	.534
1974—Memphis	.613
Rochester x‡	.611
1975—Tidewater	.610
1976—Rochester	.638
Syracuse (2nd)†	.590
1977—Pawtucket	.571
Charleston (2nd)‡	.557
1978—Charleston	.607
Richmond (4th)†	.511
1979—Columbus‡	.612
1980—Columbus‡	.593
1981—Columbus‡	.633
1982—Richmond	.590
Tidewater (3rd)†	.540
1983—Columbus	.593
Tidewater (4th)†	.511
1984—Columbus	.590
Pawtucket (4th)†	.536
1985—Syracuse	.564
Tidewater (4th)†	.540
1986—Richmond‡	.571
1987—Tidewater	.579
Columbus†	.550
1988—Rochester z	.546
Tidewater	.546

*Won split-season playoff. †Won four-team playoff. ‡Won championship and four-team playoff. §Defeated Havana in game to decide fourth place, then won four-team playoff. xLeague was divided into Northern, Southern divisions. yLeague divided into American, National divisions. z League divided into Eastern, Western divisions; won playoffs. (NOTE—Known as Eastern League in 1884, New York State League in 1885, International League in 1886-87, International Association in 1888, International League in 1889-90, Eastern Association in 1891, and Eastern League from 1892 until 1912.)

STANDING OF CLUBS AT CLOSE OF SEASON, SEPTEMBER 1

EASTERN DIVISION

Club	W.	L.	T.	Pct.	G.B.
Syracuse (Blue Jays)	83	62	0	.572	......
Rochester (Orioles)	72	73	0	.497	11
Scranton-Wilkes Barre (Phillies)	64	79	0	.448	18
Pawtucket (Red Sox)	62	84	0	.425	21½

WESTERN DIVISION

Club	W.	L.	T.	Pct.	G.B.
Richmond (Braves)	81	65	0	.555	......
Tidewater (Mets)	77	69	0	.527	4
Columbus (Yankees)	77	69	0	.527	4
Toledo (Tigers)	69	76	0	.476	11½

COMPOSITE STANDING OF CLUBS AT CLOSE OF SEASON, SEPTEMBER 1

Club	Syr.	Rich.	Tide.	Col.	Roch.	Tol.	SWB	Paw.	W.	L.	T.	Pct.	G.B.
Syracuse (Blue Jays)	....	5	7	7	9	8	10	12	83	62	0	.572	......
Richmond (Braves)	7	....	9	9	6	10	8	8	81	65	0	.555	2½
Tidewater (Mets)	5	9	....	7	7	9	7	9	77	69	0	.527	6½
Columbus (Yankees)	5	9	11	....	8	10	6	6	77	69	0	.527	6½
Rochester (Orioles)	8	6	5	4	....	7	9	9	72	73	0	.497	11
Toledo (Tigers)	4	8	9	8	5	....	5	9	69	76	0	.476	14
Scranton-Wilkes (Phillies)	8	4	5	6	9	7	....	9	64	79	0	.448	18
Pawtucket (Red Sox)	6	4	3	6	10	3	9	....	62	84	0	.425	21½

Tidewater club represented Norfolk and Portsmouth, Va.

Major league affiliations in parentheses.

Playoffs—Richmond defeated Syracuse, three games to one, to win league championship. Indianapolis (American Association) defeated Richmond, four games to none, for Alliance championship.

Regular-Season Attendance—Columbus, 518,355; Pawtucket, 278,129; Richmond, 455,686; Rochester, 284,394; Scranton-Wilkes Barre, 444,400; Syracuse, 233,078; Tidewater, 216,429; Toledo, 182,776. Total— 2,613,247. Playoffs (4 games)—25,905. Alliance playoffs (4 games)—13,341. AAA All-Star Game—14,131.

Managers—Columbus, Bucky Dent (through August 17), Richard Down (August 18 through end of season); Pawtucket, Ed Nottle; Richmond, Jim Beauchamp; Rochester, Greg Biagini; Scranton-Wilkes Barre, Bill Dancy; Syracuse, Bob Bailor; Tidewater, Mike Cubbage; Toledo, John Wockenfuss. Managerial records of teams with more than one manager: Columbus, Dent 68-62, Down 9-7.

All-Star Team—1B—Hal Morris, Columbus; 2B—Mark Lemke, Richmond; 3B—Tom O'Malley, Tidewater; SS—Randy Velarde, Columbus; OF—Butch Davis, Rochester; Glenallen Hill, Syracuse; Greg Tubbs, Richmond; C—Frank Cabrera, Syracuse-Richmond; DH—Kevin Maas, Columbus; Starting Pitcher—Alex Sanchez, Syracuse; Relief Pitcher—Mark Eichhorn, Richmond; Most Valuable Player—Tom O'Malley, Tidewater; Most Valuable Pitcher—Alex Sanchez, Syracuse; Rookie of the Year—Frank Cabrera, Syracuse-Richmond; Manager of the Year—Bob Bailor, Syracuse.

(Compiled by Howe Sportsdata International, Boston, Mass.)

CLUB BATTING

Club	Pct.	G.	AB.	R.	OR.	H.	TB.	2B.	3B.	HR.	RBI.	SH.	SF.	HP.	BB.	Int. BB.	SO.	SB.	CS.	LOB.
Columbus	.263	146	4792	640	608	1260	1910	258	43	102	584	44	39	44	451	9	936	97	55	993
Syracuse	.257	145	4789	625	524	1230	1815	234	48	85	565	36	42	31	487	24	844	152	71	988
Tidewater	.255	146	4745	603	547	1210	1734	223	23	85	553	53	36	40	547	23	790	86	32	1093
Scr'ntn-W'lkes Br	.251	143	4597	547	623	1152	1656	199	46	71	490	66	36	37	457	36	801	125	77	961
Rochester	.250	145	4680	616	553	1168	1715	239	55	66	560	34	46	45	513	30	804	115	69	976
Richmond	.247	146	4665	549	496	1154	1658	210	42	70	502	67	34	32	474	41	775	78	55	1009
Pawtucket	.247	146	4652	560	631	1147	1705	205	16	107	511	58	41	42	478	25	813	119	62	973
Toledo	.243	145	4713	547	619	1144	1656	219	37	73	500	60	40	40	535	36	744	103	45	1034

INDIVIDUAL BATTING

(Leading Qualifiers for Batting Championship—394 or More Plate Appearances)

*Bats lefthanded.   †Switch-hitter.

Player and Club	Pct.	G.	AB.	R.	H.	TB.	2B.	3B.	HR.	RBI.	SH.	SF.	HP.	BB.	Int. BB.	SO.	SB.	CS.
Morris, Harold, Columbus*	.326	111	417	70	136	213	24	1	17	66	3	4	4	28	2	47	5	3
Hill, Glenallen, Syracuse	.321	125	483	86	155	279	31	15	21	72	3	4	5	34	0	107	21	7
Davis, Wallace, Rochester	.303	127	479	81	145	222	29	9	10	64	2	5	6	28	4	57	19	8
Tubbs, Gregory, Richmond	.301	115	405	64	122	166	10	11	4	35	5	0	1	47	0	49	19	15
Cabrera, Francisco, Richmond	.300	116	434	59	130	198	31	5	9	72	1	8	3	20	2	72	4	4
O'Malley, Thomas, Tidewater*	.295	132	492	64	145	219	29	0	15	84	0	4	3	67	10	63	3	1
Contreras, Joaquin, Tidewater†	.287	127	401	49	115	171	20	6	8	43	2	2	2	38	3	92	11	4
Wielgman, Richard, Toledo*	.286	120	384	49	110	163	32	3	5	57	5	2	2	47	2	58	8	5
Stanicek, Stephen, Scr'ntn-W'lkes Br	.285	103	368	43	105	163	25	3	9	54	2	5	2	29	0	54	0	3
Hulett, Timothy, Rochester	.280	122	461	61	129	194	32	12	3	50	1	5	9	38	1	81	2	5

Departmental Leaders: G—Lemke, 146; AB—Lemke, 518; R—Hill, 86; H—Hill, 155; TB—Hill, 279; 2B—Tolman, 33; 3B—Hill, 15; HR—Hill, 21; RBI—O'Malley, 84; SH—T. Barrett, Dowell, 10; SF—Cabrera, 8; HP—D. Williams, 14; BB—McKnight, 79; IBB—Lancellotti, Lovullo, Mizerock, O'Malley, 10; SO—Denson, 116; SB—T. Barrett, 44; CS—Tubbs, 15.

(All Players—Listed Alphabetically)

Player and Club	Pct.	G.	AB.	R.	H.	TB.	2B.	3B.	HR.	RBI.	SH.	SF.	HP.	BB.	Int. BB.	SO.	SB.	CS.
Adduci, James, Scr'ntn-W'lkes Br*	.231	74	251	31	58	89	9	2	6	30	0	2	1	15	3	51	2	2
Alicea, Edwin, Richmond†	.286	4	7	1	2	2	0	0	0	1	0	0	0	1	0	2	0	0
Alvarez, Jesus, 20 Col-88 Tol*	.281	108	270	33	76	109	12	3	5	46	3	4	1	55	6	38	2	1
Anderson, Brady, Rochester*	.200	21	70	14	14	22	1	2	1	8	0	0	2	12	1	13	2	2
Austin, Dominic, Toledo	.192	16	52	4	10	14	2	1	0	2	0	0	1	6	0	14	3	0
Azocar, Oscar, Columbus*	.292	37	130	14	38	56	9	3	1	12	1	0	1	7	0	10	3	1
Bailey, Mark, Tidewater†	.242	72	190	17	46	61	7	1	2	25	2	2	3	35	0	35	0	1
Barrett, Martin, Pawtucket	.286	11	35	4	10	13	1	1	0	4	1	0	1	5	0	1	0	1
Barrett, Thomas, Scr'ntn-W'lkes Br†	.278	120	443	65	123	149	14	6	0	25	10	3	3	51	4	47	44	13
Bean, William, Toledo*	.315	76	267	43	84	114	14	2	4	29	4	2	7	27	0	35	7	2
Beatty, Blaine, Tidewater*	.300	27	20	2	6	7	1	0	0	2	3	0	0	0	0	3	0	0
Beauchamp, Kash, Richmond	.237	91	278	26	66	102	15	3	5	29	1	1	3	13	0	45	4	3
Becker, Timothy, Columbus	.223	27	103	5	23	29	4	1	0	8	1	1	0	1	0	7	0	1
Bell, Juan, Rochester†	.262	116	408	50	107	140	15	6	2	32	2	4	1	39	0	92	17	10
Bell, Terence, Richmond	.100	8	20	0	2	2	0	0	0	0	0	0	0	1	0	3	0	0
Blocker, Terry, Richmond*	.192	8	26	3	5	5	0	0	0	1	0	0	0	1	0	3	1	2
Bootay, Kevin, Scranton-Wilkes Barre	.132	23	53	3	7	8	1	1	0	4	1	1	0	7	0	12	5	2
Boudreaux, Eric, Scr'ntn-W'lkes Br	.000	19	1	0	0	0	0	0	0	0	0	0	0	0	0	1	0	0
Bradshaw, Kevin, Toledo	.000	7	4	0	0	0	0	0	0	0	0	0	0	0	0	3	0	0
Brink, Bradford, Scr'ntn-W'lkes Br	.000	3	1	0	0	0	0	0	0	0	0	0	0	1	0	1	0	0

Player and Club	Pct.	G.	AB.	R.	H.	TB.	2B.	3B.	HR.	RBI.	SH.	SF.	HP.	BB.	Int. BB.	SO.	SB.	CS.
Brower, Robert, Columbus	.253	26	95	15	24	33	3	0	2	8	2	0	6	0	12	7	3
Brown, Anthony, Tidewater*	.270	128	455	41	123	183	23	2	11	60	1	5	3	23	1	77	13	6
Brown, Kevin, Tidewater*	.176	13	17	1	3	4	1	0	0	0	2	0	0	0	0	4	0	0
Brumley, Michael, Toledo†	.231	8	26	4	6	12	2	2	0	1	0	0	1	3	1	11	1	0
Bullock, Eric, Scr'ntn-W'lkes Br*	.274	80	281	37	77	112	10	8	3	40	2	3	1	18	5	30	16	7
Burks, Ellis, Pawtucket	.143	5	21	4	3	4	1	0	0	0	0	0	0	2	0	3	0	0
Butera, Salvatore, Syracuse	.211	25	71	3	15	23	5	0	1	7	1	0	0	5	0	10	0	0
Cabrera, Francisco, 113 Syr-3 Rmd...	.300	116	434	59	130	198	31	5	9	72	1	8	3	20	2	72	4	4
Campusano, Silvestre, Syracuse	.242	112	356	46	86	131	19	4	6	30	3	2	1	44	0	81	17	4
Cannizzaro, Chris, Pawtucket†	.265	75	253	33	67	99	15	1	5	31	5	3	4	36	0	27	5	3
Carrasco, Norman, Toledo	.151	21	53	4	8	8	0	0	0	2	4	1	1	1	0	7	1	0
Carreon, Mark, Tidewater	.279	32	122	22	34	41	4	0	1	21	0	4	0	13	1	20	8	3
Carter, Gary, Tidewater	.188	5	16	2	3	6	0	0	1	3	0	0	0	2	0	1	0	0
Cijntje, Sherwin, Rochester*	.200	27	55	6	11	15	2	1	0	7	1	0	1	7	0	8	8	1
Cimo, Matthew, Scr'ntn-W'lkes Br	.241	85	216	32	52	85	7	4	6	22	5	2	2	14	0	51	3	3
Clary, Martin, Richmond	.083	15	12	2	1	1	0	0	0	0	1	0	0	2	0	8	0	0
Contreras, Joaquin, Tidewater†	.287	127	401	49	115	171	20	6	8	43	2	2	2	38	3	92	11	4
Cuyler, Milton, Toledo†	.169	24	83	4	14	21	3	2	0	6	3	1	0	8	0	27	4	1
Datz, Jeffrey, Toledo	.247	77	247	26	61	83	13	0	3	18	4	1	2	16	0	28	0	1
Davis, Wallace, Richmond	.303	127	479	81	145	222	29	9	10	64	2	5	6	28	4	57	19	8
Dean, Kevin, Richmond	.167	2	6	1	1	1	0	0	0	0	0	0	0	0	0	2	0	0
DeButch, Michael, Tidewater	.248	95	315	41	78	108	16	1	4	19	5	1	1	41	0	63	6	3
DeJesus, Ivan, Toledo	.185	18	27	3	5	8	1	1	0	2	2	0	0	5	0	5	0	0
DeLaCruz, Hector, Syracuse	.179	66	179	18	32	48	8	1	2	16	2	1	1	20	0	43	9	12
Denson, Andrew, Richmond	.255	138	463	50	118	177	32	0	9	59	1	5	12	42	2	116	0	1
Dickerson, Bobby, Columbus	.185	24	65	8	12	16	4	0	0	5	0	1	1	2	0	15	0	1
Dillard, Gordon, Scr'ntn-W'lkes Br	.200	28	15	0	3	3	0	0	0	1	2	0	0	0	0	1	0	0
DiMascio, Daniel, Toledo	.228	80	215	15	49	70	9	0	4	23	0	1	1	9	0	43	1	1
Dorsett, Brian, Columbus	.250	110	388	45	97	171	21	1	17	62	2	5	5	31	2	87	2	2
Dowell, Kenneth, Tidewater	.179	74	140	14	25	31	6	0	0	4	10	0	2	25	0	21	0	0
Drummond, Timothy, Tidewater	.000	35	1	0	0	0	0	0	0	0	0	0	0	0	0	1	0	0
Ducey, Robert, Syracuse	.103	10	29	0	3	5	0	1	0	3	0	1	0	0	0	13	0	0
Dulin, Timothy, Rochester	.252	120	389	48	98	136	21	1	5	38	8	4	1	45	2	46	8	4
Dunbar, Thomas, Richmond*	.213	27	80	4	17	24	2	1	1	15	1	4	0	3	0	9	1	1
Earl, Scott, 16 Tol-73 Col	.231	89	247	32	57	76	10	0	3	30	4	2	2	27	0	56	4	4
Eave, Gary Louis, Richmond	.048	23	21	0	1	1	0	0	0	0	3	0	0	0	0	8	0	0
Edens, Thomas, 18 Tdw-7 SWB	.000	25	5	0	0	0	0	0	0	0	2	0	0	0	0	2	0	0
Eichhorn, Mark, Richmond	.000	25	2	0	0	0	0	0	0	0	0	0	0	0	0	0	0	0
Escobar, Jose, Syracuse	.232	46	142	12	33	38	3	1	0	14	5	2	0	7	0	27	2	0
Estrada, Eduardo, Pawtucket	.154	12	39	6	6	8	0	1	0	0	0	0	4	0	0	6	1	0
Farmer, Bryan, Richmond*	.500	42	2	0	1	1	0	0	0	1	0	0	0	0	0	0	0	0
Faulkner, Craig, Rochester	.000	3	7	1	0	0	0	0	0	0	0	0	0	0	0	2	0	0
Felix, Junior, Syracuse†	.276	21	87	17	24	35	4	2	1	10	1	1	0	9	0	18	13	3
Finley, Steven, Rochester*	.160	7	25	2	4	4	0	0	0	2	0	0	1	1	0	5	3	0
Fishel, John, Columbus	.218	103	308	35	67	103	16	1	6	31	2	3	3	30	0	76	6	3
Frohwirth, Todd, Scr'ntn-W'lkes Br..	.000	21	4	0	0	0	0	0	0	0	2	0	0	0	0	2	0	0
Gant, Ronald, Richmond	.262	63	225	42	59	109	13	2	11	27	0	1	0	29	1	42	7	2
Garcia, Leonardo, Toledo*	.215	100	311	25	67	93	12	7	0	27	5	1	0	33	3	26	3	1
Gardner, Jeffrey, Toledo*	.279	101	269	28	75	86	11	0	0	24	4	3	0	25	1	27	0	0
Garrison, Webster, Syracuse	.285	50	151	18	43	52	7	1	0	9	4	0	2	18	1	25	3	2
Geren, Robert, Columbus	.253	27	95	11	24	36	4	1	2	13	2	1	1	5	0	25	1	0
Gonzalez, Angel, Pawtucket	.259	73	232	22	60	87	8	2	5	25	9	2	0	14	2	28	4	11
Green, Otis, Syracuse*	.265	87	306	45	81	109	11	1	5	28	0	3	1	32	2	55	14	6
Green, Robert, Columbus	.087	8	23	1	2	2	0	0	0	1	0	0	0	0	0	11	0	0
Greene, Thomas, Richmond	.136	26	22	2	3	4	1	0	0	1	5	0	0	3	0	7	0	0
Griffin, David, 18 Tol-91 Col	.272	109	371	51	101	162	23	1	12	54	0	4	3	49	3	66	2	0
Gross, Kip, Tidewater	.231	13	13	0	3	4	1	0	0	1	0	0	0	0	0	7	0	0
Gutierrez, Joaquin, Pawtucket	.228	100	329	25	75	89	8	0	2	21	5	1	0	23	0	43	1	2
Harris, Walter, Rochester	.219	74	233	39	51	67	9	2	1	24	3	1	6	39	0	40	19	8
Hayden, Alan, Tidewater*	.130	8	23	6	3	5	2	0	0	0	2	0	0	3	0	4	4	0
Hayes, Charles, Scr'ntn-W'lkes Br	.407	7	27	4	11	19	3	1	1	3	0	0	1	0	0	3	1	0
Heath, Kelly, Syracuse	.205	29	88	14	18	26	3	1	1	6	1	0	0	26	0	26	3	2
Henry, Dwayne, Richmond	.000	41	3	0	0	0	0	0	0	0	0	0	0	0	0	2	0	0
Hernandez, Manuel, Tidewater	.000	7	7	0	0	0	0	0	0	0	0	0	0	0	0	0	0	0
Hill, Glenallen, Syracuse	.321	125	483	86	155	279	31	15	21	72	3	4	5	34	0	107	21	7
Hoiles, Chris, Rochester	.245	96	322	41	79	130	19	1	10	51	2	4	4	31	1	58	1	2
Horn, Samuel, Pawtucket*	.232	51	164	15	38	73	9	1	8	27	0	3	0	20	2	46	0	0
Hughes, Keith, Rochester*	.274	83	285	44	78	112	20	4	2	43	0	2	1	44	3	47	4	5
Hulett, Timothy, Rochester	.280	122	461	61	129	194	32	12	3	50	1	5	9	38	1	81	2	5
Infante, Alexis, Syracuse	.208	67	250	39	52	57	5	0	0	17	4	1	0	25	0	33	10	2
Jackson, Kenneth, Scr'ntn-W'lkes Br.	.225	59	178	30	40	55	5	2	2	15	2	0	2	29	2	41	6	4
Jarrell, Joseph, Rochester	.125	6	16	0	2	3	1	0	0	3	0	1	0	0	0	5	0	0
Jefferson, Stanley, 68 Col-16 Roch†	.259	84	321	43	83	124	14	9	3	36	2	3	1	35	0	49	18	8
Jones, LaBarry, Richmond*	.263	125	429	49	113	163	16	5	8	55	4	4	2	38	7	57	12	9
Justice, David, Richmond*	.261	115	391	47	102	168	24	3	12	58	1	3	3	59	4	66	12	8
Kiefer, Steven, Columbus	.276	80	286	48	79	130	18	6	7	38	0	3	6	23	0	72	3	1
Lancellotti, Richard, Pawtucket*	.254	109	350	50	89	156	16	0	17	56	0	4	6	61	10	80	2	2
Lawton, Marcus, 70 Tide-42 Col†	.236	112	292	39	69	93	12	0	4	32	3	3	2	27	1	62	17	8
Legg, Gregory, Scranton-W Barre	.248	109	379	41	94	110	10	0	2	33	5	2	3	36	1	44	5	5
Leiper, Timothy, Toledo*	.239	101	376	43	90	116	13	2	3	31	7	1	3	28	0	33	3	6
Lemke, Mark, Richmond†	.276	146	518	69	143	194	22	7	5	61	5	6	0	66	8	45	4	8
Liddell, David, Tidewater	.151	24	73	8	11	19	2	0	2	7	0	0	2	9	0	25	0	1
Lombardi, Phillip, Tidewater†	.261	113	403	50	105	166	19	0	14	73	1	3	6	61	0	59	1	1
Lovullo, Salvatore, Toledo†	.230	112	409	48	94	151	23	2	10	52	7	4	1	44	10	57	2	1
Lundblade, Frederick, Tidewater	.171	46	111	13	19	45	5	0	7	20	1	2	0	14	1	25	0	0
Lusader, Scott, Toledo*	.242	44	153	17	37	54	9	1	2	15	1	3	0	23	0	31	6	3
Lyons, Barry, Tidewater	.100	5	20	1	2	4	0	1	0	2	0	0	0	0	0	5	0	0
Maas, Kevin, Columbus*	.320	83	291	42	93	138	23	2	6	45	0	4	1	40	0	73	2	3
Machado, Julio, Tidewater	.000	14	1	0	0	0	0	0	0	0	0	0	0	0	0	0	0	0
Maddux, Michael, Scranton-W Barre..	.000	19	9	0	0	0	0	0	0	0	3	0	0	0	0	4	0	0
Madrid, Alexander, Scranton-W Barre	.000	16	7	0	0	0	0	0	0	0	1	0	0	0	0	5	0	0
Malave, Omar, Syracuse	.217	8	23	1	5	6	1	0	0	1	0	0	0	2	0	5	0	0

Player and Club	Pct.	G.	AB.	R.	H.	TB.	2B.	3B.	HR.	RBI.	SH.	SF.	HP.	BB.	Int. BB.	SO.	SB.	CS.
Martin, John, Scranton-Wilkes Barre .	.333	7	3	0	1	1	0	0	0	0	0	0	0	0	0	1	0	0
Marzano, John, Pawtucket................	.211	106	322	27	68	103	11	0	8	36	4	2	4	15	1	53	1	4
Mathews, Edward, Richmond.............	.000	37	1	0	0	0	0	.0	0	0	0	0	0	0	0	1	0	0
McKnight, Jefferson, Tidewater†	.249	116	425	84	106	156	19	2	9	48	3	1	1	79	1	56	3	0
Melendez, Francisco, Rochester*	.258	126	454	59	117	172	24	2	9	78	2	7	2	63	4	70	5	5
Mercker, Kent, Richmond*	.074	27	27	0	2	2	0	0	0	1	3	0	0	2	0	12	0	0
Meulens, Hensley, Columbus	.289	14	45	8	13	20	4	0	1	3	0	0	0	8	0	13	0	0
Michel, Domingo, Toledo.................	.224	47	143	16	32	41	4	1	1	4	2	0	3	24	1	29	4	1
Miller-Jones, Gary, Pawtucket†	.233	100	309	41	72	104	14	0	6	32	4	4	1	25	2	66	2	4
Miller, Darrell, Columbus.................	.243	76	218	23	53	82	7	5	4	26	5	1	4	22	0	46	2	0
Miller, Keith A., Tidewater...............	.266	48	184	33	49	64	8	2	1	15	0	0	2	18	0	24	12	2
Miller, N. Keith, Scranton-W.B.†	.264	138	474	75	125	202	24	7	13	62	4	2	4	75	7	101	8	11
Mitchell, John, Tidewater.................	.091	27	22	1	2	2	0	0	0	0	7	0	0	0	0	7	0	0
Mizerock, John, Richmond*...............	.224	112	352	36	79	100	11	2	2	35	7	3	2	36	10	35	1	0
Moore, Bradley, Scranton-W Barre	1.000	62	1	1	1	1	0	0	0	0	0	0	0	0	0	0	0	0
Moore, William, Rochester	.199	70	221	25	44	69	11	1	4	28	0	3	2	32	1	61	0	2
Moritz, Christopher, Pawtucket..........	.247	38	81	14	20	23	3	0	0	5	5	0	1	8	0	27	11	1
Morris, Harold, Columbus*...............	.326	111	417	70	136	213	24	1	17	66	3	4	4	28	2	47	5	3
Myers, Gregory, Syracuse*	.270	24	89	8	24	33	6	0	1	11	1	0	0	4	0	9	0	0
Naehring, Timothy, Pawtucket	.275	79	273	32	75	102	16	1	3	31	2	7	3	27	1	41	2	3
Nezelek, Andrew, Richmond*	.400	49	5	0	2	2	0	0	0	0	0	0	0	0	0	1	0	0
Nieto, Thomas, Scranton-W Barre	.191	46	136	8	26	32	3	0	1	7	2	0	2	12	2	30	0	0
O'Malley, Thomas, Tidewater*..........	.295	132	492	64	145	219	29	0	15	84	0	4	3	67	10	63	3	1
O'Neal, Randall, Scranton-W Barre	.200	18	5	0	1	1	0	0	0	0	1	0	0	0	1	0	0	0
Olander, James, Scranton-W Barre	.252	111	274	35	69	103	17	4	3	29	8	2	3	27	1	69	5	7
Orsag, James, Pawtucket*................	.182	19	55	5	10	15	2	0	1	7	0	1	0	4	0	19	2	0
Padget, Chris, Rochester*...............	.245	118	404	44	99	154	20	4	9	51	3	3	3	46	9	65	2	3
Pardo, Alberto, Scranton-W Barre† .	.239	103	306	32	73	114	20	3	5	30	3	0	3	36	5	56	4	2
Pederson, Stuart, Syracuse*.............	.268	109	340	43	91	140	19	3	8	45	2	4	3	51	9	53	1	2
Pedrique, Alfredo, Toledo	.207	56	193	15	40	51	8	0	1	21	3	1	3	16	0	32	2	1
Perkins, Harold, Rochester†	.282	55	174	19	49	73	7	4	3	11	3	0	3	19	2	27	4	6
Pettis, Gary, Toledo†	.333	6	21	6	7	11	1	0	1	3	0	0	0	7	0	2	4	3
Pina, John, Pawtucket..................	.285	71	260	32	74	131	15	0	14	45	3	1	0	22	2	68	2	1
Plumb, David, Richmond.................	.000	3	4	0	0	0	0	0	0	0	0	0	0	0	0	1	0	0
Posey, John, 5 Roch-3 Scranton-WB .	.250	8	20	2	5	9	1	0	1	2	1	0	0	4	0	2	0	0
Puleo, Charles, Richmond..............	.000	11	6	0	0	0	0	0	0	0	2	0	0	0	0	1	0	0
Quintana, Carlos, Pawtucket............	.287	82	272	45	78	126	11	2	11	52	0	5	0	53	1	39	6	0
Rayford, Floyd, Scranton-W Barre	.193	57	150	8	29	46	8	0	3	22	1	3	0	9	0	31	0	0
Redfield, Joseph, Scranton-W Barre ..	.241	123	428	45	103	155	13	6	9	49	4	4	6	40	0	74	21	8
Reed, Darren, Tidewater..............	.268	133	444	57	119	173	30	6	4	50	1	4	11	60	1	70	11	2
Richards, Russell, Richmond*	.455	29	11	2	5	5	0	0	0	1	2	0	0	3	0	3	0	0
Richie, Robert, Toledo*..............	.293	69	215	42	63	96	9	3	6	26	2	6	0	30	2	40	3	4
Rios, Carlos, Richmond	.213	27	61	8	13	17	2	1	0	6	3	0	2	7	0	6	0	0
Ritchie, Wallace, Scranton-W Barre*.	.133	34	15	0	2	3	1	0	0	2	0	0	0	0	0	3	0	0
Rivera, German, Richmond	.250	1	4	0	1	1	0	0	0	2	0	0	0	0	0	1	0	0
Rivera, Luis, Pawtucket.................	.251	43	175	22	44	56	9	0	1	13	4	0	1	11	0	23	5	3
Roberts, John, Pawtucket..............	.226	102	248	34	56	64	6	1	0	9	8	0	2	46	1	37	27	8
Romano, Thomas, Rochester	.202	35	109	18	22	33	8	0	1	12	0	0	1	5	0	13	6	0
Romine, Kevin, Pawtucket	.300	27	90	9	27	36	3	0	2	7	0	0	0	15	0	13	0	2
Rosario, Victor, Scranton-W Barre	.258	56	151	16	39	46	7	0	0	16	3	1	1	4	0	29	3	1
Ruffin, Bruce, Scranton-Wilkes Barre	.091	9	11	0	1	1	0	0	0	0	0	0	0	0	0	4	0	0
Ryal, Mark, Scranton-Wilkes Barre* ..	.281	59	210	16	59	79	14	0	2	21	2	5	0	12	1	31	1	6
Salcedo, Ronnie, Scranton-W Barre*.	.276	69	170	22	47	70	8	0	5	18	0	1	3	37	5	20	2	3
Salinas, Manuel, Tidewater*	.158	13	19	0	3	3	0	0	0	1	0	0	0	1	1	1	0	0
Sanchez, Zoilo, Tidewater..............	.167	2	6	1	1	4	0	0	1	2	0	0	0	0	0	3	0	0
Sanders, Deion, Columbus*	.278	70	259	38	72	113	12	7	5	30	4	3	1	22	1	48	16	7
Savage, John, Tidewater.................	.000	33	1	0	0	0	0	0	0	0	0	0	0	0	0	0	0	0
Sax, David, Columbus	.313	21	64	10	20	23	3	0	0	5	1	1	1	9	1	10	0	0
Schu, Richard, Rochester	.223	28	94	11	21	32	6	1	1	10	0	2	1	16	1	21	3	2
Sebra, Robert, Scranton-W Barre......	.200	12	10	0	2	2	0	0	0	1	2	0	0	0	0	5	0	0
See, Laurence, Toledo	.227	110	321	43	73	122	18	2	9	44	0	5	3	43	4	65	4	1
Shaddy, Christopher, Richmond	.234	135	483	57	113	159	23	4	5	42	9	2	3	42	2	107	3	2
Sharts, Stephen, Scranton-W Barre* ..	.500	52	2	0	1	1	0	0	0	0	0	0	0	0	0	0	0	0
Shelton, Michael, Scranton-W Barre ..	.250	10	4	0	1	1	0	0	0	1	2	0	0	0	0	2	0	0
Shipley, Craig, Tidewater†	.206	44	131	6	27	34	1	0	2	9	2	2	0	7	0	22	0	0
Smith, Alexander, Richmond	.207	88	242	16	50	62	8	2	0	15	6	2	0	23	4	35	1	0
Smith, Dana, Rochester	.000	8	5	0	0	0	0	0	0	0	0	0	0	0	0	0	0	0
Soff, Raymond, Tidewater...............	.000	12	1	0	0	0	0	0	0	0	0	0	0	0	0	1	0	0
Sojo, Luis, Syracuse....................	.276	121	482	54	133	172	20	5	3	54	4	5	1	21	0	42	9	14
Sprague, Edward, Syracuse	.208	86	288	23	60	91	14	1	5	33	1	3	5	18	2	73	0	0
Stanicek, Stephen, Scranton-W Barre	.285	103	368	43	105	163	25	3	9	54	2	5	2	29	0	54	0	3
Stanton, Michael, Richmond*...........	.000	13	1	0	0	0	0	0	0	0	0	0	0	0	0	0	0	0
Stone, Jeffrey, Pawtucket*	.281	57	196	30	55	81	10	2	4	22	2	1	4	10	2	34	16	3
Strange, Douglas, Toledo†	.247	83	304	38	75	118	15	2	8	42	2	2	2	34	2	49	8	3
Tabaka, Jeffrey, Scranton-W Barre ..	.200	6	5	1	1	1	0	0	0	1	1	0	0	0	0	1	0	0
Tackett, Jeffrey, Rochester.............	.181	67	199	13	36	47	3	1	2	17	2	2	1	19	0	45	3	1
Tapani, Kevin, Tidewater	.200	17	10	0	2	2	0	0	0	1	3	0	0	0	0	4	0	0
Thornton, Louis, Tidewater*...........	.271	71	229	34	62	82	10	2	2	20	0	2	1	29	6	39	6	3
Tolman, Timothy, Syracuse	.252	122	420	63	106	161	33	2	6	57	2	3	4	71	0	71	8	3
Tremblay, Gary, Pawtucket	.150	63	153	16	23	37	3	1	3	14	2	2	1	17	0	35	0	1
Trujillo, Michael, 14 Tol-9 Tide........	.000	23	1	0	0	0	0	0	0	0	0	0	0	0	0	1	0	0
Tubbs, Gregory, Richmond	.301	115	405	64	122	166	10	11	4	35	5	0	1	47	0	49	19	15
Turner, Shane, Rochester*	.222	59	194	31	43	57	6	1	2	19	4	1	1	19	1	33	6	4
Valera, Julio, Tidewater	.333	2	3	1	1	1	0	0	0	0	1	0	0	0	0	0	0	0
Velarde, Randy, Columbus	.266	103	387	59	103	168	26	3	11	53	1	0	5	38	0	105	3	5
Virgil, Osvaldo, Syracuse...............	.260	43	146	15	38	54	4	0	4	18	0	1	4	12	0	20	0	1
Wade, Scott, Pawtucket.................	.238	104	345	39	82	142	20	2	12	35	2	1	0	34	1	81	6	3
Walewander, James, Toledo†	.225	133	484	53	109	151	15	3	7	38	6	4	6	60	3	72	32	10
Walker, Cleotha, Syracuse†	.239	123	431	61	103	160	11	5	12	63	1	4	1	58	8	61	37	10
Wasinger, Mark, Columbus	.249	110	353	42	88	114	17	3	1	31	6	1	4	38	0	45	7	4
West, David, Tidewater*................	.333	12	12	3	4	6	2	0	0	0	1	0	0	0	0	4	0	0
Wetherby, Jeffrey, Richmond*	.268	50	157	19	42	54	9	0	1	16	1	1	1	21	1	17	5	2

Player and Club	Pct.	G.	AB.	R.	H.	TB.	2B.	3B.	HR.	RBI.	SH.	SF.	HP.	BB.	Int. BB.	SO.	SB.	CS.
Whited, Edward, Richmond	.245	89	298	41	73	108	15	1	6	32	4	0	3	27	2	56	8	2
Whitehurst, Walter, Tidewater	.143	21	14	0	2	2	0	0	0	1	1	0	1	0	0	5	0	0
Wieligman, Richard, Toledo*	.286	120	384	49	110	163	32	3	5	57	5	2	2	47	2	58	8	5
Williams, Bernabe, Columbus†	.216	50	162	21	35	51	8	1	2	16	3	2	2	25	1	38	11	5
Williams, Dana, Pawtucket	.256	104	356	47	91	120	17	0	4	28	2	2	14	23	0	28	20	7
Williams, Kenneth R., Toledo	.255	14	51	8	13	24	2	0	3	8	0	0	1	5	0	9	2	0
Wine, Robert, Richmond	.163	29	92	9	15	24	6	0	1	6	2	1	0	7	0	32	0	0
Woodard, Michael, Columbus*	.229	40	140	17	32	39	7	0	0	7	3	0	4	0	18	1	2
Young, Delwyn, Toledo†	.220	19	50	4	11	17	1	1	1	6	0	1	7	1	15	1	0
Ziem, Stephen, Richmond	.200	18	5	1	1	1	0	0	0	0	0	0	0	0	0	3	0	0
Zupcic, Robert, Pawtucket	.255	27	94	8	24	36	7	1	1	11	0	2	0	3	0	15	1	3

The following pitchers, listed alphabetically by club, with games in parentheses, had no plate appearances, primarily through use of designated hitters:

COLUMBUS—Cary, Charles (11); Chapin, Darrin (27); Christopher, Michael (13); Davidson, Robert (22); Eiland, David (18); Fulton, William (26); Galvez, Balvino (24); Grapenthin, Richard (6); Guidry, Ronald (7); Habyan, John (8); Jones, James (20); Leiter, Mark (22); Mmahat, Kevin (15); Mohorcic, Dale (16); Nielsen, Scott (19); Noles, Dickie (42); Parker, Clayton (5); Pena, Hipolito (26); Rub, Jerry (17); Schulze, Donald (14).

PAWTUCKET—Araujo, Anazario (32); Bast, Steven (18); Bolton, Thomas (26); Boyd, Dennis (2); Chadwick, Ray (7); Curry, Stephen (7); Dalton, Michael (26); Dopson, John (2); Ellsworth, Steven (14); Hetzel, Eric (12); Kiecker, Dana (28); Leister, John (38); Rochford, Michael (37); Shikles, Larry (1); Trautwein, John (53); Woodward, Robert (40).

RICHMOND—Deitz, Timothy (1); Kilner, John (12); LeMasters, James (1); Marak, Paul (2); McKeon, Joel (11).

ROCHESTER—Bautista, Jose (15); Bell, Eric (7); Culkar, Steven (23); DuBois, Brian (4); Habyan, John (7); Harnisch, Peter (12); Huismann, Mark (16); Johnson, David (18); Jones, Michael (31); Mejia, Cesar (18); Mesa, Jose (7); Raczka, Michael (44); Schilling, Curtis (27); Schwarz, Jeffrey (9); Smith, Michael (Mississippi) (11); Smith, Michael (Texas) (36); Stanhope, Chester (28); Thorpe, Paul (14); Tibbs, Jay (4); Weston, Michael (23).

SCRANTON-WILKES BARRE—Clay, Danny (33); Combs, Patrick (3); Freeman, Marvin (5); McElroy, Charles (14); Ontiveros, Steven (1); Service, Scott (23).

SYRACUSE—Bair, Douglas (19); Blair, William (19); Buice, DeWayne (31); Castillo, Antonio (27); Cummings, Steven (19); Gilles, Thomas (29); Gozzo, Mauro (12); Guzman, Juan (14); Hernandez, Xavier (15); MacDonald, Robert (12); Musselman, Jeffrey (10); Nunez, Jose (40); O'Connor, Jack (18); Ross, Mark (26); Sanchez, Alex (28); Stottlemyre, Todd (10); Wapnick, Steven (6); Wills, Frank (14); Wishnevski, Robert (16).

TIDEWATER—Barton, Shawn (38); Innis, Jeffrey (25); Nielsen, Scott (21); Scherrer, William (20).

TOLEDO—Atherton, Keith (6); Beard, David (12); Bockus, Randy (32); Cooper, David (20); DuBois, Brian (3); Grapenthin, Richard (9); Hansen, Michael (9); Havens, Bradley (16); Holman, Shawn (51); Hudson, Charles (1); Link, Robert (55); Nosek, Randall (1); Nunez, Edwin (13); Palmer, David (10); Pena, Ramon (33); Ritz, Kevin (16); Schwabe, Michael (13); Searcy, Stephen (9); Vesling, Donald (7); Wenson, Paul (16); Williams, Kenneth L. (22).

GRAND SLAM HOME RUNS—Strange, 2; Contreras, Geren, Hill, Hoiles, Horn, Legg, Lundblade, N. Keith Miller (Scranton-Wilkes Barre), Quintana, Rayford, Velarde, Whited, Wieligman, 1 each.

AWARDED FIRST BASE ON CATCHER'S INTERFERENCE—DiMascio (Bailey); Lovullo (Hoiles); McKnight (Prince); Morris (Rayford); Walker (Scott).

CLUB FIELDING

Club	Pct.	G.	PO.	A.	E.	DP.	PB.	Club	Pct.	G.	PO.	A.	E.	DP.	PB.
Scranton-Wilkes Barre	.978	143	3638	1469	116	130	16	Columbus	.972	146	3751	1607	155	129	17
Tidewater	.975	146	3743	1629	138	130	12	Rochester	.972	145	3743	1477	153	141	11
Richmond	.974	146	3733	1461	136	142	15	Syracuse	.969	145	3808	1481	167	144	22
Pawtucket	.972	146	3705	1369	145	121	13	Toledo	.969	145	3793	1604	171	149	15

INDIVIDUAL FIELDING

*Throws lefthanded.

FIRST BASEMEN

Player and Club	Pct.	G.	PO.	A.	E.	DP.	Player and Club	Pct.	G.	PO.	A.	E.	DP.
Adduci, Scranton-Wilkes Barre*	.995	50	390	23	2	39	Miller-Jones, Pawtucket	1.000	8	43	2	0	4
Alvarez, 6 Columbus-17 Toledo	.989	23	164	11	2	22	D. Miller, Columbus	1.000	14	100	6	0	12
Bailey, Tidewater	1.000	5	36	4	0	1	N.K. Miller, Scranton-W.B.	1.000	8	76	6	0	8
Bean, Toledo*	.985	16	121	8	2	6	Mizerock, Richmond	1.000	1	3	0	0	0
Brown, Tidewater	1.000	5	9	1	0	0	Morris, Columbus*	.989	67	582	65	7	40
Cabrera, Richmond	1.000	1	5	0	0	0	O'Malley, Tidewater	1.000	7	47	4	0	1
Carreon, Tidewater*	1.000	1	2	0	0	0	Orsag, Pawtucket	.983	8	53	6	1	2
Carter, Tidewater	.923	2	12	0	1	0	Padget, Rochester	.994	18	169	11	1	15
Denson, Richmond	.988	136	1111	78	14	126	Pardo, Scranton-Wilkes Barre	1.000	2	12	3	0	4
Estrada, Pawtucket	1.000	3	17	3	0	4	Quintana, Pawtucket	.994	42	321	21	2	26
Fishel, Columbus	1.000	5	35	6	0	5	Redfield, Scranton-W.B.	.994	18	166	13	1	16
Green, Syracuse	.990	59	552	34	6	51	Romine, Pawtucket	.929	2	12	1	1	1
Griffin, 13 Toledo-67 Columbus	.994	80	721	51	5	64	Ryal, Scranton-Wilkes Barre*	1.000	8	20	1	0	4
Hoiles, Rochester	1.000	1	6	0	0	0	Salinas, Richmond	.964	5	23	4	1	2
Hughes, Tidewater	1.000	2	12	1	0	3	Schu, Rochester	1.000	4	35	0	0	2
Justice, Richmond*	1.000	1	3	1	0	0	See, Toledo	.990	38	293	12	3	23
Lancellotti, Pawtucket*	.990	91	704	51	8	70	Smith, Richmond	.977	7	40	2	1	1
Leiper, Toledo	1.000	1	14	0	0	3	Stanicek, Scranton-W.B.	.984	65	557	43	10	46
Lombardi, Tidewater	.990	68	539	50	6	49	Thornton, Tidewater	.968	10	57	4	2	2
Lovullo, Toledo	.973	9	67	5	2	7	Tolman, Syracuse	.991	90	787	66	8	74
Lyons, Tidewater	.971	4	30	3	1	4	Tremblay, Pawtucket	1.000	1	3	0	0	0
McKnight, Tidewater	.995	76	584	47	3	55	Wetherby, Richmond*	.981	10	51	2	1	2
MELENDEZ, Rochester*	.992	123	1063	81	9	109	Wieligman, Toledo*	.993	62	553	33	4	60
Michel, Toledo	1.000	5	48	4	0	5							

SECOND BASEMEN

Player and Club	Pct.	G.	PO.	A.	E.	DP.	Player and Club	Pct.	G.	PO.	A.	E.	DP.
Alicea, Richmond	.857	2	3	3	1	0	Dulin, Rochester	.977	120	231	364	14	78
Austin, Toledo	.957	16	27	61	4	8	Earl, Columbus	.983	17	25	34	1	4
M. Barrett, Pawtucket	.959	11	22	25	2	3	Escobar, Syracuse	.951	19	40	58	5	12
T. BARRETT, Scranton-W.B.	.985	114	247	331	9	76	Gardner, Tidewater	.979	90	145	234	8	47
Cannizzaro, Pawtucket	.965	52	105	115	8	24	Garrison, Syracuse	.968	38	62	87	5	14
Carrasco, Toledo	.982	9	18	36	1	4	Gutierrez, Pawtucket	1.000	7	13	11	0	3
DeButch, Tidewater	.968	11	13	17	1	4	Heath, Syracuse	.969	29	63	92	5	26
Dickerson, Columbus	.935	6	11	18	2	5	Hulett, Rochester	.946	13	27	43	4	8
Dowell, Tidewater	.971	20	29	37	2	6	Infante, Syracuse	.973	55	102	153	7	39

SECOND BASEMEN—Continued

Player and Club	Pct.	G.	PO.	A.	E.	DP.
Jackson, Scranton-Wilkes Barre	.800	2	2	2	1	1
Legg, Scranton-Wilkes Barre	.969	21	35	58	3	11
Lemke, Richmond	.979	146	299	417	15	105
Lovullo, Toledo	.965	48	103	146	9	30
Malave, Syracuse	1.000	3	4	11	0	4
McKnight, Tidewater	.957	25	34	56	4	8
Miller-Jones, Pawtucket	.969	84	152	195	11	42
K.A. Miller, Tidewater	.971	24	52	84	4	22
N.K. Miller, Scranton-W.B.	.973	14	32	40	2	10
Pedrique, Toledo	1.000	1	4	1	0	0
Perkins, Rochester	.941	7	7	9	1	2
Salcedo, Scranton-Wilkes Barre	1.000	1	0	1	0	1
Salinas, Tidewater	1.000	6	10	4	0	2
Shaddy, Richmond	.750	2	2	1	1	0
Shipley, Tidewater	1.000	6	8	8	0	1
Sojo, Syracuse	1.000	1	1	1	0	0
Tolman, Syracuse	1.000	1	2	1	0	0
Turner, Rochester	.927	10	23	28	4	5
Walewander, Toledo	.966	85	159	240	14	52
Walker, Syracuse	.951	9	15	24	2	5
Wasinger, Columbus	.978	104	220	302	12	73
Williams, Pawtucket	.929	3	5	8	1	0
Woodard, Columbus	.943	32	45	88	8	10

THIRD BASEMEN

Player and Club	Pct.	G.	PO.	A.	E.	DP.
Alvarez, Toledo	.864	48	26	69	15	7
Barrett, Scranton-Wilkes Barre	1.000	1	2	4	0	0
Cannizzaro, Pawtucket	1.000	2	1	1	0	0
Carrasco, Toledo	1.000	5	3	3	0	1
DeButch, Tidewater	.909	7	1	9	1	1
DeLaCruz, Syracuse	.913	51	39	108	14	12
Dickerson, Columbus	.938	11	4	11	1	2
Dowell, Tidewater	1.000	4	1	2	0	1
Earl, Columbus	.895	15	1	16	2	2
Escobar, Syracuse	.846	5	2	9	2	0
Estrada, Pawtucket	.958	8	12	11	1	0
Gant, Richmond	1.000	8	3	13	0	1
Gonzalez, Pawtucket	.887	62	42	84	16	8
Griffin, Columbus	.962	9	10	15	1	4
Gutierrez, Pawtucket	.917	61	29	93	11	8
Hayes, Scranton-Wilkes Barre ..	1.000	7	8	8	0	0
Hulett, Rochester	.950	86	61	167	12	23
Infante, Syracuse	.909	6	2	8	1	0
Jarrell, Rochester	1.000	2	1	5	0	0
Kiefer, Columbus	.915	75	53	131	17	10
Legg, Scranton-Wilkes Barre	.968	42	28	63	3	4
Leiper, Toledo	.833	2	1	4	1	0
Lovullo, Toledo	.942	52	29	84	7	7
Malave, Syracuse	1.000	3	2	3	0	1
McKnight, Tidewater	.950	10	4	15	1	0
Meulens, Columbus	.927	14	11	27	3	1
Michel, Toledo	.000	1	0	0	1	0
Miller, Tidewater	.875	4	2	5	1	0
Naehring, Pawtucket	.979	20	13	33	1	3
O'MALLEY, Tidewater	.966	121	80	231	11	18
Pedrique, Toledo	1.000	2	1	1	0	0
Perkins, Rochester	.865	22	14	31	7	5
Rayford, Scranton-W.B.	1.000	3	1	2	0	0
Redfield, Scranton-W.B.	.928	96	85	185	21	18
Rios, Richmond	1.000	2	1	0	0	0
G. Rivera, Richmond	1.000	1	0	2	0	0
L. Rivera, Pawtucket	1.000	4	6	7	0	0
Schu, Rochester	.915	24	15	39	5	2
See, Toledo	.600	3	0	3	2	0
Shipley, Tidewater	.900	15	8	37	5	2
Smith, Richmond	.970	57	30	100	4	14
Sprague, Syracuse	.889	86	51	149	25	11
Strange, Toledo	.951	52	47	109	8	8
Tackett, Rochester	1.000	1	0	2	0	0
Turner, Rochester	.966	26	16	40	2	6
Velarde, Columbus	.924	31	17	68	7	9
Walewander, Toledo	.667	1	0	4	2	0
Wasinger, Columbus	.857	7	1	11	2	0
Whited, Richmond	.958	86	62	142	9	5

SHORTSTOPS

Player and Club	Pct.	G.	PO.	A.	E.	DP.
Barrett, Scranton-Wilkes Barre	1.000	3	4	0	0	0
Becker, Columbus	.958	27	44	70	5	11
Bell, Rochester	.931	113	190	297	36	66
Bradshaw, Toledo	.920	8	9	14	2	2
Brumley, Toledo	.957	9	18	27	2	4
Carrasco, Toledo	.947	69	78	208	16	36
DeJesus, Toledo	1.000	16	6	26	0	7
Dickerson, Columbus	.941	4	5	11	1	3
Dowell, Tidewater	.922	48	48	117	14	26
Earl, 16 Tol-44 Col	.939	60	88	159	16	36
Escobar, Syracuse	.939	24	39	68	7	21
Gutierrez, Pawtucket	.972	33	61	79	4	22
Hulett, Rochester	.883	25	37	54	12	15
Infante, Syracuse	.692	5	4	5	4	0
Jackson, Scranton-Wilkes Barre	.959	58	62	146	9	31
Legg, Scranton-Wilkes Barre	.969	40	50	108	5	27
Lovullo, Toledo	.952	12	18	22	2	7
McKnight, Tidewater	.921	28	29	53	7	12
Miller, Tidewater	.947	5	3	15	1	2
Moritz, Pawtucket	.966	30	40	73	4	12
Naehring, Pawtucket	.930	62	105	159	20	39
Pedrique, Toledo	.960	54	88	176	11	33
Redfield, Scranton-WB	1.000	4	13	8	0	2
Rios, Richmond	.947	19	37	52	5	16
Rivera, Pawtucket	.946	37	53	104	9	13
Rosario, Scranton-Wilkes Barre	.944	52	58	127	11	23
Shaddy, Richmond	.933	134	194	373	41	86
Shipley, Tidewater	.990	28	32	65	1	11
Smith, Rochester	1.000	8	2	3	0	0
SOJO, Syracuse	.957	120	169	347	23	77
Strange, Toledo	.943	33	61	88	9	29
Velarde, Columbus	.960	78	133	227	15	40
Walewander, Toledo	.884	13	23	38	8	7

OUTFIELDERS

Player and Club	Pct.	G.	PO.	A.	E.	DP.
Adduci, Scranton-Wilkes Barre°	.964	14	26	1	1	0
Anderson, Rochester°	1.000	2	1	0	0	0
Azocar, Columbus°	.977	21	41	2	1	0
Bean, Toledo°	.983	60	110	6	2	2
Beauchamp, Richmond	1.000	73	144	3	0	0
Blocker, Richmond°	.955	8	20	1	1	0
Bootay, Scranton-Wilkes Barre	.903	14	27	1	3	0
Brower, Columbus	1.000	17	36	1	0	0
Brown, Tidewater	.975	82	151	6	4	1
Bullock, Scranton-WB°	.992	72	119	4	1	1
Burks, Pawtucket	1.000	5	16	0	0	0
Campusano, Syracuse	.981	111	256	9	5	2
Cannizzaro, Pawtucket	.833	3	4	1	1	0
Carreon, Tidewater°	1.000	12	24	0	0	0
Cijntje, Rochester°	1.000	20	44	2	0	0
Cimo, Scranton-Wilkes Barre ...	1.000	73	107	6	0	1
Contreras, Tidewater°	.984	121	239	7	4	3
Cuyler, Toledo	.962	24	48	3	2	1
Davis, Rochester	.978	111	258	8	6	0
DeButch, Tidewater	1.000	9	13	1	0	0
DeLaCruz, Syracuse	1.000	8	7	2	0	0
Denson, Richmond	1.000	1	5	0	0	0
DiMascio, Toledo	.750	5	3	0	1	0
Dowell, Tidewater	1.000	1	1	0	0	0
Ducey, Syracuse	.933	10	14	0	1	0
Dunbar, Richmond°	1.000	11	17	0	0	0
Estrada, Pawtucket	1.000	2	1	0	0	0
Felix, Syracuse	.977	21	42	0	1	0
Finley, Rochester°	1.000	5	17	2	0	1
Fishel, Columbus	.980	94	144	3	3	1
Gant, Richmond	.956	52	108	1	5	0
Garcia, Richmond°	.973	90	138	4	4	1
O. Green, Syracuse°	1.000	25	48	2	0	0
R. Green, Columbus	.986	72	137	4	2	1
Harris, Rochester	1.000	6	11	0	0	0
Hayden, Tidewater°	.972	123	242	3	7	1
Hill, Syracuse	.972	79	168	6	5	1
Hughes, Rochester°	1.000	2	0	1	0	0
Jarrell, Rochester	1.000	2	0	0	0	0
Jefferson, 61 Col-16 Roc	.989	99	181	3	2	0
Jones, Richmond	.975	106	219	12	6	3
Justice, Richmond°	1.000	4	10	1	0	0
Lancellotti, Pawtucket°	1.000	4	10	1	0	0
Lawton, 55 Tdw-41 Col	.983	96	169	6	3	0
Leiper, Toledo	.990	97	188	6	2	1
Lusader, Rochester	.964	48	78	3	3	0
Maas, Columbus°	1.000	7	14	1	0	0
McKnight, Tidewater	1.000	34	45	2	0	1
Michel, Toledo	1.000	11	9	2	0	0
D. Miller, Columbus	1.000	2	0	1	0	0
K.A. Miller, Tidewater	.949	15	32	5	2	2
N.K. Miller, Scranton-WB	.976	39	77	4	2	2
Moore, Rochester°	.966	45	54	2	2	0
Morris, Columbus°	.953	104	208	5	1	1
OLANDER, Scranton-WB	.9953	104	208	5	1	1
Padget, Rochester	.989	51	87	4	1	1

OUTFIELDERS—Continued

Player and Club	Pct.	G.	PO.	A.	E.	DP.	Player and Club	Pct.	G.	PO.	A.	E.	DP.
Pederson, Syracuse°	.953	58	96	6	5	2	Smith, Richmond	1.000	1	1	0	0	0
Perkins, Rochester	.950	14	19	0	1	1	Stone, Pawtucket	.973	34	70	1	2	0
Pettis, Toledo	1.000	4	9	1	0	1	Thornton, Tidewater	.990	48	91	7	1	0
Pina, Pawtucket	.972	66	134	6	4	2	Tubbs, Richmond	.9950	99	199	3	1	0
Quintana, Pawtucket	1.000	36	77	6	0	1	Turner, Rochester	.953	19	37	4	2	1
Reed, Tidewater	.980	129	232	19	5	3	Wade, Pawtucket	.986	91	202	15	3	1
Richie, Toledo°	.990	40	96	2	1	2	Walker, Syracuse	.994	96	162	6	1	0
Roberts, Pawtucket	.989	84	170	5	2	1	Wetherby, Richmond°	1.000	19	26	3	0	0
Romano, Rochester	.957	25	43	2	2	0	Wieligman, Toledo°	.938	46	75	1	5	0
Romine, Pawtucket	1.000	19	37	3	0	0	B. Williams, Columbus	.991	50	112	2	1	0
Ryal, Scranton-Wilkes Barre° ...	1.000	48	97	3	0	0	D. Williams, Pawtucket	.996	96	221	6	1	1
Salcedo, Scranton-WB	.969	53	61	2	2	0	K. Williams, Toledo	1.000	14	27	1	0	1
Sanchez, Tidewater	1.000	2	4	0	0	0	Young, Toledo	1.000	5	7	0	0	0
Sanders, Columbus°	.976	69	165	0	4	0	Zupcic, Pawtucket	1.000	24	61	4	0	1
See, Toledo	.952	11	19	1	1	0							

CATCHERS

Player and Club	Pct.	G.	PO.	A.	E.	DP.	PB.	Player and Club	Pct.	G.	PO.	A.	E.	DP.	PB.
Bailey, Tidewater	.989	55	255	13	3	5	4	D. Miller, Columbus	.960	30	128	15	6	0	2
Bell, Richmond	1.000	8	31	1	0	0	0	N.K. Miller, Scranton-WB	1.000	1	5	0	0	0	0
Butera, Syracuse	.994	25	155	13	1	2	4	MIZEROCK, Richmond	.991	109	675	69	7	9	9
Cabrera, 87 Syr-1 Rmd	.980	88	549	35	12	8	13	Myers, Syracuse	.985	12	60	7	1	0	2
Carter, Tidewater	1.000	4	14	1	0	0	1	Nieto, Scranton-WB	.974	44	236	25	7	2	9
Datz, Toledo	.981	74	419	55	9	9	7	Pardo, Scranton-WB	.984	82	420	19	7	3	5
DiMascio, Toledo	.977	48	223	30	6	3	6	Plumb, Richmond	1.000	3	6	1	0	0	0
Dorsett, Columbus	.987	86	482	47	7	6	9	Posey, 5 Roc-3 SWB	1.000	8	33	6	0	0	0
Faulkner, Rochester	1.000	3	14	2	0	0	0	Rayford, Scranton-WB	.982	26	156	12	3	1	2
Geren, Columbus	.987	23	137	18	2	3	6	Sax, Columbus	.989	15	77	10	1	0	0
Hoiles, Rochester	.985	80	425	33	7	4	6	See, Toledo	.977	36	187	21	5	3	2
Liddell, Tidewater	.993	24	127	10	1	1	1	Tackett, Rochester	.977	65	339	40	9	2	5
Lombardi, Tidewater	.987	60	288	27	4	6	5	Tremblay, Pawtucket	.991	61	282	41	3	4	3
Lundblade, Tidewater	.984	24	115	8	2	1	1	Virgil, Syracuse	1.000	28	155	10	0	4	3
Lyons, Tidewater	1.000	5	13	2	0	0	0	Wine, Richmond	.995	29	182	12	1	0	6
Marzano, Pawtucket	.985	105	574	62	10	7	10								

PITCHERS

Player and Club	Pct.	G.	PO.	A.	E.	DP.	Player and Club	Pct.	G.	PO.	A.	E.	DP.
Araujo, Pawtucket	.952	32	4	16	1	0	Guzman, Syracuse	1.000	14	1	2	0	1
Atherton, Toledo	1.000	6	1	1	0	0	Habyan, 7 Roc-8 Col	.947	15	12	6	1	0
Bair, Syracuse	1.000	19	1	7	0	0	Hansen, Syracuse	1.000	9	3	8	0	0
Barton, Tidewater°	.923	38	2	10	1	0	Harnisch, Rochester	1.000	12	9	6	0	0
Bast, Pawtucket°	.944	18	3	14	1	1	Havens, Toledo°	.889	16	2	6	1	0
Bautista, Rochester	1.000	15	7	8	0	1	Henry, Richmond	.889	41	2	6	1	0
Beard, Toledo	1.000	12	7	10	0	0	M. Hernandez, Tidewater	.857	7	2	4	1	0
Beatty, Tidewater°	.941	27	11	37	3	2	X. Hernandez, Syracuse	1.000	15	8	16	0	0
Bell, Rochester°	1.000	7	1	8	0	0	Hetzel, Pawtucket	1.000	12	3	5	0	0
Blair, Syracuse	.882	19	8	7	2	0	Holman, Toledo	1.000	51	8	19	0	4
Bockus, Toledo	.974	32	7	30	1	2	Huismann, Rochester	.833	16	0	5	1	0
Bolton, Pawtucket°	.987	25	8	24	0	2	Innis, Tidewater	1.000	25	4	9	0	0
Boudreaux, Scranton-W.B.	1.000	19	6	12	0	0	Johnson, Rochester	.870	18	8	12	3	1
Boyd, Pawtucket	1.000	2	0	1	0	0	J. JONES, Columbus	1.000	20	13	28	0	0
Brink, Scranton-Wilkes Barre....	1.000	3	1	2	0	0	M. Jones, Rochester°	.929	31	3	10	1	1
Brown, Tidewater°	.960	13	10	14	1	2	Kiecker, Pawtucket	.974	28	6	31	1	4
Buice, Syracuse	.923	31	3	9	1	0	Kilner, Richmond°	1.000	12	1	1	0	0
Cary, Columbus°	1.000	11	1	10	0	0	Legg, Scranton-Wilkes Barre	1.000	2	0	1	0	0
Castillo, Syracuse°	1.000	27	1	6	0	0	Leister, Pawtucket	1.000	38	4	7	0	1
Chadwick, Pawtucket	1.000	7	0	2	0	0	Leiter, Columbus	.950	22	6	13	1	1
Chapin, Columbus	.917	27	2	9	1	3	Link, Toledo	.833	55	1	9	2	0
Christopher, Columbus	1.000	13	5	5	0	1	MacDonald, Syracuse°	.714	12	1	4	2	0
Cimo, Scranton-Wilkes Barre	1.000	1	0	1	0	0	Machado, Tidewater	1.000	14	1	3	0	0
Clary, Richmond	.850	13	5	12	3	1	Maddux, Scranton-Wilkes Barre	1.000	19	9	19	0	0
Clay, Scranton-Wilkes Barre	.947	33	7	11	1	0	Madrid, Scranton-Wilkes Barre.	.923	16	7	5	1	0
Combs, Scranton-Wilkes Barre°	1.000	3	1	3	0	0	Marak, Richmond	1.000	2	0	2	0	0
Cooper, Toledo	1.000	20	2	1	0	0	Martin, Scranton-Wilkes Barre .	.750	7	0	3	1	0
Culkar, Rochester	1.000	23	1	2	0	0	Mathews, Richmond	.917	36	3	8	1	0
Cummings, Syracuse	.913	19	7	14	2	1	McElroy, Scranton-W.B.°	1.000	14	2	2	0	0
Curry, Pawtucket	.900	7	3	6	1	0	McKeon, Richmond°	1.000	11	2	2	0	0
Dalton, Pawtucket°	.944	26	6	11	1	0	Mejia, Rochester	.923	18	5	7	1	0
Davidson, Columbus	.938	22	8	7	1	0	Mercker, Richmond°	.846	27	5	17	4	1
Dillard, Scranton-Wilkes Barre°	.949	28	7	30	2	2	Mesa, Rochester	1.000	7	0	2	0	0
Dopson, Pawtucket	1.000	2	1	1	0	0	Mitchell, Tidewater	.947	26	17	37	3	3
Drummond, Tidewater	.909	35	4	6	1	0	Mmahat, Columbus°	1.000	15	7	17	0	1
DuBois, 4 Roc-3 Tol°	.800	7	0	4	1	0	Mohorcic, Columbus	.800	16	2	6	2	0
Eave, Richmond	.944	23	11	23	2	3	Moore, Scranton-Wilkes Barre..	.935	61	5	24	2	2
Edens, 18 Tdw-7 SWB	1.000	25	14	14	0	2	Musselman, Syracuse°	1.000	10	1	8	0	1
Eichhorn, Richmond	1.000	25	1	8	0	0	Nezelek, Richmond	.875	48	9	12	3	2
Eiland, Columbus	.968	18	11	19	1	2	Nielsen, 19 Col.-21 Tidewater...	.946	40	16	19	2	2
Ellsworth, Pawtucket	.933	14	1	13	1	0	Noles, Columbus	.958	42	4	19	1	4
Farmer, Richmond°	.955	42	3	18	1	0	E. Nunez, Toledo	1.000	13	3	7	0	1
Freeman, Scranton-W.B.	1.000	5	1	5	0	1	J. Nunez, Syracuse	1.000	40	6	9	0	0
Frohwirth, Scranton-W.B.	.889	21	2	6	1	1	O'Connor, Syracuse°	1.000	18	2	5	0	0
Fulton, Columbus	.842	26	5	11	3	1	O'Neal, Scranton-Wilkes Barre..	1.000	18	8	13	0	0
Galvez, Columbus	.958	24	9	14	1	1	Palmer, Toledo	.875	10	5	9	2	0
Gardner, Tidewater	1.000	1	1	1	0	0	Parker, Columbus°	1.000	5	6	3	0	0
Gilles, Syracuse	1.000	29	9	12	0	2	H. Pena, Columbus°	.800	26	2	2	1	0
Gozzo, Syracuse	.800	12	7	5	3	0	R. Pena, Toledo	1.000	33	4	7	0	2
Grapenthin, 6 Columbus-9 Tol. ..	.909	15	1	9	1	1	Puleo, Richmond	.833	11	2	8	2	0
Greene, Richmond	1.000	26	7	14	0	0	Raczka, Rochester°	.909	44	1	9	1	2
Gross, Tidewater	.917	12	9	13	2	0	Richards, Richmond	.941	27	11	21	2	5
Guidry, Columbus°	1.000	7	0	6	0	0	Ritchie, Scranton-W.B.°	1.000	34	11	14	0	1

PITCHERS—Continued

Player and Club	Pct.	G.	PO.	A.	E.	DP.	Player and Club	Pct.	G.	PO.	A.	E.	DP.
Ritz, Toledo	.957	16	9	13	1	0	Stanhope, Rochester	.913	28	5	16	2	1
Rochford, Pawtucket*	.840	37	7	14	4	2	Stanton, Richmond*	1.000	13	1	2	0	1
Ross, Syracuse	.895	26	6	11	2	2	Stottlemyre, Syracuse	.750	10	3	6	3	0
Rub, Columbus*	1.000	17	1	2	0	0	Tabaka, Scranton-W.B.*	1.000	6	2	5	0	0
Ruffin, Scranton-Wilkes Barre*	1.000	9	0	11	0	0	Tapani, Tidewater	.923	17	9	15	2	2
Sanchez, Syracuse	.900	28	13	23	4	3	Thorpe, Rochester	1.000	14	2	6	0	0
Savage, Tidewater	1.000	33	1	8	0	1	Tibbs, Rochester	1.000	4	4	3	0	1
Scherrer, Tidewater*	1.000	20	2	7	0	0	Trautwein, Pawtucket	1.000	53	7	11	0	1
Schilling, Rochester	.935	27	11	32	3	4	Trujillo, 14 Tol-9 Tdw	.926	23	8	17	2	3
Schulze, Columbus	.939	14	11	20	2	3	Valera, Tidewater	1.000	2	1	0	0	0
Schwabe, Toledo	1.000	13	5	11	0	1	Vesling, Toledo*	1.000	11	4	16	0	0
Searcy, Toledo*	1.000	9	2	4	0	1	Wenson, Toledo	1.000	16	0	8	0	0
Sebra, Scranton-Wilkes Barre ..	.947	11	6	12	1	1	West, Tidewater*	.923	12	3	9	1	1
Service, Scranton-Wilkes Barre	1.000	23	1	4	0	1	Weston, Rochester	.960	23	8	16	1	0
Sharts, Scranton-Wilkes Barre*	1.000	52	2	10	0	2	Whitehurst, Tidewater	.963	21	9	17	1	1
Shelton, Scranton-Wilkes Barre	.875	10	2	5	1	0	Williams, Toledo*	.848	22	6	22	5	2
Shikles, Pawtucket	1.000	1	1	0	0	0	Wills, Syracuse	1.000	14	1	3	0	0
M. Smith (Miss.), Rochester	1.000	11	2	3	0	0	Wishnevski, Syracuse	1.000	16	10	17	0	0
M. Smith (Tex.), Rochester	.875	36	2	12	2	0	Woodward, Pawtucket	.900	40	4	5	1	0
Soff, Tidewater	.800	12	2	2	1	1	Ziem, Richmond	.917	18	10	12	2	0

The following players did not have any fielding statistics at the positions indicated or appeared only as a designated hitter, pinch-hitter or pinch-runner: Bradshaw, 3b; Dean, dh; Deitz, p; DeLaCruz, 1b, p; Dickerson, 1b; Fishel, 3b; Gardner, of; Horn, dh, ph; Hudson, p; Hulett, p; Jackson, 3b; LeMasters, p; McKnight, c; Nosek, p; Olander, p; Ontiveros, p; Salinas, ss; Schwarz, p; Tackett, of; Thornton, 3b; Turner, ss; Wapnick, p.

CLUB PITCHING

Club	ERA.	G.	CG.	ShO.	Sv.	IP.	H.	R.	ER.	HR.	HB.	BB.	Int. BB.	SO.	WP.	Bk.
Richmond	3.07	146	13	9	50	1244.1	1058	496	425	60	33	499	26	854	63	15
Syracuse	3.13	145	19	16	32	1269.1	1106	524	441	80	28	463	14	874	54	20
Tidewater	3.30	146	29	14	33	1247.2	1184	547	457	61	27	396	27	748	43	13
Rochester	3.31	145	24	12	30	1247.2	1187	553	459	100	26	423	9	752	49	19
Toledo	3.67	145	17	14	32	1264.1	1186	619	515	84	52	551	37	808	53	23
Columbus	3.67	146	19	8	42	1250.1	1194	608	510	75	44	459	35	809	40	27
Pawtucket	3.96	146	30	10	27	1235.0	1266	631	543	109	33	483	20	820	45	17
Scranton-Wilkes Barre	4.19	143	20	9	31	1212.2	1207	623	564	98	43	505	44	802	61	11

PITCHERS' RECORDS
(Leading Qualifiers for Earned-Run Average Leadership — 117 or More Innings)

*Throws lefthanded.

Pitcher—Club	W.	L.	Pct.	ERA.	G.	GS.	CG.	GF.	ShO.	Sv.	IP.	H.	R.	ER.	HR.	HB.	BB.	Int. BB.	SO.	WP.
J. Nunez, Syracuse	11	11	.500	2.21	40	12	0	20	0	7	134.1	116	51	33	4	2	55	2	122	3
Rochford, Pawtucket*	9	6	.600	2.37	37	18	9	9	2	2	163.1	139	52	43	6	3	63	0	82	0
Eave, Richmond	13	3	.813	2.80	23	23	1	0	0	0	141.1	111	48	44	6	6	57	1	93	4
Bolton, Pawtucket*	12	5	.706	2.89	25	22	5	2	2	1	143.1	140	57	46	13	4	47	2	99	0
Mitchell, Tidewater	11	11	.500	3.03	26	26	7	0	0	0	178.1	169	78	60	5	4	57	2	86	8
Sanchez, Syracuse	13	7	.650	3.13	28	27	1	0	1	0	169.2	125	68	59	14	1	74	0	141	11
Mercker, Richmond*	9	12	.429	3.20	27	27	4	0	0	0	168.2	107	66	60	17	3	95	4	144	7
Schilling, Rochester	13	11	.542	3.21	27	27	9	0	3	0	185.1	176	76	66	11	1	59	0	109	5
Whitehurst, Tidewater	8	7	.533	3.25	21	20	3	1	1	0	133.0	123	54	48	5	1	32	2	95	3
Beatty, Tidewater*	12	10	.545	3.31	27	27	6	0	3	0	185.0	173	86	68	14	1	43	0	90	3

Departmental Leaders: G—Moore, 61; W—Eave, Sanchez, Schilling, 13; L—Dillard, 16; Pct.—Eave, .813; GS—Five pitchers tied with 27; CG—Rochford, Schilling, 9; GF—Nezelek, 37; ShO—Beatty, Schilling, 3; Sv.—Eichhorn, Noles, 19; IP—Schilling, 185.1; H—Richards, 178; R—Dillard, 92; ER—Dillard, 88; HR—Dillard, 20; HB—Holman, 10; BB—Mercker, 95; IBB—Moore, 10; SO—Mercker, 144; WP—Leister, 12.

(All Pitchers—Listed Alphabetically)

Pitcher—Club	W.	L.	Pct.	ERA.	G.	GS.	CG.	GF.	ShO.	Sv.	IP.	H.	R.	ER.	HR.	HB.	BB.	Int. BB.	SO.	WP.
Araujo, Pawtucket	4	14	.222	5.83	32	16	2	15	0	4	105.0	139	78	68	14	4	33	2	52	2
Atherton, Toledo	1	2	.333	1.38	6	0	0	4	0	1	13.0	7	4	2	0	1	10	0	12	1
Bair, Syracuse	2	0	1.000	0.72	19	0	0	16	0	7	25.0	11	3	2	0	0	16	0	16	0
Barton, Tidewater*	0	3	.000	4.28	38	0	0	20	0	5	33.2	41	22	16	3	3	9	2	27	1
Bast, Pawtucket*	6	4	.600	4.37	18	17	0	0	0	0	105.0	121	59	51	19	2	46	1	75	4
Bautista, Rochester	4	4	.500	2.83	15	13	3	1	1	0	98.2	84	41	31	10	3	26	1	47	4
Beard, Toledo	3	4	.429	2.55	12	11	1	1	0	0	60.0	49	21	17	4	0	14	1	50	2
Beatty, Tidewater*	12	10	.545	3.31	27	27	6	0	3	0	185.0	173	86	68	14	1	43	0	90	3
Bell, Rochester*	1	2	.333	4.99	7	7	0	0	0	0	39.2	40	24	22	5	0	15	0	27	4
Blair, Syracuse	5	6	.455	3.97	19	17	3	2	1	0	106.2	94	55	47	10	2	38	1	76	1
Bockus, Toledo	6	4	.600	3.91	32	14	1	10	0	3	119.2	124	63	52	9	5	52	4	58	7
Bolton, Pawtucket*	12	5	.706	2.89	25	22	5	2	2	1	143.1	140	57	46	13	4	47	2	99	0
Boudreaux, Scranton-Wil. Bar.	5	1	.833	3.83	19	1	0	2	0	0	40.0	44	17	17	5	1	14	1	18	1
Boyd, Pawtucket	0	0	.000	0.00	2	2	0	0	0	0	7.0	4	0	0	0	0	0	0	11	0
Brink, Scranton-Wilkes Barre	0	1	.000	4.09	3	3	0	0	0	0	11.0	11	7	5	0	0	4	0	3	0
Brown, Tidewater*	6	6	.500	4.44	13	13	4	0	0	0	75.0	81	41	37	2	0	31	0	46	2
Buice, Syracuse	4	2	.667	2.47	31	1	0	16	0	5	51.0	34	15	14	3	0	28	5	59	1
Cary, Columbus*	1	1	.500	3.09	11	2	0	6	0	0	23.1	17	9	8	1	0	13	1	27	1
Castillo, Syracuse*	1	3	.250	2.81	27	0	0	19	0	5	41.2	33	15	13	7	0	15	2	37	1
Chadwick, Pawtucket	2	3	.400	6.39	7	7	0	0	0	0	38.0	52	29	27	5	0	24	1	30	1
Chapin, Columbus	2	4	.333	2.93	27	0	0	21	0	1	40.0	33	15	13	3	1	15	4	38	3
Christopher, Columbus	5	6	.455	4.81	13	11	1	0	0	0	73.0	95	45	39	6	3	21	3	42	0
Cimo, Scranton-Wilkes Barre	0	0	.000	36.00	1	0	0	1	0	0	1.0	5	4	4	0	0	0	0	0	0
Clary, Richmond	7	5	.583	2.04	15	15	4	0	0	0	101.2	87	33	23	3	2	28	0	70	2
Clay, Scranton-Wilkes Barre	5	6	.455	4.58	33	7	0	17	0	2	72.2	75	46	37	4	9	51	1	49	5
Combs, Scranton-Wilkes Barre ..	3	0	1.000	0.37	3	3	2	0	1	0	24.1	15	4	1	0	0	7	0	20	1
Cooper, Toledo	2	2	.500	3.22	20	1	0	11	0	2	36.1	24	15	13	0	2	16	1	27	3
Culkar, Rochester	2	2	.500	3.99	23	1	0	9	0	2	29.1	28	14	13	2	3	8	0	19	2
Cummings, Syracuse	7	5	.583	3.14	19	17	3	1	1	0	106.0	97	46	37	1	4	41	2	60	6
Curry, Pawtucket	0	5	.000	5.59	7	6	1	0	0	0	38.2	49	27	24	6	1	12	0	19	2

Pitcher—Club	W.	L.	Pct.	ERA.	G.	GS.	CG.	GF.	ShO.	Sv.	IP.	H.	R.	ER.	HR.	HB.	BB.	Int. BB.	SO.	WP.
Dalton, Pawtucket°	1	3	.250	5.12	26	3	1	10	1	4	45.2	55	26	26	2	2	16	0	20	1
Davidson, Columbus	8	5	.615	1.83	22	7	2	9	1	2	93.1	71	26	19	2	3	30	2	56	0
Deitz, Richmond	0	0	.000	0.00	1	0	0	1	0	0	0.2	0	0	0	0	0	3	0	0	0
DeLaCruz, Syracuse	0	0	.000	0.00	1	0	0	1	0	0	1.0	0	0	0	0	1	0	0	0	1
Dillard, Scranton-Wilkes Barre°	6	16	.273	5.02	28	26	4	0	1	0	157.2	174	92	88	20	2	64	2	96	5
Dopson, Pawtucket	0	2	.000	7.27	2	2	0	0	0	0	8.2	13	9	7	1	0	1	0	9	2
Drummond, Tidewater	5	1	.833	3.27	35	0	0	14	0	0	63.1	63	29	23	3	4	26	5	42	5
DuBois, 4 Roc-3 Tol°	4	2	.667	2.00	7	7	0	0	0	0	54.0	41	14	12	6	0	18	0	29	2
Eave, Richmond	13	3	.813	2.80	23	23	1	0	0	0	141.1	111	48	44	6	6	57	1	93	4
Edens, 18 Tdw-7 SWB	2	6	.250	4.44	25	14	0	3	0	1	107.1	121	59	53	5	5	39	4	47	4
Eichhorn, Richmond	1	0	1.000	1.32	25	0	0	24	0	19	41.0	29	6	6	0	2	6	0	33	0
Eiland, Columbus	9	4	.692	3.76	18	18	2	0	0	0	103.0	107	47	43	10	1	21	0	45	1
Ellsworth, Pawtucket	1	8	.111	5.02	14	10	0	3	0	0	66.1	73	45	37	9	1	29	0	35	2
Farmer, Richmond°	5	2	.714	2.43	42	0	0	15	0	2	63.0	61	22	17	1	0	20	3	15	4
Freeman, Scranton-WB	1	1	.500	4.50	5	5	0	0	0	0	14.0	11	8	7	1	0	5	0	8	5
Frohwirth, Scranton-WB	3	2	.600	2.23	21	0	0	17	0	7	32.1	29	11	8	1	1	13	3	29	0
Fulton, Columbus	2	3	.400	4.41	26	1	0	19	0	6	49.0	56	35	24	5	1	25	2	30	4
Galvez, Columbus	5	4	.556	4.92	24	15	1	2	0	1	100.2	103	62	55	10	5	52	1	59	6
Gardner, Tidewater	0	0	.000	9.00	1	0	0	0	0	0	2.0	3	2	2	0	0	0	0	1	0
Gilles, Syracuse	4	4	.500	3.55	29	8	2	12	1	1	83.2	85	38	33	5	2	28	2	41	6
Gozzo, Syracuse	5	1	.833	2.76	12	7	2	2	1	2	62.0	56	22	19	3	0	19	0	34	2
Grapenthin, 6 Col-9 Tol	3	2	.600	3.41	15	1	0	5	0	1	37.0	37	19	14	2	2	14	0	13	1
Greene, Richmond	9	12	.429	3.61	26	26	2	0	1	0	152.0	136	74	61	9	2	50	0	125	10
Gross, Tidewater	4	4	.500	3.97	12	12	0	0	0	0	70.1	72	33	31	3	1	17	0	39	1
Guidry, Columbus°	1	5	.167	4.18	7	7	1	0	0	0	32.1	30	21	15	6	1	14	0	20	1
Guzman, Syracuse	1	1	.500	3.98	14	0	0	4	0	0	20.1	13	9	9	0	0	30	0	28	5
Habyan, 7 Roc-8 Col	3	5	.375	3.98	15	13	2	2	0	0	83.2	103	44	37	4	1	14	0	52	3
Hansen, Toledo	3	4	.429	5.09	9	9	4	0	0	0	53.0	62	33	30	4	3	26	2	23	3
Harnisch, Rochester	5	5	.500	2.58	12	12	3	0	1	0	87.1	60	27	25	7	4	35	0	59	3
Havens, Toledo°	5	3	.625	2.64	16	8	1	4	1	2	58.0	56	19	17	5	3	17	1	59	0
Henry, Richmond	11	5	.688	2.44	41	6	0	20	0	1	84.2	43	28	23	4	3	61	3	101	7
M. Hernandez, Tidewater	2	2	.500	1.69	7	6	2	0	1	0	42.2	32	11	8	0	0	7	0	30	1
X. Hernandez, Syracuse	5	6	.455	3.53	15	15	2	0	1	0	99.1	95	42	39	7	2	22	0	47	4
Hetzel, Pawtucket	4	4	.500	2.48	12	12	4	0	1	0	80.0	65	27	22	5	1	32	2	79	4
Holman, Toledo	3	1	.750	1.91	51	0	0	31	0	11	89.2	74	21	19	2	10	36	2	38	3
Hudson, Toledo	0	0	.000	4.50	1	0	0	0	0	0	4.0	3	2	2	1	0	1	0	4	0
Huismann, Rochester	2	1	.667	1.71	16	0	0	13	0	8	21.0	9	4	4	1	1	3	1	20	0
Hulett, Rochester	0	0	.000	0.00	1	0	0	1	0	0	0.2	0	0	0	0	0	0	0	0	0
Innis, Tidewater	3	1	.750	2.12	25	0	0	18	0	10	29.2	28	9	7	0	1	8	2	14	1
Johnson, Rochester	7	6	.538	3.26	18	14	2	2	0	1	105.0	104	45	38	4	4	31	2	60	4
J. Jones, Columbus	8	6	.571	3.77	20	20	4	0	1	0	124.0	110	54	52	9	2	31	1	94	1
M. Jones, Rochester°	9	7	.563	3.35	31	17	2	7	0	2	129.0	127	65	48	12	3	42	0	80	3
Kiecker, Pawtucket	8	9	.471	3.67	28	19	3	3	0	0	147.1	163	83	60	12	4	36	2	87	6
Kilner, Richmond°	1	0	1.000	7.78	12	0	0	3	0	0	19.2	23	18	17	2	1	12	0	18	1
Legg, Scranton-Wilkes Barre	0	0	.000	27.00	2	0	0	0	0	0	2.0	8	6	6	0	0	1	0	1	0
Leister, Pawtucket	7	7	.500	3.93	38	9	4	14	1	1	128.1	101	58	56	2	3	70	3	104	12
Leiter, Columbus	9	6	.600	5.00	22	12	2	0	0	0	90.0	102	50	50	5	5	34	2	70	3
LeMasters, Richmond	0	1	.000	18.00	1	1	0	0	0	0	2.0	4	5	4	1	0	2	0	0	0
Link, Toledo	6	4	.600	4.34	55	0	0	32	0	5	91.1	89	56	44	13	3	40	6	73	5
MacDonald, Syracuse°	1	0	1.000	5.63	12	0	0	4	0	0	16.0	16	10	10	0	1	6	0	12	0
Machado, Tidewater	1	2	.333	0.62	14	1	0	9	0	5	29.0	16	2	2	0	0	17	2	37	2
Maddux, Scranton-Wilkes Bar	7	7	.500	3.66	19	17	3	1	0	0	123.0	119	55	50	7	7	26	2	100	8
Madrid, Scranton-Wilkes Bar.	3	6	.333	4.84	16	10	1	2	0	0	67.0	64	37	36	10	2	30	3	51	5
Marak, Richmond	0	1	.000	9.00	2	1	0	0	0	0	4.0	8	4	4	1	0	4	1	2	1
Martin, Scranton-Wilkes Bar.	0	3	.000	13.78	7	3	0	0	0	0	16.1	28	26	25	1	0	17	1	11	3
Mathews, Richmond	2	5	.286	3.88	36	1	0	13	0	3	67.1	70	31	29	7	0	18	1	33	5
McElroy, Scranton-Wilkes Bar.°	1	2	.333	2.93	14	0	0	9	0	3	15.1	13	6	5	1	1	11	1	12	0
McKeon, Richmond°	0	0	.000	3.38	11	0	0	3	0	1	10.2	9	4	4	0	1	5	1	4	1
Mejia, Rochester	3	6	.333	4.86	18	11	0	2	0	0	66.2	77	39	36	10	0	36	0	32	4
Mercker, Richmond°	9	12	.429	3.20	27	27	4	0	0	0	168.2	107	66	60	17	3	95	4	144	7
Mesa, Rochester	0	2	.000	5.40	7	1	0	4	0	0	10.0	10	6	6	2	0	6	0	3	1
Mitchell, Tidewater	11	11	.500	3.03	26	26	7	0	2	0	178.1	169	78	60	5	4	57	2	86	8
Mmahat, Columbus°	3	4	.429	3.84	15	15	1	0	0	0	82.0	70	44	35	4	3	49	0	50	2
Mohorcic, Columbus	1	2	.333	1.01	16	0	0	11	0	3	26.2	18	12	3	1	0	10	4	12	3
Moore, Scranton-W Barre	6	10	.375	3.34	61	1	0	25	0	5	97.0	86	41	36	4	6	49	10	67	4
Musselman, Syracuse°	5	2	.714	3.77	10	10	0	0	0	0	57.1	62	24	24	4	1	24	0	30	1
Nezelek, Richmond	4	5	.444	2.44	48	0	0	37	0	12	77.1	65	25	21	0	3	35	6	30	8
Nielsen, 19 Col-21 Tide	6	11	.353	3.21	40	10	2	27	1	10	109.1	93	46	39	4	3	39	5	47	1
Noles, Columbus	5	2	.714	3.70	42	1	0	33	0	19	87.2	77	43	36	1	7	34	7	66	4
Nosek, Toledo	0	0	.000	36.00	1	1	0	0	0	0	1.0	2	4	4	0	0	4	0	0	1
E. Nunez, Toledo	1	5	.167	2.58	13	8	1	3	0	1	59.1	47	20	17	7	2	18	2	53	1
J. Nunez, Syracuse	11	11	.500	2.21	40	12	0	20	0	7	134.1	116	51	33	4	2	55	2	122	3
O'Connor, Columbus	1	2	.333	2.84	18	1	0	4	0	0	25.1	21	8	8	1	0	11	0	13	2
O'Neal, Scranton-W Barre	4	4	.500	2.53	18	11	5	2	2	1	96.0	82	33	27	7	0	23	2	71	4
Olander, Scranton-W Barre	0	0	.000	Infin	1	0	0	0	0	0	0.0	2	4	4	0	0	2	0	0	1
Ontiveros, Scranton-WB	0	0	.000	0.00	1	1	0	0	0	0	3.1	3	0	0	0	0	2	0	0	1
Palmer, Toledo	2	4	.333	3.93	10	10	0	0	0	0	55.0	49	34	24	3	2	23	0	33	2
Parker, Columbus	3	0	1.000	1.66	5	5	1	0	1	0	38.0	25	9	7	1	0	10	2	25	2
H. Pena, Columbus°	1	2	.333	6.06	26	0	0	9	0	1	32.2	44	29	22	4	1	22	2	26	3
R. Pena, Toledo	5	2	.714	2.51	33	1	0	18	0	7	61.0	57	24	17	6	1	15	6	51	1
Puleo, Richmond	5	1	.833	3.34	11	11	2	0	0	0	62.0	59	26	23	4	1	15	1	57	4
Raczka, Rochester°	1	6	.143	5.13	44	1	0	27	0	2	66.2	75	47	38	11	2	31	3	50	3
Richards, Richmond	11	11	.500	3.81	27	27	0	0	0	0	167.2	178	76	71	4	5	54	1	85	6
Ritchie, Scranton-WB°	7	4	.636	4.18	34	20	4	6	1	0	135.2	143	70	63	16	2	38	2	73	3
Ritz, Toledo	7	8	.467	3.16	16	16	1	0	0	0	102.2	95	48	36	3	8	60	1	74	4
Rochford, Pawtucket°	9	6	.600	2.37	37	18	9	9	2	2	163.1	139	52	43	6	3	43	2	76	0
Ross, Syracuse	8	5	.615	2.94	26	8	2	7	0	0	95.0	102	43	31	4	3	11	0	58	1
Rub, Columbus°	0	0	.000	1.21	17	0	0	6	0	0	22.1	12	3	3	0	1	13	0	15	1
Ruffin, Scranton-W Barre°	5	1	.833	4.68	9	9	0	0	0	0	50.0	44	28	26	2	2	39	1	44	9
Sanchez, Syracuse	13	7	.650	3.13	28	27	1	0	1	0	169.2	125	68	59	14	1	74	0	141	11
Savage, Tidewater	3	2	.600	3.59	33	1	0	21	0	6	42.2	41	21	17	2	1	21	2	28	3
Scherrer, Tidewater°	2	0	1.000	3.03	20	0	0	7	0	0	29.2	25	10	10	2	1	18	1	17	0

Pitcher—Club	W.	L.	Pct.	ERA.	G.	GS.	CG.	GF.	ShO.	Sv.	IP.	H.	R.	ER.	HR.	HB.	BB.	Int. BB.	SO.	WP.
Schilling, Rochester	13	11	.542	3.21	27	27	9	0	3	0	185.1	176	76	66	11	1	59	0	109	5
Schulze, Columbus	8	4	.667	2.05	14	14	2	0	1	0	92.0	71	27	21	3	5	28	3	62	1
Schwabe, Toledo	5	3	.625	2.60	13	5	1	4	0	0	62.1	60	20	18	2	1	10	4	32	5
Schwarz, Rochester	0	2	.000	5.84	9	0	0	4	0	2	12.1	5	9	8	0	1	16	0	12	2
Searcy, Toledo*	2	3	.400	7.54	9	9	0	0	0	0	37.0	41	36	31	2	1	37	2	26	2
Sebra, Scranton-W Barre	3	4	.429	4.73	11	11	1	0	0	0	64.2	61	36	34	9	2	21	1	56	1
Service, Scranton-W Barre	3	1	.750	2.16	23	0	0	15	0	6	33.1	27	8	8	2	2	23	6	23	0
Sharts, Scranton-W Barre*	1	2	.333	3.33	52	0	0	21	0	6	54.0	51	22	20	1	2	17	2	18	2
Shelton, Scranton-W Barre	0	3	.000	6.35	10	3	0	3	0	1	28.1	35	20	20	3	1	13	4	21	1
Shikles, Pawtucket	0	1	.000	6.75	1	1	0	0	0	0	5.1	9	5	4	1	0	3	0	4	0
M. Smith, (Tex.) Roch	2	4	.333	3.21	36	1	0	22	0	7	56.0	45	23	20	6	1	22	1	48	2
M. Smith, (Miss.), Roch	1	4	.200	5.75	11	1	0	7	0	1	20.1	29	13	13	1	0	11	1	14	1
Soff, Tidewater	1	0	1.000	2.30	12	0	0	4	0	0	15.2	16	4	4	1	2	2	0	6	2
Stanhope, Rochester	5	4	.556	4.25	28	12	2	7	0	0	91.0	113	57	43	7	1	30	0	57	3
Stanton, Richmond*	2	0	1.000	0.00	13	0	0	11	0	8	20.0	6	0	0	0	1	13	2	20	0
Stottlemyre, Syracuse	3	2	.600	3.23	10	9	2	1	0	0	55.2	46	23	20	4	2	15	0	45	0
Tabaka, Scranton-W Barre*	0	4	.000	6.32	6	6	0	0	0	0	31.1	32	26	22	2	2	23	0	15	1
Tapani, Tidewater	7	5	.583	3.47	17	17	2	0	1	0	109.0	113	49	42	6	1	25	2	63	3
Thorpe, Rochester	2	1	.667	2.66	14	0	0	6	0	1	20.1	18	7	6	0	0	6	0	12	1
Tibbs, Rochester	3	0	1.000	0.93	4	4	1	0	1	0	29.0	22	3	3	0	0	10	0	14	3
Trautwein, Pawtucket	6	8	.429	3.99	53	2	1	26	0	5	97.0	92	46	43	5	4	57	3	62	9
Trujillo, 14 Tol-9 Tide	8	5	.615	3.93	23	15	3	0	2	0	107.2	116	53	47	8	1	37	2	55	6
Valera, Tidewater	1	1	.500	2.08	2	2	0	0	0	0	13.0	8	3	3	1	1	5	0	10	1
Vesling, Toledo*	3	6	.333	3.03	11	11	3	0	2	0	71.1	62	29	24	3	5	33	0	34	1
Wapnick, Syracuse	1	0	1.000	0.69	6	1	0	4	0	0	13.0	9	1	1	0	1	5	0	10	0
Wenson, Toledo	0	3	.000	7.49	16	2	0	6	0	0	33.2	47	32	28	3	1	23	1	18	0
West, Tidewater*	7	4	.636	2.37	12	12	5	0	1	0	87.1	60	31	23	9	2	29	0	69	3
Weston, Rochester	8	3	.727	2.09	23	14	2	7	1	4	112.0	103	30	26	6	1	19	0	51	1
Whitehurst, Tidewater	8	7	.533	3.25	21	20	3	1	1	0	133.0	123	54	48	5	1	32	2	95	3
Williams, Toledo*	4	12	.250	5.38	22	20	1	0	0	0	115.1	107	81	69	6	2	78	3	74	8
Wills, Syracuse	1	0	1.000	1.59	14	0	0	11	0	5	17.0	8	7	3	1	0	8	0	13	1
Wishnevski, Syracuse	5	5	.500	3.93	16	12	2	2	1	0	89.1	83	44	39	6	9	25	0	32	8
Woodward, Pawtucket	2	5	.286	4.66	40	0	0	34	0	10	56.0	51	30	29	4	4	34	2	58	0
Ziem, Richmond	1	2	.333	2.67	18	8	0	6	0	4	60.2	62	30	18	1	3	21	2	24	3

BALKS—Havens, Schilling, 6 each; Leiter, Sanchez, 5 each; Eave, Noles, 4 each; Araujo, Bast, Cummings, Madrid, Mathews, E. Nunez, Puleo, Searcy, 3 each; Bautista, Beatty, Bell, Blair, Bockus, Cary, Chadwick, Culkar, Curry, Davidson, Galvez, Guidry, Harnisch, X. Hernandez, J. Jones, Kiecker, Link, Mercker, Mitchell, Mohorcic, Moore, Musselman, J. Nunez, Ritz, Rochford, Scherrer, Whitehurst, Woodward, Ziem, 2 each; Barton, Bolton, Buice, Castillo, Chapin, Dillard, Drummond, Eiland, Gross, Hansen, Hudson, Johnson, M. Jones, Maddux, Martin, Mmahat, O'Neal, Palmer, Parker, H. Pena, Raczka, Richards, Ross, Rub, Sharts, Stanhope, Tabaka, Tapani, Thorpe, Trujillo, Wenson, West, Wishnevski, 1 each.

COMBINATION SHUTOUTS—Eiland-Fulton, Eiland-Davidson, Davidson-Rub, Columbus; Araujo-Woodward, Bast-Bolton, Chadwick-Dalton, Pawtucket; Eave-Eichhorn 2, Mercker-Eichhorn, Eave-Henry-Nezelek, Puleo-Ziem, Mercker-Henry-Nezelek, Henry-Stanton, Eave-McKeon-Nezelek, Richmond; Weston-Huismann, Tibbs-Raczka, Mejia-M. Smith (Miss.), Harnisch-M. Smith (Tex.), Habyan-Jones, Rochester; Brink-Boudreaux-Sharts, Edens-Moore-Sharts-Service, Ritchie-Clay-McElroy, Scranton-Wilkes Barre; Sanchez-Buice 2, Sanchez-Nunez-Wills, Nunez-Guzman-Wills, Sanchez-O'Connor-Guzman-Wills, Sanchez-Bair, Cummings-Bair, Musselman-Castillo, Sanchez-Nunez, Syracuse; Tapani-Barton, Whitehurst-Innis, Beatty-Nielsen, Edens-Nielsen, Valera-Nielsen, Tidewater; Trujillo-Pena, Trujillo-Nunez, Trujillo-Holman, Nunez-Holman, Grapenthin-Holman, Williams-Pena, Beard-Bockus-Pena, Havens-Pena, Searcy-Pena, Toledo.

NO-HIT GAMES—None.

Mexican League

CLASS AAA

CHAMPIONSHIP WINNERS IN PREVIOUS YEARS

1955—Mexico City Tigers* .... .539	1971—Jalisco§ .... .558	1980—No champion y
1956—Mexico City Reds .... .692	Saltillo .... .593	1981—Mexico City Reds .... .615
1957—Yucatan .... .567	1972—Saltillo .... .636	Reynosa .... .492
Mex. C. Reds (2nd)† .... .550	Cordoba§ .... .541	1982—Ciudad Juarez x .... .570
1958—Nuevo Laredo .... .625	1973—Saltillo .... .656	Mexico City Tigers .... .508
1959—Poza Rica .... .575	Mexico City Reds x .... .590	1983—Campeche z .... .614
Mex. C. Reds (3rd)† .... .507	1974—Jalisco .... .627	Ciudad Juarez .... .535
1960—Mexico City Tigers .... .538	Mexico City Reds x .... .551	1984—Yucatan z .... .560
1961—Veracruz .... .575	1975—Tampico x .... .541	Ciudad Juarez .... .509
1962—Monterrey .... .592	Cordoba .... .649	1985—Mexico City Reds z .... .606
1963—Puebla .... .606	1976—Mexico City Reds x .... .543	Nuevo Laredo .... .5275
1964—Mexico City Reds .... .586	Union Laguna .... .547	1986—Puebla z .... .682
1965—Mexico City Tigers .... .590	1977—Mexico City Reds .... .623	Monclova .... .598
1966—Mexico City Tigers‡ .... .614	Nuevo Laredo x .... .507	1987—Mexico City Reds z .... .605
Mexico City Reds .... .571	1978—Aguascalientes x .... .589	Monterrey .... .536
1967—Jalisco .... .607	Union Laguna .... .523	1988—Mexico City Reds z .... .646
1968—Mexico City Reds .... .586	1979—Saltillo .... .704	Nuevo Laredo .... .602
1969—Reynosa .... .591	Puebla x .... .628	
1970—Aguila§ .... .580		
Mexico City Reds .... .607		

*Defeated Nuevo Laredo, two games to none, in playoff for pennant. †Won four-team playoff. ‡Won split-season playoff. §League divided into Northern, Southern divisions; won two-team playoff. xLeague divided into Northern, Southern zones; sub-divided into Eastern, Western divisions, won eight-team playoff. yA players strike on July 1 forced the cancellation of the regular season and playoff schedule. zLeague divided into Northern, Southern zones; four clubs from each zone qualified for postseason play. Won final series for league championship.

STANDING OF CLUBS AT CLOSE OF SEASON
NORTHERN ZONE

Club	N.L.	U.L.	Sal.	M.S.	S.L.	Mva.	M.I.	Cam.	Leo.	Yuc.	M.R.	M.T.	Tab.	Ags.	W.	L.	T.	Pct.	G.B.
Nuevo Laredo	..	6	8	9	7	9	11	5	3	4	6	3	4	7	82	50	0	.621	....
Union Laguna	8	..	8	7	8	10	10	0	6	3	3	3	2	5	73	59	0	.553	9
Saltillo	8	6	..	6	9	5	12	3	4	6	3	4	2	2	70	59	0	.543	10½
Monterrey Sultans	5	7	8	..	6	9	7	2	5	3	5	3	2	5	67	65	0	.508	15
San Luis	7	6	5	8	..	6	6	4	4	2	3	4	4	4	63	67	1	.485	18
Monclova	5	6	9	5	8	..	9	0	1	2	2	2	5	4	58	73	1	.443	23½
Monterrey Industrials	3	4	2	9	7	5	..	4	2	3	2	3	3	3	50	80	2	.385	31

SOUTHERN ZONE

Club	N.L.	U.L.	Sal.	M.S.	S.L.	Mva.	M.I.	Cam.	Leo.	Yuc.	M.R.	M.T.	Tab.	Ags.	W.	L.	T.	Pct.	G.B.
Campeche	1	6	2	4	2	5	6	..	6	8	7	6	10	12	75	52	2	.591	....
Leon	3	0	5	2	5	4	5	4	7	..	5	9	10	8	11	73	57	1	.562	3½
Yucatan	2	3	2	3	4	4	3	8	9	..	5	9	7	10	69	59	0	.539	6½
Mexico City Reds	0	3	3	1	7	4	4	6	5	9	..	6	8	12	68	63	0	.519	9
Mexico City Tigers	3	3	2	3	2	5	3	7	3	5	10	..	8	5	59	71	0	.454	17½
Tabasco	2	8	4	4	2	2	2	4	6	5	6	6	..	6	57	71	1	.445	18½
Aguascalientes	3	1	4	1	4	3	2	3	4	2	9	4	2	9	..	46	84	0	.354	30½

Playoffs—Nuevo Laredo defeated Monterrey Sultans, four games to three; Saltillo defeated Union Laguna, four games to one; Yucatan defeated Leon, four games to two; Campeche defeated Mexico City Reds, four games to none. Nuevo Laredo defeated Saltillo, four games to three, in Northern Zone finals; Yucatan defeated Campeche, four games to two, in Southern Zone finals. Nuevo Laredo defeated Yucatan, four games to two, in final series to capture league championship.

(Compiled by Ana Luisa Perez Talarico, League Statistician, Mexico, D.F.)

CLUB BATTING

Club	Pct.	G.	AB.	R.	OR.	H.	TB.	2B.	3B.	HR.	RBI.	SH.	SF.	HP.	BB.	Int. BB.	SO.	SB.	CS.	LOB.
Campeche	.309	129	4336	715	550	1339	1980	206	18	133	650	33	47	32	369	33	494	69	59	895
Leon	.307	131	4417	781	763	1355	2008	235	29	120	702	38	31	34	427	29	633	82	59	884
Mexico City Reds......	.304	131	4366	731	651	1327	1911	177	46	105	653	54	51	27	414	35	703	117	47	923
Union Laguna	.294	132	4342	687	614	1275	1835	206	30	98	584	76	30	48	457	49	621	86	37	965
Monterrey Indust.....	.292	132	4323	578	754	1264	1737	181	32	76	502	48	39	25	406	21	532	56	57	961
Nuevo Laredo	.292	132	4285	706	583	1250	1844	185	29	117	624	53	26	44	460	30	627	100	56	908
Monterrey Sultans ...	.292	132	4336	649	615	1264	1798	206	41	82	574	51	32	37	445	59	606	105	72	939
Aguascalientes	.289	130	4146	576	804	1199	1648	185	45	58	515	42	31	34	373	22	462	52	53	890
Saltillo	.286	129	4210	612	566	1203	1740	215	42	66	566	44	32	43	395	35	636	93	76	854
Mexico City Tigers ...	.286	131	4143	611	565	1183	1628	179	25	72	549	72	31	36	441	29	619	89	59	903
Tabasco	.279	129	4074	544	667	1137	1467	164	26	38	474	73	32	40	401	42	416	129	70	890
Monclova	.278	132	4338	611	647	1208	1664	169	46	65	527	51	33	22	481	30	695	66	56	968
San Luis	.277	131	4223	614	711	1170	1691	212	39	77	551	53	40	51	450	40	732	38	52	918
Yucatan	.272	128	4031	589	514	1095	1529	167	15	79	523	50	37	45	526	33	595	84	64	929

INDIVIDUAL BATTING
(Leading Qualifiers for Batting Championship—356 or More Plate Appearances)

Player and Club	Pct.	G.	AB.	R.	H.	TB.	2B.	3B.	HR.	RBI.	SH.	SF.	HP.	BB.	Int. BB.	SO.	SB.	CS.
Aikens, Willie, Leon	.395	128	423	108	167	320	40	1	37	131	0	2	7	104	5	67	1	2
Johnson, Roy, Campeche	.385	110	405	92	156	260	32	3	22	100	0	7	2	65	7	38	7	2
Cole, Mike, Tabasco	.375	127	459	108	172	208	16	10	0	37	1	1	4	87	8	27	100	33

Player and Club	Pct.	G.	AB.	R.	H.	TB.	2B.	3B.	HR.	RBI.	SH.	SF.	HP.	BB.	Int. BB.	SO.	SB.	CS.
Sanchez, Armando, Mexico City Reds.	.372	104	387	79	144	183	23	2	4	71	9	9	0	42	3	21	5	1
Cosey, Donald Ray, Monterrey Sultans	.361	128	507	97	183	270	24	6	17	84	2	5	2	34	3	61	6	7
Davis, Trench, Saltillo	.359	115	460	94	165	236	29	18	2	47	0	2	2	34	5	31	32	14
Valverde, Raul, Union Laguna	.358	100	355	64	127	182	21	8	6	62	5	1	4	14	0	39	5	4
Payton, Erick, Union Laguna	.353	128	467	88	165	254	27	1	20	80	4	6	6	38	16	61	28	6
Driessen, Dan, Yucatan	.351	128	436	81	153	235	44	1	12	82	0	5	3	88	13	52	0	2

Departmental Leaders: G—Stockstill, 132; AB—Gomez, 530; R—Aikens, Cole, 108; H—Cosey, 183; TB—Aikens, L. Hernandez, 320; 2B—Smith, 46; 3B—Davis, 18; HR—L. Hernandez, 39; RBI—Aikens, 131; SH—Camacho, 19; SF—Ray. Torres, 11; HP—Saiz, 13; BB—Aikens, 104; IBB—Payton, 16; SO—Mikulik, 112; SB—Cole, 100; CS—Cole, 33.

(All Players—Listed Alphabetically)

Player and Club	Pct.	G.	AB.	R.	H.	TB.	2B.	3B.	HR.	RBI.	SH.	SF.	HP.	BB.	Int. BB.	SO.	SB.	CS.
Abarca, David, Aguascalientes	.333	1	3	1	1	1	0	0	0	0	0	0	0	0	0	1	0	0
Abrego, Jesus, Nuevo Laredo	.223	74	215	31	48	59	5	3	0	28	3	0	3	28	0	31	4	1
Abril, Ramon, Union Laguna	.269	100	361	56	97	111	8	3	0	29	14	0	4	25	0	15	6	4
Acosta, Carlos, Saltillo	.266	21	64	7	17	21	4	0	0	8	0	0	0	3	0	20	3	1
Agramon, Antonio, Saltillo	.150	18	20	2	3	3	0	0	0	1	0	0	0	2	0	9	0	0
Aguilar, Enrique, Aguascalientes	.299	122	458	61	137	195	16	3	12	66	0	3	3	27	4	40	4	4
Aguilera, Antonio, Monterrey Sultans .	.279	104	408	70	114	154	14	7	4	39	5	1	2	46	7	69	31	14
Aikens, Willie, Leon	.395	128	423	108	167	320	40	1	37	131	0	2	7	104	5	67	1	2
Alfaro, Jesus, Saltillo	.234	14	47	8	11	22	3	1	2	5	0	0	0	7	1	10	0	1
Almodobar, Ricardo, M.C. Tigers	.269	98	249	28	67	80	9	2	0	21	10	0	1	16	0	40	7	10
Alonso, Hermilo, Monterrey Industrials	.268	86	220	29	59	74	8	2	1	18	2	0	0	18	0	20	2	1
Alvarez, Hector, 37 Tig-58 Ind	.294	95	211	24	62	69	7	0	0	19	3	0	0	11	0	43	13	6
Alvarez, Heriberto, Yucatan	.274	112	325	47	89	114	13	3	2	37	7	3	7	33	3	52	1	6
Alvarez, Juan Carlos, Yucatan	.221	68	195	14	43	53	5	1	1	15	7	2	2	8	0	44	4	1
Alvarez, Martin, Saltillo	.000	1	1	0	0	0	0	0	0	0	0	0	0	0	0	0	0	0
Alvarez, Ruben, Tabasco	.000	2	2	0	0	0	0	0	0	0	0	0	0	0	0	1	0	0
Amador, Arturo, Nuevo Laredo	.000	1	3	0	0	0	0	0	0	0	0	0	0	0	0	0	0	0
Arano, Jose Ramon, Saltillo	.212	82	156	18	33	42	3	3	0	14	5	1	5	15	0	27	1	3
Arce, Francisco Javier, San Luis	.299	96	314	52	94	161	17	4	14	63	0	6	7	43	6	57	2	3
Arevalo, Guadalupe, Aguascalientes ...	.333	76	243	30	81	99	12	3	0	28	2	2	2	9	1	27	1	4
Arzate, Martin, 61 Yuc-50 Leon	.268	111	362	41	97	110	11	1	0	48	5	1	1	43	0	32	6	9
Avila, Ruben, Union Laguna	.312	128	459	67	143	215	24	3	14	79	6	4	3	38	1	92	2	2
Baca, Manuel, Mexico City Reds	.314	116	417	72	131	197	15	3	15	61	3	6	2	29	4	67	0	1
Barrera, Jesus Antonio, Campeche	.260	88	246	43	64	75	8	0	1	12	4	2	1	35	0	17	6	16
Barrera, Nelson, Mexico City Reds	.283	124	460	66	130	231	16	2	27	96	0	8	5	42	11	79	2	3
Bellazetin, Jose Juan, Mexico City Tig	.312	126	426	79	133	176	25	0	6	48	4	3	1	97	8	34	12	7
Beltran, Gerardo, Mexico City Reds	.259	82	239	28	62	97	12	1	7	30	3	1	4	26	1	73	3	5
Benitez, Manuel, Mexico City Tigers ...	.317	119	423	71	134	200	19	1	15	70	1	1	10	39	2	80	6	8
Beristain, Gregorio, Mexico City Tiger	.227	22	44	4	10	10	0	0	0	5	0	1	0	8	0	7	1	2
Blancas, Gabriel, Mexico City Reds	.160	8	25	1	4	4	0	0	0	0	0	0	1	0	0	12	1	0
Bobadilla, Manuel, 78 Ind-32 Sal	.282	110	344	32	97	135	20	3	4	44	4	2	2	35	1	39	0	4
Bocanegra, Alipio, Tabasco	.250	17	16	2	4	4	0	0	0	0	0	0	0	2	0	2	1	1
Bocardo, Manuel, Monclova	.250	78	236	25	59	86	13	1	4	32	1	1	1	30	0	42	4	3
Bronson, Eddie, Saltillo	.228	16	57	4	13	18	2	0	1	8	1	0	1	1	1	8	0	1
Brown, Darrel, Monclova	.293	38	140	20	41	50	7	1	0	15	0	1	0	14	0	16	4	2
Buenrostro, Jose Luis, Leon	.256	61	121	18	31	37	4	1	0	13	1	0	1	10	0	31	0	0
Burke, Norberto, Yucatan	.240	57	150	20	36	53	6	1	3	15	0	0	2	31	2	23	0	2
Bustamante, Miguel Angel, M.C. Tig. ..	.232	58	82	9	19	23	2	1	0	5	2	1	0	13	1	20	1	0
Camacho, Adulfo, Mexico City Tigers..	.283	121	427	72	121	143	17	1	1	50	19	3	5	51	0	51	31	10
Camarero, Marco A., Nuevo Laredo.....	.200	2	5	0	1	1	0	0	0	0	1	0	0	0	0	1	0	0
Camarero, Rolando, Union Laguna	.286	2	7	1	2	2	0	0	0	1	0	0	0	1	0	1	1	0
Cangas, Rosendo, Mexico City Tigers..	.260	48	150	16	39	43	2	1	0	13	1	1	2	17	0	31	3	2
Cano, Guadalupe, Monterrey Sultans ..	.310	88	197	20	61	80	9	2	2	25	6	0	1	16	0	27	5	5
Cantu, Gerardo, Saltillo	.277	88	177	16	49	69	9	1	3	25	0	0	1	10	2	53	0	2
Castaneda, Antonio, Saltillo	.235	49	115	20	27	35	3	1	1	13	5	1	1	9	0	30	0	3
Castelan, Miguel A., 68 Leo-43 Yuc ...	.243	111	371	51	90	109	10	3	1	39	1	4	1	37	1	63	9	5
Castilla, Vinicio, Saltillo	.307	128	462	70	142	223	25	13	10	58	6	6	5	33	1	70	11	12
Castro, Eddie, 88 Ind-32 Sal	.302	120	387	61	117	191	21	1	17	70	0	5	3	75	9	83	3	4
Cazarin, Manuel, Leon	.302	122	450	75	136	198	18	1	14	60	5	5	1	30	8	48	3	4
Cepeda, Alejandro, Monclova	.221	88	199	23	44	56	5	2	1	19	4	1	0	10	0	17	1	0
Chance, Tony, Mexico City Reds	.255	67	259	41	66	113	6	4	11	42	0	1	2	17	1	66	8	3
Chapa, Victor M., Monterrey Sultans..	.300	37	80	11	24	34	2	1	2	11	0	0	0	5	0	10	1	1
Chavez, Guadalupe, Leon	.000	2	2	0	0	0	0	0	0	0	0	0	0	0	0	1	0	0
Chavez, Jose Santos, Union Laguna	.253	90	265	30	67	98	8	1	7	35	11	1	2	34	9	34	2	5
Chavez, Juan De Dios, Yucatan	.333	5	6	2	2	3	1	0	0	2	0	0	0	0	0	2	0	0
Chavez, Ricardo, Campeche	.195	31	41	6	8	9	1	0	0	2	0	2	0	4	0	8	0	0
Clayton, Leonardo, Monclova	.252	117	389	63	98	133	17	3	4	48	5	6	0	80	6	57	6	3
Clements, West, Yucatan	.275	103	334	59	92	184	18	1	24	73	0	2	5	66	4	87	3	6
Cole, Mike, Tabasco	.375	127	459	108	172	208	16	10	0	37	1	1	4	87	8	27	100	33
Contreras, Cuitlahuac, Union Laguna...	.271	71	166	27	45	63	10	1	2	23	5	1	2	20	3	36	6	0
Cosey, Donald Ray, 76 Leo-52 M.S.	.361	128	507	97	183	270	24	6	17	84	2	5	2	34	3	61	6	7
Cruz, Fernando, 12 Lag-75 Ind	.202	87	243	15	49	58	6	0	1	23	2	0	1	13	0	49	1	2
Cruz, Javier, Mexico City Tigers	.167	61	72	9	12	13	1	0	0	6	0	0	2	9	0	14	0	1
Cruz, Luis Alfonso, San Luis	.330	130	491	103	162	239	26	6	13	67	5	5	11	39	2	63	8	6
Daut, Manuel, Monclova	.271	39	96	14	26	29	3	0	0	13	3	0	3	15	0	23	1	1
David, Andre, Monterrey Industrials ...	.291	37	127	29	37	53	8	1	2	15	1	1	1	19	4	12	2	0
Davis, Trench, 24 Tab-91 Sal	.359	115	460	94	165	236	29	18	2	47	0	2	2	34	5	31	32	14
Delgado, T. 26 Yuc.-25 Ind-16 Cam..	.243	67	185	21	45	56	4	2	1	13	3	0	2	24	0	31	4	5
DeLosSantos, Carlos E., Tab	.222	103	279	34	62	70	8	0	0	18	8	1	5	26	0	25	2	4
Diaz, Luis Fernando, Nuevo Laredo	.337	117	424	101	143	231	31	3	17	65	3	0	6	62	6	61	22	6
Diaz, Remigio, Monterrey Sultans......	.273	106	326	53	89	112	7	8	0	32	9	0	0	30	0	33	25	6
Dominguez, David, San Luis	.303	131	459	70	139	226	37	1	16	89	4	10	3	58	4	79	1	3
Driessen, Dan, Yucatan	.351	128	436	81	153	235	44	1	12	82	0	5	3	88	13	52	0	2
Dunster, Donald, Monclova	.000	1	0	0	0	0	0	0	0	0	0	0	0	0	0	0	0	0
Elizondo, Fernando, Monclova	.281	119	466	55	131	172	19	5	4	60	13	4	2	25	1	30	2	4
Espino, Juan, Tabasco	.091	3	11	2	1	1	0	0	0	0	0	0	0	1	0	0	0	0
Esquer, Ramon, Leon	.238	58	126	36	30	36	2	2	0	11	2	1	1	16	1	22	5	1
Esquivias, Ruben, Union Laguna	.145	46	76	3	11	14	0	0	1	2	3	0	2	3	0	19	1	0

Player and Club	Pct.	G.	AB.	R.	H.	TB.	2B.	3B.	HR.	RBI.	SH.	SF.	HP.	BB.	Int. BB.	SO.	SB.	CS.
Estrada, Francisco, Leon	.256	43	121	14	31	35	4	0	0	8	5	0	1	10	0	4	3	0
Estrada, Hector, Mexico City Reds	.279	55	165	15	46	67	15	0	2	16	2	1	1	6	1	41	0	1
Estrada, Roberto, Tabasco	.240	53	154	14	37	46	5	2	0	19	3	1	2	8	0	20	5	2
Farmar, Damon, Nuevo Laredo	.299	98	348	53	104	154	9	1	13	54	4	2	1	34	2	90	8	6
Fernandez, Daniel, Mexico City Reds	.350	108	420	95	147	190	20	10	1	50	5	4	3	61	4	55	30	8
Flores, Jose Alberto, Union Laguna	.000	1	1	0	0	0	0	0	0	0	0	0	0	0	0	0	0	0
Flores, Jose Humberto, San Luis	.256	93	281	50	72	91	13	3	0	23	5	0	2	36	2	56	2	8
Garcia, Jesus, Mexico City Tigers	.000	10	4	4	0	0	0	0	0	0	0	0	0	0	0	1	0	0
Garcia, Jose Luis, Aguascalientes	.304	100	286	53	87	111	18	3	0	34	1	5	10	64	1	38	3	5
Garcia, Juan Manuel, Aguascalientes ..	.298	68	235	41	70	95	13	6	0	30	3	1	0	37	3	22	1	4
Garcia, Martin, 2 M.S.-69 SLP	.224	71	237	28	53	71	8	2	2	16	1	1	3	22	0	50	0	4
Garibay, Luis Alberto, Union Laguna ..	.222	11	27	1	6	6	0	0	0	2	0	0	0	2	0	8	0	0
Garibay, Roberto, San Luis	.262	79	252	28	66	86	10	2	2	21	2	4	1	13	1	54	5	1
Garza, Adolfo, 12 M.S.-91 Tabasco	.281	103	338	41	95	124	20	0	3	40	2	1	4	49	8	40	0	1
Garza, Gerardo, Nuevo Laredo	.271	119	402	60	109	175	22	1	14	52	4	2	3	19	2	52	12	2
Garzon, Eliseo, Mexico City Reds	.274	31	84	13	23	45	3	2	5	17	0	1	0	9	0	21	0	1
Garzon, Felix, Campeche	.275	128	448	49	123	163	16	0	8	66	7	5	4	29	4	59	1	0
Gassos, Genaro, Tabasco	.143	9	7	0	1	1	0	0	0	1	0	1	0	1	0	3	0	0
Gastelum, Carlos, Mexico City Reds	.268	87	269	34	72	83	8	0	1	28	8	4	2	33	1	36	0	2
Gomez, Alejandro, Monterrey Ind.	.277	130	530	75	147	170	17	3	0	42	8	5	3	32	0	49	14	12
Gonzalez, Jesus, Tabasco	.291	125	471	65	137	191	27	0	9	84	6	8	6	33	6	31	2	2
Gonzalez, Juan, Aguascalientes	.210	88	257	23	54	67	9	2	0	22	5	0	0	11	0	37	1	5
Gonzalez, Mario A., Monterrey Sultans	.217	78	184	17	40	62	6	2	4	23	4	4	1	8	0	50	2	4
Gonzalez, Noe, Leon	.335	66	227	32	76	115	15	0	8	44	2	3	0	16	1	44	1	3
Gonzalez, Pedro, Yucatan	.000	5	7	1	0	0	0	0	0	0	0	0	0	0	0	2	0	0
Grajales, Norberto, M.C. Tigers	.000	1	2	0	0	0	0	0	0	0	0	0	0	0	0	0	0	0
Green, David, Aguascalientes	.313	18	64	8	20	27	4	0	1	11	0	1	0	4	0	10	0	0
Griffith, Thomas, Nuevo Laredo	.288	16	52	11	15	21	1	1	1	5	0	1	1	3	0	13	0	2
Guerrero, Francisco, Union Laguna	.268	129	456	78	122	173	22	4	7	32	9	2	1	83	1	87	19	5
Guerrero, Jaime, Leon	.233	86	210	29	49	58	7	1	0	22	5	0	3	15	1	43	8	1
Guerrero, Leobardo, Leon	.302	82	258	50	78	99	12	3	1	40	5	1	2	31	1	20	3	4
Guerrero, Victor Hugo, San Luis	.385	13	13	2	5	5	0	0	0	0	0	0	0	0	0	2	0	1
Gutierrez, Arnoldo, Union Laguna	.240	88	192	26	46	64	9	3	1	21	2	5	2	23	0	56	2	5
Gutierrez, Felipe, Campeche	.306	67	271	53	83	118	17	0	6	31	5	2	5	13	2	26	6	5
Gutierrez, Jose Luis, Leon	.167	32	48	7	8	12	4	0	0	3	1	0	1	6	0	10	1	2
Guzman, Gelacio, Campeche	.000	1	0	1	0	0	0	0	0	0	0	0	0	0	0	0	0	0
Guzman, Marco Antonio, Campeche	.311	117	424	64	132	198	20	2	14	71	1	7	1	43	4	42	0	1
Hernandez, Leo, Campeche	.347	127	496	99	172	320	27	2	39	125	0	6	2	35	5	51	5	3
Hernandez, Miguel, M.C. Tigers	.250	116	308	35	77	96	12	2	1	35	15	2	2	43	1	40	5	1
Hernandez, Rodolfo, Monterrey Sul.	.308	119	413	63	127	189	23	0	13	84	3	7	5	58	7	48	0	6
Herrera, Isidro, Monterrey Industrials	.266	113	259	43	69	90	11	5	0	24	7	2	2	36	1	34	5	8
Herrera, Raymundo, San Luis	.063	42	32	8	2	2	0	0	0	2	1	0	2	6	0	9	2	1
Herrera, Rene, Campeche	.250	3	8	2	2	2	0	0	0	0	0	0	0	1	0	1	1	0
Herrera, Ricardo, Yucatan	.287	127	478	85	137	156	17	1	0	20	4	3	4	72	2	45	49	26
Holmes, Stan, Mexico City Reds	.317	45	161	37	51	87	8	2	8	45	0	2	2	23	1	30	1	1
Hurtado, Hector, Leon	.125	6	8	1	1	1	0	0	0	0	0	0	0	0	0	2	0	0
Jarrell, Joe, Leon	.320	99	372	64	119	190	32	3	11	64	1	3	2	17	2	61	8	5
Jimenez, Eduardo, Campeche	.312	116	385	74	120	199	25	3	16	55	0	3	12	55	2	78	15	9
Jimenez, Leopoldo, Campeche	.220	40	50	5	11	20	3	0	2	7	0	0	0	5	1	10	0	0
Johnson, Roy, Campeche	.385	110	405	92	156	260	32	3	22	100	0	7	2	65	7	38	7	2
Landreaux, Kenneth, Aguascalientes..	.292	47	168	31	49	90	10	5	7	32	0	3	1	26	4	26	6	1
Lara, Jesus, San Luis	.291	33	86	11	25	30	1	2	0	6	1	0	0	6	0	18	2	0
Lavagnino, Jose Ernesto, San Luis	.270	77	215	22	58	82	13	1	3	30	4	1	0	16	2	44	0	2
Leal, Guadalupe, Monterrey Sultans....	.311	90	289	41	90	123	19	4	2	33	5	2	0	26	5	40	6	5
Ledezma, Victor M., Aguascalientes ...	.100	15	20	3	2	5	0	0	1	2	0	0	0	8	0	2	1	1
Leyva, German, Monclova	.328	111	348	58	114	141	11	8	0	28	5	2	0	57	1	43	6	8
Lizarraga, Alejandro, 48 Ind-72 Mva .	.273	120	421	44	115	159	13	2	9	50	2	8	3	15	0	37	1	0
Lopez, Antonio, 6 Sal-48 Ags.	.323	54	186	19	60	86	10	2	4	19	0	1	2	7	0	14	5	3
Lopez, Jaime, Saltillo	.315	52	127	11	40	48	8	0	0	16	2	1	1	6	1	8	0	1
Lopez, Jesus Manuel, San Luis	.186	47	118	8	22	32	7	0	1	13	3	0	1	15	0	18	0	0
Lopez, Pablo, Saltillo	.136	13	22	1	3	4	1	0	0	1	0	0	1	0	0	4	0	0
Lopez, Salvador, Nuevo Laredo	.200	17	40	8	8	8	0	0	0	1	0	0	0	4	0	9	1	0
Loredo, Jorge Luis, Nuevo Laredo	.260	46	96	15	25	30	3	1	0	7	3	0	0	14	1	27	0	1
Luna, Jose Luis, Saltillo	.266	118	342	39	91	105	14	0	0	30	8	2	0	19	0	39	0	1
Machiria, Pablo, Mexico City Tigers	.330	126	466	66	154	234	27	7	13	85	4	6	4	27	5	39	7	1
Magana, Gabriel, Yucatan	.500	14	12	3	6	7	1	0	0	2	0	0	0	0	0	3	0	0
Martinez, Grimaldo, Monclova	.241	87	199	31	48	55	2	1	1	16	7	1	1	23	0	30	4	4
Martinez, Raul, Monterrey Sultans	.288	115	368	46	106	155	19	3	8	47	2	2	8	41	8	51	2	4
Mata, Victor, Monclova	.302	14	43	2	13	15	0	1	0	6	1	0	0	2	0	7	0	1
Mena, Evaristo, Monclova	.125	19	32	3	4	5	1	0	0	3	0	0	0	8	1	17	0	1
Mendoza, Luis Alonso, Monterrey Ind.	.308	5	13	3	4	4	0	0	0	0	0	0	0	1	0	5	0	0
Mendoza, Mario, Monterrey Sultans ..	.297	109	381	47	113	136	20	0	1	40	4	2	3	29	1	46	2	6
Mercado, Felipe, San Luis	.182	13	22	2	4	4	0	0	0	1	0	0	0	0	0	2	0	0
Mere, Pedro, Nuevo Laredo	.300	125	427	71	128	188	18	3	12	48	2	4	5	48	4	54	10	9
Meza, Alfredo, Monterrey Industrials .	.500	2	2	0	1	1	0	0	0	0	0	0	0	0	0	0	0	0
Meza, Leonel, Leon	.263	21	38	6	10	14	2	1	0	4	0	0	0	4	0	10	0	0
Mikulik, Joe, Monclova	.318	130	487	88	155	271	20	12	24	86	0	3	4	51	8	112	15	11
Miller, Eddie, Monterrey Sultans	.310	25	87	18	27	45	4	4	2	13	1	0	2	13	2	19	3	8
Mora, Andres, Monterrey Industrials ..	.316	119	427	55	135	212	15	1	20	81	0	7	3	46	6	57	0	1
Morales, Manuel, Aguascalientes	.277	81	285	35	79	93	9	1	1	16	7	0	1	16	0	5	1	10
Morales, Martin, Nuevo Laredo	.000	1	3	0	0	0	0	0	0	0	0	0	0	0	0	1	0	0
Moreno, Leonardo, San Luis	.244	41	86	14	21	23	2	0	0	3	2	1	0	10	1	7	2	4
Moreno, Lorenzo, Nuevo Laredo	.254	22	63	4	16	22	4	1	0	5	0	1	0	3	0	13	0	1
Moreno, Roberto, Monclova	.203	54	133	13	27	31	2	1	0	10	1	0	1	5	0	32	0	1
Morfin, Jorge, Campeche	.192	61	73	10	14	14	0	0	0	8	2	0	4	0	8	1	3	5
Morones, Martin, Monclova	.256	49	168	25	43	58	5	2	2	20	4	1	1	27	6	36	9	5
Navarrete, Juan, 8 Sal-97 Ind	.317	105	391	59	124	151	11	2	4	34	10	4	1	43	2	9	6	7
Navarro, Ruben, Campeche	.282	115	380	51	107	144	13	3	6	57	3	7	0	24	3	47	0	6
Noris, Rogelio, Mexico City Reds	.000	3	5	0	0	0	0	0	0	0	0	0	0	0	0	1	0	0
Nunez, Arturo, Monterrey Industrials .	.305	71	200	21	61	78	7	2	2	12	5	0	3	4	0	39	0	3
Ortiz, Alejandro, Nuevo Laredo	.294	126	436	77	128	236	19	4	27	111	0	4	2	92	10	68	8	2
Ortiz, Gregorio, Leon	.000	1	0	1	0	0	0	0	0	0	0	0	0	0	0	0	0	0

Player and Club	Pct.	G.	AB.	R.	H.	TB.	2B.	3B.	HR.	RBI.	SH.	SF.	HP.	BB.	Int. BB.	SO.	SB.	CS.
Osuna, Hector Manuel, Aguascalientes	.225	60	173	19	39	56	5	0	4	18	2	1	3	8	0	25	0	1
Pardo, Victor, Tabasco	.000	11	14	1	0	0	0	0	0	1	0	0	0	0	0	3	0	0
Payton, Erick, Union Laguna	.353	128	467	88	165	254	27	1	20	80	4	6	6	38	16	61	28	6
Pena, Luis Alberto, Campeche	.318	112	393	58	125	188	13	1	16	52	2	4	4	27	5	68	2	4
Peralta, Amado, San Luis	.275	122	375	58	103	173	26	7	10	57	3	3	5	76	15	93	2	3
Perez, Francisco, Mexico City Tigers	.000	3	2	1	0	0	0	0	0	0	0	0	0	0	0	1	0	0
Perez, Jose Luis, 44 Mva-32 Ags.	.289	76	218	26	63	79	10	0	2	22	1	3	1	29	1	45	0	1
Perez, Roberto, Yucatan	.000	2	2	0	0	0	0	0	0	0	0	0	0	0	0	1	0	0
Perez, Tovar Raul, Monterrey Sultans	.355	30	110	10	39	55	6	2	2	17	0	2	0	4	1	9	3	1
Picos, Tereso, Monterrey Sultans	.000	2	1	0	0	0	0	0	0	0	0	0	0	0	0	0	0	0
Plascencia, Obed, Nuevo Laredo	.335	82	233	29	78	107	8	0	7	42	6	0	2	16	1	29	3	6
Ponce, Hector, Campeche	.165	60	97	14	16	24	3	1	1	4	1	0	0	2	0	12	2	1
Quintero, Guadalupe, Aguascalientes	.265	59	185	25	49	67	7	1	3	22	0	1	3	16	1	23	0	2
Quintero, Victor, Tabasco	.254	101	335	41	85	100	11	2	0	31	10	3	2	26	1	26	2	2
Quiroz, Jose Julian, Mexico City Tiger.	.250	98	280	30	70	91	10	4	1	27	4	1	0	40	4	39	6	3
Rabb, John, Monterrey Sultans	.204	34	108	15	22	39	2	0	5	14	0	0	2	14	1	18	2	3
Ramirez, Efren, Tabasco	.192	47	78	6	15	22	1	0	2	15	0	0	1	9	0	25	0	0
Ramirez, Enrique, Nuevo Laredo	.279	126	451	68	126	147	14	2	1	43	12	3	1	19	0	34	7	6
Ramirez, Gustavo, Monclova	.322	54	146	20	47	63	9	2	1	20	1	0	4	6	0	17	0	1
Reyes, Enrique, 9 Lar.-83 San Luis	.220	92	232	18	51	62	6	1	1	24	7	0	3	32	1	40	1	1
Reyes, Juan, Leon	.290	121	469	77	136	241	31	1	24	101	0	5	0	22	3	109	4	1
Reyna, Luis, Aguascalientes	.335	95	337	46	113	199	20	6	18	75	0	3	5	22	5	44	26	6
Rivera, Eleazar, Campeche	.356	30	73	11	26	35	3	0	2	8	0	1	0	1	0	6	2	0
Rivero, Gener, Yucatan	.231	21	13	4	3	4	1	0	0	2	0	0	0	4	0	0	1	0
Rodriguez, Aurelio, Saltillo	.182	15	33	2	6	6	0	0	0	2	0	0	0	2	0	3	1	0
Rodriguez, Genaro, Mex. City Tigers	.309	82	217	34	67	94	10	1	5	35	0	1	3	21	2	29	3	6
Rodriguez, Guillermo, Mex. City Tigers	.297	129	498	84	148	261	27	1	28	100	1	7	5	16	4	90	4	2
Rodriguez, Juan Francisco, Yucatan	.292	127	456	81	133	157	11	2	3	46	13	4	4	61	1	19	14	5
Rodriguez, Luis, Saltillo	.235	62	136	15	32	40	6	1	0	20	2	0	0	10	0	22	0	1
Romero, Marco Antonio, N. Laredo	.291	123	450	70	131	182	19	4	8	55	4	2	3	31	3	65	5	4
Rosales, Arturo, San Luis	.285	129	484	61	138	208	32	1	12	89	2	8	8	25	2	88	2	1
Ruiz, Demetrio, Tabasco	.282	108	347	27	98	112	10	2	0	29	10	1	2	22	2	18	0	3
Saenz, Ricardo, Saltillo	.296	122	416	70	123	197	25	8	11	74	1	4	7	50	7	84	11	4
Saiz, Herminio, Union Laguna	.290	128	445	50	129	156	24	0	1	42	9	2	13	23	0	53	4	3
Salinas, Luis, Nuevo Laredo	.212	56	132	16	28	49	6	0	5	20	1	0	5	28	0	48	1	2
Samaniego, Manuel, Campeche	.429	8	7	1	3	3	0	0	0	0	0	0	0	0	0	1	0	0
Sanchez, Alejandro, Tabasco	.280	94	329	55	92	147	10	3	13	56	0	2	5	25	4	59	8	5
Sanchez, Andres, Mexico City Reds	.312	107	382	54	119	136	10	2	1	40	9	3	1	34	1	62	4	6
Sanchez, Armando, Mexico City Reds	.372	104	387	79	144	183	23	2	4	71	9	9	0	42	3	21	5	1
Sanchez, Gerardo, Nuevo Laredo	.320	132	481	89	154	222	25	5	11	84	10	6	12	59	1	30	19	8
Sanchez, Orlando, Monterrey Sultans	.303	93	333	68	101	147	15	2	9	49	1	2	0	61	11	31	9	7
Serna, Joel, Monclova	.260	121	430	42	112	151	16	1	7	57	4	2	2	37	2	81	3	4
Serratos, Miguel, Yucatan	.235	119	379	43	89	111	8	1	4	45	10	3	8	32	2	50	0	4
Simmons, Nelson, Tabasco	.310	77	239	31	74	109	11	0	8	39	0	6	0	56	9	26	0	2
Smith, Gregory, Saltillo	.332	124	455	80	151	254	46	6	15	98	0	4	5	43	9	52	28	13
Solis, Daniel, Tabasco	.221	66	131	12	29	42	5	1	2	13	3	2	3	14	1	25	0	3
Sommers, Jesus, Union Laguna	.312	129	484	85	151	238	28	1	19	84	2	5	0	57	9	66	5	1
Soto, Carlos, Monterrey Industrials	.302	88	268	39	81	132	17	2	10	48	1	4	3	32	2	32	2	0
Stevenson, Bill, Monclova	.296	22	81	13	24	33	3	0	2	11	0	0	1	11	1	18	0	0
Stockstill, David, Union Laguna	.301	132	465	98	140	234	22	6	20	82	5	8	5	88	10	40	2	4
Tatis, Bernardo, Mexico City Reds	.327	119	446	100	146	249	17	13	20	90	3	3	1	57	7	66	49	12
Tellez, Alonso, Monterrey Industrials	.327	132	498	84	163	246	38	6	11	82	0	10	4	47	6	35	7	8
Tiquet, Lazaro, Tabasco	.228	57	79	12	18	24	1	1	1	6	3	0	1	7	0	17	3	2
Tirado, Federico, Mexico City Tigers	.286	72	119	13	34	47	5	1	2	17	1	1	1	9	1	14	0	0
Tirado, Victor, Yucatan	.238	76	202	14	48	55	7	0	0	8	2	2	3	7	0	21	1	1
Torres, Eduardo, Saltillo	.276	118	362	68	100	166	8	5	16	57	3	2	7	79	3	57	6	6
Torres, Guillermo, Monterrey Ind.	.125	25	64	6	8	12	1	0	1	3	2	0	0	2	0	22	0	0
Torres, Nemesio Jaime, Tabasco	.239	32	109	8	26	32	6	0	0	12	6	2	0	5	0	10	0	0
Torres, Rafael, Aguascalientes	.265	94	283	44	75	97	12	5	0	21	6	1	1	36	0	44	2	5
Torres, Raymundo, Yucatan	.293	121	416	76	122	226	22	2	26	102	0	11	4	64	5	90	2	2
Trinidad, Ulin Sergio, Leon	.091	11	11	4	1	1	0	0	0	0	0	0	0	1	0	1	0	0
Valdez, Armando, Monterrey Ind.	.000	1	1	0	0	0	0	0	0	0	0	0	0	0	0	0	0	0
Valdez, Baltazar, Monterrey Sultans	.302	122	443	75	134	228	30	2	20	85	4	5	9	40	10	84	5	3
Valdez, Francisco, San Luis	.353	14	17	4	6	8	0	0	0	1	0	0	0	3	0	3	0	1
Valdez, Jesus, Tabasco	.287	65	188	20	54	67	10	0	1	19	2	0	1	7	1	20	0	2
Valdez, Luis Alberto, Monterrey Sul.	.260	66	215	25	56	64	6	1	0	17	3	1	3	14	0	21	6	1
Valdivia, Arturo, Monterrey Ind.	.125	7	8	0	1	1	0	0	0	1	0	1	0	0	0	2	0	0
Valencia, Carlos, Aguascalientes	.307	109	391	52	120	160	22	6	2	42	4	3	2	30	2	28	1	2
Valenzuela, Eduardo, Saltillo	.167	46	90	8	15	15	0	0	0	10	1	1	0	7	0	14	2	1
Valenzuela, Horacio, Leon	.311	103	302	42	94	143	15	5	8	48	2	3	4	29	6	30	2	3
Valenzuela, Jose Luis, Yucatan	.189	27	37	4	7	7	0	0	0	4	0	0	0	7	0	7	0	1
Valenzuela, Leonardo, Monclova	.323	114	375	69	121	185	22	6	10	61	0	3	1	52	2	60	11	7
Valle, Guadalupe, 12 Ags.-33 M.S.	.205	45	73	9	15	18	3	0	0	7	1	0	0	11	0	19	0	0
Valverde, Aaron, San Luis	.000	1	1	0	0	0	0	0	0	0	0	0	0	0	0	1	0	0
Valverde, Raul, 12 Ind.-88 Lag.	.358	100	355	64	127	182	21	8	6	62	5	1	4	14	0	39	5	4
Vargas, Rogelio, Monterrey Ind.	.000	10	5	0	0	0	0	0	0	0	0	0	0	0	0	2	0	0
Vargas, Trinidad, Yucatan	.216	42	74	9	16	21	2	0	1	9	0	1	0	5	0	19	0	1
Vazquez, Rodolfo, Mexico City Tigers.	.333	26	24	3	8	9	1	0	0	3	0	0	0	1	0	5	0	0
Vega, Ramon, Aguascalientes	.206	37	97	9	20	22	2	0	0	8	0	0	3	6	0	20	0	0
Verdugo, Vicente, Mexico City Reds	.296	131	466	71	138	165	18	3	1	52	7	5	2	20	0	41	7	3
Villa, Victor, Tabasco	.209	38	86	10	18	23	5	0	0	7	2	1	0	1	0	12	0	0
Villaescusa, Fernando, Campeche	.333	124	501	79	167	195	24	0	0	49	7	1	1	18	0	17	20	6
Villaestrigo, Braulio, Monclova	.208	12	24	7	5	6	1	0	0	1	0	0	0	5	0	8	1	0
Villagomez, David, Aguascalientes	.313	112	380	44	119	151	13	2	5	64	4	5	0	36	2	44	1	0
Villalobos, Juan Enrique, San Luis	.229	21	48	0	11	13	2	0	0	5	2	0	1	0	1	11	0	0
Villegas, Ramon, Leon	.250	1	4	0	1	1	0	0	0	1	0	0	0	0	0	1	0	0
Villela, Carlos, Monterrey Industrials	.339	79	289	39	98	118	11	3	1	27	3	2	0	22	0	27	3	2
Vizcarra, Marco Antonio, U. Laguna	.234	65	128	19	30	33	3	0	0	9	0	1	0	9	0	14	3	1
Vizcarra, Roberto, Leon	.321	131	526	93	169	220	25	4	6	44	7	2	7	47	0	35	30	18
Vizcarra, Sergio, San Luis	.300	126	486	78	146	187	13	8	4	46	11	1	4	51	3	40	9	13
Wong, Julian, Saltillo	.259	126	455	54	118	152	18	5	2	45	8	3	1	35	0	67	1	0
Yuriar, Jesus, Mexico City Reds	.265	69	181	25	48	64	6	2	2	15	5	3	1	15	0	32	7	0

Player and Club	Pct.	G.	AB.	R.	H.	TB.	2B.	3B.	HR.	RBI.	SH.	SF.	HP.	BB.	Int. BB.	SO.	SB.	CS.
Zambrano, Rosario, Tabasco	.301	110	339	46	102	119	11	3	0	44	15	1	1	27	1	35	1	7
Zamudio, Rodolfo, Monterrey Sultans	.167	7	6	1	1	1	0	0	0	0	0	0	0	1	0	3	0	0
Zaragoza, Jesus, Saltillo	.000	2	1	0	0	0	0	0	0	0	0	0	0	0	0	1	0	0
Zulueta, Felix, Tabasco	.197	27	71	6	14	20	3	0	1	7	2	0	3	4	0	15	0	0
Zuniga, Armando, Mexico City Tigers	.256	113	316	45	81	98	11	3	0	24	10	3	0	32	1	59	3	6

The following pitchers, listed alphabetically by club, with games in parentheses, had no plate appearances, primarily through use of designated hitters:

AGUASCALIENTES—Acosta, Martin (30); Beltran, Eleazar (11); Cardenas, Benito (16); Cervantes, Lauro (11); Delgadillo, Gustavo (22); Dimas, Rodolfo (32); Escarrega, Ernesto (21); Espinoza, Salvador (16); Granillo, Carlos (29); Guzman, Gelacio (9); Lara, Eduardo (26); Ludy, John (5); Montalvo, Rafael (30); Montano, Francisco (1); Quinones, Enrique (30); Raygoza, Claudio (15); Rojo, Gonzalo (8); Sauceda, Ramiro (1); Soto, Alvaro (13).

CAMPECHE—Angulo, Julian (3); Beltran, Eleazar (12); Diaz, Alejandro (13); Dominguez, Herminio (20); Duarte, Florentino (7); Elias Lomeli, Jorge (1); Garcia, Rene (27); Guzman, Gelacio (12); Huerta, Luis Enrique (26); Lopez, Jose Ramon (17); Lunar, Luis (42); Onofre, Francisco (7); Padilla, Raymundo (12); Pulido, Antonio (12); Raygoza, Martin (26); Sosa, Carlos (4); Toledo, Mario (4); Toledo, Martin (1); Valenzuela, Mario (5); Velazquez, Idelfonso (28).

LEON—Gutierrez, Porfirio (15); Herrera, Roberto (3); Ibarra, Carlos (19); Jaime Granillo, Ismael (13); Jusaino, Martin (7); Martinez, Gabriel (12); Orozco, Jaime (8); Palermo, Peter (9); Purata, Julio (10); Raygoza, Jose Ramon (28); Sanchez, Martin (51); Soto, Fernando (36); Velazquez, Luis Alfonso (1); Villanueva, Luis (42).

MEXICO CITY REDS—Andresh, Kevin (9); Angulo, Julian (26); Barojas, Salome (56); Barron, Avelino (12); Castaneda, Aurelio (21); Chavarin, Jose Angel (17); Copp, Bill (6); Diaz, Alejandro (8); Fajardo, Hector (3); Hernandez, Martin (24); Leyva, Filiberto (6); Luevano, Juan (36); Martinez, Ramon (33); Mendez, Luis Fernando (27); Pulido, Alfonso (11); Ramirez, Roberto (2); Valdez, Rodolfo (21); Velazquez, Ernesto (13); Zamorano, Luis Gabriel (11).

MEXICO CITY TIGERS—Brooks, Bill (4); Garcia, Juan (32); Herrera, Calixto (16); Jimenez, Isaac (20); Kinonen, Mike (13); LaFever, Gregory (9); Lopez, Emigdio (12); Mack, Tony (16); Moreno, Angel (25); Nery, Braulio (15); Ordaz, Reynaldo (12); Rios, Jesus (25); Rodriguez, Raul (40); Valencia, Jose (5).

MONCLOVA—Arias, Daniel (14); Campos, Jorge (1); Cano, Ezequiel (27); Cosio, Mario Alberto (20); Escamilla, Sergio (14); Garcia, Rogelio (27); Hickey, James (7); Ibarra, Jose (4); Lopez, Raul (25); Pruneda, Armando (7); Rodriguez, Ignacio (13); Valenzuela, Jairo (19); Vargas, Jose (11); Vazquez, Florentino (25); Vejar, Maximino (4).

MONTERREY INDUSTRIALS—Angulo, Kenneth (7); Campos, Jorge (17); Castaneda, Patricio (3); Diaz, Octavio (46); Diaz, Scott (4); Duarte, Florentino (34); Gutierrez, Porfirio (15); Heredia, Ubaldo (9); Jacobson, Nels (3); Martinez, Gabriel (15); McKeon, Joe (6); Monroe, Ben (29); Orduno, Victor (4); Pulido, Antonio (36); Serafin, Hector (30); Solis, Miguel (8); Torres, Guadalupe (18); Valenzuela, Guillermo (6); Wadell, Tom (5); Zamudio, Aurelio (12).

MONTERREY SULTANS—Bass, Barry (16); Garza, Adrian (7); Garza, Alejandro (24); Gonzalez, Arturo (25); Lopez, Hector (11); Lopez, Jose Ramon (4); Morales, Isidro (16); Moya, Ramon (24); Navarro, Adolfo (25); Osuna, Roberto (38); Pruneda, Armando (15); Serna, Ramon (15); Tejeda, Juan (12); Telechea, Gonzalo (3); Uribe, Juan Carlos (36); Valenzuela, Ramon Loreto (2); Veliz Arballo, Francisco (16); Wheeler, Brad (7).

NUEVO LAREDO—Alvarez, Juan Jose (24); Armenta, Alejandro (1); Banning, Douglas (23); Barraza, Ernesto (34); Carranza, Javier (21); Castillo, Luis Trinidad (20); Castro, Rodrigo (31); Couch, James (19); Cortue (25); Moore, Robert (14); Moreno, Jesus (16); Quiroz, Aaron (6); Romo, Manuel (37); Simpson, Gregory (6); Tinoco, Ruben (5); Tirado, Sebastian (14); Valdez, Jose Luis (1); Villegas, Jose Angel (31).

SALTILLO—Aguilar, Miguel (28); Castellanos, Humberto (2); Castillo, Feliciano (24); Jimenez, Cesar Danilo (16); Mendez, Martin (16); Miranda, Julio Cesar (48); Munoz, Miguel (25); Padilla, Raymundo (4); Ramirez, Emilio (24); Reynoso, Armando (27); Rodriguez, Mario Alberto (35); Rojo, Gustavo (5); Solis, Ricardo (28); White, Dave (6).

SAN LUIS—Cardenas, Benito (8); Cazarez, Juan (26); Contreras, Benjamin (7); Garcia, Horacio (17); Garcia, Jorge Luis (32); Guzman, Benjamin (15); Heredia, Gilberto (24); Lizarraga, Hugo (26); Lopez, Hector (29); Meagher, Tom (21); Morales, Isidro (15); Nery, Braulio (3); Ochoa, Porfirio (53); Ontiveros, Juan (27); Osuna, Martin (20); Reyes, Jesus M. (6); Veliz Arballo, Francisco (13); Villa, Mike (43).

TABASCO—Arcos, Martin (31); Camarena, Martin (31); Cruz, Jesus (4); Enriquez, Martin (34); Garcia, Zenon (12); Herrera, Enrique (18); Jimenez, Cesar Danilo (20); Jimenez, Danilo (28); Marcos Castillejos, Jose (8); Martinez, Victor (5); Munoz, Nelson (24); Ontiveros, Juan (23); Romero, Juan (19); Sosa, Mario (26); Telechea, Gonzalo (5); Torres, Martin (29); Ulin, Miguel (4); Valenzuela, Guillermo (2); Zamudio, Aurelio (15).

UNION LAGUNA—Castaneda, Maximiliano (19); Cervantes, Lauro (21); Diaz, Garcia Cesar (9); Hernandez, Encarnacion (29); Palafox, Juan Manuel (30); Perry, Jeff (46); Pimentel, Rafael (1); Renteria, Hilario (27); Rios, Jose Luis (24); Sombra, Francisco (31); Soto, Alvaro (15); Torres, Sotero (24).

YUCATAN—Antunez, Martin (42); Colorado, Salvador (20); Cruz, Andres (22); Diaz, Cesar (26); Dozier, Thomas (24); Esquer, Mercedes (23); Ibarra, Carlos (14); Ledon, Juan Carlos (3); Puerto, Carlos (9); Purata, Julio (10); Retes, Lorenzo (25); Urrea, Leonel (26); Velez, Alberto (23).

GRAND SLAM HOME RUNS—Aikens, Farmar, A. Ortiz, J. Reyes, 2 each; Bellazetin, Cantu, Castro, Clayton, Clements, Dominguez, Jarrell, Navarro, Ge. Rodriguez, Serna, 1 each.

AWARDED FIRST BASE ON CATCHER'S INTERFERENCE—J.A. Barrera (Gastelum); Cazarin (Villa); R. Estrada (Osuna); L. Guerrero (Osuna); L. Hernandez (Bocardo); Reyna (Espino); Verdugo (M. Hernandez).

CLUB FIELDING

Club	Pct.	G.	PO.	A.	E.	DP.	PB.	Club	Pct.	G.	PO.	A.	E.	DP.	PB.
Mexico City Tigers	.973	130	3213	1400	128	126	9	Monclova	.968	132	3338	1450	159	136	14
Union Laguna	.973	132	3328	1555	137	186	14	Nuevo Laredo	.968	132	3299	1429	158	152	17
Yucatan	.972	128	3222	1375	130	104	14	Saltillo	.966	129	3247	1464	164	130	8
Mexico City Reds	.972	131	3300	1515	138	144	20	San Luis	.965	131	3266	1465	173	125	22
Campeche	.969	129	3260	1511	151	126	19	Monterrey Industrials	.964	132	3299	1335	172	124	21
Tabasco	.968	129	3063	1433	148	130	6	Aguascalientes	.964	130	3131	1403	170	113	9
Leon	.968	131	3260	1559	160	129	16	Monterrey Sultans	.963	132	3313	1274	175	116	27

Triple Plays—Aguascalientes 2, Campeche, Mexico City Tigers, Monterrey Sultans, Nuevo Laredo, Yucatan.

INDIVIDUAL FIELDING
FIRST BASEMEN

Player and Club	Pct.	G.	PO.	A.	E.	DP.	Player and Club	Pct.	G.	PO.	A.	E.	DP.
Lavagnino, San Luis	1.000	26	176	17	0	17	Navarrete, Monterrey Ind.	.992	14	110	8	1	15
Peralta, San Luis	1.000	11	80	9	0	11	B. Valdez, Monterrey Sultans	.991	32	205	16	2	24
L.F. Diaz, Nuevo Laredo	1.000	10	41	3	0	4	Arce, San Luis	.991	63	53	55	1	59
GU. RODRIGUEZ, MC Tigers	.997	128	1118	58	3	122	A. Lopez, Aguascalientes	.991	27	194	16	2	16
Tatis, Mexico City Reds	.995	59	510	35	3	59	Smith, Saltillo	.990	83	733	65	8	77
Driessen, Yucatan	.995	120	1017	70	6	84	O. Sanchez, Monterrey Sultans	.989	54	447	23	5	38
A. Garza, Tabasco	.994	88	767	39	5	85	F. Garzon, Campeche	.989	124	1118	62	13	119
Zulueta, Tabasco	.993	16	135	10	1	11	Romero, Nuevo Laredo	.988	123	1083	74	14	124
Holmes, Mexico City Reds	.993	43	408	25	3	45	Villagomez, Aguascalientes	.988	11	79	2	1	8
R. Valverde, Union Laguna	.933	16	129	9	1	15	Mora, Monterrey Industrials	.988	78	596	36	8	53
Avila, Union Laguna	.992	18	119	12	1	19	Clayton, Monclova	.987	117	1011	78	14	107

FIRST BASEMEN—Continued

Player and Club	Pct.	G.	PO.	A.	E.	DP.	Player and Club	Pct.	G.	PO.	A.	E.	DP.
J. Valdez, Tabasco	.987	29	215	15	3	26	H. Valenzuela, Leon	.983	25	115	4	2	13
Aikens, Leon	.987	66	630	48	9	68	Castro, Saltillo	.983	76	490	38	9	46
R. Hernandez, Monterrey Sul.	.987	56	427	20	6	43	Reyna, Aguascalientes	.983	88	752	63	14	64
J. Reyes, Leon	.986	57	469	26	7	47	Beltran, Mexico City Reds	.982	20	155	10	3	15
Sommers, Union Laguna	.986	103	994	62	15	132	J. Lopez, Saltillo	.980	12	46	4	1	7
Serna, Monclova	.986	18	127	13	2	17	N. Barrera, Mexico City Reds	.979	13	86	7	2	9
Rosales, San Luis	.985	39	372	25	6	34	Cantu, Saltillo	.964	16	101	6	4	8

(Fewer Than Ten Games)

Player and Club	Pct.	G.	PO.	A.	E.	DP.	Player and Club	Pct.	G.	PO.	A.	E.	DP.
Green, Aguascalientes	1.000	2	7	0	0	1	Bobadilla, Monterrey Industrials	1.000	8	30	3	0	3
Ge. Rodriguez, MC Tigers	1.000	3	18	5	0	2	G. Torres, Monterrey Industrials	1.000	6	52	3	0	5
Quiroz, Mexico City Tigers	1.000	1	5	0	0	1	Mena, Monclova	1.000	2	3	1	0	0
L. Jimenez, Campeche	1.000	1	6	1	0	0	Arano, Saltillo	1.000	3	8	1	0	0
Villaescusa, Campeche	1.000	7	14	1	0	0	P. Lopez, Saltillo	1.000	3	15	0	0	1
T. Vargas, Yucatan	1.000	1	2	0	0	0	Al. Sanchez, Tabasco	1.000	2	15	1	0	3
Burke, Yucatan	1.000	7	23	3	0	3	Abarca, Aguascalientes	1.000	1	7	0	0	0
Clements, Yucatan	1.000	8	67	14	0	6	F. Cruz, Monterrey Industrials	.980	8	47	3	1	4
Chance, Mexico City Reds	1.000	2	19	2	0	1	Pena, Campeche	.980	6	43	6	1	3
J.L. Perez, Aguascalientes	1.000	1	2	0	0	0	Blancas, Mexico City Reds	.978	6	44	0	1	9
A. Gutierrez, Union Laguna	1.000	3	6	1	0	1	J.M. Garcia, Aguascalientes	.973	7	69	3	2	6
Camacho, Nuevo Laredo	1.000	1	6	0	0	0	Valle, Aguascalientes	.935	4	25	4	2	4
Salinas, Nuevo Laredo	1.000	9	48	2	0	6	Cazarin, Leon	.857	1	5	1	1	1
Rabb, Monterrey Sultans	1.000	2	15	1	0	0							

Triple Plays—Reyna 2, Driessen, F. Garzon, Gu. Rodriguez, Romero, B. Valdez.

SECOND BASEMEN

Player and Club	Pct.	G.	PO.	A.	E.	DP.	Player and Club	Pct.	G.	PO.	A.	E.	DP.
An. Sanchez, Mexico City Reds	.991	21	49	64	1	22	Ju. Gonzalez, Aguascalientes	.965	18	39	44	3	12
J.F. RODRIGUEZ, Yucatan	.989	127	311	339	7	73	M. Garcia, San Luis	.965	49	94	153	9	32
Je. Gonzalez, Tabasco	.987	123	305	380	9	96	Mere, Nuevo Laredo	.964	119	310	338	24	108
Ar. Sanchez, Mexico City Reds	.986	101	244	333	8	86	L. Guerrero, Leon	.964	40	87	98	7	22
R. Chavez, Campeche	.983	26	27	31	1	7	R. Diaz, Monterrey Sultans	.963	63	160	127	11	36
Villaescusa, Campeche	.980	124	312	359	14	86	Contreras, Union Laguna	.963	23	59	70	5	13
R. Vizcarra, Leon	.979	77	170	208	8	57	M.A. Vizcarra, Union Laguna	.962	24	52	76	5	15
Navarrete, Monterrey Ind.	.979	66	185	182	8	43	Esquer, Leon	.952	40	80	98	9	24
Villela, Monterrey Industrials	.978	66	164	153	7	46	Zuniga, Mexico City Tigers	.951	10	22	17	2	8
Camacho, Mexico City Tigers	.975	120	289	371	17	83	Bustamante, Mexico City Tigers	.949	20	27	29	3	10
Arevalo, Aguascalientes	.975	65	146	163	8	30	Loredo, Nuevo Laredo	.947	14	23	31	3	4
Leyva, Monclova	.974	96	271	247	14	66	J.A. Barrera, Campeche	.947	11	7	11	1	2
Wong, Saltillo	.973	117	276	311	16	85	G. Martinez, Monclova	.947	57	112	101	12	25
L.A. Valdez, Monterrey Sultans	.971	68	128	140	8	31	Ra. Herrera San Luis	.943	13	18	15	2	7
Raf. Torres, Aguascalientes	.969	55	122	159	9	34	Chapa, Monterrey Sultans	.935	18	20	23	3	2
J.H. Flores, San Luis	.967	81	159	223	13	50	Arano, Saltillo	.918	18	25	20	4	5
Abril, Union Laguna	.966	97	216	295	18	98							

(Fewer Than Ten Games)

Player and Club	Pct.	G.	PO.	A.	E.	DP.	Player and Club	Pct.	G.	PO.	A.	E.	DP.
Valle, Aguascalientes	1.000	1	1	3	0	0	J. Guerrero, Leon	1.000	1	1	2	0	3
R. Camarero, Union Laguna	1.000	2	2	1	0	0	Bobadilla, Monterrey Industrials	.957	9	26	18	2	6
Cano, Monterrey Sultans	1.000	5	6	13	0	2	Magana, Yucatan	.955	7	9	12	1	5
Alonso, Monterrey Industrials	1.000	2	9	2	0	1	Tatis, Mexico City Reds	.951	7	20	19	2	2
Moreno, Monclova	1.000	5	10	17	0	1	Verdugo, Mexico City Reds	.938	3	6	9	1	1
N.J. Torres, Tabasco	1.000	1	1	2	0	0	G. Sanchez, Nuevo Laredo	.933	5	7	7	1	2
Bocanegra, Tabasco	1.000	2	3	6	0	1	Solis, Tabasco	.917	8	19	3	2	0
Je. Garcia, Mexico City Tigers	1.000	2	0	1	0	0	Mercado, San Luis	.882	6	9	6	2	0
J.D.D. Chavez, Yucatan	1.000	3	3	0	0	0	Serna, Monclova	.879	6	10	19	4	4
T. Vargas, Yucatan	1.000	2	3	4	0	1							

Triple Plays—Arevalo 2, Camacho, R. Diaz, Mere, Villaescusa.

THIRD BASEMEN

Player and Club	Pct.	G.	PO.	A.	E.	DP.	Player and Club	Pct.	G.	PO.	A.	E.	DP.
Alfaro, Saltillo	1.000	13	6	18	0	2	Zuniga, Mexico City Tigers	.925	79	61	135	16	10
Cazarin, Leon	.975	26	20	58	2	7	L. Meza, Leon	.920	10	10	13	2	5
L. Guerrero, Leon	.967	10	9	20	1	1	Vazquez, Mexico City Tigers	.917	19	3	8	1	0
T. Vargas, Yucatan	.966	12	9	19	1	2	V. Quintero, Tabasco	.916	76	50	103	14	11
R. Moreno, Monclova	.966	12	8	20	1	2	M. Garcia, San Luis	.914	17	4	28	3	2
SAIZ, Union Laguna	.957	128	114	263	17	45	Peralta, San Luis	.913	106	82	192	26	12
Serna, Monclova	.956	80	57	139	9	19	Alonso, Monterrey Industrials	.913	69	49	129	17	16
Jarrell, Leon	.953	31	25	57	4	5	N.J. Torres, Tabasco	.912	25	16	36	5	2
Solis, Tabasco	.950	52	24	91	6	17	Valle, Monterrey Sultans	.900	11	4	5	1	0
N. Barrera, Mexico City Reds	.950	112	101	219	17	32	Cepeda, Monclova	.900	52	30	87	13	7
L. Hernandez, Campeche	.946	127	120	262	22	21	Arano, Saltillo	.899	34	26	63	10	8
A. Ortiz, Nuevo Laredo	.943	123	94	223	19	26	Bobadilla, Saltillo	.899	84	47	139	21	7
N. Gonzalez, Leon	.943	66	68	132	12	15	E. Torres, Saltillo	.895	12	7	10	2	2
Aguilar, Aguascalientes	.938	122	114	232	23	24	B. Valdez, Monterrey Sul.	.885	92	67	125	25	13
Navarrete, Monterrey Ind.	.932	24	22	33	4	4	Cangas, Mexico City Tigers	.881	46	45	66	15	8
Serratos, Yucatan	.928	116	98	224	25	14	L. Jimenez, Campeche	.857	17	2	4	1	0
An. Sanchez, Mexico City Reds	.927	17	13	25	3	3	Mata, Saltillo	.846	11	10	12	4	0
Cano, Monterrey Sultans	.925	57	32	67	8	8	Arce, San Luis	.846	10	7	15	4	0
Castaneda, Saltillo	.925	37	28	58	7	8							

(Fewer Than Ten Games)

Player and Club	Pct.	G.	PO.	A.	E.	DP.	Player and Club	Pct.	G.	PO.	A.	E.	DP.
Trinidad, Leon	1.000	1	1	0	0	0	Bocanegra, Tabasco	1.000	4	2	4	0	0
J. Guerrero, Leon	1.000	1	2	3	0	1	A. Rodriguez, Saltillo	1.000	2	3	4	0	1
H. Rodriguez, Mexico City Reds	1.000	5	3	2	0	0	Leyva, Monclova	1.000	7	7	7	0	2
Ju. Gonzalez, Aguascalientes	1.000	4	4	3	0	1	Picos, Monterrey Sultans	1.000	2	1	0	0	0
Arevalo, Aguascalientes	1.000	2	0	2	0	0	M. Mendoza, Monterrey Sul.	1.000	6	3	2	0	0

Player and Club	Pct.	G.	PO.	A.	E.	DP.
Contreras, Union Laguna	1.000	9	3	11	0	0
Valencia, Aguascalientes	.944	6	7	10	1	1
Castilla, Saltillo	.941	7	7	9	1	3
Loredo, Nuevo Laredo	.913	7	4	18	2	1
Ra. Herrera, San Luis	.882	6	5	10	2	2
Bustamante, Mexico City Tigers	.875	8	2	5	1	0
Pardo, Tabasco	.818	3	1	8	2	3
Burke, Yucatan	.786	5	7	4	3	0
Chapa, Monterrey Sultans	.750	1	1	2	1	0
Benitez, Mexico City Tigers	.750	2	0	3	1	0
Tatis, Mexico City Reds	.750	5	0	3	1	0
Esquer, Leon	.750	1	1	2	1	0
Romero, Nuevo Laredo	.714	1	1	4	2	2
L.A. Cruz, San Luis	.667	1	2	0	1	0
J.D.D. Chavez, Yucatan	.500	1	0	1	1	0

Triple Plays—Aguilar, A. Ortiz, Zuniga.

SHORTSTOPS

Player and Club	Pct.	G.	PO.	A.	E.	DP.
Beristain, Mexico City Tigers	.985	20	18	46	1	11
Zuniga, Mexico City Tigers	.972	34	40	64	3	15
Ju. Gonzalez, Aguascalientes	.970	24	30	67	3	11
R. Diaz, Monterrey Sultans	.966	42	70	100	6	21
Bustamante, Mexico City Tigers	.960	24	17	31	2	9
ELIZONDO, Monclova	.956	114	196	342	25	73
F. Guerrero, Union Laguna	.951	127	268	446	37	116
Castilla, Saltillo	.951	121	217	418	33	79
Gomez, Monterrey Industrials	.951	130	204	392	31	83
En. Ramirez, Nuevo Laredo	.951	125	224	429	34	89
F. Gutierrez, Campeche	.948	67	113	236	19	53
Verdugo, Mexico City Reds	.947	128	220	480	39	92
Almodobar, Mexico City Tigers	.946	96	113	257	21	45
Man. Morales, Aguascalientes	.946	78	118	250	21	45
M.A. Vizcarra, Nuevo Laredo	.944	12	16	18	2	4
J. Guerrero, Leon	.943	80	109	239	21	49
DeLosSantos, Tabasco	.940	103	165	304	30	56
Loredo, Nuevo Laredo	.939	14	9	22	2	3
J.A. Barrera, Campeche	.939	69	118	206	21	35
Ri. Herrera, Yucatan	.937	127	205	371	39	64
M. Mendoza, Monterrey Sultans	.933	108	168	291	33	59
R. Vizcarra, Leon	.930	78	126	222	26	48
R. Moreno, Monclova	.929	31	32	86	9	10
V. Quintero, Tabasco	.916	39	48	94	13	16
Raf. Torres, Aguascalientes	.912	35	42	93	13	13
S. Vizcarra, San Luis	.894	125	212	84	35	85

(Fewer Than Ten Games)

Player and Club	Pct.	G.	PO.	A.	E.	DP.
Valle, Monterrey Sultans	1.000	1	7	1	0	0
Peralta, San Luis	1.000	1	1	1	0	2
J.H. Flores, San Luis	1.000	1	0	2	0	0
Cano, Monterrey Sultans	1.000	1	1	0	0	0
Navarrete, Monterrey Ind	1.000	1	0	2	0	1
Solis, Tabasco	1.000	2	0	11	0	1
Bocanegra, Tabasco	1.000	4	3	11	0	3
Camacho, Mexico City Tigers	1.000	5	5	6	0	1
Villaescusa, Campeche	1.000	1	0	5	0	0
Trinidad, Leon	1.000	4	4	9	0	2
Jarrell, Leon	1.000	1	0	5	0	0
L. Guerrero, Leon	1.000	2	0	4	0	0
Re. Herrera, Campeche	.923	3	4	8	1	1
Pardo, Tabasco	.917	6	3	8	1	2
Bobadilla, Monterrey Industrials	.917	3	3	8	1	1
Wong, Saltillo	.905	9	13	25	4	2
Yuriar, Mexico City Reds	.864	4	8	11	3	3
Rivero, Yucatan	.842	8	7	9	3	3
V.H. Guerrero, San Luis	.833	3	2	8	2	1
Mercado, San Luis	.750	1	1	2	1	0
Ra. Herrera, San Luis	.667	1	1	1	1	0
Arano, Saltillo	.600	5	2	1	2	1
Vazquez, Mexico City Tigers	.500	1	0	1	1	0

Triple Plays—J.A. Barrera, Ri. Herrera, M. Mendoza, Raf. Torres.

OUTFIELDERS

Player and Club	Pct.	G.	PO.	A.	E.	DP.
Lo. Moreno, Nuevo Laredo	1.000	16	16	2	0	0
S. Lopez, Nuevo Laredo	1.000	15	11	1	0	0
Brown, Monclova	1.000	14	21	0	0	0
Lara, San Luis	1.000	19	21	2	0	0
Villagomez, Aguascalientes	1.000	47	72	4	0	0
Tiquet, Tabasco	1.000	24	17	2	0	0
Arano, Saltillo	1.000	13	15	0	0	0
Agramon, Saltillo	1.000	11	5	0	0	0
Cano, Monterrey Sultans	1.000	19	27	2	0	0
ARZATE, Leon	1.000	110	216	9	0	3
L. Guerrero, Leon	1.000	22	27	3	0	0
An. Sanchez, Mexico City Reds	1.000	18	22	4	0	0
Beltran, Mexico City Reds	1.000	31	41	1	0	0
J.L. Valenzuela, Yucatan	1.000	15	22	1	0	0
Ray. Torres, Yucatan	.989	119	264	12	3	1
Castelan, Yucatan	.988	109	239	10	3	1
Stockstill, Union Laguna	.984	132	223	26	4	7
Payton, Union Laguna	.984	126	222	18	4	4
Rabb, Monterrey Sultans	.982	28	53	2	1	0
Ponce, Campeche	.982	57	51	4	1	1
Fernandez, Mexico City Reds	.982	107	263	9	5	3
J.M. Garcia, Aguascalientes	.981	54	100	2	2	0
Machiria, Mexico City Tigers	.981	124	238	14	5	1
L. Valenzuela, Monclova	.980	114	232	11	5	2
Al. Sanchez, Tabasco	.980	83	135	10	3	2
R. Valverde, Union Laguna	.979	57	91	4	2	0
G. Sanchez, Nuevo Laredo	.979	139	217	11	5	3
Cole, Tabasco	.977	127	330	17	8	4
Dominguez, San Luis	.977	127	196	15	5	0
Perez Tovar, Monterrey Sultans	.975	30	77	2	2	2
Tellez, Monterrey Industrials	.975	132	265	10	7	3
Quiroz, Mexico City Tigers	.975	74	112	3	3	0
E. Torres, Saltillo	.974	103	179	11	5	4
Acosta, Saltillo	.974	20	33	5	1	3
Benitez, Mexico City Tigers	.974	63	106	7	3	1
Farmar, Nuevo Laredo	.974	91	178	9	5	1
Morones, Monclova	.973	42	65	8	2	1
Jarrell, Leon	.973	70	96	12	3	3
Leal, Monterrey Sultans	.972	80	136	5	4	1
Her. Alvarez, Yucatan	.972	42	67	3	2	0
Mikulik, Monclova	.972	117	257	18	8	2
H. Valenzuela, Leon	.970	77	123	7	4	2
Saenz, Saltillo	.970	116	215	12	7	1
G. Martinez, Monclova	.970	20	32	0	1	0
Chance, Mexico City Reds	.969	61	87	8	3	0
Valencia, Aguascalientes	.969	97	210	10	7	1
Hec. Alvarez, Monterrey Ind	.969	80	121	2	4	0
A. Gutierrez, Union Laguna	.968	61	90	1	3	0
Navarro, Campeche	.968	112	206	6	7	0
Cepeda, Monclova	.966	18	24	4	1	0
I. Herrera, Monterrey Ind	.965	90	130	8	5	2
L.A. Cruz, San Luis	.965	124	283	17	11	1
Yuriar, Mexico City Reds	.964	52	76	5	3	1
J.S. Chavez, Union Laguna	.964	51	76	4	3	0
Lavagnino, San Luis	.963	41	47	5	2	0
J.L. Gutierrez, Leon	.962	31	46	4	2	2
L.F. Diaz, Nuevo Laredo	.961	114	209	10	9	2
Cosey, Monterrey Sultans	.960	117	178	13	8	3
Bellazetin, Mexico City Tigers	.960	125	182	9	8	3
Aguilera, Monterrey Sultans	.959	101	221	13	10	3
J.L. Perez, Aguascalientes	.958	40	65	4	3	1
Lizarraga, Monclova	.958	110	188	15	9	3
Baca, Mexico City Reds	.957	98	190	11	9	3
R. Garibay, San Luis	.954	70	115	10	6	3
Davis, Saltillo	.953	110	218	5	11	1
Zambrano, Tabasco	.951	33	37	2	2	2
Plascencia, Nuevo Laredo	.951	28	56	2	3	0
E. Jimenez, Campeche	.950	115	183	8	10	0
Simmons, Tabasco	.948	77	120	7	7	0
Buenrostro, Leon	.947	54	51	3	3	0
Miller, Monterrey Sultans	.947	20	36	0	2	0
Landreaux, Aguascalientes	.947	46	87	3	5	1
Johnson, Campeche	.945	91	176	13	11	6
J.L. Rodriguez, Saltillo	.944	28	32	2	2	0
Morfin, Campeche	.943	50	46	4	3	0
Smith, Saltillo	.943	26	32	1	2	0
M.A. Gonzalez, Monterrey Sul	.939	41	59	3	4	1
Le. Moreno, San Luis	.938	27	39	6	3	1
David, Monterrey Sultans	.938	37	56	4	4	0
J.L. Garcia, Aguascalientes	.937	92	173	4	12	0
Clements, Yucatan	.934	87	136	6	10	0
R. Estrada, Tabasco	.932	40	53	2	4	0
Tatis, Mexico City Reds	.929	50	87	5	7	0
Delgado, Campeche	.929	55	85	7	7	1
J. Valdez, Tabasco	.917	15	20	2	2	0
Ju. Gonzalez, Aguascalientes	.917	29	41	3	4	0
Castro, Monterrey Industrials	.907	55	65	3	7	0
O. Sanchez, Monterrey Sultans	.882	10	13	2	2	1
T. Vargas, Monterrey	.880	12	20	2	3	0
J. Cruz, Mexico City Tigers	.875	16	13	1	2	1
Griffith, Nuevo Laredo	.864	11	19	0	3	0

(Fewer Than Ten Games)

Player and Club	Pct.	G.	PO.	A.	E.	DP.
Amador, Nuevo Laredo	1.000	1	2	0	0	0
Zamudio, Monterrey Sultans	1.000	1	1	0	0	0
Mora, Monterrey Industrials	1.000	5	11	0	0	0
R. Vargas, Monterrey Ind	1.000	7	1	1	0	0
P. Lopez, Saltillo	1.000	4	2	1	0	0
Bronson, Saltillo	1.000	6	4	0	0	0
Gu. Rodriguez, M.C. Tigers	1.000	6	11	1	0	1
Pena, Campeche	1.000	8	8	1	0	0

Player and Club	Pct.	G.	PO.	A.	E.	DP.
V. Tirado, Yucatan	1.000	8	8	1	0	1
Simmons, Aguascalientes	.923	6	10	2	1	0
Ledezma, Aguascalientes	.909	7	10	0	1	0
Villaestrigo, Monclova	.909	7	10	0	1	0
Reyna, Aguascalientes	.900	5	8	1	1	0
L. Jimenez, Campeche	.900	6	9	0	1	0
Abrego, Nuevo Laredo	.833	6	4	1	1	0

CATCHERS

Player and Club	Pct.	G.	PO.	A.	E.	DP.	PB.
E. Garzon, Mexico City Reds	1.000	17	65	15	0	1	2
Daut, Monclova	.992	29	111	18	1	1	1
F. Estrada, Leon	.992	42	485	24	4	2	2
GASTELUM, MC Reds	.989	86	380	56	5	4	7
Vega, Aguascalientes	.988	37	133	28	2	4	0
G. Ramirez, Monclova	.986	46	191	24	3	3	5
M. Hernandez, MC Tigers	.986	116	619	78	10	8	6
R. Martinez, Monterrey Sul.	.986	112	594	93	10	9	17
Ruiz, Tabasco	.985	106	401	66	7	6	5
G. Garza, Nuevo Laredo	.985	121	629	78	11	10	15
Luna, Saltillo	.983	118	559	96	11	4	5
J.C. Alvarez, Yucatan	.983	66	302	48	6	0	7
V. Tirado, Yucatan	.983	66	306	38	6	5	5
M.A. Guzman, Campeche	.983	112	499	74	10	9	12
Esquivias, Union Laguna	.982	47	145	22	3	4	4
F. Tirado, Mexico City Tigers	.981	53	93	11	2	1	3
E. Reyes, San Luis	.980	92	462	66	11	10	12
Rivera, Campeche	.979	21	87	8	2	2	3

Player and Club	Pct.	G.	PO.	A.	E.	DP.	PB.
O. Sanchez, Monterrey Sul.	.977	13	77	8	2	0	3
Avila, Union Laguna	.977	107	450	57	12	8	10
Nunez, Monterrey Industrials.	.976	62	332	37	9	10	8
Cazarin, Leon	.976	102	383	67	11	7	14
J.M. Lopez, San Luis	.971	48	210	24	7	4	3
E. Valenzuela, Saltillo	.971	23	60	6	2	1	1
F. Cruz, Monterrey Ind.	.970	69	371	43	13	2	9
Cantu, Saltillo	.969	30	54	8	2	2	0
H. Estrada, Mexico City Reds	.967	38	133	13	5	3	5
F. Valdez, San Luis	.967	12	26	3	1	2	0
G. Quintero, Aguascalientes	.966	53	218	39	9	3	3
G. Torres, Monterrey Ind.	.963	16	71	8	3	1	2
Villa, Tabasco	.962	29	90	11	4	0	1
Bocardo, Monclova	.962	71	321	57	15	6	8
Ef. Ramirez, Yucatan	.940	18	39	8	3	0	2
Osuna, Aguascalientes	.937	53	212	27	16	2	6
M.A. Gonzalez, Mont.Sul.	.918	26	114	9	11	0	7
Villalobos, San Luis	.915	19	50	15	6	1	6

(Fewer Than Ten Games)

Player and Club	Pct.	G.	PO.	A.	E.	DP.	PB.
Abrego, Nuevo Laredo	1.000	9	31	7	0	2	0
Rabb, Monterrey Sultans	1.000	2	4	0	0	0	0
L.A. Mendoza, Mont. Ind.	1.000	1	1	0	0	0	0
J. Cruz, Mexico City Tigers	1.000	4	4	0	0	0	0
Pena, Campeche	1.000	1	8	0	0	0	0
Samaniego, Campeche	1.000	7	10	1	0	0	1
N. Barrera, Mexico City Reds	1.000	4	12	1	0	0	2

Player and Club	Pct.	G.	PO.	A.	E.	DP.	PB.
Hurtado, Leon	1.000	6	10	0	0	0	0
Soto, Monterrey Industrials	.971	6	33	1	1	0	2
Espino, Tabasco	.895	3	14	3	2	0	0
Valdivia, Monterrey Ind.	.893	9	23	2	3	0	0
L.A. Cruz, San Luis	.875	5	4	3	1	0	0
Tatis, Mexico City Reds	.600	1	3	0	2	0	4

PITCHERS

Player and Club	Pct.	G.	PO.	A.	E.	DP.
G. Torres, Monterrey Industrials	1.000	18	4	2	0	0
Mena, Monclova	1.000	13	0	5	0	0
J. Valenzuela, Monclova	1.000	19	0	7	0	0
Vargas, Monclova	1.000	11	1	6	0	1
Vazquez, Monclova	1.000	25	3	8	0	3
R. SOLIS, Saltillo	1.000	28	10	53	0	5
Nery, Mexico City Tigers	1.000	18	0	2	0	0
J. Angulo, Mexico City Reds	1.000	29	0	3	0	0
G. Martinez, Monterrey Ind.	1.000	27	3	14	0	0
J. R. Lopez, Campeche	1.000	21	1	5	0	0
A. Diaz, Campeche	1.000	21	2	9	0	1
Purata, Leon	1.000	20	4	16	0	2
G. Guzman, Campeche	1.000	21	1	3	0	0
Padilla, Campeche	1.000	16	1	1	0	0
Serna, Monterrey Sultans	1.000	15	4	7	0	1
R. L. Valenzuela, Monterrey Sul.	1.000	21	0	5	0	0
R. Osuna, Monterrey Sultans	1.000	38	10	18	0	2
H. Garcia, San Luis	1.000	17	4	2	0	1
Cazarez, San Luis	1.000	26	1	3	0	2
B. Guzman, San Luis	1.000	15	0	2	0	0
M. Osuna, San Luis	1.000	20	3	4	0	0
G. Heredia, San Luis	1.000	24	15	38	0	2
Tirado, Nuevo Laredo	1.000	14	1	5	0	1
J.A. Villegas, Nuevo Laredo	1.000	31	0	12	0	2
Romo, Nuevo Laredo	1.000	25	0	4	0	0
Ochoa, Nuevo Laredo	1.000	53	2	14	0	2
Moore, Nuevo Laredo	1.000	14	0	3	0	0
M. Castaneda, Union Laguna	1.000	19	2	2	0	0
Flores, Union Laguna	1.000	27	4	6	0	0
E. Hernandez, Union Laguna	1.000	29	8	28	0	5
S. Torres, Union Laguna	1.000	24	0	3	0	0
Antunez, Yucatan	1.000	42	1	2	0	0
Ordaz, Mexico City Tigers	1.000	12	1	3	0	0
Grajales, Mexico City Tigers	1.000	45	1	13	0	2
J. Garcia, Mexico City Tigers	1.000	32	3	5	0	0
R. Rodriguez, MC Tigers	1.000	40	0	22	0	2
A. Moreno, Mexico City Tigers	1.000	25	11	25	0	2
C. Herrera, Mexico City Tigers	1.000	16	1	3	0	1
Lara, Aguascalientes	1.000	26	2	4	0	0
Acosta, Aguascalientes	1.000	30	8	11	0	2
Quinones, Aguascalientes	1.000	30	7	9	0	1
Granillo, Aguascalientes	1.000	29	3	15	0	4
C. Razuaga, Aguascalientes	1.000	15	3	2	0	0
Delgadillo, Aguascalientes	1.000	22	11	31	0	1
Espinoza, Aguascalientes	1.000	16	5	2	0	0
Dimas, Aguascalientes	1.000	32	7	7	0	1
Z. Garcia, Tabasco	1.000	12	1	4	0	0

Player and Club	Pct.	G.	PO.	A.	E.	DP.
Camarena, Tabasco	1.000	31	12	28	0	1
M. Sosa, Tabasco	1.000	26	2	18	0	2
E. Ramirez, Saltillo	1.000	24	4	5	0	1
M. Alvarez, Saltillo	1.000	37	8	11	0	1
Ortiz, Leon	1.000	29	4	24	0	0
Barron, Mexico City Reds	1.000	12	0	4	0	2
R. Martinez, Mexico City Reds	1.000	33	2	10	0	1
A. Castaneda, Mexico City Reds	1.000	21	3	8	0	2
R. Valdez, Mexico City Reds	1.000	21	7	15	0	0
Luevano, Mexico City Reds	1.000	36	6	9	0	0
Chavarin, Mexico City Reds	1.000	17	3	3	0	0
Zamorano, Mexico City Reds	1.000	11	0	3	0	0
Velez, Yucatan	1.000	23	1	7	0	0
C. Diaz, Yucatan	1.000	26	1	6	0	1
Jaime Granillo, Leon	1.000	13	2	1	0	0
H. Lopez, Monterrey Sultans	1.000	40	3	13	0	0
Gutierrez, Monterrey Industrials	1.000	30	4	7	0	0
C.D. Jimenez, Tabasco	1.000	29	7	8	0	0
Ontiveros, Tabasco	1.000	45	3	16	0	0
A. Soto, Aguascalientes	1.000	28	6	22	0	1
Cervantes, Union Laguna	1.000	32	2	11	0	2
Cardenas, Aguascalientes	1.000	24	4	16	0	0
Esquer, Yucatan	.981	23	11	41	1	2
Chavez, Leon	.979	33	5	41	1	9
Cano, Monclova	.976	27	11	29	1	2
Dominguez, Campeche	.975	20	7	32	1	4
Huerta, Campeche	.975	26	10	29	1	2
Retes, Yucatan	.974	25	9	29	1	1
A. Cruz, Yucatan	.973	22	12	24	1	5
Dunster, Monclova	.973	26	8	28	1	1
Beltran, Aguascalientes	.973	23	8	28	1	4
L.F. Mendez, Mexico City Reds.	.972	27	10	25	1	5
M. Munoz, Saltillo	.970	25	5	27	1	2
M.A. Rodriguez, Saltillo	.969	35	9	22	1	1
Moya, Monterrey Sultans	.968	24	3	27	1	0
Renteria, Union Laguna	.968	27	8	22	1	5
F. Soto, Leon	.967	36	4	25	1	1
Serafin, Monterrey Industrials...	.964	30	5	22	1	0
Villa, San Luis	.963	43	9	17	1	3
Sombra, Union Laguna	.963	31	8	18	1	1
Navarro, Monterrey Sultans	.958	25	1	22	1	2
J. Moreno, Nuevo Laredo	.958	16	3	20	1	2
O. Diaz, Monterrey Industrials	.958	46	4	19	1	0
Monroe, Monterrey Industrials ..	.957	26	10	12	1	0
M. Raygoza, Campeche	.956	26	15	50	3	4
Enriquez, Tabasco	.955	34	5	16	1	1
I. Rodriguez, Monclova	.955	31	3	18	1	3

PITCHERS—Continued

Player and Club	Pct.	G.	PO.	A.	E.	DP.
Duarte, Monterrey Industrials ...	.955	41	5	16	1	1
Lunar, Campeche	.952	42	5	15	1	3
Morales, Monterrey Sultans	.952	31	8	12	1	0
Perry, Union Laguna	.952	46	3	17	1	1
J. J. Alvarez, Nuevo Laredo	.950	24	5	14	1	1
I. Velazquez, Campeche	.950	28	9	29	2	1
Dozier, Yucatan	.950	24	7	12	1	0
Kinonen, Mexico City Tigers	.950	13	2	17	1	1
Palafox, Union Laguna	.946	30	5	30	2	1
J. Rios, Mexico City Tigers	.944	25	7	27	2	1
Escarrega, Aguascalientes	.943	21	10	23	2	3
Bass, Monterrey Sultans	.938	16	1	14	1	0
J.R. Raygoza, Leon	.938	28	2	13	1	4
Lizarraga, San Luis	.938	26	4	11	1	2
M. Torres, Tabasco	.930	29	5	35	3	2
Miranda, Saltillo	.929	48	4	9	1	1
Mack, Mexico City Tigers	.929	16	4	9	1	0
Al. Pulido, Mexico City Reds	.929	11	3	10	1	2
Castro, Nuevo Laredo	.923	31	3	9	1	2
I. Jimenez, Mexico City Tigers ...	.921	20	5	30	3	0
C. Ibarra, Yucatan	.920	33	8	15	2	1
N. Munoz, Tabasco	.917	24	3	8	1	2
J.L. Rios, Union Laguna	.917	24	3	8	1	0
Sanchez, Leon	.917	51	3	8	1	0
Gonzalez, Monterrey Sultans	.915	25	9	34	4	3
M. Hernandez, Mexico City Reds	.913	24	4	17	2	2
R. Villegas, Leon	.909	40	3	17	2	0
R. Lopez, Monclova	.909	25	5	15	2	1
Banning, Nuevo Laredo	.906	23	9	20	3	0
Al. Garza, Monterrey Sultans	.905	24	2	17	2	0
E. Lopez, Mexico City Tigers	.900	12	1	8	1	0
Urrea, Yucatan	.900	26	4	5	1	1
Aguilar, Saltillo	.897	28	9	17	3	0
Barraza, Nuevo Laredo	.895	34	6	11	2	4
Re. Garcia, Campeche	.895	27	2	15	2	0
J.L. Garcia, San Luis	.893	32	5	20	3	1
Colorado, Yucatan	.892	20	6	27	4	1
A. Valdez, Monterrey Industrials	.889	41	7	17	3	1
Montalvo, Aguascalientes	.882	30	7	8	2	0
Romero, Tabasco	.875	19	2	5	1	0
Pruneda, Monterrey Sultans	.875	22	0	7	1	1
Carranza, Nuevo Laredo	.864	21	5	14	3	1
Zamudio, Tabasco	.861	27	5	26	5	2
Arias, Monclova	.857	14	2	4	1	1
L.T. Castillo, Nuevo Laredo	.857	20	4	14	3	2
An. Pulido, Campeche	.857	48	1	5	1	2
Veliz Arballo, San Luis	.857	29	4	14	3	3
Reynoso, Saltillo	.857	27	11	37	8	3
Cosio, Monclova	.857	20	5	7	2	1
Couch, Nuevo Laredo	.850	25	5	12	3	0
Villanueva, Leon	.833	42	1	4	1	0
Meagher, San Luis	.833	21	9	21	6	1
E. Herrera, Tabasco	.833	18	2	3	1	0
Barojas, Mexico City Reds	.833	56	8	17	5	2
F. Castillo, Saltillo	.818	24	3	6	2	2
Ro. Garcia, Monclova	.810	27	3	14	4	1
Uribe, Monterrey Sultans	.750	36	0	6	2	0
Escamilla, Monclova	.667	14	1	1	1	0
Campos, Monterrey Industrials..	.667	18	0	4	2	0

(Fewer Than Ten Games)

Player and Club	Pct.	G.	PO.	A.	E.	DP.
G. Valenzuela, Monterrey Ind.	1.000	8	1	4	0	0
Palermo, Leon	1.000	9	0	5	0	0
Copp, Mexico City Reds	1.000	6	2	3	0	0
R. Ramirez, Mexico City Reds ...	1.000	2	0	1	0	0
Fajardo, Mexico City Reds	1.000	3	1	1	0	0
Puerto, Yucatan	1.000	9	2	2	0	0
Onofre, Campeche	1.000	5	3	3	0	0
LaFever, Mexico City Tigers	1.000	9	3	6	0	0
Valencia, Mexico City Tigers	1.000	5	1	2	0	0
Go. Rojo, Aguascalientes	1.000	8	0	3	0	0
Ludy, Aguascalientes	1.000	5	5	5	0	0
J. Cruz, Tabasco	1.000	4	0	5	0	0
V. Martinez, Tabasco	1.000	5	0	2	0	0
Arcos, Tabasco	1.000	5	1	2	0	1
Marcos Castillejos, Tabasco	1.000	8	2	7	0	1
Hickey, Monclova	1.000	7	0	3	0	0
Vejar, Monclova	1.000	4	1	0	0	0
McKeon, Monterrey Industrials.	1.000	6	0	1	0	0
M. Solis, Monterrey Industrials..	1.000	8	4	4	0	0
Waddel, Monterrey Industrials ..	1.000	5	1	2	0	0
K. Angulo, Monterrey Ind.	1.000	7	0	5	0	0
Weller, Monterrey Sultans	1.000	7	3	2	0	0
Contreras, San Luis	1.000	7	1	1	0	0
L.A. Cruz, San Luis	1.000	2	0	1	0	0
A. Quiroz, Nuevo Laredo	1.000	6	0	1	0	0
Simpson, Nuevo Laredo	1.000	6	0	1	0	0
J.L. Valdez, Nuevo Laredo	1.000	1	1	0	0	0
Diaz Garcia, Union Laguna	1.000	9	0	2	0	0
U. Heredia, Monterrey Ind.	.923	9	2	10	1	0
Andresh, Mexico City Reds	.895	9	5	12	2	0
Orozco, Leon	.889	8	4	4	1	1
White, Tabasco	.846	6	4	7	2	1
Ad. Garza, Monterrey Sultans ...	.750	7	0	3	1	0
Jusaino, Leon	.667	7	1	1	1	0
Orduno, Monterrey Industrials...	.000	4	0	0	1	0
Leyva, Mexico City Reds	.000	6	0	0	1	0

Triple Play—Esquer.

CLUB PITCHING

Club	ERA.	G.	CG.	ShO.	Sv.	IP.	H.	R.	ER.	HR.	HB.	BB.	Int. BB.	SO.	WP.	Bk.
Yucatan	3.65	128	52	11	16	1074.0	1110	514	436	80	22	347	13	627	53	2
Campeche	3.76	129	43	10	18	1086.2	1201	550	454	82	34	384	32	513	69	4
Monterrey Sultans	3.82	132	36	7	17	1104.1	1195	615	469	64	37	434	42	715	65	1
Nuevo Laredo	3.89	132	32	10	22	1099.2	1123	583	475	95	46	431	25	639	63	5
Saltillo	3.94	129	34	11	21	1082.1	1167	566	474	81	44	426	58	620	48	9
Mexico City Tigers	4.09	130	47	7	12	1071.0	1124	565	487	81	35	429	50	653	46	7
Union Laguna	4.33	132	37	3	19	1109.1	1337	614	534	89	34	371	38	573	50	3
Monclova	4.47	132	54	6	14	1112.2	1292	647	553	84	34	415	38	554	47	2
Mexico City Reds	4.52	131	17	8	26	1100.0	1164	651	553	86	42	532	10	524	62	8
Tabasco	4.84	129	28	10	27	1021.0	1259	667	549	83	40	440	30	489	40	3
San Luis	5.02	131	37	6	21	1088.2	1341	711	607	84	26	454	40	673	58	8
Monterrey Industrials	5.21	132	14	2	22	1099.2	1358	754	636	85	38	494	42	750	49	7
Leon	5.28	131	26	5	27	1086.2	1232	763	637	99	37	451	17	520	62	5
Aguascalientes	5.89	130	25	5	18	1043.2	1361	804	683	93	49	437	52	521	53	9

PITCHERS' RECORDS
(Leading Qualifiers for Earned-Run Average Leadership — 106 or More Innings)

*Throws lefthanded.

Pitcher—Club	W.	L.	Pct.	ERA.	G.	GS.	CG.	GF.	ShO.	Sv.	IP.	H.	R.	ER.	HR.	HB.	Int. BB.	BB.	SO.	WP.
Esquer, Yucatan	16	4	.800	1.98	23	23	16	0	4	0	186.0	181	50	41	9	0	37	0	139	5
Gonzalez, Monterrey Ind	15	6	.714	2.17	25	25	12	0	2	0	182.2	168	68	44	9	2	41	2	129	3
Barojas, Mexico City Reds	8	8	.500	2.78	56	0	0	56	0	24	106.2	86	45	33	1	6	55	3	70	6
R. Osuna, Monterrey Ind	10	8	.556	2.87	38	18	7	20	1	5	169.1	155	73	54	4	1	76	8	123	15
G. Heredia, San Luis	14	9	.609	2.99	24	24	15	0	3	0	180.2	183	73	60	9	4	35	2	125	7
J. Rios, Mexico City Tigers	12	8	.600	3.00	25	25	10	0	2	0	183.0	168	79	61	13	3	71	9	134	3
M. Raygoza, Campeche	15	11	.577	3.04	26	26	9	0	1	0	189.2	204	87	64	11	5	45	6	79	8
L.T. Castillo, Nuevo Laredo	8	5	.615	3.05	20	16	7	4	2	0	109.1	97	40	37	8	3	31	0	70	5
Banning, Nuevo Laredo	15	4	.789	3.10	23	22	10	1	3	0	159.2	155	69	55	16	5	41	1	94	6
R. Solis, Saltillo	14	11	.560	3.12	28	27	11	1	4	1	199.0	218	85	69	7	3	50	3	115	4

Departmental Leaders: G—Barojas, 56; W—I. Velazquez, 20; L—Camarena, 16; Pct.—Esquer, .800; GS—Camarena, M. Torres, 29; CG—Dunster, 22; GF—Barojas, 56; ShO—Esquer, R. Solis, 4; Sv.—Barojas, 24; IP—Dunster, 207.2; H—I. Velazquez, 223; R—F. Soto, 122; ER—F. Soto, 101; HR—I. Velazquez, 25; HB—Cano, Navarro, 12; BB—Ortiz, 87; IBB—Miranda, M.A. Rodriquez, 10; SO—Navarro, 150; WP—Navarro, 16.

(All Pitchers—Listed Alphabetically)

Pitcher—Club	W.	L.	Pct.	ERA.	G.	GS.	CG.	GF.	ShO.	Sv.	IP.	H.	R.	ER.	HR.	HB.	BB.	Int. BB.	SO.	WP.
Acosta, Aguascalientes	3	9	.250	7.28	30	10	1	20	0	2	89.0	122	80	72	6	4	53	3	52	11
Aguilar, Saltillo	8	9	.471	4.19	28	25	3	3	2	0	129.0	131	70	60	15	4	49	3	77	5
J.J. Alvarez, Nuevo Laredo	6	5	.545	3.32	24	16	1	8	0	0	84.0	82	38	31	4	4	53	1	49	9
M. Alvarez, Saltillo	1	3	.250	4.20	37	1	0	36	0	2	40.2	42	24	19	4	2	31	9	34	5
Andresh, Mexico City Reds	5	1	.833	2.97	9	9	0	0	0	0	60.2	58	24	20	1	6	28	0	23	7
J. Angulo, 3 Cam-26 MC Reds	1	1	.500	7.02	29	1	0	28	0	0	33.1	53	39	26	4	1	21	2	24	5
K. Angulo, Monterrey Ind	0	4	.000	10.23	7	6	0	1	0	0	22.0	35	28	25	5	0	18	0	19	2
Antunez, Yucatan	2	7	.222	3.99	42	1	1	41	0	6	47.1	57	23	21	2	0	25	2	33	5
Arano, Saltillo	0	0	.000	27.00	1	0	0	1	0	0	0.1	1	1	1	0	0	3	0	0	0
Arcos, Tabasco	0	0	.000	9.72	5	1	0	4	0	0	8.1	14	9	9	0	1	5	0	2	2
Arias, Monclova	1	3	.250	6.57	14	4	1	10	0	0	37.0	64	31	27	3	1	20	2	19	5
Armenta, Nuevo Laredo	0	0	.000	0.00	1	0	0	1	0	0	1.0	1	0	0	0	0	0	0	2	0
Banning, Nuevo Laredo	15	4	.789	3.10	23	22	10	1	3	0	159.2	155	69	55	16	5	41	1	94	6
Barojas, Mexico City Reds	8	8	.500	2.78	56	0	0	56	0	24	106.2	86	45	33	1	6	55	3	70	6
Barraza, Nuevo Laredo	3	2	.600	4.72	34	4	0	30	0	0	68.2	79	54	36	2	6	52	1	44	10
Barron, Mexico City Reds	1	3	.250	7.48	12	0	0	12	0	0	21.2	30	19	18	1	0	13	1	10	1
Bass, Monterrey Sultans	3	5	.375	4.26	16	6	1	10	0	3	50.2	57	33	24	2	2	22	7	34	2
Beltran, 12 Cam-11 Ags	10	7	.588	3.91	23	23	4	0	1	0	129.0	148	69	56	14	0	52	4	41	3
Brooks, Mexico City Tigers	0	1	.000	14.29	4	2	0	2	0	0	5.2	13	9	9	0	0	6	0	3	0
Camarena, Tabasco	11	16	.407	4.62	31	29	6	2	1	0	169.1	189	102	87	18	5	79	6	83	11
Campos, 1 Mva-17 Mont. Ind.	2	0	1.000	4.40	18	0	0	18	0	0	30.2	46	19	15	0	3	15	0	17	2
Cano, Monclova	11	10	.524	3.49	27	25	11	2	1	0	180.2	187	88	70	10	12	47	5	76	2
Cardenas, 8 SLP-16 Ags	1	4	.200	6.52	24	5	1	19	0	1	58.0	87	53	42	0	6	22	1	20	11
Carranza, Nuevo Laredo	11	6	.647	3.33	21	21	6	0	1	0	140.2	130	70	52	13	3	48	0	80	10
A. Castaneda, Mexico City Reds.	4	6	.400	5.60	21	13	1	8	0	0	72.1	77	54	45	6	1	54	0	30	6
M. Castaneda, Union Laguna	3	1	.750	5.25	19	1	0	18	0	1	36.0	55	23	21	2	1	16	4	15	1
P. Castaneda, Monterrey Ind.	1	0	1.000	0.00	3	0	0	3	0	0	7.2	0	0	0	0	0	2	0	4	0
Castellanos, Saltillo	0	0	.000	4.50	2	0	0	2	0	0	2.0	2	1	1	0	0	0	0	2	0
F. Castillo, Saltillo	0	3	.000	4.72	24	1	0	23	0	0	61.0	82	39	32	8	4	19	4	15	4
L.T. Castillo, Nuevo Laredo	8	5	.615	3.05	20	16	7	4	2	0	109.1	97	40	37	8	3	31	0	70	5
Castro, Nuevo Laredo	5	1	.167	6.34	31	6	0	25	0	0	49.2	64	44	35	4	8	20	2	16	2
Cazarez, San Luis	0	0	.000	11.57	26	0	0	26	0	0	16.1	28	23	21	1	0	19	5	15	4
Cervantes, 11 Ags-21 Lag	7	7	.500	5.68	32	6	2	26	0	8	77.2	92	56	49	6	0	33	7	54	0
Chavarin, Mexico City Reds	2	1	.667	4.25	17	1	1	16	0	0	42.1	48	26	20	4	0	18	0	14	4
Chavez, Leon	11	9	.550	4.22	33	21	3	12	1	1	168.1	206	100	79	15	1	48	4	88	11
Colorado, Yucatan	7	10	.412	3.97	20	20	8	0	1	0	138.1	157	78	61	13	6	13	1	65	0
Contreras, San Luis	0	0	.000	9.00	7	1	0	6	0	0	11.0	20	12	11	2	0	9	0	5	0
Copp, Mexico City Reds	3	2	.600	2.29	6	6	1	0	1	0	39.1	28	11	10	3	0	9	0	17	0
Cosio, Monclova	5	11	.313	6.26	20	17	2	3	0	0	102.0	118	75	71	8	2	56	2	41	10
Couch, Nuevo Laredo	6	4	.600	4.74	25	19	0	6	0	1	100.2	95	67	53	17	2	48	2	62	8
A. Cruz, Yucatan	13	8	.619	3.36	22	22	15	0	2	0	160.2	147	66	60	14	1	56	1	112	9
J. Cruz, Tabasco	0	2	.000	14.46	4	2	0	2	0	0	9.1	25	19	15	1	2	12	1	2	1
L.A. Cruz, San Luis	0	0	.000	0.00	2	0	0	2	0	1	3.2	3	0	0	0	0	0	0	4	0
Delgadillo, Aguascalientes	8	9	.471	4.29	22	22	4	0	1	0	138.1	169	73	66	14	5	40	5	40	4
A. Diaz, 8 MC Reds-13 Cam	1	6	.143	5.40	21	2	1	19	0	0	58.1	72	36	35	5	2	31	2	17	2
C. Diaz, Tabasco	3	4	.429	4.47	26	2	0	24	0	3	52.1	65	33	26	6	3	16	0	20	4
G.C. Diaz, Union Laguna	1	0	1.000	9.56	9	0	0	9	0	0	16.0	28	17	17	5	2	6	0	10	3
O. Diaz, Monterrey Industrials	1	4	.200	5.65	46	8	0	38	0	0	94.0	118	74	59	5	0	70	7	69	8
Diez, Monterrey Industrials	1	1	.500	8.74	4	3	0	1	0	0	11.1	22	17	11	3	2	5	0	12	0
Dimas, Aguascalientes	2	4	.333	5.05	32	0	0	32	0	1	71.1	86	46	40	6	3	28	7	25	4
Dominguez, Campeche	6	7	.462	3.32	20	20	4	0	2	0	130.0	150	64	48	8	1	40	2	64	5
Dozier, Yucatan	15	4	.789	3.13	24	23	11	1	2	0	181.1	159	68	63	9	4	58	1	133	11
Duarte, 7 Cam-34 Mont. Ind.	5	4	.556	4.40	41	7	2	34	0	0	102.1	119	58	50	8	8	33	2	48	1
Dunster, Monclova	15	11	.577	3.42	26	26	22	0	1	0	207.2	222	94	79	15	2	36	4	87	5
Elias Lomeli, Campeche	0	0	.000	0.00	1	0	0	1	0	0	1.0	0	0	0	0	0	0	0	0	0
Enriquez, Tabasco	4	10	.286	5.84	34	13	3	21	0	4	114.0	137	85	74	5	1	52	4	59	5
Escamilla, Monclova	3	3	.500	2.83	14	1	0	13	0	2	35.0	30	14	11	2	2	12	3	14	2
Escarrega, Aguascalientes	5	11	.313	5.59	21	20	7	1	0	0	114.1	147	87	71	12	6	40	5	33	2
Espinoza, Aguascalientes	0	2	.000	8.44	16	1	0	15	0	1	16.0	20	17	15	3	0	13	2	7	2
Esquer, Yucatan	16	4	.800	1.98	23	23	16	0	4	0	186.0	181	50	41	9	0	37	0	139	5
Fajardo, Mexico City Reds	0	0	.000	6.30	3	0	0	3	0	0	10.0	8	7	7	1	7	0	0	6	0
Flores, Union Laguna	2	3	.400	4.90	27	2	1	23	0	1	90.0	114	57	49	10	3	34	1	31	4
H. Garcia, San Luis	2	1	.667	6.07	17	2	0	15	0	0	43.0	53	32	29	0	3	28	2	17	2
J.L. Garcia, San Luis	10	11	.476	4.73	32	28	4	4	0	0	158.0	206	90	83	14	0	64	7	106	4
J. Garcia, Mexico City Tigers	1	4	.200	4.14	32	2	1	30	0	3	63.0	59	35	29	6	3	27	3	36	4
Re. Garcia, Campeche	5	4	.556	3.54	27	9	4	18	0	1	76.1	87	38	30	3	2	39	3	50	7
Ro. Garcia, Monclova	4	4	.500	4.71	27	3	2	24	0	2	70.2	75	44	37	5	2	23	7	35	5
Z. Garcia, Tabasco	0	1	.000	9.35	12	0	0	12	0	0	26.0	44	33	27	3	2	13	3	5	2
Ad. Garza, Monterrey Sultans	0	0	.000	10.00	7	0	0	7	0	0	9.0	16	13	10	1	1	5	2	1	0
Al. Garza, Monterrey Sultans	2	6	.250	3.24	24	6	0	18	0	0	75.0	84	34	27	2	1	45	2	53	9
Gonzalez, Monterrey Sultans	15	6	.714	2.17	25	25	12	0	2	0	182.2	168	68	44	9	2	41	2	129	3
Grajales, Mexico City Tigers	3	3	.500	3.90	45	1	0	44	0	5	60.0	71	32	26	6	1	20	3	45	5
Granillo, Aguascalientes	6	13	.316	6.24	29	23	3	6	0	2	137.0	177	109	95	16	3	48	4	87	3
Gutierrez, 15 Leo-15 Mont. Ind.	3	3	.500	5.99	30	10	0	20	0	0	79.2	102	69	53	5	4	47	5	51	5
B. Guzman, San Luis	0	2	.000	9.26	15	4	0	11	0	0	23.1	46	24	24	3	0	7	1	12	2
G. Guzman, 9 Ags-12 Cam	0	3	.000	9.77	21	5	1	16	0	0	31.1	62	37	34	3	0	12	1	13	2
G. Heredia, San Luis	14	9	.609	2.99	24	24	15	0	3	0	180.2	183	73	60	9	4	35	2	125	7
U. Heredia, Monterrey Ind	1	5	.167	4.67	9	9	2	0	0	0	54.0	68	31	28	4	2	17	5	50	3
E. Hernandez, Union Laguna	10	8	.556	4.37	29	26	4	3	0	1	146.1	187	83	71	9	4	54	6	64	5
M. Hernandez, MC Reds	8	13	.381	5.57	24	22	3	2	1	0	119.2	153	82	74	5	3	51	0	57	9
C. Herrera, Mexico City Tigers	0	2	.000	7.13	16	0	0	16	0	0	24.0	37	22	19	3	4	19	4	11	3
E. Herrera, Tabasco	1	1	.500	7.94	18	1	0	17	0	1	28.1	43	31	25	4	4	16	0	20	3
R. Herrera, Leon	0	0	.000	13.50	3	0	0	3	0	0	3.1	8	5	5	1	0	2	0	4	0
Hickey, Monclova	1	2	.333	5.87	7	2	0	5	0	0	15.1	19	11	10	0	1	9	0	9	0
Huerta, Campeche	12	6	.667	4.19	26	23	6	3	2	2	150.1	178	84	70	9	5	59	0	75	9
C. Ibarra, 19 Leo-14 Yuc	3	11	.214	6.62	33	16	3	17	0	3	125.0	156	107	92	8	3	53	2	50	4
J. Ibarra, Monclova	0	2	.000	10.80	4	0	0	4	0	0	1.2	5	2	2	0	0	3	0	1	0
Jacobson, Monterrey Ind	0	2	.000	7.24	3	3	0	0	0	0	13.2	16	14	11	1	0	15	0	15	2
Jaime Granillo, Leon	0	1	.000	7.78	13	1	0	12	0	1	19.2	30	18	17	4	3	9	1	6	1
C.D. Jimenez, 9 Sal-20 Tab	5	8	.385	3.91	29	11	3	18	0	10	94.1	94	50	41	8	2	50	5	51	2

374

Pitcher—Club	W.	L.	Pct.	ERA.	G.	GS.	CG.	GF.	ShO.	Sv.	IP.	H.	R.	ER.	HR.	HB.	BB.	Int. BB.	SO.	WP.
D. Jimenez, Tabasco	4	7	.364	3.94	28	11	3	13	0	7	93.2	92	48	41	7	2	50	5	51	2
I. Jimenez, Mexico City Tigers	8	9	.471	3.57	20	20	5	0	0	0	133.2	131	56	53	4	4	63	3	72	8
L. Jimenez, Campeche	0	0	.000	0.00	2	0	0	2	0	0	1.0	2	0	0	0	0	0	0	0	1
Jusaino, Leon	1	0	1.000	4.02	7	0	0	7	0	0	15.2	21	9	7	0	0	8	0	8	0
Kinonen, Mexico City Tigers	5	7	.417	3.08	13	13	5	0	0	0	84.2	81	33	29	5	2	35	1	66	5
Lara, Aguascalientes	5	2	.714	4.47	26	5	1	21	1	0	56.1	69	42	28	4	4	32	1	40	5
Ledon, Yucatan	0	0	.000	16.20	3	0	0	3	0	0	5.0	13	9	9	2	0	3	0	3	2
LeFever, Mexico City Tigers	2	6	.250	6.25	9	9	0	0	0	0	44.2	47	33	31	3	2	14	2	25	2
Leyva, Mexico City Reds	1	0	1.000	6.35	6	0	0	6	0	0	5.2	7	5	4	2	0	4	0	6	1
Lizarraga, San Luis	4	7	.364	5.07	26	17	1	9	0	0	108.1	136	67	61	8	4	47	2	48	7
E. Lopez, Mexico City Tigers	2	5	.286	3.26	12	6	0	6	0	0	47.0	47	20	17	5	2	11	2	16	2
H. Lopez, 29 SLP-11 Mon. Sul...	3	3	.500	6.81	40	2	0	38	0	2	78.0	113	64	59	6	3	39	4	37	6
J.R. Lopez, 4 Mon. Sul.-17 Cam.	3	4	.429	4.92	21	6	1	15	0	0	67.2	72	39	37	13	1	24	1	46	6
P. Lopez, Saltillo	0	0	.000	3.00	1	0	0	1	0	0	3.0	2	1	1	0	0	0	0	2	0
R. Lopez, Monclova	7	13	.350	4.55	25	25	9	0	1	0	170.0	217	95	86	18	0	57	4	96	1
Ludy, Aguascalientes	1	2	.333	6.66	5	5	0	0	0	0	25.2	44	20	19	1	2	9	0	16	2
Luevano, Mexico City Reds	5	7	.417	5.01	36	14	0	22	0	1	100.2	98	67	56	11	7	49	1	44	2
Lunar, Campeche	4	8	.333	2.77	42	5	1	37	0	12	87.2	68	31	27	3	8	43	5	62	11
Mack, Mexico City Tigers	2	8	.200	6.27	16	6	3	10	0	1	56.0	67	46	39	9	2	16	4	23	0
Marcos Castillejos, Tabasco	4	2	.667	3.46	8	7	1	1	0	0	39.0	56	16	15	2	0	2	0	11	0
G. Martinez, 12 Leo-15 M.I.	3	5	.375	4.72	27	9	1	18	0	0	97.1	129	61	51	3	6	25	0	45	3
R. Martinez, Mex. C. Reds	3	3	.667	3.59	33	10	3	23	1	1	97.2	96	48	39	10	1	41	2	53	6
V. Martinez, Tabasco	0	2	.000	10.61	5	0	0	5	0	0	9.1	18	11	11	2	1	3	0	5	0
McKeon, Monterrey Ind	2	1	.667	7.56	6	3	0	3	0	0	16.2	25	14	14	2	0	11	2	21	0
Meagher, San Luis	9	10	.474	4.26	21	21	11	0	0	0	143.2	154	85	68	13	4	52	1	115	8
Mena, Monclova	1	0	1.000	7.40	13	0	0	13	0	0	24.1	43	23	20	3	2	9	0	8	0
L.F. Mendez, Mexico City Reds ..	13	6	.684	4.09	27	27	4	0	3	0	163.0	151	79	74	10	6	79	0	90	3
M. Mendez, Saltillo	0	1	.000	8.37	16	0	0	16	0	0	23.2	28	22	22	3	4	12	0	8	1
Miranda, Saltillo	11	3	.786	3.90	48	1	1	47	0	14	80.2	72	41	35	5	3	55	10	77	6
Monroe, Monterrey Ind	8	9	.471	5.14	26	19	1	7	0	2	133.0	163	85	76	10	3	44	1	117	2
Montalvo, Aguascalientes	3	3	.500	3.86	30	0	0	30	0	10	53.2	55	27	23	2	5	15	8	42	0
Montano, Aguascalientes	0	0	.000	6.75	1	0	0	1	0	0	1.1	3	3	1	0	1	0	0	0	0
Moore, Nuevo Laredo	4	4	.500	1.71	14	0	0	14	0	2	31.2	28	10	6	1	1	12	4	26	3
Morales, 15 SLP-16 Mon. Sul...	3	9	.250	8.11	31	15	0	16	0	0	77.2	123	90	70	13	3	31	4	45	2
A. Moreno, Mexico City Tigers	15	8	.652	3.84	25	25	15	0	1	0	189.2	195	90	81	14	9	70	8	124	9
J. Moreno, Nuevo Laredo	11	3	.786	3.95	16	16	8	0	0	0	116.1	119	54	51	13	2	26	3	66	2
Moya, Monterrey Sultans	10	10	.500	4.12	24	24	7	0	1	0	142.0	185	83	65	14	4	38	3	54	3
M. Munoz, Saltillo	13	8	.619	3.90	25	24	6	1	1	0	143.0	165	71	62	10	3	27	3	67	2
N. Munoz, Tabasco	2	2	.500	6.75	24	0	0	24	0	10	26.2	22	21	20	2	1	22	0	28	2
Navarro, Monterrey Sultans	8	9	.471	3.48	25	25	8	0	1	0	163.0	154	83	63	11	12	63	3	150	16
Nery, 3 SLP-15 MC Tigers	0	0	.000	5.28	18	0	0	18	0	2	15.1	25	11	9	0	0	10	0	10	0
Ochoa, San Luis	8	2	.800	2.54	53	1	0	52	0	10	99.1	98	30	28	2	2	27	6	54	3
Onofre, Campeche	1	0	1.000	2.84	5	0	0	5	0	0	12.2	12	6	4	0	1	5	1	2	1
Ontiveros, 27 SLP-18 Tab	5	2	.714	4.30	45	0	0	45	0	5	88.0	114	59	42	5	0	30	6	34	3
Ordaz, Mexico City Tigers	1	0	1.000	1.90	12	1	1	11	1	1	23.2	20	6	5	0	1	8	2	2	0
Orduno, Monterrey Ind	0	0	.000	14.29	4	0	0	4	0	0	5.2	14	11	9	0	0	5	4	0	0
Orozco, Leon	6	2	.750	3.20	8	8	4	0	0	0	56.1	62	33	20	2	0	14	0	16	0
Ortiz, Leon	10	5	.667	4.72	29	23	3	6	1	0	129.2	137	83	68	12	6	87	0	70	14
M. Osuna, San Luis	1	0	1.000	5.59	20	0	0	20	0	0	38.2	50	32	24	3	1	18	2	21	0
R. Osuna, Monterrey Sultans	10	8	.556	2.87	38	18	7	20	1	5	169.1	155	73	54	4	1	76	8	123	15
Padilla, 4 Sal-12 Cam.	1	3	.250	8.71	16	1	0	15	0	0	20.2	23	21	20	4	2	16	3	11	1
Palafox, Union Laguna	7	8	.467	4.56	30	27	7	3	1	1	167.2	222	98	85	14	8	58	5	66	7
Palermo, Leon	3	4	.429	5.40	9	9	2	0	0	0	45.0	55	30	27	4	2	24	0	25	0
Perry, Union Laguna	12	9	.571	3.21	46	9	6	37	1	6	126.1	111	52	45	5	6	46	10	130	11
Pimentel, Union Laguna	0	0	.000	0.00	1	0	0	1	0	0	0.1	0	0	0	0	0	0	0	0	0
Pruneda, 7 Mva-15 Mon. Sul.	0	8	.000	5.29	22	11	0	11	0	0	68.0	85	56	40	6	2	31	2	19	5
Puerto, Yucatan	1	0	1.000	2.16	9	1	0	8	0	0	16.2	17	7	4	1	1	9	1	4	2
Al. Pulido, Mexico City Reds	5	0	1.000	2.91	11	9	3	2	0	0	65.0	66	27	21	7	0	14	0	19	1
An. Pulido, 36 M.I.-12 Cam	3	6	.333	4.18	48	0	0	48	0	19	64.2	74	38	30	2	3	18	6	44	1
Purata, 10 Yuc-10 Leo	8	6	.571	4.15	20	17	3	3	1	0	110.2	122	61	51	13	3	42	0	68	6
Quinones, Aguascalientes	2	11	.154	6.85	30	18	2	12	0	0	115.2	143	98	88	9	10	77	7	73	4
Quintero, Union Laguna	0	0	.000	3.00	2	0	0	2	0	0	3.0	2	0	0	0	0	4	0	0	0
A. Quiroz, Nuevo Laredo	0	0	.000	0.82	6	1	0	5	0	2	11.0	7	1	1	0	0	11	0	11	0
J.J. Quiroz, M.C. Tigers	0	0	.000	12.46	9	0	0	9	0	0	4.1	10	6	6	1	0	5	1	5	0
E. Ramirez, Saltillo	1	1	.500	4.25	24	2	0	22	0	0	48.2	53	26	23	3	1	25	1	32	5
R. Ramirez, Mexico City Reds	0	0	.000	4.91	2	1	0	1	0	0	3.2	4	2	2	0	1	2	0	2	0
C. Raygoza, Aguascalientes	1	0	1.000	6.66	15	0	0	15	0	0	25.2	39	25	19	2	2	16	2	6	4
J.R. Raygoza, Leon	3	2	.600	6.79	28	1	0	27	0	1	51.2	76	45	39	5	2	29	0	16	4
M. Raygoza, Campeche	15	11	.577	3.04	26	26	9	0	1	0	189.2	204	90	64	11	5	45	6	79	3
Renteria, Union Laguna	14	6	.700	3.86	27	26	9	1	0	1	172.2	177	87	74	14	4	44	1	101	1
Retes, Yucatan	6	9	.400	5.43	25	17	1	8	0	0	106.0	140	74	64	9	3	52	3	39	5
Reyes, San Luis	0	0	.000	9.35	6	1	0	5	0	0	8.2	18	15	9	2	0	5	1	2	2
Reynoso, Saltillo	13	9	.591	3.48	27	25	7	2	2	0	160.1	155	78	62	10	8	64	7	107	11
J. Rios, Mexico City Tigers	12	8	.600	3.00	25	25	10	0	4	0	183.0	168	79	61	13	3	71	9	134	3
J.L. Rios, Union Laguna	5	0	1.000	2.77	24	1	1	23	1	0	68.1	81	23	21	4	3	14	0	29	4
I. Rodriguez, Monclova	8	10	.444	3.58	31	20	7	11	2	1	135.2	136	63	54	6	4	70	0	101	11
M.A. Rodriguez, Saltillo	6	6	.500	3.78	35	13	3	22	0	4	128.2	147	70	54	10	10	53	10	55	4
R. Rodriguez, M.C. Tigers	8	9	.471	4.71	40	17	7	23	1	2	124.1	142	78	65	11	2	44	4	77	5
Go. Rojo, Aguascalientes	1	1	.500	11.05	8	0	0	8	0	0	7.1	16	11	9	2	1	3	0	1	0
Gu. Rojo, Saltillo	0	0	.000	2.45	5	0	0	5	0	0	3.2	1	2	1	0	0	6	0	1	1
Romero, Tabasco	0	2	.000	4.37	19	2	0	17	0	0	45.1	59	29	22	3	6	18	1	14	2
Romo, Nuevo Laredo	1	3	.250	8.65	25	3	0	22	0	2	26.0	38	28	25	7	2	23	0	17	0
Sanchez, Leon	10	7	.588	4.33	51	0	0	51	0	14	79.0	74	42	38	6	5	35	5	53	15
Sauceda, Aguascalientes	0	0	.000	16.20	1	0	0	1	0	0	1.2	5	3	3	0	0	0	2	0	0
Serafin, Monterrey Ind	7	12	.368	4.52	30	25	4	5	0	0	171.1	181	99	86	17	4	58	2	104	12
Serna, Monterrey Sultans	7	4	.636	4.66	15	15	1	0	0	0	75.1	75	46	39	3	7	41	2	49	8
Simpson, Nuevo Laredo	2	0	.000	11.25	6	1	0	5	0	0	12.0	17	16	15	0	1	7	2	8	1
M. Solis, Monterrey Ind	0	4	.000	8.80	8	5	0	3	0	0	30.2	48	34	30	2	2	19	4	14	3
R. Solis, Saltillo	14	11	.560	3.12	28	27	11	1	4	1	199.0	218	85	69	7	3	50	3	115	4
Sombra, Union Laguna	9	12	.429	4.43	31	28	5	3	0	0	152.1	202	89	75	12	3	57	5	69	9
C. Sosa, Campeche	0	0	.000	2.57	4	0	0	4	0	0	7.0	9	2	2	0	0	3	0	2	0
M. Sosa, Tabasco	12	7	.632	3.77	26	21	6	5	2	0	143.1	163	76	60	9	5	47	2	66	2

Pitcher—Club	W.	L.	Pct.	ERA	G.	GS.	CG.	GF.	ShO.	Sv.	IP.	H.	R.	ER.	HR.	HB.	BB.	Int. BB.	SO.	WP.
A. Soto, 15 Lag-13 Ags	5	12	.294	5.37	28	18	6	10	0	1	119.0	154	80	71	10	0	28	4	49	5
F. Soto, Leon	11	8	.579	5.44	36	23	8	13	1	1	167.0	218	122	101	16	6	45	2	49	2
Tejeda, Monterrey Sultans	0	0	.000	2.04	12	0	0	12	0	0	17.2	15	6	4	0	1	4	0	12	3
Telechea, 3 Mon. Sul.-5 Tab	0	2	.000	3.86	8	0	0	8	0	0	11.2	15	5	5	1	0	8	3	5	0
Tinoco, Nuevo Laredo	0	0	.000	8.59	5	1	0	4	0	0	7.1	10	8	7	2	0	4	0	3	0
Tiquet, Tabasco	0	0	.000	0.00	1	0	0	1	0	0	1.0	0	0	0	0	0	0	0	1	0
Tirado, Nuevo Laredo	3	4	.429	6.47	14	4	0	10	0	0	32.0	42	30	23	3	1	19	1	24	2
Mario Toledo, Campeche	0	0	.000	2.25	4	0	0	4	0	0	4.0	4	1	1	0	0	3	0	4	0
Martin Toledo, Campeche	0	0	.000	0.00	1	0	0	0	0	0	0.0	0	0	0	0	0	0	0	0	0
G. Torres, Monterrey Ind	2	1	.667	9.33	18	4	0	14	0	0	36.2	60	41	38	4	0	28	0	17	1
M. Torres, Tabasco	15	8	.652	3.48	29	29	10	0	1	0	196.2	215	90	76	16	5	76	6	86	4
S. Torres, Union Laguna	2	2	.500	8.66	24	0	0	24	0	0	17.2	25	19	17	3	0	9	0	7	3
Ulin, Tabasco	0	1	.000	16.50	4	0	0	4	0	0	6.0	16	11	11	0	0	2	0	3	2
Uribe, Monterrey Sultans	8	5	.615	4.36	36	1	0	35	0	9	43.1	48	30	21	2	1	25	5	28	1
Urrea, Yucatan	0	3	.000	6.88	26	2	0	24	0	0	34.0	43	30	26	2	2	15	2	11	4
A. Valdez, Monterrey Ind	11	7	.611	4.10	41	9	1	32	1	5	116.1	124	61	53	8	2	62	7	91	3
J.L. Valdez, Nuevo Laredo	0	0	.000	18.00	1	0	0	1	0	0	1.0	2	2	2	1	0	1	0	0	0
R. Valdez, Mexico City Reds	6	9	.400	5.82	21	17	1	4	0	0	102.0	128	78	66	13	6	49	2	41	6
Valencia, Mexico City Tigers	0	1	.000	9.00	5	3	0	2	0	0	14.0	18	15	14	1	0	14	2	5	0
G. Valenzuela, 2 Tab-6 Ind	2	4	.333	8.36	8	8	1	0	0	0	37.2	64	42	35	5	3	10	1	15	1
J. Valenzuela, Monclova	0	0	.000	5.28	19	2	0	17	0	1	46.0	56	30	27	4	4	13	1	16	1
M. Valenzuela, Campeche	0	0	.000	9.00	5	0	0	5	0	0	5.0	6	5	5	0	1	9	0	2	10
R.L. Valenzuela, Monterrey Sul	2	0	1.000	5.09	21	2	0	19	0	0	35.1	41	25	20	3	1	14	1	8	1
Vargas, Monclova	1	0	1.000	4.50	11	0	0	11	0	1	18.0	28	12	9	1	0	13	4	11	0
Vazquez, Monclova	1	3	.250	7.23	25	1	0	24	0	6	42.1	53	40	34	7	0	33	1	33	1
Vejar, Monclova	0	0	.000	1.69	4	0	0	4	0	0	5.1	7	1	1	0	1	3	0	1	3
E. Velazquez, M.C. Reds	0	0	.000	8.41	13	0	0	13	0	0	20.1	34	21	19	5	2	16	0	9	3
I. Velazquez, Campeche	20	6	.769	3.81	28	26	14	2	1	1	200.2	223	100	85	25	6	44	4	71	4
L.A. Velazquez, Leon	0	0	.000	11.57	1	1	0	0	0	0	2.1	3	3	3	0	2	0	0	1	0
Velez, Yucatan	2	2	.500	3.61	23	4	1	19	0	0	47.1	40	23	19	4	1	25	0	23	4
Veliz Arballo, 16 M.S.-13 SLP	3	7	.300	4.80	29	11	3	18	1	0	90.0	106	57	48	6	2	47	4	52	3
Villa, San Luis	11	7	.611	3.22	43	4	3	39	0	16	114.2	105	50	41	4	1	57	5	95	5
Villanueva, Leon	0	1	.000	4.32	42	0	0	42	0	3	25.0	32	14	12	3	0	15	2	20	3
J.A. Villegas, Nuevo Laredo	5	1	.833	3.28	31	1	0	30	0	5	49.1	59	22	18	2	6	18	2	13	2
R. Villegas, Leon	9	6	.600	4.44	40	15	3	25	1	6	117.2	130	73	58	13	4	35	1	61	0
Wadell, Monterrey Ind	1	4	.200	4.03	5	5	1	0	0	0	22.1	31	18	10	2	1	12	1	15	2
Wheeler, Monterrey Sultans	1	1	.500	3.07	7	1	0	6	0	0	14.2	24	9	5	1	1	2	1	12	0
White, Saltillo	2	3	.400	4.10	6	6	1	0	0	0	41.2	48	24	19	2	1	12	0	15	0
Zambrano, Tabasco	0	0	.000	0.00	1	0	0	1	0	0	1.0	0	0	0	0	0	1	0	2	0
Zamorano, Mexico City Reds	0	0	.000	5.29	11	0	0	11	0	1	17.0	21	10	10	1	0	8	0	4	1
Zamudio, 12 Mon. Ind.-15 Tab	3	15	.167	4.98	27	24	2	3	0	0	132.0	164	88	73	13	7	67	4	56	3

BALKS—Delgadillo, 4; Re. Garcia, Luevano, M.A. Rodriguez, 3 each; Aguilar, M. Castaneda, L.F. Mendez, An. Pulido, J. Rios, F. Soto, Zamudio, 2 each; M. Alvarez, Banning, Barraza, Cano, Cardenas, L.T. Castillo, Cazarez, Chavez, O. Diaz, J.L. Garcia, Grajales, Granillo, Gutierrez, B. Guzman, G. Heredia, M. Hernandez, Huerta, C. Ibarra, I. Jimenez, Kinonen, Lara, H. Lopez, Marcos Castillejos, R. Martinez, McKeon, Meagher, M. Mendez, Moya, Nery, Ochoa, Ontiveros, Palermo, Puerto, A. Quiroz, J.J. Quiroz, Quinones, E. Ramirez, C. Raygoza, Retes, I. Rodriguez, Romero, Serafin, R. Solis, Sombra, R. Valdez, Veliz Arballo, 1 each.

COMBINATION SHUTOUTS—Delgadillo-Quinones, Granillo-Acosta-Cardenas, Lara-Dimas, Aguascalientes; Beltran-Huerta, Huerta-Lunar, Lunar-Padilla, Campeche; Andresh-R. Martinez-Barojas, L.F. Mendez-Chavarin, Mexico City Reds; I. Jimenez-Grajales, LaFever-Grajales-R. Rodriguez, Mexico City Tigers; Hickey-Duarte, Monclova; G. Martinez-A. Valdez, Monterrey Industrials; Al. Garza-Uribe, Moya-Morales-Uribe, Monterrey Sultans; J.J. Alvarez-Castro, Carranza-J.A. Villegas, Couch-Ochoa, Romo-Ochoa, Nuevo Laredo; Aguilar-Miranda, E. Ramirez-M. Munoz-M.A. Rodriguez-M. Alvarez, Saltillo; J.L. Garcia-Villa, Meagher-Villa, San Luis; Camarena-C.D. Jimenez 2, Camarena-N. Munoz, Marcos Castillejos-C.D. Jimenez, Zamudio-C.D. Jimenez, Tabasco; Esquer-Antunez, Yucatan.

NO-HIT GAMES—None.

Pacific Coast League

CLASS AAA

Leading Batter
BRUCE FIELDS
Calgary

League President
BILL CUTLER

Leading Pitcher
JEFF BITTIGER
Vancouver

CHAMPIONSHIP WINNERS IN PREVIOUS YEARS

1903—Los Angeles .630	1936—Portland‡ .549	1968—Tulsa a .642
1904—Tacoma .589	1937—Sacramento .573	Spokane .586
Tacoma§ .571	San Diego (3rd)† .545	1969—Tacoma a .589
Los Angeles§ .571	1938—Los Angeles .590	Eugene .603
1905—Tacoma .583	Sacramento (3rd)† .537	1970—Spokane a .644
Los Angeles* .604	1939—Seattle .589	Hawaii .671
1906—Portland .657	Sacramento (4th)† .500	1971—Salt Lake City .534
1907—Los Angeles .608	1940—Seattle‡ .629	Tacoma .545
1908—Los Angeles .585	1941—Seattle‡ .598	1972—Albuquerque .622
1909—San Francisco .623	1942—Sacramento .590	Eugene .534
1910—Portland .567	Seattle (3rd)† .539	1973—Tucson .583
1911—Portland .589	1943—Los Angeles .710	Spokane .563
1912—Oakland .591	S. Francisco (2nd)† .574	1974—Spokane a .549
1913—Portland .559	1944—Los Angeles .586	Albuquerque .535
1914—Portland .574	S. Francisco (3rd)† .509	1975—Salt Lake City .556
1915—San Francisco .570	1945—Portland .622	Hawaii a .611
1916—Los Angeles .601	S. Francisco (4th)† .525	1976—Salt Lake City .625
1917—San Francisco .561	1946—San Francisco‡ .628	Hawaii a .531
1918—Vernon .569	1947—Los Angeles†† .567	1977—Phoenix a .579
Los Angeles (2nd) x .548	1948—Oakland‡ .606	Hawaii .541
1919—Vernon .613	1949—Hollywood‡ .583	1978—Tacoma b .584
1920—Vernon .556	1950—Oakland .590	Albuquerque b .557
1921—Los Angeles .574	1951—Seattle‡ .593	1979—Albuquerque .581
1922—San Francisco .638	1952—Hollywood .606	Salt Lake City c .541
1923—San Francisco .617	1953—Hollywood .589	1980—Albuquerque* .578
1924—Seattle .545	1954—San Diego y .604	Hawaii .539
1925—San Francisco .643	1955—Seattle .552	1981—Albuquerque* .712
1926—Los Angeles .599	1956—Los Angeles .637	Tacoma .561
1927—Oakland .615	1957—San Francisco .601	1982—Albuquerque* .594
1928—San Francisco* .630	1958—Phoenix .578	Spokane .545
Sacramento§§ .626	1959—Salt Lake City .552	1983—Albuquerque* .594
San Francisco§§ .626	1960—Spokane .601	Portland* .528
1929—Mission .643	1961—Tacoma .630	1984—Hawaii .621
Hollywood* .592	1962—San Diego .604	Edmonton* .486
1930—Los Angeles .576	1963—Spokane .620	1985—Vancouver* .552
Hollywood* .650	Oklahoma City a .632	Phoenix .563
1931—Hollywood .626	1964—Arkansas .609	1986—Vancouver .616
San Francisco* .608	San Diego a .576	Las Vegas* .563
1932—Portland .587	1965—Oklahoma City a .628	1987—Calgary .596
1933—Los Angeles .610	Portland .547	Albuquerque* .542
1934—Los Angeles z .786	1966—Seattle a .561	1988—Vancouver .599
Los Angeles z .689	Tulsa .578	Las Vegas* .529
1935—Los Angeles .648	1967—San Diego a .574	
San Francisco* .608	Spokane .541	

*Won split-season playoff. †Won four-team playoff. ‡Won pennant and four-team playoff. §Tied for second-half title with Tacoma winning playoff. §§Tied for second-half title, with Sacramento winning playoff. ††Ended regular season in tie with San Francisco and won one-game playoff for pennant, then won four-club playoff. xWon playoff from first-place Vernon and awarded championship. yDefeated Hollywood in one-game playoff for pennant. zWon both halves, no playoff. aLeague was divided into Northern, Southern divisions in 1963, 1969-70-71, and Eastern, Western divisions in 1964 through 1968 and 1972 through 1977, won two-team playoff. bLeague divided into Eastern and Western divisions, Tacoma and Albuquerque declared co-champions following cancellation of four-team playoff due to continuing rain and wet grounds. cWon second-half title and defeated Hawaii in four-team playoff.

STANDING OF CLUBS AT CLOSE OF FIRST HALF, JUNE 17

NORTHERN DIVISION						SOUTHERN DIVISION					
Club	W.	L.	T.	Pct.	G.B.	Club	W.	L.	T.	Pct.	G.B.
Vancouver (White Sox)	41	30	0	.577	......	Colorado Springs (Indians)	44	26	0	.629	......
Tacoma (Athletics)	39	33	0	.542	2½	Las Vegas (Padres)	36	35	0	.507	8½
Portland (Twins)	36	36	0	.500	5½	Albuquerque (Dodgers)	36	35	0	.507	8½
Edmonton (Angels)	32	37	0	.464	8	Phoenix (Giants)	36	36	0	.500	9
Calgary (Mariners)	28	43	0	.394	13	Tucson (Astros)	27	44	0	.380	17½

STANDING OF CLUBS AT CLOSE OF SECOND HALF, AUGUST 30

NORTHERN DIVISION						SOUTHERN DIVISION					
Club	W.	L.	T.	Pct.	G.B.	Club	W.	L.	T.	Pct.	G.B.
Calgary (Mariners)	42	29	0	.592	......	Albuquerque (Dodgers)	44	27	0	.620	......
Tacoma (Athletics)	38	33	0	.535	4	Las Vegas (Padres)	38	34	0	.528	6½
Portland (Twins)	36	36	0	.500	6½	Colorado Springs (Indians)	34	38	0	.472	10½
Edmonton (Angels)	33	39	0	.458	9½	Phoenix (Giants)	31	40	0	.437	13
Vancouver (White Sox)	32	39	0	.451	10	Tucson (Astros)	29	42	0	.408	15

COMPOSITE STANDING OF CLUBS AT CLOSE OF SEASON, AUGUST 30

Club	Alb.	C.S.	Tac.	L.V.	Van.	Port.	Cal.	Phoe.	Edm.	Tuc.	W.	L.	T.	Pct.	G.B.
Albuquerque (Dodgers)	....	11	6	10	7	8	9	8	11	10	80	62	0	.563	......
Colorado Springs (Indians)	5	....	9	9	8	10	9	9	6	13	78	64	0	.549	2
Tacoma (Athletics)	10	7	....	8	8	7	6	12	8	11	77	66	0	.538	3½
Las Vegas (Padres)	6	7	8	....	9	10	8	8	9	9	74	69	0	.517	6½
Vancouver (White Sox)	8	8	7	7	....	8	10	10	6	9	73	69	0	.514	7
Portland (Twins)	8	6	9	6	8	....	9	8	9	9	72	72	0	.500	9
Calgary (Mariners)	7	7	10	7	6	7	....	8	10	8	70	72	0	.493	10
Phoenix (Giants)	7	7	4	8	6	8	8	....	11	8	67	76	0	.469	13½
Edmonton (Angels)	5	8	8	7	10	7	6	5	....	9	65	76	0	.461	14½
Tucson (Astros)	6	3	5	7	7	7	7	8	6	....	56	86	0	.394	24

Major league affiliations in parentheses.

Playoffs—Vancouver defeated Calgary, three games to none; Albuquerque defeated Colorado Springs, three games to two; Vancouver defeated Albuquerque, three games to one, to win league championship.

Regular-Season Attendance—Albuquerque, 318,896; Calgary, 316,616; Colorado Springs, 203,955; Edmonton, 230,728; Las Vegas, 315,517; Phoenix, 199,157; Portland, 188,459; Tacoma, 313,007; Tucson, 186,270; Vancouver, 281,812. Total—2,554,417. Playoffs (12 games)—54,335. AAA All-Star Game—19,500.

Managers—Albuquerque, Kevin Kennedy; Calgary, Rich Morales; Colorado Springs, Mike Hargrove; Edmonton, Tom Kotchman; Las Vegas, Steve Smith; Phoenix, Gordon McKenzie; Portland, Phil Roof; Tacoma, Brad Fischer; Tucson, Bob Skinner; Vancouver, Marv Foley.

All-Star Team—1B—Kelvin Torve, Portland; 2B—Joey Cora, Las Vegas; 3B—Matt Williams, Phoenix; SS—Paul Zuvella, Colorado Springs; OF—Bruce Fields, Calgary; Jerald Clark, Las Vegas; Mike Huff, Albuquerque; C—Sandy Alomar, Las Vegas; DH—Jim Wilson, Calgary; RHP—Ramon Martinez, Albuquerque; LHP—Bryan Clark, Tacoma; Rel—Steve Olin, Colorado Springs; Most Valuable Player—Sandy Alomar, Las Vegas; Manager of the Year—Mike Hargrove, Colorado Springs.

(Compiled by Howe Sportsdata International, Boston, Mass.)

CLUB BATTING

Club	Pct.	G.	AB.	R.	OR.	H.	TB.	2B.	3B.	HR.	RBI.	SH.	SF.	HP.	BB.	Int. BB.	SO.	SB.	CS.	LOB.
Colorado Springs	.292	142	4825	781	730	1408	2168	254	43	140	715	30	34	30	482	25	838	92	72	991
Calgary	.289	142	4816	789	784	1392	2100	305	35	111	720	26	53	42	487	16	796	97	57	983
Albuquerque	.287	141	4752	733	639	1365	1949	244	50	80	663	55	43	41	454	23	749	161	96	970
Las Vegas	.272	143	4864	739	732	1323	2025	269	47	113	681	41	51	31	554	32	939	97	50	1041
Portland	.269	144	4754	613	664	1278	1898	248	45	94	556	33	45	42	501	28	842	78	62	1009
Edmonton	.265	141	4563	648	658	1208	1785	212	52	87	594	36	36	28	550	17	818	111	59	1004
Tucson	.260	142	4676	628	681	1215	1687	227	40	55	557	61	48	30	517	31	759	98	56	984
Tacoma	.254	143	4662	650	621	1186	1748	226	30	92	595	52	38	68	613	27	1001	76	61	1083
Phoenix	.252	143	4739	592	635	1195	1837	229	52	103	541	55	36	45	386	25	862	103	75	902
Vancouver	.248	141	4480	498	527	1111	1572	202	35	63	449	41	39	25	449	32	819	118	82	921

INDIVIDUAL BATTING
(Leading Qualifiers for Batting Championship—389 or More Plate Appearances)

*Bats lefthanded.   †Switch-hitter.

Player and Club	Pct.	G.	AB.	R.	H.	TB.	2B.	3B.	HR.	RBI.	SH.	SF.	HP.	BB.	Int. BB.	SO.	SB.	CS.
Fields, Bruce, Calgary*	.351	101	407	88	143	217	36	4	10	48	3	1	2	44	1	52	14	12
Brown, Michael, Edmonton	.340	101	373	53	127	211	33	6	13	70	1	1	1	40	0	64	6	3
Zuvella, Paul, Colorado Springs	.331	96	387	61	128	187	23	3	10	66	1	1	1	24	0	27	8	6
Huff, Michael, Albuquerque	.318	115	471	75	150	223	29	7	10	78	4	5	2	38	0	75	32	10
Hengel, David, Colorado Springs	.316	95	354	53	112	181	13	1	18	82	0	5	6	35	2	56	1	2
Wilson, James, Calgary	.314	138	519	79	163	271	30	0	26	133	0	11	6	54	2	102	8	3
Rodriguez, Victor, Portland	.314	120	465	63	146	216	34	3	10	50	1	2	4	35	2	45	2	1
Clark, Jerald, Las Vegas	.313	107	419	84	131	232	27	4	22	83	0	5	5	38	3	91	5	2
Cora, Jose, Las Vegas†	.310	119	507	79	157	190	25	4	0	37	4	1	8	42	3	31	40	15
Sharperson, Michael, Albuquerque	.309	98	359	81	111	149	15	7	3	48	4	3	2	66	2	46	17	12

Departmental Leaders: G—J. Wilson, 138; AB—Alomar, 523; R—Jennings, 99; H—J. Wilson, 163; TB—J. Wilson, 271; 2B—Torve, 41; 3B—Coachman, Noce, 10; HR—D. Gonzalez, 27; RBI—J. Wilson, 133; SH—Bordick, 15; SF—J. Wilson, Yurtin, 11; HP—Jennings, 16; BB—Jennings, 93; IBB—Robidoux, 9; SO—S. Howard, 135; SB—Cora, 40; CS—L. Johnson, 18.

(All Players—Listed Alphabetically)

Player and Club	Pct.	G.	AB.	R.	H.	TB.	2B.	3B.	HR.	RBI.	SH.	SF.	HP.	BB.	Int. BB.	SO.	SB.	CS.
Abner, Shawn, Las Vegas	.269	56	223	31	60	99	11	2	8	31	2	1	1	17	0	53	3	3
Allaire, Karl, 2 Tuc.-94 Edm*	.264	96	273	34	72	91	5	4	2	35	5	2	0	36	1	53	10	5
Allred, Dale, Colorado Springs*	.277	11	47	8	13	19	3	0	1	4	0	0	2	1	0	10	0	3
Alomar, Santos, Las Vegas	.306	131	523	88	160	248	33	8	13	101	2	3	2	42	5	58	3	1
Anderson, Kent, Edmonton	.333	4	12	3	4	4	0	0	1	0	0	0	0	4	0	1	1	0
Anthony, Eric, Tucson*	.217	12	46	10	10	22	3	0	3	11	0	0	0	6	0	11	0	0
Arndt, Larry, Tacoma	.280	130	489	62	137	174	23	4	2	50	14	1	2	53	2	111	11	8
Baerga, Carlos, Las Vegas†	.275	132	520	63	143	205	28	2	10	74	0	6	6	30	5	98	6	6

Player and Club	Pct.	G.	AB.	R.	H.	TB.	2B.	3B.	HR.	RBI.	SH.	SF.	HP.	BB.	Int. BB.	SO.	SB.	CS.
Baker, Douglas, Portland†	.237	84	312	38	74	98	10	4	2	27	1	5	3	36	2	52	8	9
Bando, Christopher, Tacoma†	.250	31	84	11	21	34	4	0	3	18	0	1	2	20	0	18	0	0
Barrett, Timothy, Albuquerque*	.000	47	4	1	0	0	0	0	0	0	0	0	0	0	0	2	0	0
Bass, Kevin, Tucson†	.294	6	17	1	5	6	1	0	0	2	0	1	0	1	0	2	0	0
Bathe, William, Phoenix	.348	76	270	30	94	143	21	5	6	40	0	1	5	19	0	35	1	5
Bean, William, Albuquerque*	.222	3	9	1	2	4	0	1	0	3	0	0	0	2	0	0	0	0
Beane, William, Tacoma	.318	38	151	19	48	68	6	1	4	23	0	1	0	12	3	25	4	1
Benes, Andrew, Las Vegas	.000	5	1	0	0	0	0	0	0	0	0	0	0	0	0	1	0	0
Benjamin, Michael, Phoenix	.259	113	363	44	94	132	17	6	3	36	12	2	6	18	1	82	10	4
Bichette, Dante, Edmonton	.243	61	226	39	55	103	11	2	11	40	1	2	2	24	0	39	4	5
Bierley, Brad, Portland*	.281	95	278	38	78	122	22	5	4	34	2	2	7	38	6	55	8	2
Bitker, Joseph, 18 L.V.-24 Tac	.000	42	1	0	0	0	0	0	0	0	0	0	0	0	0	0	0	0
Blair, Paul, Phoenix†	.235	53	179	19	42	46	4	0	0	11	5	1	2	10	0	23	7	2
Blankenship, Lance, Tacoma	.296	25	98	25	29	47	8	2	2	9	2	1	1	19	0	15	5	3
Boever, Daniel, Calgary	.182	12	33	2	6	7	1	0	0	1	0	1	1	3	0	9	0	1
Bordick, Michael, Tacoma	.240	136	487	55	117	139	17	1	1	43	15	2	7	58	0	51	4	9
Bowie, James, Calgary*	.268	100	336	28	90	114	12	0	4	37	0	4	2	17	0	45	2	2
Brady, Brian, Edmonton*	.236	62	203	22	48	77	10	2	5	28	2	1	0	18	1	45	4	1
Brantley, Jeffrey, Phoenix	1.000	7	1	0	1	1	0	0	0	0	0	0	0	0	0	0	0	0
Brantley, Michael, Calgary	.247	49	178	33	44	74	12	3	4	21	0	3	1	19	1	27	5	3
Brenly, Robert, Phoenix	.255	27	98	11	25	34	3	0	2	11	0	2	0	8	0	12	3	0
Brennan, William, Albuquerque	.000	34	5	0	0	0	0	0	0	0	0	0	0	5	0	1	0	0
Briley, Gregory, Calgary*	.340	25	94	27	32	54	8	1	4	20	0	0	2	13	1	10	14	2
Brilinski, Tyler, Tacoma*	.245	75	233	36	57	89	15	1	5	27	1	1	1	22	2	66	1	0
Brito, Bernardo, Portland	.254	111	355	51	90	182	12	7	22	74	2	2	4	31	4	111	1	3
Brito, Jorge, Tacoma	.200	5	15	2	3	4	1	0	0	0	0	0	0	2	0	6	0	1
Brown, Michael, Edmonton	.340	101	373	53	127	211	33	6	13	70	1	1	1	40	0	64	6	3
Brundage, David, Calgary*	.261	27	69	13	18	20	2	0	0	5	2	0	0	9	0	17	3	0
Buhner, Jay, Calgary	.311	56	196	43	61	108	12	1	11	45	0	3	0	44	1	56	4	4
Burkett, John, Phoenix	.125	28	24	0	3	3	0	0	0	1	1	0	0	0	0	9	0	0
Burtt, Dennis, Albuquerque†	.000	28	12	1	0	0	0	0	0	0	1	0	0	2	0	4	0	1
Bustabad, Juan, Albuquerque*	.200	15	20	1	4	7	1	1	0	1	0	0	0	0	0	3	0	0
Byers, Randall, Las Vegas*	.328	16	61	12	20	40	5	3	3	13	0	1	0	6	2	8	0	0
Camacho, Ernie, Phoenix	.000	40	1	0	0	0	0	0	0	0	0	0	0	0	0	0	0	0
Candaele, Casey, Tucson†	.218	68	206	22	45	53	6	1	0	17	4	1	0	20	4	37	6	3
Cano, Joselito, Tucson	.444	15	9	0	4	4	0	0	0	0	2	0	0	0	0	1	0	0
Christensen, John, Portland	.270	127	429	58	116	176	18	3	12	63	2	7	9	46	1	83	5	5
Clark, Jerald, Las Vegas	.313	107	419	84	131	232	27	4	22	83	0	5	5	38	3	81	5	2
Clements, Patrick, Las Vegas	.400	18	5	0	2	2	0	0	0	2	1	0	0	0	0	1	0	0
Close, Casey, Calgary	.330	95	324	53	107	163	27	4	7	56	1	4	5	36	1	42	3	3
Coachman, Dean, Edmonton	.285	127	477	69	136	179	17	10	2	43	0	5	1	51	1	62	14	4
Cochrane, David, Calgary†	.272	32	125	22	34	62	10	0	6	35	0	2	1	11	0	36	2	1
Cockrell, Alan, Portland	.268	127	433	60	116	170	15	3	11	61	5	6	2	57	0	127	8	5
Colombino, Carlo, Tucson	.202	40	129	15	26	33	2	1	1	12	1	1	2	4	0	18	3	0
Comstock, Keith, 28 L.V.-5 Cal*	.000	33	1	0	0	0	0	0	0	0	0	0	0	0	0	0	0	0
Cook, Dennis, Phoenix*	.500	12	10	1	5	6	1	0	0	0	0	0	0	0	0	1	0	0
Cooper, Gary, Tucson	.271	118	376	51	102	134	23	3	1	50	1	5	4	48	2	69	5	7
Cooper, Craig, Las Vegas	.249	53	177	27	44	71	10	1	5	29	0	5	0	18	1	30	1	0
Cora, Jose, Las Vegas†	.310	119	507	79	157	190	25	4	0	37	4	1	8	42	3	31	40	15
Crew, Kenneth, Tucson	.333	34	3	0	1	1	0	0	0	1	0	0	0	0	0	1	0	0
Dalena, Peter, Colorado Springs*	.329	98	340	52	112	161	24	5	5	59	1	4	2	27	4	35	1	0
Davidson, Mark, 30 Por.-39 Tuc	.245	69	237	26	58	86	9	2	5	24	1	1	3	27	0	46	2	2
Davis, Douglas, Edmonton	.265	54	147	17	39	56	6	1	3	22	3	0	2	18	0	40	0	0
Davis, Kevin, Vancouver	.318	7	22	2	7	10	0	0	1	1	0	0	0	0	0	4	0	1
Davis, Mark, Vancouver	.130	39	123	13	16	22	4	1	0	8	0	0	5	13	0	38	6	2
DeAngelis, Steven, Edmonton*	.208	11	24	2	5	13	0	1	2	8	0	0	0	4	0	4	0	0
Debus, Jon Albuquerque	.265	59	136	17	36	53	14	0	1	23	1	2	0	12	3	35	0	1
DeLima, Rafael, Portland*	.274	127	464	54	127	161	19	3	3	33	2	0	2	37	0	79	18	15
DeWolf, Robert, Las Vegas*	.267	23	60	10	16	20	2	1	0	5	2	0	1	5	0	15	0	0
Diaz, Mario, Calgary	.339	37	127	22	43	59	8	1	2	19	0	1	1	8	0	7	1	4
Dietrick, Patrick, Tacoma	.256	117	391	55	100	141	17	6	4	50	6	2	9	27	0	82	4	7
Dominguez, Jose, Phoenix	.000	11	1	0	0	0	0	0	0	0	0	0	0	0	0	0	0	0
Downs, Kelly, Phoenix	.200	3	5	0	1	1	0	0	0	0	0	0	0	0	0	1	0	0
Dravecky, David, Phoenix*	.000	1	4	0	0	0	0	0	0	0	0	0	0	0	0	3	0	0
Dugas, Shanie, Albuquerque*	.277	63	202	26	56	84	15	2	3	27	2	3	1	20	3	46	5	1
Dunbar, Thomas, Tucson*	.308	13	52	7	16	24	3	1	1	4	0	0	0	1	0	8	0	1
Dunlap, Joseph, Calgary	.177	39	124	8	22	25	3	0	0	9	2	1	1	9	0	23	1	1
Dunster, Donald, Tucson	.000	4	1	0	0	0	0	0	0	0	0	0	0	0	0	0	0	0
Eccles, John, Portland	.150	29	80	10	12	25	4	0	3	5	1	1	1	10	0	24	0	0
Eppard, James, Edmonton*	.274	90	292	40	80	104	16	1	2	34	2	4	1	45	2	37	5	5
Fields, Bruce, Calgary*	.351	101	407	88	143	217	36	4	10	48	3	1	2	44	1	52	14	12
Fischer, Jeffrey, Albuquerque	.100	28	20	0	2	2	0	0	0	0	2	0	0	0	0	6	0	0
Fletcher, Darrin, Albuquerque*	.273	100	315	34	86	119	16	1	5	44	2	6	2	30	0	38	1	5
Forrester, Thomas, Vancouver*	.202	110	356	32	72	108	16	1	6	50	4	4	2	37	5	78	4	3
Freeland, Dean, Phoenix	.000	3	1	0	0	0	0	0	0	0	0	0	0	0	0	1	0	0
Frobel, Douglas, Vancouver*	.111	29	90	7	10	18	2	0	2	8	0	1	0	7	1	33	1	0
Fulton, Gregory, Calgary†	.282	96	301	34	85	117	25	2	1	40	2	4	2	21	3	48	1	1
Gainey, Telmanch, Colorado Springs*..	.276	101	341	59	94	146	13	3	11	50	0	0	0	48	4	87	8	6
Gerhart, Kenneth, Phoenix	.193	93	269	24	52	84	6	4	6	29	6	0	1	14	2	61	10	5
Giles, Brian, Colorado Springs	.296	105	318	58	94	157	23	5	10	40	3	1	2	53	2	82	4	6
Gilmore, Terrance, Las Vegas	.125	29	16	2	2	5	1	1	0	3	2	1	0	2	0	6	0	0
Goff, Jerry, Calgary*	.233	76	253	40	59	108	16	0	11	50	1	2	3	23	1	62	1	0
Gonzalez, Denio, Colorado Springs	.288	128	420	86	121	223	17	2	27	76	3	4	4	70	0	92	4	2
Gonzalez, Jose, Albuquerque	.267	50	180	32	48	80	12	4	4	31	1	0	3	16	0	39	10	7
Green, Gary, Las Vegas	.209	62	191	18	40	46	6	0	0	18	2	4	0	20	1	32	2	1
Gross, Gregory, Tucson*	.250	21	72	7	18	20	0	1	0	5	0	0	0	6	0	8	0	1
Gunderson, Eric, Phoenix	.125	15	8	1	1	1	0	0	0	0	2	0	0	0	0	1	0	0
Gwynn, Christopher, Albuquerque*	.326	26	89	14	29	40	9	1	0	12	1	1	2	7	0	7	3	2
Hale, Walter, Portland*	.273	108	411	49	112	152	16	9	2	34	5	1	1	35	2	55	3	2
Ham, Michael, Phoenix	.220	16	41	4	9	12	1	1	0	5	1	0	1	8	0	11	0	0
Hansen, David, Albuquerque*	.267	6	30	6	8	15	1	0	2	10	0	0	2	5	0	3	0	0
Hansen, Roger, Calgary	.190	35	84	8	16	19	3	0	0	8	0	1	0	10	0	16	0	1

Player and Club	Pct.	G.	AB.	R.	H.	TB.	2B.	3B.	HR.	RBI.	SH.	SF.	HP.	BB.	Int. BB.	SO.	SB.	CS.
Hartley, Michael, Albuquerque	.667	58	3	0	2	2	0	0	0	1	1	0	0	0	0	1	0	0
Hayes, Charles, Phoenix	.284	61	229	25	65	103	15	1	7	27	0	2	0	15	1	48	5	5
Hearron, Jeffrey, Las Vegas	.203	55	143	15	29	50	9	0	4	25	1	1	2	19	0	34	0	0
Heathcock, Jeffrey, Tucson	.158	28	19	1	3	4	1	0	0	2	2	0	0	2	0	4	0	0
Hecht, Steven, Phoenix°	.444	3	9	3	4	5	1	0	0	0	0	0	0	1	0	0	2	1
Hengel, David, Colorado Springs	.316	95	354	53	112	181	13	1	18	82	0	5	6	35	2	56	1	2
Henley, Daniel, Albuquerque	.339	18	59	14	20	22	2	0	0	9	0	0	1	3	0	9	3	1
Heredia, Hector, Albuquerque	.000	26	2	0	0	0	0	0	0	0	0	0	0	1	0	0	0	0
Hernandez, Carlos, Albuquerque	.214	4	14	1	3	3	0	0	0	1	0	0	0	2	1	1	0	0
Higgins, Mark, Colorado Springs	.329	72	213	34	70	117	15	1	10	34	0	1	0	16	0	46	0	2
Hill, Donald, Tacoma†	.261	58	180	26	47	70	7	2	4	23	1	2	2	33	1	18	4	2
Hinzo, Thomas, Colorado Springs†	.254	102	410	65	104	134	13	7	1	35	2	0	7	31	2	68	22	16
Hoffman, Hunter, Calgary°	1.000	1	1	1	1	4	0	0	1	1	0	0	0	0	0	0	0	0
Holmes, Darren, Albuquerque	.143	9	7	0	1	2	1	0	0	0	0	0	0	0	0	3	0	0
Holmes, Stanley, Edmonton	.158	14	38	1	6	6	0	0	0	1	0	0	1	0	2	6	0	0
Howard, Steven, Tacoma	.243	107	341	51	83	136	10	2	13	60	1	7	11	64	1	135	15	4
Howard, Thomas, Las Vegas†	.300	80	303	45	91	124	18	3	3	31	3	1	0	30	1	56	22	11
Hubbard, Trent, Tucson†	.220	21	50	3	11	13	2	0	0	2	0	0	1	1	0	10	3	3
Huff, Michael, Albuquerque	.318	115	471	75	150	223	29	7	10	78	4	5	2	38	0	75	32	10
Ilsley, Blaise, Tucson°	.222	20	9	1	2	2	0	0	0	0	1	0	0	0	0	4	0	0
Jackson, Charles, Tucson	.309	69	243	33	75	106	14	4	3	27	4	3	0	31	1	31	9	4
Jennings, Douglas, Tacoma°	.274	137	497	99	136	214	35	5	11	64	2	8	16	93	7	95	10	12
Johnson, Lance, Vancouver°	.304	106	408	69	124	149	11	7	0	28	0	4	0	46	0	36	33	18
Jones, Gary, Tacoma°	.219	11	32	5	7	16	1	1	2	5	0	0	3	0	10	1	0
Jordan, Scott, Tucson	.189	58	164	25	31	42	3	1	2	16	5	0	2	29	1	30	7	5
Jose, Felix, Tacoma†	.287	104	387	59	111	179	26	0	14	63	1	2	3	41	8	82	11	7
Jurak, Edward, Phoenix	.295	52	173	23	51	61	7	0	1	17	0	2	2	19	0	16	4	2
Keedy, Patrick, Colorado Springs	.333	3	9	1	3	4	1	0	0	1	0	0	0	2	0	3	0	0
Kelley, Anthony, Tucson	.167	12	12	1	2	2	0	0	0	0	1	0	0	0	0	4	0	0
Kerfeld, Charles, Tucson	.000	53	1	0	0	0	0	0	0	0	1	0	0	0	0	1	0	0
Kesselmark, Joseph, Albuquerque°	.400	2	10	4	4	5	1	0	0	1	0	0	1	0	0	1	0	0
Kile, Darryl, Tucson	.000	6	2	0	0	0	0	0	0	0	0	0	0	0	0	2	0	0
Kingery, Michael, Calgary°	.290	107	396	72	115	167	22	9	4	47	2	2	2	47	2	52	7	4
Kirby, Wayne, Albuquerque°	.342	78	310	62	106	140	18	8	0	30	5	1	1	26	1	27	29	14
Knabenshue, Christopher, Las Vegas°.	.258	115	306	68	79	158	17	4	18	50	4	0	1	83	3	112	0	3
Knapp, Michael, Edmonton	.264	51	144	15	38	49	8	0	1	22	3	1	4	15	0	27	0	4
Komminsk, Brad, Colorado Springs	.289	54	190	30	55	99	17	0	9	34	0	4	2	18	0	40	7	1
Kosco, Andrew, Calgary°	.333	3	12	5	4	9	2	0	1	3	0	0	0	1	0	3	0	0
Laga, Michael, Phoenix°	.241	126	449	55	108	215	20	9	23	68	0	2	5	27	6	96	2	3
Lampkin, Thomas, Colorado Springs°..	.321	63	209	26	67	95	10	3	4	32	2	1	2	10	1	18	4	2
Landreaux, Kenneth, Albuquerque°	.243	56	189	25	46	65	9	2	2	26	0	3	1	13	1	32	7	0
Leonard, Mark, Phoenix°	.269	27	78	7	21	25	4	0	0	6	0	1	0	9	1	15	1	1
Levis, Jesse, Colorado Springs°	.000	1	1	0	0	0	0	0	0	0	0	0	0	0	0	0	0	0
Litton, Gregory, Phoenix	.180	30	89	6	16	30	4	2	2	6	0	2	0	8	0	24	1	3
Lombardozzi, Stephen, Tucson	.257	114	401	66	103	143	21	2	5	46	3	3	2	55	6	62	9	3
Lopez, Luis, Albuquerque	.493	19	75	17	37	50	7	0	2	16	0	2	1	6	0	7	1	0
Lusader, Scott, Tucson°	.248	33	121	15	30	41	3	1	2	13	1	1	1	17	0	24	5	4
Lynch, Joseph, Las Vegas	.000	45	1	0	0	0	0	0	0	0	0	0	0	0	0	1	0	0
Mack, Shane, Las Vegas	.225	24	80	10	18	26	3	1	1	8	0	1	1	14	0	19	4	2
Magallanes, Everardo, Colo. Springs°..	.250	12	44	2	11	15	1	0	1	3	1	0	0	4	0	3	1	0
Manto, Jeffrey, Edmonton	.277	127	408	89	113	213	25	3	23	67	3	4	9	91	5	81	4	4
Marquez, Edwin, Edmonton	.293	32	75	10	22	29	4	0	1	10	1	0	0	11	0	14	2	2
Martinez, Carlos, Vancouver	.391	18	64	12	25	36	3	1	2	9	0	2	0	5	0	14	2	2
Martinez, Edgar, Calgary	.345	32	113	30	39	59	11	0	3	23	1	2	3	22	1	13	2	2
Martinez, Ramon, Albuquerque	.143	18	7	0	1	1	0	0	0	1	2	0	0	0	0	4	0	0
Mason, Roger, Tucson	.154	25	13	2	2	2	0	0	0	1	2	0	0	0	0	5	0	0
Mayberry, Gregory, Albuquerque	.100	15	10	1	1	1	0	0	0	0	2	0	0	0	0	7	0	0
Maysey, Matthew, Las Vegas	.263	28	19	2	5	6	1	0	0	1	1	0	0	0	0	4	0	0
McCament, Randall, Phoenix	.000	22	2	1	0	0	0	0	0	0	0	0	0	0	0	0	0	0
McClellan, Paul, Phoenix	.000	9	4	0	0	0	0	0	0	0	1	0	0	0	0	0	0	0
McConnell, Walter, Albuquerque°	.263	52	133	18	35	47	3	0	3	17	0	1	1	23	1	26	0	0
McElroy, Glen, Vancouver	.000	1	2	0	0	0	0	0	0	0	0	0	0	2	0	0	0	0
McGinnis, Russell, Tacoma	.276	110	380	42	105	151	25	0	7	60	2	5	6	45	0	78	0	1
McGuire, William, Calgary	.276	83	268	39	74	112	17	0	7	38	4	2	2	28	1	46	1	3
McLemore, Mark, Edmonton†	.244	114	430	60	105	128	13	2	2	34	2	3	1	49	1	67	26	11
McNamara, James, Phoenix°	.174	27	69	3	12	15	3	0	0	4	2	0	0	4	0	13	1	2
McPhail, Marlin, Phoenix	.279	115	365	41	102	148	15	5	7	47	6	5	2	33	3	66	15	9
Meadows, Michael, Tucson°	.246	53	179	32	44	75	9	2	6	27	3	0	1	37	2	51	12	2
Meads, David, Tucson°	.000	1	1	0	0	0	0	0	0	0	0	0	0	0	0	1	0	0
Medina, Luis, Colorado Springs	.175	51	166	17	29	46	8	0	3	19	0	1	0	19	0	50	0	2
Mercado, Orlando, Portland	.296	57	196	17	58	92	20	1	4	29	0	4	1	16	1	30	0	1
Merullo, Matthew, Vancouver°	.222	3	9	0	2	3	1	0	0	2	1	0	0	2	0	0	0	0
Meyer, Brian, Tucson	.667	58	3	1	2	2	0	0	0	0	0	0	0	1	0	0	0	0
Meyers, Paul, Phoenix	.222	93	252	30	56	76	9	4	1	30	7	2	1	23	0	40	6	6
Michel, Domingo, Albuquerque	.311	78	238	35	74	113	12	3	7	38	1	2	7	25	0	52	7	11
Mikulik, Joseph, Tucson	.294	8	17	2	5	5	0	0	0	3	0	1	1	0	0	5	0	0
Morman, Russell, Vancouver	.278	61	216	18	60	79	14	1	1	23	0	1	1	18	2	41	1	6
Mulholland, Terence, Phoenix	.143	13	7	0	1	1	0	0	0	0	1	0	0	0	0	4	0	0
Munoz, Michael, Albuquerque°	.000	60	0	0	0	0	0	0	0	0	0	0	0	0	0	0	0	0
Murphy, Daniel, Las Vegas	.125	27	8	1	1	1	0	0	0	0	2	0	0	0	0	5	0	0
Murray, Stephen, Calgary	.178	15	45	8	8	11	0	0	1	6	2	0	0	6	0	14	2	0
Naveda, Edgar, Portland	.236	33	110	17	26	44	10	1	2	11	2	0	7	0	14	2	1
Neidlinger, James, Albuquerque†	.067	34	15	1	1	1	0	0	0	0	4	0	0	0	0	4	0	0
Nelson, James, Edmonton	.220	44	127	10	28	41	5	1	2	13	0	1	1	8	0	29	0	1
Nelson, Robert, Las Vegas°	.265	56	185	35	49	83	11	1	7	26	0	3	1	38	4	59	0	0
Nichols, Carl, Tucson	.256	104	340	45	87	128	27	1	4	27	3	2	1	35	3	76	0	0
Noce, Paul, Calgary	.278	134	510	95	142	199	28	10	3	42	4	3	5	41	0	96	22	5
Nolte, Eric, Las Vegas°	.000	23	12	0	0	0	0	0	0	0	2	0	0	1	0	3	0	0
Olker, Joseph, Phoenix	.000	29	12	1	0	0	0	0	0	0	4	0	0	1	0	8	0	0
Olson, Gregory, Portland	.235	79	247	38	58	88	6	2	6	38	3	5	3	45	2	27	3	2
Ortiz, Javier, 70 Alb-11 Tuc.	.254	81	260	47	66	109	10	0	11	36	1	0	4	36	1	63	2	2
Otto, David, Tacoma°	.750	29	4	0	3	3	0	0	0	1	0	0	0	0	0	0	0	0

380

Player and Club	Pct.	G.	AB.	R.	H.	TB.	2B.	3B.	HR.	RBI.	SH.	SF.	HP.	BB.	Int. BB.	SO.	SB.	CS.
Ouellette, Philip, Tucson†	.208	35	106	13	22	26	2	1	0	7	1	0	1	16	1	22	0	1
Pankovits, James, Albuquerque	.251	82	295	39	74	102	10	3	4	37	2	4	3	22	1	49	12	7
Paris, Kelly, Vancouver†	.226	68	235	29	53	80	15	0	4	26	4	6	0	25	2	39	5	2
Parker, Richard, Phoenix	.265	18	68	5	18	24	2	2	0	11	1	0	1	2	0	14	1	2
Pena, Jose, Phoenix	.222	32	108	6	24	32	3	1	1	9	1	0	0	4	0	18	2	2
Perezchica, Antonio, Phoenix	.231	94	307	40	71	112	11	3	8	33	2	7	5	15	0	65	5	4
Pino, Rolando, Portland	.266	35	109	17	29	51	8	1	4	13	0	1	0	19	1	29	4	3
Portugal, Mark, Tucson	.235	19	17	2	4	5	1	0	0	4	1	0	1	1	0	2	0	0
Pryor, Buddy, Tacoma	.179	54	151	15	27	39	4	1	2	10	3	2	1	20	0	41	1	0
Puikunas, Edmund, Phoenix	.000	48	2	0	0	0	0	0	0	0	1	0	0	0	0	1	0	0
Quinzer, Paul, Las Vegas	.000	21	1	1	0	0	0	0	0	0	0	0	0	1	0	0	0	0
Quirk, James, Tacoma*	.170	14	47	5	8	13	2	0	1	5	0	0	0	3	0	12	0	0
Ralston, Robert, Portland	.283	59	205	24	58	68	8	1	0	11	4	0	0	14	0	14	2	5
Ramsey, Michael James, Edmonton†	.249	102	313	42	78	98	8	3	2	26	1	3	1	20	0	41	12	3
Reboulet, Jeffery, Portland	.246	26	65	9	16	17	1	0	0	3	0	2	0	12	0	11	2	1
Reid, Jessie, Tacoma*	.226	124	411	55	93	163	16	3	16	58	1	0	3	74	3	85	5	5
Remlinger, Michael, Phoenix*	.333	11	3	0	1	1	0	0	0	0	0	0	0	0	0	1	0	0
Renteria, Richard, Calgary	.295	65	234	34	69	101	17	0	5	36	1	6	1	15	1	11	4	3
Roberts, Peter, Las Vegas*	.000	43	9	0	0	0	0	0	0	0	1	0	0	0	0	3	0	0
Robidoux, William, Vancouver*	.317	73	246	36	78	134	19	2	11	42	1	3	0	38	9	46	3	1
Rodriguez, Victor, Portland	.314	120	465	63	146	216	34	3	10	50	1	2	4	35	2	45	2	1
Rohde, David, Tucson†	.291	75	234	35	68	84	7	3	1	30	7	5	1	32	1	30	11	5
Rojas, Homar, Albuquerque	.000	1	3	0	0	0	0	0	0	1	0	0	0	0	0	0	0	0
Royer, Stanley, Tacoma	.263	6	19	2	5	6	1	0	0	2	0	0	0	2	0	6	0	0
Runge, Paul, Las Vegas	.253	119	375	56	95	137	14	5	6	50	4	4	1	69	0	77	8	2
Salas, Mark, Colorado Springs*	.315	46	146	27	46	78	10	2	6	20	2	1	1	16	6	16	0	0
Schaefer, Jeffrey, Vancouver	.228	88	294	32	67	93	13	2	3	22	5	1	1	21	0	29	10	10
Scott, Richard, Tacoma	.188	79	256	23	48	60	7	1	1	23	3	4	3	22	0	65	0	1
Sharperson, Michael, Albuquerque	.309	98	359	81	111	149	15	7	3	48	4	3	2	66	2	46	17	12
Sheaffer, Danny, Colorado Springs	.282	107	401	62	113	152	26	2	3	47	7	3	1	24	0	39	6	12
Shelby, John, Albuquerque†	.286	32	126	20	36	61	7	3	4	21	0	1	2	6	0	33	12	3
Sinatro, Matthew, 34 Tuc.-12 Cal.	.258	46	128	13	33	39	6	0	0	12	5	1	1	16	0	21	1	1
Skurla, John, Phoenix*	.206	30	68	7	14	22	2	0	2	9	0	0	1	3	0	17	0	0
Smajstrla, Craig, Tucson	.249	110	378	46	94	123	15	7	0	35	5	2	2	30	0	35	12	4
Smith, Brick, Tacoma	.111	11	27	2	3	3	0	0	0	3	0	1	0	7	0	8	0	0
Smith, Keith, Vancouver†	.213	114	356	29	76	96	9	4	1	18	8	3	4	33	2	55	6	5
Smithberg, Roger, Las Vegas	.071	22	14	0	1	1	0	0	0	0	3	0	0	0	0	9	0	0
Sosa, Samuel, Vancouver	.367	13	49	7	18	24	3	0	1	5	0	0	0	7	0	6	3	1
Speier, Chris, Phoenix	.273	9	22	5	6	7	1	0	0	4	1	0	0	8	1	7	1	0
Spilman, Harry, Tucson*	.274	69	230	29	63	92	12	1	5	38	2	4	2	18	2	21	1	2
Springer, Dennis, Albuquerque	.000	8	4	0	0	0	0	0	0	0	1	0	0	0	0	1	0	0
Springer, Steven, Vancouver	.277	137	520	61	144	195	21	3	8	56	7	5	3	26	1	83	8	8
Steels, James, Phoenix*	.272	103	368	68	100	147	21	4	6	45	4	6	5	42	4	49	23	12
Stevens, Lee, Edmonton*	.247	127	446	72	110	199	29	9	14	74	0	2	4	61	3	115	5	3
Sullivan, Marc, Vancouver	.189	84	259	18	49	61	7	1	1	14	2	0	0	23	0	67	0	2
Swan, Russell, Phoenix*	.200	14	5	1	1	1	0	0	0	0	1	0	0	0	0	1	0	0
Szekely, Joseph, Albuquerque*	.235	66	170	22	40	54	11	0	1	17	2	0	1	11	3	33	2	3
Tanner, Bruce, 3 Tac.-20 Phx.*	.000	23	4	0	0	0	0	0	0	0	0	0	0	0	0	2	0	0
Tate, Stuart, Phoenix	.000	54	3	0	0	0	0	0	0	0	1	0	0	0	0	1	0	0
Taylor, Dwight, Colorado Springs*	.279	85	272	46	76	87	4	2	1	18	5	1	1	17	0	44	21	10
Taylor, William, Las Vegas	.333	47	6	1	2	2	0	0	0	0	0	0	0	1	0	4	0	0
Tejada, Wilfredo, Phoenix	.212	62	189	14	40	54	8	3	0	14	2	1	1	5	0	31	0	3
Thomas, James, Edmonton†	.235	79	230	18	54	71	8	3	1	21	4	2	0	13	1	32	5	5
Tillman, Kerry, 22 Phx.-43 Tuc.	.285	65	249	35	71	107	19	4	3	32	0	1	2	11	2	29	10	3
Tingley, Ronald, Colorado Springs	.261	66	207	28	54	84	8	2	6	39	1	6	1	19	1	49	2	1
Tolentino, Jose, Tucson*	.272	128	408	61	111	167	27	1	9	64	3	10	3	62	6	72	2	4
Toliver, Freddie, 8 Por.-6 L.V.	.667	14	6	1	4	4	0	0	0	1	2	0	0	0	0	0	0	0
Torve, Kelvin, Portland*	.291	137	499	62	145	214	41	2	8	62	3	5	4	52	7	59	10	7
Traxler, Brian, Albuquerque*	.301	64	239	33	72	97	10	3	3	30	0	3	1	17	2	17	0	2
Valle, David, Calgary	.000	2	6	0	0	0	0	0	0	0	0	0	0	0	0	1	0	0
Venable, William, Edmonton*	.271	95	329	52	89	114	14	4	1	45	7	4	1	46	2	59	13	3
Villa, Michael, Phoenix*	.000	14	2	0	0	0	0	0	0	0	0	0	0	0	0	1	0	0
Vizcaino, Jose, Albuquerque†	.283	129	434	60	123	144	10	4	1	44	12	3	1	33	2	41	16	14
Vizquel, Omar, Calgary	.214	7	28	3	6	8	2	0	0	3	0	0	1	3	0	4	0	2
Vosberg, Edward, 24 Tuc.-12 Alb.*	.375	36	8	2	3	6	1	1	0	3	0	1	0	1	0	0	0	0
Wagner, Daniel, Vancouver	.238	23	80	4	19	25	4	1	0	9	1	3	0	1	0	12	3	0
Walker, Michael A., Calgary	.000	19	1	0	0	0	0	0	0	0	0	0	0	0	0	0	0	0
Walsh, David, Albuquerque*	.500	6	4	0	2	2	0	0	0	0	0	0	0	0	0	2	0	0
Washington, Ronald, Tucson	.320	92	331	40	106	148	19	4	5	58	3	5	1	15	1	40	2	2
Weaver, James, 100 Van.-15 Phx.*	.216	115	388	44	84	139	19	6	8	35	2	0	1	52	2	100	19	9
Weiss, Walter, Tacoma†	.111	2	9	1	1	2	1	0	0	0	0	0	0	0	0	1	0	0
Wells, Terry, Tucson*	.000	26	1	0	0	0	0	0	0	0	0	0	0	0	0	1	0	0
Wetteland, John, Albuquerque	.125	11	8	1	1	1	0	0	0	0	3	0	0	0	0	5	0	0
Willard, Gerald, Vancouver*	.276	90	283	32	78	119	18	1	7	38	0	4	0	43	5	56	0	2
Williams, Dana, Vancouver	.333	4	15	2	5	8	3	0	0	2	0	0	0	1	0	1	0	0
Williams, Edward, Vancouver	.246	35	114	12	28	39	8	0	1	13	0	0	2	15	0	18	1	1
Williams, Matthew, Phoenix	.320	76	284	61	91	193	20	2	26	61	0	1	3	32	4	51	9	3
Wilson, James, Calgary	.314	138	519	79	163	271	30	6	26	133	0	11	6	54	2	102	8	3
Wilson, Trevor, Phoenix*	.111	24	9	0	1	1	0	0	0	1	0	0	0	0	0	5	0	0
Woodard, Michael, Colorado Springs*.	.289	26	90	10	26	32	4	1	0	8	2	0	0	5	0	5	1	1
Woodson, Tracy, Albuquerque	.292	89	325	49	95	158	21	0	14	59	0	3	4	32	2	40	2	1
Wotus, Ronald, Las Vegas	.257	41	109	17	28	32	4	0	0	10	1	2	1	24	0	14	4	2
Wright, George, 117 Phx.-12 Van.†..	.242	129	446	66	108	168	32	2	8	39	1	1	5	63	3	69	3	7
Wrona, William, Las Vegas	.223	100	318	41	71	101	15	3	3	33	3	3	2	37	1	51	2	2
Young, Michael, Colorado Springs†	.308	72	260	55	80	151	21	4	14	48	0	1	0	42	2	68	2	0
Yurtin, Jeffrey, Las Vegas*	.276	115	373	49	103	174	33	4	10	60	2	11	0	39	3	85	1	2
Zuvella, Paul, Colorado Springs	.331	96	387	61	128	187	23	3	10	66	1	1	1	24	0	27	8	6

The following pitchers, listed alphabetically by club, with games in parentheses, had no plate appearances, primarily through use of designated hitters.

ALBUQUERQUE—Crews, Timothy (2); Falcone, Peter (2); Searage, Raymond (2).

CALGARY—Campbell, Michael (16); DeLeon, Luis (35); Dobie, Reginald (15); Doyle, Richard (16); Dunne, Michael (9); Hanson, Erik (8); Harris, Eugene (5); Helton, Keith (8); Hensley, Charles (17); Hull, Jeffrey (19); McLaughlin, Colin (40); Melendez, Jose (17); Niedenfuer,

Thomas (13); Oliverio, Stephen (9); Powell, Dennis (18); Price, Bryan (5); Rice, Patrick (17); Ridenour, Dana (18); Shaw, Theodore (27); Solano, Julio (43); Spagnola, Glenn (4); Taylor, Terry (10); Wilkinson, William (2); Zavaras, Clinton (21).

COLORADO SPRINGS—Allen, Neil (21); Atherton, Keith (4); Bearse, Kevin (13); Bystrom, Martin (9); Curtis, Michael (1); Davis, Joel (33); Davis, Steven (18); Edwards, Jeffrey (8); Gordon, Donald (63); Hilton, Stan (3); Kaiser, Jeffrey (31); Nichols, Rodney (10); Odekirk, Richard (3); Olin, Steven (42); Palmer, David (8); Scott, Charles (2); Seanez, Rudy (1); Shaw, Theodore (3); Skalski, Joe (10); Walker, Michael C. (28); Ward, Colby (14); Wickander, Kevin (45); Wojna, Edward (19).

EDMONTON—Buckels, Gary (24); Burcham, Timothy (1); Charland, Colin (25); Clark, Terry (21); Cliburn, Stewart (25); Corbett, Sherman (52); Fetters, Michael (26); Lazorko, Jack (21); Lovelace, Vance (37); Monteleone, Richard (13); Trudeau, Kevin (17); Ward, Colby (27); Willis, Carl (36); Young, Clifford (31).

LAS VEGAS—Ghelfi, Anthony (18); Leiper, David (11).

PHOENIX—Davis, Ronald (17); Samuels, Roger (14).

PORTLAND—Booker, Gregory (14); Casian, Lawrence (28); Cook, Michael (43); Davins, James (26); Drummond, Timothy (10); Dyer, Michael (15); Gonzalez, German (17); Guthrie, Mark (7); Hernandez, Manuel (24); Kepshire, Kurt (16); Oliveras, Francisco (17); Shields, Stephen (9); Soff, Raymond (29); St. Claire, Randy (27); Straker, Lester (28); Tapani, Kevin (6); Tunnell, Lee (25); Williams, Jimmy (16).

TACOMA—Bordi, Richard (41); Clark, Bryan (29); Corsi, James (24); Dawley, William (22); Holcomb, Scott (10); Klink, Joseph (6); Lambert, Reese (36); Law, Joseph (31); Norris, Michael (23); Perez, William (1); Shaver, Jeffrey (21); Shotkoski, David (11); Snyder, Brian (48); Walton, Bruce (32); Weber, Weston (6); Young, Matthew (2).

TUCSON—Childress, Rodney (50); Johnson, Mitchell (7); Schatzeder, Daniel (12).

VANCOUVER—Bittiger, Jeffrey (17); Blasucci, Anthony (26); Chadwick, Ray (6); Davis, John (35); Drees, Thomas (26); Hardy, John (36); Hibbard, Gregory (9); Kutzler, Jerry (12); Little, Douglas (10); Long, William (3); McCarthy, Thomas (17); McDowell, Jack (16); Patterson, Kenneth (2); Pawlowski, John (30); Peterson, Adam (25); Rodriguez, Ricardo (13); Segura, Jose (44).

GRAND SLAM HOME RUNS—Cockrell, 2; Bathe, Byers, Cochrane, Davidson, Forrester, D. Gonzalez, S. Howard, Manto, Marquez, McGuire, McLemore, Perezchica, Reid, Robidoux, Scott, Washington, M. Williams, J. Wilson, Yurtin, 1 each.

AWARDED FIRST BASE ON CATCHER'S INTERFERENCE—Eccles (Quirk); Fletcher (Tingley); Hengel (Szekely); Sharperson (Lampkin).

CLUB FIELDING

Club	Pct.	G.	PO.	A.	E.	DP.	PB.	Club	Pct.	G.	PO.	A.	E.	DP.	PB.
Vancouver	.977	141	3618	1458	121	124	11	Albuquerque	.972	141	3661	1519	150	127	20
Edmonton	.977	141	3543	1534	122	149	14	Tucson	.971	142	3676	1468	154	110	15
Portland	.976	144	3748	1618	133	143	14	Colorado Springs	.970	142	3653	1553	159	156	13
Phoenix	.975	143	3765	1593	135	131	18	Las Vegas	.970	143	3774	1553	167	117	7
Calgary	.974	142	3647	1450	138	150	30	Tacoma	.968	143	3719	1600	177	134	14

Triple Plays—Portland 2, Las Vegas.

INDIVIDUAL FIELDING

*Throws lefthanded.

FIRST BASEMEN

Player and Club	Pct.	G.	PO.	A.	E.	DP.	Player and Club	Pct.	G.	PO.	A.	E.	DP.
Allaire, Edmonton	1.000	1	12	0	0	1	Litton, Phoenix	1.000	1	10	1	0	2
Arndt, Tacoma	1.000	2	14	1	0	1	Manto, Edmonton	1.000	9	56	1	0	6
Baker, Portland	1.000	1	5	0	0	0	Martinez, Vancouver	.995	18	178	10	1	12
Bathe, Phoenix	1.000	4	22	0	0	1	McConnell, Albuquerque	.955	4	19	2	1	2
Bierley, Portland	1.000	2	10	0	0	2	McGinnis, Tacoma	.992	14	118	4	1	9
Blair, Phoenix	1.000	4	37	3	0	1	McNamara, Phoenix	1.000	1	12	0	0	0
Bowie, Calgary*	.988	97	746	67	10	84	McPhail, Vancouver	1.000	1	6	0	0	3
Brenly, Phoenix	1.000	1	6	0	0	2	Meadows, Tucson*	1.000	3	13	0	0	1
Brilinski, Tacoma*	.992	42	338	34	3	38	Medina, Colorado Springs*	.990	12	96	4	1	10
Brundage, Calgary*	1.000	4	24	1	0	4	Michel, Albuquerque	.991	40	325	23	3	23
Candaele, Tucson	1.000	1	1	0	0	0	Morman, Vancouver	.982	23	156	12	3	15
Clark, Las Vegas	.944	2	16	1	1	0	J. Nelson, Edmonton	1.000	1	4	2	0	1
Cochrane, Calgary	1.000	6	45	5	0	7	R. Nelson, Las Vegas*	.986	49	451	31	7	41
Cockrell, Portland	.979	11	84	8	2	8	Pryor, Tacoma	1.000	2	11	1	0	2
Cook, Portland	1.000	1	1	0	0	0	Quirk, Tacoma	1.000	2	22	0	0	1
C. Cooper, Las Vegas	.991	48	433	20	4	37	Robidoux, Vancouver	.990	56	440	41	5	38
G. Cooper, Tucson	1.000	1	7	0	0	1	Runge, Las Vegas	1.000	10	71	7	0	4
Dalena, Colorado Springs	.988	96	779	54	10	89	Skurla, Phoenix*	.964	3	24	3	1	2
Davis, Edmonton	1.000	1	6	0	0	1	Smith, Tucson	1.000	6	44	1	0	2
Debus, Albuquerque	.989	12	78	13	1	7	Spilman, Tucson	.983	21	164	11	3	12
Diaz, Calgary	1.000	2	2	0	0	0	Steels, Phoenix*	1.000	3	5	1	0	0
Eccles, Portland	1.000	6	36	2	0	9	Stevens, Edmonton*	.990	73	553	33	6	61
Eppard, Edmonton*	.992	69	583	52	5	69	Sullivan, Vancouver	1.000	1	0	0	0	0
Forrester, Vancouver*	.983	48	369	28	7	33	Tillman, 2 Phoenix-10 Tucson ...	.974	12	67	9	2	7
Fulton, Calgary	.988	27	156	5	2	18	Tingley, Colorado Springs	.000	1	0	0	1	0
Goff, Calgary	.979	18	128	10	3	16	Tolentino, Tucson*	.994	116	985	69	6	73
Hansen, Calgary	1.000	2	7	0	0	0	TORVE, Portland	.998	131	1206	102	2	111
Hayes, Phoenix	1.000	3	19	0	0	3	Traxler, Albuquerque*	.994	62	552	61	4	55
Higgins, Colorado Springs	.982	54	408	27	8	46	Willard, Vancouver	1.000	2	13	0	0	0
Holmes, Edmonton	1.000	3	21	2	0	1	Williams, Vancouver	1.000	2	7	0	0	1
Jennings, Tacoma*	.986	91	792	30	12	72	Wilson, Calgary	.984	7	58	5	1	5
Jurak, Phoenix	.969	11	57	5	2	4	Woodson, Albuquerque	.990	35	260	34	3	26
Kingery, Calgary*	1.000	7	44	2	0	4	Wotus, Phoenix	1.000	3	18	2	0	1
Laga, Phoenix*	.995	121	1064	93	6	99	Yurtin, Las Vegas	.989	42	344	32	4	22

Triple Plays—Torve, Yurtin.

SECOND BASEMEN

Player and Club	Pct.	G.	PO.	A.	E.	DP.	Player and Club	Pct.	G.	PO.	A.	E.	DP.
Arndt, Tacoma	.968	17	35	55	3	15	Gonzalez, Colorado Springs	.941	2	7	9	1	3
Blair, Phoenix	.973	19	39	34	2	7	Hale, Portland	.982	104	214	332	10	77
Blankenship, Tacoma	.984	24	39	81	2	10	Hayes, Phoenix	1.000	2	4	2	0	0
Bordick, Tacoma	.974	67	162	208	10	50	Hecht, Phoenix	1.000	3	9	7	0	1
Briley, Calgary	1.000	7	16	19	0	6	Henley, Albuquerque	.926	11	17	33	4	7
Candaele, Tucson	.945	10	17	35	3	4	Hill, Tacoma	.966	34	69	102	6	26
Coachman, Edmonton	.947	25	57	68	7	16	Hinzo, Colorado Springs	.976	102	206	325	13	86
Cora, Las Vegas	.958	111	230	324	24	71	Huff, Albuquerque	1.000	3	7	5	0	1
Davis, Vancouver	.778	1	3	4	2	1	Jones, Tacoma	1.000	5	8	3	0	1
Diaz, Calgary	.976	19	39	42	2	12	Jurak, Phoenix	.969	8	13	18	1	6
Dugas, Albuquerque	.982	30	39	70	2	18	Litton, Phoenix	.969	17	30	33	2	9
Dunlap, Calgary	1.000	3	5	10	0	3	Lombardozzi, Tucson	.969	98	163	274	14	43
Fulton, Calgary	.909	13	21	29	5	8	Magallanes, Colorado Springs	1.000	4	6	11	0	3
Giles, Colorado Springs	.988	17	40	41	1	10	Martinez, Calgary	.933	8	10	18	2	4

SECOND BASEMEN—Continued

Player and Club	Pct.	G.	PO.	A.	E.	DP.	Player and Club	Pct.	G.	PO.	A.	E.	DP.
McLEMORE, Edmonton	.983	114	264	323	10	95	Runge, Las Vegas	.983	13	25	33	1	8
Murray, Calgary	.958	15	29	40	3	12	Schaefer, Vancouver	.996	58	124	144	1	34
Naveda, Portland	1.000	3	2	6	0	1	Sharperson, Albuquerque	.968	56	87	154	8	36
Noce, Calgary	.987	52	85	147	3	32	Smajstrla, Tucson	.969	43	81	108	6	17
Pankovits, Albuquerque	.951	55	114	157	14	29	Speier, Phoenix	.900	2	3	6	1	2
Perezchica, Phoenix	.983	77	144	199	6	51	Springer, Vancouver	.980	85	173	265	9	51
Pryor, Tacoma	.957	4	10	12	1	2	Thomas, Edmonton	.957	6	10	12	1	5
Ralston, Portland	.965	38	69	126	7	26	Woodard, Colorado Springs	.946	23	39	66	6	12
Reboulet, Portland	.971	6	14	19	1	8	Wotus, Phoenix	.987	31	74	76	2	22
Renteria, Calgary	.980	41	78	116	4	26	Wrona, Las Vegas	.971	29	55	81	4	16

Triple Play—Hale.

THIRD BASEMEN

Player and Club	Pct.	G.	PO.	A.	E.	DP.	Player and Club	Pct.	G.	PO.	A.	E.	DP.
Arndt, Tacoma	.933	104	60	191	18	17	MANTO, Edmonton	.943	117	84	265	21	22
Baerga, Las Vegas	.916	125	92	256	32	20	Martinez, Calgary	.833	27	12	38	10	4
Beane, Tacoma	.833	7	3	7	2	1	McConnell, Albuquerque	.938	34	14	47	4	3
Bierley, Portland	.909	11	7	23	3	2	McPhail, Vancouver	.892	18	4	29	4	3
Blair, Phoenix	.938	14	5	25	2	0	Naveda, Portland	.913	21	15	27	4	2
Bordick, Tacoma	.938	10	5	25	2	2	Noce, Calgary	1.000	2	1	3	0	0
Brenley, Phoenix	.750	6	1	8	3	0	Olson, Portland	.800	2	1	3	1	0
Briley, Calgary	.857	19	5	25	5	3	Pankovits, Albuquerque	.857	10	3	19	2	0
Candaele, Tucson	.926	14	9	16	2	0	Paris, Vancouver	.917	66	33	111	13	10
Coachman, Edmonton	.955	27	14	50	3	4	Parker, Phoenix	1.000	12	10	29	0	4
Cochrane, Calgary	.907	21	13	26	4	3	Pryor, Tacoma	.870	16	11	36	7	3
Colombino, Tucson	.944	40	20	64	5	3	Ralston, Portland	.897	9	6	20	3	1
Cooper, Tucson	1.000	3	1	0	0	0	Reboulet, Portland	1.000	5	6	6	0	0
Fulton, Calgary	.923	47	26	58	7	4	Renteria, Calgary	.946	26	24	46	4	6
Giles, Colorado Springs	.990	39	25	71	1	8	Rodriguez, Portland	.941	99	62	194	16	15
Goff, Calgary	.872	14	13	21	5	5	Royer, Tacoma	.765	6	4	9	4	0
Gonzalez, Colorado Springs	.923	105	65	175	20	15	Runge, Las Vegas	.889	14	12	28	5	5
Hale, Portland	1.000	2	3	1	0	0	Sharperson, Albuquerque	.967	38	17	71	3	5
D. Hansen, Albuquerque	.786	6	3	8	3	0	Sheaffer, Colorado Springs	.818	10	3	6	2	1
R. Hansen, Calgary	.667	2	1	1	1	0	Smajstrla, Tucson	.908	47	20	49	7	5
Hayes, Phoenix	.910	33	12	69	8	7	Springer, Vancouver	.935	54	41	102	10	8
Henley, Albuquerque	1.000	4	4	8	0	1	Thomas, Edmonton	1.000	4	0	1	0	0
Hill, Tacoma	.000	2	0	0	1	0	Washington, Tucson	.951	33	21	57	4	3
Hubbard, Tucson	.938	8	6	9	1	1	E. Williams, Vancouver	.733	8	1	10	4	1
Jackson, Tucson	.860	24	15	34	8	4	M. Williams, Phoenix	.957	64	38	162	9	14
Jones, Tacoma	.813	5	3	10	3	0	Woodson, Albuquerque	.931	59	36	98	10	10
Jurak, Phoenix	.915	25	12	42	5	1	Wotus, Phoenix	1.000	5	5	3	0	0
Keedy, Colorado Springs	1.000	2	1	5	0	0	Wrona, Las Vegas	.750	1	2	1	1	0
Litton, Phoenix	1.000	4	2	7	0	0	Yurtin, Las Vegas	.957	5	2	20	1	0
Lopez, Albuquerque	.955	8	9	12	1	0							

SHORTSTOPS

Player and Club	Pct.	G.	PO.	A.	E.	DP.	Player and Club	Pct.	G.	PO.	A.	E.	DP.
Allaire, 2 Tuc.-87 Edm	.974	89	105	235	9	62	Noce, Calgary	.974	87	120	253	10	64
Anderson, Edmonton	.960	4	7	17	1	7	Parker, Phoenix	1.000	2	4	3	0	1
Arndt, Tacoma	1.000	7	6	11	0	3	Perezchica, Phoenix	.947	10	11	25	2	3
Baker, Portland	.971	79	134	295	13	72	Pino, Portland	.950	30	56	78	7	13
Benjamin, Phoenix	.970	109	149	332	15	70	Ralston, Portland	.881	9	10	27	5	7
Blair, Phoenix	.914	8	19	13	3	2	Reboulet, Portland	.900	12	17	37	6	7
Bordick, Tacoma	.933	64	94	198	21	41	Renteria, Calgary	.889	4	4	4	1	2
Bustabad, Albuquerque	.842	8	7	9	3	3	Rodriguez, Portland	.981	16	16	36	1	9
Candaele, Tucson	1.000	2	0	4	0	1	Rohde, Tucson	.963	74	108	232	13	36
Cochrane, Calgary	1.000	4	10	12	0	2	Runge, Las Vegas	.924	18	17	44	5	4
Cora, Las Vegas	.930	9	15	25	3	7	Schaefer, Vancouver	.940	30	52	88	9	19
Davis, Vancouver	.941	5	6	10	1	3	Scott, Tacoma	.952	79	117	259	19	52
Diaz, Calgary	.885	15	23	31	7	4	Sharperson, Albuquerque	.921	12	10	25	3	5
Dunlap, Calgary	.975	35	64	95	4	23	Smith, Vancouver	.968	110	181	307	16	59
Giles, Colorado Springs	.958	44	82	125	9	32	Speier, Phoenix	1.000	5	7	6	0	1
Green, Las Vegas	.929	61	71	177	19	26	Thomas, Edmonton	.942	59	66	160	14	29
Hayes, Phoenix	1.000	3	1	3	0	0	Vizcaino, Albuquerque	.951	128	191	390	30	82
Henley, Albuquerque	1.000	2	5	6	0	4	Vizquel, Calgary	1.000	7	15	14	0	8
Jackson, Tucson	.833	8	12	18	6	10	Washington, Tucson	.937	58	67	155	15	24
Jurak, Phoenix	.667	1	0	2	1	0	Weiss, Tacoma	.750	1	0	3	1	0
Litton, Phoenix	.882	6	6	9	2	1	Williams, Phoenix	.964	20	19	35	2	6
Lombardozzi, Tucson	.947	3	7	11	1	5	Wrona, Las Vegas	.963	71	77	213	11	37
Magallanes, Colorado Springs	.947	8	10	26	2	4	ZUVELLA, Colorado Springs	.975	96	139	321	12	71
Naveda, Portland	.889	3	6	2	1	3							

Triple Plays—Baker, Green, Pino.

OUTFIELDERS

Player and Club	Pct.	G.	PO.	A.	E.	DP.	Player and Club	Pct.	G.	PO.	A.	E.	DP.
Abner, Las Vegas	.993	55	129	6	1	1	Briley, Calgary	1.000	1	1	0	0	0
Allred, Colorado Springs°	1.000	11	27	1	0	0	Brito, Portland	.977	64	83	2	2	0
Alomar, Las Vegas	1.000	1	4	0	0	0	Brown, Edmonton	.988	77	156	10	2	3
Anthony, Tucson°	1.000	11	21	0	0	0	Brundage, Calgary°	1.000	21	40	1	0	0
Baker, Portland	1.000	3	4	0	0	0	Buhner, Calgary	.981	56	97	8	2	2
Bass, Tucson	1.000	4	8	0	0	0	Byers, Las Vegas	.933	9	13	1	1	1
Bathe, Phoenix	1.000	7	10	0	0	0	Candaele, Tucson	1.000	37	67	4	0	1
Bean, Albuquerque°	1.000	3	7	0	0	0	Christensen, Portland	.987	82	143	10	2	1
Beane, Tacoma	1.000	22	28	0	0	0	Clark, Las Vegas	.967	102	197	7	7	0
Bichette, Edmonton	.990	59	92	9	1	3	Close, Calgary	.979	92	181	10	4	2
Bierley, Portland	.965	72	135	3	5	0	Cochrane, Calgary	.500	2	1	0	1	0
Blair, Phoenix	.917	9	20	2	2	1	Cockrell, Portland	.981	81	144	7	3	1
Boever, Calgary	.778	9	6	1	2	0	Cooper, Tucson	.986	100	202	2	3	0
Brady, Edmonton°	.958	54	66	3	3	0	Davidson, 29 Por.-38 Tuc	1.000	67	145	9	0	2
Brantley, Calgary	.990	46	97	5	1	2	Davis, Vancouver	1.000	37	64	2	0	1

OUTFIELDERS—Continued

Player and Club	Pct.	G.	PO.	A.	E.	DP.
DeAngelis, Edmonton*	1.000	4	2	0	0	0
DeLima, Portland*	.973	124	245	9	7	1
DeWolf, Las Vegas*	1.000	18	20	1	0	0
Dietrick, Tacoma	.970	114	251	8	8	1
Dunbar, Tucson*	1.000	12	22	1	0	0
Eppard, Edmonton*	.941	7	16	0	1	0
Fields, Calgary	.967	98	201	5	7	0
Forrester, Vancouver*	.971	27	33	0	1	0
Frobel, Vancouver	.978	23	44	1	1	0
Fulton, Calgary	1.000	17	28	0	0	0
Gainey, Colorado Springs	.965	81	134	3	5	0
Gerhart, Phoenix	.978	83	128	8	3	3
Giles, Colorado Springs	.889	6	8	0	1	0
Goff, Calgary	1.000	3	4	0	0	0
Gonzalez, Albuquerque	.981	50	98	3	2	1
Gross, Tacoma	1.000	9	11	1	0	0
Gwynn, Albuquerque*	1.000	21	27	0	0	0
Hayes, Phoenix	1.000	27	40	2	0	1
Hearron, Las Vegas	1.000	2	1	0	0	0
Hengel, Colorado Springs	.980	83	138	11	3	1
S. Howard, Tacoma	.967	90	170	7	6	4
T. Howard, Las Vegas	.989	75	178	7	2	0
Hubbard, Tucson	1.000	10	7	0	0	0
Huff, Albuquerque	.991	113	202	8	2	0
Jackson, Tucson	.972	36	67	3	2	0
Jennings, Tacoma*	.964	37	50	4	2	0
Johnson, Vancouver*	.982	106	261	7	5	2
Jordan, Tucson	.987	51	142	7	2	3
Jose, Tacoma	.951	93	186	7	10	0
Jurak, Phoenix	1.000	2	2	0	0	0
Kesselmark, Albuquerque*	1.000	2	4	0	0	0
KINGERY, Calgary*	.996	99	245	8	1	2
Kirby, Albuquerque	.987	76	149	8	2	2
Knabenshue, Las Vegas	.972	93	169	5	5	1
Komminsk, Colorado Springs	.992	54	119	0	1	0
Kosco, Calgary	1.000	3	3	0	1	0
Landreaux, Albuquerque	1.000	40	60	3	0	0
Leonard, Phoenix	.909	21	29	1	3	0
Lopez, Albuquerque	1.000	6	13	0	0	0
Lusader, Tucson*	.953	33	80	2	4	0
Mack, Las Vegas	.984	20	59	3	1	0
McPhail, Vancouver	.978	91	169	6	4	1
Meadows, Tucson*	.971	49	96	5	3	0
Medina, Colorado Springs*	.925	34	45	4	4	0
Meyers, Phoenix	.994	88	164	6	1	2
Michel, Albuquerque	1.000	26	43	0	0	0
Mikulik, Tucson	1.000	5	9	0	0	0
Morman, Vancouver	1.000	5	7	0	0	0
Naveda, Portland	.952	8	20	0	1	0
Nichols, Tucson	1.000	6	11	1	0	0
Ortiz, 61 Alb.-11 Tuc.	.945	72	130	7	8	1
Pankovits, Albuquerque	.938	13	15	0	1	0
Parker, Phoenix	.917	7	11	0	1	0
Pryor, Tacoma	1.000	4	5	0	0	0
Ramsey, Edmonton*	.961	99	189	9	8	3
Reboulet, Portland	1.000	1	1	0	0	0
Reid, Tacoma*	.974	86	145	5	4	0
Runge, Las Vegas	1.000	29	39	0	0	0
Schaefer, Vancouver	1.000	1	1	0	0	0
Sheaffer, Colorado Springs	.945	77	133	5	8	3
Shelby, Albuquerque	.987	30	75	2	1	0
Skurla, Tucson	1.000	20	24	0	0	0
Smajstrla, Tucson	.900	7	9	0	1	0
Sosa, Vancouver	1.000	13	43	1	0	0
Steels, Phoenix*	.972	97	165	6	5	0
Stevens, Edmonton*	.989	64	82	7	1	0
Taylor, Colorado Springs*	.989	80	182	6	2	1
Thomas, Edmonton	1.000	3	3	0	0	0
Tillman, 19 Phx.-35 Tuc	.967	54	86	2	3	0
Tolentino, Tucson*	1.000	10	10	2	0	0
Venable, Edmonton	.990	84	189	7	2	0
Wagner, Vancouver	1.000	23	44	0	0	0
Weaver, 99 Van-14 Phx*	.973	113	211	9	6	2
D. Williams, Vancouver	.933	4	14	0	1	0
Woodard, Colorado Springs	.000	2	0	0	1	0
Wright, 99 Phx-12 Van	.978	111	220	5	5	1
Young, Colorado Springs	1.000	26	39	1	0	0
Yurtin, Las Vegas	1.000	48	110	7	0	4

CATCHERS

Player and Club	Pct.	G.	PO.	A.	E.	DP.	PB.
Alomar, Las Vegas	.984	116	702	47	12	5	3
Bando, Tacoma	.987	26	134	16	2	0	1
Bathe, Phoenix	.992	18	113	11	1	4	2
Beane, Tacoma	1.000	5	30	1	0	0	3
Brenly, Phoenix	.988	13	71	8	1	0	1
Brito, Tacoma	1.000	5	31	5	0	0	0
Cochrane, Calgary	.944	2	17	0	1	0	0
Davis, Edmonton	.997	48	251	34	1	6	3
Debus, Albuquerque	1.000	5	19	4	0	0	0
Eccles, Portland	.993	22	129	13	1	0	3
Fletcher, Albuquerque	.987	98	632	63	9	5	9
Goff, Calgary	.983	42	201	32	4	2	14
Ham, Phoenix	.991	16	102	9	1	1	1
Hansen, Calgary	1.000	18	78	2	0	3	5
Hearron, Las Vegas	.989	35	168	15	2	2	4
Hernandez, Albuquerque	.897	4	23	3	3	2	1
Hubbard, Tucson	1.000	2	7	0	0	0	0
Knapp, Edmonton	.985	51	243	20	4	4	5
Lampkin, Colorado Springs	.976	56	305	21	8	1	6
Marquez, Edmonton	.967	26	136	10	5	1	3
McElroy, Vancouver	1.000	1	7	0	0	0	0
McGinnis, Tacoma	.975	88	507	45	14	2	8
McGuire, Calgary	.987	83	467	55	7	5	10
McNamara, Phoenix	.981	23	93	12	2	2	0
Mercado, Portland	.981	53	295	19	6	1	5
Merullo, Vancouver	.952	3	19	1	1	1	3
Nelson, Edmonton	.987	37	210	16	3	1	3
Nichols, Tucson	.983	99	542	76	11	9	11
Olson, Portland	.992	70	439	29	4	4	6
Ouellette, Tucson	.980	25	133	16	3	2	2
Pena, Phoenix	.979	30	171	18	4	3	1
Pryor, Tacoma	.993	26	133	17	1	1	2
Quirk, Tacoma	.974	9	67	7	2	0	0
Rojas, Albuquerque	1.000	1	1	0	0	0	2
Salas, Colorado Springs	.989	15	86	5	1	3	1
Sheaffer, Colorado Springs	1.000	23	100	11	0	1	1
Sinatro, 31 Tuc.-12 Cal	.977	43	224	28	6	2	3
SULLIVAN, Vancouver	.996	73	409	41	2	2	2
Szekely, Albuquerque	.984	52	286	16	5	3	8
Tejada, Phoenix	.987	61	409	38	6	4	13
Tingley, Colorado Springs	.973	65	349	45	11	4	5
Torve, Portland	1.000	1	1	0	0	0	0
Valle, Calgary	1.000	2	6	0	0	0	0
Willard, Vancouver	.998	71	422	56	1	12	6

Triple Play—Olson.

PITCHERS

Player and Club	Pct.	G.	PO.	A.	E.	DP.
Allen, Colorado Springs	.969	21	11	20	1	3
Atherton, Colorado Springs	1.000	4	1	0	0	0
Barrett, Albuquerque	.938	47	6	9	1	2
Bearse, Colorado Springs*	.958	13	3	20	1	1
Benes, Las Vegas	.667	5	0	2	1	0
Bitker, 18 LV-24 Tac.	.813	42	4	9	3	0
Bittiger, Vancouver	.923	17	5	19	2	0
Blair, Phoenix	1.000	1	0	1	0	0
Blasucci, Vancouver*	1.000	26	0	2	0	0
Booker, Portland	.889	14	3	5	1	1
Bordi, Tacoma	1.000	41	1	12	0	0
Brantley, Phoenix	1.000	7	4	1	0	0
Brennan, Albuquerque	.946	34	14	21	2	1
Buckels, Edmonton	1.000	24	0	4	0	0
Burkett, Phoenix	.930	28	11	29	3	0
Burtt, Albuquerque	.844	28	13	14	5	2
Bystrom, Colorado Springs	1.000	9	1	2	0	0
Camacho, Phoenix	1.000	40	2	11	0	0
Campbell, Calgary	1.000	16	3	6	0	0
Cano, Tucson	.957	15	14	8	1	0
Casian, Portland*	.927	28	4	34	3	2
Chadwick, Vancouver	.800	6	2	2	1	0
Charland, Edmonton*	.952	25	6	14	1	1
Childress, Tucson	1.000	50	2	11	0	1
B. CLARK, Tacoma*	1.000	28	10	43	0	3
T. Clark, Edmonton	.933	21	12	16	2	3
Clements, Las Vegas*	1.000	18	3	10	0	0
Cliburn, Edmonton	1.000	25	1	7	0	1
Close, Calgary	1.000	1	1	0	0	0
Comstock, 28 LV-5 Cal.*	.917	33	3	8	1	0
D. Cook, Phoenix*	.889	12	1	7	1	0
M. Cook, Portland	.909	42	1	9	1	0
Corbett, Edmonton*	1.000	52	4	10	0	3
Corsi, Tacoma	1.000	23	1	9	0	2
Crew, Tucson	.933	34	2	12	1	1
Crews, Albuquerque	1.000	2	0	1	0	0
Davins, Edmonton	.889	25	2	6	1	0
D. Davis, Edmonton	1.000	2	0	1	0	0
Joel Davis, Colorado Springs	.900	33	14	13	3	2
John Davis, Vancouver	.917	35	3	8	1	1
M. Davis, Vancouver	1.000	1	0	1	0	0
R. Davis, Phoenix	.750	17	0	3	1	0
S. Davis, Colorado Springs*	.933	18	4	10	1	0
Dawley, Tacoma	1.000	22	1	1	0	1
DeLeon, Calgary	.923	33	5	7	1	0
Dobie, Calgary	.957	15	7	15	1	1

PITCHERS—Continued

Player and Club	Pct.	G.	PO.	A.	E.	DP.	Player and Club	Pct.	G.	PO.	A.	E.	DP.
Dominguez, Phoenix	.833	11	0	5	1	0	Niedenfuer, Calgary	.857	13	3	3	1	0
Downs, Phoenix	1.000	3	1	1	0	0	Nolte, Las Vegas*	.947	23	3	15	1	1
Doyle, Calgary	1.000	16	1	5	0	0	Norris, Tacoma	1.000	23	5	10	0	0
Dravecky, Phoenix*	1.000	1	2	2	0	0	Odekirk, Colorado Springs*	1.000	3	0	3	0	0
Drees, Vancouver*	.923	26	9	27	3	1	Olin, Colorado Springs	1.000	42	0	6	0	0
Drummond, Portland	.800	10	1	3	1	0	Oliveras, Portland	.905	17	3	16	2	0
Dunne, Calgary	.867	9	5	8	2	1	Oliverio, Calgary	1.000	9	3	4	0	0
Dunster, Tucson	1.000	4	0	4	0	0	Olker, Phoenix*	.889	29	1	15	2	1
Dyer, Portland	.900	15	7	11	2	0	Otto, Tacoma*	.968	29	8	22	1	1
Edwards, Colorado Springs*	1.000	8	1	1	0	0	Palmer, Colorado Springs	.938	8	7	8	1	0
Falcone, Albuquerque*	1.000	2	0	1	0	0	Patterson, Vancouver*	.000	2	0	0	1	0
Fetters, Edmonton	.919	26	3	31	3	1	Pawlowski, Vancouver	.913	29	7	14	2	2
Fischer, Albuquerque	.970	28	14	18	1	0	Peterson, Vancouver	.864	25	8	11	3	0
Forrester, Vancouver*	1.000	6	2	1	0	0	Portugal, Tucson	.963	17	10	16	1	0
Freeland, Phoenix	1.000	3	2	2	0	0	Powell, Calgary*	1.000	18	2	6	0	0
Ghelfi, Las Vegas	.833	18	3	7	2	0	Price, Calgary*	1.000	5	0	3	0	0
Gilmore, Las Vegas	1.000	29	12	22	0	1	Puikunas, Phoenix*	1.000	48	2	9	0	0
Gonzalez, Portland	1.000	17	2	1	0	0	Quinzer, Las Vegas	1.000	21	1	5	0	0
Gordon, Colorado Springs	.935	63	8	21	2	3	Remlinger, Phoenix*	.778	11	3	4	2	0
Gunderson, Phoenix*	.962	14	3	22	1	1	Rice, Calgary	1.000	17	2	7	0	0
Guthrie, Portland*	1.000	7	2	5	0	0	Ridenour, Calgary	1.000	18	3	8	0	0
Hanson, Calgary	.727	8	3	5	3	1	Roberts, Las Vegas*	1.000	43	6	8	0	1
Hardy, Vancouver	1.000	36	4	14	0	0	Rodriguez, Vancouver	.958	13	13	10	1	2
Harris, Calgary	1.000	5	0	3	0	1	Samuels, Phoenix*	.800	14	1	3	1	0
Hartley, Albuquerque	.857	58	4	8	2	0	Scott, Colorado Springs	1.000	2	0	1	0	0
Heathcock, Tucson	.929	28	13	26	3	4	Searage, Albuquerque*	.667	2	0	2	1	0
Helton, Calgary*	1.000	8	0	2	0	0	Segura, Vancouver	.955	44	7	14	1	0
Hensley, Calgary*	.750	17	2	1	1	0	Shaver, Tacoma	.973	19	15	21	1	2
Heredia, Albuquerque	.857	26	2	4	1	0	Shaw, 2 CS-25 Cal.	.974	27	11	26	1	3
Hernandez, Portland	.955	24	14	28	2	3	Shields, Portland	1.000	9	4	2	0	0
Hibbard, Vancouver*	1.000	9	1	12	0	0	Shotkoski, Tacoma	1.000	11	0	1	0	0
Hilton, Colorado Springs	1.000	3	0	1	0	0	Skalski, Colorado Springs	.556	10	1	4	4	1
Holcomb, Tacoma*	1.000	10	0	2	0	1	Smith, Tacoma*	1.000	1	1	0	0	0
Holmes, Albuquerque	1.000	9	3	2	0	0	Smithberg, Las Vegas	.976	22	9	31	1	2
Hull, Calgary	1.000	19	2	4	0	1	Snyder, Tacoma*	.900	48	4	14	2	2
Ilsley, Tucson*	.958	20	10	13	1	3	Soff, Portland	.947	29	5	13	1	1
Johnson, Tucson	1.000	7	3	1	0	1	Solano, Calgary	.909	43	6	4	1	0
Kaiser, Colorado Springs*	.833	31	4	11	3	0	Spagnola, Calgary	1.000	4	1	3	0	0
Kelley, Tucson	.905	12	4	15	2	1	Springer, Albuquerque	.909	8	5	5	1	1
Kepshire, Portland	.909	16	6	4	1	0	St. Claire, Portland	1.000	27	2	4	0	0
Kerfeld, Tucson	.889	53	2	6	1	1	Straker, Portland	.923	28	10	14	2	2
Kile, Tucson	.800	6	1	3	1	1	Swan, Phoenix*	.958	14	4	19	1	2
Kutzler, Vancouver	1.000	12	8	9	0	0	Tanner, 3 Tacoma-20 Phoenix	.960	23	7	17	1	2
Lambert, Tacoma*	.929	36	2	11	1	1	Tapani, Portland	1.000	6	3	5	0	0
Law, Tacoma	.970	31	8	24	1	0	Tate, Phoenix	.950	54	6	13	1	1
Lazorko, Edmonton	1.000	21	10	24	0	3	T. Taylor, Calgary	1.000	10	1	11	0	3
Leiper, Las Vegas	1.000	11	1	2	0	0	W. Taylor, Las Vegas	.889	47	5	11	2	0
Little, Vancouver	.917	10	1	10	1	2	Toliver, 8 Portland-5 Las Vegas	.818	13	2	7	2	0
Long, Vancouver	1.000	3	1	5	0	0	Trudeau, Edmonton	.750	17	0	9	3	0
Lovelace, Edmonton*	.923	37	2	10	1	0	Tunnell, Portland	.938	25	6	9	1	0
Lynch, Las Vegas	.917	44	2	9	1	0	Villa, Phoenix	1.000	14	1	7	0	0
Martinez, Albuquerque	.941	18	7	9	1	0	Vosberg, 23 Tuc.-12 Alb.*	.857	35	3	27	5	1
Mason, Tucson	.926	25	11	14	2	0	M.A. Walker, Calgary	1.000	18	6	11	0	3
Mayberry, Albuquerque	.950	15	6	13	1	1	M.C. Walker, Colorado Springs	.829	28	17	17	7	3
Maysey, Las Vegas	.926	28	10	15	2	0	Walsh, Albuquerque*	1.000	6	1	5	0	0
McCament, Phoenix	1.000	22	2	3	0	1	Walton, Tacoma	.895	32	4	13	2	0
McCarthy, Vancouver	1.000	17	5	7	0	0	Ward, 27 Edm.-14 CS	1.000	41	5	13	0	2
McClellan, Phoenix	1.000	9	5	5	0	0	Weber, Tacoma*	1.000	6	1	5	0	0
McDowell, Vancouver	1.000	16	3	9	0	0	Wells, Tucson*	.833	26	1	4	1	0
McLaughlin, Calgary	.923	40	2	10	1	0	Wetteland, Albuquerque	1.000	10	4	12	0	1
Melendez, Calgary	.900	17	2	7	1	1	Wickander, Colorado Springs*	.778	45	0	7	2	2
Meyer, Tucson	1.000	58	6	6	0	2	Wilkinson, Calgary*	1.000	2	0	1	0	0
Meyers, Phoenix*	1.000	1	0	1	0	0	Williams, Portland*	.750	16	0	3	1	0
Monteleone, Edmonton	.909	13	10	10	2	0	Willis, Edmonton	.931	36	7	20	2	2
Mulholland, Phoenix*	.765	13	1	12	4	1	Wilson, Phoenix*	.906	23	10	19	3	1
Munoz, Albuquerque*	.889	60	11	21	4	0	Wojna, Colorado Springs	.900	19	4	14	2	2
Murphy, Las Vegas	.905	27	8	11	2	0	C. Young, Edmonton*	.973	31	11	25	1	2
Neidlinger, Albuquerque	1.000	34	15	17	0	0	M. Young, Tacoma*	1.000	2	1	1	0	0
Nichols, Colorado Springs	1.000	10	2	11	0	0	Zavaras,	.913	21	9	12	2	0

The following players did not have any fielding statistics at the positions indicated or appeared only as a designated hitter, pinch-hitter or pinch-runner: Benamin, 2b; Bierley, p; Bowie, p; Burcham, p; Bustabad, 2b; Curtis, p; Dalena, p; Dunlap, of; Eccles, 3b; Green, 1b; Hill, ss, p; Hoffman, ph; Jennings, p; Klink, p; Levis, ph; Litton, c; McPhail, p; Meads, p; Murray, p; Pankovits, ss; Perez, p; V. Rodriguez, 2b; Rohde, 3b; Salas, 1b, of; Schatzeder, p; Seanez, p; Speier, 3b; Szekely, 3b, of; D. Taylor, p; Torve, p; M. Williams, of; Wrona, of; Yurtin, p.

CLUB PITCHING

Club	ERA.	G.	CG.	ShO.	Sv.	IP.	H.	R.	ER.	HR.	HB.	BB.	Int. BB.	SO.	WP.	Bk.
Vancouver	3.44	141	24	19	39	1206.0	1064	527	461	66	43	468	16	834	46	21
Tacoma	3.68	143	16	13	37	1239.2	1184	621	507	72	28	510	28	862	57	30
Phoenix	4.03	143	14	11	41	1255.0	1219	635	562	106	59	613	25	920	62	48
Albuquerque	4.09	141	14	10	36	1220.1	1267	639	554	102	14	453	21	932	58	12
Portland	4.11	144	11	8	36	1249.1	1279	664	571	91	25	467	9	826	40	34
Tucson	4.36	142	18	11	24	1225.1	1303	681	593	65	37	440	33	817	41	29
Edmonton	4.50	141	22	11	26	1181.0	1248	658	591	109	43	487	40	802	64	18
Colorado Springs	4.52	142	19	9	40	1217.2	1365	730	612	95	51	492	17	798	57	17
Las Vegas	4.61	143	20	9	32	1258.0	1399	732	645	110	32	479	37	840	57	28
Calgary	5.20	142	7	4	39	1215.2	1353	784	703	122	50	584	30	792	76	23

PITCHERS' RECORDS
(Leading Qualifiers for Earned-Run Average Leadership—115 or More Innings)

*Throws lefthanded.

Pitcher—Club	W.	L.	Pct.	ERA	G.	GS.	CG.	GF.	ShO.	Sv.	IP.	H.	R.	ER.	HR.	HB.	BB.	Int. BB.	SO.	WP.
Bittiger, Vancouver	9	5	.643	2.12	17	17	6	0	4	0	123.0	93	31	29	5	4	40	0	122	3
S. Davis, Colorado Springs*	12	2	.857	2.45	18	18	5	0	2	0	121.0	113	36	33	4	4	40	1	75	4
Peterson, Vancouver	14	5	.737	2.72	25	24	6	0	1	0	172.0	141	60	52	12	5	71	0	116	2
Wojna, Colorado Springs	9	4	.692	2.87	19	19	4	0	2	0	122.1	116	50	39	7	2	36	1	81	5
Wilson, Phoenix*	7	7	.500	3.12	23	20	2	2	0	0	115.1	109	49	40	5	2	76	1	77	5
B. Clark, Tacoma*	15	7	.682	3.14	28	28	4	0	2	0	174.2	154	77	61	4	3	85	0	112	4
Pawlowski, Vancouver	5	13	.278	3.30	29	16	1	6	0	0	122.2	120	51	45	5	3	51	2	88	6
Drees, Vancouver*	12	11	.522	3.37	26	26	4	0	3	0	168.1	142	76	63	12	4	72	2	66	2
Fischer, Albuquerque	12	10	.545	3.47	28	26	5	0	2	0	171.0	186	78	66	16	3	35	3	112	2
Mason, Tucson	7	12	.368	3.54	25	25	5	0	1	0	155.0	125	71	61	7	2	46	1	105	5

Departmental Leaders: G—Gordon, 63; W—B. Clark, 15; L—M.C. Walker, 15; Pct.—S. Davis, .857; GS—Eight pitchers tied with 28; CG—Bittiger, Fetters, Peterson, 6; GF—Hartley, 50; ShO—Bittiger, 4; Sv.—Olin, 24; IP—Heathcock, 183.1; H—Heathcock, 202; R—M.C. Walker, 124; ER—M.C. Walker, 108; HR—M.C. Walker, 21; HB—M.C. Walker, 14; BB—M.C. Walker, 93; IBB—Childress, Corbett, Munoz, 8; SO—Fetters, 144; WP—Otto, 18.

(All Pitchers—Listed Alphabetically)

Pitcher—Club	W.	L.	Pct.	ERA	G.	GS.	CG.	GF.	ShO.	Sv.	IP.	H.	R.	ER.	HR.	HB.	BB.	Int. BB.	SO.	WP.
Allen, Colorado Springs	5	3	.625	3.42	21	15	0	2	0	0	100.0	105	57	38	9	2	27	0	52	8
Atherton, Colorado Springs	0	1	.000	9.28	4	0	0	0	0	0	10.2	20	11	11	1	0	5	0	6	0
Barrett, Albuquerque	4	2	.667	3.99	47	0	0	13	0	0	67.2	67	32	30	5	1	25	1	46	5
Bearse, Colorado Springs*	5	2	.714	3.94	13	13	2	0	2	0	89.0	87	44	39	9	2	32	0	51	1
Benes, Las Vegas	2	1	.667	8.10	5	5	0	0	0	0	26.2	41	29	24	8	0	12	0	29	2
Bierley, Portland	0	0	.000	0.00	1	0	0	1	0	0	1.0	1	0	0	0	0	0	0	1	0
Bitker, 18 LV-24 Tac	3	4	.429	3.67	42	0	2	16	0	3	73.2	67	38	30	4	3	20	2	48	4
Bittiger, Vancouver	9	5	.643	2.12	17	17	6	0	4	0	123.0	93	31	29	5	4	40	0	122	3
Blair, Phoenix	0	0	.000	0.00	1	0	0	1	0	0	2.0	0	0	0	0	0	2	0	3	0
Blasucci, Vancouver*	3	1	.750	3.75	26	0	0	16	0	4	36.0	24	16	15	3	1	24	3	42	1
Booker, Portland	0	3	.000	6.07	14	11	0	0	0	0	46.0	57	35	31	4	2	22	0	23	1
Bordi, Tacoma	4	6	.400	3.61	41	10	3	25	1	11	97.1	82	46	39	7	0	28	2	75	0
Bowie, Calgary*	0	0	.000	13.50	1	0	0	0	0	0	2.0	7	5	3	1	0	1	0	0	0
Brantley, Phoenix	1	1	.500	1.26	7	0	0	5	0	3	14.1	6	2	2	1	1	6	0	20	0
Brennan, Albuquerque	6	9	.400	5.23	34	17	2	2	0	0	129.0	149	87	75	7	1	57	0	104	15
Buckels, Edmonton	0	3	.000	8.51	24	0	0	18	0	5	24.1	29	23	23	4	1	19	2	14	2
Burcham, Edmonton	0	0	.000	13.50	1	0	0	1	0	0	1.1	2	2	2	0	0	1	1	0	0
Burkett, Phoenix	10	11	.476	5.05	28	28	2	0	1	0	167.2	197	111	94	19	8	59	3	105	2
Burtt, Albuquerque	3	5	.375	5.94	28	14	0	4	0	1	109.0	141	81	72	14	1	42	1	38	8
Bystrom, Colorado Springs	4	1	.800	6.00	9	1	0	3	0	0	15.0	31	20	10	0	2	9	0	10	1
Camacho, Phoenix	3	0	1.000	1.47	40	0	0	24	0	13	55.0	33	10	9	3	5	16	2	59	2
Campbell, Calgary	6	5	.545	4.13	16	16	1	0	0	0	96.0	102	48	44	14	3	29	1	61	2
Cano, Tucson	5	5	.500	2.84	15	15	1	0	1	0	95.0	87	37	30	3	1	27	0	57	1
Casian, Portland*	7	12	.368	4.52	28	27	0	0	0	0	169.1	201	97	85	13	6	63	0	65	5
Chadwick, Vancouver	0	1	.000	7.30	6	2	0	1	0	0	12.1	11	10	10	1	2	12	0	8	1
Charland, Edmonton*	5	10	.333	5.49	25	21	2	1	0	0	136.0	150	87	83	19	3	75	5	107	6
Childress, Tucson	2	5	.286	4.48	50	0	0	16	0	1	78.1	90	46	39	7	0	33	8	48	2
B. Clark, Tacoma*	15	7	.682	3.14	28	28	4	0	2	0	174.2	154	77	61	4	3	85	0	112	4
T. Clark, Edmonton	11	5	.688	3.58	21	20	4	1	2	0	138.1	130	62	55	7	6	33	5	90	8
Clements, Las Vegas*	3	1	.750	4.09	18	6	0	4	0	2	55.0	57	31	25	5	1	24	5	34	3
Cliburn, Edmonton	1	4	.200	5.40	25	1	0	13	0	3	33.1	42	24	20	4	2	16	3	19	2
Close, Calgary	0	0	.000	0.00	1	0	0	1	0	0	2.0	1	0	0	0	0	2	0	0	0
Comstock, 28 LV-5 Cal.*	9	2	.818	2.93	33	0	0	27	0	10	55.1	45	19	18	3	2	21	3	64	4
D. Cook, Phoenix*	7	4	.636	3.12	12	12	3	0	1	0	78.0	73	29	27	4	1	19	0	85	4
M. Cook, Portland	5	3	.625	3.66	42	0	0	36	0	12	64.0	53	29	26	1	1	35	0	55	5
Corbett, Edmonton*	6	7	.462	4.41	52	0	0	35	0	9	63.1	58	33	31	11	2	45	8	43	2
Corsi, Tacoma	2	3	.400	4.13	23	0	0	18	0	8	28.1	40	17	13	1	1	9	4	23	2
Crew, Tucson	3	2	.600	4.71	34	0	0	12	0	2	57.1	59	33	30	4	4	23	5	55	1
Crews, Albuquerque	0	1	.000	7.71	2	0	0	2	0	0	2.1	3	2	2	0	0	0	0	2	0
Curtis, Colorado Springs*	0	1	.000	22.50	1	0	0	0	0	0	2.0	8	6	5	0	0	1	0	1	1
Dalena, Colorado Springs	0	0	.000	7.71	2	0	0	2	0	0	2.1	5	4	2	3	0	0	0	0	0
Davins, Portland	2	4	.333	5.58	25	0	0	15	0	2	40.1	53	28	25	6	2	15	0	26	0
D. Davis, Edmonton	0	0	.000	3.00	2	0	0	2	0	0	3.0	4	1	1	1	0	1	0	2	0
Joel Davis, Colorado Springs	6	9	.400	6.99	33	15	0	7	0	0	110.2	157	96	86	13	2	42	1	60	5
John Davis, Vancouver	4	3	.571	2.37	35	0	0	27	0	11	49.1	33	24	13	2	3	33	2	57	8
M. Davis, Vancouver	0	0	.000	0.00	1	0	0	1	0	0	1.0	0	0	0	0	0	0	0	0	0
R. Davis, Phoenix	0	1	.000	2.96	17	0	0	9	0	0	24.1	18	8	8	0	0	16	0	27	1
S. Davis, Colorado Springs*	12	2	.857	2.45	18	18	5	0	2	0	121.0	113	36	33	4	4	40	1	75	4
Dawley, Tacoma	3	1	.750	2.56	22	0	0	10	0	3	38.2	34	11	11	3	2	18	1	44	2
DeLeon, Calgary	4	4	.500	5.15	33	5	0	13	0	2	71.2	83	50	41	6	4	36	4	63	2
Dobie, Calgary	4	4	.500	4.60	15	14	0	0	0	0	72.1	69	41	37	3	3	39	3	41	1
Dominguez, Phoenix	1	2	.333	3.86	11	0	0	2	0	0	18.2	23	9	8	1	0	13	2	12	2
Downs, Phoenix	1	1	.500	8.68	3	3	0	0	0	0	9.1	11	9	9	1	0	5	0	9	0
Doyle, Calgary	2	2	.500	7.62	16	0	0	7	0	2	26.0	36	22	22	4	3	13	1	7	1
Dravecky, Phoenix*	1	0	1.000	2.00	1	1	1	0	0	0	9.0	7	2	2	0	0	0	0	3	0
Drees, Vancouver*	12	11	.522	3.37	26	26	4	0	3	0	168.1	142	76	63	12	4	72	2	66	2
Drummond, Portland	1	1	.500	3.27	10	0	0	5	0	1	22.0	19	9	8	1	0	8	0	21	1
Dunne, Calgary	4	0	1.000	3.31	9	9	0	0	0	0	51.2	54	26	19	3	3	25	0	19	2
Dunster, Tucson	0	1	.000	7.31	4	2	0	0	0	0	16.0	22	13	13	2	1	2	0	5	1
Dyer, Portland	3	6	.333	4.43	15	15	2	0	0	0	89.1	80	56	44	8	2	51	0	63	3
Edwards, Colorado Springs	1	1	.500	7.45	8	0	0	4	0	0	9.2	10	9	8	0	0	7	0	8	2
Falcone, Albuquerque*	0	0	.000	33.75	2	0	0	0	0	0	1.1	4	5	5	1	0	5	0	1	0
Fetters, Edmonton	12	8	.600	3.80	26	26	6	0	2	0	168.0	160	80	71	11	7	72	2	144	16
Fischer, Albuquerque	12	10	.545	3.47	28	26	5	0	2	0	171.0	186	78	66	16	3	35	3	112	2
Forrester, Vancouver*	0	0	.000	9.64	6	0	0	4	0	0	9.1	12	10	10	0	0	6	0	7	1
Freeland, Phoenix	1	2	.333	8.53	3	3	0	0	0	0	12.2	19	12	12	2	1	11	0	10	1
Ghelfi, Las Vegas	3	2	.600	5.05	18	3	0	7	0	0	41.0	51	29	23	3	4	23	0	28	1
Gilmore, Las Vegas	8	10	.444	4.70	29	28	4	1	1	1	172.1	199	100	90	17	4	25	3	108	2
Gonzalez, Portland	1	1	.500	3.91	17	0	0	9	0	0	25.1	26	11	11	3	0	13	0	24	3
Gordon, Colorado Springs	8	5	.615	5.08	63	2	0	19	0	1	106.1	149	75	60	8	7	36	5	76	5
Gunderson, Phoenix*	2	4	.333	5.04	14	14	2	0	1	0	85.2	93	51	48	7	2	36	2	56	7

Pitcher—Club	W.	L.	Pct.	ERA.	G.	GS.	CG.	GF.	ShO.	Sv.	IP.	H.	R.	ER.	HR.	HB.	BB.	Int. BB.	SO.	WP.
Guthrie, Portland*	3	4	.429	3.65	7	7	1	0	0	0	44.1	45	21	18	4	0	16	0	35	2
Hanson, Calgary	4	2	.667	6.87	8	8	1	0	0	0	38.0	51	30	29	1	2	11	0	37	4
Hardy, Vancouver	7	0	1.000	1.40	36	0	0	12	0	0	70.2	43	12	11	1	3	12	3	46	0
Harris, Calgary	0	0	.000	0.00	5	0	0	4	0	2	6.0	4	0	0	0	0	1	0	4	0
Hartley, Albuquerque	7	4	.636	2.79	58	0	0	50	0	18	77.1	53	31	24	4	2	34	2	76	4
Heathcock, Tucson	11	10	.524	3.73	28	28	4	0	2	0	183.1	202	90	76	8	6	30	2	73	4
Helton, Calgary*	2	0	1.000	5.02	8	0	0	1	0	0	14.1	17	9	8	0	1	9	0	10	3
Hensley, Calgary*	0	1	.000	7.94	17	0	0	5	0	0	17.0	22	16	15	3	0	10	4	19	3
Heredia, Albuquerque	2	3	.400	3.96	26	0	0	21	0	10	36.1	41	19	16	6	0	11	1	36	0
Hernandez, Portland	9	8	.529	3.91	24	19	2	3	0	0	140.1	124	71	61	13	2	38	0	83	0
Hibbard, Vancouver*	2	3	.400	2.64	9	9	2	0	1	0	58.0	47	24	17	3	1	11	0	45	5
Hill, Tacoma	0	0	.000	0.00	1	0	0	1	0	0	1.0	1	0	0	0	1	0	0	0	0
Hilton, Colorado Springs	1	0	1.000	5.40	3	0	0	1	0	0	5.0	6	3	3	0	0	2	0	1	0
Holcomb, Tacoma*	0	3	.000	11.93	10	1	0	3	0	1	14.1	16	21	19	2	0	19	1	12	2
Holmes, Albuquerque	1	4	.200	7.45	9	8	0	1	0	0	38.2	50	32	32	8	0	18	1	31	2
Hull, Calgary	3	2	.600	5.80	19	2	0	5	0	1	45.0	62	31	29	10	1	20	0	29	1
Ilsley, Tucson*	4	9	.308	5.85	20	17	1	0	0	0	103.0	120	68	67	12	6	23	2	49	2
Jennings, Tacoma*	0	0	.000	3.00	2	0	0	2	0	0	3.0	4	1	1	0	0	0	0	1	0
Johnson, Tucson	0	1	.000	1.20	7	0	0	0	0	0	15.0	12	2	2	0	0	6	1	8	0
Kaiser, Colorado Springs*	3	6	.333	4.37	31	1	0	12	0	3	45.1	64	29	22	1	1	18	1	46	3
Kelley, Tucson	3	6	.333	4.42	12	12	1	0	1	0	71.1	81	44	35	0	2	21	0	44	2
Kepshire, Portland	2	1	.667	5.59	16	0	0	5	0	0	29.0	34	20	18	1	0	15	2	22	1
Kerfeld, Tucson	3	11	.214	5.52	53	0	0	31	0	4	73.1	89	56	45	1	1	55	3	77	6
Kile, Tucson	2	1	.667	5.96	6	6	1	0	1	0	25.2	33	20	17	1	1	13	0	18	1
Klink, Tacoma*	0	0	.000	0.00	6	0	0	5	0	0	6.2	2	0	0	0	1	2	0	5	0
Kutzler, Vancouver	5	5	.500	3.83	12	12	2	0	0	0	80.0	76	37	34	6	7	20	1	36	0
Lambert, Tacoma*	2	0	1.000	4.71	36	0	0	12	0	0	63.0	67	36	33	3	0	36	3	49	6
Law, Tacoma	11	8	.579	3.78	31	28	4	1	0	0	171.1	169	87	72	16	2	84	4	114	4
Lazorko, Edmonton	8	5	.615	5.23	21	21	3	0	1	0	129.0	158	84	75	16	6	35	2	79	2
Leiper, Las Vegas*	2	2	.500	5.85	11	0	0	8	0	3	20.0	23	15	13	1	0	10	2	12	1
Little, Vancouver	1	1	.500	4.74	10	2	0	1	0	0	24.2	29	16	13	2	1	10	0	9	2
Long, Vancouver	1	2	.333	2.77	3	3	2	0	1	0	26.0	17	8	8	2	0	2	0	14	0
Lovelace, Edmonton*	0	7	.000	5.92	37	1	0	14	0	2	48.2	42	42	32	5	3	55	0	40	12
Lynch, Las Vegas	3	4	.429	5.15	44	0	0	20	0	4	71.2	111	45	41	9	0	12	1	27	0
Martinez, Albuquerque	10	2	.833	2.79	18	18	2	0	1	0	113.0	92	40	35	6	1	50	0	127	5
Mason, Tucson	7	12	.368	3.54	25	25	5	0	1	0	155.0	125	71	61	7	2	46	1	105	5
Mayberry, Albuquerque	8	4	.667	3.96	15	15	3	0	2	0	91.0	74	41	40	6	3	41	1	47	4
Maysey, Las Vegas	8	12	.400	4.08	28	28	4	0	1	0	176.1	173	94	80	19	2	84	3	96	12
McCament, Phoenix	3	0	1.000	3.62	22	0	0	6	0	1	37.1	40	15	15	4	2	12	1	13	1
McCarthy, Vancouver	2	4	.333	5.40	17	0	0	14	0	7	26.2	27	17	16	1	0	10	1	17	4
McClellan, Phoenix	3	4	.429	4.92	9	9	0	0	0	0	56.2	56	34	31	6	4	29	1	25	4
McDowell, Vancouver	5	6	.455	6.13	16	16	1	0	0	0	86.2	97	60	59	6	3	50	0	65	2
McLaughlin, Calgary	2	3	.400	5.36	40	4	0	16	0	3	87.1	98	54	52	4	2	62	2	58	6
McPhail, Vancouver	0	0	.000	0.00	1	0	0	0	0	0	0.1	1	0	0	0	0	1	0	0	0
Meads, Tucson*	0	0	.000	0.00	1	1	0	0	0	0	3.0	1	0	0	0	0	1	0	2	0
Melendez, Calgary	1	2	.333	5.75	17	2	0	4	0	0	40.2	42	27	26	6	3	19	2	24	1
Meyer, Tucson	5	4	.556	2.80	58	0	0	48	0	15	80.1	81	36	25	2	5	33	4	56	3
Meyers, Phoenix*	0	0	.000	0.00	1	0	0	1	0	0	1.0	0	0	0	0	0	1	0	0	0
Monteleone, Edmonton	3	6	.333	3.47	13	8	2	4	0	0	57.0	50	23	22	3	2	16	1	47	2
Mulholland, Phoenix*	4	5	.444	2.99	13	10	3	0	0	0	78.1	67	30	26	3	3	26	2	61	2
Munoz, Albuquerque*	6	4	.600	3.08	60	0	0	27	0	6	79.0	72	32	27	2	0	40	8	81	6
Murphy, Las Vegas	6	9	.400	4.20	27	21	3	2	2	2	133.0	129	75	62	9	3	78	1	93	12
Murray, Calgary	0	0	.000	4.50	1	0	0	1	0	0	2.0	2	1	1	0	2	0	2	1	0
Neidlinger, Albuquerque	8	6	.571	4.06	34	18	1	5	0	1	139.2	164	77	63	8	1	37	1	97	2
Nichols, Colorado Springs	8	1	.889	3.58	10	10	2	0	1	0	65.1	57	28	26	2	1	30	0	41	1
Niedenfuer, Calgary	1	2	.333	5.30	13	2	0	7	0	0	18.2	23	13	11	2	2	7	0	11	2
Nolte, Las Vegas*	6	9	.400	5.18	23	21	3	1	0	0	116.1	121	74	67	7	3	54	2	89	13
Norris, Tacoma	6	6	.500	3.18	23	12	2	3	1	1	82.0	78	39	29	6	6	27	3	72	2
Odekirk, Colorado Springs	0	0	.000	2.51	3	1	0	1	0	0	14.1	10	7	4	1	0	5	0	12	2
Olin, Colorado Springs	4	1	.800	3.22	42	0	0	38	0	24	50.1	34	18	18	6	3	15	3	46	0
Oliveras, Portland	6	4	.600	4.98	17	13	3	2	1	0	97.2	108	54	54	11	1	24	1	54	2
Oliverio, Calgary	0	0	.000	6.20	9	0	0	0	0	0	20.1	24	18	14	1	0	12	0	14	6
Olker, Phoenix*	8	6	.571	4.08	29	18	0	0	0	0	123.2	113	62	56	14	11	84	0	86	4
Otto, Tacoma*	10	13	.435	3.67	29	28	2	0	1	0	169.0	164	84	69	6	1	61	3	122	18
Palmer, Colorado Springs	2	2	.500	4.23	8	7	0	1	0	0	38.1	35	21	18	0	2	21	0	28	3
Patterson, Vancouver*	0	1	.000	1.00	2	2	0	0	0	0	9.0	6	2	1	0	1	1	0	17	2
Pawlowski, Vancouver	5	13	.278	3.30	29	16	1	6	0	0	122.2	120	51	45	5	3	51	2	88	6
Perez, Tacoma	0	0	.000	5.40	1	0	0	0	0	0	1.2	2	1	1	1	0	1	0	0	0
Peterson, Vancouver	14	5	.737	2.72	25	24	6	0	1	0	172.0	141	60	52	12	5	71	0	116	2
Portugal, Tacoma	7	5	.583	3.78	17	17	5	0	0	0	116.2	107	55	49	6	3	32	1	90	3
Powell, Calgary*	3	2	.600	2.13	18	0	0	14	0	6	25.1	21	10	6	0	1	12	0	15	0
Price, Calgary*	0	1	.000	5.54	5	3	0	1	0	0	13.0	17	8	8	1	0	9	0	10	1
Puikunas, Phoenix*	4	2	.667	5.30	48	0	0	18	0	2	74.2	84	52	44	10	5	46	3	52	7
Quinzer, Las Vegas	2	0	1.000	3.62	21	0	0	12	0	5	32.1	36	15	13	2	1	8	3	24	1
Remlinger, Phoenix*	1	6	.143	9.21	11	10	0	0	0	0	43.0	51	47	44	8	2	52	0	28	5
Rice, Calgary	6	3	.667	4.85	17	5	0	3	0	1	55.2	63	32	30	8	0	21	1	35	1
Ridenour, Calgary	2	1	.667	5.50	18	0	0	8	0	1	37.2	43	27	23	3	3	14	1	25	5
Roberts, Las Vegas*	6	6	.500	5.79	43	4	0	11	0	3	91.2	108	59	59	12	7	42	6	62	2
Rodriguez, Albuquerque	2	5	.286	6.31	13	12	0	1	0	0	61.1	90	47	43	4	5	22	0	26	2
Samuels, Phoenix*	0	3	.000	3.20	14	0	0	10	0	2	19.2	14	7	7	1	1	4	1	18	0
Schatzeder, Tucson*	0	2	.000	3.94	11	1	0	5	0	1	16.0	15	8	7	1	1	10	1	15	0
Scott, Colorado Springs	0	0	.000	8.53	7	1	0	0	0	0	6.1	14	8	6	1	0	3	0	4	0
Seanez, Colorado Springs	0	0	.000	0.00	1	0	0	1	0	0	1.0	1	0	0	0	0	0	0	0	0
Searage, Albuquerque*	0	1	.000	2.25	2	2	0	0	0	0	8.0	8	3	2	0	0	2	0	7	1
Segura, Vancouver	1	2	.333	2.30	44	0	0	32	0	17	66.2	50	21	17	0	0	19	2	52	1
Shaver, Calgary	6	7	.462	3.44	19	15	1	0	0	0	102.0	91	47	39	7	3	40	4	47	6
Shaw, 2 Colo. Spr.-25 Cal.	5	10	.333	5.18	27	24	3	1	1	0	154.2	152	95	89	17	3	76	3	97	8
Shields, Portland	2	2	.500	4.95	9	3	0	5	0	1	20.0	23	13	11	2	2	7	0	18	0
Shotkoski, Tacoma	0	0	.000	9.70	11	0	0	5	0	0	21.1	34	29	23	0	2	14	0	8	3
Skalski, Colorado Springs	2	6	.250	5.89	10	9	1	0	0	0	44.1	43	30	29	4	4	25	0	32	2
Smith, Vancouver	0	0	.000	22.50	1	0	0	1	0	0	2.0	5	5	5	1	0	1	0	0	0
Smithberg, Las Vegas	7	7	.500	4.47	22	22	4	0	0	0	137.0	159	79	68	9	4	35	2	58	3

Pitcher—Club	W.	L.	Pct.	ERA.	G.	GS.	CG.	GF.	ShO.	Sv.	IP.	H.	R.	ER.	HR.	HB.	BB.	Int. BB.	SO.	WP.
Snyder, Tacoma*	6	0	1.000	2.13	48	0	0	26	0	12	72.0	59	21	17	2	1	28	1	48	2
Soff, Portland	6	4	.600	3.81	29	6	0	15	0	5	85.0	83	38	36	6	2	27	1	59	1
Solano, Calgary	5	5	.500	3.93	43	0	0	39	0	20	52.2	63	28	23	6	0	24	3	36	8
Spagnola, Calgary	0	2	.000	7.90	4	2	0	0	0	0	13.2	16	12	12	1	1	7	0	10	0
Springer, Albuquerque	4	1	.800	4.83	8	7	0	0	0	0	41.0	58	28	22	5	0	14	0	18	1
St. Claire, Portland	4	0	1.000	3.18	27	1	0	17	0	3	45.1	39	21	16	1	0	17	1	48	6
Straker, Portland	8	9	.471	4.26	28	23	0	1	0	0	148.0	169	84	70	9	3	57	1	83	3
Swan, Phoenix*	4	3	.571	3.36	14	13	1	0	0	0	83.0	75	37	31	8	3	29	0	49	2
Tanner, 3 Tacoma-20 Phoe.	1	6	.143	2.77	23	5	0	9	0	1	61.2	57	24	19	7	1	23	1	21	1
Tapani, Portland	4	2	.667	2.20	6	6	1	0	0	0	41.0	38	15	10	4	0	12	1	30	0
Tate, Phoenix	3	7	.300	3.53	54	0	0	43	0	16	66.1	64	31	26	5	4	37	5	77	7
D. Taylor, Colo. Springs*	0	0	.000	13.50	1	0	0	1	0	0	2.0	4	3	3	1	0	1	0	1	0
T. Taylor, Calgary	2	3	.400	5.25	10	10	0	0	0	0	48.0	57	33	28	4	3	24	1	31	5
W. Taylor, Las Vegas	7	4	.636	5.13	47	0	0	22	0	1	79.0	93	48	45	5	2	27	5	71	1
Toliver, 8 Port.-5 Las Vegas	8	2	.800	2.57	13	13	4	0	2	0	84.0	72	32	24	2	2	31	0	72	3
Torve, Portland	0	0	.000	9.00	1	0	0	1	0	0	1.0	2	1	1	0	0	0	0	1	0
Trudeau, Edmonton	3	3	.500	3.41	17	12	3	2	0	0	87.0	79	35	33	2	0	26	3	47	4
Tunnell, Portland	2	4	.333	2.71	25	5	0	10	0	4	66.1	56	24	20	2	1	23	2	58	2
Villa, Phoenix	2	3	.400	2.97	14	0	0	8	0	3	30.1	24	10	10	0	2	18	1	29	5
Vosberg, 23 Tuc.-12 Alb.*	6	8	.429	6.02	35	14	0	5	0	1	107.2	139	78	72	11	3	54	7	86	8
M.A. Walker, Calgary	6	7	.462	6.44	18	17	2	0	1	0	88.0	119	74	63	15	2	37	3	46	7
M.C. Walker, Colo. Springs	6	15	.286	5.79	28	28	4	0	0	0	168.0	193	124	108	21	14	93	0	97	12
Walsh, Albuquerque*	1	2	.333	5.00	6	6	0	0	0	0	27.0	27	15	15	1	1	17	0	18	2
Walton, Tacoma	8	6	.571	3.76	32	14	1	7	1	0	107.2	118	59	45	7	1	27	1	76	3
Ward, 27 Edm.-14 Colo. Sp	4	2	.667	5.19	41	1	0	18	0	2	78.0	99	56	45	5	6	40	4	57	2
Weber, Tacoma	0	0	.000	7.36	6	0	0	2	0	0	11.0	8	9	9	1	1	7	0	6	0
Wells, Tucson*	0	5	.000	5.77	26	4	0	9	0	0	48.1	57	32	31	2	1	36	0	47	3
Wetteland, Albuquerque	5	3	.625	3.65	10	10	1	0	0	0	69.0	61	28	28	11	0	20	0	73	0
Wickander, Colo. Springs*	1	3	.250	2.95	45	0	0	26	0	11	42.2	40	14	14	2	4	27	5	41	1
Wilkinson, Calgary*	0	2	.000	5.40	2	2	0	0	0	0	6.2	8	4	4	0	0	7	0	1	2
Williams, Portland*	3	2	.600	4.18	16	0	0	8	0	3	23.2	24	15	11	0	0	18	0	22	2
Willis, Edmonton	5	7	.417	3.69	36	10	0	12	0	5	112.1	137	54	46	9	1	36	3	47	4
Wilson, Phoenix*	7	7	.500	3.12	23	20	2	0	0	0	115.1	109	49	40	5	2	76	1	77	5
Wojna, Colorado Springs	9	4	.692	2.87	19	19	4	0	2	0	122.1	116	50	39	7	2	36	1	81	5
C. Young, Edmonton*	8	9	.471	4.79	31	21	2	3	1	0	139.0	158	80	74	16	5	32	1	89	3
M. Young, Tacoma*	1	1	.500	2.45	2	2	0	0	0	0	11.0	8	4	3	0	0	5	0	6	0
Yurtin, Las Vegas	0	0	.000	.000	1	0	0	1	0	0	1.0	1	0	0	0	0	0	0	1	0
Zavaras, Calgary	6	9	.400	6.04	21	19	1	1	0	0	110.1	105	77	74	10	8	56	1	89	3

BALKS—Drees, 10; B. Clark, Olker, 9 each; Straker, 8; Wilson, 7; Cano, Murphy, Norris, 6 each; Allen, Hernandez, Nolte, 5 each; Dyer, Martinez, Puikunas, Smithberg, Villa, Vosberg, C. Young, 4 each; Charland, Childress, Crew, DeLeon, Lovelace, Maysey, Mulholland, Segura, Swan, W. Taylor, Willis, Zavaras, 3 each; Barrett, Benes, Booker, Burkett, Camacho, Casian, D. Cook, Dobie, Downs, Doyle, Dunne, Dunster, Fetters, Freeland, Ghelfi, Gonzalez, Heathcock, Helton, Kelley, Kepshire, Kerfeld, Law, McClellan, Nichols, Oliveras, Oliverio, Otto, Pawlowski, Shaver, Shaw, Tanner, Tate, Toliver, Tunnell, M.A. Walker, Walsh, Walton, Ward, Wells, Wickander, 2 each; Bearse, Bitker, Blasucci, Bordi, Brennan, Campbell, T. Clark, Corsi, John Davis, S. Davis, Dawley, Dravecky, Forrester, Gilmore, Gordon, Gunderson, Hardy, Hartley, Heredia, Kaiser, Kile, Lambert, Lazorko, Long, McDowell, McLaughlin, Meyer, Neidlinger, Portugal, Ridenour, Roberts, Samuels, Scott, Snyder, St. Claire, Tapani, D. Taylor, Trudeau, Weber, Williams, 1 each.

COMBINATION SHUTOUTS—Walsh-Neidlinger, Wetteland-Heredia, Martinez-Munoz, Neidlinger-Munoz-Hartley, Mayberry-Hartley, Albuquerque; Walker-Solano, Dobie-Helton, Calgary; Allen-Olin, Palmer-Ward, Colorado Springs; Monteleone-Young-Ward, Clark-Willis, Clark-Corbett, Fetters-Corbett, Charland-Corbett, Edmonton; Clements-Roberts-Bitker, Murphy-Clements-Lynch-Bitker, Roberts-Leiper, Maysey-Quinzer-Lynch, Las Vegas; Olker-Tate, Downs-Camacho-Tate, Cook-Mulholland-Tate, Wilson-Camacho, Gunderson-Brantley, Swan-Tate, Swan-Camacho, Remlinger-Dominguez-Camacho, Phoenix; Casian-Cook 2, Casian-Tunnell, Tunnell-Cook-Shields, Booker-Straker-Cook, Booker-Hernandez, Portland; Law-Snyder, Law-Snyder-Corsi, Shaver-Snyder, Walton-Snyder, Law-Bordi, Walton-Norris-Bitker-Snyder, Norris-Bordi, Tacoma; Heathcock-Meyer 2, Portugal-Meyer, Cano-Meyer, Mason-Kerfeld, Tucson; Kutzler-Segura 2, Peterson-Segura 2, Peterson-McCarthy, Pawlowski-Hardy, Little-Davis, Pawlowski-Davis, McDowell-Segura, Vancouver.

NO-HIT GAMES—Drees, Vancouver, defeated Calgary, 1-0, May 23; Drees, Vancouver, defeated Edmonton, 1-0 (first game), May 28; Drees, Vancouver, defeated Las Vegas, 5-0 (first game), August 16; Mason, Tucson, nine innings vs. Las Vegas, August 20 (lost 1-0 in 11 innings).

Eastern League

CLASS AA

Leading Batter
JIM LEYRITZ
Albany

League President
CHARLES ESHBACH

Leading Pitcher
STEVE ADKINS
Albany

CHAMPIONSHIP WINNERS IN PREVIOUS YEARS

1923—Williamsport .661	1948—Scranton† .636	1971—Three Rivers .569
1924—Williamsport .654	1949—Albany .664	Elmira b .561
1925—York§ .583	Binghamton (4th)‡ .500	1972—West Haven b .600
Williamsport§ .583	1950—Wilkes-Barre‡ .652	Three Rivers .559
1926—Scranton .627	1951—Wilkes-Barre .612	1973—Reading b .551
1927—Harrisburg .630	Scranton (2nd)† .562	Pittsfield .551
1928—Harrisburg .603	1952—Albany .603	1974—Thetford Mines (2nd)c .536
1929—Binghamton .597	Binghamton (2nd)‡ .562	Pittsfield (2nd) .496
1930—Wilkes-Barre .572	1953—Reading .682	1975—Reading .613
1931—Harrisburg .597	Binghamton (2nd)‡ .636	Bristol* .587
1932—Wilkes-Barre .561	1954—Wilkes-Barre .576	1976—Three Rivers .601
1933—Binghamton .690	Albany (3rd)‡ .540	West Haven d .576
1934—Binghamton .694	1955—Reading .613	1977—West Haven e .623
Williamsport* .603	Allentown (2nd)‡ .565	Three Rivers .551
1935—Scranton .657	1956—Schenectady† .609	1978—Reading .642
Binghamton* .580	1957—Binghamton .607	Bristol* .580
1936—Scranton* .609	Reading (3rd)‡ .529	1979—West Haven f .597
Elmira .629	1958—Lancaster x .568	1980—Holyoke* .561
1937—Elmira† .622	Binghamton (6th)‡ .493	Waterbury .540
1938—Binghamton .622	1959—Springfield† .607	1981—Glens Falls .615
Elmira (3rd)‡ .522	1960—Williamsport y .551	Bristol* .577
1939—Scranton† .571	Springfield (3rd)y .496	1982—West Haven* .614
1940—Scranton .568	1961—Springfield .612	Lynn .590
Binghamton (2nd)‡ .554	1962—Williamsport .593	1983—Lynn .554
1941—Wilkes-Barre .630	Elmira (2nd)‡ .514	New Britain‡ .518
Elmira (3rd)‡ .514	1963—Charleston .593	1984—Waterbury .543
1942—Albany .600	1964—Elmira .586	Vermont‡ .536
Scranton (2nd)‡ .593	1965—Pittsfield .607	1985—Albany .540
1943—Scranton .630	1966—Elmira .633	Vermont‡ .514
Elmira (2nd)‡ .568	1967—Binghamton z .586	1986—Reading .566
1944—Hartford .723	Elmira .532	Vermont‡ .554
Binghamton (4th)‡ .474	1968—Pittsfield .604	1987—Pittsfield .630
1945—Utica .615	Reading (2nd)‡ .579	Harrisburg‡ .550
Albany (3rd)‡ .564	1969—York .640	1988—Glens Falls .584
1946—Scranton† .691	1970—Waterbury a .560	Albany‡ .522
1947—Utica† .652	Reading a .553	

*Won split-season playoff. †Won championship and four-team playoff. ‡Won four-team playoff. §Tied for pennant, York winning playoff. xLeague was divided into Northern, Southern divisions and played a split season; Lancaster over-all season leader. yPlayoff finals canceled after one game because of rain with Williamsport and Springfield declared playoff co-champions. zLeague was divided into Eastern, Western divisions; Binghamton won playoff. aTied for pennant, Waterbury winning playoff. bLeague was divided into American, National divisions; won playoff. cLeague was divided into American and National divisions; won four-team playoff. dLeague was divided into Northern, Southern divisions, won playoff. eLeague was divided into New England and Canadian-American divisions; won playoff. fWon both halves of split season (no playoffs). (NOTE—Known as New York-Pennsylvania League prior to 1938.)

STANDING OF CLUBS AT CLOSE OF SEASON, AUGUST 31

Club	Alb.	Har.	C.A.	Read.	Hag.	Lon.	Wpt.	N.B.	W.	L.	T.	Pct.	G.B.
Albany (Yankees)	....	11	13	12	16	13	12	15	92	48	0	.657	....
Harrisburg (Pirates)	9	....	12	10	8	12	10	10	71	65	0	.522	19
Canton-Akron (Indians)	7	8	....	13	11	10	11	10	70	69	0	.504	21½
Reading (Phillies)	8	10	7	....	9	11	11	12	68	71	0	.489	23½
Hagerstown (Orioles)	4	12	9	10	....	10	13	9	67	72	0	.482	24½
London (Tigers)	7	8	9	9	10	....	10	10	63	76	0	.453	28½
Williamsport (Mariners)	8	10	9	9	7	10	....	10	63	77	0	.450	29
New Britain (Red Sox)	5	6	10	8	11	10	10	....	60	76	0	.441	30

London club represented London, Ont., Can.

Major league affiliations in parentheses.

Playoffs—Harrisburg defeated Canton-Akron, three games to two; Albany defeated Reading, three games to one; Albany defeated Harrisburg, three games to one, to win league championship.

Regular-Season Attendance—Albany, 192,862; Canton-Akron, 204,001; Hagerstown, 161,630; Harrisburg, 200,196; London, 167,679; New Britain, 100,943; Reading, 178,734; Williamsport, 66,767. Total—1,272,812. Playoffs—(13 games) 27,595. All-Star Game—1,847.

Managers—Albany, Buck Showalter; Canton-Akron, Bob Molinaro; Hagerstown, Jim Schaffer; Harrisburg, Dave Trembley; London, Chris Chambliss; New Britain, Butch Hobson; Reading, Mike Hart; Williamsport, Jay Ward.

All-Star Team—1B—Rob Sepanek, Albany; 2B—Andy Stankiewicz, Albany; 3B—Leo Gomez, Hagerstown; SS—Travis Fryman, London; OF—Wes Chamberlain, Harrisburg; Beau Allred, Canton-Akron; Joey Belle, Canton-Akron; DH—Troy Neel, Canton-Akron; RHP—Rodney Imes, Albany; LHP—Steve Adkins, Albany; RP—Daryl Irvine, New Britain; Most Valuable Player—Wes Chamberlain, Harrisburg; Pitcher of the Year—Rodney Imes, Albany; Manager of the Year—Buck Showalter, Albany.

(Compiled by Howe Sportsdata International, Boston, Mass.)

CLUB BATTING

Club	Pct.	G.	AB.	R.	OR.	H.	TB.	2B.	3B.	HR.	RBI.	SH.	SF.	HP.	BB.	Int. BB.	SO.	SB.	CS.	LOB.
Albany	.268	140	4356	642	453	1166	1686	186	23	96	580	37	43	62	523	31	797	154	64	961
Harrisburg	.264	136	4292	553	522	1131	1620	182	29	83	502	19	31	39	342	18	678	114	60	844
Canton-Akron	.262	139	4377	584	558	1147	1635	174	25	88	534	33	47	36	568	28	758	126	78	951
London	.248	139	4493	557	610	1113	1612	183	23	90	496	26	33	41	437	20	808	134	56	928
Hagerstown	.244	139	4457	536	539	1087	1497	179	30	57	477	29	36	38	484	20	898	137	61	940
Reading	.242	139	4365	545	601	1058	1449	154	30	59	492	27	33	43	499	28	790	121	76	928
Williamsport	.235	140	4480	515	570	1053	1506	199	28	66	454	34	46	48	421	33	915	110	59	900
New Britain	.232	136	4243	445	534	984	1352	186	28	42	395	61	34	45	452	15	802	75	59	909

INDIVIDUAL BATTING

(Leading Qualifiers for Batting Championship—378 or More Plate Appearances)

*Bats lefthanded.   †Switch-hitter.

Player and Club	Pct.	G.	AB.	R.	H.	TB.	2B.	3B.	HR.	RBI.	SH.	SF.	HP.	BB.	Int. BB.	SO.	SB.	CS.
Leyritz, James, Albany	.315	114	375	53	118	170	18	2	10	66	2	5	9	65	5	51	2	1
Chamberlain, Wesley, Harrisburg	.306	129	471	65	144	239	26	3	21	87	0	7	2	32	4	82	11	10
Allred, Dale, Canton-Akron*	.303	118	412	67	125	200	23	5	14	75	2	8	2	56	2	88	16	5
Maas, Jason, Albany*	.296	114	382	57	113	147	19	0	5	39	4	2	2	61	3	74	24	7
Neel, Troy, Canton-Akron*	.292	124	404	58	118	206	21	2	21	73	0	5	9	51	6	87	5	9
Clark, Phillip, London	.290	104	373	43	108	155	15	4	8	42	2	1	8	31	1	49	2	2
Shields, Thomas, Harrisburg	.288	123	417	66	120	156	13	4	5	47	2	3	9	25	3	62	17	5
Bellino, Frank, Reading*	.285	133	453	55	129	188	25	2	10	77	0	2	3	57	7	60	2	1
Burdick, Kevin, Harrisburg	.285	96	369	40	105	144	16	1	7	34	5	1	2	23	2	23	5	3
Gomez, Leonardo, Hagerstown	.281	134	448	71	126	209	23	3	18	78	0	5	5	89	6	102	2	2

Departmental Leaders: G—Martinez, 137; AB—Martinez, 509; R—Stankiewicz, 74; H—Chamberlain, 144; TB—Chamberlain, 239; 2B—Fryman, 30; 3B—Parker, 9; HR—Sepanek, 22; RBI—Chamberlain, 87; SH—Milstien, 10; SF—Stankiewicz, 11; HP—Four players tied with 9; BB—Gomez, 89; IBB—Martinez, 13; SO—J. Smith, 117; SB—Stankiewicz, 41; CS—Housie, 14.

(All Players—Listed Alphabetically)

Player and Club	Pct.	G.	AB.	R.	H.	TB.	2B.	3B.	HR.	RBI.	SH.	SF.	HP.	BB.	Int. BB.	SO.	SB.	CS.
Agostinelli, Salvatore, Reading	.244	79	258	27	63	72	6	0	1	23	1	2	1	32	1	24	7	4
Aldrich, Thomas, London	.228	113	382	36	87	127	11	1	9	43	2	4	3	29	1	61	2	1
Allred, Dale, Canton-Akron*	.303	118	412	67	125	200	23	5	14	75	2	8	2	56	2	88	16	5
Alou, Moises, Harrisburg	.293	54	205	36	60	78	5	2	3	19	0	2	0	17	1	38	8	4
Anderson, Bernard, London*	.171	31	105	17	18	24	0	0	2	8	0	2	0	11	1	12	2	0
Arendas, Daniel, Albany*	.258	30	97	10	25	31	3	0	1	11	0	0	4	10	1	16	2	2
Austin, Dominic, London	.255	83	298	46	76	94	10	1	2	19	4	3	1	44	2	48	30	6
Azocar, Oscar, Albany*	.279	92	362	50	101	132	15	2	4	47	8	4	0	10	4	31	11	6
Balthazar, Doyle, London	.233	62	193	17	45	72	6	0	7	20	1	1	1	18	0	36	5	1
Banister, Jeffery, Harrisburg	.238	102	336	48	80	129	13	0	12	48	1	2	4	30	0	57	2	1
Becker, Timothy, Albany	.247	90	291	36	72	95	16	2	1	34	4	6	3	10	0	25	14	8
Belle, Joseph, Canton-Akron	.282	89	312	48	88	168	20	0	20	69	0	2	4	32	5	82	8	4
Bellino, Frank, Reading*	.285	133	453	55	129	188	25	2	10	77	0	2	3	57	7	60	2	1
Bettendorf, David, Hagerstown*	.276	132	489	54	135	181	20	1	8	60	0	3	1	52	5	74	4	5
Beyeler, Arnold, London	.100	5	10	0	1	1	0	0	0	1	1	0	0	0	0	3	0	0
Boever, Daniel, Canton-Akron	.265	51	132	16	35	50	5	2	2	13	0	1	3	11	0	15	5	3
Bowie, James, Williamsport*	.262	11	42	3	11	16	5	0	0	1	0	0	0	5	0	7	0	0
Bradshaw, Kevin, London	.250	2	4	1	1	1	0	0	0	0	0	0	0	0	0	0	0	0
Brocki, Michael, Williamsport	.189	21	74	15	14	20	3	0	1	8	3	0	0	14	0	14	10	3
Brumfield, Harvey, Reading*	.273	62	187	25	51	65	8	0	2	28	0	1	1	21	3	34	12	8
Brundage, David, Williamsport*	.273	93	322	60	88	124	18	3	4	28	1	1	2	60	3	57	16	6
Bruske, James, Canton-Akron	.239	51	134	17	32	40	5	0	1	7	2	1	1	19	1	28	3	1
Brusky, Brad, Williamsport	.000	33	1	0	0	0	0	0	0	0	0	0	0	0	0	0	0	0
Buford, Don, Hagerstown†	.192	100	333	51	64	90	8	3	4	24	4	2	1	42	0	54	30	4
Burdick, Kevin, Harrisburg	.285	96	369	40	105	144	16	1	7	34	5	1	2	23	2	23	5	3
Calvert, Christopher, Reading	.247	64	178	14	44	62	6	3	2	20	1	3	4	10	0	29	4	3
Chamberlain, Wesley, Harrisburg	.306	129	471	65	144	239	26	3	21	87	0	7	2	32	4	82	11	10
Chance, Anthony, 49 Hrb-67 Hag.	.262	71	260	35	68	116	16	4	8	46	0	2	5	14	0	69	11	3
Cijntje, Sherwin, 57 Hag-17 Can*	.252	74	238	42	60	65	3	1	0	12	1	2	1	30	2	41	19	12
Citari, Joseph, Reading	.223	87	269	38	60	103	16	0	9	42	0	1	7	45	1	74	1	1
Clark, Phillip, London	.290	104	373	43	108	155	15	4	8	42	2	1	8	31	1	49	2	2
Conroy, Timothy, Harrisburg*	.000	4	2	0	0	0	0	0	0	0	0	0	0	0	0	0	0	0
Cook, Jeffrey, Harrisburg†	.286	18	63	11	18	21	1	0	0	3	1	0	0	9	0	11	7	0

Player and Club	Pct.	G	AB	R	H	TB	2B	3B	HR	RBI	SH	SF	HP	BB	Int. BB	SO	SB	CS
Cooper, Scott, New Britain*	.247	124	421	50	104	153	24	2	7	39	5	5	6	55	2	84	1	1
Crowley, Terrence, Harrisburg†	.248	30	101	9	25	28	1	1	0	9	2	1	1	5	0	11	2	0
Cuyler, Milton, London†	.262	98	366	69	96	139	8	7	7	34	4	0	4	47	2	74	32	5
Davis, Harry, Williamsport	.209	39	139	15	29	45	6	2	2	18	1	2	2	7	0	27	4	5
DeCillis, Dean, London	.245	98	375	47	92	123	14	1	5	46	1	0	2	31	0	47	4	4
Diaz, William, Williamsport	.191	32	115	9	22	32	5	1	1	13	0	2	1	8	0	34	0	1
Dickerson, Bobby, Albany	.255	21	55	8	14	19	2	0	1	5	1	0	2	0	0	12	1	0
Doyle, Richard, Williamsport	.000	26	0	0	0	0	0	0	0	0	0	0	0	0	0	0	0	0
Dunlap, Joseph, Williamsport	.207	71	237	27	49	62	7	0	2	15	5	1	3	26	1	33	7	0
Eberle, Michael, Hagerstown	.202	88	272	21	55	70	12	0	1	21	5	4	4	19	2	60	2	3
Edge, Gregory, Reading†	.244	24	78	8	19	20	1	0	0	4	1	1	0	6	1	3	0	2
Edmonds, Bobby Joe, Reading	.198	26	101	9	20	28	1	2	1	8	0	0	0	7	0	25	5	4
Edwards, Jeffrey, Canton-Akron*	.000	39	1	0	0	0	0	0	0	0	0	0	0	0	0	0	0	0
Estrada, Eduardo, New Britain	.095	7	21	0	2	4	0	1	0	2	0	1	0	3	0	3	0	0
Fagnant, Ray, New Britain	.000	3	8	0	0	0	0	0	0	0	0	0	0	0	0	3	0	0
Faulkner, Craig, Hagerstown	.210	81	272	27	57	93	8	2	8	30	0	2	2	22	1	97	0	2
Ferretti, Samuel, Canton-Akron	.250	5	4	1	1	1	0	0	0	1	0	0	0	0	0	0	0	1
Finley, Steven, Hagerstown*	.417	11	48	11	20	25	3	1	0	7	0	1	0	4	0	3	4	0
Foley, Martin, Reading	.202	85	257	26	52	66	4	2	2	25	5	2	5	13	0	53	5	6
Foster, Lindsay, Canton-Akron†	.265	70	181	27	48	51	3	0	0	8	3	1	1	14	0	33	15	6
Fryman, Travis, London	.265	118	426	52	113	172	30	1	9	56	2	4	8	19	0	78	5	3
Fulton, Gregory, Williamsport†	.067	4	15	1	1	1	0	0	0	0	0	0	0	1	0	1	0	0
Garcia, Carlos, Harrisburg	.282	54	188	28	53	77	5	5	3	25	0	1	0	8	0	36	6	4
Gilles, Mark, Canton-Akron	.000	16	1	0	0	0	0	0	0	0	0	0	0	0	0	1	0	0
Goff, Jerry, Williamsport*	.185	33	119	9	22	36	5	0	3	8	0	0	1	14	2	42	1	1
Gomez, Leonardo, Hagerstown	.281	134	448	71	126	209	23	3	18	78	0	5	5	89	6	102	2	2
Green, Robert, Albany	.259	71	232	30	60	96	12	0	8	39	1	6	0	31	0	60	1	3
Grotewold, Jeffrey, Reading*	.200	25	80	9	16	18	2	0	0	11	0	2	0	8	0	14	0	0
Hall, Andrew, Harrisburg	.167	7	18	4	3	7	1	0	1	2	0	1	0	2	0	4	0	0
Haney, Todd, Williamsport	.269	115	401	59	108	142	20	4	2	31	7	3	5	49	2	43	13	8
Hansen, Roger, Williamsport	.237	14	38	6	9	11	2	0	0	4	0	0	1	5	0	8	0	0
Hartman, Edward, Harrisburg	.262	68	214	27	56	88	10	2	6	33	1	1	3	15	0	39	2	1
Henderson, Ramon, Reading	.217	92	290	31	63	72	9	0	0	22	4	1	2	31	1	56	1	0
Hithe, Victor, Hagerstown	.277	124	451	67	125	160	21	7	0	44	2	2	5	36	0	85	29	12
Holtz, Gerald, Reading*	.227	103	321	44	73	102	15	4	2	30	2	4	2	75	3	61	11	6
Holyfield, Vince, Reading	.243	70	255	35	62	88	3	1	7	29	2	3	4	15	2	66	21	8
Hooper, Jeffrey, Williamsport	.224	70	259	23	58	91	9	0	8	43	0	1	4	9	1	72	0	1
Housie, Wayne, London†	.237	127	434	56	103	139	17	2	5	28	3	3	4	52	3	90	23	14
Howard, Christopher, Williamsport	.253	86	296	30	75	115	13	0	9	36	2	0	5	28	0	79	0	1
Jackson, Leverne, New Britain	.260	114	338	40	88	119	18	2	3	30	3	3	1	58	1	71	11	10
Jose, Manuel, London†	.243	112	367	45	89	138	21	5	6	43	5	2	1	25	0	91	11	11
Kelly, Michael, New Britain	.271	62	214	20	58	80	12	2	2	30	2	0	0	18	0	32	2	1
Kerkes, Kevin, Williamsport	.165	24	79	6	13	17	0	2	0	7	0	1	0	15	1	12	2	1
Khoury, Scott, Canton-Akron*	.168	45	113	11	19	29	3	2	1	14	1	3	0	23	1	16	2	2
Kosco, Andrew, Williamsport*	.188	56	181	15	34	46	9	0	1	19	0	2	1	12	2	48	1	0
Latmore, Robert, Hagerstown	.227	104	348	30	79	108	15	1	4	33	2	2	0	22	0	73	1	2
Leiper, Timothy, London†	.366	27	101	13	37	46	6	0	1	9	0	1	1	13	1	10	0	2
Leiva, Jose, Canton-Akron	.216	38	116	15	25	31	4	1	0	7	2	1	2	13	1	12	14	6
Lennon, Patrick, Williamsport	.262	66	248	32	65	92	14	2	3	31	0	5	0	23	2	53	7	4
Lewis, Mark, Canton-Akron	.200	7	25	4	5	6	1	0	0	1	0	0	0	1	0	3	0	0
Leyritz, James, Albany*	.315	114	375	53	118	170	18	2	10	66	2	5	9	65	5	51	2	1
Liebert, Allen, Canton-Akron*	.240	89	258	28	62	97	8	0	9	40	0	3	0	27	2	64	0	1
Livingstone, Scott, London*	.217	124	452	46	98	160	18	1	14	71	0	6	2	52	4	67	1	1
Longmire, Anthony, Harrisburg*	.291	37	127	15	37	53	7	0	3	22	1	0	1	12	0	21	1	0
Lovell, Donald, London*	.255	31	94	12	24	29	5	0	0	9	0	1	0	10	0	7	0	1
Lyden, Mitchell, Albany	.238	53	181	24	43	63	2	0	6	21	1	0	2	12	3	51	1	0
Maas, Jason, Albany*	.296	114	382	57	113	147	19	0	5	39	4	2	2	61	3	74	24	7
Magallanes, Everardo, Canton-Akron*	.278	74	241	26	67	72	5	0	0	18	4	3	1	37	0	24	1	6
Magrann, Thomas, Canton-Akron	.246	108	334	36	82	108	10	2	4	42	1	4	3	45	1	45	7	9
Marchese, Joseph, New Britain	.180	75	211	13	38	41	3	0	0	11	6	1	1	9	0	18	4	3
Martinez, Constantino, Williamsport*	.257	137	509	51	131	203	29	2	13	64	1	8	0	59	13	54	7	1
McDougal, Julius, 73 Can-45 N. Brit.†	.215	118	382	40	82	97	9	0	2	28	5	3	3	44	1	71	14	9
McElroy, Charles, Reading*	1.000	32	1	0	1	1	0	0	0	0	0	0	0	0	0	0	0	0
McKinley, Timothy, Harrisburg	.163	57	135	11	22	25	3	0	0	10	2	0	0	19	0	26	0	0
Merced, Orlando, Harrisburg†	.240	95	341	43	82	124	16	4	6	48	1	4	2	32	6	65	13	3
Meulens, Hensley, Albany	.257	104	335	55	86	131	8	2	11	45	0	1	9	61	0	108	3	2
Miller, Johan, Williamsport*	.333	3	9	1	3	3	0	0	0	2	0	0	0	0	0	0	0	0
Milstien, David, New Britain	.252	106	345	34	87	97	10	0	0	27	10	2	2	23	0	50	5	5
Mims, Larry, Hagerstown†	.222	7	18	4	4	4	0	0	0	0	0	0	0	2	0	1	0	1
Morandini, Michael, Reading*	.351	48	188	39	66	95	12	1	5	29	1	0	1	23	4	32	5	5
Moritz, Christopher, New Britain	.187	43	123	10	23	27	4	0	0	6	3	1	3	9	2	21	2	1
Neel, Troy, Canton-Akron*	.292	124	404	58	118	206	21	2	21	73	0	5	9	51	6	87	5	9
Nichols, Ty, Hagerstown*	.210	114	410	37	86	117	14	4	3	38	4	6	2	26	2	90	5	2
Orsag, James, 56 N.B.-3 Can*	.195	59	174	20	34	49	10	1	1	16	3	3	1	32	1	51	8	6
Osborne, Jeffrey, Williamsport*	.271	19	59	9	16	20	1	0	1	4	0	1	0	8	0	13	0	0
Padilla, Livio, New Britain	.158	71	215	12	34	45	6	1	1	18	4	3	3	17	1	61	1	4
Parker, Richard, Reading	.237	103	388	59	92	126	7	9	3	32	2	3	5	42	0	62	17	13
Peguero, Julio, Harrisburg†	.246	76	284	34	70	92	14	1	2	21	1	0	2	29	0	39	14	12
Perez, Julio, Harrisburg	.244	83	246	34	60	77	3	0	3	18	1	0	6	19	0	40	8	1
Pina, John, New Britain	.260	46	154	22	40	56	10	0	2	26	0	3	3	26	0	47	4	5
Posey, John, 10 Hag-60 Rea	.205	70	224	25	46	64	7	1	3	25	1	0	4	21	1	34	2	0
Pratt, Todd, New Britain	.228	109	338	30	77	102	17	1	2	35	1	5	7	44	1	66	1	2
Ramos, John, Albany	.273	105	359	55	98	146	21	0	9	60	2	7	4	40	2	65	7	5
Randle, Randy, New Britain	.239	105	351	41	84	118	12	8	2	25	5	1	0	31	2	79	13	8
Razook, Mark, Williamsport	.238	77	256	30	61	86	7	3	4	24	1	4	7	17	1	71	0	2
Rodriguez, Carlos, Albany	.252	36	107	15	27	35	4	2	0	8	3	1	0	13	0	4	1	1
Roman, Daniel, Albany	.195	15	41	2	8	8	0	0	0	5	2	0	0	0	0	8	0	0
Rosario, Victor, Reading	.235	64	213	16	50	67	8	0	3	16	2	0	0	10	0	33	7	6
Rossy, Elam, Harrisburg	.252	78	238	20	60	84	16	1	2	25	0	2	3	27	0	19	2	4
Rowland, Donald, London	.381	7	21	4	8	9	1	0	0	3	1	0	0	1	0	2	0	0
Ruiz, Benny, Canton-Akron	.111	22	54	2	6	6	0	0	0	4	3	1	0	1	0	6	0	0
Sanders, Deion, Albany*	.286	33	119	28	34	43	2	2	1	6	1	0	7	11	1	20	17	5

Player and Club	Pct.	G.	AB.	R.	H.	TB.	2B.	3B.	HR.	RBI.	SH.	SF.	HP.	BB.	Int. BB.	SO.	SB.	CS.
Scarsone, Steven, Reading	.179	75	240	30	43	60	5	0	4	22	5	4	1	15	2	67	2	2
Scott, Charles, Canton-Akron	.000	26	3	0	0	0	0	0	0	0	0	0	0	0	0	1	0	0
Segui, David, Hagerstown†	.324	44	173	22	56	75	14	1	1	27	1	2	2	16	0	16	0	0
Sepanek, Robert, Albany°	.264	112	367	56	97	180	15	1	22	77	1	2	1	55	6	99	1	2
Service, Scott, Reading	.500	23	2	0	1	1	0	0	0	0	0	0	0	0	0	0	0	0
Shaw, Scott, Albany	.242	75	240	26	58	76	12	0	2	26	1	2	2	22	0	42	2	0
Shields, Thomas, Harrisburg	.288	123	417	66	120	156	13	4	5	47	2	3	9	25	3	62	17	5
Simonds, Daniel, Hagerstown	.246	46	114	7	28	32	2	1	0	7	5	0	2	9	0	7	2	2
Skeete, Rafel, Hagerstown°	.208	51	159	17	33	42	7	1	0	13	2	2	4	28	1	42	21	6
Smith, Dana, Hagerstown	.223	77	233	29	52	65	5	1	2	23	2	1	2	46	0	46	2	4
Smith, Jackson, Williamsport	.211	134	437	39	92	130	21	1	5	33	4	8	6	35	2	117	1	6
Snyder, Cory, Canton-Akron	.455	4	11	3	5	5	0	0	0	2	0	0	1	0	1	1	0	0
Sommers, Scott, New Britain°	.208	59	144	11	30	37	5	1	0	10	1	1	4	21	1	16	1	3
Spann, Emmanuel, London	.204	27	93	8	19	28	3	0	2	10	0	1	4	6	0	34	3	1
Stanicek, Peter, Hagerstown†	.253	47	154	15	39	46	7	0	0	13	0	1	1	26	1	27	6	1
Stankiewicz, Andrew, Albany	.267	133	498	74	133	175	26	2	4	49	3	11	8	57	2	59	41	9
Strijek, Randy, Hagerstown	.194	22	72	3	14	17	3	0	0	6	2	1	1	4	0	15	0	0
Swain, Robert, Canton-Akron	.256	108	347	42	89	115	12	4	2	32	7	2	3	32	2	47	5	1
Tatis, Bernardo, Harrisburg†	.286	19	70	12	20	30	5	1	1	6	0	0	0	7	0	17	7	1
Taylor, Dwight, Canton-Akron°	.278	9	36	8	10	13	3	0	0	1	0	0	0	2	0	3	0	0
Toale, John, London°	.244	86	234	25	57	84	9	0	6	32	0	4	1	26	2	52	1	0
Torres, Ricardo, Albany	.000	24	1	0	0	0	0	0	0	0	0	0	0	0	0	0	0	0
Turner, Shane, Reading°	.199	46	141	18	28	38	5	1	1	11	0	0	2	27	1	27	13	3
Twardoski, Michael, Canton-Akron°	.274	113	380	56	104	127	19	2	0	36	4	4	0	77	2	47	7	7
Uribe, Jorge, Williamsport	.220	52	159	21	35	55	3	1	5	24	3	3	4	12	1	32	3	5
Valdez, Efrain, Canton-Akron°	.000	44	1	0	0	0	0	0	0	0	1	0	0	0	0	0	0	0
Vatcher, James, Reading	.327	48	171	27	56	85	11	3	4	32	0	4	1	26	1	29	2	0
Vaughn, Maurice, New Britain°	.278	73	245	28	68	107	15	0	8	38	1	1	3	25	3	47	1	3
Vizcaino, Reyes, Harrisburg	.158	17	57	5	9	12	1	1	0	6	0	1	0	4	0	21	0	0
Ward, Turner, Canton-Akron†	.301	30	93	19	28	35	5	1	0	3	0	0	0	15	0	16	1	2
Webster, Casey, Canton-Akron	.276	123	406	47	112	153	17	0	8	58	1	4	5	65	3	71	13	7
Wedge, Eric, New Britain	.200	14	40	3	8	10	2	0	0	2	2	0	0	5	0	10	0	0
Williams, Bernabe, Albany†	.252	91	314	63	79	139	11	8	11	42	3	1	6	60	4	72	26	13
Williams, Jeffrey, 30 Rea.-18 Wpt.° *	.242	48	165	16	40	51	5	3	0	12	0	0	0	12	0	26	6	3
Williams, Ted, Williamsport†	.247	133	477	59	118	158	21	5	3	40	6	5	6	20	2	97	37	13
Wooden, Mark, Williamsport	.000	46	2	0	0	0	0	0	0	0	0	0	0	0	0	1	0	0
Yacopino, Edward, Harrisburg°	.264	94	337	35	89	133	19	2	7	33	1	4	4	19	2	50	9	4
Young, Delwyn, 48 Lon-29 Can†	.229	77	266	41	61	118	15	3	12	33	0	1	0	37	4	66	20	5
Zambrano, Eduardo, New Britain	.219	54	169	15	37	56	8	1	3	11	4	0	4	14	0	27	3	1
Zambrano, Roberto, New Britain	.291	68	230	43	67	116	13	6	8	28	0	1	4	23	3	31	0	2
Zupcic, Robert, New Britain	.217	94	346	37	75	97	12	2	2	28	7	2	1	19	0	55	15	1

The following pitchers, listed alphabetically by club, with games in parentheses, had no plate appearances, primarily through use of designated hitters:

ALBANY—Adkins, Steven (16); Chapin, Darrin (7); Christopher, Michael (8); Clayton, Royal (25); Davidson, Robert (12); DeLeon, Pedro (17); Fulton, William (10); Green, John (20); Howard, Christian (24); Imes, Rodney (24); Kamieniecki, Scott (24); Layana, Timothy (40); Mmahat, Kevin (8); Pena, Hipolito (4); Rub, Jerry (18); Sherlock, Glenn (1); Tirado, Aristarco (11).

CANTON-AKRON—Bearse, Kevin (14); Collins, Allen (11); Dixon, Kenneth (4); Ferlenda, Gregory (12); Gonzales, Todd (12); Keliipuleole, Carl (27); Kramer, Thomas (10); Kuzniar, Paul (26); McMichael, Gregory (26); Nagy, Charles (15); Ogden, Todd (6); Poehl, Michael (3); Shaw, Jeffrey (32); Stoddard, Timothy (5); Surhoff, Richard (21).

HAGERSTOWN—Bell, Eric (9); Borgatti, Michael (1); Cavers, Michael (12); Culkar, Steven (26); DeLaRosa, Francisco (18); Dixon, Kenneth (6); DuBois, Brian (15); Garces, Robinson (32); Githens, John (27); Householder, Brian (8); Linskey, Michael (18); Mejia, Cesar (11); Mesa, Jose (3); Myers, Chris (6); Pinder, Christopher (9); Sander, Michael (32); Schwarz, Jeffrey (17); Sonberg, Erik (7); Stanhope, Chester (6); Thorpe, Paul (39); Williams, Robert (12).

HARRISBURG—Adams, Steven (28); Belinda, Stanley (32); Lind, Orlando (6); Melton, Lawrence (23); Murphy, Peter (26); Richardson, Keith (21); Ruskin, Scott (12); Russell, Robert (44); Sampen, William (12); Smith, Willie (12); Tomlin, Randy (5); Tracy, James (44); Webb, Benjamin (23); York, Michael (18).

LONDON—Aldred, Scott (20); Cooper, David (25); Everson, Gregory (47); Haas, Robert (18); Hansen, Michael (18); Hursey, Darrin (27); Nosek, Randall (22); O'Neill, Daniel (20); Ramos, Jose (33); Rightnowar, Ronald (36); Schwabe, Michael (8); Vesling, Donald (13); Wenson, Paul (27); Wilkins, Michael (11); Williams, Kenneth (3).

NEW BRITAIN—Araujo, Anazario (1); Bast, Steven (8); Boyd, Dennis (1); Carista, Michael (24); Crouch, Zachary (15); Dalton, Michael (18); Gabriele, Daniel (26); Gale, Richard (2); Irvine, Daryl (54); Kuzniar, Paul (12); Manzanillo, Josias (26); Plympton, Jeffrey (38); Riley, Edward (1); Shikles, Larry (27); Stewart, Hector (41); Wacha, Charles (15); Walters, David (34).

READING—Ayrault, Robert (12); Boudreaux, Eric (7); Brantley, Clifford (11); Buonantony, Richard (3); Carreno, Amalio (31); Christopher, Frederic (32); Combs, Patrick (19); Farr, Michael (1); Fynan, Kevin (11); Grimsley, Jason (26); Magee, Warren (20); Malone, Charles (33); Mauser, Timothy (11); McDonald, Shelby (7); Scanlan, Robert (31); Sharts, Stephen (10); Sims, Mark (12); Tabaka, Jeffrey (21); Williams, Cary (1).

WILLIAMSPORT—Balabon, Richard (4); Blueberg, James (6); Burba, David (25); DeLucia, Richard (10); Gardiner, Michael (30); Goff, Michael (8); Helton, Keith (41); Hull, Jeffrey (11); Jones, Calvin (5); Melendez, Jose (11); Nelson, Jeffrey (15); Price, Bryan (10); Rice, Patrick (13); Ridenour, Dana (6); Rojas, Ricardo (18); Runge, Scott (2); Ryan, Jody (6); Spagnola, Glenn (21); Taylor, Scott (10).

GRAND SLAM HOME RUNS—Citari, Gomez, Webster, 2 each; Bellino, Brocki, Chamberlain, Faulkner, Green, Livingstone, Martinez, Morandini, Posey, B. Williams, 1 each.

AWARDED FIRST BASE ON CATCHER'S INTERFERENCE—Banister (Eberle); Bruske (Howard); Cook (Padilla); DeCillis (Agostinelli); T. Williams (Agostinelli).

CLUB FIELDING

Club	Pct.	G.	PO.	A.	E.	DP.	PB.	Club	Pct.	G.	PO.	A.	E.	DP.	PB.
Albany	.977	140	3475	1404	113	132	14	Hagerstown	.972	139	3564	1450	147	128	13
Williamsport	.973	140	3591	1448	139	129	34	London	.970	139	3533	1507	157	139	20
Canton-Akron	.972	139	3528	1507	147	155	24	New Britain	.968	136	3445	1407	162	129	26
Harrisburg	.972	136	3349	1216	133	96	17	Reading	.966	139	3492	1407	170	137	20

Triple Plays—Hagerstown, New Britain, Reading.

INDIVIDUAL FIELDING
FIRST BASEMEN

°Throws lefthanded.

Player and Club	Pct.	G.	PO.	A.	E.	DP.	Player and Club	Pct.	G.	PO.	A.	E.	DP.
Aldrich, London	.990	107	892	75	10	100	Bettendorf, Hagerstown	.995	86	741	43	4	63
Banister, Harrisburg	1.000	1	8	2	0	1	Boever, Canton-Akron	.989	12	81	6	1	8

FIRST BASEMEN—Continued

Player and Club	Pct.	G.	PO.	A.	E.	DP.	Player and Club	Pct.	G.	PO.	A.	E.	DP.
Brundage, Williamsport*	1.000	3	23	1	0	3	Neel, Canton-Akron	.993	14	125	16	1	18
Citari, Reading	.997	80	631	72	2	70	Orsag, New Britain	.986	29	250	25	4	17
DeCillis, London	1.000	2	12	2	0	2	Osborne, Harrisburg	.986	9	66	3	1	6
Eberle, Hagerstown	1.000	1	2	0	0	0	Pratt, New Britain	1.000	15	137	6	0	6
Estrada, New Britain	1.000	3	24	3	0	2	Roman, Albany	1.000	3	15	1	0	0
Faulkner, Hagerstown	1.000	12	69	8	0	5	Segui, Hagerstown*	.998	43	381	30	1	48
Grotewold, Reading	.989	11	83	8	1	9	Sepanek, Albany*	.990	112	962	70	10	101
Hartman, Harrisburg	.984	60	442	36	8	37	Shaw, Albany	.994	22	163	7	1	15
Henderson, Reading	.995	26	186	21	1	20	Sommers, New Britain	1.000	29	243	9	0	29
Khoury, Canton-Akron*	.991	13	100	10	1	9	Swain, Canton-Akron	.947	2	16	2	1	5
Latmore, Hagerstown	1.000	1	7	0	0	1	Toale, London	.965	18	123	13	5	7
Leiper, London	1.000	8	83	4	0	4	Turner, Reading	.987	28	207	17	3	20
Lovell, London*	.976	11	78	5	2	10	Twardoski, Canton-Akron*	.990	103	850	74	9	96
Lyden, Albany	1.000	4	28	1	0	1	Vaughn, New Britain	.983	66	541	45	10	58
Magrann, Canton-Akron	.944	3	13	4	1	0	Vizcaino, Harrisburg	.979	16	127	10	3	9
MARTINEZ, Williamsport	.995	137	1260	81	7	106	Webster, Canton-Akron	1.000	2	17	0	0	2
Merced, Harrisburg	.982	52	413	28	8	36							

Triple Plays—Bettendorf, Turner, Vaughn.

SECOND BASEMEN

Player and Club	Pct.	G.	PO.	A.	E.	DP.	Player and Club	Pct.	G.	PO.	A.	E.	DP.
Austin, London	.964	74	169	202	14	47	Kelly, New Britain	1.000	1	0	1	0	0
Beyeler, London	1.000	3	2	6	0	1	Latmore, Hagerstown	.948	15	41	51	5	15
Boever, Canton-Akron	1.000	1	1	1	0	1	Magallanes, Canton-Akron	.982	59	146	175	6	53
Bradshaw, London	1.000	1	1	2	0	0	Marchese, New Britain	.969	71	151	191	11	52
Brocki, Williamsport	.982	21	43	68	2	15	Milstien, New Britain	.964	31	49	84	5	20
Burdick, Harrisburg	.985	92	170	217	6	39	Nichols, Hagerstown	.974	103	229	266	13	69
Crowley, Harrisburg	.975	30	45	70	3	11	Perez, Harrisburg	.985	16	22	42	1	9
DeCillis, London	.982	64	94	176	5	43	Randle, New Britain	.959	45	70	118	8	18
Diaz, Williamsport	1.000	1	1	2	0	0	Rowland, London	.917	2	5	6	1	1
Dickerson, Albany	.750	2	1	2	1	0	Scarsone, Reading	.971	72	168	197	11	52
Dunlap, Williamsport	1.000	4	7	15	0	6	Shaw, Albany	1.000	7	12	18	0	3
Edge, Reading	1.000	6	14	25	0	4	Stanicek, Hagerstown	.980	20	43	55	2	7
Ferretti, Canton-Akron	1.000	1	2	4	0	1	STANKIEWICZ, Albany	.993	132	242	369	4	85
Foley, Reading	.963	65	126	164	11	43	Strijek, Hagerstown	.900	2	2	7	1	0
Foster, Canton-Akron	.959	15	22	25	2	6	Swain, Canton-Akron	.977	74	153	181	8	49
Haney, Williamsport	.967	114	213	313	18	71	Turner, Reading	1.000	1	2	0	0	0
Henderson, Reading	1.000	2	5	5	0	0							

Triple Plays—Edge, Nichols, Randle.

THIRD BASEMEN

Player and Club	Pct.	G.	PO.	A.	E.	DP.	Player and Club	Pct.	G.	PO.	A.	E.	DP.
Balthazar, London	1.000	1	0	1	0	0	Livingstone, London	.936	116	90	247	23	17
Boever, Canton-Akron	.600	1	3	0	2	0	Merced, Harrisburg	.857	4	2	4	1	0
Clark, London	1.000	1	0	1	0	0	Meulens, Albany	.892	99	67	172	29	17
Cooper, New Britain	.932	122	91	212	22	22	Milstien, New Britain	.904	21	15	32	5	3
DeCillis, London	.920	8	9	14	2	3	Parker, Reading	.858	52	29	74	17	6
Diaz, Williamsport	.936	24	28	45	5	3	Perez, Harrisburg	.938	17	9	21	2	3
Dickerson, Albany	1.000	1	0	1	0	0	Randle, New Britain	1.000	1	1	2	0	0
Dunlap, Williamsport	.960	47	36	84	5	10	Razook, Williamsport	.932	63	37	113	11	7
Estrada, New Britain	1.000	1	2	6	0	1	Roman, Albany	.867	10	4	9	2	3
Foley, Reading	.806	15	6	19	6	2	Rossy, Harrisburg	.971	16	10	24	1	2
Foster, Canton-Akron	.875	2	3	4	1	1	Rowland, London	.750	3	0	3	1	0
Fulton, Williamsport	.857	2	0	6	1	0	Shaw, Albany	.931	32	17	50	5	6
Gomez, Hagerstown	.933	116	78	256	24	25	Shields, Harrisburg	.931	101	70	187	19	12
Henderson, Reading	.908	65	37	91	13	8	Swain, Canton-Akron	.913	19	7	35	4	2
Howard, Williamsport	1.000	1	0	1	0	0	Toale, London	.795	12	5	26	8	4
Latmore, Hagerstown	.892	25	18	56	9	3	Turner, Reading	.871	17	7	20	4	2
Lennon, Williamsport	.739	7	2	15	6	0	WEBSTER, Canton-Akron	.947	120	93	248	19	38
Leyritz, Albany	1.000	1	0	2	0	0							

Triple Play—Cooper.

SHORTSTOPS

Player and Club	Pct.	G.	PO.	A.	E.	DP.	Player and Club	Pct.	G.	PO.	A.	E.	DP.
Becker, Albany	.977	88	156	273	10	65	Moritz, New Britain	.914	35	50	89	13	19
DeCillis, London	.920	16	30	51	7	11	Nichols, Hagerstown	.923	9	13	23	3	4
Dickerson, Albany	.955	18	26	38	3	8	Parker, Reading	.912	10	18	13	3	3
Dunlap, Williamsport	.938	6	13	17	2	5	Perez, Harrisburg	.900	2	4	5	1	1
Edge, Reading	.886	18	34	44	10	11	Randle, New Britain	1.000	6	12	11	0	3
Foster, Canton-Akron	.944	44	77	109	11	18	Rodriguez, Albany	.968	36	46	107	5	20
Fryman, London	.952	116	192	346	27	80	Rosario, Reading	.953	64	91	171	13	40
Fulton, Williamsport	1.000	1	3	3	0	0	Rossy, Harrisburg	.958	62	97	151	11	31
Garcia, Harrisburg	.968	54	84	131	7	23	Rowland, London	.923	2	2	10	1	3
Gomez, Hagerstown	.667	1	1	1	1	0	Ruiz, Canton-Akron	.978	20	39	50	2	21
Latmore, Hagerstown	.944	43	61	126	11	26	Scarsone, Reading	1.000	3	3	3	0	0
Lewis, Canton-Akron	.956	7	15	28	2	5	Shields, Harrisburg	.961	20	33	41	3	9
Livingstone, London	.933	8	10	18	2	2	D. Smith, Hagerstown	.974	71	109	186	8	45
Magallanes, Canton-Akron	.868	11	9	24	5	4	J. SMITH, Williamsport	.957	134	210	374	26	83
McDougal, 66 Can-43 New Br	.940	109	165	307	30	69	Strijek, Hagerstown	.925	20	26	60	7	5
Milstien, New Britain	.948	59	71	168	13	26	Swain, Canton-Akron	1.000	4	8	10	0	0
Morandini, Reading	.955	48	73	137	10	38	Tatis, Harrisburg	1.000	1	1	1	0	1

Triple Play—Rosario.

OUTFIELDERS

Player and Club	Pct.	G.	PO.	A.	E.	DP.	Player and Club	Pct.	G.	PO.	A.	E.	DP.
Allred, Canton-Akron*	.963	109	204	7	8	1	Azocar, Albany*	.976	91	158	2	4	0
Alou, Harrisburg	.978	52	89	1	2	0	Belle, Canton-Akron	.979	82	136	4	3	1
Anderson, London*	.966	31	50	6	2	1	Bellino, Reading	.949	55	87	7	5	1
Arendas, Albany*	.955	30	41	1	2	0	Bettendorf, Hagerstown	.972	25	34	1	1	0
Austin, London	.909	6	10	0	1	0	Boever, Canton-Akron	.982	34	54	2	1	1

OUTFIELDERS—Continued

Player and Club	Pct.	G.	PO.	A.	E.	DP.
Bowie, Williamsport°	1.000	3	3	0	0	0
Brumfield, Reading°	.991	53	106	5	1	2
Brundage, Williamsport°	.990	87	193	9	2	2
Bruske, Canton-Akron	1.000	44	75	4	0	1
Buford, Hagerstown	.964	94	153	10	6	0
Chamberlain, Harrisburg	.936	120	205	14	15	0
Chance, 2 Harrisburg-64 Hager.	.973	66	135	8	4	1
Cijntje, 51 Hager.-17 Can.°	.959	68	134	5	6	0
Clark, London	1.000	5	1	0	0	0
Cook, Harrisburg	.963	16	25	1	1	0
Cuyler, London	.973	98	272	13	8	2
Davis, Williamsport	.981	28	51	1	1	0
DeCillis, London	1.000	1	4	0	0	0
Dunlap, Williamsport	1.000	9	13	2	0	0
Edmonds, Reading	.933	25	42	0	3	0
Ferretti, Canton-Akron	1.000	1	1	0	0	0
Finley, Hagerstown°	.925	11	35	2	3	0
Foley, Reading	1.000	3	3	0	0	0
Foster, Canton-Akron	1.000	3	4	0	0	0
Goff, Williamsport	1.000	1	1	0	0	0
Green, Albany	.989	66	83	7	1	1
HITHE, Hagerstown	.983	121	222	11	4	1
Holtz, Reading	.962	101	195	6	8	4
Holyfield, Reading	.930	68	126	7	10	1
Hooper, Williamsport	1.000	1	1	0	0	0
Housie, London	.980	120	238	13	5	4
Jackson, New Britain	.982	96	209	6	4	1
Jose, London	.953	70	131	11	7	2
Kelly, New Britain	.947	60	119	6	7	2
Kerkes, Williamsport	.974	24	37	1	1	0
Kosco, Williamsport	1.000	45	66	4	0	1
Latmore, Hagerstown	.889	8	6	2	1	0
Leiper, London	.977	19	43	0	1	0
Leiva, Canton-Akron	.980	30	46	2	1	0
Lennon, Williamsport	.897	41	65	5	8	0
Leyritz, Albany	1.000	28	50	2	0	0
Longmire, Harrisburg	.969	31	62	1	2	0
Lovell, London°	1.000	3	10	0	0	0
Maas, Albany	.971	81	131	5	4	1
McDougal, Canton-Akron	1.000	2	2	0	0	0
Merced, Harrisburg	.952	13	20	0	1	0
Mims, Hagerstown	1.000	5	5	0	0	0
Neel, Canton-Akron	.952	78	114	6	6	2
Osborne, Harrisburg	1.000	1	3	0	0	0
Parker, Reading	.976	41	76	4	2	2
Peguero, Harrisburg	.988	71	163	6	2	1
Pina, New Britain	.970	45	95	3	3	0
Ramos, Albany	.950	12	17	2	1	1
Randle, New Britain	1.000	21	46	1	0	0
Sanders, Albany°	1.000	33	79	3	0	0
Skeete, Hagerstown°	.969	51	120	4	4	1
Snyder, Canton-Akron	1.000	4	5	2	0	0
Spann, London	1.000	27	51	4	0	0
Stanicek, Hagerstown	1.000	2	6	0	0	0
Tatis, Harrisburg	1.000	16	36	1	0	0
Taylor, Canton-Akron°	1.000	8	15	0	0	0
Twardoski, Canton-Akron°	.833	6	4	1	1	0
Uribe, Williamsport	.960	51	88	8	4	3
Vatcher, Reading	.988	48	76	5	1	1
Ward, Canton-Akron	1.000	1	2	0	0	0
B. Williams, Albany	.974	90	180	5	5	0
J. Williams, 28 Read.-16 Wil.°	.978	44	82	8	2	0
T. Williams, Williamsport	.972	130	268	10	8	3
Yacopino, Harrisburg°	.978	90	173	7	4	1
Young, 47 London-28 Can.	.993	75	146	1	1	0
E. Zambrano, New Britain	.984	53	120	4	2	1
R. Zambrano, New Britain	.972	54	95	8	3	1
Zupcic, New Britain	.971	94	186	12	6	6

Triple Play—Hithe.

CATCHERS

Player and Club	Pct.	G.	PO.	A.	E.	DP.	PB.
Agostinelli, Reading	.985	73	468	48	8	6	4
Balthazar, London	.989	51	237	22	3	2	15
BANISTER, Harrisburg	.988	85	550	29	7	3	13
Calvert, Reading	.968	13	84	6	3	1	5
Clark, London	.988	87	504	55	7	8	5
Eberle, Hagerstown	.987	86	503	47	7	4	9
Fagnant, New Britain	.600	2	2	1	2	0	1
Faulkner, Hagerstown	.974	13	70	5	2	0	2
Goff, Williamsport	.971	28	179	21	6	2	7
Hall, Harrisburg	1.000	7	32	7	0	1	0
Hansen, Williamsport	.933	4	13	1	1	0	0
Hooper, Williamsport	.972	31	186	21	6	6	5
Howard, Williamsport	.984	75	443	56	8	7	21
Leyritz, Albany	.993	67	371	37	3	3	10
Liebert, Canton-Akron	.979	56	258	28	6	2	10
Lyden, Albany	1.000	2	6	0	0	0	0
Magrann, Canton-Akron	.986	97	552	71	9	8	14
McKinley, Harrisburg	.985	57	313	22	5	1	4
Miller, Williamsport	1.000	2	9	1	0	0	1
Padilla, New Britain	.982	69	340	42	7	6	14
Posey, 10 Hag.-58 Read.	.983	68	411	50	8	5	12
Pratt, New Britain	.968	65	298	36	11	2	11
Ramos, Albany	.983	78	544	44	10	2	4
Sherlock, Albany	1.000	1	2	0	0	0	0
Simonds, Hagerstown	.981	43	231	25	5	7	1
Toale, London	1.000	7	13	1	0	1	0
Wedge, New Britain	1.000	14	83	9	0	1	0

Triple Plays—Eberle, Pratt.

PITCHERS

Player and Club	Pct.	G.	PO.	A.	E.	DP.
Adams, Harrisburg	.970	28	5	27	1	3
Adkins, Albany°	.875	16	4	10	2	2
Aldred, London°	.962	20	3	22	1	0
Ayrault, Reading	1.000	2	0	1	0	0
Balabon, Williamsport	.800	4	1	3	1	0
Bast, New Britain°	1.000	8	2	13	0	0
Bearse, Canton-Akron°	1.000	14	10	18	0	1
Belinda, Harrisburg	1.000	32	3	6	0	0
Bell, Hagerstown°	1.000	9	3	5	0	0
Bellino, Reading	1.000	1	0	1	0	0
Blueberg, Williamsport	.857	6	3	3	1	0
Boudreaux, Reading	.667	7	2	0	1	0
Brantley, Reading	1.000	11	6	6	0	0
Brusky, Williamsport	1.000	33	4	6	0	0
Buonantony, Reading	1.000	3	1	1	0	0
Burba, Williamsport	.972	25	10	25	1	3
Carista, New Britain	.963	24	15	11	1	1
Carreno, Reading	1.000	31	7	14	0	1
Cavers, Hagerstown°	1.000	12	6	10	0	2
Chapin, Albany	1.000	7	0	1	0	0
F. Christopher, Reading°	.929	32	4	9	1	0
M. Christopher, Albany	1.000	8	3	7	0	0
Clayton, Albany	.978	25	15	29	1	2
Collins, Canton-Akron	.714	11	1	4	2	1
Combs, Reading°	.974	19	17	21	1	4
Conroy, Harrisburg°	1.000	4	1	3	0	0
Cooper, London	1.000	25	3	4	0	0
Crouch, New Britain°	1.000	15	6	13	0	1
Culkar, Hagerstown	1.000	26	0	6	0	0
Dalton, New Britain°	.833	18	1	4	1	2
Davidson, Albany	.769	12	5	5	3	0
DeLaRosa, Hagerstown	1.000	18	0	2	0	0
DeLeon, Albany	1.000	17	7	9	0	1
DeLucia, Williamsport	1.000	10	3	11	0	0
Dixon, 6 Hag-4 Can.	1.000	10	2	4	0	0
Doyle, Williamsport	.867	26	3	10	2	0
DuBois, Hagerstown°	.871	15	6	21	4	3
Edwards, Canton-Akron°	1.000	39	3	8	0	1
Everson, London	1.000	47	17	17	0	2
Ferlenda, Canton-Akron	1.000	12	2	0	0	0
Foley, Reading	1.000	1	0	1	0	0
Fulton, Albany	1.000	10	5	12	0	3
Fynan, Reading	1.000	11	1	3	0	0
Gabriele, New Britain	.813	26	8	5	3	0
Garces, Hagerstown°	.923	32	2	10	1	0
Gardiner, Williamsport	.857	30	2	10	2	0
Gilles, Canton-Akron	.947	16	7	11	1	0
Githens, Canton-Akron	.938	27	3	12	1	3
Goff, Williamsport	1.000	8	2	1	0	0
Gonzales, Canton-Akron°	.909	12	2	8	1	0
Green, Albany	.875	20	2	5	1	0
GRIMSLEY, Reading	.982	26	19	37	1	2
Haas, London	.875	18	5	9	2	1
Hansen, London	.900	18	9	18	3	0
Helton, Williamsport°	1.000	41	3	10	0	1
Householder, Hagerstown°	1.000	8	1	4	0	1
Howard, Albany°	1.000	24	1	3	0	0
Hull, Williamsport	1.000	11	4	5	0	0
Hursey, London°	.927	27	7	31	3	0
Imes, Albany	.949	24	10	27	2	1
Irvine, New Britain	.969	54	2	29	1	0
Jones, Williamsport	1.000	5	0	2	0	0
Kamieniecki, Albany	.926	24	10	15	2	3
Keliipuleole, Canton-Akron	.957	27	6	16	1	0
Kramer, Canton-Akron	.875	10	2	5	1	1
Kuzniar, 26 Can-12 New Br	1.000	38	5	10	0	0
Latmore, Hagerstown	1.000	2	0	1	0	0
Layana, Albany	.952	40	3	17	1	0
Lind, Harrisburg	1.000	6	4	8	0	0
Linskey, Hagerstown°	.864	18	5	14	3	1

PITCHERS—Continued

Player and Club	Pct.	G.	PO.	A.	E.	DP.
Magee, Reading	.909	20	6	4	1	0
Malone, Reading	.800	33	6	2	2	0
Manzanillo, New Britain	.897	26	11	24	4	0
Mauser, Reading	.889	11	6	10	2	0
McDonald, Reading	.875	7	0	7	1	0
McElroy, Reading*	.900	32	2	7	1	1
McMichael, Canton-Akron	.961	26	16	33	2	4
Mejia, Hagerstown	.867	11	5	8	2	1
Melendez, Williamsport	.917	11	2	9	1	1
Melton, Harrisburg	.875	23	6	8	2	3
Mesa, Hagerstown	1.000	3	1	0	0	0
Mmahat, Albany*	1.000	8	4	11	0	2
Murphy, Harrisburg	.773	26	6	11	5	0
Myers, Hagerstown*	1.000	6	2	3	0	1
Nagy, Canton-Akron	.923	15	9	15	2	0
Nelson, Williamsport	.957	15	5	17	1	0
Nosek, London	1.000	22	4	11	0	1
O'Neill, London*	1.000	20	0	2	0	1
Ogden, Canton-Akron	1.000	6	2	6	0	2
Pinder, Hagerstown	1.000	9	0	8	0	0
Plympton, New Britain	.933	38	4	10	1	0
Poehl, Canton-Akron	1.000	3	2	4	0	0
Price, Williamsport*	1.000	10	5	7	0	0
Ramos, London*	.941	33	2	14	1	0
Rice, Williamsport	1.000	13	1	7	0	1
Richardson, Harrisburg	.950	21	6	13	1	3
Ridenour, Williamsport	1.000	6	2	2	0	0
Rightnowar, London	.870	36	7	13	3	2
Rojas, Williamsport	1.000	17	5	8	0	1
Rub, Albany*	1.000	18	1	4	0	0
Ruskin, Harrisburg*	.938	12	3	12	1	0
Russell, Harrisburg*	1.000	44	5	8	0	0
Ryan, Williamsport	1.000	6	0	4	0	0
Sampen, Harrisburg	.926	26	8	17	2	3
Sander, Hagerstown	1.000	32	12	9	0	0

Player and Club	Pct.	G.	PO.	A.	E.	DP.
Scanlan, Reading	.917	31	5	17	2	0
Schwabe, London	1.000	8	2	4	0	0
Schwarz, Hagerstown	.813	17	1	12	3	1
Scott, Canton-Akron	.931	24	12	15	2	4
Service, Reading	.952	23	7	13	1	0
Sharts, Reading*	1.000	10	0	8	0	0
Shaw, Canton-Akron	.947	30	14	22	2	2
Shikles, New Britain	.953	27	18	23	2	3
Sims, Reading*	1.000	12	3	14	0	0
W. Smith, Harrisburg	1.000	12	2	2	0	0
Sonberg, Hagerstown*	1.000	7	2	4	0	0
Spagnola, Williamsport	.962	21	11	14	1	1
Stanhope, Hagerstown	1.000	6	2	7	0	1
Stewart, New Britain	.929	41	2	11	1	0
Stoddard, Canton-Akron	1.000	5	1	1	0	0
Surhoff, Canton-Akron	1.000	21	2	0	0	0
Tabaka, Reading*	.955	21	7	14	1	2
Taylor, Williamsport	1.000	10	0	7	0	1
Thorpe, Hagerstown	.882	39	3	12	2	1
Tirado, Albany	1.000	11	2	6	0	1
Tomlin, Harrisburg*	1.000	5	4	3	0	1
Torres, Albany	.955	24	6	15	1	1
Tracy, Harrisburg	.842	44	5	11	3	0
Valdez, Canton-Akron*	.944	44	6	11	1	0
Vesling, London*	.958	13	9	14	1	3
Wacha, New Britain	1.000	15	1	3	0	1
Walters, New Britain	.941	34	8	8	1	1
Webb, Harrisburg	.889	23	4	12	2	1
Wenson, London	1.000	27	1	5	0	0
Wilkins, London	1.000	11	8	9	0	1
K. Williams, London*	1.000	3	1	0	0	0
R. Williams, Hagerstown	.900	12	4	5	1	0
Wooden, Williamsport*	1.000	46	5	7	0	1
York, Harrisburg	.923	18	11	13	2	0

The following players did not have any fielding statistics at the positions indicated or appeared only as a designated hitter, pinch-hitter or pinch-runner: Araujo, p; Borgatti, p; Boyd, p; Bradshaw, 3b; Brundage, p; Bruske, ss, p; Farr, p; Faulkner, 3b; Foley, ss; Gale, p; Khoury, of; Liebert, of; Pena, p; Perez, c; Riley, p; Roman, 2b; Runge, p; Scott, of; Shaw, of; D. Smith, p; Sommers, p; Swain, of; C. Williams, of.

CLUB PITCHING

Club	ERA.	G.	CG.	ShO.	Sv.	IP.	H.	R.	ER.	HR.	HB.	BB.	Int. BB.	SO.	WP.	Bk.
Albany	2.98	140	39	19	32	1158.1	1027	453	383	59	27	394	26	910	50	18
New Britain	3.38	136	19	16	33	1149.0	1065	534	431	62	43	462	41	701	65	12
Harrisburg	3.43	136	26	11	28	1116.1	1063	512	425	75	43	369	20	862	52	17
Canton-Akron	3.44	139	28	19	27	1176.0	1111	558	449	55	60	464	28	789	79	8
Hagerstown	3.49	139	23	12	21	1188.0	1111	539	461	65	46	455	10	814	46	15
Williamsport	3.65	140	19	9	30	1197.0	1164	570	485	87	41	466	32	794	44	22
Reading	3.95	139	31	10	20	1164.0	1006	601	511	96	50	617	16	862	82	12
London	3.97	139	27	10	25	1177.2	1192	610	519	82	42	499	20	714	54	12

PITCHERS' RECORDS
(Leading Qualifiers for Earned-Run Average Leadership — 112 or More Innings)

*Throws lefthanded.

Pitcher—Club	W.	L.	Pct.	ERA.	G.	GS.	CG.	GF.	ShO.	Sv.	IP.	H.	R.	ER.	HR.	HB.	BB.	Int. BB.	SO.	WP.
Adkins, Albany*	12	1	.923	2.07	16	16	7	0	5	0	117.2	67	31	27	5	1	58	1	132	2
York, Harrisburg	11	5	.688	2.31	18	18	3	0	2	0	121.0	105	37	31	6	2	40	2	106	8
DuBois, Hagerstown*	6	4	.600	2.49	15	15	6	0	2	0	112.0	93	36	31	5	1	18	0	82	4
Imes, Albany	17	6	.739	2.73	24	24	9	0	1	0	171.2	143	56	52	11	4	41	4	128	3
Hansen, London	5	6	.455	2.81	18	17	3	0	0	0	118.2	111	58	37	6	1	37	2	67	2
Linskey, Hagerstown*	10	6	.625	2.81	18	18	7	0	4	0	128.0	108	45	40	6	4	35	0	90	4
Grimsley, Reading	11	8	.579	2.98	26	26	8	0	2	0	172.0	121	65	57	13	10	109	4	134	12
Clayton, Albany	16	4	.800	2.98	25	25	6	0	0	0	175.0	166	72	58	8	4	48	2	74	5
Spagnola, Williamsport	8	5	.615	3.06	21	21	4	0	2	0	126.2	113	50	43	11	6	36	1	69	5
Burba, Williamsport	11	7	.611	3.16	25	25	5	0	1	0	156.2	138	69	55	7	3	55	0	89	4

Departmental Leaders: G—Irvine, 54; W—Imes, 17; L—Hursey, 13; Pct.—Adkins, .923; GS—Five pitchers tied with 26; CG—Imes, 9; GF—Irvine, 45; ShO—Adkins, McMichael, 5; Sv.—Layana, 17; IP—Clayton, 175.0; H—Hursey, 183; R—Hursey, 92; ER—Hursey, Scanlan, 76; HR—Combs, 16; HB—Shaw, 14; BB—Grimsley, 109; IBB—Edwards, Manzanillo, 7; SO—Kamieniecki, 140; WP—Manzanillo, 16.

(All Pitchers—Listed Alphabetically)

Pitcher—Club	W.	L.	Pct.	ERA.	G.	GS.	CG.	GF.	ShO.	Sv.	IP.	H.	R.	ER.	HR.	HB.	BB.	Int. BB.	SO.	WP.
Adams, Harrisburg	8	2	.800	3.94	28	12	4	5	1	0	102.2	109	48	45	6	1	22	0	45	2
Adkins, Albany*	12	1	.923	2.07	16	16	7	0	5	0	117.2	67	31	27	5	1	58	1	132	2
Aldred, London*	10	6	.625	3.84	20	20	3	0	1	0	122.0	98	55	52	11	5	59	0	97	9
Araujo, New Britain	1	0	1.000	0.00	1	1	1	0	1	0	7.0	3	0	0	0	0	0	0	8	0
Ayrault, Reading	0	0	.000	1.04	2	1	0	0	0	0	8.2	3	1	1	0	0	4	0	8	0
Balabon, Williamsport	1	0	1.000	4.84	4	4	1	0	1	0	22.1	20	13	12	1	0	12	0	14	0
Bast, New Britain*	3	4	.429	2.43	8	8	1	0	1	0	59.1	50	16	16	3	4	12	2	32	1
Bearse, Canton-Akron*	9	3	.750	2.05	14	14	6	0	2	0	101.0	90	29	23	2	1	16	1	67	2
Belinda, Harrisburg	1	4	.200	2.33	32	0	0	28	0	13	38.2	32	13	10	1	1	25	3	33	4
Bell, Hagerstown*	4	2	.667	1.88	9	7	0	1	0	1	43.0	32	11	9	3	1	11	1	35	0
Bellino, Reading	0	0	.000	9.00	1	0	0	1	0	0	2.0	2	2	2	1	0	1	0	0	0
Blueberg, Williamsport	1	3	.250	6.67	6	6	0	0	0	0	29.2	43	29	22	6	2	14	1	20	1
Borgatti, Hagerstown	0	0	.000	0.00	1	0	0	1	0	0	3.0	2	0	0	0	0	0	0	1	0
Boudreaux, Reading	0	0	.000	5.84	7	0	0	0	0	0	12.1	15	13	8	3	1	0	0	11	3
Boyd, New Britain	1	0	1.000	1.80	1	1	0	0	0	0	5.0	3	1	1	0	1	0	0	8	0
Brantley, Reading	3	4	.429	3.31	11	9	0	1	0	1	49.0	49	24	18	1	2	28	0	35	2
Brundage, Williamsport*	0	0	.000	0.00	1	0	0	1	0	0	0.1	0	0	0	0	0	1	0	0	0

Pitcher—Club	W.	L.	Pct.	ERA.	G.	GS.	CG.	GF.	ShO.	Sv.	IP.	H.	R.	ER.	HR.	HB.	BB.	Int. BB.	SO.	WP.
Bruske, Canton-Akron	0	0	.000	13.50	2	0	0	2	0	0	2.0	3	3	3	0	0	2	0	1	1
Brusky, Williamsport	2	5	.286	3.70	33	0	0	15	0	2	56.0	52	28	23	3	3	22	3	41	0
Buonantony, Reading	0	0	.000	3.86	3	0	0	0	0	0	7.0	5	3	3	0	1	6	0	4	2
Burba, Williamsport	11	7	.611	3.16	25	25	5	0	1	0	156.2	138	69	55	7	3	55	0	89	4
Carista, New Britain	3	11	.214	3.79	24	20	4	1	1	0	123.1	122	62	52	8	7	45	2	69	5
Carreno, Reading	5	7	.417	4.34	31	11	2	11	1	1	101.2	99	57	49	9	4	41	2	56	9
Cavers, Hagerstown*	7	4	.636	3.81	12	12	2	0	0	0	75.2	89	38	32	2	3	33	0	26	4
Chapin, Albany	1	0	1.000	0.00	7	0	0	7	0	3	8.2	5	0	0	0	1	1	0	16	2
F. Christopher, Reading*	2	3	.400	4.53	32	2	0	5	0	0	51.2	38	26	26	6	0	46	0	50	7
M. Christopher, Albany	6	1	.857	2.52	8	8	3	0	0	0	53.2	48	17	15	1	1	7	0	33	0
Clayton, Albany	16	4	.800	2.98	25	25	6	0	0	0	175.0	166	72	58	8	4	48	2	74	5
Collins, Canton-Akron	2	3	.400	2.38	11	3	0	3	0	1	34.0	22	10	9	0	4	15	0	26	4
Combs, Reading*	8	7	.533	3.38	19	19	4	0	0	0	125.0	104	57	47	16	4	40	2	77	5
Conroy, Harrisburg*	3	0	1.000	2.08	4	4	1	0	0	0	26.0	15	6	6	2	0	10	1	21	1
Cooper, London	2	2	.500	4.13	25	0	0	21	0	6	32.2	37	16	15	4	0	12	2	18	6
Crouch, New Britain*	3	7	.300	3.26	15	14	1	0	0	0	77.1	73	35	28	5	2	21	2	41	4
Culkar, Hagerstown	6	2	.750	1.34	26	0	0	19	0	1	47.0	33	7	7	1	3	15	1	45	1
Dalton, New Britain*	3	1	.750	2.48	18	1	1	7	1	3	32.2	25	13	9	0	2	15	3	15	1
Davidson, Albany	2	0	1.000	2.87	12	3	0	4	0	2	31.1	36	20	10	1	1	7	1	26	2
DeLaRosa, Hagerstown	1	1	.500	4.55	18	0	0	15	0	8	29.2	27	15	15	1	0	20	0	34	0
DeLeon, Albany	3	7	.300	5.53	17	7	0	4	0	0	57.0	79	37	35	5	3	25	4	51	10
DeLucia, Williamsport	3	4	.429	3.79	10	10	0	0	0	0	54.2	59	28	23	5	1	13	0	41	5
Dixon, 6 Hag-4 Can	1	0	1.000	1.86	10	4	0	3	0	0	38.2	25	11	8	0	1	9	0	29	2
Doyle, Williamsport	2	2	.500	2.89	26	0	0	14	0	5	43.2	45	14	14	1	3	13	2	37	2
DuBois, Hagerstown*	6	4	.600	2.49	15	15	6	0	2	0	112.0	93	36	31	5	1	18	0	82	4
Edwards, Canton-Akron*	3	2	.600	4.14	39	0	0	29	0	10	50.0	47	23	23	0	7	29	7	49	9
Everson, London	4	3	.571	2.94	47	0	0	33	0	9	82.2	78	30	27	6	5	12	0	74	4
Farr, Reading	0	0	.000	0.00	1	0	0	1	0	0	1.0	0	0	0	0	0	0	0	0	0
Ferlenda, Canton-Akron	2	1	.667	2.00	12	1	1	4	0	0	27.0	18	10	6	1	1	17	1	25	2
Foley, Reading	0	0	.000	9.00	1	0	0	1	0	0	1.0	1	1	1	0	0	2	0	0	0
Fulton, Albany	3	5	.375	4.42	10	10	4	0	0	0	53.0	63	32	26	1	0	24	1	29	2
Fynan, Reading	0	0	.000	4.35	11	0	0	5	1	0	20.2	16	10	10	2	0	12	0	11	1
Gabriele, New Britain	5	11	.313	4.67	26	22	3	2	1	0	125.1	126	83	65	14	3	65	4	82	4
Gale, New Britain	0	0	.000	0.00	2	0	0	1	0	0	5.1	2	1	0	0	0	1	0	3	1
Garces, Hagerstown*	1	6	.143	3.47	32	4	0	11	0	1	83.0	75	39	32	9	4	46	1	76	6
Gardiner, Williamsport	4	6	.400	2.84	30	3	1	14	0	2	63.1	54	25	20	6	1	32	6	60	4
Gilles, Canton-Akron	4	5	.444	4.58	16	7	0	3	0	0	59.0	77	36	30	7	4	22	1	33	4
Githens, Hagerstown	0	9	.000	4.43	27	10	0	9	0	0	101.2	98	57	50	4	8	38	1	60	3
Goff, Williamsport	3	0	1.000	3.86	8	0	0	5	0	0	14.0	16	7	6	1	1	9	3	6	0
Gonzales, Canton-Akron*	5	3	.625	3.43	12	11	0	1	0	0	60.1	62	36	23	3	0	28	1	38	4
Green, Albany	2	1	.667	2.68	20	1	0	15	0	3	40.1	32	15	12	0	2	14	2	22	1
Grimsley, Reading	11	8	.579	2.98	26	26	8	0	1	0	172.0	121	65	57	13	10	109	4	134	12
Haas, London	3	11	.214	5.64	18	18	2	0	0	0	103.2	107	69	65	13	11	51	1	75	5
Hansen, London	5	6	.455	2.81	18	17	3	0	0	0	118.2	111	58	37	6	1	37	2	67	2
Helton, Williamsport*	3	4	.429	1.47	41	0	0	30	0	14	61.1	54	16	10	4	1	24	5	42	0
Householder, Hagerstown*	1	1	.500	3.23	8	8	0	0	0	0	30.2	22	11	11	2	2	14	0	23	1
Howard, Albany*	0	1	.000	3.44	24	0	0	10	0	0	51.2	68	43	36	3	3	26	0	43	3
Hull, Williamsport	2	6	.250	6.27	11	10	0	0	0	0	51.2	83	43	36	9	2	76	0	82	3
Hursey, London*	8	13	.381	3.97	27	26	5	0	1	0	172.1	143	56	76	12	4	41	4	128	3
Imes, Reading	17	6	.739	2.73	24	24	9	0	1	0	171.2	143	56	52	11	4	43	2	50	9
Irvine, New Britain	4	6	.400	1.28	54	1	0	45	0	16	91.1	74	24	13	0	3	23	2	50	1
Jones, Williamsport	0	0	.000	12.15	5	0	0	3	0	0	6.2	13	9	9	1	0	4	0	5	1
Kamieniecki, Albany	10	4	.526	3.70	24	23	6	1	3	1	151.0	142	67	62	13	2	57	1	140	5
Keliipuleole, Canton-Akron	5	5	.500	3.94	27	10	1	6	1	2	89.0	90	43	39	7	7	35	3	64	8
Kramer, Canton-Akron	1	6	.143	6.23	10	8	1	0	0	0	43.1	58	34	30	6	0	20	0	26	3
Kuzniar, 26 Can-12 New Br	4	5	.444	3.12	38	6	0	23	0	8	83.2	59	34	29	2	7	57	3	55	10
Latmore, Hagerstown	0	0	.000	0.00	2	0	0	2	0	0	2.1	2	0	0	0	0	1	0	2	1
Layana, Albany	7	4	.636	1.73	40	1	0	37	0	17	67.2	53	17	13	2	3	15	3	48	2
Lind, Harrisburg	4	0	1.000	1.96	6	6	3	0	2	0	41.1	31	10	9	3	0	12	0	39	1
Linskey, Hagerstown*	10	6	.625	2.81	18	18	7	0	4	0	128.0	108	45	40	6	4	35	0	90	4
Magee, Reading	0	2	.000	7.90	20	0	0	11	0	0	27.1	37	27	24	0	1	18	0	25	2
Malone, Reading	5	7	.417	4.16	33	16	2	14	1	2	106.0	64	61	49	12	4	106	1	107	5
Manzanillo, New Britain	9	10	.474	3.66	26	26	3	0	1	0	147.2	129	78	60	11	5	85	7	93	16
Mauser, Reading	7	4	.636	3.63	11	11	4	0	2	0	72.0	62	36	29	5	1	33	0	54	3
McDonald, Reading	0	2	.000	2.89	7	0	0	6	0	0	18.2	12	6	6	1	0	9	1	12	3
McElroy, Reading*	3	1	.750	2.68	32	0	0	24	0	12	47.0	39	14	14	0	3	14	2	39	3
McMichael, Canton-Akron	11	11	.500	3.49	26	26	8	0	5	0	170.0	164	81	66	10	6	64	1	101	9
Mejia, Hagerstown	6	1	.857	3.68	11	11	2	0	0	0	73.1	73	31	30	2	5	27	0	42	1
Melendez, Williamsport	3	4	.429	2.45	11	11	0	0	0	0	73.1	54	23	20	7	2	22	1	56	0
Melton, Harrisburg	4	7	.364	3.97	23	9	0	6	0	0	70.1	75	42	31	10	6	27	1	52	5
Mesa, Hagerstown	0	0	.000	1.38	3	3	0	0	0	0	13.0	9	2	2	0	0	4	0	12	0
Mmahat, Albany*	5	1	.833	1.58	8	8	1	0	1	0	51.1	35	11	9	0	2	19	0	48	3
Murphy, Harrisburg	5	6	.455	2.36	26	7	1	7	0	2	84.0	87	37	22	2	5	21	2	54	6
Myers, Hagerstown*	4	2	.667	2.56	6	6	4	0	2	0	45.2	41	16	13	1	0	12	0	25	0
Nagy, Canton-Akron	4	5	.444	3.35	15	14	2	0	0	0	94.0	102	44	35	4	2	32	0	65	7
Nelson, Williamsport	7	5	.583	3.31	15	15	2	0	0	0	92.1	72	41	34	2	4	53	1	61	9
Nosek, London	8	10	.444	4.95	22	22	3	0	1	0	123.2	113	75	68	5	3	100	1	62	14
O'Neill, London*	3	1	.750	2.70	20	0	0	9	0	0	26.2	24	10	8	0	4	20	1	27	0
Ogden, Canton-Akron	0	4	.000	11.35	6	6	0	0	0	0	23.0	40	33	29	0	4	20	0	7	1
Pena, Albany*	0	0	.000	1.42	4	0	0	2	0	0	6.1	5	1	1	0	0	2	0	5	0
Pinder, Hagerstown*	2	1	.667	3.31	9	0	0	3	0	0	16.1	15	9	6	0	0	12	0	5	1
Plympton, New Britain	4	4	.500	3.72	38	6	0	17	0	5	72.2	72	36	30	3	5	39	5	63	4
Poehl, Canton-Akron	2	1	.667	0.56	3	3	1	0	1	0	16.0	12	1	1	0	1	3	0	7	1
Price, Williamsport*	3	1	.750	4.97	10	2	0	2	0	1	29.0	32	18	16	4	0	15	2	24	0
Ramos, London*	2	5	.286	4.36	33	2	0	17	0	1	64.0	72	38	31	3	0	31	2	31	5
Rice, Williamsport	4	1	.800	2.28	13	5	2	0	1	0	47.1	39	13	12	0	0	12	2	40	2
Richardson, Harrisburg	8	10	.444	4.59	21	21	3	0	1	0	117.2	131	63	60	15	9	39	0	96	6
Ridenour, Williamsport	1	0	1.000	1.64	6	0	0	4	0	0	11.0	13	3	2	0	0	3	0	13	2
Rightnowar, London	2	8	.200	5.00	36	7	2	14	0	5	108.0	132	63	60	10	4	34	4	46	2
Riley, New Britain	0	1	.000	8.31	1	1	0	0	0	0	4.1	4	4	4	1	0	2	0	1	0
Rojas, Williamsport	6	7	.462	4.03	17	14	3	0	1	0	82.2	85	42	37	8	2	30	1	53	1
Rub, Albany*	1	2	.333	3.18	18	1	0	9	0	3	22.2	20	9	8	1	1	12	0	23	4

396

Pitcher—Club	W.	L.	Pct.	ERA.	G.	GS.	CG.	GF.	ShO.	Sv.	IP.	H.	R.	ER.	HR.	HB.	BB.	Int. BB.	SO.	WP.
Runge, Williamsport	0	1	.000	13.50	2	0	0	1	0	0	2.2	4	4	4	0	0	6	1	0	0
Ruskin, Harrisburg*	2	3	.400	4.86	12	10	2	0	0	0	63.0	64	38	34	5	1	32	0	56	2
Russell, Harrisburg*	3	6	.333	4.22	44	0	0	26	0	5	59.2	64	31	28	2	4	17	2	52	0
Ryan, Williamsport	0	2	.000	4.35	6	3	0	2	0	1	31.0	34	17	15	1	2	9	0	16	1
Sampen, Harrisburg	11	9	.550	3.21	26	26	6	0	0	0	165.2	148	75	59	8	5	40	3	134	6
Sander, Hagerstown	9	10	.474	4.49	32	14	1	8	0	1	120.1	122	70	60	15	6	48	2	62	8
Scanlan, Reading	6	10	.375	5.78	31	17	4	8	1	0	118.1	124	88	76	9	5	58	1	63	12
Schwabe, London	3	0	1.000	1.07	8	2	0	5	0	2	25.1	25	7	3	1	2	5	2	22	2
Schwarz, Hagerstown	0	6	.000	3.91	17	9	0	5	0	1	69.0	66	45	30	3	4	41	0	78	7
Scott, Canton-Akron	10	3	.769	2.82	24	9	2	5	0	1	95.2	76	36	30	4	2	23	2	67	2
Service, Reading	6	6	.500	3.26	23	10	1	9	1	1	85.2	71	36	31	8	8	23	0	82	3
Sharts, Reading*	2	2	.500	1.53	10	0	0	0	0	0	17.2	12	5	3	0	0	1	0	4	1
Shaw, Canton-Akron	7	10	.412	3.62	30	22	6	3	3	0	154.1	134	84	62	9	14	67	3	95	7
Shikles, New Britain	8	10	.444	3.49	27	19	4	3	0	2	142.0	134	68	55	5	5	38	3	67	3
Sims, Reading*	2	1	.667	2.75	12	0	0	10	0	2	19.2	22	6	6	2	1	6	0	10	0
D. Smith, Hagerstown	0	0	.000	0.00	1	0	0	1	0	0	2.0	0	0	0	0	0	0	0	0	0
W. Smith, Harrisburg	3	0	1.000	2.45	12	0	0	6	0	0	18.1	11	5	5	1	3	10	0	21	0
Sommers, New Britain	0	0	.000	4.50	1	0	0	1	0	0	2.0	3	1	1	0	0	1	0	1	0
Sonberg, Hagerstown*	2	3	.400	6.98	7	6	0	0	0	0	29.2	39	24	23	2	2	20	0	22	1
Spagnola, Williamsport	8	5	.615	3.06	21	21	4	0	2	0	126.2	113	50	43	11	6	36	1	69	5
Stanhope, Hagerstown	1	3	.250	2.88	6	6	1	0	0	0	40.2	38	14	13	2	1	12	0	21	0
Stewart, New Britain*	7	0	1.000	2.06	41	1	0	22	0	1	70.0	61	18	16	3	1	20	3	53	3
Stoddard, Canton-Akron	0	0	.000	0.90	5	1	0	4	0	1	10.0	3	3	1	0	0	2	0	9	0
Surhoff, Canton-Akron	3	0	1.000	0.73	21	0	0	14	0	4	24.2	17	3	2	0	0	7	2	26	4
Tabaka, Reading*	8	7	.533	4.65	21	17	6	1	1	0	100.2	109	59	52	8	4	54	3	80	9
Taylor, Williamsport	1	4	.200	5.75	10	7	1	1	0	0	40.2	49	26	26	6	1	20	1	22	2
Thorpe, Hagerstown	4	5	.444	3.71	39	0	0	34	0	7	53.1	53	25	22	3	0	20	3	31	1
Tirado, Albany	1	2	.333	5.26	11	2	0	4	0	0	25.2	25	19	15	4	1	10	2	21	0
Tomlin, Harrisburg*	2	2	.500	0.84	5	5	1	0	0	0	32.0	18	6	3	0	1	6	0	31	0
Torres, Albany	6	4	.600	2.66	24	11	3	9	2	1	91.1	79	35	27	3	2	37	2	79	6
Tracy, Harrisburg	2	4	.333	3.42	44	0	0	29	0	8	71.0	63	37	27	5	1	21	3	52	3
Valdez, Canton-Akron*	2	4	.333	2.15	44	2	0	18	0	1	75.1	60	26	18	1	4	33	3	55	4
Vesling, London*	5	4	.556	3.81	13	13	3	0	1	0	80.1	93	40	34	7	4	24	1	44	1
Wacha, New Britain	3	2	.600	4.97	15	2	0	4	0	0	38.0	45	23	21	2	1	18	3	23	3
Walters, New Britain	3	6	.333	4.18	34	7	1	10	1	2	94.2	105	54	44	6	1	43	4	59	6
Webb, Harrisburg	4	7	.364	4.71	23	18	2	3	0	0	105.0	110	64	55	9	4	47	3	70	8
Wenson, London	2	3	.400	3.50	27	1	1	13	0	1	43.2	48	23	17	1	1	22	3	29	0
Wilkins, London	6	4	.600	3.38	11	11	5	0	3	0	69.1	69	34	26	3	4	25	1	38	1
K. Williams, London*	0	0	.000	0.00	3	0	0	0	0	0	4.2	2	0	0	0	0	2	0	0	0
R. Williams, Hagerstown	2	6	.250	6.65	12	8	0	2	0	0	44.2	60	39	33	4	0	27	0	18	3
Wooden, Williamsport	1	7	.125	4.14	46	4	0	26	0	5	100.0	115	52	46	10	5	35	3	42	2
York, Harrisburg	11	5	.688	2.31	18	18	3	0	2	0	121.0	105	37	31	6	2	40	2	106	8

BALKS—Melendez, 6; Burba, Schwarz, 5 each; Layana, 4; Clayton, DeLeon, Dixon, Edwards, Fulton, Hull, Magee, 3 each; Adams, Aldred, Balabon, Bast, Belinda, Combs, Cooper, Hursey, Manzanillo, Melton, Murphy, Richardson, Rightnowar, Ruskin, Russell, Torres, Wacha, Walters, 2 each; Bearse, Bell, Boudreaux, Brantley, Carista, Cavers, F. Christopher, Crouch, Culkar, Doyle, Everson, Garces, Gardiner, Goff, Green, Haas, Householder, Howard, Imes, Keliipuleole, Kuzniar, Lind, Linskey, Malone, Mauser, McDonald, McMichael, Nelson, Nosek, Pinder, Ryan, Scanlan, Scott, Shikles, Tracy, Webb, Wenson, R. Williams, Wooden, 1 each.

COMBINATION SHUTOUTS—Kamieniecki-Chapin, Imes-Torres, Mmahat-Layana, Imes-Tirado, Adkins-Layana-Green, Imes-Pena, Imes-DeLeon, Albany; Shaw-Edwards-Keliipuleole, Gilles-Edwards, Bearse-Edwards, Poehl-Surhoff-Edwards, Scott-Edwards, Collins-Nagy-Shaw-Edwards, Scott-Valdez-Edwards, Canton-Akron; Mesa-Sander-Culkar-Thorpe, Householder-Bell-Thorpe, Householder-Bell, Bell-Garces-Thorpe, Hagerstown; Sampen-Belinda, Adams-Belinda, York-Belinda, Richardson-Tracy, York-Tracy, Tomlin-Tracy, Sampen-Webb-Smith, Harrisburg; Vesling-Rightnowar, Aldred-Everson, London; Crouch-Irvine 2, Bast-Dalton, Manzanillo-Shikles, Shikles-Irvine, Shikles-Crouch-Plympton, Carista-Irvine, Plympton-Wacha, Manzanillo-Stewart-Kuzniar, New Britain; Mauser-Fynan, Reading; Burba-Helton, Spagnola-Helton, Rojas-Doyle, Williamsport.

NO-HIT GAMES—Gabriele, New Britain, defeated Williamsport, 1-0, April 21; Grimsley, Reading, defeated Harrisburg, 3-0 (first game), May 3; Manzanillo, New Britain, defeated Reading, 3-0 (second game), July 12; Mauser, Reading, defeated New Britain, 9-0 (second game), August 30.

Southern League

CLASS AA

Leading Batter
SCOTT LEIUS
Orlando

League President
JIMMY BRAGAN

Leading Pitcher
PETE DELKUS
Orlando

CHAMPIONSHIP WINNERS IN PREVIOUS YEARS

1904—Macon .598	1938—Savannah .574	1965—Columbus .572
1905—Macon .625	Macon (2nd)† .570	1966—Mobile .629
1906—Savannah .637	1939—Columbus .601	1967—Birmingham .604
1907—Charleston .620	Augusta (2nd)† .597	1968—Asheville .614
1908—Jacksonville .694	1940—Savannah .627	1969—Charlotte .579
1909—Chattanooga* .738	Columbus (2nd)† .583	1970—Columbus .569
Augusta .702	1941—Macon .643	1971—Did not operate as league—clubs
1910—Columbus .588	Columbia (2nd)† .636	were members of Dixie Association.
1911—Columbus* .681	1942—Charleston .620	1972—Asheville .583
Columbia .710	Macon (2nd)† .585	Montgomery§ .561
1912—Jacksonville* .679	1943-45—Did not operate.	1973—Montgomery§ .580
Columbus .632	1946—Columbus .568	Jacksonville .559
1913—Savannah .754	Augusta (4th)† .547	1974—Jacksonville .565
Savannah .593	1947—Columbus .575	Knoxville§ .533
1914—Savannah* .667	Savannah (2nd)† .563	1975—Orlando .587
Albany .650	1948—Charleston .572	Montgomery§ .545
1915—Macon .588	Greenville (3rd)† .549	1976—Montgomery x .591
Columbus* .686	1949—Macon‡ .623	Orlando .540
1916—Augusta* .617	1950—Macon‡ .588	1977—Montgomery x .628
Columbia .631	1951—Montgomery .607	Jacksonville .522
1917—Charleston .741	1952—Columbia .649	1978—Knoxville x .611
Columbia* .667	Montgomery (3rd)† .558	Savannah .500
1918—Did not operate.	1953—Jacksonville .679	1979—Columbus .587
1919—Columbia .585	Savannah (2nd)† .571	Nashville x .576
1920—Columbia .633	1954—Jacksonville .593	1980—Memphis .576
1921—Columbia .642	Savannah (2nd)† .571	Charlotte x .500
1922—Charleston .625	1955—Columbia .636	1981—Nashville .566
1923—Charlotte* .653	Augusta (3rd)† .543	Orlando x .556
Macon .580	1956—Jacksonville‡ .621	1982—Jacksonville .576
1924—Augusta .612	1957—Augusta .636	Nashville x .535
1925—Spartanburg .620	Charlotte (2nd)† .562	1983—Birmingham x .628
1926—Greenville .662	1958—Augusta .550	Jacksonville .531
1927—Greenville .622	Macon (3rd)† .500	1984—Charlotte x .510
1928—Asheville .664	1959—Knoxville .557	Knoxville .483
1929—Asheville .605	Gastonia (4th)† .504	1985—Charlotte .545
Knoxville* .634	1960—Columbia .597	Huntsville x .542
1930—Greenville* .620	Savannah (3rd)† .561	1986—Huntsville .553
Macon .643	1961—Asheville .635	Columbus x .500
1931-35—Did not operate.	1962—Savannah .662	1987—Charlotte .586
1936—Jacksonville .652	Macon (3rd)† .576	Birmingham x .476
Columbus* .650	1963—Augusta* .661	1988—Greenville .604
1937—Columbus .572	Lynchburg .662	Chattanooga x .566
Savannah (3rd)† .565	1964—Lynchburg .579	

*Won split-season playoff. †Won four-club playoff. ‡Won championship and four-club playoff. §League was divided into Eastern and Western divisions; won playoff. xLeague was divided into Eastern and Western divisions and played split season; won playoff.

STANDING OF CLUBS AT CLOSE OF FIRST HALF, JUNE 18

EASTERN DIVISION

Club	W.	L.	T.	Pct.	G.B.
Orlando (Twins)	40	31	1	.563	......
Jacksonville (Expos)	37	33	1	.529	2½
Columbus (Astros)	32	40	0	.444	8½
Charlotte (Cubs)	30	41	0	.423	10
Greenville (Braves)	29	41	0	.414	10½

SOUTHERN DIVISION

Club	W.	L.	T.	Pct.	G.B.
Birmingham (White Sox)	53	18	0	.746	......
Knoxville (Blue Jays)	37	34	0	.521	16
Huntsville (Athletics)	37	35	0	.514	16½
Chattanooga (Reds)	33	38	0	.465	20
Memphis (Royals)	27	44	0	.380	26

STANDING OF CLUBS AT CLOSE OF SECOND HALF, AUGUST 31

EASTERN DIVISION

Club	W.	L.	T.	Pct.	G.B.
Greenville (Braves)	41	28	0	.594	......
Charlotte (Cubs)	40	32	2	.556	2½
Columbus (Astros)	39	32	0	.549	3
Orlando (Twins)	39	34	0	.534	4
Jacksonville (Expos)	31	43	0	.419	12½

SOUTHERN DIVISION

Club	W.	L.	T.	Pct.	G.B.
Huntsville (Athletics)	45	26	0	.634	......
Birmingham (White Sox)	35	37	1	.486	10
Memphis (Royals)	32	40	0	.444	13½
Knoxville (Blue Jays)	30	42	0	.417	15½
Chattanooga (Reds)	25	43	1	.368	18½

COMPOSITE STANDING OF CLUBS AT CLOSE OF SEASON, AUGUST 31

Club	Birm.	Hunt.	Orl.	Grn.	Col.	Char.	Jax.	Knox.	Chat.	Mem.	W.	L.	T.	Pct.	G.B.
Birmingham (White Sox)	....	5	9	7	13	12	8	10	11	13	88	55	1	.615	......
Huntsville (Athletics)	11	....	9	7	9	8	11	9	8	10	82	61	0	.573	6
Orlando (Twins)	7	7	....	10	8	11	8	10	10	8	79	65	0	.549	9½
Greenville (Braves)	9	8	6	....	4	8	11	7	8	9	70	69	0	.504	16
Columbus (Astros)	3	7	8	12	....	7	8	9	8	9	71	72	0	.497	17
Charlotte (Cubs)	3	8	5	8	9	....	8	8	10	11	70	73	2	.490	18
Jacksonville (Expos)	8	5	8	5	8	8	....	11	10	5	68	76	1	.472	20½
Knoxville (Blue Jays)	6	7	6	9	7	8	5	....	9	10	67	76	0	.469	21
Chattanooga (Reds)	5	8	6	6	8	6	6	6	....	9	58	81	1	.417	28
Memphis (Royals)	3	6	8	7	6	5	11	6	7	....	59	84	0	.413	29

Major league affiliations in parentheses.

Playoffs—Birmingham defeated Huntsville, three games to one; Greenville defeated Orlando, three games to one; Birmingham defeated Greenville, three games to none, to win league championship.

Regular-Season Attendance—Birmingham, 281,754; Charlotte, 157,720; Chattanooga, 156,677; Columbus, 95,689; Greenville, 211,347; Huntsville, 220,941; Jacksonville, 220,803; Knoxville, 69,776; Memphis, 175,334; Orlando, 97,803. Totals—1,687,844. Playoffs (11 games)—20,555. All-Star Game—3,554.

Managers—Birmingham, Ken Berry; Charlotte, Jim Essian; Chattanooga, Jim Tracy; Columbus, Tom Wiedenhauer; Greenville, Buddy Bailey; Huntsville, Jeff Newman; Jacksonville, Alan Bannister; Knoxville, Barry Foote; Memphis, Jeff Cox; Orlando, Ron Gardenhire.

All-Star Team—1B—Paul Sorrento, Orlando; 2B—Greg Smith, Charlotte; 3B—Robin Ventura, Birmingham; SS—Scott Leius, Orlando; C—Kelly Mann, Charlotte; Jimmy Kremers, Greenville; OF—Eric Anthony, Columbus; Harvey Pulliam, Memphis; Marquis Grissom, Jacksonville; Derrick May, Charlotte; Dann Howitt, Huntsville; DH—Bob Hamelin, Memphis; LHP—Mark Guthrie, Orlando; Wayne Edwards, Birmingham; RHP—Darryl Kile, Columbus; Relief Pitcher—Joe Klink, Huntsville; Outstanding Pitcher—Laddie Renfroe, Charlotte; Most Valuable Player—Eric Anthony, Columbus; Manager of the Year—Jeff Newman, Huntsville.

(Compiled by Howe Sportsdata International, Boston, Mass.)

CLUB BATTING

Club	Pct.	G.	AB.	R.	OR.	H.	TB.	2B.	3B.	HR.	RBI.	SH.	SF.	HP.	BB.	Int. BB.	SO.	SB.	CS.	LOB.
Charlotte	.264	145	4655	677	713	1231	1815	226	26	102	604	75	33	68	482	22	720	169	72	988
Birmingham	.260	144	4672	770	604	1213	1671	210	52	48	641	68	52	57	659	36	896	264	120	1034
Orlando	.256	145	4694	725	666	1202	1730	195	33	89	651	43	50	64	724	29	921	114	54	1163
Huntsville	.255	143	4619	748	701	1176	1804	211	42	111	673	86	48	42	757	12	954	155	69	1121
Chattanooga	.247	140	4458	584	675	1100	1588	196	44	68	537	51	51	33	471	25	803	95	47	958
Knoxville	.245	143	4545	591	584	1112	1691	178	46	103	509	35	33	51	401	12	903	112	61	881
Columbus	.243	143	4544	608	592	1105	1561	153	33	79	536	38	29	38	656	29	1018	188	92	1055
Greenville	.237	139	4415	556	533	1046	1551	170	25	95	499	39	37	36	490	32	889	99	72	933
Jacksonville	.236	145	4508	529	569	1066	1530	193	44	61	457	47	37	27	504	22	861	168	92	917
Memphis	.234	143	4550	553	704	1066	1589	185	37	88	485	37	25	38	497	23	973	98	58	963

INDIVIDUAL BATTING

(Leading Qualifiers for Batting Championship—389 or More Plate Appearances)

*Bats lefthanded.   †Switch-hitter.

Player and Club	Pct.	G.	AB.	R.	H.	TB.	2B.	3B.	HR.	RBI.	SH.	SF.	HP.	BB.	Int. BB.	SO.	SB.	CS.
Leius, Scott, Orlando	.303	99	346	49	105	143	22	2	4	45	3	2	0	38	0	74	3	2
Anthony, Eric, Columbus*	.300	107	403	67	121	225	16	2	28	79	0	3	3	35	1	127	14	9
Pappas, Erik, Charlotte	.299	119	354	69	106	187	31	1	16	49	4	2	8	66	1	50	7	8
Smith, Gregory, Charlotte†	.296	126	467	59	138	188	23	6	5	64	9	4	6	42	1	52	38	13
May, Derrick, Charlotte*	.295	136	491	72	145	208	26	5	9	70	1	0	5	33	4	76	19	7
Lanoux, Carol, Orlando*	.294	109	354	41	104	142	20	0	6	53	1	5	4	50	8	49	1	1
Pulliam, Harvey, Memphis	.290	116	417	67	121	195	28	8	10	67	0	3	5	44	4	65	5	5
Jefferson, Reginald, Chattanooga†	.287	135	487	66	140	216	19	3	17	80	0	4	7	43	5	73	2	3
Grebeck, Craig, Birmingham	.287	143	533	85	153	201	25	4	5	80	11	7	4	63	4	77	14	15
Amaral, Richard, Birmingham	.285	122	432	90	123	162	15	6	4	48	7	4	2	88	2	66	57	14

Departmental Leaders: G—Grebeck, Rhodes, 143; AB—Grebeck, McRae, 533; R—Amaral, 90; H—Grebeck, 153; TB—Howitt, 253; 2B—Sorrento, 35; 3B—Nelson, 13; HR—Anthony, 28; RBI—Sorrento, 112; SH—Escobar, 25; SF—Br. Hunter, Jorgensen, 9; HP—Whiten, 11; BB—G. Jones, 107; IBB—Ventura, 12; SO—R. Martinez, 137; SB—Penigar, 64; CS—Penigar, 22.

(All Pitchers—Listed Alphabetically)

Player and Club	Pct.	G.	AB.	R.	H.	TB.	2B.	3B.	HR.	RBI.	SH.	SF.	HP.	BB.	Int. BB.	SO.	SB.	CS.
Acta, Manuel, Columbus	.130	36	77	8	10	15	2	0	1	9	1	0	2	5	0	15	1	0
Afenir, Troy, Huntsville	.253	65	225	31	57	113	15	1	13	45	0	4	1	28	0	63	1	3
Akins, Sidney, Greenville	.000	2	1	0	0	0	0	0	0	0	0	0	0	0	0	0	0	0
Alborano, Peter, Memphis*	.250	15	60	9	15	18	1	1	0	6	0	0	2	5	0	9	0	0
Alcala, Julio, Memphis	.240	113	417	38	100	119	16	0	1	27	4	1	2	19	1	66	3	5
Alicea, Edwin, Greenville†	.219	124	352	59	77	126	7	3	12	47	3	3	3	68	3	89	22	7
Alva, John, Greenville	.208	112	384	33	80	102	13	0	3	26	6	4	2	27	2	69	4	6
Amaral, Richard, Birmingham	.285	122	432	90	123	162	15	6	4	48	7	4	2	88	2	66	57	14

Player and Club	Pct.	G.	AB.	R.	H.	TB.	2B.	3B.	HR.	RBI.	SH.	SF.	HP.	BB.	Int. BB.	SO.	SB.	CS.
Ansley, Willie, Columbus	.250	30	104	16	26	29	3	0	0	7	2	0	0	26	0	37	6	1
Anthony, Eric, Columbus*	.300	107	403	67	121	225	16	2	28	79	0	3	3	35	5	127	14	9
Arnold, Timothy, Orlando	.227	69	220	17	50	63	10	0	1	31	0	5	7	19	0	34	3	0
Avery, Steven, Greenville*	.000	13	12	0	0	0	0	0	0	0	0	0	0	1	0	10	0	0
Bafia, Robert, Charlotte	.278	79	273	38	76	121	13	1	10	39	0	3	5	15	1	55	5	3
Baldwin, Jeffrey, Columbus*	.273	96	256	31	70	86	13	0	1	23	0	1	2	39	3	54	3	6
Balsley, Darren, Knoxville	.000	14	1	0	0	0	0	0	0	0	0	0	0	0	0	1	0	0
Batiste, Kevin, Knoxville	.222	81	279	36	62	89	8	8	1	25	5	0	2	40	2	81	20	13
Beeler, Robert, Chattanooga	.198	45	131	8	26	33	4	0	1	5	3	1	0	16	2	28	0	1
Bell, Derek, Knoxville	.242	136	513	72	124	206	22	6	16	75	0	4	6	26	4	92	15	7
Bell, Michael, Greenville*	.244	132	472	63	115	165	26	3	6	57	1	1	2	62	6	91	10	5
Bell, Terence, Greenville	.000	2	4	0	0	0	0	0	0	0	0	0	0	0	0	2	0	0
Benavides, Alfredo, Chattanooga	.250	88	284	25	71	91	14	3	0	27	2	3	2	22	0	46	1	4
Bennett, Christopher, Jacksonville	.000	25	2	0	0	0	0	0	0	0	1	0	0	0	0	0	0	0
Bertolani, Jerry, Birmingham	.239	75	243	34	58	90	16	2	4	33	1	6	6	25	0	56	2	3
Blackwell, Larry, Orlando	.236	96	288	52	68	86	2	5	2	31	9	3	3	58	0	59	29	12
Blocker, Terry, Greenville*	.268	59	205	33	55	85	7	4	5	22	1	2	0	17	1	29	2	3
Bombard, Richard, Chattanooga	.000	1	1	0	0	0	0	0	0	0	0	0	0	0	0	1	0	0
Borrelli, Dean, Huntsville	.154	5	13	0	2	3	1	0	0	2	1	0	1	2	0	6	0	0
Boskie, Shawn, Charlotte	.130	32	23	3	3	5	2	0	0	1	3	0	0	4	0	4	0	0
Bottenfield, Kent, Jacksonville†	.000	25	18	0	0	0	0	0	0	0	0	0	0	0	0	8	0	0
Bowen, Kenneth, Memphis†	.190	38	100	14	19	24	5	0	0	4	3	0	0	14	0	25	1	1
Bowen, Ryan, Columbus	.038	29	26	3	1	1	0	0	0	1	0	1	3	0	0	10	0	0
Brito, Jorge, Huntsville	.219	24	73	13	16	22	2	2	0	8	2	0	0	20	0	23	1	1
Brosius, Scott, Huntsville	.271	128	461	68	125	172	22	2	7	60	6	6	5	58	3	62	4	6
Brown, Don, Chattanooga	.235	49	162	23	38	54	7	0	3	11	6	1	1	21	1	36	19	4
Brown, Kurt, Birmingham	.167	2	6	0	1	1	0	0	0	0	0	0	0	0	0	2	1	0
Browning, Michael, Columbus	.500	52	2	0	1	1	0	0	0	0	0	0	0	0	0	0	0	0
Brumfield, Jacob, Memphis	.228	104	346	43	79	100	14	2	1	25	5	0	3	53	0	74	28	12
Bruno, Joseph, Chattanooga	.000	41	1	0	0	0	0	0	0	1	0	0	0	0	0	0	0	0
Bullinger, James, Charlotte	.216	124	320	34	69	93	13	1	3	28	6	0	2	39	2	56	3	0
Bundy, Lorenzo, Greenville*	.223	52	166	20	37	58	7	1	4	23	0	1	2	24	4	25	1	2
Cakora, Matthew, Charlotte*	.000	34	1	0	0	0	0	0	0	0	0	0	0	0	0	1	0	0
Cano, Joselito, Columbus	.000	3	2	0	0	0	0	0	0	0	0	0	0	0	0	1	0	0
Canseco, Jose, Huntsville	.207	9	29	2	6	6	0	0	0	3	0	0	0	5	0	11	1	0
Canseco, Osvaldo, Huntsville	.233	91	317	52	74	131	17	2	12	52	2	4	5	51	0	88	1	2
Capello, Peter, Memphis	.143	16	49	3	7	8	1	0	0	1	0	1	0	2	0	16	0	0
Carriger, Ricky, Jacksonville	.000	14	1	0	0	0	0	0	0	0	0	0	0	0	0	1	0	0
Carter, Jeffrey, Jacksonville	.000	6	6	0	0	0	0	0	0	0	1	0	0	1	0	1	0	0
Carver, Billy Paul, Columbus	.000	1	3	0	0	0	0	0	0	0	0	0	0	0	0	1	0	0
Casarotti, Richard, Greenville†	.220	70	218	23	48	61	7	0	2	25	4	3	3	19	0	52	1	5
Casey, Timothy, Huntsville*	.249	72	229	47	57	111	12	3	12	50	1	1	3	46	0	70	1	3
Castillo, Frank, Charlotte	.000	10	5	0	0	0	0	0	0	0	0	0	0	0	0	3	0	0
Chambers, Travis, Jacksonville*	.000	40	4	0	0	0	0	0	0	0	1	0	0	0	0	1	0	0
Cianfrocco, Angelo, Jacksonville	.245	132	429	46	105	162	22	7	7	50	0	5	1	37	1	126	3	7
Clements, Anthony, Memphis	.213	112	342	35	73	100	8	5	3	21	4	0	2	34	0	97	13	5
Coffman, Kevin, Charlotte	.000	8	5	0	0	0	0	0	0	0	0	0	0	0	0	2	0	0
Colbrunn, Gregory, Jacksonville	.275	55	178	21	49	71	11	1	3	18	0	1	2	13	0	33	0	1
Cole, Stewart, Memphis	.214	90	299	30	64	96	8	3	6	32	4	2	0	25	0	67	11	3
Colombino, Carlo, Columbus	.186	84	285	27	53	66	5	1	2	24	7	1	9	19	0	45	3	2
Corbell, Charles, Huntsville	1.000	9	1	2	1	1	0	0	0	0	0	0	0	0	0	0	0	0
Cordero, Wilfredo, Jacksonville*	.215	39	121	9	26	43	6	1	3	17	3	1	0	12	0	33	1	2
Costello, Fred, Columbus	.000	30	2	0	0	0	0	0	0	0	0	0	0	0	0	2	0	0
Credeur, Todd, Columbus*	.182	21	11	0	2	2	0	0	0	2	0	0	0	1	0	7	0	0
Cruz, Luis, Charlotte	.263	81	240	37	63	76	8	1	1	16	6	0	1	7	1	28	6	5
Czajkowski, James, Greenville	.000	17	1	0	0	0	0	0	0	0	1	0	0	0	0	0	0	0
Davidson, Jackie, Charlotte†	.091	25	11	0	1	2	1	0	0	0	2	0	0	2	0	3	0	0
Davis, Kevin, Birmingham	.237	85	279	38	66	92	13	5	1	37	0	2	1	16	1	67	5	3
Davis, Mark, Birmingham	.255	56	192	35	49	80	10	3	5	26	3	0	1	25	1	52	16	7
Davis, Steven, Chattanooga*	.169	22	65	7	11	17	1	1	1	5	0	1	0	7	0	18	0	0
DeFrancesco, Anthony, Chattanooga	.225	74	209	29	47	69	11	1	3	18	3	0	2	29	3	37	1	0
Deitz, Timothy, Greenville	.000	30	2	0	0	0	0	0	0	0	0	0	0	0	0	1	0	0
DelRosario, Maximo, Greenville	.000	49	1	0	0	0	0	0	0	0	0	0	0	0	0	1	0	0
DeShields, Delino, Jacksonville*	.270	93	307	55	83	114	10	6	3	35	4	3	1	76	0	80	37	12
Diaz, Carlos, Knoxville	.250	100	320	28	80	112	12	1	6	36	4	3	3	17	0	55	3	1
Diaz, Jose, Knoxville	.170	43	106	14	18	21	0	0	1	5	3	0	0	18	0	23	1	1
Dodd, William, Chattanooga	.000	35	2	0	0	0	0	0	0	0	1	0	0	0	0	1	0	0
Doran, Mark, Birmingham	.284	23	74	13	21	27	2	2	0	7	1	1	2	6	0	24	3	1
Duke, Douglas, Jacksonville	.182	22	66	6	12	17	3	1	0	6	0	2	0	8	0	15	0	0
Dull, Michael, Jacksonville*	.178	43	107	9	19	30	4	2	1	11	1	1	1	17	2	16	0	0
Dunbar, Thomas, Greenville*	.303	35	89	12	27	42	2	2	3	13	0	0	0	17	3	7	1	2
Eccles, John, Orlando	.281	50	153	24	43	71	4	0	8	26	1	1	3	20	0	45	0	1
Escalera, Carlos, Memphis	.225	52	169	15	38	43	2	0	1	20	1	2	3	7	0	31	2	1
Escobar, Angel, Huntsville†	.245	136	458	77	112	147	20	6	1	54	25	4	3	90	0	89	10	10
Estes, Joel, Columbus*	.000	17	3	0	0	0	0	0	0	0	0	0	0	0	0	2	0	0
Eusebio, Antonio, Columbus	.187	65	203	20	38	46	6	1	0	18	0	0	3	38	1	47	7	3
Farmer, Howard, Jacksonville	.067	26	30	2	2	2	0	0	0	0	3	0	0	0	0	14	0	1
Firova, Daniel, Charlotte	.269	34	78	6	21	27	6	0	0	8	1	4	1	6	0	11	1	3
Forney, Jeffrey, Chattanooga	.000	1	0	0	0	0	0	0	0	0	0	0	0	0	0	0	0	0
Fox, Blane, Columbus*	.209	41	86	7	18	21	3	0	0	8	1	1	1	14	0	20	3	1
Fox, Eric, Columbus*	.251	139	498	84	125	190	10	5	15	51	11	2	0	72	1	85	49	15
Frazier, Louis, Columbus†	.230	135	460	65	106	130	10	1	4	31	2	1	2	76	2	101	43	14
Frobel, Douglas, Birmingham*	.213	27	80	7	17	29	4	1	2	14	1	2	1	5	2	12	4	3
Gakeler, Daniel, Jacksonville	.200	14	10	0	2	2	0	0	0	0	1	0	0	0	0	5	0	0
Garbey, Barbaro, Jacksonville	.289	67	201	19	58	75	11	0	2	24	0	2	4	19	1	22	3	4
Garcia, Cornelio, Birmingham*	.271	128	461	74	125	158	12	9	1	57	8	4	4	62	0	94	35	12
Garcia, Victor, Charlotte	.274	67	215	42	59	99	13	0	9	44	2	2	4	16	1	35	4	1
Garrison, Webster, Knoxville	.271	54	203	38	55	77	6	2	4	14	1	1	0	33	0	38	18	6
Gavin, David, Huntsville	.229	17	48	9	11	17	1	1	1	5	1	2	1	1	0	12	0	0
Germann, Mark, Chattanooga	.246	100	369	49	81	114	11	5	4	41	3	8	0	35	1	40	0	1
Gilbert, Patrick, Huntsville	.227	70	220	25	50	70	10	2	2	22	3	0	1	31	0	49	2	3
Givler, Douglas, Columbus	.286	48	7	1	2	2	0	0	0	0	0	1	0	0	0	1	0	0

Player and Club	Pct.	G.	AB.	R.	H.	TB.	2B.	3B.	HR.	RBI.	SH.	SF.	HP.	BB.	Int. BB.	SO.	SB.	CS.
Gomez, Patrick, Charlotte*	.000	2	2	1	0	0	0	0	0	0	0	0	0	0	0	1	0	0
Grebeck, Craig, Birmingham	.287	143	533	85	153	201	25	4	5	80	11	7	4	63	4	77	14	15
Green, David, Greenville	.271	34	118	15	32	56	9	0	5	22	1	3	0	9	2	18	1	2
Griffin, Tyrone, Charlotte†	.231	45	143	25	33	48	6	0	3	21	0	1	2	25	1	29	8	5
Grissom, Marquis, Jacksonville	.299	78	278	43	83	115	15	4	3	31	1	3	7	24	1	31	24	6
Grovom, Carl, Chattanooga*	.000	6	3	0	0	0	0	0	0	0	0	0	0	0	0	2	0	0
Hamelin, Robert, Memphis*	.308	68	211	45	65	135	12	5	16	47	0	1	5	52	7	52	3	6
Harrison, Phillip, Charlotte*	.154	27	26	2	4	4	0	0	0	3	5	0	0	1	0	9	1	0
Hayden, Alan, Chattanooga*	.302	33	116	22	35	40	3	1	0	11	3	0	1	13	0	15	9	7
Hemond, Scott, Huntsville	.265	132	490	89	130	183	26	6	5	62	13	6	7	62	0	77	45	17
Hennis, Randall, Columbus	.125	28	24	3	3	4	1	0	0	1	1	0	0	2	0	9	0	0
Henry, Floyd, Chattanooga*	.000	7	4	0	0	0	0	0	0	0	1	1	0	0	0	0	0	0
Hernandez, Cesar, Jacksonville	.212	81	222	25	47	67	9	1	3	13	1	0	0	22	2	60	11	4
Hickey, James, Columbus	.267	27	15	0	4	6	2	0	0	3	0	0	0	1	0	5	0	0
Hill, Milton, Chattanooga	.000	51	3	0	0	0	0	0	0	0	1	0	0	0	0	1	0	0
Hill, Orsino, Charlotte*	.261	82	241	44	63	107	14	0	10	34	2	2	2	32	1	53	6	1
Hirsch, Jeffrey, Charlotte†	.200	18	15	1	3	3	0	0	0	0	2	0	0	1	0	3	0	0
Holcomb, Scott, Huntsville	.000	29	0	0	0	0	0	0	0	0	1	0	0	0	0	0	0	0
Holmes, Stanley, Huntsville	.167	14	48	1	8	14	3	0	1	4	0	0	1	7	0	9	0	0
Hood, Dennis, Greenville	.252	136	464	68	117	180	20	5	11	44	3	3	8	48	4	124	32	14
Houston, Melvin, Birmingham	.244	131	434	54	106	148	20	2	6	41	10	4	1	54	3	43	29	19
Howitt, Dann, Huntsville*	.281	138	509	78	143	253	28	2	26	111	2	6	3	68	7	107	2	1
Hubbard, Trent, Columbus†	.264	104	348	55	92	124	7	8	3	37	4	2	2	43	3	53	28	6
Hunter, Bertram, Columbus†	.182	50	154	16	28	31	1	1	0	13	1	1	0	30	5	42	10	5
Hunter, Brian, Greenville	.253	124	451	57	114	194	19	2	19	82	1	9	7	33	2	61	5	4
Ilsley, Blaise, Columbus*	.200	5	5	0	1	1	0	0	0	0	0	0	0	0	0	3	0	0
Jacas, David, Orlando	.300	56	217	45	65	92	12	3	3	26	2	3	4	23	1	34	14	3
Jefferson, James, Chattanooga	.000	34	2	0	0	0	0	0	0	0	0	0	0	0	0	1	0	0
Jefferson, Reginald, Chattanooga†	.287	135	487	66	140	216	19	3	17	80	0	4	7	43	5	73	2	3
Jeffery, Scott, Chattanooga	.333	13	12	3	4	6	2	0	0	3	3	0	0	1	0	2	0	0
Jeter, Shawn, Knoxville*	.273	101	308	39	84	106	9	2	3	25	2	1	1	27	0	65	8	4
Jimenez, German, Greenville*	.067	24	15	0	1	1	0	0	0	1	1	0	0	1	0	2	0	0
Jirschele, Michael, Memphis	.190	44	142	11	27	34	4	0	1	19	0	2	2	27	0	39	2	4
Jones, Christopher C., Chattanooga	.251	103	378	47	95	147	18	2	10	54	0	1	3	23	1	68	10	2
Jones, Gary, Huntsville*	.275	96	287	67	79	98	10	3	1	45	3	3	4	107	1	61	16	4
Jordan, Scott, Columbus	.270	50	137	24	37	59	8	4	2	19	0	0	2	41	0	24	10	5
Jorgensen, Terry, Orlando	.263	135	514	84	135	211	27	5	13	101	0	9	5	76	4	78	1	1
Kaiser, Keith, Chattanooga†	.211	28	19	2	4	6	0	1	0	5	2	1	1	4	0	8	0	0
Kallevig, Gregory, Charlotte	.100	33	20	1	2	3	1	0	0	0	2	0	0	1	0	9	0	0
Kating, James, Huntsville	.276	59	192	25	53	70	11	0	2	17	3	2	3	28	0	27	0	0
Kile, Darryl, Columbus	.091	21	22	0	2	2	0	0	0	1	0	1	0	7	0	7	0	0
Kilner, John, Greenville*	.000	30	1	0	0	0	0	0	0	0	0	0	0	0	0	1	0	0
Kremers, James, Greenville*	.235	121	388	41	91	160	19	1	16	58	2	2	0	34	5	95	5	5
Kuld, Peter, Huntsville	.209	60	191	23	40	80	9	2	9	34	4	2	1	13	0	53	1	1
Ladnier, Deric, Memphis†	.248	49	165	29	41	56	9	0	2	20	0	3	0	12	1	36	0	1
Landrum, Cedric, Charlotte*	.255	123	361	72	92	125	11	2	6	37	5	2	5	48	0	54	45	9
Lane, Brian, Chattanooga	.252	130	464	59	117	177	19	4	11	89	1	4	8	46	4	95	6	4
Lanoux, Carol, Orlando*	.294	109	354	41	104	142	20	0	6	53	1	5	4	50	8	49	1	1
Lazor, Joseph, Chattanooga	.100	21	10	0	1	1	0	0	0	2	1	1	0	2	0	6	0	0
Leary, Robert, Jacksonville	.212	48	113	8	24	39	7	1	2	10	3	0	0	7	0	34	0	0
Lee, Terry, Chattanooga	.260	51	177	23	46	74	13	0	5	27	1	4	1	13	0	32	0	0
Leius, Scott, Orlando	.303	99	346	49	105	143	22	2	4	45	3	2	0	38	0	74	3	2
LeMasters, James, Greenville	.059	32	17	1	1	2	1	0	0	1	0	0	0	5	0	7	0	0
Leon, Danilo, Jacksonville	.071	18	14	1	1	1	0	0	0	0	0	0	0	1	0	5	0	0
Lewis, Darren, Huntsville	.323	9	31	7	10	16	1	1	1	7	2	0	1	2	0	4	0	1
Lewis, John, Charlotte*	.258	57	128	14	33	44	4	2	1	7	2	0	3	23	1	18	5	2
Lewis, Richie, Jacksonville	.250	17	12	2	3	3	0	0	0	1	1	0	0	0	0	4	0	0
Little, Douglas, Birmingham	.000	19	0	0	0	0	0	0	0	0	1	0	0	0	0	0	0	0
Lombardozzi, Christopher, Chatta.*	.262	111	325	44	85	118	20	2	3	38	3	4	2	39	2	46	0	2
Lonigro, Gregory, Chattanooga	.220	80	232	26	51	76	13	3	2	22	3	2	1	16	0	28	1	1
Lopez, Robert, Chattanooga*	.333	3	3	0	1	1	0	0	0	0	0	2	0	0	0	1	0	0
Loynd, Michael, Columbus	.000	26	14	0	0	0	0	0	0	0	5	0	0	0	0	7	0	0
Mack, Quinn, Jacksonville*	.257	122	378	46	97	140	19	3	6	40	4	1	1	27	2	55	5	7
Malave, Omar, Knoxville	.222	29	72	7	16	20	4	0	0	8	1	2	1	7	0	10	1	0
Maldonado, Phillip, Greenville	.200	9	20	0	4	4	0	0	0	1	0	0	1	3	1	3	0	0
Mann, Kelly, Charlotte	.246	117	345	37	85	125	14	1	8	56	8	8	9	33	1	60	1	1
Marak, Paul, Greenville	.143	43	14	0	2	3	1	0	0	2	2	0	0	0	0	3	0	0
Marchok, Christopher, Jacksonville*	.000	65	1	0	0	0	0	0	0	0	0	0	0	0	0	0	0	0
Martinez, Domingo, Knoxville	.246	120	415	56	102	155	19	2	10	53	1	5	9	42	3	82	2	2
Martinez, Reynaldo, Memphis*	.243	127	399	55	97	190	20	2	23	62	4	4	1	63	7	137	3	3
May, Derrick, Charlotte*	.295	136	491	72	145	208	26	5	9	70	1	0	5	33	4	76	19	7
McElroy, Glen, Birmingham	.200	26	70	7	14	15	1	0	0	9	2	0	0	5	0	8	1	2
McRae, Brian, Memphis†	.227	138	533	72	121	170	18	4	5	42	7	1	8	43	1	94	23	6
Mead, Timber, Chattanooga	.000	20	12	0	0	0	0	0	0	1	1	1	0	1	0	5	0	0
Merullo, Matthew, Birmingham*	.294	33	119	19	35	50	6	0	3	23	2	3	0	16	2	15	0	1
Michno, Thomas, Charlotte	.273	37	11	4	3	5	2	0	0	0	2	0	0	0	0	3	0	0
Minutelli, Gino, Chattanooga*	.000	6	3	0	0	0	0	0	0	0	0	0	0	1	0	0	0	0
Mordecai, Michael, Greenville	.375	4	8	0	3	3	0	0	0	0	0	0	0	1	0	1	0	0
Morgan, Kenneth, Orlando*	.246	132	452	66	111	162	11	5	10	65	2	6	4	61	4	130	16	11
Morris, Angel, Memphis	.203	102	301	27	61	93	14	0	6	29	2	1	1	60	2	61	0	0
Morris, Richard, Greenville	.254	117	342	56	87	128	11	3	8	38	2	3	6	68	0	78	5	9
Morrison, Brian, Knoxville	.154	8	26	1	4	4	0	0	0	2	0	0	0	0	0	9	0	0
Moscrey, Michael, Chattanooga*	.190	26	21	2	4	4	0	0	0	2	1	0	1	0	0	7	0	0
Mota, Jose, Huntsville†	.136	27	81	15	11	12	1	0	0	6	5	1	1	30	0	15	3	2
Mount, Charles, Birmingham	.000	43	2	0	0	0	0	0	0	0	0	0	0	0	0	2	0	0
Mullins, Ronald, Chattanooga	.500	9	2	1	1	1	0	0	0	0	0	0	0	0	0	0	0	0
Mulvaney, Michael, Chattanooga	.180	14	50	6	9	11	2	0	0	5	0	0	0	13	0	0	0	0
Munoz, Pedro, Knoxville	.267	122	442	54	118	198	15	4	19	65	0	4	2	20	2	85	10	4
Myers, Gregory, Knoxville*	.333	29	90	11	30	55	10	0	5	19	0	1	0	16	1	0	0	0
Nago, Garret, Columbus†	.256	41	86	12	22	35	1	0	4	13	0	1	2	20	0	21	0	0
Natal, Robert, Jacksonville	.206	46	141	12	29	39	8	1	0	11	2	3	0	9	0	24	2	1
Naveda, Edgar, Orlando	.283	70	230	36	65	98	12	3	5	30	2	1	2	22	0	32	2	1

Player and Club	Pct.	G.	AB.	R.	H.	TB.	2B.	3B.	HR.	RBI.	SH.	SF.	HP.	BB.	Int. BB.	SO.	SB.	CS.
Nelson, Jerome, Chattanooga†	.268	111	384	67	103	153	15	13	3	36	5	3	4	53	1	50	18	11
Nichols, Howard, Charlotte	.298	44	124	18	37	57	8	0	4	20	0	0	5	12	1	20	1	1
Oliverio, Stephen, Columbus	.000	18	9	0	0	0	0	0	0	0	4	0	0	2	0	5	0	0
Pacho, Juan, Greenville	.247	65	215	33	53	59	6	0	0	13	5	0	2	8	0	27	0	2
Pappas, Erik, Charlotte	.299	119	354	69	106	187	31	1	16	49	4	2	8	66	1	50	7	8
Parks, Derek, Orlando	.189	31	95	16	18	27	3	0	2	10	0	0	6	19	0	27	1	0
Pearson, Kevin, Chattanooga	.272	45	147	12	40	57	12	1	1	16	0	1	1	10	0	19	1	0
Pedre, Jorge, Memphis	.234	38	141	17	33	44	5	0	2	16	1	2	0	9	0	18	0	0
Penigar, Charles Lee, Birmingham†	.246	133	427	77	105	129	13	4	1	55	5	2	0	74	5	100	64	22
Perez, Yorkis, Jacksonville*	.000	21	2	0	0	0	0	0	0	0	0	0	0	0	0	1	0	0
Peters, Timothy, Jacksonville	.000	40	2	0	0	0	0	0	0	0	0	0	0	0	0	0	0	0
Plumb, David, Greenville	.226	40	106	9	24	36	6	0	2	6	2	1	0	18	0	28	1	1
Polley, Dale, Greenville	.261	28	23	2	6	7	1	0	0	2	1	0	0	1	0	9	0	0
Pruitt, Darrell, Greenville	.224	87	232	28	52	62	8	1	0	14	0	1	1	21	2	22	1	6
Pryor, Buddy, Huntsville	.308	7	26	1	8	9	1	0	0	1	0	0	0	2	0	6	0	0
Puleo, Charles, Greenville	1.000	2	1	0	1	1	0	0	0	1	0	0	0	0	0	0	0	0
Pulliam, Harvey, Memphis	.290	116	417	67	121	195	28	8	10	67	0	3	5	44	4	65	5	5
Quinlan, Thomas, Knoxville	.210	139	452	62	95	170	21	3	16	57	3	4	9	41	0	118	6	4
Raether, Eric, Jacksonville	.000	33	2	0	0	0	0	0	0	0	0	0	0	0	0	0	0	0
Randle, Michael, Orlando*	.250	120	432	73	108	121	7	3	0	27	8	3	6	68	1	82	21	10
Reboulet, Jeffery, Orlando	.216	81	291	43	63	70	5	1	0	26	2	3	1	49	0	33	11	6
Redington, Thomas, Greenville	.245	33	110	9	27	40	4	0	3	13	0	2	0	7	0	22	1	1
Reese, Kyle, Memphis	.111	15	27	1	3	6	0	0	1	6	0	0	0	0	0	13	0	0
Renfroe, Cohen, Charlotte†	.167	78	6	1	1	1	0	0	0	0	4	0	0	0	0	3	1	0
Rhodes, Karl, Columbus*	.258	143	520	81	134	181	25	5	4	63	0	3	3	93	3	105	18	12
Richardson, Allen, Orlando*	.275	89	265	44	73	102	14	3	3	35	6	3	9	43	1	44	1	2
Rivera, Hector, Jacksonville	.000	5	3	0	0	0	0	0	0	0	0	0	0	0	0	2	0	0
Rivera, Pablo, Charlotte	.265	101	287	33	76	105	5	0	8	43	5	1	2	31	2	24	4	4
Rivers, Kenneth, Knoxville	.217	40	92	3	20	24	4	0	0	4	0	0	1	3	0	13	0	1
Robinson, Marteese, Huntsville	.338	16	65	9	22	28	6	0	0	9	0	0	0	3	0	7	3	0
Robinson, Ronald, Chattanooga	.000	1	2	0	0	0	0	0	0	0	0	0	0	0	0	1	0	0
Roby, Ellis, Greenville†	.137	29	51	3	7	8	1	0	0	3	0	0	0	8	0	17	0	0
Rodgers, Darrell, Chattanooga	.000	39	10	1	0	0	0	0	0	1	1	1	1	2	0	5	0	0
Rodriguez, Boi, Jacksonville*	.247	130	388	53	96	154	19	6	9	50	1	5	2	53	3	58	6	3
Rodriguez, Rosario, Chattanooga	.000	28	4	0	0	0	0	0	0	0	0	0	0	0	0	0	0	0
Rohde, David, Columbus†	.280	67	254	40	71	86	5	2	2	27	5	2	1	41	0	25	15	5
Rojas, Melquiades, Jacksonville	.000	34	15	0	0	0	0	0	0	0	1	0	0	0	0	6	0	0
Rosario, David, Charlotte*	.400	55	5	0	2	2	0	0	0	0	1	0	0	0	0	1	0	0
Roth, Kris, Charlotte	.000	10	0	1	0	0	0	0	0	0	0	0	0	1	0	0	0	0
Sabino, Miguel, Greenville*	.220	15	41	3	9	12	1	1	0	2	1	0	1	1	0	4	5	0
Salinas, Manuel, Memphis*	.278	54	216	20	60	83	11	3	2	18	0	2	1	12	0	14	3	1
Sanchez, Pedro, Columbus†	.268	131	444	48	119	169	19	5	7	54	3	2	1	40	3	88	15	13
Sanders, Earl, Knoxville	.000	27	1	0	0	0	0	0	0	0	0	0	0	0	0	1	0	0
Santana, Miguel, Jacksonville†	.215	76	251	39	54	60	2	2	0	18	5	0	2	37	0	39	34	16
Savarino, William, Huntsville*	.244	13	41	3	10	11	1	0	0	7	0	0	0	2	0	9	0	0
Scheid, Richard, Charlotte*	.000	17	3	0	0	0	0	0	0	0	1	0	0	1	0	1	0	0
Schunk, Jerry, Knoxville	.241	95	270	32	65	98	13	4	4	31	8	5	3	17	0	19	6	3
Servais, Scott, Columbus	.236	63	199	20	47	55	5	0	1	22	1	4	3	19	0	42	0	3
Shotkoski, David, Huntsville	.000	23	1	0	0	0	0	0	0	0	0	0	0	0	0	1	0	0
Simms, Michael, Columbus	.257	109	378	64	97	184	21	3	20	81	0	6	2	66	4	110	12	6
Singley, Joseph, Birmingham	.170	20	47	2	8	9	1	0	0	4	3	0	2	2	0	25	2	1
Sipe, Patrick, Jacksonville*	.197	34	117	3	23	28	2	0	1	14	0	0	0	8	1	21	0	0
Small, Jeffrey, Charlotte	.263	28	99	12	26	35	6	0	1	10	1	1	2	5	0	18	3	3
Smith, Gregory, Charlotte†	.296	126	467	59	138	188	23	6	5	64	9	4	6	42	1	52	38	13
Snyder, Doug, Orlando*	.139	54	137	25	19	34	4	1	3	16	5	0	0	50	2	61	8	3
Sorrento, Paul, Orlando*	.255	140	509	81	130	250	35	2	27	112	0	4	7	84	7	119	1	1
Sossamon, Timothy, Jacksonville	.000	19	1	0	0	0	0	0	0	0	1	0	0	0	0	0	0	0
Spehr, Timothy, Memphis	.194	61	216	22	42	75	9	0	8	23	1	1	2	16	0	59	1	3
Stanton, Michael, Greenville*	.667	47	3	0	2	2	0	0	0	2	0	0	0	0	0	1	0	0
Stockam, Douglas, Greenville*	.333	53	3	1	1	1	0	0	0	0	0	0	0	0	0	0	0	0
Suero, Williams, Knoxville	.259	87	324	42	84	123	17	5	4	29	2	0	3	34	0	50	7	4
Sullivan, Glenn, Charlotte*	.254	129	355	51	90	145	19	6	8	50	3	3	6	38	4	38	10	6
Taubensee, Edward, Chattanooga*	.189	45	127	11	24	35	2	0	3	13	1	3	0	11	2	28	0	0
Tellez, Alonso, Jacksonville	.235	26	102	3	24	28	4	0	0	9	0	0	1	1	0	16	1	1
Torres, Philip, Columbus	.000	33	2	0	0	0	0	0	0	0	0	0	0	0	0	1	0	0
Trafton, Todd, Birmingham	.259	107	351	57	91	150	17	3	12	56	4	3	8	38	4	82	10	4
Tubbs, Gregory, Greenville	.185	11	27	4	5	5	0	0	0	1	0	0	0	8	0	4	3	0
Upshaw, Lee, Greenville*	.300	14	10	2	3	3	0	0	0	2	0	0	2	0	0	3	0	0
Vanderwal, John, Jacksonville*	.253	71	217	30	55	86	9	2	6	24	0	2	1	22	1	51	2	3
Ventura, Robin, Birmingham*	.278	129	454	75	126	164	25	2	3	67	4	6	6	93	12	51	9	7
Waggoner, Aubrey, Birmingham*	.228	114	302	66	69	116	23	6	4	35	2	1	9	76	1	74	25	12
Wagner, Daniel, Birmingham	.251	92	303	41	76	100	11	5	1	44	9	6	4	25	1	34	9	7
Wakamatsu, Donald, Birmingham	.254	92	287	45	73	94	15	0	2	45	5	5	7	32	0	54	7	6
Walker, Bernard, Chattanooga*	.238	92	277	50	66	87	10	4	1	23	2	1	1	57	3	82	27	7
Ward, Kevin, Huntsville	.310	27	84	20	26	47	4	4	3	18	0	3	1	29	0	18	15	0
Weber, Weston, Huntsville	.000	15	1	0	0	0	0	0	0	0	0	0	0	0	0	0	0	0
Webster, Leonard, Orlando	.236	59	191	29	45	58	7	0	2	17	2	2	3	44	1	20	2	0
Weems, Danny, Greenville	.143	13	14	1	2	3	1	0	0	0	0	0	0	0	0	7	0	0
Wells, Terry, Columbus*	.000	23	3	0	0	0	0	0	0	0	2	0	0	2	0	1	0	0
Wendell, Steven, Greenville*	.000	1	0	0	0	0	0	0	0	0	0	0	0	1	0	0	0	0
Whiten, Mark, Knoxville	.258	129	423	75	109	170	13	6	12	47	0	2	11	60	1	114	11	10
Willard, Gerald, Birmingham*	.300	5	10	5	3	4	1	0	0	1	0	0	0	7	1	2	0	0
Williams, Fred, Jacksonville	.159	43	88	12	14	25	2	3	1	4	1	0	0	18	0	21	5	0
Williams, Roger, Charlotte	.000	6	1	0	0	0	0	0	0	0	0	0	1	0	0	1	0	0
Wilson, Phillip, Jacksonville†	.210	24	81	11	17	23	3	0	1	6	0	0	1	10	1	12	4	3
Zosky, Edward, Charlotte	.221	56	208	21	46	63	5	3	2	14	2	1	0	10	0	32	1	1

The following pitchers, listed alphabetically by club, with games in parentheses, had no plate appearances, primarily through use of designated hitters:

BIRMINGHAM—Alvarez, Wilson (6); Blasucci, Anthony (13); Chadwick, Ray (11); Diaz, Victor (6); Edwards, Wayne (24); Groom, Wedsel (26); Hall, Gardner (27); Hudek, John (18); Kutzler, Jerry (14); Manzanillo, Ravelo (23); Menendez, Antonio (27); Middaugh, Scott (1); Ollom, Michael (11); Reynolds, David (28); Stephens, Ronald (8).

CHARLOTTE—Parmenter, Gary (12); Zarranz, Fernando (9).

CHATTANOOGA—Sierra, Ulises (3).

COLUMBUS—August, Samuel (2); Johnson, Gregory (10); Vargas, Jose (1).

GREENVILLE—Kirk, Timothy (6); Mathews, Edward (5).

HUNTSVILLE—Ariola, Anthony (10); Berg, Richard (25); Chiamparino, Scott (17); Klink, Joseph (57); Lambert, Reese (13); Maye, Stephen (10); Norris, Michael (1); Schock, William (29); Stancel, Mark (44); Stocker, Robert (44); Taylor, William (5); Veres, David (29); Wernig, Patrick (18); Young, Raymond (29).

JACKSONVILLE—Dixon, Edward (14); Pacillo, Patrick (2).

KNOXVILLE—Blumberg, Robert (2); Gilles, Thomas (12); Gozzo, Mauro (18); Guzman, Juan (22); Hall, Darren (13); Hernandez, Xavier (4); Horsman, Vincent (4); Jones, Christopher N. (39); Jones, Dennis (27); Linton, Douglas (14); MacDonald, Robert (43); Mills, Michael (12); Newcomb, Joe (24); Rogers, James (32); Shea, John (31); Wapnick, Steven (12); Williams, Gregory (14); Wishnevski, Robert (14).

MEMPHIS—Campbell, James (49); Clark, Dera (30); Cole, Victor (13); Crouch, Matthew (8); Duffy, John (46); Encarnacion, Luis (20); Filson, Peter (10); Lee, Mark (25); Magnante, Michael (26); Moeller, Dennis (5); Parnell, Mark (2); Pickens, Kevin (7); Stottlemyre, Melvin (16); Tresemer, Michael (30); Vasquez, Aguedo (64); Walker, Steven (39).

ORLANDO—Abbott, Paul (17); Bangtson, Patrick (29); Banks, Willie (1); Bianchi, Ben (6); Brinkman, Gregory (24); Bronkey, Jeffery (16); Davins, James (3); Delkus, Peter (76); Guthrie, Mark (14); North, Mark (7); Pittman, Park (34); Redding, Michael (31); Satzinger, Jeffrey (57); Simons, Douglas (14); Wassenaar, Robert (13); Williams, Jimmy (43).

GRAND SLAM HOME RUNS—Morgan, 3; Casey, 2; Afenir, Anthony, Cole, M. Davis, DeFrancesco, V. Garcia, Germann, Hemond, Howitt, Jorgensen, Landrum, Mann, May, Merullo, Reese, Sanchez, Simms, Sorrento, Trafton, 1 each.

AWARDED FIRST BASE ON CATCHER'S INTERFERENCE—M. Bell 3 (DeFrancesco, A. Morris, Reese); Farmer (Nago); Firova (Borrelli); C. Jones, Chattanooga (Servais); Randle (Savarino); Rhodes (Spehr); Sullivan (Eusebio); Ventura (Kremers).

CLUB FIELDING

Club	Pct.	G.	PO.	A.	E.	DP.	PB.	Club	Pct.	G.	PO.	A.	E.	DP.	PB.
Columbus	.969	143	3645	1432	163	126	19	Huntsville	.963	143	3714	1489	198	122	21
Greenville	.967	139	3540	1579	174	116	21	Chattanooga	.963	140	3479	1346	187	107	23
Knoxville	.967	143	3587	1565	176	117	22	Memphis	.963	143	3607	1450	197	112	25
Birmingham	.965	144	3748	1517	190	123	15	Orlando	.962	145	3711	1556	206	128	13
Charlotte	.963	145	3645	1475	195	110	16	Jacksonville	.962	145	3649	1477	205	103	20

Triple Plays—Columbus, Greenville.

INDIVIDUAL FIELDING
FIRST BASEMEN

*Throws lefthanded.

Player and Club	Pct.	G.	PO.	A.	E.	DP.	Player and Club	Pct.	G.	PO.	A.	E.	DP.
Acta, Columbus	1.000	6	33	1	0	0	Lanoux, Orlando	1.000	1	11	0	0	0
Afenir, Huntsville	1.000	2	13	2	0	2	Lee, Chattanooga	.962	6	24	1	1	3
Bafia, Charlotte	1.000	10	50	3	0	9	Malave, Knoxville	1.000	4	36	4	0	0
Bell, Greenville*	.990	131	1209	94	13	97	Mann, Charlotte	1.000	1	2	0	0	0
Brosius, Huntsville	1.000	3	23	1	0	1	Martinez, Knoxville	.987	114	929	93	13	74
Bundy, Jacksonville	.987	34	285	20	4	22	Morris, Memphis	.986	42	339	21	5	25
Capello, Memphis	.971	4	32	1	1	2	Pappas, Charlotte	.991	21	98	13	1	5
Cianfrocco, Jacksonville	1.000	1	1	0	0	0	Pearson, Chattanooga	1.000	6	44	1	0	4
Dull, Jacksonville	.992	28	251	10	2	12	Pedre, Memphis	1.000	4	28	0	0	3
Eccles, Orlando	.977	15	117	12	3	8	Richardson, Orlando	1.000	4	30	2	0	2
Firova, Charlotte	.962	5	21	4	1	5	Robinson, Huntsville	1.000	16	120	5	0	11
Garbey, Jacksonville	.974	29	218	11	6	16	Rodriguez, Jacksonville	.991	34	303	17	3	24
C. Garcia, Birmingham*	.987	123	985	86	14	88	Salinas, Memphis	.983	39	310	28	6	22
V. Garcia, Charlotte	.987	26	138	13	2	10	Schunk, Knoxville	.994	21	147	15	1	17
Germann, Chattanooga	1.000	1	6	0	0	3	Simms, Columbus	.990	109	938	44	10	75
Hamelin, Memphis*	.985	60	487	27	8	37	Sipe, Jacksonville*	.992	26	230	22	2	13
Holmes, Huntsville	1.000	1	2	0	0	1	Snyder, Orlando	.980	6	39	9	1	3
HOWITT, Huntsville	.992	108	877	71	8	77	Sorrento, Orlando	.979	124	1070	41	24	103
Be. Hunter, Columbus	.986	34	266	14	4	24	Sullivan, Charlotte*	.990	124	842	61	9	65
Br. Hunter, Greenville	1.000	11	110	9	0	9	Trafton, Birmingham	.994	23	160	6	1	16
Jefferson, Chattanooga*	.985	132	1004	79	16	84	Ventura, Birmingham	1.000	2	10	2	0	1
Jeter, Knoxville	.980	14	93	6	2	8	Wakamatsu, Birmingham	.979	7	44	3	1	4
Kating, Huntsville	.976	25	189	14	5	17	Williams, Jacksonville	1.000	1	2	0	0	0

Triple Plays—Bell, Simms.

SECOND BASEMEN

Player and Club	Pct.	G.	PO.	A.	E.	DP.	Player and Club	Pct.	G.	PO.	A.	E.	DP.
Acta, Columbus	.967	19	35	53	3	10	Malave, Knoxville	1.000	1	3	1	0	1
ALCALA, Memphis	.971	107	195	277	14	56	Mordecai, Greenville	1.000	1	3	2	0	1
Alicea, Greenville	.929	48	89	119	16	21	Morris, Greenville	.943	18	41	41	5	7
Amaral, Birmingham	.980	67	145	154	6	38	Mota, Huntsville	.957	26	57	54	5	12
Bafia, Charlotte	1.000	1	0	1	0	0	Naveda, Orlando	.980	34	48	102	3	10
Bertolani, Birmingham	.955	25	48	57	5	16	Pacho, Greenville	1.000	2	3	3	0	1
Bowen, Memphis	.947	27	32	57	5	5	Pappas, Charlotte	1.000	2	3	3	0	0
Brosius, Huntsville	.946	76	167	215	22	37	Pearson, Chattanooga	.911	12	16	25	4	4
Casarotti, Greenville	.948	69	122	170	16	38	Reboulet, Orlando	.971	30	59	77	4	25
Cianfrocco, Jacksonville	.958	6	9	14	1	2	Richardson, Orlando	.960	79	174	213	16	43
Cole, Memphis	.943	8	12	21	2	4	Robinson, Huntsville	1.000	1	3	2	0	0
Cruz, Charlotte	.933	24	36	47	6	16	Roby, Greenville	.935	12	18	25	3	4
Davis, Birmingham	.973	35	55	89	4	20	Rodriguez, Jacksonville	.795	13	10	21	8	2
Frazier, Columbus	.968	98	207	254	15	47	Rohde, Columbus	.958	4	6	17	1	2
Garrison, Knoxville	.972	54	107	167	8	26	Salinas, Memphis	1.000	5	13	19	0	3
Germann, Chattanooga	.949	21	39	36	4	6	Sanchez, Columbus	1.000	4	7	4	0	1
Grebeck, Birmingham	.958	26	54	59	5	13	Santana, Jacksonville	.929	6	7	6	1	2
Griffin, Charlotte	1.000	1	1	0	0	0	Schunk, Knoxville	1.000	6	10	11	0	2
Houston, Jacksonville	.967	118	182	323	17	56	Small, Charlotte	1.000	1	1	0	0	0
Hubbard, Columbus	.939	36	53	85	9	14	Smith, Charlotte	.968	126	253	348	20	59
Jones, Huntsville	.954	50	86	140	11	25	Suero, Knoxville	.961	86	146	228	15	49
Lanoux, Orlando	.966	13	26	31	2	6	Ventura, Birmingham	.000	1	0	0	0	0
Lombardozzi, Chattanooga	.930	60	103	111	16	23	Williams, Jacksonville	.985	14	23	43	1	4
Lonigro, Chattanooga	.969	69	130	154	9	42							

Triple Plays—Acta, Casarotti.

THIRD BASEMEN

Player and Club	Pct.	G.	PO.	A.	E.	DP.
Acta, Columbus	1.000	2	0	3	0	0
Alicea, Greenville	.868	44	24	75	15	6
Amaral, Birmingham	1.000	1	0	2	0	0
Bafia, Charlotte	.886	67	39	109	19	8
Bertolani, Birmingham	.000	1	0	0	1	0
Brosius, Memphis	.912	45	26	78	10	8
Capello, Memphis	.862	12	9	16	4	2
Cianfrocco, Jacksonville	.889	114	89	207	37	17
Cole, Memphis	.918	58	45	112	14	5
Colombino, Columbus	.972	79	47	129	5	12
Cruz, Charlotte	1.000	2	1	0	0	0
Davis, Birmingham	.769	3	3	7	3	0
Escalera, Memphis	.867	8	3	10	2	1
Garbey, Jacksonville	1.000	1	1	1	0	0
Garcia, Charlotte	.857	11	8	16	4	1
Germann, Chattanooga	1.000	3	0	11	0	3
Grebeck, Birmingham	.931	29	28	53	6	4
Griffin, Charlotte	.898	39	38	68	12	3
Hemond, Huntsville	.919	106	81	170	22	16
Hubbard, Columbus	.864	10	8	11	3	2
Jirschele, Memphis	.957	43	39	96	6	11
Jorgensen, Orlando	.919	131	99	274	33	21
Ladnier, Memphis	.909	22	20	30	5	5
Lane, Chattanooga	.922	125	94	223	27	18
Lanoux, Orlando	1.000	12	6	25	0	6
Lombardozzi, Chattanooga	.971	14	8	26	1	2
Malave, Knoxville	1.000	4	4	3	0	0
Mordecai, Greenville	1.000	2	1	4	0	1
A. Morris, Memphis	.500	4	1	1	2	0
R. Morris, Greenville	.854	54	29	88	20	8
Mulvaney, Chattanooga	.750	2	0	3	1	1
Naveda, Orlando	1.000	4	6	3	0	2
Nichols, Charlotte	.808	13	9	12	5	0
Pacho, Greenville	.914	18	11	21	3	2
Pappas, Charlotte	1.000	6	2	6	0	0
Pearson, Chattanooga	1.000	1	0	1	0	0
Quinlan, Knoxville	.909	132	81	259	34	21
Redington, Greenville	.940	33	19	90	7	4
Roby, Greenville	.875	4	3	4	1	1
Rodriguez, Jacksonville	.912	35	27	56	8	8
Rohde, Columbus	.908	60	57	101	16	14
Salinas, Memphis	1.000	3	2	10	0	1
Schunk, Knoxville	1.000	10	8	20	0	2
Small, Charlotte	.933	22	17	25	3	1
Trafton, Birmingham	1.000	3	2	0	0	0
VENTURA, Birmingham	.930	116	98	247	26	21
Wakamatsu, Birmingham	.000	1	0	0	2	0

SHORTSTOPS

Player and Club	Pct.	G.	PO.	A.	E.	DP.
Alcala, Memphis	.909	7	5	15	2	1
ALVA, Greenville	.953	107	140	305	22	58
Amaral, Birmingham	.900	38	53	100	17	14
Bafia, Charlotte	1.000	3	5	7	0	2
Benavides, Chattanooga	.947	86	129	230	20	46
Bertolani, Birmingham	.903	26	48	73	13	18
Brosius, Huntsville	.939	7	9	22	2	5
Bullinger, Charlotte	.947	118	188	281	26	60
Clements, Memphis	.919	112	163	288	40	47
Cole, Memphis	.914	26	36	60	9	15
Cordero, Jacksonville	.957	38	62	93	7	19
Cruz, Charlotte	.910	44	53	78	13	18
DeShields, Jacksonville	.910	91	127	218	34	32
Diaz, Knoxville	.934	42	70	113	13	18
Escobar, Huntsville	.930	136	205	377	44	74
Frazier, Columbus	.926	28	34	54	7	10
Germann, Chattanooga	.962	57	98	129	9	26
Grebeck, Birmingham	.960	88	152	252	17	53
Houston, Jacksonville	.925	13	13	36	4	4
Leius, Orlando	.948	93	148	257	22	55
Lonigro, Chattanooga	1.000	2	2	1	0	1
Morris, Greenville	1.000	1	1	0	0	0
Naveda, Orlando	.813	9	8	18	6	3
Pacho, Greenville	.986	47	65	152	3	21
Pearson, Chattanooga	1.000	2	0	1	0	0
Reboulet, Orlando	.928	49	68	151	17	18
Richardson, Orlando	1.000	1	0	1	0	1
Rohde, Columbus	1.000	4	7	9	0	1
Salinas, Memphis	.941	7	9	23	2	1
Sanchez, Columbus	.930	122	176	317	37	67
Schunk, Knoxville	.916	55	67	152	20	25
Small, Charlotte	.923	7	17	7	2	1
Trafton, Birmingham	1.000	1	1	0	0	0
Williams, Jacksonville	.955	8	8	13	1	2
Zosky, Knoxville	.966	56	94	135	8	24

Triple Plays — Alva, Sanchez.

OUTFIELDERS

Player and Club	Pct.	G.	PO.	A.	E.	DP.
Afenir, Huntsville	.970	20	31	1	1	0
Alborano, Memphis*	.800	7	4	0	1	0
Ansley, Columbus	1.000	30	63	1	0	1
Anthony, Columbus*	.961	104	178	17	8	3
Baldwin, Columbus*	.946	60	82	6	5	3
Batiste, Knoxville	.956	78	172	3	8	0
Bell, Knoxville	.962	126	216	12	9	4
Bertolani, Birmingham	.964	13	25	2	1	2
Blackwell, Orlando	.963	94	175	9	7	1
Blocker, Greenville*	.980	57	92	5	2	1
Brown, Chattanooga	.916	42	67	9	7	2
Brumfield, Memphis	.965	93	217	2	8	2
J. Canseco, Huntsville	1.000	5	9	0	0	0
O. Canseco, Huntsville	.975	85	148	8	4	3
Casey, Huntsville*	1.000	1	1	0	0	0
Cruz, Charlotte	1.000	9	10	0	0	0
K. Davis, Birmingham	.750	8	11	1	4	1
M. Davis, Birmingham	.972	47	102	1	3	0
S. Davis, Chattanooga	.959	20	45	2	2	0
Doran, Birmingham	.968	19	30	0	1	0
Dunbar, Greenville*	1.000	14	20	4	0	0
Forney, Chattanooga	1.000	1	1	0	0	0
B. Fox, Columbus*	.952	17	19	1	1	0
E. Fox, Huntsville*	.984	139	306	10	5	3
Frazier, Columbus	1.000	14	21	0	0	0
Frobel, Birmingham	.960	16	23	1	1	0
Garcia, Charlotte	1.000	3	4	0	0	0
Gavin, Huntsville	.952	14	20	0	1	0
Gilbert, Huntsville	.962	66	101	1	4	0
Green, Greenville	.923	24	23	1	2	0
Grissom, Jacksonville	.980	77	141	7	3	2
Hayden, Chattanooga*	.957	30	44	1	2	0
Hernandez, Jacksonville	.913	69	109	7	11	3
Hill, Charlotte	.967	73	112	6	4	1
Hood, Birmingham	.973	135	275	9	8	0
Howitt, Huntsville	.989	36	88	3	1	1
Hubbard, Columbus	.980	33	46	2	1	1
Be. Hunter, Columbus	.971	19	32	1	1	2
Br. Hunter, Greenville	.973	110	138	6	4	0
Jacas, Orlando	.962	53	120	5	5	1
Jeter, Knoxville	.977	70	125	4	3	1
C. Jones, Chattanooga	.967	102	197	8	7	1
G. Jones, Huntsville	.969	34	60	2	2	0
Jordan, Columbus	.989	47	86	6	1	2
Kating, Huntsville	.935	19	27	2	2	0
Landrum, Charlotte	.967	112	226	5	8	0
Lee, Chattanooga	1.000	31	42	2	0	1
D. Lewis, Huntsville	1.000	9	16	0	0	0
J. Lewis, Charlotte	1.000	40	47	0	0	0
Lombardozzi, Chattanooga	.926	16	25	0	2	0
Mack, Jacksonville*	.971	111	157	8	5	3
Malave, Knoxville	1.000	2	2	0	0	0
Martinez, Memphis*	.975	113	257	18	7	4
May, Charlotte	.950	130	239	8	13	0
McRae, Memphis	.981	134	249	11	5	5
Morgan, Orlando*	.963	131	219	16	9	1
Morris, Greenville	1.000	14	26	1	0	1
Munoz, Greenville	.983	46	55	3	1	0
Naveda, Orlando	1.000	17	24	0	0	0
NELSON, Chattanooga	.996	106	235	3	1	2
Nichols, Charlotte	.857	7	5	1	1	0
Pappas, Charlotte	.967	45	52	7	2	0
Pearson, Chattanooga	.955	21	36	6	2	0
Penigar, Birmingham	.948	116	228	11	13	3
Pruitt, Memphis	.975	73	110	8	3	0
Pulliam, Memphis	.971	86	157	8	5	2
Randle, Orlando*	.987	116	209	11	3	2
Reboulet, Orlando	.667	4	2	0	1	0
Reese, Memphis	1.000	1	1	0	0	0
Reynolds, Birmingham	1.000	2	0	1	0	0
Rhodes, Columbus*	.962	142	262	15	11	5
Rivera, Birmingham	.924	87	117	5	10	3
Roby, Greenville	1.000	6	1	0	0	0
Rodriguez, Jacksonville	.903	29	27	1	3	0
Sabino, Greenville*	1.000	15	20	0	0	0
Salinas, Memphis	1.000	2	2	0	0	0
Santana, Jacksonville	.951	67	108	9	6	0
Schunk, Knoxville	1.000	2	1	0	0	0
Snyder, Orlando	.963	44	74	4	3	0
Tellez, Jacksonville	1.000	26	38	0	0	0
Trafton, Birmingham	.978	63	129	6	3	0
Tubbs, Greenville	1.000	10	16	0	0	0

OUTFIELDERS—Continued

Player and Club	Pct.	G.	PO.	A.	E.	DP.
Vanderwal, Jacksonville*	.987	59	72	3	1	2
Waggoner, Birmingham	.983	103	227	4	4	0
Wagner, Birmingham	.984	85	123	3	2	0
Walker, Chattanooga	.956	74	149	4	7	0
Ward, Huntsville	1.000	25	42	5	0	0
Whiten, Knoxville	.968	122	223	17	8	3
Wilson, Jacksonville	.966	22	28	0	1	0

Triple Play—Anthony.

CATCHERS

Player and Club	Pct.	G.	PO.	A.	E.	DP.	PB.
Afenir, Huntsville	.981	18	98	8	2	0	2
Arnold, Orlando	.978	60	397	46	10	8	7
Beeler, Chattanooga	.964	43	244	26	10	1	7
Borrelli, Huntsville	.955	5	16	5	1	0	1
Brito, Huntsville	.984	24	164	25	3	1	0
Brown, Birmingham	1.000	2	4	1	0	1	1
Carver, Columbus	.889	1	7	1	1	0	0
Colbrunn, Jacksonville	.988	50	304	34	4	2	6
DeFrancesco, Chattanooga	.974	69	416	41	12	5	9
Diaz, Knoxville	.984	96	608	75	11	8	15
Duke, Jacksonville	.983	20	157	14	3	2	2
Eccles, Orlando	.992	16	105	17	1	1	0
Escalera, Memphis	.961	40	212	34	10	4	10
Eusebio, Columbus	.983	57	355	46	7	8	9
Firova, Charlotte	1.000	11	45	12	0	2	2
Garcia, Charlotte	.971	9	31	3	1	0	2
Hemond, Huntsville	.961	32	191	28	9	4	9
Hubbard, Columbus	.992	35	214	24	2	1	3
Kremers, Greenville	.989	107	649	86	8	5	19
Kuld, Huntsville	.993	59	379	45	3	5	8
Leary, Jacksonville	1.000	42	265	23	0	3	10
Maldonado, Greenville	1.000	9	40	7	0	0	2
Mann, Charlotte	.987	106	610	84	9	7	10
McElroy, Birmingham	.992	25	116	9	1	1	1
Merullo, Birmingham	.994	24	149	10	1	2	4
Morris, Memphis	.989	38	238	32	3	7	4
Myers, Knoxville	.993	24	130	12	1	0	1
Nago, Columbus	.938	3	25	5	2	0	0
Natal, Jacksonville	.981	45	324	37	7	3	2
Pappas, Charlotte	.979	46	244	32	6	2	2
Parks, Orlando	.980	23	135	12	3	3	3
Pedre, Memphis	.977	20	117	10	3	1	4
Plumb, Greenville	.989	33	163	21	2	1	0
Pryor, Huntsville	.952	7	36	4	2	0	0
Reese, Memphis	.929	12	39	0	3	0	1
Rivers, Knoxville	.990	38	172	18	2	4	6
Savarino, Huntsville	.982	8	51	4	1	1	1
Servais, Columbus	.992	52	330	45	3	5	7
Singley, Birmingham	.971	20	80	19	3	2	1
Spehr, Memphis	.984	47	274	36	5	1	6
Taubensee, Chattanooga	.976	40	213	31	6	0	7
Trafton, Birmingham	.981	12	48	4	1	0	1
WAKAMATSU, Birmingham	.990	83	459	54	5	2	7
Webster, Orlando	.988	52	293	46	4	2	3
Willard, Birmingham	.955	5	38	4	2	0	0

PITCHERS

Player and Club	Pct.	G.	PO.	A.	E.	DP.
Abbott, Orlando	.786	17	3	8	3	1
Akins, Greenville	1.000	2	2	2	0	0
Alvarez, Birmingham*	1.000	6	0	4	0	0
Ariola, Columbus	.800	10	3	1	1	0
August, Columbus	1.000	2	3	2	0	0
Avery, Greenville*	1.000	13	7	14	0	1
Balsley, Knoxville	.750	13	2	1	1	0
Bangtson, Orlando	.816	29	9	22	7	3
Banks, Orlando	.000	1	0	0	1	0
Bennett, Jacksonville	.714	25	1	9	4	1
Berg, Huntsville	1.000	25	1	4	0	0
Blasucci, Birmingham	1.000	13	3	0	0	0
Blumberg, Knoxville*	1.000	2	0	1	0	0
Bombard, Chattanooga	1.000	1	1	0	0	0
Boskie, Charlotte	.867	28	8	31	6	2
Bottenfield, Jacksonville	.956	25	9	34	2	1
Bowen, Columbus	.955	27	4	17	1	2
Brinkman, Orlando	.906	24	9	20	3	0
Bronkey, Orlando	.875	16	4	10	2	0
Browning, Columbus	.938	52	2	13	1	1
Bruno, Chattanooga	1.000	41	5	5	0	0
Cakora, Charlotte*	1.000	34	6	7	0	0
Campbell, Memphis*	.957	49	12	10	1	1
Cano, Columbus	1.000	3	0	2	0	1
Carriger, Jacksonville	.900	14	4	5	1	0
Carter, Jacksonville	.923	6	2	10	1	1
Castillo, Charlotte	1.000	10	8	8	0	0
Chadwick, Birmingham	.714	11	4	2	0	0
Chambers, Jacksonville	1.000	40	3	8	0	0
Chiamparino, Huntsville	.882	17	3	12	2	0
Clark, Memphis	.842	30	4	12	3	0
Coffman, Charlotte	1.000	7	1	6	0	0
Cole, Memphis	.875	13	6	8	2	0
Corbell, Huntsville	.900	9	4	5	1	0
Costello, Columbus	1.000	30	1	8	0	2
Credeur, Columbus*	.917	21	1	10	1	0
Crouch, Memphis	1.000	8	1	7	0	0
Czajkowski, Greenville	1.000	17	2	6	0	1
Davidson, Charlotte	1.000	25	2	19	0	1
Davins, Orlando	1.000	3	0	2	0	0
Deitz, Greenville	1.000	30	4	11	0	0
Delkus, Orlando	.875	76	8	20	4	2
DelRosario, Greenville	1.000	49	3	18	0	2
Diaz, Birmingham*	1.000	6	0	1	0	0
Dixon, Jacksonville	.750	14	1	2	1	0
Dodd, Chattanooga	.900	35	3	6	1	0
Duffy, Memphis*	.963	46	3	23	1	1
Edwards, Birmingham*	.881	24	12	25	5	1
Encarnacion, Memphis	1.000	20	3	9	0	0
Estes, Columbus*	1.000	17	0	5	0	0
Farmer, Jacksonville	.981	26	16	35	1	2
Filson, Memphis*	.909	10	3	7	1	0
Gakeler, Knoxville	.917	14	6	16	2	1
Gilles, Knoxville	.923	12	2	10	1	2
Givier, Columbus	1.000	48	5	12	0	2
Gomez, Charlotte*	1.000	2	3	7	0	0
Gozzo, Knoxville	.947	18	7	11	1	0
Groom, Birmingham*	.929	26	9	30	3	2
Grovom, Chattanooga*	.818	6	0	9	2	0
Guthrie, Orlando*	.955	14	1	20	1	1
Guzman, Knoxville	1.000	22	4	3	0	0
D. Hall, Knoxville	1.000	13	2	7	0	0
G. Hall, Birmingham*	.915	27	11	32	4	3
HARRISON, Charlotte*	1.000	27	4	31	0	2
Hennis, Columbus	.972	28	9	26	1	4
Henry, Chattanooga*	1.000	7	2	1	0	0
Hernandez, Knoxville	1.000	4	1	5	0	0
Hickey, Columbus	1.000	26	7	10	0	1
Hill, Chattanooga	1.000	51	2	5	0	1
Hirsch, Charlotte	.944	17	4	13	1	2
Holcomb, Huntsville*	.944	29	3	14	1	1
Horsman, Birmingham*	1.000	4	1	0	0	0
Hudek, Birmingham	1.000	18	1	1	0	1
Ilsley, Columbus*	.889	4	2	6	1	1
Jefferson, Chattanooga	.909	34	6	14	2	0
Jeffery, Chattanooga*	.933	12	2	12	1	1
Jimenez, Greenville*	.949	24	8	29	2	4
Johnson, Columbus	1.000	10	0	3	0	1
C. Jones, Knoxville	.939	39	10	21	2	3
D. Jones, Knoxville*	.947	27	6	12	1	1
Kaiser, Chattanooga	.892	28	7	26	4	1
Kallevig, Charlotte	.957	33	13	31	2	1
Kile, Columbus	1.000	20	4	11	0	1
Kilner, Greenville*	.769	30	4	6	3	0
Kirk, Greenville*	1.000	6	1	2	0	0
Klink, Huntsville*	1.000	57	6	10	0	1
Kutzler, Birmingham	.947	14	2	16	1	1
Lambert, Huntsville*	.900	13	4	5	1	1
Lazor, Chattanooga*	.750	21	2	16	6	0
Lee, Memphis*	1.000	25	7	20	0	1
LeMasters, Greenville	.953	32	15	26	2	1
Leon, Jacksonville	.958	18	6	17	1	2
Lewis, Jacksonville	.765	17	3	10	4	0
Linton, Huntsville	.867	14	10	16	4	0
Little, Birmingham	.933	19	2	12	1	2
Lopez, Chattanooga	1.000	3	1	4	0	1
Loynd, Birmingham*	.880	26	7	15	3	1
MacDonald, Knoxville*	1.000	43	6	20	0	1
Magnante, Memphis*	.953	26	7	34	2	2
Manzanillo, Birmingham*	.969	22	5	26	1	2
Marak, Greenville	.960	43	10	14	1	1
Marchok, Jacksonville*	.931	64	5	22	2	3
Martinez, Memphis*	1.000	1	1	0	0	0
Mathews, Greenville	.667	5	1	1	1	0
Maye, Huntsville	1.000	10	2	1	0	0
Mead, Chattanooga	1.000	20	9	17	0	1
Menendez, Birmingham	.905	27	5	14	2	0
Michno, Charlotte	.914	37	17	15	3	2
Mills, Knoxville	1.000	12	1	5	0	0
Minutelli, Chattanooga*	.857	6	1	5	1	0
Moeller, Memphis*	1.000	5	1	6	0	0
Moscrey, Chattanooga*	.964	26	5	22	1	0
Mount, Birmingham	.880	43	6	16	3	2
Mullins, Chattanooga	.800	9	2	2	1	1
Newcomb, Knoxville	1.000	24	2	13	0	0
Norris, Huntsville	.000	1	0	0	1	0
North, Orlando*	1.000	7	0	3	0	0
Oliverio, Columbus	.938	18	3	12	1	0

PITCHERS—Continued

Player and Club	Pct.	G.	PO.	A.	E.	DP.	Player and Club	Pct.	G.	PO.	A.	E.	DP.
Ollom, Birmingham	1.000	11	1	0	0	0	Simons, Orlando*	1.000	14	2	9	0	0
Pacillo, Jacksonville	1.000	2	1	1	0	0	Sossamon, Jacksonville	1.000	19	1	4	0	0
Parmenter, Charlotte	.800	12	0	4	1	1	Stancel, Huntsville	.900	44	4	14	2	3
Perez, Jacksonville*	1.000	20	0	8	0	0	Stanton, Greenville*	1.000	47	3	11	0	2
Peters, Jacksonville	.875	40	3	11	2	0	Stephens, Birmingham	1.000	8	10	5	0	0
Pickens, Memphis	1.000	7	1	2	0	0	Stockam, Greenville*	.824	53	5	9	3	0
Pittman, Orlando	.818	34	1	8	2	0	Stocker, Huntsville	.957	44	8	14	1	2
Polley, Greenville*	.908	28	9	50	6	1	Stottlemyre, Memphis	1.000	16	1	1	0	0
Puleo, Greenville	1.000	2	1	1	0	1	Torres, Columbus	.875	33	2	5	1	0
Raether, Jacksonville	1.000	33	3	7	0	1	Tresemer, Memphis	.818	30	2	13	4	3
Redding, Orlando	.895	31	3	14	2	1	Upshaw, Greenville*	.944	14	2	15	1	1
Renfroe, Charlotte	.962	78	10	15	1	1	Vargas, Columbus	1.000	1	0	2	0	0
Reynolds, Birmingham	.923	27	2	10	1	3	Vasquez, Memphis	.833	64	3	12	3	0
Rivera, Jacksonville	.889	5	3	5	1	0	Veres, Huntsville	.968	29	8	22	1	0
Robinson, Chattanooga	1.000	1	0	1	0	0	Walker, Memphis	.903	39	5	23	3	1
Rodgers, Chattanooga	.976	39	19	22	1	3	Wapnick, Knoxville	1.000	12	2	1	0	0
Rodriguez, Chattanooga*	.923	28	1	11	1	0	Wassenaar, Orlando	1.000	13	3	15	0	2
Rogers, Knoxville	.925	32	10	27	3	2	Weber, Huntsville	.846	15	1	10	2	0
Rojas, Jacksonville	.885	34	4	19	3	0	Weems, Greenville	.875	13	3	11	2	0
Rosario, Charlotte*	.786	55	3	8	3	0	Wells, Columbus*	1.000	23	1	6	0	0
Roth, Charlotte	.875	10	2	5	1	1	Wendell, Greenville	1.000	1	0	1	0	0
Sanders, Knoxville	.938	27	3	12	1	0	Wernig, Huntsville*	.844	18	7	20	5	1
Satzinger, Orlando	.875	57	5	16	3	2	G. Williams, Knoxville	1.000	14	8	5	0	0
Scheid, Charlotte*	1.000	17	1	9	0	0	J. Williams, Orlando*	.889	43	1	7	1	0
Schock, Huntsville	.952	29	10	30	2	3	R. Williams, Charlotte	1.000	6	0	1	0	0
Shea, Knoxville*	.895	31	6	28	4	1	Wishnevski, Knoxville	.955	14	5	16	1	1
Shotkoski, Huntsville	1.000	23	0	3	0	0	Young, Huntsville	.789	29	8	22	8	1
Sierra, Chattanooga	1.000	3	0	3	0	0							

The following players did not have any fielding statistics at the positions indicated or appeared only as a designated hitter, pinch-hitter or pinch-runner: Alva, 3b; Amaral, of; T. Bell, dh, ph; Bianchi, p; Blocker, p; Bullinger, 3b, p; O. Canseco, p; Cianfrocco, of; Colombino, 2b; Firova, p; Fox, p; Holmes, p; Houston, p; Howitt, p; Jordan, 3b; Kating, 3b; D. Martinez, 3b, c; McElroy, of; Middaugh, p; A. Morris, p; Morrison, dh, ph; Pappas, ss, p; Parnell, p; Penigar, p; Reese, 3b, p; Renfroe, of; Richardson, 3b; Suero, of; Sullivan, of; Taylor, p; Trafton, 2b, p; Zarranz, p.

CLUB PITCHING

Club	ERA.	G.	CG.	ShO.	Sv.	IP.	H.	R.	ER.	HR.	HB.	BB.	Int. BB.	SO.	WP.	Bk.
Greenville	3.19	139	11	6	39	1180.0	1062	533	418	85	27	437	20	838	64	17
Jacksonville	3.25	145	11	12	33	1216.1	967	569	439	44	53	581	12	1029	73	32
Birmingham	3.56	144	28	8	35	1249.1	1104	604	494	81	47	526	13	868	55	27
Columbus	3.56	143	14	9	37	1215.0	1075	592	481	83	38	591	26	905	84	28
Knoxville	3.64	143	14	13	26	1195.2	1044	584	483	67	39	637	26	886	73	24
Orlando	3.96	145	7	1	45	1237.0	1198	666	544	107	47	553	9	876	64	14
Memphis	4.34	143	6	6	30	1202.1	1194	704	580	93	52	516	14	869	80	26
Charlotte	4.38	145	17	3	23	1215.0	1251	713	591	102	62	628	74	883	69	31
Huntsville	4.38	143	9	10	39	1238.0	1242	701	603	102	38	599	12	924	89	32
Chattanooga	4.38	140	7	2	26	1159.2	1180	675	565	80	51	573	36	860	100	42

PITCHERS' RECORDS
(Leading Qualifiers for Earned-Run Average Leadership — 115 or More Innings)

*Throws lefthanded.

Pitcher—Club	W.	L.	Pct.	ERA.	G.	GS.	CG.	GF.	ShO.	Sv.	IP.	H.	R.	ER.	HR.	HB.	BB.	Int. BB.	SO.	WP.
Delkus, Orlando	8	8	.500	1.87	76	0	0	50	0	10	139.2	119	40	29	10	5	28	2	63	0
LeMasters, Greenville	7	5	.583	2.19	32	21	3	1	0	0	147.2	137	53	36	10	7	36	3	107	5
Farmer, Jacksonville	12	9	.571	2.20	26	26	5	0	2	0	184.0	122	59	45	5	4	50	0	151	6
Kile, Columbus	11	6	.647	2.58	20	20	6	0	2	0	125.2	74	47	36	5	6	68	1	108	5
Shea, Knoxville*	9	12	.429	2.70	31	29	3	1	1	0	190.1	183	79	57	14	6	57	1	96	4
Marak, Greenville	8	7	.533	3.03	43	14	0	10	0	5	121.2	102	53	41	7	3	47	1	81	5
Renfroe, Charlotte	19	7	.731	3.14	78	2	1	58	1	15	132.0	127	52	46	12	1	34	10	85	2
Menendez, Birmingham	10	4	.714	3.19	27	18	2	6	1	1	144.0	123	61	51	14	4	53	2	115	7
Edwards, Birmingham*	10	4	.714	3.19	24	19	5	1	0	1	158.0	131	69	56	6	5	65	1	122	6
Rodgers, Chattanooga	7	4	.364	3.29	39	13	1	7	0	0	132.0	137	65	48	6	3	51	3	86	9

Departmental Leaders: G—Renfroe, 78; W—Renfroe, 19; L—Bottenfield, 17; Pct.—Upshaw, .800; GS—Rogers, 30; CG—G. Hall, 9; GF—Renfroe, 58; ShO—Seven pitchers tied with 2; Sv.—Klink, 26; IP—G. Hall, 190.2; H—Boskie, 196; R—Kaiser, 110; ER—Kaiser, 97; HR—Schock, 24; HB—Boskie, 19; BB—Rogers, 132; IBB—Davidson, Michno, Renfroe, 10; SO—Boskie, 164; WP—Veres, 16.

(All Players—Listed Alphabetically)

Pitcher—Club	W.	L.	Pct.	ERA.	G.	GS.	CG.	GF.	ShO.	Sv.	IP.	H.	R.	ER.	HR.	HB.	BB.	Int. BB.	SO.	WP.
Abbott, Orlando	9	3	.750	4.37	17	17	1	0	0	0	90.2	71	48	44	6	0	48	0	102	7
Akins, Greenville	1	0	1.000	7.71	2	1	0	0	0	0	7.0	11	6	6	2	0	2	0	5	0
Alvarez, Birmingham*	2	1	.667	3.03	6	6	0	0	0	0	35.2	32	12	12	2	1	16	0	18	1
Ariola, Huntsville*	5	2	.714	3.41	10	10	2	0	0	0	60.2	58	25	23	4	1	24	0	33	3
August, Columbus	0	0	.000	3.12	2	2	0	0	0	0	8.2	4	3	3	1	0	6	0	8	1
Avery, Greenville	6	3	.667	2.77	13	13	1	0	0	0	84.1	68	32	26	3	1	34	0	75	4
Balsley, Knoxville	3	3	.500	7.36	13	1	0	2	0	0	22.0	20	19	18	2	1	13	1	21	2
Bangtson, Orlando	15	10	.600	4.76	29	27	2	0	0	0	158.2	181	96	84	8	5	81	1	72	6
Banks, Orlando	1	0	1.000	5.14	1	1	0	0	0	0	7.0	10	4	4	0	0	0	0	9	2
Bennett, Jacksonville	4	2	.667	2.40	25	8	0	8	0	3	63.2	42	29	17	3	3	20	0	52	3
Berg, Huntsville	3	2	.600	3.62	25	0	0	12	0	2	32.1	36	14	13	3	0	19	0	20	4
Bianchi, Huntsville	1	1	.500	6.75	6	1	0	1	0	0	10.2	13	9	8	1	0	13	1	4	1
Blasucci, Birmingham*	2	0	1.000	1.13	13	0	0	11	0	5	16.0	7	2	2	0	0	6	0	17	0
Blocker, Greenville*	0	0	.000	0.00	1	0	0	1	0	0	1.0	0	0	0	0	0	0	0	0	0
Blumberg, Knoxville*	0	1	.000	1.80	2	2	0	0	0	0	10.0	10	4	2	0	0	6	0	4	0
Bombard, Chattanooga	1	0	1.000	0.00	1	1	0	0	0	0	2.0	1	0	0	0	0	2	1	3	0
Boskie, Charlotte	11	8	.579	4.38	28	28	5	0	0	0	181.0	196	105	88	10	19	84	3	164	11
Bottenfield, Jacksonville	3	17	.150	5.26	25	25	1	0	0	0	138.2	137	101	81	13	9	73	2	91	6
Bowen, Columbus	8	6	.571	4.25	27	27	1	0	1	0	139.2	123	83	66	11	8	116	0	136	12
Brinkman, Orlando	5	8	.385	4.74	24	16	0	2	0	0	114.0	124	73	60	18	5	30	1	49	6
Bronkey, Orlando	1	2	.333	5.40	16	13	0	1	0	0	61.2	74	53	37	2	6	35	1	47	7
Browning, Columbus	9	6	.600	2.86	52	0	0	49	0	20	66.0	67	24	21	4	0	19	4	43	7

Pitcher—Club	W.	L.	Pct.	ERA.	G.	GS.	CG.	GF.	ShO.	Sv.	IP.	H.	R.	ER.	HR.	HB.	BB.	Int. BB.	SO.	WP.
Bruno, Chattanooga	6	2	.750	3.42	41	0	0	35	0	10	55.1	42	23	21	3	3	35	7	38	4
Bullinger, Charlotte	0	0	.000	0.00	2	0	0	2	0	0	3.0	2	0	0	0	0	3	0	5	1
Cakora, Charlotte*	0	6	.000	6.21	34	0	0	13	0	0	42.0	47	33	29	4	2	32	5	32	3
Campbell, Memphis*	7	10	.412	4.50	49	9	0	25	0	2	104.0	96	58	52	5	6	38	1	78	1
Cano, Columbus	1	1	.500	3.18	3	3	0	0	0	0	17.0	16	8	6	1	1	4	0	12	1
O. Canseco, Huntsville	0	0	.000	7.20	3	0	0	3	0	0	5.0	5	4	4	1	1	1	0	1	1
Carriger, Jacksonville	0	0	.000	5.08	14	0	0	3	0	0	28.1	32	18	16	1	1	14	0	29	2
Carter, Jacksonville	1	4	.200	2.50	6	6	1	0	0	0	36.0	23	11	10	2	0	14	1	21	2
Castillo, Charlotte	3	4	.429	3.84	10	10	4	0	0	0	68.0	73	35	29	7	1	12	3	43	1
Chadwick, Birmingham	2	1	.667	3.91	11	1	0	9	0	3	23.0	22	12	10	2	3	11	1	16	1
Chambers, Jacksonville	2	2	.500	2.93	40	4	0	19	0	2	61.1	49	26	20	1	2	32	0	67	5
Chiamparino, Huntsville	8	6	.571	4.60	17	17	2	0	1	0	101.2	109	60	52	8	4	29	0	87	8
Clark, Memphis	5	5	.500	4.40	30	13	1	5	1	1	106.1	103	63	52	11	8	29	0	93	15
Coffman, Charlotte	0	3	.000	3.74	7	4	0	1	0	0	21.2	15	15	9	0	2	26	2	12	5
Cole, Memphis	1	9	.100	6.36	13	13	0	0	0	0	63.2	67	53	45	4	5	51	1	52	4
Corbell, Huntsville	2	3	.400	6.96	9	6	0	1	0	1	32.1	53	29	25	3	3	10	0	28	0
Costello, Columbus	4	5	.444	3.33	30	0	0	17	0	3	54.0	39	22	20	5	0	21	1	39	5
Credeur, Columbus*	2	4	.333	4.20	21	12	0	3	0	0	70.2	53	38	33	11	3	42	1	68	4
Crouch, Memphis	2	2	.500	4.40	8	8	1	0	0	0	45.0	39	28	22	1	3	18	1	39	4
Czajkowski, Greenville	1	6	.143	5.56	17	4	0	3	0	0	34.0	39	31	21	4	1	16	0	18	0
Davidson, Charlotte	1	7	.125	5.42	25	16	0	4	0	0	91.1	120	66	55	5	2	59	10	55	7
Davins, Orlando	0	1	.000	3.86	3	3	0	0	0	0	14.0	10	8	6	0	1	9	0	7	0
Deitz, Greenville	1	6	.143	3.29	30	0	0	12	0	3	41.0	33	18	15	2	1	24	0	45	8
Delkus, Orlando	8	8	.500	1.87	76	0	0	50	0	10	139.2	119	40	29	10	5	28	2	63	0
DelRosario, Greenville	3	6	.333	4.67	49	0	0	25	0	5	54.0	58	39	28	6	1	23	2	33	2
Diaz, Birmingham*	0	1	.000	2.00	6	0	0	5	0	2	9.0	4	2	2	0	0	6	0	5	0
Dixon, Jacksonville	3	1	.750	0.81	14	3	0	5	0	1	33.1	23	6	3	0	3	0	0	29	1
Dodd, Chattanooga	3	2	.600	5.25	35	2	0	13	0	0	58.1	57	38	34	1	0	44	0	53	7
Duffy, Memphis*	3	5	.375	4.51	46	9	0	16	0	2	115.2	123	74	58	12	3	43	0	88	6
Edwards, Birmingham*	10	4	.714	3.19	24	19	5	1	0	1	158.0	131	69	56	6	5	65	1	122	6
Encarnacion, Memphis	4	4	.500	2.09	20	0	0	9	0	2	47.1	32	21	11	4	1	20	1	44	3
Estes, Columbus*	2	3	.400	4.91	17	0	0	13	0	0	22.0	32	18	12	3	0	12	1	12	0
Farmer, Jacksonville	12	9	.571	2.20	26	26	5	0	2	0	184.0	122	59	45	5	4	50	0	151	6
Filson, Memphis*	6	2	.750	4.14	10	9	0	0	0	0	58.2	67	34	27	10	2	18	0	31	3
Firova, Charlotte	0	0	.000	0.00	2	0	0	2	0	0	2.0	1	0	0	0	0	1	0	0	0
Fox, Columbus*	0	0	.000	15.43	1	0	0	0	0	0	2.1	3	5	4	1	0	7	0	2	1
Gakeler, Jacksonville	5	4	.556	2.39	14	14	2	0	1	0	86.2	70	31	23	1	3	39	1	76	6
Gilles, Knoxville	5	1	.833	2.94	12	4	0	4	0	0	52.0	42	23	17	1	3	14	1	27	2
Givler, Columbus	5	5	.500	2.69	48	1	0	23	0	9	90.1	75	31	27	0	2	50	8	58	6
Gomez, Charlotte*	1	0	1.000	2.51	2	2	0	0	0	0	14.1	14	5	4	0	0	3	0	11	4
Gozzo, Knoxville	7	0	1.000	2.98	18	6	2	6	1	0	60.1	59	27	20	1	1	12	1	37	2
Groom, Birmingham*	13	8	.619	4.52	26	26	3	0	1	0	167.1	172	101	84	13	2	78	1	94	11
Grovom, Chattanooga*	2	3	.400	4.54	6	6	1	0	0	0	33.2	34	21	17	3	0	19	0	33	7
Guthrie, Orlando*	8	3	.727	1.97	14	14	0	0	0	0	96.0	75	32	21	4	2	38	0	103	3
Guzman, Knoxville	1	4	.200	6.23	22	8	0	7	0	0	47.2	34	36	33	2	2	60	0	50	8
D. Hall, Knoxville	0	2	.000	3.66	13	0	0	4	0	0	19.2	21	12	8	2	1	10	0	13	3
G. Hall, Birmingham*	12	8	.600	3.45	27	27	9	0	0	0	190.2	173	97	73	9	9	68	0	147	13
Harrison, Charlotte*	6	9	.400	4.74	27	25	2	0	0	0	148.0	131	88	78	18	4	85	5	132	3
Hennis, Columbus	9	9	.500	3.58	28	28	2	0	0	0	171.0	151	75	68	6	6	78	1	101	11
Henry, Chattanooga	1	3	.250	3.42	7	7	0	0	0	0	26.1	22	12	10	2	0	12	1	19	2
Hernandez, Knoxville	1	1	.500	4.13	4	4	1	0	1	0	24.0	25	11	11	0	1	11	0	17	1
Hickey, Columbus	2	6	.250	4.61	26	6	1	3	0	0	82.0	90	51	42	9	2	19	1	41	3
Hill, Chattanooga	6	5	.545	2.06	51	0	0	42	0	13	70.0	49	19	16	4	0	28	6	63	1
Hirsch, Charlotte	2	4	.333	5.81	17	11	0	4	0	1	57.1	56	48	37	5	6	46	1	41	6
Holcomb, Huntsville*	4	3	.571	3.38	29	5	0	7	0	2	77.1	67	40	29	3	0	39	2	69	5
Holmes, Huntsville	0	0	.000	20.25	1	0	0	0	0	0	2.2	7	6	6	2	0	4	0	1	1
Horsman, Knoxville*	0	0	.000	1.80	4	0	0	3	0	1	5.0	3	1	1	0	0	3	1	3	0
Houston, Jacksonville	0	0	.000	0.00	1	0	0	1	0	0	1.0	0	0	0	0	0	0	0	0	0
Howitt, Huntsville	0	0	.000	0.00	2	0	0	2	0	0	2.0	2	1	0	0	0	0	0	2	0
Hudek, Birmingham	1	1	.500	4.24	18	0	0	16	0	11	17.0	14	8	8	2	0	9	0	10	0
Ilsley, Columbus*	1	1	.500	1.31	4	4	0	0	0	0	20.2	19	10	3	0	0	5	0	11	2
Jefferson, Chattanooga	2	5	.286	3.06	34	0	0	9	0	1	64.2	69	36	22	5	1	28	2	49	6
Jeffery, Chattanooga	4	5	.444	5.56	12	11	0	0	0	0	69.2	76	49	43	7	4	29	1	48	7
Jimenez, Greenville*	11	7	.611	3.48	24	22	2	0	1	0	137.0	141	64	53	9	1	36	1	86	6
Johnson, Columbus	2	1	.667	2.04	10	0	0	2	0	0	17.2	12	7	4	1	1	9	0	15	1
C. Jones, Knoxville	9	7	.563	3.35	39	10	2	15	1	2	102.0	83	46	38	11	1	49	5	82	4
D. Jones, Knoxville*	1	6	.143	5.33	27	12	0	5	0	0	81.0	68	57	48	4	4	90	1	84	12
Kaiser, Chattanooga	5	13	.278	5.53	28	26	5	0	1	0	158.0	169	110	97	16	3	86	3	105	15
Kallevig, Charlotte	7	10	.412	3.61	33	20	3	6	2	0	157.0	162	82	63	9	11	50	9	71	2
Kile, Columbus	11	6	.647	2.58	20	20	6	0	2	0	125.2	74	47	36	5	6	68	1	108	5
Kilner, Columbus*	2	2	.500	2.44	30	7	0	15	0	6	66.1	51	25	18	2	0	29	0	60	2
Kirk, Greenville	1	1	.500	7.24	6	1	0	0	0	0	13.2	18	13	11	5	0	6	0	9	0
Klink, Huntsville*	4	4	.500	2.82	57	0	0	53	0	26	60.2	46	19	19	2	2	23	0	59	6
Kutzler, Birmingham	9	4	.692	3.62	14	14	4	0	0	0	99.1	95	50	40	5	4	27	0	85	2
Lambert, Huntsville*	1	1	.500	0.00	13	0	0	5	0	0	27.1	14	6	0	1	0	9	0	27	0
Lazor, Chattanooga*	4	8	.333	3.44	21	16	0	3	0	0	96.2	88	50	37	3	3	51	6	93	8
Lee, Memphis*	5	11	.313	5.21	25	24	0	1	0	0	122.2	149	84	71	13	5	44	2	79	6
LeMasters, Greenville	4	3	.583	2.19	32	21	3	3	1	0	147.2	137	53	36	10	7	36	3	107	5
Leon, Jacksonville	7	4	.636	4.63	18	18	1	0	0	0	95.1	85	62	49	2	9	55	0	64	10
Lewis, Jacksonville	4	5	.556	2.58	17	17	0	0	0	0	94.1	80	37	27	2	2	55	0	105	8
Linton, Knoxville	5	4	.556	2.60	14	13	3	0	2	0	90.0	68	28	26	2	2	23	2	93	6
Little, Birmingham	4	2	.667	1.29	19	0	0	16	0	6	35.0	28	10	5	0	2	14	3	27	0
Lopez, Chattanooga	2	1	.667	3.86	3	3	0	0	0	0	21.0	25	13	9	2	0	11	0	15	0
Loynd, Columbus	8	8	.500	3.40	26	25	3	0	0	0	145.2	134	73	55	7	4	59	1	121	9
MacDonald, Knoxville*	3	5	.375	3.29	43	0	0	27	0	9	63.0	52	27	23	0	2	23	2	58	0
Magnante, Memphis*	8	9	.471	3.66	26	26	4	0	1	0	157.1	137	70	64	10	9	53	3	118	8
Manzanillo, Birmingham*	8	7	.533	3.90	22	22	2	0	0	0	129.1	105	66	56	11	6	72	0	89	2
Marak, Greenville	8	7	.533	3.03	43	14	0	10	0	5	121.2	102	53	41	7	3	47	1	81	5
Marchok, Jacksonville*	6	6	.500	1.89	64	0	0	23	0	9	76.0	40	25	16	1	6	39	4	61	9
Martinez, Memphis*	0	0	.000	27.00	1	0	0	1	0	0	0.1	1	1	1	0	0	1	0	0	0
Mathews, Greenville	1	0	1.000	1.04	5	0	0	3	0	1	8.2	5	1	1	0	0	4	0	5	2
Maye, Huntsville	1	2	.333	3.57	10	0	0	4	0	0	17.2	14	11	7	3	0	10	0	6	2
Mead, Chattanooga	5	11	.313	4.98	20	20	5	0	1	0	112.0	119	67	62	8	6	49	3	81	9

Pitcher—Club	W.	L.	Pct.	ERA.	G.	GS.	CG.	GF.	ShO.	Sv.	IP.	H.	R.	ER.	HR.	HB.	BB.	Int. BB.	SO.	WP.
Menendez, Birmingham	10	4	.714	3.19	27	18	2	6	1	1	144.0	123	61	51	14	4	53	2	115	7
Michno, Charlotte	5	7	.417	3.36	37	10	1	8	0	0	104.1	95	50	39	7	6	62	10	75	4
Middaugh, Birmingham	1	0	1.000	0.00	1	0	0	0	0	0	1.2	0	0	0	0	0	1	0	2	0
Mills, Knoxville	0	1	.000	4.18	12	0	0	5	0	0	23.2	23	12	11	1	1	19	3	16	2
Minutelli, Chattanooga*	1	1	.500	5.28	6	6	1	0	0	0	29.0	28	19	17	1	6	23	0	20	8
Moeller, Memphis*	1	1	.500	2.84	5	5	0	0	0	0	25.1	16	9	8	2	1	10	0	21	0
Morris, Memphis	0	0	.000	12.27	4	0	4	0	4	0	3.2	6	10	5	2	1	6	0	1	0
Moscrey, Chattanooga*	8	13	.381	5.50	26	25	3	1	0	0	145.2	166	100	89	10	14	75	1	96	7
Mount, Birmingham	5	4	.556	4.20	43	1	0	26	0	5	85;2	83	48	40	9	3	44	1	41	7
Mullins, Chattanooga	0	2	.000	5.64	9	1	0	1	0	0	22.1	28	19	14	2	4	16	0	11	3
Newcomb, Knoxville	0	6	.000	4.32	24	1	0	14	0	4	41.2	48	26	20	2	2	15	2	21	0
Norris, Huntsville	1	0	1.000	0.00	1	1	0	0	0	0	5.1	6	0	0	0	0	3	0	3	0
North, Orlando*	2	1	.667	4.09	7	5	0	0	0	0	33.0	34	19	15	2	1	15	0	24	3
Oliverio, Columbus	2	8	.200	4.72	18	13	0	0	0	0	74.1	89	50	39	9	4	19	1	34	4
Ollom, Birmingham	1	2	.333	7.11	11	0	0	6	0	1	19.0	25	19	15	2	1	8	0	12	1
Pacillo, Jacksonville	0	1	.000	3.60	2	2	0	0	0	0	10.0	10	6	4	0	0	3	0	8	0
Pappas, Charlotte	0	0	.000	0.00	1	0	0	1	0	0	1.0	0	0	0	0	1	1	0	0	0
Parmenter, Charlotte	0	3	.000	10.19	12	1	0	5	0	1	17.2	26	23	20	6	1	9	1	7	1
Parnell, Memphis	0	0	.000	3.00	2	0	0	1	0	0	3.0	3	1	1	0	0	4	0	1	1
Penigar, Birmingham	0	0	.000	0.00	3	0	0	3	0	0	4.0	2	0	0	0	0	0	0	3	0
Perez, Jacksonville*	4	3	.571	3.60	20	0	0	3	0	0	35.0	25	16	14	0	0	34	1	50	1
Peters, Jacksonville	3	4	.429	4.44	40	0	0	28	0	6	52.2	61	34	26	0	2	29	2	35	2
Pickens, Memphis	1	2	.333	3.45	7	0	0	2	0	1	15.2	11	9	6	1	0	14	0	12	2
Pittman, Orlando	5	9	.357	4.59	34	15	0	16	0	11	102.0	82	60	52	10	6	72	1	103	10
Polley, Greenville*	6	15	.286	3.35	28	26	3	0	2	0	163.2	142	75	61	11	4	58	1	106	6
Puleo, Greenville	0	0	.000	4.50	2	2	0	0	0	0	6.0	6	3	3	0	0	3	0	5	1
Raether, Jacksonville	0	0	.000	3.35	33	1	0	22	0	6	45.2	42	20	17	5	4	27	0	34	1
Redding, Orlando	3	1	.750	3.86	31	5	1	7	0	2	77.0	74	42	33	6	4	34	0	44	5
Reese, Memphis	0	0	.000	36.00	1	0	0	0	0	0	1.0	3	4	4	0	0	3	0	0	0
Renfroe, Charlotte	19	7	.731	3.14	78	2	1	58	1	15	132.0	127	52	46	12	1	34	10	85	2
Reynolds, Birmingham	4	5	.444	2.56	27	2	1	17	0	1	63.1	45	22	18	3	3	26	2	38	3
Rivera, Jacksonville	1	2	.333	5.33	5	5	0	0	0	0	27.0	24	17	16	3	0	17	0	22	2
Robinson, Chattanooga	0	0	.000	1.80	1	1	0	0	0	0	5.0	3	1	1	0	0	1	0	5	0
Rodgers, Chattanooga	4	7	.364	3.27	39	13	1	7	0	0	132.0	137	65	48	6	3	51	3	86	9
Rodriguez, Chattanooga*	3	0	1.000	4.47	28	0	0	11	0	2	44.1	48	24	22	6	4	18	2	36	6
Rogers, Knoxville	12	10	.545	4.56	32	30	1	0	0	0	158.0	136	89	80	12	5	132	1	120	14
Rojas, Jacksonville	10	7	.588	2.49	34	12	1	17	1	5	112.0	62	39	31	1	5	57	0	104	8
Rosario, Charlotte*	8	0	1.000	3.42	55	4	0	15	0	6	79.0	73	35	30	6	1	50	9	77	9
Roth, Charlotte	2	1	.667	7.85	10	2	0	3	0	0	18.1	24	17	16	0	2	22	2	12	2
Sanders, Knoxville	1	7	.125	4.53	27	0	0	20	0	5	49.2	46	33	25	2	1	35	3	40	8
Satzinger, Orlando	3	6	.333	4.57	57	1	0	22	0	8	110.1	105	69	56	17	6	52	1	82	3
Scheid, Charlotte*	4	1	.800	4.08	17	6	1	2	0	0	46.1	43	30	21	8	2	27	2	37	7
Schock, Huntsville	9	7	.563	4.74	29	29	1	0	0	0	178.1	193	102	94	24	7	69	1	98	13
Shea, Knoxville*	9	12	.429	2.70	31	29	3	1	1	0	190.1	183	79	57	14	6	57	1	96	4
Shotkoski, Huntsville	3	2	.600	2.84	23	0	0	12	0	1	31.2	37	15	10	2	0	11	1	21	2
Sierra, Chattanooga	1	0	1.000	5.93	3	3	1	0	0	0	13.2	19	9	9	1	0	5	0	12	1
Simons, Orlando*	7	3	.700	3.81	14	14	3	0	0	0	87.1	83	39	37	7	2	37	0	58	1
Sossamon, Jacksonville	2	6	.250	6.11	19	4	0	5	0	1	35.1	40	32	24	4	3	20	1	29	1
Stancel, Huntsville	6	3	.667	5.25	44	1	0	18	0	3	72.0	78	47	42	5	3	42	5	38	5
Stanton, Greenville*	4	1	.800	1.58	47	0	0	36	0	19	51.1	32	10	9	1	0	31	3	58	4
Stephens, Birmingham	4	3	.571	3.68	8	8	2	0	1	0	51.1	42	24	21	2	4	21	2	27	1
Stockam, Greenville*	7	4	.636	2.33	53	0	0	20	0	0	73.1	58	25	19	5	2	31	6	45	2
Stocker, Huntsville	4	1	.800	4.25	44	0	0	11	0	4	91.0	88	49	43	11	3	47	1	77	6
Stottlemyre, Memphis	3	0	1.000	1.59	16	0	0	11	0	6	22.2	15	4	4	0	0	9	0	18	1
Taylor, Huntsville	0	0	.000	15.95	5	0	0	1	0	0	7.1	15	13	13	1	0	8	0	5	3
Torres, Columbus	2	0	1.000	2.85	33	0	0	14	0	3	53.2	43	21	17	3	0	24	5	56	5
Trafton, Birmingham	0	0	.000	Infin	1	0	0	0	0	0	0.0	1	1	1	0	1	0	0	0	0
Tresemer, Memphis	3	9	.250	4.39	30	17	0	7	0	3	106.2	123	63	52	11	0	43	1	59	5
Upshaw, Greenville*	8	2	.800	2.75	14	14	0	0	0	0	95.0	78	36	29	5	2	30	2	70	14
Vargas, Columbus	1	0	1.000	1.29	1	1	1	0	0	0	7.0	7	1	1	0	0	2	0	2	2
Vasquez, Memphis	8	6	.571	4.02	64	0	0	49	0	11	94.0	99	52	42	2	4	46	4	48	5
Veres, Huntsville	8	11	.421	4.86	29	28	2	1	1	0	159.1	160	93	86	15	4	83	1	105	16
Walker, Memphis	2	9	.182	4.53	39	10	0	6	0	2	109.1	104	66	55	5	5	66	0	86	14
Wapnick, Knoxville	1	0	1.000	0.49	12	0	0	9	0	2	18.1	12	1	1	1	0	7	0	20	0
Wassenaar, Orlando	5	5	.500	4.85	13	13	0	0	0	0	81.2	93	51	44	13	4	26	0	47	9
Weber, Huntsville	3	2	.600	5.29	15	2	0	4	0	0	34.0	34	25	20	2	1	29	0	17	0
Weems, Birmingham	3	4	.429	4.97	13	13	2	0	0	0	70.2	74	44	39	10	4	30	1	28	4
Wells, Columbus*	2	3	.400	4.63	23	1	0	5	0	2	46.2	44	25	24	4	1	31	1	38	5
Wendell, Greenville	0	0	.000	9.82	1	0	0	0	0	0	3.2	7	5	4	3	0	1	0	3	0
Wernig, Huntsville*	7	6	.538	5.15	18	17	0	0	0	0	92.2	108	64	53	10	6	33	1	64	2
G. Williams, Knoxville	3	5	.375	3.55	14	12	2	1	1	0	71.0	61	32	28	6	2	33	2	51	1
J. Williams, Orlando*	6	4	.600	3.04	43	0	0	39	0	14	53.1	50	23	18	3	0	35	1	62	1
R. Williams, Charlotte	1	1	.500	6.53	6	4	0	1	0	0	20.2	33	16	15	4	0	8	1	16	0
Wishnevski, Knoxville	6	1	.857	2.31	14	11	0	2	0	0	66.1	50	23	17	4	4	26	0	36	4
Young, Huntsville	13	6	.684	3.93	29	27	2	0	2	0	146.2	112	78	64	2	3	109	0	163	12
Zarranz, Chattanooga	2	0	.000	11.70	9	0	0	4	0	0	10.0	13	13	13	1	1	14	1	8	1

BALKS—Young, 12; Farmer, 10; Hirsch, 9; Lee, Manzanillo, 8 each; Abbott, Scheid, 7 each; Guthrie, Kile, Shea, 6 each; Dodd, Guzman, Klink, Lazor, Leon, Mead, 5 each; Edwards, Hill, Kaiser, Marchok, Minutelli, Oliverio, Satzinger, 4 each; Bianchi, Bronkey, Browning, Deitz, Groom, Hickey, LeMasters, Lopez, Peters, Pittman, Rodriguez, Rogers, Schock, Stottlemyre, Walker, Weber, 3 each; Akins, Bombard, Bottenfield, Campbell, Cano, Clark, Corbell, Credeur, Crouch, Davidson, DelRosario, Duffy, Givler, Gomez, Jeffery, Lewis, Little, Mathews, Menendez, Michno, Moscrey, Newcomb, Ollom, Perez, Polley, Reese, Rosario, Simons, Torres, Upshaw, Veres, J. Williams, 2 each; Alvarez, Ariola, Bangtson, Bennett, Boskie, Brinkman, Bruno, O. Canseco, Carter, Chadwick, Coffman, Cole, Davins, Delkus, Diaz, Estes, Gakeler, Gilles, Gozzo, G. Hall, Harrison, Hennis, Holcomb, Ilsley, Jefferson, C. Jones, D. Jones, Kallevig, Kutzler, Lambert, Linton, Loynd, MacDonald, Parmenter, Renfroe, Reynolds, Rodgers, Rojas, Stockam, Tresemer, Wapnick, Wernig, G. Williams, R. Williams, 1 each.

COMBINATION SHUTOUTS—Edwards-Mount, Manzanillo-Menendez, Reynolds-Hudek, Menendez-Hudek, Groom-Reynolds-Hudek, Birmingham; Mead-Dodd-Bruno, Rodgers-Hill, Chattanooga; Loynd-Browning 2, Kile-Browning-Costello, Credeur-Givler-Browning, Credeur-Costello, Hickey-Johnson-Torres-Browning, Columbus; Polley-Deitz, Jimenez-Polley-Stanton, Greenville; Veres-Maye-Shotkoski, Wernig-Corbell, Corbell-Stancel, Norris-Klink, Young-Shotkoski, Chiamparino-Berg, Huntsville; Dixon-Marchok-Rojas, Lewis-Dixon, Bottenfield-Marchok-Rojas, Farmer-Peters, Rojas-Marchok-Raether, Farmer-Marchok, Rojas-Chambers, Rojas-Perez-Bennett, Jacksonville; Wishnevski-MacDonald-Jones, Jones-Gozzo, Wishnevski-MacDonald, Guzman-Balsley-Newcomb, Rogers-MacDonald, Knoxville; Magnante-Encarnacion, Magnante-Vasquez, Magnante-Stottlemyre, Filson-Walker, Memphis; Simons-Delkus, Orlando.

NO-HIT GAMES—None.

Texas League

CLASS AA

Leading Batter
BOB ROSE
Midland

League President
CARL SAWATSKI

Leading Pitcher
JULIO VALERA
Jackson

CHAMPIONSHIP WINNERS IN PREVIOUS YEARS

Year	Team	Pct
1888	Dallas	.671
1889	Houston	.551
1890	Galveston	.705
1892	Houston	.741
	Houston	.613
1895	Dallas	.754
	Fort Worth*	.750
1896	Fort Worth	.757
	Houston*	.679
	Galveston	.548
1897	San Antonio†	.657
	Galveston†	.717
1898	League disbanded.	
1899	Galveston	.632
	Galveston	.762
1900-01	Did not operate.	
1902	Corsicana	.866
	Corsicana	.682
1903	Paris-Waco	.615
	Dallas*	.648
1904	Corsicana*	.615
	Fort Worth	.800
1905	Fort Worth	.545
1906	Fort Worth	.677
	Cleburne x	.609
1907	Austin	.629
1908	San Antonio	.664
1909	Houston	.601
1910	Dallas†	.586
	Houston†	.586
1911	Austin	.575
1912	Houston	.626
1913	Houston	.620
1914	Houston†	.671
	Waco†	.671
1915	Waco	.592
1916	Waco	.587
1917	Dallas	.600
1918	Dallas	.584
1919	Shreveport*	.677
	Fort Worth	.651
1920	Fort Worth	.703
	Fort Worth	.750
1921	Fort Worth	.691
	Fort Worth	.662
1922	Fort Worth	.694
	Fort Worth	.711
1923	Fort Worth	.632
1924	Fort Worth	.689
	Fort Worth	.763
1925	Fort Worth	.711
	Fort Worth y	.653
1926	Dallas	.574

Year	Team	Pct
1927	Wichita Falls	.654
	Wichita Falls	.731
1928	Houston*	.679
	Wichita Falls	.620
1929	Dallas*	.588
	Wichita Falls	.697
1930	Wichita Falls	.632
	Fort Worth*	.625
1931	Houston a	.734
	Houston	.640
1932	Beaumont*	.727
	Dallas	.727
1933	Houston	.623
	San Antonio (4th)§	.523
1934	Galveston‡	.579
1935	Oklahoma City‡	.590
1936	Dallas	.604
	Tulsa (3rd)§	.519
1937	Oklahoma City	.635
	Fort Worth (3rd)§	.535
1938	Beaumont	.635
1939	Houston	.606
	Fort Worth (4th)§	.540
1940	Houston‡	.652
1941	Houston	.673
	Dallas (4th)§	.519
1942	Beaumont	.605
	Shreveport (2nd)§	.576
1943-44-45	Did not operate.	
1946	Fort Worth	.656
	Dallas (2nd)§	.591
1947	Houston‡	.623
1948	Fort Worth‡	.601
1949	Fort Worth	.649
	Tulsa (2nd)§	.584
1950	Beaumont	.595
	San Antonio (4th)§	.513
1951	Houston‡	.619
1952	Dallas	.571
	Shreveport (3rd)§	.522
1953	Dallas‡	.571
1954	Shreveport	.559
	Houston (2nd)§	.553
1955	Dallas	.581
	Shreveport (3rd)§	.540
1956	Houston‡	.623
1957	Dallas	.662
	Houston (2nd)§	.630
1958	Fort Worth	.582
	Cor. Christi (3rd)§	.507
1959	Victoria	.589
	Austin (2nd)§	.548
1960	Rio Grande Valley	.590
	Tulsa (3rd)	.528

Year	Team	Pct
1961	Amarillo	.643
	San Antonio (3rd)§	.532
1962	El Paso	.571
	Tulsa (2nd)§	.550
1963	San Antonio	.564
	Tulsa (3rd)§	.529
1964	San Antonio‡	.607
1965	Tulsa	.574
	Albuquerque b	.550
1966	Arkansas	.579
1967	Albuquerque	.557
1968	Arkansas	.586
	El Paso b	.562
1969	Amarillo	.593
	Memphis b	.504
1970	Albuquerque a	.615
	Memphis	.507
1971	Did not operate as league—clubs were members of Dixie Association.	
1972	Alexandria	.600
	El Paso b	.557
1973	San Antonio	.590
	Memphis b	.558
1974	Victoria b	.581
	El Paso	.555
1975	Lafayette c	.558
	Midland c	.604
1976	Amarillo b	.600
	Shreveport	.515
1977	El Paso	.600
	Arkansas d	.485
1978	El Paso d	.593
	Jackson	.567
1979	Arkansas d	.571
	Midland	.563
1980	Arkansas d	.596
	San Antonio	.544
1981	San Antonio	.571
	Jackson d	.507
1982	El Paso	.559
	Tulsa d	.515
1983	Jackson	.507
	Beaumont d	.500
1984	Beaumont	.654
	Jackson d	.610
1985	El Paso	.632
	Jackson d	.537
1986	El Paso d	.630
	Jackson	.533
1987	Wichita d	.515
	Jackson	.515
1988	El Paso	.552
	Tulsa	.522

*Won split-season playoff. †No playoff for title. ‡Finished first and won four-club playoff. §Won four-club playoff. xTitle to Cleburne by default. yTied with Dallas in second half and won playoff for championship. zFort Worth disbanded. aTied with Beaumont at end of first half and won title in best-of-five series played as part of second half schedule. bLeague divided into Eastern, Western divisions; won two-team playoff. cLeague divided into Eastern, Western divisions; declared co-champions when playoffs were not completed. dLeague divided into Eastern and Western divisions and played split-season; won playoffs. NOTE—Championship awarded to winner of four-team playoff, 1933-51; first-place team and playoff winner co-champions, 1952-64.

STANDING OF CLUBS AT CLOSE OF FIRST HALF, JUNE 16

EASTERN DIVISION

Club	W.	L.	T.	Pct.	G.B.
Arkansas (Cardinals)	40	28	0	.588	....
Tulsa (Rangers)	38	30	0	.559	2
Shreveport (Giants)	35	33	0	.515	5
Jackson (Mets)	31	37	0	.456	9

WESTERN DIVISION

Club	W.	L.	T.	Pct.	G.B.
Wichita (Padres)	36	30	0	.545	....
Midland (Angels)	34	32	0	.515	2
El Paso (Brewers)	30	38	0	.441	7
San Antonio (Dodgers)	26	42	0	.382	11

STANDING OF CLUBS AT CLOSE OF SECOND HALF, AUGUST 28

EASTERN DIVISION

Club	W.	L.	T.	Pct.	G.B.
Shreveport (Giants)	40	28	0	.588	....
Arkansas (Cardinals)	39	28	0	.582	½
Tulsa (Rangers)	35	33	0	.515	5
Jackson (Mets)	30	37	0	.448	9½

WESTERN DIVISION

Club	W.	L.	T.	Pct.	G.B.
Wichita (Padres)	37	33	0	.529	....
Midland (Angels)	36	34	0	.514	1
El Paso (Brewers)	33	35	0	.485	3
San Antonio (Dodgers)	23	45	0	.338	13

COMPOSITE STANDING OF CLUBS AT CLOSE OF SEASON, AUGUST 28

Club	Ark.	Shrv.	Wich.	Tul.	Mid.	ElP.	Jax.	S.A.	W.	L.	T.	Pct.	G.B.
Arkansas (Cardinals)	....	17	6	18	7	6	19	6	79	56	0	.585	....
Shreveport (Giants)	15	....	5	17	7	5	20	6	75	61	0	.551	4½
Wichita (Padres)	4	5	....	5	15	19	5	20	73	63	0	.537	6½
Tulsa (Rangers)	14	15	5	....	5	8	20	6	73	63	0	.537	6½
Midland (Angels)	3	3	17	5	....	18	3	21	70	66	0	.515	9½
El Paso (Brewers)	4	5	13	2	14	....	3	22	63	73	0	.463	16½
Jackson (Mets)	12	12	5	12	7	7	....	6	61	74	0	.452	18
San Antonio (Dodgers)	4	4	12	4	11	10	4	....	49	87	0	.360	30½

Arkansas club represented Little Rock, Ark.

Major league affiliations in parentheses.

Playoffs—Arkansas defeated Shreveport, two games to none; Arkansas defeated Wichita, four games to three, to win league championship.

Regular-Season Attendance—Arkansas, 296,428; El Paso, 228,261; Jackson, 87,153; Midland, 135,518; San Antonio, 158,402; Shreveport, 210,669; Tulsa, 218,755; Wichita, 176,424. Total—1,511,610. Playoffs (9 games)—19,692. All-Star Game—4,290.

Managers—Arkansas, Gaylen Pitts; El Paso, Marc Bombard; Jackson, Steve Swisher; Midland, Max Oliveras; San Antonio, John Shoemaker; Shreveport, Bill Evers; Tulsa, Tommy Thompson; Wichita, Pat Kelly.

All-Star Team—1B—Chris Cron, Midland; 2B—Geronimo Pena, Arkansas; 3B—Dean Palmer, Tulsa; SS—Gary DiSarcina, Midland; OF—Ray Lankford, Arkansas; Juan Gonzalez, Tulsa; Warren Newson, Wichita; C—Carlos Hernandez, San Antonio and Tim McIntosh, El Paso; DH—Bob Rose, Midland; P—Andy Benes, Wichita; Omar Oliveras, Wichita; Mike Perez, Arkansas; Dave Osteen, Arkansas; Julio Valera, Jackson; Most Valuable Player—Ray Lankford, Arkansas; Pitcher of the Year—Andy Benes, Wichita; Manager of the Year—Gaylen Pitts, Arkansas.

(Compiled by Howe Sportsdata International, Boston, Mass.)

CLUB BATTING

Club	Pct.	G.	AB.	R.	OR.	H.	TB.	2B.	3B.	HR.	RBI.	SH.	SF.	HP.	BB.	Int. BB.	SO.	SB.	CS.	LOB.
Midland	.295	136	4572	768	696	1349	2030	255	48	110	693	55	53	47	482	37	836	94	55	946
El Paso	.277	135	4549	678	782	1261	1794	202	41	83	618	28	39	36	476	33	725	118	59	975
Arkansas	.275	134	4338	710	568	1195	1715	228	41	70	629	51	46	37	445	36	679	143	64	879
San Antonio	.267	136	4591	585	655	1226	1679	195	33	64	508	46	32	40	455	31	624	92	72	970
Shreveport	.264	136	4427	603	551	1169	1593	201	38	49	532	63	56	25	480	35	727	155	78	937
Wichita	.259	136	4383	621	622	1136	1697	195	45	92	556	55	49	36	547	31	815	141	68	969
Tulsa	.258	136	4399	586	598	1134	1701	203	38	96	537	43	38	43	449	12	922	95	82	926
Jackson	.248	135	4392	469	548	1091	1481	189	18	55	419	48	42	39	391	33	759	103	52	911

INDIVIDUAL BATTING
(Leading Qualifiers for Batting Championship—367 or More Plate Appearances)
*Bats lefthanded. †Switch-hitter.

Player and Club	Pct.	G.	AB.	R.	H.	TB.	2B.	3B.	HR.	RBI.	SH.	SF.	HP.	BB.	Int. BB.	SO.	SB.	CS.
Rose, Robert, Midland	.359	99	351	64	126	190	21	5	11	73	3	8	6	50	3	62	3	2
Sambo, Ramon, El Paso†	.322	115	466	80	150	174	10	4	2	34	6	2	2	50	4	99	47	13
Aldrete, Richard, Shreveport*	.321	118	392	48	126	154	17	1	3	56	3	6	1	20	3	45	3	4
Lankford, Raymond, Arkansas*	.317	134	498	98	158	243	28	12	11	98	0	7	4	65	6	57	38	10
Ashley, Shon, El Paso	.315	113	394	65	124	194	26	1	14	65	0	3	4	36	3	92	2	5
Newson, Warren, Wichita*	.304	128	427	94	130	216	20	6	18	70	1	5	0	103	10	99	20	9
Grunhard, Daniel, Midland*	.304	105	388	64	118	196	26	8	12	57	1	4	0	38	4	60	8	5
Cron, Christopher, Midland	.301	128	491	80	148	253	33	3	22	103	1	6	14	39	5	126	0	1
McIntosh, Timothy, El Paso	.300	120	463	72	139	226	30	3	17	93	2	9	8	29	3	72	5	4
Hernandez, Carlos, San Antonio	.300	99	370	37	111	157	16	3	8	41	1	3	7	12	0	46	2	3

Departmental Leaders: G—Lankford, 134; AB—Faries, 513; R—Gilkey, 104; H—Lankford, 158; TB—J. Gonzalez, 254; 2B—Cron, 33; 3B—Lankford, 12; HR—Palmer, 25; RBI—Cron, 103; SH—Peters, 11; SF—Hollins, 10; HP—Hillemann, 16; BB—Newson, 103; IBB—Newson, 10; SO—Palmer, 152; SB—Gilkey, 53; CS—Gilkey, 22.

(All Players—Listed Alphabetically)

Player and Club	Pct.	G.	AB.	R.	H.	TB.	2B.	3B.	HR.	RBI.	SH.	SF.	HP.	BB.	Int. BB.	SO.	SB.	CS.
Akins, Sidney, Arkansas	1.000	12	2	1	2	3	1	0	0	0	0	0	0	0	0	0	0	0
Aldrete, Richard, Shreveport*	.321	118	392	48	126	154	17	1	3	56	3	6	1	20	3	45	3	4
Alexander, Gary, Tulsa	.232	131	466	59	108	182	25	2	15	64	1	7	2	59	1	103	9	11
Alfaro, Jesus, El Paso	.271	70	221	38	60	98	13	2	7	41	2	2	0	43	5	48	0	0
Alfredson, Thomas, Midland	.221	19	68	11	15	29	4	2	2	13	1	0	1	3	1	24	0	1
Alicea, Miguel, Midland	.000	11	1	0	0	0	0	0	0	0	0	0	0	0	0	1	0	0
Alyea, Brant, Jackson	.250	37	120	13	30	55	5	1	6	20	0	2	1	3	0	23	0	0
Amaro, Ruben, Midland†	.382	29	110	28	42	64	9	2	3	9	2	1	10	1	19	7	1	
Armstrong, Kevin, San Antonio	.087	26	23	0	2	3	1	0	0	3	2	1	0	1	0	11	0	0
Arnold, Tony, San Antonio	.000	8	2	0	0	0	0	0	0	0	1	0	0	0	0	2	0	0
Ashley, Shon, El Paso	.315	113	394	65	124	194	26	1	14	65	0	3	4	36	3	92	2	5
Barns, Jeffrey, Midland	.296	70	226	32	67	83	7	3	1	20	1	2	13	2	30	3	4	
Basso, Michael, Wichita	.203	66	202	23	41	54	4	0	3	18	1	3	1	16	0	31	0	1
Bauer, Peter, Jackson	.091	15	11	2	1	1	0	0	0	0	0	0	0	0	0	5	0	0
Beasley, Christopher, Midland	1.000	16	1	0	1	1	0	0	0	0	0	0	0	0	0	0	1	0

Player and Club	Pct.	G.	AB.	R.	H.	TB.	2B.	3B.	HR.	RBI.	SH.	SF.	HP.	BB.	Int. BB.	SO.	SB.	CS.
Beck, Rodney, Shreveport	.250	16	12	0	3	4	1	0	0	0	3	0	0	0	0	0	0	0
Benes, Andrew, Wichita	.071	16	14	2	1	1	0	0	0	1	1	0	1	1	0	6	0	0
Benitez, Manuel, San Antonio	.206	13	34	1	7	8	1	0	0	6	0	1	1	5	0	7	0	0
Bivens, William, Arkansas	.063	13	16	1	1	1	0	0	0	1	3	0	0	0	0	13	0	0
Blair, Paul, Shreveport†	.218	50	142	18	31	37	6	0	0	13	2	1	1	10	1	13	6	4
Bogar, Timothy, Jackson	.266	112	406	44	108	143	13	5	4	45	3	5	7	41	4	57	8	3
Bones, Ricardo, Wichita	.154	24	13	1	2	2	0	0	0	0	2	0	0	2	0	4	0	0
Bonilla, George, Shreveport°	.143	43	7	0	1	2	1	0	0	2	0	0	0	1	0	2	0	0
Brewer, Rodney, Arkansas	.277	128	470	71	130	189	25	2	10	93	0	3	7	46	3	46	2	3
Brocail, Douglas, Wichita°	.333	24	18	3	6	6	0	0	0	0	2	0	0	1	0	6	0	0
Brooks, Brian, Wichita°	.173	36	81	7	14	24	1	3	1	4	2	0	1	2	0	23	4	3
Brown, Adam, San Antonio°	.282	42	124	19	35	59	6	0	6	20	1	0	3	13	1	20	1	0
Brown, Kevin, Jackson°	.118	8	17	0	2	2	0	0	0	1	0	0	0	0	0	4	0	0
Bumgarner, Jeffrey, Jackson	.000	12	6	0	0	0	0	0	0	0	2	0	0	0	0	5	0	0
Burcham, Timothy, Midland	.000	45	1	0	0	0	0	0	0	0	0	0	0	0	0	0	0	0
Bustabad, Juan, San Antonio°	.200	59	175	16	35	41	4	1	0	15	1	0	0	13	1	20	3	2
Campbell, Kevin, San Antonio	.000	17	1	0	0	0	0	0	0	0	0	0	0	0	0	0	0	0
Carr, Charles, Jackson†	.241	116	444	45	107	122	13	1	0	22	7	2	1	27	2	66	47	20
Carter, Dennis, Arkansas	.217	83	207	27	45	72	9	0	6	32	1	2	2	11	0	67	2	2
Carter, Jeffrey, Shreveport†	.290	127	445	77	129	162	16	4	3	52	8	5	4	63	2	47	33	16
Carter, Larry, Shreveport	.182	14	11	0	2	2	0	0	0	0	1	0	1	0	0	4	0	0
Cedeno, Vinicio, Midland	.000	53	1	0	0	0	0	0	0	0	0	0	0	0	0	0	0	0
Cerny, Scott, Midland	.300	74	253	36	76	81	5	0	0	19	6	4	1	21	0	22	3	2
Chavez, Rafael, Wichita	.167	38	6	0	1	1	0	0	0	0	1	0	0	0	0	2	0	0
Cisarik, Brian, Wichita°	.263	122	372	49	98	134	15	3	5	44	2	4	1	77	5	65	23	13
Citari, Joseph, El Paso	.228	30	101	13	23	29	3	0	1	10	1	0	1	16	0	29	1	1
Colbert, Craig, Shreveport	.259	106	363	47	94	140	19	3	7	34	2	2	0	23	5	67	3	7
Conley, Virgil, Jackson°	.000	1	1	0	0	0	0	0	0	0	0	0	0	0	0	1	0	0
Conner, Gregory, Shreveport	.192	25	78	11	15	23	2	0	2	6	0	1	0	5	0	23	2	0
Connolly, Stephen, Shreveport	.000	38	13	0	0	0	0	0	0	0	4	0	0	0	0	8	0	0
Cooper, Craig, Wichita	.293	54	184	24	54	88	9	5	5	28	3	6	0	17	0	36	1	0
Cron, Christopher, Midland	.301	128	491	80	148	253	33	3	22	103	1	6	14	39	5	126	0	1
Cuevas, Angelo, Jackson°	.283	100	350	46	99	137	20	3	4	45	1	6	2	42	3	51	6	4
Curnow, Robert, Wichita	.000	4	8	1	0	0	0	0	0	0	2	0	0	1	0	4	0	0
Dabney, Ty, El Paso°	.160	16	50	6	8	10	2	0	0	5	0	1	0	6	0	10	1	0
David, Andre, El Paso°	.293	84	297	52	87	135	16	4	8	57	0	6	4	48	3	20	6	2
Davis, Mark, Midland	.241	19	58	9	14	18	1	0	1	7	3	0	1	6	0	18	6	1
DeAngelis, Steven, Midland°	.307	41	153	32	47	68	10	1	3	27	0	1	0	20	1	24	1	3
DeButch, Michael, Jackson	.264	31	87	24	23	33	4	0	2	6	0	1	0	30	0	20	9	6
Decker, Steven, Shreveport	.324	44	142	19	46	57	8	0	1	18	1	1	0	11	0	24	0	3
DeWolf, Robert, Wichita°	.241	70	187	29	45	79	14	1	6	29	1	3	0	25	6	32	5	7
Diaz, Alexis, Jackson†	.274	23	95	11	26	39	5	1	2	9	0	0	0	3	0	11	3	4
Diaz, Edgar, El Paso	.308	23	78	16	24	24	0	0	0	6	0	0	0	15	0	7	3	2
DiSarcina, Gary, Midland	.286	126	441	65	126	170	18	7	4	54	7	5	4	24	3	54	11	6
Dixon, Andrew, Shreveport°	.282	106	333	58	94	117	12	4	1	32	2	6	1	28	0	38	43	11
Dominguez, Jose, Shreveport	.000	40	6	0	0	0	0	0	0	0	1	0	0	1	0	3	0	0
Doran, Mark, Midland	.273	47	143	27	39	51	6	0	2	14	0	2	4	16	1	35	5	4
Drahman, Brian, El Paso	.000	19	1	0	0	0	0	0	0	0	0	0	0	0	0	0	0	0
Edge, Gregory, El Paso†	.243	97	371	46	90	107	9	4	0	34	4	3	2	34	1	16	10	6
Edwards, Jovon, Jackson°	.125	9	16	2	2	5	0	0	1	1	0	0	0	2	0	3	1	0
Escalera, Ruben, El Paso	.271	31	107	10	29	39	2	1	2	11	1	0	0	16	1	10	0	5
Falcone, Peter, San Antonio°	.444	17	9	0	4	5	1	0	0	4	0	1	0	0	0	4	0	0
Faries, Paul, Wichita	.265	130	513	79	136	195	25	8	6	52	2	1	2	47	0	52	41	13
Fariss, Monty, Tulsa	.272	132	497	72	135	181	27	2	5	52	8	6	0	64	0	112	12	6
Farmer, Kevin, Wichita	.258	13	31	0	8	8	0	0	0	3	0	1	0	2	0	5	0	0
Fassero, Jeffrey, Arkansas°	.100	6	10	1	1	4	0	0	1	1	1	0	0	0	0	4	0	0
Fortugno, Timothy, El Paso°	.000	10	1	0	0	0	0	0	0	0	0	0	0	0	0	1	0	0
Fox, Michael, Arkansas	.289	16	45	7	13	16	3	0	0	4	0	1	0	5	1	4	1	0
Francois, Manuel, San Antonio†	.273	91	275	30	75	104	14	6	1	24	3	2	2	25	4	54	6	5
Freeland, Dean, Shreveport	.200	18	20	4	4	4	0	0	0	2	0	0	0	0	0	2	0	0
Freiling, Howard, Jackson°	.277	115	415	34	115	151	19	1	5	44	1	2	5	20	5	51	0	1
Garner, Darrin, Tulsa	.261	116	410	59	107	127	14	3	0	33	7	3	7	48	1	60	11	10
Garner, Kevin, Wichita°	.249	103	350	51	87	165	17	2	19	63	3	2	2	30	1	102	0	0
Gay, Scott, Shreveport	.167	18	6	0	1	1	0	0	0	0	1	0	0	0	0	3	0	0
Gerhart, Kenneth, Shreveport	.200	16	60	9	12	20	2	0	2	8	1	0	0	7	0	18	1	1
Gideon, Ronnie, Jackson°	.333	12	9	1	3	4	1	0	0	2	0	1	0	1	0	4	0	0
Gilkey, Bernard, Arkansas	.278	131	500	104	139	188	25	3	6	57	8	5	2	70	2	54	53	22
Givens, Brian, Jackson	.077	13	13	0	1	1	0	0	0	0	0	0	0	0	0	6	0	0
Gonzalez, Juan, Tulsa	.293	133	502	73	147	254	30	7	21	85	1	4	9	31	3	98	1	8
Gonzalez, Otto, Midland	.313	55	160	26	50	91	15	1	8	36	1	3	0	20	3	52	0	3
Graham, Everett, Midland°	.238	65	210	30	50	78	12	2	4	25	3	0	1	23	3	30	9	3
Graves, Christopher, Midland†	.259	55	201	37	52	83	6	5	5	18	1	0	0	23	4	49	13	6
Gross, Kip, Jackson	.148	16	27	2	4	4	0	0	0	1	2	1	0	0	0	7	0	0
Grunhard, Daniel, Midland°	.304	105	388	64	118	196	26	8	12	57	1	4	0	38	4	60	8	5
Guerrero, Epifano, El Paso°	.270	128	470	66	127	200	24	8	11	73	0	7	2	42	8	51	12	4
Gunderson, Eric, Shreveport	.227	12	22	2	5	6	1	0	0	2	0	0	0	0	0	6	0	0
Hall, Andrew, Midland	.263	8	19	1	5	10	2	0	1	6	2	0	0	1	1	4	0	0
Ham, Michael, Shreveport	.125	3	8	1	1	1	0	0	0	2	0	0	0	0	0	1	0	0
Hansen, David, San Antonio°	.297	121	464	72	138	185	21	4	6	52	0	5	2	50	5	44	3	2
Harris, Gregory, Wichita°	.500	10	2	1	1	1	0	0	0	0	0	0	0	0	0	0	0	0
Haselman, William, Tulsa	.270	107	352	38	95	137	17	2	7	36	1	2	3	40	0	88	5	10
Hayden, Alan, Jackson°	.424	9	33	7	14	14	0	0	0	2	0	0	0	7	0	2	3	2
Hendricks, Steven, Wichita	.214	24	70	6	15	21	3	0	1	8	0	1	0	5	0	10	0	0
Henley, Daniel, San Antonio	.268	72	213	20	57	72	6	3	1	23	3	2	2	23	1	24	3	3
Heredia, Gilbert, Shreveport	.000	7	2	0	0	0	0	0	0	0	0	0	0	0	0	0	0	0
Hernandez, Carlos, San Antonio	.300	99	370	37	111	157	16	3	8	41	1	3	7	12	0	46	2	3
Hernandez, Jeremy, Wichita	.000	4	1	0	0	0	0	0	0	0	0	0	0	0	0	0	0	0
Hernandez, Robert, Jackson°	.200	5	10	0	2	2	0	0	0	0	0	0	0	0	0	1	0	0
Hershiser, Gordon, San Antonio	.000	36	4	0	0	0	0	0	0	0	0	0	0	0	0	2	0	0
Hill, Stephen, Arkansas°	.000	15	2	0	0	0	0	0	0	0	0	0	0	0	0	1	0	0
Hillemann, Charles, Wichita	.243	124	412	62	100	142	15	6	5	37	0	8	7	16	50	2	105	27	4
Hinkle, Michael, Arkansas	.241	21	29	5	7	8	1	0	0	2	7	0	1	0	5	0	0

Player and Club	Pct.	G.	AB.	R.	H.	TB.	2B.	3B.	HR.	RBI.	SH.	SF.	HP.	BB.	Int. BB.	SO.	SB.	CS.
Hollins, David, Wichita†	.275	131	459	69	126	190	29	4	9	79	1	10	5	63	4	88	8	3
Holmes, Darren, San Antonio	.250	18	20	2	5	6	1	0	0	1	1	0	0	0	0	5	0	0
Holsman, Richard, Wichita°	.038	24	26	1	1	1	0	0	0	0	0	0	0	0	0	9	0	0
Hostetler, Thomas, Shreveport	.100	11	10	2	1	1	0	0	0	0	3	0	0	0	0	2	1	0
Howie, Mark, Midland	.331	86	272	51	90	126	20	2	4	51	0	1	2	35	1	24	6	6
Jackson, Kenneth, Tulsa	.308	5	13	0	4	4	0	0	0	0	0	0	0	1	0	3	0	1
Jackson, Ronald, Tulsa	.211	6	19	2	4	4	0	0	0	1	0	0	0	1	0	6	0	0
Jaster, Scott, Jackson	.136	13	44	2	6	7	1	0	0	1	0	0	0	4	0	8	0	0
Jelic, Christopher, Jackson	.257	86	249	32	64	98	11	1	7	37	1	3	1	43	3	37	0	1
Johnson, Erik, Shreveport	.228	87	246	28	56	78	5	4	3	29	4	1	23	3	37	3	2
Joiner, David, Jackson	.234	54	167	16	39	45	6	0	0	9	3	2	0	8	0	20	0	2
Jones, Gary, El Paso†	.239	13	46	5	11	12	1	0	0	4	0	0	0	0	0	8	0	0
Jones, Geary, Jackson	.179	21	56	4	10	18	5	0	1	5	1	0	2	4	0	16	0	0
Kesselmark, Joseph, San Antonio°	.287	133	488	77	140	196	27	4	7	52	3	4	3	66	4	45	6	5
Kinnunen, Michael, San Antonio°	.000	5	1	0	0	0	0	0	0	0	0	0	0	0	0	1	0	0
Kirby, Wayne, San Antonio°	.214	44	140	14	30	35	3	1	0	7	2	1	1	18	0	17	11	6
Knapp, Michael, Wichita	.328	20	64	7	21	29	2	0	2	6	1	0	2	3	0	8	0	0
Kyles, Stanley, 18 Shr-2 ElP	.000	20	1	0	0	0	0	0	0	0	0	0	0	0	0	1	0	0
Lankford, Raymond, Arkansas°	.317	134	498	98	158	243	28	12	11	98	0	7	4	65	6	57	38	10
Lara, Crucito, Jackson†	.242	35	128	13	31	40	3	0	2	10	3	0	0	6	1	28	2	0
Leonard, Mark, Shreveport°	.311	63	219	29	68	119	15	3	10	52	0	3	3	33	8	40	1	5
Lepley, John, Arkansas°	.000	59	3	0	0	0	0	0	0	0	0	1	0	0	0	2	0	0
LeVasseur, Thomas, Wichita	.270	87	296	41	80	107	16	4	1	36	2	3	0	38	0	33	8	7
Lewis, James, Wichita	.000	63	5	0	0	0	0	0	0	0	0	0	0	0	0	4	0	0
Liddell, David, Jackson	.178	62	191	15	34	45	8	0	1	8	5	0	3	23	1	58	0	2
Lopez, Eduardo, Shreveport	.286	3	7	0	2	2	0	0	0	0	1	0	0	0	0	2	0	0
Lopez, Luis, San Antonio	.266	99	327	46	87	134	17	0	10	51	0	2	5	38	4	39	1	0
Loubier, Stephen, Wichita	.000	15	10	0	0	0	0	0	0	0	1	0	0	0	0	5	0	0
Loy, Darren, Tulsa	.214	20	70	8	15	17	2	0	0	2	2	0	0	3	0	13	0	0
Lynch, David, Tulsa	.000	39	1	0	0	0	0	0	0	0	0	0	0	0	0	0	0	0
Machado, Julio, Jackson	.333	32	3	0	1	1	0	0	0	0	1	0	0	0	0	0	0	0
Mangham, Eric, Jackson	.266	108	335	48	89	115	16	2	2	29	6	3	5	31	0	49	10	14
Marquez, Isidro, San Antonio	1.000	39	1	0	1	1	0	0	0	1	1	0	0	0	0	0	0	0
Marte, Alexis, Tulsa°	.236	48	140	21	33	38	1	2	0	7	5	0	1	22	0	27	6	3
Martinez, Luis, San Antonio	.191	37	115	12	22	28	4	1	0	6	2	0	6	11	0	19	4	5
Martinez, Julian, Arkansas	.255	128	451	57	115	178	30	3	9	59	3	7	0	29	0	102	14	6
Mattox, Frank, El Paso†	.264	59	235	27	62	81	13	3	0	20	0	1	3	14	1	34	6	4
Mayberry, Gregory, San Antonio	.111	11	9	1	1	4	0	0	1	1	2	0	0	0	0	3	0	0
McCament, Randall, Shreveport	.500	13	2	0	1	1	0	0	0	0	0	0	0	0	0	0	0	0
McClellan, Paul, Shreveport	.227	12	22	2	5	6	1	0	0	3	0	1	1	1	0	4	0	0
McCollom, James, Midland	.212	10	33	5	7	13	0	0	2	8	0	0	4	2	7	0	0
McConnell, Walter, San Antonio°	.298	48	178	33	53	86	12	0	7	35	1	2	0	27	0	19	0	2
McCoy, Timothy, Midland	.000	7	1	0	0	0	0	0	0	0	0	0	0	0	0	0	0	0
McDevitt, Terrance, Wichita°	.207	21	58	4	12	18	1	1	1	6	3	0	0	9	0	8	0	2
McGrath, Charles, Arkansas	.000	8	7	0	0	0	0	0	0	0	1	0	0	1	0	2	0	0
McIntosh, Timothy, El Paso	.300	120	463	72	139	226	30	3	17	93	2	9	8	29	3	72	5	4
Meagher, Thomas, Shreveport	.250	5	4	0	1	1	0	0	0	0	0	0	0	0	0	1	0	0
Meier, Kevin, Shreveport	.286	6	7	0	2	3	1	0	0	0	0	0	0	0	0	4	0	0
Meizoso, Agustin, Jackson°	.000	29	2	0	0	0	0	0	0	0	0	0	0	0	0	1	0	0
Melvin, Scott, Arkansas	.433	8	30	6	13	16	0	0	1	6	0	1	0	3	0	4	0	0
Mendez, Jesus, Arkansas°	.286	93	245	31	70	100	18	3	2	40	0	2	0	30	7	20	0	2
Micheu, Tony, Tulsa	.261	8	23	4	6	9	0	0	1	4	1	0	1	1	0	4	0	0
Millay, Garrick, Tulsa	.244	120	385	46	94	140	20	1	8	55	3	8	9	65	3	49	2	5
Miller, Lemmie, San Antonio	.236	37	55	2	13	16	3	0	0	4	0	0	1	2	0	8	0	2
Mims, Larry, Wichita	.258	11	31	1	8	8	0	0	0	2	0	0	2	2	0	2	0	2
Monell, Johnny, Jackson†	.310	80	232	27	72	100	6	2	6	29	1	2	1	13	4	28	6	1
Monico, Mario, El Paso°	.333	25	81	17	27	36	6	0	1	18	0	3	2	21	2	13	1	3
Moran, Frank, Arkansas	.165	58	115	16	19	21	2	0	0	9	3	1	3	14	0	23	0	0
Mota, Jose, Wichita†	.321	41	109	11	35	45	5	1	1	9	4	0	0	17	0	21	3	2
Mumaw, Stephen, Arkansas°	.205	28	39	4	8	8	0	0	0	1	1	0	2	0	11	0	0
Nelson, James, Midland	.275	16	40	5	11	18	1	0	2	8	0	1	0	6	0	6	1	0
Newson, Warren, Wichita°	.304	128	427	94	130	216	20	6	18	70	1	5	0	103	10	99	20	9
Nichols, Scott, Arkansas	.240	20	50	11	12	13	1	0	0	7	0	2	0	7	0	12	0	0
Nichting, Christopher, San Antonio	.190	26	21	1	4	4	0	0	0	0	3	0	0	0	0	7	0	0
Nivens, Toby, Jackson	.067	26	30	0	2	2	0	0	0	0	2	0	0	2	0	14	0	0
Offerman, Jose, San Antonio†	.288	68	278	47	80	98	6	3	2	22	3	0	1	40	4	39	32	13
Oglivie, Benjamin, El Paso°	.333	2	9	3	3	6	0	0	1	3	0	0	1	0	0	0	0	0
Olivares, Omar, Wichita	.370	30	27	5	10	14	1	0	1	5	3	0	0	3	0	5	0	0
Orton, John, Midland	.233	99	344	51	80	142	20	6	10	53	6	7	7	37	1	102	2	1
Osteen, David, Arkansas	.233	27	30	3	7	9	2	0	0	3	6	2	0	0	7	0	0
Owens, Mark, Shreveport°	.247	89	271	30	67	110	18	2	7	36	2	4	1	47	2	60	2	0
Oyster, Jeffrey, Arkansas	.000	58	2	1	0	0	0	0	0	0	0	0	0	0	4	1	0	0
Palmer, Dean, Tulsa	.251	133	498	82	125	242	32	5	25	90	3	4	4	41	4	152	15	5
Patterson, David, Shreveport	.276	112	344	49	95	122	19	1	2	45	2	4	1	57	4	31	2	8
Pellegrino, Anthony, Wichita	.264	46	106	12	28	40	4	1	2	12	0	1	2	9	0	10	0	0
Pena, Geronimo, Arkansas†	.296	77	267	61	79	138	16	8	9	44	3	4	8	38	3	68	14	6
Pena, Jose, Shreveport	.243	50	177	18	43	60	12	1	1	7	2	1	3	10	0	26	5	0
Perez, Michael, Arkansas	.000	57	4	0	0	0	0	0	0	0	0	1	0	0	0	3	0	0
Peters, Reed, Midland	.293	120	413	85	121	168	27	1	6	48	11	6	0	73	1	57	15	8
Petralli, Eugene, Tulsa°	.231	5	13	2	3	6	0	0	1	1	0	0	0	2	0	0	0	0
Picota, Lenin, Arkansas	.083	19	12	1	1	1	0	0	0	0	1	0	0	0	0	5	0	0
Pitz, Michael, San Antonio	.000	34	10	0	0	0	0	0	0	0	1	2	0	0	0	2	0	0
Plummer, Dale, Jackson	.167	25	6	1	1	1	0	0	0	0	0	0	0	0	0	4	0	0
Polka, Fredric, Jackson°	.227	8	22	0	5	6	1	0	0	3	1	0	0	3	0	5	1	0
Postier, Paul, Tulsa	.218	45	147	13	32	37	5	0	0	12	3	1	0	3	0	29	1	0
Potestio, Frank, Arkansas	.111	9	9	0	1	1	0	0	0	0	0	0	0	0	0	3	0	0
Quinzer, Paul, Wichita	.000	19	1	0	0	0	0	0	0	0	0	0	0	0	0	1	0	0
Ramsey, Michael James, El Paso†	.222	12	45	2	10	13	3	0	0	3	0	0	0	6	0	5	0	0
Rauth, Christopher, Jackson	.095	22	21	0	2	2	0	0	0	1	1	0	0	2	0	8	0	0
Remlinger, Michael, Shreveport°	.056	16	18	3	1	1	0	0	0	1	1	0	0	3	0	6	0	0
Repoz, Craig, Jackson	.216	104	296	35	64	93	19	2	2	20	3	2	5	43	3	83	9	2
Rincon, Andrew, Arkansas	.500	11	2	1	1	4	0	0	1	1	0	0	0	0	0	0	0	0
Ritchie, Gregory, Shreveport°	.238	97	332	53	79	101	14	4	0	35	7	7	1	46	0	61	30	7

Player and Club	Pct.	G.	AB.	R.	H.	TB.	2B.	3B.	HR.	RBI.	SH.	SF.	HP.	BB.	Int. BB.	SO.	SB.	CS.
Robertson, Douglas, Shreveport†	.000	52	3	0	0	0	0	0	0	0	0	0	0	0	0	0	0	0
Robertson, Michael, Arkansas	.259	119	398	60	103	137	18	5	2	43	1	0	5	36	4	67	7	4
Roca, Gilberto, Jackson	.239	37	113	7	27	30	3	0	0	8	1	0	0	5	1	15	0	0
Rodriguez, Richard, Wichita*	.200	54	5	0	1	1	0	0	0	0	1	0	0	0	0	0	0	0
Rohrmeier, Daniel, Tulsa	.319	57	210	24	67	93	3	4	5	27	4	0	1	11	0	20	5	8
Rojas, Homar, San Antonio	.301	36	93	13	28	35	5	1	0	5	0	0	0	8	0	9	1	1
Rose, Robert, Midland	.359	99	351	64	126	190	21	5	11	73	3	8	6	50	3	62	3	2
Salinas, Manuel, Jackson*	.250	48	168	13	42	47	5	0	0	22	0	3	1	7	2	11	1	1
Sambo, Ramon, El Paso†	.322	115	466	80	150	174	10	4	2	34	6	2	2	50	4	99	47	13
Samson, Frederick, Tulsa	.170	17	47	6	8	13	3	1	0	1	0	0	3	0	10	0	0
Sanchez, Zoilo, Jackson	.280	111	386	49	108	170	29	0	11	57	0	9	7	28	2	64	5	3
Santana, Miguel, San Antonio†	.259	17	54	7	14	17	1	1	0	3	1	0	1	1	0	10	2	2
Scarpetta, Daniel, San Antonio*	.000	17	1	0	0	0	0	0	0	0	0	0	0	0	0	0	0	0
Scott, Timothy, San Antonio	.333	50	3	1	1	1	0	0	0	0	1	0	0	1	0	1	0	0
Scruggs, Anthony, Tulsa	.195	60	195	19	38	50	3	3	1	21	2	1	2	22	0	60	3	1
Senne, Michael, Shreveport	.194	20	36	4	7	9	2	0	0	4	1	1	0	3	1	6	0	1
Silver, Roy, Arkansas†	.348	103	296	53	103	146	23	4	4	44	0	4	1	21	7	16	2	3
Skeete, Rafael, El Paso*	.251	49	167	34	42	53	5	3	0	11	3	0	4	21	0	50	12	5
Skurla, John, Shreveport*	.283	81	297	46	84	141	16	10	7	50	1	6	0	35	4	65	11	2
Smith, David, El Paso	.268	128	447	50	120	150	15	3	3	60	4	2	2	30	0	59	2	3
Soltero, Saul, Wichita	.250	12	4	0	1	1	0	0	0	0	0	0	0	0	0	1	0	0
Sosa, Samuel, Tulsa	.297	66	273	45	81	125	15	4	7	31	2	2	3	15	0	52	16	11
Springer, Dennis, San Antonio	.000	19	24	0	0	0	0	0	0	0	1	0	0	1	0	15	0	0
Stephens, Carl Ray, Arkansas	.262	112	363	49	95	130	14	0	7	44	4	3	4	44	2	61	2	1
Stevenson, William, Jackson*	.167	2	6	0	1	1	0	0	0	1	0	0	0	1	0	3	0	0
Stone, Brian, Arkansas	.125	9	8	0	1	1	0	0	0	0	3	0	0	1	0	2	0	0
Swan, Russell, Shreveport*	.150	11	20	1	3	3	0	0	0	0	1	0	0	0	0	5	0	0
Talamantez, Gregory, Jackson	.125	9	8	0	1	1	0	0	0	0	1	0	0	0	0	1	0	0
Threadgill, George, Tulsa	.245	32	110	11	27	37	6	2	0	14	0	1	16	0	27	8	3
Tillman, Kerry, Tulsa	.179	9	28	2	5	5	0	0	0	1	0	1	0	1	0	7	1	0
Torricelli, Timothy, El Paso	.217	73	240	34	52	75	9	1	4	24	5	0	2	15	0	34	1	0
Trautwein, David, Jackson	.333	44	9	1	3	4	1	0	0	1	0	0	0	0	0	4	0	0
Traxler, Brian, San Antonio*	.346	63	228	37	79	113	7	0	9	44	3	4	0	22	1	20	1	0
Valdez, Amilcar, San Antonio	.213	12	47	9	10	15	2	0	1	5	0	0	0	3	0	9	0	0
Valdez, Rafael, Wichita	.200	7	5	1	1	1	0	0	0	0	2	0	0	0	0	0	0	0
Valentin, Jose, Wichita†	.245	18	49	8	12	19	1	0	2	5	3	0	0	5	1	12	1	0
Valera, Julio, Jackson	.217	19	23	2	5	6	1	0	0	3	0	0	2	0	5	0	0
Vargas, Hediberto, Midland	.333	40	129	22	43	68	10	0	5	31	0	3	0	17	0	22	0	0
Villanueva, Juan, Jackson	.214	59	168	21	36	51	10	1	1	9	2	1	2	20	2	32	2	0
Walsh, David, San Antonio*	.000	38	4	0	0	0	0	0	0	0	0	0	0	0	0	2	0	0
Walters, Daniel, Wichita	.273	89	300	30	82	115	15	0	6	45	3	2	3	25	2	31	0	2
Walters, Darryel, Arkansas	.283	74	258	42	73	132	15	4	12	46	0	0	0	38	2	67	4	2
Weissman, Craig, Arkansas	.000	40	4	0	0	0	0	0	0	0	0	0	0	0	0	2	0	0
Welborn, Todd, Jackson	.000	23	4	0	0	0	0	0	0	0	0	0	0	0	0	2	0	0
Wheeler, Bradley, El Paso*	.000	9	1	0	0	0	0	0	0	0	0	0	0	0	0	1	0	0
White, Michael, San Antonio*	.227	131	463	40	105	141	21	3	3	53	1	1	0	33	6	70	6	7
Wilson, Craig, Arkansas	.317	55	224	41	71	88	12	1	1	40	3	1	1	21	1	14	8	5
Wood, Brian, Wichita*	.000	2	1	0	0	0	0	0	0	0	0	0	0	0	0	1	0	0
Wood, Edward, Shreveport*	.258	114	349	44	90	105	13	1	0	43	10	3	6	51	2	72	9	7
Wray, James, San Antonio	.000	17	2	0	0	0	0	0	0	0	0	0	0	0	0	0	0	0

The following pitchers, listed alphabetically by club, with games in parentheses, had no plate appearances, primarily through use of designated hitters:

EL PASO—Austin, James (23); Chapman, Mark (45); Clutterbuck, Bryan (4); Costello, Michael (8); Elvira, Narciso (7); Ferreira, Anthony (3); Fleming, Keith (14); Henry, Douglas (1); Higuera, Teodoro (1); Hunter, James (19); Miglio, John (11); Mills, Michael (18); Monson, Steven (20); Moraw, Carl (22); Navarro, Jaime (11); Puig, Edward (47); Schrom, Kenneth (5); Tirado, Aristarco (15); Veres, Randolf (8); Waddell, Thomas (6); Watkins, Timothy (26).

JACKSON—Stringfellow, Thornton (10).

MIDLAND—Buckels, Gary (32); Butcher, Michael (15); DiMichele, Frank (33); Graybill, David (17); Hernandez, Roberto (12); Lewis, Scott (25); Martinez, David (22); Merejo, Luis (54); Morehouse, Richard (5); Pardo, Lawrence (5); Richardson, Jeffrey (19); Townsend, James (4); Trudeau, Kevin (13); Young, Shane (10).

TULSA—Alvarez, Wilson (7); Bohanon, Brian (11); Bryant, Phillip (32); Castillo, Felipe (25); Hoover, John (21); Lamle, Adam (10); Lankard, Steven (35); Malloy, Robert (34); Manuel, Barry (11); Mathews, Terry (10); Morse, Scott (8); Moyer, Jamie (2); Petkovsek, Mark (21); Rockman, Marvin (40); Rosenthal, Wayne (31); Thomas, Mitchell (1).

GRAND SLAM HOME RUNS—Alfaro, Bogar, Citari, Cron, Cuevas, Dixon, Freiling, K. Garner, Kesselmark, Lara, McIntosh, Palmer, Patterson, G. Pena, Rohrmeier, Skurla, Traxler, Daniel Walters, Darryel Walters, 1 each.

AWARDED FIRST BASE ON CATCHER'S INTERFERENCE—Gunderson (C. Hernandez); Kesselmark (Knapp); Leonard (Roca); Liddell (Decker); Newson (C. Hernandez); Owens (Roca).

CLUB FIELDING

Club	Pct.	G.	PO.	A.	E.	DP.	PB.	Club	Pct.	G.	PO.	A.	E.	DP.	PB.
Wichita	.972	136	3493	1514	146	124	10	Arkansas	.967	134	3364	1466	163	126	15
Shreveport	.971	136	3533	1465	149	102	13	Tulsa	.967	136	3478	1550	174	135	15
Jackson	.968	135	3514	1551	166	119	15	San Antonio	.966	136	3564	1402	173	89	13
Midland	.968	136	3497	1581	169	145	19	El Paso	.965	135	3453	1527	181	155	20

Triple Play—Wichita.

INDIVIDUAL FIELDING

*Throws lefthanded.

FIRST BASEMEN

Player and Club	Pct.	G.	PO.	A.	E.	DP.	Player and Club	Pct.	G.	PO.	A.	E.	DP.
Aldrete, Shreveport*	.992	72	546	49	5	48	Cooper, Wichita	.995	41	336	31	2	25
Alexander, Tulsa	.992	128	1164	105	10	109	Cron, Midland	.988	101	920	70	12	86
Alfaro, El Paso	.987	53	423	39	6	54	David, El Paso*	.986	58	461	22	7	51
Alyea, Jackson	.875	2	7	0	1	0	Decker, Shreveport	1.000	1	1	0	0	0
Barns, Midland	1.000	1	12	0	0	1	Edge, El Paso	1.000	1	1	0	0	0
Brewer, Arkansas*	.990	128	1084	97	12	106	Escalera, El Paso	1.000	3	24	2	0	2
Cisarik, Wichita*	.989	89	731	55	9	67	Fox, Arkansas	1.000	2	19	0	0	3
Citari, El Paso	.986	30	261	21	4	29	FREILING, Jackson*	.994	109	980	90	7	85
Colbert, Shreveport	1.000	1	11	2	0	0	Gonzalez, Midland	1.000	3	8	1	0	1

FIRST BASEMEN—Continued

Player and Club	Pct.	G.	PO.	A.	E.	DP.	Player and Club	Pct.	G.	PO.	A.	E.	DP.
Graham, Midland*	.983	8	56	3	1	5	Orton, Midland	.968	3	26	4	1	2
Hendricks, Wichita	.978	18	132	4	3	9	Owens, Shreveport	.909	1	9	1	1	0
Jelic, Jackson	.983	21	166	12	3	13	Patterson, Shreveport	.997	40	290	21	1	19
Kesselmark, San Antonio*	.900	2	8	1	1	1	Pellegrino, Wichita	1.000	1	9	0	0	1
Knapp, Midland	1.000	1	5	1	0	0	Postier, Tulsa	.983	6	54	4	1	8
Lopez, San Antonio	.975	24	177	20	5	8	Salinas, Jackson	.990	12	91	8	1	5
McCollom, Midland	.987	8	68	6	1	8	Skeete, El Paso*	1.000	1	4	0	0	0
McConnell, San Antonio	.989	43	336	30	4	25	Skurla, Shreveport	.994	39	304	21	2	24
Melvin, Arkansas	1.000	1	8	0	0	1	Tillman, Tulsa	1.000	5	37	3	0	5
Mendez, Arkansas*	1.000	9	52	1	0	4	Traxler, San Antonio*	.993	61	529	52	4	35
Millay, Tulsa	1.000	3	2	0	0	1	Valdez, San Antonio	.975	12	110	6	3	6
Nelson, Midland	1.000	1	4	0	0	1	Vargas, Midland	1.000	20	195	12	0	22

Triple Play—Cisarik.

SECOND BASEMEN

Player and Club	Pct.	G.	PO.	A.	E.	DP.	Player and Club	Pct.	G.	PO.	A.	E.	DP.
Barns, Midland	.953	29	57	85	7	18	Joiner, Jackson	.963	35	73	107	7	21
Blair, Shreveport	.935	7	11	18	2	4	Lara, Jackson	.940	20	42	52	6	16
Bustabad, San Antonio	1.000	19	31	41	0	7	Mattox, El Paso	.968	45	94	151	8	34
Carter, Shreveport	.961	119	244	352	24	63	McDevitt, Wichita	.929	7	16	23	3	4
Cerny, Midland	.968	73	137	224	12	45	Melvin, Arkansas	1.000	2	3	6	0	0
DeButch, Jackson	.977	9	16	26	1	6	Mims, Wichita	.962	11	17	34	2	2
Diaz, Jackson	.968	18	25	65	3	10	Moran, Arkansas	.952	6	9	11	1	2
Edge, El Paso	.981	30	68	89	3	24	Mota, Wichita	1.000	6	15	30	0	5
FARIES, Wichita	.979	115	258	337	13	70	Pena, Arkansas	.965	77	177	208	14	55
Farmer, Wichita	1.000	4	1	8	0	0	Postier, Tulsa	.968	12	25	36	2	6
Francois, San Antonio	.938	68	120	151	18	27	Rose, Midland	.963	16	28	49	3	9
Garner, Tulsa	.977	115	246	397	15	86	Salinas, Jackson	.986	14	26	43	1	4
Guerrero, El Paso	.955	64	132	185	15	45	Sambo, El Paso	.800	3	5	3	2	1
Henley, San Antonio	.977	61	125	130	6	17	Samson, Tulsa	.963	7	11	15	1	3
Howie, Midland	.970	34	53	111	5	21	Santana, San Antonio	1.000	3	6	7	0	1
Jackson, Tulsa	.941	3	5	11	1	3	Villanueva, Jackson	.944	44	90	111	12	25
Johnson, Shreveport	.917	17	33	44	7	8	Wilson, Arkansas	.961	53	124	149	11	36

THIRD BASEMEN

Player and Club	Pct.	G.	PO.	A.	E.	DP.	Player and Club	Pct.	G.	PO.	A.	E.	DP.
Alexander, Tulsa	1.000	2	2	3	0	1	McConnell, San Antonio	1.000	3	0	3	0	1
Alfaro, El Paso	.810	7	7	10	4	1	Melvin, Arkansas	.818	5	4	5	2	2
Barns, Midland	.957	20	6	38	2	1	Millay, Tulsa	1.000	1	0	1	0	0
Blair, Shreveport	1.000	1	0	4	0	1	Moran, Arkansas	.982	25	13	41	1	4
Bustabad, San Antonio	.968	11	8	22	1	1	Mota, Wichita	1.000	6	2	7	0	0
Colbert, Shreveport	.941	41	21	59	5	4	Owens, Shreveport	.942	36	20	61	5	5
Cron, Midland	.921	23	12	46	5	5	Palmer, Tulsa	.905	118	79	208	30	14
Dabney, El Paso	.857	3	1	5	1	0	Patterson, Shreveport	.952	69	38	121	8	6
DeButch, Jackson	1.000	1	2	1	0	0	Pellegrino, Wichita	.931	21	20	34	4	5
Edge, El Paso	1.000	1	0	1	0	0	Postier, Tulsa	.980	21	13	37	1	7
Guerrero, El Paso	.889	54	26	78	13	7	Repoz, Jackson	.932	85	55	164	16	12
HANSEN, San Antonio	.949	114	92	208	16	12	Robertson, Arkansas	.935	116	63	237	21	24
Henley, San Antonio	1.000	6	2	13	0	1	Rose, Midland	.942	86	74	154	14	17
Hollins, Wichita	.920	117	77	209	25	17	Salinas, Jackson	.875	14	12	16	4	3
Howie, Midland	.857	17	10	20	5	2	Samson, Tulsa	1.000	2	0	1	0	0
Jelic, Jackson	.930	35	28	65	7	4	Smith, El Paso	.909	72	48	111	16	14
Johnson, Shreveport	1.000	5	1	4	0	0	Torricelli, El Paso	.875	7	1	13	2	1
Joiner, Jackson	1.000	8	5	16	0	0	Valentin, Wichita	1.000	1	0	1	0	0
Jones, El Paso	1.000	2	0	2	0	0	Villanueva, Jackson	.000	1	0	0	1	0
LeVasseur, Wichita	.500	1	0	1	1	0	Wilson, Arkansas	.800	2	3	1	1	0
Lopez, San Antonio	1.000	9	5	16	0	1							

SHORTSTOPS

Player and Club	Pct.	G.	PO.	A.	E.	DP.	Player and Club	Pct.	G.	PO.	A.	E.	DP.
Barns, Midland	.917	13	13	42	5	9	Lara, Jackson	.970	15	18	47	2	7
Blair, Shreveport	.910	34	56	105	16	19	LeVasseur, Wichita	.958	86	137	278	18	53
Bogar, Jackson	.949	104	185	351	29	61	J. Martinez, Arkansas	.932	126	163	396	41	76
Bustabad, San Antonio	.945	25	23	63	5	6	L. Martinez, San Antonio	.927	37	50	90	11	15
Colbert, Shreveport	.927	56	88	142	18	29	McDevitt, Wichita	.889	11	14	42	7	10
DeButch, Jackson	1.000	6	4	20	0	1	Moran, Arkansas	.902	11	12	25	4	3
A. Diaz, Jackson	.889	2	5	3	1	3	Mota, Wichita	.978	13	19	26	1	7
E. Diaz, Jackson	.941	22	49	78	8	20	Offerman, San Antonio	.932	68	106	168	20	28
DiSARCINA, Midland	.954	126	206	411	30	81	Palmer, Tulsa	.917	4	6	5	1	1
Edge, El Paso	.969	58	106	173	9	47	Pellegrino, Wichita	.900	3	4	5	1	0
Faries, Wichita	.941	17	26	54	5	7	Salinas, Jackson	.846	5	3	8	2	2
Fariss, Tulsa	.928	132	260	401	51	94	Samson, Tulsa	1.000	1	1	2	0	0
Francois, San Antonio	.902	13	21	25	5	5	Smith, El Paso	.942	59	85	175	16	42
Henley, San Antonio	.833	2	4	1	1	0	Valentin, Wichita	.897	16	26	44	8	12
Jackson, Tulsa	.750	1	0	3	1	2	Villanueva, Jackson	.933	7	13	15	2	2
Johnson, Shreveport	.966	60	82	148	8	23							

Triple Play—LeVasseur.

OUTFIELDERS

Player and Club	Pct.	G.	PO.	A.	E.	DP.	Player and Club	Pct.	G.	PO.	A.	E.	DP.
Aldrete, Shreveport*	.800	2	4	0	1	0	Colbert, Shreveport	1.000	2	2	0	0	0
Alexander, Tulsa	1.000	3	7	0	0	0	Conner, Shreveport	.963	22	25	1	1	0
Alfredson, Midland	1.000	17	24	2	0	0	Cuevas, Jackson	.983	93	166	4	3	2
Alyea, Jackson	1.000	13	20	0	0	0	Dabney, El Paso	1.000	6	6	2	0	0
Amaro, Midland	.947	20	34	2	2	0	David, El Paso*	.974	16	32	5	1	1
Ashley, El Paso	.952	109	183	17	10	0	Davis, Midland	1.000	18	37	1	0	0
Benitez, San Antonio	1.000	1	2	0	0	0	DeAngelis, Midland*	.962	13	21	4	1	0
Brooks, Wichita*	1.000	23	30	2	0	0	DeButch, Jackson	1.000	12	19	0	0	0
Carr, Jackson	.973	113	280	11	8	2	DeWolf, Wichita*	.980	51	94	4	2	1
D. Carter, Arkansas	.980	70	96	2	2	0	Diaz, Jackson	1.000	4	5	0	0	0
Cisarik, Wichita*	1.000	27	44	2	0	0	Dixon, Shreveport*	.973	79	177	6	5	1

OUTFIELDERS—Continued

Player and Club	Pct.	G.	PO.	A.	E.	DP.	Player and Club	Pct.	G.	PO.	A.	E.	DP.
Doran, Midland	.991	45	109	4	1	2	Millay, Tulsa	.956	76	125	5	6	1
Edge, El Paso	.963	14	25	1	1	1	Miller, San Antonio	.944	12	15	2	1	1
Edwards, Jackson*	1.000	1	1	0	0	0	Monell, Jackson	.977	54	81	4	2	1
Escalera, El Paso*	1.000	28	61	1	0	1	Monico, El Paso*	1.000	13	15	2	0	1
Farmer, Wichita	1.000	1	2	0	0	0	Mota, Wichita	1.000	13	21	1	0	1
Francois, San Antonio	.833	6	5	0	1	0	Newson, Wichita*	.976	126	191	15	5	0
Garner, Wichita	.968	72	113	7	4	4	Nichols, Arkansas	1.000	1	1	0	0	0
Gerhart, Shreveport	1.000	16	36	4	0	0	Peters, Midland	.946	120	199	10	12	1
Gilkey, Arkansas	.966	131	236	22	9	2	Ramsey, El Paso*	.941	11	16	0	1	0
J. Gonzalez, Tulsa	.972	133	292	15	9	2	Repoz, Jackson	.926	13	22	3	2	0
O. Gonzalez, Midland	1.000	1	1	0	0	0	Ritchie, Shreveport*	.981	94	204	8	4	2
Graham, Midland*	.954	50	79	4	4	2	Robertson, Arkansas	1.000	5	8	0	0	0
Graves, Midland	.961	51	92	7	4	1	Rohrmeier, Tulsa	.940	56	91	3	6	0
Grunhard, Midland*	.937	90	139	9	10	4	Sambo, El Paso	.981	78	141	10	3	1
Hayden, Jackson*	1.000	9	13	0	0	0	Sanchez, Jackson	.949	97	163	5	9	0
HILLEMANN, Wichita	.994	123	293	14	2	3	Santana, San Antonio	.962	12	22	3	1	0
Howie, Midland	.900	17	17	1	2	0	Scruggs, Tulsa	.991	57	108	4	1	0
Jaster, Jackson	.971	13	33	1	1	0	Senne, Shreveport	1.000	11	10	0	0	0
Kesselmark, San Antonio*	.989	123	250	15	3	2	Silver, Arkansas	1.000	26	38	2	0	1
Kirby, San Antonio	.952	41	77	3	4	1	Skeete, El Paso*	.923	48	103	5	9	0
Lankford, Arkansas*	.972	134	367	9	11	2	Skurla, Shreveport*	1.000	45	109	4	0	0
Leonard, Shreveport	1.000	60	90	5	0	1	Sosa, Tulsa	.967	66	110	7	4	0
Lopez, San Antonio	1.000	30	31	4	0	1	Threadgill, Tulsa	1.000	4	5	1	0	0
Mangham, San Antonio	.958	93	131	6	6	1	Torricelli, El Paso	1.000	1	1	0	0	0
Marte, Tulsa*	1.000	21	34	3	0	0	Walters, El Paso	.969	70	118	9	4	0
Martinez, Arkansas	1.000	1	1	0	0	0	White, San Antonio	.965	129	241	7	9	0
McIntosh, El Paso	.915	34	41	2	4	1	Wood, Shreveport*	.986	107	200	4	3	0
Mendez, Arkansas*	.991	70	106	4	1	0							

CATCHERS

Player and Club	Pct.	G.	PO.	A.	E.	DP.	PB.	Player and Club	Pct.	G.	PO.	A.	E.	DP.	PB.
Barns, Midland	1.000	1	2	0	0	0	1	Liddell, Jackson	.988	62	347	53	5	6	6
Basso, Midland	.981	66	316	40	7	7	7	E. Lopez, Shreveport	.933	2	14	0	1	0	0
Brown, San Antonio	.971	24	155	14	5	6	2	L. Lopez, San Antonio	1.000	2	1	0	0	0	0
Curnow, Wichita	1.000	4	11	2	0	0	0	Loy, Tulsa	.992	20	110	14	1	0	2
Decker, Shreveport	.980	42	229	22	5	1	4	McIntosh, El Paso	.974	76	433	57	13	10	10
Edge, El Paso	1.000	1	1	0	0	0	0	Micheu, Wichita	1.000	8	43	3	0	1	1
Farmer, Wichita	1.000	7	33	3	0	2	0	Nelson, Midland	.986	16	66	7	1	2	3
Fox, Arkansas	.971	13	61	5	2	0	2	Nichols, Arkansas	.988	19	75	7	1	1	4
Gonzalez, Midland	.974	26	131	18	4	2	3	ORTON, Midland	.994	78	440	52	3	12	8
Hall, Midland	1.000	7	27	3	0	0	0	Owens, Shreveport	.981	51	289	24	6	2	4
Ham, Shreveport	1.000	3	21	3	0	0	1	Pena, Shreveport	.988	50	300	39	4	4	4
Haselman, Tulsa	.984	104	508	63	9	5	12	Petralli, Tulsa	1.000	2	6	1	0	1	0
Hernandez, San Antonio	.976	95	629	90	18	5	7	Polka, Wichita	.945	7	47	5	3	1	2
Jackson, Tulsa	.976	6	34	6	1	0	0	Roca, Jackson	.982	33	194	27	4	1	5
Jelic, Jackson	.990	18	85	10	1	1	0	Rojas, San Antonio	.984	24	159	20	3	0	4
Ga. Jones, El Paso	.988	11	74	11	1	1	3	Stephens, Arkansas	.985	108	545	63	9	8	9
Ge. Jones, Jackson	.982	20	100	11	2	2	2	Torricelli, El Paso	1.000	58	337	37	0	6	7
Knapp, Midland	.950	19	100	15	6	0	4	Walters, Wichita	.987	75	424	35	6	4	3
LeVasseur, Wichita	1.000	1	1	0	0	1	0								

PITCHERS

Player and Club	Pct.	G.	PO.	A.	E.	DP.	Player and Club	Pct.	G.	PO.	A.	E.	DP.
Akins, Arkansas	1.000	12	1	1	0	0	Fleming, El Paso	.667	14	0	2	1	0
Alexander, Tulsa	1.000	3	1	0	0	0	Fortugno, El Paso*	1.000	10	0	6	0	1
Alicea, Midland	1.000	11	1	2	0	0	Freeland, Shreveport	.880	18	8	14	3	0
Alvarez, Tulsa*	.882	7	6	9	2	1	Gay, Shreveport	1.000	18	7	12	0	1
Armstrong, San Antonio	.830	26	15	24	8	0	Gideon, Jackson*	1.000	11	2	3	0	0
Arnold, San Antonio	1.000	8	1	13	0	0	Givens, Jackson*	.917	13	7	15	2	0
Austin, El Paso	.950	22	8	11	1	2	Graybill, Midland	1.000	17	6	7	0	0
Bauer, Jackson	.929	15	5	8	1	0	Gross, Jackson	.927	16	13	25	3	1
Beasley, Midland	.929	16	13	26	3	1	Gunderson, Shreveport*	1.000	11	2	17	0	0
Beck, Shreveport	.893	16	7	18	3	2	Harris, Wichita*	1.000	10	0	2	0	0
Benes, Wichita	1.000	16	8	10	0	2	Henry, El Paso	1.000	1	1	0	0	0
Bivens, Arkansas	.900	13	5	4	1	0	Heredia, Shreveport	.667	7	0	2	1	0
Bohanon, Tulsa*	.955	11	7	14	1	1	J. Hernandez, Wichita	1.000	4	2	2	0	0
Bones, Wichita	.958	24	7	16	1	2	R. Hernandez, Midland	.941	12	4	12	1	2
Bonilla, Shreveport*	.958	43	6	17	1	1	Hershiser, San Antonio	1.000	36	2	13	0	2
Brocail, Wichita	.926	23	10	15	2	0	Higuera, El Paso*	1.000	2	2	0	0	0
Brown, Jackson*	.800	8	4	4	2	0	Hill, Arkansas	.800	15	3	1	1	0
Bryant, Tulsa	.750	32	2	10	4	0	Hinkle, Arkansas	.983	21	18	40	1	3
Buckels, Midland	.833	32	2	3	1	1	Holmes, San Antonio	.917	17	15	18	3	2
Bumgarner, Jackson	.800	12	5	7	3	0	Holsman, Wichita*	.880	24	3	19	3	1
Burcham, Midland	.970	45	13	19	1	1	HOOVER, Tulsa	1.000	21	15	25	0	3
Butcher, Midland	.846	15	5	6	2	0	Hostetler, Shreveport	.923	11	3	9	1	0
Campbell, San Antonio	1.000	17	1	2	0	0	Hunter, El Paso	.912	19	9	22	3	1
Carter, Shreveport	1.000	14	2	9	0	0	Kinnunen, San Antonio*	1.000	5	2	1	0	0
Castillo, Tulsa	.919	25	12	22	3	0	Kyles, 18 Shr-2 ElP	.900	20	2	7	1	1
Cedeno, Midland	1.000	53	6	9	0	0	Lamle, Tulsa*	1.000	10	1	2	0	2
Chapman, El Paso	.900	45	4	5	1	1	Lankard, Tulsa	.952	35	6	14	1	1
Chavez, Wichita	.929	37	1	12	1	0	Lepley, Arkansas*	.909	59	5	15	2	1
Clutterbuck, El Paso	1.000	4	0	4	0	1	J. Lewis, Wichita	.842	63	9	7	3	0
Conley, Jackson*	1.000	1	0	1	0	0	S. Lewis, Midland	.889	25	11	13	3	0
Connolly, Shreveport*	1.000	38	5	19	0	2	Loubier, Wichita	.941	15	4	12	1	3
Costello, El Paso	.857	8	1	11	2	1	Lynch, Tulsa*	1.000	39	2	8	0	0
DiMichele, Midland*	.955	33	2	19	1	0	Machado, Jackson	.900	32	4	5	1	1
Dominguez, Shreveport	.905	40	3	16	2	0	Malloy, Tulsa	1.000	34	7	21	0	3
Drahman, El Paso	.833	19	2	3	1	1	Manuel, Tulsa	.733	11	5	6	4	0
Elvira, El Paso*	.818	7	1	8	2	0	Marquez, San Antonio	.958	39	8	15	1	0
Falcone, San Antonio*	1.000	17	0	6	0	0	Martinez, Midland	1.000	22	5	9	0	0
Fassero, Arkansas*	.800	6	1	3	1	0	Mathews, Tulsa	.917	10	4	7	1	1
Ferreira, El Paso*	1.000	3	1	4	0	1	Mayberry, San Antonio	.800	11	4	8	3	0

PITCHERS—Continued

Player and Club	Pct.	G.	PO.	A.	E.	DP.	Player and Club	Pct.	G.	PO.	A.	E.	DP.
McCament, Shreveport	1.000	13	1	5	0	0	Richardson, Midland	1.000	19	2	3	0	0
McClellan, Shreveport	.938	12	4	11	1	0	Rincon, Arkansas	.750	11	2	1	1	0
McCoy, Midland*	1.000	7	0	3	0	0	Robertson, Shreveport	.833	52	4	6	2	1
McGrath, Arkansas	.714	8	2	3	2	0	Rockman, Tulsa	.917	40	1	10	1	0
Meagher, Shreveport	1.000	5	1	2	0	0	Rodriguez, Wichita*	1.000	54	7	15	0	1
Meier, Shreveport	1.000	6	2	5	0	0	Rosenthal, Tulsa	.944	31	6	11	1	0
Meizoso, Jackson*	1.000	29	4	6	0	0	Scarpetta, San Antonio*	1.000	17	0	3	0	0
Merejo, Midland	.957	54	5	17	1	4	Schrom, El Paso	1.000	5	1	6	0	0
Miglio, El Paso*	.875	11	0	7	1	1	Scott, San Antonio	.938	48	6	9	1	1
Mills, El Paso	.786	18	2	9	3	1	Soltero, Wichita	.800	12	2	2	1	0
Monson, El Paso	.939	20	6	25	2	1	Springer, San Antonio	.966	19	14	14	1	1
Moraw, El Paso	1.000	22	1	12	0	1	Stone, Arkansas	.857	9	3	3	1	0
Morehouse, Midland	1.000	5	2	1	0	0	Stringfellow, Jackson*	.500	10	1	0	1	0
Morse, Tulsa	.833	8	5	5	2	0	Swan, Shreveport*	1.000	11	5	12	0	1
Moyer, Tulsa*	.714	2	2	3	2	1	Talamantez, Jackson	.929	9	4	9	1	0
Mumaw, Arkansas	.965	26	16	39	2	7	Thomas, Tulsa	1.000	1	0	1	0	0
Navarro, El Paso	1.000	11	6	14	0	0	Tirado, El Paso	.923	15	3	9	1	0
Nichting, San Antonio	.974	26	13	25	1	0	Townsend, Midland*	1.000	4	1	0	0	0
Nivens, Jackson	.964	25	9	18	1	3	Trautwein, Jackson	.950	44	6	13	1	1
Olivares, Wichita	.931	26	25	42	5	2	Trudeau, Midland	.900	13	9	9	2	0
Osteen, Arkansas	1.000	27	18	17	0	2	Valdez, Wichita	1.000	6	1	7	0	2
Oyster, Arkansas	.840	58	7	14	4	2	Valera, Jackson	1.000	19	11	24	0	3
Pardo, Midland	1.000	5	1	1	0	1	Veres, El Paso	.947	8	7	11	1	2
Perez, Arkansas	.933	57	5	9	1	0	Waddell, El Paso	1.000	6	1	2	0	0
Petkovsek, Tulsa	.977	21	18	25	1	4	Walsh, San Antonio*	.938	38	2	13	1	1
Picota, Arkansas	.952	19	3	17	1	0	Watkins, El Paso	.963	26	10	16	1	1
Pitz, San Antonio	.944	34	10	24	2	2	Weissman, Arkansas	.833	40	3	2	1	0
Plummer, Jackson	1.000	25	5	13	0	1	Welborn, Jackson	.938	23	2	13	1	2
Potestio, Arkansas	.909	9	4	6	1	0	Wheeler, El Paso*	1.000	9	1	5	0	0
Puig, El Paso*	1.000	47	3	14	0	2	Wood, Wichita	1.000	2	0	1	0	0
Quinzer, Wichita	.833	19	1	4	1	0	Wray, San Antonio*	.750	17	0	3	1	0
Rauth, Jackson	.935	22	10	33	3	1	Young, Midland*	1.000	10	1	6	0	0
Remlinger, Shreveport*	.909	16	6	14	2	0							

The following players did not have any fielding statistics at the positions indicated or appeared only as a designated hitter, pinch-hitter or pinch-runner: Amaro, 2b; Ashley, 1b; Barns, of; Basso, 3b; J. Carter, of; DeWolf, p; Edge, p; Hendricks, 3b; Robert Hernandez, ph, dh; K. Jackson, 3b; LeVasseur, p; McDevitt, 3b; Ogilvie, dh; Silver, c; Stevenson, dh.

CLUB PITCHING

Club	ERA.	G.	CG.	ShO.	Sv.	IP.	H.	R.	ER.	HR.	HB.	BB.	Int. BB.	SO.	WP.	Bk.
Jackson	3.42	135	26	9	23	1171.1	1092	548	445	67	47	421	41	754	71	25
Shreveport	3.49	136	17	11	37	1177.2	1116	551	457	60	34	456	25	796	77	33
Arkansas	3.80	134	16	8	39	1121.1	1135	568	474	76	38	378	9	656	64	23
Tulsa	3.92	136	15	11	38	1159.1	1166	598	505	63	44	417	15	679	49	21
Wichita	4.14	136	19	11	31	1164.1	1186	622	536	90	30	473	54	757	68	21
San Antonio	4.23	136	17	9	21	1188.0	1196	655	558	98	36	513	42	907	84	30
Midland	4.52	136	15	5	34	1165.2	1280	696	586	65	41	524	36	727	79	36
El Paso	5.07	135	18	1	36	1151.0	1390	782	649	100	33	543	26	811	75	26

PITCHERS' RECORDS
(Leading Qualifiers for Earned-Run Average Leadership — 109 or More Innings)

*Throws lefthanded.

Pitcher—Club	W.	L.	Pct.	ERA.	G.	GS.	CG.	GF.	ShO.	Sv.	IP.	H.	R.	ER.	HR.	HB.	BB.	Int. BB.	SO.	WP.
Valera, Jackson	10	6	.625	2.49	19	19	6	0	2	0	137.1	123	47	38	4	8	36	2	107	10
Gross, Jackson	6	5	.545	2.49	16	16	4	0	0	0	112.0	96	47	31	9	2	13	0	60	4
Springer, San Antonio	6	8	.429	3.15	19	19	4	0	1	0	140.0	128	58	49	13	4	46	2	89	3
Hoover, Tulsa	9	6	.600	3.38	21	17	2	4	1	1	125.0	116	53	47	6	7	37	1	77	6
Olivares, Wichita	12	11	.522	3.39	26	26	6	0	1	0	185.2	175	87	70	10	10	61	6	79	10
Petkovsek, Tulsa	8	5	.615	3.47	21	21	1	0	0	0	140.0	144	63	54	7	3	35	0	66	5
Osteen, Arkansas	15	5	.750	3.49	27	27	3	0	2	0	165.0	179	77	64	12	4	33	0	72	12
Armstrong, San Antonio	8	8	.500	3.77	26	26	3	0	2	0	157.2	151	82	66	15	3	63	3	82	9
Rauth, Jackson	6	13	.316	3.81	22	22	4	0	0	0	148.2	157	73	63	13	10	43	5	74	3
Holmes, San Antonio	5	8	.385	3.83	17	16	3	1	2	1	110.1	102	59	47	5	3	44	2	81	8

Departmental Leaders: G—J. Lewis, 63; W—Osteen, 15; L—Nichting, 14; Pct.—Gunderson, .800; GS—Osteen, 27; CG—Mumaw, 7; GF—Perez, 51; ShO—Benes, 3; Sv.—Perez, 33; IP—Olivares, 185.2; H—S. Lewis, 195; R—S. Lewis, 121; ER—S. Lewis, 89; HR—Bones, 22; HB—Olivares, Pitz, Rauth, 10; BB—Nichting, 101; IBB—Rodriguez, 11; SO—Nichting, 136; WP—Holsman, 17.

(All Pitchers—Listed Alphabetically)

Pitcher—Club	W.	L.	Pct.	ERA.	G.	GS.	CG.	GF.	ShO.	Sv.	IP.	H.	R.	ER.	HR.	HB.	BB.	Int. BB.	SO.	WP.
Akins, Arkansas	2	1	.667	2.76	12	0	0	2	0	0	16.1	17	8	5	1	1	5	0	6	4
Alexander, Tulsa	0	0	.000	2.25	3	0	0	3	0	0	4.0	4	1	1	0	0	3	0	4	0
Alicea, Midland*	0	3	.000	5.79	11	1	0	3	0	1	23.1	33	18	15	4	0	7	1	17	1
Alvarez, Tulsa*	2	2	.500	2.06	7	7	1	0	1	0	48.0	40	14	11	1	0	16	3	29	1
Armstrong, San Antonio	8	8	.500	3.77	26	26	3	0	2	0	157.2	151	82	66	15	3	63	3	82	9
Arnold, San Antonio	2	5	.286	5.91	8	8	1	0	1	0	42.2	55	34	28	6	0	11	3	19	1
Austin, El Paso	3	10	.231	5.82	22	13	2	5	0	1	85.0	121	60	55	6	4	34	1	69	4
Bauer, Jackson	3	2	.600	5.40	15	5	0	7	0	0	43.1	47	27	26	0	1	17	2	28	2
Beasley, Midland	8	4	.667	3.88	16	15	4	1	1	0	104.1	101	53	45	2	4	33	0	48	6
Beck, Shreveport	7	3	.700	3.55	16	14	4	0	1	0	99.0	108	45	39	6	3	16	3	74	3
Benes, Wichita	8	4	.667	2.16	16	16	5	3	3	0	108.1	79	32	26	6	2	39	1	115	1
Bivens, Arkansas	5	4	.556	4.87	13	12	1	0	0	0	68.1	68	41	37	6	3	27	0	41	3
Bohanon, Tulsa*	5	0	1.000	2.20	11	11	1	0	1	0	73.2	59	20	18	3	3	27	0	44	2
Bones, Wichita	10	9	.526	5.74	24	24	2	0	0	0	136.1	162	103	87	22	2	47	5	88	7
Bonilla, Shreveport*	7	3	.700	2.88	43	1	0	19	0	2	84.1	65	28	27	4	2	27	4	56	2
Brocail, Wichita	5	9	.357	5.21	23	22	1	0	1	0	134.2	158	88	78	11	1	50	4	95	9
Brown, Jackson*	5	2	.714	2.26	8	8	2	0	2	0	51.2	51	15	13	0	4	11	0	40	4
Bryant, Tulsa	6	5	.545	5.25	32	9	0	0	0	0	94.1	108	62	55	4	3	44	2	35	8
Buckels, Midland	2	1	.667	1.47	32	0	0	25	0	12	36.2	24	7	6	0	0	14	2	32	3
Bumgarner, Jackson	2	7	.222	6.78	12	11	1	0	0	0	65.0	80	53	49	6	3	35	1	35	9

Pitcher—Club	W.	L.	Pct.	ERA.	G.	GS.	CG.	GF.	ShO.	Sv.	IP.	H.	R.	ER.	HR.	HB.	BB.	Int. BB.	SO.	WP.
Burcham, Midland	6	4	.600	3.77	45	6	1	15	0	6	107.1	101	56	45	4	2	59	6	91	10
Butcher, Midland	2	6	.250	6.55	15	15	0	0	0	0	68.2	92	54	50	6	3	41	1	49	7
Campbell, San Antonio	1	5	.167	6.67	17	0	0	7	0	2	27.0	29	22	20	3	0	16	1	28	1
Carter, Shreveport	5	4	.556	4.81	14	13	1	0	0	0	67.1	67	39	36	6	4	21	0	52	2
Castillo, Tulsa	8	12	.400	4.42	25	25	6	0	2	0	156.2	171	95	77	7	6	47	1	66	5
Cedeno, Midland	8	3	.727	4.14	53	1	0	17	0	0	91.1	86	43	42	7	4	61	2	77	8
Chapman, El Paso	2	5	.286	5.37	45	0	0	28	0	3	68.2	85	48	41	9	1	37	2	55	9
Chavez, Wichita	1	5	.167	5.33	37	2	0	12	0	3	76.0	84	51	45	4	2	32	9	43	9
Clutterbuck, El Paso	0	2	.000	6.35	4	4	0	0	0	0	17.0	23	14	12	2	0	9	0	8	0
Conley, Jackson*	0	1	.000	9.00	1	1	0	0	0	0	3.0	8	5	3	1	0	0	0	0	0
Connolly, Shreveport*	8	3	.727	3.01	38	9	2	10	1	1	104.2	110	43	35	3	3	35	5	45	3
Costello, El Paso	3	4	.429	6.80	8	7	0	1	0	0	41.0	61	37	31	6	3	28	0	20	3
DeWolf, Wichita*	0	1	.000	18.00	1	1	0	0	0	0	2.0	6	4	4	0	1	0	0	1	0
DiMichele, Midland*	5	5	.500	3.57	33	14	1	7	0	0	93.1	100	44	37	3	4	57	1	55	9
Dominguez, Shreveport	2	9	.182	4.90	40	3	0	19	0	6	75.1	95	57	41	1	2	36	3	31	10
Drahman, El Paso	3	4	.429	7.26	19	0	0	8	0	2	31.0	52	31	25	3	1	11	1	23	3
Edge, El Paso	0	0	.000	Infin.	1	0	0	0	0	0	0.0	1	1	1	0	0	0	0	0	0
Elvira, El Paso*	2	2	.500	7.64	7	7	0	0	0	0	33.0	48	34	28	4	1	23	0	18	4
Falcone, San Antonio*	3	4	.429	5.65	17	10	0	0	0	0	65.1	72	46	41	5	2	39	0	62	6
Fassero, Arkansas*	4	1	.800	1.64	6	6	2	0	1	0	44.0	32	11	8	1	1	12	0	38	1
Ferreira, El Paso*	2	1	.667	4.76	3	3	0	0	0	0	17.0	17	10	9	2	0	6	0	5	1
Fleming, El Paso	0	2	.000	8.15	14	1	0	5	0	1	17.2	26	16	16	4	2	8	1	11	2
Fortugno, El Paso*	0	3	.000	7.96	10	4	0	2	0	0	26.0	29	24	23	3	1	21	2	22	4
Freeland, Shreveport	3	4	.429	4.48	17	11	0	4	0	0	76.1	74	41	38	5	1	40	1	40	4
Gay, Shreveport	3	7	.300	4.99	18	11	1	6	0	1	70.1	78	48	39	4	6	28	1	53	12
Gideon, Jackson*	1	1	.500	1.61	11	1	0	7	0	1	28.0	14	6	5	1	0	12	3	16	0
Givens, Jackson*	3	5	.375	3.39	13	13	2	0	0	0	85.0	76	39	32	4	3	55	5	68	11
Graybill, Midland	4	4	.500	4.72	17	6	0	5	0	1	61.0	76	39	32	3	3	19	3	32	1
Gross, Jackson	6	5	.545	2.49	16	16	4	0	0	0	112.0	96	47	31	9	2	13	0	60	4
Gunderson, Shreveport*	8	2	.800	2.72	11	11	2	0	1	0	72.2	68	24	22	1	1	23	0	61	1
Harris, Wichita*	1	0	1.000	3.38	10	0	0	4	0	1	18.2	20	9	7	1	0	5	1	10	0
Henry, El Paso	0	0	.000	13.50	1	1	0	0	0	0	2.0	3	3	3	1	0	3	0	2	0
Heredia, Shreveport	1	0	1.000	2.55	7	2	1	1	0	0	24.2	28	10	7	1	1	4	0	8	2
J. Hernandez, Wichita	2	1	.667	8.53	4	3	0	0	0	0	19.0	30	18	18	6	0	8	0	9	4
R. Hernandez, Midland	2	7	.222	6.89	12	12	0	0	0	0	64.0	94	57	49	4	2	30	0	42	4
Hershiser, San Antonio	0	3	.000	3.86	36	3	0	20	0	6	58.1	55	32	25	6	0	21	4	52	8
Higuera, El Paso*	0	1	.000	1.80	1	1	0	0	0	0	5.0	5	2	1	0	0	1	0	4	0
Hill, Arkansas*	2	2	.500	6.98	15	1	0	6	0	0	19.1	18	17	15	4	0	7	1	13	2
Hinkle, Arkansas	9	4	.692	4.10	21	21	0	0	0	0	131.2	139	69	60	15	4	25	1	71	3
Holmes, San Antonio	5	8	.385	3.83	17	16	3	1	2	1	110.1	102	59	47	5	3	44	2	81	8
Holsman, Wichita*	10	9	.526	4.33	24	24	2	0	1	0	143.1	134	83	69	9	6	84	4	110	17
Hoover, Tulsa	9	6	.600	3.38	21	17	2	4	1	1	125.0	116	53	47	6	7	37	1	77	6
Hostetler, Shreveport	5	4	.556	3.42	11	11	2	0	1	0	73.2	72	35	28	6	2	24	3	60	3
Hunter, El Paso	7	10	.412	4.19	19	19	4	0	0	0	124.2	149	70	58	9	4	45	1	68	5
Kinnunen, San Antonio*	0	0	.000	3.52	5	0	0	2	0	0	7.2	5	3	3	2	0	3	0	3	1
Kyles, 18 Shr-2 EIP	1	0	1.000	3.41	20	0	0	9	0	1	29.0	28	16	11	1	0	12	0	14	4
Lamle, Tulsa	0	0	.000	6.17	10	0	0	6	0	0	23.1	34	24	16	0	0	13	0	14	0
Lankard, Tulsa	3	4	.429	3.12	35	0	0	21	0	10	66.1	63	27	23	4	2	13	0	46	1
Lepley, Arkansas*	4	6	.400	3.39	59	0	0	18	0	6	69.0	63	40	26	4	3	27	1	55	4
LeVasseur, Wichita	0	0	.000	0.00	1	0	0	1	0	0	1.0	1	0	0	0	0	0	0	0	0
J. Lewis, Wichita	8	4	.667	2.70	63	0	0	50	0	18	83.1	83	28	25	3	3	33	5	53	2
S. Lewis, Midland	11	12	.478	4.93	25	25	4	0	1	0	162.1	195	121	89	15	8	55	9	104	12
Loubier, Wichita	2	4	.333	3.96	15	11	1	0	1	0	75.0	80	37	33	6	0	29	2	44	4
Lynch, Tulsa*	8	0	1.000	0.87	39	0	0	24	0	7	51.2	39	7	5	2	2	24	0	53	3
Machado, Jackson	3	5	.375	2.84	32	0	0	16	0	3	57.0	42	23	18	0	2	27	4	67	1
Malloy, Tulsa	10	9	.526	4.67	34	16	2	10	1	3	125.1	142	75	65	8	5	35	3	54	4
Manuel, Tulsa	3	4	.429	7.48	11	11	0	0	0	0	49.1	49	44	41	5	9	39	0	40	3
Marquez, San Antonio	1	4	.200	4.33	39	0	0	21	0	4	62.1	61	33	30	2	2	34	6	52	6
Martinez, Midland	9	5	.643	5.19	22	22	1	0	0	0	109.1	117	76	63	8	3	59	3	53	4
Mathews, Tulsa	2	5	.286	6.15	10	10	1	0	0	0	45.1	53	40	31	3	2	24	1	32	6
Mayberry, San Antonio	4	6	.400	4.71	11	11	1	0	1	0	63.0	74	37	33	4	4	24	0	49	8
McCament, Shreveport	4	2	.667	2.13	13	0	0	8	0	1	25.1	22	6	6	1	2	5	1	13	2
McClellan, Shreveport	8	3	.727	2.24	12	12	2	0	0	0	84.1	56	26	21	4	1	35	0	56	5
McCoy, Midland*	1	0	1.000	8.36	7	2	1	2	1	0	14.0	17	13	13	2	0	12	0	11	0
McGrath, Arkansas	5	3	.625	2.63	8	8	1	0	0	0	54.2	51	17	16	1	2	13	0	37	1
Meagher, Shreveport	1	4	.200	5.04	5	5	1	0	0	0	25.0	35	17	14	4	2	13	0	13	3
Meier, Shreveport	3	2	.600	4.74	6	6	1	0	0	0	38.0	34	24	20	7	0	7	0	23	1
Meizoso, Jackson*	2	3	.400	3.94	29	0	0	17	0	2	45.2	41	26	20	2	0	28	0	40	2
Merejo, Midland	5	4	.556	3.30	54	0	0	26	0	2	71.0	82	32	26	0	4	20	6	29	2
Miglio, El Paso*	1	0	1.000	3.63	11	0	0	2	0	0	22.1	30	15	9	1	0	8	0	20	1
Mills, El Paso	3	3	.500	4.68	18	4	0	3	0	0	57.2	61	43	30	4	1	32	4	29	3
Monson, El Paso	9	5	.643	5.68	20	20	6	0	0	0	126.2	159	91	80	13	2	58	3	104	8
Moraw, El Paso	1	1	.500	4.46	22	3	0	8	0	0	42.1	45	22	21	4	1	24	3	27	4
Morehouse, Midland	0	1	.000	7.80	5	4	0	1	0	0	15.0	19	14	13	0	0	10	0	5	1
Morse, Tulsa	3	3	.500	4.05	8	8	0	0	0	0	40.0	34	22	18	5	0	16	0	31	1
Moyer, Tulsa*	1	1	.500	5.11	2	2	1	0	1	0	12.1	16	8	7	1	0	3	0	9	1
Mumaw, Arkansas*	10	11	.476	3.93	26	25	7	0	2	0	153.1	154	74	67	7	4	55	1	69	8
Navarro, El Paso	5	2	.714	2.47	11	11	1	0	0	0	76.2	61	29	21	3	1	35	1	78	5
Nichting, San Antonio	4	14	.222	5.03	26	26	2	0	0	0	154.0	160	96	86	13	6	101	6	136	14
Nivens, Jackson	6	11	.353	4.04	25	25	5	0	0	0	160.1	154	81	72	15	4	49	9	82	12
Olivares, Wichita	12	11	.522	3.39	26	26	6	0	1	0	185.2	175	87	70	10	10	61	6	79	10
Osteen, Arkansas	15	5	.750	3.49	27	27	3	0	2	0	165.0	179	77	64	12	4	33	0	72	12
Oyster, Arkansas	5	3	.625	2.68	58	1	0	22	0	3	77.1	78	29	23	4	2	32	0	44	5
Pardo, Midland	0	0	.000	4.50	5	0	0	0	0	0	8.0	7	4	4	1	2	7	0	2	3
Perez, Arkansas	4	6	.400	3.64	57	0	0	51	0	33	76.2	68	34	31	5	2	32	2	74	3
Petkovsek, Tulsa	8	5	.615	3.47	21	21	1	0	0	0	140.0	144	63	54	7	3	35	0	66	5
Picota, Arkansas	4	4	.500	5.07	19	13	0	3	0	0	65.2	77	44	37	7	3	27	0	30	6
Pitz, San Antonio	6	9	.400	4.30	34	17	2	7	0	0	134.0	145	80	64	14	10	32	2	85	9
Plummer, Jackson	5	0	1.000	2.03	25	5	2	8	1	2	71.0	60	17	16	5	1	21	3	36	1
Potestio, Arkansas	4	2	.667	3.23	9	9	2	0	0	0	55.2	52	25	20	2	2	24	0	33	2
Puig, El Paso*	1	3	.250	3.66	47	0	0	43	0	29	64.0	62	30	26	5	1	22	0	47	3
Quinzer, Wichita	1	2	.333	3.15	19	1	0	6	0	1	40.0	37	20	14	5	0	15	2	30	0

Pitcher—Club	W.	L.	Pct.	ERA.	G.	GS.	CG.	GF.	ShO.	Sv.	IP.	H.	R.	ER.	HR.	HB.	BB.	Int. BB.	SO.	WP.
Rauth, Jackson	6	13	.316	3.81	22	22	4	0	0	0	148.2	157	73	63	13	10	43	5	74	3
Remlinger, Shreveport*	4	6	.400	2.98	16	16	0	0	0	0	90.2	68	43	30	2	3	73	0	92	16
Richardson, Midland	0	1	.000	1.59	19	0	0	18	0	10	22.2	9	4	4	1	0	5	0	12	2
Rincon, Arkansas	1	0	1.000	4.21	11	0	0	2	0	0	25.2	28	14	12	1	2	12	1	14	2
Robertson, Shreveport	4	2	.667	3.00	52	0	0	43	0	25	63.0	50	26	21	2	0	38	3	50	2
Rockman, Tulsa	3	3	.500	3.06	40	0	0	22	0	7	50.0	50	20	17	5	2	17	1	30	2
Rodriguez, Wichita*	8	3	.727	3.63	54	0	0	38	0	8	74.1	74	30	30	3	2	37	11	40	4
Rosenthal, Tulsa	2	4	.333	3.06	31	0	0	22	0	10	50.0	40	20	17	2	0	21	3	47	0
Scarpetta, San Antonio*	2	4	.333	4.66	17	0	0	5	0	0	19.1	20	11	10	2	0	8	0	19	1
Schrom, El Paso	1	2	.333	2.65	5	5	1	0	0	0	34.0	36	19	10	3	1	10	1	19	0
Scott, San Antonio	4	2	.667	3.71	48	0	0	28	0	4	68.0	71	30	28	3	0	36	5	64	1
Soltero, Wichita	0	0	.000	9.00	12	0	0	5	0	0	20.0	33	21	20	2	0	9	2	10	0
Springer, San Antonio	6	8	.429	3.15	19	19	4	0	1	0	140.0	128	58	49	13	4	46	2	89	3
Stone, Arkansas	3	2	.600	5.15	9	9	0	0	0	0	43.2	51	29	25	1	2	25	2	29	7
Stringfellow, Jackson*	1	0	1.000	4.91	10	0	0	6	0	0	14.2	15	11	8	1	1	10	1	9	1
Swan, Shreveport*	2	3	.400	2.63	11	11	0	0	0	0	75.1	62	25	22	2	1	22	1	56	3
Talamantez, Jackson	2	4	.333	3.95	9	9	0	0	0	0	41.0	49	29	18	3	4	17	2	19	3
Thomas, Tulsa	0	0	.000	6.75	1	1	0	0	0	0	4.0	4	3	3	0	0	3	0	2	1
Tirado, El Paso	3	3	.500	6.36	15	6	0	1	0	0	52.1	66	41	37	4	1	32	1	42	3
Townsend, Midland*	0	1	.000	14.73	4	0	0	0	0	0	3.2	7	7	6	1	0	5	0	5	0
Trautwein, Jackson	6	6	.500	1.65	44	0	0	38	0	13	71.0	50	20	13	2	3	18	2	39	4
Trudeau, Midland	4	5	.444	3.62	13	13	0	0	0	0	87.0	89	42	35	4	2	17	1	43	3
Valdez, Wichita	5	0	1.000	1.94	6	6	2	0	0	0	41.2	28	10	9	1	1	24	2	26	1
Valera, Jackson	10	6	.625	2.49	19	19	6	0	2	0	137.1	123	47	38	4	8	36	2	107	10
Veres, El Paso	2	3	.400	4.78	8	8	0	0	0	0	43.1	43	29	23	3	1	25	1	41	4
Waddell, El Paso	3	0	1.000	0.00	6	0	0	6	0	0	6.0	6	1	0	0	1	2	1	3	1
Walsh, San Antonio*	2	6	.250	3.72	38	0	0	15	0	2	55.2	47	26	23	4	2	30	5	63	7
Watkins, El Paso	11	6	.647	4.93	26	18	5	3	0	0	138.2	176	95	76	8	5	61	3	84	7
Weissman, Arkansas	1	2	.333	5.07	40	2	0	14	0	3	55.0	60	39	31	5	3	22	0	30	1
Welborn, Jackson	0	3	.000	4.91	23	0	0	10	0	2	36.2	29	29	20	1	1	29	2	34	4
Wheeler, El Paso*	0	0	.000	6.62	9	0	0	1	0	0	17.2	21	15	13	3	1	5	0	11	0
Wood, Wichita	0	1	.000	1.80	2	0	0	1	0	0	5.0	2	1	1	0	0	0	0	4	0
Wray, San Antonio*	1	1	.500	1.99	17	0	0	14	0	2	22.2	21	6	5	1	0	5	3	23	1
Young, Midland*	3	0	1.000	4.76	10	0	0	1	0	1	22.2	31	12	12	0	0	13	1	20	6

BALKS—S. Lewis, 9; Falcone, Freeland, Holmes, Martinez, 6 each; Robertson, Wheeler, 5 each; Alvarez, Brocail, Brown, Burcham, Connolly, Gross, Nichting, Pitz, Rauth, Scott, 4 each; Armstrong, Bones, Chavez, Elvira, Gay, Graybill, Holsman, Hoover, Manuel, Mathews, McClellan, Merejo, Oyster, Picota, Potestio, Rincon, Talamantez, Watkins, 3 each; Bauer, Beck, Benes, Bivens, Butcher, Chapman, Clutterbuck, DiMichele, Hinkle, Kyles, Lankard, Lynch, Meizoso, Miglio, Monson, Mumaw, Nivens, Remlinger, Schrom, Swan, 2 each; Akins, Beasley, Bohanon, Bonilla, Bryant, Bumgarner, Carter, Cedeno, Dominguez, Fassero, Ferreira, Fleming, Givens, Gunderson, Harris, R. Hernandez, Lepley, Machado, Marquez, Mayberry, McCoy, McGrath, Mills, Morehouse, Morse, Moyer, Navarro, Olivares, Perez, Quinzer, Rodriguez, Scarpetta, Soltero, Tirado, Trautwein, Trudeau, Valdez, Young, 1 each.

COMBINATION SHUTOUTS—Stone-Oyster-Perez, Hinkle-Perez, Picota-Oyster-Perez, Arkansas; Veres-Puig, El Paso; Gross-Meizoso-Trautwein, Rauth-Welborn-Plummer, Valera-Machado-Trautwein, Jackson; Trudeau-DiMichele-Buckels, DiMichele-Cedeno-Buckels-Merejo, Midland; Mayberry-Scott, Falcone-Campbell, Armstrong-Wray, San Antonio; McClellan-Bonilla, Swan-Dominguez-McCament, Remlinger-Connolly-Robertson, Gay-Bonilla-Connolly-Kyles, Hostetler-Carter-Robertson, Carter-Connolly-Gay-Robertson, Carter-Gay, Shreveport; Bryant-Lynch, Malloy-Hoover, Morse-Rosenthal, Bohanon-Malloy, Tulsa; Holsman-Rodriguez, Olivares-Rodriguez, Bones-Lewis, Valdez-Rodriguez, Wichita.

NO-HIT GAME—Fassero, Arkansas, defeated Jackson, 5-0, June 12.

California League

CLASS A

CHAMPIONSHIP WINNERS IN PREVIOUS YEARS

1914—Fresno	.571	1961—Reno	.743	1976—Salinas§	.650
1915—Modesto	.857	Reno	.643	Reno§	.547
1916-40—Did not operate.		1962—San José§	.686	1977—Salinas	.564
1941—Fresno	.643	Reno	.587	Lodi§	.579
S. Barbara (2nd)*	.597	1963—Modesto	.589	1978—Visalia§	.698
1942—Santa Barbara†	.642	Stockton§	.687	Lodi	.607
1943-44-45—Did not operate.		1964—Fresno	.638	1979—San José§	.636
1946—Stockton‡	.600	Fresno	.600	Reno	.525
1947—Stockton‡	.679	1965—San Jose	.586	1980—Stockton§	.638
1948—Fresno	.607	Stockton§	.614	Visalia	.507
S. Barbara (3rd)*	.529	1966—Modesto	.577	1981—Visalia	.621
1949—Bakersfield	.612	Modesto	.671	Lodi§	.521
San Jose (4th)*	.543	1967—San José§	.676	1982—Modesto§	.671
1950—Ventura	.607	Modesto	.586	Visalia	.586
Modesto (2nd)*	.586	1968—San Jose	.629	1983—Visalia	.621
1951—Santa Barbara‡	.599	Fresno§	.623	Redwood§	.529
1952—Fresno‡	.629	1969—Stockton§	.600	1984—Modesto§	.597
1953—San Jose‡	.664	Visalia	.614	Bakersfield	.486
1954—Modesto‡	.623	1970—Bakersfield	.667	1985—Fresno§	.575
1955—Stockton	.733	Bakersfield	.671	Stockton	.566
Fresno§	.718	1971—Visalia§	.583	1986—Palm Springs	.613
1956—Fresno‡	.650	Fresno	.500	Stockton§	.585
1957—Visalia x	.622	1972—Modesto§	.547	1987—Fresno§	.559
Salinas (4th)*	.504	Bakersfield	.629	Reno	.535
1958—Fresno*	.639	1973—Lodi§	.657	1988—Stockton	.657
Bakersfield	.672	Bakersfield	.571	Riverside§	.599
1959—Bakersfield	.592	1974—Fresno§	.607		
Modesto§	.643	San Jose	.579		
1960—Reno	.614	1975—Reno	.614		
Reno	.657	Reno	.614		

*Won four-club playoff. †League disbanded June 28. ‡Won championship and four-club playoff. §Won split-season playoff. xWon both halves of split-season.

STANDING OF CLUBS AT CLOSE OF FIRST HALF, JUNE 18

NORTHERN DIVISION						SOUTHERN DIVISION					
Club	W.	L.	T.	Pct.	G.B.	Club	W.	L.	T.	Pct.	G.B.
San Jose (Giants)	46	25	0	.648	....	Bakersfield (Dodgers)	41	30	0	.577	....
Stockton (Brewers)	41	30	0	.577	5	San Bernardino (Mariners)	37	34	0	.521	4
Reno (Independent)	31	40	0	.437	15	Riverside (Padres)	37	34	0	.521	4
Modesto (Athletics)	28	43	0	.394	18	Visalia (Twins)	35	36	0	.493	6
Salinas (Independent)	25	46	0	.352	21	Palm Springs (Angels)	34	37	0	.479	7

STANDING OF CLUBS AT CLOSE OF SECOND HALF, AUGUST 30

NORTHERN DIVISION						SOUTHERN DIVISION					
Club	W.	L.	T.	Pct.	G.B.	Club	W.	L.	T.	Pct.	G.B.
Stockton (Brewers)	48	23	0	.676	....	San Bernardino (Mariners)	46	25	0	.648	....
Reno (Independent)	37	34	0	.521	11	Visalia (Twins)	41	30	0	.577	5
San Jose (Giants)	35	36	0	.493	13	Bakersfield (Dodgers)	41	30	0	.577	5
Modesto (Athletics)	28	43	0	.394	20	Riverside (Padres)	27	44	0	.380	19
Salinas (Independent)	26	45	0	.366	22	Palm Springs (Angels)	26	45	0	.366	20

COMPOSITE STANDING OF CLUBS AT CLOSE OF SEASON, AUGUST 30

Club	Sto.	S.B.	Bak.	S.J.	Vis.	Reno	Riv.	P.S.	Mod.	Sal.	W.	L.	T.	Pct.	G.B.
Stockton (Brewers)	....	6	6	10	8	11	10	11	13	14	89	53	0	.627	....
San Bernardino (Mariners)	6	....	12	7	7	7	11	14	8	11	83	59	0	.585	6
Bakersfield (Dodgers)	6	8	....	7	12	6	12	14	9	8	82	60	0	.577	7
San Jose (Giants)	11	5	5	....	7	13	7	10	10	13	81	61	0	.570	8
Visalia (Twins)	4	13	8	5	....	6	11	12	8	9	76	66	0	.535	13
Reno (Independent)	10	5	6	7	6	....	6	4	12	12	68	74	0	.479	21
Riverside (Padres)	2	11	6	5	9	6	....	8	8	7	64	78	0	.451	25
Palm Springs (Angels)	1	6	8	2	8	8	12	....	10	5	60	82	0	.423	29
Modesto (Athletics)	7	4	3	10	6	8	4	2	....	12	56	86	0	.394	33
Salinas (Independent)	6	1	4	8	3	9	5	7	8	....	51	91	0	.359	38

Major league affiliations in parentheses.

Playoffs—Bakersfield defeated San Bernardino, three games to one; Stockton defeated San Jose, three games to two; Bakersfield defeated Stockton, three games to none, to win league championship.

Regular-Season Attendance—Bakersfield, 123,572; Modesto, 87,256; Palm Springs, 69,521; Reno, 75,842; Riverside, 80,154; Salinas, 47,609; San Bernardino, 184,791; San Jose, 108,458; Stockton, 72,734; Visalia, 83,946. Total—933,883. Playoffs (12 games)—26,821. All-Star Game—2,180.

Managers—Bakersfield, Tim Johnson; Modesto, Lenn Sakata (through June 8), Keith Lieppman (June 9-11), Ted Kubiak (June 12 through end of season); Palm Springs, Bill Lachemann; Reno, Eli Grba; Riverside, Steve Lubratich; Salinas, Tim Ireland; San Bernardino, Ralph Dick; San Jose, Duane Espy; Stockton, Dave Huppert; Visalia, Scott Ullger. Managerial records of teams with more than one manager: Modesto, Sakata 23-37, Lieppman 2-2, Kubiak 31-47.

All-Star Team—1B—John Jaha, Stockton; Eric Karros, Bakersfield; 2B—Steve Hecht, San Jose; 3B—Ernie Carr, Bakersfield; SS—Jose Offerman, Bakersfield; OF—Braulio Castillo, Bakersfield; Jerry Brooks, Bakersfield; Mike Humphreys, Riverside; C—Jim Campanis, San Bernardino; DH—Ruben Gonzalez, San Bernardino; P—Steve Lienhard, San Jose; Jim Blueberg, San Bernardino; Jim Wray, Bakersfield; Rafael Valdez, Riverside; Most Valuable Player—John Jaha, Stockton; Pitcher of the Year—Steve Lienhard, San Jose; Rookie of the Year—Eric Karros, Bakersfield; Manager of the Year—Duane Espy, San Jose.

(Compiled by Howe Sportsdata International, Boston, Mass.)

CLUB BATTING

Club	Pct.	G.	AB.	R.	OR.	H.	TB.	2B.	3B.	HR.	RBI.	SH.	SF.	HP.	BB.	Int. BB.	SO.	SB.	CS.	LOB.
Bakersfield	.256	142	4799	669	605	1227	1879	258	32	110	596	21	36	56	495	16	1035	174	97	980
Visalia	.255	142	4718	680	600	1202	1647	192	32	63	587	37	53	59	517	18	861	184	83	999
San Bernardino	.252	142	4727	636	547	1190	1754	203	32	99	545	32	35	49	542	12	852	142	87	1013
Reno	.250	142	4555	638	673	1137	1625	206	36	70	544	32	45	43	523	18	815	113	91	945
Riverside	.247	142	4771	598	599	1177	1580	176	34	53	503	28	49	55	512	22	858	152	80	1040
Stockton	.247	142	4645	654	496	1145	1600	204	40	57	564	57	49	58	676	25	925	120	90	1096
San Jose	.243	142	4553	600	498	1105	1531	199	31	55	512	15	43	62	515	13	979	233	119	907
Palm Springs	.231	142	4556	529	654	1053	1363	155	34	29	444	39	33	69	486	13	1101	165	61	983
Modesto	.225	142	4656	510	636	1049	1422	157	21	58	440	49	23	55	562	14	1060	93	81	1052
Salinas	.218	142	4469	459	665	976	1279	149	32	30	381	35	32	36	526	19	1059	100	94	949

INDIVIDUAL BATTING
(Leading Qualifiers for Batting Championship—383 or More Plate Appearances)

*Bats lefthanded. †Switch-hitter.

Player and Club	Pct.	G.	AB.	R.	H.	TB.	2B.	3B.	HR.	RBI.	SH.	SF.	HP.	BB.	Int. BB.	SO.	SB.	CS.
Gonzalez, Ruben, San Bernardino	.308	135	507	74	156	271	34	0	27	101	1	4	9	56	6	64	4	2
Karros, Eric, Bakersfield	.303	142	545	86	165	252	40	1	15	86	0	4	2	63	3	99	18	7
Lewis, Darren, Modesto	.298	129	503	74	150	195	23	5	4	39	2	4	11	59	0	84	27	22
Castillo, Braulio, Bakersfield	.298	126	494	83	147	245	28	8	18	82	0	5	15	42	1	132	31	22
Jaha, John, Stockton	.292	140	479	83	140	251	26	5	25	91	2	13	5	112	6	115	8	11
Brooks, Jerome, Bakersfield	.290	141	565	70	164	253	39	1	16	87	0	8	6	25	0	79	9	6
Humphreys, Michael, Riverside	.288	117	420	77	121	188	26	1	13	66	3	5	7	72	4	79	23	10
McWilliam, Timothy, Riverside	.283	119	428	56	121	171	26	3	6	60	2	6	7	47	3	55	2	1
Valdez, Frank, Visalia	.283	132	453	71	128	190	24	4	10	59	5	5	11	49	3	127	15	11
Guerrero, Juan, San Jose	.281	108	409	61	115	182	24	2	13	78	0	5	7	36	1	68	7	5
McDonald, Michael, San Bernardino*	.281	125	466	82	131	223	28	5	18	56	0	3	3	58	0	99	7	2

Departmental Leaders: G—Karros, 142; AB—J. Brooks, 565; R—Brown, 95; H—Karros, 165; TB—R. Gonzalez, 271; 2B—Karros, 40; 3B—Castillo, Hecht, W. Lee, Shaw, 8; HR—R. Gonzalez, 27; RBI—R. Gonzalez, 101; SH—Raley, 12; SF—Jaha, 13; HP—Castillo, R. Jones, 15; BB—Jaha, 112; IBB—R. Jones, 7; SO—Finken, 141; SB—W. Lee, 66; CS—Taylor, 28.

(All Players—Listed Alphabetically)

Player and Club	Pct.	G.	AB.	R.	H.	TB.	2B.	3B.	HR.	RBI.	SH.	SF.	HP.	BB.	Int. BB.	SO.	SB.	CS.
Alfonzo, Edgar, Palm Springs	.240	77	242	31	58	81	10	2	3	27	3	3	3	40	1	37	8	3
Alicea, Miguel, Palm Springs	.000	30	1	0	0	0	0	0	0	0	0	0	0	0	0	0	0	0
Ayrault, Robert, Reno	.000	28	13	0	0	0	0	0	0	0	0	0	0	0	0	5	0	0
Balfanz, John, Reno*	.229	109	376	56	86	140	24	0	10	59	1	4	5	53	4	69	5	4
Barbara, Daniel, San Bernardino	.190	23	42	2	8	8	0	0	0	2	0	0	0	5	0	10	1	0
Barton, Shawn, Reno	.229	115	407	48	93	119	16	2	2	54	4	11	4	31	1	37	10	6
Beals, Bryan, Bakersfield†	.223	39	130	27	29	36	7	0	0	2	3	0	4	17	0	35	16	1
Benoit, Dickens, Salinas	.229	83	262	36	60	74	9	1	1	19	0	1	8	20	1	69	12	3
Bigham, Scott, Riverside	.251	134	522	74	131	150	13	3	0	53	5	3	6	47	0	65	17	12
Bluhm, William, Reno	.259	97	301	40	78	108	4	7	4	31	2	2	4	31	0	63	11	5
Boddie, Eric, Bakersfield*	.186	81	231	34	43	62	9	2	2	12	0	0	5	37	0	89	5	1
Booth, David, San Jose†	.125	6	8	1	1	1	0	0	0	1	2	0	0	1	0	4	0	0
Borg, Gary, Stockton*	.266	129	458	66	122	169	28	2	5	65	2	3	2	79	1	85	5	6
Bosco, Michael, Reno	.237	135	477	69	113	147	15	5	3	48	5	0	7	45	2	74	11	13
Bour, Jeffrey, Reno†	.000	3	5	0	0	0	0	0	0	0	0	0	0	0	0	3	0	0
Brady, Patrick, 126 Sal-8 SJ	.232	134	461	53	107	143	24	3	2	29	1	2	0	87	1	95	5	10
Brito, Jorge, Modesto	.241	16	54	8	13	18	2	0	1	6	1	0	1	5	0	14	0	0
Brocki, Michael, San Bernardino	.249	108	374	61	93	118	16	3	1	24	5	1	4	59	3	52	28	14
Brooks, Jerome, Bakersfield	.290	141	565	70	164	253	39	1	16	87	0	8	6	25	0	79	9	6
Brooks, Monte, Riverside†	.129	59	171	16	22	23	1	0	0	6	3	0	4	17	1	48	10	6
Brown, Jarvis, Visalia	.240	141	545	95	131	176	21	6	4	46	4	4	13	73	0	112	49	13
Burlingame, Gregory, San Bernardino*	.000	31	1	0	0	0	0	0	0	0	0	0	0	0	0	0	0	0
Campanis, James, San Bernardino	.255	133	455	49	116	175	26	0	11	58	0	3	14	51	1	96	0	2
Capellan, Carlos, Visalia	.261	140	498	64	130	163	14	5	3	64	6	3	22	2	37	17	9
Carcione, Thomas, Modesto	.222	89	270	32	60	83	5	3	4	27	2	0	2	38	1	76	2	2
Carlson, William, San Jose	.271	92	325	40	88	135	20	3	7	50	0	6	3	22	0	63	10	7
Carpenter, Douglas, Reno	.234	16	47	5	11	17	2	2	0	5	2	0	0	10	0	12	1	2
Carr, Ernest, Bakersfield*	.254	132	531	78	135	212	36	7	9	64	1	3	1	44	2	84	2	5
Carr, Terence, Reno	.255	130	466	59	119	155	24	3	2	38	4	2	7	39	1	94	6	10
Carrasco, Claudio, 13 Reno-47 PS†	.254	60	213	37	54	77	6	4	3	25	1	1	2	25	0	47	6	1
Carter, Frederick, Palm Springs	.213	59	202	30	43	57	11	0	1	26	0	4	7	28	2	45	4	0
Carter, Richard, San Jose	.000	13	1	0	0	0	0	0	0	0	0	0	0	0	0	0	0	0
Cassels, Christopher, Stockton	.242	128	450	40	109	154	18	3	7	74	2	3	8	42	3	116	2	5
Castillo, Braulio, Bakersfield	.298	126	494	83	147	245	28	8	18	82	0	5	15	42	1	132	31	22
Chimelis, Joel, Modesto	.190	69	211	18	40	44	1	0	1	14	3	1	3	33	0	41	2	3
Clark, Isaiah, Riverside	.256	132	492	42	126	161	16	5	3	66	1	9	7	34	2	40	4	3
Clayton, Royce, San Jose	.120	28	92	5	11	13	2	0	0	4	0	1	0	13	0	27	10	1
Conner, Gregory, San Jose	.184	55	185	25	34	53	5	1	4	18	1	2	5	18	0	70	9	5
Cooper, James, San Jose	.256	105	418	60	107	137	21	3	1	36	1	0	10	21	0	104	60	15
Correia, Ronald, Modesto	.209	107	339	31	71	86	9	3	0	26	4	1	12	34	0	64	7	7
Daughtry, Dorian, San Bernardino	.118	11	17	2	2	3	1	0	0	0	0	0	0	0	0	6	0	0
Decker, Steven, San Jose	.289	64	225	27	65	86	12	0	3	46	0	5	0	44	3	36	8	5
DeLaRosa, Cesar, Palm Springs†	.211	127	445	37	94	120	11	3	3	35	7	0	4	17	0	139	7	6
Dominguez, Frank, Reno	.259	96	324	36	84	129	23	2	6	45	2	9	4	21	1	65	2	7
Dotzler, Michael, Visalia*	.190	77	242	16	46	75	11	0	6	32	5	3	0	17	0	83	0	1
Duffin, Thomas, San Bernardino	.200	38	80	8	16	21	5	0	0	11	1	1	3	11	0	11	0	0
Ealy, Thomas, San Jose	.259	115	394	50	102	146	24	1	6	50	0	1	6	45	0	86	11	11
Escalera, Ruben, Stockton*	.114	12	44	4	5	5	0	0	0	3	1	0	1	5	0	10	0	0
Farmer, Kevin, Riverside	.213	81	301	34	64	82	7	1	3	34	1	3	0	30	1	58	4	3
Farmer, Reggie, Riverside*	.227	24	88	9	20	22	2	0	0	3	0	0	1	12	1	26	7	2
Fernandez, Daniel, San Jose	.176	50	136	17	24	27	0	0	1	9	0	0	1	25	0	35	3	3
Finken, Steven, Bakersfield	.248	125	428	53	106	190	23	2	19	66	3	3	3	70	2	141	12	9
Flippo, Robert, Bakersfield	.102	19	49	4	5	9	1	0	1	2	0	1	0	2	0	14	0	0
Foster, Bryan, Stockton	.161	29	87	8	14	17	1	1	0	8	0	1	0	6	0	33	1	0
Franklin, John, Salinas	.131	30	61	7	8	12	2	1	0	2	0	0	1	6	2	20	1	1

Player and Club	Pct.	G.	AB.	R.	H.	TB.	2B.	3B.	HR.	RBI.	SH.	SF.	HP.	BB.	Int. BB.	SO.	SB.	CS.
Fraticelli, Carl, Visalia†	.205	27	83	15	17	19	0	1	0	1	0	0	0	17	0	18	0	2
Fujimoto, Kenji, Visalia	.209	60	134	15	28	39	8	0	1	8	2	0	1	14	0	29	1	1
Furcal, Lorenzo, Modesto	.102	19	49	2	5	8	0	1	0	2	0	0	0	8	0	22	0	1
Gavin, David, Modesto	.236	70	259	21	61	90	4	2	7	26	0	1	2	12	0	55	12	9
Gay, Jeffrey, Palm Springs*	.279	73	247	19	69	86	9	1	2	33	2	2	1	10	0	45	1	2
Gilbert, Shawn, Visalia	.249	125	453	52	113	138	17	1	2	43	6	3	3	54	1	70	42	16
Giles, Troy, Palm Springs	.182	55	159	9	29	33	4	0	0	12	1	2	4	12	0	74	1	1
Goins, Scott, San Jose	.229	124	424	57	97	139	21	3	5	40	1	4	8	61	0	104	6	6
Gonzalez, Ruben, San Bernardino	.308	135	507	74	156	271	34	0	27	101	1	4	9	56	6	64	4	2
Gonzalez, Jesus, Bakersfield	.000	4	6	1	0	0	0	0	0	1	0	0	0	1	0	4	0	0
Graves, Christopher, Palm Springs†	.260	68	254	49	66	83	9	4	0	20	5	2	4	33	0	65	19	5
Gray, Steven, Salinas	.111	18	9	2	1	1	0	0	0	0	1	0	0	0	0	7	1	2
Grilione, David, Bakersfield†	.136	11	22	3	3	9	0	0	2	5	0	0	0	1	0	10	0	0
Guerrero, Juan, San Jose	.281	108	409	61	115	182	24	2	13	78	0	5	7	36	1	68	7	5
Guerrero, Michael, Stockton†	.235	44	136	12	32	37	5	0	0	13	5	1	0	12	0	15	3	1
Hahn, Brent, Salinas	.130	27	77	5	10	11	1	0	0	3	0	1	0	8	0	23	1	2
Hall, Gregory, Riverside	.250	22	80	11	20	26	3	0	1	7	1	1	0	9	0	14	2	0
Ham, Michael, San Jose	.194	32	93	10	18	21	3	0	0	9	1	1	1	10	0	35	0	0
Haney, Todd, San Bernardino	.252	25	107	10	27	32	5	0	0	7	0	1	0	7	0	14	2	3
Hansen, Todd, Riverside*	.000	28	1	0	0	0	0	0	0	0	1	0	0	0	0	0	0	0
Harper, Milton, Reno*	.275	118	397	71	109	213	27	1	25	78	0	5	1	80	5	78	5	3
Hartsock, Brian, Reno*	.256	100	309	44	79	116	13	0	8	51	1	2	0	52	3	43	3	3
Hecht, Steven, San Jose*	.265	127	501	83	133	175	17	8	3	43	1	3	4	52	3	57	56	25
Hill, Steven, San Bernardino	.280	112	396	58	111	142	19	3	2	44	1	5	0	43	0	61	23	11
Hillman, Joseph, Modesto	.236	78	250	39	59	76	6	1	3	23	5	3	3	58	2	49	1	5
Hirtensteiner, Richard, P Springs*	.224	36	125	11	28	33	5	0	0	11	0	2	1	15	0	34	1	1
Hoffman, John, San Bernardino	.125	8	16	1	2	3	1	0	0	0	0	0	0	2	0	3	0	0
Huebner, John, Bakersfield*	.000	3	8	0	0	0	0	0	0	0	0	0	0	0	0	1	0	0
Humphreys, Michael, Riverside	.288	117	420	77	121	188	26	1	13	66	3	5	7	72	4	79	23	10
Jacas, David, Visalia	.307	77	287	55	88	121	15	3	4	43	0	1	5	34	1	55	19	10
Jaha, John, Stockton	.292	140	479	83	140	251	26	5	25	91	2	13	5	112	6	115	8	11
James, Todd, Palm Springs*	.000	11	1	0	0	0	0	0	0	0	0	0	0	0	0	1	0	0
Jones, James, San Jose†	.275	135	458	76	126	163	15	5	4	49	2	4	10	67	1	91	22	12
Jones, Robert, Stockton	.248	137	520	83	129	204	37	7	8	68	4	10	15	42	7	108	15	17
Kaiser, Jeffrey, Salinas†	.153	96	255	25	39	47	6	1	0	13	4	1	3	34	0	101	6	4
Karros, Eric, Bakersfield	.303	142	545	86	165	252	40	1	15	86	0	4	2	63	3	99	18	7
Kating, James, Modesto	.148	7	27	2	4	4	0	0	0	2	1	1	0	3	1	5	0	0
Kemp, Joseph, Modesto*	.286	13	49	9	14	18	1	0	1	5	1	0	0	5	1	12	0	1
King, Bryan, San Bernardino	.244	135	451	48	110	126	6	2	2	39	10	3	2	46	0	52	26	8
Kmak, Joseph, Reno	.274	78	248	39	68	100	10	5	4	34	0	1	5	40	1	41	8	4
Knoblauch, Charles, Visalia	.364	18	77	20	28	38	10	0	0	21	1	1	1	6	0	11	4	0
Kosco, Andrew, San Bernardino*	.243	50	177	22	43	90	9	1	12	27	0	2	4	12	0	48	0	0
Kuoda, Masa, Salinas	.212	124	373	31	79	94	5	5	0	28	2	0	5	20	1	93	6	13
Laya, Jesus, Salinas	.267	7	15	1	4	4	0	0	0	0	0	0	0	2	0	3	0	0
Lee, Gregory, Salinas	.136	9	22	2	3	3	0	0	0	2	1	0	0	8	0	8	2	0
Lee, Wiley, Palm Springs*	.267	135	509	86	136	179	18	8	3	57	8	3	14	47	1	88	66	10
Lewis, Darren, Modesto	.298	129	503	74	150	195	23	5	4	39	2	4	11	59	0	84	27	22
Listach, Patrick, Stockton	.229	132	480	73	110	135	11	4	2	34	7	1	4	58	1	106	37	19
Logan, Todd, Visalia*	.313	45	128	16	40	63	4	2	5	26	1	1	0	27	1	19	1	3
Lutticken, Robert, Riverside	.200	65	210	17	42	51	1	1	2	20	3	0	7	12	0	46	1	1
Malseed, James, San Jose	.170	110	341	33	58	84	13	2	3	25	3	3	3	50	1	82	7	4
Marabell, Scott, Bakersfield	.200	16	45	5	9	16	1	0	2	6	0	0	1	4	0	12	0	1
Marquez, Edwin, Palm Springs	.260	63	223	27	58	92	14	1	6	26	4	1	4	24	0	59	2	0
Martin, Christopher, Reno	.000	4	12	0	0	0	0	0	0	2	0	1	0	0	0	4	0	0
Martinez, Luis, Bakersfield	.230	56	196	15	45	56	8	0	1	16	7	2	3	4	0	25	10	11
Martinez, Ramon, Palm Springs	.192	103	317	40	61	71	8	1	0	20	0	4	5	43	0	58	4	4
Marx, William, Riverside	.000	30	3	0	0	0	0	0	0	0	0	0	0	0	0	2	0	0
Marzan, Jose, Visalia	.259	130	436	64	113	151	19	2	5	71	4	7	9	58	3	58	9	2
Masteller, Dan, Visalia*	.254	53	181	24	46	62	5	1	3	16	0	1	1	18	2	36	0	0
Matos, Francisco, Modesto	.205	65	200	14	41	51	5	1	1	23	0	1	0	12	0	41	6	5
McBride, Loy, Visalia	.232	128	479	65	111	175	19	6	11	63	2	6	3	34	3	98	19	11
McCollom, James, Palm Springs	.267	8	30	4	8	11	1	1	0	5	0	0	0	3	0	7	0	0
McDonald, Michael, San Bernardino*	.281	125	466	82	131	223	28	5	18	56	0	3	3	58	0	99	7	2
McDonald, Thomas, San Jose	.197	41	137	14	27	40	4	0	3	17	1	4	0	20	2	27	1	2
McGrew, Charles, Modesto*	.158	22	76	9	12	13	1	0	0	8	1	0	1	16	0	19	0	1
McNamara, James, 49 Sal.-19 SJ*	.250	68	220	11	55	68	10	0	1	18	1	1	0	23	2	37	3	2
McWilliam, Timothy, Riverside	.283	119	428	56	121	171	26	3	6	60	2	6	7	47	3	55	2	1
Mercedes, Henry, Modesto	.081	16	37	6	3	6	0	0	1	3	0	0	0	7	0	22	0	0
Merchant, Mark, San Bernardino†	.210	119	429	65	90	142	15	2	11	46	0	4	2	61	1	101	17	6
Meredith, Steven, Reno	.197	28	66	7	13	18	2	0	1	7	2	2	0	7	0	19	4	1
Miller, William, Bakersfield*	.231	33	78	10	18	19	1	0	0	9	1	0	1	6	0	9	2	0
Mims, Larry, Riverside†	.227	13	44	5	10	10	0	0	0	5	1	1	0	9	0	8	5	2
Molina, Mario, Palm Springs*	.209	44	134	16	28	41	4	0	3	18	0	1	1	15	0	44	1	0
Montoyo, Carlos, Stockton	.248	129	448	69	111	137	22	2	0	48	6	4	11	102	3	40	13	9
Morales, Richard, San Bernardino	.327	42	55	11	18	23	1	2	0	5	0	0	1	11	0	6	0	0
Morrow, Christian, Bakersfield*	.150	38	107	9	16	24	5	0	1	4	0	0	0	14	2	18	3	4
Nalls, Gary, Reno	.263	118	419	64	110	149	19	7	2	37	1	2	6	37	0	91	15	13
Nilsson, David, Stockton*	.244	125	472	59	115	158	16	6	5	56	4	4	1	51	1	75	2	1
Nina, Julio, Modesto*	.085	17	47	6	4	5	1	0	0	3	1	0	2	11	1	25	0	1
Oedewaldt, Larry, Stockton†	.209	31	91	14	19	25	2	2	0	9	3	0	0	15	0	23	0	3
Offerman, Jose, Bakersfield†	.306	62	245	53	75	98	9	4	2	22	0	1	2	35	2	48	37	13
Ohnoutka, Brian, Riverside	.000	19	1	0	0	0	0	0	0	0	0	0	1	0	0	2	0	0
Ortegon, Ronnie, Palm Springs*	.221	121	390	32	86	106	13	2	1	42	2	3	5	57	4	74	2	2
Ortiz, Joe, Modesto	.257	12	35	0	9	10	1	0	0	2	0	0	0	0	0	15	0	1
Ozawa, Kouichi, Visalia	.286	24	42	5	12	16	1	0	1	6	0	0	2	2	0	9	0	0
Palma, Brian, Reno*	.167	6	12	1	2	2	0	0	0	0	1	0	0	2	0	5	0	0
Parry, Robert, Modesto	.269	110	413	48	111	163	24	2	8	54	2	2	4	31	0	68	4	3
Pimentel, Edward, Salinas†	.219	43	151	12	33	43	5	1	1	16	4	1	2	11	0	25	2	5
Pittenger, Jon, Visalia†	.173	17	52	6	9	12	3	0	0	3	1	0	1	0	0	5	0	0
Preston, Steven, Stockton†	.056	10	18	4	1	1	0	0	0	0	0	1	0	0	0	6	2	1
Pritikin, James, San Bernardino*	.207	113	329	32	68	95	9	3	4	24	2	0	2	26	1	89	7	7
Pye, Edward, Bakersfield	.258	129	488	59	126	175	21	2	8	47	3	0	6	41	1	87	19	9

Player and Club	Pct.	G.	AB.	R.	H.	TB.	2B.	3B.	HR.	RBI.	SH.	SF.	HP.	BB.	Int. BB.	SO.	SB.	CS.
Raley, Timothy, Stockton*	.264	123	439	67	116	143	14	5	1	46	12	2	2	84	0	64	14	4
Reichle, Darrin, Riverside†	1.000	27	1	0	1	1	0	0	0	1	0	0	0	0	0	0	0	0
Resetar, Gary, Visalia*	.305	42	151	21	46	55	6	0	1	25	0	3	0	23	1	15	0	0
Rice, Lance, Bakersfield†	.222	126	406	41	90	122	15	1	5	53	1	5	3	53	2	83	1	4
Robinson, Marteese, Modesto	.162	18	68	4	11	14	3	0	0	7	1	2	0	8	0	15	0	1
Rodriguez, Edgar, Palm Springs	.245	86	302	29	74	104	11	5	3	31	2	1	3	33	3	72	7	4
Rodriguez, Henry, Bakersfield*	.222	3	9	2	2	5	0	0	1	2	0	0	0	0	0	3	0	0
Romero, Charles, Palm Springs†	.265	113	411	48	109	125	12	2	0	32	1	2	7	43	1	84	35	18
Ronson, Tod, Salinas*	.223	94	301	30	67	92	13	3	2	34	0	4	1	48	1	89	4	7
Royer, Stanley, Modesto	.252	127	476	54	120	183	28	1	11	69	2	2	1	58	3	132	3	2
Santana, Andres, San Jose†	.261	18	69	14	18	21	3	0	0	3	0	1	0	8	1	16	10	6
Savarino, William, Modesto*	.197	61	193	13	38	44	3	0	1	17	3	0	0	17	2	28	1	1
Senne, Michael, Salinas	.286	26	91	10	26	33	4	0	1	12	0	2	0	4	0	12	1	1
Shaw, Kerry, Salinas†	.241	128	461	54	111	151	12	8	4	43	2	2	2	44	2	72	14	9
Shevlin, James, Salinas	.264	31	87	7	23	25	2	0	0	6	2	0	0	12	0	21	0	1
Simmons, Enoch, Modesto	.000	2	5	0	0	0	0	0	0	0	0	0	0	0	0	2	0	0
Skeels, Andrew, Riverside*	.241	126	432	52	104	142	18	4	4	52	0	5	3	64	3	104	4	0
Smith, David, Visalia	.244	29	82	17	20	30	4	0	2	7	0	1	5	14	0	12	6	3
Smith, Robert, Stockton	.251	119	379	56	95	128	20	2	3	34	6	3	8	40	0	84	16	13
Snyder, Randall, Stockton†	.188	34	101	10	19	25	4	1	0	9	3	4	1	15	2	31	2	0
Sparks, Gregory, Salinas*	.258	108	356	38	92	145	24	1	9	54	0	5	1	44	4	92	1	5
Standiford, Mark, Salinas	.232	51	164	21	38	58	5	0	5	25	2	3	4	31	1	39	2	2
Stargell, Timothy, San Bernardino	.282	34	131	24	37	59	8	1	4	23	3	2	2	11	0	23	2	5
Sturdivant, David, Palm Springs*	.095	46	105	6	10	14	1	0	1	7	1	1	3	17	1	33	0	0
Suzuki, Yasu, Salinas	.187	111	327	22	61	72	3	1	2	19	7	2	1	16	0	70	5	9
Sveum, Dale, Stockton†	.186	11	43	5	8	11	0	0	1	5	0	1	0	6	1	14	0	0
Tartabull, Jose, San Bernardino	.236	69	263	34	62	80	4	4	2	26	3	1	0	29	0	29	5	6
Taylor, William C., Riverside†	.255	131	530	81	135	171	16	7	2	31	2	3	4	64	1	105	60	28
Teel, Garett, Bakersfield	.500	2	2	0	1	2	1	0	0	1	0	0	0	0	0	0	0	0
Teixeira, Vincent, 2 Vis-22 Sal.	.158	24	76	7	12	14	2	0	0	3	0	0	1	13	0	25	1	1
Thomas, Keith, Modesto*	.212	93	330	36	70	97	5	2	6	29	3	0	2	24	1	102	19	10
Threadgill, Christopher, P Springs	.159	62	164	18	26	30	2	1	0	9	2	1	1	24	1	54	2	3
Twitty, Douglas, Modesto	.233	12	43	4	10	14	4	0	0	3	1	0	1	3	0	14	1	0
Uribe, Jorge, San Bernardino	.261	56	161	21	42	69	6	3	5	19	1	0	0	18	0	41	4	9
Valdez, Frank, Visalia	.283	132	453	71	128	190	24	4	10	59	5	5	11	49	3	127	15	11
Valentin, Jose, Riverside†	.194	114	381	40	74	124	10	5	10	41	5	2	5	37	1	93	8	7
Velasquez, Guillermo, Riverside*	.279	139	544	73	152	213	30	2	9	69	0	10	2	51	4	91	4	3
Velez, Jose, Palm Springs	.213	38	122	9	26	36	7	0	1	14	0	0	0	9	0	33	0	2
Vice, Darryl, Modesto†	.184	78	255	24	47	56	9	0	0	8	8	0	5	45	1	51	3	5
Vidmar, Donald, Palm Springs*	.000	30	3	0	0	0	0	0	0	0	0	0	0	0	0	1	0	0
Villanueva, Juan, Riverside	.279	34	122	11	34	45	5	0	2	9	0	1	2	7	0	24	1	2
Weber, Weston, Modesto	.000	11	2	0	0	0	0	0	0	0	0	0	0	0	0	2	0	0
Webster, Leonard, Visalia	.268	63	231	36	62	84	7	0	5	39	0	5	1	27	1	27	2	1
Weiss, Walter, Modesto†	.375	5	8	1	3	3	0	0	0	1	0	1	1	4	0	1	0	0
Westbrook, Michael, Reno*	.253	112	403	57	102	122	12	1	2	31	7	2	0	39	0	55	27	16
Westbrooks, Elanis, San Jose	.231	82	247	24	57	76	10	3	1	23	1	3	2	15	1	50	13	11
White, Derrick, Bakersfield	.224	69	214	36	48	94	14	4	8	29	2	4	4	36	1	62	9	4
Whitney, Jeffrey, Reno	.000	28	3	0	0	0	0	0	0	0	1	0	0	0	0	2	0	0
Williams, Matthew, Salinas	.145	99	283	19	41	49	8	0	0	22	5	6	2	22	1	66	5	4
Witmeyer, Ronald, Modesto*	.204	134	457	54	93	141	22	1	8	43	5	4	4	70	1	101	5	1
Wong, Kaha, Reno	.264	74	227	33	60	74	14	0	0	18	0	2	0	26	0	46	3	3
Woods, Anthony, San Bernardino†	.216	105	269	32	58	74	10	3	0	31	4	5	1	35	0	47	16	12
Yamaguchi, Yuji, Salinas	.271	99	303	51	82	114	14	6	2	29	4	1	5	60	1	74	28	13
Yojo, Minoru, Visalia*	.209	64	158	23	33	39	4	1	0	14	0	3	1	17	0	37	0	0
Yoshinaga, Yoshi, Salinas*	.232	82	211	18	49	59	5	1	1	13	0	0	5	25	2	45	0	1

The following pitchers, listed alphabetically by club, with games in parentheses, had no plate appearances, primarily through use of designated hitters:

BAKERSFIELD—Bene, William (7); Biberdorf, Cameron (51); Bustillos, Albert (19); Calhoun, Raymond (15); Campbell, Kevin (31); Dawson, David (27); Gastelum, Macario (23); Hartsock, Jeffrey (26); James, Michael (27); Marquez, Isidro (17); Parham, William (10); Piscetta, Robert (43); Poole, James (1); Snedeker, Sean (22); Tapia, Jose (1); Tudor, John (1); Wengert, William (21); Wray, James (41).

MODESTO—Alexander, Robert (35); Baez, Pedro (33); Dye, Steven (48); Eskew, Daniel (15); Gorski, Gary (27); Green, Daryl (39); Guzeman, Johnny (5); Kopyta, Jeffrey (18); Lardizabal, Ruben (44); MacLeod, Kevin (9); McDonald, Kirk (25); Pena, Pedro (3); Perez, William (31); Richert, Peter (1); Slusarski, Joseph (27); Taylor, William E. (9); Towey, Steven (13); Veilleux, Brian (30); Young, Matthew (3).

PALM SPRINGS—Beasley, Christopher (10); Bisceglia, James (36); Bryan, Frank (10); DeJaynes, Paul (10); Graybill, David (12); Hernandez, Roberto (7); McCoy, Timothy (28); McGuire, Stephen (5); Morehouse, Richard (16); Mutz, Frank (15); Neal, David (24); Richardson, Jeffrey (24); Search, Michael (2); Townsend, James (29); Vann, Brandy (29).

RENO—Anderson, Michael (5); Bilello, John (11); Candelaria, Jorge (12); Carrasco, Carlos (28); Clark, Garry (24); Fortugno, Timothy (5); Hayes, Christopher (1); Johnson, Ranfred (1); Johnson, Sean (2); Malone, Rubio (38); Maye, Stephen (13); Odekirk, Richard (4); Strong, Joseph (53); Sullivan, Brian (24); Villanueva, Gilbert (19); Warren, Michael (33); Wheeler, Bradley (5).

RIVERSIDE—Estrada, Jay (42); Gollehon, Christopher (4); Harrison, Brian (43); Hernandez, Jeremy (9); Lewis, Anthony (29); Lifgren, Kelly (20); Loubier, Stephen (11); McKeon, Brian (1); Soltero, Saul (15); Valdez, Rafael (21); Young, Michael (11).

SALINAS—Adriance, Daniel (9); Anderson, Michael (13); Bunner, James (4); Cantrell, David (32); Carter, Larry (9); Chikida, Honen (41); Gay, Scott (9); Horan, David (23); Johnson, Dominick (17); Kaseda, Yuki (33); Messer, Douglas (27); Nelson, Scott (7); Page, Gregory (14); Pena, James (8); Taguchi, Shigeki (63); Velasquez, Raymond (66); Vuz, John (21).

SAN BERNARDINO—Ambos, William (33); Balabon, Richard (27); Baldwin, Brian (28); Blueberg, James (22); Evers, Troy (27); Felix, Nicholas (4); Goff, Michael (43); Hancock, Leland (26); Jones, Calvin (5); Newlin, James (19); Poissant, Rodney (4); Rivas, Oscar (8); Runge, Scott (38); Ryan, Jody (11); Stange, Kurt (20); Swift, William (2).

SAN JOSE—Beck, Rodney (13); Brock, Don (31); Brummett, Gregory (2); Buffolino, Rocco (25); Dewey, Mark (59); Downs, Kelly (1); Dravecky, David (2); Fye, Christopher (14); Hickerson, Bryan (21); Hostetler, Thomas (16); Lienhard, Stephen (31); Meier, Kevin (19); Pena, James (16); Phillips, Lane (10); Reed, Steve (2); Sharko, Gary (13); Terrill, James (55); Vuz, John (7).

STOCKTON—Ambrose, Mark (25); Austin, James (8); Cangemi, Jamie (26); Ciszkowski, Jeffrey (2); Derksen, Robert (4); Drahman, Brian (12); Durant, Richard (24); Elvira, Narciso (17); Fleming, Keith (11); Fortugno, Timothy (13); George, Christopher (55); Henry, Douglas (4); Hetrick, Kent (13); Ignasiak, Michael (28); Lane, Heath (11); Monson, Steven (6); Moraw, Carl (13); Perez, Leonardo (5); Shibata, Keith (14); Sparks, Steven (23); Watts, Robert (24).

VISALIA—Ard, John (28); Banks, Willie (27); Brinkman, Gregory (6); Erickson, Scott (12); McClure, LaRue (1); Meyer, Basil (58); North, Mark (8); Sagawa, Kivoshi (15); Simons, Douglas (14); Stowell, Steven (58); Strube, Robert (12); Swanson, Chad (30); Townsend, Howard (29); Trombley, Michael (6); Tsamis, George (15); Wassenaar, Robert (28); White, Frederick (30).

GRAND SLAM HOME RUNS—Hartsock, Valdez, 2 each; Balfanz, Barton, Brown, Dotzler, Ealy, R. Gonzalez, Hillman, Humphreys, Lutticken, 1 each.

AWARDED FIRST BASE ON CATCHER'S INTERFERENCE—W. Lee 4 (Campanis 3, Nilsson); Bigham 3 (Marquez, Oedewaldt, Rice); Bluhm (Williams); Gilbert (Skeels); M. McDonald (Oedewaldt); Stargell (Gay).

CLUB FIELDING

Club	Pct.	G.	PO.	A.	E.	DP.	PB.	Club	Pct.	G.	PO.	A.	E.	DP.	PB.
Stockton	.969	142	3783	1472	166	113	27	Salinas	.961	142	3627	1471	205	149	30
Visalia	.966	142	3730	1590	185	144	34	Bakersfield	.961	142	3782	1523	218	115	35
San Bernardino	.964	142	3764	1558	196	147	38	San Jose	.960	142	3719	1518	217	140	22
Modesto	.963	142	3751	1489	200	131	16	Palm Springs	.959	142	3644	1623	226	145	36
Riverside	.962	142	3759	1378	202	138	26	Reno	.955	142	3603	1455	237	135	26

Triple Play—Salinas.

INDIVIDUAL FIELDING
*Throws lefthanded.
FIRST BASEMEN

Player and Club	Pct.	G.	PO.	A.	E.	DP.	Player and Club	Pct.	G.	PO.	A.	E.	DP.
Alfonzo, Palm Springs	1.000	2	1	1	0	0	Marzan, Visalia	.988	126	1063	81	14	106
Ayrault, Reno	1.000	1	9	1	0	2	Masteller, Visalia*	1.000	1	5	2	0	1
Balfanz, Reno	.971	18	152	13	5	9	McBride, Visalia	1.000	1	6	0	0	0
Bluhm, Reno	1.000	2	14	0	0	3	McCollom, Palm Springs	1.000	7	53	7	0	3
Borg, Stockton*	.984	18	168	12	3	13	M. McDonald, San Bernardino	.979	6	45	2	1	3
Brady, 11 Sal.-1 SJ	.961	12	70	3	3	6	T. McDonald, San Jose	1.000	7	50	4	0	4
Campanis, San Bernardino	.977	6	36	6	1	4	McNamara, Salinas	1.000	7	32	2	0	3
Carlson, San Jose	.981	55	473	33	10	52	Molina, Palm Springs*	.958	3	21	2	1	4
Carr, Bakersfield	1.000	2	9	1	0	0	Morales, San Bernardino	1.000	1	1	0	0	0
Decker, San Jose	.972	5	32	3	1	3	ORTEGON, Palm Springs*	.9932	108	952	70	7	95
Dotzler, Visalia	.989	12	79	10	1	9	Ortiz, Modesto	1.000	3	31	1	0	3
Duffin, San Bernardino	.953	13	60	1	3	2	Rodriguez, Bakersfield*	1.000	1	8	0	0	0
Finken, Bakersfield	1.000	2	4	0	0	1	Ronson, Salinas	1.000	2	3	0	0	0
Franklin, Salinas	.957	4	19	3	1	2	Savarino, Modesto	.895	2	17	0	2	0
Goins, San Jose	.992	79	704	41	6	65	Shaw, Salinas	.984	26	172	13	3	18
Gonzalez, San Bernardino	.987	129	1172	77	16	123	Smith, Visalia	.917	3	11	0	1	3
Hahn, Salinas	.972	5	31	4	1	3	Sparks, Salinas*	.978	69	521	49	13	70
Hall, Riverside	.961	5	44	5	2	4	Velazquez, Riverside	.984	135	1073	95	19	115
Harper, Reno*	.987	116	951	79	14	100	Velez, Palm Springs	.981	29	244	16	5	32
Hillman, Modesto	.978	10	84	5	2	5	Williams, Salinas	.992	36	220	34	2	22
Humphreys, Riverside	1.000	1	2	0	0	1	Witmeyer, Modesto	.989	130	1111	100	13	103
Jaha, Stockton	.9930	126	1081	61	8	88	Wong, Reno	1.000	6	49	1	0	5
Karros, Bakersfield	.988	139	1232	110	16	105	Yojo, Visalia	1.000	18	103	9	0	11
Lutticken, Riverside	1.000	2	17	2	0	0	Yoshinaga, Salinas	.967	13	54	4	2	5
Martinez, Palm Springs	1.000	1	4	1	0	1							

Triple Play—Franklin.

SECOND BASEMEN

Player and Club	Pct.	G.	PO.	A.	E.	DP.	Player and Club	Pct.	G.	PO.	A.	E.	DP.
Alfonzo, Palm Springs	.989	15	31	57	1	17	W. Lee, Palm Springs	.966	129	285	392	24	93
Barton, Reno	.956	64	127	154	13	38	Listach, Stockton	.967	83	179	229	14	40
Beals, Bakersfield	1.000	2	1	5	0	0	Martin, Reno	.900	4	10	8	2	4
Bigham, Riverside	.966	130	241	301	19	75	Martinez, Palm Springs	1.000	2	0	3	0	0
Bluhm, Reno	.889	2	3	5	1	1	Matos, Modesto	.923	5	4	8	1	3
Bosco, Reno	.833	16	24	31	11	10	Meredith, Reno	.961	19	52	46	4	13
Brocki, San Bernardino	.985	84	176	225	6	59	Mims, Riverside	.980	8	23	27	1	7
Brooks, Riverside	1.000	4	7	9	0	0	Montoyo, Stockton	.984	40	75	109	3	22
CAPELLAN, Visalia	.970	125	267	347	19	84	Nilsson, Stockton	1.000	1	2	1	0	1
Carr, Bakersfield	1.000	2	4	3	0	0	Ozawa, Visalia	.667	6	1	1	1	0
Carrasco, 13 Reno-2 PS	.917	15	30	36	6	7	Pimental, Salinas	.967	43	97	106	7	36
Correia, Modesto	.954	47	92	95	9	17	Preston, Stockton	1.000	8	15	14	0	3
Finken, Bakersfield	.987	17	29	49	1	8	Pye, Bakersfield	.955	124	215	360	27	77
Foster, Stockton	.924	19	21	40	5	5	Robinson, Modesto	.915	18	49	48	9	11
Fraticelli, Visalia	.981	22	37	65	2	15	Shaw, Salinas	1.000	1	1	1	0	0
Furcal, Modesto	.943	8	10	23	2	4	Shevlin, Salinas	.909	4	6	4	1	1
Goins, San Jose	.969	6	12	19	1	3	Standiford, Salinas	.943	28	66	50	7	14
Gray, Salinas	.900	4	7	2	1	1	Stargell, San Bernardino	.933	28	49	76	9	19
Guerrero, San Jose	.926	13	21	29	4	3	Tartabull, San Bernardino	1.000	1	1	1	0	0
Haney, San Bernardino	.976	25	47	74	3	14	Teixeira, Salinas	.988	22	43	40	1	5
Hecht, Salinas	.949	124	253	382	34	88	Vice, Modesto	.970	76	160	222	12	43
Hill, San Bernardino	.882	7	9	6	2	1	Villanueva, Riverside	1.000	3	3	4	0	1
Kaiser, Salinas	.946	36	67	55	7	17	Westbrook, Reno	.926	30	61	64	10	6
Kuoda, Salinas	.986	23	29	41	1	14	Woods, San Bernardino	.976	7	15	26	1	7
G. Lee, Salinas	.952	9	21	19	2	5							

THIRD BASEMEN

Player and Club	Pct.	G.	PO.	A.	E.	DP.	Player and Club	Pct.	G.	PO.	A.	E.	DP.
Alfonzo, Palm Springs	.928	40	32	97	10	8	Foster, Stockton	.875	8	2	12	2	1
Balfanz, Reno	.895	82	67	155	26	19	Franklin, Salinas	.667	6	2	2	2	0
Barton, Reno	.900	10	8	19	3	1	Goins, San Jose	.831	26	14	35	10	5
Bluhm, Reno	.848	19	10	18	5	4	J. Guerrero, San Jose	.911	82	60	145	20	15
Bosco, Reno	.935	22	24	48	5	2	M. Guerrero, Stockton	.937	24	14	45	4	7
Brady, Salinas	.931	40	38	56	7	12	Hahn, Salinas	.250	3	0	1	3	1
Brocki, San Bernardino	.915	24	26	39	6	3	Hill, San Bernardino	.893	62	43	133	21	11
J. Brooks, Bakersfield	.667	2	1	1	1	0	Hillman, Modesto	.500	2	1	1	2	0
M. Brooks, Riverside	.851	16	13	27	7	2	Humphreys, Riverside	1.000	1	0	1	0	0
Capellan, Visalia	.929	6	3	10	1	2	Jaha, Stockton	1.000	1	0	1	0	0
Carr, Bakersfield	.882	105	86	190	37	11	Jones, San Jose	.894	36	26	84	13	7
Carrasco, Palm Springs	.957	30	32	56	4	9	Kaiser, Salinas	.833	9	1	4	1	1
Cassels, Stockton	.878	90	62	118	25	15	Karros, Bakersfield	.750	3	6	3	3	0
Clark, Riverside	.914	125	96	214	29	25	Lutticken, Riverside	1.000	1	0	1	0	0
Correia, Modesto	.941	8	6	10	1	0	Martinez, Palm Springs	.883	76	48	163	28	19
Duffin, San Bernardino	.872	19	15	19	5	0	Marzan, Visalia	.889	4	0	8	1	3
Finken, Bakersfield	.903	36	30	63	10	5	Matos, Modesto	.918	19	14	42	5	2

THIRD BASEMEN—Continued

Player and Club	Pct.	G.	PO.	A.	E.	DP.	Player and Club	Pct.	G.	PO.	A.	E.	DP.
Meredith, Reno	.636	3	0	7	4	0	Standiford, Salinas	.901	32	24	40	7	4
Nilsson, Stockton	.909	26	21	59	8	6	Teixeira, Visalia	.667	1	0	2	1	0
Ozawa, Visalia	.400	2	0	2	3	0	Valdez, Visalia	.907	123	80	222	31	16
Pittenger, Visalia	1.000	12	12	20	0	2	Velez, Palm Springs	1.000	1	0	1	0	0
ROYER, Modesto	.933	114	99	220	23	19	Villanueva, Riverside	1.000	2	1	4	0	0
Savarino, Modesto	1.000	1	1	0	0	0	Wong, Reno	.878	15	13	30	6	3
Shaw, Salinas	.926	52	48	102	12	13	Woods, San Bernardino	.878	54	25	104	18	9
Shevlin, Salinas	.825	25	13	39	11	5							

SHORTSTOPS

Player and Club	Pct.	G.	PO.	A.	E.	DP.	Player and Club	Pct.	G.	PO.	A.	E.	DP.
Alfonzo, Palm Springs	1.000	2	0	1	0	0	Kaiser, Salinas	.939	54	68	148	14	31
Barton, Reno	.910	43	66	116	18	17	KING, San Bernardino	.955	135	213	424	30	100
Bluhm, Reno	.818	3	3	6	2	0	Knoblauch, Visalia	.882	18	23	52	10	8
Bosco, Reno	.939	98	169	265	28	66	Kuoda, Salinas	.952	100	136	265	20	55
Brady, Salinas	.500	1	1	0	1	0	Listach, Stockton	.928	46	71	122	15	24
Brooks, Riverside	1.000	4	4	9	0	2	L. Martinez, Bakersfield	.953	55	85	161	12	29
Capellan, Visalia	.933	4	6	8	1	1	R. Martinez, Palm Springs	.921	14	20	38	5	7
Carrasco, Palm Springs	1.000	2	0	3	0	0	Matos, Modesto	.876	37	54	87	20	21
Chimelis, Modesto	.917	68	107	179	26	37	Meredith, Reno	1.000	1	1	0	0	0
Clayton, San Jose	.939	28	53	71	8	20	Montoyo, Stockton	.965	83	118	215	12	31
Correia, Modesto	.949	39	59	90	8	24	Offerman, Bakersfield	.901	61	94	179	30	32
DeLaRosa, Palm Springs	.932	126	201	398	44	83	Ozawa, Visalia	1.000	2	0	3	0	0
Finken, Bakersfield	.908	24	43	56	10	17	Pye, Bakersfield	.762	6	5	11	5	2
Foster, Stockton	1.000	3	3	6	0	3	Santana, San Jose	.895	18	22	46	8	10
Furcal, Modesto	.912	10	14	17	3	5	Valentin, Riverside	.924	113	227	333	46	70
Gilbert, Visalia	.938	123	204	382	39	91	Villanueva, Riverside	.940	26	48	61	7	19
Goins, San Jose	1.000	1	2	1	0	1	Weiss, Modesto	1.000	5	6	9	0	5
Gray, Salinas	.750	1	4	2	2	2	Westbrooks, San Jose	1.000	1	0	2	0	0
Guerrero, Stockton	.940	22	36	58	6	7	Woods, San Bernardino	.952	18	16	24	2	1
Jones, San Jose	.910	96	153	261	41	57							

Triple Play—Kuoda.

OUTFIELDERS

Player and Club	Pct.	G.	PO.	A.	E.	DP.	Player and Club	Pct.	G.	PO.	A.	E.	DP.
Alfonzo, Palm Springs	.875	7	7	0	1	0	Malseed, San Jose	.974	106	182	9	5	1
Beals, Bakersfield	.927	25	33	5	3	1	Marabell, Bakersfield	1.000	1	3	0	0	0
Benoit, Salinas	.957	70	104	7	5	2	Marquez, Palm Springs	.973	19	35	1	1	1
Bluhm, Reno	.944	65	111	7	7	1	Martinez, Palm Springs	1.000	6	7	2	0	0
Boddie, Bakersfield	.955	77	119	7	6	2	Marzan, Visalia	1.000	2	3	0	0	0
Booth, San Jose	.500	4	1	0	1	0	Masteller, Visalia*	.948	39	53	2	3	0
Borg, Stockton*	.985	68	125	9	2	1	McBride, Visalia	.972	119	166	5	5	1
Bour, Reno	1.000	3	1	0	0	0	McCollom, Palm Springs	1.000	1	5	0	0	0
Brady, 84 Sal.-3 SJ	.971	87	193	8	6	0	M. McDonald, San Bernardino	.953	110	175	8	9	0
J. Brooks, Bakersfield	.963	138	246	15	10	3	T. McDonald, San Jose	.939	17	27	4	2	1
M. Brooks, Riverside	.982	28	52	4	1	2	McWilliam, Riverside	.976	109	239	4	6	3
Brown, Visalia	.981	141	291	16	6	7	Merchant, San Bernardino	.963	111	205	3	8	1
Capellan, Visalia	1.000	7	10	0	0	0	Meredith, Reno	.667	2	1	1	1	0
Carpenter, Reno	1.000	14	24	0	0	0	Miller, Bakersfield*	.968	17	28	2	1	0
Carr, Reno	.987	128	222	6	3	1	Mims, Riverside	1.000	1	2	0	0	1
Carter, Palm Springs	.971	50	95	5	3	2	Morrow, Bakersfield*	1.000	25	39	0	0	0
Castillo, Bakersfield	.956	125	232	9	11	3	Nalls, Reno	.954	115	153	13	8	1
Conner, San Jose	.971	26	29	5	1	3	Nina, Modesto*	.957	10	21	1	1	0
Cooper, San Jose	.977	104	246	13	6	2	Ortegon, Palm Springs*	1.000	5	5	0	0	0
Correia, Modesto	.933	13	26	2	2	0	Parry, Modesto	.993	77	131	8	1	0
Daughtry, San Bernardino	1.000	7	3	0	0	0	Pritikin, San Bernardino	.966	97	160	12	6	1
Ealy, San Jose	.952	109	171	7	9	2	Raley, Stockton	.951	114	169	5	9	1
Escalera, Stockton*	1.000	9	12	0	0	0	E. Rodriguez, Palm Springs	.830	30	42	2	9	1
K. Farmer, Riverside	.977	41	81	3	2	3	Romero, Palm Springs	.955	113	183	8	9	1
R. Farmer, Riverside*	.968	24	59	2	2	0	Ronson, Salinas	.981	86	143	8	3	2
Finken, Bakersfield	1.000	20	32	2	0	0	Savarino, Modesto	1.000	2	7	0	0	0
Franklin, Salinas	.800	11	22	2	6	1	Senne, Salinas	1.000	21	33	2	0	1
Fujimoto, Visalia	.935	40	41	2	3	0	Shaw, Salinas	1.000	1	1	0	0	0
Gavin, Modesto	.964	54	101	5	4	1	Shevlin, Salinas	1.000	1	1	0	0	0
Giles, Palm Springs	.965	50	77	6	3	0	D. Smith, Visalia	1.000	12	19	2	0	0
Graves, Palm Springs	.970	68	159	4	5	0	R. Smith, Stockton	.980	115	188	12	4	2
Gray, Salinas	1.000	4	3	0	0	0	Sparks, Salinas*	1.000	8	11	0	0	0
Grilione, Bakersfield	1.000	4	4	0	0	0	Suzuki, Salinas	.956	97	172	2	8	1
Hall, Riverside	1.000	3	3	1	0	0	Tartabull, San Bernardino	.989	52	85	7	1	2
Hartsock, Reno	.949	38	56	0	3	0	Taylor, Riverside	.964	117	182	7	7	1
Hillman, Modesto	.971	51	67	1	2	0	Thomas, Modesto	.929	81	124	7	10	1
Hirtensteiner, Palm Springs*	.975	36	75	3	2	1	Threadgill, Palm Springs	.940	57	73	6	5	1
Humphreys, Riverside	.974	116	249	9	7	3	Twitty, Modesto	.947	12	17	1	1	0
Jacas, Visalia	.956	77	121	9	6	2	Uribe, San Bernardino	.988	43	76	7	1	4
J. Jones, San Jose	.900	3	9	0	1	0	Westbrook, Reno	.963	80	146	8	6	3
R. JONES, Stockton	.988	126	233	5	3	1	Westbrooks, San Jose	.967	67	138	7	5	2
Kating, Modesto	1.000	5	9	0	0	0	White, Bakersfield	.933	24	27	1	2	0
Kemp, Modesto*	1.000	9	13	0	0	0	Woods, San Bernardino	1.000	8	19	0	0	0
Kosco, San Bernardino	.898	32	48	5	6	0	Yamaguchi, Salinas	.963	89	149	7	6	2
Lewis, Modesto	.985	126	311	6	5	2	Yojo, Visalia	.960	16	22	2	1	1

CATCHERS

Player and Club	Pct.	G.	PO.	A.	E.	DP.	PB.	Player and Club	Pct.	G.	PO.	A.	E.	DP.	PB.
Barbara, San Bernardino	.986	20	64	4	1	1	1	Fernandez, San Jose	.997	48	264	32	1	4	8
Brito, Modesto	.991	15	97	16	1	3	4	Flippo, Bakersfield	.975	19	112	6	3	0	4
Campanis, San Bernardino	.982	120	770	87	16	6	34	Gay, Palm Springs	.953	28	151	13	8	1	7
CARCIONE, Modesto	.990	86	526	67	6	7	7	Gonzalez, Bakersfield	.944	4	16	1	1	1	0
Decker, San Jose	.986	54	385	48	6	5	8	Hahn, Salinas	.985	14	59	6	1	1	2
Dominguez, Reno	.976	77	491	70	14	3	12	Ham, San Jose	.973	30	191	26	6	0	5
Dotzler, Visalia	.983	53	358	41	7	3	14	Hoffman, San Bernardino	1.000	6	21	2	0	0	1
Farmer, Riverside	1.000	12	66	8	0	1	1	Huebner, Bakersfield	.929	3	13	0	1	0	0

CATCHERS—Continued

Player and Club	Pct.	G.	PO.	A.	E.	DP.	PB.	Player and Club	Pct.	G.	PO.	A.	E.	DP.	PB.
Kmak, Reno	.990	65	459	60	5	4	10	Palma, Reno	1.000	1	2	0	0	0	2
Laya, Salinas	1.000	5	22	2	0	0	0	Resetar, Visalia	.982	42	295	37	6	2	15
Logan, Visalia	1.000	7	18	2	0	0	1	Rice, Bakersfield	.987	124	880	103	13	4	31
Lutticken, Riverside	.982	41	295	27	6	1	5	Rodriguez, Palm Springs	.985	43	230	31	4	1	14
Marabell, Bakersfield	1.000	6	26	1	0	0	0	Savarino, Modesto	.988	29	148	16	2	3	1
Marquez, Palm Springs	.961	41	261	32	12	0	6	Skeels, Riverside	.980	95	633	68	14	7	20
McGrew, Modesto	.959	6	43	4	2	1	1	Snyder, Stockton	.974	33	228	31	7	0	7
McNamara, 44 Sal.-18 SJ	.982	62	392	56	8	3	12	Sturdivant, Palm Springs	.976	42	227	20	6	1	9
Mercedes, Modesto	.957	15	81	9	4	2	3	Teel, Bakersfield	1.000	2	8	0	0	0	0
Morales, San Bernardino	1.000	35	108	2	0	0	2	Webster, Visalia	.990	51	352	57	4	5	4
Nilsson, Stockton	.983	88	701	65	13	6	13	Williams, Salinas	.988	63	343	55	5	7	12
Oedewaldt, Stockton	.983	27	200	25	4	1	7	Wong, Reno	1.000	4	17	3	0	0	2
Ortiz, Modesto	1.000	8	26	11	0	0	0	Yoshinaga, Salinas	.993	41	243	26	2	6	5

PITCHERS

Player and Club	Pct.	G.	PO.	A.	E.	DP.	Player and Club	Pct.	G.	PO.	A.	E.	DP.
Adriance, Salinas*	1.000	9	2	3	0	0	Hickerson, San Jose*	1.000	21	5	12	0	0
Alexander, Modesto	1.000	35	7	18	0	1	Horan, Salinas	.970	23	13	19	1	2
Alicea, Palm Springs	.875	30	1	6	1	1	Hostetler, San Jose	.917	16	3	8	1	0
Ambos, San Bernardino	1.000	33	4	18	0	1	Ignasiak, Stockton	.952	28	11	29	2	0
Ambrose, Stockton	.927	25	7	31	3	1	M. James, Bakersfield	.900	27	13	14	3	0
Anderson, 5 Reno-13 Salinas	.864	18	7	12	3	0	T. James, Palm Springs*	.500	11	1	0	1	0
Ard, Visalia	.957	28	18	26	2	3	D. Johnson, Salinas	.944	17	7	10	1	2
Austin, Stockton	1.000	7	3	8	0	0	R. Johnson, Reno	1.000	1	1	3	0	2
Ayrault, Reno	1.000	24	6	12	0	2	Jones, San Bernardino	1.000	5	3	1	0	2
Baez, Modesto	.895	33	7	10	2	0	Kaseda, Salinas*	.951	33	7	32	2	4
Balabon, San Bernardino	.784	22	8	32	11	2	Kopyta, Modesto	.900	18	4	5	1	0
Baldwin, San Bernardino	1.000	28	2	6	0	1	Lane, Stockton	.900	11	4	5	1	0
Banks, Visalia	.821	27	14	18	7	3	Lardizabal, Modesto	1.000	4	1	1	0	0
Beasley, Palm Springs	.966	10	7	21	1	1	Lewis, Riverside	.821	29	7	16	5	4
Beck, San Jose	.958	13	5	18	1	2	Lienhard, San Jose	.938	31	10	35	3	5
Bene, Bakersfield	.667	7	1	1	1	0	Lifgren, Riverside	.875	20	10	11	3	0
Biberdorf, Bakersfield	.958	51	7	16	1	0	Loubier, Riverside	.909	11	9	11	2	2
Bilello, Reno	.846	11	8	3	2	2	Lutticken, Riverside	1.000	3	1	0	0	0
Bisceglia, Palm Springs*	1.000	36	0	3	0	0	MacLeod, Modesto*	1.000	9	0	8	0	0
Blueberg, San Bernardino	.781	22	12	13	7	0	Malone, Reno	.917	38	4	18	2	2
Brady, Salinas	1.000	3	1	1	0	0	Marquez, Bakersfield	1.000	17	5	12	0	0
Brinkman, Visalia	1.000	6	1	3	0	0	Marx, Riverside	1.000	29	15	20	0	1
Brock, San Jose	1.000	31	3	14	0	1	Maye, Reno	.938	13	4	11	1	2
Brummett, San Jose	1.000	2	2	3	0	0	McCoy, Palm Springs*	.878	28	12	31	6	0
Bryan, Palm Springs	1.000	10	3	2	0	0	McDonald, Modesto	.846	25	6	16	4	2
Buffolino, San Jose	1.000	25	2	6	0	1	McGuire, Palm Springs	.857	5	0	6	1	0
Bunner, Salinas	1.000	4	0	1	0	1	Meier, San Jose	1.000	19	6	17	0	0
Burlingame, San Bernardino*	.941	31	9	23	2	3	Messer, Salinas*	.875	26	3	25	4	3
Bustillos, Bakersfield	1.000	19	23	14	0	2	Meyer, Visalia	.920	58	5	18	2	1
Calhoun, Bakersfield	.875	15	4	3	1	0	Monson, Stockton	1.000	6	1	5	0	1
Campbell, Bakersfield	.955	31	9	12	1	0	Moraw, Stockton	1.000	13	0	3	0	0
Candelaria, Reno	.950	12	9	10	1	1	Morehouse, Palm Springs	.889	16	7	17	3	0
Cangemi, Stockton	1.000	26	3	9	0	0	Mutz, Palm Springs	1.000	15	2	4	0	1
Cantrell, Salinas	.828	32	10	14	5	2	Neal, Palm Springs*	.828	24	4	20	5	2
Carrasco, Reno	.867	28	6	20	4	0	Nelson, Salinas*	.625	7	0	10	6	1
L. Carter, Salinas	1.000	9	4	16	0	1	Newlin, San Bernardino	.909	19	6	4	1	0
R. Carter, San Bernardino	1.000	13	0	2	0	1	North, Visalia	1.000	8	2	14	0	1
Chikida, Salinas*	.857	41	7	5	2	2	Odekirk, Reno*	1.000	4	3	3	0	0
Clark, Reno	.867	24	9	17	4	2	Ohnoutka, Riverside	.810	18	7	10	4	0
Dawson, Bakersfield	.909	27	5	15	2	1	Page, Salinas	1.000	14	5	9	0	2
DeJaynes, Palm Springs	1.000	10	2	2	0	0	Parham, Bakersfield	1.000	10	0	7	0	0
Derksen, Stockton	1.000	4	1	1	0	0	J. Pena, 8 Sal-16 SJ*	.969	24	4	27	1	2
Dewey, San Jose	1.000	59	6	13	0	0	P. Pena, Modesto	.833	3	0	5	1	0
Downs, San Jose	1.000	1	0	1	0	0	L. Perez, Stockton	1.000	5	1	6	0	0
Drahman, Stockton	1.000	12	1	3	0	0	W. Perez, Modesto	1.000	31	2	10	0	2
Dravecky, San Jose*	1.000	2	2	4	0	1	Phillips, San Jose	.941	10	7	9	1	1
Durant, Stockton	1.000	20	1	3	0	1	Piscetta, Bakersfield	.867	43	4	9	2	1
Dye, Modesto	.964	48	7	20	1	5	Reichle, Riverside	1.000	26	7	12	0	0
Elvira, Stockton*	.944	17	6	28	2	0	Richardson, Palm Springs	1.000	24	6	5	0	0
Erickson, Visalia	.957	12	10	12	1	1	Rivas, San Bernardino*	.000	8	0	0	1	0
Eskew, Modesto	.933	15	6	8	1	1	Runge, San Bernardino	.875	38	2	5	1	1
Estrada, Riverside	.762	42	6	10	5	1	Ryan, San Bernardino	1.000	11	0	2	0	0
Evers, San Bernardino	1.000	27	8	21	0	3	Sagawa, Visalia	1.000	15	0	2	0	0
Farmer, Riverside	1.000	1	1	0	0	0	Search, Palm Springs*	1.000	2	0	1	0	0
Felix, San Bernardino*	1.000	4	0	2	0	0	Sharko, San Jose	1.000	13	1	2	0	0
Fleming, Stockton	1.000	11	1	8	0	2	Shibata, Stockton*	1.000	14	0	8	0	0
Fortugno, 5 Reno-13 Stock*	.647	18	1	10	6	0	Simons, Visalia	1.000	14	5	9	0	0
Fye, San Jose*	1.000	14	4	14	0	1	Slusarski, Modesto	.906	27	5	24	3	1
Gastelum, Bakersfield	.875	23	2	5	1	0	Snedeker, Bakersfield	.971	22	11	22	1	1
Gay, Salinas	1.000	9	3	13	0	1	Soltero, Riverside	1.000	15	2	5	0	0
George, Salinas	.889	55	2	14	2	0	S. Sparks, Modesto	.897	23	10	25	4	1
Goff, San Bernardino	1.000	43	2	7	0	0	Stange, San Bernardino	.958	20	9	14	1	2
Gollehon, Riverside	1.000	4	1	0	0	0	Stowell, Modesto	1.000	58	0	11	0	1
Gorski, Modesto	.938	24	19	11	2	0	Strong, Reno	.813	53	4	9	3	1
Graybill, Palm Springs	.917	12	5	6	1	0	Strube, Visalia	1.000	12	0	5	0	0
Green, Modesto	.895	39	8	9	2	3	Sullivan, Reno*	.947	24	5	13	1	0
Guzeman, Modesto*	.667	5	1	1	1	0	Swanson, Visalia	1.000	30	6	5	0	1
HANCOCK, San Bernardino*	1.000	26	15	32	0	4	Swift, San Bernardino	1.000	2	1	2	0	0
Hansen, Riverside	.927	28	12	26	3	3	Taguchi, Salinas*	.923	63	3	21	2	1
Harrison, Riverside*	.875	42	3	11	2	0	Tapia, Salinas	1.000	1	0	1	0	0
Hartsock, Bakersfield	1.000	26	19	24	0	0	Taylor, Modesto	1.000	9	0	1	0	0
Henry, Stockton	1.000	4	1	0	0	1	Terrill, San Jose*	.840	55	4	17	4	1
J. Hernandez, Riverside	1.000	9	6	3	0	0	Towey, Modesto	1.000	13	2	4	0	0
R. Hernandez, Palm Springs	.900	7	3	6	1	0	H. Townsend, Visalia*	1.000	29	2	7	0	0
Hetrick, Stockton	.833	13	3	12	3	0	J. Townsend, Palm Springs*	.769	29	0	10	3	2

PITCHERS—Continued

Player and Club	Pct.	G.	PO.	A.	E.	DP.	Player and Club	Pct.	G.	PO.	A.	E.	DP.
Trombley, Visalia	1.000	6	3	12	0	2	Wassenaar, Visalia	.938	28	4	11	1	3
Tsamis, Visalia*	.909	15	7	23	3	1	Watts, Stockton	1.000	24	3	16	0	1
Tudor, Bakersfield*	1.000	1	0	4	0	1	Weber, Modesto	.944	11	3	14	1	1
Valdez, Riverside	.958	21	11	12	1	2	Wengert, Bakersfield	.846	21	5	6	2	0
Vann, Palm Springs	.917	29	10	23	3	2	Wheeler, Reno*	1.000	5	3	3	0	2
Veilleux, Modesto*	.875	30	5	9	2	0	White, Visalia	.864	29	4	15	3	0
Velasquez, Salinas	.864	66	4	15	3	3	Whitney, Reno	.935	28	8	21	2	3
Vidmar, Palm Springs	.952	30	22	18	2	3	Wray, Bakersfield	1.000	41	4	14	0	0
Villanueva, Reno*	.929	19	2	11	1	0	Ma. Young, Modesto*	1.000	3	1	2	0	0
Vuz, 21 Sal-7 SJ	.889	28	4	12	2	2	Mi. Young, Riverside*	.750	11	1	5	2	0
Warren, Reno	.933	33	6	22	2	2							

The following players did not have any fielding statistics at the positions indicated or appeared only as a designated hitter, pinch-hitter or pinch-runner: Alfonzo, c, p; Bluhm, p; Borg, p; M. Brooks, p; Capellan, p; Carlson, of; E. Carr, p; Cassels, of; Ciszkowski, p; Clark, 2b; Dominguez, 3b; Duffin, of; Hayes, p; S. Johnson, p; Laya, 1b; Listach, 3b; Malseed, p; McClure, p; McKeon, p; Montoyo, 3b; Ortegon, p; Pimental, ss; Poissant, p; Poole, p; Reed, p; Richert, p; H. Rodriguez, of; Ronson, 3b, p; Simmons, dh; Skeels, of, p; G. Sparks, p; Sturdivant, p; Sveum, dh; Vidmar, 1b; Villanueva, of; Williams, 3b, p; Yoshinaga, of.

CLUB PITCHING

Club	ERA.	G.	CG.	ShO.	Sv.	IP.	H.	R.	ER.	HR.	HB.	BB.	Int. BB.	SO.	WP.	Bk.
Stockton	2.77	142	17	20	44	1261.0	1029	496	388	41	52	555	17	1114	74	14
San Jose	2.82	142	20	19	41	1239.2	1094	498	389	53	29	445	8	934	59	15
San Bernardino	2.95	142	23	11	34	1254.2	1088	547	411	76	66	461	20	946	68	14
Bakersfield	3.38	142	11	9	46	1260.2	1110	605	473	58	36	573	12	1013	77	14
Visalia	3.37	142	21	13	24	1243.1	1130	600	466	78	54	543	16	1026	102	20
Riverside	3.46	142	26	13	27	1253.0	1100	599	482	49	55	544	14	963	83	31
Modesto	3.69	142	7	5	34	1250.1	1182	636	512	78	43	530	15	887	94	26
Palm Springs	3.68	142	26	6	23	1214.2	1244	654	497	51	70	466	5	824	73	17
Reno	3.84	142	28	7	21	1201.0	1188	673	512	79	79	520	25	941	71	43
Salinas	4.07	142	12	8	30	1209.0	1096	665	547	61	58	717	38	897	124	24

PITCHERS' RECORDS
(Leading Qualifiers for Earned-Run Average Leadership — 114 or More Innings)

*Throws lefthanded.

Pitcher—Club	W.	L.	Pct.	ERA.	G.	GS.	CG.	GF.	ShO.	Sv.	IP.	H.	R.	ER.	HR.	HB.	BB.	Int. BB.	SO.	WP.
Lienhard, San Jose	12	3	.800	1.79	31	17	5	5	3	3	156.0	122	41	31	3	3	32	0	89	4
Blueberg, San Bernardino	11	6	.647	2.12	22	22	6	0	3	0	148.2	98	50	35	8	5	48	1	135	10
Meier, San Jose	11	6	.647	2.24	19	19	5	0	4	0	140.1	110	43	35	5	2	32	0	95	3
Valdez, Riverside	10	5	.667	2.26	21	21	5	0	3	0	143.1	89	40	36	4	4	58	1	137	6
S. Sparks, Stockton	13	5	.722	2.41	23	22	3	0	2	0	164.0	125	55	44	6	10	53	0	126	6
Whitney, Reno	9	7	.563	2.50	28	17	9	7	2	1	151.0	145	58	42	14	1	26	1	88	6
Hickerson, San Jose*	11	6	.647	2.55	21	21	1	0	1	0	134.0	111	52	38	1	1	57	0	110	3
Balabon, San Bernardino	10	6	.625	2.57	22	22	2	0	0	0	157.2	142	58	45	9	5	41	2	129	11
Ambrose, Stockton	11	5	.688	2.58	25	25	3	0	0	0	153.1	140	53	44	3	3	69	0	121	8
Banks, Visalia	12	9	.571	2.59	27	27	7	0	4	0	174.0	122	70	50	5	10	85	0	173	22

Departmental Leaders: G—Velasquez, 66; W—Ard, Slusarski, S. Sparks, 13; L—Neal, 16; Pct.—Beck, .846; GS—Ard, Hansen, Ignasiak, 28; CG—Whitney, 9; GF—Dewey, 57; ShO—Banks, Evers, Ignasiak, Meier, 4; Sv.—Dewey, 30; IP—Hansen, 198.0; H—Vidmar, 194; R—Vann, 97; ER—Hansen, Vann, 79; HR—Slusarski, 15; HB—Candelaria, 15; BB—Reichle, 100; IBB—Velasquez, 9; SO—Banks, 173; WP—Banks, 22.

(All Pitchers—Listed Alphabetically)

Pitcher—Club	W.	L.	Pct.	ERA.	G.	GS.	CG.	GF.	ShO.	Sv.	IP.	H.	R.	ER.	HR.	HB.	BB.	Int. BB.	SO.	WP.
Adriance, Salinas*	0	1	.000	4.35	9	0	0	3	0	0	10.1	13	5	5	0	2	7	2	8	1
Alexander, Modesto	9	5	.643	3.01	35	8	1	14	1	1	104.2	96	41	35	7	1	29	0	84	6
Alfonzo, Palm Springs	0	0	.000	0.00	1	0	0	0	0	0	0.0	0	0	0	0	0	0	0	0	0
Alicea, Palm Springs	3	1	.750	2.11	30	1	0	19	0	7	59.2	53	20	14	1	2	9	1	51	0
Ambos, San Bernardino	6	1	.857	2.95	33	6	0	5	0	2	106.2	93	41	35	6	13	49	2	60	8
Ambrose, Stockton	11	5	.688	2.58	25	25	3	0	0	0	153.1	140	53	44	3	3	69	0	121	8
Anderson, 5 Reno-13 Sal.	0	8	.000	6.14	18	12	0	3	0	0	70.1	70	61	48	9	3	50	1	54	10
Ard, Visalia	13	7	.650	3.29	28	28	4	0	0	0	186.0	155	87	68	13	10	84	0	153	4
Austin, Stockton	3	3	.500	2.61	7	7	0	0	0	0	48.1	51	19	14	3	0	14	0	44	2
Ayrault, Reno	7	4	.636	3.78	24	14	3	5	1	0	109.2	104	56	46	7	11	57	3	91	3
Baez, Modesto	2	11	.154	4.64	33	14	0	6	0	1	116.1	120	80	60	11	1	54	0	76	7
Balabon, San Bernardino	10	6	.625	2.57	22	22	2	0	0	0	157.2	142	58	45	9	5	41	2	129	11
Baldwin, San Bernardino	1	3	.250	2.62	28	0	0	14	0	2	44.2	45	24	13	1	2	14	2	32	5
Banks, Visalia	12	9	.571	2.59	27	27	7	0	4	0	174.0	122	70	50	5	10	85	0	173	22
Beasley, Palm Springs	4	3	.571	2.66	10	10	3	0	0	0	71.0	60	31	21	1	8	18	0	44	5
Beck, San Jose	11	2	.846	2.40	13	13	4	0	0	0	97.1	91	29	26	5	1	26	0	88	2
Bene, Bakersfield	0	2	.000	11.48	7	5	0	2	0	0	13.1	14	20	17	1	2	29	0	11	8
Biberdorf, Bakersfield	8	6	.571	3.39	51	2	0	19	0	5	109.0	87	51	41	8	1	51	2	90	5
Bilello, Reno	1	7	.125	5.47	11	9	1	0	0	0	54.1	64	46	33	3	5	34	2	22	3
Bisceglia, Palm Springs*	1	4	.200	5.48	36	0	0	20	0	2	47.2	58	40	29	2	5	28	1	34	10
Blueberg, San Bernardino	11	6	.647	2.12	22	22	6	0	3	0	148.2	98	50	35	8	5	48	1	135	10
Bluhm, Reno	0	0	.000	0.00	1	0	0	0	0	0	2.1	4	2	0	0	0	2	0	1	0
Borg, Stockton*	0	0	.000	0.00	1	0	0	0	0	0	1.0	0	0	0	0	0	2	0	1	0
Brady, Salinas	0	0	.000	9.00	3	0	0	2	0	0	6.0	12	8	6	0	0	6	0	2	0
Brinkman, Visalia	0	1	.000	0.00	6	0	0	2	0	0	10.0	3	2	0	0	1	6	0	6	0
Brock, San Jose	2	3	.400	2.62	31	3	0	12	0	3	82.1	77	36	24	3	2	44	1	70	15
Brooks, Riverside	0	0	.000	3.00	1	0	0	0	0	0	3.0	5	1	1	0	1	2	0	3	0
Brummett, San Jose	0	1	.000	5.59	2	2	0	0	0	0	9.2	15	7	6	2	1	8	0	5	0
Bryan, Palm Springs	0	3	.000	3.10	10	0	0	6	0	0	20.1	18	10	7	2	0	5	0	12	1
Buffolino, San Jose	0	0	.000	2.47	25	1	0	14	0	0	47.1	43	15	13	3	2	12	0	37	1
Bunner, Salinas	0	0	.000	4.91	4	0	0	3	0	0	7.1	10	5	4	1	0	1	0	3	1
Burlingame, San Bernardino	7	4	.636	3.90	31	16	2	5	1	0	124.2	147	64	54	7	2	41	3	63	1
Bustillos, Bakersfield	8	4	.667	3.17	19	19	2	0	1	0	125.0	115	53	44	7	1	42	0	80	3
Calhoun, Bakersfield	1	0	1.000	3.09	15	1	0	4	0	0	32.0	32	14	11	1	0	18	0	24	0
Campbell, Bakersfield	5	3	.625	2.54	31	0	0	17	0	6	60.1	43	23	17	1	0	28	1	63	3
Candelaria, Reno	4	3	.571	4.40	12	11	1	0	0	0	71.2	62	45	35	3	15	42	0	66	8
Cangemi, Stockton	4	2	.667	3.00	26	5	0	9	0	4	78.0	63	35	26	3	5	43	2	63	2
Cantrell, Salinas	2	12	.143	5.03	32	15	0	6	0	1	96.2	99	67	54	3	6	59	2	37	11

Pitcher—Club	W.	L.	Pct.	ERA.	G.	GS.	CG.	GF.	ShO.	Sv.	IP.	H.	R.	ER.	HR.	HB.	BB.	Int. BB.	SO.	WP.
Capellan, Visalia	0	0	.000	0.00	1	0	0	1	0	0	0.2	0	0	0	0	0	0	0	0	0
Carr, Bakersfield	0	1	.000	18.00	1	0	0	1	0	0	1.0	1	2	2	0	0	2	1	1	1
Carrasco, Reno	6	6	.500	4.89	28	17	3	6	0	0	119.2	129	80	65	5	8	69	3	79	12
L. Carter, Salinas	6	2	.750	2.00	9	9	1	0	0	0	63.0	32	22	14	2	4	27	2	56	2
R. Carter, San Bernardino	0	1	.000	4.74	13	0	0	9	0	0	24.2	22	19	13	5	1	13	0	23	0
Chikida, Salinas*	2	3	.400	5.52	41	4	0	14	0	1	91.1	88	61	56	8	6	84	0	61	20
Ciszkowski, Stockton	0	1	.000	17.36	2	1	0	0	0	0	4.2	12	14	9	1	2	6	0	5	1
Clark, Reno	6	8	.429	2.16	24	10	2	4	0	1	96.0	103	42	23	6	2	18	4	70	2
Dawson, Bakersfield	4	7	.364	3.00	27	7	1	10	0	1	81.0	66	39	27	7	1	41	0	34	5
DeJaynes, Palm Springs	0	0	.000	2.40	10	0	0	8	0	1	15.0	11	5	4	2	0	2	0	8	0
Derksen, Stockton	0	0	.000	1.23	4	0	0	3	0	0	7.1	6	3	1	0	1	4	0	5	0
Dewey, San Jose	1	6	.143	3.15	59	0	0	57	0	30	68.2	62	35	24	2	7	23	5	60	3
Downs, San Jose	0	0	.000	0.00	1	1	0	0	0	0	5.0	1	0	0	0	0	4	0	7	0
Drahman, Stockton	3	2	.600	3.25	12	0	0	10	0	4	27.2	22	11	10	0	2	9	0	30	2
Dravecky, San Jose*	2	0	1.000	1.69	2	2	2	0	1	0	16.0	13	3	3	1	0	1	0	8	0
Durant, Stockton	4	2	.667	3.99	20	1	0	11	0	4	49.2	50	26	22	2	3	25	0	44	2
Dye, Modesto	1	12	.077	3.67	48	0	0	34	0	7	68.2	65	38	28	2	8	31	2	36	2
Elvira, Stockton*	8	5	.615	3.04	17	17	6	0	2	0	115.1	92	45	39	5	5	43	0	135	11
Erickson, Visalia	3	4	.429	2.97	12	12	2	0	0	0	78.2	79	29	26	3	0	22	0	59	3
Eskew, Modesto	3	5	.375	4.06	15	15	0	0	0	0	75.1	70	39	34	3	3	31	0	58	12
Estrada, Riverside	5	8	.385	2.97	42	0	0	39	0	11	66.2	73	29	22	4	2	18	2	56	3
Evers, San Bernardino	12	9	.571	3.69	27	27	4	0	4	0	166.0	170	80	68	11	8	43	3	112	3
Farmer, Riverside	0	1	.000	4.50	1	0	0	1	0	0	2.0	2	1	1	0	0	0	0	0	0
Felix, San Bernardino*	1	0	1.000	1.00	4	1	0	3	0	0	9.0	7	8	1	2	1	2	0	8	1
Fleming, Stockton	4	0	1.000	0.00	11	0	0	9	0	3	23.1	7	2	0	0	0	11	1	25	1
Fortugno, 5 Rno-13 Stk*	4	4	.500	1.97	18	7	1	3	0	1	68.2	37	26	15	2	7	40	3	90	4
Fye, San Jose*	4	7	.364	5.54	14	13	0	0	0	0	76.1	85	52	47	2	2	62	0	52	14
Gastelum, Bakersfield	2	1	.667	5.81	23	6	0	7	0	0	57.1	50	42	37	3	1	36	1	55	6
Gay, Salinas	3	2	.600	3.25	9	8	0	1	0	1	52.2	38	22	19	1	5	21	1	47	0
George, Stockton	7	7	.500	2.15	55	0	0	52	0	22	79.2	61	30	19	1	1	37	8	85	8
Goff, San Bernardino	2	3	.400	1.93	43	0	0	39	0	17	46.2	20	15	10	3	3	27	0	38	2
Gollehon, Riverside	0	0	.000	4.70	4	0	0	2	0	0	7.2	6	5	4	0	0	9	0	9	2
Gorski, Modesto	7	6	.538	3.91	24	21	1	0	0	0	135.2	134	72	59	12	4	48	2	75	14
Graybill, Palm Springs	7	2	.778	2.61	12	8	4	0	1	0	69.0	64	31	20	1	5	16	0	41	7
Green, Modesto	3	6	.333	3.10	39	11	0	22	0	13	104.2	83	46	36	8	1	49	2	80	6
Guzeman, Modesto*	0	2	.000	4.86	5	3	0	1	0	0	16.2	23	11	9	0	0	13	0	12	2
Hancock, San Bernardino*	12	7	.632	2.60	26	26	5	0	0	0	173.0	131	69	50	5	5	82	2	119	11
Hansen, Riverside	8	8	.500	3.59	28	28	7	0	2	0	198.0	187	89	79	13	4	71	2	113	7
Harrison, Riverside*	2	7	.222	4.18	42	2	0	28	0	10	71.0	69	42	33	3	4	43	4	81	9
Hartsock, Bakersfield	12	5	.706	2.63	26	26	5	0	2	0	164.0	123	64	48	5	4	62	0	146	11
Hayes, Reno	0	0	.000	54.00	1	0	0	0	0	0	0.1	2	2	2	1	0	0	0	0	0
Henry, Stockton	0	1	.000	0.00	4	3	0	0	0	0	11.0	9	4	0	0	0	3	0	9	0
J. Hernandez, Riverside	5	2	.714	1.75	9	9	4	0	1	0	67.0	55	17	13	2	4	11	0	65	2
R. Hernandez, Palm Springs	1	4	.200	4.64	7	7	0	0	0	0	42.2	49	27	22	2	2	16	0	33	4
Hetrick, Stockton	6	5	.545	3.48	13	11	1	0	1	0	67.1	58	30	26	1	2	38	1	70	9
Hickerson, San Jose*	11	6	.647	2.55	21	21	1	0	1	0	134.0	111	52	38	1	1	57	0	110	3
Horan, Salinas	4	12	.250	4.24	23	22	1	0	0	0	127.1	133	75	60	5	7	82	2	72	17
Hostetler, San Jose	9	4	.692	2.59	16	16	2	0	0	0	111.1	99	44	32	5	1	26	0	103	1
Ignasiak, Stockton	11	6	.647	2.72	28	28	4	0	0	0	179.0	140	67	54	4	5	97	0	142	12
M. James, Bakersfield	11	8	.579	3.78	27	27	1	0	1	0	159.2	144	82	67	11	12	78	1	127	13
T. James, Palm Springs*	2	1	.667	1.88	11	1	0	4	0	0	24.0	21	11	5	0	3	18	1	21	1
D. Johnson, Salinas	6	4	.600	3.81	17	14	1	1	0	0	87.1	75	42	37	4	5	63	0	60	15
R. Johnson, Reno	0	0	.000	9.00	1	0	0	1	0	0	2.0	3	2	2	0	0	3	0	0	0
S. Johnson, Reno*	0	0	.000	0.00	2	1	0	1	0	0	5.0	2	1	0	0	0	2	0	2	0
Jones, San Bernardino	2	0	1.000	0.73	5	0	0	4	0	1	12.1	8	1	1	0	0	7	0	15	0
Kaseda, Salinas*	10	8	.556	2.82	33	20	8	6	3	2	169.1	147	63	53	8	4	63	7	167	7
Kopyta, Modesto	2	3	.400	2.80	18	0	0	11	0	1	35.1	38	15	11	1	1	21	1	29	5
Lane, Stockton	0	1	.000	3.54	11	1	0	5	0	1	28.0	21	14	11	3	3	15	2	14	2
Lardizabal, Modesto	1	2	.333	5.64	4	4	0	0	0	0	22.1	32	14	14	2	0	4	0	10	0
Lewis, Riverside	4	6	.400	4.42	29	9	0	8	0	1	95.2	108	67	47	0	6	55	0	52	10
Lienhard, San Jose	12	3	.800	1.79	31	17	5	5	3	3	156.0	122	41	31	3	3	32	0	89	4
Lifgren, Riverside	5	11	.313	4.02	20	20	1	0	0	0	121.0	120	78	54	7	11	46	1	74	8
Loubier, Riverside	7	3	.700	1.55	11	11	4	0	1	0	87.1	51	24	15	1	3	26	0	55	2
Lutticken, Riverside	0	0	.000	0.00	3	0	0	3	0	0	4.0	3	0	0	0	0	1	0	4	1
MacLeod, Modesto*	0	3	.000	5.75	9	7	0	0	0	0	36.0	31	27	23	3	1	38	0	32	9
Malone, Reno*	6	3	.667	3.72	38	4	0	19	0	0	82.1	82	50	34	5	3	53	3	89	3
Malseed, San Jose	1	0	1.000	18.00	1	0	0	1	0	0	1.0	3	2	2	0	0	1	0	1	0
Marquez, Bakersfield	6	0	1.000	0.75	17	0	0	16	0	8	36.0	21	5	3	0	2	11	0	44	2
Marx, Riverside	4	12	.250	4.66	29	10	2	9	0	1	119.2	106	71	62	3	6	56	2	71	5
Maye, Reno	3	5	.375	4.21	13	6	2	4	0	0	57.2	59	28	27	3	6	13	0	39	0
McClure, Visalia	0	0	.000	6.00	1	0	0	1	0	1	3.0	4	2	2	0	0	3	0	4	0
McCoy, Palm Springs*	5	7	.417	3.16	28	15	2	9	0	3	122.1	119	54	43	3	4	44	0	112	6
McDonald, Modesto	2	6	.250	4.22	25	8	0	5	0	0	79.0	92	52	37	4	6	31	1	39	5
McGuire, Palm Springs	2	2	.500	3.55	5	5	1	0	0	0	33.0	39	19	13	5	2	10	0	19	0
McKeon, Riverside	0	0	.000	4.50	1	0	0	0	0	0	2.0	2	1	1	0	0	2	0	1	0
Meier, San Jose	11	6	.647	2.24	19	19	5	0	4	0	140.1	110	43	35	5	2	32	0	95	3
Messer, Salinas*	3	13	.188	4.26	26	20	0	1	0	0	114.0	118	72	54	4	4	64	3	70	5
Meyer, Visalia	3	8	.273	3.22	58	0	0	41	0	12	72.2	64	36	26	4	0	40	4	63	7
Monson, Stockton	3	2	.600	2.06	6	6	0	0	0	0	39.1	31	13	9	0	0	18	0	32	0
Moraw, Stockton	1	1	.500	1.85	13	0	0	7	0	1	24.1	15	6	5	0	0	11	0	24	0
Morehouse, Palm Springs	4	9	.308	3.20	16	16	4	0	1	0	112.1	113	53	40	8	3	41	1	61	4
Mutz, Palm Springs	0	2	.000	6.99	15	2	0	5	0	0	37.1	48	35	29	2	7	23	1	29	3
Neal, Palm Springs*	3	16	.158	5.53	24	23	0	0	0	0	123.2	141	92	76	3	4	92	0	76	12
Nelson, Salinas*	0	6	.000	10.50	7	6	0	0	0	0	24.0	30	35	28	2	1	32	2	9	10
Newlin, San Bernardino	1	2	.333	1.57	19	0	0	9	0	4	28.2	13	6	5	3	1	15	1	25	1
North, Visalia*	3	3	.500	3.93	8	8	0	0	0	0	50.1	58	33	22	2	6	18	1	33	2
Odekirk, Reno*	0	0	.000	2.38	4	1	0	1	0	0	11.1	9	3	3	1	1	4	1	6	0
Ohnoutka, Riverside	2	4	.333	3.90	18	5	0	9	0	0	64.2	62	33	28	4	3	19	2	48	2
Ortegon, Palm Springs*	0	0	.000	0.00	1	0	0	0	0	0	2.0	3	2	0	0	0	1	0	1	0
Page, Salinas	2	3	.400	3.28	14	3	0	9	0	1	35.2	29	16	13	4	0	12	0	24	1
Parham, Bakersfield	4	4	.500	5.01	10	10	0	0	0	0	50.1	56	34	28	1	2	23	1	31	2
J. Pena, 8 Sal-16 SJ*	7	12	.368	2.83	24	21	1	1	1	0	140.0	112	60	44	12	2	49	0	118	3

Pitcher—Club	W.	L.	Pct.	ERA.	G.	GS.	CG.	GF.	ShO.	Sv.	IP.	H.	R.	ER.	HR.	HB.	BB.	Int. BB.	SO.	WP.
P. Pena, Modesto	0	0	.000	6.48	3	0	0	1	0	0	8.1	7	8	6	0	1	7	0	5	3
L. Perez, Stockton	0	0	.000	4.09	5	5	0	0	0	0	22.0	18	10	10	1	2	5	0	18	0
W. Perez, Modesto	2	4	.333	3.36	31	0	0	21	0	7	56.1	48	24	21	6	0	33	5	37	3
Phillips, San Jose	4	5	.444	5.05	10	10	0	0	0	0	51.2	47	35	29	2	2	24	0	34	4
Piscetta, Bakersfield	5	5	.500	2.51	43	1	0	17	0	3	75.1	70	35	21	2	2	42	1	72	4
Poissant, San Bernardino	0	0	.000	1.50	4	0	0	3	0	1	6.0	3	2	1	0	2	2	0	7	0
Poole, Bakersfield*	0	0	.000	0.00	1	0	0	1	0	0	1.2	2	1	0	0	0	0	0	1	0
Reed, San Jose	0	0	.000	0.00	2	0	0	1	0	0	2.0	0	0	0	0	0	1	0	3	0
Reichle, Riverside	10	10	.500	4.15	26	26	3	0	1	0	149.2	121	81	69	5	4	100	0	158	19
Richardson, Palm Springs	4	2	.667	4.05	24	0	0	19	0	5	26.2	19	15	12	3	3	9	0	25	5
Richert, Modesto*	0	0	.000	0.00	1	0	0	1	0	0	1.0	0	0	0	0	0	0	0	1	0
Rivas, San Bernardino*	1	0	1.000	1.93	8	0	0	2	0	1	9.1	8	5	2	0	0	4	0	9	0
Ronson, Salinas	0	0	.000	9.00	1	0	0	0	0	0	2.0	2	2	2	1	0	2	0	3	0
Runge, San Bernardino	7	6	.538	2.40	38	0	0	31	0	8	60.0	43	25	16	5	1	26	3	62	4
Ryan, San Bernardino	1	0	1.000	4.32	11	0	0	3	0	0	16.2	18	11	8	3	3	3	1	10	0
Sagawa, Visalia	0	0	.000	7.59	15	0	0	9	0	0	21.1	27	18	18	3	3	22	0	19	6
Search, Palm Springs*	0	0	.000	0.00	2	0	0	2	0	1	3.1	1	1	0	0	0	0	0	0	0
Sharko, San Jose	0	1	.000	2.96	13	1	0	6	0	0	24.1	21	9	8	1	0	8	0	16	1
Shibata, Stockton*	3	0	1.000	1.78	14	1	0	6	0	1	35.1	22	11	7	4	0	11	0	30	2
Simons, Visalia*	6	2	.750	1.49	14	14	1	0	0	0	90.2	77	33	15	4	5	33	1	79	4
Skeels, Riverside	0	0	.000	0.00	1	0	0	1	0	0	2.0	0	0	0	0	0	0	0	1	0
Slusarski, Modesto	13	10	.565	3.18	27	27	4	0	1	0	184.0	155	78	65	15	8	50	0	160	13
Snedeker, Bakersfield	12	6	.667	3.37	22	22	2	0	0	0	139.0	132	67	52	4	3	45	1	112	4
Soltero, Riverside	2	0	1.000	0.00	15	0	0	12	0	4	25.1	15	0	0	1	5	0	0	22	1
G. Sparks, Salinas*	0	0	.000	0.00	2	0	0	2	0	0	2.0	2	0	0	0	1	0	1	0	0
S. Sparks, Stockton	13	5	.722	2.41	23	22	3	0	2	0	164.0	125	55	44	6	10	53	0	126	6
Stange, San Bernardino	8	11	.421	4.42	20	20	4	0	0	0	110.0	112	69	54	10	12	42	0	95	11
Stowell, Visalia*	7	5	.583	3.84	58	0	0	30	0	6	75.0	68	38	32	3	3	42	4	66	10
Strong, Reno	8	1	.889	3.58	53	0	0	47	0	18	73.0	62	35	29	4	3	22	2	79	2
Strube, Visalia*	3	3	.500	4.05	12	11	0	0	0	0	53.1	50	35	24	7	3	45	1	40	5
Sturdivant, Palm Springs	0	0	.000	0.00	1	0	0	1	0	0	1.0	1	0	0	0	0	0	0	1	0
Sullivan, Reno*	6	7	.462	2.57	24	13	4	6	1	0	98.0	89	43	28	2	3	33	0	91	4
Swanson, Visalia	4	1	.800	2.92	30	4	1	12	0	2	64.2	57	23	21	5	4	19	1	42	6
Swift, San Bernardino	1	0	1.000	0.00	2	0	0	0	0	0	10.0	8	0	0	0	0	2	0	4	0
Taguchi, Salinas*	5	7	.417	4.60	63	0	0	28	0	5	92.0	93	51	47	8	3	35	6	66	3
Tapia, Bakersfield	0	0	.000	18.00	1	0	0	1	0	0	1.0	2	2	2	0	1	0	0	2	0
Taylor, Modesto	2	0	1.000	2.92	9	0	0	8	0	2	12.1	13	4	4	1	1	7	0	15	0
Terrill, San Jose*	5	6	.455	2.86	55	1	0	26	0	5	72.1	75	32	23	3	2	23	2	55	4
Towey, Modesto	0	1	.000	5.68	13	2	0	2	0	0	25.1	16	16	16	2	3	17	0	19	1
H. Townsend, Visalia*	1	3	.250	2.28	29	0	0	7	0	0	43.1	36	13	11	2	0	17	0	45	2
J. Townsend, Palm Springs*	3	1	.750	2.50	29	0	0	19	0	3	54.0	47	26	15	0	5	28	0	42	1
Trombley, Visalia	2	2	.500	2.14	6	6	2	0	1	0	42.0	31	12	10	2	3	11	0	36	2
Tsamis, Visalia*	6	3	.667	3.05	15	13	3	1	0	0	94.1	85	36	32	10	2	34	0	87	9
Tudor, Bakersfield*	0	0	.000	1.35	1	1	0	0	0	0	6.2	4	2	1	0	2	0	0	6	0
Valdez, Riverside	10	5	.667	2.26	21	21	5	0	3	0	143.1	89	40	36	6	4	58	1	137	6
Vann, Palm Springs	11	14	.440	4.21	29	27	4	1	0	0	169.0	185	97	79	8	7	58	0	95	3
Veillleux, Modesto*	6	4	.600	3.09	30	8	0	9	0	2	87.1	90	38	30	0	1	27	1	57	1
Velasquez, Salinas	4	7	.364	4.26	66	0	0	50	0	15	82.1	68	42	39	1	5	66	9	101	8
Vidmar, Palm Springs	10	13	.435	3.39	30	26	8	3	2	0	180.2	194	85	68	8	10	48	0	119	11
Villanueva, Reno*	1	4	.200	6.62	19	7	0	5	0	0	50.1	54	44	37	3	4	42	0	30	10
Vuz, 21 Sal-7 SJ	6	2	.750	2.82	28	15	1	6	1	0	105.1	74	44	33	6	5	73	1	68	13
Warren, Reno	7	12	.368	4.57	33	18	2	7	0	1	132.0	132	81	67	13	13	59	4	112	11
Wassenaar, Visalia	6	7	.462	3.49	28	4	0	14	0	3	80.0	88	38	31	5	3	29	2	60	9
Watts, Stockton	6	4	.600	4.28	24	7	0	9	0	3	69.1	77	42	33	4	4	22	2	40	4
Weber, Modesto	3	6	.333	3.26	11	11	0	0	0	0	69.0	60	32	25	1	3	34	1	49	4
Wengert, Bakersfield	2	7	.222	4.73	21	15	0	0	0	0	91.1	104	59	48	7	4	44	0	66	7
Wheeler, Reno*	2	1	.667	3.74	5	4	0	1	0	0	21.2	24	10	9	2	2	12	0	12	1
White, Visalia	7	8	.467	6.79	29	15	1	2	1	0	103.1	126	95	78	10	2	48	1	59	11
Whitney, Reno	9	7	.563	2.50	28	17	9	7	2	1	151.0	145	58	42	14	1	26	1	88	6
Williams, Salinas	0	0	.000	0.00	1	0	0	0	0	0	1.0	1	0	0	0	0	0	0	1	0
Wray, Bakersfield*	2	1	.667	1.27	41	0	0	35	0	24	56.2	44	12	8	1	0	18	3	50	1
Ma. Young, Modesto*	0	0	.000	0.75	3	3	0	0	0	0	12.0	9	1	1	0	0	6	0	13	1
Mi. Young, Riverside*	0	1	.000	7.04	11	1	0	3	0	0	26	20	18	1	2	1	23	0	13	6

BALKS—Carrasco, 10; Marx, 8; Mi. Young, 7; Villanueva, 6; Candelaria, Hostetler, D. Johnson, H. Townsend, 5 each; Anderson, Ard, Balabon, R. Carter, Chikida, Erickson, Estrada, MacLeod, McCoy, Neal, J. Pena, Snedeker, Veilleux, Velasquez, 4 each; Alexander, Ambrose, Ayrault, Biberdorf, Fortugno, Graybill, Malone, McDonald, Tsamis, Whitney, 3 each; Bilello, Bisceglia, Cangemi, Cantrell, Durant, Eskew, George, Hancock, Hansen, Hartsock, Hayes, Hickerson, Jones, Kaseda, Lewis, Lifgren, Loubier, Reichle, Towey, Vuz, Warren, 2 each; Baez, Banks, Beasley, Beck, Blueberg, Bustillos, Derksen, Dye, Elvira, Gastelum, Gorski, Guzeman, Harrison, Hetrick, Ignasiak, Lardizabal, Lienhard, Maye, Messer, Nelson, Newlin, North, Ohnoutka, Parham, W. Perez, Piscetta, Richardson, Sharko, Simons, Slusarski, Strong, Strube, Taguchi, Terrill, J. Townsend, Vann, Weber, Wengert, Wheeler, 1 each.

COMBINATION SHUTOUTS—Hartsock-Campbell, Wengert-Campbell, Snedeker-Wray, Bustillos-Piscetta, James-Piscetta-Marquez, Bakersfield; Veilleux-Guzman, Green-Dye, Slusarski-Veilleux, Modesto; Beasley-Bryan, Vidmar-Townsend, Palm Springs; Ayrault-Warren-Strong, Sullivan-Strong, Villanueva-Strong, Reno; Valdez-Soltero-Harrison, Reichle-Marx, Reichle-Soltero, Valdez-Ohnoutka, Lifgren-Harrison, Riverside; Gay-Velasquez, Johnson-Page, Cantrell-Taguchi, Horan-Page, Salinas; Swift-Goff, Balabon-Baldwin-Burlingame-Goff, Hancock-Newlin, San Bernardino; Meier-Terrill, Hickerson-Lienhard-Terrill, Beck-Buffolino, Lienhard-Terrill, Hostetler-Dewey, Hickerson-Brock-Dewey, Meier-Buffolino-Dewey, Hickerson-Brock, Pena-Dewey, San Jose; Monson-Moraw, Ignasiak-Cangemi, Sparks-Durant, Hetrick-George, Ambrose-Durant, Ambrose-George, Hetrick-Fortugno-Cangemi, Austin-George, Sparks-Watts, Sparks-Drahman, Henry-Durant-George, Stockton; Ard-Townsend-Brinkman-Stowell, Strube-Wassenaar, Simons-Meyer, Banks-Meyer, Banks-Townsend-Meyer, Erickson-Stowell-Meyer, Erickson-Stowell, Visalia.

NO-HIT GAMES—Banks, Visalia, defeated Palm Springs, 1-0, May 24; Valdez, Riverside, defeated Reno, 2-0 (perfect game), July 20.

Carolina League

CLASS A

CHAMPIONSHIP WINNERS IN PREVIOUS YEARS

1945—Danville	.681	1962—Durham	.636	1974—Salem	.671
1946—Greensboro	.599	Wilson	.600	Salem	.582
Raleigh (2nd)†	.563	Kinston (2nd)†	.593	1975—Rocky Mount	.667
1947—Burlington	.613	1963—Kinston§	.538	Rocky Mount	.614
Raleigh (3rd)†	.574	Greensboro§	.590	1976—Winston-Salem	.618
1948—Raleigh	.592	Wilson (2nd)†	.535	Winston-Salem	.551
Martinsville (2nd)†	.570	1964—Kinston§	.572	1977—Lynchburg	.591
1949—Danville	.601	Winston-Salem§†	.590	Peninsula‡	.556
Burlington (4th)†	.500	1965—Peninsula§	.597	1978—Peninsula	.696
1950—Winston-Salem*	.693	Durham§	.580	Lynchburg‡	.614
1951—Durham	.600	Tidewater†	.528	1979—Winston-Salem a	.607
Wins-Salem (2nd)†	.583	1966—Kinston§	.547	1980—Peninsula‡	.714
1952—Raleigh	.581	Winston-Salem§	.586	Durham	.600
Reidsville (4th)†	.536	Rocky Mount†	.533	1981—Peninsula	.522
1953—Raleigh	.593	1967—Durham x (West.)	.536	Hagerstown‡	.507
Danville (2nd)†	.572	Raleigh (East.)	.542	1982—Alexandria‡	.597
1954—Fayetteville*	.628	1968—Salem (West.)	.607	Durham	.588
1955—HP-Thomasville	.580	Ral-Dur (East.)	.597	1983—Lynchburg‡	.691
Danville (2nd)†	.533	HP-Thom. y (W.)	.493	Winston-Salem	.529
1956—HP-Thomasville	.591	1969—Rocky M (East.)	.569	1984—Lynchburg‡	.645
Fayetteville (4th)†	.523	Salem (West.)	.542	Durham	.486
1957—Durham	.632	Ral-Dur z (East.)	.560	1985—Lynchburg	.679
HP-Thomasville	.622	1970—Winston-Salem‡	.586	Winston-Salem‡	.417
1958—Danville	.576	Burlington	.597	1986—Hagerstown	.655
Burlington (4th)†	.511	1971—Peninsula‡	.647	Winston-Salem‡	.594
1959—Raleigh	.600	Kinston	.623	1987—Salem‡	.576
Wilson (2nd)†	.550	1972—Salem‡	.657	Kinston	.536
1960—Greensboro‡	.636	Burlington	.632	1988—Kinston‡	.629
Burlington	.586	1973—Lynchburg	.588	Lynchburg	.486
1961—Wilson	.594	Winston-Salem	.557		

*Won championship and four-club playoff. †Won four-club playoff. ‡Won split-season playoff. §League was divided into Eastern, Western divisions. xWon eight-club, two-division playoff. yWon eight-club, two-division playoff against Raleigh-Durham. zWon eight-club, two-division playoff against Burlington. aWon both halves of split-season (no playoffs).

STANDING OF CLUBS AT CLOSE OF FIRST HALF, JUNE 17

NORTHERN DIVISION

Club	W.	L.	T.	Pct.	G.B.
Lynchburg (Red Sox)	35	34	0	.507	......
Frederick (Orioles)	34	36	0	.486	1½
Salem (Pirates)	33	36	0	.478	2
Prince William (Yankees)	30	39	0	.435	5

SOUTHERN DIVISION

Club	W.	L.	T.	Pct.	G.B.
Durham (Braves)	47	23	0	.671	......
Kinston (Indians)	42	25	0	.627	3½
Winston-Salem (Cubs)	35	35	0	.500	12
Peninsula (Independent)	20	48	0	.294	26

STANDING OF CLUBS AT CLOSE OF SECOND HALF, AUGUST 30

NORTHERN DIVISION

Club	W.	L.	T.	Pct.	G.B.
Prince William (Yankees)	42	27	0	.609	......
Frederick (Orioles)	39	29	0	.574	2½
Lynchburg (Red Sox)	35	32	0	.522	6
Salem (Pirates)	30	39	0	.435	12

SOUTHERN DIVISION

Club	W.	L.	T.	Pct.	G.B.
Durham (Braves)	37	31	0	.544	......
Kinston (Indians)	34	35	0	.493	3½
Winston-Salem (Cubs)	29	36	0	.446	6½
Peninsula (Independent)	24	41	1	.369	11½

COMPOSITE STANDING OF CLUBS AT CLOSE OF SEASON, AUGUST 30

Club	Dur.	Kin.	Fre.	P.W.	Lyn.	W.S.	Sal.	Pen.	W.	L.	T.	Pct.	G.B.
Durham (Braves)	....	11	11	13	11	12	13	13	84	54	1	.609	......
Kinston (Indians)	9	...	15	8	7	13	11	13	76	60	0	.559	7
Frederick (Orioles)	9	5	....	14	10	11	12	12	73	65	0	.529	11
Prince William (Yankees)	7	11	6	...	11	11	13	13	72	66	0	.522	12
Lynchburg (Red Sox)	8	13	8	9	...	9	9	14	70	66	0	.515	13
Winston-Salem (Cubs)	8	6	9	9	11	....	11	10	64	71	0	.474	18½
Salem (Pirates)	7	5	8	6	10	9	....	14	63	75	0	.457	21
Peninsula (Independent)	6	5	8	7	6	6	6	....	44	89	1	.331	37½

Peninsula club represented Hampton, Va.

Major league affiliations in parentheses.

Playoffs—Prince William defeated Lynchburg, two games to one; Prince William defeated Durham, three games to one, to win league championship.

Regular-Season Attendance—Durham, 272,202; Prince William, 175,077; Frederick, 165,930; Salem, 121,581; Winston-Salem, 89,360; Kinston, 88,154; Lynchburg, 74,375; Peninsula, 20,059. Total—1,006,738. Playoffs (7 games)—18,449. All-Star Game—5,120.

Managers—Durham, Grady Little; Frederick, Jerry Narron; Kinston, Ken Bolek; Lynchburg, Gary Allenson; Peninsula, Jim Thrift; Prince William, Mark Weidemaier (through May 20), Stump Merrill (May 21 through end of season); Salem, Rocky Bridges; Winston-Salem, Jay Loviglio. Managerial record of team with more than one manager: Prince William, Weidemaier (18-23), Merrill (54-43).

All-Star Team—1B—David Segui, Frederick; 2B—Luis Mercedes, Frederick; 3B—John Wehner, Salem; SS—Mark Lewis, Kinston; C—Brian Deak, Durham; OF—Phil Plantier, Lynchburg; Moises Alou, Salem; Andy Tomberlin, Durham; DH—Don Sparks, Prince William; Starting Pitcher (tie)—Mike Draper, Prince William; Pat Gomez, Winston-Salem; Randy Tomlin, Salem; Pitcher of the Year—Charles Nagy, Kinston; Most Valuable Player—Phil Plantier, Lynchburg; Manager of the Year—Grady Little, Durham.

(Compiled by Howe Sportsdata International, Boston, Mass.)

CLUB BATTING

Club	Pct.	G.	AB.	R.	OR.	H.	TB.	2B.	3B.	HR.	RBI.	SH.	SF.	HP.	BB.	Int. BB.	SO.	SB.	CS.	LOB.
Salem	.261	138	4535	587	623	1183	1690	205	34	78	516	14	39	41	396	15	929	175	77	949
Frederick	.255	138	4496	592	579	1145	1558	185	30	56	521	36	38	40	491	22	821	207	74	983
Prince William	.250	138	4373	574	534	1092	1543	207	29	62	510	46	32	60	508	23	868	145	58	989
Durham	.247	139	4538	669	491	1121	1695	193	21	113	570	33	29	41	507	26	938	168	89	904
Lynchburg	.241	136	4314	606	546	1039	1527	192	22	84	538	31	37	58	562	25	840	53	41	1002
Winston-Salem	.240	135	4200	480	509	1009	1372	170	20	·51	423	55	37	59	438	22	909	130	66	903
Kinston	.240	136	4328	552	501	1039	1437	164	18	66	461	52	34	64	490	29	802	150	78	944
Peninsula	.232	134	4266	484	761	990	1371	138	24	65	425	27	34	44	427	17	974	208	82	859

INDIVIDUAL BATTING
(Leading Qualifiers for Batting Championship—378 or More Plate Appearances)

*Bats lefthanded.   †Switch-hitter.

Player and Club	Pct.	G.	AB.	R.	H.	TB.	2B.	3B.	HR.	RBI.	SH.	SF.	HP.	BB.	Int. BB.	SO.	SB.	CS.
Mercedes, Luis, Frederick	.309	108	401	62	124	155	12	5	3	36	2	2	3	30	2	62	29	11
Wehner, John, Salem	.301	137	515	69	155	241	32	6	14	73	0	1	1	42	4	81	21	10
Plantier, Phillip, Lynchburg*	.300	131	443	73	133	242	26	1	27	105	0	4	7	74	7	122	4	5
Tomberlin, Andy, Durham*	.281	119	363	63	102	167	13	2	16	61	3	1	5	54	7	82	35	12
Sparks, Donald, Prince William	.281	115	449	52	126	178	32	1	6	65	0	4	2	24	2	85	1	2
DeJardin, Robert, Prince William†	.278	131	475	66	132	156	19	1	1	36	15	3	10	52	2	69	38	11
Pennington, Kenneth, Durham	.275	127	462	70	127	191	34	0	10	64	2	5	3	32	1	71	17	5
Meadows, Scott, Frederick	.272	99	371	59	101	132	17	4	2	41	1	7	3	42	0	56	12	7
Ross, Sean, Durham*	.271	127	420	71	114	179	24	4	11	49	2	1	5	24	4	83	22	12
Martin, Albert, Durham*	.271	128	457	84	124	183	26	3	9	48	0	3	3	34	0	107	27	14
Bell, Leonard, Winston-Salem	.271	127	439	53	119	176	24	3	9	68	2	4	3	50	2	126	4	4

Departmental Leaders: G—Wehner, 137; AB—Wehner, 515; R—Martin, 84; H—Wehner, 155; TB—Plantier, 242; 2B—Pennington, 34; 3B—P. Kelly, 7; HR—Plantier, 27; RBI—Plantier, 105; SH—DeJardin, 15; SF—Todd, 8; HP—Crockett, 24; BB—Masse, 89; IBB—Plantier, Tomberlin, 7; SO—L. Bell, 126; SB—Lofton, 62; CS—Lofton, 21.

(All Players—Listed Alphabetically)

Player and Club	Pct.	G.	AB.	R.	H.	TB.	2B.	3B.	HR.	RBI.	SH.	SF.	HP.	BB.	Int. BB.	SO.	SB.	CS.
Adachi, Wataru, Peninsula*	.500	21	2	0	1	1	0	0	0	0	0	0	0	1	0	1	0	0
Ahalt, Dell, Frederick	.100	8	20	3	2	2	0	0	0	3	1	1	0	3	0	10	0	0
Allison, James, Kinston*	.250	93	240	40	60	81	7	1	4	25	1	2	3	42	3	31	11	7
Alou, Moises, Salem	.302	86	321	50	97	172	29	2	14	53	0	2	3	35	2	69	12	5
Arguelles, Fernando, Salem	.204	19	54	6	11	13	2	0	0	2	1	0	1	3	0	13	0	0
Aspray, Michael, Winston-Salem	.000	26	2	0	0	0	0	0	0	0	0	0	0	0	0	1	0	0
Baker, Michael, Lynchburg	.204	79	216	27	44	50	3	0	1	16	8	0	1	25	0	24	9	5
Barczi, Scott, Salem	.261	98	299	37	78	104	15	1	3	44	0	7	7	40	1	70	7	2
Bautista, Hector, Frederick*	.273	7	22	2	6	8	2	0	0	4	0	0	0	3	0	3	0	0
Bautista, Ramon, Kinston	.236	117	406	59	96	121	17	1	2	31	7	3	8	45	1	104	18	13
Bell, Leonard, Winston-Salem	.271	127	439	53	119	176	24	3	9	68	2	4	3	50	2	126	4	4
Bell, Terence, Peninsula	.284	34	102	13	29	39	4	0	2	9	1	1	4	14	0	19	0	1
Blackwell, Barry, Kinston	.252	39	119	13	30	44	6	1	2	12	0	2	4	13	0	32	1	1
Bridges, Jason, Prince William	.207	71	213	22	44	67	11	3	2	18	0	1	3	13	1	48	0	2
Brooks, Brian, Kinston*	.237	53	156	17	37	47	5	1	1	17	1	2	4	22	1	30	3	3
Brow, Dennis 26 PW-35 Pen	.187	61	187	12	35	40	2	0	1	8	0	0	1	11	0	44	2	3
Bruske, James, Kinston	.290	63	217	29	63	92	12	1	5	36	2	2	3	34	1	44	13	5
Buheller, Timothy, Lynchburg*	.218	92	261	59	57	74	9	4	0	22	2	1	4	51	1	30	6	6
Butts, David, Durham*	.253	84	257	33	65	105	6	2	10	30	0	1	0	20	1	37	3	5
Canan, Richard, Winston-Salem	.246	110	366	44	90	118	12	2	4	31	1	3	6	24	1	76	12	7
Casarotti, Richard, Durham†	.283	55	198	34	56	77	12	0	3	23	1	2	0	20	0	47	8	7
Champ, Jeffrey, Peninsula	.160	35	94	6	15	16	1	0	0	5	1	2	0	5	0	35	4	0
Champion, Brian, Durham*	.254	96	327	43	83	114	13	0	6	48	4	1	4	38	4	70	4	2
Cloninger, Gregory, Durham*	.000	1	2	0	0	0	0	0	0	0	0	0	0	0	0	2	0	0
Cohoon, Donald, Winston-Salem†	.250	93	292	31	73	93	11	0	3	23	1	2	3	31	4	82	8	5
Cortes, Hernan, Peninsula*	.260	105	308	42	80	131	14	5	9	46	0	1	1	34	3	69	17	7
Crockett, Russell, Winston-Salem	.241	131	452	52	109	127	14	2	0	37	10	3	24	26	0	69	22	5
Crowley, Dennis, Peninsula	.153	26	72	11	11	12	1	0	0	3	0	0	1	12	0	18	2	2
Crowley, Terrence, Salem†	.276	78	272	27	75	106	7	3	6	35	0	3	1	21	0	28	8	6
Cruz, Luis, Winston-Salem	.161	8	31	4	5	6	1	0	0	2	0	0	2	0	0	6	1	1
Cuevas, Johnny, Durham	.143	5	14	1	2	5	0	0	1	3	0	0	1	0	0	4	0	0
Deak, Brian, Durham	.235	113	327	44	77	150	10	0	21	64	3	2	9	66	2	111	3	3
Dean, Kevin, Durham	.207	45	135	23	28	45	6	1	3	10	0	3	34	1	47	15	4
Degifico, Vincent, Lynchburg*	.556	7	27	7	15	23	2	0	2	8	0	1	0	4	0	4	0	0
DeJardin, Robert, Prince William†	.278	131	475	66	132	156	19	1	1	36	15	3	10	52	2	69	38	11
Delpiano, Marc, Kinston	.000	1	3	0	0	0	0	0	0	0	0	0	0	0	0	1	0	0
Devereaux, Todd, Prince William*	.258	31	66	13	17	24	4	0	1	6	4	0	1	15	0	8	2	1
Devlin, Paul, Lynchburg†	.158	52	146	18	23	36	8	1	1	13	2	0	6	21	0	25	0	0
Dewey, Todd, Durham†	.170	79	224	25	38	46	5	0	1	11	3	0	0	21	0	48	5	2
Duffy, Darrin, Winston-Salem	.201	121	343	44	69	95	13	2	3	24	10	5	4	65	0	78	19	3
Easley, Michael, Kinston*	.444	6	18	4	8	9	1	0	0	4	0	0	0	3	0	2	0	1
Ehrhard, Rodney, Prince William	.237	87	224	39	53	77	10	1	4	28	4	2	0	37	1	70	5	4
Epley, Daren, Kinston*	.240	121	387	35	93	135	18	3	6	43	5	1	1	60	5	60	6	6
Erhardt, Herbert, Prince William*	.286	4	14	0	4	4	0	0	0	0	0	0	0	1	0	2	0	0
Erickson, Donald, Peninsula	.226	10	31	4	7	8	1	0	0	2	0	0	3	0	11	2	2
Falkner, Richard, Kinston	.237	111	371	43	88	128	11	1	9	50	1	4	8	30	2	66	8	2
Ferran, Alexander, Kinston*	.209	34	91	13	19	26	1	0	2	9	0	0	2	8	0	16	0	2
Ferretti, Samuel, Kinston	.232	101	323	48	75	106	17	1	4	39	7	2	6	26	1	49	9	3
Firova, Daniel, Winston-Salem	.240	26	75	3	18	20	2	0	0	6	1	0	0	2	0	14	1	0
Fleita, Oneri, Frederick*	.238	97	290	25	69	97	11	1	5	29	4	3	2	24	3	66	0	2
Fortuna, Michael, Salem†	.195	16	41	5	8	10	2	0	0	3	1	0	0	7	0	17	3	2
Fowler, Michael, Durham	.267	63	180	37	48	86	9	1	9	29	1	1	4	34	4	39	7	3
Frost, Jerald, Durham	.166	90	217	23	36	39	3	0	0	8	3	0	2	21	0	52	9	8
Garcia, Carlos, Salem	.283	81	304	45	86	127	12	4	7	44	1	5	4	18	0	51	19	6
Gast, Joseph, Peninsula*	.000	37	1	0	0	0	0	0	0	0	0	0	0	0	0	0	0	0
Gilbert, Roy, Frederick†	.239	111	352	39	84	101	9	1	2	38	3	1	4	17	1	34	35	6
Gomez, Fabio, Kinston	.267	17	45	5	12	15	0	0	1	5	0	0	1	0	12	1	0
Goselin, Scott, Durham	.188	23	69	7	13	14	1	0	0	6	0	0	7	0	16	0	2

Player and Club	Pct.	G.	AB.	R.	H.	TB.	2B.	3B.	HR.	RBI.	SH.	SF.	HP.	BB.	Int. BB.	SO.	SB.	CS.
Gray, David, Lynchburg	.188	41	85	14	16	26	4	0	2	7	0	0	2	16	0	27	1	1
Gutierrez, Ricardo, Frederick	.232	127	456	48	106	135	16	2	3	41	1	5	3	39	2	86	15	10
Gwinn, Anthony, Prince William	.231	5	13	1	3	4	1	0	0	0	0	0	0	2	0	1	0	1
Haggerty, Roger, Lynchburg	.258	96	318	33	82	99	9	1	2	37	4	4	1	33	2	51	1	1
Hannon, Phillip, Winston-Salem†	.233	121	403	41	94	122	15	2	3	40	9	1	1	30	1	73	19	8
Harms, Thomas, Frederick	.227	97	295	43	67	91	14	2	2	28	3	1	4	42	0	79	15	4
Harris, Robert, Salem	.253	57	217	25	55	67	7	1	1	16	2	1	4	14	1	56	8	8
Hartman, Edward, Salem	.250	20	68	9	17	24	7	0	0	9	0	0	0	16	0	22	2	0
Hayden, Paris, Frederick	.208	64	154	14	32	47	9	0	2	13	3	0	3	9	1	43	5	3
Hewes, Patrick, 6 PW-60 Pen	.210	66	181	11	38	44	6	0	0	13	1	4	5	24	2	26	2	1
Hunter, Robert, 11 PW-47 Pen	.217	58	207	30	45	57	7	1	1	12	4	2	3	22	0	62	31	5
Huyler, Michael, Salem	.250	44	148	19	37	59	6	2	4	21	2	2	1	16	0	19	11	2
Jaster, Scott, Peninsula	.245	74	274	37	67	115	11	2	11	48	0	2	2	21	0	58	9	6
Jensen, John, Winston-Salem*	.240	69	217	20	52	68	8	1	2	23	0	1	2	22	1	63	5	5
Jewett, Trent, Salem	.150	28	80	6	12	16	1	0	1	5	0	1	1	5	0	33	1	2
Johnson, Brian, Winston-Salem	.226	68	212	24	48	66	6	0	4	24	0	2	2	19	0	50	5	4
Johnson, Dodd, Peninsula	.267	123	434	47	116	153	15	2	6	48	0	5	6	52	4	81	6	5
Katahira, Tetsuya, Peninsula	.216	70	236	24	51	63	3	0	3	23	1	1	3	8	1	47	3	1
Kelly, Michael, Lynchburg	.287	67	244	27	70	100	17	2	3	33	0	4	1	11	1	21	5	1
Kelly, Patrick, Prince William	.266	124	436	61	116	160	21	7	3	45	4	7	8	32	1	79	31	9
Kennedy, Daniel, Winston-Salem	.059	14	17	1	1	1	0	0	0	1	1	0	0	1	0	4	0	0
Keshock, Christopher, Peninsula	.067	8	15	0	1	1	0	0	0	1	0	0	0	2	0	4	0	0
Khoury, Scott, Kinston*	.206	24	63	4	13	15	2	0	0	4	0	1	0	9	1	8	0	1
Knoblauh, Jay, Peninsula	.213	60	211	20	45	66	8	2	3	19	0	2	2	11	0	47	9	1
Kuld, Peter, Kinston	.206	24	63	6	13	20	1	0	2	3	1	0	1	4	0	22	0	0
Lehman, Michael, Frederick	.241	71	220	34	53	78	12	2	3	21	1	0	0	35	3	35	0	0
Levis, Jesse, Kinston*	.299	27	87	11	26	38	6	0	2	11	0	0	2	12	0	15	1	0
Lewis, John, Winston-Salem*	.244	53	164	20	40	56	8	1	2	17	2	0	1	29	0	25	5	5
Lewis, Mark, Kinston	.269	93	349	50	94	119	16	3	1	32	3	5	2	34	4	50	17	9
Livesey, Jeffrey, Prince William	.203	70	197	17	40	58	12	0	2	17	2	1	1	9	0	48	1	0
Lofton, Rodney, Frederick	.243	127	473	65	115	128	9	2	0	29	7	3	2	56	1	72	62	21
Longmire, Anthony, Lynchburg	.323	14	62	8	20	28	3	1	1	6	0	0	0	1	0	13	0	0
Lyden, Mitchell, Prince William	.276	30	105	17	29	54	2	1	7	28	0	0	1	8	0	26	1	0
Makemson, Jay, Peninsula	.000	11	1	0	0	0	0	0	0	0	0	0	0	0	0	1	0	0
Maldonado, Phillip, Durham	.202	54	114	9	23	31	2	0	2	16	3	0	4	21	0	24	2	1
Maloney, Richard, Lynchburg	.223	118	350	41	78	96	8	5	0	21	5	0	1	48	0	37	5	2
Martin, Albert, Durham*	.271	128	457	84	124	183	26	3	9	48	0	3	3	34	0	107	27	14
Martinez, Gilberto, Lynchburg	.229	103	371	43	85	115	21	0	3	43	2	6	10	23	1	48	2	3
Masse, William, Prince William	.239	124	377	70	90	148	17	4	11	50	3	4	13	89	4	57	16	4
McGee, Timothy, Peninsula	.158	7	19	1	3	3	0	0	0	1	0	0	0	1	0	1	0	0
Meadows, Scott, Frederick	.272	99	371	59	101	132	17	4	2	41	1	7	3	42	0	56	12	7
Mercedes, Luis, Frederick	.309	108	401	62	124	155	12	5	3	36	2	2	3	30	2	62	29	11
Merejo, Domingo, Salem*	.242	118	471	69	114	171	18	3	11	54	1	5	3	34	1	86	23	6
Mims, Larry, Frederick	.182	7	22	1	4	4	0	0	0	2	0	0	0	1	0	9	1	3
Minch, John, Kinston	.209	36	86	6	18	20	2	0	0	8	2	0	2	4	1	12	0	0
Molero, Juan, Lynchburg	.167	65	186	20	31	44	5	1	2	13	0	2	3	17	0	58	0	1
Molina, Albert, Salem†	.248	77	258	30	64	80	6	2	2	23	3	4	0	18	4	33	3	3
Mota, Carlos, Kinston	.000	1	2	0	0	0	0	0	0	0	0	0	0	0	0	0	0	0
Murrell, Rodney, Peninsula*	.253	25	83	13	21	31	7	0	1	7	1	0	0	10	0	18	4	0
Naehring, Timothy, Lynchburg	.301	56	209	24	63	84	7	1	4	37	1	3	0	23	0	30	2	0
Odor, Rouglas, Kinston	.117	28	60	4	7	7	0	0	0	2	2	0	3	3	0	12	3	0
Ogata, Kohichi, Peninsula	.239	98	335	50	80	120	9	5	7	28	6	3	3	66	0	95	41	11
Osborne, Jeffrey, Salem*	.397	15	58	12	23	31	5	0	1	4	0	1	0	5	0	18	0	0
Papageorge, Gregory, Peninsula	.265	13	34	5	9	14	2	0	1	3	1	0	0	3	1	12	0	0
Paris, Juan, Lynchburg	.229	54	118	12	27	35	4	2	0	9	2	0	1	3	1	26	0	3
Paulino, Luis, Frederick	.248	72	226	26	56	75	9	2	2	25	7	2	2	25	2	45	7	2
Pennington, Kenneth, Durham	.275	127	462	70	127	191	34	0	10	64	2	5	3	32	1	71	17	5
Pennye, Darwin, Salem	.262	114	446	54	117	161	16	5	6	44	0	3	5	26	0	76	20	4
Perez, Hector, Peninsula*	.208	13	48	1	10	11	1	0	0	9	0	1	0	3	0	14	0	1
Phillips, Vincent, Prince William*	.265	132	437	63	116	157	19	2	6	60	5	3	3	77	6	84	22	7
Pike, Mark, Kinston	.238	104	357	43	85	103	16	1	0	17	10	1	6	24	0	64	40	15
Pilkinton, Lemuel, Peninsula	.270	109	374	43	101	156	15	2	12	57	0	6	4	30	1	94	3	1
Plantier, Phillip, Lynchburg*	.300	131	443	73	133	242	26	1	27	105	0	4	7	74	7	122	4	5
Powers, Tad, Peninsula	.000	66	1	0	0	0	0	0	0	0	0	0	0	0	0	0	0	0
Powers, Scott, Lynchburg	.218	91	285	39	62	85	12	1	3	31	2	1	1	34	1	63	2	3
Ramos, Kenneth, Kinston†	.143	8	21	6	3	3	0	0	0	0	1	0	0	5	0	2	2	0
Richardson, James, Kinston†	.223	98	309	35	69	94	11	1	4	34	6	3	5	46	5	32	4	4
Rivero, Martin, Winston-Salem	.200	57	145	12	29	39	4	0	2	13	4	0	0	11	0	55	2	1
Robbins, Douglas, Frederick	.310	57	174	29	54	82	7	3	5	30	1	2	5	32	0	35	2	1
Rodriguez, Gabriel, Winston-Salem*	1.000	36	1	0	1	2	1	0	0	0	0	0	0	0	0	0	0	0
Roman, Daniel, Prince William	.056	9	18	1	1	1	0	0	0	0	0	1	0	0	0	6	0	1
Rose, Peter, Frederick*	.179	24	67	3	12	15	3	0	0	7	0	0	1	0	0	15	1	1
Ross, Sean, Durham*	.271	127	420	71	114	179	24	4	11	49	2	1	5	24	4	83	22	12
Segui, David, Frederick†	.317	83	284	43	90	139	19	0	10	50	0	3	4	41	3	32	2	1
Seymour, Winston, Salem*	.232	70	237	22	55	66	11	0	0	23	0	3	1	25	1	54	1	5
Shamburg, Kenneth, Frederick	.254	52	201	27	51	80	8	0	7	40	0	3	0	24	0	34	2	0
Shepherd, Ray, Peninsula	.174	7	23	1	4	5	1	0	0	4	0	0	0	0	0	7	1	1
Simonds, Daniel, Frederick	.194	23	62	8	12	16	2	1	0	7	0	0	0	4	0	14	1	0
Sims, Gregory, Salem	.178	27	90	10	16	21	5	0	0	6	0	3	0	12	0	28	6	6
Sparks, Donald, Prince William	.281	115	449	52	126	178	32	1	6	65	0	4	2	24	2	85	1	2
Stephan, Todd, Peninsula*	.000	36	0	0	0	0	0	0	0	0	0	0	0	0	1	0	0	0
Stout, Jeffrey, Salem	.258	24	89	10	23	24	1	0	0	3	0	0	1	0	0	8	9	1
Strickland, Robert, Winston-Salem*	.250	88	260	25	65	101	18	0	6	39	0	5	0	31	3	43	1	5
Tenacen, Francisco, Winston-Salem	.230	63	187	21	43	66	3	4	4	17	2	2	5	13	4	52	6	1
Thigpen, Leonard, Peninsula†	.175	110	337	26	59	74	3	0	4	24	4	2	4	34	1	103	15	11
Tingle, Darrell, Peninsula	.172	67	233	13	40	50	5	1	1	17	1	1	3	16	1	62	10	6
Todd, Theron, Durham*	.254	127	422	60	107	167	21	3	11	79	2	8	1	32	1	62	6	7
Tomberlin, Andy, Durham*	.281	119	363	63	102	167	13	2	16	63	1	5	2	54	7	82	35	12
Tresh, Michael, Peninsula†	.269	65	253	36	68	87	17	1	0	20	1	0	0	21	2	33	12	5
Turgeon, David, Prince William	.260	121	438	36	114	148	23	1	3	45	1	5	4	39	3	75	1	1
Valentin, John, Lynchburg	.246	75	264	47	65	100	7	2	8	34	2	2	2	41	1	40	5	2
Valverde, Miguel, Salem	.209	47	163	19	34	39	3	1	0	12	0	0	1	15	0	45	7	6
Vargas, Hector, 5 PW-84 Pen	.258	89	299	46	77	101	9	3	3	27	1	3	2	38	2	45	35	13

Player and Club	Pct.	G.	AB.	R.	H.	TB.	2B.	3B.	HR.	RBI.	SH.	SF.	HP.	BB.	Int. BB.	SO.	SB.	CS.
Vizcaino, Reyes, Salem	.251	100	342	55	86	130	17	3	7	36	0	4	4	41	1	109	14	3
Voigt, John, Frederick	.264	127	406	61	107	173	26	5	10	77	2	5	4	62	4	106	17	2
Wallin, Leslie, Lynchburg*	.207	128	397	49	82	135	18	1	11	51	0	4	5	63	4	103	1	1
Weeks, Thomas, Prince William*	.236	76	225	27	53	71	9	0	3	31	0	4	1	26	2	36	6	1
Wehner, John, Salem	.301	137	515	69	155	241	32	6	14	73	0	1	1	42	4	81	21	10
Weidie, Stuart, Lynchburg†	.254	117	422	76	107	161	20	5	8	45	3	2	9	73	3	94	15	7
Whitfield, Kenneth, Kinston	.239	104	343	57	82	148	9	3	17	55	3	4	1	46	4	87	8	2
Wilkins, Richard, Winston-Salem*	.249	132	445	61	111	173	24	1	12	54	2	7	8	50	6	87	6	3
Williams, Gerald, Prince William	.229	134	454	63	104	174	19	6	13	69	5	1	7	51	1	120	15	10
Wilson, Craig, Lynchburg	.239	105	322	38	77	118	20	0	7	34	3	3	5	50	3	74	0	2
Woods, Eric, Winston-Salem*	.249	108	361	48	90	109	12	2	1	28	10	4	2	50	0	55	19	13
Zazueta, Mauricio, Prince William	.262	30	103	15	27	35	4	2	0	5	1	0	0	16	0	25	5	3

The following pitchers, listed alphabetically by club, with games in parentheses, had no plate appearances, primarily through use of designated hitters:

DURHAM—Avery, Steven (14); Boltz, Brian (11); Burlingame, Dennis (11); Cuesta, Jaime (11); Currin, Wesley (33); Czajkowski, James (32); DelRosario, Maximo (7); Johnson, Lloyd (32); Kirk, Timothy (22); Nied, David (12); Richey, Rodney (19); Rivera, Bienvenido (23); Smith, Chad (13); Stoker, Michael (24); Tilmon, Patton (33); Trlicek, Richard (1); Turner, Matthew (53); Watson, Preston (19); Wendell, Steven (3); Ziem, Stephen (28).

FREDERICK—Bell, Brent (16); Borgatti, Michael (23); Bowden, Mark (4); Burdick, Stacey (9); Cavers, Michael (16); Constant, Andres (29); DeLaRosa, Francisco (23); Deutsch, Michael (25); Jones, Stacy (15); Kerr, Zachary (6); Linskey, Michael (9); McDonald, Benjamin (2); Miller, David (28); Mondile, Steven (38); Myers, Chris (22); Palermo, Peter (3); Pena, Jaime (1); Rhodes, Arthur (7); Riddle, David (6); Telford, Anthony (9); Williams, Robert (24).

KINSTON—Carriger, Ricky (17); Casano, Andrew (6); Cole, Christopher (1); Curtis, Michael (16); Ferlenda, Gregory (26); Gilles, Mark (19); Gonzales, Todd (5); Kallevig, Dane (1); Kiser, Garland (6); Kramer, Thomas (18); Mutis, Jeffrey (16); Nagy, Charles (13); Ogden, Todd (14); Oliveras, David (17); Ortiz, Angel (18); Piatt, Douglas (20); Roscoe, Gregory (20); Scaglione, Anthony (31); Seanez, Rudy (25); Shepherd, Keith (8); Surhoff, Richard (20).

LYNCHBURG—Birriel, Jose (9); Burgo, Dale (9); Davis, Freddie (44); Dolan, John (5); Dzafic, Bernhard (34); Fischer, Thomas (28); Haley, Bart (46); Livernois, Derek (26); Morton, Kevin (9); Owen, David (27); Pratts, Alberto (8); Richardson, Ronnie (17); Skripko, Scott (30); Taylor, Scott (19).

PENINSULA—Bauer, David (7); Bushing, Christopher (35); Cummings, Brian (11); Fine, Thomas (13); Kirk, Timothy (12); Lombardi, Alphonso (4); Machado, Julio (4); McMurtrie, Daniel (6); Michael, Matthew (29); Morrison, Anthony (26); Murphy, Brian (5); Reichard, Clyde (1); Ritter, Christopher (10); Ritter, Reggie (15); Rose, Mark (1); Siebert, Richard (20).

PRINCE WILLIAM—Cook, Andrew (25); DeLeon, Pedro (11); Draper, Michael (25); Greer, Kenneth (29); Johnson, Jeffrey (25); Marris, Mark (26); Mills, Alan (26); Nielsen, Gerald (39); Ohlms, Mark (37); Polak, Richard (7); Prybylinski, Bruce (28); Seminara, Frank (21); Stanford, Donald (14); Taylor, Wade (25).

SALEM—Ausanio, Joseph (54); Blohm, Peter (10); Buckholz, Steven (5); Downs, Ronald (36); Duncan, Calvin (26); Fansler, Stanley (7); Miller, Paul (26); Minor, Blas (39); Pacholec, Joseph (26); Richardson, Keith (5); Ruskin, Scott (14); Santiago, Delvy (1); Schlopy, Clifford (29); Smith, Todd (21); Smith, Willie (23); Tomlin, Randy (21).

WINSTON-SALEM—Caballero, Eduardo (23); Campos, Frank (2); Castillo, Frank (18); Coffman, Kevin (7); Gardner, John (6); Gomez, Patrick (23); Melvin, William (27); Michno, Thomas (7); Mullino, Ray (36); Parker, Stephen (21); Parmenter, Gary (7); Ritter, Reggie (1); Strauss, Julio (50); Zarranz, Fernando (19).

GRAND SLAM HOME RUNS—L. Bell, Merejo, Naehring, Williams, 2 each; Champion, Jaster, Knoblauh, Plantier, Valentin, Voight, 1 each.

AWARDED FIRST BASE ON CATCHER'S INTERFERENCE—Weeks 3 (Wilkins 2, Firova); Mercedes 2 (Wilkins 2); Allison (Paulino); Crockett (Champ); Hayden (Deak); Jensen (Minch); P. Kelly (T. Bell); Todd (Lehman); Wilson (Livesey).

CLUB FIELDING

Club	Pct.	G.	PO.	A.	E.	DP.	PB.	Club	Pct.	G.	PO.	A.	E.	DP.	PB.
Prince William	.970	138	3469	1540	157	116	12	Kinston	.962	136	3489	1358	192	121	23
Lynchburg	.967	136	3396	1372	164	112	18	Salem	.961	138	3475	1421	201	111	25
Durham	.964	139	3618	1584	192	121	11	Winston-Salem	.961	135	3420	1452	200	123	17
Frederick	.964	138	3540	1524	189	125	21	Peninsula	.956	134	3378	1248	212	100	30

Triple Plays—Frederick, Kinston.

INDIVIDUAL FIELDING
*Throws lefthanded.
FIRST BASEMEN

Player and Club	Pct.	G.	PO.	A.	E.	DP.	Player and Club	Pct.	G.	PO.	A.	E.	DP.
Bell, Winston-Salem	.986	114	1030	72	16	95	Lyden, Prince William	.994	18	149	6	1	17
Brow, Peninsula	1.000	16	84	9	0	9	Maldonado, Durham	.981	13	97	8	2	8
Champion, Durham	.990	87	769	38	8	65	Meadows, Frederick	1.000	11	71	10	0	5
Cohoon, Winston-Salem	1.000	1	1	0	0	0	Minch, Kinston	.968	11	83	9	3	8
Cortes, Peninsula*	.972	73	496	53	16	35	Osborne, Salem	.962	8	70	5	3	4
Degifico, Lynchburg	1.000	1	8	0	0	1	Pilkinton, Peninsula	.990	24	183	15	2	22
Devereaux, Prince William*	1.000	1	8	1	0	1	Richardson, Kinston	.980	7	41	7	1	2
Devlin, Lynchburg	.955	4	21	0	1	1	Segui, Frederick*	.995	82	707	47	4	66
Dewey, Durham	.989	12	81	6	1	3	Seymour, Salem*	.983	37	323	26	6	30
Easley, Kinston	.926	3	24	1	2	3	Shamburg, Frederick	.983	37	328	21	6	26
Epley, Kinston*	.985	118	934	85	16	91	Sparks, Prince William	.967	5	55	3	2	7
Erhardt, Prince William	1.000	2	16	3	0	0	Strickland, Winston-Salem	.971	21	157	9	5	10
Fleita, Frederick*	.978	16	128	7	3	9	Tomberlin, Durham*	1.000	33	304	8	0	25
Fowler, Durham	.947	10	70	1	4	6	Turgeon, Prince William	.987	80	758	49	11	56
Gray, Lynchburg	.980	22	143	5	3	9	Vizcaino, Salem	.983	88	732	54	14	59
Haggerty, Lynchburg	1.000	2	2	1	0	1	Voigt, Frederick	1.000	1	5	0	0	0
Hartman, Salem	.965	6	52	3	2	3	WALLIN, Lynchburg*	.992	125	909	63	8	80
Johnson, Kinston	.967	31	218	20	8	20	Weeks, Prince William	.979	36	310	11	7	23
Khoury, Kinston*	.962	4	23	2	1	3							

Triple Plays—Epley, Shamburg.

SECOND BASEMEN

Player and Club	Pct.	G.	PO.	A.	E.	DP.	Player and Club	Pct.	G.	PO.	A.	E.	DP.
Baker, Lynchburg	.959	76	144	163	13	35	T. Crowley, Salem	.966	76	142	168	11	37
Bautista, Kinston	.945	116	194	267	27	69	Dewey, Durham	.889	4	6	10	2	1
Butts, Durham	.980	38	57	93	3	14	Duffy, Winston-Salem	1.000	3	7	7	0	2
Casarotti, Durham	.957	54	110	157	12	27	Ehrhard, Prince William	.800	1	4	0	1	0
Cohoon, Winston-Salem	.750	2	2	1	1	1	Erickson, Peninsula	.902	10	18	19	4	4
CROCKETT, Winston-Salem	.973	123	270	354	17	70	Ferretti, Kinston	.934	24	43	56	7	10
D. Crowley, Peninsula	.963	26	43	62	4	10	Goselin, Durham	1.000	17	35	40	0	11

SECOND BASEMEN—Continued

Player and Club	Pct.	G.	PO.	A.	E.	DP.
Kelly, Prince William	.961	122	244	372	25	76
Lofton, Frederick	.974	41	81	105	5	20
Maloney, Durham	.964	46	80	108	7	29
Mercedes, Frederick	.953	101	204	305	25	63
Molero, Lynchburg	1.000	3	8	4	0	1
Molina, Salem	.985	40	95	98	3	18
Murrell, Peninsula	.980	24	44	56	2	16
Odor, Kinston	1.000	8	10	15	0	2

Player and Club	Pct.	G.	PO.	A.	E.	DP.
Ogata, Peninsula	.982	78	140	183	6	29
Powers, Lynchburg	.958	69	140	181	14	39
Rivero, Winston-Salem	.894	19	18	24	5	5
Roman, Prince William	1.000	2	3	10	0	1
Stout, Salem	.934	24	37	48	6	10
Tresh, Peninsula	1.000	3	7	8	0	3
Turgeon, Prince William	1.000	3	3	6	0	0
Vargas, Peninsula	1.000	1	2	2	0	2
Zazueta, Prince William	.983	13	25	34	1	8

Triple Plays—Bautista, Mercedes.

THIRD BASEMEN

Player and Club	Pct.	G.	PO.	A.	E.	DP.
Ahalt, Frederick	.952	8	3	17	1	0
Butts, Durham	.923	42	20	76	8	10
Canan, Winston-Salem	.860	56	36	112	24	7
Cohoon, Winston-Salem	.902	81	34	150	20	14
Dewey, Durham	.750	9	3	6	3	1
Erhardt, Prince William	1.000	2	1	6	0	0
Ferretti, Kinston	.892	34	11	63	9	5
Gomez, Kinston	.841	16	7	30	7	3
Goselin, Durham	.875	7	4	10	2	1
Haggerty, Lynchburg	.895	80	47	141	22	13
Johnson, Peninsula	.902	43	25	58	9	3
Lofton, Frederick	.905	67	56	134	20	13
Maloney, Durham	.778	3	0	7	2	0
Masse, Prince William	.333	1	1	0	2	0
Meadows, Frederick	.842	39	27	69	18	6
Molero, Lynchburg	.890	57	43	86	16	10

Player and Club	Pct.	G.	PO.	A.	E.	DP.
Molina, Salem	.955	6	6	15	1	1
Murrell, Peninsula	1.000	1	0	1	0	0
Odor, Kinston	1.000	1	0	1	0	0
Ogata, Peninsula	.800	14	9	7	4	0
Pennington, Durham	.877	96	48	223	38	16
Powers, Lynchburg	1.000	9	3	8	0	2
Richardson, Kinston	.916	93	75	176	23	16
Rivero, Winston-Salem	.556	4	1	4	4	1
Rose, Frederick	.871	23	15	39	8	7
Shamburg, Frederick	.860	13	12	25	6	2
SPARKS, Prince William	.930	111	67	224	22	24
Thigpen, Peninsula	.500	3	1	1	2	0
Tingle, Peninsula	.833	5	6	4	2	0
Turgeon, Prince William	.821	15	3	20	5	1
Vargas, 4 PW-80 Pen	.902	84	64	93	17	7
Wehner, Salem	.911	134	89	278	36	24
Zazueta, Prince William	1.000	7	7	15	0	0

Triple Play—Lofton.

SHORTSTOPS

Player and Club	Pct.	G.	PO.	A.	E.	DP.
Baker, Lynchburg	1.000	1	1	1	0	0
Butts, Durham	.938	5	3	12	1	2
Cloninger, Durham	1.000	1	2	2	0	1
Crockett, Winston-Salem	.667	1	0	2	1	0
DeJardin, Prince William	.941	131	195	398	37	74
Delpiano, Kinston	1.000	1	1	2	0	0
Duffy, Winston-Salem	.933	117	180	351	38	70
Ferretti, Kinston	.967	36	48	71	4	15
Frost, Durham	.916	83	101	225	30	38
Garcia, Salem	.926	81	137	262	32	45
GUTIERREZ, Frederick	.943	127	190	372	34	68
Huyler, Salem	.930	44	53	120	13	15
Lewis, Kinston	.921	89	130	244	32	60
Lofton, Frederick	.860	13	12	37	8	6

Player and Club	Pct.	G.	PO.	A.	E.	DP.
Maloney, Durham	.934	76	76	208	20	40
Molina, Salem	.951	13	21	37	3	8
Naehring, Lynchburg	.944	50	72	131	12	28
Odor, Kinston	.932	18	18	37	4	9
Ogata, Peninsula	.974	8	13	24	1	5
Powers, Lynchburg	.889	13	16	32	6	7
Rivero, Winston-Salem	.929	21	34	57	7	16
Roman, Prince William	1.000	5	2	6	0	0
Tingle, Peninsula	.929	62	91	156	19	23
Tresh, Peninsula	.937	62	120	162	19	39
Turgeon, Prince William	1.000	2	2	6	0	1
Valentin, Lynchburg	.953	74	105	220	16	37
Vargas, Peninsula	.806	6	7	18	6	5
Zazueta, Prince William	.952	5	9	11	1	2

OUTFIELDERS

Player and Club	Pct.	G.	PO.	A.	E.	DP.
Allison, Kinston*	.956	60	82	4	4	0
Alou, Lynchburg	.947	86	166	12	10	3
Bautista, Frederick*	1.000	6	9	1	0	0
Bridges, Prince William	1.000	30	33	1	0	0
Brooks, Kinston*	.933	43	70	0	5	0
Brow, 6 PW-2 Pen	1.000	8	7	0	0	0
Bruske, Kinston	.983	61	114	2	2	1
Buheller, Lynchburg*	.987	80	149	7	2	1
Canan, Winston-Salem	.972	42	66	3	2	0
Cortes, Peninsula*	.786	14	21	1	6	0
Crockett, Winston-Salem	1.000	13	10	1	0	0
Cruz, Winston-Salem	.933	8	13	1	1	0
Dean, Durham	.986	42	68	4	1	1
Devereaux, Prince William*	1.000	10	12	1	0	0
Duffy, Winston-Salem	1.000	1	2	1	0	0
Falkner, Kinston	.959	96	136	4	6	0
Ferran, Kinston*	1.000	11	9	1	0	0
Fowler, Durham	.975	45	79	0	2	0
Gilbert, Frederick	.982	105	211	8	4	1
Hannon, Winston-Salem	.988	119	235	7	3	2
Harms, Frederick	.986	89	136	6	2	1
Harris, Salem	.988	47	76	3	1	0
Hayden, Frederick	.966	55	80	6	3	1
Hunter, 6 PW-47 Pen	.951	53	130	7	7	2
Jaster, Peninsula	.954	69	139	7	7	1
Jensen, Winston-Salem	.961	62	93	6	4	1
Johnson, Peninsula	.915	27	51	3	5	1
Katahira, Peninsula	.939	68	116	8	8	0
Kelly, Lynchburg	.980	64	144	4	3	2
Keshock, Peninsula	1.000	4	4	0	0	0
Khoury, Kinston*	1.000	1	1	0	0	0
Knoblauh, Peninsula	.945	61	133	5	8	1

Player and Club	Pct.	G.	PO.	A.	E.	DP.
Lewis, Winston-Salem	.958	48	66	3	3	2
Lofton, Frederick	1.000	8	7	0	0	0
Longmire, Salem	1.000	10	14	3	0	0
Maldonado, Durham	1.000	4	5	1	0	0
Martin, Durham*	.962	90	169	7	7	1
Martinez, Lynchburg	.986	40	66	4	1	2
Masse, Prince William	.987	122	212	18	3	4
Meadows, Frederick	.957	53	86	4	4	1
Merejo, Winston-Salem*	.931	117	177	13	14	6
Mims, Frederick	1.000	6	12	0	0	0
Paris, Lynchburg	.986	42	68	2	1	0
Pennington, Durham	1.000	6	6	1	0	0
Pennye, Salem	.967	112	196	7	7	2
Perez, Peninsula*	.958	13	23	0	1	0
Phillips, Prince William*	.985	127	197	6	3	2
Pike, Kinston	.983	96	229	8	4	3
Plantier, Lynchburg	.949	97	140	10	8	1
Ramos, Kinston*	1.000	7	6	0	0	0
Ross, Durham*	.983	90	165	4	3	1
Shepherd, Peninsula	.938	6	15	0	1	0
Sims, Salem	1.000	13	25	2	0	1
Strickland, Winston-Salem	1.000	5	2	1	0	0
Tenacen, Winston-Salem	.950	27	19	0	1	0
Thigpen, Peninsula	.966	106	239	14	9	4
Todd, Durham*	.978	98	171	5	4	1
Tomberlin, Durham*	.993	77	138	8	1	3
Valverde, Salem	.952	35	57	2	3	0
VOIGT, Frederick	.990	123	184	16	2	3
Weidie, Lynchburg	.977	112	203	6	5	1
Whitfield, Kinston	.948	62	87	5	5	1
Williams, Prince William	.974	134	292	7	8	2
Woods, Winston-Salem*	.953	100	152	12	8	5

CATCHERS

Player and Club	Pct.	G.	PO.	A.	E.	DP.	PB.
Arguelles, Salem	.983	19	106	12	2	1	1
Barczi, Salem	.982	97	673	74	14	4	17
Bell, Peninsula	.978	29	161	15	4	0	2
Blackwell, Kinston	.996	32	235	30	1	2	2
Champ, Peninsula	.982	30	139	21	3	0	7

Player and Club	Pct.	G.	PO.	A.	E.	DP.	PB.
Cuevas, Salem	1.000	4	26	3	0	0	0
Deak, Durham	.987	95	599	60	9	8	7
Devlin, Lynchburg	.993	43	263	18	2	1	3
Dewey, Durham	.988	42	208	33	3	1	3
EHRHARD, Prince William	.991	74	373	65	4	3	5

CATCHERS—Continued

Player and Club	Pct.	G.	PO.	A.	E.	DP.	PB.
Firova, Winston-Salem	.967	22	124	22	5	1	4
Gray, Lynchburg	1.000	12	42	3	0	1	1
Gwinn, Prince William	.966	5	24	4	1	0	0
Hewes, 5 PW-47 Pen	.978	52	309	41	8	3	10
Jewett, Salem	.988	28	138	21	2	1	7
Johnson, Kinston	.985	65	411	39	7	1	15
Kennedy, Winston-Salem	.957	12	40	5	2	1	2
Kuld, Kinston	.994	24	141	12	1	1	3
Lehman, Frederick	.987	57	340	42	5	4	11
Levis, Kinston	.982	12	95	17	2	0	1
Livesey, Prince William	.983	67	299	43	6	0	7
Lyden, Prince William	.984	11	59	3	1	0	0
Maldonado, Durham	1.000	18	60	9	0	0	1
McGee, Peninsula	1.000	5	31	8	0	1	0
Minch, Kinston	.971	19	129	7	4	2	2
Mota, Kinston	1.000	1	6	0	0	0	0
Papageorge, Peninsula	.986	10	61	8	1	0	2
Paulino, Frederick	.985	64	408	51	7	6	4
Pilkinton, Peninsula	.986	29	189	17	3	1	9
Robbins, Frederick	.981	10	46	5	1	0	4
Simonds, Frederick	.963	22	108	22	5	2	2
Wilkins, Winston-Salem	.979	117	764	78	18	8	11
Wilson, Lynchburg	.984	97	600	66	11	7	14

PITCHERS

Player and Club	Pct.	G.	PO.	A.	E.	DP.
Adachi, Peninsula	.913	20	11	10	2	1
Aspray, Winston-Salem	.968	26	10	20	1	3
Ausanio, Salem	.933	54	6	8	1	0
Avery, Durham*	.938	14	2	13	1	0
Bauer, Peninsula	1.000	7	3	10	0	3
Bell, Frederick	1.000	16	4	2	0	0
Birriel, Lynchburg*	1.000	9	2	3	0	0
Blohm, Salem	1.000	10	1	8	0	1
Boltz, Durham*	.833	11	0	10	2	0
Borgatti, Frederick	.857	23	0	6	1	1
Bowden, Frederick*	1.000	4	0	3	0	0
Buckholz, Salem	1.000	5	4	6	0	0
Burdick, Frederick	.750	9	1	2	1	0
Burgo, Lynchburg	1.000	9	3	6	0	0
Burlingame, Durham	.947	11	9	9	1	0
Bushing, Peninsula	.889	35	7	9	2	2
Caballero, Winston-Salem	.909	23	8	12	2	0
Campos, Winston-Salem	1.000	2	2	0	0	0
Carriger, Kinston	.778	17	3	4	2	0
Castillo, Winston-Salem	.900	18	7	20	3	0
Cavers, Frederick*	.962	16	10	15	1	0
Coffman, Winston-Salem	.900	7	1	8	1	0
Constant, Frederick	.926	29	7	18	2	1
Cook, Prince William	.929	25	6	33	3	3
Cuesta, Durham*	1.000	11	1	7	0	1
Cummings, Peninsula	.923	11	6	6	1	0
Currin, Durham*	.778	33	3	4	2	0
Curtis, Kinston*	1.000	16	4	14	0	1
Czajkowski, Durham	1.000	32	1	7	0	2
Davis, Lynchburg	.897	44	6	20	3	0
DeLaRosa, Frederick	1.000	23	2	3	0	0
DeLeon, Prince William	1.000	11	4	5	0	0
DelRosario, Durham	1.000	7	1	6	0	0
Deutsch, Frederick	.958	25	7	16	1	1
Dolan, Lynchburg	1.000	5	1	0	0	0
Downs, Salem	.944	36	8	9	1	0
Draper, Prince William	.931	25	6	21	2	1
Duncan, Salem	.900	26	6	12	2	2
Dzafic, Lynchburg	1.000	34	1	11	0	0
Fansler, Salem	.778	7	5	2	2	1
Ferlenda, Kinston	1.000	26	5	2	0	0
Fine, Peninsula	.875	13	6	8	2	4
Fischer, Lynchburg*	.951	28	8	31	2	3
Gardner, Winston-Salem	.750	6	2	1	1	0
Gast, Peninsula*	.958	36	7	16	1	0
Gilles, Kinston	.882	19	4	11	2	0
Gomez, Winston-Salem*	.941	23	7	25	2	3
Gonzales, Kinston*	1.000	5	1	6	0	0
Greer, Prince William	1.000	29	8	16	0	0
Haley, Lynchburg	.875	46	3	11	2	1
J. Johnson, Prince William*	.921	25	5	30	3	0
L. Johnson, Durham*	1.000	32	2	17	0	1
Jones, Frederick	.857	15	4	2	1	0
Kerr, Frederick	.923	6	3	9	1	2
Khoury, Kinston*	1.000	1	1	0	0	0
Kirk, 12 Pen-20 Dur*	.917	32	3	19	2	1
Kiser, Kinston*	1.000	6	0	2	0	1
Kramer, Kinston	.969	18	15	16	1	0
Linskey, Frederick*	.909	9	0	10	1	2
LIVERNOIS, Lynchburg	1.000	26	8	26	0	4
Lombardi, Peninsula*	1.000	4	2	1	0	0
Machado, Peninsula	1.000	4	0	1	0	0
Makemson, Peninsula	.733	10	6	5	4	0
Marris, Prince William	1.000	26	3	13	0	1
McDonald, Frederick	1.000	2	1	1	0	0
McMurtrie, Peninsula	1.000	6	1	2	0	0
Melvin, Winston-Salem	.900	27	4	23	3	3
Michael, Peninsula*	1.000	29	2	10	0	0
D. Miller, Frederick	.923	28	11	25	3	5
P. Miller, Salem	.912	26	13	18	3	0
Mills, Prince William	1.000	26	2	6	0	0
Minor, Lynchburg	.963	39	10	16	1	1
Mondile, Frederick	.886	38	10	21	4	0
Morrison, Peninsula*	.833	21	4	11	3	0
Morton, Lynchburg*	1.000	9	0	6	0	0
Mullino, Winston-Salem	1.000	36	9	18	0	0
Mutis, Kinston	.968	16	11	19	1	1
Myers, Frederick*	1.000	22	6	21	0	4
Nagy, Kinston	.950	13	8	11	1	0
Nied, Durham	.857	12	3	9	2	0
Nielsen, Prince William*	.923	39	2	10	1	0
Ogden, Kinston	1.000	14	7	8	0	2
Ohlms, Prince William	.933	37	5	9	1	1
Oliveras, Kinston	.909	17	7	3	1	0
Ortiz, Kinston*	.933	18	3	11	1	0
Owen, Lynchburg*	.933	27	8	48	4	0
Pacholec, Salem	1.000	26	11	17	0	0
Palermo, Frederick	1.000	3	0	1	0	0
Parker, Winston-Salem*	1.000	21	5	7	0	0
Parmenter, Winston-Salem	.000	7	0	0	1	0
Piatt, Kinston	1.000	20	6	4	0	0
Polak, Prince William	1.000	7	1	5	0	0
Powers, Peninsula	.906	66	8	21	3	4
Pratts, Lynchburg	.857	8	5	1	0	
Prybylinski, Prince William	1.000	28	3	6	0	0
Rhodes, Frederick*	1.000	7	0	6	0	0
K. Richardson, Salem	1.000	5	0	5	0	1
R. Richardson, Lynchburg	.935	17	9	20	2	3
Richey, Durham	.923	19	4	8	1	1
Riddle, Frederick	1.000	6	0	2	0	0
C. Ritter, Peninsula	.870	10	6	14	3	0
R. Ritter, 15 Pen-1 WinS	1.000	16	7	5	0	1
Rivera, Durham	.958	23	6	17	1	1
Rodriguez, Winston-Salem*	.952	36	1	19	1	2
Roscoe, Kinston	.923	20	1	11	1	2
Ruskin, Salem*	.850	14	3	14	3	0
Scaglione, Kinston	.885	31	7	16	3	1
Schlopy, Salem*	.909	29	5	15	2	2
Seanez, Kinston	.952	25	8	12	1	0
Seminara, Prince William	.929	21	3	10	1	0
Shepherd, Kinston	1.000	8	2	3	0	0
Siebert, Peninsula	1.000	20	3	9	0	1
Skripko, Lynchburg	.815	30	9	13	5	3
C. Smith, Durham*	1.000	13	0	13	0	0
T. Smith, Salem	.667	7	2	0	1	0
W. Smith, Salem	1.000	23	2	10	0	0
Stanford, Prince William	.875	14	3	4	1	0
Stephan, Peninsula	.917	35	4	7	1	0
Stoker, Durham	.912	24	9	22	3	0
Strauss, Winston-Salem	1.000	50	5	7	0	0
Surhoff, Kinston	.929	20	3	10	1	1
S. Taylor, Lynchburg*	.941	19	0	16	1	1
W. Taylor, Prince William	.977	25	9	33	1	2
Telford, Frederick	.900	9	3	6	1	0
Tilmon, Durham	.973	33	7	29	1	1
Tomlin, Salem*	.941	21	14	18	2	0
Trlicek, Durham	1.000	1	0	1	0	0
Turner, Durham	.917	53	2	9	1	2
Watson, Durham	.833	19	1	4	1	0
Wendell, Durham	.714	3	1	4	2	0
R. Williams, Frederick	.917	24	5	6	1	1
Zarranz, Winston-Salem	1.000	19	3	8	0	1
Ziem, Durham	1.000	28	5	11	0	1

Triple Play—McDonald.

The following players did not have any fielding statistics at the positions indicated or appeared only as a designated hitter, pinch-hitter or pinch-runner: Allison, p; Brow, p; Casano, p; Cole, p; Dewey, of; Easley, 3b; Ferretti, p; Fortuna, dh, ph, pr; Gast, of; D. Johnson, p; Kallevig, p; Martinez, p; Michno, p; Minch, 3b; Molero, p; Morrison, of; Murphy, p; Paris, p; Pena, p; Pilkinton, p; Reichard, p; Rivero, c, p; M. Rose, p; Ross, ss; Santiago, p; Stephan, of; Tomberlin, p; G. Williams, p.

CLUB PITCHING

Club	ERA.	G.	CG.	ShO.	Sv.	IP.	H.	R.	ER.	HR.	HB.	BB.	Int. BB.	SO.	WP.	Bk.
Durham	3.02	139	9	12	45	1206.0	1098	491	405	76	50	396	32	889	63	16
Kinston	3.10	136	24	13	33	1163.0	954	501	400	53	45	530	22	1019	82	22
Winston-Salem	3.12	135	31	8	30	1140.0	1050	509	395	60	43	458	19	900	78	27
Prince William	3.44	138	18	11	26	1156.1	999	534	442	51	52	434	20	783	92	27
Frederick	3.51	138	25	9	25	1180.0	1134	579	460	78	52	457	25	872	62	29
Lynchburg	3.68	138	28	15	28	1132.0	1070	546	463	65	56	410	29	876	50	36
Salem	3.83	138	13	12	29	1158.1	1134	623	493	114	55	497	23	909	75	19
Peninsula	5.12	134	11	6	18	1126.0	1179	761	641	78	54	637	9	833	89	55

PITCHERS' RECORDS
(Leading Qualifiers for Earned-Run Average Leadership — 112 or More Innings)

*Throws lefthanded.

Pitcher—Club	W.	L.	Pct.	ERA.	G.	GS.	CG.	GF.	ShO.	Sv.	IP.	H.	R.	ER.	HR.	HB.	BB.	Int. BB.	SO.	WP.
Mullino, Winston-Salem	6	7	.462	2.32	36	10	1	13	0	5	112.1	89	45	29	4	5	39	1	93	13
Turner, Durham	9	9	.500	2.44	53	3	0	19	0	1	118.0	95	38	32	11	5	47	9	114	5
Castillo, Winston-Salem	9	6	.600	2.51	18	18	8	0	1	0	129.1	118	42	36	5	3	24	1	114	1
Kramer, Kinston	9	5	.643	2.60	18	17	5	1	1	0	131.2	97	44	38	7	4	42	3	89	4
Gomez, Winston-Salem*	11	6	.647	2.75	23	21	3	0	1	0	137.2	115	59	42	6	5	60	2	127	8
D. Miller, Frederick	13	4	.765	2.88	28	21	3	2	0	0	153.1	141	66	49	8	10	43	2	96	5
J. Johnson, Prince William*	4	10	.286	2.92	25	24	0	0	0	0	138.2	125	59	45	7	0	55	1	99	14
Constant, Frederick	10	4	.714	3.04	29	14	2	9	1	0	127.1	117	57	43	10	5	38	3	109	7
Draper, Prince William	14	8	.636	3.11	25	24	6	0	1	0	153.1	147	66	53	7	6	42	4	84	12
Tilmon, Durham	11	4	.733	3.24	33	23	0	6	0	4	144.1	145	63	52	6	9	44	2	92	5

Departmental Leaders: G—Powers, 66; W—Draper, 14; L—Aspray, 15; Pct.—D. Miller, .765; GS—Fischer, Owen, 27; CG—Aspray, 10; GF—Ausanio, 51; ShO—Nagy, 4; Sv.—Ausanio, 20; IP—Aspray, 177.0; H—Aspray, 203; R—Aspray, 95; ER—Fischer, 91; HR—Pacholec, 19; HB—Owen, 13; BB—Seanez, 111; IBB—Davis, 10; SO—Livernois, 151; WP—Melvin, 17.

(All Pitchers—Listed Alphabetically)

Pitcher—Club	W.	L.	Pct.	ERA.	G.	GS.	CG.	GF.	ShO.	Sv.	IP.	H.	R.	ER.	HR.	HB.	BB.	Int. BB.	SO.	WP.
Adachi, Peninsula	7	8	.467	3.85	20	20	3	0	1	0	138.0	129	70	59	12	5	57	0	119	7
Allison, Kinston*	0	0	.000	13.50	3	0	0	2	0	0	3.1	5	5	5	0	0	5	0	2	0
Aspray, Winston-Salem	8	15	.348	3.86	26	24	10	0	1	0	177.0	203	95	76	13	5	40	2	99	11
Ausanio, Salem	5	4	.556	2.12	54	0	0	51	0	20	89.0	51	29	21	9	3	44	6	97	5
Avery, Durham*	6	4	.600	1.45	13	13	3	0	1	0	86.2	59	22	14	5	1	20	1	90	4
Bauer, Peninsula	1	4	.200	3.08	7	3	0	1	0	0	26.1	33	21	9	2	1	11	0	10	3
Bell, Frederick	2	0	1.000	7.85	16	0	0	6	0	0	39.0	45	36	34	5	10	26	0	25	4
Birriel, Lynchburg*	1	4	.200	4.24	9	1	0	4	0	0	23.1	23	12	11	1	1	13	2	21	1
Blohm, Salem	0	7	.000	6.09	10	10	0	0	0	0	54.2	76	47	37	15	0	17	0	29	1
Boltz, Durham*	3	3	.500	3.04	11	10	1	0	1	0	50.1	63	23	17	3	0	7	2	33	4
Borgatti, Frederick	7	0	1.000	0.86	23	0	0	21	0	9	41.2	34	6	4	0	1	9	1	24	1
Bowden, Frederick*	1	0	1.000	1.04	4	0	0	2	0	0	8.2	9	3	1	0	0	4	1	8	1
Brow, Peninsula	0	0	.000	9.00	1	0	0	1	0	0	1.0	2	3	1	0	0	1	0	1	1
Buckholz, Salem	2	3	.400	5.10	5	5	0	0	0	0	30.0	33	19	17	4	4	13	0	21	7
Burdick, Frederick	3	3	.500	2.45	9	3	0	5	0	2	25.2	14	10	7	1	0	22	2	33	3
Burgo, Lynchburg	2	3	.400	3.09	9	9	1	0	1	0	46.2	39	18	16	4	0	14	1	38	1
Burlingame, Durham	4	0	1.000	0.50	11	11	2	0	2	0	54.1	28	8	3	1	0	5	1	42	2
Bushing, Peninsula	2	7	.222	4.33	35	14	1	13	1	3	99.2	96	64	48	4	8	79	0	99	10
Caballero, Winston-Salem	5	6	.455	3.65	23	17	2	1	0	0	111.0	117	56	45	11	4	38	0	75	4
Campos, Winston-Salem	0	0	.000	1.50	2	0	0	1	0	0	6.0	2	1	1	0	0	2	0	2	1
Carriger, Kinston	2	4	.333	2.22	17	0	0	11	0	4	24.1	15	9	6	2	0	12	1	27	5
Casano, Kinston	1	0	1.000	6.43	6	0	0	3	0	0	7.0	9	5	5	0	2	4	0	7	1
Castillo, Winston-Salem	9	6	.600	2.51	18	18	8	0	1	0	129.1	118	42	36	5	3	24	1	114	1
Cavers, Frederick*	4	8	.333	2.41	16	16	4	0	0	0	101.0	92	46	27	5	2	34	2	65	7
Coffman, Winston-Salem	2	3	.400	4.50	7	7	1	0	0	0	36.0	23	24	18	0	3	34	0	47	12
Cole, Kinston	1	0	1.000	0.00	1	1	1	0	1	0	7.0	4	0	0	0	0	1	0	5	0
Constant, Frederick	10	4	.714	3.04	29	14	2	9	1	0	127.1	117	57	43	10	5	38	3	109	7
Cook, Prince William	8	12	.400	3.29	25	24	5	0	1	0	153.0	123	68	56	7	6	49	0	83	6
Cuesta, Durham*	1	2	.333	4.38	11	1	0	1	0	1	24.2	20	18	12	4	1	15	0	11	3
Cummings, Peninsula	1	7	.125	6.52	11	9	0	0	0	0	58.0	65	49	42	6	5	30	0	48	5
Currin, Durham*	2	3	.400	3.50	33	1	0	12	0	1	36.0	37	18	14	3	4	13	1	33	3
Curtis, Kinston*	6	0	1.000	1.18	16	6	2	3	1	0	61.0	28	11	8	2	1	15	1	49	5
Czajkowski, Durham	2	3	.400	0.99	32	0	0	23	0	14	45.1	33	8	5	2	2	10	2	34	2
Davis, Lynchburg	3	2	.600	2.37	44	0	0	29	0	13	79.2	60	29	21	1	2	32	10	51	3
DeLaRosa, Frederick	3	4	.429	2.38	23	0	0	19	0	5	22.2	17	9	6	1	2	11	2	31	0
DeLeon, Prince William	3	2	.600	2.87	11	5	0	2	0	1	37.2	31	15	12	2	2	16	0	33	6
DelRosario, Durham	0	0	.000	0.64	7	0	0	3	0	2	14.0	6	1	1	0	0	4	2	8	0
Deutsch, Frederick	4	9	.308	4.94	25	19	2	1	0	0	129.1	147	87	71	12	3	50	1	81	8
Dolan, Lynchburg	2	1	.667	7.62	5	1	0	1	0	0	13.0	17	13	11	3	2	2	0	12	0
Downs, Salem	3	5	.375	5.38	36	1	0	13	0	1	78.2	105	53	47	8	3	40	6	42	4
Draper, Prince William	14	8	.636	3.11	25	24	6	0	1	0	153.1	147	66	53	7	6	42	4	84	12
Duncan, Salem	2	4	.333	5.11	26	4	0	10	0	2	68.2	64	49	39	4	6	33	1	55	5
Dzafic, Lynchburg	4	2	.667	2.88	34	0	0	20	0	4	56.1	57	23	18	1	3	14	2	15	0
Fansler, Salem	0	3	.000	4.88	7	7	0	0	0	0	24.0	28	19	13	6	3	19	0	13	1
Ferlenda, Kinston	2	6	.250	2.23	26	0	0	21	0	5	44.1	30	19	11	2	0	18	3	41	3
Ferretti, Kinston	0	0	.000	0.00	1	0	0	1	0	0	0.2	1	0	0	0	0	1	0	0	0
Fine, Peninsula	0	11	.000	6.35	13	13	0	0	0	0	66.2	69	56	47	2	6	57	0	26	6
Fischer, Lynchburg*	12	13	.480	4.78	28	27	7	0	2	0	171.1	178	94	91	12	6	79	1	138	12
Gardner, Winston-Salem	0	1	.000	2.16	6	0	0	3	0	0	8.1	5	5	2	0	1	13	2	7	0
Gast, Peninsula*	2	9	.182	4.83	36	16	2	13	0	3	130.1	148	74	70	9	8	47	0	97	16
Gilles, Kinston	6	3	.667	2.53	19	1	1	11	0	2	53.1	39	17	15	5	3	18	3	28	1
Gomez, Winston-Salem*	11	6	.647	2.75	23	21	3	0	1	0	137.2	115	59	42	6	5	60	2	127	8
Gonzales, Kinston*	0	2	.000	3.04	5	5	0	0	0	0	26.2	32	10	9	0	1	13	1	20	1
Greer, Prince William	7	3	.700	4.19	29	13	1	9	2	1	111.2	101	56	52	3	7	22	0	44	4
Haley, Lynchburg*	4	5	.444	3.28	46	0	0	34	0	9	60.1	64	31	22	5	4	27	6	39	4
D. Johnson, Peninsula	0	0	.000	18.00	1	0	0	1	0	0	1.0	4	2	2	0	0	1	0	1	0
J. Johnson, Prince William*	4	10	.286	2.92	25	24	0	0	0	0	138.2	125	59	45	7	0	55	1	99	14
L. Johnson, Durham*	6	2	.750	1.74	32	3	0	10	0	4	77.2	79	22	15	2	0	16	3	41	3
Jones, Frederick	5	6	.455	4.90	15	15	3	0	1	0	82.2	93	57	45	11	2	35	0	58	3

Pitcher—Club	W.	L.	Pct.	ERA.	G.	GS.	CG.	GF.	ShO.	Sv.	IP.	H.	R.	ER.	HR.	HB.	BB.	Int. BB.	SO.	WP.
Kallevig, Kinston	0	1	.000	12.00	1	1	0	0	0	0	3.0	6	4	4	0	0	3	0	4	0
Kerr, Frederick	3	3	.500	2.96	6	6	4	0	0	0	45.2	40	19	15	2	2	14	0	31	3
Khoury, Kinston*	0	0	.000	0.00	1	0	0	1	0	0	1.0	1	0	0	0	0	2	0	0	0
Kirk, 12 Pen-20 Dur*	4	5	.444	3.23	32	6	1	15	1	4	75.1	54	35	27	4	2	20	1	73	1
Kiser, Kinston*	0	1	.000	7.11	6	0	0	1	0	0	12.2	14	10	10	1	2	7	0	7	0
Kramer, Kinston	9	5	.643	2.60	18	17	5	1	1	0	131.2	97	44	38	7	4	42	3	89	4
Linskey, Frederick*	2	2	.500	0.88	9	9	3	0	2	0	61.1	47	7	6	0	2	16	2	46	1
Livernois, Lynchburg	10	8	.556	3.50	26	23	7	2	2	0	159.1	147	75	62	8	10	48	2	151	10
Lombardi, Peninsula*	0	1	.000	8.22	4	0	0	1	0	0	7.2	15	7	7	0	0	6	0	6	1
Machado, Peninsula	1	0	1.000	0.00	4	0	0	3	0	2	3.2	2	0	0	0	1	2	0	1	0
Makemson, Peninsula	2	3	.400	6.44	10	8	0	1	0	0	43.1	47	33	31	2	5	30	0	30	2
Marris, Prince William	6	7	.462	5.48	26	18	0	3	0	1	111.2	101	71	68	5	3	65	1	74	9
Martinez, Lynchburg	0	0	.000	0.00	1	0	0	1	0	0	1.0	1	0	0	0	0	1	0	0	0
McDonald, Frederick	0	0	.000	2.00	2	2	0	0	0	0	9.0	10	2	2	0	0	4	0	9	1
McMurtrie, Peninsula	1	1	.500	12.21	6	3	0	1	0	0	14.0	16	19	19	1	1	21	0	5	11
Melvin, Winston-Salem	6	9	.400	4.69	27	23	2	2	0	0	126.2	140	79	66	7	6	81	1	76	17
Michael, Peninsula*	3	5	.375	8.20	29	3	0	6	0	0	45.0	50	43	41	2	0	50	0	35	8
Michno, Winston-Salem	0	0	.000	1.26	7	0	0	4	0	2	14.1	10	2	2	0	1	2	0	15	0
D. Miller, Frederick	13	4	.765	2.88	28	21	3	2	0	0	153.1	141	66	49	8	10	43	2	96	5
P. Miller, Salem	6	12	.333	4.17	26	20	2	0	1	0	133.2	138	86	62	17	8	64	0	82	8
Mills, Prince William	6	1	.857	0.91	26	0	0	26	0	7	39.2	22	5	4	0	5	13	1	44	6
Minor, Salem	3	5	.375	3.63	39	4	0	25	0	6	86.2	91	43	35	6	2	31	6	62	3
Molero, Lynchburg	0	0	.000	9.00	2	0	0	1	0	0	2.0	3	2	2	1	0	1	0	4	0
Mondile, Frederick	2	4	.333	3.58	38	0	0	24	0	6	78.0	77	41	31	0	7	34	3	45	6
Morrison, Peninsula*	3	7	.300	6.50	21	8	1	8	0	1	62.1	68	53	45	5	3	57	0	59	1
Morton, Lynchburg*	4	5	.444	2.35	9	9	4	0	2	0	65.0	42	20	17	2	2	17	0	68	3
Mullino, Winston-Salem	6	7	.462	2.32	36	10	1	13	0	5	112.1	89	45	29	4	5	39	1	93	13
Murphy, Peninsula	0	0	.000	6.00	5	0	0	1	0	0	9.0	9	9	6	0	0	6	0	3	3
Mutis, Kinston*	7	3	.700	2.62	16	15	5	1	2	0	99.2	87	42	29	6	2	20	0	68	3
Myers, Frederick*	8	10	.444	3.99	22	21	4	1	0	0	140.0	138	65	62	14	2	53	2	118	2
Nagy, Kinston	8	4	.667	1.51	13	13	6	0	4	0	95.1	69	22	16	0	4	24	0	99	3
Nied, Durham	5	2	.714	6.63	12	12	0	0	0	0	58.1	74	47	43	10	5	23	1	38	1
Nielsen, Prince William*	3	2	.600	2.19	39	0	0	16	0	4	49.1	26	14	12	0	6	25	0	45	6
Ogden, Kinston	4	5	.444	3.78	14	11	0	1	0	0	78.2	77	40	33	6	2	34	2	29	8
Ohlms, Prince William	2	5	.286	2.58	37	0	0	29	0	6	52.1	48	25	15	1	3	25	4	37	6
Oliveras, Kinston.	3	4	.429	4.11	17	14	0	1	0	1	61.1	41	33	28	0	3	65	0	69	14
Ortiz, Kinston	5	3	.625	4.10	18	13	0	2	0	1	90.0	73	48	41	8	2	42	0	85	4
Owen, Lynchburg*	13	9	.591	3.26	27	27	4	0	1	0	168.1	152	73	61	10	13	68	1	107	6
Pacholec, Salem	12	7	.632	3.87	26	26	2	0	1	0	158.0	150	83	68	19	3	65	1	150	12
Palermo, Frederick	0	1	.000	0.00	3	0	0	2	0	0	4.1	5	3	0	0	0	5	0	5	0
Paris, Lynchburg	0	0	.000	54.00	1	0	0	0	0	0	1.0	7	6	6	0	0	1	0	1	2
Parker, Winston-Salem*	4	5	.444	1.86	21	9	4	3	1	0	72.2	60	22	15	0	0	26	1	63	2
Parmenter, Winston-Salem.	0	0	.000	9.90	7	1	0	4	0	0	10.0	17	14	11	3	0	8	2	9	1
Pena, Frederick*	0	0	.000	0.00	1	0	0	0	0	0	1.0	0	0	0	0	0	0	0	0	0
Piatt, Kinston	2	0	1.000	2.51	20	0	0	12	0	1	28.2	24	8	8	1	3	8	0	31	1
Pilkinton, Peninsula	0	0	.000	27.00	1	0	0	1	0	0	1.0	2	3	3	1	0	1	0	2	0
Polak, Prince William	1	2	.333	5.46	7	4	0	2	0	1	29.2	31	20	18	5	1	15	0	22	2
Powers, Peninsula	7	2	.778	3.18	66	0	0	45	0	5	99.0	93	45	35	8	4	36	6	70	1
Pratts, Lynchburg	1	1	.500	8.34	8	2	0	3	0	0	22.2	38	23	21	4	2	9	0	16	0
Prybylinski, Prince William	4	1	.800	2.84	28	1	0	13	0	1	69.2	57	30	22	5	1	18	1	70	5
Reichard, Peninsula	0	0	.000	27.00	1	0	0	1	0	0	1.0	3	3	3	0	0	1	0	1	0
Rhodes, Frederick*	2	2	.500	5.18	7	6	0	0	0	0	24.1	19	16	14	2	0	19	0	28	4
K. Richardson, Salem	4	0	1.000	0.84	5	5	2	0	0	0	32.0	30	3	3	0	0	10	0	26	0
R. Richardson, Lynchburg	5	4	.556	2.97	17	16	4	1	0	0	91.0	81	37	30	3	5	26	0	50	3
Richey, Durham	3	3	.500	4.20	19	0	0	14	0	3	30.0	20	14	14	3	2	17	2	30	2
Riddle, Frederick	0	1	.000	4.30	6	1	0	2	0	0	14.2	15	9	7	1	0	9	0	7	2
C. Ritter, Peninsula	1	6	.143	4.98	10	10	2	0	0	0	65.0	69	43	36	1	5	21	0	48	1
R. Ritter, 15 Pen-1 WnS	2	2	.500	3.18	16	2	0	11	0	3	28.1	27	15	10	1	0	19	3	21	1
Rivera, Durham	5	7	.417	4.49	23	22	1	0	0	0	102.1	113	55	51	6	5	51	1	58	10
Rivero, Winston-Salem	0	0	.000	18.00	1	0	0	1	0	0	1.0	0	2	2	0	0	5	0	3	0
Rodriguez, Winston-Salem*	4	3	.571	2.00	36	3	0	18	0	2	67.2	49	25	15	3	4	40	2	60	3
Roscoe, Kinston	5	1	.833	4.40	20	4	1	8	0	2	61.1	61	36	30	6	1	17	2	62	7
Rose, Peninsula	0	1	.000	7.71	1	1	0	0	0	0	4.2	6	5	4	3	0	7	0	2	0
Ruskin, Salem*	4	5	.444	2.23	14	13	3	1	0	1	84.2	71	35	21	5	4	33	0	92	6
Santiago, Salem	0	0	.000	0.00	1	0	0	0	0	0	1.0	0	0	0	0	0	4	0	0	0
Scaglione, Kinston	5	4	.556	3.46	31	8	2	11	0	3	104.0	103	51	40	4	9	43	3	102	6
Schlopy, Salem*	5	8	.385	4.83	29	12	1	8	0	1	98.2	108	64	53	8	8	39	1	71	7
Seanez, Kinston	8	10	.444	4.14	25	25	1	0	0	0	113.0	94	66	52	0	5	111	1	149	13
Seminara, Prince William	2	4	.333	3.68	21	0	0	12	0	2	36.2	26	23	15	0	5	22	3	23	5
Shepherd, Kinston	1	2	.333	2.86	8	2	0	3	0	0	28.1	25	11	9	2	0	15	0	23	2
Siebert, Peninsula	2	5	.286	9.26	20	5	0	5	0	0	45.2	63	51	47	9	4	28	0	15	7
Skripko, Lynchburg	4	6	.400	4.80	30	12	1	8	0	1	90.0	100	57	48	5	5	33	1	66	3
C. Smith, Durham*	4	3	.571	3.01	13	12	0	0	0	0	68.2	65	28	23	8	2	28	0	43	2
T. Smith, Salem	1	1	.500	4.02	7	1	0	4	0	0	15.2	12	7	7	1	2	16	0	12	3
W. Smith, Salem	4	5	.444	2.94	23	9	0	13	0	4	64.1	46	26	21	4	2	40	2	58	6
Stanford, Prince William	3	1	.750	5.22	14	0	0	9	0	1	29.1	30	19	17	0	2	11	3	21	2
Stephan, Peninsula	6	8	.429	4.72	35	16	1	6	1	1	145.0	150	87	76	10	3	63	1	103	5
Stoker, Kinston	8	6	.571	4.44	24	20	1	2	1	0	117.2	127	69	58	5	4	47	1	82	11
Strauss, Winston-Salem	5	7	.417	2.95	50	2	0	39	0	17	79.1	74	28	26	7	5	30	2	67	5
Surhoff, Salem	1	2	.333	2.03	20	0	0	18	0	14	26.2	19	10	6	1	1	12	1	23	1
S. Taylor, Lynchburg*	5	3	.625	2.89	19	9	0	4	0	1	81.0	61	33	26	7	1	25	3	99	3
W. Taylor, Prince William	9	8	.529	3.34	25	25	4	0	1	0	142.2	131	63	53	9	5	56	2	104	9
Telford, Frederick	2	1	.667	4.21	9	5	0	2	0	1	25.2	25	15	12	1	2	12	0	19	2
Tilmon, Durham	11	4	.733	3.24	33	23	0	6	0	4	144.1	145	63	52	6	9	44	2	92	5
Tomberlin, Durham*	0	0	.000	18.00	1	0	0	1	0	0	1.0	2	2	2	0	0	2	0	0	0
Tomlin, Salem*	12	6	.667	3.25	21	21	3	0	2	0	138.2	131	60	50	11	3	43	0	99	7
Trlicek, Durham.	0	0	.000	1.13	1	1	0	0	0	0	8.0	3	1	1	0	1	1	0	4	0
Turner, Durham	9	9	.500	2.44	53	0	0	19	0	1	118.0	95	38	32	11	5	47	9	114	5
Watson, Durham	3	0	1.000	1.50	19	1	0	11	0	3	54.0	37	10	9	1	4	17	1	42	2
Wendell, Durham	2	0	1.000	1.13	3	3	0	0	0	0	24.0	13	4	3	0	0	6	0	27	0
G. Williams, Prince William	0	0	.000	0.00	1	0	0	1	0	0	1.0	0	0	0	0	0	0	0	1	0
R. Williams, Frederick	2	3	.400	4.84	24	0	0	17	0	2	44.2	49	25	24	5	2	22	4	34	2

Pitcher—Club	W.	L.	Pct.	ERA.	G.	GS.	CG.	GF.	ShO.	Sv.	IP.	H.	R.	ER.	HR.	HB.	BB.	Int. BB.	SO.	WP.
Zarranz, Winston-Salem	4	3	.571	1.70	19	0	0	15	0	4	47.2	27	10	9	1	2	14	2	42	0
Ziem, Durham	9	0	1.000	1.66	28	0	0	18	0	7	48.2	39	10	9	2	3	11	2	25	1

BALKS—Stephan, 8; Aspray, Cook, Gast, C. Ritter, 7 each; Fine, Gomez, Oliveras, 6 each; Adachi, Bell, Bushing, Owen, R. Richardson, Rodriguez, Skripko, W. Taylor, 5 each; Constant, Duncan, Jones, Livernois, Melvin, Ruskin, Seminara, 4 each; Boltz, Makemson, Pacholec, Powers, Rivera, Scaglione, Siebert, Stoker, S. Taylor, Turner, 3 each; Birriel, Burdick, Cavers, Dolan, Downs, Ferlenda, Fischer, Haley, J. Johnson, Lombardi, McDonald, D. Miller, Mutis, Myers, Ogden, Parmenter, Polak, Riddle, Roscoe, W. Smith, Stanford, 2 each; Allison, Avery, Bauer, Bowden, Burgo, Burlingame, Caballero, Castillo, Cummings, Davis, DeLeon, Deutsch, Draper, Dzafic, Fansler, Greer, Kallevig, Khoury, Kramer, Marris, Martinez, McMurtrie, Michael, P. Miller, Minor, Mondile, Morrison, Murphy, Paris, Parker, Pratts, Prybylinski, Rhodes, Schlopy, Seanez, C. Smith, Watson, 1 each.

COMBINATION SHUTOUTS—Rivera-Turner, Burlingame-Turner-Currin, Burlingame-Tilmon, Avery-Johnson-Czajkowski, Johnson-Currin-Turner, Tilmon-Turner-Johnson, Stoker-Johnson-Kirk, Smith-Turner, Durham; Myers-Constant-Mondile, Myers-Borgatti, Miller-Borgatti, Myers-Williams, Rhodes-Mondile, Frederick; Seanez-Piatt-Surhoff, Ogden-Curtis-Ferlenda, Curtis-Carriger, Shepherd-Ferlenda, Kinston; Owen-Skripko-Haley, Owen-Dzafic, Burgo-Dzafic, Skripko-Davis, Richardson-Davis, Taylor-Haley, Richardson-Taylor, Lynchburg; Adachi-Stephan, Bushing-Powers, Peninsula; Johnson-Prybylinski, Cook-Nielsen, Taylor-Prybylinski-Marris-Ohlms, Johnson-Mills, Polak-Mills, Draper-Nielsen-Mills, Taylor-Ohlms, Prince William; Tomlin-Ruskin, Richardson-Downs, Tomlin-Downs-Schlopy-Ausanio, Smith-Ausanio, Fansler-Downs-Ausanio, Miller-Duncan, Ruskin-Ausanio, Pacholec-Ausanio, Salem; Gomez-Michno-Rodriguez, Melvin-Strauss, Gomez-Strauss, Mullino-Zarranz, Winston-Salem.

NO-HIT GAMES—Burlingame, Durham, defeated Frederick, 4-0 (first game, perfect game), April 9; Tomlin, Salem, defeated Kinston, 1-0, May 28.

Florida State League

CLASS A

CHAMPIONSHIP WINNERS IN PREVIOUS YEARS

1919—Sanford* .... .605	1951—DeLand§ .... .643	1970—Miami b .... .662
Orlando* .... .703	1952—DeLand x .... .704	St. Petersburg .... .600
1920—Tampa .... .654	Palatka (3rd)‡ .... .569	1971—Miami b .... .667
Tampa .... .722	1953—Daytona Beach† .... .657	Daytona Beach .... .586
1921—Orlando .... .635	DeLand .... .703	1972—Miami c .... .562
1922—St. Petersburg .... .503	1954—Jacksonville Beach .... .629	Daytona Beach .... .606
St. Petersburg .... .618	Lakeland† .... .594	1973—St. Petersburg d .... .575
1923—Orlando .... .667	1955—Orlando .... .671	West Palm Beach d .... .580
Orlando .... .678	Orlando .... .643	1974—West Palm Beach d .... .598
1924—Lakeland .... .695	1956—Cocoa .... .614	Fort Lauderdale .... .626
Lakeland .... .683	Cocoa .... .671	1975—St. Petersburg d .... .652
1925—St. Petersburg .... .667	1957—Palatka .... .629	Miami .... .581
Tampa† .... .696	Tampa† .... .681	1976—Tampa .... .559
1926—Sanford .... .647	1958—St. Petersburg .... .732	Lakeland d .... .536
Sanford .... .623	St. Petersburg .... .681	1977—Lakeland d .... .616
1927—Orlando† .... .600	1959—Tampa .... .591	West Palm Beach .... .583
Miami .... .661	St. Petersburg† .... .612	1978—Lakeland§ .... .565
1928-35—Did not operate.	1960—Lakeland .... .731	Miami§ .... .539
1936—Gainesville .... .542	Palatka† .... .614	1979—Fort Lauderdale .... .643
St. Augustine (4th)† .... .492	1961—Tampa† .... .710	Winter Haven e .... .577
1937—Gainesville§ .... .616	Sarasota .... .696	1980—Daytona Beach .... .628
1938—Leesburg .... .626	1962—Sarasota .... .689	Fort Lauderdale d .... .606
Gainesville (2nd)‡ .... .615	Fort Lauderdale† .... .623	1981—Fort Myers .... .554
1939—Sanford§ .... .787	1963—Sarasota .... .645	Daytona Beach f .... .504
1940—Daytona Beach .... .619	Sarasota .... .667	1982—Fort Lauderdale f .... .621
Orlando (4th)‡ .... .507	1964—Fort Lauderdale† .... .629	Tampa .... .546
1941—St. Augustine .... .659	St. Petersburg .... .594	1983—Daytona Beach .... .634
Leesburg (4th)‡ .... .488	1965—Fort Lauderdale .... .627	Vero Beach f .... .515
1942-45—Did not operate.	Fort Lauderdale .... .634	1984—Tampa .... .532
1946—Orlando§ .... .681	1966—Leesburg† .... .781	Fort Lauderdale f .... .521
1947—St. Augustine .... .625	St. Petersburg .... .700	1985—Fort Myers g .... .590
Gainesville (2nd)‡ .... .584	1967—St. Petersburg y .... .691	Fort Lauderdale .... .550
1948—Gainesville .... .643	Orlando .... .638	1986—St. Petersburg g .... .647
Daytona Beach (2nd)‡ ...... .616	1968—Miami .... .613	West Palm Beach .... .593
1949—Gainesville .... .635	Orlando z .... .579	1987—Fort Lauderdale g .... .616
St. Augustine (3rd)‡ .... .556	1969—Miami a .... .606	Osceola .... .576
1950—Orlando .... .629	Orlando .... .606	1988—Osceola .... .606
DeLand (3rd)‡ .... .590		St. Lucie h .... .532

*Split-season playoff abandoned after each team won three games. †Won split-season playoff. ‡Won four-club playoff. §Won championship and four-club playoff. xWon both halves of split season. yLeague divided into Eastern and Western divisions with split season. St. Petersburg and Orlando won both halves of split season; St. Petersburg won playoff. zLeague divided into Eastern and Western divisions. Miami won regular-season pennant on basis of highest won-lost percentage. Orlando won four-club playoff involving first two teams in each division. aLeague divided into Southern and Central divisions. Miami won playoff between division leaders. (NOTE—Pennant awarded to playoff winner in 1936.) bLeague divided into Eastern and Western divisions. Miami won regular-season pennant on basis of highest won-loss percentage, and also won four-club playoff involving first two teams in each division. cLeague divided into Eastern and Western divisions. Won four-club playoff involving first two teams in each division. dLeague divided into Northern and Southern divisions. Won four-club playoff involving first two teams in each division. eLeague divided into Northern and Southern divisions. Same two clubs won both halves; won playoffs. fWon split-season playoff. gLeague divided into Western, Central and Southern divisions. Won four-club playoff. hLeague divided into Eastern, Western and Central divisions; played split-season. Won six-club playoff.

STANDING OF CLUBS AT CLOSE OF FIRST HALF, JUNE 16

EASTERN DIVISION

Club	W.	L.	T.	Pct.	G.B.
St. Lucie (Mets)	42	28	0	.600	......
West Palm Beach (Expos)	39	31	0	.557	3
Vero Beach (Dodgers)	39	31	0	.557	3
Fort Lauderdale (Yankees)	33	37	0	.471	9
Miami (Independent)	16	53	0	.232	25½

WESTERN DIVISION

Club	W.	L.	T.	Pct.	G.B.
Port Charlotte (Rangers)	40	30	0	.571	......
Sarasota (White Sox)	38	31	0	.551	1½
St. Petersburg (Cardinals)	35	35	0	.500	5
Clearwater (Phillies)	34	36	0	.486	6
Dunedin (Blue Jays)	33	37	0	.471	7

CENTRAL DIVISION

Club	W.	L.	T.	Pct.	G.B.
Baseball City (Royals)	42	27	0	.609	......
Lakeland (Tigers)	39	31	0	.557	3½
Osceola (Astros)	36	33	0	.522	6
Winter Haven (Red Sox)	22	48	0	.314	20½

STANDING OF CLUBS AT CLOSE OF SECOND HALF, AUGUST 31

EASTERN DIVISION

Club	W.	L.	T.	Pct.	G.B.
St. Lucie (Mets)	37	27	0	.578	......
West Palm Beach (Expos)	35	33	0	.515	4
Vero Beach (Dodgers)	31	35	0	.470	7
Miami (Independent)	27	38	0	.415	10½
Fort Lauderdale (Yankees)	28	40	0	.412	11

WESTERN DIVISION

Club	W.	L.	T.	Pct.	G.B.
Sarasota (White Sox)	41	26	0	.612	......
St. Petersburg (Cardinals)	40	29	0	.580	2
Dunedin (Blue Jays)	36	34	0	.514	6½
Port Charlotte (Rangers)	35	34	0	.507	7
Clearwater (Phillies)	23	43	0	.348	17½

CENTRAL DIVISION

Club	W.	L.	T.	Pct.	G.B.
Lakeland (Tigers)	38	29	0	.567	......
Osceola (Astros)	36	32	0	.529	2½
Baseball City (Royals)	36	34	0	.514	3½
Winter Haven (Red Sox)	30	39	0	.435	9

COMPOSITE STANDING OF CLUBS AT CLOSE OF SEASON, AUGUST 31

Club	St.L.	Sar.	Lak.	B.C.	St.P.	P.C.	WPB	Osc.	V.B.	Dun.	Ft.L.	Clw.	W.H.	Mia.	W.	L.	T.	Pct.	G.B.
St. Lucie (Mets)	....	3	4	5	5	4	8	3	10	4	10	5	5	13	79	55	0	.590	......
Sarasota (White Sox)	4	....	6	5	8	6	5	5	4	10	6	10	5	5	79	57	0	.581	1
Lakeland (Tigers)	4	2	....	8	2	6	3	13	5	4	4	5	17	4	77	60	0	.562	3½
Baseball City (Royals)	3	3	12	....	6	5	4	11	5	3	4	4	12	6	78	61	0	.561	3½
St. Petersburg (Cardinals)	3	10	5	2	....	10	3	4	3	10	4	8	6	7	75	64	0	.540	6½
Port Charlotte (Rangers)	4	10	2	3	8	....	8	3	6	8	5	7	3	8	75	64	0	.540	6½
West Palm Beach (Expos)	8	3	5	4	5	0	....	2	10	3	13	5	6	10	74	64	0	.536	7
Osceola (Astros)	5	2	6	8	4	5	6	....	4	3	3	7	14	5	72	65	0	.526	8½
Vero Beach (Dodgers)	7	4	2	3	5	2	7	4	....	5	11	4	7	9	70	66	0	.515	10
Dunedin (Blue Jays)	4	7	4	5	6	9	5	5	3	....	5	10	3	3	69	71	0	.493	13
Fort Lauderdale (Yankees)	6	2	4	4	3	5	5	5	3	....	7	4	9	61	77	0	.442	20
Clearwater (Phillies)	1	6	3	4	8	9	3	1	4	8	1	....	2	7	57	79	0	.419	23
Winter Haven (Red Sox)	2	3	3	8	2	5	2	6	1	5	4	6	....	5	52	87	0	.374	29½
Miami (Independent)	4	2	4	2	1	0	5	3	6	5	7	1	3	....	43	91	0	.321	36

Major league affiliations in parentheses.

Playoffs—St. Petersburg defeated Baseball City, two games to none; Port Charlotte defeated Sarasota, two games to one; St. Petersburg defeated Lakeland, two games to one; Port Charlotte defeated St. Lucie, two games to one; Port Charlotte defeated St. Petersburg, two games to one, to win league championship.

Regular-Season Attendance—Baseball City, 39,220; Clearwater, 68,591; Dunedin, 41,231; Fort Lauderdale, 43,307; Lakeland, 54,409; Miami, 14,972; Osceola, 53,566; Port Charlotte, 122,060; Sarasota, 52,061; St. Lucie, 66,041; St. Petersburg, 202,383; Vero Beach, 87,178; West Palm Beach, 84,316; Winter Haven, 28,009. Total—957,344. Playoffs (14 games)—8,236. All-Star Game—2,362.

Managers—Baseball City, Luis Silverio; Clearwater, Glenn Gulliver; Dunedin, Doug Ault; Fort Lauderdale, Clete Boyer; Lakeland, John Lipon; Miami, Jim Gattis; Osceola, Rick Sweet; Port Charlotte, Bobby Jones; St. Lucie, Clint Hurdle; St. Petersburg, Dave Bialas; Sarasota, Tony Franklin; Vero Beach, Joe Alvarez; West Palm Beach, Felipe Alou; Winter Haven, Dave Holt.

All-Star Team—1B—Henri Rodriguez, Vero Beach; 2B—Paco Burgos, Port Charlotte; 3B—Chris Donnels, St. Lucie; SS—Will Cordero, West Palm Beach; OF—Rodney McCray, Sarasota; Jim Vatcher, Clearwater; Jaime Roseboro, St. Lucie; C—Jim Baxter, Lakeland; Ed Fulton, St. Petersburg; DH—Vincent Degifico, Winter Haven; RHP—Mike Miller, St. Lucie; Ron Stephens, Sarasota; LHP—Wally Trice, Osceola; Rheal Cormier, St. Petersburg; REL—Mark Grater, St. Petersburg; Jim Poole, Vero Beach; Most Valuable Player—Chris Donnels, St. Lucie; Manager of the Year—John Lipon, Lakeland.

(Compiled by Howe Sportsdata International, Boston, Mass.)

CLUB BATTING

Club	Pct.	G.	AB.	R.	OR.	H.	TB.	2B.	3B.	HR.	RBI.	SH.	SF.	HP.	BB.	Int. BB.	SO.	SB.	CS.	LOB.
Baseball City	.271	139	4567	698	615	1237	1674	180	61	45	578	43	41	42	489	18	737	245	120	897
St. Lucie	.264	134	4333	605	501	1142	1586	198	39	56	516	51	46	54	464	34	721	250	95	872
Sarasota	.260	136	4371	576	486	1137	1456	183	32	24	489	68	28	44	523	18	723	142	82	991
Vero Beach	.260	135	4365	580	500	1134	1491	172	31	41	501	43	50	41	388	29	637	171	74	853
Port Charlotte	.260	139	4504	578	548	1170	1554	172	61	30	504	39	59	41	583	27	818	119	85	1068
Osceola	.255	137	4505	587	557	1148	1542	172	51	40	506	54	69	59	483	18	826	156	72	974
Lakeland	.253	136	4431	508	418	1122	1477	151	39	42	448	52	36	41	452	24	746	119	72	975
St. Petersburg	.248	139	4472	546	526	1111	1416	155	30	30	477	34	56	47	548	22	684	167	107	1007
Dunedin	.244	140	4476	541	543	1090	1611	182	36	89	482	23	33	44	410	13	952	124	75	886
Fort Lauderdale	.242	138	4390	531	585	1064	1402	188	24	34	460	58	47	35	484	19	832	109	65	935
Miami	.239	134	4125	428	650	984	1416	161	26	73	376	30	29	31	452	17	947	85	83	871
West Palm Beach	.238	138	4507	484	439	1071	1419	162	33	40	423	40	36	54	431	37	714	155	65	957
Clearwater	.237	136	4410	463	582	1044	1417	195	32	38	410	43	37	47	368	17	738	99	51	918
Winter Haven	.230	139	4501	461	636	1037	1460	170	23	69	385	49	24	47	399	13	848	89	55	921

INDIVIDUAL BATTING
(Leading Qualifiers for Batting Championship—378 or More Plate Appearances)

*Bats lefthanded. †Switch-hitter.

Player and Club	Pct.	G.	AB.	R.	H.	TB.	2B.	3B.	HR.	RBI.	SH.	SF.	HP.	BB.	Int. BB.	SO.	SB.	CS.
Mota, Andres, Osceola	.319	131	505	68	161	202	21	4	4	69	3	10	11	42	3	61	28	9
Donnels, Chris, St. Lucie*	.313	117	386	70	121	197	23	1	17	78	2	3	6	83	15	65	18	4
Vatcher, James, Clearwater	.301	92	349	51	105	157	30	5	4	46	0	2	2	41	0	49	7	3
Caceres, Edgar, Sarasota†	.295	106	373	45	110	134	16	4	0	50	9	2	2	24	4	38	8	3
Burgos, Francisco, Port Charlotte†	.292	130	483	51	141	181	26	7	0	64	7	8	4	21	3	51	4	8
Hall, Joseph, St. Petersburg	.292	134	504	72	147	162	9	3	0	54	3	9	8	62	2	57	45	28
Valdez, Amilcar, Vero Beach	.285	104	347	48	99	154	32	1	7	56	4	3	0	29	0	65	1	1
Rodriguez, Henry, Vero Beach*	.284	126	433	53	123	188	33	1	10	73	1	6	2	48	11	58	7	6
Griffin, Mark, Vero Beach*	.282	129	440	59	124	154	8	8	2	52	3	8	7	29	6	58	35	15
Fernandez, Joey, St. Petersburg*	.282	107	362	39	102	153	22	4	7	50	2	4	1	44	2	48	0	2

Departmental Leaders: G—Rodgers, 140; AB—Rodgers, 525; R—R. Moore, 85; H—Mota, 161; TB—Yan, 218; 2B—H. Rodriguez, 33; 3B—McDaniel, 11; HR—Yan, 24; RBI—Donnels, 78; SH—C. Rodriguez, 21; SF—Fulton, 15; HP—Mota, 11; BB—McCray, 96; IBB—Donnels, 15; SO—Yan, 130; SB—Rodgers, 60; CS—Hall, 28.

(All Players—Listed Alphabetically)

Player and Club	Pct.	G.	AB.	R.	H.	TB.	2B.	3B.	HR.	RBI.	SH.	SF.	HP.	BB.	Int. BB.	SO.	SB.	CS.
Abell, Todd, Port Charlotte	.211	14	38	2	8	8	0	0	0	5	0	0	0	2	0	9	1	0
Abreu, Franklin, St. Petersburg	.201	90	254	18	51	54	3	0	0	19	2	6	0	26	0	48	4	5
Acta, Manuel, Osceola	.000	5	11	1	0	0	0	0	0	0	0	0	0	3	0	4	0	0
Adler, Marcus, Lakeland	.254	94	256	29	65	83	8	5	0	27	8	4	2	42	1	31	4	3
Alborano, Peter, Baseball City*	.337	77	279	39	94	115	9	6	0	40	2	2	1	21	2	24	8	4
Alcantara, Roberto, Miami*	.136	14	22	3	3	3	0	0	0	0	0	0	0	4	0	7	0	0
Alou, Jose, West Palm Beach	.224	95	245	27	55	67	7	1	1	23	7	2	3	18	0	37	5	5
Alyea, Brant, 62 St.L-13 P.C.	.273	75	289	32	79	104	14	1	3	45	1	4	1	17	2	40	0	2
Anglero, Jose, Baseball City	.268	94	276	28	74	96	6	5	2	29	3	4	1	23	0	49	7	5
Arendas, Daniel, Fort Lauderdale*	.347	28	101	23	35	47	8	2	0	11	0	0	2	13	2	13	4	2
Argo, William, Vero Beach†	.217	85	184	15	40	48	6	1	0	11	2	2	2	15	1	29	8	6
Bagwell, Jeffrey, Winter Haven	.310	64	210	27	65	88	13	2	2	19	3	1	3	23	0	25	1	1
Barberie, Bret, West Palm Beach†	.267	124	457	63	122	158	16	4	4	34	5	4	10	64	7	39	10	4
Barefoot, Michael, Miami	.175	21	63	5	11	12	1	0	0	1	2	0	0	16	0	15	1	1
Barragan, James, Clearwater*	.281	112	392	46	110	150	20	4	4	41	0	3	0	38	4	46	0	0
Barron, Anthony, Vero Beach	.244	105	324	45	79	108	7	5	4	40	2	3	4	17	1	90	26	12
Batiste, Kimothy, Clearwater	.234	114	385	36	90	119	12	4	3	33	11	1	4	17	1	67	13	7

Player and Club	Pct.	G.	AB.	R.	H.	TB.	2B.	3B.	HR.	RBI.	SH.	SF.	HP.	BB.	Int. BB.	SO.	SB.	CS.
Baxter, James, Lakeland	.251	91	263	32	66	96	16	1	4	22	4	2	4	30	0	80	0	2
Bernardo, Rick, 38 P.C.-62 Mia*	.251	100	319	35	80	102	15	2	1	34	4	2	2	32	5	74	5	7
Berry, Sean, Baseball City	.266	116	399	67	106	151	19	7	4	44	5	5	6	44	1	68	37	11
Beyerler, Arnold, Lakeland	.284	87	303	34	86	100	8	0	2	33	12	5	3	27	1	31	7	10
Billmeyer, Michael, Port Charlotte*.....	.164	25	73	6	12	12	0	0	0	3	0	0	0	10	0	15	0	0
Bishop, James, Miami	.230	54	165	18	38	58	11	0	3	18	0	0	1	24	0	54	0	3
Blosser, Gregory, Winter Haven*	.255	28	94	6	24	33	1	1	2	14	0	1	1	8	0	14	1	0
Bohringer, Helmut, Vero Beach	.242	30	62	6	15	17	2	0	0	10	1	1	0	5	0	13	0	1
Bonchek, Jeffery, Miami†	.212	21	52	6	11	12	1	0	0	1	0	0	1	10	1	14	1	0
Bourne, Kendrick, Clearwater†	.202	36	109	8	22	30	6	1	0	7	1	0	3	7	1	38	0	2
Bournigal, Rafael, Vero Beach	.264	132	484	74	128	144	11	1	1	37	5	3	3	33	0	21	18	13
Boyce, Thomas, Miami†	.276	49	152	19	42	51	3	0	2	13	0	3	2	19	3	34	1	2
Bridges, Jason, Fort Lauderdale	.250	1	4	0	1	1	0	0	0	2	0	0	0	0	0	3	0	0
Brogna, Rico, Lakeland*	.235	128	459	47	108	157	20	7	5	51	3	3	2	38	6	82	2	4
Brown, Kurt, Sarasota	.272	90	287	26	78	99	13	1	2	30	7	1	6	30	0	51	0	1
Brummer, Jeffrey, Vero Beach*	.306	46	62	13	19	23	1	0	1	6	1	1	0	11	1	13	8	3
Bruzdewicz, Timothy, Dunedin*	.000	13	1	0	0	0	0	0	0	0	0	0	0	0	0	0	0	0
Burgos, Francisco, Port Charlotte†	.292	130	483	51	141	181	26	7	0	64	7	8	4	21	3	51	4	8
Busby, LeWayne, Sarasota	.213	49	155	17	33	44	2	3	1	13	0	0	0	19	0	32	2	5
Byrd, James, Winter Haven†	.197	126	447	42	88	118	17	2	3	25	11	0	4	25	0	104	22	10
Cabrera, Basilio, Lakeland	.248	126	496	68	123	167	13	8	5	41	4	3	8	33	1	94	45	13
Caceres, Edgar, Sarasota†	.295	106	373	45	110	134	16	4	0	50	9	2	2	24	4	38	8	3
Calvert, Arthur, St. Petersburg	.232	70	237	25	55	74	8	1	3	24	4	2	2	19	0	53	2	1
Campbell, Darrin, Sarasota	.225	29	89	10	20	26	6	0	0	3	2	0	2	4	0	23	0	0
Caraballo, Edgardo, Baseball City	.333	3	9	0	3	3	0	0	0	0	0	0	0	0	0	2	0	0
Carlin, Michael, Clearwater†	.228	36	92	10	21	24	3	0	0	6	5	0	9	0	0	23	2	1
Carmona, Gregorio, St. Petersburg†	.224	116	348	52	78	91	4	3	1	30	5	3	2	72	0	84	31	17
Cartaya, Joel, Port Charlotte†	.279	86	330	41	92	121	8	9	1	36	6	7	2	30	2	23	10	15
Carver, Billy Paul, Osceola	.165	45	139	8	23	27	1	0	1	10	10	1	0	4	0	25	1	1
Cedeno, Domingo, Dunedin	.214	9	28	3	6	8	0	1	0	1	0	0	0	3	0	10	0	1
Cedeno, Ramon, Osceola	.303	67	221	27	67	92	6	5	3	28	1	1	1	9	1	41	2	1
Cerny, Martin, Miami*	.000	36	1	0	0	0	0	0	0	0	0	0	0	0	0	0	0	0
Chadwick, Ray, Sarasota†	.000	1	1	0	0	0	0	0	0	0	0	0	0	0	0	0	0	0
Christian, Ricardo, St. Petersburg	.231	117	308	48	71	96	12	5	1	30	2	2	0	27	1	75	27	18
Cinnella, Douglas, West Palm Beach	.000	32	1	0	0	0	0	0	0	0	1	0	0	0	0	1	0	0
Cobb, Mark, Clearwater	.189	60	212	17	40	50	3	2	1	12	1	1	1	13	0	48	3	1
Colbrunn, Gregory, West Palm Beach..	.237	59	228	20	54	62	8	0	0	25	0	2	2	6	1	29	3	1
Cole, Alexander, St. Petersburg*	.188	8	32	2	6	6	0	0	0	1	0	0	0	3	0	7	4	1
Colston, Frank, Miami*	.200	15	45	4	9	10	1	0	0	2	0	0	0	1	0	10	0	0
Conine, Jeffrey, Baseball City	.273	113	425	68	116	184	12	7	14	60	0	3	3	40	2	91	32	13
Cordero, Wilfredo, West Palm Beach..	.277	78	289	37	80	114	12	2	6	29	1	2	3	33	2	58	2	5
Crosby, Todd, St. Petersburg†	.258	105	368	60	95	118	11	3	2	31	8	3	2	68	1	40	12	2
Cruz, Bernardo, Sarasota	.204	30	93	8	19	24	1	2	0	8	4	1	0	6	0	17	5	3
Davis, Russell, Fort Lauderdale	.184	48	147	8	27	40	5	1	2	22	4	0	0	11	0	38	3	1
Davis, Steven, St. Lucie*	.263	66	217	29	57	83	16	2	2	27	0	2	3	29	0	49	20	4
Degifico, Vincent, Winter Haven*	.279	108	326	38	91	152	14	1	15	52	0	0	2	50	4	50	0	1
Delas, Michael, Lakeland	.267	5	15	1	4	4	0	0	0	5	0	1	0	2	0	4	0	0
DeLeon, Huascar, Baseball City	.255	30	102	13	26	36	8	1	0	10	1	0	5	3	0	20	0	2
Delgado, Alexander, Winter Haven	.225	78	285	27	64	71	7	0	0	16	5	0	1	17	0	30	7	3
Dellicarri, Joseph, St. Lucie	.262	44	107	17	28	43	3	0	4	18	4	1	2	14	0	18	1	3
DeYoung, Robin, West Palm Beach†...	.000	39	1	0	0	0	0	0	0	0	0	0	0	0	0	1	0	0
Diaz, Alexis, St. Lucie†	.255	102	416	54	106	140	11	10	1	33	5	3	3	20	3	38	43	16
Diaz, Jose, Dunedin	.235	57	196	31	46	70	8	2	4	24	0	0	3	19	0	37	5	5
Diaz, Serafin, St. Lucie*	.285	96	256	37	73	108	11	0	8	42	2	3	1	37	4	26	2	1
Diez, Scott, 15 WPB-21 St.L.*	.000	36	2	0	0	0	0	0	0	0	0	0	0	0	0	2	0	0
Donnels, Chris, St. Lucie*	.313	117	386	70	121	197	23	1	17	78	2	3	6	83	15	65	18	4
Dostal, Bruce, Vero Beach*	.247	118	348	58	86	112	10	5	2	24	1	1	3	43	2	49	41	6
Doster, Zachery, 63 Mia-18 Lak	.220	81	246	25	54	69	4	1	3	18	1	0	3	29	2	64	2	3
Duke, Douglas, West Palm Beach	.216	45	148	14	32	51	10	0	3	17	1	2	1	16	1	22	0	0
Dziadkowiec, Andrew, Dunedin*	.274	108	376	40	103	137	14	1	6	53	1	5	2	42	2	34	3	2
Ebel, Dino, Vero Beach	.246	94	272	31	67	84	8	0	3	34	6	4	10	24	1	42	4	3
Echemendia, Idalberto, WPB	.197	61	157	11	31	34	3	0	0	15	1	2	0	10	0	27	2	0
Elci, Lee, St. Petersburg	.132	15	38	4	5	6	1	0	0	5	0	0	2	3	0	8	0	0
Elli, Rocky, St. Lucie*	.000	26	3	0	0	0	0	0	0	0	0	0	0	0	0	0	0	0
Elliot, Terrill, St. Petersburg	.260	40	104	9	27	33	1	1	1	7	0	0	0	10	0	7	0	0
Erhardt, Herbert, Fort Lauderdale*	.252	99	329	29	83	94	8	0	1	34	4	2	0	25	0	58	1	2
Erickson, Steven, Fort Lauderdale	.200	35	100	13	20	24	2	1	0	8	3	2	0	14	1	23	5	1
Escalera, Carlos, Baseball City	.294	59	211	34	62	88	16	2	2	33	0	0	2	16	1	38	7	6
Eusebio, Antonio, Osceola	.286	52	175	22	50	62	6	3	0	30	1	3	1	19	0	27	5	3
Fagnant, Ray, Winter Haven	.150	10	20	2	3	7	1	0	1	2	1	0	0	2	0	3	0	0
Faulk, James, West Palm Beach*	.251	96	362	41	91	129	13	5	5	42	0	1	1	32	4	56	31	10
Federico, Joseph, St. Petersburg*	.136	33	103	8	14	19	5	0	0	13	0	0	1	20	1	24	0	0
Fernandez, Joey, St. Petersburg*	.282	107	362	39	102	153	22	4	7	50	2	4	1	44	2	48	0	2
Flaherty, John, Winter Haven	.260	95	334	31	87	117	14	2	4	28	2	3	2	20	1	44	1	0
Fletcher, Robert, Sarasota*	.281	118	449	66	126	158	16	5	2	55	8	3	3	48	0	42	24	8
Foley, Martin, Clearwater	.286	2	7	0	2	2	0	0	0	1	0	0	1	0	0	0	0	0
Fox, Blane, 21 Osc.-11 St.L.*	.256	32	86	8	22	26	4	0	0	5	0	1	4	0	1	17	5	2
Fox, Michael, St. Petersburg	.256	23	82	10	21	27	6	0	0	11	1	0	1	7	0	9	0	0
Fregosi, James, West Palm Beach	.148	21	61	3	9	13	4	0	0	3	1	1	0	10	0	13	1	0
Freidman, Jason, Winter Haven*	.194	21	62	5	12	16	0	2	0	5	0	0	0	2	0	12	0	0
Frye, Paul, West Palm Beach	.254	47	173	18	44	58	12	1	0	17	0	2	5	16	1	27	1	0
Fuller, Paul, Sarasota	.229	84	245	32	56	78	14	1	2	29	1	2	0	39	2	52	1	4
Fulton, Charles, St. Petersburg*	.243	125	432	38	105	150	23	2	6	75	0	15	0	51	5	64	0	2
Galindo, Luis, Lakeland	.257	120	444	56	114	121	7	0	0	39	4	1	3	56	2	63	4	7
Garman, Patrick, Port Charlotte	.288	62	215	31	62	92	11	2	5	36	0	3	3	37	2	43	1	1
Glasker, Stephen, Port Charlotte*	.220	72	250	22	55	73	9	3	1	26	1	8	1	21	3	54	11	7
Gonzalez, David, Baseball City	.300	33	120	16	36	45	4	1	1	14	2	2	0	10	0	20	4	1
Gonzalez, Carlos, Baseball City	.217	18	23	4	5	6	1	0	0	5	0	1	1	3	1	6	0	0
Gonzalez, Clifford, Sarasota*	.283	73	223	33	63	82	7	3	2	20	2	1	2	23	4	23	12	5
Gonzalez, Javier, St. Lucie	.246	56	175	26	43	59	7	0	3	16	4	3	5	10	0	39	1	0
Gonzalez, Jesus, Vero Beach	.289	40	90	12	26	32	1	1	1	12	0	2	2	12	0	13	3	2
Gonzalez, Luis, Osceola*	.286	86	287	46	82	130	16	7	6	38	1	4	4	37	5	49	2	1

Player and Club	Pct.	G.	AB.	R.	H.	TB.	2B.	3B.	HR.	RBI.	SH.	SF.	HP.	BB.	Int. BB.	SO.	SB.	CS.
Goshay, Henry, Dunedin	.156	70	77	14	12	13	1	0	0	2	0	0	1	2	1	21	3	3
Graham, Steven, St. Petersburg*	.289	15	45	7	13	17	4	0	0	5	0	1	3	1	4	0	1	1
Green, John, Fort Lauderdale	.000	21	1	0	0	0	0	0	0	0	0	0	0	0	0	1	0	0
Green, Stephen, 78 VB-22 Lak.	.301	100	312	40	94	112	11	2	1	35	6	3	0	26	1	55	8	3
Griffin, Mark, Vero Beach*	.282	129	440	59	124	154	8	8	2	52	3	8	7	29	6	58	35	15
Grotewold, Jeffrey, Clearwater*	.279	91	301	32	84	123	17	2	6	55	0	4	1	32	4	43	8	2
Gutierrez, Dimas, Miami	.213	46	150	13	32	39	5	1	0	11	1	2	4	3	0	18	4	2
Gwinn, Anthony, Fort Lauderdale	.188	40	96	7	18	23	5	0	0	11	1	1	0	6	0	24	0	0
Hailey, Freddie, Fort Lauderdale	.293	93	229	35	67	90	15	1	2	29	2	3	2	53	0	40	8	3
Hall, Joseph, St. Petersburg	.292	134	504	72	147	162	9	3	0	54	3	9	8	60	2	57	45	28
Hamilton, Michael, Port Charlotte	.000	2	5	0	0	0	0	0	0	0	0	0	0	0	0	3	0	0
Hanks, Christopher, Winter Haven	.045	13	22	0	1	1	0	0	0	1	0	0	0	1	0	5	0	0
Hare, Shawn, Lakeland*	.324	93	290	32	94	124	16	4	2	36	2	1	2	41	4	32	11	5
Harris, Russell, Osceola†	.264	97	314	57	83	111	13	6	1	32	4	5	1	84	1	43	16	6
Hartzog, Cullen, Fort Lauderdale	.000	17	0	0	0	0	0	0	0	0	1	0	0	1	0	0	0	0
Henderson, William, Lakeland	.252	65	202	12	51	65	5	0	3	20	0	1	5	17	0	32	0	2
Hernandez, Cesar, West Palm Beach†	.285	42	158	16	45	62	8	3	1	15	1	2	5	13	0	42	16	4
Hernandez, Keith, St. Lucie*	.375	4	16	1	6	7	1	0	0	1	0	0	1	0	0	4	0	0
Hernandez, Rodolfo, St. Lucie	.250	115	348	49	87	105	8	5	0	23	11	2	2	22	0	50	14	10
Hines, Timothy, St. Lucie*	.233	34	86	7	20	23	1	1	0	6	3	0	5	7	0	23	0	0
Howard, David, Baseball City†	.236	83	267	36	63	85	7	3	3	30	3	2	1	23	1	44	12	2
Hunter, Bertram, Osceola†	.242	85	343	52	83	113	10	7	2	25	5	4	2	31	0	98	29	7
Iglesias, Luis, Miami	.232	97	293	37	68	118	18	1	10	40	3	2	7	50	0	61	7	7
Ingram, Riccardo, Lakeland	.241	109	365	40	88	125	13	3	6	30	0	3	1	29	1	56	5	2
Jackson, Ronald, Port Charlotte	.269	33	104	13	28	45	9	1	2	23	1	1	2	10	0	16	0	1
Jaster, Scott, St. Lucie	.214	33	98	9	21	30	3	0	2	11	0	5	2	14	1	22	4	2
Jenkins, Bernard, Osceola	.292	63	240	33	70	102	10	5	4	30	0	0	4	21	0	51	5	7
Jimenez, Alejandro, St. Lucie*	.327	42	153	16	50	61	11	0	0	16	1	2	0	13	2	13	3	1
Johnson, Charles, St. Petersburg	.246	121	467	61	115	136	10	1	3	41	3	2	6	43	4	45	34	23
Johnson, Lindsey, Miami	.212	80	217	22	46	62	7	0	3	18	4	4	3	29	0	62	2	6
Johnson, Thomas, Baseball City*	.249	111	370	47	92	124	8	9	2	53	2	3	0	37	1	60	19	12
Jones, Geary, St. Lucie	.122	13	41	1	5	8	3	0	0	3	1	0	0	3	0	13	0	0
Jones, Ross, West Palm Beach	.000	42	2	0	0	0	0	0	0	0	0	0	0	0	0	1	0	0
Jordan, Brian, St. Petersburg†	.349	11	43	7	15	27	4	1	2	11	0	0	2	0	0	8	0	2
Kaub, Keith, Miami	.280	9	25	4	7	19	0	0	4	5	0	0	2	1	0	8	0	1
Kelley, Dean, Fort Lauderdale*	.230	110	404	52	93	126	20	2	3	36	6	5	2	23	2	60	10	7
Kelly, Jimy, Dunedin	.185	104	340	28	63	79	7	3	1	28	7	6	1	25	0	67	5	9
Kingwood, Tyrone, West Palm Beach	.256	74	277	32	71	95	7	4	3	32	1	4	0	11	1	52	19	7
Kirkpatrick, Stephen, Clearwater*	.205	126	479	40	98	126	14	1	4	30	5	2	0	34	1	48	14	12
Kline, Douglas, West Palm Beach	.000	27	1	0	0	0	0	0	0	0	0	0	0	0	0	0	0	0
Knapp, John, Vero Beach	.000	26	3	1	0	0	0	0	0	0	0	0	0	1	0	1	0	0
Knecht, Robert, Baseball City*	.295	58	200	41	59	74	5	2	2	27	1	1	2	39	0	31	12	14
Knoblauh, Jay, Fort Lauderdale	.238	39	126	19	30	51	7	1	4	14	0	0	1	12	0	36	1	0
Knorr, Randy, Dunedin	.262	33	122	13	32	56	6	0	6	23	0	2	0	6	0	21	0	2
Koenig, Gary, Baseball City	.130	13	23	1	3	3	0	0	0	2	0	0	1	0	0	12	0	0
Kosco, Bryn, West Palm Beach†	.227	60	203	16	46	61	10	1	1	22	0	4	5	42	0	42	2	2
Koslofski, Kevin, Baseball City*	.259	116	343	65	89	117	10	3	4	33	5	3	5	51	2	57	41	14
Kotchman, Randy, Miami†	.276	44	127	17	35	37	2	0	0	9	2	0	0	19	0	20	4	8
Kramer, Mark, Miami*	.284	67	243	36	69	114	9	9	6	27	1	2	1	23	2	33	3	7
Kraus, Ralph, Fort Lauderdale*	.247	123	393	45	97	123	14	3	2	35	7	5	0	53	2	86	18	12
Kuld, Peter, Miami	.167	13	36	3	6	16	1	0	3	4	0	0	2	0	0	11	0	1
Laboy, Carlos, Osceola	.188	84	256	25	48	80	6	4	6	29	2	3	4	9	0	87	2	2
Lake, Kenneth, Miami	.207	52	169	18	35	62	10	1	5	14	2	3	0	16	1	55	5	3
Lara, Crucito, St. Lucie†	.246	59	191	23	47	65	12	0	2	26	6	2	1	13	0	32	2	4
Laseke, Eric, Winter Haven	.241	97	303	37	73	96	12	1	3	21	7	2	4	26	1	38	7	3
Lau, David, St. Lucie	.148	15	27	1	4	5	1	0	0	1	3	0	2	0	0	8	0	0
Laureano, Francisco, Baseball City	.260	132	457	71	119	148	17	3	2	66	9	7	2	88	2	63	25	13
Lavender, Robert, Port Charlotte*	.212	116	321	40	68	111	14	7	5	47	2	11	2	70	3	63	6	4
Law, Travis, Port Charlotte	.262	119	439	61	115	137	15	2	1	34	1	0	4	58	1	72	26	11
Leach, Christopher, Winter Haven*	.165	63	133	11	22	26	4	0	0	5	3	1	1	23	2	36	1	1
Leake, Jon, Miami	.244	12	45	3	11	13	0	1	0	3	0	0	1	0	0	14	1	0
Leary, Robert, West Palm Beach	.238	9	21	2	5	9	1	0	1	2	0	0	1	0	0	3	0	0
Letterio, Shane, Fort Lauderdale	.255	106	364	41	93	129	16	4	4	32	0	4	1	19	1	60	15	10
Lewis, Alan, Vero Beach*	.245	124	335	39	82	106	15	3	1	43	3	7	1	30	2	26	1	0
Lewis, Daniel, Osceola*	.250	86	264	33	66	88	11	1	3	28	2	1	5	33	3	59	7	3
Lindsey, Douglas, Clearwater	.195	36	118	8	23	26	3	0	0	9	0	2	0	5	0	18	0	0
Losa, William, Port Charlotte	.226	90	265	27	60	88	12	2	4	23	0	2	5	33	0	84	2	1
Mackie, Scott, Miami	.214	27	84	3	18	24	1	1	1	3	0	0	1	4	0	27	3	3
Magallanes, William, Sarasota	.295	71	241	31	71	89	7	1	3	31	0	1	2	26	2	64	5	1
Magnuson, Brett, Vero Beach*	.243	120	354	47	86	128	16	1	8	48	2	3	4	48	3	68	5	2
Maksudian, Michael, Miami*	.313	83	288	36	90	143	18	4	9	42	0	2	0	28	2	42	6	4
Maldonado, Carlos A., Lakeland†	.286	3	7	0	2	2	0	0	0	0	0	0	0	0	0	1	0	0
Manuel, Ferral, Port Charlotte	.100	9	10	1	1	1	0	0	0	0	0	0	0	0	0	6	0	1
Marigny, Ronald, Lakeland	.259	106	378	43	98	131	13	4	4	42	4	1	3	33	3	67	8	6
Marrs, Terry, Winter Haven	.177	63	158	7	28	35	3	2	0	11	1	0	4	9	0	43	6	7
Marsh, Thomas, Clearwater	.170	43	141	12	24	31	2	1	1	10	4	0	2	7	0	30	5	2
Marshall, John, Port Charlotte*	.333	5	9	0	3	3	0	0	0	0	0	0	0	0	0	2	0	0
Marte, Alexis, Port Charlotte*	.197	22	61	16	12	12	0	0	0	2	0	1	0	15	0	6	6	1
Matilla, Pedro, Winter Haven	.222	22	45	3	10	16	3	0	1	5	1	0	0	3	0	12	0	0
Maurer, Robert, Port Charlotte*	.276	132	456	69	126	180	18	9	6	51	0	4	8	86	6	109	3	4
Mayne, Brent, Baseball City*	.542	7	24	5	13	18	3	1	0	8	0	0	0	2	0	2	0	0
Mazey, Randy, Miami†	.218	29	87	8	19	24	2	0	1	4	0	1	2	23	1	9	1	0
McCall, Roy, Clearwater	.173	32	98	8	17	24	7	0	0	11	2	1	0	17	0	37	0	0
McCray, Rodney, Sarasota	.265	124	422	81	112	142	19	4	1	34	4	2	9	96	3	81	44	22
McDaniel, Terrence, St. Lucie	.231	105	351	70	81	141	17	11	7	43	0	5	8	71	1	106	43	19
McElroy, Glen, Sarasota	.000	2	7	3	0	0	0	0	0	0	0	0	0	0	0	3	0	0
Mello, John, West Palm Beach	.227	33	128	9	29	46	10	2	1	10	1	0	2	7	0	22	4	0
Melvin, Scott, St. Petersburg	.255	112	376	50	96	121	16	3	1	44	3	5	7	55	3	56	5	1
Metoyer, Tony, Miami	.000	33	2	1	0	0	0	0	0	1	0	0	1	0	0	1	0	0
Minch, John, Miami	.286	14	42	0	12	18	3	0	1	7	0	0	0	5	0	8	0	0
Montalvo, Robert, Dunedin	.146	14	41	3	6	7	1	0	0	4	0	0	0	12	0	13	0	0
Monzon, Jose, Dunedin	.250	16	48	4	12	16	2	1	0	7	0	0	0	5	0	11	0	0

Player and Club	Pct.	G.	AB.	R.	H.	TB.	2B.	3B.	HR.	RBI.	SH.	SF.	HP.	BB.	Int. BB.	SO.	SB.	CS.
Moore, Kerwin, Baseball City	.364	4	11	3	4	7	0	0	1	2	0	0	0	1	0	2	0	0
Moore, Sean, Winter Haven	.074	12	27	0	2	2	0	0	0	0	0	0	1	2	0	10	1	3
Moore, Robert, Baseball City	.271	131	483	85	131	162	21	5	0	42	6	3	6	51	1	35	34	19
Morandini, Michael, Clearwater*	.302	17	63	14	19	25	4	1	0	4	0	1	1	7	1	8	3	1
Morris, Roderick, Port Charlotte*	.270	93	341	42	92	111	9	5	0	26	4	2	0	39	0	53	19	9
Morrison, Brian, Dunedin	.243	117	387	40	94	164	22	0	16	52	0	3	1	37	0	102	3	3
Mota, Andres, Osceola	.319	131	505	68	161	202	21	4	4	69	3	10	11	42	3	61	28	9
Munoz, Jose, Vero Beach*	.257	105	300	39	77	94	15	1	0	24	5	3	1	14	0	31	6	2
Munoz, Omer, West Palm Beach	.272	68	246	22	67	69	2	0	0	27	8	0	1	5	0	17	8	5
Murillo, Javier, Miami	.212	31	99	6	21	25	4	0	0	4	1	2	2	16	0	27	1	2
Natal, Robert, West Palm Beach	.125	15	48	5	6	9	0	0	1	2	0	0	2	9	1	9	1	0
Naughton, Daniel, St. Lucie	.205	35	83	7	17	22	5	0	0	5	0	0	0	12	0	16	4	2
Nelloms, Sylvester, Fort Lauderdale*	.216	95	301	42	65	96	10	3	5	37	1	5	2	34	0	66	11	4
Nichols, Scott, St. Petersburg	.198	35	86	7	17	25	5	0	1	5	1	1	4	11	0	19	1	0
Noelke, Michael, St. Lucie	.080	9	25	3	2	4	2	0	0	0	0	0	0	5	0	8	1	1
Nunez, Bernardino, Dunedin	.271	85	306	41	83	127	16	2	8	35	1	3	2	6	0	82	9	5
Nyssen, Daniel, Osceola	.241	87	286	32	69	94	10	3	3	31	4	5	2	17	0	45	7	3
Ocasio, Javier, Sarasota	.250	101	316	32	79	93	10	2	0	36	10	3	3	32	1	46	14	6
Ollom, Michael, Sarasota	.000	15	1	0	0	0	0	0	0	0	0	0	0	0	0	0	0	0
Ortiz, Hector, Vero Beach	.141	42	85	5	12	14	0	1	0	4	4	0	2	6	0	15	0	0
Ortiz, Joseph, Osceola	.206	115	394	47	81	112	18	2	3	52	5	12	5	42	2	63	6	3
Payton, Raymond, Sarasota	.195	51	185	20	36	51	7	1	2	25	1	1	1	14	0	40	1	3
Pedre, Jorge, Baseball City	.327	55	208	39	68	104	17	2	5	40	0	3	4	13	1	31	1	2
Peel, Jack, Sarasota	.277	76	253	32	70	88	14	2	0	31	4	1	6	24	0	46	5	5
Pegues, Steven, Lakeland	.254	55	193	24	49	60	7	2	0	15	0	1	2	7	0	19	12	4
Pena, Geronimo, St. Petersburg†	.190	6	21	2	4	5	1	0	0	2	0	0	3	3	0	6	2	3
Penn, Trevor, West Palm Beach*	.262	132	443	54	116	147	14	4	3	34	1	5	10	72	7	44	26	6
Perez, Gorky, Osceola*	.175	23	57	2	10	11	1	0	0	3	1	1	1	2	0	5	1	1
Polanco, Radhames, St. Lucie	.292	30	96	10	28	35	3	2	0	12	1	1	1	9	0	20	0	1
Popplewell, Thomas, Fort Lauderdale	.000	33	1	0	0	0	0	0	0	0	0	0	0	0	0	0	0	0
Powell, Alonzo, West Palm Beach	.317	12	41	7	13	26	4	3	1	8	0	1	0	7	2	3	1	1
Pujols, Ruben, Baseball City	.182	6	11	2	2	3	1	0	0	3	0	0	0	0	0	5	0	0
Raley, Daniel, Lakeland*	.133	17	45	3	6	7	1	0	0	4	0	1	0	8	1	7	0	1
Reaves, Scott, Clearwater	.202	74	248	18	50	60	8	1	0	11	0	1	2	22	0	46	1	2
Redman, Timothy, St. Petersburg	.167	3	12	0	2	2	0	0	0	0	0	0	0	2	0	2	0	0
Reese, Kyle, Baseball City	.224	29	67	4	15	17	2	0	0	7	0	0	2	4	0	12	3	0
Renteria, Edinson, Osceola†	.238	99	340	42	81	98	11	3	0	23	7	4	9	41	0	46	13	9
Reynolds, David, Sarasota	.000	14	1	0	0	0	0	0	0	0	0	0	0	0	0	1	0	0
Rhodes, Michael, Fort Lauderdale	.214	59	187	24	40	49	9	0	0	12	1	3	0	21	0	53	11	4
Richardi, Richard, Osceola†	.333	6	12	1	4	4	0	0	0	1	0	0	0	0	0	2	1	0
Ricker, Troy, West Palm Beach	.177	111	355	37	63	97	11	1	7	28	4	1	5	27	2	102	16	11
Rivers, Mickey, Winter Haven†	.224	104	330	25	74	81	3	2	0	18	3	1	3	8	0	60	14	4
Robertson, Roderick, Clearwater†	.265	118	385	49	102	130	14	1	4	32	10	5	4	26	1	51	24	10
Roca, Gilberto, St. Lucie	.304	24	79	8	24	31	5	1	0	8	0	0	1	0	0	9	0	0
Roche, Faustino, St. Lucie*	.283	80	304	46	86	99	11	1	0	17	5	2	1	25	1	24	37	12
Rodgers, Paul, Dunedin	.269	140	525	80	141	168	14	5	1	35	4	2	2	61	1	95	60	18
Rodriguez, Carlos, Fort Lauderdale	.241	102	353	48	85	102	15	1	0	26	21	3	3	49	1	25	9	8
Rodriguez, Henry, Vero Beach*	.284	126	433	53	123	188	33	1	10	73	1	6	2	48	11	58	7	6
Rohrmeier, Daniel, 25 Sar.-18 P.C.	.259	43	139	20	36	49	5	1	2	15	1	2	1	19	0	23	1	1
Roman, Daniel, Fort Lauderdale	.268	60	183	25	49	60	8	0	1	29	2	0	4	11	1	25	6	2
Rosario, Melvin, Fort Lauderdale	.228	89	268	30	61	89	13	0	5	30	2	1	6	32	0	87	2	5
Roseboro, Jamie, St. Lucie	.309	95	337	60	104	132	17	4	1	48	0	3	6	31	3	35	54	8
Rowland, Donald, Lakeland	.222	16	54	11	12	13	1	0	0	5	0	1	0	7	0	8	1	1
Ruckman, Scott, Dunedin	.275	94	313	35	86	125	17	2	6	35	2	4	8	12	0	42	3	1
Russell, Frederick, Baseball City†	.100	5	10	1	1	1	0	0	0	0	0	0	0	1	0	3	0	0
Sable, Luke, Port Charlotte	.245	94	319	40	78	89	3	4	0	23	2	2	1	18	0	34	6	9
Samson, Frederick, Port Charlotte	.310	26	87	18	27	32	5	0	0	5	5	4	1	0	0	15	4	3
Santana, Jose, Osceola†	.182	6	11	2	2	2	0	0	0	1	0	0	0	2	0	3	1	0
Santangelo, Frank, WPB†	.214	57	173	18	37	41	4	0	0	14	6	0	4	23	1	12	3	3
Scannell, Lawrence, Winter Haven	.191	47	115	8	22	28	3	0	1	8	1	3	9	0	24	0	1
Scott, Shawn, Dunedin	.208	67	154	10	32	37	1	2	0	10	1	1	0	12	0	41	7	7
Scruggs, Anthony, Port Charlotte	.294	60	197	29	58	84	9	4	3	34	2	4	2	38	1	50	15	5
Seeburger, John, Fort Lauderdale*	.235	129	451	39	106	142	19	1	5	55	3	8	9	33	5	91	5	1
Servais, Scott, Osceola	.268	46	153	16	41	56	9	0	2	23	0	5	2	16	2	35	0	2
Shore, Jeffrey, Port Charlotte	.208	47	120	15	25	33	4	2	0	6	1	0	1	15	0	44	0	0
Silverstein, Allan, Dunedin	.000	28	0	0	0	0	0	0	0	0	0	0	0	0	0	1	0	0
Silvestri, David, Osceola	.254	129	437	67	111	139	20	1	2	50	8	10	6	68	1	72	28	13
Singley, Joseph, Sarasota	.286	3	7	1	2	2	0	0	0	0	0	0	0	0	0	2	0	1
Sloniger, Chris, Miami	.197	77	203	17	40	49	6	0	1	14	4	1	0	30	1	55	4	2
Smith, Charles, West Palm Beach*	.198	39	86	10	17	18	1	0	0	6	0	0	0	14	1	23	1	0
Smith, Lawrence, Miami	.220	34	100	9	22	26	4	0	0	4	1	0	0	9	0	40	8	5
Smith, Timothy, Miami	.313	8	16	1	5	9	1	0	1	3	0	1	3	2	0	2	0	1
Spann, Emmanuel, Lakeland	.246	87	281	45	69	118	11	4	10	52	4	5	5	32	2	69	8	4
Spehr, Timothy, Baseball City	.250	18	64	8	16	24	5	0	1	7	2	0	0	5	0	17	1	0
Spoolstra, Scott, Miami*	.154	14	26	3	4	10	0	0	2	4	0	0	0	4	0	4	1	0
Sprague, Edward, Dunedin	.219	52	192	21	42	76	9	2	7	23	0	2	7	16	2	40	1	1
Stairs, Matthew, West Palm Beach	.189	36	111	12	21	29	3	1	1	9	1	1	0	9	0	18	0	0
Stocker, Steven, Clearwater	.267	10	30	4	8	10	2	0	0	4	0	1	2	6	0	6	0	0
Strong, Michael, Lakeland	.220	40	91	5	20	23	3	0	0	3	1	0	0	12	0	20	0	1
Suero, Williams, Dunedin	.291	51	206	35	60	86	10	5	2	17	1	0	3	16	0	32	9	3
Sullivan, Carl, Sarasota	.237	108	371	45	88	126	22	2	4	51	5	4	3	28	2	64	6	9
Szynal, Jon, Clearwater*	.087	8	23	1	2	4	0	1	0	4	0	0	0	0	0	3	0	0
Tatum, Willie, Winter Haven†	.206	118	393	44	81	108	13	1	4	37	0	3	7	42	1	88	12	6
Taveras, Marcos, Dunedin	.187	87	134	20	25	31	3	0	1	12	2	0	1	20	0	41	7	6
Taylor, David, Miami	.195	38	87	13	17	22	2	0	1	7	2	1	0	32	1	22	1	0
Tedder, Scott, Sarasota*	.272	121	386	56	105	123	18	0	0	38	9	4	2	73	1	65	14	9
Tepper, Marc, Miami*	.250	29	92	8	23	30	2	1	1	7	0	0	0	4	0	12	7	0
Thomas, Frank, Sarasota	.277	55	188	27	52	75	9	1	4	30	0	1	3	31	0	33	0	1
Thomas, Orlando, St. Petersburg	.286	5	7	1	2	2	0	0	0	0	0	0	0	1	0	3	0	0
Thoutsis, Paul, St. Petersburg*	.288	74	243	21	70	92	10	3	2	21	0	3	5	22	2	17	0	1
Toney, Anthony, Lakeland†	.164	47	122	11	20	22	0	1	0	8	1	3	1	22	1	19	12	5
Tonucci, Norman, Dunedin	.234	21	64	5	15	19	1	0	1	9	0	1	0	6	0	24	1	2

Player and Club	Pct.	G.	AB.	R.	H.	TB.	2B.	3B.	HR.	RBI.	SH.	SF.	HP.	BB.	Int. BB.	SO.	SB.	CS.
Torborg, Douglas, Miami	.333	36	6	2	2	2	0	0	0	0	1	0	0	0	0	1	0	0
Townley, Jason, Dunedin	.213	51	155	16	33	44	8	0	1	12	2	0	1	20	0	42	0	0
Tresh, Michael, Fort Lauderdale†	.263	67	243	35	64	91	12	3	3	20	5	2	1	27	0	31	7	3
Trevino, Antonio, Clearwater	.226	98	340	37	77	113	12	6	4	36	3	8	7	22	0	57	9	3
Valdez, Amilcar, Vero Beach	.285	104	347	48	99	154	32	1	7	56	4	3	0	29	0	65	1	1
Valentin, John, Winter Haven	.270	55	215	27	58	82	13	1	3	18	2	3	1	13	0	29	4	4
Vargas, Hector, Fort Lauderdale	.321	19	53	6	17	21	2	1	0	3	0	1	0	3	0	15	2	2
Vatcher, James, Clearwater	.301	92	349	51	105	157	30	5	4	46	0	2	2	41	0	49	7	3
Vaughan, Richard, Dunedin	.176	11	17	1	3	6	0	0	1	3	0	0	0	0	0	3	0	0
Vella, Gregory, Dunedin*	.245	111	331	31	81	124	21	5	4	25	1	0	2	43	2	63	6	3
Verdugo, Luis, Miami	.258	104	329	27	85	148	24	0	13	45	1	1	1	34	2	87	0	1
Viltz, Corey, West Palm Beach	.185	26	92	10	17	24	2	1	1	9	0	0	0	12	0	24	3	1
Waid, Patrick, Miami†	.293	17	58	4	17	19	0	1	0	1	2	0	0	6	0	15	4	4
Walker, Duane, Miami	.000	5	5	1	0	0	0	0	0	0	0	0	0	0	0	2	0	0
Walker, Chris, Clearwater*	.233	82	257	23	60	94	18	2	4	33	0	1	5	32	4	59	0	0
Wardlow, Joseph, Port Charlotte*	.314	54	156	22	49	62	9	2	0	25	6	3	1	32	2	18	3	4
Watson, DeJon, Baseball City*	.216	55	185	21	40	63	9	4	2	23	2	2	1	24	3	44	2	0
Whitehead, Christopher, Winter Haven	.241	120	407	55	98	150	17	1	11	27	2	1	1	57	1	111	4	7
Wiley, Craig, Lakeland†	.182	14	33	1	6	9	3	0	0	3	2	0	0	7	0	4	0	0
Williams, Cary, Clearwater	.267	52	187	35	50	70	14	0	2	14	1	2	9	16	0	31	9	4
Williams, Paul, Winter Haven	.228	82	263	25	60	112	14	1	12	41	2	5	2	26	1	44	0	0
Wilson, Todd, Miami	.154	16	39	2	6	7	1	0	0	2	0	0	0	0	0	16	0	0
Wright, Tom, Miami	.000	2	5	0	0	0	0	0	0	0	0	0	0	0	0	0	0	0
Yan, Julian, Dunedin	.250	133	460	68	115	218	21	5	24	72	1	4	10	47	5	130	2	4
Young, Mark, Dunedin	.000	4	1	2	0	0	0	0	0	0	0	0	0	0	0	0	0	0
Zaksek, John, Sarasota*	.250	1	4	0	1	1	0	0	0	0	1	0	0	0	0	0	0	0
Zambrano, Jose, Winter Haven	.219	49	146	12	32	45	4	3	1	14	2	2	2	15	0	36	4	2
Zambrano, Roberto, Winter Haven	.253	46	166	29	42	76	14	1	6	18	0	1	4	18	2	28	2	2
Zawaski, Vince, St. Lucie	.165	41	109	18	18	33	3	0	4	7	1	0	6	13	0	34	0	3
Zayas, Carlos, Clearwater	.206	62	194	14	40	49	6	0	1	14	0	2	3	13	0	30	0	1
Zeihen, Robert, Fort Lauderdale*	.252	128	420	51	106	133	16	4	1	46	2	6	2	64	5	57	6	8
Zinter, Alan, St. Lucie†	.239	48	159	17	38	57	10	0	3	32	1	5	1	18	2	31	0	1

The following pitchers, listed alphabetically by club, with games in parentheses, had no plate appearances, primarily through use of designated hitters:

BASEBALL CITY—Adams, Joseph (8); Adams, Kenneth (20); Alicano, Alberto (2); Cole, Victor (9); DeLeon, Jesus (19); Filson, Peter (8); Gross, John (8); Hopper, Bradley (19); Hudson, James (12); Johnston, Joel (26); Jundy, Lorin (34); Maldonado, Carlos C. (28); McCormack, Brian (43); McCormick, John (6); Moeller, Dennis (12); Nelson, Douglas (34); Pickens, Kevin (28); Sanchez, Israel (3); Shaw, Kevin (11); Shepherd, Keith (11); Stonikas, William (22); Stottlemyre, Melvin (13).

CLEARWATER—Ashby, Andrew (6); Brantley, Clifford (8); Buonantony, Richard (11); Carroll, James (1); Carter, Andrew (12); Christopher, Fredrick (5); Combs, Patrick (6); Coulter, Darrell (10); Elam, Todd (11); Fynan, Kevin (22); Holdridge, David (24); Langley, Wesley (25); LaRosa, John (22); Limbach, Chris (11); Mauser, Timothy (16); McDonald, Shelby (33); Peek, Timothy (8); Rambo, Matthew (9); Sims, Mark (27); Thomas, Royal (27).

DUNEDIN—Boucher, Denis (33); Burgos, Enrique (8); Cromwell, Nathaniel (31); Hall, Darren (16); Hentgen, Patrick (29); Horsman, Vincent (59); Leiter, Alois (3); Linton, Douglas (9); Lloyd, Graeme (2); Mills, Michael (3); Newcomb, Joe (4); Ogliaruso, Michael (13); Sanders, Earl (12); Seal, Michael (21); Taylor, Michael L. (3); Timlin, Michael (33); Wanish, John (5); Wapnick, Steven (24); Williams, Gregory (20); Woide, Steven (27).

FORT LAUDERDALE—Adkins, Steven (11); Garcia, Victor (29); Gogolewski, Douglas (23); Hoffman, Jeffrey (23); Hook, Michael (34); Howard, Christian (13); Leiter, Mark (6); Manon, Ramon (22); Martel, Edward (26); Mills, Alan (22); Morrison, Anthony (10); Munoz, Roberto (3); Ralph, Curtis (15); Rodriguez, Gabriel (13); Stanford, Donald (24).

LAKELAND—Cook, Ronald (31); Haas, Robert (10); Jones, Michael (29); Kiely, John (36); Knudsen, Kurt (45); Lumley, Michael (27); Meacham, Russell (11); Morhardt, Darryl (1); Morris, John (3); O'Neill, Daniel (21); Richards, David (28); Rivera, Lino (13); Robinson, Jeffrey (4); Searcy, Stephen (9); Steward, Charles (31); Stone, Eric (25); Wilkins, Michael (16); Willis, Marty (29).

MIAMI—Burgos, Enrique (15); Clarkin, Michael (22); Farr, Michael (8); Felden, Keith (18); Figueroa, Fernando (13); Garcia, Longobardo (14); Ghelfi, Andrew (7); Grayson, Michael (10); Lamle, Adam (14); Mack, Tony (19); Mallea, Luis (4); Merriman, Brett (5); Mullins, Ronald (26); Ponder, Kevin (39); Prieto, Arnoldo (8); Rivard, John (11); Singelyn, Scott (2).

OSCEOLA—Allen, Harold (26); Bauer, Peter (2); Bond, Daven (27); Campusano, Teofilo (1); Credeur, Todd (17); Farmer, Gordon (7); Hartgraves, Dean (7); Ilsley, Blaise (2); Kerfeld, Charles (5); Marrero, Rogelio (1); Normand, Guy (31); Osuna, Alfonso (46); Porter, Brian (1); Potts, David (16); Rhoden, Richard (5); Rosario, Eliezel (22); Sheehan, John (41); Simon, Richard (19); Tafoya, Dennis (55); Trice, Walter (28); Vargas, Jose (18).

PORT CHARLOTTE—Alexander, Gerald (14); Alvarez, Wilson (13); Bohanon, Brian (11); Castillo, Felipe (1); Evans, Brian (49); Hurst, Jonathan (20); Keon, Kevin (10); Kerfut, George (12); Lipscomb, Bruce (32); Manuel, Barry (15); Mathews, Terry (10); Morse, Scott (15); Ohman, Edward (23); Pavlik, Roger (26); Reitzel, Michael (21); Rosenthal, Wayne (20); Shaw, Cedric (25); Sipple, John (29); Taylor, D. Michael (43).

ST. LUCIE—Bross, Terrence (35); Bumgarner, Jeffrey (8); Castillo, Alberto (1); Gideon, Ronnie (17); Givens, Brian (1); Griffin, Terry (33); Harriger, Dennis (11); Hernandez, Robert (3); Hillman, Eric (19); LaRose, Steven (41); Machado, Julio (4); Marina, Juan (13); Meizoso, Agustin (10); Miller, Michael (26); Plummer, Dale (10); Proctor, David (22); Schourek, Peter (2); Valera, Julio (6); Whitlock, Michael (3).

ST. PETERSBURG—Becker, Gregory (56); Bivens, William (10); Buonantony, Richard (1); Burgos, John (1); Conroy, James (16); Cormier, Rheal (26); Grater, Mark (56); Hathaway, Shawn (29); Hernandez, Jeremy (3); Hoffman, Richard (27); Majer, Steffen (10); Pierson, Lawrence (52); Plemel, Lee (21); Russo, Anthony (30); Sherrill, Timothy (52); Smith, Kenneth (32).

SARASOTA—Cauley, Chris (3); Chavez, Samuel (7); Cortes, Argenis (23); DeLaCruz, Carlos (15); Drahman, Brian (7); Gennings, Brian (10); Gohmann, Kenneth (10); Hall, Todd (20); Hasler, Curtis (25); Hudek, John (27); Kennedy, Bo (25); King, Eric (1); Knackert, Brent (35); Mehrtens, Patrick (6); Middaugh, Scott (6); Morris, James (2); Resnikoff, Robert (52); Sonberg, Erik (6); Stephens, Ronald (17).

VERO BEACH—Bustillos, Albert (7); Coleman, Dale (45); Heinle, Dana (25); Hoffman, Kevin (7); Kamanaka, Masaaki (33); Kawabata, Yasuhiro (11); Luckham, Kenneth (6); Noch, Douglas (21); Opperman, Daniel (19); Patrick, Tim (2); Poole, James (60); Sampson, Michael (16); Shinall, Zakary (47); Takaheshi, Koji (13); Tudor, John (1); Vanzytveld, Jeffrey (27).

WEST PALM BEACH—Barnes, Brian (7); Bennett, Christopher (18); Boyd, Daryl (31); Brito, Mario (23); Carter, Jeffrey (7); Cavalier, Kevin (25); Clarkin, Michael (10); Henion, Scott (37); Kerrigan, Robert (7); Perez, Yorkis (18); Rivera, Hector (16); Sossamon, Timothy (11); Sullivan, Brian (2); Wainhouse, David (13).

WINTER HAVEN—Abril, Odie (35); Allen, Tracy (2); Brown, Paul (38); Conroy, Brian (8); Dedos, Felix (12); Dennison, James (11); Dzafic, Bernhard (6); Estrada, Peter (3); Florence, Donald (30); Harris, Reginald (30); Kite, Daniel (21); Landry, Howard (31); Morrison, James (4); Rush, Andrew (4); Ryan, Kenneth (24); Sanders, Alan (4); Stange, Timothy (24); Stewart, Hector (19); Thompson, Michael (11); Wacha, Charles (32).

GRAND SLAM HOME RUNS—L. Gonzalez, 2; Brown, Busby, Cabrera, A. Diaz, Ebel, Kelly, Morrison, Pedre, Roman, Rosario, P. Williams, J. Zambrano, 1 each.

AWARDED FIRST BASE ON CATCHER'S INTERFERENCE—Brummer (Zinter); Cabrera (Eusebio); Carmona (Losa); Dziadkowiec (Lindsey); D. Lewis (Zinter); Maurer (Knorr); Mota (Losa); Reaves (Verdugo); C. Rodriguez (Carver); Shore (Monzon).

CLUB FIELDING

Club	Pct.	G.	PO.	A.	E.	DP.	PB.
Vero Beach	.973	135	3472	1496	139	110	25
West Palm Beach	.970	138	3630	1519	159	127	17
Lakeland	.967	136	3549	1480	169	138	25
St. Petersburg	.967	139	3625	1578	177	142	8
St. Lucie	.966	134	3510	1452	176	128	18
Clearwater	.965	136	3505	1503	183	141	21
Sarasota	.964	136	3505	1345	180	118	12
Port Charlotte	.964	139	3615	1529	191	126	34
Osceola	.964	137	3632	1640	196	140	15
Fort Lauderdale	.964	138	3520	1397	184	118	26
Miami	.964	134	3263	1369	173	87	33
Baseball City	.964	139	3602	1495	191	141	27
Winter Haven	.964	139	3585	1516	192	137	33
Dunedin	.961	140	3562	1480	205	117	28

Triple Plays—Lakeland, Osceola, Vero Beach.

INDIVIDUAL FIELDING

*Throws lefthanded.

FIRST BASEMEN

Player and Club	Pct.	G.	PO.	A.	E.	DP.
Acta, Osceola	1.000	3	24	2	0	3
Adler, Lakeland	.979	13	89	3	2	13
Bagwell, Winter Haven	1.000	1	1	0	0	0
BARRAGAN, Clearwater*	.991	103	905	54	9	89
Bernardo, 8 P.C.-60 Mia*	.995	68	535	46	3	34
Bishop, Miami	.986	23	200	13	3	16
Brogna, Lakeland*	.989	126	1098	83	13	103
Colston, Miami	1.000	3	9	1	0	2
Conine, Baseball City	.980	98	830	65	18	80
Degifico, Winter Haven	.993	18	120	13	1	16
Diaz, St. Lucie	.980	43	317	21	7	33
Donnels, St. Lucie	.981	19	149	7	3	10
Duke, West Palm Beach	1.000	3	4	0	0	0
Elci, St. Petersburg	1.000	5	41	5	0	2
Erhardt, Fort Lauderdale	.975	24	186	13	5	20
Escalera, Baseball City	.938	2	15	0	1	2
Federico, St. Petersburg	.991	31	305	20	3	30
Fernandez, St. Petersburg	.978	26	252	19	6	22
Flaherty, Winter Haven	1.000	2	10	0	0	2
B. Fox, Osceola*	1.000	12	111	5	0	19
M. Fox, St. Petersburg	.972	18	159	15	5	19
Fregosi, West Palm Beach	1.000	3	23	3	0	3
Freidman, Winter Haven*	.988	18	151	8	2	20
Fuller, Sarasota	1.000	2	1	0	0	0
Fulton, St. Petersburg	.950	2	19	0	1	1
C. Gonzalez, Baseball City	1.000	1	4	0	0	0
J. Gonzalez, Vero Beach	1.000	2	6	0	0	0
Green, Lakeland	1.000	1	8	1	0	3
Grotewold, Clearwater	.995	24	190	17	1	21
Gutierrez, Miami	1.000	16	124	6	0	11
Hanks, Winter Haven	.875	3	7	0	1	0
Hare, Lakeland*	1.000	2	2	0	0	1
Harris, Osceola	1.000	1	3	0	0	0
Henderson, Lakeland	1.000	4	18	1	0	3
Hernandez, St. Lucie*	1.000	3	23	0	0	1
Jimenez, St. Lucie*	.995	39	358	24	2	35
Johnson, Miami	.900	3	8	1	1	0
Kaub, Miami	1.000	7	54	3	0	3
Knapp, Vero Beach	.889	1	8	0	1	0
Lara, St. Lucie	1.000	1	2	0	0	0
Lavender, Port Charlotte*	.972	6	34	1	1	4
A. Lewis, Vero Beach	1.000	2	20	2	0	1
D. Lewis, Osceola*	.971	17	158	7	5	13
Magnusson, Vero Beach	1.000	6	20	0	0	2
Maksudian, Miami	.952	3	20	0	1	1
Maurer, Port Charlotte*	.988	128	1094	105	14	105
Mello, West Palm Beach	1.000	7	66	7	0	9
Melvin, St. Petersburg	.993	47	391	21	3	33
Minch, Miami	1.000	1	14	0	0	0
Mota, Osceola	.986	18	136	4	2	17
Munoz, West Palm Beach	1.000	3	37	2	0	2
Nichols, St. Petersburg	1.000	3	22	6	0	1
Ortiz, Osceola	.990	91	842	61	9	65
Pedre, Baseball City	1.000	1	4	1	0	0
Peel, Sarasota	.978	27	253	14	6	20
Penn, West Palm Beach*	.985	129	1140	80	18	93
Reese, Baseball City	.966	6	26	2	1	3
Ricker, West Palm Beach	1.000	1	5	0	0	0
Rodriguez, Vero Beach*	.990	120	1071	66	12	87
Roman, Fort Lauderdale	.982	16	98	12	2	6
Ruckman, Baseball City	1.000	4	29	1	0	1
Seeburger, Fort Lauderdale	.982	102	846	61	17	76
Servais, Osceola	1.000	6	47	1	0	6
Silvestri, Osceola	1.000	2	17	2	0	0
Sloniger, Miami	1.000	1	9	0	0	1
Tatum, Winter Haven	.980	108	885	78	20	90
Taylor, Miami	1.000	1	7	0	0	1
Tedder, Sarasota*	.993	63	504	46	4	45
Tepper, Miami*	.973	22	167	10	5	6
F. Thomas, Sarasota	.985	51	420	31	7	38
O. Thomas, St. Petersburg	1.000	1	1	0	0	0
Thoutsis, St. Petersburg	.987	17	147	8	2	13
Trevino, Clearwater	1.000	6	46	3	0	6
Valdez, Vero Beach	.993	17	139	13	1	12
Vella, Dunedin*	.995	22	177	16	1	15
Verdugo, Miami	.979	7	44	2	1	4
Walker, Clearwater	.964	6	54	0	2	5
Watson, Baseball City*	.991	39	403	20	4	41
Williams, Winter Haven	1.000	3	17	1	0	0
Yan, Dunedin	.979	120	982	77	23	83
Zawaski, St. Lucie	.984	39	300	14	5	27
Zayas, Clearwater	.941	6	30	2	2	4
Zinter, St. Lucie	.938	9	68	7	5	8

Triple Plays—Brogna, Rodriguez.

SECOND BASEMEN

Player and Club	Pct.	G.	PO.	A.	E.	DP.
Abreu St. Petersburg	.958	30	55	106	7	34
Adler, Lakeland	1.000	3	1	5	0	0
Anglero, Baseball City	.972	18	29	41	2	11
Bagwell, Winter Haven	1.000	1	2	1	0	0
Barberie, West Palm Beach	.974	122	247	343	16	73
Barefoot, Miami	1.000	4	4	9	0	1
Berry, Baseball City	1.000	1	0	1	0	0
Beyeler, Lakeland	.968	84	177	284	15	67
Bohringer, Vero Beach	.964	7	10	17	1	4
Bournigal, Vero Beach	.986	74	118	222	5	45
Burgos, Port Charlotte	.955	120	247	325	27	68
Byrd, Winter Haven	.963	44	104	133	9	28
Caceres, Sarasota	1.000	2	6	5	0	3
Carlin, Clearwater	.982	23	55	54	2	12
CROSBY, St. Petersburg	.983	102	200	309	9	51
Davis, Fort Lauderdale	.840	5	10	11	4	3
Delgado, Winter Haven	.959	46	97	114	9	32
Dellicarri, St. Lucie	.921	18	24	34	5	10
Diaz, Dunedin	.964	49	111	132	9	29
Ebel, Vero Beach	1.000	4	2	5	0	1
Fletcher, Sarasota	.956	112	192	331	24	64
Fregosi, West Palm Beach	1.000	1	1	2	0	0
Hall, St. Petersburg	1.000	1	1	1	0	1
Harris, Osceola	.968	65	154	213	12	60
Hernandez, St. Lucie	.973	111	211	321	15	61
Howard, Baseball City	1.000	1	1	0	0	0
Kelley, Fort Lauderdale	.960	108	207	295	21	61
Kotchman, Miami	.846	5	5	6	2	1
Lara, St. Lucie	.969	20	35	60	3	11
Laseke, Winter Haven	.975	58	101	130	6	29
Laureano, Baseball City	.962	129	250	382	25	97
Letterio, Miami	.966	79	132	207	12	36
Lewis, Vero Beach	1.000	1	0	1	0	0
Maldonado, Lakeland	.933	3	4	10	1	1
Marigny, Lakeland	.963	35	61	95	6	19
Mello, West Palm Beach	1.000	3	8	7	0	2
Melvin, St. Petersburg	1.000	4	11	11	0	2
J. Munoz, Vero Beach	.961	75	112	183	12	33
O. Munoz, West Palm Beach	.978	9	18	27	1	9
Murillo, Vero Beach	.967	27	52	64	4	5
Noelke, St. Lucie	.875	2	4	3	1	0
Ocasio, Sarasota	.967	29	37	50	3	8
Pena, St. Petersburg	.966	6	9	19	1	4
Renteria, Osceola	.961	72	140	226	15	35
Richardi, Osceola	1.000	1	1	1	0	0
Robertson, Clearwater	.960	98	198	311	21	71
Roman, Fort Lauderdale	.934	14	32	39	5	11
Rowland, Lakeland	.962	14	24	27	2	6
Ruckman, Dunedin	1.000	2	3	1	0	0
Sable, Port Charlotte	.976	11	16	25	1	4
Santangelo, West Palm Beach	.966	4	9	19	1	2
Scott, Dunedin	.949	45	71	97	9	19
Sloniger, Miami	.962	28	54	73	5	15
Smith, Miami	1.000	2	2	3	0	1
Stairs, West Palm Beach	1.000	5	5	8	0	0
Suero, Dunedin	.961	51	92	155	10	12
Tresh, Fort Lauderdale	.955	13	27	36	3	4
Trevino, Clearwater	.932	15	29	40	5	8
Valentin, Winter Haven	1.000	1	5	8	0	3
Vatcher, Clearwater	.971	7	10	23	1	4
Wardlow, Port Charlotte	.978	11	17	28	1	5

Triple Plays—Bohringer, Marigny.

THIRD BASEMEN

Player and Club	Pct.	G.	PO.	A.	E.	DP.
Abell, Port Charlotte	.923	7	6	6	1	2
Abreu, St. Petersburg	.902	27	18	37	6	2
Acta, Osceola	1.000	1	2	2	0	0
Adler, Lakeland	.897	78	51	115	19	14
Alou, West Palm Beach	1.000	1	0	2	0	1
Anglero, Baseball City	.927	35	33	56	7	5
Bagwell, Winter Haven	.929	59	50	108	12	10
Barefoot, Miami	.333	2	0	1	2	0
Batiste, Clearwater	.952	8	5	15	1	0
Berry, Baseball City	.919	104	75	198	24	17
Bishop, Miami	.625	2	1	4	3	1
Bohringer, Vero Beach	.840	16	7	14	4	1
Bonchek, Miami	.920	20	22	24	4	2
Boyce, Miami	.818	16	5	13	4	2
Burgos, Port Charlotte	.667	1	1	1	1	1
CACERES, Sarasota	.943	94	64	152	13	8
Campbell, Sarasota	1.000	1	0	1	0	0
Caraballo, Baseball City	1.000	2	1	2	0	0
Carlin, Clearwater	.000	1	0	0	1	0
Carmona, St. Petersburg	1.000	1	0	1	0	0
Colston, Miami	.500	1	0	1	1	0
Crosby, St. Petersburg	1.000	3	2	4	0	0
Davis, Fort Lauderdale	.865	39	22	61	13	6
Delgado, Winter Haven	.958	23	20	49	3	4
Dellicarri, St. Lucie	1.000	3	7	5	0	3
J. Diaz, Dunedin	1.000	6	7	7	0	2
S. Diaz, St. Lucie	.917	6	5	6	1	0
Donnels, St. Lucie	.922	94	93	202	25	18
Ebel, Vero Beach	1.000	16	10	18	0	3
Echemendia, West Palm Beach..	.833	5	2	3	1	0
Erhardt, Fort Lauderdale	.902	59	38	81	13	8
Escalera, Baseball City	1.000	4	2	2	0	1
Foley, Clearwater	.667	2	1	1	1	0
Fregosi, West Palm Beach	.942	18	13	36	3	3
Garman, Port Charlotte	.931	58	38	110	11	7
Gonzalez, Baseball City	1.000	2	1	6	0	0
Gutierrez, Miami	.974	19	14	24	1	0
Hall, St. Petersburg	.915	71	46	138	17	14
Harris, Osceola	.947	16	8	28	2	3
Hernandez, St. Lucie	.000	1	0	0	1	0
Howard, Baseball City	1.000	1	1	0	0	0
Kosco, West Palm Beach	.949	59	51	99	8	6
Kotchman, Miami	.967	35	27	32	2	2
Lara, St. Lucie	1.000	13	9	12	0	1
Leake, Miami	.886	12	12	19	4	3
Letterio, Miami	1.000	3	2	5	0	2
Lewis, Vero Beach	.926	115	75	201	22	18
Maksudian, Miami	1.000	3	0	5	0	0
Marigny, Lakeland	.915	51	24	84	10	6
Marshall, Port Charlotte	1.000	3	3	2	0	0
Mello, West Palm Beach	.897	26	27	43	8	4
Melvin, St. Petersburg	.931	46	33	88	9	9
Metoyer, Miami	1.000	1	1	0	0	0
Mota, Osceola	.886	108	70	179	32	18
J. Munoz, Vero Beach	.852	12	7	16	4	1
O. Munoz, West Palm Beach	.949	18	15	41	3	8
Murillo, Miami	.750	4	1	5	2	0
Nichols, St. Petersburg	1.000	1	2	1	0	0
Ocasio, Sarasota	.897	17	10	25	4	4
Ortiz, Osceola	.500	1	0	1	1	0
Peel, Sarasota	.846	33	21	45	12	4
Polanco, St. Lucie	.952	24	22	37	3	4
Raley, Lakeland	.939	17	8	23	2	3
Reaves, Clearwater	.880	74	47	129	24	18
Renteria, Osceola	.796	15	6	33	10	3
Richardi, Osceola	1.000	4	0	3	0	0
Roman, Fort Lauderdale	.808	11	10	11	5	2
Ruckman, Dunedin	.883	82	43	145	25	19
Sable, Port Charlotte	.899	43	30	68	11	6
Sloniger, Miami	.911	34	23	59	8	2
Spann, Lakeland	.571	3	1	3	3	1
Sprague, Dunedin	.895	52	33	86	14	4
Stairs, West Palm Beach	.954	24	14	48	3	7
Tonucci, Dunedin	.900	3	4	5	1	1
Tresh, Fort Lauderdale	.893	34	18	49	8	3
Trevino, Clearwater	.913	53	36	79	11	6
Valdez, Vero Beach	1.000	15	7	18	0	0
Vargas, Baseball City	.889	3	3	5	1	1
Vatcher, Clearwater	.600	2	0	3	2	0
Vella, Dunedin*	1.000	1	1	0	0	0
Wardlow, Port Charlotte	.894	41	27	74	12	5
Whitehead, Winter Haven	.910	64	41	111	15	13
Wiley, Lakeland	1.000	1	1	0	0	0

Triple Plays—Adler, Lewis.

SHORTSTOPS

Player and Club	Pct.	G.	PO.	A.	E.	DP.
Abell, Port Charlotte	1.000	5	9	15	0	3
Abreu, St. Petersburg	.961	34	48	76	5	13
Anglero, Baseball City	.929	44	66	144	16	27
Barefoot, Miami	.942	16	23	42	4	8
Batiste, Clearwater	.931	103	163	294	34	67
Berry, Baseball City	1.000	1	1	0	0	0
Beyeler, Lakeland	1.000	2	5	7	0	1
Bournigal, Vero Beach	.963	67	101	156	10	28
Burgos, Port Charlotte	.250	1	1	0	3	0
Busby, Sarasota	.933	48	89	134	16	35
Byrd, Winter Haven	.921	84	152	244	34	53
Caceres, Sarasota	.914	10	13	19	3	2
Carmona, St. Petersburg	.916	116	152	372	48	69
Cartaya, Port Charlotte	.927	85	135	248	30	47
Cedeno, Dunedin	.968	9	9	21	1	3
Cordero, West Palm Beach	.922	77	121	224	29	48
Cruz, Sarasota	.925	29	59	65	10	18
Davis, Fort Lauderdale	.667	1	1	1	1	0
Delgado, Winter Haven	1.000	13	15	31	0	5
Dellicarri, St. Lucie	.922	24	38	56	8	14
A. Diaz, St. Lucie	.932	86	137	244	28	50
J. Diaz, Dunedin	.957	6	8	14	1	2
Ebel, Vero Beach	.965	80	113	221	12	37
Galindo, Lakeland	.956	120	219	394	28	92
Gonzalez, Baseball City	.944	31	47	71	7	17
Harris, Osceola	.692	2	3	6	4	0
Hernandez, St. Lucie	1.000	1	0	3	0	0
Howard, Baseball City	.951	70	123	224	18	47
Iglesias, Miami	.937	96	149	252	27	43
Kelly, Dunedin	.933	104	169	305	34	62
Lara, St. Lucie	.914	26	42	75	11	15
Letterio, Miami	.929	19	25	54	6	6
Marigny, Lakeland	.926	17	29	46	6	7
Montalvo, Dunedin	.922	14	21	26	4	6
Morandini, Clearwater	.975	15	20	59	2	11
Mota, Osceola	.500	1	0	2	2	0
J. Munoz, Vero Beach	1.000	8	4	11	0	2
O. Munoz, West Palm Beach	.964	39	59	100	6	14
Noelke, St. Lucie	1.000	1	1	0	0	0
Ocasio, Sarasota	.952	54	65	152	11	23
Renteria, Osceola	.911	13	21	30	5	10
Robertson, Clearwater	.951	21	37	61	5	15
RODRIGUEZ, Fort Lauderdale	.970	101	180	279	14	63
Roman, Fort Lauderdale	.932	7	19	22	3	5
Russell, Baseball City	1.000	4	1	6	0	1
Sable, Port Charlotte	.898	28	47	67	13	18
Samson, Port Charlotte	.968	26	48	74	4	15
Santangelo, West Palm Beach	.910	25	23	48	7	12
Scott, Dunedin	.796	16	14	25	10	3
Silvestri, Osceola	.956	124	221	473	32	93
Sloniger, Miami	.909	5	4	6	1	2
Smith, Miami	.833	3	1	4	1	0
Stairs, West Palm Beach	.923	6	2	10	1	1
Tresh, Fort Lauderdale	.939	22	36	57	6	12
Trevino, Clearwater	.875	1	1	6	1	2
Valentin, Winter Haven	.956	54	94	169	12	32
Vargas, Fort Lauderdale	.948	15	35	38	4	7

Triple Play—Silvestri.

OUTFIELDERS

Player and Club	Pct.	G.	PO.	A.	E.	DP.
Alborano, Baseball City*	.978	69	84	5	2	1
Alcantara, Miami*	.929	12	12	1	1	0
Alou, West Palm Beach	.985	81	129	6	2	2
Alyea, 2 P.C.-3 St.L.	1.000	5	10	0	0	0
Arendas, Fort Lauderdale*	1.000	12	21	0	0	0
Argo, Vero Beach	.986	54	65	3	1	1
Barron, Vero Beach	.985	93	184	14	3	3
Bernardo, Miami*	1.000	2	4	0	0	0
Berry, Baseball City	1.000	13	24	0	0	0
Bishop, Miami	.938	13	15	0	1	0
Blosser, Winter Haven*	.933	25	52	4	4	0
Bourne, Clearwater	1.000	25	36	0	0	0
Boyce, Miami	1.000	34	53	3	0	0
Bridges, Fort Lauderdale	1.000	1	1	0	0	0
Brummer, Vero Beach*	1.000	25	30	0	0	0
Cabrera, Miami	.984	124	232	11	4	1
Calvert, St. Petersburg	.979	59	92	2	2	0
Carlin, Clearwater	.929	9	13	0	1	0
Cedeno, Osceola	.937	61	97	7	7	1
Cerny, Miami*	1.000	1	1	0	0	0
Christian, St. Petersburg	.979	109	179	7	4	2
Cobb, Clearwater	.944	60	111	8	7	2
Cole, St. Petersburg*	1.000	8	13	0	0	0
Davis, St. Lucie	.976	59	116	6	3	1

OUTFIELDERS—Continued

Player and Club	Pct.	G.	PO.	A.	E.	DP.
A. Diaz, St. Lucie	1.000	11	14	0	0	0
S. Diaz, St. Lucie	1.000	10	16	2	0	0
Dostal, Vero Beach	.966	100	160	8	6	2
Doster, 54 Mia-14 Lak	.948	68	140	5	8	3
Echemendia, West Palm Beach..	1.000	2	1	0	0	0
Elci, St. Petersburg	1.000	3	1	1	0	0
Escalera, Baseball City	1.000	7	11	0	0	0
Faulk, West Palm Beach*	.969	89	146	9	5	3
Fletcher, Sarasota	1.000	1	1	0	0	0
Fox, 5 Osc.-7 St.L.*	.938	12	13	2	1	1
Frye, West Palm Beach	1.000	20	15	0	0	0
Glasker, Port Charlotte*	.986	65	132	6	2	2
Gonzalez, Sarasota	.986	38	67	5	1	2
Goshay, Dunedin	.953	56	39	2	2	0
Graham, St. Petersburg*	.962	13	22	3	1	0
Green, 66 VB-21 Lakeland	.994	87	160	8	1	1
Griffin, Vero Beach	.981	121	247	6	5	0
Grotewold, Clearwater	.958	17	23	0	1	0
Gutierrez, Miami	1.000	10	11	0	0	0
Hailey, Fort Lauderdale	.977	83	159	8	4	2
Hall, St. Petersburg	.950	67	143	8	8	2
Hare, Lakeland*	.986	65	140	4	2	0
Hernandez, West Palm Beach	1.000	32	53	6	0	1
Howard, Baseball City	1.000	8	16	1	0	0
Hunter, Osceola	.972	83	168	8	5	0
Ingram, Lakeland	.969	79	119	5	4	1
Jaster, St. Lucie	.961	26	47	2	2	1
Jenkins, Osceola	.978	62	128	6	3	1
C. Johnson, St. Petersburg	.979	121	321	11	7	3
L. Johnson, Miami	1.000	1	2	0	0	0
T. Johnson, Baseball City*	.964	110	207	8	8	3
Jordan, St. Petersburg	1.000	11	22	2	0	2
Kingwood, West Palm Beach	.969	67	121	4	4	0
Kirkpatrick, Clearwater	.9869	119	288	14	4	3
Knoblauh, Fort Lauderdale	.926	17	23	2	2	1
Koenig, Baseball City	1.000	2	3	0	0	0
Koslofski, Baseball City	.967	115	224	7	8	3
Kramer, Miami*	.994	66	154	2	1	0
Kraus, Fort Lauderdale*	.980	97	192	9	4	2
Laboy, Osceola*	.954	73	121	4	6	2
Lake, Miami	.958	52	111	3	5	1
Laseke, Winter Haven	.960	37	69	3	3	0
Lavender, Port Charlotte*	.973	67	104	3	3	0
Law, Port Charlotte	.977	117	245	12	6	1
Leach, Winter Haven*	.978	56	85	4	2	0
Lewis, Osceola*	.953	54	80	2	4	0
Mackie, Miami	1.000	25	50	4	0	0
Magallanes, Sarasota	.979	63	133	5	3	1
Maksudian, Miami	1.000	62	83	3	0	0
Marrs, Winter Haven	.992	54	110	7	1	1
Marsh, Clearwater	.990	42	97	1	1	0
Marte, Port Charlotte*	1.000	11	21	1	0	0
Mazey, Miami*	.981	25	50	3	1	1
McCRAY, Sarasota	.9870	123	296	9	4	2
McDaniel, St. Lucie	.983	101	214	16	4	5
Mello, West Palm Beach	1.000	3	1	0	0	0
K. Moore, Baseball City	1.000	4	7	0	0	0
R. Moore, Baseball City	.978	129	304	11	7	3
S. Moore, Winter Haven	1.000	8	12	1	0	0
Morris, Port Charlotte*	.964	92	182	7	7	1
Morrison, Dunedin	.943	99	136	14	9	2
Mota, Osceola	.889	8	7	1	1	0
Munoz, Vero Beach	1.000	9	8	0	0	0
Murillo, Miami	1.000	1	2	0	0	0
Naughton, St. Lucie	.971	29	32	2	1	0
Nelloms, Fort Lauderdale	.987	77	145	6	2	0
Nichols, St. Petersburg	1.000	18	37	1	0	1
Noelke, St. Lucie	1.000	6	6	1	0	0
Nunez, Dunedin	.970	82	153	10	5	1
Nyssen, Osceola	1.000	81	145	3	0	0
Ocasio, Sarasota	1.000	1	0	1	0	0
Payton, Sarasota	1.000	38	79	1	0	0
Pegues, Lakeland	.983	54	115	3	2	1
Perez, Lakeland	.939	21	28	3	2	0
Polanco, St. Lucie	1.000	2	1	0	0	0
Reese, Baseball City	.800	3	4	0	1	0
Rhodes, Fort Lauderdale	.904	34	43	4	5	0
Ricker, West Palm Beach	.974	110	212	13	6	4
Rivers, Winter Haven	.973	99	202	12	6	2
Roche, St. Lucie*	.968	76	142	7	5	1
Rodgers, Dunedin	.983	139	287	8	5	3
Rodriguez, Vero Beach*	1.000	3	1	0	0	0
Rohrmeier, 16 Sar.-3 P Char...	.975	19	39	0	1	0
Roseboro, St. Lucie	.986	92	208	5	3	1
Santana, Osceola*	1.000	5	5	0	0	0
Scannell, Winter Haven	.969	43	92	3	3	0
Scruggs, Port Charlotte	.973	58	100	7	3	4
Shore, Port Charlotte	.966	19	26	2	1	0
Sloniger, Miami*	1.000	8	8	0	0	0
C. Smith, West Palm Beach*	1.000	29	32	2	0	0
L. Smith, Miami	.971	26	30	4	1	1
T. Smith, Miami*	1.000	7	8	0	0	0
Spann, Lakeland	.992	72	119	6	1	0
Spoolstra, Miami*	1.000	1	3	0	0	0
Sullivan, Sarasota	.949	93	178	7	10	4
Szynal, Clearwater	.889	6	7	1	1	0
Tatum, Winter Haven	.962	78	70	5	3	2
Taveras, Dunedin	.971	58	93	7	3	3
Tedder, Sarasota*	.986	43	67	2	1	0
Thoutsis, St. Petersburg	1.000	8	16	0	0	0
Toney, Lakeland	1.000	7	7	0	0	0
Torborg, Miami*	1.000	8	19	0	0	0
Trevino, Clearwater	.970	85	153	9	5	1
Vatcher, Clearwater	.928	55	61	3	5	2
Vella, Dunedin*	.977	26	43	0	1	0
Viltz, West Palm Beach*	.958	16	23	0	1	0
Waid, Miami	1.000	5	8	0	0	0
Walker, Miami	1.000	2	1	0	0	0
Watson, Baseball City*	.981	55	95	6	2	0
Whitehead, Winter Haven	.985	52	124	7	2	2
Williams, Clearwater	.957	12	20	2	1	0
Wilson, Miami	1.000	1	1	0	0	0
Wright, Miami	1.000	1	1	0	0	0
Zaksek, Sarasota*	.961	49	63	10	3	0
J. Zambrano, Winter Haven	.959	43	67	4	3	0
R. Zambrano, Winter Haven	1.000	1	1	0	0	0
Zayas, Clearwater	.986	122	263	10	4	1
Zeihen, Fort Lauderdale*	.889	6	7	1	1	0
Zinter, St. Lucie						

Triple Play—Cedeno.

CATCHERS

Player and Club	Pct.	G.	PO.	A.	E.	DP.	PB.
Argo, Vero Beach	.973	20	32	4	1	0	4
Baxter, Lakeland	.972	89	496	61	16	9	14
Billmeyer, Port Charlotte	.994	22	147	14	1	3	3
Brown, Sarasota	.978	89	539	45	13	8	7
Campbell, Sarasota	.956	22	96	12	5	2	0
Carver, Baseball City	.990	45	242	47	3	5	3
Colbrunn, West Palm Beach	.988	57	376	49	5	4	4
Colston, Miami	1.000	2	4	1	0	0	0
Delas, Lakeland	1.000	4	17	2	0	0	1
DeLeon, Baseball City	.974	25	143	6	4	0	7
Duke, West Palm Beach	.988	41	267	50	4	4	7
DZIADKOWIEC, Dunedin	.990	70	457	53	5	5	13
Echemendia, WP Beach	.970	30	144	16	5	2	2
Elci, St. Petersburg	1.000	3	5	0	0	1	0
Elliot, St. Petersburg	.971	37	145	23	5	1	3
Erickson, Fort Lauderdale	.988	29	151	17	2	1	3
Escalera, Baseball City	.984	45	212	30	4	6	7
Eusebio, Osceola	.985	51	290	40	5	1	5
Fagnant, Winter Haven	.958	7	22	1	1	0	3
Flaherty, Winter Haven	.979	72	359	60	9	3	19
Fox, St. Petersburg	1.000	2	6	1	0	0	0
Fuller, Sarasota	.973	38	163	14	5	1	5
Fulton, St. Petersburg	.985	103	520	73	9	9	3
C. Gonzalez, Baseball City	1.000	4	7	0	0	0	0
Ja. Gonzalez, St. Lucie	.986	55	328	34	5	6	1
Je. Gonzalez, Vero Beach	.976	30	141	22	4	2	7
Grotewold, Clearwater	.993	24	119	16	1	1	4
Gwinn, Fort Lauderdale	.961	39	148	25	7	3	4
Henderson, Lakeland	.996	41	214	23	1	3	6
Hines, St. Lucie	.988	33	136	23	2	1	5
Jackson, Port Charlotte	.989	29	171	9	2	4	6
Johnson, Miami	.979	69	365	48	9	5	14
Jones, St. Lucie	.969	13	53	10	2	0	4
Knorr, Dunedin	.990	24	186	20	2	1	4
Koenig, Baseball City	1.000	10	14	0	0	0	1
Kuld, Miami	.941	11	67	13	5	0	1
Lau, St. Lucie	.986	15	66	7	1	0	1
Leary, West Palm Beach	1.000	9	40	5	0	1	2
Lindsey, Clearwater	.983	35	190	35	4	3	4
Losa, Port Charlotte	.975	73	420	43	12	7	16
Mackie, Miami	1.000	1	1	0	0	0	0
Magnusson, Vero Beach	.982	82	381	58	8	1	10
Maksudian, Miami	.972	13	56	13	2	1	4
Manuel, Port Charlotte	.952	7	19	1	1	0	2
Matilla, Winter Haven	.972	17	57	13	2	0	1
Mayne, Baseball City	1.000	7	31	2	0	1	0
McCall, Clearwater	.976	31	178	28	5	2	6
McElroy, Sarasota	1.000	1	6	0	0	0	0
Minch, Miami	.983	13	51	6	1	1	6
Monzon, Dunedin	.977	14	118	10	3	0	2
Natal, West Palm Beach	.968	15	68	24	3	2	2
Nichols, St. Petersburg	1.000	9	24	2	0	1	0
H. Ortiz, Vero Beach	.970	40	174	23	6	1	3
J. Ortiz, Osceola	.983	26	156	21	3	4	4

CATCHERS—Continued

Player and Club	Pct.	G.	PO.	A.	E.	DP.	PB.	Player and Club	Pct.	G.	PO.	A.	E.	DP.	PB.
Pedre, Baseball City	.967	39	179	24	7	1	5	Taylor, Miami	.976	35	184	21	5	0	4
Pujols, Baseball City	1.000	2	11	0	0	0	0	Thomas, St. Petersburg	1.000	3	3	0	0	0	1
Redman, St. Petersburg	1.000	3	23	1	0	0	1	Tonucci, Dunedin	1.000	6	32	2	0	0	2
Reese, Baseball City	.899	21	72	8	9	1	6	Townley, Dunedin	.981	33	184	18	4	2	7
Roca, St. Lucie	1.000	14	76	16	0	2	6	Valdez, Vero Beach	.913	8	18	3	2	0	1
Rosario, Fort Lauderdale	.984	88	536	99	10	5	19	Vaughan, Dunedin	1.000	4	8	0	0	0	0
Ruckman, Dunedin	1.000	1	2	0	0	0	0	Verdugo, Miami	.963	9	43	9	2	0	4
Servais, Osceola	.973	24	121	23	4	1	3	Wiley, Lakeland	.983	9	53	5	1	0	2
Shore, Port Charlotte	.975	22	108	11	3	1	7	Williams, Winter Haven	.982	62	344	42	7	5	10
Spehr, Baseball City	.986	12	63	7	1	1	1	Zayas, Clearwater	.977	43	225	31	6	3	6
Stocker, Clearwater	1.000	8	36	12	0	1	1	Zinter, St. Lucie	.985	21	121	13	2	1	1
Strong, Lakeland	.986	17	66	5	1	0	3								

Triple Play—Carver.

PITCHERS

Player and Club	Pct.	G.	PO.	A.	E.	DP.	Player and Club	Pct.	G.	PO.	A.	E.	DP.
Abril, Winter Haven	.920	35	9	14	2	2	Givens, St. Lucie*	1.000	1	0	1	0	0
J. Adams, Baseball City	1.000	8	3	3	0	0	Gogolewski, Fort Lauderdale	.889	23	6	18	3	4
K. Adams, Baseball City	1.000	20	2	3	0	0	Gohmann, Sarasota	1.000	10	3	0	0	0
Adkins, Fort Lauderdale*	.571	11	3	1	3	0	Grater, St. Petersburg	.810	56	6	11	4	1
Alexander, Port Charlotte*	1.000	14	6	7	0	0	Grayson, Miami	.900	10	3	6	1	1
Alicano, Baseball City*	1.000	2	0	2	0	0	Green, Fort Lauderdale	1.000	21	0	6	0	0
H. Allen, Osceola*	.927	26	7	31	3	1	Griffin, St. Lucie	.824	33	10	18	6	3
T. Allen, Winter Haven	1.000	2	0	1	0	0	Gross, Baseball City	.667	8	2	2	2	1
Alvarez, Port Charlotte*	.909	13	1	9	1	0	Haas, Lakeland	.944	10	7	10	1	1
Ashby, Clearwater	1.000	6	3	7	0	0	D. Hall, Dunedin	.923	16	4	8	1	0
Barnes, West Palm Beach*	1.000	7	4	14	0	1	T. Hall, Sarasota*	.931	20	7	20	2	1
Becker, St. Petersburg*	1.000	56	5	14	0	2	Harriger, St. Lucie	.889	11	4	12	2	1
Bennett, West Palm Beach	.900	18	2	7	1	1	Harris, Winter Haven	1.000	30	7	8	0	1
Bivens, St. Petersburg	1.000	10	1	8	0	0	Hartgraves, Osceola*	.875	7	2	5	1	0
Bohanon, Port Charlotte*	.947	11	3	15	1	2	Hartzog, Fort Lauderdale	.875	17	7	7	2	0
Bond, Osceola	.875	27	10	18	4	0	Hasler, Sarasota	.972	25	12	23	1	3
Boucher, Dunedin*	.945	33	5	47	3	2	Hathaway, St. Petersburg	.930	29	19	21	3	3
Boyd, West Palm Beach	.905	31	7	12	2	0	Heinle, Vero Beach	.909	25	2	8	1	0
Brantley, Clearwater	.800	8	1	3	1	0	Henion, West Palm Beach	1.000	37	3	7	0	0
Brito, West Palm Beach	.914	23	13	19	3	0	Hentgen, Dunedin	.950	29	1	18	1	1
Bross, St. Lucie	.818	35	1	8	1	0	J. Hernandez, St. Petersburg	1.000	3	4	2	0	0
Brown, Winter Haven*	1.000	38	5	13	0	1	R. Hernandez, St. Lucie*	.500	3	0	1	1	0
Bruzdewicz, Dunedin*	1.000	13	1	5	0	0	Hillman, St. Lucie*	.909	19	0	10	1	0
Bumgarner, St. Lucie	.889	8	3	5	1	1	J. Hoffman, Fort Lauderdale	.857	23	2	10	2	2
Buonantony, 1 St.P.-11 Clw.	.900	12	2	7	1	1	K. Hoffman, Vero Beach*	.909	9	1	9	1	0
E. Burgos, 8 Dun.-15 Mia.*	.769	23	1	9	3	0	R. Hoffman, St. Petersburg	.892	27	9	24	4	2
J. Burgos, St. Petersburg*	1.000	5	1	2	0	0	Holdridge, Clearwater	.895	24	4	13	2	2
Bustillos, Vero Beach	1.000	7	1	10	0	0	Hook, Fort Lauderdale*	.913	34	6	15	2	2
Campusano, Osceola*	1.000	1	0	1	0	0	Hopper, Baseball City	.958	19	6	17	1	0
Carroll, Clearwater	1.000	3	0	1	0	0	Horsman, Dunedin*	.944	35	3	14	1	0
A. Carter, Clearwater*	.818	12	2	7	2	2	Howard, Fort Lauderdale*	.750	13	1	2	1	0
J. Carter, West Palm Beach	.900	7	2	7	1	0	Hudek, Sarasota	1.000	27	3	3	0	0
Carver, Osceola	1.000	1	0	2	0	0	Hudson, Baseball City	1.000	12	3	6	0	0
Castillo, Port Charlotte	1.000	1	1	1	0	0	Hurst, Port Charlotte	.867	19	9	4	2	0
Cauley, Sarasota	1.000	3	1	0	0	0	Ilsley, Osceola*	1.000	2	1	0	0	0
Cavalier, West Palm Beach	.750	25	2	1	1	0	Johnston, Baseball City	.913	26	7	14	2	0
CERNY, Miami*	1.000	35	8	25	0	3	M. Jones, Lakeland	.810	29	6	11	4	0
Chavez, Sarasota*	1.000	7	2	6	0	0	R. Jones, West Palm Beach	.833	42	3	7	2	0
Christopher, Clearwater*	1.000	5	1	3	0	2	Jundy, Baseball City	.929	34	4	9	1	0
Cinnella, West Palm Beach	.952	32	18	22	2	4	Kamanaka, Vero Beach	.824	33	7	7	3	2
Clarkin, 22 Mia.-10 WPB	.968	32	8	22	1	0	Kawabata, Vero Beach	1.000	11	2	13	0	0
Cole, Baseball City	1.000	9	5	10	0	1	Kennedy, Sarasota	.905	25	12	26	4	1
Coleman, Vero Beach	.905	45	3	16	2	0	Keon, Port Charlotte	1.000	10	1	5	0	0
Combs, Clearwater*	1.000	6	3	9	0	0	Kerfeld, Osceola	1.000	5	0	1	0	0
B. Conroy, Winter Haven	1.000	8	2	2	0	1	Kerfut, Port Charlotte	1.000	12	0	4	0	0
J. Conroy, St. Petersburg	.800	16	1	3	1	0	Kerrigan, West Palm Beach	1.000	7	0	5	0	0
Cook, Lakeland*	.895	31	7	10	2	1	Kiely, Lakeland	.875	36	3	11	2	0
Cormier, St. Petersburg*	.966	26	4	24	1	0	King, Sarasota	.000	1	0	0	1	0
Cortes, Sarasota	.769	23	5	5	3	0	Kite, Winter Haven	.737	21	3	11	5	0
Credeur, Osceola*	.750	17	1	2	1	0	Kline, West Palm Beach	.931	27	6	21	2	0
Cromwell, Dunedin*	.971	31	7	26	1	2	Knackert, Sarasota	.875	35	6	15	3	0
Dedos, Winter Haven	1.000	12	0	2	0	0	Knapp, Vero Beach	.920	23	5	18	2	0
DeLaCruz, Sarasota	.879	14	9	20	4	0	Knudsen, Lakeland	.750	45	2	4	2	0
DeLeon, Baseball City	.944	19	6	11	1	1	Lamle, Miami*	.912	14	3	28	3	0
Dennison, Winter Haven*	.882	11	7	8	2	1	Landry, Winter Haven*	.885	31	4	19	3	0
DeYoung, West Palm Beach	.957	39	7	15	1	1	Langley, Clearwater*	1.000	25	5	14	0	2
Diez, 15 WPB-21 St.L.*	1.000	36	5	13	0	1	LaRosa, Clearwater*	1.000	22	1	8	0	0
Drahman, Sarasota	1.000	7	0	3	0	0	LaRose, St. Lucie	1.000	41	6	9	0	1
Dzafic, Winter Haven	1.000	6	2	2	0	0	A. Leiter, Dunedin*	1.000	3	0	1	0	0
Elam, Fort Lauderdale	1.000	3	3	6	0	0	M. Leiter, Fort Lauderdale	1.000	6	0	1	0	0
Elli, St. Lucie*	1.000	26	7	23	0	1	Limbach, Clearwater*	.889	11	1	7	1	0
Estrada, Winter Haven	1.000	7	5	5	0	0	Linton, Dunedin	1.000	9	2	3	0	0
Evans, Port Charlotte	.882	49	4	11	2	1	Lipscomb, Port Charlotte	1.000	32	9	13	0	3
Farmer, Osceola	1.000	7	3	8	0	0	Luckham, Vero Beach	1.000	6	1	3	0	0
Farr, Miami	1.000	8	0	2	0	0	Lumley, Lakeland	.795	27	11	24	9	1
Felden, Miami	1.000	18	5	6	0	0	Machado, St. Lucie	1.000	4	0	2	0	0
Figueroa, Miami*	1.000	13	4	12	0	1	Mack, Miami	.867	18	1	12	2	1
Filson, Baseball City*	1.000	8	2	11	0	1	Majer, St. Petersburg	.900	10	2	7	1	0
Florence, Winter Haven*	.917	51	11	22	3	1	Maldonado, Baseball City	.778	28	3	4	2	0
Fynan, Clearwater	1.000	22	4	10	0	1	Mallea, Miami	1.000	4	1	0	0	0
L. Garcia, Miami	1.000	14	4	16	0	0	Manon, Fort Lauderdale	.897	22	9	17	3	1
V. Garcia, Fort Lauderdale*	.957	29	3	19	1	1	Manuel, Port Charlotte	.938	15	4	11	1	1
Gennings, Sarasota	1.000	10	1	4	0	0	Marina, St. Lucie	1.000	12	7	7	0	0
Ghelfi, Miami	.929	7	2	11	1	1	Marrero, Osceola*	1.000	1	0	1	0	0
Gideon, St. Lucie*	.833	17	3	7	2	0	Martel, Fort Lauderdale	1.000	26	8	23	0	1

PITCHERS—Continued

Player and Club	Pct.	G.	PO.	A.	E.	DP.	Player and Club	Pct.	G.	PO.	A.	E.	DP.
Mathews, Port Charlotte	.947	10	5	13	1	1	Rodriguez, Fort Lauderdale	1.000	13	3	1	0	0
Mauser, Clearwater	.773	16	7	10	5	1	Rosario, Osceola*	.667	2	0	2	1	0
McCormack, Baseball City	1.000	43	0	8	0	0	Rosenthal, Port Charlotte	.917	20	3	8	1	0
McCormick, Baseball City*	1.000	6	1	2	0	0	Rush, Winter Haven	1.000	4	0	1	0	0
McDonald, Clearwater	.833	33	5	10	3	0	Russo, St. Petersburg	1.000	24	2	8	0	2
Meacham, Lakeland	1.000	11	6	9	0	0	Ryan, Winter Haven	1.000	24	8	18	0	3
Mehrtens, Sarasota*	1.000	6	2	1	0	0	Sampson, Vero Beach	1.000	16	5	4	0	1
Meizoso, St. Lucie*	.667	10	1	1	1	0	Sanchez, Baseball City*	.750	3	0	3	1	0
Merriman, Miami*	.750	5	0	3	1	0	A. Sanders, Winter Haven	1.000	4	1	1	0	0
Metoyer, Miami	.931	31	13	41	4	2	E. Sanders, Dunedin	1.000	12	1	4	0	0
Middaugh, Sarasota	1.000	6	0	1	0	0	Schourek, St. Lucie*	1.000	2	1	1	0	0
Miller, St. Lucie	.955	26	10	32	2	2	Seal, Dunedin*	.917	21	1	10	1	3
A. Mills, Fort Lauderdale	1.000	22	3	6	0	0	Searcy, Lakeland*	.909	9	1	9	1	0
Moeller, Baseball City*	1.000	12	1	11	0	0	C. Shaw, Port Charlotte*	.922	25	9	50	5	3
Morhardt, Lakeland	1.000	1	0	1	0	0	K. Shaw, Baseball City	1.000	11	0	6	0	0
Jo. Morris, Lakeland	1.000	3	1	3	0	0	Sheehan, Osceola	1.000	41	5	9	0	1
A. Morrison, Fort Lauderdale*	1.000	10	1	2	0	0	Shepherd, Baseball City	.882	11	8	7	2	1
J. Morrison, Winter Haven	1.000	4	0	1	0	0	Sherrill, St. Petersburg*	.900	52	4	5	1	0
Morse, Port Charlotte	1.000	15	10	20	0	0	Shinall, Vero Beach	.957	47	3	19	1	1
Mullins, Miami	.714	26	2	3	2	0	Silverstein, Dunedin	1.000	28	3	9	0	2
Munoz, Fort Lauderdale	1.000	3	5	3	0	0	Simon, Osceola	.957	19	8	14	1	0
Nelson, Baseball City	.905	34	5	14	2	1	Sims, Clearwater*	.975	27	5	34	1	2
Newcomb, Dunedin	1.000	4	2	1	0	0	Singelyn, Miami	.000	2	0	0	1	0
Noch, Vero Beach	1.000	21	9	15	0	1	Sipple, Port Charlotte*	.933	29	6	22	2	0
Normand, Osceola*	.815	31	4	18	5	1	Smith, St. Petersburg	.955	29	16	26	2	2
O'Neill, Lakeland*	1.000	21	1	3	0	0	Sonberg, Sarasota*	.500	6	0	1	1	1
Ogliaruso, Dunedin	.938	13	5	10	1	0	Sossamon, West Palm Beach	1.000	11	2	6	0	0
Ohman, Port Charlotte	1.000	23	0	5	0	0	Stanford, Fort Lauderdale	1.000	24	0	4	0	0
Ollom, Sarasota	.667	15	1	1	1	0	Stange, Winter Haven	1.000	24	5	6	0	0
Opperman, Vero Beach	.786	19	4	7	3	0	Stephens, Sarasota	.967	17	15	14	1	2
Ortiz, Osceola	1.000	1	1	2	0	0	Steward, Lakeland	.944	31	4	13	1	0
Osuna, Osceola*	1.000	46	4	12	0	0	Stewart, Winter Haven*	1.000	19	2	4	0	0
Patrick, Vero Beach*	1.000	2	0	1	0	0	Stone, Lakeland	.885	25	7	16	3	1
Pavlik, Port Charlotte	.978	26	19	25	1	1	Stonikas, Baseball City	1.000	22	1	10	0	4
Peek, Clearwater	.667	8	0	2	1	0	Stottlemyre, Baseball City	.750	13	4	2	2	0
Perez, West Palm Beach*	.875	18	1	6	1	0	B. Sullivan, West Palm Beach*	1.000	2	1	1	0	0
Pickens, Baseball City	.950	27	9	10	1	0	Tafoya, Osceola	1.000	55	9	17	0	1
Pierson, St. Petersburg	.958	52	6	17	1	1	Takaheshi, Vero Beach	1.000	13	2	9	0	0
Plemel, St. Petersburg	1.000	21	8	12	0	0	D.M. Taylor, Port Charlotte	.906	43	5	24	3	2
Plummer, St. Lucie	1.000	10	1	3	0	0	M.L. Taylor, Dunedin*	.750	3	1	2	1	0
Ponder, Miami	.962	39	6	19	1	1	Thomas, Clearwater	.972	27	8	27	1	1
Poole, Vero Beach*	.963	60	9	17	1	0	Thompson, Winter Haven	1.000	11	3	0	0	0
Popplewell, Fort Lauderdale	.941	32	9	7	1	0	Timlin, Dunedin	.781	33	7	18	7	0
Porter, Osceola	1.000	1	0	1	0	0	Torborg, Miami*	.949	26	6	31	2	1
Potts, Osceola	.900	16	3	6	1	1	Trice, Osceola*	.904	28	11	36	5	2
Prieto, Miami	1.000	4	2	0	0	0	Tudor, Vero Beach*	.000	1	0	0	1	0
Proctor, St. Lucie	.897	22	10	16	3	0	Valera, St. Lucie	1.000	6	1	9	0	0
Ralph, Fort Lauderdale	.889	15	4	4	1	0	Vanzytveld, Vero Beach	.918	26	16	29	4	0
Rambo, Clearwater*	.882	9	3	12	2	2	Vargas, Osceola	1.000	18	2	4	0	0
Reitzel, Port Charlotte*	1.000	21	2	11	0	1	Wacha, Winter Haven	.739	32	7	10	6	0
Resnikoff, Sarasota*	.933	52	1	13	1	0	Wainhouse, West Palm Beach	.882	13	6	9	2	1
Reynolds, Sarasota	1.000	13	2	13	0	2	Wanish, Dunedin	1.000	5	0	2	0	0
Rhoden, Osceola	1.000	5	3	5	0	0	Wapnick, Dunedin	1.000	24	4	8	0	3
Richards, Lakeland*	1.000	28	0	12	0	0	Wilkins, Lakeland	.919	16	15	19	3	4
Rivard, Miami*	.800	11	1	3	1	0	Williams, Dunedin	.963	20	6	20	1	2
H. Rivera, West Palm Beach	.960	16	10	14	1	1	Willis, Lakeland	1.000	29	4	8	0	0
L. Rivera, Lakeland	1.000	13	2	6	0	1	Woide, Dunedin*	.882	27	2	13	2	1
Robinson, Lakeland	1.000	4	0	1	0	0							

The following players did not have any fielding statistics at the positions indicated or appeared only as a designated hitter, pinch-hitter or pinch-runner: Abreu, p; Adler, of; Alcantara, 3b; Bauer, p; Busby, 3b; Chadwick, p; Christian, 3b; Coulter, p; Elci, 3b; Erickson, 3b; Federico, of; Fulton, 3b; L. Gonzalez, dh, ph; Goshay, 2b; Hamilton, ph, dh; L. Johnson, p; Kirkpatrick, p; Knecht, dh; Lara, of; Laseke, p; Lavender, p; A. Lewis, p; Lloyd, p; Metoyer, of; M. Mills, p; Ja. Morris, p; Ocasio, 1b; Powell, dh; Santangelo, of; Scott, 3b, of; Singley, dh, ph; C. Sullivan, p; Taveras, p; Tedder, p; Vaughan, p; Whitehead, p; Whitlock, p; Young, 3b.

CLUB PITCHING

Club	ERA.	G.	CG.	ShO.	Sv.	IP.	H.	R.	ER.	HR.	HB.	BB.	Int. BB.	SO.	WP.	Bk.
Lakeland	2.50	136	11	15	38	1183.0	971	418	329	27	41	477	28	831	40	27
West Palm Beach	2.67	138	17	19	39	1210.0	1040	439	359	28	40	416	27	874	47	25
Sarasota	3.00	136	22	14	41	1168.1	1035	486	389	45	62	400	20	765	57	23
St. Lucie	3.04	134	22	11	34	1170.0	1106	501	395	43	60	402	14	737	55	16
St. Petersburg	3.12	139	13	12	42	1208.1	1178	526	419	47	28	335	23	700	47	23
Port Charlotte	3.14	139	10	15	42	1205.0	1097	548	420	53	60	480	24	824	74	31
Vero Beach	3.20	135	9	14	35	1157.1	1063	500	411	54	36	460	57	733	68	21
Osceola	3.21	137	15	11	33	1210.2	1179	557	432	41	37	410	8	775	61	31
Dunedin	3.26	140	4	14	43	1187.1	1059	543	430	46	36	522	19	977	110	41
Fort Lauderdale	3.51	138	16	7	28	1173.1	1132	585	457	47	51	468	12	802	76	19
Baseball City	3.67	139	5	6	34	1200.2	1209	615	490	62	49	480	32	696	94	20
Clearwater	3.68	136	28	12	25	1168.1	1128	582	478	51	34	509	7	717	69	19
Winter Haven	3.89	139	11	7	33	1195.0	1132	636	516	48	44	613	24	747	91	28
Miami	4.39	134	24	8	14	1087.2	1162	650	530	59	49	502	11	745	90	37

PITCHERS' RECORDS
(Leading Qualifiers for Earned-Run Average Leadership — 112 or More Innings)

*Throws lefthanded.

Pitcher—Club	W.	L.	Pct.	ERA.	G.	GS.	CG.	GF.	ShO.	Sv.	IP.	H.	R.	ER.	HR.	HB.	BB.	Int. BB.	SO.	WP.
Stephens, Sarasota	10	4	.714	1.47	17	17	5	0	4	0	122.2	107	31	20	1	3	34	5	83	4
Wilkins, Lakeland	7	5	.583	1.66	16	16	4	0	1	0	119.1	95	24	22	2	1	25	0	72	1
Cormier, St. Petersburg*	12	7	.632	2.23	26	26	4	0	2	0	169.2	141	63	42	9	0	33	2	122	4
Kline, West Palm Beach	11	6	.647	2.29	27	20	3	2	2	1	129.2	109	40	33	4	3	36	3	96	3

Pitcher—Club	W.	L.	Pct.	ERA.	G.	GS.	CG.	GF.	ShO.	Sv.	IP.	H.	R.	ER.	HR.	HB.	BB.	Int. BB.	SO.	WP.
Proctor, St. Lucie	7	6	.538	2.36	22	21	3	1	0	0	133.1	104	50	35	7	5	73	0	85	10
Miller, St. Lucie	13	6	.684	2.38	26	26	8	0	2	0	200.1	177	64	53	4	12	28	0	130	2
Trice, Osceola*	16	4	.800	2.57	28	27	7	0	3	0	182.1	179	68	52	6	6	39	0	94	5
Hentgen, Dunedin	9	8	.529	2.68	29	28	0	0	0	0	151.1	123	53	45	5	2	71	1	148	16
Lumley, Lakeland	8	9	.471	2.69	27	24	0	2	0	1	130.1	108	50	39	1	13	56	2	76	9
C. Shaw, Port Charlotte*	10	6	.625	2.72	25	24	4	0	3	0	148.2	135	60	45	8	9	54	2	82	5

Departmental Leaders: G—Poole, 60; W—Trice, 16; L—Metoyer, 14; Pct.—Bross, Trice, .800; GS—Cromwell, 30; CG—Thomas, 11; GF—Poole, 50; ShO—Stephens, 4; Sv.—Grater, 32; IP—Miller, 200.1; H—Metoyer, 198; R—Holdridge, 100; ER—Holdridge, 84; HR—Holdridge, Landry, 11; HB—Hasler, 19; BB—Kite, 102; IBB—Coleman, 10; SO—Cromwell, 161; WP—Cromwell, 25.

(All Pitchers—Listed Alphabetically)

Pitcher—Club	W.	L.	Pct.	ERA.	G.	GS.	CG.	GF.	ShO.	Sv.	IP.	H.	R.	ER.	HR.	HB.	BB.	Int. BB.	SO.	WP.
Abreu, St. Petersburg	0	0	.000	10.80	5	0	0	5	0	0	5.0	9	6	6	2	0	2	0	5	0
Abril, Winter Haven	3	9	.250	3.99	35	12	3	12	1	0	117.1	117	58	52	6	7	52	3	65	11
J. Adams, Baseball City	0	0	.000	2.70	8	0	0	6	0	0	10.0	7	3	3	0	1	10	0	2	2
K. Adams, Baseball City	0	3	.000	7.81	20	4	0	9	0	1	27.2	20	30	24	1	3	45	0	17	21
Adkins, Fort Lauderdale*	3	3	.500	2.36	11	4	0	4	0	3	45.2	40	15	12	2	1	14	0	48	2
Alexander, Port Charlotte	2	3	.400	1.70	14	6	0	5	0	2	53.0	36	12	10	1	2	16	0	41	5
Alicano, Baseball City*	0	0	.000	0.00	2	0	0	1	0	0	4.0	0	0	0	0	0	1	0	3	1
H. Allen, Osceola*	12	11	.522	3.34	26	25	2	1	0	0	159.0	157	78	59	1	0	57	0	123	15
T. Allen, Winter Haven	0	1	.000	7.71	2	1	0	1	0	0	2.1	4	2	2	0	0	5	0	1	0
Alvarez, Port Charlotte*	7	4	.636	2.11	13	13	3	0	2	0	81.0	68	29	19	2	4	21	0	51	4
Ashby, Clearwater	1	4	.200	1.24	6	6	2	0	1	0	43.2	28	9	6	0	0	21	0	44	4
Barnes, West Palm Beach*	4	3	.571	0.72	7	7	4	0	3	0	50.0	25	9	4	0	0	16	0	67	4
Bauer, Osceola	0	0	.000	0.00	2	0	0	1	0	0	1.2	2	0	0	0	0	1	0	1	0
Becker, St. Petersburg*	4	3	.571	2.34	56	0	0	14	0	3	77.0	71	25	20	4	1	14	0	52	6
Bennett, West Palm Beach	2	1	.667	0.91	18	0	0	13	0	4	29.2	20	3	3	0	1	5	0	29	1
Bivens, St. Petersburg	7	0	1.000	2.23	10	10	1	0	1	0	64.2	50	17	16	3	0	20	0	47	2
Bohanon, Port Charlotte*	0	3	.000	1.81	11	7	0	3	0	1	54.2	40	16	11	1	2	20	0	33	1
Bond, Osceola	9	10	.474	3.62	27	26	1	0	0	0	154.1	155	80	62	5	6	71	0	78	10
Boucher, Dunedin*	10	10	.500	3.06	33	28	1	1	1	0	164.2	142	80	56	6	6	58	2	117	13
Boyd, West Palm Beach	4	7	.364	3.56	31	10	1	7	0	1	93.2	90	43	37	3	4	37	1	58	7
Brantley, Clearwater	0	5	.000	4.35	8	8	1	0	0	0	49.2	60	31	24	0	3	19	1	33	6
Brito, West Palm Beach	11	8	.579	2.89	23	23	4	0	1	0	149.1	134	64	48	2	4	49	2	90	5
Bross, St. Lucie	8	2	.800	2.79	35	0	0	26	0	11	58.0	39	21	18	1	1	26	3	47	3
Brown, Winter Haven*	3	9	.250	4.20	38	9	0	13	0	2	105.0	112	64	49	5	2	57	3	79	4
Bruzdewicz, Dunedin*	1	1	.500	2.63	13	1	0	5	0	1	24.0	17	11	7	0	0	15	0	17	0
Bumgarner, St. Lucie	4	3	.571	4.07	8	8	1	0	0	0	48.2	61	28	22	2	3	14	0	25	4
Buonantony, 1 St.P.-11 Clw.	3	3	.500	4.86	12	5	0	4	0	0	33.1	35	20	18	2	1	27	1	16	4
E. Burgos, 8 Dun-15 Mia*	3	1	.750	3.24	23	1	0	14	0	0	33.1	28	21	12	0	0	33	5		
J. Burgos, St. Petersburg*	1	0	1.000	6.0	4	0	0	0	0	0	6.0	4	0	0	0	0	4	0	0	0
Bustillos, Vero Beach	2	4	.333	2.93	7	7	1	0	0	0	43.0	42	19	14	4	1	11	0	30	4
Campusano, Osceola	0	0	.000	0.00	1	0	0	1	0	0	3.2	1	0	0	0	0	5	0	5	0
Carroll, Clearwater	0	0	.000	6.75	3	0	0	2	0	0	4.0	4	3	3	1	0	2	0	0	0
A. Carter, Clearwater*	1	5	.167	4.85	12	12	2	0	1	0	68.2	73	46	37	3	6	32	0	31	5
J. Carter, West Palm Beach	4	1	.800	2.57	7	7	0	0	0	0	35.0	36	14	10	0	1	8	0	29	1
Carver, Osceola	0	1	.000	9.00	1	1	0	0	0	0	1.0	1	1	1	0	0	2	0	0	0
Castillo, Port Charlotte	1	0	1.000	0.00	1	1	0	0	0	0	5.0	4	0	0	0	1	0	0	5	0
Cauley, Sarasota	0	1	.000	20.25	3	0	0	1	0	0	2.2	7	9	6	1	0	5	1	0	0
Cavalier, West Palm Beach	1	1	.500	2.65	25	0	0	15	0	5	34.0	29	10	10	1	0	11	2	24	0
Cerny, Miami*	2	7	.222	6.80	35	5	1	15	0	3	82.0	107	73	62	4	4	42	1	56	7
Chadwick, Sarasota	0	0	.000	2.25	1	0	0	0	0	0	4.0	4	3	1	0	0	4	0	4	1
Chavez, Sarasota*	3	3	.500	3.35	7	6	1	1	0	1	40.1	39	15	15	1	1	8	0	19	1
Christopher, Clearwater*	2	1	.667	0.79	5	0	0	2	0	0	11.1	1	2	1	0	0	6	0	9	1
Cinnella, West Palm Beach	6	10	.375	3.84	32	20	3	5	0	1	133.2	140	72	57	5	4	42	2	83	5
Clarkin, 22 Mia-10 WPB	5	3	.625	3.42	32	2	0	14	0	0	71.0	65	30	27	3	4	28	1	45	3
Cole, Baseball City	3	1	.750	3.86	9	9	0	0	0	0	42.0	43	23	18	2	1	22	0	30	2
Coleman, Vero Beach	3	5	.375	2.54	45	4	0	17	0	5	106.1	88	38	30	4	1	45	10	74	9
Combs, Clearwater*	2	1	.667	1.30	6	6	0	0	0	0	41.2	35	8	6	0	1	11	0	24	0
B. Conroy, Winter Haven	3	3	.500	2.95	8	6	2	1	2	0	39.2	38	19	13	3	4	11	0	30	3
J. Conroy, St. Petersburg	1	0	1.000	6.29	16	0	0	9	0	0	24.1	25	17	17	2	0	20	3	13	2
Cook, Lakeland*	7	5	.583	3.10	31	13	1	10	1	2	107.1	108	48	37	5	2	48	1	58	3
Cormier, St. Petersburg*	12	7	.632	2.23	26	26	4	0	2	0	169.2	141	63	42	9	0	33	2	122	4
Cortes, Sarasota	6	2	.750	2.72	23	9	1	4	1	0	82.2	66	31	25	2	1	24	0	59	2
Coulter, Clearwater	0	2	.000	3.74	10	1	1	5	0	3	21.2	25	11	9	2	0	9	0	15	1
Credeur, Osceola*	1	1	.500	1.67	17	0	0	8	0	0	32.1	18	12	6	0	1	20	0	28	2
Cromwell, Dunedin*	12	6	.667	3.62	31	30	0	0	0	0	151.2	136	70	61	5	4	84	0	161	25
Dedos, Winter Haven	0	0	.000	2.95	12	0	0	4	0	1	18.1	19	12	6	1	1	10	2	7	3
DeLaCruz, Sarasota	8	4	.667	2.78	14	13	1	0	1	0	81.0	64	38	25	1	6	36	0	53	9
DeLeon, Baseball City	5	5	.500	3.91	19	15	2	1	0	0	99.0	118	51	43	7	2	27	0	43	6
Dennison, Winter Haven*	1	2	.333	5.40	11	5	0	0	0	0	33.1	38	24	20	3	0	20	0	17	4
DeYoung, West Palm Beach*	1	2	.333	3.05	39	1	0	12	0	2	73.2	58	27	25	0	4	37	2	60	6
Diez, 15 WPB-21 St.L.*	5	6	.455	2.28	36	4	1	18	0	7	71.0	68	26	18	2	2	47	2	47	2
Drahman, Sarasota	0	1	.000	3.24	7	2	0	3	0	1	16.2	18	9	6	1	1	5	1	9	1
Dzafic, Winter Haven	0	0	.000	4.73	6	0	0	5	0	0	13.1	18	8	7	0	0	4	1	3	1
Elam, Clearwater	4	3	.571	2.97	11	11	2	0	1	0	69.2	53	23	23	3	1	32	0	58	7
Elli, St. Lucie*	9	6	.600	3.42	26	24	3	1	0	0	152.2	151	72	58	5	11	66	0	82	10
Estrada, Winter Haven	1	3	.250	5.18	7	6	0	0	0	0	33.0	35	22	19	0	2	11	1	13	1
Evans, Port Charlotte	4	3	.571	2.05	49	0	0	32	0	9	66.0	56	25	15	2	3	23	4	47	5
Farmer, Osceola	2	3	.400	2.66	7	6	0	1	0	1	40.2	45	14	12	3	1	21	0	27	2
Farr, Miami	0	3	.000	5.63	8	2	0	4	0	0	16.0	17	12	10	0	1	14	0	15	5
Felden, Miami	0	4	.000	5.98	18	6	0	8	0	0	52.2	57	47	35	6	3	35	0	32	9
Figueroa, Miami*	1	5	.167	2.40	13	3	1	5	0	1	41.1	34	13	11	1	2	17	0	15	2
Filson, Baseball City*	4	0	1.000	3.33	8	8	0	0	0	0	46.0	47	20	17	0	2	12	0	20	3
Florence, Winter Haven*	2	7	.222	2.88	51	2	0	31	0	15	93.2	81	46	30	1	2	34	3	71	7
Fynan, Clearwater	3	4	.429	3.93	22	3	0	13	0	5	55.0	53	30	24	3	2	18	0	33	3
L. Garcia, Miami	2	4	.333	3.69	14	13	2	0	1	0	78.0	73	45	32	7	1	37	0	63	7
V. Garcia, Fort Lauderdale*	6	7	.462	3.38	29	10	0	6	0	0	104.0	109	53	39	7	0	43	2	52	7
Gennings, Sarasota	0	1	.000	6.45	10	2	0	7	0	0	22.1	28	17	16	5	0	16	0	8	2
Ghelfi, Miami	1	6	.143	4.54	7	7	1	0	0	0	39.2	52	26	20	3	2	13	1	13	2
Gideon, St. Lucie*	0	3	.000	2.32	17	0	0	9	0	0	31.0	26	9	8	0	0	15	3	24	0

Pitcher—Club	W.	L.	Pct.	ERA.	G.	GS.	CG.	GF.	ShO.	Sv.	IP.	H.	R.	ER.	HR.	HB.	BB.	Int. BB.	SO.	WP.
Givens, St. Lucie*	0	1	.000	0.00	1	1	0	0	0	0	5.0	7	6	0	1	0	1	0	8	0
Gogolewski, Fort Lauderdale	6	12	.333	3.63	23	21	2	2	1	0	131.1	140	71	53	2	9	49	1	73	6
Gohmann, Sarasota	0	0	.000	0.42	10	0	0	5	0	2	21.2	10	1	1	0	3	4	0	11	0
Grater, St. Petersburg	3	8	.273	1.87	56	0	0	49	0	32	67.1	44	23	14	1	7	24	4	59	2
Grayson, Miami	0	0	.000	2.18	10	2	0	4	0	0	20.2	23	7	5	0	1	7	2	11	2
Green, Fort Lauderdale	0	3	.000	3.40	21	0	0	11	0	3	42.1	43	21	16	1	7	6	0	20	2
Griffin, St. Lucie	8	8	.500	2.98	33	10	2	8	0	2	111.2	117	52	37	5	10	22	2	41	2
Gross, Baseball City	1	3	.250	3.89	8	7	0	0	0	0	44.0	48	31	19	4	1	20	2	27	1
Haas, Lakeland	4	1	.800	2.03	10	10	1	0	1	0	62.0	50	16	14	1	6	16	0	46	1
D. Hall, Dunedin	1	4	.200	3.53	16	14	0	0	0	0	51.0	46	25	20	2	3	21	0	42	3
T. Hall, Sarasota*	7	7	.500	3.13	20	16	2	2	1	0	118.0	99	49	41	4	8	48	1	73	7
Harriger, St. Lucie	5	3	.625	3.19	11	11	0	0	0	0	67.2	72	33	24	6	2	17	0	17	1
Harris, Winter Haven	10	13	.435	3.99	29	26	1	2	0	0	153.1	144	81	68	6	7	77	2	85	7
Hartgraves, Osceola*	3	3	.500	2.95	7	6	1	0	1	0	39.2	36	20	13	0	2	12	0	21	4
Hartzog, Fort Lauderdale	7	7	.500	3.38	17	17	3	0	0	0	109.1	92	52	41	4	2	40	2	107	5
Hasler, Sarasota	14	8	.636	3.39	25	25	4	0	3	0	164.2	166	75	62	7	19	32	1	84	4
Hathaway, St. Petersburg	9	8	.529	3.11	29	24	2	0	2	0	159.1	186	67	55	5	0	24	1	50	1
Heinle, Vero Beach	3	1	.750	1.51	25	0	0	8	0	1	59.2	51	18	10	1	1	33	9	37	7
Henion, West Palm Beach	6	1	.857	1.37	37	0	0	26	0	13	59.0	38	9	9	1	0	14	6	33	0
Hentgen, Dunedin	9	8	.529	2.68	29	28	0	0	0	0	151.1	123	53	45	5	2	71	1	148	16
J. Hernandez, St. Petersburg	0	2	.000	7.71	3	3	0	0	0	0	14.0	17	14	12	0	0	5	0	5	2
R. Hernandez, St. Lucie*	0	0	.000	9.00	3	0	0	2	0	0	5.0	5	5	5	0	0	4	0	4	0
Hillman, St. Lucie*	6	6	.500	5.50	19	14	1	1	0	0	88.1	96	59	54	3	3	53	0	67	15
J. Hoffman, Fort Lauderdale	0	3	.000	5.19	23	0	0	12	0	0	50.1	58	35	29	1	2	19	0	19	6
K. Hoffman, Vero Beach*	4	0	1.000	3.18	9	9	0	0	0	0	51.0	38	20	18	2	1	28	1	37	4
R. Hoffman, St. Petersburg	11	12	.478	3.40	27	27	3	0	1	0	161.1	150	76	61	2	8	66	3	96	12
Holdridge, Clearwater	7	10	.412	5.71	24	24	3	0	0	0	132.1	147	100	84	11	8	77	0	77	16
Hook, Fort Lauderdale*	6	5	.545	3.67	34	9	0	15	0	2	73.2	62	35	30	5	0	40	0	57	3
Hopper, Baseball City	4	2	.667	3.69	19	9	0	6	0	1	75.2	85	40	31	4	4	26	1	37	5
Horsman, Dunedin*	5	6	.455	2.51	35	1	0	23	0	8	79.0	72	24	22	3	1	27	3	60	3
Howard, Fort Lauderdale*	2	0	1.000	1.78	13	0	0	6	0	0	25.1	19	6	5	1	1	13	3	25	0
Hudek, Sarasota	1	3	.250	1.67	27	0	0	25	0	15	43.0	22	10	8	1	2	13	2	39	1
Hudson, Baseball City	1	0	1.000	2.23	12	2	0	1	0	0	36.1	31	16	9	1	5	7	1	18	0
Hurst, Port Charlotte	4	6	.400	4.45	19	11	0	4	0	1	58.2	67	44	29	5	3	32	0	37	6
Ilsley, Osceola*	0	0	.000	6.43	2	2	0	0	0	0	7.0	8	5	5	2	0	6	0	6	0
Johnson, Miami	0	0	.000	6.75	1	0	0	1	0	0	1.1	2	1	1	1	0	1	0	2	0
Johnston, Baseball City	9	4	.692	4.92	26	26	0	0	0	0	131.2	135	84	72	6	11	63	2	76	8
M. Jones, Lakeland	9	6	.600	2.53	29	7	0	8	0	3	92.1	84	39	26	2	3	39	2	66	4
R. Jones, West Palm Beach	7	4	.636	2.84	42	3	0	16	0	1	69.2	67	31	22	3	2	31	3	70	0
Jundy, Baseball City	2	7	.222	3.55	34	0	0	17	0	4	71.0	72	43	28	4	1	33	4	47	5
Kamanaka, Vero Beach	3	3	.500	3.61	33	6	0	17	0	3	92.1	90	43	37	6	7	22	1	52	5
Kawabata, Vero Beach	5	3	.625	3.00	11	11	1	0	1	0	69.0	62	25	23	3	2	26	1	47	2
Kennedy, St. Petersburg	14	7	.667	3.01	25	25	3	0	0	0	161.2	137	62	54	9	4	57	1	86	8
Keon, Port Charlotte	1	2	.333	9.51	10	3	0	2	0	0	23.2	35	27	25	3	5	24	1	14	2
Kerfeld, Osceola	0	0	.000	1.17	5	0	0	2	0	0	7.2	4	2	1	0	0	3	0	8	0
Kerfut, Port Charlotte	3	0	1.000	5.57	12	0	0	2	0	0	21.0	32	15	13	0	1	9	1	12	2
Kerrigan, West Palm Beach	0	0	.000	0.00	7	0	0	6	0	3	12.1	9	0	0	0	3	2	0	8	0
Kiely, Lakeland	4	3	.571	2.40	36	0	0	22	0	8	63.2	52	26	17	2	0	27	4	56	1
King, Sarasota	1	0	1.000	1.00	1	1	1	0	0	0	9.0	9	1	1	0	0	0	0	7	0
Kirkpatrick, Clearwater	0	0	.000	6.00	2	0	0	2	0	0	3.0	3	2	2	0	0	1	0	1	1
Kite, Winter Haven	4	9	.308	4.11	21	20	1	0	1	0	107.1	71	59	49	3	0	102	0	96	21
Kline, West Palm Beach	11	6	.647	2.29	27	20	3	2	2	1	129.2	109	40	33	4	3	36	3	96	3
Knackert, Sarasota	8	5	.615	2.94	35	12	2	22	0	12	98.0	85	41	32	3	4	35	0	80	4
Knapp, Vero Beach	7	9	.438	3.91	23	18	1	0	0	0	122.0	140	69	53	9	3	44	2	52	6
Knudsen, Lakeland	3	2	.600	2.15	45	0	0	26	0	10	54.1	43	16	13	1	1	22	7	68	2
Lamle, Miami*	6	4	.600	3.15	14	12	4	0	0	0	85.2	88	34	30	8	5	29	2	46	4
Landry, Winter Haven*	9	10	.474	3.99	31	27	1	0	0	0	169.0	169	81	75	11	2	69	1	86	1
Langley, Clearwater*	5	3	.625	4.00	25	6	1	14	1	2	74.1	70	38	33	2	2	48	0	66	3
LaRosa, Clearwater*	2	1	.667	2.80	22	2	0	16	0	1	61.0	49	21	19	2	3	27	0	39	3
LaRose, St. Lucie	6	2	.750	2.32	41	0	0	30	0	10	62.0	49	23	16	1	4	25	3	52	2
Laseke, Winter Haven	0	0	.000	0.00	1	0	0	1	0	0	0.2	0	0	0	0	0	0	0	1	0
Lavender, Port Charlotte*	0	0	.000	0.00	1	0	0	1	0	0	1.0	1	0	0	0	0	0	0	0	0
A. Leiter, Dunedin*	0	2	.000	5.63	3	3	0	0	0	0	8.0	11	5	5	0	0	5	0	4	0
M. Leiter, Fort Lauderdale	2	2	.500	1.53	6	4	1	1	0	1	35.1	27	9	6	1	2	5	0	22	0
Lewis, Vero Beach	0	0	.000	0.00	1	0	0	1	0	0	1.0	0	0	0	1	0	0	0	0	0
Limbach, Clearwater*	2	3	.400	4.76	11	1	0	6	0	0	22.2	24	13	12	1	0	13	1	16	1
Linton, Dunedin	1	2	.333	2.96	9	1	0	5	0	2	27.1	27	12	9	1	0	9	0	35	1
Lipscomb, Port Charlotte	4	4	.500	3.20	32	0	0	13	0	3	68.1	71	29	22	7	1	26	3	46	5
Lloyd, Dunedin*	0	0	.000	10.13	2	0	0	0	0	0	2.2	6	3	3	0	0	1	0	1	1
Luckham, Vero Beach	0	0	.000	0.64	6	0	0	2	0	0	14.0	9	2	1	1	2	0	3	1
Lumley, Lakeland	8	9	.471	2.69	27	24	0	2	0	1	130.1	108	50	39	1	13	56	2	76	9
Machado, St. Lucie	1	0	1.000	0.00	4	0	0	3	0	2	10.2	5	0	0	0	3	0	14	0
Mack, Miami	3	6	.333	4.58	18	8	1	9	0	1	59.0	61	33	30	3	3	19	2	42	2
Majer, St. Petersburg	4	2	.667	4.47	10	9	1	0	1	0	54.1	56	28	27	2	2	17	0	34	3
Maldonado, Baseball City	11	3	.786	1.17	28	0	0	19	0	9	76.2	47	14	10	3	1	24	4	66	2
Mallea, Miami	1	2	.333	3.46	4	2	0	1	0	0	13.0	10	5	5	1	0	10	1	7	0
Manon, Fort Lauderdale	7	9	.438	3.53	22	22	6	0	3	0	122.1	91	62	48	5	9	53	0	100	4
Manuel, Port Charlotte	4	7	.364	4.72	15	14	0	0	0	0	76.1	77	43	40	6	8	30	0	51	6
Marina, St. Lucie	2	3	.400	4.69	12	8	0	2	0	0	55.2	68	34	29	1	5	18	0	30	1
Marrero, Osceola*	0	0	.000	0.00	1	0	0	0	0	0	2.2	3	0	0	0	0	1	0	1	0
Martel, Fort Lauderdale	10	8	.556	4.04	26	24	4	1	1	0	144.2	151	76	65	4	5	39	0	86	8
Mathews, Port Charlotte	4	2	.667	3.64	10	10	0	0	0	0	59.1	55	28	24	2	2	17	0	30	2
Mauser, Clearwater	6	7	.462	2.69	16	16	5	0	0	0	107.0	105	40	32	4	5	40	0	73	2
McCormack, Baseball City	4	4	.500	3.20	43	0	0	36	0	12	56.1	58	24	20	2	2	22	6	37	1
McCormick, Baseball City*	1	2	.333	8.20	6	6	0	0	0	0	26.1	39	26	24	3	2	10	0	12	1
McDonald, Clearwater	3	8	.273	3.19	33	1	0	25	0	7	73.1	63	34	26	3	0	32	2	54	5
Meacham, Lakeland	5	4	.556	1.95	11	9	4	1	2	0	64.2	59	15	14	3	2	12	2	39	0
Mehrtens, Sarasota*	0	0	.000	5.00	6	0	0	2	0	0	9.0	9	5	5	0	3	7	0	3	0
Meizoso, St. Lucie*	0	1	.000	3.50	10	1	0	7	0	2	18.0	17	8	7	2	1	4	0	17	3
Merriman, Miami*	0	4	.000	8.05	5	5	0	0	0	0	19.0	30	21	17	1	4	17	0	8	1
Metoyer, Miami	9	14	.391	3.80	31	26	9	4	1	1	187.1	198	89	79	6	3	59	0	127	12
Middaugh, Sarasota	0	0	.000	3.18	6	0	0	4	0	0	11.1	13	4	4	1	3	1	0	4	2

Pitcher—Club	W.	L.	Pct.	ERA.	G.	GS.	CG.	GF.	ShO.	Sv.	IP.	H.	R.	ER.	HR.	HB.	BB.	Int. BB.	SO.	WP.
Miller, St. Lucie	13	6	.684	2.38	26	26	8	0	2	0	200.1	177	64	53	4	12	28	0	130	2
A. Mills, Fort Lauderdale	1	4	.200	3.77	22	0	0	15	0	6	31.0	40	15	13	0	4	9	1	25	3
M. Mills, Dunedin	0	0	.000	0.00	3	0	0	2	0	1	4.1	2	0	0	0	1	0	0	5	0
Moeller, Baseball City*	9	0	1.000	1.77	12	11	2	1	0	0	71.0	59	17	14	2	1	20	1	64	1
Morhardt, Lakeland	1	0	1.000	0.00	1	0	0	1	0	0	1.0	1	0	0	0	0	1	0	1	0
Ja. Morris, Sarasota*	0	1	.000	10.13	2	0	0	1	0	0	2.2	3	3	3	0	0	2	0	4	1
Jo. Morris, Lakeland	0	0	.000	2.25	3	3	0	0	0	0	8.0	7	2	2	0	0	2	0	2	0
A. Morrison, Fort Lauderdale*	0	2	.000	2.12	10	0	0	7	0	1	17.0	9	7	4	0	0	15	0	13	3
J. Morrison, Winter Haven	0	1	.000	22.50	4	0	0	1	0	0	4.0	8	10	10	0	0	9	0	3	3
Morse, Port Charlotte	8	4	.667	3.09	15	15	2	0	1	0	93.1	77	37	32	6	1	23	1	74	2
Mullins, Miami	1	8	.111	6.40	26	4	0	8	0	0	52.0	48	49	37	3	4	53	1	54	11
Munoz, Fort Lauderdale	1	2	.333	4.73	3	3	0	0	0	0	13.1	16	8	7	2	0	7	0	2	0
Nelson, Baseball City	12	7	.632	3.83	34	5	0	12	0	0	105.2	112	50	45	7	2	25	7	40	4
Newcomb, Dunedin	1	0	1.000	2.45	4	0	0	3	0	2	7.1	8	2	2	0	0	2	0	1	0
Noch, Vero Beach	9	7	.563	3.98	21	15	1	0	0	0	101.2	104	50	45	3	4	31	5	52	2
Normand, Osceola*	4	4	.500	3.80	31	12	2	10	1	1	104.1	109	54	44	5	3	46	0	59	6
O'Neill, Lakeland*	4	1	.800	0.98	21	0	0	18	0	10	27.2	14	4	3	0	0	12	4	29	0
Ogliaruso, Dunedin	3	6	.333	5.09	13	10	1	2	1	0	58.1	60	40	33	6	4	28	1	33	7
Ohman, Port Charlotte	1	2	.333	4.10	23	0	0	14	0	2	26.1	34	15	12	1	1	11	2	20	3
Ollom, Sarasota	1	1	.500	5.31	15	0	0	6	0	1	20.1	20	13	12	1	0	12	1	25	1
Opperman, Vero Beach	0	7	.000	3.54	19	19	0	0	0	0	61.0	51	26	24	4	4	24	1	35	4
Ortiz, Osceola	0	0	.000	0.00	1	0	0	0	0	0	4.0	2	0	0	0	1	0	1	0
Osuna, Osceola*	3	4	.429	2.66	46	0	0	26	0	7	67.2	50	27	20	2	2	27	4	62	5
Patrick, Vero Beach*	0	1	.000	9.72	2	2	0	0	0	0	8.1	14	9	9	1	1	4	0	3	2
Pavlik, Port Charlotte	3	8	.273	3.41	26	22	1	2	1	1	118.2	92	60	45	5	8	72	1	98	12
Peek, Clearwater	1	0	1.000	5.89	8	0	0	4	0	0	18.1	23	13	12	1	1	6	0	13	0
Perez, West Palm Beach*	7	6	.538	2.76	18	12	0	3	0	1	94.2	62	34	29	2	3	54	0	85	5
Pickens, Baseball City	4	8	.333	4.25	27	12	1	4	0	1	101.2	117	56	48	5	6	39	2	66	12
Pierson, St. Petersburg	7	4	.636	2.34	52	2	0	14	0	1	80.2	78	34	21	3	3	17	5	28	2
Plemel, St. Petersburg	3	5	.375	3.46	21	11	1	4	0	0	75.1	83	37	29	4	1	13	1	38	2
Plummer, St. Lucie	1	0	1.000	5.93	10	0	0	8	0	3	13.2	20	10	9	2	1	7	1	8	1
Ponder, Miami	7	8	.467	2.96	39	10	2	24	0	8	97.1	85	39	32	4	2	32	1	72	2
Poole, Vero Beach*	11	4	.733	1.61	60	0	0	50	0	19	78.1	57	16	14	0	2	24	7	93	3
Popplewell, Fort Lauderdale	3	5	.375	4.01	32	14	0	5	0	0	119.0	119	67	53	6	3	60	1	70	9
Porter, Osceola	0	0	.000	6.00	1	0	0	0	0	0	6.0	6	4	4	0	1	0	0	2	1
Potts, Osceola	3	3	.500	2.93	16	5	0	2	0	0	46.0	51	23	15	2	1	10	1	35	1
Prieto, Miami	0	0	.000	4.32	4	0	0	1	0	0	8.1	9	8	4	1	0	3	0	8	2
Proctor, St. Lucie	7	6	.538	2.36	22	21	3	1	0	0	133.1	104	50	35	7	5	73	0	85	10
Ralph, Fort Lauderdale	6	2	.750	3.94	15	10	0	3	0	0	59.1	66	42	26	4	6	37	0	31	11
Rambo, Clearwater*	2	4	.333	5.74	9	8	0	1	0	0	42.1	51	34	27	0	1	31	0	24	5
Reitzel, Port Charlotte*	5	2	.714	3.76	21	5	0	5	0	1	55.0	58	28	23	0	3	26	2	33	1
Resnikoff, Sarasota*	1	5	.167	2.66	52	0	0	23	0	8	67.2	57	26	20	3	1	27	6	74	6
Reynolds, Sarasota	4	2	.667	3.66	13	7	2	5	1	1	51.2	48	26	21	4	2	22	1	25	1
Rhoden, Osceola	1	1	.500	2.00	5	5	1	0	1	0	27.0	23	9	6	2	0	5	0	26	0
Richards, Lakeland*	7	3	.700	1.80	28	10	0	9	0	1	100.0	69	24	20	1	4	50	1	76	2
Rivard, Miami*	0	1	.000	3.63	11	1	0	5	0	0	17.1	20	14	7	1	1	12	0	16	3
H. Rivera, West Palm Beach	7	3	.700	1.83	16	16	2	0	1	0	103.1	85	25	21	1	3	28	1	61	2
L. Rivera, Lakeland	3	0	1.000	0.00	13	0	0	8	0	1	19.2	10	3	0	0	0	9	1	13	0
Robinson, Lakeland	0	0	.000	6.55	4	0	0	0	0	0	11.0	12	8	8	1	0	4	0	5	0
Rodriguez, Fort Lauderdale	0	1	.000	0.98	13	0	0	12	0	3	18.1	18	2	2	1	0	10	0	27	2
Rosario, Osceola	0	1	.000	9.82	2	1	0	0	0	0	3.2	5	4	4	0	0	1	0	2	0
Rosenthal, Port Charlotte	2	1	.667	2.22	20	0	0	16	0	10	24.1	13	8	6	1	0	8	1	26	1
Rush, Winter Haven	0	2	.000	9.31	4	2	0	1	0	0	9.2	13	14	10	1	2	12	0	3	1
Russo, St. Petersburg	1	4	.200	3.33	24	0	0	9	0	0	48.2	48	22	18	0	4	22	1	40	2
Ryan, Winter Haven	8	8	.500	3.15	24	22	3	1	0	0	137.0	114	58	48	5	7	81	0	78	8
Sampson, Vero Beach	6	2	.750	3.57	16	11	1	4	1	0	68.0	50	28	27	2	1	29	1	43	4
Sanchez, Baseball City*	1	0	1.000	0.00	3	0	0	2	0	0	8.0	7	3	0	0	0	2	0	4	0
A. Sanders, Winter Haven	0	1	.000	6.28	4	1	0	0	0	0	14.1	18	12	10	1	0	2	0	8	1
E. Sanders, Dunedin	2	2	.500	3.52	12	1	0	8	0	3	23.0	12	11	9	1	1	14	0	25	5
Schourek, St. Lucie*	0	0	.000	2.25	2	1	0	1	0	0	4.0	3	1	1	0	0	2	0	4	0
Seal, Dunedin*	3	1	.750	3.53	21	0	0	16	0	3	35.2	32	17	14	2	1	15	2	27	4
Searcy, Lakeland*	2	3	.400	2.56	9	9	0	0	0	0	52.2	40	21	15	0	0	33	0	44	4
C. Shaw, Port Charlotte*	10	6	.625	2.72	25	24	4	0	3	0	148.2	135	60	45	8	9	54	2	82	5
K. Shaw, Baseball City	3	1	.750	2.53	11	11	0	0	0	0	53.1	42	22	15	3	1	15	0	26	8
Sheehan, Osceola	3	3	.500	4.44	41	0	0	31	0	12	50.2	54	32	25	3	3	19	2	33	2
Shepherd, Baseball City	1	7	.125	4.94	11	10	0	0	0	0	47.1	45	33	26	3	2	32	0	20	3
Sherrill, St. Petersburg*	4	0	1.000	2.12	52	0	0	21	0	6	68.0	52	19	16	3	0	23	3	48	2
Shinall, Vero Beach	5	7	.417	2.51	47	4	1	23	0	7	86.0	71	32	24	4	2	29	7	69	4
Silverstein, Dunedin	2	4	.333	7.04	28	1	0	16	0	1	55.0	68	47	43	6	0	36	1	44	3
Simon, Osceola	6	8	.429	3.79	19	19	1	0	0	0	121.0	126	60	51	5	5	33	0	66	5
Sims, Clearwater*	2	6	.250	2.49	27	6	0	13	0	7	83.0	86	34	23	3	2	20	1	45	3
Singelyn, Miami	0	1	.000	17.18	2	2	0	0	0	0	3.2	8	7	7	0	2	4	0	2	1
Sipple, Port Charlotte*	6	3	.667	2.76	29	6	0	10	0	4	71.2	63	26	22	0	3	24	1	64	4
Smith, St. Petersburg	8	9	.471	4.53	29	25	1	1	0	0	131.0	163	78	66	7	2	33	0	57	3
Sonberg, Sarasota*	1	2	.333	6.28	6	1	0	1	0	0	14.1	20	15	10	0	1	8	0	11	1
Sossamon, West Palm Beach	0	1	.000	1.13	11	1	0	6	0	3	24.0	15	3	3	0	1	7	1	21	0
Stanford, Fort Lauderdale	1	2	.333	2.32	24	0	0	22	0	9	31.0	32	9	8	1	0	9	2	25	5
Stange, Winter Haven*	1	0	1.000	3.00	24	0	0	13	0	1	33.0	34	16	11	0	2	10	0	20	2
Stephens, Sarasota	10	4	.714	1.47	17	17	5	0	4	0	122.2	107	31	20	1	3	34	5	83	4
Steward, Lakeland	3	3	.500	2.83	31	3	0	9	0	1	76.1	57	29	24	4	1	34	1	48	9
Stewart, Winter Haven*	1	3	.250	2.35	19	0	0	15	0	6	30.2	25	13	8	0	0	10	2	28	4
Stone, Lakeland	5	9	.357	3.56	25	25	1	0	0	0	129.0	100	65	51	2	5	63	2	101	4
Stonikas, Baseball City	2	2	.500	2.28	22	0	0	15	0	2	43.1	47	15	11	2	2	16	0	16	5
Stottlemyre, Baseball City	1	2	.333	4.94	13	2	0	6	0	4	23.2	30	14	13	1	1	9	2	25	3
B. Sullivan, West Palm Beach*	0	1	.000	3.72	2	2	0	0	0	0	9.2	14	4	4	0	0	2	0	7	1
C. Sullivan, Sarasota	0	0	.000	4.50	1	0	0	1	0	0	2.0	3	2	1	0	0	0	0	3	0
Tafoya, Osceola	7	7	.500	2.55	55	0	0	34	0	12	98.2	83	35	28	3	3	25	1	70	0
Takaheshi, Vero Beach	0	4	.000	5.18	13	2	0	4	0	0	33.0	35	24	19	2	1	27	7	26	2
Taveras, Dunedin	0	0	.000	0.00	1	0	0	0	0	0	1.0	0	0	0	0	0	0	0	0	0
D.M. Taylor, Port Charlotte	6	4	.600	2.55	43	2	0	20	0	8	99.0	83	46	28	3	4	44	3	64	8
M.L. Taylor, Dunedin*	1	1	.500	3.09	3	2	0	1	0	0	11.2	11	6	4	0	0	12	0	3	1
Tedder, Sarasota*	0	0	.000	0.00	1	0	0	1	0	0	1.0	1	0	0	0	0	0	0	1	0

Pitcher—Club	W.	L.	Pct.	ERA.	G.	GS.	CG.	GF.	ShO.	Sv.	IP.	H.	R.	ER.	HR.	HB.	BB.	Int. BB.	SO.	WP.
Thomas, Clearwater	11	9	.550	3.33	27	21	11	0	3	0	154.0	141	70	57	7	1	39	1	49	1
Thompson, Winter Haven	2	0	1.000	5.82	11	0	0	4	0	0	21.2	31	15	14	0	0	11	0	12	4
Timlin, Dunedin	5	8	.385	3.25	33	7	1	16	0	7	88.2	90	44	32	2	5	36	2	64	10
Torborg, Miami*	6	11	.353	4.74	26	25	3	0	1	0	150.0	175	91	79	6	8	66	0	111	11
Trice, Osceola*	16	4	.800	2.57	28	27	7	0	3	0	182.1	179	68	52	6	6	39	0	94	5
Tudor, Vero Beach*	1	0	1.000	1.80	1	1	0	0	0	0	5.0	1	1	1	1	0	0	0	5	0
Valera, St. Lucie	4	2	.667	1.00	6	6	3	0	2	0	45.0	34	5	5	1	0	6	1	45	0
Vanzytveld, Vero Beach	10	9	.526	3.60	26	26	3	0	0	0	157.2	160	80	63	7	3	81	5	75	9
Vargas, Osceola	2	1	.667	4.35	18	2	0	4	0	0	49.2	61	29	24	2	3	16	0	27	3
Vaughan, Dunedin	0	0	.000	0.00	2	0	0	2	0	0	2.0	1	0	0	0	0	1	0	1	0
Wacha, Winter Haven	4	6	.400	2.20	32	0	0	22	0	8	57.1	42	21	14	2	5	26	6	41	4
Wainhouse, West Palm Beach	1	5	.167	4.07	13	13	0	0	0	0	66.1	75	35	30	4	8	19	0	26	6
Wanish, Dunedin	1	0	1.000	1.69	5	0	0	2	0	2	10.2	8	3	2	0	1	7	0	5	1
Wapnick, Dunedin	4	0	1.000	2.05	24	1	0	11	0	7	66.0	48	19	15	2	3	22	1	59	9
Whitehead, Winter Haven	0	0	.000	9.00	1	0	0	1	0	0	1.0	1	1	1	0	1	0	0	0	1
Whitlock, St. Lucie*	0	0	.000	11.57	3	0	0	3	0	0	2.1	1	3	3	0	0	4	0	1	1
Wilkins, Lakeland	7	5	.583	1.66	16	16	4	0	1	0	119.1	95	24	22	2	1	25	0	72	1
Williams, Dunedin	3	5	.375	2.32	20	9	0	8	0	3	81.1	63	26	21	3	2	27	1	60	5
Willis, Lakeland	5	5	.500	3.39	29	3	0	11	0	1	63.2	62	28	24	2	3	26	1	31	0
Woide, Dunedin*	3	5	.375	3.21	27	3	1	12	0	4	70.0	68	38	25	2	2	22	2	51	2

BALKS—Reitzel, 9; Boucher, 8; Cormier, Silverstein, 7 each; Abril, L. Garcia, Lipscomb, Lumley, Mack, Opperman, Stone, 6 each; Johnston, Metoyer, Osuna, Pierson, Rivard, Simon, Trice, 5 each; Cromwell, T. Hall, Harris, Hentgen, Horsman, Kline, Miller, Noch, Pavlik, Perez, Potts, Rhoden, Ryan, Searcy, Stephens, 4 each; Becker, Brown, Elam, Filson, V. Garcia, Green, M. Jones, Knudsen, Langley, LaRose, Mullins, H. Rivera, Timlin, Wainhouse, 3 each; K. Adams, Bennett, Bond, Brantley, Brito, Bruzdewicz, E. Burgos, A. Carter, Cerny, Cinnella, Clarkin, Coleman, B. Conroy, J. Conroy, Credeur, DeLaCruz, Dennison, Diez, Elli, Fynan, Grayson, Hartzog, Hasler, Kerfut, Kiely, Knackert, Manon, Martel, McCormack, A. Mills, Morse, Ollom, Ponder, Proctor, Reynolds, C. Shaw, Shinall, Sipple, Stottlemyre, Tafoya, Thompson, Williams, 2 each; Abreu, Adkins, Ashby, Bohanon, Bross, Bustillos, Cauley, Cavalier, Cole, Combs, DeLeon, DeYoung, Dzafic, Farr, Florence, Gideon, Gohmann, Haas, D. Hall, Hathaway, Heinle, Henion, R. Hernandez, Hillman, J. Hoffman, K. Hoffman, R. Hoffman, Holdridge, Hook, Hopper, Hudek, Jundy, Kamanaka, Knapp, Landry, LaRosa, A. Leiter, M. Leiter, Majer, Manuel, Mauser, McCormick, McDonald, Moeller, Munoz, Normand, Patrick, Rambo, Resnikoff, Rosenthal, Russo, Seal, Singelyn, Smith, Sossamon, Stewart, C. Sullivan, D.M. Taylor, M.L. Taylor, Torborg, Vanzytveld, Vargas, Wacha, Wapnick, Wilkins, Willis, Woide, 1 each.

COMBINATION SHUTOUTS—Moeller-Hudson-Nelson-Stonikas, Hopper-Nelson-McCormack, Nelson-Maldonado-Stottlemyre, Filson-Maldonado, Cole-Maldonado, Cole-Jundy, Baseball City; Combs-Sims, Combs-McDonald, Mauser-Langley, Elam-Sims, Buonantony-Langley, Clearwater; Cromwell-Wapnick 2, Williams-Boucher-Mills, Boucher-Williams, Hall-Linton-Timlin, Boucher-Timlin-Horsman, Cromwell-Newcomb-Horsman, Boucher-Timlin, Cromwell-Newcomb, Cromwell-Seal, Hentgen-Horsman, Boucher-Wanish-Seal, Dunedin; Hook-Green, Martel-Leiter-Rodriguez, Fort Lauderdale; Wilkins-Kiely, Stone-Jones, Haas-Willis-Knudsen-O'Neill, Lumley-Willis, Richards-Jones-Steward, Richards-Jones-Cook-Knudsen, Robinson-Richards, Lumley-Knudsen, Willis-Rivera, Lumley-Knudsen-Steward-Rivera-Cook, Lakeland; Garcia-Ponder, Miami; Allen-Tafoya, Trice-Osuna-Sheehan, Bond-Osuna, Normand-Tafoya, Bond-Tafoya, Osceola; Hurst-Evans-Rosenthal, Bohanon-Rosenthal-Evans, Bohanon-Sipple, Manuel-Taylor, Sipple-Alexander, Reitzel-Kerfut-Evans, Alexander-Taylor, Mathews-Kerfut-Taylor, Port Charlotte; Marina-Plummer, Hillman-LaRose, Proctor-Diez-LaRose, Elli-LaRose, Miller-LaRose, Elli-Bross-LaRose, Griffin-Bross, St. Lucie; Burgos-Pierson-Grater, Bivens-Smith-Sherrill-Grater; Hoffman-Becker-Sherrill-Grater; Cormier-Grater-Pierson, Smith-Sherrill, St. Petersburg; Cortes-Hudek, Knackert-Reynolds, Kennedy-Resnikoff-Ollom, Sarasota; Kawabata-Poole 2, Kawabata-Shinall-Poole, Sampson-Kamanaka, Noch-Kamanaka, Sampson-Coleman-Poole, Vanzytveld-Shinall-Poole, Vanzytveld-Poole, Hoffman-Kamanaka, Knapp-Shinall, Hoffman-Poole, Shinall-Coleman, Vero Beach; Carter-Kline, Cinnella-Kline-Bennett, Rivera-DeYoung-Sossamon-Diez-Bennett, Brito-Henion-Sossamon-Diez, Rivera-Jones-Cavalier, Kline-Diez, Wainhouse-Perez, Brito-Henion, Rivera-Henion, Cinnella-Kerrigan, Kline-Kerrigan, Jones-Kerrigan, West Palm Beach; Brown-Dedos, Kite-Wacha, Ryan-Brown, Winter Haven.

NO-HIT GAMES—Haas, Lakeland, defeated Clearwater, 5-0, April 14; Manon, Fort Lauderdale, defeated Dunedin, 3-0 (second game), May 1; Kite, Winter Haven, defeated Dunedin, 14-0, July 25; Hartgraves, Osceola, defeated Winter Haven, 3-0 (six innings), August 21.

Midwest League

CLASS A

CHAMPIONSHIP WINNERS IN PREVIOUS YEARS

1947—Belleville	.667	1963—Clinton	.710	1976—Waterloo a	.600
Belleville	.672	Clinton	.629	Cedar Rapids	.595
1948—West Frankfort*	.708	1964—Clinton	.667	1977—Waterloo	.580
1949—Centralia	.627	Fox Cities z	.667	Burlington a	.511
Paducah (4th)†	.454	1965—Burlington	.667	1978—Appleton a	.708
1950—Centralia‡	.675	Burlington	.677	Burlington	.500
1951—Paris§	.700	1966—Fox Cities z	.689	1979—Waterloo	.600
Danville (4th)†	.432	Cedar Rapids	.762	Quad Cities a	.579
1952—Danville x	.685	1967—Wisconsin Rapids	.685	1980—Waterloo a	.610
Decatur (3rd)†	.584	Appleton z	.587	Quad Cities	.532
1953—Decatur*	.576	1968—Decatur	.656	1981—Wausau a	.636
1954—Decatur	.587	Quad Cities z	.648	Quad Cities	.570
Danville (2nd)‡	.528	1969—Appleton	.648	1982—Madison	.626
1955—Dubuque*	.587	Appleton	.690	Appleton b	.579
1956—Paris y	.656	1970—Quincy z	.691	1983—Appleton c	.635
Dubuque	.603	Quad Cities	.581	Springfield	.576
1957—Decatur y	.683	1971—Appleton	.642	1984—Appleton c	.640
Clinton	.623	Quad Cities a	.548	Springfield	.504
1958—Michigan City	.623	1972—Appleton	.598	1985—Kenosha b	.568
Waterloo z	.613	Danville	.584	Peoria	.536
1959—Waterloo	.613	1973—Wisconsin Rapids a	.562	1986—Springfield	.621
Waterloo	.613	Danville	.537	Waterloo b	.557
1960—Waterloo	.629	1974—Appleton	.593	1987—Springfield	.671
Waterloo	.677	Danville a	.517	Kenosha b	.586
1961—Waterloo	.613	1975—Waterloo a	.727	1988—Cedar Rapids a	.621
Quincy z	.594	Quad Cities	.624	Kenosha	.579
1962—Dubuque z	.667				
Waterloo	.625				

*Won championship and four-club playoff. †Won four-club playoff. ‡Playoff finals canceled because of bad weather. §Won both halves of split-season. xWon first half of split-season and tied Paris for second-half title. yWon first-half title and four-team playoff. zWon split-season playoff. aLeague divided into Northern and Southern divisions and played split-season. Playoff winner. bLeague divided into Northern, Central and Southern divisions. Playoff winner. cLeague divided into Northern, Central and Southern divisions; regular-season and playoff winner. (NOTE—Known as Illinois State League in 1947-48 and Mississippi-Ohio Valley League from 1949 through 1955.)

STANDING OF CLUBS AT CLOSE OF FIRST HALF, JUNE 16

NORTHERN DIVISION						SOUTHERN DIVISION					
Club	W.	L.	T.	Pct.	G.B.	Club	W.	L.	T.	Pct.	G.B.
South Bend (White Sox)	44	18	0	.710	......	Cedar Rapids (Reds)	41	27	0	.603	......
Wausau (Mariners)	35	26	0	.574	8½	Peoria (Cubs)	42	28	0	.600	......
Rockford (Expos)	34	32	0	.515	12	Quad City (Angels)	34	34	0	.500	7
Kenosha (Twins)	31	30	0	.508	12½	Springfield (Cardinals)	32	35	0	.478	8½
Madison (Athletics)	32	31	0	.508	12½	Burlington (Braves)	30	38	0	.441	11
Appleton (Royals)	31	33	0	.484	14	Waterloo (Independent)	26	40	0	.394	14
Beloit (Brewers)	23	40	0	.365	21½	Clinton (Giants)	23	46	0	.333	18½

STANDING OF CLUBS AT CLOSE OF SECOND HALF, AUGUST 28

NORTHERN DIVISION						SOUTHERN DIVISION					
Club	W.	L.	T.	Pct.	G.B.	Club	W.	L.	T.	Pct.	G.B.
Rockford (Expos)	40	27	0	.597	......	Springfield (Cardinals)	41	27	0	.603	......
South Bend (White Sox)	41	29	0	.586	½	Quad City (Angels)	38	29	0	.567	2½
Beloit (Brewers)	39	32	0	.549	3	Cedar Rapids (Reds)	39	30	0	.565	2½
Appleton (Royals)	36	35	0	.507	6	Peoria (Cubs)	38	31	0	.551	3½
Kenosha (Twins)	32	36	0	.471	8½	Clinton (Giants)	32	38	0	.457	10
Wausau (Mariners)	31	42	0	.425	12	Burlington (Brewers)	30	39	0	.435	11½
Madison (Athletics)	27	41	0	.397	13½	Waterloo (Independent)	21	49	0	.300	21

COMPOSITE STANDING OF CLUBS AT CLOSE OF SEASON, AUGUST 28

Club	S.B.	C.R.	Peo.	Roc.	Spr.	Q.C.	App.	Wau.	Ken.	Bel.	Mad.	Bur.	Cln.	Wat.	W.	L.	T.	Pct.	G.B.
South Bend (White Sox)	....	6	5	6	5	7	9	8	5	8	8	4	8	85	47	0	.644	......
Cedar Rapids (Reds)	0	....	6	6	10	6	4	7	6	6	2	9	10	8	80	57	0	.584	7½
Peoria (Cubs)	3	5	....	3	11	10	2	3	7	5	5	7	7	9	80	59	0	.576	8½
Rockford (Expos)	6	2	5	....	2	5	9	4	11	6	10	6	5	3	74	59	0	.556	11½
Springfield (Cardinals)	3	4	3	6	....	5	0	4	5	8	5	8	10	12	73	62	0	.541	13½
Quad City (Angels)	1	8	3	3	9	....	3	8	3	4	2	8	8	12	72	63	0	.533	14½
Appleton (Royals)	5	4	6	5	6	4	....	6	6	5	6	7	4	3	67	68	0	.496	19½
Wausau (Mariners)	6	1	5	10	4	0	8	....	3	5	8	4	6	6	66	68	0	.493	20
Kenosha (Twins)	7	1	1	2	2	4	8	8	....	7	7	5	5	6	63	66	0	.488	20½
Beloit (Brewers)	5	2	3	6	0	4	9	7	6	....	7	3	4	6	62	72	0	.463	24
Madison (Athletics)	5	6	3	4	1	5	7	5	6	7	....	3	4	3	59	72	0	.450	25½
Burlington (Braves)	2	5	7	2	6	6	1	4	3	5	3	....	9	7	60	77	0	.438	27½
Clinton (Giants)	4	4	7	3	4	5	4	2	3	4	4	5	....	6	55	84	0	.396	33½
Waterloo (Independent)	0	6	5	3	2	2	4	2	2	2	5	6	8	....	47	89	0	.346	40

Quad City's home games played in Davenport, Ia.

Major league affiliations in parentheses.

Playoffs—Springfield defeated Cedar Rapids, two games to none; South Bend defeated Rockford, two games to none; South Bend defeated Springfield, three games to none, to win league championship.

Regular-Season Attendance—Appleton, 76,223; Beloit, 93,166; Burlington, 82,936; Cedar Rapids, 181,189; Clinton, 68,487; Kenosha, 63,392; Madison, 84,064; Peoria, 225,757; Quad City, 191,825; Rockford, 139,338; South Bend, 203,197; Springfield, 164,012; Waterloo, 93,555; Wausau, 49,302. Total—1,716,443. Playoffs—17,724. All-Star Game—3,742.

Managers—Appleton, Brian Poldberg; Beloit, Alex Tavares; Burlington, Jim Saul; Cedar Rapids, Dave Miley; Clinton, Keith Bodie; Kenosha, Steve Liddle; Madison, Jim Nettles; Peoria, Brad Mills; Quad City, Eddie Rodriguez; Rockford, Mike Quade; South Bend, Rick Patterson; Springfield, Dan Radison; Waterloo, Jaime Moreno; Wausau, Tommy Jones.

All-Star Team—1B—Adam Casillas, Cedar Rapids; 2B—Cesar Bernhardt, South Bend; 3B—Tom Redington, Burlington; SS—Jeff Branson, Cedar Rapids; OF—Derek Lee, South Bend; Terrel Hansen, Rockford; J.T. Bruett, Kenosha; C—Bert Heffernan, Beloit; DH—Rob Lukachyk, South Bend; LHP—Sam Chavez, South Bend; RHP—Glenn Carter, Quad City; LH Reliever—Scott Radinsky, South Bend; RH Reliever—Dale Kisten, Springfield; Most Valuable Player—Tom Redington, Burlington; Manager of the Year—Dave Miley, Cedar Rapids.

(Compiled by Howe Sportsdata International, Boston, Mass.)

CLUB BATTING

Club	Pct.	G.	AB.	R.	OR.	H.	TB.	2B.	3B.	HR.	RBI.	SH.	SF.	HP.	BB.	Int. BB.	SO.	SB.	CS.	LOB.
South Bend	.261	132	4243	638	466	1106	1550	196	43	54	532	54	44	52	524	33	820	202	137	872
Cedar Rapids	.258	137	4571	640	504	1180	1714	206	23	94	579	36	42	40	498	19	840	142	77	968
Springfield	.249	135	4410	584	527	1096	1542	164	24	78	503	29	41	46	513	21	804	137	79	949
Wausau	.244	134	4287	614	632	1048	1480	168	27	70	528	44	26	66	553	21	933	156	75	961
Quad City	.244	135	4312	548	489	1052	1484	193	22	65	462	34	31	53	460	24	941	117	87	911
Beloit	.241	134	4267	510	544	1029	1418	171	31	52	447	39	35	47	474	21	821	127	105	917
Peoria	.240	139	4513	572	477	1084	1467	171	43	42	506	83	37	62	477	28	870	144	70	959
Appleton	.237	135	4384	546	589	1040	1401	149	28	52	473	24	46	72	426	13	840	90	68	954
Rockford	.237	133	4380	571	517	1037	1526	184	34	79	512	33	31	80	503	30	1037	127	56	968
Burlington	.234	137	4540	513	622	1061	1496	172	13	79	447	30	30	49	477	11	845	103	69	929
Kenosha	.231	129	4157	496	522	962	1311	158	25	47	417	24	33	58	512	20	894	192	91	938
Madison	.231	131	4234	517	567	978	1393	155	19	74	447	28	27	47	470	17	1019	142	65	898
Waterloo	.222	136	4388	506	709	975	1374	156	16	69	424	53	24	40	547	20	1131	162	94	888
Clinton	.218	139	4417	471	561	965	1254	135	32	30	370	69	32	59	457	22	923	150	109	865

INDIVIDUAL BATTING

(Leading Qualifiers for Batting Championship—378 or More Plate Appearances)

*Bats lefthanded. †Switch-hitter.

Player and Club	Pct.	G.	AB.	R.	H.	TB.	2B.	3B.	HR.	RBI.	SH.	SF.	HP.	BB.	Int. BB.	SO.	SB.	CS.
Casillas, Adam, Cedar Rapids*	.321	134	455	70	146	192	28	3	4	69	2	5	3	98	5	32	4	8
Bernhardt, Cesar, South Bend	.300	127	493	73	148	206	26	7	6	81	2	8	5	32	2	40	18	12
Heffernan, Bertram, Beloit*	.296	127	425	53	126	160	20	1	4	59	3	4	4	70	4	57	9	8
Farmer, Reginald, Waterloo*	.295	95	342	55	101	147	15	2	9	42	8	5	1	48	1	116	34	12
Paulino, Elvin, Peoria*	.295	119	414	57	122	179	29	2	8	72	2	5	9	61	4	63	5	4
Aylward, James, Quad City	.293	130	478	55	140	203	30	0	11	77	1	5	5	44	3	46	4	4
Lukachyk, Robert, South Bend*	.291	122	430	60	125	158	16	4	3	63	5	6	2	35	7	78	18	15
Lee, Derek, South Bend*	.286	125	448	89	128	199	24	7	11	48	4	2	9	87	4	83	45	26
Payton, David, Springfield	.284	121	398	69	113	163	23	3	7	49	1	4	7	54	1	55	8	6
Branson, Jeffery, Cedar Rapids*	.281	127	469	70	132	192	28	1	10	68	4	4	2	41	3	90	5	6
Terris, Adam, Rockford*	.281	120	413	69	116	161	21	3	6	49	2	1	5	82	6	73	1	3

Departmental Leaders: G—Arias, 136; AB—Boddie, 508; R—Lee, 89; H—Bernhardt, 148; TB—Bernhardt, 206; 2B—Vannaman, 32; 3B—Arias, 11; HR—Redington, 17; RBI—Bernhardt, Hansen, 81; SH—E. Williams, 13; SF—Kremer, 9; HP—Hansen, 23; BB—Fiore, 101; IBB—Fiore, Griffin, 9; SO—Tinsley, 177; SB—Bruett, 61; CS—Bruett, 27.

(All Players—Listed Alphabetically)

Player and Club	Pct.	G.	AB.	R.	H.	TB.	2B.	3B.	HR.	RBI.	SH.	SF.	HP.	BB.	Int. BB.	SO.	SB.	CS.
Adames, Juan, Peoria	.222	103	324	35	72	93	9	3	2	21	8	0	1	33	2	61	3	5
Adriance, Daniel, Clinton*	.189	21	37	3	7	8	1	0	0	2	1	0	0	2	0	9	3	0
Aguilar, Mark, Madison	.204	94	279	26	57	70	7	0	2	22	3	2	6	22	0	69	5	3
Alvarez, Clemente, South Bend	.222	86	230	22	51	66	15	0	0	22	9	1	0	16	0	59	4	1
Amaro, Ruben, Quad City†	.360	59	200	50	72	98	9	4	3	27	0	1	7	42	4	25	20	8
Arias, Alejandro, Peoria	.277	136	506	74	140	178	10	11	2	64	9	2	7	49	3	67	31	6
Arrington, Warren, Peoria	.221	102	321	57	71	87	11	1	1	23	11	2	6	57	3	70	29	8
Aylward, James, Quad City	.293	130	478	55	140	203	30	0	11	77	1	5	5	44	3	46	4	4
Baldwin, Anthony, Burlington	.219	110	374	46	82	146	21	2	13	60	1	4	2	41	0	113	20	11
Barbara, Daniel, Wausau	.215	63	177	22	38	41	3	0	0	19	2	1	7	26	0	41	2	3
Beall, Michael, Appleton*	.253	110	367	39	93	126	13	1	6	59	0	8	1	41	3	39	4	2
Beeler, Robert, Cedar Rapids	.254	51	177	22	45	68	8	0	5	21	1	2	2	20	0	31	1	2
Beltre, Esteban, Rockford	.213	104	375	42	80	107	15	3	2	33	5	1	0	33	1	83	9	3
Bernhardt, Cesar, South Bend	.300	127	493	73	148	206	26	7	6	81	2	8	5	32	2	40	18	12
Bernstine, Nehames, Peoria†	.286	6	14	2	4	4	0	0	0	2	0	0	0	0	0	2	4	0
Blanks, Daryl, Burlington*	.209	93	278	21	58	69	6	1	1	12	2	0	2	20	0	46	4	6
Boddie, Rodney, Rockford†	.248	133	508	78	126	159	19	4	2	42	2	4	3	80	1	80	38	13
Boeschen, Jarrett, Burlington	.133	5	15	1	2	2	0	0	0	2	0	0	0	0	0	4	0	0
Bolick, Frank, Beloit†	.301	88	299	44	90	140	23	0	9	41	0	2	6	47	5	52	9	6
Bonner, Jeffry, Clinton*	.233	117	352	39	82	97	11	2	0	32	11	2	1	49	2	66	17	11
Borrelli, Dean, Madison	.153	20	59	2	9	13	1	0	1	6	0	0	0	4	0	18	0	0
Boyce, Thomas, Kenosha†	.188	8	16	0	3	3	0	0	0	1	0	0	0	5	0	5	0	0
Branson, Jeffery, Cedar Rapids*	.281	127	469	70	132	192	28	1	10	68	4	4	2	41	3	90	5	6
Brauning, Jeff, Clinton	.226	28	93	9	21	28	1	3	0	6	1	0	2	5	0	14	5	3
Briggs, Kenneth, Kenosha†	.263	40	137	12	36	54	6	0	4	18	3	1	3	10	0	32	1	3
Brito, Jorge, Madison	.210	43	143	20	30	45	4	1	3	14	1	0	2	22	1	46	1	0
Brock, Gregory, Beloit*	.346	16	52	10	18	26	2	0	2	10	0	0	0	2	0	11	0	2
Brock, Norman, Cedar Rapids*	.268	117	422	77	113	168	24	5	7	36	10	3	3	52	1	65	27	11
Brown, Don, Cedar Rapids	.237	72	266	41	63	92	6	4	5	32	3	4	2	30	2	55	21	8
Brown, Terence, Kenosha	.259	55	185	24	48	60	10	1	0	18	0	1	6	14	0	43	7	5
Brown, Winston, Springfield*	.233	87	236	30	55	87	15	1	5	20	2	0	1	25	4	67	5	1
Bruett, Joseph, Kenosha*	.267	120	445	82	119	139	9	1	3	29	2	1	0	89	2	64	61	27
Bryant, Scott, Cedar Rapids	.235	49	186	26	47	81	7	0	9	39	1	1	0	30	0	46	2	4
Buccheri, James, Madison	.233	115	433	56	101	116	9	3	0	35	3	3	5	26	1	61	43	12
Buchanan, Robert, Appleton	.209	16	43	4	9	10	1	0	0	5	0	1	0	5	0	12	0	0
Busby, LeWayne, South Bend	.298	55	131	21	39	48	5	2	0	17	3	0	0	18	1	24	9	4
Butcher, Arthur, Beloit*	.172	48	134	5	23	34	4	2	1	10	0	0	1	5	0	31	3	2
Byington, John, Beloit	.208	44	149	14	31	45	7	2	1	14	0	2	3	14	2	26	0	3
Campbell, Donovan, Burlington*	.244	108	394	48	96	142	19	3	7	38	1	5	1	45	1	56	15	6

Player and Club	Pct.	G.	AB.	R.	H.	TB.	2B.	3B.	HR.	RBI.	SH.	SF.	HP.	BB.	Int. BB.	SO.	SB.	CS.
Candelari, Enrico, Wausau	.219	104	310	42	68	103	18	1	5	30	2	5	4	35	1	83	6	5
Canino, Carlos, Peoria	.000	5	1	1	0	0	0	0	0	0	0	0	0	1	0	1	0	0
Capello, Peter, Appleton	.281	41	153	21	43	60	6	1	3	24	0	4	2	10	0	28	2	0
Carcione, Thomas, Madison	.214	8	28	4	6	10	1	0	1	3	0	0	0	4	0	11	0	0
Carey, Frank, Clinton⬦	.242	64	244	28	59	68	7	1	0	22	4	1	1	27	6	53	8	4
Carrasco, Claudio, Quad City†	.240	50	154	16	37	53	10	0	2	21	0	1	0	14	0	38	3	2
Casillas, Adam, Cedar Rapids⬦	.321	134	455	70	146	192	28	3	4	69	2	5	3	98	5	32	4	8
Castleberry, Kevin, Burlington⬦	.246	64	224	27	55	66	8	0	1	20	2	2	0	20	1	32	14	8
Castro, Ernest, Wausau⬦	.252	73	234	33	59	77	7	1	3	31	0	0	2	33	0	33	4	2
Chasey, Mark, South Bend⬦	.261	104	318	47	83	113	11	5	3	45	3	3	13	36	2	73	15	7
Clark, Jeffrey, Burlington⬦	.059	10	17	2	1	3	0	1	0	0	0	0	0	0	0	2	1	0
Clayton, Royce, Clinton	.236	104	385	39	91	110	13	3	0	24	4	5	4	39	0	101	28	16
Cloninger, Gregory, Burlington⬦	.218	96	316	25	69	87	6	0	4	37	1	3	2	10	1	50	0	3
Cole, Robert, Burlington	.255	118	447	53	114	140	13	2	3	30	6	1	0	34	1	65	12	12
Colescott, Robert, Springfield	.247	114	369	39	91	142	18	6	7	53	3	4	2	31	1	102	4	2
Colon, Antonio, Peoria	.056	10	18	0	1	2	1	0	0	1	1	1	2	4	0	7	1	0
Colvard, Ben, Cedar Rapids	.278	127	446	65	124	186	21	1	13	66	2	4	5	36	1	100	27	10
Coomer, Ronald, Madison	.319	61	216	28	69	96	15	0	4	28	0	1	0	30	1	34	0	1
Coppell, Shannon, Clinton	.236	125	406	48	96	123	8	8	1	31	12	2	3	37	3	83	20	17
Cruz, Bernardo, South Bend	.205	25	73	6	15	18	1	1	0	7	3	2	0	4	0	13	3	2
Cruz, Victor, Clinton	.115	14	26	0	3	5	2	0	0	4	0	1	0	4	0	7	0	1
Cuevas, Johnny, Burlington	.229	70	223	21	51	77	10	2	4	24	0	1	9	0	0	51	1	1
Cunningham, David, Waterloo	.207	119	405	62	84	101	13	2	0	30	7	3	7	91	0	74	31	11
Curnow, Robert, Waterloo	.167	56	186	14	31	41	4	0	2	9	0	2	2	11	0	64	1	1
Curtis, Chad, Quad City	.244	23	78	7	19	28	3	0	2	11	1	1	0	6	0	17	7	5
Davenport, Adell, Clinton	.236	128	436	50	103	165	16	2	14	65	5	4	13	35	2	98	1	4
Davidson, Michael, Quad City	.167	4	6	1	1	1	0	0	0	0	0	0	0	3	0	2	1	0
Davis, Brian, South Bend	.000	10	9	0	0	0	0	0	0	0	0	0	0	2	0	4	1	1
Davis, Harry, Wausau	.289	22	76	11	22	38	7	0	3	16	1	1	2	6	1	17	3	1
Davis, Mark, Burlington	.230	101	330	40	76	122	13	0	11	46	0	1	7	29	0	66	1	1
DeAngelis, Steven, Quad City⬦	.302	47	162	25	49	82	18	0	5	28	0	1	3	7	2	27	1	2
DeLeon, Huascar, Appleton	.165	43	139	11	23	40	3	1	4	15	1	1	2	7	0	44	0	0
Diaz, Stephen, Beloit	.172	15	29	0	5	5	0	0	0	1	1	0	1	1	0	12	1	0
Diaz, William, Wausau	.278	51	169	27	47	63	5	1	3	24	2	0	1	18	4	33	2	0
Dombrowski, Robert, Cedar Rapids	.222	15	45	8	10	17	4	0	1	5	0	1	1	4	0	13	2	0
Doran, Mark, Quad City	.257	10	35	4	9	13	4	0	0	4	0	0	0	3	0	9	0	0
Dunn, Steven, Kenosha⬦	.219	63	219	17	48	56	8	0	0	23	1	2	1	18	4	55	2	1
Dyer, Linton, Appleton	.252	41	103	13	26	31	5	0	0	13	0	1	3	19	1	27	1	4
Eastman, Douglas, Cedar Rapids	.266	102	320	36	85	112	14	2	3	34	3	1	2	45	1	63	19	7
Eatinger, Michael, South Bend	.250	6	24	3	6	7	1	0	0	1	0	0	0	2	0	6	1	0
Economy, Scott, Cedar Rapids	.000	38	1	0	0	0	0	0	0	0	0	0	0	0	0	0	0	0
Edmonds, James, Quad City⬦	.261	31	92	11	24	31	4	0	1	4	0	0	0	7	0	34	1	0
Edward, John, Quad City	.077	5	13	1	1	1	0	0	0	0	0	0	0	1	0	9	0	0
Elci, Lee, Springfield	.271	43	107	12	29	45	4	0	4	15	4	0	1	15	1	31	0	0
Erickson, Donald, Beloit	.237	13	38	8	9	10	1	0	0	2	1	0	1	2	0	7	1	0
Esquer, David, Quad City	.237	56	169	21	40	48	6	1	0	12	2	0	0	16	0	33	2	2
Estes, Joel, Clinton⬦	.000	39	1	0	0	0	0	0	0	0	0	0	1	0	0	0	0	0
Eveline, William, Quad City⬦	.244	74	217	34	53	72	8	1	3	27	2	1	1	25	1	35	6	5
Faccio, John, Beloit	.071	5	14	2	1	1	0	0	0	0	0	0	0	1	0	8	0	0
Farmer, Reginald, Waterloo⬦	.295	95	342	55	101	147	15	2	9	42	8	5	1	48	1	116	34	12
Fernandez, Julio, Clinton⬦	.222	53	135	12	30	36	2	2	0	5	4	1	1	21	1	30	2	5
Finn, John, Beloit	.299	73	274	49	82	107	8	7	1	20	5	2	4	38	0	27	29	11
Fiore, Michael, Springfield	.251	129	438	71	110	167	23	2	10	54	0	3	6	101	9	56	26	11
Flora, Kevin, Quad City	.218	120	372	46	81	100	8	4	1	21	5	3	6	57	2	107	30	10
Fontes, Bradley, Kenosha	.140	34	107	7	15	22	1	0	2	14	0	1	0	11	1	46	0	0
Ford, Ondra, Appleton⬦	.237	125	438	50	104	154	19	5	7	39	3	1	0	20	2	110	13	6
Foster, Kevin, Rockford	.162	44	117	9	19	29	3	2	1	15	3	0	2	18	0	44	1	0
Fowler, Donald, Waterloo	.000	41	1	0	0	0	0	0	0	0	0	0	0	0	0	1	0	0
Franco, Matthew, Peoria⬦	.224	16	58	4	13	17	4	0	0	9	0	1	1	5	0	5	0	1
Furcal, Lorenzo, Madison	.161	11	31	3	5	7	2	0	0	1	0	0	2	0	0	13	3	1
Garber, Jeffrey, Appleton	.263	117	407	63	107	152	18	3	7	50	9	8	13	54	1	77	4	1
Garcia, Jose, Kenosha	.235	123	468	58	110	160	24	4	6	49	1	5	6	18	2	69	16	8
Garcia, Librado, Beloit	.209	92	263	27	55	83	8	4	4	21	6	0	4	19	0	83	6	9
Gardiner, Michael, Wausau	.000	15	1	0	0	0	0	0	0	0	0	0	0	0	0	1	0	0
Garibaldo, Christobal, Appleton	.214	118	388	41	83	95	10	1	0	24	2	3	5	10	0	53	11	3
Gavin, David, Waterloo	.220	24	91	13	20	37	6	1	3	12	0	0	1	4	0	19	1	3
Gieseke, Mark, Waterloo†	.281	39	139	15	39	50	6	1	1	13	0	1	4	16	2	24	4	0
Glass, Steven, Burlington	.194	54	201	18	39	49	5	1	1	14	5	0	6	12	0	36	3	2
Gonzales, Lawrence, Quad City	.195	69	195	24	38	61	3	1	6	20	2	1	4	39	1	34	2	5
Graterol, Jose, Kenosha	.191	46	157	22	30	47	3	1	4	18	1	0	5	16	0	48	9	1
Gray, Steven, Clinton	.154	12	39	0	6	7	1	0	0	0	1	0	0	2	0	20	1	2
Grier, Antron, Springfield	.274	24	62	13	17	19	2	0	0	3	0	0	1	9	0	9	1	3
Griffin, Tyrone, Peoria†	.287	82	296	45	85	142	15	6	10	64	1	2	5	49	9	74	16	4
Gross, Deryk, Kenosha	.230	109	379	37	87	123	10	7	4	40	2	1	2	34	1	107	11	6
Guerrero, Michael, Beloit†	.222	51	171	28	38	48	10	0	0	13	2	2	0	13	0	33	7	4
Hall, Lamar, Burlington	.095	15	42	3	4	4	0	0	0	1	0	0	0	1	0	13	0	0
Hannahs, Mitchell, Beloit	.316	64	225	42	71	98	14	2	3	36	4	2	3	35	1	35	14	11
Hanselman, Carl, Clinton⬦	.000	15	1	1	0	0	0	0	0	0	0	0	0	0	0	0	0	0
Hansen, Terrel, Rockford	.269	125	468	60	126	204	24	3	16	81	1	7	23	25	4	120	5	2
Hargis, Daniel, Rockford	.182	13	33	1	6	8	2	0	0	0	0	0	0	0	0	15	0	1
Hart, Darrin, Waterloo	.118	7	17	1	2	2	0	0	0	0	0	0	0	0	0	8	0	0
Hart, Jeffrey, Waterloo	.000	28	1	0	0	0	0	0	0	0	0	0	0	0	0	1	0	0
Heck, Robert, Madison	.043	27	69	3	3	5	2	0	0	0	1	0	0	4	0	24	0	0
Heffernan, Bertram, Beloit⬦	.296	127	425	53	126	160	20	1	4	59	3	4	4	70	4	57	9	8
Henderson, Francisco, Appleton	.127	30	79	10	10	14	2	1	0	5	0	0	1	6	0	25	1	1
Hendricks, Steven, Waterloo	.303	62	218	31	66	116	17	0	11	50	0	1	0	15	1	21	14	6
Hilpert, Adam, Clinton	.214	43	131	13	28	31	1	0	0	13	1	1	4	16	0	26	4	5
Hoffman, Hunter, Wausau⬦	.259	87	259	43	67	106	16	1	7	38	0	4	3	31	2	75	2	0
Holbert, Ray, Waterloo	.155	117	354	37	55	64	7	1	0	20	7	1	2	41	0	99	13	13
Holland, Timothy, Waterloo	.202	113	391	42	79	113	19	0	5	32	3	2	0	34	1	82	4	4
Holley, Robert, Appleton	.243	68	230	27	56	79	12	1	3	36	1	2	3	36	0	44	1	1
Hornacek, Jay, South Bend	.254	81	244	37	62	96	13	0	7	40	4	4	4	26	1	44	7	8
Hosey, Dwayne, Madison	.245	123	470	72	115	176	16	6	11	51	2	2	8	44	3	82	33	18

Player and Club	Pct.	G.	AB.	R.	H.	TB.	2B.	3B.	HR.	RBI.	SH.	SF.	HP.	BB.	Int. BB.	SO.	SB.	CS.
Howard, Christopher, Wausau	.240	36	125	13	30	50	8	0	4	32	0	1	1	13	1	35	0	0
Huffman, Kris, Springfield†	.177	57	113	6	20	22	2	0	0	3	2	0	0	13	0	25	7	6
Hulse, Jeffery, Appleton	.241	119	419	56	101	148	13	2	10	61	0	4	15	37	3	79	3	5
Infante, Kennedy, Cedar Rapids	.241	65	241	28	58	90	9	1	7	24	1	0	3	12	1	23	1	2
Jackson, Kenneth, Beloit	.258	107	396	59	102	175	19	3	16	57	3	4	4	27	0	79	18	9
Jensen, John, Peoria*	.226	47	168	11	38	63	13	0	4	21	0	3	3	14	1	47	1	0
Kating, James, Madison	.333	16	57	7	19	33	6	1	2	10	1	0	1	8	0	4	3	1
Kaub, Keith, Rockford	.183	76	235	27	43	83	7	0	11	32	3	2	4	32	0	90	0	2
Keitges, Jeffrey, Wausau*	.275	92	316	49	87	133	16	0	10	46	0	2	6	47	5	63	1	1
Kelso, Jeffrey, Quad City	.250	3	8	0	2	2	0	0	0	1	0	0	1	0	0	4	0	0
Kemper, Harvey, Clinton*	.248	42	141	16	35	42	4	0	1	10	1	0	2	15	2	29	3	1
Kerkes, Kevin, Wausau	.191	85	215	24	41	66	11	1	4	22	5	0	4	32	0	41	2	5
Kilpatrick, Jeffrey, Quad City	.133	18	45	3	6	6	0	0	0	0	0	0	2	1	0	8	1	2
King, Michael, Waterloo*	.206	94	315	26	65	102	7	0	10	38	2	1	2	32	2	76	0	2
Kipila, Jeffrey, Waterloo	.167	10	24	3	4	8	1	0	1	1	1	0	0	5	0	5	0	1
Knoblauch, Charles, Kenosha	.286	51	196	29	56	77	13	1	2	19	1	1	1	32	0	23	9	7
Kosco, Bryn, Rockford†	.267	77	292	47	78	127	16	0	11	44	0	2	2	39	6	61	2	0
Kremer, Kenneth, Beloit*	.251	129	426	44	107	150	14	4	7	60	2	9	2	50	4	62	3	7
Krumback, Mark, Cedar Rapids†	.306	22	85	13	26	33	3	2	0	12	0	3	0	5	0	14	4	2
Kuhn, Chadwick, Waterloo*	.202	87	262	29	53	99	10	6	8	29	3	0	1	26	3	104	3	4
Kvasnicka, Jay, Kenosha*	.257	126	460	55	118	152	20	4	2	42	2	1	3	72	3	83	30	9
Laker, Timothy, Rockford	.229	14	48	4	11	14	1	1	0	4	0	0	0	3	0	6	1	0
Langiotti, Freddie, Springfield	.181	57	160	13	29	39	5	1	1	9	2	1	0	17	0	28	1	2
Lee, Derek, South Bend*	.286	125	448	89	128	199	24	7	11	48	4	2	9	87	4	83	45	26
Lombardozzi, Christopher, C.R.*	.286	4	14	1	4	4	0	0	0	1	0	0	0	4	0	1	1	0
Lonigro, Gregory, Cedar Rapids	.224	36	134	22	30	46	7	0	3	18	1	1	1	7	0	24	6	1
Looper, Edward, Springfield	.260	68	208	33	54	67	5	1	2	22	2	1	3	21	0	35	2	1
Lopez, Juan, Clinton	.181	31	94	6	17	21	4	0	0	6	2	0	0	3	0	27	0	2
Lopez, Pedro, Waterloo	.191	97	319	32	61	82	13	1	2	26	6	1	4	25	1	61	4	4
Love, Sylvester, Beloit*	.224	15	58	7	13	15	2	0	0	2	0	0	0	4	0	9	3	1
Love, William, Madison*	.246	118	378	44	93	147	12	3	12	56	4	2	5	50	5	96	3	3
Lukachyk, Robert, South Bend*	.291	122	430	60	125	158	16	4	3	63	5	6	2	35	7	78	18	15
Maclin, Lonnie, Springfield*	.248	103	315	33	78	103	10	3	3	34	4	1	2	21	0	56	18	14
Malchesky, Thomas, Springfield	.256	61	203	28	52	83	8	1	7	27	1	2	4	11	1	52	2	2
Malinak, Michael, Cedar Rapids	.162	38	136	18	22	36	3	1	3	16	1	2	4	7	0	48	0	1
Marrero, Oreste, Beloit*	.125	14	40	1	5	6	1	0	0	3	0	1	0	3	0	20	1	0
Marrero, Vilato, Beloit	.224	81	254	25	57	67	6	2	0	22	3	2	6	27	0	45	3	5
Martinez, Angel, Madison	.189	36	127	12	24	29	5	0	0	16	0	1	0	6	0	28	4	3
Martinez, Carlos, South Bend	.545	3	11	2	6	9	3	0	0	3	0	0	0	1	0	1	2	0
Mason, Robert, Rockford	.172	13	29	3	5	9	1	0	1	3	0	0	0	2	0	12	0	0
Mateo, Luis, Madison†	.144	66	174	9	25	29	2	1	0	12	1	1	1	8	0	58	2	0
Mathews, Jeremy, Wausau	.180	38	111	7	20	29	3	0	2	8	1	2	0	12	0	46	1	1
Mathiot, Michael, Kenosha	.143	45	119	14	17	22	2	0	1	6	0	0	7	15	0	44	8	4
Maynard, Ellerton, Wausau	.260	130	407	62	106	138	10	5	4	49	3	0	11	57	1	105	49	14
McDevitt, Terrance, Waterloo*	.250	68	212	24	53	57	4	0	0	20	4	1	2	44	2	36	8	5
McNaney, Scott, Waterloo	.224	58	165	15	37	44	5	1	0	10	2	0	1	28	0	47	1	2
Meadows, Scott, Waterloo	.403	19	62	14	25	32	5	1	0	6	0	1	2	8	0	13	0	0
Mealy, Anthony, Cedar Rapids	.167	15	48	5	8	19	2	0	3	5	1	0	1	2	0	22	0	0
Mehl, Steven, South Bend†	.220	72	173	32	38	49	7	2	0	8	5	0	1	31	1	36	12	7
Mendoza, Jesus, Burlington	.247	39	97	8	24	27	3	0	0	7	0	3	0	9	0	27	0	0
Mercedes, Henry, Madison	.211	51	152	11	32	41	3	0	2	13	3	0	1	22	1	46	0	0
Messerly, Michael, 70 Mad.-11 Wat.	.232	81	228	34	53	70	8	0	3	22	1	0	1	52	0	65	1	1
Meyett, Donald, Beloit*	.222	96	252	37	56	62	4	1	0	9	4	0	3	21	1	33	5	8
Michalak, Anthony, Clinton	.246	65	240	15	59	72	9	2	0	15	4	1	1	8	0	12	2	6
Milchin, Michael, Springfield*	.000	7	1	0	0	0	0	0	0	0	0	0	0	0	0	0	0	0
Miller, Johan, Wausau*	.256	54	133	16	34	47	5	1	2	22	4	0	0	22	0	24	0	0
Mitchell, Keith, Burlington	.261	127	448	64	117	170	23	0	10	49	0	4	5	70	1	65	12	7
Mordecai, Michael, Burlington	.253	65	241	39	61	77	11	1	1	22	4	2	5	33	0	43	12	5
Morris, Steven, Kenosha†	.225	16	40	9	9	11	2	0	0	0	0	0	0	7	0	15	4	1
Muhammad, Robert, Beloit	.100	9	20	2	2	2	0	0	0	1	0	0	1	2	0	12	1	2
Mulville, Duane, Cedar Rapids	.222	65	207	23	46	60	8	0	2	24	0	5	2	14	0	41	2	2
Mundy, Richard, Peoria	.000	11	15	2	0	0	0	0	0	0	0	0	1	0	0	6	1	0
Murray, Stephen, Wausau	.270	43	137	26	37	45	3	1	1	13	0	1	1	21	1	21	14	3
Murrell, Rodney, 17-Beloit-58 Mad.*	.233	75	215	22	50	61	8	0	1	24	4	4	0	29	0	32	2	3
Musolino, Michael, Quad City*	.286	88	315	38	90	136	19	0	9	56	2	3	3	40	3	35	3	3
Myers, James, Clinton	.000	3	1	0	0	0	0	0	0	0	0	0	0	0	0	1	0	0
Nelson, Darren, Quad City	.197	19	71	7	14	17	1	1	0	8	1	2	1	3	0	13	1	2
Noland, James, Waterloo*	.239	99	331	40	79	83	4	0	0	18	9	1	2	39	1	86	31	15
O'Leary, Troy, Beloit*	.183	42	115	7	21	25	4	0	0	8	0	0	0	15	1	20	1	7
Oberdank, Jeffrey, Quad City	.198	93	349	49	69	88	9	5	0	20	5	5	7	22	1	56	4	4
Oedewaldt, Larry, Beloit	.238	9	21	1	5	5	0	0	0	0	0	0	0	5	0	7	0	0
Oller, Jeffrey, Rockford*	.212	15	33	2	7	9	2	0	0	4	0	1	3	5	1	8	0	0
Ortiz, Joseph, Beloit	.231	19	52	4	12	14	2	0	0	6	0	1	0	1	0	25	1	0
Ortiz, Raymond, Kenosha*	.246	51	175	19	43	62	8	1	3	21	1	2	3	24	2	32	4	0
Paredes, Jesus, Rockford†	.214	73	238	35	51	65	8	3	0	18	4	1	1	21	1	57	20	9
Partrick, David, Quad City	.202	100	321	34	65	81	11	1	1	17	6	0	2	15	0	122	12	7
Pattin, Jon, Clinton*	.279	20	43	1	12	12	0	0	0	4	0	0	0	7	0	7	0	1
Paulino, Elvin, Peoria*	.295	119	414	57	122	179	29	2	8	72	2	5	9	61	4	63	5	4
Paynter, William, Peoria	.100	33	60	3	6	6	0	0	0	2	7	0	3	1	0	23	0	0
Payton, David, Springfield	.284	121	398	69	113	163	23	3	7	49	1	4	7	54	1	55	8	6
Payton, Raymond, South Bend	.257	33	101	10	26	43	6	1	3	10	0	0	1	5	0	26	2	2
Peguero, Jeremias, Beloit	.050	7	20	0	1	1	0	0	0	0	0	0	0	2	0	7	1	3
Perez, Beban, Quad City*	.287	93	324	42	93	106	7	3	0	18	2	0	4	34	4	68	14	14
Perry, Eric, Peoria*	.223	91	273	27	61	90	13	2	4	40	1	3	0	38	3	53	2	6
Pfaff, Richard, Beloit	.203	117	374	30	76	109	15	3	4	39	1	2	0	46	1	85	5	6
Pfaff, Robert, Burlington	.205	69	224	14	46	65	7	0	4	16	3	1	1	13	0	59	1	0
Phillips, Charles, Quad City*	.192	125	442	41	85	140	29	1	8	50	4	4	4	49	2	146	3	3
Piechowski, Timothy, Rockford*	.250	18	48	7	12	18	1	1	1	6	0	1	0	7	0	8	0	0
Pino, Rolando, Kenosha	.217	81	244	42	53	90	13	3	6	36	1	5	10	74	0	45	17	8
Pittenger, Jon, Kenosha†	.247	27	93	6	23	28	0	1	1	14	0	3	0	21	0	12	3	1
Pledger, Kinnis, South Bend*	.266	89	293	49	78	110	13	5	3	39	4	4	0	56	3	79	26	14
Pratt, Steven, Clinton	.085	23	59	4	5	9	1	0	1	6	0	1	0	5	0	14	0	0

Player and Club	Pct.	G.	AB.	R.	H.	TB.	2B.	3B.	HR.	RBI.	SH.	SF.	HP.	BB.	Int. BB.	SO.	SB.	CS.
Preston, Stephen, Appleton†	.156	40	141	17	22	24	2	0	0	10	0	0	0	21	1	26	5	1
Prusia, Gregory, Appleton	.235	85	277	40	65	85	7	2	3	25	2	4	4	21	1	55	1	4
Ramsey, Fernando, Peoria	.244	131	410	56	100	117	7	5	0	34	11	3	10	25	0	70	16	10
Razook, Mark, Wausau	.265	20	68	14	18	29	2	0	3	11	1	0	0	11	0	20	0	0
Redington, Thomas, Burlington	.299	85	298	49	89	154	14	0	17	52	0	4	7	53	5	47	4	1
Reed, Steve, Clinton	.000	61	1	0	0	0	0	0	0	0	0	0	0	0	0	1	0	0
Reed, William, Waterloo*	.000	34	1	0	0	0	0	0	0	0	0	0	0	0	0	0	0	0
Resetar, Gary, Kenosha*	.269	45	160	20	43	54	8	0	1	20	2	1	0	18	2	11	3	4
Reynoso, Henry, Beloit†	.158	15	57	6	9	9	0	0	0	2	0	0	4	0	7	4	2
Ricci, Charles, Waterloo	.000	29	2	0	0	0	0	0	0	0	0	0	0	0	0	1	0	0
Rickman, Andrew, Cedar Rapids†	.188	13	32	3	6	7	1	0	0	3	0	0	0	8	0	8	0	0
Ricks, Edward, 44 Mad-67 Water	.220	111	354	40	78	125	13	2	10	40	0	6	3	51	1	152	13	8
Robinson, Darryl, Appleton	.261	75	261	38	68	80	5	2	1	27	2	4	6	22	0	31	1	1
Robinson, Marteese, Madison	.333	71	252	33	84	127	12	2	9	44	1	4	2	18	3	24	5	1
Robles, Jorge, Wausau*	.245	129	494	62	121	141	7	5	1	40	8	4	1	69	2	46	20	16
Romero, Charles, Quad City*	.188	19	69	5	13	15	2	0	0	6	0	1	0	5	0	14	1	5
Roskom, Bryan, Kenosha	.182	91	302	26	55	79	9	0	5	25	4	6	3	14	1	88	4	3
Ross, Michael, Springfield	.268	129	477	61	128	181	17	0	12	62	1	5	9	44	1	70	4	4
Roth, Gregory, South Bend*	.274	117	368	67	101	153	18	2	10	55	4	7	2	88	7	77	9	13
Rumsey, Daniel, Clinton*	.156	53	160	22	25	48	6	1	5	14	0	2	1	19	2	39	7	4
Saccomanno, Joseph, Burlington	.193	50	166	14	32	36	4	0	0	3	0	0	12	0	22	3	2
Saetre, Damon, Wausau*	.245	55	163	23	40	52	9	0	1	18	1	0	1	23	0	35	5	3
Sanchez, Osvaldo, Waterloo*	.217	98	323	27	70	113	11	1	10	42	1	2	8	39	2	88	6	6
Sarbaugh, Mike, Beloit	.146	16	48	4	7	10	3	0	0	4	0	0	2	1	0	15	0	0
Schnurbusch, Chris, Cedar Rapids	.236	94	275	28	65	85	9	1	3	34	1	3	1	14	0	46	9	4
Schoonover, Gary, Burlington*	.234	54	167	15	39	52	7	0	2	12	2	0	0	8	1	35	0	4
Sellick, John, Springfield	.230	126	440	61	101	165	15	2	15	74	0	7	7	44	1	100	1	3
Sellner, Scott, Cedar Rapids	.267	114	416	59	111	158	19	2	8	50	5	3	6	44	1	62	7	8
Shelton, Harry, Peoria*	.226	96	270	34	61	69	6	1	0	19	6	3	0	26	1	50	13	5
Shephard, Kelvin, Rockford	.259	89	266	30	69	91	10	3	2	32	1	3	3	27	0	80	10	6
Shireman, Jeffrey, Springfield†	.248	121	379	39	94	104	7	0	1	37	6	8	1	55	1	31	8	4
Siddall, Joseph, Rockford*	.236	98	313	36	74	105	15	2	4	38	5	4	6	26	2	56	8	5
Singley, Joseph, South Bend	.115	9	26	4	3	5	2	0	0	3	0	0	1	2	0	9	0	0
Siwa, Joseph, Kenosha	.217	25	83	5	18	25	5	1	0	5	2	1	0	4	1	17	0	0
Slavin, David, Clinton*	.204	38	103	6	21	27	3	0	1	12	0	1	1	19	1	19	0	2
Smiley, Rueben, Clinton*	.208	125	451	53	94	113	13	3	0	26	7	2	5	30	0	72	22	9
Smith, Edward, South Bend	.246	115	382	52	94	142	20	2	8	49	0	4	7	43	4	84	7	9
Smith, Joel, Rockford*	.227	104	375	50	85	138	15	4	10	53	0	1	14	31	4	112	22	6
Smith, Tracy, Peoria	.179	86	229	25	41	58	5	0	0	15	9	0	2	15	0	56	7	5
Smith, Woodrow, Peoria	.224	89	303	29	68	98	11	2	5	33	1	5	3	16	0	87	0	4
Stairs, Matthew, Rockford	.284	44	141	20	40	59	9	2	2	14	2	1	2	15	3	29	5	4
Standiford, Mark, Clinton	.114	61	176	22	20	26	3	0	1	12	3	3	8	25	1	49	7	2
Stanley, Timothy, Rockford*	.136	11	22	1	3	5	1	0	0	4	0	0	1	0	4	0	2
Stargell, Timothy, Wausau	.278	90	320	57	89	150	17	4	12	43	4	2	5	37	0	63	20	10
Stillwell, Rod, Appleton†	.207	47	145	12	30	35	5	0	0	7	1	0	1	7	0	26	1	0
Sveum, Dale, Beloit†	.133	6	15	0	2	3	1	0	0	2	0	0	0	5	2	6	0	0
Tartabull, Jose, Wausau	.240	60	217	31	52	65	7	3	0	21	6	0	13	1	31	11	2
Taubensee, Edward, Cedar Rapids*	.199	59	196	25	39	68	5	0	8	22	0	2	25	4	55	4	1
Taylor, Scott, (Ill.), Peoria	.181	24	83	3	15	17	2	0	0	3	2	1	0	5	0	8	0	1
Tejada, Alejandro, Rockford	.179	28	84	3	15	18	1	1	0	5	1	0	0	6	0	23	1	0
Tejada, Eugenio, South Bend	.174	75	201	22	35	42	5	1	0	10	2	0	6	0	34	10	5
Terris, Adam, Rockford*	.281	120	413	69	116	161	21	3	6	49	2	1	5	82	6	73	1	3
Thomas, Delvin, Wausau*	.161	40	137	13	22	31	3	0	2	21	1	3	5	13	1	50	2	2
Thomas, Kelvin, Wausau*	.211	40	123	26	26	44	5	2	3	16	2	1	11	21	1	39	9	5
Tinsley, Lee, Madison†	.181	123	397	51	72	104	10	2	6	31	3	1	9	67	1	177	19	11
Tucker, Eddie, Clinton	.246	126	426	44	105	138	20	2	3	43	3	4	9	58	2	80	6	5
Vannaman, Timothy, Madison	.241	124	469	69	113	188	32	2	13	59	2	4	3	40	0	98	12	5
Vargas, Hediberto, Quad City	.297	41	138	30	41	87	10	0	12	33	0	2	2	21	1	37	1	2
Walbeck, Matthew, Peoria	.252	94	341	38	86	117	19	0	4	47	1	3	3	20	1	47	5	2
Walker, Hugh, Appleton*	.256	103	344	38	88	125	13	3	6	40	0	0	11	35	1	74	13	17
Warren, Randy, South Bend	.196	49	148	25	29	43	8	3	0	13	0	2	4	22	0	26	11	7
White, Charlie, Springfield	.248	129	504	76	125	155	10	4	4	41	1	5	2	58	1	87	50	20
Williams, Edward, Peoria*	.244	122	409	69	100	130	16	4	2	37	13	3	6	56	1	71	14	9
Williams, Kent, Quad City†	.171	13	35	1	6	7	1	0	0	0	0	0	0	0	17	0	1
Williams, Ray, Wausau	.253	40	95	13	24	32	6	1	0	8	1	0	1	13	0	31	3	2
Williams, Reginald, Clinton†	.195	68	236	38	46	68	9	2	3	18	5	1	3	29	0	66	14	9
Williams, Theodore, Burlington	.158	19	38	5	6	8	2	0	0	2	0	0	0	6	0	15	0	1
Wolff, Richard, South Bend	.571	3	7	0	4	5	1	0	0	3	0	1	0	1	0	0	0	0
Wright, Donald, Appleton	.249	124	450	66	112	143	15	5	2	33	3	5	5	75	0	90	29	22
Wright, John, Kenosha	.180	59	172	32	31	47	7	0	3	19	1	1	8	16	1	55	3	3
Zaksek, John, South Bend*	.263	52	133	17	35	38	1	1	0	15	5	0	3	11	1	24	2	4
Zane, Kelly, Rockford	.208	102	342	47	71	117	14	1	10	35	4	3	11	49	1	76	4	0

The following pitchers, listed alphabetically by club, with games in parentheses, had no plate appearances, primarily through use of designated hitters:

APPLETON—Alexander, Jonathan (6); Drezek, Karl (31); Drohan, William (9); Harvey, Gregory (26); Hoeme, Steven (29); Hofer, John (23); Huth, Jonathan (13); Magee, Byron (15); McCormick, John (20); Nocas, Luke (8); Osik, Stephen (5); Otto, Steven (43); Parnell, Mark (46); Pichardo, Hipolito (12); Pierce, Benjamin (31); Shifflett, Steven (18); Studeman, Dennis (5); Vaughn, Randall (15); Wagner, Hector (24).

BELOIT—Cangemi, James (9); Carmody, Kevin (40); Carter, Larry (17); Drake, Samuel (2); Eldred, Calvin (5); Fitzgerald, David (27); Grayson, Michael (3); Johnson, Christopher (25); Kiefer, Mark (30); Krippner, Curt (23); Landry, Gregory (10); Lane, Heath (17); Ludy, John (9); Mirabella, Paul (2); Miranda, Angel (30); Sandoval, Guillermo (30); Voit, David (4); Wahl, Timothy (7); Watts, Robert (16).

BURLINGTON—Cuesta, Jaime (1); Cummings, Brian (12); Czarnik, Christopher (41); Karasinski, David (29); Kelly, Kevin (11); Kurczewski, Tommy (3); Longuil, Richard (31); Meister, Ralph (12); Minchey, Nathan (11); Nied, David (13); Reis, David (34); Throckmorton, Bruce (1); Upshaw, Lee (12); Vazquez, Marcos (2); Watson, Preston (14); Waznik, Allan (34); Weems, Danny (13); Wendell, Steven (22); Wright, William (40).

CEDAR RAPIDS—Foster, Stephen (51); Groninger, Gerry (1); Hester, Steven (27); Jeffery, Scott (14); Marsh, Quinn (49); McCarthy, Steven (30); Myers, Michael (27); Powell, Ross (13); Risley, William (27); Rodriguez, Tomas (11); Turek, Joseph (25); Vierra, Joseph (47).

CLINTON—Breitenbucher, Karl (21); DeLaRosa, Domingo (43); Dour, Brian (10); Fye, Christopher (20); Garrison, Darren (18); Ghelfi, Andrew (14); Gibbons, William (5); Gould, Frank (1); Hancock, Christopher (18); Hernandez, Marino (8); Johnson, Dominick (8); Novoa, Rafael (13); Rambo, Daniel (12); Rogers, Kevin (29); Sharko, Gary (16).

KENOSHA—Garces, Richard (24); Johnson, Carl (18); Krol, David (16); Kryzanowski, Rusty (46); Mahomes, Patrick (25); McClure,

LaRue (33); Misuraca, Michael (9); Muh, Steven (26); Neagle, Dennis (6); Newman, Alan (18); North, Mark (19); Pomeranz, Michael (31); Rovasio, Dominick (22); Swanson, Chad (11); Trombley, Michael (12).

MADISON—Allison, Dana (13); Ariola, Anthony (19); Berg, Richard (21); Briscoe, John (21); Chitren, Stephen (20); Foley, James (35); Garcia, Apolinar (27); Golmont, Van (31); Guzman, Dionini (10); Harris, Ray (25); Lawson, James (33); MacLeod, Kevin (11); Masters, Frank (4); Maye, Stephen (16); Patrick, Bronswell (13); Stancel, Mark (8); Taylor, William (35).

PEORIA—Davis, Braz (27); Eddings, Jay (38); Espino, Francisco (12); Gomez, Henrique (3); Lopez, Marcos (28); Massicotte, Jeffrey (35); Parmenter, Gary (8); Robinson, Brett (28); Salles, John (21); Slocumb, Heath (49); Sodders, Michael (28); Stroud, Derek (40); Zarranz, Fernando (7).

QUAD CITY—Abbott, Kyle (13); Carter, Glenn (25); DeJaynes, Paul (8); Erb, Michael (25); Holzemer, Mark (25); Marchese, John (49); Martin, Justin (9); McGuire, Stephen (15); Murphy, Gary (39); Mutz, Frank (18); Pardo, Lawrence (27); Search, Michael (3); Townsend, James (9); Vanderwel, William (22); Vegely, Bruce (48); Zappelli, Mark (48).

ROCKFORD—Alleyne, Isaac (23); Bromby, Scott (6); Buzzard, Dale (9); Cornelius, Jonathan (17); Davis, Bret (38); Freed, Daniel (26); Gibbons, Michael (40); Howze, Benjamin (26); Kerrigan, Robert (45); Minchey, Nathan (15); Nabholz, Christopher (24); Oropeza, David (9); Piatt, Douglas (11); Regira, Gary (14); Shiflett, Matthew (18); Winston, Darrin (47).

SOUTH BEND—Brutcher, Lenny (16); Chavez, Samuel (20); Cooper, Virgil (16); Dabney, Frederick (26); DeLaCruz, Carlos (12); Fuller, Scott (5); Galvan, Michael (16); Hernandez, Roberto (4); Johnson, Lee (13); Jones, Barry (3); Marshall, Brett (40); Merigliano, Frank (19); Mitchener, Michael (33); Pall, Donn (2); Perschke, Gregory (13); Radinsky, Scott (53); Schrenk, Steven (16); Ventura, Jose (29).

SPRINGFIELD—Broadfoot, Scott (30); Duvall, Bradley (13); Faccio, Luis (27); Gewecke, Stephen (13); Grimes, David (62); Kisten, Dale (57); Lawrence, Scott (34); Marte, Roberto (24); Meamber, Timothy (37); Plemel, Lee (11); Richardson, David (51); Rose, Matthew (5); Sala, David (13); Satterfield, Cory (27).

WATERLOO—Borgatti, Michael (17); Cantwell, Robert (8); Figueroa, Alexis (21); Galindez, Luis (33); Hoyer, Bradley (33); Lebron, Jose (34); Morton, Ronald (47); Slomkowski, Richard (43).

WAUSAU—Backus, Todd (23); Bennett, James (24); Bryant, Erick (4); Bryant, Keith (2); Burnau, Benjamin (45); Carter, Richard (3); Eldredge, Edward (14); Felix, Nicholas (38); Furcal, Manuel (4); Liss, Thomas (8); McGuire, Michael (19); Pitcher, Scott (49); Reilley, John (43); Ryan, Jody (15); Stoerck, Scott (12); Taylor, Scott (Kan.) (16); Whitlock, Michael (29); Wilkinson, Brian (17).

GRAND SLAM HOME RUNS—Baldwin, Mitchell, Paulino, Redington, 2 each; Arias, Brito, Bryant, W. Diaz, Fontes, Garber, Griffin, Hansen, Hendricks, Holley, Howard, Jackson, Kaub, Keitges, Lonigro, Love, Maynard, Phillips, Ross, Sellick, E. Smith, J. Smith, Walbeck, 1 each.

AWARDED FIRST BASE ON CATCHER'S INTERFERENCE—W. Brown 3 (Buchanan, Cuevas, Musolino); Aylward 2 (Alvarez, Cuevas); Oberdank 2 (Hornacek, Langiotti); Ramsey 2 (Colescott, Langiotti); Adriance (Colon); Blanks (Alvarez); Coppell (Buchanan); Flora (Borrelli); Graterol (DeLeon); Hansen (DeLeon); Henderson (Singley); Kvasnicka (Colescott); Meyett (Hornacek); Roskom (DeLeon); Stargell (Laker); Zane (Briggs).

CLUB FIELDING

Club	Pct.	G.	PO.	A.	E.	DP.	PB.	Club	Pct.	G.	PO.	A.	E.	DP.	PB.
Springfield	.968	135	3537	1608	170	108	24	Beloit	.962	134	3434	1430	192	104	6
Cedar Rapids	.967	137	3608	1586	175	120	25	Waterloo	.961	136	3599	1677	213	125	25
Quad City	.966	135	3461	1304	169	113	27	Burlington	.960	137	3604	1553	216	101	21
Appleton	.965	135	3445	1477	181	109	38	Kenosha	.958	129	3349	1347	205	94	22
Peoria	.964	139	3672	1580	197	130	28	Clinton	.958	139	3658	1550	231	123	30
Rockford	.963	133	3500	1513	193	111	34	Madison	.956	131	3372	1384	221	110	24
Wausau	.963	134	3389	1394	186	110	24	South Bend	.954	132	3464	1344	231	105	19

Triple Plays—Quad City 2, Burlington, South Bend, Springfield, Waterloo, Wausau.

INDIVIDUAL FIELDING

*Throws lefthanded.

FIRST BASEMEN

Player and Club	Pct.	G.	PO.	A.	E.	DP.	Player and Club	Pct.	G.	PO.	A.	E.	DP.
Aylward, Quad City	.958	3	21	2	1	1	KREMER, Beloit*	.99306	113	919	84	7	77
Beall, Appleton*	.988	93	822	68	11	64	Kuhn, Waterloo*	.993	23	132	14	1	11
Bolick, Beloit	1.000	1	2	0	0	0	Looper, Springfield	.970	9	87	10	3	5
Brock, Beloit	.978	12	80	8	2	8	P. Lopez, Waterloo	.952	2	18	2	1	3
Busby, South Bend	1.000	1	2	0	0	0	Love, Madison*	.976	81	654	48	17	58
Candelari, Wausau	1.000	2	9	2	0	0	Lukachyk, South Bend	.980	15	94	5	2	5
Capello, Appleton	.971	3	33	0	1	2	Malinak, Cedar Rapids	1.000	3	24	2	0	4
Casillas, Cedar Rapids*	.992	132	1214	80	11	100	Marrero, Beloit*	.923	1	12	0	1	1
Chasey, South Bend*	.982	101	759	68	15	73	Mendoza, Burlington	.989	33	236	24	3	22
Cloninger, Burlington	.970	8	60	4	2	3	Messerly, Madison	.852	5	19	4	4	1
Colescott, Springfield	.970	8	61	4	2	5	Michalak, Clinton	1.000	1	35	1	0	3
Coomer, Madison	.977	5	41	2	1	1	Murray, Wausau	.938	6	42	3	3	5
Coppell, Clinton	.667	1	2	0	1	0	Murrell, 2 Bel-1 Mad	1.000	3	16	1	0	0
Davenport, Clinton	.986	117	1029	68	16	98	Nelson, Quad City	1.000	2	11	2	0	1
Davis, Burlington	.99267	101	873	76	7	60	J. Ortiz, Beloit	1.000	4	26	2	0	0
Dunn, Kenosha*	.987	63	470	54	7	28	R. Ortiz, Kenosha*	.977	49	382	46	10	39
Elci, Springfield	1.000	2	3	1	0	1	Pattin, Clinton	1.000	1	1	0	0	0
Eveline, Quad City	1.000	1	1	0	0	0	Paulino, Peoria	.985	115	1073	97	18	102
Fiore, Springfield	.986	17	136	9	2	13	Payton, South Bend	1.000	1	1	0	0	0
Gieseke, Waterloo*	.992	34	346	20	3	27	Perry, Peoria	.996	30	222	22	1	19
Glass, Burlington	1.000	16	100	6	0	7	Pfaff, Beloit*	.986	10	68	3	1	4
Gonzales, Quad City	.990	15	100	4	1	10	Phillips, Quad City*	.981	115	935	44	19	82
Grier, Springfield	1.000	1	1	1	0	0	D. Robinson, Appleton	.975	20	146	12	4	9
Hansen, Rockford	1.000	4	10	0	0	1	M. Robinson, Madison	.981	33	299	19	6	26
Hendricks, Waterloo	.995	62	552	44	3	36	Roth, South Bend	.987	10	71	5	1	6
Hoffman, Wausau	.975	27	222	15	6	21	Saetre, Wausau*	.992	46	361	33	3	39
Holley, Appleton	.984	27	239	15	4	20	Sanchez, Waterloo*	.857	1	6	0	1	0
Hornacek, South Bend	.980	6	42	7	1	6	Schnurbusch, Cedar Rapids	.939	10	41	5	3	3
Infante, Cedar Rapids	.970	4	30	2	1	4	Sellick, Springfield	.981	109	1046	93	22	74
Kating, Madison	1.000	14	115	5	0	14	E. Smith, South Bend	.973	16	102	5	3	6
Kaub, Rockford	.972	28	201	9	6	23	T. Smith, Peoria	1.000	2	5	3	0	0
Keitges, Wausau	.992	63	484	39	4	35	Terris, Rockford*	.986	112	1019	74	16	75
Kemper, Clinton*	.985	21	185	10	3	12	Vargas, Quad City	1.000	1	5	1	0	0
King, Waterloo	.977	29	278	25	7	24	Williams, Burlington	1.000	1	7	1	0	0
Kipila, Quad City	.969	9	57	5	2	7	Wright, Kenosha	.970	23	151	12	5	10

Triple Plays—Davis, Gieseke, Keitges, Phillips, E. Smith.

SECOND BASEMEN

Player and Club	Pct.	G.	PO.	A.	E.	DP.	Player and Club	Pct.	G.	PO.	A.	E.	DP.
Adames, Peoria	.953	99	184	280	23	57	Bernhardt, South Bend	.963	118	193	324	20	70
Aguilar, Madison	.896	13	15	28	5	7	BUCCHERI, Madison	.980	95	184	249	9	42
Amaro, Quad City	.934	16	26	31	4	4	Busby, South Bend	1.000	3	0	1	0	0
Aylward, Quad City	1.000	1	1	2	0	1	Candelari, Wausau	.875	2	3	4	1	0

SECOND BASEMEN—Continued

Player and Club	Pct.	G.	PO.	A.	E.	DP.	Player and Club	Pct.	G.	PO.	A.	E.	DP.
Carey, Clinton	.950	62	138	187	17	32	McDevitt, Waterloo	.944	62	107	181	17	35
Carrasco, Quad City	.961	21	33	41	3	10	McNaney, Waterloo	.959	26	45	73	5	14
Castleberry, Burlington	.943	62	120	197	19	23	Mordecai, Burlington	1.000	2	4	3	0	1
Cloninger, Burlington	.980	22	34	64	2	12	Murray, Wausau	1.000	6	14	12	0	4
V. Cruz, Clinton	.625	3	3	2	3	2	Murrell, 13 Bel-10 Mad	.973	23	53	55	3	16
Cunningham, Waterloo	.970	54	119	172	9	31	Oberdank, Quad City	.977	93	166	255	10	47
Dombrowski, Cedar Rapids	.947	3	11	7	1	3	Paredes, Rockford	.934	52	89	109	14	19
Erickson, Beloit	.889	5	14	10	3	3	Peguero, Beloit	.938	7	13	17	2	2
Esquer, Quad City	1.000	14	18	37	0	10	Pino, Kenosha	1.000	1	1	1	0	1
Fernandez, Clinton	.938	44	72	93	11	19	Preston, Appleton	.953	38	67	114	9	20
Flora, Quad City	1.000	1	0	1	0	0	Reynoso, Beloit	.921	15	34	24	5	4
Foster, Rockford	.930	15	22	31	4	4	Rickman, Cedar Rapids	.882	5	9	6	2	3
Garber, Appleton	.976	91	149	250	10	39	Robles, Wausau	.920	6	8	15	2	6
Garcia, Kenosha	.974	94	211	268	13	54	Roskom, Kenosha	.933	2	7	7	1	1
Glass, Burlington	.940	27	37	73	7	11	Ross, Springfield	.978	129	240	412	15	67
Gray, Clinton	.818	10	19	26	10	5	Roth, South Bend	.917	13	20	24	4	5
Griffin, Peoria	.968	37	74	108	6	30	Schnurbusch, Cedar Rapids	.963	18	30	48	3	12
Guerrero, Beloit	1.000	1	0	1	0	0	Schoonover, Burlington	.946	37	62	77	8	15
Hannahs, Beloit	.966	62	105	180	10	37	Sellner, Cedar Rapids	.968	112	213	361	19	61
Hart, Waterloo	1.000	6	10	25	0	3	Smith, Peoria	.953	10	15	26	2	6
Hilpert, Clinton	.943	14	17	33	3	7	Standiford, Clinton	.988	16	28	56	1	5
Holland, Waterloo	1.000	1	3	2	0	1	Stanley, Beloit	1.000	1	1	3	0	0
Huffman, Springfield	.952	11	10	30	2	5	Stargell, Wausau	.944	83	168	222	23	56
Lonigro, Cedar Rapids	1.000	6	8	18	0	5	Stillwell, Appleton	.939	9	13	18	2	2
Looper, Springfield	1.000	1	0	1	0	1	Thomas, Wausau	.954	40	81	86	8	16
Marrero, Beloit	.954	39	72	114	9	21	Williams, Burlington	1.000	1	1	0	0	0
Martinez, Madison	.917	19	29	48	7	8	Wolff, South Bend	.900	3	5	4	1	0
Mateo, Madison	.500	1	0	1	1	0	Zane, Rockford	.973	76	143	222	10	50
Mathiot, Kenosha	.926	36	61	64	10	4							

Triple Plays—Bernhardt, Cunningham, Oberdank, Ross, Stargell.

THIRD BASEMEN

Player and Club	Pct.	G.	PO.	A.	E.	DP.	Player and Club	Pct.	G.	PO.	A.	E.	DP.
Adames, Peoria	1.000	3	0	5	0	0	Krumback, Cedar Rapids	.842	19	8	40	9	3
Aguilar, Madison	.928	35	26	51	6	5	Lombardozzi, Cedar Rapids	.909	4	4	6	1	0
AYLWARD, Quad City	.941	127	86	218	19	27	Lonigro, Cedar Rapids	.934	28	22	49	5	3
Bolick, Beloit	.910	63	44	108	15	13	Lopez, Waterloo	.818	3	2	7	2	0
Boyce, Kenosha	.800	5	1	3	1	0	Lukachyk, South Bend	1.000	2	2	1	0	1
Briggs, Kenosha	.833	4	3	7	2	1	Malchesky, Springfield	.901	47	29	71	11	0
Buccheri, Madison	.830	17	14	25	8	3	Marrero, Beloit	.913	27	16	57	7	2
Byington, Beloit	.849	34	15	47	11	0	Martinez, South Bend	.750	3	0	9	3	2
Candelari, Wausau	.852	25	16	30	8	2	Mathews, Wausau	.875	30	10	53	9	3
Capello, Appleton	.955	33	24	60	4	8	McNaney, Waterloo	.922	32	32	86	10	5
Carrasco, Quad City	.750	1	0	3	1	0	Meadows, Waterloo	.839	18	15	37	10	6
Cloninger, Burlington	.933	38	20	63	6	6	Michalak, Clinton	.916	54	38	115	14	13
Coomer, Madison	.946	32	26	62	5	3	Mitchell, Burlington	1.000	1	1	1	0	0
Coppell, Clinton	.853	41	22	59	14	4	Mordecai, Burlington	.867	7	6	7	2	0
B. Cruz, South Bend	1.000	3	1	5	0	0	Mulville, Cedar Rapids	.929	5	3	10	1	0
V. Cruz, Davenport	.727	4	4	4	3	0	Murray, Wausau	.931	10	9	18	2	1
Cunningham, Waterloo	.968	47	40	110	5	8	Murrell, Madison	.935	19	15	43	4	6
Davenport, Clinton	.000	3	0	0	1	0	Payton, Springfield	.926	90	54	171	18	19
S. Diaz, Beloit	1.000	1	0	1	0	0	Pino, Kenosha	.958	8	9	14	1	3
W. Diaz, Wausau	.880	48	36	81	16	7	Pittenger, Kenosha	.980	24	19	30	1	3
Dombrowski, Cedar Rapids	.786	9	6	16	6	0	Razook, Wausau	.909	9	6	14	2	2
Eatinger, South Bend	.750	5	7	5	4	1	Redington, Burlington	.918	85	55	181	21	13
Esquer, Quad City	1.000	7	3	11	0	0	Rickman, Cedar Rapids	1.000	1	0	1	0	0
Fernandez, Clinton	1.000	4	0	1	0	0	Ricks, Waterloo	.667	2	0	2	1	0
Foster, Rockford	.852	23	7	39	8	4	D. Robinson, Madison	.924	53	23	87	9	5
Franco, Peoria	.878	16	11	32	6	3	M. Robinson, Madison	.861	36	21	72	15	6
Garber, Appleton	.892	21	21	37	7	5	Robles, Wausau	1.000	3	0	7	0	2
Garcia, Kenosha	.938	26	30	46	5	1	Roskom, Kenosha	.873	66	42	96	20	12
Glass, Burlington	.882	5	5	10	2	0	Roth, South Bend	.843	31	26	44	13	1
Gray, Clinton	1.000	1	0	2	0	0	Rumsey, Clinton	1.000	1	0	1	0	0
Griffin, Peoria	.888	34	19	68	11	3	Sarbaugh, Beloit	.909	14	7	23	3	2
Heffernan, Beloit	.000	1	0	0	1	0	Schnurbusch, Cedar Rapids	.813	34	12	49	14	0
Hilpert, Clinton	.857	26	14	28	7	0	Schoonover, Burlington	.842	8	3	13	3	0
Hoffman, Wausau	.818	24	11	34	10	4	E. Smith, South Bend	.842	96	78	135	40	16
Holbert, Waterloo	1.000	1	0	1	0	0	T. Smith, Peoria	.854	19	14	27	7	4
Holland, Waterloo	.935	49	31	98	9	8	W. Smith, Peoria	.901	74	35	138	19	13
Holley, Appleton	.914	26	20	44	6	3	Stairs, Rockford	.929	42	30	62	7	2
Huffman, Springfield	.950	12	5	14	1	2	Standiford, Clinton	.927	19	12	26	3	3
Infante, Cedar Rapids	.965	48	31	105	5	13	Stillwell, Appleton	.917	6	7	4	1	0
Kelso, Quad City	.800	3	1	3	1	0	Williams, Burlington	.667	1	1	1	1	0
Kosco, Rockford	.946	76	57	155	12	10							

Triple Plays—Aylward 2.

SHORTSTOPS

Player and Club	Pct.	G.	PO.	A.	E.	DP.	Player and Club	Pct.	G.	PO.	A.	E.	DP.
Adames, Peoria	1.000	1	0	1	0	0	Coppell, Clinton	1.000	2	0	1	0	0
Adriance, Clinton*	1.000	1	0	1	0	0	B. Cruz, South Bend	.938	24	35	55	6	14
Aguilar, Madison	.920	37	49	89	12	14	V. Cruz, Clinton	.778	3	2	5	2	1
Arias, Peoria	.944	135	210	408	37	83	Cunningham, Waterloo	.953	24	48	74	6	13
BELTRE, Rockford	.94535	104	183	336	30	61	Diaz, Wausau	1.000	2	5	4	0	2
Branson, Cedar Rapids	.94490	125	172	394	33	67	Erickson, Beloit	.800	5	5	7	3	1
Brauning, Clinton	.936	27	30	73	7	14	Esquer, Quad City	.909	23	21	39	6	7
Busby, South Bend	.959	51	70	116	8	22	Finn, Beloit	.927	73	129	203	26	45
Capello, Appleton	.929	5	3	10	1	0	Flora, Quad City	.905	118	156	280	46	59
Castleberry, Burlington	.667	1	1	1	1	0	Furcal, Madison	.841	10	15	22	7	4
Clayton, Clinton	.943	104	182	332	31	71	Garibaldo, Appleton	.941	118	178	330	32	66
Cloninger, Burlington	.962	12	21	30	2	5	Glass, Burlington	.918	12	15	30	4	6

SHORTSTOPS—Continued

Player and Club	Pct.	G.	PO.	A.	E.	DP.	Player and Club	Pct.	G.	PO.	A.	E.	DP.
Guerrero, Beloit	.906	47	72	131	21	23	Murrell, Madison	.949	23	32	61	5	15
Hall, Burlington	.964	14	19	35	2	7	Pino, Kenosha	.938	62	93	163	17	12
Hilpert, Clinton	.900	4	4	5	1	2	Preston, Appleton	1.000	2	1	2	0	1
Holbert, Waterloo	.941	116	205	302	32	58	Razook, Wausau	.879	8	9	20	4	7
Holland, Waterloo	.941	4	5	11	1	1	Redington, Burlington	1.000	1	2	2	0	1
Huffman, Springfield	.960	34	32	64	4	10	Rickman, Cedar Rapids	.889	5	6	10	2	4
Knoblauch, Kenosha	.898	50	60	124	21	20	Robles, Wausau	.939	113	170	351	34	63
Kosco, Rockford	1.000	1	1	2	0	1	Roskom, Kenosha	.925	19	29	45	6	10
Lonigro, Cedar Rapids	.958	4	9	14	1	2	Roth, South Bend	.956	10	16	27	2	6
Marrero, Beloit	.887	12	18	29	6	2	Saccomanno, Burlington	.929	50	67	141	16	20
Martinez, Madison	.935	18	30	42	5	12	Schnurbusch, Cedar Rapids	.897	9	14	21	4	6
Mateo, Madison	.874	61	77	104	26	20	Shireman, Springfield	.939	120	171	340	33	61
McDevitt, Waterloo	1.000	2	1	3	0	1	Smith, Peoria	.870	11	6	14	3	2
Michalak, Clinton	.935	8	14	15	2	1	Stanley, Rockford	.800	2	3	5	2	2
Mordecai, Burlington	.924	58	74	156	19	18	Stillwell, Appleton	.935	21	34	38	5	8
Murray, Wausau	.942	11	19	46	4	6	A. Tejada, Rockford	.836	28	32	70	20	17
							E. Tejada, South Bend	.893	69	112	146	31	32

Triple Plays—B. Cruz, Holbert, Shireman.

OUTFIELDERS

Player and Club	Pct.	G.	PO.	A.	E.	DP.	Player and Club	Pct.	G.	PO.	A.	E.	DP.
Adriance, Clinton*	.909	13	20	0	2	0	Kerkes, Wausau	.973	78	108	0	3	0
Amaro, Quad City	1.000	45	68	3	0	0	Kilpatrick, Quad City	.944	14	16	1	1	0
Arrington, Peoria	.981	71	100	5	2	0	Kuhn, Waterloo*	.899	35	56	6	7	0
Baldwin, Burlington	.968	62	116	6	4	2	Kvasnicka, Kenosha*	.950	125	204	6	11	1
Bernstine, Peoria	1.000	1	1	0	0	0	Lee, South Bend	.960	114	187	6	8	1
Blanks, Burlington*	.934	51	76	9	6	1	Looper, Springfield	.977	37	36	6	1	0
Boddie, Rockford	.981	131	232	22	5	4	Love, Beloit*	.952	15	20	0	1	0
Bolick, Beloit	1.000	1	1	0	0	0	Lukachyk, South Bend	.962	91	166	10	7	2
Bonner, Clinton	.974	112	179	9	5	1	Maclin, Springfield*	.966	95	135	7	5	1
Brock, Cedar Rapids*	.985	108	182	10	3	2	Malinak, Cedar Rapids	1.000	1	1	1	0	1
D. Brown, Cedar Rapids	.966	65	106	8	4	0	Maynard, Wausau	.977	127	240	10	6	2
T. Brown, Kenosha	.954	38	57	5	3	0	McNaney, Waterloo	1.000	2	3	0	0	0
W. Brown, Springfield	.967	58	82	6	3	0	Mehl, South Bend	.976	49	79	2	2	1
BRUETT, Kenosha*	.988	101	234	10	3	5	Messerly, 16 Mad-10 Water	.979	26	46	1	1	0
Bryant, Cedar Rapids	.976	48	79	3	2	0	Meyett, Beloit*	.986	86	133	4	2	1
Buccheri, Madison	1.000	2	1	0	0	0	Miller, Wausau	1.000	1	1	0	0	0
Butcher, Beloit*	.902	41	44	2	5	0	Mitchell, Burlington	.971	125	249	17	8	3
Campbell, Burlington*	.952	78	149	8	8	1	Morris, Kenosha	.960	15	24	0	1	0
Candelari, Wausau	.951	45	56	2	3	0	Muhammad, Beloit	1.000	7	6	0	0	0
Castro, Wausau*	.953	54	76	5	4	1	Noland, Waterloo	.952	91	175	5	9	2
Clark, Burlington	1.000	7	9	0	0	0	O'Leary, Beloit*	.982	38	55	1	1	0
Cole, Burlington	.961	108	158	14	7	1	Partrick, Quad City	.969	100	181	5	6	2
Colvard, Cedar Rapids	.964	98	152	8	6	0	D. Payton, Springfield	.974	27	36	2	1	1
Coppell, Clinton	.964	83	129	4	5	2	R. Payton, South Bend	.960	12	24	0	1	0
Cruz, Clinton	1.000	1	1	0	0	0	Perez, Quad City	.963	92	150	8	6	1
Cunningham, Waterloo	1.000	2	3	0	0	0	Pfaff, Beloit*	.969	79	119	5	4	1
Curtis, Quad City	.972	23	34	1	1	0	Phillips, Quad City*	.955	18	19	2	1	1
B. Davis, South Bend	1.000	9	3	0	0	0	Piechowski, Rockford*	1.000	16	24	0	0	0
H. Davis, Wausau	.964	21	27	0	1	0	Pledger, South Bend	.975	78	153	5	4	1
DeAngelis, Quad City*	.875	10	14	0	2	0	Prusia, Appleton	.947	47	68	3	4	0
Doran, Quad City	1.000	10	14	0	0	0	Ramsey, Peoria	.962	128	272	9	11	1
Dyer, Appleton	.857	7	10	2	2	0	Ricks, 36 Mad-62 Water	.923	98	167	13	15	3
Eastman, Cedar Rapids	.953	96	152	11	8	2	Romero, Quad City	.969	19	30	1	1	1
Edmonds, Quad City*	.942	30	47	2	3	1	Rumsey, Clinton	.906	22	29	0	3	0
Edward, Quad City*	1.000	5	9	0	0	0	Sanchez, Waterloo*	.905	60	81	14	10	3
Elci, Springfield	1.000	3	2	1	0	1	Shelton, Peoria	.961	76	93	5	4	0
Esquer, Springfield	1.000	11	21	0	0	0	Shephard, Rockford	.953	51	76	6	4	2
Eveline, Quad City	.949	54	72	3	4	1	Smiley, Clinton*	.923	123	221	7	19	0
Farmer, Waterloo*	.973	93	236	13	7	3	Smith, Rockford	.967	97	206	2	7	1
Fiore, Springfield	.958	82	130	6	6	2	Standiford, Clinton	.833	8	5	0	1	0
Ford, Appleton*	.969	122	277	9	9	2	Stillwell, Appleton	1.000	10	12	2	0	1
Garcia, Beloit	.916	81	105	4	10	1	Tartabull, Wausau	.987	51	73	3	1	0
Gavin, Waterloo	1.000	20	27	4	0	0	Thomas, Wausau*	.932	40	67	1	5	1
Gieseke, Waterloo*	.750	4	2	1	1	1	Tinsley, Madison	.972	118	274	7	8	0
Graterol, Kenosha	.917	13	19	3	2	0	Tucker, Clinton	1.000	3	3	0	0	0
Grier, Springfield	1.000	22	29	3	0	0	Vannaman, Madison	.970	120	176	16	6	5
Gross, Kenosha	.966	102	186	10	7	2	Walker, Appleton	.948	100	173	8	10	2
Hansen, Rockford	.981	117	195	14	4	3	Warren, South Bend	.964	47	103	3	4	0
Henderson, Appleton	.975	29	35	4	1	0	White, Springfield	.966	128	248	7	9	1
Hilpert, Clinton	1.000	3	2	0	0	0	E. Williams, Peoria*	.964	115	183	4	7	0
Holland, Waterloo	.975	61	102	13	3	4	K. Williams, Quad City	1.000	5	7	0	0	0
Hosey, Madison	.939	110	207	8	14	3	Ra. Williams, Wausau	.947	32	33	3	2	0
Jackson, Beloit	.961	104	170	4	7	1	Re. Williams, Clinton	.981	67	146	7	3	2
Jensen, Peoria	.969	44	61	1	2	0	D. Wright, Appleton	.960	115	178	14	8	1
Kating, Madison	1.000	2	3	0	0	0	J. Wright, Kenosha	1.000	4	4	0	0	0
Kemper, Clinton*	.947	8	18	0	1	0	Zaksek, South Bend*	.966	39	55	1	2	0

Triple Plays—Campbell, Tartabull.

CATCHERS

Player and Club	Pct.	G.	PO.	A.	E.	DP.	PB.	Player and Club	Pct.	G.	PO.	A.	E.	DP.	PB.
Alvarez, South Bend	.987	86	529	60	8	1	4	Colescott, Springfield	.983	95	548	80	11	2	16
Barbara, Wausau	.990	63	441	34	5	2	12	Colon, Peoria	.984	10	54	7	1	0	1
Beeler, Cedar Rapids	.992	49	322	30	3	1	9	Coppell, Clinton	1.000	1	1	0	0	0	0
Boeschen, Burlington	.971	5	32	2	1	0	2	Cuevas, Burlington	.978	68	453	42	11	5	7
Borrelli, Madison	.975	20	136	17	4	2	2	Curnow, Waterloo	.969	38	164	21	6	3	5
Briggs, Kenosha	.988	32	221	31	3	4	11	DeLeon, Appleton	.974	43	250	44	8	4	12
Brito, Madison	.986	41	252	28	4	1	6	Diaz, Beloit	.970	14	61	4	2	0	1
Buchanan, Appleton	.949	15	99	12	6	1	1	Dyer, Appleton	.961	27	129	20	6	1	8
Candelari, Wausau	1.000	3	6	0	0	0	0	Faccio, Clinton	1.000	5	35	3	0	0	0
Canino, Peoria	1.000	4	4	0	0	0	0	Fontes, Kenosha	.958	34	206	23	10	0	3
Carcione, Madison	.955	8	56	8	3	0	2	Gonzales, Quad City	.986	54	400	36	6	5	13

CATCHERS—Continued

Player and Club	Pct.	G.	PO.	A.	E.	DP.	PB.	Player and Club	Pct.	G.	PO.	A.	E.	DP.	PB.
Hargis, Rockford	.938	13	55	6	4	0	7	Oedewaldt, Beloit	1.000	8	60	5	0	0	0
Heck, Madison	.980	26	128	22	3	3	4	Oller, Rockford	1.000	11	37	9	0	1	2
HEFFERNAN, Beloit	.991	119	832	109	9	11	4	Ortiz, Beloit	1.000	2	5	4	0	0	1
Hornacek, South Bend	.988	60	416	62	6	4	11	Pattin, Clinton	1.000	10	53	1	0	0	1
Howard, Wausau	.989	36	253	20	3	2	4	Paynter, Peoria	.977	31	149	23	4	1	5
Hulse, Appleton	.993	61	353	63	3	4	17	Pfaff, Burlington	.986	62	418	69	7	2	12
Kaub, Rockford	1.000	1	6	0	0	0	1	Pratt, Clinton	.991	18	97	13	1	1	4
King, Waterloo	.977	17	73	12	2	2	2	Resetar, Kenosha	.983	43	322	32	6	4	7
Laker, Rockford	.960	14	91	6	4	1	4	Siddall, Rockford	.984	97	656	91	12	7	19
Langiotti, Springfield	.988	56	302	35	4	2	8	Singley, South Bend	.909	7	36	4	4	0	4
J. Lopez, Clinton	.986	26	176	28	3	3	5	Siwa, Kenosha	.984	24	224	27	4	4	1
P. Lopez, Waterloo	.976	87	455	85	13	7	18	Slavin, Clinton	1.000	7	25	3	0	1	3
Mason, Rockford	.969	12	57	6	2	0	1	Taubensee, Cedar Rapids	.980	56	400	49	9	1	4
Mercedes, Madison	.986	49	304	40	5	3	10	Taylor, Peoria	.995	23	162	28	1	2	10
Miller, Wausau	.996	48	259	16	1	2	8	Tucker, Clinton	.986	94	646	60	10	8	17
Mulville, Cedar Rapids	.983	39	261	22	5	3	12	Walbeck, Peoria	.984	93	605	72	11	2	12
Mundy, Peoria	1.000	7	22	2	0	1	0	Williams, Burlington	1.000	10	31	3	0	0	0
Musolino, Quad City	.990	88	686	70	8	2	14								

Triple Play—Musolino.

PITCHERS

Player and Club	Pct.	G.	PO.	A.	E.	DP.	Player and Club	Pct.	G.	PO.	A.	E.	DP.
Abbott, Quad City*	1.000	13	1	10	0	1	W. Gibbons, Clinton	1.000	5	0	1	0	0
Alexander, Appleton*	1.000	6	1	2	0	0	Golmont, Madison	.818	31	1	8	2	2
Alleyne, Rockford*	.750	23	1	5	2	1	Grayson, Beloit	1.000	3	0	2	0	0
Allison, Madison*	1.000	13	3	5	0	0	Grimes, Springfield	.917	62	1	21	2	3
Ariola, Madison*	.892	18	4	29	4	2	Guzman, Madison*	.923	9	4	8	1	0
Backus, Wausau*	.750	23	0	6	2	0	Hancock, Clinton*	.900	18	1	17	2	0
Bennett, Wausau*	.971	24	3	31	1	1	Hanselman, Clinton	.963	15	3	23	1	2
Berg, Madison	1.000	21	3	8	0	1	Harris, Madison*	.942	25	5	44	3	4
Borgatti, Waterloo	.931	17	10	17	2	1	Hart, Waterloo	1.000	28	4	21	0	0
Breitenbucher, Clinton	.909	21	2	8	1	0	Harvey, Appleton	.826	26	5	14	4	0
Briscoe, Madison	.861	21	7	24	5	0	M. Hernandez, Clinton*	1.000	8	0	2	0	1
Broadfoot, Springfield	1.000	30	1	9	0	0	R. Hernandez, South Bend	1.000	4	3	8	0	0
Bromby, Rockford	1.000	6	0	3	0	0	HESTER, Cedar Rapids	1.000	27	12	32	0	1
Brutcher, South Bend	1.000	16	4	9	0	0	Hoeme, Appleton	.842	29	6	10	3	0
E. Bryant, Wausau	1.000	4	2	1	0	0	Hofer, Appleton	.778	23	3	4	2	0
K. Bryant, Wausau	.500	2	0	1	1	0	Holzemer, Quad City*	.974	25	5	32	1	2
Burnau, Wausau*	.939	45	10	36	3	1	Howze, Rockford	.886	26	6	25	4	1
Buzzard, Rockford	1.000	9	0	3	0	0	Hoyer, Waterloo*	.923	33	9	15	2	2
Cangemi, Beloit	.955	9	7	14	1	0	Huth, Appleton	1.000	13	1	3	0	1
Cantwell, Waterloo*	1.000	8	0	3	0	0	Jeffery, Cedar Rapids	1.000	14	10	26	0	3
Capello, Appleton	1.000	1	0	3	0	0	Ca. Johnson, Kenosha	.750	18	4	5	3	1
Carmody, Beloit*	.909	40	5	5	1	0	Ch. Johnson, Beloit	.875	25	9	19	4	1
G. Carter, Quad City	.935	25	7	22	2	1	D. Johnson, Clinton	.900	8	3	6	1	1
L. Carter, Beloit	1.000	17	7	7	0	0	L. Johnson, South Bend	.923	13	6	6	1	0
R. Carter, Wausau	.750	3	0	3	1	0	Jones, South Bend	.500	3	0	1	1	0
Chavez, South Bend*	.961	20	3	46	2	1	Karasinski, Burlington*	.933	29	5	23	2	0
Chitren, Madison	1.000	20	1	6	0	1	Kelly, Burlington*	.667	11	0	8	4	0
Cooper, South Bend	.857	16	6	6	2	1	Kerrigan, Rockford	.938	45	2	13	1	0
Cornelius, Rockford	.917	17	6	16	2	0	Kiefer, Beloit	.977	30	10	33	1	3
Cuesta, Burlington*	1.000	1	0	2	0	0	Kisten, Springfield	.889	57	8	16	3	3
Cummings, Burlington	1.000	12	8	6	0	1	Krippner, Beloit	.941	23	18	14	2	1
Czarnik, Burlington	.850	41	5	12	3	1	Krol, Kenosha	.909	16	4	6	1	2
Dabney, South Bend*	.867	26	5	21	4	0	Kryzanowski, Kenosha	.926	46	11	14	2	4
Braz Davis, Peoria	.921	27	13	22	3	2	Kurczewski, Burlington	1.000	3	1	0	0	0
Bret Davis, Rockford	.875	38	5	16	3	0	Landry, Beloit	.900	10	0	9	1	0
DeAngelis, Quad City*	1.000	1	0	3	0	0	Lane, Beloit	.969	17	3	28	1	1
DeJaynes, Quad City	1.000	8	1	0	0	0	Lawrence, Springfield	.942	34	15	50	4	4
DeLaCruz, South Bend	.871	11	12	15	4	1	Lawson, Madison	1.000	33	5	14	0	0
DeLaRosa, Clinton	.821	43	6	17	5	0	Lebron, Waterloo	.897	34	8	18	3	2
Dour, Clinton	.941	10	3	13	1	1	Liss, Wausau*	1.000	8	0	9	0	0
Drezek, Appleton	1.000	31	5	6	0	2	Longuil, Burlington	.857	31	5	13	3	2
Drohan, Appleton	1.000	9	6	12	0	0	Lopez, Peoria	.920	28	19	27	4	2
Duvall, Springfield	.923	13	9	15	2	1	Ludy, Beloit	1.000	9	1	1	0	0
Economy, Cedar Rapids	.964	38	5	22	1	2	MacLeod, Madison*	.800	11	1	7	2	0
Eddings, Peoria	.963	38	5	21	1	0	Magee, Appleton*	1.000	15	2	3	0	0
Eldred, Beloit	.900	5	4	5	1	0	Mahomes, Kenosha	.914	25	11	21	3	1
Erb, Quad City	.964	25	7	20	1	0	Marchese, Quad City	1.000	49	3	10	0	2
Espino, Peoria	1.000	12	2	7	0	0	Marrero, Beloit	1.000	1	0	2	0	0
Estes, Clinton*	1.000	39	4	36	0	1	Marsh, Cedar Rapids	.926	49	10	15	2	2
Faccio, Springfield	1.000	27	13	24	0	2	Marshall, South Bend	.818	40	3	6	2	0
Felix, Wausau*	.938	38	3	12	1	1	Marte, Quad City	1.000	24	6	7	0	2
Figueroa, Waterloo	1.000	21	0	3	0	0	Martin, Quad City	1.000	9	1	3	0	0
Fitzgerald, Beloit*	.974	27	9	29	1	1	Massicotte, Peoria	.880	35	10	12	3	0
Foley, Madison	1.000	33	10	15	0	0	Masters, Madison	1.000	4	2	2	0	0
Foster, Cedar Rapids	.875	51	6	8	2	1	Maye, Madison	.857	16	1	5	1	0
Fowler, Waterloo	.964	41	8	19	1	2	McCarthy, Cedar Rapids*	1.000	30	2	12	0	0
Freed, Rockford	.973	26	20	51	2	3	McClure, Kenosha	1.000	33	2	7	0	0
Fuller, South Bend	1.000	5	1	1	0	0	McCormick, Appleton*	.914	20	2	30	3	1
Furcal, Wausau*	1.000	4	0	2	0	0	M. McGuire, Wausau	1.000	19	2	23	0	1
Fye, Clinton*	.879	15	5	24	4	4	S. McGuire, Quad City	.917	15	5	17	2	0
Galindez, Waterloo*	.966	33	7	21	1	1	Meamber, Springfield	.943	37	13	20	2	1
Galvan, South Bend*	1.000	16	2	2	0	0	Meister, Burlington	.500	12	0	2	2	0
Garces, Kenosha	.931	24	20	34	4	0	Merigliano, South Bend	.880	19	10	12	3	1
Garcia, Madison	.892	27	9	24	4	0	Milchin, Springfield*	1.000	6	1	8	0	0
Gardiner, Wausau	1.000	15	3	5	0	0	Minchey, 15 Rock.-11 Bur.	.903	26	9	19	3	0
Garrison, Clinton*	1.000	18	2	4	0	2	Mirabella, Beloit*	1.000	2	1	1	0	0
Gewecke, Springfield*	1.000	13	1	3	0	0	Miranda, Beloit*	1.000	43	5	10	0	1
Ghelfi, Clinton	1.000	12	1	6	0	0	Misuraca, Kenosha	.636	9	1	6	4	0
M. Gibbons, Rockford	1.000	40	3	13	0	0	Mitchener, South Bend	.852	33	4	19	4	2

PITCHERS—Continued

Player and Club	Pct.	G.	PO.	A.	E.	DP.	Player and Club	Pct.	G.	PO.	A.	E.	DP.
Morton, Waterloo	.933	47	8	20	2	1	Ryan, Wausau	1.000	15	8	12	0	0
Muh, Kenosha*	.806	26	5	24	7	1	Sala, Springfield*	1.000	13	3	2	0	0
Murphy, Quad City	.909	39	2	18	2	2	Salles, Peoria	.909	21	16	24	4	0
Murray, Wausau	1.000	7	0	2	0	0	Sandoval, Beloit	.967	30	8	21	1	0
Mutz, Quad City	1.000	18	2	4	0	0	Satterfield, Springfield	.952	27	30	29	3	2
J. Myers, Clinton	.936	32	7	37	3	4	Schrenk, South Bend	.906	16	8	21	3	1
M. Myers, Cedar Rapids	.974	27	10	28	1	4	Search, Quad City*	1.000	3	1	0	0	0
Nabholz, Rockford*	.957	24	7	38	2	2	Sharko, Clinton	.909	16	5	5	1	0
Neagle, Kenosha*	.846	6	1	10	2	0	Shifflett, Appleton	1.000	18	4	3	0	0
Newman, Kenosha*	.912	18	0	31	3	0	Shiflett, Rockford	1.000	18	2	6	0	1
Nied, Burlington	.938	13	0	15	1	0	Slocumb, Peoria	1.000	49	3	16	0	0
Nocas, Appleton	1.000	8	1	6	0	0	Slomkowski, Waterloo	.971	43	12	22	1	1
North, Kenosha*	1.000	19	1	14	0	2	Sodders, Peoria*	.980	28	15	33	1	4
Novoa, Clinton	.813	13	3	10	3	0	Stancel, Madison	.900	8	1	8	1	0
Oropeza, Rockford	1.000	9	1	4	0	1	Stoerck, Wausau	1.000	12	4	6	0	0
Osik, Appleton	1.000	5	1	0	0	0	Stroud, Peoria*	.833	40	4	6	2	0
Otto, Appleton	.978	43	7	37	1	2	Studeman, Appleton	1.000	5	0	1	0	1
Pardo, Quad City	.842	27	5	11	3	2	Swanson, Kenosha	1.000	11	7	10	0	0
Parmenter, Peoria	1.000	8	1	2	0	0	S. Taylor, Wausau	.963	16	8	18	1	0
Parnell, Appleton	1.000	46	5	10	0	2	W. Taylor, Madison	.933	35	3	11	1	1
Patrick, Madison	.818	12	4	5	2	0	Throckmorton, Burlington	1.000	1	1	0	0	0
Perschke, South Bend	1.000	13	2	5	0	1	Trombley, Kenosha	1.000	12	4	8	0	1
Piatt, Rockford	1.000	11	0	1	0	0	Turek, Cedar Rapids	.963	25	11	15	1	1
Pichardo, Appleton	1.000	12	10	15	0	0	Upshaw, Burlington*	.885	12	5	18	3	0
Pierce, Appleton*	.962	31	9	16	1	1	Vanderwel, Quad City	.857	22	2	10	2	1
Pitcher, Wausau	.909	49	4	6	1	1	Vaughn, Appleton	.900	15	4	14	2	0
Plemel, Springfield	.962	11	7	18	1	2	Vazquez, Burlington	.800	2	0	4	1	0
Pomeranz, Kenosha*	.861	31	7	24	5	0	Vegely, Quad City*	.957	48	5	17	1	1
Powell, Cedar Rapids*	.800	13	4	8	3	0	Ventura, South Bend	.893	29	6	19	3	0
Radinsky, South Bend*	.833	53	2	8	2	0	Vierra, Cedar Rapids*	.938	47	3	12	1	0
Rambo, Clinton	.905	12	6	13	2	0	Voit, Beloit	1.000	4	4	2	0	0
S. Reed, Clinton	1.000	60	1	23	0	2	Wagner, Appleton	.931	24	9	18	2	3
W. Reed, Waterloo*	.857	31	7	17	4	1	Wahl, Beloit	1.000	7	2	3	0	0
Regira, Rockford	.857	14	6	6	2	0	Watson, Burlington	.889	14	6	18	3	1
Reilley, Wausau	.955	43	4	17	1	1	Watts, Beloit	.857	16	4	8	2	0
Reis, Burlington	.906	34	12	17	3	1	Waznik, Burlington*	.750	34	2	4	2	0
Ricci, Waterloo	.930	29	22	31	4	1	Weems, Burlington	.864	13	10	9	3	2
Richardson, Springfield*	1.000	51	6	12	0	0	Wendell, Burlington	.898	22	22	22	5	1
Risley, Cedar Rapids	.897	27	9	17	3	1	Whitlock, Wausau*	.962	29	9	16	1	2
Robinson, Peoria	.919	28	9	25	3	1	Wilkinson, Wausau	1.000	17	6	5	0	0
Rodriguez, Cedar Rapids*	1.000	11	4	5	0	2	Winston, Rockford*	.923	47	2	22	2	2
Rogers, Clinton*	.892	29	3	30	4	2	Wright, Burlington	.917	40	4	7	1	0
Rovasio, Kenosha	.875	22	1	6	1	0	Zappelli, Quad City	.875	48	5	16	3	1
							Zarranz, Peoria	1.000	7	1	0	0	0

Triple Play—Murphy.

The following players did not have any fielding statistics at the positions indicated or appeared only as a designated hitter, pinch-hitter or pinch-runner: Adriance, p; Beall, p; Bennett, of; Bolick, 2b; Brauning, 3b; Busby, 3b; Carey, of; Carrasco, of; Casillas, p; Coppell, 2b, p; B. Cruz, 2b; Curnow, p; Davenport, of; Davidson, of; Drake, p; Economy, 1b; Elci, c; Eldredge, p; Estes, of; Gomez, p; Gould, p; Holley, ss; Howard, of; Jackson, 3b; Krumback, of; Kuhn, p; Langiotti, 1b; Looper, 3b, p; J. Lopez, 1b; Love, p; McDevitt, 3b; Mealy, of; Michalak, of; Miller, 3b; J. Ortiz, of; R. Ortiz, p; Pall, p; Paredes, 3b; Paulino, of; D. Payton, 2b; Reed, of; Rose, p; Ross, ss; Shelton, p; T. Smith, p; Stanley, 3b, of; Sveum, dh; Townsend, p; T. Williams, p; Zane, ss, of.

CLUB PITCHING

Club	ERA.	G.	CG.	ShO.	Sv.	IP.	H.	R.	ER.	HR.	HB.	BB.	Int. BB.	SO.	WP.	Bk.
Peoria	2.69	139	27	12	40	1224.0	1080	477	366	49	43	369	17	980	71	20
South Bend	2.75	132	17	13	41	1154.2	965	466	353	47	67	469	16	963	58	36
Rockford	3.04	133	13	11	35	1166.2	1023	517	394	38	35	480	16	901	106	33
Quad City	3.03	135	14	17	34	1153.2	937	489	389	55	53	480	17	1069	61	40
Cedar Rapids	3.05	137	16	17	38	1202.2	933	504	407	80	45	458	25	966	88	29
Springfield	3.19	135	19	11	38	1179.0	1085	527	418	56	45	427	27	847	68	13
Clinton	3.26	139	9	11	37	1219.1	1069	561	441	54	60	595	45	959	66	37
Kenosha	3.35	129	17	7	33	1116.1	912	522	415	52	61	598	30	949	76	31
Beloit	3.45	134	24	14	26	1144.2	1016	544	439	59	69	513	27	951	56	28
Madison	3.53	131	12	9	31	1124.0	1061	567	441	53	52	465	5	850	80	27
Appleton	3.55	135	14	13	42	1148.1	1063	589	453	67	60	491	9	808	85	26
Burlington	3.71	137	27	13	24	1201.1	1168	622	495	77	47	449	24	898	73	22
Wausau	4.01	134	14	13	26	1129.2	1082	632	503	97	54	521	23	933	85	32
Waterloo	4.39	136	21	2	21	1199.2	1219	709	585	101	79	526	19	644	91	29

PITCHERS' RECORDS
(Leading Qualifiers for Earned-Run Average Leadership — 112 or More Innings)

*Throws lefthanded.

Pitcher — Club	W.	L.	Pct.	ERA.	G.	GS.	CG.	GF.	ShO.	Sv.	IP.	H.	R.	ER.	HR.	HB.	BB.	Int. BB.	SO.	WP.
Ventura, South Bend	7	3	.700	1.57	29	10	2	8	2	1	115.0	74	36	20	4	8	50	1	87	4
Ariola, Madison*	9	5	.643	1.86	18	18	5	0	4	0	121.0	87	44	25	2	5	32	0	115	4
Chavez, South Bend*	15	3	.833	1.91	20	19	3	1	1	0	141.1	125	46	30	7	3	38	1	102	3
G. Carter, Quad City	15	6	.714	2.05	25	25	5	0	1	0	166.2	109	48	38	10	2	57	1	190	4
Dabney, South Bend*	11	7	.611	2.09	26	26	3	0	3	0	163.1	128	50	38	2	11	65	1	150	7
Nabholz, Rockford*	13	5	.722	2.18	24	23	3	0	3	0	161.1	132	54	39	6	0	41	0	149	11
Wendell, Burlington	9	11	.450	2.21	22	22	9	0	5	0	159.0	127	63	39	7	3	41	1	153	1
Freed, Rockford	13	8	.619	2.29	26	26	8	0	3	0	192.2	164	67	49	2	3	49	1	121	13
Kiefer, Beloit	9	6	.600	2.32	30	15	7	5	2	1	131.2	106	44	34	4	8	32	2	100	6
Salles, Peoria	9	8	.529	2.48	21	21	2	0	0	0	138.0	137	60	38	4	5	73	3	73	10

Departmental Leaders: G—Grimes, 62; W—Lopez, 18; L—W. Reed, 15; Pct.—Chavez, .833; GS—Lopez, Robinson, Rogers, Sodders, 28; CG—Ricci, Wendell, 9; GF—Kisten, 52; ShO—Wendell, 5; Sv.—Kisten, 37; IP—Sodders, 202.1; H—Lopez, 187; R—Howze, 98; ER—Minchey, 81; HR—Hester, 22; HB—W. Reed, 16; BB—Mahomes, Muh, 100; IBB—Estes, 14; SO—G. Carter, 190; WP—Minchey, 22.

(All Pitchers—Listed Alphabetically)

Pitcher—Club	W.	L.	Pct.	ERA.	G.	GS.	CG.	GF.	ShO.	Sv.	IP.	H.	R.	ER.	HR.	HB.	BB.	Int. BB.	SO.	WP.
Abbott, Quad City*	5	4	.556	2.57	13	12	0	1	0	0	73.2	55	26	21	5	4	30	0	95	3
Adriance, Clinton*	0	0	.000	0.00	1	0	0	1	0	0	1.0	2	0	0	0	0	1	0	3	1
Alexander, Appleton*	0	0	.000	0.73	6	0	0	3	0	1	12.1	4	3	1	0	0	8	0	10	3
Alleyne, Rockford*	7	3	.700	2.84	23	13	0	6	0	0	88.2	70	37	28	2	2	42	0	82	7
Allison, Madison*	2	3	.400	1.13	13	0	0	11	0	1	24.0	24	6	3	0	0	3	2	16	1
Ariola, Madison*	9	5	.643	1.86	18	18	5	0	4	0	121.0	87	44	25	2	5	32	0	115	4
Backus, Wausau*	2	2	.500	4.15	23	1	0	3	0	0	43.1	50	25	20	6	3	21	2	34	4
Beall, Appleton*	0	0	.000	7.71	2	0	0	1	0	0	2.1	1	2	2	0	0	4	0	2	0
Bennett, Wausau*	6	12	.333	4.02	24	23	2	0	0	0	127.2	125	68	57	12	4	39	1	86	2
Berg, Madison	1	1	.500	1.82	21	0	0	18	0	9	29.2	24	10	6	1	1	7	0	20	1
Borgatti, Waterloo	4	8	.333	5.06	17	15	3	1	0	0	96.0	115	63	54	9	3	24	0	68	3
Breitenbucher, Clinton	1	3	.250	2.63	21	1	0	8	0	1	51.1	46	21	15	3	2	12	3	30	0
Briscoe, Madison	7	5	.583	4.21	21	20	1	1	0	0	117.2	121	66	55	7	9	57	0	69	11
Broadfoot, Springfield	2	1	.667	4.06	30	2	0	7	0	0	51.0	65	31	23	3	1	15	2	26	4
Bromby, Rockford	0	1	.000	4.35	6	0	0	0	0	0	10.1	12	5	5	1	0	2	0	5	0
Brutcher, South Bend	5	5	.500	3.74	16	14	2	0	1	0	91.1	91	45	38	4	7	33	0	82	4
E. Bryant, Wausau	0	0	.000	10.00	4	0	0	0	0	0	9.0	18	12	10	4	0	4	0	9	0
K. Bryant, Wausau	0	2	.000	6.75	2	2	0	0	0	0	8.0	9	7	6	1	0	3	0	6	1
Burnau, Wausau*	7	7	.500	3.24	45	7	0	15	0	2	100.0	92	51	36	5	3	52	4	106	10
Buzzard, Rockford	0	1	.000	5.94	9	0	0	2	0	1	16.2	19	11	11	1	0	12	1	7	3
Cangemi, Beloit	3	4	.429	4.45	9	8	1	0	0	0	54.2	54	30	27	3	2	23	3	35	2
Cantwell, Waterloo*	0	1	.000	7.98	8	0	0	4	0	0	14.2	18	15	13	1	1	7	0	10	1
Capello, Appleton	0	0	.000	4.91	1	0	0	1	0	0	3.2	7	2	2	0	1	0	3	0	0
Carmody, Beloit*	3	2	.600	2.74	40	1	0	17	0	5	72.1	62	28	22	2	5	41	4	66	2
G. Carter, Quad City	15	6	.714	2.05	25	25	5	0	1	0	166.2	109	48	38	10	2	57	1	190	4
L. Carter, Beloit	2	2	.500	3.24	17	6	0	5	0	0	50.0	65	25	18	1	3	19	1	30	2
R. Carter, Wausau	0	1	.000	14.09	3	1	0	2	0	0	7.2	10	13	12	0	0	10	0	8	0
Casillas, Cedar Rapids	0	0	.000	11.57	3	0	0	2	0	0	2.1	3	3	3	0	0	3	0	2	1
Chavez, South Bend*	15	3	.833	1.91	20	19	3	1	1	0	141.1	125	46	30	7	3	38	1	102	3
Chitren, Madison	2	1	.667	1.19	20	0	0	18	0	7	22.2	13	3	3	1	2	4	0	17	0
Cooper, South Bend	0	1	.000	5.52	16	1	0	11	0	2	29.1	34	20	18	5	2	14	0	26	1
Coppell, Clinton	0	0	.000	27.00	1	0	0	0	0	0	0.1	1	1	1	0	0	0	0	0	0
Cornelius, Rockford	5	6	.455	4.27	17	17	0	0	0	0	84.1	71	58	40	6	11	63	0	66	13
Cuesta, Burlington*	0	0	.000	27.00	1	0	0	1	0	0	2.0	6	6	6	0	0	4	0	1	0
Cummings, Burlington	3	7	.300	5.11	12	12	2	0	1	0	75.2	83	52	43	5	3	27	0	54	5
Curnow, Waterloo	0	0	.000	5.79	3	0	0	3	0	0	4.2	2	3	3	0	1	3	0	5	0
Czarnik, Burlington	5	4	.556	2.77	41	3	0	19	0	4	84.1	79	43	26	3	2	32	1	65	6
Dabney, South Bend*	11	7	.611	2.09	26	26	3	0	0	0	163.1	128	50	38	2	11	65	1	150	7
Braz Davis, Peoria	9	13	.409	2.98	27	27	6	0	0	0	163.0	140	68	54	9	4	66	1	150	11
Bret Davis, Rockford	6	4	.600	2.98	38	3	0	10	0	0	90.2	91	41	30	4	3	25	1	83	9
DeAngelis, Quad City*	0	0	.000	9.00	1	0	0	1	0	0	2.0	2	1	0	0	0	0	0	2	0
DeJaynes, Quad City	0	0	.000	6.52	8	0	0	5	0	0	9.2	13	9	7	0	0	3	0	7	2
DeLaCruz, South Bend	7	3	.700	2.30	11	11	1	0	0	0	74.1	61	31	19	1	7	28	0	64	4
DeLaRosa, Clinton	3	5	.375	3.64	43	6	0	16	0	3	99.0	101	51	40	5	7	44	1	75	3
Dour, Clinton	2	5	.286	2.98	10	10	0	0	0	0	57.1	59	22	19	1	2	13	1	32	0
Drake, Beloit	1	1	.500	8.31	2	2	0	0	0	0	8.2	13	8	8	1	1	4	0	9	0
Drezek, Appleton*	1	2	.333	3.28	31	1	0	11	0	1	46.2	40	25	17	2	6	42	2	28	9
Drohan, Appleton	6	1	.857	1.32	9	9	1	0	0	0	54.2	41	13	8	0	0	15	0	35	2
Duvall, Springfield	2	5	.286	3.95	13	13	0	0	0	0	66.0	61	45	29	3	3	38	0	49	7
Economy, Cedar Rapids	5	1	.833	2.66	38	2	0	12	0	4	81.1	50	33	24	3	4	41	3	86	14
Eddings, Peoria	3	3	.500	1.20	38	0	0	25	0	11	75.0	61	13	10	3	5	8	2	47	1
Eldred, Beloit	2	1	.667	2.30	5	5	0	0	0	0	31.1	23	10	8	0	1	11	1	32	2
Eldredge, Wausau	1	1	.500	7.11	14	0	0	5	0	0	12.2	12	14	10	1	2	14	0	12	1
Erb, Quad City	11	4	.733	2.69	25	24	4	0	3	0	147.1	113	57	44	5	5	43	1	161	9
Espino, Peoria	1	0	1.000	3.63	12	0	0	6	0	0	22.1	19	11	9	1	2	12	0	13	3
Estes, Clinton*	2	5	.286	1.98	39	0	0	22	0	4	86.1	68	22	19	1	9	32	14	75	0
Faccio, Springfield	7	9	.438	4.63	27	27	3	0	1	0	147.2	150	84	76	7	5	61	0	126	9
Felix, Wausau*	4	5	.444	4.14	38	6	0	17	0	1	67.1	59	40	31	5	1	50	1	83	14
Figueroa, Waterloo	0	0	.000	10.61	21	0	0	8	0	0	28.0	33	33	33	5	4	24	0	16	7
Fitzgerald, Beloit*	10	9	.526	2.95	27	25	6	1	2	1	167.2	139	71	55	9	6	73	0	108	7
Foley, Madison	4	6	.400	3.98	33	11	0	12	0	1	108.2	98	56	48	7	8	63	0	80	13
Foster, Cedar Rapids	0	3	.000	2.14	51	0	0	47	0	23	59.0	46	16	14	2	5	19	6	55	5
Fowler, Waterloo	5	8	.385	2.95	41	5	0	16	0	7	119.0	109	47	39	4	6	46	1	56	3
Freed, Rockford	13	8	.619	2.29	26	26	3	0	3	0	192.2	164	67	49	2	3	49	1	121	13
Fuller, South Bend	0	0	.000	4.50	5	0	0	1	0	1	10.0	6	5	5	0	1	7	0	10	0
Furcal, Wausau*	3	1	.750	1.64	4	3	0	0	0	0	22.0	18	7	4	1	0	6	0	20	0
Fye, Madison	6	6	.500	2.48	15	8	3	1	0	0	69.0	45	28	19	2	0	46	3	54	9
Galindez, Waterloo*	2	12	.143	6.47	33	19	1	7	0	1	104.1	127	85	75	13	9	63	1	57	8
Galvan, South Bend*	4	1	.800	2.14	16	0	0	7	0	1	33.2	18	8	8	1	2	19	1	34	5
Garces, Kenosha	9	10	.474	3.41	24	24	4	0	1	0	142.2	117	70	54	5	5	62	1	84	5
Garcia, Madison	5	14	.263	4.60	27	25	3	0	2	0	139.0	146	87	71	6	15	65	0	110	9
Gardiner, Wausau	4	0	1.000	0.59	15	1	0	11	0	7	30.1	21	5	2	0	1	10	0	48	0
Garrison, Clinton*	1	1	.500	4.03	18	0	0	7	0	0	22.1	25	17	10	0	0	20	1	24	3
Gewecke, Springfield*	2	0	1.000	5.57	13	2	0	6	0	0	21.0	20	14	13	3	1	14	0	9	1
Ghelfi, Clinton	1	2	.333	2.27	12	0	0	6	0	1	35.2	30	13	9	3	1	4	1	25	0
M. Gibbons, Rockford	3	2	.600	1.76	40	0	0	19	0	2	61.1	51	17	12	2	5	11	6	63	0
W. Gibbons, Clinton	0	0	.000	2.08	5	0	0	2	0	0	8.2	11	4	2	1	0	4	0	6	3
Golmont, Madison	3	4	.429	4.05	31	0	0	5	0	2	66.2	67	41	30	1	3	37	0	67	5
Gomez, Peoria	0	0	.000	0.00	3	0	0	2	0	0	3.0	4	1	0	0	1	0	1	0	1
Gould, Clinton*	0	1	.000	15.43	1	1	0	0	0	0	2.1	2	4	4	0	0	4	0	1	0
Grayson, Beloit	0	0	.000	3.86	3	0	0	0	0	0	7.0	12	6	3	1	1	0	0	4	0
Grimes, Springfield	6	6	.500	2.00	62	0	0	22	0	1	90.0	83	27	20	3	2	30	11	67	1
Guzman, Springfield	3	3	.500	3.74	9	9	1	0	0	0	45.2	41	26	19	3	2	21	0	36	1
Hancock, Clinton*	4	7	.364	5.88	18	17	0	0	0	0	72.0	63	53	47	5	5	77	0	62	17
Hanselman, Clinton	1	11	.083	4.80	15	15	1	0	0	0	86.1	81	55	46	5	3	56	1	37	6
Harris, Madison*	6	10	.375	3.29	25	23	2	1	1	0	150.1	151	66	55	11	2	34	1	105	13
Hart, Waterloo	7	7	.500	3.27	28	13	0	4	0	0	104.2	90	49	38	5	3	40	3	53	8
Harvey, Appleton	13	7	.650	3.51	26	25	4	0	1	0	141.0	148	72	55	7	8	70	0	115	11
M. Hernandez, Clinton*	2	2	.500	7.83	8	4	0	0	0	0	23.0	30	24	20	4	0	21	0	20	0
R. Hernandez, South Bend	1	1	.500	3.33	4	4	0	0	0	0	24.1	19	9	9	1	0	7	0	17	0
Hester, Cedar Rapids	10	7	.588	3.50	27	26	4	0	2	0	167.1	152	83	65	22	3	50	2	89	5
Hoeme, Appleton	4	5	.444	3.32	29	12	0	1	0	0	89.1	83	47	33	9	7	57	0	73	10

Pitcher—Club	W.	L.	Pct.	ERA.	G.	GS.	CG.	GF.	ShO.	Sv.	IP.	H.	R.	ER.	HR.	HB.	BB.	Int. BB.	SO.	WP.
Hofer, Appleton	2	2	.500	3.48	23	0	0	11	0	2	41.1	30	19	16	5	2	25	1	25	0
Holzemer, Quad City*	12	7	.632	3.36	25	25	3	0	1	0	139.1	122	68	52	4	5	64	1	131	12
Howze, Rockford	8	12	.400	5.08	26	26	2	0	0	0	136.1	135	98	77	9	4	82	0	55	12
Hoyer, Waterloo*	1	6	.143	5.48	33	13	0	6	0	1	95.1	111	67	58	7	2	35	2	44	5
Huth, Appleton	2	2	.500	3.81	13	3	0	2	0	1	28.1	22	16	12	2	1	22	0	23	3
Jeffery, Cedar Rapids	11	3	.786	2.04	14	14	4	0	1	0	97.0	69	24	22	4	3	20	0	73	10
Ca. Johnson, Kenosha	1	1	.500	3.79	18	0	0	5	0	1	38.0	30	18	16	3	11	24	0	33	5
Ch. Johnson, Beloit	9	9	.500	3.18	25	22	2	2	1	0	138.2	118	63	49	8	13	50	0	118	5
D. Johnson, Clinton	0	4	.000	5.79	8	7	0	0	0	0	37.1	42	29	24	2	2	28	0	30	3
L. Johnson, South Bend	5	0	1.000	1.48	13	4	1	3	1	1	42.2	29	7	7	1	2	18	0	37	1
Jones, South Bend	0	0	.000	4.91	3	0	0	1	0	0	3.2	6	3	2	0	0	2	0	2	0
Karasinski, Burlington*	6	8	.429	3.42	29	16	4	3	1	1	123.2	137	53	47	9	2	33	1	61	5
Kelly, Burlington*	0	8	.000	6.06	11	10	1	1	0	0	49.0	61	40	33	4	4	34	0	29	6
Kerrigan, Rockford	5	5	.500	1.98	45	0	0	35	0	12	59.0	44	19	13	1	0	22	3	43	4
Kiefer, Beloit	9	6	.600	2.32	30	15	7	5	2	1	131.2	106	44	34	4	8	32	2	100	6
Kisten, Springfield	1	6	.143	2.91	57	0	0	52	0	37	65.0	45	30	21	7	4	31	6	61	5
Krippner, Beloit	8	9	.471	4.06	23	22	3	1	2	0	130.2	101	63	59	13	7	75	1	133	8
Krol, Kenosha	3	4	.429	4.03	16	5	0	6	0	0	60.1	65	34	27	3	5	23	4	57	2
Kryzanowski, Kenosha	4	7	.364	3.02	46	0	0	26	0	6	86.1	73	33	29	8	4	43	8	52	8
Kuhn, Waterloo*	0	0	.000	6.75	1	0	0	1	0	0	1.1	2	1	1	0	0	0	0	1	0
Kurczewski, Burlington	0	0	.000	27.00	3	0	0	1	0	0	2.2	6	8	8	1	1	8	0	3	3
Landry, Beloit	1	5	.167	6.48	10	10	0	0	0	0	41.2	52	37	30	4	2	35	0	25	5
Lane, Beloit	4	9	.308	4.55	17	16	5	1	0	0	97.0	100	61	49	4	8	37	2	59	6
Lawrence, Springfield	13	9	.591	2.58	34	23	7	2	1	0	170.2	156	64	49	3	6	44	1	98	13
Lawson, Madison	5	3	.625	3.90	33	5	0	11	0	2	83.0	72	42	36	2	2	43	2	67	11
Lebron, Waterloo	2	9	.182	4.99	34	20	3	5	0	0	124.1	131	77	69	14	6	69	0	66	9
Liss, Wausau*	2	4	.333	5.48	8	8	0	0	0	0	44.1	58	28	27	9	2	20	2	30	1
Longuil, Burlington	7	7	.500	3.78	31	5	1	16	1	5	81.0	75	43	34	6	3	41	3	73	7
Looper, Springfield	0	0	.000	0.00	1	0	0	1	0	0	1.0	1	1	0	0	0	1	0	3	1
Lopez, Peoria	18	8	.692	2.92	28	28	8	0	3	0	200.2	187	73	65	9	7	31	1	141	6
Love, Madison*	0	0	.000	0.00	1	0	0	1	0	0	1.0	0	0	0	0	0	2	0	0	0
Ludy, Beloit	0	3	.000	6.30	9	0	0	7	0	0	10.0	11	8	7	0	0	3	2	15	0
MacLeod, Madison*	4	3	.571	3.49	11	10	0	0	0	0	56.2	44	27	22	3	1	35	0	46	3
Magee, Appleton*	0	2	.000	7.11	15	0	0	6	0	1	19.0	23	22	15	2	4	13	0	14	5
Mahomes, Kenosha	13	7	.650	3.28	25	25	3	0	1	0	156.1	120	66	57	4	2	100	3	167	9
Marchese, Quad City	2	3	.400	1.82	49	0	0	23	0	6	79.0	54	20	16	2	4	40	5	77	5
Marrero, Beloit	0	0	.000	2.25	1	0	0	1	0	0	4.0	2	1	1	0	0	1	0	1	0
Marsh, Cedar Rapids	6	5	.545	2.03	49	3	0	17	0	3	111.0	83	39	25	5	6	41	2	75	8
Marshall, South Bend	1	6	.143	3.75	40	0	0	14	0	0	72.0	71	41	30	7	2	26	5	58	4
Marte, Springfield	3	3	.500	5.55	24	8	0	6	0	0	58.1	53	43	36	1	7	43	0	41	5
Martin, Quad City	0	3	.000	7.25	9	4	0	4	0	0	22.1	31	19	18	2	1	16	0	10	2
Massicotte, Peoria	3	3	.500	2.82	35	5	0	13	0	1	92.2	82	41	29	2	6	47	3	69	12
Masters, Madison	1	1	.500	14.04	4	0	0	0	0	0	8.1	20	15	13	2	1	6	0	4	0
Maye, Madison	1	4	.200	4.18	16	0	0	10	0	0	32.1	44	24	15	1	2	12	0	21	2
McCarthy, Cedar Rapids*	5	0	1.000	1.51	30	0	0	11	0	1	53.2	38	13	9	1	1	21	3	39	4
McClure, Kenosha	2	0	1.000	3.29	33	0	0	26	0	15	38.1	35	16	14	1	1	21	1	50	4
McCormick, Appleton*	8	5	.615	3.42	20	20	2	0	1	0	121.0	115	55	46	7	3	46	0	88	6
M. McGuire, Wausau	6	5	.545	4.18	19	16	1	2	0	0	94.2	89	53	44	12	3	58	0	79	5
S. McGuire, Quad City	3	6	.333	3.79	15	13	1	1	1	0	71.1	78	38	30	6	3	22	1	38	1
Meamber, Springfield	10	8	.556	3.19	37	16	4	7	2	0	138.1	141	53	49	6	2	37	2	82	5
Meister, Burlington	0	0	.000	7.58	12	0	0	6	0	0	19.0	27	17	16	1	1	8	0	17	0
Merigliano, South Bend	11	4	.733	2.91	19	19	4	0	1	0	111.1	92	46	36	3	6	47	0	101	5
Milchin, Springfield*	3	2	.600	2.14	6	6	1	0	0	0	42.0	30	14	10	3	0	11	1	44	2
Minchey, 15 Rock-11 Bur	5	12	.294	4.67	26	26	1	0	0	0	156.0	154	88	81	8	5	82	2	87	22
Mirabella, Beloit	0	0	.000	0.00	2	0	0	0	0	0	5.0	3	0	0	0	0	6	0	6	0
Miranda, Beloit*	6	5	.545	0.86	43	0	0	40	0	16	63.0	39	13	6	1	1	32	6	88	3
Misuraca, Kenosha	1	5	.167	5.28	9	9	0	0	0	0	46.0	47	32	27	9	5	15	0	30	1
Mitchener, South Bend	6	4	.600	4.15	33	8	0	12	0	3	78.0	81	44	36	4	2	52	4	41	7
Morton, Waterloo	7	7	.500	2.78	47	1	0	33	0	8	100.1	97	43	31	9	5	27	3	68	10
Muh, Kenosha*	10	11	.476	4.40	26	26	6	0	0	0	157.1	132	95	77	8	8	100	4	141	16
Murphy, Quad City	5	5	.500	2.83	39	2	0	15	0	1	70.0	55	37	22	2	7	36	1	46	6
Murray, Wausau	0	0	.000	0.00	7	0	0	6	0	0	10.0	2	0	0	2	5	1	0	13	0
Mutz, Quad City	3	2	.600	2.38	18	3	1	6	0	1	56.2	37	16	15	1	3	18	1	45	1
J. Myers, Clinton	4	12	.250	3.73	32	21	0	5	0	0	137.2	139	71	57	6	9	58	5	63	11
M. Myers, Cedar Rapids	11	9	.550	3.29	27	27	5	0	3	0	175.0	161	70	64	14	3	50	2	135	4
Nabholz, Rockford*	13	5	.722	2.18	24	23	3	0	3	0	161.1	132	54	39	6	0	41	0	149	11
Neagle, Kenosha*	2	1	.667	1.65	6	6	1	0	1	0	43.2	25	9	8	3	1	16	0	40	1
Newman, Kenosha*	3	9	.250	2.84	18	18	1	0	0	0	88.2	65	41	28	2	4	74	0	82	3
Nied, Burlington	5	6	.455	3.83	13	12	2	0	1	0	80.0	78	38	34	3	5	23	0	73	3
Nocas, Appleton	1	1	.500	5.40	8	1	0	1	0	0	15.0	13	14	9	1	0	12	0	16	1
North, Kenosha*	3	1	.750	2.43	19	6	1	0	0	0	63.0	51	18	17	0	2	26	3	48	6
Novoa, Clinton*	5	4	.556	2.54	13	10	0	0	0	0	63.2	58	20	18	1	4	18	1	61	1
Oropeza, Rockford	0	0	.000	2.25	9	1	0	5	0	0	16.0	12	5	4	1	0	7	0	11	2
Ortiz, Kenosha*	0	0	.000	0.00	1	0	0	0	0	0	1.0	0	0	0	0	0	0	0	0	0
Osik, Appleton	0	2	.000	4.87	5	3	0	1	0	0	20.1	18	12	11	1	1	9	0	18	2
Otto, Appleton	6	7	.462	3.42	43	7	2	21	1	3	113.0	114	49	43	5	3	23	2	60	3
Pall, South Bend	0	0	.000	0.00	2	0	0	0	0	0	3.1	1	0	0	0	0	4	0	4	0
Pardo, Quad City	5	9	.357	4.03	27	18	0	1	0	0	116.0	101	60	52	11	6	54	1	88	3
Parmenter, Peoria	0	2	.000	2.39	8	2	0	3	0	1	26.1	22	9	7	2	0	11	1	23	0
Parnell, Appleton	2	3	.400	2.01	46	0	0	43	0	28	53.2	37	18	12	2	5	15	0	63	1
Patrick, Madison	2	5	.286	3.64	12	10	0	1	0	0	54.1	62	29	22	4	0	14	0	32	3
Perschke, South Bend	0	2	.000	3.10	13	0	0	8	0	1	20.1	19	10	7	0	1	2	0	16	2
Piatt, Rockford	2	2	.500	3.20	11	0	0	3	0	0	19.2	19	7	7	1	1	11	1	24	2
Pichardo, Appleton	5	4	.556	2.97	12	12	0	0	0	0	75.2	58	29	25	4	5	18	0	50	5
Pierce, Appleton*	3	4	.429	3.73	31	3	0	11	0	5	62.2	47	34	26	5	4	34	1	54	6
Pitcher, Wausau	1	4	.200	2.45	49	1	0	35	0	11	69.2	58	24	19	3	4	23	2	58	4
Plemel, Springfield	5	2	.714	1.78	11	11	2	0	1	0	76.0	61	22	15	4	2	16	0	62	4
Pomeranz, Kenosha*	4	5	.444	2.99	31	7	1	11	0	4	81.1	61	41	27	2	9	47	2	54	5
Powell, Cedar Rapids*	7	4	.636	3.54	13	13	1	0	1	0	76.1	68	37	30	4	1	23	0	58	4
Radinsky, South Bend*	7	5	.583	1.75	53	0	0	49	0	31	61.2	39	21	12	1	5	19	2	83	2
Rambo, Clinton	4	4	.500	3.26	12	11	0	0	0	0	66.1	59	27	24	7	3	19	3	63	2
S. Reed, Clinton	5	3	.625	1.05	60	0	0	50	0	26	94.2	54	16	11	1	7	38	10	104	0
W. Reed, Waterloo*	6	15	.286	4.43	31	23	4	2	1	1	140.1	145	85	69	14	16	81	1	83	17

Pitcher—Club	W.	L.	Pct.	ERA.	G.	GS.	CG.	GF.	ShO.	Sv.	IP.	H.	R.	ER.	HR.	HB.	BB.	Int. BB.	SO.	WP.
Regira, Rockford	2	2	.500	2.17	14	5	0	2	0	0	45.2	37	15	11	0	2	24	2	44	6
Reilley, Wausau	3	3	.500	5.81	43	0	0	16	0	3	79.0	92	65	51	5	2	42	5	80	14
Reis, Burlington	7	5	.583	3.32	34	8	2	15	0	1	116.2	112	49	43	6	2	34	5	54	9
Ricci, Waterloo	10	12	.455	2.98	29	25	9	1	0	0	181.1	160	89	60	11	12	59	5	89	14
Richardson, Springfield°	4	2	.667	2.62	51	0	0	11	0	0	55.0	41	18	16	2	2	22	4	45	4
Risley, Cedar Rapids	9	10	.474	3.90	27	27	2	0	0	0	140.2	87	72	61	9	6	81	2	128	19
Robinson, Peoria	15	9	.625	2.79	28	28	5	0	3	0	187.1	177	80	58	4	6	56	0	160	12
Rodriguez, Cedar Rapids°	2	1	.667	8.04	11	0	0	4	0	0	15.2	13	15	14	2	2	12	1	7	0
Rogers, Clinton°	13	8	.619	2.55	29	28	4	0	0	0	169.1	128	74	48	4	6	78	1	168	5
Rose, Springfield°	0	1	.000	1.50	5	0	0	1	0	0	6.0	7	5	1	0	0	5	0	4	0
Rovasio, Kenosha	0	3	.000	2.65	22	0	0	16	0	4	37.1	26	19	11	2	1	23	1	56	6
Ryan, Wausau	7	4	.636	2.73	15	14	1	1	1	0	85.2	76	35	26	4	2	16	1	57	2
Sala, Springfield°	0	0	.000	3.74	13	0	0	5	0	0	21.2	20	10	9	2	3	15	0	17	2
Salles, Peoria	9	8	.529	2.48	21	21	2	0	0	0	138.0	137	60	38	4	5	30	1	73	10
Sandoval, Beloit	3	3	.500	4.32	30	0	0	13	0	1	75.0	64	40	36	7	5	43	4	77	6
Satterfield, Springfield	15	8	.652	2.87	27	27	2	0	1	0	169.1	151	66	54	9	7	45	0	113	5
Schrenk, South Bend	5	2	.714	4.33	16	16	1	0	1	0	79.0	71	44	38	6	8	44	1	49	9
Search, Quad City°	0	0	.000	4.05	3	0	0	0	0	0	6.2	6	3	3	1	0	2	0	10	2
Sharko, Clinton	1	1	.500	2.02	16	0	0	9	0	2	35.2	25	9	8	3	0	22	0	26	2
Shelton, Peoria	0	0	.000	0.00	1	0	0	1	0	0	1.0	0	0	0	0	0	0	0	0	0
Shifflett, Appleton	3	3	.500	4.15	18	2	0	5	0	0	39.0	34	25	18	1	2	19	2	13	8
Shiflett, Rockford	0	1	.000	3.38	18	4	0	5	0	1	32.0	29	16	12	0	1	24	0	25	3
Slocumb, Peoria	5	3	.625	1.78	49	0	0	43	0	22	55.2	31	16	11	0	1	33	4	52	6
Slomkowski, Waterloo	3	4	.429	4.54	43	2	1	24	0	3	85.1	79	50	43	8	11	48	3	28	6
Smith, Peoria	0	0	.000	0.00	2	0	0	2	0	0	2.0	0	1	0	0	0	1	0	2	0
Sodders, Peoria°	14	7	.667	2.98	28	28	6	0	1	0	202.1	180	80	67	13	5	51	1	177	7
Stancel, Madison	0	1	.000	3.24	8	0	0	7	0	3	8.1	8	7	3	0	0	4	0	5	0
Stoerck, Wausau	3	2	.600	3.49	12	11	1	1	0	0	69.2	67	30	27	8	2	21	1	36	3
Stroud, Peoria°	3	2	.600	2.62	40	0	0	12	0	2	44.2	28	18	13	1	1	20	2	58	3
Studeman, Appleton	0	1	.000	8.10	5	0	0	3	0	0	3.1	3	5	3	1	0	5	0	4	0
Swanson, Kenosha	3	1	.750	2.33	11	0	0	4	0	0	27.0	20	7	7	1	0	11	3	14	1
S. Taylor, Wausau	9	7	.563	3.22	16	16	6	0	2	0	106.1	92	49	38	5	6	37	1	65	8
W. Taylor, Madison	4	3	.571	2.47	35	0	0	23	0	6	54.2	38	18°	15	3	0	28	0	37	3
Throckmorton, Burlington	0	0	.000	4.50	1	0	0	1	0	0	2.0	2	1	1	0	0	0	0	3	0
Townsend, Quad City°	0	0	.000	1.23	9	0	0	3	0	2	7.1	6	1	1	0	1	4	0	4	0
Trombley, Kenosha	5	1	.833	3.12	12	3	0	6	0	2	49.0	45	23	17	1	3	13	0	41	4
Turek, Cedar Rapids	9	11	.450	3.74	25	25	0	0	0	0	149.0	120	77	62	10	7	77	1	138	11
Upshaw, Burlington°	5	3	.625	2.09	12	12	2	0	0	0	90.1	67	31	21	2	5	24	1	100	2
Vanderwel, Quad City	1	6	.143	4.84	22	9	0	7	0	0	48.1	43	33	26	1	4	42	0	37	9
Vaughn, Appleton	5	6	.455	4.04	15	14	0	0	0	0	75.2	76	48	34	4	2	24	0	43	4
Vazquez, Burlington	0	0	.000	6.55	2	2	0	0	0	0	11.0	13	11	8	1	0	4	0	10	1
Vegely, Quad City°	5	5	.500	3.89	48	0	0	13	0	2	69.1	68	38	30	3	5	28	3	57	1
Ventura, South Bend	7	3	.700	1.57	29	10	2	8	2	1	115.0	74	36	20	4	8	50	1	87	4
Vierra, Cedar Rapids°	5	3	.625	1.70	47	0	0	28	0	7	74.1	43	22	14	4	4	20	3	81	3
Voit, Beloit	0	0	.000	7.71	4	0	0	3	0	0	9.1	7	8	8	0	4	8	0	11	0
Wagner, Appleton	6	11	.353	4.56	24	23	3	1	0	0	130.1	149	79	66	9	6	29	1	71	6
Wahl, Beloit	0	3	.000	8.10	7	0	0	4	0	1	10.0	15	15	9	1	0	8	0	4	0
Watson, Burlington	2	6	.250	4.46	14	14	2	0	1	0	82.2	88	47	41	6	3	43	1	65	9
Watts, Beloit	1	1	.500	2.43	16	0	0	10	0	1	37.0	30	13	10	0	2	18	1	26	2
Waznik, Burlington°	2	0	1.000	4.68	34	0	0	14	0	0	32.2	30	21	17	3	3	22	3	29	3
Weems, Burlington	2	5	.286	4.29	13	10	1	2	1	0	63.0	60	39	30	12	6	22	1	31	2
Wendell, Burlington	9	11	.450	2.21	22	22	9	0	5	0	159.0	127	63	39	7	3	41	1	153	1
Whitlock, Wausau°	3	4	.429	5.25	29	10	3	8	2	2	82.1	78	61	48	7	11	55	2	49	11
Wilkinson, Wausau	5	4	.556	5.40	17	12	0	0	0	0	60.0	56	45	36	9	4	34	0	59	6
Williams, Burlington	0	0	.000	0.00	4	0	0	2	0	0	2.0	1	0	0	0	0	2	0	1	0
Winston, Rockford°	7	1	.875	1.52	47	0	0	30	0	16	65.0	52	16	11	0	0	11	0	70	7
Wright, Burlington	5	1	.833	2.10	40	0	0	29	0	13	55.2	47	23	13	2	2	19	6	45	3
Zappelli, Quad City	5	3	.625	1.85	48	0	0	41	0	22	68.0	44	15	14	2	3	21	2	71	1
Zarranz, Peoria	0	1	.000	4.50	7	0	0	5	0	2	10.0	12	6	5	1	0	2	1	14	0

BALKS—Merigliano, 11; Bret Davis, Hoyer, Newman, Salles, 9 each; G. Carter, Risley, Vegely, 8 each; Rogers, Slomkowski, 7 each; Dabney, Garces, Novoa, Wendell, 6 each; Abbott, Foster, Howze, L. Johnson, 5 each; Economy, Garcia, Guzman, Harris, Holzemer, Krippner, Lane, Misuraca, Pichardo, Regira, W. Taylor, 4 each; Borgatti, Brutcher, Cangemi, Cornelius, Czarnik, Braz Davis, DeLaCruz, DeLaRosa, Dour, Felix, Hanselman, Harvey, M. Hernandez, Karasinski, Lopez, Ludy, Mahomes, Masters, Murphy, Powell, W. Reed, Ryan, Satterfield, Shifflett, Shiflett, S. Taylor, Trombley, Turek, Vanderwel, Vaughn, Whitlock, Wilkinson, Zappelli, 3 each; Ariola, Backus, Carmody, Eldred, Erb, Freed, Galindez, Garrison, Gewecke, Hancock, Hester, Hoeme, Ch. Johnson, D. Johnson, Krol, Landry, Liss, MacLeod, Marshall, McCormick, M. McGuire, S. McGuire, Morton, Murray, Nabholz, Nocas, Otto, Patrick, Radinsky, Reis, Sharko, Stroud, Upshaw, Zarranz, 2 each; Alleyne, Bennett, Breitenbucher, Briscoe, E. Bryant, Burnau, Buzzard, L. Carter, R. Carter, Cooper, Cummings, Duvall, Eldredge, Faccio, Fitzgerald, Fowler, Fuller, Furcal, Fye, Ghelfi, Hofer, Huth, Jeffery, Ca. Johnson, Kelly, Kerrigan, Kryzanowski, Lawrence, Lebron, Longuil, Marchese, Marsh, Marte, Maye, McCarthy, Meamber, Milchin, Minchey, Miranda, Mitchener, Mutz, Nied, Parnell, Perschke, Pierce, Pitcher, Plemel, Pomeranz, Rambo, Reilley, Ricci, Richardson, Rovasio, Sandoval, Sodders, Stoerck, Vierra, Wagner, Wahl, Watson, Watts, Weems, Winston, 1 each.

COMBINATION SHUTOUTS—Drohan-Hofer-Parnell, McCormack-Nocas-Parnell, Wagner-Studeman, Harvey-Parnell, Hoeme-Parnell, Harvey-Shifflett, Hoeme-Otto-Parnell, Wagner-Parnell, Pichardo-Drezek-Parnell, Vaughn-Alexander, Appleton; Landry-Watts, Krippner-Carter-Miranda, Fitzgerald-Miranda, Johnson-Sandoval-Carmody-Carter, Kiefer-Cangemi-Carmody-Miranda, Eldred-Miranda, Mirabella-Kiefer-Carmody-Miranda, Beloit; Wendell-Czarnik, Czarnik-Longuil-Wright, Burlington; Jeffery-Vierra-Foster, Risley-McCarthy-Foster 2, Jeffery-Marsh-Vierra, Jeffery-Vierra, Myers-McCarthy-Foster, Myers-Foster, Myers-Economy-Foster, Turek-Marsh, Powell-Foster, Cedar Rapids; Rogers-Reed 2, Novoa-Reed 2, Rogers-Estes, Hancock-Fye, DeLaRosa-Estes, Myers-Estes, Rambo-Estes-Reed, Rambo-DeLaRosa, Rambo-Ghelfi, Clinton; Newman-Rovasio-Johnson, Mahomes-North, Pomeranz-McClure, Garces-Kryzanowski-Rovasio, Kenosha; Harris-Taylor, Mac-Leod-Golmont-Lawson-Chitren, Madison; Robinson-Stroud-Slocumb, Parmenter-Espino, Robinson-Slocumb, Davis-Slocumb, Sodders-Eddings, Peoria; Erb-Zappelli, Carter-Zappelli-Marchese, Carter-Zappelli, Mutz-Marchese, McGuire-Murphy-Marchese, Pardo-Vegely-Marchese, Pardo-Marchese-Vegely-Murphy, Holzemer-Marchese-Mutz, Carter-Vegely, Carter-Vegely-Vanderwel, Carter-Zappelli-Townsend, Quad City; Freed-Buzzard-Alleyne, Nabholz-Bromby-Gibbons, Alleyne-Davis-Winston, Nabholz-Davis, Nabholz-Winston, Rockford; Dabney-Radinsky 2, Ventura-Radinsky, Dabney-Mitchener, Mitchener-Radinsky, Schrenk-Ventura-Marshall, South Bend; Faccio-Grimes, Satterfield-Richardson-Kisten, Satterfield-Grimes-Richardson-Kisten, Marte-Grimes-Kisten, Lawrence-Richardson-Kisten, Springfield; Hart-Morton, Waterloo; Taylor-Gardiner-Kisten, Beloit, Bennett-Gardiner, McGuire-Pitcher, Bennett-Reilley-Burnau, Wilkinson-Burnau, Stoerck-Burnau-Pitcher, Ryan-Felix-Burnau, Ryan-Felix-Pitcher, Wausau.

NO-HIT GAMES—Krippner, Beloit, defeated Madison, 1-0, May 26; Ryan, Wausau, defeated Clinton, 2-0, July 29.

NY-Pennsylvania League

CLASS A

CHAMPIONSHIP WINNERS IN PREVIOUS YEARS

1939—Olean*	.631	1958—Wellsville	.556	1976—Elmira	.727
1940—Olean*	.625	Geneva (2nd)†	.548	Elmira	.703
1941—Jamestown	.618	1959—Wellsville†	.635	1977—Oneonta y	.671
Bradford (2nd)†	.549	1960—Erie	.643	Batavia	.600
1942—Jamestown*	.672	Wellsville (2nd)†	.535	1978—Oneonta	.729
1943—Lockport	.591	1961—Geneva	.616	Geneva z	.718
Wellsville (3rd)†	.532	Olean (4th)†	.512	1979—Geneva	.725
1944—Lockport	.608	1962—Jamestown	.580	Oneonta z	.618
Jamestown (2nd)†	.565	Auburn (3rd)†	.521	1980—Oneonta y	.662
1945—Batavia*	.677	1963—Auburn	.585	Geneva	.649
1946—Jamestown‡	.672	Batavia (3rd)†	.485	1981—Oneonta y	.658
Batavia‡	.672	1964—Auburn§	.622	Jamestown	.649
1947—Jamestown*	.690	1965—Binghamton	.677	1982—Oneonta	.566
1948—Lockport*	.603	Binghamton	.607	Niagara Falls y	.553
1949—Bradford*	.635	1966—Auburn x	.620	1983—Utica y	.649
1950—Hornell	.653	Binghamton	.646	Newark	.649
Olean (2nd)†	.568	1967—Auburn	.667	1984—Newark	.622
1951—Olean	.622	1968—Auburn	.645	Little Falls y	.587
Hornell (3rd)†	.568	Oneonta (2nd)*	.558	1985—Oneonta*	.705
1952—Hamilton	.659	1969—Oneonta	.662	Auburn	.603
Jamestown (2nd)†	.643	1970—Oneonta	.623	1986—Oneonta	.766
1953—Jamestown*	.704	1971—Oneonta	.662	St. Catharines z	.632
1954—Corning*	.621	1972—Niagara Falls	.686	1987—Geneva z	.632
1955—Hamilton*	.656	1973—Auburn	.667	Watertown	.579
1956—Wellsville*	.617	1974—Oneonta	.768	1988—Oneonta y	.632
1957—Wellsville	.632	1975—Newark	.688	Jamestown	.618
Erie (2nd)†	.598	Newark	.714		

*Won championship and four-club playoff. †Won four-club playoff. ‡Jamestown and Batavia declared co-champions; Batavia defeated Jamestown in final of four-club playoff. §Won championship and two-club playoff. xWon split-season playoff. yLeague divided into Eastern and Western Divisions; won playoff. zLeague divided into Wrigley and Yawkey Divisions; won playoff. (NOTE—Known as Pennsylvania-Ontario-New York League from 1939 through 1956.)

STANDING OF CLUBS AT CLOSE OF SEASON, SEPTEMBER 4

EASTERN DIVISION

Club	W.	L.	T.	Pct.	G.B.
Pittsfield (Mets)	53	23	0	.697	....
Oneonta (Yankees)	48	27	0	.640	4½
Watertown (Indians)	47	30	0	.610	6½
Utica (White Sox)	39	39	0	.500	15
Geneva (Cubs)	36	39	0	.480	16½
Auburn (Astros)	35	42	0	.455	18½
Elmira (Red Sox)	30	46	0	.395	23

WESTERN DIVISION

Club	W.	L.	T.	Pct.	G.B.
Jamestown (Expos)	44	32	0	.579	....
Niagara Falls (Tigers)	43	33	0	.566	1
Batavia (Phillies)	37	39	0	.487	7
Welland (Pirates)	32	44	0	.421	12
Hamilton (Cardinals)	32	44	0	.421	12
St. Catharines (Blue Jays)	31	45	0	.408	13
Erie (Orioles)	25	49	0	.338	18

COMPOSITE STANDING OF CLUBS AT CLOSE OF SEASON, SEPTEMBER 4

Club	Pit.	Ont.	Wat.	Jam.	N.F.	Uti.	Bat.	Gen.	Aub.	Wel.	Ham.	St.C.	Elm.	Eri.	W.	L.	T.	Pct.	G.B.
Pittsfield (Mets)	...	6	6	3	4	3	4	6	3	3	3	7	3	7	53	23	0	.697	....
Oneonta (Yankees)	2	...	5	3	3	5	4	4	5	3	2	2	7	3	48	27	0	.640	4½
Watertown (Indians)	2	3	...	3	4	2	3	6	7	4	3	6	2	8	47	30	0	.610	6½
Jamestown (Expos)	1	1	0	...	6	3	4	3	2	5	4	5	2	8	44	32	0	.579	9
Niagara Falls (Tigers)	1	0	0	2	...	3	4	2	1	6	7	8	3	6	43	33	0	.566	10
Utica (White Sox)	6	3	6	1	1	...	2	2	4	2	2	2	5	3	39	39	0	.500	15
Batavia (Phillies)	1	0	1	4	4	2	...	3	3	3	4	5	2	5	37	39	0	.487	16
Geneva (Cubs)	4	3	2	0	1	6	3	...	4	3	2	3	3	2	36	39	0	.480	16½
Auburn (Astros)	3	1	3	2	3	4	1	4	...	2	4	1	4	5	35	42	0	.455	18½
Welland (Pirates)	1	1	0	3	4	2	5	1	1	...	5	3	1	5	32	44	0	.421	21
Hamilton (Cardinals)	1	1	2	4	1	2	4	2	0	2	...	5	2	6	32	44	0	.421	21
St. Catharines (Blue Jays)	1	2	1	3	0	2	3	1	3	5	5	...	1	4	31	45	0	.408	22
Elmira (Red Sox)	1	3	2	2	1	3	2	5	4	3	2	1	...	1	30	46	0	.395	23
Erie (Orioles)	0	1	2	2	2	1	1	2	2	3	4	3	1	...	25	49	0	.338	27

Major league affiliations in parentheses.

Playoffs—Jamestown defeated Pittsfield, two games to one, to win league championship.

Regular-Season Attendance—Auburn, 38,155; Batavia, 38,704; Elmira, 56,595; Erie, 56,025; Geneva, 32,252; Hamilton, 60,192; Jamestown, 35,039; Niagara Falls, 54,138; Oneonta, 52,955; Pittsfield, 96,931; St. Catharines, 31,594; Utica, 56,836; Watertown, 63,928; Welland, 41,217. Totals—714,561. Playoffs (3 games)—7,779.

Managers—Auburn, Reggie Waller; Batavia, Don McCormack; Elmira, Mike Verdi; Erie, Bobby Tolan; Geneva, Bill Hayes; Hamilton, Joe Pettini; Jamestown, Don Werner; Niagara Falls, Rick Magante; Oneonta, Brian Butterfield; Pittsfield, Tim Blackwell; St. Catharines, Bob Shirley; Utica, Ron Vaughn (through July 3); Mike Gellinger (July 4 through end of season); Watertown, Brian Graham; Welland, U.L. Washington. Managerial records of teams with more than one manager: Utica, Vaughn (8-10), Gellinger (31-29).

All-Star Team—1B—Howard Prager, Auburn; 2B—(tie) Eduardo Ortega, Batavia and Mica Lewis, Auburn; 3B—Fabio Gomez, Watertown; SS—William White, Geneva; OF—Sherman Obando, Oneonta; Brian Cornelius, Niagara Falls; Jeff Goodale, Niagara Falls; Todd Mayo, Jamestown; C—(tie) Carlos Mota, Watertown and Eric Albright, Niagara Falls; RHP—John Johnstone, Pittsfield; Shannon Jones, Geneva; LHP—Greg Langbehn, Pittsfield; Mike Gardella, Oneonta; DH—Marc Tepper, Watertown; Manager of the Year—Tim Blackwell, Pittsfield.

(Compiled by Howe Sportsdata International, Boston, Mass.)

CLUB BATTING

Club	Pct.	G.	AB.	R.	OR.	H.	TB.	2B.	3B.	HR.	RBI.	SH.	SF.	HP.	BB.	Int. BB.	SO.	SB.	CS.	LOB.
Pittsfield	.273	76	2516	390	284	687	979	111	41	33	326	31	21	24	245	7	534	134	49	511
Oneonta	.272	75	2510	404	284	683	959	114	27	36	330	25	24	38	256	12	443	106	45	521
Watertown	.269	77	2622	408	312	706	990	109	17	47	359	31	34	32	232	11	542	77	29	523
Niagara Falls	.263	76	2546	425	343	670	977	124	18	49	361	29	31	28	303	14	560	84	43	536
Auburn	.254	77	2519	362	426	639	931	110	28	42	304	23	26	27	240	11	662	173	60	480
Geneva	.249	75	2510	344	353	625	913	118	16	46	301	34	18	44	302	11	516	64	48	579
Utica	.243	78	2610	338	359	635	852	102	26	21	289	20	15	30	256	6	618	98	60	520
Welland	.242	76	2512	305	346	608	820	87	19	29	252	7	16	14	203	10	624	127	48	500
Erie	.242	74	2455	307	447	594	865	111	17	42	264	26	10	21	284	9	540	72	26	550
Jamestown	.241	76	2469	337	291	595	868	100	22	43	271	7	24	31	247	9	663	170	69	455
Batavia	.233	76	2554	305	299	596	825	94	12	37	253	25	20	23	239	8	545	63	36	532
Hamilton	.230	76	2425	284	339	558	800	101	21	33	235	3	23	22	247	5	580	99	54	484
St. Catharines	.223	76	2530	275	337	564	813	97	7	46	237	10	14	22	231	10	711	48	37	510
Elmira	.220	76	2446	267	331	538	754	95	14	31	216	34	14	31	223	6	631	106	69	464

INDIVIDUAL BATTING
(Leading Qualifiers for Batting Championship—211 or More Plate Appearances)

*Bats lefthanded.   †Switch-hitter.

Player and Club	Pct.	G.	AB.	R.	H.	TB.	2B.	3B.	HR.	RBI.	SH.	SF.	HP.	BB.	Int. BB.	SO.	SB.	CS.
Tepper, Marc, Watertown*	.347	68	245	37	85	120	16	2	5	46	1	1	0	24	1	33	2	1
Prager, Howard, Auburn*	.335	73	251	54	84	129	15	3	8	58	1	4	2	36	3	45	21	4
Gomez, Fabio, Watertown	.331	73	296	64	98	148	15	4	9	57	2	2	1	15	2	56	6	3
Harris, Keith, Utica	.326	57	193	30	63	80	6	4	1	27	0	4	4	21	1	36	14	12
White, William, Geneva	.323	68	254	44	82	112	19	1	3	29	2	1	3	43	0	36	16	5
Cornelius, Brian, Niagara Falls*	.319	68	273	47	87	109	13	0	3	24	3	0	0	22	3	44	11	9
Obando, Sherman, Oneonta	.312	70	276	50	86	133	23	3	6	45	1	2	6	16	1	45	8	5
Hudson, Deryk, Jamestown	.311	61	222	23	69	105	14	2	6	43	0	5	2	21	2	34	6	3
Hines, Timothy, Pittsfield*	.309	55	194	26	60	77	11	3	0	23	2	1	2	16	0	42	6	6
Butterfield, Christi, Pittsfield†	.304	71	260	51	79	132	13	8	8	47	2	3	5	30	2	63	14	6

Departmental Leaders: G—Kimberlin, Pennyfeather, Reimink, 75; AB—Gomez, 296; R—Gomez, 64; H—Gomez, 98; TB—Gomez, 148; 2B—Obando, 23; 3B—Butterfield, Howard, 8; HR—Kent, 13; RBI—Prager, 58; SH—Kimberlin, 11; SF—Albright, 7; HP—Hill, 13; BB—Benitez, Reimink, 50; IBB—Snow, 6; SO—Mobley, 108; SB—P. Howell, 45; CS—Jenkins, 13.

(All Players—Listed Alphabetically)

Player and Club	Pct.	G.	AB.	R.	H.	TB.	2B.	3B.	HR.	RBI.	SH.	SF.	HP.	BB.	Int. BB.	SO.	SB.	CS.
Abare, William, St. Catharines*	.172	54	180	12	31	39	5	0	1	5	0	0	0	32	0	76	0	0
Albright, Eric, Niagara Falls	.282	66	238	46	67	111	13	2	9	42	0	7	1	35	1	51	6	4
Allen, James, Hamilton	.286	4	14	3	4	4	0	0	0	1	0	0	1	1	0	4	1	0
Alvarez, David, Elmira*	.121	16	33	3	4	4	0	0	0	1	0	1	0	1	0	8	0	0
Ausmus, Bradley, Oneonta	.261	52	165	29	43	52	6	0	1	18	2	0	0	22	0	28	6	4
Bailey, Robert, Welland†	.281	18	57	11	16	20	1	0	1	6	2	0	0	6	0	11	5	1
Banton, Scott, Hamilton	.219	66	215	21	47	55	5	0	1	13	0	1	1	29	0	46	16	7
Barnwell, Richard, Oneonta	.289	69	256	58	74	107	17	5	2	29	4	2	6	33	1	57	39	9
Battell, Mark, Hamilton	.241	54	174	16	42	66	10	1	4	23	0	3	5	17	1	47	6	3
Beacom, Christopher, St. Catharines*	.247	71	275	26	68	89	9	0	4	24	7	1	1	27	1	47	2	5
Beasley, Anthony, Erie	.279	65	247	39	69	88	12	2	1	14	5	0	4	25	0	31	19	4
Beltran, Angel, Welland	.203	41	128	11	26	34	5	0	1	12	0	0	0	4	1	23	2	1
Benitez, Luis, Geneva	.183	58	191	27	35	40	3	1	0	18	2	0	3	50	0	41	2	4
Bennett, Albert, Batavia	.188	29	80	8	15	20	2	0	1	10	0	2	3	1	0	27	4	2
Bennett, Brian, Auburn	.000	2	6	0	0	0	0	0	0	0	0	0	2	0	0	3	0	0
Berlin, Randolph, Hamilton	.281	44	167	25	47	74	8	2	5	19	0	1	1	10	0	46	6	3
Berthel, Daniel, Erie	.234	55	192	30	45	80	11	0	8	25	0	1	3	24	0	48	7	3
Bieser, Steven, Batavia†	.240	25	75	13	18	26	3	1	1	13	2	2	2	12	0	20	2	1
Biggers, Alan, Hamilton	.205	18	39	5	8	10	2	0	0	2	0	0	1	2	0	7	3	0
Brannon, Clifford, Hamilton	.249	69	257	29	64	84	6	4	2	26	0	5	0	22	0	70	16	5
Braxton, Glen, Utica*	.133	5	15	1	2	2	0	0	0	1	0	1	0	4	0	8	0	2
Brewington, Michael, Welland*	.293	40	133	22	39	56	9	1	2	11	1	0	1	10	2	31	14	4
Brown, Dana, Batavia	.274	62	237	37	65	87	12	2	2	24	2	0	2	22	1	25	18	7
Brubaker, Franklin, Oneonta	.000	15	1	0	0	0	0	0	0	0	0	0	0	0	0	1	0	0
Bruehl, Darin, Auburn	.171	33	82	8	14	25	2	0	3	10	2	1	1	8	0	40	1	2
Butterfield, Christian, Pittsfield†	.304	71	260	51	79	132	13	8	8	47	2	3	5	30	2	63	14	4
Cameron, Stanton, Pittsfield	.257	71	253	35	65	110	13	1	10	50	1	1	4	41	2	71	7	2
Campas, Michael, Hamilton†	.214	53	182	19	39	49	5	1	1	14	0	1	2	22	1	36	4	1
Caraballo, Nelson, Welland	.111	6	18	2	2	2	0	0	0	0	0	0	0	3	0	8	0	0
Castillo, Alberto, Pittsfield	.236	34	123	13	29	40	8	0	1	13	0	2	2	7	0	26	2	0
Churchill, Timothy, Batavia	.222	49	167	20	37	55	6	0	4	23	0	3	3	8	0	32	0	1
Cole, Mark, Niagara Falls†	.000	1	1	0	0	0	0	0	0	0	0	0	0	0	0	1	0	0
Coleman, Kenneth, Utica†	.178	27	90	16	16	16	0	0	0	4	0	1	1	14	0	17	9	2
Colon, Antonio, Geneva	.208	15	48	6	10	13	3	0	0	4	0	0	1	4	0	8	0	0
Cornelius, Brian, Niagara Falls*	.319	68	273	47	87	109	13	0	3	24	3	0	0	22	3	44	11	9
Cramer, William, Jamestown	.229	31	109	16	25	28	3	0	0	14	0	3	2	4	0	17	2	2
Cromer, Roy, Hamilton	.263	35	137	18	36	48	6	3	0	16	2	1	1	17	0	30	4	4
Cruz, Ivan, Niagara Falls*	.274	64	226	43	62	98	11	2	7	40	0	1	3	27	4	29	2	0
Cummings, Brian, Batavia*	.284	53	190	21	54	88	7	0	9	33	0	0	1	11	1	26	1	0
Davis, Brian, Utica	.185	46	135	20	25	34	3	0	2	12	2	0	1	8	0	49	6	1
Davis, Russell, Oneonta	.288	65	236	33	68	106	7	5	7	42	1	2	1	19	0	44	3	3
Davison, Scotty, Jamestown	.239	59	230	29	55	71	10	3	0	18	2	1	0	12	0	57	19	5
DeJardin, Bradford, Watertown*	.248	42	117	20	29	37	2	0	2	10	0	3	1	19	1	38	5	2
Delgado, Carlos, St. Catharines*	.180	31	89	9	16	21	5	0	0	11	0	0	1	23	1	39	0	0
Delgado, Pablo, Geneva	.139	13	36	2	5	5	0	0	0	3	0	0	0	3	0	8	2	1
Dellicarri, Joseph, Pittsfield	.375	7	24	3	9	10	1	0	0	5	0	0	0	4	0	1	0	0
Devereaux, Todd, Oneonta*	.364	3	11	1	4	4	0	0	0	0	0	0	0	0	0	4	0	0
Diaz, German, Geneva*	.000	2	1	0	0	0	0	0	0	0	0	0	0	0	0	0	0	0
Dixon, Colin, Elmira	.297	37	128	21	38	55	4	2	3	19	2	3	1	20	0	27	3	0
Dorante, Luis, Elmira	.161	35	87	11	14	26	3	0	3	10	0	1	3	12	0	20	2	3
Dukes, Willie, Elmira	.119	18	59	3	7	12	5	0	0	1	0	0	1	3	0	24	1	2

Player and Club	Pct.	G.	AB.	R.	H.	TB.	2B.	3B.	HR.	RBI.	SH.	SF.	HP.	BB.	Int. BB.	SO.	SB.	CS.
Durkin, Martin, Watertown†	.263	51	152	24	40	60	11	0	3	20	0	3	0	12	1	36	6	0
Eatinger, Michael, Utica	.291	21	86	13	25	38	5	1	2	11	1	0	0	5	0	11	1	0
Ebright, Christopher, Geneva°	.254	69	244	41	62	109	14	3	9	45	1	0	1	37	4	42	4	0
Elder, Isaac, Jamestown†	.238	46	143	22	34	41	4	0	1	10	1	0	3	19	0	62	15	6
Erdman, Bradley, Geneva	.176	26	85	6	15	17	2	0	0	3	0	1	0	6	1	26	1	1
Escobar, John, Batavia	.197	60	193	16	38	45	2	1	1	13	0	3	1	15	0	42	1	3
Etheredge, Jeffrey, Batavia†	.136	30	88	18	12	19	2	1	1	2	1	0	0	22	0	41	9	2
Fernandez, Jose, Hamilton°	.200	52	165	24	33	57	7	1	5	23	0	3	1	25	1	47	3	2
Ferran, Alexander, Watertown°	.198	69	253	34	50	77	9	3	4	34	7	3	2	26	0	47	8	1
Foggie, Cornell, Watertown°	.238	46	126	18	30	41	6	1	1	13	3	1	1	14	1	17	5	0
Fortuna, Michael, Welland†	.192	42	130	12	25	37	1	1	3	19	0	3	0	11	1	43	2	1
Francisco, Ramirez, Jamestown†	.077	9	26	1	2	2	0	0	0	0	0	0	0	5	0	9	1	0
Francisco, Rene, Geneva	.277	63	260	36	72	95	12	4	1	18	6	2	0	15	0	38	11	8
Furch, John, Utica	.223	61	224	22	50	72	8	1	4	26	0	0	2	18	0	75	1	2
Garcia, Oscar, St. Catharines	.219	25	96	8	21	22	1	0	0	1	0	0	1	1	0	48	1	0
Garcia, Tomas, Welland	.292	17	72	9	21	23	2	0	0	3	0	0	0	5	0	15	5	2
Golden, Brian, Hamilton	.000	29	0	0	0	0	0	0	0	0	1	0	0	0	0	0	0	0
Gomez, Fabio, Watertown	.331	73	296	64	98	148	15	4	9	57	2	2	1	15	2	56	6	3
Goodale, Jeffrey, Niagara Falls	.268	66	239	38	64	112	17	5	7	49	0	6	5	34	2	59	8	4
Grace, Michael, Jamestown	.000	4	4	1	0	0	0	0	0	0	0	0	0	1	0	1	0	0
Graham, Steven, Hamilton°	.277	51	202	33	56	92	11	2	7	30	0	2	0	9	1	31	14	9
Grayum, Richard, Geneva°	.290	69	259	43	75	119	16	2	8	33	6	4	0	38	2	57	0	5
Gremillion, Jeffrey, Welland	.212	22	66	9	14	18	0	2	0	4	0	0	1	9	0	16	3	2
Gryskevich, Larry, Hamilton°	.134	34	97	6	13	21	4	2	0	8	0	0	0	6	0	35	1	2
Hancock, Jeffrey, Watertown	.242	56	182	31	44	49	2	0	1	25	4	1	11	15	0	59	6	2
Hanks, Christopher, Elmira	.238	52	181	14	43	55	7	1	1	16	1	2	3	11	1	38	3	5
Harris, Keith, Utica	.326	57	193	30	63	80	6	4	1	27	0	4	4	21	1	36	14	12
Hart, Brian, Watertown	.172	15	29	4	5	6	1	0	0	3	0	0	2	1	0	5	0	0
Hayes, Mark, Hamilton	.168	34	95	12	16	26	1	0	3	6	0	0	0	19	0	28	2	4
Hedge, Patrick, Erie	.207	53	169	14	35	49	9	1	1	23	1	1	1	18	0	53	3	1
Heiderscheit, Patrick, Jamestown°	.000	22	1	0	0	0	0	0	0	0	0	0	0	0	0	0	0	0
Henderson, David, Auburn	.226	69	230	36	52	79	10	4	3	24	0	5	10	16	1	68	14	4
Henderson, Derek, Pittsfield	.263	47	152	24	40	58	11	2	1	19	2	2	1	14	0	36	6	1
Henderson, Valentine, Welland	.257	71	280	46	72	89	7	2	2	18	1	0	3	23	1	69	34	9
Hernandez, Enrique, Oneonta	.223	29	94	12	21	31	4	0	2	7	0	0	1	15	0	21	1	1
Hernandez, Henry, Hamilton°	.315	35	108	16	34	54	11	3	1	9	0	1	1	16	0	23	0	1
Herrera, Jose, Oneonta	.207	8	29	4	6	6	0	0	0	1	2	0	0	1	1	7	0	0
Hicks, Aman, Erie°	.205	44	151	19	31	53	3	2	5	16	1	0	0	8	1	42	3	5
Hicks, Anthony, Hamilton	.156	42	128	11	20	28	3	1	1	11	0	1	1	4	0	37	5	6
Hildreth, Bradley, Erie	.231	65	229	29	53	63	10	0	0	22	3	1	2	21	0	43	3	1
Hill, Lewellyn, Oneonta†	.213	48	164	36	35	58	5	3	4	24	0	1	13	14	0	60	7	2
Hines, Timothy, Pittsfield°	.309	55	194	26	60	77	11	3	0	23	2	1	2	16	0	42	6	6
Hoffner, Jamie, Pittsfield°	.285	39	123	19	35	53	7	4	1	14	2	1	1	10	0	31	1	2
Holifield, Rickey, St. Catharines°	.220	60	209	22	46	67	7	1	4	21	0	2	1	15	1	74	4	7
Holmes, William, Welland°	.261	27	92	12	24	37	4	0	3	15	0	2	0	16	1	15	1	1
Horowitz, Edward, Erie	.222	40	126	10	28	37	7	1	0	14	1	0	2	20	0	31	3	2
Howard, Timothy, Pittsfield†	.281	63	228	35	64	86	6	8	0	31	2	3	2	19	2	22	13	9
Howell, David, Oneonta°	.257	60	206	27	53	72	7	3	2	24	3	1	1	27	2	33	10	2
Howell, Patrick, Pittsfield	.290	56	231	41	67	80	4	3	1	26	6	1	3	7	0	46	45	10
Hoy, Peter, Elmira°	.000	27	1	0	0	0	0	0	0	0	0	0	0	0	0	0	0	0
Hudson, Deryk, Jamestown	.311	61	222	23	69	105	14	2	6	43	0	5	2	21	2	34	6	3
Hurst, Joseph, Niagara Falls	.283	55	198	41	56	95	9	0	10	38	1	3	1	25	0	59	9	3
Hyde, Mickey, Batavia	.249	53	177	11	44	56	6	3	0	13	1	0	1	10	0	51	2	2
Infante, Thomas, Hamilton°	.000	24	1	0	0	0	0	0	0	0	0	0	0	0	0	0	1	0
Ingram, Jeffrey, Utica	.292	50	171	19	50	62	6	0	2	20	1	1	4	14	0	32	1	7
James, Joseph, Watertown°	.233	59	206	29	48	87	12	3	7	31	0	4	4	16	1	57	0	0
Jenkins, Garrett, Elmira	.194	73	248	27	48	62	6	1	2	16	5	2	6	11	0	85	25	13
Johnson, Avery, Watertown	.250	11	32	2	8	8	0	0	0	2	0	0	0	6	0	9	0	1
Johnson, Deron, Welland	.245	55	200	19	49	81	15	4	3	31	1	3	3	10	1	51	8	6
Johnson, Kevin, Jamestown	.198	42	121	17	24	37	3	2	2	11	0	1	0	15	0	52	11	3
Johnson, Luther, Auburn°	.253	59	182	29	46	82	12	3	6	29	1	1	0	28	3	45	10	5
Keating, David, Niagara Falls	.290	55	200	37	58	82	6	3	4	33	2	2	4	16	0	63	12	5
Keefer, Paul, Welland	.305	48	164	27	50	58	4	2	0	11	1	0	0	20	0	18	4	8
Kent, Jeffrey, St. Catharines	.224	73	268	34	60	115	14	1	13	37	0	4	6	33	2	81	5	1
Kimberlin, Keith, Niagara Falls†	.246	75	285	50	70	86	13	0	1	24	11	4	6	32	1	47	15	5
Kobza, Gregory, Utica°	.215	68	219	28	47	73	11	3	3	31	0	3	4	39	3	61	6	6
Krause, Ronald, Jamestown°	.300	19	70	9	21	22	1	0	0	10	0	0	2	6	0	23	5	2
Lake, Kenneth, Jamestown	.234	73	261	45	61	111	13	2	11	39	0	3	4	34	2	87	19	7
Laker, Timothy, Jamestown	.222	58	216	25	48	65	9	1	2	24	0	3	2	16	1	40	8	4
Lewis, Mica, Auburn	.261	67	230	45	60	79	9	2	2	16	2	3	0	33	0	59	24	4
Lewis, Ronnie, Auburn	.257	30	74	7	19	20	1	0	0	2	0	1	0	9	0	27	8	3
Limoncelli, Jeffrey, Elmira	.190	9	21	4	4	4	0	0	0	0	0	0	1	5	0	3	0	1
Linden, Mark, Geneva	.225	68	227	30	51	66	10	1	1	12	2	1	8	25	0	65	10	7
Lofton, Kenneth, Auburn°†	.264	34	110	21	29	34	3	1	0	8	1	4	0	14	0	30	26	5
Lowery, Josh, Batavia	.247	49	162	21	40	59	8	1	3	20	0	2	1	22	0	39	3	4
Lozinski, Anthony, Batavia	.053	7	19	1	1	1	0	0	0	0	0	0	0	0	0	5	0	0
Madsen, Lance, Auburn	.265	59	196	25	52	92	9	2	9	33	3	1	2	12	2	60	9	3
Makarewicz, Scott, Auburn	.241	61	216	22	52	81	17	0	4	24	5	1	4	14	0	43	2	0
Maldonado, Carlos, Niagara Falls†	.100	7	20	7	2	3	1	0	0	1	0	1	0	10	0	9	0	0
Manahan, Austin, Welland	.213	50	178	18	38	58	3	4	3	16	0	1	1	17	0	51	12	1
Mason, Felton, Jamestown	.145	19	62	6	9	10	1	0	0	0	0	0	0	2	0	26	3	0
Matilla, Pedro, Elmira	.265	14	34	9	9	15	4	1	0	3	0	0	0	14	0	7	0	0
May, Lee, Pittsfield†	.237	25	97	14	23	31	5	0	1	7	0	1	0	5	0	24	8	1
Mayo, Todd, Jamestown°	.303	68	238	55	72	98	17	3	1	18	1	1	4	37	0	20	37	9
McNeely, Jeffrey, Elmira	.250	61	208	20	52	65	7	0	2	21	1	0	4	26	0	54	16	8
Meek, Richard, Erie	.200	42	110	10	22	27	3	1	0	8	1	1	4	16	1	23	4	1
Mendonca, Robert, Batavia	.197	46	152	21	30	38	8	0	0	12	1	1	3	19	0	31	1	0
Mercedes, Hector, St. Catharines†	.156	37	122	14	19	22	3	0	0	7	0	0	0	10	0	39	0	1
Merejo, Jesus, Utica	.227	37	128	14	29	35	6	0	0	10	2	0	0	11	0	32	3	1
Metts, Carey, Erie	.231	44	147	22	34	56	10	0	4	19	0	1	0	19	0	39	2	1
Michael, Steven, Elmira	.240	67	192	23	46	73	14	2	3	23	4	1	3	14	2	58	3	0
Middlekauff, Craig, Niagara Falls°	.259	11	27	3	7	11	1	0	1	7	0	1	0	3	0	5	0	0

Player and Club	Pct.	G.	AB.	R.	H.	TB.	2B.	3B.	HR.	RBI.	SH.	SF.	HP.	BB.	Int. BB.	SO.	SB.	CS.
Miller, Orlando, Oneonta	.291	58	213	29	62	74	5	2	1	25	3	1	3	6	0	38	8	2
Millette, Joe, Batavia	.238	11	42	4	10	13	3	0	0	4	0	0	0	4	0	6	3	0
Mobley, Anton, St. Catharines	.224	73	277	30	62	99	13	0	8	31	0	3	2	15	3	108	5	8
Moccia, Mario, Niagara Falls	.253	37	95	11	24	30	4	1	0	19	1	3	0	9	0	21	1	1
Monegro, Miguel, Elmira	.167	19	48	5	8	10	2	0	0	5	1	0	1	3	0	11	1	0
Moore, Barton, Elmira	.182	65	203	24	37	50	4	0	3	14	8	1	0	24	1	79	26	10
Moore, Cary, Erie	.220	43	127	9	28	37	3	3	0	10	2	0	0	9	0	40	4	0
Morrison, James, Elmira	.229	41	48	11	11	14	1	1	0	2	0	0	0	9	0	19	3	4
Mosley, Anthony, Elmira†	.000	27	1	0	0	0	0	0	0	0	0	0	0	0	0	0	0	0
Mota, Carlos, Watertown	.300	62	217	30	65	91	6	1	6	35	2	3	1	12	1	37	6	4
Mundy, Richard, Geneva	.245	44	139	15	34	49	5	2	2	17	3	0	10	7	0	43	6	2
Munoz, Luis, Elmira	.207	65	213	20	44	63	11	1	2	16	3	0	0	10	0	47	6	3
Murphy, Micah, Geneva*	.175	50	143	16	25	41	11	1	1	11	3	1	2	14	0	36	0	2
Murray, Glenn, Jamestown	.300	3	10	1	3	4	1	0	0	1	0	0	0	1	0	1	0	0
Navarro, Norberto, Pittsfield	.280	46	157	26	44	54	6	2	0	14	3	1	0	18	0	30	13	3
Nelson, Erik, Welland	.209	27	91	5	19	21	0	1	0	5	0	0	3	2	1	31	2	1
Nicosia, Steven, Erie	.260	60	196	19	51	58	7	0	0	23	2	3	2	12	0	31	20	4
O'Halloran, Gregory, St. Catharines*	.283	69	265	31	75	107	13	2	5	27	0	1	2	21	2	33	7	4
Obando, Sherman, Oneonta	.312	70	276	50	86	133	23	3	6	45	1	2	6	16	1	45	8	5
Odor, Rouglas, Watertown	.272	52	195	30	53	78	9	2	4	24	2	2	2	17	1	34	10	1
Ortega, Eduardo, Batavia*	.284	63	243	25	69	74	5	0	0	10	10	1	1	11	0	33	6	7
Oster, Paul, Oneonta†	.299	53	197	27	59	82	13	2	2	29	3	5	1	16	0	26	7	6
Ostopowicz, Richard, Pittsfield	.200	19	45	5	9	14	2	0	1	7	1	0	0	2	0	15	0	0
Owens, Michael, Batavia*	.223	49	179	31	40	77	7	0	10	33	1	2	3	17	3	60	0	1
Parese, Billy, St. Catharines	.176	70	262	27	46	53	7	0	0	10	1	0	2	23	0	38	7	3
Patterson, Gregg, Geneva*	.105	9	19	0	2	2	0	0	0	0	0	0	0	3	1	7	0	0
Pedersen, Donald, Niagara Falls*	.218	40	110	5	24	37	13	0	0	14	0	1	2	10	0	25	0	1
Pennyfeather, William, Welland	.190	75	289	34	55	76	10	1	3	26	1	6	2	12	1	75	18	5
Perez, Eulogio, Batavia	.120	15	50	5	6	6	0	0	0	3	0	1	0	5	0	17	0	0
Perozo, Ender, Elmira†	.215	29	93	6	20	26	3	0	1	7	3	0	2	4	0	24	0	4
Peterson, Robert, Welland	.184	16	38	0	7	7	0	0	0	2	0	0	0	10	0	16	0	0
Pipik, Gary, Jamestown†	.129	34	85	7	11	17	1	1	1	3	0	1	3	4	0	30	6	4
Piskor, Stephen, Pittsfield*	.216	13	37	5	8	11	3	0	0	0	0	0	0	1	0	14	0	0
Plemmons, Ronald, Utica*	.241	69	257	37	62	88	12	4	2	24	0	1	2	34	0	47	7	6
Prager, Howard, Auburn*	.335	73	251	54	84	129	15	3	8	58	1	4	2	36	3	45	21	4
Pride, Curtis, Pittsfield*	.259	55	212	35	55	86	7	3	6	23	2	1	2	25	1	47	9	2
Ramirez, John, Jamestown	.295	13	44	9	13	21	2	0	2	11	0	0	0	4	0	12	2	2
Redman, Timothy, Hamilton	.221	38	113	7	25	27	2	0	0	14	0	2	3	12	0	20	2	1
Reed, Toncie, Auburn†	.274	67	241	41	66	100	12	5	4	35	0	4	1	18	1	64	7	6
Reimink, Robert, Niagara Falls†	.254	75	291	52	74	103	17	3	2	31	3	0	0	50	3	58	15	4
Reynolds, Douglas, Erie	.189	35	106	19	20	37	5	0	4	13	2	0	0	21	0	30	0	0
Richardson, Michael, Erie*	.345	32	113	18	39	64	7	0	6	23	0	1	0	14	2	21	0	0
Riemer, Timothy, Watertown*	.273	13	11	2	3	3	0	0	0	1	0	0	0	2	0	3	0	0
Riley, Paul, Auburn	.196	35	97	9	19	23	2	1	0	10	0	0	1	15	0	41	5	2
Rodriguez, Buenaventura, Jam.*	.211	67	213	32	45	71	9	4	3	23	2	2	5	24	1	79	21	10
Rodriguez, Jose, Welland†	.185	26	81	7	15	20	3	1	0	9	0	0	1	11	0	36	3	1
Rosado, Edwin, Batavia†	.222	44	144	15	32	41	6	0	1	8	3	0	1	13	1	22	3	3
Rosario, Julio, Elmira	.231	50	143	12	33	41	3	1	1	16	4	1	1	3	0	19	2	2
Rose, Peter, Erie*	.276	58	228	30	63	92	13	5	2	26	2	0	1	12	1	34	1	2
Rosfelder, Christopher, Elmira*	.214	55	145	13	31	36	5	0	0	8	1	0	2	21	1	28	2	3
Ross, Joseph, Oneonta	.156	15	32	3	5	6	1	0	0	2	0	0	0	5	0	2	0	1
Sanders, Lance, Utica	.109	16	46	3	5	8	3	0	0	3	0	1	0	8	0	20	0	1
Santana, Jose, Auburn†	.264	61	208	23	55	75	6	4	2	19	1	0	1	12	0	46	26	11
Santangelo, Frank, Jamestown†	.500	2	6	0	3	4	1	0	0	0	0	0	0	1	0	1	0	0
Scott, Gary, Geneva*	.280	48	175	33	49	91	10	1	10	42	0	2	9	22	2	23	4	1
Scott, Kevin, Auburn	.245	60	204	24	50	67	10	2	1	24	5	2	2	13	0	52	13	5
Segui, Daniel, Pittsfield	.276	59	199	32	55	74	6	5	1	23	6	2	2	26	0	41	8	5
Sellers, Rick, Niagara Falls	.254	29	71	17	18	29	3	1	2	6	2	0	0	17	0	22	3	0
Seymour, Winston, Welland*	.256	35	129	13	33	43	4	0	2	18	0	0	1	8	0	18	1	1
Shannon, Daniel, Hamilton*	.220	50	168	16	37	50	5	1	2	15	1	1	1	8	0	42	12	2
Shingledecker, Gary, Erie	.231	50	143	13	33	43	5	1	1	12	3	0	1	20	1	23	3	1
Singley, Joseph, Utica	.280	30	107	15	30	39	6	0	1	14	3	0	0	8	0	31	2	0
Small, Robert, Jamestown*	.224	38	125	7	28	44	4	0	4	12	0	0	1	5	1	37	1	0
Snow, Jack, Oneonta†	.292	73	274	41	80	126	18	2	8	51	2	4	2	29	6	35	4	1
Spencer, John, Elmira	.267	54	195	21	52	75	10	2	3	16	1	2	3	17	1	52	12	9
Stacey, Albert, Geneva*	.248	71	246	27	61	92	7	0	8	42	3	4	6	22	0	45	5	4
Stairs, Matthew, Jamestown	.256	14	43	8	11	15	1	0	1	5	0	0	0	3	0	5	1	2
Stocker, Steven, Batavia	.182	17	55	5	10	16	4	1	0	1	0	0	0	3	0	15	0	0
Strickland, Dedrick, Oneonta†	.353	18	17	9	6	6	0	0	0	7	0	0	0	15	0	3	0	1
Tagliaferri, Eugene, Niagara Falls	.173	33	110	10	19	30	2	0	3	15	2	0	3	5	0	54	1	1
Tatarian, Dean, Utica	.287	49	167	29	48	64	10	0	2	25	1	1	4	20	0	38	10	2
Taylor, Samuel, Auburn†	.265	47	147	17	39	53	7	2	1	20	2	1	2	20	1	9	2	1
Tejada, Alejandro, 13 Jam-36 Utica	.212	49	151	14	32	37	2	0	1	10	5	1	0	11	0	41	12	5
Tepper, Marc, Watertown*	.347	68	245	37	85	120	16	2	5	46	1	1	0	24	1	33	2	1
Tesmer, James, Pittsfield	.214	40	140	15	30	38	6	1	0	12	0	2	0	7	0	18	1	3
Thomas, Mark, Welland	.283	32	106	18	30	43	4	0	3	16	0	1	0	11	0	41	5	2
Thompson, Robert, Utica†	.214	18	56	6	12	17	2	0	1	10	0	0	1	5	0	8	0	1
Thompson, Ryan, St. Catharines	.273	74	278	39	76	110	14	1	6	36	0	3	4	16	0	60	9	6
Torres, Freddy, Niagara Falls	.223	54	148	17	33	36	1	1	0	15	3	2	2	9	0	16	1	4
Trujillo, Jose, Hamilton	.293	26	92	20	27	42	12	0	1	7	0	0	2	25	1	16	4	3
Trusky, Kenneth, Welland*	.339	32	115	13	39	51	6	0	2	20	0	0	0	6	0	20	6	0
Tucholski, Thomas, Welland	.091	4	11	1	1	2	1	0	0	0	0	0	0	0	0	5	0	0
Uhrhan, Kevin, Elmira	.000	21	2	0	0	0	0	0	0	0	0	0	0	1	0	1	0	0
Urbon, Joseph, Batavia*	.192	32	104	5	20	24	4	0	0	4	1	0	0	3	0	25	4	0
Valentin, Edwin, Auburn†	.214	57	192	18	41	45	2	1	0	12	1	0	1	12	1	39	7	6
Vanscoyoc, Aaron, Oneonta†	.237	65	224	35	53	63	7	0	1	16	3	0	3	20	1	25	3	5
Vargas, Gonzalo, St. Catharines†	.188	19	48	6	9	13	1	0	1	7	0	0	0	7	0	18	0	0
Vazquez, Jose, Oneonta†	.243	40	115	10	28	33	1	2	0	9	1	1	2	4	18	0	7	3
Wakefield, Timothy, Welland	.206	36	63	7	13	20	4	0	1	9	0	1	0	3	0	21	1	1
Walker, Dennis, Utica	.230	72	256	28	59	75	6	5	0	20	2	3	1	18	1	72	11	6
Wearing, Melvin, Erie	.251	60	171	26	43	81	6	1	10	22	1	2	1	45	3	51	0	1
Wedge, Eric, Elmira	.234	41	145	20	34	65	6	2	7	22	0	0	0	15	0	21	1	1

Player and Club	Pct.	G.	AB.	R.	H.	TB.	2B.	3B.	HR.	RBI.	SH.	SF.	HP.	BB.	Int. BB.	SO.	SB.	CS.
Welch, Douglas, Geneva	.257	51	183	18	47	62	6	0	3	26	2	2	1	12	1	40	3	8
White, William, Geneva	.323	68	254	44	82	112	19	1	3	29	2	1	3	43	0	36	16	5
Wiley, Craig, Niagara Falls†	.357	5	14	1	5	5	0	0	0	3	0	1	0	5	0	0	0	2
Williams, Daniel, Watertown	.295	52	190	25	56	71	6	0	3	31	1	6	3	13	2	23	0	1
Williams, Flavio, Welland	.282	25	71	9	20	24	4	0	0	7	0	0	0	6	0	10	1	1
Wilson, Mark, Hamilton	.141	24	71	3	10	13	3	0	0	7	0	1	1	2	0	14	0	1
Wilson, Nigel, St. Catharines*	.217	42	161	17	35	56	5	2	4	18	1	0	4	11	0	50	8	2
Witherspoon, Richard, Elmira	.167	9	18	0	3	3	0	0	0	0	0	0	0	0	0	6	0	1
Wolak, Jerome, Utica	.274	57	223	28	61	84	13	5	0	24	1	0	4	12	0	35	12	4
Woodruff, Patrick, Batavia	.320	16	50	11	16	27	2	0	3	7	1	1	0	6	1	16	4	2
Woods, Tyrone, Jamestown	.263	63	209	23	55	96	6	4	9	29	0	3	2	20	1	59	8	9
Young, Donald, Watertown†	.253	71	257	45	65	81	8	1	2	17	5	3	4	25	0	59	17	12
Young, Erik, Watertown	.237	41	114	13	27	33	6	0	0	11	1	2	0	15	0	29	6	1
Zaksek, John, Utica*	.214	32	117	16	25	34	3	3	0	17	0	0	1	14	1	17	7	3
Zinter, Alan, Pittsfield†	.366	12	41	11	15	25	2	1	2	12	0	1	0	12	0	4	0	1

The following pitchers, listed alphabetically by club, with games in parentheses, had no plate appearances, primarily through use of designated hitters:

AUBURN—Brown, Duane (2); Campusano, Teofilo (19); Desapio, James (19); Emm, Arthur (15); Gonzales, Benjamin (24); Hyson, Cole (15); Jones, Todd (11); Marrero, Rogelio (20); McDowell, Michael (15); Perez, Francisco (11); Porter, Brian (7); Reynolds, Shane (6); Small, Mark (10); Wall, Donnell (12).

BATAVIA—Agado, David (2); Ayrault, Robert (4); Bratlien, Erik (19); Corsaro, Robby (22); Elliott, Donald (8); Fletcher, Edward (14); Gaddy, Robert (16); Goergen, Todd (7); Gunderson, Gregory (13); Parris, Steven (13); Patterson, Jeffrey (9); Repoz, Jeffrey (2); Stevens, Matthew (16); Sullivan, Michael (24); West, Darin (10).

ELMIRA—Diaz, Johnny (2); Konopki, Mark (6); Locker, John (19); Morelli, Frank (1); Morton, Kevin (3); Quantrill, Paul (20); Riley, Edward (17); Rivera, Carlos (2); Rush, Andrew (15); Sanders, Alan (16); Thompson, Michael (3).

ERIE—Bowen, John (7); Brown, Daniel (3); Brown, David (17); Doman, Robert (10); Eck, Harold (1); Hemmerly, John (26); Kerr, Zachary (9); Leinen, Patrick (18); Martin, Thomas (7); Oquist, Michael (15); Pena, Jaime (19); Rhodes, Arthur (5); Riddle, David (14); Rupp, Mark (2); Smith, Rick (12); Somerville, Robert (3); Wheatcroft, Robert (7); Williams, Steven (19).

GENEVA—Beer, Darrin (13); Bush, Kalani (15); Cesari, Jeffrey (20); Espino, Francisco (13); Gore, Keven (14); Jones, Shannon (14); Ludwig, Jeffrey (18); Swartzbaugh, David (18); Sweeney, James (23); Willis, Travis (16).

HAMILTON—Boss, David (15); Bowlan, Mark (16); Brooks, Rodney (15); Cassidy, Michael (6); Cebuhar, John (17); Gorton, Chris (20); Green, Donald (35); Grubb, Sean (32); Keller, Clyde (1); Lata, Timothy (23); Milchin, Michael (8); Tukes, Stanley (14).

JAMESTOWN—Archibald, Daniel (24); Barnes, Brian (2); Buzzard, Dale (25); Ciaglo, Paul (4); Eddy, James (11); Hutto, Paul (2); Kilgo, Raymond (30); Klancnik, Joseph (18); Logan, Joseph (15); Regira, Gary (5); Sommer, David (13); Thigpen, Arthur (2); Thoden, John (1); Wessel, Troy (18); Whitehead, Steven (12); Young, Bryan (18).

NIAGARA FALLS—Betances, Marcos (9); DeSilva, John (4); Doherty, John (26); Ettles, Mark (5); Garcia, Michael (7); Gonzales, Francisco (10); Heins, James (17); Herrmann, Timothy (15); Langston, Keith (13); Logue, Matthew (26); Marcero, Douglas (15); Marshall, Randall (6); Nute, Scott (13); Pinto, Gustavo (18); Shea, Kurt (11); Wilson, David (5).

ONEONTA—Canestro, Arthur (22); Chase, Scott (16); Gardella, Michael (28); Hutton, Mark (12); Juarbe, Kenneth (13); Malone, Todd (18); Moody, James (30); Petlick, Joel (1); Rhodes, Ricky (13); Seminara, Frank (11); Stanford, Lawrence (15).

PITTSFIELD—Butler, Christopher (1); Dorn, Chris (6); Freitas, Michael (13); Harriger, Dennis (3); Johnson, Paul (24); Johnston, Craig (7); Johnstone, John (15); Langbehn, Gregory (14); McCann, Joseph (13); Medina, Luciano (9); Richmond, Ryan (18); Telgheder, David (13); Vazquez, Edgardo (3); Vitko, Joseph (15); Willoughby, Mark (16).

ST. CATHARINES—Bicknell, Greg (17); Blumberg, Robert (17); Brown, Daren (18); Dodd, Daniel (5); Hutson, Scott (5); Jockish, Michael (20); Kizziah, Daren (17); Kulina, Kenneth (2); Martin, Gregg (19); McCutcheon, Gregory (19); Nelinbach, Rodney (8); Santana, Ernesto (10); Stock, Sterling (20); Wanish, John (15).

UTICA—Burroughs, Kenneth (9); Capparelli, Richard (12); Cooper, Virgil (10); Davino, Michael (19); Galvan, Michael (2); Gorman, David (13); Keyser, Brian (14); Long, Richard (20); Mehrtens, Patrick (16); Middaugh, Scott (11); Pershke, Gregory (14); Ruffin, Johnny (15); Smith, John (1); Stevens, Scott (22); Van Winkle, David (17).

WATERTOWN—Alexander, Charles (1); Allen, Scott (10); Bevenour, Keith (10); Dipoto, Gerald (14); Egloff, Bruce (22); Kiser, Garland (12); Kovach, Ty (15); Merriman, Brett (14); Neill, Scott (19); Piatt, Douglas (15); Roscoe, Gregory (9); Ryan, Robert (7); Vespe, William (17).

WELLAND—Arvesen, Scott (5); Bird, David (17); Broome, Kimberly (13); Byerly, Rodney (16); Deller, Thomas (28); Doss, Raymond (13); Kuder, Jeffrey (14); Latham, John (15); Magria, Javier (14); Masters, Wayne (13); Slaughter, Garland (4); Wagner, Paul (13); Way, Ronald (23).

GRAND SLAM HOME RUNS—Wedge, 2; Albright, Butterfield, Cruz, Ebright, Graham, Middlekauf, Mota, G. Scott, Spencer, Stacy, Vargas, Welch, Zinter, 1 each.

AWARDED FIRST BASE ON CATCHER'S INTERFERENCE—An. Hicks 3 (Cramer, Mota, Nelson); Holmes 2 (O. Garcia 2); Bruehl (Colon); Cornelius (Nelson); Erdman (O'Halloran); Etheredge (Horowitz); Murphy (E. Hernandez); Obando (Colon); White (Rosado).

CLUB FIELDING

Club	Pct.	G.	PO.	A.	E.	DP.	PB.	Club	Pct.	G.	PO.	A.	E.	DP.	PB.
Niagara Falls	.969	76	1995	800	90	66	13	Hamilton	.954	76	1936	659	125	45	7
Oneonta	.966	75	1955	738	95	44	16	St. Catharines	.952	76	1997	761	139	57	24
Elmira	.960	76	1993	752	113	51	19	Watertown	.952	77	2045	812	144	53	21
Batavia	.959	76	2024	837	122	68	11	Erie	.952	74	1909	722	133	61	15
Utica	.959	78	2069	771	122	39	20	Jamestown	.951	76	2005	880	148	68	19
Pittsfield	.956	76	1976	838	129	62	13	Welland	.946	76	1938	698	151	42	40
Geneva	.954	75	1986	801	133	43	15	Auburn	.942	77	1982	788	170	68	23

INDIVIDUAL FIELDING
FIRST BASEMEN

*Throws lefthanded.

Player and Club	Pct.	G.	PO.	A.	E.	DP.	Player and Club	Pct.	G.	PO.	A.	E.	DP.
Abare, St. Catharines*	.965	51	421	25	16	27	Dixon, Elmira	1.000	3	12	2	0	1
Alvarez, Elmira	.973	11	68	5	2	5	Dorante, Elmira	.958	3	23	0	1	0
Battell, Hamilton	.987	20	142	10	2	12	Furch, Utica	.985	31	245	20	4	11
Beacom, St. Catharines	.984	25	236	9	4	21	Graham, Hamilton*	1.000	1	1	0	0	0
Berlin, Hamilton	.979	6	38	8	1	2	Grayum, Geneva	1.000	1	12	0	0	0
Brewington, Welland*	.981	7	48	5	1	3	Gremillion, Welland	1.000	1	1	0	0	1
Bruehl, Auburn	1.000	1	2	0	0	1	Gryskevich, Hamilton*	1.000	6	32	4	0	1
Cameron, Pittsfield	.969	24	209	12	7	19	Hanks, Elmira	.977	32	238	19	6	17
Churchill, Batavia	.987	44	362	25	5	30	Hernandez, Hamilton*	.968	32	224	20	8	8
Cruz, Niagara Falls*	.989	54	439	30	5	43	Hoffner, Pittsfield	.992	39	346	18	3	25
Cummings, Batavia	.931	3	26	1	2	1	Holmes, Welland*	.988	27	226	18	3	14
DeJardin, Watertown*	.941	2	16	0	1	2	Horowitz, Erie	1.000	11	77	3	0	11

FIRST BASEMEN—Continued

Player and Club	Pct.	G.	PO.	A.	E.	DP.
Howell, Oneonta*	1.000	4	23	3	0	1
Hudson, Jamestown	.979	10	85	10	2	7
James, Watertown	1.000	1	0	1	0	0
Johnson, Welland	.929	4	39	0	3	1
Kobza, Utica	.987	49	359	28	5	18
Lake, Jamestown	1.000	5	46	2	0	4
Metts, Erie	.977	7	38	4	1	2
Michael, Elmira	.988	36	238	19	3	18
Moccia, Niagara Falls	.985	17	128	6	2	9
Moore, Erie	1.000	2	5	0	0	0
Munoz, Elmira	1.000	6	31	4	0	0
Murphy, Geneva*	.981	27	197	13	4	11
Owens, Batavia*	.982	35	306	16	6	22
Pedersen, Niagara Falls*	.989	12	86	3	1	6
Prager, Auburn*	.983	69	543	37	10	54
Richardson, Erie*	.972	22	166	8	5	14
Riley, Auburn	.978	6	42	2	1	1
Rodriguez, Jamestown*	.979	66	549	56	13	49
Rosfelder, Elmira	.929	3	12	1	1	0
Scott, Auburn	.984	9	59	3	1	5
Segui, Pittsfield	1.000	1	2	0	0	1
Seymour, Welland*	.969	35	264	19	9	13
Shannon, Hamilton	.943	17	109	6	7	12
Shingledecker, Erie	1.000	1	2	0	0	0
SNOW, Oneonta*	.991	73	590	53	6	34
Stacey, Geneva*	.980	52	474	20	10	26
Tatarian, Utica	1.000	4	30	2	0	1
Tepper, Watertown*	.968	53	455	36	16	30
Tesmer, Pittsfield	.989	18	165	9	2	10
Thomas, Welland	1.000	3	24	4	0	1
Wakefield, Welland	1.000	1	2	0	0	0
Wearing, Erie	.985	43	304	18	5	28
Williams, Watertown	.988	26	228	23	3	17

SECOND BASEMEN

Player and Club	Pct.	G.	PO.	A.	E.	DP.
Beacom, St. Catharines	1.000	1	2	1	0	0
Beasley, Erie	.935	46	96	104	14	27
BENITEZ, Geneva	.969	53	92	124	7	16
Berlin, Hamilton	.909	13	18	22	4	2
Biggers, Hamilton	.889	2	3	5	1	1
Campas, Hamilton	.961	39	73	73	6	7
Cole, Niagara Falls	1.000	1	1	0	0	0
Coleman, Utica	.961	27	57	66	5	13
Cramer, Jamestown	.833	1	1	4	1	0
Davison, Jamestown	.944	7	13	21	2	5
Durkin, Watertown	.942	33	56	75	8	10
Eatinger, Utica	.964	18	37	43	3	5
Escobar, Batavia	.935	18	35	52	6	12
Fortuna, Welland	1.000	5	8	7	0	3
Francisco, Jamestown	.978	9	17	27	1	5
Garcia, Welland	.897	14	22	30	6	5
Hancock, Watertown	.964	47	74	116	7	21
Da. Henderson, Auburn	.980	8	20	28	1	7
De. Henderson, Pittsfield	.714	2	0	5	2	0
Hildreth, Erie	1.000	1	2	1	0	1
Howard, Pittsfield	.951	57	101	171	14	26
Hudson, Jamestown	.971	30	64	71	4	16
Johnson, Jamestown	.875	2	4	3	1	0
Keefer, Welland	.955	39	78	72	7	12
Lewis, Auburn	.954	47	87	122	10	27
Limoncelli, Elmira	1.000	5	5	8	0	1
Linden, Geneva	.970	24	42	56	3	7
Maldonado, Niagara Falls	.966	7	13	15	1	4
Merejo, Utica	.960	32	59	61	5	8
Miller, Oneonta	.948	41	70	94	9	11
Monegro, Elmira	.958	17	25	43	3	7
B. Moore, Elmira	.934	61	112	169	20	19
C. Moore, Erie	.857	7	8	22	5	4
Munoz, Elmira	1.000	8	9	8	0	3
Navarro, Pittsfield	1.000	5	8	10	0	3
Odor, Watertown	.953	8	21	20	2	4
Ortega, Batavia	.951	63	111	180	15	37
Parese, St. Catharines	.931	70	123	176	22	29
Ramirez, Jamestown	.946	13	18	35	3	3
Reimink, Niagara Falls	.976	30	50	71	3	12
Rodriguez, Welland	1.000	1	3	2	0	1
Santangelo, Jamestown	.833	2	5	5	2	1
Segui, Pittsfield	.957	13	16	50	3	8
Shingledecker, Erie	.946	28	56	66	7	17
Stairs, Jamestown	.939	11	13	33	3	6
Tatarian, Utica	1.000	5	8	5	0	2
Tejada, Jamestown	.974	8	17	21	1	5
Torres, Niagara Falls	.983	49	71	98	3	21
Trujillo, Hamilton	.950	26	45	70	6	15
Valentin, Auburn	.939	27	50	58	7	12
Vargas, St. Catharines	1.000	5	12	6	0	3
Vazquez, Oneonta	.952	40	58	99	8	16
Wakefield, Welland	.958	7	15	8	1	2
Williams, Welland	.925	19	17	20	3	2

THIRD BASEMEN

Player and Club	Pct.	G.	PO.	A.	E.	DP.
Ausmus, Oneonta	1.000	1	1	1	0	0
Battell, Hamilton	.864	30	20	37	9	1
Beacom, St. Catharines	.971	34	22	46	2	6
Berlin, Hamilton	.839	21	14	38	10	5
Biggers, Hamilton	.857	12	5	7	2	1
Butterfield, Pittsfield	.828	41	41	70	23	5
Campas, Hamilton	.914	13	14	18	3	1
Cramer, Jamestown	.842	5	5	11	3	1
Davis, Oneonta	.870	65	27	87	17	11
Dixon, Elmira	.958	32	24	45	3	1
Dorante, Elmira	.500	1	0	1	1	0
Durkin, Watertown	.778	12	2	12	4	0
Eatinger, Utica	.875	2	3	4	1	0
Erdman, Geneva	.600	4	1	5	4	0
Escobar, Batavia	.929	40	25	66	7	5
Fortuna, Welland	.883	25	18	50	9	6
Gomez, Watertown	.845	67	49	120	31	9
Goodale, Niagara Falls	1.000	3	1	2	0	0
Grace, Jamestown	.833	4	0	5	1	0
Grayum, Geneva	.818	6	4	14	4	2
Da. Henderson, Auburn	1.000	1	3	0	0	1
De. Henderson, Pittsfield	.000	1	0	0	1	0
Herrera, Oneonta	.929	7	5	8	1	0
Hildreth, Erie	1.000	1	1	1	0	0
Horowitz, Erie	1.000	2	0	3	0	0
Hudson, Jamestown	.700	12	6	8	6	2
Kent, St. Catharines	.899	35	35	72	12	6
Kobza, Utica	.852	12	6	17	4	0
Lewis, Auburn	.750	3	1	2	1	0
Linden, Geneva	.795	29	14	48	16	3
Mendonca, Batavia	.910	44	28	63	9	11
Miller, Oneonta	1.000	6	4	8	0	1
Moccia, Niagara Falls	1.000	1	1	0	0	0
B. Moore, Elmira	1.000	3	4	3	0	0
C. Moore, Erie	.833	17	10	15	5	0
Munoz, Elmira	.973	17	8	28	1	2
Murray, Jamestown	.500	1	0	1	1	0
Perozo, Elmira	.956	25	19	24	2	0
Reimink, Niagara Falls	.939	46	37	71	7	5
Riley, Auburn	.881	22	17	35	7	5
Rodriguez, Welland	.830	19	11	28	8	1
Rosario, Elmira	1.000	3	1	3	0	0
Rose, Erie	.916	52	46	96	13	8
G. Scott, Geneva	.868	42	23	69	14	3
K. Scott, Auburn	.868	30	27	32	9	4
Segui, Pittsfield	.928	35	24	66	7	4
Shingledecker, Erie	.800	13	8	20	7	2
Stairs, Jamestown	.571	2	2	3	2	0
Tagliaferri, Niagara Falls	.829	31	11	57	14	5
Tejada, Jamestown	.500	1	0	1	1	0
Thomas, Welland	.818	23	18	36	12	1
Torres, Niagara Falls	1.000	1	1	0	0	0
Valentin, Auburn	.924	32	16	69	7	9
Vargas, St. Catharines	.800	8	9	3	3	1
Wakefield, Welland	.839	11	6	20	5	0
WALKER, Utica	.929	68	61	108	13	8
D. Williams, Watertown	.929	6	2	11	1	0
F. Williams, Welland	1.000	2	1	1	0	0
Wilson, Hamilton	.706	9	5	7	5	0
Woods, Jamestown	.882	55	37	98	18	9

SHORTSTOPS

Player and Club	Pct.	G.	PO.	A.	E.	DP.
Bailey, Welland	.907	18	27	41	7	5
Beasley, Erie	.912	16	19	33	5	8
Berlin, Hamilton	.957	6	16	16	1	2
Biggers, Hamilton	.900	2	4	5	1	0
Cromer, Hamilton	.932	35	66	85	11	21
Davison, Jamestown	.906	50	64	147	22	25
Dellicarri, Pittsfield	.955	4	7	14	1	3
Escobar, Batavia	.840	4	9	12	4	2
Fortuna, Welland	.852	5	7	16	4	2
Gomez, Watertown	1.000	4	4	9	0	2
Hancock, Watertown	.958	11	19	27	2	5
Hart, Watertown	.914	14	13	19	3	4
Hayes, Hamilton	.863	34	35	66	16	5
Da. Henderson, Auburn	.895	59	82	149	27	25
De. Henderson, Pittsfield	.904	35	60	81	15	15
Herrera, Oneonta	1.000	1	1	6	0	1

SHORTSTOPS—Continued

Player and Club	Pct.	G.	PO.	A.	E.	DP.	Player and Club	Pct.	G.	PO.	A.	E.	DP.
Hildreth, Erie	.927	61	80	147	18	34	C. Moore, Erie	.938	4	7	8	1	0
Howard, Pittsfield	1.000	2	3	1	0	1	Munoz, Elmira	.940	36	54	72	8	13
Hudson, Jamestown	.929	6	13	13	2	2	Navarro, Pittsfield	.911	36	55	118	17	22
Johnson, Watertown	.846	10	11	22	6	3	Odor, Watertown	.934	48	72	125	14	22
Kent, St. Catharines	.911	38	68	106	17	19	Perez, Batavia	.928	15	18	46	5	5
Kimberlin, Niagara Falls	.944	75	133	223	21	47	Perozo, Elmira	.917	4	6	5	1	1
Krause, Jamestown	.935	19	41	60	7	13	Rosario, Elmira	.907	47	53	93	15	19
Lewis, Auburn	.837	21	30	47	15	17	Sanders, Utica	.903	16	21	35	6	7
Linden, Geneva	.933	3	2	12	1	2	Scott, Geneva	.952	7	12	8	1	2
Lowery, Batavia	.895	49	58	139	23	27	Spencer, Elmira	1.000	2	2	4	0	1
Manahan, Welland	.926	50	66	135	16	19	Tatarian, Utica	.920	25	31	49	7	3
Mercedes, St. Catharines	.925	37	58	102	13	15	Tejada, 3 Jam-36 Utica	.950	39	56	97	8	16
Merejo, Utica	.929	4	3	10	1	1	Torres, Niagara Falls	1.000	1	2	4	0	2
Miller, Oneonta	1.000	12	21	22	0	4	VANSCOYOC, Oneonta	.950	65	107	157	14	20
Millette, Batavia	.914	10	14	39	5	4	Vargas, St. Catharines	.444	4	1	3	5	0
Monegro, Elmira	1.000	1	3	0	0	0	White, Geneva	.943	67	106	211	19	21
B. Moore, Elmira	1.000	1	0	1	0	0	Williams, Welland	.875	6	8	13	3	2

OUTFIELDERS

Player and Club	Pct.	G.	PO.	A.	E.	DP.	Player and Club	Pct.	G.	PO.	A.	E.	DP.
Allen, Hamilton	1.000	4	7	0	0	0	Linden, Geneva	.923	8	11	1	1	0
Banton, Hamilton	.969	65	87	6	3	2	Lofton, Auburn*	.837	28	37	4	8	0
Barnwell, Oneonta	.975	49	71	6	2	2	Madsen, Auburn	.956	52	83	3	4	0
Bennett, Batavia	.907	24	34	5	4	1	Mason, Jamestown	.867	14	13	0	2	0
Berthel, Erie	.932	53	92	4	7	0	May, Pittsfield	.955	25	40	2	2	0
Bieser, Batavia	1.000	10	11	0	0	0	Mayo, Jamestown*	.973	64	98	9	3	1
Biggers, Hamilton	1.000	2	1	0	0	0	McNeely, Elmira	.935	60	96	5	7	0
Brannon, Hamilton*	.966	69	138	4	5	0	Meek, Erie	.943	38	47	3	3	1
Braxton, Utica*	1.000	1	1	0	0	0	Michael, Elmira	.971	23	31	3	1	0
Brewington, Welland*	.931	16	27	0	2	0	Middlekauff, Niagara Falls	1.000	5	7	0	0	0
Brown, Batavia*	.983	54	114	5	2	2	Miller, Oneonta	1.000	1	1	0	0	0
Butterfield, Pittsfield	.974	25	37	1	1	0	Mobley, St. Catharines	.971	72	154	11	5	1
Cameron, Pittsfield	.978	49	81	6	2	1	Monegro, Elmira	1.000	1	2	0	0	0
Cornelius, Niagara Falls	.975	66	112	7	3	0	Moore, Erie	.889	10	8	0	1	0
Davis, Utica	.958	42	64	5	3	0	Morrison, Elmira	1.000	22	17	2	0	1
DeJardin, Watertown*	.974	36	38	0	1	0	Munoz, Elmira	1.000	3	5	1	0	0
Delgado, Geneva	1.000	12	18	0	0	0	Nelson, Welland	1.000	1	1	0	0	0
Devereaux, Oneonta*	1.000	2	3	0	0	0	Nicosia, Erie	.941	58	93	2	6	2
Dukes, Batavia	.818	15	8	1	2	0	Obando, Oneonta	.893	37	50	0	6	0
Durkin, Watertown	.889	7	7	1	1	0	Oster, Oneonta*	.970	51	88	8	3	2
Ebright, Geneva*	.961	67	94	5	4	0	Ostopowicz, Pittsfield	1.000	15	22	0	0	0
Elder, Jamestown*	.938	38	55	6	4	0	Owens, Batavia*	1.000	8	9	1	0	0
Etheredge, Batavia	.962	26	47	3	2	0	Pennyfeather, Welland	.931	75	170	6	13	2
Ferran, Watertown*	.937	69	109	9	8	3	Perozo, Elmira	1.000	3	4	0	0	0
Foggie, Watertown*	.923	42	48	0	4	0	Pipik, Jamestown	.871	22	23	4	4	0
Francisco, Geneva	.930	59	119	1	9	0	PLEMMONS, Utica	.992	66	125	3	1	0
Goodale, Niagara Falls	.981	54	93	8	2	1	Pride, Pittsfield	.964	54	105	3	4	1
Graham, Hamilton*	.989	50	89	4	1	1	Reed, Auburn*	.932	56	93	3	7	0
Grayum, Geneva	.975	53	74	5	2	0	Reimink, Niagara Falls	1.000	7	7	1	0	0
Gremillion, Welland	.958	18	21	2	1	0	Riley, Auburn	1.000	3	3	1	0	0
Hanks, Elmira	1.000	5	2	0	0	0	Rodriguez, Welland	1.000	6	9	0	0	0
Harris, Utica	.957	52	110	2	5	0	Santana, Auburn*	.898	52	93	4	11	0
Hedge, Erie	.964	48	79	1	3	0	Scott, Auburn	1.000	7	3	1	0	0
De. Henderson, Pittsfield	1.000	4	5	1	0	0	Shannon, Hamilton	1.000	18	23	2	0	1
V. Henderson, Welland	.965	70	103	7	4	1	Spencer, Pittsfield	.901	53	76	6	9	1
Am. Hicks, Erie*	.970	36	64	1	2	0	Stacey, Geneva*	1.000	4	2	0	0	0
An. Hicks, Hamilton	1.000	16	21	1	0	1	Strickland, Oneonta	.950	12	19	0	1	0
Hill, Oneonta	.966	44	82	3	3	0	Taylor, Batavia*	.968	38	59	1	2	0
Holifield, St. Catharines*	.983	58	115	4	2	0	Tesmer, Pittsfield	.875	8	6	1	1	0
Howard, Pittsfield	1.000	1	1	0	0	0	Thomas, Welland	.750	4	3	0	1	0
D. Howell, Oneonta*	.930	44	64	2	5	0	Thompson, St. Catharines	.961	72	111	11	5	1
P. Howell, Pittsfield	.975	56	113	5	3	1	Trusky, Niagara Falls	1.000	20	35	3	0	0
Hurst, Niagara Falls*	.959	50	91	2	4	0	Urbon, Batavia*	1.000	26	52	3	0	2
Hyde, Batavia	.975	44	73	5	2	1	Welch, Geneva	.932	32	52	3	4	0
Jenkins, Elmira	.929	71	135	9	11	2	M. Wilson, Hamilton	.929	14	26	0	2	0
D. Johnson, Welland	1.000	21	33	0	0	0	N. Wilson, St. Catharines*	.929	30	37	2	3	0
K. Johnson, Jamestown	.930	38	47	6	4	0	Witherspoon, Elmira	1.000	1	1	0	0	0
L. Johnson, Auburn*	.893	45	70	5	9	0	Wolak, Utica	.938	54	88	2	6	0
Keating, Niagara Falls*	.949	52	106	5	6	0	Woodruff, Batavia	1.000	13	21	3	0	1
Lake, Jamestown	.949	68	87	7	5	2	D. Young, Watertown	.970	70	95	2	3	0
Lewis, Auburn	1.000	15	15	0	0	0	E. Young, Watertown	.933	33	41	1	3	0
Limoncelli, Elmira	1.000	2	2	0	0	0	Zaksek, Utica*	.987	31	71	3	1	2

CATCHERS

Player and Club	Pct.	G.	PO.	A.	E.	DP.	PB.	Player and Club	Pct.	G.	PO.	A.	E.	DP.
Albright, Niagara Falls	.983	60	439	71	9	8	8	Hanks, Elmira	.963	7	26	0	1	0	3
Ausmus, Oneonta	.984	52	400	42	7	1	7	Hernandez, Oneonta	.982	20	149	19	3	1	7
Battell, Hamilton	.857	2	6	0	1	0	0	Hines, Pittsfield	.969	39	220	32	8	1	5
Beltran, Welland	.971	34	239	29	8	4	14	Horowitz, Erie	.970	22	148	15	5	0	3
Bennett, Auburn	1.000	2	9	3	0	0	0	Ingram, Utica	.980	47	353	39	8	4	9
Bieser, Batavia	.981	12	93	8	2	2	2	Laker, Jamestown	.984	55	437	61	8	5	16
Bruehl, Auburn	.979	31	199	29	5	1	12	Lozinski, Batavia	1.000	7	52	4	0	1	0
Caraballo, Welland	.952	6	36	4	2	0	1	Makarewicz, Auburn	.982	39	280	49	6	3	5
Castillo, Pittsfield	.991	25	186	26	2	3	3	Matilla, Elmira	.968	12	83	8	3	0	3
Colon, Erie	.953	15	112	9	6	0	3	Metts, Erie	.982	27	197	27	4	0	6
Cramer, Jamestown	.982	18	147	18	3	1	2	Mota, Watertown	.976	59	472	51	13	2	15
Delgado, St. Catharines	.974	10	63	13	2	1	3	Mundy, Geneva	.975	44	344	49	10	4	9
Dorante, Elmira	.976	32	216	30	6	1	6	Nelson, Welland	.972	26	187	21	6	0	10
Erdman, Geneva	.976	21	142	21	4	2	3	O'HALLORAN, St. Catharines	.988	48	356	40	5	4	15
Fernandez, Hamilton	.985	47	369	35	6	4	2	Peterson, Welland	.984	15	108	15	2	0	13
Garcia, St. Catharines	.981	19	143	16	3	0	6	Piskor, Pittsfield	.939	7	42	4	3	0	0

CATCHERS—Continued

Player and Club	Pct.	G.	PO.	A.	E.	DP.	Player and Club	Pct.	G.	PO.	A.	E.	DP.
Redman, Hamilton	.990	32	262	29	3	5	Small, Jamestown	.971	6	34	0	1	0
Reynolds, Erie	.977	33	230	26	6	4	Stocker, Batavia	.986	17	131	11	2	1
Riemer, Watertown	.969	10	30	1	1	0	Tesmer, Pittsfield	1.000	3	9	0	0	3
Rosado, Batavia	.980	44	301	40	7	3	Thompson, Utica	.973	16	92	17	3	1
Rosfelder, Elmira	1.000	1	2	0	0	0	Tucholski, Welland	1.000	3	29	3	0	2
Ross, Oneonta	.989	13	81	9	1	1	Wedge, Elmira	.994	36	283	30	2	7
Scott, Auburn	.978	17	79	10	2	1	Wiley, Niagara Falls	1.000	1	7	0	0	0
Sellers, Niagara Falls	.993	21	116	19	1	5	Williams, Watertown	.994	19	139	20	1	5
Singley, Utica	.968	21	154	25	6	8	Zinter, Pittsfield	1.000	6	33	3	0	2

PITCHERS

Player and Club	Pct.	G.	PO.	A.	E.	DP.	Player and Club	Pct.	G.	PO.	A.	E.	DP.
Alexander, Watertown*	1.000	1	1	0	0	0	Infante, Hamilton	1.000	24	3	8	0	1
Allen, Watertown*	.958	10	1	22	1	0	Jockish, St. Catharines*	1.000	20	0	4	0	0
Archibald, Jamestown	.889	24	6	10	2	0	Johnson, Pittsfield	1.000	24	0	13	0	1
Arvesen, Welland	1.000	5	0	2	0	0	Johnston, Pittsfield*	1.000	7	0	2	0	0
Ayrault, Batavia	1.000	4	1	3	0	1	Johnstone, Pittsfield	.889	15	7	17	3	0
Barnes, Jamestown*	1.000	2	0	1	0	0	S. Jones, Geneva	.833	14	3	7	2	0
Beer, Geneva	.882	13	3	12	2	1	T. Jones, Auburn*	.842	11	4	12	3	1
Betances, Niagara Falls	.889	9	3	5	1	1	Juarbe, Oneonta*	.900	13	4	14	2	1
Bevenour, Watertown*	1.000	10	1	3	0	0	Kerr, Erie	.938	9	3	12	1	1
Bicknell, St. Catharines	1.000	17	10	8	0	1	Keyser, Utica	.909	14	3	17	2	0
Bird, Welland	.750	17	0	9	3	0	Kilgo, Jamestown*	.962	30	9	16	1	2
Blumberg, St. Catharines*	1.000	17	2	11	0	0	Kiser, Jamestown	.941	12	1	15	1	0
Boss, Hamilton	.917	15	3	8	1	0	Kizziah, St. Catharines	.861	17	7	24	5	0
Bowen, Erie*	1.000	7	0	1	0	1	Klancnik, Jamestown	1.000	18	1	2	0	0
Bowlan, Hamilton	.958	16	10	13	1	0	Konopki, Elmira	1.000	6	1	1	0	0
Bratlien, Batavia	.941	19	3	13	1	0	Kovach, Watertown	.909	15	12	8	2	1
Brooks, Hamilton	.500	5	2	0	2	0	Kuder, Welland*	.846	14	0	11	2	0
Broome, Welland*	1.000	13	1	3	0	0	Kulina, St. Catharines*	1.000	2	0	1	0	0
Dan. Brown, Erie	.000	3	0	0	1	0	LANGBEHN, Pittsfield*	1.000	14	6	21	0	2
Dar. Brown, St. Catharines	.615	18	1	7	5	0	Langston, Niagara Falls	.700	13	3	4	3	0
Dav. Brown, Erie	.500	17	0	2	2	0	Lata, Hamilton	1.000	23	11	10	0	2
Du. Brown, Auburn	.333	2	1	0	2	0	Latham, Welland*	.800	15	3	9	3	0
Brubaker, Oneonta	1.000	14	1	5	0	0	Leinen, Erie*	.889	16	4	20	3	1
Burroughs, Utica	1.000	9	1	5	0	1	Locker, Elmira	1.000	19	4	4	0	0
Bush, Geneva	.957	15	5	17	1	0	Logan, Jamestown	.963	15	11	15	1	2
Butler, Pittsfield	1.000	1	0	1	0	0	Logue, Niagara Falls	.875	26	4	3	1	1
Buzzard, Jamestown	1.000	25	5	7	0	0	Long, Utica*	.800	20	1	11	3	0
Byerly, Welland*	1.000	16	2	11	0	0	Ludwig, Geneva	.750	18	2	4	2	0
Campusano, Auburn*	.800	19	0	8	2	1	Magria, Welland	1.000	14	0	5	0	0
Canestro, Oneonta*	.955	22	3	18	1	0	Malone, Oneonta*	1.000	18	1	9	0	0
Capparelli, Utica	.714	12	2	3	2	0	Marcero, Niagara Falls*	1.000	15	3	13	0	1
Cassidy, Hamilton*	.909	6	4	6	1	0	Marrero, Auburn*	.857	20	3	15	3	1
Cebuhar, Hamilton*	.917	17	2	9	1	2	Marshall, Niagara Falls*	1.000	6	2	4	0	0
Cesari, Geneva	1.000	20	4	15	0	2	G. Martin, St. Catharines	.875	19	5	9	2	0
Chase, Oneonta*	1.000	16	3	4	0	0	T. Martin, Erie*	1.000	7	0	5	0	0
Ciaglo, Jamestown*	.857	4	3	3	1	0	Masters, Welland	1.000	13	2	4	0	0
Cooper, Utica	.706	10	6	6	5	0	McCann, Pittsfield	1.000	13	3	5	0	0
Corsaro, Batavia	.923	22	3	9	1	0	McCutcheon, St. Catharines	.929	19	4	22	2	0
Davino, Utica	.857	19	2	10	2	0	McDowell, Auburn	.500	15	0	3	3	0
Deller, Welland*	1.000	28	3	4	0	0	Medina, Pittsfield	.600	9	2	1	2	0
Desapio, Auburn*	.750	19	0	12	4	0	Meek, Erie	1.000	4	1	3	0	0
DeSilva, Niagara Falls	1.000	4	3	7	0	1	Mehrtens, Utica*	.828	16	4	20	5	0
Dipoto, Watertown	.947	14	5	13	1	2	Merriman, Watertown	.897	14	8	18	3	2
Dodd, St. Catharines	1.000	5	1	1	0	1	Michael, Elmira	1.000	4	1	2	0	0
Doherty, Niagara Falls	1.000	26	5	11	0	2	Middaugh, Utica	1.000	11	2	16	0	0
Dorn, Pittsfield	1.000	6	3	3	0	1	Milchin, Hamilton*	.889	8	5	3	1	0
Doss, Welland	.846	13	2	9	2	1	Moody, Oneonta	.833	30	3	7	2	0
Eck, Erie*	1.000	1	0	1	0	0	Morrison, Elmira	1.000	5	3	4	0	0
Eddy, Jamestown	.967	11	4	25	1	2	Morton, Elmira*	.800	3	2	2	1	0
Egloff, Watertown	.750	22	1	2	1	0	Mosley, Elmira*	1.000	26	4	6	0	0
Elliott, Batavia	.800	8	3	5	2	0	Neill, Watertown	.900	19	3	6	1	0
Emm, Auburn	1.000	15	3	5	0	1	Nelinbach, St. Catharines	1.000	8	0	1	0	0
Espino, Geneva	1.000	13	3	8	0	0	Nute, Niagara Falls*	.857	11	0	6	1	0
Ettles, Niagara Falls	1.000	5	1	3	0	1	Oquist, Erie	.950	15	8	11	1	0
Fletcher, Batavia	.923	14	5	7	1	1	Parris, Batavia	.850	13	4	13	3	2
Freitas, Pittsfield	1.000	13	3	15	0	2	G. Patterson, Geneva*	1.000	2	1	5	0	0
Gaddy, Batavia*	1.000	16	4	9	0	0	J. Patterson, Batavia	1.000	9	3	11	0	0
Galvan, Utica*	.800	2	1	3	1	0	Pena, Erie*	.875	19	0	7	1	0
Garcia, Niagara Falls	1.000	4	4	13	0	0	Perez, Auburn	.917	11	5	6	1	1
Gardella, Oneonta*	1.000	28	1	2	0	0	Pershke, Utica	1.000	14	1	4	0	0
Goergen, Batavia	1.000	7	2	12	0	1	Piatt, Watertown	.909	15	3	7	1	0
Golden, Hamilton	1.000	29	2	2	0	0	Pinto, Niagara Falls	1.000	18	1	6	0	0
B. Gonzales, Auburn	.833	24	3	2	1	0	Porter, Auburn	.909	7	4	6	1	0
F. Gonzales, Niagara Falls*	.875	10	0	7	1	0	Quantrill, Elmira	1.000	20	3	12	0	2
Gore, Geneva	.833	14	1	4	1	0	Regira, Jamestown	.667	5	1	1	1	0
Gorman, Utica	.875	13	2	12	2	0	Reynolds, Auburn*	.909	6	5	5	1	0
Gorton, Hamilton	1.000	20	2	4	0	0	A. Rhodes, Erie*	1.000	5	0	5	0	0
Green, Hamilton*	.900	35	2	7	1	0	R. Rhodes, Oneonta	1.000	12	5	4	0	0
Grubb, Hamilton	.900	32	4	5	1	1	Richmond, Pittsfield	1.000	18	6	14	0	2
Gunderson, Batavia	1.000	13	2	8	0	0	Riddle, Erie	1.000	14	2	6	0	0
Harriger, Pittsfield	1.000	3	2	10	0	0	Riley, Elmira*	1.000	17	5	11	0	0
Heiderscheit, Jamestown	.900	21	2	7	1	1	Roscoe, Watertown	1.000	9	3	5	0	0
Heins, Niagara Falls	1.000	17	5	5	0	0	Rosfelder, Elmira	1.000	2	2	1	0	1
Hemmerly, Erie*	1.000	26	0	8	0	0	Ruffin, Utica	.917	15	7	15	2	0
Herrmann, Niagara Falls	1.000	15	6	12	0	2	Rupp, Erie	1.000	2	0	1	0	0
Hoy, Elmira	.976	26	12	29	1	3	Rush, Elmira	.957	15	8	14	1	0
Hutson, St. Catharines	.778	5	1	6	2	0	Ryan, Watertown*	1.000	7	1	8	0	1
Hutton, Oneonta	1.000	12	5	8	0	0	Sanders, Elmira	.944	16	7	10	1	1
Hyson, Auburn	.917	15	4	7	1	0	Santana, St. Catharines	.667	10	0	2	1	0

PITCHERS—Continued

Player and Club	Pct.	G.	PO.	A.	E.	DP.
Seminara, Oneonta	.889	11	9	15	3	2
Shea, Niagara Falls	.900	11	2	7	1	1
Slaughter, Welland	.667	4	0	2	1	0
Small, Auburn	1.000	10	1	1	0	0
J. Smith, Utica	1.000	1	0	3	0	0
R. Smith, Erie*	1.000	12	2	1	0	0
Somerville, Erie	1.000	3	0	1	0	0
Sommer, Jamestown	.885	13	7	16	3	2
Stanford, Oneonta	.968	15	5	25	1	4
M. Stevens, Batavia	.917	16	2	9	1	0
S. Stevens, Utica	.917	22	4	7	1	0
Stock, St. Catharines	.875	20	5	9	2	1
Sullivan, Batavia	.750	24	2	4	2	0
Swartzbaugh, Geneva	1.000	18	6	18	0	0
Sweeney, Geneva	.929	23	5	8	1	2
Telgheder, Pittsfield	1.000	13	2	8	0	1
Thigpen, Jamestown	1.000	2	0	1	0	0
Thoden, Jamestown	1.000	1	1	3	0	1
Thompson, Elmira	1.000	3	1	0	0	0
Tukes, Hamilton	.818	14	3	6	2	0
Uhrhan, Elmira	1.000	19	4	4	0	0
Van Winkle, Utica	.667	17	2	2	2	0
Vazquez, Pittsfield	.909	3	1	9	1	0
Vespe, Watertown	1.000	17	4	4	0	0
Vitko, Pittsfield	1.000	5	3	5	0	1
Wagner, Welland	1.000	13	7	8	0	2
Wakefield, Welland	.750	18	3	3	2	1
Wall, Auburn	1.000	12	6	7	0	1
Wanish, St. Catharines	.833	15	1	4	1	0
Way, Welland*	.800	23	5	3	2	0
Wessel, Jamestown	.600	18	0	3	2	0
West, Batavia*	.875	10	1	6	1	0
Wheatcroft, Erie	1.000	7	3	0	0	0
Whitehead, Jamestown	.765	12	5	8	4	1
Williams, Erie*	.929	19	3	10	1	0
Willis, Geneva	.971	16	6	27	1	1
Willoughby, Pittsfield*	.750	16	1	5	2	1
Wilson, Niagara Falls	1.000	5	1	0	0	0
Young, Jamestown	1.000	18	6	13	0	1

The following players did not have any fielding statistics at the positions indicated or appeared only as a designated hitter, pinch-hitter or pinch-runner: Agado, p; Alvarez, of; Battell, ss; Brannon, p; Bruehl, p; Butterfield, 2b; Campas, ss; G. Diaz, dh, ph; J. Diaz, p; Doman, p; Dorante, of; Fortuna, of; Re. Francisco, p; Gryskevich, of; Horowitz, p; D. Howell, p; Hutto, p; Keefer, 3b; Keller, p; Lake, 2b, 3b; Limoncelli, 3b; Logue, ss; Madsen, 3b; Metts, of; Morelli, c; Ostopowicz, ss, p; Petlick, p; Piskor, p; Redman, 3b; Repoz, p; R. Rhodes, of; Rivera, p; Segui, p; Sellers, of; Tejada, of; Tucholski, 3b; Uhrhan, of; M. Wilson, 2b.

CLUB PITCHING

Club	ERA.	G.	CG.	ShO.	Sv.	IP.	H.	R.	ER.	HR.	HB.	BB.	Int. BB.	SO.	WP.	Bk.
Pittsfield	2.86	76	15	10	23	658.2	595	284	209	22	23	178	9	475	24	11
Jamestown	2.90	76	4	5	26	668.1	599	291	215	21	28	295	12	613	34	11
Batavia	2.93	76	12	10	15	674.2	583	299	220	72	22	181	11	558	24	8
Watertown	3.00	77	13	4	21	681.2	598	312	227	22	23	260	5	662	58	16
Oneonta	3.14	75	6	6	26	651.2	583	284	227	30	21	250	11	615	34	14
Welland	3.19	76	4	4	17	646.0	576	346	229	32	27	298	4	598	62	17
St. Catharines	3.43	76	5	5	14	665.2	628	337	254	42	22	229	6	551	48	14
Elmira	3.47	76	17	3	8	664.1	655	331	256	37	30	238	5	596	27	22
Geneva	3.48	75	16	2	11	662.0	615	353	256	41	37	191	18	606	42	17
Utica	3.56	78	2	5	19	689.2	588	359	273	37	32	339	3	597	48	15
Hamilton	3.57	76	2	6	21	645.1	616	339	256	37	29	240	17	620	32	25
Niagara Falls	4.05	76	6	6	18	665.0	650	343	299	40	23	231	9	555	30	17
Auburn	4.29	77	11	2	17	660.2	701	426	315	42	41	327	10	555	60	20
Erie	4.84	74	6	4	10	636.1	711	447	342	60	29	251	9	568	48	19

PITCHERS' RECORDS
(Leading Qualifiers for Earned-Run Average Leadership — 62 or More Innings)

*Throws lefthanded.

Pitcher—Club	W.	L.	Pct.	ERA.	G.	GS.	CG.	GF.	ShO.	Sv.	IP.	H.	R.	ER.	HR.	HB.	BB.	Int. BB.	SO.	WP.
Canestro, Oneonta*	7	2	.778	1.05	22	8	1	6	1	0	77.1	51	11	9	3	2	20	3	61	1
Kilgo, Jamestown*	6	3	.667	1.39	30	3	0	21	0	8	64.2	46	16	10	3	0	20	1	74	4
Moody, Oneonta	4	3	.571	1.40	30	0	0	16	0	4	64.1	46	13	10	4	0	17	2	81	0
S. Jones, Geneva	6	2	.750	1.53	14	14	2	0	1	0	94.0	54	22	16	3	3	28	0	113	8
Sommer, Jamestown	6	4	.600	1.68	13	13	2	0	1	0	80.1	63	18	15	1	3	30	0	72	4
Wall, Auburn	7	0	1.000	1.79	12	8	3	2	1	1	65.1	45	17	13	2	3	12	0	69	2
Langbehn, Pittsfield*	10	3	.769	1.80	14	14	3	0	2	0	100.0	76	33	20	1	2	35	3	70	2
Young, Jamestown	5	2	.714	1.94	18	10	0	8	0	4	65.0	63	18	14	2	5	14	0	62	6
Seminara, Oneonta	7	2	.778	2.06	11	10	3	0	1	0	70.0	51	25	16	0	3	18	0	70	1
Bird, Welland*	6	7	.462	2.20	17	9	1	5	0	0	65.1	59	27	16	2	4	31	1	77	6

Departmental Leaders: G—Green, 35; W—Johnstone, 11; L—McCutcheon, 12; Pct.—Wall, 1.000; GS—McCutcheon, 19; CG—Beer, Quantrill, Willis, 5; GF—Gardella, 26; ShO—Marcero, 3; Sv.—Gardella, 19; IP—Hoy, 118.0; H—McCutcheon, 129; R—McCutcheon, 60; ER—Pena, 50; HR—Fletcher, 13; HB—Bush, Rush, 9; BB—Mehrtens, 54; IBB—Cesari, 6; SO—S. Jones, 113; WP—McCutcheon, 12.

(All Pitchers—Listed Alphabetically)

Pitcher—Club	W.	L.	Pct.	ERA.	G.	GS.	CG.	GF.	ShO.	Sv.	IP.	H.	R.	ER.	HR.	HB.	BB.	Int. BB.	SO.	WP.
Agado, Batavia	0	0	.000	0.00	2	0	0	1	0	0	3.2	2	0	0	0	0	5	0	1	0
Alexander, Watertown*	0	0	.000	5.40	1	1	0	0	0	0	3.1	5	2	2	0	0	1	0	3	1
Allen, Watertown*	2	5	.286	3.34	10	10	2	0	0	0	59.1	64	30	22	3	0	15	0	44	2
Archibald, Jamestown	4	0	1.000	3.14	24	3	0	15	0	7	51.2	54	23	18	0	1	22	4	47	3
Arvesen, Welland	1	0	1.000	3.38	5	1	0	2	0	1	13.1	8	6	5	0	0	6	0	16	2
Ayrault, Batavia	2	1	.667	1.38	4	3	2	1	1	0	26.0	13	5	4	2	2	7	0	20	0
Barnes, Jamestown*	1	0	1.000	1.00	2	2	0	0	0	0	9.0	4	1	1	0	0	3	0	15	1
Beer, Geneva	5	6	.455	2.64	13	11	5	1	1	0	75.0	75	34	22	3	2	6	0	72	2
Betances, Niagara Falls	1	3	.250	7.61	9	9	0	0	0	0	36.2	40	34	31	4	2	28	0	35	3
Bevenour, Watertown*	1	0	1.000	4.00	10	1	0	5	0	1	27.0	29	15	12	2	1	17	0	28	3
Bicknell, St. Catharines	6	5	.545	4.19	17	11	1	2	0	0	86.0	80	56	40	6	4	35	0	60	9
Bird, Welland*	6	7	.462	2.20	17	9	1	5	0	0	65.1	59	27	16	2	4	31	1	77	6
Blumberg, St. Catharines*	3	5	.375	2.36	17	14	0	1	0	1	87.2	63	32	23	4	2	28	0	102	3
Boss, Hamilton	4	4	.500	4.22	15	13	0	1	0	0	70.1	63	39	33	5	6	37	1	56	4
Bowen, Erie*	0	0	.000	6.75	7	0	4	0	0	0	9.1	11	7	7	0	2	10	0	10	2
Bowlan, Hamilton	4	5	.444	5.01	16	14	0	0	0	0	73.2	98	50	41	3	4	16	1	73	4
Brannon, Hamilton	0	0	.000	9.00	2	0	0	2	0	0	2.0	3	2	2	0	0	0	1	0	0
Bratlien, Batavia	4	6	.400	3.59	19	12	4	4	0	1	95.1	80	50	38	12	4	13	1	97	0
Brooks, Hamilton	0	2	.000	2.27	5	5	0	0	0	0	31.2	25	15	8	2	0	4	0	35	0
Broome, Welland*	4	0	1.000	1.57	13	2	0	7	0	1	34.1	23	10	6	3	2	9	0	24	2
Dan. Brown, Erie	0	1	.000	4.50	3	0	0	0	0	0	4.0	2	5	2	0	1	3	0	3	1
Dar. Brown, St. Catharines	4	3	.571	3.93	18	10	0	0	0	0	75.2	82	41	33	4	3	26	0	67	4
Dav. Brown, Erie	0	3	.000	8.31	17	1	0	3	0	1	21.2	25	33	20	1	2	31	2	21	11

Pitcher—Club	W.	L.	Pct.	ERA.	G.	GS.	CG.	GF.	ShO.	Sv.	IP.	H.	R.	ER.	HR.	HB.	BB.	Int. BB.	SO.	WP.
Du. Brown, Auburn	0	1	.000	3.12	2	1	1	0	0	0	8.2	6	6	3	0	0	5	0	9	0
Brubaker, Oneonta	5	2	.714	3.20	14	0	0	5	0	0	39.1	37	17	14	1	1	12	1	21	2
Bruehl, Auburn	0	0	.000	9.00	1	0	0	1	0	0	1.0	1	3	1	0	0	3	0	1	1
Burroughs, Utica	0	2	.000	7.45	9	5	0	4	0	0	19.1	21	23	16	1	1	33	0	12	8
Bush, Geneva	3	4	.429	3.77	15	14	1	0	0	0	90.2	93	50	38	7	9	14	3	50	2
Butler, Pittsfield	0	0	.000	27.00	1	0	0	0	0	0	0.1	2	3	1	0	0	1	0	0	0
Buzzard, Jamestown	1	4	.200	3.59	25	0	0	15	0	5	42.2	42	24	17	1	0	30	2	44	0
Byerly, Welland	1	4	.200	4.21	16	6	0	6	0	2	51.1	58	36	24	4	2	13	1	41	1
Campusano, Auburn*	2	3	.400	4.62	19	6	0	10	0	2	60.1	67	43	31	2	7	37	0	41	10
Canestro, Oneonta*	7	2	.778	1.05	22	8	1	6	1	0	77.1	51	11	9	3	2	20	3	61	1
Capparelli, Utica	2	0	1.000	3.42	12	0	0	8	0	0	23.2	20	11	9	1	1	12	0	30	2
Cassidy, Hamilton*	4	1	.800	1.64	6	6	0	0	0	0	38.1	22	10	7	1	3	10	0	33	0
Cebuhar, Hamilton*	4	4	.500	3.27	17	10	1	2	1	0	71.2	66	32	26	5	8	25	1	77	6
Cesari, Geneva	3	3	.500	4.32	20	1	0	15	0	5	41.2	51	25	20	2	3	16	6	23	0
Chase, Oneonta*	0	2	.000	3.97	16	0	0	12	0	2	34.0	42	21	15	2	1	21	1	18	2
Ciaglo, Jamestown*	0	2	.000	4.19	4	4	0	0	0	0	19.1	16	15	9	0	0	13	0	21	1
Cooper, Utica	4	3	.571	4.18	10	10	0	0	0	0	56.0	52	28	26	3	0	29	0	33	3
Corsaro, Batavia	0	5	.000	2.95	22	0	0	15	0	5	39.2	31	20	13	7	0	13	3	33	2
Davino, Utica	6	1	.857	2.82	19	1	0	8	0	2	54.1	42	25	17	1	2	12	1	63	0
Deller, Welland	1	1	.500	2.36	28	0	0	18	0	7	42.0	31	20	11	3	3	20	0	48	3
Desapio, Auburn*	4	4	.500	3.76	19	8	1	6	0	1	69.1	98	50	29	4	2	24	1	37	3
DeSilva, Niagara Falls	3	0	1.000	1.88	4	4	0	0	0	0	24.0	15	5	5	0	2	8	0	24	3
Diaz, Elmira*	0	0	.000	0.00	1	0	0	1	0	0	0.2	2	1	0	0	0	0	0	2	0
Dipoto, Watertown	6	5	.545	3.61	14	14	1	0	0	0	87.1	75	42	35	3	4	39	0	98	10
Dodd, St. Catharines	0	1	.000	4.91	5	0	0	3	0	0	11.0	17	12	6	1	0	6	2	7	1
Doherty, Niagara Falls	1	1	.500	0.95	26	1	0	25	0	14	47.1	30	7	5	1	3	6	2	45	2
Doman, Erie*	0	1	.000	4.26	10	0	0	5	0	2	12.2	21	7	6	1	1	2	0	13	0
Dorn, Pittsfield	4	1	.800	3.35	6	6	0	0	0	0	37.2	42	19	14	1	1	11	0	22	3
Doss, Welland	4	4	.500	1.76	13	9	1	0	1	0	56.1	36	20	11	1	4	36	1	48	5
Eck, Erie*	0	0	.000	8.10	1	0	0	0	0	0	3.1	8	4	3	0	0	1	0	5	1
Eddy, Jamestown	8	1	.889	2.22	11	11	1	0	0	0	69.0	74	19	17	3	6	17	0	43	0
Egloff, Watertown	1	1	.500	2.59	22	0	0	17	0	8	48.2	33	19	14	2	1	24	1	63	9
Elliott, Batavia	4	1	.800	1.42	8	8	0	0	0	0	57.0	45	21	9	2	0	14	1	48	4
Emm, Auburn	1	4	.200	3.95	15	1	0	8	0	2	41.0	44	23	18	1	2	12	2	24	4
Espino, Geneva	2	4	.333	4.40	13	5	2	6	0	1	47.0	45	28	23	0	7	14	0	38	10
Ettles, Niagara Falls	3	0	1.000	1.02	5	0	0	3	0	1	17.2	12	3	2	0	0	2	0	21	1
Fletcher, Batavia	7	5	.583	3.28	14	14	3	0	0	0	82.1	77	41	30	13	3	28	0	58	3
Francisco, Geneva	0	0	.000	0.00	1	0	0	1	0	0	0.1	0	0	0	0	0	0	0	0	1
Freitas, Pittsfield	3	0	1.000	4.05	13	2	0	8	0	0	33.1	37	19	15	2	0	5	1	16	2
Gaddy, Batavia*	4	6	.400	2.97	16	11	1	3	1	0	75.2	61	29	25	9	0	22	0	72	1
Galvan, Utica*	0	0	.000	0.00	2	0	0	1	0	0	4.1	1	0	0	0	1	0	4	0
Garcia, Niagara Falls	5	1	.833	1.56	7	6	1	0	0	0	40.1	27	12	7	3	3	7	0	39	0
Gardella, Oneonta*	2	0	1.000	1.67	28	0	0	26	0	19	37.2	23	8	7	2	0	15	0	66	1
Goergen, Batavia	2	3	.400	3.57	7	7	0	0	0	0	35.1	31	16	14	4	1	6	0	22	0
Golden, Hamilton	2	2	.500	4.34	29	0	0	8	0	1	37.1	37	23	18	2	0	26	4	53	5
B. Gonzales, Batavia	3	5	.375	4.02	24	0	0	21	0	6	40.1	46	23	18	2	2	15	5	41	5
F. Gonzales, Niagara Falls*	3	3	.500	3.79	10	5	1	3	1	0	38.0	36	20	16	2	0	16	1	35	0
Gore, Geneva	1	2	.333	4.29	14	1	0	8	0	0	35.2	29	20	17	3	0	24	1	38	3
Gorman, Utica	1	3	.250	5.88	13	4	0	6	0	0	33.2	38	29	22	3	5	23	0	17	4
Gorton, Hamilton	0	3	.000	3.00	20	0	0	19	0	13	27.0	23	14	9	1	2	11	3	29	0
Green, Hamilton*	2	4	.333	3.13	35	0	0	9	0	1	37.1	34	23	13	2	0	22	2	50	5
Grubb, Hamilton	3	4	.429	3.24	32	0	0	14	0	2	41.2	38	18	15	0	1	13	3	42	1
Gunderson, Batavia	0	1	.000	3.28	13	0	0	8	0	3	24.2	27	11	9	2	3	8	1	17	0
Harriger, Pittsfield	2	0	1.000	1.71	3	3	1	0	1	0	21.0	20	4	4	0	1	0	0	17	0
Heiderscheit, Jamestown	2	2	.500	3.73	21	3	0	5	0	1	50.2	49	38	21	2	0	26	1	43	0
Heins, Niagara Falls	3	2	.600	5.11	17	1	0	5	0	1	44.0	43	28	25	2	3	20	0	34	2
Hemmerly, Erie*	2	5	.286	5.11	26	2	0	18	0	5	44.0	53	30	25	4	1	15	1	28	2
Herrmann, Niagara Falls	7	4	.636	4.21	15	15	1	0	0	0	87.2	98	47	41	4	3	24	0	61	1
Horowitz, Erie	0	0	.000	32.40	1	0	0	1	0	0	1.2	3	6	6	1	0	5	0	2	1
Howell, Oneonta*	0	0	.000	9.00	1	0	0	1	0	0	2.0	3	2	2	0	2	1	0	1	0
Hoy, Elmira	6	10	.375	2.82	26	12	3	6	0	1	118.0	109	52	37	6	4	37	1	73	3
Hutson, St. Catharines	3	1	.750	1.70	5	5	2	0	2	0	37.0	22	7	7	2	2	2	0	29	0
Hutto, Jamestown	0	0	.000	4.50	2	0	0	0	0	0	2.0	1	1	1	1	0	0	0	4	0
Hutton, Oneonta	6	2	.750	4.07	12	12	0	0	0	0	66.1	70	39	30	1	1	24	0	62	5
Hyson, Auburn	4	5	.444	3.69	15	12	2	2	0	1	78.0	77	42	32	7	5	36	1	78	4
Infante, Hamilton	1	4	.200	3.56	24	3	1	12	0	4	48.0	54	32	19	4	0	11	1	29	0
Jockish, St. Catharines*	2	3	.400	3.91	20	0	0	18	0	5	23.0	25	12	10	0	1	15	0	23	2
Johnson, Pittsfield	0	1	.000	1.85	24	0	0	23	0	18	39.0	33	11	8	2	1	5	1	30	1
Johnston, Pittsfield*	2	1	.667	3.00	7	0	0	5	0	1	15.0	13	9	5	0	1	3	0	19	0
Johnstone, Pittsfield	11	2	.846	2.77	15	15	2	0	1	0	104.0	101	47	32	4	3	28	1	60	4
S. Jones, Geneva	6	2	.750	1.53	14	14	2	0	1	0	94.0	54	22	16	3	3	28	0	113	8
T. Jones, Auburn*	2	3	.400	5.44	11	9	1	1	0	0	49.2	47	39	30	2	2	42	1	71	9
Juarbe, Oneonta*	7	3	.700	2.82	13	13	1	0	0	0	73.1	60	28	23	3	5	26	0	73	6
Keller, Hamilton	1	0	1.000	0.00	1	1	0	0	0	0	2.0	0	0	0	0	0	0	0	3	0
Kerr, Erie	3	2	.600	3.12	9	8	0	0	0	0	57.2	64	26	20	6	1	12	0	51	6
Keyser, Utica	4	4	.500	2.98	14	13	2	0	0	0	93.2	79	37	31	6	4	22	0	70	5
Kilgo, Jamestown	6	3	.667	1.39	30	3	0	21	0	8	64.2	46	16	10	3	0	21	0	74	4
Kiser, Watertown*	7	1	.875	3.41	12	9	2	0	0	0	74.0	66	36	28	4	2	18	0	74	5
Kizziah, St. Catharines	3	3	.500	2.50	17	11	1	4	1	0	79.1	72	35	22	1	3	25	1	34	5
Klancnik, Jamestown	1	1	.500	7.56	18	0	0	3	0	0	25.0	32	26	21	3	7	18	1	26	5
Konopki, Elmira	0	1	.000	6.59	6	1	0	4	0	1	13.2	20	14	10	2	0	10	2	2
Kovach, Watertown	7	4	.636	3.61	15	15	3	0	0	1	94.2	88	53	38	2	3	45	0	72	7
Kuder, Welland*	0	7	.000	5.05	14	11	1	2	0	0	57.0	65	42	32	2	3	24	0	48	8
Kulina, St. Catharines*	0	2	.000	6.75	2	1	0	0	0	0	4.0	4	7	3	1	0	2	0	3	0
Langbehn, Pittsfield*	10	3	.769	1.80	14	14	3	0	2	0	100.0	76	33	20	1	2	35	3	70	2
Langston, Niagara Falls	4	4	.500	3.95	13	10	0	2	0	0	57.0	67	31	25	3	1	17	1	47	3
Lata, Hamilton	4	5	.444	3.69	23	9	0	5	0	0	75.2	72	35	31	4	1	26	1	59	2
Latham, Welland*	2	6	.250	3.25	15	12	0	1	0	0	74.2	64	41	27	4	2	44	0	66	9
Leinen, Erie*	2	9	.182	3.55	16	15	2	0	0	0	101.1	95	56	40	11	4	34	3	82	3
Locker, Elmira	1	2	.333	3.29	19	0	0	8	0	0	27.1	24	11	10	1	1	16	2	27	2
Logan, Jamestown	4	7	.364	2.88	15	13	1	0	0	0	84.1	67	32	27	3	2	30	1	77	1
Logue, Niagara Falls	1	4	.200	4.28	26	0	0	16	0	1	40.0	36	21	19	4	2	5	0	39	1

Pitcher—Club	W.	L.	Pct.	ERA.	G.	GS.	CG.	GF.	ShO.	Sv.	IP.	H.	R.	ER.	HR.	HB.	BB.	Int. BB.	SO.	WP.
Long, Utica*	3	3	.500	3.63	20	0	0	11	0	2	52.0	44	28	21	0	4	29	2	54	2
Ludwig, Geneva	3	2	.600	4.74	18	1	1	8	0	1	43.2	49	32	23	5	1	15	1	37	0
Magria, Welland	3	6	.333	4.47	14	9	0	2	0	1	58.1	52	42	29	4	3	35	0	50	5
Malone, Oneonta*	3	5	.375	6.45	18	5	0	3	0	1	51.2	78	42	37	6	1	29	4	49	7
Marcero, Niagara Falls*	5	4	.556	3.15	15	15	3	0	3	0	94.1	80	33	33	4	2	22	1	72	1
Marrero, Auburn*	1	3	.250	6.35	20	3	0	7	0	2	51.0	61	47	36	3	8	41	0	35	7
Marshall, Niagara Falls*	0	2	.000	7.82	6	0	0	2	0	0	12.2	18	11	11	3	0	3	0	14	0
G. Martin, St. Catharines	4	3	.571	4.10	19	3	0	8	0	1	52.2	51	25	24	6	0	27	1	61	4
T. Martin, Erie*	0	5	.000	6.64	7	7	0	0	0	0	40.2	42	39	30	2	1	25	0	44	11
Masters, Welland	1	0	1.000	1.17	13	0	0	5	0	1	30.2	24	9	4	0	0	12	0	32	1
McCann, Pittsfield	4	2	.667	3.04	13	6	1	4	1	2	56.1	43	23	19	5	1	17	0	47	4
McCutcheon, St. Catharines	4	12	.250	3.55	19	19	1	0	0	0	114.0	129	60	45	7	2	21	0	85	12
McDowell, Auburn	1	4	.200	12.58	15	2	0	4	0	0	34.1	58	56	48	10	0	34	0	22	7
Medina, Pittsfield	0	2	.000	6.48	9	3	0	3	0	0	25.0	31	24	18	0	0	6	0	14	1
Meek, Erie	0	0	.000	3.60	4	0	0	4	0	0	5.0	4	2	2	1	0	3	0	2	0
Mehrtens, Utica*	4	6	.400	3.77	16	16	0	0	0	0	93.0	75	49	39	8	7	54	0	66	2
Merriman, Watertown	7	5	.583	2.64	14	14	2	0	2	0	92.0	75	50	27	1	8	44	0	64	3
Michael, Elmira	0	2	.000	5.74	4	2	0	1	0	0	15.2	11	12	10	0	0	10	0	9	4
Middaugh, Elmira	4	4	.500	2.90	11	11	0	0	0	0	62.0	57	26	20	5	4	22	0	50	6
Milchin, Hamilton*	1	2	.333	2.18	8	8	0	0	0	0	41.1	35	11	10	2	2	9	0	46	0
Moody, Oneonta	4	3	.571	1.40	30	0	0	16	0	4	64.1	46	13	10	4	0	17	2	81	0
Morrison, Elmira	0	2	.000	6.60	5	4	0	0	0	0	15.0	20	11	11	2	0	10	0	12	0
Morton, Elmira*	1	1	.500	1.88	3	3	2	0	0	0	24.0	11	6	5	0	1	6	0	32	1
Mosley, Elmira*	1	4	.200	3.14	26	1	0	20	0	4	48.2	47	23	17	0	2	20	1	45	2
Neill, Watertown	3	2	.600	1.82	19	0	0	15	0	5	34.2	31	11	7	0	1	10	0	29	2
Nelinbach, St. Catharines	0	0	.000	3.95	8	0	0	6	0	0	13.2	7	6	6	2	0	7	0	12	0
Nute, Niagara Falls*	1	1	.500	2.17	11	0	0	2	0	1	29.0	26	11	7	1	0	20	0	16	1
Oquist, Erie	7	4	.636	3.59	15	15	1	0	1	0	97.2	86	43	39	7	3	25	0	109	1
Ostopowicz, Pittsfield	0	0	.000	Infin.	1	0	0	0	0	0	0.0	0	3	3	0	1	3	0	0	0
Parris, Batavia	3	5	.375	3.92	13	10	1	1	0	0	66.2	69	38	29	6	4	20	1	46	4
G. Patterson, Geneva*	0	1	.000	6.23	2	2	0	0	0	0	8.2	5	6	6	1	1	5	0	8	0
J. Patterson, Batavia	2	4	.333	2.87	9	7	1	2	1	1	53.1	44	19	17	4	1	11	0	41	2
Pena, Erie*	1	7	.125	8.82	19	7	0	6	0	0	51.0	80	57	50	5	4	28	2	27	5
Perez, Auburn	4	3	.571	2.83	11	11	0	0	0	0	60.1	51	28	19	3	1	35	0	46	2
Pershke, Utica	0	0	.000	1.59	14	0	0	14	0	9	17.0	5	3	3	0	1	4	0	20	0
Petlick, Oneonta	1	0	1.000	9.00	1	0	0	0	0	0	2.0	1	2	2	0	0	2	0	1	0
Piatt, Watertown	4	2	.667	0.51	15	0	0	15	0	6	35.0	21	5	2	0	0	9	4	43	2
Pinto, Niagara Falls	3	1	.750	6.30	18	0	0	11	0	0	30.0	37	23	21	4	0	18	2	24	3
Piskor, Pittsfield	0	0	.000	9.00	1	0	0	0	0	0	2.0	2	2	2	1	0	2	0	1	0
Porter, Auburn	3	4	.429	3.28	7	7	2	0	0	0	46.2	47	20	17	2	4	6	0	35	2
Quantrill, Elmira	5	4	.556	3.43	20	7	5	7	0	2	76.0	90	37	29	5	6	12	2	57	1
Regira, Jamestown	1	0	1.000	2.77	5	0	0	3	0	0	13.0	8	5	4	1	0	7	0	19	1
Repoz, Batavia	0	0	.000	10.13	2	0	0	1	0	0	2.2	3	3	3	1	0	2	0	1	0
Reynolds, Auburn	3	2	.600	2.31	6	6	1	0	0	0	35.0	36	16	9	1	4	14	0	23	1
A. Rhodes, Erie*	2	0	1.000	1.16	5	5	1	0	0	0	31.0	13	7	4	1	0	10	0	45	2
R. Rhodes, Oneonta	2	3	.400	4.70	12	12	0	0	0	0	53.2	46	35	28	3	1	35	0	52	3
Richmond, Pittsfield	8	4	.667	3.26	18	12	3	4	0	0	94.0	85	42	34	3	8	27	0	56	3
Riddle, Erie	2	4	.333	4.24	14	1	0	10	0	2	23.1	34	19	11	3	0	11	1	26	0
Riley, Elmira*	4	6	.400	3.13	17	15	2	0	1	0	92.0	81	42	32	2	2	50	0	102	3
Rivera, Elmira	0	0	.000	15.00	2	0	0	0	0	0	3.0	7	5	5	0	2	1	0	0	0
Roscoe, Watertown	6	1	.857	2.78	9	9	2	0	0	0	58.1	50	21	18	3	2	13	0	75	7
Rosfelder, Elmira	0	0	.000	2.25	2	0	0	1	0	0	4.0	5	1	1	1	0	1	0	1	0
Ruffin, Utica	4	8	.333	3.36	15	15	0	0	0	0	88.1	67	43	33	3	1	46	0	92	8
Rupp, Erie	0	0	.000	2.70	2	0	0	1	0	0	3.1	2	1	1	0	1	0	0	3	0
Rush, Elmira	4	4	.500	2.55	15	14	1	1	0	0	81.1	69	30	23	3	9	39	0	85	4
Ryan, Watertown*	1	1	.500	3.60	7	1	0	5	0	1	20.0	23	8	8	2	0	5	0	16	2
Sanders, Elmira	6	8	.429	3.22	16	13	4	0	1	0	100.2	99	50	36	10	3	20	0	100	2
Santana, St. Catharines	0	1	.000	9.45	10	0	0	8	0	0	13.1	23	15	14	4	0	5	0	9	1
Segui, Pittsfield	0	0	.000	0.00	1	0	0	0	0	0	2.0	1	0	0	0	0	0	0	1	0
Seminara, Oneonta	7	2	.778	2.06	11	10	3	0	1	0	70.0	51	25	16	0	3	18	0	70	1
Shea, Niagara Falls	3	2	.600	5.70	11	10	0	1	0	0	53.2	66	40	34	4	2	22	0	36	8
Slaughter, Welland	0	0	.000	5.14	4	0	0	2	0	1	7.0	8	7	4	1	0	9	0	4	1
Small, Auburn	0	1	.000	5.03	10	3	0	4	0	2	19.2	17	13	11	3	1	11	0	23	3
J. Smith, Utica	0	1	.000	4.50	1	1	0	0	0	0	6.0	7	4	3	0	0	3	0	3	0
R. Smith, Erie*	0	2	.000	6.95	12	1	0	7	0	0	22.0	28	21	17	1	1	16	0	18	1
Somerville, Erie	0	0	.000	8.10	3	0	0	0	0	0	3.1	6	4	3	0	0	2	0	0	1
Sommer, Jamestown	6	4	.600	1.68	13	13	2	0	1	0	80.1	63	18	15	1	3	30	0	72	4
Stanford, Oneonta	4	3	.571	3.83	15	15	1	0	1	0	80.0	75	41	34	5	4	30	0	60	6
M. Stevens, Batavia	5	1	.833	1.97	16	4	0	6	0	0	45.2	35	11	10	2	2	13	2	48	2
S. Stevens, Utica	4	3	.571	1.96	22	0	0	17	0	4	46.0	40	25	10	4	1	13	0	51	4
Stock, St. Catharines	2	5	.286	3.12	20	2	0	7	0	1	49.0	44	22	17	3	4	18	2	39	3
Sullivan, Batavia	4	1	.800	2.96	24	0	0	18	0	5	45.2	41	22	15	6	1	13	1	42	5
Swartzbaugh, Geneva	2	3	.400	4.92	18	10	0	1	0	0	75.0	81	59	41	5	1	35	1	77	8
Sweeney, Geneva	7	5	.583	2.16	23	1	0	18	0	4	50.0	41	22	12	5	2	13	3	57	3
Telgheder, Pittsfield	5	3	.625	2.45	13	7	4	4	1	2	58.2	43	18	16	2	2	9	1	65	2
Thigpen, Jamestown	0	0	.000	0.00	3	0	0	2	0	0	3.0	1	0	0	0	0	1	0	3	0
Thoden, Jamestown	0	1	.000	2.25	1	1	0	0	0	0	4.0	4	1	1	0	0	1	0	4	1
Thompson, Elmira	0	1	.000	12.00	3	2	0	1	0	0	6.0	15	10	8	2	0	1	0	6	1
Tukes, Hamilton	2	4	.333	4.56	14	8	0	2	0	0	47.1	46	35	24	6	2	30	0	34	5
Uhrman, Elmira	2	1	.667	5.17	19	2	0	9	0	0	38.1	45	26	22	3	2	12	0	35	2
Van Winkle, Utica	3	1	.750	5.13	17	2	0	8	0	2	40.1	40	28	23	2	2	26	0	32	4
Vazquez, Pittsfield	0	2	.000	6.75	3	2	0	0	0	0	10.2	18	11	8	0	0	4	0	6	0
Vespe, Watertown	2	3	.400	2.66	17	3	1	5	0	0	47.1	38	20	14	0	1	20	0	53	5
Vitko, Pittsfield	2	1	.667	0.91	5	5	1	0	1	0	29.2	24	6	3	1	2	8	0	29	1
Wagner, Welland	4	5	.444	4.47	13	10	1	0	0	0	50.1	54	34	25	4	1	15	0	34	4
Wakefield, Welland	1	1	.500	3.40	18	1	0	11	0	2	39.2	30	17	15	1	2	21	0	42	9
Wall, Auburn	7	0	1.000	1.79	12	8	3	2	1	1	65.1	45	17	13	2	3	12	0	69	2
Wanish, St. Catharines	0	1	.000	1.86	15	0	0	14	0	6	19.1	9	7	4	1	1	12	0	20	4
Way, Welland*	4	3	.571	2.74	23	6	1	10	1	1	65.2	64	35	20	3	1	23	1	64	5
Wessel, Jamestown	1	3	.250	5.67	18	1	0	4	0	1	27.0	28	26	17	0	1	23	2	29	3
West, Batavia*	0	0	.000	2.14	10	0	0	4	0	0	21.0	24	13	5	2	0	6	1	12	1
Wheatcroft, Erie	3	2	.600	3.40	7	6	1	0	1	0	42.1	43	21	16	5	6	7	0	32	0

Pitcher—Club	W.	L.	Pct.	ERA.	G.	GS.	CG.	GF.	ShO.	Sv.	IP.	H.	R.	ER.	HR.	HB.	BB.	Int. BB.	SO.	WP.
Whitehead, Jamestown..............	4	2	.667	3.43	12	12	0	0	0	0	57.2	47	28	22	1	3	40	0	33	5
Williams, Erie*	3	4	.429	5.90	19	6	1	8	1	0	61.0	91	59	40	10	5	10	0	47	0
Willis, Geneva	4	7	.364	3.41	16	15	5	1	0	0	100.1	92	55	38	7	8	21	3	93	5
Willoughby, Pittsfield*	2	1	.667	2.10	16	1	0	9	0	1	30.0	24	10	7	0	0	14	2	23	1
Wilson, Niagara Falls...................	0	1	.000	12.08	5	0	0	0	0	0	12.2	19	17	17	1	0	13	2	13	1
Young, Jamestown......................	5	2	.714	1.94	18	10	0	8	0	4	65.0	63	18	14	2	5	14	0	62	6

BALKS—Locker, 10; Stock, Vespe, 6 each; McDowell, Milchin, 5 each; Dipoto, Freitas, Hoy, Infante, Riddle, 4 each; Beer, Canestro, Cesari, Ciaglo, Corsaro, Doss, F. Gonzales, Keyser, Lata, Logue, Marrero, Pena, Pershke, Porter, Seminara, Wall, Willis, 3 each; Betances, Bicknell, Blumberg, Boss, Bowlan, Broome, Byerly, Cebuhar, Davino, Doherty, Egloff, Golden, Gorman, Gorton, Heins, Hemmerly, Hutton, Hyson, Kiser, Kuder, Latham, Long, Magria, Marshall, T. Martin, McCutcheon, Medina, Moody, G. Patterson, J. Patterson, Quantrill, Rosfelder, Telgheder, Thoden, Wheatcroft, 2 each; Allen, Arvesen, Barnes, Bowen, Bush, Campusano, Capparelli, Cassidy, Chase, Cooper, Deller, Desapio, DeSilva, Eck, Eddy, Espino, Ettles, Fletcher, Gaddy, Gore, Green, Heiderscheit, Horowitz, Jockish, Johnston, Johnstone, T. Jones, Juarbe, Kilgo, Kizziah, Konopki, Langston, Leinen, Logan, Ludwig, Malone, Masters, Oquist, Reynolds, A. Rhodes, Riley, Rush, Ryan, Segui, Slaughter, Sommer, Stanford, Swartzbaugh, Sweeney, Thompson, Tukes, Van Winkle, West, 1 each.

COMBINATION SHUTOUTS—Wall-Emm, Auburn; Elliott-Sullivan-Stevens, Elliott-Sullivan, Elliott-Corsaro, Gaddy-Sullivan, Patterson-Stevens, Goergen-Sullivan, Stevens-Gunderson, Batavia; Rush-Quantrill, Elmira; Riddle-Hemmerly, Erie; Milchin-Boss, Boss-Golden-Green-Brooks, Bowlan-Gorton, Cassidy-Golden-Gorton, Boss-Gorton, Hamilton; Young-Thigpen-Archibald, Eddy-Archibald, Eddy-Kilgo, Whitehead-Kilgo, Jamestown; Langston-Doherty, Garcia-Logue-Doherty, Niagara Falls; Hutton-Moody-Gardella, Rhodes-Canestro-Moody, Canestro-Moody, Oneonta; Langbehn-Telgheder-Richmond, McCann-Johnson, Telgheder-Johnson, Pittsfield; Bicknell-Wanish, Brown-Martin, St. Catharines; Ruffin-Pershke, Van Winkle-Long-Stevens, Mehrtens-Pershke, Keyser-Van Winkle, Middaugh-Davino, Utica; Vespe-Piatt, Dipoto-Neill, Watertown; Broome-Byerly, Doss-Arvesen, Welland.

NO-HIT GAMES—Marcero, Niagara Falls, defeated Elmira, 5-0, August 26; Doss, Welland, defeated Batavia, 1-0, August 28.

Northwest League

CLASS A

CHAMPIONSHIP WINNERS IN PREVIOUS YEARS

1901—Portland .... .675	1948—Spokane .... .614	1971—Tri-City a .... .625
1902—Butte .... .608	1949—Yakima .... .660	Bend .... .538
1903—Butte .... .578	Vancouver (2nd)† .... .615	1972—Lewiston a .... .675
1904—Boise .... .625	1950—Yakima .... .613	Walla Walla .... .513
1905—Vancouver .... .586	1951—Spokane .... .655	1973—Walla Walla b .... .638
Everett* .... .667	1952—Victoria .... .631	Portland .... .563
1906—Tacoma .... .600	1953—Salem .... .635	1974—Bellingham .... .619
1907—Aberdeen .... .625	Spokane* .... .590	Eugene c .... .571
1908—Vancouver .... .578	1954—Vancouver* .... .636	1975—Portland .... .545
1909—Seattle .... .653	Lewiston .... .629	Eugene d .... .684
1910—Spokane .... .596	1955—Salem .... .646	1976—Portland .... .556
1911—Vancouver .... .628	Eugene* .... .639	Walla Walla d .... .639
1912—Seattle .... .600	1956—Yakima .... .691	1977—Bellingham e .... .618
1913—Vancouver .... .600	Yakima .... .619	Portland .... .667
1914—Vancouver .... .632	1957—Eugene .... .576	1978—Grays Harbor f .... .671
1915—Seattle .... .564	Wenatchee* .... .647	Eugene .... .514
1916—Spokane .... .622	1958—Lewiston .... .621	1979—Central Oregon d .... .606
1917—Great Falls .... .592	Yakima* .... .594	Walla Walla .... .571
1918—Seattle .... .588	1959—Salem .... .623	1980—Bellingham g .... .643
1919—Seattle .... .590	Yakima* .... .563	Bellingham .... .557
1920—Victoria .... .600	1960—Yakima .... .638	Eugene g .... .529
1921—Yakima .... .710	Yakima .... .562	1981—Medford d .... .600
Yakima† .... .660	1961—Lewiston* .... .621	Bellingham .... .557
1922—Calgary† .... .600	Yakima .... .600	1982—Medford .... .757
1923-36—Did not operate.	1962—Wenatchee* .... .574	Salem d .... .486
1937—Wenatchee .... .603	Tri-City .... .580	1983—Medford h .... .735
Tacoma* .... .627	1963—Lewiston .... .594	Bellingham .... .588
1938—Yakima .... .583	Yakima* .... .613	1984—Tri-Cities h .... .622
Bellingham (2nd)† .... .511	1964—Eugene .... .636	Medford .... .608
1939—Wenatchee .... .601	Yakima* .... .611	1985—Everett h .... .541
Tacoma (2nd)† .... .533	1965—Lewiston .... .667	Eugene .... .541
1940—Spokane .... .587	Tri-City* .... .681	1986—Bellingham h .... .608
Tacoma (4th)† .... .500	1966—Tri-City .... .679	Eugene .... .608
1941—Spokane .... .669	1967—Medford .... .607	1987—Spokane c .... .711
1942—Vancouver .... .594	1968—Tri-City .... .600	Everett .... .653
1943-45—Did not operate.	1969—Rogue Valley .... .633	1988—Southern Oregon .... .605
1946—Wenatchee .... .622	1970—Lewiston a .... .538	Spokane d .... .553
1947—Spokane .... .566	Coos Bay-No. Bend .... .563	

*Won split-season playoff. †Won four-club playoff. §League disbanded June 18. aLeague divided into Northern and Southern divisions, declared champion under league rules. bLeague divided into Eastern and Western divisions, declared champion under league rules. cLeague divided into Eastern and Western divisions; won two-team playoff. dLeague divided into Northern and Southern divisions; won two-team playoff. eLeague divided into Affiliate and Independent divisions; won two-team playoff. fDeclared league champion after winning one-game playoff. Balance of playoff canceled due to rain and wet grounds. gDeclared co-champion after winning one game. Balance of playoff canceled due to rain and wet grounds. hLeague divided into Washington and Oregon divisions; won two-team playoff. (NOTE—Known as Pacific Northwest League 1901-02, Pacific National League 1903-04, Northwestern League 1905-18, Pacific Coast International League 1919-22 and Western International League 1937-54.)

STANDING OF CLUBS AT CLOSE OF SEASON, SEPTEMBER 1

NORTHERN DIVISION

Club	W.	L.	T.	Pct.	G.B.
Spokane (Padres)	41	34	0	.547	....
Boise (Independent)	35	40	0	.467	6
Bellingham (Mariners)	32	43	0	.427	9
Everett (Giants)	31	44	0	.413	10

SOUTHERN DIVISION

Club	W.	L.	T.	Pct.	G.B.
Southern Oregon (Athletics)	45	30	0	.600	....
Eugene (Royals)	43	33	0	.566	2½
Salem (Dodgers)	41	35	0	.539	4½
Bend (Angels)	33	42	0	.440	12

COMPOSITE STANDING OF CLUBS AT CLOSE OF SEASON, SEPTEMBER 1

Club	S.O.	Eug.	Spo.	Sal.	Boi.	Bend	Bel.	Ev.	W.	L.	T.	Pct.	G.B.
Southern Oregon (Athletics)	....	5	4	5	7	10	8	6	45	30	0	.600	....
Eugene (Royals)	5	....	5	8	7	2	9	7	43	33	0	.566	2½
Spokane (Padres)	6	5	....	6	9	6	5	4	41	34	0	.547	4
Salem (Dodgers)	5	8	4	....	6	7	5	6	41	35	0	.539	4½
Boise (Independent)	3	3	7	4	....	5	6	7	35	40	0	.467	10
Bend (Angels)	5	8	4	3	5	....	4	4	33	42	0	.440	12
Bellingham (Mariners)	2	1	4	5	4	6	....	10	32	43	0	.427	13
Everett (Giants)	4	3	6	4	2	6	6	....	31	44	0	.413	14

Southern Oregon played home games in Medford and Cline Falls.

Major league affiliations in parentheses.

Playoffs—Spokane defeated Southern Oregon, two games to one, to win league championship.

Regular-Season Attendance—Bellingham, 31,685; Bend, 40,526; Boise, 127,594; Eugene, 141,134; Everett, 70,714; Salem, 30,049; Southern Oregon, 69,641; Spokane, 124,844. Total—636,187. Playoffs (3 games)—5,309.

Managers—Bellingham, Paul Carey; Bend, Don Long; Boise, Mal Fichman; Eugene, Paul Kirsch; Everett, Joe Strain; Salem, Tom Beyers; Southern Oregon, Grady Fuson; Spokane, Bruce Bochy.

All-Star Team—1B—Fred Cooley, Southern Oregon; 2B—Kevin Higgins, Spokane; 3B—Craig Paquette, Southern Oregon; SS—Tim Wallace, Boise; OF—Kevin Long, Eugene; Darrell Sherman, Spokane; Steve Hosey, Everett; C—Mike Piazza, Salem; DH—Dave Staton, Spokane; RHP—Ricky Davis, Spokane; LHP—Kerry Knox, Spokane; Manager of the Year—Bruce Bochy, Spokane.

478

(Compiled by Howe Sportsdata International, Boston, Mass.)

CLUB BATTING

Club	Pct.	G.	AB.	R.	OR.	H.	TB.	2B.	3B.	HR.	RBI.	SH.	SF.	HP.	BB.	Int. BB.	SO.	SB.	CS.	LOB.
Spokane	.277	75	2557	438	400	709	928	110	8	31	386	11	32	46	330	10	496	131	35	592
Eugene	.259	76	2625	421	383	681	927	128	8	34	337	14	26	31	369	18	588	159	42	621
Southern Oregon	.259	75	2595	432	343	672	975	113	14	54	361	12	23	26	363	6	657	75	46	594
Salem	.255	76	2541	371	387	649	911	97	30	35	305	23	13	26	282	8	558	113	52	538
Boise	.253	75	2547	390	351	645	858	97	13	30	320	30	22	33	338	9	518	76	28	598
Bend	.241	75	2541	400	433	613	888	91	14	52	339	10	22	45	327	5	659	44	26	584
Everett	.236	75	2551	356	435	601	837	94	17	36	303	17	26	56	292	12	593	76	35	573
Bellingham	.227	75	2470	286	362	561	805	97	9	43	239	8	12	50	272	8	675	67	29	556

INDIVIDUAL BATTING

(Leading Qualifiers for Batting Championship—205 or More Plate Appearances)

*Bats lefthanded.   †Switch-hitter.

Player and Club	Pct.	G.	AB.	R.	H.	TB.	2B.	3B.	HR.	RBI.	SH.	SF.	HP.	BB.	Int. BB.	SO.	SB.	CS.
Staton, David, Spokane	.362	70	260	52	94	163	18	0	17	72	0	2	8	39	4	49	1	1
Paquette, Craig, Southern Oregon	.336	71	277	53	93	163	22	3	14	56	0	1	2	30	4	46	9	4
Higgins, Kevin, Spokane*	.332	71	295	54	98	119	9	3	2	52	1	9	5	30	1	13	2	4
Collins, Sean, Eugene	.322	66	233	51	75	95	14	0	2	41	3	4	2	35	0	39	31	2
Sherman, Darrell, Spokane*	.318	70	258	70	82	97	13	1	0	29	2	4	13	58	2	29	58	7
Wallace, Timothy, Boise†	.316	75	301	57	95	113	10	1	2	32	2	1	4	38	0	29	14	2
Peters, Rex, Salem†	.313	76	268	52	84	112	9	2	5	40	1	4	4	56	3	45	14	2
Long, Kevin, Eugene*	.312	69	260	54	81	111	19	1	3	45	1	6	1	36	6	40	15	3
Cooley, Fred, Southern Oregon	.306	69	258	51	79	140	18	2	13	62	0	2	0	36	0	62	1	2
Solseth, David, Eugene*	.303	62	234	32	71	111	18	2	6	44	0	2	4	36	4	34	2	1

Departmental Leaders: G—Jo. Alvarez, Peters, 76; AB—Wallace, 301; R—Sherman, 70; H—Higgins, 98; TB—Paquette, Staton, 163; 2B—Paquette, 22; 3B—Jo. Alvarez, Carroll, 6; HR—Staton, 17; RBI—Staton, 72; SH—Carroll, Perez, 6; SF—Higgins, 9; HP—Sherman, 13; BB—Johnson, 67; IBB—Long, 6; SO—Hosey, 84; SB—Sherman, 58; CS—Johnson, 12.

(All Players—Listed Alphabetically)

Player and Club	Pct.	G.	AB.	R.	H.	TB.	2B.	3B.	HR.	RBI.	SH.	SF.	HP.	BB.	Int. BB.	SO.	SB.	CS.
Abbott, Kurt, Southern Oregon	.100	5	10	2	1	1	0	0	0	1	0	1	0	0	0	3	1	0
Alvarez, Javier, Eugene	.276	24	58	8	16	20	1	0	1	7	0	0	0	6	0	12	0	0
Alvarez, Jorge, Salem	.268	76	291	46	78	122	14	6	6	33	1	0	3	49	1	58	22	11
Armas, Marco, Southern Oregon	.316	36	136	18	43	61	5	2	3	22	1	1	0	6	0	42	1	0
Bailey, Lash, Bellingham	.287	72	258	33	74	113	19	1	6	36	0	0	6	29	2	72	1	0
Barton, Jeffery, Eugene*	.275	68	269	34	74	93	11	1	2	47	1	5	2	27	1	45	3	2
Beard, Garrett, Salem	.241	75	274	38	66	99	11	2	6	54	0	3	4	31	1	58	6	4
Bellinger, Clayton, Everett	.200	51	185	29	37	59	8	1	4	16	1	0	1	19	0	47	3	2
Bethea, Stephen, Spokane†	.219	62	215	36	47	59	7	1	1	22	2	0	1	41	0	45	4	2
Billingsley, Rodney, Spokane	.236	39	140	19	33	44	5	0	2	22	2	2	2	13	0	50	1	0
Boddie, Eric, Salem	.265	31	102	14	27	35	3	1	1	12	0	1	2	11	0	25	3	3
Boggs, Scott, Boise*	.385	14	13	1	5	5	0	0	0	0	0	0	0	4	0	4	0	0
Boyce, Joseph, Boise*	.263	63	198	29	52	75	9	1	4	32	3	1	0	27	0	38	3	3
Brakebill, Mark, Bellingham	.278	47	144	16	40	59	12	2	1	26	0	0	10	19	0	37	8	4
Brito, Francisco, Bend	.208	27	106	7	22	26	2	1	0	10	2	1	0	5	0	17	1	0
Buchanan, Robert, Eugene	.242	31	66	11	16	17	1	0	0	8	0	2	1	15	0	12	1	0
Carroll, Donald, Salem*	.263	67	236	50	62	107	15	6	6	28	6	1	2	31	1	70	15	7
Cayson, Tony, Bellingham	.125	29	64	6	8	8	0	0	0	1	1	0	0	7	0	16	6	2
Centala, Scott, Eugene	.000	27	2	0	0	0	0	0	0	0	0	0	0	0	0	0	2	0
Cespedes, Teodoro, Everett	.000	2	4	0	0	0	0	0	0	0	0	0	0	0	0	2	0	0
Chevalier, Boanerge, Bellingham†	.179	48	156	12	28	30	2	0	0	7	1	0	0	20	0	22	14	5
Cluff, Paul, Boise	.270	43	159	28	43	47	4	0	0	22	2	2	1	23	0	15	4	1
Coleman, DeRico, Spokane	.273	55	198	34	54	58	2	1	0	26	1	0	3	18	1	35	19	5
Collins, Ronald, Eugene	.203	45	148	16	30	43	4	0	3	21	2	2	2	22	0	40	6	4
Collins, Sean, Eugene	.322	66	233	51	75	95	14	0	2	41	3	4	2	35	0	39	31	2
Conte, Michael, Southern Oregon	.302	61	245	64	74	101	12	0	5	28	0	1	4	27	2	40	19	4
Cook, Stanley, Boise*	.241	65	228	38	55	71	9	0	3	25	0	0	2	31	1	44	5	4
Cooley, Fred, Southern Oregon	.306	69	258	51	79	140	18	2	13	62	0	2	0	36	0	62	1	2
Crowe, Ronald, Everett	.275	69	273	43	75	107	18	1	4	35	0	5	8	14	1	38	2	3
Daughtry, Dorian, Bellingham	.273	14	55	6	15	21	1	1	1	4	0	0	0	2	0	15	1	1
Davis, Douglas, Bellingham	.179	23	67	7	12	27	3	0	4	7	0	1	0	5	0	25	1	0
Doucet, Eric, Boise	.205	37	73	11	15	17	2	0	0	2	4	0	0	11	1	28	0	0
Eagar, Bradley, Southern Oregon	.235	37	119	9	28	32	1	0	1	14	1	2	0	3	0	31	1	1
Easley, Damion, Bend	.298	36	131	34	39	58	5	1	4	21	0	0	4	25	0	21	9	4
Edward, John, Bend	.208	8	24	3	5	5	0	0	0	3	0	0	1	1	0	10	0	1
Forrester, Gary, Salem†	.167	27	72	6	12	13	1	0	0	7	3	0	0	11	0	17	4	1
Furcal, Lorenzo, Southern Oregon	.183	38	104	16	19	28	2	2	1	6	0	0	0	17	0	26	3	3
Gieseke, Mark, Spokane†	.385	3	13	3	5	6	1	0	0	2	0	0	1	0	0	1	0	0
Gil, Jose, Bend*	.000	1	3	0	0	0	0	0	0	0	0	0	1	0	0	0	0	0
Gilcrist, John, Eugene	.264	59	212	34	56	76	11	0	3	19	0	0	2	20	2	43	19	4
Gonzalez, Jesus, Salem	.118	4	17	2	2	2	0	0	0	2	0	0	0	1	0	3	0	0
Goodlow, Sebastian, Salem	.206	45	126	7	26	32	4	1	0	10	0	1	0	3	0	37	2	3
Grahovac, Michael, Everett	.168	46	161	12	27	37	2	1	2	13	1	2	4	9	0	44	0	1
Griffith, Thomas, Boise†	.216	45	102	18	22	30	1	2	1	14	2	1	1	15	0	28	5	2
Gurchiek, Christopher, Boise	.273	10	22	1	6	6	0	0	0	3	1	1	0	2	0	7	0	0
Hall, Kevin, Everett	.212	33	104	19	22	38	2	1	4	14	0	0	3	21	1	36	2	2
Hanlin, Richard, Bellingham	.206	42	131	12	27	41	2	0	4	12	1	1	2	13	0	44	2	2
Harris, Franklyn, Southern Oregon	.204	17	54	6	11	17	3	0	1	10	0	1	2	7	0	15	0	0
Higgins, Kevin, Spokane*	.332	71	295	54	98	119	9	3	2	52	1	9	5	30	1	13	2	4
Hirtensteiner, Richard, Bend*	.281	26	89	22	25	33	5	0	1	13	0	3	3	18	0	22	1	2
Hosey, Steven, Everett	.288	73	288	44	83	142	14	3	13	59	0	2	10	27	2	84	15	3
Johnson, Randall, Everett	.273	68	245	50	67	84	6	1	3	27	2	1	3	67	0	69	19	12
Jones, Robert, Bend	.249	66	257	36	64	99	12	1	7	37	0	2	3	24	1	58	4	3
Jones, Victor, Boise†	.167	15	12	2	2	2	0	0	0	1	0	0	1	2	0	5	0	0
Kapano, Corey, Bend	.251	63	227	34	57	85	10	0	6	27	1	1	2	48	2	67	0	3
Kasper, Kevin, Everett	.239	38	113	16	27	32	5	0	0	16	3	2	4	21	1	24	7	0
Kelso, Jeffrey, Bend	.221	58	213	30	47	72	13	0	4	35	1	1	3	20	0	79	4	2
Kemper, Harvey, Boise*	.221	25	86	6	19	24	2	0	1	12	0	0	3	15	1	21	0	1

Player and Club	Pct.	G.	AB.	R.	H.	TB.	2B.	3B.	HR.	RBI.	SH.	SF.	HP.	BB.	Int. BB.	SO.	SB.	CS.
Kilpatrick, Jeffrey, Bend	.156	24	96	7	15	16	1	0	0	10	0	0	1	8	0	26	4	0
King, David, Eugene	.348	44	161	24	56	90	11	1	7	28	0	1	3	16	1	34	1	0
Kipila, Jeffery, Bend	.269	66	238	48	64	121	10	1	15	49	0	4	4	45	1	63	3	0
Lasher, Matthew, Bend	.242	28	95	18	23	25	2	0	0	11	0	0	0	20	0	18	2	1
Laya, Jesus, Everett	.251	65	247	22	62	71	5	2	0	30	1	1	1	24	1	36	3	1
Lemuth, Stephen, Southern Oregon*	.213	32	80	6	17	27	4	0	2	12	0	0	2	14	0	37	3	3
Lewis, Ronald, Bend†	.143	5	14	2	2	2	0	0	0	0	0	0	1	1	0	6	0	0
Long, Kevin, Eugene*	.312	69	260	54	81	111	19	1	3	45	1	6	1	36	6	40	15	3
Lydy, Scott, Southern Oregon	.209	67	230	37	48	72	11	2	3	28	3	4	3	31	0	72	8	5
MacMillan, Darrell, Boise	.253	49	154	21	39	53	6	1	2	26	2	3	1	13	1	22	1	1
Malone, Jackson, Boise	.226	56	168	18	38	52	5	0	3	27	5	2	4	26	0	28	5	3
Mancini, Joseph, Boise*	.183	45	126	9	23	30	7	0	0	14	2	1	0	15	1	41	1	0
Marrero, Oreste, Boise*	.276	54	203	38	56	99	8	1	11	43	0	4	0	30	3	60	1	2
Martin, Steven, Spokane	.251	60	207	38	52	65	5	1	2	23	2	4	1	23	0	55	24	9
Martinez, Angel, Everett	.208	15	53	9	11	15	1	0	1	3	0	0	0	10	0	15	3	0
Martinez, Pablo, Spokane†	.250	2	8	3	2	2	0	0	0	0	0	0	0	0	0	0	1	0
Mathews, Jeremy, Bellingham	.192	38	130	10	25	37	6	0	2	8	0	0	1	11	0	59	2	1
Mattia, Tony, Boise*	.259	15	54	5	14	16	2	0	0	4	0	0	1	2	0	18	0	0
Mattingly, Steve, Boise	.195	17	41	3	8	10	2	0	0	5	0	0	1	3	0	18	0	0
McDonald, Michael, Everett	.177	43	141	18	25	32	4	0	1	15	2	5	5	16	0	39	4	1
McFarlin, Jason, Everett*	.260	37	131	17	34	44	4	3	0	12	2	2	1	5	1	25	7	3
McGee, Anthony, Spokane	.206	43	141	20	29	35	6	0	0	17	0	2	0	20	0	27	1	0
McMurray, Brock, Salem	.328	36	134	23	44	67	12	4	1	25	0	0	1	20	0	23	4	4
Mentzer, Troy, Everett	.193	29	88	12	17	21	1	0	1	12	2	2	2	12	1	19	1	2
Mercedes, Henry, Southern Oregon	.164	22	61	6	10	12	0	1	0	1	0	0	1	10	0	24	0	2
Molina, Mario, Bend*	.139	20	72	8	10	14	1	0	1	11	0	0	0	8	0	23	0	1
Montes, Daniel, Everett†	.177	20	62	4	11	13	2	0	0	2	0	0	1	3	0	15	1	1
Moore, Kerwin, Eugene‡	.221	65	226	44	50	69	9	2	2	25	1	0	2	36	0	75	20	6
Morrow, Christian, Salem*	.323	27	93	20	30	45	3	3	2	16	0	0	1	12	2	11	4	2
Murphy, Patrick, Eugene	.264	64	201	23	53	63	7	0	1	19	1	1	5	32	1	40	6	3
Nelson, Darren, Bend	.239	13	46	4	11	16	2	0	1	8	0	2	1	2	0	9	1	1
Neville, David, Bend	.233	28	90	8	21	26	3	1	0	11	1	0	3	7	0	31	0	0
Ortiz, Hector, Salem	.229	44	140	13	32	37	3	1	0	12	2	0	1	4	0	24	2	1
Ortiz, Joseph, Southern Oregon	.143	5	14	0	2	2	0	0	0	2	0	0	0	1	0	2	0	1
Palyan, Vincent, Everett	.277	56	202	37	56	79	13	2	2	24	1	0	1	22	0	28	4	2
Paquette, Craig, Southern Oregon	.336	71	277	53	93	163	22	3	14	56	0	1	2	30	4	46	9	4
Pardo, Benigno, Eugene	.000	11	1	0	0	0	0	0	0	0	0	0	0	0	0	0	0	0
Parker, Richard, Bend	.244	36	131	15	32	45	5	1	2	16	0	1	0	15	0	37	1	1
Paul, Corey, Bellingham*	.237	59	198	25	47	63	7	0	3	25	0	4	0	43	1	73	2	3
Perez, Jose, Salem†	.242	55	178	27	43	50	5	1	0	13	6	1	4	17	0	27	10	6
Peters, Rex, Salem†	.313	76	268	52	84	112	9	2	5	40	1	4	4	56	3	45	14	2
Piazza, Michael, Salem	.268	57	198	22	53	88	11	0	8	25	0	1	2	13	0	51	0	0
Pirkl, Gregory, Bellingham	.257	70	265	31	68	98	6	0	8	36	1	3	3	23	2	51	4	1
Reyan, Julio, Bellingham	.256	62	227	22	58	83	10	0	5	27	0	1	3	23	3	60	6	1
Richardson, Milton, Eugene	.152	34	79	10	12	16	1	0	1	6	2	0	0	7	0	30	5	1
Rijo, Rafael, Salem	.228	73	281	33	64	74	4	3	0	18	4	1	1	6	0	76	20	6
Ritchie, David, Eugene†	.238	40	130	28	31	37	6	0	0	13	2	1	2	32	2	44	12	2
Ritter, Kenneth, Southern Oregon	.196	53	148	31	29	43	3	1	3	13	2	0	1	50	0	50	3	1
Rittman, Alvin, Bellingham	.159	41	113	14	18	26	5	0	1	6	0	0	6	13	0	32	1	1
Roa, Pedro, Bellingham	.157	33	102	11	16	19	1	1	0	5	1	0	0	3	0	30	2	1
Rodriguez, Ruben, Boise	.262	67	206	40	54	75	12	3	1	21	4	2	8	31	1	43	15	1
Romay, Guillermo, Bellingham	.116	37	112	9	13	18	3	1	0	5	1	1	1	16	0	39	3	0
Romero, Jose, Spokane	.000	1	0	0	0	0	0	0	0	0	0	0	0	0	0	0	0	0
Rudstrom, Thomas, Bend	.157	24	89	11	14	15	1	0	0	7	0	1	3	5	0	21	0	0
Rupp, Robert, Spokane	.242	57	207	33	50	77	15	0	4	30	0	1	2	28	0	47	2	0
Russell, Frederick, Eugene†	.185	45	162	15	30	42	7	1	1	11	0	0	1	10	1	51	2	4
Ryan, Colin, Eugene	.208	37	106	11	22	25	3	0	0	8	1	1	3	18	0	27	2	1
Salmon, Timothy, Bend	.245	55	196	37	48	82	6	5	6	31	1	2	6	33	0	61	2	4
Sherman, Darrell, Spokane*	.318	70	258	70	82	97	13	1	0	29	2	4	13	58	2	29	58	7
Shockey, Scott, Southern Oregon*	.339	32	112	21	38	52	5	0	3	26	1	2	2	18	0	19	2	4
Simmons, Enoch, Southern Oregon	.222	69	257	31	57	71	9	1	1	23	2	2	6	32	0	69	10	7
Smith, David, Bellingham	.221	63	240	30	53	75	10	0	4	23	0	1	6	12	0	50	5	1
Sobczyk, Robert, Boise	.190	36	105	10	20	24	1	0	1	9	0	0	1	10	0	17	2	1
Solseth, David, Eugene*	.303	62	234	32	71	111	18	2	6	44	0	2	4	36	4	34	2	1
Span, Brian, Spokane	.213	47	136	19	29	37	5	0	1	19	0	2	3	7	0	57	4	1
Specyalski, Brian, Bend†	.262	54	202	36	53	62	5	2	0	15	3	4	5	19	1	31	5	2
Sperry, Christopher, Salem†	.136	17	22	3	3	3	0	0	0	0	0	0	0	8	0	8	1	1
Staton, David, Spokane	.362	70	260	52	94	163	18	0	17	72	0	2	8	39	4	49	1	1
Strebeck, Richard, Southern Oregon	.217	18	46	8	10	13	3	0	0	5	0	1	1	5	0	15	0	0
Stupur, Daniel, Salem*	.211	43	109	15	23	25	2	0	0	10	0	0	0	9	0	25	4	1
Tamarez, Carlos, Southern Oregon†	.105	7	19	2	2	2	0	0	0	1	0	0	0	2	0	7	0	0
Taylor, Terry, Bend*	.240	16	50	11	12	17	2	0	1	6	0	0	0	11	0	13	1	0
Thompson, Kirk, Eugene*	.252	42	131	27	33	40	7	0	0	13	1	2	2	25	0	20	19	2
Thrams, Jeffrey, Boise	.212	19	52	7	11	12	1	0	0	2	1	0	2	0	0	8	1	1
Threadgill, Henry, Bend*	.234	13	47	9	11	22	2	0	3	8	0	0	2	4	0	5	3	1
Toole, Matthew, Spokane	.333	3	12	0	4	4	0	0	0	3	0	0	0	1	0	1	1	0
Tunison, Richard, Eugene†	.228	58	215	33	49	72	9	1	4	29	0	2	3	23	1	47	18	9
Turang, Brian, Bellingham	.285	60	207	42	59	87	10	3	4	11	2	0	12	33	0	50	9	6
Twardy, Glenn, Bellingham	.000	17	1	0	0	0	0	0	0	0	0	0	0	0	0	0	0	0
Varni, Patrick, Boise	.297	27	91	15	27	40	10	0	1	12	2	3	1	18	0	18	1	1
Waggoner, James, Southern Oregon*	.270	54	200	35	54	64	7	0	1	18	1	1	0	35	0	40	5	6
Wallace, Timothy, Boise†	.316	75	301	57	95	113	10	1	2	32	2	1	4	38	0	29	14	2
Warren, Glenn, Everett	.110	27	73	10	8	11	1	1	0	2	1	0	1	6	0	19	6	1
Weaver, Trent, Southern Oregon	.267	50	176	27	46	59	7	0	2	30	1	4	2	29	0	42	6	3
Welch, Bryce, Everett	.173	32	104	4	18	22	4	0	0	8	0	1	1	8	2	30	1	0
Welsh, Scot, Spokane*	.283	59	198	23	56	69	13	0	0	22	0	0	6	23	1	41	9	4
Williams, Kent, Bend†	.304	31	125	20	38	47	4	1	1	10	1	0	2	8	0	41	3	0
Williams, Reginald, Boise†	.268	42	153	33	41	57	5	1	3	14	1	2	0	24	0	29	18	5
Young, Jason, Everett	.246	36	130	19	32	45	5	1	2	18	1	3	9	18	2	38	1	1

The following pitchers, listed alphabetically by club, with games in parentheses, had no plate appearances, primarily through use of designated hitters:

BELLINGHAM—Backus, Todd (4); Bryant, Keith (17); Darwin, Jeffery (12); Gordon, Anthony (15); Gutierrez, James (13); LeBlanc, Michael (24); Liss, Thomas (6); Lodding, Richard (15); Lodgek, Scott (14); Loe, Darin (21); Rivas, Oscar (16); Salkeld, Roger (8); Wiggs, Johnny (22); Woodson, Walter (12).

BEND—Adams, David (14); Bennett, Erik (15); Cobb, Marvin (23); Haffner, Lester (20); Helm, Wayne (15); Jones, James (5); Martin, Justin (2); Martinez, Filiberto (12); Moore, Marcus (14); Reyes, Juan (13); Rice, David (11); Swingle, Paul (9); Warrecker, William (18); Warren, Joe (21).

BOISE—Arola, Bruce (28); Bilello, John (16); Candelaria, Jorge (12); Cerny, Christopher (13); Currie, Brian (30); Forrest, Christopher (6); Gyarmati, Jeffrey (18); King, Steven (16); Larson, Michael (28); Lomeli, Michael (20); Matas, James (6); Olson, Daniel (28); Tafoya, Rodney (13); Wurm, Garry (31).

EUGENE—Ahern, Brian (13); Baldwin, Kirk (11); Jacobs, Develon (20); Karchner, Matthew (8); Lindsey, Donald (19); Pierce, Edward (27); Rogers, Rodney (16); Schaefer, Christopher (15); Talbert, Louis (16); Webster, Michael (11); Wiley, Warren (21).

EVERETT—Aleys, Maximo (16); Brummett, Gregory (14); Callahan, Stephen (26); Dour, Brian (4); Ebert, Scott (14); Gustafson, Edward (25); Hancock, Christopher (11); Hanselman, Carl (11); Henrikson, Daniel (24); Hernandez, Marino (3); Hocking, William (2); Jones, Kevin (24); Lund, Greg (12); Novoa, Rafael (3); Quezada, Edward (13); Schiller, John (22).

SALEM—Bene, William (7); Branconier, Paul (15); Enno, Clayton (12); Fletcher, Robert (9); Gonzalez, Lawrence (19); Kries, John (19); Luckham, Kenneth (17); Miller, William (9); Nina, Rubin (15); Pascual, Jorge (23); Perez, Pedro (23); Robinson, Napolean (23); Taveras, Ramon (13).

SOUTHERN OREGON—Allison, Dana (11); Annee, Timothy (15); Chitren, Stephen (2); Cormier, Russell (9); Erwin, Scott (15); Gibbs, James (12); Grimes, Michael (15); Guzmon, Dionini (5); Kracl, Darin (15); Latter, David (28); Osteen, Gavin (16); Pena, Pedro (15); Rizza, Gerald (15); Smith, Todd (21); Towey, Steven (7); Venuto, Nicholas (26).

SPOKANE—Banks, Lance (24); Buckley, Joseph (22); Cunningham, Troy (18); Davis, Richard (15); Deville, Daniel (23); Devore, Paul (1); Diaz, Luis (1); Florie, Bryce (14); Gollehon, Christopher (12); Johnson, William (16); Knox, Kerry (12); McKeon, Brian (2); Phelan, John (20); Sheridan, Robert (5); Towers, Kevin (1); Zinter, Edward (17).

GRAND SLAM HOME RUNS—Bailey, Bethea, Cooley, R. Jones, Marrero, Paquette, Paul, Pirkl, 1 each.

AWARDED FIRST BASE ON CATCHER'S INTERFERENCE—Barton 3 (Hall, Piazza, Pirkl); Bellinger 2 (Harris 2); S. Collins (Sperry); Nelson (Harris); Palyan (Pirkl); Rupp (Pirkl); Salmon (Pirkl).

CLUB FIELDING

Club	Pct.	G.	PO.	A.	E.	DP.	PB.	Club	Pct.	G.	PO.	A.	E.	DP.	PB.
Southern Oregon	.963	75	2019	837	110	60	20	Bend	.948	75	1937	744	146	70	10
Boise	.955	75	1981	819	132	73	19	Everett	.947	75	1995	807	157	73	44
Eugene	.952	76	2042	785	143	66	21	Salem	.946	76	1985	787	157	75	19
Spokane	.949	75	1959	786	148	62	16	Bellingham	.944	75	1957	785	164	63	22

INDIVIDUAL FIELDING

*Throws lefthanded.

FIRST BASEMEN

Player and Club	Pct.	G.	PO.	A.	E.	DP.	Player and Club	Pct.	G.	PO.	A.	E.	DP.
Armas, Southern Oregon	1.000	4	22	1	0	2	McMurray, Salem	1.000	1	6	1	0	1
Bailey, Bellingham	.986	72	596	39	9	51	Mentzer, Everett	1.000	1	11	0	0	1
Boggs, Boise	1.000	1	3	0	0	1	Molina, Bend	.962	10	97	3	4	10
Collins, Eugene	.947	5	35	1	2	3	Nelson, Bend	1.000	1	9	3	0	3
Cooley, Southern Oregon	.997	40	349	30	1	29	Neville, Bend	.976	6	38	2	1	5
Davis, Bellingham	1.000	8	55	2	0	3	Palyan, Everett	1.000	1	5	1	0	0
Gieseke, Spokane*	1.000	1	9	1	0	1	PETERS, Salem*	.991	76	672	23	6	65
Kemper, Boise*	1.000	2	6	0	0	1	Ritter, Southern Oregon	.992	16	124	3	1	6
King, Eugene	.970	22	192	5	6	15	Rupp, Spokane	.969	47	384	25	13	39
Kipila, Bend	.974	60	454	34	13	48	Shockey, Southern Oregon*	.986	24	200	14	3	13
Lasher, Bend	1.000	2	6	0	0	0	Span, Spokane	1.000	1	3	0	0	1
Laya, Everett	.983	64	535	38	10	59	Taylor, Bend	1.000	1	3	0	0	0
Mancini, Eugene	.953	9	75	6	4	11	Tunison, Eugene	.988	55	455	21	6	39
Marrero, Boise*	.980	53	475	18	10	40	Welch, Everett	.989	13	85	3	1	5
Mattia, Boise	.983	13	107	9	2	9	Welish, Spokane*	.978	31	254	10	6	17
McDonald, Everett	1.000	1	8	1	0	1							

SECOND BASEMEN

Player and Club	Pct.	G.	PO.	A.	E.	DP.	Player and Club	Pct.	G.	PO.	A.	E.	DP.
Ja. Alvarez, Eugene	.957	20	29	37	3	8	Montes, Everett	1.000	8	15	16	0	7
Jo. ALVAREZ, Salem	.964	75	184	213	15	60	Paquette, Southern Oregon	.955	8	9	12	1	2
Bethea, Spokane	.970	8	11	21	1	2	Rittman, Bellingham	1.000	3	4	4	0	1
Boggs, Boise	1.000	3	3	3	0	0	Roa, Bellingham	.942	33	57	88	9	15
Boyce, Boise	.937	10	25	34	4	7	Russell, Eugene	.933	7	9	19	2	2
Brito, Bend	.969	5	12	19	1	3	Specyalski, Bend	.950	43	88	119	11	28
Cluff, Boise	.971	40	62	106	5	29	Sperry, Salem	1.000	2	1	3	0	0
R. Collins, Eugene	1.000	1	2	1	0	0	Stupur, Salem	1.000	1	2	3	0	1
S. Collins, Eugene	.939	61	138	155	19	32	Taylor, Bend	.925	11	24	25	4	9
Crowe, Everett	.953	31	68	95	8	21	Thrams, Boise	1.000	3	2	4	0	2
Furcal, Southern Oregon	.974	34	64	88	4	14	Threadgill, Bend	.894	12	18	24	5	7
Gil, Bend	.800	1	3	1	1	0	Turang, Bellingham	.931	48	84	131	16	26
Higgins, Spokane	.942	69	140	200	21	45	Varni, Boise	.962	24	45	55	4	14
Johnson, Everett	.933	3	7	7	1	1	Waggoner, Southern Oregon	.667	1	1	1	1	0
Kasper, Everett	.970	5	18	14	1	7	Weaver, Southern Oregon	.932	37	55	96	11	15
Lasher, Bend	.974	8	13	24	1	4	Young, Everett	.982	33	63	97	3	19
Martinez, Southern Oregon	1.000	10	13	21	0	8							

THIRD BASEMEN

Player and Club	Pct.	G.	PO.	A.	E.	DP.	Player and Club	Pct.	G.	PO.	A.	E.	DP.
Armas, Southern Oregon	.742	11	7	16	8	0	Mathews, Bellingham	.881	38	27	69	13	4
Beard, Salem	.852	74	50	146	34	11	Mercedes, Southern Oregon	1.000	1	0	1	0	0
Bethea, Spokane	.880	9	3	19	3	3	Murphy, Eugene	.880	63	22	103	17	8
Boggs, Boise	1.000	3	0	3	0	1	Nelson, Bend	.923	7	6	18	2	2
Boyce, Boise	.789	31	16	44	16	4	PAQUETTE, Southern Oregon	.936	59	35	125	11	12
Brakebill, Bellingham	.838	40	29	64	18	4	Span, Spokane	1.000	2	2	0	0	0
R. Collins, Eugene	.809	22	10	28	9	0	Specyalski, Bend	.833	5	2	3	1	0
S. Collins, Eugene	1.000	1	1	1	0	0	Sperry, Salem	.500	1	0	1	1	0
Cooley, Southern Oregon	.857	4	0	6	1	0	Staton, Spokane	.854	64	30	116	25	6
Crowe, Everett	.872	27	18	50	10	4	Stupur, Salem	.778	4	3	4	2	0
Johnson, Everett	.836	37	23	74	19	6	Thrams, Boise	.852	13	9	14	4	2
Kapano, Bend	.854	61	33	84	20	11	Toole, Spokane	1.000	3	3	9	0	0
Kipila, Bend	.778	3	2	5	2	1	Varni, Boise	1.000	1	1	0	0	0
Lasher, Bend	.800	1	1	3	1	0	Weaver, Southern Oregon	.846	9	1	10	2	1
Malone, Boise	.884	37	18	58	10	7	Welch, Everett	.854	17	11	24	6	2

SHORTSTOPS

Player and Club	Pct.	G.	PO.	A.	E.	DP.	Player and Club	Pct.	G.	PO.	A.	E.	DP.
Abbott, Southern Oregon	.929	4	6	7	1	1	P. Martinez, Spokane	1.000	2	6	7	0	0
Ja. Alvarez, Eugene	.923	4	4	8	1	4	Montes, Everett	.872	9	19	22	6	4
Jo. Alvarez, Salem	1.000	2	0	6	0	0	Paquette, Southern Oregon	.921	8	17	18	3	7
Bellinger, Everett	.874	42	57	110	24	22	Perez, Salem	.882	55	65	144	28	34
Bethea, Spokane	.944	26	43	93	8	13	Ritchie, Eugene	.882	38	43	114	21	14
Brito, Bend	.947	22	18	54	4	12	Rittman, Bellingham	.922	38	54	100	13	26
Chevalier, Bellingham	.903	48	72	114	20	21	Russell, Eugene	.908	38	51	106	16	21
Easley, Bend	.863	33	49	89	22	23	Specyalski, Bend	.905	8	11	27	4	2
Forrester, Salem	.884	25	32	82	15	15	Tamarez, Southern Oregon	.938	7	9	21	2	1
Furcal, Southern Oregon	.833	1	0	5	1	0	Taylor, Bend	1.000	1	1	1	0	0
Kasper, Everett	.887	32	44	90	17	20	WAGGONER, Southern Oregon	.952	54	88	169	13	32
Lasher, Bend	.911	14	14	27	4	4	Wallace, Boise	.934	75	105	250	25	47
Martin, Spokane	.842	47	55	110	31	22	Weaver, Southern Oregon	1.000	3	2	12	0	0
A. Martinez, Southern Oregon	.946	7	8	27	2	4							

OUTFIELDERS

Player and Club	Pct.	G.	PO.	A.	E.	DP.	Player and Club	Pct.	G.	PO.	A.	E.	DP.
Armas, Southern Oregon	.923	11	11	1	1	1	Long, Eugene*	.955	66	100	5	5	1
Barton, Spokane	.952	68	114	5	6	1	Lydy, Southern Oregon	.949	66	109	3	6	3
Bethea, Spokane	.867	11	12	1	2	0	Mancini, Boise	.909	8	10	0	1	0
Boddie, Salem	.942	30	62	3	4	0	Mattingly, Boise	.667	3	2	0	1	0
Carroll, Salem*	.949	62	87	6	5	1	McDonald, Everett	.944	38	51	0	3	0
Cayson, Bellingham	.893	22	22	3	3	1	McFarlin, Everett*	.932	37	77	5	6	0
Coleman, Spokane	.948	44	53	2	3	1	McMurray, Salem	.956	28	38	5	2	2
Conte, Southern Oregon	.987	50	71	4	1	2	Moore, Eugene	.956	63	127	3	6	0
COOK, Boise*	1.000	62	109	6	0	1	Morrow, Salem*	.919	17	30	4	3	0
Crowe, Everett	1.000	1	3	0	0	0	Palyan, Everett	.932	45	63	5	5	0
Daughtry, Bellingham	.964	14	24	3	1	2	Paul, Bellingham*	.908	58	56	3	6	0
Edward, Bend	.833	6	5	0	1	0	Richardson, Eugene	1.000	29	18	1	0	0
Gilcrist, Eugene	.962	57	97	4	4	2	Rijo, Salem	.970	73	155	9	5	2
Goodlow, Salem	.878	36	35	1	5	0	Ritter, Southern Oregon	.972	27	34	1	1	0
Griffith, Boise	.973	41	62	9	2	5	Rodriguez, Boise	.946	66	79	8	5	2
Gurchiek, Boise	.786	7	9	2	3	0	Romay, Bellingham	.937	37	58	1	4	0
Hanlin, Bellingham	.937	42	87	2	6	1	Salmon, Bend	.958	54	84	7	4	1
Hirtensteiner, Bend*	.974	22	36	2	1	0	Sherman, Spokane*	.980	69	137	9	3	1
Hosey, Everett*	.974	73	143	8	4	0	Simmons, Southern Oregon	.970	69	128	1	4	0
Johnson, Everett	.938	17	29	1	2	0	Smith, Bellingham	.922	61	93	2	8	0
R. Jones, Bend	.950	53	111	2	6	0	Span, Spokane	.974	37	35	3	1	1
V. Jones, Boise	.909	9	9	1	1	1	Thompson, Eugene	.902	35	34	3	4	0
Kelso, Bend	.967	58	85	4	3	0	Turang, Bellingham	.882	9	13	2	2	0
Kemper, Boise*	.964	18	26	1	1	0	Warren, Everett	.976	24	40	0	1	0
Kilpatrick, Bend	.900	20	15	3	2	0	Welish, Spokane*	1.000	6	12	0	0	0
Lasher, Bend	1.000	1	2	0	0	0	K. Williams, Bend	.864	13	19	0	3	0
Lemuth, Southern Oregon	.862	20	23	2	4	0	R. Williams, Boise	.971	41	64	3	2	1
Lewis, Bend	1.000	5	10	0	0	0							

CATCHERS

Player and Club	Pct.	G.	PO.	A.	E.	DP.	PB.	Player and Club	Pct.	G.	PO.	A.	E.	DP.	PB.
Billingsley, Spokane	.980	37	272	29	6	1	8	H. Ortiz, Salem	.961	41	268	24	12	2	10
Buchanan, Eugene	.978	31	213	9	5	1	4	J. Ortiz, Southern Oregon	.957	3	20	2	1	0	1
Doucet, Salem	.995	36	187	28	1	2	5	Parker, Bend	.986	36	305	38	5	3	6
Eagar, Southern Oregon	.990	37	270	21	3	2	11	Piazza, Salem	.977	35	230	21	6	1	4
Gonzalez, Salem	.944	4	31	3	2	0	2	Pirkl, Bellingham	.973	40	296	23	9	2	9
Grahovac, Everett	.965	38	277	26	11	3	29	Reyan, Bellingham	.979	39	291	28	7	1	13
Hall, Everett	.977	24	160	8	4	0	9	Rudstrom, Bend	.995	23	184	22	1	0	2
Harris, Southern Oregon	.961	15	110	13	5	1	3	Ryan, Eugene	.984	37	269	33	5	3	13
MacMillan, Boise	.977	26	154	15	4	0	7	Sobczyk, Boise	.985	36	295	28	5	4	7
McGEE, Spokane	.990	42	346	31	4	0	8	Solseth, Eugene	.979	25	166	23	4	1	4
Mentzer, Everett	.979	23	129	12	3	2	6	Sperry, Salem	.944	6	17	0	1	0	3
Mercedes, Southern Oregon	.979	21	129	14	3	1	3	Strebeck, Southern Oregon	.972	13	62	8	2	0	2
Neville, Bend	.980	17	138	10	3	2	2								

PITCHERS

Player and Club	Pct.	G.	PO.	A.	E.	DP.	Player and Club	Pct.	G.	PO.	A.	E.	DP.
Adams, Bend	1.000	14	6	9	0	0	Deville, Spokane	1.000	23	5	11	0	0
Ahern, Eugene	.957	13	4	18	1	0	Dour, Everett	1.000	4	0	2	0	0
Aleys, Everett*	.963	16	7	19	1	4	Ebert, Everett	.818	14	4	5	2	1
Allison, Southern Oregon*	.800	11	1	3	1	1	Enno, Salem*	1.000	12	0	6	0	0
Annee, Southern Oregon*	.833	15	0	5	1	1	Erwin, Southern Oregon	.929	15	4	9	1	0
Arola, Boise	1.000	28	0	3	0	0	Fletcher, Salem*	1.000	9	0	1	0	0
Backus, Bellingham*	.667	4	1	1	1	0	Florie, Spokane	.867	14	3	10	2	0
Baldwin, Eugene*	.875	11	0	7	1	1	Forrest, Boise	.667	6	0	4	2	0
Banks, Spokane	.857	24	1	5	1	1	Gibbs, Southern Oregon	1.000	12	2	1	0	0
Bennett, Bend	1.000	15	4	13	0	0	Gollehon, Spokane	.500	12	0	1	1	0
Bilello, Boise	.885	16	4	19	3	0	Gonzalez, Salem	.750	19	1	2	1	1
Branconier, Salem	1.000	15	3	14	0	0	Gordon, Bellingham*	.833	15	1	9	2	0
Brummett, Everett	.870	14	8	12	3	0	Grimes, Southern Oregon	.966	15	10	18	1	1
Bryant, Bellingham	.857	17	2	4	1	1	Gustafson, Everett	1.000	25	3	8	0	1
Buckley, Spokane*	.917	22	1	10	1	2	Gutierrez, Everett	.850	13	3	14	3	0
Callahan, Everett*	1.000	26	0	5	0	0	Guzman, Spokane	.500	1	1	0	1	0
Candelaria, Boise	.792	12	5	14	5	0	Guzman, Southern Oregon*	1.000	5	0	2	0	0
Centala, Eugene	.833	27	1	4	1	0	Gyarmati, Boise	.700	18	3	4	3	0
Cerny, Boise*	1.000	13	0	1	0	0	Haffner, Bend	1.000	20	2	7	0	1
Cobb, Bend	1.000	23	2	0	0	0	Hancock, Everett*	.800	11	1	7	2	0
Cormier, Southern Oregon	1.000	9	0	2	0	0	Hanselman, Everett	1.000	11	3	5	0	0
Cunningham, Spokane	.714	18	1	4	2	0	Helm, Bend	.929	15	4	9	1	0
Currie, Boise*	1.000	30	0	4	0	0	Henrikson, Everett*	.875	24	1	6	1	1
Darwin, Bellingham	.933	12	6	8	1	1	Hernandez, Everett*	1.000	3	0	2	0	0
Davis, Spokane	.875	15	6	15	3	1	Jacobs, Eugene	.929	20	3	10	1	1

PITCHERS—Continued

Player and Club	Pct.	G.	PO.	A.	E.	DP.	Player and Club	Pct.	G.	PO.	A.	E.	DP.
Johnson, Spokane	.750	16	1	2	1	0	Pena, Southern Oregon	.760	15	7	12	6	0
J. Jones, Bend	.750	5	1	2	1	0	Perez, Salem	.875	23	3	4	1	0
K. Jones, Everett	1.000	24	3	9	0	0	Phelan, Spokane	1.000	20	5	14	0	2
Karchner, Eugene	1.000	8	1	5	0	1	Pierce, Eugene*	1.000	27	0	2	0	0
King, Boise	.800	16	1	11	3	0	Quezada, Everett	1.000	13	1	3	0	0
Knox, Spokane*	.944	12	4	13	1	0	Reyes, Bend	1.000	13	1	2	0	0
Kracl, Southern Oregon	.909	15	3	7	1	0	Rice, Bend	.875	11	1	6	1	0
Kries, Salem*	1.000	19	0	6	0	0	Rivas, Bellingham*	.923	16	2	10	1	0
Larson, Boise	.889	28	2	6	1	0	Rizza, Southern Oregon	1.000	14	1	5	0	0
Latter, Southern Oregon	1.000	28	1	10	0	0	Robinson, Salem	.818	23	2	7	2	2
LeBlanc, Bellingham	1.000	24	2	2	0	0	Rogers, Eugene	1.000	16	0	3	0	0
Lindsey, Eugene*	.889	19	2	6	1	0	Salkeld, Bellingham	.692	8	6	3	4	1
Liss, Bellingham*	.833	6	3	2	1	0	SCHAEFER, Eugene	1.000	15	6	26	0	1
Lodding, Bellingham	1.000	15	5	9	0	1	Schiller, Everett	1.000	22	2	7	0	1
Lodgek, Bellingham	.636	14	2	5	4	0	Sheridan, Spokane	.667	5	1	1	1	1
Loe, Bellingham	1.000	21	0	5	0	0	Smith, Southern Oregon	1.000	21	4	2	0	0
Lomeli, Boise	.957	20	2	20	1	0	Swingle, Bend	1.000	9	0	2	0	0
Luckham, Salem	.700	17	0	7	3	0	Tafoya, Boise*	.933	12	3	11	1	0
Lund, Everett	.833	12	2	8	2	1	Talbert, Eugene	.929	16	2	11	1	3
Martin, Bend	1.000	2	0	1	0	0	Taveras, Salem	.938	13	3	12	1	2
Martinez, Bend*	.840	12	6	15	4	1	Twardy, Bellingham	1.000	17	3	4	0	1
Matas, Salem	.818	6	2	7	2	1	Venuto, Southern Oregon	.917	26	5	6	1	1
McKeon, Spokane	1.000	2	0	3	0	0	Warrecker, Bend*	1.000	18	0	3	0	0
Miller, Salem	1.000	9	0	5	0	1	Warren, Bend	.786	21	6	5	3	1
Moore, Bend	.806	14	8	17	6	2	Webster, Eugene*	.750	11	0	3	1	0
Nina, Salem*	.870	15	2	18	3	0	Wiggs, Bellingham*	1.000	22	1	15	0	0
Novoa, Everett*	.750	3	1	2	1	0	Wiley, Eugene	1.000	21	5	6	0	0
Olson, Boise	.833	28	1	4	1	0	Woodson, Bellingham	.900	12	2	16	2	4
Osteen, Southern Oregon*	.857	16	4	2	1	1	Wurm, Boise	1.000	31	0	6	0	1
Pardo, Eugene*	.875	11	3	4	1	1	Zinter, Spokane	.923	17	6	6	1	2
Pascual, Salem	1.000	23	3	3	0	0							

The following players did not have any fielding statistics at the positions indicated or appeared only as a designated hitter, pinch-hitter or pinch-runner: Bene, p; Boggs, of; Cayson, 3b; Cespedes, of; Chitren, p; Devore, p; Diaz, p; Forrester, p; Hall, of; Hocking, p; A. Martinez, 3b; Ritter, c; Romero, ph; Span, 2b; Stupur, p; Towers, p; Towey, p.

CLUB PITCHING

Club	ERA.	G.	CG.	ShO.	Sv.	IP.	H.	R.	ER.	HR.	HB.	BB.	Int. BB.	SO.	WP.	Bk.
Boise	3.39	75	3	6	15	660.1	634	351	249	35	55	273	18	627	64	27
Bellingham	3.57	75	1	6	15	652.1	589	362	259	23	30	307	8	578	53	24
Southern Oregon	3.72	75	2	9	15	673.0	589	343	278	51	32	295	9	582	45	33
Eugene	3.76	76	5	6	15	680.2	667	383	284	31	45	315	2	661	73	27
Spokane	3.94	75	4	8	15	653.0	666	400	286	37	28	295	9	610	53	41
Salem	3.97	76	2	4	20	661.2	664	387	292	43	30	349	17	528	53	15
Everett	4.38	75	4	1	13	665.0	631	435	324	49	59	396	5	555	86	22
Bend	4.70	75	9	2	8	645.2	691	433	337	46	34	343	8	603	73	34

PITCHERS' RECORDS
(Leading Qualifiers for Earned-Run Average Leadership—61 or More Innings)

*Throws lefthanded.

Pitcher—Club	W.	L.	Pct.	ERA.	G.	GS.	CG.	GF.	ShO.	Sv.	IP.	H.	R.	ER.	HR.	HB.	BB.	Int. BB.	SO.	WP.
Davis, Spokane	9	2	.818	1.35	15	14	2	1	2	1	93.0	71	22	14	2	0	13	0	106	5
Lomeli, Boise	5	2	.714	2.06	20	10	0	0	0	0	70.0	60	28	16	6	4	19	0	52	5
Taveras, Salem	7	1	.875	2.07	13	13	1	0	1	0	78.1	69	27	18	2	4	29	1	61	3
Lodgek, Bellingham	4	4	.500	2.42	14	14	1	0	1	0	74.1	68	32	20	1	3	31	0	71	5
Schaefer, Eugene	7	4	.636	2.47	15	15	3	0	1	0	105.2	96	45	29	1	10	34	0	70	5
Candelaria, Boise	6	5	.545	2.54	12	12	2	0	1	0	74.1	61	35	21	1	15	33	1	62	8
Knox, Spokane*	8	2	.800	2.63	12	12	1	0	0	0	75.1	74	30	22	7	1	10	0	76	1
Pena, Southern Oregon	5	2	.714	2.69	15	11	1	0	1	0	70.1	52	26	21	5	3	25	0	53	2
Zinter, Spokane	6	4	.600	2.70	17	7	0	5	0	2	73.1	64	25	22	2	1	37	0	89	6
Brummett, Everett	4	2	.667	2.88	14	10	1	2	0	0	72.0	63	34	23	1	6	24	0	76	6
King, Boise	8	3	.727	2.88	14	14	2	0	0	0	93.2	86	36	30	2	9	29	0	105	13

Departmental Leaders: G—Wurm, 31; W—Kracl, 10; L—Ebert, 9; Pct.—Kracl, .909; GS—Bilello, 16; CG—Helm, Martinez, Schaefer, 3; GF—Centala, 25; ShO—Davis, 2; Sv.—Centala, Wiggs, 9; IP—Schaefer, 105.2; H—Branconier, 104; R—Florie, Helm, 66; ER—Helm, 63; HR—Grimes, 11; HB—Candelaria, 15; BB—Ebert, 60; IBB—Currie, 6; SO—Davis, 106; WP—Ebert, 20.

(All Pitchers—Listed Alphabetically)

Pitcher—Club	W.	L.	Pct.	ERA.	G.	GS.	CG.	GF.	ShO.	Sv.	IP.	H.	R.	ER.	HR.	HB.	BB.	Int. BB.	SO.	WP.
Adams, Bend	2	6	.250	4.91	14	12	0	0	0	0	73.1	82	55	40	8	2	45	1	75	7
Ahern, Eugene	4	5	.444	3.41	13	13	0	0	0	0	71.1	78	36	27	3	6	23	0	54	9
Aleys, Everett*	5	5	.500	3.09	16	15	1	1	0	0	84.1	76	48	29	3	9	37	1	68	18
Allison, Southern Oregon*	0	2	.000	1.84	11	2	0	6	0	4	29.1	17	8	6	0	1	4	0	27	2
Annee, Southern Oregon*	1	3	.250	7.41	15	0	0	5	0	0	17.0	15	14	14	0	3	11	0	16	2
Arola, Boise	2	0	1.000	6.10	28	0	0	7	0	2	38.1	54	31	26	6	2	17	4	33	3
Backus, Bellingham*	0	0	.000	1.04	4	0	0	2	0	2	8.2	6	1	1	0	2	2	0	9	0
Baldwin, Eugene*	1	4	.200	6.70	11	10	0	0	0	0	41.2	50	36	31	5	0	28	0	26	2
Banks, Spokane	2	1	.667	3.19	24	0	0	13	0	1	36.2	39	25	13	3	3	11	2	19	4
Bene, Salem	0	2	.000	9.22	7	4	0	0	0	0	13.2	13	18	14	1	3	27	0	13	10
Bennett, Bend	6	8	.429	3.47	15	15	2	0	0	0	96.0	96	58	37	4	3	36	0	96	8
Bilello, Boise	4	7	.364	3.30	16	16	1	0	0	0	90.0	94	44	33	2	4	32	1	92	5
Branconier, Salem	5	6	.455	4.91	15	15	0	0	0	0	88.0	104	58	48	4	3	29	0	51	1
Brummett, Everett	4	2	.667	2.88	14	10	1	2	0	0	72.0	63	34	23	1	6	24	0	76	6
Bryant, Bellingham	2	1	.667	2.67	17	0	0	5	0	0	30.1	21	14	9	1	1	10	0	22	2
Buckley, Spokane*	1	3	.250	4.75	22	1	0	8	0	1	41.2	56	34	22	3	1	20	2	41	4
Callahan, Everett*	6	3	.667	2.25	26	0	0	24	0	6	36.0	32	14	9	3	2	8	0	25	0
Candelaria, Boise	6	5	.545	2.54	12	12	2	0	1	0	74.1	61	35	21	1	15	33	1	62	8
Centala, Eugene	4	3	.571	2.25	27	0	0	25	0	9	52.0	38	16	13	1	2	20	1	87	2

Pitcher—Club	W.	L.	Pct.	ERA.	G.	GS.	CG.	GF.	ShO.	Sv.	IP.	H.	R.	ER.	HR.	HB.	BB.	Int. BB.	SO.	WP.
Cerny, Boise*	0	0	.000	4.63	13	0	0	3	0	0	11.2	8	6	6	0	0	13	1	14	5
Chitren, Southern Oregon	0	0	.000	1.80	2	0	0	1	0	0	5.0	3	2	1	0	0	2	0	3	0
Cobb, Bend	2	3	.400	5.84	23	0	0	21	0	4	24.2	27	17	16	3	1	16	1	23	4
Cormier, Southern Oregon	3	2	.600	4.00	9	6	0	2	0	1	36.0	35	18	16	2	2	13	0	37	3
Cunningham, Spokane	1	2	.333	6.15	18	3	0	9	0	3	41.0	55	33	28	6	0	15	0	33	2
Currie, Boise*	2	5	.286	2.45	30	0	0	22	0	5	29.1	33	19	8	0	0	14	6	35	4
Darwin, Bellingham	1	7	.125	4.92	12	12	0	0	0	0	64.0	73	42	35	3	3	24	0	47	4
Davis, Spokane	9	2	.818	1.35	15	14	2	1	2	1	93.0	71	22	14	2	0	13	0	106	5
Deville, Spokane	4	2	.667	2.58	23	1	0	17	0	5	52.1	43	21	15	2	2	17	0	49	1
Devore, Spokane	0	0	.000	0.00	1	0	0	1	0	0	3.2	2	1	0	0	1	2	1	6	1
Diaz, Spokane	0	0	.000	0.00	1	0	0	1	0	0	2.0	2	0	0	0	0	1	0	0	0
Dour, Everett	1	1	.500	2.40	4	2	0	1	0	0	15.0	11	7	4	0	3	2	0	11	1
Ebert, Everett	4	9	.308	6.13	14	14	1	0	0	0	69.0	67	61	47	6	13	60	1	42	20
Enno, Salem*	2	4	.333	2.70	12	12	0	0	0	0	56.2	52	32	17	0	0	43	0	56	3
Erwin, Southern Oregon	6	3	.667	3.36	15	15	0	0	0	0	83.0	68	36	31	9	1	43	1	83	6
Fletcher, Salem*	1	0	1.000	1.69	9	0	0	6	0	3	10.2	8	2	2	0	0	8	1	15	1
Florie, Spokane	4	5	.444	7.08	14	14	0	0	0	0	61.0	79	66	48	2	4	40	1	50	11
Forrest, Boise	1	0	1.000	6.86	6	6	0	0	0	0	21.0	30	25	16	3	0	19	0	16	4
Forrester, Salem	0	0	.000	10.80	1	0	0	1	0	0	1.2	3	2	2	1	0	1	0	3	0
Gibbs, Southern Oregon	0	1	.000	5.40	12	0	0	2	0	1	21.2	22	21	13	2	2	16	0	18	1
Gollehon, Spokane	0	1	.000	4.40	12	0	0	7	0	0	14.1	6	10	7	0	1	20	0	19	0
Gonzalez, Salem	1	1	.500	5.11	19	0	0	9	0	1	44.0	51	39	25	6	1	46	2	33	5
Gordon, Bellingham*	2	3	.400	4.85	15	5	0	4	0	0	39.0	37	33	21	1	0	34	1	34	4
Grimes, Southern Oregon	6	6	.500	4.23	15	14	1	0	1	0	87.1	81	44	41	11	4	23	0	70	2
Gustafson, Everett	2	6	.250	3.12	25	2	0	14	0	4	52.0	40	25	18	5	4	25	2	59	8
Gutierrez, Bellingham	1	5	.167	3.90	13	11	0	1	0	0	57.2	68	44	25	4	1	24	0	33	1
Guzman, Spokane	1	0	1.000	3.60	1	1	0	0	0	0	5.0	6	3	2	0	0	1	0	1	0
Guzman, Southern Oregon*	3	1	.750	2.63	5	5	0	0	0	0	27.1	23	16	8	0	0	12	0	26	2
Gyarmati, Boise	0	2	.000	3.29	18	1	0	3	0	0	41.0	41	21	15	0	5	15	0	23	1
Haffner, Bend	4	1	.800	2.43	20	0	0	12	0	3	29.2	25	10	8	0	3	18	0	24	1
Hancock, Everett*	2	5	.286	5.64	11	11	0	0	0	0	52.2	47	52	33	3	2	53	0	50	13
Hanselman, Everett	2	4	.333	4.96	11	10	0	0	0	0	52.2	44	32	29	7	6	35	0	43	2
Helm, Bend	3	7	.300	6.14	15	15	3	0	1	0	92.1	100	66	63	7	7	48	2	98	9
Henrikson, Everett*	2	2	.500	4.13	24	0	0	7	0	3	52.1	42	26	24	2	1	43	0	50	4
Hernandez, Everett*	0	2	.000	5.14	3	3	0	0	0	0	14.0	11	9	8	0	0	14	0	9	1
Hocking, Everett*	0	0	.000	16.20	2	0	0	0	0	0	3.1	8	6	6	0	0	0	0	3	1
Jacobs, Eugene	4	2	.667	3.30	20	5	1	5	1	1	71.0	73	34	26	3	4	20	0	50	3
Johnson, Spokane	3	4	.429	4.33	16	12	1	2	0	1	72.2	70	53	35	5	7	40	1	70	8
J. Jones, Bend	1	1	.500	7.36	5	0	0	3	0	0	11.0	19	14	9	1	2	3	0	11	2
K. Jones, Everett	1	2	.333	2.20	24	0	0	6	0	0	49.0	43	22	12	3	2	31	1	33	4
Karchner, Eugene	1	1	.500	3.90	8	5	0	0	0	0	30.0	30	19	13	1	5	8	0	25	7
King, Boise	8	3	.727	2.88	16	15	0	0	0	0	93.2	86	36	30	2	9	29	0	105	13
Knox, Spokane*	8	2	.800	2.63	12	12	1	0	0	0	75.1	74	30	22	7	1	10	0	76	1
Kracl, Southern Oregon	10	1	.909	3.69	15	15	0	0	0	0	90.1	87	47	37	4	6	43	0	68	7
Kries, Salem*	5	0	1.000	3.16	19	0	0	10	0	0	37.0	28	15	13	1	1	21	2	27	2
Larson, Boise	1	3	.250	3.79	28	0	0	7	0	1	40.1	30	20	17	6	3	17	1	36	2
Latter, Southern Oregon	1	1	.500	2.29	28	1	0	13	0	1	51.0	38	20	13	2	1	20	4	52	1
LeBlanc, Bellingham	2	2	.500	3.13	24	0	0	21	0	4	37.1	33	20	13	0	1	14	1	28	4
Lindsey, Eugene*	3	1	.750	3.41	19	8	1	3	0	0	66.0	69	36	25	2	6	27	0	76	10
Liss, Bellingham*	3	2	.600	3.69	6	6	0	0	0	0	31.2	29	16	13	1	1	18	0	32	2
Lodding, Bellingham	4	5	.444	3.75	15	9	0	2	0	0	60.0	45	29	25	4	4	39	1	36	6
Lodgek, Bellingham	4	4	.500	2.42	14	14	1	0	1	0	74.1	68	32	20	1	3	31	0	71	5
Loe, Bellingham	3	3	.500	5.98	21	0	0	8	0	0	40.2	34	34	27	4	4	27	2	45	4
Lomeli, Boise	5	2	.714	2.06	20	10	0	0	0	0	70.0	60	28	16	6	4	19	0	52	5
Luckham, Salem	6	7	.462	4.54	17	10	0	3	0	0	71.1	74	47	36	6	7	30	1	49	5
Lund, Everett	2	1	.667	5.48	12	5	1	1	0	0	44.1	51	31	27	8	6	19	0	26	3
Martin, Bend	0	2	.000	10.57	2	2	0	0	0	0	7.2	12	10	9	2	2	4	0	6	0
Martinez, Bend*	6	4	.600	4.52	12	12	3	0	1	0	75.2	85	47	38	7	4	25	0	61	4
Matas, Boise	1	3	.250	6.41	6	6	0	0	0	0	26.2	28	23	19	0	2	18	0	30	4
McKeon, Spokane	0	0	.000	9.64	5	0	0	1	0	1	4.2	8	5	5	0	0	1	0	3	0
Miller, Salem	1	0	1.000	6.16	9	2	0	3	0	0	19.0	22	23	13	3	2	12	0	15	4
Moore, Bend	2	5	.286	4.52	14	14	1	0	0	0	81.2	84	53	41	2	5	51	1	74	14
Nina, Salem*	5	6	.455	4.63	15	15	1	0	0	0	89.1	102	50	46	10	3	26	2	48	3
Novoa, Everett*	0	1	.000	4.80	3	3	0	0	0	0	15.0	20	11	8	2	1	8	0	20	3
Olson, Boise	0	3	.000	4.10	28	0	0	9	0	0	37.1	31	23	17	4	5	24	2	43	5
Osteen, Southern Oregon*	2	2	.500	3.50	16	6	0	3	0	0	46.1	44	24	18	3	3	29	0	42	9
Pardo, Eugene*	0	0	.000	11.63	11	2	0	3	0	0	21.2	32	31	28	3	0	23	0	18	5
Pascual, Salem	3	3	.500	3.47	23	0	0	14	0	6	49.1	45	22	19	3	4	25	3	65	6
Pena, Southern Oregon	5	2	.714	2.69	15	11	1	0	1	0	70.1	52	26	21	5	3	25	0	53	2
Perez, Salem	2	2	.500	2.79	23	3	0	9	0	4	58.0	40	23	18	4	0	30	2	51	6
Phelan, Spokane	2	5	.286	6.24	20	5	0	5	0	0	57.2	72	54	40	5	3	49	1	36	5
Pierce, Eugene*	2	2	.500	2.77	27	0	0	24	0	4	39.0	24	19	12	0	3	26	0	71	9
Quezada, Everett	0	0	.000	10.02	13	0	0	6	0	0	20.2	32	26	23	3	2	15	0	13	1
Reyes, Salem	2	0	1.000	2.74	13	0	0	7	0	0	23.0	19	12	7	1	0	9	0	16	2
Rice, Bend	0	0	.000	9.00	11	1	0	1	0	0	23.0	31	23	23	3	3	19	2	9	5
Rivas, Bellingham*	4	1	.800	1.02	16	0	0	3	0	0	35.1	26	7	4	0	3	4	0	40	2
Rizza, Southern Oregon	2	0	1.000	6.75	14	0	0	5	0	0	22.2	22	18	17	4	3	8	1	13	4
Robinson, Salem	3	3	.500	3.50	23	2	0	18	0	6	43.2	48	25	17	2	2	20	3	40	4
Rogers, Eugene	2	3	.400	4.20	16	0	0	2	0	0	30.0	33	22	14	3	2	23	0	40	5
Salkeld, Bellingham	2	2	.500	1.29	8	6	0	1	0	0	42.0	27	17	6	0	4	10	0	55	3
Schaefer, Eugene	7	4	.636	2.47	15	15	3	0	1	0	105.2	96	45	29	1	10	34	0	70	5
Schiller, Everett	0	1	.000	6.61	22	0	0	9	0	0	32.2	44	31	24	3	2	22	0	27	1
Sheridan, Salem	0	3	.000	6.88	5	5	0	0	0	0	17.0	16	17	13	0	3	18	1	10	3
Smith, Southern Oregon	3	2	.600	3.45	21	0	0	18	0	5	28.2	25	14	11	2	2	13	0	37	1
Stupur, Salem	0	0	.000	36.00	1	0	0	1	0	0	1.0	5	4	4	0	0	2	0	0	1
Swingle, Bend	1	0	1.000	2.95	9	0	0	2	0	0	18.1	7	9	6	0	0	19	0	26	5
Tafoya, Boise*	3	4	.429	3.26	12	9	0	1	0	0	47.0	47	29	17	4	2	14	0	44	1
Talbert, Eugene	8	3	.727	3.98	16	7	0	0	0	0	63.1	53	37	28	4	3	40	0	63	6
Taveras, Salem	7	1	.875	2.07	13	13	1	0	1	0	78.1	69	27	18	2	4	29	1	61	3
Towers, Spokane	0	0	.000	5.40	1	0	0	1	0	0	1.2	3	1	1	0	0	1	0	2	1
Towey, Southern Oregon	0	2	.000	5.73	7	0	0	4	0	1	11.0	10	7	7	2	0	8	1	12	1
Twardy, Bellingham	1	1	.500	6.16	17	0	0	10	0	0	30.2	31	23	21	1	1	27	0	14	10

Pitcher—Club	W.	L.	Pct.	ERA.	G.	GS.	CG.	GF.	ShO.	Sv.	IP.	H.	R.	ER.	HR.	HB.	BB.	Int. BB.	SO.	WP.
Venuto, Southern Oregon	3	2	.600	4.89	26	0	0	14	0	2	46.0	47	28	25	5	1	25	2	25	5
Warrecker, Bend*	1	2	.333	4.55	18	0	0	8	0	0	31.2	38	20	16	5	0	21	1	31	5
Warren, Bend	3	3	.500	3.75	21	4	0	12	0	1	57.2	66	37	24	3	2	29	0	53	7
Webster, Eugene*	2	4	.333	6.41	11	11	0	0	0	0	46.1	59	41	33	5	3	36	0	40	6
Wiggs, Bellingham*	0	3	.000	1.58	22	0	0	17	0	9	40.0	28	8	7	1	0	2	2	59	3
Wiley, Eugene	5	1	.833	1.05	21	0	0	9	0	1	42.2	32	11	5	0	1	7	1	41	4
Woodson, Bellingham	3	4	.429	4.75	12	12	0	0	0	0	60.2	63	42	32	2	2	27	1	53	3
Wurm, Boise	2	3	.400	2.04	31	0	0	20	0	7	39.2	31	11	9	1	4	9	2	42	4
Zinter, Spokane	6	4	.600	2.70	17	7	0	5	0	2	73.1	64	25	22	2	1	37	0	89	6

BALKS—Zinter, 11; Lindsey, Tafoya, 9 each; King, Latter, Woodson, 8 each; Adams, 7; Banks, Bennett, Moore, Warrecker, 6 each; Ahern, Cormier, Gibbs, Grimes, Helm, Lodding, 5 each; Brummett, Gustafson, Henrikson, Jacobs, Sheridan, 4 each; Candelaria, Cunningham, Johnson, Knox, Kries, Lodgek, Lomeli, Robinson, Salkeld, Taveras, Wiley, 3 each; Deville, Devore, Enno, Erwin, Fletcher, Guzman, Hocking, LeBlanc, Phelan, Pierce, Schaefer, Smith, Towey, 2 each; Aleys, Allison, Arola, Baldwin, Buckley, Callahan, Cobb, Davis, Ebert, Florie, Forrest, Gordon, Haffner, Hanselman, Hernandez, J. Jones, K. Jones, Kracl, Larson, Liss, Matas, Miller, Novoa, Pascual, Pena, Schiller, Swingle, Talbert, Twardy, Venuto, 1 each.

COMBINATION SHUTOUTS—Gutierrez-Loe-LeBlanc-Rivas, Darwin-Rivas-LeBlanc, Liss-Wiggs, Gordon-Bryant-LeBlanc, Woodson-Rivas-LeBlanc, Bellingham; Candelaria-Lomeli-Wurm, King-Wurm, Lomeli-Larson, Tafoya-Wurm, Matas-Olson-Wurm, Boise; Talbert-Pierce 2, Lindsey-Centala, Ahern-Wiley, Eugene; Aleys-Gustafson, Everett; Branconier-Miller, Branconier-Pascual, Enno-Pascual-Fletcher, Salem; Grimes-Latter-Smith, Erwin-Venuto, Erwin-Osteen, Grimes-Smith, Erwin-Latter-Smith, Pena-Latter, Kracl-Towey-Latter, Southern Oregon; Davis-Gollehon-Deville, Knox-Buckley, Knox-Banks-Zinter, Davis-Buckley, Deville-Cunningham, Florie-Banks, Spokane.

NO-HIT GAMES—Helm, Bend, defeated Everett, 10-0, July 2; Aleys, Everett, defeated Bend, 4-1, July 21.

South Atlantic League

CLASS A

CHAMPIONSHIP WINNERS IN PREVIOUS YEARS

1948—Lincolnton* .627	1967—Spartanburg .730	1979—Greenwood‡ .565
1949—Newton-Conover .667	Spartanburg .567	Spartanburg .525
Ruth'ford Co. (2nd)† .627	1968—Spartanburg .597	1980—Greensboro .590
1950—Newton-Conover .627	Greenwood‡ .597	Charleston .561
Lenoir (2nd)† .626	1969—Greenwood‡ .587	1981—Greensboro‡ .695
1951—Morganton .645	Shelby .565	Greenwood .549
Shelby (2nd)† .604	1970—Greenville .576	1982—Greensboro‡ .681
1952—Lincolnton .649	Greenville .619	Florence .546
Shelby (2nd)† .645	1971—Greenwood .631	1983—Columbia .620
1953-59—League inactive.	Greenwood .759	Gastonia‡ .587
1960—Lexington .707	1972—Spartanburg‡ .788	1984—Charleston .549
Salisbury (2nd)† .650	Greenville .652	Asheville‡ .510
1961—Salisbury .627	1973—Spartanburg‡ .646	1985—Florence‡ .599
Shelby (4th)† .481	Gastonia .619	Greensboro .540
1962—Statesville .563	1974—Gastonia .606	1986—Columbia‡ .682
Statesville .700	Gastonia .672	Asheville .643
1963—Greenville† .576	1975—Spartanburg .543	1987—Asheville .655
Salisbury .631	Spartanburg .614	Myrtle Beach‡ .597
1964—Rock Hill .672	1976—Asheville .544	1988—Charleston (S.C.) .616
Salisbury‡ .631	Greenwood‡ .600	Spartanburg‡ .500
1965—Salisbury .641	1977—Greenwood .557	
Rock Hill‡ .603	Gastonia‡ .590	
1966—Spartanburg .682	1978—Greenwood .614	
Spartanburg .767	Greenwood .565	

*Won championship and four-club playoff. †Won four-club playoff. ‡Won split-season playoff. (NOTE—Known as Western Carolina League from 1948 through 1962 and known as Western Carolinas League through 1979.)

STANDING OF CLUBS AT CLOSE OF FIRST HALF, JUNE 16

NORTHERN DIVISION

Club	W.	L.	T.	Pct.	G.B.
Gastonia (Rangers)	44	26	0	.629	......
Greensboro (Reds)	42	26	1	.618	1
Spartanburg (Phillies)	35	36	0	.493	9½
Fayetteville (Tigers)	34	35	0	.493	9½
Asheville (Astros)	30	36	0	.455	12
Charleston (W.Va.) (Cubs)	25	38	1	.397	15½

SOUTHERN DIVISION

Club	W.	L.	T.	Pct.	G.B.
Augusta (Pirates)	44	28	0	.611	......
Columbia (Mets)	38	31	0	.551	4½
Savannah (Cardinals)	32	37	0	.464	10½
Charleston (S.C.) (Padres)	32	39	0	.451	11½
Sumter (Braves)	30	40	0	.429	13
Myrtle Beach (Blue Jays)	29	43	0	.403	15

STANDING OF CLUBS AT CLOSE OF SECOND HALF, AUGUST 31

NORTHERN DIVISION

Club	W.	L.	T.	Pct.	G.B.
Gastonia (Rangers)	48	22	0	.686	......
Asheville (Astros)	38	34	0	.528	11
Greensboro (Reds)	36	34	0	.514	12
Fayetteville (Tigers)	36	34	0	.514	12
Charleston (W.Va.) (Cubs)	33	38	0	.465	15½
Spartanburg (Phillies)	27	43	0	.386	21

SOUTHERN DIVISION

Club	W.	L.	T.	Pct.	G.B.
Charleston (S.C.) (Padres)	40	29	0	.580	......
Savannah (Cardinals)	37	33	0	.529	3½
Columbia (Mets)	35	36	0	.493	6
Augusta (Pirates)	33	39	0	.458	8½
Myrtle Beach (Blue Jays)	30	40	0	.429	10½
Sumter (Braves)	30	41	0	.423	11

COMPOSITE STANDING OF CLUBS AT CLOSE OF SEASON, AUGUST 31

Club	Gas.	Gbr.	Aug.	Col.	ChSC	Fay.	Sav.	Ash.	Spar.	ChWV	Sum.	M.B.	W.	L.	T.	Pct.	G.B.
Gastonia (Rangers)	....	6	8	5	5	9	8	14	16	11	5	5	92	48	0	.657	......
Greensboro (Reds)	10	....	7	7	8	3	8	8	5	6	8	8	78	60	1	.565	13
Augusta (Pirates)	2	2	....	10	9	9	9	3	4	6	10	13	77	67	0	.535	17
Columbia (Mets)	4	3	6	....	9	7	7	7	6	3	12	9	73	67	0	.521	19
Charleston (S.C.) (Padres)	5	3	7	8	....	6	8	5	5	6	10	9	72	68	0	.514	20
Fayetteville (Tigers)	7	8	1	2	3	....	4	8	8	14	8	7	70	69	0	.504	21½
Savannah (Cardinals)	2	7	7	6	9	6	....	4	5	4	8	11	69	70	0	.496	22½
Asheville (Astros)	2	10	7	3	5	7	5	....	9	7	5	8	68	70	0	.493	23
Spartanburg (Phillies)	2	8	6	4	5	7	4	8	....	7	7	4	62	79	0	.440	30½
Charleston (W.Va.) (Cubs)	4	7	4	7	3	5	6	7	9	....	5	1	58	76	1	.433	31
Sumter (Braves)	5	4	7	8	4	2	8	4	3	9	....	5	60	81	0	.426	32½
Myrtle Beach (Blue Jays)	5	2	6	7	3	8	2	6	8	5	....	....	59	83	0	.415	34

Major league affiliations in parentheses.

Playoffs—Augusta defeated Charleston (S.C.), two games to one; Augusta defeated Gastonia, three games to one, to win league championship.

Regular-Season Attendance—Asheville, 96,178; Augusta, 119,153; Charleston (S.C.), 78,438; Charleston (W.Va.), 130,293; Columbia, 85,862; Fayetteville, 65,931; Gastonia, 51,290; Greensboro, 157,927; Myrtle Beach, 68,779; Savannah, 76,287; Spartanburg, 94,120; Sumter, 36,706. Total—1,060,964. Playoffs (7 games)—6,897. All-Star Game—7,218.

Managers—Asheville, Jim Coveney; Augusta, Stan Cliburn; Charleston (S.C.), Jack Krol; Charleston (W.Va.), Greg Mahlberg; Columbia, Bill Stein; Fayetteville, Gene Roof; Gastonia, Orlando Gomez; Greensboro, Gary Denbo; Myrtle Beach, Mike Fischlin; Savannah, Keith Champion; Spartanburg, Mel Roberts; Sumter, Ned Yost.

All-Star Team—1B—Mike Mulvaney, Greensboro; 2B—Jeff Frey, Gastonia; 3B—Keith Raisanen, Augusta; SS—(tie) Andujar Cedeno, Asheville and Reggie Sanders, Greensboro; OF—Willie Ansley, Asheville; OF—Kevin Belcher, Gastonia; OF—Mauricio Nunez, Savannah; C—Todd Hundley, Columbia; DH—Trey McCoy, Gastonia; RHP—John Ericks, Savannah; LHP—Pedro Martinez, Charleston (S.C.); Manager—Orlando Gomez, Gastonia; Most Valuable Player—Mike Mulvaney, Greensboro; Most Outstanding Pitcher—Pedro Martinez, Charleston (S.C.).

(Compiled by Howe Sportsdata International, Boston, Mass.)

CLUB BATTING

Club	Pct.	G.	AB.	R.	OR.	H.	TB.	2B.	3B.	HR.	RBI.	SH.	SF.	HP.	BB.	Int. BB.	SO.	SB.	CS.	LOB.
Columbia	.257	140	4556	636	564	1169	1613	196	31	62	536	34	39	72	458	19	871	150	63	965
Greensboro	.252	139	4522	672	610	1139	1571	188	35	58	579	23	31	58	595	17	911	134	65	1046
Gastonia	.251	140	4572	642	517	1146	1682	205	29	91	565	57	49	40	534	33	918	118	84	989
Augusta	.246	144	4646	709	619	1145	1604	218	32	59	606	51	38	42	694	13	1125	193	96	1051
Fayetteville	.246	139	4504	614	643	1107	1475	164	24	52	522	67	33	55	609	18	878	150	76	1039
Myrtle Beach	.243	142	4646	638	711	1131	1583	176	18	80	549	23	33	29	611	11	1043	108	73	1037
Asheville	.242	138	4343	673	666	1051	1465	175	13	71	527	41	38	42	635	5	1060	303	122	926
Spartanburg	.237	141	4488	527	559	1064	1425	171	26	46	463	42	42	41	522	8	942	95	57	1022
Sumter	.236	141	4570	587	680	1080	1474	197	31	45	479	47	56	53	512	14	983	172	83	960
Charleston (S.C.)	.235	140	4583	573	611	1077	1479	187	16	61	491	45	33	59	545	17	953	153	72	1037
Savannah	.226	139	4326	556	524	976	1339	153	15	60	462	44	32	75	563	18	846	171	81	979
Charleston (W.Va.)	.223	135	4313	450	573	962	1253	147	15	38	383	66	28	39	493	13	859	84	65	978

INDIVIDUAL BATTING

(Leading Qualifiers for Batting Championship—389 or More Plate Appearances)

°Bats lefthanded. †Switch-hitter.

Player and Club	Pct.	G.	AB.	R.	H.	TB.	2B.	3B.	HR.	RBI.	SH.	SF.	HP.	BB.	Int. BB.	SO.	SB.	CS.
Frye, Jeffrey, Gastonia	.313	125	464	85	145	180	26	3	1	40	5	1	1	72	5	53	33	13
Ansley, Willie, Asheville	.309	103	340	81	105	141	14	2	6	55	4	5	4	73	0	90	53	16
Giannelli, Raymond, Myrtle Beach°	.301	127	458	76	138	211	17	1	18	84	1	8	5	78	4	53	2	6
Cedeno, Andujar, Asheville	.300	126	487	76	146	223	23	6	14	93	2	5	1	29	0	124	23	10
Gardner, Glen, Sumter°	.298	132	480	68	143	191	28	1	6	71	1	3	7	59	5	63	28	10
Cudjo, Lavell, Greensboro	.295	119	417	78	123	153	10	7	2	36	3	1	9	65	3	95	28	11
Berry, Mark, Greensboro	.286	98	318	54	91	128	23	1	4	55	0	4	3	76	1	32	2	5
Witkowski, Matthew, Char. (S.C.)	.283	119	448	67	127	155	18	5	0	44	8	1	4	65	4	81	26	15
Morrisette, James, Columbia	.283	133	446	79	126	198	27	3	13	60	2	5	15	55	0	79	19	8
Raley, Daniel, Fayetteville°	.281	104	363	58	102	145	16	3	7	60	10	6	3	74	5	29	10	2

Departmental Leaders: G—Kuehl, 139; AB—DeLaRosa, 535; R—M. Young, 94; H—A. Cedeno, 146; TB—Kuehl, 232; 2B—McCoy, 31; 3B—Ventress, 11; HR—Cronk, 22; RBI—Mulvaney, 112; SH—Rosario, 16; SF—Simmons, 11; HP—Ferguson, 30; BB—Ferguson, 132; IBB—Hundley, 10; SO—Estep, Roberson, 149; SB—Lamphere, 67; CS—H. Fuller, 28.

(All Players—Listed Alphabetically)

Player and Club	Pct.	G.	AB.	R.	H.	TB.	2B.	3B.	HR.	RBI.	SH.	SF.	HP.	BB.	Int. BB.	SO.	SB.	CS.
Aceto, Theodore, Columbia	.237	30	76	10	18	20	0	1	0	5	0	1	3	8	0	16	1	1
Acosta, Jose, Augusta°	.250	28	4	0	1	1	0	0	0	0	0	0	0	0	0	1	0	0
Adams, Brian, Spartanburg	.217	20	69	6	15	19	4	0	0	8	1	1	0	4	0	21	0	0
Adams, Lionel, Sumter	.100	4	10	0	1	2	1	0	0	1	0	0	1	0	0	2	0	0
Andrade, Jose, Charleston (W.Va.)	.159	59	176	9	28	29	1	0	0	9	4	1	2	15	0	38	1	2
Ansley, Willie, Asheville	.309	103	340	81	105	141	14	2	6	55	4	5	4	73	0	90	53	16
Antigua, Felix, Augusta	.256	50	180	23	46	52	6	0	0	14	0	1	2	13	0	19	0	0
Arguelles, Fernando, Augusta	.175	31	97	5	17	22	5	0	0	8	3	1	3	7	0	31	0	0
Arland, Mark, Greensboro	.200	76	240	35	48	71	9	1	4	25	0	1	10	37	1	76	9	4
Avent, Steven, Spartanburg	.140	16	43	5	6	9	0	0	1	4	1	0	1	6	0	10	0	0
Baez, Igor, Greensboro	.191	30	94	10	18	25	4	0	1	8	0	0	1	7	0	18	0	0
Baez, Kevin, Columbia	.254	123	426	59	108	150	25	1	5	44	9	3	6	58	3	53	11	9
Bailey, Robert, Augusta†	.200	51	185	20	37	44	3	2	0	14	0	0	0	37	0	44	9	3
Baxter, David, Greensboro†	.258	32	128	21	33	35	0	1	0	14	0	1	1	17	0	30	12	2
Beams, Michael, Asheville	.239	118	397	47	95	159	17	1	15	68	7	5	5	60	0	96	14	5
Belbru, Juan, Savannah	.199	91	271	22	54	81	6	0	7	37	2	2	2	14	0	73	12	6
Belcher, Kevin, Gastonia	.296	93	338	61	100	165	21	1	14	59	4	7	5	31	0	62	13	11
Benitez, Luis, Charleston (W.Va.)	.167	35	102	6	17	17	0	0	0	9	2	0	1	17	0	25	2	3
Bennett, Brian, Asheville	.217	43	120	11	26	32	6	0	0	8	2	0	0	16	0	44	2	0
Berry, Anthony, Gastonia°	.169	43	118	16	20	33	4	0	3	16	0	1	4	18	0	35	4	1
Berry, Mark, Greensboro	.286	98	318	54	91	128	23	1	4	55	0	4	3	76	1	32	2	5
Biggers, Alan, Savannah	.171	17	41	2	7	7	0	0	0	2	1	0	1	1	0	10	1	1
Borders, Todd, Charleston (W.Va.)	.125	18	40	6	5	6	1	0	0	2	2	0	0	11	0	18	0	1
Brenner, Michael, Greensboro	.095	11	21	0	2	4	0	1	0	0	0	0	0	5	0	12	0	0
Brewington, Michael, Augusta°	.250	22	88	10	22	32	5	1	1	11	0	0	0	8	0	21	4	1
Briggs, David, Charleston (S.C.)	.175	77	268	12	47	56	6	0	1	22	2	1	3	12	1	53	2	1
Brooks, Eric, Myrtle Beach	.259	75	270	33	70	80	7	0	1	35	2	2	2	32	0	48	2	1
Calzado, Lorenzo, Savannah	.133	23	83	9	11	16	5	0	0	4	0	1	0	1	0	28	1	0
Campos, Rafael, Asheville	.169	89	267	25	45	56	6	1	1	15	4	2	3	48	0	65	1	2
Caraballo, Nelson, Augusta	.097	12	31	2	3	3	0	0	0	3	0	0	4	0	0	12	0	0
Caraballo, Ramon, Sumter†	.263	45	171	22	45	68	10	5	1	32	1	3	2	16	0	38	9	4
Carlin, Michael, Spartanburg†	.198	30	101	9	20	23	3	0	0	6	3	1	1	6	0	26	5	1
Carter, Edward, Savannah°	.193	111	290	42	56	57	1	0	0	23	6	1	0	43	3	24	21	5
Castillo, Benigno, Fayetteville	.225	104	306	45	69	105	10	1	8	36	4	0	11	44	0	77	2	8
Cedeno, Andujar, Asheville	.300	126	487	76	146	223	23	6	14	93	2	5	1	29	0	124	23	10
Cedeno, Domingo, Myrtle Beach	.200	9	35	4	7	7	0	0	0	2	1	0	0	3	0	12	1	1
Chance, Anthony, Augusta	.136	5	22	3	3	9	1	1	1	5	0	0	0	0	0	5	0	0
Charno, Joseph, Asheville°	.229	97	293	40	67	124	13	1	14	47	0	3	4	42	3	90	2	5
Churchill, Timothy, Spartanburg	.190	47	158	12	30	38	5	0	1	25	3	5	4	4	0	27	0	0
Cifarelli, Gerard, Charleston (S.C.)	.213	80	230	21	49	66	12	1	1	29	3	5	7	39	0	35	0	1
Cole, Mark, Fayetteville	.237	49	156	23	37	52	8	2	1	11	2	1	2	19	0	25	1	0
Cole, Marvin, Charleston (W.Va.)	.234	76	274	21	64	75	6	1	1	16	4	0	2	22	1	6	3	8
Colon, Cristobal, Gastonia†	.226	125	473	58	107	141	9	8	3	49	11	4	2	10	0	95	8	5
Conley, Gregory, Charleston (S.C.)	.241	111	390	32	94	126	15	1	5	41	0	6	3	37	0	99	2	2
Craig, Dale, Charleston (W.Va.)	.086	13	35	3	3	3	0	0	0	1	1	1	0	5	0	13	1	0
Cronk, Douglas, Gastonia°	.251	133	478	72	120	209	17	3	22	77	0	7	3	74	5	132	4	1
Cudjo, Lavell, Greensboro	.295	119	417	78	123	153	10	7	2	36	3	1	9	65	3	95	28	11
Culberson, Calvain, Sumter	.190	111	369	44	70	100	11	2	5	38	3	6	3	56	0	66	18	7
David, Gregory, Myrtle Beach°	.221	110	371	45	82	125	23	1	6	47	0	3	0	64	4	80	2	4
Davidson, Michael, Fayetteville	.239	59	176	22	42	57	8	2	1	19	5	0	1	37	0	21	3	2
DeLaRosa, Juan, Myrtle Beach	.256	132	535	66	137	210	28	6	11	74	1	4	2	9	1	124	19	10
Delas, Michael, Fayetteville	.245	96	318	32	78	105	9	0	6	43	3	3	5	43	1	72	2	3
DeLoach, Bobby, Savannah	.220	110	368	43	81	135	16	4	10	40	1	4	4	32	1	94	12	11
DeLosSantos, Pedro, Asheville	.202	100	336	36	68	92	9	0	5	22	3	0	2	24	0	87	15	3

Player and Club	Pct.	G.	AB.	R.	H.	TB.	2B.	3B.	HR.	RBI.	SH.	SF.	HP.	BB.	Int. BB.	SO.	SB.	CS.
Eklund, Troy, Gastonia	.196	47	143	20	28	40	9	0	1	10	5	1	4	18	2	35	3	2
Ellison, Paul, Spartanburg	.189	62	175	13	33	35	2	0	0	10	3	0	4	31	0	45	0	1
Erickson, Donald, Fayetteville	.262	67	233	38	61	73	7	1	1	19	4	1	4	29	0	47	6	2
Estep, Christopher, Augusta	.221	121	393	76	87	149	23	3	11	53	2	0	5	80	0	149	28	8
Fanning, Steven, Savannah	.265	112	407	59	108	140	13	2	5	40	5	0	5	44	1	94	7	1
Federico, Joseph, Savannah*	.227	93	317	39	72	116	19	2	7	43	2	3	3	48	3	89	2	2
Ferguson, James, Savannah	.251	126	339	79	85	103	13	1	1	30	13	0	30	132	0	37	18	12
Fernandez, Reynaldo, Asheville*	.233	66	210	16	49	62	7	0	2	24	0	2	0	14	0	59	0	2
Fowler, Michael, Sumter	.196	40	148	23	29	51	10	0	4	18	1	4	0	11	0	40	1	2
Franco, Matthew, Char. (W.Va.)*	.271	109	377	42	102	135	16	1	5	48	5	4	0	57	0	40	2	2
Frye, Jeffrey, Gastonia	.313	125	464	85	145	180	26	3	1	40	5	1	1	72	5	53	33	13
Fuller, Harry, Asheville*	.261	133	482	88	126	144	12	0	2	52	5	4	3	80	0	70	50	28
Fuller, Jon, Greensboro	.190	30	84	8	16	20	4	0	0	10	0	4	0	8	0	18	0	0
Gant, Ronald, Sumter	.385	12	39	13	15	24	4	1	1	5	0	0	0	11	2	3	4	2
Gardner, Glen, Sumter*	.298	132	480	68	143	191	28	1	6	71	1	3	7	59	5	63	28	10
Giannelli, Raymond, Myrtle Beach*	.301	127	458	76	138	211	17	1	18	84	1	8	5	78	4	53	2	6
Gonzalez, Wallace, Sumter	.000	1	1	0	0	0	0	0	0	0	0	0	0	0	0	0	0	0
Goselin, Scott, Sumter	.260	65	223	22	58	69	6	1	1	27	3	2	1	21	1	33	5	2
Graves, Kenley, Columbia	.169	22	59	6	10	12	2	0	0	3	0	0	0	7	0	18	0	0
Grier, Antron, Savannah	.236	74	275	33	65	72	4	0	1	18	1	2	4	27	1	51	17	11
Hall, Lamar, Sumter	.281	39	139	13	39	45	2	2	0	11	2	2	0	6	0	24	3	4
Hamilton, Michael, Gastonia	.179	14	28	3	5	6	1	0	0	4	0	0	0	1	0	7	0	1
Harding, Greg, Myrtle Beach	.257	99	342	43	88	135	12	1	11	53	0	5	0	31	0	44	7	1
Harper, Gregory, Sumter	.180	45	139	13	25	33	8	0	0	9	3	2	1	12	0	59	3	0
Harris, Franklyn, Columbia	.300	4	10	1	3	4	1	0	0	2	0	0	0	2	0	2	0	0
Harris, James, Columbia	.229	10	35	2	8	9	1	0	0	4	0	0	0	6	0	5	0	0
Harris, Robert, Augusta	.281	8	32	3	9	11	2	0	0	9	0	0	0	0	0	9	3	1
Harris, Vincent, Charleston (S.C.)†	.232	128	456	86	106	116	8	1	0	13	4	1	3	92	0	81	60	20
Henry, Carlos, Asheville*	.277	30	94	12	26	32	3	0	1	16	0	3	0	26	0	18	6	2
Hernandez, Jose, Gastonia	.219	91	215	35	47	69	7	6	1	16	8	0	0	33	0	67	9	2
Hodge, Timothy, Myrtle Beach*	.228	123	377	58	86	109	11	0	4	39	3	3	2	75	1	142	9	7
Honeywell, Brent, Augusta	.000	26	1	0	0	0	0	0	0	0	0	0	0	0	0	1	0	0
Howard, Ronald, Fayetteville†	.212	87	288	53	61	82	13	1	2	22	3	0	3	47	1	63	17	9
Howard, Timothy, Columbia†	.281	15	57	8	16	17	1	0	0	4	0	0	1	1	0	9	3	1
Hundley, Todd, Columbia†	.269	125	439	67	118	182	23	4	11	66	1	5	8	54	10	67	6	3
Huyler, Michael, Augusta	.238	82	261	30	62	79	15	1	0	28	7	5	0	19	1	39	5	3
Infante, Kennedy, Greensboro	.221	21	68	7	15	18	3	0	0	3	1	0	0	7	0	12	2	1
Javier, Vicente, Greensboro†	.203	59	128	11	26	30	4	0	0	13	3	0	1	9	0	28	4	3
Jerich, William, Augusta	.218	73	243	35	53	69	11	1	1	20	6	0	1	30	0	61	4	3
Jimenez, Alejandro, Columbia*	.284	56	190	34	54	88	11	1	7	39	0	3	1	14	0	31	3	1
Johnson, Dante, Greensboro	.217	21	69	4	15	18	3	0	0	7	0	0	2	0	0	17	0	0
Joiner, David, Columbia	.269	12	26	4	7	7	0	0	0	0	0	0	1	2	0	3	0	0
Jones, Eugene, Greensboro	.251	115	406	68	102	140	19	2	5	62	1	3	5	36	1	58	16	3
Keller, Clyde, Savannah	.000	28	0	5	0	0	0	0	0	0	0	0	0	1	0	0	1	0
Keller, Steven, Spartanburg†	.226	116	402	34	91	122	18	2	3	45	3	2	2	48	0	65	1	2
Kindred, Vincent, Savannah	.225	74	231	29	52	92	12	2	8	38	1	2	4	33	0	59	4	2
Klesko, Ryan, Sumter*	.289	25	90	17	26	35	6	0	1	12	1	1	0	11	1	14	1	0
Krumback, Mark, Greensboro†	.266	54	184	24	49	62	4	3	1	20	1	1	1	20	0	43	7	4
Kuehl, John, Charleston (S.C.)†	.258	139	534	84	138	232	30	2	20	98	2	5	10	48	5	126	8	2
Lamphere, Lawrence, Asheville†	.223	134	479	89	107	134	24	0	1	42	3	5	7	65	2	117	67	21
Lemle, Robert, Columbia	.279	66	229	41	64	71	3	2	0	14	2	3	1	29	0	46	38	9
Leonard, Mathew, Char. (W.Va.)*	.153	21	59	5	9	11	2	0	0	4	0	0	0	1	0	18	0	1
Lester, James, Charleston (S.C.)	.317	36	120	22	38	55	8	0	3	24	2	3	2	16	0	18	1	0
Lewis, Joseph, Gastonia*	.233	37	103	13	24	29	5	0	0	10	1	1	0	16	1	19	1	0
Lewis, Mica, Asheville	.186	55	156	35	29	38	6	0	1	16	2	2	2	43	0	45	13	7
Linares, Antonio, Spartanburg	.245	101	347	34	85	105	9	4	1	27	3	1	0	19	0	47	5	5
Lindsey, Douglas, Spartanburg	.228	39	136	14	31	47	7	0	3	17	1	1	0	23	2	31	2	2
Lofton, Kenneth, Asheville*	.329	22	82	14	27	32	2	0	1	9	2	0	1	12	0	10	14	6
Lopez, Luis, Charleston (S.C.)†	.222	127	460	50	102	122	15	1	1	29	7	3	2	17	0	85	12	9
Lopez, Steve, Sumter	.211	96	336	38	71	108	18	2	5	36	4	2	4	20	0	116	3	0
Macaluso, Nicholas, Spartanburg*	.221	90	326	35	72	100	11	1	5	47	1	4	3	52	1	88	1	1
Maisonueve, Samuel, Columbia	.245	30	49	11	12	12	0	0	0	2	2	0	2	9	0	5	1	0
Malchesky, Thomas, Savannah	.160	9	25	0	4	4	0	0	0	1	0	1	1	2	0	12	0	0
Marsh, Thomas, Spartanburg	.253	79	288	42	73	123	18	1	10	42	2	5	3	29	2	66	8	5
Marshall, John, Spartanburg*	.207	57	203	17	42	48	3	0	1	15	1	2	0	13	0	32	0	0
Martin, Darryl, Fayetteville	.248	129	505	67	125	171	20	1	8	65	9	5	6	37	1	80	17	8
Martinez, Luis, Savannah†	.237	67	236	28	56	74	12	0	2	29	2	1	1	19	1	32	8	4
Martinez, Pablo, Charleston (S.C.)†	.175	31	80	13	14	16	2	0	0	4	3	1	0	11	0	21	0	1
Martinez, Rafael, Myrtle Beach	.227	74	260	32	59	80	9	3	2	24	3	0	4	15	0	53	8	5
Massarelli, John, Asheville	.248	90	246	43	61	87	3	2	3	21	2	2	3	35	0	42	25	6
May, Lee, Columbia†	.205	80	264	36	54	67	6	2	1	19	3	0	1	23	0	79	19	6
McCoy, Homer, Gastonia	.280	130	461	79	129	218	31	2	18	89	0	10	6	72	4	81	7	4
McCutchen, James, Gastonia	.216	119	370	38	80	100	15	1	1	25	7	4	2	50	5	84	12	18
McDonald, Kevin, Myrtle Beach	.154	10	13	1	2	2	0	0	0	0	0	0	0	3	0	3	0	1
McGraw, Jeffrey, Asheville*	.185	12	27	5	5	9	1	0	1	4	1	0	1	14	0	4	0	0
McKeon, Kasey, Fayetteville†	.077	5	13	2	1	2	1	0	0	0	0	0	0	2	0	6	0	0
McNabb, Glen, Augusta	.265	124	452	60	120	150	21	3	1	56	7	6	3	55	0	75	14	20
Mendazona, Michael, Gastonia	.188	49	133	14	25	27	2	0	0	11	3	0	0	11	0	16	1	0
Mendez, Eddie, Myrtle Beach	.236	93	296	31	70	87	12	1	1	16	1	0	4	22	1	73	3	8
Mendez, Julio, Savannah	.170	101	283	31	48	60	4	1	2	24	4	3	3	36	1	43	7	5
Mendoza, Jesus, Sumter	.243	11	37	5	9	11	2	0	0	2	0	0	0	6	1	10	0	0
Merchant, Mark, Augusta†	.322	15	59	11	19	27	6	1	0	8	0	1	0	7	1	13	3	1
Millette, Joe, Spartanburg	.239	60	209	27	50	60	4	3	0	18	3	3	7	28	0	36	4	2
Minaya, Roberto, Sumter	.222	120	460	44	102	124	10	3	2	34	4	4	5	23	0	70	12	12
Montalvo, Robert, Myrtle Beach	.189	52	148	15	28	30	2	0	0	10	1	0	0	32	0	37	1	2
Monzon, Jose, Myrtle Beach	.236	50	165	18	39	49	7	0	1	10	0	0	0	19	0	31	3	2
Morandini, Michael, Spartanburg*	.338	63	231	43	78	102	19	1	1	30	4	2	3	35	0	45	18	9
Morrisette, James, Columbia	.283	133	446	79	126	198	27	3	13	60	2	5	15	55	0	79	19	8
Mulvaney, Michael, Greensboro	.266	122	459	62	122	204	23	1	19	112	0	8	3	37	5	71	1	3
Murphy, James C., Charleston (W.Va.)	.225	113	387	38	87	105	11	2	1	28	3	2	7	21	1	89	9	8
Murphy, James K., Fayetteville*	.244	78	234	23	57	76	6	2	3	33	1	4	0	25	2	53	1	2
Neely, Jeffrey, Augusta	.250	55	4	0	1	1	0	0	0	0	1	0	0	0	0	2	0	0

Player and Club	Pct.	G.	AB.	R.	H.	TB.	2B.	3B.	HR.	RBI.	SH.	SF.	HP.	BB.	Int. BB.	SO.	SB.	CS.
Noelke, Michael, Columbia	.253	32	95	7	24	33	3	0	2	11	4	0	2	10	0	25	1	2
Nunez, Mauricio, Savannah	.308	95	347	43	107	147	20	1	6	59	1	7	2	31	2	39	32	7
Olah, Robert, Columbia	.259	133	506	63	131	189	28	6	6	67	0	3	6	32	2	89	3	1
Oller, Jeffrey, Gastonia°	.263	97	331	37	87	137	10	2	12	48	1	4	1	28	7	77	2	3
Olmstead, Reed, Spartanburg°	.238	115	403	46	96	147	30	0	7	50	4	5	5	39	2	106	0	0
Osborne, Jeffrey, Augusta°	.300	74	267	46	80	130	15	4	9	44	0	0	1	34	2	63	6	2
Ozuna, Mateo, Savannah	.208	114	365	46	76	89	9	2	0	25	4	2	5	21	0	62	24	8
Padilla, Freddy, Fayetteville	.152	29	79	4	12	15	3	0	0	6	0	0	0	1	0	14	0	1
Parese, Billy, Myrtle Beach	.240	8	25	2	6	6	0	0	0	0	0	0	0	2	0	10	1	0
Pegues, Steven, Fayetteville	.309	70	269	35	83	109	11	6	1	38	1	3	2	15	2	52	16	10
Pennye, Darwin, Augusta	.357	27	112	21	40	52	10	1	0	18	0	2	0	13	1	17	3	4
Perez, Eduardo, Sumter	.232	114	401	39	93	129	21	0	5	44	4	5	5	44	1	68	2	6
Perozo, Daniel, Greensboro	.255	45	137	18	35	49	6	4	0	10	1	0	0	10	0	33	2	1
Pesavento, Patrick, Fayetteville°	.248	71	226	45	56	59	3	0	0	23	5	1	0	64	0	35	12	9
Pettengill, Timothy, Savannah	.233	88	270	31	63	104	14	0	9	35	0	3	6	28	2	45	5	4
Piechowski, Timothy, Gastonia°	.225	73	213	31	48	70	11	1	3	25	3	3	2	29	1	29	6	3
Pierce, Dominic, Gastonia	.258	41	97	16	25	35	8	1	0	8	2	0	1	14	1	18	3	2
Piskor, Stephen, Columbia°	.231	8	26	2	6	8	2	0	0	2	0	0	1	0	0	9	0	0
Polanco, Radhames, Columbia	.208	68	240	28	50	71	10	1	3	27	1	2	1	15	0	54	1	0
Provence, Todd, Myrtle Beach	.229	42	140	24	32	61	8	0	7	26	0	1	3	26	0	51	5	1
Raisanen, Keith, Augusta	.263	125	437	67	115	183	19	2	15	92	0	7	8	68	1	113	5	5
Raley, Daniel, Fayetteville°	.281	104	363	58	102	145	16	3	7	60	10	6	3	74	5	29	10	2
Reis, Paulo, Sumter	.229	133	476	78	109	135	18	4	0	29	7	5	11	83	0	83	22	14
Relaford, Winston, Sumter†	.258	67	236	41	61	71	6	2	0	6	2	1	3	28	0	58	31	6
Rendina, Michael, Fayetteville°	.116	28	86	9	10	14	4	0	0	5	3	0	0	11	1	19	0	0
Riesgo, Nikco, Charleston, (S.C.)	.239	119	402	74	96	165	25	1	13	53	3	3	10	73	3	81	34	13
Rizzo, Thomas, Sumter	.207	77	237	30	49	67	11	2	1	22	7	3	4	34	1	62	7	2
Roach, Brett, Fayetteville	.191	45	136	10	26	35	4	1	1	12	0	1	1	17	1	31	2	3
Roberson, Kevin, Charleston (W.Va.)†	.254	126	429	49	109	169	19	1	13	57	2	3	5	70	4	149	3	6
Rodriguez, Ahmed, Savannah†	.125	3	8	1	1	1	0	0	0	0	0	0	0	0	0	3	0	0
Rodriguez, Ivan, Gastonia	.238	112	386	38	92	137	22	1	7	42	5	4	2	21	0	58	2	5
Romero, Armando, Augusta†	.224	121	388	58	87	131	26	3	4	55	3	6	6	67	4	74	8	5
Rosa, Julio, Fayetteville	.232	62	168	23	39	50	6	1	1	15	3	2	8	19	0	38	1	3
Rosado, Edwin, Spartanburg†	.111	21	63	4	7	9	0	1	0	3	0	1	0	8	0	12	0	1
Rosario, Jossy, Charleston (W.Va.)	.194	94	319	39	62	81	14	1	1	26	16	1	0	19	1	32	6	3
Rowland, Richard, Fayetteville	.272	108	375	43	102	148	17	1	9	59	3	3	3	54	2	98	4	1
Rush, Edward, Greensboro	.258	128	407	72	105	128	11	6	0	42	5	2	5	76	0	66	6	7
Sanders, Reginald, Greensboro	.289	81	315	53	91	146	18	5	9	53	1	1	3	29	2	63	21	7
Santacruz, Nick, Spartanburg	.233	39	90	16	21	26	3	1	0	8	2	1	0	29	0	26	0	2
Saunders, Douglas, Columbia	.263	115	377	53	99	137	18	4	4	38	4	3	3	35	2	78	5	5
Seal, Michael, Myrtle Beach°	.000	19	1	0	0	0	0	0	0	0	0	0	0	0	0	0	0	0
Shelton, Benjamin, Augusta	.246	122	386	67	95	143	16	4	8	50	0	3	8	87	1	132	18	4
Shermet, David, Asheville	.220	103	300	52	66	93	18	0	3	32	4	0	5	54	0	90	18	9
Simmons, Randolph, Sumter°	.240	129	466	71	112	184	21	6	13	71	0	11	2	57	2	132	23	12
Sims, Gregory, Augusta	.233	95	296	71	69	91	11	1	3	40	8	4	6	91	0	84	46	19
Smith, Edward, Myrtle Beach	.059	10	17	0	1	1	0	0	0	0	0	0	0	3	0	11	0	0
Smith, Gregory, Charleston (S.C.)	.259	116	417	49	108	159	25	1	8	63	2	1	6	54	0	86	1	4
Smith, Woodrow, Charleston (W.Va.)	.205	18	73	6	15	25	4	0	2	7	1	2	1	0	0	14	1	3
Sodders, Randy, Charleston (W.Va.)	.186	22	70	3	13	13	0	0	0	2	1	0	0	8	0	13	1	1
Songini, Michael, Greensboro°	.245	117	359	54	88	118	11	2	5	40	3	1	9	66	2	48	4	5
Span, Brian, Charleston (S.C.)	.163	40	129	8	21	30	3	0	2	9	1	0	0	10	0	54	2	1
Spurgeon, Scott, Asheville	.111	12	27	2	3	7	1	0	1	3	0	0	1	0	0	9	0	0
St. Peter, William, Charleston (W.Va.)	.215	97	311	33	67	86	13	0	2	25	3	2	3	39	1	56	4	5
Stevanus, Michael, Augusta†	.250	27	16	1	4	6	0	1	0	5	0	0	0	3	0	8	0	0
Stout, Jeffrey, Augusta	.268	75	183	31	49	51	2	0	0	15	11	1	3	22	0	14	19	7
Sutko, Glenn, Greensboro	.234	109	333	44	78	120	21	0	7	41	0	3	4	47	1	105	1	3
Swain, Thayer, Gastonia	.297	60	212	25	63	85	7	0	5	35	2	2	7	34	2	47	9	13
Szynal, Jon, Spartanburg°	.193	68	202	20	39	45	3	0	1	16	1	3	1	35	0	37	1	1
Taylor, Michael, Myrtle Beach	.221	121	403	62	89	103	4	2	2	36	7	2	1	74	0	80	8	7
Taylor, Scott, Charleston (W.Va.)	.253	73	229	23	58	63	5	0	0	19	3	2	3	23	0	22	2	1
Tenhunfeld, Joseph, Spartanburg	.274	50	168	19	46	64	6	0	4	17	0	1	2	17	0	36	0	0
Terzarial, Anthony, Greensboro	.234	83	308	44	72	91	14	1	1	27	3	1	2	33	1	70	17	7
Tesmer, James, Columbia	.429	2	7	1	3	3	0	0	0	1	0	0	1	0	0	1	0	0
Thomas, Mark, Savannah	.189	32	90	11	17	29	3	0	3	12	0	0	3	0	0	45	5	2
Thomas, Orlando, Savannah	.176	68	170	14	30	41	5	0	2	14	1	1	4	50	3	51	0	1
Toney, Anthony, Fayetteville†	.297	50	185	35	55	62	5	1	0	18	4	1	2	28	1	24	40	6
Tonucci, Norman, Myrtle Beach	.252	38	127	21	32	50	3	0	5	19	0	1	0	22	0	36	0	0
Toole, Matthew Charleston, (S.C.)	.219	59	215	15	47	53	6	0	0	13	2	1	1	11	0	54	1	1
Torres, Freddy, Fayetteville	.217	34	92	8	20	22	2	0	0	6	2	0	0	15	0	12	3	4
Trusky, Kenneth, Augusta°	.243	26	103	11	25	35	4	0	2	12	0	1	0	5	0	16	4	2
Uribe, Miliciades, Charleston (W.Va.)°	.246	86	280	35	69	90	14	2	1	26	2	1	2	35	1	48	6	4
Uribe, Relito, Myrtle Beach	.134	34	67	3	9	11	2	0	0	2	1	0	0	7	0	25	0	3
Urman, Michael, Sumter	.205	36	112	6	23	27	4	0	0	11	4	2	4	14	0	42	0	0
Valverde, Miguel, Augusta	.209	45	158	18	33	39	4	1	0	12	0	1	1	22	1	48	8	4
Vaughan, Richard, Myrtle Beach	.200	32	100	10	20	39	7	0	4	16	0	1	1	6	0	32	0	2
Ventress, Leroy, Spartanburg	.279	136	516	91	144	180	14	11	0	33	4	1	2	59	1	109	42	24
Verstandig, Mark, Charleston, (S.C.)°	.282	32	78	7	22	31	6	0	1	10	4	1	1	26	1	17	0	1
Wakefield, Timothy, Augusta	.235	11	34	5	8	12	2	1	0	5	0	0	0	1	0	14	1	1
Walker, Duane, Fayetteville	.235	69	217	26	51	67	8	1	2	21	4	1	0	24	1	70	13	3
Walker, Lonnie, Columbia	.252	96	329	38	83	106	9	1	4	42	2	3	6	33	1	73	14	11
Waller, Casey, Spartanburg†	.257	55	202	25	52	87	9	1	8	31	1	2	3	18	0	40	1	0
Wardlow, Joseph, Gastonia°	.111	3	9	1	1	1	0	0	0	1	0	0	0	1	0	2	0	0
Washington, Kraig, Char. (W.Va.)	.178	11	45	6	8	8	0	0	0	2	0	0	0	3	0	3	0	0
Weinheimer, Wayne, Char., (W.Va.)	.228	107	369	37	84	120	18	0	6	43	2	4	3	49	2	95	5	3
Welish, Scot, Charleston, (S.C.)°	.208	40	120	13	25	32	2	1	1	15	0	1	6	14	0	25	0	0
Whalen, Shawn, Charleston, (S.C.)°	.182	62	236	20	43	68	6	2	5	24	2	0	1	20	3	37	3	1
Wiley, Craig, Fayetteville†	.253	21	79	13	20	26	3	0	1	11	1	1	0	20	0	12	0	0
Williams, Eric, Charleston, (W.Va.)°	.196	114	378	37	74	107	14	5	3	35	5	2	5	59	0	86	8	8
Williams, Flavio, Augusta	.347	44	124	24	43	53	8	1	2	16	0	1	8	18	0	15	0	1
Williams, Jerrone, Char. (W.Va.)†	.244	91	360	52	88	110	9	2	3	24	10	3	4	30	1	95	26	6
Witkowski, Matthew, Char. (S.C.)	.283	119	448	67	127	155	18	5	0	44	8	1	4	65	4	81	26	15
Wolfer, James, Greensboro°	.213	21	47	5	10	11	1	0	0	1	0	0	1	8	0	16	0	0

Player and Club	Pct.	G.	AB.	R.	H.	TB.	2B.	3B.	HR.	RBI.	SH.	SF.	HP.	BB.	Int. BB.	SO.	SB.	CS.
Woodruff, Patrick, Spartanburg	.227	38	128	13	29	31	2	0	0	7	1	1	0	16	0	29	7	1
Young, Derrick, Columbia	.265	131	461	59	122	157	15	4	4	59	4	6	3	42	0	88	24	6
Young, Mark, Myrtle Beach	.274	129	496	94	136	187	24	3	7	56	2	3	4	81	0	98	37	12
Zawaski, Vince, Columbia	.254	65	209	27	53	72	11	1	2	26	0	2	10	23	1	41	1	0
Zayas, Pedro, Spartanburg	.143	9	28	2	4	5	1	0	0	4	0	0	0	3	0	8	0	0

The following pitchers, listed alphabetically by club, with games in parentheses, had no plate appearances, primarily through use of designated hitters:

ASHEVILLE—Dovey, Troy (24); Dunnum, Rick (37); Farmer, Gordon (19); Gardner, Christopher (15); Griffiths, Brian (22); Gutierrez, Anthony (5); Hartgraves, Dean (19); Johnson, Gregory (42); Perez, Francisco (22); Ponte, Edward (42); Reynolds, Shane (8); Rosario, Eliezel (19); Scheckla, Rodney (31); Windes, Rodney (53).

AUGUSTA—Andersh, Kevin (14); Blohm, Peter (18); Brown, Scott (5); Buckholz, Steven (17); Byerly, Rodney (1); Copp, William (3); Felix, Antonio (27); Huseby, Kenneth (22); Kuder, Jeffrey (4); McDowell, Timothy (21); Odom, Timothy (14); Underwood, Robert (23); Valdez, Ramon (1).

CHARLESTON (S.C.)—Beavers, Mark (13); Bond, David (5); Brucato, Robert (19); Bryand, Renay (48); Cantwell, Robert (25); Florie, Bryce (12); Hart, Jeffrey (4); Haslock, Christopher (56); Hernandez, Jeremy (10); Knox, Kerry (2); Martinez, Pedro (28); Murdock, Joseph (30); Sager, Anthony (26); Tucker, Vance (25); Tukes, Stanley (2); Wood, Brian (53).

CHARLESTON (W.Va.)—Burns, Daren (19); Cakora, Matthew (12); Campos, Frank (38); DiBartolomeo, Stephen (20); Doss, Jason (33); Eddings, Jay (5); Gardner, John (32); Goodwin, David (41); Lutz, Christopher (23); Rasp, Ronnie (54); Reed, Sean (24); Smalls, Roberto (23); Teague, Scott (5); Whitson, Anthony (27).

COLUMBIA—Brady, Michael (15); Corbin, Archie (27); Dorn, Chris (10); Fine, Thomas (12); Hill, Christopher (29); Hillman, Eric (9); Newton, Stephen (36); Perez, Vladimir (25); Reich, Andrew (20); Rogers, Bryan (14); Schourek, Peter (27); Vasquez, Julian (37); Wenrick, John (44); Young, Anthony (22).

FAYETTEVILLE—Belcher, Glenn (5); Berrios, Hector (25); Betances, Marcos (5); Brader, Timothy (49); DeSilva, John (10); Ettles, Mark (19); Ferm, Edward (16); Gohr, Gregory (4); Ingram, Linty (28); Koller, Michael (26); Marshall, Randall (34); Meacham, Russell (16); Nozling, Paul (39); Rivera, Lino (38); Rowland, Donald (2); Rudolph, Blaine (40); Shea, Kurt (16); Shoup, Eric (6); Thomas, Robert (3); Torres, Leonardo (43).

GASTONIA—Allen, Steven (51); Brown, Robert (18); Compres, Fidel (8); Cunningham, Everett (27); Gore, Bryan (24); Hvizda, James (62); MacNeil, Timothy (22); McCray, Eric (22); McGraw, Frank (1); Nen, Robb (24); Oliver, Darren (24); Randle, Carl (17); Romero, Ronaldo (22); Spencer, Kyle (43); Valdez, Francisco (26); Wilkinson, Spencer (1).

GREENSBORO—Anderson, Michael (25); Ayala, Robert (22); Dempster, Kurtis (10); Garcia, Victoriano (43); Grovom, Carl (11); Landy, Brian (26); Malley, Michael (39); McAuliffe, David (50); Nordstrom, Carl (44); Sanford, Meredith (25); Satre, Jason (27); Spradlin, Jerry (42).

MYRTLE BEACH—Bradley, Eric (6); Brady, Michael (35); Brown, Timothy (34); Bruzdewicz, Timothy (23); Burgos, Enrique (16); Cross, Jesse (36); DePastino, Andrew (29); Dodd, Daniel (13); Hutson, Scott (12); Johnson, Curtis (40); Johnson, Dane (4); Lloyd, Graeme (1); Ogliaruso, Michael (21); Olivares, Jose (39); Ward, Anthony (16); Weathers, David (31); Wilson, Terry (18).

SAVANNAH—Brooks, Rodney (9); Burgos, John (4); Clark, Mark (27); Ericks, John (28); Harvick, Brad (31); Hayes, James (1); Hensley, Michael (15); Hershman, William (7); Hitt, Daniel (63); Majer, Steffen (15); Ozuna, Gabriel (59); Rose, Matthew (8); Sala, David (11); Sherrill, Timothy (3); Stone, Brian (25); Taylor, Andrew (29); Weese, Dean (54).

SPARTANBURG—Ashby, Andrew (17); Backs, Jason (25); Borland, Toby (47); Carter, Andrew (15); Coulter, Darrell (17); Dell, Timothy (18); Elam, Todd (21); Elliott, Donald (7); Garcia, Reginald (2); Kent, Troy (5); LaRosa, John (12); Limbach, Chris (8); Lindsey, Darrell (27); McCarthy, Gregory (24); Peek, Timothy (19); Rambo, Matthew (14); Tracy, Richard (5); Wilson, Gary (34).

SUMTER—Bruck, Thomas (2); Calderone, Jeffrey (23); DeLeon, Roberto (34); Dickman, David (9); Duncan, Robert (29); Grove, Scott (28); Johnson, Lloyd (11); Kelly, Kevin (13); Maldonado, Johnny (48); Meier, Jeffrey (39); Meister, Ralph (9); Mitchell, Glenn (30); Murray, Matthew (12); Richey, Rodney (33); Smith, Chad (15); Thomas, Ronald (3); Trlicek, Richard (15); Vazquez, Marcos (25); Wohlers, Mark (14).

GRAND SLAM HOME RUNS—Beams, Kuehl, Raisanen, Sanders, 2 each; A. Berry, R. Caraballo, Castillo, Colon, Davidson, Delas, DeLoach, Gardner, Harding, Hundley, Jones, Martin, Mulvaney, Raley, Songini, L. Walker, Weinheimer, Zawaski, 1 each.

AWARDED FIRST BASE ON CATCHER'S INTERFERENCE—Rendina 2 (Andrade 2); Ventress 2 (I. Rodriguez, S. Taylor); Avent (Hundley); Estep (Sutko); Lamphere (Antigua); Macaluso (Hundley); Marsh (Bennett); E. Mendez (Bennett); Morrisette (Sutko); Raisanen (Sutko); D. Walker (Hundley).

CLUB FIELDING

Club	Pct.	G.	PO.	A.	E.	DP.	PB.	Club	Pct.	G.	PO.	A.	E.	DP.	PB.
Gastonia	.963	140	3680	1564	199	140	53	Charleston (W.Va.)	.961	135	3474	1538	206	137	18
Columbia	.963	140	3575	1412	193	118	20	Augusta	.958	144	3718	1454	229	104	22
Fayetteville	.963	139	3621	1513	199	133	26	Myrtle Beach	.956	142	3641	1416	230	108	47
Savannah	.962	139	3517	1353	191	87	10	Asheville	.954	138	3487	1561	242	124	24
Sumter	.961	141	3662	1610	212	145	20	Greensboro	.954	139	3534	1247	232	87	39
Spartanburg	.961	141	3576	1560	208	108	31	Charleston (S.C.)	.945	140	3659	1472	296	121	29

Triple Plays—Asheville, Columbia.

INDIVIDUAL FIELDING

FIRST BASEMEN

*Throws lefthanded.

Player and Club	Pct.	G.	PO.	A.	E.	DP.	Player and Club	Pct.	G.	PO.	A.	E.	DP.
Baez, Greensboro	.909	2	9	1	1	0	Jones, Greensboro	1.000	8	42	3	0	5
Beams, Asheville	.972	25	200	7	6	21	Keller, Spartanburg	1.000	2	8	0	0	0
Berry, Greensboro	.993	48	390	24	3	26	Klesko, Sumter*	.979	18	173	11	4	15
Brewington, Augusta*	.950	3	18	1	1	3	Kuehl, Charleston (S.C.)	.985	68	556	49	9	56
Calzado, Savannah	.966	23	180	19	7	15	Leonard, Charleston (W.Va.)*	.958	5	44	2	2	3
Charno, Asheville	1.000	3	11	0	0	2	Lopez, Sumter	.990	72	673	45	7	66
Churchill, Spartanburg	.988	45	401	25	5	30	Marshall, Spartanburg	1.000	1	2	0	0	0
Cifarelli, Charleston (S.C.)	.944	2	17	0	1	1	L. Martinez, Savannah	.988	25	161	10	2	10
Conley, Charleston (S.C.)	.963	10	74	4	3	6	R. Martinez, Myrtle Beach	1.000	1	2	0	0	0
CRONK, Gastonia*	.989	122	1120	94	14	111	McCoy, Gastonia	.994	21	142	12	1	10
David, Myrtle Beach	.983	108	867	54	16	65	McGraw, Asheville*	.991	11	101	4	1	8
DeLoach, Savannah	1.000	1	5	0	0	0	Mendoza, Sumter	.990	11	94	5	1	13
DeLosSantos, Asheville	.968	7	55	6	2	8	Mulvaney, Greensboro	.980	86	631	49	14	44
Federico, Savannah*	.982	93	750	48	15	45	Murphy, Fayetteville	.961	22	140	8	6	14
Fernandez, Asheville*	.986	52	408	16	6	36	Neely, Augusta	1.000	1	5	0	0	1
Fowler, Sumter	.961	5	46	3	2	4	Nunez, Savannah	1.000	3	21	1	0	1
Franco, Charleston (W.Va.)	1.000	6	51	2	0	9	Olah, Columbia	.988	77	612	47	8	52
Gardner, Sumter	.986	14	137	8	2	13	Olmstead, Spartanburg*	.988	86	738	58	10	56
Hamilton, Savannah	1.000	1	4	0	0	0	Osborne, Augusta	.995	19	178	7	1	14
Harding, Myrtle Beach	.988	42	303	23	4	24	Perez, Sumter	1.000	14	139	7	0	9
Henry, Asheville*	.993	30	276	20	2	11	Raisanen, Augusta	1.000	1	0	1	0	0
Jimenez, Columbia*	.980	36	261	33	6	20	Raley, Fayetteville	.989	90	781	54	9	77
Johnson, Greensboro	1.000	1	4	0	0	0	Rendina, Fayetteville*	.984	26	234	13	4	20
Joiner, Columbia	.833	3	5	0	1	0	Roach, Fayetteville	.971	9	62	6	2	7

FIRST BASEMEN—Continued

Player and Club	Pct.	G.	PO.	A.	E.	DP.
Saunders, Columbia	1.000	1	1	1	0	0
Shelton, Augusta*	.975	117	976	69	27	71
Shermet, Asheville	.986	26	210	9	3	18
Smith, Charleston (S.C.)*	.987	43	363	19	5	30
Spurgeon, Asheville	1.000	2	13	2	0	3
Tenhunfeld, Spartanburg	.983	13	111	6	2	5
Tesmer, Columbia	1.000	1	8	1	0	3
M. Thomas, Augusta	.950	6	35	3	2	1
O. Thomas, Savannah	1.000	1	6	0	0	0
Uribe, Charleston (W.Va.)*	.988	36	324	17	4	27
Urman, Sumter	.980	7	44	6	1	7
Wakefield, Augusta	1.000	2	23	0	0	4
Weinheimer, Charleston (W.Va.)	.977	94	872	51	22	82
Welish, Charleston (S.C.)*	.995	23	167	17	1	9
Wiley, Fayetteville	1.000	1	9	0	0	2
Zawaski, Columbia	.989	33	259	10	3	22

Triple Play—Shermet.

SECOND BASEMEN

Player and Club	Pct.	G.	PO.	A.	E.	DP.
Aceto, Columbia	1.000	4	5	15	0	1
Belbru, Savannah	1.000	1	1	0	0	0
Benitez, Charleston (W.Va.)	.930	33	42	91	10	21
Brenner, Greensboro	.850	5	6	11	3	1
Campos, Asheville	.952	36	60	80	7	11
Carlin, Spartanburg	.958	29	63	73	6	12
Mark Cole, Fayetteville	.970	47	90	139	7	30
Marvin Cole, Charleston (W.Va.)	.953	57	125	178	15	43
Erickson, Fayetteville	1.000	9	17	34	0	7
Fanning, Savannah	1.000	2	2	7	0	0
Ferguson, Savannah	.979	41	60	80	3	12
FRYE, Gastonia	.977	125	242	340	14	82
Goselin, Sumter	.938	6	14	14	2	2
Hernandez, Gastonia	.935	20	33	39	5	15
R. Howard, Fayetteville	.964	74	149	195	13	41
T. Howard, Columbia	.971	7	14	19	1	2
Javier, Greensboro	.935	15	13	16	2	5
Joiner, Columbia	1.000	6	7	14	0	4
Keller, Savannah	1.000	1	1	0	0	0
Krumback, Greensboro	1.000	1	2	1	0	1
Lamphere, Asheville	.970	77	146	238	12	43
Lester, Charleston (S.C.)	.921	7	17	18	3	7
Lewis, Asheville	.958	34	67	114	8	28
Macaluso, Spartanburg	.939	69	130	165	19	34
Maisonueve, Columbia	.953	17	20	21	2	6
Marshall, Spartanburg	.906	12	20	28	5	4
P. Martinez, Charleston (S.C.)	.857	3	10	8	3	1
R. Martinez, Myrtle Beach	.897	9	18	17	4	1
McCutchen, Gastonia	1.000	1	0	1	0	1
McNabb, Augusta	.951	124	235	284	27	60
Mendez, Savannah	1.000	2	1	2	0	0
Noelke, Columbia	.935	7	14	15	2	5
Ozuna, Savannah	.938	104	181	242	28	42
Parese, Myrtle Beach	.938	8	15	15	2	1
Pierce, Gastonia	1.000	1	0	1	0	0
Reis, Sumter	.971	131	292	421	21	94
Rizzo, Sumter	.903	6	13	15	3	5
Rosa, Fayetteville	.949	15	34	41	4	12
Rosario, Charleston (W.Va.)	.976	35	66	98	4	19
Rush, Greensboro	.956	71	107	154	12	33
Santacruz, Spartanburg	.902	12	16	30	5	4
Saunders, Columbia	.961	113	222	291	21	61
Sodders, Charleston (W.Va.)	.980	21	37	59	2	15
Songini, Greensboro	.943	60	92	141	14	20
Stevanus, Augusta	.960	5	12	12	1	4
Stout, Augusta	.986	18	32	37	1	4
Taylor, Myrtle Beach	.968	119	242	303	18	70
Toole, Charleston (S.C.)	.978	14	19	26	1	8
Waller, Spartanburg	.973	20	49	61	3	8
Wardlow, Gastonia	1.000	1	1	0	0	0
Washington, Charleston (W.Va.)	1.000	2	7	7	0	4
Williams, Augusta	.974	10	17	21	1	3
Witkowski, Charleston (S.C.)	.930	119	263	321	44	67
Wolfer, Greensboro	1.000	1	5	1	0	0
Young, Myrtle Beach	.882	14	15	30	6	2

Triple Play—Saunders.

THIRD BASEMEN

Player and Club	Pct.	G.	PO.	A.	E.	DP.
Adams, Sumter	.900	4	3	6	1	0
Biggers, Savannah	.600	6	0	3	2	0
Brenner, Greensboro	.857	6	3	3	1	0
Campos, Asheville	.932	49	27	111	10	10
Cedeno, Asheville	1.000	1	0	2	0	0
Cifarelli, Charleston (S.C.)	.879	15	7	22	4	3
DeLosSantos, Asheville	.872	82	45	200	36	13
Erickson, Fayetteville	.899	54	32	93	14	9
Ferguson, Savannah	.950	62	56	135	10	10
Franco, Charleston (W.Va.)	.916	83	57	182	22	10
Gardner, Sumter	.890	97	55	171	28	23
Giannelli, Myrtle Beach	.911	88	65	161	22	12
Goselin, Sumter	.936	38	14	74	6	8
Hall, Sumter	1.000	1	0	1	0	0
Harris, Columbia	.944	9	5	12	1	2
Hernandez, Gastonia	.910	42	25	66	9	5
Howard, Fayetteville	.941	8	3	13	1	2
Infante, Greensboro	.881	21	11	26	5	0
Javier, Greensboro	.889	18	14	18	4	0
Keller, Spartanburg	.929	65	36	134	13	7
Krumback, Greensboro	.916	30	31	45	7	5
Kuehl, Charleston (S.C.)	.826	52	20	75	20	4
Lamphere, Asheville	1.000	1	3	1	0	0
Lester, Charleston (S.C.)	.879	24	10	48	8	5
Lewis, Asheville	.848	14	8	20	5	1
Lopez, Sumter	1.000	2	1	1	0	0
Macaluso, Spartanburg	.902	18	7	30	4	2
Malchesky, Savannah	1.000	9	6	7	0	1
Marshall, Spartanburg	.900	30	21	87	12	8
P. Martinez, Charleston (S.C.)	1.000	14	9	23	0	1
R. Martinez, Myrtle Beach	.000	2	0	0	2	0
Mendez, Savannah	.917	68	35	120	14	9
Morrisette, Columbia	.877	71	68	124	27	13
Mulvaney, Greensboro	.908	32	30	49	8	2
OLLER, Gastonia	.893	97	49	201	30	22
Osborne, Augusta	.667	1	1	1	1	0
Ozuna, Savannah	.833	7	5	10	3	1
Padilla, Fayetteville	.898	28	12	41	6	2
Pierce, Gastonia	.872	28	15	26	6	3
Polanco, Columbia	.912	62	32	102	13	7
Raisanen, Augusta	.900	86	57	149	23	9
Raley, Fayetteville	.909	10	8	12	2	1
Reis, Sumter	1.000	2	1	4	0	0
Roach, Fayetteville	.952	38	29	50	4	4
Romero, Augusta	.667	1	1	1	1	0
Rosa, Fayetteville	.870	7	8	12	3	2
Shermet, Asheville	.800	1	3	1	1	1
Smith, Charleston (W.Va.)	.855	18	13	34	8	5
Songini, Greensboro	.814	42	34	49	19	1
Span, Charleston (S.C.)	1.000	1	2	1	0	0
Spurgeon, Asheville	1.000	2	0	2	0	0
St. Peter, Charleston (W.Va.)	.920	38	33	71	9	6
Stout, Augusta	.914	36	22	52	7	3
Taylor, Charleston (W.Va.)	1.000	2	2	2	0	1
Tonucci, Myrtle Beach	.964	14	7	20	1	2
Toole, Charleston (S.C.)	.900	45	37	80	13	9
Torres, Charleston (S.C.)	1.000	1	0	1	0	0
Uribe, Myrtle Beach	1.000	3	0	2	0	0
Wakefield, Augusta	.769	6	4	6	3	1
Waller, Spartanburg	.916	30	23	53	7	5
Wardlow, Gastonia	.600	3	1	2	2	2
Wiley, Fayetteville	.931	14	8	19	2	1
Williams, Augusta	.929	33	19	46	5	8
Young, Myrtle Beach	.865	40	24	72	15	6

SHORTSTOPS

Player and Club	Pct.	G.	PO.	A.	E.	DP.
Aceto, Columbia	.906	24	13	35	5	4
BAEZ, Columbia	.934	121	181	327	36	60
Bailey, Augusta	.888	51	61	137	25	25
Caraballo, Sumter	.920	44	57	151	18	28
A. Cedeno, Asheville	.895	125	182	344	62	70
D. Cedeno, Myrtle Beach	.821	9	12	20	7	3
Mark Cole, Fayetteville	1.000	2	2	4	0	1
Marvin Cole, Charleston (W.Va.)	.903	15	25	40	7	9
Colon, Gastonia	.915	125	183	320	47	69
DeLosSantos, Asheville	.906	11	16	32	5	4
Erickson, Fayetteville	1.000	8	5	22	0	2
Fanning, Savannah	.897	97	136	230	42	31
Ferguson, Savannah	.885	20	20	34	7	7
Franco, Charleston (W.Va.)	1.000	2	3	4	0	1
Hall, Sumter	.894	37	45	115	19	21
Hernandez, Gastonia	.969	27	33	62	3	14
Howard, Columbia	1.000	1	2	5	0	2
Huyler, Augusta	.927	82	113	229	27	32
Javier, Greensboro	.884	24	25	36	8	8
Joiner, Columbia	1.000	2	4	4	0	3
Lester, Charleston (S.C.)	.920	5	10	13	2	1
Lewis, Asheville	.895	3	4	13	2	0

SHORTSTOPS—Continued

Player and Club	Pct.	G.	PO.	A.	E.	DP.
Lopez, Charleston (S.C.)	.895	126	256	373	74	78
P. Martinez, Charleston (S.C.)	.894	12	12	30	5	0
R. Martinez, Myrtle Beach	.924	66	111	193	25	32
Mendez, Savannah	.971	30	34	68	3	8
Millette, Spartanburg	.914	60	90	166	24	30
Montalvo, Myrtle Beach	.960	52	61	133	8	21
Morandini, Spartanburg	.966	61	87	198	10	26
Noelke, Columbia	.889	7	6	18	3	2
Pesavento, Fayetteville	.945	71	110	214	19	47
Rizzo, Sumter	.910	63	95	189	28	40
Rodriguez, Savannah	.750	2	4	5	3	0
Rosa, Fayetteville	.963	40	65	117	7	21
Rosario, Charleston (W.Va.)	.908	66	102	173	28	44
Rush, Greensboro	.944	55	77	143	13	15
Sanders, Greensboro	.875	77	125	169	42	34
Santacruz, Spartanburg	.917	22	32	67	9	11
Saunders, Columbia	1.000	3	2	2	0	1
St. Peter, Charleston (W.Va.)	.942	56	96	149	15	25
Stout, Augusta	.959	21	27	43	3	7
Taylor, Myrtle Beach	1.000	2	4	3	0	1
Torres, Fayetteville	.918	31	47	87	12	21
Uribe, Myrtle Beach	.869	31	30	56	13	9
Washington, Charleston (W.Va.)	.907	9	11	28	4	8

Triple Play—A. Cedeno.

OUTFIELDERS

Player and Club	Pct.	G.	PO.	A.	E.	DP.
Ansley, Asheville	.974	97	179	12	5	1
Arland, Greensboro	.968	71	144	5	5	2
Baxter, Greensboro	1.000	11	16	1	0	0
Beams, Asheville	.935	85	119	10	9	1
Belbru, Savannah	.939	84	129	10	9	2
Belcher, Gastonia	.978	93	172	5	4	2
Berry, Gastonia	.971	29	32	1	1	0
Biggers, Savannah	1.000	1	3	0	0	0
Brewington, Augusta*	.966	13	28	0	1	0
Briggs, Charleston (S.C.)	.978	70	128	6	3	0
Carter, Savannah*	.981	100	148	8	3	1
Castillo, Fayetteville	.944	96	170	15	11	2
Chance, Augusta	.818	4	8	1	2	0
Cudjo, Greensboro	.970	111	208	21	7	3
Culberson, Sumter	.974	107	211	17	6	6
Davidson, Fayetteville	.889	36	56	0	7	0
DeLaRosa, Myrtle Beach	.974	132	276	20	8	3
DeLoach, Savannah	.971	70	93	6	3	1
Eklund, Gastonia	.949	45	68	6	4	3
Estep, Augusta	.970	120	214	10	7	2
Fowler, Sumter	.926	18	25	0	2	0
Franco, Charleston (W.Va.)	1.000	3	2	1	0	0
Fuller, Asheville	.967	128	214	21	8	5
Gant, Sumter	.909	12	19	1	2	0
Gardner, Sumter	1.000	6	5	1	0	0
Grier, Savannah	.985	73	126	7	2	2
R. Harris, Augusta	.917	7	11	0	1	0
V. Harris, Charleston (S.C.)	.967	127	243	18	9	1
Hernandez, Gastonia	1.000	4	10	2	0	0
Hodge, Myrtle Beach	.943	119	156	9	10	4
Howard, Columbia	1.000	7	11	0	0	0
Hundley, Columbia	1.000	1	3	0	0	0
Jerich, Augusta	.974	69	105	6	3	0
Johnson, Greensboro	.964	20	26	1	1	1
Jones, Greensboro	.959	100	154	10	7	0
Kindred, Savannah	1.000	38	49	1	0	1
Krumback, Greensboro	.960	13	24	0	1	0
Lamphere, Asheville	.982	37	48	6	1	1
Lemle, Columbia	.975	61	113	4	3	1
J. Lewis, Gastonia	.875	7	6	1	1	0
M. Lewis, Asheville	1.000	2	1	0	0	0
Linares, Savannah	.931	101	137	11	11	2
Lofton, Asheville*	.951	22	38	1	2	0
Marsh, Spartanburg	.945	78	128	10	8	3
Martin, Fayetteville	.951	125	200	13	11	1
May, Columbia	.963	77	174	6	7	0
McCoy, Gastonia	.846	42	41	3	8	1
McCutchen, Gastonia	.964	116	181	9	7	2
McDonald, Myrtle Beach	1.000	8	6	0	0	0
Mendez, Myrtle Beach	.978	87	127	7	3	0
Merchant, Augusta	1.000	14	23	0	0	0
Minaya, Sumter	.984	118	234	10	4	2
Morrisette, Columbia	.942	53	77	4	5	1
Murphy, Charleston (W.Va.)	.983	107	160	10	3	0
Noelke, Columbia	1.000	13	12	1	0	0
Nunez, Savannah	.978	91	171	4	4	1
Osborne, Augusta	.947	10	17	1	1	0
Pegues, Fayetteville	.985	70	127	8	2	2
Pennye, Augusta	.931	27	49	5	4	0
Perozo, Greensboro	.955	44	80	5	4	0
Piechowski, Gastonia*	.978	65	82	8	2	3
Provence, Myrtle Beach	.945	41	63	6	4	0
Raisanen, Augusta	1.000	1	0	1	0	0
Relaford, Sumter	.984	43	59	2	1	0
Riesgo, Charleston (S.C.)	.940	76	134	7	9	0
Roach, Fayetteville	1.000	2	2	0	0	0
Roberson, Charleston (W.Va.)	.970	116	210	18	7	7
Shermet, Asheville	.964	65	96	11	4	0
Simmons, Sumter*	.976	127	195	12	5	1
Sims, Augusta	.972	91	205	5	6	3
E. Smith, Myrtle Beach	1.000	9	8	0	0	0
G. Smith, Charleston (S.C.)*	.946	61	96	9	6	2
Span, Charleston (S.C.)	.883	34	67	1	9	0
Swain, Gastonia	1.000	42	70	0	0	0
Szynal, Spartanburg	.950	61	68	8	4	1
Tenhunfeld, Spartanburg	.926	22	24	1	2	0
Terzarial, Greensboro	.967	64	133	3	5	2
Thomas, Augusta	.957	21	21	1	1	0
Toney, Fayetteville	.986	44	72	1	1	0
Trusky, Augusta	.969	26	56	6	2	0
Uribe, Charleston (W.Va.)*	.897	21	25	1	3	0
Valverde, Augusta	.923	41	96	0	8	0
Ventress, Spartanburg	.980	133	247	2	5	2
D. Walker, Fayetteville	.984	65	120	4	2	2
L. Walker, Columbia	.966	93	138	5	5	0
Whalen, Charleston (S.C.)*	.966	62	142	1	5	1
E. WILLIAMS, Char. (W.Va.)*	.990	99	186	6	2	0
J. Williams, Charleston (W.Va.)	.975	67	147	7	4	1
Woodruff, Spartanburg	.989	38	90	4	1	1
D. Young, Columbia	.973	129	209	7	6	1
M. Young, Myrtle Beach	.951	54	90	7	5	4

CATCHERS

Player and Club	Pct.	G.	PO.	A.	E.	DP.	PB.
Adams, Spartanburg	.975	19	131	22	4	3	3
Andrade, Charleston (W.Va.)	.978	59	314	48	8	4	6
Antigua, Augusta	.969	22	140	18	5	2	8
Arguelles, Augusta	.977	23	154	16	4	0	3
Avent, Spartanburg	.985	11	58	7	1	2	5
Baez, Greensboro	.967	14	78	11	3	0	2
Bennett, Asheville	.987	41	261	34	4	4	10
Borders, Charleston (W.Va.)	1.000	5	12	0	0	0	1
Brooks, Myrtle Beach	.978	63	462	38	11	2	21
Caraballo, Augusta	.968	12	54	6	2	0	1
Charno, Spartanburg	.975	28	133	21	4	3	5
Cifarelli, Charleston (S.C.)	.956	39	213	24	11	1	9
Conley, Charleston (S.C.)	.976	95	627	76	17	6	18
Craig, Charleston (W.Va.)	.989	13	82	5	1	0	0
Delas, Fayetteville	.983	58	375	25	7	3	11
Ellison, Spartanburg	.989	56	388	46	5	7	12
Fuller, Greensboro	.975	29	181	13	5	1	8
Graves, Columbia	1.000	20	108	9	0	0	4
Hamilton, Gastonia	.966	10	50	7	2	3	1
Harper, Sumter	.974	45	261	43	8	7	4
Harris, Columbia	1.000	4	29	1	0	0	1
Hundley, Columbia	.986	120	826	91	13	12	12
Leonard, Charleston (W.Va.)	1.000	3	4	0	0	0	0
Lewis, Gastonia	.981	12	47	4	1	2	3
Lindsey, Spartanburg	.978	33	240	32	6	4	5
Martinez, Savannah	.995	27	168	18	1	3	2
Massarelli, Asheville	.981	82	505	57	11	11	9
McKeon, Fayetteville	.963	4	21	5	1	0	3
Mendazona, Gastonia	.991	46	289	26	3	2	15
Monzon, Myrtle Beach	.985	46	354	42	6	3	20
Noelke, Columbia	1.000	3	12	0	0	0	1
Osborne, Augusta	1.000	1	2	0	0	0	0
Perez, Sumter	.978	88	621	89	16	13	11
Pettengill, Savannah	.989	62	389	46	5	3	2
Piskor, Columbia	.982	8	51	3	1	2	2
Roach, Fayetteville	1.000	3	6	3	0	0	0
Rodriguez, Gastonia	.986	96	691	96	11	6	34
ROMERO, Augusta	.989	98	628	73	8	6	10
Rosado, Spartanburg	.981	21	129	26	3	1	6
Rowland, Charleston (S.C.)	.982	77	527	66	11	6	11
Spurgeon, Asheville	1.000	1	3	0	0	0	0
Sutko, Greensboro	.986	99	676	77	11	4	22
Taylor, Charleston (W.Va.)	.984	69	364	62	7	12	11
Thomas, Savannah	.991	66	498	59	5	2	6
Tonucci, Myrtle Beach	.921	6	33	2	3	2	2
Urman, Sumter	.987	12	69	8	1	3	5
Vaughan, Myrtle Beach	.984	32	222	24	4	3	4
Verstandig, Charleston (S.C.)	.991	17	97	12	1	3	2
Wiley, Fayetteville	1.000	5	28	5	0	1	1
Wolfer, Greensboro	.973	16	92	16	3	0	7
Zayas, Spartanburg	.938	4	25	5	2	0	0

Triple Play—Hundley.

PITCHERS

Player and Club	Pct.	G.	PO.	A.	E.	DP.
Acosta, Augusta*	.926	28	2	23	2	1
Allen, Gastonia	.976	51	13	28	1	2
Andersh, Augusta*	.969	14	4	27	1	3
Anderson, Greensboro	.962	25	12	13	1	1
Ashby, Spartanburg	.903	17	12	16	3	1
Ayala, Greensboro	.868	22	7	26	5	1
Backs, Spartanburg	.964	25	7	20	1	5
Beavers, Charleston (S.C.)*	.722	13	2	11	5	2
Belcher, Fayetteville	1.000	5	0	2	0	1
Bennett, Asheville	1.000	1	0	1	0	0
Berrios, Fayetteville*	.857	25	5	7	2	0
Betances, Fayetteville	1.000	5	0	4	0	0
Blohm, Augusta	.943	18	7	26	2	4
Bond, Charleston (S.C.)*	1.000	5	0	3	0	0
Borland, Spartanburg	.963	47	5	21	1	2
Brader, Fayetteville*	.944	49	7	10	1	2
Bradley, Myrtle Beach	.667	6	0	2	1	0
Brady, 35 MB-15 Col.	1.000	50	6	3	0	0
Brooks, Savannah	.923	9	4	8	1	0
R. Brown, Gastonia	.933	18	1	13	1	0
T. Brown, Myrtle Beach	.966	34	12	16	1	2
Brucato, Charleston (S.C.)	.920	19	9	14	2	2
Bruck, Sumter	1.000	2	0	1	0	0
Bruzdewicz, Myrtle Beach*	1.000	23	1	6	0	0
Bryand, Charleston (S.C.)*	.885	48	3	20	3	1
Buckholz, Augusta	.914	17	9	23	3	1
E. Burgos, Myrtle Beach*	1.000	16	1	3	0	1
J. Burgos, Savannah*	1.000	4	0	3	0	0
Burns, Charleston (W.Va.)	.857	19	2	10	2	1
Cakora, Charleston (W.Va.)*	1.000	12	1	2	0	0
Calderone, Sumter	.857	23	2	4	1	0
Campos, Charleston (W.Va.)	.902	38	7	30	4	2
Cantwell, Charleston (S.C.)*	.900	25	0	9	1	2
Carter, Spartanburg	1.000	15	2	13	0	0
CLARK, Savannah	.972	27	11	24	1	0
Compres, Gastonia	.750	8	1	2	1	0
Copp, Augusta*	1.000	3	0	7	0	0
Corbin, Columbia	.889	27	7	17	3	1
Coulter, Spartanburg	1.000	17	2	6	0	1
Cross, Myrtle Beach	.611	36	4	7	7	0
Cunningham, Gastonia	.921	27	10	25	3	4
DeLeon, Sumter*	.917	34	1	10	1	0
Dell, Spartanburg	.913	18	3	18	2	0
Dempster, Greensboro	1.000	10	4	4	0	0
DePastino, Myrtle Beach	.840	29	7	14	4	1
DeSilva, Fayetteville	.818	9	3	5	4	2
DiBartolomeo, Char. (W.Va.)	1.000	20	3	6	0	0
Dickman, Sumter	1.000	9	1	1	0	1
Dodd, Myrtle Beach	1.000	13	3	5	0	1
Dorn, Columbia	1.000	10	1	14	0	0
Doss, Charleston (W.Va.)	.786	33	5	6	3	0
Dovey, Asheville	.952	24	5	15	1	2
Duncan, Sumter	1.000	29	2	9	0	1
Dunnum, Asheville	.846	36	6	27	6	2
Eddings, Charleston (W.Va.)	1.000	5	1	3	0	0
Elam, Spartanburg	.875	21	4	10	2	0
Elliott, Spartanburg	.714	7	3	2	2	0
Ericks, Savannah	.939	28	13	18	2	1
Ettles, Fayetteville	1.000	19	0	4	0	0
Farmer, Asheville	.917	18	6	16	2	1
Felix, Augusta	.920	27	11	12	2	0
Ferm, Fayetteville	.952	16	6	14	1	1
Fine, Columbia	.875	12	1	6	1	0
Florie, Charleston (S.C.)	.692	12	0	9	4	0
R. Garcia, Spartanburg	1.000	2	0	2	0	1
V. Garcia, Greensboro	1.000	43	2	6	0	0
C. Gardner, Asheville	.842	15	4	12	3	0
J. Gardner, Charleston (W.Va.)	.938	32	11	34	3	3
Gohr, Fayetteville	1.000	4	1	0	0	0
Goodwin, Charleston (W.Va.)	.960	41	14	34	2	4
Gore, Gastonia*	1.000	24	1	11	0	0
Griffiths, Asheville	.933	22	6	8	1	0
Grove, Sumter	.969	28	8	23	1	2
Grovom, Greensboro*	.850	11	6	11	3	0
Gutierrez, Asheville*	.667	5	0	2	1	1
Hart, Charleston (S.C.)	1.000	4	0	1	0	0
Hartgraves, Asheville*	1.000	19	4	18	0	0
Harvick, Savannah*	.964	31	7	20	1	0
Haslock, Charleston (S.C.)	.944	56	4	13	1	1
Hensley, Savannah	.889	15	3	13	2	1
Hernandez, Charleston (S.C.)	.938	10	5	10	1	0
Hershman, Savannah	.667	7	0	2	1	0
Hill, Columbia*	.939	29	8	23	2	1
Hillman, Columbia	.800	9	0	4	1	0
Hitt, Savannah*	1.000	63	5	20	0	0
Honeywell, Augusta*	1.000	26	4	7	0	0
Huseby, Augusta	.917	22	7	15	2	0
Hutson, Myrtle Beach	.833	12	2	8	2	2
Hvizda, Gastonia	.941	62	6	10	1	0
Ingram, Fayetteville	.935	28	8	35	3	1
C. Johnson, Myrtle Beach	.842	40	6	10	3	2
D. Johnson, Myrtle Beach	1.000	4	2	0	0	0
G. Johnson, Asheville	.857	42	0	6	1	0
L. Johnson, Sumter*	1.000	11	0	5	0	0
Keller, Savannah	.917	18	11	11	2	1
Kelly, Sumter*	.692	13	2	7	4	0
Kent, Spartanburg	.600	6	0	3	2	0
Knox, Charleston (S.C.)*	1.000	2	1	1	0	0
Koller, Fayetteville	.814	26	6	29	8	4
Kuder, Augusta*	1.000	4	0	1	0	0
Landy, Greensboro*	.958	26	3	20	1	0
LaRosa, Spartanburg*	1.000	12	2	5	0	2
Limbach, Spartanburg*	1.000	8	0	2	0	0
Lindsey, Spartanburg	.918	27	23	33	5	1
Lloyd, Myrtle Beach*	.000	1	0	0	1	0
Lutz, Charleston (W.Va.)	.905	23	3	16	2	1
MacNeil, Gastonia	1.000	22	5	6	0	2
Majer, Savannah	1.000	15	3	3	0	0
Maldonado, Sumter	.880	48	6	16	3	1
Malley, Greensboro*	.905	39	6	13	2	1
Marshall, Fayetteville*	.909	34	2	8	1	0
Martinez, Charleston (S.C.)*	.867	27	5	34	6	1
McAuliffe, Greensboro	.875	50	2	5	1	0
McCarthy, Spartanburg*	.923	24	6	18	2	1
McCray, Gastonia*	.968	22	2	28	1	1
McDowell, Augusta	.949	21	14	23	2	3
McGraw, Gastonia*	1.000	1	0	1	0	0
Meacham, Fayetteville	.909	16	9	21	3	3
Meier, Sumter	.944	39	6	11	1	2
Meister, Sumter	1.000	9	1	3	0	0
Mitchell, Sumter	.944	30	7	10	1	1
Murdock, Charleston (S.C.)*	.917	30	3	19	2	1
Murray, Sumter	1.000	12	3	10	0	0
Neely, Augusta	1.000	54	8	14	0	1
Nen, Gastonia	.854	24	16	19	6	1
Newton, Columbia	.938	36	7	8	1	3
Nordstrom, Greensboro	1.000	43	4	9	0	0
Nozling, Fayetteville*	.889	39	0	8	1	0
Odom, Augusta	.833	14	4	11	3	1
Ogliaruso, Myrtle Beach	.846	21	9	13	4	2
Olivares, Myrtle Beach*	.857	39	2	16	3	1
Oliver, Gastonia*	.957	24	11	34	2	2
Ozuna, Savannah	.895	59	3	14	2	2
Peek, Spartanburg	.889	19	2	6	1	1
F. Perez, Asheville	1.000	22	3	10	0	0
V. Perez, Columbia	.867	25	4	9	2	0
Ponte, Asheville	.909	42	7	13	2	4
Rambo, Spartanburg*	1.000	14	2	8	0	0
Randle, Gastonia	1.000	17	1	11	0	0
Rasp, Charleston (W.Va.)	1.000	54	1	5	0	1
Reed, Charleston (W.Va.)*	1.000	24	1	7	0	2
Reich, Columbia	.912	20	7	24	3	1
Reynolds, Asheville	.900	8	3	6	1	2
Richey, Sumter	.857	33	2	4	1	0
Rivera, Fayetteville	.944	38	7	10	1	3
Rogers, Columbia	1.000	14	5	11	0	1
Romero, Columbia	.864	22	7	12	3	0
Rosario, Asheville*	.789	19	4	11	4	0
Rose, Savannah*	.500	8	0	1	1	0
Rudolph, Fayetteville	.875	40	9	12	3	2
Sager, Charleston (S.C.)	.925	26	9	28	3	4
Sala, Savannah*	.875	11	1	6	1	0
Sanford, Greensboro	.909	25	9	11	2	0
Satre, Greensboro	.778	27	10	11	6	1
Scheckla, Asheville	.933	31	4	10	1	0
Schourek, Greensboro*	.941	27	9	23	2	0
Seal, Myrtle Beach*	1.000	19	0	7	0	0
Shea, Fayetteville	.846	16	2	9	2	2
Shoup, Fayetteville	1.000	6	0	2	0	0
Smalls, Charleston (W.Va.)	.889	23	5	19	3	0
Smith, Sumter*	.857	15	1	17	3	1
Spencer, Gastonia	1.000	43	7	16	0	1
Spradlin, Greensboro	.800	42	6	6	3	1
Stevanus, Augusta	1.000	22	0	6	0	1
Stone, Savannah	.933	25	6	8	1	0
Taylor, Savannah	.857	29	6	18	4	1
Teague, Charleston (W.Va.)*	1.000	5	0	6	0	0
Rob. Thomas, Fayetteville	1.000	3	0	1	0	1
Ron. Thomas, Sumter*	.667	3	0	2	1	0
Torres, Fayetteville	.850	43	5	12	3	1
Tracy, Spartanburg	1.000	5	0	4	0	0
Trlicek, Sumter	.955	15	8	13	1	1
Tucker, Charleston (S.C.)	.944	25	12	5	1	1
Tukes, Charleston (S.C)	.000	2	0	0	1	0
Underwood, Augusta*	.917	23	0	11	1	1
F. Valdez, Gastonia	.848	26	12	16	5	1
R. Valdez, Augusta*	1.000	1	1	0	0	0
Vasquez, Columbia	.900	37	2	7	1	1
Vazquez, Sumter	.909	25	14	26	4	2
Ward, Myrtle Beach*	1.000	16	4	13	0	0
Weathers, Myrtle Beach	.857	31	6	30	6	1
Weese, Savannah	.900	54	5	4	1	3
Wenrick, Columbia	.955	44	6	15	1	0
Whitson, Charleston (W.Va.)	1.000	27	4	14	0	1

PITCHERS—Continued

Player and Club	Pct.	G.	PO.	A.	E.	DP.	Player and Club	Pct.	G.	PO.	A.	E.	DP.
G. Wilson, Spartanburg	.957	34	4	18	1	1	Wohlers, Sumter	.818	14	1	8	2	1
T. Wilson, Myrtle Beach	1.000	18	6	6	0	0	Wood, Charleston (S.C.)	1.000	53	10	14	0	1
Windes, Asheville*	.824	53	3	11	3	0	Young, Columbia	.829	21	11	23	7	1

The following players did not have any fielding statistics at the positions indicated or appeared only as a designated hitter, pinch-hitter or pinch-runner: K. Baez, of; S. Brown, p; Byerly, p; Culberson, p; Gonzalez, ph; Hamilton, 3b, p; Hayes, p; Jimenez, of; Joiner, 3b; Lester, of; S. Lopez, of; McKeon, of; J. Mendez, p; James K. Murphy (Fayetteville), p; Noelke, 1b; Oller, 2b, ss; Provence, 1b; Raley, 2b; Roach, p; D. Rowland, p; Shelton, of; Sherrill, p; Verstandig, p; Weese, of; Wilkinson, p.

CLUB PITCHING

Club	ERA.	G.	CG.	ShO.	Sv.	IP.	H.	R.	ER.	HR.	HB.	BB.	Int. BB.	SO.	WP.	Bk.
Savannah	2.86	139	16	20	32	1172.1	1007	524	372	47	48	475	6	1013	79	17
Gastonia	2.88	140	7	17	49	1226.2	927	517	392	50	70	576	21	1078	97	38
Spartanburg	3.24	141	13	10	29	1192.0	1019	559	429	55	62	555	4	971	85	25
Columbia	3.35	140	23	10	31	1191.2	1054	564	443	62	44	546	18	1012	57	18
Charleston (S.C.)	3.41	140	16	12	34	1219.2	1149	611	462	61	42	505	23	919	62	18
Charleston (W.Va.)	3.42	135	16	11	31	1158.0	1072	573	440	45	44	551	12	730	85	25
Augusta	3.46	144	35	13	25	1239.1	1155	619	477	36	50	569	27	946	97	26
Greensboro	3.61	139	13	11	41	1178.0	1014	610	473	64	44	604	2	993	101	22
Fayetteville	3.80	139	7	12	36	1207.0	1166	643	509	67	62	538	15	914	76	35
Asheville	4.03	138	20	5	31	1162.1	1131	666	521	68	37	577	19	875	100	34
Myrtle Beach	4.07	142	6	5	36	1213.2	1162	711	549	78	57	675	24	1026	89	36
Sumter	4.14	141	7	7	37	1220.2	1191	680	562	90	45	600	15	912	67	19

PITCHERS' RECORDS
(Leading Qualifiers for Earned-Run Average Leadership — 115 or More Innings)

*Throws lefthanded.

Pitcher—Club	W.	L.	Pct.	ERA.	G.	GS.	CG.	GF.	ShO.	Sv.	IP.	H.	R.	ER.	HR.	HB.	BB.	Int. BB.	SO.	WP.
Martinez, Charleston (S.C.)*	14	8	.636	1.97	27	27	5	0	2	0	187.0	147	53	41	5	2	64	1	158	4
Ericks, Savannah	11	10	.524	2.04	28	28	1	0	0	0	167.1	90	59	38	4	9	101	0	211	11
Blohm, Augusta	13	4	.765	2.32	18	18	12	0	2	0	135.2	123	48	35	3	6	35	1	97	6
Nen, Gastonia	7	4	.636	2.41	24	24	1	0	1	0	138.1	96	47	37	7	6	76	0	146	15
Clark, Savannah	14	9	.609	2.44	27	27	4	0	2	0	173.2	143	61	47	8	1	52	0	132	11
McCray, Gastonia*	7	7	.500	2.52	22	22	0	0	0	0	121.2	95	51	34	5	3	55	0	110	9
Cunningham, Gastonia	9	5	.643	2.52	27	20	3	2	1	1	139.1	112	47	39	5	10	43	1	118	10
Buckholz, Augusta	9	4	.692	2.57	17	17	3	0	1	0	119.0	109	45	34	5	5	46	2	70	6
Dunnum, Asheville	6	6	.500	2.63	36	18	4	7	1	0	144.0	121	60	42	5	3	53	2	114	17
Sanford, Greensboro	12	6	.667	2.81	25	25	3	0	1	0	153.2	112	52	48	8	2	64	0	160	6

Departmental Leaders: G—Hitt, 63; W—Clark, Martinez, Sager, F. Valdez, 14; L—Satre, Weathers, Whitson, 13; Pct.—V. Garcia, .909; GS—Weathers, 31; CG—Blohm, 12; GF—Hvizda, 54; ShO—Lutz, 8; Sv.—Hvizda, 35; IP—Martinez, 187.0; H—Grove, 172; R—T. Brown, 103; ER—Satre, 85; HR—T. Brown, 18; HB—Ingram, 13; BB—Felix, 123; IBB—Haslock, 9; SO—Ericks, 211; WP—Malley, 23.

(All Pitchers—Listed Alphabetically)

Pitcher—Club	W.	L.	Pct.	ERA.	G.	GS.	CG.	GF.	ShO.	Sv.	IP.	H.	R.	ER.	HR.	HB.	BB.	Int. BB.	SO.	WP.
Acosta, Augusta*	5	5	.500	5.29	28	3	1	15	0	1	81.2	95	56	48	4	0	35	3	59	3
Allen, Gastonia	6	2	.750	2.02	51	0	0	20	0	3	89.0	60	33	20	1	10	31	5	84	2
Andersh, Augusta*	5	5	.500	5.02	14	14	0	0	0	0	75.1	96	58	42	5	6	29	0	48	7
Anderson, Greensboro	11	6	.647	2.86	25	25	4	0	2	0	154.1	117	64	49	7	8	72	0	154	9
Ashby, Spartanburg	5	9	.357	2.87	17	17	3	0	1	0	106.2	95	48	34	8	5	49	0	100	8
Ayala, Greensboro	5	8	.385	4.10	22	19	1	1	0	0	105.1	97	73	48	7	4	50	0	70	10
Backs, Savannah	7	8	.467	4.24	25	19	2	4	0	1	121.0	104	63	57	5	12	72	0	99	8
Beavers, Charleston (S.C.)*	5	5	.500	4.14	13	12	0	1	0	0	45.2	48	26	21	0	2	42	0	24	4
Belcher, Fayetteville	1	1	.500	6.00	5	0	0	1	0	0	9.0	12	7	6	1	1	5	0	4	3
Bennett, Asheville	0	0	.000	0.00	1	0	0	1	0	0	2.0	0	0	0	0	0	1	0	0	0
Berrios, Fayetteville*	4	2	.667	4.88	25	7	0	5	0	0	59.0	66	38	32	4	3	28	1	36	1
Betances, Fayetteville	0	2	.000	5.49	5	5	0	0	0	0	19.2	15	14	12	0	1	17	0	7	0
Blohm, Augusta	13	4	.765	2.32	18	18	12	0	2	0	135.2	123	48	35	3	6	35	1	97	6
Bond, Charleston (S.C.)*	0	0	.000	12.54	5	4	0	0	0	0	18.2	31	26	26	1	1	15	0	12	1
Borland, Spartanburg	4	5	.444	2.97	47	0	0	46	0	9	66.2	62	29	22	3	7	35	1	48	15
Brader, Fayetteville*	7	3	.700	4.07	49	0	0	28	0	6	73.0	71	41	33	6	3	28	4	34	8
Bradley, Myrtle Beach	3	0	1.000	2.45	6	0	0	1	0	0	7.1	8	2	2	1	1	0	0	7	0
Brady, 35 MB-15 Col.	3	1	.750	1.78	50	0	0	39	0	18	60.2	48	14	12	0	5	32	4	74	2
Brooks, Savannah	3	4	.429	3.44	9	9	1	0	0	0	49.2	51	25	19	1	0	24	1	33	3
R. Brown, Gastonia	6	1	.857	2.54	18	4	0	6	0	0	63.2	58	21	18	3	1	12	0	36	4
S. Brown, Augusta	0	2	.000	9.28	5	2	0	3	0	0	10.2	16	17	11	0	1	5	0	11	4
T. Brown, Myrtle Beach	3	12	.200	4.47	34	22	1	6	0	1	151.0	165	103	75	18	11	65	2	95	8
Brucato, Charleston (S.C.)	7	6	.538	3.24	19	17	1	0	0	0	97.1	96	53	35	6	1	48	0	63	11
Bruck, Sumter	0	1	.000	2.25	2	1	0	1	0	0	8.0	8	4	2	2	0	3	0	3	0
Bruzdewicz, Myrtle Beach*	2	4	.333	4.26	23	0	0	9	0	0	44.1	39	30	21	4	2	37	3	37	1
Bryand, Charleston (S.C.)*	8	5	.615	3.53	48	1	0	21	0	3	91.2	90	46	36	9	3	40	5	70	1
Buckholz, Augusta	9	4	.692	2.57	17	17	3	0	1	0	119.0	109	45	34	5	5	46	2	70	6
E. Burgos, Myrtle Beach*	0	2	.000	2.70	16	1	0	10	0	1	16.2	16	11	5	0	2	20	2	15	3
J. Burgos, Savannah*	3	0	1.000	0.66	4	4	1	0	1	0	27.1	16	4	2	0	7	10	2	22	7
Burns, Charleston (W.Va.)	1	5	.167	3.38	19	2	0	4	0	1	64.0	71	39	24	2	9	21	1	51	4
Byerly, Charleston*	0	0	.000	4.50	1	0	0	0	0	0	2.0	2	1	1	0	0	2	0	2	0
Cakora, Charleston (W.Va.)*	2	1	.667	1.83	25	0	0	12	0	2	19.2	18	4	4	0	1	5	0	20	2
Calderone, Sumter	2	2	.500	5.66	23	0	0	9	0	0	35.0	39	27	22	2	6	22	2	38	1
Campos, Charleston (W.Va.)	2	11	.154	3.44	38	18	2	7	0	2	131.0	113	67	50	4	8	87	1	82	11
Cantwell, Charleston (S.C.)*	0	3	.000	4.66	25	5	0	11	0	0	63.2	86	44	33	5	1	28	0	36	0
Carter, Spartanburg*	6	5	.545	3.28	15	15	1	0	0	0	90.2	73	38	33	5	3	51	0	72	7
Clark, Savannah	14	9	.609	2.44	27	27	4	0	2	0	173.2	143	61	47	8	1	52	0	132	11
Compres, Gastonia	0	1	.000	0.92	8	0	0	4	0	1	19.2	12	4	2	1	2	5	0	13	0
Copp, Augusta*	0	1	.000	3.00	3	2	0	0	0	0	15.0	18	9	5	0	4	12	0	9	0
Corbin, Columbia	9	9	.500	4.51	27	23	4	3	2	1	153.2	149	86	77	16	5	72	0	130	2
Coulter, Spartanburg	1	5	.167	4.73	17	2	0	5	0	0	45.2	51	36	24	2	2	29	0	28	2
Cross, Myrtle Beach	7	8	.467	3.51	36	13	0	17	0	4	100.0	61	46	39	7	6	81	0	139	13
Culberson, Sumter	0	0	.000	18.00	1	0	0	1	0	0	1.0	3	2	2	0	0	1	0	0	1
Cunningham, Gastonia	9	5	.643	2.52	27	20	3	2	1	1	139.1	112	47	39	5	10	43	1	118	10
DeLeon, Sumter*	2	4	.333	3.22	34	7	0	9	0	1	86.2	92	40	31	7	0	30	1	56	1

494

Pitcher—Club	W.	L.	Pct.	ERA.	G.	GS.	CG.	GF.	ShO.	Sv.	IP.	H.	R.	ER.	HR.	HB.	BB.	Int. BB.	SO.	WP.
Dell, Spartanburg	6	5	.545	3.00	18	18	1	0	1	0	99.0	85	48	33	4	1	34	0	84	5
Dempster, Greensboro	2	3	.400	7.55	10	8	0	1	0	0	31.0	35	32	26	1	5	48	0	29	7
DePastino, Myrtle Beach	7	8	.467	4.03	29	29	0	0	0	0	145.0	127	79	65	6	8	108	3	128	16
DeSilva, Fayetteville	2	2	.500	2.73	9	9	1	0	0	0	52.2	40	23	16	4	0	21	0	54	2
DiBartolomeo, Charl. (W.Va.)	4	2	.667	2.05	20	0	0	10	0	1	48.1	34	26	11	4	1	27	1	27	8
Dickman, Sumter	0	1	.000	10.13	9	0	0	6	0	0	13.1	11	18	15	0	4	30	0	5	2
Dodd, Myrtle Beach	2	0	1.000	4.32	13	0	0	4	0	1	33.1	41	24	16	3	1	11	0	24	5
Dorn, Columbia	4	1	.800	1.88	10	6	0	3	0	0	48.0	51	16	10	0	0	18	0	19	2
Doss, Charleston (W.Va.)	7	6	.538	3.13	33	15	0	4	0	1	118.0	98	48	41	4	2	72	5	78	10
Dovey, Asheville	7	8	.467	4.57	24	18	2	3	1	1	106.1	96	70	54	6	4	66	1	74	8
Duncan, Sumter	3	7	.300	4.93	29	1	0	15	0	0	49.1	61	36	27	4	1	19	1	31	1
Dunnum, Asheville	6	6	.500	2.63	36	18	4	7	1	0	144.0	121	60	42	5	3	53	2	114	17
Eddings, Charleston (W.Va.)	0	0	.000	1.93	5	0	3	0	0	0	9.1	11	2	2	0	0	2	0	6	0
Elam, Spartanburg	3	4	.429	2.62	21	7	0	12	0	4	68.2	41	29	20	1	2	26	0	64	10
Elliott, Spartanburg	2	3	.400	2.47	7	7	1	0	1	0	43.2	46	19	12	1	0	14	0	36	4
Ericks, Savannah	11	10	.524	2.04	28	28	1	0	0	0	167.1	90	59	38	4	9	101	0	211	11
Ettles, Fayetteville	2	2	.500	2.28	19	0	0	11	0	4	27.2	28	9	7	1	1	9	2	34	1
Farmer, Asheville	9	2	.818	2.95	18	18	5	0	0	0	119.0	82	50	39	8	6	58	1	122	7
Felix, Augusta	9	12	.429	3.98	27	27	4	0	0	0	160.2	137	85	71	3	11	123	2	161	13
Ferm, Fayetteville	6	10	.375	3.96	16	16	2	0	2	0	91.0	90	49	40	2	4	45	0	48	10
Fine, Columbia	3	3	.500	4.10	12	6	1	4	0	2	48.1	40	27	22	5	4	27	0	45	5
Florie, Charleston (S.C.)	1	7	.125	6.95	12	12	0	0	0	0	44.0	54	47	34	2	1	42	0	22	10
R. Garcia, Spartanburg	0	0	.000	0.00	2	0	0	0	0	0	5.0	2	0	0	0	0	0	0	4	0
V. Garcia, Greensboro	10	1	.909	2.75	43	0	0	20	0	5	85.0	54	36	26	5	5	39	0	108	2
C. Gardner, Asheville	3	8	.273	3.84	15	15	2	0	0	0	77.1	76	53	33	5	1	58	0	49	8
J. Gardner, Charleston (W.Va.)	3	4	.429	2.81	32	13	1	14	0	5	102.2	72	42	32	0	5	69	0	84	13
Gohr, Fayetteville	0	2	.000	7.15	4	4	0	0	0	0	11.1	11	9	9	3	0	6	0	10	0
Goodwin, Charleston (W.Va.)	7	6	.538	3.76	41	10	0	15	0	3	131.2	138	71	55	2	4	49	0	49	9
Gore, Gastonia*	5	2	.714	3.96	24	4	0	6	0	0	52.1	42	28	23	3	2	18	2	49	4
Griffiths, Asheville	6	9	.400	6.14	22	22	0	0	0	0	110.0	125	85	75	13	4	76	0	95	21
Grove, Sumter	9	11	.450	4.20	28	28	2	0	0	0	160.2	172	89	75	13	4	65	1	96	6
Grovom, Greensboro*	3	3	.500	4.37	11	11	0	0	0	0	59.2	53	33	29	2	1	34	0	45	11
Gutierrez, Asheville*	1	3	.250	7.08	5	4	0	1	0	0	20.1	18	17	16	2	2	23	0	17	4
Hamilton, Gastonia	1	0	1.000	5.40	2	0	0	1	0	0	3.1	0	2	2	0	1	4	0	2	3
Hart, Charleston (S.C.)	0	0	.000	11.57	4	0	0	2	0	0	7.0	11	9	9	2	1	2	0	5	0
Hartgraves, Asheville	5	8	.385	4.11	19	19	4	0	0	0	120.1	140	66	55	6	4	49	2	87	5
Harvick, Savannah*	5	9	.357	4.58	31	14	1	5	0	0	108.0	125	74	55	5	6	35	1	60	3
Haslock, Charleston (S.C.)	8	4	.667	1.78	56	0	0	34	0	10	101.1	68	26	20	3	6	38	9	91	8
Hayes, Savannah	1	0	1.000	3.60	1	1	0	0	0	0	5.0	4	2	2	0	0	5	0	5	3
Hensley, Savannah	4	7	.364	4.06	15	15	2	0	0	0	84.1	88	43	38	2	7	36	0	60	11
Hernandez, Charleston (S.C.)	3	5	.375	3.53	10	10	2	0	1	0	58.2	65	37	23	2	3	16	1	39	1
Hershman, Savannah	0	2	.000	7.07	7	3	0	2	0	0	14.0	28	19	11	1	1	9	0	13	5
Hill, Columbia*	11	7	.611	3.04	29	25	2	1	1	0	165.2	140	74	56	5	4	78	1	157	9
Hillman, Columbia*	2	1	.667	1.87	9	7	0	2	0	1	33.2	28	17	7	1	4	21	0	33	1
Hitt, Savannah*	4	2	.667	2.38	63	0	0	21	0	4	64.1	61	25	17	2	1	15	2	42	1
Honeywell, Augusta*	8	3	.727	2.98	26	0	0	13	0	1	48.1	42	19	16	1	1	24	4	46	4
Huseby, Augusta	3	5	.375	4.28	22	15	2	5	1	0	109.1	109	64	52	3	1	47	0	81	10
Hutson, Myrtle Beach	2	4	.333	6.85	12	7	0	0	0	0	46.0	59	42	35	6	2	18	1	30	1
Hvizda, Gastonia	8	2	.800	1.19	62	0	0	54	0	35	90.2	52	19	12	3	3	22	2	84	3
Ingram, Fayetteville	7	10	.412	3.44	28	23	2	1	1	0	154.1	144	73	59	9	13	58	2	132	7
C. Johnson, Myrtle Beach	4	4	.500	4.16	40	0	0	23	0	9	88.2	80	53	41	5	4	49	0	91	4
D. Johnson, Myrtle Beach	0	0	.000	1.59	4	0	0	0	0	0	5.2	5	1	1	0	0	4	0	5	2
G. Johnson, Asheville	1	4	.200	2.81	42	0	0	37	0	20	48.0	35	22	15	1	1	24	3	53	3
L. Johnson, Sumter*	3	2	.600	2.10	11	0	0	6	0	3	25.2	20	7	6	0	0	7	1	25	4
Keller, Savannah	4	5	.444	1.64	18	9	2	3	2	0	76.2	47	23	14	4	3	15	0	66	2
Kelly, Sumter*	2	2	.500	5.32	13	13	0	0	0	0	66.0	69	43	39	5	4	49	0	48	5
Kent, Spartanburg	1	0	1.000	1.84	6	0	0	2	0	1	14.2	9	4	3	1	0	7	0	9	0
Knox, Charleston (S.C.)*	0	0	.000	2.45	2	2	0	0	0	0	11.0	9	3	3	0	3	1	0	11	1
Koller, Fayetteville	5	9	.357	3.35	26	26	0	0	0	0	153.0	149	69	57	8	9	49	0	107	12
Kuder, Augusta*	0	1	.000	13.97	4	2	0	0	0	0	9.2	15	17	15	2	1	12	0	11	5
Landy, Greensboro*	6	9	.400	4.19	26	16	2	2	0	0	124.2	149	89	58	11	5	52	0	54	5
LaRosa, Spartanburg	1	3	.250	2.42	12	0	0	12	0	4	22.1	12	7	6	0	0	11	0	16	2
Limbach, Spartanburg*	0	0	.000	1.20	8	0	0	4	0	0	15.0	14	6	2	1	0	7	0	12	2
Lindsey, Spartanburg	8	12	.400	3.33	27	27	2	0	0	0	167.1	168	87	62	11	5	52	0	108	4
Lloyd, Myrtle Beach*	0	0	.000	5.40	1	1	0	0	0	0	5.0	5	4	3	1	0	4	0	3	1
Lutz, Charleston (W.Va.)	6	10	.375	3.38	23	23	5	0	3	0	128.0	123	61	48	6	6	41	0	101	4
MacNeil, Gastonia	4	2	.667	5.98	22	1	0	12	0	3	43.2	40	39	29	1	3	38	5	32	9
Majer, Savannah	1	0	1.000	1.00	15	0	0	3	0	0	27.0	18	4	3	2	7	0	22	0	(overflow)
Maldonado, Sumter	3	6	.333	4.73	48	0	0	32	0	11	66.2	62	36	35	4	6	38	3	59	2
Malley, Greensboro*	8	4	.667	3.61	39	7	1	12	0	1	97.1	86	54	39	3	0	58	1	77	23
Marshall, Fayetteville*	5	3	.625	3.22	34	3	0	7	0	0	64.1	62	32	23	3	0	21	3	61	3
Martinez, Char. (S.C.)*	14	8	.636	1.97	27	27	5	0	2	0	187.0	147	53	41	5	2	41	1	158	4
McAuliffe, Greensboro	3	4	.429	1.39	50	0	0	45	0	28	58.1	29	13	9	3	1	30	1	54	3
McCarthy, Spartanburg*	5	8	.385	4.18	24	15	2	4	1	0	112.0	90	58	52	3	9	80	0	115	8
McCray, Gastonia*	7	7	.500	2.52	22	22	0	0	0	0	121.2	95	51	34	5	3	55	0	110	9
McDowell, Augusta	6	8	.429	2.85	21	19	5	1	1	1	142.1	125	58	45	2	7	54	2	103	14
McGraw, Gastonia*	0	0	.000	1.80	1	1	0	0	0	0	5.0	3	1	1	0	0	0	0	0	0
Meacham, Fayetteville	10	3	.769	2.29	16	15	2	1	0	0	102.0	103	33	26	4	1	23	0	74	2
Meier, Sumter	4	8	.333	4.33	39	0	0	10	0	0	68.2	62	39	33	4	2	35	4	53	4
Meister, Sumter	1	3	.250	5.35	9	4	1	2	0	0	35.1	43	22	21	2	0	20	0	25	4
Mendez, Savannah	0	0	.000	27.00	1	0	0	1	0	0	2.0	8	6	6	0	0	2	0	2	0
Mitchell, Sumter	1	3	.250	6.35	30	3	0	17	0	0	56.2	67	47	40	9	2	44	1	44	10
Murdock, Char. (S.C.)*	9	3	.750	3.09	30	21	2	4	0	0	148.1	136	69	51	9	4	41	1	93	4
Murphy, Fayetteville	0	0	.000	0.00	1	0	0	1	0	0	1.0	0	0	0	0	0	0	0	0	0
Murray, Sumter	3	5	.375	4.33	12	12	0	0	0	0	72.2	62	37	35	10	1	22	0	69	4
Neely, Augusta	10	8	.556	1.22	54	0	0	50	0	19	95.2	62	17	13	0	4	26	8	93	3
Nen, Gastonia	7	4	.636	2.41	24	24	1	0	1	0	138.1	96	47	37	7	6	76	0	146	15
Newton, Columbia	5	5	.500	3.97	36	9	0	19	0	2	77.0	64	42	34	4	4	47	1	71	6
Nordstrom, Greensboro	4	1	.800	3.02	43	0	0	23	0	5	80.1	66	34	27	5	5	47	0	80	7
Nozling, Fayetteville*	2	1	.667	4.21	39	0	0	14	0	2	66.1	52	37	31	1	6	48	0	48	6
Odom, Augusta	5	4	.556	4.14	14	14	3	0	0	0	82.2	79	51	38	2	1	42	0	34	8
Ogliaruso, Myrtle Beach	9	8	.529	3.64	21	21	2	0	0	0	123.2	119	67	50	6	2	52	1	84	6

Pitcher—Club	W.	L.	Pct.	ERA.	G.	GS.	CG.	GF.	ShO.	Sv.	IP.	H.	R.	ER.	HR.	HB.	BB.	Int. BB.	SO.	WP.
Olivares, Myrtle Beach°	3	9	.250	4.29	39	3	0	16	0	5	86.0	78	49	41	3	2	60	5	97	11
Oliver, Gastonia°	8	7	.533	3.16	24	23	2	0	1	0	122.1	86	54	43	4	5	82	1	108	15
Ozuna, Savannah	3	5	.375	1.58	59	0	0	52	0	28	74.0	48	21	13	2	3	19	2	94	3
Peek, Spartanburg	3	1	.750	1.99	19	1	0	13	0	3	45.1	32	15	10	4	3	20	1	42	1
F. Perez, Asheville	3	3	.500	5.85	22	1	0	5	0	2	47.2	57	36	31	3	1	25	2	29	2
V. Perez, Columbia	3	5	.375	2.99	25	8	0	13	0	5	81.1	66	32	27	3	1	34	1	63	4
Ponte, Asheville	11	3	.786	3.27	42	0	0	21	0	2	82.2	69	42	30	2	4	38	2	62	6
Rambo, Spartanburg°	7	4	.636	4.46	14	11	1	2	0	0	70.2	57	40	35	3	11	45	0	51	7
Randle, Gastonia	1	2	.333	3.55	17	0	0	7	0	1	33.0	24	17	13	2	4	31	0	32	1
Rasp, Charleston (W.Va.)	8	3	.727	2.87	54	0	0	45	0	15	75.1	68	29	24	3	3	23	1	55	5
Reed, Charleston (W.Va.)°	5	2	.714	2.86	24	5	0	3	0	1	63.0	53	25	20	2	0	33	1	45	6
Reich, Columbia	11	5	.688	2.36	20	13	3	1	2	0	114.1	90	42	30	1	6	44	0	61	2
Reynolds, Asheville	5	3	.625	3.68	8	8	2	0	1	0	51.1	53	25	21	2	1	21	0	33	1
Richey, Sumter	0	1	.000	1.93	33	0	0	32	0	19	42.0	21	11	9	3	2	18	0	62	3
Rivera, Fayetteville	4	1	.800	2.86	38	0	0	33	0	19	56.2	57	28	18	1	5	24	0	50	4
Roach, Fayetteville	0	0	.000	9.00	1	0	0	1	0	0	1.0	1	1	1	0	0	1	0	0	0
Rogers, Columbia	3	2	.600	3.12	14	4	0	6	0	3	43.1	36	16	15	1	2	14	0	36	0
Romero, Gastonia	5	5	.500	4.82	22	15	0	2	0	0	84.0	81	56	45	4	7	60	1	62	9
Rosario, Asheville°	7	7	.500	3.61	19	15	1	3	0	1	102.1	115	55	41	7	0	25	1	61	8
Rose, Savannah°	0	0	.000	7.62	8	0	0	2	0	0	13.0	12	12	11	0	0	13	0	15	1
Rowland, Fayetteville	0	0	.000	4.50	2	0	0	2	0	0	2.0	3	1	1	0	0	2	0	2	0
Rudolph, Fayetteville	2	3	.400	4.97	40	5	0	12	0	5	87.0	83	56	48	5	1	45	1	81	4
Sager, Charleston (S.C.)	14	9	.609	3.38	26	25	6	0	2	0	167.2	166	77	63	4	7	40	1	105	10
Sala, Savannah°	2	4	.333	5.98	11	11	1	0	0	0	52.2	70	43	35	6	3	31	0	33	6
Sanford, Greensboro	12	6	.667	2.81	25	25	3	0	1	0	153.2	112	52	48	8	2	64	0	160	6
Satre, Greensboro	7	13	.350	5.72	27	27	2	0	0	0	133.2	128	95	85	7	5	87	0	106	14
Scheckla, Asheville	0	1	.000	6.00	31	0	0	16	0	1	60.0	78	49	40	5	4	29	1	31	6
Schourek, Columbia°	5	9	.357	2.85	27	19	5	3	1	1	136.0	120	66	43	11	2	66	2	131	5
Seal, Myrtle Beach°	0	5	.000	2.53	19	0	0	11	0	1	32.0	37	10	9	2	1	15	3	29	4
Shea, Fayetteville	3	5	.375	5.43	16	16	0	0	0	0	66.1	74	53	40	4	3	45	0	28	10
Sherrill, Savannah°	0	0	.000	3	3	0	0	3	0	2	3.2	3	0	0	0	0	2	0	6	0
Shoup, Fayetteville	1	0	1.000	2.00	6	0	0	2	0	0	9.0	8	2	2	0	1	6	0	13	0
Smalls, Char. (W.Va.)	5	11	.313	4.33	23	23	1	0	0	0	108.0	106	71	52	3	4	72	1	49	8
Smith, Sumter°	8	3	.727	3.06	15	15	0	0	0	0	94.0	85	41	32	5	1	37	0	55	1
Spencer, Gastonia	11	5	.688	2.22	43	2	0	18	0	5	85.0	63	35	21	3	9	35	4	105	5
Spradlin, Greensboro	7	2	.778	2.76	42	1	0	22	0	2	94.2	88	35	29	5	3	23	0	56	4
Stevanus, Augusta	0	0	.000	4.02	22	0	0	12	0	3	47.0	47	28	21	2	4	27	1	33	3
Stone, Savannah	6	3	.667	2.59	25	6	1	6	0	0	59.0	38	19	17	1	4	32	0	69	3
Taylor, Savannah	4	9	.308	3.30	29	12	2	9	0	0	103.2	103	63	38	8	3	34	0	56	6
Teague, Char. (W.Va.)°	2	2	.500	2.87	5	5	1	0	0	0	31.1	33	15	10	4	1	13	0	16	0
Rob. Thomas, Fayetteville	0	0	.000	11.57	3	0	0	2	0	0	4.2	8	8	6	0	0	7	0	2	0
Ron. Thomas, Sumter°	1	0	1.000	3.05	3	3	0	0	0	0	20.2	23	8	7	0	0	6	0	19	2
Torres, Fayetteville	9	10	.474	3.94	43	10	0	11	0	0	96.0	89	60	42	10	11	52	2	91	4
Tracy, Spartanburg	0	0	.000	2.38	5	0	0	3	0	0	11.1	9	3	3	0	1	3	0	8	0
Trlicek, Sumter	6	5	.545	2.59	15	15	0	0	0	0	93.2	73	40	27	7	4	40	1	72	3
Tucker, Charleston (S.C.)	1	2	.333	6.39	25	3	0	7	0	0	63.1	75	62	45	11	4	41	0	31	4
Tukes, Charleston (S.C.)	0	0	.000	4.91	2	1	0	0	0	0	7.1	8	7	4	0	0	9	0	5	0
Underwood, Augusta°	4	4	.500	2.70	23	10	5	9	0	0	96.2	73	44	29	4	1	46	3	76	10
F. Valdez, Gastonia	14	3	.824	3.13	26	24	1	1	1	0	135.1	99	57	47	8	4	62	0	97	7
R. Valdez, Augusta°	0	1	.000	1.17	1	1	0	0	0	0	7.2	7	2	1	0	1	2	0	9	1
Vasquez, Columbia	1	5	.167	3.88	37	0	0	25	0	7	58.0	47	30	25	3	4	32	1	61	5
Vazquez, Sumter	10	10	.500	3.27	25	25	4	0	1	0	156.2	144	78	57	9	4	56	0	98	4
Verstandig, Char. (S.C.)	0	0	.000	0.00	1	0	0	1	0	0	1.1	2	0	0	0	2	0	0	1	0
Ward, Myrtle Beach°	2	5	.286	5.22	16	13	1	1	0	1	69.0	73	49	40	6	2	36	0	46	3
Weathers, Myrtle Beach	11	13	.458	3.86	31	31	2	0	0	0	172.2	163	99	74	3	7	86	2	111	12
Weese, Savannah	4	1	.800	0.81	54	0	0	16	0	2	67.0	54	19	6	0	5	36	0	78	8
Wenrick, Columbia	6	8	.429	4.09	44	3	0	22	0	4	88.0	94	49	40	7	3	29	8	55	7
Whitson (W.Va.)	6	13	.316	4.72	27	21	6	2	0	0	127.2	134	73	67	12	4	37	1	67	5
Wilkinson, Gastonia	0	0	.000	162.00	1	0	0	0	0	0	0.1	4	6	6	0	0	2	0	0	1
G. Wilson, Spartanburg	3	7	.300	2.19	34	2	0	21	0	7	86.1	69	29	21	3	1	20	2	75	2
T. Wilson, Myrtle Beach	2	1	.667	6.00	18	1	0	7	0	0	42.0	52	35	28	6	1	24	1	34	1
Windes, Asheville°	4	5	.444	3.68	53	0	0	24	0	4	71.0	66	36	29	3	2	31	4	48	4
Wohlers, Sumter	2	7	.222	6.49	14	14	0	0	0	0	68.0	74	55	49	3	4	59	0	51	10
Wood, Charleston (S.C.)	7	7	.500	1.53	53	0	0	42	0	20	105.2	57	26	18	2	3	36	5	153	3
Young, Columbia	9	6	.600	3.49	21	17	8	2	1	0	129.0	115	60	50	5	4	55	1	127	7

BALKS—C. Gardner, 10; T. Brown, 9; F. Valdez, 8; Gore, 7; Andersh, Lutz, 6 each; Backs, C. Johnson, Lindsey, Malley, McCray, Newton, Nozling, 5 each; Cunningham, Dell, DePastino, Huseby, Nen, Olivares, Ponte, Reynolds, Satre, Whitson, 4 each; Acosta, Betances, Burns, Clark, Cross, DeLeon, DeSilva, Ferm, J. Gardner, Grove, Hartgraves, Hernandez, Ingram, Keller, McDowell, Meacham, Rasp, Sanford, Scheckla, Schourek, Shea, Torres, Trlicek, Young, 3 each; Allen, Anderson, Ayala, S. Brown, Brucato, Cantwell, Dodd, Dunnum, Ericks, Ettles, Farmer, Florie, V. Garcia, Griffiths, Hutson, Hvizda, Kent, Koller, Landy, Majer, Martinez, McCarthy, Mitchell, Oliver, Rudolph, Smalls, Spencer, Vasquez, Vazquez, Ward, Wood, 2 each; Belcher, Bond, Borland, Brader, Brady, R. Brown, Bruck, Bryand, Buckholz, Byerly, Cakora, Calderone, Carter, Dempster, DiBartolomeo, Dovey, Eddings, Elam, Felix, Fine, Harvick, Haslock, Hensley, Hill, G. Johnson, Knox, Kuder, LaRosa, Maldonado, Meister, Murray, Neely, Nordstrom, Odom, Ogliaruso, Ozuna, Peek, F. Perez, V. Perez, Rambo, Reich, Rivera, Rogers, Romero, Rosario, Rose, Sager, Sala, Seal, Stevanus, Stone, Teague, R. Valdez, Weathers, Weese, G. Wilson, T. Wilson, Wohlers, 1 each.

COMBINATION SHUTOUTS—Farmer-Perez, Dovey-Windes, Asheville; Andersh-Neely, Felix-Acosta-Neely, Andersh-Stevanus, McDowell-Acosta, Buckholz-Underwood, Felix-Neely, Huseby-Neely, Felix-Honeywell-Neely, Augusta; Sager-Wood 2, Sager-Haslock, Martinez-Haslock, Brucato-Bryand, Martinez-Wood, Beavers-Bryand, Charleston (S.C.); Lutz-Doss-Cakora, Lutz-Goodwin, Campos-Rasp, Smalls-Burns, Reed-Rasp, Goodwin-Rasp, Doss-Campos, Doss-DiBartolomeo, Charleston (W.Va.); Young-Hillman, Hill-Brady, Schourek-Brady, Columbia; Koller-Marshall-Torres-Brader, Shea-Rudolph-Rivera, Meacham-Brader, Torres-Rivera, Torres-Marshall-Rivera, Ingram-Torres, Rudolph-Torres-Rivera, Berrios-Torres-Rudolph, Ferm-Ettles, Fayetteville; McCray-Allen-Hvizda 2, Oliver-Cunningham-Hvizda, Oliver-Cunningham, Cunningham-Randle-Spencer, McCray-Randle, Romero-Allen-Hvizda, Nen-Spencer-Allen-Hvizda, Valdez-Allen, McCray-Compres-Allen-Hvizda-Gore, Cunningham-Hvizda, Oliver-Allen-Hvizda, Romero-Hvizda, Gastonia; Sanford-Spradlin-McAuliffe, Sanford-Nordstrom-McAuliffe, Satre-Spradlin-Malley, Dempster-Spradlin, Sanford-Spradlin-Malley-Nordstrom, Sanford-Garcia, Sanford-McAuliffe, Anderson-McAuliffe, Greensboro; Brown-Dodd, Weathers-Cross-Brady, Cross-Johnson-Brady, Cross-Brown-Burgos-Brady, Cross-Bradley, Myrtle Beach; Stone-Ozuna 2, Burgos-Hitt-Ozuna, Clark-Hitt, Ericks-Stone, Ericks-Weese, Ericks-Ozuna, Ericks-Weese-Ozuna 2, Clark-Weese, Ericks-Witt-Weese-Ozuna, Brooks-Rose-Weese-Ozuna, Ericks-Taylor-Hitt-Ozuna, Clark-Hitt-Ozuna, Clark-Weese-Hitt-Ozuna, Savannah; Dell-Coulter-Borland, Lindsey-Elam, Peek-Rambo, Rambo-Wilson-Borland, Lindsey-Wilson, Spartanburg; Wohlers-Johnson-Richey, Grove-Maldonado-Johnson-Richey, Vazquez-Richey, Grove-Maldonado-Duncan-Richey, Trlicek-Maldonado-Richey, Trlicek-Maldonado, Sumter.

NO-HIT GAMES—Sanford, Greensboro, defeated Myrtle Beach, 7-0, June 2; Dell, Spartanburg, defeated Greensboro, 2-0 (seven innings), June 13; Valdez, Gastonia, defeated Asheville, 7-0, July 2; Anderson, Greensboro, defeated Columbia, 5-0 (first game, six innings), July 27; Keller, Savannah, defeated Augusta, 4-0, August 22.

Appalachian League

SUMMER CLASS A CLASSIFICATION

CHAMPIONSHIP WINNERS IN PREVIOUS YEARS

1921—Greenville .608	1950—Bluefield .600	1972—Bristol a .588
Johnson City* .627	Bluefield z .745	Covington .586
1922—Bristol .557	1951—Kingsport‡ .659	1973—Kingsport .757
1923—Knoxville .635	1952—Johnson City .595	1974—Bristol a .754
1924—Knoxville* .642	Welch (3rd)† .509	Bluefield .536
Bristol .607	1953—Welch* .705	1975—Marion .515
1925—Greenville .667	Johnson City .672	Johnson City a .603
1926-36—Did not operate.	1954—Bluefield‡ .619	1976—Johnson City a .714
1937—Elizabethton .559	1955—Salem** .689	Bluefield .600
Pennington Gap* .580	1956—Did not operate.	1977—Kingsport .623
1938—Elizabethton .664	1957—Bluefield .701	1978—Elizabethton .594
Greenville (3rd)† .571	1958—Johnson City .662	1979—Paintsville .800
1939—Elizabethton‡ .597	1959—Morristown .603	1980—Paintsville .657
1940—Johnson City§ .726	1960—Wytheville .614	1981—Paintsville .657
Elizabethton .750	1961—Middlesboro .591	1982—Bluefield a .681
1941—Johnson City .614	1962—Bluefield .671	Johnson City .478
Elizabethton* .661	1963—Bluefield .652	1983—Paintsville .653
1942—Bristol .667	1964—Johnson City .662	1984—Elizabethton b .580
Bristol x .660	1965—Salem .614	Pulaski .536
1943—Bristol .755	1966—Marion .623	1985—Bristol c .638
Bristol y .617	1967—Bluefield .627	1986—Johnson City .667
1944—Kingsport‡ .575	1968—Marion .583	Pulaski b .621
1945—Kingsport‡ .670	1969—Pulaski a .576	1987—Burlington b .729
1946—New River‡ .675	Johnson City .544	Johnson City .609
1947—Pulaski .648	1970—Bluefield .638	1988—Kingsport b .644
New River (3rd)† .516	1971—Bluefield a .609	Burlington .529
1948—Pulaski‡ .680	Kingsport .559	
1949—Bluefield‡ .721		

*Won split-season playoff. †Won four-team playoff. ‡Won championship and four-team playoff. §Johnson City, first-half winner, won playoff involving six clubs. xWon both halves and defeated second-place Elizabethton in playoff. yWon both halves, but Erwin won four-team playoff. zWon both halves, but Bristol won two-club playoff. **Salem and Johnson City declared playoff co-champions when weather forced cancellation of final series. aLeague was divided into Northern, Southern divisions; declared league champion, based on highest won-lost percentage. bLeague was divided into Northern, Southern divisions; won playoff for league championship. cBristol declared league champion based on regular-season record.

STANDING OF CLUBS AT CLOSE OF SEASON, AUGUST 28

NORTHERN DIVISION

Club	W.	L.	T.	Pct.	G.B.
Pulaski (Braves)	42	26	0	.618	......
Princeton (Pirates)	32	37	0	.464	10½
Burlington (Indians)	31	37	0	.456	11
Martinsville (Phillies)	29	38	0	.433	12½
Bluefield (Orioles)	27	41	0	.397	15

SOUTHERN DIVISION

Club	W.	L.	T.	Pct.	G.B.
Elizabethton (Twins)	47	21	0	.691	......
Johnson City (Cardinals)	38	32	0	.543	10
Wytheville (Cubs)	34	35	0	.493	13½
Kingsport (Mets)	35	37	0	.486	14
Bristol (Tigers)	28	39	0	.418	18½

COMPOSITE STANDING OF CLUBS AT CLOSE OF SEASON, AUGUST 28

Club	Eliz.	Pul.	J.C.	Wyt.	Kng.	Prn.	Bur.	Mar.	Bri.	Blu.	W.	L.	T.	Pct.	G.B.
Elizabethton (Twins)	..	6	7	4	5	4	4	6	4	7	47	21	0	.691	......
Pulaski (Braves)	2	..	5	7	6	4	4	5	3	6	42	26	0	.618	5
Johnson City (Cardinals)	1	3	..	4	6	5	4	7	4	4	38	32	0	.543	10
Wytheville (Cubs)	3	1	2	..	3	5	5	3	7	5	34	35	0	.493	13½
Kingsport (Mets)	3	2	2	5	..	5	4	5	3	6	35	37	0	.486	14
Princeton (Pirates)	3	4	3	3	3	..	4	3	5	4	32	37	0	.464	15½
Burlington (Indians)	2	4	4	3	4	2	..	4	5	3	31	37	0	.456	16
Martinsville (Phillies)	2	2	4	5	3	3	4	..	3	3	29	38	0	.433	17½
Bristol (Tigers)	4	3	1	1	5	5	3	3	..	3	28	39	0	.418	18½
Bluefield (Orioles)	1	1	4	3	2	4	5	3	4	..	27	41	0	.397	20

Major league affiliations in parentheses.

Playoffs—Elizabethton defeated Pulaski, two games to none, to win league championship.

Regular-Season Attendance—Bluefield, 25,548; Bristol, 20,008; Burlington, 55,695; Elizabethton, 17,952; Johnson City, 33,450; Kingsport, 38,791; Martinsville, 58,189; Princeton, 33,754; Pulaski, 11,284; Wytheville, 16,839. Totals—311,510. Playoffs (2 games)—927.

Managers—Bluefield, Mike Young; Bristol, Ruben Amaro; Burlington, Jim Gabella; Elizabethton, Ray Smith; Johnson City, Mark DeJohn; Kingsport, Jim Eschen; Martinsville, Rollie Dearmas; Princeton, Julio Garcia; Pulaski, Fred Koenig; Wytheville, Steve Roadcap.

All-Star Team—1B-Tom Hardgrove, Martinsville; 2B-Bruce Schreiber, Princeton; SS-Manny Alexander, Bluefield; 3B-T.R. Lewis, Bluefield; C-Brook Fordyce, Kingsport; DH—James Harris, Kingsport; OF-Rex Delanuez, Elizabethton; Mike House, Elizabethton; Melvin Nieves, Pulaski; RHP-Mike Misuraca, Elizabethton; LHP-Roger Hailey, Pulaski; Player of the Year-Mike House, Elizabethton; Manager of the Year-Ray Smith, Elizabethton.

(Compiled by Howe Sportsdata International, Boston, Mass.)

CLUB BATTING

Club	Pct.	G.	AB.	R.	OR.	H.	TB.	2B.	3B.	HR.	RBI.	SH.	SF.	HP.	BB.	Int. BB.	SO.	SB.	CS.	LOB.
Elizabethton	.275	68	2231	424	251	614	919	107	18	54	359	5	32	33	309	11	392	53	21	510
Pulaski	.275	68	2221	384	287	611	843	111	14	31	323	48	29	26	257	16	382	119	53	486
Bluefield	.269	68	2315	389	478	622	917	120	8	53	327	12	19	29	244	4	506	65	46	494
Kingsport	.268	72	2292	382	380	615	938	122	9	61	313	34	23	29	245	7	479	146	48	449
Princeton	.259	69	2276	316	364	590	839	110	35	23	269	3	14	19	241	11	453	67	43	504
Martinsville	.246	67	2204	286	338	543	771	102	9	36	238	11	16	23	247	3	575	52	28	500

Club	Pct.	G.	AB.	R.	OR.	H.	TB.	2B.	3B.	HR.	RBI.	SH.	SF.	HP.	BB.	Int. BB.	SO.	SB.	CS.	LOB.
Wytheville	.244	69	2291	380	454	560	838	79	20	53	307	13	16	41	308	8	478	78	22	520
Burlington	.244	68	2178	315	321	531	741	94	7	34	258	21	13	41	237	11	486	105	40	465
Johnson City	.240	70	2170	312	277	521	724	81	7	36	266	15	15	21	293	10	528	85	52	490
Bristol	.234	67	2159	296	334	506	746	83	26	35	246	9	9	26	235	10	529	91	32	447

INDIVIDUAL BATTING

(Leading Qualifiers for Batting Championship—194 or More Plate Appearances)

*Bats lefthanded.   †Switch-hitter.

Player and Club	Pct.	G.	AB.	R.	H.	TB.	2B.	3B.	HR.	RBI.	SH.	SF.	HP.	BB.	Int. BB.	SO.	SB.	CS.
House, Michael, Elizabethton	.376	63	221	54	83	140	21	0	12	68	0	6	5	42	3	43	1	1
Harris, James, Kingsport	.367	58	210	37	77	114	12	2	7	55	0	8	2	21	0	28	19	5
Schreiber, Bruce, Princeton	.348	64	224	31	78	115	15	8	2	38	0	2	0	20	2	31	7	4
Kelly, Patrick, Pulaski*	.331	50	163	25	54	60	4	1	0	21	8	0	5	18	2	17	5	7
Fordyce, Brook, Kingsport	.327	69	226	45	74	116	15	0	9	38	3	2	1	30	1	26	10	6
Stiegele, Robert, Bluefield	.324	55	179	37	58	100	13	1	9	31	0	2	4	34	1	35	5	1
Delanuez, Rexford, Elizabethton	.321	55	193	47	62	104	11	2	9	37	0	2	2	37	0	36	6	0
McCoy, Brent, Pulaski†	.316	63	225	43	71	94	11	3	2	59	7	4	1	32	0	20	17	5
Castellano, Pedro, Wytheville	.311	66	244	55	76	128	17	4	9	42	1	3	3	46	2	44	5	2
Alexander, Manuel, Bluefield	.310	65	274	49	85	108	13	2	2	34	0	2	3	20	1	49	19	8

Departmental Leaders: G—McClinton, 70; AB—M. Alexander, 274; R—Castellano, Diaz, 55; H—M. Alexander, 85; TB—House, 140; 2B—House, 21; 3B—DeLosSantos, Schreiber, 8; HR—Hardgrove, 13; RBI—House, 68; SH—Kelly 8; SF—Harris, 8; HP—Gentile, 9; BB—Lloyd, 59; IBB—Curley, 5; SO—Schmidt, 71; SB—Heath, 40; CS—Heath, 17.

(All Players—Listed Alphabetically)

Player and Club	Pct.	G.	AB.	R.	H.	TB.	2B.	3B.	HR.	RBI.	SH.	SF.	HP.	BB.	Int. BB.	SO.	SB.	CS.
Adams, Brian, Martinsville	.300	4	10	2	3	4	1	0	0	0	0	0	0	2	1	1	0	0
Adkins, Adrian, Princeton	.000	3	7	0	0	0	0	0	0	0	0	0	0	0	0	3	0	0
Alexander, Eric, Bluefield	.293	26	75	14	22	26	1	0	1	8	0	0	4	19	0	18	2	1
Alexander, Manuel, Bluefield	.310	65	274	49	85	108	13	2	2	34	0	2	3	20	1	49	19	8
Allen, James, Johnson City	.256	51	160	20	41	46	2	0	1	18	2	0	0	26	0	27	6	5
Andujar, Juan, Johnson City†	.254	67	240	40	61	91	9	0	7	31	1	3	4	21	0	61	12	5
Antigua, Felix, Princeton	.306	24	85	8	26	35	6	0	1	13	0	0	6	0	6	11	1	2
Aponte, Nelwin, Wytheville	.095	7	21	2	2	3	1	0	0	0	0	0	0	2	0	5	0	1
Bailey, Troy, Wytheville*	.268	57	190	36	51	61	3	2	1	20	1	0	1	34	2	45	24	1
Batiste, Christopher, Bluefield	.245	35	98	10	24	26	2	0	0	8	1	1	2	7	0	39	1	4
Bean, Kenneth, Martinsville	.105	17	38	1	4	5	1	0	0	1	1	0	2	0	0	17	1	1
Bell, David, Johnson City	.226	25	84	7	19	24	2	0	1	6	0	1	0	7	0	18	5	3
Benitez, Christian, Bluefield	.236	52	182	34	43	51	6	1	0	12	0	1	2	21	0	31	11	3
Boeschen, Jarrett, Pulaski	.188	6	16	2	3	4	1	0	0	0	0	0	0	1	0	0	0	0
Borders, Todd, Wytheville	.167	3	6	0	1	1	0	0	0	0	0	0	0	0	0	4	0	0
Brannon, Clifford, Johnson City	.250	1	4	0	1	2	1	0	0	0	0	0	0	0	0	0	0	0
Briggs, Kenneth, Elizabethton†	.154	3	13	2	2	3	1	0	0	0	0	0	0	0	0	1	0	0
Brito, Luis, Martinsville†	.313	9	16	1	5	5	0	0	0	1	0	0	0	3	0	3	0	0
Brown, Ronald, Wytheville	.187	35	123	13	23	32	2	2	1	10	0	1	1	6	0	20	0	0
Brown, Stacy, Burlington*	.165	46	115	20	19	26	2	1	1	9	4	0	0	28	3	40	11	0
Buhe, Timothy, Kingsport	.236	57	165	29	39	47	6	1	0	12	4	1	2	34	0	35	11	3
Caines, Arthuro, Bristol	.250	58	192	17	48	80	6	4	6	24	0	0	2	23	2	59	6	4
Cairo, Sergio, Bluefield	.266	57	207	30	55	78	13	2	2	40	1	2	2	13	0	19	1	7
Calzado, Lorenzo, Johnson City	.287	51	171	22	49	74	4	3	5	21	0	1	1	17	1	44	2	1
Cancel, Daniel, Wytheville	.291	52	196	54	57	89	6	1	8	27	1	1	3	43	0	44	22	6
Canino, Carlos, Wytheville	.100	7	10	0	1	1	0	0	0	2	0	1	0	2	0	6	0	0
Carmona, William, Martinsville	.286	5	7	1	2	2	0	0	0	1	0	0	0	3	0	0	0	0
Carson, Paul, Martinsville	.140	22	57	5	8	9	1	0	0	5	0	2	2	7	0	18	0	1
Carter, Terry, Burlington	.000	2	3	0	0	0	0	0	0	0	0	0	0	0	0	2	0	0
Casado, Cancio, Martinsville	.333	6	9	2	3	5	0	1	0	0	0	0	0	0	0	2	0	0
Castellano, Pedro, Wytheville	.311	66	244	55	76	128	17	4	9	42	1	3	3	46	2	44	5	2
Castillo, Alberto, Kingsport	.257	27	74	15	19	32	4	0	3	12	0	0	1	11	1	14	2	1
Charbonnet, Mark, Burlington*	.231	41	169	24	39	54	3	0	4	16	2	1	1	4	0	51	13	2
Clark, Jeffrey, Pulaski*	.282	51	181	34	51	65	9	1	1	23	2	5	0	24	3	15	19	5
Coleman, Paul, Johnson City	.233	53	172	26	40	60	11	0	3	24	0	1	3	16	0	58	7	1
Cordova, Martin, Elizabethton	.284	38	148	32	42	74	2	3	8	29	0	0	3	14	1	29	2	1
Cosman, James, Martinsville*	.226	14	31	2	7	14	1	0	2	4	0	0	0	6	0	7	0	0
Cotton, John, Burlington*	.207	64	227	36	47	60	5	1	2	22	4	1	3	22	0	56	20	3
Craig, Dale, Wytheville	.192	13	26	2	5	8	1	1	0	2	1	0	1	1	0	8	1	1
Cruz, Ismael, Martinsville†	.271	43	155	18	42	48	4	1	0	16	1	0	0	20	0	24	5	4
Cunningham, Earl, Wytheville	.258	49	182	20	47	78	6	2	7	38	0	1	8	12	3	40	3	1
Curley, Timothy, Princeton*	.263	62	243	40	64	100	15	6	3	26	0	1	1	36	5	44	13	3
Current, Matthew, Martinsville*	.288	33	104	14	30	38	8	0	0	13	0	1	1	14	0	9	1	1
Curtis, John, Princeton	.209	47	177	19	37	52	5	5	0	17	1	2	0	12	0	33	4	3
Dalson, Kevin, Wytheville*	.201	56	164	22	33	40	7	0	0	11	1	1	2	21	0	20	6	0
Daniels, Lance, Bristol	.159	24	63	4	10	13	3	0	0	4	0	0	1	5	0	25	0	0
Davis, Allen, Bluefield	.205	43	127	17	26	30	4	0	0	12	1	1	1	22	0	47	4	0
Davis, Michael, Burlington*	.274	63	212	26	58	84	8	0	6	31	0	2	7	13	1	33	3	1
Davis, Nicky, Kingsport*	.252	64	206	24	52	99	15	1	10	34	1	2	4	24	3	54	2	2
Davis, Robert, Bristol	.130	37	100	9	13	15	2	0	0	5	1	0	6	10	0	58	7	2
Delanuez, Rexford, Elizabethton	.321	55	193	47	62	104	11	2	9	37	0	2	2	37	0	36	6	0
DeLosSantos, Alberto, Princeton	.262	52	202	32	53	81	6	8	2	14	0	1	2	6	1	30	10	6
Delpiano, Marc, Burlington	.227	42	97	17	22	24	2	0	0	9	2	1	6	13	0	12	4	5
Devares, Cesar, Bluefield	.214	12	42	3	9	13	4	0	0	7	0	0	0	1	0	5	0	0
Diaz, Alberto, Kingsport	.278	68	273	55	76	103	19	1	2	19	2	0	1	17	0	24	31	11
Dixon, Steven, Johnson City*	.000	19	1	0	0	0	0	0	0	0	0	0	0	0	0	1	0	0
Dunn, Steven, Elizabethton	.305	57	210	34	64	100	12	3	6	42	1	4	0	22	2	41	0	2
Edwards, Calvin, Johnson City	.169	29	71	6	12	15	1	1	0	6	1	0	0	9	0	15	1	1
Fayne, Jeffrey, Johnson City†	.215	60	186	27	40	57	9	1	2	19	2	1	2	29	1	51	7	7
Fielitz, William, Johnson City	.191	31	89	9	17	21	4	0	0	10	0	0	2	5	0	38	1	0
Ford, Calvin, Wytheville	.191	44	136	21	26	39	4	0	3	19	2	0	3	19	1	42	2	0
Fordyce, Brook, Kingsport	.327	69	226	45	74	116	15	0	9	38	3	2	1	30	1	26	10	6
Foster Lamar, Martinsville*	.252	37	123	17	31	40	3	0	2	12	0	2	3	7	0	26	1	0
Fowler, John, Bluefield†	.300	62	220	43	66	112	19	0	9	39	1	0	0	16	1	39	7	6

Player and Club	Pct.	G.	AB.	R.	H.	TB.	2B.	3B.	HR.	RBI.	SH.	SF.	HP.	BB.	Int. BB.	SO.	SB.	CS.
Frias, Israel, Bluefield	.218	27	78	10	17	30	4	0	3	8	1	0	0	8	0	21	0	1
Fults, Nathan, Pulaski	.143	10	28	2	4	4	0	0	0	0	1	0	1	0	0	10	0	2
Gamble, Freddie, Bristol*	.205	50	146	14	30	39	5	2	0	8	1	0	1	7	0	19	3	1
Garcia, Amadeo, Elizabethton	.248	34	101	14	25	31	4	1	0	11	0	0	2	12	0	19	3	1
Garzon, Eliseo, Princeton	.189	12	37	2	7	11	1	0	1	2	0	0	1	4	0	9	0	0
Gentile, Randy, Elizabethton	.270	61	211	32	57	80	8	3	3	38	0	4	9	24	0	30	5	1
Giles, Brian, Burlington*	.310	36	129	18	40	47	7	0	0	20	0	1	1	11	2	19	6	3
Giordano, Marc, Princeton*	.261	15	23	3	6	8	2	0	0	2	0	0	1	0	0	9	1	0
Greene, William, Princeton*	.324	39	136	22	44	64	6	4	2	24	0	0	2	9	1	29	4	4
Guzik, Robbi, Kingsport	.247	52	146	10	36	44	6	1	0	15	7	2	1	5	0	31	6	2
Hall, Christopher, Bristol	.244	41	135	17	33	36	3	0	0	10	2	1	0	15	0	27	1	1
Hardgrove, Thomas, Martinsville*	.286	61	206	40	59	111	11	1	13	45	1	2	3	29	0	56	0	1
Harris, James, Kingsport	.367	58	210	37	77	114	12	2	7	55	0	8	2	21	0	28	19	5
Hart, Brian, Burlington	.203	21	64	5	13	17	4	0	0	1	1	0	1	2	1	14	2	0
Hartmann, Reid, Kingsport†	.295	66	227	46	67	108	14	0	9	39	4	3	6	24	1	52	16	3
Heath, Lee, Pulaski†	.263	65	236	50	62	75	11	1	0	21	4	1	3	44	0	60	40	17
Hinde, Michael, Elizabethton*	.192	38	120	19	23	46	3	1	6	15	0	1	2	15	1	47	4	0
Holmes, William, Princeton*	.293	40	147	24	43	73	15	0	5	28	0	1	3	15	0	24	0	0
House, Michael, Elizabethton	.376	63	221	54	83	140	21	0	12	68	0	6	5	42	3	43	1	1
Howard, David, Princeton†	.232	45	151	18	35	52	9	1	2	14	0	1	2	28	0	36	3	5
Huff, Bradford, Wytheville	.212	42	132	17	28	35	5	1	0	11	1	0	1	11	0	19	2	0
Hutchinson, Sean, Pulaski	.205	18	39	5	8	17	3	0	2	8	3	1	0	2	0	9	0	0
Ibarguen, Enrique, Bristol†	.195	49	154	29	30	41	4	2	1	14	1	1	3	25	0	52	13	3
Jackson, Jeffrey, Martinsville	.227	48	163	16	37	50	5	1	2	21	0	1	2	14	1	66	11	2
Jimenez, Roberto, Burlington	.246	21	65	10	16	26	7	0	1	8	2	0	0	3	0	16	0	1
Johnson, Avery, Burlington	.286	24	91	15	26	31	5	0	0	9	1	0	1	13	0	19	4	5
Kelly, Patrick, Pulaski*	.331	50	163	25	54	60	4	1	0	21	8	0	5	18	2	17	5	7
Kennedy, Daniel, Wytheville	.237	12	38	4	9	12	0	0	1	3	0	0	0	3	0	3	0	2
Kessinger, Keith, Bluefield	.273	28	99	17	27	37	4	0	2	9	2	0	1	8	0	12	1	0
Kinyoun, Travis, Bristol†	.232	53	151	21	35	55	6	1	4	27	1	1	3	30	1	29	4	1
Kraft, Michael, Johnson City*	.283	62	198	33	56	90	13	0	7	37	2	3	0	30	1	28	5	1
Kupsey, John, Pulaski	.250	53	160	39	40	64	9	0	5	22	6	0	5	16	1	45	5	1
Lachman, Thomas, Burlington	.184	17	49	3	9	14	2	0	1	3	1	0	2	5	0	13	0	0
Lane, Nolan, Burlington	.265	65	234	37	62	96	15	2	5	34	0	1	5	27	1	46	14	8
Leon, Jose, Elizabethton	.253	23	75	8	19	21	2	0	0	8	0	2	0	6	0	4	0	0
Levis, Jesse, Burlington*	.344	27	93	11	32	48	4	0	4	16	0	1	2	10	3	7	1	0
Lewis, Kenneth, Bristol	.324	44	136	29	44	64	13	2	1	15	0	0	2	26	0	30	19	6
Lewis, Theodore, Bluefield	.331	40	151	31	50	93	11	1	10	32	0	2	0	9	0	21	0	2
Little, Michael, Wytheville	.217	51	157	26	34	61	1	1	8	25	0	1	4	15	0	41	1	2
Llanos, Aurelio, Martinsville†	.182	33	99	10	18	32	5	0	3	6	0	1	1	10	0	50	3	0
Lloyd, Michael, Elizabethton	.219	66	233	54	51	73	13	0	3	28	2	5	3	59	0	40	9	3
Lopez, Javier, Pulaski	.261	51	153	27	40	59	8	1	3	27	0	3	1	5	0	35	3	2
Lowe, Christopher, Martinsville	.217	42	152	13	33	42	9	0	0	11	0	1	1	20	0	50	5	5
Lugo, Angel, Elizabethton	.148	19	61	8	9	9	0	0	0	2	0	0	0	4	0	16	1	1
Lytle, Wade, Princeton	.173	18	52	8	9	14	2	0	1	4	1	0	1	2	0	20	0	0
Maldonado, Carlos, Bristol†	.205	38	122	14	25	35	5	1	1	11	3	2	1	10	0	21	1	0
Manahan, Austin, Princeton	.233	19	73	8	17	25	5	0	1	8	0	1	0	6	1	24	1	1
Masteller, Dan, Elizabethton*	.342	9	38	8	13	19	0	0	2	9	0	0	0	6	0	2	2	2
McClinton, Timothy, Kingsport	.278	70	230	38	64	103	13	1	8	29	3	2	3	24	1	63	16	4
McCoy, Brent, Pulaski†	.316	63	225	43	71	94	11	3	2	39	7	4	1	32	0	20	17	5
McCreary, Robert, Elizabethton†	.279	62	229	38	64	85	11	2	2	28	0	4	0	24	4	13	0	2
McKeon, Kasey, Bristol†	.242	39	120	17	29	36	4	0	1	13	0	1	0	9	1	25	1	2
Meddaugh, Dean, Burlington*	.169	30	71	9	12	14	2	0	0	6	0	0	2	8	0	16	2	3
Medina, Facanel, Martinsville	.200	29	110	12	22	25	3	0	0	7	1	0	1	4	0	27	12	2
Medina, Ricardo, Wytheville	.264	51	163	17	43	50	7	0	0	18	2	2	0	17	0	29	1	0
Merrill, Lawrence, Johnson City*	.000	1	3	0	0	0	0	0	0	0	0	0	0	0	0	2	0	0
Meyer, Richard, Martinsville	.233	38	129	13	30	41	7	2	0	12	1	0	0	8	0	28	1	3
Milene, Jeffrey, Elizabethton	.167	14	36	4	6	7	1	0	0	2	0	0	0	4	0	7	0	0
Minnifield, Wallace, Kingsport	.223	41	121	18	27	44	5	0	4	21	0	1	1	7	0	38	6	3
Montero, Sixto, Martinsville*	.000	2	3	0	0	0	0	0	0	1	0	0	0	0	0	1	0	0
Morris, Steven, Elizabethton†	.247	45	146	42	36	46	5	1	1	13	1	2	4	31	0	30	20	6
Mota, William, Elizabethton†	.339	32	115	17	39	54	10	1	1	14	0	2	2	2	0	13	0	0
Nebraska, David, Burlington	.171	28	76	7	13	17	4	0	0	9	2	1	0	7	0	24	1	0
Nieves, Melvin, Pulaski†	.277	64	231	43	64	113	16	3	9	46	3	4	1	30	4	59	6	4
Norwood, Aaron, Bluefield	.136	42	110	14	15	16	1	0	0	2	4	0	2	7	0	32	5	2
O'Neal, Kelley, Bristol*	.231	60	208	31	48	77	6	7	3	24	0	1	1	15	1	47	9	2
Ochs, Anthony, Johnson City	.233	65	202	30	47	69	7	0	5	32	2	2	7	45	3	56	11	3
Ortiz, Ramon, Burlington	.209	31	67	11	14	15	1	0	0	4	2	0	2	4	0	13	6	2
Ostopowicz, Richard, Kingsport	.246	19	57	12	14	21	4	0	1	4	1	0	1	7	0	15	4	0
Paynter, William, Wytheville	.261	28	92	18	24	39	2	2	3	12	2	0	2	4	0	16	3	1
Pemberton, Rudy, Bristol	.271	56	214	40	58	89	9	2	6	39	0	1	4	14	0	43	19	3
Perez, Eulogio, Martinsville	.201	40	134	18	27	48	10	1	3	17	1	4	0	12	0	40	0	4
Phillips, Jimmy, Martinsville*	.233	42	146	18	34	54	11	0	3	18	0	1	2	19	0	33	0	0
Pichardo, Francisco, Elizabethton	.242	13	33	5	8	12	2	1	0	4	1	0	0	2	0	10	0	1
Pisacreta, Michael, Pulaski	.254	50	138	20	35	54	7	0	4	24	2	1	1	15	0	27	0	2
Pitcavage, Joel, Princeton	.200	6	20	1	4	4	0	0	0	0	0	0	0	5	0	4	0	1
Pough, Clyde, Burlington	.258	67	225	39	58	99	15	1	8	37	0	2	3	36	0	64	9	5
Ratliff, Daryl, Princeton	.245	66	208	28	51	53	2	0	0	21	0	1	0	24	1	31	10	3
Rendina, Michael, Bristol*	.272	62	224	34	61	107	13	0	11	34	0	1	1	28	3	36	5	3
Reyes, Juan, Bristol	.210	22	62	6	13	17	0	2	0	5	0	0	0	6	0	26	3	3
Rodriguez, Ahmed, Johnson City†	.164	58	165	19	27	44	5	0	4	17	3	1	1	21	1	53	3	5
Rodriguez, Jose B., Princeton†	.284	21	74	15	21	25	4	0	0	7	0	0	0	10	0	15	4	1
Rodriguez, Roman, Princeton	.227	60	229	27	52	67	8	2	1	27	1	2	3	24	0	51	7	5
Roso, James, Bluefield	.307	48	153	32	47	69	10	0	4	25	1	3	4	22	1	25	0	3
Rudolph, Mason, Kingsport	.157	20	51	7	8	16	2	0	2	4	0	0	0	0	0	22	0	0
Sample, Deron, Kingsport	.400	32	5	1	2	2	0	0	0	0	0	0	0	3	0	1	0	0
Savinon, Odalis, Johnson City	.271	59	207	33	56	62	3	0	1	19	0	1	1	26	0	52	10	9
Schmidt, Keith, Bluefield*	.227	55	194	28	44	71	10	1	5	32	0	3	2	17	0	71	6	6
Schreiber, Bruce, Princeton*	.348	64	224	31	78	115	15	8	2	38	0	2	0	20	2	31	7	4
Seibert, Malcolm, Bristol*	.000	10	1	0	0	0	0	0	0	0	0	0	0	0	0	0	0	0
Siwa, Joseph, Elizabethton	.257	9	35	5	9	13	1	0	1	10	0	1	0	5	0	9	0	0
Snover, Daniel, Pulaski	.241	63	216	43	52	69	9	1	2	33	5	5	5	32	3	24	10	3

Player and Club	Pct.	G.	AB.	R.	H.	TB.	2B.	3B.	HR.	RBI.	SH.	SF.	HP.	BB.	Int. BB.	SO.	SB.	CS.
Sodders, Randy, Wytheville	.217	18	60	12	13	20	2	1	1	6	0	0	0	12	0	7	2	0
Stephens, John, Johnson City*	.253	66	217	40	55	69	10	2	0	25	4	1	0	41	3	24	15	10
Stiegele, Robert, Bluefield	.324	55	179	37	58	100	13	1	9	31	0	2	4	34	1	35	5	1
Swail, Steven, Pulaski	.218	31	78	12	17	21	4	0	0	6	1	0	0	8	0	16	2	0
Talford, Calvin, Martinsville	.241	10	29	0	7	7	0	0	0	0	0	0	0	0	0	11	0	0
Tarasco, Anthony, Pulaski*	.340	49	156	22	53	71	8	2	2	22	2	2	0	21	2	20	7	2
Tejada, Francisco, Martinsville	.500	5	12	2	6	10	1	0	1	4	0	0	0	2	0	3	0	0
Thomas, Corey, Martinsville	.268	26	97	18	26	35	2	2	1	6	1	0	2	12	0	17	2	3
Thompson, Jeffrey, Kingsport†	.200	10	25	4	5	5	0	0	0	3	1	0	0	3	0	11	4	0
Thornton, Eric, Kingsport*	.156	41	90	13	14	17	1	1	0	6	4	0	3	6	0	19	8	3
Torres, Jessie, Princeton	.252	39	115	24	29	42	5	1	2	15	0	2	2	29	0	30	1	3
Torres, Paul, Wytheville	.236	54	191	34	45	77	9	1	7	38	0	2	6	32	0	55	2	4
Torres, Ramon, Burlington*	.250	40	116	20	29	41	5	2	1	10	1	0	2	14	0	32	5	2
Valencia, Gilbert, Martinsville*	.287	47	150	24	43	58	9	0	2	13	1	1	0	28	0	27	5	0
Vargas, Julio, Martinsville	.270	30	89	15	24	28	4	0	0	5	0	0	2	19	1	19	1	0
Vazquez, Edgardo, Kingsport	.000	18	1	0	0	0	0	0	0	0	0	0	0	0	0	0	0	0
Wacker, Wade, Elizabethton†	.154	3	13	1	2	2	0	0	0	1	0	0	0	0	0	2	0	0
Washington, Kyle, Kingsport	.222	62	185	28	41	67	6	1	6	20	3	1	3	29	0	46	11	5
Welch, Daniel, Martinsville	.311	39	135	24	42	60	6	0	4	17	2	1	1	13	0	37	4	1
Welch, Kenneth, Burlington	.293	31	75	7	22	28	3	0	1	14	1	0	1	5	0	10	4	0
West, Robert, Princeton	.192	22	73	6	14	18	4	0	0	9	0	2	1	5	0	19	1	2
White, Clinton, Wytheville	.263	48	160	23	42	64	6	2	4	22	1	3	6	18	0	30	4	1
Williams, Earl, Bluefield	.270	43	126	20	34	57	5	0	6	28	0	2	2	20	0	42	3	2
Wilson, Bradley, Bristol*	.221	43	131	14	29	42	4	3	1	13	0	1	1	12	2	31	0	1
Wright, Brian, Pulaski*	.284	58	201	17	57	73	11	1	1	28	2	3	3	9	1	25	5	3

The following pitchers, listed alphabetically by club, with games in parentheses, had no plate appearances, primarily through use of designated hitters:

BLUEFIELD—Anderson, Matthew (14); Bautista, Juan (7); Belen, Matires (28); Heiden, Shawn (9); Marett, John (11); Martin, Thomas (8); Medina, Victor (21); Moore, Daryl (12); Pennington, Brad (15); Sieradzki, Allen (17); Sutton, Douglas (3); Taylor, Thomas (11); Teixeira, Joseph (19); Wheatcroft, Robert (10).

BRISTOL—Betances, Marcos (4); Bowman, Michael (8); Braley, Jeffrey (23); Checo, Pedro (14); Coleman, Matthew (15); Garcia, Michael (8); Guzman, Jose (12); Maietta, Ronald (9); Martinez, Ivan (6); Matchett, Stephen (7); Neidlinger, Joseph (14); Rodriguez, Eddy (24); Rodriguez, Jose H. (12); Rountree, Brian (12); Stefani, Mario (19).

BURLINGTON—Alexander, Charles (3); Allen, Scott (5); Baker, Andrew (8); Cole, Christopher (9); DeLaCruz, Anthony (22); Elston, Cary (11); Gonzales, Michael (21); Neill, Scott (2); Person, Robert (10); Pettiford, Cecil (11); Rivera, Roberto (18); Tillman, Tommy (10); Ventura, Reynaldo (18); Woodfin, Olonzo (17).

ELIZABETHTON—Asp, Bryan (1); Benson, Thomas (8); Best, Jayson (12); Bigham, David (9); Diaz, Sandy (12); Freeman, Richard (5); Harrington, Jody (9); Johnson, Karl (13); Lipson, Marc (10); Misuraca, Michael (13); Neagle, Dennis (6); Nedin, Timothy (14); Taylor, Kerry (9); Wiese, Phillip (14).

JOHNSON CITY—Baker, Ernie (15); Botkin, Alan (11); Cimorelli, Frank (12); Corry, Steven (2); Espinal, William (32); Eversgerd, Bryan (16); Fletcher, Dennis (22); Halama, Scott (6); Ortiz, Jose (7); Oswalt, Jeffrey (4); Pacheco, Albert (13); Shackle, Richard (15); Weber, Ron (15); Wiseman, Dennis (12).

KINGSPORT—Auchard, Daniel (8); Butler, Christopher (15); Carrasco, Hector (12); Engle, Thomas (13); Fidler, Andrew (6); Johnston, Craig (15); Lehnerz, Michael (7); Medina, Luciano (5); Polanco, Nicolas (21); Scheffler, James (18); Scott, Craig (22); Thomas, Michael (6).

MARTINSVILLE—Bauer, Albert (19); Carrillo, Francisco (5); Dafforn, Michael (16); Goedhart, Darrell (15); Gray, Elliott (22); Hurst, Charles (15); Lovdal, Stewart (22); McKnight, Gregory (7); Patterson, Jeffrey (7); Randall, Mark (27); Ross, David (18); Shive, Charles (12); Wells, Robert (4); Wiegandt, Scott (9).

PRINCETON—Dooley, Marvin (15); Hamilton, Zane (22); Martinez, Ramon (25); Mooney, Troy (10); Parkinson, Eric (14); Perez, Rafael (7); Redmond, Andre (13); Santiago, Delvy (14); Valdez, Ramon (12); Watson, David (14); Woods, Kelly (17).

PULASKI—Adams, Thomas (10); Arnold, Gregory (10); Brown, Terrance (13); Calderone, Jeffrey (5); Hailey, Roger (12); Jewett, Earl (14); Parker, Jarrod (16); Ritter, Darren (14); Roy, Walter (14); Schafer, William (25); Sottile, Shaun (21); Strange, Donald (27); Thompson, Alan (21); Throckmorton, Bruce (2); Wohlers, Mark (14).

WYTHEVILLE—Correa, Amilcar (16); DiBartolomeo, Stephen (4); Fowler, Edward (12); Gelb, Jac (15); Gillespie, Donald (16); Mill, Fredrick (16); Hollins, Jessie (22); Jaques, Eric (28); Kessler, Gregory (13); Mack, Raymond (11); Perez, Leopoldo (13); Taylor, Aaron (15); Teague, Scott (7).

GRAND SLAM HOME RUNS—Allen, Andujar, Cairo, Cancel, Cordova, Diaz, Kinyoun, Lane, Lopez, McCoy, Nieves, Paynter, Schmidt, Schreiber, 1 each.

AWARDED FIRST BASE ON CATCHER'S INTERFERENCE—Charbonnet (Ochs); Hall (Garzon); Hartmann (Lopez); Holmes (Swail); Lowe (Mota); Redina (Swail).

CLUB FIELDING

Club	Pct.	G.	PO.	A.	E.	DP.	PB.	Club	Pct.	G.	PO.	A.	E.	DP.	PB.
Elizabethton	.964	68	1718	714	92	51	16	Princeton	.947	69	1725	695	135	57	34
Pulaski	.954	68	1728	698	116	57	24	Bristol	.946	67	1682	712	137	54	18
Johnson City	.952	70	1716	725	124	63	10	Martinsville	.945	67	1704	758	142	63	19
Wytheville	.950	69	1767	724	132	43	26	Burlington	.943	68	1710	711	146	63	22
Kingsport	.948	72	1793	733	138	41	20	Bluefield	.939	68	1712	705	156	50	18

INDIVIDUAL FIELDING

*Throws lefthanded.

FIRST BASEMEN

Player and Club	Pct.	G.	PO.	A.	E.	DP.	Player and Club	Pct.	G.	PO.	A.	E.	DP.
Caines, Bristol	.885	6	45	1	6	4	Lytle, Princeton	1.000	2	2	0	0	0
Calzado, Johnson City	.974	38	324	19	9	30	Medina, Wytheville	.990	50	369	31	4	22
Castellano, Wytheville	.500	1	1	0	1	1	Ochs, Johnson City	1.000	3	15	2	0	3
Castillo, Kingsport	1.000	1	1	0	0	0	Ortiz, Burlington	1.000	1	3	0	0	1
Daniels, Bristol	1.000	1	12	0	0	0	Ostopowicz, Kingsport	1.000	3	3	0	0	0
M. Davis, Burlington*	.983	62	477	41	9	51	Paynter, Wytheville	1.000	1	2	0	0	0
N. Davis, Kingsport	.984	41	291	18	5	19	Phillips, Martinsville*	.979	23	213	15	5	18
DUNN, Elizabethton*	.994	57	480	36	3	42	Pisacreta, Pulaski	.980	16	96	4	2	14
Fowler, Bluefield	.974	40	255	12	7	26	Rendina, Bristol*	.991	59	504	42	5	40
Garcia, Elizabethton	1.000	1	1	0	0	0	Rudolph, Kingsport	1.000	2	5	0	0	2
Hardgrove, Martinsville	.969	45	387	26	13	38	Torres, Wytheville	.984	25	238	14	4	16
Harris, Kingsport	.987	36	279	21	4	17	Welch, Burlington	.964	15	78	3	3	5
Holmes, Princeton*	.993	36	276	22	2	25	White, Wytheville	.500	2	1	0	1	1
House, Elizabethton*	.991	11	101	4	1	7	Williams, Bluefield	.978	39	303	14	7	19
Howard, Princeton	.978	35	255	15	6	26	Wilson, Bristol	1.000	4	27	3	0	3
Kinyoun, Bristol	1.000	1	1	0	0	0	Wright, Pulaski	.990	57	478	25	5	36
Kraft, Johnson City	.977	32	274	18	7	25							

SECOND BASEMEN

Player and Club	Pct.	G.	PO.	A.	E.	DP.
Aponte, Wytheville	.875	4	10	11	3	2
Benitez, Bluefield	.932	48	76	129	15	17
Brito, Martinsville	1.000	1	1	1	0	0
Brown, Wytheville	.919	21	36	55	8	12
Cairo, Bluefield	.667	1	1	1	1	0
Cordova, Elizabethton	1.000	1	0	2	0	0
Cotton, Burlington	.905	64	124	153	29	30
Cruz, Martinsville	.950	40	71	121	10	21
Dalson, Wytheville	.962	8	9	16	1	4
DeLosSantos, Princeton	.889	5	13	19	4	4
Delpiano, Burlington	.920	9	10	13	2	5
Diaz, Kingsport	.936	67	108	184	20	23
Edwards, Johnson City	.929	24	36	56	7	14
Ford, Wytheville	.952	28	53	66	6	10
Gamble, Bristol	.942	32	44	69	7	10
Hart, Burlington	1.000	1	2	2	0	0
Hartmann, Kingsport	.970	11	11	21	1	4
Kelly, Pulaski	.984	11	25	38	1	7
Kessinger, Bluefield	.980	18	37	62	2	9
Lloyd, Elizabethton	.962	66	134	172	12	34
Lugo, Elizabethton	.857	4	2	4	1	0
Maldonado, Bristol	.972	24	45	61	3	11
Medina, Martinsville	.918	29	40	94	12	22
Minnifield, Kingsport	.667	1	2	2	2	0
Reyes, Bristol	.929	19	32	60	7	14
Rodriguez, Johnson City	.947	51	70	126	11	24
Schreiber, Princeton	.964	64	149	145	11	36
SNOVER, Pulaski	.983	60	104	181	5	32
Sodders, Wytheville	.925	17	22	40	5	4
Stephens, Johnson City	1.000	1	1	0	0	0
Stiegele, Bluefield	1.000	5	7	14	0	4

THIRD BASEMEN

Player and Club	Pct.	G.	PO.	A.	E.	DP.
Brown, Wytheville	.743	14	8	18	9	1
Canino, Wytheville	1.000	1	0	1	0	0
Casado, Martinsville	1.000	4	0	1	0	0
Castellano, Wytheville	.925	33	23	51	6	2
Cordova, Elizabethton	.765	5	5	8	4	0
Dalson, Wytheville	.938	11	10	20	2	0
DeLosSantos, Princeton	.881	20	17	42	8	3
Delpiano, Burlington	1.000	1	0	3	0	0
Edwards, Johnson City	1.000	2	1	1	0	0
Fordyce, Kingsport	.667	3	0	2	1	0
Foster, Martinsville	.905	33	21	65	9	9
Fowler, Bluefield	.875	5	3	4	1	0
GENTILE, Elizabethton	.924	59	35	98	11	11
Hall, Bristol	.938	34	21	55	5	3
Harris, Kingsport	.900	18	12	15	3	1
Hartmann, Kingsport	.888	47	25	78	13	4
Ibarguen, Bristol	1.000	2	1	0	0	0
Kelly, Pulaski	.841	30	16	53	13	6
Kessinger, Bluefield	1.000	8	8	12	0	1
Kupsey, Pulaski	.802	42	28	53	20	3
Lewis, Bluefield	.740	36	24	50	26	3
Lugo, Elizabethton	.800	6	2	6	2	0
Lytle, Princeton	.800	7	4	8	3	0
Maldonado, Bristol	.875	9	3	11	2	1
McClinton, Kingsport	.796	20	14	25	10	3
McKeon, Bristol	.818	3	1	8	2	1
Medina, Wytheville	.000	1	0	0	1	0
Merrill, Johnson City	.667	1	2	0	1	0
Meyer, Martinsville	.795	36	17	53	18	2
O'Neal, Bristol	.913	28	15	27	4	3
Ochs, Johnson City	.917	4	3	8	1	1
Pough, Burlington	.863	59	42	116	25	7
J. Rodriguez, Princeton	1.000	2	0	1	0	0
R. Rodriguez, Princeton	.853	41	31	85	20	9
Sodders, Wytheville	.500	3	0	1	1	0
Stephens, Johnson City	.911	65	55	120	17	9
Stiegele, Bluefield	.908	28	27	42	7	2
Torres, Wytheville	.907	14	14	25	4	3
Welch, Burlington	.926	13	7	18	2	4
Wright, Pulaski	1.000	1	0	1	0	0

SHORTSTOPS

Player and Club	Pct.	G.	PO.	A.	E.	DP.
Alexander, Bluefield	.908	64	140	177	32	37
Andujar, Johnson City	.924	66	93	175	22	38
Aponte, Wytheville	.833	3	5	5	2	1
Brito, Martinsville	1.000	6	6	11	0	2
Buhe, Kingsport	.898	56	83	136	25	16
Casado, Martinsville	1.000	1	0	2	0	0
Castellano, Wytheville	.928	37	67	87	12	9
Dalson, Wytheville	.931	36	62	126	14	20
Delpiano, Burlington	.922	31	30	77	9	12
Gamble, Bristol	.950	8	13	25	2	4
Greene, Princeton	.843	35	33	69	19	16
Hall, Bristol	.900	5	5	13	2	4
Hart, Burlington	.906	20	41	36	8	14
Hartmann, Kingsport	.873	16	16	32	7	3
Ibarguen, Bristol	.852	37	54	96	26	17
Johnson, Burlington	.904	22	32	53	9	4
Kelly, Pulaski	.915	9	15	28	4	4
Kessinger, Bluefield	1.000	2	0	3	0	0
Lugo, Elizabethton	.938	7	10	20	2	2
Lytle, Princeton	.500	1	1	1	1	0
Maldonado, Bristol	1.000	3	2	6	0	0
Manahan, Princeton	.904	19	35	50	9	9
McCoy, Pulaski	.902	58	84	156	26	38
McCREARY, Elizabethton	.925	62	97	185	23	36
Montero, Martinsville	1.000	1	1	1	0	0
O'Neal, Bristol	.900	20	36	54	10	7
Perez, Martinsville	.932	40	62	130	14	30
A. Rodriguez, Johnson City	1.000	6	9	12	0	5
J. Rodriguez, Princeton	1.000	1	0	1	0	0
R. Rodriguez, Princeton	.939	17	39	54	6	10
Snover, Pulaski	.833	4	4	11	3	2
Stiegele, Bluefield	.929	4	7	6	1	0
Thomas, Martinsville	.891	26	46	69	14	9
Thompson, Kingsport	1.000	9	10	13	0	3
Welch, Burlington	.737	3	4	10	5	2

OUTFIELDERS

Player and Club	Pct.	G.	PO.	A.	E.	DP.
Alexander, Bluefield	.978	26	42	2	1	0
Allen, Johnson City	.919	29	34	0	3	0
Bailey, Wytheville	.969	56	92	1	3	0
Batiste, Bluefield	.771	33	25	2	8	0
Bean, Martinsville	.920	10	22	1	2	1
Bell, Johnson City	.895	22	32	2	4	0
Brown, Burlington	.926	39	48	2	4	0
Caines, Bristol	.914	51	90	6	9	0
Cairo, Bluefield	.955	56	101	6	5	0
Cancel, Wytheville	.929	52	87	4	7	0
Carmona, Martinsville	1.000	3	1	0	0	0
Carson, Martinsville	.857	16	18	0	3	0
Charbonnet, Burlington°	.962	22	23	2	1	0
Clark, Pulaski	.978	50	86	2	2	0
Coleman, Johnson City	.913	49	91	4	9	1
Cordova, Elizabethton	1.000	5	1	1	0	0
Cunningham, Wytheville	.883	36	52	1	7	1
Curley, Princeton°	.933	62	91	7	7	0
Curtis, Princeton	.985	47	63	3	1	0
Daniels, Bristol	.789	14	14	1	4	0
A. Davis, Bluefield	.938	42	56	4	4	0
R. Davis, Bristol	.980	32	47	3	1	1
Delanuez, Elizabethton	.951	54	72	6	4	0
DeLosSantos, Princeton	1.000	3	1	0	0	0
Fayne, Johnson City	.977	57	75	11	2	2
Ford, Wytheville	1.000	13	10	0	0	0
Fordyce, Kingsport	1.000	14	8	1	0	0
Foster, Martinsville	1.000	1	1	0	0	0
Frias, Bluefield	1.000	1	4	0	0	0
Fults, Pulaski	.778	10	6	1	2	0
Gamble, Bristol	1.000	9	15	0	0	0
Garcia, Elizabethton	.905	27	35	3	4	0
Giles, Burlington°	.982	31	52	3	1	0
Guzik, Kingsport	.891	51	44	5	6	0
Harris, Kingsport	.333	2	1	0	2	0
Heath, Pulaski	.949	63	125	4	7	0
Hinde, Elizabethton°	.962	16	25	0	1	0
House, Elizabethton°	.943	46	50	0	3	0
Jackson, Martinsville	.975	42	75	4	2	0
Kelly, Pulaski	1.000	1	1	0	0	0
Kinyoun, Bristol	1.000	1	1	0	0	0
Kraft, Johnson City	.917	7	10	1	1	0
Lane, Burlington	.951	59	114	2	6	0
Lewis, Bristol	.947	44	86	4	5	1
Little, Wytheville	.944	43	63	5	4	0
Llanos, Martinsville	.936	30	41	3	3	0
Lowe, Martinsville	.986	42	67	4	1	0
Lugo, Elizabethton	1.000	1	2	0	0	0
Masteller, Elizabethton°	1.000	7	10	1	0	0
McClinton, Kingsport	.933	44	55	1	4	0
McKeon, Bristol	.500	3	1	0	1	0
Meddaugh, Burlington	.977	30	39	3	1	1
Minnifield, Kingsport	.953	37	54	7	3	1
Morris, Elizabethton	1.000	43	48	2	0	0

OUTFIELDERS—Continued

Player and Club	Pct.	G.	PO.	A.	E.	DP.
Nieves, Pulaski	.885	47	45	1	6	0
Norwood, Bluefield	.912	40	48	4	5	1
O'Neal, Bristol	.909	5	10	0	1	0
Ortiz, Burlington	.857	18	17	1	3	0
Ostopowicz, Kingsport	.933	19	26	2	2	0
Pemberton, Bristol	.946	53	84	4	5	2
Pichardo, Elizabethton	.933	11	14	0	1	0
Pisacreta, Pulaski	1.000	17	17	1	0	0
Pitcavage, Princeton	.917	6	11	0	1	0
Ratliff, Princeton	.967	65	110	9	4	3
Rendina, Bristol*	1.000	2	6	0	0	0
Rodriguez, Princeton	.944	7	16	1	1	0
SAVINON, Johnson City	.980	59	96	4	2	0
Schmidt, Bluefield	.813	11	12	1	3	0
Stiegele, Bluefield	.903	19	24	4	3	0
Talford, Martinsville	1.000	6	4	0	0	0
Tarasco, Pulaski	.942	30	45	4	3	2
Thornton, Kingsport	.957	34	38	6	2	0
P. Torres, Wytheville	.857	14	11	1	2	0
R. Torres, Burlington*	.980	27	47	3	1	0
Valencia, Martinsville*	.983	41	51	7	1	1
Vazquez, Kingsport	1.000	3	2	0	0	0
Wacker, Elizabethton	.500	3	3	0	3	0
Washington, Kingsport	.967	58	115	4	4	0
Welch, Martinsville	.944	30	46	5	3	2
West, Princeton	.844	19	24	3	5	0
White, Wytheville	.786	12	11	0	3	0
Wright, Pulaski	1.000	1	1	0	0	0

CATCHERS

Player and Club	Pct.	G.	PO.	A.	E.	DP.	PB.
Adams, Martinsville	.947	4	14	4	1	0	2
Adkins, Princeton	1.000	1	1	0	0	0	1
Antigua, Princeton	.985	23	168	24	3	1	7
Boeschen, Pulaski	1.000	6	34	5	0	0	1
Briggs, Elizabethton	1.000	3	25	3	0	0	1
Canino, Wytheville	1.000	3	3	0	0	0	2
Carter, Burlington	1.000	1	4	0	0	0	3
Castillo, Kingsport	.994	19	138	18	1	1	3
Cosman, Martinsville	.982	7	51	3	1	0	3
Craig, Wytheville	1.000	11	46	6	0	0	4
Current, Martinsville	.983	31	197	29	4	1	6
Devares, Bluefield	.959	11	59	12	3	0	4
Fielitz, Johnson City	1.000	24	142	14	0	1	4
FORDYCE, Kingsport	.991	50	303	25	3	1	11
Frias, Bluefield	.960	21	129	16	6	0	5
Garzon, Princeton	.936	12	83	5	6	0	7
Harris, Kingsport	1.000	2	5	2	0	0	0
Howard, Princeton	1.000	1	13	1	0	0	0
Huff, Wytheville	.995	25	161	21	1	0	9
Hutchinson, Pulaski	.988	12	76	3	1	0	8
Jimenez, Burlington	.983	21	105	14	2	3	4
Kennedy, Wytheville	.958	12	83	9	4	0	5
Kinyoun, Bristol	.965	36	225	24	9	6	9
Leon, Elizabethton	.995	23	188	26	1	0	3
Levis, Burlington	.991	27	189	27	2	2	4
Lopez, Pulaski	.983	38	264	26	5	4	7
McKeon, Bristol	.964	21	112	22	5	1	6
Milene, Elizabethton	.989	12	79	7	1	0	3
Mota, Elizabethton	.979	27	199	29	5	2	9
Nebraska, Burlington	.959	28	121	21	6	2	11
Ochs, Johnson City	.964	51	318	32	13	2	6
Paynter, Wytheville	.985	27	172	25	3	1	6
Roso, Bluefield	.979	43	288	43	7	2	9
Rudolph, Kingsport	.956	18	79	8	4	0	6
Siwa, Elizabethton	1.000	8	62	5	0	0	0
Swail, Pulaski	.987	30	141	15	2	1	8
Tejada, Martinsville	1.000	3	22	0	0	0	0
Torres, Princeton	.982	38	247	25	5	1	19
Vargas, Martinsville	.965	29	197	23	8	2	8
Wilson, Bristol	.991	20	92	19	1	2	3

PITCHERS

Player and Club	Pct.	G.	PO.	A.	E.	DP.
Adams, Pulaski	1.000	10	0	2	0	0
Alexander, Burlington	1.000	3	2	1	0	0
Allen, Burlington*	1.000	5	11	7	0	2
Anderson, Bluefield*	.900	14	2	7	1	0
Arnold, Pulaski*	1.000	10	0	2	0	0
Auchard, Kingsport*	.500	8	0	1	1	0
A. Baker, Burlington	.917	8	6	5	1	0
E. Baker, Johnson City	1.000	15	1	7	0	1
Baur, Martinsville	1.000	19	1	7	0	2
Bautista, Bluefield	.917	7	1	2	0	0
Belen, Bluefield	.917	28	2	9	1	2
Benson, Elizabethton	.833	8	1	4	1	0
Best, Elizabethton	.875	12	6	8	2	0
Betances, Bristol	.800	4	2	2	1	0
Bigham, Elizabethton*	1.000	9	2	1	0	1
Botkin, Johnson City*	1.000	11	1	14	0	0
Bowman, Bristol	.857	8	3	3	1	0
Braley, Bristol	1.000	23	1	11	0	2
Brown, Pulaski	.917	13	9	13	2	2
Butler, Kingsport	.974	15	16	22	1	1
Calderone, Pulaski	1.000	5	0	2	0	0
Carrasco, Kingsport	.786	12	5	6	3	0
Carrillo, Martinsville	1.000	5	0	1	0	0
Checo, Bristol	.750	14	2	4	2	0
Cimorelli, Johnson City	.895	12	1	16	2	2
Cole, Burlington	1.000	9	12	10	0	0
Coleman, Bristol	1.000	14	8	14	0	1
Correa, Wytheville	1.000	16	2	2	0	0
Corry, Johnson City	1.000	2	1	1	0	0
Dafforn, Martinsville	.750	16	0	3	1	0
DeLaCruz, Burlington	1.000	22	6	3	0	1
Diaz, Elizabethton	.909	12	4	6	1	1
DiBartolomeo, Wytheville	1.000	4	0	3	0	0
Dixon, Johnson City*	.900	18	3	15	2	2
Dooley, Princeton	.947	15	7	11	1	1
Elston, Burlington	.864	11	11	8	3	1
Engle, Kingsport	.750	13	1	2	1	0
Espinal, Johnson City	.929	32	3	10	1	0
Eversgerd, Johnson City*	1.000	16	2	10	0	0
Fidler, Kingsport*	1.000	6	2	0	0	1
Fletcher, Johnson City	.833	22	1	4	1	0
Fowler, Wytheville	.857	12	4	8	2	0
Freeman, Elizabethton	1.000	5	2	0	0	0
Garcia, Bristol	1.000	8	1	2	0	0
Gelb, Wytheville	.905	15	6	13	2	1
Gillespie, Wytheville*	.667	16	4	2	3	0
Giordano, Princeton*	1.000	9	6	15	0	3
Goedhart, Martinsville	.667	15	8	6	7	2
Gonzales, Burlington	.844	21	17	10	5	0
Gray, Martinsville	1.000	22	4	9	0	0
Guzman, Bristol	.850	12	5	12	3	2
Hailey, Pulaski*	1.000	12	3	13	0	0
Halama, Johnson City	.500	6	1	0	1	0
Hamilton, Princeton	.923	21	5	7	1	0
Harrington, Elizabethton*	.800	9	3	5	2	0
Heiden, Bluefield	1.000	9	2	0	0	0
Hill, Wytheville	.889	16	3	13	2	1
Hollins, Wytheville	.833	22	2	3	1	0
Hurst, Martinsville	.833	15	5	10	3	0
Jaques, Wytheville	1.000	28	2	6	0	0
Jewett, Pulaski	1.000	14	3	8	0	1
Johnson, Elizabethton	1.000	13	1	9	0	0
Johnston, Kingsport*	.833	15	3	2	1	0
Kessler, Wytheville	.947	13	6	12	1	0
Lehnerz, Kingsport	.889	7	2	6	1	0
Lipson, Elizabethton	1.000	10	2	3	0	0
Lovdal, Martinsville	.750	22	2	7	3	1
Mack, Wytheville	.833	11	4	6	2	0
Maietta, Bristol	1.000	9	1	2	0	0
Marett, Bluefield	.900	11	2	7	1	0
Martin, Bluefield*	.833	8	5	5	2	2
Martinez, Princeton	.750	25	2	4	2	0
Matchett, Bristol	.000	7	0	0	1	0
McKnight, Martinsville*	1.000	7	1	1	0	0
L. Medina, Kingsport	1.000	5	7	2	0	0
V. Medina, Bluefield	1.000	21	3	8	0	1
MISURACA, Elizabethton	1.000	13	5	24	0	4
Mooney, Princeton	.875	10	6	8	2	0
Moore, Bluefield*	.923	12	2	10	1	0
Neagle, Elizabethton*	1.000	6	0	2	0	0
Nedin, Elizabethton*	.833	14	4	6	2	1
Neidlinger, Bristol	.944	14	5	12	1	0
Neill, Burlington	1.000	2	1	2	0	0
Ortiz, Johnson City	.667	7	1	1	1	0
Oswalt, Johnson City*	.667	3	0	2	1	0
Pacheco, Johnson City	.783	13	3	15	5	1
Parker, Pulaski	.778	16	3	4	2	2
Parkinson, Princeton	.885	14	6	17	3	1
Patterson, Martinsville	.867	7	4	9	2	0
Pennington, Bluefield*	.840	15	7	14	4	1
L. Perez, Wytheville	1.000	13	3	3	0	0
R. Perez, Princeton	1.000	7	0	5	0	0
Person, Burlington	.857	10	2	4	1	0
Pettiford, Martinsville	.947	11	5	13	1	0
Polanco, Kingsport	.923	21	2	10	1	1
Randall, Martinsville	1.000	27	1	4	0	1
Redmond, Princeton	.750	12	0	3	1	0
Ritter, Pulaski	1.000	14	2	9	0	0
Rivera, Burlington*	.941	18	3	13	1	0
E. Rodriguez, Bristol*	1.000	24	0	1	0	0
J. Rodriguez, Bristol	.966	12	5	23	1	1
Ross, Martinsville*	1.000	18	2	2	0	0

PITCHERS—Continued

Player and Club	Pct.	G.	PO.	A.	E.	DP.	Player and Club	Pct.	G.	PO.	A.	E.	DP.
Rountree, Bristol	.900	12	3	6	1	0	Teixeira, Bluefield	.909	19	3	7	1	1
Roy, Pulaski	1.000	14	1	7	0	0	Thomas, Kingsport*	1.000	6	0	7	0	0
Sample, Kingsport	.833	29	3	7	2	0	Thompson, Pulaski*	1.000	21	2	1	0	0
Santiago, Princeton	.957	14	7	15	1	0	Throckmorton, Pulaski	1.000	2	0	1	0	0
Schafer, Pulaski	.917	25	4	7	1	2	Tillman, Burlington*	.963	10	11	15	1	0
Scheffler, Kingsport	.833	18	2	8	2	1	Valdez, Princeton*	.938	12	3	12	1	3
Scott, Kingsport	.895	22	10	7	2	0	Vazquez, Kingsport	.974	17	11	26	1	1
Seibert, Bristol*	.600	9	1	2	2	0	Ventura, Burlington	.800	18	5	7	3	1
Shackle, Johnson City	1.000	15	5	9	0	0	Watson, Princeton*	.857	14	0	6	1	1
Shive, Martinsville	.929	12	2	11	1	0	Weber, Johnson City*	.875	15	3	4	1	0
Sieradzki, Bluefield	.857	17	2	4	1	0	West, Princeton	1.000	2	0	1	0	0
Sottile, Pulaski	.833	21	3	7	2	1	Wheatcroft, Bluefield	1.000	10	4	8	0	1
Stefani, Bristol	.714	19	1	4	2	1	Wiegandt, Martinsville*	.947	9	2	16	1	1
Strange, Pulaski	.889	27	5	3	1	0	Wiese, Elizabethton*	.958	14	4	19	1	0
A. Taylor, Wytheville	.941	15	8	8	1	0	Wiseman, Johnson City	1.000	12	9	11	0	1
K. Taylor, Elizabethton	.929	9	4	9	1	0	Wohlers, Pulaski	.889	14	2	6	1	0
T. Taylor, Bluefield	1.000	11	1	4	0	0	Woodfin, Burlington*	.905	17	9	10	2	0
Teague, Wytheville*	1.000	7	2	5	0	0	Woods, Princeton*	1.000	17	0	2	0	0

The following players did not have any fielding statistics at the positions indicated or appeared only as a designated hitter, pinch-hitter or pinch-runner: Asp, p; Borders, ph, dh; Brannon, dh; M. Coleman, of; Daniels, p; Delpiano, p; Harris, p; Hutchinson, 3b; Lachmann, dh, ph; I. Martinez, p; Morris, 2b; O'Neal, 2b; Person, of; Reyes, of; Sample, of; Stiegele, p; Sutton, p; Washington, 1b; K. Welch, of; Wells, p; Williams, of.

CLUB PITCHING

Club	ERA.	G.	CG.	ShO.	Sv.	IP.	H.	R.	ER.	HR.	HB.	BB.	Int. BB.	SO.	WP.	Bk.
Elizabethton	3.27	68	19	8	12	572.2	457	251	208	30	31	275	7	564	50	19
Johnson City	3.38	70	6	5	15	572.0	544	277	215	26	16	233	16	453	36	29
Pulaski	3.39	68	3	7	16	576.0	511	287	217	35	22	217	15	518	39	26
Burlington	3.74	68	14	5	14	570.0	565	321	237	42	39	243	7	448	37	17
Martinsville	3.91	67	5	5	13	568.0	587	338	247	57	24	225	9	459	32	30
Bristol	4.13	67	7	4	12	560.2	567	334	257	23	33	253	10	412	60	13
Kingsport	4.14	72	9	2	16	597.2	572	380	275	50	24	310	11	519	50	24
Princeton	4.18	69	9	4	15	575.0	580	364	267	48	28	281	6	505	61	21
Wytheville	5.64	69	4	4	15	589.0	667	454	369	57	39	241	0	472	58	38
Bluefield	5.95	68	1	1	14	570.2	663	478	377	48	32	338	10	458	59	26

PITCHERS' RECORDS
(Leading Qualifiers for Earned-Run Average Leadership—58 or More Innings)

*Throws lefthanded.

Pitcher—Club	W.	L.	Pct.	ERA.	G.	GS.	CG.	GF.	ShO.	Sv.	IP.	H.	R.	ER.	HR.	HB.	BB.	Int. BB.	SO.	WP.
Hailey, Pulaski*	7	3	.700	1.41	12	12	3	0	1	0	70.1	47	14	11	2	2	27	0	73	7
Nedin, Elizabethton*	6	2	.750	1.58	14	7	5	6	1	2	74.0	45	17	13	2	6	33	0	102	8
Shackle, Johnson City	4	5	.444	1.67	15	10	1	2	1	0	59.1	40	15	11	3	0	16	1	60	2
Best, Elizabethton	7	1	.875	2.36	12	9	1	2	0	1	61.0	34	23	16	5	3	31	0	66	5
Wiese, Elizabethton*	10	0	1.000	2.48	14	13	4	1	1	0	98.0	79	31	27	5	1	25	0	101	9
J. Rodriguez, Bristol	4	6	.400	2.49	12	12	4	0	1	0	76.0	55	30	21	1	9	28	0	49	3
Gonzales, Burlington	7	5	.583	2.51	21	1	1	8	0	0	64.2	70	29	18	2	1	23	2	27	3
Butler, Kingsport	5	5	.500	2.51	15	13	6	0	1	0	89.2	77	38	25	7	2	30	1	61	10
Misuraca, Elizabethton	10	3	.769	2.53	13	13	9	0	2	0	103.0	92	34	29	3	5	33	0	89	8
Wiseman, Johnson City	4	3	.571	2.65	12	12	1	0	1	0	74.2	74	34	22	2	2	16	0	52	4

Departmental Leaders: G—Espinal, 32; W—Misuraca, Wiese, 10; L—Dooley, Hurst, Kessler, Pennington, 7; Pct.—Wiese, 1.000; GS—Dooley, Gelb, 15; CG—Misuraca, 9; GF—Jaques, 26; ShO—Misuraca, 2; Sv.—Randall, 13; IP—Misuraca, 103.0; H—A. Taylor, 116; R—A. Taylor, 80; ER—A. Taylor, 65; HR—A. Taylor, 13; HB—Woodfin, 15; BB—Pennington, 74; IBB—R. Martinez, Schafer, 5; SO—Gelb, 110; WP—Pennington, Redmond, 14.

(All Pitchers—Listed Alphabetically)

Pitcher—Club	W.	L.	Pct.	ERA.	G.	GS.	CG.	GF.	ShO.	Sv.	IP.	H.	R.	ER.	HR.	HB.	BB.	Int. BB.	SO.	WP.
Adams, Pulaski	3	0	1.000	4.50	10	1	0	3	0	0	20.0	16	13	10	3	1	6	1	16	0
Alexander, Burlington	1	0	1.000	2.79	3	3	0	0	0	0	9.2	9	4	3	1	1	4	0	7	0
Allen, Burlington*	2	0	1.000	1.55	5	5	0	0	0	0	29.0	28	8	5	1	0	5	0	29	0
Anderson, Bluefield*	0	4	.000	8.66	14	5	0	4	0	0	35.1	60	48	34	5	10	18	3	35	5
Arnold, Pulaski*	2	0	1.000	6.00	10	0	0	3	0	0	12.0	11	12	8	2	1	11	0	9	4
Asp, Elizabethton	0	0	.000	5.40	1	0	0	0	0	0	1.2	4	1	1	0	0	1	0	2	0
Auchard, Kingsport*	0	0	.000	6.75	8	0	0	1	0	0	9.1	10	13	7	1	1	7	0	11	3
A. Baker, Burlington	2	4	.333	4.46	8	8	1	0	1	0	34.1	29	21	17	3	1	18	0	38	10
E. Baker, Johnson City*	3	1	.750	1.57	15	0	0	4	0	0	23.0	22	5	4	2	1	4	1	14	0
Baur, Martinsville	2	1	.667	4.24	19	0	0	5	0	0	40.1	37	24	19	5	3	15	1	33	4
Bautista, Bluefield	0	0	.000	6.75	7	0	0	6	0	0	16.0	22	13	12	3	1	12	0	6	1
Belen, Bluefield	5	3	.625	5.32	28	1	0	22	0	7	45.2	50	37	27	1	0	33	4	23	2
Benson, Elizabethton	2	1	.667	6.23	8	2	0	5	0	1	21.2	27	18	15	3	0	14	0	14	0
Best, Elizabethton	7	1	.875	2.36	12	9	1	2	0	1	61.0	34	23	16	5	3	31	0	66	5
Betances, Bristol	0	0	.000	5.54	4	0	0	1	0	0	13.0	17	11	8	1	1	7	0	8	1
Bigham, Elizabethton*	0	2	.000	3.47	9	2	0	4	0	0	23.1	12	11	9	3	2	17	1	24	4
Botkin, Johnson City*	3	3	.500	4.27	11	11	0	0	0	0	59.0	63	32	28	3	3	26	0	53	3
Bowman, Bristol	1	1	.500	4.05	8	5	0	1	0	0	26.2	29	20	12	3	0	17	0	18	4
Braley, Bristol	1	5	.167	2.05	23	0	0	19	0	6	26.1	23	10	6	1	0	15	2	25	2
Brown, Pulaski	7	3	.700	4.83	13	13	0	0	0	0	69.0	70	48	37	3	6	27	2	40	2
Butler, Kingsport	5	5	.500	2.51	15	13	6	0	1	0	89.2	77	38	25	7	2	30	1	61	10
Calderone, Pulaski	1	0	1.000	0.00	5	0	0	4	0	0	7.2	3	0	0	0	0	0	0	14	0
Carrasco, Kingsport	1	6	.143	5.74	12	10	0	1	0	0	53.1	69	49	34	6	1	34	1	55	4
Carrillo, Martinsville	0	0	.000	1.64	6	0	0	1	0	0	11.0	8	3	2	1	2	4	1	8	1
Checo, Bristol	1	5	.167	4.18	14	1	0	8	0	1	23.2	34	17	11	1	3	17	0	15	0
Cimorelli, Johnson City	2	4	.333	4.57	12	12	1	0	0	0	65.0	78	40	33	4	3	17	1	36	3
Cole, Burlington	3	3	.500	3.09	9	7	4	0	0	0	55.1	52	27	19	4	1	9	0	36	1
Coleman, Bristol	4	2	.667	4.06	14	10	1	2	1	0	68.2	70	39	31	3	6	27	0	31	11
Correa, Wytheville	3	1	.750	5.22	16	2	0	8	0	1	29.1	31	23	17	2	1	16	0	30	5
Corry, Johnson City	0	1	.000	12.46	2	1	0	0	0	0	4.1	11	6	6	1	0	4	0	4	0
Dafforn, Martinsville	1	0	1.000	13.05	16	0	0	7	0	0	20.0	36	31	29	6	1	21	1	22	3

Pitcher—Club	W.	L.	Pct.	ERA.	G.	GS.	CG.	GF.	ShO.	Sv.	IP.	H.	R.	ER.	HR.	HB.	BB.	Int. BB.	SO.	WP.
Daniels, Bristol	0	0	.000	18.00	1	0	0	1	0	0	2.0	4	6	4	0	0	3	0	1	2
DeLaCruz, Burlington	2	0	1.000	0.74	22	0	0	21	0	11	24.1	17	3	2	1	1	14	0	24	1
Delpiano, Burlington	0	0	.000	0.00	1	0	0	1	0	0	1.0	0	0	0	0	0	2	0	0	0
Diaz, Elizabethton	5	3	.625	5.37	12	7	0	1	0	0	55.1	56	41	33	4	5	43	3	46	5
DiBartolomeo, Wytheville	1	0	1.000	0.00	4	0	0	4	0	2	8.0	2	0	0	0	1	0	0	6	0
Dixon, Johnson City*	1	3	.250	6.02	18	3	0	5	0	0	43.1	50	34	29	1	2	23	2	29	4
Dooley, Princeton	2	7	.222	4.60	15	15	2	0	0	0	78.1	94	55	40	7	2	27	0	50	6
Elston, Burlington	0	4	.000	8.53	11	7	0	1	0	0	38.0	41	51	36	9	6	44	0	39	2
Engle, Kingsport	3	4	.429	6.66	13	12	0	1	0	0	52.2	62	55	39	10	3	47	0	50	2
Espinal, Johnson City	2	2	.500	2.13	32	0	0	24	0	12	42.1	31	11	10	1	0	20	2	34	4
Eversgerd, Johnson City*	2	3	.400	3.64	16	1	0	5	0	0	29.2	30	16	12	1	0	12	1	19	2
Fidler, Kingsport*	1	0	1.000	2.31	6	1	0	1	0	1	11.2	5	6	3	0	0	11	0	14	3
Fletcher, Johnson City	9	0	1.000	2.60	22	0	0	12	0	2	27.2	24	10	8	3	0	13	3	34	1
Fowler, Wytheville	4	2	.667	5.28	12	5	0	2	0	0	46.0	52	29	27	6	3	15	0	30	3
Freeman, Elizabethton	0	0	.000	4.70	5	1	0	2	0	0	15.1	15	8	8	0	2	11	0	14	1
Garcia, Bristol	0	3	.000	4.60	8	0	0	3	0	0	15.2	17	9	8	0	0	4	1	13	1
Gelb, Wytheville	9	4	.692	3.42	15	15	1	0	1	0	102.2	87	46	39	7	7	25	0	110	3
Gillespie, Wytheville*	0	2	.000	13.14	16	1	0	5	0	0	24.2	43	41	36	5	2	23	0	19	8
Giordano, Princeton*	3	2	.600	4.11	9	5	0	4	0	0	35.0	33	22	16	0	1	26	0	18	7
Goedhart, Martinsville	5	5	.500	3.00	15	12	0	1	0	0	72.0	67	43	24	7	4	31	0	50	4
Gonzales, Burlington	7	5	.583	2.51	21	1	1	8	0	0	64.2	70	29	18	2	1	23	2	27	3
Gray, Martinsville	1	3	.250	4.20	22	5	1	6	1	0	49.1	54	25	23	4	0	24	1	34	3
Guzman, Bristol	2	5	.286	4.29	12	12	1	0	0	0	65.0	67	41	31	3	3	40	0	47	8
Hailey, Pulaski*	7	3	.700	1.41	12	12	3	0	1	0	70.1	47	14	11	2	2	27	0	73	7
Halama, Johnson City	1	1	.500	2.70	6	0	0	5	0	1	6.2	6	4	2	0	1	4	3	6	0
Hamilton, Princeton	0	2	.000	2.77	21	1	0	9	0	0	52.0	53	30	16	6	2	20	0	44	4
Harrington, Elizabethton*	1	4	.200	9.72	9	3	0	4	0	0	25.0	24	30	27	2	3	29	1	22	5
Harris, Kingsport	0	0	.000	0.00	1	0	0	1	0	0	2.0	3	2	0	0	0	1	0	2	0
Heiden, Bluefield	2	2	.500	8.73	9	6	0	0	0	0	33.0	35	32	32	4	3	30	0	31	8
Hill, Wytheville	1	4	.200	8.17	16	5	0	6	0	0	50.2	65	50	46	4	4	25	0	36	9
Hollins, Wytheville	3	1	.750	4.84	22	3	0	6	0	0	48.1	59	44	26	4	6	23	0	31	12
Hurst, Martinsville	5	7	.417	3.66	15	14	3	0	0	0	83.2	99	49	34	8	2	16	0	68	4
Jaques, Wytheville*	2	3	.400	1.25	28	0	0	26	0	11	36.0	27	6	5	1	1	7	0	47	3
Jewett, Pulaski	2	1	.667	3.53	14	7	0	1	0	0	43.1	44	20	17	3	1	9	0	37	3
Johnson, Elizabethton	1	3	.250	2.05	13	0	0	12	0	3	22.0	15	7	5	0	1	9	2	14	1
Johnston, Kingsport*	1	1	.500	2.89	15	1	0	8	0	1	18.2	18	8	6	2	1	11	1	21	1
Kessler, Wytheville	3	7	.300	6.00	13	11	2	2	0	0	66.0	80	56	44	4	6	17	0	35	4
Lehnerz, Kingsport	2	1	.667	5.09	7	7	0	0	0	0	35.1	30	26	20	3	3	20	0	23	4
Lipson, Elizabethton	1	0	1.000	5.02	10	0	0	9	0	3	14.1	8	8	8	1	0	8	0	14	2
Lovdal, Martinsville	2	3	.400	5.57	22	0	0	9	0	0	32.1	32	28	20	5	2	22	3	14	3
Mack, Wytheville	0	5	.000	8.83	11	6	1	2	0	0	34.2	43	38	34	3	1	31	0	20	4
Maietta, Bristol	2	1	.667	3.71	9	3	0	1	0	0	26.2	25	12	11	3	2	15	1	32	4
Marett, Bluefield	2	3	.400	4.82	11	7	0	1	0	0	52.1	-58	33	28	5	3	28	1	35	1
Martin, Bluefield*	3	3	.500	4.62	8	8	0	0	0	0	39.0	36	28	20	3	0	25	0	31	2
I. Martinez, Bristol	0	0	.000	9.00	6	0	0	2	0	0	9.0	16	10	9	0	0	4	0	5	1
R. Martinez, Princeton	4	3	.571	4.71	25	0	0	23	0	8	28.2	34	17	15	5	1	11	5	20	2
Matchett, Bristol	1	0	1.000	2.89	7	2	0	2	0	0	18.2	17	9	6	1	1	7	0	17	4
McKnight, Martinsville*	2	2	.500	2.28	7	3	0	2	0	0	23.2	19	7	6	2	1	10	0	20	0
L. Medina, Kingsport	3	1	.750	3.81	5	4	1	0	0	0	26.0	26	14	11	3	1	8	0	19	3
V. Medina, Bluefield	2	2	.500	5.88	21	0	0	6	0	1	49.0	59	38	32	7	2	28	0	34	2
Misuraca, Elizabethton	10	3	.769	2.53	13	13	9	0	2	0	103.0	92	34	29	3	5	33	0	89	8
Mooney, Princeton	3	1	.750	4.30	10	5	0	0	0	0	37.2	36	26	18	5	1	23	0	20	5
Moore, Bluefield*	3	6	.333	5.28	12	9	1	2	1	1	58.0	76	46	34	4	3	12	0	45	2
Neagle, Elizabethton*	1	2	.333	4.50	6	3	0	3	0	1	22.0	20	11	11	1	1	8	0	32	1
Nedin, Elizabethton*	6	2	.750	1.58	14	7	5	6	1	2	74.0	45	17	13	2	6	33	0	102	8
Neidlinger, Bristol	1	3	.250	7.88	14	5	0	5	0	0	37.2	55	38	33	2	2	12	0	22	5
Neill, Burlington	1	1	.500	4.50	2	1	0	0	0	0	6.0	6	4	3	0	0	0	0	5	1
Ortiz, Johnson City	0	0	.000	10.24	7	0	0	1	0	0	9.2	12	13	11	1	1	6	1	11	1
Oswalt, Johnson City*	1	0	1.000	2.30	3	3	1	0	0	0	15.2	11	5	4	0	1	7	0	7	1
Pacheco, Johnson City	3	3	.500	3.57	13	13	0	0	0	0	70.2	65	37	28	5	2	38	0	57	7
Parker, Pulaski	3	2	.600	3.68	16	8	0	2	0	0	58.2	56	33	24	5	1	24	2	47	3
Parkinson, Princeton	1	4	.200	4.35	14	8	1	2	0	1	60.0	67	39	29	6	2	33	1	59	3
Patterson, Martinsville	2	4	.333	3.61	7	7	0	0	0	0	42.1	35	23	17	3	2	12	0	44	3
Pennington, Bluefield*	2	7	.222	6.58	15	14	0	0	0	0	64.1	50	58	47	2	6	74	0	81	14
L. Perez, Wytheville	2	0	1.000	5.18	13	3	0	4	0	1	33.0	32	20	19	5	2	20	0	34	1
R. Perez, Princeton	3	0	1.000	2.49	7	2	1	2	1	0	25.1	21	11	7	1	0	9	0	29	4
Person, Burlington	0	1	.000	3.18	10	5	0	3	0	1	34.0	23	13	12	1	5	17	0	19	5
Pettiford, Burlington	4	2	.667	3.59	11	10	1	0	0	0	67.2	61	35	27	6	6	26	0	71	5
Polanco, Kingsport	3	3	.500	4.55	21	2	1	6	0	1	55.1	59	36	28	5	3	15	2	30	1
Randall, Martinsville	2	2	.500	2.51	27	0	0	23	0	13	32.1	37	14	9	2	1	7	2	21	3
Redmond, Princeton	0	2	.000	6.84	12	1	0	2	0	0	26.1	19	30	20	1	4	37	0	29	14
Ritter, Pulaski	6	5	.545	3.62	14	13	0	0	0	0	64.2	58	37	26	2	5	21	1	55	3
Rivera, Burlington*	3	4	.429	3.51	18	2	1	8	0	2	51.1	44	24	20	4	1	16	3	42	0
E. Rodriguez, Bristol*	1	2	.333	3.07	24	0	0	11	0	2	29.1	24	14	10	0	1	7	0	35	2
J. Rodriguez, Bristol	4	6	.400	2.49	12	12	4	0	1	0	76.0	55	30	21	1	9	28	0	49	3
Ross, Martinsville*	3	2	.600	3.55	18	5	0	5	0	0	45.2	34	24	18	4	1	29	0	52	2
Rountree, Bristol	3	5	.375	4.82	12	12	1	0	0	0	65.1	65	38	35	2	2	30	3	54	8
Roy, Pulaski	2	1	.667	2.12	14	2	0	3	0	0	29.2	26	9	7	1	0	6	0	23	4
Sample, Kingsport	3	6	.333	2.78	29	1	0	24	0	10	35.2	23	16	11	2	1	24	1	42	3
Santiago, Princeton	6	6	.500	3.67	14	14	2	0	0	0	90.2	84	47	37	9	6	31	0	81	2
Schafer, Pulaski	3	5	.375	2.30	25	0	0	12	0	5	43.0	31	17	11	3	1	25	5	43	2
Scheffler, Kingsport	3	4	.429	4.18	18	5	0	7	0	1	51.2	51	32	24	3	2	30	2	50	2
Scott, Kingsport	2	2	.500	4.14	22	1	0	8	0	2	54.1	39	29	25	4	5	31	3	53	6
Seibert, Bristol	2	1	.667	2.66	9	4	0	4	0	1	20.1	11	7	6	1	1	9	0	18	1
Shackle, Johnson City	4	5	.444	1.67	15	10	1	2	1	0	59.1	40	15	11	3	0	16	1	60	2
Shive, Martinsville	2	4	.333	4.24	12	12	1	0	0	0	63.2	77	40	30	5	4	17	0	43	1
Sieradzki, Bluefield	1	3	.250	5.30	17	1	0	10	0	2	37.1	43	27	22	1	0	14	1	27	6
Sottile, Pulaski	1	3	.250	2.57	21	4	0	8	0	0	49.0	43	24	14	3	2	20	1	46	4
Stefani, Bristol	5	0	1.000	3.68	19	0	0	3	0	2	36.2	38	23	15	1	2	18	1	29	3
Stiegele, Bluefield	0	0	.000	9.00	1	0	0	0	0	0	2.0	4	2	2	0	1	0	1	1	1
Strange, Pulaski	3	0	1.000	2.45	27	0	0	20	0	5	33.0	27	9	9	1	0	6	2	39	4
Sutton, Bluefield	0	0	.000	31.50	3	0	0	2	0	0	2.0	0	7	7	0	0	11	0	4	8

Pitcher—Club	W.	L.	Pct.	ERA.	G.	GS.	CG.	GF.	ShO.	Sv.	IP.	H.	R.	ER.	HR.	HB.	BB.	Int. BB.	SO.	WP.
A. Taylor, Wytheville	5	6	.455	7.37	15	13	0	0	0	0	79.1	116	80	65	13	6	27	0	47	5
K. Taylor, Elizabethton	3	0	1.000	1.50	9	8	0	0	0	0	36.0	26	11	6	1	2	22	0	24	1
T. Taylor, Bluefield	1	3	.250	6.48	11	10	0	0	0	0	41.2	56	42	30	4	0	29	1	36	1
Teague, Wytheville*	1	0	1.000	3.26	7	5	0	0	0	0	30.1	30	21	11	3	0	11	0	27	1
Teixeira, Bluefield	2	2	.500	4.14	19	0	0	10	0	2	45.2	58	32	21	3	2	12	0	33	1
Thomas, Kingsport*	1	2	.333	6.52	6	3	0	3	0	0	19.1	13	16	14	1	1	17	0	17	1
Thompson, Pulaski*	1	2	.333	5.04	21	0	0	6	0	1	25.0	30	14	14	1	0	9	1	23	1
Throckmorton, Pulaski	0	0	.000	1.93	2	0	0	1	0	1	4.2	1	1	1	0	0	0	0	3	0
Tillman, Burlington*	2	5	.286	4.06	10	9	4	1	1	0	51.0	61	30	23	4	1	11	0	40	0
Valdez, Princeton*	5	2	.714	2.71	12	12	3	0	1	0	73.0	56	30	22	3	2	32	0	83	4
Vazquez, Kingsport	7	2	.778	3.05	17	12	1	2	0	0	82.2	87	40	28	3	0	24	0	71	7
Ventura, Burlington	3	5	.375	3.63	18	4	2	6	0	0	52.0	70	32	21	1	0	19	2	23	4
Watson, Princeton*	2	6	.250	6.35	14	6	0	5	0	0	39.2	51	37	28	4	4	19	0	40	7
Weber, Johnson City*	3	3	.500	1.54	15	4	2	6	0	0	41.0	27	15	7	1	0	31	1	37	4
Wells, Martinsville	0	0	.000	4.50	4	0	0	2	0	0	6.0	8	5	3	1	0	2	0	3	1
West, Princeton	0	0	.000	21.00	2	0	0	1	0	0	3.0	8	8	7	0	1	4	0	0	1
Wheatcroft, Bluefield	4	3	.571	5.29	10	7	0	3	0	1	49.1	56	35	29	6	1	11	0	36	5
Wiegandt, Martinsville*	2	5	.286	2.56	9	9	0	0	0	0	45.2	44	22	13	4	1	15	0	47	0
Wiese, Elizabethton*	10	0	1.000	2.48	14	13	4	1	1	0	98.0	79	31	27	5	1	25	0	101	9
Wiseman, Johnson City	4	3	.571	2.65	12	12	1	0	1	0	74.2	74	34	22	2	2	16	0	52	4
Wohlers, Pulaski	1	1	.500	5.48	14	8	0	2	0	0	46.0	48	36	28	5	2	28	0	50	2
Woodfin, Burlington*	1	3	.250	5.40	17	6	0	5	0	0	51.2	54	40	31	5	15	35	0	48	5
Woods, Princeton*	3	2	.600	4.26	17	0	0	12	0	1	25.1	24	12	12	1	2	9	0	32	2

BALKS—Pacheco, 12; Scheffler, 9; Goedhart, Pennington, 8 each; Hollins, 7; Dooley, Misuraca, Ross, Wheatcroft, 6 each; Brown, Carrasco, Kessler, Mack, V. Medina, Parkinson, Ritter, A. Taylor, Vazquez, 5 each; Correa, Elston, Patterson, 4 each; Bautista, Best, Cimorelli, Espinal, Hill, Jaques, R. Perez, J. Rodriguez, Watson, Wiseman, 3 each; Baur, Calderone, Checo, Dixon, Engle, Gillespie, Guzman, Hurst, Jewitt, Mooney, Nedin, Parker, L. Perez, Pettiford, Rivera, Schafer, Seibert, Shive, Sottile, Thompson, Tillman, Ventura, Weber, Wiese, 2 each; Adams, Alexander, Allen, Anderson, Auchard, Benson, Botkin, Bowman, Braley, Carrillo, Corry, Dafforn, DeLaCruz, Delpiano, Diaz, DiBartolomeo, Fletcher, Garcia, Gelb, Gonzales, Gray, Hailey, Hamilton, Harrington, Johnson, Johnston, Lipson, Lovdal, Martin, I. Martinez, Neagle, Polanco, Randall, Roy, Shackle, Sieradzki, Strange, Teixeira, Valdez, Wells, 1 each.

COMBINATION SHUTOUTS—J. Rodriguez-E. Rodriguez, Guzman-Stefani-E. Rodriguez, Bristol; Baker-Neill-Rivera, Allen-Rivera-DeLa-Cruz, Allen-Elston, Burlington; Misuraca-Harrington, Diaz-Neagle, Neagle-Harrington, Taylor-Lipson, Elizabethton; Weber-Espinal 2, Pacheco-Baker-Espinal, Johnson City; Carrasco-Sample, Kingsport; Patterson-Randall, Hurst-Randall, Patterson-Ross-Randall, Ross-Gray-Goedhart-Randall, Martinsville; Giordano-Woods, Parkinson-Martinez, Princeton; Hailey-Schafer 2, Brown-Thompson-Schafer, Wohlers-Jewett-Roy-Sottile, Parker-Roy, Ritter-Adams, Pulaski; Gelb-Jaques 2, Kessler-Fowler-Taylor-Hill, Wytheville.

NO-HIT GAMES—None.

Arizona League

SUMMER CLASS A CLASSIFICATION

CHAMPIONSHIP WINNERS IN PREVIOUS YEARS

1988—Peoria Brewers...................... .690

STANDING OF CLUBS AT CLOSE OF SEASON, AUGUST 31

Club	Brew.	Ath.	Mar.	Pad.	Car.	Ang.	W.	L.	T.	Pct.	G.B.
Brewers	....	8	7	9	7	10	41	15	0	.732	....
Athletics	4	....	6	6	7	6	29	27	0	.518	12
Mariners	4	6	....	6	5	7	28	28	0	.500	13
Padres	2	4	5	....	8	6	25	31	0	.446	16
Cardinals	3	4	7	4	....	6	24	31	0	.436	16½
Angels	2	5	3	6	4	....	20	35	0	.364	20½

Games played in Mesa, Peoria, Scottsdale and Tempe.

Club names are major league affiliations.

Playoffs—None.

Regular-Season Attendance—No total official attendance figures reported.

Managers—Angels, Nate Oliver; Athletics, Casey Parsons; Brewers, Jeff Nate; Cardinals, Luis Melendez; Mariners, Dave Myers; Padres, Lonnie Keeter.

All-Star Team—1B—Leon Glenn, Brewers; 2B—Henry Reynoso, Brewers; 3B—Luis Lanfranco, Athletics; SS—Justin McCray, Brewers; OF—Sean Twitty, Mariners; Kelvin Thomas, Mariners; Brian Stephens, Mariners; Francisco Garcia, Cardinals; C—Troy Clemons, Cardinals; DH—Scott Henry, Athletics; LHP—Jeff Kinder, Brewers; Russell Garside, Padres; RHP—Rob Callistro, Mariners; LHRP—Manuel Furcal, Mariners; RHRP—Reggie Leslie, Brewers; Most Valuable Player—Leon Glenn, Brewers; Managers of the Year—Casey Parsons, Athletics; Dave Myers, Mariners.

(Compiled by Howe Sportsdata International, Boston, Mass.)

CLUB BATTING

Club	Pct.	G.	AB.	R.	OR.	H.	TB.	2B.	3B.	HR.	RBI.	SH.	SF.	HP.	BB.	Int. BB.	SO.	SB.	CS.	LOB.
Brewers	.296	56	1968	398	234	583	784	83	26	22	297	7	32	28	236	9	387	122	56	404
Athletics	.276	56	2023	383	288	558	751	79	30	18	311	7	30	19	282	7	417	75	20	479
Angels	.266	56	1887	275	363	501	618	58	22	5	230	10	19	26	165	8	390	116	48	362
Mariners	.250	56	1927	271	307	482	685	83	33	18	226	5	22	25	155	6	454	59	32	369
Cardinals	.246	55	1898	292	353	466	580	65	14	7	228	3	18	22	197	6	389	97	36	364
Padres	.215	56	1880	232	306	405	496	50	13	5	166	2	14	23	181	4	427	102	29	380

INDIVIDUAL BATTING

(Leading Qualifiers for Batting Championship—162 or More Plate Appearances)

*Bats lefthanded.   †Switch-hitter.

Player and Club	Pct.	G.	AB.	R.	H.	TB.	2B.	3B.	HR.	RBI.	SH.	SF.	HP.	BB.	Int. BB.	SO.	SB.	CS.
Glenn, Leon, Brewers*	.382	51	212	42	81	126	10	7	7	50	0	2	2	14	5	46	21	9
Arredondo, Roberto, Padres*	.338	52	195	33	66	86	11	3	1	30	0	1	3	18	1	31	10	4
Reynoso, Henry, Brewers†	.333	38	165	40	55	61	4	1	0	19	1	4	2	12	0	17	24	7
Garcia, Francisco, Cardinals	.322	50	171	21	55	62	5	1	0	23	0	2	2	9	2	21	14	4
Hendley, Brett, Athletics*	.311	56	206	55	64	96	9	4	5	43	0	1	0	56	1	62	11	1
Pueschner, Craig, Padres	.308	46	172	22	53	66	6	2	1	22	1	2	5	16	0	35	6	2
Ledinsky, Raymond, Angels	.304	45	161	28	49	60	7	2	0	25	0	4	5	22	1	29	9	5
Powell, Gordon, Brewers	.304	49	171	30	52	72	11	3	1	23	0	2	2	7	0	33	6	3
Delpozo, Roberto, Mariners	.298	51	188	22	56	78	10	3	2	27	1	0	2	15	1	32	8	3
McCray, Justin, Brewers	.296	52	159	33	47	65	11	2	1	23	1	2	4	29	0	36	9	6

Departmental Leaders: G—Hendley, 56; AB—Glenn, 212; R—Hendley, 55; H—Glenn, 81; TB—Glenn, 126; 2B—Amparo, Tahan, 14; 3B—K. Thomas, 9; HR—Glenn, 7; RBI—Glenn, 50; SH—Munoz, Tamarez, Wallace, 2; SF—Tahan, 6; HP—Williams, 8; BB—Hendley, 56; IBB—Glenn, 5; SO—Hendley, 62; SB—P. Martinez, 29; CS—Glenn, 9.

(All Players—Listed Alphabetically)

Player and Club	Pct.	G.	AB.	R.	H.	TB.	2B.	3B.	HR.	RBI.	SH.	SF.	HP.	BB.	Int. BB.	SO.	SB.	CS.
Abbott, Kurt, Athletics	.271	36	155	27	42	53	5	3	0	25	0	4	2	8	2	40	0	1
Amparo, Nestor, Mariners*	.260	49	173	23	45	64	14	1	1	17	1	3	0	15	1	50	3	1
Arredondo, Roberto, Padres*	.338	52	195	33	66	86	11	3	1	30	0	1	3	18	1	31	10	4
Ayala, Adan, Padres†	.208	49	144	18	30	39	7	1	0	17	0	3	0	9	1	28	7	0
Beck, Brian, Padres*	.214	52	201	24	43	57	4	2	2	23	0	2	1	14	0	56	9	0
Beck, Wynn, Athletics*	.370	9	27	8	10	19	2	2	1	7	0	1	1	6	0	3	0	0
Bierwiler, Richard, Padres	.208	40	120	11	25	26	1	0	0	9	0	2	3	9	0	24	4	0
Borse, Paul, Angels	.244	43	160	22	39	51	8	2	0	18	1	2	4	13	1	38	19	4
Boudreau, Thomas, Mariners	.220	13	41	4	9	12	3	0	0	9	0	1	1	6	0	12	0	0
Bream, Scott, Padres	.175	28	97	15	17	22	3	1	0	8	0	0	1	18	0	22	9	5
Brito, Francisco, Angels	.300	15	50	5	15	16	1	0	0	4	1	0	0	2	0	5	3	3
Burrola, Michael, Brewers	.333	3	12	1	4	4	0	0	0	4	0	0	0	0	0	4	0	0
Campa, Eric, Athletics	.290	11	31	4	9	9	0	0	0	6	0	0	1	5	0	4	4	0
Candelario, Francisco, Mariners	.260	23	73	7	19	29	5	1	1	9	0	0	1	2	0	22	2	0
Carrasquillo, Angel, Angels*	.248	38	125	14	31	37	4	1	0	24	1	0	0	12	2	26	5	3
Clemens, Troy, Cardinals*	.267	47	146	18	39	52	6	2	1	26	0	2	1	12	0	19	4	2
Curtis, Chad, Angels	.303	32	122	30	37	58	4	4	3	20	1	2	2	14	2	20	17	2
Davis, Danny, Cardinals†	.400	2	5	0	2	2	0	0	0	0	0	0	0	1	0	1	0	1
Davis, Jerry, Cardinals	.125	25	40	5	5	6	1	0	0	4	0	0	1	7	0	18	1	1
Delpozo, Roberto, Mariners	.298	51	188	22	56	78	10	3	2	27	1	0	2	15	1	32	8	3

Player and Club	Pct.	G.	AB.	R.	H.	TB.	2B.	3B.	HR.	RBI.	SH.	SF.	HP.	BB.	Int. BB.	SO.	SB.	CS.
Dempsey, John, Cardinals*	.186	22	59	7	11	13	0	1	0	9	0	1	0	9	0	10	2	1
Donald, Tremayne, Cardinals	.281	34	96	19	27	34	3	2	0	4	0	0	12	0	23	6	3
Duran, Ignacio, Cardinals	.235	48	153	13	36	44	4	2	0	21	0	0	2	6	0	40	0	2
Ealy, Tracey, Cardinals	.242	47	157	37	38	40	2	0	0	16	1	1	5	18	0	33	17	6
Eldridge, Rodney, Angels	.262	12	42	8	11	15	1	0	1	7	0	1	0	4	0	6	2	0
Ellsworth, Ben, Cardinals	.206	43	160	20	33	41	5	0	1	15	1	0	1	16	0	17	6	3
Figueroa, Tito, Athletics	.333	4	6	1	2	2	0	0	0	1	0	0	0	1	0	1	1	0
Foster, Bryan, Brewers†	.000	2	3	2	0	0	0	0	0	0	0	0	0	1	0	1	1	0
French, Deron, Cardinals	.190	35	105	15	20	22	2	0	0	7	0	0	1	7	0	27	8	1
Garcia, Francisco, Cardinals	.322	50	171	21	55	62	5	1	0	23	0	2	9	2	21	14	4
Garrett, Clifton, Angels*	.320	34	75	17	24	28	2	1	0	7	0	0	2	15	0	12	7	4
Gil, Jose, Angels*	.265	31	68	9	18	20	2	0	0	5	1	0	2	8	0	18	6	3
Glenn, Leon, Brewers*	.382	51	212	42	81	126	10	7	7	50	0	2	14	5	46	21	9
Guerrero, Michael, Brewers†	.277	11	47	10	13	21	3	1	1	11	1	2	1	6	0	5	3	2
Harris, Eric, Padres	.157	41	115	13	18	18	0	0	0	3	1	1	1	6	0	41	12	1
Harris, Kenneth, Brewers	.298	31	84	12	25	29	4	0	0	14	0	0	1	10	0	20	2	3
Hayes, Mark, Cardinals	.308	9	26	6	8	11	3	0	0	4	0	0	3	0	5	1	1
Hays, Kevin, Cardinals	.188	27	48	9	9	9	0	0	0	2	0	0	4	12	0	10	0	1
Henderson, Lee, Padres	.210	35	105	13	22	25	3	0	0	7	0	0	2	19	1	20	3	3
Hendley, Brett, Athletics*	.311	56	206	55	64	96	9	4	5	43	0	1	0	56	1	62	11	1
Henry, Scott, Athletics*	.279	49	172	34	48	67	5	4	2	37	0	3	4	32	0	36	3	1
Heredia, Eddy, Brewers†	.279	29	43	12	12	12	0	0	0	7	0	0	1	7	0	11	0	3
Jackson, Lorenzo, Angels†	.143	5	21	4	3	5	0	1	0	2	0	0	1	0	9	1	0
Jefferson, Ronald, Brewers	.000	15	2	0	0	0	0	0	0	0	0	0	0	0	0	0	0	0
Johnson, Michael, Brewers	.146	22	48	8	7	8	1	0	0	4	0	0	2	4	0	17	1	0
Jordan, Timmy, Cardinals*	.211	36	109	11	23	26	3	0	0	7	0	1	0	8	0	22	6	2
Jorge, Genaro, Angels*	.176	8	17	1	3	3	0	0	0	1	0	0	1	0	9	0	0
Joyce, James, Padres	.225	30	80	11	18	20	2	0	0	3	0	1	1	12	0	16	2	3
Kidwiler, Jeffrey, Mariners	.171	37	123	14	21	23	2	0	0	15	0	4	4	7	0	24	1	3
Kluge, Matthew, Mariners	.239	15	46	4	11	12	1	0	0	1	0	0	1	2	0	8	0	0
Krokroskia, Sean, Athletics	.269	49	197	54	53	76	11	3	2	21	0	2	3	28	0	38	7	2
Landinez, Carlos, Cardinals	.253	47	146	25	37	45	3	1	1	16	0	0	2	19	1	41	10	0
Lanfranco, Luis, Athletics	.282	49	195	30	55	80	12	5	1	38	0	0	1	20	1	32	4	5
Lasher, Matthew, Angels	.387	10	31	3	12	13	1	0	0	6	0	0	1	3	0	1	1	2
LeBlanc, Winston, Mariners	.177	18	62	4	11	13	0	1	0	7	0	1	0	4	0	19	1	0
Ledinsky, Raymond, Angels	.304	45	161	28	49	60	7	2	0	25	0	4	5	22	1	29	9	5
Leslie, Reginald, Brewers	.000	22	1	0	0	0	0	0	0	0	0	0	0	0	0	0	0	0
Lewis, Anthony, Cardinals	.246	51	187	32	46	62	10	0	2	27	0	4	0	11	1	45	11	3
Lewis, Ronald, Angels†	.250	8	24	3	6	7	1	0	0	4	0	1	0	3	0	7	7	0
Lofthus, Kevin, Athletics	.290	8	31	8	9	15	3	0	1	5	0	1	0	4	1	6	1	0
Love, Sylvester, Brewers*	.390	15	59	18	23	27	2	1	0	7	1	0	0	8	0	6	11	1
Lyons, Mario, Athletics	.285	42	137	32	39	52	5	4	0	11	1	0	1	24	1	26	15	3
Magarity, Jeremy, Cardinals	.000	15	0	1	0	0	0	0	0	0	0	0	0	1	0	0	0	0
Mangual, Victor, Brewers	1.000	24	1	1	1	1	0	0	0	0	0	0	0	0	0	0	0	0
Marimon, Zenith, Athletics*	.222	23	45	5	10	10	0	0	0	3	0	0	1	9	1	8	0	1
Marrero, Oreste, Brewers*	.409	10	44	13	18	29	0	1	3	16	0	1	0	2	0	5	2	2
Martinez, Angel, Athletics	.258	16	66	12	17	22	2	0	1	8	0	1	1	7	0	13	4	1
Martinez, Luis, Athletics	.170	13	47	9	8	9	1	0	0	5	0	0	3	0	5	1	0
Martinez, Pablo, Padres†	.236	45	178	31	42	47	3	1	0	12	0	0	2	22	1	25	29	4
McCray, Justin, Brewers	.296	52	159	33	47	65	11	2	1	23	1	2	4	29	0	36	9	6
McCreadie, Brant, Brewers	.177	32	79	7	14	18	2	1	0	5	0	1	0	6	0	23	1	1
McNair, Fredrick, Mariners	.282	36	142	24	40	62	6	2	4	18	0	2	2	7	0	38	4	2
Mejia, Rodolfo, Angels	.000	4	2	0	0	0	0	0	0	0	0	0	0	0	0	2	0	0
Merrill, Lawrence, Cardinals*	.247	34	81	9	20	22	2	0	0	2	1	0	1	7	0	22	1	0
Moscat, Rafael, Athletics	.211	27	76	7	16	19	1	1	0	4	1	1	2	3	0	11	5	1
Muhammad, Robert, Brewers	.274	37	124	21	34	54	9	1	3	21	1	4	0	15	0	18	5	2
Munoz, Orlando, Angels†	.222	39	135	18	30	38	4	2	0	18	2	1	1	10	0	21	5	5
Mussett, Jose, Angels	.267	27	86	16	23	30	3	2	0	9	0	0	1	4	1	22	4	7
Parks, Bryan, Brewers	.306	36	98	16	30	36	4	1	0	9	0	2	2	15	0	21	5	2
Peacock, Richard, Padres	.100	25	70	7	7	11	1	0	1	5	0	0	3	0	27	2	1
Pedro, Derrick, Brewers	.354	29	79	12	28	34	2	2	0	9	0	1	0	5	1	5	1	2
Perez, Tirson, Padres	.133	29	60	5	8	9	1	0	0	2	0	0	0	5	0	19	0	0
Peterson, Andrew, Angels	.153	21	59	6	9	10	1	0	0	4	0	0	0	4	0	14	0	1
Powell, Gordon, Brewers	.304	49	171	30	52	72	11	3	1	23	0	2	2	7	0	33	6	3
Pueschner, Craig, Padres	.308	46	172	22	53	66	6	2	1	22	1	2	5	16	0	35	6	2
Raasch, Glen, Mariners	.223	45	157	19	35	55	8	3	2	22	0	2	3	18	0	42	1	3
Raven, Luis, Angels	.207	43	145	15	30	43	6	2	1	20	0	3	1	8	0	43	3	0
Reynoso, Henry, Brewers†	.333	38	165	40	55	61	4	1	0	19	1	4	2	12	0	17	24	7
Robertson, William, Brewers	.259	53	201	40	52	82	9	3	5	32	0	5	7	26	0	47	7	5
Romero, Jose, Padres	.210	47	167	12	35	45	4	3	0	15	0	0	3	0	36	4	6
Sammons, Lee, Athletics	.255	36	106	26	27	28	1	0	0	15	0	4	0	29	0	25	10	1
Sanchez, Joaquin, Athletics	.182	6	11	0	2	4	0	1	0	4	0	0	0	1	0	5	0	0
Santana, Jose, Athletics*	.286	42	140	24	40	40	0	0	0	16	1	2	1	12	0	23	14	2
Santarini, John, Mariners*	.253	27	91	18	23	28	5	0	0	5	1	1	0	3	1	3	5	0
Sarbaugh, Michael, Brewers	.357	4	14	3	5	5	0	0	0	3	0	1	1	3	0	2	0	0
Sass, James, Brewers	.326	12	43	12	14	19	2	0	1	14	0	1	1	8	0	8	6	0
Savinon, Odalis, Cardinals	.333	4	12	2	4	6	2	0	0	1	0	1	0	1	0	1	0	1
Scott, Robert, Brewers	.000	6	1	0	0	0	0	0	0	0	0	0	0	0	0	1	0	0
Seda, Israel, Mariners†	.099	24	71	3	7	8	1	0	0	6	0	1	0	4	0	23	2	3
Shannon, Samuel, Padres	.130	51	146	16	19	23	4	0	0	9	0	2	4	20	0	38	4	0
Sierra, Domingo, Angels	.338	37	130	13	44	48	2	1	0	16	0	2	2	6	1	15	7	3
Snyder, Randall, Brewers†	.283	19	60	14	17	21	2	1	0	8	1	1	0	11	2	14	5	2
Staydohar, David, Angels	.208	21	72	6	15	21	2	2	0	2	0	0	3	0	21	2	0
Stela, Jose, Angels	.299	31	77	12	23	27	4	0	0	9	1	1	3	0	7	2	1
Stephens, Brian, Mariners*	.273	35	132	22	36	60	9	3	3	24	0	1	1	13	1	26	2	1
Street, Bryan, Angels	.219	19	32	4	7	9	2	0	0	4	0	0	0	8	0	14	1	0
Taft, Timothy, Angels	.361	32	72	12	26	31	3	1	0	7	1	0	0	8	0	6	1	3
Tahan, Kevin, Cardinals	.294	50	170	39	50	80	14	5	2	42	0	6	1	35	2	20	10	4
Tallent, Ronald, Angels	.146	19	41	5	6	8	0	1	0	2	0	0	2	0	22	0	0
Tamarez, Carlos, Athletics	.233	37	129	17	30	35	3	1	0	9	2	4	0	13	0	37	1	1
Terrell, James, Mariners	.247	42	146	19	36	50	7	2	1	13	0	3	0	10	0	35	1	1
Thomas, Delvin, Mariners	.284	20	88	14	25	41	4	3	2	14	0	1	0	2	0	6	4	4

Player and Club	Pct.	G.	AB.	R.	H.	TB.	2B.	3B.	HR.	RBI.	SH.	SF.	HP.	BB.	Int. BB.	SO.	SB.	CS.
Thomas, Kelvin, Mariners*	.296	21	71	20	21	47	2	9	2	17	0	2	1	10	1	27	4	1
Tredway, Edward, Athletics*	.292	48	168	18	49	61	7	1	1	29	1	4	1	4	0	24	4	0
Turvey, Joseph, Cardinals*	.111	17	27	3	3	3	0	0	0	2	0	1	3	0	0	14	0	0
Twitty, Douglas, Athletics	.374	33	139	27	52	74	10	0	4	35	0	2	0	17	0	21	0	1
Twitty, Sean, Mariners	.250	46	160	22	40	52	4	4	0	10	0	0	1	9	0	48	9	3
Verstraete, John, Padres	.067	14	30	1	2	2	0	0	0	1	0	0	0	7	0	9	1	0
Villaman, Alberto, Brewers†	.164	22	55	6	9	9	0	0	0	4	0	0	0	3	0	19	0	0
Walker, Jimmy, Brewers	.308	18	52	12	16	22	4	1	0	9	0	1	1	2	0	9	0	1
Wallace, William, Athletics†	.203	34	79	9	16	20	2	1	0	8	2	1	0	12	0	20	4	1
Weldin, David, Brewers*	.236	39	110	33	26	29	3	0	0	9	1	2	1	42	1	18	12	5
Williams, Landon, Mariners	.288	49	163	32	47	51	2	1	0	12	2	0	8	23	1	39	12	7
Zimbauer, Jason, Brewers	.000	13	1	0	0	0	0	0	0	0	0	0	0	0	0	1	0	0

The following pitchers, listed alphabetically by club, with games in parentheses, had no plate appearances, primarily through use of designated hitters:

ANGELS—Canney, Douglas (1); Castillo, Roberto (16); Fritz, John (14); Goode, Ricky (8); Heredia, Julian (14); Linares, Juan (3); Martin, Justin (12); Pinkowski, Tim (12); Rivera, Carlos (18); Search, Michael (10); Severino, Blas (16); Walker, Jewell (8).

ATHLETICS—Brimhall, Bradley (4); Grott, William (9); Gulledge, Hugh (17); Lardizabal, Ruben (9); List, Paul (13); Lynch, Jeffrey (1); Macarty, Scott (12); Martinez, Reynaldo (27); Mejia, Leandro (14); Meyer, Michael (11); Miller, Russell (13); Orr, Daniel (7); Peck, Steven (12); Rizza, Gerard (9); Ross, Gary (13); Russell, Todd (13).

BREWERS—Cornell, Daren (3); Henry, Kevin (14); Hooper, Michael (7); Kellogg, Geoffrey (15); Kinder, Jeffrey (13); Lluberes, Luis (12); Potts, James (16).

CARDINALS—Arias, Jose (19); Cassidy, Michael (14); Corona, John (28); Corry, Steven (15); Driscol, Robert (7); Fletcher, Dennis (7); Gaston, Russell (8); Glover, Gregory (13); Hammond, Allan (4); Hayes, James (4); Oswalt, Jeffrey (6); Rodriguez, Manuel (17); Spiller, Derron (2); Tolbert, Mark (29).

MARINERS—Ballesteros, Valentine (8); Beiras, Michael (20); Callistro, Robert (12); Czarkowski, Mark (21); DeJesus, Melvin (5); Furcal, Manuel (18); Garcia, Marcos (13); Gistlinck, Gregory (2); Kostich, William (17); Magill, James (13); Pena, Antonio (11); Robertson, Clyde (11).

PADRES—Banks, Lance (1); Borgos, Jose (8); Davila, Jose (11); Diaz, Luis (20); Garside, Russell (13); Guzman, Pedro (26); McKeon, Brian (13); Pickett, Dan (20); Santiago, Rafael (12); Thompson, Charles (14); Thompson, William (1).

GRAND SLAM HOME RUN—Stephens.

AWARDED FIRST BASE ON CATCHER'S INTERFERENCE—Pueschner 2 (Clemens, Kluge).

CLUB FIELDING

Club	Pct.	G.	PO.	A.	E.	DP.	PB.	Club	Pct.	G.	PO.	A.	E.	DP.	PB.
Brewers	.960	56	1506	589	88	46	15	Angels	.944	55	1448	625	124	41	21
Athletics	.957	56	1501	615	95	58	21	Cardinals	.940	55	1474	594	132	35	16
Padres	.951	56	1479	607	108	30	15	Mariners	.938	56	1496	614	139	31	16

*Throws lefthanded.

INDIVIDUAL FIELDING
FIRST BASEMEN

Player and Club	Pct.	G.	PO.	A.	E.	DP.	Player and Club	Pct.	G.	PO.	A.	E.	DP.
Amparo, Mariners*	.967	46	405	32	15	23	Henry, Athletics	1.000	4	44	2	0	5
Arredondo, Padres*	.978	49	448	41	11	25	Kidwiler, Mariners	.977	8	69	15	2	4
Ayala, Padres	1.000	2	7	0	0	0	Ledinsky, Angels	1.000	3	20	1	0	2
Beck, Padres*	1.000	1	12	1	0	0	Lewis, Cardinals	1.000	1	3	0	0	0
Bierwiler, Padres	.980	4	45	5	1	3	Marimon, Athletics	1.000	10	33	3	0	3
Boudreau, Mariners	.938	4	15	0	1	0	Marrero, Brewers*	1.000	6	61	1	0	11
Carrasquillo, Angels	.977	32	276	23	7	17	McCreadie, Brewers	1.000	4	14	2	0	2
Clemens, Cardinals	1.000	1	1	0	0	0	Muhammad, Brewers	1.000	2	9	1	0	0
Davis, Cardinals	1.000	1	6	0	0	0	Mussett, Angels	1.000	2	1	0	0	0
Delpozo, Mariners	.941	3	16	0	1	1	Peterson, Angels	1.000	5	16	4	0	1
Eldridge, Angels	.980	11	89	9	2	6	Santana, Angels*	.981	11	94	9	2	10
GLENN, Brewers	.991	50	408	30	4	32	Seda, Mariners	1.000	1	2	0	0	0
Harris, Brewers	1.000	1	1	0	0	0	Taft, Angels	1.000	1	1	0	0	0
Hays, Cardinals	1.000	9	49	6	0	3	Tahan, Cardinals	.979	50	440	37	10	31
Henderson, Padres	1.000	1	7	0	0	0	Villaman, Brewers	1.000	1	2	0	0	0
Hendley, Athletics	.989	50	423	36	5	47							

SECOND BASEMEN

Player and Club	Pct.	G.	PO.	A.	E.	DP.	Player and Club	Pct.	G.	PO.	A.	E.	DP.
Abbott, Athletics	.978	8	26	19	1	7	A. Martinez, Athletics	.962	12	15	35	2	8
Ayala, Padres	1.000	3	4	3	0	0	P. Martinez, Padres	.983	12	25	32	1	3
Bierwiler, Padres	.875	5	1	6	1	1	McCray, Brewers	.969	6	11	20	1	3
Borse, Angels	.951	8	14	25	2	5	Merrill, Cardinals	1.000	2	0	1	0	0
Campa, Athletics	.833	2	0	5	1	0	Moscat, Athletics	.966	22	34	52	3	12
Cornell, Brewers	1.000	1	0	1	0	0	Muhammad, Brewers	.964	10	22	31	2	4
Curtis, Angels	.935	20	33	54	6	7	Reynoso, Brewers	.922	37	55	98	13	19
Donald, Cardinals	.951	21	37	41	4	9	Seda, Mariners	.818	6	8	10	4	1
Ellsworth, Cardinals	.914	9	14	18	3	4	SHANNON, Padres	.941	47	94	96	12	16
Gil, Angels	.912	18	26	36	6	4	Sierra, Angels	.985	16	27	40	1	8
Guerrero, Brewers	.968	6	15	15	1	7	Tamarez, Cardinals	.962	15	33	42	3	10
Harris, Padres	1.000	1	0	1	0	0	Thomas, Mariners	.926	12	28	22	4	3
Landinez, Cardinals	.937	37	54	80	9	10	Wallace, Athletics	.892	8	18	15	4	4
Lasher, Angels	1.000	4	9	7	0	2	Williams, Mariners	.919	37	72	98	15	16
LeBlanc, Mariners	1.000	3	6	7	0	4							

THIRD BASEMEN

Player and Club	Pct.	G.	PO.	A.	E.	DP.	Player and Club	Pct.	G.	PO.	A.	E.	DP.
Abbott, Athletics	.909	5	3	7	1	2	Hayes, Cardinals	1.000	2	0	2	0	0
Ayala, Padres	.667	1	2	2	2	0	Henry, Athletics	.857	9	8	16	4	0
Bierwiler, Padres	.667	5	1	9	5	0	Kidwiler, Mariners	1.000	3	1	6	0	0
Campa, Athletics	1.000	1	1	0	0	0	Landinez, Cardinals	1.000	3	0	4	0	0
DELPOZO, Mariners	.904	44	38	66	11	5	Lanfranco, Athletics	.848	42	39	67	19	6
Duran, Cardinals	.886	38	19	82	13	6	LeBlanc, Mariners	.909	8	5	15	2	0
Gil, Angels	.000	1	0	0	1	0	Martinez, Padres	.943	18	14	36	3	5

THIRD BASEMEN—Continued

Player and Club	Pct.	G.	PO.	A.	E.	DP.	Player and Club	Pct.	G.	PO.	A.	E.	DP.
McCreadie, Brewers	.857	17	5	13	3	2	Romero, Padres	.897	38	27	60	10	2
McNair, Mariners	.714	4	4	6	4	0	Sarbaugh, Brewers	.960	4	3	21	1	1
Merrill, Cardinals	.894	29	8	34	5	0	Seda, Mariners	.667	1	1	1	1	0
Peterson, Angels	.826	10	4	15	4	0	Sierra, Angels	.860	20	14	23	6	0
Powell, Brewers	.853	43	31	68	17	7	Wallace, Athletics	1.000	2	0	1	0	0
Raven, Angels	.816	32	17	54	16	7							

SHORTSTOPS

Player and Club	Pct.	G.	PO.	A.	E.	DP.	Player and Club	Pct.	G.	PO.	A.	E.	DP.
ABBOTT, Athletics	.922	25	30	64	8	7	LeBlanc, Mariners	.760	5	6	13	6	1
Bierwiler, Padres	.952	9	12	28	2	1	A. Martinez, Athletics	.960	5	9	15	1	2
Borse, Angels	.714	1	3	2	2	0	P. Martinez, Padres	.922	20	29	66	8	9
Bream, Padres	.962	26	36	65	4	7	McCray, Brewers	.936	38	62	99	11	18
Brito, Angels	.824	15	17	39	12	3	McNair, Mariners	.899	20	25	64	10	4
Campa, Athletics	.975	8	14	25	1	7	Merrill, Cardinals	1.000	1	0	3	0	0
Cornell, Brewers	.500	1	0	1	1	0	Moscat, Athletics	.500	2	0	1	1	1
Duran, Cardinals	.837	9	15	21	7	3	Muhammad, Brewers	1.000	1	0	3	0	0
Ellsworth, Cardinals	.845	36	60	87	27	18	Munoz, Angels	.943	36	62	103	10	22
Foster, Brewers	1.000	1	1	2	0	0	Peterson, Angels	1.000	1	2	0	0	0
Guerrero, Brewers	.926	6	12	13	2	0	Reynoso, Brewers	.800	2	1	3	1	0
Hayes, Cardinals	.941	7	16	16	2	3	Romero, Padres	1.000	1	0	1	0	0
Hays, Cardinals	1.000	1	0	3	0	0	Seda, Mariners	.915	9	16	27	4	5
Heredia, Brewers	.863	23	19	44	10	10	Shannon, Padres	.769	3	6	4	3	0
Kidwiler, Mariners	.908	26	30	88	12	11	Tamarez, Athletics	.925	22	30	68	8	18
Landinez, Cardinals	.826	7	6	13	4	4	Wallace, Athletics	.750	3	0	3	1	1
Lasher, Angels	.880	6	7	15	3	1	Williams, Mariners	1.000	2	3	3	0	3

OUTFIELDERS

Player and Club	Pct.	G.	PO.	A.	E.	DP.	Player and Club	Pct.	G.	PO.	A.	E.	DP.
Ayala, Padres	.923	11	9	3	1	0	Muhammad, Brewers	.958	22	42	4	2	0
Beck, Padres°	.955	50	81	4	4	0	Mussett, Angels	.904	18	41	6	5	0
Bierwiler, Padres	.833	5	5	0	1	0	Peacock, Padres	.950	21	19	0	1	0
Borse, Angels	.986	37	65	3	1	1	Pedro, Brewers	1.000	22	18	0	0	0
Boudreau, Mariners	1.000	7	3	0	0	0	Perez, Padres	.958	24	45	1	2	0
Burrola, Brewers	1.000	3	2	0	0	0	Peterson, Angels	1.000	2	2	1	0	0
Curtis, Angels	1.000	15	29	4	0	1	Pueschner, Padres	.967	46	115	2	4	1
Davis, Cardinals	1.000	19	14	2	0	0	Raven, Angels	.857	5	4	2	1	1
Delpozo, Mariners	1.000	1	1	0	0	0	ROBERTSON, Brewers	.989	48	84	4	1	0
Ealy, Cardinals	.935	46	72	0	5	0	Sammons, Athletics	.958	34	42	4	2	0
French, Cardinals	1.000	27	27	0	0	0	Sanchez, Athletics	.500	6	2	0	2	0
Garcia, Cardinals	.861	38	59	3	10	0	Santana, Angels°	.936	26	41	3	3	0
Garrett, Angels°	1.000	29	41	1	0	1	Santarini, Mariners°	1.000	27	25	1	0	0
E. Harris, Padres	.938	31	44	1	3	0	Sass, Brewers	1.000	12	19	3	0	0
K. Harris, Brewers	1.000	28	39	3	0	0	Savinon, Cardinals	1.000	4	7	0	0	0
Henry, Athletics	.857	12	11	1	2	0	Seda, Mariners	1.000	2	3	0	0	0
Jordan, Cardinals	.938	20	30	0	2	0	Sierra, Angels	.500	1	1	0	1	0
Jorge, Angels°	1.000	6	5	0	0	0	Staydohar, Angels	1.000	17	31	4	0	0
Krokroskia, Athletics	.978	49	87	4	2	1	Stephens, Mariners	.966	34	53	3	2	1
Ledinsky, Angels	.891	30	45	4	6	0	Terrell, Mariners	.946	41	48	5	3	0
A. Lewis, Cardinals	.942	45	59	6	4	0	Thomas, Athletics°	.864	20	36	2	6	0
R. Lewis, Angels	1.000	4	5	0	0	0	D. Twitty, Athletics	1.000	33	39	1	0	0
Love, Brewers°	.967	10	29	0	1	0	S. Twitty, Mariners	.942	44	65	0	4	0
Lyons, Athletics	.945	41	63	6	4	0	Verstraete, Padres	1.000	6	2	1	0	0
Magarity, Cardinals	1.000	1	1	0	0	0	Walker, Brewers	.955	14	17	4	1	0
McCray, Brewers	1.000	4	4	0	0	0	Wallace, Athletics	1.000	14	11	0	0	0
McNair, Mariners	1.000	7	14	0	0	0	Weldin, Brewers°	1.000	32	53	4	0	0

CATCHERS

Player and Club	Pct.	G.	PO.	A.	E.	DP.	PB.	Player and Club	Pct.	G.	PO.	A.	E.	DP.	PB.
Ayala, Padres	.966	26	128	13	5	0	5	Martinez, Athletics	.987	10	66	11	1	0	5
Candelario, Mariners	.981	22	146	9	3	1	5	Mejia, Angels	.800	3	4	0	1	0	1
Clemens, Cardinals	.978	44	281	32	7	0	11	Parks, Brewers	.988	26	150	21	2	0	5
Dempsey, Cardinals	.900	4	24	3	3	0	2	Raasch, Mariners	.978	26	201	21	5	0	8
Figueroa, Athletics	.909	2	7	3	1	0	1	Santarini, Mariners°	1.000	1	1	0	0	0	0
Hays, Cardinals	1.000	13	59	7	0	1	5	Snyder, Angels	.985	18	116	13	2	1	5
Henderson, Padres	.959	27	150	36	8	1	4	Stela, Angels	.973	31	148	30	5	1	6
Hendley, Athletics	.833	4	5	0	1	0	4	Street, Angels	1.000	18	67	10	0	1	5
Henry, Athletics	1.000	11	41	4	0	0	6	Taft, Angels	.954	30	128	18	7	1	7
Johnson, Brewers	.987	19	72	5	1	0	3	Tallent, Angels	.962	7	24	1	1	0	2
Joyce, Padres	.948	13	77	14	5	0	6	TREDWAY, Athletics	.983	47	324	28	6	0	5
Kluge, Mariners	.975	15	111	5	3	0	3	Turvey, Cardinals	.961	14	64	10	3	0	2
Marimon, Athletics	1.000	1	3	0	0	0	0	Villaman, Brewers	1.000	14	95	10	0	0	2

PITCHERS

Player and Club	Pct.	G.	PO.	A.	E.	DP.	Player and Club	Pct.	G.	PO.	A.	E.	DP.
Arias, Cardinals	.870	19	6	14	3	0	Furcal, Mariners°	1.000	18	1	7	0	0
Ballesteros, Mariners°	1.000	8	0	2	0	0	Garcia, Mariners	.971	13	18	16	1	0
Beiras, Mariners	.909	20	3	7	1	0	Garside, Padres°	.824	13	2	12	3	0
Brimhall, Athletics	1.000	4	1	1	0	0	Gaston, Cardinals	1.000	8	1	3	0	0
Callistro, Mariners	.857	12	4	14	3	0	Gil, Angels	1.000	1	0	1	0	0
Cassidy, Cardinals°	1.000	4	3	9	0	1	Glover, Cardinals	.800	13	1	3	1	0
Castillo, Angels	.889	16	6	2	1	0	Goode, Angels	.500	8	1	0	1	0
Corona, Cardinals°	.938	28	5	10	1	0	Grott, Athletics°	.714	9	1	4	2	0
Corry, Cardinals	.857	15	6	12	3	0	Gulledge, Athletics	.667	17	1	5	3	0
Czarkowski, Mariners°	.950	21	2	17	1	0	Guzman, Padres	.882	26	5	10	2	0
Davila, Padres	1.000	11	2	2	0	0	Hammond, Cardinals	1.000	4	0	1	0	0
Diaz, Padres	.923	20	6	6	1	0	Hayes, Cardinals	.500	4	1	0	1	0
Driscol, Cardinals°	1.000	7	2	6	0	0	Henry, Brewers°	.800	14	1	3	1	0
Fletcher, Cardinals	.800	7	2	2	1	0	Heredia, Angels	.938	14	8	22	2	2
Fritz, Angels	.882	14	6	9	2	0	Hooper, Brewers	1.000	7	0	1	0	0

PITCHERS—Continued

Player and Club	Pct.	G.	PO.	A.	E.	DP.	Player and Club	Pct.	G.	PO.	A.	E.	DP.
JEFFERSON, Brewers	1.000	13	10	17	0	3	Oswalt, Cardinals*	.889	6	4	4	1	0
Kellogg, Brewers	.875	15	2	5	1	0	Peck, Athletics	1.000	12	3	2	0	0
Kinder, Brewers*	.857	13	1	5	1	0	Pena, Mariners	.625	11	1	9	6	0
Kostich, Mariners*	.923	17	3	9	1	1	Pickett, Padres*	.955	20	4	17	1	1
Lardizabal, Athletics	1.000	9	4	8	0	0	Pinkowski, Angels	.833	12	3	2	1	0
Leslie, Brewers	.875	22	3	4	1	0	Potts, Brewers	1.000	16	3	6	0	0
Linares, Angels*	1.000	3	0	4	0	0	Rivera, Angels	.909	18	0	10	1	2
List, Athletics	1.000	13	1	1	0	0	Rizza, Athletics	.800	9	0	4	1	0
Lluberes, Brewers	.800	12	5	3	2	1	Robertson, Mariners	1.000	11	1	3	0	1
Lynch, Athletics	1.000	1	0	2	0	0	Rodriguez, Cardinals	.857	17	4	2	1	0
Macarty, Athletics*	.857	12	6	1	0	0	Ross, Athletics	1.000	3	1	1	0	0
Magarity, Cardinals	.944	14	8	9	1	1	Russell, Athletics	.857	13	7	11	3	2
Magill, Mariners	.680	13	6	11	8	1	Santiago, Padres*	1.000	12	6	9	0	0
Mangual, Brewers	.750	20	4	5	3	0	Scott, Brewers	.500	5	0	1	1	0
Martin, Angels	.889	12	5	11	2	0	Search, Angels*	.909	10	3	7	1	1
Martinez, Athletics	1.000	27	7	7	0	1	Severino, Angels	.909	16	1	9	1	0
McKeon, Padres	.786	13	2	9	3	0	C. Thompson, Padres	.947	14	7	11	1	0
Mejia, Athletics	.941	14	4	12	1	1	Tolbert, Cardinals	.933	30	6	8	1	1
Meyer, Athletics	1.000	11	1	2	0	0	Walker, Angels	.800	8	2	2	1	0
Miller, Athletics	1.000	13	8	7	0	0	Zimbauer, Brewers	.875	12	5	2	1	0
Orr, Athletics	1.000	7	1	3	0	0							

The following players did not have any fielding statistics at the positions indicated or appeared only as a designated hitter, pinch-hitter or pinch-runner: Ayala, p; Banks, p; W. Beck, dh, ph; Borgos, p; Campa, p; Canney, p; Carrasquillo, of; Cornell, 3b; D. Davis, dh, ph; DeJesus, p; Donald, ss, of; Duran, 1b; Gil, of; Gistlinck, p; Hendley, of; Jackson, dh; Johnson, of; Joyce, of; Kidwiler, p; Landinez, of; A. Lewis, 2b, p; Lofthus, dh; Lyons, p; Macarty, of; McCray, 3b; Mejia, of; Merrill, p; Moscat, c; Munoz, 2b; Mussett, 2b; Pedro, 3b; Perez, 2b, p; Shannon, 3b; Snyder, p; Spiller, p; Taft, 3b, of, p; Tallent, p; W. Thompson, p; Tredway, of; Villaman, of; Wallace, p.

CLUB PITCHING

Club	ERA.	G.	CG.	ShO.	Sv.	IP.	H.	R.	ER.	HR.	HB.	BB.	Int. BB.	SO.	WP.	Bk.
Brewers	3.10	56	5	5	12	502.0	473	234	173	13	26	164	3	431	33	19
Mariners	3.84	56	3	3	15	498.2	471	307	213	11	27	189	4	445	38	25
Padres	4.09	56	5	4	7	493.0	508	306	224	16	32	172	10	368	14	34
Athletics	4.14	56	1	4	7	500.1	479	288	230	12	17	245	5	442	29	27
Cardinals	4.56	55	4	4	10	491.1	501	353	249	14	17	230	11	414	44	21
Angels	5.20	55	5	1	7	482.2	563	363	279	9	24	216	7	364	48	47

PITCHERS' RECORDS
(Leading Qualifiers for Earned-Run Average Leadership — 48 or More Innings)

*Throws lefthanded.

Pitcher—Club	W.	L.	Pct.	ERA.	G.	GS.	CG.	GF.	ShO.	Sv.	IP.	H.	R.	ER.	HR.	HB.	BB.	Int. BB.	SO.	WP.
Lluberes, Brewers	8	0	1.000	1.33	12	11	1	1	0	0	74.1	66	16	11	3	2	15	0	54	2
Martinez, Athletics	5	3	.625	1.82	27	0	0	25	0	5	49.1	32	17	10	0	0	22	3	38	0
McKeon, Padres	4	4	.500	2.01	13	10	2	3	1	1	71.2	70	33	16	2	1	16	0	59	2
Czarkowski, Mariners*	2	0	1.000	2.04	21	0	0	13	0	5	61.2	46	16	14	1	1	9	0	42	3
Callistro, Mariners	5	2	.714	2.62	12	12	1	0	0	0	75.2	69	41	22	0	6	22	0	78	3
Kellogg, Brewers	4	3	.571	2.67	15	7	0	1	0	1	54.0	43	28	16	2	1	28	0	45	2
Garcia, Mariners	4	5	.444	2.75	13	13	2	0	1	0	78.2	65	42	24	0	4	32	0	54	5
Zimbauer, Brewers	7	1	.875	2.78	12	12	0	0	0	0	71.1	57	25	22	3	1	24	0	72	5
Miller, Athletics	4	3	.571	2.81	13	11	1	0	0	0	64.0	77	31	20	1	0	17	0	64	5
Jefferson, Brewers	7	2	.778	2.82	13	13	3	0	1	0	89.1	92	45	28	3	10	15	0	68	3

Departmental Leaders: G—Tolbert, 29; W—Lluberes, 8; L—Magill, Martin, C. Thompson, 7; Pct.—Lluberes, 1.000; GS—Fritz, C. Thompson, 14; CG—Corry, Heredia, Jefferson, 3; GF—Martinez, 25; ShO—Corry, 2; Sv.—Leslie, 7; IP—Heredia, 92.1; H—Heredia, 109; R—Martin, 63; ER—Martin, 51; HR—Diaz, Heredia, 5; HB—C. Thompson, 5; BB—List, Severino, 41; IBB—Corona, Guzman, Tolbert, 4; SO—Callistro, 78; WP—Martin, 13.

(All Pitchers—Listed Alphabetically)

Pitcher—Club	W.	L.	Pct.	ERA.	G.	GS.	CG.	GF.	ShO.	Sv.	IP.	H.	R.	ER.	HR.	HB.	BB.	Int. BB.	SO.	WP.
Arias, Cardinals	4	3	.571	5.07	19	7	0	2	0	0	55.0	52	45	31	2	1	35	0	47	8
Ayala, Padres	0	0	.000	0.00	1	1	0	0	0	0	6.0	3	1	0	0	1	1	0	7	0
Ballesteros, Mariners*	1	2	.333	4.94	8	4	0	2	0	0	23.2	25	15	13	1	0	17	0	20	3
Banks, Mariners	0	1	.000	9.00	1	0	0	0	0	0	1.0	2	2	1	0	0	3	0	1	0
Beiras, Mariners	1	4	.200	7.09	20	0	0	15	0	4	33.0	43	32	26	2	1	20	2	33	2
Borgos, Padres	0	0	.000	3.48	8	0	0	7	0	0	10.1	6	5	4	0	0	10	0	4	1
Brimhall, Athletics	0	0	.000	7.04	4	0	0	0	0	0	7.2	9	6	6	0	1	4	0	9	0
Callistro, Mariners	5	2	.714	2.62	12	12	1	0	0	0	75.2	69	41	22	0	6	22	0	78	3
Campa, Athletics	0	0	.000	4.50	1	0	0	1	0	0	4	2	2	2	0	0	2	0	1	0
Canney, Angels*	0	0	.000	27.00	1	0	0	0	0	0	0.1	1	1	1	0	0	0	0	0	0
Cassidy, Cardinals*	3	0	1.000	1.80	4	4	0	0	0	0	25.0	18	7	5	1	1	10	0	20	0
Castillo, Angels	4	3	.571	3.10	16	1	0	12	0	2	29.0	32	12	10	0	1	6	1	20	1
Corona, Cardinals*	0	1	.000	5.17	28	0	0	18	0	5	38.1	48	25	22	1	1	14	4	31	0
Corry, Cardinals	3	5	.375	4.09	15	9	3	1	2	0	72.2	68	46	33	0	0	25	1	70	3
Czarkowski, Mariners*	2	0	1.000	2.04	21	0	0	13	0	5	61.2	46	16	14	1	1	9	0	42	3
Davila, Padres	0	1	.000	15.88	11	0	0	5	0	0	11.1	22	25	20	0	1	14	0	5	1
DeJesus, Mariners	0	0	.000	12.00	5	0	0	3	0	0	6.0	7	10	8	0	3	10	0	8	1
Diaz, Padres	3	1	.750	4.54	20	0	0	8	0	0	41.2	48	29	21	5	4	18	1	17	0
Driscol, Cardinals*	1	4	.200	5.20	7	4	0	1	0	0	27.2	30	17	16	0	0	8	0	27	2
Fletcher, Cardinals	1	0	1.000	2.19	7	1	0	5	0	2	12.1	10	6	3	0	1	4	1	18	3
Fritz, Angels	4	5	.444	4.13	14	14	0	0	0	0	85.0	86	50	39	0	3	38	1	70	10
Furcal, Mariners*	5	0	1.000	3.21	18	0	0	11	0	5	28.0	28	11	10	0	5	10	0	28	3
Garcia, Mariners	4	5	.444	2.75	13	13	2	0	1	0	78.2	65	42	24	0	4	32	0	54	5
Garside, Padres*	7	4	.636	3.43	13	12	2	1	1	0	78.2	67	36	30	1	2	23	2	66	1
Gaston, Cardinals	2	3	.400	4.84	8	7	0	0	0	0	35.1	33	29	19	1	1	27	0	42	7
Gil, Angels	0	0	.000	4.50	3	0	0	0	0	0	2.0	3	6	5	0	0	7	0	1	2
Gistlinck, Mariners	0	0	.000	36.00	2	0	0	0	0	0	1.0	4	4	4	0	1	3	0	1	0
Glover, Cardinals*	0	2	.000	11.34	13	0	0	2	0	0	16.2	25	31	21	0	3	24	1	16	3
Goode, Angels	0	0	.000	5.84	4	0	0	0	0	0	12.1	15	12	8	0	1	15	1	9	3
Grott, Athletics*	3	1	.750	2.31	9	5	0	0	0	0	35.0	29	10	9	0	2	9	0	44	1

Pitcher—Club	W.	L.	Pct.	ERA.	G.	GS.	CG.	GF.	ShO.	Sv.	IP.	H.	R.	ER.	HR.	HB.	BB.	Int. BB.	SO.	WP.
Gulledge, Athletics	0	1	.000	6.75	17	2	0	4	0	0	34.2	38	31	26	0	2	29	0	24	2
Guzman, Padres	4	6	.400	4.65	26	4	0	20	0	4	62.0	63	40	32	3	3	11	4	39	0
Hammond, Cardinals	0	0	.000	4.26	4	0	0	0	0	0	6.1	6	5	3	1	0	2	0	3	1
Hayes, Cardinals	1	0	1.000	2.79	4	3	0	0	0	0	19.1	14	11	6	1	0	16	0	17	5
Henry, Brewers*	2	0	1.000	3.57	14	1	0	5	0	0	22.2	27	15	9	0	1	3	0	22	3
Heredia, Angels	3	4	.429	4.29	14	13	3	1	0	0	92.1	109	55	44	5	1	21	0	74	2
Hooper, Brewers	0	0	.000	8.18	7	1	0	1	0	0	11.0	13	12	10	0	2	5	0	10	0
Jefferson, Brewers	7	2	.778	2.82	13	13	3	0	1	0	89.1	92	45	28	3	10	15	0	68	3
Kellogg, Brewers	4	3	.571	2.67	15	7	0	1	0	1	54.0	45	28	16	2	1	28	0	45	2
Kidwiler, Mariners	0	0	.000	27.00	1	0	0	1	0	0	0.1	1	2	1	0	0	1	0	0	0
Kinder, Brewers*	7	1	.875	3.62	13	6	1	5	0	2	54.2	55	23	22	0	0	20	0	37	4
Kostich, Mariners*	2	3	.400	5.44	17	3	0	4	0	0	49.2	54	38	30	4	1	13	2	53	1
Lardizabal, Athletics	2	1	.667	4.79	9	4	0	1	0	0	41.1	48	24	22	1	0	7	1	28	2
Leslie, Brewers	4	2	.667	1.71	22	1	0	18	0	7	47.1	32	11	9	0	3	14	1	56	4
Lewis, Cardinals	0	0	.000	0.00	2	0	0	2	0	0	1.1	2	0	0	0	0	1	0	1	0
Linares, Angels*	0	1	.000	9.39	3	0	0	0	0	0	7.2	12	8	8	0	1	5	1	6	1
List, Athletics	0	1	.000	6.41	12	0	0	5	0	0	19.2	7	18	14	1	0	41	0	36	5
Lluberes, Brewers	8	0	1.000	1.33	12	11	1	1	0	0	74.1	66	16	11	3	2	15	0	54	2
Lynch, Athletics	0	0	.000	27.00	1	0	0	0	0	0	1.0	2	4	3	0	0	2	0	0	0
Lyons, Athletics	0	0	.000	45.00	1	0	0	0	0	0	1.0	3	5	5	0	0	3	0	0	0
Macarty, Athletics*	2	5	.286	4.87	12	9	0	1	0	0	40.2	36	25	22	4	0	29	1	47	2
Magarity, Cardinals	4	5	.444	3.98	14	12	1	0	0	0	72.1	78	43	32	2	2	21	0	41	4
Magill, Mariners	2	7	.222	3.39	13	13	0	0	0	0	66.1	63	54	25	0	6	36	0	61	8
Mangual, Brewers	1	3	.250	5.02	20	3	0	14	0	1	37.2	37	30	21	1	2	19	0	34	7
Martin, Angels	2	7	.222	6.17	12	12	1	0	0	0	74.1	92	63	51	1	3	29	0	53	13
Martinez, Athletics	5	3	.625	1.82	27	0	0	25	0	5	49.1	32	17	10	0	0	22	3	38	0
McKeon, Padres	4	4	.500	2.01	13	10	2	3	1	1	71.2	70	33	16	2	1	16	0	59	2
Mejia, Athletics	5	1	.833	4.93	14	9	0	1	0	0	65.2	71	40	36	1	1	19	0	37	3
Merrill, Cardinals	0	1	.000	6.75	1	0	0	1	0	0	1.1	2	1	1	0	0	1	0	0	0
Meyer, Athletics	0	2	.000	5.29	11	0	0	5	0	0	17.0	18	15	10	1	1	13	0	16	4
Miller, Athletics	4	3	.571	2.81	13	11	1	0	0	0	64.0	77	31	20	1	0	17	0	64	5
Orr, Athletics	0	0	.000	1.04	7	0	0	2	0	0	8.2	4	4	1	0	3	4	0	8	2
Oswalt, Cardinals*	1	1	.500	3.95	6	4	0	0	0	0	27.1	25	16	12	0	2	12	0	24	2
Peck, Athletics	1	3	.250	3.04	12	1	0	6	0	1	23.2	21	10	8	1	1	7	0	22	0
Pena, Mariners	4	5	.444	4.61	11	11	0	0	0	0	56.2	48	35	29	2	3	15	0	54	6
Perez, Padres	0	0	.000	0.00	1	0	0	1	0	0	1.2	2	0	0	0	0	1	0	0	0
Pickett, Padres*	1	2	.333	3.72	20	3	0	6	0	1	55.2	62	32	23	3	2	27	1	53	1
Pinkowski, Angels	1	5	.167	5.94	12	3	0	6	0	1	33.1	40	26	22	2	2	7	0	26	2
Potts, Brewers	1	3	.250	5.87	16	1	0	4	0	1	30.2	40	22	20	1	1	14	2	25	1
Rivera, Angels	1	4	.200	5.44	18	4	0	8	0	0	51.1	56	44	31	0	7	19	2	37	2
Rizza, Athletics	1	0	1.000	3.68	9	0	0	3	0	1	22.0	22	10	9	0	2	5	0	10	2
Robertson, Mariners	2	0	1.000	3.50	11	0	0	4	0	1	18.0	18	7	7	1	1	6	0	13	3
Rodriguez, Cardinals	2	3	.400	6.29	17	4	0	6	0	1	34.1	37	33	24	4	1	19	0	25	3
Ross, Athletics	0	1	.000	9.00	3	2	0	0	0	0	5.0	3	5	5	1	0	5	0	3	0
Russell, Athletics	6	5	.545	3.39	13	13	0	0	0	0	61.0	55	31	23	1	4	27	0	55	1
Santiago, Padres*	3	5	.375	3.34	12	12	1	0	0	0	72.2	74	44	27	2	6	25	2	59	3
Scott, Brewers	0	0	.000	5.63	5	0	0	2	0	0	8.0	9	7	5	0	3	7	0	7	2
Search, Angels*	1	1	.500	2.00	10	0	0	9	0	3	18.0	11	4	4	0	1	3	0	20	0
Severino, Angels	4	4	.500	5.07	16	8	1	5	0	1	60.1	73	47	34	1	3	41	1	42	5
Snyder, Brewers	0	0	.000	0.00	1	0	0	0	0	0	1.0	0	0	0	0	0	0	0	1	0
Spiller, Cardinals*	0	0	.000	19.29	2	0	0	0	0	0	2.1	5	6	5	0	0	4	0	1	0
Taft, Angels	0	1	.000	13.50	2	0	0	1	0	0	1.1	3	3	2	0	1	1	0	0	0
Tallent, Angels	0	0	.000	9.00	1	0	0	1	0	0	2.0	3	2	2	0	0	1	0	0	2
C. Thompson, Padres	3	7	.300	5.74	14	14	0	0	0	0	78.1	88	59	50	0	12	23	0	54	5
W. Thompson, Padres	0	0	.000	0.00	1	0	0	0	0	0	2.0	1	0	0	0	0	0	0	4	0
Tolbert, Cardinals	2	3	.400	3.30	29	0	0	13	0	1	43.2	48	32	16	1	4	16	4	31	3
Walker, Angels	0	0	.000	12.15	8	0	0	2	0	0	13.1	27	30	18	0	0	23	0	6	5
Wallace, Athletics	0	0	.000	0.00	1	0	0	1	0	0	1.0	0	0	0	0	0	0	0	0	0
Zimbauer, Brewers	7	1	.875	2.78	12	12	0	0	0	0	71.1	57	25	22	3	1	24	0	72	5

BALKS—Arias, Fritz, 12 each; Heredia, 11; Davila, Diaz, Macarty, Pinkowski, Zimbauer, 7 each; Mejia, Severino, 6 each; Kellogg, Kostich, 5 each; Callistro, Castillo, Pickett, C. Thompson, 4 each; Beiras, DeJesus, Linares, Magill, Mangual, McKeon, 3 each; Ballesteros, Banks, Brimhall, Furcal, Garcia, Garside, Gil, Grott, Gulledge, Magarity, Martinez, Potts, Rodriguez, Santiago, Tolbert, 2 each; Ayala, Borgos, Corry, Guzman, Hammond, Hayes, Henry, Lardizabal, Leslie, List, Miller, Pena, Rivera, Rizza, Ross, Russell, Search, 1 each.

COMBINATION SHUTOUTS—Severino-Rivera-Goode-Castillo, Angels; Russell-Rizza-Meyer, Macarty-Rizza, Lardizabal-Rizza, Russell-Brimhall-Gulledge, Athletics; Zimbauer-Kellogg-Henry, Lluberes-Kinder, Zimbauer-Kellogg-Leslie, Lluberes-Leslie, Brewers; Magarity-Corona, Gaston-Tolbert, Cardinals; Ballesteros-Kostich-Beiras, Magill-Ballesteros, Mariners; Garside-Diaz, McKeon-Guzman, Padres.

NO-HIT GAME—Garcia, Mariners, defeated Padres, 4-0, July 20.

Gulf Coast League

SUMMER CLASS A CLASSIFICATION

CHAMPIONSHIP WINNERS IN PREVIOUS YEARS

1964—Sarasota Braves .... .610	1974—Chicago N.L. .... .702	1984—White Sox .... .651
1965—Bradenton Astros .... .632	1975—Texas .... .774	Rangers b .... .571
1966—New York A.L. .... .667	1976—Texas .... .704	1985—Yankees c .... .705
1967—Kansas City .... .614	1977—Chicago-A.L .... .731	Rangers .... .532
1968—Oakland .... .650	1978—Texas .... .600	1986—Reds .... .548
1969—Montreal .... .585	1979—Houston .... .635	Dodgers b .... .541
1970—Chicago A.L. .... .600	1980—Kansas City-Blue .... .635	1987—Dodgers b .... .683
1971—Kansas City .... .755	1981—Kansas City-Gold .... .688	Royals .... .635
1972—Chicago N.L. a .... .651	1982—New York-A.L. .... .667	1988—Yankees b .... .714
Kansas City a .... .651	1983—Texas .... .645	Royals .... .619
1973—Texas .... .732	Los Angeles b .... .617	

(Note—Known as Sarasota Rookie League in 1964 and Florida Rookie League in 1965.) aDeclared co-champions; no playoff. bLeague divided into Northern and Southern divisions; won one-game playoff for league championship. cYankees declared champion based on winning percentage when one-game playoff against Rangers was rained out.

STANDING OF CLUBS AT CLOSE OF SEASON, AUGUST 28

NORTHERN DIVISION

Club	W.	L.	T.	Pct.	G.B.
Dodgers	40	23	0	.635	......
Reds	37	26	0	.587	3
Royals	35	28	0	.556	5
Indians	34	29	0	.540	6
Red Sox	27	36	0	.429	13
Astros	16	47	0	.254	24

SOUTHERN DIVISION

Club	W.	L.	T.	Pct.	G.B.
Yankees	41	22	0	.651	......
White Sox	40	23	0	.635	1
Braves	37	26	1	.587	4
Rangers	33	30	2	.524	8
Expos	28	35	3	.444	13
Twins	27	36	0	.429	14
Mets	25	38	2	.397	16
Pirates	21	42	0	.333	20

COMPOSITE STANDING OF CLUBS AT CLOSE OF SEASON, AUGUST 28

Club	Yan.	WS	Dod.	Rds.	Brv.	Roy.	Ind.	Rng.	Exp.	Twi.	RS	Met.	Pir.	Ast.	W.	L.	T.	Pct.	G.B.
Yankees	..	5	0	0	5	0	0	4	8	7	0	5	7	0	41	22	0	.651	......
White Sox	4	..	0	0	0	0	7	6	7	0	6	6	0	40	23	0	.635	1
Dodgers	0	0	..	6	0	8	8	0	0	0	7	0	11	40	23	0	.635	1
Reds	0	0	6	..	0	7	7	0	0	8	0	0	9	37	26	0	.587	4
Braves	4	5	0	0	..	0	0	6	3	6	0	7	6	0	37	26	1	.587	4
Royals	0	0	5	6	0	..	7	0	0	6	0	0	11	35	28	0	.556	6
Indians	0	0	5	5	0	6	..	0	0	0	10	0	8	34	29	0	.540	7
Rangers	5	2	0	0	3	0	0	..	7	4	0	7	5	0	33	30	2	.524	8
Expos	1	3	0	6	0	0	2	..	7	0	5	4	0	28	35	3	.444	13
Twins	2	2	0	3	0	5	2	..	0	7	0	6	0	27	36	0	.429	14
Red Sox	0	0	5	5	0	6	3	0	0	0	..	0	8	27	36	0	.429	14
Mets	4	3	0	0	2	0	2	4	2	0	..	8	0	25	38	2	.397	16
Pirates	2	3	0	0	3	0	4	5	3	0	1	..	0	21	42	0	.333	20
Astros	0	2	4	0	1	4	0	0	0	5	0	0	..	16	47	0	.254	25

Games played in Bradenton and Sarasota, Fla.

Club names are major league affiliations.

Playoffs—Yankees (Southern Division winner) defeated Dodgers (Northern Division winner), two games to one, to win league championship.

Regular-Season Attendance—No total official attendance figures reported.

Managers—Astros, Julio Linares; Braves, Jim Procopio; Dodgers, Jerry Royster; Expos, Jerry Weinstein; Indians, Mike Brown; Mets, John Tamargo; Pirates, Woody Huyke; Rangers, Chino Cadahia; Reds, Sam Mejias; Red Sox, Felix Maldonado; Royals, Carlos Tosca; Twins, Joel Lepel; White Sox, Ed Pebley; Yankees, Jack Gillis.

All-Star Team—1B—Harry Guanchez, Royals; 2B—Oswaldo Apolinero, Braves; 3B—Butch Huskey, Mets; SS—Andres Rodriguez, Yankees; OF—Kenneth Powell, Rangers; Greg Blosser, Red Sox; Ken Ramos, Indians; DH—Freddy Gonzalez, Dodgers; C—Pedro Matilla, Red Sox; Starting Pitchers—Pedro Astacio, Dodgers; Sterling Hitchcock, Yankees; Relief Pitcher—Mike Soper, Indians; Manager of the Year—Jack Gillis, Yankees.

(Compiled by Howe Sportsdata International, Boston, Mass.)

CLUB BATTING

Club	Pct.	G.	AB.	R.	OR.	H.	TB.	2B.	3B.	HR.	RBI.	SH.	SF.	HP.	BB.	Int. BB.	SO.	SB.	CS.	LOB.
Dodgers	.268	63	2108	303	203	565	734	71	31	12	253	17	20	25	224	4	393	145	53	435
Reds	.254	63	2121	285	250	539	698	76	22	13	227	22	21	32	238	6	412	82	49	502
Braves	.254	64	2145	343	290	545	765	98	31	20	287	27	23	28	219	10	457	119	60	412
Yankees	.254	63	2155	337	220	547	762	84	40	17	287	16	26	19	263	3	434	53	29	483
White Sox	.250	63	2008	309	189	502	657	83	21	10	240	18	26	24	237	2	393	153	66	396
Royals	.247	63	2101	292	240	518	657	63	23	10	236	23	17	33	208	2	436	92	43	447
Indians	.246	63	2123	290	288	522	658	78	26	2	240	23	16	26	268	9	365	66	46	485
Pirates	.242	63	2078	270	365	503	688	68	27	21	213	11	14	27	166	4	422	101	40	391
Rangers	.241	65	2095	267	278	505	658	77	23	10	204	4	28	22	197	4	340	80	42	413
Red Sox	.239	63	2098	223	269	501	667	65	16	23	192	20	12	22	211	6	381	31	16	466
Expos	.232	66	2059	262	312	478	641	77	19	16	212	12	17	20	266	3	491	96	54	431
Twins	.229	63	2022	273	344	463	633	85	26	11	227	6	17	27	251	1	522	126	22	440
Astros	.217	63	2078	208	351	450	588	69	21	9	160	4	10	34	169	6	510	111	51	406
Mets	.216	65	2029	231	294	439	614	74	34	11	187	13	21	23	195	1	469	112	43	392

INDIVIDUAL BATTING
(Leading Qualifiers for Batting Championship—170 or More Plate Appearances)

*Bats lefthanded.   †Switch-hitter.

Player and Club	Pct.	G.	AB.	R.	H.	TB.	2B.	3B.	HR.	RBI.	SH.	SF.	HP.	BB.	Int. BB.	SO.	SB.	CS.
Gonzalez, Freddy, Dodgers	.380	51	158	26	60	91	13	6	2	24	0	1	2	17	0	24	7	8
Guanchez, Harry, Royals	.332	59	208	36	69	84	11	2	0	28	1	2	10	22	0	33	6	2
Young, Eric, Dodgers	.330	56	197	53	65	92	11	5	2	22	1	1	3	33	1	16	41	10
Apolinario, Oswaldo, Braves	.326	59	227	54	74	87	7	3	0	28	4	2	3	14	1	37	26	10
Eiterman, Thomas, Indians	.324	40	148	28	48	60	6	3	0	27	0	3	3	24	0	13	5	5
Curtis, Craig, Astros*	.323	51	186	25	60	79	8	4	1	14	1	0	1	25	1	45	28	5
Howard, Johnny, Twins*	.317	47	167	20	53	76	10	5	1	28	0	3	0	19	1	32	0	2
Miranda, Giovanni, Royals	.311	55	193	38	60	70	4	3	0	24	2	4	1	19	0	15	23	9
Ramos, Kenneth, Indians*	.311	54	193	41	60	74	7	2	1	14	3	2	3	39	1	18	17	7
Rodriguez, Andres, Yankees	.302	56	212	28	64	75	7	2	0	18	3	1	0	9	0	34	3	3

Departmental Leaders: G—Ra. Jimenez, Santiago, 62; AB—Ra. Jimenez, 250; R—Apolinario, 54; H—Apolinario, 74; TB—Ra. Jimenez, 114; 2B—Roble, 18; 3B—Easley, 11; HR—Ra. Jimenez, 7; RBI—Ra. Jimenez, 46; SH—Several players tied with 4; SF—Abell, Mathis, 6; HP—Guanchez, 10; BB—K. Ramos, 39; IBB—Easley, 5; SO—Gerald, 80; SB—E. Young, 41; CS—Gerrod Davis, 11.

(All Players—Listed Alphabetically)

Player and Club	Pct.	G.	AB.	R.	H.	TB.	2B.	3B.	HR.	RBI.	SH.	SF.	HP.	BB.	Int. BB.	SO.	SB.	CS.
Abell, Todd, Rangers	.284	44	155	17	44	58	8	3	0	16	1	6	2	15	0	22	1	2
Adams, Gary, Expos*	.200	30	85	11	17	22	2	0	1	7	0	0	1	8	0	25	3	1
Adams, Thomas, Braves	.000	10	1	0	0	0	0	0	0	0	0	0	0	0	0	0	0	0
Adkins, Adrian, Pirates	.167	2	6	1	1	3	0	1	0	0	0	0	0	1	0	1	0	0
Alvarez, David, Red Sox*	.311	19	61	10	19	33	3	1	3	9	0	0	0	8	0	7	0	0
Andrews, Jay, Royals†	.234	48	167	14	39	56	7	5	0	16	2	1	5	11	0	37	6	3
Andujar, Hector, Indians	.202	32	94	8	19	20	1	0	0	3	1	0	2	6	0	18	2	0
Andujar, Robert, White Sox	.154	10	26	4	4	4	0	0	0	1	0	0	2	2	0	9	2	0
Anglada, Raymundo, Astros	.203	43	128	7	26	30	4	0	0	5	2	1	3	5	1	31	4	1
Angotti, Donald, Astros	.205	18	44	6	9	12	1	1	0	0	0	0	5	0	9	0	2
Apolinario, Oswaldo, Braves	.326	59	227	54	74	87	7	3	0	28	4	2	3	14	1	37	26	10
Ashley, Billy, Dodgers	.238	48	160	23	38	51	6	2	1	19	0	3	2	19	1	42	9	1
Atwater, Tyrone, Expos*	.304	44	125	20	38	42	2	1	0	9	2	1	0	16	0	26	7	3
Aude, Richard, Pirates	.216	24	88	13	19	22	3	0	0	7	0	1	3	5	0	17	2	0
Awkard, Herman, Red Sox	.143	24	49	5	7	7	0	0	0	1	0	0	1	4	0	20	1	1
Bagwell, Jeffrey, Red Sox	.316	5	19	3	6	7	1	0	0	3	0	0	0	3	0	0	0	0
Batista, Gervasio, Red Sox*	.167	7	12	1	2	2	0	0	0	0	0	0	0	0	0	2	0	0
Baxter, David, Reds†	.237	24	76	15	18	19	1	0	0	7	2	1	1	10	0	19	6	3
Berge, Torrin, Reds*	.253	35	99	8	25	28	3	0	0	12	2	3	0	10	0	15	1	1
Berroa, Fabricio, Braves	.333	1	3	1	1	2	1	0	0	2	0	0	0	0	0	1	0	0
Blackwell, Eric, Dodgers*	.232	45	125	12	29	37	1	2	1	14	0	1	2	8	0	25	16	2
Blosser, Gregory, Red Sox*	.288	40	146	17	42	61	7	3	2	20	0	2	1	25	1	19	3	0
Boggetto, Bradley, Dodgers*	.667	15	3	2	2	2	0	0	0	0	0	0	0	2	0	0	0	0
Bohringer, Helmut, Dodgers	.258	13	31	4	8	9	1	0	0	2	2	1	0	3	0	3	2	0
Brenner, Michael, Reds	.197	21	61	9	12	20	1	2	1	6	0	0	1	5	0	23	3	2
Brooks, Bradley, Twins	.167	24	6	1	1	1	0	0	0	0	0	0	1	0	1	0	0
Brown, Alvin, Twins	.194	27	72	2	14	14	0	0	0	5	0	0	2	9	0	22	1	2
Brown, Anthony, Pirates	.294	22	85	12	25	30	3	1	0	11	0	0	0	7	0	7	6	1
Brown, Jimmy, Dodgers†	.143	5	7	0	1	1	0	0	0	1	0	0	0	0	0	3	0	0
Brown, Michael, Pirates*	.221	39	140	18	31	40	5	2	0	11	0	1	2	19	0	28	2	3
Brummer, Jeffrey, Dodgers*	.350	8	20	5	7	7	0	0	0	1	0	1	1	4	1	3	5	1
Bruno, Christopher, Royals*	.275	48	91	17	25	34	4	1	1	10	2	1	0	16	2	22	9	5
Brust, David, Braves*	.258	51	186	27	48	77	11	3	4	33	0	2	0	19	1	33	6	4
Bryant, Jody, Twins*	.105	35	86	11	9	17	1	2	1	13	1	2	2	9	0	39	3	0
Buell, Jeffrey, White Sox*	.254	37	122	20	31	37	6	0	0	13	1	1	1	16	2	27	2	2
Bullett, Scott, Pirates†	.255	46	165	24	42	58	7	3	1	16	1	0	5	12	2	31	15	5
Burroughs, Eric, Reds*	.347	29	121	20	42	49	1	3	0	10	1	1	1	2	0	30	7	3
Burton, Michael, Rangers	.293	56	191	33	56	94	12	4	6	26	0	3	9	20	1	27	1	2
Byers, Jerome, Royals	.202	39	99	18	20	29	4	1	1	9	4	1	1	10	0	32	2	1
Calcina, Luciano, Expos†	.000	1	4	0	0	0	0	0	0	0	0	0	0	0	0	3	0	0
Camarillo, Roberto, Rangers	.170	34	100	13	17	18	1	0	0	6	1	0	0	10	0	36	0	1
Campusano, Genaro, Pirates	.245	30	98	9	24	41	5	0	4	15	0	1	2	2	0	29	1	1
Canate, Emisael, Indians	.208	11	24	4	5	7	2	0	0	0	0	0	0	0	0	8	0	0
Caraballo, Edgardo, Royals	.238	46	160	18	38	47	6	0	1	25	0	4	6	16	0	18	4	4
Caraballo, Ramon, Braves†	.247	20	77	9	19	27	3	1	1	10	1	1	0	10	0	14	5	4
Cardenas, Daniel, Dodgers	.261	55	199	28	52	85	7	7	4	36	0	4	3	13	1	51	5	6
Carroll, Kevin, Mets	.209	37	110	12	23	31	6	1	0	11	1	1	0	15	0	28	2	3
Carter, Terry, Indians	.214	28	84	7	18	21	3	0	0	10	2	1	0	10	0	22	1	0
Castellano, Miguel, Rangers	.247	59	215	27	53	77	12	3	2	26	0	2	0	23	0	22	19	4
Castillo, Dennis, Rangers	.220	46	141	22	31	41	6	2	0	13	0	0	1	17	0	19	9	3
Castro, Frendy, Yankees	.212	25	52	10	11	14	0	0	1	4	1	0	4	4	0	10	1	3
Cepicky, Scott, White Sox*	.316	40	133	14	42	54	8	2	0	23	0	1	2	12	0	13	5	6
Chiusano, Michael, Dodgers	.140	22	50	5	7	9	2	0	0	3	0	0	1	0	11	0	0
Coker, Shane, Reds	.261	45	153	26	40	57	6	4	1	10	2	1	2	7	0	31	14	5
Coleman, Kenneth, White Sox†	.434	22	76	23	33	43	6	2	0	13	1	3	13	0	7	18	6
Colon, Felix, Red Sox	.224	58	214	29	48	77	9	1	6	21	1	1	4	22	2	43	2	1
Cooper, Timothy, Yankees	.182	34	110	16	20	23	3	0	0	11	3	2	3	14	1	30	2	1
Coughlin, Kevin, White Sox*	.257	24	74	11	19	21	2	0	0	13	0	0	0	12	0	8	9	2
Cramer, William, Expos	.800	2	5	2	4	4	0	0	0	2	0	0	0	0	0	0	0	0
Crowder, Kevin, Red Sox	.163	19	43	0	7	7	0	0	0	5	1	1	0	3	1	14	0	0
Curtis, Craig, Astros*	.323	51	186	25	60	79	8	4	1	14	1	0	1	25	1	45	28	5
D'Ambrosio, Andrew, White Sox	.185	26	65	10	12	21	2	2	1	7	0	1	2	12	0	21	1	0
Dallas, Gershon, Astros	.213	47	174	21	37	45	8	0	0	11	0	1	4	8	1	25	8	5
Davis, Gerald, Yankees	.000	1	1	0	0	0	0	0	0	0	0	0	0	0	0	0	0	0
Davis, Gerrod, Mets*	.246	52	195	26	48	64	6	5	0	18	0	0	2	12	0	33	7	11
DeJardin, Bradford, Indians*	.392	16	51	15	20	22	2	0	0	10	0	0	3	17	1	11	4	0
DeLeon, Jorge, Rangers	.164	21	67	5	11	11	0	0	0	4	0	0	6	0	16	3	1
Diaz, Jose, Yankees	.333	1	3	0	1	1	0	0	0	0	0	0	0	1	0	0	0	0
Dickerson, Darnell, Royals	.190	41	100	20	19	26	3	2	0	8	0	0	0	14	0	33	4	2
Diggs, Corey, Astros	.215	41	135	10	29	35	4	1	0	16	0	1	1	10	0	25	4	2
Dismuke, James, Reds*	.184	34	98	6	18	22	1	0	1	5	0	0	3	8	2	19	0	1

Player and Club	Pct.	G.	AB.	R.	H.	TB.	2B.	3B.	HR.	RBI.	SH.	SF.	HP.	BB.	Int. BB.	SO.	SB.	CS.
Dixon, Colin, Red Sox	.276	24	87	10	24	31	2	1	1	7	0	0	3	8	0	10	0	1
Doffek, Scott, Dodgers*	.281	41	135	17	38	44	4	1	0	16	2	2	2	14	0	13	6	2
Doyle, Bernard, Red Sox*	.130	18	46	0	6	7	1	0	0	4	2	0	0	2	0	8	0	1
Dukes, Willie, Red Sox	.248	34	117	11	29	39	4	0	2	8	0	1	1	9	0	32	6	1
Easley, Michael, Indians*	.290	57	214	34	62	98	14	11	0	32	0	1	4	25	5	23	3	7
Eatinger, Michael, White Sox	.257	30	105	17	27	40	6	2	1	16	1	2	0	13	0	14	7	4
Egan, Scott, White Sox	.250	3	8	1	2	3	1	0	0	0	0	0	0	0	0	1	0	0
Eiterman, Thomas, Indians	.324	40	148	28	48	60	6	3	0	27	0	3	3	24	0	13	5	5
Ellis, Christopher, Expos	.120	15	25	2	3	3	0	0	0	2	0	0	2	3	0	11	0	1
Ellis, Jason, Braves	.143	6	14	3	2	3	1	0	0	1	0	0	0	1	0	3	0	1
Encarnacion, Juan, Astros	.192	46	156	16	30	54	8	5	2	19	0	0	3	17	0	49	14	2
Etheridge, Christopher, Expos	.095	18	21	1	2	2	0	0	0	1	0	0	1	2	0	5	0	0
Eusebio, Pedro, Braves*	.229	17	48	6	11	20	3	0	2	6	0	1	0	4	0	13	0	2
Fagnant, Ray, Red Sox	.143	6	14	1	2	3	1	0	0	1	1	0	0	3	0	4	0	0
Feliz, Janeiro, Pirates	.202	43	114	17	23	31	5	0	1	12	1	2	0	19	0	36	8	2
Fields, Kenneth, Red Sox	.252	31	119	6	30	32	2	0	0	5	4	0	0	7	0	18	1	0
Fimbres, Javier, Twins	.244	32	86	13	21	30	4	1	1	15	0	0	5	14	0	14	1	1
Fox, Andrew, Yankees*	.248	40	141	26	35	57	9	2	3	25	0	2	2	31	1	29	6	1
Francisco, Ramirez, Expos†	.333	7	21	2	7	11	2	1	0	0	0	0	0	2	0	4	2	0
Freidman, Jason, Red Sox*	.250	32	116	8	29	37	4	2	0	9	1	0	2	5	1	13	0	2
Frese, Todd, Rangers	.250	6	4	2	1	1	0	0	0	0	0	0	0	1	0	0	0	0
Fully, Edwards, Mets	.270	26	74	8	20	26	4	1	0	7	0	1	1	9	0	14	5	2
Fulton, Robert, Indians*	.269	38	104	14	28	35	2	1	1	18	1	1	0	11	0	21	2	2
Fults, Nathan, Braves	.236	39	144	13	34	44	4	3	0	21	2	4	1	7	0	32	4	4
Gaither, Horace, White Sox*	.297	47	158	30	47	58	7	2	0	11	3	3	0	17	0	13	29	8
Ganino, Eric, Dodgers	.229	29	83	8	19	22	1	1	0	11	0	0	1	5	0	10	0	0
Garcia, Luis, Pirates	.195	22	82	8	16	17	1	0	0	6	0	0	2	2	0	11	2	4
Garcia, Miguel, Indians	.143	28	77	8	11	12	1	0	0	3	1	0	1	7	0	18	1	0
Garcia, Omar, Mets	.255	32	98	15	25	30	3	1	0	8	0	1	1	10	0	22	6	2
Garcia, Silvestre, Astros	.220	48	177	17	39	53	7	2	1	15	0	1	4	6	0	34	7	5
Garcia, Tomas, Pirates	.277	33	112	21	31	35	2	1	0	9	2	0	0	8	0	15	23	3
Garland, Timothy, Yankees	.327	32	107	20	35	40	3	1	0	20	0	3	1	11	0	19	5	3
Garzon, Eliseo, Pirates	.311	13	45	5	14	23	5	2	0	6	0	0	1	4	0	5	0	1
Gerald, Edward, Royals	.184	61	217	30	40	56	1	6	1	21	1	0	1	30	0	80	15	5
Gianni, Gaetano, Reds	.184	22	49	6	9	10	1	0	0	4	2	1	0	9	0	16	0	1
Gilliam, Sean, Yankees	.272	41	162	19	44	64	6	4	2	29	0	4	2	12	1	32	5	1
Gonzalez, Agustin, Reds	.208	21	48	6	10	10	0	0	0	4	1	0	1	14	0	8	1	1
Gonzalez, David, Royals	.250	31	108	20	27	38	6	1	1	16	2	0	0	8	0	15	9	2
Gonzalez, Freddy, Dodgers	.380	51	158	26	60	91	13	6	2	24	0	1	2	17	0	24	7	8
Gonzalez, Pedro, Dodgers	.245	34	94	16	23	28	5	0	0	13	0	0	0	14	0	16	3	1
Gonzalez, Wallace, Braves	.380	16	50	6	19	28	4	1	1	8	0	0	0	4	0	10	3	3
Graham, Timothy, Red Sox	.246	41	134	12	33	42	5	2	0	7	3	1	1	18	0	32	4	2
Grant, Lawrence, Red Sox	.193	42	140	11	27	30	0	0	1	7	1	0	0	16	0	23	0	1
Graterol, Jose, Twins	.267	3	15	5	4	8	1	0	1	1	0	0	0	0	0	4	2	0
Greene, William, Pirates*	.279	23	86	17	24	48	3	3	5	11	0	0	1	9	1	7	6	3
Gremillion, Jeffrey, Pirates	.250	9	32	7	8	12	1	0	1	8	0	0	3	2	0	7	5	0
Griesser, Grant, Royals	.310	19	58	5	18	22	2	1	0	8	1	1	2	3	0	9	1	0
Guanchez, Harry, Royals	.332	59	208	36	69	84	11	2	0	28	1	2	10	22	0	33	6	2
Gumpf, John, Twins	.204	48	157	18	32	45	4	3	1	20	1	0	3	21	0	55	4	0
Guzman, Ramon, White Sox	.191	23	68	3	13	17	2	1	0	5	0	1	2	3	0	16	4	2
Hairston, John, White Sox†	.213	22	47	16	10	15	1	2	0	4	0	1	0	13	0	17	7	1
Hamm, Stacy, Indians	.221	31	77	16	17	20	3	0	0	5	2	0	2	10	0	21	0	4
Hanel, Marcus, Pirates	.231	28	78	11	18	23	3	1	0	8	4	0	0	6	0	18	2	1
Harrell, Steven, Indians*	.438	11	16	6	7	11	2	1	0	0	0	0	0	9	0	5	2	0
Haughney, Trevor, Rangers*	.301	26	73	11	22	23	1	0	0	3	0	1	0	11	0	8	2	1
Hayes, Michael Ray, Pirates	.245	29	94	8	23	25	2	0	0	12	1	0	2	10	0	17	4	3
Heilgeist, James, Expos	.158	14	38	5	6	8	0	1	0	2	0	0	0	9	0	15	1	2
Henderson, Pedro, Indians	.222	41	117	9	26	30	2	1	0	11	0	0	0	11	0	38	3	3
Herron, Pressley, Expos	.279	46	147	23	41	47	4	1	0	9	1	0	1	9	0	23	21	2
Hinson, Dean, Pirates	.197	22	61	6	12	18	3	0	1	4	0	1	0	3	0	18	0	0
Hoerner, Troy, Twins	.206	36	102	13	21	33	3	3	1	16	0	2	1	22	0	37	0	1
Hollis, Jackson, Reds*	.300	29	80	14	24	33	4	1	1	11	0	3	1	24	1	16	4	3
Holum, Brett, Astros*	.283	49	159	16	45	54	5	2	0	16	0	3	2	23	2	23	7	4
Horne, Tyrone, Expos*	.206	24	68	7	14	21	3	2	0	13	0	0	0	11	0	29	4	4
Houk, Thomas, Twins	.285	47	158	26	45	64	15	2	0	23	0	3	1	28	0	26	1	3
Howard, Johnny, Twins*	.317	47	167	20	53	76	10	5	1	28	0	3	0	19	1	32	0	2
Hughes, Troy, Braves	.218	36	110	17	24	29	5	0	0	10	1	1	1	11	0	29	8	4
Hunter, Brian, Astros	.170	51	206	15	35	37	2	0	0	13	0	0	1	7	0	42	12	6
Hurlbutt, Robert, Astros	.100	6	10	1	1	1	0	0	0	0	0	0	0	2	0	1	0	1
Huskey, Robert, Mets	.263	54	190	27	50	86	14	2	6	34	0	0	1	14	0	36	4	1
Indriago, Juan, Royals†	.154	31	65	11	10	12	0	1	0	4	2	0	0	12	0	21	3	2
Isava, Jesus, Royals†	.188	10	16	1	3	3	0	0	0	1	0	0	0	1	0	4	0	0
James, Steven, White Sox*	.222	29	81	15	18	25	1	0	2	11	0	1	1	17	0	22	5	2
Jarvis, John, Yankees*	.189	23	53	9	10	16	1	1	1	3	0	0	0	3	0	13	0	0
Jennings, Lance, Royals	.238	47	164	15	39	45	3	0	1	15	2	1	1	9	0	34	0	2
Jimenez, Ramon, Yankees*	.268	62	250	42	67	114	12	7	7	46	0	1	0	27	0	53	3	2
Jimenez, Roberto, Indians	.158	19	57	8	9	12	3	0	0	3	2	1	0	5	0	11	1	0
Jiminez, Vincent, Braves	.250	33	108	9	27	34	7	0	0	19	1	1	2	8	1	24	3	1
Johnson, Brian, Yankees	.361	17	61	7	22	25	1	1	0	8	0	0	1	4	0	5	0	1
Johnson, Darron, Royals	.273	40	132	15	36	57	9	0	4	20	1	1	0	10	0	19	2	0
Johnson, Kevin, Expos	.182	7	22	4	4	5	1	0	0	0	0	0	1	5	0	9	1	0
Johnson, Marcel, Mets	.190	53	184	23	35	53	4	4	2	14	0	1	4	13	0	40	5	2
Johnson, Scott, Indians	.193	34	109	8	21	24	3	0	0	14	3	1	2	7	0	15	0	0
Jones, Christopher, Royals	.207	32	111	12	23	24	1	0	0	11	0	0	2	10	0	28	2	2
Jones, Maurice, Astros	.167	48	162	18	27	35	4	2	0	5	1	0	4	11	0	66	11	7
Klesko, Ryan, Braves*	.404	17	57	14	23	39	5	4	1	16	0	1	0	6	2	6	4	3
Kluss, Dennis, Indians	.228	59	202	23	46	57	7	2	0	24	2	1	2	35	0	23	9	6
Koenig, Gary, Royals	.320	10	25	6	8	9	1	0	0	3	0	0	0	5	0	5	1	1
Krause, Ronald, Expos*	.282	39	124	20	35	45	4	3	0	15	1	4	1	31	1	24	6	3
Kremblas, Frank, Reds	.230	60	213	32	49	64	10	1	1	18	1	2	1	28	1	44	8	4
Krkovski, Tony, Braves	.219	27	73	14	16	23	5	1	0	7	0	0	0	5	0	29	5	1
Lanfranco, Lepido, Astros	.190	21	58	5	11	14	0	0	1	8	0	0	0	5	0	21	1	0

Player and Club	Pct.	G.	AB.	R.	H.	TB.	2B.	3B.	HR.	RBI.	SH.	SF.	HP.	BB.	Int. BB.	SO.	SB.	CS.
Lewis, Joseph, Rangers°	.222	41	108	11	24	27	3	0	0	12	0	4	1	9	1	15	3	2
Limoncelli, Jeffrey, Red Sox	.182	14	44	6	8	8	0	0	0	2	2	0	0	4	0	7	0	0
Lohry, Adin, Yankees°	.266	38	124	24	33	43	4	3	0	12	0	0	0	28	0	34	5	2
Longmire, Anthony, Pirates†	.000	2	5	0	0	0	0	0	0	0	0	0	0	1	0	1	0	0
Lopez, Bartolome, Astros	.233	31	90	6	21	28	1	0	2	6	0	1	2	2	0	26	0	3
Lora, Jose, Red Sox	.177	28	96	10	17	19	0	1	0	2	1	1	0	6	0	28	0	0
Lott, Billy, Dodgers	.193	46	150	18	29	39	2	4	0	9	1	0	1	10	0	48	5	1
Lucin, Anthony, Astros	.194	25	67	6	13	15	2	0	0	6	0	1	2	3	0	17	0	1
Machuca, Victor, Reds†	.264	20	53	10	14	16	2	0	0	2	0	0	0	14	0	5	2	2
Maldonado, Ricardo, Expos	.194	55	160	15	31	37	3	0	1	15	1	2	1	17	0	41	1	2
Manuel, Ferral, Rangers	.250	7	12	1	3	3	0	0	0	1	0	0	3	2	0	2	0	1
Marabella, Antonio, Expos°	.286	32	98	14	28	41	5	1	2	14	2	1	0	13	0	7	1	1
Martin, Eugene, Braves	.186	41	145	19	27	34	2	1	1	12	3	3	2	17	0	31	10	4
Martin, Jon, Pirates	.500	1	4	0	2	2	0	0	0	1	0	0	0	1	0	1	1	2
Martin, Todd, White Sox	.250	23	84	14	21	21	0	0	0	5	1	0	0	8	0	18	10	5
Martinez, Erasmo, Dodgers	.133	17	30	0	4	4	0	0	0	0	0	0	1	3	0	11	0	1
Martinez, John, Indians†	.247	32	89	4	22	28	4	1	0	8	0	1	0	5	0	17	0	1
Marze, Dickey, Braves	.276	52	181	44	50	83	13	4	4	22	4	1	2	37	1	32	14	2
Mason, Felton, Expos	.191	23	68	9	13	19	1	1	1	9	0	1	7	0	0	27	12	4
Mathis, Wayne, Mets°	.218	54	197	24	43	57	5	3	1	17	4	6	7	22	0	41	20	6
Matilla, Pedro, Red Sox	.285	41	130	18	37	57	5	0	5	23	2	2	1	20	1	19	0	0
Matos, Malvin, Rangers	.254	43	134	15	34	38	4	0	0	10	1	1	0	6	0	24	6	3
McKamie, Sean, Dodgers	.316	42	133	20	42	45	3	0	0	15	4	2	2	23	0	22	13	2
McKinnon, Willie, Twins	.220	26	50	5	11	12	1	0	0	4	0	0	3	0	0	10	2	0
McLin, Joseph, Pirates	.244	13	41	8	10	15	0	1	1	3	0	0	0	6	0	12	3	0
McMillan, Stuart, Braves	.164	25	67	8	11	15	0	2	0	10	0	2	2	15	0	22	4	3
McNeely, Jeffrey, Red Sox	.406	9	32	10	13	16	1	1	0	4	0	1	0	7	0	3	5	1
Mendez, Miguel, Braves	.288	28	104	15	30	47	3	4	2	16	0	1	2	6	0	16	5	3
Meyer, Paul, Mets	.151	31	106	3	16	23	2	1	1	7	0	1	5	0	0	23	2	0
Milholland, Eric, White Sox	.000	1	1	0	0	0	0	0	0	0	0	0	0	0	0	1	0	0
Miranda, Giovanni, Royals	.311	55	193	38	60	70	4	3	0	24	2	4	1	19	0	15	23	9
Mitchell, Antonio, Pirates	.275	13	40	4	11	11	0	0	0	1	0	1	0	4	0	10	1	0
Mitchell, Timothy, Red Sox°	.205	29	73	12	15	22	7	0	0	8	0	0	2	16	0	16	1	2
Molina, Carlos, Reds	.272	35	92	14	25	37	7	1	1	14	0	0	7	8	0	23	1	3
Mompres, Danilo, Mets	.239	56	197	16	47	69	14	4	0	18	1	4	3	18	1	39	9	3
Montero, Jorge, Astros	.209	42	129	19	27	45	6	3	2	10	0	0	1	11	0	46	7	4
Monzon, Daniel, White Sox	.250	25	72	17	18	23	3	1	0	10	2	2	1	15	0	12	3	0
Moore, Devren, Mets	.200	49	160	18	32	50	3	6	1	14	0	1	0	22	0	56	12	6
Moore, Lawrence, Reds†	.000	4	13	1	0	0	0	0	0	1	1	0	0	1	0	1	3	0
Moore, Sean, Red Sox	.267	28	86	10	23	35	4	1	2	13	0	2	0	4	0	12	2	1
Moore, Timothy, Twins°	.168	37	95	10	16	19	3	0	0	10	0	0	0	24	0	26	19	1
Morgan, Dennis, Braves°	.231	17	52	6	12	12	0	0	0	3	0	0	1	0	0	12	0	2
Mota, William, Twins†	.220	14	41	5	9	10	1	0	0	5	1	1	0	2	0	6	1	1
Mouton, Brian, Rangers	.213	53	183	21	39	54	4	4	1	17	1	2	1	13	0	35	4	1
Moye, Wayne, White Sox°	.213	19	47	5	10	14	0	2	0	3	1	1	0	4	0	17	3	3
Murray, Glenn, Expos	.172	27	87	10	15	25	6	2	0	7	0	1	2	6	0	30	8	1
Niemeyer, Bryan, Red Sox	.000	2	2	0	0	0	0	0	0	0	0	0	0	0	0	1	0	0
Noriega, Reynaldo, Yankees†	.296	39	125	29	37	53	4	6	0	16	3	3	1	33	0	27	7	2
Norman, Kenneth, Twins†	.218	43	124	17	27	35	4	2	0	13	0	0	4	7	0	37	21	1
Norris, Randy, White Sox	.250	34	76	13	19	22	1	1	0	8	1	0	1	10	0	21	10	2
Nunez, Alejandro, Twins†	.223	48	188	24	42	49	5	1	0	7	0	0	1	15	0	49	30	5
Nunez, Rogelio, White Sox	.226	38	106	8	24	25	1	0	0	10	3	1	0	1	0	21	8	4
Ochoa, Rafael, White Sox	.150	17	40	5	6	6	0	0	0	5	0	1	0	6	0	13	1	0
Ortega, Hector, Expos	.077	5	13	3	1	1	0	0	0	0	0	0	0	3	0	5	1	1
Ortiz, Ramon, Indians	.400	3	10	2	4	5	1	0	0	0	0	0	0	2	0	2	1	1
Oster, Paul, Yankees†	.000	1	2	0	0	0	0	0	0	0	0	0	0	0	0	2	0	0
Palys, Michael, Indians	.186	27	70	11	13	16	3	0	0	5	2	1	1	14	1	16	1	3
Penn, Shannon, Rangers†	.218	47	147	19	32	36	2	1	0	8	0	1	1	20	0	27	17	7
Perez, Guillermo, Reds†	.186	16	43	7	8	9	1	0	0	3	0	0	1	3	0	16	1	0
Perez, Joseph, Indians°	.237	17	59	8	14	16	2	0	0	8	1	0	0	1	0	16	5	0
Perozo, Ender, Red Sox†	.267	23	75	8	20	28	5	0	1	6	0	0	4	7	0	15	0	1
Phillips, James, Pirates	.333	2	6	2	2	4	0	1	0	1	0	0	0	2	0	1	0	0
Pichardo, Francisco, Twins†	.250	30	80	3	20	22	2	0	0	4	0	1	0	5	0	18	8	1
Pierce, Dominic, Rangers	.233	36	120	10	28	39	6	1	1	13	0	2	0	7	1	14	0	4
Pitcavage, Joel, Pirates	.324	20	68	9	22	25	3	0	0	5	0	1	0	5	0	8	1	0
Powell, Kenneth, Rangers	.257	53	179	27	46	57	7	2	0	21	0	2	2	22	1	35	6	5
Puchales, Javier, Dodgers°	.333	41	120	15	40	42	2	0	0	9	2	0	2	4	0	14	8	6
Quijada, Edward, Astros	.253	25	75	10	19	27	6	1	0	10	0	1	2	19	1	19	2	3
Quinones, Eliezer, Reds	.278	38	115	22	32	42	7	0	1	15	0	2	0	12	1	15	8	2
Ramirez, Francisco, Twins	.181	29	72	6	13	17	4	0	0	7	1	2	1	5	0	19	0	0
Ramos, Jorge, White Sox	.213	46	141	17	30	35	2	0	1	17	3	1	5	8	0	26	9	4
Ramos, Kenneth, Indians°	.311	54	193	41	60	74	7	2	1	14	3	2	3	39	1	18	17	7
Ramsey, Jeffrey, Expos°	.234	60	192	20	45	66	6	3	3	24	0	2	1	24	1	31	8	5
Reyes, Freddy, Mets	.042	9	24	2	1	1	0	0	0	0	2	0	0	2	0	9	0	0
Reyes, Glen, Astros†	.175	33	97	8	17	18	1	0	0	9	0	0	3	10	0	27	6	2
Reyes, Victor, Rangers	.080	15	25	3	2	4	0	1	0	2	0	0	7	0	5	6	0	0
Rittman, Arness, Mets	.191	43	136	13	26	32	2	2	0	12	1	2	1	10	0	20	13	6
Rivera, David, Twins†	.248	48	145	28	36	44	6	1	0	9	0	0	0	15	0	23	30	1
Rivera, Hector, Expos	.172	30	64	7	11	13	2	0	0	3	1	0	2	5	0	15	1	5
Roberts, Mark, Reds†	.273	26	88	12	24	27	3	0	0	7	1	0	0	5	0	10	2	2
Robertson, Jason, Yankees°	.285	58	214	27	61	83	12	5	0	31	0	4	0	28	0	28	4	4
Roble, Josman, Braves°	.282	56	202	37	57	88	18	2	3	37	2	2	3	25	4	47	7	4
Robles, Roberto, Pirates	.259	31	112	11	29	50	3	3	4	21	0	2	1	5	0	38	4	2
Rodriguez, Abimael, Expos	.238	36	80	9	19	24	3	1	0	10	1	1	1	11	0	18	2	5
Rodriguez, Andres, Yankees	.302	56	212	28	64	75	7	2	0	18	3	1	0	9	0	34	3	3
Rodriguez, Hector, Pirates	.237	53	198	22	47	59	4	4	0	17	1	1	3	11	0	45	2	1
Rodriguez, Luis, Expos	.238	48	143	23	34	40	6	0	0	10	2	2	2	20	0	28	8	0
Rogers, Keith, Pirates°	.271	21	70	13	19	34	3	3	2	6	0	2	1	12	1	23	4	3
Rolfes, Michael, Braves°	.000	17	0	0	0	0	0	0	0	0	0	0	1	1	0	0	0	0
Romano, Scott, Yankees	.215	51	195	28	42	59	9	1	2	24	3	2	2	22	0	38	4	2
Ronca, Joseph, Pirates	.218	45	179	21	39	50	6	1	1	18	0	1	0	8	0	19	7	4
Rudolph, Mason, Mets	.177	21	62	3	11	13	2	0	0	1	3	0	0	0	0	24	1	0
Salcido, Mario, Braves	.250	17	44	7	11	13	2	0	0	5	4	1	2	3	0	6	1	0

Player and Club	Pct.	G.	AB.	R.	H.	TB.	2B.	3B.	HR.	RBI.	SH.	SF.	HP.	BB.	Int. BB.	SO.	SB.	CS.
Sanders, Lance, White Sox	.238	10	21	3	5	8	1	1	0	4	0	0	0	8	0	5	2	0
Santana, Jose, Indians	.200	35	115	10	23	30	5	1	0	21	0	1	0	8	0	13	1	3
Santiago, Angelo, Expos	.248	62	202	26	50	86	14	2	6	32	0	3	2	29	1	63	3	3
Schiel, Robert, Twins	.190	43	137	24	26	38	6	0	2	14	0	1	4	24	0	36	1	1
Semke, Jay, Reds°	.262	44	141	15	37	50	5	1	2	26	1	5	1	16	0	24	5	2
Sena, Sean, Dodgers	.183	38	104	8	19	21	2	0	0	5	3	1	1	10	0	19	3	2
Shepherd, Michael, Braves	.000	27	1	0	0	0	0	0	0	0	0	0	0	0	0	1	0	0
Sheppard, Donald, White Sox	.183	26	82	11	15	19	4	0	0	4	1	0	0	7	0	28	4	4
Smith, Charles, Expos°	.273	7	22	5	6	7	1	0	0	3	0	0	0	4	0	5	1	0
Solimine, Joseph, White Sox	.203	25	69	11	14	23	6	0	1	10	0	0	1	15	0	14	1	1
Strickland, Dedrick, Yankees†	.100	4	10	1	1	1	0	0	0	0	0	0	1	1	0	1	1	0
Sugimoto, Craig, Expos	.200	51	150	11	30	40	7	0	1	14	0	2	0	17	0	21	1	2
Sweeney, Michael, Braves	.259	13	54	9	14	17	1	1	0	9	1	0	0	3	0	16	2	1
Taylor, David, Twins	.287	39	122	24	35	61	10	5	2	15	1	0	0	16	0	41	0	0
Tena, Paulino, Rangers	.271	59	229	30	62	77	11	2	0	26	0	5	1	6	0	31	9	4
Teter, Craig, White Sox	.284	43	134	15	38	62	11	2	3	21	0	4	2	9	0	25	6	8
Texidor, Jose, Rangers	.000	8	11	0	0	0	0	0	0	0	0	0	0	2	0	2	0	1
Thomas, Colovito, Braves	.226	27	93	14	21	24	1	1	0	4	2	0	2	11	0	13	9	1
Thomas, Frank, White Sox	.365	17	52	8	19	27	5	0	1	11	0	2	1	11	0	3	1	0
Thome, James, Indians°	.237	55	186	22	44	55	5	3	0	22	3	2	1	21	1	33	6	4
Thompson, Jeffrey, Mets†	.203	45	133	23	27	30	3	0	0	10	1	0	0	30	0	32	11	2
Troncoso, Nolberto, Dodgers	.300	48	150	28	45	55	8	1	0	27	0	0	2	29	0	29	20	5
Tucker, Robert, Astros†	.160	16	25	2	4	6	2	0	0	5	0	0	0	2	0	4	0	1
Tucker, Tony, Twins	.235	38	119	18	28	38	5	1	1	18	1	3	1	12	0	27	2	2
Turner, Brian, Yankees°	.207	50	188	29	39	55	7	3	1	28	2	3	2	20	0	30	5	2
Turrentine, Richard, Yankees	.169	34	130	21	22	33	5	3	0	10	1	1	0	13	0	43	2	2
Tyson, Kevin, Braves	.136	33	103	11	14	19	2	0	1	8	2	0	0	14	0	31	2	3
Valentin, Alfredo, White Sox	.222	28	99	16	22	30	6	1	0	15	0	2	0	4	0	15	4	2
Vann, Troy, Red Sox	.190	27	79	9	15	19	0	2	0	7	1	0	0	5	0	18	0	0
Vasquez, Russell, Dodgers	.235	45	132	11	31	39	3	1	1	21	2	2	0	9	0	22	1	3
Vazquez, Pedro, Royals†	.235	51	187	16	44	45	1	0	0	17	3	1	4	12	0	31	7	2
Velez, Noel, Reds	.260	51	177	20	46	60	6	1	2	19	0	0	1	12	0	28	3	7
Virden, Mikel, Expos†	.253	35	95	13	24	32	5	0	1	10	0	0	1	14	0	26	4	2
Vitko, Joseph, Mets	.000	8	1	0	0	0	0	0	0	0	0	0	0	0	0	0	0	0
Walling, Michael, Braves	.000	20	1	0	0	0	0	0	0	0	0	0	0	0	0	0	0	0
Ward, Turner, Indians†	.200	4	15	2	3	3	0	0	0	1	0	0	0	2	0	2	1	0
Watson, Todd, Reds°	.290	61	224	21	65	90	10	6	1	41	4	1	5	30	1	27	8	2
Whims, Charles, Dodgers°	.222	11	27	4	6	11	0	1	1	5	0	0	3	0	12	1	1
Wiley, James, Yankees°	.200	16	15	1	3	6	1	1	0	2	0	0	0	1	0	7	0	0
Williams, Anthony, Mets°	.216	44	162	18	35	49	6	4	0	16	0	2	2	13	0	52	15	3
Williams, Barry, White Sox†	.143	5	21	2	3	4	1	0	0	0	0	0	0	1	0	6	2	0
Williams, Clifford, Rangers	.000	1	1	0	0	0	0	0	0	0	0	0	0	0	0	0	0	0
Williams, Timothy, Pirates	.159	22	69	3	11	12	1	0	0	4	1	0	1	2	0	18	4	2
Witherspoon, Richard, Red Sox	.229	9	35	1	8	11	1	1	0	7	0	0	1	1	0	7	0	0
Woods, Terre, Red Sox	.281	28	96	11	27	30	3	0	0	9	0	0	1	1	0	5	4	1
Wright, Benny, Reds	.232	53	177	21	41	55	7	2	1	12	4	1	6	20	0	42	5	5
Young, Eric, Dodgers	.330	56	197	53	65	92	11	5	2	22	1	1	3	33	1	16	41	10
Young, Ronald, Indians†	.167	13	12	2	2	2	0	0	0	1	0	0	0	0	7	1	0
Zambrano, Jose, Red Sox	.212	10	33	4	7	7	0	0	0	4	0	0	0	7	0	4	2	0

The following pitchers, listed alphabetically by club, with games in parentheses, had no plate appearances, primarily through use of designated hitters:

ASTROS—Allen, David (13); Brown, Duane (13); Emm, Arthur (5); Gutierrez, Anthony (12); Hampton, Mark (11); Juden, Jeffrey (9); Metheney, David (2); Munoz, Julio (9); Navarro, Luis (7); Prats, Mario (17); Rinaldi, Kevin (21); Rivas, Limbert (27); Scott, Tyrone (12); Wheeler, Kenneth (14).

BRAVES—Bruck, Thomas (12); Chiles, Barry (3); Cullens, Eric (17); Dickman, David (7); Gabriele, Michael (15); Gallaher, Anthony (12); Grebe, Brett (12); Maye, Anthony (7); Murray, Matthew (2); Roa, Joseph (13); Steinmetz, Robert (10); Thomas, Ronald (5).

DODGERS—Astacio, Pedro (12); Bishop, Craig (9); Braase, John (21); Calderon, Edmund (18); Cantres, Jorge (15); Daniel, Anthony (18); Delahoya, Javier (9); Hoffman, Kevin (5); Mesa, Baltazar (11); Patrick, Tim (7); Takaheshi, Koji (3); Tatis, Fausto (11).

EXPOS—Ashley, Duane (7); Aucoin, Derek (7); Barry, Jeffrey (10); Bochtler, Douglas (9); Diaz, Rafael (11); Eddy, James (5); Espinosa, Carlos (20); Fier, Michael (12); Hutto, Paul (25); Lane, Kevin (28); Martinez, Martin (10); Perez, Julio (10); Romberg, Michael (11); Thigpen, Arthur (14); Torres, Fernando (11); Tuss, Jeffrey (13).

INDIANS—Kallevig, Dane (11); McElfish, Shawn (27); Mirabella, Gennaro (18); Morrison, Teryl (12); Paxton, Gregory (8); Ryan, Robert (8); Soper, Michael (32); Stevens, Jeffrey (23); Walden, Alan (11); Wechsberg, Von (9); Wertz, William (12).

METS—Anaya, Michael (12); Benson, Nathaniel (15); Bristow, Richard (19); Castillo, Juan (14); Langan, Richard (8); Lindsay, Darian (22); Martinez, Jose (11); Ramirez, Hector (16); Rees, Robert (11); Thomas, Michael (8); Torres, Jose (2); Wilson, Thomas (5).

PIRATES—Arias, Julio (9); Broadwater, Thomas (11); Brown, Scott (12); DeLosSantos, Mariano (13); Fajardo, Hector (10); Francescon, Louis (12); Hawkins, Rodney (18); Hope, John (4); Lyle, Jeffrey (9); Mays, Keith (11); Pagan, Joseph (13); Perez, Rafael (2); Roeder, Steven (12); Rychel, Kevin (13); Scoates, Richard (7); Shade, Derek (11); Smith, Todd (2); Sparks, Shane (7).

RANGERS—Alexander, Gerald (6); Arner, Michael (13); Ayala, Jason (4); Barreiro, Fernando (14); Buckley, Travis (16); Castro, Confessor (8); Correa, Edwin (4); DeVaughan, Todd (3); Fowler, Kevin (23); Gamez, Robert (23); Giberti, David (4); Keon, Kevin (4); Kerfut, George (4); MacNeil, Timothy (14); McGough, Keith (15); McMurtry, Craig (14); Mileski, Thomas (10); Moyer, Jamie (3); Phillips, Brad (14); Randle, Carl (13); Scheetz, Brian (5); St. Pe, Irving (8); Washington, Tyrone (6).

REDS—Cecil, Timothy (13); Diaz, Rafael J. (10); Hook, Christopher (14); King, Douglas (13); Linares, Yfrain (15); Manon, Ramon (11); Minutelli, Gino (1); Nieves, Ernesto (25); Perez, Jose (14); Plemmons, Scott (12); Ray, John (11); Stevens, Dale (19); Vasquez, Ricardo (14); Wyatt, Charles (9).

RED SOX—Allen, Tracy (9); Budrewicz, Timothy (3); Conroy, Brian (7); Delgado, Richard (17); Dennison, James (5); Gonzales, Melvin (14); Hansell, Gregory (10); Malzone, John (15); Morton, Kevin (2); Quantrill, Paul (2); Ring, David (11); Santamaria, Silverio (16); Santiago, Cedric (15); Scott, Rennie (13).

ROYALS—Aranguren, Ismael (16); Baez, Francisco (18); Berumen, Andres (12); Bowling, Stanley (14); Bryans, Jason (7); Chrisman, James (8); Connor, John (21); Dunn, William (19); Foster, Clinton (1); Gross, John (6); Harvey, Todd (17); Malena, Ramon (22); Milton, Herbert (12); Reno, Brent (22); West, Eric (12).

TWINS—Abel, Jackie (22); Alvarez, Alejandro (12); Arias, Jose (7); Bethancourt, Jose (15); Chmielewski, Shon (15); Lipson, Marc (23); Mieses, Melanio (15); Pulido, Juan (22); Reyes, Elvis (18); Robles, Scott (12).

WHITE SOX—Bittiger, Jeffrey (2); Borgula, Thomas (14); Caridad, Roland (13); Chafin, John (4); Conover, Kevin (17); Garcia, Ramon (14); Gennings, Brian (5); Hulme, Patrick (15); Hunter, Robert (10); Johnson, Ernie (5); Jones, Barry (8); King, Eric (2); Matznick, Daniel (12); McDowell, Jack (4); Mongiello, Michael (8); Robinson, James (10); Ruiz, Jorge (11); Thoma, Scott (20); Tolar, Kevin (13).

YANKEES—Brubaker, Franklin (2); Candelaria, John (2); Chase, Scott (1); Dacosta, William (4); Gietzen, Peter (18); Haller, James (24);

Hitchcock, Sterling (13); Johnston, Daniel (16); Mauldin, James (8); Munoz, Roberto (2); Perez, Cesar (11); Perry, Stevie (15); Polak, Richard (8); Quirico, Rafael (17); Rojas, Ubaldo (14); Springer, Russell (6).

GRAND SLAM HOME RUNS—Bruno, Bryant, Castro, S. Garcia, Huskey, D. Johnson, Maldonado, Molina, Robles, Solimine, Taylor, Turner, 1 each.

AWARDED FIRST BASE ON CATCHER'S INTERFERENCE—Blosser (John Martinez); Ramsey (Jarvis); Robertson (R. Nunez); R. Tucker (P. Gonzalez).

CLUB FIELDING

Club	Pct.	G.	PO.	A.	E.	DP.	PB.	Club	Pct.	G.	PO.	A.	E.	DP.	PB.
Royals	.965	63	1658	679	86	50	13	Indians	.951	63	1683	742	125	50	13
Yankees	.963	63	1683	684	91	40	20	Red Sox	.951	63	1662	746	125	42	12
Dodgers	.963	63	1676	663	91	46	16	Pirates	.948	63	1604	708	126	59	25
White Sox	.960	63	1635	707	97	64	22	Twins	.946	63	1603	729	132	66	40
Rangers	.959	65	1671	664	100	45	37	Astros	.938	63	1638	663	151	43	26
Braves	.956	64	1699	737	113	56	30	Mets	.938	65	1639	710	154	49	19
Reds	.953	63	1667	739	118	51	10	Expos	.938	66	1672	689	156	34	21

Triple Plays—Braves, Royals, Twins.

INDIVIDUAL FIELDING

*Throws lefthanded.

FIRST BASEMEN

Player and Club	Pct.	G.	PO.	A.	E.	DP.	Player and Club	Pct.	G.	PO.	A.	E.	DP.
Alvarez, Red Sox	.982	14	102	10	2	7	Holum, Astros	.977	23	202	6	5	11
Batista, Red Sox*	1.000	3	7	0	0	0	Howard, Twins*	.984	43	411	22	7	40
Berge, Reds*	.985	25	186	9	3	19	Huskey, Mets	1.000	3	23	1	0	1
Boggetto, Dodgers	1.000	1	7	0	0	0	James, White Sox*	.800	1	7	1	2	0
Brooks, Twins	1.000	5	15	0	0	1	JIMENEZ, Yankees*	.991	62	540	29	5	33
Brown, Pirates*	.951	32	263	29	15	23	D. Johnson, Royals	.976	11	79	4	2	4
Bruno, Royals*	1.000	1	2	0	0	0	M. Johnson, Mets	.976	36	302	20	8	22
Brust, Braves	.989	8	81	5	1	5	S. Johnson, Indians	.982	21	148	13	3	11
Buell, White Sox*	.974	34	274	26	8	29	Lopez, Astros	.963	10	75	4	3	2
Bullett, Pirates*	.946	6	52	1	3	6	Maldonado, Expos	.926	4	23	2	2	1
Burton, Rangers	.990	52	481	37	5	30	McLin, Pirates	.987	8	73	4	1	7
Campusano, Pirates	1.000	2	15	0	0	2	Mitchell, Red Sox*	.988	12	81	4	1	7
Castellano, Rangers	.955	9	58	5	3	5	Perozo, Red Sox	1.000	1	2	0	0	0
Cepicky, White Sox	.991	11	102	4	1	6	Phillips, Pirates	1.000	2	22	2	0	1
Crowder, Red Sox	.950	7	35	3	2	1	Pierce, Rangers	1.000	6	45	4	0	5
Curtis, Astros*	.968	35	282	17	10	23	Ramsey, Expos	.926	3	21	4	2	1
D'Ambrosio, White Sox	.984	11	60	2	1	6	Roble, Braves*	.972	56	515	37	16	44
Dismuke, Reds	.983	28	215	16	4	16	Rodriguez, Pirates	.982	13	105	6	2	8
Dixon, Red Sox	1.000	5	52	2	0	1	Rudolph, Mets	1.000	1	3	1	0	1
Easley, Indians	.980	9	84	13	2	10	Santana, Indians	.992	30	239	14	2	16
Eiterman, Indians	1.000	12	107	9	0	7	Santiago, Expos	.963	56	430	32	18	14
Eusebio, Braves*	.979	5	41	5	1	1	Sugimoto, Expos	.976	10	77	3	2	5
Fimbres, Twins	.983	16	113	2	2	13	Taylor, Twins	.984	6	59	3	1	5
Freidman, Red Sox*	.990	30	284	25	3	16	Thomas, White Sox	.986	15	130	8	2	18
Garcia, Mets	.960	30	250	14	11	22	Troncoso, Dodgers	.989	44	344	21	4	32
Garzon, Pirates	1.000	1	10	1	0	2	Tucker, Pirates	1.000	1	13	0	0	0
Gonzalez, Dodgers	1.000	22	166	10	0	11	Turner, Yankees*	1.000	2	9	0	0	0
Gremillion, Pirates	1.000	1	2	0	0	0	Vasquez, Dodgers	1.000	7	25	0	0	0
Guanchez, Royals	.983	57	471	35	9	43	Watson, Reds	.975	20	189	8	5	10
Gumpf, Twins	1.000	1	4	0	0	1							

Triple Plays—Brust, Guanchez.

SECOND BASEMEN

Player and Club	Pct.	G.	PO.	A.	E.	DP.	Player and Club	Pct.	G.	PO.	A.	E.	DP.
Anglada, Astros	.981	24	48	57	2	13	Holum, Astros	1.000	1	1	4	0	0
Apolinario, Braves	.969	58	105	149	8	32	Houk, Twins	1.000	1	2	5	0	0
Atwater, Expos	.929	21	37	41	6	5	Indriago, Royals	.984	11	34	28	1	7
Awkard, Red Sox	.900	4	7	2	1	0	Kluss, Indians	.966	47	100	126	8	26
Bagwell, Red Sox	1.000	1	0	1	0	0	Kremblas, Reds	.957	39	86	115	9	27
Berroa, Braves	.500	1	1	0	1	0	Krkovski, Braves	.973	10	16	20	1	1
Bohringer, Dodgers	1.000	3	4	5	0	0	Limoncelli, Red Sox	.911	11	18	23	4	3
Brenner, Reds	.961	11	24	25	2	6	Machuca, Royals	.935	19	28	44	5	7
Brown, Dodgers	1.000	5	3	4	0	1	Marabella, Expos	1.000	1	0	1	0	0
Calcina, Expos	1.000	1	1	0	0	0	Miranda, Royals	1.000	9	11	29	0	1
Camarillo, Rangers	.905	5	6	13	2	2	Mompres, Mets	.952	33	59	80	7	19
Caraballo, Braves	.500	1	0	1	1	0	Monzon, White Sox	.955	13	33	30	3	11
Castillo, Rangers	.967	25	43	44	3	7	Moore, Reds	1.000	1	2	2	0	0
Coleman, White Sox	.990	22	43	61	1	13	Noriega, Yankees	.949	31	67	82	8	13
Colon, Red Sox	.944	4	10	7	1	0	Penn, Rangers	.965	42	68	71	5	15
Diaz, Yankees	1.000	1	2	2	0	1	Reyes, Astros	.903	29	47	55	11	9
Diggs, Astros	.919	19	32	36	6	5	Rittman, Mets	.929	16	30	35	5	6
Doffek, Dodgers	.984	16	33	27	1	5	Rivera, Twins	.948	43	87	131	12	30
Eatinger, White Sox	.953	28	52	70	6	18	A. Rodriguez, Expos	.945	19	23	29	3	2
Feliz, Pirates	.952	27	59	80	7	12	H. Rodriguez, Pirates	.000	1	0	0	1	0
Fields, Red Sox	.950	27	51	82	7	19	L. Rodriguez, Expos	.944	25	52	49	6	5
Francisco, Expos	.967	7	9	20	1	2	Ronca, Pirates	.875	5	7	14	3	6
Frese, Rangers	1.000	1	2	0	0	0	Schiel, Twins	.946	26	49	73	7	21
Gaither, White Sox	1.000	3	4	7	0	2	Sena, Dodgers	1.000	1	2	2	0	1
L. Garcia, Rangers	.900	3	4	5	1	1	Thompson, Mets	.949	24	38	55	5	11
M. Garcia, Indians	.940	26	42	52	6	8	Turrentine, Yankees	.905	33	68	66	14	12
T. Garcia, Pirates	.959	31	64	100	7	23	Vasquez, Dodgers	1.000	1	0	1	0	0
Gonzalez, Dodgers	1.000	1	1	0	0	0	VAZQUEZ, Royals	.970	46	117	109	7	32
Grant, Red Sox	.955	19	34	51	4	5	Young, Dodgers	.939	47	104	128	15	22
Herron, Expos	.923	6	14	22	3	3	Zambrano, Red Sox	.800	1	2	2	1	0

Triple Plays—Krkovski, Rivera, Vazquez.

THIRD BASEMEN

Player and Club	Pct.	G.	PO.	A.	E.	DP.	Player and Club	Pct.	G.	PO.	A.	E.	DP.
Abell, Rangers	.889	3	4	4	1	0	Marabella, Expos	.859	28	9	52	10	1
Anglada, Astros	.887	17	15	32	6	4	E. Martin, Braves	1.000	1	0	1	0	0
Atwater, Expos	.852	8	5	18	4	0	T. Martin, White Sox	1.000	1	0	1	0	0
Aude, Pirates	.821	23	23	32	12	4	Martinez, Dodgers	.929	15	1	12	1	0
Bagwell, Red Sox	.867	5	2	11	2	0	Mathis, Mets	1.000	1	1	1	0	0
Bohringer, Dodgers	1.000	8	4	18	0	0	Mendez, Braves	.926	28	17	70	7	4
Brust, Braves	.914	27	23	41	6	6	Miranda, Royals	1.000	7	4	7	0	0
Bryant, Twins	.857	2	4	2	1	1	Monzon, White Sox	.909	9	9	11	2	1
Caraballo, Royals	.910	42	31	80	11	5	Morgan, Braves	.781	8	7	18	7	2
Castellano, Rangers	.846	6	3	8	2	1	Murray, Expos	.805	16	7	26	8	0
Colon, Red Sox	.893	10	11	14	3	4	Ortega, Expos	.800	5	2	6	2	0
Cooper, Yankees	.833	24	10	35	9	2	Palys, Indians	.000	1	0	0	1	0
Crowder, Red Sox	.900	10	5	13	2	0	Perez, Reds	.811	14	9	21	7	0
D'Ambrosio, White Sox	.667	4	1	9	5	0	Perozo, Red Sox	.967	10	5	24	1	1
Dixon, Red Sox	.851	19	21	36	10	2	Pierce, Rangers	.667	1	1	1	1	0
Doffek, Dodgers	.750	8	3	9	4	1	Pitcavage, Pirates	1.000	1	0	3	0	0
Easley, Indians	.903	46	40	100	15	3	Quijada, Astros	.885	25	21	48	9	5
Eatinger, White Sox	1.000	2	0	7	0	0	Ramos, White Sox	.919	24	15	53	6	7
Feliz, Pirates	1.000	1	0	3	0	1	Rittman, Mets	.862	21	28	53	13	2
Fields, Red Sox	.875	4	4	3	1	1	Rivera, Expos	1.000	1	0	4	0	0
Fox, Yankees	.920	40	37	78	10	6	Roberts, Reds	1.000	13	9	31	0	3
Gaither, White Sox	.891	29	13	36	6	6	H. Rodriguez, Pirates	.881	40	29	75	14	8
Garcia, Astros	.875	1	2	5	1	0	L. Rodriguez, Expos	.927	14	18	20	3	2
Gonzalez, Dodgers	.909	10	4	16	2	2	Romano, Yankees	.667	1	0	2	1	0
Grant, Red Sox	.833	3	3	7	2	0	Rudolph, Mets	1.000	1	0	1	0	0
Holum, Astros	.870	24	26	54	12	5	Sanders, White Sox	1.000	1	0	1	0	0
Houk, Twins	.886	37	29	72	13	9	Schiel, Twins	.938	7	6	9	1	0
Huskey, Mets	.871	46	50	105	23	6	Sugimoto, Expos	.875	2	3	4	1	0
Indriago, Royals	.750	1	2	1	1	1	Taylor, Twins	.766	27	16	33	15	1
Jones, Astros	.886	17	11	28	5	1	TENA, Rangers	.911	59	41	143	18	8
Kluss, Indians	1.000	6	3	7	0	0	Thome, Indians	.860	17	14	29	7	2
Kremblas, Reds	.500	1	1	0	1	0	Vasquez, Dodgers	.938	40	30	60	6	7
Krkovski, Braves	.833	5	1	4	1	0	Velez, Reds	.899	46	39	95	15	4
Limoncelli, Red Sox	1.000	2	2	0	0	0	Woods, Red Sox	.741	9	4	16	7	1
Lopez, Astros	1.000	1	0	1	0	0	Zambrano, Red Sox	1.000	1	0	1	0	0

SHORTSTOPS

Player and Club	Pct.	G.	PO.	A.	E.	DP.	Player and Club	Pct.	G.	PO.	A.	E.	DP.
Abell, Rangers	.942	42	61	102	10	22	T. Martin, White Sox	.935	22	40	60	7	18
Andujar, Indians	.872	32	61	89	22	21	Martinez, Dodgers	1.000	1	0	2	0	1
Anglada, Astros	.923	3	4	8	1	2	Marze, Braves	.900	47	70	129	22	23
Apolinario, Braves	.882	3	8	7	2	1	Mathis, Mets	.900	21	30	51	9	6
Atwater, Expos	.839	7	9	17	5	1	McKamie, Dodgers	.906	40	54	91	15	11
Brenner, Reds	.870	8	12	28	6	6	Miranda, Royals	.961	28	42	81	5	12
Brown, Pirates	.905	14	17	40	6	5	Mompres, Mets	.825	24	35	59	20	12
Brust, Braves	.957	6	12	10	1	4	Monzon, White Sox	1.000	1	1	0	0	0
Camarillo, Rangers	.913	27	31	64	9	8	Noriega, Yankees	.971	8	11	23	1	4
Caraballo, Braves	.950	14	30	46	4	8	Nunez, Twins	.924	48	61	171	19	32
Colon, Red Sox	.925	42	76	135	17	14	Perez, Reds	1.000	1	1	1	0	0
Diggs, Astros	.904	22	23	43	7	2	Ramos, White Sox	.920	22	39	64	9	10
Feliz, Pirates	.917	13	14	30	4	5	Rittman, Mets	1.000	1	1	0	0	0
Frese, Rangers	1.000	1	0	2	0	1	Roberts, Reds	.833	2	0	5	1	2
Gaither, White Sox	.919	14	27	41	6	13	Ab. Rodriguez, Expos	.851	15	13	27	7	5
L. Garcia, Pirates	.946	19	28	60	5	16	AN. RODRIGUEZ, Yankees	.955	56	81	155	11	17
S. Garcia, Astros	.865	45	76	110	29	20	L. Rodriguez, Expos	.909	13	13	37	5	5
Gonzalez, Royals	.962	28	37	89	5	13	Sanders, White Sox	.897	9	6	20	3	4
Grant, Red Sox	.904	21	37	66	11	12	Schiel, Twins	.923	13	17	43	5	8
Greene, Pirates	.961	17	25	49	3	6	Sena, Dodgers	.936	35	40	92	9	18
Houk, Twins	.833	8	10	15	5	4	Thome, Indians	.922	40	51	115	14	16
Indriago, Royals	.945	12	19	33	3	5	Thompson, Mets	.941	24	36	76	7	14
Krause, Expos	.922	39	62	104	14	11	Turrentine, Yankees	.500	1	2	0	2	1
Kremblas, Reds	.917	3	2	9	1	2	Wright, Reds	.885	53	63	183	32	28
J. Martin, Pirates	.857	1	2	4	1	0							

Triple Plays—Apolinario, Gonzalez.

OUTFIELDERS

Player and Club	Pct.	G.	PO.	A.	E.	DP.	Player and Club	Pct.	G.	PO.	A.	E.	DP.
Adams, Expos☆	.944	20	17	0	1	0	Dallas, Astros	.983	27	54	5	1	0
Andrews, Royals	.887	43	52	3	7	0	Davis, Mets☆	.933	51	106	6	8	2
Andujar, White Sox	1.000	10	15	0	0	0	DeJardin, Indians☆	.955	12	18	3	1	0
Ashley, Dodgers	.914	42	50	3	5	1	Dickerson, Royals	.956	39	39	4	2	0
Awkard, Red Sox	.857	11	11	1	2	0	Doyle, Red Sox☆	.960	13	23	1	1	0
Baxter, Reds	.983	22	52	6	1	1	Dukes, Red Sox	.895	20	30	4	4	0
Blackwell, Dodgers	1.000	33	42	3	0	0	Eiterman, Indians	.975	25	35	4	1	3
Blosser, Red Sox☆	.933	34	54	2	4	1	Encarnacion, Astros	.986	39	65	4	1	1
Brown, Pirates	1.000	4	1	3	0	0	Fully, Mets	.971	24	29	5	1	0
Brummer, Dodgers☆	1.000	7	14	0	0	0	Fulton, Indians☆	.969	22	31	0	1	0
Bruno, Royals☆	1.000	41	50	1	0	0	Fults, Braves	.984	38	60	3	1	1
Brust, Braves	1.000	6	11	1	0	0	Garland, Yankees	.931	30	25	2	2	0
Bryant, Twins	1.000	24	22	0	0	0	Gerald, Royals	.966	60	141	3	5	1
Bullett, Pirates☆	.958	34	89	3	4	0	Gianni, Reds	1.000	15	20	3	0	0
Burroughs, Reds☆	.958	27	64	4	3	0	Gilliam, Yankees	1.000	7	2	0	0	0
Byers, Royals	1.000	33	50	0	0	0	Gonzalez, Dodgers	1.000	4	1	0	0	0
Canate, Indians	.857	6	6	0	1	0	Graham, Red Sox	.987	38	75	3	1	2
Caraballo, Braves	.900	5	9	0	1	0	Gremillion, Pirates	1.000	7	10	0	0	0
Cardenas, Reds	.981	54	97	5	2	1	Gumpf, Twins	.962	43	70	6	3	3
Castellano, Rangers	.950	48	70	6	4	1	Guzman, White Sox	1.000	23	34	0	0	0
Castillo, Rangers	.900	9	9	0	1	0	Hairston, White Sox	.955	14	21	0	1	0
Coker, Reds	.959	37	46	1	2	0	Hamm, Indians	.980	25	46	2	1	0
Coughlin, White Sox☆	1.000	24	26	1	0	0	Harrell, Indians☆	.714	5	5	0	2	0

OUTFIELDERS—Continued

Player and Club	Pct.	G.	PO.	A.	E.	DP.	Player and Club	Pct.	G.	PO.	A.	E.	DP.
Haughney, Rangers	.974	22	37	1	1	1	Palys, Indians	1.000	19	38	4	0	1
Hayes, Pirates	.971	25	33	1	1	0	Perez, Indians*	1.000	12	14	0	0	0
Heilgeist, Expos	1.000	12	19	1	0	0	Perozo, Red Sox	.958	11	20	3	1	1
Henderson, Indians	.965	34	51	4	2	1	Pichardo, Twins	.981	30	47	4	1	0
Herron, Expos	.968	38	56	4	2	1	Pitcavage, Pirates	1.000	13	16	0	0	0
Hoerner, Twins	.919	20	32	2	3	1	Powell, Rangers	.982	44	55	1	1	0
Hollis, Mets	1.000	27	53	1	0	1	Puchales, Dodgers*	.988	35	79	2	1	0
Horne, Expos	.958	18	21	2	1	0	Quinones, Reds	.956	31	43	0	2	0
Hughes, Braves	.966	35	52	5	2	1	Ramos, Indians*	.978	50	86	5	2	0
Hunter, Astros	.980	51	95	4	2	0	Ramsey, Expos	.970	51	96	2	3	1
James, White Sox*	.500	2	1	0	1	0	Rivera, Expos	.929	27	38	1	3	0
Johnson, Expos	1.000	7	10	0	0	0	Roberts, Reds	1.000	12	15	1	0	0
Jones, Astros	.943	47	77	6	5	2	Robertson, Yankees*	.969	58	90	3	3	0
Kluss, Indians	1.000	5	13	0	0	0	Robles, Pirates	.984	30	57	5	1	2
Lohry, Yankees	1.000	2	1	0	0	0	Rogers, Pirates*	1.000	12	25	2	0	2
Lopez, Astros	1.000	11	12	1	0	0	Romano, Yankees	.947	49	81	8	5	2
Lora, Red Sox	.949	26	55	1	3	1	Ronca, Pirates	.948	39	67	6	4	2
Lott, Dodgers	.984	39	60	0	1	0	Salcido, Braves	1.000	15	23	3	0	0
Martin, Braves	.973	39	70	3	2	1	Semke, Reds	1.000	40	76	3	0	0
Mason, Expos	.907	22	37	2	4	0	Sheppard, White Sox	1.000	25	38	0	0	0
Mathis, Mets	.938	31	60	1	4	0	Smith, Expos*	1.000	4	3	0	0	0
Matos, Rangers	.923	40	53	7	5	2	Strickland, Yankees	1.000	2	3	1	0	0
McKinnon, Twins	.926	20	25	0	2	0	Sweeney, Braves	.944	13	17	0	1	0
McMillan, Braves	.976	24	41	0	1	0	Teter, White Sox	.982	40	52	4	1	0
McNeely, Red Sox	1.000	9	13	1	0	1	Texidor, Rangers	.800	8	4	0	1	0
Mitchell, Pirates	.957	11	22	0	1	0	Thomas, Braves	.953	27	60	1	3	0
Montero, Astros	.920	29	41	5	4	1	Troncoso, Dodgers	1.000	3	2	0	0	0
D. Moore, Mets	.947	48	80	9	5	0	Tucker, Twins	1.000	22	36	6	0	1
L. Moore, Reds	.875	3	6	1	1	0	TURNER, Yankees*	1.000	49	54	4	0	0
S. Moore, Red Sox	.950	20	35	3	2	0	Valentin, White Sox	1.000	28	30	2	0	0
T. Moore, Twins*	.962	34	47	3	2	1	Vann, Red Sox	.978	23	44	1	1	0
Mouton, Rangers	.952	40	57	2	3	0	Virden, Expos	1.000	31	50	5	0	2
Moye, White Sox*	.958	13	23	0	1	0	Watson, Reds	1.000	3	4	0	0	0
Murray, Expos	1.000	1	3	0	0	0	A. Williams, Mets*	.975	44	76	3	2	1
Norman, Twins	.941	35	29	3	2	0	B. Williams, White Sox	1.000	5	7	1	0	1
Norris, White Sox	.957	28	19	3	1	0	T. Williams, Pirates	.960	19	23	1	1	0
Ochoa, White Sox	.778	13	6	1	2	0	Young, Indians	1.000	2	2	0	0	0
Ortiz, Indians	1.000	3	8	0	0	0	Zambrano, Red Sox	1.000	7	11	0	0	0

CATCHERS

Player and Club	Pct.	G.	PO.	A.	E.	DP.	PB.	Player and Club	Pct.	G.	PO.	A.	E.	DP.	PB.
Adkins, Pirates	1.000	1	4	0	0	0	0	Jarvis, Yankees	.987	22	130	20	2	3	3
Angotti, Astros	.984	17	113	13	2	0	3	Jennings, Royals	.988	47	300	41	4	2	9
Brown, Twins	.921	23	102	14	10	0	15	Jimenez, Indians	.950	19	99	14	6	1	2
Brust, Braves	.875	1	6	1	1	0	2	Jiminez, Braves	.986	19	117	19	2	2	12
Campusano, Pirates	.972	20	122	16	4	4	8	B. Johnson, Yankees	.990	11	84	14	1	0	5
Carroll, Mets	.967	37	194	38	8	0	6	M. Johnson, Mets	.833	1	4	1	1	0	0
Carter, Indians	.973	27	154	24	5	1	4	Koenig, Royals	1.000	8	40	3	0	0	1
Castro, Yankees	.970	25	136	27	5	0	4	Kremblas, Reds	.976	15	72	10	2	1	2
Cepicky, White Sox	.986	12	61	10	1	0	3	Lanfranco, Astros	.985	21	116	16	2	2	3
Chiusano, Dodgers	.974	21	131	19	4	1	9	Lewis, Rangers	.986	40	253	34	4	1	11
Cramer, Expos	1.000	2	4	0	0	0	1	Lohry, Yankees	.992	27	219	32	2	2	8
DeLeon, Rangers	.960	21	154	14	7	0	18	Lucin, Astros	.971	25	114	22	4	0	12
Egan, White Sox	1.000	3	21	3	0	0	2	Maldonado, Expos	.964	47	264	30	11	4	6
C. Ellis, Expos	.857	6	11	1	2	0	2	Manuel, Rangers	.963	7	46	6	2	0	5
J. Ellis, Braves	.950	6	18	1	1	0	1	Martinez, Indians	.957	32	158	22	8	2	7
Etheridge, Expos	.984	16	55	7	1	1	4	Matilla, Red Sox	.977	40	259	76	8	4	4
Fagnant, Red Sox	.946	6	32	3	2	0	1	Meyer, Mets	.952	3	18	2	1	0	1
Fimbres, Twins	.942	13	51	14	4	0	9	MOLINA, Reds	.990	33	186	21	2	1	4
Ganino, Dodgers	.985	28	175	25	3	0	5	Mota, Twins	.974	14	65	10	2	2	4
Garcia, Mets	1.000	1	4	1	0	0	0	Nunez, White Sox	.983	38	245	45	5	2	9
Garzon, Pirates	.978	8	35	10	1	0	0	Ramirez, Twins	.983	29	153	21	3	1	11
Gianni, Mets	.970	6	28	4	1	1	1	F. Reyes, Mets	.983	9	49	8	1	0	1
A. Gonzalez, Reds	.983	21	107	10	2	1	3	V. Reyes, Rangers	.985	14	59	6	1	0	3
P. Gonzalez, Dodgers	.971	30	175	27	6	2	2	Rudolph, Mets	.966	19	100	14	4	0	11
W. Gonzalez, Braves	.969	13	54	9	2	1	6	Solimine, White Sox	.982	22	149	14	3	0	8
Griesser, Royals	.990	14	87	12	1	0	2	Sugimoto, Expos	.977	21	120	10	3	1	8
Hanel, Pirates	.977	28	152	19	4	3	10	Taylor, Pirates	1.000	1	2	0	0	0	1
Hinson, Pirates	.965	18	97	12	4	1	7	Tucker, Astros	.982	16	47	7	1	0	6
Hurlbutt, Astros	.966	6	26	2	1	0	2	Tyson, Braves	.983	31	197	39	4	3	9
Isava, Royals	.923	5	12	0	1	0	1	Woods, Red Sox	.976	19	106	14	3	3	7

PITCHERS

Player and Club	Pct.	G.	PO.	A.	E.	DP.	Player and Club	Pct.	G.	PO.	A.	E.	DP.
Abel, Twins	.889	22	2	6	1	0	Benson, Mets	.700	15	3	4	3	1
Adams, Braves	1.000	10	3	6	0	0	Berumen, Royals	1.000	12	5	5	0	0
D. Allen, Astros	.857	13	2	4	1	0	Bethancourt, Twins	.800	15	1	11	3	1
T. Allen, Red Sox	.909	9	5	5	1	0	Bishop, Dodgers*	1.000	9	0	2	0	0
Alvarez, Twins	1.000	12	5	8	0	0	Bittiger, White Sox	1.000	2	1	4	0	0
Anaya, Mets	.846	12	4	7	2	1	Bochtler, Expos	.727	9	2	6	3	0
Jo. Arias, Twins	.500	7	0	2	2	0	Boggetto, Dodgers	.909	12	7	13	2	1
Ju. Arias, Pirates*	1.000	9	0	3	0	0	Borgula, White Sox	.714	14	2	3	2	0
Arner, Rangers	1.000	13	5	6	0	0	Bowling, Royals	.667	14	0	2	1	0
ASTACIO, Dodgers	1.000	12	5	19	0	1	Braase, Dodgers	1.000	21	3	5	0	0
Aucoin, Astros	.800	7	1	3	1	0	Bristow, Mets	1.000	19	1	2	0	1
Ayala, Rangers	1.000	4	1	2	0	0	Broadwater, Pirates	.833	11	1	4	1	1
Baez, Royals*	.846	18	0	11	2	0	Brooks, Twins	.875	19	2	5	1	0
Barreiro, Rangers	1.000	14	1	2	0	0	D. Brown, Astros	.864	13	5	14	3	0
Barry, Expos*	1.000	10	0	2	0	0	S. Brown, Pirates	1.000	12	2	4	0	0
							Brubaker, Yankees	1.000	2	0	3	0	0

PITCHERS—Continued

Player and Club	Pct.	G.	PO.	A.	E.	DP.
Bruck, Braves	1.000	12	3	12	0	0
Bryans, Royals	.833	7	2	3	1	0
Buckley, Rangers	.900	16	2	7	1	0
Budrewicz, Red Sox	.667	3	0	2	1	0
Calderon, Dodgers	1.000	18	2	2	0	0
Candelaria, Yankees*	1.000	2	2	2	0	0
Cantres, Dodgers	.500	15	0	2	2	0
Caridad, White Sox	1.000	13	1	2	0	0
Castillo, Mets	.950	14	4	15	1	0
Castro, Rangers	1.000	8	2	4	0	0
Cecil, Reds	.920	13	5	18	2	1
Chafin, White Sox	1.000	4	4	5	0	1
Chase, Yankees*	1.000	1	1	1	0	0
Chiles, Braves	.667	3	0	2	1	1
Chmielewski, Twins	.900	15	4	5	1	0
Chrisman, Royals	.750	8	1	2	1	0
Connor, Royals	.923	21	0	12	1	0
Conover, White Sox*	1.000	17	1	3	0	0
Conroy, Red Sox	.909	7	3	7	1	1
Correa, Rangers	1.000	4	1	1	0	0
Cullens, Braves	1.000	17	6	14	0	2
Dacosta, Yankees	1.000	4	1	3	0	0
Daniel, Dodgers*	.857	16	2	4	1	1
Delahoya, Dodgers	1.000	9	3	9	0	0
Delgado, Red Sox	1.000	17	6	14	0	1
DeLosSantos, Pirates	1.000	13	1	5	0	0
Dennison, Red Sox*	.889	5	0	8	1	0
DeVaughan, Rangers	1.000	3	2	2	0	0
Rafael Diaz, Expos	.917	11	8	14	2	1
Rafael J. Diaz, Reds*	1.000	10	0	9	0	1
Dickman, Braves	.714	7	2	3	2	0
Dunn, Royals	.909	19	3	7	1	0
Eddy, Royals	.909	5	4	6	1	0
Emm, Astros	1.000	5	0	9	0	0
Espinosa, Expos	.909	20	3	7	1	2
Fajardo, Pirates	.750	10	1	2	1	0
Fier, Expos*	.950	12	1	18	1	1
Fowler, Rangers	1.000	23	3	5	0	0
Francescon, Pirates*	.909	12	5	15	2	0
Gabriele, Braves	.750	15	1	5	2	0
Gallaher, Braves	.600	12	2	1	2	1
Gamez, Rangers*	.846	23	1	10	2	1
Garcia, White Sox	1.000	14	1	9	0	0
Gennings, White Sox	.714	5	0	5	2	0
Giberti, Rangers*	1.000	4	0	4	0	0
Gietzen, Yankees*	.889	18	4	4	1	0
Gonzales, Red Sox	.917	14	0	11	1	0
Grebe, Braves	1.000	12	2	10	0	2
Gross, Royals	.900	6	2	7	1	0
Gutierrez, Astros*	.750	12	0	6	2	0
Haller, Yankees*	.938	24	3	12	1	0
Hampton, Astros	.867	11	5	8	2	0
Hansell, Red Sox	.846	10	4	7	2	0
Harvey, Royals*	.813	17	0	13	3	0
Hawkins, Pirates	.667	18	0	2	1	0
Hitchcock, Yankees*	1.000	13	2	14	0	1
Hoffman, Dodgers*	1.000	5	0	2	0	0
Hook, Reds	1.000	14	3	3	0	0
Hope, Pirates	1.000	4	0	4	0	0
Hulme, White Sox	1.000	15	2	9	0	0
Hunter, White Sox	.909	10	4	6	1	0
Hutto, Expos	.800	25	3	5	2	0
Johnson, White Sox*	1.000	5	0	1	0	0
Johnston, Yankees	1.000	16	1	9	0	1
Jones, White Sox	.833	8	0	5	1	0
Juden, Astros	.600	9	2	4	4	0
Kallevig, Indians	.885	11	6	17	3	1
Keon, Rangers	.500	4	1	0	1	0
Kerfut, Rangers	.800	4	0	4	1	0
D. King, Reds*	.864	13	6	13	3	0
E. King, White Sox	1.000	2	1	7	0	1
Lane, Expos	.769	28	2	8	3	0
Linares, Reds	.857	15	3	9	2	0
Lindsay, Mets*	.950	22	7	12	1	0
Lipson, Twins	.833	23	2	3	1	0
Lyle, Pirates	1.000	9	2	1	0	0
MacNeil, Rangers	.900	14	1	17	2	0
Malena, Royals	.857	22	2	4	1	0
Malzone, Red Sox	1.000	15	6	9	0	0
Manon, Reds	1.000	11	1	3	0	0
J. Martinez, Mets	1.000	11	2	5	0	1
M. Martinez, Expos	.810	10	3	14	4	0
Matznick, White Sox	.769	12	1	9	3	0
Mauldin, Yankees	1.000	8	0	8	0	0
Maye, Braves	1.000	7	0	2	0	0
Mays, Pirates	.846	11	3	8	2	1
McDowell, White Sox	.857	4	2	4	1	0
McElfish, Indians*	.938	27	3	12	1	0
McGough, Rangers	.800	15	0	4	1	0
McMurtry, Rangers	1.000	4	0	2	0	0
Mesa, Dodgers	.727	10	0	8	3	0
Metheney, Astros	1.000	2	0	1	0	1
Mieses, Twins	1.000	15	2	5	0	0
Mileski, Rangers	1.000	10	0	1	0	0
Milton, Royals	.889	12	3	5	1	0
Mirabella, Indians	.750	18	2	10	4	0
Mongiello, White Sox	1.000	8	3	8	0	2
Morrison, Indians	.600	12	3	0	2	0
Morton, Red Sox*	1.000	2	1	0	0	0
Moyer, Rangers*	1.000	3	1	0	0	0
J. Munoz, Astros	.895	9	3	14	2	1
R. Munoz, Yankees	1.000	2	1	2	0	0
Navarro, Astros*	1.000	7	0	5	0	0
Niemeyer, Red Sox	.857	9	5	1	1	0
Nieves, Reds	1.000	25	3	2	0	0
Pagan, Pirates	.880	13	9	13	3	2
Patrick, Dodgers*	1.000	7	1	6	0	1
Paxton, Indians	.833	8	1	4	1	0
C. Perez, Yankees	1.000	11	2	5	0	0
Jo. Perez, Reds*	1.000	14	3	4	0	0
Ju. Perez, Expos	.800	10	4	0	1	0
R. Perez, Pirates	1.000	2	1	0	0	0
Perry, Yankees*	1.000	15	0	5	0	0
Phillips, Rangers	1.000	14	0	5	0	1
Plemmons, Reds	1.000	12	2	4	0	0
Polak, Yankees	.667	8	3	3	3	1
Prats, Astros*	.750	17	0	3	1	0
Pulido, Twins*	.833	22	3	2	1	0
Quantrill, Red Sox	1.000	2	1	2	0	0
Quirico, Yankees*	.850	17	6	11	3	1
Ramirez, Mets	.846	15	3	8	2	2
Randle, Rangers	.905	13	6	13	2	0
Ray, Reds	.833	11	1	4	1	0
Rees, Mets	.875	11	3	4	1	0
Reno, Royals	1.000	22	5	5	0	0
Reyes, Twins	1.000	18	2	6	0	1
Rinaldi, Astros*	.778	21	2	5	2	1
Ring, Red Sox	1.000	11	1	8	0	0
Rivas, Astros	.810	27	4	13	4	1
Roa, Braves	.933	13	7	7	1	0
Robinson, White Sox	.833	10	4	6	2	0
Robles, Twins	.882	12	3	12	2	1
Roeder, Pirates	.857	12	3	3	1	0
Rojas, Yankees*	.923	14	2	10	1	1
Rolfes, Braves*	.920	16	1	22	2	2
Romberg, Expos	1.000	11	2	5	0	0
Ruiz, White Sox	1.000	11	1	3	0	0
Ryan, Indians*	.900	8	4	14	2	0
Rychel, Pirates	.875	13	4	17	3	1
Santamaria, Red Sox	.750	16	3	6	3	0
Santiago, Red Sox*	1.000	15	1	10	0	0
Scheetz, Rangers	1.000	5	2	2	0	1
R. Scott, Red Sox	1.000	13	3	5	0	0
T. Scott, Astros*	.500	12	0	3	3	0
Shade, Pirates	1.000	11	1	3	0	1
Shepherd, Braves	.895	27	3	14	2	0
Smith, Pirates	.714	2	2	3	2	0
Soper, Indians	1.000	32	1	8	0	0
Sparks, Pirates	1.000	7	2	5	0	0
Springer, Yankees	1.000	6	0	1	0	0
St. Pe, Rangers	1.000	8	1	0	0	0
Steinmetz, Braves	1.000	10	1	4	0	0
D. Stevens, Reds	1.000	19	2	8	0	1
J. Stevens, Indians*	1.000	23	1	8	0	1
Takaheshi, Dodgers	.750	3	0	3	1	0
Tatis, Dodgers	.727	11	2	6	3	0
Thigpen, Royals	.929	14	1	12	1	2
Thoma, White Sox	1.000	20	1	4	0	0
M. Thomas, Mets*	1.000	8	1	2	0	0
R. Thomas, Braves*	1.000	5	3	2	0	0
Tolar, White Sox*	.947	13	2	16	1	2
Torres, Expos	.000	11	0	0	1	0
Tuss, Expos	.857	13	6	6	2	0
Vasquez, Reds	.500	14	0	2	2	0
Vitko, Mets	1.000	8	4	8	0	0
Walden, Indians	.938	11	3	12	1	1
Walling, Braves	.889	20	3	5	1	0
Washington, Rangers	.500	6	0	1	1	0
Wechsberg, Indians	1.000	9	4	2	0	0
Wertz, Indians	.889	12	2	6	1	0
West, Royals	.818	12	3	6	2	1
Wheeler, Astros	.833	14	1	9	2	0
Wiley, Yankees	.917	11	3	8	1	0
Wilson, Mets	.750	5	1	2	1	0
Wyatt, Reds	.750	9	0	3	1	0

The following players did not have any fielding statistics at the positions indicated or appeared only as a designated hitter, pinch-hitter or pinch-runner: Alexander, p; Anglada, of; Ashley, p; Bryant, 2b; Gerald Davis, of; Foster, p; Hairston, p; Hamm, ss; Hayes, p; Houk, p; Kluss, ss; Langan, p; Longmire, of; E. Martinez, of; Marze, of; Minutelli, p; T. Mitchell, of; M. Murray, p; Oster, of; Rittman, c; Ab. Rodriguez, 3b; Rogers, p; Schiel, p; Scoates, p; Sena, 3b; J. Torres, p; Troncoso, 3b; Ru. Vasquez, ss; E. Young, 3b, c.

CLUB PITCHING

Club	ERA.	G.	CG.	ShO.	Sv.	IP.	H.	R.	ER.	HR.	HB.	BB.	Int. BB.	SO.	WP.	Bk.
White Sox	2.36	63	3	10	18	545.0	402	189	143	10	19	238	4	482	41	22
Dodgers	2.61	63	6	10	18	558.2	447	203	162	14	27	220	2	480	36	18
Yankees	2.81	63	0	7	22	561.0	425	220	175	8	30	219	1	588	48	23
Reds	3.19	63	2	7	21	555.2	522	250	197	16	28	210	7	365	38	33
Red Sox	3.23	63	5	3	15	554.0	524	269	199	4	28	194	4	393	39	20
Indians	3.27	63	2	7	17	561.0	558	288	204	9	33	233	5	407	55	24
Braves	3.32	64	3	7	14	566.1	499	290	209	18	17	226	5	398	44	10
Royals	3.32	63	2	8	18	552.2	491	240	204	11	26	208	12	437	41	10
Mets	3.54	65	12	4	9	546.1	529	294	215	10	25	187	4	350	50	15
Rangers	3.59	63	2	7	21	557.0	473	278	222	16	29	198	6	505	42	14
Expos	3.67	66	2	2	15	557.1	568	312	227	18	21	214	5	435	51	18
Astros	4.17	63	3	4	5	546.0	553	351	253	15	30	253	3	415	81	45
Twins	4.18	63	4	1	12	534.1	563	344	248	19	21	212	2	377	78	22
Pirates	4.53	63	3	2	10	534.2	523	365	269	17	28	300	1	393	50	36

PITCHERS' RECORDS
(Leading Qualifiers for Earned-Run Average Leadership — 50 or More Innings)

*Throws lefthanded.

Pitcher—Club	W.	L.	Pct.	ERA.	G.	GS.	CG.	GF.	ShO.	Sv.	IP.	H.	R.	ER.	HR.	HB.	BB.	Int. BB.	SO.	WP.
Shepherd, Braves	3	3	.500	1.43	27	0	0	19	0	6	50.1	27	11	8	2	1	15	1	34	4
Santiago, Red Sox*	1	2	.333	1.44	15	4	1	7	0	0	50.0	34	14	8	0	3	16	2	38	3
Delahoya, Dodgers	4	3	.571	1.46	9	8	2	1	1	0	55.1	28	13	9	0	4	19	0	70	3
Hitchcock, Yankees*	9	1	.900	1.64	13	13	0	0	0	0	76.2	48	16	14	1	4	27	0	98	5
Tolar, White Sox*	6	2	.750	1.65	13	12	1	0	0	0	60.0	29	16	11	0	1	54	0	58	10
Kallevig, Indians	5	4	.556	1.66	11	11	1	0	1	0	65.0	57	20	12	0	3	17	0	40	2
Manon, Reds	6	1	.857	1.67	11	6	1	3	1	0	54.0	53	15	10	3	0	8	1	27	1
Arner, Rangers	7	0	1.000	1.71	13	12	0	0	0	0	63.1	47	15	12	1	3	9	1	75	1
Randle, Rangers	5	2	.714	1.72	13	11	1	0	1	0	68.0	46	21	13	1	7	31	1	76	3
Cecil, Reds	8	1	.889	1.87	13	11	1	1	1	0	72.1	59	23	15	2	3	19	0	56	6

Departmental Leaders: G—Soper, 32; W—Hitchcock, 9; L—J. Munoz, 9; Pct.—Hunter, 1.000; GS—Castillo, Hitchcock, Rychel, 13; CG—Robles, 3; GF—Soper, 32; ShO—Several pitchers tied with 1; Sv.—Soper, 15; IP—Castillo, 84.1; H—Bethancourt, 95; R—Chmielewski, 51; ER—Chmielewski, 38; HR—Alvarez, Chmielewski, Tuss, 5; HB—Rychel, 9; BB—Tolar, 54; IBB—Dunn, 3; SO—Hitchcock, 98; WP—D. Brown, Reyes, T. Scott, 14.

(All Pitchers—Listed Alphabetically)

Pitcher—Club	W.	L.	Pct.	ERA.	G.	GS.	CG.	GF.	ShO.	Sv.	IP.	H.	R.	ER.	HR.	HB.	BB.	Int. BB.	SO.	WP.
Abel, Twins	2	1	.667	2.75	22	0	0	9	0	3	36.0	27	14	11	0	3	18	0	17	6
Adams, Braves	4	2	.667	4.06	10	2	0	1	0	0	31.0	32	16	14	2	0	12	0	10	4
Alexander, Rangers	0	0	.000	0.00	6	0	0	5	0	4	6.1	3	0	0	0	0	9	0	9	0
D. Allen, Astros	1	2	.333	5.13	13	0	0	6	0	0	26.1	29	20	15	4	4	20	0	15	4
T. Allen, Red Sox	3	1	.750	3.65	9	6	0	0	0	0	37.0	32	20	15	0	0	18	1	37	4
Alvarez, Twins	3	7	.300	5.64	12	12	0	0	0	0	59.0	66	43	37	5	1	21	0	46	8
Anaya, Braves	3	5	.375	4.05	12	12	2	0	0	0	73.1	71	43	33	0	3	23	0	47	5
Aranguren, Royals*	3	0	1.000	3.40	16	6	0	5	0	0	45.0	39	20	17	0	3	24	0	38	2
Jo. Arias, Twins	3	2	.600	4.45	7	4	1	0	0	0	28.1	35	17	14	1	0	6	0	23	2
Ju. Arias, Pirates*	2	2	.500	1.32	9	0	0	6	0	1	13.2	7	6	2	0	0	7	0	10	1
Arner, Rangers	7	0	1.000	1.71	13	12	0	0	0	0	63.1	47	15	12	1	3	9	1	75	1
Ashley, Expos	0	0	.000	18.00	1	0	0	0	0	0	1.0	1	2	2	0	0	2	0	2	0
Astacio, Dodgers	7	3	.700	3.17	12	12	1	0	1	0	76.2	77	30	27	3	4	12	0	52	4
Aucoin, Expos	2	1	.667	2.66	7	3	0	1	0	1	23.2	24	10	7	2	0	12	0	27	3
Ayala, Rangers*	2	0	1.000	5.84	4	1	0	1	0	0	12.1	13	8	8	0	1	4	0	9	1
Baez, Royals*	4	4	.500	2.67	18	8	1	1	1	1	57.1	46	22	17	0	0	9	1	52	3
Barreiro, Rangers	1	1	.500	6.04	14	0	0	8	0	1	22.1	18	15	15	2	3	11	0	18	1
Barry, Expos*	1	2	.333	3.38	10	0	0	0	0	0	13.1	11	11	5	0	3	9	1	14	2
Benson, Mets	2	3	.400	2.91	15	5	1	3	0	0	52.2	49	24	17	1	4	22	1	23	0
Berumen, Royals	2	4	.333	4.78	12	10	0	0	0	0	49.0	57	29	26	2	4	17	1	24	6
Bethancourt, Twins	2	6	.250	3.82	15	12	0	0	0	0	75.1	95	48	32	1	1	29	0	41	5
Bishop, Dodgers*	1	0	1.000	1.65	9	4	0	3	0	0	27.1	21	6	5	1	2	11	0	31	0
Bittiger, White Sox	1	1	.500	0.75	2	2	0	0	0	0	12.0	7	3	1	0	0	0	0	10	0
Bochtler, Expos	2	2	.500	3.21	9	9	1	0	0	0	47.2	46	22	17	0	0	20	1	45	3
Boggetto, Dodgers	5	4	.556	3.62	12	12	1	0	1	0	69.2	67	33	28	4	3	35	1	40	4
Borgula, White Sox	4	0	1.000	3.57	14	0	0	2	0	0	22.2	28	14	9	1	3	11	0	20	1
Bowling, Royals	0	1	.000	3.96	14	0	0	4	0	2	25.0	29	12	11	0	1	12	1	19	2
Braase, Dodgers	2	0	1.000	2.34	21	0	0	15	0	6	42.1	32	11	11	0	1	8	1	38	6
Bristow, Mets	3	3	.500	2.78	19	4	1	11	0	5	45.1	42	26	14	1	2	15	1	36	4
Broadwater, Pirates	0	1	.000	4.79	11	1	0	3	0	0	20.2	23	25	11	2	0	25	0	16	4
Brooks, Twins	1	0	1.000	6.35	19	0	0	11	0	0	28.1	31	25	20	1	2	16	0	19	7
D. Brown, Astros	3	7	.300	2.55	13	12	2	1	1	0	74.0	70	30	21	2	3	22	0	50	14
S. Brown, Pirates	2	2	.500	3.12	12	0	0	12	0	5	17.1	17	6	6	0	1	3	1	23	0
Brubaker, Yankees	2	0	1.000	0.00	2	2	0	0	0	0	11.0	6	0	0	0	0	3	0	7	0
Bruck, Braves	2	2	.500	2.66	12	5	1	5	1	2	40.2	32	21	12	0	1	17	0	34	2
Bryans, Braves	1	2	.333	2.08	7	7	1	0	0	0	34.2	26	9	8	0	3	11	0	30	2
Buckley, Rangers	3	3	.500	3.40	16	4	0	2	0	0	50.1	41	28	19	1	0	24	1	34	3
Budrewicz, Red Sox	2	2	.500	5.29	3	3	0	0	0	0	17.0	15	12	10	0	1	9	0	9	1
Calderon, Dodgers	1	1	.500	3.11	18	1	0	14	0	6	37.2	28	15	13	1	1	25	0	43	0
Candelaria, Yankees*	1	0	1.000	0.00	2	0	0	2	0	0	8.0	6	0	0	0	0	1	0	12	0
Cantres, Dodgers	5	2	.714	2.83	15	0	0	10	0	2	35.0	31	14	11	2	0	21	0	24	2
Caridad, White Sox	1	1	.500	3.33	13	0	0	8	0	1	27.0	20	12	10	1	2	15	0	24	6
Castillo, Mets	4	7	.364	2.88	14	13	2	0	1	0	84.1	84	41	27	1	7	29	0	59	13
Castro, Rangers	2	2	.500	3.50	8	6	0	0	0	0	36.0	30	16	14	2	1	12	0	29	6
Cecil, Reds	8	1	.889	1.87	13	11	1	1	1	0	72.1	59	23	15	2	3	19	0	56	6
Chafin, White Sox	1	0	1.000	1.80	4	1	0	1	0	0	15.0	14	4	3	0	0	6	0	12	1
Chase, Yankees*	0	0	.000	0.00	1	0	0	0	0	0	1.0	0	0	0	0	0	0	0	0	0
Chiles, Braves	1	0	1.000	1.50	3	0	0	1	0	0	6.0	2	5	1	1	0	5	0	4	1
Chmielewski, Twins	3	5	.375	5.23	15	11	0	0	0	0	65.1	86	51	38	5	1	18	0	43	9
Chrisman, Royals	3	0	1.000	2.40	8	0	0	2	0	1	15.0	12	5	4	0	1	6	0	15	1
Connor, Royals	3	3	.500	3.26	21	4	0	6	0	1	58.0	51	23	21	0	1	11	2	28	2
Conover, White Sox*	1	0	1.000	2.04	17	0	0	15	0	5	17.2	10	4	4	1	0	7	1	23	0
Conroy, Red Sox	4	2	.667	2.25	7	7	2	0	0	0	44.0	33	15	11	0	2	9	0	31	2

Pitcher—Club	W.	L.	Pct.	ERA.	G.	GS.	CG.	GF.	ShO.	Sv.	IP.	H.	R.	ER.	HR.	HB.	BB.	Int. BB.	SO.	WP.
Correa, Rangers	0	2	.000	8.64	4	4	0	0	0	0	8.1	8	9	8	2	1	7	0	10	1
Cullens, Braves	3	3	.500	3.49	17	4	0	4	0	1	49.0	47	35	19	0	3	22	0	32	5
Dacosta, Yankees	1	0	1.000	3.29	4	2	0	0	0	0	13.2	9	8	5	0	0	8	0	10	3
Daniel, Dodgers°	2	2	.500	3.89	16	2	0	7	0	0	34.2	40	21	15	0	0	13	0	25	3
Delahoya, Dodgers	4	3	.571	1.46	9	8	2	1	1	0	55.1	28	13	9	0	4	19	0	70	3
Delgado, Red Sox	3	6	.333	3.69	17	5	1	8	0	2	61.0	71	37	25	1	8	11	0	36	3
DeLosSantos, Pirates	2	2	.500	5.79	13	4	0	6	0	2	37.1	41	27	24	2	2	19	0	24	5
Dennison, Red Sox°	3	2	.600	1.55	5	5	0	0	0	0	29.0	25	9	5	0	0	10	0	23	0
DeVaughan, Rangers	0	0	.000	5.40	3	0	0	0	0	0	5.0	5	4	3	0	1	1	0	3	1
Rafael, Diaz, Expos	2	8	.200	3.67	11	8	1	1	0	0	54.0	62	27	22	1	1	9	0	50	3
Rafael J. Diaz, Reds°	2	1	.667	3.31	10	4	0	2	0	0	32.2	39	15	12	0	0	6	0	20	0
Dickman, Braves	1	0	1.000	5.82	7	2	0	1	0	1	17.0	18	12	11	1	0	9	0	11	3
Dunn, Royals	3	2	.600	4.54	19	0	0	5	0	2	33.2	32	18	17	1	2	19	3	41	1
Eddy, Expos	1	0	1.000	1.96	5	2	0	0	0	0	18.1	17	5	4	0	0	2	0	8	1
Emm, Astros	1	1	.500	4.03	5	5	1	0	1	0	29.0	33	14	13	1	0	7	0	14	2
Espinosa, Expos	3	1	.750	3.97	20	7	0	4	0	0	59.0	57	33	26	3	1	23	0	22	1
Fajardo, Pirates	0	5	.000	5.97	10	6	0	0	0	0	34.2	38	24	23	0	0	20	0	19	1
Fier, Expos°	5	3	.625	2.03	12	12	0	0	0	0	71.0	59	24	16	1	4	25	0	57	7
Foster, Royals	0	0	.000	40.50	1	0	0	0	0	0	0.2	1	3	3	0	0	4	0	1	1
Fowler, Rangers	0	4	.000	4.36	23	0	0	18	0	9	33.0	31	17	16	1	1	2	0	25	1
Francescon, Pirates°	4	3	.571	3.03	12	9	2	1	1	0	65.1	51	29	22	0	3	25	0	55	4
Gabriele, Braves	4	2	.667	5.13	15	8	0	2	0	1	54.1	60	43	31	2	1	20	1	33	6
Gallaher, Braves	1	2	.333	3.86	12	6	0	2	0	0	35.0	24	18	15	0	2	26	0	19	2
Gamez, Rangers°	2	1	.667	3.76	23	1	0	5	0	2	40.2	35	17	17	0	0	18	0	44	3
Garcia, White Sox	6	4	.600	3.06	14	7	2	2	1	0	53.0	34	21	18	1	2	17	0	52	1
Gennings, White Sox	0	1	.000	0.00	5	0	0	2	0	0	10.1	9	1	0	0	1	2	0	6	3
Giberti, Rangers°	0	1	.000	9.00	4	0	0	0	0	0	7.0	9	7	7	0	0	5	0	6	2
Gietzen, Yankees°	0	2	.000	5.40	18	2	0	9	0	1	40.0	36	28	24	0	2	20	0	57	6
Gonzales, Red Sox	0	1	.000	3.03	14	2	0	9	0	2	32.2	30	12	11	0	0	13	0	15	0
Grebe, Braves	4	3	.571	2.86	12	9	0	1	0	0	56.2	53	24	18	2	1	25	0	26	2
Gross, Royals	3	2	.600	2.36	6	6	0	0	0	0	34.1	29	11	9	0	1	7	1	40	2
Gutierrez, Astros°	1	3	.250	5.02	12	1	0	4	0	0	37.2	38	23	21	0	2	26	0	33	5
Hairston, White Sox	0	0	.000	3.00	1	0	0	0	0	0	3.0	2	1	1	0	0	2	0	1	0
Haller, Yankees°	5	4	.556	2.36	24	0	0	22	0	8	45.2	29	15	12	1	2	21	1	60	7
Hampton, Astros	0	2	.000	4.79	11	8	0	1	0	0	35.2	38	31	19	1	4	14	0	22	6
Hansell, Red Sox	3	2	.600	2.53	10	8	0	2	0	2	57.0	51	23	16	1	4	23	0	44	3
Harvey, Royals°	2	3	.400	4.18	17	0	0	2	0	0	32.1	31	18	15	1	1	14	2	23	2
Hawkins, Pirates	3	0	1.000	3.70	18	0	0	16	0	0	24.1	28	12	10	0	0	11	0	17	3
Hayes, Pirates	0	0	.000	27.00	1	0	0	0	0	0	2.0	4	6	6	1	1	4	0	1	0
Hitchcock, Yankees°	9	1	.900	1.64	13	13	0	0	0	0	76.2	48	16	14	1	4	27	0	98	5
Hoffman, Dodgers°	2	1	.667	3.71	5	1	0	2	0	1	17.0	11	10	7	0	1	8	0	30	4
Hook, Reds	4	1	.800	3.18	14	9	0	1	0	0	51.0	43	19	18	1	4	17	0	39	4
Hope, Reds	0	1	.000	4.80	4	3	0	0	0	0	15.0	15	12	8	0	1	6	0	14	0
Houk, Twins	0	0	.000	0.00	2	0	0	2	0	0	4.0	0	0	0	0	1	0	0	3	0
Hulme, White Sox	1	1	.500	1.51	15	0	0	3	0	1	35.2	17	6	6	1	0	18	0	27	0
Hunter, White Sox	8	0	1.000	1.11	10	9	0	0	0	0	48.2	35	10	6	1	2	11	0	45	2
Hutto, Expos	0	1	.000	1.55	25	1	0	14	0	4	40.2	32	12	7	1	0	15	0	36	4
Johnson, White Sox°	0	1	.000	4.50	5	0	0	1	0	0	10.0	9	5	5	0	0	4	0	10	1
Johnston, Yankees	4	2	.667	2.59	16	1	0	11	0	5	41.2	29	18	12	2	4	20	0	33	4
Jones, White Sox	0	1	.000	1.47	7	4	0	2	0	1	18.1	12	7	3	0	1	5	0	14	0
Juden, Astros	1	4	.200	3.40	9	8	0	0	0	0	39.2	33	21	15	0	3	17	0	49	7
Kallevig, Indians	5	4	.556	1.66	11	11	1	0	1	0	65.0	57	20	12	0	3	17	0	40	2
Keon, Rangers	1	1	.500	1.35	4	0	0	0	0	0	6.2	3	1	1	0	0	2	0	5	2
Kerfut, Rangers	1	1	.500	2.87	4	3	1	0	0	0	15.2	13	8	5	1	2	4	0	16	0
D. King, Reds°	3	3	.500	3.12	13	9	0	3	0	1	52.0	48	22	18	2	3	23	0	35	3
E. King, White Sox	1	1	.500	4.09	2	2	0	0	0	0	11.0	13	8	5	0	1	3	1	8	2
Lane, Expos	2	5	.286	2.88	28	0	0	21	0	6	34.1	36	20	11	1	1	13	1	33	4
Langan, Mets	0	1	.000	9.00	8	0	0	6	0	0	9.0	12	11	9	0	1	10	0	4	2
Linares, Reds	3	5	.375	3.63	15	12	0	0	0	0	67.0	66	33	27	0	7	29	1	53	8
Lindsay, Mets°	2	1	.667	3.14	22	2	2	9	1	3	51.2	47	24	18	2	1	8	1	22	4
Lipson, Twins	4	1	.800	1.42	23	0	0	19	0	7	31.2	23	6	5	0	1	6	1	32	9
Lyle, Pirates	0	1	.000	4.74	9	0	0	3	0	0	19.0	23	11	10	3	0	7	0	10	2
MacNeil, Rangers	3	5	.375	3.76	14	12	0	0	0	0	67.0	60	44	28	1	5	27	1	49	11
Malena, Royals	2	2	.500	2.63	22	0	0	20	0	3	27.1	22	12	8	3	0	1	1	28	1
Malzone, Red Sox	3	5	.375	4.74	15	9	1	3	0	1	62.2	73	38	33	1	0	13	0	45	3
Manon, Reds	6	1	.857	1.67	11	6	1	3	1	0	54.0	53	15	10	3	0	8	1	27	1
J. Martinez, Mets	1	4	.200	6.55	11	4	1	4	0	0	34.1	54	35	25	2	1	4	1	22	2
M. Martinez, Expos	2	4	.333	4.67	10	10	0	0	0	0	52.0	56	39	27	0	3	23	1	44	7
Matznick, White Sox	2	3	.400	3.12	12	11	0	1	0	0	52.0	46	27	18	0	3	28	0	47	7
Mauldin, Yankees	3	2	.600	2.48	8	7	0	0	0	0	36.1	23	12	10	0	3	19	0	33	4
Maye, Braves	0	1	.000	10.03	7	0	0	3	0	0	11.2	12	13	13	1	1	16	0	5	1
Mays, Pirates	0	3	.000	6.93	11	6	0	0	0	0	37.2	47	38	29	2	1	22	0	18	4
McDowell, White Sox	2	0	1.000	0.75	4	4	0	0	0	0	24.0	19	2	2	0	1	4	0	25	2
McElfish, Indians°	5	2	.714	2.78	27	0	0	9	0	0	71.1	75	31	22	1	5	26	2	37	2
McGough, Rangers	3	0	1.000	3.20	15	0	0	5	0	0	19.2	16	9	7	1	1	6	1	14	0
McMurtry, Rangers	0	1	.000	1.13	4	2	0	0	0	0	8.0	3	2	1	0	0	2	0	10	0
Mesa, Dodgers	3	3	.500	3.08	10	9	1	0	1	0	52.2	37	23	18	2	4	30	0	33	3
Metheney, Astros	1	0	1.000	8.31	2	0	0	0	0	0	4.1	8	4	4	0	0	1	0	1	0
Mieses, Reds	2	6	.250	5.71	15	9	0	3	0	0	52.0	66	48	33	3	1	26	0	23	7
Mileski, Rangers	0	1	.000	14.46	10	0	0	8	0	0	9.1	19	15	15	2	0	4	0	4	1
Milton, Royals	5	2	.714	3.32	12	12	0	0	0	0	59.2	48	24	22	0	3	30	0	60	5
Minutelli, Reds°	0	0	.000	0.00	1	1	0	0	0	0	1.0	0	0	0	0	0	1	0	0	0
Mirabella, Indians	5	5	.500	4.48	18	2	0	4	0	0	64.1	70	42	32	2	2	23	1	53	4
Mongiello, White Sox	1	3	.250	3.58	8	4	0	3	0	2	32.2	28	16	13	2	2	13	0	28	3
Morrison, Indians	1	2	.333	6.27	12	7	0	4	0	1	47.1	53	47	33	1	7	30	0	34	11
Morton, Red Sox°	1	0	1.000	0.00	2	1	0	1	0	1	6.0	2	0	0	0	1	1	0	11	0
Moyer, Rangers°	1	0	1.000	1.64	3	3	0	0	0	0	11.0	8	4	2	0	2	1	0	18	0
J. Munoz, Astros	0	9	.000	4.18	9	9	0	0	0	0	51.2	53	34	24	2	2	13	0	26	4
R. Munoz, Yankees	1	1	.500	3.48	2	2	0	0	0	0	10.1	5	4	4	0	0	4	0	13	1
Murray, Braves	1	0	1.000	0.00	2	0	0	0	0	0	7.0	3	0	0	0	1	0	0	10	0
Navarro, Astros°	0	2	.000	3.16	7	4	0	3	0	0	25.2	23	11	9	0	2	11	0	10	2
Niemeyer, Red Sox	1	1	.500	5.16	9	1	0	5	0	0	22.2	22	14	13	1	0	12	0	18	1
Nieves, Reds	0	3	.000	2.27	25	0	0	24	0	13	31.2	27	12	8	1	2	10	2	30	3

Pitcher—Club	W.	L.	Pct.	ERA	G.	GS.	CG.	GF.	ShO.	Sv.	IP.	H.	R.	ER.	HR.	HB.	BB.	Int. BB.	SO.	WP.
Pagan, Pirates	5	5	.500	3.82	13	12	1	0	0	0	70.2	68	47	30	4	2	40	0	38	8
Patrick, Dodgers°	4	1	.800	0.24	7	5	1	2	1	1	37.2	18	7	1	0	0	12	0	39	2
Paxton, Indians	1	1	.500	3.71	8	8	0	0	0	0	26.2	26	13	11	0	1	10	0	24	2
C. Perez, Yankees	1	0	1.000	2.88	11	3	0	6	0	3	25.0	13	8	8	1	3	9	0	23	1
Jo. Perez, Reds°	0	1	.000	3.58	14	0	0	5	0	0	27.2	23	15	11	1	2	22	0	13	2
Ju. Perez, Expos	0	1	.000	10.69	10	2	0	4	0	0	16.0	26	19	19	1	3	9	0	14	3
R. Perez, Pirates	0	0	.000	2.45	2	0	0	0	0	0	3.2	3	1	1	0	0	1	0	3	0
Perry, Yankees°	2	2	.500	4.73	15	1	0	4	0	1	32.1	32	20	17	0	2	24	0	29	5
Phillips, Rangers	1	2	.333	1.88	14	2	0	6	0	3	28.2	21	11	6	0	2	12	1	16	1
Plemmons, Reds	3	1	.750	2.25	12	1	0	3	0	2	36.0	27	11	9	1	0	12	1	25	0
Polak, Yankees	3	0	1.000	1.84	8	3	0	4	0	1	29.1	22	9	6	0	0	6	0	32	1
Prats, Astros°	1	1	.500	3.22	17	0	0	10	0	1	36.1	28	16	13	1	2	15	0	40	6
Pulido, Twins°	3	0	1.000	2.25	22	0	0	11	0	2	36.0	22	9	9	0	3	14	0	46	6
Quantrill, Red Sox	0	0	.000	0.00	2	0	0	2	0	2	5.0	2	0	0	0	0	0	0	5	0
Quirico, Yankees°	2	2	.500	3.82	17	7	0	1	0	1	63.2	61	32	27	2	3	20	0	55	0
Ramirez, Mets	0	5	.000	4.50	15	5	0	8	0	0	42.0	35	29	21	3	0	24	0	14	8
Randle, Rangers	5	2	.714	1.72	13	11	1	0	1	0	68.0	46	21	13	1	7	31	1	76	3
Ray, Reds	6	2	.750	2.72	11	10	0	0	0	0	56.1	55	22	17	1	2	13	0	28	5
Rees, Mets	2	5	.286	4.81	11	7	2	4	1	1	48.2	52	26	26	3	0	17	0	29	5
Reno, Royals	1	0	1.000	1.27	22	0	0	15	0	7	35.1	24	6	5	0	1	11	0	12	3
Reyes, Twins	1	2	.333	4.29	18	3	0	2	0	0	50.1	42	38	24	0	4	42	1	46	14
Rinaldi, Astros°	3	3	.500	4.78	21	2	0	12	0	0	49.0	49	38	26	1	2	23	1	33	8
Ring, Red Sox	0	2	.000	2.63	11	3	0	5	0	2	37.2	42	16	11	0	3	19	1	28	0
Rivas, Astros	3	3	.500	4.82	27	0	0	21	0	4	52.1	63	42	28	2	1	27	2	43	4
Roa, Braves	2	2	.500	2.89	13	4	0	4	0	0	37.1	40	18	12	2	0	10	1	21	3
Robinson, White Sox	4	0	1.000	1.47	10	7	0	1	0	0	43.0	26	7	7	0	0	16	0	32	1
Robles, Twins	3	6	.333	3.22	12	12	3	0	0	0	67.0	68	44	24	2	3	15	0	37	5
Roeder, Pirates	0	4	.000	4.92	12	5	0	5	0	0	40.1	32	20	18	0	6	26	0	32	7
Rogers, Pirates°	0	0	.000	9.00	1	0	0	0	0	0	1.0	1	2	1	0	1	2	0	1	0
Rojas, Yankees°	1	2	.333	2.86	14	2	0	6	0	0	44.0	41	21	14	0	2	15	0	39	5
Rolfes, Braves°	5	1	.833	3.39	16	10	1	4	1	2	63.2	62	30	24	2	1	20	0	58	4
Romberg, Expos	1	1	.500	7.98	11	0	0	6	0	2	14.2	19	14	13	2	1	6	1	11	2
Ruiz, White Sox	1	2	.333	5.09	11	0	0	2	0	0	23.0	24	17	13	0	0	8	0	18	0
Ryan, Indians°	2	3	.400	2.05	8	6	0	1	0	0	48.1	40	18	11	1	0	9	0	35	3
Rychel, Pirates	1	6	.143	3.09	13	13	0	0	0	0	67.0	52	40	23	0	9	31	0	79	6
Santamaria, Red Sox	3	5	.375	2.95	16	6	0	9	0	0	58.0	54	32	19	0	5	30	0	35	8
Santiago, Red Sox°	2	2	.333	1.44	15	4	1	7	0	0	50.0	34	14	8	0	3	16	2	38	3
Scheetz, Rangers	1	0	1.000	1.29	5	0	0	3	0	2	7.0	1	1	1	0	0	4	0	8	1
Schiel, Twins	0	0	.000	9.00	1	0	0	0	0	0	1.0	2	1	1	0	1	0	0	1	0
Scoates, Pirates	1	2	.333	9.37	7	1	0	2	0	0	16.1	17	17	17	1	1	16	0	9	3
R. Scott, Red Sox	1	5	.167	5.77	13	6	0	7	0	3	34.1	38	27	22	0	1	10	0	17	5
T. Scott, Astros°	0	6	.000	6.23	12	6	0	2	0	0	30.1	37	34	21	0	1	32	0	34	14
Shade, Pirates	1	2	.333	5.40	11	1	0	4	0	0	26.2	26	21	16	0	0	23	0	14	2
Shepherd, Braves	3	3	.500	1.43	27	0	0	19	0	6	50.1	27	11	8	2	1	15	1	34	4
Smith, Pirates	0	1	.000	3.38	2	2	0	0	0	0	10.2	9	5	4	0	0	5	0	7	0
Soper, Indians	5	2	.714	1.05	32	0	0	32	0	15	42.2	41	9	5	0	1	9	1	33	1
Sparks, Pirates	0	2	.000	7.15	7	0	0	2	0	0	11.1	21	16	9	2	0	7	0	3	0
Springer, Yankees	3	0	1.000	1.50	6	6	0	0	0	0	24.0	14	8	4	0	1	10	0	34	1
St. Pe, Rangers	0	1	.000	6.00	8	1	0	1	0	0	21.0	25	15	14	0	1	6	0	18	2
Steinmetz, Braves	3	2	.600	2.08	10	8	1	0	0	0	47.2	30	12	11	2	4	16	0	54	5
D. Stevens, Reds	1	3	.250	3.21	19	0	0	11	0	5	42.0	39	16	15	2	1	15	1	22	1
J. Stevens, Indians°	1	2	.333	4.07	23	0	0	10	0	1	42.0	45	24	19	1	1	19	1	29	4
Takaheshi, Dodgers	1	0	1.000	0.00	3	0	0	2	0	1	12.1	7	0	0	0	2	4	0	11	0
Tatis, Dodgers	3	3	.500	2.54	11	9	0	1	0	1	60.1	50	20	17	1	5	22	0	44	5
Thigpen, Expos	4	0	1.000	2.56	14	0	0	8	0	1	31.2	23	11	9	1	0	17	0	21	3
Thoma, White Sox	0	2	.000	2.77	20	0	0	17	0	8	26.0	20	8	8	0	0	14	2	27	1
M. Thomas, Mets°	2	0	1.000	1.44	8	3	0	5	0	0	31.1	23	5	5	0	2	14	0	34	2
R. Thomas, Braves°	1	1	.500	3.60	5	3	0	1	0	0	20.0	20	11	8	0	1	5	0	13	2
Tolar, White Sox°	6	2	.750	1.65	13	12	1	0	0	0	60.0	29	16	11	0	1	54	0	58	10
F. Torres, Expos	0	2	.000	7.11	11	0	0	5	0	0	12.2	19	14	10	0	0	7	0	4	1
J. Torres, Mets	0	0	.000	0.00	2	0	0	1	0	0	1.2	2	0	0	0	0	1	0	2	0
Tuss, Expos	3	4	.429	4.28	13	12	0	0	0	0	67.1	80	49	32	5	4	22	0	47	7
Vasquez, Reds	0	3	.000	4.94	14	0	0	8	0	0	23.2	31	22	13	2	1	11	1	11	4
Vitko, Mets	4	1	.800	3.29	8	5	1	2	0	0	41.0	28	20	15	0	1	16	0	33	4
Walden, Indians	4	2	.667	3.79	11	10	0	1	0	0	57.0	65	42	24	2	6	38	0	33	8
Walling, Braves	3	1	.750	2.77	20	1	0	13	0	1	39.0	37	22	12	0	1	8	2	34	4
Washington, Rangers	0	2	.000	8.71	6	3	0	1	0	0	10.1	18	11	10	1	0	6	0	9	1
Wechsberg, Indians	1	3	.250	3.56	9	8	0	0	0	0	30.1	29	19	12	1	3	16	0	33	7
Wertz, Indians	4	3	.571	3.14	12	11	1	0	1	0	66.0	57	23	23	0	4	36	0	56	11
West, Royals	3	3	.500	4.17	12	10	0	1	0	0	45.1	34	28	21	3	5	35	0	31	7
Wheeler, Astros	1	4	.200	4.00	14	8	0	0	0	0	54.0	51	33	24	1	4	25	0	45	5
Wiley, Yankees	2	4	.429	2.88	11	10	0	0	0	0	56.1	50	21	18	1	4	12	0	53	5
Wilson, Mets	2	3	.400	1.45	5	5	0	0	0	0	31.0	30	10	5	0	3	0	0	25	1
Wyatt, Reds	1	1	.500	25.92	1	0	0	0	0	0	8.1	12	25	24	0	3	6	0	6	1

BALKS—D. Brown, Cecil, Rivas, 10 each; Quirico, 8; D. Allen, Paxton, 6 each; Alvarez, Buckley, Grebe, Mays, J. Munoz, Rinaldi, Shade, Wechsberg, 5 each; Rafael J. Diaz (Reds), Francescon, Garcia, Malzone, Mauldin, Nieves, Ray, Rychel, Soper, Sparks, 4 each; Benson, Bethancourt, Braase, Castillo, Conroy, Fier, Hansell, Hoffman, Hunter, Milton, Patrick, Ju. Perez, Plemmons, Prats, Pulido, Reyes, Robinson, Thoma, Vitko, Walden, 3 each; T. Allen, Jo. Arias, Arner, Astacio, Baez, Borgula, Broadwater, S. Brown, Calderon, Chmielewski, Correa, Daniel, Rafael Diaz (Expos), Giberti, Hawkins, Hook, Hutto, Juden, Linares, McElfish, Mieses, Niemeyer, Pagan, Ramirez, Rees, Rojas, Romberg, Ruiz, Ryan, Scoates, Wiley, Wilson, 2 each; Aucoin, Barreiro, Bochtler, Boggetto, Brooks, Bryans, Budrewicz, Candelaria, Chrisman, Cullens, Delahoya, Delgado, Dennison, DeVaughan, Eddy, Espinosa, Foster, Gallaher, Gennings, Gietzen, Gonzales, Gross, Gutierrez, Haller, Hampton, Harvey, Hope, Hulme, Johnston, Kerfut, D. King, E. King, Lane, Lyle, Manon, M. Martinez, Matznick, Minutelli, Mirabella, Mongiello, R. Munoz, Navarro, Jo. Perez, R. Perez, Perry, Polak, Ring, Robles, Rogers, Santamaria, T. Scott, Shepherd, Steinmetz, J. Stevens, Tatis, Walling, 1 each.

COMBINATION SHUTOUTS—Navarro-Rinaldi, Juden-Allen-Rinaldi, Astros; Murray-Cullens-Shepherd, Steinmetz-Cullens-Chiles, Steinmetz-Shields-Shepherd, Rolfes-Walling, Rolfes-Dickman-Roa, Braves; Astacio-Calderon, Patrick-Cantres, Mesa-Braase, Bishop-Tatis, Daniel-Cantres, Dodgers; Martinez-Hutto, Fier-Romberg, Expos; Wertz-Soper 2, Kallevig-Stevens-Soper, Paxton-Ryan-McElfish-Soper, Walden-McElfish, Indians; Martinez-Lindsay-Rees, Mets; Francescon-Roeder, Pirates; Randle-Phillips, Buckley-Fowler, Correa-Randle-Phillips, Moyer-McMurtry-Arner-Fowler, Arner-Gamez, Arner-Phillips-Fowler, Rangers; Ray-Wyatt-Stevens, Cecil-Nieves, Linares-King, Hook-Plemmons, Cecil-Stevens-Nieves, Reds; Malzone-Hansell, Hansell-Malzone, Allen-Ring, Red Sox; Aranguren-Reno 2, Connor-Malena, Gross-Baez, Baez-Reno, Milton-Dunn-Reno, West-Bowling-Malena, Royals; Robles-Lipson, Twins; Matznick-Mongiello 2, Matznick-Hulme-Thoma-Conover, McDowell-Jones-Conover, Hunter-Garcia-Thoma, Tolar-Hulme, Hunter-Hulme-Conover, Tolar-Hulme-Caridad, Tolar-Ruiz-Conover, White Sox; Hitchcock-Rojas 2, Brubaker-Chase-Perez, Hitchcock-Johnston, Candelaria-Quirico-Haller, Hitchcock-Haller, Dacosta-Haller, Yankees.

NO-HIT GAME—Garcia, White Sox, defeated Mets, 2-0, August 3.

Pioneer League

SUMMER CLASS A CLASSIFICATION

CHAMPIONSHIP WINNERS IN PREVIOUS YEARS

1939—Twin Falls*	.581	1955—Boise	.588	1973—Billings	.629
1940—Salt Lake City	.608	Magic Valley (4th)*	.489	1974—Idaho Falls	.569
Ogden (4th)*	.492	1956—Boise	.561	1975—Great Falls	.577
1941—Boise	.623	1957—Salt Lake City	.650	1976—Great Falls	.577
Ogden (2nd)*	.598	Billings†	.582	1977—Lethbridge	.629
1942—Pocatello†	.690	1958—Great Falls	.582	1978—Billings x	.735
Boise	.683	Boise†	.615	1979—Helena	.623
1943-44-45—Did not operate.		1959—Boise	.633	Lethbridge y	.559
1946—Twin Falls‡	.585	Billings (2nd)*	.523	1980—Lethbridge y	.743
Salt Lake City†	.585	1960—Boise	.686	Billings	.629
1947—Salt Lake City	.618	Idaho Falls	.650	1981—Calgary	.657
Twin Falls†	.600	1961—Boise	.638	Butte y	.557
1948—Pocatello	.611	Great Falls*	.571	1982—Medicine Hat y	.629
Twin Falls (2nd)*	.595	1962—Boise§	.565	Idaho Falls	.600
1949—Twin Falls	.624	Billings†	.706	1983—Billings y	.614
Pocatello (3rd)*	.595	1963—Idaho Falls	.702	Calgary	.600
1950—Pocatello	.635	Magic Valley†	.643	1984—Billings	.691
Billings (3rd)*	.571	1964—Treasure Valley	.615	Helena y	.647
1951—Salt Lake City	.618	1965—Treasure Valley	.530	1985—Great Falls	.771
Great Falls (3rd)*	.559	1966—Ogden	.591	Salt Lake City y	.657
1952—Pocatello	.595	1967—Ogden	.621	1986—Salt Lake City z	.643
Idaho Falls (2nd)*	.573	1968—Ogden	.609	Great Falls	.571
1953—Ogden	.679	1969—Ogden	.620	1987—Salt Lake City z	.700
Salt Lake C. (4th)*	.527	1970—Idaho Falls	.629	Helena	.657
1954—Salt Lake City	.595	1971—Great Falls	.643	1988—Great Falls z	.754
Great Falls (4th)*	.530	1972—Billings	.694	Butte	.629

*Won four-club playoff. †Won split-season playoff. ‡Ended first half in tie with Salt Lake City and won one-game playoff. §Ended first half in tie with Billings and Great Falls and won playoff. xBillings (first place) defeated Idaho Falls (second place) in First Place-Second Place playoff. yLeague divided into Northern and Southern divisions; won two-club playoff. zWon two-club playoff.

STANDING OF CLUBS AT CLOSE OF SEASON, AUGUST 30

NORTHERN DIVISION

Club	W.	L.	T.	Pct.	G.B.
Great Falls (Dodgers)	53	14	0	.791	......
Helena (Brewers)	38	30	0	.559	15½
Billings (Reds)	26	41	0	.388	27
Medicine Hat (Blue Jays)	23	46	0	.333	31

SOUTHERN DIVISION

Club	W.	L.	T.	Pct.	G.B.
Butte (Rangers)	41	25	0	.621	......
Salt Lake City (Independent)	33	36	0	.478	12½
Pocatello (Giants)	29	38	0	.433	12½
Idaho Falls (Braves)	27	40	0	.403	14½

COMPOSITE STANDING OF CLUBS AT CLOSE OF SEASON, AUGUST 30

Club	GF.	But.	Hel.	SLC.	Poc.	IF.	Bil.	MH	W.	L.	T.	Pct.	G.B.
Great Falls (Dodgers)	....	5	9	5	6	7	9	12	53	14	0	.791	......
Butte (Rangers)	1	....	4	10	7	10	4	5	41	25	0	.621	11½
Helena (Brewers)	5	3	....	5	3	6	9	7	38	30	0	.559	15½
Salt Lake City (Independent)	2	3	2	....	8	8	3	7	33	36	0	.478	21
Pocatello (Giants)	1	6	4	6	....	4	5	3	29	38	0	.433	24
Idaho Falls (Braves)	0	3	1	6	8	....	5	4	27	40	0	.403	26
Billings (Reds)	3	3	4	4	2	2	....	8	26	41	0	.388	27
Medicine Hat (Blue Jays)	2	2	6	0	4	3	6	....	23	46	0	.333	31

Major league affiliations in parentheses.

Playoffs—Great Falls defeated Butte, three games to none, to win league championship.

Regular-Season Attendance—Billings, 77,405; Butte, 26,711; Great Falls, 69,637; Helena, 39,645; Idaho Falls, 65,773; Medicine Hat, 13,624; Pocatello, 17,117; Salt Lake City, 173,256. Total—483,168. Playoffs (3 games)—5,550.

Managers—Billings, Dave Keller; Butte, Bump Wills; Great Falls, Joe Vavra; Helena, Dusty Rhodes; Idaho Falls, Cloyd Boyer; Medicine Hat, Ralph Wheeler; Pocatello, Deron McCue; Salt Lake City, Barry Moss.

All-Star Team—1B—Bo Dodson, Helena; 2B—Ramces Guerrero, Helena; 3B—Mike Grace, Salt Lake City; SS—Tim Barker, Great Falls; OF—Scott Pose, Billings; Dan Peltier, Butte; Shawn Holtzclaw, Medicine Hat; C—Barry Winford, Butte; DH—Tom Goodwin, Great Falls; P—Kiki Jones, Great Falls; Jamie McAndrew, Great Falls; Tony Valle, Idaho Falls.

(Compiled by Howe Sportsdata International, Boston, Mass.)

CLUB BATTING

Club	Pct.	G.	AB.	R.	OR.	H.	TB.	2B.	3B.	HR.	RBI.	SH.	SF.	HP.	BB.	Int. BB.	SO.	SB.	CS.	LOB.
Salt Lake City	.305	69	2475	413	475	756	1064	136	23	42	357	16	18	32	241	7	528	58	46	542
Great Falls	.294	67	2216	431	197	652	948	105	28	45	352	16	18	23	316	7	442	171	57	491
Butte	.292	66	2203	400	316	644	942	111	26	45	346	6	15	27	260	6	458	95	40	454
Billings	.272	67	2293	349	387	623	799	96	16	16	287	24	10	33	258	9	475	103	45	506
Helena	.268	68	2213	367	332	592	820	82	19	36	311	56	21	27	301	6	443	70	27	513
Idaho Falls	.258	67	2282	367	396	589	877	96	21	50	323	11	16	35	278	4	583	61	31	519
Pocatello	.258	67	2198	309	384	567	829	106	21	38	261	28	19	27	211	6	455	85	60	431
Medicine Hat	.230	69	2282	282	431	525	702	76	25	17	235	17	20	33	282	3	636	56	35	529

INDIVIDUAL BATTING

(Leading Qualifiers for Batting Championship—189 or More Plate Appearances)

*Bats lefthanded. †Switch-hitter.

Player and Club	Pct.	G.	AB.	R.	H.	TB.	2B.	3B.	HR.	RBI.	SH.	SF.	HP.	BB.	Int. BB.	SO.	SB.	CS.
Winford, Barry, Butte	.359	61	198	54	71	100	15	1	4	31	1	1	1	39	0	24	10	2
Pose, Scott, Billings*	.352	60	210	52	74	85	7	2	0	25	1	1	1	54	3	31	26	3
Grace, Michael, Salt Lake City	.350	63	240	37	84	123	17	2	6	37	1	1	5	28	3	31	4	6
Giustino, Gerard, Salt Lake City	.350	51	200	37	70	112	17	2	7	36	0	2	5	13	0	34	0	1
O'Donnell, Stephen, Great Falls	.345	60	223	46	77	113	11	2	7	44	1	1	3	31	1	55	8	5
Newkirk, Craig, Butte*	.339	58	180	21	61	82	10	4	1	34	1	1	0	27	0	24	6	1
O'Leary, Troy, Helena*	.338	68	263	54	89	144	16	3	11	56	9	3	2	28	1	43	9	8
Howard, Matthew, Great Falls	.333	59	186	39	62	83	8	2	3	34	5	2	9	21	0	14	23	8
Waid, Patrick, Salt Lake City	.332	60	247	48	82	119	11	4	6	32	2	2	2	17	0	43	10	9
Miller, Roger, Pocatello	.332	57	199	39	66	98	8	3	6	38	2	4	4	19	1	14	8	5

Departmental Leaders: G—Karczewski, O'Leary, 68; AB—Harris, 264; R—Goodwin, 55; H—O'Leary, 89; TB—O'Leary, 144; 2B—Giustino, Grace, Karczewski, 17; 3B—Harris, 8; HR—Guerrero, 13; RBI—O'Leary, 56; SH—Brown, 10; SF—Harring, Holtzclaw, 5; HP—Gill, 14; BB—Pose, 54; IBB—Grace, Pose, 3; SO—Beaulac, 85; SB—Goodwin, 60; CS—Barker, M. Garcia, Karczewski, Waid, 9.

(All Players—Listed Alphabetically)

Player and Club	Pct.	G.	AB.	R.	H.	TB.	2B.	3B.	HR.	RBI.	SH.	SF.	HP.	BB.	Int. BB.	SO.	SB.	CS.
Adams, Lionel, Idaho Falls	.297	25	91	18	27	54	9	0	6	21	0	2	2	7	0	31	0	0
Ahrens, Kelly, Pocatello	.224	34	107	13	24	42	6	0	4	19	0	2	3	16	0	43	1	1
Allen, Richard, Billings	.321	26	84	13	27	33	6	0	0	17	0	2	1	8	0	17	3	1
Baar, Bryan, Great Falls	.288	48	139	31	40	81	9	1	10	38	0	1	1	27	0	35	1	1
Baranoski, James, Idaho Falls	.105	7	19	5	2	8	0	0	2	5	0	0	2	2	0	4	0	1
Barker, Timothy, Great Falls	.313	59	201	54	63	99	9	6	5	36	1	1	2	37	0	55	25	9
Beaulac, Joseph, Salt Lake City*	.282	64	252	39	71	103	11	3	5	37	1	4	4	27	0	85	3	1
Bible, Michael, Salt Lake City	.310	50	171	21	53	75	7	3	3	37	2	0	4	12	1	35	2	2
Booth, David, Pocatello†	.263	44	137	27	36	55	7	3	2	13	2	1	0	13	1	44	5	2
Bowers, Brent, Medicine Hat*	.222	54	207	16	46	52	2	2	0	13	0	1	0	19	0	55	6	2
Brauning, Jeff, Pocatello	.244	36	135	23	33	41	6	1	0	12	1	1	3	15	0	18	12	5
Brown, Reginald, Helena†	.266	61	214	47	57	64	7	0	0	23	10	1	1	32	0	27	19	6
Burton, Christopher, Idaho Falls*	.269	55	208	39	56	67	8	0	1	21	3	2	1	19	0	50	15	4
Cala, Craig, Pocatello	.319	44	141	38	45	83	10	2	8	18	0	1	2	34	0	33	6	6
Carlton, Andrew, Medicine Hat	.238	29	84	11	20	31	2	3	1	8	0	0	2	15	0	29	0	1
Cedeno, Domingo, Medicine Hat	.232	53	194	28	45	62	6	4	1	20	3	1	3	23	0	65	6	6
Cerny, Mark, Billings*	.298	49	161	32	48	66	10	4	0	20	2	1	0	18	0	39	12	2
Chiaramonte, John, Pocatello	.000	21	1	0	0	0	0	0	0	0	0	0	0	0	0	1	0	0
Charpia, Reed, Helena*	.279	56	179	24	50	64	6	1	2	19	7	0	1	19	0	25	5	1
Clinton, James, Butte	.219	60	137	14	30	37	7	0	0	15	0	0	2	12	2	37	3	3
Cole, Todd, Medicine Hat	.173	22	52	4	9	9	0	0	0	4	1	1	2	12	1	21	0	0
Collier, Anthony, Great Falls*	.341	50	173	30	59	82	11	3	2	24	1	1	1	10	1	33	7	5
Cox, Darron, Billings	.274	49	157	20	43	49	6	0	0	18	2	0	5	21	0	34	11	3
Crispin, Luis, Pocatello†	.172	18	58	2	10	12	0	1	0	4	0	0	3	0	0	15	1	1
Crowley, Brian, Butte	.247	33	73	11	18	24	4	1	0	6	1	1	0	3	0	24	1	0
Crump, Gerald, Medicine Hat*	.210	26	81	9	17	26	3	3	0	7	3	1	0	8	0	25	1	0
DeLoach, Lee, Butte	.242	28	66	5	16	16	0	0	0	5	0	0	6	1	0	17	3	1
Deutsch, John, Great Falls*	.296	64	223	38	66	97	11	1	6	43	0	3	0	48	2	48	9	3
Diaz, Angel, Helena	.244	61	213	29	52	70	7	4	1	20	4	2	4	9	1	33	5	3
Diggs, Antonio, Helena†	.243	51	148	24	36	39	1	1	0	14	0	5	1	14	0	29	5	3
Dodson, Brian, Helena*	.310	65	216	38	67	100	13	1	6	42	1	3	4	52	2	52	5	1
Dombrowski, Robert, Billings	.208	23	77	9	16	22	6	0	0	5	0	0	0	10	0	18	2	5
Duke, Andy, Billings	.231	44	134	16	31	43	6	0	2	16	0	0	1	18	0	45	5	2
Eklund, Troy, Butte	.273	6	22	2	6	10	1	0	1	4	0	1	0	2	0	4	0	0
Ellis, Jason, Idaho Falls	.333	2	3	0	1	1	0	0	0	0	0	0	0	0	0	1	0	0
Evans, Phillip, Salt Lake City	.200	36	110	13	22	27	5	0	0	6	3	0	2	15	0	37	0	1
Flinn, Geoffrey, Butte*	.296	54	162	34	48	68	9	1	3	31	1	1	5	28	0	33	13	5
Floyd, Daniel, Great Falls	.182	20	44	4	8	12	2	1	0	4	1	0	2	2	0	18	0	0
Fowler, Yale, Great Falls	.220	40	100	17	22	30	5	0	1	9	1	0	1	18	1	29	1	1
Frias, Pedro, Pocatello†	.196	58	189	18	37	51	7	2	1	10	3	0	1	14	0	35	13	6
Garcia, Manuel, Butte	.264	61	212	42	56	90	9	2	7	30	1	1	6	30	0	66	15	9
Garcia, Patricio, Medicine Hat	.252	34	107	14	27	39	5	2	1	15	0	4	2	5	0	31	1	3
Garczyk, Ed, Salt Lake City	.323	35	130	27	42	48	6	0	0	11	0	2	0	9	0	27	8	5
Gill, Christopher, Billings	.291	57	196	42	57	72	5	2	2	25	0	1	14	23	1	21	12	6
Gillum, Kenneth, Billings*	.225	28	102	13	23	36	2	1	3	22	0	0	1	10	0	25	4	2
Giustino, Gerard, Salt Lake City	.350	51	200	37	70	112	17	2	7	36	0	2	5	13	0	34	0	1
Glenn, Leon, Helena*	.000	6	15	0	0	0	0	0	0	0	0	0	0	0	0	4	0	0
Gonzalez, Agustin, Billings	.167	4	6	0	1	1	0	0	0	0	0	0	0	1	0	2	0	0
Goodwin, Thomas, Great Falls*	.308	63	240	55	74	98	12	3	2	33	1	2	2	28	1	30	60	8
Gould, Frank, Pocatello	.000	13	1	0	0	0	0	0	0	0	0	0	0	0	0	1	0	0
Grace, Michael, Salt Lake City	.350	63	240	37	84	123	17	2	6	37	1	1	5	28	3	31	4	6
Gray, Steven, Pocatello	.159	26	88	2	14	14	0	0	0	3	0	1	1	3	0	23	6	4
Green, Darryl, Salt Lake City	.241	12	29	4	7	8	1	0	0	2	0	0	0	1	0	6	0	0
Guerrero, Ramces, Idaho Falls	.258	47	132	29	34	78	5	0	13	32	0	3	2	35	1	50	2	2
Harr, Matthew, Pocatello	.224	48	156	23	35	47	7	1	1	19	7	4	2	19	0	29	7	7
Harring, Kenneth, Idaho Falls	.322	54	199	34	64	89	8	4	3	31	2	5	1	19	0	26	11	4
Harris, Donald, Butte	.284	65	264	50	75	116	7	8	6	37	0	3	6	12	0	54	14	4
Harvell, Roderick, Great Falls*	.328	45	134	26	44	49	3	1	0	12	1	0	1	14	0	17	17	7
Haugen, Troy, Helena†	.265	57	181	32	48	69	7	4	2	20	3	2	2	34	0	45	6	1
Hays, Daren, Butte*	.316	62	212	34	67	102	16	2	5	50	0	1	1	21	0	35	3	3
Heckel, Walter, Medicine Hat*	.240	59	221	38	53	62	9	0	0	15	1	0	1	47	0	67	21	7
Henderson, Harry, Billings*	.225	51	178	15	40	53	4	0	3	22	0	0	0	10	2	41	1	2
Hoffman, Trevor, Billings	.249	61	201	22	50	58	5	0	1	20	5	3	3	19	1	40	1	6
Hollis, Jackson, Billings*	.292	19	65	10	19	27	5	0	1	12	1	0	0	15	1	18	1	1
Holtzclaw, Shawn, Medicine Hat*	.277	64	242	29	67	102	15	4	4	40	0	5	2	20	1	54	3	3
Houston, Tyler, Idaho Falls*	.244	50	176	30	43	66	11	0	4	24	0	0	1	25	1	41	4	0
Howard, Matthew, Great Falls	.333	59	186	39	62	83	8	2	3	34	5	2	9	21	0	14	23	8
Huntey, Clark, Pocatello	.222	21	72	11	16	22	4	1	0	6	1	0	0	8	0	21	1	0
Irish, Jeffrey, Medicine Hat	.139	22	72	16	10	14	1	0	1	5	0	0	2	10	0	24	0	0
Jaime, Juan, Medicine Hat	.295	38	132	16	39	47	5	0	1	19	0	3	1	18	0	19	4	1
Jones, Heath, Pocatello	.205	35	117	8	24	32	5	0	1	12	0	1	2	10	1	22	0	2

Player and Club	Pct.	G.	AB.	R.	H.	TB.	2B.	3B.	HR.	RBI.	SH.	SF.	HP.	BB.	Int. BB.	SO.	SB.	CS.
Kappesser, Robert, Helena	.139	32	72	13	10	13	1	1	0	1	2	0	0	14	0	24	3	0
Karczewski, Raymond, SLC†	.260	68	254	39	66	92	17	3	1	30	1	0	2	27	1	56	12	9
Kidd, Dennis, Salt Lake City°	.333	12	39	10	13	23	2	1	2	7	1	1	0	3	0	6	1	1
Kuhlman, Eric, Idaho Falls	.000	15	2	0	0	0	0	0	0	0	0	0	0	0	0	2	0	0
Lewis, Joseph, Butte°	.385	11	26	6	10	13	3	0	0	5	0	0	2	0	0	4	1	0
Loeb, Marc, Medicine Hat	.290	21	62	6	18	18	0	0	0	8	1	1	3	12	0	12	0	0
Loera, Javier, Great Falls	.120	14	25	3	3	6	0	0	1	3	0	0	1	1	0	11	1	0
Lopez, Alfred, Idaho Falls	.222	37	81	13	18	21	1	1	0	8	1	0	3	19	0	27	0	1
Marquez, Edgar, Medicine Hat	.213	22	47	6	10	10	0	0	0	3	1	0	0	2	0	22	0	0
Marshall, Randolph, Butte°	.267	56	172	27	46	70	13	1	3	26	0	0	0	22	0	27	2	0
Matsukubo, Shingo, Salt Lake City°..	.167	6	6	0	1	1	0	0	0	0	0	0	0	0	0	3	0	0
May, Shawn, Pocatello†	.202	29	99	10	20	22	2	0	0	6	0	0	0	6	0	21	1	6
McDonald, Kevin, Medicine Hat	.111	6	9	2	1	1	0	0	0	1	0	0	0	3	0	4	1	0
Mengel, Brad, Medicine Hat	.238	42	147	17	35	46	7	2	0	14	1	0	6	12	0	36	3	1
Mesa, Audy, Pocatello	.274	30	106	11	29	42	7	0	2	8	1	0	1	1	0	20	1	3
Micheu, Tony, Butte	.343	15	35	8	12	13	1	0	0	8	0	1	2	7	0	8	0	2
Miller, Roger, Pocatello	.332	57	199	39	66	98	8	3	6	38	2	4	4	19	1	14	8	5
Miller, Steven, Medicine Hat	.235	22	68	10	16	24	5	0	1	7	0	0	0	16	0	11	2	1
Miller, William A., Great Falls°	.286	11	28	2	8	9	1	0	0	4	0	1	0	4	0	8	0	0
Miller, William J., Idaho Falls	.209	45	139	20	29	47	3	0	5	18	0	0	2	12	0	51	0	1
Montes, Daniel, Pocatello†	.299	25	87	13	26	34	6	1	0	12	1	0	1	8	0	16	5	3
Morrow, Timmy, Butte	.271	60	225	40	61	84	7	2	4	27	1	2	1	12	1	44	13	5
Newkirk, Craig, Butte	.339	58	180	21	61	82	10	4	1	34	1	1	0	27	0	24	6	1
Nichols, Brian, Billings	.267	39	146	16	39	48	9	0	0	18	4	0	3	9	0	20	2	3
Nyquist, Michael, Salt Lake City	.167	12	24	2	4	4	0	0	0	2	0	1	0	2	0	7	0	0
O'Donnell, Stephen, Great Falls	.345	60	223	46	77	113	11	2	7	44	1	1	3	31	1	55	8	5
O'Leary, Troy, Helena°	.338	68	263	54	89	144	16	3	11	56	9	3	2	28	1	43	9	8
Oliva, Jose, Butte	.211	41	114	18	24	44	2	3	4	13	0	2	1	14	1	41	4	3
Olmeda, Jose, Idaho Falls†	.248	61	230	36	57	77	5	6	1	27	0	1	0	31	0	40	9	4
Parker, Stacy, Butte	.333	6	9	1	3	3	0	0	0	1	0	0	1	1	0	3	0	0
Parrotte, Brian, Billings°	.262	39	122	19	32	42	4	0	2	12	3	0	1	7	1	31	6	2
Peltier, Daniel, Butte°	.402	33	122	35	49	79	7	1	7	28	0	1	2	25	2	16	10	1
Perozo, Daniel, Billings	.261	50	161	30	42	54	6	3	0	12	5	0	2	9	0	41	15	4
Pose, Scott, Billings°	.352	60	210	52	74	85	7	2	0	25	1	1	1	54	3	31	26	3
Powell, Gordon, Helena	.250	5	8	1	2	2	0	0	0	1	0	0	0	1	0	4	0	0
Pullins, Jimmie, Idaho Falls	.194	51	139	26	27	43	5	1	3	15	3	0	4	23	0	46	1	3
Ramirez, John, Salt Lake City	.367	38	150	23	55	74	11	1	2	26	1	2	2	11	0	13	2	3
Reagan, Kyle, Billings°	.241	40	137	18	33	46	6	2	1	18	1	1	1	8	0	21	2	1
Reid, Dante, Medicine Hat°	.151	22	53	1	8	8	0	0	0	5	1	0	0	6	0	23	0	2
Reynoso, Henry, Helena†	.200	5	10	0	2	2	0	0	0	0	0	0	0	0	0	1	1	0
Rigsby, Ricky, Idaho Falls	.251	59	199	31	50	82	10	5	4	33	0	1	5	21	0	61	8	1
Roberts, Lonell, Medicine Hat	.141	29	78	2	11	12	1	0	0	6	1	0	1	7	0	27	3	3
Roebuck, Joseph, Helena	.213	60	174	22	37	60	6	1	5	29	4	1	6	12	0	47	3	0
Rojas, Wilberto, Medicine Hat	.223	55	197	22	44	71	7	1	6	26	0	3	6	17	0	56	1	1
Rolen, Steven, Pocatello	.330	56	203	33	67	108	14	3	7	33	5	2	5	13	1	31	9	3
Rooney, Andrew, Medicine Hat°	.248	49	145	24	36	52	7	3	1	13	1	0	2	16	0	30	4	3
Roper, Brian, Butte	.175	17	40	3	7	7	0	0	0	3	0	0	1	3	0	14	0	2
Sanderson, Shaun, Salt Lake City	.342	28	79	14	27	40	5	1	2	10	0	0	2	11	0	13	2	0
Sarbaugh, Michael, Helena	.333	24	84	17	28	42	8	0	2	9	1	1	2	7	0	16	0	1
Sass, James, Helena	.217	34	83	13	18	21	1	1	0	11	3	2	0	18	1	15	1	1
Seals, Billy, Great Falls†	.254	27	63	8	16	25	3	0	2	8	0	1	0	6	0	15	0	0
Sims, Daniel, Idaho Falls°	.315	50	184	27	58	66	6	1	0	23	0	0	1	20	0	25	6	4
Smeltzer, Schuyler, Salt Lake City°..	.217	22	69	14	15	25	4	0	2	6	0	1	0	10	0	22	0	1
Snyder, Randall, Helena†	.316	24	79	13	25	33	2	0	2	13	0	1	0	12	1	13	0	1
Sparrow, Christopher, Idaho Falls	.262	54	191	19	50	71	10	1	3	29	1	0	4	22	0	52	0	0
Speakes, Joseph, Pocatello	.265	55	189	20	50	76	12	1	4	27	4	0	1	16	1	51	3	4
Sweeney, Michael, Idaho Falls	.097	14	31	4	3	8	2	0	1	1	0	0	1	5	0	21	0	0
Tannahill, Kevin, Helena	.254	33	71	14	18	23	2	0	1	11	3	1	0	20	0	23	2	1
Tarchione, Travis, Salt Lake City	.324	63	256	45	83	107	13	1	3	49	3	2	2	19	0	39	7	6
Teel, Garett, Great Falls	.140	37	93	9	13	18	2	0	1	5	3	0	0	15	0	12	1	1
Thomas, Donald, Idaho Falls	.297	22	74	16	22	35	5	1	2	14	0	0	3	5	1	13	3	1
Tripodi, Max, Salt Lake City°	.275	54	189	36	52	74	9	2	3	27	1	0	1	35	2	62	5	1
Troup, James, Salt Lake City	.300	17	30	4	9	9	0	0	0	2	0	0	1	1	0	9	2	0
Vollmer, Gustavo, Pocatello	.351	27	97	18	34	49	5	2	2	17	1	0	0	12	1	14	5	1
Vondran, Steven, Billings	.308	43	156	22	48	64	9	2	1	25	0	0	0	18	0	31	0	2
Waid, Patrick, Salt Lake City	.332	60	247	48	82	119	11	4	6	32	2	2	2	17	0	43	10	9
Waldenberger, David, Idaho Falls†	.256	47	168	18	43	59	8	1	2	19	1	2	3	11	1	40	2	5
Weldin, Daniel, Helena°	.100	13	20	1	2	2	0	0	0	1	0	1	0	4	0	5	0	0
White, Craig, Great Falls°	.274	45	117	29	32	49	8	3	1	26	1	3	0	24	0	17	7	4
White, Darrin, Helena°	.279	59	183	25	51	72	5	2	4	35	4	2	4	25	0	40	6	1
Williams, Wayne, Medicine Hat	.235	15	34	5	8	10	0	1	0	5	0	0	0	8	1	7	0	0
Willis, Steve, Pocatello	.063	5	16	0	1	1	0	0	0	0	0	0	1	0	0	3	1	1
Wilson, Norbert, Medicine Hat°	.100	19	50	6	5	6	1	0	0	1	1	0	0	6	0	18	0	1
Winford, Barry, Butte	.359	61	198	54	71	100	15	1	4	31	1	1	1	39	0	24	10	2
Wismer, Michael, Great Falls	.304	48	161	35	49	81	10	5	4	24	0	2	0	24	0	28	8	4
Wright, Brian, Idaho Falls°	.333	4	15	2	5	5	0	0	0	2	0	0	0	2	0	1	0	0
Zona, Jeffrey, Idaho Falls	.000	23	1	0	0	0	0	0	0	0	0	0	0	0	0	1	0	0

The following pitchers, listed alphabetically by club, with games in parentheses, had no plate appearances, primarily through use of designated hitters:

BILLINGS—Bates, Eric (24); Blankenship, Robert (13); Borcherding, Mark (13); Dempster, Kurtis (8); Doty, Sean (18); Fry, Brian (17); Galloway, Gilbert (22); Keim, Christopher (11); Pugh, Timothy (13); Rodriguez, Tomas (15); Teegarden, Travis (16); Wilburn, Ema (20).

BUTTE—Asche, Scott (9); Bickhardt, Eric (18); Borges, Jose (6); Eischen, Joseph (12); Franklin, Jay (21); Graves, John (26); Matsumura, Takaaki (4); Ohman, Edward (1); Perez, David (18); Romero, Brian (10); Rowley, Stephen (11); Shiflett, Christian (15); Steiner, Brian (11); Sugiura, Koji (6); Young, Mark (8).

GREAT FALLS—Bielanin, Raymond (13); Brosnan, Jason (13); Calhoun, Raymond (7); Crane, Richard (16); Cummings, Audelle (17); Fletcher, Robert (2); Frame, Michael (16); Helmick, Anthony (13); Humber, Frank (24); Jones, Keith (12); Madsen, Eril (23); McAndrew, Jamie (13); Parisotto, Barry (14); Potthoff, Michael (15).

HELENA—Andrzejewski, Joseph (11); Brakeley, William (6); Correa, Ramser (2); Drake, Samuel (7); Federico, Gustavo (14); Kimball, Scott (11); Kinder, Jeffrey (5); Landry, Gregory (13); Muscat, Scott (18); Patton, Eric (19); Potts, James (2); Rehwinkel, Patrick (3); Rugg, Russell (10); Vancho, Robert (10); Voit, David (29); Wilson, Timothy (17).

IDAHO FALLS—Eckhardt, Thomas (9); Gore, Lee (18); Haeberle, Kevin (8); Kortright, James (16); Lemon, Donald (9); Newman, Thomas (12); Osmon, David (14); Parker, Michael (18); Rogers, Douglas (13); Valle, Pascual (13); White, Andrew (13).

MEDICINE HAT—Bradley, Eric (21); Evaschuk, Brad (19); Fritz, James (17); Gordon, Scott (16); Kulina, Kenneth (21); Mooney, Jeffrey (21); Small, Aaron (15); Steed, Ricky (7); Taylor, Michael (17); Tovar, Carlos (19); Tyson, Allen (18).

POCATELLO—Carrico, John (12); Hernandez, Marino (10); Herring, Vincent (18); Hillman, Stewart (14); Lund, Greg (2); Musselwhite, Darren (28); Quintel, Mark (23); Rambo, Daniel (2); Rapp, Patrick (16); Ruiz, Jose (14); Taylor, Robert (29).

SALT LAKE CITY—Alexander, David (17); Ashworth, Michael (16); Bray, Scott (28); Deushane, Mark (8); Fukushima, Akihiro (16); Rivard, John (5); Ryan, Daniel (5); Singelyn, Scott (10); Skyrd, Christopher (6); St. John, Anthony (26); Steinkamp, Michael (10); Stewart, John (15); Studstill, Thomas (17); Taguchi, Shigeki (14); Wells, William (3); Woodard, Thane (2).

GRAND SLAM HOME RUNS—Marshall, 2; Ahrens, Baar, Giustino, Henderson, Holtzclaw, W.J. Miller (Idaho Falls), Peltier, Rigsby, Snyder, 1 each.

AWARDED FIRST BASE ON CATCHER'S INTERFERENCE—Crump 4 (Kappesser 2, Ahrens, Sanderson); Snyder 2 (R. Miller, Nichols); Adams (Bible); Burton (Floyd); Charpia (Jaime); Fowler (Jaime); Harring (Jaime); Montes (W.J. Miller, Idaho Falls); Roper (Tannahill); Smeltzer (Jaime).

CLUB FIELDING

Club	Pct.	G.	PO.	A.	E.	DP.	PB.	Club	Pct.	G.	PO.	A.	E.	DP.	PB.
Great Falls	.969	67	1728	742	78	66	14	Butte	.955	66	1677	717	114	71	14
Pocatello	.960	67	1733	737	104	59	10	Billings	.947	67	1743	707	138	55	16
Helena	.958	68	1752	734	109	58	11	Idaho Falls	.943	67	1719	741	150	48	25
Salt Lake City	.956	69	1820	769	119	60	10	Medicine Hat	.940	69	1796	736	161	56	15

Triple Plays—Billings 2.

INDIVIDUAL FIELDING

*Throws lefthanded.

FIRST BASEMEN

Player and Club	Pct.	G.	PO.	A.	E.	DP.	Player and Club	Pct.	G.	PO.	A.	E.	DP.
Baranoski, Idaho Falls	.946	4	31	4	2	1	R. Miller, Pocatello	.977	10	82	4	2	7
Beaulac, Salt Lake City*	.974	22	170	15	5	16	W. Miller, Idaho Falls	.979	6	44	2	1	3
Cala, Pocatello	.958	3	23	0	1	3	Nichols, Billings	1.000	1	1	0	0	1
Clinton, Butte	.988	22	74	5	1	8	O'Donnell, Great Falls	1.000	10	50	3	0	7
Crump, Idaho Falls	.986	25	188	17	3	16	Reagan, Billings	.960	32	229	14	10	24
DEUTSCH, Great Falls*	.988	64	550	40	7	53	Roebuck, Helena	.986	8	60	8	1	5
Dodson, Helena*	.986	63	509	43	8	49	Rojas, Medicine Hat	.976	46	339	33	9	30
Flinn, Butte	.984	9	57	4	1	4	Rolen, Pocatello	.955	3	19	2	1	5
Giustino, Salt Lake City	.982	26	252	14	5	15	Rooney, Medicine Hat	.846	3	20	2	4	1
Guerrero, Idaho Falls	.989	9	77	9	1	3	Smeltzer, Salt Lake City	.987	22	149	7	2	17
Hays, Butte	.875	2	6	1	1	1	Sparrow, Idaho Falls	.980	51	422	24	9	34
Henderson, Billings*	.985	35	258	11	4	19	Tarchione, Salt Lake City	.982	6	54	2	1	6
Huntey, Pocatello	.987	18	140	8	2	14	Troup, Salt Lake City	1.000	1	1	1	0	0
Jones, Pocatello	.983	33	273	15	5	22	Vondran, Billings	1.000	8	68	7	0	6
Marshall, Butte	.981	55	432	39	9	56	Willis, Pocatello	.978	5	42	2	1	2
Mengel, Medicine Hat	.875	2	7	0	1	2	Wright, Idaho Falls	1.000	4	35	4	0	2

Triple Plays—Henderson 2.

SECOND BASEMEN

Player and Club	Pct.	G.	PO.	A.	E.	DP.	Player and Club	Pct.	G.	PO.	A.	E.	DP.
Brauning, Pocatello	1.000	1	0	2	0	0	Harr, Pocatello	.968	38	82	101	6	26
Charpia, Helena	1.000	2	0	4	0	0	Harring, Idaho Falls	.970	42	70	123	6	17
Clinton, Butte	.818	5	7	2	2	0	Haugen, Helena	.973	47	98	122	6	28
Cole, Medicine Hat	1.000	1	1	0	0	0	Heckel, Medicine Hat	.952	58	121	158	14	30
Crispin, Pocatello	1.000	3	1	5	0	1	HOWARD, Great Falls	.983	55	108	173	5	36
DeLoach, Great Falls	.985	22	24	43	1	10	Mesa, Pocatello	.926	21	32	56	7	13
Diaz, Helena	1.000	1	3	4	0	3	Miller, Medicine Hat	.961	13	30	43	3	6
Diggs, Helena	.960	28	50	47	4	9	Montes, Pocatello	.938	11	25	35	4	7
Dombrowski, Billings	.904	18	33	33	7	5	Newkirk, Butte	1.000	1	0	1	0	0
Flinn, Butte	.977	11	13	30	1	11	Parrotte, Billings	.966	14	23	34	2	5
Garcia, Butte	.930	61	106	147	19	37	Pose, Billings	.850	7	6	11	3	1
Garczyk, Salt Lake City	.964	33	76	110	7	26	Ramirez, Salt Lake City	.930	38	101	97	15	22
Gill, Billings	.981	39	101	111	4	25	Reynoso, Helena	.762	4	6	10	5	1
Guerrero, Idaho Falls	.955	33	50	77	6	12	White, Great Falls	.824	5	3	11	3	2

THIRD BASEMEN

Player and Club	Pct.	G.	PO.	A.	E.	DP.	Player and Club	Pct.	G.	PO.	A.	E.	DP.
Adams, Idaho Falls	.848	14	10	29	7	0	Mengel, Medicine Hat	.906	40	42	83	13	8
Allen, Billings	.857	25	19	41	10	5	Miller, Medicine Hat	.941	7	5	11	1	1
Brauning, Pocatello	.923	6	1	11	1	0	Montes, Pocatello	1.000	9	4	22	0	6
Carlton, Medicine Hat	.840	25	23	45	13	1	NEWKIRK, Butte	.950	56	26	89	6	10
Charpia, Helena	.907	44	33	64	10	7	O'Donnell, Great Falls	.924	57	21	101	10	7
Clinton, Butte	1.000	3	1	0	0	0	Oliva, Butte	1.000	2	0	1	0	0
Crispin, Pocatello	.870	9	5	15	3	0	Parrotte, Billings	.904	22	9	38	5	4
DeLoach, Great Falls	.000	1	0	0	1	0	Powell, Helena	.667	2	1	1	1	0
Dombrowski, Billings	.700	3	1	6	3	1	Rolen, Pocatello	.928	46	42	87	10	6
Flinn, Butte	.829	16	9	25	7	1	Sanderson, Salt Lake City	.800	10	4	16	5	0
Floyd, Great Falls	1.000	1	0	1	0	0	Sarbaugh, Helena	1.000	20	13	42	0	4
Gill, Billings	1.000	2	1	3	0	0	Teel, Great Falls	.500	3	1	0	1	0
Grace, Salt Lake City	.912	63	46	109	15	15	Thomas, Idaho Falls	1.000	3	3	7	0	1
Harring, Idaho Falls	1.000	8	2	15	0	2	Vondran, Billings	.836	22	20	36	11	2
Haugen, Helena	.917	7	5	6	1	0	Waldenberger, Idaho Falls	.910	44	26	85	11	4
Howard, Great Falls	.938	6	6	9	1	0	White, Great Falls	1.000	9	5	12	0	1

SHORTSTOPS

Player and Club	Pct.	G.	PO.	A.	E.	DP.	Player and Club	Pct.	G.	PO.	A.	E.	DP.
Barker, Great Falls	.909	57	75	165	24	36	Diggs, Helena	.886	9	17	22	5	4
Brauning, Pocatello	.930	9	17	23	3	6	Flinn, Butte	.883	15	19	34	7	8
Brown, Helena	.930	57	85	166	19	25	Frias, Pocatello	.912	58	78	171	24	32
Cedeno, Medicine Hat	.906	53	100	141	25	25	Gill, Billings	1.000	8	11	22	0	2
Charpia, Helena	.966	5	15	13	1	7	Harr, Pocatello	1.000	1	2	1	0	0
Clinton, Butte	.911	27	41	82	12	24	Harring, Idaho Falls	.923	7	11	13	2	3
Cole, Medicine Hat	.912	20	30	32	6	11	Haugen, Helena	.889	1	2	6	1	1

CATCHERS—Continued

Player and Club	Pct.	G.	PO.	A.	E.	DP.
Hoffman, Billings	.911	60	116	140	25	30
KARCZEWSKI, Salt Lake City	.952	68	105	212	16	39
Montes, Pocatello	1.000	2	3	3	0	0
Oliva, Butte	.897	38	38	93	15	22
Olmeda, Idaho Falls	.916	60	81	180	24	28
Parrotte, Billings	.857	3	1	5	1	1
Sanderson, Salt Lake City	1.000	1	2	1	0	0
Thomas, Idaho Falls	.889	2	2	6	1	0
Waldenberger, Idaho Falls	.667	2	1	3	2	0
White, Great Falls	.929	19	26	39	5	10

Triple Plays—Hoffman 2.

OUTFIELDERS

Player and Club	Pct.	G.	PO.	A.	E.	DP.
Beaulac, Salt Lake City*	.935	44	53	5	4	1
Bible, Salt Lake City	.939	22	27	4	2	0
Booth, Pocatello	.913	38	65	8	7	1
Bowers, Medicine Hat	.988	41	80	4	1	1
Brauning, Pocatello	.905	13	19	0	2	0
Burton, Idaho Falls	.931	53	86	9	7	2
Cala, Pocatello	1.000	25	41	0	0	0
Cerny, Billings*	.945	44	65	4	4	1
Clinton, Butte	.800	8	4	0	1	0
Collier, Great Falls*	.974	36	37	0	1	0
Crowley, Butte	.857	25	18	0	3	0
DIAZ, Helena	.989	61	85	3	1	0
Diggs, Helena	1.000	9	3	1	0	0
Duke, Butte	.946	35	49	4	3	1
Fowler, Great Falls	1.000	38	32	2	0	0
Garcia, Medicine Hat	.939	28	45	1	3	1
Gillum, Billings	.861	25	29	2	5	0
Giustino, Salt Lake City	.917	8	11	0	1	0
Goodwin, Great Falls	.986	49	67	3	1	2
Gray, Pocatello	.947	25	36	0	2	0
Guerrero, Idaho Falls	1.000	2	2	0	0	0
Harr, Pocatello	1.000	8	8	1	0	0
Harris, Butte	.984	65	115	7	2	3
Harvell, Great Falls*	.950	42	36	2	2	0
Hays, Butte	1.000	25	24	0	0	0
Hollis, Billings	.941	18	28	4	2	1
Holtzclaw, Medicine Hat*	.957	55	106	6	5	0
Kappesser, Helena	1.000	1	1	0	0	0
Kidd, Salt Lake City*	.938	12	14	1	1	0
Loera, Great Falls	1.000	13	11	0	0	0
Marquez, Medicine Hat	1.000	20	31	1	0	0
May, Pocatello	1.000	24	30	1	0	1
McDonald, Medicine Hat	1.000	3	5	1	0	0
W.A. Miller, Great Falls*	.800	9	4	0	1	0
W.J. Miller, Idaho Falls	1.000	2	1	0	0	0
Morrow, Butte	.965	58	77	5	3	0
Nyquist, Salt Lake City	1.000	12	5	2	0	0
O'Leary, Helena*	.970	68	92	6	3	1
Peltier, Butte*	.941	31	28	4	2	0
Perozo, Billings	.967	47	85	2	3	0
Pose, Billings	.960	52	88	8	4	1
Pullins, Idaho Falls	.911	51	85	7	9	0
Reid, Medicine Hat*	.875	14	20	1	3	0
Rigsby, Idaho Falls	.853	41	53	5	10	1
Roberts, Medicine Hat	.955	25	42	0	2	0
Roebuck, Helena	1.000	49	59	4	0	1
Rolen, Pocatello	1.000	1	6	0	0	0
Rooney, Medicine Hat	.982	27	52	2	1	0
Sanderson, Salt Lake City	1.000	2	5	1	0	0
Sass, Helena	.870	31	18	2	3	0
Sims, Idaho Falls*	.889	48	55	9	8	1
Speakes, Pocatello	.974	54	73	3	2	1
Sweeney, Helena	.895	14	17	0	2	0
Tarchione, Salt Lake City	.778	7	7	0	2	0
Thomas, Idaho Falls	.882	16	15	0	2	0
Tripodi, Salt Lake City	.947	53	67	4	4	0
Troup, Salt Lake City	1.000	15	19	1	0	0
Vollmer, Pocatello	.961	27	44	5	2	1
Waid, Salt Lake City	.967	60	111	5	4	1
Weldin, Helena*	1.000	12	6	1	0	0
White, Great Falls	1.000	1	1	0	0	0
Wilson, Medicine Hat*	.913	17	21	0	2	0
Wismer, Great Falls	.974	47	71	5	2	1

Triple Play—Cerny.

CATCHERS

Player and Club	Pct.	G.	PO.	A.	E.	DP.	PB.
Ahrens, Pocatello	.981	31	231	31	5	3	6
BAAR, Great Falls	.993	40	252	27	2	1	5
Baranoski, Idaho Falls	.667	2	2	0	1	0	0
Bible, Salt Lake City	.964	23	125	10	5	0	3
Clinton, Butte	1.000	3	11	0	0	0	0
Cox, Billings	.982	32	192	24	4	0	6
Ellis, Idaho Falls	1.000	2	6	0	0	0	0
Evans, Salt Lake City	.986	37	254	32	4	3	7
Floyd, Great Falls	.971	18	92	8	3	0	5
Gonzalez, Billings	.950	4	18	1	1	0	0
Green, Salt Lake City	.938	12	54	6	4	2	0
Houston, Idaho Falls	.970	24	148	15	5	2	14
Huntey, Pocatello	1.000	4	32	1	0	0	1
Irish, Medicine Hat	.955	22	133	16	7	1	4
Jaime, Medicine Hat	.940	25	161	27	12	1	4
Kappesser, Helena	.957	29	224	23	11	0	6
Lewis, Butte	1.000	4	19	2	0	0	3
Loeb, Medicine Hat	.971	15	86	14	3	1	3
Lopez, Idaho Falls	.963	36	211	20	9	1	5
Micheu, Butte	1.000	8	40	8	0	0	1
R. Miller, Pocatello	.990	36	256	36	3	2	3
W. Miller, Idaho Falls	.941	18	85	11	6	1	6
Nichols, Billings	.983	37	253	39	5	3	9
Rigsby, Idaho Falls	.940	8	45	2	3	0	0
Roper, Butte	.978	15	83	5	2	0	0
Sanderson, Salt Lake City	.967	11	78	9	3	0	0
Seals, Great Falls	1.000	2	7	0	0	0	0
Snyder, Helena	.955	21	145	24	8	0	3
Tannahill, Helena	.954	12	58	4	3	0	1
Teel, Great Falls	.991	30	213	16	2	1	4
Vondran, Billings	1.000	1	3	0	0	0	1
White, Helena	.971	20	119	15	4	0	1
Williams, Medicine Hat	.988	12	71	9	1	0	4
Winford, Butte	.991	51	390	32	4	3	10

PITCHERS

Player and Club	Pct.	G.	PO.	A.	E.	DP.
Alexander, Salt Lake City	.882	17	2	13	2	0
Andrzejewski, Helena	.750	11	3	0	1	0
Asche, Butte*	.857	9	1	5	1	0
Ashworth, Salt Lake City	.960	16	6	18	1	0
Bates, Billings	1.000	24	2	12	0	0
Bickhardt, Butte	1.000	17	1	6	0	0
Bielanin, Great Falls	1.000	13	3	1	0	0
Blankenship, Billings	.944	13	4	13	1	1
Borcherding, Billings	.889	13	4	12	2	1
Borges, Butte*	1.000	6	3	3	0	1
Bradley, Medicine Hat	.833	21	1	4	1	0
Brakeley, Helena*	.889	6	2	6	1	0
Bray, Salt Lake City	1.000	28	4	3	0	0
Brosnan, Great Falls*	1.000	13	3	11	0	1
Calhoun, Great Falls	1.000	7	2	5	0	1
Carrico, Pocatello*	.800	12	2	6	2	0
Chiaramonte, Pocatello	.875	21	1	6	1	1
Correa, Helena	1.000	2	0	2	0	0
Crane, Great Falls*	1.000	16	0	1	0	0
Cummings, Great Falls	1.000	17	0	3	0	0
Dempster, Billings	.875	8	2	5	1	0
Deushane, Salt Lake City	.778	8	2	5	2	0
Doty, Billings	1.000	18	6	4	0	1
Drake, Helena	.800	7	1	3	1	0
Eckhardt, Idaho Falls	.625	9	2	3	3	0
Eischen, Butte*	.733	12	1	10	4	0
Evaschuk, Medicine Hat	.692	19	2	7	4	2
Federico, Helena	.893	14	7	18	3	3
Frame, Great Falls	.900	16	2	7	1	2
Franklin, Butte	.917	21	4	7	1	0
Fritz, Medicine Hat	.783	17	7	11	5	0
Fry, Billings*	.773	17	3	14	5	1
Fukushima, Salt Lake City	.923	16	1	11	1	1
Galloway, Billings	.769	21	2	8	3	2
Gordon, Medicine Hat	.941	16	6	10	1	0
Gore, Idaho Falls*	1.000	18	1	1	0	0
Gould, Pocatello*	.909	13	1	9	1	0
Graves, Butte	.889	26	8	8	2	0
Haeberle, Idaho Falls	1.000	8	2	10	0	1
Helmick, Great Falls	.938	13	6	9	1	1
Hernandez, Pocatello*	1.000	10	0	8	0	0
Herring, Pocatello*	1.000	18	1	4	0	0
Hillman, Pocatello	.905	14	3	16	2	1
Humber, Great Falls*	.900	24	3	6	1	0
Jones, Great Falls	1.000	12	6	12	0	3
Keim, Billings*	.889	11	3	5	1	0
Kimball, Helena	.857	11	4	8	2	0
Kinder, Helena*	1.000	5	0	1	0	1

PITCHERS—Continued

Player and Club	Pct.	G.	PO.	A.	E.	DP.	Player and Club	Pct.	G.	PO.	A.	E.	DP.
Kortright, Idaho Falls	1.000	16	4	4	0	1	Rugg, Helena°	1.000	10	3	2	0	0
Kuhlman, Idaho Falls	.880	13	5	17	3	0	Ruiz, Pocatello°	.250	14	0	1	3	0
Kulina, Medicine Hat°	1.000	21	5	9	0	1	Ryan, Salt Lake City°	1.000	5	0	1	0	1
Landry, Helena	.929	13	2	11	1	1	Shiflett, Butte	.923	15	6	6	1	0
Lemon, Idaho Falls	1.000	9	6	4	0	1	Singelyn, Salt Lake City	.600	10	3	0	2	0
Lund, Pocatello	1.000	2	0	1	0	0	Skyrd, Salt Lake City	1.000	6	0	2	0	0
Madsen, Great Falls	1.000	23	4	4	0	1	Small, Medicine Hat	.850	15	5	12	3	1
Matsumura, Butte	.500	4	1	0	1	0	St. John, Salt Lake City	.842	26	4	12	3	0
McAndrew, Great Falls	.769	13	4	6	3	0	Steed, Medicine Hat	.857	7	1	5	1	0
Mooney, Medicine Hat	.813	21	6	7	3	0	Steiner, Butte°	.944	11	3	14	1	0
MUSCAT, Helena	1.000	18	7	13	0	1	Steinkamp, Salt Lake City	1.000	10	2	15	0	2
Musselwhite, Pocatello	1.000	28	3	13	0	0	Stewart, Salt Lake City°	1.000	15	1	5	0	0
Newman, Idaho Falls	.000	12	0	0	1	0	Studstill, Salt Lake City	.933	17	2	12	1	1
Osmon, Idaho Falls	1.000	14	4	14	0	0	Taguchi, Salt Lake City°	1.000	14	0	3	0	0
Parisotto, Great Falls	1.000	14	3	10	0	1	M. Taylor, Medicine Hat°	.692	17	2	7	4	0
Parker, Idaho Falls	.923	18	6	6	1	1	R. Taylor, Pocatello	1.000	29	3	6	0	0
Patton, Helena	.917	19	7	4	1	0	Teegarden, Billings	.889	16	3	5	1	0
Perez, Butte	.933	17	5	23	2	1	Tovar, Medicine Hat	.667	19	2	6	4	0
Potthoff, Great Falls	1.000	14	0	7	0	1	Tyson, Medicine Hat	.786	18	0	11	3	0
Pugh, Billings	.826	13	0	19	4	1	Valle, Idaho Falls	.786	13	5	6	3	0
Quintel, Pocatello°	.667	23	0	2	1	0	Vancho, Helena	.923	10	3	9	1	1
Rambo, Pocatello	1.000	2	1	1	0	0	Voit, Helena	.923	29	2	10	1	1
Rapp, Pocatello	.955	16	6	15	1	2	Wells, Salt Lake City	1.000	3	3	2	0	0
Rehwinkel, Helena	1.000	3	0	1	0	0	White, Idaho Falls	.750	13	2	4	2	0
Rivard, Salt Lake City°	.500	5	0	2	2	0	Wilburn, Helena	.824	20	6	8	3	1
Rodriguez, Billings°	.750	15	1	2	1	0	Wilson, Helena	.818	17	4	5	2	0
Rogers, Idaho Falls	.846	13	3	8	2	0	Woodard, Salt Lake City	1.000	2	0	1	0	0
Romero, Butte°	.778	10	4	3	2	1	Young, Butte	.833	18	0	5	1	0
Rowley, Butte	1.000	11	2	11	0	1	Zona, Idaho Falls	.889	22	3	5	1	0

The following players did not have any fielding statistics at the positions indicated or appeared only as a designated hitter, pinch-hitter or pinch-runner: Baar, 1b; Cole, 3b; Crowley, p; Eklund, of; Fletcher, p; Flinn, of; Gill, 1b; Grace, p; Loeb, p; Lopez, 3b; Matsukubo, of; May, p; R. Miller, p; Morrow, p; Newkirk, p; Nichols, p; Ohman, p; S. Parker, of; Potts, p; Sugiura, p; Tannahill, 3b.

CLUB PITCHING

Club	ERA.	G.	CG.	ShO.	Sv.	IP.	H.	R.	ER.	HR.	HB.	BB.	Int. BB.	SO.	WP.	Bk.
Great Falls	2.41	67	3	13	26	576.0	456	197	154	20	21	232	2	565	37	21
Butte	4.01	66	5	5	15	559.0	580	316	249	26	36	272	2	534	65	44
Helena	4.22	68	6	4	17	584.0	593	332	274	43	35	323	11	538	71	36
Billings	4.80	67	4	1	13	581.0	609	387	310	49	32	299	2	445	61	26
Medicine Hat	4.87	69	0	1	10	598.2	646	431	324	31	29	315	12	443	55	26
Idaho Falls	4.88	67	4	1	15	573.0	639	396	311	35	27	226	6	482	56	43
Pocatello	5.00	67	5	2	17	577.2	676	384	321	48	25	194	7	521	47	26
Salt Lake City	6.05	69	6	1	13	606.2	749	475	408	37	32	286	6	497	78	35

PITCHERS' RECORDS
(Leading Qualifiers for Earned-Run Average Leadership—56 or More Innings)

°Throws lefthanded.

Pitcher—Club	W.	L.	Pct.	ERA.	G.	GS.	CG.	GF.	ShO.	Sv.	IP.	H.	R.	ER.	HR.	HB.	BB.	Int. BB.	SO.	WP.
R. Taylor, Pocatello	3	2	.600	1.25	29	1	0	20	0	10	57.2	46	12	8	0	2	11	2	74	2
Jones, Great Falls	8	0	1.000	1.58	12	12	2	0	2	0	62.2	40	15	11	2	3	21	0	63	2
McAndrew, Great Falls	11	0	1.000	1.65	13	13	1	0	0	0	76.1	49	16	14	5	4	27	0	72	2
Helmick, Great Falls	4	3	.571	2.05	13	10	0	2	0	2	66.0	38	20	15	3	3	28	0	63	2
Parisotto, Great Falls	9	1	.900	2.09	14	12	0	1	0	1	73.1	62	21	17	1	2	17	0	68	4
Brosnan, Great Falls°	6	2	.750	2.55	13	13	0	0	0	0	67.0	41	24	19	1	3	55	0	89	10
Steiner, Butte°	6	2	.750	2.95	11	11	0	0	0	0	58.0	65	21	19	1	1	31	0	46	10
Carrico, Pocatello°	7	3	.700	3.07	12	12	0	0	0	0	70.1	56	28	24	5	1	21	0	67	8
Kuhlman, Idaho Falls	2	8	.200	3.64	13	13	0	0	0	0	76.2	80	44	31	2	5	19	0	53	4
Bates, Billings	4	2	.667	3.68	24	0	0	6	0	1	66.0	62	33	27	2	1	29	0	43	7

Departmental Leaders: G—R. Taylor, Voit, 29; W—McAndrew, 11; L—Gordon, Hillman, Kuhlman, 8; Pct.—McAndrew, 1.000; GS—Ashworth, 15; CG—Ashworth, Hillman, Rowley, 3; GF—Bray, 27; ShO—Drake, Jones, Rowley, 2; Sv.—Voit, 11; IP—Ashworth, 95.1; H—Federico, 111; R—Gordon, 61; ER—Ashworth, St. John, 48; HR—Gould, 10; HB—Wilburn, 9; BB—Andrzejewski, 59; IBB—Voit, 5; SO—Brosnan, 89; WP—Valle, 17.

(All Pitchers—Listed Alphabetically)

Pitcher—Club	W.	L.	Pct.	ERA.	G.	GS.	CG.	GF.	ShO.	Sv.	IP.	H.	R.	ER.	HR.	HB.	BB.	Int. BB.	SO.	WP.
Alexander, Salt Lake City	3	1	.750	6.21	17	1	0	9	0	1	33.1	46	29	23	2	3	12	0	18	4
Andrzejewski, Helena	3	2	.600	6.13	11	10	0	1	0	0	39.2	29	30	27	2	5	59	0	50	16
Asche, Butte°	3	1	.750	4.26	9	4	1	2	0	0	31.2	31	17	15	1	2	12	0	31	1
Ashworth, Salt Lake City	4	7	.364	4.53	16	15	3	0	1	0	95.1	107	56	48	7	3	23	1	60	8
Bates, Billings	4	2	.667	3.68	24	0	0	6	0	1	66.0	62	33	27	2	1	29	0	43	7
Bickhardt, Butte	3	0	1.000	2.33	17	1	0	3	0	1	46.1	37	13	12	1	3	21	0	52	2
Bielanin, Great Falls	0	0	.000	1.65	13	0	0	9	0	2	16.1	14	8	3	0	1	8	0	18	3
Blankenship, Billings	3	7	.300	5.78	13	13	1	0	0	0	67.0	94	53	43	8	2	22	0	44	6
Borcherding, Billings	4	4	.500	3.97	13	13	1	0	0	0	68.0	72	45	30	6	4	28	0	40	1
Borges, Butte°	1	1	.500	5.46	6	6	0	0	0	0	29.2	35	25	18	0	9	9	0	21	1
Bradley, Medicine Hat	2	3	.400	2.43	21	0	0	18	0	7	33.1	37	16	9	3	0	12	2	45	6
Brakeley, Helena°	2	1	.667	4.81	6	6	1	0	0	0	33.2	36	19	18	5	1	17	0	39	5
Bray, Salt Lake City	6	2	.750	5.31	28	0	0	27	0	6	42.1	46	26	25	3	0	21	4	54	6
Brosnan, Great Falls°	6	2	.750	2.55	13	13	0	0	0	0	67.0	41	24	19	1	3	55	0	89	10
Calhoun, Great Falls	0	1	.000	1.59	7	0	0	3	0	2	17.0	21	4	3	0	0	11	1	11	1
Carrico, Pocatello°	7	3	.700	3.07	12	12	0	0	0	0	70.1	56	28	24	5	1	21	0	67	8
Chiaramonte, Pocatello	0	1	.000	8.23	21	0	0	8	0	2	27.1	44	26	25	4	2	20	0	33	5
Correa, Helena	0	0	.000	0.00	2	1	0	1	0	0	3.0	3	0	0	0	0	2	0	2	1
Crane, Great Falls°	3	0	1.000	3.33	16	0	0	4	0	1	24.1	23	15	9	0	0	21	0	25	2
Crowley, Butte	0	0	.000	27.00	1	0	0	0	0	0	1.1	1	1	1	0	1	1	0	0	2

Pitcher—Club	W.	L.	Pct.	ERA	G.	GS.	CG.	GF.	ShO.	Sv.	IP.	H.	R.	ER.	HR.	HB.	BB.	Int. BB.	SO.	WP.
Cummings, Great Falls	1	0	1.000	4.01	17	0	0	7	0	3	24.2	23	11	11	3	3	5	0	24	2
Dempster, Billings	3	3	.500	5.95	8	8	0	0	0	0	42.1	44	28	28	3	7	23	0	39	8
Deushane, Salt Lake City	2	2	.500	6.33	8	8	1	0	0	0	42.2	54	31	30	1	7	21	0	31	5
Doty, Billings	3	2	.600	6.58	18	0	0	15	0	2	26.0	23	20	19	2	1	16	1	21	1
Drake, Helena	2	0	1.000	2.88	7	6	2	0	2	0	34.1	26	13	11	4	0	12	0	40	2
Eckhardt, Idaho Falls	0	2	.000	4.43	9	1	0	5	0	1	22.1	27	21	11	0	3	18	2	13	5
Eischen, Butte°	3	7	.300	5.30	12	12	0	0	0	0	52.2	50	45	31	4	6	38	0	57	13
Evaschuk, Medicine Hat	2	1	.667	7.30	19	1	0	6	0	1	40.2	59	48	33	2	5	32	1	31	4
Federico, Helena	5	4	.556	4.50	14	13	0	0	0	0	80.0	111	53	40	7	5	25	0	34	7
Fletcher, Great Falls°	0	0	.000	0.00	2	0	0	0	0	0	2.0	0	0	0	0	0	1	0	4	0
Frame, Great Falls	3	1	.750	1.59	16	4	0	7	0	3	39.2	33	9	7	1	0	15	2	33	4
Franklin, Butte	1	3	.250	9.90	21	1	0	15	0	2	30.0	47	34	33	2	3	16	0	31	9
Fritz, Medicine Hat	1	7	.125	6.02	17	11	0	5	0	0	61.1	77	50	41	2	2	37	0	28	8
Fry, Billings°	2	2	.500	4.08	17	5	0	5	0	1	53.0	40	28	24	9	0	26	0	33	2
Fukushima, Salt Lake City	3	5	.375	5.10	16	7	1	2	0	0	60.0	66	39	34	3	0	30	0	50	10
Galloway, Billings	1	1	.500	9.00	21	0	0	12	0	1	26.0	35	33	26	3	1	28	0	23	8
Gordon, Medicine Hat	4	8	.333	4.53	16	12	0	2	0	0	87.1	92	61	44	5	4	27	1	57	8
Gore, Idaho Falls°	1	3	.250	4.60	18	0	0	8	0	1	31.1	40	19	16	1	0	11	2	34	2
Gould, Pocatello°	3	4	.429	5.76	13	9	0	0	0	0	54.2	58	39	35	10	5	24	0	41	2
Grace, Salt Lake City	0	0	.000	0.00	1	0	0	1	0	0	0.2	1	0	0	0	0	0	0	2	0
Graves, Butte	4	3	.571	2.96	26	1	0	14	0	4	48.2	40	21	16	4	1	20	0	52	1
Haeberle, Idaho Falls	1	2	.333	5.04	8	2	0	4	0	1	25.0	26	19	14	1	1	12	0	16	4
Helmick, Great Falls	4	3	.571	2.05	13	10	0	2	0	2	66.0	38	20	15	3	3	28	0	63	2
Hernandez, Pocatello°	2	2	.500	6.30	10	9	0	0	0	0	50.0	62	37	35	8	1	26	0	57	6
Herring, Pocatello°	1	2	.333	5.25	18	0	0	7	0	1	24.0	24	17	14	1	1	14	0	44	2
Hillman, Pocatello	4	8	.333	4.77	14	13	3	0	0	0	88.2	105	60	47	6	1	13	1	70	1
Humber, Great Falls°	3	1	.750	3.13	24	0	0	18	0	8	31.2	35	15	11	2	0	8	0	31	3
Jones, Great Falls	8	0	1.000	1.58	12	12	2	0	2	0	62.2	40	15	11	2	3	21	0	63	2
Keim, Billings°	0	4	.000	4.88	11	5	0	3	0	1	31.1	28	19	17	2	0	23	0	33	3
Kimball, Helena	1	3	.250	3.89	11	4	0	4	0	1	39.1	43	22	17	2	1	14	2	43	3
Kinder, Helena°	0	1	.000	4.05	5	0	0	4	0	1	6.2	7	4	3	1	1	3	0	9	1
Kortright, Idaho Falls	2	4	.333	6.86	16	4	0	4	0	1	39.1	51	35	30	5	0	16	0	19	2
Kuhlman, Idaho Falls	2	8	.200	3.64	13	13	0	0	0	0	76.2	80	44	31	2	5	19	0	53	4
Kulina, Medicine Hat°	2	2	.500	3.56	21	1	0	14	0	1	55.2	59	29	22	1	0	24	3	58	3
Landry, Helena	5	5	.500	4.64	13	10	1	1	0	0	64.0	62	40	33	5	3	46	0	54	8
Lemon, Idaho Falls	2	1	.667	6.47	9	6	0	1	0	0	40.1	50	31	29	6	1	17	0	20	2
Loeb, Medicine Hat	0	0	.000	0.00	1	0	0	1	0	0	1.0	0	0	0	0	0	1	0	1	0
Lund, Pocatello	0	1	.000	10.13	2	2	0	0	0	0	8.0	9	9	9	2	1	7	0	3	1
Madsen, Great Falls	3	3	.500	5.13	23	1	0	8	0	2	40.1	45	24	23	1	0	15	0	32	1
Matsumura, Butte	0	0	.000	9.35	4	0	0	1	0	0	8.2	12	10	9	0	0	7	0	3	2
May, Pocatello	0	0	.000	0.00	1	0	0	1	0	0	0.2	1	0	0	0	0	0	0	1	0
McAndrew, Great Falls	11	0	1.000	1.65	13	13	1	0	0	0	76.1	49	16	14	5	4	27	0	72	2
Miller, Pocatello	0	0	.000	9.00	1	0	0	0	0	0	1.0	1	1	1	0	0	2	0	0	0
Mooney, Medicine Hat	3	2	.600	2.82	21	1	0	12	0	1	51.0	54	28	16	2	1	17	0	28	3
Morrow, Butte	0	0	.000	18.00	1	0	0	1	0	0	1.0	3	2	2	0	0	2	0	0	0
Muscat, Helena	3	3	.500	4.02	18	2	0	5	0	1	53.2	46	33	24	2	4	34	1	39	6
Musselwhite, Pocatello	4	5	.444	4.62	28	6	1	12	1	3	64.1	95	45	33	2	0	11	2	45	5
Newkirk, Butte	0	0	.000	10.80	2	0	0	0	0	0	1.2	2	2	2	1	0	0	0	3	0
Newman, Idaho Falls	0	3	.000	8.46	12	3	0	7	0	0	22.1	35	25	21	2	1	12	0	19	5
Nichols, Billings	0	0	.000	0.00	1	0	0	1	0	0	1.0	0	0	0	0	0	0	0	1	0
Ohman, Butte	0	0	.000	0.00	1	0	0	1	0	0	1.0	1	0	0	0	0	0	0	1	0
Osmon, Idaho Falls	4	3	.571	2.45	14	6	2	3	1	0	51.1	39	20	14	3	5	15	0	36	0
Parisotto, Great Falls	9	1	.900	2.09	14	12	0	1	0	1	73.1	62	21	17	1	2	17	0	68	4
Parker, Idaho Falls	0	2	.000	6.45	18	0	0	10	0	2	37.2	39	31	27	2	2	19	0	36	2
Patton, Helena	6	2	.750	2.98	19	1	1	10	1	1	48.1	35	20	16	0	1	35	1	54	8
Perez, Butte	3	2	.600	2.50	17	4	1	3	0	1	54.0	57	30	15	2	2	19	0	45	0
Potthoff, Great Falls	2	2	.500	2.86	14	2	0	5	0	2	34.2	32	15	11	2	1	10	0	32	1
Potts, Helena	0	0	.000	0.00	2	0	0	0	0	0	4.1	3	1	0	0	0	2	0	1	0
Pugh, Billings	2	6	.250	3.94	13	13	2	0	0	0	77.2	81	44	34	4	5	25	0	72	4
Quintel, Pocatello°	1	3	.250	6.59	23	1	0	9	0	1	27.1	38	24	20	1	2	20	1	23	7
Rambo, Pocatello	0	1	.000	1.29	2	2	0	0	0	0	14.0	11	2	2	0	0	3	0	11	0
Rapp, Pocatello	4	6	.400	5.30	16	12	1	1	0	0	73.0	90	54	43	5	8	29	1	40	6
Rehwinkel, Helena	1	0	1.000	8.31	3	0	0	0	0	0	4.1	6	4	4	1	0	4	0	3	0
Rivard, Salt Lake City°	0	3	.000	13.50	5	4	0	0	0	0	14.2	29	24	22	2	0	7	0	17	1
Rodriguez, Billings°	0	1	.000	2.30	15	0	0	12	0	6	27.1	19	11	7	0	0	18	0	27	4
Rogers, Idaho Falls	3	4	.429	4.50	13	9	2	3	0	1	58.0	70	42	29	4	3	17	1	59	7
Romero, Butte°	5	0	1.000	1.79	10	7	0	3	0	0	45.1	36	11	9	0	3	23	1	41	4
Rowley, Butte	4	2	.667	4.12	11	11	3	0	2	0	59.0	52	32	27	5	8	37	0	62	9
Rugg, Butte	4	0	1.000	3.65	10	2	0	3	0	0	24.2	20	13	10	4	1	16	0	33	1
Ruiz, Pocatello°	0	0	.000	14.58	14	0	0	4	0	0	16.2	36	30	27	4	1	11	0	13	2
Ryan, Salt Lake City°	0	1	.000	8.16	5	3	0	0	0	0	14.1	19	15	13	2	0	12	0	10	4
Shiflett, Butte	5	2	.714	4.24	15	8	0	1	0	1	57.1	67	36	27	3	3	24	0	53	7
Singelyn, Salt Lake City	4	3	.571	7.78	10	6	0	0	0	0	37.0	44	34	32	1	5	26	0	36	8
Skyrd, Salt Lake City	0	0	.000	13.50	6	0	0	0	0	0	10.0	15	19	15	0	0	16	0	10	3
Small, Medicine Hat	1	7	.125	5.86	15	14	0	0	0	0	70.2	80	55	46	2	3	31	1	40	9
St. John, Salt Lake City	5	4	.556	5.54	26	7	0	7	0	1	78.0	90	56	48	4	6	36	0	79	4
Steed, Medicine Hat	0	2	.000	3.38	7	6	0	0	0	0	16.0	14	10	6	1	1	11	0	11	2
Steiner, Butte°	6	2	.750	2.95	11	11	0	0	0	0	58.0	65	21	19	1	1	31	0	46	10
Steinkamp, Salt Lake City	3	3	.500	5.61	10	9	1	0	0	0	59.1	84	49	37	4	7	10	0	24	2
Stewart, Salt Lake City°	1	2	.333	4.68	15	1	0	5	0	2	32.2	35	24	17	1	1	16	1	37	5
Studstill, Salt Lake City	2	1	.667	3.86	17	4	0	10	0	3	46.2	54	29	20	2	0	17	0	31	9
Sugiura, Butte	0	0	.000	11.42	6	0	0	2	0	0	8.2	21	13	11	1	0	4	0	8	2
Taguchi, Salt Lake City°	0	1	.000	8.57	14	1	0	1	0	0	21.0	27	20	20	3	0	27	0	24	6
M. Taylor, Medicine Hat°	5	5	.500	4.43	17	9	0	3	0	0	69.0	58	45	34	5	4	47	1	40	2
R. Taylor, Pocatello	3	2	.600	1.25	29	1	0	20	0	10	57.2	46	12	8	0	2	11	2	74	2
Teegarden, Billings	1	4	.200	8.07	16	3	0	2	0	0	32.1	45	40	29	5	2	23	0	28	6
Tovar, Medicine Hat	0	7	.000	6.10	19	10	0	5	0	0	62.0	61	52	42	4	3	53	1	59	7
Tyson, Medicine Hat	3	2	.600	6.22	18	4	0	3	0	0	50.2	55	37	35	4	6	30	2	45	3
Valle, Idaho Falls	4	4	.500	5.12	13	12	0	1	0	0	65.0	65	46	37	4	3	36	1	83	17
Vancho, Helena	1	5	.167	6.04	10	8	1	1	0	0	44.2	57	33	30	5	1	20	1	38	7
Voit, Helena	2	0	1.000	2.91	29	0	0	24	0	11	46.1	46	17	15	1	7	12	5	59	1
Wells, Salt Lake City	0	1	.000	11.20	3	3	0	0	0	0	13.2	23	18	17	2	0	9	0	11	1

Pitcher—Club	W.	L.	Pct.	ERA.	G.	GS.	CG.	GF.	ShO.	Sv.	IP.	H.	R.	ER.	HR.	HB.	BB.	Int. BB.	SO.	WP.
White, Idaho Falls	5	3	.625	4.40	13	11	0	2	0	0	61.1	75	37	30	1	2	23	0	55	2
Wilburn, Billings	3	5	.375	3.71	20	7	0	7	0	1	63.0	66	33	26	5	9	38	1	42	11
Wilson, Helena	3	4	.429	4.11	17	5	0	8	0	2	57.0	63	30	26	4	5	22	1	40	5
Woodard, Salt Lake City	0	0	.000	12.60	2	0	0	1	0	0	5.0	9	8	7	0	0	3	0	3	2
Young, Butte	3	2	.600	0.72	18	0	0	15	0	6	25.0	21	3	2	1	2	8	1	29	2
Zona, Idaho Falls	3	1	.750	4.68	22	0	0	15	0	8	42.1	42	26	22	4	1	11	0	39	4

BALKS—Eischen, 11; Gore, Shiflett, 10 each; Ashworth, Franklin, Muscat, Musselwhite, Osmon, Patton, 7 each; Andrzejewski, Pugh, 6 each; Chiaramonte, Fritz, Kuhlman, Newman, Parisotto, Small, Tovar, Wells, 5 each; Bielanin, Brosnan, Carrico, Galloway, Parker, Rivard, White, Wilburn, 4 each; Borcherding, Bray, Fry, Kimball, Lemon, Potthoff, Rowley, Rugg, St. John, Steed, Tyson, Vancho, 3 each; Alexander, Bickhardt, Borges, Dempster, Deushane, Fletcher, Gordon, Gould, Helmick, Hernandez, Hillman, Keim, Kortright, Mooney, Romero, Ruiz, Skyrd, Steiner, Steinkamp, Taguchi, Voit, 2 each; Asche, Blankenship, Brakeley, Crowley, Drake, Federico, Haeberle, Landry, Loeb, Lund, Madsen, Matsumura, Rambo, Ryan, Singelyn, Studstill, Sugiura, Teegarden, Valle, Wilson, Young, Zona, 1 each.

COMBINATION SHUTOUTS—Dempster-Bates-Doty-Galloway, Billings; Shiflett-Graves-Ohman, Shiflett-Graves, Romero-Graves, Butte; Helmick-Potthoff-Calhoun, McAndrew-Parisotto, Brosnan-Bielanin, Jones-Potthoff-Humber, Brosnan-Frame-Madsen-Cummings, Frame-Humber, McAndrew-Cummings, Parisotto-Helmick, Frame-Potthoff, McAndrew-Madsen, Brosnan-Cummings, Great Falls; Federico-Muscat, Helena; Taylor-Tyson, Medicine Hat; Rambo-Rapp, Pocatello.

NO-HIT GAMES—None.

Index to Minor League Clubs, Cities

1990 A.L. EAST DIVISION SLATE . . .

1990	EAST						
	AT MILWAUKEE	AT DETROIT	AT CLEVELAND	AT TORONTO	AT BALTIMORE	AT NEW YORK	AT BOSTON
MILWAUKEE ...		April 27*, 28*, **29**, 30* August 14*, 15*, 16*	June 15*, 16*, **17** Sept. 17*, 18*, 19*	June 1*, 2, **3** August 27*, 28*, 29	June 12*, 13*, 14* Sept. 21*, 22*, **23**	June 26*, 27*, 28 August 23*, 24*, 25, **26**	April 13*, 14, **15**, 16 Sept. 10*, 11*, 12*
DETROIT	May 7*, 8*, 9 Sept. 7*, 8*, **9**		June 5*, 6*, 7* August 10*, 11*, **12**, 13*	May 4*, 5, **6** August 7*, 8*, 9*	April 19*, 20*, 21, **22** Sept. 10*, 11*, 12*	April 6*, 7, **8** July 30*, 31* August 1*, 2*	April 9, 10, 11 August 3*, 4, **5**
CLEVELAND ...	June 22*, 23*, **24**, 25* August 20*, 21*, 22	June 12*, 13*, 14* August 17*, 18*, **19**		April 23*, 24*, 25*, 26 Sept. 21*, 22, **23**	June 26*, 27*, 28 August 24*, 25*, **26**	April 3, 4*, 5* August 3*, 4*, **5**, 6	June 8*, 9, **10**, 11* Sept. 25*, 26*
TORONTO	June 8*, 9*, **10**, 11* Sept. 24*, 25*, 26*	May 10*, 11*, 12*, **13** Sept. 3, 4*, 5*	April 30* May 1*, 2* August 31* Sept. 1*, **2**		April 6*, 7, **8** July 30*, 31* August 1†	June 15*, 16*, **17** August 20*, 21*, 22*	June 25*, 26*, 27*, 28* Sept. 28*, 29, **30**
BALTIMORE	June 4*, 5*, 6*, 7 August 31* Sept. 1*, **2**	April 13*, 14, **15** July 23*, 24*, 25	June 19*, 20*, 21* Sept. 27*, 28*, 29, **30**	April 16, 17*, 18* Sept. 13*, 14*, 15, **16***		June 1*, 2*, **3** Sept. 24*, 25*, 26*	June 22*, 23, **24** August 20*, 21*, 22
NEW YORK	June 18*, 19*, 20 Sept. 28*, 29, **30**	April 17*, 18 Sept. 13*, 14*, 15*, **16**	April 10*, 11* July 27 (Tn)*, 28*, **29**	June 21*, 22*, 23, **24** Sept. 17*, 18*, 19*	June 8*, 9*, **10** August 27*, 28*, 29*, 30*		June 4*, 5*, 6*, 7* August 31* Sept. 1, **2***
BOSTON	April 20*, 21, **22** July 23*, 24*, 25	April 2, 4, 5 July 26*, 27*, 28, **29**	June 1*, 2*, **3** August 27*, 28*, 29*, 30*	June 19*, 20* August 23*, 24*, 25, **26**	June 15*, 16, **17**, 18* Sept. 17*, 18*, 19*	June 12*, 13*, 14* Sept. 21*, 22, **23**	
SEATTLE	May 21*, 22 July 19*, 20*, 21*, **22**	June 8 (Tn)*, 9*, **10** Sept. 25*, 26*	May 18*, 19, **20** July 3*, 4, 5*	May 15*, 16*, 17 July 6*, 7, **8**	April 27*, 28*, **29** Sept. 3, 4*, 5*	April 24*, 25*, 26* August 17*, 18, **19**	April 30* May 1*, 2* Sept. 7*, 8, **9**
OAKLAND	May 18*, 19*, **20** July 3*, 4*, 5	June 18*, 19*, 20 August 24*, 25, **26***	May 15*, 16* July 6 (Tn)*, 7*, **8***	May 21, 22 June 29*, 30 July **1**, 2	April 24*, 25*, 26* August 17*, 18*, **19**	April 30* May 1*, 2* Sept. 7*, 8*, **9**	April 27*, 28, **29** Sept. 3*, 4*, 5*
CALIFORNIA ...	May 15*, 16*, 17 July 6*, 7*, **8**	June 15*, 16, **17** August 20*, 21*, 22	May 21*, 22* June 29*, 30* July **1**, 2*	May 18*, 19, **20** July 3*, 4*, 5*	April 30* May 1*, 2* Sept. 7*, 8*, **9**	April 27*, 28, **29** Sept. 3, 5*, 6*	April 24*, 25*, 26* August 17*, 18, **19**
TEXAS	April 6, 7, **8** July 30*, 31* August 1	May 23*, 24* July 12*, 13*, 14*, **15**	May 4*, 5, **6** August 7*, 8*, 9*	April 10, 11*, 12* July 27*, 28, **29**	May 18*, 19*, **20** July 16*, 17*, 18*	April 13*, 14, **15** Sept. 10*, 11*, 12*	May 21*, 22* June 29*, 30 July **1**, 2
KANSAS CITY ..	April 24*, 25*, 26 August 17*, 18, **19**	May 21*, 22* July 5*, 6*, 7*, **8**	April 6, 7, **8** July 30*, 31* August 1*	April 20*, 21, **22** July 24*, 25*, 26*	April 2, 4*, **5*** August 3*, 4*, 5*	May 18*, 19, **20*** July 16*, 17*, 18	May 23*, 24* July 12*, 13*, 14, **15**
MINNESOTA ...	May 4*, 5, **6** Sept. 3, 4*, 5*	May 1*, 2*, 3 Sept. 28*, 29, **30**	April 27*, 28, **29** August 14*, 15*, 16*	June 5*, 6*, 7* August 10*, 11, **12**	May 21*, 22* July 12*, 13*, 14*, **15**	May 15*, 16*, 17* July 6*, 7, **8**	May 18*, 19, **20** July 16*, 17*, 18*
CHICAGO	April 10*, 11 August 2*, 3*, 4*, **5**	May 25*, 26, **27** July 16*, 17*, 18*	April 20*, 21, **22** Sept. 10*, 11*, 12*	May 7*, 8*, 9* Sept. 7*, 8, **9**	May 23*, 24* July 19*, 20*, 21*, **22**	May 21*, 22* July 12*, 13*, 14, **15**	April 6, 7, **8** July 30*, 31* August 1*
1990	81 HOME DATES 50 NIGHTS	80 HOME DATES 53 NIGHTS	79 HOME DATES 58 NIGHTS	81 HOME DATES 47 NIGHTS	81 HOME DATES 63 NIGHTS	81 HOME DATES 55 NIGHTS	81 HOME DATES 49 NIGHTS

*NIGHT GAME
NIGHT GAME: Any game starting after 5:00 p.m.
HEAVY BLACK FIGURES DENOTE SUNDAY

AND COMPLETE WEST SCHEDULES

1990	WEST						
	AT SEATTLE	**AT OAKLAND**	**AT CALIFORNIA**	**AT TEXAS**	**AT KANSAS CITY**	**AT MINNESOTA**	**AT CHICAGO**
MILWAUKEE...	May 28, 29*, 30* June 29*, 30* July 1	May 23*, 24 July 12*, 13*, 14, **15**	May 25*, 26*, **27** July 16*, 17*, 18	April 17*, 18*, 19* Sept. 14*, 15*, **16**	May 1*, 2*, 3* August 10*, 11*, **12**	May 11*, 12*, **13** August 6*, 7*, 8*	April 2, 4, 5 July 27*, 28*, **29**
DETROIT.........	June 1*, 2*, **3** August 28*, 29*, 30*	June 25*, 26*, 27 Sept. 21*, 22, **23**	June 21*, 22*, 23*, **24** Sept. 18*, 19*	May 15*, 16*, 17* July 20*, 21*, **22***	May 28*, 29*, 30* June 29*, 30* July 1	April 23*, 24*, 25* August 31* Sept. 1*, 2	May 18*, 19*, **20** July 2*, 3*, 4*
CLEVELAND ...	May 23*, 24* July 12*, 13*, 14*, **15**	May 25*, 26, **27** July 16*, 17, 18	May 28, 29*, 30* July 20*, 21*, **22**	May 11*, 12*, **13*** Sept. 3*, 4*, 5*	April 16*, 17*, 18* Sept. 14*, 15*, **16**	May 8*, 9*, 10* Sept. 7*, 8, **9**	April 13, 14*, **15** July 23*, 24*, 25
TORONTO	May 25*, 26*, **27** July 16*, 17*, 18	May 28*, 29*, 30 July 20*, 21*, **22**	May 23*, 24* July 12*, 13*, 14*, **15**	April 3*, 5 August 2*, 3*, 4*, **5***	April 13*, 14, **15** Sept. 10*, 11*, 12*	June 12*, 13*, 14* August 17*, 18*, **19**	April 27*, 28*, **29** August 13*, 14*, 15*
BALTIMORE....	May 4*, 5*, **6** August 13*, 14*, 15*	May 11*, 12, **13** August 7*, 8, 9	May 7*, 8*, 9* August 10*, 11*, **12**	May 25*, 26*, **27** July 3*, 4*, 5*	April 9, 11*, 12* July 27*, 28, **29**	May 28, 29*, 30* June 29*, 30* July 1*	May 15*, 16*, 17* July 6*, 7*, **8**
NEW YORK	May 11*, 12*, **13** August 7*, 8*, 9*	May 7*, 8, 9 August 10*, 11, **12**	May 4*, 5*, **6** August 13*, 14*, 15*	April 20*, 21*, **22** July 23*, 24*, 25*	May 25*, 26*, **27** July 2*, 3*, 4*	May 23*, 24* July 19*, 20*, 21*, **22**	May 28*, 29*, 30* June 29*, 30* July 1
BOSTON	May 7*, 8*, 9* August 10*, 11*, **12**	May 4*, 5, **6** August 13*, 14*, 15	May 11*, 12*, **13** August 7*, 8*, 9*	May 28*, 29*, 30* July 6*, 7*, **8***	May 14*, 15*, 16* July 20*, 21*, **22***	May 25*, 26*, **27** July 3*, 4, 5	April 17*, 18* Sept. 13*, 14*, 15*, **16**
SEATTLE.........		April 19*, 20*, 21, **22** July 30*, 31* August 1	April 9*, 10*, 11* Sept. 13*, 14*, 15*, **16**	June 22*, 23*, **24*** August 20*, 21*, 22*	June 18*, 19*, 20* August 23*, 24*, 25*, **26**	April 6*, 7*, **8** July 24*, 25*, 26	June 5*, 6*, 7 Sept. 28*, 29*, **30**
OAKLAND	April 13*, 14*, **15** Sept. 10*, 11*, 12		April 17*, 18* August 2*, 3*, 4*, **5**	June 5*, 6*, 7* Sept. 27*, 28*, 29*, **30**	May 31* June 1*, 2*, **3** Sept. 24*, 25*, 26*	April 3*, 4*, 5 July 27*, 28*, **29**	June 14*, 15*, 16*, **17** August 20*, 21*, 22*
CALIFORNIA ...	April 3*, 4*, 5 July 27*, 28*, **29**	April 6*, 7, **8** July 23*, 24*, 25, 26		June 1*, 2*, **3***, 4* Sept. 24*, 25*, 26*	June 5*, 6*, 7 Sept. 21*, 22, **23**	April 20*, 21, **22** July 30*, 31* August 1	June 18*, 19*, 20* August 23*, 24*, 25*, **26**
TEXAS	June 14*, 15*, 16*, **17** Sept. 17*, 18*, 19*	June 11*, 12, 13 August 31* Sept. 1, **2**	June 8*, 9*, **10** August 27*, 28*, 29*		April 27*, 28, **29** August 13*, 14*, 15*	June 25*, 26*, 27*, **28** Sept. 21*, 22*, **23**	April 30* May 1*, 2*, **3*** August 10*, 11, **12**
KANSAS CITY	June 26*, 27*, 28 August 31* Sept. 1*, **2**	June 8*, 9, **10** August 28*, 29*, 30	June 11*, 12*, 13* Sept. 27*, 28*, 29*, **30**	May 8*, 9*, 10* Sept. 6*, 7*, 8*, **9**		June 21*, 22*, 23*, **24** Sept. 17*, 18*, 19*	May 11*, 12*, **13** Sept. 3*, 4*, 5*
MINNESOTA ...	April 16*, 17*, 18* August 2*, 3, 4*, **5**	April 9*, 10*, 11 Sept. 13*, 14*, 15, **16**	April 12*, 13*, 14*, **15** Sept. 10*, 11*, 12*	June 18*, 19*, 20* August 24*, 25*, **26***	June 15*, 16*, **17** August 20*, 21*, 22*		May 31* June 1*, 2*, **3*** Sept. 25*, 26*
CHICAGO.........	June 11*, 12*, 13 Sept. 20*, 21*, 22*, **23**	June 22*, 23, **24** Sept. 17*, 18*, 19	June 25*, 26*, 27 August 31* Sept. 1, **2**	April 24*, 25*, 26* August 17*, 18*, **19***	May 4*, 5*, **6** August 6*, 7*, 8*, 9*	June 8*, 9*, **10** August 27*, 28*, 29*, 30	
1990	81 HOME DATES 61 NIGHTS	81 HOME DATES 37 NIGHTS	81 HOME DATES 64 NIGHTS	81 HOME DATES 75 NIGHTS	81 HOME DATES 63 NIGHTS	81 HOME DATES 60 NIGHTS	81 HOME DATES 62 NIGHTS

JULY 10—ALL-STAR GAME AT WRIGLEY FIELD IN CHICAGO
AUGUST 6—HALL OF FAME GAME AT COOPERSTOWN, N.Y. (Montreal Expos vs. Baltimore Orioles)

1990 N.L. EAST DIVISION SLATE . . .

1990	EAST					
	AT CHICAGO	AT MONTREAL	AT NEW YORK	AT PHILADELPHIA	AT PITTSBURGH	AT ST. LOUIS
CHICAGO		June 18*, 19*, 20* / July 26*, 27*, 28*, **29** / Sept. 3, 4*	April 17*, 18*, 19 / August 10*, 11*, **12** / Sept. 28*, 29, **30**	April 3*, 4*, 5 / June 14*, 15*, 16*, **17*** / Sept. 5*, 6	April 13*, 14, **15** / June 4*, 5*, 6* / Sept. 25*, 26*, 27*	June 1*, 2*, **3** / July 23*, 24*, 25* / Sept. 14*, 15*, **16**
MONTREAL	June 25*, 26, 27, 28 / August 3, 4*, **5** / Sept. 10*, 11		April 20*, 21, **22** / June 4*, 5*, 6* / Sept. 18*, 19*, 20	April 6*, 7*, **8** / June 11*, 12*, 13* / Sept. 21*, 22*, **23**	June 1*, 2*, **3** / August 7*, 8*, 9* / Sept. 7*, 8*, **9**	April 9*, 10*, 11 / June 14*, 15*, 16*, **17** / Sept. 5*, 6
NEW YORK	April 6, 7, **8** / June 11*, 12, 13 / Sept. 21, 22, **23**	April 13*, 14, **15*** / July 31* / August 1*, 2 / Sept. 25*, 26*, 27*		June 1*, 2*, **3** / July 23*, 24*, 25* / Sept. 7*, 8*, **9**	April 3*, 4*, 5 / June 14*, 15*, 16*, **17** / Sept. 5*, 6*	June 25*, 26*, 27* / August 3*, 4, **5**, 6* / Sept. 3, 4*
PHILADELPHIA	April 9*, 10, 11 / June 7*, 8, 9, **10** / Sept. 12, 13	April 16*, 17*, 18* / August 10*, 11*, **12** / Sept. 28*, 29*, **30**	June 22*, 23*, **24** / August 7*, 8, 9* / Sept. 14*, 15, **16**		June 25*, 26*, 27* / July 26*, 27*, 28*, **29** / Sept. 3, 4*	April 20*, 21*, **22** / June 4*, **5**, 6* / Sept. 18*, 19*, 20*
PITTSBURGH	April 20, 21*, **22** / July 31* / August 1, 2 / Sept. 18*, 19, 20	June 22*, 23*, **24** / July 23*, 24*, 25* / Sept. 14*, 15*, **16**	April 9, 11, 12 / June 7*, 8*, 9*, **10** / Sept. 12*, 13*	June 18*, 19*, 20 / August 3*, 4*, **5**, 6* / Sept. 10*, 11		April 6*, 7*, **8** / June 11*, 12*, 13* / Sept. 28*, 29, **30**
ST. LOUIS	June 22, 23, **24** / August 7*, 8, 9 / Sept. 7, 8, **9***	April 3, 4*, **5*** / June 7*, 8*, 9*, **10** / Sept. 12*, 13*	June 18*, 19*, 20 / July 26*, 27*, 28, **29*** / Sept. 10*, 11*	April 13*, 14*, **15** / July 31* / August 1*, 2* / Sept. 24*, 25*, 26*	April 16*, 17*, 18* / August 10*, 11*, **12** / Sept. 21*, 22*, **23**	
ATLANTA	May 7*, 8, 9 / August 17, 18, **19**	May 2*, 3* / June 29*, 30* / July **1**, 2*	April 24*, 25* / July 19*, 20*, 21*, **22**	May 24*, 25*, 26*, **27** / July 3*, 4*	May 4*, 5*, **6** / August 14*, 15*, 16	May 11*, 12*, **13** / August 20*, 21*, 22*
CINCINNATI	May 21*, 22 / August 30*, 31 / Sept. 1, **2**	May 24*, 25, 26, **27** / July 3*, 4*	May 2*, 3* / June 28*, 29*, 30 / July **1**	April 24*, 25* / July 5*, 6*, 7*, **8**	May 9*, 10* / August 23*, 24*, 25*, **26**	May 4*, 5*, **6**, 7* / August 14*, 15
HOUSTON	May 25, 26, **27** / August 13*, 14, 15	April 30* / May 1* / July 5*, 6*, 7*, **8**	May 4, 5, **6**, 7* / July 3*, 4*	May 2*, 3* / June 29*, 30* / July **1**, 2*	May 11*, 12*, **13*** / August 20*, 21*, 22	May 15*, 16 / August 16*, 17*, 18*, **19**
LOS ANGELES	May 23, 24 / July 12*, 13, 14, **15**	May 8*, 9*, 10 / August 31* / Sept. 1*, **2**	May 11*, 12, **13** / August 14*, 15*, 16	May 4*, 5*, **6** / August 28*, 29*, 30*	May 28, 29*, 30 / July 20*, 21*, **22**	May 25*, 26*, **27** / July 16*, 17*, 18*
SAN DIEGO	May 4, 5, **6** / July 16*, 17, 18	May 22*, 23* / August 24*, 25*, **26**, 27*	May 24*, 25*, 26*, **27** / August 28*, 29*	May 28*, 29*, 30* / August 31* / Sept. 1*, **2**	May 7*, 8* / July 12*, 13*, 14, **15**	May 9*, 10 / July 19*, 20*, 21*, **22**
SAN FRAN.	May 28, 29*, 30 / July 20, 21, **22**	May 4*, 5, **6**, 7* / August 28*, 29*	May 8*, 9* / August 30*, 31* / Sept. 1, **2**	May 11*, 12*, **13** / August 14*, 15*, 16	May 25*, 26*, **27** / July 16*, 17*, 18*	May 23*, 24 / July 12*, 13*, 14*, **15***
1990	81 HOME DATES 18 NIGHTS	81 HOME DATES 62 NIGHTS	81 HOME DATES 53 NIGHTS	81 HOME DATES 64 NIGHTS	81 HOME DATES 62 NIGHTS	81 HOME DATES 60 NIGHTS

*NIGHT GAMES
NIGHT GAME: Any game starting after 5:00 p.m.
HEAVY BLACK FIGURES DENOTE SUNDAY

AND COMPLETE WEST SCHEDULES

1990	WEST					
	AT ATLANTA	AT CINCINNATI	AT HOUSTON	AT LOS ANGELES	AT SAN DIEGO	AT SAN FRANCISCO
CHICAGO.........	May 14*, 15*, 16* August 24*, 25*, **26**	May 11*, 12*, **13** August 20*, 21*, 22*	May 17*, 18*, 19*, **20** August 28*, 29*	April 27*, 28*, **29*** July 2*, 3*, 4*	April 24*, 25*, 26 June 29*, 30* July **1**	May 1*, 2 July 6*, 7, **8-8**
MONTREAL	May 28, 30* July 12*, 13*, 14*, **15**	April 27*, 28, **29** July 16*, 17*, 18*	April 24*, 25* July 19*, 20*, 21*, **22**	May 14*, 15*, 16* August 17*, 18*, **19**	May 11*, 12*, **13** August 14*, 15*, 16	May 18*, 19*, **20** August 20*, 21*, 22
NEW YORK	April 30* May 1* July 5*, 6*, 7*, **8**	May 28*, 29* July 12*, 13*, 14*, **15**	April 27*, 28*, **29** July 16*, 17*, 18*	May 21*, 22 August 23*, 24*, 25, **26**	May 18*, 19*, **20** August 20*, 21*, 22	May 14*, 15*, 16 August 17*, 18, **19***
PHILADELPHIA	April 27*, 28*, **29** July 16*, 17*, 18*	April 30* May 1 July 19*, 20*, 21, **22**	May 8*, 9* July 12*, 13*, 14*, **15**	May 18*, 19*, **20** August 20*, 21*, 22*	May 14*, 15*, 16 August 17*, 18*, **19**	May 21*, 22 August 23*, 24*, 25, **26**
PITTSBURGH..	May 17*, 18*, 19*, **20*** August 28*, 29*	May 14*, 15*, 16* August 17*, 18*, **19**	May 21*, 22*, 23* August 31* Sept. 1*, **2**	May 1*, 2* July 5*, 6*, 7*, **8**	April 27*, 28*, **29** July 2*, 3*, 4*	April 24*, 25*, 26 June 29*, 30 July **1**
ST. LOUIS	May 21*, 22* August 30*, 31* Sept 1*, **2**	May 17*, 18*, 19*, **20** August 28*, 29*	May 28, 29*, 30* August 24*, 25*, **26**	April 24*, 25*, 26* June 29*, 30* July **1**	May 1*, 2 July 5, 6*, 7*, **8**	April 27*, 28*, **29** July 2*, 3*, 4
ATLANTA.......		April 20*, 21, **22** June 12*, 13*, 14* Sept. 25*, 26*, 27*	April 17*, 18* August 2*, 3*, 4*, **5** Sept. 28*, 29, **30**	June 4*, 5*, 6* July 26*, 27*, 28*, **29** Sept. 5*, 6*	May 31* June 1*, 2*, **3** July 30*, 31* Sept. 7*, 8*, **9**	April 2*, 3*, 4 June 15*, 16, **17** Sept. 10*, 11*, 12
CINCINNATI ...	April 13*, 14*, **15**, 16* June 19*, 20*, 21* Sept. 3, 4*		April 9*, 10*, 11* June 7*, 8*, 9*, **10** Sept. 19*, 20*	May 31* June 1*, 2*, **3** July 30*, 31* Sept. 7*, 8*, **9**	April 6*, 7*, **8** July 23*, 24*, 25 Sept. 21*, 22*, **23**	June 4*, 5*, 6 July 26*, 27*, 28, **29** Sept. 5*, 6
HOUSTON.......	April 6*, 7*, **8** July 23*, 24*, 25* Sept. 21*, 22*, **23**	April 2*, 4*, 5 June 15*, 16*, **17** Sept. 11*, 12*, 13*		April 19*, 20*, 21*, **22** June 18*, 19*, 20* Sept. 3*, 4*	June 4*, 5*, 6 July 26*, 27*, 28*, **29** Sept. 5*, 6*	May 31* June 1*, 2, **3** July 30*, 31 Sept. 7*, 8, **9**
LOS ANGELES	June 25*, 26*, 27* August 10*, 11*, **12**, 13* Sept. 17*, 18*	June 22*, 23*, **24*** August 7*, 8*, 9* Sept. 14*, 15*, **16**	April 13*, 14, **15** June 11*, 12*, 13* Sept. 24*, 25*, 26*		April 10*, 11*, 12 June 8*, 9*, **10** Sept. 10*, 11*, 12*	April 17*, 18 August 2*, 3*, 4, **5** Sept. 28*, 29, **30**
SAN DIEGO.....	June 22*, 23*, **24** August 7*, 8*, 9* Sept. 14*, 15*, **16**	April 17*, 18* August 2*, 3*, 4*, **5** Sept. 28*, 29, **30**	June 25*, 26*, 27*, 28 August 10*, 11*, **12*** Sept. 17*, 18*	April 2*, 3*, 4*, 5* June 15*, 16, **17** Sept. 19*, 20*		April 13*, 14, **15** June 18*, 19*, 20 Sept. 24*, 25*, 26
SAN FRAN......	April 10*, 11*, 12* June 8*, 9*, **10**, 11* Sept. 19*, 20*	June 25*, 26*, 27 August 10*, 11*, **12**, 13* Sept. 17*, 18	June 22*, 23, **24** August 6*, 7*, 8 Sept. 14*, 15*, **16**	April 6*, 7*, **8** July 23*, 24*, 25* Sept. 21*, 22*, **23**	April 20*, 21*, **22***, 23* June 12*, 13*, 14 Sept. 3*, 4*	
1990	81 HOME DATES 67 NIGHTS	81 HOME DATES 60 NIGHTS	81 HOME DATES 63 NIGHTS	81 HOME DATES 65 NIGHTS	81 HOME DATES 59 NIGHTS	80 HOME DATES 41 NIGHTS

JULY 10—ALL-STAR GAME AT WRIGLEY FIELD IN CHICAGO
AUGUST 6—HALL OF FAME GAME AT COOPERSTOWN, N.Y. (Montreal Expos vs. Baltimore Orioles)

Index to Contents

AMERICAN LEAGUE

NATIONAL LEAGUE

1989 Game Scores

1989 Game Scores

NATIONAL ASSOCIATION (MINOR LEAGUE) AVERAGES

Thank you for your purchase! We appreciate your support of *The Sporting News* books. We would like to know more about you and your interests so that we can continue to provide you with books that meet as many of your needs as possible. . . . Please take a few minutes and fill out our questionnaire. Thanks for your help!

Greg Wiley
Book Publisher

*Which *TSN* titles have you purchased?

In 1990 _____ _____ _____

In 1989 _____ _____ _____

In 1988 _____ _____ _____

*Have you purchased any of the following titles from other publishers?

☐ The Baseball Encyclopedia   ☐ Diamond Appraised
☐ Bill James Abstract 1988   ☐ Total Baseball
☐ Dickson Baseball Dictionary   ☐ The Babe—Life in Pictures
☐ The Elias Baseball Analyst   ☐ The Baseball Hall Of Fame
☐ The Heart Of The Order   50th Anniversary Issue
☐ Summer Of 1949

*How do you purchase *TSN* books?

☐ Waldenbooks   ☐ *TSN* Ads
☐ B. Dalton   ☐ *TSN* Mailings
☐ Crown   ☐ Other Book Stores

*Could you make some suggestions for improving *TSN* books or services?

_____

_____

*What's your favorite *TSN* book(s)? _____

_____

*What's your favorite section? _____

_____

*What's your least favorite section? _____

_____

*Do you subscribe to *The Sporting News*?   ☐ Yes ☐ No

*Education: ☐ High School   ☐ Graduate Degree
              ☐ Some College   ☐ Attending High School
              ☐ College Graduate   ☐ Attending College

*Age: ☐ Under 15   ☐ 19-23   ☐ 31-42   ☐ 56+
             ☐ 15-18   ☐ 24-30   ☐ 43-55

*Would you like to receive our book mailings announcing new titles? If so please provide us with your name and address.

Name _____

Address _____

City/State/Zip _____

Call **1-800-669-5700** if you would like subscription information.